S0-ARO-483

Baker
Topical Guide
to the Bible

Baker Topical Guide to the Bible

Walter A. Elwell
General Editor

Douglas Buckwalter
Associate Editor

A Division of Baker Book House Co
Grand Rapids, Michigan 49516

© 1991 by Baker Books

Published by Baker Books
a division of Baker Book House Company
P.O. Box 6287, Grand Rapids, MI 49516-6287

Previously published as *Topical Analysis of the Bible*
Published in 2000 as *Baker Topical Guide to the Bible*

Printed in the United States of America

All rights reserved. No part of this publication may be reproduced, stored in a retrieval system, or transmitted in any form or by any means—for example, electronic, photocopy, recording—without the prior written permission of the publisher. The only exception is brief quotations in printed reviews.

ISBN 0-8010-2255-X

Scripture quotations are from the HOLY BIBLE, NEW INTERNATIONAL VERSION®. NIV®. Copyright © 1973, 1978, 1984 by International Bible Society. Used by permission of Zondervan Publishing House. All rights reserved.

For current information about all releases from Baker Book House, visit our web site:
http://www.bakerbooks.com

Contents

Contents

Acknowledgments

Special thanks are due to many people who played a significant part in bringing this work to completion. It is appropriate to mention some of them here—Carol Rebell, Julie Pearson, Vivian Youngberg, and Allan Fisher.

Doug Buckwalter is to be thanked especially for the indexes, as well as for everything else he did. Without his untiring effort this book would not have been possible.

Finally, gratitude is due to Wheaton College for giving me a sabbatical leave in the spring of 1989 in order to finish the first draft of this reference work.

Walter A. Elwell

Introduction

We live in a society that is gradually losing its sense of direction. Traditional Christian values, morals, attitudes, and ideas are slowly being eroded and are being replaced by a destructive relativism that will leave nothing but disorder in its wake. Moreover, polls taken throughout the last twenty years show a continual, appalling decline in knowledge of what the Bible teaches. If this were only a diminishing understanding of highly abstruse matters, that would be one thing, but it concerns instead the most fundamental knowledge of Scripture, such as the ability to name the Ten Commandments. In one poll 44 percent of the public could not identify Jesus' statement to Nicodemus (even though the choices were listed), and those who claimed church membership were not far behind at 37 percent. The ignorance of one denominational group was even greater than that of the general public, with 47 percent saying they did not know the answer. Interestingly enough, this does not imply any massive loss of faith in the Bible. Almost 75 percent of the public said they believe that the Bible is the Word of God, and 84 percent said the Ten Commandments are still valid for today—they just do not happen to know what they are!

In the light of this, Baker Book House is offering a reference work that will make the theological content of the Bible more accessible to the interested reader. Its purpose is to arrange the basic teachings of the Scriptures into a set of recognizable topics and present a full or representative collection of biblical passages that speak about each of those topics.

How to Use This Book

The reader may wish to scan the table of contents in order to get a sense of what is in each chapter. In this way the larger topics may be seen as parts of a whole. Then, for a more detailed look, a reader may consult the abbreviated outlines at the beginning of each chapter or the complete outline in the appendix. If the reader then wishes to pursue related ideas which are part of a single, larger topic, he or she may consult the index. There, the various topics are arranged alphabetically, and references to each are cited. (Some topics are found necessarily in several contexts.) Using these resources, the reader may conveniently locate whatever topic is desired.

The wording used in the headings is usually that of the New International Version (NIV) of the Bible, although in some instances theological terminology (e.g., omnipotence, millennium) not found in the NIV is used because of its familiarity. For example, if one wishes to consider God's omnipotence, one might look in the index under "omnipotence," "all-powerful," or "power." Or one might be directed to the same information by scanning the complete outline. There, the reader will find headings such as "The Divine Name Represents God's Power and Authority," "Powerful God," "God Is Omnipotent" (all from chap. 1, The Personal God); "Jesus Possesses God's Attributes: Omnipotence," "Power" (both in chap. 2, Jesus Christ); "The Holy Spirit's Divine Qualities: Power" (in chap. 3, The Holy Spirit); and "God's Power Is Revealed" (in chap. 5, The Revelation of God).

Arrangement of Material

The fifteen chapters are arranged in a manner that will be familiar to most students of theology, although the outline will not look like that of any systematic theology in particular. We had hoped to find a consensus in selection and ordering of topics, but after examining more than seventy-five systematic theologies, of which no two were alike, we decided to construct our own outline. This outline is not necessarily better than all the others, but it does serve the purpose of arranging the material comprehensively for easy reference. There is an obvious order of progression in the sequence that is used:

God (Father, Son, Holy Spirit, works of God, revelation)
The created order (angels, humanity [men and women])
Salvation (sin, salvation)
The Christian life (sanctification, Christian living)
Church life (church, sacraments)
Eschatology (death, second coming, last judgment, eternal future)

Perhaps a word needs to be said about the internal arrangement of some of these sections. In the first category revelation was put at the end of the section, but not because it is of least importance. In some ways it is of the most importance, being the source of all we know about God and his dealings with us. But it seemed best to us to speak first about the foundational topic of who God is, then to identify his works, then to focus on his revelatory work. In the second section, separate material was added on what the Bible says specifically about women. Obviously, this is not to imply that humanity in general is a separate topic from women in particular or that everything in chapter 7 on humanity does not apply to women as well as men. Women were discussed separately only because at this time in the history of the church it might be helpful to have such a collection of material for quick reference. (In the first draft of this book, chapter 8 was incorporated in one larger chapter on humanity.) The need of the present moment also provides the rationale for treating the subject more comprehensively than is usually done in strictly theological reference works covering such topics as marriage, family, and historical leadership. In the fourth section, sanctification and Christian living were differentiated primarily for practical reasons. Putting the material together would have made a chapter that was much too long, so the entries were divided into separate chapters along basically theoretical (sanctification) and practical (Christian living) lines.

Theological Perspective

The theological perspective of this work is taken from historic Protestant Christian orthodoxy. Some of the particular emphases to be found are the following:

A traditional doctrine of the Trinity is reflected throughout the work. God is defined as Father, Son, and Holy Spirit. Consequently, when God's works (e.g., creation) are in view, the work of the Son and the Spirit is noted along with that of the Father. There are, of course, separate chapters on the Son and the Holy Spirit, but this is to make the material easy to locate, not to imply that the Son and the Holy Spirit are less than God.

Throughout this volume there is an emphasis on God as person. This, too, is part of historic orthodoxy and is perhaps an emphasis that is needed today more than ever. In the face of New Age thinking and neo-Hegelian theologies—which would postulate a pantheizing approach to thinking about God and, in effect, depersonalize him—it needs to be reasserted that God is not to be identified as an impersonal Force, or Ground, or *Geist.* Although God is the one who is infinitely beyond us, he is available to us in a personal way as Father, Friend, and Redeemer. He solicits our prayers because he can hear and answer them. He communes with us because he cares for us and desires our fellowship. He entered the human race as one of us so that we can see his desire to relate personally to us embodied concretely. God is not a person exactly as we are, certainly, but he is not less a person than we are, or less able to interact. There is a great mystery in this that cannot be fully explained, but it should not be weakened on that account. The uniform testimony of Scripture is that God can be known personally by those who will approach him in the proper way—in love, purity of heart, and humility of spirit.

The full deity of Christ the Son is also emphasized in this book. In order to establish this point, we have used numerous quotes from the Gospels, but without making any distinction as to what some scholars consider authentic or inauthentic. The existing text of the Bible is used just as it stands. This is, no doubt, out of line with some current developmental Christologies or extreme theories of NT authorship that assume multiple layers of material in the Gospels. But a decision had to be made, and it was thought best to use the text as it is. Consequently, the Synoptics and John are used as truly reflective of what Jesus thought and said. If someone is inclined to discredit some of this material as being secondary and as coming from a later time in the life of the church, let it at least be acknowledged that the Jesus reflected in this volume is the Jesus who exists de facto in the Gospels as we now have them. When all is said and done, this is the only real Jesus that we can know.

Both the OT and the NT are used on an equal footing in the citations, which are arranged in canonical order. Here again, historic orthodoxy has postulated the essential unity of Scripture. This is not to say that everything is precisely equivalent to everything else, but the earliest church did retain the OT as its own and built its theology on it. For this reason, the whole of the Bible is used as the inspired Word of God to define the doctrines under discussion.

There are some matters (mostly ecclesiastical and eschatological) on which Christians have traditionally differed. A sincere effort was made to stay as neutral as possible on these topics by including all of the material relating to them. The reader may then sort out what seems misplaced from his or her point of view. For example, some Christians believe that Christ's second coming will have two phases seven (or three and one-half) years apart; others believe that Christ will return only once. All the material relating to this is put in the appropriate spot as a single topic ("The Second Coming of Jesus," pp. 746–54). Readers may arrange it as they will. Another example is the "Gifts of the Spirit" (pp. 156–58). There are those who believe that these supernatural endowments ended with the close of the NT period, whereas others believe they are valid for today. Those who view them as valid for the church in our day are provided with the list as well as the reasons God gave the gifts. Those who do not look for them today are able to consider what God did for the church at its inception.

On some matters, it was not possible to be neutral because to arrange the material required making a decision. Two examples of this will suffice. First, as part of the doctrine of the church ("Metaphors and Names for the People of God, the Church," pp. 687–94), should OT references to God's people have been used? There is no easy answer to this question, but for the sake of completeness the OT references were included. However, they were kept separate from the NT references. So for those who see no continuity in the people of God between OT and NT, the OT references may be used merely to refer to Israel. For those who *do* see a unity to the people of God, both the OT and NT references may be considered together. Second, a premillennial arrangement of material was chosen in the section on eschatology. Amillenarians will have no difficulty in grouping all the material together in order to have it depict a general resurrection and judgment, whereas premillenarians can take it as it stands.

In spite of our best efforts, however, it could still be observed that this work has not achieved absolute neutrality and might have been arranged differently. All we can do is plead for understanding in this matter. It is not our intention that this volume be a source of conflict about controversial matters, but rather an aid to the believer in understanding the Bible and growing spiritually. If we are to have differences, let us have them charitably.

Methodology

Despite the fact that about thirty-five thousand Scripture references are to be found in this work, it was not possible to be exhaustive in citing the references to each topic. Where all of the references could be used reasonably, that was done. When there were too many to use, a selection was made that attempted to reflect the overall nature of the material.

We tried not to overuse any references; a single reference, however, has many ideas in it. When we concluded this was so, we used the same citation in as many places as were appropriate. We also tried to avoid overlapping the category headings, but again, it was not always possible. Our usual procedure was to put similar citations under one heading and then to provide the necessary cross-reference. However, when an idea was being looked at in two or more slightly different ways, similar citations were kept separate, trying to reflect those shades of difference in the headings.

We tried to make the wording of each heading

conform to the actual texts cited under it, but this too was not always possible. Occasionally, we have selected passages whose general meaning, rather than a specific word, relates them to a heading. (For example, in the section on God as Teacher, Ps. 119:102 does not call God a teacher per se, but says God has taught us. "Providence Provides for Believers" [p. 210] is another good example of this.) Most often, however, the exact wording or idea of a heading will be found in the references cited under it. In some instances, the NIV uses a different English translation than it ordinarily does, giving the appearance that a particular word in a heading is not found in the text, when, in fact, it is. For example, under "The Human Mind" (p. 335) the NIV translates the Greek word for *mind* with the English word *thinking*. In other places the heading itself seems out of line with the verses presented. An example of this is "Human Kidneys" (p. 334), where the Hebrew or Greek word for "kidney" is translated variously by the NIV as "heart" or "mind"; or again, "Human Bowels" (p. 331), where the NIV translates the Hebrew or Greek as "churning," "heart," "affection," "compassion," or "pity." It was felt best, in cases such as these, to keep the category heading which best reflected the Hebrew or Greek text. To clarify these instances for the reader, we have included some of the words from the NIV parenthetically in these headings and have marked them as alternate English translations (ET).

In some cases, we have selected passages where the general sense is to be found, rather than a specific word (e.g., in the section on God as teacher, Ps. 119:102 does not call God a Teacher per se, but says that God has taught us). Most often, however, the exact wording or idea will be found.

Abbreviations

Ar	Aramaic
chap.	chapter
Col	Colossians
Dan	Daniel
Deut	Deuteronomy
Eccles	Ecclesiastes
Eph	Ephesians
ET	English translation
Exod	Exodus
Ezek	Ezekiel
Gal	Galatians
Gen	Genesis
Gk	Greek
Hab	Habakkuk
Hag	Haggai
Hb	Hebrew
Heb	Hebrews
Hos	Hosea
Isa	Isaiah
Jer	Jeremiah
Jon	Jonah
Josh	Joshua
Judg	Judges
Lam	Lamentations
Lev	Leviticus
Mal	Malachi
Matt	Matthew
Mic	Micah
NT	New Testament
Nah	Nahum
Neh	Nehemiah
NIV	New International Version
Num	Numbers
OT	Old Testament
Obad	Obadiah
Phil	Philippians
Philem	Philemon
Prov	Proverbs
Ps	Psalms
Rev	Revelation
RSV	Revised Standard Version
Rom	Romans
Song of Songs	Song of Songs
Zech	Zechariah
Zeph	Zephaniah
1 Chron	1 Chronicles
2 Chron	2 Chronicles
1 Cor	1 Corinthians
2 Cor	2 Corinthians
1 Pet	1 Peter
2 Pet	2 Peter
1 Sam	1 Samuel
2 Sam	2 Samuel
1 Thess	1 Thessalonians
2 Thess	2 Thessalonians
1 Tim	1 Timothy
2 Tim	2 Timothy

1

The Personal God

I
The Person of God

A. The Existence of God

1. God's Existence Supported by Direct Affirmation

Exod 3 [14]God said to Moses, "I AM WHO I AM. This is what you are to say to the Israelites: 'I AM has sent me to you.'"

[15]God also said to Moses, "Say to the Israelites, 'The LORD, the God of your fathers—the God of Abraham, the God of Isaac and the God of Jacob—has sent me to you.' This is my name forever, the name by which I am to be remembered from generation to generation."

Isa 43 [10]"You are my witnesses," declares the LORD, "and my servant whom I have chosen, so that you may know and believe me and understand that I am he. Before me no god was formed, nor will there be one after me."

2. God's Existence Supported by His Work

Gen 1 [1]In the beginning God created the heavens and the earth.

1 Kings 18 [24]"Then you call on the name of your god, and I will call on the name of the LORD. The god who answers by fire—he is God."

Then all the people said, "What you say is good."

[25]Elijah said to the prophets of Baal, "Choose one of the bulls and prepare it first, since there are so many of you. Call on the name of your god, but do not light the fire." [26]So they took the bull given them and prepared it.

Then they called on the name of Baal from morning till

noon. "O Baal, answer us!" they shouted. But there was no response; no one answered. And they danced around the altar they had made.

27At noon Elijah began to taunt them. "Shout louder!" he said. "Surely he is a god! Perhaps he is deep in thought, or busy, or traveling. Maybe he is sleeping and must be awakened." 28So they shouted louder and slashed themselves with swords and spears, as was their custom, until their blood flowed. 29Midday passed, and they continued their frantic prophesying until the time for the evening sacrifice. But there was no response, no one answered, no one paid attention.

30Then Elijah said to all the people, "Come here to me." They came to him, and he repaired the altar of the LORD, which was in ruins. 31Elijah took twelve stones, one for each of the tribes descended from Jacob, to whom the word of the LORD had come, saying, "Your name shall be Israel." 32With the stones he built an altar in the name of the LORD, and he dug a trench around it large enough to hold two seahs of seed. 33He arranged the wood, cut the bull into pieces and laid it on the wood. Then he said to them, "Fill four large jars with water and pour it on the offering and on the wood."

34"Do it again," he said, and they did it again.

"Do it a third time," he ordered, and they did it the third time. 35The water ran down around the altar and even filled the trench.

36At the time of sacrifice, the prophet Elijah stepped forward and prayed: "O LORD, God of Abraham, Isaac and Israel, let it be known today that you are God in Israel and that I am your servant and have done all these things at your command. 37Answer me, O LORD, answer me, so these people will know that you, O LORD, are God, and that you are turning their hearts back again."

38Then the fire of the LORD fell and burned up the sacrifice, the wood, the stones and the soil, and also licked up the water in the trench.

39When all the people saw this, they fell prostrate and cried, "The LORD—he is God! The LORD—he is God!"

Ps 9 16The LORD is known by his justice; the wicked are ensnared by the work of their hands.

Ps 100 3Know that the LORD is God. It is he who made us, and we are his; we are his people, the sheep of his pasture.

Ps 105 2Sing to him, sing praise to him; tell of all his wonderful acts. . . .

5Remember the wonders he has done, his miracles, and the judgments he pronounced. . . .

16He called down famine on the land and destroyed all their supplies of food; 17and he sent a man before them—Joseph, sold as a slave. 18They bruised his feet with shackles, his neck was put in irons, 19till what he foretold came to pass, till the word of the LORD proved him true. 20The king sent and released him, the ruler of peoples set him free. 21He made him master of his household, ruler over all he possessed, 22to instruct his princes as he pleased and teach his elders wisdom. . . . 26He sent Moses his servant, and Aaron, whom he had chosen. 27They performed his miraculous signs among them, his wonders in the land of Ham. . . . 43He brought out his people with rejoicing, his chosen ones with shouts of joy; 44he gave them the lands of the nations, and they fell heir to what others had toiled for—45that they might keep his precepts and observe his laws.

Praise the LORD.

2 Cor 1 21Now it is God who makes both us and you stand firm in Christ. He anointed us. . . .

Heb 3 4For every house is built by someone, but God is the builder of everything.

3. God's Existence Supported by Human Intuition

Ps 10 4In his pride the wicked does not seek him; in all his thoughts there is no room for God.

Ps 14 1The fool says in his heart, "There is no God." They are corrupt, their deeds are vile; there is no one who does good.

Eccles 3 11He has made everything beautiful in its time. He has also set eternity in the hearts of men; yet they cannot fathom what God has done from beginning to end.

John 1 1In the beginning was the Word, and the Word was with God, and the Word was God.

2He was with God in the beginning.

3Through him all things were made; without him nothing was made that has been made. 4In him was life, and that life was the light of men. 5The light shines in the darkness, but the darkness has not understood it.

John 1 9The true light that gives light to every man was coming into the world.

Rom 1 19since what may be known about God is plain to them, because God has made it plain to them. 20For since the creation of the world God's invisible qualities—his eternal power and divine nature—have been clearly seen, being understood from what has been made, so that men are without excuse. . . .

28Furthermore, since they did not think it worthwhile to retain the knowledge of God, he gave them over to a depraved mind, to do what ought not to be done. . . . 32Although they know God's righteous decree that those who do such things deserve death, they not only continue to do these very things but also approve of those who practice them.

Rom 2 14(Indeed, when Gentiles, who do not have the law, do by nature things required by the law, they are a law for themselves, even though they do not have the law, 15since they show that the requirements of the law are written on their hearts, their consciences also bearing witness, and their thoughts now accusing, now even defending them.)

4. God's Existence Supported by His People

Ps 105 41He opened the rock, and water gushed out; like a river it flowed in the desert. 42For he remembered his holy promise given to his servant Abraham. 43He brought out his people with rejoicing, his chosen ones with shouts of joy; 44he gave them the lands of the nations, and they fell heir to what others had toiled for—45that they might keep his precepts and observe his laws. Praise the LORD.

Isa 40 9You who bring good tidings to Zion, go up on a high mountain. You who bring good tidings to Jerusalem, lift up your voice with a shout, lift it up, do not be afraid; say to the towns of Judah, "Here is your God!" 10See, the Sovereign LORD comes with power, and his arm rules for him. See, his reward is with him, and his recompense accompanies him. 11He tends his flock like a shepherd: He gathers the lambs in his arms and carries them close to his heart; he gently leads those that have young.

1 Cor 8 3But the man who loves God is known by God.

1 John 2 3We know that we have come to know him if we obey his commands.

1 John 4 7Dear friends, let us love one another, for love comes from God. Everyone who loves has been born of God and knows God. 8Whoever does not love does not know God, because God is love.

5. God's Existence Supported by the Nations

Ps 68 32Sing to God, O kingdoms of the earth, sing praise to the LORD, 33to him who rides the ancient skies above, who thunders with mighty voice.

Ps 117 1Praise the LORD, all you nations; extol him, all you peoples.

Ps 148 7Praise the LORD from the earth, you great sea creatures and all ocean depths, . . . 11kings of the earth and all nations, you princes and all rulers on earth, 12young men and maidens, old men and children. 13Let them praise the name of the LORD, for his name alone is exalted; his splendor is above the earth and the heavens.

Isa 41 1"Be silent before me, you islands! Let the nations renew their strength! Let them come forward and speak; let us meet together at the place of judgment. 2Who has stirred up one from the east, calling him in righteousness to his service? He hands nations over to him and subdues kings before him. He turns them to dust with his sword, to windblown chaff with his bow. 3He pursues them and moves on unscathed, by a path his feet have not traveled before. 4Who has done this and carried it through, calling forth the generations from the beginning? I, the LORD—with the first of them and with the last—I am he."

Mal 1 11"My name will be great among the nations, from the rising to the setting of the sun. In every place incense and pure offerings will be brought to my name, because my name will be great among the nations," says the LORD Almighty.

Acts 17 26"From one man he made every nation of men, that they should inhabit the whole earth; and he determined the times set for them and the exact places where they should live.

27God did this so that men would seek him and perhaps reach out for him and find him, though he is not far from each one of us."

6. God's Existence Supported by Nature

Job 12 7"But ask the animals, and they will teach you, or the birds of the air, and they will tell you; 8or speak to the earth, and it will teach you, or let the fish of the sea inform you. 9Which of all these does not know that the hand of the LORD has done this?"
Ps 8 1O LORD, our LORD, how majestic is your name in all the earth! You have set your glory above the heavens.
Ps 19 1The heavens declare the glory of God; the skies proclaim the work of his hands. 2Day after day they pour forth speech; night after night they display knowledge. 3There is no speech or language where their voice is not heard. 4Their voice goes out into all the earth, their words to the ends of the world. In the heavens he has pitched a tent for the sun, 5which is like a bridegroom coming forth from his pavilion, like a champion rejoicing to run his course. 6It rises at one end of the heavens and makes its circuit to the other; nothing is hidden from its heat.
Ps 50 6And the heavens proclaim his righteousness, for God himself is judge.
Ps 69 34Let heaven and earth praise him, the seas and all that move in them. . . .
Ps 93 1The LORD reigns, he is robed in majesty; the LORD is robed in majesty and is armed with strength. The world is firmly established; it cannot be moved. 2Your throne was established long ago; you are from all eternity.

3The seas have lifted up, O LORD, the seas have lifted up their voice; the seas have lifted up their pounding waves. 4Mightier than the thunder of the great waters, mightier than the breakers of the sea—the LORD on high is mighty.
Ps 104 10He makes springs pour water into the ravines; it flows between the mountains. 11They give water to all the beasts of the field; the wild donkeys quench their thirst. 12The birds of the air nest by the waters; they sing among the branches. 13He waters the mountains from his upper chambers; the earth is satisfied by the fruit of his work. 14He makes grass grow for the cattle, and plants for man to cultivate—bringing forth food from the earth: 15wine that gladdens the heart of man, oil to make his face shine, and bread that sustains his heart. 16The trees of the LORD are well watered, the cedars of Lebanon that he planted. 17There the birds make their nests; the stork has its home in the pine trees. 18The high mountains belong to the wild goats; the crags are a refuge for the coneys.

19The moon marks off the seasons, and the sun knows when to go down. 20You bring darkness, it becomes night, and all the beasts of the forest prowl. 21The lions roar for their prey and seek their food from God. 22The sun rises, and they steal away; they return and lie down in their dens. 23Then man goes out to his work, to his labor until evening.

24How many are your works, O LORD! In wisdom you made them all; the earth is full of your creatures. 25There is the sea, vast and spacious, teeming with creatures beyond number—living things both large and small.
Ps 148 7Praise the LORD from the earth, you great sea creatures and all ocean depths, 8lightning and hail, snow and clouds, stormy winds that do his bidding, 9you mountains and all hills, fruit trees and all cedars, 10wild animals and all cattle, small creatures and flying birds. . . . 13Let them praise the name of the LORD, for his name alone is exalted; his splendor is above the earth and the heavens.
Acts 14 15"Men, why are you doing this? We too are only men, human like you. We are bringing you good news, telling you to turn from these worthless things to the living God, who made heaven and earth and sea and everything in them. 16In the past, he let all nations go their own way. 17Yet he has not left himself without testimony: He has shown kindness by giving you rain from heaven and crops in their seasons; he provides you with plenty of food and fills your hearts with joy."

B. The One and Only God

1. God Is the Only God

Exod 8 10"Tomorrow," Pharaoh said.

Moses replied, "It will be as you say, so that you may know there is no one like the LORD our God."
Exod 15 11"Who among the gods is like you, O LORD? Who is like you—majestic in holiness, awesome in glory, working wonders?"
Exod 18 9Jethro was delighted to hear about all the good things the LORD had done for Israel in rescuing them from the hand of the Egyptians. 10He said, "Praise be to the LORD, who rescued you from the hand of the Egyptians and of Pharaoh, and who rescued the people from the hand of the Egyptians. 11Now I know that the LORD is greater than all other gods, for he did this to those who had treated Israel arrogantly."
Exod 20 3"You shall have no other gods before me."
Exod 34 14"Do not worship any other god, for the LORD, whose name is Jealous, is a jealous God."
Deut 4 35You were shown these things so that you might know that the LORD is God; besides him there is no other.
Deut 6 4Hear, O Israel: The LORD our God, the LORD is one.
Deut 32 39"See now that I myself am He! There is no god besides me. I put to death and I bring to life, I have wounded and I will heal, and no one can deliver out of my hand."
2 Sam 7 22"How great you are, O Sovereign LORD! There is no one like you, and there is no God but you, as we have heard with our own ears."
2 Sam 22 32"For who is God besides the LORD? And who is the Rock except our God?"
1 Kings 8 22Then Solomon stood before the altar of the LORD in front of the whole assembly of Israel, spread out his hands toward heaven 23and said: "O LORD, God of Israel, there is no God like you in heaven above or on earth below—you who keep your covenant of love with your servants who continue wholeheartedly in your way."
1 Kings 8 59"And may these words of mine, which I have prayed before the LORD, be near to the LORD our God day and night, that he may uphold the cause of his servant and the cause of his people Israel according to each day's need, 60so that all the peoples of the earth may know that the LORD is God and that there is no other."
2 Kings 5 15Then Naaman and all his attendants went back to the man of God. He stood before him and said, "Now I know that there is no God in all the world except in Israel. Please accept now a gift from your servant."
2 Kings 19 15And Hezekiah prayed to the LORD: "O LORD, God of Israel, enthroned between the cherubim, you alone are God over all the kingdoms of the earth. You have made heaven and earth."
Neh 9 6"You alone are the LORD. You made the heavens, even the highest heavens, and all their starry host, the earth and all that is on it, the seas and all that is in them. You give life to everything, and the multitudes of heaven worship you."
Ps 18 31For who is God besides the LORD? And who is the Rock except our God?
Ps 35 10My whole being will exclaim, "Who is like you, O LORD? You rescue the poor from those too strong for them, the poor and needy from those who rob them."
Ps 86 8Among the gods there is none like you, O Lord; no deeds can compare with yours. 9All the nations you have made will come and worship before you, O LORD; they will bring glory to your name. 10For you are great and do marvelous deeds; you alone are God.
Ps 95 3For the LORD is the great God, the great King above all gods.
Ps 96 4For great is the LORD and most worthy of praise; he is to be feared above all gods. 5For all the gods of the nations are idols, but the LORD made the heavens. 6Splendor and majesty are before him; strength and glory are in his sanctuary.
Ps 113 4The LORD is exalted over all the nations, his glory above the heavens. 5Who is like the LORD our God, the One who sits enthroned on high, 6who stoops down to look on the heavens and the earth? 7He raises the poor from the dust and lifts the needy from the ash heap; 8he seats them with princes, with the princes of their people. 9He settles the barren woman in her home as a happy mother of children. Praise the LORD.
Ps 135 5I know that the LORD is great, that our LORD is greater than all gods. 6The LORD does whatever pleases him, in the heavens and on the earth, in the seas and all their depths. 7He makes clouds rise from the ends of the earth; he sends lightning with the rain and brings out the wind from his storehouses.

Isa 37 [16]"O LORD Almighty, God of Israel, enthroned between the cherubim, you alone are God over all the kingdoms of the earth. You have made heaven and earth. . . . [20]Now, O LORD our God, deliver us from his hand, so that all kingdoms on earth may know that you alone, O LORD, are God."
Isa 40 [25]"To whom will you compare me? Or who is my equal?" says the Holy One. [26]Lift your eyes and look to the heavens: Who created all these? He who brings out the starry host one by one, and calls them each by name. Because of his great power and mighty strength, not one of them is missing.
Isa 43 [3]"For I am the LORD, your God, the Holy One of Israel, your Savior; I give Egypt for your ransom, Cush and Seba in your stead. . . . [10]You are my witnesses," declares the LORD, "and my servant whom I have chosen, so that you may know and believe me and understand that I am he. Before me no god was formed, nor will there be one after me. [11]I, even I, am the LORD, and apart from me there is no savior."
Isa 44 [6]"This is what the LORD says—Israel's King and Redeemer, the LORD Almighty: I am the first and I am the last; apart from me there is no God. . . . [8]Do not tremble, do not be afraid. Did I not proclaim this and foretell it long ago? You are my witnesses. Is there any God besides me? No, there is no other Rock; I know not one."
Isa 45 [21]"Declare what is to be, present it—let them take counsel together. Who foretold this long ago, who declared it from the distant past? Was it not I, the LORD? And there is no God apart from me, a righteous God and a Savior; there is none but me."
Isa 46 [9]"Remember the former things, those of long ago; I am God, and there is no other; I am God, and there is none like me."
Isa 49 [26]"I will make your oppressors eat their own flesh; they will be drunk on their own blood, as with wine. Then all mankind will know that I, the LORD, am your Savior, your Redeemer, the Mighty One of Jacob."
Hos 13 [4]"But I am the LORD your God, who brought you out of Egypt. You shall acknowledge no God but me, no Savior except me."
Mic 7 [18]Who is a God like you, who pardons sin and forgives the transgression of the remnant of his inheritance? You do not stay angry forever but delight to show mercy.
Zech 14 [9]The LORD will be king over the whole earth. On that day there will be one LORD, and his name the only name.
Mal 2 [10]Have we not all one Father? Did not one God create us? Why do we profane the covenant of our fathers by breaking faith with one another?
Matt 23 [9]"And do not call anyone on earth 'father,' for you have one Father, and he is in heaven."
John 8 [41]"You are doing the things your own father does."
"We are not illegitimate children," they protested. "The only Father we have is God himself."
John 17 [3]"Now this is eternal life: that they may know you, the only true God, and Jesus Christ, whom you have sent."
Rom 3 [30]since there is only one God, who will justify the circumcised by faith and the uncircumcised through that same faith.
1 Cor 8 [4]So then, about eating food sacrificed to idols: We know that an idol is nothing at all in the world and that there is no God but one. [5]For even if there are so-called gods, whether in heaven or on earth (as indeed there are many "gods" and many "lords"), [6]yet for us there is but one God, the Father, from whom all things came and for whom we live; and there is but one Lord, Jesus Christ, through whom all things came and through whom we live.
Gal 3 [20]A mediator, however, does not represent just one party; but God is one.
Eph 4 [6]one God and Father of all, who is over all and through all and in all.
1 Tim 2 [5]For there is one God and one mediator between God and men, the man Christ Jesus. . . .
1 Tim 6 [15]which God will bring about in his own time—God, the blessed and only Ruler, the King of kings and Lord of lords. . . .
James 2 [19]You believe that there is one God. Good! Even the demons believe that—and shudder.

2. All Other Gods Are Idols

Exod 20 [4]"You shall not make for yourself an idol in the form of anything in heaven above or on the earth beneath or in the waters below. [5]You shall not bow down to them or worship them; for I, the LORD your God, am a jealous God, punishing the children for the sin of the fathers to the third and fourth generation of those who hate me. . . ."
Exod 20 [23]"Do not make any gods to be alongside me; do not make for yourselves gods of silver or gods of gold."
Exod 23 [13]"Be careful to do everything I have said to you. Do not invoke the names of other gods; do not let them be heard on your lips."
Lev 19 [4]"'Do not turn to idols or make gods of cast metal for yourselves. I am the LORD your God.'"
Lev 26 [1]"'Do not make idols or set up an image or a sacred stone for yourselves, and do not place a carved stone in your land to bow down before it. I am the LORD your God.'"
Lev 26 [30]"I will destroy your high places, cut down your incense altars and pile your dead bodies on the lifeless forms of your idols, and I will abhor you."
Deut 4 [19]And when you look up to the sky and see the sun, the moon and the stars—all the heavenly array—do not be enticed into bowing down to them and worshiping things the LORD your God has apportioned to all the nations under heaven. . . . [35]You were shown these things so that you might know that the LORD is God; besides him there is no other.
Deut 16 [21]Do not set up any wooden Asherah pole beside the altar you build to the LORD your God, [22]and do not erect a sacred stone, for these the LORD your God hates.
Deut 27 [15]"Cursed is the man who carves an image or casts an idol—a thing detestable to the LORD, the work of the craftsman's hands—and sets it up in secret."
Then all the people shall say, "Amen!"
Ps 81 [9]"You shall have no foreign god among you; you shall not bow down to an alien god."
Ps 89 [6]For who in the skies above can compare with the LORD? Who is like the LORD among the heavenly beings?
Ps 96 [5]For all the gods of the nations are idols, but the LORD made the heavens.
Ps 97 [6]The heavens proclaim his righteousness, and all the peoples see his glory.
[7]All who worship images are put to shame, those who boast in idols—worship him, all you gods!
[8]Zion hears and rejoices and the villages of Judah are glad because of your judgments, O LORD. [9]For you, O LORD, are the Most High over all the earth; you are exalted far above all gods.
Ps 115 [4]But their idols are silver and gold, made by the hands of men. [5]They have mouths, but cannot speak, eyes, but they cannot see; [6]they have ears, but cannot hear, noses, but they cannot smell; [7]they have hands, but cannot feel, feet, but they cannot walk; nor can they utter a sound with their throats. [8]Those who make them will be like them, and so will all who trust in them.
Ps 118 [8]It is better to take refuge in the LORD than to trust in man. [9]It is better to take refuge in the LORD than to trust in princes.
Ps 135 [15]The idols of the nations are silver and gold, made by the hands of men. [16]They have mouths, but cannot speak, eyes, but they cannot see; [17]they have ears, but cannot hear, nor is there breath in their mouths. [18]Those who make them will be like them, and so will all who trust in them.
Isa 19 [1]An oracle concerning Egypt: See, the LORD rides on a swift cloud and is coming to Egypt. The idols of Egypt tremble before him, and the hearts of the Egyptians melt within them.
Isa 40 [18]To whom, then, will you compare God? What image will you compare him to? [19]As for an idol, a craftsman casts it, and a goldsmith overlays it with gold and fashions silver chains for it. [20]A man too poor to present such an offering selects wood that will not rot. He looks for a skilled craftsman to set up an idol that will not topple.
[21]Do you not know? Have you not heard? Has it not been told you from the beginning? Have you not understood since the earth was founded? [22]He sits enthroned above the circle of the earth, and its people are like grasshoppers. He stretches out the heavens like a canopy, and spreads them out like a tent to live in. [23]He brings princes to naught and reduces the rulers of this world to nothing. [24]No sooner are they planted, no sooner are they sown, no sooner do they take root in the ground, than he blows on them and they wither, and a whirlwind sweeps them away like chaff.
[25]"To whom will you compare me? Or who is my equal?" says the Holy One. [26]Lift your eyes and look to the heavens:

Who created all these? He who brings out the starry host one by one, and calls them each by name. Because of his great power and mighty strength, not one of them is missing.
Isa 41 22"Bring in your idols to tell us what is going to happen. Tell us what the former things were, so that we may consider them and know their final outcome. Or declare to us the things to come, 23tell us what the future holds, so we may know that you are gods. Do something, whether good or bad, so that we will be dismayed and filled with fear. 24But you are less than nothing and your works are utterly worthless; he who chooses you is detestable."
Isa 42 17"But those who trust in idols, who say to images, 'You are our gods,' will be turned back in utter shame."
Isa 43 10"You are my witnesses," declares the LORD, "and my servant whom I have chosen, so that you may know and believe me and understand that I am he. Before me no god was formed, nor will there be one after me."
Isa 44 9All who make idols are nothing, and the things they treasure are worthless. Those who would speak up for them are blind; they are ignorant, to their own shame. 10Who shapes a god and casts an idol, which can profit him nothing? 11He and his kind will be put to shame; craftsmen are nothing but men. Let them all come together and take their stand; they will be brought down to terror and infamy.

12The blacksmith takes a tool and works with it in the coals; he shapes an idol with hammers, he forges it with the might of his arm. He gets hungry and loses his strength; he drinks no water and grows faint. 13The carpenter measures with a line and makes an outline with a marker; he roughs it out with chisels and marks it with compasses. He shapes it in the form of man, of man in all his glory, that it may dwell in a shrine. 14He cut down cedars, or perhaps took a cypress or oak. He let it grow among the trees of the forest, or planted a pine, and the rain made it grow. 15It is man's fuel for burning; some of it he takes and warms himself, he kindles a fire and bakes bread. But he also fashions a god and worships it; he makes an idol and bows down to it. 16Half of the wood he burns in the fire; over it he prepares his meal, he roasts his meat and eats his fill. He also warms himself and says, "Ah! I am warm; I see the fire." 17From the rest he makes a god, his idol; he bows down to it and worships. He prays to it and says, "Save me; you are my god." 18They know nothing, they understand nothing; their eyes are plastered over so they cannot see, and their minds closed so they cannot understand. 19No one stops to think, no one has the knowledge or understanding to say, "Half of it I used for fuel; I even baked bread over its coals, I roasted meat and I ate. Shall I make a detestable thing from what is left? Shall I bow down to a block of wood?" 20He feeds on ashes, a deluded heart misleads him; he cannot save himself, or say, "Is not this thing in my right hand a lie?"
Isa 45 5"I am the LORD, and there is no other; apart from me there is no God. I will strengthen you, though you have not acknowledged me, 6so that from the rising of the sun to the place of its setting men may know there is none besides me. I am the LORD, and there is no other. . . ."

14This is what the LORD says: "The products of Egypt and the merchandise of Cush, and those tall Sabeans—they will come over to you and will be yours; they will trudge behind you, coming over to you in chains. They will bow down before you and plead with you, saying, 'Surely God is with you, and there is no other; there is no other god.'"

15Truly you are a God who hides himself, O God and Savior of Israel. 16All the makers of idols will be put to shame and disgraced; they will go off into disgrace together. 17But Israel will be saved by the LORD with an everlasting salvation; you will never be put to shame or disgraced, to ages everlasting.

18For this is what the LORD says—he who created the heavens, he is God; he who fashioned and made the earth, he founded it; he did not create it to be empty, but formed it to be inhabited—he says: "I am the LORD, and there is no other."
Isa 46 1Bel bows down, Nebo stoops low; their idols are borne by beasts of burden. The images that are carried about are burdensome, a burden for the weary. 2They stoop and bow down together; unable to rescue the burden, they themselves go off into captivity.

3"Listen to me, O house of Jacob, all you who remain of the house of Israel, you whom I have upheld since you were conceived, and have carried since your birth. 4Even to your old age and gray hairs I am he, I am he who will sustain you. I have made you and I will carry you; I will sustain you and I will rescue you.

5"To whom will you compare me or count me equal? To whom will you liken me that we may be compared? 6Some pour out gold from their bags and weigh out silver on the scales; they hire a goldsmith to make it into a god, and they bow down and worship it. 7They lift it to their shoulders and carry it; they set it up in its place, and there it stands. From that spot it cannot move. Though one cries out to it, it does not answer; it cannot save him from his troubles."
Jer 10 11"Tell them this: 'These gods, who did not make the heavens and the earth, will perish from the earth and from under the heavens.'"
Hos 8 5"Throw out your calf-idol, O Samaria! My anger burns against them. How long will they be incapable of purity? 6They are from Israel! This calf—a craftsman has made it; it is not God. It will be broken in pieces, that calf of Samaria."
Acts 14 11When the crowd saw what Paul had done, they shouted in the Lycaonian language, "The gods have come down to us in human form!" 12Barnabas they called Zeus, and Paul they called Hermes because he was the chief speaker. 13The priest of Zeus, whose temple was just outside the city, brought bulls and wreaths to the city gates because he and the crowd wanted to offer sacrifices to them.

14But when the apostles Barnabas and Paul heard of this, they tore their clothes and rushed out into the crowd, shouting: 15"Men, why are you doing this? We too are only men, human like you. We are bringing you good news, telling you to turn from these worthless things to the living God, who made heaven and earth and sea and everything in them."
Acts 17 29"Therefore since we are God's offspring, we should not think that the divine being is like gold or silver or stone—an image made by man's design and skill."
Rom 1 25They exchanged the truth of God for a lie, and worshiped and served created things rather than the Creator—who is forever praised. Amen.
1 Cor 8 4So then, about eating food sacrificed to idols: We know that an idol is nothing at all in the world and that there is no God but one.
1 Thess 1 9for they themselves report what kind of reception you gave us. They tell how you turned to God from idols to serve the living and true God. . . .

C. The Name of God

1. The Idea of the Divine Name

a) The Divine Name Designates God Himself

Exod 3 15God also said to Moses, "Say to the Israelites, 'The LORD, the God of your fathers—the God of Abraham, the God of Isaac and the God of Jacob—has sent me to you.' This is my name forever, the name by which I am to be remembered from generation to generation."
Exod 6 3"I appeared to Abraham, to Isaac and to Jacob as God Almighty, but by my name the LORD I did not make myself known to them."
Exod 15 3"The LORD is a warrior; the LORD is his name."
1 Kings 8 42". . . for men will hear of your great name and your mighty hand and your outstretched arm—when he comes and prays toward this temple. . . ."
1 Kings 18 24"Then you call on the name of your god, and I will call on the name of the LORD. The god who answers by fire—he is God."

Then all the people said, "What you say is good."
Ps 20 1May the LORD answer you when you are in distress; may the name of the God of Jacob protect you.
Ps 54 1Save me, O God, by your name; vindicate me by your might.
Ps 83 18Let them know that you, whose name is the LORD—that you alone are the Most High over all the earth.
Isa 18 7At that time gifts will be brought to the LORD Almighty from a people tall and smooth-skinned, from a people feared far and wide, an aggressive nation of strange speech, whose land is divided by rivers—the gifts will be brought to Mount Zion, the place of the Name of the LORD Almighty.
Isa 30 27See, the Name of the LORD comes from afar, with burning anger and dense clouds of smoke; his lips are full of wrath, and his tongue is a consuming fire.

Isa 42 [8]"I am the LORD; that is my name! I will not give my glory to another or my praise to idols."
Isa 47 [4]Our Redeemer—the LORD Almighty is his name—is the Holy One of Israel.
Isa 48 [2]". . . you who call yourselves citizens of the holy city and rely on the God of Israel—the LORD Almighty is his name. . . ."
Jer 32 [18]"You show love to thousands but bring the punishment for the fathers' sins into the laps of their children after them. O great and powerful God, whose name is the LORD Almighty. . . ."
Jer 33 [2]"This is what the LORD says, he who made the earth, the LORD who formed it and established it—the LORD is his name. . . ."
Jer 44 [26]"But hear the word of the LORD, all Jews living in Egypt: 'I swear by my great name,' says the LORD, 'that no one from Judah living anywhere in Egypt will ever again invoke my name or swear, "As surely as the Sovereign LORD lives."'"
Jer 49 [13]"I swear by myself," declares the LORD, "that Bozrah will become a ruin and an object of horror, of reproach and of cursing; and all its towns will be in ruins forever."
Ezek 43 [8]"When they placed their threshold next to my threshold and their doorposts beside my doorposts, with only a wall between me and them, they defiled my holy name by their detestable practices. So I destroyed them in my anger."
Amos 5 [27]"Therefore I will send you into exile beyond Damascus," says the LORD, whose name is God Almighty.
Zech 14 [9]The LORD will be king over the whole earth. On that day there will be one LORD, and his name the only name.
Mal 2 [2]"If you do not listen, and if you do not set your heart to honor my name," says the LORD Almighty, "I will send a curse upon you, and I will curse your blessings. Yes, I have already cursed them, because you have not set your heart to honor me."
1 Tim 6 [1]All who are under the yoke of slavery should consider their masters worthy of full respect, so that God's name and our teaching may not be slandered.
Rev 3 [12]"Him who overcomes I will make a pillar in the temple of my God. Never again will he leave it. I will write on him the name of my God and the name of the city of my God, the new Jerusalem, which is coming down out of heaven from my God; and I will also write on him my new name."

b) The Divine Name Is the Greatest Name

(1) The Divine Name Endures Forever

Ps 135 [13]Your name, O LORD, endures forever, your renown, O LORD, through all generations.

(2) The Divine Name Is Awesome

Deut 28 [58]If you do not carefully follow all the words of this law, which are written in this book, and do not revere this glorious and awesome name—the LORD your God . . .
Ps 99 [3]Let them praise your great and awesome name—he is holy.
Ps 111 [9]He provided redemption for his people; he ordained his covenant forever—holy and awesome is his name.

(3) The Divine Name Is beyond Human Understanding

Judg 13 [18]He replied, "Why do you ask my name? It is beyond understanding."

(4) The Divine Name Is Exalted

Ps 138 [2]I will bow down toward your holy temple and will praise your name for your love and your faithfulness, for you have exalted above all things your name and your word.
Ps 148 [13]Let them praise the name of the LORD, for his name alone is exalted; his splendor is above the earth and the heavens.

(5) The Divine Name Is Glorious

Deut 28 [58]If you do not carefully follow all the words of this law, which are written in this book, and do not revere this glorious and awesome name—the LORD your God . . .
Neh 9 [5]And the Levites—Jeshua, Kadmiel, Bani, Hashabneiah, Sherebiah, Hodiah, Shebaniah and Pethahiah—said: "Stand up and praise the LORD your God, who is from everlasting to everlasting."

"Blessed be your glorious name, and may it be exalted above all blessing and praise."
Ps 66 [2]Sing the glory of his name; make his praise glorious!
Ps 79 [9]Help us, O God our Savior, for the glory of your name; deliver us and forgive our sins for your name's sake.

(6) The Divine Name Is Good

Ps 52 [9]I will praise you forever for what you have done; in your name I will hope, for your name is good. I will praise you in the presence of your saints.
Ps 54 [6]I will sacrifice a freewill offering to you; I will praise your name, O LORD, for it is good.

(7) The Divine Name Is Great

Josh 7 [9]"The Canaanites and the other people of the country will hear about this and they will surround us and wipe out our name from the earth. What then will you do for your own great name?"
1 Sam 12 [22]"For the sake of his great name the LORD will not reject his people, because the LORD was pleased to make you his own."
2 Chron 6 [32]"As for the foreigner who does not belong to your people Israel but has come from a distant land because of your great name and your mighty hand and your outstretched arm—when he comes and prays toward this temple . . ."
Ps 76 [1]In Judah God is known; his name is great in Israel.
Ps 99 [3]Let them praise your great and awesome name—he is holy.
Jer 44 [26]"But hear the word of the LORD, all Jews living in Egypt: 'I swear by my great name,' says the LORD, 'that no one from Judah living anywhere in Egypt will ever again invoke my name or swear, "As surely as the Sovereign LORD lives."'"
Ezek 36 [23]"'I will show the holiness of my great name, which has been profaned among the nations, the name you have profaned among them. Then the nations will know that I am the LORD, declares the Sovereign LORD, when I show myself holy through you before their eyes.'"
Mal 1 [11]"My name will be great among the nations, from the rising to the setting of the sun. In every place incense and pure offerings will be brought to my name, because my name will be great among the nations," says the LORD Almighty.

(8) The Divine Name Is Holy

Ps 30 [4]Sing to the LORD, you saints of his; praise his holy name.
Ps 33 [21]In him our hearts rejoice, for we trust in his holy name.
Ps 97 [12]Rejoice in the LORD, you who are righteous, and praise his holy name.
Ps 103 [1]Praise the LORD, O my soul; all my inmost being, praise his holy name.
Ps 105 [3]Glory in his holy name; let the hearts of those who seek the LORD rejoice.
Ps 106 [47]Save us, O LORD our God, and gather us from the nations, that we may give thanks to your holy name and glory in your praise.
Ps 111 [9]He provided redemption for his people; he ordained his covenant forever—holy and awesome is his name.
Isa 57 [15]For this is what the high and lofty One says—he who lives forever, whose name is holy: "I live in a high and holy place, but also with him who is contrite and lowly in spirit, to revive the spirit of the lowly and to revive the heart of the contrite."
Ezek 39 [7]"'I will make known my holy name among my people Israel. I will no longer let my holy name be profaned, and the nations will know that I the LORD am the Holy One in Israel.'"

(9) The Divine Name Is Jealously Preserved

Exod 20 [7]"You shall not misuse the name of the LORD your God, for the LORD will not hold anyone guiltless who misuses his name."
Exod 34 [14]"Do not worship any other god, for the LORD, whose name is Jealous, is a jealous God."
Lev 18 [21]"'Do not give any of your children to be sacrificed to Molech, for you must not profane the name of your God. I am the LORD.'"
Lev 19 [12]"'Do not swear falsely by my name and so profane the name of your God. I am the LORD.'"
Lev 20 [3]"'I will set my face against that man and I will cut him off from his people; for by giving his children to Molech, he has defiled my sanctuary and profaned my holy name.'"
Lev 24 [10]Now the son of an Israelite mother and an Egyptian father went out among the Israelites, and a fight broke out in the camp between him and an Israelite. [11]The son of the Israelite woman blasphemed the Name with a curse; so they brought him to Moses. (His mother's name was Shelomith, the

daughter of Dibri the Danite.) [12]They put him in custody until the will of the LORD should be made clear to them.

[13]Then the LORD said to Moses: [14]"Take the blasphemer outside the camp. All those who heard him are to lay their hands on his head, and the entire assembly is to stone him. [15]Say to the Israelites: 'If anyone curses his God, he will be held responsible; [16]anyone who blasphemes the name of the LORD must be put to death. The entire assembly must stone him. Whether an alien or native-born, when he blasphemes the Name, he must be put to death.'"

Ezek 20 [9]"'But for the sake of my name I did what would keep it from being profaned in the eyes of the nations they lived among and in whose sight I had revealed myself to the Israelites by bringing them out of Egypt.'"

Ezek 20 [21]"'But the children rebelled against me: They did not follow my decrees, they were not careful to keep my laws—although the man who obeys them will live by them—and they desecrated my Sabbaths. So I said I would pour out my wrath on them and spend my anger against them in the desert. [22]But I withheld my hand, and for the sake of my name I did what would keep it from being profaned in the eyes of the nations in whose sight I had brought them out.'"

Ezek 36 [20]"And wherever they went among the nations they profaned my holy name, for it was said of them, 'These are the LORD's people, and yet they had to leave his land.'"

Ezek 39 [7]"'I will make known my holy name among my people Israel. I will no longer let my holy name be profaned, and the nations will know that I the LORD am the Holy One in Israel.' . . . [25]"Therefore this is what the Sovereign LORD says: I will now bring Jacob back from captivity and will have compassion on all the people of Israel, and I will be zealous for my holy name."

(10) The Divine Name Is Majestic

Ps 8 [1]O LORD, our Lord, how majestic is your name in all the earth! You have set your glory above the heavens. . . . [9]O LORD, our Lord, how majestic is your name in all the earth!

Mic 5 [4]He will stand and shepherd his flock in the strength of the LORD, in the majesty of the name of the LORD his God. And they will live securely, for then his greatness will reach to the ends of the earth.

(11) The Divine Name Is Trustworthy

1 Sam 12 [22]"For the sake of his great name the LORD will not reject his people, because the LORD was pleased to make you his own."

Ps 23 [3]he restores my soul. He guides me in paths of righteousness for his name's sake.

Ps 31 [3]Since you are my rock and my fortress, for the sake of your name lead and guide me.

Ps 33 [21]In him our hearts rejoice, for we trust in his holy name.

Ps 119 [132]Turn to me and have mercy on me, as you always do to those who love your name.

Ps 124 [8]Our help is in the name of the LORD, the Maker of heaven and earth.

Ps 143 [11]For your name's sake, O LORD, preserve my life; in your righteousness, bring me out of trouble.

Isa 50 [10]Who among you fears the LORD and obeys the word of his servant? Let him who walks in the dark, who has no light, trust in the name of the LORD and rely on his God.

c) The Divine Name Reveals God's Nature

Gen 21 [33]Abraham planted a tamarisk tree in Beersheba, and there he called upon the name of the LORD, the Eternal God.

Exod 3 [14]God said to Moses, "I AM WHO I AM. This is what you are to say to the Israelites: 'I AM has sent me to you.'"

[15]God also said to Moses, "Say to the Israelites, 'The LORD, the God of your fathers—the God of Abraham, the God of Isaac and the God of Jacob—has sent me to you.' This is my name forever, the name by which I am to be remembered from generation to generation.

[16]"Go, assemble the elders of Israel and say to them, 'The LORD, the God of your fathers—the God of Abraham, Isaac and Jacob—appeared to me and said: I have watched over you and have seen what has been done to you in Egypt.'"

Exod 33 [19]And the LORD said, "I will cause all my goodness to pass in front of you, and I will proclaim my name, the LORD, in your presence. I will have mercy on whom I will have mercy, and I will have compassion on whom I will have compassion."

Exod 34 [14]"Do not worship any other god, for the LORD, whose name is Jealous, is a jealous God."

1 Chron 29 [16]"O LORD our God, as for all this abundance that we have provided for building you a temple for your Holy Name, it comes from your hand, and all of it belongs to you."

Ps 48 [10]Like your name, O God, your praise reaches to the ends of the earth; your right hand is filled with righteousness.

Ps 106 [8]Yet he saved them for his name's sake, to make his mighty power known.

Ps 124 [8]Our help is in the name of the LORD, the Maker of heaven and earth.

Prov 18 [10]The name of the LORD is a strong tower; the righteous run to it and are safe.

Isa 63 [16]But you are our Father, though Abraham does not know us or Israel acknowledge us; you, O LORD, are our Father, our Redeemer from of old is your name.

Amos 4 [13]He who forms the mountains, creates the wind, and reveals his thoughts to man, he who turns dawn to darkness, and treads the high places of the earth—the LORD God Almighty is his name.

d) The Divine Name Signifies God's Presence

Exod 23 [21]"Pay attention to him and listen to what he says. Do not rebel against him; he will not forgive your rebellion, since my Name is in him."

Deut 12 [5]But you are to seek the place the LORD your God will choose from among all your tribes to put his Name there for his dwelling. To that place you must go. . . .

Deut 12 [11]Then to the place the LORD your God will choose as a dwelling for his Name—there you are to bring everything I command you: your burnt offerings and sacrifices, your tithes and special gifts, and all the choice possessions you have vowed to the LORD.

Deut 14 [23]Eat the tithe of your grain, new wine and oil, and the firstborn of your herds and flocks in the presence of the LORD your God at the place he will choose as a dwelling for his Name, so that you may learn to revere the LORD your God always. [24]But if that place is too distant and you have been blessed by the LORD your God and cannot carry your tithe (because the place where the LORD will choose to put his Name is so far away) . . .

Deut 16 [5]You must not sacrifice the Passover in any town the LORD your God gives you [6]except in the place he will choose as a dwelling for his Name. There you must sacrifice the Passover in the evening, when the sun goes down, on the anniversary of your departure from Egypt. [7]Roast it and eat it at the place the LORD your God will choose. Then in the morning return to your tents. . . . [11]And rejoice before the LORD your God at the place he will choose as a dwelling for his Name—you, your sons and daughters, your menservants and maidservants, the Levites in your towns, and the aliens, the fatherless and the widows living among you.

2 Sam 7 [13]"'He is the one who will build a house for my Name, and I will establish the throne of his kingdom forever.'"

1 Kings 9 [3]The LORD said to him: "I have heard the prayer and plea you have made before me; I have consecrated this temple, which you have built, by putting my Name there forever. My eyes and my heart will always be there."

1 Kings 11 [36]"'I will give one tribe to his son so that David my servant may always have a lamp before me in Jerusalem, the city where I chose to put my Name.'"

2 Kings 21 [4]He built altars in the temple of the LORD, of which the LORD had said, "In Jerusalem I will put my Name."

2 Kings 21 [7]He took the carved Asherah pole he had made and put it in the temple, of which the LORD had said to David and to his son Solomon, "In this temple and in Jerusalem, which I have chosen out of all the tribes of Israel, I will put my Name forever."

2 Kings 23 [27]So the LORD said, "I will remove Judah also from my presence as I removed Israel, and I will reject Jerusalem, the city I chose, and this temple, about which I said, 'There shall my Name be.'"

2 Chron 7 [16]"I have chosen and consecrated this temple so that my Name may be there forever. My eyes and my heart will always be there."

Neh 1 [9]"'. . . but if you return to me and obey my commands, then even if your exiled people are at the farthest horizon, I will gather them from there and bring them to the place I have chosen as a dwelling for my Name.'"

Ps 75 [1]We give thanks to you, O God, we give thanks, for your Name is near; men tell of your wonderful deeds.
Isa 18 [7]At that time gifts will be brought to the LORD Almighty from a people tall and smooth-skinned, from a people feared far and wide, an aggressive nation of strange speech, whose land is divided by rivers—the gifts will be brought to Mount Zion, the place of the Name of the LORD Almighty.

e) The Divine Name Represents God's Power and Authority

Deut 18 [19]"If anyone does not listen to my words that the prophet speaks in my name, I myself will call him to account."
Ps 118 [10]All the nations surrounded me, but in the name of the LORD I cut them off. [11]They surrounded me on every side, but in the name of the LORD I cut them off. [12]They swarmed around me like bees, but they died out as quickly as burning thorns; in the name of the LORD I cut them off.
Ps 118 [26]Blessed is he who comes in the name of the LORD. From the house of the LORD we bless you.
Ps 124 [8]Our help is in the name of the LORD, the Maker of heaven and earth.
Prov 18 [10]The name of the LORD is a strong tower; the righteous run to it and are safe.
Jer 11 [21]"Therefore this is what the LORD says about the men of Anathoth who are seeking your life and saying, 'Do not prophesy in the name of the LORD or you will die by our hands.' . . ."
Jer 29 [9]"They are prophesying lies to you in my name. I have not sent them," declares the LORD.
Jer 51 [57]"I will make her officials and wise men drunk, her governors, officers and warriors as well; they will sleep forever and not awake," declares the King, whose name is the LORD Almighty.
Ezek 39 [7]"'I will make known my holy name among my people Israel. I will no longer let my holy name be profaned, and the nations will know that I the LORD am the Holy One in Israel.'"
Ezek 39 [25]"Therefore this is what the Sovereign LORD says: I will now bring Jacob back from captivity and will have compassion on all the people of Israel, and I will be zealous for my holy name."
Ezek 43 [8]"When they placed their threshold next to my threshold and their doorposts beside my doorposts, with only a wall between me and them, they defiled my holy name by their detestable practices. So I destroyed them in my anger."
Dan 9 [6]"We have not listened to your servants the prophets, who spoke in your name to our kings, our princes and our fathers, and to all the people of the land."
Amos 5 [8](he who made the Pleiades and Orion, who turns blackness into dawn and darkens day into night, who calls for the waters of the sea and pours them out over the face of the land—the LORD is his name. . . .)
Amos 9 [6]he who builds his lofty palace in the heavens and sets its foundation on the earth, who calls for the waters of the sea and pours them out over the face of the land—the LORD is his name.

f) The Divine Name Identifies God's People

Deut 18 [5]for the LORD your God has chosen them and their descendants out of all your tribes to stand and minister in the LORD's name always.
Deut 28 [10]Then all the peoples on earth will see that you are called by the name of the LORD, and they will fear you.
2 Chron 7 [14]". . . if my people, who are called by my name, will humble themselves and pray and seek my face and turn from their wicked ways, then will I hear from heaven and will forgive their sin and will heal their land."
Ezra 5 [1]Now Haggai the prophet and Zechariah the prophet, a descendant of Iddo, prophesied to the Jews in Judah and Jerusalem in the name of the God of Israel, who was over them.
Ps 61 [5]For you have heard my vows, O God; you have given me the heritage of those who fear your name.
Ps 118 [26]Blessed is he who comes in the name of the LORD. From the house of the LORD we bless you.
Isa 43 [6]"I will say to the north, 'Give them up!' and to the south, 'Do not hold them back.' Bring my sons from afar and my daughters from the ends of the earth—[7]everyone who is called by my name, whom I created for my glory, whom I formed and made."
Mic 4 [5]All the nations may walk in the name of their gods; we will walk in the name of the LORD our God for ever and ever.
Mic 5 [4]He will stand and shepherd his flock in the strength of the LORD, in the majesty of the name of the LORD his God. And they will live securely, for then his greatness will reach to the ends of the earth.

g) People Respond to the Divine Name

(1) They Are Protected by the Divine Name

Ps 20 [1]May the LORD answer you when you are in distress; may the name of the God of Jacob protect you.
Prov 18 [10]The name of the LORD is a strong tower; the righteous run to it and are safe.

(2) They Are Saved by the Divine Name

Ps 54 [1]Save me, O God, by your name; vindicate me by your might.
Joel 2 [32]"And everyone who calls on the name of the LORD will be saved; for on Mount Zion and in Jerusalem there will be deliverance, as the LORD has said, among the survivors whom the LORD calls."
Rom 10 [13]for, "Everyone who calls on the name of the Lord will be saved."

(3) They Bless Others in the Divine Name

2 Sam 6 [18]After he had finished sacrificing the burnt offerings and fellowship offerings, he blessed the people in the name of the LORD Almighty.
Ps 129 [8]May those who pass by not say, "The blessing of the LORD be upon you; we bless you in the name of the LORD."

(4) They Call on the Divine Name

1 Kings 18 [24]"Then you call on the name of your god, and I will call on the name of the LORD. The god who answers by fire—he is God."

Then all the people said, "What you say is good."
Ps 80 [18]Then we will not turn away from you; revive us, and we will call on your name.
Ps 99 [6]Moses and Aaron were among his priests, Samuel was among those who called on his name; they called on the LORD and he answered them.
Ps 105 [1]Give thanks to the LORD, call on his name; make known among the nations what he has done.
Ps 116 [4]Then I called on the name of the LORD: "O LORD, save me!"
Ps 116 [13]I will lift up the cup of salvation and call on the name of the LORD.
Ps 116 [17]I will sacrifice a thank offering to you and call on the name of the LORD.
Isa 12 [4]In that day you will say: "Give thanks to the LORD, call on his name; make known among the nations what he has done, and proclaim that his name is exalted."
Zech 13 [9]"This third I will bring into the fire; I will refine them like silver and test them like gold. They will call on my name and I will answer them; I will say, 'They are my people,' and they will say, 'The LORD is our God.'"

(5) They Confess the Divine Name

1 Kings 8 [33]"When your people Israel have been defeated by an enemy because they have sinned against you, and when they turn back to you and confess your name, praying and making supplication to you in this temple, [34]then hear from heaven and forgive the sin of your people Israel and bring them back to the land you gave to their fathers.

[35]"When the heavens are shut up and there is no rain because your people have sinned against you, and when they pray toward this place and confess your name and turn from their sin because you have afflicted them, [36]then hear from heaven and forgive the sin of your servants, your people Israel. Teach them the right way to live, and send rain on the land you gave your people for an inheritance."
2 Chron 6 [24]"When your people Israel have been defeated by an enemy because they have sinned against you and when they turn back and confess your name, praying and making supplication before you in this temple. . . .

[26]"When the heavens are shut up and there is no rain because your people have sinned against you, and when they pray toward this place and confess your name and turn from their sin because you have afflicted them. . . ."

2 Tim 2 [19]Nevertheless, God's solid foundation stands firm, sealed with this inscription: "The Lord knows those who are his," and, "Everyone who confesses the name of the Lord must turn away from wickedness."
Heb 13 [15]Through Jesus, therefore, let us continually offer to God a sacrifice of praise—the fruit of lips that confess his name.

(6) They Extol and Exalt the Divine Name

Ps 20 [5]We will shout for joy when you are victorious and will lift up our banners in the name of our God. May the LORD grant all your requests.
Ps 34 [3]Glorify the LORD with me; let us exalt his name together.
Ps 145 [2]Every day I will praise you and extol your name for ever and ever.
Ps 148 [13]Let them praise the name of the LORD, for his name alone is exalted; his splendor is above the earth and the heavens.
Isa 12 [4]In that day you will say: "Give thanks to the LORD, call on his name; make known among the nations what he has done, and proclaim that his name is exalted."
Isa 24 [15]Therefore in the east give glory to the LORD; exalt the name of the LORD, the God of Israel, in the islands of the sea.

(7) They Fear and Revere the Divine Name

1 Kings 8 [43]". . . then hear from heaven, your dwelling place, and do whatever the foreigner asks of you, so that all the peoples of the earth may know your name and fear you, as do your own people Israel, and may know that this house I have built bears your Name."
Ps 61 [5]For you have heard my vows, O God; you have given me the heritage of those who fear your name.
Ps 86 [11]Teach me your way, O LORD, and I will walk in your truth; give me an undivided heart, that I may fear your name.
Ps 102 [15]The nations will fear the name of the LORD, all the kings of the earth will revere your glory.
Isa 59 [19]From the west, men will fear the name of the LORD, and from the rising of the sun, they will revere his glory. For he will come like a pent-up flood that the breath of the LORD drives along.
Mic 6 [9]Listen! The LORD is calling to the city—and to fear your name is wisdom—"Heed the rod and the One who appointed it."
Mal 1 [14]"Cursed is the cheat who has an acceptable male in his flock and vows to give it, but then sacrifices a blemished animal to the Lord. For I am a great king," says the LORD Almighty, "and my name is to be feared among the nations."
Mal 4 [2]"But for you who revere my name, the sun of righteousness will rise with healing in its wings. And you will go out and leap like calves released from the stall."
Rev 11 [18]"The nations were angry; and your wrath has come. The time has come for judging the dead, and for rewarding your servants the prophets and your saints and those who reverence your name, both small and great—and for destroying those who destroy the earth."

(8) They Give Thanks to the Divine Name

Ps 106 [47]Save us, O LORD our God, and gather us from the nations, that we may give thanks to your holy name and glory in your praise.

(9) They Glory in and Glorify the Divine Name

1 Chron 16 [10]Glory in his holy name; let the hearts of those who seek the LORD rejoice.
Ps 29 [2]Ascribe to the LORD the glory due his name; worship the LORD in the splendor of his holiness.
Ps 86 [9]All the nations you have made will come and worship before you, O LORD; they will bring glory to your name. . . . [12]I will praise you, O Lord my God, with all my heart; I will glorify your name forever.
Ps 105 [3]Glory in his holy name; let the hearts of those who seek the LORD rejoice.
Ps 115 [1]Not to us, O LORD, not to us but to your name be the glory, because of your love and faithfulness.

(10) They Honor the Divine Name

Isa 26 [13]O LORD, our God, other lords besides you have ruled over us, but your name alone do we honor.
Jer 3 [17]"At that time they will call Jerusalem The Throne of the LORD, and all nations will gather in Jerusalem to honor the name of the LORD. No longer will they follow the stubbornness of their evil hearts."
Mal 2 [2]"If you do not listen, and if you do not set your heart to honor my name," says the LORD Almighty, "I will send a curse upon you, and I will curse your blessings. Yes, I have already cursed them, because you have not set your heart to honor me."
Mal 3 [16]Then those who feared the LORD talked with each other, and the LORD listened and heard. A scroll of remembrance was written in his presence concerning those who feared the LORD and honored his name.

(11) They Hope in the Divine Name

Ps 52 [9]I will praise you forever for what you have done; in your name I will hope, for your name is good. I will praise you in the presence of your saints.

(12) They Know and Make Known the Divine Name

Exod 9 [16]"But I have raised you up for this very purpose, that I might show you my power and that my name might be proclaimed in all the earth."
Deut 32 [3]I will proclaim the name of the LORD. Oh, praise the greatness of our God!
1 Kings 8 [43]". . . then hear from heaven, your dwelling place, and do whatever the foreigner asks of you, so that all the peoples of the earth may know your name and fear you, as do your own people Israel, and may know that this house I have built bears your Name."
Ps 22 [22]I will declare your name to my brothers; in the congregation I will praise you.
Ps 102 [21]So the name of the LORD will be declared in Zion and his praise in Jerusalem. . . .

(13) They Love the Divine Name

Ps 5 [11]But let all who take refuge in you be glad; let them ever sing for joy. Spread your protection over them, that those who love your name may rejoice in you.
Ps 69 [36]the children of his servants will inherit it, and those who love his name will dwell there.
Ps 119 [132]Turn to me and have mercy on me, as you always do to those who love your name.
Isa 56 [6]And foreigners who bind themselves to the LORD to serve him, to love the name of the LORD, and to worship him, all who keep the Sabbath without desecrating it and who hold fast to my covenant . . .

(14) They Make the Divine Name Their Heart's Desire

Isa 26 [8]Yes, LORD, walking in the way of your laws, we wait for you; your name and renown are the desire of our hearts.

(15) They Praise the Divine Name

Ps 30 [4]Sing to the LORD, you saints of his; praise his holy name.
Ps 44 [8]In God we make our boast all day long, and we will praise your name forever.
Ps 61 [8]Then will I ever sing praise to your name and fulfill my vows day after day.
Ps 74 [21]Do not let the oppressed retreat in disgrace; may the poor and needy praise your name.
Ps 97 [12]Rejoice in the LORD, you who are righteous, and praise his holy name.
Ps 99 [3]Let them praise your great and awesome name—he is holy.
Ps 103 [1]Praise the LORD, O my soul; all my inmost being, praise his holy name.
Ps 113 [1]Praise the LORD. Praise, O servants of the LORD, praise the name of the LORD. [2]Let the name of the LORD be praised, both now and forevermore. [3]From the rising of the sun to the place where it sets, the name of the LORD is to be praised.
Ps 145 [1]I will exalt you, my God the King; I will praise your name for ever and ever. . . . [21]My mouth will speak in praise of the LORD. Let every creature praise his holy name for ever and ever.
Ps 149 [3]Let them praise his name with dancing and make music to him with tambourine and harp.

(16) They Rejoice in the Divine Name

Ps 89 [16]They rejoice in your name all day long; they exult in your righteousness.

(17) They Remember the Divine Name

Ps 119 [55]In the night I remember your name, O LORD, and I will keep your law.

(18) They Seek the Divine Name

Ps 83 [16]Cover their faces with shame so that men will seek your name, O LORD.

(19) They Sing about and to the Divine Name

2 Sam 22 [50]"Therefore I will praise you, O LORD, among the nations; I will sing praises to your name."
Ps 7 [17]I will give thanks to the LORD because of his righteousness and will sing praise to the name of the LORD Most High.
Ps 18 [49]Therefore I will praise you among the nations, O LORD; I will sing praises to your name.
Ps 66 [2]Sing the glory of his name; make his praise glorious!
Ps 68 [4]Sing to God, sing praise to his name, extol him who rides on the clouds—his name is the LORD—and rejoice before him.
Ps 69 [30]I will praise God's name in song and glorify him with thanksgiving.
Ps 92 [1]It is good to praise the LORD and make music to your name, O Most High. . . .
Rom 15 [9]so that the Gentiles may glorify God for his mercy, as it is written: "Therefore I will praise you among the Gentiles; I will sing hymns to your name."

(20) They Stand in Awe of the Divine Name

Mal 2 [5]"My covenant was with him, a covenant of life and peace, and I gave them to him; this called for reverence and he revered me and stood in awe of my name."

(21) They Swear by the Divine Name

Gen 14 [22]But Abram said to the king of Sodom, "I have raised my hand to the LORD, God Most High, Creator of heaven and earth, and have taken an oath. . . ."
Gen 31 [53]"May the God of Abraham and the God of Nahor, the God of their father, judge between us."
So Jacob took an oath in the name of the Fear of his father Isaac.
Deut 6 [13]Fear the LORD your God, serve him only and take your oaths in his name.
Deut 10 [20]Fear the LORD your God and serve him. Hold fast to him and take your oaths in his name.
1 Sam 20 [42]Jonathan said to David, "Go in peace, for we have sworn friendship with each other in the name of the LORD, saying, 'The LORD is witness between you and me, and between your descendants and my descendants forever.'" Then David left, and Jonathan went back to the town.
Ps 63 [11]But the king will rejoice in God; all who swear by God's name will praise him, while the mouths of liars will be silenced.
Jer 12 [16]"And if they learn well the ways of my people and swear by my name, saying, 'As surely as the LORD lives'—even as they once taught my people to swear by Baal—then they will be established among my people."
Jer 44 [26]"But hear the word of the LORD, all Jews living in Egypt: 'I swear by my great name,' says the LORD, 'that no one from Judah living anywhere in Egypt will ever again invoke my name or swear, "As surely as the Sovereign LORD lives."'"
Zech 5 [4]"The LORD Almighty declares, 'I will send it out, and it will enter the house of the thief and the house of him who swears falsely by my name. It will remain in his house and destroy it, both its timbers and its stones.'"
Heb 6 [13]When God made his promise to Abraham, since there was no one greater for him to swear by, he swore by himself. . . .

(22) They Trust in the Divine Name

Ps 20 [7]Some trust in chariots and some in horses, but we trust in the name of the LORD our God.
Ps 33 [21]In him our hearts rejoice, for we trust in his holy name.
Isa 50 [10]Who among you fears the LORD and obeys the word of his servant? Let him who walks in the dark, who has no light, trust in the name of the LORD and rely on his God.
Zeph 3 [12]But I will leave within you the meek and humble, who trust in the name of the LORD.

(23) They Walk in the Divine Name

Zech 10 [12]"I will strengthen them in the LORD and in his name they will walk," declares the LORD.

h) The Divine Name Relates to Jesus' Name

See p. 132b, The Name of Christ

2. The Single Names of God

1) Almighty (Hb: Shaddai)

Gen 49 [25]". . . because of your father's God, who helps you, because of the Almighty, who blesses you with blessings of the heavens above, blessings of the deep that lies below, blessings of the breast and womb."
Num 24 [4]". . . the oracle of the one who hears the words of God, who sees a vision from the Almighty, who falls prostrate and whose eyes are opened . . ."
Num 24 [16]". . . the oracle of one who hears the words of God, who has knowledge from the Most High, who sees a vision from the Almighty, who falls prostrate, and whose eyes are opened . . ."
Ruth 1 [20]"Don't call me Naomi," she told them. "Call me Mara, because the Almighty has made my life very bitter. [21]I went away full, but the LORD has brought me back empty. Why call me Naomi? The LORD has afflicted me; the Almighty has brought misfortune upon me."
Job 8 [3]"Does God pervert justice? Does the Almighty pervert what is right?"
Job 8 [5]"But if you will look to God and plead with the Almighty . . ."
Job 11 [7]"Can you fathom the mysteries of God? Can you probe the limits of the Almighty?"
Job 22 [23]"If you return to the Almighty, you will be restored: If you remove wickedness far from your tent [24]and assign your nuggets to the dust, your gold of Ophir to the rocks in the ravines, [25]then the Almighty will be your gold, the choicest silver for you. [26]Surely then you will find delight in the Almighty and will lift up your face to God."
Job 33 [4]"The Spirit of God has made me; the breath of the Almighty gives me life."
Job 34 [10]"So listen to me, you men of understanding. Far be it from God to do evil, from the Almighty to do wrong. . . . [12]It is unthinkable that God would do wrong, that the Almighty would pervert justice."
Ps 68 [14]When the Almighty scattered the kings in the land, it was like snow fallen on Zalmon.
Ps 91 [1]He who dwells in the shelter of the Most High will rest in the shadow of the Almighty.
Isa 13 [6]Wail, for the day of the LORD is near; it will come like destruction from the Almighty.
Ezek 1 [24]When the creatures moved, I heard the sound of their wings, like the roar of rushing waters, like the voice of the Almighty, like the tumult of an army. When they stood still, they lowered their wings.
Joel 1 [15]Alas for that day! For the day of the LORD is near; it will come like destruction from the Almighty.

2) Almighty (Gk: Pantokrator)

Rev 1 [8]"I am the Alpha and the Omega," says the Lord God, "who is, and who was, and who is to come, the Almighty."

3) God (Hb: El)

Gen 16 [13]She gave this name to the LORD who spoke to her: "You are the God who sees me," for she said, "I have now seen the One who sees me."
Exod 34 [14]"Do not worship any other god, for the LORD, whose name is Jealous, is a jealous **God**."
Num 23 [19]"God is not a man, that he should lie, nor a son of man, that he should change his mind. Does he speak and then not act? Does he promise and not fulfill?"
Deut 4 [24]For the LORD your God is a consuming fire, a jealous God.
Deut 32 [4]He is the Rock, his works are perfect, and all his ways are just. A faithful God who does no wrong, upright and just is he.
2 Sam 22 [33]"It is God who arms me with strength and makes my way perfect."
Neh 9 [31]"But in your great mercy you did not put an end to

them or abandon them, for you are a gracious and merciful God."
Job 5 8"But if it were I, I would appeal to God; I would lay my cause before him."
Job 8 3"Does God pervert justice? Does the Almighty pervert what is right?"
Job 8 5"But if you will look to God and plead with the Almighty . . ."
Job 8 13"Such is the destiny of all who forget God; so perishes the hope of the godless."
Job 8 20"Surely God does not reject a blameless man or strengthen the hands of evildoers."
Job 34 10"So listen to me, you men of understanding. Far be it from God to do evil, from the Almighty to do wrong."
Ps 5 4You are not a God who takes pleasure in evil; with you the wicked cannot dwell.
Ps 18 30As for God, his way is perfect; the word of the LORD is flawless. He is a shield for all who take refuge in him.
Ps 19 1The heavens declare the glory of God; the skies proclaim the work of his hands.
Ps 31 5Into your hands I commit my spirit; redeem me, O LORD, the God of truth.
Ps 136 26Give thanks to the God of heaven. His love endures forever.
Ps 139 23Search me, O God, and know my heart; test me and know my anxious thoughts.
Ps 150 1Praise the LORD. Praise God in his sanctuary; praise him in his mighty heavens.
Isa 5 16But the LORD Almighty will be exalted by his justice, and the holy God will show himself holy by his righteousness.
Isa 43 12"I have revealed and saved and proclaimed—I, and not some foreign god among you. You are my witnesses," declares the LORD, "that I am God."
Jer 51 56"A destroyer will come against Babylon; her warriors will be captured, and their bows will be broken. For the LORD is a God of retribution; he will repay in full."
Hos 1 10"Yet the Israelites will be like the sand on the seashore, which cannot be measured or counted. In the place where it was said to them, 'You are not my people,' they will be called 'sons of the living God.'"
Hos 11 9"I will not carry out my fierce anger, nor will I turn and devastate Ephraim. For I am God, and not man—the Holy One among you. I will not come in wrath."
Jon 4 2He prayed to the LORD, "O LORD, is this not what I said when I was still at home? That is why I was so quick to flee to Tarshish. I knew that you are a gracious and compassionate God, slow to anger and abounding in love, a God who relents from sending calamity."
Mic 7 18Who is a God like you, who pardons sin and forgives the transgression of the remnant of his inheritance? You do not stay angry forever but delight to show mercy.
Nah 1 2The LORD is a jealous and avenging God; the LORD takes vengeance and is filled with wrath. The LORD takes vengeance on his foes and maintains his wrath against his enemies.

4) God (Ar: Elah)

Ezra 5 1Now Haggai the prophet and Zechariah the prophet, a descendant of Iddo, prophesied to the Jews in Judah and Jerusalem in the name of the God of Israel, who was over them.
Ezra 5 8The king should know that we went to the district of Judah, to the temple of the great God. The people are building it with large stones and placing the timbers in the walls. The work is being carried on with diligence and is making rapid progress under their direction.
Ezra 6 9Whatever is needed—young bulls, rams, male lambs for burnt offerings to the God of heaven, and wheat, salt, wine and oil, as requested by the priests in Jerusalem—must be given them daily without fail, 10 so that they may offer sacrifices pleasing to the God of heaven and pray for the well-being of the king and his sons.
Ezra 7 12Artaxerxes, king of kings, To Ezra the priest, a teacher of the Law of the God of heaven: Greetings.
Ezra 7 26Whoever does not obey the law of your God and the law of the king must surely be punished by death, banishment, confiscation of property, or imprisonment.
Dan 2 47The king said to Daniel, "Surely your **God** is the **God** of gods and the Lord of kings and a revealer of mysteries, for you were able to reveal this mystery."
Dan 6 22"My God sent his angel, and he shut the mouths of the lions. They have not hurt me, because I was found innocent in his sight. Nor have I ever done any wrong before you, O king."
23The king was overjoyed and gave orders to lift Daniel out of the den. And when Daniel was lifted from the den, no wound was found on him, because he had trusted in his God. . . .
25Then King Darius wrote to all the peoples, nations and men of every language throughout the land: "May you prosper greatly!
26"I issue a decree that in every part of my kingdom people must fear and reverence the God of Daniel. For he is the living God and he endures forever; his kingdom will not be destroyed, his dominion will never end."

5) God (Hb: Eloah)

Deut 32 15Jeshurun grew fat and kicked; filled with food, he became heavy and sleek. He abandoned the God who made him and rejected the Rock his Savior.
Neh 9 17"They refused to listen and failed to remember the miracles you performed among them. They became stiff-necked and in their rebellion appointed a leader in order to return to their slavery. But you are a forgiving God, gracious and compassionate, slow to anger and abounding in love. Therefore you did not desert them. . . ."
Job 4 17"'Can a mortal be more righteous than God? Can a man be more pure than his Maker?'"
Job 11 7"Can you fathom the mysteries of God? Can you probe the limits of the Almighty?"
Job 19 26"And after my skin has been destroyed, yet in my flesh I will see God. . . ."
Job 22 12"Is not God in the heights of heaven? And see how lofty are the highest stars!"
Job 33 12"But I tell you, in this you are not right, for God is greater than man."
Job 37 22"Out of the north he comes in golden splendor; God comes in awesome majesty."
Ps 50 22"Consider this, you who forget God, or I will tear you to pieces, with none to rescue. . . ."
Prov 30 5"Every word of God is flawless; he is a shield to those who take refuge in him."
Isa 44 8"Do not tremble, do not be afraid. Did I not proclaim this and foretell it long ago? You are my witnesses. Is there any God besides me? No, there is no other Rock; I know not one."

6) God (Hb: Elohim)

Gen 1 1In the beginning God created the heavens and the earth. 2Now the earth was formless and empty, darkness was over the surface of the deep, and the Spirit of God was hovering over the waters. . . .
27So God created man in his own image, in the image of God he created him; male and female he created them.
28God blessed them and said to them, "Be fruitful and increase in number; fill the earth and subdue it. Rule over the fish of the sea and the birds of the air and over every living creature that moves on the ground."
29Then God said, "I give you every seed-bearing plant on the face of the whole earth and every tree that has fruit with seed in it. They will be yours for food. . . ."
31God saw all that he had made, and it was very good. And there was evening, and there was morning—the sixth day.
Gen 9 6"Whoever sheds the blood of man, by man shall his blood be shed; for in the image of God has God made man."
Gen 24 3"I want you to swear by the LORD, the God of heaven and the God of earth, that you will not get a wife for my son from the daughters of the Canaanites, among whom I am living. . . . 7The LORD, the God of heaven, who brought me out of my father's household and my native land and who spoke to me and promised me on oath, saying, 'To your offspring I will give this land'—he will send his angel before you so that you can get a wife for my son from there."
Exod 20 2"I am the LORD your God, who brought you out of Egypt, out of the land of slavery."
Num 27 16"May the LORD, the God of the spirits of all mankind, appoint a man over this community. . . ."

Deut 2 7The Lord your God has blessed you in all the work of your hands. He has watched over your journey through this vast desert. These forty years the LORD your God has been with you, and you have not lacked anything.
Deut 2 30But Sihon king of Heshbon refused to let us pass through. For the LORD your God had made his spirit stubborn and his heart obstinate in order to give him into your hands, as he has now done. 33. . . the LORD our God delivered him over to us and we struck him down, together with his sons and his whole army.
Deut 3 22"Do not be afraid of them; the LORD your God himself will fight for you."
Deut 4 35You were shown these things so that you might know that the LORD is God; besides him there is no other.
Deut 23 5However, the LORD your God would not listen to Balaam but turned the curse into a blessing for you, because the LORD your God loves you.
Josh 24 19Joshua said to the people, "You are not able to serve the LORD. He is a holy **God**; he is a jealous God. He will not forgive your rebellion and your sins."
1 Sam 6 20and the men of Beth Shemesh asked, "Who can stand in the presence of the LORD, this holy God? To whom will the ark go up from here?"
1 Sam 17 26David asked the men standing near him, "What will be done for the man who kills this Philistine and removes this disgrace from Israel? Who is this uncircumcised Philistine that he should defy the armies of the living God?"
Ps 7 9O righteous **God**, who searches minds and hearts, bring to an end the violence of the wicked and make the righteous secure. 10My shield is **God** Most High, who saves the upright in heart. 11**God** is a righteous judge, a God who expresses his wrath every day.
Ps 42 9I say to God my Rock, "Why have you forgotten me? Why must I go about mourning, oppressed by the enemy?"
Ps 47 7For God is the King of all the earth; sing to him a psalm of praise. 8God reigns over the nations; God is seated on his holy throne. 9The nobles of the nations assemble as the people of the God of Abraham, for the kings of the earth belong to God; he is greatly exalted.
Ps 50 6And the heavens proclaim his righteousness, for God himself is judge.
Ps 77 13Your ways, O God, are holy. What god is so great as our God? 14You are the God who performs miracles; you display your power among the peoples.
Ps 99 9Exalt the LORD our God and worship at his holy mountain, for the LORD our God is holy.
Eccles 12 13Now all has been heard; here is the conclusion of the matter: Fear God and keep his commandments, for this is the whole duty of man. 14For God will bring every deed into judgment, including every hidden thing, whether it is good or evil.
Isa 37 16"O LORD Almighty, God of Israel, enthroned between the cherubim, you alone are God over all the kingdoms of the earth. You have made heaven and earth."
Isa 40 28Do you not know? Have you not heard? The LORD is the everlasting God, the Creator of the ends of the earth. He will not grow tired or weary, and his understanding no one can fathom.
Isa 41 13"For I am the LORD, your God, who takes hold of your right hand and says to you, Do not fear; I will help you."
Isa 45 21"Declare what is to be, present it—let them take counsel together. Who foretold this long ago, who declared it from the distant past? Was it not I, the LORD? And there is no **God** apart from me, a righteous God and a Savior; there is none but me."
Isa 46 9"Remember the former things, those of long ago; I am God, and there is no other; I am **God**, and there is none like me."
Isa 49 5And now the LORD says—he who formed me in the womb to be his servant to bring Jacob back to him and gather Israel to himself, for I am honored in the eyes of the LORD and my God has been my strength . . .
Isa 52 10The LORD will lay bare his holy arm in the sight of all the nations, and all the ends of the earth will see the salvation of our God.
Jer 3 23"Surely the idolatrous commotion on the hills and mountains is a deception; surely in the LORD our God is the salvation of Israel."
Jer 32 27"I am the LORD, the God of all mankind. Is anything too hard for me?"

7) God (Gk: Theos)

Matt 1 23"The virgin will be with child and will give birth to a son, and they will call him Immanuel"—which means, "God with us."
Matt 5 8"Blessed are the pure in heart, for they will see God. 9Blessed are the peacemakers, for they will be called sons of God."
Matt 23 22"And he who swears by heaven swears by God's throne and by the one who sits on it."
Mark 10 27Jesus looked at them and said, "With man this is impossible, but not with God; all things are possible with God."
Mark 12 29"The most important one," answered Jesus, "is this: 'Hear, O Israel, the Lord our God, the Lord is one. 30Love the Lord your God with all your heart and with all your soul and with all your mind and with all your strength.'"
Luke 1 47"and my spirit rejoices in God my Savior. . . ."
John 3 16"For God so loved the world that he gave his one and only Son, that whoever believes in him shall not perish but have eternal life."
John 4 24"God is spirit, and his worshipers must worship in spirit and in truth."
Acts 17 24"The God who made the world and everything in it is the Lord of heaven and earth and does not live in temples built by hands."
Rom 1 20For since the creation of the world God's invisible qualities—his eternal power and divine nature—have been clearly seen, being understood from what has been made, so that men are without excuse.

21For although they knew God, they neither glorified him as God nor gave thanks to him, but their thinking became futile and their foolish hearts were darkened. . . . 25They exchanged the truth of God for a lie, and worshiped and served created things rather than the Creator—who is forever praised. Amen.
Rom 4 21being fully persuaded that God had power to do what he had promised.
Rom 11 33Oh, the depth of the riches of the wisdom and knowledge of God! How unsearchable his judgments, and his paths beyond tracing out! 34"Who has known the mind of the Lord? Or who has been his counselor?" 35"Who has ever given to God, that God should repay him?" 36For from him and through him and to him are all things. To him be the glory forever! Amen.
1 Cor 2 10but God has revealed it to us by his Spirit.

The Spirit searches all things, even the deep things of God. 11For who among men knows the thoughts of a man except the man's spirit within him? In the same way no one knows the thoughts of God except the Spirit of God. 12We have not received the spirit of the world but the Spirit who is from God, that we may understand what God has freely given us.
1 Cor 15 28When he has done this, then the Son himself will be made subject to him who put everything under him, so that God may be all in all.
2 Cor 4 6For God, who said, "Let light shine out of darkness," made his light shine in our hearts to give us the light of the knowledge of the glory of God in the face of Christ.
2 Cor 13 14May the grace of the Lord Jesus Christ, and the love of God, and the fellowship of the Holy Spirit be with you all.
Gal 3 20A mediator, however, does not represent just one party; but God is one.
Eph 4 6one God and Father of all, who is over all and through all and in all.
Col 1 9For this reason, since the day we heard about you, we have not stopped praying for you and asking God to fill you with the knowledge of his will through all spiritual wisdom and understanding.
1 Tim 6 15which God will bring about in his own time—God, the blessed and only Ruler, the King of kings and Lord of Lords, 16who alone is immortal and who lives in unapproachable light, whom no one has seen or can see. To him be honor and might forever. Amen.
Heb 11 6And without faith it is impossible to please God,

because anyone who comes to him must believe that he exists and that he rewards those who earnestly seek him.
James 2 [19]You believe that there is one God. Good! Even the demons believe that—and shudder.
James 4 [8]Come near to God and he will come near to you. Wash your hands, you sinners, and purify your hearts, you double-minded.
1 Pet 5 [5]Young men, in the same way be submissive to those who are older. All of you, clothe yourselves with humility toward one another, because, "God opposes the proud but gives grace to the humble."
2 Pet 3 [5]But they deliberately forget that long ago by God's word the heavens existed and the earth was formed out of water and by water.
1 John 3 [20]whenever our hearts condemn us. For God is greater than our hearts, and he knows everything.
Rev 21 [3]And I heard a loud voice from the throne saying, "Now the dwelling of God is with men, and he will live with them. They will be his people, and God himself will be with them and be their God."

8) Lord (Hb: Adon)

Ps 136 [3]Give thanks to the Lord of lords: His love endures forever.
Isa 10 [33]See, the Lord, the LORD Almighty, will lop off the boughs with great power. The lofty trees will be felled, the tall ones will be brought low.
Mal 3 [1]"See, I will send my messenger, who will prepare the way before me. Then suddenly the Lord you are seeking will come to his temple; the messenger of the covenant, whom you desire, will come," says the LORD Almighty.

9) Lord (Hb: Adonai)

Exod 34 [9]"O Lord, if I have found favor in your eyes," he said, "then let the Lord go with us. Although this is a stiff-necked people, forgive our wickedness and our sin, and take us as your inheritance."
Josh 7 [8]"O Lord, what can I say, now that Israel has been routed by its enemies?"
Judg 6 [15]"But Lord," Gideon asked, "how can I save Israel? My clan is the weakest in Manasseh, and I am the least in my family."
Neh 4 [14]After I looked things over, I stood up and said to the nobles, the officials and the rest of the people, "Don't be afraid of them. Remember the Lord, who is great and awesome, and fight for your brothers, your sons and your daughters, your wives and your homes."
Job 28 [28]"And he said to man, 'The fear of the Lord—that is wisdom, and to shun evil is understanding.'"
Ps 2 [4]The One enthroned in heaven laughs; the Lord scoffs at them.
Ps 35 [23]Awake, and rise to my defense! Contend for me, my God and Lord.
Ps 54 [4]Surely God is my help; the Lord is the one who sustains me.
Ps 68 [17]The chariots of God are tens of thousands and thousands of thousands; the Lord has come from Sinai into his sanctuary.
Ps 86 [3]Have mercy on me, O Lord, for I call to you all day long. [4]Bring joy to your servant, for to you, O Lord, I lift up my soul. [5]You are forgiving and good, O Lord, abounding in love to all who call to you.
Ps 130 [6]My soul waits for the Lord more than watchmen wait for the morning, more than watchmen wait for the morning.
Ps 147 [5]Great is our Lord and mighty in power; his understanding has no limit.
Isa 6 [1]In the year that King Uzziah died, I saw the Lord seated on a throne, high and exalted, and the train of his robe filled the temple.
Dan 9 [4]I prayed to the Lord my God and confessed: "O LORD, the great and awesome God, who keeps his covenant of love with all who love him and obey his commands. . . ."
Dan 9 [19]"O Lord, listen! O Lord, forgive! O Lord, hear and act! For your sake, O my God, do not delay, because your city and your people bear your Name."
Hos 12 [14]But Ephraim has bitterly provoked him to anger; his Lord will leave upon him the guilt of his bloodshed and will repay him for his contempt.
Mic 4 [13]"Rise and thresh, O Daughter of Zion, for I will give you horns of iron; I will give you hoofs of bronze and you will break to pieces many nations." You will devote their ill-gotten gains to the LORD, their wealth to the LORD of all the earth.
Zech 4 [14]So he said, "These are the two who are anointed to serve the Lord of all the earth."
Mal 1 [12]"But you profane it by saying of the Lord's table, 'It is defiled,' and of its food, 'It is contemptible.'"

10) Lord (Hb: Yah)

Exod 15 [2]"The LORD is my strength and my song; he has become my salvation. He is my God, and I will praise him, my father's God, and I will exalt him."
Ps 68 [4]Sing to God, sing praise to his name, extol him who rides on the clouds—his name is the LORD—and rejoice before him.
Ps 94 [12]Blessed is the man you discipline, O LORD, the man you teach from your law. . . .
Ps 104 [35]But may sinners vanish from the earth and the wicked be no more. Praise the LORD, O my soul. Praise the LORD.
Ps 115 [17]It is not the dead who praise the LORD, those who go down to silence; [18]it is we who extol the LORD, both now and forevermore. Praise the LORD.
Ps 118 [14]The LORD is my strength and my song; he has become my salvation.
Ps 118 [17]I will not die but live, and will proclaim what the LORD has done. [18]The LORD has chastened me severely, but he has not given me over to death. [19]Open for me the gates of righteousness; I will enter and give thanks to the LORD.
Ps 135 [4]For the LORD has chosen Jacob to be his own, Israel to be his treasured possession.

11) Lord (Hb: Yahweh)

Gen 4 [26]Seth also had a son, and he named him Enosh. At that time men began to call on the name of the LORD.
Exod 3 [14]God said to Moses, "I AM who I AM. This is what you are to say to the Israelites: 'I AM has sent me to you.'"

[15]God also said to Moses, "Say to the Israelites, 'The LORD, the God of your fathers—the God of Abraham, the God of Isaac and the God of Jacob—has sent me to you.' This is my name forever, the name by which I am to be remembered from generation to generation."
Exod 6 [2]God also said to Moses, "I am the LORD. [3]I appeared to Abraham, to Isaac and to Jacob as God Almighty, but by my name the LORD I did not make myself known to them."
Exod 15 [11]"Who among the gods is like you, O LORD? Who is like you—majestic in holiness, awesome in glory, working wonders?"
Exod 20 [2]"I am the LORD your God, who brought you out of Egypt, out of the land of slavery."
Exod 33 [19]And the LORD said, "I will cause all my goodness to pass in front of you, and I will proclaim my name, the LORD, in your presence. I will have mercy on whom I will have mercy, and I will have compassion on whom I will have compassion."
Exod 34 [5]Then the LORD came down in the cloud and stood there with him and proclaimed his name, the LORD. [6]And he passed in front of Moses, proclaiming, "The LORD, the LORD, the compassionate and gracious God, slow to anger, abounding in love and faithfulness, [7]maintaining love to thousands, and forgiving wickedness, rebellion and sin. Yet he does not leave the guilty unpunished; he punishes the children and their children for the sin of the fathers to the third and fourth generation."
Deut 10 [17]For the LORD your God is God of gods and Lord of lords, the great God, mighty and awesome, who shows no partiality and accepts no bribes.
Deut 28 [10]Then all the peoples on earth will see that you are called by the name of the LORD, and they will fear you.
Judg 8 [23]But Gideon told them, "I will not rule over you, nor will my son rule over you. The LORD will rule over you."
1 Sam 12 [12]"But when you saw that Nahash king of the Ammonites was moving against you, you said to me, 'No, we want a king to rule over us'—even though the LORD your God was your king."

1 Kings 2 3"and observe what the LORD your God requires: Walk in his ways, and keep his decrees and commands, his laws and requirements, as written in the Law of Moses, so that you may prosper in all you do and wherever you go. . . ."
2 Chron 7 11When Solomon had finished the temple of the LORD and the royal palace, and had succeeded in carrying out all he had in mind to do in the temple of the LORD and in his own palace, 12the LORD appeared to him at night and said:

"I have heard your prayer and have chosen this place for myself as a temple for sacrifices.

13"When I shut up the heavens so that there is no rain, or command locusts to devour the land or send a plague among my people, 14if my people, who are called by my name, will humble themselves and pray and seek my face and turn from their wicked ways, then will I hear from heaven and will forgive their sin and will heal their land. 15Now my eyes will be open and my ears attentive to the prayers offered in this place. 16I have chosen and consecrated this temple so that my Name may be there forever. My eyes and my heart will always be there."
Ps 10 16The LORD is King for ever and ever; the nations will perish from his land.
Ps 103 6The LORD works righteousness and justice for all the oppressed.
Ps 110 1The **LORD** says to my Lord: "Sit at my right hand until I make your enemies a footstool for your feet."
Ps 130 3If you, O **LORD**, kept a record of sins, O Lord, who could stand? 4But with you there is forgiveness; therefore you are feared. 5I wait for the LORD, my soul waits, and in his word I put my hope.
Ps 146 10The **LORD** reigns forever, your God, O Zion, for all generations. Praise the LORD.
Prov 1 7The fear of the LORD is the beginning of knowledge, but fools despise wisdom and discipline.
Isa 33 22For the LORD is our judge, the LORD is our lawgiver, the LORD is our king; it is he who will save us.
Isa 43 3"For I am the LORD, your God, the Holy One of Israel, your Savior; I give Egypt for your ransom, Cush and Seba in your stead."
Isa 45 24"They will say of me, 'In the LORD alone are righteousness and strength.'" All who have raged against him will come to him and be put to shame.
Jer 14 9Why are you like a man taken by surprise, like a warrior powerless to save? You are among us, O LORD, and we bear your name; do not forsake us!
Jer 31 31"The time is coming," declares the LORD, "when I will make a new covenant with the house of Israel and with the house of Judah. 32It will not be like the covenant I made with their forefathers when I took them by the hand to lead them out of Egypt, because they broke my covenant, though I was a husband to them," declares the LORD. 33"This is the covenant I will make with the house of Israel after that time," declares the LORD. "I will put my law in their minds and write it on their hearts. I will be their God, and they will be my people. 34No longer will a man teach his neighbor, or a man his brother, saying, 'Know the LORD,' because they will all know me, from the least of them to the greatest," declares the LORD. "For I will forgive their wickedness and will remember their sins no more."
Jer 32 27"I am the LORD, the God of all mankind. Is anything too hard for me?"
Dan 9 14"The LORD did not hesitate to bring the disaster upon us, for the LORD our God is righteous in everything he does; yet we have not obeyed him."
Amos 5 8(he who made the Pleiades and Orion, who turns blackness into dawn and darkens day into night, who calls for the waters of the sea and pours them out over the face of the land—the LORD is his name. . . .)
Mal 3 6"I the LORD do not change. So you, O descendants of Jacob, are not destroyed."

12) Lord (Gk: Kurios)

Matt 9 38"Ask the Lord of the harvest, therefore, to send out workers into his harvest field."
Matt 11 25At that time Jesus said, "I praise you, Father, LORD of heaven and earth, because you have hidden these things from the wise and learned, and revealed them to little children."
Mark 5 19Jesus did not let him, but said, "Go home to your family and tell them how much the Lord has done for you, and how he has had mercy on you."
Mark 12 29"The most important one," answered Jesus, "is this: 'Hear, O Israel, the Lord our God, the Lord is one. 30Love the Lord your God with all your heart and with all your soul and with all your mind and with all your strength.'"
Mark 13 20"If the Lord had not cut short those days, no one would survive. But for the sake of the elect, whom he has chosen, he has shortened them."
Luke 1 15". . . for he will be great in the sight of the LORD. He is never to take wine or other fermented drink, and he will be filled with the Holy Spirit even from birth. 16Many of the people of Israel will he bring back to the Lord their God."
Luke 5 17One day as he was teaching, Pharisees and teachers of the law, who had come from every village of Galilee and from Judea and Jerusalem, were sitting there. And the power of the Lord was present for him to heal the sick.
Luke 10 21At that time Jesus, full of joy through the Holy Spirit, said, "I praise you, Father, Lord of heaven and earth, because you have hidden these things from the wise and learned, and revealed them to little children. Yes, Father, for this was your good pleasure."
Luke 20 37"But in the account of the bush, even Moses showed that the dead rise, for he calls the Lord 'the God of Abraham, and the God of Isaac, and the God of Jacob.'"
John 12 38This was to fulfill the word of Isaiah the prophet: "Lord, who has believed our message and to whom has the arm of the Lord been revealed?"
Acts 1 24Then they prayed, "Lord, you know everyone's heart. Show us which of these two you have chosen. . . ."
Acts 17 24"The God who made the world and everything in it is the Lord of heaven and earth and does not live in temples built by hands."
Rom 4 8"Blessed is the man whose sin the Lord will never count against him."
Rom 9 28"For the Lord will carry out his sentence on earth with speed and finality."
Rom 15 11And again, "Praise the Lord, all you Gentiles, and sing praises to him, all you peoples."
1 Cor 2 16"For who has known the mind of the Lord that he may instruct him?" But we have the mind of Christ.
1 Cor 10 9We should not test the Lord, as some of them did—and were killed by snakes.
2 Cor 10 17But, "Let him who boasts boast in the Lord."
2 Thess 1 9They will be punished with everlasting destruction and shut out from the presence of the Lord and from the majesty of his power. . . .
1 Tim 6 15which God will bring about in his own time—God, the blessed and only Ruler, the King of kings and Lord of lords . . .
2 Tim 1 18May the Lord grant that he will find mercy from the Lord on that day! You know very well in how many ways he helped me in Ephesus.
Heb 7 21but he became a priest with an oath when God said to him: "The Lord has sworn and will not change his mind: 'You are a priest forever.'"
Heb 8 2and who serves in the sanctuary, the true tabernacle set up by the Lord, not by man.
James 1 7That man should not think he will receive anything from the Lord. . . .
James 3 9With the tongue we praise our Lord and Father, and with it we curse men, who have been made in God's likeness.
James 5 11As you know, we consider blessed those who have persevered. You have heard of Job's perseverance and have seen what the Lord finally brought about. The Lord is full of compassion and mercy.
2 Pet 3 8But do not forget this one thing, dear friends: With the Lord a day is like a thousand years, and a thousand years are like a day.
Jude 5Though you already know all this, I want to remind you that the Lord delivered his people out of Egypt, but later destroyed those who did not believe.
Rev 4 11"You are worthy, our Lord and God, to receive glory and honor and power, for you created all things, and by your will they were created and have their being."

13) *Most High (Hb: Elyon)*

Num 24 [16]". . . the oracle of one who hears the words of God, who has knowledge from the Most High, who sees a vision from the Almighty, who falls prostrate, and whose eyes are opened . . ."

Deut 32 [8]When the Most High gave the nations their inheritance, when he divided all mankind, he set up boundaries for the peoples according to the number of the sons of Israel.

Ps 9 [2]I will be glad and rejoice in you; I will sing praise to your name, O Most High.

Ps 82 [6]"I said, 'You are "gods"; you are all sons of the Most High.'"

Ps 83 [18]Let them know that you, whose name is the LORD—that you alone are the Most High over all the earth.

Ps 87 [5]Indeed, of Zion it will be said, "This one and that one were born in her, and the Most High himself will establish her."

Ps 97 [9]For you, O LORD, are the Most High over all the earth; you are exalted far above all gods.

Ps 107 [11]for they had rebelled against the words of God and despised the counsel of the Most High.

Isa 14 [14]"I will ascend above the tops of the clouds; I will make myself like the Most High."

Dan 7 [18]"'But the saints of the Most High will receive the kingdom and will possess it forever—yes, for ever and ever.'"

Dan 7 [22]". . . until the Ancient of Days came and pronounced judgment in favor of the saints of the Most High, and the time came when they possessed the kingdom."

Dan 7 [25]"'He will speak against the Most High and oppress his saints and try to change the set times and the laws. The saints will be handed over to him for a time, times and half a time.'"

Dan 7 [27]"'Then the sovereignty, power and greatness of the kingdoms under the whole heaven will be handed over to the saints, the people of the Most High. His kingdom will be an everlasting kingdom, and all rulers will worship and obey him.'"

14) *Most High (Ar: Illai)*

Dan 4 [17]"'The decision is announced by messengers, the holy ones declare the verdict, so that the living may know that the Most High is sovereign over the kingdoms of men and gives them to anyone he wishes and sets over them the lowliest of men.'"

Dan 4 [24]"This is the interpretation, O king, and this is the decree the Most High has issued against my lord the king: [25]You will be driven away from people and will live with the wild animals; you will eat grass like cattle and be drenched with the dew of heaven. Seven times will pass by for you until you acknowledge that the Most High is sovereign over the kingdoms of men and gives them to anyone he wishes. . . ."

[32]"You will be driven away from people and will live with the wild animals; you will eat grass like cattle. Seven times will pass by for you until you acknowledge that the Most High is sovereign over the kingdoms of men and gives them to anyone he wishes."

[34]At the end of that time, I, Nebuchadnezzar, raised my eyes toward heaven, and my sanity was restored. Then I praised the Most High; I honored and glorified him who lives forever. His dominion is an eternal dominion; his kingdom endures from generation to generation.

Dan 7 [25]"'He will speak against the Most High and oppress his saints and try to change the set times and the laws. The saints will be handed over to him for a time, times and half a time.'"

15) *Most High (Gk: Hupsistos)*

Luke 1 [32]"He will be great and will be called the Son of the Most High. The Lord God will give him the throne of his father David. . . ."

Luke 1 [35]The angel answered, "The Holy Spirit will come upon you, and the power of the Most High will overshadow you. So the holy one to be born will be called the Son of God."

Luke 1 [76]"And you, my child, will be called a prophet of the Most High; for you will go on before the Lord to prepare the way for him. . . ."

Luke 6 [35]"But love your enemies, do good to them, and lend to them without expecting to get anything back. Then your reward will be great, and you will be sons of the Most High, because he is kind to the ungrateful and wicked."

Acts 7 [48]"However, the Most High does not live in houses made by men. As the prophet says . . ."

16) *Sovereign Lord (Gk: Despotes)*

Luke 2 [29]"Sovereign Lord, as you have promised, you now dismiss your servant in peace."

Acts 4 [24]When they heard this, they raised their voices together in prayer to God. "Sovereign Lord," they said, "you made the heaven and the earth and the sea, and everything in them."

2 Pet 2 [1]But there were also false prophets among the people, just as there will be false teachers among you. They will secretly introduce destructive heresies, even denying the sovereign Lord who bought them—bringing swift destruction on themselves.

Rev 6 [10]They called out in a loud voice, "How long, Sovereign Lord, holy and true, until you judge the inhabitants of the earth and avenge our blood?"

3. The Compound Names of God

1) *El Elohe Israel (Hb: El Elohe Yisrael)*

Gen 33 [20]There he set up an altar and called it El Elohe Israel.

2) *God Almighty (Hb: Elohim Sabaoth)*

Amos 5 [27]"Therefore I will send you into exile beyond Damascus," says the LORD, whose name is God Almighty.

3) *God Almighty (Hb: El Shaddai)*

Gen 17 [1]When Abram was ninety-nine years old, the LORD appeared to him and said, "I am God Almighty; walk before me and be blameless."

Gen 28 [3]"May God Almighty bless you and make you fruitful and increase your numbers until you become a community of peoples."

Gen 35 [11]And God said to him, "I am God Almighty; be fruitful and increase in number. A nation and a community of nations will come from you, and kings will come from your body."

Gen 43 [14]"And may God Almighty grant you mercy before the man so that he will let your other brother and Benjamin come back with you. As for me, if I am bereaved, I am bereaved."

Gen 48 [3]Jacob said to Joseph, "God Almighty appeared to me at Luz in the land of Canaan, and there he blessed me. . . ."

Exod 6 [3]"I appeared to Abraham, to Isaac and to Jacob as God Almighty, but by my name the LORD I did not make myself known to them."

Ezek 10 [5]The sound of the wings of the cherubim could be heard as far away as the outer court, like the voice of God Almighty when he speaks.

4) *God Almighty (Gk: Theos Pantokrator)*

Rev 16 [14]They are spirits of demons performing miraculous signs, and they go out to the kings of the whole world, to gather them for the battle on the great day of God Almighty.

Rev 19 [15]Out of his mouth comes a sharp sword with which to strike down the nations. "He will rule them with an iron scepter." He treads the winepress of the fury of the wrath of God Almighty.

5) *God Most High (Hb: El Elyon)*

Gen 14 [18]Then Melchizedek king of Salem brought out bread and wine. He was priest of God Most High, [19]and he blessed Abram, saying, "Blessed be Abram by God Most High, Creator of heaven and earth. [20]And blessed be God Most High, who delivered your enemies into your hand." Then Abram gave him a tenth of everything.

Ps 78 [35]They remembered that God was their Rock, that God Most High was their Redeemer.

6) *God Most High (Hb: Elohim Elyon)*

Ps 57 [2]I cry out to God Most High, to God, who fulfills his purpose for me.

7) *Lord, Lord (Hb: Yah, Yahweh)*

Isa 12 [2]"Surely God is my salvation; I will trust and not be afraid. The LORD, the LORD, is my strength and my song; he has become my salvation."

8) Lord Almighty (Hb: Yahweh Sabaoth)

1 Sam 1 3Year after year this man went up from his town to worship and sacrifice to the LORD Almighty at Shiloh, where Hophni and Phinehas, the two sons of Eli, were priests of the LORD.

1 Sam 1 11And she made a vow, saying, "O LORD Almighty, if you will only look upon your servant's misery and remember me, and not forget your servant but give her a son, then I will give him to the LORD for all the days of his life, and no razor will ever be used on his head."

1 Sam 4 4So the people sent men to Shiloh, and they brought back the ark of the covenant of the LORD Almighty, who is enthroned between the cherubim. And Eli's two sons, Hophni and Phinehas, were there with the ark of the covenant of God.

2 Sam 6 2He and all his men set out from Baalah of Judah to bring up from there the ark of God, which is called by the Name, the name of the LORD Almighty, who is enthroned between the cherubim that are on the ark.

2 Sam 7 26". . . so that your name will be great forever. Then men will say, 'The LORD Almighty is God over Israel!' And the house at your servant David will be established before you."

27"O LORD Almighty, God of Israel, you have revealed this to your servant, saying, 'I will build a house for you.' So your servant has found courage to offer you this prayer."

1 Chron 17 24". . . so that it will be established and that your name will be great forever. Then men will say, 'The LORD Almighty, the God over Israel, is Israel's God!' And the house of your servant David will be established before you."

Ps 24 10Who is he, this King of glory? The LORD Almighty—he is the King of glory.

Ps 46 7The LORD Almighty is with us; the God of Jacob is our fortress.

Isa 6 3And they were calling to one another: "Holy, holy, holy is the LORD Almighty; the whole earth is full of his glory." . . .

5"Woe to me!" I cried. "I am ruined! For I am a man of unclean lips, and I live among a people of unclean lips, and my eyes have seen the King, the LORD Almighty."

Isa 37 16"O LORD Almighty, God of Israel, enthroned between the cherubim, you alone are God over all the kingdoms of the earth. You have made heaven and earth."

Isa 44 6"This is what the LORD says—Israel's King and Redeemer, the LORD Almighty: I am the first and I am the last; apart from me there is no God."

Jer 46 18"As surely as I live," declares the King, whose name is the LORD Almighty, "one will come who is like Tabor among the mountains, like Carmel by the sea."

Zech 10 3"My anger burns against the shepherds, and I will punish the leaders; for the LORD Almighty will care for his flock, the house of Judah, and make them like a proud horse in battle."

Zech 14 16Then the survivors from all the nations that have attacked Jerusalem will go up year after year to worship the King, the LORD Almighty, and to celebrate the Feast of Tabernacles. 17If any of the peoples of the earth do not go up to Jerusalem to worship the King, the LORD Almighty, they will have no rain.

9) Lord Almighty (Gk: Kurios Pantokrator)

2 Cor 6 18"I will be a Father to you, and you will be my sons and daughters, says the Lord Almighty."

10) Lord Almighty (Gk: Kurios Sabaoth)

Rom 9 29It is just as Isaiah said previously: "Unless the Lord Almighty had left us descendants, we would have become like Sodom, we would have been like Gomorrah."

James 5 4Look! The wages you failed to pay the workmen who mowed your fields are crying out against you. The cries of the harvesters have reached the ears of the Lord Almighty.

11) Lord God (Hb: Yahweh Elohim)

Gen 3 8Then the man and his wife heard the sound of the LORD God as he was walking in the garden in the cool of the day, and they hid from the LORD God among the trees of the garden.

Neh 9 7"You are the LORD God, who chose Abram and brought him out of Ur of the Chaldeans and named him Abraham."

Ps 68 18When you ascended on high, you led captives in your train; you received gifts from men, even from the rebellious—that you, O LORD God, might dwell there.

Jon 4 6Then the LORD God provided a vine and made it grow up over Jonah to give shade for his head to ease his discomfort, and Jonah was very happy about the vine.

12) Lord God (Gk: Kurios Theos)

Luke 1 32"He will be great and will be called the Son of the Most High. The Lord God will give him the throne of his father David. . . ."

Rev 1 8"I am the Alpha and the Omega," says the Lord God, "who is, and who was, and who is to come, the Almighty."

Rev 22 5There will be no more night. They will not need the light of a lamp or the light of the sun, for the Lord God will give them light. And they will reign for ever and ever.

13) Lord God Almighty (Hb: Yahweh Elohim Sabaoth)

1 Kings 19 10He replied, "I have been very zealous for the LORD God Almighty. The Israelites have rejected your covenant, broken down your altars, and put your prophets to death with the sword. I am the only one left, and now they are trying to kill me too."

Ps 80 4O LORD God Almighty, how long will your anger smolder against the prayers of your people? . . . 19Restore us, O LORD God Almighty; make your face shine upon us, that we may be saved.

Ps 89 8O LORD God Almighty, who is like you? You are mighty, O LORD, and your faithfulness surrounds you.

Jer 5 14Therefore this is what the LORD God Almighty says: "Because the people have spoken these words, I will make my words in your mouth a fire and these people the wood it consumes."

Jer 15 16When your words came, I ate them; they were my joy and my heart's delight, for I bear your name, O LORD God Almighty.

Hos 12 5the LORD God Almighty, the LORD is his name of renown!

Amos 4 13He who forms the mountains, creates the wind, and reveals his thoughts to man, he who turns dawn to darkness, and treads the high places of the earth—the LORD God Almighty is his name.

14) Lord God Almighty (Gk: Kurios Theos Pantokrator)

Rev 4 8Each of the four living creatures had six wings and was covered with eyes all around, even under his wings. Day and night they never stop saying: "Holy, holy, holy is the Lord God Almighty, who was, and is, and is to come."

Rev 11 16And the twenty-four elders, who were seated on their thrones before God, fell on their faces and worshiped God, 17saying: "We give thanks to you, Lord God Almighty, the One who is and who was, because you have taken your great power and have begun to reign."

Rev 15 3and sang the song of Moses the servant of God and the song of the Lamb: "Great and marvelous are your deeds, Lord God Almighty. Just and true are your ways, King of the ages."

Rev 16 7And I heard the altar respond: "Yes, Lord God Almighty, true and just are your judgments."

Rev 19 6Then I heard what sounded like a great multitude, like the roar of rushing waters and like loud peals of thunder, shouting: "Hallelujah! For our Lord God Almighty reigns."

Rev 21 22I did not see a temple in the city, because the Lord God Almighty and the Lamb are its temple.

15) Lord God Most High (Hb: Yahweh El Elyon)

Gen 14 22But Abram said to the king of Sodom, "I have raised my hand to the LORD, God Most High, Creator of heaven and earth, and have taken an oath . . ."

16) Lord Most High (Hb: Yahweh Elyon)

Ps 7 17I will give thanks to the LORD because of his righteousness and will sing praise to the name of the LORD Most High.

Ps 47 2How awesome is the LORD Most High, the great King over all the earth!

Ps 97 9For you, O LORD, are the Most High over all the earth; you are exalted far above all gods.

17) *Lord, the Lord Almighty (Hb: Adon Yahweh Sabaoth)*

Isa 1 [24]Therefore the Lord, the LORD Almighty, the Mighty One of Israel, declares: "Ah, I will get relief from my foes and avenge myself on my enemies."

18) *Lord, the Lord Almighty (Hb: Adonai Yahweh Sabaoth)*

Ps 69 [6]May those who hope in you not be disgraced because of me, O Lord, the LORD Almighty; may those who seek you not be put to shame because of me, O God of Israel.
Isa 22 [5]The Lord, the LORD Almighty, has a day of tumult and trampling and terror in the Valley of Vision, a day of battering down walls and of crying out to the mountains. . . .

[12]The Lord, the LORD Almighty, called you on that day to weep and to wail, to tear out your hair and put on sackcloth. . . .

[14]The LORD Almighty has revealed this in my hearing: "Till your dying day this sin will not be atoned for," says the Lord, the LORD Almighty.

[15]This is what the Lord, the LORD Almighty, says: "Go, say to this steward, to Shebna, who is in charge of the palace . . ."
Jer 46 [10]"But that day belongs to the Lord, the LORD Almighty—a day of vengeance, for vengeance on his foes."
Jer 50 [25]"The LORD has opened his arsenal and brought out the weapons of his wrath, for the Sovereign LORD Almighty has work to do in the land of the Babylonians."
Jer 50 [31]"See, I am against you, O arrogant one," declares the Lord, the LORD Almighty, "for your day has come, the time for you to be punished."

19) *Mighty One, God, the Lord (Hb: El, Elohim, Yahweh)*

Josh 22 [22]"The Mighty One, God, the LORD! The Mighty One, God, the LORD! He knows! And let Israel know! If this has been in rebellion or disobedience to the LORD, do not spare us this day."
Ps 50 [1]The Mighty One, God, the LORD, speaks and summons the earth from the rising of the sun to the place where it sets.

20) *Most High God (Ar: Elah Illai)*

Dan 3 [26]Nebuchadnezzar then approached the opening of the blazing furnace and shouted, "Shadrach, Meshach and Abednego, servants of the Most High God, come out! Come here!" So Shadrach, Meshach and Abednego came out of the fire. . . .
Dan 4 [2]It is my pleasure to tell you about the miraculous signs and wonders that the Most High God has performed for me.
Dan 5 [18]"O king, the Most High God gave your father Nebuchadnezzar sovereignty and greatness and glory and splendor."
Dan 5 [21]"He was driven away from people and given the mind of an animal; he lived with the wild donkeys and ate grass like cattle; and his body was drenched with the dew of heaven, until he acknowledged that the Most High God is sovereign over the kingdoms of men and sets over them anyone he wishes."

21) *Most High God (Gk: Hupsistos Theos)*

Mark 5 [7]He shouted at the top of his voice, "What do you want with me, Jesus, Son of the Most High God? Swear to God that you won't torture me!"
Acts 16 [17]This girl followed Paul and the rest of us, shouting, "These men are servants of the Most High God, who are telling you the way to be saved."
Heb 7 [1]This Melchizedek was king of Salem and priest of God Most High. He met Abraham returning from the defeat of the kings and blessed him. . . .

22) *Sovereign Lord (Hb: Adonai Yahweh)*

Deut 9 [26]I prayed to the LORD and said, "O Sovereign LORD, do not destroy your people, your own inheritance that you redeemed by your great power and brought out of Egypt by a mighty hand."
Josh 7 [7]And Joshua said, "Ah, Sovereign LORD, why did you ever bring this people across the Jordan to deliver us into the hands of the Amorites to destroy us? If only we had been content to stay on the other side of the Jordan!"
Judg 6 [22]When Gideon realized that it was the angel of the LORD, he exclaimed, "Ah, Sovereign LORD! I have seen the angel of the LORD face to face!"
2 Sam 7 [28]"O Sovereign LORD, you are God! Your words are trustworthy, and you have promised these good things to your servant."
Isa 25 [8]he will swallow up death forever. The Sovereign LORD will wipe away the tears from all faces; he will remove the disgrace of his people from all the earth. The LORD has spoken.
Ezek 9 [8]While they were killing and I was left alone, I fell facedown, crying out, "Ah, Sovereign LORD! Are you going to destroy the entire remnant of Israel in this outpouring of your wrath on Jerusalem?"
Amos 6 [8]The Sovereign LORD has sworn by himself—the LORD God Almighty declares: "I abhor the pride of Jacob and detest his fortress; I will deliver up the city and everything in it.
Amos 7 [2]When they had stripped the land clean, I cried out, "Sovereign LORD, forgive! How can Jacob survive? He is so small!"
Zech 9 [14]Then the LORD will appear over them; his arrow will flash like lightning. The Sovereign LORD will sound the trumpet; he will march in the storms of the south. . . .

23) *Sovereign Lord (Hb: Yahweh Adonai)*

Hab 3 [19]The Sovereign LORD is my strength; he makes my feet like the feet of a deer, he enables me to go on the heights.

24) *Sovereign Lord Almighty (Hb: Adonai Yahweh Sabaoth)*

See Lord, the Lord Almighty (Hb: Adonai Yahweh Sabaoth)

4. Descriptive Names of God

1) *Ancient of Days*

Dan 7 [9]"As I looked, thrones were set in place, and the Ancient of Days took his seat. His clothing was as white as snow; the hair of his head was white like wool. His throne was flaming with fire, and its wheels were all ablaze."
Dan 7 [13]"In my vision at night I looked, and there before me was one like a son of man, coming with the clouds of heaven. He approached the Ancient of Days and was led into his presence."
Dan 7 [22]". . . until the Ancient of Days came and pronounced judgment in favor of the saints of the Most High, and the time came when they possessed the kingdom."

2) *Avenging God*

See p. 21b, Jealous and Avenging God

3) *Awesome God*

See p. 20a, Great and Awesome God; p. 20b, Great, Mighty, and Awesome God

4) *Blessed God*

1 Tim 1 [11]that conforms to the glorious gospel of the blessed God, which he entrusted to me.

5) *Compassionate and Gracious God*

Exod 34 [6]And he passed in front of Moses, proclaiming, "The LORD, the LORD, the compassionate and gracious God, slow to anger, abounding in love and faithfulness. . . ."
Ps 86 [15]But you, O LORD, are a compassionate and gracious God, slow to anger, abounding in love and faithfulness.
Ps 103 [8]The LORD is compassionate and gracious, slow to anger, abounding in love.
Ps 111 [4]He has caused his wonders to be remembered; the LORD is gracious and compassionate.
Ps 145 [8]The LORD is gracious and compassionte, slow to anger and rich in love.
Jon 4 [2]He prayed to the LORD, "O LORD, is this not what I said when I was still at home? That is why I was so quick to flee to Tarshish. I knew that you are a gracious and compassionate God, slow to anger and abounding in love, a God who relents from sending calamity."

6) *Eternal God*

Gen 21 [33]Abraham planted a tamarisk tree in Beersheba, and there he called upon the name of the LORD, the Eternal God.
Deut 33 [27]"The eternal God is your refuge, and underneath are

the everlasting arms. He will drive out your enemy before you, saying, 'Destroy him!'"

Rom 16 26but now revealed and made known through the prophetic writings by the command of the eternal God, so that all nations might believe and obey him . . .

7) *Everlasting God*

Isa 40 28Do you not know? Have you not heard? The LORD is the everlasting God, the Creator of the ends of the earth. He will not grow tired or weary, and his understanding no one can fathom.

8) *Faithful God*

Deut 7 9Know therefore that the LORD your God is God; he is the faithful God, keeping his covenant of love to a thousand generations of those who love him and keep his commands.

Deut 32 4He is the Rock, his works are perfect, and all his ways are just. A faithful God who does no wrong, upright and just is he.

9) *Faithful Holy One*

Hos 11 12Ephraim has surrounded me with lies, the house of Israel with deceit. And Judah is unruly against God, even against the faithful Holy One.

10) *Fear of Isaac*

Gen 31 42"If the God of my father, the God of Abraham and the Fear of Isaac, had not been with me, you would surely have sent me away empty-handed. But God has seen my hardship and the toil of my hands, and last night he rebuked you."

Gen 31 53"May the God of Abraham and the God of Nahor, the God of their father, judge between us."

So Jacob took an oath in the name of the Fear of his father Isaac.

11) *Forgiving God*

Neh 9 17"They refused to listen and failed to remember the miracles you performed among them. They became stiff-necked and in their rebellion appointed a leader in order to return to their slavery. But you are a forgiving God, gracious and compassionate, slow to anger and abounding in love. Therefore you did not desert them. . . ."

Ps 99 8O LORD our God, you answered them; you were to Israel a forgiving God, though you punished their misdeeds.

12) *God before Whom My Fathers Abraham and Isaac Walked*

Gen 48 15Then he blessed Joseph and said, "May the God before whom my fathers Abraham and Isaac walked, the God who has been my shepherd all my life to this day . . ."

13) *God My Maker*

Job 35 10"But no one says, 'Where is God my Maker, who gives songs in the night . . . ?'"

14) *God of Abraham*

Ps 47 9The nobles of the nations assemble as the people of the God of Abraham, for the kings of the earth belong to God; he is greatly exalted.

15) *God of Abraham and the God of Nahor*

Gen 31 53"May the God of Abraham and the God of Nahor, the God of their father, judge between us."

16) *God of Abraham, Isaac, and Israel*

1 Kings 18 36At the time of sacrifice, the prophet Elijah stepped forward and prayed: "O LORD, God of Abraham, Isaac and Israel, let it be known today that you are God in Israel and that I am your servant and have done all these things at your command."

1 Chron 29 18"O LORD, God of our fathers Abraham, Isaac and Israel, keep this desire in the hearts of your people forever, and keep their hearts loyal to you."

2 Chron 30 6At the king's command, couriers went throughout Israel and Judah with letters from the king and from his officials, which read:

"People of Israel, return to the LORD, the God of Abraham, Isaac and Israel, that he may return to you who are left, who have escaped from the hand of the kings of Assyria."

17) *God of Abraham, Isaac, and Jacob*

Exod 3 6Then he said, "I am the God of your father, the God of Abraham, the God of Isaac and the God of Jacob." At this, Moses hid his face, because he was afraid to look at God.

Exod 3 15God also said to Moses, "Say to the Israelites, 'The LORD, the God of your fathers—the God of Abraham, the God of Isaac and the God of Jacob—has sent me to you.' This is my name forever, the name by which I am to be remembered from generation to generation.

16"Go, assemble the elders of Israel and say to them, 'The LORD, the God of your fathers—the God of Abraham, Isaac and Jacob—appeared to me and said: I have watched over you and have seen what has been done to you in Egypt.'"

Mark 12 26"Now about the dead rising—have you not read in the book of Moses, in the account of the bush, how God said to him, 'I am the God of Abraham, the God of Isaac, and the God of Jacob'?"

Acts 7 32"'I am the God of your fathers, the God of Abraham, Isaac and Jacob.' Moses trembled with fear and did not dare to look."

18) *God of All Comfort*

2 Cor 1 3Praise be to the God and Father of our Lord Jesus Christ, the Father of compassion and the God of all comfort. . . .

19) *God of All Grace*

1 Pet 5 10And the God of all grace, who called you to his eternal glory in Christ, after you have suffered a little while, will himself restore you and make you strong, firm and steadfast.

20) *God of All Mankind*

Jer 32 27"I am the LORD, the God of all mankind. Is anything too hard for me?"

21) *God of All the Earth*

Isa 54 5"For your Maker is your husband—the LORD Almighty is his name—the Holy One of Israel is your Redeemer; he is called the God of all the earth."

22) *God of Bethel*

Gen 31 13"'I am the God of Bethel, where you anointed a pillar and where you made a vow to me. Now leave this land at once and go back to your native land.'"

23) *God of Glory*

Ps 29 3The voice of the LORD is over the waters; the God of glory thunders, the LORD thunders over the mighty waters.

Acts 7 2To this he replied, "Brothers and fathers, listen to me! The God of glory appeared to our father Abraham while he was still in Mesopotamia, before he lived in Haran."

24) *God of Gods*

Deut 10 17For the LORD your God is God of gods and Lord of lords, the great God, mighty and awesome, who shows no partiality and accepts no bribes.

Ps 136 2Give thanks to the God of gods. His love endures forever.

Dan 2 47The king said to Daniel, "Surely your God is the God of gods and the Lord of kings and a revealer of mysteries, for you were able to reveal this mystery."

Dan 11 36"The king will do as he pleases. He will exalt and magnify himself above every god and will say unheard-of things against the God of gods. He will be successful until the time of wrath is completed, for what has been determined must take place."

25) *God of Heaven*

Gen 24 7"The LORD, the God of heaven, who brought me out of my father's household and my native land and who spoke to me and promised me on oath, saying, 'To your offspring I will give this land'—he will send his angel before you so that you can get a wife for my son from there."

2 Chron 36 23"This is what Cyrus king of Persia says: 'The LORD, the God of heaven, has given me all the kingdoms of the earth and he has appointed me to build a temple for him at Jerusalem in Judah. Anyone of his people among you—may the LORD his God be with him, and let him go up.'"

Ezra 1 [2]"This is what Cyrus king of Persia says: 'The LORD, the God of heaven, has given me all the kingdoms of the earth and he has appointed me to build a temple for him at Jerusalem in Judah.'"
Ezra 5 [12]"But because our fathers angered the God of heaven, he handed them over to Nebuchadnezzar the Chaldean, King of Babylon, who destroyed this temple and deported the people to Babylon."
Neh 1 [5]Then I said: "O LORD, God of heaven, the great and awesome God, who keeps his covenant of love with those who love him and obey his commands. . . ."
Ps 136 [26]Give thanks to the God of heaven. *His love endures forever.*
Dan 2 [37]"You, O king, are the king of kings. The God of heaven has given you dominion and power and might and glory. . . ."
Jon 1 [9]He answered, "I am a Hebrew and I worship the LORD, the God of heaven, who made the sea and the land."
Rev 11 [13]At that very hour there was a severe earthquake and a tenth of the city collapsed. Seven thousand people were killed in the earthquake, and the survivors were terrified and gave glory to the God of heaven.

26) God of Heaven and Earth

Gen 24 [3]"I want you to swear by the LORD, the God of heaven and the God of earth, that you will not get a wife for my son from the daughters of the Canaanites, among whom I am living. . . ."
Josh 2 [11]"When we heard of it, our hearts melted and everyone's courage failed because of you, for the LORD your God is God in heaven above and on the earth below."
Ezra 5 [11]This is the answer they gave us: "We are the servants of the God of heaven and earth, and we are rebuilding the temple that was built many years ago, one that a great king of Israel built and finished."

27) God of Israel

Ps 68 [35]You are awesome, O God, in your sanctuary; the God of Israel gives power and strength to his people. Praise be to God!
Ps 69 [6]May those who hope in you not be disgraced because of me, O Lord, the LORD Almighty; may those who seek you not be put to shame because of me, O God of Israel.
Matt 15 [31]The people were amazed when they saw the mute speaking, the crippled made well, the lame walking and the blind seeing. And they praised the God of Israel.

28) God of Jacob

2 Sam 23 [1]These are the last words of David: "The oracle of David son of Jesse, the oracle of the man exalted by the Most High, the man anointed by the God of Jacob, Israel's singer of songs . . ."
Ps 20 [1]May the LORD answer you when you are in distress; may the name of the God of Jacob protect you.
Ps 24 [6]Such is the generation of those who seek him, who seek your face, O God of Jacob.
Ps 46 [11]The LORD Almighty is with us; the God of Jacob is our fortress.
Ps 75 [9]As for me, I will declare this forever; I will sing praise to the God of Jacob.
Ps 81 [1]Sing for joy to God our strength; shout aloud to the God of Jacob! [4]. . . this is a decree for Israel, an ordinance of the God of Jacob.
Ps 84 [8]Hear my prayer, O LORD God Almighty; listen to me, O God of Jacob.
Mic 4 [2]Many nations will come and say, "Come, let us go up to the mountain of the LORD, to the house of the God of Jacob. He will teach us his ways, so that we may walk in his paths." The law will go out from Zion, the word of the LORD from Jerusalem.
Acts 7 [46]". . . who enjoyed God's favor and asked that he might provide a dwelling place for the God of Jacob."

29) God of Justice

Isa 30 [18]Yet the LORD longs to be gracious to you; he rises to show you compassion. For the LORD is a God of justice. Blessed are all who wait for him!

30) God of Love and Peace

2 Cor 13 [11]Finally, brothers, good-by. Aim for perfection, listen to my appeal, be of one mind, live in peace. And the God of love and peace will be with you.

31) God of My Father Abraham

Gen 32 [9]Then Jacob prayed, "O God of my father Abraham, God of my father Isaac, O LORD, who said to me, 'Go back to your country and your relatives, and I will make you prosper.' . . ."

32) God of My Father Isaac

Gen 32 [9]Then Jacob prayed, "O God of my father Abraham, God of my father Isaac, O LORD, who said to me, 'Go back to your country and your relatives, and I will make you prosper . . .'"

33) God of My Fathers

Dan 2 [23]"I thank and praise you, O God of my fathers: You have given me wisdom and power, you have made known to me what we asked of you, you have made known to us the dream of the king."

34) God of My Life

Ps 42 [8]By day the LORD directs his love, at night his song is with me—a prayer to the God of my life.

35) God of Our Fathers

Ezra 7 [27]Praise be to the LORD, the God of our fathers, who has put it into the king's heart to bring honor to the house of the LORD in Jerusalem in this way. . . .
Acts 5 [30]"The God of our fathers raised Jesus from the dead—whom you had killed by hanging him on a tree."

36) God of Peace

Rom 15 [33]The God of peace be with you all. Amen.
Rom 16 [20]The God of peace will soon crush Satan under your feet. The grace of our LORD Jesus be with you.
1 Thess 5 [23]May God himself, the God of peace, sanctify you through and through. May your whole spirit, soul and body be kept blameless at the coming of our LORD Jesus Christ.
Heb 13 [20]May the God of peace, who through the blood of the eternal covenant brought back from the dead our LORD Jesus, that great Shepherd of the sheep . . .

37) God of the Hebrews

Exod 3 [18]"The elders of Israel will listen to you. Then you and the elders are to go to the king of Egypt and say to him, 'The LORD, the God of the Hebrews, has met with us. Let us take a three-day journey into the desert to offer sacrifices to the LORD our God.'"

38) God of the Living

Matt 22 [31]"But about the resurrection of the dead—have you not read what God said to you, [32]'I am the God of Abraham, the God of Isaac, and the God of Jacob'? He is not the God of the dead but of the living."

39) God of the Spirits of All Mankind

Num 16 [22]But Moses and Aaron fell facedown and cried out, "O God, God of the spirits of all mankind, will you be angry with the entire assembly when only one man sins?"
Num 27 [16]"May the LORD, the God of the spirits of all mankind, appoint a man over this community. . . ."

40) God of the Spirits of the Prophets

Rev 22 [6]The angel said to me, "These words are trustworthy and true. The Lord, the God of the spirits of the prophets, sent his angel to show his servants the things that must soon take place."

41) God of Their Fathers

1 Chron 29 [20]Then David said to the whole assembly, "Praise the LORD your God." So they all praised the LORD, the God of their fathers; they bowed low and fell prostrate before the LORD and the king.
2 Chron 20 [33]The high places, however, were not removed, and the people still had not set their hearts on the God of their fathers.

2 Chron 28 [6]In one day Pekah son of Remaliah killed a hundred and twenty thousand soldiers in Judah—because Judah had forsaken the LORD, the God of their fathers.

42) God of Truth

Ps 31 [5]Into your hands I commit my spirit; redeem me, O LORD, the God of truth.
Isa 65 [16]"Whoever invokes a blessing in the land will do so by the God of truth; he who takes an oath in the land will swear by the God of truth. For the past troubles will be forgotten and hidden from my eyes."

43) God of Your Father

Gen 31 [29]"I have the power to harm you; but last night the God of your father said to me, 'Be careful not to say anything to Jacob, either good or bad.'"
Gen 43 [23]"It's all right," he said. "Don't be afraid. Your God, the God of your father, has given you treasure in your sacks; I received your silver." Then he brought Simeon out to them.
Gen 46 [3]"I am God, the God of your father," he said. "Do not be afraid to go down to Egypt, for I will make you into a great nation there."
Gen 50 [17]"'This is what you are to say to Joseph: I ask you to forgive your brothers the sins and the wrongs they committed in treating you so badly.' Now please forgive the sins of the servants of the God of your father." When their message came to him, Joseph wept.

44) God of Your Father Abraham

Gen 26 [24]That night the LORD appeared to him and said, "I am the God of your father Abraham. Do not be afraid, for I am with you; I will bless you and will increase the number of your descendents for the sake of my servant Abraham."

45) God of Your Fathers

Deut 6 [3]Hear, O Israel, and be careful to obey so that it may go well with you and that you may increase greatly in a land flowing with milk and honey, just as the LORD, the God of your fathers, promised you.
Ezra 10 [11]"Now make confession to the LORD, the God of your fathers, and do his will. Separate yourselves from the peoples around you and from your foreign wives."

46) God over All the Kingdoms of the Earth

Isa 37 [16]"O LORD Almighty, God of Israel, enthroned between the cherubim, you alone are God over all the kingdoms of the earth. You have made heaven and earth."

47) God Who Avenges

Ps 94 [1]O LORD, the God who avenges, O God who avenges, shine forth.

48) God Who Has Been My Shepherd

Gen 48 [15]Then he blessed Joseph and said, "May the God before whom my fathers Abraham and Isaac walked, the God who has been my shepherd all my life to this day . . ."

49) God Who Sees Me

Gen 16 [13]She gave this name to the LORD who spoke to her: "You are the God who sees me," for she said, "I have now seen the One who sees me."

50) Gracious and Compassionate God

See p. 17b, Compassionate and Gracious God

51) Gracious and Merciful God

Neh 9 [31]"But in your great mercy you did not put an end to them or abandon them, for you are a gracious and merciful God."

52) Gracious and Righteous God

Ps 116 [5]The LORD is gracious and righteous; our God is full of compassion.

53) Great and Awesome God

Deut 7 [21]Do not be terrified by them, for the LORD your God, who is among you, is a great and awesome God.
Neh 1 [5]Then I said: "O LORD, God of heaven, the great and awesome God, who keeps his covenant of love with those who love him and obey his commands . . ."
Dan 9 [4]I prayed to the LORD my God and confessed: "O Lord, the great and awesome God, who keeps his covenant of love with all who love him and obey his commands . . ."

54) Great and Powerful God

Jer 32 [18]"You show love to thousands but bring the punishment for the fathers' sins into the laps of their children after them. O great and powerful God, whose name is the LORD Almighty . . ."

55) Great God

Deut 10 [17]For the LORD your God is God of gods and Lord of lords, the great God, mighty and awesome, who shows no partiality and accepts no bribes.
Neh 8 [6]Ezra praised the LORD, the great God; and all the people lifted their hands and responded, "Amen! Amen!" Then they bowed down and worshiped the LORD with their faces to the ground.
Ps 95 [3]For the LORD is the great God, the great King above all gods.
Dan 2 [45]"This is the meaning of the vision of the rock cut out of a mountain, but not by human hands—a rock that broke the iron, the bronze, the clay, the silver and the gold to pieces.

"The great God has shown the king what will take place in the future. The dream is true and the interpretation is trustworthy."

56) Great, Mighty, and Awesome God

Deut 10 [17]For the LORD your God is God of gods and Lord of lords, the great God, mighty and awesome, who shows no partiality and accepts no bribes.
Neh 9 [32]"Now therefore, O our God, the great, mighty and awesome God, who keeps his covenant of love, do not let all this hardship seem trifling in your eyes—the hardship that has come upon us, upon our kings and leaders, upon our priests and prophets, upon our fathers and all your people, from the days of the kings of Assyria until today."

57) Holy God

Josh 24 [19]Joshua said to the people, "You are not able to serve the LORD. He is a holy God; he is a jealous God. He will not forgive your rebellion and your sins."
1 Sam 6 [20]and the men of Beth Shemesh asked, "Who can stand in the presence of the LORD, this holy God? To whom will the ark go up from here?"

58) Holy One

Job 6 [10]"Then I would still have this consolation—my joy in unrelenting pain—that I had not denied the words of the Holy One."
Prov 9 [10]"The fear of the LORD is the beginning of wisdom, and knowledge of the Holy One is understanding."
Isa 40 [25]"To whom will you compare me? Or who is my equal?" says the Holy One.
Isa 43 [15]"I am the LORD, your Holy One, Israel's Creator, your King."
Hos 11 [9]"I will not carry out my fierce anger, nor will I turn and devastate Ephraim. For I am God, and not man—the Holy One among you. I will not come in wrath."
Hab 1 [12]O LORD, are you not from everlasting? My God, my Holy One, we will not die. O LORD, you have appointed them to execute judgment; O Rock, you have ordained them to punish.

59) Holy One of Israel

2 Kings 19 [22]"'Who is it you have insulted and blasphemed? Against whom have you raised your voice and lifted your eyes in pride? Against the Holy One of Israel!'"
Ps 71 [22]I will praise you with the harp for your faithfulness, O my God; I will sing praise to you with the lyre, O Holy One of Israel.
Ps 78 [41]Again and again they put God to the test; they vexed the Holy One of Israel.
Ps 89 [18]Indeed, our shield belongs to the LORD, our king to the Holy One of Israel.
Isa 5 [19]to those who say, "Let God hurry, let him hasten his work so we may see it. Let it approach, let the plan of the Holy One of Israel come, so we may know it."

Isa 10 [20]In that day the remnant of Israel, the survivors of the house of Jacob, will no longer rely on him who struck them down but will rely on the LORD, the Holy One of Israel.
Isa 12 [6]"Shout aloud and sing for joy, people of Zion, for great is the Holy One of Israel among you."
Isa 17 [7]In that day men will look to their Maker and turn their eyes to the Holy One of Israel.
Isa 30 [11]"Leave this way, get off this path, and stop confronting us with the Holy One of Israel!"
Isa 41 [14]"Do not be afraid, O worm Jacob, O little Israel, for I myself will help you," declares the LORD, your Redeemer, the Holy One of Israel. . . .

[16]"You will winnow them, the wind will pick them up, and a gale will blow them away. But you will rejoice in the LORD and glory in the Holy One of Israel."
Isa 43 [14]This is what the LORD says—your Redeemer, the Holy One of Israel: "For your sake I will send to Babylon and bring down as fugitives all the Babylonians, in the ships in which they took pride."
Isa 49 [7]This is what the LORD says—the Redeemer and Holy One of Israel—to him who was despised and abhorred by the nation, to the servant of rulers: "Kings will see you and rise up, princes will see and bow down, because of the LORD, who is faithful, the Holy One of Israel, who has chosen you."
Isa 54 [5]"For your Maker is your husband—the LORD Almighty is his name—the Holy One of Israel is your Redeemer; he is called the God of all the earth."
Isa 60 [9]"Surely the islands look to me; in the lead are the ships of Tarshish, bringing your sons from afar, with their silver and gold, to the honor of the LORD your God, the Holy One of Israel, for he has endowed you with splendor."
Jer 50 [29]"Summon archers against Babylon, all those who draw the bow. Encamp all around her; let no one escape. Repay her for her deeds; do to her as she has done. For she has defied the LORD, the Holy One of Israel."
Jer 51 [5]"For Israel and Judah have not been forsaken by their God, the LORD Almighty, though their land is full of guilt before the Holy One of Israel."
Ezek 39 [7]"'I will make known my holy name among my people Israel. I will no longer let my holy name be profaned, and the nations will know that I the LORD am the Holy One in Israel.'"

60) Holy One of Jacob

Isa 29 [23]"When they see among them their children, the work of my hands, they will keep my name holy; they will acknowledge the holiness of the Holy One of Jacob, and will stand in awe of the God of Israel."

61) I Am

Exod 3 [13]Moses said to God, "Suppose I go to the Israelites and say to them, 'The God of your fathers has sent me to you,' and they ask me, 'What is his name?' Then what shall I tell them?"

[14]God said to Moses, "I AM WHO I AM. This is what you are to say to the Israelites: 'I AM has sent me to you.'"
John 8 [56]"Your father Abraham rejoiced at the thought of seeing my day; he saw it and was glad."

[57]"You are not yet fifty years old," the Jews said to him, "and you have seen Abraham!"

[58]"I tell you the truth," Jesus answered, "before Abraham was born, I am!"

62) Immortal God

Rom 1 [23]and exchanged the glory of the immortal God for images made to look like mortal man and birds and animals and reptiles.

63) Invisible God

Col 1 [15]He is the image of the invisible God, the firstborn over all creation.

64) Jealous God

Exod 20 [4]"You shall not make for yourself an idol in the form of anything in heaven above or on the earth beneath or in the waters below. [5]You shall not bow down to them or worship them; for I, the LORD your God, am a jealous God, punishing the children for the sin of the fathers to the third and fourth generation of those who hate me, [6]but showing love to a thousand generations of those who love me and keep my commandments."
Exod 34 [14]"Do not worship any other god, for the LORD, whose name is Jealous, is a jealous God."
Deut 4 [24]For the LORD your God is a consuming fire, a jealous God.
Josh 24 [19]Joshua said to the people, "You are not able to serve the LORD. He is a holy God; he is a jealous God. He will not forgive your rebellion and your sins. [20]If you forsake the LORD and serve foreign gods, he will turn and bring disaster on you and make an end of you, after he has been good to you."

65) Jealous and Avenging God

Nah 1 [2]The LORD is a jealous and avenging God; the LORD takes vengeance and is filled with wrath. The LORD takes vengeance on his foes and maintains his wrath against his enemies.

66) Just and Mighty One

Job 34 [17]"Can he who hates justice govern? Will you condemn the just and mighty One?"

67) Living God

Deut 5 [26]For what mortal man has ever heard the voice of the living God speaking out of fire, as we have, and survived?
Ps 42 [2]My soul thirsts for God, for the living God. When can I go and meet with God?
Ps 84 [2]My soul yearns, even faints, for the courts of the LORD; my heart and my flesh cry out for the living God.
Jer 10 [10]But the LORD is the true God; he is the living God, the eternal King. When he is angry, the earth trembles; the nations cannot endure his wrath.
Dan 6 [26]"I issue a decree that in every part of my kingdom people must fear and reverence the God of Daniel. For he is the living God and he endures forever; his kingdom will not be destroyed, his dominion will never end."
Acts 14 [15]"Men, why are you doing this? We too are only men, human like you. We are bringing you good news, telling you to turn from these worthless things to the living God, who made heaven and earth and sea and everything in them."
1 Tim 4 [10](and for this we labor and strive), that we have put our hope in the living God, who is the Savior of all men, and especially of those who believe.

68) Living and True God

1 Thess 1 [9]for they themselves report what kind of reception you gave us. They tell how you turned to God from idols to serve the living and true God. . . .

69) Living God, the Lord Almighty

Jer 23 [36]"But you must not mention 'the oracle of the LORD' again, because every man's own word becomes his oracle and so you distort the words of the living God, the LORD Almighty, our God."

70) Lord Almighty, My King and My God

Ps 84 [3]Even the sparrow has found a home, and the swallow a nest for herself, where she may have her young—a place near your altar, O LORD Almighty, my King and my God.

71) Lord Almighty, the God of Israel

2 Sam 7 [27]"O LORD Almighty, God of Israel, you have revealed this to your servant, saying, 'I will build a house for you.' So your servant has found courage to offer you this prayer."
Isa 37 [16]"O LORD Almighty, God of Israel, enthroned between the cherubim, you alone are God over all the kingdoms of the earth. You have made heaven and earth."
Jer 27 [21]". . . yes, this is what the LORD Almighty, the God of Israel, says about the things that are left in the house of the LORD and in the palace of the King of Judah and in Jerusalem . . ."
Jer 32 [14]"'This is what the LORD Almighty, the God of Israel, says: Take these documents, both the sealed and unsealed copies of the deed of purchase, and put them in a clay jar so they will last a long time. [15]For this is what the LORD Almighty, the God of Israel, says: Houses, fields and vineyards will again be bought in this land.'"

72) Lord God Almighty, the God of Israel

1 Chron 17 [24]". . . so that it will be established and that your name will be great forever. Then men will say, 'The LORD

Almighty, the God over Israel, is Israel's God!' And the house of your servant David will be established before you."

Ps 59 [5]O LORD God Almighty, the God of Israel, rouse yourself to punish all the nations; show no mercy to wicked traitors.

Jer 35 [17]"Therefore, this is what the LORD God Almighty, the God of Israel, says: 'Listen! I am going to bring on Judah and on everyone living in Jerusalem every disaster I pronounced against them. I spoke to them, but they did not listen; I called to them, but they did not answer.'"

73) Lord God, the God of Israel

Ps 72 [18]Praise be to the LORD God, the God of Israel, who alone does marvelous deeds.

74) Lord My God

Num 22 [18]But Balaam answered them, "Even if Balak gave me his palace filled with silver and gold, I could not do anything great or small to go beyond the command of the LORD my God."

Deut 4 [5]See, I have taught you decrees and laws as the LORD my God commanded me, so that you may follow them in the land you are entering to take possession of it.

2 Chron 2 [4]"Now I am about to build a temple for the Name of the LORD my God and to dedicate it to him for burning fragrant incense before him, for setting out the consecrated bread regularly, and for making burnt offerings every morning and evening and on Sabbaths and New Moons and at the appointed feasts of the LORD our God. This is a lasting ordinance for Israel."

Ps 13 [3]Look on me and answer, O LORD my God. Give light to my eyes, or I will sleep in death. . . .

75) Lord of All the Earth

Josh 3 [11]"See, the ark of the covenant of the Lord of all the earth will go into the Jordan ahead of you. . . . [13]And as soon as the priests who carry the ark of the LORD—the Lord of all the earth—set foot in the Jordan, its waters flowing downstream will be cut off and stand up in a heap."

Ps 97 [5]The mountains melt like wax before the LORD, before the Lord of all the earth.

Mic 4 [13]"Rise and thresh, O Daughter of Zion, for I will give you horns of iron; I will give you hoofs of bronze and you will break to pieces many nations." You will devote their ill-gotten gains to the LORD, their wealth to the Lord of all the earth.

Zech 4 [14]So he said, "These are the two who are anointed to serve the Lord of all the earth."

Rev 11 [4]These are the two olive trees and the two lampstands that stand before the Lord of the earth.

76) Lord of Heaven

Dan 5 [23]"Instead, you have set yourself up against the Lord of heaven. You had the goblets from his temple brought to you, and you and your nobles, your wives and your concubines drank wine from them. You praised the gods of silver and gold, of bronze, iron, wood and stone, which cannot see or hear or understand. But you did not honor the God who holds in his hand your life and all your ways."

77) Lord of Heaven and Earth

Luke 10 [21]At that time Jesus, full of joy through the Holy Spirit, said, "I praise you, Father, Lord of heaven and earth, because you have hidden these things from the wise and learned, and revealed them to little children. Yes, Father, for this was your good pleasure."

Acts 17 [24]"The God who made the world and everything in it is the Lord of heaven and earth and does not live in temples built by hands."

78) Lord of Kings

Dan 2 [47]The king said to Daniel, "Surely your God is the God of gods and the Lord of kings and a revealer of mysteries, for you were able to reveal this mystery."

79) Lord of Lords

Deut 10 [17]For the LORD your God is God of gods and Lord of lords, the great God, mighty and awesome, who shows no partiality and accepts no bribes.

Ps 136 [3]Give thanks to the Lord of lords: *His love endures forever.*

Rev 17 [14]"They will make war against the Lamb, but the Lamb will overcome them because he is Lord of lords and King of kings—and with him will be his called, chosen and faithful followers."

Rev 19 [16]On his robe and on his thigh he has this name written: KING OF KINGS AND LORD OF LORDS.

80) Lord of the Harvest

Matt 9 [37]Then he said to his disciples, "The harvest is plentiful but the workers are few. [38]Ask the Lord of the harvest, therefore, to send out workers into his harvest field."

81) Lord of the Whole World

Zech 6 [5]The angel answered me, "These are the four spirits of heaven, going out from standing in the presence of the Lord of the whole world."

82) Lord Our God

Deut 1 [6]The LORD our God said to us at Horeb, "You have stayed long enough at this mountain." . . .

[19]Then, as the LORD our God commanded us, we set out from Horeb and went toward the hill country of the Amorites through all that vast and dreadful desert that you have seen, and so we reached Kadesh Barnea. [20]Then I said to you, "You have reached the hill country of the Amorites, which the LORD our God is giving us."

Deut 2 [29]". . . as the descendants of Esau, who live in Seir, and the Moabites, who live in Ar, did for us—until we cross the Jordan into the land the LORD our God is giving us."

Deut 5 [24]And you said, "The LORD our God has shown us his glory and his majesty, and we have heard his voice from the fire. Today we have seen that a man can live even if God speaks with him. [25]But now, why should we die? This great fire will consume us, and we will die if we hear the voice of the LORD our God any longer. . . . [27]Go near and listen to all that the LORD our God says. Then tell us whatever the LORD our God tells you. We will listen and obey."

Deut 6 [4]Hear, O Israel: The LORD our God, the LORD is one. . . . [20]In the future, when your son asks you, "What is the meaning of the stipulations, decrees and laws the LORD our God has commanded you?" . . . [24]"The LORD commanded us to obey all these decrees and to fear the LORD our God, so that we might always prosper and be kept alive, as is the case today. [25]And if we are careful to obey all this law before the LORD our God, as he has commanded us, that will be our righteousness."

2 Kings 19 [19]"Now, O LORD our God, deliver us from his hand, so that all kingdoms on earth may know that you alone, O LORD, are God."

Ps 20 [7]Some trust in chariots and some in horses, but we trust in the name of the LORD our God.

83) Lord Our Maker

Job 35 [10]"But no one says, 'Where is God my Maker, who gives songs in the night . . . ?'"

Ps 95 [6]Come, let us bow down in worship, let us kneel before the LORD our Maker. . . .

84) Lord Our Righteousness

Jer 23 [6]"In his days Judah will be saved and Israel will live in safety. This is the name by which he will be called: The LORD Our Righteousness."

85) Lord, the God of Israel

Josh 24 [23]"Now then," said Joshua, "throw away the foreign gods that are among you and yield your hearts to the LORD, the God of Israel."

Ruth 2 [12]"May the LORD repay you for what you have done. May you be richly rewarded by the LORD, the God of Israel, under whose wings you have come to take refuge."

1 Chron 16 [36]Praise be to the LORD, the God of Israel, from everlasting to everlasting.

2 Chron 6 [4]Then he said: "Praise be to the LORD, the God of Israel, who with his hands has fulfilled what he promised with his mouth to my father David. . . ."

Ps 41 [13]Praise be to the LORD, the God of Israel, from everlasting to everlasting. Amen and Amen.

Isa 37 [21]Then Isaiah son of Amoz sent a message to Hezekiah:

"This is what the LORD, the God of Israel, says: Because you have prayed to me concerning Sennacherib king of Assyria, [22]this is the word the LORD has spoken against him: The Virgin Daughter of Zion despises and mocks you. The Daughter of Jerusalem tosses her head as you flee."

Jer 24 [5]"This is what the LORD, the God of Israel, says: 'Like these good figs, I regard as good the exiles from Judah, whom I sent away from this place to the land of the Babylonians.'"

Jer 25 [15]This is what the LORD, the God of Israel, said to me: "Take from my hand this cup filled with the wine of my wrath and make all the nations to whom I send you drink it."

Luke 1 [68]"Praise be to the Lord, the God of Israel, because he has come and has redeemed his people."

86) Lord, the God of Your Father David

Isa 38 [5]"Go and tell Hezekiah, 'This is what the LORD, the God of your father David, says: I have heard your prayer and seen your tears; I will add fifteen years to your life.'"

87) Lord Their God

Ezek 28 [26]"'They will live there in safety and will build houses and plant vineyards; they will live in safety when I inflict punishment on all their neighbors who maligned them. Then they will know that I am the LORD their God.'"

88) Lord Your God

Gen 27 [20]Isaac asked his son, "How did you find it so quickly, my son?"

"The LORD your God gave me success," he replied.

Deut 1 [32]In spite of this, you did not trust in the LORD your God. . . ."

Deut 2 [7]The LORD your God has blessed you in all the work of your hands. He has watched over your journey through this vast desert. These forty years the LORD your God has been with you, and you have not lacked anything.

Deut 8 [10]When you have eaten and are satisfied, praise the LORD your God for the good land he has given you.

Deut 11 [1]Love the LORD your God and keep his requirements, his decrees, his laws and his commands always.

Josh 1 [9]"Have I not commanded you? Be strong and courageous. Do not be terrified; do not be discouraged, for the LORD your God will be with you wherever you go." . . .

[11]"Go through the camp and tell the people, 'Get your supplies ready. Three days from now you will cross the Jordan here to go in and take possession of the land the LORD your God is giving you for your own.'" . . .

[13]"Remember the command that Moses the servant of the LORD gave you: 'The LORD your God is giving you rest and has granted you this land.' [15]. . . until the LORD gives them rest, as he has done for you, and until they too have taken possession of the land that the LORD your God is giving them. After that, you may go back and occupy your own land, which Moses the servant of the LORD gave you east of the Jordan toward the sunrise." . . .

[17]"Just as we fully obeyed Moses, so we will obey you. Only may the LORD your God be with you as he was with Moses."

1 Sam 12 [12]"But when you saw that Nahash king of the Ammonites was moving against you, you said to me, 'No, we want a king to rule over us'—even though the LORD your God was your king. . . . [14]If you fear the LORD and serve and obey him and do not rebel against his commands, and if both you and the king who reigns over you follow the LORD your God—good!" . . .

[19]The people all said to Samuel, "Pray to the LORD your God for your servants so that we will not die, for we have added to all our other sins the evil of asking for a king."

89) Loving God

Ps 59 [9]O my strength, I watch for you; you, O God, are my fortress, [10]my loving God. God will go before me and will let me gloat over those who slander me.

Ps 59 [17]O my Strength, I sing praise to you; you, O God, are my fortress, my loving God.

Ps 144 [2]He is my loving God and my fortress, my stronghold and my deliverer, my shield, in whom I take refuge, who subdues peoples under me.

90) Majestic Glory

2 Pet 1 [17]For he received honor and glory from God the Father when the voice came to him from the Majestic Glory, saying, "This is my Son, whom I love; with him I am well pleased."

91) Majesty in Heaven

Heb 8 [1]The point of what we are saying is this: We do have such a high priest, who sat down at the right hand of the throne of the Majesty in heaven. . . .

92) Merciful God

Deut 4 [31]For the LORD your God is a merciful God; he will not abandon or destroy you or forget the covenant with your forefathers, which he confirmed to them by oath.

93) Mighty God

Isa 9 [6]For to us a child is born, to us a son is given, and the government will be on his shoulders. And he will be called Wonderful Counselor, Mighty God, Everlasting Father, Prince of Peace.

Isa 10 [21]A remnant will return, a remnant of Jacob will return to the Mighty God.

Luke 22 [69]"But from now on, the Son of Man will be seated at the right hand of the mighty God."

94) Mighty One

Isa 10 [33]See, the Lord, the LORD Almighty, will lop off the boughs with great power. The lofty trees will be felled, the tall ones will be brought low. [34]He will cut down the forest thickets with an ax; Lebanon will fall before the Mighty One.

Isa 33 [21]There the LORD will be our Mighty One. It will be like a place of broad rivers and streams. No galley with oars will ride them, no mighty ship will sail them.

Mark 14 [62]"I am," said Jesus. "And you will see the Son of Man sitting at the right hand of the Mighty One and coming on the clouds of heaven."

Luke 1 [49]". . . for the Mighty One has done great things for me—holy is his name."

95) Mighty One of Israel

Isa 1 [24]Therefore the Lord, the LORD Almighty, the Mighty One of Israel, declares: "Ah, I will get relief from my foes and avenge myself on my enemies."

96) Mighty One of Jacob

Gen 49 [24]"But his bow remained steady, his strong arms stayed limber, because of the hand of the Mighty One of Jacob, because of the Shepherd, the Rock of Israel. . . ."

Ps 132 [2]He swore an oath to the LORD and made a vow to the Mighty One of Jacob: [3]"I will not enter my house or go to my bed— [4]I will allow no sleep to my eyes, no slumber to my eyelids, [5]till I find a place for the LORD, a dwelling for the Mighty One of Jacob."

Isa 49 [26]"I will make your oppressors eat their own flesh; they will be drunk on their own blood, as with wine. Then all mankind will know that I, the LORD, am your Savior, your Redeemer, the Mighty One of Jacob."

Isa 60 [16]"You will drink the milk of nations and be nursed at royal breasts. Then you will know that I, the LORD, am your Savior, your Redeemer, the Mighty One of Jacob."

97) Most High over All the Earth

Ps 83 [18]Let them know that you, whose name is the LORD—that you alone are the Most High over all the earth.

Ps 97 [9]For you, O LORD, are the Most High over all the earth; you are exalted far above all gods.

98) One Enthroned in Heaven

Ps 2 [4]The One enthroned in heaven laughs; the Lord scoffs at them.

99) One of Sinai

Judg 5 [5]"The mountains quaked before the LORD, the One of Sinai, before the LORD, the God of Israel."

Ps 68 [8]the earth shook, the heavens poured down rain, before God, the One of Sinai, before God, the God of Israel.

100) One to Be Feared

Ps 76 11Make vows to the LORD your God and fulfill them; let all the neighboring lands bring gifts to the One to be feared.

101) One Who Goes with You

Deut 20 4"For the LORD your God is the one who goes with you to fight for you against your enemies to give you victory."

102) One Who Remembered Us

Ps 136 23to the One who remembered us in our low estate *His love endures forever.*

103) One Who Sits Enthroned on High

Ps 113 5Who is like the LORD our God, the One who sits enthroned on high . . . ?

104) Powerful God

See p. 20b, Great and Powerful God

105) Pride of Jacob

Amos 8 7The LORD has sworn by the Pride of Jacob: "I will never forget anything they have done."

106) Righteous God

Ps 4 1Answer me when I call to you, O my righteous God. Give me relief from my distress; be merciful to me and hear my prayer.
Ps 7 9O righteous God, who searches minds and hearts, bring to an end the violence of the wicked and make the righteous secure.
Isa 45 21"Declare what is to be, present it—let them take counsel together. Who foretold this long ago, who declared it from the distant past? Was it not I, the LORD? And there is no God apart from me, a righteous God and a Savior; there is none but me."

107) Righteous One

Prov 21 12The Righteous One takes note of the house of the wicked and brings the wicked to ruin.
Isa 24 16From the ends of the earth we hear singing: "Glory to the Righteous One." But I said, "I waste away, I waste away! Woe to me! The treacherous betray! With treachery the treacherous betray!"

108) The Lord Is a God of Retribution

Jer 51 56"A destroyer will come against Babylon; her warriors will be captured, and their bows will be broken. For the LORD is a God of retribution; he will repay in full."

109) The Lord Is Just

2 Chron 12 6The leaders of Israel and the king humbled themselves and said, "The LORD is just."

110) The Lord Is My Banner

Exod 17 15Moses built an altar and called it The LORD is my Banner.

111) The Lord Is My Shepherd

Ps 23 1The LORD is my shepherd, I shall not be in want.

112) The Lord Is Peace

Judg 6 24So Gideon built an altar to the LORD there and called it The LORD is Peace. To this day it stands in Ophrah of the Abiezrites.

113) The Lord Is There

Ezek 48 35"The distance all around will be 18,000 cubits.
"And the name of the city from that time on will be: THE LORD IS THERE."

114) The Lord Will Provide

Gen 22 14So Abraham called that place The LORD Will Provide. And to this day it is said, "On the mountain of the LORD it will be provided."

115) The Lord Who Heals You

Exod 15 26He said, "If you listen carefully to the voice of the LORD your God and do what is right in his eyes, if you pay attention to his commands and keep all his decrees, I will not bring on you any of the diseases I brought on the Egyptians, for I am the LORD, who heals you."

116) The Lord Who Makes You Holy

Exod 31 13"Say to the Israelites, 'You must observe my Sabbaths. This will be a sign between me and you for the generations to come, so you may know that I am the LORD, who makes you holy.'"

117) The Lord Who Strikes the Blow

Ezek 7 9"I will not look on you with pity or spare you; I will repay you in accordance with your conduct and the detestable practices among you. Then you will know that it is I the LORD who strikes the blow."

118) True God

2 Chron 15 3"For a long time Israel was without the true God, without a priest to teach and without the law."
Jer 10 10But the LORD is the true God; he is the living God, the eternal King. When he is angry, the earth trembles; the nations cannot endure his wrath.
John 17 3"Now this is eternal life: that they may know you, the only true God, and Jesus Christ, whom you have sent."

119) Wise God

Rom 16 27to the only wise God be glory forever through Jesus Christ! Amen.

D. Designations, Descriptive Titles, and Figures of Speech for God

1. Abba

Mark 14 36"*Abba*, Father," he said, "everything is possible for you. Take this cup from me. Yet not what I will, but what you will."
Rom 8 15For you did not receive a spirit that makes you a slave again to fear, but you received the Spirit of sonship. And by him we cry, "*Abba*, Father."
Gal 4 6Because you are sons, God sent the Spirit of his Son into our hearts, the Spirit who calls out, "*Abba*, Father."

2. Alpha and Omega

Rev 1 8"I am the Alpha and the Omega," says the Lord God, "who is, and who was, and who is to come, the Almighty."
Rev 21 6He said to me: "It is done. I am the Alpha and the Omega, the Beginning and the End. To him who is thirsty I will give to drink without cost from the spring of the water of life."

3. Architect

Heb 11 10For he was looking forward to the city with foundations, whose architect and builder is God.

4. Banner

Exod 17 14Then the LORD said to Moses, "Write this on a scroll as something to be remembered and make sure that Joshua hears it, because I will completely blot out the memory of Amalek from under heaven."
15Moses built an altar and called it The LORD is my Banner. 16He said, "For hands were lifted up to the throne of the LORD. The LORD will be at war against the Amalekites from generation to generation."

5. Bear Robbed of Her Cubs

Hos 13 8"Like a bear robbed of her cubs, I will attack them and rip them open. Like a lion I will devour them; a wild animal will tear them apart."

6. Beginning and End

Rev 21 6He said to me: "It is done. I am the Alpha and the Omega, the Beginning and the End. To him who is thirsty I will give to drink without cost from the spring of the water of life."

7. Birds Hovering Overhead

Isa 31 5"Like birds hovering overhead, the LORD Almighty will shield Jerusalem; he will shield it and deliver it, he will 'pass over' it and will rescue it."

8. Blessed and Only Ruler

1 Tim 6 [15]which God will bring about in his own time—God, the blessed and only Ruler, the King of kings and Lord of lords . . .

9. Bridegroom

Isa 62 [5]As a young man marries a maiden, so will your sons marry you; as a bridegroom rejoices over his bride, so will your God rejoice over you.

10. Builder

Heb 11 [10]For he was looking forward to the city with foundations, whose architect and builder is God.

11. Cart

Amos 2 [13]"Now then, I will crush you as a cart crushes when loaded with grain."

12. Confidence

Ps 71 [5]For you have been my hope, O Sovereign LORD, my confidence since my youth.
Prov 3 [25]Have no fear of sudden disaster or of the ruin that overtakes the wicked, [26]for the LORD will be your confidence and will keep your foot from being snared.

13. Consuming Fire

Deut 4 [24]For the LORD your God is a consuming fire, a jealous God.
Heb 12 [29]for our "God is a consuming fire."

14. Creator

Deut 32 [6]Is this the way you repay the LORD, O foolish and unwise people? Is he not your Father, your Creator, who made you and formed you?
Eccles 12 [1]Remember your Creator in the days of your youth, before the days of trouble come and the years approach when you will say, "I find no pleasure in them". . . .
Matt 19 [4]"Haven't you read," he replied, "that at the beginning the Creator 'made them male and female' . . . ?"
Rom 1 [25]They exchanged the truth of God for a lie, and worshiped and served created things rather than the Creator—who is forever praised. Amen.

15. Creator of Heaven and Earth

Gen 14 [19]and he blessed Abram, saying, "Blessed be Abram by God Most High, Creator of heaven and earth."
Gen 14 [22]But Abram said to the king of Sodom, "I have raised my hand to the LORD, God Most High, Creator of heaven and earth, and have taken an oath. . . ."

16. Creator of Israel

Isa 43 [15]"I am the LORD, your Holy One, Israel's Creator, your King."

17. Creator of the Ends of the Earth

Isa 40 [28]Do you not know? Have you not heard? The LORD is the everlasting God, the Creator of the ends of the earth. He will not grow tired or weary, and his understanding no one can fathom.

18. Defender

Ps 68 [5]A father to the fatherless, a defender of widows, is God in his holy dwelling.
Prov 23 [10]Do not move an ancient boundary stone or encroach on the fields of the fatherless, [11]for their Defender is strong; he will take up their case against you.

19. Deliverer

2 Sam 22 [2]He said: "The LORD is my rock, my fortress and my deliverer. . . ."
Ps 40 [17]Yet I am poor and needy; may the Lord think of me. You are my help and my deliverer; O my God, do not delay.
Ps 144 [2]He is my loving God and my fortress, my stronghold and my deliverer, my shield, in whom I take refuge, who subdues peoples under me.

20. Devouring Fire

Deut 9 [3]But be assured today that the LORD your God is the one who goes across ahead of you like a devouring fire. He will destroy them; he will subdue them before you. And you will drive them out and annihilate them quickly, as the LORD has promised you.

21. Dew

Hos 14 [5]"I will be like the dew to Israel; he will blossom like a lily. Like a cedar of Lebanon he will send down his roots. . . ."

22. Dwelling Place

Ps 90 [1]Lord, you have been our dwelling place throughout all generations.
Ps 91 [9]If you make the Most High your dwelling—even the LORD, who is my refuge . . .

23. Eagle

Exod 19 [4]"'You yourselves have seen what I did to Egypt, and how I carried you on eagles' wings and brought you to myself.'"
Deut 32 [10]In a desert land he found him, in a barren and howling waste. He shielded him and cared for him; he guarded him as the apple of his eye, [11]like an eagle that stirs up its nest and hovers over its young, that spreads its wings to catch them and carries them on its pinions. [12]The LORD alone led him; no foreign god was with him.

24. Enemy

Jer 30 [14]"'All your allies have forgotten you; they care nothing for you. I have struck you as an enemy would and punished you as would the cruel, because your guilt is so great and your sins so many.'"
Lam 2 [4]Like an enemy he has strung his bow; his right hand is ready. Like a foe he has slain all who were pleasing to the eye; he has poured out his wrath like fire on the tent of the Daughter of Zion. [5]The Lord is like an enemy; he has swallowed up Israel. He has swallowed up all her palaces and destroyed her strongholds. He has multiplied mourning and lamentation for the Daughter of Judah.

25. Eternal King

Jer 10 [10]But the LORD is the true God; he is the living God, the eternal King. When he is angry, the earth trembles; the nations cannot endure his wrath.

26. Ever-Present Help

Ps 46 [1]God is our refuge and strength, an ever-present help in trouble.

27. Faithful Creator

1 Pet 4 [19]So then, those who suffer according to God's will should commit themselves to their faithful Creator and continue to do good.

28. Father

Deut 1 [30]"The LORD your God, who is going before you, will fight for you, as he did for you in Egypt, before your very eyes, [31]and in the desert. There you saw how the LORD your God carried you, as a father carries his son, all the way you went until you reached this place."
Deut 32 [6]Is this the way you repay the LORD, O foolish and unwise people? Is he not your Father, your Creator, who made you and formed you?
Job 38 [28]"Does the rain have a father? Who fathers the drops of dew?"

Ps 68 [5]A father to the fatherless, a defender of widows, is God in his holy dwelling.
Ps 89 [26]"He will call out to me, 'You are my Father, my God, the Rock my Savior.'"
Ps 103 [13]As a father has compassion on his children, so the LORD has compassion on those who fear him. . . .
Isa 63 [16]But you are our Father, though Abraham does not know us or Israel acknowledge us; you, O LORD, are our Father, our Redeemer from of old is your name.
Isa 64 [8]Yet, O LORD, you are our Father. We are the clay, you are the potter; we are all the work of your hand.
Jer 3 [4]"Have you not just called to me: 'My Father, my friend from my youth . . . ?'"
Jer 3 [19]"I myself said, 'How gladly would I treat you like sons and give you a desirable land, the most beautiful inheritance of any nation.' I thought you would call me 'Father' and not turn away from following me."
Mal 1 [6]"A son honors his father, and a servant his master. If I am a father, where is the honor due me? If I am a master, where is the respect due me?" says the LORD Almighty. "It is you, O priests, who show contempt for my name.

"But you ask, 'How have we shown contempt for your name?'"
Mal 2 [10]Have we not all one Father? Did not one God create us? Why do we profane the covenant of our fathers by breaking faith with one another?
Matt 6 [9]"This, then, is how you should pray: 'Our Father in heaven, hallowed be your name. . . .'"
Mark 13 [32]"No one knows about that day or hour, not even the angels in heaven, nor the Son, but only the Father."
Luke 10 [21]At that time Jesus, full of joy through the Holy Spirit, said, "I praise you, Father, Lord of heaven and earth, because you have hidden these things from the wise and learned, and revealed them to little children. Yes, Father, for this was your good pleasure.

[22]"All things have been committed to me by my Father. No one knows who the Son is except the Father, and no one knows who the Father is except the Son and those to whom the Son chooses to reveal him."
John 20 [17]Jesus said, "Do not hold on to me, for I have not yet returned to the Father. Go instead to my brothers and tell them, 'I am returning to my Father and your Father, to my God and your God.'"
Acts 2 [33]"Exalted to the right hand of God, he has received from the Father the promised Holy Spirit and has poured out what you now see and hear."
Eph 4 [6]one God and Father of all, who is over all and through all and in all.
Phil 4 [20]To our God and Father be glory for ever and ever. Amen.
1 Pet 1 [17]Since you call on a Father who judges each man's work impartially, live your lives as strangers here in reverent fear.
1 John 3 [1]How great is the love the Father has lavished on us, that we should be called children of God! And that is what we are! The reason the world does not know us is that it did not know him.

29. Father of Compassion

2 Cor 1 [3]Praise be to the God and Father of our Lord Jesus Christ, the Father of compassion and the God of all comfort. . . .

30. Father of Our Lord Jesus Christ

Rom 15 [6]so that with one heart and mouth you may glorify the God and Father of our Lord Jesus Christ.
2 Cor 1 [3]Praise be to the God and Father of our Lord Jesus Christ, the Father of compassion and the God of all comfort. . . .
Eph 1 [3]Praise be to the God and Father of our Lord Jesus Christ, who has blessed us in the heavenly realms with every spiritual blessing in Christ.
Col 1 [3]We always thank God, the Father of our Lord Jesus Christ, when we pray for you. . . .
1 Pet 1 [3]Praise be to the God and Father of our Lord Jesus Christ! In his great mercy he has given us new birth into a living hope through the resurrection of Jesus Christ from the dead. . . .

31. Father of Our Spirits

Heb 12 [9]Moreover, we have all had human fathers who disciplined us and we respected them for it. How much more should we submit to the Father of our spirits and live!

32. Father of the Heavenly Lights

James 1 [17]Every good and perfect gift is from above, coming down from the Father of the heavenly lights, who does not change like shifting shadows.

33. Feathers

Ps 91 [4]He will cover you with his feathers, and under his wings you will find refuge; his faithfulness will be your shield and rampart.

34. First and Last

Isa 41 [4]"Who has done this and carried it through, calling forth the generations from the beginning? I, the LORD—with the first of them and with the last—I am he."
Isa 44 [6]"This is what the LORD says—Israel's King and Redeemer, the LORD Almighty: I am the first and I am the last; apart from me there is no God."
Isa 48 [12]"Listen to me, O Jacob, Israel, whom I have called: I am he; I am the first and I am the last."

35. Foe

Lam 2 [4]Like an enemy he has strung his bow; his right hand is ready. Like a foe he has slain all who were pleasing to the eye; he has poured out his wrath like fire on the tent of the Daughter of Zion.

36. Fortress

2 Sam 22 [2]He said: "The LORD is my rock, my fortress and my deliverer. . . ."
Ps 46 [11]The LORD Almighty is with us; the God of Jacob is our fortress.
Ps 48 [3]God is in her citadels; he has shown himself to be her fortress.
Ps 59 [17]O my Strength, I sing praise to you; you, O God, are my fortress, my loving God.
Ps 62 [2]He alone is my rock and my salvation; he is my fortress, I will never be shaken.
Ps 71 [3]Be my rock of refuge, to which I can always go; give the command to save me, for you are my rock and my fortress.
Ps 91 [2]I will say of the LORD, "He is my refuge and my fortress, my God, in whom I trust."
Ps 144 [2]He is my loving God and my fortress, my stronghold and my deliverer, my shield, in whom I take refuge, who subdues peoples under me.
Isa 17 [10]You have forgotten God your Savior; you have not remembered the Rock, your fortress. Therefore, though you set out the finest plants and plant imported vines . . .
Jer 16 [19]O LORD, my strength and my fortress, my refuge in time of distress, to you the nations will come from the ends of the earth and say, "Our fathers possessed nothing but false gods, worthless idols that did them no good."

37. Fortress of Salvation

Ps 28 [8]The LORD is the strength of his people, a fortress of salvation for his anointed one.

38. Friend from Youth

Jer 3 [4]"Have you not just called to me: 'My Father, my friend from my youth . . . ?'"

39. Gardener

John 15 [1]"I am the true vine, and my Father is the gardener."

40. Glorious Crown

Isa 28 [5]In that day the LORD Almighty will be a glorious crown, a beautiful wreath for the remnant of his people.

41. Glorious Father

Eph 1 [17]I keep asking that the God of our Lord Jesus Christ, the glorious Father, may give you the Spirit of wisdom and revelation, so that you may know him better.

42. Glorious Sword

Deut 33 [29]"Blessed are you, O Israel! Who is like you, a people saved by the LORD? He is your shield and helper and your glorious sword. Your enemies will cower before you, and you will trample down their high places."

43. Glory

Ps 89 [17]For you are their glory and strength, and by your favor you exalt our horn.

44. Great King

Ps 48 [1]Great is the LORD, and most worthy of praise, in the city of our God, his holy mountain. [2]It is beautiful in its loftiness, the joy of the whole earth. Like the utmost heights of Zaphon is Mount Zion, the city of the Great King. [3]God is in her citadels; he has shown himself to be her fortress.

45. Great King above All Gods

Ps 95 [3]For the LORD is the great God, the great King above all gods.

46. Great King over All the Earth

Ps 47 [2]How awesome is the LORD Most High, the great King over all the earth!

47. Green Pine Tree

Hos 14 [8]"O Ephraim, what more have I to do with idols? I will answer him and care for him. I am like a green pine tree; your fruitfulness comes from me."

48. Guide

Ps 48 [14]For this God is our God for ever and ever; he will be our guide even to the end.

49. Heaven

Dan 4 [26]"The command to leave the stump of the tree with its roots means that your kingdom will be restored to you when you acknowledge that Heaven rules."

50. Heavenly Father

Matt 6 [14]"For if you forgive men when they sin against you, your heavenly Father will also forgive you. [15]But if you do not forgive men their sins, your Father will not forgive your sins."

51. Help

Ps 30 [10]"Hear, O LORD, and be merciful to me; O LORD, be my help."
Ps 33 [20]We wait in hope for the LORD; he is our help and our shield.
Ps 54 [4]Surely God is my help; the Lord is the one who sustains me.
Ps 70 [5]Yet I am poor and needy; come quickly to me, O God. You are my help and my deliverer; O LORD, do not delay.
Ps 115 [9]O house of Israel, trust in the LORD—he is their help and shield. [10]O house of Aaron, trust in the LORD—he is their help and shield. [11]You who fear him, trust in the LORD—he is their help and shield.
Ps 146 [5]Blessed is he whose help is the God of Jacob, whose hope is in the LORD his God. . . .

52. Helper

Deut 33 [29]"Blessed are you, O Israel! Who is like you, a people saved by the LORD? He is your shield and helper and your glorious sword. Your enemies will cower before you, and you will trample down their high places."
Ps 10 [14]But you, O God, do see trouble and grief; you consider it to take it in hand. The victim commits himself to you; you are the helper of the fatherless.
Ps 27 [9]Do not hide your face from me, do not turn your servant away in anger; you have been my helper. Do not reject me or forsake me, O God my Savior.
Ps 118 [7]The LORD is with me; he is my helper. I will look in triumph on my enemies.
Heb 13 [6]So we say with confidence, "The Lord is my helper; I will not be afraid. What can man do to me?"

53. He Who Calls

Rom 9 [11]Yet, before the twins were born or had done anything good or bad—in order that God's purpose in election might stand: [12]not by works but by him who calls—she was told, "The older will serve the younger."
Gal 1 [6]I am astonished that you are so quickly deserting the one who called you by the grace of Christ and are turning to a different gospel . . .
Gal 5 [8]That kind of persuasion does not come from the one who calls you.
1 Thess 5 [24]The one who calls you is faithful and he will do it.
1 Pet 1 [15]But just as he who called you is holy, so be holy in all you do . . .
1 Pet 2 [9]But you are a chosen people, a royal priesthood, a holy nation, a people belonging to God, that you may declare the praises of him who called you out of darkness into his wonderful light.

54. Hiding Place

Ps 32 [7]You are my hiding place; you will protect me from trouble and surround me with songs of deliverance.

55. Holy Father

John 17 [11]"I will remain in the world no longer, but they are still in the world, and I am coming to you. Holy Father, protect them by the power of your name—the name you gave me—so that they may be one as we are one."

56. Hope

Ps 65 [5]You answer us with awesome deeds of righteousness, O God our Savior, the hope of all the ends of the earth and of the farthest seas. . . .
Ps 71 [5]For you have been my hope, O Sovereign LORD, my confidence since my youth.

57. Hope of Israel

Jer 14 [8]O Hope of Israel, its Savior in times of distress, why are you like a stranger in the land, like a traveler who stays only a night?
Jer 17 [13]O LORD, the hope of Israel, all who forsake you will be put to shame. Those who turn away from you will be written in the dust because they have forsaken the LORD, the spring of living water.

58. Hope of Their Fathers

Jer 50 [7]"Whoever found them devoured them; their enemies said, 'We are not guilty, for they sinned against the LORD, their true pasture, the LORD, the hope of their fathers.'"

59. Horn of Salvation

2 Sam 22 [3]". . . my God is my rock, in whom I take refuge, my shield and the horn of my salvation. He is my stronghold, my refuge and my savior—from violent men you save me."

60. Husband

Isa 54 [5]"For your Maker is your husband—the LORD Almighty is his name—the Holy One of Israel is your Redeemer; he is called the God of all the earth."
Jer 3 [14]"Return, faithless people," declares the LORD, "for I am your husband. I will choose you—one from a town and two from a clan—and bring you to Zion."
Jer 31 [32]"It will not be like the covenant I made with their forefathers when I took them by the hand to lead them out of Egypt, because they broke my covenant, though I was a husband to them," declares the LORD.
Ezek 16 [32]"'You adulterous wife! You prefer strangers to your own husband!'"
Hos 2 [16]"In that day," declares the LORD, "you will call me 'my husband'; you will no longer call me 'my master.'"

61. Inheritance

Num 18 [20]The LORD said to Aaron, "You will have no inheritance in their land, nor will you have any share among them; I am your share and your inheritance among the Israelites."
Deut 10 [9](That is why the Levites have no share or inheritance among their brothers; the LORD is their inheritance, as the LORD your God told them.)
Deut 18 [2]They shall have no inheritance among their brothers; the LORD is their inheritance, as he promised them.
Josh 13 [33]But to the tribe of Levi, Moses had given no inheritance; the LORD, the God of Israel, is their inheritance, as he promised them.
Ezek 44 [28]"'I am to be the only inheritance the priests have. You are to give them no possession in Israel; I will be their possession.'"

62. Judge

Job 9 [15]"Though I were innocent, I could not answer him; I could only plead with my Judge for mercy."
Isa 33 [22]For the LORD is our judge, the LORD is our lawgiver, the LORD is our king; it is he who will save us.
John 8 [50]"I am not seeking glory for myself; but there is one who seeks it, and he is the judge."
James 4 [12]There is only one Lawgiver and Judge, the one who is able to save and destroy. But you—who are you to judge your neighbor?
James 5 [9]Don't grumble against each other, brothers, or you will be judged. The Judge is standing at the door!
See also p. 165b, God as Judge

63. Judge of All Men

Heb 12 [23]to the church of the firstborn, whose names are written in heaven. You have come to God, the judge of all men, to the spirits of righteous men made perfect. . . .

64. Judge of the Earth

Gen 18 [25]"Far be it from you to do such a thing—to kill the righteous with the wicked, treating the righteous and the wicked alike. Far be it from you! Will not the Judge of all the earth do right?"
Ps 94 [2]Rise up, O Judge of the earth; pay back to the proud what they deserve.

65. Keeper

Ps 121 [5]The LORD is your keeper; the LORD is your shade on your right hand (RSV).

66. King

Ps 5 [2]Listen to my cry for help, my King and my God, for to you I pray.
Ps 10 [16]The LORD is King for ever and ever; the nations will perish from his land.
Ps 29 [10]The LORD sits enthroned over the flood; the LORD is enthroned as King forever.
Ps 84 [3]Even the sparrow has found a home, and the swallow a nest for herself, where she may have her young—a place near your altar, O LORD Almighty, my King and my God.
Ps 99 [4]The King is mighty, he loves justice—you have established equity; in Jacob you have done what is just and right.
Ps 145 [1]I will exalt you, my God the King; I will praise your name for ever and ever.
Isa 6 [5]"Woe to me!" I cried. "I am ruined! For I am a man of unclean lips, and I live among a people of unclean lips, and my eyes have seen the King, the LORD Almighty."
Isa 33 [22]For the LORD is our judge, the LORD is our lawgiver, the LORD is our king; it is he who will save us.
Isa 43 [15]"I am the LORD, your Holy One, Israel's Creator, your King."
Zech 14 [9]The LORD will be king over the whole earth. On that day there will be one LORD, and his name the only name.

67. King Eternal

Jer 10 [10]"But the LORD is the true God; he is the living God, the eternal King. When he is angry, the earth trembles; the nations cannot endure his wrath."
1 Tim 1 [17]Now to the King eternal, immortal, invisible, the only God, be honor and glory for ever and ever. Amen.

68. King from of Old

Ps 74 [12]But you, O God, are my king from of old; you bring salvation upon the earth.

69. King of All the Earth

Ps 47 [7]For God is the king of all the earth; sing to him a psalm of praise.

70. King of Glory

Ps 24 [7]Lift up your heads, O you gates; be lifted up, you ancient doors, that the King of glory may come in. [8]Who is this King of glory? The LORD strong and mighty, the LORD mighty in battle. [9]Lift up your heads, O you gates; lift them up, you ancient doors, that the King of glory may come in. [10]Who is he, this King of glory? The LORD Almighty—he is the King of glory.

71. King of Heaven

Dan 4 [37]Now I, Nebuchadnezzar, praise and exalt and glorify the King of heaven, because everything he does is right and all his ways are just. And those who walk in pride he is able to humble.

72. King of Israel

Isa 44 [6]"This is what the LORD says—Israel's King and Redeemer, the LORD Almighty: I am the first and I am the last; apart from me there is no God."
Zeph 3 [15]The LORD has taken away your punishment, he has turned back your enemy. The LORD, the King of Israel, is with you; never again will you fear any harm.

73. King of Kings

1 Tim 6 [15]which God will bring about in his own time—God, the blessed and only Ruler, the King of kings and Lord of Lords . . .

74. King of the Ages

Rev 15 [3]and sang the song of Moses the servant of God and the song of the Lamb: "Great and marvelous are your deeds, Lord God Almighty. Just and true are your ways, King of the ages."

75. King of the Nations

Jer 10 [7]Who should not revere you, O King of the nations? This is your due. Among all the wise men of the nations and in all their kingdoms, there is no one like you.

76. Lamp

2 Sam 22 [29]"You are my lamp, O LORD; the LORD turns my darkness into light."

77. Lawgiver

Isa 33 [22]For the LORD is our judge, the LORD is our lawgiver, the LORD is our king; it is he who will save us.
James 4 [12]There is only one Lawgiver and Judge, the one who is able to save and destroy. But you—who are you to judge your neighbor?

78. Leader

2 Chron 13 [12]"God is with us; he is our leader. His priests with their trumpets will sound the battle cry against you. Men of Israel, do not fight against the LORD, the God of your fathers, for you will not succeed."

79. Leopard

Hos 13 [7]"So I will come upon them like a lion, like a leopard I will lurk by the path."

80. Life

Deut 30 [19]This day I call heaven and earth as witnesses against you that I have set before you life and death, blessings and curses. Now choose life, so that you and your children may live [20]and that you may love the LORD your God, listen to his voice, and hold fast to him. For the LORD is your life, and he will give you many years in the land he swore to give to your fathers, Abraham, Isaac and Jacob.

81. Light

Ps 27 [1]The LORD is my light and my salvation—whom shall I fear? The LORD is the stronghold of my life—of whom shall I be afraid?
Isa 60 [19]"The sun will no more be your light by day, nor will the brightness of the moon shine on you, for the LORD will be your everlasting light, and your God will be your glory. [20]Your sun will never set again, and your moon will wane no more; the LORD will be your everlasting light, and your days of sorrow will end."
Mic 7 [8]Do not gloat over me, my enemy! Though I have fallen, I will rise. Though I sit in darkness, the LORD will be my light.
1 John 1 [5]This is the message we have heard from him and declare to you: God is light; in him there is no darkness at all.

82. Lion

Isa 31 [4]This is what the LORD says to me: "As a lion growls, a great lion over his prey—and though a whole band of shepherds is called together against him, he is not frightened by their shouts or disturbed by their clamor—so the LORD Almighty will come down to do battle on Mount Zion and on its heights."
Hos 5 [14]"For I will be like a lion to Ephraim, like a great lion to Judah. I will tear them to pieces and go away; I will carry them off, with no one to rescue them."
Hos 11 [10]"They will follow the LORD; he will roar like a lion. When he roars, his children will come trembling from the west."
Hos 13 [7]"So I will come upon them like a lion, like a leopard I will lurk by the path. [8]Like a bear robbed of her cubs, I will attack them and rip them open. Like a lion I will devour them; a wild animal will tear them apart."
Amos 3 [8]The lion has roared—who will not fear? The Sovereign LORD has spoken—who can but prophesy?

83. Love

1 John 4 [8]Whoever does not love does not know God, because God is love.
1 John 4 [16]And so we know and rely on the love God has for us. God is love. Whoever lives in love lives in God, and God in him.

84. Maker

Job 4 [17]"'Can a mortal be more righteous than God? Can a man be more pure than his Maker?'"
Ps 95 [6]Come, let us bow down in worship, let us kneel before the LORD our Maker. . . .
Ps 149 [2]Let Israel rejoice in their Maker; let the people of Zion be glad in their King.
Isa 17 [7]In that day men will look to their Maker and turn their eyes to the Holy One of Israel.
Isa 54 [5]"For your Maker is your husband—the LORD Almighty is his name—the Holy One of Israel is your Redeemer; he is called the God of all the earth."

85. Maker of All Things

Prov 22 [2]Rich and poor have this in common: The LORD is the Maker of them all.
Eccles 11 [5]As you do not know the path of the wind, or how the body is formed in a mother's womb, so you cannot understand the work of God, the Maker of all things.
Jer 10 [16]He who is the Portion of Jacob is not like these, for he is the Maker of all things, including Israel, the tribe of his inheritance—the LORD Almighty is his name.

86. Maker of Heaven and Earth

Ps 115 [15]May you be blessed by the LORD, the Maker of heaven and earth.
Ps 121 [2]My help comes from the LORD, the Maker of heaven and earth.
Ps 134 [3]May the LORD, the Maker of heaven and earth, bless you from Zion.
Ps 146 [6]the Maker of heaven and earth, the sea, and everything in them—the LORD, who remains faithful forever.

87. Master

Hos 2 [16]"In that day," declares the LORD, "you will call me 'my husband'; you will no longer call me 'my master.'"
Mal 1 [6]"A son honors his father, and a servant his master. If I am a father, where is the honor due me? If I am a master, where is the respect due me?" says the LORD Almighty. "It is you, O priests, who show contempt for my name.

"But you ask, 'How have we shown contempt for your name?'"

88. Mighty Man

Isa 42 [13]The LORD will march out like a mighty man, like a warrior he will stir up his zeal; with a shout he will raise the battle cry and will triumph over his enemies.

89. Mighty Warrior

Jer 20 [11]But the LORD is with me like a mighty warrior; so my persecutors will stumble and not prevail. They will fail and be thoroughly disgraced; their dishonor will never be forgotten.

90. Moth

Hos 5 [12]"I am like a moth to Ephraim, like rot to the people of Judah."

91. Mother

Isa 49 [13]"Shout for joy, O heavens; rejoice, O earth; burst into song, O mountains! For the LORD comforts his people and will have compassion on the afflicted ones. . . . [15]Can a mother forget the baby at her breast and have no compassion on the child she has borne? Though she may forget, I will not forget you!"
Isa 66 [13]"As a mother comforts her child, so will I comfort you; and you will be comforted over Jerusalem."

92. Name

Exod 23 [21]"Pay attention to him and listen to what he says. Do not rebel against him; he will not forgive your rebellion, since my Name is in him."
Deut 12 [5]But you are to seek the place the LORD your God will choose from among all your tribes to put his Name there for his dwelling. To that place you must go. . . . [7]There, in the presence of the LORD your God, you and your families shall eat and shall rejoice in everything you have put your hand to, because the LORD your God has blessed you.

1 Kings 8 [29]"May your eyes be open toward this temple night and day, this place of which you said, 'My Name shall be there,' so that you will hear the prayer your servant prays toward this place."
2 Chron 33 [4]He built altars in the temple of the LORD, of which the LORD had said, "My Name will remain in Jerusalem forever."
Ezra 6 [12]May God, who has caused his Name to dwell there, overthrow any king or people who lifts a hand to change this decree or to destroy this temple in Jerusalem.

I Darius have decreed it. Let it be carried out with diligence.
Ps 75 [1]We give thanks to you, O God, we give thanks, for your Name is near; men tell of your wonderful deeds.

93. Portion

Ps 73 [26]My flesh and my heart may fail, but God is the strength of my heart and my portion forever.
Ps 119 [57]You are my portion, O LORD; I have promised to obey your words.
Ps 142 [5]I cry to you, O LORD; I say, "You are my refuge, my portion in the land of the living."
Lam 3 [24]I say to myself, "The LORD is my portion; therefore I will wait for him."

94. Portion of Jacob

Jer 51 [19]"He who is the Portion of Jacob is not like these, for he is the Maker of all things, including the tribe of his inheritance—the LORD Almighty is his name."

95. Potter

Isa 29 [16]You turn things upside down, as if the potter were thought to be like the clay! Shall what is formed say to him who formed it, "He did not make me"? Can the pot say of the potter, "He knows nothing"?
Isa 45 [9]"Woe to him who quarrels with his Maker, to him who is but a potsherd among the potsherds on the ground. Does the clay say to the potter, 'What are you making?' Does your work say, 'He has no hands'?"
Isa 64 [8]Yet, O LORD, you are our Father. We are the clay, you are the potter; we are all the work of your hand.
Jer 18 [1]This is the word that came to Jeremiah from the LORD: [2]"Go down to the potter's house, and there I will give you my message." [3]So I went down to the potter's house, and I saw him working at the wheel. [4]But the pot he was shaping from the clay was marred in his hands; so the potter formed it into another pot, shaping it as seemed best to him.

[5]Then the word of the LORD came to me: [6]"O house of Israel, can I not do with you as this potter does?" declares the LORD. "Like clay in the hand of the potter, so are you in my hand, O house of Israel."
Rom 9 [21]Does not the potter have the right to make out of the same lump of clay some pottery for noble purposes and some for common use?

96. Praise of Israel

Ps 22 [3]Yet you are enthroned as the Holy One; you are the praise of Israel.

97. Redeemer

Job 19 [25]"I know that my Redeemer lives, and that in the end he will stand upon the earth."
Ps 19 [14]May the words of my mouth and the meditation of my heart be pleasing in your sight, O LORD, my Rock and my Redeemer.
Ps 78 [35]They remembered that God was their Rock, that God Most High was their Redeemer.
Isa 43 [14]This is what the LORD says—your Redeemer, the Holy One of Israel: "For your sake I will send to Babylon and bring down as fugitives all the Babylonians, in the ships in which they took pride."
Isa 44 [6]"This is what the LORD says—Israel's King and Redeemer, the LORD Almighty: I am the first and I am the last; apart from me there is no God."
Isa 44 [24]"This is what the LORD says—your Redeemer, who formed you in the womb: I am the LORD, who has made all things, who alone stretched out the heavens, who spread out the earth by myself. . . ."
Isa 47 [4]Our Redeemer—the LORD Almighty is his name—is the Holy One of Israel.
Isa 49 [26]"I will make your oppressors eat their own flesh; they will be drunk on their own blood, as with wine. Then all mankind will know that I, the LORD, am your Savior, your Redeemer, the Mighty One of Jacob."
Isa 54 [5]"For your Maker is your husband—the LORD Almighty is his name—the Holy One of Israel is your Redeemer; he is called the God of all the earth. . . . [8]In a surge of anger I hid my face from you for a moment, but with everlasting kindness I will have compassion on you," says the LORD your Redeemer.
Isa 59 [20]"The Redeemer will come to Zion, to those in Jacob who repent of their sins," declares the LORD.
Isa 60 [16]"You will drink the milk of nations and be nursed at royal breasts. Then you will know that I, the LORD, am your Savior, your Redeemer, the Mighty One of Jacob."
Jer 50 [34]"Yet their Redeemer is strong; the LORD Almighty is his name. He will vigorously defend their cause so that he may bring rest to their land, but unrest to those who live in Babylon."

98. Redeemer of Old

Isa 63 [16]But you are our Father, though Abraham does not know us or Israel acknowledge us; you, O LORD, are our Father, our Redeemer from of old is your name.

99. Refuge

Deut 33 [27]"The eternal God is your refuge, and underneath are the everlasting arms. He will drive out your enemy before you, saying, 'Destroy him!'"
2 Sam 22 [3]". . . my God is my rock, in whom I take refuge, my shield and the horn of my salvation. He is my stronghold, my refuge and my savior—from violent men you save me."
2 Sam 22 [31]"As for God, his way is perfect; the word of the LORD is flawless. He is a shield for all who take refuge in him."
Ps 7 [1]O LORD my God, I take refuge in you; save and deliver me from all who pursue me. . . .
Ps 9 [9]The LORD is a refuge for the oppressed, a stronghold in times of trouble.
Ps 14 [6]You evildoers frustrate the plans of the poor, but the LORD is their refuge.
Ps 46 [1]God is our refuge and strength, an ever-present help in trouble.
Ps 59 [16]But I will sing of your strength, in the morning I will sing of your love; for you are my fortress, my refuge in times of trouble.
Ps 62 [7]My salvation and my honor depend on God; he is my mighty rock, my refuge. [8]Trust in him at all times, O people; pour out your hearts to him, for God is our refuge.
Ps 73 [28]But as for me, it is good to be near God. I have made the Sovereign LORD my refuge; I will tell of all your deeds.
Ps 142 [5]I cry to you, O LORD; I say, "You are my refuge, my portion in the land of the living."
Isa 25 [4]You have been a refuge for the poor, a refuge for the needy in his distress, a shelter from the storm and a shade from the heat. For the breath of the ruthless is like a storm driving against a wall. . . .
Isa 57 [13]"When you cry out for help, let your collection of idols save you! The wind will carry all of them off, a mere breath will blow them away. But the man who makes me his refuge will inherit the land and possess my holy mountain."
Jer 16 [19]O LORD, my strength and my fortress, my refuge in time of distress, to you the nations will come from the ends of the earth and say, "Our fathers possessed nothing but false gods, worthless idols that did them no good."
Jer 17 [17]Do not be a terror to me; you are my refuge in the day of disaster.
Joel 3 [16]The LORD will roar from Zion and thunder from Jerusalem; the earth and the sky will tremble. But the LORD will be a refuge for his people, a stronghold for the people of Israel.
Nah 1 [7]The LORD is good, a refuge in times of trouble. He cares for those who trust in him. . . .

100. Revealer of Mysteries

Dan 2 [29]"As you were lying there, O king, your mind turned to things to come, and the revealer of mysteries showed you what is going to happen."
Dan 2 [47]The king said to Daniel, "Surely your God is the God of gods and the Lord of kings and a revealer of mysteries, for you were able to reveal this mystery."

101. Reward

Gen 15 [1]After this, the word of the LORD came to Abram in a vision: "Do not be afraid, Abram. I am your shield, your very great reward."

102. Righteous Father

John 17 [25]"Righteous Father, though the world does not know you, I know you, and they know that you have sent me."

103. Righteous Judge

Ps 7 [11]God is a righteous judge, a God who expresses his wrath every day.

104. Roar

Jer 25 [30]"Now prophesy all these words against them and say to them: 'The LORD will roar from on high; he will thunder from his holy dwelling and roar mightily against his land. He will shout like those who tread the grapes, shout against all who live on the earth.'"
Amos 1 [2]He said: "The LORD roars from Zion and thunders from Jerusalem; the pastures of the shepherds dry up, and the top of Carmel withers."

105. Rock

Deut 32 [4]He is the Rock, his works are perfect, and all his ways are just. A faithful God who does no wrong, upright and just is he.
Deut 32 [15]Jeshurun grew fat and kicked; filled with food, he became heavy and sleek. He abandoned the God who made him and rejected the Rock his Savior.
Deut 32 [18]You deserted the Rock, who fathered you; you forgot the God who gave you birth.
Deut 32 [30]How could one man chase a thousand, or two put ten thousand to flight, unless their Rock had sold them, unless the LORD had given them up? [31]For their rock is not like our Rock, as even our enemies concede.
1 Sam 2 [2]"There is no one holy like the LORD; there is no one besides you; there is no Rock like our God."
2 Sam 22 [2]He said: "The LORD is my rock, my fortress and my deliverer; [3]my God is my rock, in whom I take refuge, my shield and the horn of my salvation. He is my stronghold, my refuge and my savior—from violent men you save me."
2 Sam 22 [32]"For who is God besides the LORD? And who is the Rock except our God?"
2 Sam 22 [47]"The LORD lives! Praise be to my Rock! Exalted be God, the Rock, my Savior!"
Ps 19 [14]May the words of my mouth and the meditation of my heart be pleasing in your sight, O LORD, my Rock and my Redeemer.
Ps 31 [2]Turn your ear to me, come quickly to my rescue; be my rock of refuge, a strong fortress to save me. [3]Since you are my rock and my fortress, for the sake of your name lead and guide me.
Ps 62 [6]He alone is my rock and my salvation; he is my fortress, I will not be shaken. [7]My salvation and my honor depend on God; he is my mighty rock, my refuge.
Ps 92 [15]proclaiming, "The LORD is upright; he is my Rock, and there is no wickedness in him."
Ps 144 [1]Praise be to the LORD my Rock, who trains my hands for war, my fingers for battle.
Isa 17 [10]You have forgotten God your Savior; you have not remembered the Rock, your fortress. Therefore, though you set out the finest plants and plant imported vines . . .
Isa 44 [8]"Do not tremble, do not be afraid. Did I not proclaim this and foretell it long ago? You are my witnesses. Is there any God besides me? No, there is no other Rock; I know not one."

106. Rock Eternal

Isa 26 [4]Trust in the LORD forever, for the LORD, the LORD, is the Rock eternal.

107. Rock of Israel

Gen 49 [24]"But his bow remained steady, his strong arms stayed limber, because of the hand of the Mighty One of Jacob, because of the Shepherd, the Rock of Israel. . . ."
2 Sam 23 [3]"The God of Israel spoke, the Rock of Israel said to me: 'When one rules over men in righteousness, when he rules in the fear of God . . .'"
Isa 30 [29]And you will sing as on the night you celebrate a holy festival; your hearts will rejoice as when people go up with flutes to the mountain of the LORD, to the Rock of Israel.

108. Rock of Our Salvation

Ps 95 [1]Come, let us sing for joy to the LORD; let us shout aloud to the Rock of our salvation.

109. Rock That Makes Men Fall

Isa 8 [14]". . . and he will be a sanctuary; but for both houses of Israel he will be a stone that causes men to stumble and a rock that makes them fall. And for the people of Jerusalem he will be a trap and a snare."

110. Rot

Hos 5 [12]"I am like a moth to Ephraim, like rot to the people of Judah."

111. Ruler of All Things

1 Chron 29 [12]"Wealth and honor come from you; you are the ruler of all things. In your hands are strength and power to exalt and give strength to all."

112. Salvation

Exod 15 [2]"The LORD is my strength and my song; he has become my salvation. He is my God, and I will praise him, my father's God, and I will exalt him."
Ps 27 [1]The LORD is my light and my salvation—whom shall I fear? The LORD is the stronghold of my life—of whom shall I be afraid?
Ps 62 [2]He alone is my rock and my salvation; he is my fortress, I will never be shaken.
Ps 118 [14]The LORD is my strength and my song; he has become my salvation . . . [21]I will give you thanks, for you answered me; you have become my salvation.
Isa 12 [2]"Surely God is my salvation; I will trust and not be afraid. The LORD, the LORD, is my strength and my song; he has become my salvation."

113. Sanctuary

Isa 8 [13]"The LORD Almighty is the one you are to regard as holy, he is the one you are to fear, he is the one you are to dread, [14]and he will be a sanctuary; but for both houses of Israel he will be a stone that causes men to stumble and a rock that makes them fall. And for the people of Jerusalem he will be a trap and a snare."

114. Savior

Deut 32 [15]Jeshurun grew fat and kicked; filled with food, he became heavy and sleek. He abandoned the God who made him and rejected the Rock his Savior.
2 Sam 22 [3]". . . my God is my rock, in whom I take refuge, my shield and the horn of my salvation. He is my stronghold, my refuge and my savior—from violent men you save me."
2 Sam 22 [47]"The LORD lives! Praise be to my Rock! Exalted be God, the Rock, my Savior!"
Ps 27 [9]Do not hide your face from me, do not turn your servant away in anger; you have been my helper. Do not reject me or forsake me, O God my Savior.
Ps 38 [22]Come quickly to help me, O Lord my Savior.
Ps 42 [11]Why are you downcast, O my soul? Why so disturbed

within me? Put your hope in God, for I will yet praise him, my Savior and my God.
Ps 68 [19]Praise be to the Lord, to God our Savior, who daily bears our burdens.
Ps 89 [26]"He will call out to me, 'You are my Father, my God, the Rock my Savior.'"
Isa 45 [21]"Declare what is to be, present it—let them take counsel together. Who foretold this long ago, who declared it from the distant past? Was it not I, the LORD? And there is no God apart from me, a righteous God and a Savior; there is none but me."
Jer 14 [8]O Hope of Israel, its Savior in times of distress, why are you like a stranger in the land, like a traveler who stays only a night?
Hos 13 [4]"But I am the LORD your God, who brought you out of Egypt. You shall acknowledge no God but me, no Savior except me."
Mic 7 [7]But as for me, I watch in hope for the LORD, I wait for God my Savior; my God will hear me.
Hab 3 [18]yet I will rejoice in the LORD, I will be joyful in God my Savior.
Luke 1 [47]". . . and my spirit rejoices in God my Savior. . . ."
1 Tim 1 [1]Paul, an apostle of Christ Jesus by the command of God our Savior and of Christ Jesus our hope . . .
Jude [25]to the only God our Savior be glory, majesty, power and authority, through Jesus Christ our Lord, before all ages, now and forevermore! Amen.

115. Savior of All Men

1 Tim 4 [10](and for this we labor and strive), that we have put our hope in the living God, who is the Savior of all men, and especially of those who believe.

116. Savior of Israel

Isa 45 [15]Truly you are a God who hides himself, O God and Savior of Israel.

117. Shade

Ps 121 [5]The LORD watches over you—the LORD is your shade at your right hand; [6]the sun will not harm you by day, nor the moon by night.
Isa 25 [4]You have been a refuge for the poor, a refuge for the needy in his distress, a shelter from the storm and a shade from the heat. For the breath of the ruthless is like a storm driving against a wall [5]and like the heat of the desert. You silence the uproar of foreigners; as heat is reduced by the shadow of a cloud, so the song of the ruthless is stilled.

118. Share

Num 18 [20]The LORD said to Aaron, "You will have no inheritance in their land, nor will you have any share among them; I am your share and your inheritance among the Israelites."

119. Shelter

Isa 25 [4]You have been a refuge for the poor, a refuge for the needy in his distress, a shelter from the storm and a shade from the heat. For the breath of the ruthless is like a storm driving against a wall. . . .

120. Shepherd

Gen 49 [24]"But his bow remained steady, his strong arms stayed limber, because of the hand of the Mighty One of Jacob, because of the Shepherd, the Rock of Israel. . . ."
Ps 23 [1]The LORD is my shepherd, I shall not be in want.
Ps 28 [9]Save your people and bless your inheritance; be their shepherd and carry them forever.
Eccles 12 [11]The words of the wise are like goads, their collected sayings like firmly embedded nails—given by one Shepherd.
Isa 40 [11]He tends his flock like a shepherd: He gathers the lambs in his arms and carries them close to his heart; he gently leads those that have young.
Ezek 34 [11]"'For this is what the Sovereign LORD says: I myself will search for my sheep and look after them. [12]As a shepherd looks after his scattered flock when he is with them, so will I look after my sheep. I will rescue them from all the places where they were scattered on a day of clouds and darkness. [13]I will bring them out from the nations and gather them from the countries, and I will bring them into their own land. I will pasture them on the mountains of Israel, in the ravines and in all the settlements in the land. [14]I will tend them in a good pasture, and the mountain heights of Israel will be their grazing land. There they will lie down in good grazing land, and there they will feed in a rich pasture on the mountains of Israel. [15]I myself will tend my sheep and have them lie down, declares the Sovereign LORD. [16]I will search for the lost and bring back the strays. I will bind up the injured and strengthen the weak, but the sleek and the strong I will destroy. I will shepherd the flock with justice.'"

121. Shepherd of Israel

Ps 80 [1]Hear us, O Shepherd of Israel, you who lead Joseph like a flock; you who sit enthroned between the cherubim, shine forth. . . .

122. Shield

Gen 15 [1]After this, the word of the LORD came to Abram in a vision: "Do not be afraid, Abram. I am your shield, your very great reward."
Deut 33 [29]"Blessed are you, O Israel! Who is like you, a people saved by the LORD? He is your shield and helper and your glorious sword. Your enemies will cower before you, and you will trample down their high places."
2 Sam 22 [3]". . . my God is my rock, in whom I take refuge, my shield and the horn of my salvation. He is my stronghold, my refuge and my savior—from violent men you save me."
2 Sam 22 [31]"As for God, his way is perfect; the word of the LORD is flawless. He is a shield for all who take refuge in him."
Ps 7 [10]My shield is God Most High, who saves the upright in heart.
Ps 28 [7]The LORD is my strength and my shield; my heart trusts in him, and I am helped. My heart leaps for joy and I will give thanks to him in song.
Ps 33 [20]We wait in hope for the LORD; he is our help and our shield.
Ps 59 [11]But do not kill them, O Lord our shield, or my people will forget. In your might make them wander about, and bring them down.
Ps 84 [11]For the LORD God is a sun and shield; the LORD bestows favor and honor; no good thing does he withhold from those whose walk is blameless.
Ps 115 [9]O house of Israel, trust in the LORD—he is their help and shield. [10]O house of Aaron, trust in the LORD—he is their help and shield. [11]You who fear him, trust in the LORD—he is their help and shield.
Ps 144 [2]He is my loving God and my fortress, my stronghold and my deliverer, my shield, in whom I take refuge, who subdues peoples under me.
Prov 2 [6]For the LORD gives wisdom, and from his mouth come knowledge and understanding. [7]He holds victory in store for the upright, he is a shield to those whose walk is blameless. . . .
Prov 30 [5]"Every word of God is flawless; he is a shield to those who take refuge in him."

123. Snare

Isa 8 [14]". . . and he will be a sanctuary; but for both houses of Israel he will be a stone that causes men to stumble and a rock that makes them fall. And for the people of Jerusalem he will be a trap and a snare."

124. Song

Exod 15 [2]"The LORD is my strength and my song; he has become my salvation. He is my God, and I will praise him, my father's God, and I will exalt him."
Isa 12 [2]"Surely God is my salvation; I will trust and not be afraid. The LORD, the LORD, is my strength and my song; he has become my salvation."

125. Source of Strength

Isa 28 [6]He will be a spirit of justice to him who sits in judgment, a source of strength to those who turn back the battle at the gate.

126. Spirit of Justice

Isa 28 [5]In that day the LORD Almighty will be a glorious crown, a beautiful wreath for the remnant of his people. [6]He will be a spirit of justice to him who sits in judgment, a source of strength to those who turn back the battle at the gate

127. Spring of Living Water

Jer 2 [13]"My people have committed two sins: They have forsaken me, the spring of living water, and have dug their own cisterns, broken cisterns that cannot hold water."
Jer 17 [13]O LORD, the hope of Israel, all who forsake you will be put to shame. Those who turn away from you will be written in the dust because they have forsaken the LORD, the spring of living water.

128. Stone That Causes Men to Stumble

Isa 8 [14]". . . and he will be a sanctuary; but for both houses of Israel he will be a stone that causes men to stumble and a rock that makes them fall. And for the people of Jerusalem he will be a trap and a snare."

129. Strength

Exod 15 [2]"The LORD is my strength and my song; he has become my salvation. He is my God, and I will praise him, my father's God, and I will exalt him."
Ps 18 [1]I love you, O LORD, my strength.
Ps 28 [7]The LORD is my strength and my shield; my heart trusts in him, and I am helped. My heart leaps for joy and I will give thanks to him in song.
Ps 46 [1]God is our refuge and strength, an ever-present help in trouble.
Ps 59 [9]O my Strength, I watch for you; you, O God, are my fortress. . . . [17]O my Strength, I sing praise to you; you, O God, are my fortress, my loving God.
Ps 81 [1]Sing for joy to God our strength; shout aloud to the God of Jacob!
Ps 89 [17]For you are their glory and strength, and by your favor you exalt our horn.
Isa 33 [2]O LORD, be gracious to us; we long for you. Be our strength every morning, our salvation in time of distress.
Isa 49 [5]And now the LORD says—he who formed me in the womb to be his servant to bring Jacob back to him and gather Israel to himself, for I am honored in the eyes of the LORD and my God has been my strength . . .
Jer 16 [19]O LORD, my strength and my fortress, my refuge in time of distress, to you the nations will come from the ends of the earth and say, "Our fathers possessed nothing but false gods, worthless idols that did them no good."
Hab 3 [19]The Sovereign LORD is my strength; he makes my feet like the feet of a deer, he enables me to go on the heights.

130. Strength of His People

Ps 28 [8]The LORD is the strength of his people, a fortress of salvation for his anointed one.

131. Strength of My Heart

Ps 73 [26]My flesh and my heart may fail, but God is the strength of my heart and my portion forever.

132. Strong Deliverer

Ps 140 [7]O Sovereign LORD, my strong deliverer, who shields my head in the day of battle . . .

133. Strong Fortress

Ps 31 [2]Turn your ear to me, come quickly to my rescue; be my rock of refuge, a strong fortress to save me. [3]Since you are my rock and my fortress, for the sake of your name lead and guide me.

134. Stronghold

2 Sam 22 [3]". . . my God is my rock, in whom I take refuge, my shield and the horn of my salvation. He is my stronghold, my refuge and my savior—from violent men you save me."
Ps 9 [9]The LORD is a refuge for the oppressed, a stronghold in times of trouble.
Ps 43 [2]You are God my stronghold. Why have you rejected me? Why must I go about mourning, oppressed by the enemy?
Ps 144 [2]He is my loving God and my fortress, my stronghold and my deliverer, my shield, in whom I take refuge, who subdues peoples under me.
Joel 3 [16]The LORD will roar from Zion and thunder from Jerusalem; the earth and the sky will tremble. But the LORD will be a refuge for his people, a stronghold for the people of Israel.

135. Stronghold of My Life

Ps 27 [1]The LORD is my light and my salvation—whom shall I fear? The LORD is the stronghold of my life—of whom shall I be afraid?

136. Strong Tower

Ps 61 [3]For you have been my refuge, a strong tower against the foe.
Prov 18 [10]The name of the LORD is a strong tower; the righteous run to it and are safe.

137. Sun

Ps 84 [11]For the LORD God is a sun and shield; the LORD bestows favor and honor; no good thing does he withhold from those whose walk is blameless.

138. Sun of Righteousness

Mal 4 [2]"But for you who revere my name, the sun of righteousness will rise with healing in its wings. And you will go out and leap like calves released from the stall."

139. Support

Ps 18 [18]They confronted me in the day of my disaster, but the LORD was my support.

140. Teacher

Ps 25 [9]He guides the humble in what is right and teaches them his way.
Ps 27 [11]Teach me your way, O LORD; lead me in a straight path because of my oppressors.
Ps 94 [12]Blessed is the man you discipline, O LORD, the man you teach from your law. . . .
Ps 119 [102]I have not departed from your laws, for you yourself have taught me.
Ps 119 [171]May my lips overflow with praise, for you teach me your decrees.

141. The Cruel

Jer 30 [14]"All your allies have forgotten you; they care nothing for you. I have struck you as an enemy would and punished you as would the cruel, because your guilt is so great and your sins so many."

142. Thunder

2 Sam 22 [14]"The LORD thundered from heaven; the voice of the Most High resounded."
Ps 29 [3]The voice of the LORD is over the waters; the God of glory thunders, the LORD thunders over the mighty waters.
Ps 68 [33]to him who rides the ancient skies above, who thunders with mighty voice.
Joel 2 [11]The LORD thunders at the head of his army; his forces are beyond number, and mighty are those who obey his com-

mand. The day of the LORD is great; it is dreadful. Who can endure it?

143. Trap

Isa 8 14"... and he will be a sanctuary; but for both houses of Israel he will be a stone that causes men to stumble and a rock that makes them fall. And for the people of Jerusalem he will be a trap and a snare."

144. True Pasture

Jer 50 7"Whoever found them devoured them; their enemies said, 'We are not guilty, for they sinned against the LORD, their true pasture, the LORD, the hope of their fathers.'"

145. Upright One

Ps 25 8Good and upright is the LORD; therefore he instructs sinners in his ways.
Isa 26 7The path of the righteous is level; O upright One, you make the way of the righteous smooth.

146. Wall of Fire

Zech 2 5"'And I myself will be a wall of fire around it,' declares the LORD, 'and I will be its glory within.'"

147. Warrior

Exod 15 3"The LORD is a warrior; the LORD is his name."
Ps 24 8Who is this King of glory? The LORD strong and mighty, the LORD mighty in battle.
Isa 42 13The LORD will march out like a mighty man, like a warrior he will stir up his zeal; with a shout he will raise the battle cry and will triumph over his enemies.

148. Watcher of Men

Job 7 20"If I have sinned, what have I done to you, O watcher of men? Why have you made me your target? Have I become a burden to you?"

149. Wild Animal

Hos 13 8"Like a bear robbed of her cubs, I will attack them and rip them open. Like a lion I will devour them; a wild animal will tear them apart."

150. Wings

Exod 19 4"'You yourselves have seen what I did to Egypt, and how I carried you on eagles' wings and brought you to myself.'"
Ruth 2 12"May the LORD repay you for what you have done. May you be richly rewarded by the LORD, the God of Israel, under whose wings you have come to take refuge."
Ps 17 8Keep me as the apple of your eye; hide me in the shadow of your wings....
Ps 36 7How priceless is your unfailing love! Both high and low among men shall find refuge in the shadow of your wings.
Ps 57 1Have mercy on me, O God, have mercy on me, for in you my soul takes refuge. I will take refuge in the shadow of your wings until the disaster has passed.
Ps 61 4I long to dwell in your tent forever and take refuge in the shelter of your wings.
Ps 63 7Because you are my help, I sing in the shadow of your wings.
Matt 23 37"O Jerusalem, Jerusalem, you who kill the prophets and stone those sent to you, how often I have longed to gather your children together, as a hen gathers her chicks under her wings, but you were not willing."

151. Woman

Isa 42 14"For a long time I have kept silent, I have been quiet and held myself back. But now, like a woman in childbirth, I cry out, I gasp and pant."

152. Wreath

Isa 28 5In that day the LORD Almighty will be a glorious crown, a beautiful wreath for the remnant of his people.

E. Anthropomorphisms for God

1. Arm

Deut 33 27"The eternal God is your refuge, and underneath are the everlasting arms. He will drive out your enemy before you, saying, 'Destroy him!'"
2 Chron 6 32"As for the foreigner who does not belong to your people Israel but has come from a distant land because of your great name and your mighty hand and your outstretched arm—when he comes and prays toward this temple..."
Job 40 9"Do you have an arm like God's, and can your voice thunder like his?"
Ps 44 3It was not by their sword that they won the land, nor did their arm bring them victory; it was your right hand, your arm, and the light of your face, for you loved them.
Ps 77 15With your mighty arm you redeemed your people, the descendants of Jacob and Joseph.
Ps 89 10You crushed Rahab like one of the slain; with your strong arm you scattered your enemies. . . . 13Your arm is endued with power; your hand is strong, your right hand exalted.
Ps 98 1Sing to the LORD a new song, for he has done marvelous things; his right hand and his holy arm have worked salvation for him.
Isa 52 10The LORD will lay bare his holy arm in the sight of all the nations, and all the ends of the earth will see the salvation of our God.
Isa 59 1Surely the arm of the LORD is not too short to save, nor his ear too dull to hear. . . . 16He saw that there was no one, he was appalled that there was no one to intervene; so his own arm worked salvation for him, and his own righteousness sustained him.
Isa 63 12who sent his glorious arm of power to be at Moses' right hand, who divided the waters before them, to gain for himself everlasting renown...
Jer 27 5"With my great power and outstretched arm I made the earth and its people and the animals that are on it, and I give it to anyone I please."

2. Back

Exod 33 21Then the LORD said, "There is a place near me where you may stand on a rock. 22When my glory passes by, I will put you in a cleft in the rock and cover you with my hand until I have passed by. 23Then I will remove my hand and you will see my back; but my face must not be seen."
Jer 18 17"Like a wind from the east, I will scatter them before their enemies; I will show them my back and not my face in the day of their disaster."

3. Beauty

Ps 27 4One thing I ask of the LORD, this is what I seek; that I may dwell in the house of the LORD all the days of my life, to gaze upon the beauty of the LORD and to seek him in his temple.

4. Bodily Form

Gen 18 1The LORD appeared to Abraham near the great trees of Mamre while he was sitting at the entrance to his tent in the heat of the day.
Gen 35 9After Jacob returned from Paddan Aram, God appeared to him again and blessed him.
Gen 48 3Jacob said to Joseph, "God Almighty appeared to me at Luz in the land of Canaan, and there he blessed me...."
Exod 24 9Moses and Aaron, Nadab and Abihu, and the seventy elders of Israel went up 10and saw the God of Israel. Under his feet was something like a pavement made of sapphire, clear as the sky itself. 11But God did not raise his hand against these leaders of the Israelites; they saw God, and they ate and drank.
2 Chron 7 11When Solomon had finished the temple of the LORD and the royal palace, and had succeeded in carrying out all he had in mind to do in the temple of the LORD and in his own palace, 12the LORD appeared to him at night and said: "I have heard your prayer and have chosen this place for myself as a temple for sacrifices."

Isa 6 [1]In the year that King Uzziah died, I saw the Lord seated on a throne, high and exalted, and the train of his robe filled the temple.
Ezek 1 [26]Above the expanse over their heads was what looked like a throne of sapphire, and high above on the throne was a figure like that of a man. [27]I saw that from what appeared to be his waist up he looked like glowing metal, as if full of fire, and that from there down he looked like fire; and brilliant light surrounded him. [28]Like the appearance of a rainbow in the clouds on a rainy day, so was the radiance around him.

This was the appearance of the likeness of the glory of the LORD. When I saw it, I fell facedown, and I heard the voice of one speaking.
Ezek 8 [1]In the sixth year, in the sixth month on the fifth day, while I was sitting in my house and the elders of Judah were sitting before me, the hand of the Sovereign LORD came upon me there. [2]I looked, and I saw a figure like that of a man. From what appeared to be his waist down he was like fire, and from there up his appearance was as bright as glowing metal. [3]He stretched out what looked like a hand and took me by the hair of my head. The Spirit lifted me up between earth and heaven and in visions of God he took me to Jerusalem, to the entrance to the north gate of the inner court, where the idol that provokes to jealousy stood.
Dan 7 [9]"As I looked, thrones were set in place, and the Ancient of Days took his seat. His clothing was as white as snow; the hair of his head was white like wool. His throne was flaming with fire, and its wheels were all ablaze. [10]A river of fire was flowing, coming out from before him. Thousands upon thousands attended him; ten thousand times ten thousand stood before him. The court was seated, and the books were opened."
Amos 9 [1]I saw the Lord standing by the altar, and he said: "Strike the tops of the pillars so that the thresholds shake. Bring them down on the heads of all the people; those who are left I will kill with the sword. Not one will get away, none will escape."
Rev 4 [2]At once I was in the Spirit, and there before me was a throne in heaven with someone sitting on it. [3]And the one who sat there had the appearance of jasper and carnelian. A rainbow, resembling an emerald, encircled the throne.

5. Breath

2 Sam 22 [16]"The valleys of the sea were exposed and the foundations of the earth laid bare at the rebuke of the LORD, at the blast of breath from his nostrils."
Job 15 [30]"He will not escape the darkness; a flame will wither his shoots, and the breath of God's mouth will carry him away."
Job 33 [4]"The Spirit of God has made me; the breath of the Almighty gives me life."
Job 37 [10]"The breath of God produces ice, and the broad waters become frozen."
Ps 33 [6]By the word of the LORD were the heavens made, their starry host by the breath of his mouth.
Isa 11 [4]but with righteousness he will judge the needy, with justice he will give decisions for the poor of the earth. He will strike the earth with the rod of his mouth; with the breath of his lips he will slay the wicked.
Isa 30 [28]His breath is like a rushing torrent, rising up to the neck. He shakes the nations in the sieve of destruction; he places in the jaws of the peoples a bit that leads them astray.
Isa 30 [33]Topheth has long been prepared; it has been made ready for the king. Its fire pit has been made deep and wide, with an abundance of fire and wood; the breath of the LORD, like a stream of burning sulfur, sets it ablaze.

6. Ears

2 Sam 22 [7]"In my distress I called to the LORD; I called out to my God. From his temple he heard my voice; my cry came to his ears."
2 Kings 19 [28]"'Because you rage against me and your insolence has reached my ears, I will put my hook in your nose and my bit in your mouth, and I will make you return by the way you came.'"
2 Chron 7 [15]"Now my eyes will be open and my ears attentive to the prayers offered in this place."
Neh 1 [6]". . . let your ear be attentive and your eyes open to hear the prayer your servant is praying before you day and night for your servants, the people of Israel. I confess the sins we Israelites, including myself and my father's house, have committed against you."
Ps 34 [15]The eyes of the LORD are on the righteous and his ears are attentive to their cry. . . .
Ps 102 [2]Do not hide your face from me when I am in distress. Turn your ear to me; when I call, answer me quickly.
Ps 116 [2]Because he turned his ear to me, I will call on him as long as I live.
Isa 59 [1]Surely the arm of the LORD is not too short to save, nor his ear too dull to hear.
1 Pet 3 [12]"For the eyes of the Lord are on the righteous and his ears are attentive to their prayer, but the face of the Lord is against those who do evil."

7. Eyes

Deut 11 [12]It is a land the LORD your God cares for; the eyes of the LORD your God are continually on it from the beginning of the year to its end.
1 Kings 8 [29]"May your eyes be open toward this temple night and day, this place of which you said, 'My Name shall be there,' so that you will hear the prayer your servant prays toward this place."
2 Chron 16 [9]"For the eyes of the LORD range throughout the earth to strengthen those whose hearts are fully committed to him. You have done a foolish thing, and from now on you will be at war."
Ps 33 [18]But the eyes of the LORD are on those who fear him, on those whose hope is in his unfailing love. . . .
Ps 34 [15]The eyes of the LORD are on the righteous and his ears are attentive to their cry. . . .
Ps 139 [16]your eyes saw my unformed body. All the days ordained for me were written in your book before one of them came to be.
Prov 15 [3]The eyes of the LORD are everywhere, keeping watch on the wicked and the good.
Prov 22 [12]The eyes of the LORD keep watch over knowledge, but he frustrates the words of the unfaithful.
Amos 9 [4]"Though they are driven into exile by their enemies, there I will command the sword to slay them. I will fix my eyes upon them for evil and not for good."
Heb 4 [13]Nothing in all creation is hidden from God's sight. Everything is uncovered and laid bare before the eyes of him to whom we must give account.
1 Pet 3 [12]"For the eyes of the Lord are on the righteous and his ears are attentive to their prayer, but the face of the Lord is against those who do evil."

8. Face

Gen 32 [30]So Jacob called the place Peniel, saying, "It is because I saw God face to face, and yet my life was spared."
Exod 33 [11]The LORD would speak to Moses face to face, as a man speaks with his friend. Then Moses would return to the camp, but his young aide Joshua son of Nun did not leave the tent.
Exod 33 [20]"But," he said, "you cannot see my face, for no one may see me and live. . . . [23]Then I will remove my hand and you will see my back; but my face must not be seen."
Num 6 [25]"'. . . the LORD make his face shine upon you and be gracious to you; [26]the LORD turn his face toward you and give you peace.'"
Num 12 [8]"With him I speak face to face, clearly and not in riddles; he sees the form of the LORD. Why then were you not afraid to speak against my servant Moses?"
Deut 5 [4]The LORD spoke to you face to face out of the fire on the mountain.
Deut 34 [10]Since then, no prophet has risen in Israel like Moses, whom the LORD knew face to face. . . .
1 Chron 16 [11]Look to the LORD and his strength; seek his face always.
2 Chron 7 [14]". . . if my people, who are called by my name, will humble themselves and pray and seek my face and turn from their wicked ways, then will I hear from heaven and will forgive their sin and will heal their land."

Ps 27 [8]My heart says of you, "Seek his face!" Your face, LORD, I will seek. [9]Do not hide your face from me, do not turn your servant away in anger; you have been my helper. Do not reject me or forsake me, O God my Savior.
Ps 34 [16]the face of the LORD is against those who do evil, to cut off the memory of them from the earth.
Ps 67 [1]May God be gracious to us and bless us and make his face shine upon us. . . .
Ps 80 [19]Restore us, O LORD God Almighty; make your face shine upon us, that we may be saved.
Ps 105 [4]Look to the LORD and his strength; seek his face always.
Ps 119 [135]Make your face shine upon your servant and teach me your decrees.
1 Pet 3 [12]"For the eyes of the Lord are on the righteous and his ears are attentive to their prayer, but the face of the Lord is against those who do evil."

9. Feet

Gen 3 [8]Then the man and his wife heard the sound of the LORD God as he was walking in the garden in the cool of the day, and they hid from the LORD God among the trees of the garden.
Exod 24 [9]Moses and Aaron, Nadab and Abihu, and the seventy elders of Israel went up [10]and saw the God of Israel. Under his feet was something like a pavement made of sapphire, clear as the sky itself.
2 Sam 22 [10]"He parted the heavens and came down; dark clouds were under his feet."
Isa 66 [1]This is what the LORD says: "Heaven is my throne, and the earth is my footstool. Where is the house you will build for me? Where will my resting place be?"
Nah 1 [3]The LORD is slow to anger and great in power; the LORD will not leave the guilty unpunished. His way is in the whirlwind and the storm, and clouds are the dust of his feet.

10. Fingers

Exod 8 [19]The magicians said to Pharaoh, "This is the finger of God." But Pharaoh's heart was hard and he would not listen, just as the LORD had said.
Exod 31 [18]When the LORD finished speaking to Moses on Mount Sinai, he gave him the two tablets of the Testimony, the tablets of stone inscribed by the finger of God.
Deut 9 [10]The LORD gave me two stone tablets inscribed by the finger of God. On them were all the commandments the LORD proclaimed to you on the mountain out of the fire, on the day of the assembly.
Ps 8 [3]When I consider your heavens, the work of your fingers, the moon and the stars, which you have set in place . . .
Luke 11 [20]"But if I drive out demons by the finger of God, then the kingdom of God has come to you."

11. Give Birth

Deut 32 [18]You deserted the Rock, who fathered you; you forgot the God who gave you birth.
Job 38 [28]"Does the rain have a father? Who fathers the drops of dew? [29]From whose womb comes the ice? Who gives birth to the frost from the heavens . . . ?"
Isa 46 [3]"Listen to me, O house of Jacob, all you who remain of the house of Israel, you whom I have upheld since you were conceived, and have carried since your birth. [4]Even to your old age and gray hairs I am he, I am he who will sustain you. I have made you and I will carry you; I will sustain you and I will rescue you."

12. Hair

Dan 7 [9]"As I looked, thrones were set in place, and the Ancient of Days took his seat. His clothing was as white as snow; the hair of his head was white like wool. His throne was flaming with fire, and its wheels were all ablaze."

13. Hand

Exod 15 [6]"Your right hand, O LORD, was majestic in power. Your right hand, O LORD, shattered the enemy."
Exod 33 [22]"When my glory passes by, I will put you in a cleft in the rock and cover you with my hand until I have passed by. [23]Then I will remove my hand and you will see my back; but my face must not be seen."
Ezra 7 [9]He had begun his journey from Babylon on the first day of the first month, and he arrived in Jerusalem on the first day of the fifth month, for the gracious hand of his God was on him.
Ps 8 [6]You made him ruler over the works of your hands; you put everything under his feet. . . .
Ps 21 [8]Your hand will lay hold on all your enemies; your right hand will seize your foes.
Ps 31 [15]My times are in your hands; deliver me from my enemies and from those who pursue me.
Ps 44 [2]With your hand you drove out the nations and planted our fathers; you crushed the peoples and made our fathers flourish. [3]It was not by their sword that they won the land, nor did their arm bring them victory; it was your right hand, your arm, and the light of your face, for you loved them.
Ps 63 [8]My soul clings to you; your right hand upholds me.
Ps 89 [13]Your arm is endued with power; your hand is strong, your right hand exalted.
Ps 95 [4]In his hand are the depths of the earth, and the mountain peaks belong to him. [5]The sea is his, for he made it, and his hands formed the dry land.
Ps 118 [16]"The LORD's right hand is lifted high; the LORD's right hand has done mighty things!"
Ps 138 [7]Though I walk in the midst of trouble, you preserve my life; you stretch out your hand against the anger of my foes, with your right hand you save me. [8]The LORD will fulfill his purpose for me; your love, O LORD, endures forever—do not abandon the works of your hands.
Ps 139 [10]even there your hand will guide me, your right hand will hold me fast.
Prov 30 [4]"Who has gone up to heaven and come down? Who has gathered up the wind in the hollow of his hands? Who has wrapped up the waters in his cloak? Who has established all the ends of the earth? What is his name, and the name of his son? Tell me if you know!"
Isa 1 [25]"I will turn my hand against you; I will thoroughly purge away your dross and remove all your impurities."
Isa 62 [3]You will be a crown of splendor in the LORD's hand, a royal diadem in the hand of your God.
Isa 64 [8]Yet, O LORD, you are our Father. We are the clay, you are the potter; we are all the work of your hand.
Hab 3 [4]His splendor was like the sunrise; rays flashed from his hand, where his power was hidden.
Acts 13 [11]"Now the hand of the Lord is against you. You are going to be blind, and for a time you will be unable to see the light of the sun."

Immediately mist and darkness came over him, and he groped about, seeking someone to lead him by the hand.
Heb 1 [10]He also says, "In the beginning, O Lord, you laid the foundations of the earth, and the heavens are the work of your hands."

14. Head

Dan 7 [9]"As I looked, thrones were set in place, and the Ancient of Days took his seat. His clothing was as white as snow; the hair of his head was white like wool. His throne was flaming with fire, and its wheels were all ablaze."

15. Hearing

Num 11 [18]"Tell the people: 'Consecrate yourselves in preparation for tomorrow, when you will eat meat. The LORD heard you when you wailed, "If only we had meat to eat! We were better off in Egypt!" Now the LORD will give you meat, and you will eat it.'"
Ps 69 [33]The LORD hears the needy and does not despise his captive people.
Ps 94 [9]Does he who implanted the ear not hear? Does he who formed the eye not see?
Ps 116 [1]I love the LORD, for he heard my voice; he heard my cry for mercy.
Isa 59 [2]But your iniquities have separated you from your God;

your sins have hidden his face from you, so that he will not hear.

16. Heart

Gen 6 [6]The LORD was grieved that he had made man on the earth, and his heart was filled with pain.
2 Chron 7 [16]"I have chosen and consecrated this temple so that my Name may be there forever. My eyes and my heart will always be there."
Hos 11 [8]"How can I give you up, Ephraim? How can I hand you over, Israel? How can I treat you like Admah? How can I make you like Zeboiim? My heart is changed within me; all my compassion is aroused."

17. Laughter

Ps 2 [4]The One enthroned in heaven laughs; the Lord scoffs at them.
Ps 37 [13]but the Lord laughs at the wicked, for he knows their day is coming.
Ps 59 [8]But you, O LORD, laugh at them; you scoff at all those nations.

18. Lips

Ps 89 [34]"I will not violate my covenant or alter what my lips have uttered."
Isa 11 [4]but with righteousness he will judge the needy, with justice he will give decisions for the poor of the earth. He will strike the earth with the rod of his mouth; with the breath of his lips he will slay the wicked.
Isa 30 [27]See, the Name of the LORD comes from afar, with burning anger and dense clouds of smoke; his lips are full of wrath, and his tongue is a consuming fire.

19. Mouth

Deut 8 [3]He humbled you, causing you to hunger and then feeding you with manna, which neither you nor your fathers had known, to teach you that man does not live on bread alone but on every word that comes from the mouth of the LORD.
2 Sam 22 [9]"Smoke rose from his nostrils; consuming fire came from his mouth, burning coals blazed out of it."
Job 15 [30]"He will not escape the darkness; a flame will wither his shoots, and the breath of God's mouth will carry him away."
Ps 33 [6]By the word of the LORD were the heavens made, their starry host by the breath of his mouth.
Isa 40 [5]"And the glory of the LORD will be revealed, and all mankind together will see it. For the mouth of the LORD has spoken."
Isa 45 [23]"By myself I have sworn, my mouth has uttered in all integrity a word that will not be revoked: Before me every knee will bow; by me every tongue will swear."
Isa 48 [3]"I foretold the former things long ago, my mouth announced them and I made them known; then suddenly I acted, and they came to pass."

20. Nostrils

2 Sam 22 [9]"Smoke rose from his nostrils; consuming fire came from his mouth, burning coals blazed out of it."
2 Sam 22 [16]"The valleys of the sea were exposed and the foundations of the earth laid bare at the rebuke of the LORD, at the blast of breath from his nostrils."

21. Palm of Hand

Isa 49 [16]"See, I have engraved you on the palms of my hands; your walls are ever before me."

22. Remembering

1 Sam 1 [19]Early the next morning they arose and worshiped before the LORD and then went back to their home at Ramah. Elkanah lay with Hannah his wife, and the LORD remembered her.
Ps 78 [39]He remembered that they were but flesh, a passing breeze that does not return.
Ps 98 [3]He has remembered his love and his faithfulness to the house of Israel; all the ends of the earth have seen the salvation of our God.
Ps 105 [42]For he remembered his holy promise given to his servant Abraham.
Ps 106 [45]for their sake he remembered his covenant and out of his great love he relented.
Ps 136 [23]to the One who remembered us in our low estate *His love endures forever.*

23. Shoulders

Deut 33 [12]About Benjamin he said: "Let the beloved of the LORD rest secure in him, for he shields him all day long, and the one the LORD loves rests between his shoulders."

24. Seeing

Ps 10 [11]He says to himself, "God has forgotten; he covers his face and never sees."
Ps 33 [13]From heaven the LORD looks down and sees all mankind. . . .

25. Sitting

Ps 29 [10]The LORD sits enthroned over the flood; the LORD is enthroned as King forever.

26. Smelling

Gen 8 [21]The LORD smelled the pleasing aroma and said in his heart: "Never again will I curse the ground because of man, even though every inclination of his heart is evil from childhood. And never again will I destroy all living creatures, as I have done."

27. Standing

Amos 7 [7]This is what he showed me: The Lord was standing by a wall that had been built true to plumb, with a plumb line in his hand.
Amos 9 [1]I saw the Lord standing by the altar, and he said: "Strike the tops of the pillars so that the thresholds shake. Bring them down on the heads of all the people; those who are left I will kill with the sword. Not one will get away, none will escape."

28. Tongue

Isa 30 [27]See, the Name of the LORD comes from afar, with burning anger and dense clouds of smoke; his lips are full of wrath, and his tongue is a consuming fire.

29. Voice

Exod 3 [4]When the LORD saw that he had gone over to look, God called to him from within the bush, "Moses! Moses!"
And Moses said, "Here I am."
Exod 19 [19]and the sound of the trumpet grew louder and louder. Then Moses spoke and the voice of God answered him.
Deut 4 [12]Then the LORD spoke to you out of the fire. You heard the sound of words but saw no form; there was only a voice.
1 Kings 19 [12]After the earthquake came a fire, but the LORD was not in the fire. And after the fire came a gentle whisper. [13]When Elijah heard it, he pulled his cloak over his face and went out and stood at the mouth of the cave.
Then a voice said to him, "What are you doing here, Elijah?"
Job 37 [5]"God's voice thunders in marvelous ways; he does great things beyond our understanding."
Ps 29 [3]The voice of the LORD is over the waters; the God of glory thunders, the LORD thunders over the mighty waters. [4]The voice of the LORD is powerful; the voice of the LORD is majestic. [5]The voice of the Lord breaks the cedars; the LORD breaks in pieces the cedars of Lebanon. . . . [7]The voice of the LORD strikes with flashes of lightning. [8]The voice of the LORD shakes the desert; the LORD shakes the Desert of Kadesh. [9]The voice of the LORD twists the oaks and strips the forests bare. And in his temple all cry, "Glory!"

Ezek 10 [5]The sound of the wings of the cherubim could be heard as far away as the outer court, like the voice of God Almighty when he speaks.
Ezek 43 [2]and I saw the glory of the God of Israel coming from the east. His voice was like the roar of rushing waters, and the land was radiant with his glory.
Luke 3 [22]and the Holy Spirit descended on him in bodily form like a dove. And a voice came from heaven: "You are my Son, whom I love; with you I am well pleased."
Acts 7 [31]"When he saw this, he was amazed at the sight. As he went over to look more closely, he heard the Lord's voice. . . ."
Heb 12 [18]You have not come to a mountain that can be touched and that is burning with fire; to darkness, gloom and storm; [19]to a trumpet blast or to such a voice speaking words that those who heard it begged that no further word be spoken to them, [20]because they could not bear what was commanded: "If even an animal touches the mountain, it must be stoned." [21]The sight was so terrifying that Moses said, "I am trembling with fear."

30. Waist

Ezek 1 [27]I saw that from what appeared to be his waist up he looked like glowing metal, as if full of fire, and that from there down he looked like fire; and brilliant light surrounded him.
Ezek 8 [2]I looked, and I saw a figure like that of a man. From what appeared to be his waist down he was like fire, and from there up his appearance was as bright as glowing metal.

31. Walking

Gen 3 [8]Then the man and his wife heard the sound of the LORD God as he was walking in the garden in the cool of the day, and they hid from the LORD God among the trees of the garden.

32. Watching

Gen 31 [49]It was also called Mizpah, because he said, "May the LORD keep watch between you and me when we are away from each other."
Ps 1 [6]For the LORD watches over the way of the righteous, but the way of the wicked will perish.
Ps 11 [4]The LORD is in his holy temple; the LORD is on his heavenly throne. He observes the sons of men; his eyes examine them.
Ps 66 [7]He rules forever by his power, his eyes watch the nations—let not the rebellious rise up against him.

F. God's Dwelling Place

1. God Dwells in Heaven

Deut 4 [36]From heaven he made you hear his voice to discipline you. On earth he showed you his great fire, and you heard his words from out of the fire.
Deut 4 [39]Acknowledge and take to heart this day that the LORD is God in heaven above and on the earth below. There is no other.
Deut 26 [15]"Look down from heaven, your holy dwelling place, and bless your people Israel and the land you have given us as you promised on oath to our forefathers, a land flowing with milk and honey."
1 Sam 2 [10]". . . those who oppose the LORD will be shattered. He will thunder against them from heaven; the LORD will judge the ends of the earth.

"He will give strength to his king and exalt the horn of his anointed."
1 Kings 8 [30]"Hear the supplication of your servant and of your people Israel when they pray toward this place. Hear from heaven, your dwelling place, and when you hear, forgive. [32]. . . then hear from heaven and act. Judge between your servants, condemning the guilty and bringing down on his own head what he has done. Declare the innocent not guilty, and so establish his innocence. [34]. . . then hear from heaven and forgive the sin of your people Israel and bring them back to the land you gave to their fathers. [36]. . . then hear from heaven and forgive the sin of your servants, your people Israel. Teach them the right way to live, and send rain on the land you gave your people for an inheritance. [39]. . . then hear from heaven, your dwelling place. Forgive and act; deal with each man according to all he does, since you know his heart (for you alone know the hearts of all men). [43]. . . then hear from heaven, your dwelling place, and do whatever the foreigner asks of you, so that all the peoples of the earth may know your name and fear you, as do your own people Israel, and may know that this house I have built bears your Name. [45]. . . then hear from heaven their prayer and their plea, and uphold their cause. [49]. . . then from heaven, your dwelling place, hear their prayer and their plea, and uphold their cause."
2 Chron 6 [21]"Hear the supplications of your servant and of your people Israel when they pray toward this place. Hear from heaven, your dwelling place; and when you hear, forgive."
2 Chron 20 [5]Then Jehoshaphat stood up in the assembly of Judah and Jerusalem at the temple of the LORD in the front of the new courtyard [6]and said: "O LORD, God of our fathers, are you not the God who is in heaven? You rule over all the kingdoms of the nations. Power and might are in your hand, and no one can withstand you."
Job 22 [12]"Is not God in the heights of heaven? And see how lofty are the highest stars!"
Ps 14 [2]The LORD looks down from heaven on the sons of men to see if there are any who understand, any who seek God.
Ps 20 [6]Now I know that the LORD saves his anointed; he answers him from his holy heaven with the saving power of his right hand.
Ps 33 [13]From heaven the LORD looks down and sees all mankind. . . .
Ps 73 [25]Whom have I in heaven but you? And earth has nothing I desire besides you.
Ps 102 [19]"The LORD looked down from his sanctuary on high, from heaven he viewed the earth. . . ."
Ps 103 [19]The LORD has established his throne in heaven, and his kingdom rules over all.
Eccles 5 [2]Do not be quick with your mouth, do not be hasty in your heart to utter anything before God. God is in heaven and you are on earth, so let your words be few.
Isa 63 [15]Look down from heaven and see from your lofty throne, holy and glorious. Where are your zeal and your might? Your tenderness and compassion are withheld from us.
Lam 3 [49]My eyes will flow unceasingly, without relief, [50]until the LORD looks down from heaven and sees.
Matt 6 [9]"This, then, is how you should pray: 'Our Father in heaven, hallowed be your name. . . .'"
Matt 10 [32]"Whoever acknowledges me before men, I will also acknowledge him before my Father in heaven. [33]But whoever disowns me before men, I will disown him before my Father in heaven."
Matt 16 [17]Jesus replied, "Blessed are you, Simon son of Jonah, for this was not revealed to you by man, but by my Father in heaven."
Acts 7 [49]"'Heaven is my throne, and the earth is my footstool. What kind of house will you build for me? says the Lord. Or where will my resting place be?'"
Acts 7 [55]But Stephen, full of the Holy Spirit, looked up to heaven and saw the glory of God, and Jesus standing at the right hand of God. [56]"Look," he said, "I see heaven open and the Son of Man standing at the right hand of God."
Heb 8 [1]The point of what we are saying is this: We do have such a high priest, who sat down at the right hand of the throne of the Majesty in heaven. . . .
Rev 4 [1]After this I looked, and there before me was a door standing open in heaven. And the voice I had first heard speaking to me like a trumpet said, "Come up here, and I will show you what must take place after this." [2]At once I was in the Spirit, and there before me was a throne in heaven with someone sitting on it.

2. Heaven Cannot Contain God

1 Kings 8 [27]"But will God really dwell on earth? The heavens, even the highest heaven, cannot contain you. How much less this temple I have built!"
2 Chron 2 [6]"But who is able to build a temple for him, since the heavens, even the highest heavens, cannot contain him?

Who then am I to build a temple for him, except as a place to burn sacrifices before him?"
2 Chron 6 [18]"But will God really dwell on earth with men? The heavens, even the highest heavens, cannot contain you. How much less this temple I have built!"
Ps 148 [13]Let them praise the name of the LORD, for his name alone is exalted; his splendor is above the earth and the heavens.
See also p. 60a, God Is Omnipotent

G. The Knowability of God

1. God Is Known by Various Ways

a) God Is Known by His Initiative

Gen 3 [8]Then the man and his wife heard the sound of the LORD God as he was walking in the garden in the cool of the day, and they hid from the LORD God among the trees of the garden. [9]But the LORD God called to the man, "Where are you?"
Exod 33 [17]And the LORD said to Moses, "I will do the very thing you have asked, because I am pleased with you and I know you by name."
Jer 1 [5]"Before I formed you in the womb I knew you, before you were born I set you apart; I appointed you as a prophet to the nations."
Matt 11 [27]"All things have been committed to me by my Father. No one knows the Son except the Father, and no one knows the Father except the Son and those to whom the Son chooses to reveal him."
Rom 1 [19]since what may be known about God is plain to them, because God has made it plain to them.
Gal 4 [8]Formerly, when you did not know God, you were slaves to those who by nature are not gods. [9]But now that you know God—or rather are known by God—how is it that you are turning back to those weak and miserable principles? Do you wish to be enslaved by them all over again?
Eph 1 [17]I keep asking that the God of our Lord Jesus Christ, the glorious Father, may give you the Spirit of wisdom and revelation, so that you may know him better.
1 John 5 [20]We know also that the Son of God has come and has given us understanding, so that we may know him who is true. And we are in him who is true—even in his Son Jesus Christ. He is the true God and eternal life.

b) God Is Known by His Works

Exod 7 [5]"And the Egyptians will know that I am the LORD when I stretch out my hand against Egypt and bring the Israelites out of it."
Exod 9 [29]Moses replied, "When I have gone out of the city, I will spread out my hands in prayer to the LORD. The thunder will stop and there will be no more hail, so you may know that the earth is the LORD's."
Deut 4 [34]Has any god ever tried to take for himself one nation out of another nation by testings, by miraculous signs and wonders, by war, by a mighty hand and an outstretched arm, or by great and awesome deeds, like all the things the LORD your God did for you in Egypt before your very eyes?

[35]You were shown these things so that you might know that the LORD is God; besides him there is no other.
Deut 6 [21]tell him: "We were slaves of Pharaoh in Egypt, but the LORD brought us out of Egypt with a mighty hand. [22]Before our eyes the LORD sent miraculous signs and wonders—great and terrible—upon Egypt and Pharaoh and his whole household."
Josh 3 [10]"This is how you will know that the living God is among you and that he will certainly drive out before you the Canaanites, Hittites, Hivites, Perizzites, Girgashites, Amorites and Jebusites."
Ps 46 [8]Come and see the works of the LORD, the desolations he has brought on the earth. [9]He makes wars cease to the ends of the earth; he breaks the bow and shatters the spear, he burns the shields with fire. [10]"Be still, and know that I am God; I will be exalted among the nations, I will be exalted in the earth."
Ps 66 [5]Come and see what God has done, how awesome his works in man's behalf! [6]He turned the sea into dry land, they passed through the waters on foot—come, let us rejoice in him. [7]He rules forever by his power, his eyes watch the nations—let not the rebellious rise up against him.
Ps 77 [10]Then I thought, "To this I will appeal: the years of the right hand of the Most High." [11]I will remember the deeds of the LORD; yes, I will remember your miracles of long ago. [12]I will meditate on all your works and consider all your mighty deeds.

[13]Your ways, O God, are holy. What god is so great as our God? [14]You are the God who performs miracles; you display your power among the peoples. [15]With your mighty arm you redeemed your people, the descendants of Jacob and Joseph.
Ps 98 [2]The LORD has made his salvation known and revealed his righteousness to the nations.
Ps 103 [7]He made known his ways to Moses, his deeds to the people of Israel. . . .
Ps 111 [2]Great are the works of the LORD; they are pondered by all who delight in them. [3]Glorious and majestic are his deeds, and his righteousness endures forever. [4]He has caused his wonders to be remembered; the LORD is gracious and compassionate. [5]He provides food for those who fear him; he remembers his covenant forever. [6]He has shown his people the power of his works, giving them the lands of other nations. [7]The works of his hands are faithful and just; all his precepts are trustworthy.
John 10 [25]Jesus answered, "I did tell you, but you do not believe. The miracles I do in my Father's name speak for me, [26]but you do not believe because you are not my sheep. [27]My sheep listen to my voice; I know them, and they follow me. [28]I give them eternal life, and they shall never perish; no one can snatch them out of my hand. [29]My Father, who has given them to me, is greater than all; no one can snatch them out of my Father's hand. [30]I and the Father are one."
John 14 [11]"Believe me when I say that I am in the Father and the Father is in me; or at least believe on the evidence of the miracles themselves."

c) God Is Known by Fellowship with Him

John 10 [14]"I am the good shepherd; I know my sheep and my sheep know me— [15]just as the Father knows me and I know the Father—and I lay down my life for the sheep."
John 17 [3]"Now this is eternal life: that they may know you, the only true God, and Jesus Christ, whom you have sent."
1 Cor 2 [9]However, as it is written: "No eye has seen, no ear has heard, no mind has conceived what God has prepared for those who love him"— [10]but God has revealed it to us by his Spirit.

The Spirit searches all things, even the deep things of God. [11]For who among men knows the thoughts of a man except the man's spirit within him? In the same way no one knows the thoughts of God except the Spirit of God. [12]We have not received the spirit of the world but the Spirit who is from God, that we may understand what God has freely given us. [13]This is what we speak, not in words taught us by human wisdom but in words taught by the Spirit, expressing spiritual truths in spiritual words. [14]The man without the Spirit does not accept the things that come from the Spirit of God, for they are foolishness to him, and he cannot understand them, because they are spiritually discerned. [15]The spiritual man makes judgments about all things, but he himself is not subject to any man's judgment: [16]"For who has known the mind of the Lord that he may instruct him?" But we have the mind of Christ.
Col 1 [10]And we pray this in order that you may live a life worthy of the Lord and may please him in every way: bearing fruit in every good work, growing in the knowledge of God. . . .
1 Pet 1 [8]Though you have not seen him, you love him; and even though you do not see him now, you believe in him and are filled with an inexpressible and glorious joy. . . .
1 John 1 [3]We proclaim to you what we have seen and heard, so that you also may have fellowship with us. And our fellowship is with the Father and with his Son, Jesus Christ.
1 John 4 [12]No one has ever seen God; but if we love one another, God lives in us and his love is made complete in us.

[13]We know that we live in him and he in us, because he has given us of his Spirit. [14]And we have seen and testify that the Father has sent his Son to be the Savior of the world. [15]If anyone acknowledges that Jesus is the Son of God, God lives in

him and he in God. 16And so we know and rely on the love God has for us.

God is love. Whoever lives in love lives in God, and God in him.

d) God Is Known by Human Intuition

Eccles 3 11He has made everything beautiful in its time. He has also set eternity in the hearts of men; yet they cannot fathom what God has done from beginning to end.
Rom 1 19since what may be known about God is plain to them, because God has made it plain to them. 20For since the creation of the world God's invisible qualities—his eternal power and divine nature—have been clearly seen, being understood from what has been made, so that men are without excuse. . . . 28Furthermore, since they did not think it worthwhile to retain the knowledge of God, he gave them over to a depraved mind, to do what ought not to be done. . . . 32Although they know God's righteous decree that those who do such things deserve death, they not only continue to do these very things but also approve of those who practice them.
Rom 2 14(Indeed, when Gentiles, who do not have the law, do by nature things required by the law, they are a law for themselves, even though they do not have the law, 15since they show that the requirements of the law are written on their hearts, their consciences also bearing witness, and their thoughts now accusing, now even defending them.)

e) God Is Known by the Natural Order

Ps 8 1O LORD, our Lord, how majestic is your name in all the earth!

You have set your glory above the heavens. 2From the lips of children and infants you have ordained praise because of your enemies, to silence the foe and the avenger.

3When I consider your heavens, the work of your fingers, the moon and the stars, which you have set in place, 4what is man that you are mindful of him, the son of man that you care for him? 5You made him a little lower than the heavenly beings and crowned him with glory and honor.

6You made him ruler over the works of your hands; you put everything under his feet: 7all flocks and herds, and the beasts of the field, 8the birds of the air, and the fish of the sea, all that swim the paths of the seas.

9O LORD, our Lord, how majestic is your name in all the earth!
Ps 19 1The heavens declare the glory of God; the skies proclaim the work of his hands. 2Day after day they pour forth speech; night after night they display knowledge. 3There is no speech or language where their voice is not heard. 4Their voice goes out into all the earth, their words to the ends of the world.

In the heavens he has pitched a tent for the sun, 5which is like a bridegroom coming forth from his pavilion, like a champion rejoicing to run his course. 6It rises at one end of the heavens and makes its circuit to the other; nothing is hidden from its heat.
Isa 40 25"To whom will you compare me? Or who is my equal?" says the Holy One. 26Lift your eyes and look to the heavens: Who created all these? He who brings out the starry host one by one, and calls them each by name. Because of his great power and mighty strength, not one of them is missing.

2. God Is Approachable

Exod 24 9Moses and Aaron, Nadab and Abihu, and the seventy elders of Israel went up 10and saw the God of Israel. Under his feet was something like a pavement made of sapphire, clear as the sky itself. 11But God did not raise his hand against these leaders of the Israelites; they saw God, and they ate and drank.
Deut 4 7What other nation is so great as to have their gods near them the way the LORD our God is near us whenever we pray to him?
Ps 17 15And I—in righteousness I will see your face; when I awake, I will be satisfied with seeing your likeness.
Ps 24 3Who may ascend the hill of the LORD? Who may stand in his holy place? 4He who has clean hands and a pure heart, who does not lift up his soul to an idol or swear by what is false.
Ps 27 4One thing I ask of the LORD, this is what I seek: that I may dwell in the house of the LORD all the days of my life, to gaze upon the beauty of the LORD and to seek him in his temple.
Ps 34 8Taste and see that the LORD is good; blessed is the man who takes refuge in him.
Ps 43 3Send forth your light and your truth, let them guide me; let them bring me to your holy mountain, to the place where you dwell.
Ps 65 4Blessed are those you choose and bring near to live in your courts! We are filled with the good things of your house, of your holy temple.
Ps 145 18The LORD is near to all who call on him, to all who call on him in truth. 19He fulfills the desires of those who fear him; he hears their cry and saves them.
Isa 55 3"Give ear and come to me; hear me, that your soul may live. I will make an everlasting covenant with you, my faithful love promised to David."
Jer 9 23This is what the LORD says: "Let not the wise man boast of his wisdom or the strong man boast of his strength or the rich man boast of his riches, 24but let him who boasts boast about this: that he understands and knows me, that I am the LORD, who exercises kindness, justice and righteousness on earth, for in these I delight," declares the LORD.
Jer 31 34"No longer will a man teach his neighbor, or a man his brother, saying, 'Know the LORD,' because they will all know me, from the least of them to the greatest," declares the LORD. "For I will forgive their wickedness and will remember their sins no more."
Matt 5 8"Blessed are the pure in heart, for they will see God."
Matt 6 6"But when you pray, go into your room, close the door and pray to your Father, who is unseen. Then your Father, who sees what is done in secret, will reward you."
John 17 3"Now this is eternal life: that they may know you, the only true God, and Jesus Christ, whom you have sent."
Acts 14 27On arriving there, they gathered the church together and reported all that God had done through them and how he had opened the door of faith to the Gentiles.
Acts 17 24"The God who made the world and everything in it is the Lord of heaven and earth and does not live in temples built by hands. 25And he is not served by human hands, as if he needed anything, because he himself gives all men life and breath and everything else. 26From one man he made every nation of men, that they should inhabit the whole earth; and he determined the times set for them and the exact places where they should live. 27God did this so that men would seek him and perhaps reach out for him and find him, though he is not far from each one of us."
Rom 5 1Therefore, since we have been justified through faith, we have peace with God through our Lord Jesus Christ, 2through whom we have gained access by faith into this grace in which we now stand. And we rejoice in the hope of the glory of God.
Eph 2 13But now in Christ Jesus you who once were far away have been brought near through the blood of Christ. . . . 17He came and preached peace to you who were far away and peace to those who were near. 18For through him we both have access to the Father by one Spirit.
Col 1 21Once you were alienated from God and were enemies in your minds because of your evil behavior. 22But now he has reconciled you by Christ's physical body through death to present you holy in his sight, without blemish and free from accusation. . . .
Heb 7 18The former regulation is set aside because it was weak and useless 19(for the law made nothing perfect), and a better hope is introduced, by which we draw near to God. . . . 25Therefore he is able to save completely those who come to God through him, because he always lives to intercede for them.
Heb 11 6And without faith it is impossible to please God, because anyone who comes to him must believe that he exists and that he rewards those who earnestly seek him.
James 4 8Come near to God and he will come near to you. Wash your hands, you sinners, and purify your hearts, you double-minded.
1 Pet 3 18For Christ died for sins once for all, the righteous for the unrighteous, to bring you to God. He was put to death in the body but made alive by the Spirit. . . .

1 John 3 [2]Dear friends, now we are children of God, and what we will be has not yet been made known. But we know that when he appears, we shall be like him, for we shall see him as he is.
Rev 22 [17]The Spirit and the bride say, "Come!" And let him who hears say, "Come!" Whoever is thirsty, let him come; and whoever wishes, let him take the free gift of the water of life.

3. God Is Incomprehensible

Job 9 [10]"He performs wonders that cannot be fathomed, miracles that cannot be counted. [11]When he passes me, I cannot see him; when he goes by, I cannot perceive him."
Job 11 [7]"Can you fathom the mysteries of God? Can you probe the limits of the Almighty? [8]They are higher than the heavens—what can you do? They are deeper than the depths of the grave—what can you know? [9]Their measure is longer than the earth and wider than the sea."
Job 23 [8]"But if I go to the east, he is not there; if I go to the west, I do not find him.[9]When he is at work in the north, I do not see him; when he turns to the south, I catch no glimpse of him."
Job 26 [14]"And these are but the outer fringe of his works; how faint the whisper we hear of him! Who then can understand the thunder of his power?"
Job 33 [13]"Why do you complain to him that he answers none of man's words? [14]For God does speak—now one way, now another—though man may not perceive it."
Job 36 [26]"How great is God—beyond our understanding! The number of his years is past finding out."
Job 37 [5]"God's voice thunders in marvelous ways; he does great things beyond our understanding."
Job 37 [23]"The Almighty is beyond our reach and exalted in power; in his justice and great righteousness, he does not oppress."
Ps 92 [5]How great are your works, O LORD, how profound your thoughts!
Ps 139 [1]O LORD, you have searched me and you know me. [2]You know when I sit and when I rise; you perceive my thoughts from afar. [3]You discern my going out and my lying down; you are familiar with all my ways. [4]Before a word is on my tongue you know it completely, O LORD. [5]You hem me in—behind and before; you have laid your hand upon me. [6]Such knowledge is too wonderful for me, too lofty for me to attain.
Ps 145 [3]Great is the LORD and most worthy of praise; his greatness no one can fathom.
Prov 30 [4]"Who has gone up to heaven and come down? Who has gathered up the wind in the hollow of his hands? Who has wrapped up the waters in his cloak? Who has established all the ends of the earth? What is his name, and the name of his son? Tell me if you know!"
Eccles 3 [11]He has made everything beautiful in its time. He has also set eternity in the hearts of men; yet they cannot fathom what God has done from beginning to end.
Eccles 11 [5]As you do not know the path of the wind, or how the body is formed in a mother's womb, so you cannot understand the work of God, the Maker of all things.
Isa 40 [13]Who has understood the mind of the LORD, or instructed him as his counselor?
Isa 40 [28]Do you not know? Have you not heard? The LORD is the everlasting God, the Creator of the ends of the earth. He will not grow tired or weary, and his understanding no one can fathom.
Isa 55 [8]"For my thoughts are not your thoughts, neither are your ways my ways," declares the LORD. [9]"As the heavens are higher than the earth, so are my ways higher than your ways and my thoughts than your thoughts."
John 1 [18]No one has ever seen God, but God the One and Only, who is at the Father's side, has made him known.
Rom 11 [33]Oh, the depth of the riches of the wisdom and knowledge of God! How unsearchable his judgments, and his paths beyond tracing out! [34]"Who has known the mind of the Lord? Or who has been his counselor?"
1 Cor 2 [10]but God has revealed it to us by his Spirit. The Spirit searches all things, even the deep things of God. [11]For who among men knows the thoughts of a man except the man's spirit within him? In the same way no one knows the thoughts of God except the Spirit of God.
1 Cor 2 [16]"For who has known the mind of the Lord that he may instruct him?" But we have the mind of Christ.
1 John 4 [12]No one has ever seen God; but if we love one another, God lives in us and his love is made complete in us.

H. God's Glory as His Being

Exod 15 [11]"Who among the gods is like you, O LORD? Who is like you—majestic in holiness, awesome in glory, working wonders?"
Exod 24 [17]To the Israelites the glory of the LORD looked like a consuming fire on top of the mountain.
Exod 40 [34]Then the cloud covered the Tent of Meeting, and the glory of the LORD filled the tabernacle. [35]Moses could not enter the Tent of Meeting because the cloud had settled upon it, and the glory of the LORD filled the tabernacle.
Lev 9 [23]Moses and Aaron then went into the Tent of Meeting. When they came out, they blessed the people; and the glory of the LORD appeared to all the people.
Num 14 [21]"Nevertheless, as surely as I live and as surely as the glory of the LORD fills the whole earth . . ."
Deut 5 [24]And you said, "The LORD our God has shown us his glory and his majesty, and we have heard his voice from the fire. Today we have seen that a man can live even if God speaks with him."
1 Kings 8 [11]And the priests could not perform their service because of the cloud, for the glory of the LORD filled his temple.
1 Chron 16 [24]Declare his glory among the nations, his marvelous deeds among all peoples.
Neh 9 [5]And the Levites—Jeshua, Kadmiel, Bani, Hashabneiah, Sherebiah, Hodiah, Shebaniah and Pethahiah—said: "Stand up and praise the LORD your God, who is from everlasting to everlasting."

"Blessed be your glorious name, and may it be exalted above all blessing and praise."
Ps 8 [1]O LORD, our Lord, how majestic is your name in all the earth! You have set your glory above the heavens.
Ps 19 [1]The heavens declare the glory of God; the skies proclaim the work of his hands.
Ps 29 [1]Ascribe to the LORD, O mighty ones, ascribe to the LORD glory and strength. [2]Ascribe to the LORD the glory due his name; worship the LORD in the splendor of his holiness. [3]The voice of the LORD is over the waters; the God of glory thunders, the LORD thunders over the mighty waters.
Ps 63 [2]I have seen you in the sanctuary and beheld your power and your glory.
Ps 96 [8]Ascribe to the LORD the glory due his name; bring an offering and come into his courts.
Ps 111 [3]Glorious and majestic are his deeds, and his righteousness endures forever.
Ps 138 [4]May all the kings of the earth praise you, O LORD, when they hear the words of your mouth. [5]May they sing of the ways of the LORD, for the glory of the LORD is great.
Isa 6 [1]In the year that King Uzziah died, I saw the Lord seated on a throne, high and exalted, and the train of his robe filled the temple. [2]Above him were seraphs, each with six wings: With two wings they covered their faces, with two they covered their feet, and with two they were flying. [3]And they were calling to one another: "Holy, holy, holy is the LORD Almighty; the whole earth is full of his glory." [4]At the sound of their voices the doorposts and thresholds shook and the temple was filled with smoke.
Isa 42 [8]"I am the LORD; that is my name! I will not give my glory to another or my praise to idols."
Isa 58 [8]"Then your light will break forth like the dawn, and your healing will quickly appear; then your righteousness will go before you, and the glory of the LORD will be your rear guard."
Isa 60 [1]"Arise, shine, for your light has come, and the glory of the LORD rises upon you. [2]See, darkness covers the earth and thick darkness is over the peoples, but the LORD rises upon you and his glory appears over you."
Isa 66 [18]"And I, because of their actions and their imagina-

tions, am about to come and gather all nations and tongues, and they will come and see my glory.

[19]"I will set a sign among them, and I will send some of those who survive to the nations—to Tarshish, to the Libyans and Lydians (famous as archers), to Tubal and Greece, and to the distant islands that have not heard of my fame or seen my glory. They will proclaim my glory among the nations."

Hab 2 [14]"For the earth will be filled with the knowledge of the glory of the LORD, as the waters cover the sea."

Hag 2 [7]"'I will shake all nations, and the desired of all nations will come, and I will fill this house with glory,' says the LORD Almighty."

Zech 2 [5]"'And I myself will be a wall of fire around it,' declares the LORD, 'and I will be its glory within.'"

Luke 2 [9]An angel of the Lord appeared to them, and the glory of the Lord shone around them, and they were terrified. . . .

[14]"Glory to God in the highest, and on earth peace to men on whom his favor rests."

John 17 [22]"I have given them the glory that you gave me, that they may be one as we are one. . . ."

Rom 6 [4]We were therefore buried with him through baptism into death in order that, just as Christ was raised from the dead through the glory of the Father, we too may live a new life.

2 Cor 4 [6]For God, who said, "Let light shine out of darkness," made his light shine in our hearts to give us the light of the knowledge of the glory of God in the face of Christ.

Heb 1 [3]The Son is the radiance of God's glory and the exact representation of his being, sustaining all things by his powerful word. After he had provided purification for sins, he sat down at the right hand of the Majesty in heaven.

2 Pet 1 [17]For he received honor and glory from God the Father when the voice came to him from the Majestic Glory, saying, "This is my Son, whom I love; with him I am well pleased."

Rev 21 [23]The city does not need the sun or the moon to shine on it, for the glory of God gives it light, and the Lamb is its lamp.

I. The Greatness of God

Deut 3 [24]"O Sovereign LORD, you have begun to show to your servant your greatness and your strong hand. For what god is there in heaven or on earth who can do the deeds and mighty works you do?"

Deut 10 [17]For the LORD your God is God of gods and Lord of lords, the great God, mighty and awesome, who shows no partiality and accepts no bribes.

Deut 32 [3]I will proclaim the name of the LORD. Oh, praise the greatness of our God! [4]He is the Rock, his works are perfect, and all his ways are just. A faithful God who does no wrong, upright and just is he.

2 Sam 7 [22]"How great you are, O Sovereign LORD! There is no one like you, and there is no God but you, as we have heard with our own ears."

1 Kings 8 [42]". . . for men will hear of your great name and your mighty hand and your outstretched arm—when he comes and prays toward this temple. . . ."

1 Chron 16 [25]For great is the LORD and most worthy of praise; he is to be feared above all gods.

1 Chron 29 [10]David praised the LORD in the presence of the whole assembly, saying, "Praise be to you, O LORD, God of our father Israel, from everlasting to everlasting. [11]Yours, O LORD, is the greatness and the power and the glory and the majesty and the splendor, for everything in heaven and earth is yours. Yours, O LORD, is the kingdom; you are exalted as head over all. [12]Wealth and honor come from you; you are the ruler of all things. In your hands are strength and power to exalt and give strength to all. [13]Now, our God, we give you thanks, and praise your glorious name."

Neh 1 [5]Then I said: "O LORD, God of heaven, the great and awesome God, who keeps his covenant of love with those who love him and obey his commands. . . ."

Neh 8 [6]Ezra praised the LORD, the great God; and all the people lifted their hands and responded, "Amen! Amen!" Then they bowed down and worshiped the LORD with their faces to the ground.

Job 33 [12]"But I tell you, in this you are not right, for God is greater than man."

Ps 48 [1]Great is the LORD, and most worthy of praise, in the city of our God, his holy mountain.

Ps 77 [13]Your ways, O God, are holy. What god is so great as our God?

Ps 95 [3]For the LORD is the great God, the great King above all gods.

Ps 96 [4]For great is the LORD and most worthy of praise; he is to be feared above all gods.

Ps 104 [1]Praise the LORD, O my soul. O LORD my God, you are very great; you are clothed with splendor and majesty.

Ps 135 [5]I know that the LORD is great, that our Lord is greater than all gods. [6]The LORD does whatever pleases him, in the heavens and on the earth, in the seas and all their depths. [7]He makes clouds rise from the ends of the earth; he sends lightning with the rain and brings out the wind from his storehouses.

Ps 138 [5]May they sing of the ways of the LORD, for the glory of the LORD is great.

Ps 145 [3]Great is the LORD and most worthy of praise; his greatness no one can fathom. [4]One generation will commend your works to another; they will tell of your mighty acts. [5]They will speak of the glorious splendor of your majesty, and I will meditate on your wonderful works. [6]They will tell of the power of your awesome works, and I will proclaim your great deeds.

Ps 150 [2]Praise him for his acts of power; praise him for his surpassing greatness.

Isa 12 [6]"Shout aloud and sing for joy, people of Zion, for great is the Holy One of Israel among you."

Jer 32 [18]"You show love to thousands but bring the punishment for the fathers' sins into the laps of their children after them. O great and powerful God, whose name is the LORD Almighty . . ."

Mal 1 [11]"My name will be great among the nations, from the rising to the setting of the sun. In every place incense and pure offerings will be brought to my name, because my name will be great among the nations," says the LORD Almighty.

John 10 [29]"My Father, who has given them to me, is greater than all; no one can snatch them out of my Father's hand."

Heb 6 [13]When God made his promise to Abraham, since there was no one greater for him to swear by, he swore by himself. . . .

1 John 3 [20]whenever our hearts condemn us. For God is greater than our hearts, and he knows everything.

1 John 4 [4]You, dear children, are from God and have overcome them, because the one who is in you is greater than the one who is in the world.

J. The Fatherhood of God

1. Divine Fatherhood

Gal 1 [1]Paul, an apostle—sent not from men nor by man, but by Jesus Christ and God the Father, who raised him from the dead . . .

Gal 1 [4]who gave himself for our sins to rescue us from the present evil age, according to the will of our God and Father . . .

Eph 1 [2]Grace and peace to you from God our Father and the Lord Jesus Christ.

Eph 5 [20]always giving thanks to God the Father for everything, in the name of our Lord Jesus Christ.

Col 1 [12]giving thanks to the Father, who has qualified you to share in the inheritance of the saints in the kingdom of light.

1 Thess 1 [3]We continually remember before our God and Father your work produced by faith, your labor prompted by love, and your endurance inspired by hope in our Lord Jesus Christ.

1 Thess 3 [13]May he strengthen your hearts so that you will be blameless and holy in the presence of our God and Father when our Lord Jesus comes with all his holy ones.

2 Thess 2 [16]May our Lord Jesus Christ himself and God our Father, who loved us and by his grace gave us eternal encouragement and good hope . . .

Heb 12 [9]Moreover, we have all had human fathers who disciplined us and we respected them for it. How much more should we submit to the Father of our spirits and live!

James 1 [17]Every good and perfect gift is from above, coming down from the Father of the heavenly lights, who does not change like shifting shadows.

2. God as Father over Creation

Num 16 22But Moses and Aaron fell facedown and cried out, "O God, God of the spirits of all mankind, will you be angry with the entire assembly when only one man sins?"
Acts 17 28"'For in him we live and move and have our being.' As some of your own poets have said, 'We are his offspring.'"

29"Therefore since we are God's offspring, we should not think that the divine being is like gold or silver or stone—an image made by man's design and skill."
1 Cor 8 6yet for us there is but one God, the Father, from whom all things came and for whom we live; and there is but one Lord, Jesus Christ, through whom all things came and through whom we live.
Eph 3 14For this reason I kneel before the Father, 15from whom his whole family in heaven and on earth derives its name.
Eph 4 6one God and Father of all, who is over all and through all and in all.
Heb 12 9Moreover, we have all had human fathers who disciplined us and we respected them for it. How much more should we submit to the Father of our spirits and live!

3. God as Father of Israel

Exod 4 22"Then say to Pharaoh, 'This is what the LORD says: Israel is my firstborn son. . . .'"
Deut 14 1You are the children of the LORD your God. Do not cut yourselves or shave the front of your heads for the dead. . . .
Deut 32 6Is this the way you repay the LORD, O foolish and unwise people? Is he not your Father, your Creator, who made you and formed you?
Ps 89 26"He will call out to me, 'You are my Father, my God, the Rock my Savior.'"
Isa 63 7I will tell of the kindnesses of the LORD, the deeds for which he is to be praised, according to all the LORD has done for us—yes, the many good things he has done for the house of Israel, according to his compassion and many kindnesses. 8He said, "Surely they are my people, sons who will not be false to me"; and so he became their Savior. 9In all their distress he too was distressed, and the angel of his presence saved them. In his love and mercy he redeemed them; he lifted them up and carried them all the days of old.
Isa 63 16But you are our Father, though Abraham does not know us or Israel acknowledge us; you, O LORD, are our Father, our Redeemer from of old is your name.
Isa 64 8Yet, O LORD, you are our Father. We are the clay, you are the potter; we are all the work of your hand.
Jer 3 4"Have you not just called to me: 'My Father, my friend from my youth . . .'?"
Jer 3 19"I myself said, 'How gladly would I treat you like sons and give you a desirable land, the most beautiful inheritance of any nation.' I thought you would call me 'Father' and not turn away from following me."
Jer 31 9"They will come with weeping; they will pray as I bring them back. I will lead them beside streams of water on a level path where they will not stumble, because I am Israel's father, and Ephraim is my firstborn son."
Hos 1 10"Yet the Israelites will be like the sand on the seashore, which cannot be measured or counted. In the place where it was said to them, 'You are not my people,' they will be called 'sons of the living God.'"
Hos 11 1"When Israel was a child, I loved him, and out of Egypt I called my son."
Mal 1 1An oracle: The word of the LORD to Israel through Malachi. . . .

6"A son honors his father, and a servant his master. If I am a father, where is the honor due me? If I am a master, where is the respect due me?" says the LORD Almighty. "It is you, O priests, who show contempt for my name.

"But you ask, 'How have we shown contempt for your name?'"
Mal 2 10Have we not all one Father? Did not one God create us? Why do we profane the covenant of our fathers by breaking faith with one another?
Mal 3 17"They will be mine," says the LORD Almighty, "in the day when I make up my treasured possession. I will spare them, just as in compassion a man spares his son who serves him."
Rom 9 3For I could wish that I myself were cursed and cut off from Christ for the sake of my brothers, those of my own race, 4the people of Israel. Theirs is the adoption as sons; theirs the divine glory, the covenants, the receiving of the law, the temple worship and the promises.

4. God as Father of Jesus Christ

Matt 3 17And a voice from heaven said, "This is my Son, whom I love; with him I am well pleased."
Matt 11 27"All things have been committed to me by my Father. No one knows the Son except the Father, and no one knows the Father except the Son and those to whom the Son chooses to reveal him."
Mark 9 7Then a cloud appeared and enveloped them, and a voice came from the cloud: "This is my Son, whom I love. Listen to him!"
Mark 14 36"*Abba*, Father," he said, "everything is possible for you. Take this cup from me. Yet not what I will, but what you will."
Luke 2 49"Why were you searching for me?" he asked. "Didn't you know I had to be in my Father's house?"
Luke 23 46Jesus called out with a loud voice, "Father, into your hands I commit my spirit." When he had said this, he breathed his last.
John 1 14The Word became flesh and made his dwelling among us. We have seen his glory, the glory of the One and Only, who came from the Father, full of grace and truth.
John 5 17Jesus said to them, "My Father is always at his work to this very day, and I, too, am working." 18For this reason the Jews tried all the harder to kill him; not only was he breaking the Sabbath, but he was even calling God his own Father, making himself equal with God.

19Jesus gave them this answer: "I tell you the truth, the Son can do nothing by himself; he can do only what he sees his Father doing, because whatever the Father does the Son also does. 20For the Father loves the Son and shows him all he does. Yes, to your amazement he will show him even greater things than these. 21For just as the Father raises the dead and gives them life, even so the Son gives life to whom he is pleased to give it. 22Moreover, the Father judges no one, but has entrusted all judgment to the Son, 23that all may honor the Son just as they honor the Father. He who does not honor the Son does not honor the Father, who sent him."
John 8 28So Jesus said, "When you have lifted up the Son of Man, then you will know that I am the one I claim to be and that I do nothing on my own but speak just what the Father has taught me."
John 10 25Jesus answered, "I did tell you, but you do not believe. The miracles I do in my Father's name speak for me. . . . 30I and the Father are one."
John 14 6Jesus answered, "I am the way and the truth and the life. No one comes to the Father except through me. 7If you really knew me, you would know my Father as well. From now on, you do know him and have seen him."

8Philip said, "Lord, show us the Father and that will be enough for us."

9Jesus answered: "Don't you know me, Philip, even after I have been among you such a long time? Anyone who has seen me has seen the Father. How can you say, 'Show us the Father'? 10Don't you believe that I am in the Father, and that the Father is in me? The words I say to you are not just my own. Rather, it is the Father, living in me, who is doing his work. 11Believe me when I say that I am in the Father and the Father is in me; or at least believe on the evidence of the miracles themselves. 12I tell you the truth, anyone who has faith in me will do what I have been doing. He will do even greater things than these, because I am going to the Father. 13And I will do whatever you ask in my name, so that the Son may bring glory to the Father."
John 14 20"On that day you will realize that I am in my Father, and you are in me, and I am in you. 21Whoever has my commands and obeys them, he is the one who loves me. He who

loves me will be loved by my Father, and I too will love him and show myself to him."

John 20 [17]Jesus said, "Do not hold on to me, for I have not yet returned to the Father. Go instead to my brothers and tell them, 'I am returning to my Father and your Father, to my God and your God.'"

2 Cor 11 [31]The God and Father of the Lord Jesus, who is to be praised forever, knows that I am not lying.

Eph 1 [3]Praise be to the God and Father of our Lord Jesus Christ, who has blessed us in the heavenly realms with every spiritual blessing in Christ.

Col 1 [3]We always thank God, the Father of our Lord Jesus Christ, when we pray for you. . . .

Heb 1 [5]For to which of the angels did God ever say, "You are my Son; today I have become your Father"? Or again, "I will be his Father, and he will be my Son"?

5. God as Father of Believers

Ps 89 [26]"He will call out to me, 'You are my Father, my God, the Rock my Savior.'"

Ps 103 [13]As a father has compassion on his children, so the LORD has compassion on those who fear him. . . .

Isa 43 [6]"I will say to the north, 'Give them up!' and to the south, 'Do not hold them back.' Bring my sons from afar and my daughters from the ends of the earth— [7]everyone who is called by my name, whom I created for my glory, whom I formed and made."

Matt 6 [8]"Do not be like them, for your Father knows what you need before you ask him.

[9]"This, then, is how you should pray: 'Our Father in heaven, hallowed be your name. . . .'"

Matt 6 [14]"For if you forgive men when they sin against you, your heavenly Father will also forgive you. [15]But if you do not forgive men their sins, your Father will not forgive your sins. . . . [17]But when you fast, put oil on your head and wash your face, [18]so that it will not be obvious to men that you are fasting, but only to your Father, who is unseen; and your Father, who sees what is done in secret, will reward you."

Matt 6 [26]"Look at the birds of the air; they do not sow or reap or store away in barns, and yet your heavenly Father feeds them. Are you not much more valuable than they? . . . [32]For the pagans run after all these things, and your heavenly Father knows that you need them."

Matt 7 [11]"If you, then, though you are evil, know how to give good gifts to your children, how much more will your Father in heaven give good gifts to those who ask him!"

John 1 [12]Yet to all who received him, to those who believed in his name, he gave the right to become children of God— [13]children born not of natural descent, nor of human decision or a husband's will, but born of God.

Rom 1 [7]To all in Rome who are loved by God and called to be saints: Grace and peace to you from God our Father and from the Lord Jesus Christ.

Rom 8 [15]For you did not receive a spirit that makes you a slave again to fear, but you received the Spirit of sonship. And by him we cry, "*Abba*, Father." [16]The Spirit himself testifies with our spirit that we are God's children. [17]Now if we are children, then we are heirs—heirs of God and co-heirs with Christ, if indeed we share in his sufferings in order that we may also share in his glory.

1 Cor 1 [3]Grace and peace to you from God our Father and the Lord Jesus Christ.

2 Cor 1 [3]Praise be to the God and Father of our Lord Jesus Christ, the Father of compassion and the God of all comfort. . . .

Gal 3 [26]You are all sons of God through faith in Christ Jesus. . . .

Gal 4 [6]Because you are sons, God sent the Spirit of his Son into our hearts, the Spirit who calls out, "*Abba*, Father."

2 Thess 2 [16]May our Lord Jesus Christ himself and God our Father, who loved us and by his grace gave us eternal encouragement and good hope . . .

James 1 [27]Religion that God our Father accepts as pure and faultless is this: to look after orphans and widows in their distress and to keep oneself from being polluted by the world.

James 3 [9]With the tongue we praise our Lord and Father, and with it we curse men, who have been made in God's likeness.

1 Pet 1 [17]Since you call on a Father who judges each man's work impartially, live your lives as strangers here in reverent fear.

1 John 1 [3]We proclaim to you what we have seen and heard, so that you also may have fellowship with us. And our fellowship is with the Father and with his Son, Jesus Christ.

1 John 2 [1]My dear children, I write this to you so that you will not sin. But if anybody does sin, we have one who speaks to the Father in our defense—Jesus Christ, the Righteous One.

1 John 3 [1]How great is the love the Father has lavished on us, that we should be called children of God! And that is what we are! The reason the world does not know us is that it did not know him.

II
The Nature of God as Person

A. *God Is a Person*

1. God Thinks and Knows

1 Sam 2 [3]"Do not keep talking so proudly or let your mouth speak such arrogance, for the LORD is a God who knows, and by him deeds are weighed."

1 Chron 28 [9]"And you, my son Solomon, acknowledge the God of your father, and serve him with wholehearted devotion and with a willing mind, for the LORD searches every heart and understands every motive behind the thoughts. If you seek him, he will be found by you; but if you forsake him, he will reject you forever."

Job 28 [20]"Where then does wisdom come from? Where does understanding dwell? [21]It is hidden from the eyes of every living thing, concealed even from the birds of the air. . . . [23]God understands the way to it and he alone knows where it dwells, [24]for he views the ends of the earth and sees everything under the heavens."

Ps 139 [1]O LORD, you have searched me and you know me. [2]You know when I sit and when I rise; you perceive my thoughts from afar. [3]You discern my going out and my lying down; you are familiar with all my ways. [4]Before a word is on my tongue you know it completely, O LORD. [5]You hem me in—behind and before; you have laid your hand upon me. [6]Such knowledge is too wonderful for me, too lofty for me to attain.

Jer 17 [10]"I the LORD search the heart and examine the mind, to reward a man according to his conduct, according to what his deeds deserve."

Acts 1 [24]Then they prayed, "Lord, you know everyone's heart. Show us which of these two you have chosen. . . ."

2 Cor 4 [2]Rather, we have renounced secret and shameful ways; we do not use deception, nor do we distort the word of God. On the contrary, by setting forth the truth plainly we commend ourselves to every man's conscience in the sight of God.

2 Cor 12 [3]And I know that this man—whether in the body or apart from the body I do not know, but God knows . . .

Gal 4 [9]But now that you know God—or rather are known by God—how is it that you are turning back to those weak and miserable principles? Do you wish to be enslaved by them all over again?

Phil 3 [15]All of us who are mature should take such a view of things. And if on some point you think differently, that too God will make clear to you.

2 Tim 2 [19]Nevertheless, God's solid foundation stands firm, sealed with this inscription: "The Lord knows those who are his," and, "Everyone who confesses the name of the Lord must turn away from wickedness."

Heb 4 [13]Nothing in all creation is hidden from God's sight. Everything is uncovered and laid bare before the eyes of him to whom we must give account.

1 John 3 [20]whenever our hearts condemn us. For God is greater than our hearts, and he knows everything.

2. God Formulates Plans and Acts on Them

Isa 14 [26]"This is the plan determined for the whole world; this is the hand stretched out over all nations. [27]For the LORD Almighty has purposed, and who can thwart him? His hand is stretched out, and who can turn it back?"
Isa 46 [10]"I make known the end from the beginning, from ancient times, what is still to come. I say: My purpose will stand, and I will do all that I please."
Isa 55 [11]". . . so is my word that goes out from my mouth: It will not return to me empty, but will accomplish what I desire and achieve the purpose for which I sent it."
Acts 2 [23]"This man was handed over to you by God's set purpose and foreknowledge; and you, with the help of wicked men, put him to death by nailing him to the cross."
Rom 4 [20]Yet he did not waver through unbelief regarding the promise of God, but was strengthened in his faith and gave glory to God, [21]being fully persuaded that God had power to do what he had promised.
Rom 8 [28]And we know that in all things God works for the good of those who love him, who have been called according to his purpose. [29]For those God foreknew he also predestined to be conformed to the likeness of his Son, that he might be the firstborn among many brothers. [30]And those he predestined, he also called; those he called, he also justified; those he justified, he also glorified.
1 Cor 1 [1]Paul, called to be an apostle of Christ Jesus by the will of God, and our brother Sosthenes . . .
Gal 1 [3]Grace and peace to you from God our Father and the Lord Jesus Christ, [4]who gave himself for our sins to rescue us from the present evil age, according to the will of our God and Father. . . .
Eph 1 [1]Paul, an apostle of Christ Jesus by the will of God,
To the saints in Ephesus, the faithful in Christ Jesus. . . .
[9]And he made known to us the mystery of his will according to his good pleasure, which he purposed in Christ. . . .
Eph 2 [10]For we are God's workmanship, created in Christ Jesus to do good works, which God prepared in advance for us to do.
Eph 3 [10]His intent was that now, through the church, the manifold wisdom of God should be made known to the rulers and authorities in the heavenly realms, [11]according to his eternal purpose which he accomplished in Christ Jesus our Lord.

3. God Makes Ethical Judgments

Prov 5 [21]For a man's ways are in full view of the LORD, and he examines all his paths.
Jer 20 [12]O LORD Almighty, you who examine the righteous and probe the heart and mind, let me see your vengeance upon them, for to you I have committed my cause.
Acts 10 [42]"He commanded us to preach to the people and to testify that he is the one whom God appointed as judge of the living and the dead."
Acts 17 [31]"For he has set a day when he will judge the world with justice by the man he has appointed. He has given proof of this to all men by raising him from the dead."
Rom 2 [16]This will take place on the day when God will judge men's secrets through Jesus Christ, as my gospel declares.
1 Cor 3 [17]If anyone destroys God's temple, God will destroy him; for God's temple is sacred, and you are that temple.
1 Cor 4 [5]Therefore judge nothing before the appointed time; wait till the Lord comes. He will bring to light what is hidden in darkness and will expose the motives of men's hearts. At that time each will receive his praise from God.
2 Cor 11 [31]The God and Father of the Lord Jesus, who is to be praised forever, knows that I am not lying.
1 Thess 2 [11]For you know that we dealt with each of you as a father deals with his own children, [12]encouraging, comforting and urging you to live lives worthy of God, who calls you into his kingdom and glory.
1 Pet 4 [5]But they will have to give account to him who is ready to judge the living and the dead.

4. God Feels Emotion

Gen 6 [6]The LORD was grieved that he had made man on the earth, and his heart was filled with pain.
Exod 20 [5]"You shall not bow down to them or worship them; for I, the LORD your God, am a jealous God, punishing the children for the sin of the fathers to the third and fourth generation of those who hate me, [6]but showing love to a thousand generations of those who love me and keep my commandments."
Deut 32 [35]"It is mine to avenge; I will repay. In due time their foot will slip; their day of disaster is near and their doom rushes upon them."

[36]The LORD will judge his people and have compassion on his servants when he sees their strength is gone and no one is left, slave or free. [37]He will say: "Now where are their gods, the rock they took refuge in, [38]the gods who ate the fat of their sacrifices and drank the wine of their drink offerings? Let them rise up to help you! Let them give you shelter!

[39]"See now that I myself am He! There is no god besides me. I put to death and I bring to life, I have wounded and I will heal, and no one can deliver out of my hand. [40]I lift my hand to heaven and declare: As surely as I live forever, [41]when I sharpen my flashing sword and my hand grasps it in judgment, I will take vengeance on my adversaries and repay those who hate me. [42]I will make my arrows drunk with blood, while my sword devours flesh: the blood of the slain and the captives, the heads of the enemy leaders."

[43]Rejoice, O nations, with his people, for he will avenge the blood of his servants; he will take vengeance on his enemies and make atonement for his land and people.
Neh 9 [31]"But in your great mercy you did not put an end to them or abandon them, for you are a gracious and merciful God."
Job 19 [11]"His anger burns against me; he counts me among his enemies."
Ps 5 [5]The arrogant cannot stand in your presence; you hate all who do wrong. [6]You destroy those who tell lies; bloodthirsty and deceitful men the LORD abhors.
Ps 11 [5]The LORD examines the righteous, but the wicked and those who love violence his soul hates.
Ps 104 [31]May the glory of the LORD endure forever; may the LORD rejoice in his works. . . .
Ps 111 [4]He has caused his wonders to be remembered; the LORD is gracious and compassionate.
Isa 1 [24]Therefore the Lord, the LORD Almighty, the Mighty One of Israel, declares: "Ah, I will get relief from my foes and avenge myself on my enemies."
Isa 62 [4]No longer will they call you Deserted, or name your land Desolate. But you will be called Hephzibah, and your land Beulah; for the LORD will take delight in you, and your land will be married. [5]As a young man marries a maiden, so will your sons marry you; as a bridegroom rejoices over his bride, so will your God rejoice over you.
Jer 31 [3]The LORD appeared to us in the past, saying: "I have loved you with an everlasting love; I have drawn you with loving-kindness."
Lam 2 [3]In fierce anger he has cut off every horn of Israel. He has withdrawn his right hand at the approach of the enemy. He has burned in Jacob like a flaming fire that consumes everything around it.
Ezek 5 [13]"Then my anger will cease and my wrath against them will subside, and I will be avenged. And when I have spent my wrath upon them, they will know that I the LORD have spoken in my zeal."
Zeph 3 [8]"Therefore wait for me," declares the LORD, "for the day I will stand up to testify. I have decided to assemble the nations, to gather the kingdoms and to pour out my wrath on them—all my fierce anger. The whole world will be consumed by the fire of my jealous anger."
Rom 9 [13]Just as it is written: "Jacob I loved, but Esau I hated."
2 Cor 9 [7]Each man should give what he has decided in his heart to give, not reluctantly or under compulsion, for God loves a cheerful giver.
Eph 5 [6]Let no one deceive you with empty words, for because of such things God's wrath comes on those who are disobedient.
Phil 2 [27]Indeed he was ill, and almost died. But God had mercy on him, and not on him only but also on me, to spare me sorrow upon sorrow.

James 5 [11]As you know, we consider blessed those who have persevered. You have heard of Job's perseverance and have seen what the Lord finally brought about. The Lord is full of compassion and mercy.
1 John 4 [16]And so we know and rely on the love God has for us. God is love. Whoever lives in love lives in God, and God in him.

5. God Responds to Requests from Others

Exod 3 [7]The LORD said, "I have indeed seen the misery of my people in Egypt. I have heard them crying out because of their slave drivers, and I am concerned about their suffering. [8]So I have come down to rescue them from the hand of the Egyptians and to bring them up out of that land into a good and spacious land, a land flowing with milk and honey—the home of the Canaanites, Hittites, Amorites, Perizzites, Hivites and Jebusites."
Exod 6 [5]"Moreover, I have heard the groaning of the Israelites, whom the Egyptians are enslaving, and I have remembered my covenant."
Job 34 [28]"They caused the cry of the poor to come before him, so that he heard the cry of the needy."
Ps 81 [10]"I am the LORD your God, who brought you up out of Egypt. Open wide your mouth and I will fill it."
Ps 91 [14]"Because he loves me," says the LORD, "I will rescue him; I will protect him, for he acknowledges my name. [15]He will call upon me, and I will answer him; I will be with him in trouble, I will deliver him and honor him."
Ps 119 [26]"I recounted my ways and you answered me; teach me your decrees."
Prov 16 [1]To man belong the plans of the heart, but from the LORD comes the reply of the tongue.
Isa 58 [9]"Then you will call, and the LORD will answer; you will cry for help, and he will say: Here am I. If you do away with the yoke of oppression, with the pointing finger and malicious talk . . ."
Zech 13 [9]"This third I will bring into the fire; I will refine them like silver and test them like gold. They will call on my name and I will answer them; I will say, 'They are my people,' and they will say, 'The LORD is our God.'"
John 9 [31]"We know that God does not listen to sinners. He listens to the godly man who does his will."
2 Cor 1 [3]Praise be to the God and Father of our Lord Jesus Christ, the Father of compassion and the God of all comfort, [4]who comforts us in all our troubles, so that we can comfort those in any trouble with the comfort we ourselves have received from God.
2 Cor 9 [8]And God is able to make all grace abound to you, so that in all things at all times, having all that you need, you will abound in every good work.
Phil 4 [6]Do not be anxious about anything, but in everything, by prayer and petition, with thanksgiving, present your requests to God. [7]And the peace of God, which transcends all understanding, will guard your hearts and your minds in Christ Jesus. . . . [19]And my God will meet all your needs according to his glorious riches in Christ Jesus.
James 4 [8]Come near to God and he will come near to you. Wash your hands, you sinners, and purify your hearts, you double-minded. . . . [10]Humble yourselves before the Lord, and he will lift you up.
1 John 5 [14]This is the confidence we have in approaching God: that if we ask anything according to his will, he hears us. [15]And if we know that he hears us—whatever we ask—we know that we have what we asked of him.

6. God Has Aesthetic Capacities

Gen 1 [31]God saw all that he had made, and it was very good. And there was evening, and there was morning—the sixth day.
Ps 27 [4]One thing I ask of the LORD, this is what I seek: that I may dwell in the house of the LORD all the days of my life, to gaze upon the beauty of the LORD and to seek him in his temple.
Ps 104 [24]How many are your works, O LORD! In wisdom you made them all; the earth is full of your creatures.
Eccles 3 [11]He has made everything beautiful in its time. He has also set eternity in the hearts of men; yet they cannot fathom what God has done from beginning to end.
Isa 28 [5]In that day the LORD Almighty will be a glorious crown, a beautiful wreath for the remnant of his people.
Ezek 31 [2]"Son of man, say to Pharaoh king of Egypt and to his hordes: 'Who can be compared with you in majesty? [3]Consider Assyria, once a cedar in Lebanon, with beautiful branches overshadowing the forest; it towered on high, its top above the thick foliage. [4]The waters nourished it, deep springs made it grow tall; their streams flowed all around its base and sent their channels to all the trees of the field. [5]So it towered higher than all the trees of the field; its boughs increased and its branches grew long, spreading because of abundant waters. [6]All the birds of the air nested in its boughs, all the beasts of the field gave birth under its branches; all the great nations lived in its shade. [7]It was majestic in beauty, with its spreading boughs, for its roots went down to abundant waters. [8]The cedars in the garden of God could not rival it, nor could the pine trees equal its boughs, nor could the plane trees compare with its branches—no tree in the garden of God could match its beauty. [9]I made it beautiful with abundant branches, the envy of all the trees of Eden in the garden of God.'"
1 Tim 4 [4]For everything God created is good, and nothing is to be rejected if it is received with thanksgiving. . . .

B. God Is a Spirit

Ps 139 [7]Where can I go from your Spirit? Where can I flee from your presence? [8]If I go up to the heavens, you are there; if I make my bed in the depths, you are there. [9]If I rise on the wings of the dawn, if I settle on the far side of the sea, [10]even there your hand will guide me, your right hand will hold me fast.

[11]If I say, "Surely the darkness will hide me and the light become night around me," [12]even the darkness will not be dark to you; the night will shine like the day, for darkness is as light to you.
Isa 31 [3]But the Egyptians are men and not God; their horses are flesh and not spirit. When the LORD stretches out his hand, he who helps will stumble, he who is helped will fall; both will perish together.
John 4 [24]"God is spirit, and his worshipers must worship in spirit and in truth."
Acts 7 [48]"However, the Most High does not live in houses made by men. As the prophet says: [49]'Heaven is my throne, and the earth is my footstool. What kind of house will you build for me? says the Lord. Or where will my resting place be? [50]Has not my hand made all these things?'"
2 Cor 3 [17]Now the Lord is the Spirit, and where the Spirit of the Lord is, there is freedom. [18]And we, who with unveiled faces all reflect the Lord's glory, are being transformed into his likeness with ever-increasing glory, which comes from the Lord, who is the Spirit.

C. God Is Invisible

Deut 4 [11]You came near and stood at the foot of the mountain while it blazed with fire to the very heavens, with black clouds and deep darkness.[12]Then the LORD spoke to you out of the fire. You heard the sound of words but saw no form; there was only a voice. [13]He declared to you his covenant, the Ten Commandments, which he commanded you to follow and then wrote them on two stone tablets. [14]And the LORD directed me at that time to teach you the decrees and laws you are to follow in the land that you are crossing the Jordan to possess.

[15]You saw no form of any kind the day the LORD spoke to you at Horeb out of the fire. Therefore watch yourselves very carefully. . . .
Job 9 [11]"When he passes me, I cannot see him; when he goes by, I cannot perceive him."
Job 23 [8]"But if I go to the east, he is not there; if I go to the west, I do not find him. [9]When he is at work in the north, I do not see him; when he turns to the south, I catch no glimpse of him."

John 1 [18]No one has ever seen God, but God the One and Only, who is at the Father's side, has made him known.
John 5 [37]"And the Father who sent me has himself testified concerning me. You have never heard his voice nor seen his form. . . ."
John 6 [46]"No one has seen the Father except the one who is from God; only he has seen the Father."
Rom 1 [20]For since the creation of the world God's invisible qualities—his eternal power and divine nature—have been clearly seen, being understood from what has been made, so that men are without excuse.
Col 1 [15]He is the image of the invisible God, the firstborn over all creation.
1 Tim 1 [17]Now to the King eternal, immortal, invisible, the only God, be honor and glory for ever and ever. Amen.
1 Tim 6 [15]which God will bring about in his own time—God, the blessed and only Ruler, the King of kings and Lord of lords, [16]who alone is immortal and who lives in unapproachable light, whom no one has seen or can see. To him be honor and might forever. Amen.
Heb 11 [27]By faith he left Egypt, not fearing the king's anger; he persevered because he saw him who is invisible.

D. God Is Alive

Josh 3 [10]"This is how you will know that the living God is among you and that he will certainly drive out before you the Canaanites, Hittites, Hivites, Perizzites, Girgashites, Amorites and Jebusites."
1 Sam 17 [26]David asked the men standing near him, "What will be done for the man who kills this Philistine and removes this disgrace from Israel? Who is this uncircumcised Philistine that he should defy the armies of the living God?"
Ps 84 [2]My soul yearns, even faints, for the courts of the LORD; my heart and my flesh cry out for the living God.
Isa 37 [4]"It may be that the LORD your God will hear the words of the field commander, whom his master, the king of Assyria, has sent to ridicule the living God, and that he will rebuke him for the words the LORD your God has heard. Therefore pray for the remnant that still survives."
Isa 37 [17]"Give ear, O LORD, and hear; open your eyes, O LORD, and see; listen to all the words Sennacherib has sent to insult the living God."
Jer 10 [10]But the LORD is the true God; he is the living God, the eternal King. When he is angry, the earth trembles; the nations cannot endure his wrath.
Dan 4 [34]At the end of that time, I, Nebuchadnezzar, raised my eyes toward heaven, and my sanity was restored. Then I praised the Most High; I honored and glorified him who lives forever. His dominion is an eternal dominion; his kingdom endures from generation to generation.
Dan 6 [26]"I issue a decree that in every part of my kingdom people must fear and reverence the God of Daniel. For he is the living God and he endures forever; his kingdom will not be destroyed, his dominion will never end."
Hos 1 [10]"Yet the Israelites will be like the sand on the seashore, which cannot be measured or counted. In the place where it was said to them, 'You are not my people,' they will be called 'sons of the living God.'"
Matt 16 [16]Simon Peter answered, "You are the Christ, the Son of the living God."
John 5 [26]"For as the Father has life in himself, so he has granted the Son to have life in himself."
Acts 14 [15]"Men, why are you doing this? We too are only men, human like you. We are bringing you good news, telling you to turn from these worthless things to the living God, who made heaven and earth and sea and everything in them."
2 Cor 3 [3]You show that you are a letter from Christ, the result of our ministry, written not with ink but with the Spirit of the living God, not on tablets of stone but on tablets of human hearts.
1 Thess 1 [9]for they themselves report what kind of reception you gave us. They tell how you turned to God from idols to serve the living and true God. . . .
1 Tim 3 [15]if I am delayed, you will know how people ought to conduct themselves in God's household, which is the church of the living God, the pillar and foundation of the truth.
Heb 3 [12]See to it, brothers, that none of you has a sinful, unbelieving heart that turns away from the living God.
Heb 9 [14]How much more, then, will the blood of Christ, who through the eternal Spirit offered himself unblemished to God, cleanse our consciences from acts that lead to death, so that we may serve the living God!
Rev 7 [2]Then I saw another angel coming up from the east, having the seal of the living God. He called out in a loud voice to the four angels who had been given power to harm the land and sea. . . .

E. God Is Perfect

Deut 32 [4]He is the Rock, his works are perfect, and all his ways are just. A faithful God who does no wrong, upright and just is he.
2 Sam 22 [31]"As for God, his way is perfect; the word of the LORD is flawless. He is a shield for all who take refuge in him."
Job 37 [16]"Do you know how the clouds hang poised, those wonders of him who is perfect in knowledge?"
Ps 19 [7]The law of the LORD is perfect, reviving the soul. The statutes of the LORD are trustworthy, making wise the simple.
Prov 30 [5]"Every word of God is flawless; he is a shield to those who take refuge in him."
Matt 5 [48]"Be perfect, therefore, as your heavenly Father is perfect."
Rom 12 [2]Do not conform any longer to the pattern of this world, but be transformed by the renewing of your mind. Then you will be able to test and approve what God's will is—his good, pleasing and perfect will.

F. God Is Active

1. God Is Active in Nature

Gen 1 [1]In the beginning God created the heavens and the earth.
Neh 9 [6]"You alone are the LORD. You made the heavens, even the highest heavens, and all their starry host, the earth and all that is on it, the seas and all that is in them. You give life to everything, and the multitudes of heaven worship you."
Job 9 [8]"He alone stretches out the heavens and treads on the waves of the sea."
Ps 24 [1]The earth is the LORD's, and everything in it, the world, and all who live in it; [2]for he founded it upon the seas and established it upon the waters.
Ps 33 [6]By the word of the LORD were the heavens made, their starry host by the breath of his mouth.
Ps 95 [3]For the LORD is the great God, the great King above all gods. [4]In his hand are the depths of the earth, and the mountain peaks belong to him. [5]The sea is his, for he made it, and his hands formed the dry land.
Ps 104 [1]Praise the LORD, O my soul.

O LORD my God, you are very great; you are clothed with splendor and majesty. [2]He wraps himself in light as with a garment; he stretches out the heavens like a tent [3]and lays the beams of his upper chambers on their waters. He makes the clouds his chariot and rides on the wings of the wind. [4]He makes winds his messengers, flames of fire his servants.

[5]He set the earth on its foundations; it can never be moved. [6]You covered it with the deep as with a garment; the waters stood above the mountains. [7]But at your rebuke the waters fled, at the sound of your thunder they took to flight; [8]they flowed over the mountains, they went down into the valleys, to the place you assigned for them. [9]You set a boundary they cannot cross; never again will they cover the earth.

[10]He makes springs pour water into the ravines; it flows between the mountains. [11]They give water to all the beasts of the field; the wild donkeys quench their thirst. [12]The birds of the air nest by the waters; they sing among the branches. [13]He waters the mountains from his upper chambers; the earth is satisfied by the fruit of his work. [14]He makes grass grow for the cattle, and plants for man to cultivate—bringing forth food from the earth: [15]wine that gladdens the heart of man, oil to make his face shine, and bread that sustains his heart. [16]The

trees of the LORD are well watered, the cedars of Lebanon that he planted. 17There the birds make their nests; the stork has its home in the pine trees. 18The high mountains belong to the wild goats; the crags are a refuge for the coneys.

19The moon marks off the seasons, and the sun knows when to go down. 20You bring darkness, it becomes night, and all the beasts of the forest prowl. 21The lions roar for their prey and seek their food from God. 22The sun rises, and they steal away; they return and lie down in their dens. 23Then man goes out to his work, to his labor until evening.

24How many are your works, O LORD! In wisdom you made them all; the earth is full of your creatures. 25There is the sea, vast and spacious, teeming with creatures beyond number—living things both large and small. 26There the ships go to and fro, and the leviathan, which you formed to frolic there.

27These all look to you to give them their food at the proper time. 28When you give it to them, they gather it up; when you open your hand, they are satisfied with good things. 29When you hide your face, they are terrified; when you take away their breath, they die and return to the dust. 30When you send your Spirit, they are created, and you renew the face of the earth.

31May the glory of the LORD endure forever; may the LORD rejoice in his works—32he who looks at the earth, and it trembles, who touches the mountains, and they smoke.

Ps 119 89Your word, O LORD, is eternal; it stands firm in the heavens. 90Your faithfulness continues through all generations; you established the earth, and it endures. 91Your laws endure to this day, for all things serve you.

Eccles 11 5As you do not know the path of the wind, or how the body is formed in a mother's womb, so you cannot understand the work of God, the Maker of all things.

Isa 42 5This is what God the LORD says—he who created the heavens and stretched them out, who spread out the earth and all that comes out of it, who gives breath to its people, and life to those who walk on it: 6"I, the LORD, have called you in righteousness; I will take hold of your hand. I will keep you and will make you to be a covenant for the people and a light for the Gentiles, 7to open eyes that are blind, to free captives from prison and to release from the dungeon those who sit in darkness.

8"I am the LORD; that is my name! I will not give my glory to another or my praise to idols."

Isa 44 24"This is what the LORD says—your Redeemer, who formed you in the womb: I am the LORD, who has made all things, who alone stretched out the heavens, who spread out the earth by myself. . . ."

Isa 45 12"It is I who made the earth and created mankind upon it. My own hands stretched out the heavens; I marshaled their starry hosts."

Amos 4 13He who forms the mountains, creates the wind, and reveals his thoughts to man, he who turns dawn to darkness, and treads the high places of the earth—the LORD God Almighty is his name.

Heb 1 10He also says, "In the beginning, O Lord, you laid the foundations of the earth, and the heavens are the work of your hands."

Heb 3 4For every house is built by someone, but God is the builder of everything.

Heb 11 3By faith we understand that the universe was formed at God's command, so that what is seen was not made out of what was visible.

Rev 14 7He said in a loud voice, "Fear God and give him glory, because the hour of his judgment has come. Worship him who made the heavens, the earth, the sea and the springs of water."

2. God Is Active in Israel's History

Gen 12 1The LORD had said to Abram, "Leave your country, your people and your father's household and go to the land I will show you. 2I will make you into a great nation and I will bless you; I will make your name great, and you will be a blessing. 3I will bless those who bless you, and whoever curses you I will curse; and all peoples on earth will be blessed through you."

Gen 17 3Abram fell facedown, and God said to him, 4"As for me, this is my covenant with you: You will be the father of many nations. . . . 7I will establish my covenant as an everlasting covenant between me and you and your descendants after you for the generations to come, to be your God and the God of your descendants after you."

Gen 22 17"I will surely bless you and make your descendants as numerous as the stars in the sky and as the sand on the seashore. Your descendants will take possession of the cities of their enemies, 18and through your offspring all nations on earth will be blessed, because you have obeyed me."

Exod 19 4"'You yourselves have seen what I did to Egypt, and how I carried you on eagles' wings and brought you to myself. 5Now if you obey me fully and keep my covenant, then out of all nations you will be my treasured possession. Although the whole earth is mine, 6you will be for me a kingdom of priests and a holy nation.' These are the words you are to speak to the Israelites."

Exod 29 45"Then I will dwell among the Israelites and be their God.46They will know that I am the LORD their God, who brought them out of Egypt so that I might dwell among them. I am the LORD their God."

Deut 2 7The LORD your God has blessed you in all the work of your hands. He has watched over your journey through this vast desert. These forty years the LORD your God has been with you, and you have not lacked anything.

Deut 6 10When the LORD your God brings you into the land he swore to your fathers, to Abraham, Isaac and Jacob, to give you—a land with large, flourishing cities you did not build, 11houses filled with all kinds of good things you did not provide, wells you did not dig, and vineyards and olive groves you did not plant—then when you eat and are satisfied, 12be careful that you do not forget the LORD, who brought you out of Egypt, out of the land of slavery.

Deut 32 9For the LORD's portion is his people, Jacob his allotted inheritance.

10In a desert land he found him, in a barren and howling waste. He shielded him and cared for him; he guarded him as the apple of his eye. . . .

Josh 1 5"No one will be able to stand up against you all the days of your life. As I was with Moses, so I will be with you; I will never leave you nor forsake you."

Judg 2 18Whenever the LORD raised up a judge for them, he was with the judge and saved them out of the hands of their enemies as long as the judge lived; for the LORD had compassion on them as they groaned under those who oppressed and afflicted them.

2 Sam 7 10"'And I will provide a place for my people Israel and will plant them so that they can have a home of their own and no longer be disturbed. Wicked people will not oppress them anymore, as they did at the beginning 11and have done ever since the time I appointed leaders over my people Israel. I will also give you rest from all your enemies.

"'The LORD declares to you that the LORD himself will establish a house for you: 12When your days are over and you rest with your fathers, I will raise up your offspring to succeed you, who will come from your own body, and I will establish his kingdom. 13He is the one who will build a house for my Name, and I will establish the throne of his kingdom forever. 14I will be his father, and he will be my son. When he does wrong, I will punish him with the rod of men, with floggings inflicted by men. 15But my love will never be taken away from him, as I took it away from Saul, whom I removed from before you. 16Your house and your kingdom will endure forever before me; your throne will be established forever.'"

2 Kings 5 15Then Naaman and all his attendants went back to the man of God. He stood before him and said, "Now I know that there is no God in all the world except in Israel. Please accept now a gift from your servant."

Ps 77 15With your mighty arm you redeemed your people, the descendants of Jacob and Joseph.

Ps 89 3You said, "I have made a covenant with my chosen one, I have sworn to David my servant, 4'I will establish your line forever and make your throne firm through all generations.'"

Ps 130 8He himself will redeem Israel from all their sins.

Isa 5 1I will sing for the one I love a song about his vineyard: My loved one had a vineyard on a fertile hillside. 2He dug it up and cleared it of stones and planted it with the choicest vines.

He built a watchtower in it and cut out a winepress as well. Then he looked for a crop of good grapes, but it yielded only bad fruit.

[3]"Now you dwellers in Jerusalem and men of Judah, judge between me and my vineyard. [4]What more could have been done for my vineyard than I have done for it? When I looked for good grapes, why did it yield only bad? [5]Now I will tell you what I am going to do to my vineyard: I will take away its hedge, and it will be destroyed; I will break down its wall, and it will be trampled. [6]I will make it a wasteland, neither pruned nor cultivated, and briers and thorns will grow there. I will command the clouds not to rain on it."

[7]The vineyard of the LORD Almighty is the house of Israel, and the men of Judah are the garden of his delight. And he looked for justice, but saw bloodshed; for righteousness, but heard cries of distress.

Jer 31 [31]"The time is coming," declares the LORD, "when I will make a new covenant with the house of Israel and with the house of Judah. [32]It will not be like the covenant I made with their forefathers when I took them by the hand to lead them out of Egypt, because they broke my covenant, though I was a husband to them," declares the LORD. [33]"This is the covenant I will make with the house of Israel after that time," declares the LORD. "I will put my law in their minds and write it on their hearts. I will be their God, and they will be my people. [34]No longer will a man teach his neighbor, or a man his brother, saying, 'Know the LORD,' because they will all know me, from the least of them to the greatest," declares the LORD. "For I will forgive their wickedness and will remember their sins no more."

Hos 11 [1]"When Israel was a child, I loved him, and out of Egypt I called my son."

Rom 11 [23]And if they do not persist in unbelief, they will be grafted in, for God is able to graft them in again. [24]After all, if you were cut out of an olive tree that is wild by nature, and contrary to nature were grafted into a cultivated olive tree, how much more readily will these, the natural branches, be grafted into their own olive tree!

[25]I do not want you to be ignorant of this mystery, brothers, so that you may not be conceited: Israel has experienced a hardening in part until the full number of the Gentiles has come in. [26]And so all Israel will be saved, as it is written: "The deliverer will come from Zion; he will turn godlessness away from Jacob. [27] And this is my covenant with them when I take away their sins."

3. God Is Active in Other Nations and in the Whole World

Deut 32 [8]When the Most High gave the nations their inheritance, when he divided all mankind, he set up boundaries for the peoples according to the number of the sons of Israel.

2 Kings 19 [15]And Hezekiah prayed to the LORD: "O LORD, God of Israel, enthroned between the cherubim, you alone are God over all the kingdoms of the earth. You have made heaven and earth."

Job 12 [13]"To God belong wisdom and power; counsel and understanding are his. [14]What he tears down cannot be rebuilt; the man he imprisons cannot be released. . . . [17]He leads counselors away stripped and makes fools of judges. [18]He takes off the shackles put on by kings and ties a loincloth around their waist. [19]He leads priests away stripped and overthrows men long established. [20]He silences the lips of trusted advisers and takes away the discernment of elders. [21]He pours contempt on nobles and disarms the mighty. [22]He reveals the deep things of darkness and brings deep shadows into the light. [23]He makes nations great, and destroys them; he enlarges nations, and disperses them. [24]He deprives the leaders of the earth of their reason; he sends them wandering through a trackless waste. [25]They grope in darkness with no light; he makes them stagger like drunkards."

Ps 2 [10]Therefore, you kings, be wise; be warned, you rulers of the earth. [11]Serve the LORD with fear and rejoice with trembling. [12]Kiss the Son, lest he be angry and you be destroyed in your way, for his wrath can flare up in a moment. Blessed are all who take refuge in him.

Ps 22 [27]All the ends of the earth will remember and turn to the LORD, and all the families of the nations will bow down before him, [28]for dominion belongs to the LORD and he rules over the nations.

Ps 66 [7]He rules forever by his power, his eyes watch the nations—let not the rebellious rise up against him.

Ps 75 [6]No one from the east or the west or from the desert can exalt a man. [7]But it is God who judges: He brings one down, he exalts another.

Prov 8 [15]"By me kings reign and rulers make laws that are just; [16]by me princes govern, and all nobles who rule on earth."

Dan 2 [21]"He changes times and seasons; he sets up kings and deposes them. He gives wisdom to the wise and knowledge to the discerning."

Dan 2 [37]"You, O king, are the king of kings. The God of heaven has given you dominion and power and might and glory; [38]in your hands he has placed mankind and the beasts of the field and the birds of the air. Wherever they live, he has made you ruler over them all. You are that head of gold."

Dan 4 [17]"'The decision is announced by messengers, the holy ones declare the verdict, so that the living may know that the Most High is sovereign over the kingdoms of men and gives them to anyone he wishes and sets over them the lowliest of men.'"

Dan 4 [32]"You will be driven away from people and will live with the wild animals; you will eat grass like cattle. Seven times will pass by for you until you acknowledge that the Most High is sovereign over the kingdoms of men and gives them to anyone he wishes." . . .

[34]At the end of that time, I, Nebuchadnezzar, raised my eyes toward heaven, and my sanity was restored. Then I praised the Most High; I honored and glorified him who lives forever. His dominion is an eternal dominion; his kingdom endures from generation to generation. [35]All the peoples of the earth are regarded as nothing. He does as he pleases with the powers of heaven and the peoples of the earth. No one can hold back his hand or say to him: "What have you done?"

Acts 17 [26]"From one man he made every nation of men, that they should inhabit the whole earth; and he determined the times set for them and the exact places where they should live."

Rom 13 [1]Everyone must submit himself to the governing authorities, for there is no authority except that which God has established. The authorities that exist have been established by God. [2]Consequently, he who rebels against the authority is rebelling against what God has instituted, and those who do so will bring judgment on themselves. [3]For rulers hold no terror for those who do right, but for those who do wrong. Do you want to be free from fear of the one in authority? Then do what is right and he will commend you. [4]For he is God's servant to do you good. But if you do wrong, be afraid, for he does not bear the sword for nothing. He is God's servant, an agent of wrath to bring punishment on the wrongdoer. [5]Therefore, it is necessary to submit to the authorities, not only because of possible punishment but also because of conscience.

[6]This is also why you pay taxes, for the authorities are God's servants, who give their full time to governing. [7]Give everyone what you owe him: If you owe taxes, pay taxes; if revenue, then revenue; if respect, then respect; if honor, then honor.

4. God Is Active in Human Lives

Gen 1 [26]Then God said, "Let us make man in our image, in our likeness, and let them rule over the fish of the sea and the birds of the air, over the livestock, over all the earth, and over all the creatures that move along the ground." [27]So God created man in his own image, in the image of God he created him; male and female he created them.

[28]God blessed them and said to them, "Be fruitful and increase in number; fill the earth and subdue it. Rule over the fish of the sea and the birds of the air and over every living creature that moves on the ground."

Gen 2 [7]the LORD God formed the man from the dust of the ground and breathed into his nostrils the breath of life, and the man became a living being.

Gen 9 [5]"And for your lifeblood I will surely demand an accounting. I will demand an accounting from every animal.

And from each man, too, I will demand an accounting for the life of his fellow man. 6Whoever sheds the blood of man, by man shall his blood be shed; for in the image of God has God made man. 7As for you, be fruitful and increase in number; multiply on the earth and increase upon it."

1 Sam 2 6"The LORD brings death and makes alive; he brings down to the grave and raises up. 7The LORD sends poverty and wealth; he humbles and he exalts. 8He raises the poor from the dust and lifts the needy from the ash heap; he seats them with princes and has them inherit a throne of honor. "For the foundations of the earth are the LORD's; upon them he has set the world."

Job 14 5"Man's days are determined; you have decreed the number of his months and have set limits he cannot exceed."

Ps 8 3When I consider your heavens, the work of your fingers, the moon and the stars, which you have set in place, 4what is man that you are mindful of him, the son of man that you care for him? 5You made him a little lower than the heavenly beings and crowned him with glory and honor. 6You made him ruler over the works of your hands; you put everything under his feet: 7all flocks and herds, and the beasts of the field, 8the birds of the air, and the fish of the sea, all that swim the paths of the seas.

Eccles 3 11He has made everything beautiful in its time. He has also set eternity in the hearts of men; yet they cannot fathom what God has done from beginning to end.

Matt 5 45". . . that you may be sons of your Father in heaven. He causes his sun to rise on the evil and the good, and sends rain on the righteous and the unrighteous."

Luke 6 35"But love your enemies, do good to them, and lend to them without expecting to get anything back. Then your reward will be great, and you will be sons of the Most High, because he is kind to the ungrateful and wicked."

Acts 14 17"Yet he has not left himself without testimony: He has shown kindness by giving you rain from heaven and crops in their seasons; he provides you with plenty of food and fills your hearts with joy."

Acts 17 29"Therefore since we are God's offspring, we should not think that the divine being is like gold or silver or stone—an image made by man's design and skill. 30In the past God overlooked such ignorance, but now he commands all people everywhere to repent."

1 Tim 2 3This is good, and pleases God our Savior, 4who wants all men to be saved and to come to a knowledge of the truth. 5For there is one God and one mediator between God and men, the man Christ Jesus, 6who gave himself as a ransom for all men—the testimony given in its proper time.

2 Pet 3 9The Lord is not slow in keeping his promise, as some understand slowness. He is patient with you, not wanting anyone to perish, but everyone to come to repentance.

5. God Is Active in Jesus' Life

Matt 1 23"The virgin will be with child and will give birth to a son, and they will call him Immanuel"—which means, "God with us."

Matt 3 17And a voice from heaven said, "This is my Son, whom I love; with him I am well pleased."

John 3 16"For God so loved the world that he gave his one and only Son, that whoever believes in him shall not perish but have eternal life. 17For God did not send his Son into the world to condemn the world, but to save the world through him."

John 4 34"My food," said Jesus, "is to do the will of him who sent me and to finish his work."

John 5 19Jesus gave them this answer: "I tell you the truth, the Son can do nothing by himself; he can do only what he sees his Father doing, because whatever the Father does the Son also does. 20For the Father loves the Son and shows him all he does. Yes, to your amazement he will show him even greater things than these. 21For just as the Father raises the dead and gives them life, even so the Son gives life to whom he is pleased to give it. 22Moreover, the Father judges no one, but has entrusted all judgment to the Son, 23that all may honor the Son just as they honor the Father. He who does not honor the Son does not honor the Father, who sent him. . . . 30By myself I can do nothing; I judge only as I hear, and my judgment is just, for I seek not to please myself but him who sent me."

John 6 27"Do not work for food that spoils, but for food that endures to eternal life, which the Son of Man will give you. On him God the Father has placed his seal of approval."

John 8 42Jesus said to them, "If God were your Father, you would love me, for I came from God and now am here. I have not come on my own; but he sent me."

John 10 17"The reason my Father loves me is that I lay down my life—only to take it up again. 18No one takes it from me, but I lay it down of my own accord. I have authority to lay it down and authority to take it up again. This command I received from my Father."

John 13 3Jesus knew that the Father had put all things under his power, and that he had come from God and was returning to God. . . .

John 16 27"No, the Father himself loves you because you have loved me and have believed that I came from God."

John 17 11"I will remain in the world no longer, but they are still in the world, and I am coming to you. Holy Father, protect them by the power of your name—the name you gave me—so that they may be one as we are one."

Acts 2 22"Men of Israel, listen to this: Jesus of Nazareth was a man accredited by God to you by miracles, wonders and signs, which God did among you through him, as you yourselves know. 23This man was handed over to you by God's set purpose and foreknowledge; and you, with the help of wicked men, put him to death by nailing him to the cross. 24But God raised him from the dead, freeing him from the agony of death, because it was impossible for death to keep its hold on him. . . .

36"Therefore let all Israel be assured of this: God has made this Jesus, whom you crucified, both Lord and Christ."

Acts 10 36"You know the message God sent to the people of Israel, telling the good news of peace through Jesus Christ, who is Lord of all. 37You know what has happened throughout Judea, beginning in Galilee after the baptism that John preached—38how God anointed Jesus of Nazareth with the Holy Spirit and power, and how he went around doing good and healing all who were under the power of the devil, because God was with him.

39"We are witnesses of everything he did in the country of the Jews and in Jerusalem. They killed him by hanging him on a tree, 40but God raised him from the dead on the third day and caused him to be seen. . . . 42He commanded us to preach to the people and to testify that he is the one whom God appointed as judge of the living and the dead."

Acts 17 31"For he has set a day when he will judge the world with justice by the man he has appointed. He has given proof of this to all men by raising him from the dead."

Rom 3 25God presented him as a sacrifice of atonement, through faith in his blood. He did this to demonstrate his justice, because in his forbearance he had left the sins committed beforehand unpunished—26he did it to demonstrate his justice at the present time, so as to be just and the one who justifies those who have faith in Jesus.

1 Cor 15 15More than that, we are then found to be false witnesses about God, for we have testified about God that he raised Christ from the dead. But he did not raise him if in fact the dead are not raised.

2 Cor 5 19that God was reconciling the world to himself in Christ, not counting men's sins against them. And he has committed to us the message of reconciliation. . . . 21God made him who had no sin to be sin for us, so that in him we might become the righteousness of God.

Gal 4 4But when the time had fully come, God sent his Son, born of a woman, born under law. . . .

Eph 1 4For he chose us in him before the creation of the world to be holy and blameless in his sight. In love 5he predestined us to be adopted as his sons through Jesus Christ, in accordance with his pleasure and will. . . . 9And he made known to us the mystery of his will according to his good pleasure, which he purposed in Christ, 10to be put into effect when the times will have reached their fulfillment—to bring all things in heaven and on earth together under one head, even Christ.

Eph 3 11according to his eternal purpose which he accomplished in Christ Jesus our Lord.

Phil 2 9Therefore God exalted him to the highest place and gave him the name that is above every name, 10that at the

name of Jesus every knee should bow, in heaven and on earth and under the earth, 11and every tongue confess that Jesus Christ is Lord, to the glory of God the Father.
Heb 1 8But about the Son he says, "Your throne, O God, will last for ever and ever, and righteousness will be the scepter of your kingdom. 9You have loved righteousness and hated wickedness; therefore God, your God, has set you above your companions by anointing you with the oil of joy."

6. God Is Active in the Church

Matt 16 18"And I tell you that you are Peter, and on this rock I will build my church, and the gates of Hades will not overcome it."
Luke 2 28Simeon took him in his arms and praised God, saying: 29"Sovereign Lord, as you have promised, you now dismiss your servant in peace. 30For my eyes have seen your salvation, 31which you have prepared in the sight of all people, 32a light for revelation to the Gentiles and for glory to your people Israel."

33The child's father and mother marveled at what was said about him.
Acts 10 41"He was not seen by all the people, but by witnesses whom God had already chosen—by us who ate and drank with him after he rose from the dead."
Acts 13 2While they were worshiping the Lord and fasting, the Holy Spirit said, "Set apart for me Barnabas and Saul for the work to which I have called them."
Acts 20 28"Keep watch over yourselves and all the flock of which the Holy Spirit has made you overseers. Be shepherds of the church of God, which he bought with his own blood."
Rom 5 8But God demonstrates his own love for us in this: While we were still sinners, Christ died for us.
1 Cor 12 28And in the church God has appointed first of all apostles, second prophets, third teachers, then workers of miracles, also those having gifts of healing, those able to help others, those with gifts of administration, and those speaking in different kinds of tongues.
2 Cor 5 20We are therefore Christ's ambassadors, as though God were making his appeal through us. We implore you on Christ's behalf: Be reconciled to God.
Eph 1 11In him we were also chosen, having been predestined according to the plan of him who works out everything in conformity with the purpose of his will. . . . 22And God placed all things under his feet and appointed him to be head over everything for the church, 23which is his body, the fullness of him who fills everything in every way.
Eph 2 10For we are God's workmanship, created in Christ Jesus to do good works, which God prepared in advance for us to do. . . . 19Consequently, you are no longer foreigners and aliens, but fellow citizens with God's people and members of God's household, 20built on the foundation of the apostles and prophets, with Christ Jesus himself as the chief cornerstone. 21In him the whole building is joined together and rises to become a holy temple in the Lord. 22And in him you too are being built together to become a dwelling in which God lives by his Spirit.
Eph 3 1For this reason I, Paul, the prisoner of Christ Jesus for the sake of you Gentiles—

2Surely you have heard about the administration of God's grace that was given to me for you, 3that is, the mystery made known to me by revelation, as I have already written briefly. 4In reading this, then, you will be able to understand my insight into the mystery of Christ, 5which was not made known to men in other generations as it has now been revealed by the Spirit to God's holy apostles and prophets. 6This mystery is that through the gospel the Gentiles are heirs together with Israel, members together of one body, and sharers together in the promise in Christ Jesus.

7I became a servant of this gospel by the gift of God's grace given me through the working of his power. 8Although I am less than the least of all God's people, this grace was given me: to preach to the Gentiles the unsearchable riches of Christ, 9and to make plain to everyone the administration of this mystery, which for ages past was kept hidden in God, who created all things. 10His intent was that now, through the church, the manifold wisdom of God should be made known to the rulers and authorities in the heavenly realms, 11according to his eternal purpose which he accomplished in Christ Jesus our Lord. 12In him and through faith in him we may approach God with freedom and confidence. 13I ask you, therefore, not to be discouraged because of my sufferings for you, which are your glory.
Phil 2 12Therefore, my dear friends, as you have always obeyed—not only in my presence, but now much more in my absence—continue to work out your salvation with fear and trembling, 13for it is God who works in you to will and to act according to his good purpose.
Col 3 12Therefore, as God's chosen people, holy and dearly loved, clothe yourselves with compassion, kindness, humility, gentleness and patience.
2 Thess 2 13But we ought always to thank God for you, brothers loved by the Lord, because from the beginning God chose you to be saved through the sanctifying work of the Spirit and through belief in the truth.
1 Pet 2 9But you are a chosen people, a royal priesthood, a holy nation, a people belonging to God, that you may declare the praises of him who called you out of darkness into his wonderful light.
1 John 3 2Dear friends, now we are children of God, and what we will be has not yet been made known. But we know that when he appears, we shall be like him, for we shall see him as he is.

7. God Is Active in (Future) World History

Ps 2 6"I have installed my King on Zion, my holy hill." 7I will proclaim the decree of the LORD: He said to me, "You are my Son; today I have become your Father. 8Ask of me, and I will make the nations your inheritance, the ends of the earth your possession. 9You will rule them with an iron scepter; you will dash them to pieces like pottery."
Isa 9 6For to us a child is born, to us a son is given, and the government will be on his shoulders. And he will be called Wonderful Counselor, Mighty God, Everlasting Father, Prince of Peace. 7Of the increase of his government and peace there will be no end. He will reign on David's throne and over his kingdom, establishing and upholding it with justice and righteousness from that time on and forever. The zeal of the LORD Almighty will accomplish this.
Dan 7 13"In my vision at night I looked, and there before me was one like a son of man, coming with the clouds of heaven. He approached the Ancient of Days and was led into his presence. 14He was given authority, glory and sovereign power; all peoples, nations and men of every language worshiped him. His dominion is an everlasting dominion that will not pass away, and his kingdom is one that will never be destroyed."
Joel 3 2"I will gather all nations and bring them down to the Valley of Jehoshaphat. There I will enter into judgment against them concerning my inheritance, my people Israel, for they scattered my people among the nations and divided up my land."
Matt 25 31"When the Son of Man comes in his glory, and all the angels with him, he will sit on his throne in heavenly glory. 32All the nations will be gathered before him, and he will separate the people one from another as a shepherd separates the sheep from the goats. 33He will put the sheep on his right and the goats on his left.

34"Then the King will say to those on his right, 'Come, you who are blessed by my Father; take your inheritance, the kingdom prepared for you since the creation of the world. 35For I was hungry and you gave me something to eat, I was thirsty and you gave me something to drink, I was a stranger and you invited me in, 36I needed clothes and you clothed me, I was sick and you looked after me, I was in prison and you came to visit me.'

37"Then the righteous will answer him, 'Lord, when did we see you hungry and feed you, or thirsty and give you something to drink? 38When did we see you a stranger and invite you in, or needing clothes and clothe you? 39When did we see you sick or in prison and go to visit you?'

40"The King will reply, 'I tell you the truth, whatever you did for one of the least of these brothers of mine, you did for me.'

41"Then he will say to those on his left, 'Depart from me, you who are cursed, into the eternal fire prepared for the devil and his angels. 42For I was hungry and you gave me nothing to eat, I was thirsty and you gave me nothing to drink, 43I was a stranger and you did not invite me in, I needed clothes and you did not clothe me, I was sick and in prison and you did not look after me.'

44"They also will answer, 'Lord, when did we see you hungry or thirsty or a stranger or needing clothes or sick or in prison, and did not help you?'

45"He will reply, 'I tell you the truth, whatever you did not do for one of the least of these, you did not do for me.'

46"Then they will go away to eternal punishment, but the righteous to eternal life."

Luke 1 31"You will be with child and give birth to a son, and you are to give him the name Jesus. 32He will be great and will be called the Son of the Most High. The Lord God will give him the throne of his father David, 33and he will reign over the house of Jacob forever; his kingdom will never end."

Acts 3 19"Repent, then, and turn to God, so that your sins may be wiped out, that times of refreshing may come from the Lord, 20and that he may send the Christ, who has been appointed for you—even Jesus. 21He must remain in heaven until the time comes for God to restore everything, as he promised long ago through his holy prophets."

1 Cor 15 22For as in Adam all die, so in Christ all will be made alive. 23But each in his own turn: Christ, the firstfruits; then, when he comes, those who belong to him. 24Then the end will come, when he hands over the kingdom to God the Father after he has destroyed all dominion, authority and power. 25For he must reign until he has put all his enemies under his feet. 26The last enemy to be destroyed is death. 27For he "has put everything under his feet." Now when it says that "everything" has been put under him, it is clear that this does not include God himself, who put everything under Christ. 28When he has done this, then the Son himself will be made subject to him who put everything under him, so that God may be all in all.

Eph 1 9And he made known to us the mystery of his will according to his good pleasure, which he purposed in Christ, 10to be put into effect when the times will have reached their fulfillment—to bring all things in heaven and on earth together under one head, even Christ.

11In him we were also chosen, having been predestined according to the plan of him who works out everything in conformity with the purpose of his will. . . .

Rev 11 15The seventh angel sounded his trumpet, and there were loud voices in heaven, which said: "The kingdom of the world has become the kingdom of our Lord and of his Christ, and he will reign for ever and ever." 16And the twenty-four elders, who were seated on their thrones before God, fell on their faces and worshiped God, 17saying: "We give thanks to you, Lord God Almighty, the One who is and who was, because you have taken your great power and have begun to reign."

Rev 21 22I did not see a temple in the city, because the Lord God Almighty and the Lamb are its temple. 23The city does not need the sun or the moon to shine on it, for the glory of God gives it light, and the Lamb is its lamp. 24The nations will walk by its light, and the kings of the earth will bring their splendor into it. 25On no day will its gates ever be shut, for there will be no night there. 26The glory and honor of the nations will be brought into it.

G. God Is Transcendent

Deut 4 39Acknowledge and take to heart this day that the LORD is God in heaven above and on the earth below. There is no other.

Deut 10 14To the LORD your God belong the heavens, even the highest heavens, the earth and everything in it.

1 Kings 8 27"But will God really dwell on earth? The heavens, even the highest heaven, cannot contain you. How much less this temple I have built!"

2 Chron 2 6"But who is able to build a temple for him, since the heavens, even the highest heavens, cannot contain him? Who then am I to build a temple for him, except as a place to burn sacrifices before him?"

Ps 11 4The LORD is in his holy temple; the LORD is on his heavenly throne. He observes the sons of men; his eyes examine them.

Ps 95 3For the LORD is the great God, the great King above all gods.

Ps 99 2Great is the LORD in Zion; he is exalted over all the nations. 3Let them praise your great and awesome name—he is holy.

Ps 103 19The LORD has established his throne in heaven, and his kingdom rules over all.

Ps 113 5Who is like the LORD our God, the One who sits enthroned on high, 6who stoops down to look on the heavens and the earth?

Ps 123 1I lift up my eyes to you, to you whose throne is in heaven.

Isa 6 1In the year that King Uzziah died, I saw the Lord seated on a throne, high and exalted, and the train of his robe filled the temple.

Isa 33 5The LORD is exalted, for he dwells on high; he will fill Zion with justice and righteousness.

Isa 55 8"For my thoughts are not your thoughts, neither are your ways my ways," declares the LORD. 9"As the heavens are higher than the earth, so are my ways higher than your ways and my thoughts than your thoughts."

Isa 57 15For this is what the high and lofty One says—he who lives forever, whose name is holy: "I live in a high and holy place, but also with him who is contrite and lowly in spirit, to revive the spirit of the lowly and to revive the heart of the contrite."

Matt 23 22"And he who swears by heaven swears by God's throne and by the one who sits on it."

Luke 2 14"Glory to God in the highest, and on earth peace to men on whom his favor rests."

Acts 7 49"'Heaven is my throne, and the earth is my footstool. What kind of house will you build for me? says the Lord. Or where will my resting place be?'"

Acts 17 24"The God who made the world and everything in it is the Lord of heaven and earth and does not live in temples built by hands. 25And he is not served by human hands, as if he needed anything, because he himself gives all men life and breath and everything else."

Rom 9 5Theirs are the patriarchs, and from them is traced the human ancestry of Christ, who is God over all, forever praised! Amen.

Eph 4 6one God and Father of all, who is over all and through all and in all.

H. God Is Immanent

Gen 2 7the LORD God formed the man from the dust of the ground and breathed into his nostrils the breath of life, and the man became a living being.

Exod 29 45"Then I will dwell among the Israelites and be their God. 46They will know that I am the LORD their God, who brought them out of Egypt so that I might dwell among them. I am the LORD their God."

Deut 4 7What other nation is so great as to have their gods near them the way the LORD our God is near us whenever we pray to him?

Deut 4 39Acknowledge and take to heart this day that the LORD is God in heaven above and on the earth below. There is no other.

Job 33 4"The Spirit of God has made me; the breath of the Almighty gives me life."

Job 34 14"If it were his intention and he withdrew his spirit and breath, 15all mankind would perish together and man would return to the dust."

Ps 33 13From heaven the LORD looks down and sees all mankind; 14from his dwelling place he watches all who live on earth—15he who forms the hearts of all, who considers everything they do.

Ps 104 29When you hide your face, they are terrified; when you take away their breath, they die and return to the dust. 30When you send your Spirit, they are created, and you renew the face of the earth.

Ps 139 1O LORD, you have searched me and you know me. 2You know when I sit and when I rise; you perceive my thoughts from afar. 3You discern my going out and my lying down; you are familiar with all my ways. 4Before a word is on my tongue you know it completely, O LORD. 5You hem me in—behind and before; you have laid your hand upon me. 6Such knowledge is too wonderful for me, too lofty for me to attain.

7Where can I go from your Spirit? Where can I flee from your presence? 8If I go up to the heavens, you are there; if I make my bed in the depths, you are there. 9If I rise on the wings of the dawn, if I settle on the far side of the sea, 10even there your hand will guide me, your right hand will hold me fast.

Isa 57 15For this is what the high and lofty One says—he who lives forever, whose name is holy: "I live in a high and holy place, but also with him who is contrite and lowly in spirit, to revive the spirit of the lowly and to revive the heart of the contrite."

Isa 63 11Then his people recalled the days of old, the days of Moses and his people—where is he who brought them through the sea, with the shepherd of his flock? Where is he who set his Holy Spirit among them, 12who sent his glorious arm of power to be at Moses' right hand, who divided the waters before them, to gain for himself everlasting renown, 13who led them through the depths? Like a horse in open country, they did not stumble; 14like cattle that go down to the plain, they were given rest by the Spirit of the LORD. This is how you guided your people to make for yourself a glorious name.

Jer 23 23"Am I only a God nearby," declares the LORD, "and not a God far away? 24Can anyone hide in secret places so that I cannot see him?" declares the LORD. "Do not I fill heaven and earth?" declares the Lord.

Mic 1 3Look! The LORD is coming from his dwelling place; he comes down and treads the high places of the earth.

Matt 5 45". . . that you may be sons of your Father in heaven. He causes his sun to rise on the evil and the good, and sends rain on the righteous and the unrighteous."

Matt 6 25"Therefore I tell you, do not worry about your life, what you will eat or drink; or about your body, what you will wear. Is not life more important than food, and the body more important than clothes? 26Look at the birds of the air; they do not sow or reap or store away in barns, and yet your heavenly Father feeds them. Are you not much more valuable than they? 27Who of you by worrying can add a single hour to his life?

28"And why do you worry about clothes? See how the lilies of the field grow. They do not labor or spin. 29Yet I tell you that not even Solomon in all his splendor was dressed like one of these. 30If that is how God clothes the grass of the field, which is here today and tomorrow is thrown into the fire, will he not much more clothe you, O you of little faith?"

Matt 10 29"Are not two sparrows sold for a penny? Yet not one of them will fall to the ground apart from the will of your Father. 30And even the very hairs of your head are all numbered."

Acts 17 27"God did this so that men would seek him and perhaps reach out for him and find him, though he is not far from each one of us. 28'For in him we live and move and have our being.' As some of your own poets have said, 'We are his offspring.'"

Rom 11 36For from him and through him and to him are all things. To him be the glory forever! Amen.

1 Cor 3 23and you are of Christ, and Christ is of God.

1 Cor 12 6There are different kinds of working, but the same God works all of them in all men.

1 Cor 15 28When he has done this, then the Son himself will be made subject to him who put everything under him, so that God may be all in all.

Eph 4 6one God and Father of all, who is over all and through all and in all.

Col 1 17He is before all things, and in him all things hold together.

Rev 21 3And I heard a loud voice from the throne saying, "Now the dwelling of God is with men, and he will live with them. They will be his people, and God himself will be with them and be their God. 4He will wipe every tear from their eyes. There will be no more death or mourning or crying or pain, for the old order of things has passed away."

III
The Attributes of God

A. God Is a Unity (Is One)

Exod 15 11"Who among the gods is like you, O Lord? Who is like you—majestic in holiness, awesome in glory, working wonders?"

Deut 4 35You were shown these things so that you might know that the LORD is God; besides him there is no other. . . . 39Acknowledge and take to heart this day that the LORD is God in heaven above and on the earth below. There is no other.

Deut 6 4Hear, O Israel: The LORD our God, the LORD is one.

Deut 32 39"See now that I myself am He! There is no god besides me. I put to death and I bring to life, I have wounded and I will heal, and no one can deliver out of my hand."

2 Sam 7 22"How great you are, O Sovereign LORD! There is no one like you, and there is no God but you, as we have heard with our own ears."

1 Kings 8 60". . . so that all the peoples of the earth may know that the LORD is God and that there is no other."

Ps 86 10For you are great and do marvelous deeds; you alone are God.

Isa 42 8"I am the LORD; that is my name! I will not give my glory to another or my praise to idols."

Isa 44 6"This is what the LORD says—Israel's King and Redeemer, the LORD Almighty: I am the first and I am the last; apart from me there is no God."

Isa 45 5"I am the LORD, and there is no other; apart from me there is no God. I will strengthen you, though you have not acknowledged me, 6so that from the rising of the sun to the place of its setting men may know there is none besides me. I am the LORD, and there is no other."

Joel 2 27"Then you will know that I am in Israel, that I am the LORD your God, and that there is no other; never again will my people be shamed."

Zech 14 9The LORD will be king over the whole earth. On that day there will be one LORD, and his name the only name.

John 5 44"How can you believe if you accept praise from one another, yet make no effort to obtain the praise that comes from the only God?"

John 17 3"Now this is eternal life: that they may know you, the only true God, and Jesus Christ, whom you have sent."

1 Cor 8 4So then, about eating food sacrificed to idols: We know that an idol is nothing at all in the world and that there is no God but one. 5For even if there are so-called gods, whether in heaven or on earth (as indeed there are many "gods" and many "lords"), 6yet for us there is but one God, the Father, from whom all things came and for whom we live; and there is but one Lord, Jesus Christ, through whom all things came and through whom we live.

Gal 3 20A mediator, however, does not represent just one party; but God is one.

Eph 4 5one Lord, one faith, one baptism; 6one God and Father of all, who is over all and through all and in all.

1 Tim 1 17Now to the King eternal, immortal, invisible, the only God, be honor and glory for ever and ever. Amen.

1 Tim 2 5For there is one God and one mediator between God and men, the man Christ Jesus. . . .

1 Tim 6 15which God will bring about in his own time—God, the blessed and only Ruler, the King of kings and Lord of lords . . .

James 2 19You believe that there is one God. Good! Even the demons believe that—and shudder.

B. God Is Compassionate

Exod 33 19And the LORD said, "I will cause all my goodness to pass in front of you, and I will proclaim my name, the LORD, in your presence. I will have mercy on whom I will have mercy, and I will have compassion on whom I will have compassion."

Exod 34 6And he passed in front of Moses, proclaiming, "The LORD, the LORD, the compassionate and gracious God, slow to anger, abounding in love and faithfulness . . ."

Deut 30 [2]and when you and your children return to the LORD your God and obey him with all your heart and with all your soul according to everything I command you today, [3]then the LORD your God will restore your fortunes and have compassion on you and gather you again from all the nations where he scattered you.
2 Kings 13 [23]But the LORD was gracious to them and had compassion and showed concern for them because of his covenant with Abraham, Isaac and Jacob. To this day he has been unwilling to destroy them or banish them from his presence.
2 Chron 30 [9]"If you return to the LORD, then your brothers and your children will be shown compassion by their captors and will come back to this land, for the LORD your God is gracious and compassionate. He will not turn his face from you if you return to him."
Neh 9 [17]"They refused to listen and failed to remember the miracles you performed among them. They became stiff-necked and in their rebellion appointed a leader in order to return to their slavery. But you are a forgiving God, gracious and compassionate, slow to anger and abounding in love. Therefore you did not desert them. . . ."
Ps 86 [15]But you, O LORD, are a compassionate and gracious God, slow to anger, abounding in love and faithfulness.
Ps 102 [13]You will arise and have compassion on Zion, for it is time to show favor to her; the appointed time has come.
Ps 103 [2]Praise the LORD, O my soul, and forget not all his benefits . . . [4]who redeems your life from the pit and crowns you with love and compassion. . . . [13]As a father has compassion on his children, so the LORD has compassion on those who fear him. . . .
Ps 145 [8]The LORD is gracious and compassionate, slow to anger and rich in love. [9]The LORD is good to all; he has compassion on all he has made.
Isa 49 [10]"They will neither hunger nor thirst, nor will the desert heat or the sun beat upon them. He who has compassion on them will guide them and lead them beside springs of water."
Isa 63 [7]I will tell of the kindnesses of the LORD, the deeds for which he is to be praised, according to all the LORD has done for us—yes, the many good things he has done for the house of Israel, according to his compassion and many kindnesses.
Jer 12 [15]"But after I uproot them, I will again have compassion and will bring each of them back to his own inheritance and his own country."
Lam 3 [22]Because of the LORD's great love we are not consumed, for his compassions never fail.
Hos 2 [19]"I will betroth you to me forever; I will betroth you in righteousness and justice, in love and compassion."
Joel 2 [18]Then the LORD will be jealous for his land and take pity on his people.
Jon 4 [2]He prayed to the LORD, "O LORD, is this not what I said when I was still at home? That is why I was so quick to flee to Tarshish. I knew that you are a gracious and compassionate God, slow to anger and abounding in love, a God who relents from sending calamity."
Mic 7 [18]Who is a God like you, who pardons sin and forgives the transgression of the remnant of his inheritance? You do not stay angry forever but delight to show mercy. [19]You will again have compassion on us; you will tread our sins underfoot and hurl all our iniquities into the depths of the sea.
2 Cor 1 [3]Praise be to the God and Father of our Lord Jesus Christ, the Father of compassion and the God of all comfort. . . .
James 5 [11]As you know, we consider blessed those who have persevered. You have heard of Job's perseverance and have seen what the Lord finally brought about. The Lord is full of compassion and mercy.

C. God Is Eternal

Gen 21 [33]Abraham planted a tamarisk tree in Beersheba, and there he called upon the name of the LORD, the Eternal God.
Deut 32 [40]"I lift my hand to heaven and declare: As surely as I live forever. . . ."
Deut 33 [27]"The eternal God is your refuge, and underneath are the everlasting arms. He will drive out your enemy before you, saying, 'Destroy him!'"
1 Chron 16 [36]Praise be to the LORD, the God of Israel, from everlasting to everlasting. Then all the people said "Amen" and "Praise the LORD."
Neh 9 [5]And the Levites—Jeshua, Kadmiel, Bani, Hashabneiah, Sherebiah, Hodiah, Shebaniah and Pethahiah—said: "Stand up and praise the LORD your God, who is from everlasting to everlasting."

"Blessed be your glorious name, and may it be exalted above all blessing and praise."
Job 36 [26]"How great is God—beyond our understanding! The number of his years is past finding out."
Ps 29 [10]The LORD sits enthroned over the flood; the LORD is enthroned as King forever.
Ps 33 [11]But the plans of the LORD stand firm forever, the purposes of his heart through all generations.
Ps 41 [13]Praise be to the LORD, the God of Israel, from everlasting to everlasting. Amen and Amen.
Ps 45 [6]Your throne, O God, will last for ever and ever; a scepter of justice will be the scepter of your kingdom.
Ps 48 [14]For this God is our God for ever and ever; he will be our guide even to the end.
Ps 90 [1]Lord, you have been our dwelling place throughout all generations. [2]Before the mountains were born or you brought forth the earth and the world, from everlasting to everlasting you are God. . . . [4]For a thousand years in your sight are like a day that has just gone by, or like a watch in the night.
Ps 93 [2]Your throne was established long ago; you are from all eternity.
Ps 102 [25]"In the beginning you laid the foundations of the earth, and the heavens are the work of your hands. [26]They will perish, but you remain; they will all wear out like a garment. Like clothing you will change them and they will be discarded. [27]But you remain the same, and your years will never end."
Isa 26 [4]Trust in the LORD forever, for the LORD, the LORD, is the Rock eternal.
Isa 40 [28]Do you not know? Have you not heard? The LORD is the everlasting God, the Creator of the ends of the earth. He will not grow tired or weary, and his understanding no one can fathom.
Isa 41 [4]"Who has done this and carried it through, calling forth the generations from the beginning? I, the LORD—with the first of them and with the last—I am he."
Isa 44 [6]"This is what the LORD says—Israel's King and Redeemer, the LORD Almighty: I am the first and I am the last; apart from me there is no God."
Isa 57 [15]For this is what the high and lofty One says—he who lives forever, whose name is holy: "I live in a high and holy place, but also with him who is contrite and lowly in spirit, to revive the spirit of the lowly and to revive the heart of the contrite."
Lam 5 [19]You, O LORD, reign forever; your throne endures from generation to generation.
Dan 4 [34]At the end of that time, I, Nebuchadnezzar, raised my eyes toward heaven, and my sanity was restored. Then I praised the Most High; I honored and glorified him who lives forever.

His dominion is an eternal dominion; his kingdom endures from generation to generation.
Hab 1 [12]O LORD, are you not from everlasting? My God, my Holy One, we will not die. O LORD, you have appointed them to execute judgment; O Rock, you have ordained them to punish.
Hab 3 [6]He stood, and shook the earth; he looked, and made the nations tremble. The ancient mountains crumbled and the age-old hills collapsed. His ways are eternal.
Rom 1 [20]For since the creation of the world God's invisible qualities—his eternal power and divine nature—have been clearly seen, being understood from what has been made, so that men are without excuse.
Rom 16 [26]but now revealed and made known through the prophetic writings by the command of the eternal God, so that all nations might believe and obey him . . .
1 Cor 2 [7]No, we speak of God's secret wisdom, a wisdom that has been hidden and that God destined for our glory before time began.
Eph 1 [4]For he chose us in him before the creation of the world to be holy and blameless in his sight. . . .

1 Tim 1 [17]Now to the King eternal, immortal, invisible, the only God, be honor and glory for ever and ever. Amen.
1 Tim 6 [15]which God will bring about in his own time—God, the blessed and only Ruler, the King of kings and Lord of lords, [16]who alone is immortal and who lives in unapproachable light, whom no one has seen or can see. To him be honor and might forever. Amen.
Heb 1 [10]He also says, "In the beginning, O Lord, you laid the foundations of the earth, and the heavens are the work of your hands. [11]They will perish, but you remain; they will all wear out like a garment. [12]You will roll them up like a robe; like a garment they will be changed. But you remain the same, and your years will never end."
2 Pet 3 [8]But do not forget this one thing, dear friends: With the Lord a day is like a thousand years, and a thousand years are like a day.
Rev 1 [8]"I am the Alpha and the Omega," says the Lord God, "who is, and who was, and who is to come, the Almighty."
Rev 4 [8]Each of the four living creatures had six wings and was covered with eyes all around, even under his wings. Day and night they never stop saying: "Holy, holy, holy is the Lord God Almighty, who was, and is, and is to come." [9]Whenever the living creatures give glory, honor and thanks to him who sits on the throne and who lives for ever and ever . . .

D. God Is Faithful and Trustworthy

Exod 34 [6]And he passed in front of Moses, proclaiming, "The LORD, the LORD, the compassionate and gracious God, slow to anger, abounding in love and faithfulness. . . ."
Deut 7 [9]Know therefore that the LORD your God is God; he is the faithful God, keeping his covenant of love to a thousand generations of those who love him and keep his commands.
Deut 32 [4]He is the Rock, his works are perfect, and all his ways are just. A faithful God who does no wrong, upright and just is he.
2 Sam 7 [28]"O Sovereign LORD, you are God! Your words are trustworthy, and you have promised these good things to your servant."
1 Kings 8 [56]"Praise be to the LORD, who has given rest to his people Israel just as he promised. Not one word has failed of all the good promises he gave through his servant Moses."
2 Chron 6 [15]"You have kept your promise to your servant David my father; with your mouth you have promised and with your hand you have fulfilled it—as it is today."
Ps 25 [10]All the ways of the LORD are loving and faithful for those who keep the demands of his covenant.
Ps 33 [4]For the word of the LORD is right and true; he is faithful in all he does.
Ps 36 [5]Your love, O LORD, reaches to the heavens, your faithfulness to the skies.
Ps 57 [3]He sends from heaven and saves me, rebuking those who hotly pursue me; God sends his love and his faithfulness.
Ps 86 [15]But you, O LORD, are a compassionate and gracious God, slow to anger, abounding in love and faithfulness.
Ps 89 [2]I will declare that your love stands firm forever, that you established your faithfulness in heaven itself.
Ps 91 [4]He will cover you with his feathers, and under his wings you will find refuge; his faithfulness will be your shield and rampart.
Ps 92 [1]It is good to praise the LORD and make music to your name, O Most High, [2]to proclaim your love in the morning and your faithfulness at night. . . .
Ps 100 [5]For the LORD is good and his love endures forever; his faithfulness continues through all generations.
Ps 115 [1]Not to us, O LORD, not to us but to your name be the glory, because of your love and faithfulness.
Ps 138 [8]The LORD will fulfill his purpose for me; your love, O LORD, endures forever—do not abandon the works of your hands.
Ps 146 [6]the Maker of heaven and earth, the sea, and everything in them—the LORD, who remains faithful forever.
Isa 25 [1]O LORD, you are my God; I will exalt you and praise your name, for in perfect faithfulness you have done marvelous things, things planned long ago.
Isa 49 [7]This is what the LORD says—the Redeemer and Holy One of Israel—to him who was despised and abhorred by the nation, to the servant of rulers: "Kings will see you and rise up, princes will see and bow down, because of the LORD, who is faithful, the Holy One of Israel, who has chosen you."
Lam 3 [22]Because of the LORD's great love we are not consumed, for his compassions never fail. [23]They are new every morning; great is your faithfulness.
Hos 2 [19]"I will betroth you to me forever; I will betroth you in righteousness and justice, in love and compassion."
1 Cor 1 [9]God, who has called you into fellowship with his Son Jesus Christ our Lord, is faithful.
1 Cor 10 [13]No temptation has seized you except what is common to man. And God is faithful; he will not let you be tempted beyond what you can bear. But when you are tempted, he will also provide a way out so that you can stand up under it.
2 Cor 1 [18]But as surely as God is faithful, our message to you is not "Yes" and "No." [19]For the Son of God, Jesus Christ, who was preached among you by me and Silas and Timothy, was not "Yes" and "No," but in him it has always been "Yes." [20]For no matter how many promises God has made, they are "Yes" in Christ. And so through him the "Amen" is spoken by us to the glory of God.
1 Thess 5 [23]May God himself, the God of peace, sanctify you through and through. May your whole spirit, soul and body be kept blameless at the coming of our Lord Jesus Christ. [24]The one who calls you is faithful and he will do it.
2 Thess 3 [3]But the Lord is faithful, and he will strengthen and protect you from the evil one.
2 Tim 2 [13]If we are faithless, he will remain faithful, for he cannot disown himself.
Heb 10 [23]Let us hold unswervingly to the hope we profess, for he who promised is faithful.
1 Pet 4 [19]So then, those who suffer according to God's will should commit themselves to their faithful Creator and continue to do good.
1 John 1 [9]If we confess our sins, he is faithful and just and will forgive us our sins and purify us from all unrighteousness.

E. God Is Good

Gen 1 [31]God saw all that he had made, and it was very good. And there was evening, and there was morning—the sixth day.
Exod 33 [19]And the LORD said, "I will cause all my goodness to pass in front of you, and I will proclaim my name, the LORD, in your presence. I will have mercy on whom I will have mercy, and I will have compassion on whom I will have compassion."
2 Chron 5 [13]The trumpeters and singers joined in unison, as with one voice, to give praise and thanks to the LORD. Accompanied by trumpets, cymbals and other instruments, they raised their voices in praise to the LORD and sang: "He is good; his love endures forever."

Then the temple of the LORD was filled with a cloud. . . .
2 Chron 6 [41]"Now arise, O LORD God, and come to your resting place, you and the ark of your might. May your priests, O LORD God, be clothed with salvation, may your saints rejoice in your goodness."
2 Chron 30 [18]Although most of the many people who came from Ephraim, Manasseh, Issachar and Zebulun had not purified themselves, yet they ate the Passover, contrary to what was written. But Hezekiah prayed for them, saying, "May the LORD, who is good, pardon everyone. . . ."
Ps 25 [7]Remember not the sins of my youth and my rebellious ways; according to your love remember me, for you are good, O LORD.

[8]Good and upright is the LORD; therefore he instructs sinners in his ways.
Ps 31 [19]How great is your goodness, which you have stored up for those who fear you, which you bestow in the sight of men on those who take refuge in you.
Ps 34 [8]Taste and see that the LORD is good; blessed is the man who takes refuge in him.
Ps 52 [9]I will praise you forever for what you have done; in your name I will hope, for your name is good. I will praise you in the presence of your saints.
Ps 73 [1]Surely God is good to Israel, to those who are pure in heart.

Ps 84 [11]For the LORD God is a sun and shield; the LORD bestows favor and honor; no good thing does he withhold from those whose walk is blameless.
Ps 100 [5]For the LORD is good and his love endures forever; his faithfulness continues through all generations.
Ps 106 [1]Praise the LORD.
Give thanks to the LORD, for he is good; his love endures forever.
Ps 107 [1]Give thanks to the Lord, for he is good; his love endures forever.
Ps 118 [1]Give thanks to the LORD, for he is good; his love endures forever.
Ps 119 [68]You are good, and what you do is good; teach me your decrees.
Ps 135 [3]Praise the LORD, for the LORD is good; sing praise to his name, for that is pleasant.
Ps 145 [7]They will celebrate your abundant goodness and joyfully sing of your righteousness. . . . [9]The LORD is good to all; he has compassion on all he has made. . . . [15]The eyes of all look to you, and you give them their food at the proper time. [16]You open your hand and satisfy the desires of every living thing.
Jer 33 [10]"This is what the LORD says: 'You say about this place, "It is a desolate waste, without men or animals." Yet in the towns of Judah and the streets of Jerusalem that are deserted, inhabited by neither men nor animals, there will be heard once more [11]the sounds of joy and gladness, the voices of bride and bridegroom, and the voices of those who bring thank offerings to the house of the LORD, saying, "Give thanks to the LORD Almighty, for the LORD is good; his love endures forever." For I will restore the fortunes of the land as they were before,' says the LORD."
Lam 3 [25]The LORD is good to those whose hope is in him, to the one who seeks him. . . .
Nah 1 [7]The LORD is good, a refuge in times of trouble. He cares for those who trust in him. . . .
Matt 5 [45]". . . that you may be sons of your Father in heaven. He causes his sun to rise on the evil and the good, and sends rain on the righteous and the unrighteous."
Matt 7 [11]"If you, then, though you are evil, know how to give good gifts to your children, how much more will your Father in heaven give good gifts to those who ask him!"
Matt 19 [17]"Why do you ask me about what is good?" Jesus replied. "There is only One who is good. If you want to enter life, obey the commandments."
Mark 10 [18]"Why do you call me good?" Jesus answered. "No one is good—except God alone."
Acts 14 [17]"Yet he has not left himself without testimony: He has shown kindness by giving you rain from heaven and crops in their seasons; he provides you with plenty of food and fills your hearts with joy."
Rom 8 [32]He who did not spare his own Son, but gave him up for us all—how will he not also, along with him, graciously give us all things?
2 Thess 1 [11]With this in mind, we constantly pray for you, that our God may count you worthy of his calling, and that by his power he may fulfill every good purpose of yours and every act prompted by your faith.
James 1 [5]If any of you lacks wisdom, he should ask God, who gives generously to all without finding fault, and it will be given to him. . . . [17]Every good and perfect gift is from above, coming down from the Father of the heavenly lights, who does not change like shifting shadows.
2 Pet 1 [3]His divine power has given us everything we need for life and godliness through our knowledge of him who called us by his own glory and goodness.

F. God Is Gracious

Exod 34 [6]And he passed in front of Moses, proclaiming, "The LORD, the LORD, the compassionate and gracious God, slow to anger, abounding in love and faithfulness. . . ."
2 Kings 13 [23]But the LORD was gracious to them and had compassion and showed concern for them because of his covenant with Abraham, Isaac and Jacob. To this day he has been unwilling to destroy them or banish them from his presence.
2 Chron 30 [9]"If you return to the LORD, then your brothers and your children will be shown compassion by their captors and will come back to this land, for the LORD your God is gracious and compassionate. He will not turn his face from you if you return to him."
Ezra 9 [8]"But now, for a brief moment, the LORD our God has been gracious in leaving us a remnant and giving us a firm place in his sanctuary, and so our God gives light to our eyes and a little relief in our bondage."
Neh 9 [17]"They refused to listen and failed to remember the miracles you performed among them. They became stiff-necked and in their rebellion appointed a leader in order to return to their slavery. But you are a forgiving God, gracious and compassionate, slow to anger and abounding in love. Therefore you did not desert them. . . ."
Neh 9 [31]"But in your great mercy you did not put an end to them or abandon them, for you are a gracious and merciful God."
Ps 86 [15]But you, O LORD, are a compassionate and gracious God, slow to anger, abounding in love and faithfulness.
Ps 111 [4]He has caused his wonders to be remembered; the LORD is gracious and compassionate.
Ps 116 [5]The LORD is gracious and righteous; our God is full of compassion.
Ps 145 [9]The LORD is good to all; he has compassion on all he has made.
Isa 30 [18]Yet the LORD longs to be gracious to you; he rises to show you compassion. For the LORD is a God of justice. Blessed are all who wait for him!
Joel 2 [13]Rend your heart and not your garments. Return to the LORD your God, for he is gracious and compassionate, slow to anger and abounding in love, and he relents from sending calamity.
Jon 4 [2]He prayed to the LORD, "O LORD, is this not what I said when I was still at home? That is why I was so quick to flee to Tarshish. I knew that you are a gracious and compassionate God, slow to anger and abounding in love, a God who relents from sending calamity."
Rom 11 [5]So too, at the present time there is a remnant chosen by grace. [6]And if by grace, then it is no longer by works; if it were, grace would no longer be grace.
2 Cor 9 [8]And God is able to make all grace abound to you, so that in all things at all times, having all that you need, you will abound in every good work.
2 Cor 12 [9]But he said to me, "My grace is sufficient for you, for my power is made perfect in weakness." Therefore I will boast all the more gladly about my weaknesses, so that Christ's power may rest on me.
Eph 1 [6]to the praise of his glorious grace, which he has freely given us in the One he loves. [7]In him we have redemption through his blood, the forgiveness of sins, in accordance with the riches of God's grace. . . .
Eph 2 [7]in order that in the coming ages he might show the incomparable riches of his grace, expressed in his kindness to us in Christ Jesus.
Col 1 [6]. . . All over the world this gospel is bearing fruit and growing, just as it has been doing among you since the day you heard it and understood God's grace in all its truth.
2 Thess 2 [16]May our Lord Jesus Christ himself and God our Father, who loved us and by his grace gave us eternal encouragement and good hope, [17]encourage your hearts and strengthen you in every good deed and word.
2 Tim 1 [8]So do not be ashamed to testify about our Lord, or ashamed of me his prisoner. But join with me in suffering for the gospel, by the power of God, [9]who has saved us and called us to a holy life—not because of anything we have done but because of his own purpose and grace. This grace was given us in Christ Jesus before the beginning of time. . . .
Titus 2 [11]For the grace of God that brings salvation has appeared to all men. [12]It teaches us to say "No" to ungodliness and worldly passions, and to live self-controlled, upright and godly lives in this present age, [13]while we wait for the blessed hope—the glorious appearing of our great God and Savior, Jesus Christ. . . .
Heb 4 [16]Let us then approach the throne of grace with confidence, so that we may receive mercy and find grace to help us in our time of need.

James 4 [6]But he gives us more grace. That is why Scripture says: "God opposes the proud but gives grace to the humble."
1 Pet 4 [10]Each one should use whatever gift he has received to serve others, faithfully administering God's grace in its various forms.
1 Pet 5 [10]And the God of all grace, who called you to his eternal glory in Christ, after you have suffered a little while, will himself restore you and make you strong, firm and steadfast. . . . [12]With the help of Silas, whom I regard as a faithful brother, I have written to you briefly, encouraging you and testifying that this is the true grace of God. Stand fast in it.

G. God Is Holy

Exod 15 [11]"Who among the gods is like you, O LORD? Who is like you—majestic in holiness, awesome in glory, working wonders?"
Lev 11 [44]"'I am the LORD your God; consecrate yourselves and be holy, because I am holy. Do not make yourselves unclean by any creature that moves about on the ground. [45]I am the LORD who brought you up out of Egypt to be your God; therefore be holy, because I am holy.'"
Deut 32 [4]He is the Rock, his works are perfect, and all his ways are just. A faithful God who does no wrong, upright and just is he.
Josh 24 [19]Joshua said to the people, "You are not able to serve the LORD. He is a holy God; he is a jealous God. He will not forgive your rebellion and your sins."
1 Sam 2 [2]"There is no one holy like the LORD; there is no one besides you; there is no Rock like our God."
1 Sam 6 [20]and the men of Beth Shemesh asked, "Who can stand in the presence of the LORD, this holy God? To whom will the ark go up from here?"
1 Chron 16 [10]Glory in his holy name; let the hearts of those who seek the LORD rejoice.
Job 6 [10]"Then I would still have this consolation—my joy in unrelenting pain—that I had not denied the words of the Holy One."
Ps 5 [4]You are not a God who takes pleasure in evil; with you the wicked cannot dwell.
Ps 18 [30]As for God, his way is perfect; the word of the LORD is flawless. He is a shield for all who take refuge in him.
Ps 22 [3]Yet you are enthroned as the Holy One; you are the praise of Israel.
Ps 30 [4]Sing to the LORD, you saints of his; praise his holy name.
Ps 92 [15]proclaiming, "The LORD is upright; he is my Rock, and there is no wickedness in him."
Prov 9 [10]"The fear of the LORD is the beginning of wisdom, and knowledge of the Holy One is understanding."
Isa 6 [3]And they were calling to one another: "Holy, holy, holy is the LORD Almighty; the whole earth is full of his glory."
Isa 40 [25]"To whom will you compare me? Or who is my equal?" says the Holy One.
Isa 43 [15]"I am the LORD, your Holy One, Israel's Creator, your King."
Isa 52 [10]The LORD will lay bare his holy arm in the sight of all the nations, and all the ends of the earth will see the salvation of our God.
Isa 57 [15]For this is what the high and lofty One says—he who lives forever, whose name is holy: "I live in a high and holy place, but also with him who is contrite and lowly in spirit, to revive the spirit of the lowly and to revive the heart of the contrite."
Ezek 39 [7]"'I will make known my holy name among my people Israel. I will no longer let my holy name be profaned, and the nations will know that I the LORD am the Holy One in Israel.'"
Hos 11 [9]"I will not carry out my fierce anger, nor will I turn and devastate Ephraim. For I am God, and not man—the Holy One among you. I will not come in wrath."
Hab 1 [13]Your eyes are too pure to look on evil; you cannot tolerate wrong. Why then do you tolerate the treacherous? Why are you silent while the wicked swallow up those more righteous than themselves?
Luke 1 [49]". . . for the Mighty One has done great things for me—holy is his name."
John 17 [11]"I will remain in the world no longer, but they are still in the world, and I am coming to you. Holy Father, protect them by the power of your name—the name you gave me—so that they may be one as we are one."
Heb 12 [10]Our fathers disciplined us for a little while as they thought best; but God disciplines us for our good, that we may share in his holiness. . . .

[28]Therefore, since we are receiving a kingdom that cannot be shaken, let us be thankful, and so worship God acceptably with reverence and awe, [29]for our "God is a consuming fire."
James 1 [13]When tempted, no one should say, "God is tempting me." For God cannot be tempted by evil, nor does he tempt anyone; [14]but each one is tempted when, by his own evil desire, he is dragged away and enticed.
1 Pet 1 [15]But just as he who called you is holy, so be holy in all you do; [16]for it is written: "Be holy, because I am holy."
1 John 1 [5]This is the message we have heard from him and declare to you: God is light; in him there is no darkness at all.
Rev 4 [8]Each of the four living creatures had six wings and was covered with eyes all around, even under his wings. Day and night they never stop saying: "Holy, holy, holy is the Lord God Almighty, who was, and is, and is to come."
Rev 6 [10]They called out in a loud voice, "How long, Sovereign Lord, holy and true, until you judge the inhabitants of the earth and avenge our blood?"

H. God Is Impartial

Deut 10 [17]For the LORD your God is God of gods and Lord of lords, the great God, mighty and awesome, who shows no partiality and accepts no bribes.
2 Chron 19 [7]"Now let the fear of the LORD be upon you. Judge carefully, for with the LORD our God there is no injustice or partiality or bribery."
Job 34 [19]". . . who shows no partiality to princes and does not favor the rich over the poor, for they are all the work of his hands?"
Job 36 [5]"God is mighty, but does not despise men; he is mighty, and firm in his purpose."
Matt 5 [45]". . . that you may be sons of your Father in heaven. He causes his sun to rise on the evil and the good, and sends rain on the righteous and the unrighteous."
Acts 10 [34]Then Peter began to speak: "I now realize how true it is that God does not show favoritism [35]but accepts men from every nation who fear him and do what is right."
Rom 2 [6]God "will give to each person according to what he has done." . . . [11]For God does not show favoritism.
Rom 10 [12]For there is no difference between Jew and Gentile—the same Lord is Lord of all and richly blesses all who call on him. . . .
Gal 2 [6]As for those who seemed to be important—whatever they were makes no difference to me; God does not judge by external appearance—those men added nothing to my message.
Eph 6 [9]And masters, treat your slaves in the same way. Do not threaten them, since you know that he who is both their Master and yours is in heaven, and there is no favoritism with him.
Col 3 [25]Anyone who does wrong will be repaid for his wrong, and there is no favoritism.
James 3 [17]But the wisdom that comes from heaven is first of all pure; then peace-loving, considerate, submissive, full of mercy and good fruit, impartial and sincere.
1 Pet 1 [17]Since you call on a Father who judges each man's work impartially, live your lives as strangers here in reverent fear.

I. God Is Just

Exod 34 [6]And he passed in front of Moses, proclaiming, "The LORD, the LORD, the compassionate and gracious God, slow to anger, abounding in love and faithfulness, [7]maintaining love to thousands, and forgiving wickedness, rebellion and sin. Yet he does not leave the guilty unpunished; he punishes the children and their children for the sin of the fathers to the third and fourth generation."

Deut 32 [4]He is the Rock, his works are perfect, and all his ways are just. A faithful God who does no wrong, upright and just is he.
2 Chron 12 [6]The leaders of Israel and the king humbled themselves and said, "The LORD is just."
Neh 9 [33]"In all that has happened to us, you have been just; you have acted faithfully, while we did wrong."
Job 34 [17]"Can he who hates justice govern? Will you condemn the just and mighty One? [18]Is he not the One who says to kings, 'You are worthless,' and to nobles, 'You are wicked,' [19]who shows no partiality to princes and does not favor the rich over the poor, for they are all the work of his hands? [20]They die in an instant, in the middle of the night; the people are shaken and they pass away; the mighty are removed without human hand.

[21]"His eyes are on the ways of men; he sees their every step. [22]There is no dark place, no deep shadow, where evildoers can hide. [23]God has no need to examine men further, that they should come before him for judgment. [24]Without inquiry he shatters the mighty and sets up others in their place. [25]Because he takes note of their deeds, he overthrows them in the night and they are crushed. [26]He punishes them for their wickedness where everyone can see them, [27]because they turned from following him and had no regard for any of his ways. [28]They caused the cry of the poor to come before him, so that he heard the cry of the needy. [29]But if he remains silent, who can condemn him? If he hides his face, who can see him? Yet he is over man and nation alike, [30]to keep a godless man from ruling, from laying snares for the people."
Ps 33 [5]The LORD loves righteousness and justice; the earth is full of his unfailing love. . . . [13]From heaven the LORD looks down and sees all mankind; [14]from his dwelling place he watches all who live on earth—[15]he who forms the hearts of all, who considers everything they do.
Ps 36 [6]Your righteousness is like the mighty mountains, your justice like the great deep. O LORD, you preserve both man and beast.
Ps 45 [6]Your throne, O God, will last for ever and ever; a scepter of justice will be the scepter of your kingdom.
Ps 58 [11]Then men will say, "Surely the righteous still are rewarded; surely there is a God who judges the earth."
Ps 96 [13]they will sing before the LORD, for he comes, he comes to judge the earth. He will judge the world in righteousness and the peoples in his truth.
Ps 97 [2]Clouds and thick darkness surround him; righteousness and justice are the foundation of his throne.
Ps 140 [12]I know that the LORD secures justice for the poor and upholds the cause of the needy.
Isa 30 [18]Yet the LORD longs to be gracious to you; he rises to show you compassion. For the LORD is a God of justice. Blessed are all who wait for him!
Isa 61 [8]"For I, the LORD, love justice; I hate robbery and iniquity. In my faithfulness I will reward them and make an everlasting covenant with them."
Ezek 18 [4]"For every living soul belongs to me, the father as well as the son—both alike belong to me. The soul who sins is the one who will die."
Zeph 3 [5]The LORD within her is righteous; he does no wrong. Morning by morning he dispenses his justice, and every new day he does not fail, yet the unrighteous know no shame.
Matt 25 [21]"His master replied, 'Well done, good and faithful servant! You have been faithful with a few things; I will put you in charge of many things. Come and share your master's happiness!'"
Luke 18 [7]"And will not God bring about justice for his chosen ones, who cry out to him day and night? Will he keep putting them off? [8]I tell you, he will see that they get justice, and quickly. However, when the Son of Man comes, will he find faith on the earth?"
Acts 17 [31]"For he has set a day when he will judge the world with justice by the man he has appointed. He has given proof of this to all men by raising him from the dead."
Rom 1 [32]Although they know God's righteous decree that those who do such things deserve death, they not only continue to do these very things but also approve of those who practice them.
Rom 2 [7]To those who by persistence in doing good seek glory, honor and immortality, he will give eternal life.
Rom 3 [25]God presented him as a sacrifice of atonement, through faith in his blood. He did this to demonstrate his justice, because in his forbearance he had left the sins committed beforehand unpunished—[26]he did it to demonstrate his justice at the present time, so as to be just and the one who justifies those who have faith in Jesus.
2 Thess 1 [8]He will punish those who do not know God and do not obey the gospel of our Lord Jesus.
1 John 1 [9]If we confess our sins, he is faithful and just and will forgive us our sins and purify us from all unrighteousness.
Rev 16 [5]Then I heard the angel in charge of the waters say: "You are just in these judgments, you who are and who were, the Holy One, because you have so judged; [6]for they have shed the blood of your saints and prophets, and you have given them blood to drink as they deserve."

J. God Is Love

Exod 34 [6]And he passed in front of Moses, proclaiming, "The LORD, the LORD, the compassionate and gracious God, slow to anger, abounding in love and faithfulness, [7]maintaining love to thousands, and forgiving wickedness, rebellion and sin. Yet he does not leave the guilty unpunished; he punishes the children and their children for the sin of the fathers to the third and fourth generation."
Deut 7 [6]For you are a people holy to the LORD your God. The LORD your God has chosen you out of all the peoples on the face of the earth to be his people, his treasured possession.

[7]The LORD did not set his affection on you and choose you because you were more numerous than other peoples, for you were the fewest of all peoples. [8]But it was because the LORD loved you and kept the oath he swore to your forefathers that he brought you out with a mighty hand and redeemed you from the land of slavery, from the power of Pharaoh king of Egypt. . . . [13]He will love you and bless you and increase your numbers. He will bless the fruit of your womb, the crops of your land—your grain, new wine and oil—the calves of your herds and the lambs of your flocks in the land that he swore to your forefathers to give you.
Deut 10 [15]Yet the LORD set his affection on your forefathers and loved them, and he chose you, their descendants, above all the nations, as it is today. . . . [18]He defends the cause of the fatherless and the widow, and loves the alien, giving him food and clothing.
Deut 23 [5]However, the LORD your God would not listen to Balaam but turned the curse into a blessing for you, because the LORD your God loves you.
1 Chron 16 [34]Give thanks to the LORD, for he is good; his love endures forever.
Job 7 [17]"What is man that you make so much of him, that you give him so much attention . . . ?"
Ps 32 [10]Many are the woes of the wicked, but the LORD's unfailing love surrounds the man who trusts in him.
Ps 36 [7]How priceless is your unfailing love! Both high and low among men find refuge in the shadow of your wings.
Ps 42 [8]By day the LORD directs his love, at night his song is with me—a prayer to the God of my life.
Ps 59 [17]O my Strength, I sing praise to you; you, O God, are my fortress, my loving God.
Ps 63 [3]Because your love is better than life, my lips will glorify you.
Ps 86 [5]You are forgiving and good, O Lord, abounding in love to all who call to you.
Ps 103 [17]But from everlasting to everlasting the LORD's love is with those who fear him, and his righteousness with their children's children. . . .
Ps 106 [1]Praise the LORD. Give thanks to the LORD, for he is good; his love endures forever.
Ps 107 [1]Give thanks to the LORD, for he is good; his love endures forever. . . . [8]Let them give thanks to the LORD for his unfailing love and his wonderful deeds for men. . . .

[43]Whoever is wise, let him heed these things and consider the great love of the LORD.
Ps 136 [1]Give thanks to the LORD, for he is good. *His love endures forever.* [2]Give thanks to the God of gods. *His love endures forever.* [3]Give thanks to the Lord of lords: *His love*

endures forever. [4]to him who alone does great wonders, *His love endures forever.* [5]who by his understanding made the heavens, *His love endures forever.* . . . [26]Give thanks to the God of heaven. *His love endures forever.*

Ps 138 [2]I will bow down toward your holy temple and will praise your name for your love and your faithfulness, for you have exalted above all things your name and your word. . . . [8]The LORD will fulfill his purpose for me; your love, O LORD, endures forever—do not abandon the works of your hands.

Ps 145 [8]The LORD is gracious and compassionate, slow to anger and rich in love. . . . [17]The LORD is righteous in all his ways and loving toward all he has made.

Ps 146 [8]the LORD gives sight to the blind, the LORD lifts up those who are bowed down, the LORD loves the righteous.

Isa 38 [17]Surely it was for my benefit that I suffered such anguish. In your love you kept me from the pit of destruction; you have put all my sins behind your back.

Jer 31 [3]The LORD appeared to us in the past, saying: "I have loved you with an everlasting love; I have drawn you with loving-kindness."

Jer 33 [11]"'. . . the sounds of joy and gladness, the voices of bride and bridegroom, and the voices of those who bring thank offerings to the house of the LORD, saying, "Give thanks to the LORD Almighty, for the LORD is good; his love endures forever." For I will restore the fortunes of the land as they were before,' says the LORD."

Joel 2 [13]Rend your heart and not your garments. Return to the LORD your God, for he is gracious and compassionate, slow to anger and abounding in love, and he relents from sending calamity.

Jon 4 [2]He prayed to the LORD, "O LORD, is this not what I said when I was still at home? That is why I was so quick to flee to Tarshish. I knew that you are a gracious and compassionate God, slow to anger and abounding in love, a God who relents from sending calamity."

Mal 1 [2]"I have loved you," says the LORD.

"But you ask, 'How have you loved us?'"

"Was not Esau Jacob's brother?" the LORD says. "Yet I have loved Jacob. . . ."

Matt 3 [17]And a voice from heaven said, "This is my Son, whom I love; with him I am well pleased."

John 3 [16]"For God so loved the world that he gave his one and only Son, that whoever believes in him shall not perish but have eternal life."

John 5 [20]"For the Father loves the Son and shows him all he does. Yes, to your amazement he will show him even greater things than these."

John 14 [23]Jesus replied, "If anyone loves me, he will obey my teaching. My Father will love him, and we will come to him and make our home with him."

John 16 [27]"No, the Father himself loves you because you have loved me and have believed that I came from God."

John 17 [24]"Father, I want those you have given me to be with me where I am, and to see my glory, the glory you have given me because you loved me before the creation of the world."

Rom 5 [8]But God demonstrates his own love for us in this: While we were still sinners, Christ died for us.

Rom 8 [38]For I am convinced that neither death nor life, neither angels nor demons, neither the present nor the future, nor any powers, [39]neither height nor depth, nor anything else in all creation, will be able to separate us from the love of God that is in Christ Jesus our Lord.

2 Cor 13 [11]Finally, brothers, good-by. Aim for perfection, listen to my appeal, be of one mind, live in peace. And the God of love and peace will be with you.

Eph 2 [4]But because of his great love for us, God, who is rich in mercy, [5]made us alive with Christ even when we were dead in transgressions—it is by grace you have been saved.

Titus 3 [4]But when the kindness and love of God our Savior appeared, [5]he saved us, not because of righteous things we had done, but because of his mercy. He saved us through the washing of rebirth and renewal by the Holy Spirit. . . .

Heb 12 [6]". . . because the Lord disciplines those he loves, and he punishes everyone he accepts as a son."

1 John 3 [1]How great is the love the Father has lavished on us, that we should be called children of God! And that is what we are! The reason the world does not know us is that it did not know him.

1 John 4 [7]Dear friends, let us love one another, for love comes from God. Everyone who loves has been born of God and knows God. [8]Whoever does not love does not know God, because God is love. [9]This is how God showed his love among us: He sent his one and only Son into the world that we might live through him. [10]This is love: not that we loved God, but that he loved us and sent his Son as an atoning sacrifice for our sins. [11]Dear friends, since God so loved us, we also ought to love one another.

Jude [21]Keep yourselves in God's love as you wait for the mercy of our Lord Jesus Christ to bring you to eternal life.

K. God Is Merciful

Exod 33 [19]And the LORD said, "I will cause all my goodness to pass in front of you, and I will proclaim my name, the LORD, in your presence. I will have mercy on whom I will have mercy, and I will have compassion on whom I will have compassion."

Deut 4 [31]For the LORD your God is a merciful God; he will not abandon or destroy you or forget the covenant with your forefathers, which he confirmed to them by oath.

Deut 13 [17]None of those condemned things shall be found in your hands, so that the LORD will turn from his fierce anger; he will show you mercy, have compassion on you, and increase your numbers, as he promised on oath to your forefathers, [18]because you obey the LORD your God, keeping all his commands that I am giving you today and doing what is right in his eyes.

Neh 9 [31]"But in your great mercy you did not put an end to them or abandon them, for you are a gracious and merciful God."

Ps 25 [6]Remember, O LORD, your great mercy and love, for they are from of old.

Ps 78 [38]Yet he was merciful; he forgave their iniquities and did not destroy them. Time after time he restrained his anger and did not stir up his full wrath.

Isa 55 [7]Let the wicked forsake his way and the evil man his thoughts. Let him turn to the LORD, and he will have mercy on him, and to our God, for he will freely pardon.

Isa 63 [9]In all their distress he too was distressed, and the angel of his presence saved them. In his love and mercy he redeemed them; he lifted them up and carried them all the days of old.

Jer 3 [12]"Go, proclaim this message toward the north: 'Return, faithless Israel,' declares the LORD, 'I will frown on you no longer, for I am merciful,' declares the LORD, 'I will not be angry forever.'"

Lam 3 [22]Because of the LORD's great love we are not consumed, for his compassions never fail. [23]They are new every morning; great is your faithfulness.

Dan 9 [9]"The Lord our God is merciful and forgiving, even though we have rebelled against him. . . ."

Mic 7 [18]Who is a God like you, who pardons sin and forgives the transgression of the remnant of his inheritance? You do not stay angry forever but delight to show mercy.

Zech 1 [16]"Therefore, this is what the LORD says: 'I will return to Jerusalem with mercy, and there my house will be rebuilt. And the measuring line will be stretched out over Jerusalem,' declares the LORD Almighty."

Luke 1 [50]"His mercy extends to those who fear him, from generation to generation."

Luke 6 [35]"But love your enemies, do good to them, and lend to them without expecting to get anything back. Then your reward will be great, and you will be sons of the Most High, because he is kind to the ungrateful and wicked. [36]Be merciful, just as your Father is merciful."

Luke 18 [10]"Two men went up to the temple to pray, one a Pharisee and the other a tax collector. . . .

[13]"But the tax collector stood at a distance. He would not even look up to heaven, but beat his breast and said, 'God, have mercy on me, a sinner.'

[14]"I tell you that this man, rather than the other, went home justified before God. For everyone who exalts himself will be humbled, and he who humbles himself will be exalted."

Rom 9 [16]It does not, therefore, depend on man's desire or

effort, but on God's mercy. . . . [23]What if he did this to make the riches of his glory known to the objects of his mercy, whom he prepared in advance for glory . . . ?
Rom 11 [30]Just as you who were at one time disobedient to God have now received mercy as a result of their disobedience, [31]so they too have now become disobedient in order that they too may now receive mercy as a result of God's mercy to you. [32]For God has bound all men over to disobedience so that he may have mercy on them all.
Eph 2 [4]But because of his great love for us, God, who is rich in mercy . . .
Heb 4 [16]Let us then approach the throne of grace with confidence, so that we may receive mercy and find grace to help us in our time of need.
James 5 [11]As you know, we consider blessed those who have persevered. You have heard of Job's perseverance and have seen what the Lord finally brought about. The Lord is full of compassion and mercy.
1 Pet 1 [3]Praise be to the God and Father of our Lord Jesus Christ! In his great mercy he has given us new birth into a living hope through the resurrection of Jesus Christ from the dead. . . .
Jude [21]Keep yourselves in God's love as you wait for the mercy of our Lord Jesus Christ to bring you to eternal life.

L. God Is Omnipotent

Gen 17 [1]When Abram was ninety-nine years old, the LORD appeared to him and said, "I am God Almighty; walk before me and be blameless."
Gen 18 [14]"Is anything too hard for the LORD? I will return to you at the appointed time next year and Sarah will have a son."
Exod 9 [16]"'But I have raised you up for this very purpose, that I might show you my power and that my name might be proclaimed in all the earth.'"
Exod 15 [6]"Your right hand, O LORD, was majestic in power. Your right hand, O LORD, shattered the enemy."
Josh 4 [24]"He did this so that all the peoples of the earth might know that the hand of the LORD is powerful and so that you might always fear the LORD your God."
1 Sam 14 [6]Jonathan said to his young armor-bearer, "Come, let's go over to the outpost of those uncircumcised fellows. Perhaps the LORD will act in our behalf. Nothing can hinder the LORD from saving, whether by many or by few."
Job 42 [2]"I know that you can do all things; no plan of yours can be thwarted."
Ps 93 [4]Mightier than the thunder of the great waters, mightier than the breakers of the sea—the LORD on high is mighty.
Ps 111 [6]He has shown his people the power of his works, giving them the lands of other nations.
Ps 115 [3]Our God is in heaven; he does whatever pleases him.
Ps 135 [5]I know that the LORD is great, that our Lord is greater than all gods. [6]The LORD does whatever pleases him, in the heavens and on the earth, in the seas and all their depths.
Isa 14 [24]The LORD Almighty has sworn, "Surely, as I have planned, so it will be, and as I have purposed, so it will stand. [25]I will crush the Assyrian in my land; on my mountains I will trample him down. His yoke will be taken from my people, and his burden removed from their shoulders."

[26]This is the plan determined for the whole world; this is the hand stretched out over all nations. [27]For the LORD Almighty has purposed, and who can thwart him? His hand is stretched out, and who can turn it back?
Isa 44 [24]"This is what the LORD says—your Redeemer, who formed you in the womb: I am the LORD, who has made all things, who alone stretched out the heavens, who spread out the earth by myself. . . ."
Isa 45 [11]"This is what the LORD says—the Holy One of Israel, and its Maker: Concerning things to come, do you question me about my children, or give me orders about the work of my hands? [12]It is I who made the earth and created mankind upon it. My own hands stretched out the heavens; I marshaled their starry hosts. [13]I will raise up Cyrus in my righteousness: I will make all his ways straight. He will rebuild my city and set my exiles free, but not for a price or reward, says the LORD Almighty."
Isa 46 [4]"Even to your old age and gray hairs I am he, I am he who will sustain you. I have made you and I will carry you; I will sustain you and I will rescue you."
Jer 32 [17]"Ah, Sovereign LORD, you have made the heavens and the earth by your great power and outstretched arm. Nothing is too hard for you. [18]You show love to thousands but bring the punishment for the fathers' sins into the laps of their children after them. O great and powerful God, whose name is the LORD Almighty, [19]great are your purposes and mighty are your deeds. Your eyes are open to all the ways of men; you reward everyone according to his conduct and as his deeds deserve. [20]You performed miraculous signs and wonders in Egypt and have continued them to this day, both in Israel and among all mankind, and have gained the renown that is still yours. [21]You brought your people Israel out of Egypt with signs and wonders, by a mighty hand and an outstretched arm and with great terror. [22]You gave them this land you had sworn to give their forefathers, a land flowing with milk and honey. [23]They came in and took possession of it, but they did not obey you or follow your law; they did not do what you commanded them to do. So you brought all this disaster upon them."
Jer 32 [27]"I am the LORD, the God of all mankind. Is anything too hard for me?"
Matt 19 [26]Jesus looked at them and said, "With man this is impossible, but with God all things are possible."
Mark 14 [36]"*Abba*, Father," he said, "everything is possible for you. Take this cup from me. Yet not what I will, but what you will."
Luke 1 [37]"For nothing is impossible with God."
Acts 4 [24]When they heard this, they raised their voices together in prayer to God. "Sovereign Lord," they said, "you made the heaven and the earth and the sea, and everything in them. [25]You spoke by the Holy Spirit through the mouth of your servant, our father David: 'Why do the nations rage and the peoples plot in vain? [26]The kings of the earth take their stand and the rulers gather together against the Lord and against his Anointed One.' [27]Indeed Herod and Pontius Pilate met together with the Gentiles and the people of Israel in this city to conspire against your holy servant Jesus, whom you anointed. [28]They did what your power and will had decided beforehand should happen. [29]Now, Lord, consider their threats and enable your servants to speak your word with great boldness. [30]Stretch out your hand to heal and perform miraculous signs and wonders through the name of your holy servant Jesus."

[31]After they prayed, the place where they were meeting was shaken. And they were all filled with the Holy Spirit and spoke the word of God boldly.
Rom 4 [20]Yet he did not waver through unbelief regarding the promise of God, but was strengthened in his faith and gave glory to God, [21]being fully persuaded that God had power to do what he had promised.
Eph 1 [11]In him we were also chosen, having been predestined according to the plan of him who works out everything in conformity with the purpose of his will. . . .
Rev 4 [8]Each of the four living creatures had six wings and was covered with eyes all around, even under his wings. Day and night they never stop saying: "Holy, holy, holy is the Lord God Almighty, who was, and is, and is to come."
Rev 19 [6]Then I heard what sounded like a great multitude, like the roar of rushing waters and like loud peals of thunder, shouting: "Hallelujah! For our Lord God Almighty reigns."

M. God Is Omnipresent

Gen 16 [13]She gave this name to the LORD who spoke to her: "You are the God who sees me," for she said, "I have now seen the One who sees me."
Deut 2 [7]The LORD your God has blessed you in all the work of your hands. He has watched over your journey through this vast desert. These forty years the LORD your God has been with you, and you have not lacked anything.
Deut 4 [7]What other nation is so great as to have their gods near them the way the LORD our God is near us whenever we pray to him?
1 Kings 8 [27]"But will God really dwell on earth? The heavens, even the highest heaven, cannot contain you. How much less this temple I have built!"

Ps 46 [1]God is our refuge and strength, an ever-present help in trouble.
Ps 139 [7]Where can I go from your Spirit? Where can I flee from your presence? [8]If I go up to the heavens, you are there; if I make my bed in the depths, you are there. [9]If I rise on the wings of the dawn, if I settle on the far side of the sea, [10]even there your hand will guide me, your right hand will hold me fast. . . .

[17]How precious to me are your thoughts, O God! How vast is the sum of them! [18]Were I to count them, they would outnumber the grains of sand. When I awake, I am still with you.
Ps 145 [18]The LORD is near to all who call on him, to all who call on him in truth.
Isa 66 [1]This is what the LORD says: "Heaven is my throne, and the earth is my footstool. Where is the house you will build for me? Where will my resting place be?"
Jer 23 [23]"Am I only a God nearby," declares the LORD, "and not a God far away? [24]Can anyone hide in secret places so that I cannot see him?" declares the LORD. "Do not I fill heaven and earth?" declares the LORD.
Matt 28 [20]". . . and teaching them to obey everything I have commanded you. And surely I am with you always, to the very end of the age."
Acts 17 [24]"The God who made the world and everything in it is the Lord of heaven and earth and does not live in temples built by hands. . . . [27]God did this so that men would seek him and perhaps reach out for him and find him, though he is not far from each one of us. [28]'For in him we live and move and have our being.' As some of your own poets have said, 'We are his offspring.'"
Heb 4 [13]Nothing in all creation is hidden from God's sight. Everything is uncovered and laid bare before the eyes of him to whom we must give account.

N. God Is Omniscient

Gen 6 [5]The LORD saw how great man's wickedness on the earth had become, and that every inclination of the thoughts of his heart was only evil all the time.
Exod 3 [7]The LORD said, "I have indeed seen the misery of my people in Egypt. I have heard them crying out because of their slave drivers, and I am concerned about their suffering."
1 Kings 8 [39]". . . then hear from heaven, your dwelling place. Forgive and act; deal with each man according to all he does, since you know his heart (for you alone know the hearts of all men). . . ."
2 Kings 19 [27]"'But I know where you stay and when you come and go and how you rage against me.'"
2 Chron 16 [9]"For the eyes of the LORD range throughout the earth to strengthen those whose hearts are fully committed to him. You have done a foolish thing, and from now on you will be at war."
Job 9 [4]"His wisdom is profound, his power is vast. Who has resisted him and come out unscathed?"
Job 12 [13]"To God belong wisdom and power; counsel and understanding are his."
Job 28 [12]"But where can wisdom be found? Where does understanding dwell? [13]Man does not comprehend its worth; it cannot be found in the land of the living. [14]The deep says, 'It is not in me'; the sea says, 'It is not with me.' [15]It cannot be bought with the finest gold, nor can its price be weighed in silver. [16]It cannot be bought with the gold of Ophir, with precious onyx or sapphires. [17]Neither gold nor crystal can compare with it, nor can it be had for jewels of gold. [18]Coral and jasper are not worthy of mention; the price of wisdom is beyond rubies. [19]The topaz of Cush cannot compare with it; it cannot be bought with pure gold.

[20]"Where then does wisdom come from? Where does understanding dwell? [21]It is hidden from the eyes of every living thing, concealed even from the birds of the air. [22]Destruction and Death say, 'Only a rumor of it has reached our ears.' [23]God understands the way to it and he alone knows where it dwells, [24]for he views the ends of the earth and sees everything under the heavens. [25]When he established the force of the wind and measured out the waters, [26]when he made a decree for the rain and a path for the thunderstorm, [27]then he looked at wisdom and appraised it; he confirmed it and tested it. [28]And he said to man, 'The fear of the Lord—that is wisdom, and to shun evil is understanding.'"
Job 37 [16]"Do you know how the clouds hang poised, those wonders of him who is perfect in knowledge?"
Ps 7 [9]O righteous God, who searches minds and hearts, bring to an end the violence of the wicked and make the righteous secure.
Ps 33 [13]From heaven the LORD looks down and sees all mankind; [14]from his dwelling place he watches all who live on earth—[15]he who forms the hearts of all, who considers everything they do.
Ps 94 [11]The LORD knows the thoughts of man; he knows that they are futile.
Ps 104 [24]How many are your works, O LORD! In wisdom you made them all; the earth is full of your creatures.
Ps 139 [1]O LORD, you have searched me and you know me. [2]You know when I sit and when I rise; you perceive my thoughts from afar. [3]You discern my going out and my lying down; you are familiar with all my ways. [4]Before a word is on my tongue you know it completely, O LORD.

[5]You hem me in—behind and before; you have laid your hand upon me. [6]Such knowledge is too wonderful for me, too lofty for me to attain.

[7]Where can I go from your Spirit? Where can I flee from your presence? [8]If I go up to the heavens, you are there; if I make my bed in the depths, you are there. [9]If I rise on the wings of the dawn, if I settle on the far side of the sea, [10]even there your hand will guide me, your right hand will hold me fast.
Ps 147 [4]He determines the number of the stars and calls them each by name. [5]Great is our Lord and mighty in power; his understanding has no limit.
Prov 3 [19]By wisdom the LORD laid the earth's foundations, by understanding he set the heavens in place; [20]by his knowledge the deeps were divided, and the clouds let drop the dew.
Prov 5 [21]For a man's ways are in full view of the LORD, and he examines all his paths.
Prov 15 [3]The eyes of the LORD are everywhere, keeping watch on the wicked and the good. . . . [11]Death and Destruction lie open before the LORD—how much more the hearts of men!
Isa 31 [2]Yet he too is wise and can bring disaster; he does not take back his words. He will rise up against the house of the wicked, against those who help evildoers.
Isa 40 [28]Do you not know? Have you not heard? The LORD is the everlasting God, the Creator of the ends of the earth. He will not grow tired or weary, and his understanding no one can fathom.
Isa 44 [7]"Who then is like me? Let him proclaim it. Let him declare and lay out before me what has happened since I established my ancient people, and what is yet to come—yes, let him foretell what will come. [8]Do not tremble, do not be afraid. Did I not proclaim this and foretell it long ago? You are my witnesses. Is there any God besides me? No, there is no other Rock; I know not one."

[9]All who make idols are nothing, and the things they treasure are worthless. Those who would speak up for them are blind; they are ignorant, to their own shame. [10]Who shapes a god and casts an idol, which can profit him nothing? . . .

[24]"This is what the LORD says—your Redeemer, who formed you in the womb: I am the LORD, who has made all things, who alone stretched out the heavens, who spread out the earth by myself, [25]who foils the signs of false prophets and makes fools of diviners, who overthrows the learning of the wise and turns it into nonsense, [26]who carries out the words of his servants and fulfills the predictions of his messengers, who says of Jerusalem, 'It shall be inhabited,' of the towns of Judah, 'They shall be built,' and of their ruins, 'I will restore them,' [27]who says to the watery deep, 'Be dry, and I will dry up your streams,' [28]who says of Cyrus, 'He is my shepherd and will accomplish all that I please; he will say of Jerusalem, "Let it be rebuilt," and of the temple, "Let its foundations be laid."'"
Isa 46 [9]"Remember the former things, those of long ago; I am God, and there is no other; I am God, and there is none like

me. [10]I make known the end from the beginning, from ancient times, what is still to come. I say: My purpose will stand, and I will do all that I please. [11]From the east I summon a bird of prey; from a far-off land, a man to fulfill my purpose. What I have said, that will I bring about; what I have planned, that will I do."

Jer 10 [7]Who should not revere you, O King of the nations? This is your due. Among all the wise men of the nations and in all their kingdoms, there is no one like you. . . . [12]But God made the earth by his power; he founded the world by his wisdom and stretched out the heavens by his understanding.

Jer 17 [10]"I the LORD search the heart and examine the mind, to reward a man according to his conduct, according to what his deeds deserve."

Ezek 11 [5]Then the Spirit of the LORD came upon me, and he told me to say: "This is what the LORD says: That is what you are saying, O house of Israel, but I know what is going through your mind."

Dan 2 [20]and said: "Praise be to the name of God for ever and ever; wisdom and power are his. [21]He changes times and seasons; he sets up kings and deposes them. He gives wisdom to the wise and knowledge to the discerning. [22]He reveals deep and hidden things; he knows what lies in darkness, and light dwells with him."

Matt 6 [8]"Do not be like them, for your Father knows what you need before you ask him. . . . [32]For the pagans run after all these things, and your heavenly Father knows that you need them."

Matt 10 [29]"Are not two sparrows sold for a penny? Yet not one of them will fall to the ground apart from the will of your Father. [30]And even the very hairs of your head are all numbered."

Acts 1 [24]Then they prayed, "Lord, you know everyone's heart. Show us which of these two you have chosen. . . ."

Acts 2 [23]"This man was handed over to you by God's set purpose and foreknowledge; and you, with the help of wicked men, put him to death by nailing him to the cross."

Acts 15 [8]God, who knows the heart, showed that he accepted them by giving the Holy Spirit to them, just as he did to us."

Acts 15 [17]"'. . . that the remnant of men may seek the Lord, and all the Gentiles who bear my name, says the Lord, who does these things' [18]that have been known for ages."

Rom 11 [33]Oh, the depth of the riches of the wisdom and knowledge of God! How unsearchable his judgments, and his paths beyond tracing out!

Rom 16 [25]Now to him who is able to establish you by my gospel and the proclamation of Jesus Christ, according to the revelation of the mystery hidden for long ages past, [26]but now revealed and made known through the prophetic writings by the command of the eternal God, so that all nations might believe and obey him— [27]to the only wise God be glory forever through Jesus Christ! Amen.

1 Cor 1 [18]For the message of the cross is foolishness to those who are perishing, but to us who are being saved it is the power of God. . . . [21]For since in the wisdom of God the world through its wisdom did not know him, God was pleased through the foolishness of what was preached to save those who believe. [24]. . . but to those whom God has called, both Jews and Greeks, Christ the power of God and the wisdom of God. [25]For the foolishness of God is wiser than man's wisdom, and the weakness of God is stronger than man's strength.

1 Cor 2 [7]No, we speak of God's secret wisdom, a wisdom that has been hidden and that God destined for our glory before time began.

Eph 1 [7]In him we have redemption through his blood, the forgiveness of sins, in accordance with the riches of God's grace [8]that he lavished on us with all wisdom and understanding.

Eph 3 [10]His intent was that now, through the church, the manifold wisdom of God should be made known to the rulers and authorities in the heavenly realms. . . .

Heb 4 [13]Nothing in all creation is hidden from God's sight. Everything is uncovered and laid bare before the eyes of him to whom we must give account.

James 1 [5]If any of you lacks wisdom, he should ask God, who gives generously to all without finding fault, and it will be given to him.

James 3 [17]But the wisdom that comes from heaven is first of all pure; then peace-loving, considerate, submissive, full of mercy and good fruit, impartial and sincere.

1 John 3 [19]This then is how we know that we belong to the truth, and how we set our hearts at rest in his presence [20]whenever our hearts condemn us. For God is greater than our hearts, and he knows everything.

Rev 7 [12]saying: "Amen! Praise and glory and wisdom and thanks and honor and power and strength be to our God for ever and ever. Amen!"

O. God Is Patient, Longsuffering, and Forbearing

Exod 34 [6]And he passed in front of Moses, proclaiming, "The LORD, the LORD, the compassionate and gracious God, slow to anger, abounding in love and faithfulness, [7]maintaining love to thousands, and forgiving wickedness, rebellion and sin. Yet he does not leave the guilty unpunished; he punishes the children and their children for the sin of the fathers to the third and fourth generation."

Num 14 [18]"'The LORD is slow to anger, abounding in love and forgiving sin and rebellion. Yet he does not leave the guilty unpunished; he punishes the children for the sin of the fathers to the third and fourth generation.'"

Neh 9 [17]"They refused to listen and failed to remember the miracles you performed among them. They became stiff-necked and in their rebellion appointed a leader in order to return to their slavery. But you are a forgiving God, gracious and compassionate, slow to anger and abounding in love. Therefore you did not desert them. . . ."

Ps 78 [38]Yet he was merciful; he forgave their iniquities and did not destroy them. Time after time he restrained his anger and did not stir up his full wrath.

Ps 103 [8]The LORD is compassionate and gracious, slow to anger, abounding in love. [10]. . . he does not treat us as our sins deserve or repay us according to our iniquities.

Isa 7 [13]Then Isaiah said, "Hear now, you house of David! Is it not enough to try the patience of men? Will you try the patience of my God also?"

Jer 11 [7]"'From the time I brought your forefathers up from Egypt until today, I warned them again and again, saying, "Obey me."'"

Hos 11 [9]"I will not carry out my fierce anger, nor will I turn and devastate Ephraim. For I am God, and not man—the Holy One among you. I will not come in wrath."

Nah 1 [3]The LORD is slow to anger and great in power; the LORD will not leave the guilty unpunished. His way is in the whirlwind and the storm, and clouds are the dust of his feet.

Matt 23 [37]"O Jerusalem, Jerusalem, you who kill the prophets and stone those sent to you, how often I have longed to gather your children together, as a hen gathers her chicks under her wings, but you were not willing."

Acts 13 [18]". . . he endured their conduct for about forty years in the desert. . . ."

Rom 2 [4]Or do you show contempt for the riches of his kindness, tolerance and patience, not realizing that God's kindness leads you toward repentance?

Rom 3 [25]God presented him as a sacrifice of atonement, through faith in his blood. He did this to demonstrate his justice, because in his forbearance he had left the sins committed beforehand unpunished. . . .

Rom 9 [22]What if God, choosing to show his wrath and make his power known, bore with great patience the objects of his wrath—prepared for destruction?

Rom 15 [5]May the God who gives endurance and encouragement give you a spirit of unity among yourselves as you follow Christ Jesus. . . .

1 Pet 3 [20]who disobeyed long ago when God waited patiently in the days of Noah while the ark was being built. In it only a few people, eight in all, were saved through water. . . .

2 Pet 3 [9]The Lord is not slow in keeping his promise, as some understand slowness. He is patient with you, not wanting anyone to perish, but everyone to come to repentance. . . . [15]Bear in mind that our Lord's patience means salvation, just as our dear brother Paul also wrote you with the wisdom that God gave him.

P. God Is Righteous

Gen 18 [25]"Far be it from you to do such a thing—to kill the righteous with the wicked, treating the righteous and the wicked alike. Far be it from you! Will not the Judge of all the earth do right?"

Ezra 9 [15]"O LORD, God of Israel, you are righteous! We are left this day as a remnant. Here we are before you in our guilt, though because of it not one of us can stand in your presence."

Job 4 [17]"'Can a mortal be more righteous than God? Can a man be more pure than his Maker?'"

Job 37 [23]"The Almighty is beyond our reach and exalted in power; in his justice and great righteousness, he does not oppress."

Ps 7 [9]O righteous God, who searches minds and hearts, bring to an end the violence of the wicked and make the righteous secure.

Ps 11 [7]For the LORD is righteous, he loves justice; upright men will see his face.

Ps 25 [8]Good and upright is the LORD; therefore he instructs sinners in his ways.

Ps 33 [4]For the word of the LORD is right and true; he is faithful in all he does. [5]The LORD loves righteousness and justice; the earth is full of his unfailing love.

Ps 36 [6]Your righteousness is like the mighty mountains, your justice like the great deep. O LORD, you preserve both man and beast.

Ps 89 [14]Righteousness and justice are the foundation of your throne; love and faithfulness go before you.

Ps 92 [12]The righteous will flourish like a palm tree, they will grow like a cedar of Lebanon; [13]planted in the house of the LORD, they will flourish in the courts of our God. [14]They will still bear fruit in old age, they will stay fresh and green, [15]proclaiming, "The LORD is upright; he is my Rock, and there is no wickedness in him."

Ps 98 [2]The LORD has made his salvation known and revealed his righteousness to the nations.

Ps 119 [137]Righteous are you, O LORD, and your laws are right. . . . [142]Your righteousness is everlasting and your law is true.

Ps 129 [4]But the LORD is righteous; he has cut me free from the cords of the wicked.

Ps 145 [7]They will celebrate your abundant goodness and joyfully sing of your righteousness. . . . [17]The LORD is righteous in all his ways and loving toward all he has made.

Isa 28 [17]"I will make justice the measuring line and righteousness the plumb line; hail will sweep away your refuge, the lie, and water will overflow your hiding place."

Isa 45 [21]"Declare what is to be, present it—let them take counsel together. Who foretold this long ago, who declared it from the distant past? Was it not I, the LORD? And there is no God apart from me, a righteous God and a Savior; there is none but me."

Jer 9 [24]". . . but let him who boasts boast about this: that he understands and knows me, that I am the LORD, who exercises kindness, justice and righteousness on earth, for in these I delight," declares the LORD.

Jer 12 [1]You are always righteous, O LORD, when I bring a case before you. Yet I would speak with you about your justice: Why does the way of the wicked prosper? Why do all the faithless live at ease?

Dan 9 [7]"Lord, you are righteous, but this day we are covered with shame—the men of Judah and people of Jerusalem and all Israel, both near and far, in all the countries where you have scattered us because of our unfaithfulness to you. . . . [14]The LORD did not hesitate to bring the disaster upon us, for the LORD our God is righteous in everything he does; yet we have not obeyed him."

Hos 14 [9]Who is wise? He will realize these things. Who is discerning? He will understand them. The ways of the LORD are right; the righteous walk in them, but the rebellious stumble in them.

Zeph 3 [5]The LORD within her is righteous; he does no wrong. Morning by morning he dispenses his justice, and every new day he does not fail, yet the unrighteous know no shame.

John 17 [25]"Righteous Father, though the world does not know you, I know you, and they know that you have sent me."

Rom 1 [17]For in the gospel a righteousness from God is revealed, a righteousness that is by faith from first to last, just as it is written: "The righteous will live by faith."

Rom 3 [21]But now a righteousness from God, apart from law, has been made known, to which the Law and the Prophets testify.

2 Tim 4 [8]Now there is in store for me the crown of righteousness, which the Lord, the righteous Judge, will award to me on that day—and not only to me, but also to all who have longed for his appearing.

Q. God Is Self-Existent

Exod 3 [14]God said to Moses, "I AM WHO I AM. This is what you are to say to the Israelites: 'I AM has sent me to you.'"

Deut 32 [40]"I lift my hand to heaven and declare: As surely as I live forever. . . ."

Isa 43 [10]"You are my witnesses," declares the LORD, "and my servant whom I have chosen, so that you may know and believe me and understand that I am he. Before me no god was formed, nor will there be one after me."

Isa 44 [6]"This is what the LORD says—Israel's King and Redeemer, the LORD Almighty: I am the first and I am the last; apart from me there is no God."

Jer 10 [10]But the LORD is the true God; he is the living God, the eternal King. When he is angry, the earth trembles; the nations cannot endure his wrath.

John 5 [26]"For as the Father has life in himself, so he has granted the Son to have life in himself."

Acts 17 [24]"The God who made the world and everything in it is the Lord of heaven and earth and does not live in temples built by hands. [25]And he is not served by human hands, as if he needed anything, because he himself gives all men life and breath and everything else."

Rom 11 [36]For from him and through him and to him are all things. To him be the glory forever! Amen.

Col 1 [16]For by him all things were created: things in heaven and on earth, visible and invisible, whether thrones or powers or rulers or authorities; all things were created by him and for him.

R. God Is Truthful

Num 23 [19]"God is not a man, that he should lie, nor a son of man, that he should change his mind. Does he speak and then not act? Does he promise and not fulfill?"

1 Sam 15 [29]"He who is the Glory of Israel does not lie or change his mind; for he is not a man, that he should change his mind."

Ps 12 [6]And the words of the LORD are flawless, like silver refined in a furnace of clay, purified seven times.

Ps 26 [3]for your love is ever before me, and I walk continually in your truth.

Ps 31 [5]Into your hands I commit my spirit; redeem me, O LORD, the God of truth.

Ps 33 [4]For the word of the LORD is right and true; he is faithful in all he does.

Ps 40 [10]I do not hide your righteousness in my heart; I speak of your faithfulness and salvation. I do not conceal your love and your truth from the great assembly.

Ps 43 [3]Send forth your light and your truth, let them guide me; let them bring me to your holy mountain, to the place where you dwell.

Ps 86 [11]Teach me your way, O LORD, and I will walk in your truth; give me an undivided heart, that I may fear your name.

Ps 132 [11]The LORD swore an oath to David, a sure oath that he will not revoke: "One of your own descendants I will place on your throne. . . ."

Isa 45 [19]"I have not spoken in secret, from somewhere in a land of darkness; I have not said to Jacob's descendants, 'Seek me in vain.' I, the LORD, speak the truth; I declare what is right."

Isa 65 [16]"Whoever invokes a blessing in the land will do so by the God of truth; he who takes an oath in the land will swear by the God of truth. For the past troubles will be forgotten and hidden from my eyes."

Jer 10 [10] But the LORD is the true God; he is the living God, the eternal King. When he is angry, the earth trembles; the nations cannot endure his wrath.

Dan 9 [13]"Just as it is written in the Law of Moses, all this disaster has come upon us, yet we have not sought the favor of the LORD our God by turning from our sins and giving attention to your truth."

John 3 [33]The man who has accepted it has certified that God is truthful.

John 7 [28]Then Jesus, still teaching in the temple courts, cried out, "Yes, you know me, and you know where I am from. I am not here on my own, but he who sent me is true. You do not know him. . . ."

John 8 [26]"I have much to say in judgment of you. But he who sent me is reliable, and what I have heard from him I tell the world."

John 14 [16]"And I will ask the Father, and he will give you another Counselor to be with you forever—[17]the Spirit of truth. The world cannot accept him, because it neither sees him nor knows him. But you know him, for he lives with you and will be in you."

John 17 [3]"Now this is eternal life: that they may know you, the only true God, and Jesus Christ, whom you have sent."

John 17 [17]"Sanctify them by the truth; your word is truth."

Rom 1 [25]They exchanged the truth of God for a lie, and worshiped and served created things rather than the Creator—who is forever praised. Amen.

Rom 3 [4]Not at all! Let God be true, and every man a liar. As it is written: "So that you may be proved right when you speak and prevail when you judge."

Rom 15 [8]For I tell you that Christ has become a servant of the Jews on behalf of God's truth, to confirm the promises made to the patriarchs. . . .

Titus 1 [2]a faith and knowledge resting on the hope of eternal life, which God, who does not lie, promised before the beginning of time . . .

Heb 6 [18]God did this so that, by two unchangeable things in which it is impossible for God to lie, we who have fled to take hold of the hope offered to us may be greatly encouraged.

1 John 5 [20]We know also that the Son of God has come and has given us understanding, so that we may know him who is true. And we are in him who is true—even in his Son Jesus Christ. He is the true God and eternal life.

[21]Dear children, keep yourselves from idols.

Rev 6 [10]They called out in a loud voice, "How long, Sovereign Lord, holy and true, until you judge the inhabitants of the earth and avenge our blood?"

Rev 15 [3]and sang the song of Moses the servant of God and the song of the Lamb: "Great and marvelous are your deeds, Lord God Almighty. Just and true are your ways, King of the ages."

S. God Is Unchangeable

Gen 18 [25]"Far be it from you to do such a thing—to kill the righteous with the wicked, treating the righteous and the wicked alike. Far be it from you! Will not the Judge of all the earth do right?"

Num 23 [19]"God is not a man, that he should lie, nor a son of man, that he should change his mind. Does he speak and then not act? Does he promise and not fulfill? [20]I have received a command to bless; he has blessed, and I cannot change it."

1 Sam 15 [29]"He who is the Glory of Israel does not lie or change his mind; for he is not a man, that he should change his mind."

2 Sam 22 [31]"As for God, his way is perfect; the word of the LORD is flawless. He is a shield for all who take refuge in him."

1 Kings 8 [56]"Praise be to the LORD, who has given rest to his people Israel just as he promised. Not one word has failed of all the good promises he gave through his servant Moses."

Job 23 [13]"But he stands alone, and who can oppose him? He does whatever he pleases. [14]He carries out his decree against me, and many such plans he still has in store."

Ps 33 [11]But the plans of the LORD stand firm forever, the purposes of his heart through all generations.

Ps 102 [26]"They will perish, but you remain; they will all wear out like a garment. Like clothing you will change them and they will be discarded. [27]But you remain the same, and your years will never end."

Ps 103 [17]But from everlasting to everlasting the LORD's love is with those who fear him, and his righteousness with their children's children. . . .

Prov 19 [21]Many are the plans in a man's heart, but it is the LORD's purpose that prevails.

Eccles 3 [14]I know that everything God does will endure forever; nothing can be added to it and nothing taken from it. God does it so that men will revere him.

Isa 14 [24]The LORD Almighty has sworn, "Surely, as I have planned, so it will be, and as I have purposed, so it will stand."

Isa 31 [2]Yet he too is wise and can bring disaster; he does not take back his words. He will rise up against the house of the wicked, against those who help evildoers.

Isa 46 [9]"Remember the former things, those of long ago; I am God, and there is no other; I am God, and there is none like me. [10]I make known the end from the beginning, from ancient times, what is still to come. I say: My purpose will stand, and I will do all that I please."

Mal 3 [6]"I the LORD do not change. So you, O descendants of Jacob, are not destroyed."

Matt 24 [35]"Heaven and earth will pass away, but my words will never pass away."

John 5 [17]Jesus said to them, "My Father is always at his work to this very day, and I, too, am working."

Acts 4 [28]"They did what your power and will had decided beforehand should happen."

2 Cor 1 [20]For no matter how many promises God has made, they are "Yes" in Christ. And so through him the "Amen" is spoken by us to the glory of God.

Heb 6 [17]Because God wanted to make the unchanging nature of his purpose very clear to the heirs of what was promised, he confirmed it with an oath. [18]God did this so that, by two unchangeable things in which it is impossible for God to lie, we who have fled to take hold of the hope offered to us may be greatly encouraged.

James 1 [17]Every good and perfect gift is from above, coming down from the Father of the heavenly lights, who does not change like shifting shadows.

T. God Possesses Freedom (Sovereignty)

Gen 24 [3]"I want you to swear by the LORD, the God of heaven and the God of earth, that you will not get a wife for my son from the daughters of the Canaanites, among whom I am living. . . ."

Deut 4 [39]Acknowledge and take to heart this day that the LORD is God in heaven above and on the earth below. There is no other.

1 Sam 2 [6]"The LORD brings death and makes alive; he brings down to the grave and raises up. [7]The LORD sends poverty and wealth; he humbles and he exalts. [8]He raises the poor from the dust and lifts the needy from the ash heap; he seats them with princes and has them inherit a throne of honor.

"For the foundations of the earth are the LORD's; upon them he has set the world."

2 Sam 7 [28]"O Sovereign LORD, you are God! Your words are trustworthy, and you have promised these good things to your servant."

2 Kings 19 [15]And Hezekiah prayed to the LORD: "O LORD, God of Israel, enthroned between the cherubim, you alone are God over all the kingdoms of the earth. You have made heaven and earth."

Job 9 [12]"If he snatches away, who can stop him? Who can say to him, 'What are you doing?'"

Job 41 [11]"Who has a claim against me that I must pay? Everything under heaven belongs to me."

Ps 24 [1]The earth is the LORD's, and everything in it, the world, and all who live in it. . . . [10]Who is he, this King of glory? The LORD Almighty—he is the King of glory.
Ps 50 [10]". . . for every animal of the forest is mine, and the cattle on a thousand hills. [11]I know every bird in the mountains, and the creatures of the field are mine. [12]If I were hungry I would not tell you, for the world is mine, and all that is in it."
Ps 75 [6]No one from the east or the west or from the desert can exalt a man. [7]But it is God who judges: He brings one down, he exalts another.
Ps 95 [3]For the LORD is the great God, the great King above all gods. [4]In his hand are the depths of the earth, and the mountain peaks belong to him. [5]The sea is his, for he made it, and his hands formed the dry land.
Ps 99 [1]The LORD reigns, let the nations tremble; he sits enthroned between the cherubim, let the earth shake.
Ps 115 [3]Our God is in heaven; he does whatever pleases him.
Ps 135 [6]The LORD does whatever pleases him, in the heavens and on the earth, in the seas and all their depths.
Ps 146 [10]The LORD reigns forever, your God, O Zion, for all generations. Praise the LORD.
Eccles 3 [14]I know that everything God does will endure forever; nothing can be added to it and nothing taken from it. God does it so that men will revere him.
Eccles 9 [1]So I reflected on all this and concluded that the righteous and the wise and what they do are in God's hands, but no man knows whether love or hate awaits him.
Isa 45 [9]"Woe to him who quarrels with his Maker, to him who is but a potsherd among the potsherds on the ground. Does the clay say to the potter, 'What are you making?' Does your work say, 'He has no hands'?"
Isa 46 [10]"I make known the end from the beginning, from ancient times, what is still to come. I say: My purpose will stand, and I will do all that I please."
Isa 61 [1]The Spirit of the Sovereign LORD is on me, because the LORD has anointed me to preach good news to the poor. He has sent me to bind up the brokenhearted, to proclaim freedom for the captives and release from darkness for the prisoners. . . . [11]For as the soil makes the sprout come up and a garden causes seeds to grow, so the Sovereign LORD will make righteousness and praise spring up before all nations.
Jer 18 [6]"O house of Israel, can I not do with you as this potter does?" declares the LORD. "Like clay in the hand of the potter, so are you in my hand, O house of Israel."
Lam 5 [19]You, O LORD, reign forever; your throne endures from generation to generation.
Dan 4 [35]All the peoples of the earth are regarded as nothing. He does as he pleases with the powers of heaven and the peoples of the earth. No one can hold back his hand or say to him: "What have you done?"
Dan 6 [26]"I issue a decree that in every part of my kingdom people must fear and reverence the God of Daniel. For he is the living God and he endures forever; his kingdom will not be destroyed, his dominion will never end."
Mal 1 [14]"Cursed is the cheat who has an acceptable male in his flock and vows to give it, but then sacrifices a blemished animal to the Lord. For I am a great king," says the LORD Almighty, "and my name is to be feared among the nations."
Matt 6 [9]"This, then, is how you should pray: 'Our Father in heaven, hallowed be your name, [10]your kingdom come, your will be done on earth as it is in heaven.'"
Matt 11 [25]At that time Jesus said, "I praise you, Father, Lord of heaven and earth, because you have hidden these things from the wise and learned, and revealed them to little children. [26]Yes, Father, for this was your good pleasure."
John 19 [11]Jesus answered, "You would have no power over me if it were not given to you from above. Therefore the one who handed me over to you is guilty of a greater sin."
Acts 4 [24]When they heard this, they raised their voices together in prayer to God. "Sovereign Lord," they said, "you made the heaven and the earth and the sea, and everything in them. [25]You spoke by the Holy Spirit through the mouth of your servant, our father David: 'Why do the nations rage and the peoples plot in vain? [26]The kings of the earth take their stand and the rulers gather together against the Lord and against his Anointed One.' [27]Indeed Herod and Pontius Pilate met together with the Gentiles and the people of Israel in this city to conspire against your holy servant Jesus, whom you anointed. [28]They did what your power and will had decided beforehand should happen."
Rom 14 [11]It is written: "'As surely as I live,' says the Lord, 'every knee will bow before me; every tongue will confess to God.'"
Eph 1 [11]In him we were also chosen, having been predestined according to the plan of him who works out everything in conformity with the purpose of his will. . . .
Eph 4 [6]one God and Father of all, who is over all and through all and in all.
Heb 1 [3]The Son is the radiance of God's glory and the exact representation of his being, sustaining all things by his powerful word. After he had provided purification for sins, he sat down at the right hand of the Majesty in heaven.
James 4 [12]There is only one Lawgiver and Judge, the one who is able to save and destroy. But you—who are you to judge your neighbor?
Rev 1 [5]and from Jesus Christ, who is the faithful witness, the firstborn from the dead, and the ruler of the kings of the earth.

To him who loves us and has freed us from our sins by his blood, [6]and has made us to be a kingdom and priests to serve his God and Father—to him be glory and power for ever and ever! Amen.

U. God Shows Loving-kindness

Exod 15 [13]"In your unfailing love you will lead the people you have redeemed. In your strength you will guide them to your holy dwelling."
Ps 6 [4]Turn, O LORD, and deliver me; save me because of your unfailing love.
Ps 18 [50]He gives his king great victories; he shows unfailing kindness to his anointed, to David and his descendants forever.
Ps 89 [30]"If his sons forsake my law and do not follow my statutes, [31]if they violate my decrees and fail to keep my commands, [32]I will punish their sin with the rod, their iniquity with flogging; [33]but I will not take my love from him, nor will I ever betray my faithfulness. [34]I will not violate my covenant or alter what my lips have uttered."
Ps 103 [8]The LORD is compassionate and gracious, slow to anger, abounding in love. [9]He will not always accuse, nor will he harbor his anger forever; [10]he does not treat us as our sins deserve or repay us according to our iniquities.
Isa 27 [2]In that day—"Sing about a fruitful vineyard: [3]I, the LORD, watch over it; I water it continually. I guard it day and night so that no one may harm it. [4]I am not angry. If only there were briers and thorns confronting me! I would march against them in battle; I would set them all on fire. [5]Or else let them come to me for refuge; let them make peace with me, yes, let them make peace with me."
Isa 54 [7]"For a brief moment I abandoned you, but with deep compassion I will bring you back. [8]In a surge of anger I hid my face from you for a moment, but with everlasting kindness I will have compassion on you," says the LORD your Redeemer.
Isa 57 [16]"I will not accuse forever, nor will I always be angry, for then the spirit of man would grow faint before me—the breath of man that I have created."
Isa 63 [7]I will tell of the kindnesses of the LORD, the deeds for which he is to be praised, according to all the LORD has done for us—yes, the many good things he has done for the house of Israel, according to his compassion and many kindnesses.
Jer 9 [24]". . . but let him who boasts boast about this: that he understands and knows me, that I am the LORD, who exercises kindness, justice and righteousness on earth, for in these I delight," declares the LORD.
Jer 31 [3]The LORD appeared to us in the past, saying: "I have loved you with an everlasting love; I have drawn you with loving-kindness."
Ezek 16 [42]"'Then my wrath against you will subside and my jealous anger will turn away from you; I will be calm and no longer angry.'"
Hos 11 [9]"I will not carry out my fierce anger, nor will I turn

and devastate Ephraim. For I am God, and not man—the Holy One among you. I will not come in wrath."
Mic 7 8Do not gloat over me, my enemy! Though I have fallen, I will rise. Though I sit in darkness, the LORD will be my light.
Luke 6 35"But love your enemies, do good to them, and lend to them without expecting to get anything back. Then your reward will be great, and you will be sons of the Most High, because he is kind to the ungrateful and wicked."
Rom 2 4Or do you show contempt for the riches of his kindness, tolerance and patience, not realizing that God's kindness leads you toward repentance?
Rom 11 22Consider therefore the kindness and sternness of God: sternness to those who fell, but kindness to you, provided that you continue in his kindness. Otherwise, you also will be cut off.
Eph 2 6And God raised us up with Christ and seated us with him in the heavenly realms in Christ Jesus, 7in order that in the coming ages he might show the incomparable riches of his grace, expressed in his kindness to us in Christ Jesus.
Titus 3 4But when the kindness and love of God our Savior appeared, 5he saved us, not because of righteous things we had done, but because of his mercy. He saved us through the washing of rebirth and renewal by the Holy Spirit. . . .

IV
God as Trinity

A. The Oneness of God

See p. 53b, God Is a Unity

B. The Triunity of God

1. The Trinity in OT Allusions

a) The Plurality of the Godhead

Gen 1 26Then God said, "Let us make man in our image, in our likeness, and let them rule over the fish of the sea and the birds of the air, over the livestock, over all the earth, and over all the creatures that move along the ground."
Gen 3 22And the LORD God said, "The man has now become like one of us, knowing good and evil. He must not be allowed to reach out his hand and take also from the tree of life and eat, and live forever."
Gen 11 7"Come, let us go down and confuse their language so they will not understand each other."
2 Sam 23 2"The Spirit of the LORD spoke through me; his word was on my tongue. 3The God of Israel spoke, the Rock of Israel said to me: 'When one rules over men in righteousness, when he rules in the fear of God. . . .'"
Prov 30 4"Who has gone up to heaven and come down? Who has gathered up the wind in the hollow of his hands? Who has wrapped up the waters in his cloak? Who has established all the ends of the earth? What is his name, and the name of his son? Tell me if you know!"
Isa 48 16"Come near me and listen to this: From the first announcement I have not spoken in secret; at the time it happens, I am there."
And now the Sovereign LORD has sent me, with his Spirit.
Isa 63 8He said, "Surely they are my people, sons who will not be false to me"; and so he became their Savior. 9In all their distress he too was distressed, and the angel of his presence saved them. In his love and mercy he redeemed them; he lifted them up and carried them all the days of old. 10Yet they rebelled and grieved his Holy Spirit. So he turned and became their enemy and he himself fought against them.
11Then his people recalled the days of old, the days of Moses and his people—where is he who brought them through the sea, with the shepherd of his flock? Where is he who set his Holy Spirit among them . . . ?

b) The Triple Use of the Divine Name

Num 6 24""'The LORD bless you and keep you; 25the LORD make his face shine upon you and be gracious to you; 26the LORD turn his face toward you and give you peace.'"
27"So they will put my name on the Israelites, and I will bless them."
Ps 29 3The voice of the LORD is over the waters; the God of glory thunders, the LORD thunders over the mighty waters. 4The voice of the LORD is powerful; the voice of the LORD is majestic. 5The voice of the LORD breaks the cedars; the LORD breaks in pieces the cedars of Lebanon.
Isa 6 1In the year that King Uzziah died, I saw the Lord seated on a throne, high and exalted, and the train of his robe filled the temple. 2Above him were seraphs, each with six wings: With two wings they covered their faces, with two they covered their feet, and with two they were flying. 3And they were calling to one another: "Holy, holy, holy is the LORD Almighty; the whole earth is full of his glory."

c) The Son in the OT

(1) Abraham's Visitor

See p. 69b, The Preexistent Christ in Theophany

(2) Angel of God

See p. 69b, The Preexistent Christ in Theophany

(3) Angel of the Lord

See p. 69b, The Preexistent Christ in Theophany

(4) Commander of the Lord's Army

See p. 69b, The Preexistent Christ in Theophany

(5) Messiah

See p. 71a, The Preexistent Christ in Theology

(6) Wisdom

See p. 71a, The Preexistent Christ in Theology

(7) Word

See p. 71a, The Preexistent Christ in Theology

d) The Spirit in the OT

See p. 146a, The Holy Spirit in the OT

2. The Trinity in NT Teaching

Matt 3 16As soon as Jesus was baptized, he went up out of the water. At that moment heaven was opened, and he saw the Spirit of God descending like a dove and lighting on him. 17And a voice from heaven said, "This is my Son, whom I love; with him I am well pleased."
Matt 12 18"Here is my servant whom I have chosen, the one I love, in whom I delight; I will put my Spirit on him, and he will proclaim justice to the nations."
Matt 12 28"But if I drive out demons by the Spirit of God, then the kingdom of God has come upon you."
Matt 22 43He said to them, "How is it then that David, speaking by the Spirit, calls him 'Lord'? For he says, 44'The Lord said to my Lord: "Sit at my right hand until I put your enemies under your feet."'"
Matt 28 19"Therefore go and make disciples of all nations, baptizing them in the name of the Father and of the Son and of the Holy Spirit. . . ."
Luke 1 35The angel answered, "The Holy Spirit will come upon you, and the power of the Most High will overshadow you. So the holy one to be born will be called the Son of God."
Luke 3 21When all the people were being baptized, Jesus was baptized too. And as he was praying, heaven was opened 22and the Holy Spirit descended on him in bodily form like a dove. And a voice came from heaven: "You are my Son, whom I love; with you I am well pleased."
Luke 24 49"I am going to send you what my Father has promised; but stay in the city until you have been clothed with power from on high."
John 1 33"I would not have known him, except that the one who sent me to baptize with water told me, 'The man on whom you see the Spirit come down and remain is he who will baptize with the Holy Spirit.' 34I have seen and I testify that this is the Son of God."
John 3 34"For the one whom God has sent speaks the words of God, for God gives the Spirit without limit. 35The Father loves the Son and has placed everything in his hands."
John 14 11"Believe me when I say that I am in the Father and

the Father is in me; or at least believe on the evidence of the miracles themselves. 12I tell you the truth, anyone who has faith in me will do what I have been doing. He will do even greater things than these, because I am going to the Father. 13And I will do whatever you ask in my name, so that the Son may bring glory to the Father. 14You may ask me for anything in my name, and I will do it.

15"If you love me, you will obey what I command. 16And I will ask the Father, and he will give you another Counselor to be with you forever—17the Spirit of truth. The world cannot accept him, because it neither sees him nor knows him. But you know him, for he lives with you and will be in you. 18I will not leave you as orphans; I will come to you. 19Before long, the world will not see me anymore, but you will see me. Because I live, you also will live. 20On that day you will realize that I am in my Father, and you are in me, and I am in you. 21Whoever has my commands and obeys them, he is the one who loves me. He who loves me will be loved by my Father, and I too will love him and show myself to him."

22Then Judas (not Judas Iscariot) said, "But, Lord, why do you intend to show yourself to us and not to the world?"

23Jesus replied, "If anyone loves me, he will obey my teaching. My Father will love him, and we will come to him and make our home with him. 24He who does not love me will not obey my teaching. These words you hear are not my own; they belong to the Father who sent me.

25"All this I have spoken while still with you. 26But the Counselor, the Holy Spirit, whom the Father will send in my name, will teach you all things and will remind you of everything I have said to you."

John 15 26"When the Counselor comes, whom I will send to you from the Father, the Spirit of truth who goes out from the Father, he will testify about me."

John 16 7"But I tell you the truth: It is for your good that I am going away. Unless I go away, the Counselor will not come to you; but if I go, I will send him to you. 8When he comes, he will convict the world of guilt in regard to sin and righteousness and judgment: 9in regard to sin, because men do not believe in me; 10in regard to righteousness, because I am going to the Father, where you can see me no longer; 11and in regard to judgment, because the prince of this world now stands condemned.

12"I have much more to say to you, more than you can now bear. 13But when he, the Spirit of truth, comes, he will guide you into all truth. He will not speak on his own; he will speak only what he hears, and he will tell you what is yet to come. 14He will bring glory to me by taking from what is mine and making it known to you. 15All that belongs to the Father is mine. That is why I said the Spirit will take from what is mine and make it known to you."

John 20 21Again Jesus said, "Peace be with you! As the Father has sent me, I am sending you." 22And with that he breathed on them and said, "Receive the Holy Spirit."

Acts 2 32"God has raised this Jesus to life, and we are all witnesses of the fact. 33Exalted to the right hand of God, he has received from the Father the promised Holy Spirit and has poured out what you now see and hear. . . ."

38Peter replied, "Repent and be baptized, every one of you, in the name of Jesus Christ for the forgiveness of your sins. And you will receive the gift of the Holy Spirit. 39The promise is for you and your children and for all who are far off—for all whom the Lord our God will call."

Acts 10 36"You know the message God sent to the people of Israel, telling the good news of peace through Jesus Christ, who is Lord of all. 37You know what has happened throughout Judea, beginning in Galilee after the baptism that John preached—38how God anointed Jesus of Nazareth with the Holy Spirit and power, and how he went around doing good and healing all who were under the power of the devil, because God was with him."

Rom 8 9You, however, are controlled not by the sinful nature but by the Spirit, if the Spirit of God lives in you. And if anyone does not have the Spirit of Christ, he does not belong to Christ. 10But if Christ is in you, your body is dead because of sin, yet your spirit is alive because of righteousness. 11And if the Spirit of him who raised Jesus from the dead is living in you, he who raised Christ from the dead will also give life to your mortal bodies through his Spirit, who lives in you. . . .

26In the same way, the Spirit helps us in our weakness. We do not know what we ought to pray for, but the Spirit himself intercedes for us with groans that words cannot express. 27And he who searches our hearts knows the mind of the Spirit, because the Spirit intercedes for the saints in accordance with God's will.

Rom 15 16to be a minister of Christ Jesus to the Gentiles with the priestly duty of proclaiming the gospel of God, so that the Gentiles might become an offering acceptable to God, sanctified by the Holy Spirit.

1 Cor 6 15Do you not know that your bodies are members of Christ himself? Shall I then take the members of Christ and unite them with a prostitute? Never! . . . 19Do you not know that your body is a temple of the Holy Spirit, who is in you, whom you have received from God? You are not your own. . . .

1 Cor 12 4There are different kinds of gifts, but the same Spirit. 5There are different kinds of service, but the same Lord. 6There are different kinds of working, but the same God works all of them in all men.

2 Cor 1 20For no matter how many promises God has made, they are "Yes" in Christ. And so through him the "Amen" is spoken by us to the glory of God. 21Now it is God who makes both us and you stand firm in Christ. He anointed us, 22set his seal of ownership on us, and put his Spirit in our hearts as a deposit, guaranteeing what is to come.

2 Cor 13 14May the grace of the Lord Jesus Christ, and the love of God, and the fellowship of the Holy Spirit be with you all.

Gal 4 4But when the time had fully come, God sent his Son, born of a woman, born under law. . . . 6Because you are sons, God sent the Spirit of his Son into our hearts, the Spirit who calls out, "*Abba*, Father."

Eph 2 13But now in Christ Jesus you who once were far away have been brought near through the blood of Christ. . . . 18For through him we both have access to the Father by one Spirit. . . . 22And in him you too are being built together to become a dwelling in which God lives by his Spirit.

Eph 3 14For this reason I kneel before the Father, 15from whom his whole family in heaven and on earth derives its name. 16I pray that out of his glorious riches he may strengthen you with power through his Spirit in your inner being, 17so that Christ may dwell in your hearts through faith. And I pray that you, being rooted and established in love, 18may have power, together with all the saints, to grasp how wide and long and high and deep is the love of Christ, 19and to know this love that surpasses knowledge—that you may be filled to the measure of all the fullness of God.

Eph 4 4There is one body and one Spirit—just as you were called to one hope when you were called—5one Lord, one faith, one baptism; 6one God and Father of all, who is over all and through all and in all.

2 Thess 2 13But we ought always to thank God for you, brothers loved by the Lord, because from the beginning God chose you to be saved through the sanctifying work of the Spirit and through belief in the truth. 14He called you to this through our gospel, that you might share in the glory of our Lord Jesus Christ.

Titus 3 4But when the kindness and love of God our Savior appeared, 5he saved us, not because of righteous things we had done, but because of his mercy. He saved us through the washing of rebirth and renewal by the Holy Spirit, 6whom he poured out on us generously through Jesus Christ our Savior. . . .

Heb 9 14How much more, then, will the blood of Christ, who through the eternal Spirit offered himself unblemished to God, cleanse our consciences from acts that lead to death, so that we may serve the living God!

1 Pet 1 2who have been chosen according to the foreknowledge of God the Father, through the sanctifying work of the Spirit, for obedience to Jesus Christ and sprinkling by his blood: Grace and peace be yours in abundance.

1 Pet 3 18For Christ died for sins once for all, the righteous for

the unrighteous, to bring you to God. He was put to death in the body but made alive by the Spirit. . . .
1 John 4 [2]This is how you can recognize the Spirit of God: Every spirit that acknowledges that Jesus Christ has come in the flesh is from God. . . . [13]We know that we live in him and he in us, because he has given us of his Spirit. [14]And we have seen and testify that the Father has sent his Son to be the Savior of the world.
Jude [20]But you, dear friends, build yourselves up in your most holy faith and pray in the Holy Spirit. [21]Keep yourselves in God's love as you wait for the mercy of our Lord Jesus Christ to bring you to eternal life.

C. The Deity of the Persons of the Godhead

1. The Deity of the Father

See p. 42b, The Fatherhood of God

2. The Deity of the Son

See p. 88a, The Deity of Christ

3. The Deity of the Holy Spirit

See p. 139a, The Deity of the Holy Spirit

2

Jesus Christ

I
Christ in the OT

A. The Preexistent Christ

1. The Preexistent Christ in Theophany

a) Abraham's Visitor

Gen 18 [1]The LORD appeared to Abraham near the great trees of
Mamre while he was sitting at the entrance to his tent in the
heat of the day. [2]Abraham looked up and saw three men standing nearby. When he saw them, he hurried from the entrance of
his tent to meet them and bowed low to the ground.
[3]He said, "If I have found favor in your eyes, my lord, do
not pass your servant by. [4]Let a little water be brought, and
then you may all wash your feet and rest under this tree. [5]Let
me get you something to eat, so you can be refreshed and then
go on your way—now that you have come to your servant."
"Very well," they answered, "do as you say."
[6]So Abraham hurried into the tent to Sarah. "Quick," he
said, "get three seahs of fine flour and knead it and bake some
bread."
[7]Then he ran to the herd and selected a choice, tender calf
and gave it to a servant, who hurried to prepare it. [8]He then
brought some curds and milk and the calf that had been prepared, and set these before them. While they ate, he stood near
them under a tree.
[9]"Where is your wife Sarah?" they asked him.
"There, in the tent," he said.
[10]Then the LORD said, "I will surely return to you about this
time next year, and Sarah your wife will have a son."
Now Sarah was listening at the entrance to the tent, which
was behind him. [11]Abraham and Sarah were already old and
well advanced in years, and Sarah was past the age of childbearing. [12]So Sarah laughed to herself as she thought, "After I
am worn out and my master is old, will I now have this pleasure?"
[13]Then the LORD said to Abraham, "Why did Sarah laugh
and say, 'Will I really have a child, now that I am old?' [14]Is anything too hard for the LORD? I will return to you at the
appointed time next year and Sarah will have a son."
[15]Sarah was afraid, so she lied and said, "I did not laugh."
But he said, "Yes, you did laugh."
[16]When the men got up to leave, they looked down toward
Sodom, and Abraham walked along with them to see them on
their way. [17]Then the LORD said, "Shall I hide from Abraham
what I am about to do? [18]Abraham will surely become a great
and powerful nation, and all nations on earth will be blessed
through him. [19]For I have chosen him, so that he will direct his

children and his household after him to keep the way of the LORD by doing what is right and just, so that the LORD will bring about for Abraham what he has promised him."

20Then the LORD said, "The outcry against Sodom and Gomorrah is so great and their sin so grievous 21that I will go down and see if what they have done is as bad as the outcry that has reached me. If not, I will know."

22The men turned away and went toward Sodom, but Abraham remained standing before the LORD. 23Then Abraham approached him and said: "Will you sweep away the righteous with the wicked? 24What if there are fifty righteous people in the city? Will you really sweep it away and not spare the place for the sake of the fifty righteous people in it? 25Far be it from you to do such a thing—to kill the righteous with the wicked, treating the righteous and the wicked alike. Far be it from you! Will not the Judge of all the earth do right?"

26The LORD said, "If I find fifty righteous people in the city of Sodom, I will spare the whole place for their sake."

27Then Abraham spoke up again: "Now that I have been so bold as to speak to the Lord, though I am nothing but dust and ashes, 28what if the number of the righteous is five less than fifty? Will you destroy the whole city because of five people?"

"If I find forty-five there," he said, "I will not destroy it."

29Once again he spoke to him, "What if only forty are found there?"

He said, "For the sake of forty, I will not do it."

30Then he said, "May the Lord not be angry, but let me speak. What if only thirty can be found there?"

He answered, "I will not do it if I find thirty there."

31Abraham said, "Now that I have been so bold as to speak to the Lord, what if only twenty can be found there?"

He said, "For the sake of twenty, I will not destroy it."

32Then he said, "May the Lord not be angry, but let me speak just once more. What if only ten can be found there?"

He answered, "For the sake of ten, I will not destroy it."

33When the LORD had finished speaking with Abraham, he left, and Abraham returned home.

Gen 19 24Then the LORD rained down burning sulfur on Sodom and Gomorrah—from the LORD out of the heavens.

b) Angel of God

Gen 31 11"The angel of God said to me in the dream, 'Jacob.' I answered, 'Here I am.' 12And he said, 'Look up and see that all the male goats mating with the flock are streaked, speckled or spotted, for I have seen all that Laban has been doing to you. 13I am the God of Bethel, where you anointed a pillar and where you made a vow to me. Now leave this land at once and go back to your native land.'"

Gen 48 15Then he blessed Joseph and said, "May the God before whom my fathers Abraham and Isaac walked, the God who has been my shepherd all my life to this day, 16the Angel who has delivered me from all harm—may he bless these boys. May they be called by my name and the names of my fathers Abraham and Isaac, and may they increase greatly upon the earth."

Exod 23 20"See, I am sending an angel ahead of you to guard you along the way and to bring you to the place I have prepared. 21Pay attention to him and listen to what he says. Do not rebel against him; he will not forgive your rebellion, since my Name is in him."

Dan 3 25He said, "Look! I see four men walking around in the fire, unbound and unharmed, and the fourth looks like a son of the gods." . . .

28Then Nebuchadnezzar said, "Praise be to the God of Shadrach, Meshach and Abednego, who has sent his angel and rescued his servants! They trusted in him and defied the king's command and were willing to give up their lives rather than serve or worship any god except their own God."

c) Angel of His Presence

Isa 63 8He said, "Surely they are my people, sons who will not be false to me"; and so he became their Savior. 9In all their distress he too was distressed, and the angel of his presence saved them. In his love and mercy he redeemed them; he lifted them up and carried them all the days of old. 10Yet they rebelled and grieved his Holy Spirit. So he turned and became their enemy and he himself fought against them.

11Then his people recalled the days of old, the days of Moses and his people—where is he who brought them through the sea, with the shepherd of his flock? Where is he who set his Holy Spirit among them? . . .

d) Angel of the Lord

Gen 16 7The angel of the LORD found Hagar near a spring in the desert; it was the spring that is beside the road to Shur. 8And he said, "Hagar, servant of Sarai, where have you come from, and where are you going?"

"I'm running away from my mistress Sarai," she answered.

9Then the angel of the LORD told her, "Go back to your mistress and submit to her." 10The angel added, "I will so increase your descendants that they will be too numerous to count."

11The angel of the LORD also said to her: "You are now with child and you will have a son. You shall name him Ishmael, for the LORD has heard of your misery. 12He will be a wild donkey of a man; his hand will be against everyone and everyone's hand against him, and he will live in hostility toward all his brothers."

13She gave this name to the Lord who spoke to her: "You are the God who sees me," for she said, "I have now seen the One who sees me." 14That is why the well was called Beer Lahai Roi; it is still there, between Kadesh and Bered.

Gen 22 11But the angel of the LORD called out to him from heaven, "Abraham! Abraham!"

"Here I am," he replied.

12"Do not lay a hand on the boy," he said. "Do not do anything to him. Now I know that you fear God, because you have not withheld from me your son, your only son."

13Abraham looked up and there in a thicket he saw a ram caught by its horns. He went over and took the ram and sacrificed it as a burnt offering instead of his son. 14So Abraham called that place The LORD Will Provide. And to this day it is said, "On the mountain of the LORD it will be provided."

15The angel of the LORD called to Abraham from heaven a second time 16and said, "I swear by myself, declares the LORD, that because you have done this and have not withheld your son, your only son, 17I will surely bless you and make your descendants as numerous as the stars in the sky and as the sand on the seashore. Your descendants will take possession of the cities of their enemies, 18and through your offspring all nations on earth will be blessed, because you have obeyed me."

Exod 3 2There the angel of the LORD appeared to him in flames of fire from within a bush. Moses saw that though the bush was on fire it did not burn up. 3So Moses thought, "I will go over and see this strange sight—why the bush does not burn up."

4When the LORD saw that he had gone over to look, God called to him from within the bush, "Moses! Moses!"

And Moses said, "Here I am."

5"Do not come any closer," God said. "Take off your sandals, for the place where you are standing is holy ground."

6Then he said, "I am the God of your father, the God of Abraham, the God of Isaac and the God of Jacob." At this, Moses hid his face, because he was afraid to look at God.

Judg 2 1The angel of the LORD went up from Gilgal to Bokim and said, "I brought you up out of Egypt and led you into the land that I swore to give to your forefathers. I said, 'I will never break my covenant with you, 2and you shall not make a covenant with the people of this land, but you shall break down their altars.' Yet you have disobeyed me. Why have you done this? 3Now therefore I tell you that I will not drive them out before you; they will be thorns in your sides and their gods will be a snare to you."

4When the angel of the LORD had spoken these things to all the Israelites, the people wept aloud, 5and they called that place Bokim. There they offered sacrifices to the LORD. 6After Joshua had dismissed the Israelites, they went to take possession of the land, each to his own inheritance.

Judg 6 11The angel of the LORD came and sat down under the oak in Ophrah that belonged to Joash the Abiezrite, where his son Gideon was threshing wheat in a winepress to keep it from the Midianites. 12When the angel of the LORD appeared to Gideon, he said, "The LORD is with you, mighty warrior."

13"But sir," Gideon replied, "if the LORD is with us, why has all this happened to us? Where are all his wonders that our fathers told us about when they said, 'Did not the LORD bring us up out of Egypt?' But now the LORD has abandoned us and put us into the hand of Midian."

14The LORD turned to him and said, "Go in the strength you have and save Israel out of Midian's hand. Am I not sending you?"

15"But Lord," Gideon asked, "how can I save Israel? My clan is the weakest in Manasseh, and I am the least in my family."

16The LORD answered, "I will be with you, and you will strike down all the Midianites together."

17Gideon replied, "If now I have found favor in your eyes, give me a sign that it is really you talking to me. 18Please do not go away until I come back and bring my offering and set it before you."

And the LORD said, "I will wait until you return."

19Gideon went in, prepared a young goat, and from an ephah of flour he made bread without yeast. Putting the meat in a basket and its broth in a pot, he brought them out and offered them to him under the oak.

20The angel of God said to him, "Take the meat and the unleavened bread, place them on this rock, and pour out the broth." And Gideon did so. 21With the tip of the staff that was in his hand, the angel of the LORD touched the meat and the unleavened bread. Fire flared from the rock, consuming the meat and the bread. And the angel of the LORD disappeared. 22When Gideon realized that it was the angel of the LORD, he exclaimed, "Ah, Sovereign LORD! I have seen the angel of the LORD face to face!"

23But the LORD said to him, "Peace! Do not be afraid. You are not going to die."

24So Gideon built an altar to the LORD there and called it The LORD is Peace. To this day it stands in Ophrah of the Abiezrites.

Judg 13 20As the flame blazed up from the altar toward heaven, the angel of the LORD ascended in the flame. Seeing this, Manoah and his wife fell with their faces to the ground. 21When the angel of the LORD did not show himself again to Manoah and his wife, Manoah realized that it was the angel of the LORD. 22"We are doomed to die!" he said to his wife. "We have seen God!"

e) Commander of the Lord's Army

Josh 5 13Now when Joshua was near Jericho, he looked up and saw a man standing in front of him with a drawn sword in his hand. Joshua went up to him and asked, "Are you for us or for our enemies?"

14"Neither," he replied, "but as commander of the army of the LORD I have now come." Then Joshua fell facedown to the ground in reverence, and asked him, "What message does my Lord have for his servant?"

15The commander of the LORD's army replied, "Take off your sandals, for the place where you are standing is holy." And Joshua did so.

Josh 6 2Then the LORD said to Joshua, "See, I have delivered Jericho into your hands, along with its king and its fighting men."

2. The Preexistent Christ in Theology

a) Elohim

Ps 45 6Your throne, O God, will last for ever and ever; a scepter of justice will be the scepter of your kingdom. 7You love righteousness and hate wickedness; therefore God, your God, has set you above your companions by anointing you with the oil of joy.

b) Jehovah (Yahweh)

Isa 40 3A voice of one calling: "In the desert prepare the way for the LORD; make straight in the wilderness a highway for our God."

Isa 44 6"This is what the LORD says—Israel's King and Redeemer, the LORD Almighty: I am the first and I am the last; apart from me there is no God."

Isa 48 12"Listen to me, O Jacob, Israel, whom I have called: I am he; I am the first and I am the last. 13My own hand laid the foundations of the earth, and my right hand spread out the heavens; when I summon them, they all stand up together.

14"Come together, all of you, and listen: Which of the idols has foretold these things? The LORD's chosen ally will carry out his purpose against Babylon; his arm will be against the Babylonians. 15I, even I, have spoken; yes, I have called him. I will bring him, and he will succeed in his mission.

16"Come near me and listen to this: "From the first announcement I have not spoken in secret; at the time it happens, I am there."

And now the Sovereign LORD has sent me, with his Spirit.

Jer 23 5"The days are coming," declares the LORD, "when I will raise up to David a righteous Branch, a King who will reign wisely and do what is just and right in the land. 6In his days Judah will be saved and Israel will live in safety. This is the name by which he will be called: The LORD Our Righteousness."

Hos 1 7"Yet I will show love to the house of Judah; and I will save them—not by bow, sword or battle, or by horses and horsemen, but by the LORD their God."

Joel 2 32"And everyone who calls on the name of the LORD will be saved; for on Mount Zion and in Jerusalem there will be deliverance, as the LORD has said, among the survivors whom the LORD calls."

c) Member of the Godhead

Gen 1 26Then God said, "Let us make man in our image, in our likeness, and let them rule over the fish of the sea and the birds of the air, over the livestock, over all the earth, and over all the creatures that move along the ground."

Gen 3 22And the LORD God said, "The man has now become like one of us, knowing good and evil. He must not be allowed to reach out his hand and take also from the tree of life and eat, and live forever."

Gen 11 7"Come, let us go down and confuse their language so they will not understand each other."

Ps 2 2The kings of the earth take their stand and the rulers gather together against the LORD and against his Anointed One. 3"Let us break their chains," they say, "and throw off their fetters."

4The One enthroned in heaven laughs; the Lord scoffs at them. 5Then he rebukes them in his anger and terrifies them in his wrath, saying, 6"I have installed my King on Zion, my holy hill."

Ps 45 6Your throne, O God, will last for ever and ever; a scepter of justice will be the scepter of your kingdom. 7You love righteousness and hate wickedness; therefore God, your God, has set you above your companions by anointing you with the oil of joy.

d) Messiah

Ps 110 1The LORD says to my Lord: "Sit at my right hand until I make your enemies a footstool for your feet."

Isa 7 14"Therefore the Lord himself will give you a sign: The virgin will be with child and will give birth to a son, and will call him Immanuel."

Isa 9 6For to us a child is born, to us a son is given, and the government will be on his shoulders. And he will be called Wonderful Counselor, Mighty God, Everlasting Father, Prince of Peace. 7Of the increase of his government and peace there will be no end. He will reign on David's throne and over his kingdom, establishing and upholding it with justice and righteousness from that time on and forever. The zeal of the LORD Almighty will accomplish this.

Jer 23 5"The days are coming," declares the LORD, "when I will raise up to David a righteous Branch, a King who will reign wisely and do what is just and right in the land. 6In his days Judah will be saved and Israel will live in safety. This is the name by which he will be called: The LORD Our Righteousness."

Mic 5 2"But you, Bethlehem Ephrathah, though you are small among the clans of Judah, out of you will come for me one who will be ruler over Israel, whose origins are from of old, from ancient times."

Zech 13 [7]"Awake, O sword, against my shepherd, against the man who is close to me!" declares the LORD Almighty. "Strike the shepherd, and the sheep will be scattered, and I will turn my hand against the little ones."
Mal 3 [1]"See, I will send my messenger, who will prepare the way before me. Then suddenly the Lord you are seeking will come to his temple; the messenger of the covenant, whom you desire, will come," says the LORD Almighty.

e) Son of God

Ps 2 [2]The kings of the earth take their stand and the rulers gather together against the LORD and against his Anointed One. [3]"Let us break their chains," they say, "and throw off their fetters."

[4]The One enthroned in heaven laughs; the Lord scoffs at them. [5]Then he rebukes them in his anger and terrifies them in his wrath, saying, [6]"I have installed my King on Zion, my holy hill."

[7]I will proclaim the decree of the LORD:

He said to me, "You are my Son; today I have become your Father. [8]Ask of me, and I will make the nations your inheritance, the ends of the earth your possession. [9]You will rule them with an iron scepter; you will dash them to pieces like pottery."

[10]Therefore, you kings, be wise; be warned, you rulers of the earth. [11]Serve the LORD with fear and rejoice with trembling. [12]Kiss the Son, lest he be angry and you be destroyed in your way, for his wrath can flare up in a moment. Blessed are all who take refuge in him.
Prov 30 [4]"Who has gone up to heaven and come down? Who has gathered up the wind in the hollow of his hands? Who has wrapped up the waters in his cloak? Who has established all the ends of the earth? What is his name, and the name of his son? Tell me if you know!"

f) Wisdom

Job 28 [23]"God understands the way to it and he alone knows where it dwells, [24]for he views the ends of the earth and sees everything under the heavens. [25]When he established the force of the wind and measured out the waters, [26]when he made a decree for the rain and a path for the thunderstorm, [27]then he looked at wisdom and appraised it; he confirmed it and tested it."
Prov 3 [19]By wisdom the LORD laid the earth's foundations, by understanding he set the heavens in place. . . .
Prov 8 [1]Does not wisdom call out? Does not understanding raise her voice? . . .

[12]"I, wisdom, dwell together with prudence; I possess knowledge and discretion. [13]To fear the LORD is to hate evil; I hate pride and arrogance, evil behavior and perverse speech. [14]Counsel and sound judgment are mine; I have understanding and power. [15]By me kings reign and rulers make laws that are just; [16]by me princes govern, and all nobles who rule on earth. [17]I love those who love me, and those who seek me find me. [18]With me are riches and honor, enduring wealth and prosperity. [19]My fruit is better than fine gold; what I yield surpasses choice silver. [20]I walk in the way of righteousness, along the paths of justice, [21]bestowing wealth on those who love me and making their treasuries full.

[22]"The LORD brought me forth as the first of his works, before his deeds of old; [23]I was appointed from eternity, from the beginning, before the world began. [24]When there were no oceans, I was given birth, when there were no springs abounding with water; [25]before the mountains were settled in place, before the hills, I was given birth, [26]before he made the earth or its fields or any of the dust of the world. [27]I was there when he set the heavens in place, when he marked out the horizon on the face of the deep, [28]when he established the clouds above and fixed securely the fountains of the deep, [29]when he gave the sea its boundary so the waters would not overstep his command, and when he marked out the foundations of the earth. [30]Then I was the craftsman at his side. I was filled with delight day after day, rejoicing always in his presence, [31]rejoicing in his whole world and delighting in mankind.

[32]"Now then, my sons, listen to me; blessed are those who keep my ways. [33]Listen to my instruction and be wise; do not ignore it. [34]Blessed is the man who listens to me, watching daily at my doors, waiting at my doorway. [35]For whoever finds me finds life and receives favor from the LORD. [36]But whoever fails to find me harms himself; all who hate me love death." (cf. Matt 11:19; Luke 7:35; 11:49; Heb 1:2)

g) Word

Ps 33 [6]By the word of the LORD were the heavens made, their starry host by the breath of his mouth.
Ps 107 [20]He sent forth his word and healed them; he rescued them from the grave.
Ps 119 [89]Your word, O LORD, is eternal; it stands firm in the heavens.
Ps 147 [15]He sends his command to the earth; his word runs swiftly. [16]He spreads the snow like wool and scatters the frost like ashes. [17]He hurls down his hail like pebbles. Who can withstand his icy blast? [18]He sends his word and melts them; he stirs up his breezes, and the waters flow.

B. Christ in Prophecy

See p. 78b, Prophecies concerning Christ

C. Christ in Type

1. Persons as Types of Christ

a) Aaron

Exod 28 [1]"Have Aaron your brother brought to you from among the Israelites, along with his sons Nadab and Abihu, Eleazar and Ithamar, so they may serve me as priests."
Heb 5 [4]No one takes this honor upon himself; he must be called by God, just as Aaron was. [5]So Christ also did not take upon himself the glory of becoming a high priest. But God said to him, "You are my Son; today I have become your Father."

b) Adam

Rom 5 [14]Nevertheless, death reigned from the time of Adam to the time of Moses, even over those who did not sin by breaking a command, as did Adam, who was a pattern of the one to come.
1 Cor 15 [45]So it is written: "The first man Adam became a living being"; the last Adam, a life-giving spirit.

c) David

2 Sam 8 [15]David reigned over all Israel, doing what was just and right for all his people.
Ps 89 [19]Once you spoke in a vision, to your faithful people you said: "I have bestowed strength on a warrior; I have exalted a young man from among the people. [20]I have found David my servant; with my sacred oil I have anointed him."
Ezek 37 [24]"'My servant David will be king over them, and they will all have one shepherd. They will follow my laws and be careful to keep my decrees.'"
Matt 1 [1]A record of the genealogy of Jesus Christ the son of David, the son of Abraham . . .
Acts 13 [22]"After removing Saul, he made David their king. He testified concerning him: 'I have found David son of Jesse a man after my own heart; he will do everything I want him to do.'"

d) Jonah

Jon 1 [17]But the LORD provided a great fish to swallow Jonah, and Jonah was inside the fish three days and three nights.
Matt 12 [40]"For as Jonah was three days and three nights in the belly of a huge fish, so the Son of Man will be three days and three nights in the heart of the earth."

e) Melchizedek

Gen 14 [18]Then Melchizedek king of Salem brought out bread and wine. He was priest of God Most High, [19]and he blessed Abram, saying, "Blessed be Abram by God Most High, Creator of heaven and earth. [20]And blessed be God Most High, who delivered your enemies into your hand." Then Abram gave him a tenth of everything.

Heb 5 [8]Although he was a son, he learned obedience from what he suffered [9]and, once made perfect, he became the source of eternal salvation for all who obey him [10]and was designated by God to be high priest in the order of Melchizedek.
Heb 7 [1]This Melchizedek was king of Salem and priest of God Most High. He met Abraham returning from the defeat of the kings and blessed him, [2]and Abraham gave him a tenth of everything. First, his name means "king of righteousness"; then also, "king of Salem" means "king of peace." [3]Without father or mother, without genealogy, without beginning of days or end of life, like the Son of God he remains a priest forever.

[4]Just think how great he was: Even the patriarch Abraham gave him a tenth of the plunder! [5]Now the law requires the descendants of Levi who become priests to collect a tenth from the people—that is, their brothers—even though their brothers are descended from Abraham. [6]This man, however, did not trace his descent from Levi, yet he collected a tenth from Abraham and blessed him who had the promises. [7]And without doubt the lesser person is blessed by the greater. [8]In the one case, the tenth is collected by men who die; but in the other case, by him who is declared to be living. [9]One might even say that Levi, who collects the tenth, paid the tenth through Abraham, [10]because when Melchizedek met Abraham, Levi was still in the body of his ancestor.

[11]If perfection could have been attained through the Levitical priesthood (for on the basis of it the law was given to the people), why was there still need for another priest to come—one in the order of Melchizedek, not in the order of Aaron? [12]For when there is a change of the priesthood, there must also be a change of the law. [13]He of whom these things are said belonged to a different tribe, and no one from that tribe has ever served at the altar. [14]For it is clear that our LORD descended from Judah, and in regard to that tribe Moses said nothing about priests. [15]And what we have said is even more clear if another priest like Melchizedek appears, [16]one who has become a priest not on the basis of a regulation as to his ancestry but on the basis of the power of an indestructible life. [17]For it is declared: "You are a priest forever, in the order of Melchizedek."

f) Moses

Num 12 [7]"But this is not true of my servant Moses; he is faithful in all my house."
Deut 18 [15]The LORD your God will raise up for you a prophet like me from among your own brothers. You must listen to him.
Acts 3 [20]". . . and that he may send the Christ, who has been appointed for you—even Jesus. [21]He must remain in heaven until the time comes for God to restore everything, as he promised long ago through his holy prophets. [22]For Moses said, 'The LORD your God will raise up for you a prophet like me from among your own people; you must listen to everything he tells you.'"
Heb 3 [2]He was faithful to the one who appointed him, just as Moses was faithful in all God's house. [3]Jesus has been found worthy of greater honor than Moses, just as the builder of a house has greater honor than the house itself. [4]For every house is built by someone, but God is the builder of everything. [5]Moses was faithful as a servant in all God's house, testifying to what would be said in the future. [6]But Christ is faithful as a son over God's house. And we are his house, if we hold on to our courage and the hope of which we boast.

g) Solomon

1 Kings 10 [1]When the queen of Sheba heard about the fame of Solomon and his relation to the name of the LORD, she came to test him with hard questions. [2]Arriving at Jerusalem with a very great caravan—with camels carrying spices, large quantities of gold, and precious stones—she came to Solomon and talked with him about all that she had on her mind. [3]Solomon answered all her questions; nothing was too hard for the king to explain to her. [4]When the queen of Sheba saw all the wisdom of Solomon and the palace he had built, [5]the food on his table, the seating of his officials, the attending servants in their robes, his cupbearers, and the burnt offerings he made at the temple of the LORD, she was overwhelmed.
Matt 12 [42]"The Queen of the South will rise at the judgment with this generation and condemn it; for she came from the ends of the earth to listen to Solomon's wisdom, and now one greater than Solomon is here."

2. Objects as Types of Christ

a) Bronze Snake

Num 21 [9]So Moses made a bronze snake and put it up on a pole. Then when anyone was bitten by a snake and looked at the bronze snake, he lived.
John 3 [14]"Just as Moses lifted up the snake in the desert, so the Son of Man must be lifted up, [15]that everyone who believes in him may have eternal life."

b) Manna

Exod 16 [11]The LORD said to Moses, [12]"I have heard the grumbling of the Israelites. Tell them, 'At twilight you will eat meat, and in the morning you will be filled with bread. Then you will know that I am the LORD your God.'"

[13]That evening quail came and covered the camp, and in the morning there was a layer of dew around the camp. [14]When the dew was gone, thin flakes like frost on the ground appeared on the desert floor. [15]When the Israelites saw it, they said to each other, "What is it?" For they did not know what it was.

Moses said to them, "It is the bread the LORD has given you to eat."
John 6 [32]Jesus said to them, "I tell you the truth, it is not Moses who has given you the bread from heaven, but it is my Father who gives you the true bread from heaven. [33]For the bread of God is he who comes down from heaven and gives life to the world."

[34]"Sir," they said, "from now on give us this bread."

[35]Then Jesus declared, "I am the bread of life. He who comes to me will never go hungry, and he who believes in me will never be thirsty."

c) Passover Lamb

Exod 12 [3]"Tell the whole community of Israel that on the tenth day of this month each man is to take a lamb for his family, one for each household. [4]If any household is too small for a whole lamb, they must share one with their nearest neighbor, having taken into account the number of people there are. You are to determine the amount of lamb needed in accordance with what each person will eat. [5]The animals you choose must be year-old males without defect, and you may take them from the sheep or the goats. [6]Take care of them until the fourteenth day of the month, when all the people of the community of Israel must slaughter them at twilight. . . .

[46]"It must be eaten inside one house; take none of the meat outside the house. Do not break any of the bones."
Num 9 [12]"They must not leave any of it till morning or break any of its bones. When they celebrate the Passover, they must follow all the regulations."
Ps 34 [20]he protects all his bones, not one of them will be broken.
John 19 [36]These things happened so that the scripture would be fulfilled: "Not one of his bones will be broken." . . .
1 Cor 5 [7]Get rid of the old yeast that you may be a new batch without yeast—as you really are. For Christ, our Passover lamb, has been sacrificed.

d) Rock of Horeb

Exod 17 [6]"I will stand there before you by the rock at Horeb. Strike the rock, and water will come out of it for the people to drink." So Moses did this in the sight of the elders of Israel.
1 Cor 10 [3]They all ate the same spiritual food [4]and drank the same spiritual drink; for they drank from the spiritual rock that accompanied them, and that rock was Christ.

e) Veil

Exod 40 [21]Then he brought the ark into the tabernacle and hung the shielding curtain and shielded the ark of the Testimony, as the LORD commanded him.

2 Chron 3 14He made the curtain of blue, purple and crimson yarn and fine linen, with cherubim worked into it.

Heb 10 19Therefore, brothers, since we have confidence to enter the Most Holy Place by the blood of Jesus, 20by a new and living way opened for us through the curtain, that is, his body . . .

D. Christ in Parallel

1. Persons as Parallels to Christ

a) Abel

Gen 4 8Now Cain said to his brother Abel, "Let's go out to the field." And while they were in the field, Cain attacked his brother Abel and killed him. . . . 10The LORD said, "What have you done? Listen! Your brother's blood cries out to me from the ground."

Heb 12 24to Jesus the mediator of a new covenant, and to the sprinkled blood that speaks a better word than the blood of Abel.

b) Eliakim

Isa 22 20"In that day I will summon my servant, Eliakim son of Hilkiah. 21I will clothe him with your robe and fasten your sash around him and hand your authority over to him. He will be a father to those who live in Jerusalem and to the house of Judah. 22I will place on his shoulder the key to the house of David; what he opens no one can shut, and what he shuts no one can open."

Rev 3 7"To the angel of the church in Philadelphia write: These are the words of him who is holy and true, who holds the key of David. What he opens no one can shut, and what he shuts no one can open."

c) Elijah

Luke 4 24"I tell you the truth," he continued, "no prophet is accepted in his hometown. 25I assure you that there were many widows in Israel in Elijah's time, when the sky was shut for three and a half years and there was a severe famine throughout the land. 26Yet Elijah was not sent to any of them, but to a widow in Zarephath in the region of Sidon."

d) Elisha

2 Kings 4 42A man came from Baal Shalishah, bringing the man of God twenty loaves of barley bread baked from the first ripe grain, along with some heads of new grain. "Give it to the people to eat," Elisha said.

43"How can I set this before a hundred men?" his servant asked.

But Elisha answered, "Give it to the people to eat. For this is what the LORD says: 'They will eat and have some left over.'" 44Then he set it before them, and they ate and had some left over, according to the word of the LORD.

Mark 6 35By this time it was late in the day, so his disciples came to him. "This is a remote place," they said, "and it's already very late. 36Send the people away so they can go to the surrounding countryside and villages and buy themselves something to eat."

37But he answered, "You give them something to eat."

They said to him, "That would take eight months of a man's wages! Are we to go and spend that much on bread and give it to them to eat?"

38"How many loaves do you have?" he asked. "Go and see."

When they found out, they said, "Five—and two fish."

39Then Jesus directed them to have all the people sit down in groups on the green grass. 40So they sat down in groups of hundreds and fifties. 41Taking the five loaves and the two fish and looking up to heaven, he gave thanks and broke the loaves. Then he gave them to his disciples to set before the people. He also divided the two fish among them all. 42They all ate and were satisfied, 43and the disciples picked up twelve basketfuls of broken pieces of bread and fish. 44The number of the men who had eaten was five thousand.

Luke 4 23Jesus said to them, "Surely you will quote this proverb to me: 'Physician, heal yourself! Do here in your hometown what we have heard that you did in Capernaum.'

24"I tell you the truth," he continued, "no prophet is accepted in his hometown. . . . 27And there were many in Israel with leprosy in the time of Elisha the prophet, yet not one of them was cleansed—only Naaman the Syrian."

e) Isaac

Gen 22 1Some time later God tested Abraham. He said to him, "Abraham!"

"Here I am," he replied.

2Then God said, "Take your son, your only son, Isaac, whom you love, and go to the region of Moriah. Sacrifice him there as a burnt offering on one of the mountains I will tell you about."

John 3 16"For God so loved the world that he gave his one and only Son, that whoever believes in him shall not perish but have eternal life."

Heb 11 17By faith Abraham, when God tested him, offered Isaac as a sacrifice. He who had received the promises was about to sacrifice his one and only son, 18even though God had said to him, "It is through Isaac that your offspring will be reckoned." 19Abraham reasoned that God could raise the dead, and figuratively speaking, he did receive Isaac back from death.

f) Joshua

Josh 1 5"No one will be able to stand up against you all the days of your life. As I was with Moses, so I will be with you; I will never leave you nor forsake you.

6"Be strong and courageous, because you will lead these people to inherit the land I swore to their forefathers to give them."

Heb 4 8For if Joshua had given them rest, God would not have spoken later about another day. 9There remains, then, a Sabbath-rest for the people of God. . . .

g) Kinsman-Redeemer

Ruth 3 9"Who are you?" he asked.

"I am your servant Ruth," she said. "Spread the corner of your garment over me, since you are a kinsman-redeemer."

Ruth 4 14The women said to Naomi: "Praise be to the LORD, who this day has not left you without a kinsman-redeemer. May he become famous throughout Israel!"

Gal 3 13Christ redeemed us from the curse of the law by becoming a curse for us, for it is written: "Cursed is everyone who is hung on a tree."

h) Noah

Gen 5 29He named him Noah and said, "He will comfort us in the labor and painful toil of our hands caused by the ground the LORD has cursed."

2 Cor 1 5For just as the sufferings of Christ flow over into our lives, so also through Christ our comfort overflows.

2. Offices as Parallels to Christ

a) King

Matt 2 2and asked, "Where is the one who has been born king of the Jews? We saw his star in the east and have come to worship him."

Luke 1 32"He will be great and will be called the Son of the Most High. The LORD God will give him the throne of his father David, 33and he will reign over the house of Jacob forever; his kingdom will never end."

Rev 19 16On his robe and on his thigh he has this name written: KING OF KINGS AND LORD OF LORDS.

b) Priest

Heb 2 17For this reason he had to be made like his brothers in every way, in order that he might become a merciful and faithful high priest in service to God, and that he might make atonement for the sins of the people.

Heb 3 1Therefore, holy brothers, who share in the heavenly calling, fix your thoughts on Jesus, the apostle and high priest whom we confess.

Heb 5 6And he says in another place, "You are a priest forever, in the order of Melchizedek."

Heb 8 [1]The point of what we are saying is this: We do have such a high priest, who sat down at the right hand of the throne of the Majesty in heaven, [2]and who serves in the sanctuary, the true tabernacle set up by the Lord, not by man.
Heb 9 [7]But only the high priest entered the inner room, and that only once a year, and never without blood, which he offered for himself and for the sins the people had committed in ignorance. . . .

[11]When Christ came as high priest of the good things that are already here, he went through the greater and more perfect tabernacle that is not man-made, that is to say, not a part of this creation. [12]He did not enter by means of the blood of goats and calves; but he entered the Most Holy Place once for all by his own blood, having obtained eternal redemption. . . .

[24]For Christ did not enter a man-made sanctuary that was only a copy of the true one; he entered heaven itself, now to appear for us in God's presence.
Heb 10 [21]and since we have a great priest over the house of God . . .

c) Prophet

Deut 18 [15]The LORD your God will raise up for you a prophet like me from among your own brothers. You must listen to him.
Luke 24 [19]"What things?" he asked.

"About Jesus of Nazareth," they replied. "He was a prophet, powerful in word and deed before God and all the people."
Acts 3 [20]". . . and that he may send the Christ, who has been appointed for you—even Jesus. [21]He must remain in heaven until the time comes for God to restore everything, as he promised long ago through his holy prophets. [22]For Moses said, 'The Lord your God will raise up for you a prophet like me from among your own people; you must listen to everything he tells you.'"
Heb 1 [1]In the past God spoke to our forefathers through the prophets at many times and in various ways, [2]but in these last days he has spoken to us by his Son, whom he appointed heir of all things, and through whom he made the universe.
Rev 1 [5]and from Jesus Christ, who is the faithful witness, the firstborn from the dead, and the ruler of the kings of the earth.

To him who loves us and has freed us from our sins by his blood. . . .

3. Events as Parallels to Christ

a) Clothing of Adam and Eve

Gen 3 [21]The LORD God made garments of skin for Adam and his wife and clothed them.
Job 29 [14]"I put on righteousness as my clothing; justice was my robe and my turban."
Ps 132 [9]"May your priests be clothed with righteousness; may your saints sing for joy."
Isa 61 [10]I delight greatly in the LORD; my soul rejoices in my God. For he has clothed me with garments of salvation and arrayed me in a robe of righteousness, as a bridegroom adorns his head like a priest, and as a bride adorns herself with her jewels.
Rom 13 [14]Rather, clothe yourselves with the Lord Jesus Christ, and do not think about how to gratify the desires of the sinful nature.
Gal 3 [27]for all of you who were baptized into Christ have clothed yourselves with Christ.
Rev 19 [7]"Let us rejoice and be glad and give him glory! For the wedding of the Lamb has come, and his bride has made herself ready. [8]Fine linen, bright and clean, was given her to wear." (Fine linen stands for the righteous acts of the saints.)

b) Creation

Rom 8 [19]The creation waits in eager expectation for the sons of God to be revealed. [20]For the creation was subjected to frustration, not by its own choice, but by the will of the one who subjected it, in hope [21]that the creation itself will be liberated from its bondage to decay and brought into the glorious freedom of the children of God.
2 Cor 4 [6]For God, who said, "Let light shine out of darkness," made his light shine in our hearts to give us the light of the knowledge of the glory of God in the face of Christ.
2 Cor 5 [17]Therefore, if anyone is in Christ, he is a new creation; the old has gone, the new has come!
Gal 6 [15]Neither circumcision nor uncircumcision means anything; what counts is a new creation.
2 Pet 3 [13]But in keeping with his promise we are looking forward to a new heaven and a new earth, the home of righteousness.
Rev 22 [1]Then the angel showed me the river of the water of life, as clear as crystal, flowing from the throne of God and of the Lamb [2]down the middle of the great street of the city. On each side of the river stood the tree of life, bearing twelve crops of fruit, yielding its fruit every month. And the leaves of the tree are for the healing of the nations. [3]No longer will there be any curse. The throne of God and of the Lamb will be in the city, and his servants will serve him. [4]They will see his face, and his name will be on their foreheads. [5]There will be no more night. They will not need the light of a lamp or the light of the sun, for the Lord God will give them light. And they will reign for ever and ever.

c) Exodus

Matt 2 [14]So he got up, took the child and his mother during the night and left for Egypt, [15]where he stayed until the death of Herod. And so was fulfilled what the Lord had said through the prophet: "Out of Egypt I called my son."
1 Cor 10 [1]For I do not want you to be ignorant of the fact, brothers, that our forefathers were all under the cloud and that they all passed through the sea. [2]They were all baptized into Moses in the cloud and in the sea. [3]They all ate the same spiritual food [4]and drank the same spiritual drink; for they drank from the spiritual rock that accompanied them, and that rock was Christ. [5]Nevertheless, God was not pleased with most of them; their bodies were scattered over the desert.

[6]Now these things occurred as examples to keep us from setting our hearts on evil things as they did. [7]Do not be idolaters, as some of them were; as it is written: "The people sat down to eat and drink and got up to indulge in pagan revelry." [8]We should not commit sexual immorality, as some of them did—and in one day twenty-three thousand of them died. [9]We should not test the Lord, as some of them did—and were killed by snakes. [10]And do not grumble, as some of them did—and were killed by the destroying angel.

[11]These things happened to them as examples and were written down as warnings for us, on whom the fulfillment of the ages has come.
Heb 3 [7]So, as the Holy Spirit says: "Today, if you hear his voice, [8]do not harden your hearts as you did in the rebellion, during the time of testing in the desert, [9]where your fathers tested and tried me and for forty years saw what I did. [10]That is why I was angry with that generation, and I said, 'Their hearts are always going astray, and they have not known my ways.' [11]So I declared on oath in my anger, 'They shall never enter my rest.'"

[12]See to it, brothers, that none of you has a sinful, unbelieving heart that turns away from the living God. [13]But encourage one another daily, as long as it is called Today, so that none of you may be hardened by sin's deceitfulness. [14]We have come to share in Christ if we hold firmly till the end the confidence we had at first. [15]As has just been said: "Today, if you hear his voice, do not harden your hearts as you did in the rebellion."

[16]Who were they who heard and rebelled? Were they not all those Moses led out of Egypt? [17]And with whom was he angry for forty years? Was it not with those who sinned, whose bodies fell in the desert? [18]And to whom did God swear that they would never enter his rest if not to those who disobeyed? [19]So we see that they were not able to enter, because of their unbelief.
Jude [4]For certain men whose condemnation was written about long ago have secretly slipped in among you. They are godless men, who change the grace of our God into a license for immorality and deny Jesus Christ our only Sovereign and Lord.

[5]Though you already know all this, I want to remind you

that the Lord delivered his people out of Egypt, but later destroyed those who did not believe.

d) Flood

1 Pet 3 [18]For Christ died for sins once for all, the righteous for the unrighteous, to bring you to God. He was put to death in the body but made alive by the Spirit, [19]through whom also he went and preached to the spirits in prison [20]who disobeyed long ago when God waited patiently in the days of Noah while the ark was being built. In it only a few people, eight in all, were saved through water, [21]and this water symbolizes baptism that now saves you also—not the removal of dirt from the body but the pledge of a good conscience toward God. It saves you by the resurrection of Jesus Christ, [22]who has gone into heaven and is at God's right hand—with angels, authorities and powers in submission to him.

e) Wilderness Wanderings

Heb 4 [1]Therefore, since the promise of entering his rest still stands, let us be careful that none of you be found to have fallen short of it. [2]For we also have had the gospel preached to us, just as they did; but the message they heard was of no value to them, because those who heard did not combine it with faith. [3]Now we who have believed enter that rest, just as God has said, "So I declared on oath in my anger, 'They shall never enter my rest.'" And yet his work has been finished since the creation of the world. [4]For somewhere he has spoken about the seventh day in these words: "And on the seventh day God rested from all his work." [5]And again in the passage above he says, "They shall never enter my rest."

[6]It still remains that some will enter that rest, and those who formerly had the gospel preached to them did not go in, because of their disobedience. [7]Therefore God again set a certain day, calling it Today, when a long time later he spoke through David, as was said before: "Today, if you hear his voice, do not harden your hearts." [8]For if Joshua had given them rest, God would not have spoken later about another day. [9]There remains, then, a Sabbath-rest for the people of God; [10]for anyone who enters God's rest also rests from his own work, just as God did from his. [11]Let us, therefore, make every effort to enter that rest, so that no one will fall by following their example of disobedience.

4. Objects as Parallels to Christ

a) Ark

Gen 7 [13]On that very day Noah and his sons, Shem, Ham and Japheth, together with his wife and the wives of his three sons, entered the ark. . . . [15]Pairs of all creatures that have the breath of life in them came to Noah and entered the ark. [16]The animals going in were male and female of every living thing, as God had commanded Noah. Then the LORD shut him in.

1 Pet 3 [20]who disobeyed long ago when God waited patiently in the days of Noah while the ark was being built. In it only a few people, eight in all, were saved through water, [21]and this water symbolizes baptism that now saves you also—not the removal of dirt from the body but the pledge of a good conscience toward God. It saves you by the resurrection of Jesus Christ. . . .

b) Cities of Refuge

Num 35 [6]"Six of the towns you give the Levites will be cities of refuge, to which a person who has killed someone may flee. In addition, give them forty-two other towns."

Matt 11 [28]"Come to me, all you who are weary and burdened, and I will give you rest."

Heb 6 [18]God did this so that, by two unchangeable things in which it is impossible for God to lie, we who have fled to take hold of the hope offered to us may be greatly encouraged.

1 Pet 5 [7]Cast all your anxiety on him because he cares for you.

c) Jacob's Ladder

Gen 28 [12]He had a dream in which he saw a stairway resting on the earth, with its top reaching to heaven, and the angels of God were ascending and descending on it.

John 1 [51]He then added, "I tell you the truth, you shall see heaven open, and the angels of God ascending and descending on the Son of Man."

d) Tree of Life

Gen 2 [9]And the LORD God made all kinds of trees grow out of the ground—trees that were pleasing to the eye and good for food. In the middle of the garden were the tree of life and the tree of the knowledge of good and evil.

John 1 [4]In him was life, and that life was the light of men.

Rev 22 [1]Then the angel showed me the river of the water of life, as clear as crystal, flowing from the throne of God and of the Lamb [2]down the middle of the great street of the city. On each side of the river stood the tree of life, bearing twelve crops of fruit, yielding its fruit every month. And the leaves of the tree are for the healing of the nations.

5. Levitical Cultus as Parallel to Christ

a) Place of Worship

(1) Tabernacle

Exod 40 [2]"Set up the tabernacle, the Tent of Meeting, on the first day of the first month." . . .

[34]Then the cloud covered the Tent of Meeting, and the glory of the LORD filled the tabernacle.

Col 2 [9]For in Christ all the fullness of the Deity lives in bodily form. . . .

Heb 9 [11]When Christ came as high priest of the good things that are already here, he went through the greater and more perfect tabernacle that is not man-made, that is to say, not a part of this creation.

(2) Temple

1 Kings 6 [1]In the four hundred and eightieth year after the Israelites had come out of Egypt, in the fourth year of Solomon's reign over Israel, in the month of Ziv, the second month, he began to build the temple of the LORD. . . . [38]In the eleventh year in the month of Bul, the eighth month, the temple was finished in all its details according to its specifications. He had spent seven years building it.

John 2 [19]Jesus answered them, "Destroy this temple, and I will raise it again in three days." . . .

[21]But the temple he had spoken of was his body.

b) Furniture

(1) Bronze Basin

Exod 30 [18]"Make a bronze basin, with its bronze stand, for washing. Place it between the Tent of Meeting and the altar, and put water in it. [19]Aaron and his sons are to wash their hands and feet with water from it. [20]Whenever they enter the Tent of Meeting, they shall wash with water so that they will not die. Also, when they approach the altar to minister by presenting an offering made to the LORD by fire . . ."

Zech 13 [1]"On that day a fountain will be opened to the house of David and the inhabitants of Jerusalem, to cleanse them from sin and impurity."

Eph 5 [26]to make her holy, cleansing her by the washing with water through the word, [27]and to present her to himself as a radiant church, without stain or wrinkle or any other blemish, but holy and blameless.

(2) Golden Altar

Exod 40 [5]"Place the gold altar of incense in front of the ark of the Testimony and put the curtain at the entrance to the tabernacle. . . ."

[26]Moses placed the gold altar in the Tent of Meeting in front of the curtain [27]and burned fragrant incense on it, as the LORD commanded him.

Heb 13 [15]Through Jesus, therefore, let us continually offer to God a sacrifice of praise—the fruit of lips that confess his name.

Rev 8 [3]Another angel, who had a golden censer, came and stood at the altar. He was given much incense to offer, with the prayers of all the saints, on the golden altar before the throne.

(3) Golden Candlestick

Exod 25 [31]"Make a lampstand of pure gold and hammer it out, base and shaft; its flowerlike cups, buds and blossoms shall be of one piece with it."

John 8 12When Jesus spoke again to the people, he said, "I am the light of the world. Whoever follows me will never walk in darkness, but will have the light of life."

(4) Mercy Seat

Exod 25 17"Make an atonement cover of pure gold—two and a half cubits long and a cubit and a half wide. 18And make two cherubim out of hammered gold at the ends of the cover. 19Make one cherub on one end and the second cherub on the other; make the cherubim of one piece with the cover, at the two ends. 20The cherubim are to have their wings spread upward, overshadowing the cover with them. The cherubim are to face each other, looking toward the cover. 21Place the cover on top of the ark and put in the ark the Testimony, which I will give you. 22There, above the cover between the two cherubim that are over the ark of the Testimony, I will meet with you and give you all my commands for the Israelites."

Rom 3 25God presented him as a sacrifice of atonement, through faith in his blood. He did this to demonstrate his justice, because in his forbearance he had left the sins committed beforehand unpunished. . . .

Heb 4 16Let us then approach the throne of grace with confidence, so that we may receive mercy and find grace to help us in our time of need.

(5) Table and Bread of the Presence

Exod 25 23"Make a table of acacia wood—two cubits long, a cubit wide and a cubit and a half high. 24Overlay it with pure gold and make a gold molding around it. 25Also make around it a rim a handbreadth wide and put a gold molding on the rim. 26Make four gold rings for the table and fasten them to the four corners, where the four legs are. 27The rings are to be close to the rim to hold the poles used in carrying the table. 28Make the poles of acacia wood, overlay them with gold and carry the table with them. 29And make its plates and dishes of pure gold, as well as its pitchers and bowls for the pouring out of offerings. 30Put the bread of the Presence on this table to be before me at all times."

John 1 16From the fullness of his grace we have all received one blessing after another.

John 6 48"I am the bread of life."

c) Objects for Sacrifice

(1) Incense

Lev 16 12"He is to take a censer full of burning coals from the altar before the LORD and two handfuls of finely ground fragrant incense and take them behind the curtain. 13He is to put the incense on the fire before the LORD, and the smoke of the incense will conceal the atonement cover above the Testimony, so that he will not die."

Ps 141 2May my prayer be set before you like incense; may the lifting up of my hands be like the evening sacrifice.

John 17 9"I pray for them. I am not praying for the world, but for those you have given me, for they are yours."

(2) Red Heifer

Num 19 2"This is a requirement of the law that the LORD has commanded: Tell the Israelites to bring you a red heifer without defect or blemish and that has never been under a yoke. 3Give it to Eleazar the priest; it is to be taken outside the camp and slaughtered in his presence. 4Then Eleazar the priest is to take some of its blood on his finger and sprinkle it seven times toward the front of the Tent of Meeting. 5While he watches, the heifer is to be burned—its hide, flesh, blood and offal. 6The priest is to take some cedar wood, hyssop and scarlet wool and throw them onto the burning heifer. . . .

9"A man who is clean shall gather up the ashes of the heifer and put them in a ceremonially clean place outside the camp. They shall be kept by the Israelite community for use in the water of cleansing; it is for purification from sin."

Heb 9 13The blood of goats and bulls and the ashes of a heifer sprinkled on those who are ceremonially unclean sanctify them so that they are outwardly clean. 14How much more, then, will the blood of Christ, who through the eternal Spirit offered himself unblemished to God, cleanse our consciences from acts that lead to death, so that we may serve the living God!

(3) Scapegoat

Lev 16 20"When Aaron has finished making atonement for the Most Holy Place, the Tent of Meeting and the altar, he shall bring forward the live goat. 21He is to lay both hands on the head of the live goat and confess over it all the wickedness and rebellion of the Israelites—all their sins—and put them on the goat's head. He shall send the goat away into the desert in the care of a man appointed for the task. 22The goat will carry on itself all their sins to a solitary place; and the man shall release it in the desert."

Isa 53 6We all, like sheep, have gone astray, each of us has turned to his own way; and the LORD has laid on him the iniquity of us all. . . . 12Therefore I will give him a portion among the great, and he will divide the spoils with the strong, because he poured out his life unto death, and was numbered with the transgressors. For he bore the sin of many, and made intercession for the transgressors.

Heb 10 4because it is impossible for the blood of bulls and goats to take away sins.

5Therefore, when Christ came into the world, he said: "Sacrifice and offering you did not desire, but a body you prepared for me; 6with burnt offerings and sin offerings you were not pleased."

d) Kinds of Offering

(1) Atonement

Lev 16 15"He shall then slaughter the goat for the sin offering for the people and take its blood behind the curtain and do with it as he did with the bull's blood: He shall sprinkle it on the atonement cover and in front of it. 16In this way he will make atonement for the Most Holy Place because of the uncleanness and rebellion of the Israelites, whatever their sins have been. He is to do the same for the Tent of Meeting, which is among them in the midst of their uncleanness."

Heb 9 12He did not enter by means of the blood of goats and calves; but he entered the Most Holy Place once for all by his own blood, having obtained eternal redemption. . . . 24For Christ did not enter a man-made sanctuary that was only a copy of the true one; he entered heaven itself, now to appear for us in God's presence.

(2) Burnt

Lev 1 2"Speak to the Israelites and say to them: 'When any of you brings an offering to the LORD, bring as your offering an animal from either the herd or the flock. . . . 4He is to lay his hand on the head of the burnt offering, and it will be accepted on his behalf to make atonement for him.'"

Heb 10 8First he said, "Sacrifices and offerings, burnt offerings and sin offerings you did not desire, nor were you pleased with them" (although the law required them to be made). 9Then he said, "Here I am, I have come to do your will." He sets aside the first to establish the second. 10And by that will, we have been made holy through the sacrifice of the body of Jesus Christ once for all.

(3) Peace

Lev 3 1"'If someone's offering is a fellowship offering, and he offers an animal from the herd, whether male or female, he is to present before the LORD an animal without defect.'"

Eph 2 14For he himself is our peace, who has made the two one and has destroyed the barrier, the dividing wall of hostility, 15by abolishing in his flesh the law with its commandments and regulations. His purpose was to create in himself one new man out of the two, thus making peace, 16and in this one body to reconcile both of them to God through the cross, by which he put to death their hostility.

(4) Sin

Lev 4 2"Say to the Israelites: 'When anyone sins unintentionally and does what is forbidden in any of the LORD's commands—

3"'If the anointed priest sins, bringing guilt on the people, he must bring to the LORD a young bull without defect as a sin offering for the sin he has committed. 12 . . . that is, all the rest of the bull—he must take outside the camp to a place ceremonially clean, where the ashes are thrown, and burn it in a wood fire on the ash heap.'"

Heb 13 11The high priest carries the blood of animals into the Most Holy Place as a sin offering, but the bodies are burned outside the camp. 12And so Jesus also suffered outside the city gate to make the people holy through his own blood.

(5) Trespass (Guilt)

Lev 6 [1]The LORD said to Moses: [2]"If anyone sins and is unfaithful to the LORD by deceiving his neighbor about something entrusted to him or left in his care or stolen, or if he cheats him, [3]or if he finds lost property and lies about it, or if he swears falsely, or if he commits any such sin that people may do—[4]when he thus sins and becomes guilty, he must return what he has stolen or taken by extortion, or what was entrusted to him, or the lost property he found, [5]or whatever it was he swore falsely about. He must make restitution in full, add a fifth of the value to it and give it all to the owner on the day he presents his guilt offering. [6]And as a penalty he must bring to the priest, that is, to the LORD, his guilt offering, a ram from the flock, one without defect and of the proper value. [7]In this way the priest will make atonement for him before the LORD, and he will be forgiven for any of these things he did that made him guilty."

Isa 53 [10]Yet it was the LORD's will to crush him and cause him to suffer, and though the LORD makes his life a guilt offering, he will see his offspring and prolong his days, and the will of the LORD will prosper in his hand.

e) Feasts

(1) Day of Atonement

Exod 30 [10]"Once a year Aaron shall make atonement on its horns. This annual atonement must be made with the blood of the atoning sin offering for the generations to come. It is most holy to the LORD."

Lev 23 [26]The LORD said to Moses, [27]"The tenth day of this seventh month is the Day of Atonement. Hold a sacred assembly and deny yourselves, and present an offering made to the LORD by fire. [28]Do no work on that day, because it is the Day of Atonement, when atonement is made for you before the LORD your God. [29]Anyone who does not deny himself on that day must be cut off from his people. [30]I will destroy from among his people anyone who does any work on that day. [31]You shall do no work at all. This is to be a lasting ordinance for the generations to come, wherever you live. [32]It is a sabbath of rest for you, and you must deny yourselves. From the evening of the ninth day of the month until the following evening you are to observe your sabbath."

Rom 3 [25]God presented him as a sacrifice of atonement, through faith in his blood. He did this to demonstrate his justice, because in his forbearance he had left the sins committed beforehand unpunished. . . .

Rom 11 [26]And so all Israel will be saved, as it is written: "The deliverer will come from Zion; he will turn godlessness away from Jacob. [27]And this is my covenant with them when I take away their sins."

(2) Day of Firstfruits

Exod 23 [16]"Celebrate the Feast of Harvest with the firstfruits of the crops you sow in your field.

"Celebrate the Feast of Ingathering at the end of the year, when you gather in your crops from the field."

Num 28 [26]"'On the day of firstfruits, when you present to the LORD an offering of new grain during the Feast of Weeks, hold a sacred assembly and do no regular work.'"

1 Cor 15 [20]But Christ has indeed been raised from the dead, the firstfruits of those who have fallen asleep. [21]For since death came through a man, the resurrection of the dead comes also through a man. [22]For as in Adam all die, so in Christ all will be made alive. [23]But each in his own turn: Christ, the firstfruits; then, when he comes, those who belong to him.

(3) Day of Sounding Trumpets

Lev 23 [24]"Say to the Israelites: 'On the first day of the seventh month you are to have a day of rest, a sacred assembly commemorated with trumpet blasts.'"

Num 29 [1]"'On the first day of the seventh month hold a sacred assembly and do no regular work. It is a day for you to sound the trumpets.'"

Matt 24 [31]"And he will send his angels with a loud trumpet call, and they will gather his elect from the four winds, from one end of the heavens to the other."

(4) Passover

Exod 12 [3]"Tell the whole community of Israel that on the tenth day of this month each man is to take a lamb for his family, one for each household. . . . [5]The animals you choose must be year-old males without defect, and you may take them from the sheep or the goats. [6]Take care of them until the fourteenth day of the month, when all the people of the community of Israel must slaughter them at twilight. [7]Then they are to take some of the blood and put it on the sides and tops of the doorframes of the houses where they eat the lambs. [8]That same night they are to eat the meat roasted over the fire, along with bitter herbs, and bread made without yeast. . . . [11]This is how you are to eat it: with your cloak tucked into your belt, your sandals on your feet and your staff in your hand. Eat it in haste; it is the LORD's Passover. . . .

[14]"This is a day you are to commemorate; for the generations to come you shall celebrate it as a festival to the LORD—a lasting ordinance."

Lev 23 [5]"The LORD's Passover begins at twilight on the fourteenth day of the first month."

1 Cor 5 [7]Get rid of the old yeast that you may be a new batch without yeast—as you really are. For Christ, our Passover lamb, has been sacrificed.

(5) Tabernacles

Lev 23 [34]"Say to the Israelites: 'On the fifteenth day of the seventh month the LORD's Feast of Tabernacles begins, and it lasts for seven days. [35]The first day is a sacred assembly; do no regular work. [36]For seven days present offerings made to the LORD by fire, and on the eighth day hold a sacred assembly and present an offering made to the LORD by fire. It is the closing assembly; do no regular work.'"

Zech 14 [16]Then the survivors from all the nations that have attacked Jerusalem will go up year after year to worship the King, the LORD Almighty, and to celebrate the Feast of Tabernacles. [17]If any of the peoples of the earth do not go up to Jerusalem to worship the King, the LORD Almighty, they will have no rain. [18]If the Egyptian people do not go up and take part, they will have no rain. The LORD will bring on them the plague he inflicts on the nations that do not go up to celebrate the Feast of Tabernacles. [19]This will be the punishment of Egypt and the punishment of all the nations that do not go up to celebrate the Feast of Tabernacles.

[20]On that day HOLY TO THE LORD will be inscribed on the bells of the horses, and the cooking pots in the LORD's house will be like the sacred bowls in front of the altar. [21]Every pot in Jerusalem and Judah will be holy to the LORD Almighty, and all who come to sacrifice will take some of the pots and cook in them. And on that day there will no longer be a Canaanite in the house of the LORD Almighty.

John 1 [14]The Word became flesh and made his dwelling among us. We have seen his glory, the glory of the One and Only, who came from the Father, full of grace and truth.

II
Prophecies concerning Christ

A. Christological Prophecies and Fulfillments

1. Circumstances and Events Related to Christ's Birth

a) Christ to Be a Human Being

(1) Prophecy

Gen 3 [15]"And I will put enmity between you and the woman, and between your offspring and hers; he will crush your head, and you will strike his heel."

(2) Fulfillment

Gal 4 [4]But when the time had fully come, God sent his Son, born of a woman, born under law. . . .

b) Christ to Be Incarnate God

(1) Prophecy

Ps 2 [7]I will proclaim the decree of the LORD: He said to me, "You are my Son; today I have become your Father."

Ps 110 [1]The LORD says to my Lord: "Sit at my right hand until I make your enemies a footstool for your feet."

Isa 9 [6]For to us a child is born, to us a son is given, and the government will be on his shoulders. And he will be called Wonderful Counselor, Mighty God, Everlasting Father, Prince of Peace. [7]Of the increase of his government and peace there will be no end. He will reign on David's throne and over his kingdom, establishing and upholding it with justice and righteousness from that time on and forever. The zeal of the LORD Almighty will accomplish this.

Mic 5 [2]"But you, Bethlehem Ephrathah, though you are small among the clans of Judah, out of you will come for me one who will be ruler over Israel, whose origins are from of old, from ancient times."

(2) Fulfillment

Matt 1 [23]"The virgin will be with child and will give birth to a son, and they will call him Immanuel"—which means, "God with us."

John 1 [14]The Word became flesh and made his dwelling among us. We have seen his glory, the glory of the One and Only, who came from the Father, full of grace and truth.

Rom 9 [5]Theirs are the patriarchs, and from them is traced the human ancestry of Christ, who is God over all, forever praised! Amen.

Heb 1 [8]But about the Son he says, "Your throne, O God, will last for ever and ever, and righteousness will be the scepter of your kingdom."

c) Christ to Be a Descendant of Abraham

(1) Prophecy

Gen 12 [3]"I will bless those who bless you, and whoever curses you I will curse; and all peoples on earth will be blessed through you."

Gen 18 [18]"Abraham will surely become a great and powerful nation, and all nations on earth will be blessed through him."

Gen 22 [18]". . . and through your offspring all nations on earth will be blessed, because you have obeyed me."

(2) Fulfillment

Acts 3 [25]"And you are heirs of the prophets and of the covenant God made with your fathers. He said to Abraham, 'Through your offspring all peoples on earth will be blessed.'"

Gal 3 [8]The Scripture foresaw that God would justify the Gentiles by faith, and announced the gospel in advance to Abraham: "All nations will be blessed through you." . . . [16]The promises were spoken to Abraham and to his seed. The Scripture does not say "and to seeds," meaning many people, but "and to your seed," meaning one person, who is Christ.

d) Christ to Be a Descendant of Isaac

(1) Prophecy

Gen 21 [12]But God said to him, "Do not be so distressed about the boy and your maidservant. Listen to whatever Sarah tells you, because it is through Isaac that your offspring will be reckoned."

Gen 26 [2]The LORD appeared to Isaac and said, "Do not go down to Egypt; live in the land where I tell you to live. . . . [4]I will make your descendants as numerous as the stars in the sky and will give them all these lands, and through your offspring all nations on earth will be blessed. . . ."

(2) Fulfillment

Gal 3 [16]The promises were spoken to Abraham and to his seed. The Scripture does not say "and to seeds," meaning many people, but "and to your seed," meaning one person, who is Christ.

e) Christ to Be a Descendant of Jacob

(1) Prophecy

Gen 28 [13]There above it stood the LORD, and he said: "I am the LORD, the God of your father Abraham and the God of Isaac. I will give you and your descendants the land on which you are lying. [14]Your descendants will be like the dust of the earth, and you will spread out to the west and to the east, to the north and to the south. All peoples on earth will be blessed through you and your offspring."

(2) Fulfillment

Matt 1 [2]Abraham was the father of Isaac, Isaac the father of Jacob, Jacob the father of Judah and his brothers . . . [16]and Jacob the father of Joseph, the husband of Mary, of whom was born Jesus, who is called Christ.

Luke 3 [23]Now Jesus himself was about thirty years old when he began his ministry. He was the son, so it was thought, of Joseph, the son of Heli . . . [34]the son of Jacob, the son of Isaac, the son of Abraham, the son of Terah, the son of Nahor. . . .

f) Christ to Be a Descendant of Judah

(1) Prophecy

Gen 49 [10]"The scepter will not depart from Judah, nor the ruler's staff from between his feet, until he comes to whom it belongs and the obedience of the nations is his."

(2) Fulfillment

Heb 7 [14]For it is clear that our Lord descended from Judah, and in regard to that tribe Moses said nothing about priests.

g) Christ to Be a Descendant of Jesse

(1) Prophecy

Isa 11 [1]A shoot will come up from the stump of Jesse; from his roots a Branch will bear fruit. . . . [10]In that day the Root of Jesse will stand as a banner for the peoples; the nations will rally to him, and his place of rest will be glorious.

(2) Fulfillment

Rom 15 [12]And again, Isaiah says, "The Root of Jesse will spring up, one who will arise to rule over the nations; the Gentiles will hope in him."

h) Christ to Be a Descendant of David

(1) Prophecy

2 Sam 7 [12]"'When your days are over and you rest with your fathers, I will raise up your offspring to succeed you, who will come from your own body, and I will establish his kingdom. [13]He is the one who will build a house for my Name, and I will establish the throne of his kingdom forever. . . . [16]Your house and your kingdom will endure forever before me; your throne will be established forever.'"

Ps 89 [3]You said, "I have made a covenant with my chosen one, I have sworn to David my servant, [4]'I will establish your line forever and make your throne firm through all generations.'"

Ps 89 [20]"I have found David my servant; with my sacred oil I have anointed him. . . . [27]I will also appoint him my firstborn, the most exalted of the kings of the earth. [28]I will maintain my love to him forever, and my covenant with him will never fail. [29]I will establish his line forever, his throne as long as the heavens endure."

Ps 132 [11]The LORD swore an oath to David, a sure oath that he will not revoke: "One of your own descendants I will place on your throne. . . ."

Jer 23 [5]"The days are coming," declares the LORD, "when I will raise up to David a righteous Branch, a King who will reign wisely and do what is just and right in the land."

Jer 33 [14]"'The days are coming,' declares the LORD, 'when I will fulfill the gracious promise I made to the house of Israel and to the house of Judah. [15]In those days and at that time I will make a righteous Branch sprout from David's line; he will do what is just and right in the land.'"

(2) Fulfillment

Matt 21 [9]The crowds that went ahead of him and those that followed shouted, "Hosanna to the Son of David!" "Blessed is he who comes in the name of the Lord!" "Hosanna in the highest!"

Matt 22 [42]"What do you think about the Christ? Whose son is he?"

"The son of David," they replied.

John 7 [42]"Does not the Scripture say that the Christ will come from David's family and from Bethlehem, the town where David lived?"

Acts 13 [22]"After removing Saul, he made David their king. He testified concerning him: 'I have found David son of Jesse a man after my own heart; he will do everything I want him to do.'

[23]"From this man's descendants God has brought to Israel the Savior Jesus, as he promised."
Rom 1 [3]regarding his Son, who as to his human nature was a descendant of David . . .

i) The Time of Christ's Coming

(1) Prophecy

Gen 49 [10]"The scepter will not depart from Judah, nor the ruler's staff from between his feet, until he comes to whom it belongs and the obedience of the nations is his."
Dan 9 [24]"Seventy 'sevens' are decreed for your people and your holy city to finish transgression, to put an end to sin, to atone for wickedness, to bring in everlasting righteousness, to seal up vision and prophecy and to anoint the most holy.

[25]"Know and understand this: From the issuing of the decree to restore and rebuild Jerusalem until the Anointed One, the ruler, comes, there will be seven 'sevens,' and sixty-two 'sevens.' It will be rebuilt with streets and a trench, but in times of trouble."
Hag 2 [6]"This is what the LORD Almighty says: 'In a little while I will once more shake the heavens and the earth, the sea and the dry land. [7]I will shake all nations, and the desired of all nations will come, and I will fill this house with glory,' says the LORD Almighty. [8]'The silver is mine and the gold is mine,' declares the LORD Almighty. [9]'The glory of this present house will be greater than the glory of the former house,' says the LORD Almighty. 'And in this place I will grant peace,' declares the LORD Almighty."

(2) Fulfillment

Matt 1 [20]But after he had considered this, an angel of the Lord appeared to him in a dream and said, "Joseph son of David, do not be afraid to take Mary home as your wife, because what is conceived in her is from the Holy Spirit. [21]She will give birth to a son, and you are to give him the name Jesus, because he will save his people from their sins."
Luke 2 [3]And everyone went to his own town to register. [4]So Joseph also went up from the town of Nazareth in Galilee to Judea, to Bethlehem the town of David, because he belonged to the house and line of David. [5]He went there to register with Mary, who was pledged to be married to him and was expecting a child.
Heb 12 [25]See to it that you do not refuse him who speaks. If they did not escape when they refused him who warned them on earth, how much less will we, if we turn away from him who warns us from heaven? [26]At that time his voice shook the earth, but now he has promised, "Once more I will shake not only the earth but also the heavens." [27]The words "once more" indicate the removing of what can be shaken—that is, created things—so that what cannot be shaken may remain.

[28]Therefore, since we are receiving a kingdom that cannot be shaken, let us be thankful, and so worship God acceptably with reverence and awe, [29]for our "God is a consuming fire."

j) Christ to Be Born of a Virgin

(1) Prophecy

Isa 7 [14]"Therefore the Lord himself will give you a sign: The virgin will be with child and will give birth to a son, and will call him Immanuel."

(2) Fulfillment

Matt 1 [22]All this took place to fulfill what the Lord had said through the prophet: [23]"The virgin will be with child and will give birth to a son, and they will call him Immanuel"—which means, "God with us."

[24]When Joseph woke up, he did what the angel of the Lord had commanded him and took Mary home as his wife. [25]But he had no union with her until she gave birth to a son. And he gave him the name Jesus.

k) Christ to Be Born in Bethlehem

(1) Prophecy

Mic 5 [2]"But you, Bethlehem Ephrathah, though you are small among the clans of Judah, out of you will come for me one who will be ruler over Israel, whose origins are from of old, from ancient times."

(2) Fulfillment

Matt 2 [1]After Jesus was born in Bethlehem in Judea, during the time of King Herod, Magi from the east came to Jerusalem. . . .
Luke 2 [4]So Joseph also went up from the town of Nazareth in Galilee to Judea, to Bethlehem the town of David, because he belonged to the house and line of David. [5]He went there to register with Mary, who was pledged to be married to him and was expecting a child. [6]While they were there, the time came for the baby to be born, [7]and she gave birth to her firstborn, a son. She wrapped him in cloths and placed him in a manger, because there was no room for them in the inn.
John 7 [42]"Does not the Scripture say that the Christ will come from David's family and from Bethlehem, the town where David lived?"

l) Infant Jesus to Be Taken to Egypt

(1) Prophecy

Hos 11 [1]"When Israel was a child, I loved him, and out of Egypt I called my son."

(2) Fulfillment

Matt 2 [14]So he got up, took the child and his mother during the night and left for Egypt, [15]where he stayed until the death of Herod. And so was fulfilled what the LORD had said through the prophet: "Out of Egypt I called my son."

m) Herod's Killing of the Infants

(1) Prophecy

Jer 31 [15]This is what the LORD says: "A voice is heard in Ramah, mourning and great weeping, Rachel weeping for her children and refusing to be comforted, because her children are no more."

(2) Fulfillment

Matt 2 [16]When Herod realized that he had been outwitted by the Magi, he was furious, and he gave orders to kill all the boys in Bethlehem and its vicinity who were two years old and under, in accordance with the time he had learned from the Magi. [17]Then what was said through the prophet Jeremiah was fulfilled:

[18]"A voice is heard in Ramah, weeping and great mourning, Rachel weeping for her children and refusing to be comforted, because they are no more."

n) Jesus Would Grow up in Nazareth

(1) Prophecy

Judg 13 [3]The angel of the LORD appeared to her and said, "You are sterile and childless, but you are going to conceive and have a son. [5]. . . because you will conceive and give birth to a son. No razor may be used on his head, because the boy is to be a Nazirite, set apart to God from birth, and he will begin the deliverance of Israel from the hands of the Philistines."
Isa 11 [1]A shoot will come up from the stump of Jesse; from his roots a Branch will bear fruit.
Isa 53 [2]He grew up before him like a tender shoot, and like a root out of dry ground. He had no beauty or majesty to attract us to him, nothing in his appearance that we should desire him.

(2) Fulfillment

Matt 2 [21]So he got up, took the child and his mother and went to the land of Israel. [22]But when he heard that Archelaus was reigning in Judea in place of his father Herod, he was afraid to go there. Having been warned in a dream, he withdrew to the district of Galilee, [23]and he went and lived in a town called Nazareth. So was fulfilled what was said through the prophets: "He will be called a Nazarene."

2. John the Baptist, a Forerunner in the Spirit of Elijah

a) Prophecy

Isa 40 [3]A voice of one calling: "In the desert prepare the way for the LORD; make straight in the wilderness a highway for our God. [4]Every valley shall be raised up, every mountain and hill made low; the rough ground shall become level, the rugged places a plain. [5]And the glory of the LORD will be revealed, and

all mankind together will see it. For the mouth of the LORD has spoken."
Mal 3 [1]"See, I will send my messenger, who will prepare the way before me. Then suddenly the Lord you are seeking will come to his temple; the messenger of the covenant, whom you desire, will come," says the LORD Almighty.
Mal 4 [5]"See, I will send you the prophet Elijah before that great and dreadful day of the LORD comes."

b) Fulfillment

Matt 3 [1]In those days John the Baptist came, preaching in the Desert of Judea [2]and saying, "Repent, for the kingdom of heaven is near."
Matt 11 [11]"I tell you the truth: Among those born of women there has not risen anyone greater than John the Baptist; yet he who is least in the kingdom of heaven is greater than he. [12]From the days of John the Baptist until now, the kingdom of heaven has been forcefully advancing, and forceful men lay hold of it. [13]For all the Prophets and the Law prophesied until John. [14]And if you are willing to accept it, he is the Elijah who was to come."
Mark 9 [13]"But I tell you, Elijah has come, and they have done to him everything they wished, just as it is written about him."
Luke 1 [17]"And he will go on before the Lord, in the spirit and power of Elijah, to turn the hearts of the fathers to their children and the disobedient to the wisdom of the righteous—to make ready a people prepared for the Lord."

3. Circumstances and Events Related to Christ's Ministry

a) Christ to Be a Prophet

(1) Prophecy

Deut 18 [15]The LORD your God will raise up for you a prophet like me from among your own brothers. You must listen to him. . . .

[17]The LORD said to me: "What they say is good. [18]I will raise up for them a prophet like you from among their brothers; I will put my words in his mouth, and he will tell them everything I command him. [19]If anyone does not listen to my words that the prophet speaks in my name, I myself will call him to account."

(2) Fulfillment

Matt 21 [11]The crowds answered, "This is Jesus, the prophet from Nazareth in Galilee."
Luke 24 [19]"What things?" he asked.

"About Jesus of Nazareth," they replied. "He was a prophet, powerful in word and deed before God and all the people."
John 4 [19]"Sir," the woman said, "I can see that you are a prophet."
Acts 3 [22]"For Moses said, 'The Lord your God will raise up for you a prophet like me from among your own people; you must listen to everything he tells you.'"
Acts 7 [37]"This is that Moses who told the Israelites, 'God will send you a prophet like me from your own people.'"

b) Christ to Be the Servant of God

(1) Prophecy

Isa 42 [1]"Here is my servant, whom I uphold, my chosen one in whom I delight; I will put my Spirit on him and he will bring justice to the nations. [2]He will not shout or cry out, or raise his voice in the streets. [3]A bruised reed he will not break, and a smoldering wick he will not snuff out. In faithfulness he will bring forth justice; [4]he will not falter or be discouraged till he establishes justice on earth. In his law the islands will put their hope."

(2) Fulfillment

Matt 12 [15]Aware of this, Jesus withdrew from that place. Many followed him, and he healed all their sick, [16]warning them not to tell who he was. [17]This was to fulfill what was spoken through the prophet Isaiah: [18]"Here is my servant whom I have chosen, the one I love, in whom I delight; I will put my Spirit on him, and he will proclaim justice to the nations. [19]He will not quarrel or cry out; no one will hear his voice in the streets. [20]A bruised reed he will not break, and a smoldering wick he will not snuff out, till he leads justice to victory. [21]In his name the nations will put their hope."

c) Christ to Be the Messiah

(1) Prophecy

Ps 2 [2]The kings of the earth take their stand and the rulers gather together against the LORD and against his Anointed One.
Dan 9 [24]"Seventy 'sevens' are decreed for your people and your holy city to finish transgression, to put an end to sin, to atone for wickedness, to bring in everlasting righteousness, to seal up vision and prophecy and to anoint the most holy.

[25]"Know and understand this: From the issuing of the decree to restore and rebuild Jerusalem until the Anointed One, the ruler, comes, there will be seven 'sevens,' and sixty-two 'sevens.' It will be rebuilt with streets and a trench, but in times of trouble."

(2) Fulfillment

Mark 8 [27]Jesus and his disciples went on to the villages around Caesarea Philippi. On the way he asked them, "Who do people say I am?"

[28]They replied, "Some say John the Baptist; others say Elijah; and still others, one of the prophets."

[29]"But what about you?" he asked. "Who do you say I am?"

Peter answered, "You are the Christ."
Acts 2 [36]"Therefore let all Israel be assured of this: God has made this Jesus, whom you crucified, both Lord and Christ."
Acts 18 [28]For he vigorously refuted the Jews in public debate, proving from the Scriptures that Jesus was the Christ.

d) Christ to Be a Savior

(1) Prophecy

Isa 59 [20]"The Redeemer will come to Zion, to those in Jacob who repent of their sins," declares the LORD.
Isa 62 [11]The LORD has made proclamation to the ends of the earth: "Say to the Daughter of Zion, 'See, your Savior comes! See, his reward is with him, and his recompense accompanies him.'"

(2) Fulfillment

Luke 2 [11]"Today in the town of David a Savior has been born to you; he is Christ the Lord."
John 4 [42]They said to the woman, "We no longer believe just because of what you said; now we have heard for ourselves, and we know that this man really is the Savior of the world."
Acts 5 [31]"God exalted him to his own right hand as Prince and Savior that he might give repentance and forgiveness of sins to Israel."
1 John 4 [14]And we have seen and testify that the Father has sent his Son to be the Savior of the world.

e) Christ to Preach the Good News

(1) Prophecy

Isa 61 [1]The Spirit of the Sovereign LORD is on me, because the LORD has anointed me to preach good news to the poor. He has sent me to bind up the brokenhearted, to proclaim freedom for the captives and release from darkness for the prisoners. . . .

(2) Fulfillment

Matt 11 [5]"The blind receive sight, the lame walk, those who have leprosy are cured, the deaf hear, the dead are raised, and the good news is preached to the poor."
Mark 1 [14]After John was put in prison, Jesus went into Galilee, proclaiming the good news of God.
Luke 4 [14]Jesus returned to Galilee in the power of the Spirit, and news about him spread through the whole countryside. [15]He taught in their synagogues, and everyone praised him.

[16]He went to Nazareth, where he had been brought up, and on the Sabbath day he went into the synagogue, as was his custom. And he stood up to read. [17]The scroll of the prophet Isaiah was handed to him. Unrolling it, he found the place where it is written: [18]"The Spirit of the Lord is on me, because he has anointed me to preach good news to the poor. He has sent me to proclaim freedom for the prisoners and recovery of sight for the blind, to release the oppressed, [19]to proclaim the year of the Lord's favor."

[20]Then he rolled up the scroll, gave it back to the attendant and sat down. The eyes of everyone in the synagogue were fas-

tened on him, [21]and he began by saying to them, "Today this scripture is fulfilled in your hearing."

Luke 8 [1]After this, Jesus traveled about from one town and village to another, proclaiming the good news of the kingdom of God. The Twelve were with him. . . .

f) Christ to Speak in Parables

(1) Prophecy

Isa 6 [9]He said, "Go and tell this people: 'Be ever hearing, but never understanding; be ever seeing, but never perceiving.' [10]Make the heart of this people calloused; make their ears dull and close their eyes. Otherwise they might see with their eyes, hear with their ears, understand with their hearts, and turn and be healed."

(2) Fulfillment

Matt 13 [13]"This is why I speak to them in parables: Though seeing, they do not see; though hearing, they do not hear or understand. [14]In them is fulfilled the prophecy of Isaiah: 'You will be ever hearing but never understanding; you will be ever seeing but never perceiving. [15]For this people's heart has become calloused; they hardly hear with their ears, and they have closed their eyes. Otherwise they might see with their eyes, hear with their ears, understand with their hearts and turn, and I would heal them.'"

g) Christ to Function as a (High) Priest

(1) Prophecy

Ps 110 [4]The LORD has sworn and will not change his mind: "You are a priest forever, in the order of Melchizedek."

Isa 53 [12]Therefore I will give him a portion among the great, and he will divide the spoils with the strong, because he poured out his life unto death, and was numbered with the transgressors. For he bore the sin of many, and made intercession for the transgressors.

Zech 6 [12]"Tell him this is what the LORD Almighty says: 'Here is the man whose name is the Branch, and he will branch out from his place and build the temple of the LORD. [13]It is he who will build the temple of the LORD, and he will be clothed with majesty and will sit and rule on his throne. And he will be a priest on his throne. And there will be harmony between the two.'"

(2) Fulfillment

Luke 23 [34]Jesus said, "Father, forgive them, for they do not know what they are doing." And they divided up his clothes by casting lots.

Rom 8 [34]Who is he that condemns? Christ Jesus, who died—more than that, who was raised to life—is at the right hand of God and is also interceding for us.

Heb 5 [5]So Christ also did not take upon himself the glory of becoming a high priest. But God said to him: "You are my Son; today I have become your Father." [6]And he says in another place: "You are a priest forever, in the order of Melchizedek."

[7]During the days of Jesus' life on earth, he offered up prayers and petitions with loud cries and tears to the one who could save him from death, and he was heard because of his reverent submission. [8]Although he was a son, he learned obedience from what he suffered, [9]and, once made perfect, he became the source of eternal salvation for all who obey him [10]and was designated by God to be high priest in the order of Melchizedek.

Heb 6 [19]We have this hope as an anchor for the soul, firm and secure. It enters the inner sanctuary behind the curtain, [20]where Jesus, who went before us, has entered on our behalf. He has become a high priest forever, in the order of Melchizedek.

Heb 7 [15]And what we have said is even more clear if another priest like Melchizedek appears, [16]one who has become a priest not on the basis of a regulation as to his ancestry but on the basis of the power of an indestructible life. [17]For it is declared: "You are a priest forever, in the order of Melchizedek."

[18]The former regulation is set aside because it was weak and useless [19](for the law made nothing perfect), and a better hope is introduced, by which we draw near to God.

[20]And it was not without an oath! Others became priests without any oath, [21]but he became a priest with an oath when God said to him: "The Lord has sworn and will not change his mind: 'You are a priest forever.'" [22]Because of this oath, Jesus has become the guarantee of a better covenant.

[23]Now there have been many of those priests, since death prevented them from continuing in office; [24]but because Jesus lives forever, he has a permanent priesthood. [25]Therefore he is able to save completely those who come to God through him, because he always lives to intercede for them.

[26]Such a high priest meets our need—one who is holy, blameless, pure, set apart from sinners, exalted above the heavens. [27]Unlike the other high priests, he does not need to offer sacrifices day after day, first for his own sins, and then for the sins of the people. He sacrificed for their sins once for all when he offered himself. [28]For the law appoints as high priests men who are weak; but the oath, which came after the law, appointed the Son, who has been made perfect forever.

Heb 9 [11]When Christ came as high priest of the good things that are already here, he went through the greater and more perfect tabernacle that is not man-made, that is to say, not a part of this creation. [12]He did not enter by means of the blood of goats and calves; but he entered the Most Holy Place once for all by his own blood, having obtained eternal redemption. [13]The blood of goats and bulls and the ashes of a heifer sprinkled on those who are ceremonially unclean sanctify them so that they are outwardly clean. [14]How much more, then, will the blood of Christ, who through the eternal Spirit offered himself unblemished to God, cleanse our consciences from acts that lead to death, so that we may serve the living God!

Heb 9 [24]For Christ did not enter a man-made sanctuary that was only a copy of the true one; he entered heaven itself, now to appear for us in God's presence.

1 John 2 [1]My dear children, I write this to you so that you will not sin. But if anybody does sin, we have one who speaks to the Father in our defense—Jesus Christ, the Righteous One.

h) Christ to Be a King

(1) Prophecy

Ps 2 [6]"I have installed my King on Zion, my holy hill."

Ps 132 [11]The LORD swore an oath to David, a sure oath that he will not revoke: "One of your own descendants I will place on your throne. . . ."

Jer 23 [5]"The days are coming," declares the LORD, "when I will raise up to David a righteous Branch, a King who will reign wisely and do what is just and right in the land. [6]In his days Judah will be saved and Israel will live in safety. This is the name by which he will be called: The LORD Our Righteousness."

Ezek 37 [24]"'My servant David will be king over them, and they will all have one shepherd. They will follow my laws and be careful to keep my decrees. [25]They will live in the land I gave to my servant Jacob, the land where your fathers lived. They and their children and their children's children will live there forever, and David my servant will be their prince forever.'"

(2) Fulfillment

Matt 2 [5]"In Bethlehem in Judea," they replied, "for this is what the prophet has written:

[6]"'But you, Bethlehem, in the land of Judah, are by no means least among the rulers of Judah; for out of you will come a ruler who will be the shepherd of my people Israel.'"

Luke 1 [32]"He will be great and will be called the Son of the Most High. The Lord God will give him the throne of his father David, [33]and he will reign over the house of Jacob forever; his kingdom will never end."

John 1 [49]Then Nathanael declared, "Rabbi, you are the Son of God; you are the King of Israel."

John 18 [33]Pilate then went back inside the palace, summoned Jesus and asked him, "Are you the king of the Jews?" . . .

[36]Jesus said, "My kingdom is not of this world. If it were, my servants would fight to prevent my arrest by the Jews. But now my kingdom is from another place."

[37]"You are a king, then!" said Pilate.

Jesus answered, "You are right in saying I am a king. In fact, for this reason I was born, and for this I came into the world, to testify to the truth. Everyone on the side of truth listens to me."

i) Christ to Minister in Galilee

(1) Prophecy

Isa 9 [1]Nevertheless, there will be no more gloom for those who were in distress. In the past he humbled the land of Zebulun and the land of Naphtali, but in the future he will honor Galilee of the Gentiles, by the way of the sea, along the Jordan—

[2]The people walking in darkness have seen a great light; on those living in the land of the shadow of death a light has dawned.

(2) Fulfillment

Matt 4 [12]When Jesus heard that John had been put in prison, he returned to Galilee. [13]Leaving Nazareth, he went and lived in Capernaum, which was by the lake in the area of Zebulun and Naphtali—[14]to fulfill what was said through the prophet Isaiah: [15]"Land of Zebulun and land of Naphtali, the way to the sea, along the Jordan, Galilee of the Gentiles—[16]the people living in darkness have seen a great light; on those living in the land of the shadow of death a light has dawned."

j) Christ to Be Anointed by God's Spirit

(1) Prophecy

Isa 11 [2]The Spirit of the LORD will rest on him—the Spirit of wisdom and of understanding, the Spirit of counsel and of power, the Spirit of knowledge and of the fear of the LORD. . . .
Isa 42 [1]"Here is my servant, whom I uphold, my chosen one in whom I delight; I will put my Spirit on him and he will bring justice to the nations."
Isa 61 [1]The Spirit of the Sovereign LORD is on me, because the LORD has anointed me to preach good news to the poor. He has sent me to bind up the brokenhearted, to proclaim freedom for the captives and release from darkness for the prisoners. . . .

(2) Fulfillment

Matt 3 [16]As soon as Jesus was baptized, he went up out of the water. At that moment heaven was opened, and he saw the Spirit of God descending like a dove and lighting on him.
John 3 [34]"For the one whom God has sent speaks the words of God, for God gives the Spirit without limit."
Acts 4 [27]"Indeed Herod and Pontius Pilate met together with the Gentiles and the people of Israel in this city to conspire against your holy servant Jesus, whom you anointed."

k) Christ to Have a Healing Ministry

(1) Prophecy

Isa 53 [4]Surely he took up our infirmities and carried our sorrows, yet we considered him stricken by God, smitten by him, and afflicted.

(2) Fulfillment

Matt 4 [23]Jesus went throughout Galilee, teaching in their synagogues, preaching the good news of the kingdom, and healing every disease and sickness among the people. [24]News about him spread all over Syria, and people brought to him all who were ill with various diseases, those suffering severe pain, the demon-possessed, those having seizures, and the paralyzed, and he healed them.
Matt 8 [16]When evening came, many who were demon-possessed were brought to him, and he drove out the spirits with a word and healed all the sick. [17]This was to fulfill what was spoken through the prophet Isaiah: "He took up our infirmities and carried our diseases."
Mark 6 [56]And wherever he went—into villages, towns or countryside—they placed the sick in the marketplaces. They begged him to let them touch even the edge of his cloak, and all who touched him were healed.
Luke 6 [17]He went down with them and stood on a level place. A large crowd of his disciples was there and a great number of people from all over Judea, from Jerusalem, and from the coast of Tyre and Sidon, [18]who had come to hear him and to be healed of their diseases. Those troubled by evil spirits were cured, [19]and the people all tried to touch him, because power was coming from him and healing them all.

l) Christ to Work Miracles

(1) Prophecy

Isa 35 [5]Then will the eyes of the blind be opened and the ears of the deaf unstopped. [6]Then will the lame leap like a deer, and the mute tongue shout for joy. Water will gush forth in the wilderness and streams in the desert.

(2) Fulfillment

Matt 11 [4]Jesus replied, "Go back and report to John what you hear and see: [5]The blind receive sight, the lame walk, those who have leprosy are cured, the deaf hear, the dead are raised, and the good news is preached to the poor. [6]Blessed is the man who does not fall away on account of me."
Matt 15 [30]Great crowds came to him, bringing the lame, the blind, the crippled, the mute and many others, and laid them at his feet; and he healed them.
Matt 21 [14]The blind and the lame came to him at the temple, and he healed them.
John 6 [1]Some time after this, Jesus crossed to the far shore of the Sea of Galilee (that is, the Sea of Tiberias), [2]and a great crowd of people followed him because they saw the miraculous signs he had performed on the sick.
John 20 [30]Jesus did many other miraculous signs in the presence of his disciples, which are not recorded in this book. [31]But these are written that you may believe that Jesus is the Christ, the Son of God, and that by believing you may have life in his name.

m) Christ to Be a Light to the Gentiles

(1) Prophecy

Isa 9 [2]The people walking in darkness have seen a great light; on those living in the land of the shadow of death a light has dawned.
Isa 49 [6]he says: "It is too small a thing for you to be my servant to restore the tribes of Jacob and bring back those of Israel I have kept. I will also make you a light for the Gentiles, that you may bring my salvation to the ends of the earth."

(2) Fulfillment

Luke 2 [32]". . . a light for revelation to the Gentiles and for glory to your people Israel."
Acts 13 [47]"For this is what the Lord has commanded us: 'I have made you a light for the Gentiles, that you may bring salvation to the ends of the earth.'"

n) Christ to Cleanse the Temple

(1) Prophecy

Ps 69 [9]for zeal for your house consumes me, and the insults of those who insult you fall on me.

(2) Fulfillment

Matt 21 [12]Jesus entered the temple area and drove out all who were buying and selling there. He overturned the tables of the money changers and the benches of those selling doves. [13]"It is written," he said to them, "'My house will be called a house of prayer,' but you are making it a 'den of robbers.'"
John 2 [13]When it was almost time for the Jewish Passover, Jesus went up to Jerusalem. [14]In the temple courts he found men selling cattle, sheep and doves, and others sitting at tables exchanging money. [15]So he made a whip out of cords, and drove all from the temple area, both sheep and cattle; he scattered the coins of the money changers and overturned their tables. [16]To those who sold doves he said, "Get these out of here! How dare you turn my Father's house into a market!"

[17]His disciples remembered that it is written: "Zeal for your house will consume me."

o) Christ to Enter Jerusalem in Triumph

(1) Prophecy

Zech 9 [9]Rejoice greatly, O Daughter of Zion! Shout, Daughter of Jerusalem! See, your king comes to you, righteous and having salvation, gentle and riding on a donkey, on a colt, the foal of a donkey.

(2) Fulfillment

Matt 21 [4]This took place to fulfill what was spoken through the prophet: [5]"Say to the Daughter of Zion, 'See, your king comes to you, gentle and riding on a donkey, on a colt, the foal of a donkey.'"

[6]The disciples went and did as Jesus had instructed them. [7]They brought the donkey and the colt, placed their cloaks on them, and Jesus sat on them. [8]A very large crowd spread their cloaks on the road, while others cut branches from the trees and spread them on the road. [9]The crowds that went ahead of

him and those that followed shouted, "Hosanna to the Son of David!" "Blessed is he who comes in the name of the Lord!" "Hosanna in the highest!"

[10]When Jesus entered Jerusalem, the whole city was stirred and asked, "Who is this?"

4. Circumstances and Events Related to Christ's Death

a) Christ Would Be Despised by Men

(1) Prophecy

Ps 22 [6]But I am a worm and not a man, scorned by men and despised by the people.
Isa 49 [7]This is what the LORD says—the Redeemer and Holy One of Israel—to him who was despised and abhorred by the nation, to the servant of rulers: "Kings will see you and rise up, princes will see and bow down, because of the LORD, who is faithful, the Holy One of Israel, who has chosen you."
Isa 53 [2]He grew up before him like a tender shoot, and like a root out of dry ground. He had no beauty or majesty to attract us to him, nothing in his appearance that we should desire him. [3]He was despised and rejected by men, a man of sorrows, and familiar with suffering. Like one from whom men hide their faces he was despised, and we esteemed him not.

(2) Fulfillment

Luke 19 [14]"But his subjects hated him and sent a delegation after him to say, 'We don't want this man to be our king.'"
Luke 23 [18]With one voice they cried out, "Away with this man! Release Barabbas to us!"
John 1 [11]He came to that which was his own, but his own did not receive him.

b) People and Rulers Would Conspire against Christ

(1) Prophecy

Ps 2 [1]Why do the nations conspire and the peoples plot in vain? [2]The kings of the earth take their stand and the rulers gather together against the LORD and against his Anointed One.

(2) Fulfillment

Matt 12 [14]But the Pharisees went out and plotted how they might kill Jesus.

c) Christ Would Suffer in This Life

(1) Prophecy

Isa 52 [14]Just as there were many who were appalled at him—his appearance was so disfigured beyond that of any man and his form marred beyond human likeness. . . .
Isa 53 [3]He was despised and rejected by men, a man of sorrows, and familiar with suffering. Like one from whom men hide their faces he was despised, and we esteemed him not.

(2) Fulfillment

Luke 22 [15]And he said to them, "I have eagerly desired to eat this Passover with you before I suffer."
Luke 22 [44]And being in anguish, he prayed more earnestly, and his sweat was like drops of blood falling to the ground.
Heb 4 [15]For we do not have a high priest who is unable to sympathize with our weaknesses, but we have one who has been tempted in every way, just as we are—yet was without sin.

d) Christ Would Be Betrayed by a Friend

(1) Prophecy

Ps 41 [9]Even my close friend, whom I trusted, he who shared my bread, has lifted up his heel against me.
Ps 55 [12]If an enemy were insulting me, I could endure it; if a foe were raising himself against me, I could hide from him. [13]But it is you, a man like myself, my companion, my close friend, [14]with whom I once enjoyed sweet fellowship as we walked with the throng at the house of God.

(2) Fulfillment

Luke 22 [3]Then Satan entered Judas, called Iscariot, one of the Twelve. [4]And Judas went to the chief priests and the officers of the temple guard and discussed with them how he might betray Jesus.
John 6 [64]"Yet there are some of you who do not believe." For Jesus had known from the beginning which of them did not believe and who would betray him.
John 6 [70]Then Jesus replied, "Have I not chosen you, the Twelve? Yet one of you is a devil!" [71](He meant Judas, the son of Simon Iscariot, who, though one of the Twelve, was later to betray him.)
John 13 [18]"I am not referring to all of you; I know those I have chosen. But this is to fulfill the scripture: 'He who shares my bread has lifted up his heel against me.'"

e) Christ Would Be Sold for Thirty Pieces of Silver

(1) Prophecy

Zech 11 [12]I told them, "If you think it best, give me my pay; but if not, keep it." So they paid me thirty pieces of silver.

(2) Fulfillment

Matt 26 [14]Then one of the Twelve—the one called Judas Iscariot—went to the chief priests [15]and asked, "What are you willing to give me if I hand him over to you?" So they counted out for him thirty silver coins.

f) The Silver Would Buy a Potter's Field

(1) Prophecy

Zech 11 [13]And the LORD said to me, "Throw it to the potter"—the handsome price at which they priced me! So I took the thirty pieces of silver and threw them into the house of the LORD to the potter.

(2) Fulfillment

Matt 27 [3]When Judas, who had betrayed him, saw that Jesus was condemned, he was seized with remorse and returned the thirty silver coins to the chief priests and the elders. [4]"I have sinned," he said, "for I have betrayed innocent blood."

"What is that to us?" they replied. "That's your responsibility."

[5]So Judas threw the money into the temple and left. Then he went away and hanged himself.

[6]The chief priests picked up the coins and said, "It is against the law to put this into the treasury, since it is blood money." [7]So they decided to use the money to buy the potter's field as a burial place for foreigners. [8]That is why it has been called the Field of Blood to this day. [9]Then what was spoken by Jeremiah the prophet was fulfilled: "They took the thirty silver coins, the price set on him by the people of Israel, [10]and they used them to buy the potter's field, as the Lord commanded me."

g) Christ Would Be Forsaken

(1) Prophecy

Zech 13 [7]"Awake, O sword, against my shepherd, against the man who is close to me!" declares the LORD Almighty. "Strike the shepherd, and the sheep will be scattered, and I will turn my hand against the little ones."

(2) Fulfillment

Matt 26 [31]Then Jesus told them, "This very night you will all fall away on account of me, for it is written: 'I will strike the shepherd, and the sheep of the flock will be scattered.'"
John 16 [32]"But a time is coming, and has come, when you will be scattered, each to his own home. You will leave me all alone. Yet I am not alone, for my Father is with me."

h) Christ Would Be Silent before His Accusers

(1) Prophecy

Isa 53 [7]He was oppressed and afflicted, yet he did not open his mouth; he was led like a lamb to the slaughter, and as a sheep before her shearers is silent, so he did not open his mouth.

(2) Fulfillment

Matt 27 [12]When he was accused by the chief priests and the elders, he gave no answer.
Luke 23 [9]He plied him with many questions, but Jesus gave him no answer.

i) Christ Would Be Beaten

(1) Prophecy

Isa 52 [14]Just as there were many who were appalled at

him—his appearance was so disfigured beyond that of any man and his form marred beyond human likeness. . . .

(2) Fulfillment

Matt 27 [26]Then he released Barabbas to them. But he had Jesus flogged, and handed him over to be crucified.

j) Christ Would Be Spit Upon

(1) Prophecy

Isa 50 [5]The Sovereign LORD has opened my ears, and I have not been rebellious; I have not drawn back. [6]I offered my back to those who beat me, my cheeks to those who pulled out my beard; I did not hide my face from mocking and spitting.

(2) Fulfillment

Matt 26 [67]Then they spit in his face and struck him with their fists. Others slapped him. . . .
Matt 27 [30]They spit on him, and took the staff and struck him on the head again and again.

k) Christ Would Be Hit in the Face

(1) Prophecy

Mic 5 [1]Marshal your troops, O city of troops, for a siege is laid against us. They will strike Israel's ruler on the cheek with a rod.

(2) Fulfillment

Matt 27 [30]They spit on him, and took the staff and struck him on the head again and again.

l) Christ Would Be Crucified

(1) Prophecy

Ps 22 [16]Dogs have surrounded me; a band of evil men has encircled me, they have pierced my hands and my feet.

(2) Fulfillment

Matt 26 [2]"As you know, the Passover is two days away—and the Son of Man will be handed over to be crucified."
John 3 [14]"Just as Moses lifted up the snake in the desert, so the Son of Man must be lifted up. . . ."

m) Christ Would Be Given Gall and Vinegar

(1) Prophecy

Ps 69 [21]They put gall in my food and gave me vinegar for my thirst.

(2) Fulfillment

Matt 27 [34]There they offered Jesus wine to drink, mixed with gall; but after tasting it, he refused to drink it.
Matt 27 [48]Immediately one of them ran and got a sponge. He filled it with wine vinegar, put it on a stick, and offered it to Jesus to drink.
Luke 23 [36]The soldiers also came up and mocked him. They offered him wine vinegar. . . .

n) Christ's Garments Would Be Divided Up

(1) Prophecy

Ps 22 [18]They divide my garments among them and cast lots for my clothing.

(2) Fulfillment

Matt 27 [35]When they had crucified him, they divided up his clothes by casting lots.

o) Christ Would Be Reviled and Mocked

(1) Prophecy

Ps 22 [7]All who see me mock me; they hurl insults, shaking their heads: [8]"He trusts in the LORD; let the LORD rescue him. Let him deliver him, since he delights in him."
Ps 22 [12]Many bulls surround me; strong bulls of Bashan encircle me. [13]Roaring lions tearing their prey open their mouths wide against me.

(2) Fulfillment

Matt 27 [39]Those who passed by hurled insults at him, shaking their heads. . . .

[41]In the same way the chief priests, the teachers of the law and the elders mocked him. [42]"He saved others," they said, "but he can't save himself! He's the King of Israel! Let him come down now from the cross, and we will believe in him."

Mark 15 [31]In the same way the chief priests and the teachers of the law mocked him among themselves. "He saved others," they said, "but he can't save himself! [32]Let this Christ, this King of Israel, come down now from the cross, that we may see and believe." Those crucified with him also heaped insults on him.
Luke 23 [35]The people stood watching, and the rulers even sneered at him. They said, "He saved others; let him save himself if he is the Christ of God, the Chosen One."

[36]The soldiers also came up and mocked him. They offered him wine vinegar. . . .

p) Christ Would Die Surrounded by Criminals

(1) Prophecy

Isa 53 [12]Therefore I will give him a portion among the great, and he will divide the spoils with the strong, because he poured out his life unto death, and was numbered with the transgressors. For he bore the sin of many, and made intercession for the transgressors.

(2) Fulfillment

Matt 27 [38]Two robbers were crucified with him, one on his right and one on his left.
Mark 15 [27]They crucified two robbers with him, one on his right and one on his left.
Luke 22 [36]He said to them, "But now if you have a purse, take it, and also a bag; and if you don't have a sword, sell your cloak and buy one. [37]It is written: 'And he was numbered with the transgressors'; and I tell you that this must be fulfilled in me. Yes, what is written about me is reaching its fulfillment."

q) Christ Would Die for the Sin of the World

(1) Prophecy

Isa 53 [5]But he was pierced for our transgressions, he was crushed for our iniquities; the punishment that brought us peace was upon him, and by his wounds we are healed. . . . [8]By oppression and judgment he was taken away. And who can speak of his descendants? For he was cut off from the land of the living; for the transgression of my people he was stricken. . . .

[10]Yet it was the LORD's will to crush him and cause him to suffer, and though the LORD makes his life a guilt offering, he will see his offspring and prolong his days, and the will of the LORD will prosper in his hand. . . . [12]Therefore I will give him a portion among the great, and he will divide the spoils with the strong, because he poured out his life unto death, and was numbered with the transgressors. For he bore the sin of many, and made intercession for the transgressors.
Dan 9 [26]"After the sixty-two 'sevens,' the Anointed One will be cut off and will have nothing. The people of the ruler who will come will destroy the city and the sanctuary. The end will come like a flood: War will continue until the end, and desolations have been decreed."

(2) Fulfillment

Matt 27 [50]And when Jesus had cried out again in a loud voice, he gave up his spirit.
Acts 8 [30]Then Philip ran up to the chariot and heard the man reading Isaiah the prophet. "Do you understand what you are reading?" Philip asked.

[31]"How can I," he said, "unless someone explains it to me?" So he invited Philip to come up and sit with him.

[32]The eunuch was reading this passage of Scripture: "He was led like a sheep to the slaughter, and as a lamb before the shearer is silent, so he did not open his mouth. [33]In his humiliation he was deprived of justice. Who can speak of his descendants? For his life was taken from the earth."

[34]The eunuch asked Philip, "Tell me, please, who is the prophet talking about, himself or someone else?" [35]Then Philip began with that very passage of Scripture and told him the good news about Jesus.
1 Cor 15 [3]For what I received I passed on to you as of first importance: that Christ died for our sins according to the Scriptures. . . .
Gal 1 [3]Grace and peace to you from God our Father and the Lord Jesus Christ, [4]who gave himself for our sins to rescue us

from the present evil age, according to the will of our God and Father. . . .

1 Pet 2 23When they hurled their insults at him, he did not retaliate; when he suffered, he made no threats. Instead, he entrusted himself to him who judges justly. 24He himself bore our sins in his body on the tree, so that we might die to sins and live for righteousness; by his wounds you have been healed.

r) None of Christ's Bones Would Be Broken

(1) Prophecy

Ps 34 20he protects all his bones, not one of them will be broken.

(2) Fulfillment

John 19 32The soldiers therefore came and broke the legs of the first man who had been crucified with Jesus, and then those of the other. 33But when they came to Jesus and found that he was already dead, they did not break his legs. . . . 36These things happened so that the scripture would be fulfilled: "Not one of his bones will be broken." . . .

s) Christ's Body Would Be Pierced

(1) Prophecy

Zech 12 10"And I will pour out on the house of David and the inhabitants of Jerusalem a spirit of grace and supplication. They will look on me, the one they have pierced, and they will mourn for him as one mourns for an only child, and grieve bitterly for him as one grieves for a firstborn son."

(2) Fulfillment

John 19 34Instead, one of the soldiers pierced Jesus' side with a spear, bringing a sudden flow of blood and water. 37. . . and, as another scripture says, "They will look on the one they have pierced."

t) Christ Would Be Buried with the Rich

(1) Prophecy

Isa 53 9He was assigned a grave with the wicked, and with the rich in his death, though he had done no violence, nor was any deceit in his mouth.

(2) Fulfillment

Matt 27 57As evening approached, there came a rich man from Arimathea, named Joseph, who had himself become a disciple of Jesus. 58Going to Pilate, he asked for Jesus' body, and Pilate ordered that it be given to him. 59Joseph took the body, wrapped it in a clean linen cloth, 60and placed it in his own new tomb that he had cut out of the rock. He rolled a big stone in front of the entrance to the tomb and went away.

5. Circumstances Related to Christ's Resurrection and Return

a) Christ's Resurrection

(1) Prophecy

Ps 16 9Therefore my heart is glad and my tongue rejoices; my body also will rest secure, 10because you will not abandon me to the grave, nor will you let your Holy One see decay.

Ps 49 15But God will redeem my life from the grave; he will surely take me to himself.

Hos 6 1"Come, let us return to the LORD. He has torn us to pieces but he will heal us; he has injured us but he will bind up our wounds. 2After two days he will revive us; on the third day he will restore us, that we may live in his presence."

(2) Fulfillment

Matt 28 5The angel said to the women, "Do not be afraid, for I know that you are looking for Jesus, who was crucified. 6He is not here; he has risen, just as he said. Come and see the place where he lay. 7Then go quickly and tell his disciples: 'He has risen from the dead and is going ahead of you into Galilee. There you will see him.' Now I have told you."

Mark 16 6"Don't be alarmed," he said. "You are looking for Jesus the Nazarene, who was crucified. He has risen! He is not here. See the place where they laid him. 7But go, tell his disciples and Peter, 'He is going ahead of you into Galilee. There you will see him, just as he told you.'"

Luke 24 5In their fright the women bowed down with their faces to the ground, but the men said to them, "Why do you look for the living among the dead? 6He is not here; he has risen! Remember how he told you, while he was still with you in Galilee: 7'The Son of Man must be delivered into the hands of sinful men, be crucified and on the third day be raised again.'"

John 20 26A week later his disciples were in the house again, and Thomas was with them. Though the doors were locked, Jesus came and stood among them and said, "Peace be with you!" 27Then he said to Thomas, "Put your finger here; see my hands. Reach out your hand and put it into my side. Stop doubting and believe."

Acts 1 3After his suffering, he showed himself to these men and gave many convincing proofs that he was alive. He appeared to them over a period of forty days and spoke about the kingdom of God.

Acts 2 24"But God raised him from the dead, freeing him from the agony of death, because it was impossible for death to keep its hold on him."

Rom 1 4and who through the Spirit of holiness was declared with power to be the Son of God by his resurrection from the dead: Jesus Christ our Lord.

Rom 6 4We were therefore buried with him through baptism into death in order that, just as Christ was raised from the dead through the glory of the Father, we too may live a new life.

1 Cor 15 20But Christ has indeed been raised from the dead, the firstfruits of those who have fallen asleep.

Heb 13 20May the God of peace, who through the blood of the eternal covenant brought back from the dead our Lord Jesus, that great Shepherd of the sheep . . .

Rev 1 5and from Jesus Christ, who is the faithful witness, the firstborn from the dead, and the ruler of the kings of the earth.

To him who loves us and has freed us from our sins by his blood. . . .

b) Christ's Ascension

(1) Prophecy

Ps 16 11You have made known to me the path of life; you will fill me with joy in your presence, with eternal pleasures at your right hand.

Ps 68 18When you ascended on high, you led captives in your train; you received gifts from men, even from the rebellious—that you, O LORD God, might dwell there.

(2) Fulfillment

Luke 24 51While he was blessing them, he left them and was taken up into heaven.

Acts 1 9After he said this, he was taken up before their very eyes, and a cloud hid him from their sight.

1 Tim 3 16Beyond all question, the mystery of godliness is great: He appeared in a body, was vindicated by the Spirit, was seen by angels, was preached among the nations, was believed on in the world, was taken up in glory.

1 Pet 1 21Through him you believe in God, who raised him from the dead and glorified him, and so your faith and hope are in God.

c) Christ's Exaltation

(1) Prophecy

Ps 110 1The LORD says to my Lord: "Sit at my right hand until I make your enemies a footstool for your feet."

2The LORD will extend your mighty scepter from Zion; you will rule in the midst of your enemies. 3Your troops will be willing on your day of battle. Arrayed in holy majesty, from the womb of the dawn you will receive the dew of your youth.

4The LORD has sworn and will not change his mind: "You are a priest forever, in the order of Melchizedek."

5The Lord is at your right hand; he will crush kings on the day of his wrath. 6He will judge the nations, heaping up the dead and crushing the rulers of the whole earth. 7He will drink from a brook beside the way; therefore he will lift up his head.

Ps 118 22The stone the builders rejected has become the capstone. . . .

(2) Fulfillment

Acts 2 32"God has raised this Jesus to life, and we are all witnesses of the fact. 33Exalted to the right hand of God, he has received from the Father the promised Holy Spirit and has poured out what you now see and hear."

Acts 5 31"God exalted him to his own right hand as Prince and Savior that he might give repentance and forgiveness of sins to Israel."

Acts 7 55But Stephen, full of the Holy Spirit, looked up to heaven and saw the glory of God, and Jesus standing at the right hand of God. 56"Look," he said, "I see heaven open and the Son of Man standing at the right hand of God."

Eph 1 20which he exerted in Christ when he raised him from the dead and seated him at his right hand in the heavenly realms. . . .

Phil 2 9Therefore God exalted him to the highest place and gave him the name that is above every name, 10that at the name of Jesus every knee should bow, in heaven and on earth and under the earth, 11and every tongue confess that Jesus Christ is Lord, to the glory of God the Father.

Col 3 1Since, then, you have been raised with Christ, set your hearts on things above, where Christ is seated at the right hand of God.

Heb 1 3The Son is the radiance of God's glory and the exact representation of his being, sustaining all things by his powerful word. After he had provided purification for sins, he sat down at the right hand of the Majesty in heaven.

Heb 8 1The point of what we are saying is this: We do have such a high priest, who sat down at the right hand of the throne of the Majesty in heaven. . . .

Heb 10 12But when this priest had offered for all time one sacrifice for sins, he sat down at the right hand of God.

1 Pet 3 22who has gone into heaven and is at God's right hand—with angels, authorities and powers in submission to him.

Rev 3 21"To him who overcomes, I will give the right to sit with me on my throne, just as I overcame and sat down with my Father on his throne."

Rev 5 13Then I heard every creature in heaven and on earth and under the earth and on the sea, and all that is in them, singing: "To him who sits on the throne and to the Lamb be praise and honor and glory and power, for ever and ever!"

d) Christ's Second Coming

(1) Prophecy

2 Sam 7 13"'He is the one who will build a house for my Name, and I will establish the throne of his kingdom forever.'"

Ps 50 2From Zion, perfect in beauty, God shines forth. 3Our God comes and will not be silent; a fire devours before him, and around him a tempest rages. 4He summons the heavens above, and the earth, that he may judge his people: 5"Gather to me my consecrated ones, who made a covenant with me by sacrifice."

Isa 9 6For to us a child is born, to us a son is given, and the government will be on his shoulders. And he will be called Wonderful Counselor, Mighty God, Everlasting Father, Prince of Peace. 7Of the increase of his government and peace there will be no end. He will reign on David's throne and over his kingdom, establishing and upholding it with justice and righteousness from that time on and forever. The zeal of the LORD Almighty will accomplish this.

Isa 16 5In love a throne will be established; in faithfulness a man will sit on it—one from the house of David—one who in judging seeks justice and speeds the cause of righteousness.

Isa 66 18"And I, because of their actions and their imaginations, am about to come and gather all nations and tongues, and they will come and see my glory."

Jer 30 9"'Instead, they will serve the LORD their God and David their king, whom I will raise up for them.'"

Dan 7 13"In my vision at night I looked, and there before me was one like a son of man, coming with the clouds of heaven. He approached the Ancient of Days and was led into his presence. 14He was given authority, glory and sovereign power; all peoples, nations and men of every language worshiped him. His dominion is an everlasting dominion that will not pass away, and his kingdom is one that will never be destroyed."

(2) Fulfillment

Matt 25 31"When the Son of Man comes in his glory, and all the angels with him, he will sit on his throne in heavenly glory."

Mark 8 38"If anyone is ashamed of me and my words in this adulterous and sinful generation, the Son of Man will be ashamed of him when he comes in his Father's glory with the holy angels."

Luke 12 40"You also must be ready, because the Son of Man will come at an hour when you do not expect him."

John 14 3"And if I go and prepare a place for you, I will come back and take you to be with me that you also may be where I am."

Acts 1 11"Men of Galilee," they said, "why do you stand here looking into the sky? This same Jesus, who has been taken from you into heaven, will come back in the same way you have seen him go into heaven."

1 Cor 1 8He will keep you strong to the end, so that you will be blameless on the day of our Lord Jesus Christ.

Phil 1 6being confident of this, that he who began a good work in you will carry it on to completion until the day of Christ Jesus.

1 Thess 3 13May he strengthen your hearts so that you will be blameless and holy in the presence of our God and Father when our Lord Jesus comes with all his holy ones.

1 Thess 4 13Brothers, we do not want you to be ignorant about those who fall asleep, or to grieve like the rest of men, who have no hope. 14We believe that Jesus died and rose again and so we believe that God will bring with Jesus those who have fallen asleep in him. 15According to the Lord's own word, we tell you that we who are still alive, who are left till the coming of the Lord, will certainly not precede those who have fallen asleep. 16For the Lord himself will come down from heaven, with a loud command, with the voice of the archangel and with the trumpet call of God, and the dead in Christ will rise first. 17After that, we who are still alive and are left will be caught up together with them in the clouds to meet the Lord in the air. And so we will be with the Lord forever.

1 Thess 5 2for you know very well that the day of the Lord will come like a thief in the night.

2 Thess 1 7and give relief to you who are troubled, and to us as well. This will happen when the Lord Jesus is revealed from heaven in blazing fire with his powerful angels.

Titus 2 13while we wait for the blessed hope—the glorious appearing of our great God and Savior, Jesus Christ. . . .

2 Pet 3 10But the day of the Lord will come like a thief. The heavens will disappear with a roar; the elements will be destroyed by fire, and the earth and everything in it will be laid bare.

Rev 19 11I saw heaven standing open and there before me was a white horse, whose rider is called Faithful and True. With justice he judges and makes war. 12His eyes are like blazing fire, and on his head are many crowns. He has a name written on him that no one knows but he himself. 13He is dressed in a robe dipped in blood, and his name is the Word of God. 14The armies of heaven were following him, riding on white horses and dressed in fine linen, white and clean. 15Out of his mouth comes a sharp sword with which to strike down the nations. "He will rule them with an iron scepter." He treads the winepress of the fury of the wrath of God Almighty. 16On his robe and on his thigh he has this name written: KING OF KINGS AND LORD OF LORDS.

17And I saw an angel standing in the sun, who cried in a loud voice to all the birds flying in midair, "Come, gather together for the great supper of God, 18so that you may eat the flesh of kings, generals, and mighty men, of horses and their riders, and the flesh of all people, free and slave, small and great."

19Then I saw the beast and the kings of the earth and their armies gathered together to make war against the rider on the horse and his army. 20But the beast was captured, and with him the false prophet who had performed the miraculous signs on his behalf. With these signs he had deluded those who had received the mark of the beast and worshiped his image. The two of them were thrown alive into the fiery lake of burning sulfur. 21The rest of them were killed with the sword that came out of the mouth of the rider on the horse, and all the birds gorged themselves on their flesh.

B. *The Appeal to OT Prophecies in the NT*

1. Jesus' Appeal to OT Prophecies

Matt 26 [23]Jesus replied, "The one who has dipped his hand into the bowl with me will betray me. [24]The Son of Man will go just as it is written about him. But woe to that man who betrays the Son of Man! It would be better for him if he had not been born."
Mark 9 [12]Jesus replied, "To be sure, Elijah does come first, and restores all things. Why then is it written that the Son of Man must suffer much and be rejected? [13]But I tell you, Elijah has come, and they have done to him everything they wished, just as it is written about him."
Luke 18 [31]Jesus took the Twelve aside and told them, "We are going up to Jerusalem, and everything that is written by the prophets about the Son of Man will be fulfilled. [32]He will be handed over to the Gentiles. They will mock him, insult him, spit on him, flog him and kill him. [33]On the third day he will rise again."
Luke 22 [37]"It is written: 'And he was numbered with the transgressors'; and I tell you that this must be fulfilled in me. Yes, what is written about me is reaching its fulfillment."
Luke 24 [44]He said to them, "This is what I told you while I was still with you: Everything must be fulfilled that is written about me in the Law of Moses, the Prophets and the Psalms."

[45]Then he opened their minds so they could understand the Scriptures. [46]He told them, "This is what is written: The Christ will suffer and rise from the dead on the third day, [47]and repentance and forgiveness of sins will be preached in his name to all nations, beginning at Jerusalem."

2. The Apostles' Appeal to OT Prophecies

Acts 3 [18]"But this is how God fulfilled what he had foretold through all the prophets, saying that his Christ would suffer."
Acts 10 [43]"All the prophets testify about him that everyone who believes in him receives forgiveness of sins through his name."
Acts 17 [2]As his custom was, Paul went into the synagogue, and on three Sabbath days he reasoned with them from the Scriptures, [3]explaining and proving that the Christ had to suffer and rise from the dead. "This Jesus I am proclaiming to you is the Christ," he said.
Acts 18 [28]For he vigorously refuted the Jews in public debate, proving from the Scriptures that Jesus was the Christ.
Acts 24 [14]"However, I admit that I worship the God of our fathers as a follower of the Way, which they call a sect. I believe everything that agrees with the Law and that is written in the Prophets. . . ."
Acts 26 [22]"But I have had God's help to this very day, and so I stand here and testify to small and great alike. I am saying nothing beyond what the prophets and Moses said would happen—[23]that the Christ would suffer and, as the first to rise from the dead, would proclaim light to his own people and to the Gentiles."
Acts 28 [23]They arranged to meet Paul on a certain day, and came in even larger numbers to the place where he was staying. From morning till evening he explained and declared to them the kingdom of God and tried to convince them about Jesus from the Law of Moses and from the Prophets.

III
The Deity of Christ

A. *Jesus' Claims to Deity*

1. Claims Relating to God

a) Jesus Claimed Equality with God

Matt 10 [40]"He who receives you receives me, and he who receives me receives the one who sent me."
Matt 11 [27]"All things have been committed to me by my Father. No one knows the Son except the Father, and no one knows the Father except the Son and those to whom the Son chooses to reveal him."
Matt 28 [19]"Therefore go and make disciples of all nations, baptizing them in the name of the Father and of the Son and of the Holy Spirit. . . ."
John 3 [35]"The Father loves the Son and has placed everything in his hands."
John 5 [17]Jesus said to them, "My Father is always at his work to this very day, and I, too, am working." [18]For this reason the Jews tried all the harder to kill him; not only was he breaking the Sabbath, but he was even calling God his own Father, making himself equal with God. . . .

[22]"Moreover, the Father judges no one, but has entrusted all judgment to the Son, [23]that all may honor the Son just as they honor the Father. He who does not honor the Son does not honor the Father, who sent him."
John 6 [62]"What if you see the Son of Man ascend to where he was before!"
John 8 [19]Then they asked him, "Where is your father?"

"You do not know me or my Father," Jesus replied. "If you knew me, you would know my Father also."
John 8 [58]"I tell you the truth," Jesus answered, "before Abraham was born, I am!"
John 10 [30]"I and the Father are one.

[36]". . . what about the one whom the Father set apart as his very own and sent into the world? Why then do you accuse me of blasphemy because I said, 'I am God's Son'? [37]Do not believe me unless I do what my Father does. [38]But if I do it, even though you do not believe me, believe the miracles, that you may know and understand that the Father is in me, and I in the Father."
John 12 [44]Then Jesus cried out, "When a man believes in me, he does not believe in me only, but in the one who sent me. [45]When he looks at me, he sees the one who sent me."
John 14 [1]"Do not let your hearts be troubled. Trust in God; trust also in me. . . ."

[7]"If you really knew me, you would know my Father as well. From now on, you do know him and have seen him."

[8]Philip said, "Lord, show us the Father and that will be enough for us."

[9]Jesus answered: "Don't you know me, Philip, even after I have been among you such a long time? Anyone who has seen me has seen the Father. How can you say, 'Show us the Father'? [10]Don't you believe that I am in the Father, and that the Father is in me? The words I say to you are not just my own. Rather, it is the Father, living in me, who is doing his work. [11]Believe me when I say that I am in the Father and the Father is in me; or at least believe on the evidence of the miracles themselves."
John 15 [23]"He who hates me hates my Father as well. [24]If I had not done among them what no one else did, they would not be guilty of sin. But now they have seen these miracles, and yet they have hated both me and my Father."
John 16 [28]"I came from the Father and entered the world; now I am leaving the world and going back to the Father."
John 17 [10]"All I have is yours, and all you have is mine. And glory has come to me through them. [21]. . . that all of them may be one, Father, just as you are in me and I am in you. May they also be in us so that the world may believe that you have sent me. [22]I have given them the glory that you gave me, that they may be one as we are one: [23]I in them and you in me. May they be brought to complete unity to let the world know that you sent me and have loved them even as you have loved me."

b) Jesus Claimed the Rights of God

(1) Jesus Claimed to Forgive Sins

Matt 26 [28]"This is my blood of the covenant, which is poured out for many for the forgiveness of sins."
Mark 2 [1]A few days later, when Jesus again entered Capernaum, the people heard that he had come home. [2]So many gathered that there was no room left, not even outside the door, and he preached the word to them. [3]Some men came, bringing to him a paralytic, carried by four of them. [4]Since they could not get him to Jesus because of the crowd, they made an opening in the roof above Jesus and, after digging through it, lowered the mat the paralyzed man was lying on.

[5]When Jesus saw their faith, he said to the paralytic, "Son, your sins are forgiven."

[6]Now some teachers of the law were sitting there, thinking to themselves, [7]"Why does this fellow talk like that? He's blaspheming! Who can forgive sins but God alone?"

[8]Immediately Jesus knew in his spirit that this was what they were thinking in their hearts, and he said to them, "Why are you thinking these things? [9]Which is easier: to say to the paralytic, 'Your sins are forgiven,' or to say, 'Get up, take your mat and walk'? [10]But that you may know that the Son of Man has authority on earth to forgive sins. . . ." He said to the paralytic, [11]"I tell you, get up, take your mat and go home." [12]He got up, took his mat and walked out in full view of them all. This amazed everyone and they praised God, saying, "We have never seen anything like this!"

Luke 7 [48]Then Jesus said to her, "Your sins are forgiven."

[49]The other guests began to say among themselves, "Who is this who even forgives sins?"

(2) Jesus Claimed to Give Life

Mark 5 [41]He took her by the hand and said to her, *"Talitha koum!"* (which means, "Little girl, I say to you, get up!"). [42]Immediately the girl stood up and walked around (she was twelve years old). At this they were completely astonished.

Luke 23 [42]Then he said, "Jesus, remember me when you come into your kingdom."

[43]Jesus answered him, "I tell you the truth, today you will be with me in paradise."

John 5 [21]"For just as the Father raises the dead and gives them life, even so the Son gives life to whom he is pleased to give it. . . . [25]I tell you the truth, a time is coming and has now come when the dead will hear the voice of the Son of God and those who hear will live. . . .

[28]"Do not be amazed at this, for a time is coming when all who are in their graves will hear his voice [29]and come out—those who have done good will rise to live, and those who have done evil will rise to be condemned."

John 6 [33]"For the bread of God is he who comes down from heaven and gives life to the world."

John 10 [10]"The thief comes only to steal and kill and destroy; I have come that they may have life, and have it to the full."

John 11 [25]Jesus said to her, "I am the resurrection and the life. He who believes in me will live, even though he dies. . . ."

John 14 [6]Jesus answered, "I am the way and the truth and the life. No one comes to the Father except through me."

(3) Jesus Claimed to Judge

John 5 [22]"Moreover, the Father judges no one, but has entrusted all judgment to the Son. . . . [27]And he has given him authority to judge because he is the Son of Man."

John 8 [15]"You judge by human standards; I pass judgment on no one. [16]But if I do judge, my decisions are right, because I am not alone. I stand with the Father, who sent me."

(4) Jesus Claimed to Grant Spiritual Blessings

Luke 24 [49]"I am going to send you what my Father has promised; but stay in the city until you have been clothed with power from on high."

John 1 [12]Yet to all who received him, to those who believed in his name, he gave the right to become children of God. . . .

John 14 [13]"And I will do whatever you ask in my name, so that the Son may bring glory to the Father. [14]You may ask me for anything in my name, and I will do it. . . .

[27]"Peace I leave with you; my peace I give you. I do not give to you as the world gives. Do not let your hearts be troubled and do not be afraid."

John 17 [13]"I am coming to you now, but I say these things while I am still in the world, so that they may have the full measure of my joy within them."

(5) Jesus Did Miracles

Matt 11 [4]Jesus replied, "Go back and report to John what you hear and see: [5]The blind receive sight, the lame walk, those who have leprosy are cured, the deaf hear, the dead are raised, and the good news is preached to the poor. [6]Blessed is the man who does not fall away on account of me."

John 5 [36]"I have testimony weightier than that of John. For the very work that the Father has given me to finish, and which I am doing, testifies that the Father has sent me."

John 10 [37]"Do not believe me unless I do what my Father does. [38]But if I do it, even though you do not believe me, believe the miracles, that you may know and understand that the Father is in me, and I in the Father."

John 15 [24]"If I had not done among them what no one else did, they would not be guilty of sin. But now they have seen these miracles, and yet they have hated both me and my Father."

(6) Jesus Cleansed the Temple

Matt 21 [12]Jesus entered the temple area and drove out all who were buying and selling there. He overturned the tables of the money changers and the benches of those selling doves. [13]"It is written," he said to them, "'My house will be called a house of prayer,' but you are making it a 'den of robbers.'"

(7) Jesus Claimed to Establish God's Kingdom

Matt 4 [23]Jesus went throughout Galilee, teaching in their synagogues, preaching the good news of the kingdom, and healing every disease and sickness among the people.

Matt 6 [33]"But seek first his kingdom and his righteousness, and all these things will be given to you as well."

Matt 7 [21]"Not everyone who says to me, 'Lord, Lord,' will enter the kingdom of heaven, but only he who does the will of my Father who is in heaven."

Matt 12 [28]"But if I drive out demons by the Spirit of God, then the kingdom of God has come upon you."

Matt 21 [31]"Which of the two did what his father wanted?"

"The first," they answered.

Jesus said to them, "I tell you the truth, the tax collectors and the prostitutes are entering the kingdom of God ahead of you."

Matt 25 [34]"Then the King will say to those on his right, 'Come, you who are blessed by my Father; take your inheritance, the kingdom prepared for you since the creation of the world.'"

Mark 1 [14]After John was put in prison, Jesus went into Galilee, proclaiming the good news of God. [15]"The time has come," he said. "The kingdom of God is near. Repent and believe the good news!"

Luke 12 [32]"Do not be afraid, little flock, for your Father has been pleased to give you the kingdom."

(8) Jesus Exorcised Demons

Mark 1 [27]The people were all so amazed that they asked each other, "What is this? A new teaching—and with authority! He even gives orders to evil spirits and they obey him."

Luke 11 [14]Jesus was driving out a demon that was mute. When the demon left, the man who had been mute spoke, and the crowd was amazed. [15]But some of them said, "By Beelzebub, the prince of demons, he is driving out demons." [16]Others tested him by asking for a sign from heaven.

[17]Jesus knew their thoughts and said to them: "Any kingdom divided against itself will be ruined, and a house divided against itself will fall. [18]If Satan is divided against himself, how can his kingdom stand? I say this because you claim that I drive out demons by Beelzebub. [19]Now if I drive out demons by Beelzebub, by whom do your followers drive them out? So then, they will be your judges. [20]But if I drive out demons by the finger of God, then the kingdom of God has come to you."

(9) Jesus Claimed to Defeat Satan

Luke 4 [1]Jesus, full of the Holy Spirit, returned from the Jordan and was led by the Spirit in the desert, [2]where for forty days he was tempted by the devil. He ate nothing during those days, and at the end of them he was hungry.

[3]The devil said to him, "If you are the Son of God, tell this stone to become bread."

[4]Jesus answered, "It is written: 'Man does not live on bread alone.'"

[5]The devil led him up to a high place and showed him in an instant all the kingdoms of the world. [6]And he said to him, "I will give you all their authority and splendor, for it has been given to me, and I can give it to anyone I want to. [7]So if you worship me, it will all be yours."

[8]Jesus answered, "It is written: 'Worship the Lord your God and serve him only.'"

[9]The devil led him to Jerusalem and had him stand on the

highest point of the temple. "If you are the Son of God," he said, "throw yourself down from here. [10]For it is written: 'He will command his angels concerning you to guard you carefully; [11]they will lift you up in their hands, so that you will not strike your foot against a stone.'"

[12]Jesus answered, "It says: 'Do not put the Lord your God to the test.'"

[13]When the devil had finished all this tempting, he left him until an opportune time.

John 12 [31]"Now is the time for judgment on this world; now the prince of this world will be driven out."

(10) Jesus Claimed to Be Lord of the Sabbath

Mark 2 [27]Then he said to them, "The Sabbath was made for man, not man for the Sabbath. [28]So the Son of Man is Lord even of the Sabbath."

(11) Jesus Claimed to Be David's Lord

Luke 20 [41]Then Jesus said to them, "How is it that they say the Christ is the Son of David? [42]David himself declares in the Book of Psalms: 'The Lord said to my Lord: "Sit at my right hand [43]until I make your enemies a footstool for your feet."' [44]David calls him 'Lord.' How then can he be his son?"

c) Jesus Claimed the Authority of God

(1) General Statements

Matt 7 [28]When Jesus had finished saying these things, the crowds were amazed at his teaching, [29]because he taught as one who had authority, and not as their teachers of the law.

Matt 21 [23]Jesus entered the temple courts, and, while he was teaching, the chief priests and the elders of the people came to him. "By what authority are you doing these things?" they asked. "And who gave you this authority?"

[24]Jesus replied, "I will also ask you one question. If you answer me, I will tell you by what authority I am doing these things. [25]John's baptism—where did it come from? Was it from heaven, or from men?"

They discussed it among themselves and said, "If we say, 'From heaven,' he will ask, 'Then why didn't you believe him?' [26]But if we say, 'From men'—we are afraid of the people, for they all hold that John was a prophet."

[27]So they answered Jesus, "We don't know."

Then he said, "Neither will I tell you by what authority I am doing these things."

Matt 28 [18]Then Jesus came to them and said, "All authority in heaven and on earth has been given to me."

Mark 1 [22]The people were amazed at his teaching, because he taught them as one who had authority, not as the teachers of the law.

John 3 [31]"The one who comes from above is above all; the one who is from the earth belongs to the earth, and speaks as one from the earth. The one who comes from heaven is above all."

John 17 [2]"For you granted him authority over all people that he might give eternal life to all those you have given him."

(2) Particular Sayings

Matt 5 [18]"I tell you the truth, until heaven and earth disappear, not the smallest letter, not the least stroke of a pen, will by any means disappear from the Law until everything is accomplished. [19]Anyone who breaks one of the least of these commandments and teaches others to do the same will be called least in the kingdom of heaven, but whoever practices and teaches these commands will be called great in the kingdom of heaven. [20]For I tell you that unless your righteousness surpasses that of the Pharisees and the teachers of the law, you will certainly not enter the kingdom of heaven."

Matt 5 [21]"You have heard that it was said to the people long ago, 'Do not murder, and anyone who murders will be subject to judgment.' [22]But I tell you that anyone who is angry with his brother will be subject to judgment. Again, anyone who says to his brother, 'Raca,' is answerable to the Sanhedrin. But anyone who says, 'You fool!' will be in danger of the fire of hell."

Matt 5 [26]"I tell you the truth, you will not get out until you have paid the last penny."

Matt 5 [27]"You have heard that it was said, 'Do not commit adultery.' [28]But I tell you that anyone who looks at a woman lustfully has already committed adultery with her in his heart."

Matt 5 [31]"It has been said, 'Anyone who divorces his wife must give her a certificate of divorce.' [32]But I tell you that anyone who divorces his wife, except for marital unfaithfulness, causes her to become an adulteress, and anyone who marries the divorced woman commits adultery."

Matt 5 [33]"Again, you have heard that it was said to the people long ago, 'Do not break your oath, but keep the oaths you have made to the Lord.' [34]But I tell you, Do not swear at all: either by heaven, for it is God's throne; [35]or by the earth, for it is his footstool; or by Jerusalem, for it is the city of the Great King."

Matt 5 [38]"You have heard that it was said, 'Eye for eye, and tooth for tooth.' [39]But I tell you, Do not resist an evil person. If someone strikes you on the right cheek, turn to him the other also."

Matt 5 [43]"You have heard that it was said, 'Love your neighbor and hate your enemy.' [44]But I tell you: Love your enemies and pray for those who persecute you. . . ."

Matt 6 [2]"So when you give to the needy, do not announce it with trumpets, as the hypocrites do in the synagogues and on the streets, to be honored by men. I tell you the truth, they have received their reward in full."

Matt 6 [25]"Therefore I tell you, do not worry about your life, what you will eat or drink; or about your body, what you will wear. Is not life more important than food, and the body more important than clothes?"

Matt 6 [29]"Yet I tell you that not even Solomon in all his splendor was dressed like one of these."

Matt 7 [22]"Many will say to me on that day, 'Lord, Lord, did we not prophesy in your name, and in your name drive out demons and perform many miracles?' [23]Then I will tell them plainly, 'I never knew you. Away from me, you evildoers!'"

Matt 8 [11]"I say to you that many will come from the east and the west, and will take their places at the feast with Abraham, Isaac and Jacob in the kingdom of heaven. [12]But the subjects of the kingdom will be thrown outside, into the darkness, where there will be weeping and gnashing of teeth."

Matt 10 [15]"I tell you the truth, it will be more bearable for Sodom and Gomorrah on the day of judgment than for that town."

Matt 10 [23]"When you are persecuted in one place, flee to another. I tell you the truth, you will not finish going through the cities of Israel before the Son of Man comes."

Matt 10 [42]"And if anyone gives even a cup of cold water to one of these little ones because he is my disciple, I tell you the truth, he will certainly not lose his reward."

Matt 12 [6]"I tell you that one greater than the temple is here."

Matt 12 [36]"But I tell you that men will have to give account on the day of judgment for every careless word they have spoken."

Matt 13 [17]"For I tell you the truth, many prophets and righteous men longed to see what you see but did not see it, and to hear what you hear but did not hear it."

Matt 17 [12]"But I tell you, Elijah has already come, and they did not recognize him, but have done to him everything they wished. In the same way the Son of Man is going to suffer at their hands."

Matt 17 [20]He replied, "Because you have so little faith. I tell you the truth, if you have faith as small as a mustard seed, you can say to this mountain, 'Move from here to there' and it will move. Nothing will be impossible for you."

Matt 18 [3]And he said: "I tell you the truth, unless you change and become like little children, you will never enter the kingdom of heaven."

Matt 18 [13]"And if he finds it, I tell you the truth, he is happier about that one sheep than about the ninety-nine that did not wander off."

Matt 18 [18]"I tell you the truth, whatever you bind on earth will be bound in heaven, and whatever you loose on earth will be loosed in heaven.

[19]"Again, I tell you that if two of you on earth agree about anything you ask for, it will be done for you by my Father in heaven. [20]For where two or three come together in my name, there am I with them."

Matt 19 [9]"I tell you that anyone who divorces his wife, except for marital unfaithfulness, and marries another woman commits adultery."

Matt 19 [23]Then Jesus said to his disciples, "I tell you the truth, it is hard for a rich man to enter the kingdom of heaven.

[24]Again I tell you, it is easier for a camel to go through the eye of a needle than for a rich man to enter the kingdom of God."
Matt 21 [31]"Which of the two did what his father wanted?"

"The first," they answered.

Jesus said to them, "I tell you the truth, the tax collectors and the prostitutes are entering the kingdom of God ahead of you."
Matt 21 [43]"Therefore I tell you that the kingdom of God will be taken away from you and given to a people who will produce its fruit."
Matt 23 [36]"I tell you the truth, all this will come upon this generation."
Matt 24 [2]"Do you see all these things?" he asked. "I tell you the truth, not one stone here will be left on another; every one will be thrown down."

[3]As Jesus was sitting on the Mount of Olives, the disciples came to him privately. "Tell us," they said, "when will this happen, and what will be the sign of your coming and of the end of the age?". . .

[34]"I tell you the truth, this generation will certainly not pass away until all these things have happened. [35]Heaven and earth will pass away, but my words will never pass away."
Matt 25 [12]"But he replied, 'I tell you the truth, I don't know you.'"
Matt 25 [40]"The King will reply, 'I tell you the truth, whatever you did for one of the least of these brothers of mine, you did for me.'"
Mark 3 [28]"I tell you the truth, all the sins and blasphemies of men will be forgiven them. [29]But whoever blasphemes against the Holy Spirit will never be forgiven; he is guilty of an eternal sin."
Mark 5 [41]He took her by the hand and said to her, *"Talitha koum!"* (which means, "Little girl, I say to you, get up!").
Mark 8 [12]He sighed deeply and said, "Why does this generation ask for a miraculous sign? I tell you the truth, no sign will be given to it."
Mark 9 [1]And he said to them, "I tell you the truth, some who are standing here will not taste death before they see the kingdom of God come with power."
Mark 9 [41]"I tell you the truth, anyone who gives you a cup of water in my name because you belong to Christ will certainly not lose his reward."
Mark 10 [15]"I tell you the truth, anyone who will not receive the kingdom of God like a little child will never enter it."
Mark 10 [29]"I tell you the truth," Jesus replied, "no one who has left home or brothers or sisters or mother or father or children or fields for me and the gospel [30]will fail to receive a hundred times as much in this present age (homes, brothers, sisters, mothers, children and fields—and with them, persecutions) and in the age to come, eternal life. [31]But many who are first will be last, and the last first."
Mark 11 [23]"I tell you the truth, if anyone says to this mountain, 'Go, throw yourself into the sea,' and does not doubt in his heart but believes that what he says will happen, it will be done for him. [24]Therefore I tell you, whatever you ask for in prayer, believe that you have received it, and it will be yours. [25]And when you stand praying, if you hold anything against anyone, forgive him, so that your Father in heaven may forgive you your sins."
Mark 12 [43]Calling his disciples to him, Jesus said, "I tell you the truth, this poor widow has put more into the treasury than all the others."
Mark 13 [30]"I tell you the truth, this generation will certainly not pass away until all these things have happened. [31]Heaven and earth will pass away, but my words will never pass away.

[32]"No one knows about that day or hour, not even the angels in heaven, nor the Son, but only the Father. . . . [37]What I say to you, I say to everyone: 'Watch!'"
Mark 14 [9]"I tell you the truth, wherever the gospel is preached throughout the world, what she has done will also be told, in memory of her."
Mark 14 [18]While they were reclining at the table eating, he said, "I tell you the truth, one of you will betray me—one who is eating with me."
Mark 14 [25]"I tell you the truth, I will not drink again of the fruit of the vine until that day when I drink it anew in the kingdom of God."
Mark 14 [30]"I tell you the truth," Jesus answered, "today—yes, tonight—before the rooster crows twice you yourself will disown me three times."
Luke 4 [24]"I tell you the truth," he continued, "no prophet is accepted in his hometown. [25]I assure you that there were many widows in Israel in Elijah's time, when the sky was shut for three and a half years and there was a severe famine throughout the land. [26]Yet Elijah was not sent to any of them, but to a widow in Zarephath in the region of Sidon. [27]And there were many in Israel with leprosy in the time of Elisha the prophet, yet not one of them was cleansed—only Naaman the Syrian."
Luke 6 [27]"But I tell you who hear me: Love your enemies, do good to those who hate you, [28]bless those who curse you, pray for those who mistreat you."
Luke 7 [28]"I tell you, among those born of women there is no one greater than John; yet the one who is least in the kingdom of God is greater than he."
Luke 7 [47]"Therefore, I tell you, her many sins have been forgiven—for she loved much. But he who has been forgiven little loves little."
Luke 10 [24]"For I tell you that many prophets and kings wanted to see what you see but did not see it, and to hear what you hear but did not hear it."
Luke 11 [9]"So I say to you: Ask and it will be given to you; seek and you will find; knock and the door will be opened to you."
Luke 12 [4]"I tell you, my friends, do not be afraid of those who kill the body and after that can do no more. [5]But I will show you whom you should fear: Fear him who, after the killing of the body, has power to throw you into hell. Yes, I tell you, fear him."
Luke 12 [8]"I tell you, whoever acknowledges me before men, the Son of Man will also acknowledge him before the angels of God."
Luke 12 [37]"It will be good for those servants whose master finds them watching when he comes. I tell you the truth, he will dress himself to serve, will have them recline at the table and will come and wait on them."
Luke 12 [43]"It will be good for that servant whom the master finds doing so when he returns. [44]I tell you the truth, he will put him in charge of all his possessions."
Luke 13 [23]Someone asked him, "Lord, are only a few people going to be saved?"

He said to them, [24]"Make every effort to enter through the narrow door, because many, I tell you, will try to enter and will not be able to."
Luke 13 [35]"Look, your house is left to you desolate. I tell you, you will not see me again until you say, 'Blessed is he who comes in the name of the Lord.'"
Luke 16 [9]"I tell you, use worldly wealth to gain friends for yourselves, so that when it is gone, you will be welcomed into eternal dwellings."
Luke 23 [43]Jesus answered him, "I tell you the truth, today you will be with me in paradise."
John 1 [51]He then added, "I tell you the truth, you shall see heaven open, and the angels of God ascending and descending on the Son of Man."
John 3 [3]In reply Jesus declared, "I tell you the truth, no one can see the kingdom of God unless he is born again." . . .

[5]Jesus answered, "I tell you the truth, no one can enter the kingdom of God unless he is born of water and the Spirit."
John 3 [11]"I tell you the truth, we speak of what we know, and we testify to what we have seen, but still you people do not accept our testimony."
John 5 [19]Jesus gave them this answer: "I tell you the truth, the Son can do nothing by himself; he can do only what he sees his Father doing, because whatever the Father does the Son also does. . . .

[24]"I tell you the truth, whoever hears my word and believes him who sent me has eternal life and will not be condemned; he has crossed over from death to life. [25]I tell you the truth, a time is coming and has now come when the dead will hear the voice of the Son of God and those who hear will live."
John 6 [26]Jesus answered, "I tell you the truth, you are looking

for me, not because you saw miraculous signs but because you ate the loaves and had your fill."

John 6 [32]Jesus said to them, "I tell you the truth, it is not Moses who has given you the bread from heaven, but it is my Father who gives you the true bread from heaven."

John 6 [47]"I tell you the truth, he who believes has everlasting life."

John 6 [53]Jesus said to them, "I tell you the truth, unless you eat the flesh of the Son of Man and drink his blood, you have no life in you."

John 8 [34]Jesus replied, "I tell you the truth, everyone who sins is a slave to sin."

John 8 [51]"I tell you the truth, if anyone keeps my word, he will never see death."

John 8 [58]"I tell you the truth," Jesus answered, "before Abraham was born, I am!"

John 10 [1]"I tell you the truth, the man who does not enter the sheep pen by the gate, but climbs in by some other way, is a thief and a robber. . . ."

[7]Therefore Jesus said again, "I tell you the truth, I am the gate for the sheep."

John 12 [24]"I tell you the truth, unless a kernel of wheat falls to the ground and dies, it remains only a single seed. But if it dies, it produces many seeds. [25]The man who loves his life will lose it, while the man who hates his life in this world will keep it for eternal life."

John 13 [16]"I tell you the truth, no servant is greater than his master, nor is a messenger greater than the one who sent him."

John 13 [20]"I tell you the truth, whoever accepts anyone I send accepts me; and whoever accepts me accepts the one who sent me."

John 13 [21]After he had said this, Jesus was troubled in spirit and testified, "I tell you the truth, one of you is going to betray me."

John 13 [38]Then Jesus answered, "Will you really lay down your life for me? I tell you the truth, before the rooster crows, you will disown me three times!"

John 14 [12]"I tell you the truth, anyone who has faith in me will do what I have been doing. He will do even greater things than these, because I am going to the Father."

John 16 [20]"I tell you the truth, you will weep and mourn while the world rejoices. You will grieve, but your grief will turn to joy. . . . [23]In that day you will no longer ask me anything. I tell you the truth, my Father will give you whatever you ask in my name."

John 21 [18]"I tell you the truth, when you were younger you dressed yourself and went where you wanted; but when you are old you will stretch out your hands, and someone else will dress you and lead you where you do not want to go."

d) Jesus Described Himself as God's Counterpart on Earth

Matt 11 [25]At that time Jesus said, "I praise you, Father, Lord of heaven and earth, because you have hidden these things from the wise and learned, and revealed them to little children. [26]Yes, Father, for this was your good pleasure.

[27]"All things have been committed to me by my Father. No one knows the Son except the Father, and no one knows the Father except the Son and those to whom the Son chooses to reveal him."

John 3 [16]"For God so loved the world that he gave his one and only Son, that whoever believes in him shall not perish but have eternal life."

John 5 [19]Jesus gave them this answer: "I tell you the truth, the Son can do nothing by himself; he can do only what he sees his Father doing, because whatever the Father does the Son also does. [20]For the Father loves the Son and shows him all he does. Yes, to your amazement he will show him even greater things than these. [21]For just as the Father raises the dead and gives them life, even so the Son gives life to whom he is pleased to give it. [22]Moreover, the Father judges no one, but has entrusted all judgment to the Son, [23]that all may honor the Son just as they honor the Father. He who does not honor the Son does not honor the Father, who sent him."

John 8 [19]Then they asked him, "Where is your father?"

"You do not know me or my Father," Jesus replied. "If you knew me, you would know my Father also." . . . [38]"I am telling you what I have seen in the Father's presence, and you do what you have heard from your father."

John 10 [36]". . . what about the one whom the Father set apart as his very own and sent into the world? Why then do you accuse me of blasphemy because I said, 'I am God's Son'?"

John 17 [25]"Righteous Father, though the world does not know you, I know you, and they know that you have sent me. [26]I have made you known to them, and will continue to make you known in order that the love you have for me may be in them and that I myself may be in them."

e) Jesus Accepted Prayer, Praise, and Worship

Matt 2 [2]and asked, "Where is the one who has been born king of the Jews? We saw his star in the east and have come to worship him."

Matt 8 [2]A man with leprosy came and knelt before him and said, "Lord, if you are willing, you can make me clean."

Matt 9 [18]While he was saying this, a ruler came and knelt before him and said, "My daughter has just died. But come and put your hand on her, and she will live."

Matt 14 [33]Then those who were in the boat worshiped him, saying, "Truly you are the Son of God."

Matt 15 [25]The woman came and knelt before him. "Lord, help me!" she said.

Matt 18 [20]"For where two or three come together in my name, there am I with them."

Matt 28 [9]Suddenly Jesus met them. "Greetings," he said. They came to him, clasped his feet and worshiped him. . . .

[17]When they saw him, they worshiped him; but some doubted.

Mark 5 [6]When he saw Jesus from a distance, he ran and fell on his knees in front of him. [7]He shouted at the top of his voice, "What do you want with me, Jesus, Son of the Most High God? Swear to God that you won't torture me!"

Luke 23 [42]Then he said, "Jesus, remember me when you come into your kingdom."

[43]Jesus answered him, "I tell you the truth, today you will be with me in paradise."

Luke 24 [52]Then they worshiped him and returned to Jerusalem with great joy.

John 5 [23]". . . that all may honor the Son just as they honor the Father. He who does not honor the Son does not honor the Father, who sent him."

John 14 [14]"You may ask me for anything in my name, and I will do it."

f) Jesus Found the Source of Power within Himself

Matt 9 [6]"But so that you may know that the Son of Man has authority on earth to forgive sins. . . ." Then he said to the paralytic, "Get up, take your mat and go home."

John 5 [26]"For as the Father has life in himself, so he has granted the Son to have life in himself."

John 10 [17]"The reason my Father loves me is that I lay down my life—only to take it up again. [18]No one takes it from me, but I lay it down of my own accord. I have authority to lay it down and authority to take it up again. This command I received from my Father."

John 10 [28]"I give them eternal life, and they shall never perish; no one can snatch them out of my hand."

g) Jesus Never Showed Any Consciousness of Sin

John 8 [46]"Can any of you prove me guilty of sin? If I am telling the truth, why don't you believe me?"

John 14 [30]"I will not speak with you much longer, for the prince of this world is coming. He has no hold on me. . . ."

John 17 [4]"I have brought you glory on earth by completing the work you gave me to do."

2. Claims Relating to Human Beings

a) Jesus Promised Peace and Rest to Those Who Trust Him

Matt 11 [28]"Come to me, all you who are weary and burdened, and I will give you rest. [29]Take my yoke upon you and learn from me, for I am gentle and humble in heart, and you will find rest for your souls. [30]For my yoke is easy and my burden is light."

John 6 [29]Jesus answered, "The work of God is this: to believe in the one he has sent."

John 7 [38]"Whoever believes in me, as the Scripture has said, streams of living water will flow from within him."

John 14 [27]"Peace I leave with you; my peace I give you. I do not give to you as the world gives. Do not let your hearts be troubled and do not be afraid."

John 16 [33]"I have told you these things, so that in me you may have peace. In this world you will have trouble. But take heart! I have overcome the world."

John 20 [19]On the evening of that first day of the week, when the disciples were together, with the doors locked for fear of the Jews, Jesus came and stood among them and said, "Peace be with you!"

b) Jesus Claimed Power over All Life, Space, and Time

Matt 16 [27]"For the Son of Man is going to come in his Father's glory with his angels, and then he will reward each person according to what he has done."

Matt 18 [20]"For where two or three come together in my name, there am I with them."

Matt 24 [1]Jesus left the temple and was walking away when his disciples came up to him to call his attention to its buildings. [2]"Do you see all these things?" he asked. "I tell you the truth, not one stone here will be left on another; every one will be thrown down."

[3]As Jesus was sitting on the Mount of Olives, the disciples came to him privately. "Tell us," they said, "when will this happen, and what will be the sign of your coming and of the end of the age?"

[4]Jesus answered: "Watch out that no one deceives you. [5]For many will come in my name, claiming, 'I am the Christ,' and will deceive many. [6]You will hear of wars and rumors of wars, but see to it that you are not alarmed. Such things must happen, but the end is still to come. [7]Nation will rise against nation, and kingdom against kingdom. There will be famines and earthquakes in various places. [8]All these are the beginning of birth pains.

[9]"Then you will be handed over to be persecuted and put to death, and you will be hated by all nations because of me. [10]At that time many will turn away from the faith and will betray and hate each other, [11]and many false prophets will appear and deceive many people. [12]Because of the increase of wickedness, the love of most will grow cold, [13]but he who stands firm to the end will be saved. [14]And this gospel of the kingdom will be preached in the whole world as a testimony to all nations, and then the end will come.

[15]"So when you see standing in the holy place 'the abomination that causes desolation,' spoken of through the prophet Daniel—let the reader understand—[16]then let those who are in Judea flee to the mountains. [17]Let no one on the roof of his house go down to take anything out of the house. [18]Let no one in the field go back to get his cloak. [19]How dreadful it will be in those days for pregnant women and nursing mothers! [20]Pray that your flight will not take place in winter or on the Sabbath. [21]For then there will be great distress, unequaled from the beginning of the world until now—and never to be equaled again. [22]If those days had not been cut short, no one would survive, but for the sake of the elect those days will be shortened. [23]At that time if anyone says to you, 'Look, here is the Christ!' or, 'There he is!' do not believe it. [24]For false Christs and false prophets will appear and perform great signs and miracles to deceive even the elect—if that were possible. [25]See, I have told you ahead of time.

[26]"So if anyone tells you, 'There he is, out in the desert,' do not go out; or, 'Here he is, in the inner rooms,' do not believe it. [27]For as lightning that comes from the east is visible even in the west, so will be the coming of the Son of Man. [28]Wherever there is a carcass, there the vultures will gather.

[29]"Immediately after the distress of those days 'the sun will be darkened, and the moon will not give its light; the stars will fall from the sky, and the heavenly bodies will be shaken.'

[30]"At that time the sign of the Son of Man will appear in the sky, and all the nations of the earth will mourn. They will see the Son of Man coming on the clouds of the sky, with power and great glory. [31]And he will send his angels with a loud trumpet call, and they will gather his elect from the four winds, from one end of the heavens to the other.

[32]"Now learn this lesson from the fig tree: As soon as its twigs get tender and its leaves come out, you know that summer is near. [33]Even so, when you see all these things, you know that it is near, right at the door. [34]I tell you the truth, this generation will certainly not pass away until all these things have happened. [35]Heaven and earth will pass away, but my words will never pass away.

[36]"No one knows about that day or hour, not even the angels in heaven, nor the Son, but only the Father. [37]As it was in the days of Noah, so it will be at the coming of the Son of Man. [38]For in the days before the flood, people were eating and drinking, marrying and giving in marriage, up to the day Noah entered the ark; [39]and they knew nothing about what would happen until the flood came and took them all away. That is how it will be at the coming of the Son of Man. [40]Two men will be in the field; one will be taken and the other left. [41]Two women will be grinding with a hand mill; one will be taken and the other left.

[42]"Therefore keep watch, because you do not know on what day your Lord will come. [43]But understand this: If the owner of the house had known at what time of night the thief was coming, he would have kept watch and would not have let his house be broken into. [44]So you also must be ready, because the Son of Man will come at an hour when you do not expect him.

[45]"Who then is the faithful and wise servant, whom the master has put in charge of the servants in his household to give them their food at the proper time? [46]It will be good for that servant whose master finds him doing so when he returns. [47]I tell you the truth, he will put him in charge of all his possessions. [48]But suppose that servant is wicked and says to himself, 'My master is staying away a long time,' [49]and he then begins to beat his fellow servants and to eat and drink with drunkards. [50]The master of that servant will come on a day when he does not expect him and at an hour he is not aware of. [51]He will cut him to pieces and assign him a place with the hypocrites, where there will be weeping and gnashing of teeth."

Matt 28 [18]Then Jesus came to them and said, "All authority in heaven and on earth has been given to me. [20] . . . and teaching them to obey everything I have commanded you. And surely I am with you always, to the very end of the age."

John 14 [23]Jesus replied, "If anyone loves me, he will obey my teaching. My Father will love him, and we will come to him and make our home with him."

c) Jesus Claimed to Determine People's Eternal Destiny

Matt 7 [21]"Not everyone who says to me, 'Lord, Lord,' will enter the kingdom of heaven, but only he who does the will of my Father who is in heaven. [22]Many will say to me on that day, 'Lord, Lord, did we not prophesy in your name, and in your name drive out demons and perform many miracles?' [23]Then I will tell them plainly, 'I never knew you. Away from me, you evildoers!'"

Matt 10 [32]"Whoever acknowledges me before men, I will also acknowledge him before my Father in heaven. [33]But whoever disowns me before men, I will disown him before my Father in heaven."

Matt 11 [6]"Blessed is the man who does not fall away on account of me."

Matt 25 [31]"When the Son of Man comes in his glory, and all the angels with him, he will sit on his throne in heavenly glory. [32]All the nations will be gathered before him, and he will separate the people one from another as a shepherd separates the sheep from the goats. [33]He will put the sheep on his right and the goats on his left.

[34]"Then the King will say to those on his right, 'Come, you who are blessed by my Father; take your inheritance, the kingdom prepared for you since the creation of the world. [35]For I was hungry and you gave me something to eat, I was thirsty and you gave me something to drink, I was a stranger and you invited me in, [36]I needed clothes and you clothed me, I was sick

and you looked after me, I was in prison and you came to visit me.'

37“Then the righteous will answer him, 'Lord, when did we see you hungry and feed you, or thirsty and give you something to drink? 38When did we see you a stranger and invite you in, or needing clothes and clothe you? 39When did we see you sick or in prison and go to visit you?'

40“The King will reply, 'I tell you the truth, whatever you did for one of the least of these brothers of mine, you did for me.'

41“Then he will say to those on his left, 'Depart from me, you who are cursed, into the eternal fire prepared for the devil and his angels. 42For I was hungry and you gave me nothing to eat, I was thirsty and you gave me nothing to drink, 43I was a stranger and you did not invite me in, I needed clothes and you did not clothe me, I was sick and in prison and you did not look after me.'

44“They also will answer, 'Lord, when did we see you hungry or thirsty or a stranger or needing clothes or sick or in prison, and did not help you?'

45“He will reply, 'I tell you the truth, whatever you did not do for one of the least of these, you did not do for me.'

46“Then they will go away to eternal punishment, but the righteous to eternal life.”

Mark 8 34Then he called the crowd to him along with his disciples and said: “If anyone would come after me, he must deny himself and take up his cross and follow me. 35For whoever wants to save his life will lose it, but whoever loses his life for me and for the gospel will save it. 36What good is it for a man to gain the whole world, yet forfeit his soul? 37Or what can a man give in exchange for his soul? 38If anyone is ashamed of me and my words in this adulterous and sinful generation, the Son of Man will be ashamed of him when he comes in his Father's glory with the holy angels.”

John 3 16“For God so loved the world that he gave his one and only Son, that whoever believes in him shall not perish but have eternal life.”

John 5 24“I tell you the truth, whoever hears my word and believes him who sent me has eternal life and will not be condemned; he has crossed over from death to life.”

John 10 28“I give them eternal life, and they shall never perish; no one can snatch them out of my hand. 29My Father, who has given them to me, is greater than all; no one can snatch them out of my Father's hand.”

John 12 32“But I, when I am lifted up from the earth, will draw all men to myself.”

d) Jesus Claimed Final Authority over People

John 4 24“God is spirit, and his worshipers must worship in spirit and in truth.”

25The woman said, “I know that Messiah” (called Christ) “is coming. When he comes, he will explain everything to us.”

26Then Jesus declared, “I who speak to you am he.”

John 6 35Then Jesus declared, “I am the bread of life. He who comes to me will never go hungry, and he who believes in me will never be thirsty.”

John 8 12When Jesus spoke again to the people, he said, “I am the light of the world. Whoever follows me will never walk in darkness, but will have the light of life.” . . .

23But he continued, “You are from below; I am from above. You are of this world; I am not of this world. 24I told you that you would die in your sins; if you do not believe that I am the one I claim to be, you will indeed die in your sins.” . . .

28So Jesus said, “When you have lifted up the Son of Man, then you will know that I am the one I claim to be and that I do nothing on my own but speak just what the Father has taught me.” . . .

58“I tell you the truth,” Jesus answered, “before Abraham was born, I am!”

John 10 7Therefore Jesus said again, “I tell you the truth, I am the gate for the sheep. . . . 9I am the gate; whoever enters through me will be saved. He will come in and go out, and find pasture.”

John 10 11“I am the good shepherd. The good shepherd lays down his life for the sheep. . . . 14I am the good shepherd; I know my sheep and my sheep know me. . . .”

John 11 25Jesus said to her, “I am the resurrection and the life. He who believes in me will live, even though he dies. . . .”

John 13 18“I am not referring to all of you; I know those I have chosen. But this is to fulfill the scripture: 'He who shares my bread has lifted up his heel against me.'

19“I am telling you now before it happens, so that when it does happen you will believe that I am He. 20I tell you the truth, whoever accepts anyone I send accepts me; and whoever accepts me accepts the one who sent me.”

John 14 6Jesus answered, “I am the way and the truth and the life. No one comes to the Father except through me.”

John 15 1“I am the true vine, and my Father is the gardener. . . .

5“I am the vine; you are the branches. If a man remains in me and I in him, he will bear much fruit; apart from me you can do nothing.”

3. Claims Relating to Jesus' Mission

a) Jesus Came to Be People's Savior

Matt 9 12On hearing this, Jesus said, “It is not the healthy who need a doctor, but the sick. 13But go and learn what this means: 'I desire mercy, not sacrifice.' For I have not come to call the righteous, but sinners.”

Matt 15 24He answered, “I was sent only to the lost sheep of Israel.”

Matt 18 12“What do you think? If a man owns a hundred sheep, and one of them wanders away, will he not leave the ninety-nine on the hills and go to look for the one that wandered off? 13And if he finds it, I tell you the truth, he is happier about that one sheep than about the ninety-nine that did not wander off. 14In the same way your Father in heaven is not willing that any of these little ones should be lost.”

Mark 2 17On hearing this, Jesus said to them, “It is not the healthy who need a doctor, but the sick. I have not come to call the righteous, but sinners.”

Luke 15 1Now the tax collectors and “sinners” were all gathering around to hear him. 2But the Pharisees and the teachers of the law muttered, “This man welcomes sinners and eats with them.”

3Then Jesus told them this parable: 4“Suppose one of you has a hundred sheep and loses one of them. Does he not leave the ninety-nine in the open country and go after the lost sheep until he finds it? 5And when he finds it, he joyfully puts it on his shoulders 6and goes home. Then he calls his friends and neighbors together and says, 'Rejoice with me; I have found my lost sheep.' 7I tell you that in the same way there will be more rejoicing in heaven over one sinner who repents than over ninety-nine righteous persons who do not need to repent.

8“Or suppose a woman has ten silver coins and loses one. Does she not light a lamp, sweep the house and search carefully until she finds it? 9And when she finds it, she calls her friends and neighbors together and says, 'Rejoice with me; I have found my lost coin.' 10In the same way, I tell you, there is rejoicing in the presence of the angels of God over one sinner who repents.”

11Jesus continued: “There was a man who had two sons. 12The younger one said to his father, 'Father, give me my share of the estate.' So he divided his property between them.

13“Not long after that, the younger son got together all he had, set off for a distant country and there squandered his wealth in wild living. 14After he had spent everything, there was a severe famine in that whole country, and he began to be in need. 15So he went and hired himself out to a citizen of that country, who sent him to his fields to feed pigs. 16He longed to fill his stomach with the pods that the pigs were eating, but no one gave him anything.

17“When he came to his senses, he said, 'How many of my father's hired men have food to spare, and here I am starving to death! 18I will set out and go back to my father and say to him: Father, I have sinned against heaven and against you. 19I am no longer worthy to be called your son; make me like one of your hired men.' 20So he got up and went to his father.

“But while he was still a long way off, his father saw him and was filled with compassion for him; he ran to his son, threw his arms around him and kissed him.

[21]"The son said to him, 'Father, I have sinned against heaven and against you. I am no longer worthy to be called your son.'

[22]"But the father said to his servants, 'Quick! Bring the best robe and put it on him. Put a ring on his finger and sandals on his feet. [23]Bring the fattened calf and kill it. Let's have a feast and celebrate. [24]For this son of mine was dead and is alive again; he was lost and is found.' So they began to celebrate.

[25]"Meanwhile, the older son was in the field. When he came near the house, he heard music and dancing. [26]So he called one of the servants and asked him what was going on. [27]'Your brother has come,' he replied, 'and your father has killed the fattened calf because he has him back safe and sound.'

[28]"The older brother became angry and refused to go in. So his father went out and pleaded with him. [29]But he answered his father, 'Look! All these years I've been slaving for you and never disobeyed your orders. Yet you never gave me even a young goat so I could celebrate with my friends. [30]But when this son of yours who has squandered your property with prostitutes comes home, you kill the fattened calf for him!'

[31]"'My son,' the father said, 'you are always with me, and everything I have is yours. [32]But we had to celebrate and be glad, because this brother of yours was dead and is alive again; he was lost and is found.'"

Luke 19 [10]"For the Son of Man came to seek and to save what was lost."

John 3 [14]"Just as Moses lifted up the snake in the desert, so the Son of Man must be lifted up, [15]that everyone who believes in him may have eternal life.

[16]"For God so loved the world that he gave his one and only Son, that whoever believes in him shall not perish but have eternal life. [17]For God did not send his Son into the world to condemn the world, but to save the world through him. [18]Whoever believes in him is not condemned, but whoever does not believe stands condemned already because he has not believed in the name of God's one and only Son."

John 3 [36]"Whoever believes in the Son has eternal life, but whoever rejects the Son will not see life, for God's wrath remains on him."

John 6 [51]"I am the living bread that came down from heaven. If anyone eats of this bread, he will live forever. This bread is my flesh, which I will give for the life of the world."

John 8 [12]When Jesus spoke again to the people, he said, "I am the light of the world. Whoever follows me will never walk in darkness, but will have the light of life."

John 10 [16]"I have other sheep that are not of this sheep pen. I must bring them also. They too will listen to my voice, and there shall be one flock and one shepherd. . . . [28]I give them eternal life, and they shall never perish; no one can snatch them out of my hand."

John 12 [47]"As for the person who hears my words but does not keep them, I do not judge him. For I did not come to judge the world, but to save it."

b) Jesus Came to Make God Known

Mark 1 [14]After John was put in prison, Jesus went into Galilee, proclaiming the good news of God.

Mark 1 [38]Jesus replied, "Let us go somewhere else—to the nearby villages—so I can preach there also. That is why I have come."

Luke 10 [22]"All things have been committed to me by my Father. No one knows who the Son is except the Father, and no one knows who the Father is except the Son and those to whom the Son chooses to reveal him."

Luke 14 [7]When he noticed how the guests picked the places of honor at the table, he told them this parable: [8]"When someone invites you to a wedding feast, do not take the place of honor, for a person more distinguished than you may have been invited. [9]If so, the host who invited both of you will come and say to you, 'Give this man your seat.' Then, humiliated, you will have to take the least important place. [10]But when you are invited, take the lowest place, so that when your host comes, he will say to you, 'Friend, move up to a better place.' Then you will be honored in the presence of all your fellow guests. [11]For everyone who exalts himself will be humbled, and he who humbles himself will be exalted." . . .

[23]"Then the master told his servant, 'Go out to the roads and country lanes and make them come in, so that my house will be full. [24]I tell you, not one of those men who were invited will get a taste of my banquet.'"

John 5 [17]Jesus said to them, "My Father is always at his work to this very day, and I, too, am working."

John 6 [38]"For I have come down from heaven not to do my will but to do the will of him who sent me."

John 7 [16]Jesus answered, "My teaching is not my own. It comes from him who sent me. [17]If anyone chooses to do God's will, he will find out whether my teaching comes from God or whether I speak on my own. [18]He who speaks on his own does so to gain honor for himself, but he who works for the honor of the one who sent him is a man of truth; there is nothing false about him."

John 8 [26]"I have much to say in judgment of you. But he who sent me is reliable, and what I have heard from him I tell the world." . . . [38]"I am telling you what I have seen in the Father's presence, and you do what you have heard from your father." . . .

[42]Jesus said to them, "If God were your Father, you would love me, for I came from God and now am here. I have not come on my own; but he sent me."

John 12 [49]"For I did not speak of my own accord, but the Father who sent me commanded me what to say and how to say it. [50]I know that his command leads to eternal life. So whatever I say is just what the Father has told me to say."

John 15 [15]"I no longer call you servants, because a servant does not know his master's business. Instead, I have called you friends, for everything that I learned from my Father I have made known to you."

John 16 [25]"Though I have been speaking figuratively, a time is coming when I will no longer use this kind of language but will tell you plainly about my Father. . . . [28]I came from the Father and entered the world; now I am leaving the world and going back to the Father."

c) Jesus Came to Sum Up the Entire OT

Matt 5 [17]"Do not think that I have come to abolish the Law or the Prophets; I have not come to abolish them but to fulfill them. [18]I tell you the truth, until heaven and earth disappear, not the smallest letter, not the least stroke of a pen, will by any means disappear from the Law until everything is accomplished."

Matt 11 [4]Jesus replied, "Go back and report to John what you hear and see: [5]The blind receive sight, the lame walk, those who have leprosy are cured, the deaf hear, the dead are raised, and the good news is preached to the poor. [6]Blessed is the man who does not fall away on account of me."

Matt 13 [16]"But blessed are your eyes because they see, and your ears because they hear. [17]For I tell you the truth, many prophets and righteous men longed to see what you see but did not see it, and to hear what you hear but did not hear it."

Mark 1 [14]After John was put in prison, Jesus went into Galilee, proclaiming the good news of God. [15]"The time has come," he said. "The kingdom of God is near. Repent and believe the good news!"

Luke 4 [17]The scroll of the prophet Isaiah was handed to him. Unrolling it, he found the place where it is written: [18]"The Spirit of the Lord is on me, because he has anointed me to preach good news to the poor. He has sent me to proclaim freedom for the prisoners and recovery of sight for the blind, to release the oppressed, [19]to proclaim the year of the Lord's favor."

[20]Then he rolled up the scroll, gave it back to the attendant and sat down. The eyes of everyone in the synagogue were fastened on him, [21]and he began by saying to them, "Today this scripture is fulfilled in your hearing."

Luke 10 [23]Then he turned to his disciples and said privately, "Blessed are the eyes that see what you see. [24]For I tell you that many prophets and kings wanted to see what you see but did not see it, and to hear what you hear but did not hear it."

Luke 24 [27]And beginning with Moses and all the Prophets, he explained to them what was said in all the Scriptures concerning himself.

Luke 24 [44]He said to them, "This is what I told you while I was still with you: Everything must be fulfilled that is written about me in the Law of Moses, the Prophets and the Psalms."

[45]Then he opened their minds so they could understand the Scriptures.

John 5 [39]"You diligently study the Scriptures because you think that by them you possess eternal life. These are the Scriptures that testify about me, [40]yet you refuse to come to me to have life."

B. NT Claims to Jesus' Deity

1. Jesus Is Considered Equal with God

Acts 2 [38]Peter replied, "Repent and be baptized, every one of you, in the name of Jesus Christ for the forgiveness of your sins. And you will receive the gift of the Holy Spirit."

1 Cor 1 [3]Grace and peace to you from God our Father and the Lord Jesus Christ.

1 Cor 12 [4]There are different kinds of gifts, but the same Spirit. [5]There are different kinds of service, but the same Lord. [6]There are different kinds of working, but the same God works all of them in all men.

2 Cor 13 [14]May the grace of the Lord Jesus Christ, and the love of God, and the fellowship of the Holy Spirit be with you all.

Gal 1 [3]Grace and peace to you from God our Father and the Lord Jesus Christ. . . .

Eph 4 [4]There is one body and one Spirit—just as you were called to one hope when you were called—[5]one Lord, one faith, one baptism; [6]one God and Father of all, who is over all and through all and in all.

Eph 6 [23]Peace to the brothers, and love with faith from God the Father and the Lord Jesus Christ.

Phil 2 [6]Who, being in very nature God, did not consider equality with God something to be grasped . . .

Col 1 [19]For God was pleased to have all his fullness dwell in him. . . .

Col 2 [9]For in Christ all the fullness of the Deity lives in bodily form. . . .

Col 3 [1]Since, then, you have been raised with Christ, set your hearts on things above, where Christ is seated at the right hand of God.

1 Thess 3 [11]Now may our God and Father himself and our Lord Jesus clear the way for us to come to you.

2 Thess 2 [16]May our Lord Jesus Christ himself and God our Father, who loved us and by his grace gave us eternal encouragement and good hope, [17]encourage your hearts and strengthen you in every good deed and word.

1 John 2 [23]No one who denies the Son has the Father; whoever acknowledges the Son has the Father also.

1 John 5 [20]We know also that the Son of God has come and has given us understanding, so that we may know him who is true. And we are in him who is true—even in his Son Jesus Christ. He is the true God and eternal life.

Rev 20 [6]Blessed and holy are those who have part in the first resurrection. The second death has no power over them, but they will be priests of God and of Christ and will reign with him for a thousand years.

Rev 22 [3]No longer will there be any curse. The throne of God and of the Lamb will be in the city, and his servants will serve him.

2. Jesus Possesses God's Attributes

a) Eternality

John 1 [1]In the beginning was the Word, and the Word was with God, and the Word was God. [2]He was with God in the beginning. . . .

[15]John testifies concerning him. He cries out, saying, "This was he of whom I said, 'He who comes after me has surpassed me because he was before me.'"

Acts 3 [15]"You killed the author of life, but God raised him from the dead. We are witnesses of this."

Col 1 [17]He is before all things, and in him all things hold together.

Heb 1 [11]"They will perish, but you remain; they will all wear out like a garment."

Rev 1 [8]"I am the Alpha and the Omega," says the Lord God, "who is, and who was, and who is to come, the Almighty."

Rev 1 [17]When I saw him, I fell at his feet as though dead. Then he placed his right hand on me and said: "Do not be afraid. I am the First and the Last. [18]I am the Living One; I was dead, and behold I am alive for ever and ever! And I hold the keys of death and Hades."

b) Faithfulness

2 Thess 3 [3]But the Lord is faithful, and he will strengthen and protect you from the evil one.

2 Tim 2 [13]if we are faithless, he will remain faithful, for he cannot disown himself.

Heb 2 [17]For this reason he had to be made like his brothers in every way, in order that he might become a merciful and faithful high priest in service to God, and that he might make atonement for the sins of the people.

Heb 3 [6]But Christ is faithful as a son over God's house. And we are his house, if we hold on to our courage and the hope of which we boast.

Rev 1 [5]and from Jesus Christ, who is the faithful witness, the firstborn from the dead, and the ruler of the kings of the earth.

To him who loves us and has freed us from our sins by his blood. . . .

Rev 3 [14]"To the angel of the church in Laodicea write: These are the words of the Amen, the faithful and true witness, the ruler of God's creation."

Rev 19 [11]I saw heaven standing open and there before me was a white horse, whose rider is called Faithful and True. With justice he judges and makes war.

c) Goodness

John 10 [11]"I am the good shepherd. The good shepherd lays down his life for the sheep."

Acts 10 [38]". . . how God anointed Jesus of Nazareth with the Holy Spirit and power, and how he went around doing good and healing all who were under the power of the devil, because God was with him."

1 Pet 2 [2]Like newborn babies, crave pure spiritual milk, so that by it you may grow up in your salvation, [3]now that you have tasted that the Lord is good.

d) Grace

John 1 [14]The Word became flesh and made his dwelling among us. We have seen his glory, the glory of the One and Only, who came from the Father, full of grace and truth. . . . [17]For the law was given through Moses; grace and truth came through Jesus Christ.

Acts 15 [11]"No! We believe it is through the grace of our Lord Jesus that we are saved, just as they are."

2 Cor 8 [9]For you know the grace of our Lord Jesus Christ, that though he was rich, yet for your sakes he became poor, so that you through his poverty might become rich.

1 Tim 1 [14]The grace of our Lord was poured out on me abundantly, along with the faith and love that are in Christ Jesus.

Heb 4 [16]Let us then approach the throne of grace with confidence, so that we may receive mercy and find grace to help us in our time of need.

e) Holiness

Mark 1 [24]"What do you want with us, Jesus of Nazareth? Have you come to destroy us? I know who you are—the Holy One of God!"

Luke 1 [35]The angel answered, "The Holy Spirit will come upon you, and the power of the Most High will overshadow you. So the holy one to be born will be called the Son of God."

John 6 [69]"We believe and know that you are the Holy One of God."

Acts 3 [14]"You disowned the Holy and Righteous One and asked that a murderer be released to you."

Acts 4 [27]"Indeed Herod and Pontius Pilate met together with the Gentiles and the people of Israel in this city to conspire against your holy servant Jesus, whom you anointed."

Heb 4 [15]For we do not have a high priest who is unable to sympathize with our weaknesses, but we have one who has been tempted in every way, just as we are—yet was without sin.

Heb 7 [26]Such a high priest meets our need—one who is holy, blameless, pure, set apart from sinners, exalted above the heavens.

1 Pet 2 [22]"He committed no sin, and no deceit was found in his mouth."

Rev 3 [7]"To the angel of the church in Philadelphia write: These are the words of him who is holy and true, who holds the key of David. What he opens no one can shut, and what he shuts no one can open."

f) Justice

Rev 19 [11]I saw heaven standing open and there before me was a white horse, whose rider is called Faithful and True. With justice he judges and makes war.

g) Love

John 15 [9]"As the Father has loved me, so have I loved you. Now remain in my love."

Rom 8 [35]Who shall separate us from the love of Christ? Shall trouble or hardship or persecution or famine or nakedness or danger or sword? . . . [38]For I am convinced that neither death nor life, neither angels nor demons, neither the present nor the future, nor any powers, [39]neither height nor depth, nor anything else in all creation, will be able to separate us from the love of God that is in Christ Jesus our Lord.

2 Cor 5 [14]For Christ's love compels us, because we are convinced that one died for all, and therefore all died.

Eph 3 [17]so that Christ may dwell in your hearts through faith. And I pray that you, being rooted and established in love, [18]may have power, together with all the saints, to grasp how wide and long and high and deep is the love of Christ. . . .

1 John 3 [16]This is how we know what love is: Jesus Christ laid down his life for us. And we ought to lay down our lives for our brothers.

h) Mercy

Heb 2 [17]For this reason he had to be made like his brothers in every way, in order that he might become a merciful and faithful high priest in service to God, and that he might make atonement for the sins of the people.

Heb 4 [16]Let us then approach the throne of grace with confidence, so that we may receive mercy and find grace to help us in our time of need.

Jude [21]Keep yourselves in God's love as you wait for the mercy of our Lord Jesus Christ to bring you to eternal life.

i) Omnipotence

Isa 9 [6]For to us a child is born, to us a son is given, and the government will be on his shoulders. And he will be called Wonderful Counselor, Mighty God, Everlasting Father, Prince of Peace.

Matt 28 [18]Then Jesus came to them and said, "All authority in heaven and on earth has been given to me."

1 Cor 1 [24]but to those whom God has called, both Jews and Greeks, Christ the power of God and the wisdom of God.

1 Cor 15 [24]Then the end will come, when he hands over the kingdom to God the Father after he has destroyed all dominion, authority and power.

Eph 1 [19]and his incomparably great power for us who believe. That power is like the working of his mighty strength, [20]which he exerted in Christ when he raised him from the dead and seated him at his right hand in the heavenly realms, [21]far above all rule and authority, power and dominion, and every title that can be given, not only in the present age but also in the one to come.

Col 2 [10]and you have been given fullness in Christ, who is the head over every power and authority.

Heb 1 [3]The Son is the radiance of God's glory and the exact representation of his being, sustaining all things by his powerful word. After he had provided purification for sins, he sat down at the right hand of the Majesty in heaven.

1 Pet 3 [22]who has gone into heaven and is at God's right hand—with angels, authorities and powers in submission to him.

2 Pet 1 [16]We did not follow cleverly invented stories when we told you about the power and coming of our Lord Jesus Christ, but we were eyewitnesses of his majesty.

Rev 1 [8]"I am the Alpha and the Omega," says the Lord God, "who is, and who was, and who is to come, the Almighty."

Rev 12 [10]Then I heard a loud voice in heaven say: "Now have come the salvation and the power and the kingdom of our God, and the authority of his Christ. For the accuser of our brothers, who accuses them before our God day and night, has been hurled down."

j) Omnipresence

Matt 18 [20]"For where two or three come together in my name, there am I with them."

John 3 [13]"No one has ever gone into heaven except the one who came from heaven—the Son of Man."

Eph 1 [22]And God placed all things under his feet and appointed him to be head over everything for the church, [23]which is his body, the fullness of him who fills everything in every way.

k) Omniscience

Matt 11 [27]"All things have been committed to me by my Father. No one knows the Son except the Father, and no one knows the Father except the Son and those to whom the Son chooses to reveal him."

Acts 1 [24]Then they prayed, "Lord, you know everyone's heart. Show us which of these two you have chosen. . . ."

1 Cor 4 [5]Therefore judge nothing before the appointed time; wait till the Lord comes. He will bring to light what is hidden in darkness and will expose the motives of men's hearts. At that time each will receive his praise from God.

Col 2 [2]My purpose is that they may be encouraged in heart and united in love, so that they may have the full riches of complete understanding, in order that they may know the mystery of God, namely, Christ, [3]in whom are hidden all the treasures of wisdom and knowledge.

Rev 2 [19]"I know your deeds, your love and faith, your service and perseverance, and that you are now doing more than you did at first."

Rev 2 [23]"I will strike her children dead. Then all the churches will know that I am he who searches hearts and minds, and I will repay each of you according to your deeds."

l) Patience

1 Tim 1 [16]But for that very reason I was shown mercy so that in me, the worst of sinners, Christ Jesus might display his unlimited patience as an example for those who would believe on him and receive eternal life.

m) Righteousness

2 Tim 4 [8]Now there is in store for me the crown of righteousness, which the Lord, the righteous Judge, will award to me on that day—and not only to me, but also to all who have longed for his appearing.

Heb 1 [8]But about the Son he says, "Your throne, O God, will last for ever and ever, and righteousness will be the scepter of your kingdom."

Heb 7 [1]This Melchizedek was king of Salem and priest of God Most High. He met Abraham returning from the defeat of the kings and blessed him, [2]and Abraham gave him a tenth of everything. First, his name means "king of righteousness"; then also, "king of Salem" means "king of peace." . . .

[17]For it is declared, "You are a priest forever, in the order of Melchizedek." . . .

[26]Such a high priest meets our need—one who is holy, blameless, pure, set apart from sinners, exalted above the heavens.

1 Pet 3 [18]For Christ died for sins once for all, the righteous for the unrighteous, to bring you to God. He was put to death in the body but made alive by the Spirit. . . .

1 John 2 [1]My dear children, I write this to you so that you will not sin. But if anybody does sin, we have one who speaks to the Father in our defense—Jesus Christ, the Righteous One. . . .

[29]If you know that he is righteous, you know that everyone who does what is right has been born of him.

Rev 19 [11]I saw heaven standing open and there before me was a white horse, whose rider is called Faithful and True. With justice he judges and makes war.

n) Self-Existence

John 1 [1]In the beginning was the Word, and the Word was with God, and the Word was God.
2 Cor 8 [9]For you know the grace of our Lord Jesus Christ, that though he was rich, yet for your sakes he became poor, so that you through his poverty might become rich.
Phil 2 [6]Who, being in very nature God, did not consider equality with God something to be grasped . . .
Heb 7 [16]one who has become a priest not on the basis of a regulation as to his ancestry but on the basis of the power of an indestructible life.

o) Truthfulness

John 1 [14]The Word became flesh and made his dwelling among us. We have seen his glory, the glory of the One and Only, who came from the Father, full of grace and truth. . . . [17]For the law was given through Moses; grace and truth came through Jesus Christ.
John 14 [6]Jesus answered, "I am the way and the truth and the life. No one comes to the Father except through me."
John 18 [37]"You are a king, then!" said Pilate.
Jesus answered, "You are right in saying I am a king. In fact, for this reason I was born, and for this I came into the world, to testify to the truth. Everyone on the side of truth listens to me."
2 Cor 11 [10]As surely as the truth of Christ is in me, nobody in the regions of Achaia will stop this boasting of mine.
Eph 4 [21]Surely you heard of him and were taught in him in accordance with the truth that is in Jesus.
1 John 5 [20]We know also that the Son of God has come and has given us understanding, so that we may know him who is true. And we are in him who is true—even in his Son Jesus Christ. He is the true God and eternal life.
Rev 3 [7]"To the angel of the church in Philadelphia write: These are the words of him who is holy and true, who holds the key of David. What he opens no one can shut, and what he shuts no one can open. . . .
[14]"To the angel of the church in Laodicea write: These are the words of the Amen, the faithful and true witness, the ruler of God's creation."
Rev 19 [11]I saw heaven standing open and there before me was a white horse, whose rider is called Faithful and True. With justice he judges and makes war.

p) Unchangeability

Heb 1 [11]"They will perish, but you remain; they will all wear out like a garment. [12]You will roll them up like a robe; like a garment they will be changed. But you remain the same, and your years will never end."
Heb 13 [8]Jesus Christ is the same yesterday and today and forever.

q) Wisdom

1 Cor 1 [24]but to those whom God has called, both Jews and Greeks, Christ the power of God and the wisdom of God.
1 Cor 1 [30]It is because of him that you are in Christ Jesus, who has become for us wisdom from God—that is, our righteousness, holiness and redemption.
Col 2 [2]My purpose is that they may be encouraged in heart and united in love, so that they may have the full riches of complete understanding, in order that they may know the mystery of God, namely, Christ, [3]in whom are hidden all the treasures of wisdom and knowledge.
Rev 5 [12]In a loud voice they sang: "Worthy is the Lamb, who was slain, to receive power and wealth and wisdom and strength and honor and glory and praise!"

3. Jesus Does the Work of God

a) God's Work Related to the Created Order

(1) Jesus Created

See p. 181b, The Son and Creation

(2) Jesus Sustains

John 1 [3]Through him all things were made; without him nothing was made that has been made. [4]In him was life, and that life was the light of men.
Col 1 [17]He is before all things, and in him all things hold together.
Heb 1 [3]The Son is the radiance of God's glory and the exact representation of his being, sustaining all things by his powerful word. After he had provided purification for sins, he sat down at the right hand of the Majesty in heaven.

(3) Jesus Rules

1 Cor 15 [27]For he "has put everything under his feet." Now when it says that "everything" has been put under him, it is clear that this does not include God himself, who put everything under Christ.
Phil 2 [9]Therefore God exalted him to the highest place and gave him the name that is above every name, [10]that at the name of Jesus every knee should bow, in heaven and on earth and under the earth, [11]and every tongue confess that Jesus Christ is Lord, to the glory of God the Father.
Rev 1 [5]and from Jesus Christ, who is the faithful witness, the firstborn from the dead, and the ruler of the kings of the earth.
To him who loves us and has freed us from our sins by his blood . . .
Rev 3 [14]"To the angel of the church in Laodicea write: These are the words of the Amen, the faithful and true witness, the ruler of God's creation."

b) God's Work Related to Mankind

(1) Jesus Judges All Mankind

Acts 10 [42]"He commanded us to preach to the people and to testify that he is the one whom God appointed as judge of the living and the dead."
Acts 17 [31]"For he has set a day when he will judge the world with justice by the man he has appointed. He has given proof of this to all men by raising him from the dead."
Rom 2 [16]This will take place on the day when God will judge men's secrets through Jesus Christ, as my gospel declares.
2 Cor 5 [10]For we must all appear before the judgment seat of Christ, that each one may receive what is due him for the things done while in the body, whether good or bad.
2 Tim 4 [1]In the presence of God and of Christ Jesus, who will judge the living and the dead, and in view of his appearing and his kingdom, I give you this charge. . . .

(2) Jesus Punishes the Wicked

1 Thess 5 [2]for you know very well that the day of the Lord will come like a thief in the night. [3]While people are saying, "Peace and safety," destruction will come on them suddenly, as labor pains on a pregnant woman, and they will not escape.
2 Thess 1 [6]God is just: He will pay back trouble to those who trouble you [7]and give relief to you who are troubled, and to us as well. This will happen when the Lord Jesus is revealed from heaven in blazing fire with his powerful angels. [8]He will punish those who do not know God and do not obey the gospel of our Lord Jesus. [9]They will be punished with everlasting destruction and shut out from the presence of the Lord and from the majesty of his power. . . .
2 Thess 2 [8]And then the lawless one will be revealed, whom the Lord Jesus will overthrow with the breath of his mouth and destroy by the splendor of his coming.
Rev 6 [14]The sky receded like a scroll, rolling up, and every mountain and island was removed from its place.
[15]Then the kings of the earth, the princes, the generals, the rich, the mighty, and every slave and every free man hid in caves and among the rocks of the mountains. [16]They called to the mountains and the rocks, "Fall on us and hide us from the face of him who sits on the throne and from the wrath of the Lamb! [17]For the great day of their wrath has come, and who can stand?"
Rev 11 [18]"The nations were angry; and your wrath has come. The time has come for judging the dead, and for rewarding your servants the prophets and your saints and those who reverence your name, both small and great—and for destroying those who destroy the earth."
Rev 21 [8]"But the cowardly, the unbelieving, the vile, the murderers, the sexually immoral, those who practice magic arts, the idolaters and all liars—their place will be in the fiery lake of burning sulfur. This is the second death."

(3) Jesus Rewards the Righteous

1 Cor 9 [25]Everyone who competes in the games goes into strict training. They do it to get a crown that will not last; but we do it to get a crown that will last forever.

Col 3 [4]When Christ, who is your life, appears, then you also will appear with him in glory.

1 Thess 4 [17]After that, we who are still alive and are left will be caught up together with them in the clouds to meet the Lord in the air. And so we will be with the Lord forever.

2 Thess 1 [10]on the day he comes to be glorified in his holy people and to be marveled at among all those who have believed. This includes you, because you believed our testimony to you.

2 Tim 4 [8]Now there is in store for me the crown of righteousness, which the Lord, the righteous Judge, will award to me on that day—and not only to me, but also to all who have longed for his appearing.

1 Pet 1 [3]Praise be to the God and Father of our Lord Jesus Christ! In his great mercy he has given us new birth into a living hope through the resurrection of Jesus Christ from the dead, [4]and into an inheritance that can never perish, spoil or fade—kept in heaven for you, [5]who through faith are shielded by God's power until the coming of the salvation that is ready to be revealed in the last time.

Rev 2 [10]"Do not be afraid of what you are about to suffer. I tell you, the devil will put some of you in prison to test you, and you will suffer persecution for ten days. Be faithful, even to the point of death, and I will give you the crown of life."

Rev 7 [17]"For the Lamb at the center of the throne will be their shepherd; he will lead them to springs of living water. And God will wipe away every tear from their eyes."

Rev 11 [18]"The nations were angry; and your wrath has come. The time has come for judging the dead, and for rewarding your servants the prophets and your saints and those who reverence your name, both small and great—and for destroying those who destroy the earth."

c) God's Work Related to the Problem of Sin

(1) Jesus Overcomes Evil

Col 2 [15]And having disarmed the powers and authorities, he made a public spectacle of them, triumphing over them by the cross.

Heb 2 [14]Since the children have flesh and blood, he too shared in their humanity so that by his death he might destroy him who holds the power of death—that is, the devil. . . .

1 John 3 [8]He who does what is sinful is of the devil, because the devil has been sinning from the beginning. The reason the Son of God appeared was to destroy the devil's work.

Rev 17 [14]"They will make war against the Lamb, but the Lamb will overcome them because he is Lord of lords and King of kings—and with him will be his called, chosen and faithful followers."

(2) Jesus Appeases God's Wrath

Rom 3 [23]for all have sinned and fall short of the glory of God, [24]and are justified freely by his grace through the redemption that came by Christ Jesus. [25]God presented him as a sacrifice of atonement, through faith in his blood. He did this to demonstrate his justice, because in his forbearance he had left the sins committed beforehand unpunished. . . .

Rom 5 [8]But God demonstrates his own love for us in this: While we were still sinners, Christ died for us.

[9]Since we have now been justified by his blood, how much more shall we be saved from God's wrath through him! [10]For if, when we were God's enemies, we were reconciled to him through the death of his Son, how much more, having been reconciled, shall we be saved through his life! [11]Not only is this so, but we also rejoice in God through our Lord Jesus Christ, through whom we have now received reconciliation.

2 Cor 5 [21]God made him who had no sin to be sin for us, so that in him we might become the righteousness of God.

Gal 3 [13]Christ redeemed us from the curse of the law by becoming a curse for us, for it is written: "Cursed is everyone who is hung on a tree."

Eph 2 [13]But now in Christ Jesus you who once were far away have been brought near through the blood of Christ.

[14]For he himself is our peace, who has made the two one and has destroyed the barrier, the dividing wall of hostility, [15]by abolishing in his flesh the law with its commandments and regulations. His purpose was to create in himself one new man out of the two, thus making peace, [16]and in this one body to reconcile both of them to God through the cross, by which he put to death their hostility.

Heb 9 [11]When Christ came as high priest of the good things that are already here, he went through the greater and more perfect tabernacle that is not man-made, that is to say, not a part of this creation. [12]He did not enter by means of the blood of goats and calves; but he entered the Most Holy Place once for all by his own blood, having obtained eternal redemption. [13]The blood of goats and bulls and the ashes of a heifer sprinkled on those who are ceremonially unclean sanctify them so that they are outwardly clean. [14]How much more, then, will the blood of Christ, who through the eternal Spirit offered himself unblemished to God, cleanse our consciences from acts that lead to death, so that we may serve the living God!

1 Pet 3 [18]For Christ died for sins once for all, the righteous for the unrighteous, to bring you to God. He was put to death in the body but made alive by the Spirit. . . .

1 John 4 [10]This is love: not that we loved God, but that he loved us and sent his Son as an atoning sacrifice for our sins.

(3) Jesus Justifies People before God

Acts 13 [39]"Through him everyone who believes is justified from everything you could not be justified from by the law of Moses."

Rom 3 [23]for all have sinned and fall short of the glory of God, [24]and are justified freely by his grace through the redemption that came by Christ Jesus.

Rom 3 [26]he did it to demonstrate his justice at the present time, so as to be just and the one who justifies those who have faith in Jesus.

Rom 4 [23]The words "it was credited to him" were written not for him alone, [24]but also for us, to whom God will credit righteousness—for us who believe in him who raised Jesus our Lord from the dead. [25]He was delivered over to death for our sins and was raised to life for our justification.

Rom 5 [9]Since we have now been justified by his blood, how much more shall we be saved from God's wrath through him!

Rom 8 [1]Therefore, there is now no condemnation for those who are in Christ Jesus, [2]because through Christ Jesus the law of the Spirit of life set me free from the law of sin and death. [3]For what the law was powerless to do in that it was weakened by the sinful nature, God did by sending his own Son in the likeness of sinful man to be a sin offering. And so he condemned sin in sinful man. . . .

Gal 2 [16]". . . know that a man is not justified by observing the law, but by faith in Jesus Christ. So we, too, have put our faith in Christ Jesus that we may be justified by faith in Christ and not by observing the law, because by observing the law no one will be justified.

[17]"If, while we seek to be justified in Christ, it becomes evident that we ourselves are sinners, does that mean that Christ promotes sin? Absolutely not!"

1 John 1 [7]But if we walk in the light, as he is in the light, we have fellowship with one another, and the blood of Jesus, his Son, purifies us from all sin.

(4) Jesus Reconciles People to God

Rom 5 [10]For if, when we were God's enemies, we were reconciled to him through the death of his Son, how much more, having been reconciled, shall we be saved through his life! [11]Not only is this so, but we also rejoice in God through our Lord Jesus Christ, through whom we have now received reconciliation.

2 Cor 5 [18]All this is from God, who reconciled us to himself through Christ and gave us the ministry of reconciliation. . . .

Eph 2 [14]For he himself is our peace, who has made the two one and has destroyed the barrier, the dividing wall of hostility, [15]by abolishing in his flesh the law with its commandments and regulations. His purpose was to create in himself one new man out of the two, thus making peace, [16]and in this one body to reconcile both of them to God through the cross, by which he put to death their hostility.

Col 1 [20]and through him to reconcile to himself all things, whether things on earth or things in heaven, by making peace through his blood, shed on the cross.

(5) Jesus Forgives Sin

Acts 5 [31]"God exalted him to his own right hand as Prince and Savior that he might give repentance and forgiveness of sins to Israel."

Eph 1 [7]In him we have redemption through his blood, the forgiveness of sins, in accordance with the riches of God's grace. . . .

Col 3 [13]Bear with each other and forgive whatever grievances you may have against one another. Forgive as the Lord forgave you.

(6) Jesus Saves People

Acts 4 [12]"Salvation is found in no one else, for there is no other name under heaven given to men by which we must be saved."

1 Thess 5 [9]For God did not appoint us to suffer wrath but to receive salvation through our Lord Jesus Christ.

1 Tim 1 [15]Here is a trustworthy saying that deserves full acceptance: Christ Jesus came into the world to save sinners—of whom I am the worst.

1 John 4 [14]And we have seen and testify that the Father has sent his Son to be the Savior of the world.

d) God's Work Related to Believers

(1) Jesus Gives Life to Believers

Gal 2 [20]"I have been crucified with Christ and I no longer live, but Christ lives in me. The life I live in the body, I live by faith in the Son of God, who loved me and gave himself for me."

Eph 2 [4]But because of his great love for us, God, who is rich in mercy, [5]made us alive with Christ even when we were dead in transgressions—it is by grace you have been saved. [6]And God raised us up with Christ and seated us with him in the heavenly realms in Christ Jesus. . . .

Col 3 [4]When Christ, who is your life, appears, then you also will appear with him in glory.

1 Thess 5 [10]He died for us so that, whether we are awake or asleep, we may live together with him.

2 Tim 2 [11]Here is a trustworthy saying: If we died with him, we will also live with him. . . .

1 John 4 [9]This is how God showed his love among us: He sent his one and only Son into the world that we might live through him.

1 John 5 [12]He who has the Son has life; he who does not have the Son of God does not have life.

(2) Jesus Gives Revelation to Believers

2 Cor 12 [1]I must go on boasting. Although there is nothing to be gained, I will go on to visions and revelations from the Lord.

Gal 1 [12]I did not receive it from any man, nor was I taught it; rather, I received it by revelation from Jesus Christ.

(3) Jesus Indwells Believers

2 Cor 13 [5]Examine yourselves to see whether you are in the faith; test yourselves. Do you not realize that Christ Jesus is in you—unless, of course, you fail the test?

Eph 3 [17]so that Christ may dwell in your hearts through faith. And I pray that you, being rooted and established in love . . .

(4) Jesus Empowers Believers

2 Cor 12 [9]But he said to me, "My grace is sufficient for you, for my power is made perfect in weakness." Therefore I will boast all the more gladly about my weaknesses, so that Christ's power may rest on me.

Phil 4 [13]I can do everything through him who gives me strength.

Col 1 [29]To this end I labor, struggling with all his energy, which so powerfully works in me.

1 Tim 1 [12]I thank Christ Jesus our Lord, who has given me strength, that he considered me faithful, appointing me to his service.

(5) Jesus Speaks through Believers

2 Cor 13 [3]since you are demanding proof that Christ is speaking through me. He is not weak in dealing with you, but is powerful among you.

(6) Jesus Calls for Ministry from Believers

Acts 26 [16]"'Now get up and stand on your feet. I have appeared to you to appoint you as a servant and as a witness of what you have seen of me and what I will show you. [17]I will rescue you from your own people and from the Gentiles. I am sending you to them [18]to open their eyes and turn them from darkness to light, and from the power of Satan to God, so that they may receive forgiveness of sins and a place among those who are sanctified by faith in me.'"

2 Cor 5 [20]We are therefore Christ's ambassadors, as though God were making his appeal through us. We implore you on Christ's behalf: Be reconciled to God.

(7) Jesus Sanctifies Believers

1 Cor 1 [30]It is because of him that you are in Christ Jesus, who has become for us wisdom from God—that is, our righteousness, holiness and redemption.

Eph 5 [25]Husbands, love your wives, just as Christ loved the church and gave himself up for her [26]to make her holy, cleansing her by the washing with water through the word, [27]and to present her to himself as a radiant church, without stain or wrinkle or any other blemish, but holy and blameless.

Heb 2 [11]Both the one who makes men holy and those who are made holy are of the same family. So Jesus is not ashamed to call them brothers.

Heb 13 [12]And so Jesus also suffered outside the city gate to make the people holy through his own blood.

(8) Jesus Intercedes for Believers

Rom 8 [34]Who is he that condemns? Christ Jesus, who died—more than that, who was raised to life—is at the right hand of God and is also interceding for us.

Eph 3 [12]In him and through faith in him we may approach God with freedom and confidence.

Col 3 [17]And whatever you do, whether in word or deed, do it all in the name of the Lord Jesus, giving thanks to God the Father through him.

Heb 7 [25]Therefore he is able to save completely those who come to God through him, because he always lives to intercede for them.

1 John 2 [1]My dear children, I write this to you so that you will not sin. But if anybody does sin, we have one who speaks to the Father in our defense—Jesus Christ, the Righteous One.

(9) Jesus Preserves Believers

Rom 8 [34]Who is he that condemns? Christ Jesus, who died—more than that, who was raised to life—is at the right hand of God and is also interceding for us.

1 Cor 1 [8]He will keep you strong to the end, so that you will be blameless on the day of our Lord Jesus Christ.

2 Tim 1 [12]That is why I am suffering as I am. Yet I am not ashamed, because I know whom I have believed, and am convinced that he is able to guard what I have entrusted to him for that day.

Heb 2 [18]Because he himself suffered when he was tempted, he is able to help those who are being tempted.

(10) Jesus Transforms the Bodies of Believers

1 Cor 15 [50]I declare to you, brothers, that flesh and blood cannot inherit the kingdom of God, nor does the perishable inherit the imperishable. [51]Listen, I tell you a mystery: We will not all sleep, but we will all be changed. . . .

Phil 3 [20]But our citizenship is in heaven. And we eagerly await a Savior from there, the Lord Jesus Christ, [21]who, by the power that enables him to bring everything under his control, will transform our lowly bodies so that they will be like his glorious body.

(11) Jesus Leads Believers

Rev 7 [17]"For the Lamb at the center of the throne will be their shepherd; he will lead them to springs of living water. And God will wipe away every tear from their eyes."

e) God's Work Related to Scripture

1 Pet 1 [10]Concerning this salvation, the prophets, who spoke of the grace that was to come to you, searched intently and with the greatest care, [11]trying to find out the time and circumstances to which the Spirit of Christ in them was pointing when he predicted the sufferings of Christ and the glories that would follow.

4. Jesus Is Identified with God

a) Jesus and God's Being

Heb 1 [3]The Son is the radiance of God's glory and the exact representation of his being, sustaining all things by his powerful word. After he had provided purification for sins, he sat down at the right hand of the Majesty in heaven.

b) Jesus and God's Glory

2 Cor 3 [18]And we, who with unveiled faces all reflect the Lord's glory, are being transformed into his likeness with ever-increasing glory, which comes from the Lord, who is the Spirit.
Heb 1 [3]The Son is the radiance of God's glory and the exact representation of his being, sustaining all things by his powerful word. After he had provided purification for sins, he sat down at the right hand of the Majesty in heaven.

c) Jesus and God's Image

2 Cor 4 [4]The god of this age has blinded the minds of unbelievers, so that they cannot see the light of the gospel of the glory of Christ, who is the image of God.
Col 1 [15]He is the image of the invisible God, the firstborn over all creation.

d) Jesus and God's Name

John 1 [1]In the beginning was the Word, and the Word was with God, and the Word was God. . . . [18]No one has ever seen God, but God the One and Only, who is at the Father's side, has made him known.
John 20 [28]Thomas said to him, "My Lord and my God!" . . . [31]But these are written that you may believe that Jesus is the Christ, the Son of God, and that by believing you may have life in his name.
Acts 9 [20]At once he began to preach in the synagogues that Jesus is the Son of God.
Acts 20 [28]"Keep watch over yourselves and all the flock of which the Holy Spirit has made you overseers. Be shepherds of the church of God, which he bought with his own blood."
Rom 9 [5]Theirs are the patriarchs, and from them is traced the human ancestry of Christ, who is God over all, forever praised! Amen.
Col 2 [9]For in Christ all the fullness of the Deity lives in bodily form. . . .
1 Thess 1 [9]for they themselves report what kind of reception you gave us. They tell how you turned to God from idols to serve the living and true God, [10]and to wait for his Son from heaven, whom he raised from the dead—Jesus, who rescues us from the coming wrath.
1 Tim 3 [16]Beyond all question, the mystery of godliness is great: He appeared in a body, was vindicated by the Spirit, was seen by angels, was preached among the nations, was believed on in the world, was taken up in glory.
Titus 2 [13]while we wait for the blessed hope—the glorious appearing of our great God and Savior, Jesus Christ . . .
Heb 1 [5]For to which of the angels did God ever say, "You are my Son; today I have become your Father"? Or again, "I will be his Father, and he will be my Son"? . . . [8]But about the Son he says, "Your throne, O God, will last for ever and ever, and righteousness will be the scepter of your kingdom."
2 Pet 2 [1]But there were also false prophets among the people, just as there will be false teachers among you. They will secretly introduce destructive heresies, even denying the sovereign Lord who bought them—bringing swift destruction on themselves.
1 John 5 [20]We know also that the Son of God has come and has given us understanding, so that we may know him who is true. And we are in him who is true—even in his Son Jesus Christ. He is the true God and eternal life.

e) Jesus and God's Nature

Phil 2 [6]Who, being in very nature God, did not consider equality with God something to be grasped. . . .

5. Jesus Is Paralleled with God

1) The Glory Is of God and Christ

Rom 5 [1]Therefore, since we have been justified through faith, we have peace with God through our Lord Jesus Christ, [2]through whom we have gained access by faith into this grace in which we now stand. And we rejoice in the hope of the glory of God.
1 Cor 2 [8]None of the rulers of this age understood it, for if they had, they would not have crucified the Lord of glory.
1 Pet 4 [13]But rejoice that you participate in the sufferings of Christ, so that you may be overjoyed when his glory is revealed. [14]If you are insulted because of the name of Christ, you are blessed, for the Spirit of glory and of God rests on you.
2 Pet 1 [17]For he received honor and glory from God the Father when the voice came to him from the Majestic Glory, saying, "This is my Son, whom I love; with him I am well pleased."

2) The Glory of God Is in Christ

2 Cor 4 [6]For God, who said, "Let light shine out of darkness," made his light shine in our hearts to give us the light of the knowledge of the glory of God in the face of Christ.

3) Majesty Is of God and Christ

Heb 1 [3]The Son is the radiance of God's glory and the exact representation of his being, sustaining all things by his powerful word. After he had provided purification for sins, he sat down at the right hand of the Majesty in heaven.
2 Pet 1 [16]We did not follow cleverly invented stories when we told you about the power and coming of our Lord Jesus Christ, but we were eyewitnesses of his majesty. [17]For he received honor and glory from God the Father when the voice came to him from the Majestic Glory, saying, "This is my Son, whom I love; with him I am well pleased."

4) The Spirit Is of God and Christ

Rom 8 [9]You, however, are controlled not by the sinful nature but by the Spirit, if the Spirit of God lives in you. And if anyone does not have the Spirit of Christ, he does not belong to Christ.
Phil 1 [19]for I know that through your prayers and the help given by the Spirit of Jesus Christ, what has happened to me will turn out for my deliverance.
1 Thess 4 [8]Therefore, he who rejects this instruction does not reject man but God, who gives you his Holy Spirit.
1 Pet 1 [11]trying to find out the time and circumstances to which the Spirit of Christ in them was pointing when he predicted the sufferings of Christ and the glories that would follow. [12]It was revealed to them that they were not serving themselves but you, when they spoke of the things that have now been told you by those who have preached the gospel to you by the Holy Spirit sent from heaven. Even angels long to look into these things.

5) Only God Is Wise and Christ Is Our Wisdom

1 Cor 1 [21]For since in the wisdom of God the world through its wisdom did not know him, God was pleased through the foolishness of what was preached to save those who believe. [22]Jews demand miraculous signs and Greeks look for wisdom, [23]but we preach Christ crucified: a stumbling block to Jews and foolishness to Gentiles, [24]but to those whom God has called, both Jews and Greeks, Christ the power of God and the wisdom of God.

6) The Power Is of God and Christ

1 Cor 5 [4]When you are assembled in the name of our Lord Jesus and I am with you in spirit, and the power of our Lord Jesus is present, [5]hand this man over to Satan, so that the sinful nature may be destroyed and his spirit saved on the day of the Lord.
2 Cor 6 [7]in truthful speech and in the power of God; with weapons of righteousness in the right hand and in the left. . . .
2 Cor 12 [9]But he said to me, "My grace is sufficient for you, for my power is made perfect in weakness." Therefore I will boast all the more gladly about my weaknesses, so that Christ's power may rest on me.

7) Christ Is the Power of God

1 Cor 1 [24]but to those whom God has called, both Jews and Greeks, Christ the power of God and the wisdom of God.

8) The Truth Is of God and Christ

Rom 1 [25]They exchanged the truth of God for a lie, and worshiped and served created things rather than the Creator—who is forever praised. Amen.

Rom 9 [1]I speak the truth in Christ—I am not lying, my conscience confirms it in the Holy Spirit. . . .
2 Cor 11 [10]As surely as the truth of Christ is in me, nobody in the regions of Achaia will stop this boasting of mine.

9) The Authoritative Word Is of God and Christ

Matt 4 [4]Jesus answered, "It is written: 'Man does not live on bread alone, but on every word that comes from the mouth of God.'"
Col 3 [16]Let the word of Christ dwell in you richly as you teach and admonish one another with all wisdom, and as you sing psalms, hymns and spiritual songs with gratitude in your hearts to God.
1 Thess 1 [8]The Lord's message rang out from you not only in Macedonia and Achaia—your faith in God has become known everywhere. Therefore we do not need to say anything about it. . . .

10) God and Christ Love Us

Rom 5 [8]But God demonstrates his own love for us in this: while we were still sinners, Christ died for us.
Rom 8 [35]Who shall separate us from the love of Christ? Shall trouble or hardship or persecution or famine or nakedness or danger or sword?
Gal 2 [20]"I have been crucified with Christ and I no longer live, but Christ lives in me. The life I live in the body, I live by faith in the Son of God, who loved me and gave himself for me."

11) The Love of God Is in Christ

Rom 8 [39]neither height nor depth, nor anything else in all creation, will be able to separate us from the love of God that is in Christ Jesus our Lord.

12) Mercy Is from God and Christ

Rom 15 [9]so that the Gentiles may glorify God for his mercy, as it is written: "Therefore I will praise you among the Gentiles; I will sing hymns to your name."
1 Cor 7 [25]Now about virgins: I have no command from the Lord, but I give a judgment as one who by the Lord's mercy is trustworthy.
1 Tim 1 [2]To Timothy my true son in the faith: Grace, mercy and peace from God the Father and Christ Jesus our Lord.
2 Tim 1 [2]To Timothy, my dear son: Grace, mercy and peace from God the Father and Christ Jesus our Lord.
Jude [21]Keep yourselves in God's love as you wait for the mercy of our Lord Jesus Christ to bring you to eternal life.

13) The Gospel Is of God and Christ

Rom 1 [16]I am not ashamed of the gospel, because it is the power of God for the salvation of everyone who believes: first for the Jew, then for the Gentile.
2 Cor 10 [14]We are not going too far in our boasting, as would be the case if we had not come to you, for we did get as far as you with the gospel of Christ.
Gal 1 [7]which is really no gospel at all. Evidently some people are throwing you into confusion and are trying to pervert the gospel of Christ.
Phil 1 [27]Whatever happens, conduct yourselves in a manner worthy of the gospel of Christ. Then, whether I come and see you or only hear about you in my absence, I will know that you stand firm in one spirit, contending as one man for the faith of the gospel. . . .
1 Thess 2 [2]We had previously suffered and been insulted in Philippi, as you know, but with the help of our God we dared to tell you his gospel in spite of strong opposition.
1 Thess 3 [2]We sent Timothy, who is our brother and God's fellow worker in spreading the gospel of Christ, to strengthen and encourage you in your faith. . . .
2 Thess 1 [8]He will punish those who do not know God and do not obey the gospel of our Lord Jesus.

14) Salvation Is from God and Christ

Eph 5 [23]For the husband is the head of the wife as Christ is the head of the church, his body, of which he is the Savior.
Phil 3 [20]But our citizenship is in heaven. And we eagerly await a Savior from there, the Lord Jesus Christ. . . .
1 Thess 5 [9]For God did not appoint us to suffer wrath but to receive salvation through our Lord Jesus Christ.
Titus 2 [10]and not to steal from them, but to show that they can be fully trusted, so that in every way they will make the teaching about God our Savior attractive.

[11]For the grace of God that brings salvation has appeared to all men.
Titus 2 [13]while we wait for the blessed hope—the glorious appearing of our great God and Savior, Jesus Christ. . . .

15) God and Christ Rescue Us

Col 1 [13]For he has rescued us from the dominion of darkness and brought us into the kingdom of the Son he loves. . . .
1 Thess 1 [10]and to wait for his Son from heaven, whom he raised from the dead—Jesus, who rescues us from the coming wrath.

16) God and Christ Redeem Us

Gal 3 [13]Christ redeemed us from the curse of the law by becoming a curse for us, for it is written: "Cursed is everyone who is hung on a tree."
Gal 4 [4]But when the time had fully come, God sent his Son born of a woman, born under law, [5]to redeem those under law, that we might receive the full rights of sons.
Col 1 [13]For he has rescued us from the dominion of darkness and brought us into the Kingdom of the Son he loves, [14]in whom we have redemption, the forgiveness of sins.

17) God and Christ Forgive Our Sins

Col 1 [13]For he has rescued us from the dominion of darkness and brought us into the kingdom of the Son he loves, [14]in whom we have redemption, the forgiveness of sins.
Col 2 [13]When you were dead in your sins and in the uncircumcision of your sinful nature, God made you alive with Christ. He forgave us all our sins. . . .

18) We Are to Believe God and Christ

Acts 16 [31]They replied, "Believe in the Lord Jesus, and you will be saved—you and your household."
Rom 4 [1]What then shall we say that Abraham, our forefather, discovered in this matter? [2]If, in fact, Abraham was justified by works, he had something to boast about—but not before God. [3]What does the Scripture say? "Abraham believed God, and it was credited to him as righteousness."
Gal 2 [16]". . . know that a man is not justified by observing the law, but by faith in Jesus Christ. So we, too, have put our faith in Christ Jesus that we may be justified by faith in Christ and not by observing the law, because by observing the law no one will be justified.

[17]"If, while we seek to be justified in Christ, it becomes evident that we ourselves are sinners, does that mean that Christ promotes sin? Absolutely not! [18]If I rebuild what I destroyed, I prove that I am a lawbreaker. [19]For through the law I died to the law so that I might live for God."

19) We Are to Know God and Christ

Gal 4 [8]Formerly, when you did not know God, you were slaves to those who by nature are not gods. [9]But now that you know God—or rather are known by God—how is it that you are turning back to those weak and miserable principles? Do you wish to be enslaved by them all over again?
Phil 3 [10]I want to know Christ and the power of his resurrection and the fellowship of sharing in his sufferings, becoming like him in his death. . . .
2 Pet 1 [8]For if you possess these qualities in increasing measure, they will keep you from being ineffective and unproductive in your knowledge of our Lord Jesus Christ.

20) Peace Comes from God and Christ

Eph 2 [13]But now in Christ Jesus you who once were far away have been brought near through the blood of Christ.

[14]For he himself is our peace, who has made the two one and has destroyed the barrier, the dividing wall of hostility. . . .
Phil 1 [2]Grace and peace to you from God our Father and the Lord Jesus Christ.
Col 1 [2]To the holy and faithful brothers in Christ at Colosse: Grace and peace to you from God our Father.
Col 3 [15]Let the peace of Christ rule in your hearts, since as

members of one body you were called to peace. And be thankful.

1 Thess 1 [1]Paul, Silas and Timothy,

To the church of the Thessalonians in God the Father and the Lord Jesus Christ: Grace and peace to you.

1 Thess 5 [23]May God himself, the God of peace, sanctify you through and through. May your whole spirit, soul and body be kept blameless at the coming of our Lord Jesus Christ.

21) Grace Is of God and Christ

Gal 1 [6]I am astonished that you are so quickly deserting the one who called you by the grace of Christ and are turning to a different gospel. . . .

Col 1 [2]To the holy and faithful brothers in Christ at Colosse: Grace and peace to you from God our Father.

Col 1 [6]that has come to you. All over the world this gospel is bearing fruit and growing, just as it has been doing among you since the day you heard it and understood God's grace in all its truth.

Phil 1 [2]Grace and peace to you from God our Father and the Lord Jesus Christ.

Phil 4 [23]The grace of the Lord Jesus Christ be with your spirit. Amen.

1 Thess 1 [1]Paul, Silas and Timothy,

To the church of the Thessalonians in God the Father and the Lord Jesus Christ: Grace and peace to you.

1 Thess 5 [28]The grace of our Lord Jesus Christ be with you.

22) God and Christ Dwell in Us

Gal 2 [20]"I have been crucified with Christ and I no longer live, but Christ lives in me. The life I live in the body, I live by faith in the Son of God, who loved me and gave himself for me."

Eph 3 [16]I pray that out of his glorious riches he may strengthen you with power through his Spirit in your inner being, [17]so that Christ may dwell in your hearts through faith. And I pray that you, being rooted and established in love . . .

Eph 4 [6]one God and Father of all, who is over all and through all and in all.

Col 1 [27]To them God has chosen to make known among the Gentiles the glorious riches of this mystery, which is Christ in you, the hope of glory.

23) God and Christ Sanctify Us

Acts 20 [32]"Now I commit you to God and to the word of his grace, which can build you up and give you an inheritance among all those who are sanctified."

Acts 26 [15]"Then I asked, 'Who are you, Lord?'

"'I am Jesus, whom you are persecuting,' the Lord replied. . . . [17]'I will rescue you from your own people and from the Gentiles. I am sending you to them [18]to open their eyes and turn them from darkness to light, and from the power of Satan to God, so that they may receive forgiveness of sins and a place among those who are sanctified by faith in me.'"

1 Cor 1 [2]To the church of God in Corinth, to those sanctified in Christ Jesus and called to be holy, together with all those everywhere who call on the name of our Lord Jesus Christ—their Lord and ours. . . .

24) God and Christ Are Our Strength

Phil 4 [13]I can do everything through him who gives me strength.

Col 1 [10]And we pray this in order that you may live a life worthy of the Lord and may please him in every way: bearing fruit in every good work, growing in the knowledge of God, [11]being strengthened with all power according to his glorious might so that you may have great endurance and patience, and joyfully . . .

25) God and Christ Strengthen Us

2 Thess 2 [16]May our Lord Jesus Christ himself and God our Father, who loved us and by his grace gave us eternal encouragement and good hope, [17]encourage your hearts and strengthen you in every good deed and word.

26) God and Christ Comfort Us

2 Cor 1 [3]Praise be to the God and Father of our Lord Jesus Christ, the Father of compassion and the God of all comfort, [4]who comforts us in all our troubles, so that we can comfort those in any trouble with the comfort we ourselves have received from God. [5]For just as the sufferings of Christ flow over into our lives, so also through Christ our comfort overflows.

Phil 2 [1]If you have any encouragement from being united with Christ, if any comfort from his love, if any fellowship with the Spirit, if any tenderness and compassion . . .

27) We Are to Obey God and Christ

Acts 5 [29]Peter and the other apostles replied: "We must obey God rather than men!"

2 Cor 10 [5]We demolish arguments and every pretension that sets itself up against the knowledge of God, and we take captive every thought to make it obedient to Christ.

Eph 6 [5]Slaves, obey your earthly masters with respect and fear, and with sincerity of heart, just as you would obey Christ.

1 Pet 1 [1]Peter, an apostle of Jesus Christ,

To God's elect, strangers in the world, scattered throughout Pontus, Galatia, Cappadocia, Asia and Bithynia, [2]who have been chosen according to the foreknowledge of God the Father, through the sanctifying work of the Spirit, for obedience to Jesus Christ and sprinkling by his blood: Grace and peace be yours in abundance.

28) We Live by the Will of God and Christ

Eph 1 [11]In him we were also chosen, having been predestined according to the plan of him who works out everything in conformity with the purpose of his will. . . .

Eph 5 [17]Therefore do not be foolish, but understand what the Lord's will is.

29) We Live in the Presence of God and Christ

Acts 10 [33]"So I sent for you immediately, and it was good of you to come. Now we are all here in the presence of God to listen to everything the Lord has commanded you to tell us."

1 Thess 2 [19]For what is our hope, our joy, or the crown in which we will glory in the presence of our Lord Jesus when he comes? Is it not you?

2 Tim 4 [1]In the presence of God and of Christ Jesus, who will judge the living and the dead, and in view of his appearing and his kingdom, I give you this charge. . . .

30) We Are to Live Worthy of God and Christ

Col 1 [10]And we pray this in order that you may live a life worthy of the Lord and may please him in every way: bearing fruit in every good work, growing in the knowledge of God. . . .

1 Thess 2 [11]For you know that we dealt with each of you as a father deals with his own children, [12]encouraging, comforting and urging you to live lives worthy of God, who calls you into his kingdom and glory.

31) We Live in the Sight of God and Christ

2 Cor 2 [10]If you forgive anyone, I also forgive him. And what I have forgiven—if there was anything to forgive—I have forgiven in the sight of Christ for your sake. . . .

2 Cor 4 [2]Rather, we have renounced secret and shameful ways; we do not use deception, nor do we distort the word of God. On the contrary, by setting forth the truth plainly we commend ourselves to every man's conscience in the sight of God.

1 Tim 5 [21]I charge you, in the sight of God and Christ Jesus and the elect angels, to keep these instructions without partiality, and to do nothing out of favoritism.

32) We Are Servants (Slaves) of God and Christ

Rom 1 [1]Paul, a servant of Christ Jesus, called to be an apostle and set apart for the gospel of God . . .

Gal 1 [10]Am I now trying to win the approval of men, or of God? Or am I trying to please men? If I were still trying to please men, I would not be a servant of Christ.

Col 3 [23]Whatever you do, work at it with all your heart, as working for the Lord, not for men, [24]since you know that you will receive an inheritance from the Lord as a reward. It is the Lord Christ you are serving.

1 Thess 1 [9]for they themselves report what kind of reception you gave us. They tell how you turned to God from idols to serve the living and true God. . . .

33) We Boast in God and Christ

1 Cor 1 [28]He chose the lowly things of this world and the despised things—and the things that are not—to nullify the things that are, [29]so that no one may boast before him. [30]It is because of him that you are in Christ Jesus, who has become for us wisdom from God—that is, our righteousness, holiness and redemption. [31]Therefore, as it is written: "Let him who boasts boast in the Lord."
Phil 2 [16]as you hold out the word of life—in order that I may boast on the day of Christ that I did not run or labor for nothing.

34) We Hope in God and Christ

Rom 15 [13]May the God of hope fill you with all joy and peace as you trust in him, so that you may overflow with hope by the power of the Holy Spirit.
1 Cor 15 [19]If only for this life we have hope in Christ, we are to be pitied more than all men.
Eph 1 [12]in order that we, who were the first to hope in Christ, might be for the praise of his glory.
1 Tim 1 [1]Paul, an apostle of Christ Jesus by the command of God our Savior and of Christ Jesus our hope . . .

35) We Joy (Rejoice) in God and Christ

Luke 1 [46]And Mary said: "My soul glorifies the Lord [47]and my spirit rejoices in God my Savior. . . ."
Phil 1 [26]so that through my being with you again your joy in Christ Jesus will overflow on account of me.

36) We Are to Glory in God and Christ

Rom 15 [17]Therefore I glory in Christ Jesus in my service to God.
Phil 2 [11]and every tongue confess that Jesus Christ is Lord, to the glory of God the Father.
Phil 3 [3]For it is we who are the circumcision, we who worship by the Spirit of God, who glory in Christ Jesus, and who put no confidence in the flesh. . . .

37) The Fullness of God and Christ Is Ours

Eph 3 [19]and to know this love that surpasses knowledge—that you may be filled to the measure of all the fullness of God.
Eph 4 [13]until we all reach unity in the faith and in the knowledge of the Son of God and become mature, attaining to the whole measure of the fullness of Christ.

38) The Kingdom Is of God and Christ

Eph 5 [5]For of this you can be sure: No immoral, impure or greedy person—such a man is an idolater—has any inheritance in the kingdom of Christ and of God.
Col 1 [13]For he has rescued us from the dominion of darkness and brought us into the kingdom of the Son he loves. . . .
1 Thess 2 [12]encouraging, comforting and urging you to live lives worthy of God, who calls you into his kingdom and glory.

39) The Church Is of God and Christ

Gal 1 [13]For you have heard of my previous way of life in Judaism, how intensely I persecuted the church of God and tried to destroy it.
1 Thess 1 [1]Paul, Silas and Timothy,
To the church of the Thessalonians in God the Father and the Lord Jesus Christ: Grace and peace to you.
1 Thess 2 [14]For you, brothers, became imitators of God's churches in Judea, which are in Christ Jesus: You suffered from your own countrymen the same things those churches suffered from the Jews. . . .

40) The Mystery (Secret Things) Is of God and Christ

Eph 3 [4]In reading this, then, you will be able to understand my insight into the mystery of Christ. . . .
Eph 3 [8]Although I am less than the least of all God's people, this grace was given me: to preach to the Gentiles the unsearchable riches of Christ, [9]and to make plain to everyone the administration of this mystery, which for ages past was kept hidden in God, who created all things.
Col 4 [3]And pray for us, too, that God may open a door for our message, so that we may proclaim the mystery of Christ, for which I am in chains.

41) The Great Day Is of God and Christ

1 Cor 1 [8]He will keep you strong to the end, so that you will be blameless on the day of our Lord Jesus Christ.
2 Cor 1 [14]as you have understood us in part, you will come to understand fully that you can boast of us just as we will boast of you in the day of the Lord Jesus.
Phil 1 [6]being confident of this, that he who began a good work in you will carry it on to completion until the day of Christ Jesus.
1 Thess 5 [2]for you know very well that the day of the Lord will come like a thief in the night.

42) We Stand before God and Christ

Gal 1 [20]I assure you before God that what I am writing you is no lie.
1 Thess 2 [19]For what is our hope, our joy, or the crown in which we will glory in the presence of our Lord Jesus when he comes? Is it not you?

43) We Appear before the Judgment Seat of God and Christ

Rom 14 [10]You, then, why do you judge your brother? Or why do you look down on your brother? For we will all stand before God's judgment seat. [11]It is written: "'As surely as I live,' says the Lord, 'every knee will bow before me; every tongue will confess to God.'" [12]So then, each of us will give an account of himself to God.
2 Cor 5 [10]For we must all appear before the judgment seat of Christ, that each one may receive what is due him for the things done while in the body, whether good or bad.

6. Jesus Is Assigned OT Designations of God

Matt 1 [23]"The virgin will be with child and will give birth to a son, and they will call him Immanuel"—which means, "God with us." (Isa 7:14)
Matt 3 [3]This is he who was spoken of through the prophet Isaiah: "A voice of one calling in the desert, 'Prepare the way for the Lord, make straight paths for him.'" (Isa 40:3)
John 3 [31]"The one who comes from above is above all; the one who is from the earth belongs to the earth, and speaks as one from the earth. The one who comes from heaven is above all." (Ps 97:9)
John 12 [38]This was to fulfill the word of Isaiah the prophet: "Lord, who has believed our message and to whom has the arm of the Lord been revealed?"
[39]For this reason they could not believe, because, as Isaiah says elsewhere: [40]"He has blinded their eyes and deadened their hearts, so they can neither see with their eyes, nor understand with their hearts, nor turn—and I would heal them." [41]Isaiah said this because he saw Jesus' glory and spoke about him. (Isa 53:1; 6:10)
Acts 3 [14]"You disowned the Holy and Righteous One and asked that a murderer be released to you." (1 Sam 2:2)
Rom 10 [9]That if you confess with your mouth, "Jesus is Lord," and believe in your heart that God raised him from the dead, you will be saved. [10]For it is with your heart that you believe and are justified, and it is with your mouth that you confess and are saved. [11]As the Scripture says, "Anyone who trusts in him will never be put to shame." (Isa 28:16) [12]For there is no difference between Jew and Gentile—the same Lord is Lord of all and richly blesses all who call on him, [13]for, "Everyone who calls on the name of the Lord will be saved." (Joel 2:32)
Rom 14 [10]You, then, why do you judge your brother? Or why do you look down on your brother? For we will all stand before God's judgment seat. [11]It is written: "'As surely as I live,' says the Lord, 'every knee will bow before me; every tongue will confess to God.'" [12]So then, each of us will give an account of himself to God. (Isa 49:18; 45:23)
1 Cor 1 [30]It is because of him that you are in Christ Jesus, who

has become for us wisdom from God—that is, our righteousness, holiness and redemption. (Isa 45:24; Jer 23:5–6)
1 Cor 2 [8]None of the rulers of this age understood it, for if they had, they would not have crucified the Lord of glory. (Ps 24:7–10)
2 Cor 5 [10]For we must all appear before the judgment seat of Christ, that each one may receive what is due him for the things done while in the body, whether good or bad. (Eccles 12:14)
Eph 4 [7]But to each one of us grace has been given as Christ apportioned it. [8]This is why it says: "When he ascended on high, he led captives in his train and gave gifts to men." (Ps 68:18)
Phil 2 [9]Therefore God exalted him to the highest place and gave him the name that is above every name, [10]that at the name of Jesus every knee should bow, in heaven and on earth and under the earth, [11]and every tongue confess that Jesus Christ is Lord, to the glory of God the Father. (Isa 45:23)
2 Thess 1 [6]God is just: He will pay back trouble to those who trouble you [7]and give relief to you who are troubled, and to us as well. This will happen when the Lord Jesus is revealed from heaven in blazing fire with his powerful angels. [8]He will punish those who do not know God and do not obey the gospel of our Lord Jesus. [9]They will be punished with everlasting destruction and shut out from the presence of the Lord and from the majesty of his power [10]on the day he comes to be glorified in his holy people and to be marveled at among all those who have believed. This includes you, because you believed our testimony to you. (Isa 2:10–19)
2 Thess 1 [12]We pray this so that the name of our Lord Jesus may be glorified in you, and you in him, according to the grace of our God and the Lord Jesus Christ. (Isa 66:5)
Titus 2 [13]while we wait for the blessed hope—the glorious appearing of our great God and Savior, Jesus Christ. . . . (Hos 1:7)
Heb 1 [8]But about the Son he says, "Your throne, O God, will last for ever and ever, and righteousness will be the scepter of your kingdom. [9]You have loved righteousness and hated wickedness; therefore God, your God, has set you above your companions by anointing you with the oil of joy." (Ps 45:6–7)
Heb 13 [20]May the God of peace, who through the blood of the eternal covenant brought back from the dead our Lord Jesus, that great Shepherd of the sheep . . . (Isa 40:10–11)
1 Pet 3 [15]But in your hearts set apart Christ as Lord. Always be prepared to give an answer to everyone who asks you to give the reason for the hope that you have. But do this with gentleness and respect. . . . (Isa 8:13)
Rev 1 [17]When I saw him, I fell at his feet as though dead. Then he placed his right hand on me and said: "Do not be afraid. I am the First and the Last." (Isa 44:6)

7. Jesus Is Superior to Men and Angels

John 1 [17]For the law was given through Moses; grace and truth came through Jesus Christ.
Eph 1 [19]and his incomparably great power for us who believe. That power is like the working of his mighty strength, [20]which he exerted in Christ when he raised him from the dead and seated him at his right hand in the heavenly realms, [21]far above all rule and authority, power and dominion, and every title that can be given, not only in the present age but also in the one to come. [22]And God placed all things under his feet and appointed him to be head over everything for the church, [23]which is his body, the fullness of him who fills everything in every way.
Phil 2 [9]Therefore God exalted him to the highest place and gave him the name that is above every name, [10]that at the name of Jesus every knee should bow, in heaven and on earth and under the earth. . . .
Col 1 [17]He is before all things, and in him all things hold together. [18]And he is the head of the body, the church; he is the beginning and the firstborn from among the dead, so that in everything he might have the supremacy.
Col 2 [10]and you have been given fullness in Christ, who is the head over every power and authority.
Heb 1 [4]So he became as much superior to the angels as the name he has inherited is superior to theirs.

[5]For to which of the angels did God ever say, "You are my Son; today I have become your Father"? Or again, "I will be his Father, and he will be my Son"? [6]And again, when God brings his firstborn into the world, he says, "Let all God's angels worship him." . . . [13]To which of the angels did God ever say, "Sit at my right hand until I make your enemies a footstool for your feet"?
Heb 2 [5]It is not to angels that he has subjected the world to come, about which we are speaking. . . . [7]"You made him a little lower than the angels; you crowned him with glory and honor [8]and put everything under his feet." In putting everything under him, God left nothing that is not subject to him. Yet at present we do not see everything subject to him.
Heb 3 [3]Jesus has been found worthy of greater honor than Moses, just as the builder of a house has greater honor than the house itself.
1 Pet 3 [21]and this water symbolizes baptism that now saves you also—not the removal of dirt from the body but the pledge of a good conscience toward God. It saves you by the resurrection of Jesus Christ, [22]who has gone into heaven and is at God's right hand—with angels, authorities and powers in submission to him.
Rev 1 [5]and from Jesus Christ, who is the faithful witness, the firstborn from the dead, and the ruler of the kings of the earth.

To him who loves us and has freed us from our sins by his blood . . .

8. Jesus Receives Prayer, Praise, and Worship

Acts 3 [16]"By faith in the name of Jesus, this man whom you see and know was made strong. It is Jesus' name and the faith that comes through him that has given this complete healing to him, as you can all see."
Acts 7 [59]While they were stoning him, Stephen prayed, "Lord Jesus, receive my spirit." [60]Then he fell on his knees and cried out, "Lord, do not hold this sin against them." When he had said this, he fell asleep.
Acts 22 [16]"'And now what are you waiting for? Get up, be baptized and wash your sins away, calling on his name.'"
Rom 1 [7]To all in Rome who are loved by God and called to be saints: Grace and peace to you from God our Father and from the Lord Jesus Christ.
Rom 10 [9]That if you confess with your mouth, "Jesus is Lord," and believe in your heart that God raised him from the dead, you will be saved. [10]For it is with your heart that you believe and are justified, and it is with your mouth that you confess and are saved. [11]As the Scripture says, "Anyone who trusts in him will never be put to shame." [12]For there is no difference between Jew and Gentile—the same Lord is Lord of all and richly blesses all who call on him. . . .
1 Cor 11 [24]and when he had given thanks, he broke it and said, "This is my body, which is for you; do this in remembrance of me." [25]In the same way, after supper he took the cup, saying, "This cup is the new covenant in my blood; do this, whenever you drink it, in remembrance of me."
2 Cor 12 [8]Three times I pleaded with the Lord to take it away from me. [9]But he said to me, "My grace is sufficient for you, for my power is made perfect in weakness." Therefore I will boast all the more gladly about my weaknesses, so that Christ's power may rest on me.
Gal 1 [3]Grace and peace to you from God our Father and the Lord Jesus Christ, [4]who gave himself for our sins to rescue us from the present evil age, according to the will of our God and Father, [5]to whom be glory for ever and ever. Amen.
Gal 6 [18]The grace of our Lord Jesus Christ be with your spirit, brothers. Amen.
Eph 5 [21]Submit to one another out of reverence for Christ.
Phil 2 [10]that at the name of Jesus every knee should bow, in heaven and on earth and under the earth, [11]and every tongue confess that Jesus Christ is Lord, to the glory of God the Father.
2 Thess 2 [16]May our Lord Jesus Christ himself and God our Father, who loved us and by his grace gave us eternal encouragement and good hope, [17]encourage your hearts and strengthen you in every good deed and word.

1 Tim 1 [2]To Timothy my true son in the faith: Grace, mercy and peace from God the Father and Christ Jesus our Lord. . . .

[12]I thank Christ Jesus our Lord, who has given me strength, that he considered me faithful, appointing me to his service.

2 Tim 4 [18]The Lord will rescue me from every evil attack and will bring me safely to his heavenly kingdom. To him be glory for ever and ever. Amen. . . .

[22]The Lord be with your spirit. Grace be with you.

Heb 1 [6]And again, when God brings his firstborn into the world, he says, "Let all God's angels worship him."

Heb 13 [20]May the God of peace, who through the blood of the eternal covenant brought back from the dead our Lord Jesus, that great Shepherd of the sheep, [21]equip you with everything good for doing his will, and may he work in us what is pleasing to him, through Jesus Christ, to whom be glory for ever and ever. Amen.

1 Pet 3 [15]But in your hearts set apart Christ as Lord. Always be prepared to give an answer to everyone who asks you to give the reason for the hope that you have. But do this with gentleness and respect. . . .

2 Pet 3 [18]But grow in the grace and knowledge of our Lord and Savior Jesus Christ. To him be glory both now and forever! Amen.

Rev 5 [14]The four living creatures said, "Amen," and the elders fell down and worshiped.

Rev 7 [9]After this I looked and there before me was a great multitude that no one could count, from every nation, tribe, people and language, standing before the throne and in front of the Lamb. They were wearing white robes and were holding palm branches in their hands. [10]And they cried out in a loud voice: "Salvation belongs to our God, who sits on the throne, and to the Lamb."

Rev 15 [3]and sang the song of Moses the servant of God and the song of the Lamb: "Great and marvelous are your deeds, Lord God Almighty. Just and true are your ways, King of the ages. [4]Who will not fear you, O Lord, and bring glory to your name? For you alone are holy. All nations will come and worship before you, for your righteous acts have been revealed."

C. The Sinlessness of Jesus

Matt 27 [3]When Judas, who had betrayed him, saw that Jesus was condemned, he was seized with remorse and returned the thirty silver coins to the chief priests and the elders. [4]"I have sinned," he said, "for I have betrayed innocent blood."

"What is that to us?" they replied. "That's your responsibility."

John 7 [16]Jesus answered, "My teaching is not my own. It comes from him who sent me. [17]If anyone chooses to do God's will, he will find out whether my teaching comes from God or whether I speak on my own. [18]He who speaks on his own does so to gain honor for himself, but he who works for the honor of the one who sent him is a man of truth; there is nothing false about him."

John 8 [29]"The one who sent me is with me; he has not left me alone, for I always do what pleases him." . . .

[46]"Can any of you prove me guilty of sin? If I am telling the truth, why don't you believe me?" . . . [50]"I am not seeking glory for myself; but there is one who seeks it, and he is the judge."

Rom 15 [3]For even Christ did not please himself but, as it is written: "The insults of those who insult you have fallen on me."

2 Cor 5 [21]God made him who had no sin to be sin for us, so that in him we might become the righteousness of God.

Heb 1 [9]"You have loved righteousness and hated wickedness; therefore God, your God, has set you above your companions by anointing you with the oil of joy."

Heb 2 [10]In bringing many sons to glory, it was fitting that God, for whom and through whom everything exists, should make the author of their salvation perfect through suffering.

Heb 4 [15]For we do not have a high priest who is unable to sympathize with our weaknesses, but we have one who has been tempted in every way, just as we are—yet was without sin.

Heb 7 [26]Such a high priest meets our need—one who is holy, blameless, pure, set apart from sinners, exalted above the heavens. [27]Unlike the other high priests, he does not need to offer sacrifices day after day, first for his own sins, and then for the sins of the people. He sacrificed for their sins once for all when he offered himself. [28]For the law appoints as high priests men who are weak; but the oath, which came after the law, appointed the Son, who has been made perfect forever.

1 Pet 1 [19]but with the precious blood of Christ, a lamb without blemish or defect.

1 Pet 2 [22]"He committed no sin, and no deceit was found in his mouth." [23]When they hurled their insults at him, he did not retaliate; when he suffered, he made no threats. Instead, he entrusted himself to him who judges justly.

1 John 3 [5]But you know that he appeared so that he might take away our sins. And in him is no sin.

D. The Glory of Christ

Mark 9 [2]After six days Jesus took Peter, James and John with him and led them up a high mountain, where they were all alone. There he was transfigured before them. [3]His clothes became dazzling white, whiter than anyone in the world could bleach them. [4]And there appeared before them Elijah and Moses, who were talking with Jesus.

[5]Peter said to Jesus, "Rabbi, it is good for us to be here. Let us put up three shelters—one for you, one for Moses and one for Elijah." [6](He did not know what to say, they were so frightened.)

[7]Then a cloud appeared and enveloped them, and a voice came from the cloud: "This is my Son, whom I love. Listen to him!"

Luke 24 [26]"Did not the Christ have to suffer these things and then enter his glory?"

John 1 [14]The Word became flesh and made his dwelling among us. We have seen his glory, the glory of the One and Only, who came from the Father, full of grace and truth.

John 2 [11]This, the first of his miraculous signs, Jesus performed in Cana of Galilee. He thus revealed his glory, and his disciples put their faith in him.

John 11 [4]When he heard this, Jesus said, "This sickness will not end in death. No, it is for God's glory so that God's Son may be glorified through it."

John 12 [38]This was to fulfill the word of Isaiah the prophet: "Lord, who has believed our message and to whom has the arm of the Lord been revealed?"

[39]For this reason they could not believe, because, as Isaiah says elsewhere: [40]"He has blinded their eyes and deadened their hearts, so they can neither see with their eyes, nor understand with their hearts, nor turn—and I would heal them." [41]Isaiah said this because he saw Jesus' glory and spoke about him. (Isa 53:1; 6:10)

John 17 [5]"And now, Father, glorify me in your presence with the glory I had with you before the world began. . . . [22]I have given them the glory that you gave me, that they may be one as we are one. . . ."

1 Cor 2 [8]None of the rulers of this age understood it, for if they had, they would not have crucified the Lord of glory.

Gal 1 [3]Grace and peace to you from God our Father and the Lord Jesus Christ, [4]who gave himself for our sins to rescue us from the present evil age, according to the will of our God and Father, [5]to whom be glory for ever and ever. Amen.

1 Tim 3 [16]Beyond all question, the mystery of godliness is great: He appeared in a body, was vindicated by the Spirit, was seen by angels, was preached among the nations, was believed on in the world, was taken up in glory.

Heb 1 [3]The Son is the radiance of God's glory and the exact representation of his being, sustaining all things by his powerful word. After he had provided purification for sins, he sat down at the right hand of the Majesty in heaven.

1 Pet 1 [21]Through him you believe in God, who raised him from the dead and glorified him, and so your faith and hope are in God.

2 Pet 1 [16]We did not follow cleverly invented stories when we told you about the power and coming of our Lord Jesus Christ, but we were eyewitnesses of his majesty. [17]For he received honor and glory from God the Father when the voice came to him from the Majestic Glory, saying, "This is my Son, whom I love; with him I am well pleased."

Rev 1 [6]and has made us to be a kingdom and priests to serve his God and Father—to him be glory and power for ever and ever! Amen.

E. The Resurrection of Christ

See p. 86a, Christ's Resurrection

F. The Exaltation of Christ

Ps 8 [5]You made him a little lower than the heavenly beings and crowned him with glory and honor. [6]You made him ruler over the works of your hands; you put everything under his feet. . . .
Ps 89 [27]"I will also appoint him my firstborn, the most exalted of the kings of the earth."
Ps 110 [1]The LORD says to my Lord: "Sit at my right hand until I make your enemies a footstool for your feet."
Ps 118 [22]The stone the builders rejected has become the capstone; [23]the LORD has done this, and it is marvelous in our eyes.
Isa 52 [13]See, my servant will act wisely; he will be raised and lifted up and highly exalted.
John 6 [62]"What if you see the Son of Man ascend to where he was before!"
Acts 2 [33]"Exalted to the right hand of God, he has received from the Father the promised Holy Spirit and has poured out what you now see and hear."
Acts 5 [31]"God exalted him to his own right hand as Prince and Savior that he might give repentance and forgiveness of sins to Israel."
Acts 7 [55]But Stephen, full of the Holy Spirit, looked up to heaven and saw the glory of God, and Jesus standing at the right hand of God.
Rom 8 [29]For those God foreknew he also predestined to be conformed to the likeness of his Son, that he might be the firstborn among many brothers.
1 Cor 11 [3]Now I want you to realize that the head of every man is Christ, and the head of the woman is man, and the head of Christ is God.
Eph 1 [19]and his incomparably great power for us who believe. That power is like the working of his mighty strength, [20]which he exerted in Christ when he raised him from the dead and seated him at his right hand in the heavenly realms, [21]far above all rule and authority, power and dominion, and every title that can be given, not only in the present age but also in the one to come. [22]And God placed all things under his feet and appointed him to be head over everything for the church. . . .
Eph 4 [15]Instead, speaking the truth in love, we will in all things grow up into him who is the Head, that is, Christ.
Eph 5 [23]For the husband is the head of the wife as Christ is the head of the church, his body, of which he is the Savior.
Phil 2 [9]Therefore God exalted him to the highest place and gave him the name that is above every name, [10]that at the name of Jesus every knee should bow, in heaven and on earth and under the earth. . . .
Col 2 [10]and you have been given fullness in Christ, who is the head over every power and authority.
Col 3 [1]Since, then, you have been raised with Christ, set your hearts on things above, where Christ is seated at the right hand of God.
Heb 1 [3]The Son is the radiance of God's glory and the exact representation of his being, sustaining all things by his powerful word. After he had provided purification for sins, he sat down at the right hand of the Majesty in heaven. [4]So he became as much superior to the angels as the name he has inherited is superior to theirs.

[5]For to which of the angels did God ever say, "You are my Son; today I have become your Father"? Or again, "I will be his Father, and he will be my Son"? . . . [13]To which of the angels did God ever say, "Sit at my right hand until I make your enemies a footstool for your feet"?
Heb 2 [5]It is not to angels that he has subjected the world to come, about which we are speaking. . . . [7]"You made him a little lower than the angels; you crowned him with glory and honor [8]and put everything under his feet." In putting everything under him, God left nothing that is not subject to him. Yet at present we do not see everything subject to him. [9]But we see Jesus, who was made a little lower than the angels, now crowned with glory and honor because he suffered death, so that by the grace of God he might taste death for everyone.
Heb 10 [12]But when this priest had offered for all time one sacrifice for sins, he sat down at the right hand of God.
Heb 12 [2]Let us fix our eyes on Jesus, the author and perfecter of our faith, who for the joy set before him endured the cross, scorning its shame, and sat down at the right hand of the throne of God.
1 Pet 3 [22]who has gone into heaven and is at God's right hand—with angels, authorities and powers in submission to him.
Rev 3 [21]"To him who overcomes, I will give the right to sit with me on my throne, just as I overcame and sat down with my Father on his throne."

IV
The Humanity of Christ

A. Christ Was Called a Man by Many

1. John the Baptist Called Him a Man

John 1 [30]"This is the one I meant when I said, 'A man who comes after me has surpassed me because he was before me.'"

2. Jesus Called Himself a Man

Matt 8 [20]Jesus replied, "Foxes have holes and birds of the air have nests, but the Son of Man has no place to lay his head."
Matt 16 [13]When Jesus came to the region of Caesarea Philippi, he asked his disciples, "Who do people say the Son of Man is?"
Matt 16 [27]"For the Son of Man is going to come in his Father's glory with his angels, and then he will reward each person according to what he has done. [28]I tell you the truth, some who are standing here will not taste death before they see the Son of Man coming in his kingdom."
Matt 25 [31]"When the Son of Man comes in his glory, and all the angels with him, he will sit on his throne in heavenly glory."
Matt 26 [64]"Yes, it is as you say," Jesus replied. "But I say to all of you: In the future you will see the Son of Man sitting at the right hand of the Mighty One and coming on the clouds of heaven."

[65]Then the high priest tore his clothes and said, "He has spoken blasphemy! Why do we need any more witnesses? Look, now you have heard the blasphemy. [66]What do you think?"

"He is worthy of death," they answered.

[67]Then they spit in his face and struck him with their fists. Others slapped him. . . .
John 8 [40]"As it is, you are determined to kill me, a man who has told you the truth that I heard from God. Abraham did not do such things."

3. Crowds Called Him a Man

Mark 6 [2]When the Sabbath came, he began to teach in the synagogue, and many who heard him were amazed.

"Where did this man get these things?" they asked. "What's this wisdom that has been given him, that he even does miracles! [3]Isn't this the carpenter? Isn't this Mary's son and the brother of James, Joseph, Judas and Simon? Aren't his sisters here with us?" And they took offense at him.

4. The Samaritan Woman Called Him a Man

John 4 [9]The Samaritan woman said to him, "You are a Jew and I am a Samaritan woman. How can you ask me for a drink?" (For Jews do not associate with Samaritans.)

5. Jewish Leaders Called Him a Man

John 7 [27]"But we know where this man is from; when the Christ comes, no one will know where he is from."

John 8 [57]"You are not yet fifty years old," the Jews said to him, "and you have seen Abraham!"
John 9 [29]"We know that God spoke to Moses, but as for this fellow, we don't even know where he comes from."
John 10 [33]"We are not stoning you for any of these," replied the Jews, "but for blasphemy, because you, a mere man, claim to be God."

6. Pilate Called Him a Man

John 19 [5]When Jesus came out wearing the crown of thorns and the purple robe, Pilate said to them, "Here is the man!"

7. The Disciples Called Him a Man

Matt 8 [23]Then he got into the boat and his disciples followed him. [24]Without warning, a furious storm came up on the lake, so that the waves swept over the boat. But Jesus was sleeping. [25]The disciples went and woke him, saying, "Lord, save us! We're going to drown."

[26]He replied, "You of little faith, why are you so afraid?" Then he got up and rebuked the winds and the waves, and it was completely calm.

[27]The men were amazed and asked, "What kind of man is this? Even the winds and the waves obey him!"
John 21 [4]Early in the morning, Jesus stood on the shore, but the disciples did not realize that it was Jesus.

[5]He called out to them, "Friends, haven't you any fish?"

"No," they answered.

[6]He said, "Throw your net on the right side of the boat and you will find some." When they did, they were unable to haul the net in because of the large number of fish.

[7]Then the disciple whom Jesus loved said to Peter, "It is the Lord!" As soon as Simon Peter heard him say, "It is the Lord," he wrapped his outer garment around him (for he had taken it off) and jumped into the water. [8]The other disciples followed in the boat, towing the net full of fish, for they were not far from shore, about a hundred yards. [9]When they landed, they saw a fire of burning coals there with fish on it, and some bread.

[10]Jesus said to them, "Bring some of the fish you have just caught."

[11]Simon Peter climbed aboard and dragged the net ashore. It was full of large fish, 153, but even with so many the net was not torn. [12]Jesus said to them, "Come and have breakfast." None of the disciples dared ask him, "Who are you?" They knew it was the Lord. [13]Jesus came, took the bread and gave it to them, and did the same with the fish. [14]This was now the third time Jesus appeared to his disciples after he was raised from the dead.

8. Peter Called Him a Man

Acts 2 [22]"Men of Israel, listen to this: Jesus of Nazareth was a man accredited by God to you by miracles, wonders and signs, which God did among you through him, as you yourselves know."

9. Paul Called Him a Man

Acts 17 [31]"For he has set a day when he will judge the world with justice by the man he has appointed. He has given proof of this to all men by raising him from the dead."
Rom 5 [12]Therefore, just as sin entered the world through one man, and death through sin, and in this way death came to all men, because all sinned—[13]for before the law was given, sin was in the world. But sin is not taken into account when there is no law. [14]Nevertheless, death reigned from the time of Adam to the time of Moses, even over those who did not sin by breaking a command, as did Adam, who was a pattern of the one to come.

[15]But the gift is not like the trespass. For if the many died by the trespass of the one man, how much more did God's grace and the gift that came by the grace of the one man, Jesus Christ, overflow to the many! [16]Again, the gift of God is not like the result of the one man's sin: The judgment followed one sin and brought condemnation, but the gift followed many trespasses and brought justification. [17]For if, by the trespass of the one man, death reigned through that one man, how much more will those who receive God's abundant provision of grace and of the gift of righteousness reign in life through the one man, Jesus Christ.

[18]Consequently, just as the result of one trespass was condemnation for all men, so also the result of one act of righteousness was justification that brings life for all men. [19]For just as through the disobedience of the one man the many were made sinners, so also through the obedience of the one man the many will be made righteous.

[20]The law was added so that the trespass might increase. But where sin increased, grace increased all the more, [21]so that, just as sin reigned in death, so also grace might reign through righteousness to bring eternal life through Jesus Christ our Lord.
1 Cor 15 [21]For since death came through a man, the resurrection of the dead comes also through a man.
1 Cor 15 [47]The first man was of the dust of the earth, the second man from heaven. [48]As was the earthly man, so are those who are of the earth; and as is the man from heaven, so also are those who are of heaven. [49]And just as we have borne the likeness of the earthly man, so shall we bear the likeness of the man from heaven.
Phil 2 [5]Your attitude should be the same as that of Christ Jesus: . . . [7]but made himself nothing, taking the very nature of a servant, being made in human likeness. [8]And being found in appearance as a man, he humbled himself and became obedient to death—even death on a cross!
1 Tim 2 [5]For there is one God and one mediator between God and men, the man Christ Jesus. . . .

10. The Author of Hebrews Called Him a Man

Heb 2 [6]But there is a place where someone has testified: "What is man that you are mindful of him, the son of man that you care for him?"

B. Christ Shared with Humanity a Physical Nature

1. Jesus Had Physical Descent

a) He Was Born as a Baby

Matt 2 [1]After Jesus was born in Bethlehem in Judea, during the time of King Herod, Magi from the east came to Jerusalem. . . .
Luke 2 [4]So Joseph also went up from the town of Nazareth in Galilee to Judea, to Bethlehem the town of David, because he belonged to the house and line of David. [5]He went there to register with Mary, who was pledged to be married to him and was expecting a child. [6]While they were there, the time came for the baby to be born, [7]and she gave birth to her firstborn, a son. She wrapped him in cloths and placed him in a manger, because there was no room for them in the inn. . . .

[16]So they hurried off and found Mary and Joseph, and the baby, who was lying in the manger. . . .

[21]On the eighth day, when it was time to circumcise him, he was named Jesus, the name the angel had given him before he had been conceived.
Gal 4 [4]But when the time had fully come, God sent his Son, born of a woman, born under law. . . .

b) He Was a Son of Mary

Matt 12 [46]While Jesus was still talking to the crowd, his mother and brothers stood outside, wanting to speak to him.
Mark 6 [3]"Isn't this the carpenter? Isn't this Mary's son and the brother of James, Joseph, Judas and Simon? Aren't his sisters here with us?" And they took offense at him.
Acts 1 [14]They all joined together constantly in prayer, along with the women and Mary the mother of Jesus, and with his brothers.

2. Jesus Grew Physically

a) He Grew as a Child

Luke 2 [41]Every year his parents went to Jerusalem for the Feast of the Passover. [42]When he was twelve years old, they went up to the Feast, according to the custom.

Luke 2 [52]And Jesus grew in wisdom and stature, and in favor with God and men.

b) He Grew to Adulthood

Luke 3 [23]Now Jesus himself was about thirty years old when he began his ministry. He was the son, so it was thought, of Joseph, the son of Heli. . . .

John 8 [40]"As it is, you are determined to kill me, a man who has told you the truth that I heard from God. Abraham did not do such things."

John 8 [56]"Your father Abraham rejoiced at the thought of seeing my day; he saw it and was glad."

[57]"You are not yet fifty years old," the Jews said to him, "and you have seen Abraham!"

John 19 [5]When Jesus came out wearing the crown of thorns and the purple robe, Pilate said to them, "Here is the man!"

Acts 2 [22]"Men of Israel, listen to this: Jesus of Nazareth was a man accredited by God to you by miracles, wonders and signs, which God did among you through him, as you yourselves know."

3. Jesus Had Human Names

a) Carpenter

Mark 6 [3]"Isn't this the carpenter? Isn't this Mary's son and the brother of James, Joseph, Judas and Simon? Aren't his sisters here with us?" And they took offense at him.

b) Carpenter's Son

Matt 13 [53]When Jesus had finished these parables, he moved on from there. [54]Coming to his hometown, he began teaching the people in their synagogue, and they were amazed. "Where did this man get this wisdom and these miraculous powers?" they asked. [55]"Isn't this the carpenter's son? Isn't his mother's name Mary, and aren't his brothers James, Joseph, Simon and Judas? [56]Aren't all his sisters with us? Where then did this man get all these things?"

c) Jesus

Matt 1 [21]"She will give birth to a son, and you are to give him the name Jesus, because he will save his people from their sins."

Luke 2 [21]On the eighth day, when it was time to circumcise him, he was named Jesus, the name the angel had given him before he had been conceived.

d) Joseph's Son

Luke 4 [22]All spoke well of him and were amazed at the gracious words that came from his lips. "Isn't this Joseph's son?" they asked.

John 1 [45]Philip found Nathanael and told him, "We have found the one Moses wrote about in the Law, and about whom the prophets also wrote—Jesus of Nazareth, the son of Joseph."

John 6 [42]They said, "Is this not Jesus, the son of Joseph, whose father and mother we know? How can he now say, 'I came down from heaven'?"

e) King

John 18 [33]Pilate then went back inside the palace, summoned Jesus and asked him, "Are you the king of the Jews?"

[34]"Is that your own idea," Jesus asked, "or did others talk to you about me?"

[35]"Am I a Jew?" Pilate replied. "It was your people and your chief priests who handed you over to me. What is it you have done?"

[36]Jesus said, "My kingdom is not of this world. If it were, my servants would fight to prevent my arrest by the Jews. But now my kingdom is from another place."

[37]"You are a king, then!" said Pilate. Jesus answered, "You are right in saying I am a king. In fact, for this reason I was born, and for this I came into the world, to testify to the truth. Everyone on the side of truth listens to me."

f) Mary's Son

Mark 6 [3]"Isn't this the carpenter? Isn't this Mary's son and the brother of James, Joseph, Judas and Simon? Aren't his sisters here with us?" And they took offense at him.

g) Master

Luke 5 [5]Simon answered, "Master, we've worked hard all night and haven't caught anything. But because you say so, I will let down the nets."

Luke 9 [49]"Master," said John, "we saw a man driving out demons in your name and we tried to stop him, because he is not one of us."

[50]"Do not stop him," Jesus said, "for whoever is not against you is for you."

Luke 17 [11]Now on his way to Jerusalem, Jesus traveled along the border between Samaria and Galilee. [12]As he was going into a village, ten men who had leprosy met him. They stood at a distance [13]and called out in a loud voice, "Jesus, Master, have pity on us!"

h) Messiah

Luke 9 [18]Once when Jesus was praying in private and his disciples were with him, he asked them, "Who do the crowds say I am?"

[19]They replied, "Some say John the Baptist; others say Elijah; and still others, that one of the prophets of long ago has come back to life."

[20]"But what about you?" he asked. "Who do you say I am?"

Peter answered, "The Christ of God."

[21]Jesus strictly warned them not to tell this to anyone.

John 1 [40]Andrew, Simon Peter's brother, was one of the two who heard what John had said and who had followed Jesus. [41]The first thing Andrew did was to find his brother Simon and tell him, "We have found the Messiah" (that is, the Christ). [42]And he brought him to Jesus.

Jesus looked at him and said, "You are Simon son of John. You will be called Cephas" (which, when translated, is Peter).

John 4 [25]The woman said, "I know that Messiah" (called Christ) "is coming. When he comes, he will explain everything to us."

[26]Then Jesus declared, "I who speak to you am he." . . .

[28]Then, leaving her water jar, the woman went back to the town and said to the people, [29]"Come, see a man who told me everything I ever did. Could this be the Christ?" [30]They came out of the town and made their way toward him. . . .

[39]Many of the Samaritans from that town believed in him because of the woman's testimony, "He told me everything I ever did." [40]So when the Samaritans came to him, they urged him to stay with them, and he stayed two days. [41]And because of his words many more became believers.

[42]They said to the woman, "We no longer believe just because of what you said; now we have heard for ourselves, and we know that this man really is the Savior of the world."

John 11 [27]"Yes, Lord," she told him, "I believe that you are the Christ, the Son of God, who was to come into the world."

i) Physician

Luke 4 [23]Jesus said to them, "Surely you will quote this proverb to me: 'Physician, heal yourself! Do here in your hometown what we have heard that you did in Capernaum.'"

j) Prophet

Matt 21 [11]The crowds answered, "This is Jesus, the prophet from Nazareth in Galilee."

Luke 7 [16]They were all filled with awe and praised God. "A great prophet has appeared among us," they said. "God has come to help his people."

Luke 24 [17]He asked them, "What are you discussing together as you walk along?"

They stood still, their faces downcast. [18]One of them, named Cleopas, asked him, "Are you only a visitor to Jerusalem and do not know the things that have happened there in these days?"

[19]"What things?" he asked.

"About Jesus of Nazareth," they replied. "He was a prophet, powerful in word and deed before God and all the people. [20]The chief priests and our rulers handed him over to be sentenced to death, and they crucified him; [21]but we had hoped that he was the one who was going to redeem Israel. And what is more, it is the third day since all this took place."

John 4 [19]"Sir," the woman said, "I can see that you are a prophet."
John 9 [17]Finally they turned again to the blind man, "What have you to say about him? It was your eyes he opened."
The man replied, "He is a prophet."

k) Rabbi

Matt 23 [8]"But you are not to be called 'Rabbi,' for you have only one Master and you are all brothers."
Mark 10 [51]"What do you want me to do for you?" Jesus asked him.
The blind man said, "Rabbi, I want to see."
John 3 [2]He came to Jesus at night and said, "Rabbi, we know you are a teacher who has come from God. For no one could perform the miraculous signs you are doing if God were not with him."

l) Rabboni

John 20 [16]Jesus said to her, "Mary."
She turned toward him and cried out in Aramaic, "Rabboni!" (which means Teacher).

m) Son of David

Matt 12 [23]All the people were astonished and said, "Could this be the Son of David?"
Matt 21 [9]The crowds that went ahead of him and those that followed shouted.
"Hosanna to the Son of David!"
"Blessed is he who comes in the name of the Lord!"
"Hosanna in the highest!"
Mark 10 [47]When he heard that it was Jesus of Nazareth, he began to shout, "Jesus, Son of David, have mercy on me!"
[48]Many rebuked him and told him to be quiet, but he shouted all the more, "Son of David, have mercy on me!"

n) Son of Man

Matt 8 [20]Jesus replied, "Foxes have holes and birds of the air have nests, but the Son of Man has no place to lay his head."
Luke 19 [10]"For the Son of Man came to seek and to save what was lost."

o) Teacher

Matt 8 [19]Then a teacher of the law came to him and said, "Teacher, I will follow you wherever you go."
Matt 23 [10]"Nor are you to be called 'teacher,' for you have one Teacher, the Christ."
Mark 10 [17]As Jesus started on his way, a man ran up to him and fell on his knees before him. "Good teacher," he asked, "what must I do to inherit eternal life?"
Luke 7 [40]Jesus answered him, "Simon, I have something to tell you."
"Tell me, teacher," he said.
Luke 8 [49]While Jesus was still speaking, someone came from the house of Jairus, the synagogue ruler. "Your daughter is dead," he said. "Don't bother the teacher any more."
[50]Hearing this, Jesus said to Jairus, "Don't be afraid; just believe, and she will be healed."
John 3 [2]He came to Jesus at night and said, "Rabbi, we know you are a teacher who has come from God. For no one could perform the miraculous signs you are doing if God were not with him."

4. Jesus Had a Physical Body

John 1 [14]The Word became flesh and made his dwelling among us. We have seen his glory, the glory of the One and Only, who came from the Father, full of grace and truth.
John 2 [21]But the temple he had spoken of was his body.
Acts 2 [31]Seeing what was ahead, he spoke of the resurrection of the Christ, that he was not abandoned to the grave, nor did his body see decay.
Rom 8 [3]For what the law was powerless to do in that it was weakened by the sinful nature, God did by sending his own Son in the likeness of sinful man to be a sin offering. And so he condemned sin in sinful man. . . .
Phil 2 [7]but made himself nothing, taking the very nature of a servant, being made in human likeness. [8]And being found in appearance as a man, he humbled himself and became obedient to death—even death on a cross!
Col 1 [22]But now he has reconciled you by Christ's physical body through death to present you holy in his sight, without blemish and free from accusation. . . .
Col 2 [9]For in Christ all the fullness of the Deity lives in bodily form. . . .
Heb 2 [14]Since the children have flesh and blood, he too shared in their humanity so that by his death he might destroy him who holds the power of death—that is, the devil—[15]and free those who all their lives were held in slavery by their fear of death. [16]For surely it is not angels he helps, but Abraham's descendants. [17]For this reason he had to be made like his brothers in every way, in order that he might become a merciful and faithful high priest in service to God, and that he might make atonement for the sins of the people.
Heb 10 [5]Therefore, when Christ came into the world, he said: "Sacrifice and offering you did not desire, but a body you prepared for me. . . ."
Heb 10 [10]And by that will, we have been made holy through the sacrifice of the body of Jesus Christ once for all.
1 Pet 2 [24]He himself bore our sins in his body on the tree, so that we might die to sins and live for righteousness; by his wounds you have been healed.
1 John 4 [2]This is how you can recognize the Spirit of God: Every spirit that acknowledges that Jesus Christ has come in the flesh is from God. . . .
2 John [7]Many deceivers, who do not acknowledge Jesus Christ as coming in the flesh, have gone out into the world. Any such person is the deceiver and the antichrist.

5. Jesus Had Physical Limitations

a) He Needed Nourishment

Matt 4 [2]After fasting forty days and forty nights, he was hungry.
Matt 21 [18]Early in the morning, as he was on his way back to the city, he was hungry.
John 4 [7]When a Samaritan woman came to draw water, Jesus said to her, "Will you give me a drink?"
John 19 [28]Later, knowing that all was now completed, and so that the Scripture would be fulfilled, Jesus said, "I am thirsty."

b) He Needed Rest

Mark 4 [38]Jesus was in the stern, sleeping on a cushion. The disciples woke him and said to him, "Teacher, don't you care if we drown?"
Mark 6 [31]Then, because so many people were coming and going that they did not even have a chance to eat, he said to them, "Come with me by yourselves to a quiet place and get some rest."
Luke 9 [58]Jesus replied, "Foxes have holes and birds of the air have nests, but the Son of Man has no place to lay his head."
John 4 [6]Jacob's well was there, and Jesus, tired as he was from the journey, sat down by the well. It was about the sixth hour.

c) He Experienced Physical Injury and Pain

Matt 26 [67]Then they spit in his face and struck him with their fists. Others slapped him. . . .
Matt 27 [26]Then he released Barabbas to them. But he had Jesus flogged, and handed him over to be crucified.
Luke 22 [64]They blindfolded him and demanded, "Prophesy! Who hit you?"
Luke 23 [33]When they came to the place called the Skull, there they crucified him, along with the criminals—one on his right, the other on his left.
John 19 [34]Instead, one of the soldiers pierced Jesus' side with a spear, bringing a sudden flow of blood and water.
1 Pet 2 [21]To this you were called, because Christ suffered for you, leaving you an example, that you should follow in his steps. [22]"He committed no sin, and no deceit was found in his mouth." [23]When they hurled their insults at him, he did not retaliate; when he suffered, he made no threats. Instead, he entrusted himself to him who judges justly.

d) He Died

John 19 [30]When he had received the drink, Jesus said, "It is finished." With that, he bowed his head and gave up his spirit.
Acts 17 [3]explaining and proving that the Christ had to suffer and rise from the dead. "This Jesus I am proclaiming to you is the Christ," he said.
1 Cor 15 [3]For what I received I passed on to you as of first importance: that Christ died for our sins according to the Scriptures. . . .
Phil 2 [8]And being found in appearance as a man, he humbled himself and became obedient to death—even death on a cross!
Heb 2 [14]Since the children have flesh and blood, he too shared in their humanity so that by his death he might destroy him who holds the power of death—that is, the devil. . . .
1 Pet 3 [18]For Christ died for sins once for all, the righteous for the unrighteous, to bring you to God. He was put to death in the body but made alive by the Spirit. . . .
Rev 5 [12]In a loud voice they sang: "Worthy is the Lamb, who was slain, to receive power and wealth and wisdom and strength and honor and glory and praise!"

e) He Was Buried

Luke 23 [50]Now there was a man named Joseph, a member of the Council, a good and upright man, [51]who had not consented to their decision and action. He came from the Judean town of Arimathea and he was waiting for the kingdom of God. [52]Going to Pilate, he asked for Jesus' body. [53]Then he took it down, wrapped it in linen cloth and placed it in a tomb cut in the rock, one in which no one had yet been laid.
1 Cor 15 [3]For what I received I passed on to you as of first importance: that Christ died for our sins according to the Scriptures, [4]that he was buried, that he was raised on the third day according to the Scriptures. . . .

6. Jesus Was Handled by Others

Luke 8 [43]And a woman was there who had been subject to bleeding for twelve years, but no one could heal her. [44]She came up behind him and touched the edge of his cloak, and immediately her bleeding stopped.

[45]"Who touched me?" Jesus asked.

When they all denied it, Peter said, "Master, the people are crowding and pressing against you."

[46]But Jesus said, "Someone touched me; I know that power has gone out from me."

[47]Then the woman, seeing that she could not go unnoticed, came trembling and fell at his feet. In the presence of all the people, she told why she had touched him and how she had been instantly healed.
Luke 24 [39]"Look at my hands and my feet. It is I myself! Touch me and see; a ghost does not have flesh and bones, as you see I have."
John 20 [27]Then he said to Thomas, "Put your finger here; see my hands. Reach out your hand and put it into my side. Stop doubting and believe."
1 John 1 [1]That which was from the beginning, which we have heard, which we have seen with our eyes, which we have looked at and our hands have touched—this we proclaim concerning the Word of life. [2]The life appeared; we have seen it and testify to it, and we proclaim to you the eternal life, which was with the Father and has appeared to us. [3]We proclaim to you what we have seen and heard, so that you also may have fellowship with us. And our fellowship is with the Father and with his Son, Jesus Christ.

C. Christ Shared with Humanity an Emotional Nature

1. Jesus Had Unpleasant Emotions

a) He Experienced Anger

Mark 3 [5]He looked around at them in anger and, deeply distressed at their stubborn hearts, said to the man, "Stretch out your hand." He stretched it out, and his hand was completely restored.
John 2 [13]When it was almost time for the Jewish Passover, Jesus went up to Jerusalem. [14]In the temple courts he found men selling cattle, sheep and doves, and others sitting at tables exchanging money. [15]So he made a whip out of cords, and drove all from the temple area, both sheep and cattle; he scattered the coins of the money changers and overturned their tables. [16]To those who sold doves he said, "Get these out of here! How dare you turn my Father's house into a market!"

[17]His disciples remembered that it is written: "Zeal for your house will consume me."

b) He Experienced Disgust

Matt 17 [17]"O unbelieving and perverse generation," Jesus replied, "how long shall I stay with you? How long shall I put up with you? Bring the boy here to me."
Mark 8 [12]He sighed deeply and said, "Why does this generation ask for a miraculous sign? I tell you the truth, no sign will be given to it."

c) He Experienced Distress

Mark 14 [33]He took Peter, James and John along with him, and he began to be deeply distressed and troubled.
John 12 [27]"Now my heart is troubled, and what shall I say? 'Father, save me from this hour'? No, it was for this very reason I came to this hour."

d) He Experienced Loneliness

Matt 26 [38]Then he said to them, "My soul is overwhelmed with sorrow to the point of death. Stay here and keep watch with me."

e) He Experienced Sorrow

Matt 23 [37]"O Jerusalem, Jerusalem, you who kill the prophets and stone those sent to you, how often I have longed to gather your children together, as a hen gathers her chicks under her wings, but you were not willing."
Matt 26 [36]Then Jesus went with his disciples to a place called Gethsemane, and he said to them, "Sit here while I go over there and pray." [37]He took Peter and the two sons of Zebedee along with him, and he began to be sorrowful and troubled. [38]Then he said to them, "My soul is overwhelmed with sorrow to the point of death. Stay here and keep watch with me."

[39]Going a little farther, he fell with his face to the ground and prayed, "My Father, if it is possible, may this cup be taken from me. Yet not as I will, but as you will."

[40]Then he returned to his disciples and found them sleeping. "Could you men not keep watch with me for one hour?" he asked Peter. [41]"Watch and pray so that you will not fall into temptation. The spirit is willing, but the body is weak."

[42]He went away a second time and prayed, "My Father, if it is not possible for this cup to be taken away unless I drink it, may your will be done."

[43]When he came back, he again found them sleeping, because their eyes were heavy. [44]So he left them and went away once more and prayed the third time, saying the same thing.

[45]Then he returned to the disciples and said to them, "Are you still sleeping and resting? Look, the hour is near, and the Son of Man is betrayed into the hands of sinners. [46]Rise, let us go! Here comes my betrayer!"
Luke 19 [41]As he approached Jerusalem and saw the city, he wept over it [42]and said, "If you, even you, had only known on this day what would bring you peace—but now it is hidden from your eyes."
John 11 [33]When Jesus saw her weeping, and the Jews who had come along with her also weeping, he was deeply moved in spirit and troubled. [34]"Where have you laid him?" he asked.

"Come and see, Lord," they replied.

[35]Jesus wept.

2. Jesus Had Pleasant Emotions

a) He Demonstrated Affection

Matt 18 [10]"See that you do not look down on one of these little ones. For I tell you that their angels in heaven always see the face of my Father in heaven."
Mark 9 [36]He took a little child and had him stand among them. Taking him in his arms, he said to them, [37]"Whoever welcomes one of these little children in my name welcomes me; and who-

ever welcomes me does not welcome me but the one who sent me."

Luke 18 [16]But Jesus called the children to him and said, "Let the little children come to me, and do not hinder them, for the kingdom of God belongs to such as these."

b) He Demonstrated Amazement

Matt 8 [10]When Jesus heard this, he was astonished and said to those following him, "I tell you the truth, I have not found anyone in Israel with such great faith."

c) He Demonstrated Appreciation

John 12 [7]"Leave her alone," Jesus replied. "It was intended that she should save this perfume for the day of my burial."

d) He Demonstrated Compassion

Matt 9 [36]When he saw the crowds, he had compassion on them, because they were harassed and helpless, like sheep without a shepherd.

Matt 14 [14]When Jesus landed and saw a large crowd, he had compassion on them and healed their sick.

Matt 20 [34]Jesus had compassion on them and touched their eyes. Immediately they received their sight and followed him.

Mark 8 [2]"I have compassion for these people; they have already been with me three days and have nothing to eat. [3]If I send them home hungry, they will collapse on the way, because some of them have come a long distance."

Luke 7 [13]When the Lord saw her, his heart went out to her and he said, "Don't cry."

e) He Demonstrated Confidence

Mark 4 [35]That day when evening came, he said to his disciples, "Let us go over to the other side." [36]Leaving the crowd behind, they took him along, just as he was, in the boat. There were also other boats with him. [37]A furious squall came up, and the waves broke over the boat, so that it was nearly swamped. [38]Jesus was in the stern, sleeping on a cushion. The disciples woke him and said to him, "Teacher, don't you care if we drown?"

[39]He got up, rebuked the wind and said to the waves, "Quiet! Be still!" Then the wind died down and it was completely calm.

[40]He said to his disciples, "Why are you so afraid? Do you still have no faith?"

[41]They were terrified and asked each other, "Who is this? Even the wind and the waves obey him!"

f) He Demonstrated Love

Mark 10 [21]Jesus looked at him and loved him. "One thing you lack," he said. "Go, sell everything you have and give to the poor, and you will have treasure in heaven. Then come, follow me."

John 11 [5]Jesus loved Martha and her sister and Lazarus.

John 13 [1]It was just before the Passover Feast. Jesus knew that the time had come for him to leave this world and go to the Father. Having loved his own who were in the world, he now showed them the full extent of his love.

John 19 [26]When Jesus saw his mother there, and the disciple whom he loved standing nearby, he said to his mother, "Dear woman, here is your son," [27]and to the disciple, "Here is your mother." From that time on, this disciple took her into his home.

g) He Demonstrated Loyalty

John 18 [8]"I told you that I am he," Jesus answered. "If you are looking for me, then let these men go." [9]This happened so that the words he had spoken would be fulfilled: "I have not lost one of those you gave me."

h) He Demonstrated Self-Control

Matt 27 [14]But Jesus made no reply, not even to a single charge—to the great amazement of the governor.

i) He Demonstrated Sympathy

Heb 4 [15]For we do not have a high priest who is unable to sympathize with our weaknesses, but we have one who has been tempted in every way, just as we are—yet was without sin.

j) He Had a Need for Solitude

Luke 4 [42]At daybreak Jesus went out to a solitary place. The people were looking for him and when they came to where he was, they tried to keep him from leaving them.

Luke 5 [16]But Jesus often withdrew to lonely places and prayed.

k) He Had a Sense of Accomplishment

John 13 [1]It was just before the Passover Feast. Jesus knew that the time had come for him to leave this world and go to the Father. Having loved his own who were in the world, he now showed them the full extent of his love. . . . [3]Jesus knew that the Father had put all things under his power, and that he had come from God and was returning to God. . . .

John 19 [30]When he had received the drink, Jesus said, "It is finished." With that, he bowed his head and gave up his spirit.

D. Christ Shared with Humanity an Intellectual Nature

1. Jesus Was Creative in Dialogue

a) He Used Illustration

Matt 7 [3]"Why do you look at the speck of sawdust in your brother's eye and pay no attention to the plank in your own eye? [4]How can you say to your brother, 'Let me take the speck out of your eye,' when all the time there is a plank in your own eye? [5]You hypocrite, first take the plank out of your own eye, and then you will see clearly to remove the speck from your brother's eye."

Matt 10 [16]"I am sending you out like sheep among wolves. Therefore be as shrewd as snakes and as innocent as doves."

Matt 19 [24]"Again I tell you, it is easier for a camel to go through the eye of a needle than for a rich man to enter the kingdom of God."

Mark 9 [43]"If your hand causes you to sin, cut it off. It is better for you to enter life maimed than with two hands to go into hell, where the fire never goes out. . . . [45]And if your foot causes you to sin, cut it off. It is better for you to enter life crippled than to have two feet and be thrown into hell. . . . [47]And if your eye causes you to sin, pluck it out. It is better for you to enter the kingdom of God with one eye than to have two eyes and be thrown into hell, [48]where 'their worm does not die, and the fire is not quenched.'"

John 15 [1]"I am the true vine, and my Father is the gardener. [2]He cuts off every branch in me that bears no fruit, while every branch that does bear fruit he prunes so that it will be even more fruitful. [3]You are already clean because of the word I have spoken to you. [4]Remain in me, and I will remain in you. No branch can bear fruit by itself; it must remain in the vine. Neither can you bear fruit unless you remain in me.

[5]"I am the vine; you are the branches. If a man remains in me and I in him, he will bear much fruit; apart from me you can do nothing. [6]If anyone does not remain in me, he is like a branch that is thrown away and withers; such branches are picked up, thrown into the fire and burned. [7]If you remain in me and my words remain in you, ask whatever you wish, and it will be given you. [8]This is to my Father's glory, that you bear much fruit, showing yourselves to be my disciples."

b) He Used Parable

Matt 13 [3]Then he told them many things in parables, saying: "A farmer went out to sow his seed. [4]As he was scattering the seed, some fell along the path, and the birds came and ate it up. [5]Some fell on rocky places, where it did not have much soil. It sprang up quickly, because the soil was shallow. [6]But when the sun came up, the plants were scorched, and they withered because they had no root. [7]Other seed fell among thorns, which grew up and choked the plants. [8]Still other seed fell on good soil, where it produced a crop—a hundred, sixty or thirty times what was sown. [9]He who has ears, let him hear."

[10]The disciples came to him and asked, "Why do you speak to the people in parables?"

[11]He replied, "The knowledge of the secrets of the kingdom of heaven has been given to you, but not to them. [12]Whoever has will be given more, and he will have an abundance. Whoever does not have, even what he has will be taken from

him. 13This is why I speak to them in parables: Though seeing, they do not see; though hearing, they do not hear or understand. 14In them is fulfilled the prophecy of Isaiah: 'You will be ever hearing but never understanding; you will be ever seeing but never perceiving. 15For this people's heart has become calloused; they hardly hear with their ears, and they have closed their eyes. Otherwise they might see with their eyes, hear with their ears, understand with their hearts and turn, and I would heal them.' 16But blessed are your eyes because they see, and your ears because they hear. 17For I tell you the truth, many prophets and righteous men longed to see what you see but did not see it, and to hear what you hear but did not hear it.

18"Listen then to what the parable of the sower means: 19When anyone hears the message about the kingdom and does not understand it, the evil one comes and snatches away what was sown in his heart. This is the seed sown along the path. 20The one who received the seed that fell on rocky places is the man who hears the word and at once receives it with joy. 21But since he has no root, he lasts only a short time. When trouble or persecution comes because of the word, he quickly falls away. 22The one who received the seed that fell among the thorns is the man who hears the word, but the worries of this life and the deceitfulness of wealth choke it, making it unfruitful. 23But the one who received the seed that fell on good soil is the man who hears the word and understands it. He produces a crop, yielding a hundred, sixty or thirty times what was sown."

Mark 4 30Again he said, "What shall we say the kingdom of God is like, or what parable shall we use to describe it? 31It is like a mustard seed, which is the smallest seed you plant in the ground. 32Yet when planted, it grows and becomes the largest of all garden plants, with such big branches that the birds of the air can perch in its shade."

33With many similar parables Jesus spoke the word to them, as much as they could understand. 34He did not say anything to them without using a parable. But when he was alone with his own disciples, he explained everything.

Luke 10 25On one occasion an expert in the law stood up to test Jesus. "Teacher," he asked, "what must I do to inherit eternal life?"

26"What is written in the Law?" he replied. "How do you read it?"

27He answered: "'Love the Lord your God with all your heart and with all your soul and with all your strength and with all your mind'; and, 'Love your neighbor as yourself.'"

28"You have answered correctly," Jesus replied. "Do this and you will live."

29But he wanted to justify himself, so he asked Jesus, "And who is my neighbor?"

30In reply Jesus said: "A man was going down from Jerusalem to Jericho, when he fell into the hands of robbers. They stripped him of his clothes, beat him and went away, leaving him half dead. 31A priest happened to be going down the same road, and when he saw the man, he passed by on the other side. 32So too, a Levite, when he came to the place and saw him, passed by on the other side. 33But a Samaritan, as he traveled, came where the man was; and when he saw him, he took pity on him. 34He went to him and bandaged his wounds, pouring on oil and wine. Then he put the man on his own donkey, took him to an inn and took care of him. 35The next day he took out two silver coins and gave them to the innkeeper. 'Look after him,' he said, 'and when I return, I will reimburse you for any extra expense you may have.'

36"Which of these three do you think was a neighbor to the man who fell into the hands of robbers?"

37The expert in the law replied, "The one who had mercy on him."

Jesus told him, "Go and do likewise."

c) He Used Poetry

Matt 7 1"Do not judge, or you too will be judged. 2For in the same way you judge others, you will be judged, and with the measure you use, it will be measured to you."

Matt 7 6"Do not give dogs what is sacred; do not throw your pearls to pigs. If you do, they may trample them under their feet, and then turn and tear you to pieces."

Matt 7 7"Ask and it will be given to you; seek and you will find; knock and the door will be opened to you."

Matt 23 5"Everything they do is done for men to see: They make their phylacteries wide and the tassels on their garments long; 6they love the place of honor at banquets and the most important seats in the synagogues; 7they love to be greeted in the marketplaces and to have men call them 'Rabbi.'

8"But you are not to be called 'Rabbi,' for you have only one Master and you are all brothers. 9And do not call anyone on earth 'father,' for you have one Father, and he is in heaven. 10Nor are you to be called 'teacher,' for you have one Teacher, the Christ."

Mark 4 24"Consider carefully what you hear," he continued. "With the measure you use, it will be measured to you—and even more. 25Whoever has will be given more; whoever does not have, even what he has will be taken from him."

John 3 6"Flesh gives birth to flesh, but the Spirit gives birth to spirit."

John 11 9Jesus answered, "Are there not twelve hours of daylight? A man who walks by day will not stumble, for he sees by this world's light. 10It is when he walks by night that he stumbles, for he has no light."

d) He Used Rhetoric

Matt 6 25"Therefore I tell you, do not worry about your life, what you will eat or drink; or about your body, what you will wear. Is not life more important than food, and the body more important than clothes? 26Look at the birds of the air; they do not sow or reap or store away in barns, and yet your heavenly Father feeds them. Are you not much more valuable than they? 27Who of you by worrying can add a single hour to his life?

28"And why do you worry about clothes? See how the lilies of the field grow. They do not labor or spin. 29Yet I tell you that not even Solomon in all his splendor was dressed like one of these. 30If that is how God clothes the grass of the field, which is here today and tomorrow is thrown into the fire, will he not much more clothe you, O you of little faith?"

Matt 22 23That same day the Sadducees, who say there is no resurrection, came to him with a question. . . .

29Jesus replied, "You are in error because you do not know the Scriptures or the power of God. . . . 31But about the resurrection of the dead— have you not read what God said to you, 32'I am the God of Abraham, the God of Isaac, and the God of Jacob'? He is not the God of the dead but of the living."

e) He Used the OT

Matt 6 29"Yet I tell you that not even Solomon in all his splendor was dressed like one of these."

Matt 7 12"So in everything, do to others what you would have them do to you, for this sums up the Law and the Prophets."

Matt 11 13"For all the Prophets and the Law prophesied until John. 14And if you are willing to accept it, he is the Elijah who was to come."

Matt 12 39He answered, "A wicked and adulterous generation asks for a miraculous sign! But none will be given it except the sign of the prophet Jonah. 40For as Jonah was three days and three nights in the belly of a huge fish, so the Son of Man will be three days and three nights in the heart of the earth. 41The men of Nineveh will stand up at the judgment with this generation and condemn it; for they repented at the preaching of Jonah, and now one greater than Jonah is here. 42The Queen of the South will rise at the judgment with this generation and condemn it; for she came from the ends of the earth to listen to Solomon's wisdom, and now one greater than Solomon is here."

Matt 23 35"And so upon you will come all the righteous blood that has been shed on earth, from the blood of righteous Abel to the blood of Zechariah son of Berekiah, whom you murdered between the temple and the altar."

Matt 24 15"So when you see standing in the holy place 'the abomination that causes desolation,' spoken of through the prophet Daniel—let the reader understand. . . ."

Luke 4 16He went to Nazareth, where he had been brought up, and on the Sabbath day he went into the synagogue, as was his custom. And he stood up to read. 17The scroll of the prophet Isaiah was handed to him. Unrolling it, he found the place where it is written: [18]"The Spirit of the Lord is on me, because he has anointed me to preach good news to the poor. He has sent me to proclaim freedom for the prisoners and recovery of sight for the blind, to release the oppressed, [19]to proclaim the year of the Lord's favor."

Luke 17 [26]"Just as it was in the days of Noah, so also will it be in the days of the Son of Man. [27]People were eating, drinking, marrying and being given in marriage up to the day Noah entered the ark. Then the flood came and destroyed them all.

[28]"It was the same in the days of Lot. People were eating and drinking, buying and selling, planting and building. [29]But the day Lot left Sodom, fire and sulfur rained down from heaven and destroyed them all."

John 5 [45]"But do not think I will accuse you before the Father. Your accuser is Moses, on whom your hopes are set. [46]If you believed Moses, you would believe me, for he wrote about me. [47]But since you do not believe what he wrote, how are you going to believe what I say?"

John 8 [17]"In your own Law it is written that the testimony of two men is valid. [18]I am one who testifies for myself; my other witness is the Father, who sent me."

2. Jesus Was Perceptive

a) He Had Common Sense

Mark 3 [9]Because of the crowd he told his disciples to have a small boat ready for him, to keep the people from crowding him. [10]For he had healed many, so that those with diseases were pushing forward to touch him.

Mark 6 [30]The apostles gathered around Jesus and reported to him all they had done and taught. [31]Then, because so many people were coming and going that they did not even have a chance to eat, he said to them, "Come with me by yourselves to a quiet place and get some rest."

[32]So they went away by themselves in a boat to a solitary place.

John 7 [1]After this, Jesus went around in Galilee, purposely staying away from Judea because the Jews there were waiting to take his life.

b) He Had Insight

Mark 2 [8]Immediately Jesus knew in his spirit that this was what they were thinking in their hearts, and he said to them, "Why are you thinking these things? [9]Which is easier: to say to the paralytic, 'Your sins are forgiven,' or to say, 'Get up, take your mat and walk'? [10]But that you may know that the Son of Man has authority on earth to forgive sins. . . ." He said to the paralytic, [11]"I tell you, get up, take your mat and go home." [12]He got up, took his mat and walked out in full view of them all. This amazed everyone and they praised God, saying, "We have never seen anything like this!"

Mark 10 [17]As Jesus started on his way, a man ran up to him and fell on his knees before him. "Good teacher," he asked, "what must I do to inherit eternal life?"

[18]"Why do you call me good?" Jesus answered. "No one is good—except God alone. [19]You know the commandments: 'Do not murder, do not commit adultery, do not steal, do not give false testimony, do not defraud, honor your father and mother.'"

[20]"Teacher," he declared, "all these I have kept since I was a boy."

[21]Jesus looked at him and loved him. "One thing you lack," he said. "Go, sell everything you have and give to the poor, and you will have treasure in heaven. Then come, follow me."

[22]At this the man's face fell. He went away sad, because he had great wealth.

Mark 12 [28]One of the teachers of the law came and heard them debating. Noticing that Jesus had given them a good answer, he asked him, "Of all the commandments, which is the most important?"

[29]"The most important one," answered Jesus, "is this: 'Hear, O Israel, the Lord our God, the Lord is one. [30]Love the Lord your God with all your heart and with all your soul and with all your mind and with all your strength.' [31]The second is this: 'Love your neighbor as yourself.' There is no commandment greater than these."

[32]"Well said, teacher," the man replied. "You are right in saying that God is one and there is no other but him. [33]To love him with all your heart, with all your understanding and with all your strength, and to love your neighbor as yourself is more important than all burnt offerings and sacrifices."

[34]When Jesus saw that he had answered wisely, he said to him, "You are not far from the kingdom of God." And from then on no one dared ask him any more questions.

Luke 9 [47]Jesus, knowing their thoughts, took a little child and had him stand beside him. [48]Then he said to them, "Whoever welcomes this little child in my name welcomes me; and whoever welcomes me welcomes the one who sent me. For he who is least among you all—he is the greatest."

John 2 [23]Now while he was in Jerusalem at the Passover Feast, many people saw the miraculous signs he was doing and believed in his name. [24]But Jesus would not entrust himself to them, for he knew all men. [25]He did not need man's testimony about man, for he knew what was in man.

John 6 [15]Jesus, knowing that they intended to come and make him king by force, withdrew again to a mountain by himself.

John 6 [60]On hearing it, many of his disciples said, "This is a hard teaching. Who can accept it?"

[61]Aware that his disciples were grumbling about this, Jesus said to them, "Does this offend you? [62]What if you see the Son of Man ascend to where he was before! [63]The Spirit gives life; the flesh counts for nothing. The words I have spoken to you are spirit and they are life. [64]Yet there are some of you who do not believe." For Jesus had known from the beginning which of them did not believe and who would betray him.

c) He Had a Quick Wit

Matt 22 [15]Then the Pharisees went out and laid plans to trap him in his words. [16]They sent their disciples to him along with the Herodians. "Teacher," they said, "we know you are a man of integrity and that you teach the way of God in accordance with the truth. You aren't swayed by men, because you pay no attention to who they are. [17]Tell us then, what is your opinion? Is it right to pay taxes to Caesar or not?"

[18]But Jesus, knowing their evil intent, said, "You hypocrites, why are you trying to trap me? [19]Show me the coin used for paying the tax." They brought him a denarius, [20]and he asked them, "Whose portrait is this? And whose inscription?"

[21]"Caesar's," they replied.

Then he said to them, "Give to Caesar what is Caesar's, and to God what is God's."

[22]When they heard this, they were amazed. So they left him and went away.

Mark 11 [27]They arrived again in Jerusalem, and while Jesus was walking in the temple courts, the chief priests, the teachers of the law and the elders came to him. [28]"By what authority are you doing these things?" they asked. "And who gave you authority to do this?"

[29]Jesus replied, "I will ask you one question. Answer me, and I will tell you by what authority I am doing these things. [30]John's baptism—was it from heaven, or from men? Tell me!"

[31]They discussed it among themselves and said, "If we say, 'From heaven,' he will ask, 'Then why didn't you believe him?' [32]But if we say, 'From men' . . . ." (They feared the people, for everyone held that John really was a prophet.)

[33]So they answered Jesus, "We don't know."

Jesus said, "Neither will I tell you by what authority I am doing these things."

Luke 8 [19]Now Jesus' mother and brothers came to see him, but they were not able to get near him because of the crowd. [20]Someone told him, "Your mother and brothers are standing outside, wanting to see you."

[21]He replied, "My mother and brothers are those who hear God's word and put it into practice."

d) He Had Recall

Matt 19 [3]Some Pharisees came to him to test him. They asked, "Is it lawful for a man to divorce his wife for any and every reason?"

[4]"Haven't you read," he replied, "that at the beginning the Creator 'made them male and female,' [5]and said, 'For this reason a man will leave his father and mother and be united to his

wife, and the two will become one flesh'? [6]So they are no longer two, but one. Therefore what God has joined together, let man not separate."

Matt 21 [14]The blind and the lame came to him at the temple, and he healed them. [15]But when the chief priests and the teachers of the law saw the wonderful things he did and the children shouting in the temple area, "Hosanna to the Son of David," they were indignant.

[16]"Do you hear what these children are saying?" they asked him.

"Yes," replied Jesus, "have you never read, 'From the lips of children and infants you have ordained praise'?"

Matt 22 [29]Jesus replied, "You are in error because you do not know the Scriptures or the power of God. [30]At the resurrection people will neither marry nor be given in marriage; they will be like the angels in heaven. [31]But about the resurrection of the dead—have you not read what God said to you, [32]'I am the God of Abraham, the God of Isaac, and the God of Jacob'? He is not the God of the dead but of the living."

[33]When the crowds heard this, they were astonished at his teaching.

Mark 12 [10]"Haven't you read this scripture: 'The stone the builders rejected has become the capstone; [11]the Lord has done this, and it is marvelous in our eyes'?"

Mark 12 [18]Then the Sadducees, who say there is no resurrection, came to him with a question. [19]"Teacher," they said, "Moses wrote for us that if a man's brother dies and leaves a wife but no children, the man must marry the widow and have children for his brother. [20]Now there were seven brothers. The first one married and died without leaving any children. [21]The second one married the widow, but he also died, leaving no child. It was the same with the third. [22]In fact, none of the seven left any children. Last of all, the woman died too. [23]At the resurrection whose wife will she be, since the seven were married to her?"

[24]Jesus replied, "Are you not in error because you do not know the Scriptures or the power of God? [25]When the dead rise, they will neither marry nor be given in marriage; they will be like the angels in heaven. [26]Now about the dead rising—have you not read in the book of Moses, in the account of the bush, how God said to him, 'I am the God of Abraham, the God of Isaac, and the God of Jacob'? [27]He is not the God of the dead, but of the living. You are badly mistaken!"

Luke 6 [1]One Sabbath Jesus was going through the grainfields, and his disciples began to pick some heads of grain, rub them in their hands and eat the kernels. [2]Some of the Pharisees asked, "Why are you doing what is unlawful on the Sabbath?"

[3]Jesus answered them, "Have you never read what David did when he and his companions were hungry? [4]He entered the house of God, and taking the consecrated bread, he ate what is lawful only for priests to eat. And he also gave some to his companions." [5]Then Jesus said to them, "The Son of Man is Lord of the Sabbath."

3. Jesus Was Knowledgeable

a) He Read

Luke 4 [16]He went to Nazareth, where he had been brought up, and on the Sabbath day he went into the synagogue, as was his custom. And he stood up to read.

b) He Wrote

John 8 [1]But Jesus went to the Mount of Olives. [2]At dawn he appeared again in the temple courts, where all the people gathered around him, and he sat down to teach them. [3]The teachers of the law and the Pharisees brought in a woman caught in adultery. They made her stand before the group [4]and said to Jesus, "Teacher, this woman was caught in the act of adultery. [5]In the Law Moses commanded us to stone such women. Now what do you say?" [6]They were using this question as a trap, in order to have a basis for accusing him.

But Jesus bent down and started to write on the ground with his finger. [7]When they kept on questioning him, he straightened up and said to them, "If any one of you is without sin, let him be the first to throw a stone at her." [8]Again he stooped down and wrote on the ground.

[9]At this, those who heard began to go away one at a time, the older ones first, until only Jesus was left, with the woman still standing there. [10]Jesus straightened up and asked her, "Woman, where are they? Has no one condemned you?"

[11]"No one, sir," she said.

"Then neither do I condemn you," Jesus declared. "Go now and leave your life of sin."

c) He Learned

Luke 2 [46]After three days they found him in the temple courts, sitting among the teachers, listening to them and asking them questions. [47]Everyone who heard him was amazed at his understanding and his answers.

Luke 2 [52]And Jesus grew in wisdom and stature, and in favor with God and men.

John 7 [14]Not until halfway through the Feast did Jesus go up to the temple courts and begin to teach. [15]The Jews were amazed and asked, "How did this man get such learning without having studied?"

4. Jesus Was Intelligent

a) He Was a Teacher

Matt 5 [1]Now when he saw the crowds, he went up on a mountainside and sat down. His disciples came to him, [2]and he began to teach them, saying . . .

Mark 6 [34]When Jesus landed and saw a large crowd, he had compassion on them, because they were like sheep without a shepherd. So he began teaching them many things.

Mark 14 [14]"Say to the owner of the house he enters, 'The Teacher asks: Where is my guest room, where I may eat the Passover with my disciples?'"

Luke 19 [47]Every day he was teaching at the temple. But the chief priests, the teachers of the law and the leaders among the people were trying to kill him.

Luke 24 [27]And beginning with Moses and all the Prophets, he explained to them what was said in all the Scriptures concerning himself.

John 7 [16]Jesus answered, "My teaching is not my own. It comes from him who sent me."

John 8 [2]At dawn he appeared again in the temple courts, where all the people gathered around him, and he sat down to teach them.

John 13 [13]"You call me 'Teacher' and 'Lord,' and rightly so, for that is what I am. [14]Now that I, your Lord and Teacher, have washed your feet, you also should wash one another's feet."

b) He Was a Preacher

Matt 4 [23]Jesus went throughout Galilee, teaching in their synagogues, preaching the good news of the kingdom, and healing every disease and sickness among the people.

Mark 1 [38]Jesus replied, "Let us go somewhere else—to the nearby villages—so I can preach there also. That is why I have come." [39]So he traveled throughout Galilee, preaching in their synagogues and driving out demons.

Luke 4 [43]But he said, "I must preach the good news of the kingdom of God to the other towns also, because that is why I was sent."

Luke 7 [22]So he replied to the messengers, "Go back and report to John what you have seen and heard: The blind receive sight, the lame walk, those who have leprosy are cured, the deaf hear, the dead are raised, and the good news is preached to the poor."

Luke 20 [1]One day as he was teaching the people in the temple courts and preaching the gospel, the chief priests and the teachers of the law, together with the elders, came up to him.

c) He Was a Prophet

Mark 6 [4]Jesus said to them, "Only in his hometown, among his relatives and in his own house is a prophet without honor."

Luke 13 [33]"In any case, I must keep going today and tomorrow and the next day—for surely no prophet can die outside Jerusalem!"

Luke 24 [19]"What things?" he asked.

"About Jesus of Nazareth," they replied. "He was a prophet, powerful in word and deed before God and all the people."

John 12 [49]"For I did not speak of my own accord, but the

Father who sent me commanded me what to say and how to say it. [50]I know that his command leads to eternal life. So whatever I say is just what the Father has told me to say."

E. Christ Shared with Humanity a Moral Nature

1. Jesus Was Conscious of God

a) He Was Spiritually Minded

Luke 2 [49]"Why were you searching for me?" he asked. "Didn't you know I had to be in my Father's house?"
John 8 [23]But he continued, "You are from below; I am from above. You are of this world; I am not of this world."
John 16 [28]"I came from the Father and entered the world; now I am leaving the world and going back to the Father."
John 17 [14]"I have given them your word and the world has hated them, for they are not of the world any more than I am of the world. . . . [16]They are not of the world, even as I am not of it."

b) He Sought God's Will

Matt 6 [9]"This, then, is how you should pray: 'Our Father in heaven, hallowed be your name, [10]your kingdom come, your will be done on earth as it is in heaven.'"
Matt 26 [39]Going a little farther, he fell with his face to the ground and prayed, "My Father, if it is possible, may this cup be taken from me. Yet not as I will, but as you will." . . .

[42]He went away a second time and prayed, "My Father, if it is not possible for this cup to be taken away unless I drink it, may your will be done."
John 4 [34]"My food," said Jesus, "is to do the will of him who sent me and to finish his work."
John 5 [30]"By myself I can do nothing; I judge only as I hear, and my judgment is just, for I seek not to please myself but him who sent me."
John 6 [38]"For I have come down from heaven not to do my will but to do the will of him who sent me."
John 12 [27]"Now my heart is troubled, and what shall I say? 'Father, save me from this hour'? No, it was for this very reason I came to this hour. [28]Father, glorify your name!"

Then a voice came from heaven, "I have glorified it, and will glorify it again."
John 14 [31]" . . . but the world must learn that I love the Father and that I do exactly what my Father has commanded me.

"Come now; let us leave."

c) He Had Moral Strength

Matt 26 [62]Then the high priest stood up and said to Jesus, "Are you not going to answer? What is this testimony that these men are bringing against you?" [63]But Jesus remained silent.

The high priest said to him, "I charge you under oath by the living God: Tell us if you are the Christ, the Son of God."
Matt 27 [12]When he was accused by the chief priests and the elders, he gave no answer.
Luke 4 [1]Jesus, full of the Holy Spirit, returned from the Jordan and was led by the Spirit in the desert, [2]where for forty days he was tempted by the devil. He ate nothing during those days, and at the end of them he was hungry.

[3]The devil said to him, "If you are the Son of God, tell this stone to become bread."

[4]Jesus answered, "It is written: 'Man does not live on bread alone.'"

[5]The devil led him up to a high place and showed him in an instant all the kingdoms of the world. [6]And he said to him, "I will give you all their authority and splendor, for it has been given to me, and I can give it to anyone I want to. [7]So if you worship me, it will all be yours."

[8]Jesus answered, "It is written: 'Worship the Lord your God and serve him only.'"

[9]The devil led him to Jerusalem and had him stand on the highest point of the temple. "If you are the Son of God," he said, "throw yourself down from here. [10]For it is written: 'He will command his angels concerning you to guard you carefully; [11]they will lift you up in their hands, so that you will not strike your foot against a stone.'"

[12]Jesus answered, "It says: 'Do not put the Lord your God to the test.'"

[13]When the devil had finished all this tempting, he left him until an opportune time.
John 18 [3]So Judas came to the grove, guiding a detachment of soldiers and some officials from the chief priests and Pharisees. They were carrying torches, lanterns and weapons.

[4]Jesus, knowing all that was going to happen to him, went out and asked them, "Who is it you want?"

[5]"Jesus of Nazareth," they replied.

"I am he," Jesus said. (And Judas the traitor was standing there with them.) [6]When Jesus said, "I am he," they drew back and fell to the ground.

[7]Again he asked them, "Who is it you want?"

And they said, "Jesus of Nazareth."

[8]"I told you that I am he," Jesus answered. "If you are looking for me, then let these men go."

2. Jesus Was Consistent

a) He Was Meek

Isa 53 [7]He was oppressed and afflicted, yet he did not open his mouth; he was led like a lamb to the slaughter, and as a sheep before her shearers is silent, so he did not open his mouth. [8]By oppression and judgment he was taken away. And who can speak of his descendants? For he was cut off from the land of the living; for the transgression of my people he was stricken.
Matt 11 [29]"Take my yoke upon you and learn from me, for I am gentle and humble in heart, and you will find rest for your souls."
Matt 12 [19]"He will not quarrel or cry out; no one will hear his voice in the streets."
Mark 10 [45]"For even the Son of Man did not come to be served, but to serve, and to give his life as a ransom for many."
Luke 22 [26]"But you are not to be like that. Instead, the greatest among you should be like the youngest, and the one who rules like the one who serves. [27]For who is greater, the one who is at the table or the one who serves? Is it not the one who is at the table? But I am among you as one who serves."

b) He Was Trustworthy

John 8 [14]Jesus answered, "Even if I testify on my own behalf, my testimony is valid, for I know where I came from and where I am going. But you have no idea where I come from or where I am going. . . . [17]In your own Law it is written that the testimony of two men is valid. [18]I am one who testifies for myself; my other witness is the Father, who sent me."
John 18 [37]"You are a king, then!" said Pilate.

Jesus answered, "You are right in saying I am a king. In fact, for this reason I was born, and for this I came into the world, to testify to the truth. Everyone on the side of truth listens to me."

3. Jesus Was Committed to Others

a) He Was Concerned about People's Welfare

Matt 4 [23]Jesus went throughout Galilee, teaching in their synagogues, preaching the good news of the kingdom, and healing every disease and sickness among the people.
Matt 8 [16]When evening came, many who were demon-possessed were brought to him, and he drove out the spirits with a word and healed all the sick.
Matt 9 [35]Jesus went through all the towns and villages, teaching in their synagogues, preaching the good news of the kingdom and healing every disease and sickness.
Matt 12 [15]Aware of this, Jesus withdrew from that place. Many followed him, and he healed all their sick. . . .
Matt 14 [14]When Jesus landed and saw a large crowd, he had compassion on them and healed their sick.
Matt 15 [30]Great crowds came to him, bringing the lame, the blind, the crippled, the mute and many others, and laid them at his feet; and he healed them.
Matt 19 [2]Large crowds followed him, and he healed them there.
Matt 21 [14]The blind and the lame came to him at the temple, and he healed them.
Mark 1 [32]That evening after sunset the people brought to Jesus all the sick and demon-possessed. [33]The whole town gathered at the door, [34]and Jesus healed many who had various diseases.

He also drove out many demons, but he would not let the demons speak because they knew who he was.

b) He Was Concerned about Justice

Matt 5 [23]"Therefore, if you are offering your gift at the altar and there remember that your brother has something against you, [24]leave your gift there in front of the altar. First go and be reconciled to your brother; then come and offer your gift."
Matt 12 [7]"If you had known what these words mean, 'I desire mercy, not sacrifice,' you would not have condemned the innocent."
Matt 12 [18]"Here is my servant whom I have chosen, the one I love, in whom I delight; I will put my Spirit on him, and he will proclaim justice to the nations. . . . [20]A bruised reed he will not break, and a smoldering wick he will not snuff out, till he leads justice to victory."
John 5 [30]"By myself I can do nothing; I judge only as I hear, and my judgment is just, for I seek not to please myself but him who sent me."

c) He Was Concerned about People's Eternal Destiny

Matt 6 [33]"But seek first his kingdom and his righteousness, and all these things will be given to you as well."
Mark 1 [14]After John was put in prison, Jesus went into Galilee, proclaiming the good news of God. [15]"The time has come," he said. "The kingdom of God is near. Repent and believe the good news!"
Mark 2 [17]On hearing this, Jesus said to them, "It is not the healthy who need a doctor, but the sick. I have not come to call the righteous, but sinners."
Luke 15 [7]"I tell you that in the same way there will be more rejoicing in heaven over one sinner who repents than over ninety-nine righteous persons who do not need to repent."
Luke 24 [47]" . . . and repentance and forgiveness of sins will be preached in his name to all nations, beginning at Jerusalem."
John 5 [24]"I tell you the truth, whoever hears my word and believes him who sent me has eternal life and will not be condemned; he has crossed over from death to life."
John 7 [38]"Whoever believes in me, as the Scripture has said, streams of living water will flow from within him."
John 11 [25]Jesus said to her, "I am the resurrection and the life. He who believes in me will live, even though he dies; [26]and whoever lives and believes in me will never die. Do you believe this?"
John 12 [36]"Put your trust in the light while you have it, so that you may become sons of light." When he had finished speaking, Jesus left and hid himself from them.
John 12 [44]Then Jesus cried out, "When a man believes in me, he does not believe in me only, but in the one who sent me. [45]When he looks at me, he sees the one who sent me. [46]I have come into the world as a light, so that no one who believes in me should stay in darkness."
John 20 [27]Then he said to Thomas, "Put your finger here; see my hands. Reach out your hand and put it into my side. Stop doubting and believe." . . .

[29]Then Jesus told him, "Because you have seen me, you have believed; blessed are those who have not seen and yet have believed." . . .

[31]But these are written that you may believe that Jesus is the Christ, the Son of God, and that by believing you may have life in his name.

V
Metaphors, Titles, and Names of Christ

1. Adam, The Last

1 Cor 15 [45]So it is written: "The first man Adam became a living being"; the last Adam, a life-giving spirit.

2. Advocate

1 John 2 [1]My dear children, I write this to you so that you will not sin. But if anybody does sin, we have one who speaks to the Father in our defense—Jesus Christ, the Righteous One.

3. Almighty

Rev 1 [8]"I am the Alpha and the Omega," says the Lord God, "who is, and who was, and who is to come, the Almighty."

4. Alpha and Omega

Rev 1 [8]"I am the Alpha and the Omega," says the Lord God, "who is, and who was, and who is to come, the Almighty."
Rev 22 [13]"I am the Alpha and the Omega, the First and the Last, the Beginning and the End."

5. Amen

Rev 3 [14]"To the angel of the church in Laodicea write: These are the words of the Amen, the faithful and true witness, the ruler of God's creation."

6. Angel of God's Presence

Isa 63 [9]In all their distress he too was distressed, and the angel of his presence saved them. In his love and mercy he redeemed them; he lifted them up and carried them all the days of old.

7. Anointed One

Ps 2 [2]The kings of the earth take their stand and the rulers gather together against the LORD and against his Anointed One.
Dan 9 [25]"Know and understand this: From the issuing of the decree to restore and rebuild Jerusalem until the Anointed One, the ruler, comes, there will be seven 'sevens,' and sixty-two 'sevens.' It will be rebuilt with streets and a trench, but in times of trouble."
Acts 4 [25]"You spoke by the Holy Spirit through the mouth of your servant, our father David: 'Why do the nations rage and the peoples plot in vain? [26]The kings of the earth take their stand and the rulers gather together against the Lord and against his Anointed One.' [27]Indeed Herod and Pontius Pilate met together with the Gentiles and the people of Israel in this city to conspire against your holy servant Jesus, whom you anointed."

8. Apostle

Heb 3 [1]Therefore, holy brothers, who share in the heavenly calling, fix your thoughts on Jesus, the apostle and high priest whom we confess.

9. Arm of the Lord

Isa 53 [1]Who has believed our message and to whom has the arm of the LORD been revealed? [2]He grew up before him like a tender shoot, and like a root out of dry ground. He had no beauty or majesty to attract us to him, nothing in his appearance that we should desire him.

10. Atoning Sacrifice

1 John 2 [2]He is the atoning sacrifice for our sins, and not only for ours but also for the sins of the whole world.

11. Author of Faith

Heb 12 [2]Let us fix our eyes on Jesus, the author and perfecter of our faith, who for the joy set before him endured the cross, scorning its shame, and sat down at the right hand of the throne of God.

12. Author of Life

Acts 3 [15]"You killed the author of life, but God raised him from the dead. We are witnesses of this."

13. Author of Salvation

Heb 2 [10]In bringing many sons to glory, it was fitting that God, for whom and through whom everything exists, should make the author of their salvation perfect through suffering.

14. Banner

Isa 11 [10]In that day the Root of Jesse will stand as a banner for the peoples; the nations will rally to him, and his place of rest will be glorious. . . .

[12]He will raise a banner for the nations and gather the exiles of Israel; he will assemble the scattered people of Judah from the four quarters of the earth.

15. Beginning and End

Rev 22 [13]"I am the Alpha and the Omega, the First and the Last, the Beginning and the End."

16. Beloved One

Eph 1 [6]to the praise of his glorious grace, which he has freely given us in the One he loves.

17. Branch

Isa 4 [2]In that day the Branch of the LORD will be beautiful and glorious, and the fruit of the land will be the pride and glory of the survivors in Israel.
Isa 11 [1]A shoot will come up from the stump of Jesse; from his roots a Branch will bear fruit.
Jer 23 [5]"The days are coming," declares the LORD, "when I will raise up to David a righteous Branch, a King who will reign wisely and do what is just and right in the land."
Zech 3 [8]"'Listen, O high priest Joshua and your associates seated before you, who are men symbolic of things to come: I am going to bring my servant, the Branch.'"
Zech 6 [12]"Tell him this is what the LORD Almighty says: 'Here is the man whose name is the Branch, and he will branch out from his place and build the temple of the LORD.'"

18. Bread of God

John 6 [32]Jesus said to them, "I tell you the truth, it is not Moses who has given you the bread from heaven, but it is my Father who gives you the true bread from heaven. [33]For the bread of God is he who comes down from heaven and gives life to the world."

19. Bread of Life

John 6 [35]Then Jesus declared, "I am the bread of life. He who comes to me will never go hungry, and he who believes in me will never be thirsty. . . . [48]I am the bread of life. [49]Your forefathers ate the manna in the desert, yet they died. [50]But here is the bread that comes down from heaven, which a man may eat and not die. [51]I am the living bread that came down from heaven. If anyone eats of this bread, he will live forever. This bread is my flesh, which I will give for the life of the world."

20. Bridegroom

Matt 9 [15]Jesus answered, "How can the guests of the bridegroom mourn while he is with them? The time will come when the bridegroom will be taken from them; then they will fast."
Matt 25 [1]"At that time the kingdom of heaven will be like ten virgins who took their lamps and went out to meet the bridegroom. [2]Five of them were foolish and five were wise. [3]The foolish ones took their lamps but did not take any oil with them. [4]The wise, however, took oil in jars along with their lamps. [5]The bridegroom was a long time in coming, and they all became drowsy and fell asleep.

[6]"At midnight the cry rang out: 'Here's the bridegroom! Come out to meet him!'

[7]"Then all the virgins woke up and trimmed their lamps. [8]The foolish ones said to the wise, 'Give us some of your oil; our lamps are going out.'

[9]"'No,' they replied, 'there may not be enough for both us and you. Instead, go to those who sell oil and buy some for yourselves.'

[10]"But while they were on their way to buy the oil, the bridegroom arrived. The virgins who were ready went in with him to the wedding banquet. And the door was shut.

[11]"Later the others also came. 'Sir! Sir!' they said. 'Open the door for us!'

[12]"But he replied, 'I tell you the truth, I don't know you.'

[13]"Therefore keep watch, because you do not know the day or the hour."
John 3 [29]"The bride belongs to the bridegroom. The friend who attends the bridegroom waits and listens for him, and is full of joy when he hears the bridegroom's voice. That joy is mine, and it is now complete."

21. Capstone

Matt 21 [42]Jesus said to them, "Have you never read in the Scriptures: 'The stone the builders rejected has become the capstone; the Lord has done this, and it is marvelous in our eyes'?"

22. Chief Shepherd

1 Pet 5 [4]And when the Chief Shepherd appears, you will receive the crown of glory that will never fade away.

23. Child

Isa 9 [6]For to us a child is born, to us a son is given, and the government will be on his shoulders. And he will be called Wonderful Counselor, Mighty God, Everlasting Father, Prince of Peace.
1 John 5 [1]Everyone who believes that Jesus is the Christ is born of God, and everyone who loves the father loves his child as well.

24. Chosen One

Isa 42 [1]"Here is my servant, whom I uphold, my chosen one in whom I delight; I will put my Spirit on him and he will bring justice to the nations."
Luke 23 [35]The people stood watching, and the rulers even sneered at him. They said, "He saved others; let him save himself if he is the Christ of God, the Chosen One."

25. Chosen Servant

Matt 12 [18]"Here is my servant whom I have chosen, the one I love, in whom I delight; I will put my Spirit on him, and he will proclaim justice to the nations."

26. Christ

Matt 1 [16]and Jacob the father of Joseph, the husband of Mary, of whom was born Jesus, who is called Christ.
Matt 16 [20]Then he warned his disciples not to tell anyone that he was the Christ.
Mark 14 [61]But Jesus remained silent and gave no answer.

Again the high priest asked him, "Are you the Christ, the Son of the Blessed One?"
Luke 2 [11]"Today in the town of David a Savior has been born to you; he is Christ the Lord."

Luke 9 [20]"But what about you?" he asked. "Who do you say I am?"

Peter answered, "The Christ of God."

Luke 23 [2]And they began to accuse him, saying, "We have found this man subverting our nation. He opposes payment of taxes to Caesar and claims to be Christ, a king."

Luke 23 [35]The people stood watching, and the rulers even sneered at him. They said, "He saved others; let him save himself if he is the Christ of God, the Chosen One." . . .

[39]One of the criminals who hung there hurled insults at him: "Aren't you the Christ? Save yourself and us!"

John 1 [41]The first thing Andrew did was to find his brother Simon and tell him, "We have found the Messiah" (that is, the Christ).

John 12 [34]The crowd spoke up, "We have heard from the Law that the Christ will remain forever, so how can you say, 'The Son of Man must be lifted up'? Who is this 'Son of Man'?"

Acts 2 [31]"Seeing what was ahead, he spoke of the resurrection of the Christ, that he was not abandoned to the grave, nor did his body see decay. . . .

[36]"Therefore let all Israel be assured of this: God has made this Jesus, whom you crucified, both Lord and Christ."

Acts 3 [18]"But this is how God fulfilled what he had foretold through all the prophets, saying that his Christ would suffer."

Acts 5 [42]Day after day, in the temple courts and from house to house, they never stopped teaching and proclaiming the good news that Jesus is the Christ.

Rom 5 [8]But God demonstrates his own love for us in this: While we were still sinners, Christ died for us.

Rom 9 [5]Theirs are the patriarchs, and from them is traced the human ancestry of Christ, who is God over all, forever praised! Amen.

Rom 10 [4]Christ is the end of the law so that there may be righteousness for everyone who believes.

Rom 14 [9]For this very reason, Christ died and returned to life so that he might be the Lord of both the dead and the living.

1 Cor 1 [23]but we preach Christ crucified: a stumbling block to Jews and foolishness to Gentiles, [24]but to those whom God has called, both Jews and Greeks, Christ the power of God and the wisdom of God.

1 Cor 2 [16]"For who has known the mind of the Lord that he may instruct him?" But we have the mind of Christ.

1 Cor 3 [23]and you are of Christ, and Christ is of God.

1 Cor 12 [27]Now you are the body of Christ, and each one of you is a part of it.

2 Cor 2 [17]Unlike so many, we do not peddle the word of God for profit. On the contrary, in Christ we speak before God with sincerity, like men sent from God.

Gal 3 [13]Christ redeemed us from the curse of the law by becoming a curse for us, for it is written: "Cursed is everyone who is hung on a tree."

Eph 5 [21]Submit to one another out of reverence for Christ. . . . [23]For the husband is the head of the wife as Christ is the head of the church, his body, of which he is the Savior. [24]Now as the church submits to Christ, so also wives should submit to their husbands in everything.

[25]Husbands, love your wives, just as Christ loved the church and gave himself up for her. . . . [29]After all, no one ever hated his own body, but he feeds and cares for it, just as Christ does the church. . . . [32]This is a profound mystery—but I am talking about Christ and the church.

Phil 1 [21]For to me, to live is Christ and to die is gain.

Col 3 [15]Let the peace of Christ rule in your hearts, since as members of one body you were called to peace. And be thankful.

Philem [6]I pray that you may be active in sharing your faith, so that you will have a full understanding of every good thing we have in Christ.

Heb 3 [6]But Christ is faithful as a son over God's house. And we are his house, if we hold on to our courage and the hope of which we boast.

Heb 9 [15]For this reason Christ is the mediator of a new covenant, that those who are called may receive the promised eternal inheritance—now that he has died as a ransom to set them free from the sins committed under the first covenant.

1 Pet 5 [10]And the God of all grace, who called you to his eternal glory in Christ, after you have suffered a little while, will himself restore you and make you strong, firm and steadfast. . . . [14]Greet one another with a kiss of love.

Peace to all of you who are in Christ.

1 John 5 [1]Everyone who believes that Jesus is the Christ is born of God, and everyone who loves the father loves his child as well.

Rev 11 [15]The seventh angel sounded his trumpet, and there were loud voices in heaven, which said: "The kingdom of the world has become the kingdom of our Lord and of his Christ, and he will reign for ever and ever."

27. Christ Jesus

Rom 3 [22]This righteousness from God comes through faith in Jesus Christ to all who believe. There is no difference, [23]for all have sinned and fall short of the glory of God, [24]and are justified freely by his grace through the redemption that came by Christ Jesus.

Rom 8 [1]Therefore, there is now no condemnation for those who are in Christ Jesus. . . .

Rom 15 [5]May the God who gives endurance and encouragement give you a spirit of unity among yourselves as you follow Christ Jesus. . . .

Rom 16 [3]Greet Priscilla and Aquila, my fellow workers in Christ Jesus.

1 Cor 1 [2]To the church of God in Corinth, to those sanctified in Christ Jesus and called to be holy, together with all those everywhere who call on the name of our Lord Jesus Christ—their Lord and ours. . . . [30]It is because of him that you are in Christ Jesus, who has become for us wisdom from God—that is, our righteousness, holiness and redemption.

Gal 2 [16]". . . know that a man is not justified by observing the law, but by faith in Jesus Christ. So we, too, have put our faith in Christ Jesus that we may be justified by faith in Christ and not by observing the law, because by observing the law no one will be justified."

Phil 1 [1]Paul and Timothy, servants of Christ Jesus,

To all the saints in Christ Jesus at Philippi, together with the overseers and deacons. . . . [6]being confident of this, that he who began a good work in you will carry it on to completion until the day of Christ Jesus. . . . [8]God can testify how I long for all of you with the affection of Christ Jesus.

Phil 3 [3]For it is we who are the circumcision, we who worship by the Spirit of God, who glory in Christ Jesus, and who put no confidence in the flesh. . . . [8]What is more, I consider everything a loss compared to the surpassing greatness of knowing Christ Jesus my Lord, for whose sake I have lost all things. I consider them rubbish, that I may gain Christ. . . .

Col 2 [6]So then, just as you received Christ Jesus as Lord, continue to live in him. . . .

1 Thess 5 [18]give thanks in all circumstances, for this is God's will for you in Christ Jesus.

1 Tim 1 [1]Paul, an apostle of Christ Jesus by the command of God our Savior and of Christ Jesus our hope . . .

1 Tim 2 [5]For there is one God and one mediator between God and men, the man Christ Jesus. . . .

1 Tim 3 [13]Those who have served well gain an excellent standing and great assurance in their faith in Christ Jesus.

1 Tim 4 [6]If you point these things out to the brothers, you will be a good minister of Christ Jesus, brought up in the truths of the faith and of the good teaching that you have followed.

1 Tim 5 [21]I charge you, in the sight of God and Christ Jesus and the elect angels, to keep these instructions without partiality, and to do nothing out of favoritism.

2 Tim 1 [9]who has saved us and called us to a holy life—not because of anything we have done but because of his own purpose and grace. This grace was given us in Christ Jesus before the beginning of time, [10]but it has now been revealed through the appearing of our Savior, Christ Jesus, who has destroyed death and has brought life and immortality to light through the gospel.

2 Tim 2 [10]Therefore I endure everything for the sake of the elect, that they too may obtain the salvation that is in Christ Jesus, with eternal glory.

2 Tim 3 [15]and how from infancy you have known the holy

Scriptures, which are able to make you wise for salvation through faith in Christ Jesus.

28. Commander of the Lord's Army

Josh 5 [14]"Neither," he replied, "but as commander of the army of the LORD I have now come." Then Joshua fell facedown to the ground in reverence, and asked him, "What message does my Lord have for his servant?"

[15]The commander of the LORD's army replied, "Take off your sandals, for the place where you are standing is holy." And Joshua did so.

29. Commander of the Peoples

Isa 55 [4]"See, I have made him a witness to the peoples, a leader and commander of the peoples."

30. Consolation of Israel

Luke 2 [25]Now there was a man in Jerusalem called Simeon, who was righteous and devout. He was waiting for the consolation of Israel, and the Holy Spirit was upon him.

31. Cornerstone

Eph 2 [20]built on the foundation of the apostles and prophets, with Christ Jesus himself as the chief cornerstone.
1 Pet 2 [6]For in Scripture it says: "See, I lay a stone in Zion, a chosen and precious cornerstone, and the one who trusts in him will never be put to shame."

32. David

Jer 30 [9]"'Instead, they will serve the LORD their God and David their king, whom I will raise up for them.'"
Ezek 37 [24]"'My servant David will be king over them, and they will all have one shepherd. They will follow my laws and be careful to keep my decrees. [25]They will live in the land I gave to my servant Jacob, the land where your fathers lived. They and their children and their children's children will live there forever, and David my servant will be their prince forever.'"
Hos 3 [5]Afterward the Israelites will return and seek the LORD their God and David their king. They will come trembling to the LORD and to his blessings in the last days.

33. Deliverer

Rom 11 [26]And so all Israel will be saved, as it is written: "The deliverer will come from Zion; he will turn godlessness away from Jacob."

34. Desired of All Nations

Hag 2 [7]"'I will shake all nations, and the desired of all nations will come, and I will fill this house with glory,' says the LORD Almighty."

35. Doctor

Matt 9 [12]On hearing this, Jesus said, "It is not the healthy who need a doctor, but the sick."

36. Eternal Life

1 John 5 [20]We know also that the Son of God has come and has given us understanding, so that we may know him who is true. And we are in him who is true—even in his Son Jesus Christ. He is the true God and eternal life.

37. Everlasting Father

Isa 9 [6]For to us a child is born, to us a son is given, and the government will be on his shoulders. And he will be called Wonderful Counselor, Mighty God, Everlasting Father, Prince of Peace.

38. Exact Representation of God's Being

Heb 1 [3]The Son is the radiance of God's glory and the exact representation of his being, sustaining all things by his powerful word. After he had provided purification for sins, he sat down at the right hand of the Majesty in heaven.

39. Faithful and True

Rev 19 [11]I saw heaven standing open and there before me was a white horse, whose rider is called Faithful and True. With justice he judges and makes war.

40. Faithful and True Witness

Rev 3 [14]"To the angel of the church in Laodicea write: These are the words of the Amen, the faithful and true witness, the ruler of God's creation."

41. Faithful Witness

Rev 1 [5]and from Jesus Christ, who is the faithful witness, the firstborn from the dead, and the ruler of the kings of the earth.

To him who loves us and has freed us from our sins by his blood . . .

42. First and Last

Rev 1 [17]When I saw him, I fell at his feet as though dead. Then he placed his right hand on me and said: "Do not be afraid. I am the First and the Last."
Rev 2 [8]"To the angel of the church in Smyrna write: These are the words of him who is the First and the Last, who died and came to life again."
Rev 22 [13]"I am the Alpha and the Omega, the First and the Last, the Beginning and the End."

43. Firstborn

Ps 89 [27]"I will also appoint him my firstborn, the most exalted of the kings of the earth."
Rom 8 [29]For those God foreknew he also predestined to be conformed to the likeness of his Son, that he might be the firstborn among many brothers.
Col 1 [15]He is the image of the invisible God, the firstborn over all creation. . . . [18]And he is the head of the body, the church; he is the beginning and the firstborn from among the dead, so that in everything he might have the supremacy.
Heb 1 [6]And again, when God brings his firstborn into the world, he says, "Let all God's angels worship him."
Rev 1 [5]and from Jesus Christ, who is the faithful witness, the firstborn from the dead, and the ruler of the kings of the earth.

To him who loves us and has freed us from our sins by his blood . . .

44. Firstfruits

1 Cor 15 [20]But Christ has indeed been raised from the dead, the firstfruits of those who have fallen asleep. . . . [23]But each in his own turn: Christ, the firstfruits; then, when he comes, those who belong to him.

45. Foolishness

1 Cor 1 [23]but we preach Christ crucified: a stumbling block to Jews and foolishness to Gentiles. . . .

46. Forerunner

Heb 6 [19]We have this hope as an anchor for the soul, firm and secure. It enters the inner sanctuary behind the curtain, [20]where Jesus, who went before us, has entered on our behalf. He has become a high priest forever, in the order of Melchizedek.

47. *Foundation*

1 Cor 3 [11]For no one can lay any foundation other than the one already laid, which is Jesus Christ.

48. *Fountain*

Zech 13 [1]"On that day a fountain will be opened to the house of David and the inhabitants of Jerusalem, to cleanse them from sin and impurity."

49. *Friend of Sinners*

Matt 11 [19]"The Son of Man came eating and drinking, and they say, 'Here is a glutton and a drunkard, a friend of tax collectors and "sinners."' But wisdom is proved right by her actions."

50. *Gate*

John 10 [7]Therefore Jesus said again, "I tell you the truth, I am the gate for the sheep. [8]All who ever came before me were thieves and robbers, but the sheep did not listen to them. [9]I am the gate; whoever enters through me will be saved. He will come in and go out, and find pasture."

51. *Gift of God*

John 4 [10]Jesus answered her, "If you knew the gift of God and who it is that asks you for a drink, you would have asked him and he would have given you living water."
2 Cor 9 [15]Thanks be to God for his indescribable gift!

52. *Glory of Israel*

Luke 2 [32]". . . a light for revelation to the Gentiles and for glory to your people Israel."

53. *Glory of the Lord*

Isa 40 [5]"And the glory of the LORD will be revealed, and all mankind together will see it. For the mouth of the LORD has spoken."

54. *God*

Mark 2 [1]A few days later, when Jesus again entered Capernaum, the people heard that he had come home. [2]So many gathered that there was no room left, not even outside the door, and he preached the word to them. [3]Some men came, bringing to him a paralytic, carried by four of them. [4]Since they could not get him to Jesus because of the crowd, they made an opening in the roof above Jesus and, after digging through it, lowered the mat the paralyzed man was lying on. [5]When Jesus saw their faith, he said to the paralytic, "Son, your sins are forgiven."

[6]Now some teachers of the law were sitting there, thinking to themselves, [7]"Why does this fellow talk like that? He's blaspheming! Who can forgive sins but God alone?"

[8]Immediately Jesus knew in his spirit that this was what they were thinking in their hearts, and he said to them, "Why are you thinking these things? [9]Which is easier: to say to the paralytic, 'Your sins are forgiven,' or to say, 'Get up, take your mat and walk'? [10]But that you may know that the Son of Man has authority on earth to forgive sins. . . ." He said to the paralytic, [11]"I tell you, get up, take your mat and go home." [12]He got up, took his mat and walked out in full view of them all. This amazed everyone and they praised God, saying, "We have never seen anything like this!"
Rom 9 [5]Theirs are the patriarchs, and from them is traced the human ancestry of Christ, who is God over all, forever praised! Amen.
Titus 2 [13]while we wait for the blessed hope—the glorious appearing of our great God and Savior, Jesus Christ . . .
2 Pet 1 [1]Simon Peter, a servant and apostle of Jesus Christ,

To those who through the righteousness of our God and Savior Jesus Christ have received a faith as precious as ours. . . .
1 John 5 [20]We know also that the Son of God has come and has given us understanding, so that we may know him who is true. And we are in him who is true—even in his Son Jesus Christ. He is the true God and eternal life.

55. *Good Shepherd*

John 10 [11]"I am the good shepherd. The good shepherd lays down his life for the sheep. . . .

[14]"I am the good shepherd; I know my sheep and my sheep know me. . . ."

56. *Great Shepherd*

Heb 13 [20]May the God of peace, who through the blood of the eternal covenant brought back from the dead our Lord Jesus, that great Shepherd of the sheep . . .

57. *Guarantee*

Heb 7 [22]Because of this oath, Jesus has become the guarantee of a better covenant.

58. *Head*

1 Cor 11 [3]Now I want you to realize that the head of every man is Christ, and the head of the woman is man, and the head of Christ is God.
Eph 5 [23]For the husband is the head of the wife as Christ is the head of the church, his body, of which he is the Savior.
Col 1 [18]And he is the head of the body, the church; he is the beginning and the firstborn from among the dead, so that in everything he might have the supremacy.
Col 2 [10]and you have been given fullness in Christ, who is the head over every power and authority.

59. *Heir of All Things*

Heb 1 [2]but in these last days he has spoken to us by his Son, whom he appointed heir of all things, and through whom he made the universe.

60. *Hen*

Matt 23 [37]"O Jerusalem, Jerusalem, you who kill the prophets and stone those sent to you, how often I have longed to gather your children together, as a hen gathers her chicks under her wings, but you were not willing."

61. *High Priest*

Ps 110 [4]The LORD has sworn and will not change his mind: "You are a priest forever, in the order of Melchizedek."
Heb 2 [17]For this reason he had to be made like his brothers in every way, in order that he might become a merciful and faithful high priest in service to God, and that he might make atonement for the sins of the people.
Heb 3 [1]Therefore, holy brothers, who share in the heavenly calling, fix your thoughts on Jesus, the apostle and high priest whom we confess.
Heb 4 [14]Therefore, since we have a great high priest who has gone through the heavens, Jesus the Son of God, let us hold firmly to the faith we profess.
Heb 6 [20]where Jesus, who went before us, has entered on our behalf. He has become a high priest forever, in the order of Melchizedek.

62. Holiness

1 Cor 1 30It is because of him that you are in Christ Jesus, who has become for us wisdom from God—that is, our righteousness, holiness and redemption.

63. Holy One (of God)

Ps 16 10because you will not abandon me to the grave, nor will you let your Holy One see decay.
Mark 1 24"What do you want with us, Jesus of Nazareth? Have you come to destroy us? I know who you are—the Holy One of God!"
Luke 1 35The angel answered, "The Holy Spirit will come upon you, and the power of the Most High will overshadow you. So the holy one to be born will be called the Son of God."
John 6 69"We believe and know that you are the Holy One of God."
Acts 2 27"'. . . because you will not abandon me to the grave, nor will you let your Holy One see decay.'"

64. Holy Servant

Acts 4 27"Indeed Herod and Pontius Pilate met together with the Gentiles and the people of Israel in this city to conspire against your holy servant Jesus, whom you anointed. 28They did what your power and will had decided beforehand should happen. 29Now, Lord, consider their threats and enable your servants to speak your word with great boldness. 30Stretch out your hand to heal and perform miraculous signs and wonders through the name of your holy servant Jesus."

65. Hope

1 Tim 1 1Paul, an apostle of Christ Jesus by the command of God our Savior and of Christ Jesus our hope . . .

66. Hope of Glory

Col 1 27To them God has chosen to make known among the Gentiles the glorious riches of this mystery, which is Christ in you, the hope of glory.

67. Hope of Israel

Acts 28 20"For this reason I have asked to see you and talk with you. It is because of the hope of Israel that I am bound with this chain."

68. Horn of Salvation

Luke 1 69"He has raised up a horn of salvation for us in the house of his servant David. . . ."

69. I Am

Exod 3 14God said to Moses, "I AM WHO I AM. This is what you are to say to the Israelites: 'I AM has sent me to you.'"
John 8 58"I tell you the truth," Jesus answered, "before Abraham was born, I am!"

70. Image of God

2 Cor 4 4The god of this age has blinded the minds of unbelievers, so that they cannot see the light of the gospel of the glory of Christ, who is the image of God.
Col 1 15He is the image of the invisible God, the firstborn over all creation.

71. Immanuel

Isa 7 14"Therefore the Lord himself will give you a sign: The virgin will be with child and will give birth to a son, and will call him Immanuel."
Matt 1 23"The virgin will be with child and will give birth to a son, and they will call him Immanuel"—which means, "God with us."

72. Jehovah (Yahweh)

Exod 6 3"I appeared to Abraham, to Isaac and to Jacob as God Almighty, but by my name the LORD I did not make myself known to them."
Isa 40 3A voice of one calling: "In the desert prepare the way for the LORD; make straight in the wilderness a highway for our God."

73. Jehovah (Yahweh) Our Righteousness

Jer 23 6"In his days Judah will be saved and Israel will live in safety. This is the name by which he will be called: The LORD Our Righteousness."

74. Jesus

Matt 1 16and Jacob the father of Joseph, the husband of Mary, of whom was born Jesus, who is called Christ.
Matt 1 21"She will give birth to a son, and you are to give him the name Jesus, because he will save his people from their sins."
Matt 26 71Then he went out to the gateway, where another girl saw him and said to the people there, "This fellow was with Jesus of Nazareth."
Matt 27 37Above his head they placed the written charge against him: THIS IS JESUS, THE KING OF THE JEWS.
Luke 2 21On the eighth day, when it was time to circumcise him, he was named Jesus, the name the angel had given him before he had been conceived.
Luke 23 42Then he said, "Jesus, remember me when you come into your kingdom."
John 1 45Philip found Nathanael and told him, "We have found the one Moses wrote about in the Law, and about whom the prophets also wrote—Jesus of Nazareth, the son of Joseph."
John 9 22His parents said this because they were afraid of the Jews, for already the Jews had decided that anyone who acknowledged that Jesus was the Christ would be put out of the synagogue.
John 20 31But these are written that you may believe that Jesus is the Christ, the Son of God, and that by believing you may have life in his name.
Acts 1 11"Men of Galilee," they said, "why do you stand here looking into the sky? This same Jesus, who has been taken from you into heaven, will come back in the same way you have seen him go into heaven."
Acts 4 2They were greatly disturbed because the apostles were teaching the people and proclaiming in Jesus the resurrection of the dead.
Acts 9 20At once he began to preach in the synagogues that Jesus is the Son of God.
Acts 10 38". . . how God anointed Jesus of Nazareth with the Holy Spirit and power, and how he went around doing good and healing all who were under the power of the devil, because God was with him."
Acts 13 23"From this man's descendants God has brought to Israel the Savior Jesus, as he promised."
Acts 26 15"Then I asked, 'Who are you, Lord?'"
"'I am Jesus, whom you are persecuting,' the Lord replied."
Rom 10 9That if you confess with your mouth, "Jesus is Lord," and believe in your heart that God raised him from the dead, you will be saved.
1 Cor 12 3Therefore I tell you that no one who is speaking by the Spirit of God says, "Jesus be cursed," and no one can say, "Jesus is Lord," except by the Holy Spirit.
2 Cor 4 10We always carry around in our body the death of Jesus, so that the life of Jesus may also be revealed in our body.
Gal 6 17Finally, let no one cause me trouble, for I bear on my body the marks of Jesus.

Eph 4 [21]Surely you heard of him and were taught in him in accordance with the truth that is in Jesus.
Phil 2 [10]that at the name of Jesus every knee should bow, in heaven and on earth and under the earth . . .
1 Thess 1 [10]and to wait for his Son from heaven, whom he raised from the dead—Jesus, who rescues us from the coming wrath.
1 Thess 4 [14]We believe that Jesus died and rose again and so we believe that God will bring with Jesus those who have fallen asleep in him.
Heb 2 [9]But we see Jesus, who was made a little lower than the angels, now crowned with glory and honor because he suffered death, so that by the grace of God he might taste death for everyone.
Heb 7 [22]Because of this oath, Jesus has become the guarantee of a better covenant.
Heb 7 [24]but because Jesus lives forever, he has a permanent priesthood.
2 Pet 1 [2]Grace and peace be yours in abundance through the knowledge of God and of Jesus our Lord.
1 John 1 [7]But if we walk in the light, as he is in the light, we have fellowship with one another, and the blood of Jesus, his Son, purifies us from all sin.
1 John 2 [6]Whoever claims to live in him must walk as Jesus did.
1 John 5 [1]Everyone who believes that Jesus is the Christ is born of God, and everyone who loves the father loves his child as well.
Rev 12 [17]Then the dragon was enraged at the woman and went off to make war against the rest of her offspring—those who obey God's commandments and hold to the testimony of Jesus.

75. Jesus Christ

Mark 1 [1]The beginning of the gospel about Jesus Christ, the Son of God.
John 1 [17]For the law was given through Moses; grace and truth came through Jesus Christ.
John 17 [3]"Now this is eternal life: that they may know you, the only true God, and Jesus Christ, whom you have sent."
Acts 4 [10]". . . then know this, you and all the people of Israel: It is by the name of Jesus Christ of Nazareth, whom you crucified but whom God raised from the dead, that this man stands before you healed."
Acts 16 [18]She kept this up for many days. Finally Paul became so troubled that he turned around and said to the spirit, "In the name of Jesus Christ I command you to come out of her!" At that moment the spirit left her.
1 Cor 1 [2]To the church of God in Corinth, to those sanctified in Christ Jesus and called to be holy, together with all those everywhere who call on the name of our Lord Jesus Christ—their Lord and ours: . . . [30]It is because of him that you are in Christ Jesus, who has become for us wisdom from God—that is, our righteousness, holiness and redemption.
1 Cor 2 [2]For I resolved to know nothing while I was with you except Jesus Christ and him crucified.
Gal 2 [16]". . . know that a man is not justified by observing the law, but by faith in Jesus Christ. So we, too, have put our faith in Christ Jesus that we may be justified by faith in Christ and not by observing the law, because by observing the law no one will be justified."
Phil 2 [11]and every tongue confess that Jesus Christ is Lord, to the glory of God the Father.
Titus 2 [13]while we wait for the blessed hope—the glorious appearing of our great God and Savior, Jesus Christ . . .
Titus 3 [6]whom he poured out on us generously through Jesus Christ our Savior . . .
Heb 13 [8]Jesus Christ is the same yesterday and today and forever.
Heb 13 [21]equip you with everything good for doing his will, and may he work in us what is pleasing to him, through Jesus Christ, to whom be glory for ever and ever. Amen.
2 Pet 1 [1]Simon Peter, a servant and apostle of Jesus Christ,
To those who through the righteousness of our God and Savior Jesus Christ have received a faith as precious as ours. . . .
2 Pet 1 [11]and you will receive a rich welcome into the eternal kingdom of our Lord and Savior Jesus Christ.
2 Pet 2 [20]If they have escaped the corruption of the world by knowing our Lord and Savior Jesus Christ and are again entangled in it and overcome, they are worse off at the end than they were at the beginning.
2 Pet 3 [18]But grow in the grace and knowledge of our Lord and Savior Jesus Christ. To him be glory both now and forever! Amen.

76. Judge

Acts 10 [42]"He commanded us to preach to the people and to testify that he is the one whom God appointed as judge of the living and the dead."
Rev 19 [11]I saw heaven standing open and there before me was a white horse, whose rider is called Faithful and True. With justice he judges and makes war.

77. King

Jer 23 [5]"The days are coming," declares the LORD, "when I will raise up to David a righteous Branch, a King who will reign wisely and do what is just and right in the land."
Matt 25 [34]"Then the King will say to those on his right, 'Come, you who are blessed by my Father; take your inheritance, the kingdom prepared for you since the creation of the world.'"
John 18 [36]Jesus said, "My kingdom is not of this world. If it were, my servants would fight to prevent my arrest by the Jews. But now my kingdom is from another place."
[37]"You are a king, then!" said Pilate.
Jesus answered, "You are right in saying I am a king. In fact, for this reason I was born, and for this I came into the world, to testify to the truth. Everyone on the side of truth listens to me."

78. King of Israel

John 1 [49]Then Nathanael declared, "Rabbi, you are the Son of God; you are the King of Israel."

79. King of Kings

1 Tim 6 [15]which God will bring about in his own time—God, the blessed and only Ruler, the King of kings and Lord of lords. . . .
Rev 17 [14]"They will make war against the Lamb, but the Lamb will overcome them because he is Lord of lords and King of kings—and with him will be his called, chosen and faithful followers."
Rev 19 [16]On his robe and on his thigh he has this name written: KING OF KINGS AND LORD OF LORDS.

80. King of the Ages

Rev 15 [3]and sang the song of Moses the servant of God and the song of the Lamb: "Great and marvelous are your deeds, Lord God Almighty. Just and true are your ways, King of the ages."

81. King of the Jews

Matt 2 [1]After Jesus was born in Bethlehem in Judea, during the time of King Herod, Magi from the east came to Jerusalem [2]and asked, "Where is the one who has been born king of the Jews? We saw his star in the east and have come to worship him."
Matt 27 [37]Above his head they placed the written charge against him: THIS IS JESUS, THE KING OF THE JEWS.

82. King of Zion

Ps 2 [6]"I have installed my King on Zion, my holy hill."
Matt 21 [5]"Say to the Daughter of Zion, 'See, your king comes to you, gentle and riding on a donkey, on a colt, the foal of a donkey.'"

83. King over the Whole Earth

Zech 14 [9]The LORD will be king over the whole earth. On that day there will be one LORD, and his name the only name.

84. Lamb (of God)

John 1 [29]The next day John saw Jesus coming toward him and said, "Look, the Lamb of God, who takes away the sin of the world!"
John 1 [36]When he saw Jesus passing by, he said, "Look, the Lamb of God!"
1 Pet 1 [19]but with the precious blood of Christ, a lamb without blemish or defect.
Rev 5 [6]Then I saw a Lamb, looking as if it had been slain, standing in the center of the throne, encircled by the four living creatures and the elders. He had seven horns and seven eyes, which are the seven spirits of God sent out into all the earth. . . . [8]And when he had taken it, the four living creatures and the twenty-four elders fell down before the Lamb. Each one had a harp and they were holding golden bowls full of incense, which are the prayers of the saints. . . .

[12]In a loud voice they sang: "Worthy is the Lamb, who was slain, to receive power and wealth and wisdom and strength and honor and glory and praise!"

[13]Then I heard every creature in heaven and on earth and under the earth and on the sea, and all that is in them, singing: "To him who sits on the throne and to the Lamb be praise and honor and glory and power, for ever and ever!"
Rev 6 [1]I watched as the Lamb opened the first of the seven seals. Then I heard one of the four living creatures say in a voice like thunder, "Come!"
Rev 6 [16]They called to the mountains and the rocks, "Fall on us and hide us from the face of him who sits on the throne and from the wrath of the Lamb!"
Rev 7 [9]After this I looked and there before me was a great multitude that no one could count, from every nation, tribe, people and language, standing before the throne and in front of the Lamb. They were wearing white robes and were holding palm branches in their hands. [10]And they cried out in a loud voice: "Salvation belongs to our God, who sits on the throne, and to the Lamb." . . .

[14]I answered, "Sir, you know."

And he said, "These are they who have come out of the great tribulation; they have washed their robes and made them white in the blood of the Lamb."
Rev 12 [11]"They overcame him by the blood of the Lamb and by the word of their testimony; they did not love their lives so much as to shrink from death."
Rev 13 [8]All inhabitants of the earth will worship the beast—all whose names have not been written in the book of life belonging to the Lamb that was slain from the creation of the world.
Rev 14 [1]Then I looked, and there before me was the Lamb, standing on Mount Zion, and with him 144,000 who had his name and his Father's name written on their foreheads. . . . [4]These are those who did not defile themselves with women, for they kept themselves pure. They follow the Lamb wherever he goes. They were purchased from among men and offered as firstfruits to God and the Lamb.
Rev 15 [3]and sang the song of Moses the servant of God and the song of the Lamb: "Great and marvelous are your deeds, Lord God Almighty. Just and true are your ways, King of the ages."
Rev 17 [14]"They will make war against the Lamb, but the Lamb will overcome them because he is Lord of lords and King of kings—and with him will be his called, chosen and faithful followers."
Rev 19 [7]"Let us rejoice and be glad and give him glory! For the wedding of the Lamb has come, and his bride has made herself ready. . . ."

[9]Then the angel said to me, "Write: 'Blessed are those who are invited to the wedding supper of the Lamb!'" And he added, "These are the true words of God."
Rev 21 [22]I did not see a temple in the city, because the Lord God Almighty and the Lamb are its temple. [23]The city does not need the sun or the moon to shine on it, for the glory of God gives it light, and the Lamb is its lamp.
Rev 22 [1]Then the angel showed me the river of the water of life, as clear as crystal, flowing from the throne of God and of the Lamb. . . . [3]No longer will there be any curse. The throne of God and of the Lamb will be in the city, and his servants will serve him.

85. Lamp

Rev 21 [23]The city does not need the sun or the moon to shine on it, for the glory of God gives it light, and the Lamb is its lamp.

86. Launderer's Soap

Mal 3 [2]But who can endure the day of his coming? Who can stand when he appears? For he will be like a refiner's fire or a launderer's soap.

87. Leader

Isa 55 [4]"See, I have made him a witness to the peoples, a leader and commander of the peoples."

88. Life

John 11 [25]Jesus said to her, "I am the resurrection and the life. He who believes in me will live, even though he dies. . . ."
John 14 [6]Jesus answered, "I am the way and the truth and the life. No one comes to the Father except through me."
Col 3 [4]When Christ, who is your life, appears, then you also will appear with him in glory.

89. Life-giving Spirit

1 Cor 15 [45]So it is written: "The first man Adam became a living being"; the last Adam, a life-giving spirit.

90. Light (of the World)

John 1 [1]In the beginning was the Word, and the Word was with God, and the Word was God. [2]He was with God in the beginning. . . . [4]In him was life, and that life was the light of men. [5]The light shines in the darkness, but the darkness has not understood it.

[6]There came a man who was sent from God; his name was John. [7]He came as a witness to testify concerning that light, so that through him all men might believe. [8]He himself was not the light; he came only as a witness to the light. [9]The true light that gives light to every man was coming into the world.
John 8 [12]When Jesus spoke again to the people, he said, "I am the light of the world. Whoever follows me will never walk in darkness, but will have the light of life."
John 9 [5]"While I am in the world, I am the light of the world."

91. Light for the Gentiles

Isa 49 [6]he says: "It is too small a thing for you to be my servant to restore the tribes of Jacob and bring back those of Israel I have kept. I will also make you a light for the Gentiles, that you may bring my salvation to the ends of the earth."
Luke 2 [32]". . . a light for revelation to the Gentiles and for glory to your people Israel."

92. Lion of the Tribe of Judah

Rev 5 [5]Then one of the elders said to me, "Do not weep! See, the Lion of the tribe of Judah, the Root of David, has triumphed. He is able to open the scroll and its seven seals."

93. Living One

Rev 1 [18]"I am the Living One; I was dead, and behold I am alive for ever and ever! And I hold the keys of death and Hades."

94. *Living Stone*

1 Pet 2 [4]As you come to him, the living Stone—rejected by men but chosen by God and precious to him . . .

95. *Lord*

Ps 110 [1]The LORD says to my Lord: "Sit at my right hand until I make your enemies a footstool for your feet."
Mal 3 [1]"See, I will send my messenger, who will prepare the way before me. Then suddenly the Lord you are seeking will come to his temple; the messenger of the covenant, whom you desire, will come," says the LORD Almighty.
Matt 7 [21]"Not everyone who says to me, 'Lord, Lord,' will enter the kingdom of heaven, but only he who does the will of my Father who is in heaven."
Matt 24 [42]"Therefore keep watch, because you do not know on what day your Lord will come."
Mark 2 [28]"So the Son of Man is Lord even of the Sabbath."
Luke 6 [46]"Why do you call me, 'Lord, Lord,' and do not do what I say?"
John 6 [68]Simon Peter answered him, "Lord, to whom shall we go? You have the words of eternal life."
John 13 [13]"You call me 'Teacher' and 'Lord,' and rightly so, for that is what I am."
Acts 2 [36]"Therefore let all Israel be assured of this: God has made this Jesus, whom you crucified, both Lord and Christ."
Acts 3 [19]"Repent, then, and turn to God, so that your sins may be wiped out, that times of refreshing may come from the Lord. . . ."
Rom 10 [13]for, "Everyone who calls on the name of the Lord will be saved."
1 Cor 3 [5]What, after all, is Apollos? And what is Paul? Only servants, through whom you came to believe—as the Lord has assigned to each his task.
1 Cor 4 [4]My conscience is clear, but that does not make me innocent. It is the Lord who judges me.
1 Cor 11 [23]For I received from the Lord what I also passed on to you: The Lord Jesus, on the night he was betrayed, took bread. . . . [26]For whenever you eat this bread and drink this cup, you proclaim the Lord's death until he comes.
2 Cor 5 [6]Therefore we are always confident and know that as long as we are at home in the body we are away from the Lord. [7]We live by faith, not by sight. [8]We are confident, I say, and would prefer to be away from the body and at home with the Lord.
Eph 6 [7]Serve wholeheartedly, as if you were serving the Lord, not men, [8]because you know that the Lord will reward everyone for whatever good he does, whether he is slave or free.
Col 3 [23]Whatever you do, work at it with all your heart, as working for the Lord, not for men, [24]since you know that you will receive an inheritance from the Lord as a reward. It is the Lord Christ you are serving.
1 Thess 4 [16]For the Lord himself will come down from heaven, with a loud command, with the voice of the archangel and with the trumpet call of God, and the dead in Christ will rise first. [17]After that, we who are still alive and are left will be caught up together with them in the clouds to meet the Lord in the air. And so we will be with the Lord forever.
2 Tim 2 [22]Flee the evil desires of youth, and pursue righteousness, faith, love and peace, along with those who call on the Lord out of a pure heart.
2 Tim 4 [8]Now there is in store for me the crown of righteousness, which the Lord, the righteous Judge, will award to me on that day—and not only to me, but also to all who have longed for his appearing.
Heb 2 [3]how shall we escape if we ignore such a great salvation? This salvation, which was first announced by the Lord, was confirmed to us by those who heard him.
1 Pet 2 [3]now that you have tasted that the Lord is good.
2 Pet 1 [11]and you will receive a rich welcome into the eternal kingdom of our Lord and Savior Jesus Christ.

96. *Lord God Almighty*

Rev 4 [8]Each of the four living creatures had six wings and was covered with eyes all around, even under his wings. Day and night they never stop saying: "Holy, holy, holy is the Lord God Almighty, who was, and is, and is to come."
Rev 15 [3]and sang the song of Moses the servant of God and the song of the Lamb: "Great and marvelous are your deeds, Lord God Almighty. Just and true are your ways, King of the ages."

97. *Lord Jesus*

Acts 7 [59]While they were stoning him, Stephen prayed, "Lord Jesus, receive my spirit."
Acts 8 [16]because the Holy Spirit had not yet come upon any of them; they had simply been baptized into the name of the Lord Jesus.
Acts 11 [20]Some of them, however, men from Cyprus and Cyrene, went to Antioch and began to speak to Greeks also, telling them the good news about the Lord Jesus.
Acts 15 [11]"No! We believe it is through the grace of our Lord Jesus that we are saved, just as they are."
Acts 16 [31]They replied, "Believe in the Lord Jesus, and you will be saved—you and your household."
Acts 20 [21]"I have declared to both Jews and Greeks that they must turn to God in repentance and have faith in our Lord Jesus."
1 Cor 5 [4]When you are assembled in the name of our Lord Jesus and I am with you in spirit, and the power of our Lord Jesus is present, [5]hand this man over to Satan, so that the sinful nature may be destroyed and his spirit saved on the day of the Lord.
2 Cor 11 [31]The God and Father of the Lord Jesus, who is to be praised forever, knows that I am not lying.
Col 3 [17]And whatever you do, whether in word or deed, do it all in the name of the Lord Jesus, giving thanks to God the Father through him.
1 Thess 4 [1]Finally, brothers, we instructed you how to live in order to please God, as in fact you are living. Now we ask you and urge you in the Lord Jesus to do this more and more. [2]For you know what instructions we gave you by the authority of the Lord Jesus.
2 Thess 1 [7]and give relief to you who are troubled, and to us as well. This will happen when the Lord Jesus is revealed from heaven in blazing fire with his powerful angels. [8]He will punish those who do not know God and do not obey the gospel of our Lord Jesus.
Heb 13 [20]May the God of peace, who through the blood of the eternal covenant brought back from the dead our Lord Jesus, that great Shepherd of the sheep . . .
2 Pet 1 [2]Grace and peace be yours in abundance through the knowledge of God and of Jesus our Lord.
Rev 22 [20]He who testifies to these things says, "Yes, I am coming soon."
Amen. Come, Lord Jesus.
[21]The grace of the Lord Jesus be with God's people. Amen.

98. *Lord Jesus Christ*

Acts 11 [17]"So if God gave them the same gift as he gave us, who believed in the Lord Jesus Christ, who was I to think that I could oppose God?"
Rom 5 [1]Therefore, since we have been justified through faith, we have peace with God through our Lord Jesus Christ. . . . [11]Not only is this so, but we also rejoice in God through our Lord Jesus Christ, through whom we have now received reconciliation.
Rom 6 [23]For the wages of sin is death, but the gift of God is eternal life in Christ Jesus our Lord.
Rom 7 [25]Thanks be to God—through Jesus Christ our Lord!
So then, I myself in my mind am a slave to God's law, but in the sinful nature a slave to the law of sin.
Rom 8 [39]neither height nor depth, nor anything else in all creation, will be able to separate us from the love of God that is in Christ Jesus our Lord.
Rom 13 [14]Rather, clothe yourselves with the Lord Jesus Christ, and do not think about how to gratify the desires of the sinful nature.
Rom 15 [30]I urge you, brothers, by our Lord Jesus Christ and by

the love of the Spirit, to join me in my struggle by praying to God for me.
1 Cor 1 [2]To the church of God in Corinth, to those sanctified in Christ Jesus and called to be holy, together with all those everywhere who call on the name of our Lord Jesus Christ—their Lord and ours: [3]Grace and peace to you from God our Father and the Lord Jesus Christ. . . .
[10]I appeal to you, brothers, in the name of our Lord Jesus Christ, that all of you agree with one another so that there may be no divisions among you and that you may be perfectly united in mind and thought.
1 Cor 6 [11]And that is what some of you were. But you were washed, you were sanctified, you were justified in the name of the Lord Jesus Christ and by the Spirit of our God.
Phil 3 [20]But our citizenship is in heaven. And we eagerly await a Savior from there, the Lord Jesus Christ. . . .
1 Tim 1 [12]I thank Christ Jesus our Lord, who has given me strength, that he considered me faithful, appointing me to his service.
Philem [25]The grace of the Lord Jesus Christ be with your spirit.
James 2 [1]My brothers, as believers in our glorious Lord Jesus Christ, don't show favoritism.
1 Pet 1 [3]Praise be to the God and Father of our Lord Jesus Christ! In his great mercy he has given us new birth into a living hope through the resurrection of Jesus Christ from the dead. . . .
Jude [21]Keep yourselves in God's love as you wait for the mercy of our Lord Jesus Christ to bring you to eternal life.

99. Lord of All

Acts 10 [36]"know the message God sent to the people of Israel, telling the good news of peace through Jesus Christ, who is Lord of all."
Rom 10 [12]For there is no difference between Jew and Gentile—the same Lord is Lord of all and richly blesses all who call on him. . . .

100. Lord of Glory

1 Cor 2 [8]None of the rulers of this age understood it, for if they had, they would not have crucified the Lord of glory.

101. Lord of Lords

1 Tim 6 [15]which God will bring about in his own time—God, the blessed and only Ruler, the King of kings and Lord of lords . . .
Rev 17 [14]"They will make war against the Lamb, but the Lamb will overcome them because he is Lord of lords and King of kings—and with him will be his called, chosen and faithful followers."
Rev 19 [16]On his robe and on his thigh he has this name written: KING OF KINGS AND LORD OF LORDS.

102. Lord of the Dead and the Living

Rom 14 [9]For this very reason, Christ died and returned to life so that he might be the Lord of both the dead and the living.

103. Lord of the Sabbath

Matt 12 [8]"For the Son of Man is Lord of the Sabbath."

104. Man

John 19 [5]When Jesus came out wearing the crown of thorns and the purple robe, Pilate said to them, "Here is the man!"
Acts 17 [31]"For he has set a day when he will judge the world with justice by the man he has appointed. He has given proof of this to all men by raising him from the dead."
Rom 5 [15]But the gift is not like the trespass. For if the many died by the trespass of the one man, how much more did God's grace and the gift that came by the grace of the one man, Jesus Christ, overflow to the many!
1 Tim 2 [5]For there is one God and one mediator between God and men, the man Christ Jesus. . . .

105. Man of Sorrows

Isa 53 [3]He was despised and rejected by men, a man of sorrows, and familiar with suffering. Like one from whom men hide their faces he was despised, and we esteemed him not.

106. Master

Matt 23 [8]"But you are not to be called 'Rabbi,' for you have only one Master and you are all brothers."

107. Mediator

1 Tim 2 [5]For there is one God and one mediator between God and men, the man Christ Jesus. . . .
Heb 8 [6]But the ministry Jesus has received is as superior to theirs as the covenant of which he is mediator is superior to the old one, and it is founded on better promises.
Heb 9 [15]For this reason Christ is the mediator of a new covenant, that those who are called may receive the promised eternal inheritance—now that he has died as a ransom to set them free from the sins committed under the first covenant.
Heb 12 [24]to Jesus the mediator of a new covenant, and to the sprinkled blood that speaks a better word than the blood of Abel.

108. Melchizedek

Heb 7 [1]This Melchizedek was king of Salem and priest of God Most High. He met Abraham returning from the defeat of the kings and blessed him, [2]and Abraham gave him a tenth of everything. First, his name means "king of righteousness"; then also, "king of Salem" means "king of peace." [3]Without father or mother, without genealogy, without beginning of days or end of life, like the Son of God he remains a priest forever.

109. Messenger of the Covenant

Mal 3 [1]"See, I will send my messenger, who will prepare the way before me. Then suddenly the Lord you are seeking will come to his temple; the messenger of the covenant, whom you desire, will come," says the LORD Almighty.

110. Messiah

John 1 [41]The first thing Andrew did was to find his brother Simon and tell him, "We have found the Messiah" (that is, the Christ).
John 4 [25]The woman said, "I know that Messiah" (called Christ) "is coming. When he comes, he will explain everything to us."

111. Mighty God

Isa 9 [6]For to us a child is born, to us a son is given, and the government will be on his shoulders. And he will be called Wonderful Counselor, Mighty God, Everlasting Father, Prince of Peace.

112. Morning Star

2 Pet 1 [19]And we have the word of the prophets made more certain, and you will do well to pay attention to it, as to a light shining in a dark place, until the day dawns and the morning star rises in your hearts.
Rev 22 [16]"I, Jesus, have sent my angel to give you this testimony for the churches. I am the Root and the Offspring of David, and the bright Morning Star."

113. Most Exalted of the Kings of the Earth

Ps 89 [27]"I will also appoint him my firstborn, the most exalted of the kings of the earth."

114. Nazarene

Matt 2 [23]and he went and lived in a town called Nazareth. So was fulfilled what was said through the prophets: "He will be called a Nazarene."
Mark 14 [67]When she saw Peter warming himself, she looked closely at him.
"You also were with that Nazarene, Jesus," she said.
Mark 16 [6]"Don't be alarmed," he said. "You are looking for Jesus the Nazarene, who was crucified. He has risen! He is not here. See the place where they laid him."

115. Offspring of David

Rev 22 [16]"I, Jesus, have sent my angel to give you this testimony for the churches. I am the Root and the Offspring of David, and the bright Morning Star."

116. One Greater Than Jonah

Luke 11 [29]As the crowds increased, Jesus said, "This is a wicked generation. It asks for a miraculous sign, but none will be given it except the sign of Jonah. [30]For as Jonah was a sign to the Ninevites, so also will the Son of Man be to this generation. . . . [32]The men of Nineveh will stand up at the judgment with this generation and condemn it; for they repented at the preaching of Jonah, and now one greater than Jonah is here."

117. One Greater Than Solomon

Luke 11 [31]"The Queen of the South will rise at the judgment with the men of this generation and condemn them; for she came from the ends of the earth to listen to Solomon's wisdom, and now one greater than Solomon is here."

118. One Who Is, Was, and Is to Come

Rev 1 [4]John, To the seven churches in the province of Asia: Grace and peace to you from him who is, and who was, and who is to come, and from the seven spirits before his throne. . . .
Rev 1 [8]"I am the Alpha and the Omega," says the Lord God, "who is, and who was, and who is to come, the Almighty."

119. One Who Will Baptize with the Holy Spirit

Mark 1 [7]And this was his message: "After me will come one more powerful than I, the thongs of whose sandals I am not worthy to stoop down and untie. [8]I baptize you with water, but he will baptize you with the Holy Spirit."

120. Only Begotten

John 1 [14]The Word became flesh and made his dwelling among us. We have seen his glory, the glory of the One and Only, who came from the Father, full of grace and truth.
John 3 [16]"For God so loved the world that he gave his one and only Son, that whoever believes in him shall not perish but have eternal life."
1 John 4 [9]This is how God showed his love among us: He sent his one and only Son into the world that we might live through him.

121. Overseer

1 Pet 2 [25]For you were like sheep going astray, but now you have returned to the Shepherd and Overseer of your souls.

122. Passover Lamb

1 Cor 5 [7]Get rid of the old yeast that you may be a new batch without yeast—as you really are. For Christ, our Passover lamb, has been sacrificed.

123. Peace

Eph 2 [14]For he himself is our peace, who has made the two one and has destroyed the barrier, the dividing wall of hostility, [15]by abolishing in his flesh the law with its commandments and regulations. His purpose was to create in himself one new man out of the two, thus making peace. . . .

124. Perfecter of Faith

Heb 12 [2]Let us fix our eyes on Jesus, the author and perfecter of our faith, who for the joy set before him endured the cross, scorning its shame, and sat down at the right hand of the throne of God.

125. Physician

Luke 4 [23]Jesus said to them, "Surely you will quote this proverb to me: 'Physician, heal yourself! Do here in your hometown what we have heard that you did in Capernaum.'"

126. Power

1 Cor 1 [24]but to those whom God has called, both Jews and Greeks, Christ the power of God and the wisdom of God.

127. Prince

Acts 5 [31]"God exalted him to his own right hand as Prince and Savior that he might give repentance and forgiveness of sins to Israel."

128. Prince of Peace

Isa 9 [6]For to us a child is born, to us a son is given, and the government will be on his shoulders. And he will be called Wonderful Counselor, Mighty God, Everlasting Father, Prince of Peace.

129. Prophet

Luke 24 [19]"What things?" he asked.
"About Jesus of Nazareth," they replied. "He was a prophet, powerful in word and deed before God and all the people."
John 7 [40]On hearing his words, some of the people said, "Surely this man is the Prophet."
Acts 3 [22]"For Moses said, 'The Lord your God will raise up for you a prophet like me from among your own people; you must listen to everything he tells you.'"

130. Purifier

Mal 3 [3]He will sit as a refiner and purifier of silver; he will purify the Levites and refine them like gold and silver. Then the LORD will have men who will bring offerings in righteousness. . . .
Matt 3 [12]"His winnowing fork is in his hand, and he will clear his threshing floor, gathering his wheat into the barn and burning up the chaff with unquenchable fire."

131. Rabbi

Mark 14 [45]Going at once to Jesus, Judas said, "Rabbi!" and kissed him.
John 1 [38]Turning around, Jesus saw them following and asked, "What do you want?"
They said, "Rabbi" (which means Teacher), "where are you staying?"

John 1 [49]Then Nathanael declared, "Rabbi, you are the Son of God; you are the King of Israel."
John 3 [2]He came to Jesus at night and said, "Rabbi, we know you are a teacher who has come from God. For no one could perform the miraculous signs you are doing if God were not with him."
John 6 [25]When they found him on the other side of the lake, they asked him, "Rabbi, when did you get here?"
John 9 [2]His disciples asked him, "Rabbi, who sinned, this man or his parents, that he was born blind?"

132. Rabboni

John 20 [16]Jesus said to her, "Mary."

She turned toward him and cried out in Aramaic, "Rabboni!" (which means Teacher).

133. Radiance of God's Glory

Heb 1 [3]The Son is the radiance of God's glory and the exact representation of his being, sustaining all things by his powerful word. After he had provided purification for sins, he sat down at the right hand of the Majesty in heaven.

134. Ransom

1 Tim 2 [5]For there is one God and one mediator between God and men, the man Christ Jesus, [6]who gave himself as a ransom for all men—the testimony given in its proper time.

135. Redeemer

Job 19 [25]"I know that my Redeemer lives, and that in the end he will stand upon the earth."
Isa 59 [20]"The Redeemer will come to Zion, to those in Jacob who repent of their sins," declares the LORD.

136. Redemption

1 Cor 1 [30]It is because of him that you are in Christ Jesus, who has become for us wisdom from God—that is, our righteousness, holiness and redemption.

137. Refiner

Mal 3 [3]He will sit as a refiner and purifier of silver; he will purify the Levites and refine them like gold and silver. Then the LORD will have men who will bring offerings in righteousness. . . .

138. Refiner's Fire

Mal 3 [2]But who can endure the day of his coming? Who can stand when he appears? For he will be like a refiner's fire or a launderer's soap.

139. Resurrection

John 11 [25]Jesus said to her, "I am the resurrection and the life. He who believes in me will live, even though he dies. . . ."

140. Righteous Judge

Acts 10 [42]"He commanded us to preach to the people and to testify that he is the one whom God appointed as judge of the living and the dead."
2 Tim 4 [8]Now there is in store for me the crown of righteousness, which the Lord, the righteous Judge, will award to me on that day—and not only to me, but also to all who have longed for his appearing.

141. Righteousness

1 Cor 1 [30]It is because of him that you are in Christ Jesus, who has become for us wisdom from God—that is, our righteousness, holiness and redemption.

142. Righteous One

Acts 3 [14]"You disowned the Holy and Righteous One and asked that a murderer be released to you."
Acts 7 [52]"Was there ever a prophet your fathers did not persecute? They even killed those who predicted the coming of the Righteous One. And now you have betrayed and murdered him. . . ."
Acts 22 [14]"Then he said: 'The God of our fathers has chosen you to know his will and to see the Righteous One and to hear words from his mouth.'"
1 John 2 [1]My dear children, I write this to you so that you will not sin. But if anybody does sin, we have one who speaks to the Father in our defense—Jesus Christ, the Righteous One.

143. Righteous Servant

Isa 53 [11]After the suffering of his soul, he will see the light of life and be satisfied; by his knowledge my righteous servant will justify many, and he will bear their iniquities.

144. Rising Sun

Luke 1 [76]"And you, my child, will be called a prophet of the Most High; for you will go on before the Lord to prepare the way for him, [77]to give his people the knowledge of salvation through the forgiveness of their sins, [78]because of the tender mercy of our God, by which the rising sun will come to us from heaven [79]to shine on those living in darkness and in the shadow of death, to guide our feet into the path of peace."

145. Rock

1 Cor 10 [4]and drank the same spiritual drink; for they drank from the spiritual rock that accompanied them, and that rock was Christ.
1 Pet 2 [8]and, "A stone that causes men to stumble and a rock that makes them fall." They stumble because they disobey the message—which is also what they were destined for.

146. Root of David

Rev 5 [5]Then one of the elders said to me, "Do not weep! See, the Lion of the tribe of Judah, the Root of David, has triumphed. He is able to open the scroll and its seven seals."
Rev 22 [16]"I, Jesus, have sent my angel to give you this testimony for the churches. I am the Root and the Offspring of David, and the bright Morning Star."

147. Root of Jesse

Isa 11 [10]In that day the Root of Jesse will stand as a banner for the peoples; the nations will rally to him, and his place of rest will be glorious.

148. Ruler

Mic 5 [1]Marshal your troops, O city of troops, for a siege is laid against us. They will strike Israel's ruler on the cheek with a rod.
Matt 2 [6]"'But you, Bethlehem, in the land of Judah, are by no means least among the rulers of Judah; for out of you will come a ruler who will be the shepherd of my people Israel.'"
1 Tim 6 [15]which God will bring about in his own time—God, the blessed and only Ruler, the King of kings and Lord of lords . . .

149. Ruler of God's Creation

Rev 3 [14]"To the angel of the church in Laodicea write: These are the words of the Amen, the faithful and true witness, the ruler of God's creation."

150. Ruler of the Kings of the Earth

Rev 1 [5]and from Jesus Christ, who is the faithful witness, the firstborn from the dead, and the ruler of the kings of the earth.

To him who loves us and has freed us from our sins by his blood. . . .

151. Ruler over Israel

Mic 5 [2]"But you, Bethlehem Ephrathah, though you are small among the clans of Judah, out of you will come for me one who will be ruler over Israel, whose origins are from of old, from ancient times."

152. Salvation

Luke 2 [29]"Sovereign Lord, as you have promised, you now dismiss your servant in peace. [30]For my eyes have seen your salvation, [31]which you have prepared in the sight of all people, [32]a light for revelation to the Gentiles and for glory to your people Israel."

153. Savior

Luke 2 [11]"Today in the town of David a Savior has been born to you; he is Christ the Lord."
John 4 [42]They said to the woman, "We no longer believe just because of what you said; now we have heard for ourselves, and we know that this man really is the Savior of the world."
Acts 5 [31]"God exalted him to his own right hand as Prince and Savior that he might give repentance and forgiveness of sins to Israel."
Acts 13 [23]"From this man's descendants God has brought to Israel the Savior Jesus, as he promised."
Eph 5 [23]For the husband is the head of the wife as Christ is the head of the church, his body, of which he is the Savior.
2 Tim 1 [10]but it has now been revealed through the appearing of our Savior, Christ Jesus, who has destroyed death and has brought life and immortality to light through the gospel.
Titus 2 [13]while we wait for the blessed hope—the glorious appearing of our great God and Savior, Jesus Christ . . .
Titus 3 [6]whom he poured out on us generously through Jesus Christ our Savior . . .
2 Pet 1 [11]and you will receive a rich welcome into the eternal kingdom of our Lord and Savior Jesus Christ.
2 Pet 3 [18]But grow in the grace and knowledge of our Lord and Savior Jesus Christ. To him be glory both now and forever! Amen.
1 John 4 [14]And we have seen and testify that the Father has sent his Son to be the Savior of the world.

154. Second Man

1 Cor 15 [47]The first man was of the dust of the earth, the second man from heaven.

155. Seed (of the Woman)

Gen 3 [15]"And I will put enmity between you and the woman, and between your offspring [or seed] and hers; he will crush your head, and you will strike his heel."
Gal 3 [16]The promises were spoken to Abraham and to his seed. The Scripture does not say "and to seeds," meaning many people, but "and to your seed," meaning one person, who is Christ.

156. Servant

Isa 42 [1]"Here is my servant, whom I uphold, my chosen one in whom I delight; I will put my Spirit on him and he will bring justice to the nations."
Isa 49 [3]He said to me, "You are my servant, Israel, in whom I will display my splendor."

[4]But I said, "I have labored to no purpose; I have spent my strength in vain and for nothing. Yet what is due me is in the LORD's hand, and my reward is with my God."

[5]And now the LORD says—he who formed me in the womb to be his servant to bring Jacob back to him and gather Israel to himself, for I am honored in the eyes of the LORD and my God has been my strength—[6]he says: "It is too small a thing for you to be my servant to restore the tribes of Jacob and bring back those of Israel I have kept. I will also make you a light for the Gentiles, that you may bring my salvation to the ends of the earth."

[7]This is what the LORD says—the Redeemer and Holy One of Israel—to him who was despised and abhorred by the nation, to the servant of rulers: "Kings will see you and rise up, princes will see and bow down, because of the LORD, who is faithful, the Holy One of Israel, who has chosen you."
Isa 52 [13]See, my servant will act wisely; he will be raised and lifted up and highly exalted.
Isa 53 [11]After the suffering of his soul he will see the light of life and be satisfied; by his knowledge my righteous servant will justify many, and he will bear their iniquities. (Isa 52:13–53:12)
Zech 3 [8]"'Listen, O high priest Joshua and your associates seated before you, who are men symbolic of things to come: I am going to bring my servant, the Branch.'"
Matt 12 [18]"Here is my servant whom I have chosen, the one I love, in whom I delight; I will put my Spirit on him, and he will proclaim justice to the nations."
Luke 22 [27]"For who is the greater, the one who is at the table or the one who serves? It is not the one who is at the table? But I am among you as one who serves."
Acts 3 [13]"The God of Abraham, Isaac and Jacob, the God of our fathers, has glorified his servant Jesus. You handed him over to be killed, and you disowned him before Pilate, though he had decided to let him go."
Acts 3 [25]"And you are heirs of the prophets and of the covenant God made with your fathers. He said to Abraham, 'Through your offspring all peoples on earth will be blessed.' [26]When God raised up his servant, he sent him first to you to bless you by turning each of you from your wicked ways."

157. Shepherd

Matt 2 [6]"'But you, Bethlehem, in the land of Judah, are by no means least among the rulers of Judah; for out of you will come a ruler who will be the shepherd of my people Israel.'"
1 Pet 2 [25]For you were like sheep going astray, but now you have returned to the Shepherd and Overseer of your souls.

158. Shiloh

Gen 49 [10]"The scepter will not depart from Judah, nor the ruler's staff from between his feet, until he comes to whom it belongs [until Shiloh comes], and the obedience of the nations is his."

159. Son

Ps 2 [7]I will proclaim the decree of the LORD: He said to me, "You are my Son; today I have become your Father." . . . [12]Kiss the Son, lest he be angry and you be destroyed in your way, for his wrath can flare up in a moment. Blessed are all who take refuge in him.
Isa 9 [6]For to us a child is born, to us a son is given, and the government will be on his shoulders. And he will be called Wonderful Counselor, Mighty God, Everlasting Father, Prince of Peace.
Matt 3 [17]And a voice from heaven said, "This is my Son, whom I love; with him I am well pleased."
Matt 11 [27]"All things have been committed to me by my Father. No one knows the Son except the Father, and no one knows the Father except the Son and those to whom the Son chooses to reveal him."

John 3 [35]"The Father loves the Son and has placed everything in his hands."
John 5 [22]"Moreover, the Father judges no one, but has entrusted all judgment to the Son, [23]that all may honor the Son just as they honor the Father. He who does not honor the Son does not honor the Father, who sent him."
Rom 1 [3]regarding his Son, who as to his human nature was a descendant of David . . .
Col 1 [13]For he has rescued us from the dominion of darkness and brought us into the kingdom of the Son he loves. . . .
Heb 1 [2]but in these last days he has spoken to us by his Son, whom he appointed heir of all things, and through whom he made the universe. [3]The Son is the radiance of God's glory and the exact representation of his being, sustaining all things by his powerful word. After he had provided purification for sins, he sat down at the right hand of the Majesty in heaven.
1 John 2 [23]No one who denies the Son has the Father; whoever acknowledges the Son has the Father also.

160. Son of David

Matt 15 [22]A Canaanite woman from that vicinity came to him, crying out, "Lord, Son of David, have mercy on me! My daughter is suffering terribly from demon-possession."

161. Son of God

Isa 9 [6]For to us a child is born, to us a son is given, and the government will be on his shoulders. And he will be called Wonderful Counselor, Mighty God, Everlasting Father, Prince of Peace.
Matt 4 [3]The tempter came to him and said, "If you are the Son of God, tell these stones to become bread."
Matt 8 [29]"What do you want with us, Son of God?" they shouted. "Have you come here to torture us before the appointed time?"
Luke 1 [35]The angel answered, "The Holy Spirit will come upon you, and the power of the Most High will overshadow you. So the holy one to be born will be called the Son of God."
John 1 [34]"I have seen and I testify that this is the Son of God."
John 1 [49]Then Nathanael declared, "Rabbi, you are the Son of God; you are the King of Israel."
John 5 [18]For this reason the Jews tried all the harder to kill him; not only was he breaking the Sabbath, but he was even calling God his own Father, making himself equal with God.
John 10 [36]". . . what about the one whom the Father set apart as his very own and sent into the world? Why then do you accuse me of blasphemy because I said, 'I am God's Son'?"
John 15 [10]"If you obey my commands, you will remain in my love, just as I have obeyed my Father's commands and remain in his love."
John 19 [7]The Jews insisted, "We have a law, and according to that law he must die, because he claimed to be the Son of God."
John 20 [17]Jesus said, "Do not hold on to me, for I have not yet returned to the Father. Go instead to my brothers and tell them, 'I am returning to my Father and your Father, to my God and your God.'" . . .

[30]Jesus did many other miraculous signs in the presence of his disciples, which are not recorded in this book. [31]But these are written that you may believe that Jesus is the Christ, the Son of God, and that by believing you may have life in his name.
Acts 9 [20]At once he began to preach in the synagogues that Jesus is the Son of God.
Rom 1 [4]and who through the Spirit of holiness was declared with power to be the Son of God by his resurrection from the dead: Jesus Christ our Lord.
Rom 8 [3]For what the law was powerless to do in that it was weakened by the sinful nature, God did by sending his own Son in the likeness of sinful man to be a sin offering. And so he condemned sin in sinful man. . . . [32]He who did not spare his own Son, but gave him up for us all—how will he not also, along with him, graciously give us all things?
2 Cor 11 [31]The God and Father of the Lord Jesus, who is to be praised forever, knows that I am not lying.
Gal 4 [4]But when the time had fully come, God sent his Son, born of a woman, born under law. . . .
Eph 1 [3]Praise be to the God and Father of our Lord Jesus Christ, who has blessed us in the heavenly realms with every spiritual blessing in Christ.
1 John 4 [14]And we have seen and testify that the Father has sent his Son to be the Savior of the world. [15]If anyone acknowledges that Jesus is the Son of God, God lives in him and he in God.
1 John 5 [5]Who is it that overcomes the world? Only he who believes that Jesus is the Son of God. . . . [20]We know also that the Son of God has come and has given us understanding, so that we may know him who is true. And we are in him who is true—even in his Son Jesus Christ. He is the true God and eternal life.
Rev 2 [18]"To the angel of the church in Thyatira write:

These are the words of the Son of God, whose eyes are like blazing fire and whose feet are like burnished bronze."

162. Son of Joseph

Luke 3 [23]Now Jesus himself was about thirty years old when he began his ministry. He was the son, so it was thought, of Joseph, the son of Heli. . . .
John 1 [45]Philip found Nathanael and told him, "We have found the one Moses wrote about in the Law, and about whom the prophets also wrote—Jesus of Nazareth, the son of Joseph."
John 6 [42]They said, "Is this not Jesus, the son of Joseph, whose father and mother we know? How can he now say, 'I came down from heaven'?"

163. Son of Man

Dan 7 [13]"In my vision at night I looked, and there before me was one like a son of man, coming with the clouds of heaven. He approached the Ancient of Days and was led into his presence."
Matt 8 [20]Jesus replied, "Foxes have holes and birds of the air have nests, but the Son of Man has no place to lay his head."
Matt 10 [23]"When you are persecuted in one place, flee to another. I tell you the truth, you will not finish going through the cities of Israel before the Son of Man comes."
Matt 11 [19]"The Son of Man came eating and drinking, and they say, 'Here is a glutton and a drunkard, a friend of tax collectors and "sinners."' But wisdom is proved right by her actions."
Matt 13 [37]He answered, "The one who sowed the good seed is the Son of Man. . . . [41]The Son of Man will send out his angels, and they will weed out of his kingdom everything that causes sin and all who do evil."
Matt 16 [13]When Jesus came to the region of Caesarea Philippi, he asked his disciples, "Who do people say the Son of Man is?"
Matt 17 [9]As they were coming down the mountain, Jesus instructed them, "Don't tell anyone what you have seen, until the Son of Man has been raised from the dead."
Matt 17 [22]When they came together in Galilee, he said to them, "The Son of Man is going to be betrayed into the hands of men."
Matt 24 [27]"For as lightning that comes from the east is visible even in the west, so will be the coming of the Son of Man. . . .

[30]"At that time the sign of the Son of Man will appear in the sky, and all the nations of the earth will mourn. They will see the Son of Man coming on the clouds of the sky, with power and great glory."
Matt 25 [31]"When the Son of Man comes in his glory, and all the angels with him, he will sit on his throne in heavenly glory."
Matt 26 [2]"As you know, the Passover is two days away—and the Son of Man will be handed over to be crucified."
Matt 26 [24]"The Son of Man will go just as it is written about him. But woe to that man who betrays the Son of Man! It would be better for him if he had not been born."
Matt 26 [45]Then he returned to the disciples and said to them, "Are you still sleeping and resting? Look, the hour is near, and the Son of Man is betrayed into the hands of sinners."

Mark 2 [28]"So the Son of Man is Lord even of the Sabbath."
Mark 8 [38]"If anyone is ashamed of me and my words in this adulterous and sinful generation, the Son of Man will be ashamed of him when he comes in his Father's glory with the holy angels."
Mark 9 [12]Jesus replied, "To be sure, Elijah does come first, and restores all things. Why then is it written that the Son of Man must suffer much and be rejected?"
Luke 5 [24]"But that you may know that the Son of Man has authority on earth to forgive sins. . . ." He said to the paralyzed man, "I tell you, get up, take your mat and go home."
Luke 6 [22]"Blessed are you when men hate you, when they exclude you and insult you and reject your name as evil, because of the Son of Man."
Luke 11 [30]"For as Jonah was a sign to the Ninevites, so also will the Son of Man be to this generation."
Luke 12 [8]"I tell you, whoever acknowledges me before men, the Son of Man will also acknowledge him before the angels of God."
Luke 17 [22]Then he said to his disciples, "The time is coming when you will long to see one of the days of the Son of Man, but you will not see it."
Luke 19 [10]"For the Son of Man came to seek and to save what was lost."
Luke 21 [36]"Be always on the watch, and pray that you may be able to escape all that is about to happen, and that you may be able to stand before the Son of Man."
John 1 [51]He then added, "I tell you the truth, you shall see heaven open, and the angels of God ascending and descending on the Son of Man."
John 3 [13]"No one has ever gone into heaven except the one who came from heaven—the Son of Man."
John 5 [27]"And he has given him authority to judge because he is the Son of Man."
John 6 [27]"Do not work for food that spoils, but for food that endures to eternal life, which the Son of Man will give you. On him God the Father has placed his seal of approval."
John 6 [53]Jesus said to them, "I tell you the truth, unless you eat the flesh of the Son of Man and drink his blood, you have no life in you."
John 6 [62]"What if you see the Son of Man ascend to where he was before!"
John 8 [28]So Jesus said, "When you have lifted up the Son of Man, then you will know that I am the one I claim to be and that I do nothing on my own but speak just what the Father has taught me."
John 9 [35]Jesus heard that they had thrown him out, and when he found him, he said, "Do you believe in the Son of Man?"
John 12 [23]Jesus replied, "The hour has come for the Son of Man to be glorified."
John 13 [31]When he was gone, Jesus said, "Now is the Son of Man glorified and God is glorified in him."
Acts 7 [56]"Look," he said, "I see heaven open and the Son of Man standing at the right hand of God."
Rev 1 [13]and among the lampstands was someone "like a son of man," dressed in a robe reaching down to his feet and with a golden sash around his chest.

164. Son of Mary

Matt 1 [16]and Jacob the father of Joseph, the husband of Mary, of whom was born Jesus, who is called Christ. . . .

[18]This is how the birth of Jesus Christ came about: His mother Mary was pledged to be married to Joseph, but before they came together, she was found to be with child through the Holy Spirit.
Mark 6 [3]"Isn't this the carpenter? Isn't this Mary's son and the brother of James, Joseph, Judas and Simon? Aren't his sisters here with us?" And they took offense at him.

165. Son of the Blessed One

Mark 14 [61]But Jesus remained silent and gave no answer.

Again the high priest asked him, "Are you the Christ, the Son of the Blessed One?"

166. Son of the Living God

Matt 16 [16]Simon Peter answered, "You are the Christ, the Son of the living God."

167. Son of the Most High

Luke 1 [32]"He will be great and will be called the Son of the Most High. The Lord God will give him the throne of his father David. . . ."

168. Source of Eternal Salvation

Heb 5 [9]and, once made perfect, he became the source of eternal salvation for all who obey him. . . .

169. Sovereign

Jude [4]For certain men whose condemnation was written about long ago have secretly slipped in among you. They are godless men, who change the grace of our God into a license for immorality and deny Jesus Christ our only Sovereign and Lord.

170. Stone

Matt 21 [42]Jesus said to them, "Have you never read in the Scriptures: 'The stone the builders rejected has become the capstone; the Lord has done this, and it is marvelous in our eyes'?" (Ps 118:22–23)
1 Pet 2 [4]As you come to him, the living Stone—rejected by men but chosen by God and precious to him—[5]you also, like living stones, are being built into a spiritual house to be a holy priesthood, offering spiritual sacrifices acceptable to God through Jesus Christ. [6]For in Scripture it says: "See, I lay a stone in Zion, a chosen and precious cornerstone, and the one who trusts in him will never be put to shame." [7]Now to you who believe, this stone is precious. But to those who do not believe, "The stone the builders rejected has become the capstone," [8]and, "A stone that causes men to stumble and a rock that makes them fall." They stumble because they disobey the message—which is also what they were destined for.

171. Stumbling Block

1 Cor 1 [23]but we preach Christ crucified: a stumbling block to Jews and foolishness to Gentiles. . . .
1 Pet 2 [4]As you come to him, the living Stone—rejected by men but chosen by God and precious to him—[5]you also, like living stones, are being built into a spiritual house to be a holy priesthood, offering spiritual sacrifices acceptable to God through Jesus Christ. [6]For in Scripture it says: "See, I lay a stone in Zion, a chosen and precious cornerstone, and the one who trusts in him will never be put to shame." [7]Now to you who believe, this stone is precious. But to those who do not believe, "The stone the builders rejected has become the capstone," [8]and, "A stone that causes men to stumble and a rock that makes them fall." They stumble because they disobey the message—which is also what they were destined for.

172. Sun of Righteousness

Mal 4 [2]"But for you who revere my name, the sun of righteousness will rise with healing in its wings. And you will go out and leap like calves released from the stall."

173. Teacher

Matt 19 [16]Now a man came up to Jesus and asked, "Teacher, what good thing must I do to get eternal life?"
Matt 23 [10]"Nor are you to be called 'teacher,' for you have one Teacher, the Christ."
John 11 [28]And after she had said this, she went back and called her sister Mary aside. "The Teacher is here," she said, "and is asking for you."

John 13 [13]"You call me 'Teacher' and 'Lord,' and rightly so, for that is what I am. [14]Now that I, your Lord and Teacher, have washed your feet, you also should wash one another's feet."

174. Tested Stone

Isa 28 [16]So this is what the Sovereign LORD says: "See, I lay a stone in Zion, a tested stone, a precious cornerstone for a sure foundation; the one who trusts will never be dismayed."

175. True God

1 John 5 [20]We know also that the Son of God has come and has given us understanding, so that we may know him who is true. And we are in him who is true—even in his Son Jesus Christ. He is the true God and eternal life.

176. True Light

John 1 [9]The true light that gives light to every man was coming into the world.

177. (True) Witness

Isa 55 [4]"See, I have made him a witness to the peoples, a leader and commander of the peoples."
John 18 [37]"You are a king, then!" said Pilate.

Jesus answered, "You are right in saying I am a king. In fact, for this reason I was born, and for this I came into the world, to testify to the truth. Everyone on the side of truth listens to me."
Rev 3 [14]"To the angel of the church in Laodicea write: These are the words of the Amen, the faithful and true witness, the ruler of God's creation."

178. Truth

John 14 [6]Jesus answered, "I am the way and the truth and the life. No one comes to the Father except through me."

179. Vine

John 15 [1]"I am the true vine, and my Father is the gardener."

180. Way

John 14 [6]Jesus answered, "I am the way and the truth and the life. No one comes to the Father except through me."

181. Wisdom

Prov 8 [12]"I, wisdom, dwell together with prudence; I possess knowledge and discretion."
1 Cor 1 [23]but we preach Christ crucified: a stumbling block to Jews and foolishness to Gentiles, [24]but to those whom God has called, both Jews and Greeks, Christ the power of God and the wisdom of God. . . . [30]It is because of him that you are in Christ Jesus, who has become for us wisdom from God—that is, our righteousness, holiness and redemption.

182. Wonderful Counselor

Isa 9 [6]For to us a child is born, to us a son is given, and the government will be on his shoulders. And he will be called Wonderful Counselor, Mighty God, Everlasting Father, Prince of Peace.

183. Word (of God)

John 1 [1]In the beginning was the Word, and the Word was with God, and the Word was God. . . .

[14]The Word became flesh and made his dwelling among us. We have seen his glory, the glory of the One and Only, who came from the Father, full of grace and truth.
Rev 19 [13]He is dressed in a robe dipped in blood, and his name is the Word of God.

184. Word of Life

1 John 1 [1]That which was from the beginning, which we have heard, which we have seen with our eyes, which we have looked at and our hands have touched—this we proclaim concerning the Word of life.

VI
The Name of Christ

A. Jesus' Name Is Supreme over All

Acts 4 [12]"Salvation is found in no one else, for there is no other name under heaven given to men by which we must be saved."
Phil 2 [9]Therefore God exalted him to the highest place and gave him the name that is above every name, [10]that at the name of Jesus every knee should bow, in heaven and on earth and under the earth, [11]and every tongue confess that Jesus Christ is Lord, to the glory of God the Father.
Heb 1 [4]So he became as much superior to the angels as the name he has inherited is superior to theirs.

B. The Holy Spirit Was Sent in Jesus' Name

John 14 [26]"But the Counselor, the Holy Spirit, whom the Father will send in my name, will teach you all things and will remind you of everything I have said to you."

C. Believers Experience Much in Jesus' Name

1. Believers Are Anointed in His Name

James 5 [14]Is any one of you sick? He should call the elders of the church to pray over him and anoint him with oil in the name of the Lord.

2. Believers Are Baptized into His Name

Acts 2 [38]Peter replied, "Repent and be baptized, every one of you, in the name of Jesus Christ for the forgiveness of your sins. And you will receive the gift of the Holy Spirit."
Acts 8 [16]because the Holy Spirit had not yet come upon any of them; they had simply been baptized into the name of the Lord Jesus.
Acts 10 [48]So he ordered that they be baptized in the name of Jesus Christ. Then they asked Peter to stay with them for a few days.
Acts 19 [5]On hearing this, they were baptized into the name of the Lord Jesus.

3. Believers Are Forgiven in His Name

Luke 24 [46]He told them, "This is what is written: The Christ will suffer and rise from the dead on the third day, [47]and repentance and forgiveness of sins will be preached in his name to all nations, beginning at Jerusalem."
Acts 10 [43]"All the prophets testify about him that everyone who believes in him receives forgiveness of sins through his name."
Acts 22 [16]"'And now what are you waiting for? Get up, be baptized and wash your sins away, calling on his name.'"
1 John 2 [12]I write to you, dear children, because your sins have been forgiven on account of his name.

4. Believers Are Justified in His Name

1 Cor 6 [11]And that is what some of you were. But you were washed, you were sanctified, you were justified in the name of the Lord Jesus Christ and by the Spirit of our God.

5. Believers Are Protected by His Name

John 17 [11]"I will remain in the world no longer, but they are still in the world, and I am coming to you. Holy Father, protect them by the power of your name—the name you gave me—so that they may be one as we are one. [12]While I was with them, I protected them and kept them safe by that name you gave me. None has been lost except the one doomed to destruction so that Scripture would be fulfilled."

6. Believers Assemble in His Name

Matt 18 [20]"For where two or three come together in my name, there am I with them."
1 Cor 5 [4]When you are assembled in the name of our Lord Jesus and I am with you in spirit, and the power of our Lord Jesus is present . . .

7. Believers Bear His Name

Acts 9 [15]But the Lord said to Ananias, "Go! This man is my chosen instrument to carry my name before the Gentiles and their kings and before the people of Israel."
1 Pet 4 [16]However, if you suffer as a Christian, do not be ashamed, but praise God that you bear that name.

8. Believers Believe in His Name

John 1 [12]Yet to all who received him, to those who believed in his name, he gave the right to become children of God. . . .
John 3 [18]"Whoever believes in him is not condemned, but whoever does not believe stands condemned already because he has not believed in the name of God's one and only Son."
Acts 3 [16]"By faith in the name of Jesus, this man whom you see and know was made strong. It is Jesus' name and the faith that comes through him that has given this complete healing to him, as you can all see."
1 John 3 [23]And this is his command: to believe in the name of his Son, Jesus Christ, and to love one another as he commanded us.
1 John 5 [13]I write these things to you who believe in the name of the Son of God so that you may know that you have eternal life.

9. Believers Call on His Name

Acts 9 [14]"And he has come here with authority from the chief priests to arrest all who call on your name."
Acts 9 [21]All those who heard him were astonished and asked, "Isn't he the man who raised havoc in Jerusalem among those who call on this name? And hasn't he come here to take them as prisoners to the chief priests?"
Acts 22 [16]"'And now what are you waiting for? Get up, be baptized and wash your sins away, calling on his name.'"
Rom 10 [13]for, "Everyone who calls on the name of the Lord will be saved."
1 Cor 1 [2]To the church of God in Corinth, to those sanctified in Christ Jesus and called to be holy, together with all those everywhere who call on the name of our Lord Jesus Christ—their Lord and ours. . . .

10. Believers Call on His Name for Salvation

Acts 2 [21]"'And everyone who calls on the name of the Lord will be saved.'"
Acts 4 [12]"Salvation is found in no one else, for there is no other name under heaven given to men by which we must be saved."

11. Believers Command and Make Appeals in His Name

1 Cor 1 [10]I appeal to you, brothers, in the name of our Lord Jesus Christ, that all of you agree with one another so that there may be no divisions among you and that you may be perfectly united in mind and thought.
2 Thess 3 [6]In the name of the Lord Jesus Christ, we command you, brothers, to keep away from every brother who is idle and does not live according to the teaching you received from us.

12. Believers Do Everything in His Name

Col 3 [17]And whatever you do, whether in word or deed, do it all in the name of the Lord Jesus, giving thanks to God the Father through him.

13. Believers Do Miracles and Heal in His Name

Mark 9 [39]"Do not stop him," Jesus said. "No one who does a miracle in my name can in the next moment say anything bad about me. . . ."
Acts 3 [6]Then Peter said, "Silver or gold I do not have, but what I have I give you. In the name of Jesus Christ of Nazareth, walk."
Acts 3 [16]"By faith in the name of Jesus, this man whom you see and know was made strong. It is Jesus' name and the faith that comes through him that has given this complete healing to him, as you can all see."
Acts 4 [10]". . . then know this, you and all the people of Israel: It is by the name of Jesus Christ of Nazareth, whom you crucified but whom God raised from the dead, that this man stands before you healed."
Acts 4 [30]"Stretch out your hand to heal and perform miraculous signs and wonders through the name of your holy servant Jesus."

14. Believers Drive Out Demons in His Name

Mark 9 [38]"Teacher," said John, "we saw a man driving out demons in your name and we told him to stop, because he was not one of us."
Luke 10 [17]The seventy-two returned with joy and said, "Lord, even the demons submit to us in your name."
Acts 16 [18]She kept this up for many days. Finally Paul became so troubled that he turned around and said to the spirit, "In the name of Jesus Christ I command you to come out of her!" At that moment the spirit left her.

15. Believers Give Thanks in His Name

Eph 5 [20]always giving thanks to God the Father for everything, in the name of our Lord Jesus Christ.

16. Believers Glorify His Name

2 Thess 1 [12]We pray this so that the name of our Lord Jesus may be glorified in you, and you in him, according to the grace of our God and the Lord Jesus Christ.

17. Believers Have Life in His Name

John 20 [31]But these are written that you may believe that Jesus is the Christ, the Son of God, and that by believing you may have life in his name.

18. Believers Make Requests in His Name

John 14 [13]"And I will do whatever you ask in my name, so that the Son may bring glory to the Father. [14]You may ask me for anything in my name, and I will do it."
John 16 [23]"In that day you will no longer ask me anything. I tell you the truth, my Father will give you whatever you ask in my name. [24]Until now you have not asked for anything in my name. Ask and you will receive, and your joy will be complete. . . . [26]In that day you will ask in my name. I am not saying that I will ask the Father on your behalf."

19. Believers Speak, Preach, and Teach in His Name

Acts 4 [18]Then they called them in again and commanded them not to speak or teach at all in the name of Jesus.
Acts 5 [28]"We gave you strict orders not to teach in this name,"

he said. "Yet you have filled Jerusalem with your teaching and are determined to make us guilty of this man's blood."
Acts 5 [40]His speech persuaded them. They called the apostles in and had them flogged. Then they ordered them not to speak in the name of Jesus, and let them go.
Acts 8 [12]But when they believed Philip as he preached the good news of the kingdom of God and the name of Jesus Christ, they were baptized, both men and women.
Acts 9 [27]But Barnabas took him and brought him to the apostles. He told them how Saul on his journey had seen the Lord and that the Lord had spoken to him, and how in Damascus he had preached fearlessly in the name of Jesus. [28]So Saul stayed with them and moved about freely in Jerusalem, speaking boldly in the name of the Lord.

20. Believers Suffer for His Name

Luke 21 [12]"But before all this, they will lay hands on you and persecute you. They will deliver you to synagogues and prisons, and you will be brought before kings and governors, and all on account of my name."
John 15 [20]"Remember the words I spoke to you: 'No servant is greater than his master.' If they persecuted me, they will persecute you also. If they obeyed my teaching, they will obey yours also. [21]They will treat you this way because of my name, for they do not know the One who sent me."
Acts 5 [41]The apostles left the Sanhedrin, rejoicing because they had been counted worthy of suffering disgrace for the Name.
Acts 9 [15]But the Lord said to Ananias, "Go! This man is my chosen instrument to carry my name before the Gentiles and their kings and before the people of Israel. [16]I will show him how much he must suffer for my name."
Acts 15 [26]men who have risked their lives for the name of our Lord Jesus Christ.
Acts 21 [13]Then Paul answered, "Why are you weeping and breaking my heart? I am ready not only to be bound, but also to die in Jerusalem for the name of the Lord Jesus."
1 Pet 4 [14]If you are insulted because of the name of Christ, you are blessed, for the Spirit of glory and of God rests on you.
Rev 2 [3]"You have persevered and have endured hardships for my name, and have not grown weary."

3

The Holy Spirit

I
The Personality of the Holy Spirit

A. The Spirit Has Characteristics of Personhood

1. The Spirit Has Intelligence

Isa 11 [2]The Spirit of the LORD will rest on him—the Spirit of wisdom and of understanding, the Spirit of counsel and of power, the Spirit of knowledge and of the fear of the LORD. . . .
John 14 [26]"But the Counselor, the Holy Spirit, whom the Father will send in my name, will teach you all things and will remind you of everything I have said to you."

Rom 8 [27]And he who searches our hearts knows the mind of the Spirit, because the Spirit intercedes for the saints in accordance with God's will.
1 Cor 2 [10]but God has revealed it to us by his Spirit.

The Spirit searches all things, even the deep things of God. [11]For who among men knows the thoughts of a man except the man's spirit within him? In the same way no one knows the thoughts of God except the Spirit of God. [12]We have not received the spirit of the world but the Spirit who is from God, that we may understand what God has freely given us. [13]This is what we speak, not in words taught us by human wisdom but in words taught by the Spirit, expressing spiritual truths in spiritual words.
1 Cor 12 [8]To one there is given through the Spirit the message of wisdom, to another the message of knowledge by means of the same Spirit. . . .
Eph 1 [17]I keep asking that the God of our Lord Jesus Christ, the glorious Father, may give you the Spirit of wisdom and revelation, so that you may know him better.

2. The Spirit Shows Emotion

Isa 63 [10]Yet they rebelled and grieved his Holy Spirit. So he turned and became their enemy and he himself fought against them.
Rom 15 [30]I urge you, brothers, by our Lord Jesus Christ and by the love of the Spirit, to join me in my struggle by praying to God for me.
Eph 4 [30]And do not grieve the Holy Spirit of God, with whom you were sealed for the day of redemption.

3. The Spirit Has a Will

1 Cor 12 [11]All these are the work of one and the same Spirit, and he gives them to each one, just as he determines.

B. The Spirit Is Distinguished among the Persons of the Godhead

1. The Spirit Is Distinguished from Jesus

John 14 [16]"And I will ask the Father, and he will give you another Counselor to be with you forever. . . . [26]But the Counselor, the Holy Spirit, whom the Father will send in my name, will teach you all things and will remind you of everything I have said to you."
John 15 [26]"When the Counselor comes, whom I will send to you from the Father, the Spirit of truth who goes out from the Father, he will testify about me."
John 16 [7]"But I tell you the truth: It is for your good that I am going away. Unless I go away, the Counselor will not come to you; but if I go, I will send him to you. . . . [14]He will bring glory to me by taking from what is mine and making it known to you."

2. The Spirit Is Distinguished within the Trinity

Matt 3 [16]As soon as Jesus was baptized, he went up out of the water. At that moment heaven was opened, and he saw the Spirit of God descending like a dove and lighting on him. [17]And a voice from heaven said, "This is my Son, whom I love; with him I am well pleased."
Matt 28 [19]"Therefore go and make disciples of all nations, baptizing them in the name of the Father and of the Son and of the Holy Spirit. . . ."
Rom 15 [16]to be a minister of Christ Jesus to the Gentiles with the priestly duty of proclaiming the gospel of God, so that the Gentiles might become an offering acceptable to God, sanctified by the Holy Spirit.
2 Cor 1 [21]Now it is God who makes both us and you stand firm in Christ. He anointed us, [22]set his seal of ownership on us, and put his Spirit in our hearts as a deposit, guaranteeing what is to come.
2 Cor 13 [14]May the grace of the Lord Jesus Christ, and the love of God, and the fellowship of the Holy Spirit be with you all.
Eph 3 [14]For this reason I kneel before the Father, [15]from whom his whole family in heaven and on earth derives its name. [16]I pray that out of his glorious riches he may strengthen you with power through his Spirit in your inner being, [17]so that Christ may dwell in your hearts through faith. And I pray that you, being rooted and established in love . . .
2 Thess 2 [13]But we ought always to thank God for you, brothers loved by the Lord, because from the beginning God chose you to be saved through the sanctifying work of the Spirit and through belief in the truth. [14]He called you to this through our gospel, that you might share in the glory of our Lord Jesus Christ.
1 Pet 1 [2]who have been chosen according to the foreknowledge of God the Father, through the sanctifying work of the Spirit, for obedience to Jesus Christ and sprinkling by his blood: Grace and peace be yours in abundance.
Jude [20]But you, dear friends, build yourselves up in your most holy faith and pray in the Holy Spirit. [21]Keep yourselves in God's love as you wait for the mercy of our Lord Jesus Christ to bring you to eternal life.

C. The Spirit Is Referred to with Personal Pronouns

John 14 [16]"And I will ask the Father, and he will give you another Counselor to be with you forever—[17]the Spirit of truth. The world cannot accept him, because it neither sees him nor knows him. But you know him, for he lives with you and will be in you."
John 15 [26]"When the Counselor comes, whom I will send to you from the Father, the Spirit of truth who goes out from the Father, he will testify about me."
John 16 [7]"But I tell you the truth: It is for your good that I am going away. Unless I go away, the Counselor will not come to you; but if I go, I will send him to you. [8]When he comes, he will convict the world of guilt in regard to sin and righteousness and judgment: [9]in regard to sin, because men do not believe in me; [10]in regard to righteousness, because I am going to the Father, where you can see me no longer; [11]and in regard to judgment, because the prince of this world now stands condemned.

[12]"I have much more to say to you, more than you can now bear. [13]But when he, the Spirit of truth, comes, he will guide you into all truth. He will not speak on his own; he will speak only what he hears, and he will tell you what is yet to come. [14]He will bring glory to me by taking from what is mine and making it known to you."
Eph 1 [13]And you also were included in Christ when you heard the word of truth, the gospel of your salvation. Having believed, you were marked in him with a seal, the promised Holy Spirit, [14]who is a deposit guaranteeing our inheritance until the redemption of those who are God's possession—to the praise of his glory.

D. The Spirit Is Affected as a Person

1. The Spirit Can Be Blasphemed

Matt 12 [31]"And so I tell you, every sin and blasphemy will be forgiven men, but the blasphemy against the Spirit will not be forgiven. [32]Anyone who speaks a word against the Son of Man will be forgiven, but anyone who speaks against the Holy Spirit will not be forgiven, either in this age or in the age to come."
Mark 3 [28]"I tell you the truth, all the sins and blasphemies of men will be forgiven them. [29]But whoever blasphemes against the Holy Spirit will never be forgiven; he is guilty of an eternal sin."

2. The Spirit Can Be Grieved

Isa 63 [10]Yet they rebelled and grieved his Holy Spirit. So he turned and became their enemy and he himself fought against them.
Eph 4 [30]And do not grieve the Holy Spirit of God, with whom you were sealed for the day of redemption.

3. The Spirit Can Be Insulted

Heb 10 [29]How much more severely do you think a man deserves to be punished who has trampled the Son of God under foot, who has treated as an unholy thing the blood of the covenant that sanctified him, and who has insulted the Spirit of grace?

4. The Spirit Can Be Lied To

Acts 5 [3]Then Peter said, "Ananias, how is it that Satan has so filled your heart that you have lied to the Holy Spirit and have kept for yourself some of the money you received for the land? [4]Didn't it belong to you before it was sold? And after it was sold, wasn't the money at your disposal? What made you think of doing such a thing? You have not lied to men but to God."

5. The Spirit Can Be Obeyed

Acts 10 [19]While Peter was still thinking about the vision, the Spirit said to him, "Simon, three men are looking for you. [20]So get up and go downstairs. Do not hesitate to go with them, for I have sent them."

[21]Peter went down and said to the men, "I'm the one you're looking for. Why have you come?"

6. The Spirit Can Be Quenched

1 Thess 5 [19]Do not put out the Spirit's fire. . . .

7. The Spirit Can Be Resisted

Acts 6 [9]Opposition arose, however, from members of the Synagogue of the Freedmen (as it was called)—Jews of Cyrene and Alexandria as well as the provinces of Cilicia and Asia. These men began to argue with Stephen, [10]but they could not stand up against his wisdom or the Spirit by whom he spoke.
Acts 7 [51]"You stiff-necked people, with uncircumcised hearts and ears! You are just like your fathers: You always resist the Holy Spirit!"

8. The Spirit Can Be Tested

Acts 5 [9]Peter said to her, "How could you agree to test the Spirit of the Lord? Look! The feet of the men who buried your husband are at the door, and they will carry you out also."

E. The Spirit Has Moral Capacities

1. The Spirit Convicts the World of Guilt

John 16 [8]"When he comes, he will convict the world of guilt in regard to sin and righteousness and judgment: [9]in regard to sin, because men do not believe in me; [10]in regard to righteousness, because I am going to the Father, where you can see me no longer; [11]and in regard to judgment, because the prince of this world now stands condemned."

2. The Spirit Glorifies Christ

John 16 [14]"He will bring glory to me by taking from what is mine and making it known to you."

3. The Spirit Guides into Truth

John 16 [13]"But when he, the Spirit of truth, comes, he will guide you into all truth. He will not speak on his own; he will speak only what he hears, and he will tell you what is yet to come."

4. The Spirit Intercedes

Rom 8 [26]In the same way, the Spirit helps us in our weakness. We do not know what we ought to pray for, but the Spirit himself intercedes for us with groans that words cannot express. [27]And he who searches our hearts knows the mind of the Spirit, because the Spirit intercedes for the saints in accordance with God's will.

5. The Spirit Regenerates

John 3 [3]In reply Jesus declared, "I tell you the truth, no one can see the kingdom of God unless he is born again."

[4]"How can a man be born when he is old?" Nicodemus asked. "Surely he cannot enter a second time into his mother's womb to be born!"

[5]Jesus answered, "I tell you the truth, no one can enter the kingdom of God unless he is born of water and the Spirit."

6. The Spirit Restrains Evil

Gen 6 [3]Then the LORD said, "My Spirit will not contend with man forever, for he is mortal; his days will be a hundred and twenty years.". . .

[5]The LORD saw how great man's wickedness on the earth had become, and that every inclination of the thoughts of his heart was only evil all the time.

7. The Spirit Sanctifies

Rom 15 [16]to be a minister of Christ Jesus to the Gentiles with the priestly duty of proclaiming the gospel of God, so that the Gentiles might become an offering acceptable to God, sanctified by the Holy Spirit.
1 Cor 6 [11]And that is what some of you were. But you were washed, you were sanctified, you were justified in the name of the Lord Jesus Christ and by the Spirit of our God.

F. The Spirit Is a Distinct Personality with Power

Judg 14 [6]The Spirit of the LORD came upon him in power so that he tore the lion apart with his bare hands as he might have torn a young goat. But he told neither his father nor his mother what he had done.
Judg 14 [19]Then the Spirit of the LORD came upon him in power. He went down to Ashkelon, struck down thirty of their men, stripped them of their belongings and gave their clothes to those who had explained the riddle. Burning with anger, he went up to his father's house.
Judg 15 [14]As he approached Lehi, the Philistines came toward him shouting. The Spirit of the LORD came upon him in power. The ropes on his arms became like charred flax, and the bindings dropped from his hands.
1 Sam 10 [10]When they arrived at Gibeah, a procession of prophets met him; the Spirit of God came upon him in power, and he joined in their prophesying.
1 Sam 16 [13]So Samuel took the horn of oil and anointed him in the presence of his brothers, and from that day on the Spirit of the LORD came upon David in power. Samuel then went to Ramah.
Luke 1 [35]The angel answered, "The Holy Spirit will come upon you, and the power of the Most High will overshadow you. So the holy one to be born will be called the Son of God."
Luke 4 [14]Jesus returned to Galilee in the power of the Spirit, and news about him spread through the whole countryside.
Acts 10 [38]". . . how God anointed Jesus of Nazareth with the Holy Spirit and power, and how he went around doing good and healing all who were under the power of the devil, because God was with him."
Acts 15 [28]It seemed good to the Holy Spirit and to us not to burden you with anything beyond the following requirements. . . .
Rom 15 [13]May the God of hope fill you with all joy and peace as you trust in him, so that you may overflow with hope by the power of the Holy Spirit.
1 Cor 2 [4]My message and my preaching were not with wise and persuasive words, but with a demonstration of the Spirit's power. . . .

G. The Spirit Does What Persons Do

1. The Spirit Commissions

Acts 11 [12]"The Spirit told me to have no hesitation about going with them. These six brothers also went with me, and we entered the man's house."

Acts 13 [2]While they were worshiping the Lord and fasting, the Holy Spirit said, "Set apart for me Barnabas and Saul for the work to which I have called them."...

[4]The two of them, sent on their way by the Holy Spirit, went down to Seleucia and sailed from there to Cyprus.

Acts 20 [28]"Keep watch over yourselves and all the flock of which the Holy Spirit has made you overseers. Be shepherds of the church of God, which he bought with his own blood."

2. The Spirit Communicates

2 Cor 3 [3]You show that you are a letter from Christ, the result of our ministry, written not with ink but with the Spirit of the living God, not on tablets of stone but on tablets of human hearts.

Eph 3 [5]which was not made known to men in other generations as it has now been revealed by the Spirit to God's holy apostles and prophets.

3. The Spirit Encourages

Acts 9 [31]Then the church throughout Judea, Galilee and Samaria enjoyed a time of peace. It was strengthened; and encouraged by the Holy Spirit, it grew in numbers, living in the fear of the Lord.

4. The Spirit Gives Gifts

1 Cor 12 [7]Now to each one the manifestation of the Spirit is given for the common good. [8]To one there is given through the Spirit the message of wisdom, to another the message of knowledge by means of the same Spirit, [9]to another faith by the same Spirit, to another gifts of healing by that one Spirit, [10]to another miraculous powers, to another prophecy, to another distinguishing between spirits, to another speaking in different kinds of tongues, and to still another the interpretation of tongues. [11]All these are the work of one and the same Spirit, and he gives them to each one, just as he determines.

5. The Spirit Leads

Matt 4 [1]Then Jesus was led by the Spirit into the desert to be tempted by the devil.

Acts 8 [29]The Spirit told Philip, "Go to that chariot and stay near it."

Acts 16 [6]Paul and his companions traveled throughout the region of Phrygia and Galatia, having been kept by the Holy Spirit from preaching the word in the province of Asia. [7]When they came to the border of Mysia, they tried to enter Bithynia, but the Spirit of Jesus would not allow them to.

Rom 8 [14]because those who are led by the Spirit of God are sons of God.

6. The Spirit Speaks

Matt 10 [20]". . . for it will not be you speaking, but the Spirit of your Father speaking through you."

Acts 1 [16]and said, "Brothers, the Scripture had to be fulfilled which the Holy Spirit spoke long ago through the mouth of David concerning Judas, who served as guide for those who arrested Jesus. . . ."

Acts 8 [29]The Spirit told Philip, "Go to that chariot and stay near it."

Acts 10 [19]While Peter was still thinking about the vision, the Spirit said to him, "Simon, three men are looking for you."

Acts 21 [11]Coming over to us, he took Paul's belt, tied his own hands and feet with it and said, "The Holy Spirit says, 'In this way the Jews of Jerusalem will bind the owner of this belt and will hand him over to the Gentiles.'"

1 Tim 4 [1]The Spirit clearly says that in later times some will abandon the faith and follow deceiving spirits and things taught by demons.

Heb 3 [7]So, as the Holy Spirit says: "Today, if you hear his voice . . ."

1 Pet 1 [11]trying to find out the time and circumstances to which the Spirit of Christ in them was pointing when he predicted the sufferings of Christ and the glories that would follow. [12]It was revealed to them that they were not serving themselves but you, when they spoke of the things that have now been told you by those who have preached the gospel to you by the Holy Spirit sent from heaven. Even angels long to look into these things.

Rev 2 [7]"He who has an ear, let him hear what the Spirit says to the churches. To him who overcomes, I will give the right to eat from the tree of life, which is in the paradise of God."

Rev 22 [17]The Spirit and the bride say, "Come!" And let him who hears say, "Come!" Whoever is thirsty, let him come; and whoever wishes, let him take the free gift of the water of life.

7. The Spirit Strengthens

Acts 9 [31]Then the church throughout Judea, Galilee and Samaria enjoyed a time of peace. It was strengthened; and encouraged by the Holy Spirit, it grew in numbers, living in the fear of the Lord.

Rom 8 [26]In the same way, the Spirit helps us in our weakness. We do not know what we ought to pray for, but the Spirit himself intercedes for us with groans that words cannot express.

Eph 3 [16]I pray that out of his glorious riches he may strengthen you with power through his Spirit in your inner being. . . .

8. The Spirit Teaches

Luke 12 [12]". . . for the Holy Spirit will teach you at that time what you should say."

John 14 [26]"But the Counselor, the Holy Spirit, whom the Father will send in my name, will teach you all things and will remind you of everything I have said to you."

1 Cor 2 [13]This is what we speak, not in words taught us by human wisdom but in words taught by the Spirit, expressing spiritual truths in spiritual words.

Heb 9 [8]The Holy Spirit was showing by this that the way into the Most Holy Place had not yet been disclosed as long as the first tabernacle was still standing.

9. The Spirit Testifies

John 15 [26]"When the Counselor comes, whom I will send to you from the Father, the Spirit of truth who goes out from the Father, he will testify about me."

Acts 5 [32]"We are witnesses of these things, and so is the Holy Spirit, whom God has given to those who obey him."

Rom 8 [16]The Spirit himself testifies with our spirit that we are God's children.

Heb 10 [15]The Holy Spirit also testifies to us about this. First he says . . .

1 John 4 [2]This is how you can recognize the Spirit of God: Every spirit that acknowledges that Jesus Christ has come in the flesh is from God. . . .

1 John 5 [6]This is the one who came by water and blood—Jesus Christ. He did not come by water only, but by water and blood. And it is the Spirit who testifies, because the Spirit is the truth. [7]For there are three that testify: [8]the Spirit, the water and the blood; and the three are in agreement.

H. The Spirit Gives Life

Ps 104 [30]When you send your Spirit, they are created, and you renew the face of the earth.

Isa 32 [15]till the Spirit is poured upon us from on high, and the desert becomes a fertile field, and the fertile field seems like a forest.

Isa 44 [3]"For I will pour water on the thirsty land, and streams on the dry ground; I will pour out my Spirit on your offspring, and my blessing on your descendants. [4]They will spring up like grass in a meadow, like poplar trees by flowing streams."

Ezek 37 [14]"'I will put my Spirit in you and you will live, and I will settle you in your own land. Then you will know that I the LORD have spoken, and I have done it, declares the LORD.'"

John 6 [63]"The Spirit gives life; the flesh counts for nothing. The words I have spoken to you are spirit and they are life."

Rom 8 [2]because through Christ Jesus the law of the Spirit of life set me free from the law of sin and death.

1 Pet 3 [18]For Christ died for sins once for all, the righteous for the unrighteous, to bring you to God. He was put to death in the body but made alive by the Spirit. . . .

II
The Deity of the Holy Spirit

A. The Spirit Is Considered Divine

1. The Spirit's Deity in His Own Being

a) The Spirit Is Called God

Acts 5 [3]Then Peter said, "Ananias, how is it that Satan has so filled your heart that you have lied to the Holy Spirit and have kept for yourself some of the money you received for the land? [4]Didn't it belong to you before it was sold? And after it was sold, wasn't the money at your disposal? What made you think of doing such a thing? You have not lied to men but to God."

b) The Spirit Is Called Lord

2 Cor 3 [17]Now the Lord is the Spirit, and where the Spirit of the Lord is, there is freedom. [18]And we, who with unveiled faces all reflect the Lord's glory, are being transformed into his likeness with ever-increasing glory, which comes from the Lord, who is the Spirit.

c) The Spirit Is Called the Spirit

Num 11 [17]"I will come down and speak with you there, and I will take of the Spirit that is on you and put the Spirit on them. They will help you carry the burden of the people so that you will not have to carry it alone." . . . [25]Then the LORD came down in the cloud and spoke with him, and he took of the Spirit that was on him and put the Spirit on the seventy elders. When the Spirit rested on them, they prophesied, but they did not do so again.

1 Chron 12 [18]Then the Spirit came upon Amasai, chief of the Thirty, and he said: "We are yours, O David! We are with you, O son of Jesse! Success, success to you, and success to those who help you, for your God will help you."

So David received them and made them leaders of his raiding bands.

Isa 32 [15]till the Spirit is poured upon us from on high, and the desert becomes a fertile field, and the fertile field seems like a forest.

Ezek 2 [2]As he spoke, the Spirit came into me and raised me to my feet, and I heard him speaking to me.

Ezek 8 [3]He stretched out what looked like a hand and took me by the hair of my head. The Spirit lifted me up between earth and heaven and in visions of God he took me to Jerusalem, to the entrance to the north gate of the inner court, where the idol that provokes to jealousy stood.

Mark 1 [12]At once the Spirit sent him out into the desert. . . .

John 7 [39]By this he meant the Spirit, whom those who believed in him were later to receive. Up to that time the Spirit had not been given, since Jesus had not yet been glorified.

Acts 11 [28]One of them, named Agabus, stood up and through the Spirit predicted that a severe famine would spread over the entire Roman world. (This happened during the reign of Claudius.)

Acts 20 [22]"And now, compelled by the Spirit, I am going to Jerusalem, not knowing what will happen to me there."

Acts 21 [4]Finding the disciples there, we stayed with them seven days. Through the Spirit they urged Paul not to go on to Jerusalem.

Rom 7 [6]But now, by dying to what once bound us, we have been released from the law so that we serve in the new way of the Spirit, and not in the old way of the written code.

Rom 8 [16]The Spirit himself testifies with our spirit that we are God's children.

2 Cor 3 [6]He has made us competent as ministers of a new covenant—not of the letter but of the Spirit; for the letter kills, but the Spirit gives life.

Gal 5 [16]So I say, live by the Spirit, and you will not gratify the desires of the sinful nature. [17]For the sinful nature desires what is contrary to the Spirit, and the Spirit what is contrary to the sinful nature. They are in conflict with each other, so that you do not do what you want. [18]But if you are led by the Spirit, you are not under law.

Eph 6 [18]And pray in the Spirit on all occasions with all kinds of prayers and requests. With this in mind, be alert and always keep on praying for all the saints.

1 Tim 3 [16]Beyond all question, the mystery of godliness is great: He appeared in a body, was vindicated by the Spirit, was seen by angels, was preached among the nations, was believed on in the world, was taken up in glory.

1 Pet 3 [18]For Christ died for sins once for all, the righteous for the unrighteous, to bring you to God. He was put to death in the body but made alive by the Spirit. . . .

1 John 3 [24]Those who obey his commands live in him, and he in them. And this is how we know that he lives in us: We know it by the Spirit he gave us.

1 John 4 [6]We are from God, and whoever knows God listens to us; but whoever is not from God does not listen to us. This is how we recognize the Spirit of truth and the spirit of falsehood.

Jude [19]These are the men who divide you, who follow mere natural instincts and do not have the Spirit.

d) The Spirit Is Identified with Yahweh

Num 24 [2]When Balaam looked out and saw Israel encamped tribe by tribe, the Spirit of God came upon him [3]and he uttered his oracle: "The oracle of Balaam son of Beor, the oracle of one whose eye sees clearly, [4]the oracle of one who hears the words of God, who sees a vision from the Almighty, who falls prostrate, and whose eyes are opened. . . ."

[12]Balaam answered Balak, "Did I not tell the messengers you sent me, [13]'Even if Balak gave me his palace filled with silver and gold, I could not do anything of my own accord, good or bad, to go beyond the command of the LORD—and I must say only what the LORD says'?"

Acts 7 [51]"You stiff-necked people, with uncircumcised hearts and ears! You are just like your fathers: You always resist the Holy Spirit!" (Ps 78:17, 21)

Acts 28 [25]They disagreed among themselves and began to leave after Paul had made this final statement: "The Holy Spirit spoke the truth to your forefathers when he said through Isaiah the prophet: [26]'Go to this people and say, "You will be ever hearing but never understanding; you will be ever seeing but never perceiving." [27]For this people's heart has become calloused; they hardly hear with their ears, and they have closed their eyes. Otherwise they might see with their eyes, hear with their ears, understand with their hearts and turn, and I would heal them.'" (Isa 6:9–10)

1 Cor 2 [12]We have not received the spirit of the world but the Spirit who is from God, that we may understand what God has freely given us.

Heb 3 [7]So, as the Holy Spirit says: "Today, if you hear his voice, [8]do not harden your hearts as you did in the rebellion, during the time of testing in the desert, [9]where your fathers tested and tried me and for forty years saw what I did." (Ps 95:7–11; Exod 17:7)

Heb 10 [15]The Holy Spirit also testifies to us about this. First he says: [16]"This is the covenant I will make with them after that time, says the Lord. I will put my laws in their hearts, and I will write them on their minds." [17]Then he adds: "Their sins and lawless acts I will remember no more." (Jer 31:33–34)

2 Pet 1 [21]For prophecy never had its origin in the will of man, but men spoke from God as they were carried along by the Holy Spirit. (Num 12:6)

e) The Spirit Is Spoken of as Divine

Matt 12 [32]"Anyone who speaks a word against the Son of Man will be forgiven, but anyone who speaks against the Holy Spirit will not be forgiven, either in this age or in the age to come."

Mark 3 [29]"But whoever blasphemes against the Holy Spirit will never be forgiven; he is guilty of an eternal sin."

1 Cor 3 [16]Don't you know that you yourselves are God's temple and that God's Spirit lives in you?

1 Cor 6 [19]Do you not know that your body is a temple of the Holy Spirit, who is in you, whom you have received from God? You are not your own. . . .

Eph 2 [22]And in him you too are being built together to become a dwelling in which God lives by his Spirit.

2. The Spirit's Relationship to the Other Divine Persons

a) The Spirit and the Father

(1) His Spirit

Num 11 [29]But Moses replied, "Are you jealous for my sake? I wish that all the LORD's people were prophets and that the LORD would put his Spirit on them!"
Isa 34 [16]Look in the scroll of the LORD and read: None of these will be missing, not one will lack her mate. For it is his mouth that has given the order, and his Spirit will gather them together.
Isa 48 [16]"Come near me and listen to this: From the first announcement I have not spoken in secret; at the time it happens, I am there." And now the Sovereign LORD has sent me, with his Spirit.
Zech 7 [12]"They made their hearts as hard as flint and would not listen to the law or to the words that the LORD Almighty had sent by his Spirit through the earlier prophets. So the LORD Almighty was very angry."
1 Cor 2 [10]but God has revealed it to us by his Spirit.
The Spirit searches all things, even the deep things of God.
Gal 3 [5]Does God give you his Spirit and work miracles among you because you observe the law, or because you believe what you heard?
Eph 2 [22]And in him you too are being built together to become a dwelling in which God lives by his Spirit.
Eph 3 [16]I pray that out of his glorious riches he may strengthen you with power through his Spirit in your inner being. . . .
1 Thess 4 [8]Therefore, he who rejects this instruction does not reject man but God, who gives you his Holy Spirit.
1 John 4 [12]No one has ever seen God; but if we love one another, God lives in us and his love is made complete in us.
[13]We know that we live in him and he in us, because he has given us of his Spirit.

(2) My Spirit

Gen 6 [3]Then the LORD said, "My Spirit will not contend with man forever, for he is mortal; his days will be a hundred and twenty years."
Isa 30 [1]"Woe to the obstinate children," declares the LORD, "to those who carry out plans that are not mine, forming an alliance, but not by my Spirit, heaping sin upon sin. . . ."
Isa 42 [1]"Here is my servant, whom I uphold, my chosen one in whom I delight; I will put my Spirit on him and he will bring justice to the nations."
Isa 44 [3]"For I will pour water on the thirsty land, and streams on the dry ground; I will pour out my Spirit on your offspring, and my blessing on your descendants."
Isa 59 [21]"As for me, this is my covenant with them," says the LORD. "My Spirit, who is on you, and my words that I have put in your mouth will not depart from your mouth, or from the mouths of your children, or from the mouths of their descendants from this time on and forever," says the LORD.
Ezek 36 [27]"'And I will put my Spirit in you and move you to follow my decrees and be careful to keep my laws.'"
Joel 2 [28]"And afterward, I will pour out my Spirit on all people. Your sons and daughters will prophesy, your old men will dream dreams, your young men will see visions. [29]Even on my servants, both men and women, I will pour out my Spirit in those days."
Hag 2 [5]"'This is what I covenanted with you when you came out of Egypt. And my Spirit remains among you. Do not fear.'"
Zech 4 [6]So he said to me, "This is the word of the LORD to Zerubbabel: 'Not by might nor by power, but by my Spirit,' says the LORD Almighty."
Matt 12 [18]"Here is my servant whom I have chosen, the one I love, in whom I delight; I will put my Spirit on him, and he will proclaim justice to the nations."

(3) Spirit of God

Gen 1 [2]Now the earth was formless and empty, darkness was over the surface of the deep, and the Spirit of God was hovering over the waters.
Exod 31 [3]". . . and I have filled him with the Spirit of God, with skill, ability and knowledge in all kinds of crafts. . . ."
Num 24 [2]When Balaam looked out and saw Israel encamped tribe by tribe, the Spirit of God came upon him. . . .
1 Sam 10 [10]When they arrived at Gibeah, a procession of prophets met him; the Spirit of God came upon him in power, and he joined in their prophesying.
1 Sam 11 [6]When Saul heard their words, the Spirit of God came upon him in power, and he burned with anger.
1 Sam 19 [20]so he sent men to capture him. But when they saw a group of prophets prophesying, with Samuel standing there as their leader, the Spirit of God came upon Saul's men and they also prophesied.
1 Sam 19 [23]So Saul went to Naioth at Ramah. But the Spirit of God came even upon him, and he walked along prophesying until he came to Naioth.
2 Chron 15 [1]The Spirit of God came upon Azariah son of Oded.
2 Chron 24 [20]Then the Spirit of God came upon Zechariah son of Jehoiada the priest. He stood before the people and said, "This is what God says: 'Why do you disobey the LORD's commands? You will not prosper. Because you have forsaken the LORD, he has forsaken you.'"
Job 33 [4]"The Spirit of God has made me; the breath of the Almighty gives me life."
Ezek 11 [24]The Spirit lifted me up and brought me to the exiles in Babylonia in the vision given by the Spirit of God. Then the vision I had seen went up from me. . . .
Rom 8 [9]You, however, are controlled not by the sinful nature but by the Spirit, if the Spirit of God lives in you. And if anyone does not have the Spirit of Christ, he does not belong to Christ.
Rom 8 [14]because those who are led by the Spirit of God are sons of God.
1 Cor 2 [11]For who among men knows the thoughts of a man except the man's spirit within him? In the same way no one knows the thoughts of God except the Spirit of God. . . . [14]The man without the Spirit does not accept the things that come from the Spirit of God, for they are foolishness to him, and he cannot understand them, because they are spiritually discerned.
1 Cor 3 [16]Don't you know that you yourselves are God's temple and that God's Spirit lives in you?
1 Cor 6 [11]And that is what some of you were. But you were washed, you were sanctified, you were justified in the name of the Lord Jesus Christ and by the Spirit of our God.
1 Cor 7 [40]In my judgment, she is happier if she stays as she is—and I think that I too have the Spirit of God.
1 Pet 4 [14]If you are insulted because of the name of Christ, you are blessed, for the Spirit of glory and of God rests on you.
1 John 4 [2]This is how you can recognize the Spirit of God: Every spirit that acknowledges that Jesus Christ has come in the flesh is from God. . . .

(4) Spirit of Him Who Raised Jesus from the Dead

Rom 8 [11]And if the Spirit of him who raised Jesus from the dead is living in you, he who raised Christ from the dead will also give life to your mortal bodies through his Spirit, who lives in you.

(5) Spirit of Yahweh

Judg 3 [10]The Spirit of the LORD came upon him, so that he became Israel's judge and went to war. The LORD gave Cushan-Rishathaim king of Aram into the hands of Othniel, who overpowered him.
Judg 6 [34]Then the Spirit of the LORD came upon Gideon, and he blew a trumpet, summoning the Abiezrites to follow him.
Judg 11 [29]Then the Spirit of the LORD came upon Jephthah. He crossed Gilead and Manasseh, passed through Mizpah of Gilead, and from there he advanced against the Ammonites.
Judg 13 [25]and the Spirit of the LORD began to stir him while he was in Mahaneh Dan, between Zorah and Eshtaol.
Judg 14 [6]The Spirit of the LORD came upon him in power so that he tore the lion apart with his bare hands as he might have torn a young goat. But he told neither his father nor his mother what he had done.
Judg 14 [19]Then the Spirit of the LORD came upon him in

power. He went down to Ashkelon, struck down thirty of their men, stripped them of their belongings and gave their clothes to those who had explained the riddle. Burning with anger, he went up to his father's house.

Judg 15 [14]As he approached Lehi, the Philistines came toward him shouting. The Spirit of the LORD came upon him in power. The ropes on his arms became like charred flax, and the bindings dropped from his hands.

1 Sam 10 [6]"The Spirit of the LORD will come upon you in power, and you will prophesy with them; and you will be changed into a different person."

1 Sam 16 [13]So Samuel took the horn of oil and anointed him in the presence of his brothers, and from that day on the Spirit of the LORD came upon David in power. Samuel then went to Ramah.

[14]Now the Spirit of the LORD had departed from Saul, and an evil spirit from the LORD tormented him.

2 Sam 23 [2]"The Spirit of the LORD spoke through me; his word was on my tongue."

1 Kings 18 [12]"I don't know where the Spirit of the LORD may carry you when I leave you. If I go and tell Ahab and he doesn't find you, he will kill me. Yet I your servant have worshiped the LORD since my youth."

2 Kings 2 [16]"Look," they said, "we your servants have fifty able men. Let them go and look for your master. Perhaps the Spirit of the LORD has picked him up and set him down on some mountain or in some valley."

"No," Elisha replied, "do not send them."

2 Chron 20 [14]Then the Spirit of the LORD came upon Jahaziel son of Zechariah, the son of Benaiah, the son of Jeiel, the son of Mattaniah, a Levite and descendant of Asaph, as he stood in the assembly.

Isa 11 [2]The Spirit of the LORD will rest on him—the Spirit of wisdom and of understanding, the Spirit of counsel and of power, the Spirit of knowledge and of the fear of the LORD. . . .

Isa 40 [13]Who has understood the mind [spirit] of the LORD, or instructed him as his counselor?

Isa 63 [14]like cattle that go down to the plain, they were given rest by the Spirit of the LORD. This is how you guided your people to make for yourself a glorious name.

Ezek 11 [5]Then the Spirit of the LORD came upon me, and he told me to say: "This is what the LORD says: That is what you are saying, O house of Israel, but I know what is going through your mind."

Ezek 37 [1]The hand of the LORD was upon me, and he brought me out by the Spirit of the LORD and set me in the middle of a valley; it was full of bones.

Mic 3 [8]But as for me, I am filled with power, with the Spirit of the LORD, and with justice and might, to declare to Jacob his transgression, to Israel his sin.

(6) Spirit of the Living God

2 Cor 3 [3]You show that you are a letter from Christ, the result of our ministry, written not with ink but with the Spirit of the living God, not on tablets of stone but on tablets of human hearts.

(7) Spirit of the Lord

Isa 11 [2]The Spirit of the LORD will rest on him—the Spirit of wisdom and of understanding, the Spirit of counsel and of power, the Spirit of knowledge and of the fear of the LORD. . . .

Luke 4 [18]"The Spirit of the Lord is on me, because he has anointed me to preach good news to the poor. He has sent me to proclaim freedom for the prisoners and recovery of sight for the blind, to release the oppressed. . . ."

Acts 5 [9]Peter said to her, "How could you agree to test the Spirit of the Lord? Look! The feet of the men who buried your husband are at the door, and they will carry you out also."

Acts 8 [39]When they came up out of the water, the Spirit of the Lord suddenly took Philip away, and the eunuch did not see him again, but went on his way rejoicing.

(8) Spirit of the Sovereign Lord

Isa 61 [1]The Spirit of the Sovereign LORD is on me, because the LORD has anointed me to preach good news to the poor. He has sent me to bind up the brokenhearted, to proclaim freedom for the captives and release from darkness for the prisoners. . . .

(9) Spirit of Your Father

Matt 10 [20]". . . for it will not be you speaking, but the Spirit of your Father speaking through you."

(10) Your Spirit

Neh 9 [20]"You gave your good Spirit to instruct them. You did not withhold your manna from their mouths, and you gave them water for their thirst. . . . [30]For many years you were patient with them. By your Spirit you admonished them through your prophets. Yet they paid no attention, so you handed them over to the neighboring peoples."

Ps 104 [30]When you send your Spirit, they are created, and you renew the face of the earth.

Ps 139 [7]Where can I go from your Spirit? Where can I flee from your presence?

Ps 143 [10]Teach me to do your will, for you are my God; may your good Spirit lead me on level ground.

b) The Spirit and the Son

(1) Spirit of Christ

Rom 8 [9]You, however, are controlled not by the sinful nature but by the Spirit, if the Spirit of God lives in you. And if anyone does not have the Spirit of Christ, he does not belong to Christ.

1 Pet 1 [11]trying to find out the time and circumstances to which the Spirit of Christ in them was pointing when he predicted the sufferings of Christ and the glories that would follow.

(2) Spirit of His Son

Gal 4 [6]Because you are sons, God sent the Spirit of his Son into our hearts, the Spirit who calls out, "*Abba*, Father."

(3) Spirit of Jesus

Acts 16 [7]When they came to the border of Mysia, they tried to enter Bithynia, but the Spirit of Jesus would not allow them to.

(4) Spirit of Jesus Christ

Phil 1 [19]for I know that through your prayers and the help given by the Spirit of Jesus Christ, what has happened to me will turn out for my deliverance.

3. The Spirit's Divine Qualities

a) Eternal

John 14 [16]"And I will ask the Father, and he will give you another Counselor to be with you forever. . . ."

Heb 9 [14]How much more, then, will the blood of Christ, who through the eternal Spirit offered himself unblemished to God, cleanse our consciences from acts that lead to death, so that we may serve the living God!

b) Good

Neh 9 [20]"You gave your good Spirit to instruct them. You did not withhold your manna from their mouths, and you gave them water for their thirst."

Ps 143 [10]Teach me to do your will, for you are my God; may your good Spirit lead me on level ground.

c) Holy

Ps 51 [11]Do not cast me from your presence or take your Holy Spirit from me.

Isa 63 [10]Yet they rebelled and grieved his Holy Spirit. So he turned and became their enemy and he himself fought against them.

[11]Then his people recalled the days of old, the days of Moses and his people—where is he who brought them through the sea, with the shepherd of his flock? Where is he who set his Holy Spirit among them . . . ?

Mark 1 [8]"I baptize you with water, but he will baptize you with the Holy Spirit."

Luke 1 [35]The angel answered, "The Holy Spirit will come upon you, and the power of the Most High will overshadow you. So the holy one to be born will be called the Son of God."

John 14 [26]"But the Counselor, the Holy Spirit, whom the Father will send in my name, will teach you all things and will remind you of everything I have said to you."

Acts 1 [8]"But you will receive power when the Holy Spirit comes on you; and you will be my witnesses in Jerusalem, and in all Judea and Samaria, and to the ends of the earth."

Acts 7 [51]"You stiff-necked people, with uncircumcised hearts and ears! You are just like your fathers: You always resist the Holy Spirit!"

Acts 10 [44]While Peter was still speaking these words, the Holy Spirit came on all who heard the message. [45]The circumcised believers who had come with Peter were astonished that the gift of the Holy Spirit had been poured out even on the Gentiles. [46]For they heard them speaking in tongues and praising God.

Then Peter said, [47]"Can anyone keep these people from being baptized with water? They have received the Holy Spirit just as we have."

Acts 15 [28]It seemed good to the Holy Spirit and to us not to burden you with anything beyond the following requirements. . . .

Acts 28 [25]They disagreed among themselves and began to leave after Paul had made this final statement: "The Holy Spirit spoke the truth to your forefathers when he said through Isaiah the prophet . . ."

Rom 1 [4]and who through the Spirit of holiness was declared with power to be the Son of God by his resurrection from the dead: Jesus Christ our Lord.

Rom 5 [5]And hope does not disappoint us, because God has poured out his love into our hearts by the Holy Spirit, whom he has given us.

Rom 14 [17]For the kingdom of God is not a matter of eating and drinking, but of righteousness, peace and joy in the Holy Spirit. . . .

Rom 15 [13]May the God of hope fill you with all joy and peace as you trust in him, so that you may overflow with hope by the power of the Holy Spirit.

Rom 15 [16]to be a minister of Christ Jesus to the Gentiles with the priestly duty of proclaiming the gospel of God, so that the Gentiles might become an offering acceptable to God, sanctified by the Holy Spirit.

1 Cor 6 [19]Do you not know that your body is a temple of the Holy Spirit, who is in you, whom you have received from God? You are not your own. . . .

2 Cor 6 [6]in purity, understanding, patience and kindness; in the Holy Spirit and in sincere love . . .

Eph 1 [13]And you also were included in Christ when you heard the word of truth, the gospel of your salvation. Having believed, you were marked in him with a seal, the promised Holy Spirit. . . .

Eph 4 [30]And do not grieve the Holy Spirit of God, with whom you were sealed for the day of redemption.

1 Thess 1 [5]because our gospel came to you not simply with words, but also with power, with the Holy Spirit and with deep conviction. You know how we lived among you for your sake. [6]You became imitators of us and of the Lord; in spite of severe suffering, you welcomed the message with the joy given by the Holy Spirit.

2 Tim 1 [14]Guard the good deposit that was entrusted to you—guard it with the help of the Holy Spirit who lives in us.

Titus 3 [5]he saved us, not because of righteous things we had done, but because of his mercy. He saved us through the washing of rebirth and renewal by the Holy Spirit. . . .

Heb 2 [4]God also testified to it by signs, wonders and various miracles, and gifts of the Holy Spirit distributed according to his will.

Heb 9 [8]The Holy Spirit was showing by this that the way into the Most Holy Place had not yet been disclosed as long as the first tabernacle was still standing.

Heb 10 [15]The Holy Spirit also testifies to us about this. First he says . . .

1 Pet 1 [12]It was revealed to them that they were not serving themselves but you, when they spoke of the things that have now been told you by those who have preached the gospel to you by the Holy Spirit sent from heaven. Even angels long to look into these things.

2 Pet 1 [21]For prophecy never had its origin in the will of man, but men spoke from God as they were carried along by the Holy Spirit.

Jude [20]But you, dear friends, build yourselves up in your most holy faith and pray in the Holy Spirit.

d) Holy One

1 John 2 [20]But you have an anointing from the Holy One, and all of you know the truth.

e) Love

Rom 15 [30]I urge you, brothers, by our Lord Jesus Christ and by the love of the Spirit, to join me in my struggle by praying to God for me.

Gal 5 [22]But the fruit of the Spirit is love, joy, peace, patience, kindness, goodness, faithfulness. . . .

f) Omnipresent

Ps 139 [7]Where can I go from your Spirit? Where can I flee from your presence? [8]If I go up to the heavens, you are there; if I make my bed in the depths, you are there.

John 14 [16]"And I will ask the Father, and he will give you another Counselor to be with you forever—[17]the Spirit of truth. The world cannot accept him, because it neither sees him nor knows him. But you know him, for he lives with you and will be in you."

Eph 2 [18]For through him we both have access to the Father by one Spirit.

[19]Consequently, you are no longer foreigners and aliens, but fellow citizens with God's people and members of God's household, [20]built on the foundation of the apostles and prophets, with Christ Jesus himself as the chief cornerstone. [21]In him the whole building is joined together and rises to become a holy temple in the Lord. [22]And in him you too are being built together to become a dwelling in which God lives by his Spirit.

g) Omniscient

Isa 40 [13]Who has understood the mind of the LORD, or instructed him as his counselor? [14]Whom did the LORD consult to enlighten him, and who taught him the right way? Who was it that taught him knowledge or showed him the path of understanding?

John 14 [26]"But the Counselor, the Holy Spirit, whom the Father will send in my name, will teach you all things and will remind you of everything I have said to you."

John 16 [13]"But when he, the Spirit of truth, comes, he will guide you into all truth. He will not speak on his own; he will speak only what he hears, and he will tell you what is yet to come."

1 Cor 2 [10]but God has revealed it to us by his Spirit.

The Spirit searches all things, even the deep things of God. [11]For who among men knows the thoughts of a man except the man's spirit within him? In the same way no one knows the thoughts of God except the Spirit of God.

h) One Spirit

Eph 4 [4]There is one body and one Spirit—just as you were called to one hope when you were called. . . .

i) Power

Gen 1 [2]Now the earth was formless and empty, darkness was over the surface of the deep, and the Spirit of God was hovering over the waters.

Isa 11 [2]The Spirit of the LORD will rest on him—the Spirit of wisdom and understanding, the Spirit of counsel and of power, the Spirit of knowledge and of the fear of the LORD. . . .

Zech 4 [6]So he said to me, "This is the word of the LORD to Zerubbabel: 'Not by might nor by power, but by my Spirit,' says the LORD Almighty."

Rom 15 [13]May the God of hope fill you with all joy and peace as you trust in him, so that you may overflow with hope by the power of the Holy Spirit.

Rom 15 [19]by the power of signs and miracles, through the power of the Spirit. So from Jerusalem all the way around to Illyricum, I have fully proclaimed the gospel of Christ.

1 Cor 12 [4]There are different kinds of gifts, but the same Spirit. [5]There are different kinds of service, but the same Lord. [6]There are different kinds of working, but the same God works all of them in all men.

[7]Now to each one the manifestation of the Spirit is given for the common good. . . . [11]All these are the work of one and the same Spirit, and he gives them to each one, just as he determines.

2 Cor 3 [17]Now the Lord is the Spirit, and where the Spirit of the Lord is, there is freedom. [18]And we, who with unveiled faces all reflect the Lord's glory, are being transformed into his likeness with ever-increasing glory, which comes from the Lord, who is the Spirit.
1 Pet 3 [18]For Christ died for sins once for all, the righteous for the unrighteous, to bring you to God. He was put to death in the body but made alive by the Spirit. . . .

j) Power of the Most High

Luke 1 [35]The angel answered, "The Holy Spirit will come upon you, and the power of the Most High will overshadow you. So the holy one to be born will be called the Son of God."

k) Spirit of Glory

1 Pet 4 [14]If you are insulted because of the name of Christ, you are blessed, for the Spirit of glory and of God rests on you.

l) Spirit of Grace

Heb 10 [29]How much more severely do you think a man deserves to be punished who has trampled the Son of God under foot, who has treated as an unholy thing the blood of the covenant that sanctified him, and who has insulted the Spirit of grace?

m) Spirit of Life

Rom 8 [2]because through Christ Jesus the law of the Spirit of life set me free from the law of sin and death.

n) Spirit of Truth

John 14 [16]"And I will ask the Father, and he will give you another Counselor to be with you forever—[17]the Spirit of truth. The world cannot accept him, because it neither sees him nor knows him. But you know him, for he lives with you and will be in you."
John 15 [26]"When the Counselor comes, whom I will send to you from the Father, the Spirit of truth who goes out from the Father, he will testify about me."
John 16 [13]"But when he, the Spirit of truth, comes, he will guide you into all truth. He will not speak on his own; he will speak only what he hears, and he will tell you what is yet to come."
1 John 4 [6]We are from God, and whoever knows God listens to us; but whoever is not from God does not listen to us. This is how we recognize the Spirit of truth and the spirit of falsehood.
1 John 5 [6]This is the one who came by water and blood—Jesus Christ. He did not come by water only, but by water and blood. And it is the Spirit who testifies, because the Spirit is the truth.

o) Spirit of Wisdom and Revelation

Isa 11 [2]The Spirit of the LORD will rest on him—the Spirit of wisdom and of understanding, the Spirit of counsel and of power, the Spirit of knowledge and of the fear of the LORD. . . .
Eph 1 [17]I keep asking that the God of our Lord Jesus Christ, the glorious Father, may give you the Spirit of wisdom and revelation, so that you may know him better.

B. The Spirit Is Said to Possess Equality with Divinity

1. Equality with Deity Expressed in Benediction

2 Cor 13 [14]May the grace of the Lord Jesus Christ, and the love of God, and the fellowship of the Holy Spirit be with you all.

2. Equality with Deity Expressed in Prayer

Eph 3 [16]I pray that out of his glorious riches he may strengthen you with power through his Spirit in your inner being, [17]so that Christ may dwell in your hearts through faith. And I pray that you, being rooted and established in love, [18]may have power, together with all the saints, to grasp how wide and long and high and deep is the love of Christ, [19]and to know this love that surpasses knowledge—that you may be filled to the measure of all the fullness of God.

3. Equality with Deity Expressed in Redemption

1 Pet 1 [2]who have been chosen according to the foreknowledge of God the Father, through the sanctifying work of the Spirit, for obedience to Jesus Christ and sprinkling by his blood: Grace and peace be yours in abundance.

4. Equality with Deity Expressed in the Baptismal Formula

Matt 28 [19]"Therefore go and make disciples of all nations, baptizing them in the name of the Father and of the Son and of the Holy Spirit. . . ."

5. Equality with Deity Expressed in the Church

Eph 2 [22]And in him you too are being built together to become a dwelling in which God lives by his Spirit.

6. Equality with Deity Expressed in the Distribution of Gifts

1 Cor 12 [4]There are different kinds of gifts, but the same Spirit. [5]There are different kinds of service, but the same Lord. [6]There are different kinds of working, but the same God works all of them in all men.

7. Equality with Deity Expressed in the Mystery of Christ

Eph 3 [4]In reading this, then, you will be able to understand my insight into the mystery of Christ, [5]which was not made known to men in other generations as it has now been revealed by the Spirit to God's holy apostles and prophets. [6]This mystery is that through the gospel the Gentiles are heirs together with Israel, members together of one body, and sharers together in the promise in Christ Jesus.

8. Equality with Deity Expressed in Unity

Eph 4 [4]There is one body and one Spirit—just as you were called to one hope when you were called—[5]one Lord, one faith, one baptism; [6]one God and Father of all, who is over all and through all and in all.

9. Equality with Deity Expressed in Witness

Luke 12 [11]"When you are brought before synagogues, rulers and authorities, do not worry about how you will defend yourselves or what you will say, [12]for the Holy Spirit will teach you at that time what you should say." (cf. Luke 21:12–15)

C. The Spirit Has a Divine Source

1. The Spirit Proceeds from the Father

Ps 104 [30]When you send your Spirit, they are created, and you renew the face of the earth.
Rom 8 [9]You, however, are controlled not by the sinful nature but by the Spirit, if the Spirit of God lives in you. And if anyone does not have the Spirit of Christ, he does not belong to Christ.
1 Cor 2 [11]For who among men knows the thoughts of a man except the man's spirit within him? In the same way no one knows the thoughts of God except the Spirit of God. [12]We have not received the spirit of the world but the Spirit who is from God, that we may understand what God has freely given us.

2. The Spirit Proceeds from the Son

John 16 [7]"But I tell you the truth: It is for your good that I am going away. Unless I go away, the Counselor will not come to you; but if I go, I will send him to you."
Rom 8 [9]You, however, are controlled not by the sinful nature but by the Spirit, if the Spirit of God lives in you. And if anyone does not have the Spirit of Christ, he does not belong to Christ.

3. The Spirit Proceeds from Father and Son

Luke 24 [49]"I am going to send you what my Father has promised; but stay in the city until you have been clothed with power from on high."
John 15 [26]"When the Counselor comes, whom I will send to you from the Father, the Spirit of truth who goes out from the Father, he will testify about me."
John 16 [13]"But when he, the Spirit of truth, comes, he will guide you into all truth. He will not speak on his own; he will speak only what he hears, and he will tell you what is yet to come. [14]He will bring glory to me by taking from what is mine and making it known to you. [15]All that belongs to the Father is mine. That is why I said the Spirit will take from what is mine and make it known to you."
Acts 2 [33]"Exalted to the right hand of God, he has received from the Father the promised Holy Spirit and has poured out what you now see and hear."
Gal 4 [6]Because you are sons, God sent the Spirit of his Son into our hearts, the Spirit who calls out, "*Abba*, Father."

4. The Spirit Proceeds from Heaven

1 Pet 1 [12]It was revealed to them that they were not serving themselves but you, when they spoke of the things that have now been told you by those who have preached the gospel to you by the Holy Spirit sent from heaven. Even angels long to look into these things.

D. The Spirit's Work Is Divine

1. The Spirit Anoints

Acts 10 [38]". . . how God anointed Jesus of Nazareth with the Holy Spirit and power, and how he went around doing good and healing all who were under the power of the devil, because God was with him."
1 John 2 [20]But you have an anointing from the Holy One, and all of you know the truth. . . . [27]As for you, the anointing you received from him remains in you, and you do not need anyone to teach you. But as his anointing teaches you about all things and as that anointing is real, not counterfeit—just as it has taught you, remain in him.

2. The Spirit Calls

2 Thess 2 [13]But we ought always to thank God for you, brothers loved by the Lord, because from the beginning God chose you to be saved through the sanctifying work of the Spirit and through belief in the truth. [14]He called you to this through our gospel, that you might share in the glory of our Lord Jesus Christ.

3. The Spirit Contends

Gen 6 [3]Then the LORD said, "My Spirit will not contend with man forever, for he is mortal; his days will be a hundred and twenty years."

4. The Spirit Convicts

John 16 [7]"But I tell you the truth: It is for your good that I am going away. Unless I go away, the Counselor will not come to you; but if I go, I will send him to you. [8]When he comes, he will convict the world of guilt in regard to sin and righteousness and judgment: [9]in regard to sin, because men do not believe in me; [10]in regard to righteousness, because I am going to the Father, where you can see me no longer; [11]and in regard to judgment, because the prince of this world now stands condemned."

5. The Spirit Counsels

John 14 [16]"And I will ask the Father, and he will give you another Counselor to be with you forever—[17]the Spirit of truth. The world cannot accept him, because it neither sees him nor knows him. But you know him, for he lives with you and will be in you."
John 14 [26]"But the Counselor, the Holy Spirit, whom the Father will send in my name, will teach you all things and will remind you of everything I have said to you."
John 15 [26]"When the Counselor comes, whom I will send to you from the Father, the Spirit of truth who goes out from the Father, he will testify about me."
John 16 [7]"But I tell you the truth: It is for your good that I am going away. Unless I go away, the Counselor will not come to you; but if I go, I will send him to you."

6. The Spirit Creates

Gen 1 [2]Now the earth was formless and empty, darkness was over the surface of the deep, and the Spirit of God was hovering over the waters.
[3]And God said, "Let there be light," and there was light.
Job 33 [4]"The Spirit of God has made me; the breath of the Almighty gives me life."
Ps 104 [30]When you send your Spirit, they are created, and you renew the face of the earth.
Isa 40 [12]Who has measured the waters in the hollow of his hand, or with the breadth of his hand marked off the heavens? Who has held the dust of the earth in a basket, or weighed the mountains on the scales and the hills in a balance? [13]Who has understood the mind [Spirit] of the LORD, or instructed him as his counselor? [14]Whom did the LORD consult to enlighten him, and who taught him the right way? Who was it that taught him knowledge or showed him the path of understanding?

7. The Spirit Empowers

Judg 3 [10]The Spirit of the LORD came upon him, so that he became Israel's judge and went to war. The LORD gave Cushan-Rishathaim king of Aram into the hands of Othniel, who overpowered him.
Judg 6 [34]Then the Spirit of the LORD came upon Gideon, and he blew a trumpet, summoning the Abiezrites to follow him.
Matt 12 [28]"But if I drive out demons by the Spirit of God, then the kingdom of God has come upon you."
Acts 1 [8]"But you will receive power when the Holy Spirit comes on you; and you will be my witnesses in Jerusalem, and in all Judea and Samaria, and to the ends of the earth."
Rom 15 [19]by the power of signs and miracles, through the power of the Spirit. So from Jerusalem all the way around to Illyricum, I have fully proclaimed the gospel of Christ.
Eph 3 [16]I pray that out of his glorious riches he may strengthen you with power through his Spirit in your inner being. . . .

8. The Spirit Fills

Exod 31 [3]". . . and I have filled him with the Spirit of God, with skill, ability and knowledge in all kinds of crafts. . . ."
Acts 2 [1]When the day of Pentecost came, they were all together in one place. [2]Suddenly a sound like the blowing of a violent wind came from heaven and filled the whole house where they were sitting. [3]They saw what seemed to be tongues of fire that separated and came to rest on each of them. [4]All of them were filled with the Holy Spirit and began to speak in other tongues as the Spirit enabled them.
Acts 4 [31]After they prayed, the place where they were meeting was shaken. And they were all filled with the Holy Spirit and spoke the word of God boldly.
Acts 9 [17]Then Ananias went to the house and entered it. Placing his hands on Saul, he said, "Brother Saul, the Lord—Jesus, who appeared to you on the road as you were coming here—has sent me so that you may see again and be filled with the Holy Spirit."
Acts 13 [9]Then Saul, who was also called Paul, filled with the Holy Spirit, looked straight at Elymas and said . . .
Acts 13 [52]And the disciples were filled with joy and with the Holy Spirit.
Eph 5 [18]Do not get drunk on wine, which leads to debauchery. Instead, be filled with the Spirit.

9. The Spirit Generates Christ

Luke 1 [35]The angel answered, "The Holy Spirit will come upon you, and the power of the Most High will overshadow you. So the holy one to be born will be called the Son of God."

10. The Spirit Gives Gifts

See p. 156a, Gifts of the Spirit

11. The Spirit Gives Life

John 6 [63]"The Spirit gives life; the flesh counts for nothing. The words I have spoken to you are spirit and they are life."
Rom 1 [4]and who through the Spirit of holiness was declared with power to be the Son of God by his resurrection from the dead: Jesus Christ our Lord.
1 Pet 3 [18]For Christ died for sins once for all, the righteous for the unrighteous, to bring you to God. He was put to death in the body but made alive by the Spirit. . . .

12. The Spirit Illumines

John 14 [26]"But the Counselor, the Holy Spirit, whom the Father will send in my name, will teach you all things and will remind you of everything I have said to you."

13. The Spirit Indwells

Gen 41 [38]So Pharaoh asked them, "Can we find anyone like this man, one in whom is the spirit of God?"
Num 27 [18]So the LORD said to Moses, "Take Joshua son of Nun, a man in whom is the spirit, and lay your hand on him."
Dan 4 [8]Finally, Daniel came into my presence and I told him the dream. (He is called Belteshazzar, after the name of my god, and the spirit of the holy gods is in him.)
John 14 [17]". . . the Spirit of truth. The world cannot accept him, because it neither sees him nor knows him. But you know him, for he lives with you and will be in you."
Rom 8 [9]You, however, are controlled not by the sinful nature but by the Spirit, if the Spirit of God lives in you. And if anyone does not have the Spirit of Christ, he does not belong to Christ. . . . [11]And if the Spirit of him who raised Jesus from the dead is living in you, he who raised Christ from the dead will also give life to your mortal bodies through his Spirit, who lives in you.
1 Cor 3 [16]Don't you know that you yourselves are God's temple and that God's Spirit lives in you?
1 Cor 6 [19]Do you not know that your body is a temple of the Holy Spirit, who is in you, whom you have received from God? You are not your own. . . .
Gal 4 [6]Because you are sons, God sent the Spirit of his Son into our hearts, the Spirit who calls out, "*Abba*, Father."
1 John 3 [24]Those who obey his commands live in him, and he in them. And this is how we know that he lives in us: We know it by the Spirit he gave us.

14. The Spirit Inspires

2 Tim 3 [16]All Scripture is God-breathed and is useful for teaching, rebuking, correcting and training in righteousness. . . .
2 Pet 1 [21]For prophecy never had its origin in the will of man, but men spoke from God as they were carried along by the Holy Spirit.

15. The Spirit Intercedes

Rom 8 [26]In the same way, the Spirit helps us in our weakness. We do not know what we ought to pray for, but the Spirit himself intercedes for us with groans that words cannot express. [27]And he who searches our hearts knows the mind of the Spirit, because the Spirit intercedes for the saints in accordance with God's will.

16. The Spirit Regenerates

John 3 [3]In reply Jesus declared, "I tell you the truth, no one can see the kingdom of God unless he is born again."

[4]"How can a man be born when he is old?" Nicodemus asked. "Surely he cannot enter a second time into his mother's womb to be born!"

[5]Jesus answered, "I tell you the truth, no one can enter the kingdom of God unless he is born of water and the Spirit. [6]Flesh gives birth to flesh, but the Spirit gives birth to spirit."
Titus 3 [5]he saved us, not because of righteous things we had done, but because of his mercy. He saved us through the washing of rebirth and renewal by the Holy Spirit. . . .

17. The Spirit Reveals

Luke 2 [26]It had been revealed to him by the Holy Spirit that he would not die before he had seen the Lord's Christ.
John 14 [26]"But the Counselor, the Holy Spirit, whom the Father will send in my name, will teach you all things and will remind you of everything I have said to you."
John 16 [12]"I have much more to say to you, more than you can now bear. [13]But when he, the Spirit of truth, comes, he will guide you into all truth. He will not speak on his own; he will speak only what he hears, and he will tell you what is yet to come. [14]He will bring glory to me by taking from what is mine and making it known to you. [15]All that belongs to the Father is mine. That is why I said the Spirit will take from what is mine and make it known to you."
Acts 21 [11]Coming over to us, he took Paul's belt, tied his own hands and feet with it and said, "The Holy Spirit says, 'In this way the Jews of Jerusalem will bind the owner of this belt and will hand him over to the Gentiles.'"
1 Cor 2 [9]However, as it is written: "No eye has seen, no ear has heard, no mind has conceived what God has prepared for those who love him"—[10]but God has revealed it to us by his Spirit.

The Spirit searches all things, even the deep things of God. [11]For who among men knows the thoughts of a man except the man's spirit within him? In the same way no one knows the thoughts of God except the Spirit of God. [12]We have not received the spirit of the world but the Spirit who is from God, that we may understand what God has freely given us. [13]This is what we speak, not in words taught us by human wisdom but in words taught by the Spirit, expressing spiritual truths in spiritual words.

18. The Spirit Sanctifies

Rom 15 [16]to be a minister of Christ Jesus to the Gentiles with the priestly duty of proclaiming the gospel of God, so that the Gentiles might become an offering acceptable to God, sanctified by the Holy Spirit.
1 Cor 6 [11]And that is what some of you were. But you were washed, you were sanctified, you were justified in the name of the Lord Jesus Christ and by the Spirit of our God.
2 Thess 2 [13]But we ought always to thank God for you, brothers loved by the Lord, because from the beginning God chose you to be saved through the sanctifying work of the Spirit and through belief in the truth.
1 Pet 1 [2]who have been chosen according to the foreknowledge of God the Father, through the sanctifying work of the Spirit, for obedience to Jesus Christ and sprinkling by his blood: Grace and peace be yours in abundance.

19. The Spirit Seals

2 Cor 1 [22]set his seal of ownership on us, and put his Spirit in our hearts as a deposit, guaranteeing what is to come.
2 Cor 5 [5]Now it is God who has made us for this very purpose and has given us the Spirit as a deposit, guaranteeing what is to come.
Eph 1 [13]And you also were included in Christ when you heard the word of truth, the gospel of your salvation. Having believed, you were marked in him with a seal, the promised Holy Spirit, [14]who is a deposit guaranteeing our inheritance until the redemption of those who are God's possession—to the praise of his glory.
Eph 4 [30]And do not grieve the Holy Spirit of God, with whom you were sealed for the day of redemption.

20. The Spirit Testifies

John 15 [26]"When the Counselor comes, whom I will send to you from the Father, the Spirit of truth who goes out from the Father, he will testify about me."
Acts 5 [30]"The God of our fathers raised Jesus from the dead—whom you had killed by hanging him on a tree. [31]God exalted him to his own right hand as Prince and Savior that he might give repentance and forgiveness of sins to Israel. [32]We are witnesses of these things, and so is the Holy Spirit, whom God has given to those who obey him."

Rom 8 [16]The Spirit himself testifies with our spirit that we are God's children.
Heb 10 [15]The Holy Spirit also testifies to us about this. First he says: [16]"This is the covenant I will make with them after that time, says the Lord. I will put my laws in their hearts, and I will write them on their minds." [17]Then he adds: "Their sins and lawless acts I will remember no more."

III
The Holy Spirit in the OT

A. The Spirit Is Active in the World at Large

1. The Spirit as Giver of Life

Job 33 [4]"The Spirit of God has made me; the breath of the Almighty gives me life."
Ps 104 [30]When you send your Spirit, they are created, and you renew the face of the earth.
Ezek 37 [14]"'I will put my Spirit in you and you will live, and I will settle you in your own land. Then you will know that I the LORD have spoken, and I have done it, declares the LORD.'"

2. The Spirit as Sustainer of Life

Gen 6 [3]Then the LORD said, "My Spirit will not contend with man forever, for he is mortal; his days will be a hundred and twenty years."
Job 32 [8]"But it is the spirit in a man, the breath of the Almighty, that gives him understanding."
Job 34 [14]"If it were his intention and he withdrew his spirit and breath, [15]all mankind would perish together and man would return to the dust."

B. The Spirit Was Active in Israel's History

1. The Spirit's Presence with Israel

a) The Spirit Accomplished God's Will in the World

Isa 32 [15]till the Spirit is poured upon us from on high, and the desert becomes a fertile field, and the fertile field seems like a forest.
Isa 34 [16]Look in the scroll of the LORD and read: None of these will be missing, not one will lack her mate. For it is his mouth that has given the order, and his Spirit will gather them together.
Zech 4 [6]So he said to me, "This is the word of the LORD to Zerubbabel: 'Not by might nor by power, but by my Spirit,' says the LORD Almighty."

b) The Spirit Aroused and Energized the Judges

Judg 3 [10]The Spirit of the LORD came upon him, so that he became Israel's judge and went to war. The LORD gave Cushan-Rishathaim king of Aram into the hands of Othniel, who overpowered him.
Judg 6 [34]Then the Spirit of the LORD came upon Gideon, and he blew a trumpet, summoning the Abiezrites to follow him.
Judg 11 [29]Then the Spirit of the LORD came upon Jephthah. He crossed Gilead and Manasseh, passed through Mizpah of Gilead, and from there he advanced against the Ammonites.
Judg 13 [24]The woman gave birth to a boy and named him Samson. He grew and the LORD blessed him, [25]and the Spirit of the LORD began to stir him while he was in Mahaneh Dan, between Zorah and Eshtaol.

c) The Spirit Brought a Spirit of Repentance

Ps 51 [1]Have mercy on me, O God, according to your unfailing love; according to your great compassion blot out my transgressions. . . . [11]Do not cast me from your presence or take your Holy Spirit from me.
Isa 63 [10]Yet they rebelled and grieved his Holy Spirit. So he turned and became their enemy and he himself fought against them. [11]Then his people recalled the days of old, the days of Moses and his people—where is he who brought them through the sea, with the shepherd of his flock? Where is he who set his Holy Spirit among them . . . ?

d) The Spirit Brought Messages from God

Num 24 [2]When Balaam looked out and saw Israel encamped tribe by tribe, the Spirit of God came upon him [3]and he uttered his oracle: "The oracle of Balaam son of Beor, the oracle of one whose eye sees clearly. . . ."
2 Sam 23 [2]"The Spirit of the LORD spoke through me; his word was on my tongue."
2 Chron 20 [14]Then the Spirit of the LORD came upon Jahaziel son of Zechariah, the son of Benaiah, the son of Jeiel, the son of Mattaniah, a Levite and descendant of Asaph, as he stood in the assembly.
[15]He said: "Listen, King Jehoshaphat and all who live in Judah and Jerusalem! This is what the LORD says to you: 'Do not be afraid or discouraged because of this vast army. For the battle is not yours, but God's.'"
2 Chron 24 [20]Then the Spirit of God came upon Zechariah son of Jehoiada the priest. He stood before the people and said, "This is what God says: 'Why do you disobey the LORD's commands? You will not prosper. Because you have forsaken the LORD, he has forsaken you.'"
Ezek 11 [5]Then the Spirit of the LORD came upon me, and he told me to say: "This is what the LORD says: That is what you are saying, O house of Israel, but I know what is going through your mind."
Zech 7 [12]"They made their hearts as hard as flint and would not listen to the law or to the words that the LORD Almighty had sent by his Spirit through the earlier prophets. So the LORD Almighty was very angry."

e) The Spirit Brought the Abiding Presence of God

Num 27 [18]So the LORD said to Moses, "Take Joshua son of Nun, a man in whom is the spirit, and lay your hand on him."
1 Sam 10 [6]The Spirit of the LORD will come upon you in power, and you will prophesy with them; and you will be changed into a different person. [7]Once these signs are fulfilled, do whatever your hand finds to do, for God is with you."
1 Sam 16 [13]So Samuel took the horn of oil and anointed him in the presence of his brothers, and from that day on the Spirit of the LORD came upon David in power. Samuel then went to Ramah.
Isa 59 [21]"As for me, this is my covenant with them," says the LORD. "My Spirit, who is on you, and my words that I have put in your mouth will not depart from your mouth, or from the mouths of your children, or from the mouths of their descendants from this time on and forever," says the LORD.
Hag 2 [5]"'This is what I covenanted with you when you came out of Egypt. And my Spirit remains among you. Do not fear.'"

f) The Spirit Brought the Power of God

Judg 14 [6]The Spirit of the LORD came upon him in power so that he tore the lion apart with his bare hands as he might have torn a young goat. But he told neither his father nor his mother what he had done.
Judg 14 [19]Then the Spirit of the LORD came upon him in power. He went down to Ashkelon, struck down thirty of their men, stripped them of their belongings and gave their clothes to those who had explained the riddle. Burning with anger, he went up to his father's house.
Judg 15 [14]As he approached Lehi, the Philistines came toward him shouting. The Spirit of the LORD came upon him in power. The ropes on his arms became like charred flax, and the bindings dropped from his hands. [15]Finding a fresh jawbone of a donkey, he grabbed it and struck down a thousand men.
1 Sam 10 [6]"The Spirit of the LORD will come upon you in power, and you will prophesy with them; and you will be changed into a different person. . . ."
[10]When they arrived at Gibeah, a procession of prophets

met him; the Spirit of God came upon him in power, and he joined in their prophesying.

1 Sam 11 [6]When Saul heard their words, the Spirit of God came upon him in power, and he burned with anger. [7]He took a pair of oxen, cut them into pieces, and sent the pieces by messengers throughout Israel, proclaiming, "This is what will be done to the oxen of anyone who does not follow Saul and Samuel." Then the terror of the LORD fell on the people, and they turned out as one man.

1 Sam 16 [13]So Samuel took the horn of oil and anointed him in the presence of his brothers, and from that day on the Spirit of the LORD came upon David in power. Samuel then went to Ramah.

Mic 3 [8]But as for me, I am filled with power, with the Spirit of the LORD, and with justice and might, to declare to Jacob his transgression, to Israel his sin.

g) The Spirit Gave Guidance

1 Kings 18 [12]"I don't know where the Spirit of the LORD may carry you when I leave you. If I go and tell Ahab and he doesn't find you, he will kill me. Yet I your servant have worshiped the LORD since my youth."

Ps 143 [10]Teach me to do your will, for you are my God; may your good Spirit lead me on level ground.

Isa 48 [16]"Come near me and listen to this: From the first announcement I have not spoken in secret; at the time it happens, I am there." And now the Sovereign LORD has sent me, with his Spirit.

Isa 63 [14]like cattle that go down to the plain, they were given rest by the Spirit of the LORD. This is how you guided your people to make for yourself a glorious name.

h) The Spirit Imparted Knowledge

Exod 35 [31]". . . and he has filled him with the Spirit of God, with skill, ability and knowledge in all kinds of crafts. . . ."

1 Chron 28 [12]He gave him the plans of all that the Spirit had put in his mind for the courts of the temple of the LORD and all the surrounding rooms, for the treasuries of the temple of God and for the treasuries for the dedicated things.

Isa 11 [2]The Spirit of the LORD will rest on him—the Spirit of wisdom and of understanding, the Spirit of counsel and of power, the Spirit of knowledge and of the fear of the LORD. . . .

i) The Spirit Imparted Wisdom and Skill

Gen 41 [38]So Pharaoh asked them, "Can we find anyone like this man, one in whom is the spirit of God?"

[39]Then Pharaoh said to Joseph, "Since God has made all this known to you, there is no one so discerning and wise as you."

Exod 31 [3]". . . and I have filled him with the Spirit of God, with skill, ability and knowledge in all kinds of crafts—[4]to make artistic designs for work in gold, silver and bronze, [5]to cut and set stones, to work in wood, and to engage in all kinds of craftsmanship."

Exod 35 [31]". . . and he has filled him with the Spirit of God, with skill, ability and knowledge in all kinds of crafts. . . ."

Deut 34 [9]Now Joshua son of Nun was filled with the spirit of wisdom because Moses had laid his hands on him. So the Israelites listened to him and did what the LORD had commanded Moses.

Dan 5 [11]"There is a man in your kingdom who has the spirit of the holy gods in him. In the time of your father he was found to have insight and intelligence and wisdom like that of the gods. King Nebuchadnezzar your father—your father the king, I say—appointed him chief of the magicians, enchanters, astrologers and diviners. [12]This man Daniel, whom the king called Belteshazzar, was found to have a keen mind and knowledge and understanding, and also the ability to interpret dreams, explain riddles and solve difficult problems. Call for Daniel, and he will tell you what the writing means."

[13]So Daniel was brought before the king, and the king said to him, "Are you Daniel, one of the exiles my father the king brought from Judah? [14]I have heard that the spirit of the gods is in you and that you have insight, intelligence and outstanding wisdom."

j) The Spirit Inspired People to Prophesy

Num 24 [2]When Balaam looked out and saw Israel encamped tribe by tribe, the Spirit of God came upon him [3]and he uttered his oracle: "The oracle of Balaam son of Beor, the oracle of one whose eye sees clearly. . . ."

2 Sam 23 [2]"The Spirit of the LORD spoke through me; his word was on my tongue."

1 Chron 12 [18]Then the Spirit came upon Amasai, chief of the Thirty, and he said: "We are yours, O David! We are with you, O son of Jesse! Success, success to you, and success to those who help you, for your God will help you."

So David received them and made them leaders of his raiding bands.

2 Chron 15 [1]The Spirit of God came upon Azariah son of Oded. [2]He went out to meet Asa and said to him, "Listen to me, Asa and all Judah and Benjamin. The LORD is with you when you are with him. If you seek him, he will be found by you, but if you forsake him, he will forsake you."

2 Chron 20 [14]Then the Spirit of the LORD came upon Jahaziel son of Zechariah, the son of Benaiah, the son of Jeiel, the son of Mattaniah, a Levite and descendant of Asaph, as he stood in the assembly.

[15]He said: "Listen, King Jehoshaphat and all who live in Judah and Jerusalem! This is what the LORD says to you: 'Do not be afraid or discouraged because of this vast army. For the battle is not yours, but God's.'"

2 Chron 24 [20]Then the Spirit of God came upon Zechariah son of Jehoiada the priest. He stood before the people and said, "This is what God says: 'Why do you disobey the LORD's commands? You will not prosper. Because you have forsaken the LORD, he has forsaken you.'"

Neh 9 [30]"For many years you were patient with them. By your Spirit you admonished them through your prophets. Yet they paid no attention, so you handed them over to the neighboring peoples."

Zech 7 [12]"They made their hearts as hard as flint and would not listen to the law or to the words that the LORD Almighty had sent by his Spirit through the earlier prophets. So the LORD Almighty was very angry."

k) The Spirit Moved People to Action

1 Sam 11 [6]When Saul heard their words, the Spirit of God came upon him in power, and he burned with anger. [7]He took a pair of oxen, cut them into pieces, and sent the pieces by messengers throughout Israel, proclaiming, "This is what will be done to the oxen of anyone who does not follow Saul and Samuel." Then the terror of the LORD fell on the people, and they turned out as one man.

Ezek 2 [2]As he spoke, the Spirit came into me and raised me to my feet, and I heard him speaking to me.

Ezek 3 [14]The Spirit then lifted me up and took me away, and I went in bitterness and in the anger of my spirit, with the strong hand of the LORD upon me.

l) The Spirit Produced Ecstatic Experiences

Num 11 [25]Then the LORD came down in the cloud and spoke with him, and he took of the Spirit that was on him and put the Spirit on the seventy elders. When the Spirit rested on them, they prophesied, but they did not do so again.

[26]However, two men, whose names were Eldad and Medad, had remained in the camp. They were listed among the elders, but did not go out to the Tent. Yet the Spirit also rested on them, and they prophesied in the camp. [27]A young man ran and told Moses, "Eldad and Medad are prophesying in the camp."

[28]Joshua son of Nun, who had been Moses' aide since youth, spoke up and said, "Moses, my lord, stop them!"

[29]But Moses replied, "Are you jealous for my sake? I wish that all the LORD's people were prophets and that the LORD would put his Spirit on them!"

1 Sam 19 [19]Word came to Saul: "David is in Naioth at Ramah"; [20]so he sent men to capture him. But when they saw a group of prophets prophesying, with Samuel standing there as their leader, the Spirit of God came upon Saul's men and they also prophesied. [21]Saul was told about it, and he sent more men, and they prophesied too. Saul sent men a third time, and they also prophesied. [22]Finally, he himself left for Ramah and went to the great cistern at Secu. And he asked, "Where are Samuel and David?"

"Over in Naioth at Ramah," they said.

[23]So Saul went to Naioth at Ramah. But the Spirit of God came even upon him, and he walked along prophesying until he came to Naioth. [24]He stripped off his robes and also prophesied in Samuel's presence. He lay that way all that day and night. This is why people say, "Is Saul also among the prophets?"

Ezek 8 [3]He stretched out what looked like a hand and took me by the hair of my head. The Spirit lifted me up between earth and heaven and in visions of God he took me to Jerusalem, to the entrance to the north gate of the inner court, where the idol that provokes to jealousy stood.

Ezek 11 [24]The Spirit lifted me up and brought me to the exiles in Babylonia in the vision given by the Spirit of God. Then the vision I had seen went up from me. . . .

Joel 2 [28]"And afterward, I will pour out my Spirit on all people. Your sons and daughters will prophesy, your old men will dream dreams, your young men will see visions. [29]Even on my servants, both men and women, I will pour out my Spirit in those days."

m) The Spirit Produced Miraculous Events

2 Kings 2 [13]He picked up the cloak that had fallen from Elijah and went back and stood on the bank of the Jordan. [14]Then he took the cloak that had fallen from him and struck the water with it. "Where now is the LORD, the God of Elijah?" he asked. When he struck the water, it divided to the right and to the left, and he crossed over.

[15]The company of the prophets from Jericho, who were watching, said, "The spirit of Elijah is resting on Elisha." And they went to meet him and bowed to the ground before him. [16]"Look," they said, "we your servants have fifty able men. Let them go and look for your master. Perhaps the Spirit of the LORD has picked him up and set him down on some mountain or in some valley."

"No," Elisha replied, "do not send them."

Ezek 8 [3]He stretched out what looked like a hand and took me by the hair of my head. The Spirit lifted me up between earth and heaven and in visions of God he took me to Jerusalem, to the entrance to the north gate of the inner court, where the idol that provokes to jealousy stood.

Ezek 11 [1]Then the Spirit lifted me up and brought me to the gate of the house of the LORD that faces east. There at the entrance to the gate were twenty-five men, and I saw among them Jaazaniah son of Azzur and Pelatiah son of Benaiah, leaders of the people.

Ezek 43 [5]Then the Spirit lifted me up and brought me into the inner court, and the glory of the LORD filled the temple.

2. The Spirit's Message to Israel

a) A Message of Judgment

2 Chron 24 [20]Then the Spirit of God came upon Zechariah son of Jehoiada the priest. He stood before the people and said, "This is what God says: 'Why do you disobey the LORD's commands? You will not prosper. Because you have forsaken the LORD, he has forsaken you.'"

Ezek 11 [5]Then the Spirit of the LORD came upon me, and he told me to say: "This is what the LORD says: That is what you are saying, O house of Israel, but I know what is going through your mind. [6]You have killed many people in this city and filled its streets with the dead.

[7]"Therefore this is what the Sovereign LORD says: The bodies you have thrown there are the meat and this city is the pot, but I will drive you out of it. [8]You fear the sword, and the sword is what I will bring against you, declares the Sovereign LORD. [9]I will drive you out of the city and hand you over to foreigners and inflict punishment on you. [10]You will fall by the sword, and I will execute judgment on you at the borders of Israel. Then you will know that I am the LORD. [11]This city will not be a pot for you, nor will you be the meat in it; I will execute judgment on you at the borders of Israel. [12]And you will know that I am the LORD, for you have not followed my decrees or kept my laws but have conformed to the standards of the nations around you."

Mic 3 [8]But as for me, I am filled with power, with the Spirit of the LORD, and with justice and might, to declare to Jacob his transgression, to Israel his sin.

b) A Message of Deliverance and Blessing

Num 24 [2]When Balaam looked out and saw Israel encamped tribe by tribe, the Spirit of God came upon him [3]and he uttered his oracle: "The oracle of Balaam son of Beor, the oracle of one whose eye sees clearly, [4]the oracle of one who hears the words of God, who sees a vision from the Almighty, who falls prostrate, and whose eyes are opened:

[5]"How beautiful are your tents, O Jacob, your dwelling places, O Israel!

[6]"Like valleys they spread out, like gardens beside a river, like aloes planted by the LORD, like cedars beside the waters. [7]Water will flow from their buckets; their seed will have abundant water.

"Their king will be greater than Agag; their kingdom will be exalted.

[8]"God brought them out of Egypt; they have the strength of a wild ox. They devour hostile nations and break their bones in pieces; with their arrows they pierce them. [9]Like a lion they crouch and lie down, like a lioness—who dares to rouse them?

"May those who bless you be blessed and those who curse you be cursed!"

2 Sam 23 [2]"The Spirit of the LORD spoke through me; his word was on my tongue. [3]The God of Israel spoke, the Rock of Israel said to me: 'When one rules over men in righteousness, when he rules in the fear of God, [4]he is like the light of morning at sunrise on a cloudless morning, like the brightness after rain that brings the grass from the earth.'

[5]"Is not my house right with God? Has he not made with me an everlasting covenant, arranged and secured in every part? Will he not bring to fruition my salvation and grant me my every desire?"

1 Chron 12 [18]Then the Spirit came upon Amasai, chief of the Thirty, and he said: "We are yours, O David! We are with you, O son of Jesse! Success, success to you, and success to those who help you, for your God will help you."

So David received them and made them leaders of his raiding bands.

2 Chron 15 [1]The Spirit of God came upon Azariah son of Oded. [2]He went out to meet Asa and said to him, "Listen to me, Asa and all Judah and Benjamin. The LORD is with you when you are with him. If you seek him, he will be found by you, but if you forsake him, he will forsake you. [3]For a long time Israel was without the true God, without a priest to teach and without the law. [4]But in their distress they turned to the LORD, the God of Israel, and sought him, and he was found by them. [5]In those days it was not safe to travel about, for all the inhabitants of the lands were in great turmoil. [6]One nation was being crushed by another and one city by another, because God was troubling them with every kind of distress. [7]But as for you, be strong and do not give up, for your work will be rewarded."

2 Chron 20 [14]Then the Spirit of the LORD came upon Jahaziel son of Zechariah, the son of Benaiah, the son of Jeiel, the son of Mattaniah, a Levite and descendant of Asaph, as he stood in the assembly.

[15]He said: "Listen, King Jehoshaphat and all who live in Judah and Jerusalem! This is what the LORD says to you: 'Do not be afraid or discouraged because of this vast army. For the battle is not yours, but God's. . . . [17]You will not have to fight this battle. Take up your positions; stand firm and see the deliverance the LORD will give you, O Judah and Jerusalem. Do not be afraid; do not be discouraged. Go out to face them tomorrow, and the LORD will be with you.'"

Hag 2 [5]"'This is what I covenanted with you when you came out of Egypt. And my Spirit remains among you. Do not fear.'"

3. The Spirit's Presence Withdrawn

Num 11 [25]Then the LORD came down in the cloud and spoke with him, and he took of the Spirit that was on him and put the Spirit on the seventy elders. When the Spirit rested on them, they prophesied, but they did not do so again. . . . [29]But Moses replied, "Are you jealous for my sake? I wish that all the LORD's people were prophets and that the LORD would put his Spirit on them!"

Judg 16 20Then she called, "Samson, the Philistines are upon you!"

He awoke from his sleep and thought, "I'll go out as before and shake myself free." But he did not know that the LORD had left him.

1 Sam 16 14Now the Spirit of the LORD had departed from Saul, and an evil spirit from the LORD tormented him.

1 Kings 22 24Then Zedekiah son of Kenaanah went up and slapped Micaiah in the face. "Which way did the spirit from the LORD go when he went from me to speak to you?" he asked.

Ps 51 11Do not cast me from your presence or take your Holy Spirit from me.

C. The Spirit Is Present in OT Prophecy

1. Prophecies Related to Israel

Isa 32 14The fortress will be abandoned, the noisy city deserted; citadel and watchtower will become a wasteland forever, the delight of donkeys, a pasture for flocks, 15till the Spirit is poured upon us from on high, and the desert becomes a fertile field, and the fertile field seems like a forest.

Isa 44 3"For I will pour water on the thirsty land, and streams on the dry ground; I will pour out my Spirit on your offspring, and my blessing on your descendants. 4They will spring up like grass in a meadow, like poplar trees by flowing streams. 5One will say, 'I belong to the LORD'; another will call himself by the name of Jacob; still another will write on his hand, 'The LORD's,' and will take the name Israel."

Isa 59 21"As for me, this is my covenant with them," says the LORD. "My Spirit, who is on you, and my words that I have put in your mouth will not depart from your mouth, or from the mouths of your children, or from the mouths of their descendants from this time on and forever," says the LORD.

Ezek 36 26"I will give you a new heart and put a new spirit in you; I will remove from you your heart of stone and give you a heart of flesh. 27And I will put my Spirit in you and move you to follow my decrees and be careful to keep my laws. 28You will live in the land I gave your forefathers; you will be my people, and I will be your God. 29I will save you from all your uncleanness. I will call for the grain and make it plentiful and will not bring famine upon you."

Ezek 37 14"'I will put my Spirit in you and you will live, and I will settle you in your own land. Then you will know that I the LORD have spoken, and I have done it, declares the LORD.'"

Ezek 39 25"Therefore this is what the Sovereign LORD says: I will now bring Jacob back from captivity and will have compassion on all the people of Israel, and I will be zealous for my holy name. 26They will forget their shame and all the unfaithfulness they showed toward me when they lived in safety in their land with no one to make them afraid. 27When I have brought them back from the nations and have gathered them from the countries of their enemies, I will show myself holy through them in the sight of many nations. 28Then they will know that I am the LORD their God, for though I sent them into exile among the nations, I will gather them to their own land, not leaving any behind. 29I will no longer hide my face from them, for I will pour out my Spirit on the house of Israel, declares the Sovereign LORD."

2. Prophecies Related to the Messiah

Isa 11 1A shoot will come up from the stump of Jesse; from his roots a Branch will bear fruit. 2The Spirit of the LORD will rest on him—the Spirit of wisdom and of understanding, the Spirit of counsel and of power, the Spirit of knowledge and of the fear of the LORD. . . .

Isa 42 1"Here is my servant, whom I uphold, my chosen one in whom I delight; I will put my Spirit on him and he will bring justice to the nations. 2He will not shout or cry out, or raise his voice in the streets. 3A bruised reed he will not break, and a smoldering wick he will not snuff out. In faithfulness he will bring forth justice. . . ."

Isa 61 1The Spirit of the Sovereign LORD is on me, because the LORD has anointed me to preach good news to the poor. He has sent me to bind up the brokenhearted, to proclaim freedom for the captives and release from darkness for the prisoners, 2to proclaim the year of the LORD's favor and the day of vengeance of our God, to comfort all who mourn, 3and provide for those who grieve in Zion—to bestow on them a crown of beauty instead of ashes, the oil of gladness instead of mourning, and a garment of praise instead of a spirit of despair. They will be called oaks of righteousness, a planting of the LORD for the display of his splendor.

3. Prophecies Related to Mankind

Joel 2 28"And afterward, I will pour out my Spirit on all people. Your sons and daughters will prophesy, your old men will dream dreams, your young men will see visions. 29Even on my servants, both men and women, I will pour out my Spirit in those days."

IV
The Holy Spirit and the Life of Christ

A. The Spirit and John the Baptist

1. The Spirit in John's Birth

Luke 1 41When Elizabeth heard Mary's greeting, the baby leaped in her womb, and Elizabeth was filled with the Holy Spirit.

Luke 1 67His father Zechariah was filled with the Holy Spirit and prophesied. . . .

2. The Spirit in John's Ministry

Luke 1 14"He will be a joy and delight to you, and many will rejoice because of his birth, 15for he will be great in the sight of the Lord. He is never to take wine or other fermented drink, and he will be filled with the Holy Spirit even from birth. 16Many of the people of Israel will he bring back to the Lord their God. 17And he will go on before the Lord, in the spirit and power of Elijah, to turn the hearts of the fathers to their children and the disobedient to the wisdom of the righteous—to make ready a people prepared for the Lord."

3. The Spirit in John's Preaching about Christ

Matt 3 10"The ax is already at the root of the trees, and every tree that does not produce good fruit will be cut down and thrown into the fire.

11"I baptize you with water for repentance. But after me will come one who is more powerful than I, whose sandals I am not fit to carry. He will baptize you with the Holy Spirit and with fire."

Luke 3 16John answered them all, "I baptize you with water. But one more powerful than I will come, the thongs of whose sandals I am not worthy to untie. He will baptize you with the Holy Spirit and with fire."

John 3 34"For the one whom God has sent speaks the words of God, for God gives the Spirit without limit."

B. The Spirit and Jesus in His Early Years

1. The Spirit in Jesus' Conception and Birth

Matt 1 18This is how the birth of Jesus Christ came about: His mother Mary was pledged to be married to Joseph, but before they came together, she was found to be with child through the Holy Spirit. . . . 20But after he had considered this, an angel of the Lord appeared to him in a dream and said, "Joseph son of David, do not be afraid to take Mary home as your wife, because what is conceived in her is from the Holy Spirit."

Luke 1 35The angel answered, "The Holy Spirit will come upon you, and the power of the Most High will overshadow you. So the holy one to be born will be called the Son of God."

2. The Spirit in Jesus' Temple Presentation

Luke 2 [25]Now there was a man in Jerusalem called Simeon, who was righteous and devout. He was waiting for the consolation of Israel, and the Holy Spirit was upon him. [26]It had been revealed to him by the Holy Spirit that he would not die before he had seen the Lord's Christ. [27]Moved by the Spirit, he went into the temple courts. When the parents brought in the child Jesus to do for him what the custom of the Law required . . .

C. The Spirit and Jesus during His Public Ministry

1. The Spirit in Jesus' Baptism

Matt 3 [16]As soon as Jesus was baptized, he went up out of the water. At that moment heaven was opened, and he saw the Spirit of God descending like a dove and lighting on him. [17]And a voice from heaven said, "This is my Son, whom I love; with him I am well pleased."
Luke 3 [21]When all the people were being baptized, Jesus was baptized too. And as he was praying, heaven was opened [22]and the Holy Spirit descended on him in bodily form like a dove. And a voice came from heaven: "You are my Son, whom I love; with you I am well pleased."
John 1 [32]Then John gave this testimony: "I saw the Spirit come down from heaven as a dove and remain on him. [33]I would not have known him, except that the one who sent me to baptize with water told me, 'The man on whom you see the Spirit come down and remain is he who will baptize with the Holy Spirit.'"

2. The Spirit in Jesus' Temptation

Mark 1 [12]At once the Spirit sent him out into the desert, [13]and he was in the desert forty days, being tempted by Satan. He was with the wild animals, and angels attended him.
Luke 4 [1]Jesus, full of the Holy Spirit, returned from the Jordan and was led by the Spirit in the desert, [2]where for forty days he was tempted by the devil. He ate nothing during those days, and at the end of them he was hungry.

3. The Spirit in Jesus' Teaching Ministry

Matt 12 [18]"Here is my servant whom I have chosen, the one I love, in whom I delight; I will put my Spirit on him, and he will proclaim justice to the nations."
Luke 4 [18]"The Spirit of the Lord is on me, because he has anointed me to preach good news to the poor. He has sent me to proclaim freedom for the prisoners and recovery of sight for the blind, to release the oppressed. . . ."

4. The Spirit in Jesus' Exorcisms

Matt 12 [28]"But if I drive out demons by the Spirit of God, then the kingdom of God has come upon you. . . . [31]And so I tell you, every sin and blasphemy will be forgiven men, but the blasphemy against the Spirit will not be forgiven. [32]Anyone who speaks a word against the Son of Man will be forgiven, but anyone who speaks against the Holy Spirit will not be forgiven, either in this age or in the age to come."

5. The Spirit in Jesus' Person

Luke 4 [14]Jesus returned to Galilee in the power of the Spirit, and news about him spread through the whole countryside.
Luke 10 [21]At that time Jesus, full of joy through the Holy Spirit, said, "I praise you, Father, Lord of heaven and earth, because you have hidden these things from the wise and learned, and revealed them to little children. Yes, Father, for this was your good pleasure."
John 3 [34]"For the one whom God has sent speaks the words of God, for God gives the Spirit without limit."
Acts 10 [38]". . . how God anointed Jesus of Nazareth with the Holy Spirit and power, and how he went around doing good and healing all who were under the power of the devil, because God was with him."

D. The Spirit and Jesus during and after His Passion

1. The Spirit in Jesus' Death

Heb 9 [14]How much more, then, will the blood of Christ, who through the eternal Spirit offered himself unblemished to God, cleanse our consciences from acts that lead to death, so that we may serve the living God!

2. The Spirit in Jesus' Resurrection

Rom 1 [4]and who through the Spirit of holiness was declared with power to be the Son of God by his resurrection from the dead: Jesus Christ our Lord.
Rom 8 [11]And if the Spirit of him who raised Jesus from the dead is living in you, he who raised Christ from the dead will also give life to your mortal bodies through his Spirit, who lives in you.
1 Pet 1 [11]trying to find out the time and circumstances to which the Spirit of Christ in them was pointing when he predicted the sufferings of Christ and the glories that would follow.
1 Pet 3 [18]For Christ died for sins once for all, the righteous for the unrighteous, to bring you to God. He was put to death in the body but made alive by the Spirit. . . .

3. The Spirit in the Post-Resurrection Period

Luke 24 [49]"I am going to send you what my Father has promised; but stay in the city until you have been clothed with power from on high."
John 7 [39]By this he meant the Spirit, whom those who believed in him were later to receive. Up to that time the Spirit had not been given, since Jesus had not yet been glorified.
John 15 [26]"When the Counselor comes, whom I will send to you from the Father, the Spirit of truth who goes out from the Father, he will testify about me."
John 16 [7]"But I tell you the truth: It is for your good that I am going away. Unless I go away, the Counselor will not come to you; but if I go, I will send him to you."
John 20 [22]And with that he breathed on them and said, "Receive the Holy Spirit. [23]If you forgive anyone his sins, they are forgiven; if you do not forgive them, they are not forgiven."
Acts 1 [2]until the day he was taken up to heaven, after giving instructions through the Holy Spirit to the apostles he had chosen.
Acts 1 [5]"For John baptized with water, but in a few days you will be baptized with the Holy Spirit."

E. Jesus' Statements about the Spirit

Matt 10 [20]". . . for it will not be you speaking, but the Spirit of your Father speaking through you."
Matt 12 [28]"But if I drive out demons by the Spirit of God, then the kingdom of God has come upon you. . . . [31]And so I tell you, every sin and blasphemy will be forgiven men, but the blasphemy against the Spirit will not be forgiven. [32]Anyone who speaks a word against the Son of Man will be forgiven, but anyone who speaks against the Holy Spirit will not be forgiven, either in this age or in the age to come."
Matt 28 [19]"Therefore go and make disciples of all nations, baptizing them in the name of the Father and of the Son and of the Holy Spirit. . . ."
Mark 12 [36]"David himself, speaking by the Holy Spirit, declared: 'The Lord said to my Lord: "Sit at my right hand until I put your enemies under your feet."'"
Mark 13 [11]"Whenever you are arrested and brought to trial, do not worry beforehand about what to say. Just say whatever is given you at the time, for it is not you speaking, but the Holy Spirit."
Luke 11 [13]"If you then, though you are evil, know how to give good gifts to your children, how much more will your Father in heaven give the Holy Spirit to those who ask him!"

Luke 12 10“And everyone who speaks a word against the Son of Man will be forgiven, but anyone who blasphemes against the Holy Spirit will not be forgiven.”
Luke 12 11“When you are brought before synagogues, rulers and authorities, do not worry about how you will defend yourselves or what you will say, 12for the Holy Spirit will teach you at that time what you should say.”
John 3 5Jesus answered, “I tell you the truth, no one can enter the kingdom of God unless he is born of water and the Spirit. 6Flesh gives birth to flesh, but the Spirit gives birth to spirit. . . . 8The wind blows wherever it pleases. You hear its sound, but you cannot tell where it comes from or where it is going. So it is with everyone born of the Spirit.”
John 6 63“The Spirit gives life; the flesh counts for nothing. The words I have spoken to you are spirit and they are life.”
John 7 38“Whoever believes in me, as the Scripture has said, streams of living water will flow from within him.” 39By this he meant the Spirit, whom those who believed in him were later to receive. Up to that time the Spirit had not been given, since Jesus had not yet been glorified.
John 14 16“And I will ask the Father, and he will give you another Counselor to be with you forever—17the Spirit of truth. The world cannot accept him, because it neither sees him nor knows him. But you know him, for he lives with you and will be in you.”
John 14 26“But the Counselor, the Holy Spirit, whom the Father will send in my name, will teach you all things and will remind you of everything I have said to you.”
John 15 26“When the Counselor comes, whom I will send to you from the Father, the Spirit of truth who goes out from the Father, he will testify about me.”
John 16 7“But I tell you the truth: It is for your good that I am going away. Unless I go away, the Counselor will not come to you; but if I go, I will send him to you. 8When he comes, he will convict the world of guilt in regard to sin and righteousness and judgment: 9in regard to sin, because men do not believe in me; 10in regard to righteousness, because I am going to the Father, where you can see me no longer; 11and in regard to judgment, because the prince of this world now stands condemned.

12“I have much more to say to you, more than you can now bear. 13But when he, the Spirit of truth, comes, he will guide you into all truth. He will not speak on his own; he will speak only what he hears, and he will tell you what is yet to come. 14He will bring glory to me by taking from what is mine and making it known to you. 15All that belongs to the Father is mine. That is why I said the Spirit will take from what is mine and make it known to you.”
Acts 1 8“But you will receive power when the Holy Spirit comes on you; and you will be my witnesses in Jerusalem, and in all Judea and Samaria, and to the ends of the earth.”

V
The Holy Spirit in the Church

A. The Spirit’s Coming and Baptism

1. Foretold by OT Prophets

Isa 44 3“For I will pour water on the thirsty land, and streams on the dry ground; I will pour out my Spirit on your offspring, and my blessing on your descendants.”
Ezek 39 29“I will no longer hide my face from them, for I will pour out my Spirit on the house of Israel, declares the Sovereign LORD.”
Joel 2 28“And afterward, I will pour out my Spirit on all people. Your sons and daughters will prophesy, your old men will dream dreams, your young men will see visions. 29Even on my servants, both men and women, I will pour out my Spirit in those days.”

2. Announced by John the Baptist

Matt 3 11“I baptize you with water for repentance. But after me will come one who is more powerful than I, whose sandals I am not fit to carry. He will baptize you with the Holy Spirit and with fire.”
Mark 1 8“I baptize you with water, but he will baptize you with the Holy Spirit.”
John 1 26“I baptize with water,” John replied, “but among you stands one you do not know. 27He is the one who comes after me, the thongs of whose sandals I am not worthy to untie.” . . .

32Then John gave this testimony: “I saw the Spirit come down from heaven as a dove and remain on him. 33I would not have known him, except that the one who sent me to baptize with water told me, ‘The man on whom you see the Spirit come down and remain is he who will baptize with the Holy Spirit.’”

3. Promised by Christ

Luke 24 49“I am going to send you what my Father has promised; but stay in the city until you have been clothed with power from on high.”
John 14 16“And I will ask the Father, and he will give you another Counselor to be with you forever—17the Spirit of truth. The world cannot accept him, because it neither sees him nor knows him. But you know him, for he lives with you and will be in you. 18I will not leave you as orphans; I will come to you. 19Before long, the world will not see me anymore, but you will see me. Because I live, you also will live. 20On that day you will realize that I am in my Father, and you are in me, and I am in you.”
John 15 26“When the Counselor comes, whom I will send to you from the Father, the Spirit of truth who goes out from the Father, he will testify about me.”
John 16 7“But I tell you the truth: It is for your good that I am going away. Unless I go away, the Counselor will not come to you; but if I go, I will send him to you. 8When he comes, he will convict the world of guilt in regard to sin and righteousness and judgment: 9in regard to sin, because men do not believe in me; 10in regard to righteousness, because I am going to the Father, where you can see me no longer; 11and in regard to judgment, because the prince of this world now stands condemned.

12“I have much more to say to you, more than you can now bear. 13But when he, the Spirit of truth, comes, he will guide you into all truth. He will not speak on his own; he will speak only what he hears, and he will tell you what is yet to come. 14He will bring glory to me by taking from what is mine and making it known to you. 15All that belongs to the Father is mine. That is why I said the Spirit will take from what is mine and make it known to you.”
Acts 1 5“For John baptized with water, but in a few days you will be baptized with the Holy Spirit.”
Acts 1 8“But you will receive power when the Holy Spirit comes on you; and you will be my witnesses in Jerusalem, and in all Judea and Samaria, and to the ends of the earth.”

4. Realized in History

Acts 2 1When the day of Pentecost came, they were all together in one place. 2Suddenly a sound like the blowing of a violent wind came from heaven and filled the whole house where they were sitting. 3They saw what seemed to be tongues of fire that separated and came to rest on each of them. 4All of them were filled with the Holy Spirit and began to speak in other tongues as the Spirit enabled them.
Acts 2 33“Exalted to the right hand of God, he has received from the Father the promised Holy Spirit and has poured out what you now see and hear.”
Acts 5 32“We are witnesses of these things, and so is the Holy Spirit, whom God has given to those who obey him.”
Acts 8 17Then Peter and John placed their hands on them, and they received the Holy Spirit.
Acts 10 44While Peter was still speaking these words, the Holy Spirit came on all who heard the message. 45The circumcised believers who had come with Peter were astonished that the gift of the Holy Spirit had been poured out even on the Gentiles. 46For they heard them speaking in tongues and praising God.

Then Peter said, 47“Can anyone keep these people from

being baptized with water? They have received the Holy Spirit just as we have."

Acts 11 15"As I began to speak, the Holy Spirit came on them as he had come on us at the beginning. 16Then I remembered what the Lord had said: 'John baptized with water, but you will be baptized with the Holy Spirit.' 17So if God gave them the same gift as he gave us, who believed in the Lord Jesus Christ, who was I to think that I could oppose God?"

Acts 19 6When Paul placed his hands on them, the Holy Spirit came on them, and they spoke in tongues and prophesied.

1 Cor 12 13For we were all baptized by one Spirit into one body—whether Jews or Greeks, slave or free—and we were all given the one Spirit to drink.

Gal 4 6Because you are sons, God sent the Spirit of his Son into our hearts, the Spirit who calls out, "*Abba*, Father."

Eph 4 4There is one body and one Spirit—just as you were called to one hope when you were called. . . .

5. Manifested in Believers' Lives

a) Associated with Repentance and Faith

Acts 2 37When the people heard this, they were cut to the heart and said to Peter and the other apostles, "Brothers, what shall we do?"

38Peter replied, "Repent and be baptized, every one of you, in the name of Jesus Christ for the forgiveness of your sins. And you will receive the gift of the Holy Spirit."

Acts 8 12But when they believed Philip as he preached the good news of the kingdom of God and the name of Jesus Christ, they were baptized, both men and women. 13Simon himself believed and was baptized. And he followed Philip everywhere, astonished by the great signs and miracles he saw.

14When the apostles in Jerusalem heard that Samaria had accepted the word of God, they sent Peter and John to them. 15When they arrived, they prayed for them that they might receive the Holy Spirit, 16because the Holy Spirit had not yet come upon any of them; they had simply been baptized into the name of the Lord Jesus. 17Then Peter and John placed their hands on them, and they received the Holy Spirit.

18When Simon saw that the Spirit was given at the laying on of the apostles' hands, he offered them money 19and said, "Give me also this ability so that everyone on whom I lay my hands may receive the Holy Spirit."

20Peter answered: "May your money perish with you, because you thought you could buy the gift of God with money!"

Acts 16 31They replied, "Believe in the Lord Jesus, and you will be saved—you and your household." 32Then they spoke the word of the Lord to him and to all the others in his house. 33At that hour of the night the jailer took them and washed their wounds; then immediately he and all his family were baptized. 34The jailer brought them into his house and set a meal before them; he was filled with joy because he had come to believe in God—he and his whole family.

Acts 18 8Crispus, the synagogue ruler, and his entire household believed in the Lord; and many of the Corinthians who heard him believed and were baptized.

Acts 22 16"'And now what are you waiting for? Get up, be baptized and wash your sins away, calling on his name.'"

b) Expressed Visibly in Water Baptism

Matt 28 19"Therefore go and make disciples of all nations, baptizing them in the name of the Father and of the Son and of the Holy Spirit. . . ."

Acts 2 38Peter replied, "Repent and be baptized, every one of you, in the name of Jesus Christ for the forgiveness of your sins. And you will receive the gift of the Holy Spirit." . . . 41Those who accepted his message were baptized, and about three thousand were added to their number that day.

Acts 8 12But when they believed Philip as he preached the good news of the kingdom of God and the name of Jesus Christ, they were baptized, both men and women. . . .

14When the apostles in Jerusalem heard that Samaria had accepted the word of God, they sent Peter and John to them. 15When they arrived, they prayed for them that they might receive the Holy Spirit, 16because the Holy Spirit had not yet come upon any of them; they had simply been baptized into the name of the Lord Jesus. 17Then Peter and John placed their hands on them, and they received the Holy Spirit.

Acts 9 17Then Ananias went to the house and entered it. Placing his hands on Saul, he said, "Brother Saul, the Lord—Jesus, who appeared to you on the road as you were coming here—has sent me so that you may see again and be filled with the Holy Spirit." 18Immediately, something like scales fell from Saul's eyes, and he could see again. He got up and was baptized. . . .

Acts 10 47"Can anyone keep these people from being baptized with water? They have received the Holy Spirit just as we have." 48So he ordered that they be baptized in the name of Jesus Christ. Then they asked Peter to stay with them for a few days.

Acts 16 15When she and the members of her household were baptized, she invited us to her home. "If you consider me a believer in the Lord," she said, "come and stay at my house." And she persuaded us.

Acts 19 2and asked them, "Did you receive the Holy Spirit when you believed?"

They answered, "No, we have not even heard that there is a Holy Spirit."

3So Paul asked, "Then what baptism did you receive?"

"John's baptism," they replied.

4Paul said, "John's baptism was a baptism of repentance. He told the people to believe in the one coming after him, that is, in Jesus." 5On hearing this, they were baptized into the name of the Lord Jesus. 6When Paul placed his hands on them, the Holy Spirit came on them, and they spoke in tongues and prophesied.

6. Unites Believers Universally with the Body of Christ

Rom 6 1What shall we say, then? Shall we go on sinning so that grace may increase? 2By no means! We died to sin; how can we live in it any longer? 3Or don't you know that all of us who were baptized into Christ Jesus were baptized into his death? 4We were therefore buried with him through baptism into death in order that, just as Christ was raised from the dead through the glory of the Father, we too may live a new life.

5If we have been united with him like this in his death, we will certainly also be united with him in his resurrection. 6For we know that our old self was crucified with him so that the body of sin might be done away with, that we should no longer be slaves to sin—7because anyone who has died has been freed from sin.

8Now if we died with Christ, we believe that we will also live with him. 9For we know that since Christ was raised from the dead, he cannot die again; death no longer has mastery over him. 10The death he died, he died to sin once for all; but the life he lives, he lives to God.

1 Cor 12 12The body is a unit, though it is made up of many parts; and though all its parts are many, they form one body. So it is with Christ. 13For we were all baptized by one Spirit into one body—whether Jews or Greeks, slave or free—and we were all given the one Spirit to drink.

Gal 3 26You are all sons of God through faith in Christ Jesus, 27for all of you who were baptized into Christ have clothed yourselves with Christ.

Eph 4 3Make every effort to keep the unity of the Spirit through the bond of peace. 4There is one body and one Spirit—just as you were called to one hope when you were called—5one Lord, one faith, one baptism. . . .

Col 2 11In him you were also circumcised, in the putting off of the sinful nature, not with a circumcision done by the hands of men but with the circumcision done by Christ, 12having been buried with him in baptism and raised with him through your faith in the power of God, who raised him from the dead.

1 Pet 3 18For Christ died for sins once for all, the righteous for the unrighteous, to bring you to God. He was put to death in the body but made alive by the Spirit. . . . [21]and this water symbolizes baptism that now saves you also—not the removal of dirt from the body but the pledge of a good conscience toward God. It saves you by the resurrection of Jesus Christ, [22]who has gone into heaven and is at God's right hand—with angels, authorities and powers in submission to him.

B. The Spirit's Ministry in the Church

1. The Spirit and Ministry

a) The Spirit Appoints Leaders

Acts 20 [28]"Keep watch over yourselves and all the flock of which the Holy Spirit has made you overseers. Be shepherds of the church of God, which he bought with his own blood."

b) The Spirit Bestows Gifts

1 Cor 12 [4]There are different kinds of gifts, but the same Spirit. [5]There are different kinds of service, but the same Lord. [6]There are different kinds of working, but the same God works all of them in all men.

[7]Now to each one the manifestation of the Spirit is given for the common good. [8]To one there is given through the Spirit the message of wisdom, to another the message of knowledge by means of the same Spirit, [9]to another faith by the same Spirit, to another gifts of healing by that one Spirit, [10]to another miraculous powers, to another prophecy, to another distinguishing between spirits, to another speaking in different kinds of tongues, and to still another the interpretation of tongues. [11]All these are the work of one and the same Spirit, and he gives them to each one, just as he determines.

c) The Spirit Gives Direction to Leaders

Acts 8 [29]The Spirit told Philip, "Go to that chariot and stay near it."
Acts 13 [2]While they were worshiping the Lord and fasting, the Holy Spirit said, "Set apart for me Barnabas and Saul for the work to which I have called them." . . . [4]The two of them, sent on their way by the Holy Spirit, went down to Seleucia and sailed from there to Cyprus.
Acts 16 [6]Paul and his companions traveled throughout the region of Phrygia and Galatia, having been kept by the Holy Spirit from preaching the word in the province of Asia. [7]When they came to the border of Mysia, they tried to enter Bithynia, but the Spirit of Jesus would not allow them to. [8]So they passed by Mysia and went down to Troas. [9]During the night Paul had a vision of a man of Macedonia standing and begging him, "Come over to Macedonia and help us." [10]After Paul had seen the vision, we got ready at once to leave for Macedonia, concluding that God had called us to preach the gospel to them.

d) The Spirit Provides Power for Ministry

Acts 1 [8]"But you will receive power when the Holy Spirit comes on you; and you will be my witnesses in Jerusalem, and in all Judea and Samaria, and to the ends of the earth."
Acts 4 [31]After they prayed, the place where they were meeting was shaken. And they were all filled with the Holy Spirit and spoke the word of God boldly. . . . [33]With great power the apostles continued to testify to the resurrection of the Lord Jesus, and much grace was upon them all.
1 Cor 2 [4]My message and my preaching were not with wise and persuasive words, but with a demonstration of the Spirit's power. . . .
2 Cor 3 [6]He has made us competent as ministers of a new covenant—not of the letter but of the Spirit; for the letter kills, but the Spirit gives life.
1 Thess 1 [5]because our gospel came to you not simply with words, but also with power, with the Holy Spirit and with deep conviction. You know how we lived among you for your sake.
1 Pet 1 [12]It was revealed to them that they were not serving themselves but you, when they spoke of the things that have now been told you by those who have preached the gospel to you by the Holy Spirit sent from heaven. Even angels long to look into these things.

2. The Spirit and the Sacraments

a) Baptism

Matt 28 [19]"Therefore go and make disciples of all nations, baptizing them in the name of the Father and of the Son and of the Holy Spirit. . . ."
1 Cor 12 [13]For we were all baptized by one Spirit into one body—whether Jews or Greeks, slave or free—and we were all given the one Spirit to drink.
1 Pet 3 [21]and this water symbolizes baptism that now saves you also—not the removal of dirt from the body but the pledge of a good conscience toward God. It saves you by the resurrection of Jesus Christ. . . .

b) Worship in General

Eph 5 [18]Do not get drunk on wine, which leads to debauchery. Instead, be filled with the Spirit. [19]Speak to one another with psalms, hymns and spiritual songs. Sing and make music in your heart to the Lord, [20]always giving thanks to God the Father for everything, in the name of our Lord Jesus Christ.

[21]Submit to one another out of reverence for Christ.
Phil 3 [3]For it is we who are the circumcision, we who worship by the Spirit of God, who glory in Christ Jesus, and who put no confidence in the flesh. . . .

3. The Spirit and Sustenance

a) The Spirit Encourages

Acts 9 [31]Then the church throughout Judea, Galilee and Samaria enjoyed a time of peace. It was strengthened; and encouraged by the Holy Spirit, it grew in numbers, living in the fear of the Lord.

b) The Spirit Establishes Growth and Unity

1 Cor 12 [13]For we were all baptized by one Spirit into one body—whether Jews or Greeks, slave or free—and we were all given the one Spirit to drink.
Eph 2 [19]Consequently, you are no longer foreigners and aliens, but fellow citizens with God's people and members of God's household, [20]built on the foundation of the apostles and prophets, with Christ Jesus himself as the chief cornerstone. [21]In him the whole building is joined together and rises to become a holy temple in the Lord. [22]And in him you too are being built together to become a dwelling in which God lives by his Spirit.
Eph 4 [4]There is one body and one Spirit—just as you were called to one hope when you were called. . . .

c) The Spirit Gives Wisdom

Acts 15 [28]It seemed good to the Holy Spirit and to us not to burden you with anything beyond the following requirements. . . .

d) The Spirit Indwells

1 Cor 3 [16]Don't you know that you yourselves are God's temple and that God's Spirit lives in you?

e) The Spirit Intercedes

Rom 8 [26]In the same way, the Spirit helps us in our weakness. We do not know what we ought to pray for, but the Spirit himself intercedes for us with groans that words cannot express. [27]And he who searches our hearts knows the mind of the Spirit, because the Spirit intercedes for the saints in accordance with God's will.
Eph 6 [18]And pray in the Spirit on all occasions with all kinds of prayers and requests. With this in mind, be alert and always keep on praying for all the saints.

f) The Spirit Reveals Christ's Message

Rev 2 [7]"He who has an ear, let him hear what the Spirit says to the churches. To him who overcomes, I will give the right to eat from the tree of life, which is in the paradise of God."

g) The Spirit Sanctifies

Rom 15 [16]to be a minister of Christ Jesus to the Gentiles with the priestly duty of proclaiming the gospel of God, so that the

Gentiles might become an offering acceptable to God, sanctified by the Holy Spirit.

VI The Holy Spirit in the Believer

A. The Fullness of the Spirit

1. The Reality of the Spirit's Fullness

Acts 2 [4]All of them were filled with the Holy Spirit and began to speak in other tongues as the Spirit enabled them.
Acts 4 [8]Then Peter, filled with the Holy Spirit, said to them: "Rulers and elders of the people!"
Acts 4 [31]After they prayed, the place where they were meeting was shaken. And they were all filled with the Holy Spirit and spoke the word of God boldly.
Acts 6 [3]"Brothers, choose seven men from among you who are known to be full of the Spirit and wisdom. We will turn this responsibility over to them. . . ."

[5]This proposal pleased the whole group. They chose Stephen, a man full of faith and of the Holy Spirit; also Philip, Procorus, Nicanor, Timon, Parmenas, and Nicolas from Antioch, a convert to Judaism.
Acts 7 [55]But Stephen, full of the Holy Spirit, looked up to heaven and saw the glory of God, and Jesus standing at the right hand of God.
Acts 9 [17]Then Ananias went to the house and entered it. Placing his hands on Saul, he said, "Brother Saul, the Lord—Jesus, who appeared to you on the road as you were coming here—has sent me so that you may see again and be filled with the Holy Spirit."
Acts 11 [24]He was a good man, full of the Holy Spirit and faith, and a great number of people were brought to the Lord.
Acts 13 [9]Then Saul, who was also called Paul, filled with the Holy Spirit, looked straight at Elymas and said . . .
Acts 13 [52]And the disciples were filled with joy and with the Holy Spirit.

2. The Imperative of the Spirit's Fullness

Eph 5 [18]Do not get drunk on wine, which leads to debauchery. Instead, be filled with the Spirit.

B. Fruit of the Spirit

1. Love

Gal 5 [22]But the fruit of the Spirit is love, joy, peace, patience, kindness, goodness, faithfulness. . . .
Ps 69 [16]Answer me, O Lord, out of the goodness of your love; in your great mercy turn to me.
John 3 [16]"For God so loved the world that he gave his one and only Son, that whoever believes in him shall not perish but have eternal life."
John 13 [34]"A new command I give you: Love one another. As I have loved you, so you must love one another. [35]By this all men will know that you are my disciples, if you love one another."
John 17 [26]"I have made you known to them, and will continue to make you known in order that the love you have for me may be in them and that I myself may be in them."
Rom 5 [5]And hope does not disappoint us, because God has poured out his love into our hearts by the Holy Spirit, whom he has given us. . . . [8]But God demonstrates his own love for us in this: While we were still sinners, Christ died for us.
Rom 12 [9]Love must be sincere. Hate what is evil; cling to what is good.
Rom 13 [10]Love does no harm to its neighbor. Therefore love is the fulfillment of the law.
1 Cor 13 [4]Love is patient, love is kind. It does not envy, it does not boast, it is not proud. [5]It is not rude, it is not self-seeking, it is not easily angered, it keeps no record of wrongs. [6]Love does not delight in evil but rejoices with the truth. [7]It always protects, always trusts, always hopes, always perseveres.

[8]Love never fails. But where there are prophecies, they will cease; where there are tongues, they will be stilled; where there is knowledge, it will pass away. [9]For we know in part and we prophesy in part, [10]but when perfection comes, the imperfect disappears. [11]When I was a child, I talked like a child, I thought like a child, I reasoned like a child. When I became a man, I put childish ways behind me. [12]Now we see but a poor reflection as in a mirror; then we shall see face to face. Now I know in part; then I shall know fully, even as I am fully known.

[13]And now these three remain: faith, hope and love. But the greatest of these is love.
Gal 5 [13]You, my brothers, were called to be free. But do not use your freedom to indulge the sinful nature; rather, serve one another in love. [14]The entire law is summed up in a single command: "Love your neighbor as yourself."
Eph 5 [25]Husbands, love your wives, just as Christ loved the church and gave himself up for her. . . .
1 John 3 [14]We know that we have passed from death to life, because we love our brothers. Anyone who does not love remains in death. . . .

[16]This is how we know what love is: Jesus Christ laid down his life for us. And we ought to lay down our lives for our brothers.
1 John 4 [13]We know that we live in him and he in us, because he has given us of his Spirit. . . . [16]And so we know and rely on the love God has for us.

God is love. Whoever lives in love lives in God, and God in him.

2. Joy

Gal 5 [22]But the fruit of the Spirit is love, joy, peace, patience, kindness, goodness, faithfulness. . . .
John 15 [11]"I have told you this so that my joy may be in you and that your joy may be complete."
John 16 [24]"Until now you have not asked for anything in my name. Ask and you will receive, and your joy will be complete."
Rom 14 [17]For the kingdom of God is not a matter of eating and drinking, but of righteousness, peace and joy in the Holy Spirit. . . .
Rom 15 [13]May the God of hope fill you with all joy and peace as you trust in him, so that you may overflow with hope by the power of the Holy Spirit.
Phil 4 [4]Rejoice in the Lord always. I will say it again: Rejoice!
1 Thess 1 [6]You became imitators of us and of the Lord; in spite of severe suffering, you welcomed the message with the joy given by the Holy Spirit.
1 Thess 5 [16]Be joyful always. . . .
1 Pet 1 [8]Though you have not seen him, you love him; and even though you do not see him now, you believe in him and are filled with an inexpressible and glorious joy. . . .
1 John 1 [4]We write this to make our joy complete.

3. Peace

Gal 5 [22]But the fruit of the Spirit is love, joy, peace, patience, kindness, goodness, faithfulness. . . .
John 14 [27]"Peace I leave with you; my peace I give you. I do not give to you as the world gives. Do not let your hearts be troubled and do not be afraid."
Rom 5 [1]Therefore, since we have been justified through faith, we have peace with God through our Lord Jesus Christ. . . .
Rom 8 [6]The mind of sinful man is death, but the mind controlled by the Spirit is life and peace. . . .
Rom 14 [17]For the kingdom of God is not a matter of eating and drinking, but of righteousness, peace and joy in the Holy Spirit. . . .
Eph 2 [14]For he himself is our peace, who has made the two one and has destroyed the barrier, the dividing wall of hostility, [15]by abolishing in his flesh the law with its commandments and regulations. His purpose was to create in himself one new man out of the two, thus making peace, [16]and in this one body to reconcile both of them to God through the cross, by which he put to death their hostility. [17]He came and preached peace to you who were far away and peace to those who were near.

[18]For through him we both have access to the Father by one Spirit.
Eph 4 [3]Make every effort to keep the unity of the Spirit through the bond of peace.
Phil 4 [7]And the peace of God, which transcends all understanding, will guard your hearts and your minds in Christ Jesus.
1 Thess 5 [13]Hold them in the highest regard in love because of their work. Live in peace with each other.
2 Tim 2 [22]Flee the evil desires of youth, and pursue righteousness, faith, love and peace, along with those who call on the Lord out of a pure heart.

4. Patience

Gal 5 [22]But the fruit of the Spirit is love, joy, peace, patience, kindness, goodness, faithfulness. . . .
Rom 9 [22]What if God, choosing to show his wrath and make his power known, bore with great patience the objects of his wrath—prepared for destruction?
Rom 12 [12]Be joyful in hope, patient in affliction, faithful in prayer.
Eph 4 [2]Be completely humble and gentle; be patient, bearing with one another in love.
Col 1 [11]being strengthened with all power according to his glorious might so that you may have great endurance and patience, and joyfully . . .
Col 3 [12]Therefore, as God's chosen people, holy and dearly loved, clothe yourselves with compassion, kindness, humility, gentleness and patience.
1 Thess 5 [14]And we urge you, brothers, warn those who are idle, encourage the timid, help the weak, be patient with everyone.
1 Tim 1 [16]But for that very reason I was shown mercy so that in me, the worst of sinners, Christ Jesus might display his unlimited patience as an example for those who would believe on him and receive eternal life.
2 Pet 3 [9]The Lord is not slow in keeping his promise, as some understand slowness. He is patient with you, not wanting anyone to perish, but everyone to come to repentance. . . . [15]Bear in mind that our Lord's patience means salvation, just as our dear brother Paul also wrote you with the wisdom that God gave him.

5. Kindness

Gal 5 [22]But the fruit of the Spirit is love, joy, peace, patience, kindness, goodness, faithfulness. . . .
Rom 2 [4]Or do you show contempt for the riches of his kindness, tolerance and patience, not realizing that God's kindness leads you toward repentance?
Rom 11 [22]Consider therefore the kindness and sternness of God: sternness to those who fell, but kindness to you, provided that you continue in his kindness. Otherwise, you also will be cut off.
2 Cor 6 [4]Rather, as servants of God we commend ourselves in every way: in great endurance; in troubles, hardships and distresses; . . . [6]in purity, understanding, patience and kindness; in the Holy Spirit and in sincere love. . . .
Eph 2 [6]And God raised us up with Christ and seated us with him in the heavenly realms in Christ Jesus, [7]in order that in the coming ages he might show the incomparable riches of his grace, expressed in his kindness to us in Christ Jesus.
Col 3 [12]Therefore, as God's chosen people, holy and dearly loved, clothe yourselves with compassion, kindness, humility, gentleness and patience.
Titus 3 [4]But when the kindness and love of God our Savior appeared, [5]he saved us, not because of righteous things we had done, but because of his mercy. He saved us through the washing of rebirth and renewal by the Holy Spirit. . . .
2 Pet 1 [5]For this very reason, make every effort to add to your faith goodness; and to goodness, knowledge; . . . [7]and to godliness, brotherly kindness; and to brotherly kindness, love.

6. Goodness

Gal 5 [22]But the fruit of the Spirit is love, joy, peace, patience, kindness, goodness, faithfulness. . . .
Ps 23 [6]Surely goodness and love will follow me all the days of my life, and I will dwell in the house of the LORD forever.
Rom 8 [28]And we know that in all things God works for the good of those who love him, who have been called according to his purpose.
Rom 15 [14]I myself am convinced, my brothers, that you yourselves are full of goodness, complete in knowledge and competent to instruct one another.
Eph 5 [8]For you were once darkness, but now you are light in the Lord. Live as children of light [9](for the fruit of the light consists in all goodness, righteousness and truth). . . .
Heb 6 [5]who have tasted the goodness of the word of God and the powers of the coming age . . .
1 Pet 2 [3]now that you have tasted that the Lord is good.
2 Pet 1 [3]His divine power has given us everything we need for life and godliness through our knowledge of him who called us by his own glory and goodness. . . .
[5]For this very reason, make every effort to add to your faith goodness; and to goodness, knowledge. . . .

7. Faithfulness

Gal 5 [22]But the fruit of the Spirit is love, joy, peace, patience, kindness, goodness, faithfulness. . . .
Ps 36 [5]Your love, O LORD, reaches to the heavens, your faithfulness to the skies.
Ps 89 [24]"My faithful love will be with him, and through my name his horn will be exalted. [33]. . . but I will not take my love from him, nor will I ever betray my faithfulness."
Ps 92 [1]It is good to praise the LORD and make music to your name, O Most High, [2]to proclaim your love in the morning and your faithfulness at night. . . .
Lam 3 [22]Because of the LORD's great love we are not consumed, for his compassions never fail. [23]They are new every morning; great is your faithfulness.
1 Cor 1 [9]God, who has called you into fellowship with his Son Jesus Christ our Lord, is faithful.
1 Cor 10 [13]No temptation has seized you except what is common to man. And God is faithful; he will not let you be tempted beyond what you can bear. But when you are tempted, he will also provide a way out so that you can stand up under it.
1 Thess 5 [24]The one who calls you is faithful and he will do it.
2 Thess 3 [3]But the Lord is faithful, and he will strengthen and protect you from the evil one.
Heb 3 [6]But Christ is faithful as a son over God's house. And we are his house, if we hold on to our courage and the hope of which we boast.
1 Pet 4 [19]So then, those who suffer according to God's will should commit themselves to their faithful Creator and continue to do good.

8. Gentleness

Gal 5 [22]But the fruit of the Spirit is love, joy, peace, patience, kindness, goodness, faithfulness, [23]gentleness and self-control. Against such things there is no law.
2 Cor 10 [1]By the meekness and gentleness of Christ, I appeal to you—I, Paul, who am "timid" when face to face with you, but "bold" when away!
Eph 4 [2]Be completely humble and gentle; be patient, bearing with one another in love.
Phil 4 [5]Let your gentleness be evident to all. The Lord is near.
Col 3 [12]Therefore, as God's chosen people, holy and dearly loved, clothe yourselves with compassion, kindness, humility, gentleness and patience.
1 Tim 6 [11]But you, man of God, flee from all this, and pursue righteousness, godliness, faith, love, endurance and gentleness.
1 Pet 3 [15]But in your hearts set apart Christ as Lord. Always be prepared to give an answer to everyone who asks you to give the reason for the hope that you have. But do this with gentleness and respect. . . .

9. Self-Control

Gal 5 [22]But the fruit of the Spirit is love, joy, peace, patience, kindness, goodness, faithfulness, [23]gentleness and self-control. Against such things there is no law.

1 Thess 5 [6]So then, let us not be like others, who are asleep, but let us be alert and self-controlled. . . . [8]But since we belong to the day, let us be self-controlled, putting on faith and love as a breastplate, and the hope of salvation as a helmet.
2 Tim 1 [7]For God did not give us a spirit of timidity, but a spirit of power, of love and of self-discipline.
Titus 2 [11]For the grace of God that brings salvation has appeared to all men. [12]It teaches us to say "No" to ungodliness and worldly passions, and to live self-controlled, upright and godly lives in this present age. . . .
1 Pet 1 [13]Therefore, prepare your minds for action; be self-controlled; set your hope fully on the grace to be given you when Jesus Christ is revealed.
2 Pet 1 [5]For this very reason, make every effort to add to your faith goodness; and to goodness, knowledge; [6]and to knowledge, self-control; and to self-control, perseverance; and to perseverance, godliness. . . .

C. Gifts of the Spirit

1. The Source of the Gifts

Rom 12 [6]We have different gifts, according to the grace given us. If a man's gift is prophesying, let him use it in proportion to his faith.
1 Cor 12 [4]There are different kinds of gifts, but the same Spirit. . . . [7]Now to each one the manifestation of the Spirit is given for the common good. . . . [11]All these are the work of one and the same Spirit, and he gives them to each one, just as he determines.
Heb 2 [4]God also testified to it by signs, wonders and various miracles, and gifts of the Holy Spirit distributed according to his will.

2. Identification of the Gifts

a) Acts of Mercy

Rom 12 [6]We have different gifts, according to the grace given us. If a man's gift is prophesying, let him use it in proportion to his faith. [8]. . . if it is encouraging, let him encourage; if it is contributing to the needs of others, let him give generously; if it is leadership, let him govern diligently; if it is showing mercy, let him do it cheerfully.

b) Administration

1 Cor 12 [28]And in the church God has appointed first of all apostles, second prophets, third teachers, then workers of miracles, also those having gifts of healing, those able to help others, those with gifts of administration, and those speaking in different kinds of tongues.

c) Apostleship

1 Cor 12 [28]And in the church God has appointed first of all apostles, second prophets, third teachers, then workers of miracles, also those having gifts of healing, those able to help others, those with gifts of administration, and those speaking in different kinds of tongues. [29]Are all apostles? Are all prophets? Are all teachers? Do all work miracles?
Eph 4 [11]It was he who gave some to be apostles, some to be prophets, some to be evangelists, and some to be pastors and teachers. . . .

d) Discernment of Spirits

1 Cor 12 [10]to another miraculous powers, to another prophecy, to another distinguishing between spirits, to another speaking in different kinds of tongues, and to still another the interpretation of tongues.

e) Encouragement

Rom 12 [8]if it is encouraging, let him encourage; if it is contributing to the needs of others, let him give generously; if it is leadership, let him govern diligently; if it is showing mercy, let him do it cheerfully.
1 Cor 14 [26]What then shall we say, brothers? When you come together, everyone has a hymn, or a word of instruction, a revelation, a tongue or an interpretation. All of these must be done for the strengthening of the church.

f) Evangelism

Eph 4 [11]It was he who gave some to be apostles, some to be prophets, some to be evangelists, and some to be pastors and teachers. . . .

g) Faith

1 Cor 12 [9]to another faith by the same Spirit, to another gifts of healing by that one Spirit . . .
1 Cor 13 [2]If I have the gift of prophecy and can fathom all mysteries and all knowledge, and if I have a faith that can move mountains, but have not love, I am nothing.

h) Giving Aid

Rom 12 [8]if it is encouraging, let him encourage; if it is contributing to the needs of others, let him give generously; if it is leadership, let him govern diligently; if it is showing mercy, let him do it cheerfully.
1 Cor 13 [3]If I give all I possess to the poor and surrender my body to the flames, but have not love, I gain nothing.

i) Healing

1 Cor 12 [9]to another faith by the same Spirit, to another gifts of healing by that one Spirit . . .
1 Cor 12 [28]And in the church God has appointed first of all apostles, second prophets, third teachers, then workers of miracles, also those having gifts of healing, those able to help others, those with gifts of administration, and those speaking in different kinds of tongues. [29]Are all apostles? Are all prophets? Are all teachers? Do all work miracles?

j) Helping

1 Cor 12 [28]And in the church God has appointed first of all apostles, second prophets, third teachers, then workers of miracles, also those having gifts of healing, those able to help others, those with gifts of administration, and those speaking in different kinds of tongues.

k) Interpreting Tongues

1 Cor 12 [10]to another miraculous powers, to another prophecy, to another distinguishing between spirits, to another speaking in different kinds of tongues, and to still another the interpretation of tongues.
1 Cor 12 [30]Do all have gifts of healing? Do all speak in tongues? Do all interpret?
1 Cor 14 [26]What then shall we say, brothers? When you come together, everyone has a hymn, or a word of instruction, a revelation, a tongue or an interpretation. All of these must be done for the strengthening of the church.

l) Leadership

Rom 12 [8]if it is encouraging, let him encourage; if it is contributing to the needs of others, let him give generously; if it is leadership, let him govern diligently; if it is showing mercy, let him do it cheerfully.

m) Prophecy

Rom 12 [6]We have different gifts, according to the grace given us. If a man's gift is prophesying, let him use it in proportion to his faith.
1 Cor 12 [10]to another miraculous powers, to another prophecy, to another distinguishing between spirits, to another speaking in different kinds of tongues, and to still another the interpretation of tongues.
1 Cor 12 [28]And in the church God has appointed first of all apostles, second prophets, third teachers, then workers of miracles, also those having gifts of healing, those able to help others, those with gifts of administration, and those speaking in different kinds of tongues. [29]Are all apostles? Are all prophets? Are all teachers? Do all work miracles?
1 Cor 13 [2]If I have the gift of prophecy and can fathom all mysteries and all knowledge, and if I have a faith that can move mountains, but have not love, I am nothing.
1 Cor 14 [26]What then shall we say, brothers? When you come together, everyone has a hymn, or a word of instruction, a revelation, a tongue or an interpretation. All of these must be done for the strengthening of the church. . . .

[29]Two or three prophets should speak, and the others should weigh carefully what is said. [30]And if a revelation comes

to someone who is sitting down, the first speaker should stop. [31]For you can all prophesy in turn so that everyone may be instructed and encouraged. [32]The spirits of prophets are subject to the control of prophets.
Eph 4 [11]It was he who gave some to be apostles, some to be prophets, some to be evangelists, and some to be pastors and teachers. . . .

n) Service

Rom 12 [7]If it is serving, let him serve; if it is teaching, let him teach. . . .
1 Pet 4 [11]If anyone speaks, he should do it as one speaking the very words of God. If anyone serves, he should do it with the strength God provides, so that in all things God may be praised through Jesus Christ. To him be the glory and the power for ever and ever. Amen.

o) Speaking in Various Kinds of Tongues

1 Cor 12 [10]to another miraculous powers, to another prophecy, to another distinguishing between spirits, to another speaking in different kinds of tongues, and to still another the interpretation of tongues.
1 Cor 12 [28]And in the church God has appointed first of all apostles, second prophets, third teachers, then workers of miracles, also those having gifts of healing, those able to help others, those with gifts of administration, and those speaking in different kinds of tongues. [29]Are all apostles? Are all prophets? Are all teachers? Do all work miracles? [30]Do all have gifts of healing? Do all speak in tongues? Do all interpret?
1 Cor 13 [1]If I speak in the tongues of men and of angels, but have not love, I am only a resounding gong or a clanging cymbal.
1 Cor 14 [26]What then shall we say, brothers? When you come together, everyone has a hymn, or a word of instruction, a revelation, a tongue or an interpretation. All of these must be done for the strengthening of the church.

p) Teaching (and Pastoring)

Rom 12 [7]If it is serving, let him serve; if it is teaching, let him teach. . . .
1 Cor 12 [28]And in the church God has appointed first of all apostles, second prophets, third teachers, then workers of miracles, also those having gifts of healing, those able to help others, those with gifts of administration, and those speaking in different kinds of tongues. [29]Are all apostles? Are all prophets? Are all teachers? Do all work miracles?
1 Cor 14 [26]What then shall we say, brothers? When you come together, everyone has a hymn, or a word of instruction, a revelation, a tongue or an interpretation. All of these must be done for the strengthening of the church.
Eph 4 [11]It was he who gave some to be apostles, some to be prophets, some to be evangelists, and some to be pastors and teachers. . . .

q) Uttering Knowledge

1 Cor 12 [8]To one there is given through the Spirit the message of wisdom, to another the message of knowledge by means of the same Spirit. . . .
1 Cor 13 [2]If I have the gift of prophecy and can fathom all mysteries and all knowledge, and if I have a faith that can move mountains, but have not love, I am nothing.

r) Uttering Wisdom

1 Cor 12 [8]To one there is given through the Spirit the message of wisdom, to another the message of knowledge by means of the same Spirit. . . .

s) Working Miracles

1 Cor 12 [10]to another miraculous powers, to another prophecy, to another distinguishing between spirits, to another speaking in different kinds of tongues, and to still another the interpretation of tongues.
1 Cor 12 [28]And in the church God has appointed first of all apostles, second prophets, third teachers, then workers of miracles, also those having gifts of healing, those able to help others, those with gifts of administration, and those speaking in different kinds of tongues. [29]Are all apostles? Are all prophets? Are all teachers? Do all work miracles?

3. Purpose of the Gifts

a) Gifts Are for Active Use in the Church

1 Cor 14 [26]What then shall we say, brothers? When you come together, everyone has a hymn, or a word of instruction, a revelation, a tongue or an interpretation. All of these must be done for the strengthening of the church.
1 Tim 4 [14]Do not neglect your gift, which was given you through a prophetic message when the body of elders laid their hands on you.
2 Tim 1 [6]For this reason I remind you to fan into flame the gift of God, which is in you through the laying on of my hands.

b) Gifts Are for Building Up the Body of Christ

Rom 12 [3]For by the grace given me I say to every one of you: Do not think of yourself more highly than you ought, but rather think of yourself with sober judgment, in accordance with the measure of faith God has given you. [4]Just as each of us has one body with many members, and these members do not all have the same function, [5]so in Christ we who are many form one body, and each member belongs to all the others. [6]We have different gifts, according to the grace given us. If a man's gift is prophesying, let him use it in proportion to his faith.
1 Cor 12 [12]The body is a unit, though it is made up of many parts; and though all its parts are many, they form one body. So it is with Christ. [13]For we were all baptized by one Spirit into one body—whether Jews or Greeks, slave or free—and we were all given the one Spirit to drink.

[14]Now the body is not made up of one part but of many. [15]If the foot should say, "Because I am not a hand, I do not belong to the body," it would not for that reason cease to be part of the body. [16]And if the ear should say, "Because I am not an eye, I do not belong to the body," it would not for that reason cease to be part of the body. [17]If the whole body were an eye, where would the sense of hearing be? If the whole body were an ear, where would the sense of smell be? [18]But in fact God has arranged the parts in the body, every one of them, just as he wanted them to be. [19]If they were all one part, where would the body be? [20]As it is, there are many parts, but one body.

[21]The eye cannot say to the hand, "I don't need you!" And the head cannot say to the feet, "I don't need you!" [22]On the contrary, those parts of the body that seem to be weaker are indispensable, [23]and the parts that we think are less honorable we treat with special honor. And the parts that are unpresentable are treated with special modesty, [24]while our presentable parts need no special treatment. But God has combined the members of the body and has given greater honor to the parts that lacked it, [25]so that there should be no division in the body, but that its parts should have equal concern for each other. [26]If one part suffers, every part suffers with it; if one part is honored, every part rejoices with it.

[27]Now you are the body of Christ, and each one of you is a part of it.
1 Cor 14 [3]But everyone who prophesies speaks to men for their strengthening, encouragement and comfort. [4]He who speaks in a tongue edifies himself, but he who prophesies edifies the church. [5]I would like every one of you to speak in tongues, but I would rather have you prophesy. He who prophesies is greater than one who speaks in tongues, unless he interprets, so that the church may be edified.
Eph 4 [11]It was he who gave some to be apostles, some to be prophets, some to be evangelists, and some to be pastors and teachers, [12]to prepare God's people for works of service, so that the body of Christ may be built up. . . .
Eph 4 [16]From him the whole body, joined and held together by every supporting ligament, grows and builds itself up in love, as each part does its work.

c) Gifts Are for Serving One Another

1 Pet 4 [10]Each one should use whatever gift he has received to serve others, faithfully administering God's grace in its various forms.

d) Gifts Are for the Common Good

1 Cor 12 [7]Now to each one the manifestation of the Spirit is given for the common good.

e) Gifts Are for Equipping the Saints

Eph 4 [11]It was he who gave some to be apostles, some to be prophets, some to be evangelists, and some to be pastors and teachers, [12]to prepare God's people for works of service, so that the body of Christ may be built up. . . .

D. Ministry of the Spirit

1. The Spirit Assists Believers in Worship

Phil 3 [3]For it is we who are the circumcision, we who worship by the Spirit of God, who glory in Christ Jesus, and who put no confidence in the flesh. . . .

2. The Spirit Assures Believers

Rom 8 [16]The Spirit himself testifies with our spirit that we are God's children.

3. The Spirit Baptizes Believers

John 1 [33]"I would not have known him, except that the one who sent me to baptize with water told me, 'The man on whom you see the Spirit come down and remain is he who will baptize with the Holy Spirit.'"
1 Cor 12 [13]For we were all baptized by one Spirit into one body—whether Jews or Greeks, slave or free—and we were all given the one Spirit to drink.

4. The Spirit Blesses Believers

Gal 5 [22]But the fruit of the Spirit is love, joy, peace, patience, kindness, goodness, faithfulness, [23]gentleness and self-control. Against such things there is no law.
Gal 6 [8]The one who sows to please his sinful nature, from that nature will reap destruction; the one who sows to please the Spirit, from the Spirit will reap eternal life.
1 Thess 1 [6]You became imitators of us and of the Lord; in spite of severe suffering, you welcomed the message with the joy given by the Holy Spirit.

5. The Spirit Compels Believers

Acts 20 [22]"And now, compelled by the Spirit, I am going to Jerusalem, not knowing what will happen to me there. [23]I only know that in every city the Holy Spirit warns me that prison and hardships are facing me."
2 Pet 1 [21]For prophecy never had its origin in the will of man, but men spoke from God as they were carried along by the Holy Spirit.

6. The Spirit Controls Believers' Minds

Rom 8 [5]Those who live according to the sinful nature have their minds set on what that nature desires; but those who live in accordance with the Spirit have their minds set on what the Spirit desires. [6]The mind of sinful man is death, but the mind controlled by the Spirit is life and peace. . . .

7. The Spirit Dwells in Believers

John 14 [16]"And I will ask the Father, and he will give you another Counselor to be with you forever—[17]the Spirit of truth. The world cannot accept him, because it neither sees him nor knows him. But you know him, for he lives with you and will be in you."
Rom 5 [5]And hope does not disappoint us, because God has poured out his love into our hearts by the Holy Spirit, whom he has given us.
Rom 8 [9]You, however, are controlled not by the sinful nature but by the Spirit, if the Spirit of God lives in you. And if anyone does not have the Spirit of Christ, he does not belong to Christ.
1 Cor 2 [12]We have not received the spirit of the world but the Spirit who is from God, that we may understand what God has freely given us.
1 Cor 3 [16]Don't you know that you yourselves are God's temple and that God's Spirit lives in you?
1 Cor 6 [19]Do you not know that your body is a temple of the Holy Spirit, who is in you, whom you have received from God? You are not your own. . . .
Gal 3 [2]I would like to learn just one thing from you: Did you receive the Spirit by observing the law, or by believing what you heard?
Gal 4 [6]Because you are sons, God sent the Spirit of his Son into our hearts, the Spirit who calls out, "*Abba*, Father."
James 4 [5]Or do you think Scripture says without reason that the spirit he caused to live in us envies intensely?
1 Pet 4 [14]If you are insulted because of the name of Christ, you are blessed, for the Spirit of glory and of God rests on you.
1 John 3 [24]Those who obey his commands live in him, and he in them. And this is how we know that he lives in us: We know it by the Spirit he gave us.
1 John 4 [13]We know that we live in him and he in us, because he has given us of his Spirit.

8. The Spirit Empowers Believers

Acts 1 [8]"But you will receive power when the Holy Spirit comes on you; and you will be my witnesses in Jerusalem, and in all Judea and Samaria, and to the ends of the earth."
Acts 2 [4]All of them were filled with the Holy Spirit and began to speak in other tongues as the Spirit enabled them.
Eph 3 [16]I pray that out of his glorious riches he may strengthen you with power through his Spirit in your inner being. . . .
Phil 1 [19]for I know that through your prayers and the help given by the Spirit of Jesus Christ, what has happened to me will turn out for my deliverance.
2 Tim 1 [14]Guard the good deposit that was entrusted to you—guard it with the help of the Holy Spirit who lives in us.

9. The Spirit Equips Believers for Service

1 Cor 12 [7]Now to each one the manifestation of the Spirit is given for the common good.
2 Cor 6 [4]Rather, as servants of God we commend ourselves in every way: in great endurance; in troubles, hardships and distresses; . . . [6]in purity, understanding, patience and kindness; in the Holy Spirit and in sincere love. . . .
Eph 6 [17]Take the helmet of salvation and the sword of the Spirit, which is the word of God.

10. The Spirit Fights Believers' Sinful Nature

Rom 8 [13]For if you live according to the sinful nature, you will die; but if by the Spirit you put to death the misdeeds of the body, you will live. . . .
Gal 5 [17]For the sinful nature desires what is contrary to the Spirit, and the Spirit what is contrary to the sinful nature. They are in conflict with each other, so that you do not do what you want.

11. The Spirit Fills Believers

Acts 2 [4]All of them were filled with the Holy Spirit and began to speak in other tongues as the Spirit enabled them.
Acts 4 [8]Then Peter, filled with the Holy Spirit, said to them: "Rulers and elders of the people!"
Acts 4 [31]After they prayed, the place where they were meeting was shaken. And they were all filled with the Holy Spirit and spoke the word of God boldly.
Acts 6 [3]Brothers, choose seven men from among you who are known to be full of the Spirit and wisdom. We will turn this responsibility over to them. . . .
Acts 9 [17]Then Ananias went to the house and entered it. Placing his hands on Saul, he said, "Brother Saul, the Lord—Jesus, who appeared to you on the road as you were

coming here—has sent me so that you may see again and be filled with the Holy Spirit."
Acts 11 [24]He was a good man, full of the Holy Spirit and faith, and a great number of people were brought to the Lord.
Acts 13 [9]Then Saul, who was also called Paul, filled with the Holy Spirit, looked straight at Elymas and said . . .
Eph 5 [18]Do not get drunk on wine, which leads to debauchery. Instead, be filled with the Spirit.

12. The Spirit Frees Believers

Rom 8 [2]because through Christ Jesus the law of the Spirit of life set me free from the law of sin and death.

13. The Spirit Gives Believers Access to the Father

Eph 2 [18]For through him we both have access to the Father by one Spirit.

14. The Spirit Glorifies Christ in Believers

John 16 [13]"But when he, the Spirit of truth, comes, he will guide you into all truth. He will not speak on his own; he will speak only what he hears, and he will tell you what is yet to come. [14]He will bring glory to me by taking from what is mine and making it known to you."
1 Cor 12 [3]Therefore I tell you that no one who is speaking by the Spirit of God says, "Jesus be cursed," and no one can say, "Jesus is Lord," except by the Holy Spirit.

15. The Spirit Guarantees Future Blessing to Believers

2 Cor 1 [22]set his seal of ownership on us, and put his Spirit in our hearts as a deposit, guaranteeing what is to come.
2 Cor 5 [5]Now it is God who has made us for this very purpose and has given us the Spirit as a deposit, guaranteeing what is to come.
Eph 1 [13]And you also were included in Christ when you heard the word of truth, the gospel of your salvation. Having believed, you were marked in him with a seal, the promised Holy Spirit, [14]who is a deposit guaranteeing our inheritance until the redemption of those who are God's possession—to the praise of his glory.

16. The Spirit Guides Believers

Acts 8 [29]The Spirit told Philip, "Go to that chariot and stay near it."
Acts 10 [19]While Peter was still thinking about the vision, the Spirit said to him, "Simon, three men are looking for you. [20]So get up and go downstairs. Do not hesitate to go with them, for I have sent them."
Acts 16 [6]Paul and his companions traveled throughout the region of Phrygia and Galatia, having been kept by the Holy Spirit from preaching the word in the province of Asia. [7]When they came to the border of Mysia, they tried to enter Bithynia, but the Spirit of Jesus would not allow them to.
Rom 8 [14]because those who are led by the Spirit of God are sons of God.
Gal 5 [18]But if you are led by the Spirit, you are not under law. . . . [25]Since we live by the Spirit, let us keep in step with the Spirit.

17. The Spirit Has Fellowship with Believers

2 Cor 13 [14]May the grace of the Lord Jesus Christ, and the love of God, and the fellowship of the Holy Spirit be with you all.
Phil 2 [1]If you have any encouragement from being united with Christ, if any comfort from his love, if any fellowship with the Spirit, if any tenderness and compassion . . .

18. The Spirit Helps Believers

Phil 1 [19]for I know that through your prayers and the help given by the Spirit of Jesus Christ, what has happened to me will turn out for my deliverance.

19. The Spirit Is a Gift to Believers

1 Thess 4 [8]Therefore, he who rejects this instruction does not reject man but God, who gives you his Holy Spirit.
Titus 3 [5]he saved us, not because of righteous things we had done, but because of his mercy. He saved us through the washing of rebirth and renewal by the Holy Spirit, [6]whom he poured out on us generously through Jesus Christ our Savior . . .
1 John 4 [13]We know that we live in him and he in us, because he has given us of his Spirit.

20. The Spirit Prays for and with Believers

Rom 8 [26]In the same way, the Spirit helps us in our weakness. We do not know what we ought to pray for, but the Spirit himself intercedes for us with groans that words cannot express. [27]And he who searches our hearts knows the mind of the Spirit, because the Spirit intercedes for the saints in accordance with God's will.
Eph 6 [18]And pray in the Spirit on all occasions with all kinds of prayers and requests. With this in mind, be alert and always keep on praying for all the saints.
Jude [20]But you, dear friends, build yourselves up in your most holy faith and pray in the Holy Spirit.

21. The Spirit Regenerates Believers

John 3 [5]Jesus answered, "I tell you the truth, no one can enter the kingdom of God unless he is born of water and the Spirit. [6]Flesh gives birth to flesh, but the Spirit gives birth to spirit. . . . [8]The wind blows wherever it pleases. You hear its sound, but you cannot tell where it comes from or where it is going. So it is with everyone born of the Spirit."
Gal 3 [3]Are you so foolish? After beginning with the Spirit, are you now trying to attain your goal by human effort?
1 Thess 1 [4]For we know, brothers loved by God, that he has chosen you, [5]because our gospel came to you not simply with words, but also with power, with the Holy Spirit and with deep conviction. You know how we lived among you for your sake.
Titus 3 [5]he saved us, not because of righteous things we had done, but because of his mercy. He saved us through the washing of rebirth and renewal by the Holy Spirit. . . .

22. The Spirit Seals Believers

2 Cor 1 [22]set his seal of ownership on us, and put his Spirit in our hearts as a deposit, guaranteeing what is to come.
Eph 1 [13]And you also were included in Christ when you heard the word of truth, the gospel of your salvation. Having believed, you were marked in him with a seal, the promised Holy Spirit. . . .
Eph 4 [30]And do not grieve the Holy Spirit of God, with whom you were sealed for the day of redemption.

23. The Spirit Speaks through Believers

Mark 13 [11]"Whenever you are arrested and brought to trial, do not worry beforehand about what to say. Just say whatever is given you at the time, for it is not you speaking, but the Holy Spirit."

24. The Spirit Teaches Believers

Luke 12 [12]". . . for the Holy Spirit will teach you at that time what you should say."
John 14 [26]"But the Counselor, the Holy Spirit, whom the Father will send in my name, will teach you all things and will remind you of everything I have said to you."
1 Cor 2 [13]This is what we speak, not in words taught us by human wisdom but in words taught by the Spirit, expressing spiritual truths in spiritual words.
1 John 2 [20]But you have an anointing from the Holy One, and all of you know the truth. . . . [27]As for you, the anointing you received from him remains in you, and you do not need anyone to teach you. But as his anointing teaches you about all things and as that anointing is real, not counterfeit—just as it has taught you, remain in him.

25. The Spirit Transforms Believers

2 Cor 3 [3]You show that you are a letter from Christ, the result of our ministry, written not with ink but with the Spirit of the living God, not on tablets of stone but on tablets of human hearts. . . . [18]And we, who with unveiled faces all reflect the Lord's glory, are being transformed into his likeness with ever-increasing glory, which comes from the Lord, who is the Spirit.

VII
The Holy Spirit and the World

A. The Spirit Created

See p. 181b, The Spirit and Creation

B. The Spirit Convicts

John 16 [7]"But I tell you the truth: It is for your good that I am going away. Unless I go away, the Counselor will not come to you; but if I go, I will send him to you. [8]When he comes, he will convict the world of guilt in regard to sin and righteousness and judgment: [9]in regard to sin, because men do not believe in me; [10]in regard to righteousness, because I am going to the Father, where you can see me no longer; [11]and in regard to judgment, because the prince of this world now stands condemned."

C. The Spirit Testifies and Converts

John 15 [26]"When the Counselor comes, whom I will send to you from the Father, the Spirit of truth who goes out from the Father, he will testify about me."
Rom 8 [16]The Spirit himself testifies with our spirit that we are God's children.
1 Cor 2 [11]For who among men knows the thoughts of a man except the man's spirit within him? In the same way no one knows the thoughts of God except the Spirit of God. [12]We have not received the spirit of the world but the Spirit who is from God, that we may understand what God has freely given us. [13]This is what we speak, not in words taught us by human wisdom but in words taught by the Spirit, expressing spiritual truths in spiritual words. [14]The man without the Spirit does not accept the things that come from the Spirit of God, for they are foolishness to him, and he cannot understand them, because they are spiritually discerned.
Gal 3 [3]Are you so foolish? After beginning with the Spirit, are you now trying to attain your goal by human effort?

D. The Spirit Restrains Evil

2 Thess 2 [7]For the secret power of lawlessness is already at work; but the one who now holds it back will continue to do so till he is taken out of the way.

VIII
The Holy Spirit and the Bible

***See* p. 266b, The Spirit and Scripture**

IX
Sins against the Holy Spirit

A. Blaspheming the Spirit

Mark 3 [29]"But whoever blasphemes against the Holy Spirit will never be forgiven; he is guilty of an eternal sin."

B. Grieving the Spirit

Isa 63 [10]Yet they rebelled and grieved his Holy Spirit. So he turned and became their enemy and he himself fought against them.
Eph 4 [30]And do not grieve the Holy Spirit of God, with whom you were sealed for the day of redemption.

C. Humiliating the Spirit

Heb 10 [29]How much more severely do you think a man deserves to be punished who has trampled the Son of God under foot, who has treated as an unholy thing the blood of the covenant that sanctified him, and who has insulted the Spirit of grace?

D. Lying to the Spirit

Acts 5 [3]Then Peter said, "Ananias, how is it that Satan has so filled your heart that you have lied to the Holy Spirit and have kept for yourself some of the money you received for the land?" . . .

[9]Peter said to her, "How could you agree to test the Spirit of the Lord? Look! The feet of the men who buried your husband are at the door, and they will carry you out also."

E. Quenching the Spirit

1 Thess 5 [19]Do not put out the Spirit's fire. . . .

F. Resisting the Spirit

Gen 6 [3]Then the LORD said, "My Spirit will not contend with man forever, for he is mortal; his days will be a hundred and twenty years."
Acts 6 [9]Opposition arose, however, from members of the Synagogue of the Freedmen (as it was called)—Jews of Cyrene and Alexandria as well as the provinces of Cilicia and Asia. These men began to argue with Stephen, [10]but they could not stand up against his wisdom or the Spirit by whom he spoke.
Acts 7 [51]"You stiff-necked people, with uncircumcised hearts and ears! You are just like your fathers: You always resist the Holy Spirit!"

X
Metaphors for the Holy Spirit

A. Clothing

Luke 24 [49]"I am going to send you what my Father has promised; but stay in the city until you have been clothed with power from on high."

B. Deposit

2 Cor 1 [21]Now it is God who makes both us and you stand firm in Christ. He anointed us, [22]set his seal of ownership on us, and put his Spirit in our hearts as a deposit, guaranteeing what is to come.
2 Cor 5 [5]Now it is God who has made us for this very purpose and has given us the Spirit as a deposit, guaranteeing what is to come.
Eph 1 [13]And you also were included in Christ when you heard the word of truth, the gospel of your salvation. Having believed, you were marked in him with a seal, the promised Holy Spirit, [14]who is a deposit guaranteeing our inheritance until the redemption of those who are God's possession—to the praise of his glory.

C. Dove

Matt 3 [16]As soon as Jesus was baptized, he went up out of the water. At that moment heaven was opened, and he saw the Spirit of God descending like a dove and lighting on him.

John 1 32Then John gave this testimony: "I saw the Spirit come down from heaven as a dove and remain on him."

D. Fire

Acts 2 3They saw what seemed to be tongues of fire that separated and came to rest on each of them. 4All of them were filled with the Holy Spirit and began to speak in other tongues as the Spirit enabled them.

E. Oil

1 Sam 16 13So Samuel took the horn of oil and anointed him in the presence of his brothers, and from that day on the Spirit of the LORD came upon David in power. Samuel then went to Ramah.
Luke 4 18"The Spirit of the Lord is on me, because he has anointed me to preach good news to the poor. He has sent me to proclaim freedom for the prisoners and recovery of sight for the blind, to release the oppressed. . . ."
Acts 10 38". . . how God anointed Jesus of Nazareth with the Holy Spirit and power, and how he went around doing good and healing all who were under the power of the devil, because God was with him."
2 Cor 1 21Now it is God who makes both us and you stand firm in Christ. He anointed us, 22set his seal of ownership on us, and put his Spirit in our hearts as a deposit, guaranteeing what is to come.
1 John 2 20But you have an anointing from the Holy One, and all of you know the truth. . . . 27As for you, the anointing you received from him remains in you, and you do not need anyone to teach you. But as his anointing teaches you about all things and as that anointing is real, not counterfeit—just as it has taught you, remain in him.

F. Seal

2 Cor 1 21Now it is God who makes both us and you stand firm in Christ. He anointed us, 22set his seal of ownership on us, and put his Spirit in our hearts as a deposit, guaranteeing what is to come.
Eph 1 13And you also were included in Christ when you heard the word of truth, the gospel of your salvation. Having believed, you were marked in him with a seal, the promised Holy Spirit. . . .
Eph 4 30And do not grieve the Holy Spirit of God, with whom you were sealed for the day of redemption.

G. Water

Isa 32 15till the Spirit is poured upon us from on high, and the desert becomes a fertile field, and the fertile field seems like a forest.
Isa 44 3"For I will pour water on the thirsty land, and streams on the dry ground; I will pour out my Spirit on your offspring, and my blessing on your descendants. 4They will spring up like grass in a meadow, like poplar trees by flowing streams."
John 4 14". . . but whoever drinks the water I give him will never thirst. Indeed, the water I give him will become in him a spring of water welling up to eternal life."
John 7 37On the last and greatest day of the Feast, Jesus stood and said in a loud voice, "If anyone is thirsty, let him come to me and drink. 38Whoever believes in me, as the Scripture has said, streams of living water will flow from within him." 39By this he meant the Spirit, whom those who believed in him were later to receive. Up to that time the Spirit had not been given, since Jesus had not yet been glorified.

H. Wind

John 3 8"The wind blows wherever it pleases. You hear its sound, but you cannot tell where it comes from or where it is going. So it is with everyone born of the Spirit."
Acts 2 1When the day of Pentecost came, they were all together in one place. 2Suddenly a sound like the blowing of a violent wind came from heaven and filled the whole house where they were sitting. 3They saw what seemed to be tongues of fire that separated and came to rest on each of them. 4All of them were filled with the Holy Spirit and began to speak in other tongues as the Spirit enabled them.
2 Pet 1 21For prophecy never had its origin in the will of man, but men spoke from God as they were carried along by the Holy Spirit.

4

The Works of God

I
The Decrees of God

A. *The Sovereign Reign of God*

1. God's Reign in General

a) God as Ruler

Exod 15 [18]"The LORD will reign for ever and ever."
Deut 4 [39]Acknowledge and take to heart this day that the LORD is God in heaven above and on the earth below. There is no other.
Deut 10 [14]To the LORD your God belong the heavens, even the highest heavens, the earth and everything in it. . . . [17]For the LORD your God is God of gods and Lord of lords, the great God, mighty and awesome, who shows no partiality and accepts no bribes.
2 Kings 19 [15]And Hezekiah prayed to the LORD: "O LORD, God of Israel, enthroned between the cherubim, you alone are God over all the kingdoms of the earth. You have made heaven and earth."
1 Chron 29 [11]"Yours, O LORD, is the greatness and the power and the glory and the majesty and the splendor, for everything in heaven and earth is yours. Yours, O LORD, is the kingdom; you are exalted as head over all. [12]Wealth and honor come from you; you are the ruler of all things. In your hands are strength and power to exalt and give strength to all."
2 Chron 20 [6]and said: "O LORD, God of our fathers, are you not the God who is in heaven? You rule over all the kingdoms of the nations. Power and might are in your hand, and no one can withstand you."
Job 25 [2]"Dominion and awe belong to God; he establishes order in the heights of heaven."
Job 40 [6]Then the LORD spoke to Job out of the storm: . . . **41** [11]"Who has a claim against me that I must pay? Everything under heaven belongs to me."
Ps 5 [2]Listen to my cry for help, my King and my God, for to you I pray.
Ps 10 [16]The LORD is King for ever and ever; the nations will perish from his land.
Ps 22 [27]All the ends of the earth will remember and turn to the LORD, and all the families of the nations will bow down before him, [28]for dominion belongs to the LORD and he rules over the nations.
Ps 24 [1]The earth is the LORD's, and everything in it, the world, and all who live in it. . . . [10]Who is he, this King of glory? The LORD Almighty—he is the King of glory.
Ps 29 [10]The LORD sits enthroned over the flood; the LORD is enthroned as King forever.
Ps 44 [4] You are my King and my God, who decrees victories for Jacob.
Ps 45 [6]Your throne, O God, will last for ever and ever; a scepter of justice will be the scepter of your kingdom.
Ps 47 [2] How awesome is the LORD Most High, the great King over all the earth! . . . [8]God reigns over the nations; God is seated on his holy throne. [9]The nobles of the nations assemble as the people of the God of Abraham, for the kings of the earth belong to God; he is greatly exalted.
Ps 66 [7]He rules forever by his power, his eyes watch the nations—let not the rebellious rise up against him.
Ps 67 [4]May the nations be glad and sing for joy, for you rule the peoples justly and guide the nations of the earth.

Ps 74 [12]But you, O God, are my king from of old; you bring salvation upon the earth.
Ps 83 [18]Let them know that you, whose name is the LORD—that you alone are the Most High over all the earth.
Ps 84 [3]Even the sparrow has found a home, and the swallow a nest for herself, where she may have her young—a place near your altar, O LORD Almighty, my King and my God.
Ps 89 [14]Righteousness and justice are the foundation of your throne; love and faithfulness go before you.
Ps 93 [1]The LORD reigns, he is robed in majesty; the LORD is robed in majesty and is armed with strength. The world is firmly established; it cannot be moved. [2]Your throne was established long ago; you are from all eternity.
Ps 95 [3]For the LORD is the great God, the great King above all gods.
Ps 97 [1]The LORD reigns, let the earth be glad; let the distant shores rejoice. [2]Clouds and thick darkness surround him; righteousness and justice are the foundation of his throne. . . .

[9]For you, O LORD, are the Most High over all the earth; you are exalted far above all gods.
Ps 98 [6]with trumpets and the blast of the ram's horn—shout for joy before the LORD, the King.
Ps 99 [4]The King is mighty, he loves justice—you have established equity; in Jacob you have done what is just and right. [5]Exalt the LORD our God and worship at his footstool; he is holy.
Ps 103 [19]The LORD has established his throne in heaven, and his kingdom rules over all.
Ps 113 [4]The LORD is exalted over all the nations, his glory above the heavens.
Ps 115 [3]Our God is in heaven; he does whatever pleases him.
Ps 145 [1]I will exalt you, my God the King; I will praise your name for ever and ever. . . . [13]Your kingdom is an everlasting kingdom, and your dominion endures through all generations. The LORD is faithful to all his promises and loving toward all he has made.
Ps 146 [10]The LORD reigns forever, your God, O Zion, for all generations. Praise the LORD.
Ps 149 [2]Let Israel rejoice in their Maker; let the people of Zion be glad in their King.
Isa 6 [5]"Woe to me!" I cried. "I am ruined! For I am a man of unclean lips, and I live among a people of unclean lips, and my eyes have seen the King, the LORD Almighty."
Isa 33 [22]For the LORD is our judge, the LORD is our lawgiver, the LORD is our king; it is he who will save us.
Isa 37 [16]"O LORD Almighty, God of Israel, enthroned between the cherubim, you alone are God over all the kingdoms of the earth. You have made heaven and earth."
Isa 43 [15]"I am the LORD, your Holy One, Israel's Creator, your King."
Isa 44 [6]"This is what the LORD says—Israel's King and Redeemer, the LORD Almighty: I am the first and I am the last; apart from me there is no God."
Isa 66 [1]This is what the LORD says: "Heaven is my throne, and the earth is my footstool. Where is the house you will build for me? Where will my resting place be?"
Jer 10 [10]But the LORD is the true God; he is the living God, the eternal King. When he is angry, the earth trembles; the nations cannot endure his wrath.
Lam 5 [19]You, O LORD, reign forever; your throne endures from generation to generation.
Ezek 18 [1]The word of the LORD came to me: . . . [4]"For every living soul belongs to me, the father as well as the son—both alike belong to me. The soul who sins is the one who will die."
Dan 2 [20]and said: "Praise be to the name of God for ever and ever; wisdom and power are his. [21]He changes times and seasons; he sets up kings and deposes them. He gives wisdom to the wise and knowledge to the discerning."
Dan 2 [47]The king said to Daniel, "Surely your God is the God of gods and the Lord of kings and a revealer of mysteries, for you were able to reveal this mystery."
Dan 4 [34]At the end of that time, I, Nebuchadnezzar, raised my eyes toward heaven, and my sanity was restored. Then I praised the Most High; I honored and glorified him who lives forever.

His dominion is an eternal dominion; his kingdom endures from generation to generation. [35]All the peoples of the earth are regarded as nothing. He does as he pleases with the powers of heaven and the peoples of the earth. No one can hold back his hand or say to him: "What have you done?"
Dan 6 [26]"I issue a decree that in every part of my kingdom people must fear and reverence the God of Daniel.

"For he is the living God and he endures forever; his kingdom will not be destroyed, his dominion will never end."
Mal 1 [14]"Cursed is the cheat who has an acceptable male in his flock and vows to give it, but then sacrifices a blemished animal to the Lord. For I am a great king," says the LORD Almighty, "and my name is to be feared among the nations."
Rom 11 [36]For from him and through him and to him are all things. To him be the glory forever! Amen.
1 Tim 1 [17]Now to the King eternal, immortal, invisible, the only God, be honor and glory for ever and ever. Amen.
1 Tim 6 [15]which God will bring about in his own time—God, the blessed and only Ruler, the King of kings and Lord of lords . . .
Rev 19 [6]Then I heard what sounded like a great multitude, like the roar of rushing waters and like loud peals of thunder, shouting: "Hallelujah! For our Lord God Almighty reigns."

b) God as Counselor

1 Kings 22 [5]But Jehoshaphat also said to the king of Israel, "First seek the counsel of the LORD."
Job 12 [13]"To God belong wisdom and power; counsel and understanding are his."
Ps 32 [8]I will instruct you and teach you in the way you should go; I will counsel you and watch over you.
Ps 73 [24]You guide me with your counsel, and afterward you will take me into glory.
Ps 107 [11]for they had rebelled against the words of God and despised the counsel of the Most High.
Prov 8 [14]"Counsel and sound judgment are mine; I have understanding and power."
Isa 9 [6]For to us a child is born, to us a son is given, and the government will be on his shoulders. And he will be called Wonderful Counselor, Mighty God, Everlasting Father, Prince of Peace.
Isa 28 [29]All this also comes from the LORD Almighty, wonderful in counsel and magnificent in wisdom.
John 14 [16]"And I will ask the Father, and he will give you another Counselor to be with you forever—[17]the Spirit of truth. The world cannot accept him, because it neither sees him nor knows him. But you know him, for he lives with you and will be in you."
John 14 [26]"But the Counselor, the Holy Spirit, whom the Father will send in my name, will teach you all things and will remind you of everything I have said to you."
John 15 [26]"When the Counselor comes, whom I will send to you from the Father, the Spirit of truth who goes out from the Father, he will testify about me."
John 16 [7]"But I tell you the truth: It is for your good that I am going away. Unless I go away, the Counselor will not come to you; but if I go, I will send him to you. [8]When he comes, he will convict the world of guilt in regard to sin and righteousness and judgment: [9]in regard to sin, because men do not believe in me; [10]in regard to righteousness, because I am going to the Father, where you can see me no longer; [11]and in regard to judgment, because the prince of this world now stands condemned."

c) God as Lawgiver

Gen 26 [5]". . . because Abraham obeyed me and kept my requirements, my commands, my decrees and my laws."
Exod 15 [25]Then Moses cried out to the LORD, and the LORD showed him a piece of wood. He threw it into the water, and the water became sweet.

There the LORD made a decree and a law for them, and there he tested them.
Lev 18 [4]"'You must obey my laws and be careful to follow my decrees. I am the LORD your God. [5]Keep my decrees and laws, for the man who obeys them will live by them. I am the LORD.'"
Lev 20 [22]"'Keep all my decrees and laws and follow them, so

that the land where I am bringing you to live may not vomit you out.'"
Num 19 [2]"This is a requirement of the law that the LORD has commanded: Tell the Israelites to bring you a red heifer without defect or blemish and that has never been under a yoke."
Num 31 [21]Then Eleazar the priest said to the soldiers who had gone into battle, "This is the requirement of the law that the LORD gave Moses. . . ."
Deut 6 [1]These are the commands, decrees and laws the LORD your God directed me to teach you to observe in the land that you are crossing the Jordan to possess. . . .
Deut 30 [16]For I command you today to love the LORD your God, to walk in his ways, and to keep his commands, decrees and laws; then you will live and increase, and the LORD your God will bless you in the land you are entering to possess.
1 Kings 9 [4]"As for you, if you walk before me in integrity of heart and uprightness, as David your father did, and do all I command and observe my decrees and laws . . ."
2 Kings 10 [31]Yet Jehu was not careful to keep the law of the LORD, the God of Israel, with all his heart. He did not turn away from the sins of Jeroboam, which he had caused Israel to commit.
1 Chron 16 [40]to present burnt offerings to the LORD on the altar of burnt offering regularly, morning and evening, in accordance with everything written in the Law of the LORD, which he had given Israel.
2 Chron 34 [14]While they were bringing out the money that had been taken into the temple of the LORD, Hilkiah the priest found the Book of the Law of the LORD that had been given through Moses.
Ezra 7 [12]Artaxerxes, king of kings,

To Ezra the priest, a teacher of the Law of the God of heaven: Greetings. . . . [14]You are sent by the king and his seven advisers to inquire about Judah and Jerusalem with regard to the Law of your God, which is in your hand.
Ps 1 [1]Blessed is the man who does not walk in the counsel of the wicked or stand in the way of sinners or sit in the seat of mockers. [2]But his delight is in the law of the LORD, and on his law he meditates day and night.
Ps 18 [21]For I have kept the ways of the LORD; I have not done evil by turning from my God. [22]All his laws are before me; I have not turned away from his decrees.
Ps 19 [7]The law of the LORD is perfect, reviving the soul. The statutes of the LORD are trustworthy, making wise the simple. [8]The precepts of the LORD are right, giving joy to the heart. The commands of the LORD are radiant, giving light to the eyes. [9]The fear of the LORD is pure, enduring forever. The ordinances of the LORD are sure and altogether righteous. [10]They are more precious than gold, than much pure gold; they are sweeter than honey, than honey from the comb. [11]By them is your servant warned; in keeping them there is great reward.
Ps 37 [31]The law of his God is in his heart; his feet do not slip.
Ps 119 [72]The law from your mouth is more precious to me than thousands of pieces of silver and gold.
Ps 119 [142]Your righteousness is everlasting and your law is true.
Isa 1 [10]Hear the word of the LORD, you rulers of Sodom; listen to the law of our God, you people of Gomorrah!
Isa 33 [22]For the LORD is our judge, the LORD is our lawgiver, the LORD is our king; it is he who will save us.
Isa 42 [21]It pleased the LORD for the sake of his righteousness to make his law great and glorious.
Jer 31 [33]"This is the covenant I will make with the house of Israel after that time," declares the LORD. "I will put my law in their minds and write it on their hearts. I will be their God, and they will be my people."
Ezek 20 [19]"I am the LORD your God; follow my decrees and be careful to keep my laws."
Rom 7 [22]For in my inner being I delight in God's law. . . . [25]Thanks be to God—through Jesus Christ our Lord!

So then, I myself in my mind am a slave to God's law, but in the sinful nature a slave to the law of sin.
James 4 [12]There is only one Lawgiver and Judge, the one who is able to save and destroy. But you—who are you to judge your neighbor?

d) God as Judge

Gen 18 [25]"Far be it from you to do such a thing—to kill the righteous with the wicked, treating the righteous and the wicked alike. Far be it from you! Will not the Judge of all the earth do right?"
Deut 32 [36]The LORD will judge his people and have compassion on his servants when he sees their strength is gone and no one is left, slave or free.
1 Sam 2 [9]"He will guard the feet of his saints, but the wicked will be silenced in darkness.

"It is not by strength that one prevails; [10]those who oppose the LORD will be shattered. He will thunder against them from heaven; the LORD will judge the ends of the earth.

"He will give strength to his king and exalt the horn of his anointed."
Ps 7 [11]God is a righteous judge, a God who expresses his wrath every day.
Ps 9 [4]For you have upheld my right and my cause; you have sat on your throne, judging righteously. . . .

[7]The LORD reigns forever; he has established his throne for judgment. [8]He will judge the world in righteousness; he will govern the peoples with justice.
Ps 11 [4]The LORD is in his holy temple; the LORD is on his heavenly throne. He observes the sons of men; his eyes examine them. [5]The LORD examines the righteous, but the wicked and those who love violence his soul hates. [6]On the wicked he will rain fiery coals and burning sulfur; a scorching wind will be their lot. [7]For the LORD is righteous, he loves justice; upright men will see his face.
Ps 50 [6]And the heavens proclaim his righteousness, for God himself is judge.
Ps 75 [6]No one from the east or the west or from the desert can exalt a man. [7]But it is God who judges: He brings one down, he exalts another. [8]In the hand of the LORD is a cup full of foaming wine mixed with spices; he pours it out, and all the wicked of the earth drink it down to its very dregs.
Ps 76 [8]From heaven you pronounced judgment, and the land feared and was quiet—[9]when you, O God, rose up to judge, to save all the afflicted of the land.

[10]Surely your wrath against men brings you praise, and the survivors of your wrath are restrained.

[11]Make vows to the LORD your God and fulfill them; let all the neighboring lands bring gifts to the One to be feared. [12]He breaks the spirit of rulers; he is feared by the kings of the earth.
Ps 82 [1]God presides in the great assembly; he gives judgment among the "gods." . . .

[8]Rise up, O God, judge the earth, for all the nations are your inheritance.
Ps 94 [1]O LORD, the God who avenges, O God who avenges, shine forth. [2]Rise up, O Judge of the earth; pay back to the proud what they deserve.
Ps 96 [10]Say among the nations, "The LORD reigns." The world is firmly established, it cannot be moved; he will judge the peoples with equity. [13]. . . they will sing before the LORD, for he comes, he comes to judge the earth. He will judge the world in righteousness and the peoples in his truth.
Ps 105 [7]He is the LORD our God; his judgments are in all the earth.
Prov 8 [14]"Counsel and sound judgment are mine; I have understanding and power."
Eccles 3 [17]I thought in my heart, "God will bring to judgment both the righteous and the wicked, for there will be a time for every activity, a time for every deed."
Isa 33 [22]For the LORD is our judge, the LORD is our lawgiver, the LORD is our king; it is he who will save us.
Isa 40 [1]Comfort, comfort my people, says your God. [2]Speak tenderly to Jerusalem, and proclaim to her that her hard service has been completed, that her sin has been paid for, that she has received from the LORD's hand double for all her sins. . . . [22]He sits enthroned above the circle of the earth, and its people are like grasshoppers. He stretches out the heavens like a canopy, and spreads them out like a tent to live in. [23]He brings princes to naught and reduces the rulers of this world to nothing.
Jer 11 [20]But, O LORD Almighty, you who judge righteously and

test the heart and mind, let me see your vengeance upon them, for to you I have committed my cause.

Jer 32 18“You show love to thousands but bring the punishment for the fathers' sins into the laps of their children after them. O great and powerful God, whose name is the LORD Almighty, 19great are your purposes and mighty are your deeds. Your eyes are open to all the ways of men; you reward everyone according to his conduct and as his deeds deserve.”

Ezek 7 3“The end is now upon you and I will unleash my anger against you. I will judge you according to your conduct and repay you for all your detestable practices. 4I will not look on you with pity or spare you; I will surely repay you for your conduct and the detestable practices among you. Then you will know that I am the LORD.”

Ezek 33 20“Yet, O house of Israel, you say, 'The way of the Lord is not just.' But I will judge each of you according to his own ways.”

Joel 3 12“Let the nations be roused; let them advance into the Valley of Jehoshaphat, for there I will sit to judge all the nations on every side.”

Rom 2 16This will take place on the day when God will judge men's secrets through Jesus Christ, as my gospel declares.

Rom 9 28“For the Lord will carry out his sentence on earth with speed and finality.”

Rom 14 10You, then, why do you judge your brother? Or why do you look down on your brother? For we will all stand before God's judgment seat. 11It is written: “'As surely as I live,' says the Lord, 'every knee will bow before me; every tongue will confess to God.'” 12So then, each of us will give an account of himself to God.

1 Cor 5 12What business is it of mine to judge those outside the church? Are you not to judge those inside? 13God will judge those outside. “Expel the wicked man from among you.”

Heb 10 30For we know him who said, “It is mine to avenge; I will repay,” and again, “The Lord will judge his people.”

Heb 12 23to the church of the firstborn, whose names are written in heaven. You have come to God, the judge of all men, to the spirits of righteous men made perfect. . . .

James 4 12There is only one Lawgiver and Judge, the one who is able to save and destroy. But you—who are you to judge your neighbor?

James 5 9Don't grumble against each other, brothers, or you will be judged. The Judge is standing at the door!

2. God's Reign (Kingdom) in the NT

a) John the Baptist's Announcement of the Kingdom

Matt 3 1In those days John the Baptist came, preaching in the Desert of Judea 2and saying, “Repent, for the kingdom of heaven is near.” 3This is he who was spoken of through the prophet Isaiah: “A voice of one calling in the desert, 'Prepare the way for the Lord, make straight paths for him.'”

4John's clothes were made of camel's hair, and he had a leather belt around his waist. His food was locusts and wild honey. 5People went out to him from Jerusalem and all Judea and the whole region of the Jordan. 6Confessing their sins, they were baptized by him in the Jordan River.

7But when he saw many of the Pharisees and Sadducees coming to where he was baptizing, he said to them: “You brood of vipers! Who warned you to flee from the coming wrath? 8Produce fruit in keeping with repentance. 9And do not think you can say to yourselves, 'We have Abraham as our father.' I tell you that out of these stones God can raise up children for Abraham. 10The ax is already at the root of the trees, and every tree that does not produce good fruit will be cut down and thrown into the fire.

11“I baptize you with water for repentance. But after me will come one who is more powerful than I, whose sandals I am not fit to carry. He will baptize you with the Holy Spirit and with fire. 12His winnowing fork is in his hand, and he will clear his threshing floor, gathering his wheat into the barn and burning up the chaff with unquenchable fire.”

Matt 11 7As John's disciples were leaving, Jesus began to speak to the crowd about John: “What did you go out into the desert to see? A reed swayed by the wind? 8If not, what did you go out to see? A man dressed in fine clothes? No, those who wear fine clothes are in kings' palaces. 9Then what did you go out to see? A prophet? Yes, I tell you, and more than a prophet. 10This is the one about whom it is written: 'I will send my messenger ahead of you, who will prepare your way before you.' 11I tell you the truth: Among those born of women there has not risen anyone greater than John the Baptist; yet he who is least in the kingdom of heaven is greater than he. 12From the days of John the Baptist until now, the kingdom of heaven has been forcefully advancing, and forceful men lay hold of it. 13For all the Prophets and the Law prophesied until John. 14And if you are willing to accept it, he is the Elijah who was to come.”

Mark 1 1The beginning of the gospel about Jesus Christ, the Son of God.

2It is written in Isaiah the prophet: “I will send my messenger ahead of you, who will prepare your way”—3“a voice of one calling in the desert, 'Prepare the way for the Lord, make straight paths for him.'” 4And so John came, baptizing in the desert region and preaching a baptism of repentance for the forgiveness of sins. 5The whole Judean countryside and all the people of Jerusalem went out to him. Confessing their sins, they were baptized by him in the Jordan River. 6John wore clothing made of camel's hair, with a leather belt around his waist, and he ate locusts and wild honey. 7And this was his message: “After me will come one more powerful than I, the thongs of whose sandals I am not worthy to stoop down and untie. 8I baptize you with water, but he will baptize you with the Holy Spirit.”

Luke 3 1In the fifteenth year of the reign of Tiberius Caesar—when Pontius Pilate was governor of Judea, Herod tetrarch of Galilee, his brother Philip tetrarch of Iturea and Traconitis, and Lysanias tetrarch of Abilene—2during the high priesthood of Annas and Caiaphas, the word of God came to John son of Zechariah in the desert. 3He went into all the country around the Jordan, preaching a baptism of repentance for the forgiveness of sins. 4As is written in the book of the words of Isaiah the prophet: “A voice of one calling in the desert, 'Prepare the way for the Lord, make straight paths for him. 5Every valley shall be filled in, every mountain and hill made low. The crooked roads shall become straight, the rough ways smooth. 6And all mankind will see God's salvation.'”

7John said to the crowds coming out to be baptized by him, “You brood of vipers! Who warned you to flee from the coming wrath? 8Produce fruit in keeping with repentance. And do not begin to say to yourselves, 'We have Abraham as our father.' For I tell you that out of these stones God can raise up children for Abraham. 9The ax is already at the root of the trees, and every tree that does not produce good fruit will be cut down and thrown into the fire.”

10“What should we do then?” the crowd asked.

11John answered, “The man with two tunics should share with him who has none, and the one who has food should do the same.”

12Tax collectors also came to be baptized. “Teacher,” they asked, “what should we do?”

13“Don't collect any more than you are required to,” he told them.

14Then some soldiers asked him, “And what should we do?”

He replied, “Don't extort money and don't accuse people falsely—be content with your pay.”

15The people were waiting expectantly and were all wondering in their hearts if John might possibly be the Christ. 16John answered them all, “I baptize you with water. But one more powerful than I will come, the thongs of whose sandals I am not worthy to untie. He will baptize you with the Holy Spirit and with fire. 17His winnowing fork is in his hand to clear his threshing floor and to gather the wheat into his barn, but he will burn up the chaff with unquenchable fire.” 18And with many other words John exhorted the people and preached the good news to them.

b) Jesus' Teaching concerning the Kingdom

(1) Entrance into the Kingdom

Matt 4 17From that time on Jesus began to preach, “Repent, for the kingdom of heaven is near.” . . .

23Jesus went throughout Galilee, teaching in their synagogues, preaching the good news of the kingdom, and healing every disease and sickness among the people.

Matt 5 20"For I tell you that unless your righteousness surpasses that of the Pharisees and the teachers of the law, you will certainly not enter the kingdom of heaven."

Matt 7 13"Enter through the narrow gate. For wide is the gate and broad is the road that leads to destruction, and many enter through it. 14But small is the gate and narrow the road that leads to life, and only a few find it. . . .

21"Not everyone who says to me, 'Lord, Lord,' will enter the kingdom of heaven, but only he who does the will of my Father who is in heaven. 22Many will say to me on that day, 'Lord, Lord, did we not prophesy in your name, and in your name drive out demons and perform many miracles?' 23Then I will tell them plainly, 'I never knew you. Away from me, you evildoers!'"

Matt 8 10When Jesus heard this, he was astonished and said to those following him, "I tell you the truth, I have not found anyone in Israel with such great faith. 11I say to you that many will come from the east and the west, and will take their places at the feast with Abraham, Isaac and Jacob in the kingdom of heaven. 12But the subjects of the kingdom will be thrown outside, into the darkness, where there will be weeping and gnashing of teeth."

13Then Jesus said to the centurion, "Go! It will be done just as you believed it would." And his servant was healed at that very hour.

Matt 9 35Jesus went through all the towns and villages, teaching in their synagogues, preaching the good news of the kingdom and healing every disease and sickness. 36When he saw the crowds, he had compassion on them, because they were harassed and helpless, like sheep without a shepherd. 37Then he said to his disciples, "The harvest is plentiful but the workers are few. 38Ask the Lord of the harvest, therefore, to send out workers into his harvest field."

Matt 11 12"From the days of John the Baptist until now, the kingdom of heaven has been forcefully advancing, and forceful men lay hold of it. 13For all the Prophets and the Law prophesied until John. 14And if you are willing to accept it, he is the Elijah who was to come."

Matt 13 18"Listen then to what the parable of the sower means: 19When anyone hears the message about the kingdom and does not understand it, the evil one comes and snatches away what was sown in his heart. This is the seed sown along the path. 20The one who received the seed that fell on rocky places is the man who hears the word and at once receives it with joy. 21But since he has no root, he lasts only a short time. When trouble or persecution comes because of the word, he quickly falls away. 22The one who received the seed that fell among the thorns is the man who hears the word, but the worries of this life and the deceitfulness of wealth choke it, making it unfruitful. 23But the one who received the seed that fell on good soil is the man who hears the word and understands it. He produces a crop, yielding a hundred, sixty or thirty times what was sown."

Matt 13 44"The kingdom of heaven is like treasure hidden in a field.When a man found it, he hid it again, and then in his joy went and sold all he had and bought that field.

45"Again, the kingdom of heaven is like a merchant looking for fine pearls. 46When he found one of great value, he went away and sold everything he had and bought it."

Matt 18 2He called a little child and had him stand among them. 3And he said: "I tell you the truth, unless you change and become like little children, you will never enter the kingdom of heaven."

Matt 19 23Then Jesus said to his disciples, "I tell you the truth, it is hard for a rich man to enter the kingdom of heaven. 24Again I tell you, it is easier for a camel to go through the eye of a needle than for a rich man to enter the kingdom of God."

25When the disciples heard this, they were greatly astonished and asked, "Who then can be saved?"

26Jesus looked at them and said, "With man this is impossible, but with God all things are possible."

Matt 21 28"What do you think? There was a man who had two sons. He went to the first and said, 'Son, go and work today in the vineyard.'

29"'I will not,' he answered, but later he changed his mind and went.

30"Then the father went to the other son and said the same thing. He answered, 'I will, sir,' but he did not go.

31"Which of the two did what his father wanted?"

"The first," they answered.

Jesus said to them, "I tell you the truth, the tax collectors and the prostitutes are entering the kingdom of God ahead of you. 32For John came to you to show you the way of righteousness, and you did not believe him, but the tax collectors and the prostitutes did. And even after you saw this, you did not repent and believe him."

Mark 1 14After John was put in prison, Jesus went into Galilee, proclaiming the good news of God. 15"The time has come," he said. "The kingdom of God is near. Repent and believe the good news!"

Mark 9 42"And if anyone causes one of these little ones who believe in me to sin, it would be better for him to be thrown into the sea with a large millstone tied around his neck. 43If your hand causes you to sin, cut it off. It is better for you to enter life maimed than with two hands to go into hell, where the fire never goes out. 45And if your foot causes you to sin, cut it off. It is better for you to enter life crippled than to have two feet and be thrown into hell. 47And if your eye causes you to sin, pluck it out. It is better for you to enter the kingdom of God with one eye than to have two eyes and be thrown into hell, 48where 'their worm does not die, and the fire is not quenched.'"

Mark 10 15"I tell you the truth, anyone who will not receive the kingdom of God like a little child will never enter it."

Luke 18 17"I tell you the truth, anyone who will not receive the kingdom of God like a little child will never enter it."

John 3 3In reply Jesus declared, "I tell you the truth, no one can see the kingdom of God unless he is born again."

4"How can a man be born when he is old?" Nicodemus asked. "Surely he cannot enter a second time into his mother's womb to be born!"

5Jesus answered, "I tell you the truth, no one can enter the kingdom of God unless he is born of water and the Spirit. 6Flesh gives birth to flesh, but the Spirit gives birth to spirit. 7You should not be surprised at my saying, 'You must be born again.'"

(2) The Nature and Life of the Kingdom

Matt 5 1Now when he saw the crowds, he went up on a mountainside and sat down. His disciples came to him, 2and he began to teach them, saying: 3"Blessed are the poor in spirit, for theirs is the kingdom of heaven. 4Blessed are those who mourn, for they will be comforted. 5Blessed are the meek, for they will inherit the earth. 6Blessed are those who hunger and thirst for righteousness, for they will be filled. 7Blessed are the merciful, for they will be shown mercy. 8Blessed are the pure in heart, for they will see God. 9Blessed are the peacemakers, for they will be called sons of God. 10Blessed are those who are persecuted because of righteousness, for theirs is the kingdom of heaven.

11"Blessed are you when people insult you, persecute you and falsely say all kinds of evil against you because of me. 12Rejoice and be glad, because great is your reward in heaven, for in the same way they persecuted the prophets who were before you. . . .

19"Anyone who breaks one of the least of these commandments and teaches others to do the same will be called least in the kingdom of heaven, but whoever practices and teaches these commands will be called great in the kingdom of heaven."

Matt 6 31"So do not worry, saying, 'What shall we eat?' or 'What shall we drink?' or 'What shall we wear?' 32For the pagans run after all these things, and your heavenly Father knows that you need them. 33But seek first his kingdom and his righteousness, and all these things will be given to you as well."

Matt 13 31He told them another parable: "The kingdom of heaven is like a mustard seed, which a man took and planted in his field. 32Though it is the smallest of all your seeds, yet when it grows, it is the largest of garden plants and becomes a tree, so that the birds of the air come and perch in its branches."

33He told them still another parable: "The kingdom of

heaven is like yeast that a woman took and mixed into a large amount of flour until it worked all through the dough."

Matt 18 [4]"Therefore, whoever humbles himself like this child is the greatest in the kingdom of heaven.

[5]"And whoever welcomes a little child like this in my name welcomes me. [6]But if anyone causes one of these little ones who believe in me to sin, it would be better for him to have a large millstone hung around his neck and to be drowned in the depths of the sea.

[7]"Woe to the world because of the things that cause people to sin! Such things must come, but woe to the man through whom they come! [8]If your hand or your foot causes you to sin, cut it off and throw it away. It is better for you to enter life maimed or crippled than to have two hands or two feet and be thrown into eternal fire. [9]And if your eye causes you to sin, gouge it out and throw it away. It is better for you to enter life with one eye than to have two eyes and be thrown into the fire of hell."

Matt 18 [23]"Therefore, the kingdom of heaven is like a king who wanted to settle accounts with his servants. [24]As he began the settlement, a man who owed him ten thousand talents was brought to him. [25]Since he was not able to pay, the master ordered that he and his wife and his children and all that he had be sold to repay the debt.

[26]"The servant fell on his knees before him. 'Be patient with me,' he begged, 'and I will pay back everything.' [27]The servant's master took pity on him, canceled the debt and let him go.

[28]"But when that servant went out, he found one of his fellow servants who owed him a hundred denarii. He grabbed him and began to choke him. 'Pay back what you owe me!' he demanded.

[29]"His fellow servant fell to his knees and begged him, 'Be patient with me, and I will pay you back.'

[30]"But he refused. Instead, he went off and had the man thrown into prison until he could pay the debt. [31]When the other servants saw what had happened, they were greatly distressed and went and told their master everything that had happened.

[32]"Then the master called the servant in. 'You wicked servant,' he said, 'I canceled all that debt of yours because you begged me to. [33]Shouldn't you have had mercy on your fellow servant just as I had on you?' [34]In anger his master turned him over to the jailers to be tortured, until he should pay back all he owed.

[35]"This is how my heavenly Father will treat each of you unless you forgive your brother from your heart."

Matt 19 [11]Jesus replied, "Not everyone can accept this word, but only those to whom it has been given. [12]For some are eunuchs because they were born that way; others were made that way by men; and others have renounced marriage because of the kingdom of heaven. The one who can accept this should accept it."

Matt 20 [1]"For the kingdom of heaven is like a landowner who went out early in the morning to hire men to work in his vineyard. [2]He agreed to pay them a denarius for the day and sent them into his vineyard.

[3]"About the third hour he went out and saw others standing in the marketplace doing nothing. [4]He told them, 'You also go and work in my vineyard, and I will pay you whatever is right.' [5]So they went.

"He went out again about the sixth hour and the ninth hour and did the same thing. [6]About the eleventh hour he went out and found still others standing around. He asked them, 'Why have you been standing here all day long doing nothing?'

[7]"'Because no one has hired us,' they answered.

"He said to them, 'You also go and work in my vineyard.'

[8]"When evening came, the owner of the vineyard said to his foreman, 'Call the workers and pay them their wages, beginning with the last ones hired and going on to the first.'

[9]"The workers who were hired about the eleventh hour came and each received a denarius. [10]So when those came who were hired first, they expected to receive more. But each one of them also received a denarius. [11]When they received it, they began to grumble against the landowner. [12]'These men who were hired last worked only one hour,' they said, 'and you have made them equal to us who have borne the burden of the work and the heat of the day.'

[13]"But he answered one of them, 'Friend, I am not being unfair to you. Didn't you agree to work for a denarius? [14]Take your pay and go. I want to give the man who was hired last the same as I gave you. [15]Don't I have the right to do what I want with my own money? Or are you envious because I am generous?'

[16]"So the last will be first, and the first will be last."

Matt 20 [20]Then the mother of Zebedee's sons came to Jesus with her sons and, kneeling down, asked a favor of him.

[21]"What is it you want?" he asked.

She said, "Grant that one of these two sons of mine may sit at your right and the other at your left in your kingdom."

[22]"You don't know what you are asking," Jesus said to them. "Can you drink the cup I am going to drink?"

"We can," they answered.

[23]Jesus said to them, "You will indeed drink from my cup, but to sit at my right or left is not for me to grant. These places belong to those for whom they have been prepared by my Father."

[24]When the ten heard about this, they were indignant with the two brothers. [25]Jesus called them together and said, "You know that the rulers of the Gentiles lord it over them, and their high officials exercise authority over them. [26]Not so with you. Instead, whoever wants to become great among you must be your servant, [27]and whoever wants to be first must be your slave—[28]just as the Son of Man did not come to be served, but to serve, and to give his life as a ransom for many."

Matt 23 [8]"But you are not to be called 'Rabbi,' for you have only one Master and you are all brothers. [9]And do not call anyone on earth 'father,' for you have one Father, and he is in heaven. [10]Nor are you to be called 'teacher,' for you have one Teacher, the Christ. [11]The greatest among you will be your servant. [12]For whoever exalts himself will be humbled, and whoever humbles himself will be exalted."

Luke 9 [57]As they were walking along the road, a man said to him, "I will follow you wherever you go."

[58]Jesus replied, "Foxes have holes and birds of the air have nests, but the Son of Man has no place to lay his head."

[59]He said to another man, "Follow me."

But the man replied, "Lord, first let me go and bury my father."

[60]Jesus said to him, "Let the dead bury their own dead, but you go and proclaim the kingdom of God."

[61]Still another said, "I will follow you, Lord; but first let me go back and say good-by to my family."

[62]Jesus replied, "No one who puts his hand to the plow and looks back is fit for service in the kingdom of God."

John 18 [36]Jesus said, "My kingdom is not of this world. If it were, my servants would fight to prevent my arrest by the Jews. But now my kingdom is from another place."

(3) The Kingdom as Present

Matt 4 [17]From that time on Jesus began to preach, "Repent, for the kingdom of heaven is near."

Matt 11 [11]"I tell you the truth: Among those born of women there has not risen anyone greater than John the Baptist; yet he who is least in the kingdom of heaven is greater than he. [12]From the days of John the Baptist until now, the kingdom of heaven has been forcefully advancing, and forceful men lay hold of it."

Matt 12 [28]"But if I drive out demons by the Spirit of God, then the kingdom of God has come upon you."

Matt 13 [11]He replied, "The knowledge of the secrets of the kingdom of heaven has been given to you, but not to them. [12]Whoever has will be given more, and he will have an abundance. Whoever does not have, even what he has will be taken from him. . . . [16]But blessed are your eyes because they see, and your ears because they hear. [17]For I tell you the truth, many prophets and righteous men longed to see what you see but did not see it, and to hear what you hear but did not hear it."

Matt 18 [4]"Therefore, whoever humbles himself like this child is the greatest in the kingdom of heaven."

Matt 21 [43]"Therefore I tell you that the kingdom of God will be taken away from you and given to a people who will produce its fruit."

Matt 23 13"Woe to you, teachers of the law and Pharisees, you hypocrites! You shut the kingdom of heaven in men's faces. You yourselves do not enter, nor will you let those enter who are trying to."

Luke 7 28"I tell you, among those born of women there is no one greater than John; yet the one who is least in the kingdom of God is greater than he."

Luke 9 1When Jesus had called the Twelve together, he gave them power and authority to drive out all demons and to cure diseases, 2and he sent them out to preach the kingdom of God and to heal the sick.

Luke 17 20Once, having been asked by the Pharisees when the kingdom of God would come, Jesus replied, "The kingdom of God does not come with your careful observation, 21nor will people say, 'Here it is,' or 'There it is,' because the kingdom of God is within you."

(4) The Kingdom as Future

Matt 6 9"This, then, is how you should pray: 'Our Father in heaven, hallowed be your name, 10your kingdom come, your will be done on earth as it is in heaven.'"

Matt 25 1"At that time the kingdom of heaven will be like ten virgins who took their lamps and went out to meet the bridegroom. 2Five of them were foolish and five were wise. 3The foolish ones took their lamps but did not take any oil with them. 4The wise, however, took oil in jars along with their lamps. 5The bridegroom was a long time in coming, and they all became drowsy and fell asleep.

6"At midnight the cry rang out: 'Here's the bridegroom! Come out to meet him!'

7"Then all the virgins woke up and trimmed their lamps. 8The foolish ones said to the wise, 'Give us some of your oil; our lamps are going out.'

9"'No,' they replied, 'there may not be enough for both us and you. Instead, go to those who sell oil and buy some for yourselves.'

10"But while they were on their way to buy the oil, the bridegroom arrived. The virgins who were ready went in with him to the wedding banquet. And the door was shut.

11"Later the others also came. 'Sir! Sir!' they said. 'Open the door for us!'

12"But he replied, 'I tell you the truth, I don't know you.'

13"Therefore keep watch, because you do not know the day or the hour."

Matt 25 34"Then the King will say to those on his right, 'Come, you who are blessed by my Father; take your inheritance, the kingdom prepared for you since the creation of the world. 35For I was hungry and you gave me something to eat, I was thirsty and you gave me something to drink, I was a stranger and you invited me in, 36I needed clothes and you clothed me, I was sick and you looked after me, I was in prison and you came to visit me.' . . .

40"The King will reply, 'I tell you the truth, whatever you did for one of the least of these brothers of mine, you did for me.'"

Matt 26 29"I tell you, I will not drink of this fruit of the vine from now on until that day when I drink it anew with you in my Father's kingdom."

Mark 14 25"I tell you the truth, I will not drink again of the fruit of the vine until that day when I drink it anew in the kingdom of God."

Luke 11 2He said to them, "When you pray, say: 'Father, hallowed be your name, your kingdom come.'"

Luke 13 22Then Jesus went through the towns and villages, teaching as he made his way to Jerusalem. 23Someone asked him, "Lord, are only a few people going to be saved?"

He said to them, 24"Make every effort to enter through the narrow door, because many, I tell you, will try to enter and will not be able to. 25Once the owner of the house gets up and closes the door, you will stand outside knocking and pleading, 'Sir, open the door for us.'

"But he will answer, 'I don't know you or where you come from.'

26"Then you will say, 'We ate and drank with you, and you taught in our streets.'

27"But he will reply, 'I don't know you or where you come from. Away from me, all you evildoers!'

28"There will be weeping there, and gnashing of teeth, when you see Abraham, Isaac and Jacob and all the prophets in the kingdom of God, but you yourselves thrown out. 29People will come from east and west and north and south, and will take their places at the feast in the kingdom of God. 30Indeed there are those who are last who will be first, and the first who will be last."

Luke 19 11While they were listening to this, he went on to tell them a parable, because he was near Jerusalem and the people thought that the kingdom of God was going to appear at once. 12He said: "A man of noble birth went to a distant country to have himself appointed king and then to return. 13So he called ten of his servants and gave them ten minas. 'Put this money to work,' he said, 'until I come back.'

14"But his subjects hated him and sent a delegation after him to say, 'We don't want this man to be our king.'

15"He was made king, however, and returned home. Then he sent for the servants to whom he had given the money, in order to find out what they had gained with it.

16"The first one came and said, 'Sir, your mina has earned ten more.'

17"'Well done, my good servant!' his master replied. 'Because you have been trustworthy in a very small matter, take charge of ten cities.'

18"The second came and said, 'Sir, your mina has earned five more.'

19"His master answered, 'You take charge of five cities.'

20"Then another servant came and said, 'Sir, here is your mina; I have kept it laid away in a piece of cloth. 21I was afraid of you, because you are a hard man. You take out what you did not put in and reap what you did not sow.'

22"His master replied, 'I will judge you by your own words, you wicked servant! You knew, did you, that I am a hard man, taking out what I did not put in, and reaping what I did not sow? 23Why then didn't you put my money on deposit, so that when I came back, I could have collected it with interest?'

24"Then he said to those standing by, 'Take his mina away from him and give it to the one who has ten minas.'

25"'Sir,' they said, 'he already has ten!'

26"He replied, 'I tell you that to everyone who has, more will be given, but as for the one who has nothing, even what he has will be taken away. 27But those enemies of mine who did not want me to be king over them—bring them here and kill them in front of me.'"

Luke 21 9"When you hear of wars and revolutions, do not be frightened. These things must happen first, but the end will not come right away. . . .

25"There will be signs in the sun, moon and stars. On the earth, nations will be in anguish and perplexity at the roaring and tossing of the sea. . . . 27At that time they will see the Son of Man coming in a cloud with power and great glory. . . . 31Even so, when you see these things happening, you know that the kingdom of God is near."

Luke 22 14When the hour came, Jesus and his apostles reclined at the table. 15And he said to them, "I have eagerly desired to eat this Passover with you before I suffer. 16For I tell you, I will not eat it again until it finds fulfillment in the kingdom of God."

17After taking the cup, he gave thanks and said, "Take this and divide it among you. 18For I tell you I will not drink again of the fruit of the vine until the kingdom of God comes."

c) The Church and the Kingdom

(1) Kingdom-Life in the Church

Acts 8 12But when they believed Philip as he preached the good news of the kingdom of God and the name of Jesus Christ, they were baptized, both men and women.

Acts 14 21They preached the good news in that city and won a large number of disciples. Then they returned to Lystra, Iconium and Antioch, 22strengthening the disciples and encouraging them to remain true to the faith. "We must go through many hardships to enter the kingdom of God," they said. 23Paul and Barnabas appointed elders for them in each church and, with prayer and fasting, committed them to the Lord, in whom they had put their trust.

Acts 19 8Paul entered the synagogue and spoke boldly there for three months, arguing persuasively about the kingdom of God.

9But some of them became obstinate; they refused to believe and publicly maligned the Way. So Paul left them. He took the disciples with him and had discussions daily in the lecture hall of Tyrannus. 10This went on for two years, so that all the Jews and Greeks who lived in the province of Asia heard the word of the Lord.

11God did extraordinary miracles through Paul. . . .

Acts 20 25"Now I know that none of you among whom I have gone about preaching the kingdom will ever see me again. 26Therefore, I declare to you today that I am innocent of the blood of all men. 27For I have not hesitated to proclaim to you the whole will of God. 28Keep watch over yourselves and all the flock of which the Holy Spirit has made you overseers. Be shepherds of the church of God, which he bought with his own blood. 29I know that after I leave, savage wolves will come in among you and will not spare the flock. 30Even from your own number men will arise and distort the truth in order to draw away disciples after them. 31So be on your guard! Remember that for three years I never stopped warning each of you night and day with tears."

Acts 28 23They arranged to meet Paul on a certain day, and came in even larger numbers to the place where he was staying. From morning till evening he explained and declared to them the kingdom of God and tried to convince them about Jesus from the Law of Moses and from the Prophets. . . . 31Boldly and without hindrance he preached the kingdom of God and taught about the Lord Jesus Christ.

Rom 14 17For the kingdom of God is not a matter of eating and drinking, but of righteousness, peace and joy in the Holy Spirit. . . .

1 Cor 4 20For the kingdom of God is not a matter of talk but of power.

1 Cor 6 9Do you not know that the wicked will not inherit the kingdom of God? Do not be deceived: Neither the sexually immoral nor idolaters nor adulterers nor male prostitutes nor homosexual offenders 10nor thieves nor the greedy nor drunkards nor slanderers nor swindlers will inherit the kingdom of God. 11And that is what some of you were. But you were washed, you were sanctified, you were justified in the name of the Lord Jesus Christ and by the Spirit of our God.

Gal 5 16So I say, live by the Spirit, and you will not gratify the desires of the sinful nature. . . .

19The acts of the sinful nature are obvious: sexual immorality, impurity and debauchery; 20idolatry and witchcraft; hatred, discord, jealousy, fits of rage, selfish ambition, dissensions, factions 21and envy; drunkenness, orgies, and the like. I warn you, as I did before, that those who live like this will not inherit the kingdom of God. . . .

24Those who belong to Christ Jesus have crucified the sinful nature with its passions and desires.

Eph 5 5For of this you can be sure: No immoral, impure or greedy person—such a man is an idolater—has any inheritance in the kingdom of Christ and of God.

Col 1 13For he has rescued us from the dominion of darkness and brought us into the kingdom of the Son he loves, 14in whom we have redemption, the forgiveness of sins.

Col 4 11Jesus, who is called Justus, also sends greetings. These are the only Jews among my fellow workers for the kingdom of God, and they have proved a comfort to me.

1 Thess 2 11For you know that we dealt with each of you as a father deals with his own children, 12encouraging, comforting and urging you to live lives worthy of God, who calls you into his kingdom and glory.

2 Thess 1 5All this is evidence that God's judgment is right, and as a result you will be counted worthy of the kingdom of God, for which you are suffering.

James 2 5Listen, my dear brothers: Has not God chosen those who are poor in the eyes of the world to be rich in faith and to inherit the kingdom he promised those who love him?

2 Pet 1 5For this very reason, make every effort to add to your faith goodness; and to goodness, knowledge; 6and to knowledge, self-control; and to self-control, perseverance; and to perseverance, godliness; 7and to godliness, brotherly kindness; and to brotherly kindness, love. 8For if you possess these qualities in increasing measure, they will keep you from being ineffective and unproductive in your knowledge of our Lord Jesus Christ. 9But if anyone does not have them, he is nearsighted and blind, and has forgotten that he has been cleansed from his past sins.

10Therefore, my brothers, be all the more eager to make your calling and election sure. For if you do these things, you will never fall, 11and you will receive a rich welcome into the eternal kingdom of our Lord and Savior Jesus Christ.

Rev 1 9I, John, your brother and companion in the suffering and kingdom and patient endurance that are ours in Jesus, was on the island of Patmos because of the word of God and the testimony of Jesus.

Rev 12 10Then I heard a loud voice in heaven say: "Now have come the salvation and the power and the kingdom of our God, and the authority of his Christ. For the accuser of our brothers, who accuses them before our God day and night, has been hurled down. 11They overcame him by the blood of the Lamb and by the word of their testimony; they did not love their lives so much as to shrink from death. 12Therefore rejoice, you heavens and you who dwell in them! But woe to the earth and the sea, because the devil has gone down to you! He is filled with fury, because he knows that his time is short."

(2) The Consummation of the Kingdom

Acts 1 3After his suffering, he showed himself to these men and gave many convincing proofs that he was alive. He appeared to them over a period of forty days and spoke about the kingdom of God. 4On one occasion, while he was eating with them, he gave them this command: "Do not leave Jerusalem, but wait for the gift my Father promised, which you have heard me speak about. 5For John baptized with water, but in a few days you will be baptized with the Holy Spirit."

6So when they met together, they asked him, "Lord, are you at this time going to restore the kingdom to Israel?"

7He said to them: "It is not for you to know the times or dates the Father has set by his own authority. 8But you will receive power when the Holy Spirit comes on you; and you will be my witnesses in Jerusalem, and in all Judea and Samaria, and to the ends of the earth."

1 Cor 15 24Then the end will come, when he hands over the kingdom to God the Father after he has destroyed all dominion, authority and power. 25For he must reign until he has put all his enemies under his feet. 26The last enemy to be destroyed is death. 27For he "has put everything under his feet." Now when it says that "everything" has been put under him, it is clear that this does not include God himself, who put everything under Christ. 28When he has done this, then the Son himself will be made subject to him who put everything under him, so that God may be all in all.

1 Cor 15 50I declare to you, brothers, that flesh and blood cannot inherit the kingdom of God, nor does the perishable inherit the imperishable. 51Listen, I tell you a mystery: We will not all sleep, but we will all be changed—52in a flash, in the twinkling of an eye, at the last trumpet. For the trumpet will sound, the dead will be raised imperishable, and we will be changed. 53For the perishable must clothe itself with the imperishable, and the mortal with immortality. 54When the perishable has been clothed with the imperishable, and the mortal with immortality, then the saying that is written will come true: "Death has been swallowed up in victory."

2 Tim 4 1In the presence of God and of Christ Jesus, who will judge the living and the dead, and in view of his appearing and his kingdom, I give you this charge: 2Preach the Word; be prepared in season and out of season; correct, rebuke and encourage—with great patience and careful instruction. 3For the time will come when men will not put up with sound doctrine. Instead, to suit their own desires, they will gather around them a great number of teachers to say what their itching ears want to hear. 4They will turn their ears away from the truth and turn aside to myths. 5But you, keep your head in all situations, endure hardship, do the work of an evangelist, discharge all the duties of your ministry.

Heb 12 28Therefore, since we are receiving a kingdom that cannot be shaken, let us be thankful, and so worship God acceptably with reverence and awe, 29for our "God is a consuming fire."

Rev 11 15The seventh angel sounded his trumpet, and there were loud voices in heaven, which said: "The kingdom of the world has become the kingdom of our Lord and of his Christ, and he will reign for ever and ever."

B. The Will of God

1. The Essence of God's Will

a) His Will Is Unified

Prov 19 [21]Many are the plans in a man's heart, but it is the LORD's purpose that prevails.
Rom 8 [28]And we know that in all things God works for the good of those who love him, who have been called according to his purpose.
Rom 9 [11]Yet, before the twins were born or had done anything good or bad—in order that God's purpose in election might stand . . .
Eph 1 [11]In him we were also chosen, having been predestined according to the plan of him who works out everything in conformity with the purpose of his will. . . .

b) His Will Is Unchanging

Ps 33 [11]But the plans of the LORD stand firm forever, the purposes of his heart through all generations.
Eccles 3 [14]I know that everything God does will endure forever; nothing can be added to it and nothing taken from it. God does it so that men will revere him.
Isa 25 [1]O LORD, you are my God; I will exalt you and praise your name, for in perfect faithfulness you have done marvelous things, things planned long ago.
Isa 46 [10]"I make known the end from the beginning, from ancient times, what is still to come. I say: My purpose will stand, and I will do all that I please."
Acts 2 [23]"This man was handed over to you by God's set purpose and foreknowledge; and you, with the help of wicked men, put him to death by nailing him to the cross."
Acts 4 [27]"Indeed Herod and Pontius Pilate met together with the Gentiles and the people of Israel in this city to conspire against your holy servant Jesus, whom you anointed. [28]They did what your power and will had decided beforehand should happen."
Eph 3 [11]according to his eternal purpose which he accomplished in Christ Jesus our Lord.
Heb 6 [17]Because God wanted to make the unchanging nature of his purpose very clear to the heirs of what was promised, he confirmed it with an oath.
James 1 [17]Every good and perfect gift is from above, coming down from the Father of the heavenly lights, who does not change like shifting shadows.

c) His Will Is Most Excellent

(1) The Goodness of the Divine Will

Rom 12 [2]Do not conform any longer to the pattern of this world, but be transformed by the renewing of your mind. Then you will be able to test and approve what God's will is—his good, pleasing and perfect will.
Phil 2 [13]for it is God who works in you to will and to act according to his good purpose.

(2) The Grace of the Divine Will

Eph 2 [6]And God raised us up with Christ and seated us with him in the heavenly realms in Christ Jesus, [7]in order that in the coming ages he might show the incomparable riches of his grace, expressed in his kindness to us in Christ Jesus.

(3) The Perfection of the Divine Will

Rom 12 [2]Do not conform any longer to the pattern of this world, but be transformed by the renewing of your mind. Then you will be able to test and approve what God's will is—his good, pleasing and perfect will.

(4) The Righteousness of the Divine Will

Deut 33 [21]"He chose the best land for himself; the leader's portion was kept for him. When the heads of the people assembled, he carried out the LORD's righteous will, and his judgments concerning Israel."
1 Sam 2 [22]Now Eli, who was very old, heard about everything his sons were doing to all Israel and how they slept with the women who served at the entrance to the Tent of Meeting. [23]So he said to them, "Why do you do such things? I hear from all the people about these wicked deeds of yours. [24]No, my sons, it is not a good report that I hear spreading among the LORD's people. [25]If a man sins against another man, God may mediate for him; but if a man sins against the LORD, who will intercede for him?" His sons, however, did not listen to their father's rebuke, for it was the LORD's will to put them to death.
[26]And the boy Samuel continued to grow in stature and in favor with the LORD and with men.

(5) The Wisdom of the Divine Will

Eph 3 [10]His intent was that now, through the church, the manifold wisdom of God should be made known to the rulers and authorities in the heavenly realms, [11]according to his eternal purpose which he accomplished in Christ Jesus our Lord.

d) His Will Is Ultimate

Lam 3 [37]Who can speak and have it happen if the Lord has not decreed it? [38]Is it not from the mouth of the Most High that both calamities and good things come?
Rev 4 [11]"You are worthy, our Lord and God, to receive glory and honor and power, for you created all things, and by your will they were created and have their being."

2. The Determination of God's Will

a) God Is Free to Act as He Wills

Job 23 [13]"But he stands alone, and who can oppose him? He does whatever he pleases."
Ps 115 [3]Our God is in heaven; he does whatever pleases him.
Ps 135 [6]The LORD does whatever pleases him, in the heavens and on the earth, in the seas and all their depths.
Isa 44 [24]"This is what the LORD says—your Redeemer, who formed you in the womb: I am the LORD, who has made all things, who alone stretched out the heavens, who spread out the earth by myself, . . . [28]who says of Cyrus, 'He is my shepherd and will accomplish all that I please; he will say of Jerusalem, "Let it be rebuilt," and of the temple, "Let its foundations be laid."'"
Isa 46 [10]"I make known the end from the beginning, from ancient times, what is still to come. I say: My purpose will stand, and I will do all that I please."
Dan 4 [17]"'The decision is announced by messengers, the holy ones declare the verdict, so that the living may know that the Most High is sovereign over the kingdoms of men and gives them to anyone he wishes and sets over them the lowliest of men.'"
Dan 4 [25]"You will be driven away from people and will live with the wild animals; you will eat grass like cattle and be drenched with the dew of heaven. Seven times will pass by for you until you acknowledge that the Most High is sovereign over the kingdoms of men and gives them to anyone he wishes."
Dan 4 [35]All the peoples of the earth are regarded as nothing. He does as he pleases with the powers of heaven and the peoples of the earth. No one can hold back his hand or say to him: "What have you done?"
Dan 5 [21]"He was driven away from people and given the mind of an animal; he lived with the wild donkeys and ate grass like cattle; and his body was drenched with the dew of heaven, until he acknowledged that the Most High God is sovereign over the kingdoms of men and sets over them anyone he wishes."
Rom 9 [15]For he says to Moses, "I will have mercy on whom I have mercy, and I will have compassion on whom I have compassion." . . . [18]Therefore God has mercy on whom he wants to have mercy, and he hardens whom he wants to harden.
Eph 1 [5]he predestined us to be adopted as his sons through Jesus Christ, in accordance with his pleasure and will. . . . [9]And he made known to us the mystery of his will according to his good pleasure, which he purposed in Christ. . . .
[11]In him we were also chosen, having been predestined according to the plan of him who works out everything in conformity with the purpose of his will. . . .

b) God Must Act according to His Nature

Gen 18 [25]"Far be it from you to do such a thing—to kill the righteous with the wicked, treating the righteous and the

wicked alike. Far be it from you! Will not the Judge of all the earth do right?"
Num 23 [19]"God is not a man, that he should lie, nor a son of man, that he should change his mind. Does he speak and then not act? Does he promise and not fulfill?"
1 Sam 15 [29]"He who is the Glory of Israel does not lie or change his mind; for he is not a man, that he should change his mind."
Rom 3 [26]he did it to demonstrate his justice at the present time, so as to be just and the one who justifies those who have faith in Jesus.
2 Tim 2 [13]if we are faithless, he will remain faithful, for he cannot disown himself.
Titus 1 [2]a faith and knowledge resting on the hope of eternal life, which God, who does not lie, promised before the beginning of time . . .
Heb 6 [18]God did this so that, by two unchangeable things in which it is impossible for God to lie, we who have fled to take hold of the hope offered to us may be greatly encouraged.
James 1 [13]When tempted, no one should say, "God is tempting me." For God cannot be tempted by evil, nor does he tempt anyone. . . .

3. The Expression of God's Will

a) His Will Is Partially Hidden

Deut 29 [29]The secret things belong to the LORD our God, but the things revealed belong to us and to our children forever, that we may follow all the words of this law.
Job 3 [23]"Why is life given to a man whose way is hidden, whom God has hedged in?"
Job 9 [10]"He performs wonders that cannot be fathomed, miracles that cannot be counted."
Job 28 [20]"Where then does wisdom come from? Where does understanding dwell? [21]It is hidden from the eyes of every living thing, concealed even from the birds of the air. [22]Destruction and Death say, 'Only a rumor of it has reached our ears.' [23]God understands the way to it and he alone knows where it dwells, [24]for he views the ends of the earth and sees everything under the heavens. [25]When he established the force of the wind and measured out the waters, [26]when he made a decree for the rain and a path for the thunderstorm, [27]then he looked at wisdom and appraised it; he confirmed it and tested it."
Job 38 [1]Then the LORD answered Job out of the storm. He said: [2]"Who is this that darkens my counsel with words without knowledge? [3]Brace yourself like a man; I will question you, and you shall answer me.

[4]"Where were you when I laid the earth's foundation? Tell me, if you understand. [5]Who marked off its dimensions? Surely you know! Who stretched a measuring line across it? [6]On what were its footings set, or who laid its cornerstone—[7]while the morning stars sang together and all the angels shouted for joy?

[8]"Who shut up the sea behind doors when it burst forth from the womb, [9]when I made the clouds its garment and wrapped it in thick darkness, [10]when I fixed limits for it and set its doors and bars in place, [11]when I said, 'This far you may come and no farther; here is where your proud waves halt'?

[12]"Have you ever given orders to the morning, or shown the dawn its place, [13]that it might take the earth by the edges and shake the wicked out of it? [14]The earth takes shape like clay under a seal; its features stand out like those of a garment. [15]The wicked are denied their light, and their upraised arm is broken.

[16]"Have you journeyed to the springs of the sea or walked in the recesses of the deep? [17]Have the gates of death been shown to you? Have you seen the gates of the shadow of death? [18]Have you comprehended the vast expanses of the earth? Tell me, if you know all this.

[19]"What is the way to the abode of light? And where does darkness reside? [20]Can you take them to their places? Do you know the paths to their dwellings? [21]Surely you know, for you were already born! You have lived so many years!

[22]"Have you entered the storehouses of the snow or seen the storehouses of the hail, [23]which I reserve for times of trouble, for days of war and battle? [24]What is the way to the place where the lightning is dispersed, or the place where the east winds are scattered over the earth? [25]Who cuts a channel for the torrents of rain, and a path for the thunderstorm, [26]to water a land where no man lives, a desert with no one in it, [27]to satisfy a desolate wasteland and make it sprout with grass? [28]Does the rain have a father? Who fathers the drops of dew? [29]From whose womb comes the ice? Who gives birth to the frost from the heavens [30]when the waters become hard as stone, when the surface of the deep is frozen?

[31]"Can you bind the beautiful Pleiades? Can you loose the cords of Orion? [32]Can you bring forth the constellations in their seasons or lead out the Bear with its cubs? [33]Do you know the laws of the heavens? Can you set up God's dominion over the earth?

[34]"Can you raise your voice to the clouds and cover yourself with a flood of water? [35]Do you send the lightning bolts on their way? Do they report to you, 'Here we are'? [36]Who endowed the heart with wisdom or gave understanding to the mind? [37]Who has the wisdom to count the clouds? Who can tip over the water jars of the heavens [38]when the dust becomes hard and the clods of earth stick together?

[39]"Do you hunt the prey for the lioness and satisfy the hunger of the lions [40]when they crouch in their dens or lie in wait in a thicket? [41]Who provides food for the raven when its young cry out to God and wander about for lack of food?"
Ps 78 [2]I will open my mouth in parables, I will utter hidden things, things from of old. . . .
Isa 48 [6]"You have heard these things; look at them all. Will you not admit them?

"From now on I will tell you of new things, of hidden things unknown to you."
Dan 2 [22]"He reveals deep and hidden things; he knows what lies in darkness, and light dwells with him."
Rom 11 [33]Oh, the depth of the riches of the wisdom and knowledge of God! How unsearchable his judgments, and his paths beyond tracing out! [34]"Who has known the mind of the Lord? Or who has been his counselor?"
1 Cor 2 [7]No, we speak of God's secret wisdom, a wisdom that has been hidden and that God destined for our glory before time began.
Eph 3 [9]and to make plain to everyone the administration of this mystery, which for ages past was kept hidden in God, who created all things.

b) His Will May Be Revealed

Exod 18 [15]Moses answered him, "Because the people come to me to seek God's will."
Lev 24 [12]They put him in custody until the will of the LORD should be made clear to them.
Deut 29 [29]The secret things belong to the LORD our God, but the things revealed belong to us and to our children forever, that we may follow all the words of this law.
Deut 30 [14]No, the word is very near you; it is in your mouth and in your heart so you may obey it.
2 Sam 7 [21]"For the sake of your word and according to your will, you have done this great thing and made it known to your servant."
Ps 40 [8]"I desire to do your will, O my God; your law is within my heart."
Ps 143 [10]Teach me to do your will, for you are my God; may your good Spirit lead me on level ground.
John 7 [17]"If anyone chooses to do God's will, he will find out whether my teaching comes from God or whether I speak on my own."
Rom 10 [8]But what does it say? "The word is near you; it is in your mouth and in your heart," that is, the word of faith we are proclaiming. . . .
Rom 12 [2]Do not conform any longer to the pattern of this world, but be transformed by the renewing of your mind. Then you will be able to test and approve what God's will is—his good, pleasing and perfect will.
Eph 5 [17]Therefore do not be foolish, but understand what the Lord's will is.
Col 1 [9]For this reason, since the day we heard about you, we have not stopped praying for you and asking God to fill you

with the knowledge of his will through all spiritual wisdom and understanding.

4. The Extent of God's Will: All Inclusive

See p. 189a, The Providence of God

5. The Intent of God's Will

a) His Will Is Purposeful

Gen 45 [4]Then Joseph said to his brothers, "Come close to me." When they had done so, he said, "I am your brother Joseph, the one you sold into Egypt! [5]And now, do not be distressed and do not be angry with yourselves for selling me here, because it was to save lives that God sent me ahead of you. [6]For two years now there has been famine in the land, and for the next five years there will not be plowing and reaping. [7]But God sent me ahead of you to preserve for you a remnant on earth and to save your lives by a great deliverance."

Gen 50 [19]But Joseph said to them, "Don't be afraid. Am I in the place of God? [20]You intended to harm me, but God intended it for good to accomplish what is now being done, the saving of many lives."

2 Sam 17 [14]Absalom and all the men of Israel said, "The advice of Hushai the Arkite is better than that of Ahithophel." For the LORD had determined to frustrate the good advice of Ahithophel in order to bring disaster on Absalom.

Isa 46 [8]"Remember this, fix it in mind, take it to heart, you rebels. [9]Remember the former things, those of long ago; I am God, and there is no other; I am God, and there is none like me. [10]I make known the end from the beginning, from ancient times, what is still to come. I say: My purpose will stand, and I will do all that I please. [11]From the east I summon a bird of prey; from a far-off land, a man to fulfill my purpose. What I have said, that will I bring about; what I have planned, that will I do."

Isa 55 [11]". . . so is my word that goes out from my mouth: It will not return to me empty, but will accomplish what I desire and achieve the purpose for which I sent it."

Matt 25 [34]"Then the King will say to those on his right, 'Come, you who are blessed by my Father; take your inheritance, the kingdom prepared for you since the creation of the world.'"

b) His Will Is Realized in and through Christ

Isa 53 [10]Yet it was the LORD's will to crush him and cause him to suffer, and though the LORD makes his life a guilt offering, he will see his offspring and prolong his days, and the will of the LORD will prosper in his hand. [11]After the suffering of his soul, he will see the light of life and be satisfied; by his knowledge my righteous servant will justify many, and he will bear their iniquities. [12]Therefore I will give him a portion among the great, and he will divide the spoils with the strong, because he poured out his life unto death, and was numbered with the transgressors. For he bore the sin of many, and made intercession for the transgressors.

Gal 4 [4]But when the time had fully come, God sent his Son, born of a woman, born under law, [5]to redeem those under law, that we might receive the full rights of sons.

Eph 1 [4]For he chose us in him before the creation of the world to be holy and blameless in his sight. In love [5]he predestined us to be adopted as his sons through Jesus Christ, in accordance with his pleasure and will. . . . [9]And he made known to us the mystery of his will according to his good pleasure, which he purposed in Christ, [10]to be put into effect when the times will have reached their fulfillment—to bring all things in heaven and on earth together under one head, even Christ.

Eph 3 [11]according to his eternal purpose which he accomplished in Christ Jesus our Lord.

6. God's Will in the Lives of Believers

a) An Attitude of Thanksgiving Conforms to His Will

1 Thess 5 [16]Be joyful always; [17]pray continually; [18]give thanks in all circumstances, for this is God's will for you in Christ Jesus.

b) Believers Are Given Gifts and Offices by His Will

Acts 1 [24]Then they prayed, "Lord, you know everyone's heart. Show us which of these two you have chosen [25]to take over this apostolic ministry which Judas left to go where he belongs." [26]Then they cast lots, and the lot fell to Matthias; so he was added to the eleven apostles.

1 Cor 1 [1]Paul, called to be an apostle of Christ Jesus by the will of God, and our brother Sosthenes . . .

2 Cor 1 [1]Paul, an apostle of Christ Jesus by the will of God, and Timothy our brother,

To the church of God in Corinth, together with all the saints throughout Achaia. . . .

Eph 1 [1]Paul, an apostle of Christ Jesus by the will of God,

To the saints in Ephesus, the faithful in Christ Jesus. . . .

Col 1 [1]Paul, an apostle of Christ Jesus by the will of God, and Timothy our brother . . .

2 Tim 1 [1]Paul, an apostle of Christ Jesus by the will of God, according to the promise of life that is in Christ Jesus. . . .

Heb 2 [2]For if the message spoken by angels was binding, and every violation and disobedience received its just punishment, [3]how shall we escape if we ignore such a great salvation? This salvation, which was first announced by the Lord, was confirmed to us by those who heard him. [4]God also testified to it by signs, wonders and various miracles, and gifts of the Holy Spirit distributed according to his will.

c) Believers Are Made Holy by His Will

1 Thess 4 [3]It is God's will that you should be sanctified: that you should avoid sexual immorality. . . .

Heb 10 [10]And by that will, we have been made holy through the sacrifice of the body of Jesus Christ once for all.

d) Believers Are to Do and Live according to His Will

1 Chron 13 [2]He then said to the whole assembly of Israel, "If it seems good to you and if it is the will of the LORD our God, let us send word far and wide to the rest of our brothers throughout the territories of Israel, and also to the priests and Levites who are with them in their towns and pasturelands, to come and join us."

Ezra 7 [18]You and your brother Jews may then do whatever seems best with the rest of the silver and gold, in accordance with the will of your God.

Ezra 10 [11]"Now make confession to the LORD, the God of your fathers, and do his will. Separate yourselves from the peoples around you and from your foreign wives."

Matt 7 [21]"Not everyone who says to me, 'Lord, Lord,' will enter the kingdom of heaven, but only he who does the will of my Father who is in heaven."

Matt 12 [50]"For whoever does the will of my Father in heaven is my brother and sister and mother."

Mark 3 [35]"Whoever does God's will is my brother and sister and mother."

Acts 18 [21]But as he left, he promised, "I will come back if it is God's will." Then he set sail from Ephesus.

1 Cor 4 [19]But I will come to you very soon, if the Lord is willing, and then I will find out not only how these arrogant people are talking, but what power they have.

2 Cor 8 [5]And they did not do as we expected, but they gave themselves first to the Lord and then to us in keeping with God's will.

Eph 6 [6]Obey them not only to win their favor when their eye is on you, but like slaves of Christ, doing the will of God from your heart.

Heb 10 [36]You need to persevere so that when you have done the will of God, you will receive what he has promised.

1 Pet 4 [1]Therefore, since Christ suffered in his body, arm yourselves also with the same attitude, because he who has suffered in his body is done with sin. [2]As a result, he does not live the rest of his earthly life for evil human desires, but rather for the will of God.

1 John 2 [17]The world and its desires pass away, but the man who does the will of God lives forever.

Rev 2 [26]To him who overcomes and does my will to the end, I will give authority over the nations. . . .

e) Believers Are to Make His Will Known

Matt 28 [18]Then Jesus came to them and said, "All authority in heaven and on earth has been given to me. [19]Therefore go and make disciples of all nations, baptizing them in the name of the Father and of the Son and of the Holy Spirit, [20]and teaching them to obey everything I have commanded you. And surely I am with you always, to the very end of the age."
Acts 20 [27]For I have not hesitated to proclaim to you the whole will of God.

f) Believers Are to Pray according to His Will

Matt 6 [9]"This, then, is how you should pray: 'Our Father in heaven, hallowed be your name, [10]your kingdom come, your will be done on earth as it is in heaven.'"
Rom 1 [9]God, whom I serve with my whole heart in preaching the gospel of his Son, is my witness how constantly I remember you [10]in my prayers at all times; and I pray that now at last by God's will the way may be opened for me to come to you.
Rom 15 [30]I urge you, brothers, by our Lord Jesus Christ and by the love of the Spirit, to join me in my struggle by praying to God for me. [31]Pray that I may be rescued from the unbelievers in Judea and that my service in Jerusalem may be acceptable to the saints there, [32]so that by God's will I may come to you with joy and together with you be refreshed.
1 John 5 [14]This is the confidence we have in approaching God: that if we ask anything according to his will, he hears us.

g) Believers Are to Seek, Desire, and Choose His Will

Exod 18 [15]Moses answered him, "Because the people come to me to seek God's will."
Ps 40 [8]"I desire to do your will, O my God; your law is within my heart."
Ps 143 [10]Teach me to do your will, for you are my God; may your good Spirit lead me on level ground.
John 7 [17]"If anyone chooses to do God's will, he will find out whether my teaching comes from God or whether I speak on my own."

h) Believers Are to Stand Firm in His Will

Col 4 [12]Epaphras, who is one of you and a servant of Christ Jesus, sends greetings. He is always wrestling in prayer for you, that you may stand firm in all the will of God, mature and fully assured.

i) Believers Are to Submit to His Will

Acts 21 [14]When he would not be dissuaded, we gave up and said, "The Lord's will be done."
James 4 [15]Instead, you ought to say, "If it is the Lord's will, we will live and do this or that."

j) Believers Are to Suffer according to His Will

1 Pet 3 [17]It is better, if it is God's will, to suffer for doing good than for doing evil.

k) Believers Are to Test and Approve His Will

Rom 12 [1]Therefore, I urge you, brothers, in view of God's mercy, to offer your bodies as living sacrifices, holy and pleasing to God—this is your spiritual act of worship. [2]Do not conform any longer to the pattern of this world, but be transformed by the renewing of your mind. Then you will be able to test and approve what God's will is—his good, pleasing and perfect will.

l) Believers Are to Understand and Know His Will

Lev 24 [12]They put him in custody until the will of the LORD should be made clear to them.
Acts 22 [14]"Then he said: 'The God of our fathers has chosen you to know his will and to see the Righteous One and to hear words from his mouth.'"
Eph 1 [9]And he made known to us the mystery of his will according to his good pleasure, which he purposed in Christ. . . .
Eph 5 [17]Therefore do not be foolish, but understand what the Lord's will is.
Col 1 [9]For this reason, since the day we heard about you, we have not stopped praying for you and asking God to fill you with the knowledge of his will through all spiritual wisdom and understanding.

m) God Predestined Believers according to His Will in Christ

Eph 1 [5]he predestined us to be adopted as his sons through Jesus Christ, in accordance with his pleasure and will. . . .
Eph 1 [11]In him we were also chosen, having been predestined according to the plan of him who works out everything in conformity with the purpose of his will. . . .

n) God Works His Will in Believers

Phil 2 [13]for it is God who works in you to will and to act according to his good purpose.
Heb 13 [20]May the God of peace, who through the blood of the eternal covenant brought back from the dead our Lord Jesus, that great Shepherd of the sheep, [21]equip you with everything good for doing his will, and may he work in us what is pleasing to him, through Jesus Christ, to whom be glory for ever and ever. Amen.

o) The Holy Spirit Intercedes for Believers according to His Will

Rom 8 [26]In the same way, the Spirit helps us in our weakness. We do not know what we ought to pray for, but the Spirit himself intercedes for us with groans that words cannot express. [27]And he who searches our hearts knows the mind of the Spirit, because the Spirit intercedes for the saints in accordance with God's will.

7. God's Will in the Judgment of Unbelievers

Prov 16 [4]The LORD works out everything for his own ends—even the wicked for a day of disaster.
Rom 9 [22]What if God, choosing to show his wrath and make his power known, bore with great patience the objects of his wrath—prepared for destruction?
1 Pet 2 [7]Now to you who believe, this stone is precious. But to those who do not believe, "The stone the builders rejected has become the capstone," [8]and, "A stone that causes men to stumble and a rock that makes them fall." They stumble because they disobey the message—which is also what they were destined for.
Jude [4]For certain men whose condemnation was written about long ago have secretly slipped in among you. They are godless men, who change the grace of our God into a license for immorality and deny Jesus Christ our only Sovereign and Lord.
See also p. 180a, Rejection by God

C. The Election of God

1. God's Election of Angels

1 Tim 5 [21]I charge you, in the sight of God and Christ Jesus and the elect angels, to keep these instructions without partiality, and to do nothing out of favoritism.

2. God's Election of Israel

Gen 25 [22]The babies jostled each other within her, and she said, "Why is this happening to me?" So she went to inquire of the LORD.

[23]The LORD said to her, "Two nations are in your womb, and two peoples from within you will be separated; one people will be stronger than the other, and the older will serve the younger."
Deut 4 [37]Because he loved your forefathers and chose their descendants after them, he brought you out of Egypt by his Presence and his great strength, [38]to drive out before you nations greater and stronger than you and to bring you into their land to give it to you for your inheritance, as it is today.
Deut 7 [6]For you are a people holy to the LORD your God. The

LORD your God has chosen you out of all the peoples on the face of the earth to be his people, his treasured possession. [7]The LORD did not set his affection on you and choose you because you were more numerous than other peoples, for you were the fewest of all peoples. [8]But it was because the LORD loved you and kept the oath he swore to your forefathers that he brought you out with a mighty hand and redeemed you from the land of slavery, from the power of Pharaoh king of Egypt.

Deut 10 [15]Yet the LORD set his affection on your forefathers and loved them, and he chose you, their descendants, above all the nations, as it is today.

Deut 14 [1]You are the children of the LORD your God. Do not cut yourselves or shave the front of your heads for the dead, [2]for you are a people holy to the LORD your God. Out of all the peoples on the face of the earth, the LORD has chosen you to be his treasured possession.

1 Kings 3 [8]"Your servant is here among the people you have chosen, a great people, too numerous to count or number."

1 Chron 16 [13]O descendants of Israel his servant, O sons of Jacob, his chosen ones.

Ps 33 [12]Blessed is the nation whose God is the LORD, the people he chose for his inheritance.

Ps 65 [4]Blessed are those you choose and bring near to live in your courts! We are filled with the good things of your house, of your holy temple.

Ps 105 [4]Look to the LORD and his strength; seek his face always. [5]Remember the wonders he has done, his miracles, and the judgments he pronounced, [6]O descendants of Abraham his servant, O sons of Jacob, his chosen ones. . . . [43]He brought out his people with rejoicing, his chosen ones with shouts of joy. . . .

Ps 106 [4]Remember me, O LORD, when you show favor to your people, come to my aid when you save them, [5]that I may enjoy the prosperity of your chosen ones, that I may share in the joy of your nation and join your inheritance in giving praise.

Ps 135 [4]For the LORD has chosen Jacob to be his own, Israel to be his treasured possession.

Isa 14 [1]The LORD will have compassion on Jacob; once again he will choose Israel and will settle them in their own land. Aliens will join them and unite with the house of Jacob.

Isa 41 [8]"But you, O Israel, my servant, Jacob, whom I have chosen, you descendants of Abraham my friend, [9]I took you from the ends of the earth, from its farthest corners I called you. I said, 'You are my servant'; I have chosen you and have not rejected you. [10]So do not fear, for I am with you; do not be dismayed, for I am your God. I will strengthen you and help you; I will uphold you with my righteous right hand."

Isa 43 [20]"The wild animals honor me, the jackals and the owls, because I provide water in the desert and streams in the wasteland, to give drink to my people, my chosen, [21]the people I formed for myself that they may proclaim my praise."

Isa 44 [1]"But now listen, O Jacob, my servant, Israel, whom I have chosen. [2]This is what the LORD says—he who made you, who formed you in the womb, and who will help you: Do not be afraid, O Jacob, my servant, Jeshurun, whom I have chosen."

Isa 45 [4]"For the sake of Jacob my servant, of Israel my chosen, I summon you by name and bestow on you a title of honor, though you do not acknowledge me."

Isa 49 [7]This is what the LORD says—the Redeemer and Holy One of Israel—to him who was despised and abhorred by the nation, to the servant of rulers: "Kings will see you and rise up, princes will see and bow down, because of the LORD, who is faithful, the Holy One of Israel, who has chosen you."

Isa 65 [9]"I will bring forth descendants from Jacob, and from Judah those who will possess my mountains; my chosen people will inherit them, and there will my servants live. . . .

[15]"You will leave your name to my chosen ones as a curse; the Sovereign LORD will put you to death, but to his servants he will give another name. . . .

[22]"No longer will they build houses and others live in them, or plant and others eat. For as the days of a tree, so will be the days of my people; my chosen ones will long enjoy the works of their hands."

Jer 30 [22]"'So you will be my people, and I will be your God.'"

Ezek 20 [5]". . . and say to them: 'This is what the Sovereign LORD says: On the day I chose Israel, I swore with uplifted hand to the descendants of the house of Jacob and revealed myself to them in Egypt. With uplifted hand I said to them, "I am the LORD your God."'"

Amos 3 [2]"You only have I chosen of all the families of the earth; therefore I will punish you for all your sins."

Mal 1 [2]"I have loved you," says the LORD.

"But you ask, 'How have you loved us?'

"Was not Esau Jacob's brother?" the LORD says. "Yet I have loved Jacob, [3]but Esau I have hated, and I have turned his mountains into a wasteland and left his inheritance to the desert jackals."

Acts 13 [17]"The God of the people of Israel chose our fathers; he made the people prosper during their stay in Egypt, with mighty power he led them out of that country. . . ."

Rom 9 [1]I speak the truth in Christ—I am not lying, my conscience confirms it in the Holy Spirit—[2]I have great sorrow and unceasing anguish in my heart. [3]For I could wish that I myself were cursed and cut off from Christ for the sake of my brothers, those of my own race, [4]the people of Israel. Theirs is the adoption as sons; theirs the divine glory, the covenants, the receiving of the law, the temple worship and the promises. [5]Theirs are the patriarchs, and from them is traced the human ancestry of Christ, who is God over all, forever praised! Amen.

Rom 11 [28]As far as the gospel is concerned, they are enemies on your account; but as far as election is concerned, they are loved on account of the patriarchs, [29]for God's gifts and his call are irrevocable. [30]Just as you who were at one time disobedient to God have now received mercy as a result of their disobedience, [31]so they too have now become disobedient in order that they too may now receive mercy as a result of God's mercy to you.

3. God's Election of the Place of Worship

a) God's Promise of a Place of Worship

Deut 12 [5]But you are to seek the place the LORD your God will choose from among all your tribes to put his Name there for his dwelling. To that place you must go. . . .

Deut 31 [11]". . . when all Israel comes to appear before the LORD your God at the place he will choose, you shall read this law before them in their hearing."

Josh 9 [27]That day he made the Gibeonites woodcutters and water carriers for the community and for the altar of the LORD at the place the LORD would choose. And that is what they are to this day.

b) God's Fulfillment of His Promise

(1) The Temple

1 Kings 9 [3]The LORD said to him: "I have heard the prayer and plea you have made before me; I have consecrated this temple, which you have built, by putting my Name there forever. My eyes and my heart will always be there."

2 Kings 21 [7]He took the carved Asherah pole he had made and put it in the temple, of which the LORD had said to David and to his son Solomon, "In this temple and in Jerusalem, which I have chosen out of all the tribes of Israel, I will put my Name forever."

Matt 21 [12]Jesus entered the temple area and drove out all who were buying and selling there. He overturned the tables of the money changers and the benches of those selling doves. [13]"It is written," he said to them, "'My house will be called a house of prayer,' but you are making it a 'den of robbers.'"

(2) Jerusalem

1 Kings 11 [13]"Yet I will not tear the whole kingdom from him, but will give him one tribe for the sake of David my servant and for the sake of Jerusalem, which I have chosen."

1 Kings 11 [36]"'I will give one tribe to his son so that David my servant may always have a lamp before me in Jerusalem, the city where I chose to put my Name.'"

1 Kings 14 [21]Rehoboam son of Solomon was king in Judah. He was forty-one years old when he became king, and he reigned seventeen years in Jerusalem, the city the LORD had

chosen out of all the tribes of Israel in which to put his Name. His mother's name was Naamah; she was an Ammonite.
2 Kings 23 [27]So the LORD said, "I will remove Judah also from my presence as I removed Israel, and I will reject Jerusalem, the city I chose, and this temple, about which I said, 'There shall my Name be.'"
2 Chron 6 [6]"'But now I have chosen Jerusalem for my Name to be there, and I have chosen David to rule my people Israel.'"
Neh 1 [9]"'. . . but if you return to me and obey my commands, then even if your exiled people are at the farthest horizon, I will gather them from there and bring them to the place I have chosen as a dwelling for my Name.'"
Ps 132 [13]For the LORD has chosen Zion, he has desired it for his dwelling. . . .
Zech 1 [17]"Proclaim further: This is what the LORD Almighty says: 'My towns will again overflow with prosperity, and the LORD will again comfort Zion and choose Jerusalem.'"
Zech 2 [12]"The LORD will inherit Judah as his portion in the holy land and will again choose Jerusalem."
Zech 3 [2]The LORD said to Satan, "The LORD rebuke you, Satan! The LORD, who has chosen Jerusalem, rebuke you! Is not this man a burning stick snatched from the fire?"

4. God's Election of the Messiah

Isa 42 [1]"Here is my servant, whom I uphold, my chosen one in whom I delight; I will put my Spirit on him and he will bring justice to the nations."
Luke 9 [35]A voice came from the cloud, saying, "This is my Son, whom I have chosen; listen to him."
Luke 23 [35]The people stood watching, and the rulers even sneered at him. They said, "He saved others; let him save himself if he is the Christ of God, the Chosen One."
1 Pet 1 [18]For you know that it was not with perishable things such as silver or gold that you were redeemed from the empty way of life handed down to you from your forefathers, [19]but with the precious blood of Christ, a lamb without blemish or defect. [20]He was chosen before the creation of the world, but was revealed in these last times for your sake.
1 Pet 2 [4]As you come to him, the living Stone—rejected by men but chosen by God and precious to him—[5]you also, like living stones, are being built into a spiritual house to be a holy priesthood, offering spiritual sacrifices acceptable to God through Jesus Christ. [6]For in Scripture it says: "See, I lay a stone in Zion, a chosen and precious cornerstone, and the one who trusts in him will never be put to shame."

5. God's Election to Salvation of Believers and the Believing Community

1 Kings 19 [18]"Yet I reserve seven thousand in Israel—all whose knees have not bowed down to Baal and all whose mouths have not kissed him."
Matt 11 [25]At that time Jesus said, "I praise you, Father, Lord of heaven and earth, because you have hidden these things from the wise and learned, and revealed them to little children. [26]Yes, Father, for this was your good pleasure."
Matt 13 [10]The disciples came to him and asked, "Why do you speak to the people in parables?"

[11]He replied, "The knowledge of the secrets of the kingdom of heaven has been given to you, but not to them."
Matt 22 [14]"For many are invited, but few are chosen."
Matt 24 [22]"If those days had not been cut short, no one would survive, but for the sake of the elect those days will be shortened."
Mark 13 [20]"If the Lord had not cut short those days, no one would survive. But for the sake of the elect, whom he has chosen, he has shortened them. . . . [22]For false Christs and false prophets will appear and perform signs and miracles to deceive the elect—if that were possible. . . .

[27]"And he will send his angels and gather his elect from the four winds, from the ends of the earth to the ends of the heavens."
Luke 18 [7]"And will not God bring about justice for his chosen ones, who cry out to him day and night? Will he keep putting them off?"
John 6 [37]"All that the Father gives me will come to me, and whoever comes to me I will never drive away. . . . [39]And this is the will of him who sent me, that I shall lose none of all that he has given me, but raise them up at the last day."
John 15 [16]"You did not choose me, but I chose you and appointed you to go and bear fruit—fruit that will last. Then the Father will give you whatever you ask in my name. . . .

[19]"If you belonged to the world, it would love you as its own. As it is, you do not belong to the world, but I have chosen you out of the world. That is why the world hates you."
John 17 [6]"I have revealed you to those whom you gave me out of the world. They were yours; you gave them to me and they have obeyed your word."
Acts 13 [48]When the Gentiles heard this, they were glad and honored the word of the Lord; and all who were appointed for eternal life believed.
Rom 8 [33]Who will bring any charge against those whom God has chosen? It is God who justifies.
Rom 9 [22]What if God, choosing to show his wrath and make his power known, bore with great patience the objects of his wrath—prepared for destruction? [23]What if he did this to make the riches of his glory known to the objects of his mercy, whom he prepared in advance for glory—[24]even us, whom he also called, not only from the Jews but also from the Gentiles? [25]As he says in Hosea: "I will call them 'my people' who are not my people; and I will call her 'my loved one' who is not my loved one," [26]and, "It will happen that in the very place where it was said to them, 'You are not my people,' they will be called 'sons of the living God.'"
Rom 11 [5]So too, at the present time there is a remnant chosen by grace.
Eph 1 [4]For he chose us in him before the creation of the world to be holy and blameless in his sight. In love [5]he predestined us to be adopted as his sons through Jesus Christ, in accordance with his pleasure and will. . . .
Col 3 [12]Therefore, as God's chosen people, holy and dearly loved, clothe yourselves with compassion, kindness, humility, gentleness and patience.
1 Thess 1 [4]For we know, brothers loved by God, that he has chosen you. . . .
2 Thess 2 [13]But we ought always to thank God for you, brothers loved by the Lord, because from the beginning God chose you to be saved through the sanctifying work of the Spirit and through belief in the truth.
2 Tim 2 [10]Therefore I endure everything for the sake of the elect, that they too may obtain the salvation that is in Christ Jesus, with eternal glory.
Titus 1 [1]Paul, a servant of God and an apostle of Jesus Christ for the faith of God's elect and the knowledge of the truth that leads to godliness . . .
James 1 [18]He chose to give us birth through the word of truth, that we might be a kind of firstfruits of all he created.
James 2 [5]Listen, my dear brothers: Has not God chosen those who are poor in the eyes of the world to be rich in faith and to inherit the kingdom he promised those who love him?
1 Pet 1 [1]Peter, an apostle of Jesus Christ,

To God's elect, strangers in the world, scattered throughout Pontus, Galatia, Cappadocia, Asia and Bithynia, [2]who have been chosen according to the foreknowledge of God the Father, through the sanctifying work of the Spirit, for obedience to Jesus Christ and sprinkling by his blood: Grace and peace be yours in abundance.
1 Pet 2 [9]But you are a chosen people, a royal priesthood, a holy nation, a people belonging to God, that you may declare the praises of him who called you out of darkness into his wonderful light.
1 Pet 5 [13]She who is in Babylon, chosen together with you, sends you her greetings, and so does my son Mark.
2 John [1]The elder,

To the chosen lady and her children, whom I love in the truth—and not I only, but also all who know the truth. . . .
2 John [13]The children of your chosen sister send their greetings.
Rev 17 [14]"They will make war against the Lamb, but the Lamb will overcome them because he is Lord of lords and King of

kings—and with him will be his called, chosen and faithful followers."

6. God's Election of Individuals

a) The Election of Abraham

Gen 18 [19]"For I have chosen him, so that he will direct his children and his household after him to keep the way of the LORD by doing what is right and just, so that the LORD will bring about for Abraham what he has promised him."
Neh 9 [7]"You are the LORD God, who chose Abram and brought him out of Ur of the Chaldeans and named him Abraham."

b) The Election of Jacob

Rom 9 [10]Not only that, but Rebekah's children had one and the same father, our father Isaac. [11]Yet, before the twins were born or had done anything good or bad—in order that God's purpose in election might stand: [12]not by works but by him who calls—she was told, "The older will serve the younger." [13]Just as it is written: "Jacob I loved, but Esau I hated."

c) The Election of Judah

1 Chron 28 [4]"Yet the LORD, the God of Israel, chose me from my whole family to be king over Israel forever. He chose Judah as leader, and from the house of Judah he chose my family, and from my father's sons he was pleased to make me king over all Israel."
Ps 78 [68]but he chose the tribe of Judah, Mount Zion, which he loved.

d) The Election of Moses

Ps 106 [23]So he said he would destroy them—had not Moses, his chosen one, stood in the breach before him to keep his wrath from destroying them.

e) The Election of Zerubbabel

Hag 2 [23]"'On that day,' declares the LORD Almighty, 'I will take you, my servant Zerubbabel son of Shealtiel,' declares the LORD, 'and I will make you like my signet ring, for I have chosen you,' declares the LORD Almighty."

f) The Election of Witnesses to Christ's Resurrection

Acts 10 [41]"He was not seen by all the people, but by witnesses whom God had already chosen—by us who ate and drank with him after he rose from the dead."

g) The Election of Matthias

Acts 1 [24]Then they prayed, "Lord, you know everyone's heart. Show us which of these two you have chosen. . . ." [26]Then they cast lots, and the lot fell to Matthias; so he was added to the eleven apostles.

h) The Election of Paul

Acts 9 [15]But the Lord said to Ananias, "Go! This man is my chosen instrument to carry my name before the Gentiles and their kings and before the people of Israel."
Acts 22 [13]"He stood beside me and said, 'Brother Saul, receive your sight!' And at that very moment I was able to see him.

[14]"Then he said: 'The God of our fathers has chosen you to know his will and to see the Righteous One and to hear words from his mouth.'"

7. God's Election of People to an Office

a) The Election of Priests

(1) Aaron as High Priest

Exod 28 [1]"Have Aaron your brother brought to you from among the Israelites, along with his sons Nadab and Abihu, Eleazar and Ithamar, so they may serve me as priests. . . .

[29]"Whenever Aaron enters the Holy Place, he will bear the names of the sons of Israel over his heart on the breastpiece of decision as a continuing memorial before the LORD. [30]Also put the Urim and the Thummim in the breastpiece, so they may be over Aaron's heart whenever he enters the presence of the LORD. Thus Aaron will always bear the means of making decisions for the Israelites over his heart before the LORD. . . . [34]The gold bells and the pomegranates are to alternate around the hem of the robe. [35]Aaron must wear it when he ministers. The sound of the bells will be heard when he enters the Holy Place before the LORD and when he comes out, so that he will not die.

[36]"Make a plate of pure gold and engrave on it as on a seal: HOLY TO THE LORD. [37]Fasten a blue cord to it to attach it to the turban; it is to be on the front of the turban. [38]It will be on Aaron's forehead, and he will bear the guilt involved in the sacred gifts the Israelites consecrate, whatever their gifts may be. It will be on Aaron's forehead continually so that they will be acceptable to the LORD."
Num 16 [5]Then he said to Korah and all his followers: "In the morning the LORD will show who belongs to him and who is holy, and he will have that person come near him. The man he chooses he will cause to come near him." . . .

[16]Moses said to Korah, "You and all your followers are to appear before the LORD tomorrow—you and they and Aaron. [17]Each man is to take his censer and put incense in it—250 censers in all—and present it before the LORD. You and Aaron are to present your censers also." . . . [19]When Korah had gathered all his followers in opposition to them at the entrance to the Tent of Meeting, the glory of the LORD appeared to the entire assembly. [20]The LORD said to Moses and Aaron, [21]"Separate yourselves from this assembly so I can put an end to them at once." . . .

[39]So Eleazar the priest collected the bronze censers brought by those who had been burned up, and he had them hammered out to overlay the altar, [40]as the LORD directed him through Moses. This was to remind the Israelites that no one except a descendant of Aaron should come to burn incense before the LORD, or he would become like Korah and his followers.
Num 17 [5]"The staff belonging to the man I choose will sprout, and I will rid myself of this constant grumbling against you by the Israelites." . . .

[8]The next day Moses entered the Tent of the Testimony and saw that Aaron's staff, which represented the house of Levi, had not only sprouted but had budded, blossomed and produced almonds.
1 Sam 2 [27]Now a man of God came to Eli and said to him, "This is what the LORD says: 'Did I not clearly reveal myself to your father's house when they were in Egypt under Pharaoh? [28]I chose your father out of all the tribes of Israel to be my priest, to go up to my altar, to burn incense, and to wear an ephod in my presence. I also gave your father's house all the offerings made with fire by the Israelites.'"

(2) Levi's Tribe as Priests

Deut 10 [8]At that time the LORD set apart the tribe of Levi to carry the ark of the covenant of the LORD, to stand before the LORD to minister and to pronounce blessings in his name, as they still do today.
Deut 18 [1]The priests, who are Levites—indeed the whole tribe of Levi—are to have no allotment or inheritance with Israel. They shall live on the offerings made to the LORD by fire, for that is their inheritance. [5]. . . for the LORD your God has chosen them and their descendants out of all your tribes to stand and minister in the LORD's name always.
Deut 21 [5]The priests, the sons of Levi, shall step forward, for the LORD your God has chosen them to minister and to pronounce blessings in the name of the LORD and to decide all cases of dispute and assault.
2 Chron 29 [5]and said: "Listen to me, Levites! Consecrate yourselves now and consecrate the temple of the LORD, the God of your fathers. Remove all defilement from the sanctuary. . . . [11]My sons, do not be negligent now, for the LORD has chosen you to stand before him and serve him, to minister before him and to burn incense."

b) The Election of Kings

(1) The Promise of Their Election

Deut 17 [15]be sure to appoint over you the king the LORD your God chooses. He must be from among your own brothers. Do not place a foreigner over you, one who is not a brother Israelite.

(2) Saul's Election

1 Sam 9 [15]Now the day before Saul came, the LORD had revealed this to Samuel: [16]"About this time tomorrow I will send you a man from the land of Benjamin. Anoint him leader over my people Israel; he will deliver my people from the hand of the Philistines. I have looked upon my people, for their cry has reached me."

[17]When Samuel caught sight of Saul, the LORD said to him, "This is the man I spoke to you about; he will govern my people."

1 Sam 10 [21]Then he brought forward the tribe of Benjamin, clan by clan, and Matri's clan was chosen. Finally Saul son of Kish was chosen. But when they looked for him, he was not to be found. . . .

[24]Samuel said to all the people, "Do you see the man the LORD has chosen? There is no one like him among all the people."

Then the people shouted, "Long live the king!"

2 Sam 21 [6]". . . let seven of his male descendants be given to us to be killed and exposed before the LORD at Gibeah of Saul—the Lord's chosen one."

So the king said, "I will give them to you."

(3) David's Election

1 Sam 16 [1]The LORD said to Samuel, "How long will you mourn for Saul, since I have rejected him as king over Israel? Fill your horn with oil and be on your way; I am sending you to Jesse of Bethlehem. I have chosen one of his sons to be king." . . .

[6]When they arrived, Samuel saw Eliab and thought, "Surely the LORD's anointed stands here before the LORD."

[7]But the LORD said to Samuel, "Do not consider his appearance or his height, for I have rejected him. The LORD does not look at the things man looks at. Man looks at the outward appearance, but the LORD looks at the heart."

[8]Then Jesse called Abinadab and had him pass in front of Samuel. But Samuel said, "The LORD has not chosen this one either." [9]Jesse then had Shammah pass by, but Samuel said, "Nor has the LORD chosen this one." [10]Jesse had seven of his sons pass before Samuel, but Samuel said to him, "The LORD has not chosen these." [11]So he asked Jesse, "Are these all the sons you have?"

"There is still the youngest," Jesse answered, "but he is tending the sheep."

Samuel said, "Send for him; we will not sit down until he arrives."

[12]So he sent and had him brought in. He was ruddy, with a fine appearance and handsome features.

Then the LORD said, "Rise and anoint him; he is the one."

2 Sam 6 [21]David said to Michal, "It was before the LORD, who chose me rather than your father or anyone from his house when he appointed me ruler over the LORD's people Israel—I will celebrate before the LORD."

1 Kings 8 [16]"'Since the day I brought my people Israel out of Egypt, I have not chosen a city in any tribe of Israel to have a temple built for my Name to be there, but I have chosen David to rule my people Israel.'"

1 Kings 11 [34]"'But I will not take the whole kingdom out of Solomon's hand; I have made him ruler all the days of his life for the sake of David my servant, whom I chose and who observed my commands and statutes.'"

1 Chron 28 [4]"Yet the LORD, the God of Israel, chose me from my whole family to be king over Israel forever. He chose Judah as leader, and from the house of Judah he chose my family, and from my father's sons he was pleased to make me king over all Israel."

2 Chron 6 [6]"'But now I have chosen Jerusalem for my Name to be there, and I have chosen David to rule my people Israel.'"

Ps 78 [70]He chose David his servant and took him from the sheep pens; [71]from tending the sheep he brought him to be the shepherd of his people Jacob, of Israel his inheritance.

Ps 89 [3]You said, "I have made a covenant with my chosen one, I have sworn to David my servant, [4]'I will establish your line forever and make your throne firm through all generations.'" . . .

[19]Once you spoke in a vision, to your faithful people you said: "I have bestowed strength on a warrior; I have exalted a young man from among the people. [20]I have found David my servant; with my sacred oil I have anointed him."

(4) Solomon's Election

1 Chron 28 [5]"Of all my sons—and the LORD has given me many—he has chosen my son Solomon to sit on the throne of the kingdom of the LORD over Israel. [6]He said to me: 'Solomon your son is the one who will build my house and my courts, for I have chosen him to be my son, and I will be his father. [7]I will establish his kingdom forever if he is unswerving in carrying out my commands and laws, as is being done at this time.'"

2 Chron 1 [8]Solomon answered God, "You have shown great kindness to David my father and have made me king in his place. [9]Now, LORD God, let your promise to my father David be confirmed, for you have made me king over a people who are as numerous as the dust of the earth. [10]Give me wisdom and knowledge, that I may lead this people, for who is able to govern this great people of yours?"

c) The Election of Apostles

Luke 6 [13]When morning came, he called his disciples to him and chose twelve of them, whom he also designated apostles. . . .

John 6 [70]Then Jesus replied, "Have I not chosen you, the Twelve? Yet one of you is a devil!"

John 13 [18]"I am not referring to all of you; I know those I have chosen. But this is to fulfill the scripture: 'He who shares my bread has lifted up his heel against me.'"

Acts 1 [2]until the day he was taken up to heaven, after giving instructions through the Holy Spirit to the apostles he had chosen.

Acts 1 [24]Then they prayed, "Lord, you know everyone's heart. Show us which of these two you have chosen [25]to take over this apostolic ministry, which Judas left to go where he belongs." [26]Then they cast lots, and the lot fell to Matthias; so he was added to the eleven apostles.

8. God's Election to a Task

John 15 [16]"You did not choose me, but I chose you and appointed you to go and bear fruit—fruit that will last. Then the Father will give you whatever you ask in my name."

Acts 9 [15]But the Lord said to Ananias, "Go! This man is my chosen instrument to carry my name before the Gentiles and their kings and before the people of Israel."

Acts 15 [7]After much discussion, Peter got up and addressed them: "Brothers, you know that some time ago God made a choice among you that the Gentiles might hear from my lips the message of the gospel and believe."

9. God's Election and Human Freedom

a) The Command and the Need to Choose

Deut 11 [26]See, I am setting before you today a blessing and a curse—[27]the blessing if you obey the commands of the LORD your God that I am giving you today; [28]the curse if you disobey the commands of the LORD your God and turn from the way that I command you today by following other gods, which you have not known.

Deut 30 [15]See, I set before you today life and prosperity, death and destruction. [16]For I command you today to love the LORD your God, to walk in his ways, and to keep his commands, decrees and laws; then you will live and increase, and the LORD your God will bless you in the land you are entering to possess. . . .

[19]This day I call heaven and earth as witnesses against you that I have set before you life and death, blessings and curses. Now choose life, so that you and your children may live. . . .

Josh 24 [15]"But if serving the LORD seems undesirable to you, then choose for yourselves this day whom you will serve, whether the gods your forefathers served beyond the River, or the gods of the Amorites, in whose land you are living. But as for me and my household, we will serve the LORD."

1 Chron 28 [9]"And you, my son Solomon, acknowledge the God of your father, and serve him with wholehearted devotion and with a willing mind, for the LORD searches every heart and understands every motive behind the thoughts. If you seek him, he will be found by you; but if you forsake him, he will reject you forever."

Isa 55 [1]"Come, all you who are thirsty, come to the waters; and you who have no money, come, buy and eat! Come, buy wine and milk without money and without cost. . . ."

[6]Seek the LORD while he may be found; call on him while he is near. [7]Let the wicked forsake his way and the evil man his thoughts. Let him turn to the LORD, and he will have mercy on him, and to our God, for he will freely pardon.

Jer 26 [3]"Perhaps they will listen and each will turn from his evil way. Then I will relent and not bring on them the disaster I was planning because of the evil they have done."

Ezek 18 [21]"But if a wicked man turns away from all the sins he has committed and keeps all my decrees and does what is just and right, he will surely live; he will not die. [22]None of the offenses he has committed will be remembered against him. Because of the righteous things he has done, he will live. [23]Do I take any pleasure in the death of the wicked? declares the Sovereign LORD. Rather, am I not pleased when they turn from their ways and live?"

Joel 2 [32]And everyone who calls on the name of the LORD will be saved; for on Mount Zion and in Jerusalem there will be deliverance, as the LORD has said, among the survivors whom the LORD calls.

Amos 5 [4]This is what the LORD says to the house of Israel: "Seek me and live; [5]do not seek Bethel, do not go to Gilgal, do not journey to Beersheba. For Gilgal will surely go into exile, and Bethel will be reduced to nothing." [6]Seek the LORD and live, or he will sweep through the house of Joseph like a fire; it will devour, and Bethel will have no one to quench it.

Matt 11 [28]"Come to me, all you who are weary and burdened, and I will give you rest. [29]Take my yoke upon you and learn from me, for I am gentle and humble in heart, and you will find rest for your souls. [30]For my yoke is easy and my burden is light."

Matt 23 [37]"O Jerusalem, Jerusalem, you who kill the prophets and stone those sent to you, how often I have longed to gather your children together, as a hen gathers her chicks under her wings, but you were not willing."

John 3 [16]"For God so loved the world that he gave his one and only Son, that whoever believes in him shall not perish but have eternal life."

John 5 [39]"You diligently study the Scriptures because you think that by them you possess eternal life. These are the Scriptures that testify about me, [40]yet you refuse to come to me to have life."

Acts 2 [21]"'And everyone who calls on the name of the Lord will be saved.'"

Rom 10 [11]As the Scripture says, "Anyone who trusts in him will never be put to shame." [13]. . . for, "Everyone who calls on the name of the Lord will be saved."

Rev 22 [17]The Spirit and the bride say, "Come!" And let him who hears say, "Come!" Whoever is thirsty, let him come; and whoever wishes, let him take the free gift of the water of life.

b) Hardening of the Heart

(1) God Hardens the Human Heart

Exod 4 [21]The LORD said to Moses, "When you return to Egypt, see that you perform before Pharaoh all the wonders I have given you the power to do. But I will harden his heart so that he will not let the people go."

Exod 7 [3]"But I will harden Pharaoh's heart, and though I multiply my miraculous signs and wonders in Egypt, [4]he will not listen to you. Then I will lay my hand on Egypt and with mighty acts of judgment I will bring out my divisions, my people the Israelites. . . .

[13]Yet Pharaoh's heart became hard and he would not listen to them, just as the LORD had said.

Exod 9 [12]But the LORD hardened Pharaoh's heart and he would not listen to Moses and Aaron, just as the LORD had said to Moses.

Exod 10 [1]Then the LORD said to Moses, "Go to Pharaoh, for I have hardened his heart and the hearts of his officials so that I may perform these miraculous signs of mine among them. . . ."

Exod 10 [20]But the LORD hardened Pharaoh's heart, and he would not let the Israelites go.

Exod 10 [27]But the LORD hardened Pharaoh's heart, and he was not willing to let them go.

Exod 11 [9]The LORD had said to Moses, "Pharaoh will refuse to listen to you—so that my wonders may be multiplied in Egypt." [10]Moses and Aaron performed all these wonders before Pharaoh, but the LORD hardened Pharaoh's heart, and he would not let the Israelites go out of his country.

Exod 14 [4]"And I will harden Pharaoh's heart, and he will pursue them. But I will gain glory for myself through Pharaoh and all his army, and the Egyptians will know that I am the LORD." So the Israelites did this. . . .

[8]The LORD hardened the heart of Pharaoh king of Egypt, so that he pursued the Israelites, who were marching out boldly.

Exod 14 [17]"I will harden the hearts of the Egyptians so that they will go in after them. And I will gain glory through Pharaoh and all his army, through his chariots and his horsemen."

Deut 2 [30]But Sihon king of Heshbon refused to let us pass through. For the LORD your God had made his spirit stubborn and his heart obstinate in order to give him into your hands, as he has now done.

Josh 11 [19]Except for the Hivites living in Gibeon, not one city made a treaty of peace with the Israelites, who took them all in battle. [20]For it was the LORD himself who hardened their hearts to wage war against Israel, so that he might destroy them totally, exterminating them without mercy, as the LORD had commanded Moses.

Rom 9 [17]For the Scripture says to Pharaoh: "I raised you up for this very purpose, that I might display my power in you and that my name might be proclaimed in all the earth." [18]Therefore God has mercy on whom he wants to have mercy, and he hardens whom he wants to harden.

(2) Humans Harden Their Own Hearts

Exod 8 [15]But when Pharaoh saw that there was relief, he hardened his heart and would not listen to Moses and Aaron, just as the LORD had said.

Exod 8 [32]But this time also Pharaoh hardened his heart and would not let the people go.

Exod 9 [15]"'For by now I could have stretched out my hand and struck you and your people with a plague that would have wiped you off the earth. [16]But I have raised you up for this very purpose, that I might show you my power and that my name might be proclaimed in all the earth. [17]You still set yourself against my people and will not let them go.'" . . .

[34]When Pharaoh saw that the rain and hail and thunder had stopped, he sinned again: He and his officials hardened their hearts. [35]So Pharaoh's heart was hard and he would not let the Israelites go, just as the LORD had said through Moses.

1 Sam 6 [6]"Why do you harden your hearts as the Egyptians and Pharaoh did? When he treated them harshly, did they not send the Israelites out so they could go on their way?"

2 Chron 36 [11]Zedekiah was twenty-one years old when he became king, and he reigned in Jerusalem eleven years. [12]He did evil in the eyes of the LORD his God and did not humble himself before Jeremiah the prophet, who spoke the word of the LORD. [13]He also rebelled against King Nebuchadnezzar, who had made him take an oath in God's name. He became stiff-necked and hardened his heart and would not turn to the LORD, the God of Israel.

Ps 95 [8]do not harden your hearts as you did at Meribah, as you did that day at Massah in the desert. . . .

Prov 28 [14]Blessed is the man who always fears the LORD, but he who hardens his heart falls into trouble.

Ezek 3 [4]He then said to me: "Son of man, go now to the house of Israel and speak my words to them. [5]You are not being sent to a people of obscure speech and difficult language, but to the house of Israel—[6]not to many peoples of obscure speech and difficult language, whose words you cannot understand. Surely if I had sent you to them, they would have listened to you. [7]But the house of Israel is not willing to listen to you because they are not willing to listen to me, for the whole house of Israel is hardened and obstinate."

Heb 3 [8]". . . do not harden your hearts as you did in the rebellion, during the time of testing in the desert. . . ."

Heb 3 [15]As has just been said: "Today, if you hear his voice, do not harden your hearts as you did in the rebellion."

Heb 4 [7]Therefore God again set a certain day, calling it Today, when a long time later he spoke through David, as was said before: "Today, if you hear his voice, do not harden your hearts."

(3) Sin Hardens the Human Heart

Dan 5 [20]"But when his heart became arrogant and hardened with pride, he was deposed from his royal throne and stripped of his glory."
Eph 4 [18]They are darkened in their understanding and separated from the life of God because of the ignorance that is in them due to the hardening of their hearts.
Heb 3 [13]But encourage one another daily, as long as it is called Today, so that none of you may be hardened by sin's deceitfulness.

c) Rejection by God

1 Sam 2 [25]"If a man sins against another man, God may mediate for him; but if a man sins against the LORD, who will intercede for him?" His sons, however, did not listen to their father's rebuke, for it was the LORD's will to put them to death.
1 Kings 12 [13]The king answered the people harshly. Rejecting the advice given him by the elders, [14]he followed the advice of the young men and said, "My father made your yoke heavy; I will make it even heavier. My father scourged you with whips; I will scourge you with scorpions." [15]So the king did not listen to the people, for this turn of events was from the LORD, to fulfill the word the LORD had spoken to Jeroboam son of Nebat through Ahijah the Shilonite.
2 Chron 25 [16]While he was still speaking, the king said to him, "Have we appointed you an adviser to the king? Stop! Why be struck down?"

So the prophet stopped but said, "I know that God has determined to destroy you, because you have done this and have not listened to my counsel."
Isa 29 [2]Yet I will besiege Ariel; she will mourn and lament, she will be to me like an altar hearth. [6]. . . the LORD Almighty will come with thunder and earthquake and great noise, with windstorm and tempest and flames of a devouring fire. . . .

[9]Be stunned and amazed, blind yourselves and be sightless; be drunk, but not from wine, stagger, but not from beer. [10]The LORD has brought over you a deep sleep: He has sealed your eyes (the prophets); he has covered your heads (the seers).

[11]For you this whole vision is nothing but words sealed in a scroll. And if you give the scroll to someone who can read, and say to him, "Read this, please," he will answer, "I can't; it is sealed." [12]Or if you give the scroll to someone who cannot read, and say, "Read this, please," he will answer, "I don't know how to read."

[13]The Lord says: "These people come near to me with their mouth and honor me with their lips, but their hearts are far from me. Their worship of me is made up only of rules taught by men."
Jer 6 [30]"They are called rejected silver, because the LORD has rejected them."
Mal 1 [2]"I have loved you," says the LORD.

"But you ask, 'How have you loved us?'

"Was not Esau Jacob's brother?" the LORD says. "Yet I have loved Jacob, [3]but Esau I have hated, and I have turned his mountains into a wasteland and left his inheritance to the desert jackals."
John 17 [12]"While I was with them, I protected them and kept them safe by that name you gave me. None has been lost except the one doomed to destruction so that Scripture would be fulfilled."
Rom 1 [21]For although they knew God, they neither glorified him as God nor gave thanks to him, but their thinking became futile and their foolish hearts were darkened. [22]Although they claimed to be wise, they became fools [23]and exchanged the glory of the immortal God for images made to look like mortal man and birds and animals and reptiles.

[24]Therefore God gave them over in the sinful desires of their hearts to sexual impurity for the degrading of their bodies with one another.
Rom 9 [22]What if God, choosing to show his wrath and make his power known, bore with great patience the objects of his wrath—prepared for destruction?
Rom 9 [30]What shall we say? That the Gentiles, who did not pursue righteousness, have obtained it, a righteousness that is by faith; [31]but Israel, who pursued a law of righteousness, has not attained it. [32]Why not? Because they pursued it not by faith but as if it were by works. They stumbled over the "stumbling stone." [33]As it is written: "See, I lay in Zion a stone that causes men to stumble and a rock that makes them fall, and the one who trusts in him will never be put to shame."
Rom 11 [7]What then? What Israel sought so earnestly it did not obtain, but the elect did. The others were hardened, [8]as it is written: "God gave them a spirit of stupor, eyes so that they could not see and ears so that they could not hear, to this very day."
2 Cor 13 [5]Examine yourselves to see whether you are in the faith; test yourselves. Do you not realize that Christ Jesus is in you—unless, of course, you fail the test? [6]And I trust that you will discover that we have not failed the test.
2 Thess 2 [11]For this reason God sends them a powerful delusion so that they will believe the lie [12]and so that all will be condemned who have not believed the truth but have delighted in wickedness.
2 Tim 3 [8]Just as Jannes and Jambres opposed Moses, so also these men oppose the truth—men of depraved minds, who, as far as the faith is concerned, are rejected. [9]But they will not get very far because, as in the case of those men, their folly will be clear to everyone.
Jude [4]For certain men whose condemnation was written about long ago have secretly slipped in among you. They are godless men, who change the grace of our God into a license for immorality and deny Jesus Christ our only Sovereign and Lord.

II
The Created Order of God

A. The Creator: The Triune God

1. The Father and Creation

Gen 1 [1]In the beginning God created the heavens and the earth.
Exod 20 [11]"For in six days the LORD made the heavens and the earth, the sea, and all that is in them, but he rested on the seventh day. Therefore the LORD blessed the Sabbath day and made it holy."
1 Sam 2 [8]"He raises the poor from the dust and lifts the needy from the ash heap; he seats them with princes and has them inherit a throne of honor.

"For the foundations of the earth are the LORD's; upon them he has set the world."
2 Kings 19 [15]And Hezekiah prayed to the LORD: "O LORD, God of Israel, enthroned between the cherubim, you alone are God over all the kingdoms of the earth. You have made heaven and earth."
1 Chron 16 [26]For all the gods of the nations are idols, but the LORD made the heavens.
2 Chron 2 [12]And Hiram added: "Praise be to the LORD, the God of Israel, who made heaven and earth! He has given King David a wise son, endowed with intelligence and discernment, who will build a temple for the LORD and a palace for himself."
Neh 9 [6]"You alone are the LORD. You made the heavens, even the highest heavens, and all their starry host, the earth and all that is on it, the seas and all that is in them. You give life to everything, and the multitudes of heaven worship you."
Job 26 [7]"He spreads out the northern skies over empty space; he suspends the earth over nothing."
Ps 24 [1]The earth is the LORD's, and everything in it, the world, and all who live in it; [2]for he founded it upon the seas and established it upon the waters.
Ps 33 [6]By the word of the LORD were the heavens made, their starry host by the breath of his mouth.
Ps 78 [69]He built his sanctuary like the heights, like the earth that he established forever.
Ps 90 [2]Before the mountains were born or you brought forth

the earth and the world, from everlasting to everlasting you are God.
Ps 102 [25]"In the beginning you laid the foundations of the earth, and the heavens are the work of your hands."
Ps 104 [5]He set the earth on its foundations; it can never be moved.
Ps 119 [90]Your faithfulness continues through all generations; you established the earth, and it endures. [91]Your laws endure to this day, for all things serve you.
Ps 121 [1]I lift up my eyes to the hills—where does my help come from? [2]My help comes from the LORD, the Maker of heaven and earth.
Ps 146 [5]Blessed is he whose help is the God of Jacob, whose hope is in the LORD his God, [6]the Maker of heaven and earth, the sea, and everything in them—the LORD, who remains faithful forever.
Prov 8 [22]"The LORD brought me forth as the first of his works, before his deeds of old; [23]I was appointed from eternity, from the beginning, before the world began."
Prov 30 [4]"Who has gone up to heaven and come down? Who has gathered up the wind in the hollow of his hands? Who has wrapped up the waters in his cloak? Who has established all the ends of the earth? What is his name, and the name of his son? Tell me if you know!"
Isa 40 [12]Who has measured the waters in the hollow of his hand, or with the breadth of his hand marked off the heavens? Who has held the dust of the earth in a basket, or weighed the mountains on the scales and the hills in a balance? . . .

[21]Do you not know? Have you not heard? Has it not been told you from the beginning? Have you not understood since the earth was founded? [22]He sits enthroned above the circle of the earth, and its people are like grasshoppers. He stretches out the heavens like a canopy, and spreads them out like a tent to live in. . . . [26]Lift your eyes and look to the heavens: Who created all these? He who brings out the starry host one by one, and calls them each by name. Because of his great power and mighty strength, not one of them is missing. . . . [28]Do you not know? Have you not heard? The LORD is the everlasting God, the Creator of the ends of the earth. He will not grow tired or weary, and his understanding no one can fathom.
Isa 45 [12]"It is I who made the earth and created mankind upon it. My own hands stretched out the heavens; I marshaled their starry hosts."
Isa 45 [18]For this is what the LORD says—he who created the heavens, he is God; he who fashioned and made the earth, he founded it; he did not create it to be empty, but formed it to be inhabited—he says: "I am the LORD, and there is no other."
Isa 48 [13]"My own hand laid the foundations of the earth, and my right hand spread out the heavens; when I summon them, they all stand up together."
Isa 51 [13]". . . that you forget the LORD your Maker, who stretched out the heavens and laid the foundations of the earth, that you live in constant terror every day because of the wrath of the oppressor, who is bent on destruction? For where is the wrath of the oppressor? . . . [16]I have put my words in your mouth and covered you with the shadow of my hand—I who set the heavens in place, who laid the foundations of the earth, and who say to Zion, 'You are my people.'"
Isa 66 [1]This is what the LORD says: "Heaven is my throne, and the earth is my footstool. Where is the house you will build for me? Where will my resting place be? [2]Has not my hand made all these things, and so they came into being?" declares the LORD.

"This is the one I esteem: he who is humble and contrite in spirit, and trembles at my word."
Jer 10 [12]But God made the earth by his power; he founded the world by his wisdom and stretched out the heavens by his understanding.
Jer 32 [17]"Ah, Sovereign LORD, you have made the heavens and the earth by your great power and outstretched arm. Nothing is too hard for you."
Jer 33 [2]"This is what the LORD says, he who made the earth, the LORD who formed it and established it—the LORD is his name. . . ."
Jer 51 [15]"He made the earth by his power; he founded the world by his wisdom and stretched out the heavens by his understanding."
Amos 4 [13]He who forms the mountains, creates the wind, and reveals his thoughts to man, he who turns dawn to darkness, and treads the high places of the earth—the LORD God Almighty is his name.
Amos 9 [6]he who builds his lofty palace in the heavens and sets its foundation on the earth, who calls for the waters of the sea and pours them out over the face of the land—the LORD is his name.
Mark 13 [19]". . . because those will be days of distress unequaled from the beginning, when God created the world, until now—and never to be equaled again."
Acts 4 [24]When they heard this, they raised their voices together in prayer to God. "Sovereign Lord," they said, "you made the heaven and the earth and the sea, and everything in them."
Eph 3 [9]and to make plain to everyone the administration of this mystery, which for ages past was kept hidden in God, who created all things.
Heb 3 [4]For every house is built by someone, but God is the builder of everything.
Heb 11 [3]By faith we understand that the universe was formed at God's command, so that what is seen was not made out of what was visible.
2 Pet 3 [5]But they deliberately forget that long ago by God's word the heavens existed and the earth was formed out of water and by water.
Rev 14 [7]He said in a loud voice, "Fear God and give him glory, because the hour of his judgment has come. Worship him who made the heavens, the earth, the sea and the springs of water."

2. The Son and Creation

John 1 [1]In the beginning was the Word, and the Word was with God, and the Word was God. . . .

[3]Through him all things were made; without him nothing was made that has been made. . . .

[10]He was in the world, and though the world was made through him, the world did not recognize him.
1 Cor 8 [6]yet for us there is but one God, the Father, from whom all things came and for whom we live; and there is but one Lord, Jesus Christ, through whom all things came and through whom we live.
Col 1 [15]He is the image of the invisible God, the firstborn over all creation. [16]For by him all things were created: things in heaven and on earth, visible and invisible, whether thrones or powers or rulers or authorities; all things were created by him and for him.
Heb 1 [1]In the past God spoke to our forefathers through the prophets at many times and in various ways, [2]but in these last days he has spoken to us by his Son, whom he appointed heir of all things, and through whom he made the universe. . . .

[10]He also says, "In the beginning, O Lord, you laid the foundations of the earth, and the heavens are the work of your hands."

3. The Spirit and Creation

Gen 1 [2]Now the earth was formless and empty, darkness was over the surface of the deep, and the Spirit of God was hovering over the waters.
Job 26 [13]"By his breath the skies became fair; his hand pierced the gliding serpent."
Job 33 [4]"The Spirit of God has made me; the breath of the Almighty gives me life."
Ps 33 [6]By the word of the LORD were the heavens made, their starry host by the breath of his mouth.
Ps 104 [30]When you send your Spirit, they are created, and you renew the face of the earth.

B. The Created Order

1. Creation of the Universe and All Things

Ps 89 [11]The heavens are yours, and yours also the earth; you founded the world and all that is in it.

Ps 102 [25]In the beginning you laid the foundations of the earth, and the heavens are the work of your hands.

Eccles 11 [5]As you do not know the path of the wind, or how the body is formed in a mother's womb, so you cannot understand the work of God, the Maker of all things.

Isa 44 [24]"This is what the LORD says—your Redeemer, who formed you in the womb: I am the LORD, who has made all things, who alone stretched out the heavens, who spread out the earth by myself. . . ."

Isa 45 [12]"It is I who made the earth and created mankind upon it. My own hands stretched out the heavens; I marshaled their starry hosts."

Jer 10 [16]He who is the Portion of Jacob is not like these, for he is the Maker of all things, including Israel, the tribe of his inheritance—the LORD Almighty is his name.

Acts 4 [24]When they heard this, they raised their voices together in prayer to God. "Sovereign Lord," they said, "you made the heaven and the earth and the sea, and everything in them."

Acts 14 [15]"Men, why are you doing this? We too are only men, human like you. We are bringing you good news, telling you to turn from these worthless things to the living God, who made heaven and earth and sea and everything in them."

Acts 17 [24]"The God who made the world and everything in it is the Lord of heaven and earth and does not live in temples built by hands. [25]And he is not served by human hands, as if he needed anything, because he himself gives all men life and breath and everything else. [26]From one man he made every nation of men, that they should inhabit the whole earth; and he determined the times set for them and the exact places where they should live."

Rom 11 [36]For from him and through him and to him are all things. To him be the glory forever! Amen.

1 Cor 11 [12]For as woman came from man, so also man is born of woman. But everything comes from God.

Eph 3 [9]and to make plain to everyone the administration of this mystery, which for ages past was kept hidden in God, who created all things.

Col 1 [16]For by him all things were created: things in heaven and on earth, visible and invisible, whether thrones or powers or rulers or authorities; all things were created by him and for him.

Heb 2 [10]In bringing many sons to glory, it was fitting that God, for whom and through whom everything exists, should make the author of their salvation perfect through suffering.

Heb 3 [4]For every house is built by someone, but God is the builder of everything.

Rev 4 [11]"You are worthy, our Lord and God, to receive glory and honor and power, for you created all things, and by your will they were created and have their being."

Rev 10 [6]And he swore by him who lives for ever and ever, who created the heavens and all that is in them, the earth and all that is in it, and the sea and all that is in it, and said, "There will be no more delay!"

2. Creation of the Natural World Order

a) Land and Sea

Gen 1 [9]And God said, "Let the water under the sky be gathered to one place, and let dry ground appear." And it was so. [10]God called the dry ground "land," and the gathered waters he called "seas." And God saw that it was good.

Job 12 [8]". . . or speak to the earth, and it will teach you, or let the fish of the sea inform you. [9]Which of all these does not know that the hand of the LORD has done this? [10]In his hand is the life of every creature and the breath of all mankind."

Job 38 [3]"Brace yourself like a man; I will question you, and you shall answer me.

[4]"Where were you when I laid the earth's foundation? Tell me, if you understand. [5]Who marked off its dimensions? Surely you know! Who stretched a measuring line across it? [6]On what were its footings set, or who laid its cornerstone—[7]while the morning stars sang together and all the angels shouted for joy?

[8]"Who shut up the sea behind doors when it burst forth from the womb, [9]when I made the clouds its garment and wrapped it in thick darkness, [10]when I fixed limits for it and set its doors and bars in place, [11]when I said, 'This far you may come and no farther; here is where your proud waves halt'?

[12]"Have you ever given orders to the morning, or shown the dawn its place, [13]that it might take the earth by the edges and shake the wicked out of it? [14]The earth takes shape like clay under a seal; its features stand out like those of a garment. . . .

[16]"Have you journeyed to the springs of the sea or walked in the recesses of the deep? . . . [18]Have you comprehended the vast expanses of the earth? Tell me, if you know all this."

Ps 24 [1]The earth is the LORD's, and everything in it, the world, and all who live in it; [2]for he founded it upon the seas and established it upon the waters.

Ps 33 [7]He gathers the waters of the sea into jars; he puts the deep into storehouses.

Ps 65 [6]who formed the mountains by your power, having armed yourself with strength . . .

Ps 89 [12]You created the north and the south; Tabor and Hermon sing for joy at your name.

Ps 95 [5]The sea is his, for he made it, and his hands formed the dry land.

Ps 104 [5]He set the earth on its foundations; it can never be moved. [6]You covered it with the deep as with a garment; the waters stood above the mountains. [7]But at your rebuke the waters fled, at the sound of your thunder they took to flight; [8]they flowed over the mountains, they went down into the valleys, to the place you assigned for them. [9]You set a boundary they cannot cross; never again will they cover the earth. [10]He makes springs pour water into the ravines; it flows between the mountains.

Ps 136 [3]Give thanks to the Lord of lords: *His love endures forever.* [6]. . . who spread out the earth upon the waters, *His love endures forever.*

Prov 3 [20]by his knowledge the deeps were divided, and the clouds let drop the dew.

Prov 8 [24]"When there were no oceans, I was given birth, when there were no springs abounding with water; [25]before the mountains were settled in place, before the hills, I was given birth, [26]before he made the earth or its fields or any of the dust of the world. [28]. . . when he established the clouds above and fixed securely the fountains of the deep, [29]when he gave the sea its boundary so the waters would not overstep his command, and when he marked out the foundations of the earth."

Isa 40 [12]Who has measured the waters in the hollow of his hand, or with the breadth of his hand marked off the heavens? Who has held the dust of the earth in a basket, or weighed the mountains on the scales and the hills in a balance? . . . [28]Do you not know? Have you not heard? The LORD is the everlasting God, the Creator of the ends of the earth. He will not grow tired or weary, and his understanding no one can fathom.

Jer 5 [22]"Should you not fear me?" declares the LORD. "Should you not tremble in my presence? I made the sand a boundary for the sea, an everlasting barrier it cannot cross. The waves may roll, but they cannot prevail; they may roar, but they cannot cross it."

Amos 5 [8](he who made the Pleiades and Orion, who turns blackness into dawn and darkens day into night, who calls for the waters of the sea and pours them out over the face of the land—the LORD is his name. . . .)

Jon 1 [9]He answered, "I am a Hebrew and I worship the LORD, the God of heaven, who made the sea and the land."

b) Light and Darkness

Gen 1 [3]And God said, "Let there be light," and there was light. [4]God saw that the light was good, and he separated the light from the darkness. [5]God called the light "day," and the darkness he called "night." And there was evening, and there was morning—the first day.

Job 26 [10]"He marks out the horizon on the face of the waters for a boundary between light and darkness."

Ps 74 [16]The day is yours, and yours also the night; you established the sun and moon.

Isa 45 [7]"I form the light and create darkness, I bring prosperity and create disaster; I, the LORD, do all these things."

Amos 5 [8](he who made the Pleiades and Orion, who turns blackness into dawn and darkens day into night, who calls for the waters of the sea and pours them out over the face of the land—the LORD is his name. . . .)

2 Cor 4 [6]For God, who said, "Let light shine out of darkness," made his light shine in our hearts to give us the light of the knowledge of the glory of God in the face of Christ.

c) Plant Life

Gen 1 [11]Then God said, "Let the land produce vegetation: seed-bearing plants and trees on the land that bear fruit with seed in it, according to their various kinds." And it was so. [12]The land produced vegetation: plants bearing seed according to their kinds and trees bearing fruit with seed in it according to their kinds. And God saw that it was good.

Gen 2 [4]This is the account of the heavens and the earth when they were created.

When the LORD God made the earth and the heavens—[5]and no shrub of the field had yet appeared on the earth and no plant of the field had yet sprung up, for the LORD God had not sent rain on the earth and there was no man to work the ground, [6]but streams came up from the earth and watered the whole surface of the ground—[7]the LORD God formed the man from the dust of the ground and breathed into his nostrils the breath of life, and the man became a living being.

[8]Now the LORD God had planted a garden in the east, in Eden; and there he put the man he had formed. [9]And the LORD God made all kinds of trees grow out of the ground—trees that were pleasing to the eye and good for food. In the middle of the garden were the tree of life and the tree of the knowledge of good and evil.

Ps 104 [14]He makes grass grow for the cattle, and plants for man to cultivate—bringing forth food from the earth. . . . [16]The trees of the LORD are well watered, the cedars of Lebanon that he planted.

d) Sky

Gen 1 [6]And God said, "Let there be an expanse between the waters to separate water from water." [7]So God made the expanse and separated the water under the expanse from the water above it. And it was so. [8]God called the expanse "sky." And there was evening, and there was morning—the second day.

Job 9 [8]"He alone stretches out the heavens and treads on the waves of the sea."

Job 26 [7]"He spreads out the northern skies over empty space; he suspends the earth over nothing. [8]He wraps up the waters in his clouds, yet the clouds do not burst under their weight. . . . [13]By his breath the skies became fair; his hand pierced the gliding serpent."

Job 28 [25]"When he established the force of the wind and measured out the waters, [26]when he made a decree for the rain and a path for the thunderstorm . . ."

Job 36 [27]"He draws up the drops of water, which distill as rain to the streams; [28]the clouds pour down their moisture and abundant showers fall on mankind. [29]Who can understand how he spreads out the clouds, how he thunders from his pavilion? [30]See how he scatters his lightning about him, bathing the depths of the sea."

Job 37 [16]"Do you know how the clouds hang poised, those wonders of him who is perfect in knowledge? [17]You who swelter in your clothes when the land lies hushed under the south wind, [18]can you join him in spreading out the skies, hard as a mirror of cast bronze?"

Ps 19 [1]The heavens declare the glory of God; the skies proclaim the work of his hands.

Ps 33 [6]By the word of the LORD were the heavens made, their starry host by the breath of his mouth.

Ps 104 [2]He wraps himself in light as with a garment; he stretches out the heavens like a tent [3]and lays the beams of his upper chambers on their waters. He makes the clouds his chariot and rides on the wings of the wind. [4]He makes winds his messengers, flames of fire his servants.

Ps 135 [7]He makes clouds rise from the ends of the earth; he sends lightning with the rain and brings out the wind from his storehouses.

Ps 136 [3]Give thanks to the Lord of lords: *His love endures forever.* [5]. . . who by his understanding made the heavens, *His love endures forever.*

Ps 148 [4]Praise him, you highest heavens and you waters above the skies. [5]Let them praise the name of the LORD, for he commanded and they were created.

Prov 3 [19]By wisdom the LORD laid the earth's foundations, by understanding he set the heavens in place. . . .

Prov 8 [27]"I was there when he set the heavens in place, when he marked out the horizon on the face of the deep, [28]when he established the clouds above and fixed securely the fountains of the deep. . . ."

Prov 30 [4]"Who has gone up to heaven and come down? Who has gathered up the wind in the hollow of his hands? Who has wrapped up the waters in his cloak? Who has established all the ends of the earth? What is his name, and the name of his son? Tell me if you know!"

Isa 40 [12]Who has measured the waters in the hollow of his hand, or with the breadth of his hand marked off the heavens? Who has held the dust of the earth in a basket, or weighed the mountains on the scales and the hills in a balance?

Jer 10 [13]When he thunders, the waters in the heavens roar; he makes clouds rise from the ends of the earth. He sends lightning with the rain and brings out the wind from his storehouses.

e) Sun, Moon, and Stars

Gen 1 [14]And God said, "Let there be lights in the expanse of the sky to separate the day from the night, and let them serve as signs to mark seasons and days and years, [15]and let them be lights in the expanse of the sky to give light on the earth." And it was so. [16]God made two great lights—the greater light to govern the day and the lesser light to govern the night. He also made the stars. [17]God set them in the expanse of the sky to give light on the earth, [18]to govern the day and the night, and to separate light from darkness. And God saw that it was good.

Job 9 [9]"He is the Maker of the Bear and Orion, the Pleiades and the constellations of the south."

Job 38 [1]Then the LORD answered Job out of the storm. He said: . . . [12]"Have you ever given orders to the morning, or shown the dawn its place? . . .

[19]"What is the way to the abode of light? And where does darkness reside? [20]Can you take them to their places? Do you know the paths to their dwellings? . . .

[31]"Can you bind the beautiful Pleiades? Can you loose the cords of Orion? [32]Can you bring forth the constellations in their seasons or lead out the Bear with its cubs? [33]Do you know the laws of the heavens? Can you set up God's dominion over the earth?"

Ps 8 [3]When I consider your heavens, the work of your fingers, the moon and the stars, which you have set in place, [4]what is man that you are mindful of him, the son of man that you care for him?

Ps 19 [4]Their voice goes out into all the earth, their words to the ends of the world. In the heavens he has pitched a tent for the sun, [5]which is like a bridegroom coming forth from his pavilion, like a champion rejoicing to run his course. [6]It rises at one end of the heavens and makes its circuit to the other; nothing is hidden from its heat.

Ps 74 [16]The day is yours, and yours also the night; you established the sun and moon. [17]It was you who set all the boundaries of the earth; you made both summer and winter.

Ps 104 [19]The moon marks off the seasons, and the sun knows when to go down. [20]You bring darkness, it becomes night, and all the beasts of the forest prowl. [21]The lions roar for their prey and seek their food from God. [22]The sun rises, and they steal away; they return and lie down in their dens. [23]Then man goes out to his work, to his labor until evening.

Ps 136 [3]Give thanks to the Lord of lords: *His love endures forever.* [7]. . . who made the great lights—*His love endures forever.* [8]the sun to govern the day, *His love endures forever.* [9]the moon and stars to govern the night; *His love endures forever.*

Ps 148 [3]Praise him, sun and moon, praise him, all you shining stars. . . . [5]Let them praise the name of the LORD, for he commanded and they were created.

Jer 31 [35]This is what the LORD says, he who appoints the sun to shine by day, who decrees the moon and stars to shine by

night, who stirs up the sea so that its waves roar—the LORD Almighty is his name. . . .
Amos 5 [8](he who made the Pleiades and Orion, who turns blackness into dawn and darkens day into night, who calls for the waters of the sea and pours them out over the face of the land—the LORD is his name. . . .)

3. Creation of Animal Life

Gen 1 [20]And God said, "Let the water teem with living creatures, and let birds fly above the earth across the expanse of the sky." [21]So God created the great creatures of the sea and every living and moving thing with which the water teems, according to their kinds, and every winged bird according to its kind. And God saw that it was good. [22]God blessed them and said, "Be fruitful and increase in number and fill the water in the seas, and let the birds increase on the earth."
Job 12 [7]"But ask the animals, and they will teach you, or the birds of the air, and they will tell you; [8]or speak to the earth, and it will teach you, or let the fish of the sea inform you. [9]Which of all these does not know that the hand of the LORD has done this? [10]In his hand is the life of every creature and the breath of all mankind."
Job 39 [13]"The wings of the ostrich flap joyfully, but they cannot compare with the pinions and feathers of the stork. [14]She lays her eggs on the ground and lets them warm in the sand, [15]unmindful that a foot may crush them, that some wild animal may trample them. [16]She treats her young harshly, as if they were not hers; she cares not that her labor was in vain, [17]for God did not endow her with wisdom or give her a share of good sense. [18]Yet when she spreads her feathers to run, she laughs at horse and rider. . . .

[26]"Does the hawk take flight by your wisdom and spread his wings toward the south? [27]Does the eagle soar at your command and build his nest on high?"
Ps 8 [6]You made him ruler over the works of your hands; you put everything under his feet: . . . [8]the birds of the air, and the fish of the sea, all that swim the paths of the seas.
Ps 104 [25]There is the sea, vast and spacious, teeming with creatures beyond number—living things both large and small. [26]There the ships go to and fro, and the leviathan, which you formed to frolic there.
Jer 27 [5]"With my great power and outstretched arm I made the earth and its people and the animals that are on it, and I give it to anyone I please."

4. Creation of Humankind

a) Humans Were a Special Work of God

Exod 4 [11]The LORD said to him, "Who gave man his mouth? Who makes him deaf or mute? Who gives him sight or makes him blind? Is it not I, the LORD?"
Deut 4 [32]Ask now about the former days, long before your time, from the day God created man on the earth; ask from one end of the heavens to the other. Has anything so great as this ever happened, or has anything like it ever been heard of?
Job 34 [19]". . . who shows no partiality to princes and does not favor the rich over the poor, for they are all the work of his hands?"
Job 35 [10]"But no one says, 'Where is God my Maker, who gives songs in the night, [11]who teaches more to us than to the beasts of the earth and makes us wiser than the birds of the air?'"
Ps 8 [4]what is man that you are mindful of him, the son of man that you care for him? [5]You made him a little lower than the heavenly beings and crowned him with glory and honor. [6]You made him ruler over the works of your hands; you put everything under his feet: [7]all flocks and herds, and the beasts of the field, [8]the birds of the air, and the fish of the sea, all that swim the paths of the seas.
Ps 33 [13]From heaven the LORD looks down and sees all mankind . . . [15]he who forms the hearts of all, who considers everything they do.
Ps 95 [6]Come, let us bow down in worship, let us kneel before the LORD our Maker. . . .
Ps 100 [3]Know that the LORD is God. It is he who made us, and we are his; we are his people, the sheep of his pasture.
Ps 102 [18]Let this be written for a future generation, that a people not yet created may praise the LORD. . . .
Ps 138 [8]The LORD will fulfill his purpose for me; your love, O LORD, endures forever—do not abandon the works of your hands.
Prov 22 [2]Rich and poor have this in common: The LORD is the Maker of them all.
Eccles 7 [29]"This only have I found: God made mankind upright, but men have gone in search of many schemes."
Eccles 12 [1]Remember your Creator in the days of your youth, before the days of trouble come and the years approach when you will say, "I find no pleasure in them." . . .
Isa 45 [12]"It is I who made the earth and created mankind upon it. My own hands stretched out the heavens; I marshaled their starry hosts."
Isa 54 [16]"See, it is I who created the blacksmith who fans the coals into flame and forges a weapon fit for its work. And it is I who have created the destroyer to work havoc. . . ."
Isa 64 [8]Yet, O LORD, you are our Father. We are the clay, you are the potter; we are all the work of your hand.
Jer 27 [5]"With my great power and outstretched arm I made the earth and its people and the animals that are on it, and I give it to anyone I please."
Mal 2 [10]Have we not all one Father? Did not one God create us? Why do we profane the covenant of our fathers by breaking faith with one another?
1 Pet 4 [19]So then, those who suffer according to God's will should commit themselves to their faithful Creator and continue to do good.

b) Humans Were Created as Male and Female

Gen 1 [27]So God created man in his own image, in the image of God he created him; male and female he created them.
Gen 5 [2]He created them male and female and blessed them. And when they were created, he called them "man."
Matt 19 [4]"Haven't you read," he replied, "that at the beginning the Creator 'made them male and female'? . . ."
Mark 10 [6]"But at the beginning of creation God 'made them male and female.'"

c) Humans Were Fashioned in God's Image

Gen 1 [26]Then God said, "Let us make man in our image, in our likeness, and let them rule over the fish of the sea and the birds of the air, over the livestock, over all the earth, and over all the creatures that move along the ground."

[27]So God created man in his own image, in the image of God he created him; male and female he created them.

[28]God blessed them and said to them, "Be fruitful and increase in number; fill the earth and subdue it. Rule over the fish of the sea and the birds of the air and over every living creature that moves on the ground."
Gen 5 [1]This is the written account of Adam's line.

When God created man, he made him in the likeness of God.
Gen 9 [6]"Whoever sheds the blood of man, by man shall his blood be shed; for in the image of God has God made man."
Col 3 [9]Do not lie to each other, since you have taken off your old self with its practices [10]and have put on the new self, which is being renewed in knowledge in the image of its Creator.
James 3 [9]With the tongue we praise our Lord and Father, and with it we curse men, who have been made in God's likeness. [10]Out of the same mouth come praise and cursing. My brothers, this should not be.

d) Humans Were Given Bodily Form

Gen 2 [7]the LORD God formed the man from the dust of the ground and breathed into his nostrils the breath of life, and the man became a living being.
Job 10 [8]"Your hands shaped me and made me. Will you now turn and destroy me? [9]Remember that you molded me like clay. Will you now turn me to dust again? [10]Did you not pour me out like milk and curdle me like cheese, [11]clothe me with skin and flesh and knit me together with bones and sinews?"
Job 31 [15]"Did not he who made me in the womb make them? Did not the same one form us both within our mothers?"
Job 33 [6]"I am just like you before God; I too have been taken from clay."

Ps 94 [9]Does he who implanted the ear not hear? Does he who formed the eye not see?
Ps 119 [73]Your hands made me and formed me; give me understanding to learn your commands.
Ps 139 [13]For you created my inmost being; you knit me together in my mother's womb. [14]I praise you because I am fearfully and wonderfully made; your works are wonderful, I know that full well. [15]My frame was not hidden from you when I was made in the secret place. When I was woven together in the depths of the earth, [16]your eyes saw my unformed body. All the days ordained for me were written in your book before one of them came to be.
Prov 20 [12]Ears that hear and eyes that see—the LORD has made them both.
Isa 43 [1]But now, this is what the LORD says—he who created you, O Jacob, he who formed you, O Israel: "Fear not, for I have redeemed you; I have summoned you by name; you are mine. [7]. . . everyone who is called by my name, whom I created for my glory, whom I formed and made."

e) Humans Were Made Living Beings

Gen 2 [7]the LORD God formed the man from the dust of the ground and breathed into his nostrils the breath of life, and the man became a living being.
Num 16 [22]But Moses and Aaron fell facedown and cried out, "O God, God of the spirits of all mankind, will you be angry with the entire assembly when only one man sins?"
Job 10 [12]"You gave me life and showed me kindness, and in your providence watched over my spirit."
Job 12 [10]"In his hand is the life of every creature and the breath of all mankind."
Job 27 [3]". . . as long as I have life within me, the breath of God in my nostrils . . ."
Job 33 [4]"The Spirit of God has made me; the breath of the Almighty gives me life."
Ps 119 [73]Your hands made me and formed me; give me understanding to learn your commands.
Eccles 12 [7]and the dust returns to the ground it came from, and the spirit returns to God who gave it.
Isa 42 [5]This is what God the LORD says—he who created the heavens and stretched them out, who spread out the earth and all that comes out of it, who gives breath to its people, and life to those who walk on it. . . .
Isa 57 [16]"I will not accuse forever, nor will I always be angry, for then the spirit of man would grow faint before me—the breath of man that I have created."
Jer 38 [16]But King Zedekiah swore this oath secretly to Jeremiah: "As surely as the LORD lives, who has given us breath, I will neither kill you nor hand you over to those who are seeking your life."
Dan 5 [23]"Instead, you have set yourself up against the Lord of heaven. You had the goblets from his temple brought to you, and you and your nobles, your wives and your concubines drank wine from them. You praised the gods of silver and gold, of bronze, iron, wood and stone, which cannot see or hear or understand. But you did not honor the God who holds in his hand your life and all your ways."
Zech 12 [1]This is the word of the LORD concerning Israel. The LORD, who stretches out the heavens, who lays the foundation of the earth, and who forms the spirit of man within him, declares . . .
Acts 17 [25]"And he is not served by human hands, as if he needed anything, because he himself gives all men life and breath and everything else. [26]From one man he made every nation of men, that they should inhabit the whole earth; and he determined the times set for them and the exact places where they should live."
1 Cor 15 [45]So it is written: "The first man Adam became a living being"; the last Adam, a life-giving spirit.
Heb 12 [9]Moreover, we have all had human fathers who disciplined us and we respected them for it. How much more should we submit to the Father of our spirits and live!

5. Creation of the Supernatural World Order

Ps 148 [2]Praise him, all his angels, praise him, all his heavenly hosts. . . . [5]Let them praise the name of the LORD, for he commanded and they were created.
Col 1 [16]For by him all things were created: things in heaven and on earth, visible and invisible, whether thrones or powers or rulers or authorities; all things were created by him and for him.

C. The Purpose of Creation

1. Creation Was for the Sake of God

Ps 104 [31]May the glory of the LORD endure forever; may the LORD rejoice in his works. . . .
Prov 16 [4]The LORD works out everything for his own ends—even the wicked for a day of disaster.
Rom 11 [36]For from him and through him and to him are all things. To him be the glory forever! Amen.
Col 1 [16]For by him all things were created: things in heaven and on earth, visible and invisible, whether thrones or powers or rulers or authorities; all things were created by him and for him.

2. Creation Expressed God's Sovereignty

Job 28 [24]". . . for he views the ends of the earth and sees everything under the heavens. [25]When he established the force of the wind and measured out the waters, [26]when he made a decree for the rain and a path for the thunderstorm, [27]then he looked at wisdom and appraised it; he confirmed it and tested it."
Ps 24 [1]The earth is the LORD's, and everything in it, the world, and all who live in it; [2]for he founded it upon the seas and established it upon the waters.
Ps 33 [6]By the word of the LORD were the heavens made, their starry host by the breath of his mouth. . . . [9]For he spoke, and it came to be; he commanded, and it stood firm.
Ps 50 [12]"If I were hungry I would not tell you, for the world is mine, and all that is in it."
Ps 89 [11]The heavens are yours, and yours also the earth; you founded the world and all that is in it. [12]You created the north and the south; Tabor and Hermon sing for joy at your name.
Ps 95 [5]The sea is his, for he made it, and his hands formed the dry land.
Prov 3 [19]By wisdom the LORD laid the earth's foundations, by understanding he set the heavens in place; [20]by his knowledge the deeps were divided, and the clouds let drop the dew.
Prov 30 [4]"Who has gone up to heaven and come down? Who has gathered up the wind in the hollow of his hands? Who has wrapped up the waters in his cloak? Who has established all the ends of the earth? What is his name, and the name of his son? Tell me if you know!"
Isa 45 [18]For this is what the LORD says—he who created the heavens, he is God; he who fashioned and made the earth, he founded it; he did not create it to be empty, but formed it to be inhabited—he says: "I am the LORD, and there is no other."
Isa 48 [13]"My own hand laid the foundations of the earth, and my right hand spread out the heavens; when I summon them, they all stand up together."
Jer 10 [12]But God made the earth by his power; he founded the world by his wisdom and stretched out the heavens by his understanding.
Jer 27 [5]"With my great power and outstretched arm I made the earth and its people and the animals that are on it, and I give it to anyone I please."
Heb 11 [3]By faith we understand that the universe was formed at God's command, so that what is seen was not made out of what was visible.
2 Pet 3 [5]But they deliberately forget that long ago by God's word the heavens existed and the earth was formed out of water and by water.

3. Creation Revealed God's Glory

Neh 9 [5]And the Levites—Jeshua, Kadmiel, Bani, Hashabneiah, Sherebiah, Hodiah, Shebaniah and Pethahiah—said: "Stand up and praise the LORD your God, who is from everlasting to everlasting."

"Blessed be your glorious name, and may it be exalted above all blessing and praise. [6]You alone are the LORD. You made the heavens, even the highest heavens, and all their starry host, the earth and all that is on it, the seas and all that is in them. You give life to everything, and the multitudes of heaven worship you."

Ps 19 [1]The heavens declare the glory of God; the skies proclaim the work of his hands. [2]Day after day they pour forth speech; night after night they display knowledge. [3]There is no speech or language where their voice is not heard. [4]Their voice goes out into all the earth, their words to the ends of the world. In the heavens he has pitched a tent for the sun. . . .

Ps 104 [30]When you send your Spirit, they are created, and you renew the face of the earth.

[31]May the glory of the LORD endure forever; may the LORD rejoice in his works—[32]he who looks at the earth, and it trembles, who touches the mountains, and they smoke.

Isa 43 [7]". . . everyone who is called by my name, whom I created for my glory, whom I formed and made."

Rom 1 [20]For since the creation of the world God's invisible qualities—his eternal power and divine nature—have been clearly seen, being understood from what has been made, so that men are without excuse.

2 Cor 4 [6]For God, who said, "Let light shine out of darkness," made his light shine in our hearts to give us the light of the knowledge of the glory of God in the face of Christ.

4. Creation Showed God's Majesty

Ps 8 [1]O LORD, our Lord, how majestic is your name in all the earth!

You have set your glory above the heavens. . . .

[3]When I consider your heavens, the work of your fingers, the moon and the stars, which you have set in place . . .

Ps 104 [24]How many are your works, O LORD! In wisdom you made them all; the earth is full of your creatures.

Isa 51 [12]"I, even I, am he who comforts you. Who are you that you fear mortal men, the sons of men, who are but grass, [13]that you forget the LORD your Maker, who stretched out the heavens and laid the foundations of the earth, that you live in constant terror every day because of the wrath of the oppressor, who is bent on destruction? For where is the wrath of the oppressor? . . . [16]I have put my words in your mouth and covered you with the shadow of my hand—I who set the heavens in place, who laid the foundations of the earth, and who say to Zion, 'You are my people.'"

Amos 4 [13]He who forms the mountains, creates the wind, and reveals his thoughts to man, he who turns dawn to darkness, and treads the high places of the earth—the LORD God Almighty is his name.

5. Creation Unfolded God's Purposes

Gen 1 [27]So God created man in his own image, in the image of God he created him; male and female he created them.

[28]God blessed them and said to them, "Be fruitful and increase in number; fill the earth and subdue it. Rule over the fish of the sea and the birds of the air and over every living creature that moves on the ground."

Ps 119 [90]Your faithfulness continues through all generations; you established the earth, and it endures. [91]Your laws endure to this day, for all things serve you.

Isa 42 [5]This is what God the LORD says—he who created the heavens and stretched them out, who spread out the earth and all that comes out of it, who gives breath to its people, and life to those who walk on it: [6]"I, the LORD, have called you in righteousness; I will take hold of your hand. I will keep you and will make you to be a covenant for the people and a light for the Gentiles. . . ."

Isa 45 [18]For this is what the LORD says—he who created the heavens, he is God; he who fashioned and made the earth, he founded it; he did not create it to be empty, but formed it to be inhabited—he says: "I am the LORD, and there is no other."

D. The Praise of the Creator

2 Kings 19 [15]And Hezekiah prayed to the LORD: "O LORD, God of Israel, enthroned between the cherubim, you alone are God over all the kingdoms of the earth. You have made heaven and earth."

1 Chron 16 [25]For great is the LORD and most worthy of praise; he is to be feared above all gods. [26]For all the gods of the nations are idols, but the LORD made the heavens.

2 Chron 2 [12]And Hiram added: "Praise be to the LORD, the God of Israel, who made heaven and earth! He has given King David a wise son, endowed with intelligence and discernment, who will build a temple for the LORD and a palace for himself."

Neh 9 [6]"You alone are the LORD. You made the heavens, even the highest heavens, and all their starry host, the earth and all that is on it, the seas and all that is in them. You give life to everything, and the multitudes of heaven worship you."

Job 12 [9]"Which of all these does not know that the hand of the LORD has done this? [10]In his hand is the life of every creature and the breath of all mankind."

Job 36 [24]"Remember to extol his work, which men have praised in song. [25]All mankind has seen it; men gaze on it from afar. [26]How great is God—beyond our understanding! The number of his years is past finding out.

[27]"He draws up the drops of water, which distill as rain to the streams; [28]the clouds pour down their moisture and abundant showers fall on mankind. [29]Who can understand how he spreads out the clouds, how he thunders from his pavilion?"

Ps 28 [5]Since they show no regard for the works of the LORD and what his hands have done, he will tear them down and never build them up again.

[6]Praise be to the LORD, for he has heard my cry for mercy.

Ps 40 [5]Many, O LORD my God, are the wonders you have done. The things you planned for us no one can recount to you; were I to speak and tell of them, they would be too many to declare.

Ps 90 [1]Lord, you have been our dwelling place throughout all generations. [2]Before the mountains were born or you brought forth the earth and the world, from everlasting to everlasting you are God.

Ps 92 [4]For you make me glad by your deeds, O LORD; I sing for joy at the works of your hands. [5]How great are your works, O LORD, how profound your thoughts!

Ps 103 [22]Praise the LORD, all his works everywhere in his dominion. Praise the LORD, O my soul.

Ps 104 [1]Praise the LORD, O my soul.

O LORD my God, you are very great; you are clothed with splendor and majesty. [2]He wraps himself in light as with a garment; he stretches out the heavens like a tent [3]and lays the beams of his upper chambers on their waters. He makes the clouds his chariot and rides on the wings of the wind. [4]He makes winds his messengers, flames of fire his servants.

[5]He set the earth on its foundations; it can never be moved. [6]You covered it with the deep as with a garment; the waters stood above the mountains. [7]But at your rebuke the waters fled, at the sound of your thunder they took to flight; [8]they flowed over the mountains, they went down into the valleys, to the place you assigned for them. [9]You set a boundary they cannot cross; never again will they cover the earth.

[10]He makes springs pour water into the ravines; it flows between the mountains. [11]They give water to all the beasts of the field; the wild donkeys quench their thirst. [12]The birds of the air nest by the waters; they sing among the branches. [13]He waters the mountains from his upper chambers; the earth is satisfied by the fruit of his work. [14]He makes grass grow for the cattle, and plants for man to cultivate—bringing forth food from the earth: [15]wine that gladdens the heart of man, oil to make his face shine, and bread that sustains his heart. [16]The trees of the LORD are well watered, the cedars of Lebanon that he planted. [17]There the birds make their nests; the stork has its home in the pine trees. [18]The high mountains belong to the wild goats; the crags are a refuge for the coneys.

[19]The moon marks off the seasons, and the sun knows when to go down. [20]You bring darkness, it becomes night, and all the beasts of the forest prowl. [21]The lions roar for their prey and seek their food from God. [22]The sun rises, and they steal away; they return and lie down in their dens. [23]Then man goes out to his work, to his labor until evening.

[24]How many are your works, O LORD! In wisdom you made them all; the earth is full of your creatures. [25]There is the sea, vast and spacious, teeming with creatures beyond number—living things both large and small. [26]There the ships go to and fro, and the leviathan, which you formed to frolic there.

27These all look to you to give them their food at the proper time. 28When you give it to them, they gather it up; when you open your hand, they are satisfied with good things. 29When you hide your face, they are terrified; when you take away their breath, they die and return to the dust. 30When you send your Spirit, they are created, and you renew the face of the earth.

31May the glory of the LORD endure forever; may the LORD rejoice in his works. . . .

Ps 111 2Great are the works of the LORD; they are pondered by all who delight in them. 3Glorious and majestic are his deeds, and his righteousness endures forever. 4He has caused his wonders to be remembered; the LORD is gracious and compassionate. . . . 7The works of his hands are faithful and just; all his precepts are trustworthy. 8They are steadfast for ever and ever, done in faithfulness and uprightness.

Ps 119 72The law from your mouth is more precious to me than thousands of pieces of silver and gold.

73Your hands made me and formed me; give me understanding to learn your commands.

Ps 121 2My help comes from the LORD, the Maker of heaven and earth.

Ps 145 10All you have made will praise you, O LORD; your saints will extol you.

Ps 146 5Blessed is he whose help is the God of Jacob, whose hope is in the LORD his God, 6the Maker of heaven and earth, the sea, and everything in them—the LORD, who remains faithful forever.

Ps 148 1Praise the LORD.

Praise the LORD from the heavens, praise him in the heights above. 2Praise him, all his angels, praise him, all his heavenly hosts. 3Praise him, sun and moon, praise him, all you shining stars. 4Praise him, you highest heavens and you waters above the skies. 5Let them praise the name of the LORD, for he commanded and they were created. 6He set them in place for ever and ever; he gave a decree that will never pass away.

Isa 40 12Who has measured the waters in the hollow of his hand, or with the breadth of his hand marked off the heavens? Who has held the dust of the earth in a basket, or weighed the mountains on the scales and the hills in a balance? . . .

21Do you not know? Have you not heard? Has it not been told you from the beginning? Have you not understood since the earth was founded? 22He sits enthroned above the circle of the earth, and its people are like grasshoppers. He stretches out the heavens like a canopy, and spreads them out like a tent to live in. . . .

26Lift your eyes and look to the heavens: Who created all these? He who brings out the starry host one by one, and calls them each by name. Because of his great power and mighty strength, not one of them is missing. . . . 28Do you not know? Have you not heard? The LORD is the everlasting God, the Creator of the ends of the earth. He will not grow tired or weary, and his understanding no one can fathom. 29He gives strength to the weary and increases the power of the weak. 30Even youths grow tired and weary, and young men stumble and fall; 31but those who hope in the LORD will renew their strength. They will soar on wings like eagles; they will run and not grow weary, they will walk and not be faint.

Jer 32 17"Ah, Sovereign LORD, you have made the heavens and the earth by your great power and outstretched arm. Nothing is too hard for you."

Amos 9 6he who builds his lofty palace in the heavens and sets its foundation on the earth, who calls for the waters of the sea and pours them out over the face of the land—the LORD is his name.

Acts 4 24When they heard this, they raised their voices together in prayer to God. "Sovereign Lord," they said, "you made the heaven and the earth and the sea, and everything in them."

Rom 1 20For since the creation of the world God's invisible qualities—his eternal power and divine nature—have been clearly seen, being understood from what has been made, so that men are without excuse. . . .

25They exchanged the truth of God for a lie, and worshiped and served created things rather than the Creator—who is forever praised. Amen.

1 Cor 8 6yet for us there is but one God, the Father, from whom all things came and for whom we live; and there is but one Lord, Jesus Christ, through whom all things came and through whom we live.

Col 1 15He is the image of the invisible God, the firstborn over all creation. 16For by him all things were created: things in heaven and on earth, visible and invisible, whether thrones or powers or rulers or authorities; all things were created by him and for him. 17He is before all things, and in him all things hold together.

Rev 14 7He said in a loud voice, "Fear God and give him glory, because the hour of his judgment has come. Worship him who made the heavens, the earth, the sea and the springs of water."

E. The Goodness of the Created Order

Gen 1 10God called the dry ground "land," and the gathered waters he called "seas." And God saw that it was good.

Gen 1 12The land produced vegetation: plants bearing seed according to their kinds and trees bearing fruit with seed in it according to their kinds. And God saw that it was good.

Gen 1 16God made two great lights—the greater light to govern the day and the lesser light to govern the night. He also made the stars. 17God set them in the expanse of the sky to give light on the earth, 18to govern the day and the night, and to separate light from darkness. And God saw that it was good.

Gen 1 25God made the wild animals according to their kinds, the livestock according to their kinds, and all the creatures that move along the ground according to their kinds. And God saw that it was good.

Gen 1 31God saw all that he had made, and it was very good. And there was evening, and there was morning—the sixth day.

Gen 2 3And God blessed the seventh day and made it holy, because on it he rested from all the work of creating that he had done.

Ps 104 24How many are your works, O LORD! In wisdom you made them all; the earth is full of your creatures. . . . 28When you give it to them, they gather it up; when you open your hand, they are satisfied with good things.

Ps 119 68You are good, and what you do is good; teach me your decrees.

1 Tim 4 4For everything God created is good, and nothing is to be rejected if it is received with thanksgiving. . . .

F. The Promise of a New Creation

Isa 11 1A shoot will come up from the stump of Jesse; from his roots a Branch will bear fruit. 2The Spirit of the LORD will rest on him—the Spirit of wisdom and of understanding, the Spirit of counsel and of power, the Spirit of knowledge and of the fear of the LORD—3and he will delight in the fear of the LORD.

He will not judge by what he sees with his eyes, or decide by what he hears with his ears; 4but with righteousness he will judge the needy, with justice he will give decisions for the poor of the earth. He will strike the earth with the rod of his mouth; with the breath of his lips he will slay the wicked. 5Righteousness will be his belt and faithfulness the sash around his waist.

6The wolf will live with the lamb, the leopard will lie down with the goat, the calf and the lion and the yearling together; and a little child will lead them. 7The cow will feed with the bear, their young will lie down together, and the lion will eat straw like the ox. 8The infant will play near the hole of the cobra, and the young child put his hand into the viper's nest. 9They will neither harm nor destroy on all my holy mountain, for the earth will be full of the knowledge of the LORD as the waters cover the sea.

Isa 41 18"I will make rivers flow on barren heights, and springs within the valleys. I will turn the desert into pools of water, and the parched ground into springs. 19I will put in the desert the cedar and the acacia, the myrtle and the olive. I will set pines in the wasteland, the fir and the cypress together, 20so that people may see and know, may consider and understand, that the hand of the LORD has done this, that the Holy One of Israel has created it."

Isa 65 17"Behold, I will create new heavens and a new earth. The former things will not be remembered, nor will they come to mind. [18]But be glad and rejoice forever in what I will create, for I will create Jerusalem to be a delight and its people a joy. [19]I will rejoice over Jerusalem and take delight in my people; the sound of weeping and of crying will be heard in it no more.

[20]"Never again will there be in it an infant who lives but a few days, or an old man who does not live out his years; he who dies at a hundred will be thought a mere youth; he who fails to reach a hundred will be considered accursed. [21]They will build houses and dwell in them; they will plant vineyards and eat their fruit. [22]No longer will they build houses and others live in them, or plant and others eat. For as the days of a tree, so will be the days of my people; my chosen ones will long enjoy the works of their hands. [23]They will not toil in vain or bear children doomed to misfortune; for they will be a people blessed by the LORD, they and their descendants with them. [24]Before they call I will answer; while they are still speaking I will hear. [25]The wolf and the lamb will feed together, and the lion will eat straw like the ox, but dust will be the serpent's food. They will neither harm nor destroy on all my holy mountain," says the LORD.

Isa 66 [22]"As the new heavens and the new earth that I make will endure before me," declares the LORD, "so will your name and descendants endure. [23]From one New Moon to another and from one Sabbath to another, all mankind will come and bow down before me," says the LORD.

Hos 2 [18]"In that day I will make a covenant for them with the beasts of the field and the birds of the air and the creatures that move along the ground. Bow and sword and battle I will abolish from the land, so that all may lie down in safety. [19]I will betroth you to me forever; I will betroth you in righteousness and justice, in love and compassion."

Matt 19 [28]Jesus said to them, "I tell you the truth, at the renewal of all things, when the Son of Man sits on his glorious throne, you who have followed me will also sit on twelve thrones, judging the twelve tribes of Israel."

Acts 3 [21]"He must remain in heaven until the time comes for God to restore everything, as he promised long ago through his holy prophets."

Rom 8 [18]I consider that our present sufferings are not worth comparing with the glory that will be revealed in us. [19]The creation waits in eager expectation for the sons of God to be revealed. [20]For the creation was subjected to frustration, not by its own choice, but by the will of the one who subjected it, in hope [21]that the creation itself will be liberated from its bondage to decay and brought into the glorious freedom of the children of God.

2 Pet 3 [7]By the same word the present heavens and earth are reserved for fire, being kept for the day of judgment and destruction of ungodly men.

[8]But do not forget this one thing, dear friends: With the Lord a day is like a thousand years, and a thousand years are like a day. [9]The Lord is not slow in keeping his promise, as some understand slowness. He is patient with you, not wanting anyone to perish, but everyone to come to repentance.

[10]But the day of the Lord will come like a thief. The heavens will disappear with a roar; the elements will be destroyed by fire, and the earth and everything in it will be laid bare.

[11]Since everything will be destroyed in this way, what kind of people ought you to be? You ought to live holy and godly lives [12]as you look forward to the day of God and speed its coming. That day will bring about the destruction of the heavens by fire, and the elements will melt in the heat. [13]But in keeping with his promise we are looking forward to a new heaven and a new earth, the home of righteousness.

Rev 21 [1]Then I saw a new heaven and a new earth, for the first heaven and the first earth had passed away, and there was no longer any sea. [2]I saw the Holy City, the new Jerusalem, coming down out of heaven from God, prepared as a bride beautifully dressed for her husband. [3]And I heard a loud voice from the throne saying, "Now the dwelling of God is with men, and he will live with them. They will be his people, and God himself will be with them and be their God. [4]He will wipe every tear from their eyes. There will be no more death or mourning or crying or pain, for the old order of things has passed away."

[5]He who was seated on the throne said, "I am making everything new!" Then he said, "Write this down, for these words are trustworthy and true."

[6]He said to me: "It is done. I am the Alpha and the Omega, the Beginning and the End. To him who is thirsty I will give to drink without cost from the spring of the water of life. [7]He who overcomes will inherit all this, and I will be his God and he will be my son. [8]But the cowardly, the unbelieving, the vile, the murderers, the sexually immoral, those who practice magic arts, the idolaters and all liars—their place will be in the fiery lake of burning sulfur. This is the second death."

III
The Preservation of God

A. God Is Active beyond Creation

Neh 9 [6]"You alone are the LORD. You made the heavens, even the highest heavens, and all their starry host, the earth and all that is on it, the seas and all that is in them. You give life to everything, and the multitudes of heaven worship you."

Job 34 [12]"It is unthinkable that God would do wrong, that the Almighty would pervert justice. [13]Who appointed him over the earth? Who put him in charge of the whole world? [14]If it were his intention and he withdrew his spirit and breath, [15]all mankind would perish together and man would return to the dust."

Ps 36 [5]Your love, O LORD, reaches to the heavens, your faithfulness to the skies. [6]Your righteousness is like the mighty mountains, your justice like the great deep. O LORD, you preserve both man and beast. [7]How priceless is your unfailing love! Both high and low among men find refuge in the shadow of your wings. [8]They feast on the abundance of your house; you give them drink from your river of delights. [9]For with you is the fountain of life; in your light we see light.

Ps 66 [8]Praise our God, O peoples, let the sound of his praise be heard; [9]he has preserved our lives and kept our feet from slipping.

Ps 104 [29]When you hide your face, they are terrified; when you take away their breath, they die and return to the dust. [30]When you send your Spirit, they are created, and you renew the face of the earth.

Ps 119 [89]Your word, O LORD, is eternal; it stands firm in the heavens. [90]Your faithfulness continues through all generations; you established the earth, and it endures. [91]Your laws endure to this day, for all things serve you.

Ps 145 [1]I will exalt you, my God the King; I will praise your name for ever and ever. [2]Every day I will praise you and extol your name for ever and ever.

[3]Great is the LORD and most worthy of praise; his greatness no one can fathom. [4]One generation will commend your works to another; they will tell of your mighty acts. [5]They will speak of the glorious splendor of your majesty, and I will meditate on your wonderful works. [6]They will tell of the power of your awesome works, and I will proclaim your great deeds. [7]They will celebrate your abundant goodness and joyfully sing of your righteousness.

[8]The LORD is gracious and compassionate, slow to anger and rich in love. [9]The LORD is good to all; he has compassion on all he has made. [10]All you have made will praise you, O LORD; your saints will extol you. [11]They will tell of the glory of your kingdom and speak of your might, [12]so that all men may know of your mighty acts and the glorious splendor of your kingdom. [13]Your kingdom is an everlasting kingdom, and your dominion endures through all generations.

The LORD is faithful to all his promises and loving toward all he has made. [14]The LORD upholds all those who fall and lifts up all who are bowed down. [15]The eyes of all look to you, and you give them their food at the proper time. [16]You open your hand and satisfy the desires of every living thing.

[17]The LORD is righteous in all his ways and loving toward all he has made. [18]The LORD is near to all who call on him, to all who call on him in truth. [19]He fulfills the desires of those who fear him; he hears their cry and saves them. [20]The LORD

watches over all who love him, but all the wicked he will destroy.

[21]My mouth will speak in praise of the LORD. Let every creature praise his holy name for ever and ever.

Isa 40 [28]Do you not know? Have you not heard? The LORD is the everlasting God, the Creator of the ends of the earth. He will not grow tired or weary, and his understanding no one can fathom.

Acts 17 [28]"'For in him we live and move and have our being.' As some of your own poets have said, 'We are his offspring.'"

Col 1 [17]He is before all things, and in him all things hold together.

1 Tim 6 [13]In the sight of God, who gives life to everything, and of Christ Jesus, who while testifying before Pontius Pilate made the good confession, I charge you. . . .

Heb 1 [2]but in these last days he has spoken to us by his Son, whom he appointed heir of all things, and through whom he made the universe. [3]The Son is the radiance of God's glory and the exact representation of his being, sustaining all things by his powerful word. After he had provided purification for sins, he sat down at the right hand of the Majesty in heaven.

B. Preservation Is the Work of the Triune God

1. The Father and Preservation

John 5 [17]Jesus said to them, "My Father is always at his work to this very day, and I, too, am working."

1 Tim 6 [13]In the sight of God, who gives life to everything, and of Christ Jesus, who while testifying before Pontius Pilate made the good confession, I charge you. . . .

2. The Son and Preservation

John 5 [17]Jesus said to them, "My Father is always at his work to this very day, and I, too, am working."

Col 1 [15]He is the image of the invisible God, the firstborn over all creation. . . . [17]He is before all things, and in him all things hold together.

Heb 1 [2]but in these last days he has spoken to us by his Son, whom he appointed heir of all things, and through whom he made the universe. [3]The Son is the radiance of God's glory and the exact representation of his being, sustaining all things by his powerful word. After he had provided purification for sins, he sat down at the right hand of the Majesty in heaven.

3. The Spirit and Preservation

Ps 104 [30]When you send your Spirit, they are created, and you renew the face of the earth.

C. Preservation Involves All of Creation

Col 1 [17]He is before all things, and in him all things hold together.

IV
The Providence of God

A. Providence at Work in All Creation

1. The World Is God's

Deut 10 [14]To the LORD your God belong the heavens, even the highest heavens, the earth and everything in it.

1 Chron 29 [11]"Yours, O LORD, is the greatness and the power and the glory and the majesty and the splendor, for everything in heaven and earth is yours. Yours, O LORD, is the kingdom; you are exalted as head over all."

Job 9 [5]"He moves mountains without their knowing it and overturns them in his anger. [6]He shakes the earth from its place and makes its pillars tremble. [7]He speaks to the sun and it does not shine; he seals off the light of the stars. [8]He alone stretches out the heavens and treads on the waves of the sea. [9]He is the Maker of the Bear and Orion, the Pleiades and the constellations of the south. [10]He performs wonders that cannot be fathomed, miracles that cannot be counted."

Job 12 [10]"In his hand is the life of every creature and the breath of all mankind."

Job 41 [11]"Who has a claim against me that I must pay? Everything under heaven belongs to me."

Ps 24 [1]The earth is the LORD's, and everything in it, the world, and all who live in it. . . .

Ps 47 [9]The nobles of the nations assemble as the people of the God of Abraham, for the kings of the earth belong to God; he is greatly exalted.

Ps 89 [11]The heavens are yours, and yours also the earth; you founded the world and all that is in it.

Ps 95 [3]For the LORD is the great God, the great King above all gods. [4]In his hand are the depths of the earth, and the mountain peaks belong to him. [5]The sea is his, for he made it, and his hands formed the dry land.

Ps 103 [19]The LORD has established his throne in heaven, and his kingdom rules over all.

Ps 108 [7]God has spoken from his sanctuary: "In triumph I will parcel out Shechem and measure off the Valley of Succoth. [8]Gilead is mine, Manasseh is mine; Ephraim is my helmet, Judah my scepter."

Ps 115 [16]The highest heavens belong to the LORD, but the earth he has given to man.

Ps 135 [5]I know that the LORD is great, that our Lord is greater than all gods. [6]The LORD does whatever pleases him, in the heavens and on the earth, in the seas and all their depths.

Ps 147 [15]He sends his command to the earth; his word runs swiftly.

Ps 148 [1]Praise the LORD.

Praise the LORD from the heavens, praise him in the heights above. [2]Praise him, all his angels, praise him, all his heavenly hosts. [3]Praise him, sun and moon, praise him, all you shining stars. [4]Praise him, you highest heavens and you waters above the skies. [5]Let them praise the name of the LORD, for he commanded and they were created. [6]He set them in place for ever and ever; he gave a decree that will never pass away.

[7]Praise the LORD from the earth, you great sea creatures and all ocean depths, [8]lightning and hail, snow and clouds, stormy winds that do his bidding, [9]you mountains and all hills, fruit trees and all cedars, [10]wild animals and all cattle, small creatures and flying birds, [11]kings of the earth and all nations, you princes and all rulers on earth, [12]young men and maidens, old men and children.

[13]Let them praise the name of the LORD, for his name alone is exalted; his splendor is above the earth and the heavens. [14]He has raised up for his people a horn, the praise of all his saints, of Israel, the people close to his heart.

Praise the LORD.

Dan 4 [35]All the peoples of the earth are regarded as nothing. He does as he pleases with the powers of heaven and the peoples of the earth. No one can hold back his hand or say to him: "What have you done?"

Amos 9 [5]The Lord, the LORD Almighty, he who touches the earth and it melts, and all who live in it mourn—the whole land rises like the Nile, then sinks like the river of Egypt—[6]he who builds his lofty palace in the heavens and sets its foundation on the earth, who calls for the waters of the sea and pours them out over the face of the land—the LORD is his name.

Hag 2 [8]"'The silver is mine and the gold is mine,' declares the LORD Almighty."

Acts 17 [24]"The God who made the world and everything in it is the Lord of heaven and earth and does not live in temples built by hands. [25]And he is not served by human hands, as if he needed anything, because he himself gives all men life and breath and everything else. [26]From one man he made every nation of men, that they should inhabit the whole earth; and he determined the times set for them and the exact places where they should live. [27]God did this so that men would seek him and perhaps reach out for him and find him, though he is not far from each one of us. [28]'For in him we live and move and have our being.' As some of your own poets have said, 'We are his offspring.'"

1 Cor 10 [26]for, "The earth is the Lord's, and everything in it."
Eph 1 [11]In him we were also chosen, having been predestined according to the plan of him who works out everything in conformity with the purpose of his will. . . .

2. His Providence Gives and Empowers Life

Matt 4 [4]Jesus answered, "It is written: 'Man does not live on bread alone, but on every word that comes from the mouth of God.'"
Acts 17 [28]"'For in him we live and move and have our being.' As some of your own poets have said, 'We are his offspring.'"

3. His Providence Preserves Life

Gen 45 [7]"But God sent me ahead of you to preserve for you a remnant on earth and to save your lives by a great deliverance."
Deut 30 [20]and that you may love the LORD your God, listen to his voice, and hold fast to him. For the LORD is your life, and he will give you many years in the land he swore to give to your fathers, Abraham, Isaac and Jacob.
Job 8 [20]"Surely God does not reject a blameless man or strengthen the hands of evildoers."
Ps 37 [17]for the power of the wicked will be broken, but the LORD upholds the righteous.
Ps 37 [28]For the LORD loves the just and will not forsake his faithful ones. They will be protected forever, but the offspring of the wicked will be cut off. . . .
Ps 41 [1]Blessed is he who has regard for the weak; the LORD delivers him in times of trouble. [2]The LORD will protect him and preserve his life; he will bless him in the land and not surrender him to the desire of his foes.
Ps 79 [11]May the groans of the prisoners come before you; by the strength of your arm preserve those condemned to die.
Prov 2 [8]for he guards the course of the just and protects the way of his faithful ones.
Isa 40 [28]Do you not know? Have you not heard? The LORD is the everlasting God, the Creator of the ends of the earth. He will not grow tired or weary, and his understanding no one can fathom. [29]He gives strength to the weary and increases the power of the weak. [30]Even youths grow tired and weary, and young men stumble and fall; [31]but those who hope in the LORD will renew their strength. They will soar on wings like eagles; they will run and not grow weary, they will walk and not be faint.
See also p. 189a, The Father and Preservation

B. Providence at Work in the Natural Order

1. God's Providence in the Material Universe

a) The Heavenly Bodies

(1) Eclipses

Job 9 [7]"He speaks to the sun and it does not shine; he seals off the light of the stars."
Isa 13 [10]The stars of heaven and their constellations will not show their light. The rising sun will be darkened and the moon will not give its light.
Ezek 32 [7]"'When I snuff you out, I will cover the heavens and darken their stars; I will cover the sun with a cloud, and the moon will not give its light. [8]All the shining lights in the heavens I will darken over you; I will bring darkness over your land, declares the Sovereign LORD.'"
Joel 2 [10]Before them the earth shakes, the sky trembles, the sun and moon are darkened, and the stars no longer shine.
Joel 3 [15]The sun and moon will be darkened, and the stars no longer shine.
Amos 8 [9]"In that day," declares the Sovereign LORD, "I will make the sun go down at noon and darken the earth in broad daylight."

(2) The Moon

Ps 104 [2]He wraps himself in light as with a garment; he stretches out the heavens like a tent. . . .

[19]The moon marks off the seasons, and the sun knows when to go down. [20]You bring darkness, it becomes night, and all the beasts of the forests prowl.
Isa 30 [26]The moon will shine like the sun, and the sunlight will be seven times brighter, like the light of seven full days, when the LORD binds up the bruises of his people and heals the wounds he inflicted.
Jer 31 [35]This is what the LORD says, he who appoints the sun to shine by day, who decrees the moon and stars to shine by night, who stirs up the sea so that its waves roar—the LORD Almighty is his name. . . .

(3) Stars

Job 38 [31]"Can you bind the beautiful Pleiades? Can you loose the cords of Orion? [32]Can you bring forth the constellations in their seasons or lead out the Bear with its cubs? [33]Do you know the laws of the heavens? Can you set up God's dominion over the earth?"
Isa 40 [26]Lift your eyes and look to the heavens: Who created all these? He who brings out the starry host one by one, and calls them each by name. Because of his great power and mighty strength, not one of them is missing.

(4) The Sun

Ps 104 [2]He wraps himself in light as with a garment; he stretches out the heavens like a tent. . . .

[19]The moon marks off the seasons, and the sun knows when to go down. [20]You bring darkness, it becomes night, and all the beasts of the forest prowl.
Isa 30 [26]The moon will shine like the sun, and the sunlight will be seven times brighter, like the light of seven full days, when the LORD binds up the bruises of his people and heals the wounds he inflicted.
Jer 31 [35]This is what the LORD says, he who appoints the sun to shine by day, who decrees the moon and stars to shine by night, who stirs up the sea so that its waves roar—the LORD Almighty is his name. . . .
Matt 5 [45]". . . that you may be sons of your Father in heaven. He causes his sun to rise on the evil and the good, and sends rain on the righteous and the unrighteous."

b) Day and Night and Cycles of Seasons

Gen 8 [22]"As long as the earth endures, seedtime and harvest, cold and heat, summer and winter, day and night will never cease."
Ps 65 [8]Those living far away fear your wonders; where morning dawns and evening fades you call forth songs of joy.
Ps 104 [19]The moon marks off the seasons, and the sun knows when to go down. [20]You bring darkness, it becomes night, and all the beasts of the forest prowl. [21]The lions roar for their prey and seek their food from God. [22]The sun rises, and they steal away; they return and lie down in their dens. [23]Then man goes out to his work, to his labor until evening.
Jer 31 [35]This is what the LORD says, he who appoints the sun to shine by day, who decrees the moon and stars to shine by night, who stirs up the sea so that its waves roar—the LORD Almighty is his name. . . .
Jer 33 [25]"This is what the LORD says: 'If I have not established my covenant with day and night and the fixed laws of heaven and earth, [26]then I will reject the descendants of Jacob and David my servant and will not choose one of his sons to rule over the descendants of Abraham, Isaac and Jacob. For I will restore their fortunes and have compassion on them.'"

c) The Earth's Atmosphere

(1) Clouds

Job 37 [11]"He loads the clouds with moisture; he scatters his lightning through them. [12]At his direction they swirl around over the face of the whole earth to do whatever he commands them. [13]He brings the clouds to punish men, or to water his earth and show his love."
Job 37 [15]"Do you know how God controls the clouds and makes his lightning flash? [16]Do you know how the clouds hang poised, those wonders of him who is perfect in knowledge?"
Job 38 [34]"Can you raise your voice to the clouds and cover yourself with a flood of water?"
Ps 97 [2]Clouds and thick darkness surround him; righteousness and justice are the foundation of his throne.

Ps 135 7He makes clouds rise from the ends of the earth; he sends lightning with the rain and brings out the wind from his storehouses.

Ps 147 8He covers the sky with clouds; he supplies the earth with rain and makes grass grow on the hills.

Jer 10 13When he thunders, the waters in the heavens roar; he makes clouds rise from the ends of the earth. He sends lightning with the rain and brings out the wind from his storehouses.

Ezek 30 18"'Dark will be the day at Tahpanhes when I break the yoke of Egypt; there her proud strength will come to an end. She will be covered with clouds, and her villages will go into captivity. 19So I will inflict punishment on Egypt, and they will know that I am the LORD.'"

(2) Dew

Gen 27 28"May God give you of heaven's dew and of earth's richness—an abundance of grain and new wine."

Job 38 28"Does the rain have a father? Who fathers the drops of dew?"

(3) Frost

Job 38 29"From whose womb comes the ice? Who gives birth to the frost from the heavens? . . ."

Ps 147 16He spreads the snow like wool and scatters the frost like ashes.

(4) Hail

Exod 9 18"'Therefore, at this time tomorrow I will send the worst hailstorm that has ever fallen on Egypt, from the day it was founded till now. 19Give an order now to bring your livestock and everything you have in the field to a place of shelter, because the hail will fall on every man and animal that has not been brought in and is still out in the field, and they will die.'"

20Those officials of Pharaoh who feared the word of the LORD hurried to bring their slaves and their livestock inside. 21But those who ignored the word of the LORD left their slaves and livestock in the field.

22Then the LORD said to Moses, "Stretch out your hand toward the sky so that hail will fall all over Egypt—on men and animals and on everything growing in the fields of Egypt." 23When Moses stretched out his staff toward the sky, the LORD sent thunder and hail, and lightning flashed down to the ground. So the LORD rained hail on the land of Egypt; 24hail fell and lightning flashed back and forth. It was the worst storm in all the land of Egypt since it had become a nation. 25Throughout Egypt hail struck everything in the fields—both men and animals; it beat down everything growing in the fields and stripped every tree. 26The only place it did not hail was the land of Goshen, where the Israelites were.

27Then Pharaoh summoned Moses and Aaron. "This time I have sinned," he said to them. "The LORD is in the right, and I and my people are in the wrong. 28Pray to the LORD, for we have had enough thunder and hail. I will let you go; you don't have to stay any longer."

29Moses replied, "When I have gone out of the city, I will spread out my hands in prayer to the LORD. The thunder will stop and there will be no more hail, so you may know that the earth is the LORD's. 30But I know that you and your officials still do not fear the LORD God."

31(The flax and barley were destroyed, since the barley had headed and the flax was in bloom. 32The wheat and spelt, however, were not destroyed, because they ripen later.)

33Then Moses left Pharaoh and went out of the city. He spread out his hands toward the LORD; the thunder and hail stopped, and the rain no longer poured down on the land.

Job 38 22"Have you entered the storehouses of the snow or seen the storehouses of the hail, 23which I reserve for times of trouble, for days of war and battle?"

Ps 105 32He turned their rain into hail, with lightning throughout their land; 33he struck down their vines and fig trees and shattered the trees of their country.

Ps 147 17He hurls down his hail like pebbles. Who can withstand his icy blast? 18He sends his word and melts them; he stirs up his breezes, and the waters flow.

Isa 28 2See, the Lord has one who is powerful and strong. Like a hailstorm and a destructive wind, like a driving rain and a flooding downpour, he will throw it forcefully to the ground.

Hag 2 17"'I struck all the work of your hands with blight, mildew and hail, yet you did not turn to me,' declares the LORD."

(5) Lightning

Exod 9 23When Moses stretched out his staff toward the sky, the LORD sent thunder and hail, and lightning flashed down to the ground. So the LORD rained hail on the land of Egypt; 24hail fell and lightning flashed back and forth. It was the worst storm in all the land of Egypt since it had become a nation.

Exod 19 16On the morning of the third day there was thunder and lightning, with a thick cloud over the mountain, and a very loud trumpet blast. Everyone in the camp trembled.

2 Sam 22 13"Out of the brightness of his presence bolts of lightning blazed forth. 14The LORD thundered from heaven; the voice of the Most High resounded. 15He shot arrows and scattered the enemies, bolts of lightning and routed them."

Job 36 30"See how he scatters his lightning about him, bathing the depths of the sea. . . . 32He fills his hands with lightning and commands it to strike its mark."

Job 37 3"He unleashes his lightning beneath the whole heaven and sends it to the ends of the earth."

Job 38 35"Do you send the lightning bolts on their way? Do they report to you, 'Here we are'?"

Ps 18 12Out of the brightness of his presence clouds advanced, with hailstones and bolts of lightning. 13The LORD thundered from heaven; the voice of the Most High resounded. 14He shot his arrows and scattered the enemies, great bolts of lightning and routed them.

Ps 97 4His lightning lights up the world; the earth sees and trembles.

Ps 135 7He makes clouds rise from the ends of the earth; he sends lightning with the rain and brings out the wind from his storehouses.

Ps 144 5Part your heavens, O LORD, and come down; touch the mountains, so that they smoke. 6Send forth lightning and scatter the enemies; shoot your arrows and rout them.

Jer 10 13When he thunders, the waters in the heavens roar; he makes clouds rise from the ends of the earth. He sends lightning with the rain and brings out the wind from his storehouses.

(6) Rain

Gen 7 4"Seven days from now I will send rain on the earth for forty days and forty nights, and I will wipe from the face of the earth every living creature I have made."

Deut 28 12The LORD will open the heavens, the storehouse of his bounty, to send rain on your land in season and to bless all the work of your hands. You will lend to many nations but will borrow from none.

1 Kings 18 1After a long time, in the third year, the word of the LORD came to Elijah: "Go and present yourself to Ahab, and I will send rain on the land."

2 Chron 6 26"When the heavens are shut up and there is no rain because your people have sinned against you, and when they pray toward this place and confess your name and turn from their sin because you have afflicted them, 27then hear from heaven and forgive the sin of your servants, your people Israel. Teach them the right way to live, and send rain on the land you gave your people for an inheritance."

Job 5 10"He bestows rain on the earth; he sends water upon the countryside."

Job 36 27"He draws up the drops of water, which distill as rain to the streams; 28the clouds pour down their moisture and abundant showers fall on mankind. 29Who can understand how he spreads out the clouds, how he thunders from his pavilion?"

Job 37 6"He says to the snow, 'Fall on the earth,' and to the rain shower, 'Be a mighty downpour.' 7So that all men he has made may know his work, he stops every man from his labor. 8The animals take cover; they remain in their dens. 9The tempest comes out from its chamber, the cold from the driving winds."

Job 38 25"Who cuts a channel for the torrents of rain, and a path for the thunderstorm, 26to water a land where no man lives, a desert with no one in it, 27to satisfy a desolate wasteland and make it sprout with grass? 28Does the rain have a father? Who fathers the drops of dew?"

Ps 147 [8]He covers the sky with clouds; he supplies the earth with rain and makes grass grow on the hills.
Jer 14 [22]Do any of the worthless idols of the nations bring rain? Do the skies themselves send down showers? No, it is you, O LORD our God. Therefore our hope is in you, for you are the one who does all this.
Ezek 34 [26]"'I will bless them and the places surrounding my hill. I will send down showers in season; there will be showers of blessing.'"
Joel 2 [23]Be glad, O people of Zion, rejoice in the LORD your God, for he has given you the autumn rains in righteousness. He sends you abundant showers, both autumn and spring rains, as before.
Zech 10 [1]Ask the LORD for rain in the springtime; it is the LORD who makes the storm clouds. He gives showers of rain to men, and plants of the field to everyone.
Matt 5 [45]". . . that you may be sons of your Father in heaven. He causes his sun to rise on the evil and the good, and sends rain on the righteous and the unrighteous."
Acts 14 [17]"Yet he has not left himself without testimony: He has shown kindness by giving you rain from heaven and crops in their seasons; he provides you with plenty of food and fills your hearts with joy."

(7) Rainbow

Gen 9 [12]And God said, "This is the sign of the covenant I am making between me and you and every living creature with you, a covenant for all generations to come: [13]I have set my rainbow in the clouds, and it will be the sign of the covenant between me and the earth. [14]Whenever I bring clouds over the earth and the rainbow appears in the clouds, [15]I will remember my covenant between me and you and all living creatures of every kind. Never again will the waters become a flood to destroy all life. [16]Whenever the rainbow appears in the clouds, I will see it and remember the everlasting covenant between God and all living creatures of every kind on the earth."

[17]So God said to Noah, "This is the sign of the covenant I have established between me and all life on the earth."

(8) Sky

Job 37 [18]". . . can you join him in spreading out the skies, hard as a mirror of cast bronze?"

(9) Snow

Job 37 [6]"He says to the snow, 'Fall on the earth,' and to the rain shower, 'Be a mighty downpour.'"
Job 38 [22]"Have you entered the storehouses of the snow or seen the storehouses of the hail? . . ."
Ps 147 [16]He spreads the snow like wool and scatters the frost like ashes.

(10) Thunder

Exod 9 [23]When Moses stretched out his staff toward the sky, the LORD sent thunder and hail, and lightning flashed down to the ground. So the LORD rained hail on the land of Egypt. . . .
Exod 20 [18]When the people saw the thunder and lightning and heard the trumpet and saw the mountain in smoke, they trembled with fear. They stayed at a distance [19]and said to Moses, "Speak to us yourself and we will listen. But do not have God speak to us or we will die."
Job 36 [33]"His thunder announces the coming storm; even the cattle make known its approach."
Job 37 [4]"After that comes the sound of his roar; he thunders with his majestic voice. When his voice resounds, he holds nothing back. [5]God's voice thunders in marvelous ways; he does great things beyond our understanding."
Jer 10 [13]When he thunders, the waters in the heavens roar; he makes clouds rise from the ends of the earth. He sends lightning with the rain and brings out the wind from his storehouses.

(11) Wind

Job 37 [17]"You who swelter in your clothes when the land lies hushed under the south wind, [18]can you join him in spreading out the skies, hard as a mirror of cast bronze?"
Ps 135 [7]He makes clouds rise from the ends of the earth; he sends lightning with the rain and brings out the wind from his storehouses.
Ps 147 [18]He sends his word and melts them; he stirs up his breezes, and the waters flow.
Jer 4 [11]At that time this people and Jerusalem will be told, "A scorching wind from the barren heights in the desert blows toward my people, but not to winnow or cleanse; [12]a wind too strong for that comes from me. Now I pronounce my judgments against them."
Jer 49 [36]"I will bring against Elam the four winds from the four quarters of the heavens; I will scatter them to the four winds, and there will not be a nation where Elam's exiles do not go."
Ezek 13 [13]"'Therefore this is what the Sovereign LORD says: In my wrath I will unleash a violent wind, and in my anger hailstones and torrents of rain will fall with destructive fury.'"
Mark 4 [41]They were terrified and asked each other, "Who is this? Even the wind and the waves obey him!"

d) The Earth's Landscape and Environment

(1) Earthquakes

Job 9 [6]"He shakes the earth from its place and makes its pillars tremble."
Ps 18 [7]The earth trembled and quaked, and the foundations of the mountains shook; they trembled because he was angry.
Ps 104 [31]May the glory of the LORD endure forever; may the LORD rejoice in his works—[32]he who looks at the earth, and it trembles, who touches the mountains, and they smoke.
Isa 13 [13]Therefore I will make the heavens tremble; and the earth will shake from its place at the wrath of the LORD Almighty, in the day of his burning anger.
Jer 4 [24]I looked at the mountains, and they were quaking; all the hills were swaying.
Ezek 38 [19]"'In my zeal and fiery wrath I declare that at that time there shall be a great earthquake in the land of Israel. [20]The fish of the sea, the birds of the air, the beasts of the field, every creature that moves along the ground, and all the people on the face of the earth will tremble at my presence. The mountains will be overturned, the cliffs will crumble and every wall will fall to the ground.'"

(2) Famine and Drought

Lev 26 [18]"'If after all this you will not listen to me, I will punish you for your sins seven times over. [19]I will break down your stubborn pride and make the sky above you like iron and the ground beneath you like bronze. [20]Your strength will be spent in vain, because your soil will not yield its crops, nor will the trees of the land yield their fruit.'"
Deut 28 [23]The sky over your head will be bronze, the ground beneath you iron. [24]The LORD will turn the rain of your country into dust and powder; it will come down from the skies until you are destroyed.
1 Kings 17 [1]Now Elijah the Tishbite, from Tishbe in Gilead, said to Ahab, "As the LORD, the God of Israel, lives, whom I serve, there will be neither dew nor rain in the next few years except at my word."
Ps 107 [33]He turned rivers into a desert, flowing springs into thirsty ground, [34]and fruitful land into a salt waste, because of the wickedness of those who lived there.
Jer 8 [13]"'I will take away their harvest, declares the LORD. There will be no grapes on the vine. There will be no figs on the tree, and their leaves will wither. What I have given them will be taken from them.'"
Jer 51 [36]Therefore, this is what the LORD says: "See, I will defend your cause and avenge you; I will dry up her sea and make her springs dry."
Ezek 22 [24]"Son of man, say to the land, 'You are a land that has had no rain or showers in the day of wrath.'"
Ezek 30 [12]"'I will dry up the streams of the Nile and sell the land to evil men; by the hand of foreigners I will lay waste the land and everything in it.

"'I the LORD have spoken.'"
Hos 13 [15]". . . even though he thrives among his brothers. An east wind from the LORD will come, blowing in from the desert; his spring will fail and his well dry up. His storehouse will be plundered of all its treasures."
Amos 4 [6]"I gave you empty stomachs in every city and lack of

bread in every town, yet you have not returned to me," declares the LORD.

7"I also withheld rain from you when the harvest was still three months away. I sent rain on one town, but withheld it from another. One field had rain; another had none and dried up. 8People staggered from town to town for water but did not get enough to drink, yet you have not returned to me," declares the LORD.

Nah 1 4He rebukes the sea and dries it up; he makes all the rivers run dry. Bashan and Carmel wither and the blossoms of Lebanon fade.

Hag 1 9"You expected much, but see, it turned out to be little. What you brought home, I blew away. Why?" declares the LORD Almighty. "Because of my house, which remains a ruin, while each of you is busy with his own house. 10Therefore, because of you the heavens have withheld their dew and the earth its crops. 11I called for a drought on the fields and the mountains, on the grain, the new wine, the oil and whatever the ground produces, on men and cattle, and on the labor of your hands."

(3) Fire

Isa 66 16For with fire and with his sword the LORD will execute judgment upon all men, and many will be those slain by the LORD.

Ezek 20 45The word of the LORD came to me: 46"Son of man, set your face toward the south; preach against the south and prophesy against the forest of the southland. 47Say to the southern forest: 'Hear the word of the LORD. This is what the Sovereign LORD says: I am about to set fire to you, and it will consume all your trees, both green and dry. The blazing flame will not be quenched, and every face from south to north will be scorched by it. 48Everyone will see that I the LORD have kindled it; it will not be quenched.'"

Ezek 30 8"'Then they will know that I am the LORD, when I set fire to Egypt and all her helpers are crushed.'"

Amos 7 4This is what the Sovereign LORD showed me: The Sovereign LORD was calling for judgment by fire; it dried up the great deep and devoured the land.

(4) Ice

Job 37 10"The breath of God produces ice, and the broad waters become frozen."

Job 38 29"From whose womb comes the ice? Who gives birth to the frost from the heavens 30when the waters become hard as stone, when the surface of the deep is frozen?"

(5) Mountains

Deut 4 11You came near and stood at the foot of the mountain while it blazed with fire to the very heavens, with black clouds and deep darkness.

Judg 5 5"The mountains quaked before the LORD, the One of Sinai, before the LORD, the God of Israel."

Job 9 5"He moves mountains without their knowing it and overturns them in his anger."

Ps 97 5The mountains melt like wax before the LORD, before the Lord of all the earth.

Ps 104 31May the glory of the LORD endure forever; may the LORD rejoice in his works—32he who looks at the earth, and it trembles, who touches the mountains, and they smoke.

Ps 144 5Part your heavens, O LORD, and come down; touch the mountains, so that they smoke.

Isa 64 1Oh, that you would rend the heavens and come down, that the mountains would tremble before you! 2As when fire sets twigs ablaze and causes water to boil, come down to make your name known to your enemies and cause the nations to quake before you! 3For when you did awesome things that we did not expect, you came down, and the mountains trembled before you.

Mic 1 4The mountains melt beneath him and the valleys split apart, like wax before the fire, like water rushing down a slope.

Nah 1 5The mountains quake before him and the hills melt away. The earth trembles at his presence, the world and all who live in it.

(6) Plagues and Calamities

Exod 9 1Then the LORD said to Moses, "Go to Pharaoh and say to him, 'This is what the LORD, the God of the Hebrews, says: "Let my people go, so that they may worship me." 2If you refuse to let them go and continue to hold them back, 3the hand of the LORD will bring a terrible plague on your livestock in the field—on your horses and donkeys and camels and on your cattle and sheep and goats. 4But the LORD will make a distinction between the livestock of Israel and that of Egypt, so that no animal belonging to the Israelites will die."'"

2 Chron 6 28"When famine or plague comes to the land, or blight or mildew, locusts or grasshoppers, or when enemies besiege them in any of their cities, whatever disaster or disease may come, 29and when a prayer or plea is made by any of your people Israel—each one aware of his afflictions and pains, and spreading out his hands toward this temple—30then hear from heaven, your dwelling place. Forgive, and deal with each man according to all he does, since you know his heart (for you alone know the hearts of men), 31so that they will fear you and walk in your ways all the time they live in the land you gave our fathers."

Isa 29 6the LORD Almighty will come with thunder and earthquake and great noise, with windstorm and tempest and flames of a devouring fire.

Isa 34 9Edom's streams will be turned into pitch, her dust into burning sulfur; her land will become blazing pitch! 10It will not be quenched night and day; its smoke will rise forever. From generation to generation it will lie desolate; no one will ever pass through it again. 11The desert owl and screech owl will possess it; the great owl and the raven will nest there. God will stretch out over Edom the measuring line of chaos and the plumb line of desolation. 12Her nobles will have nothing there to be called a kingdom, all her princes will vanish away. 13Thorns will overrun her citadels, nettles and brambles her strongholds. She will become a haunt for jackals, a home for owls.

Ezek 38 22"'I will execute judgment upon him with plague and bloodshed; I will pour down torrents of rain, hailstones and burning sulfur on him and on his troops and on the many nations with him.'"

Hos 2 12"I will ruin her vines and her fig trees, which she said were her pay from her lovers; I will make them a thicket, and wild animals will devour them."

Amos 4 9"Many times I struck your gardens and vineyards, I struck them with blight and mildew. Locusts devoured your fig and olive trees, yet you have not returned to me," declares the LORD.

10"I sent plagues among you as I did to Egypt. I killed your young men with the sword, along with your captured horses. I filled your nostrils with the stench of your camps, yet you have not returned to me," declares the LORD.

Nah 1 3The LORD is slow to anger and great in power; the LORD will not leave the guilty unpunished. His way is in the whirlwind and the storm, and clouds are the dust of his feet.

Luke 21 11"There will be great earthquakes, famines and pestilences in various places, and fearful events and great signs from heaven."

(7) Waters, Seas, and Floods

Gen 6 17"I am going to bring floodwaters on the earth to destroy all life under the heavens, every creature that has the breath of life in it. Everything on earth will perish."

Gen 7 11In the six hundredth year of Noah's life, on the seventeenth day of the second month—on that day all the springs of the great deep burst forth, and the floodgates of the heavens were opened. 12And rain fell on the earth forty days and forty nights.

Job 38 34"Can you raise your voice to the clouds and cover yourself with a flood of water?"

Ps 65 5You answer us with awesome deeds of righteousness, O God our Savior, the hope of all the ends of the earth and of the farthest seas. . . . 7who stilled the roaring of the seas, the roaring of their waves, and the turmoil of the nations.

Ps 89 9You rule over the surging sea; when its waves mount up, you still them.

Ps 89 25"I will set his hand over the sea, his right hand over the rivers."

Ps 104 10He makes springs pour water into the ravines; it flows between the mountains. 11They give water to all the beasts of the field; the wild donkeys quench their thirst. 12The birds of the air nest by the waters; they sing among the branches. 13He waters the mountains from his upper chambers; the earth is satisfied by the fruit of his work.

Ps 107 35He turned the desert into pools of water and the parched ground into flowing springs. . . .

Isa 30 25In the day of great slaughter, when the towers fall, streams of water will flow on every high mountain and every lofty hill.

Isa 35 4say to those with fearful hearts, "Be strong, do not fear; your God will come, he will come with vengeance; with divine retribution he will come to save you." . . . 7The burning sand will become a pool, the thirsty ground bubbling springs. In the haunts where jackals once lay, grass and reeds and papyrus will grow.

Ezek 26 19"This is what the Sovereign LORD says: When I make you a desolate city, like cities no longer inhabited, and when I bring the ocean depths over you and its vast waters cover you . . ."

Mark 4 37A furious squall came up, and the waves broke over the boat, so that it was nearly swamped. 38Jesus was in the stern, sleeping on a cushion. The disciples woke him and said to him, "Teacher, don't you care if we drown?"

39He got up, rebuked the wind and said to the waves, "Quiet! Be still!" Then the wind died down and it was completely calm. . . .

41They were terrified and asked each other, "Who is this? Even the wind and the waves obey him!"

2. God's Providence and Plant Life

Lev 26 4"'I will send you rain in its season, and the ground will yield its crops and the trees of the field their fruit.'"

Deut 11 14then I will send rain on your land in its season, both autumn and spring rains, so that you may gather in your grain, new wine and oil.

Job 38 25"Who cuts a channel for the torrents of rain, and a path for the thunderstorm, 26to water a land where no man lives, a desert with no one in it, 27to satisfy a desolate wasteland and make it sprout with grass?"

Ps 65 9You care for the land and water it; you enrich it abundantly. The streams of God are filled with water to provide the people with grain, for so you have ordained it. 10You drench its furrows and level its ridges; you soften it with showers and bless its crops. 11You crown the year with your bounty, and your carts overflow with abundance. 12The grasslands of the desert overflow; the hills are clothed with gladness. 13The meadows are covered with flocks and the valleys are mantled with grain; they shout for joy and sing.

Ps 104 14He makes grass grow for the cattle, and plants for man to cultivate—bringing forth food from the earth: 15wine that gladdens the heart of man, oil to make his face shine, and bread that sustains his heart. 16The trees of the LORD are well watered, the cedars of Lebanon that he planted.

Ps 147 8He covers the sky with clouds; he supplies the earth with rain and makes grass grow on the hills.

Isa 41 19"I will put in the desert the cedar and the acacia, the myrtle and the olive. I will set pines in the wasteland, the fir and the cypress together. . . ."

Joel 2 21Be not afraid, O land; be glad and rejoice. Surely the LORD has done great things. 22Be not afraid, O wild animals, for the open pastures are becoming green. The trees are bearing their fruit; the fig tree and the vine yield their riches.

Amos 9 13"The days are coming," declares the LORD, "when the reaper will be overtaken by the plowman and the planter by the one treading grapes. New wine will drip from the mountains and flow from all the hills."

Jon 4 6Then the LORD God provided a vine and made it grow up over Jonah to give shade for his head to ease his discomfort, and Jonah was very happy about the vine. 7But at dawn the next day God provided a worm, which chewed the vine so that it withered. 8When the sun rose, God provided a scorching east wind, and the sun blazed on Jonah's head so that he grew faint. He wanted to die, and said, "It would be better for me to die than to live."

9But God said to Jonah, "Do you have a right to be angry about the vine?"

"I do," he said. "I am angry enough to die."

10But the LORD said, "You have been concerned about this vine, though you did not tend it or make it grow. It sprang up overnight and died overnight."

Matt 6 28"And why do you worry about clothes? See how the lilies of the field grow. They do not labor or spin. 29Yet I tell you that not even Solomon in all his splendor was dressed like one of these. 30If that is how God clothes the grass of the field, which is here today and tomorrow is thrown into the fire, will he not much more clothe you, O you of little faith?"

Acts 14 17"Yet he has not left himself without testimony: He has shown kindness by giving you rain from heaven and crops in their seasons; he provides you with plenty of food and fills your hearts with joy."

3. God's Providence and Living Creatures

a) Birds

1 Kings 17 4"You will drink from the brook, and I have ordered the ravens to feed you there."

Ps 104 16The trees of the LORD are well watered, the cedars of Lebanon that he planted. 17There the birds make their nests; the stork has its home in the pine trees.

Ps 147 9He provides food for the cattle and for the young ravens when they call.

Isa 46 11"From the east I summon a bird of prey; from a far-off land, a man to fulfill my purpose. What I have said, that will I bring about; what I have planned, that will I do."

Matt 6 26"Look at the birds of the air; they do not sow or reap or store away in barns, and yet your heavenly Father feeds them. Are you not much more valuable than they?"

Matt 10 29"Are not two sparrows sold for a penny? Yet not one of them will fall to the ground apart from the will of your Father."

b) Fish

Jon 1 17But the LORD provided a great fish to swallow Jonah, and Jonah was inside the fish three days and three nights.

Matt 17 26"From others," Peter answered.

"Then the sons are exempt," Jesus said to him. 27"But so that we may not offend them, go to the lake and throw out your line. Take the first fish you catch; open its mouth and you will find a four-drachma coin. Take it and give it to them for my tax and yours."

Luke 5 4When he had finished speaking, he said to Simon, "Put out into deep water, and let down the nets for a catch."

5Simon answered, "Master, we've worked hard all night and haven't caught anything. But because you say so, I will let down the nets."

6When they had done so, they caught such a large number of fish that their nets began to break. 7So they signaled their partners in the other boat to come and help them, and they came and filled both boats so full that they began to sink.

8When Simon Peter saw this, he fell at Jesus' knees and said, "Go away from me, Lord; I am a sinful man!" 9For he and all his companions were astonished at the catch of fish they had taken. . . .

c) Land Animals

Lev 26 21"'If you remain hostile toward me and refuse to listen to me, I will multiply your afflictions seven times over, as your sins deserve. 22I will send wild animals against you, and they will rob you of your children, destroy your cattle and make you so few in number that your roads will be deserted.'"

Deut 7 20Moreover, the LORD your God will send the hornet among them until even the survivors who hide from you have perished.

Job 5 23"For you will have a covenant with the stones of the field, and the wild animals will be at peace with you."

Job 12 10"In his hand is the life of every creature and the breath of all mankind."

Job 38 39"Do you hunt the prey for the lioness and satisfy the hunger of the lions 40when they crouch in their dens or lie in wait in a thicket? 41Who provides food for the raven when its young cry out to God and wander about for lack of food?"

Job 39 5"Who let the wild donkey go free? Who untied his ropes? 6I gave him the wasteland as his home, the salt flats as

his habitat. 7He laughs at the commotion in the town; he does not hear a driver's shout. 8He ranges the hills for his pasture and searches for any green thing."
Ps 104 20You bring darkness, it becomes night, and all the beasts of the forest prowl. 21The lions roar for their prey and seek their food from God. 22The sun rises, and they steal away; they return and lie down in their dens. 23Then man goes out to his work, to his labor until evening.

24How many are your works, O LORD! In wisdom you made them all; the earth is full of your creatures. 25There is the sea, vast and spacious, teeming with creatures beyond number—living things both large and small. 26There the ships go to and fro and the leviathan, which you formed to frolic there.

27These all look to you to give them their food at the proper time. 28When you give it to them, they gather it up; when you open your hand, they are satisfied with good things. 29When you hide your face, they are terrified; when you take away their breath, they die and return to the dust. 30When you send your Spirit, they are created, and you renew the face of the earth.
Ps 147 9He provides food for the cattle and for the young ravens when they call.
Jer 5 6"Therefore a lion from the forest will attack them, a wolf from the desert will ravage them, a leopard will lie in wait near their towns to tear to pieces any who venture out, for their rebellion is great and their backslidings many."
Hos 2 18"In that day I will make a covenant for them with the beasts of the field and the birds of the air and the creatures that move along the ground. Bow and sword and battle I will abolish from the land, so that all may lie down in safety."
Joel 2 21Be not afraid, O land; be glad and rejoice. Surely the LORD has done great things. 22Be not afraid, O wild animals, for the open pastures are becoming green. The trees are bearing their fruit; the fig tree and the vine yield their riches.
Amos 7 1This is what the Sovereign LORD showed me: He was preparing swarms of locusts after the king's share had been harvested and just as the second crop was coming up.

4. The Preservation of All Life

Job 12 10"In his hand is the life of every creature and the breath of all mankind."
Ps 50 9"I have no need of a bull from your stall or of goats from your pens, 10for every animal of the forest is mine, and the cattle on a thousand hills. 11I know every bird in the mountains, and the creatures of the field are mine. 12If I were hungry I would not tell you, for the world is mine, and all that is in it."
Ps 145 13Your kingdom is an everlasting kingdom, and your dominion endures through all generations. The LORD is faithful to all his promises and loving toward all he has made. 14The LORD upholds all those who fall and lifts up all who are bowed down. 15The eyes of all look to you, and you give them their food at the proper time. 16You open your hand and satisfy the desires of every living thing.
1 Tim 6 13In the sight of God, who gives life to everything, and of Christ Jesus, who while testifying before Pontius Pilate made the good confession, I charge you. . . .

5. The Restoration of Creation

Isa 11 6The wolf will live with the lamb, the leopard will lie down with the goat, the calf and the lion and the yearling together; and a little child will lead them. 7The cow will feed with the bear, their young will lie down together, and the lion will eat straw like the ox. 8The infant will play near the hole of the cobra, and the young child put his hand into the viper's nest. 9They will neither harm nor destroy on all my holy mountain, for the earth will be full of the knowledge of the LORD as the waters cover the sea.
Isa 41 17"The poor and needy search for water, but there is none; their tongues are parched with thirst. But I the LORD will answer them; I, the God of Israel, will not forsake them. 18I will make rivers flow on barren heights, and springs within the valleys. I will turn the desert into pools of water, and the parched ground into springs. 19I will put in the desert the cedar and the acacia, the myrtle and the olive. I will set pines in the wasteland, the fir and the cypress together, 20so that people may see and know, may consider and understand, that the hand of the LORD has done this, that the Holy One of Israel has created it."
Isa 43 19"See, I am doing a new thing! Now it springs up; do you not perceive it? I am making a way in the desert and streams in the wasteland. 20The wild animals honor me, the jackals and the owls, because I provide water in the desert and streams in the wasteland, to give drink to my people, my chosen, 21the people I formed for myself that they may proclaim my praise."
Isa 55 10"As the rain and the snow come down from heaven, and do not return to it without watering the earth and making it bud and flourish, so that it yields seed for the sower and bread for the eater, 11so is my word that goes out from my mouth: It will not return to me empty, but will accomplish what I desire and achieve the purpose for which I sent it. 12You will go out in joy and be led forth in peace; the mountains and hills will burst into song before you, and all the trees of the field will clap their hands. 13Instead of the thornbush will grow the pine tree, and instead of briers the myrtle will grow. This will be for the LORD's renown, for an everlasting sign, which will not be destroyed."
Ezek 47 1The man brought me back to the entrance of the temple, and I saw water coming out from under the threshold of the temple toward the east (for the temple faced east). The water was coming down from under the south side of the temple, south of the altar. 2He then brought me out through the north gate and led me around the outside to the outer gate facing east, and the water was flowing from the south side.

3As the man went eastward with a measuring line in his hand, he measured off a thousand cubits and then led me through water that was ankle-deep. 4He measured off another thousand cubits and led me through water that was knee-deep. He measured off another thousand and led me through water that was up to the waist. 5He measured off another thousand, but now it was a river that I could not cross, because the water had risen and was deep enough to swim in—a river that no one could cross. 6He asked me, "Son of man, do you see this?"

Then he led me back to the bank of the river. 7When I arrived there, I saw a great number of trees on each side of the river. 8He said to me, "This water flows toward the eastern region and goes down into the Arabah, where it enters the Sea. When it empties into the Sea, the water there becomes fresh. 9Swarms of living creatures will live wherever the river flows. There will be large numbers of fish, because this water flows there and makes the salt water fresh; so where the river flows everything will live. 10Fishermen will stand along the shore; from En Gedi to En Eglaim there will be places for spreading nets. The fish will be of many kinds—like the fish of the Great Sea. 11But the swamps and marshes will not become fresh; they will be left for salt. 12Fruit trees of all kinds will grow on both banks of the river. Their leaves will not wither, nor will their fruit fail. Every month they will bear, because the water from the sanctuary flows to them. Their fruit will serve for food and their leaves for healing."
Acts 3 21"He must remain in heaven until the time comes for God to restore everything, as he promised long ago through his holy prophets."
Rom 8 19The creation waits in eager expectation for the sons of God to be revealed. 20For the creation was subjected to frustration, not by its own choice, but by the will of the one who subjected it, in hope 21that the creation itself will be liberated from its bondage to decay and brought into the glorious freedom of the children of God.

22We know that the whole creation has been groaning as in the pains of childbirth right up to the present time.
Rev 21 1Then I saw a new heaven and a new earth, for the first heaven and the first earth had passed away, and there was no longer any sea. 2I saw the Holy City, the new Jerusalem, coming down out of heaven from God, prepared as a bride beautifully dressed for her husband. 3And I heard a loud voice from the throne saying, "Now the dwelling of God is with men, and he will live with them. They will be his people, and God himself will be with them and be their God. 4He will wipe every tear from their eyes. There will be no more death or mourning or crying or pain, for the old order of things has passed away."
Rev 22 1Then the angel showed me the river of the water of

life, as clear as crystal, flowing from the throne of God and of the Lamb [2]down the middle of the great street of the city. On each side of the river stood the tree of life, bearing twelve crops of fruit, yielding its fruit every month. And the leaves of the tree are for the healing of the nations. [3]No longer will there be any curse. The throne of God and of the Lamb will be in the city, and his servants will serve him. [4]They will see his face, and his name will be on their foreheads. [5]There will be no more night. They will not need the light of a lamp or the light of the sun, for the Lord God will give them light. And they will reign for ever and ever.

C. Providence and the Peoples of the World

1. God's Providence in Nations

a) Providence Appoints and Removes Rulers

1 Kings 19 [15]The LORD said to him, "Go back the way you came, and go to the Desert of Damascus. When you get there, anoint Hazael king over Aram."

2 Kings 8 [12]"Why is my lord weeping?" asked Hazael.

"Because I know the harm you will do to the Israelites," he answered. "You will set fire to their fortified places, kill their young men with the sword, dash their little children to the ground, and rip open their pregnant women."

[13]Hazael said, "How could your servant, a mere dog, accomplish such a feat?"

"The LORD has shown me that you will become king of Aram," answered Elisha.

Job 12 [24]"He deprives the leaders of the earth of their reason; he sends them wandering through a trackless waste. [25]They grope in darkness with no light; he makes them stagger like drunkards."

Isa 7 [20]In that day the Lord will use a razor hired from beyond the River—the king of Assyria—to shave your head and the hair of your legs, and to take off your beards also.

Isa 10 [5]"Woe to the Assyrian, the rod of my anger, in whose hand is the club of my wrath! [6]I send him against a godless nation, I dispatch him against a people who anger me, to seize loot and snatch plunder, and to trample them down like mud in the streets. [7]But this is not what he intends, this is not what he has in mind; his purpose is to destroy, to put an end to many nations. [8]'Are not my commanders all kings?' he says. [9]'Has not Calno fared like Carchemish? Is not Hamath like Arpad, and Samaria like Damascus? [10]As my hand seized the kingdoms of the idols, kingdoms whose images excelled those of Jerusalem and Samaria—[11]shall I not deal with Jerusalem and her images as I dealt with Samaria and her idols?'"

[12]When the Lord has finished all his work against Mount Zion and Jerusalem, he will say, "I will punish the king of Assyria for the willful pride of his heart and the haughty look in his eyes. [13]For he says: 'By the strength of my hand I have done this, and by my wisdom, because I have understanding. I removed the boundaries of nations, I plundered their treasures; like a mighty one I subdued their kings. [14]As one reaches into a nest, so my hand reached for the wealth of the nations; as men gather abandoned eggs, so I gathered all the countries; not one flapped a wing, or opened its mouth to chirp.'"

[15]Does the ax raise itself above him who swings it, or the saw boast against him who uses it? As if a rod were to wield him who lifts it up, or a club brandish him who is not wood! [16]Therefore, the Lord, the LORD Almighty, will send a wasting disease upon his sturdy warriors; under his pomp a fire will be kindled like a blazing flame.

Isa 40 [23]He brings princes to naught and reduces the rulers of this world to nothing. [24]No sooner are they planted, no sooner are they sown, no sooner do they take root in the ground, than he blows on them and they wither, and a whirlwind sweeps them away like chaff.

Jer 27 [5]"'"With my great power and outstretched arm I made the earth and its people and the animals that are on it, and I give it to anyone I please. [6]Now I will hand all your countries over to my servant Nebuchadnezzar king of Babylon; I will make even the wild animals subject to him. [7]All nations will serve him and his son and his grandson until the time for his land comes; then many nations and great kings will subjugate him."'"

Dan 2 [21]"He changes times and seasons; he sets up kings and deposes them. He gives wisdom to the wise and knowledge to the discerning."

Dan 2 [37]"You, O king, are the king of kings. The God of heaven has given you dominion and power and might and glory; [38]in your hands he has placed mankind and the beasts of the field and the birds of the air. Wherever they live, he has made you ruler over them all. You are that head of gold."

Dan 4 [17]"'The decision is announced by messengers, the holy ones declare the verdict, so that the living may know that the Most High is sovereign over the kingdoms of men and gives them to anyone he wishes and sets over them the lowliest of men.'"

Dan 4 [24]"This is the interpretation, O king, and this is the decree the Most High has issued against my lord the king: [25]You will be driven away from people and will live with the wild animals; you will eat grass like cattle and be drenched with the dew of heaven. Seven times will pass by for you until you acknowledge that the Most High is sovereign over the kingdoms of men and gives them to anyone he wishes."

Dan 5 [18]"O king, the Most High God gave your father Nebuchadnezzar sovereignty and greatness and glory and splendor. [19]Because of the high position he gave him, all the peoples and nations and men of every language dreaded and feared him. Those the king wanted to put to death, he put to death; those he wanted to spare, he spared; those he wanted to promote, he promoted; and those he wanted to humble, he humbled. [20]But when his heart became arrogant and hardened with pride, he was deposed from his royal throne and stripped of his glory."

Hos 13 [11]"So in my anger I gave you a king, and in my wrath I took him away."

Rom 13 [1]Everyone must submit himself to the governing authorities, for there is no authority except that which God has established. The authorities that exist have been established by God.

b) Providence Determines National Destiny

Deut 2 [30]But Sihon king of Heshbon refused to let us pass through. For the LORD your God had made his spirit stubborn and his heart obstinate in order to give him into your hands, as he has now done.

Deut 32 [8]When the Most High gave the nations their inheritance, when he divided all mankind, he set up boundaries for the peoples according to the number of the sons of Israel.

Job 12 [23]"He makes nations great, and destroys them; he enlarges nations, and disperses them."

Ps 22 [27]All the ends of the earth will remember and turn to the LORD, and all the families of the nations will bow down before him, [28]for dominion belongs to the LORD and he rules over the nations.

Ps 33 [10]The LORD foils the plans of the nations; he thwarts the purposes of the peoples. [11]But the plans of the LORD stand firm forever, the purposes of his heart through all generations.

Ps 47 [7]For God is the King of all the earth; sing to him a psalm of praise. [8]God reigns over the nations; God is seated on his holy throne. [9]The nobles of the nations assemble as the people of the God of Abraham, for the kings of the earth belong to God; he is greatly exalted.

Ps 66 [7]He rules forever by his power, his eyes watch the nations—let not the rebellious rise up against him.

Isa 14 [24]The LORD Almighty has sworn, "Surely, as I have planned, so it will be, and as I have purposed, so it will stand. [25]I will crush the Assyrian in my land; on my mountains I will trample him down. His yoke will be taken from my people, and his burden removed from their shoulders."

[26]This is the plan determined for the whole world; this is the hand stretched out over all nations.

Isa 26 [15]You have enlarged the nation, O LORD; you have enlarged the nation. You have gained glory for yourself; you have extended all the borders of the land.

Isa 43 [14]This is what the LORD says—your Redeemer, the Holy

One of Israel: "For your sake I will send to Babylon and bring down as fugitives all the Babylonians, in the ships in which they took pride."

Isa 48 [14]"Come together, all of you, and listen: Which of the idols has foretold these things? The LORD's chosen ally will carry out his purpose against Babylon; his arm will be against the Babylonians. [15]I, even I, have spoken; yes, I have called him. I will bring him, and he will succeed in his mission."

Ezek 29 [19]"Therefore this is what the Sovereign LORD says: I am going to give Egypt to Nebuchadnezzar king of Babylon, and he will carry off its wealth. He will loot and plunder the land as pay for his army. [20]I have given him Egypt as a reward for his efforts because he and his army did it for me, declares the Sovereign LORD."

Dan 2 [37]"You, O king, are the king of kings. The God of heaven has given you dominion and power and might and glory; [38]in your hands he has placed mankind and the beasts of the field and the birds of the air. Wherever they live, he has made you ruler over them all. You are that head of gold.

[39]"After you, another kingdom will rise, inferior to yours. Next, a third kingdom, one of bronze, will rule over the whole earth. [40]Finally, there will be a fourth kingdom, strong as iron—for iron breaks and smashes everything—and as iron breaks things to pieces, so it will crush and break all the others. . . .

[44]"In the time of those kings, the God of heaven will set up a kingdom that will never be destroyed, nor will it be left to another people. It will crush all those kingdoms and bring them to an end, but it will itself endure forever."

Dan 11 [27]"The two kings, with their hearts bent on evil, will sit at the same table and lie to each other, but to no avail, because an end will still come at the appointed time."

Acts 17 [26]"From one man he made every nation of men, that they should inhabit the whole earth; and he determined the times set for them and the exact places where they should live."

c) Providence Concludes Human History

Dan 8 [9]Out of one of them came another horn, which started small but grew in power to the south and to the east and toward the Beautiful Land. [10]It grew until it reached the host of the heavens, and it threw some of the starry host down to the earth and trampled on them. [11]It set itself up to be as great as the Prince of the host; it took away the daily sacrifice from him, and the place of his sanctuary was brought low. [12]Because of rebellion, the host of the saints and the daily sacrifice were given over to it. It prospered in everything it did, and truth was thrown to the ground. . . .

[14]He said to me, "It will take 2,300 evenings and mornings; then the sanctuary will be reconsecrated." . . .

[17]As he came near the place where I was standing, I was terrified and fell prostrate. "Son of man," he said to me, "understand that the vision concerns the time of the end."

Dan 11 [35]"Some of the wise will stumble, so that they may be refined, purified and made spotless until the time of the end, for it will still come at the appointed time."

Acts 17 [31]"For he has set a day when he will judge the world with justice by the man he has appointed. He has given proof of this to all men by raising him from the dead."

2. God's Providence and "Incidental" Circumstances

Exod 21 [12]"Anyone who strikes a man and kills him shall surely be put to death. [13]However, if he does not do it intentionally, but God lets it happen, he is to flee to a place I will designate."

1 Sam 24 [3]He came to the sheep pens along the way; a cave was there, and Saul went in to relieve himself. David and his men were far back in the cave. [4]The men said, "This is the day the LORD spoke of when he said to you, 'I will give your enemy into your hands for you to deal with as you wish.'" Then David crept up unnoticed and cut off a corner of Saul's robe. . . .

[10]"This day you have seen with your own eyes how the LORD delivered you into my hands in the cave. Some urged me to kill you, but I spared you; I said, 'I will not lift my hand against my master, because he is the LORD's anointed.'"

Prov 16 [33]The lot is cast into the lap, but its every decision is from the LORD.

Jon 1 [7]Then the sailors said to each other, "Come, let us cast lots to find out who is responsible for this calamity." They cast lots and the lot fell on Jonah.

Matt 10 [29]"Are not two sparrows sold for a penny? Yet not one of them will fall to the ground apart from the will of your Father. [30]And even the very hairs of your head are all numbered."

Acts 1 [23]So they proposed two men: Joseph called Barsabbas (also known as Justus) and Matthias. [24]Then they prayed, "Lord, you know everyone's heart. Show us which of these two you have chosen [25]to take over this apostolic ministry, which Judas left to go where he belongs." [26]Then they cast lots, and the lot fell to Matthias; so he was added to the eleven apostles.

3. God's Providence in Human Existence

a) Providence and Birth

Job 10 [8]"Your hands shaped me and made me. Will you now turn and destroy me? [9]Remember that you molded me like clay. Will you now turn me to dust again? [10]Did you not pour me out like milk and curdle me like cheese, [11]clothe me with skin and flesh and knit me together with bones and sinews? [12]You gave me life and showed me kindness, and in your providence watched over my spirit."

Ps 71 [6]From birth I have relied on you; you brought me forth from my mother's womb. I will ever praise you.

Ps 139 [13]For you created my inmost being; you knit me together in my mother's womb. [14]I praise you because I am fearfully and wonderfully made; your works are wonderful, I know that full well. [15]My frame was not hidden from you when I was made in the secret place. When I was woven together in the depths of the earth, [16]your eyes saw my unformed body. All the days ordained for me were written in your book before one of them came to be.

Eccles 11 [5]As you do not know the path of the wind, or how the body is formed in a mother's womb, so you cannot understand the work of God, the Maker of all things.

Jer 1 [5]"Before I formed you in the womb I knew you, before you were born I set you apart; I appointed you as a prophet to the nations."

b) Providence and Life Work

1 Sam 16 [1]The LORD said to Samuel, "How long will you mourn for Saul, since I have rejected him as king over Israel? Fill your horn with oil and be on your way; I am sending you to Jesse of Bethlehem. I have chosen one of his sons to be king."

Esther 4 [14]"For if you remain silent at this time, relief and deliverance for the Jews will arise from another place, but you and your father's family will perish. And who knows but that you have come to royal position for such a time as this?"

Eccles 2 [24]A man can do nothing better than to eat and drink and find satisfaction in his work. This too, I see, is from the hand of God, [25]for without him, who can eat or find enjoyment?

Eccles 5 [19]Moreover, when God gives any man wealth and possessions, and enables him to enjoy them, to accept his lot and be happy in his work—this is a gift of God.

Isa 45 [1]"This is what the LORD says to his anointed, to Cyrus, whose right hand I take hold of to subdue nations before him and to strip kings of their armor, to open doors before him so that gates will not be shut: [2]I will go before you and will level the mountains; I will break down gates of bronze and cut through bars of iron. [3]I will give you the treasures of darkness, riches stored in secret places, so that you may know that I am the LORD, the God of Israel, who summons you by name. [4]For the sake of Jacob my servant, of Israel my chosen, I summon you by name and bestow on you a title of honor, though you do not acknowledge me. [5]I am the LORD, and there is no other; apart from me there is no God. I will strengthen you, though you have not acknowledged me. . . ."

Luke 1 [15]". . . for he will be great in the sight of the Lord. He is never to take wine or other fermented drink, and he will be filled with the Holy Spirit even from birth. [16]Many of the peo-

ple of Israel will he bring back to the Lord their God. [17]And he will go on before the Lord, in the spirit and power of Elijah, to turn the hearts of the fathers to their children and the disobedient to the wisdom of the righteous—to make ready a people prepared for the Lord."
Gal 1 [15]But when God, who set me apart from birth and called me by his grace, was pleased [16]to reveal his Son in me so that I might preach him among the Gentiles, I did not consult any man. . . .

c) Providence in Life's Circumstances

1 Chron 13 [2]He then said to the whole assembly of Israel, "If it seems good to you and if it is the will of the LORD our God, let us send word far and wide to the rest of our brothers throughout the territories of Israel, and also to the priests and Levites who are with them in their towns and pasturelands, to come and join us."
Job 5 [18]"For he wounds, but he also binds up; he injures, but his hands also heal."
Job 23 [14]"He carries out his decree against me, and many such plans he still has in store."
Isa 19 [22]The LORD will strike Egypt with a plague; he will strike them and heal them. They will turn to the LORD, and he will respond to their pleas and heal them.
Luke 1 [52]"He has brought down rulers from their thrones but has lifted up the humble. [53]He has filled the hungry with good things but has sent the rich away empty."
Acts 18 [21]But as he left, he promised, "I will come back if it is God's will." Then he set sail from Ephesus.
Rom 15 [32]so that by God's will I may come to you with joy and together with you be refreshed.
1 Cor 4 [19]But I will come to you very soon, if the Lord is willing, and then I will find out not only how these arrogant people are talking, but what power they have.
Heb 6 [3]And God permitting, we will do so.
James 4 [13]Now listen, you who say, "Today or tomorrow we will go to this or that city, spend a year there, carry on business and make money." [14]Why, you do not even know what will happen tomorrow. What is your life? You are a mist that appears for a little while and then vanishes. [15]Instead, you ought to say, "If it is the Lord's will, we will live and do this or that."

d) Providence and Temporal Needs

Lev 26 [4]"'I will send you rain in its season, and the ground will yield its crops and the trees of the field their fruit. [5]Your threshing will continue until grape harvest and the grape harvest will continue until planting, and you will eat all the food you want and live in safety in your land.'"
Deut 11 [14]then I will send rain on your land in its season, both autumn and spring rains, so that you may gather in your grain, new wine and oil. [15]I will provide grass in the fields for your cattle, and you will eat and be satisfied.
Deut 28 [12]The LORD will open the heavens, the storehouse of his bounty, to send rain on your land in season and to bless all the work of your hands. You will lend to many nations but will borrow from none.
1 Kings 17 [4]"You will drink from the brook, and I have ordered the ravens to feed you there."
Job 36 [31]"This is the way he governs the nations and provides food in abundance."
Ps 65 [9]You care for the land and water it; you enrich it abundantly. The streams of God are filled with water to provide the people with grain, for so you have ordained it. [10]You drench its furrows and level its ridges; you soften it with showers and bless its crops.
Ps 111 [5]He provides food for those who fear him; he remembers his covenant forever.
Ps 136 [25]and who gives food to every creature. *His love endures forever.*
Jer 5 [24]"They do not say to themselves, 'Let us fear the LORD our God, who gives autumn and spring rains in season, who assures us of the regular weeks of harvest.'"
Matt 5 [45]". . . that you may be sons of your Father in heaven. He causes his sun to rise on the evil and the good, and sends rain on the righteous and the unrighteous."
Acts 14 [16]"In the past, he let all nations go their own way. [17]Yet he has not left himself without testimony: He has shown kindness by giving you rain from heaven and crops in their seasons; he provides you with plenty of food and fills your hearts with joy."

e) Providence and Prosperity

1 Sam 15 [17]Samuel said, "Although you were once small in your own eyes, did you not become the head of the tribes of Israel? The LORD anointed you king over Israel."
2 Sam 7 [8]"Now then, tell my servant David, 'This is what the LORD Almighty says: I took you from the pasture and from following the flock to be ruler over my people Israel. [9]I have been with you wherever you have gone, and I have cut off all your enemies from before you. Now I will make your name great, like the names of the greatest men of the earth.'"
1 Kings 3 [10]The Lord was pleased that Solomon had asked for this. [11]So God said to him, "Since you have asked for this and not for long life or wealth for yourself, nor have asked for the death of your enemies but for discernment in administering justice, [12]I will do what you have asked. I will give you a wise and discerning heart, so that there will never have been anyone like you, nor will there ever be. [13]Moreover, I will give you what you have not asked for—both riches and honor—so that in your lifetime you will have no equal among kings."
Job 8 [7]"Your beginnings will seem humble, so prosperous will your future be."
Job 36 [11]"If they obey and serve him, they will spend the rest of their days in prosperity and their years in contentment."
Job 42 [10]After Job had prayed for his friends, the LORD made him prosperous again and gave him twice as much as he had before.
Ps 1 [1]Blessed is the man who does not walk in the counsel of the wicked or stand in the way of sinners or sit in the seat of mockers. [2]But his delight is in the law of the LORD, and on his law he meditates day and night. [3]He is like a tree planted by streams of water, which yields its fruit in season and whose leaf does not wither. Whatever he does prospers.
Ps 18 [32]It is God who arms me with strength and makes my way perfect. [33]He makes my feet like the feet of a deer; he enables me to stand on the heights. [34]He trains my hands for battle, my arms can bend a bow of bronze. [35]You give me your shield of victory, and your right hand sustains me; you stoop down to make me great. [36]You broaden the path beneath me, so that my ankles do not turn.

[37]I pursued my enemies and overtook them; I did not turn back till they were destroyed. [38]I crushed them so that they could not rise; they fell beneath my feet. [39]You armed me with strength for battle; you made my adversaries bow at my feet. [40]You made my enemies turn their backs in flight, and I destroyed my foes. [41]They cried for help, but there was no one to save them—to the LORD, but he did not answer. [42]I beat them as fine as dust borne on the wind; I poured them out like mud in the streets.

[43]You have delivered me from the attacks of the people; you have made me the head of nations; people I did not know are subject to me. [44]As soon as they hear me, they obey me; foreigners cringe before me. [45]They all lose heart; they come trembling from their strongholds.

[46]The LORD lives! Praise be to my Rock! Exalted be God my Savior! [47]He is the God who avenges me, who subdues nations under me, [48]who saves me from my enemies. You exalted me above my foes; from violent men you rescued me. [49]Therefore I will praise you among the nations, O LORD; I will sing praises to your name. [50]He gives his king great victories; he shows unfailing kindness to his anointed, to David and his descendants forever.
Ps 107 [41]But he lifted the needy out of their affliction and increased their families like flocks.
Ps 148 [14]He has raised up for his people a horn, the praise of all his saints, of Israel, the people close to his heart. Praise the LORD.

f) Providence and Adversity

Job 19 [8]"He has blocked my way so I cannot pass; he has shrouded my paths in darkness. [9]He has stripped me of my honor and removed the crown from my head. [10]He tears me down on every side till I am gone; he uproots my hope like a tree. 11His anger burns against me; he counts me among his enemies. 12His troops advance in force; they build a siege ramp against me and encamp around my tent.

13"He has alienated my brothers from me; my acquaintances are completely estranged from me. 14My kinsmen have gone away; my friends have forgotten me. 15My guests and my maidservants count me a stranger; they look upon me as an alien. 16I summon my servant, but he does not answer, though I beg him with my own mouth. 17My breath is offensive to my wife; I am loathsome to my own brothers. 18Even the little boys scorn me; when I appear, they ridicule me. 19All my intimate friends detest me; those I love have turned against me. 20I am nothing but skin and bones; I have escaped with only the skin of my teeth."

Job 30 1"But now they mock me, men younger than I, whose fathers I would have disdained to put with my sheep dogs. . . . 11Now that God has unstrung my bow and afflicted me, they throw off restraint in my presence."

Ps 89 45You have cut short the days of his youth; you have covered him with a mantle of shame.

Ps 107 39Then their numbers decreased, and they were humbled by oppression, calamity and sorrow; 40he who pours contempt on nobles made them wander in a trackless waste.

Isa 14 16Those who see you stare at you, they ponder your fate: "Is this the man who shook the earth and made kingdoms tremble, 17the man who made the world a desert, who overthrew its cities and would not let his captives go home?"

18All the kings of the nations lie in state, each in his own tomb. 19But you are cast out of your tomb like a rejected branch; you are covered with the slain, with those pierced by the sword, those who descend to the stones of the pit. Like a corpse trampled underfoot, 20you will not join them in burial, for you have destroyed your land and killed your people.

The offspring of the wicked will never be mentioned again. . . .

22"I will rise up against them," declares the LORD Almighty. "I will cut off from Babylon her name and survivors, her offspring and descendants," declares the LORD. 23"I will turn her into a place for owls and into swampland; I will sweep her with the broom of destruction," declares the LORD Almighty.

Isa 18 4This is what the LORD says to me: "I will remain quiet and will look on from my dwelling place, like shimmering heat in the sunshine, like a cloud of dew in the heat of harvest." 5For, before the harvest, when the blossom is gone and the flower becomes a ripening grape, he will cut off the shoots with pruning knives, and cut down and take away the spreading branches. 6They will all be left to the mountain birds of prey and to the wild animals; the birds will feed on them all summer, the wild animals all winter.

Isa 22 15This is what the Lord, the LORD Almighty, says: "Go, say to this steward, to Shebna, who is in charge of the palace: 16What are you doing here and who gave you permission to cut out a grave for yourself here, hewing your grave on the height and chiseling your resting place in the rock?

17"Beware, the LORD is about to take firm hold of you and hurl you away, O you mighty man. 18He will roll you up tightly like a ball and throw you into a large country. There you will die and there your splendid chariots will remain—you disgrace to your master's house! 19I will depose you from your office, and you will be ousted from your position."

Lam 3 1I am the man who has seen affliction by the rod of his wrath. 2He has driven me away and made me walk in darkness rather than light; 3indeed, he has turned his hand against me again and again, all day long.

4He has made my skin and my flesh grow old and has broken my bones. 5He has besieged me and surrounded me with bitterness and hardship. 6He has made me dwell in darkness like those long dead.

7He has walled me in so I cannot escape; he has weighed me down with chains. 8Even when I call out or cry for help, he shuts out my prayer. 9He has barred my way with blocks of stone; he has made my paths crooked.

10Like a bear lying in wait, like a lion in hiding, 11he dragged me from the path and mangled me and left me without help. 12He drew his bow and made me the target for his arrows.

13He pierced my heart with arrows from his quiver. 14I became the laughingstock of all my people; they mock me in song all day long. 15He has filled me with bitter herbs and sated me with gall.

16He has broken my teeth with gravel; he has trampled me in the dust. 17I have been deprived of peace; I have forgotten what prosperity is. . . .

37Who can speak and have it happen if the Lord has not decreed it? 38Is it not from the mouth of the Most High that both calamities and good things come?

Lam 4 5Those who once ate delicacies are destitute in the streets. Those nurtured in purple now lie on ash heaps. . . .

11The LORD has given full vent to his wrath; he has poured out his fierce anger. He kindled a fire in Zion that consumed her foundations.

Rev 18 14"They will say, 'The fruit you longed for is gone from you. All your riches and splendor have vanished, never to be recovered.' 15The merchants who sold these things and gained their wealth from her will stand far off, terrified at her torment. They will weep and mourn 16and cry out: 'Woe! Woe, O great city, dressed in fine linen, purple and scarlet, and glittering with gold, precious stones and pearls! 17In one hour such great wealth has been brought to ruin!'

"Every sea captain, and all who travel by ship, the sailors, and all who earn their living from the sea, will stand far off. 18When they see the smoke of her burning, they will exclaim, 'Was there ever a city like this great city?' 19They will throw dust on their heads, and with weeping and mourning cry out:

"'Woe! Woe, O great city, where all who had ships on the sea became rich through her wealth! In one hour she has been brought to ruin! 20Rejoice over her, O heaven! Rejoice, saints and apostles and prophets! God has judged her for the way she treated you.'"

g) Providence and Death

Deut 32 49"Go up into the Abarim Range to Mount Nebo in Moab, across from Jericho, and view Canaan, the land I am giving the Israelites as their own possession. 50There on the mountain that you have climbed you will die and be gathered to your people, just as your brother Aaron died on Mount Hor and was gathered to his people. 51This is because both of you broke faith with me in the presence of the Israelites at the waters of Meribah Kadesh in the Desert of Zin and because you did not uphold my holiness among the Israelites. 52Therefore, you will see the land only from a distance; you will not enter the land I am giving to the people of Israel."

1 Sam 2 25"If a man sins against another man, God may mediate for him; but if a man sins against the LORD, who will intercede for him?" His sons, however, did not listen to their father's rebuke, for it was the LORD's will to put them to death.

Job 14 5"Man's days are determined; you have decreed the number of his months and have set limits he cannot exceed."

John 21 18"I tell you the truth, when you were younger you dressed yourself and went where you wanted; but when you are old you will stretch out your hands, and someone else will dress you and lead you where you do not want to go." 19Jesus said this to indicate the kind of death by which Peter would glorify God. Then he said to him, "Follow me!"

2 Tim 4 6For I am already being poured out like a drink offering, and the time has come for my departure. 7I have fought the good fight, I have finished the race, I have kept the faith. 8Now there is in store for me the crown of righteousness, which the Lord, the righteous Judge, will award to me on that day—and not only to me, but also to all who have longed for his appearing.

2 Pet 1 13I think it is right to refresh your memory as long as I live in the tent of this body, 14because I know that I will soon put it aside, as our Lord Jesus Christ has made clear to me.

4. God's Providence in Human Actions

a) God Works through Human Decisions

Exod 12 36The LORD had made the Egyptians favorably disposed toward the people, and they gave them what they asked for; so they plundered the Egyptians.

1 Sam 24 18“You have just now told me of the good you did to me; the LORD delivered me into your hands, but you did not kill me.”

1 Chron 5 26So the God of Israel stirred up the spirit of Pul king of Assyria (that is, Tiglath-Pileser king of Assyria), who took the Reubenites, the Gadites and the half-tribe of Manasseh into exile. He took them to Halah, Habor, Hara and the river of Gozan, where they are to this day.

2 Chron 36 22In the first year of Cyrus king of Persia, in order to fulfill the word of the LORD spoken by Jeremiah, the LORD moved the heart of Cyrus king of Persia to make a proclamation throughout his realm and to put it in writing:

23“This is what Cyrus king of Persia says: ‘The LORD, the God of heaven, has given me all the kingdoms of the earth and he has appointed me to build a temple for him at Jerusalem in Judah. Anyone of his people among you—may the LORD his God be with him, and let him go up.’”

Ezra 6 22For seven days they celebrated with joy the Feast of Unleavened Bread, because the LORD had filled them with joy by changing the attitude of the king of Assyria, so that he assisted them in the work on the house of God, the God of Israel.

Ezra 7 27Praise be to the LORD, the God of our fathers, who has put it into the king’s heart to bring honor to the house of the LORD in Jerusalem in this way. . . .

Neh 6 16When all our enemies heard about this, all the surrounding nations were afraid and lost their self-confidence, because they realized that this work had been done with the help of our God.

Prov 20 24A man’s steps are directed by the LORD. How then can anyone understand his own way?

Eph 2 10For we are God’s workmanship, created in Christ Jesus to do good works, which God prepared in advance for us to do.

Phil 2 13for it is God who works in you to will and to act according to his good purpose.

James 4 13Now listen, you who say, “Today or tomorrow we will go to this or that city, spend a year there, carry on business and make money.” 14Why, you do not even know what will happen tomorrow. What is your life? You are a mist that appears for a little while and then vanishes. 15Instead, you ought to say, “If it is the Lord’s will, we will live and do this or that.”

b) God Overrules Human Intention

Gen 24 50Laban and Bethuel answered, “This is from the LORD; we can say nothing to you one way or the other.”

Gen 31 29“I have the power to harm you; but last night the God of your father said to me, ‘Be careful not to say anything to Jacob, either good or bad.’”

Gen 45 5“And now, do not be distressed and do not be angry with yourselves for selling me here, because it was to save lives that God sent me ahead of you. 6For two years now there has been famine in the land, and for the next five years there will not be plowing and reaping. 7But God sent me ahead of you to preserve for you a remnant on earth and to save your lives by a great deliverance.

8“So then, it was not you who sent me here, but God. He made me father to Pharaoh, lord of his entire household and ruler of all Egypt.”

Gen 50 19But Joseph said to them, “Don’t be afraid. Am I in the place of God? 20You intended to harm me, but God intended it for good to accomplish what is now being done, the saving of many lives.”

Num 23 7Then Balaam uttered his oracle: “Balak brought me from Aram, the king of Moab from the eastern mountains. ‘Come,’ he said, ‘curse Jacob for me; come, denounce Israel.’ 8How can I curse those whom God has not cursed? How can I denounce those whom the LORD has not denounced? . . .”

11Balak said to Balaam, “What have you done to me? I brought you to curse my enemies, but you have done nothing but bless them!”

12He answered, “Must I not speak what the LORD puts in my mouth?”

Num 24 10Then Balak’s anger burned against Balaam. He struck his hands together and said to him, “I summoned you to curse my enemies, but you have blessed them these three times. 11Now leave at once and go home! I said I would reward you handsomely, but the LORD has kept you from being rewarded.”

12Balaam answered Balak, “Did I not tell the messengers you sent me, 13‘Even if Balak gave me his palace filled with silver and gold, I could not do anything of my own accord, good or bad, to go beyond the command of the LORD—and I must say only what the LORD says’?”

Deut 23 3No Ammonite or Moabite or any of his descendants may enter the assembly of the LORD, even down to the tenth generation. 4For they did not come to meet you with bread and water on your way when you came out of Egypt, and they hired Balaam son of Beor from Pethor in Aram Naharaim to pronounce a curse on you. 5However, the LORD your God would not listen to Balaam but turned the curse into a blessing for you, because the LORD your God loves you.

2 Sam 17 14Absalom and all the men of Israel said, “The advice of Hushai the Arkite is better than that of Ahithophel.” For the LORD had determined to frustrate the good advice of Ahithophel in order to bring disaster on Absalom.

1 Kings 12 22But this word of God came to Shemaiah the man of God: 23“Say to Rehoboam son of Solomon king of Judah, to the whole house of Judah and Benjamin, and to the rest of the people, 24‘This is what the LORD says: Do not go up to fight against your brothers, the Israelites. Go home, every one of you, for this is my doing.’” So they obeyed the word of the LORD and went home again, as the LORD had ordered.

Ps 33 10The LORD foils the plans of the nations; he thwarts the purposes of the peoples. 11But the plans of the LORD stand firm forever, the purposes of his heart through all generations.

Prov 21 30There is no wisdom, no insight, no plan that can succeed against the LORD.

Isa 10 5“Woe to the Assyrian, the rod of my anger, in whose hand is the club of my wrath! 6I send him against a godless nation, I dispatch him against a people who anger me, to seize loot and snatch plunder, and to trample them down like mud in the streets. 7But this is not what he intends, this is not what he has in mind; his purpose is to destroy, to put an end to many nations.”

John 7 30At this they tried to seize him, but no one laid a hand on him, because his time had not yet come.

John 8 20He spoke these words while teaching in the temple area near the place where the offerings were put. Yet no one seized him, because his time had not yet come.

Acts 2 23“This man was handed over to you by God’s set purpose and foreknowledge; and you, with the help of wicked men, put him to death by nailing him to the cross. 24But God raised him from the dead, freeing him from the agony of death, because it was impossible for death to keep its hold on him.”

Acts 5 38“Therefore, in the present case I advise you: Leave these men alone! Let them go! For if their purpose or activity is of human origin, it will fail. 39But if it is from God, you will not be able to stop these men; you will only find yourselves fighting against God.”

c) Human Effort Is Futile without God

2 Kings 17 15They rejected his decrees and the covenant he had made with their fathers and the warnings he had given them. They followed worthless idols and themselves became worthless. They imitated the nations around them although the LORD had ordered them, “Do not do as they do,” and they did the things the LORD had forbidden them to do.

Ps 94 11The LORD knows the thoughts of man; he knows that they are futile.

Ps 127 1Unless the LORD builds the house, its builders labor in vain. Unless the LORD watches over the city, the watchmen stand guard in vain. 2In vain you rise early and stay up late, toiling for food to eat—for he grants sleep to those he loves.

Jer 2 5This is what the LORD says: “What fault did your fathers find in me, that they strayed so far from me? They followed worthless idols and became worthless themselves.”

Jer 51 58This is what the LORD Almighty says: “Babylon’s thick wall will be leveled and her high gates set on fire; the peoples exhaust themselves for nothing, the nations’ labor is only fuel for the flames.”

Hab 2 13“Has not the LORD Almighty determined that the people's labor is only fuel for the fire, that the nations exhaust themselves for nothing?"

Rom 1 21For although they knew God, they neither glorified him as God nor gave thanks to him, but their thinking became futile and their foolish hearts were darkened. 22Although they claimed to be wise, they became fools 23and exchanged the glory of the immortal God for images made to look like mortal man and birds and animals and reptiles.

Eph 4 17So I tell you this, and insist on it in the Lord, that you must no longer live as the Gentiles do, in the futility of their thinking. 18They are darkened in their understanding and separated from the life of God because of the ignorance that is in them due to the hardening of their hearts. 19Having lost all sensitivity, they have given themselves over to sensuality so as to indulge in every kind of impurity, with a continual lust for more.

d) Results Depend Ultimately on God

1 Sam 2 4"The bows of the warriors are broken, but those who stumbled are armed with strength. 5Those who were full hire themselves out for food, but those who were hungry hunger no more. She who was barren has borne seven children, but she who has had many sons pines away.

6"The LORD brings death and makes alive; he brings down to the grave and raises up. 7The LORD sends poverty and wealth; he humbles and he exalts. 8He raises the poor from the dust and lifts the needy from the ash heap; he seats them with princes and has them inherit a throne of honor.

"For the foundations of the earth are the LORD's; upon them he has set the world."

Job 34 24"Without inquiry he shatters the mighty and sets up others in their place."

Ps 30 6When I felt secure, I said, "I will never be shaken." 7O LORD, when you favored me, you made my mountain stand firm; but when you hid your face, I was dismayed.

Ps 31 14But I trust in you, O LORD; I say, "You are my God." 15My times are in your hands; deliver me from my enemies and from those who pursue me.

Ps 71 20Though you have made me see troubles, many and bitter, you will restore my life again; from the depths of the earth you will again bring me up. 21You will increase my honor and comfort me once again.

Ps 75 6No one from the east or the west or from the desert can exalt a man. 7But it is God who judges: He brings one down, he exalts another.

Ps 102 9For I eat ashes as my food and mingle my drink with tears 10because of your great wrath, for you have taken me up and thrown me aside.

Ps 113 7He raises the poor from the dust and lifts the needy from the ash heap; 8he seats them with princes, with the princes of their people. 9He settles the barren woman in her home as a happy mother of children. Praise the LORD.

Prov 16 1To man belong the plans of the heart, but from the LORD comes the reply of the tongue.

Prov 16 9In his heart a man plans his course, but the LORD determines his steps.

Prov 19 21Many are the plans in a man's heart, but it is the LORD's purpose that prevails.

Prov 21 1The king's heart is in the hand of the LORD; he directs it like a watercourse wherever he pleases.

Isa 14 26This is the plan determined for the whole world; this is the hand stretched out over all nations. 27For the LORD Almighty has purposed, and who can thwart him? His hand is stretched out, and who can turn it back?

Isa 45 7"I form the light and create darkness, I bring prosperity and create disaster; I, the LORD, do all these things."

Jer 10 23I know, O LORD, that a man's life is not his own; it is not for man to direct his steps.

1 Cor 4 6Now, brothers, I have applied these things to myself and Apollos for your benefit, so that you may learn from us the meaning of the saying, "Do not go beyond what is written." Then you will not take pride in one man over against another. 7For who makes you different from anyone else? What do you have that you did not receive? And if you did receive it, why do you boast as though you did not?

D. Providence at Work in Israel

1. God's Providence at the Inception of Israel's History

a) The Patriarchs

Gen 12 1The LORD had said to Abram, "Leave your country, your people and your father's household and go to the land I will show you.

2"I will make you into a great nation and I will bless you; I will make your name great, and you will be a blessing. 3I will bless those who bless you, and whoever curses you I will curse; and all peoples on earth will be blessed through you."

Gen 17 3Abram fell facedown, and God said to him, 4"As for me, this is my covenant with you: You will be the father of many nations. 5No longer will you be called Abram; your name will be Abraham, for I have made you a father of many nations. 6I will make you very fruitful; I will make nations of you, and kings will come from you. 7I will establish my covenant as an everlasting covenant between me and you and your descendants after you for the generations to come, to be your God and the God of your descendants after you. 8The whole land of Canaan, where you are now an alien, I will give as an everlasting possession to you and your descendants after you; and I will be their God."

Gen 17 15God also said to Abraham, "As for Sarai your wife, you are no longer to call her Sarai; her name will be Sarah. 16I will bless her and will surely give you a son by her. I will bless her so that she will be the mother of nations; kings of peoples will come from her."

Gen 22 1Some time later God tested Abraham. He said to him, "Abraham!"

"Here I am," he replied.

2Then God said, "Take your son, your only son, Isaac, whom you love, and go to the region of Moriah. Sacrifice him there as a burnt offering on one of the mountains I will tell you about." . . .

9When they reached the place God had told him about, Abraham built an altar there and arranged the wood on it. He bound his son Isaac and laid him on the altar, on top of the wood. 10Then he reached out his hand and took the knife to slay his son. 11But the angel of the LORD called out to him from heaven, "Abraham! Abraham!"

"Here I am," he replied.

12"Do not lay a hand on the boy," he said. "Do not do anything to him. Now I know that you fear God, because you have not withheld from me your son, your only son."

Gen 28 20Then Jacob made a vow, saying, "If God will be with me and will watch over me on this journey I am taking and will give me food to eat and clothes to wear 21so that I return safely to my father's house, then the LORD will be my God. . . ."

Gen 49 22"Joseph is a fruitful vine, a fruitful vine near a spring, whose branches climb over a wall. 23With bitterness archers attacked him; they shot at him with hostility. 24But his bow remained steady, his strong arms stayed limber, because of the hand of the Mighty One of Jacob, because of the Shepherd, the Rock of Israel, 25because of your father's God, who helps you, because of the Almighty, who blesses you with blessings of the heavens above, blessings of the deep that lies below, blessings of the breast and womb."

Isa 51 2". . . look to Abraham, your father, and to Sarah, who gave you birth. When I called him he was but one, and I blessed him and made him many."

b) Bondage in Egypt

Gen 15 13Then the LORD said to him, "Know for certain that your descendants will be strangers in a country not their own, and they will be enslaved and mistreated four hundred years."

Gen 45 4Then Joseph said to his brothers, "Come close to me." When they had done so, he said, "I am your brother Joseph, the one you sold into Egypt! 5And now, do not be distressed and do not be angry with yourselves for selling me here, because it was to save lives that God sent me ahead of you. 6For two years now there has been famine in the land, and for the next five years there will not be plowing and reaping. 7But God sent me ahead of you to preserve for you a remnant on earth to save your lives by a great deliverance.

[8]"So then, it was not you who sent me here, but God. He made me father to Pharaoh, lord of his entire household and ruler of all Egypt. [9]Now hurry back to my father and say to him, 'This is what your son Joseph says: God has made me lord of all Egypt. Come down to me; don't delay. [10]You shall live in the region of Goshen and be near me—you, your children and grandchildren, your flocks and herds, and all you have. [11]I will provide for you there, because five years of famine are still to come. Otherwise you and your household and all who belong to you will become destitute.'

[12]"You can see for yourselves, and so can my brother Benjamin, that it is really I who am speaking to you. [13]Tell my father about all the honor accorded me in Egypt and about everything you have seen. And bring my father down here quickly."

Gen 50 [19]But Joseph said to them, "Don't be afraid. Am I in the place of God? [20]You intended to harm me, but God intended it for good to accomplish what is now being done, the saving of many lives."

Ps 105 [14]He allowed no one to oppress them; for their sake he rebuked kings: [15]"Do not touch my anointed ones; do my prophets no harm."

[16]He called down famine on the land and destroyed all their supplies of food; [17]and he sent a man before them—Joseph, sold as a slave. [18]They bruised his feet with shackles, his neck was put in irons, [19]till what he foretold came to pass, till the word of the LORD proved him true. [20]The king sent and released him, the ruler of peoples set him free. [21]He made him master of his household, ruler over all he possessed, [22]to instruct his princes as he pleased and teach his elders wisdom.

[23]Then Israel entered Egypt; Jacob lived as an alien in the land of Ham. [24]The LORD made his people very fruitful; he made them too numerous for their foes. . . .

Acts 7 [9]"Because the patriarchs were jealous of Joseph, they sold him as a slave into Egypt. But God was with him [10]and rescued him from all his troubles. He gave Joseph wisdom and enabled him to gain the goodwill of Pharaoh king of Egypt; so he made him ruler over Egypt and all his palace."

2. God's Providence as the Nation of Israel Grew

a) Redemption from Egypt

Gen 15 [13]Then the LORD said to him, "Know for certain that your descendants will be strangers in a country not their own, and they will be enslaved and mistreated four hundred years. [14]But I will punish the nation they serve as slaves, and afterward they will come out with great possessions."

Exod 3 [21]"And I will make the Egyptians favorably disposed toward this people, so that when you leave you will not go empty-handed."

Exod 12 [35]The Israelites did as Moses instructed and asked the Egyptians for articles of silver and gold and for clothing. [36]The LORD had made the Egyptians favorably disposed toward the people, and they gave them what they asked for; so they plundered the Egyptians.

Exod 14 [4]"And I will harden Pharaoh's heart, and he will pursue them. But I will gain glory for myself through Pharaoh and all his army, and the Egyptians will know that I am the LORD." So the Israelites did this.

Deut 5 [15]"Remember that you were slaves in Egypt and that the LORD your God brought you out of there with a mighty hand and an outstretched arm. Therefore the LORD your God has commanded you to observe the Sabbath day."

Neh 9 [9]"You saw the suffering of our forefathers in Egypt; you heard their cry at the Red Sea. [10]You sent miraculous signs and wonders against Pharaoh, against all his officials and all the people of his land, for you knew how arrogantly the Egyptians treated them. You made a name for yourself, which remains to this day. [11]You divided the sea before them, so that they passed through it on dry ground, but you hurled their pursuers into the depths, like a stone into mighty waters."

Ps 77 [14]You are the God who performs miracles; you display your power among the peoples. [15]With your mighty arm you redeemed your people, the descendants of Jacob and Joseph.

[16]The waters saw you, O God, the waters saw you and writhed; the very depths were convulsed. [17]The clouds poured down water, the skies resounded with thunder; your arrows flashed back and forth. [18]Your thunder was heard in the whirlwind, your lightning lit up the world; the earth trembled and quaked. [19]Your path led through the sea, your way through the mighty waters, though your footprints were not seen.

[20]You led your people like a flock by the hand of Moses and Aaron.

Ps 105 [23]Then Israel entered Egypt; Jacob lived as an alien in the land of Ham. [24]The LORD made his people very fruitful; he made them too numerous for their foes, [25]whose hearts he turned to hate his people, to conspire against his servants. [26]He sent Moses his servant, and Aaron, whom he had chosen. [27]They performed his miraculous signs among them, his wonders in the land of Ham. [28]He sent darkness and made the land dark—for had they not rebelled against his words? [29]He turned their waters into blood, causing their fish to die. [30]Their land teemed with frogs, which went up into the bedrooms of their rulers. [31]He spoke, and there came swarms of flies, and gnats throughout their country. [32]He turned their rain into hail, with lightning throughout their land; [33]he struck down their vines and fig trees and shattered the trees of their country. [34]He spoke, and the locusts came, grasshoppers without number; [35]they ate up every green thing in their land, ate up the produce of their soil. [36]Then he struck down all the firstborn in their land, the firstfruits of all their manhood.

[37]He brought out Israel, laden with silver and gold, and from among their tribes no one faltered. [38]Egypt was glad when they left, because dread of Israel had fallen on them.

Ps 136 [10]to him who struck down the firstborn of Egypt *His love endures forever.* [11]and brought Israel out from among them *His love endures forever.* [12]with a mighty hand and outstretched arm; *His love endures forever.* [13]to him who divided the Red Sea asunder *His love endures forever.* [14]and brought Israel through the midst of it, *His love endures forever.* [15]but swept Pharaoh and his army into the Red Sea; *His love endures forever.*

Isa 63 [11]Then his people recalled the days of old, the days of Moses and his people—where is he who brought them through the sea, with the shepherd of his flock? Where is he who set his Holy Spirit among them, [12]who sent his glorious arm of power to be at Moses' right hand, who divided the waters before them, to gain for himself everlasting renown, [13]who led them through the depths? Like a horse in open country, they did not stumble; [14]like cattle that go down to the plain, they were given rest by the Spirit of the LORD. This is how you guided your people to make for yourself a glorious name.

Acts 7 [30]"After forty years had passed, an angel appeared to Moses in the flames of a burning bush in the desert near Mount Sinai. [31]When he saw this, he was amazed at the sight. As he went over to look more closely, he heard the Lord's voice: . . . [34]'I have indeed seen the oppression of my people in Egypt. I have heard their groaning and have come down to set them free. Now come, I will send you back to Egypt.'

[35]"This is the same Moses whom they had rejected with the words, 'Who made you ruler and judge?' He was sent to be their ruler and deliverer by God himself, through the angel who appeared to him in the bush. [36]He led them out of Egypt and did wonders and miraculous signs in Egypt, at the Red Sea and for forty years in the desert."

b) Sustenance in the Wilderness

Exod 16 [13]That evening quail came and covered the camp, and in the morning there was a layer of dew around the camp. [14]When the dew was gone, thin flakes like frost on the ground appeared on the desert floor. [15]When the Israelites saw it, they said to each other, "What is it?" For they did not know what it was.

Moses said to them, "It is the bread the LORD has given you to eat."

Num 11 [31]Now a wind went out from the LORD and drove quail in from the sea. It brought them down all around the camp to about three feet above the ground, as far as a day's walk in any direction.

Deut 1 [10]"The LORD your God has increased your numbers so that today you are as many as the stars in the sky."
Deut 2 [7]The LORD your God has blessed you in all the work of your hands. He has watched over your journey through this vast desert. These forty years the LORD your God has been with you, and you have not lacked anything.
Deut 8 [2]Remember how the LORD your God led you all the way in the desert these forty years, to humble you and to test you in order to know what was in your heart, whether or not you would keep his commands. [3]He humbled you, causing you to hunger and then feeding you with manna, which neither you nor your fathers had known, to teach you that man does not live on bread alone but on every word that comes from the mouth of the LORD. [4]Your clothes did not wear out and your feet did not swell during these forty years.
Deut 29 [5]During the forty years that I led you through the desert, your clothes did not wear out, nor did the sandals on your feet.
Neh 9 [15]"In their hunger you gave them bread from heaven and in their thirst you brought them water from the rock; you told them to go in and take possession of the land you had sworn with uplifted hand to give them."
Ps 78 [52]But he brought his people out like a flock; he led them like sheep through the desert. [53]He guided them safely, so they were unafraid; but the sea engulfed their enemies. [54]Thus he brought them to the border of his holy land, to the hill country his right hand had taken. [55]He drove out nations before them and allotted their lands to them as an inheritance; he settled the tribes of Israel in their homes.
Ps 105 [39]He spread out a cloud as a covering, and a fire to give light at night. [40]They asked, and he brought them quail and satisfied them with the bread of heaven. [41]He opened the rock, and water gushed out; like a river it flowed in the desert.
Ps 136 [16]to him who led his people through the desert, *His love endures forever.*
Isa 48 [21]They did not thirst when he led them through the deserts; he made water flow for them from the rock; he split the rock and water gushed out.
Amos 2 [10]"I brought you up out of Egypt, and I led you forty years in the desert to give you the land of the Amorites."
John 6 [31]"Our forefathers ate the manna in the desert; as it is written: 'He gave them bread from heaven to eat.'"

c) Guidance through the Cloud and Fire

Exod 13 [21]By day the LORD went ahead of them in a pillar of cloud to guide them on their way and by night in a pillar of fire to give them light, so that they could travel by day or night. [22]Neither the pillar of cloud by day nor the pillar of fire by night left its place in front of the people.
Exod 33 [9]As Moses went into the tent, the pillar of cloud would come down and stay at the entrance, while the LORD spoke with Moses. [10]Whenever the people saw the pillar of cloud standing at the entrance to the tent, they all stood and worshiped, each at the entrance to his tent.
Num 12 [5]Then the LORD came down in a pillar of cloud; he stood at the entrance to the Tent and summoned Aaron and Miriam. When both of them stepped forward . . .
Deut 31 [15]Then the LORD appeared at the Tent in a pillar of cloud, and the cloud stood over the entrance to the Tent.
Neh 9 [12]"By day you led them with a pillar of cloud, and by night with a pillar of fire to give them light on the way they were to take."
Neh 9 [19]"Because of your great compassion you did not abandon them in the desert. By day the pillar of cloud did not cease to guide them on their path, nor the pillar of fire by night to shine on the way they were to take."
Ps 99 [7]He spoke to them from the pillar of cloud; they kept his statutes and the decrees he gave them.

d) Conquering of the Promised Land

Exod 15 [13]"In your unfailing love you will lead the people you have redeemed. In your strength you will guide them to your holy dwelling. [14]The nations will hear and tremble; anguish will grip the people of Philistia. [15]The chiefs of Edom will be terrified, the leaders of Moab will be seized with trembling, the people of Canaan will melt away; [16]terror and dread will fall upon them. By the power of your arm they will be as still as a stone—until your people pass by, O LORD, until the people you bought pass by. [17]You will bring them in and plant them on the mountain of your inheritance—the place, O LORD, you made for your dwelling, the sanctuary, O Lord, your hands established. [18]The LORD will reign for ever and ever."
Deut 4 [37]Because he loved your forefathers and chose their descendants after them, he brought you out of Egypt by his Presence and his great strength, [38]to drive out before you nations greater and stronger than you and to bring you into their land to give it to you for your inheritance, as it is today.
Deut 7 [13]He will love you and bless you and increase your numbers. He will bless the fruit of your womb, the crops of your land—your grain, new wine and oil—the calves of your herds and the lambs of your flocks in the land that he swore to your forefathers to give you. [14]You will be blessed more than any other people; none of your men or women will be childless, nor any of your livestock without young. [15]The LORD will keep you free from every disease. He will not inflict on you the horrible diseases you knew in Egypt, but he will inflict them on all who hate you.
Josh 1 [1]After the death of Moses the servant of the LORD, the LORD said to Joshua son of Nun, Moses' aide: [2]"Moses my servant is dead. Now then, you and all these people, get ready to cross the Jordan River into the land I am about to give to them—to the Israelites. [3]I will give you every place where you set your foot, as I promised Moses. [4]Your territory will extend from the desert to Lebanon, and from the great river, the Euphrates—all the Hittite country—to the Great Sea on the west. [5]No one will be able to stand up against you all the days of your life. As I was with Moses, so I will be with you; I will never leave you nor forsake you. . . .

[8]"Do not let this Book of the Law depart from your mouth; meditate on it day and night, so that you may be careful to do everything written in it. Then you will be prosperous and successful. [9]Have I not commanded you? Be strong and courageous. Do not be terrified; do not be discouraged, for the LORD your God will be with you wherever you go."
Josh 2 [8]Before the spies lay down for the night, she went up on the roof [9]and said to them, "I know that the LORD has given this land to you and that a great fear of you has fallen on us, so that all who live in this country are melting in fear because of you. [10]We have heard how the LORD dried up the water of the Red Sea for you when you came out of Egypt, and what you did to Sihon and Og, the two kings of the Amorites east of the Jordan, whom you completely destroyed. [11]When we heard of it, our hearts melted and everyone's courage failed because of you, for the LORD your God is God in heaven above and on the earth below."
Neh 9 [25]"They captured fortified cities and fertile land; they took possession of houses filled with all kinds of good things, wells already dug, vineyards, olive groves and fruit trees in abundance. They ate to the full and were well-nourished; they reveled in your great goodness."
Ps 44 [1]We have heard with our ears, O God; our fathers have told us what you did in their days, in days long ago. [2]With your hand you drove out the nations and planted our fathers; you crushed the peoples and made our fathers flourish. [3]It was not by their sword that they won the land, nor did their arm bring them victory; it was your right hand, your arm, and the light of your face, for you loved them.
Ps 78 [54]Thus he brought them to the border of his holy land, to the hill country his right hand had taken. [55]He drove out nations before them and allotted their lands to them as an inheritance; he settled the tribes of Israel in their homes.
Ps 105 [42]For he remembered his holy promise given to his servant Abraham. [43]He brought out his people with rejoicing, his chosen ones with shouts of joy; [44]he gave them the lands of the nations, and they fell heir to what others had toiled for—[45]that they might keep his precepts and observe his laws. Praise the LORD.
Ps 136 [17]who struck down great kings, *His love endures forever.* [18]and killed mighty kings—*His love endures forever.* [19]Sihon king of the Amorites, *His love endures forever.* [20]and Og king of

Bashan—*His love endures forever.* 21and gave their land as an inheritance, *His love endures forever.* 22an inheritance to his servant Israel; *His love endures forever.*

Amos 2 9"I destroyed the Amorite before them, though he was tall as the cedars and strong as the oaks. I destroyed his fruit above and his roots below.

10"I brought you up out of Egypt, and I led you forty years in the desert to give you the land of the Amorites."

e) Period of the Judges

Judg 2 11Then the Israelites did evil in the eyes of the LORD and served the Baals. 12They forsook the LORD, the God of their fathers, who had brought them out of Egypt. They followed and worshiped various gods of the peoples around them. They provoked the LORD to anger 13because they forsook him and served Baal and the Ashtoreths. 14In his anger against Israel the LORD handed them over to raiders who plundered them. He sold them to their enemies all around, whom they were no longer able to resist. 15Whenever Israel went out to fight, the hand of the LORD was against them to defeat them, just as he had sworn to them. They were in great distress.

16Then the LORD raised up judges, who saved them out of the hands of these raiders. 17Yet they would not listen to their judges but prostituted themselves to other gods and worshiped them. Unlike their fathers, they quickly turned from the way in which their fathers had walked, the way of obedience to the LORD's commands. 18Whenever the LORD raised up a judge for them, he was with the judge and saved them out of the hands of their enemies as long as the judge lived; for the LORD had compassion on them as they groaned under those who oppressed and afflicted them. 19But when the judge died, the people returned to ways even more corrupt than those of their fathers, following other gods and serving and worshiping them. They refused to give up their evil practices and stubborn ways.

Judg 9 23God sent an evil spirit between Abimelech and the citizens of Shechem, who acted treacherously against Abimelech. 24God did this in order that the crime against Jerub-Baal's seventy sons, the shedding of their blood, might be avenged on their brother Abimelech and on the citizens of Shechem, who had helped him murder his brothers.

Ruth 1 6When she heard in Moab that the LORD had come to the aid of his people by providing food for them, Naomi and her daughters-in-law prepared to return home from there.

f) Time of the Kings

1 Sam 14 6Jonathan said to his young armor-bearer, "Come, let's go over to the outpost of those uncircumcised fellows. Perhaps the LORD will act in our behalf. Nothing can hinder the LORD from saving, whether by many or by few."

2 Sam 5 23so David inquired of the LORD, and he answered, "Do not go straight up, but circle around behind them and attack them in front of the balsam trees. 24As soon as you hear the sound of marching in the tops of the balsam trees, move quickly, because that will mean the LORD has gone out in front of you to strike the Philistine army." 25So David did as the LORD commanded him, and he struck down the Philistines all the way from Gibeon to Gezer.

1 Kings 2 1When the time drew near for David to die, he gave a charge to Solomon his son.

2"I am about to go the way of all the earth," he said. "So be strong, show yourself a man, 3and observe what the LORD your God requires: Walk in his ways, and keep his decrees and commands, his laws and requirements, as written in the Law of Moses, so that you may prosper in all you do and wherever you go, 4and that the LORD may keep his promise to me: 'If your descendants watch how they live, and if they walk faithfully before me with all their heart and soul, you will never fail to have a man on the throne of Israel.'"

1 Kings 12 15So the king did not listen to the people, for this turn of events was from the LORD, to fulfill the word the LORD had spoken to Jeroboam son of Nebat through Ahijah the Shilonite.

1 Kings 12 23"Say to Rehoboam son of Solomon king of Judah, to the whole house of Judah and Benjamin, and to the rest of the people, 24'This is what the LORD says: Do not go up to fight against your brothers, the Israelites. Go home, every one of you, for this is my doing.'" So they obeyed the word of the LORD and went home again, as the LORD had ordered.

2 Kings 18 5Hezekiah trusted in the LORD, the God of Israel. There was no one like him among all the kings of Judah, either before him or after him. 6He held fast to the LORD and did not cease to follow him; he kept the commands the LORD had given Moses. 7And the LORD was with him; he was successful in whatever he undertook. He rebelled against the king of Assyria and did not serve him.

1 Chron 29 10David praised the LORD in the presence of the whole assembly, saying, "Praise be to you, O LORD, God of our father Israel, from everlasting to everlasting. . . . 12Wealth and honor come from you; you are the ruler of all things. In your hands are strength and power to exalt and give strength to all. 13Now, our God, we give you thanks, and praise your glorious name.

14"But who am I, and who are my people, that we should be able to give as generously as this? Everything comes from you, and we have given you only what comes from your hand. 15We are aliens and strangers in your sight, as were all our forefathers. Our days on earth are like a shadow, without hope. 16O LORD our God, as for all this abundance that we have provided for building you a temple for your Holy Name, it comes from your hand, and all of it belongs to you."

2 Chron 1 11God said to Solomon, "Since this is your heart's desire and you have not asked for wealth, riches or honor, nor for the death of your enemies, and since you have not asked for a long life but for wisdom and knowledge to govern my people over whom I have made you king, 12therefore wisdom and knowledge will be given you. And I will also give you wealth, riches and honor, such as no king who was before you ever had and none after you will have."

2 Chron 13 12"God is with us; he is our leader. His priests with their trumpets will sound the battle cry against you. Men of Israel, do not fight against the LORD, the God of your fathers, for you will not succeed." . . .

18The men of Israel were subdued on that occasion, and the men of Judah were victorious because they relied on the LORD, the God of their fathers.

2 Chron 16 7At that time Hanani the seer came to Asa king of Judah and said to him: "Because you relied on the king of Aram and not on the LORD your God, the army of the king of Aram has escaped from your hand. 8Were not the Cushites and Libyans a mighty army with great numbers of chariots and horsemen? Yet when you relied on the LORD, he delivered them into your hand. 9For the eyes of the LORD range throughout the earth to strengthen those whose hearts are fully committed to him. You have done a foolish thing, and from now on you will be at war."

2 Chron 17 3The LORD was with Jehoshaphat because in his early years he walked in the ways his father David had followed. He did not consult the Baals 4but sought the God of his father and followed his commands rather than the practices of Israel. 5The LORD established the kingdom under his control; and all Judah brought gifts to Jehoshaphat, so that he had great wealth and honor.

2 Chron 20 15He said: "Listen, King Jehoshaphat and all who live in Judah and Jerusalem! This is what the LORD says to you: 'Do not be afraid or discouraged because of this vast army. For the battle is not yours, but God's. . . . 17You will not have to fight this battle. Take up your positions; stand firm and see the deliverance the LORD will give you, O Judah and Jerusalem. Do not be afraid; do not be discouraged. Go out to face them tomorrow, and the LORD will be with you.'"

2 Chron 26 3Uzziah was sixteen years old when he became king, and he reigned in Jerusalem fifty-two years. His mother's name was Jecoliah; she was from Jerusalem. 4He did what was right in the eyes of the LORD, just as his father Amaziah had done. 5He sought God during the days of Zechariah, who instructed him in the fear of God. As long as he sought the LORD, God gave him success.

2 Chron 27 6Jotham grew powerful because he walked steadfastly before the LORD his God.

2 Chron 32 21And the LORD sent an angel, who annihilated all the fighting men and the leaders and officers in the camp of the Assyrian king. So he withdrew to his own land in disgrace. And when he went into the temple of his god, some of his sons cut him down with the sword.

[22]So the LORD saved Hezekiah and the people of Jerusalem from the hand of Sennacherib king of Assyria and from the hand of all others. He took care of them on every side.

3. God's Providential Judgment of Israel

Deut 32 [15]Jeshurun grew fat and kicked; filled with food, he became heavy and sleek. He abandoned the God who made him and rejected the Rock his Savior. . . .

[19]The LORD saw this and rejected them because he was angered by his sons and daughters. [20]"I will hide my face from them," he said, "and see what their end will be; for they are a perverse generation, children who are unfaithful. . . . [22]For a fire has been kindled by my wrath, one that burns to the realm of death below. It will devour the earth and its harvests and set afire the foundations of the mountains.

[23]"I will heap calamities upon them and spend my arrows against them. [24]I will send wasting famine against them, consuming pestilence and deadly plague; I will send against them the fangs of wild beasts, the venom of vipers that glide in the dust. [25]In the street the sword will make them childless; in their homes terror will reign. Young men and young women will perish, infants and gray-haired men. [26]I said I would scatter them and blot out their memory from mankind. . . ."

Isa 3 [14]The LORD enters into judgment against the elders and leaders of his people: "It is you who have ruined my vineyard; the plunder from the poor is in your houses. [15]What do you mean by crushing my people and grinding the faces of the poor?" declares the Lord, the LORD Almighty.

Isa 5 [24]Therefore, as tongues of fire lick up straw and as dry grass sinks down in the flames, so their roots will decay and their flowers blow away like dust; for they have rejected the law of the LORD Almighty and spurned the word of the Holy One of Israel.

Jer 11 [11]"Therefore this is what the LORD says: 'I will bring on them a disaster they cannot escape. Although they cry out to me, I will not listen to them. [12]The towns of Judah and the people of Jerusalem will go and cry out to the gods to whom they burn incense, but they will not help them at all when disaster strikes.'"

Jer 25 [28]"But if they refuse to take the cup from your hand and drink, tell them, 'This is what the LORD Almighty says: You must drink it! [29]See, I am beginning to bring disaster on the city that bears my Name, and will you indeed go unpunished? You will not go unpunished, for I am calling down a sword upon all who live on the earth, declares the LORD Almighty.'"

Jer 52 [3]It was because of the LORD's anger that all this happened to Jerusalem and Judah, and in the end he thrust them from his presence.

Now Zedekiah rebelled against the king of Babylon.

Ezek 7 [2]"Son of man, this is what the Sovereign LORD says to the land of Israel: The end! The end has come upon the four corners of the land. [3]The end is now upon you and I will unleash my anger against you. I will judge you according to your conduct and repay you for all your detestable practices. [4]I will not look on you with pity or spare you; I will surely repay you for your conduct and the detestable practices among you. Then you will know that I am the LORD.

[5]"This is what the Sovereign LORD says: Disaster! An unheard-of disaster is coming. [6]The end has come! The end has come! It has roused itself against you. It has come! [7]Doom has come upon you—you who dwell in the land. The time has come, the day is near; there is panic, not joy, upon the mountains. [8]I am about to pour out my wrath on you and spend my anger against you; I will judge you according to your conduct and repay you for all your detestable practices. [9]I will not look on you with pity or spare you; I will repay you in accordance with your conduct and the detestable practices among you. Then you will know that it is I the LORD who strikes the blow."

Ezek 9 [9]He answered me, "The sin of the house of Israel and Judah is exceedingly great; the land is full of bloodshed and the city is full of injustice. They say, 'The LORD has forsaken the land, the LORD does not see.' [10]So I will not look on them with pity or spare them, but I will bring down on their own heads what they have done."

Ezek 16 [59]"'This is what the Sovereign LORD says: I will deal with you as you deserve, because you have despised my oath by breaking the covenant.'"

Ezek 18 [20]"The soul who sins is the one who will die. The son will not share the guilt of the father, nor will the father share the guilt of the son. The righteousness of the righteous man will be credited to him, and the wickedness of the wicked will be charged against him.

[21]"But if a wicked man turns away from all the sins he has committed and keeps all my decrees and does what is just and right, he will surely live; he will not die. [22]None of the offenses he has committed will be remembered against him. Because of the righteous things he has done, he will live. [23]Do I take any pleasure in the death of the wicked? declares the Sovereign LORD. Rather, am I not pleased when they turn from their ways and live?

[24]"But if a righteous man turns from his righteousness and commits sin and does the same detestable things the wicked man does, will he live? None of the righteous things he has done will be remembered. Because of the unfaithfulness he is guilty of and because of the sins he has committed, he will die.

[25]"Yet you say, 'The way of the Lord is not just.' Hear, O house of Israel: Is my way unjust? Is it not your ways that are unjust? [26]If a righteous man turns from his righteousness and commits sin, he will die for it; because of the sin he has committed he will die. [27]But if a wicked man turns away from the wickedness he has committed and does what is just and right, he will save his life. [28]Because he considers all the offenses he has committed and turns away from them, he will surely live; he will not die. . . .

[30]"Therefore, O house of Israel, I will judge you, each one according to his ways, declares the Sovereign LORD. Repent! Turn away from all your offenses; then sin will not be your downfall. [31]Rid yourselves of all the offenses you have committed, and get a new heart and a new spirit. Why will you die, O house of Israel? [32]For I take no pleasure in the death of anyone, declares the Sovereign LORD. Repent and live!"

Ezek 20 [23]"'Also with uplifted hand I swore to them in the desert that I would disperse them among the nations and scatter them through the countries, [24]because they had not obeyed my laws but had rejected my decrees and desecrated my Sabbaths, and their eyes lusted after their fathers' idols. [25]I also gave them over to statutes that were not good and laws they could not live by; [26]I let them become defiled through their gifts—the sacrifice of every firstborn—that I might fill them with horror so they would know that I am the LORD.'"

Ezek 24 [13]"'Now your impurity is lewdness. Because I tried to cleanse you but you would not be cleansed from your impurity, you will not be clean again until my wrath against you has subsided.

[14]"'I the LORD have spoken. The time has come for me to act. I will not hold back; I will not have pity, nor will I relent. You will be judged according to your conduct and your actions, declares the Sovereign LORD.'"

Ezek 39 [21]"I will display my glory among the nations, and all the nations will see the punishment I inflict and the hand I lay upon them. [22]From that day forward the house of Israel will know that I am the LORD their God. [23]And the nations will know that the people of Israel went into exile for their sin, because they were unfaithful to me. So I hid my face from them and handed them over to their enemies, and they all fell by the sword. [24]I dealt with them according to their uncleanness and their offenses, and I hid my face from them."

Hos 5 [1]"Hear this, you priests! Pay attention, you Israelites! Listen, O royal house! This judgment is against you: You have been a snare at Mizpah, a net spread out on Tabor. . . .

[4]"Their deeds do not permit them to return to their God. A spirit of prostitution is in their heart; they do not acknowledge the LORD. [5]Israel's arrogance testifies against them; the Israelites, even Ephraim, stumble in their sin; Judah also stumbles with them. [6]When they go with their flocks and herds to seek the LORD, they will not find him; he has withdrawn himself from them. . . .

[14]"For I will be like a lion to Ephraim, like a great lion to

Judah. I will tear them to pieces and go away; I will carry them off, with no one to rescue them. [15]Then I will go back to my place until they admit their guilt. And they will seek my face; in their misery they will earnestly seek me."

Amos 4 [1]Hear this word, you cows of Bashan on Mount Samaria, you women who oppress the poor and crush the needy and say to your husbands, "Bring us some drinks!" [2]The Sovereign LORD has sworn by his holiness: "The time will surely come when you will be taken away with hooks, the last of you with fishhooks. [3]You will each go straight out through breaks in the wall, and you will be cast out toward Harmon," declares the LORD. . . .

[6]"I gave you empty stomachs in every city and lack of bread in every town, yet you have not returned to me," declares the LORD.

[7]"I also withheld rain from you when the harvest was still three months away. I sent rain on one town, but withheld it from another. One field had rain; another had none and dried up. [8]People staggered from town to town for water but did not get enough to drink, yet you have not returned to me," declares the LORD.

[9]"Many times I struck your gardens and vineyards, I struck them with blight and mildew. Locusts devoured your fig and olive trees, yet you have not returned to me," declares the LORD.

[10]"I sent plagues among you as I did to Egypt. I killed your young men with the sword, along with your captured horses. I filled your nostrils with the stench of your camps, yet you have not returned to me," declares the LORD.

[11]"I overthrew some of you as I overthrew Sodom and Gomorrah. You were like a burning stick snatched from the fire, yet you have not returned to me," declares the LORD.

[12]"Therefore this is what I will do to you, Israel, and because I will do this to you, prepare to meet your God, O Israel."

Mic 6 [9]Listen! The LORD is calling to the city—and to fear your name is wisdom—"Heed the rod and the One who appointed it. [10]Am I still to forget, O wicked house, your ill-gotten treasures and the short ephah, which is accursed? [11]Shall I acquit a man with dishonest scales, with a bag of false weights? [12]Her rich men are violent; her people are liars and their tongues speak deceitfully. [13]Therefore, I have begun to destroy you, to ruin you because of your sins. [14]You will eat but not be satisfied; your stomach will still be empty. You will store up but save nothing, because what you save I will give to the sword. [15]You will plant but not harvest; you will press olives but not use the oil on yourselves, you will crush grapes but not drink the wine. [16]You have observed the statutes of Omri and all the practices of Ahab's house, and you have followed their traditions. Therefore I will give you over to ruin and your people to derision; you will bear the scorn of the nations."

Mal 3 [5]"So I will come near to you for judgment. I will be quick to testify against sorcerers, adulterers and perjurers, against those who defraud laborers of their wages, who oppress the widows and the fatherless, and deprive aliens of justice, but do not fear me," says the LORD Almighty.

4. God's Providential Restoration of Israel

Ps 14 [7]Oh, that salvation for Israel would come out of Zion! When the LORD restores the fortunes of his people, let Jacob rejoice and Israel be glad!

Ps 69 [35]for God will save Zion and rebuild the cities of Judah. Then people will settle there and possess it; [36]the children of his servants will inherit it, and those who love his name will dwell there.

Ps 95 [6]Come, let us bow down in worship, let us kneel before the LORD our Maker; [7]for he is our God and we are the people of his pasture, the flock under his care.

Today, if you hear his voice, [8]do not harden your hearts as you did at Meribah, as you did that day at Massah in the desert, [9]where your fathers tested and tried me, though they had seen what I did.

Ps 147 [12]Extol the LORD, O Jerusalem; praise your God, O Zion, [13]for he strengthens the bars of your gates and blesses your people within you. [14]He grants peace to your borders and satisfies you with the finest of wheat.

Ps 147 [19]He has revealed his word to Jacob, his laws and decrees to Israel. [20]He has done this for no other nation; they do not know his laws. Praise the LORD.

Isa 41 [13]"For I am the LORD, your God, who takes hold of your right hand and says to you, Do not fear; I will help you. [14]Do not be afraid, O worm Jacob, O little Israel, for I myself will help you," declares the LORD, your Redeemer, the Holy One of Israel.

Isa 42 [6]"I, the LORD, have called you in righteousness; I will take hold of your hand. I will keep you and will make you to be a covenant for the people and a light for the Gentiles. . . ."

Isa 46 [3]"Listen to me, O house of Jacob, all you who remain of the house of Israel, you whom I have upheld since you were conceived, and have carried since your birth. [4]Even to your old age and gray hairs I am he, I am he who will sustain you. I have made you and I will carry you; I will sustain you and I will rescue you."

Jer 30 [18]"This is what the LORD says: 'I will restore the fortunes of Jacob's tents and have compassion on his dwellings; the city will be rebuilt on her ruins, and the palace will stand in its proper place. [19]From them will come songs of thanksgiving and the sound of rejoicing. I will add to their numbers, and they will not be decreased; I will bring them honor, and they will not be disdained. [20]Their children will be as in days of old, and their community will be established before me; I will punish all who oppress them. [21]Their leader will be one of their own; their ruler will arise from among them. I will bring him near and he will come close to me, for who is he who will devote himself to be close to me?' declares the LORD.

[22]"'So you will be my people, and I will be your God.'"

Ezek 34 [11]"'For this is what the Sovereign LORD says: I myself will search for my sheep and look after them. [12]As a shepherd looks after his scattered flock when he is with them, so will I look after my sheep. I will rescue them from all the places where they were scattered on a day of clouds and darkness. [13]I will bring them out from the nations and gather them from the countries, and I will bring them into their own land. I will pasture them on the mountains of Israel, in the ravines and in all the settlements in the land. [14]I will tend them in a good pasture, and the mountain heights of Israel will be their grazing land. There they will lie down in good grazing land, and there they will feed in a rich pasture on the mountains of Israel. [15]I myself will tend my sheep and have them lie down, declares the Sovereign LORD. [16]I will search for the lost and bring back the strays. I will bind up the injured and strengthen the weak, but the sleek and the strong I will destroy. I will shepherd the flock with justice.

[17]"'As for you, my flock, this is what the Sovereign LORD says: I will judge between one sheep and another, and between rams and goats. [18]Is it not enough for you to feed on the good pasture? Must you also trample the rest of your pasture with your feet? Is it not enough for you to drink clear water? Must you also muddy the rest with your feet? [19]Must my flock feed on what you have trampled and drink what you have muddied with your feet?

[20]"'Therefore this is what the Sovereign LORD says to them: See, I myself will judge between the fat sheep and the lean sheep. [21]Because you shove with flank and shoulder, butting all the weak sheep with your horns until you have driven them away, [22]I will save my flock, and they will no longer be plundered. I will judge between one sheep and another. [23]I will place over them one shepherd, my servant David, and he will tend them; he will tend them and be their shepherd. [24]I the LORD will be their God, and my servant David will be prince among them. I the LORD have spoken.

[25]"'I will make a covenant of peace with them and rid the land of wild beasts so that they may live in the desert and sleep in the forests in safety. [26]I will bless them and the places surrounding my hill. I will send down showers in season; there will be showers of blessing. [27]The trees of the field will yield their fruit and the ground will yield its crops; the people will be secure in their land. They will know that I am the LORD, when I break the bars of their yoke and rescue them from the hands of those who enslaved them. [28]They will no longer be plundered

by the nations, nor will wild animals devour them. They will live in safety, and no one will make them afraid. 29I will provide for them a land renowned for its crops, and they will no longer be victims of famine in the land or bear the scorn of the nations. 30Then they will know that I, the LORD their God, am with them and that they, the house of Israel, are my people, declares the Sovereign LORD. 31You my sheep, the sheep of my pasture, are people, and I am your God, declares the Sovereign LORD.'"

Ezek 36 8"'But you, O mountains of Israel, will produce branches and fruit for my people Israel, for they will soon come home. 9I am concerned for you and will look on you with favor; you will be plowed and sown, 10and I will multiply the number of people upon you, even the whole house of Israel. The towns will be inhabited and the ruins rebuilt. 11I will increase the number of men and animals upon you, and they will be fruitful and become numerous. I will settle people on you as in the past and will make you prosper more than before. Then you will know that I am the LORD. 12I will cause people, my people Israel, to walk upon you. They will possess you, and you will be their inheritance; you will never again deprive them of their children.'"

Amos 9 13"The days are coming," declares the LORD, "when the reaper will be overtaken by the plowman and the planter by the one treading grapes. New wine will drip from the mountains and flow from all the hills. 14I will bring back my exiled people Israel; they will rebuild the ruined cities and live in them. They will plant vineyards and drink their wine; they will make gardens and eat their fruit. 15I will plant Israel in their own land, never again to be uprooted from the land I have given them," says the LORD your God.

Zech 8 12"The seed will grow well, the vine will yield its fruit, the ground will produce its crops, and the heavens will drop their dew. I will give all these things as an inheritance to the remnant of this people."

Mal 3 10"Bring the whole tithe into the storehouse, that there may be food in my house. Test me in this," says the LORD Almighty, "and see if I will not throw open the floodgates of heaven and pour out so much blessing that you will not have room enough for it. 11I will prevent pests from devouring your crops, and the vines in your fields will not cast their fruit," says the LORD Almighty. 12"Then all the nations will call you blessed, for yours will be a delightful land," says the LORD Almighty.

E. Providence at Work in the Lives of Believers

1. Providence Cares for Believers

Ps 71 6From birth I have relied on you; you brought me forth from my mother's womb. I will ever praise you.

Rom 8 28And we know that in all things God works for the good of those who love him, who have been called according to his purpose.

1 Pet 5 7Cast all your anxiety on him because he cares for you.

2. Providence Comforts Believers

2 Cor 1 3Praise be to the God and Father of our Lord Jesus Christ, the Father of compassion and the God of all comfort, 4who comforts us in all our troubles, so that we can comfort those in any trouble with the comfort we ourselves have received from God.

2 Cor 7 6But God, who comforts the downcast, comforted us by the coming of Titus. . . .

Phil 2 1If you have any encouragement from being united with Christ, if any comfort from his love, if any fellowship with the Spirit, if any tenderness and compassion . . .

2 Thess 2 16May our Lord Jesus Christ himself and God our Father, who loved us and by his grace gave us eternal encouragement and good hope . . .

3. Providence Delivers Believers

Gen 7 1The LORD then said to Noah, "Go into the ark, you and your whole family, because I have found you righteous in this generation. . . . 4Seven days from now I will send rain on the earth for forty days and forty nights, and I will wipe from the face of the earth every living creature I have made." . . . 7And Noah and his sons and his wife and his sons' wives entered the ark to escape the waters of the flood.

2 Kings 22 18"Tell the king of Judah, who sent you to inquire of the LORD, 'This is what the LORD, the God of Israel, says concerning the words you heard: 19Because your heart was responsive and you humbled yourself before the LORD when you heard what I have spoken against this place and its people, that they would become accursed and laid waste, and because you tore your robes and wept in my presence, I have heard you, declares the LORD. 20Therefore I will gather you to your fathers, and you will be buried in peace. Your eyes will not see all the disaster I am going to bring on this place.'"

So they took her answer back to the king.

Job 4 7"Consider now: Who, being innocent, has ever perished? Where were the upright ever destroyed?"

Job 5 17"Blessed is the man whom God corrects; so do not despise the discipline of the Almighty. . . . 19From six calamities he will rescue you; in seven no harm will befall you. 20In famine he will ransom you from death, and in battle from the stroke of the sword. 21You will be protected from the lash of the tongue, and need not fear when destruction comes."

Job 36 6"He does not keep the wicked alive but gives the afflicted their rights. 7He does not take his eyes off the righteous; he enthrones them with kings and exalts them forever."

Ps 32 7You are my hiding place; you will protect me from trouble and surround me with songs of deliverance.

Ps 33 18But the eyes of the LORD are on those who fear him, on those whose hope is in his unfailing love, 19to deliver them from death and keep them alive in famine.

Ps 34 7The angel of the LORD encamps around those who fear him, and he delivers them. . . .

17The righteous cry out, and the LORD hears them; he delivers them from all their troubles.

Ps 35 10My whole being will exclaim, "Who is like you, O LORD? You rescue the poor from those too strong for them, the poor and needy from those who rob them."

Ps 37 25I was young and now I am old, yet I have never seen the righteous forsaken or their children begging bread.

Ps 50 14"Sacrifice thank offerings to God, fulfill your vows to the Most High, 15and call upon me in the day of trouble; I will deliver you, and you will honor me."

Ps 55 18He ransoms me unharmed from the battle waged against me, even though many oppose me.

Ps 56 13For you have delivered me from death and my feet from stumbling, that I may walk before God in the light of life.

Ps 72 12For he will deliver the needy who cry out, the afflicted who have no one to help.

Ps 91 9If you make the Most High your dwelling—even the LORD, who is my refuge—10then no harm will befall you, no disaster will come near your tent.

Prov 1 33". . . but whoever listens to me will live in safety and be at ease, without fear of harm."

Prov 12 28In the way of righteousness there is life; along that path is immortality.

Eccles 8 5Whoever obeys his command will come to no harm, and the wise heart will know the proper time and procedure.

Isa 54 14"In righteousness you will be established: Tyranny will be far from you; you will have nothing to fear. Terror will be far removed; it will not come near you. 15If anyone does attack you, it will not be my doing; whoever attacks you will surrender to you."

Jer 39 16"Go and tell Ebed-Melech the Cushite, 'This is what the LORD Almighty, the God of Israel, says: I am about to fulfill my words against this city through disaster, not prosperity. At that time they will be fulfilled before your eyes. 17But I will rescue you on that day, declares the LORD; you will not be handed over to those you fear. 18I will save you; you will not fall by the sword but will escape with your life, because you trust in me, declares the LORD.'"

Ezek 18 5"Suppose there is a righteous man who does what is just and right. 6He does not eat at the mountain shrines or look to the idols of the house of Israel. He does not defile his neighbor's wife or lie with a woman during her period. 7He does not oppress anyone, but returns what he took in pledge for a loan.

He does not commit robbery but gives his food to the hungry and provides clothing for the naked. [8]He does not lend at usury or take excessive interest. He withholds his hand from doing wrong and judges fairly between man and man. [9]He follows my decrees and faithfully keeps my laws. That man is righteous; he will surely live, declares the Sovereign LORD."
Amos 5 [4]This is what the LORD says to the house of Israel: "Seek me and live. . . ."
Rom 7 [24]What a wretched man I am! Who will rescue me from this body of death? [25]Thanks be to God—through Jesus Christ our Lord!

So then, I myself in my mind am a slave to God's law, but in the sinful nature a slave to the law of sin.

8 [1]Therefore, there is now no condemnation for those who are in Christ Jesus, [2]because through Christ Jesus the law of the Spirit of life set me free from the law of sin and death.
2 Cor 1 [10]He has delivered us from such a deadly peril, and he will deliver us. On him we have set our hope that he will continue to deliver us. . . .
Gal 1 [3]Grace and peace to you from God our Father and the Lord Jesus Christ, [4]who gave himself for our sins to rescue us from the present evil age, according to the will of our God and Father. . . .
Col 1 [13]For he has rescued us from the dominion of darkness and brought us into the kingdom of the Son he loves. . . .
1 Thess 1 [10]and to wait for his Son from heaven, whom he raised from the dead—Jesus, who rescues us from the coming wrath.
2 Tim 4 [18]The Lord will rescue me from every evil attack and will bring me safely to his heavenly kingdom. To him be glory for ever and ever. Amen.
2 Pet 2 [5]if he did not spare the ancient world when he brought the flood on its ungodly people, but protected Noah, a preacher of righteousness, and seven others . . . [9]if this is so, then the Lord knows how to rescue godly men from trials and to hold the unrighteous for the day of judgment, while continuing their punishment.

4. Providence Directs Believers

Ps 37 [23]If the LORD delights in a man's way, he makes his steps firm; [24]though he stumble, he will not fall, for the LORD upholds him with his hand.
Ps 40 [5]Many, O LORD my God, are the wonders you have done. The things you planned for us no one can recount to you; were I to speak and tell of them, they would be too many to declare.
Ps 73 [23]Yet I am always with you; you hold me by my right hand. [24]You guide me with your counsel, and afterward you will take me into glory.
Ps 119 [133]Direct my footsteps according to your word; let no sin rule over me.
Ps 121 [3]He will not let your foot slip—he who watches over you will not slumber. . . .
Prov 3 [5]Trust in the LORD with all your heart and lean not on your own understanding; [6]in all your ways acknowledge him, and he will make your paths straight.
Prov 16 [9]In his heart a man plans his course, but the LORD determines his steps.
2 Thess 3 [5]May the Lord direct your hearts into God's love and Christ's perseverance.

5. Providence Dwells with Believers

Ps 9 [10]Those who know your name will trust in you, for you, LORD, have never forsaken those who seek you.
Ps 37 [28]For the LORD loves the just and will not forsake his faithful ones. They will be protected forever, but the offspring of the wicked will be cut off. . . .
Ps 41 [12]In my integrity you uphold me and set me in your presence forever.
Ps 90 [1]Lord, you have been our dwelling place throughout all generations.
Ps 94 [14]For the LORD will not reject his people; he will never forsake his inheritance.
John 10 [27]My sheep listen to my voice; I know them, and they follow me.
1 Cor 6 [19]Do you not know that your body is a temple of the Holy Spirit, who is in you, whom you have received from God? You are not your own. . . .
2 Cor 6 [16]What agreement is there between the temple of God and idols? For we are the temple of the living God. As God has said: "I will live with them and walk among them, and I will be their God, and they will be my people."

[17]"Therefore come out from them and be separate, says the Lord. Touch no unclean thing, and I will receive you." [18]"I will be a Father to you, and you will be my sons and daughters, says the Lord Almighty."
Heb 11 [16]Instead, they were longing for a better country—a heavenly one. Therefore God is not ashamed to be called their God, for he has prepared a city for them.
Heb 13 [5]Keep your lives free from the love of money and be content with what you have, because God has said, "Never will I leave you; never will I forsake you."
Rev 21 [3]And I heard a loud voice from the throne saying, "Now the dwelling of God is with men, and he will live with them. They will be his people, and God himself will be with them and be their God."

6. Providence Heals Believers

Job 5 [17]"Blessed is the man whom God corrects; so do not despise the discipline of the Almighty. [18]For he wounds, but he also binds up; he injures, but his hands also heal."
Ps 30 [2]O LORD my God, I called to you for help and you healed me.
Ps 103 [2]Praise the LORD, O my soul, and forget not all his benefits—[3]who forgives all your sins and heals all your diseases, [4]who redeems your life from the pit and crowns you with love and compassion, [5]who satisfies your desires with good things so that your youth is renewed like the eagle's.
Ps 147 [3]He heals the brokenhearted and binds up their wounds.
Jer 33 [6]"'Nevertheless, I will bring health and healing to it; I will heal my people and will let them enjoy abundant peace and security.'"
James 5 [16]Therefore confess your sins to each other and pray for each other so that you may be healed. The prayer of a righteous man is powerful and effective.
1 Pet 2 [24]He himself bore our sins in his body on the tree, so that we might die to sins and live for righteousness; by his wounds you have been healed.

7. Providence Helps Believers

Ps 17 [6]I call on you, O God, for you will answer me; give ear to me and hear my prayer.
Ps 33 [20]We wait in hope for the LORD; he is our help and our shield.
Ps 37 [40]The LORD helps them and delivers them; he delivers them from the wicked and saves them, because they take refuge in him.
Ps 46 [1]God is our refuge and strength, an ever-present help in trouble.
Ps 54 [4]Surely God is my help; the Lord is the one who sustains me.
Ps 121 [1]I lift up my eyes to the hills—where does my help come from? [2]My help comes from the LORD, the Maker of heaven and earth.
Ps 146 [5]Blessed is he whose help is the God of Jacob, whose hope is in the LORD his God. . . .
Isa 50 [7]Because the Sovereign LORD helps me, I will not be disgraced. Therefore have I set my face like flint, and I know I will not be put to shame. [8]He who vindicates me is near. Who then will bring charges against me? Let us face each other! Who is my accuser? Let him confront me! [9]It is the Sovereign LORD who helps me. Who is he that will condemn me? They will all wear out like a garment; the moths will eat them up.
Acts 26 [22]"But I have had God's help to this very day, and so I stand here and testify to small and great alike. I am saying nothing beyond what the prophets and Moses said would happen. . . ."
Rom 8 [26]In the same way, the Spirit helps us in our weakness. We do not know what we ought to pray for, but the Spirit himself intercedes for us with groans that words cannot express.

Heb 4 [16]Let us then approach the throne of grace with confidence, so that we may receive mercy and find grace to help us in our time of need.
Heb 13 [6]So we say with confidence, "The Lord is my helper; I will not be afraid. What can man do to me?"

8. Providence Honors Believers

Ps 15 [4]who despises a vile man but honors those who fear the LORD, who keeps his oath even when it hurts . . .
Ps 84 [11]For the LORD God is a sun and shield; the LORD bestows favor and honor; no good thing does he withhold from those whose walk is blameless.

9. Providence Is Active in Believers

Phil 2 [12]Therefore, my dear friends, as you have always obeyed—not only in my presence, but now much more in my absence—continue to work out your salvation with fear and trembling, [13]for it is God who works in you to will and to act according to his good purpose.

10. Providence Keeps Believers

Ps 16 [1]Keep me safe, O God, for in you I take refuge.
Ps 17 [8]Keep me as the apple of your eye; hide me in the shadow of your wings. . . .
Ps 19 [13]Keep your servant also from willful sins; may they not rule over me. Then will I be blameless, innocent of great transgression.
Fs 25 [20]Guard my life and rescue me; let me not be put to shame, for I take refuge in you.
Ps 63 [8]My soul clings to you; your right hand upholds me.
Ps 86 [2]Guard my life, for I am devoted to you. You are my God; save your servant who trusts in you.
Ps 91 [11]For he will command his angels concerning you to guard you in all your ways. . . .
Ps 97 [10]Let those who love the LORD hate evil, for he guards the lives of his faithful ones and delivers them from the hand of the wicked.
Ps 140 [4]Keep me, O LORD, from the hands of the wicked; protect me from men of violence who plan to trip my feet.
Ps 141 [3]Set a guard over my mouth, O LORD; keep watch over the door of my lips. [4]Let not my heart be drawn to what is evil, to take part in wicked deeds with men who are evildoers; let me not eat of their delicacies.
Prov 3 [26]for the LORD will be your confidence and will keep your foot from being snared.
2 Tim 1 [12]That is why I am suffering as I am. Yet I am not ashamed, because I know whom I have believed, and am convinced that he is able to guard what I have entrusted to him for that day.
1 Pet 1 [5]who through faith are shielded by God's power until the coming of the salvation that is ready to be revealed in the last time.
1 Pet 4 [19]So then, those who suffer according to God's will should commit themselves to their faithful Creator and continue to do good.
Jude [1]Jude, a servant of Jesus Christ and a brother of James,
To those who have been called, who are loved by God the Father and kept by Jesus Christ. . . .
Jude [24]To him who is able to keep you from falling and to present you before his glorious presence without fault and with great joy—[25]to the only God our Savior be glory, majesty, power and authority, through Jesus Christ our Lord, before all ages, now and forevermore! Amen.
Rev 3 [10]"Since you have kept my command to endure patiently, I will also keep you from the hour of trial that is going to come upon the whole world to test those who live on the earth."

11. Providence Leads Believers

Ps 5 [8]Lead me, O LORD, in your righteousness because of my enemies—make straight your way before me.
Ps 23 [1]The LORD is my shepherd, I shall not be in want. [2]He makes me lie down in green pastures, he leads me beside quiet waters, [3]he restores my soul. He guides me in paths of righteousness for his name's sake.
Ps 25 [5]guide me in your truth and teach me, for you are God my Savior, and my hope is in you all day long.
Ps 31 [3]Since you are my rock and my fortress, for the sake of your name lead and guide me.
Ps 43 [3]Send forth your light and your truth, let them guide me; let them bring me to your holy mountain, to the place where you dwell.
Ps 48 [14]For this God is our God for ever and ever; he will be our guide even to the end.
Ps 61 [2]From the ends of the earth I call to you, I call as my heart grows faint; lead me to the rock that is higher than I.
Ps 139 [24]See if there is any offensive way in me, and lead me in the way everlasting.
John 10 [3]"The watchman opens the gate for him, and the sheep listen to his voice. He calls his own sheep by name and leads them out."
John 16 [13]"But when he, the Spirit of truth, comes, he will guide you into all truth. He will not speak on his own; he will speak only what he hears, and he will tell you what is yet to come."
Rom 2 [4]Or do you show contempt for the riches of his kindness, tolerance and patience, not realizing that God's kindness leads you toward repentance?

12. Providence Preserves Believers

Job 10 [12]"You gave me life and showed me kindness, and in your providence watched over my spirit."
Ps 31 [23]Love the LORD, all his saints! The LORD preserves the faithful, but the proud he pays back in full.
Ps 37 [28]For the LORD loves the just and will not forsake his faithful ones. They will be protected forever, but the offspring of the wicked will be cut off. . . .
Ps 41 [2]The LORD will protect him and preserve his life; he will bless him in the land and not surrender him to the desire of his foes.
Ps 54 [1]Save me, O God, by your name; vindicate me by your might.
Ps 63 [8]My soul clings to you; your right hand upholds me.
Ps 66 [8]Praise our God, O peoples, let the sound of his praise be heard; [9]he has preserved our lives and kept our feet from slipping.
Ps 119 [116]Sustain me according to your promise, and I will live; do not let my hopes be dashed. [117]Uphold me, and I will be delivered; I will always have regard for your decrees.
Ps 138 [7]Though I walk in the midst of trouble, you preserve my life; you stretch out your hand against the anger of my foes, with your right hand you save me.
Ps 145 [20]The LORD watches over all who love him, but all the wicked he will destroy.
Ps 146 [7]He upholds the cause of the oppressed and gives food to the hungry. The LORD sets prisoners free, [8]the LORD gives sight to the blind, the LORD lifts up those who are bowed down, the LORD loves the righteous. [9]The LORD watches over the alien and sustains the fatherless and the widow, but he frustrates the ways of the wicked.
Prov 2 [8]for he guards the course of the just and protects the way of his faithful ones.
Prov 16 [7]When a man's ways are pleasing to the LORD, he makes even his enemies live at peace with him.
John 10 [28]"I give them eternal life, and they shall never perish; no one can snatch them out of my hand."
Phil 1 [6]being confident of this, that he who began a good work in you will carry it on to completion until the day of Christ Jesus.
1 Thess 5 [23]May God himself, the God of peace, sanctify you through and through. May your whole spirit, soul and body be kept blameless at the coming of our Lord Jesus Christ.

13. Providence Protects Believers

Gen 15 [1]After this, the word of the LORD came to Abram in a vision: "Do not be afraid, Abram. I am your shield, your very great reward."
1 Sam 25 [29]"Even though someone is pursuing you to take your life, the life of my master will be bound securely in the

ing by the LORD your God. But the lives of your ... hurl away as from the pocket of a sling."
... [33]"It is God who arms me with strength and makes ... way perfect."
Job 5 [11]"The lowly he sets on high, and those who mourn are lifted to safety."
Ps 4 [8]I will lie down and sleep in peace, for you alone, O LORD, make me dwell in safety.
Ps 9 [9]The LORD is a refuge for the oppressed, a stronghold in times of trouble.
Ps 12 [7]O LORD, you will keep us safe and protect us from such people forever.
Ps 16 [5]LORD, you have assigned me my portion and my cup; you have made my lot secure.
Ps 17 [7]Show the wonder of your great love, you who save by your right hand those who take refuge in you from their foes. [8]Keep me as the apple of your eye; hide me in the shadow of your wings [9]from the wicked who assail me, from my mortal enemies who surround me.
Ps 18 [35]You give me your shield of victory, and your right hand sustains me; you stoop down to make me great.
Ps 23 [1]The LORD is my shepherd, I shall not be in want. [2]He makes me lie down in green pastures, he leads me beside quiet waters, [3]he restores my soul. He guides me in paths of righteousness for his name's sake. [4]Even though I walk through the valley of the shadow of death, I will fear no evil, for you are with me; your rod and your staff, they comfort me.

[5]You prepare a table before me in the presence of my enemies. You anoint my head with oil; my cup overflows. [6]Surely goodness and love will follow me all the days of my life, and I will dwell in the house of the LORD forever.
Ps 28 [8]The LORD is the strength of his people, a fortress of salvation for his anointed one.
Ps 29 [11]The LORD gives strength to his people; the LORD blesses his people with peace.
Ps 34 [7]The angel of the LORD encamps around those who fear him, and he delivers them.

[8]Taste and see that the LORD is good; blessed is the man who takes refuge in him.
Ps 46 [5]God is within her, she will not fall; God will help her at break of day. [6]Nations are in uproar, kingdoms fall; he lifts his voice, the earth melts.

[7]The LORD Almighty is with us; the God of Jacob is our fortress.
Ps 56 [3]When I am afraid, I will trust in you. [4]In God, whose word I praise, in God I trust; I will not be afraid. What can mortal man do to me? [11]. . . in God I trust; I will not be afraid. What can man do to me? . . . [13]For you have delivered me from death and my feet from stumbling, that I may walk before God in the light of life.
Ps 57 [1]Have mercy on me, O God, have mercy on me, for in you my soul takes refuge. I will take refuge in the shadow of your wings until the disaster has passed.
Ps 59 [16]But I will sing of your strength, in the morning I will sing of your love; for you are my fortress, my refuge in times of trouble.
Ps 61 [3]For you have been my refuge, a strong tower against the foe.
Ps 91 [1]He who dwells in the shelter of the Most High will rest in the shadow of the Almighty. . . .

[3]Surely he will save you from the fowler's snare and from the deadly pestilence. [4]He will cover you with his feathers, and under his wings you will find refuge; his faithfulness will be your shield and rampart.
Ps 116 [6]The LORD protects the simplehearted; when I was in great need, he saved me.
Ps 119 [114]You are my refuge and my shield; I have put my hope in your word.
Ps 121 [3]He will not let your foot slip—he who watches over you will not slumber; [4]indeed, he who watches over Israel will neither slumber nor sleep.

[5]The LORD watches over you—the LORD is your shade at your right hand; [6]the sun will not harm you by day, nor the moon by night.

[7]The LORD will keep you from all harm—he will watch over your life; [8]the LORD will watch over your coming and going both now and forevermore.
Ps 125 [2]As the mountains surround Jerusalem, so the LORD surrounds his people both now and forevermore.
Prov 3 [25]Have no fear of sudden disaster or of the ruin that overtakes the wicked, [26]for the LORD will be your confidence and will keep your foot from being snared.
Prov 14 [26]He who fears the LORD has a secure fortress, and for his children it will be a refuge.
Prov 18 [10]The name of the LORD is a strong tower; the righteous run to it and are safe.
Prov 29 [25]Fear of man will prove to be a snare, but whoever trusts in the LORD is kept safe.
Isa 40 [11]He tends his flock like a shepherd: He gathers the lambs in his arms and carries them close to his heart; he gently leads those that have young.
Isa 41 [10]"So do not fear, for I am with you; do not be dismayed, for I am your God. I will strengthen you and help you; I will uphold you with my righteous right hand."
Isa 43 [1]But now, this is what the LORD says—he who created you, O Jacob, he who formed you, O Israel: "Fear not, for I have redeemed you; I have summoned you by name; you are mine. [2]When you pass through the waters, I will be with you; and when you pass through the rivers, they will not sweep over you. When you walk through the fire, you will not be burned; the flames will not set you ablaze."
John 17 [11]"I will remain in the world no longer, but they are still in the world, and I am coming to you. Holy Father, protect them by the power of your name—the name you gave me—so that they may be one as we are one. [12]While I was with them, I protected them and kept them safe by that name you gave me. None has been lost except the one doomed to destruction so that Scripture would be fulfilled. . . . [15]My prayer is not that you take them out of the world but that you protect them from the evil one."
2 Thess 3 [3]But the Lord is faithful, and he will strengthen and protect you from the evil one.
Heb 13 [6]So we say with confidence, "The Lord is my helper; I will not be afraid. What can man do to me?"

14. Providence Provides for Believers

Ps 5 [12]For surely, O LORD, you bless the righteous; you surround them with your favor as with a shield.
Ps 23 [5]You prepare a table before me in the presence of my enemies. You anoint my head with oil; my cup overflows. [6]Surely goodness and love will follow me all the days of my life, and I will dwell in the house of the LORD forever.
Ps 34 [9]Fear the LORD, you his saints, for those who fear him lack nothing. [10]The lions may grow weak and hungry, but those who seek the LORD lack no good thing.
2 Cor 9 [8]And God is able to make all grace abound to you, so that in all things at all times, having all that you need, you will abound in every good work.
Eph 3 [20]Now to him who is able to do immeasurably more than all we ask or imagine, according to his power that is at work within us . . .
Phil 4 [19]And my God will meet all your needs according to his glorious riches in Christ Jesus.
James 1 [17]Every good and perfect gift is from above, coming down from the Father of the heavenly lights, who does not change like shifting shadows.

15. Providence Sends Blessings to Believers

Gen 25 [11]After Abraham's death, God blessed his son Isaac, who then lived near Beer Lahai Roi.
Deut 11 [13]So if you faithfully obey the commands I am giving you today—to love the LORD your God and to serve him with all your heart and with all your soul—[14]then I will send rain on your land in its season, both autumn and spring rains, so that you may gather in your grain, new wine and oil. [15]I will provide grass in the fields for your cattle, and you will eat and be satisfied.
1 Kings 2 [3]". . . and observe what the LORD your God requires: Walk in his ways, and keep his decrees and commands, his

laws and requirements, as written in the Law of Moses, so that you may prosper in all you do and wherever you go. . . ."

2 Kings 10 30The LORD said to Jehu, "Because you have done well in accomplishing what is right in my eyes and have done to the house of Ahab all I had in mind to do, your descendants will sit on the throne of Israel to the fourth generation."

2 Chron 17 3The LORD was with Jehoshaphat because in his early years he walked in the ways his father David had followed. He did not consult the Baals 4but sought the God of his father and followed his commands rather than the practices of Israel. 5The LORD established the kingdom under his control; and all Judah brought gifts to Jehoshaphat, so that he had great wealth and honor.

Job 11 13"Yet if you devote your heart to him and stretch out your hands to him, 14if you put away the sin that is in your hand and allow no evil to dwell in your tent, 15then you will lift up your face without shame; you will stand firm and without fear. 16You will surely forget your trouble, recalling it only as waters gone by. 17Life will be brighter than noonday, and darkness will become like morning. 18You will be secure, because there is hope; you will look about you and take your rest in safety. 19You will lie down, with no one to make you afraid, and many will court your favor."

Job 22 21"Submit to God and be at peace with him; in this way prosperity will come to you."

Ps 5 12For surely, O LORD, you bless the righteous; you surround them with your favor as with a shield.

Ps 24 3Who may ascend the hill of the LORD? Who may stand in his holy place? 4He who has clean hands and a pure heart, who does not lift up his soul to an idol or swear by what is false. 5He will receive blessing from the LORD and vindication from God his Savior. 6Such is the generation of those who seek him, who seek your face, O God of Jacob.

Ps 25 10All the ways of the LORD are loving and faithful for those who keep the demands of his covenant. . . . 12Who, then, is the man that fears the LORD? He will instruct him in the way chosen for him. 13He will spend his days in prosperity, and his descendants will inherit the land.

Ps 31 19How great is your goodness, which you have stored up for those who fear you, which you bestow in the sight of men on those who take refuge in you.

Ps 65 4Blessed are those you choose and bring near to live in your courts! We are filled with the good things of your house, of your holy temple.

Ps 84 11For the LORD God is a sun and shield; the LORD bestows favor and honor; no good thing does he withhold from those whose walk is blameless.

Ps 97 11Light is shed upon the righteous and joy on the upright in heart.

Ps 103 17But from everlasting to everlasting the LORD's love is with those who fear him, and his righteousness with their children's children—18with those who keep his covenant and remember to obey his precepts.

Ps 112 1Praise the LORD.

Blessed is the man who fears the LORD, who finds great delight in his commands.

2His children will be mighty in the land; the generation of the upright will be blessed. 3Wealth and riches are in his house, and his righteousness endures forever.

Ps 144 12Then our sons in their youth will be like well-nurtured plants, and our daughters will be like pillars carved to adorn a palace. 13Our barns will be filled with every kind of provision. Our sheep will increase by thousands, by tens of thousands in our fields; 14our oxen will draw heavy loads. There will be no breaching of walls, no going into captivity, no cry of distress in our streets.

15Blessed are the people of whom this is true; blessed are the people whose God is the LORD.

Prov 3 33The LORD's curse is on the house of the wicked, but he blesses the home of the righteous.

Prov 21 21He who pursues righteousness and love finds life, prosperity and honor.

Isa 1 18"Come now, let us reason together," says the LORD. "Though your sins are like scarlet, they shall be as white as snow; though they are red as crimson, they shall be like wool. 19If you are willing and obedient, you will eat the best from the land. . . ."

Jer 33 6"'Nevertheless, I will bring health and healing to it; I will heal my people and will let them enjoy abundant peace and security.'"

Zech 3 6The angel of the LORD gave this charge to Joshua: 7"This is what the LORD Almighty says: 'If you will walk in my ways and keep my requirements, then you will govern my house and have charge of my courts, and I will give you a place among these standing here.'"

Rom 10 12For there is no difference between Jew and Gentile—the same Lord is Lord of all and richly blesses all who call on him. . . .

Eph 1 3Praise be to the God and Father of our Lord Jesus Christ, who has blessed us in the heavenly realms with every spiritual blessing in Christ.

Heb 11 6And without faith it is impossible to please God, because anyone who comes to him must believe that he exists and that he rewards those who earnestly seek him.

16. Providence Strengthens Believers

Ps 18 1I love you, O LORD, my strength. . . .

29With your help I can advance against a troop; with my God I can scale a wall. . . .

35You give me your shield of victory, and your right hand sustains me; you stoop down to make me great.

Ps 37 17for the power of the wicked will be broken, but the LORD upholds the righteous. . . .

39The salvation of the righteous comes from the LORD; he is their stronghold in time of trouble.

Ps 84 5Blessed are those whose strength is in you, who have set their hearts on pilgrimage.

Ps 118 14The LORD is my strength and my song; he has become my salvation.

Rom 14 1Accept him whose faith is weak, without passing judgment on disputable matters. . . . 4Who are you to judge someone else's servant? To his own master he stands or falls. And he will stand, for the Lord is able to make him stand.

1 Cor 10 13No temptation has seized you except what is common to man. And God is faithful; he will not let you be tempted beyond what you can bear. But when you are tempted, he will also provide a way out so that you can stand up under it.

2 Cor 3 5Not that we are competent in ourselves to claim anything for ourselves, but our competence comes from God.

2 Cor 4 7But we have this treasure in jars of clay to show that this all-surpassing power is from God and not from us. 8We are hard pressed on every side, but not crushed; perplexed, but not in despair. . . .

2 Cor 12 9But he said to me, "My grace is sufficient for you, for my power is made perfect in weakness." Therefore I will boast all the more gladly about my weaknesses, so that Christ's power may rest on me. 10That is why, for Christ's sake, I delight in weaknesses, in insults, in hardships, in persecutions, in difficulties. For when I am weak, then I am strong.

2 Thess 2 16May our Lord Jesus Christ himself and God our Father, who loved us and by his grace gave us eternal encouragement and good hope, 17encourage your hearts and strengthen you in every good deed and word.

1 Tim 1 12I thank Christ Jesus our Lord, who has given me strength, that he considered me faithful, appointing me to his service.

2 Tim 4 17But the Lord stood at my side and gave me strength, so that through me the message might be fully proclaimed and all the Gentiles might hear it. And I was delivered from the lion's mouth.

1 Pet 4 11If anyone speaks, he should do it as one speaking the very words of God. If anyone serves, he should do it with the strength God provides, so that in all things God may be praised through Jesus Christ. To him be the glory and the power for ever and ever. Amen.

17. Providence Teaches Believers

Ps 25 8Good and upright is the LORD; therefore he instructs sinners in his ways. 9He guides the humble in what is right and teaches them his way.

Ps 71 [17]Since my youth, O God, you have taught me, and to this day I declare your marvelous deeds.
John 14 [26]"But the Counselor, the Holy Spirit, whom the Father will send in my name, will teach you all things and will remind you of everything I have said to you."
Acts 2 [28]"'You have made known to me the paths of life; you will fill me with joy in your presence.'"
2 Cor 4 [6]For God, who said, "Let light shine out of darkness," made his light shine in our hearts to give us the light of the knowledge of the glory of God in the face of Christ.
1 Thess 4 [9]Now about brotherly love we do not need to write to you, for you yourselves have been taught by God to love each other.
1 John 2 [27]As for you, the anointing you received from him remains in you, and you do not need anyone to teach you. But as his anointing teaches you about all things and as that anointing is real, not counterfeit—just as it has taught you, remain in him.

F. Providence and Evil

1. Providence and Evil Actions

Exod 10 [27]But the LORD hardened Pharaoh's heart, and he was not willing to let them go.
Judg 9 [22]After Abimelech had governed Israel three years, [23]God sent an evil spirit between Abimelech and the citizens of Shechem, who acted treacherously against Abimelech. [24]God did this in order that the crime against Jerub-Baal's seventy sons, the shedding of their blood, might be avenged on their brother Abimelech and on the citizens of Shechem, who had helped him murder his brothers.
2 Sam 16 [10]But the king said, "What do you and I have in common, you sons of Zeruiah? If he is cursing because the LORD said to him, 'Curse David,' who can ask, 'Why do you do this?'"

[11]David then said to Abishai and all his officials, "My son, who is of my own flesh, is trying to take my life. How much more, then, this Benjamite! Leave him alone; let him curse, for the LORD has told him to. [12]It may be that the LORD will see my distress and repay me with good for the cursing I am receiving today."
2 Sam 24 [1]Again the anger of the LORD burned against Israel, and he incited David against them, saying, "Go and take a census of Israel and Judah." (1 Chron 21:1)
Acts 2 [23]"This man was handed over to you by God's set purpose and foreknowledge; and you, with the help of wicked men, put him to death by nailing him to the cross."
Acts 4 [27]"Indeed Herod and Pontius Pilate met together with the Gentiles and the people of Israel in this city to conspire against your holy servant Jesus, whom you anointed. [28]They did what your power and will had decided beforehand should happen."
Rom 1 [24]Therefore God gave them over in the sinful desires of their hearts to sexual impurity for the degrading of their bodies with one another. . . .

[26]Because of this, God gave them over to shameful lusts. Even their women exchanged natural relations for unnatural ones. . . .

[28]Furthermore, since they did not think it worthwhile to retain the knowledge of God, he gave them over to a depraved mind, to do what ought not to be done.
Rom 11 [32]For God has bound all men over to disobedience so that he may have mercy on them all.
2 Thess 2 [9]The coming of the lawless one will be in accordance with the work of Satan displayed in all kinds of counterfeit miracles, signs and wonders, [10]and in every sort of evil that deceives those who are perishing. They perish because they refused to love the truth and so be saved. [11]For this reason God sends them a powerful delusion so that they will believe the lie [12]and so that all will be condemned who have not believed the truth but have delighted in wickedness.

2. Providence and Evil Itself

a) Providence Directs Evil

Gen 45 [8]"So then, it was not you who sent me here, but God. He made me father to Pharaoh, lord of his entire household and ruler of all Egypt."
Gen 50 [20]"You intended to harm me, but God intended it for good to accomplish what is now being done, the saving of many lives."
Exod 4 [21]The LORD said to Moses, "When you return to Egypt, see that you perform before Pharaoh all the wonders I have given you the power to do. But I will harden his heart so that he will not let the people go."
Prov 16 [4]The LORD works out everything for his own ends—even the wicked for a day of disaster.
Isa 10 [5]"Woe to the Assyrian, the rod of my anger, in whose hand is the club of my wrath!"
John 13 [27]As soon as Judas took the bread, Satan entered into him.

"What you are about to do, do quickly," Jesus told him. . . .
Acts 2 [23]"This man was handed over to you by God's set purpose and foreknowledge; and you, with the help of wicked men, put him to death by nailing him to the cross."
Acts 3 [26]"When God raised up his servant, he sent him first to you to bless you by turning each of you from your wicked ways."
Acts 4 [27]"Indeed Herod and Pontius Pilate met together with the Gentiles and the people of Israel in this city to conspire against your holy servant Jesus, whom you anointed. [28]They did what your power and will had decided beforehand should happen."
Rom 9 [17]For the Scripture says to Pharaoh: "I raised you up for this very purpose, that I might display my power in you and that my name might be proclaimed in all the earth." [18]Therefore God has mercy on whom he wants to have mercy, and he hardens whom he wants to harden.
Rom 11 [13]I am talking to you Gentiles. Inasmuch as I am the apostle to the Gentiles, I make much of my ministry [14]in the hope that I may somehow arouse my own people to envy and save some of them. [15]For if their rejection is the reconciliation of the world, what will their acceptance be but life from the dead? . . .

[25]I do not want you to be ignorant of this mystery, brothers, so that you may not be conceited: Israel has experienced a hardening in part until the full number of the Gentiles has come in.

b) Providence Limits Evil

Job 1 [12]The LORD said to Satan, "Very well, then, everything he has is in your hands, but on the man himself do not lay a finger."

Then Satan went out from the presence of the LORD.
Job 2 [6]The LORD said to Satan, "Very well, then, he is in your hands; but you must spare his life."
Ps 124 [1]If the LORD had not been on our side—let Israel say—[2]if the LORD had not been on our side when men attacked us, [3]when their anger flared against us, they would have swallowed us alive. . . .
1 Cor 10 [13]No temptation has seized you except what is common to man. And God is faithful; he will not let you be tempted beyond what you can bear. But when you are tempted, he will also provide a way out so that you can stand up under it.
2 Thess 2 [7]For the secret power of lawlessness is already at work; but the one who now holds it back will continue to do so till he is taken out of the way.
Rev 20 [2]He seized the dragon, that ancient serpent, who is the devil, or Satan, and bound him for a thousand years. [3]He threw him into the Abyss, and locked and sealed it over him, to keep him from deceiving the nations anymore until the thousand years were ended. After that, he must be set free for a short time.

c) Providence Permits Evil

Deut 8 [2]Remember how the LORD your God led you all the way in the desert these forty years, to humble you and to test you in order to know what was in your heart, whether or not you would keep his commands.
2 Chron 32 [31]But when envoys were sent by the rulers of Babylon to ask him about the miraculous sign that had occurred in the land, God left him to test him and to know everything that was in his heart.
Ps 17 [13]Rise up, O LORD, confront them, bring them down; res-

cue me from the wicked by your sword. [14]O LORD, by your hand save me from such men, from men of this world whose reward is in this life.

You still the hunger of those you cherish; their sons have plenty, and they store up wealth for their children.

Ps 81 [11]"But my people would not listen to me; Israel would not submit to me. [12]So I gave them over to their stubborn hearts to follow their own devices."

Isa 53 [4]Surely he took up our infirmities and carried our sorrows, yet we considered him stricken by God, smitten by him, and afflicted. . . .

[10]Yet it was the LORD's will to crush him and cause him to suffer, and though the LORD makes his life a guilt offering, he will see his offspring and prolong his days, and the will of the LORD will prosper in his hand.

Hos 4 [17]"Ephraim is joined to idols; leave him alone!"

Acts 14 [16]"In the past, he let all nations go their own way."

Rom 1 [24]Therefore God gave them over in the sinful desires of their hearts to sexual impurity for the degrading of their bodies with one another. . . .

[26]Because of this, God gave them over to shameful lusts. Even their women exchanged natural relations for unnatural ones. . . .

[28]Furthermore, since they did not think it worthwhile to retain the knowledge of God, he gave them over to a depraved mind, to do what ought not to be done.

Rom 3 [25]God presented him as a sacrifice of atonement, through faith in his blood. He did this to demonstrate his justice, because in his forbearance he had left the sins committed beforehand unpunished. . . .

d) Providence Prevents Evil

Gen 20 [6]Then God said to him in the dream, "Yes, I know you did this with a clear conscience, and so I have kept you from sinning against me. That is why I did not let you touch her."

Gen 31 [24]Then God came to Laban the Aramean in a dream at night and said to him, "Be careful not to say anything to Jacob, either good or bad."

Ps 19 [13]Keep your servant also from willful sins; may they not rule over me. Then will I be blameless, innocent of great transgression.

Hos 2 [6]"Therefore I will block her path with thornbushes; I will wall her in so that she cannot find her way. [7]She will chase after her lovers but not catch them; she will look for them but not find them. Then she will say, 'I will go back to my husband as at first, for then I was better off than now.' . . .

[14]"Therefore I am now going to allure her; I will lead her into the desert and speak tenderly to her. [15]There I will give her back her vineyards, and will make the Valley of Achor a door of hope. There she will sing as in the days of her youth, as in the day she came up out of Egypt.

[16]"In that day," declares the LORD, "you will call me 'my husband'; you will no longer call me 'my master.' [17]I will remove the names of the Baals from her lips; no longer will their names be invoked. [18]In that day I will make a covenant for them with the beasts of the field and the birds of the air and the creatures that move along the ground. Bow and sword and battle I will abolish from the land, so that all may lie down in safety. [19]I will betroth you to me forever; I will betroth you in righteousness and justice, in love and compassion. [20]I will betroth you in faithfulness, and you will acknowledge the LORD."

Matt 6 [13]"'And lead us not into temptation, but deliver us from the evil one.'"

3. Temporal Judgment of the Wicked

a) Providence Avenges with Punishment

Gen 6 [13]So God said to Noah, "I am going to put an end to all people, for the earth is filled with violence because of them. I am surely going to destroy both them and the earth."

Deut 7 [10]But those who hate him he will repay to their face by destruction; he will not be slow to repay to their face those who hate him.

2 Sam 23 [6]"But evil men are all to be cast aside like thorns, which are not gathered with the hand. [7]Whoever touches thorns uses a tool of iron or the shaft of a spear; they are burned up where they lie."

Job 4 [8]"As I have observed, those who plow evil and those who sow trouble reap it. [9]At the breath of God they are destroyed; at the blast of his anger they perish."

Job 11 [11]"Surely he recognizes deceitful men; and when he sees evil, does he not take note? . . . [20]But the eyes of the wicked will fail, and escape will elude them; their hope will become a dying gasp."

Job 18 [5]"The lamp of the wicked is snuffed out; the flame of his fire stops burning. [6]The light in his tent becomes dark; the lamp beside him goes out. . . . [16]His roots dry up below and his branches wither above. [17]The memory of him perishes from the earth; he has no name in the land. . . . [21]Surely such is the dwelling of an evil man; such is the place of one who knows not God."

Job 38 [1]Then the LORD answered Job out of the storm. He said: . . . [12]"Have you ever given orders to the morning, or shown the dawn its place, [13]that it might take the earth by the edges and shake the wicked out of it? [14]The earth takes shape like clay under a seal; its features stand out like those of a garment. [15]The wicked are denied their light, and their upraised arm is broken."

Ps 1 [4]Not so the wicked! They are like chaff that the wind blows away. [5]Therefore the wicked will not stand in the judgment, nor sinners in the assembly of the righteous.

[6]For the LORD watches over the way of the righteous, but the way of the wicked will perish.

Ps 11 [6]On the wicked he will rain fiery coals and burning sulfur; a scorching wind will be their lot.

Ps 34 [16]the face of the LORD is against those who do evil, to cut off the memory of them from the earth. . . . [21]Evil will slay the wicked; the foes of the righteous will be condemned.

Ps 37 [10]A little while, and the wicked will be no more; though you look for them, they will not be found. . . .

[12]The wicked plot against the righteous and gnash their teeth at them; [13]but the Lord laughs at the wicked, for he knows their day is coming. . . .

[20]But the wicked will perish: The LORD's enemies will be like the beauty of the fields, they will vanish—vanish like smoke.

Ps 89 [30]"If his sons forsake my law and do not follow my statutes, [31]if they violate my decrees and fail to keep my commands, [32]I will punish their sin with the rod, their iniquity with flogging. . . ."

Ps 92 [9]For surely your enemies, O LORD, surely your enemies will perish; all evildoers will be scattered.

Ps 94 [23]He will repay them for their sins and destroy them for their wickedness; the LORD our God will destroy them.

Ps 119 [118]You reject all who stray from your decrees, for their deceitfulness is in vain. [119]All the wicked of the earth you discard like dross; therefore I love your statutes.

Prov 2 [22]but the wicked will be cut off from the land, and the unfaithful will be torn from it.

Prov 11 [23]The desire of the righteous ends only in good, but the hope of the wicked only in wrath.

Isa 1 [28]But rebels and sinners will both be broken, and those who forsake the LORD will perish.

Isa 9 [13]But the people have not returned to him who struck them, nor have they sought the LORD Almighty. [14]So the LORD will cut off from Israel both head and tail, both palm branch and reed in a single day. . . .

Isa 9 [18]Surely wickedness burns like a fire; it consumes briers and thorns, it sets the forest thickets ablaze, so that it rolls upward in a column of smoke. [19]By the wrath of the LORD Almighty the land will be scorched and the people will be fuel for the fire; no one will spare his brother.

Jer 23 [19]"See, the storm of the LORD will burst out in wrath, a whirlwind swirling down on the heads of the wicked."

Jer 48 [11]"Moab has been at rest from youth, like wine left on its dregs, not poured from one jar to another—she has not gone into exile. So she tastes as she did, and her aroma is unchanged. [12]But days are coming," declares the LORD, "when I will send men who pour from jars, and they will pour her out; they will empty her jars and smash her jugs."

Ezek 11 [21]"But as for those whose hearts are devoted to their vile images and detestable idols, I will bring down on their own heads what they have done, declares the Sovereign LORD."

Ezek 22 [31]"So I will pour out my wrath on them and consume them with my fiery anger, bringing down on their own heads all they have done, declares the Sovereign LORD."

Zeph 3 [1]Woe to the city of oppressors, rebellious and defiled! [2]She obeys no one, she accepts no correction. She does not trust in the LORD, she does not draw near to her God. . . .

[7]"I said to the city, 'Surely you will fear me and accept correction!' Then her dwelling would not be cut off, nor all my punishments come upon her. But they were still eager to act corruptly in all they did."

Mal 4 [1]"Surely the day is coming; it will burn like a furnace. All the arrogant and every evildoer will be stubble, and that day that is coming will set them on fire," says the LORD Almighty. "Not a root or a branch will be left to them. . . . [3]Then you will trample down the wicked; they will be ashes under the soles of your feet on the day when I do these things," says the LORD Almighty.

Matt 23 [33]"You snakes! You brood of vipers! How will you escape being condemned to hell?"

Acts 3 [22]"For Moses said, 'The Lord your God will raise up for you a prophet like me from among your own people; you must listen to everything he tells you. [23]Anyone who does not listen to him will be completely cut off from among his people.'"

Rom 1 [18]The wrath of God is being revealed from heaven against all the godlessness and wickedness of men who suppress the truth by their wickedness. . . .

1 Pet 4 [17]For it is time for judgment to begin with the family of God; and if it begins with us, what will the outcome be for those who do not obey the gospel of God? [18]And, "If it is hard for the righteous to be saved, what will become of the ungodly and the sinner?"

b) Providence Brings Calamity

Job 5 [2]"Resentment kills a fool, and envy slays the simple. [3]I myself have seen a fool taking root, but suddenly his house was cursed. [4]His children are far from safety, crushed in court without a defender. [5]The hungry consume his harvest, taking it even from among thorns, and the thirsty pant after his wealth."

Job 18 [5]"The lamp of the wicked is snuffed out; the flame of his fire stops burning. . . . [12]Calamity is hungry for him; disaster is ready for him when he falls."

Job 21 [17]"Yet how often is the lamp of the wicked snuffed out? How often does calamity come upon them, the fate God allots in his anger? [18]How often are they like straw before the wind, like chaff swept away by a gale?"

Job 24 [22]"But God drags away the mighty by his power; though they become established, they have no assurance of life. [23]He may let them rest in a feeling of security, but his eyes are on their ways. [24]For a little while they are exalted, and then they are gone; they are brought low and gathered up like all others; they are cut off like heads of grain."

Ps 36 [12]See how the evildoers lie fallen—thrown down, not able to rise!

Ps 37 [34]Wait for the LORD and keep his way. He will exalt you to inherit the land; when the wicked are cut off, you will see it. [35]I have seen a wicked and ruthless man flourishing like a green tree in its native soil, [36]but he soon passed away and was no more; though I looked for him, he could not be found. [37]Consider the blameless, observe the upright; there is a future for the man of peace. [38]But all sinners will be destroyed; the future of the wicked will be cut off.

Ps 55 [23]But you, O God, will bring down the wicked into the pit of corruption; bloodthirsty and deceitful men will not live out half their days. But as for me, I trust in you.

Ps 73 [3]For I envied the arrogant when I saw the prosperity of the wicked.

[4]They have no struggles; their bodies are healthy and strong. [5]They are free from the burdens common to man; they are not plagued by human ills. [6]Therefore pride is their necklace; they clothe themselves with violence. [7]From their callous hearts comes iniquity; the evil conceits of their minds know no limits. [8]They scoff, and speak with malice; in their arrogance they threaten oppression. [9]Their mouths lay claim to heaven, and their tongues take possession of the earth. [10]Therefore their people turn to them and drink up waters in abundance. [11]They say, "How can God know? Does the Most High have knowledge?"

[12]This is what the wicked are like—always carefree, they increase in wealth.

[13]Surely in vain have I kept my heart pure; in vain have I washed my hands in innocence. [14]All day long I have been plagued; I have been punished every morning. . . . [16]When I tried to understand all this, it was oppressive to me [17]till I entered the sanctuary of God; then I understood their final destiny.

[18]Surely you place them on slippery ground; you cast them down to ruin. [19]How suddenly are they destroyed, completely swept away by terrors! [20]As a dream when one awakes, so when you arise, O Lord, you will despise them as fantasies.

Ps 92 [6]The senseless man does not know, fools do not understand, [7]that though the wicked spring up like grass and all evildoers flourish, they will be forever destroyed.

Prov 4 [19]But the way of the wicked is like deep darkness; they do not know what makes them stumble.

Prov 6 [12]A scoundrel and villain, who goes about with a corrupt mouth . . . [14]who plots evil with deceit in his heart—he always stirs up dissension. [15]Therefore disaster will overtake him in an instant; he will suddenly be destroyed—without remedy.

Prov 21 [12]The Righteous One takes note of the house of the wicked and brings the wicked to ruin.

Eccles 8 [12]Although a wicked man commits a hundred crimes and still lives a long time, I know that it will go better with God-fearing men, who are reverent before God. [13]Yet because the wicked do not fear God, it will not go well with them, and their days will not lengthen like a shadow.

1 Thess 5 [3]While people are saying, "Peace and safety," destruction will come on them suddenly, as labor pains on a pregnant woman, and they will not escape.

c) Providence Brings Shame

Job 8 [22]"Your enemies will be clothed in shame, and the tents of the wicked will be no more."

Job 18 [19]"He has no offspring or descendants among his people, no survivor where once he lived. [20]Men of the west are appalled at his fate; men of the east are seized with horror. [21]Surely such is the dwelling of an evil man; such is the place of one who knows not God."

Ps 53 [5]There they were, overwhelmed with dread, where there was nothing to dread. God scattered the bones of those who attacked you; you put them to shame, for God despised them.

Ps 60 [6]God has spoken from his sanctuary: "In triumph I will parcel out Shechem and measure off the Valley of Succoth. . . . [8]Moab is my washbasin, upon Edom I toss my sandal; over Philistia I shout in triumph."

Jer 13 [21]What will you say when the LORD sets over you those you cultivated as your special allies? Will not pain grip you like that of a woman in labor? [22]And if you ask yourself, "Why has this happened to me?"—it is because of your many sins that your skirts have been torn off and your body mistreated.

Jer 22 [21]"I warned you when you felt secure, but you said, 'I will not listen!' This has been your way from your youth; you have not obeyed me. [22]The wind will drive all your shepherds away, and your allies will go into exile. Then you will be ashamed and disgraced because of all your wickedness."

Mic 6 [16]"You have observed the statutes of Omri and all the practices of Ahab's house, and you have followed their traditions. Therefore I will give you over to ruin and your people to derision; you will bear the scorn of the nations."

G. Providence and Suffering

1. Providence Delivers from Suffering

Gen 31 [42]"If the God of my father, the God of Abraham and the Fear of Isaac, had not been with me, you would surely have sent me away empty-handed. But God has seen my hardship and the toil of my hands, and last night he rebuked you."

2 Sam 22 [17]"He reached down from on high and took hold of me; he drew me out of deep waters. [18]He rescued me from my powerful enemy, from my foes, who were too strong for me. [19]They confronted me in the day of my disaster, but the LORD was my support. [20]He brought me out into a spacious place; he rescued me because he delighted in me."

2 Chron 30 [9]"If you return to the LORD, then your brothers and your children will be shown compassion by their captors and will come back to this land, for the LORD your God is gracious and compassionate. He will not turn his face from you if you return to him."

Job 5 [11]"The lowly he sets on high, and those who mourn are lifted to safety."

Job 11 [16]"You will surely forget your trouble, recalling it only as waters gone by. [17]Life will be brighter than noonday, and darkness will become like morning. [18]You will be secure, because there is hope; you will look about you and take your rest in safety. [19]You will lie down, with no one to make you afraid, and many will court your favor. [20]But the eyes of the wicked will fail, and escape will elude them; their hope will become a dying gasp."

Ps 30 [5]For his anger lasts only a moment, but his favor lasts a lifetime; weeping may remain for a night, but rejoicing comes in the morning. . . . [11]You turned my wailing into dancing; you removed my sackcloth and clothed me with joy. . . .

Ps 34 [19]A righteous man may have many troubles, but the LORD delivers him from them all; [20]he protects all his bones, not one of them will be broken.

Ps 37 [32]The wicked lie in wait for the righteous, seeking their very lives; [33]but the LORD will not leave them in their power or let them be condemned when brought to trial.

Ps 91 [15]"He will call upon me, and I will answer him; I will be with him in trouble, I will deliver him and honor him."

Ps 112 [4]Even in darkness light dawns for the upright, for the gracious and compassionate and righteous man. . . . [7]He will have no fear of bad news; his heart is steadfast, trusting in the LORD.

Ps 146 [7]He upholds the cause of the oppressed and gives food to the hungry. The LORD sets prisoners free, [8]the LORD gives sight to the blind, the LORD lifts up those who are bowed down, the LORD loves the righteous. [9]The LORD watches over the alien and sustains the fatherless and the widow, but he frustrates the ways of the wicked.

Isa 9 [4]For as in the day of Midian's defeat, you have shattered the yoke that burdens them, the bar across their shoulders, the rod of their oppressor.

Isa 25 [4]You have been a refuge for the poor, a refuge for the needy in his distress, a shelter from the storm and a shade from the heat. For the breath of the ruthless is like a storm driving against a wall. . . .

Jer 15 [11]The LORD said, "Surely I will deliver you for a good purpose; surely I will make your enemies plead with you in times of disaster and times of distress."

Lam 3 [31]For men are not cast off by the Lord forever. [32]Though he brings grief, he will show compassion, so great is his unfailing love. [33]For he does not willingly bring affliction or grief to the children of men.

Nah 1 [9]Whatever they plot against the LORD he will bring to an end; trouble will not come a second time. . . .

[12]This is what the LORD says: "Although they have allies and are numerous, they will be cut off and pass away. Although I have afflicted you, O Judah, I will afflict you no more. [13]Now I will break their yoke from your neck and tear your shackles away."

2. Providence Permits Suffering

Job 2 [6]The LORD said to Satan, "Very well, then, he is in your hands; but you must spare his life."

[7]So Satan went out from the presence of the LORD and afflicted Job with painful sores from the soles of his feet to the top of his head. . . .

[13]Then they sat on the ground with him for seven days and seven nights. No one said a word to him, because they saw how great his suffering was.

Job 5 [6]"For hardship does not spring from the soil, nor does trouble sprout from the ground. [7]Yet man is born to trouble as surely as sparks fly upward."

Job 14 [1]"Man born of woman is of few days and full of trouble."

Ps 42 [10]My bones suffer mortal agony as my foes taunt me, saying to me all day long, "Where is your God?"

Eccles 1 [8]All things are wearisome, more than one can say. The eye never has enough of seeing, nor the ear its fill of hearing.

Eccles 2 [22]What does a man get for all the toil and anxious striving with which he labors under the sun? [23]All his days his work is pain and grief; even at night his mind does not rest. This too is meaningless.

Eccles 5 [17]All his days he eats in darkness, with great frustration, affliction and anger.

Eccles 7 [14]When times are good, be happy; but when times are bad, consider: God has made the one as well as the other. Therefore, a man cannot discover anything about his future.

Matt 4 [24]News about him spread all over Syria, and people brought to him all who were ill with various diseases, those suffering severe pain, the demon-possessed, those having seizures, and the paralyzed, and he healed them.

Matt 8 [6]"Lord," he said, "my servant lies at home paralyzed and in terrible suffering."

Mark 5 [26]She had suffered a great deal under the care of many doctors and had spent all she had, yet instead of getting better she grew worse.

Luke 4 [38]Jesus left the synagogue and went to the home of Simon. Now Simon's mother-in-law was suffering from a high fever, and they asked Jesus to help her.

John 15 [18]"If the world hates you, keep in mind that it hated me first. [19]If you belonged to the world, it would love you as its own. As it is, you do not belong to the world, but I have chosen you out of the world. That is why the world hates you. [20]Remember the words I spoke to you: 'No servant is greater than his master.' If they persecuted me, they will persecute you also. If they obeyed my teaching, they will obey yours also."

John 16 [33]"I have told you these things, so that in me you may have peace. In this world you will have trouble. But take heart! I have overcome the world."

Acts 7 [11]"Then a famine struck all Egypt and Canaan, bringing great suffering, and our fathers could not find food."

2 Cor 11 [23]Are they servants of Christ? (I am out of my mind to talk like this.) I am more. I have worked much harder, been in prison more frequently, been flogged more severely, and been exposed to death again and again. [24]Five times I received from the Jews the forty lashes minus one. [25]Three times I was beaten with rods, once I was stoned, three times I was shipwrecked, I spent a night and a day in the open sea, [26]I have been constantly on the move. I have been in danger from rivers, in danger from bandits, in danger from my own countrymen, in danger from Gentiles; in danger in the city, in danger in the country, in danger at sea; and in danger from false brothers. [27]I have labored and toiled and have often gone without sleep; I have known hunger and thirst and have often gone without food; I have been cold and naked.

2 Cor 12 [7]To keep me from becoming conceited because of these surpassingly great revelations, there was given me a thorn in my flesh, a messenger of Satan, to torment me. [8]Three times I pleaded with the Lord to take it away from me. [9]But he said to me, "My grace is sufficient for you, for my power is made perfect in weakness." Therefore I will boast all the more gladly about my weaknesses, so that Christ's power may rest on me.

Heb 5 [8]Although he was a son, he learned obedience from what he suffered [9]and, once made perfect, he became the source of eternal salvation for all who obey him. . . .

1 Pet 1 [6]In this you greatly rejoice, though now for a little while you may have had to suffer grief in all kinds of trials.

1 Pet 4 [12]Dear friends, do not be surprised at the painful trial you are suffering, as though something strange were happening to you. [13]But rejoice that you participate in the sufferings of Christ, so that you may be overjoyed when his glory is revealed.

1 Pet 5 [9]Resist him, standing firm in the faith, because you know that your brothers throughout the world are undergoing the same kind of sufferings.

3. Providence Sends Suffering

Gen 3 [16]To the woman he said, "I will greatly increase your pains in childbearing; with pain you will give birth to children.

Your desire will be for your husband, and he will rule over you."

Exod 4 [11]The LORD said to him, "Who gave man his mouth? Who makes him deaf or mute? Who gives him sight or makes him blind? Is it not I, the LORD?"

Job 10 [17]"You bring new witnesses against me and increase your anger toward me; your forces come against me wave upon wave."

Ps 55 [19]God, who is enthroned forever, will hear them and afflict them—men who never change their ways and have no fear of God.

Ps 66 [10]For you, O God, tested us; you refined us like silver. [11]You brought us into prison and laid burdens on our backs. [12]You let men ride over our heads; we went through fire and water, but you brought us to a place of abundance.

Ps 88 [15]From my youth I have been afflicted and close to death; I have suffered your terrors and am in despair. [16]Your wrath has swept over me; your terrors have destroyed me. [17]All day long they surround me like a flood; they have completely engulfed me. [18]You have taken my companions and loved ones from me; the darkness is my closest friend.

Ps 119 [75]I know, O LORD, that your laws are righteous, and in faithfulness you have afflicted me.

Lam 1 [12]"Is it nothing to you, all you who pass by? Look around and see. Is any suffering like my suffering that was inflicted on me, that the LORD brought on me in the day of his fierce anger?

[13]"From on high he sent fire, sent it down into my bones. He spread a net for my feet and turned me back. He made me desolate, faint all the day long.

[14]"My sins have been bound into a yoke; by his hands they were woven together. They have come upon my neck and the Lord has sapped my strength. He has handed me over to those I cannot withstand."

Lam 3 [1]I am the man who has seen affliction by the rod of his wrath. [2]He has driven me away and made me walk in darkness rather than light; [3]indeed, he has turned his hand against me again and again, all day long.

John 9 [1]As he went along, he saw a man blind from birth. [2]His disciples asked him, "Rabbi, who sinned, this man or his parents, that he was born blind?"

[3]"Neither this man nor his parents sinned," said Jesus, "but this happened so that the work of God might be displayed in his life."

John 11 [4]When he heard this, Jesus said, "This sickness will not end in death. No, it is for God's glory so that God's Son may be glorified through it."

4. Providence Sustains in Suffering

2 Sam 22 [18]"He rescued me from my powerful enemy, from my foes, who were too strong for me. [19]They confronted me in the day of my disaster, but the LORD was my support."

2 Chron 30 [9]"If you return to the LORD, then your brothers and your children will be shown compassion by their captors and will come back to this land, for the LORD your God is gracious and compassionate. He will not turn his face from you if you return to him."

Job 15 [11]"Are God's consolations not enough for you, words spoken gently to you?"

Ps 23 [4]Even though I walk through the valley of the shadow of death, I will fear no evil, for you are with me; your rod and your staff, they comfort me.

Ps 37 [23]If the LORD delights in a man's way, he makes his steps firm; [24]though he stumble, he will not fall, for the LORD upholds him with his hand.

Ps 129 [1]They have greatly oppressed me from my youth—let Israel say—[2]they have greatly oppressed me from my youth, but they have not gained the victory over me. [3]Plowmen have plowed my back and made their furrows long. [4]But the LORD is righteous; he has cut me free from the cords of the wicked.

Ps 140 [12]I know that the LORD secures justice for the poor and upholds the cause of the needy.

Ps 145 [14]The LORD upholds all those who fall and lifts up all who are bowed down.

Isa 51 [12]"I, even I, am he who comforts you. Who are you that you fear mortal men, the sons of men, who are but grass, [13]that you forget the LORD your Maker, who stretched out the heavens and laid the foundations of the earth, that you live in constant terror every day because of the wrath of the oppressor, who is bent on destruction? For where is the wrath of the oppressor? [14]The cowering prisoners will soon be set free; they will not die in their dungeon, nor will they lack bread."

Isa 66 [13]"As a mother comforts her child, so will I comfort you; and you will be comforted over Jerusalem."

Jer 8 [18]O my Comforter in sorrow, my heart is faint within me.

Lam 3 [19]I remember my affliction and my wandering, the bitterness and the gall. [20]I well remember them, and my soul is downcast within me. [21]Yet this I call to mind and therefore I have hope:

[22]Because of the LORD's great love we are not consumed, for his compassions never fail. [23]They are new every morning; great is your faithfulness. [24]I say to myself, "The LORD is my portion; therefore I will wait for him."

[25]The LORD is good to those whose hope is in him, to the one who seeks him; [26]it is good to wait quietly for the salvation of the LORD. [27]It is good for a man to bear the yoke while he is young.

[28]Let him sit alone in silence, for the LORD has laid it on him.

2 Cor 1 [3]Praise be to the God and Father of our Lord Jesus Christ, the Father of compassion and the God of all comfort, [4]who comforts us in all our troubles, so that we can comfort those in any trouble with the comfort we ourselves have received from God. [5]For just as the sufferings of Christ flow over into our lives, so also through Christ our comfort overflows. [6]If we are distressed, it is for your comfort and salvation; if we are comforted, it is for your comfort, which produces in you patient endurance of the same sufferings we suffer. [7]And our hope for you is firm, because we know that just as you share in our sufferings, so also you share in our comfort.

2 Cor 6 [4]Rather, as servants of God we commend ourselves in every way: in great endurance; in troubles, hardships and distresses; [5]in beatings, imprisonments and riots; in hard work, sleepless nights and hunger; [6]in purity, understanding, patience and kindness; in the Holy Spirit and in sincere love; [7]in truthful speech and in the power of God; with weapons of righteousness in the right hand and in the left; [8]through glory and dishonor, bad report and good report; genuine, yet regarded as imposters; [9]known, yet regarded as unknown; dying, and yet we live on; beaten, and yet not killed; [10]sorrowful, yet always rejoicing; poor, yet making many rich; having nothing, and yet possessing everything.

2 Cor 12 [7]To keep me from becoming conceited because of these surpassingly great revelations, there was given me a thorn in my flesh, a messenger of Satan, to torment me. [8]Three times I pleaded with the Lord to take it away from me. [9]But he said to me, "My grace is sufficient for you, for my power is made perfect in weakness." Therefore I will boast all the more gladly about my weaknesses, so that Christ's power may rest on me. [10]That is why, for Christ's sake, I delight in weaknesses, in insults, in hardships, in persecutions, in difficulties. For when I am weak, then I am strong.

Phil 4 [19]And my God will meet all your needs according to his glorious riches in Christ Jesus.

5. Providence Teaches and Refines through Suffering

Deut 8 [5]Know then in your heart that as a man disciplines his son, so the LORD your God disciplines you.

Job 5 [17]"Blessed is the man whom God corrects; so do not despise the discipline of the Almighty. [18]For he wounds, but he also binds up; he injures, but his hands also heal."

Job 36 [8]"But if men are bound in chains, held fast by cords of affliction, [9]he tells them what they have done—that they have sinned arrogantly. [10]He makes them listen to correction and commands them to repent of their evil. . . . [12]But if they do not listen, they will perish by the sword and die without knowledge."

Ps 94 [12]Blessed is the man you discipline, O LORD, the man you

teach from your law; [13]you grant him relief from days of trouble, till a pit is dug for the wicked.
Ps 119 [67]Before I was afflicted I went astray, but now I obey your word. . . . [71]It was good for me to be afflicted so that I might learn your decrees.
Prov 3 [11]My son, do not despise the LORD's discipline and do not resent his rebuke, [12]because the LORD disciplines those he loves, as a father the son he delights in.
Isa 26 [8]Yes, LORD, walking in the way of your laws, we wait for you; your name and renown are the desire of our hearts. [9]My soul yearns for you in the night; in the morning my spirit longs for you. When your judgments come upon the earth, the people of the world learn righteousness. . . .

[16]LORD, they came to you in their distress; when you disciplined them, they could barely whisper a prayer.
Isa 48 [10]"See, I have refined you, though not as silver; I have tested you in the furnace of affliction."
Dan 11 [35]"Some of the wise will stumble, so that they may be refined, purified and made spotless until the time of the end, for it will still come at the appointed time."
Hos 5 [14]"For I will be like a lion to Ephraim, like a great lion to Judah. I will tear them to pieces and go away; I will carry them off, with no one to rescue them. [15]Then I will go back to my place until they admit their guilt. And they will seek my face; in their misery they will earnestly seek me."
Zech 13 [9]"This third I will bring into the fire; I will refine them like silver and test them like gold. They will call on my name and I will answer them; I will say, 'They are my people,' and they will say, 'The LORD is our God.'"
Mal 3 [2]But who can endure the day of his coming? Who can stand when he appears? For he will be like a refiner's fire or a launderer's soap. [3]He will sit as a refiner and purifier of silver; he will purify the Levites and refine them like gold and silver. Then the LORD will have men who will bring offerings in righteousness. . . .
Heb 12 [4]In your struggle against sin, you have not yet resisted to the point of shedding your blood. [5]And you have forgotten that word of encouragement that addresses you as sons: "My son, do not make light of the Lord's discipline, and do not lose heart when he rebukes you, [6]because the Lord disciplines those he loves, and he punishes everyone he accepts as a son."

[7]Endure hardship as discipline; God is treating you as sons. For what son is not disciplined by his father? [8]If you are not disciplined (and everyone undergoes discipline), then you are illegitimate children and not true sons. [9]Moreover, we have all had human fathers who disciplined us and we respected them for it. How much more should we submit to the Father of our spirits and live! [10]Our fathers disciplined us for a little while as they thought best; but God disciplines us for our good, that we may share in his holiness. [11]No discipline seems pleasant at the time, but painful. Later on, however, it produces a harvest of righteousness and peace for those who have been trained by it.

H. Miracles as a Special Providence of God

1. The Attestation of Miracles

Deut 4 [34]Has any god ever tried to take for himself one nation out of another nation, by testings, by miraculous signs and wonders, by war, by a mighty hand and an outstretched arm, or by great and awesome deeds, like all the things the LORD your God did for you in Egypt before your very eyes?
1 Chron 16 [11]Look to the LORD and his strength; seek his face always. [12]Remember the wonders he has done, his miracles, and the judgments he pronounced. . . .
Neh 9 [17]"They refused to listen and failed to remember the miracles you performed among them. They became stiff-necked and in their rebellion appointed a leader in order to return to their slavery. But you are a forgiving God, gracious and compassionate, slow to anger and abounding in love. Therefore you did not desert them. . . ."
Job 5 [9]"He performs wonders that cannot be fathomed, miracles that cannot be counted."
Ps 77 [11]I will remember the deeds of the LORD; yes, I will remember your miracles of long ago. . . . [14]You are the God who performs miracles; you display your power among the peoples.
Ps 78 [12]He did miracles in the sight of their fathers in the land of Egypt, in the region of Zoan.
Ps 106 [7]When our fathers were in Egypt, they gave no thought to your miracles; they did not remember your many kindnesses, and they rebelled by the sea, the Red Sea. . . . [21]They forgot the God who saved them, who had done great things in Egypt, [22]miracles in the land of Ham and awesome deeds by the Red Sea.
Ps 136 [3]Give thanks to the Lord of lords: *His love endures forever.* [4]to him who alone does great wonders, *His love endures forever.*
Matt 11 [20]Then Jesus began to denounce the cities in which most of his miracles had been performed, because they did not repent. [21]"Woe to you, Korazin! Woe to you, Bethsaida! If the miracles that were performed in you had been performed in Tyre and Sidon, they would have repented long ago in sackcloth and ashes. [22]But I tell you, it will be more bearable for Tyre and Sidon on the day of judgment than for you. [23]And you, Capernaum, will you be lifted up to the skies? No, you will go down to the depths. If the miracles that were performed in you had been performed in Sodom, it would have remained to this day."
Mark 6 [2]When the Sabbath came, he began to teach in the synagogue, and many who heard him were amazed.

"Where did this man get these things?" they asked. "What's this wisdom that has been given him, that he even does miracles!"
Luke 19 [37]When he came near the place where the road goes down the Mount of Olives, the whole crowd of disciples began joyfully to praise God in loud voices for all the miracles they had seen. . . .
John 10 [32]but Jesus said to them, "I have shown you many great miracles from the Father. For which of these do you stone me?"
John 20 [30]Jesus did many other miraculous signs in the presence of his disciples, which are not recorded in this book.
Acts 5 [12]The apostles performed many miraculous signs and wonders among the people. And all the believers used to meet together in Solomon's Colonnade.
Acts 6 [8]Now Stephen, a man full of God's grace and power, did great wonders and miraculous signs among the people.
Acts 15 [12]The whole assembly became silent as they listened to Barnabas and Paul telling about the miraculous signs and wonders God had done among the Gentiles through them.
1 Cor 12 [28]And in the church God has appointed first of all apostles, second prophets, third teachers, then workers of miracles, also those having gifts of healing, those able to help others, those with gifts of administration, and those speaking in different kinds of tongues. [29]Are all apostles? Are all prophets? Are all teachers? Do all work miracles?
2 Cor 12 [12]The things that mark an apostle—signs, wonders and miracles—were done among you with great perseverance.
Gal 3 [5]Does God give you his Spirit and work miracles among you because you observe the law, or because you believe what you heard?

2. Examples of Miracles

a) Miracles in Nature

Exod 4 [2]Then the LORD said to him, "What is that in your hand?"

"A staff," he replied.

[3]The LORD said, "Throw it on the ground."

Moses threw it on the ground and it became a snake, and he ran from it.
Exod 7 [20]Moses and Aaron did just as the LORD had commanded. He raised his staff in the presence of Pharaoh and his officials and struck the water of the Nile, and all the water was changed into blood.
Exod 8 [6]So Aaron stretched out his hand over the waters of Egypt, and the frogs came up and covered the land.
Exod 8 [24]And the LORD did this. Dense swarms of flies poured into Pharaoh's palace and into the houses of his officials, and throughout Egypt the land was ruined by the flies.

The Works of God

Exod 10 13So Moses stretched out his staff over Egypt, and the LORD made an east wind blow across the land all that day and all that night. By morning the wind had brought the locusts; 14they invaded all Egypt and settled down in every area of the country in great numbers. Never before had there been such a plague of locusts, nor will there ever be again.
Exod 14 21Then Moses stretched out his hand over the sea, and all that night the LORD drove the sea back with a strong east wind and turned it into dry land. The waters were divided, 22and the Israelites went through the sea on dry ground, with a wall of water on their right and on their left.
Exod 16 11The LORD said to Moses, 12"I have heard the grumbling of the Israelites. Tell them, 'At twilight you will eat meat, and in the morning you will be filled with bread. Then you will know that I am the LORD your God.'"

13That evening quail came and covered the camp, and in the morning there was a layer of dew around the camp. 14When the dew was gone, thin flakes like frost on the ground appeared on the desert floor. 15When the Israelites saw it, they said to each other, "What is it?" For they did not know what it was.

Moses said to them, "It is the bread the LORD has given you to eat."
Exod 17 6"I will stand there before you by the rock at Horeb. Strike the rock, and water will come out of it for the people to drink." So Moses did this in the sight of the elders of Israel.
Lev 9 24Fire came out from the presence of the LORD and consumed the burnt offering and the fat portions on the altar. And when all the people saw it, they shouted for joy and fell facedown.
Num 17 8The next day Moses entered the Tent of the Testimony and saw that Aaron's staff, which represented the house of Levi, had not only sprouted but had budded, blossomed and produced almonds.
Josh 3 14So when the people broke camp to cross the Jordan, the priests carrying the ark of the covenant went ahead of them. 15Now the Jordan is at flood stage all during harvest. Yet as soon as the priests who carried the ark reached the Jordan and their feet touched the water's edge, 16the water from upstream stopped flowing. It piled up in a heap a great distance away, at a town called Adam in the vicinity of Zarethan, while the water flowing down to the Sea of the Arabah (the Salt Sea) was completely cut off. So the people crossed over opposite Jericho.
Josh 10 13So the sun stood still, and the moon stopped, till the nation avenged itself on its enemies, as it is written in the Book of Jashar.

The sun stopped in the middle of the sky and delayed going down about a full day.
1 Kings 17 14"For this is what the LORD, the God of Israel, says: 'The jar of flour will not be used up and the jug of oil will not run dry until the day the LORD gives rain on the land.'"

15She went away and did as Elijah had told her. So there was food every day for Elijah and for the woman and her family. 16For the jar of flour was not used up and the jug of oil did not run dry, in keeping with the word of the LORD spoken by Elijah.
2 Kings 2 8Elijah took his cloak, rolled it up and struck the water with it. The water divided to the right and to the left, and the two of them crossed over on dry ground. . . . 11As they were walking along and talking together, suddenly a chariot of fire and horses of fire appeared and separated the two of them, and Elijah went up to heaven in a whirlwind.
2 Kings 2 19The men of the city said to Elisha, "Look, our lord, this town is well situated, as you can see, but the water is bad and the land is unproductive."

20"Bring me a new bowl," he said, "and put salt in it." So they brought it to him.

21Then he went out to the spring and threw the salt into it, saying, "This is what the LORD says: 'I have healed this water. Never again will it cause death or make the land unproductive.'" 22And the water has remained wholesome to this day, according to the word Elisha had spoken.
2 Kings 6 5As one of them was cutting down a tree, the iron axhead fell into the water. "Oh, my lord," he cried out, "it was borrowed!"

6The man of God asked, "Where did it fall?" When he showed him the place, Elisha cut a stick and threw it there, and made the iron float.
Ps 136 13to him who divided the Red Sea asunder *His love endures forever.* 14and brought Israel through the midst of it, *His love endures forever.*
Matt 14 22Immediately Jesus made the disciples get into the boat and go on ahead of him to the other side, while he dismissed the crowd. 23After he had dismissed them, he went up on a mountainside by himself to pray. When evening came, he was there alone, 24but the boat was already a considerable distance from land, buffeted by the waves because the wind was against it.

25During the fourth watch of the night Jesus went out to them, walking on the lake. 26When the disciples saw him walking on the lake, they were terrified. "It's a ghost," they said, and cried out in fear.

27But Jesus immediately said to them: "Take courage! It is I. Don't be afraid."

28"Lord, if it's you," Peter replied, "tell me to come to you on the water."

29"Come," he said.

Then Peter got down out of the boat, walked on the water and came toward Jesus. 30But when he saw the wind, he was afraid and, beginning to sink, cried out, "Lord, save me!"

31Immediately Jesus reached out his hand and caught him. "You of little faith," he said, "why did you doubt?"

32And when they climbed into the boat, the wind died down.
Matt 15 32Jesus called his disciples to him and said, "I have compassion for these people; they have already been with me three days and have nothing to eat. I do not want to send them away hungry, or they may collapse on the way."

33His disciples answered, "Where could we get enough bread in this remote place to feed such a crowd?"

34"How many loaves do you have?" Jesus asked.

"Seven," they replied, "and a few small fish."

35He told the crowd to sit down on the ground. 36Then he took the seven loaves and the fish, and when he had given thanks, he broke them and gave them to the disciples, and they in turn to the people. 37They all ate and were satisfied. Afterward the disciples picked up seven basketfuls of broken pieces that were left over. 38The number of those who ate was four thousand, besides women and children.
Matt 17 24After Jesus and his disciples arrived in Capernaum, the collectors of the two-drachma tax came to Peter and asked, "Doesn't your teacher pay the temple tax?"

25"Yes, he does," he replied.

When Peter came into the house, Jesus was the first to speak. "What do you think, Simon?" he asked. "From whom do the kings of the earth collect duty and taxes—from their own sons or from others?"

26"From others," Peter answered.

"Then the sons are exempt," Jesus said to him. 27"But so that we may not offend them, go to the lake and throw out your line. Take the first fish you catch; open its mouth and you will find a four-drachma coin. Take it and give it to them for my tax and yours."
Matt 21 18Early in the morning, as he was on his way back to the city, he was hungry. 19Seeing a fig tree by the road, he went up to it but found nothing on it except leaves. Then he said to it, "May you never bear fruit again!" Immediately the tree withered.
Mark 4 35That day when evening came, he said to his disciples, "Let us go over to the other side." 36Leaving the crowd behind, they took him along, just as he was, in the boat. There were also other boats with him. 37A furious squall came up, and the waves broke over the boat, so that it was nearly swamped. 38Jesus was in the stern, sleeping on a cushion. The disciples woke him and said to him, "Teacher, don't you care if we drown?"

39He got up, rebuked the wind and said to the waves, "Quiet! Be still!" Then the wind died down and it was completely calm.

40He said to his disciples, "Why are you so afraid? Do you still have no faith?"

[41]They were terrified and asked each other, "Who is this? Even the wind and the waves obey him!"

Luke 8 [22]One day Jesus said to his disciples, "Let's go over to the other side of the lake." So they got into a boat and set out. [23]As they sailed, he fell asleep. A squall came down on the lake, so that the boat was being swamped, and they were in great danger.

[24]The disciples went and woke him, saying, "Master, Master, we're going to drown!"

He got up and rebuked the wind and the raging waters; the storm subsided, and all was calm. [25]"Where is your faith?" he asked his disciples.

In fear and amazement they asked one another, "Who is this? He commands even the winds and the water, and they obey him."

John 2 [6]Nearby stood six stone water jars, the kind used by the Jews for ceremonial washing, each holding from twenty to thirty gallons.

[7]Jesus said to the servants, "Fill the jars with water"; so they filled them to the brim.

[8]Then he told them, "Now draw some out and take it to the master of the banquet."

They did so, [9]and the master of the banquet tasted the water that had been turned into wine. He did not realize where it had come from, though the servants who had drawn the water knew. Then he called the bridegroom aside [10]and said, "Everyone brings out the choice wine first and then the cheaper wine after the guests have had too much to drink; but you have saved the best till now."

John 21 [4]Early in the morning, Jesus stood on the shore, but the disciples did not realize that it was Jesus.

[5]He called out to them, "Friends, haven't you any fish?"

"No," they answered.

[6]He said, "Throw your net on the right side of the boat and you will find some." When they did, they were unable to haul the net in because of the large number of fish.

b) Miracles of Healing, Deliverance, and Restoration

2 Kings 5 [13]Naaman's servants went to him and said, "My father, if the prophet had told you to do some great thing, would you not have done it? How much more, then, when he tells you, 'Wash and be cleansed'!" [14]So he went down and dipped himself in the Jordan seven times, as the man of God had told him, and his flesh was restored and became clean like that of a young boy.

2 Kings 13 [21]Once while some Israelites were burying a man, suddenly they saw a band of raiders; so they threw the man's body into Elisha's tomb. When the body touched Elisha's bones, the man came to life and stood up on his feet.

Ps 136 [10]to him who struck down the firstborn of Egypt *His love endures forever.* [11]and brought Israel out from among them *His love endures forever.* [12]with a mighty hand and outstretched arm; *His love endures forever.*

Matt 4 [24]News about him spread all over Syria, and people brought to him all who were ill with various diseases, those suffering severe pain, the demon-possessed, those having seizures, and the paralyzed, and he healed them.

Matt 8 [16]When evening came, many who were demon-possessed were brought to him, and he drove out the spirits with a word and healed all the sick.

Matt 9 [23]When Jesus entered the ruler's house and saw the flute players and the noisy crowd, [24]he said, "Go away. The girl is not dead but asleep." But they laughed at him. [25]After the crowd had been put outside, he went in and took the girl by the hand, and she got up.

Matt 12 [15]Aware of this, Jesus withdrew from that place. Many followed him, and he healed all their sick. . . .

Matt 15 [28]Then Jesus answered, "Woman, you have great faith! Your request is granted." And her daughter was healed from that very hour.

Matt 15 [30]Great crowds came to him, bringing the lame, the blind, the crippled, the mute and many others, and laid them at his feet; and he healed them. [31]The people were amazed when they saw the mute speaking, the crippled made well, the lame walking and the blind seeing. And they praised the God of Israel.

Matt 21 [14]The blind and the lame came to him at the temple, and he healed them.

Mark 6 [55]They ran throughout that whole region and carried the sick on mats to wherever they heard he was. [56]And wherever he went—into villages, towns or countryside—they placed the sick in the marketplaces. They begged him to let them touch even the edge of his cloak, and all who touched him were healed.

Luke 22 [51]But Jesus answered, "No more of this!" And he touched the man's ear and healed him.

John 5 [8]Then Jesus said to him, "Get up! Pick up your mat and walk." [9]At once the man was cured; he picked up his mat and walked.

The day on which this took place was a Sabbath. . . .

John 11 [43]When he had said this, Jesus called in a loud voice, "Lazarus, come out!" [44]The dead man came out, his hands and feet wrapped with strips of linen, and a cloth around his face.

Jesus said to them, "Take off the grave clothes and let him go."

Acts 3 [6]Then Peter said, "Silver or gold I do not have, but what I have I give you. In the name of Jesus Christ of Nazareth, walk." [7]Taking him by the right hand, he helped him up, and instantly the man's feet and ankles became strong. [8]He jumped to his feet and began to walk. Then he went with them into the temple courts, walking and jumping, and praising God.

Acts 8 [7]With shrieks, evil spirits came out of many, and many paralytics and cripples were healed.

Acts 19 [11]God did extraordinary miracles through Paul, [12]so that even handkerchiefs and aprons that had touched him were taken to the sick, and their illnesses were cured and the evil spirits left them.

Acts 28 [8]His father was sick in bed, suffering from fever and dysentery. Paul went in to see him and, after prayer, placed his hands on him and healed him.

c) Miracles of Judgment

Exod 12 [29]At midnight the LORD struck down all the firstborn in Egypt, from the firstborn of Pharaoh, who sat on the throne, to the firstborn of the prisoner, who was in the dungeon, and the firstborn of all the livestock as well. [30]Pharaoh and all his officials and all the Egyptians got up during the night, and there was loud wailing in Egypt, for there was not a house without someone dead.

Num 16 [28]Then Moses said, "This is how you will know that the LORD has sent me to do all these things and that it was not my idea: [29]If these men die a natural death and experience only what usually happens to men, then the LORD has not sent me. [30]But if the LORD brings about something totally new, and the earth opens its mouth and swallows them, with everything that belongs to them, and they go down alive into the grave, then you will know that these men have treated the LORD with contempt."

[31]As soon as he finished saying all this, the ground under them split apart [32]and the earth opened its mouth and swallowed them, with their households and all Korah's men and all their possessions.

Josh 6 [2]Then the LORD said to Joshua, "See, I have delivered Jericho into your hands, along with its king and its fighting men. [3]March around the city once with all the armed men. Do this for six days. [4]Have seven priests carry trumpets of rams' horns in front of the ark. On the seventh day, march around the city seven times, with the priests blowing the trumpets. [5]When you hear them sound a long blast on the trumpets, have all the people give a loud shout; then the wall of the city will collapse and the people will go up, every man straight in." . . .

[20]When the trumpets sounded, the people shouted, and at the sound of the trumpet, when the people gave a loud shout, the wall collapsed; so every man charged straight in, and they took the city.

2 Kings 1 [10]Elijah answered the captain, "If I am a man of God, may fire come down from heaven and consume you and your fifty men!" Then fire fell from heaven and consumed the captain and his men.

[11]At this the king sent to Elijah another captain with his

fifty men. The captain said to him, "Man of God, this is what the king says, 'Come down at once!'"

12"If I am a man of God," Elijah replied, "may fire come down from heaven and consume you and your fifty men!" Then the fire of God fell from heaven and consumed him and his fifty men.

2 Kings 5 27"Naaman's leprosy will cling to you and to your descendants forever." Then Gehazi went from Elisha's presence and he was leprous, as white as snow.

2 Kings 6 18As the enemy came down toward him, Elisha prayed to the LORD, "Strike these people with blindness." So he struck them with blindness, as Elisha had asked.

2 Kings 19 35That night the angel of the LORD went out and put to death a hundred and eighty-five thousand men in the Assyrian camp. When the people got up the next morning—there were all the dead bodies!

Ps 136 17who struck down great kings, *His love endures forever.* 18and killed mighty kings—*His love endures forever.* 19Sihon king of the Amorites *His love endures forever.* 20and Og king of Bashan—*His love endures forever.*

Acts 13 8But Elymas the sorcerer (for that is what his name means) opposed them and tried to turn the proconsul from the faith. 9Then Saul, who was also called Paul, filled with the Holy Spirit, looked straight at Elymas and said, 10"You are a child of the devil and an enemy of everything that is right! You are full of all kinds of deceit and trickery. Will you never stop perverting the right ways of the Lord? 11Now the hand of the Lord is against you. You are going to be blind, and for a time you will be unable to see the light of the sun."

3. The Purpose of Miracles

a) Miracles Accredit God's Messengers

Deut 34 10Since then, no prophet has risen in Israel like Moses, whom the LORD knew face to face, 11who did all those miraculous signs and wonders the LORD sent him to do in Egypt—to Pharaoh and to all his officials and to his whole land. 12For no one has ever shown the mighty power or performed the awesome deeds that Moses did in the sight of all Israel.

1 Kings 18 36At the time of sacrifice, the prophet Elijah stepped forward and prayed: "O LORD, God of Abraham, Isaac and Israel, let it be known today that you are God in Israel and that I am your servant and have done all these things at your command. 37Answer me, O LORD, answer me, so these people will know that you, O LORD, are God, and that you are turning their hearts back again."

38Then the fire of the LORD fell and burned up the sacrifice, the wood, the stones and the soil, and also licked up the water in the trench.

39When all the people saw this, they fell prostrate and cried, "The LORD—he is God! The LORD—he is God!"

Acts 2 22"Men of Israel, listen to this: Jesus of Nazareth was a man accredited by God to you by miracles, wonders and signs, which God did among you through him, as you yourselves know."

Acts 2 42They devoted themselves to the apostles' teaching and to the fellowship, to the breaking of bread and to prayer. 43Everyone was filled with awe, and many wonders and miraculous signs were done by the apostles.

Acts 8 6When the crowds heard Philip and saw the miraculous signs he did, they all paid close attention to what he said. 7With shrieks, evil spirits came out of many, and many paralytics and cripples were healed. 8So there was great joy in that city.

b) Miracles Bring Glory to God

Exod 14 16"Raise your staff and stretch out your hand over the sea to divide the water so that the Israelites can go through the sea on dry ground. 17I will harden the hearts of the Egyptians so that they will go in after them. And I will gain glory through Pharaoh and all his army, through his chariots and his horsemen. 18The Egyptians will know that I am the LORD when I gain glory through Pharaoh, his chariots and his horsemen."

1 Kings 18 36At the time of sacrifice, the prophet Elijah stepped forward and prayed: "O LORD, God of Abraham, Isaac and Israel, let it be known today that you are God in Israel and that I am your servant and have done all these things at your command. 37Answer me, O LORD, answer me, so these people will know that you, O LORD, are God, and that you are turning their hearts back again."

38Then the fire of the LORD fell and burned up the sacrifice, the wood, the stones and the soil, and also licked up the water in the trench.

39When all the people saw this, they fell prostrate and cried, "The LORD—he is God! The LORD—he is God!"

Matt 15 30Great crowds came to him, bringing the lame, the blind, the crippled, the mute and many others, and laid them at his feet; and he healed them. 31The people were amazed when they saw the mute speaking, the crippled made well, the lame walking and the blind seeing. And they praised the God of Israel.

Acts 4 21After further threats they let them go. They could not decide how to punish them, because all the people were praising God for what had happened. 22For the man who was miraculously healed was over forty years old.

c) Miracles Confirm God's Message

2 Kings 20 9Isaiah answered, "This is the LORD's sign to you that the LORD will do what he has promised: Shall the shadow go forward ten steps, or shall it go back ten steps?"

10"It is a simple matter for the shadow to go forward ten steps," said Hezekiah. "Rather, have it go back ten steps."

11Then the prophet Isaiah called upon the LORD, and the LORD made the shadow go back the ten steps it had gone down on the stairway of Ahaz.

John 14 11"Believe me when I say that I am in the Father and the Father is in me; or at least believe on the evidence of the miracles themselves."

Acts 14 3So Paul and Barnabas spent considerable time there, speaking boldly for the Lord, who confirmed the message of his grace by enabling them to do miraculous signs and wonders.

Heb 2 2For if the message spoken by angels was binding, and every violation and disobedience received its just punishment, 3how shall we escape if we ignore such a great salvation? This salvation, which was first announced by the Lord, was confirmed to us by those who heard him. 4God also testified to it by signs, wonders and various miracles, and gifts of the Holy Spirit distributed according to his will.

d) Miracles Confirm Jesus' Life and Ministry

Matt 11 2When John heard in prison what Christ was doing, he sent his disciples 3to ask him, "Are you the one who was to come, or should we expect someone else?"

4Jesus replied, "Go back and report to John what you hear and see: 5The blind receive sight, the lame walk, those who have leprosy are cured, the deaf hear, the dead are raised, and the good news is preached to the poor."

John 10 25Jesus answered, "I did tell you, but you do not believe. The miracles I do in my Father's name speak for me. . . ."

John 10 37"Do not believe me unless I do what my Father does. 38But if I do it, even though you do not believe me, believe the miracles, that you may know and understand that the Father is in me, and I in the Father."

John 11 41So they took away the stone. Then Jesus looked up and said, "Father, I thank you that you have heard me. 42I knew that you always hear me, but I said this for the benefit of the people standing here, that they may believe that you sent me."

43When he had said this, Jesus called in a loud voice, "Lazarus, come out!" 44The dead man came out, his hands and feet wrapped with strips of linen, and a cloth around his face.

Jesus said to them, "Take off the grave clothes and let him go."

e) Miracles Demonstrate God's Presence

Exod 3 1Now Moses was tending the flock of Jethro his father-in-law, the priest of Midian, and he led the flock to the far side of the desert and came to Horeb, the mountain of God. 2There the angel of the LORD appeared to him in flames of fire from within a bush. Moses saw that though the bush was on fire it did not burn up. 3So Moses thought, "I will go over and see this strange sight—why the bush does not burn up."

4When the LORD saw that he had gone over to look, God called to him from within the bush, "Moses! Moses!"

And Moses said, "Here I am."

5"Do not come any closer," God said. "Take off your sandals, for the place where you are standing is holy ground." [6]Then he said, "I am the God of your father, the God of Abraham, the God of Isaac and the God of Jacob." At this, Moses hid his face, because he was afraid to look at God.

Deut 4 [34]Has any god ever tried to take for himself one nation out of another nation, by testings, by miraculous signs and wonders, by war, by a mighty hand and an outstretched arm, or by great and awesome deeds, like all the things the LORD your God did for you in Egypt before your very eyes? . . . [37]Because he loved your forefathers and chose their descendants after them, he brought you out of Egypt by his Presence and his great strength. . . .

Luke 11 [20]"But if I drive out demons by the finger of God, then the kingdom of God has come to you."

f) Miracles Promote Obedience and Faith

Exod 14 [31]And when the Israelites saw the great power the LORD displayed against the Egyptians, the people feared the LORD and put their trust in him and in Moses his servant.

Josh 4 [23]"For the LORD your God dried up the Jordan before you until you had crossed over. The LORD your God did to the Jordan just what he had done to the Red Sea when he dried it up before us until we had crossed over. [24]He did this so that all the peoples of the earth might know that the hand of the LORD is powerful and so that you might always fear the LORD your God."

Ps 105 [4]Look to the LORD and his strength; seek his face always.

[5]Remember the wonders he has done, his miracles, and the judgments he pronounced, [6]O descendants of Abraham his servant, O sons of Jacob, his chosen ones.

John 20 [30]Jesus did many other miraculous signs in the presence of his disciples, which are not recorded in this book. [31]But these are written that you may believe that Jesus is the Christ, the Son of God, and that by believing you may have life in his name.

Acts 13 [8]But Elymas the sorcerer (for that is what his name means) opposed them and tried to turn the proconsul from the faith. [9]Then Saul, who was also called Paul, filled with the Holy Spirit, looked straight at Elymas and said, . . . [11]"Now the hand of the Lord is against you. You are going to be blind, and for a time you will be unable to see the light of the sun."

Immediately mist and darkness came over him, and he groped about, seeking someone to lead him by the hand. [12]When the proconsul saw what had happened, he believed, for he was amazed at the teaching about the Lord.

Acts 16 [25]About midnight Paul and Silas were praying and singing hymns to God, and the other prisoners were listening to them. [26]Suddenly there was such a violent earthquake that the foundations of the prison were shaken. At once all the prison doors flew open, and everybody's chains came loose. [27]The jailer woke up, and when he saw the prison doors open, he drew his sword and was about to kill himself because he thought the prisoners had escaped. [28]But Paul shouted, "Don't harm yourself! We are all here!"

[29]The jailer called for lights, rushed in and fell trembling before Paul and Silas. [30]He then brought them out and asked, "Sirs, what must I do to be saved?"

[31]They replied, "Believe in the Lord Jesus, and you will be saved—you and your household." [32]Then they spoke the word of the Lord to him and to all the others in his house. [33]At that hour of the night the jailer took them and washed their wounds; then immediately he and all his family were baptized. [34]The jailer brought them into his house and set a meal before them; he was filled with joy because he had come to believe in God—he and his whole family.

Rom 15 [18]I will not venture to speak of anything except what Christ has accomplished through me in leading the Gentiles to obey God by what I have said and done—[19]by the power of signs and miracles, through the power of the Spirit. So from Jerusalem all the way around to Illyricum, I have fully proclaimed the gospel of Christ.

g) Miracles Prove God's Sovereignty

Exod 7 [5]"And the Egyptians will know that I am the LORD when I stretch out my hand against Egypt and bring the Israelites out of it."

Exod 7 [16]"Then say to him, 'The LORD, the God of the Hebrews, has sent me to say to you: Let my people go, so that they may worship me in the desert. But until now you have not listened. [17]This is what the LORD says: By this you will know that I am the LORD: With the staff that is in my hand I will strike the water of the Nile, and it will be changed into blood.'"

Exod 8 [10]"Tomorrow," Pharaoh said.

Moses replied, "It will be as you say, so that you may know there is no one like the LORD our God. [11]The frogs will leave you and your houses, your officials and your people; they will remain only in the Nile."

Deut 4 [34]Has any god ever tried to take for himself one nation out of another nation, by testings, by miraculous signs and wonders, by war, by a mighty hand and an outstretched arm, or by great and awesome deeds, like all the things the LORD your God did for you in Egypt before your very eyes?

[35]You were shown these things so that you might know that the LORD is God; besides him there is no other.

Deut 29 [5]During the forty years that I led you through the desert, your clothes did not wear out, nor did the sandals on your feet. [6]You ate no bread and drank no wine or other fermented drink. I did this so that you might know that I am the LORD your God.

Josh 3 [9]Joshua said to the Israelites, "Come here and listen to the words of the LORD your God. [10]This is how you will know that the living God is among you and that he will certainly drive out before you the Canaanites, Hittites, Hivites, Perizzites, Girgashites, Amorites and Jebusites. [11]See, the ark of the covenant of the Lord of all the earth will go into the Jordan ahead of you. [12]Now then, choose twelve men from the tribes of Israel, one from each tribe. [13]And as soon as the priests who carry the ark of the LORD—the Lord of all the earth—set foot in the Jordan, its waters flowing downstream will be cut off and stand up in a heap."

h) Miracles Strengthen God's People

Exod 6 [6]"Therefore, say to the Israelites: 'I am the LORD, and I will bring you out from under the yoke of the Egyptians. I will free you from being slaves to them, and I will redeem you with an outstretched arm and with mighty acts of judgment. [7]I will take you as my own people, and I will be your God. Then you will know that I am the LORD your God, who brought you out from under the yoke of the Egyptians.'"

Exod 10 [1]Then the LORD said to Moses, "Go to Pharaoh, for I have hardened his heart and the hearts of his officials so that I may perform these miraculous signs of mine among them [2]that you may tell your children and grandchildren how I dealt harshly with the Egyptians and how I performed my signs among them, and that you may know that I am the LORD."

Exod 29 [46]"They will know that I am the LORD their God, who brought them out of Egypt so that I might dwell among them. I am the LORD their God."

Deut 7 [17]You may say to yourselves, "These nations are stronger than we are. How can we drive them out?" [18]But do not be afraid of them; remember well what the LORD your God did to Pharaoh and to all Egypt. [19]You saw with your own eyes the great trials, the miraculous signs and wonders, the mighty hand and outstretched arm, with which the LORD your God brought you out. The LORD your God will do the same to all the peoples you now fear.

Acts 4 [13]When they saw the courage of Peter and John and realized that they were unschooled, ordinary men, they were astonished and they took note that these men had been with Jesus. [14]But since they could see the man who had been healed standing there with them, there was nothing they could say. [15]So they ordered them to withdraw from the Sanhedrin and then conferred together. [16]"What are we going to do with these men?" they asked. "Everybody living in Jerusalem knows they have done an outstanding miracle, and we cannot deny it. [17]But to stop this thing from spreading any further among the people, we must warn these men to speak no longer to anyone in this name."

[18]Then they called them in again and commanded them not to speak or teach at all in the name of Jesus. [19]But Peter and John replied, "Judge for yourselves whether it is right in God's sight to obey you rather than God. [20]For we cannot help speaking about what we have seen and heard."

5

The Revelation of God

I
The Modes of Revelation

A. Revelation through Angels

Job 33 [19]"Or a man may be chastened on a bed of pain with
constant distress in his bones, [20]so that his very being finds
food repulsive and his soul loathes the choicest meal. [21]His
flesh wastes away to nothing, and his bones, once hidden, now
stick out. [22]His soul draws near to the pit, and his life to the
messengers of death.

[23]"Yet if there is an angel on his side as a mediator, one out
of a thousand, to tell a man what is right for him, [24]to be gracious to him and say, 'Spare him from going down to the pit; I
have found a ransom for him'—[25]then his flesh is renewed like
a child's; it is restored as in the days of his youth."

Dan 4 [13]"In the visions I saw while lying in my bed, I looked,
and there before me was a messenger, a holy one, coming down
from heaven. [14]He called in a loud voice: 'Cut down the tree
and trim off its branches; strip off its leaves and scatter its fruit.
Let the animals flee from under it and the birds from its
branches. [15]But let the stump and its roots, bound with iron
and bronze, remain in the ground, in the grass of the field.

"'Let him be drenched with the dew of heaven, and let him
live with the animals among the plants of the earth. [16]Let his
mind be changed from that of a man and let him be given the
mind of an animal, till seven times pass by for him.

[17]"'The decision is announced by messengers, the holy ones
declare the verdict, so that the living may know that the Most
High is sovereign over the kingdoms of men and gives them to
anyone he wishes and sets over them the lowliest of men.'"

Dan 8 [15]While I, Daniel, was watching the vision and trying to
understand it, there before me stood one who looked like a
man. [16]And I heard a man's voice from the Ulai calling,
"Gabriel, tell this man the meaning of the vision."

Dan 9 [21]while I was still in prayer, Gabriel, the man I had
seen in the earlier vision, came to me in swift flight about the
time of the evening sacrifice. [22]He instructed me and said to
me, "Daniel, I have now come to give you insight and understanding. [23]As soon as you began to pray, an answer was
given, which I have come to tell you, for you are highly
esteemed. Therefore, consider the message and understand
the vision. . . ."

Dan 10 [5]I looked up and there before me was a man dressed in
linen, with a belt of the finest gold around his waist. [6]His body
was like chrysolite, his face like lightning, his eyes like flaming
torches, his arms and legs like the gleam of burnished bronze,
and his voice like the sound of a multitude. . . .

[10]A hand touched me and set me trembling on my hands

and knees. 11He said, "Daniel, you who are highly esteemed, consider carefully the words I am about to speak to you, and stand up, for I have now been sent to you." And when he said this to me, I stood up trembling.

Zech 1 9I asked, "What are these, my lord?"

The angel who was talking with me answered, "I will show you what they are."

10Then the man standing among the myrtle trees explained, "They are the ones the LORD has sent to go throughout the earth."

11And they reported to the angel of the LORD, who was standing among the myrtle trees, "We have gone throughout the earth and found the whole world at rest and in peace."

12Then the angel of the LORD said, "LORD Almighty, how long will you withhold mercy from Jerusalem and from the towns of Judah, which you have been angry with these seventy years?" 13So the LORD spoke kind and comforting words to the angel who talked with me.

14Then the angel who was speaking to me said, "Proclaim this word: This is what the LORD Almighty says: 'I am very jealous for Jerusalem and Zion, 15but I am very angry with the nations that feel secure. I was only a little angry, but they added to the calamity.'

16"Therefore, this is what the LORD says: 'I will return to Jerusalem with mercy, and there my house will be rebuilt. And the measuring line will be stretched out over Jerusalem,' declares the LORD Almighty.

17"Proclaim further: This is what the LORD Almighty says: 'My towns will again overflow with prosperity, and the LORD will again comfort Zion and choose Jerusalem.'"

18Then I looked up—and there before me were four horns! 19I asked the angel who was speaking to me, "What are these?"

He answered me, "These are the horns that scattered Judah, Israel and Jerusalem."

20Then the LORD showed me four craftsmen. 21I asked, "What are these coming to do?"

He answered, "These are the horns that scattered Judah so that no one could raise his head, but the craftsmen have come to terrify them and throw down these horns of the nations who lifted up their horns against the land of Judah to scatter its people."

Luke 1 11Then an angel of the Lord appeared to him, standing at the right side of the altar of incense. 12When Zechariah saw him, he was startled and was gripped with fear. 13But the angel said to him: "Do not be afraid, Zechariah; your prayer has been heard. Your wife Elizabeth will bear you a son, and you are to give him the name John. . . ."

18Zechariah asked the angel, "How can I be sure of this? I am an old man and my wife is well along in years."

19The angel answered, "I am Gabriel. I stand in the presence of God, and I have been sent to speak to you and to tell you this good news."

Acts 7 53". . . you who have received the law that was put into effect through angels but have not obeyed it."

Acts 8 26Now an angel of the Lord said to Philip, "Go south to the road—the desert road—that goes down from Jerusalem to Gaza."

Acts 23 9There was a great uproar, and some of the teachers of the law who were Pharisees stood up and argued vigorously. "We find nothing wrong with this man," they said. "What if a spirit or an angel has spoken to him?"

Acts 27 23"Last night an angel of the God whose I am and whom I serve stood beside me 24and said, 'Do not be afraid, Paul. You must stand trial before Caesar; and God has graciously given you the lives of all who sail with you.'"

Gal 3 19What, then, was the purpose of the law? It was added because of transgressions until the Seed to whom the promise referred had come. The law was put into effect through angels by a mediator.

Heb 2 2For if the message spoken by angels was binding, and every violation and disobedience received its just punishment, 3how shall we escape if we ignore such a great salvation? This salvation, which was first announced by the Lord, was confirmed to us by those who heard him.

Rev 1 1The revelation of Jesus Christ, which God gave him to show his servants what must soon take place. He made it known by sending his angel to his servant John. . . .

Rev 5 2And I saw a mighty angel proclaiming in a loud voice, "Who is worthy to break the seals and open the scroll?" . . .

11Then I looked and heard the voice of many angels, numbering thousands upon thousands, and ten thousand times ten thousand. They encircled the throne and the living creatures and the elders. 12In a loud voice they sang: "Worthy is the Lamb, who was slain, to receive power and wealth and wisdom and strength and honor and glory and praise!"

Rev 7 11All the angels were standing around the throne and around the elders and the four living creatures. They fell down on their faces before the throne and worshiped God, 12saying: "Amen! Praise and glory and wisdom and thanks and honor and power and strength be to our God for ever and ever. Amen!"

Rev 22 6The angel said to me, "These words are trustworthy and true. The Lord, the God of the spirits of the prophets, sent his angel to show his servants the things that must soon take place." . . .

8I, John, am the one who heard and saw these things. And when I had heard and seen them, I fell down to worship at the feet of the angel who had been showing them to me. 9But he said to me, "Do not do it! I am a fellow servant with you and with your brothers the prophets and of all who keep the words of this book. Worship God!"

Rev 22 16"I, Jesus, have sent my angel to give you this testimony for the churches. I am the Root and the Offspring of David, and the bright Morning Star."

B. Revelation through Christian Experience

Matt 5 13"You are the salt of the earth. But if the salt loses its saltiness, how can it be made salty again? It is no longer good for anything, except to be thrown out and trampled by men.

14"You are the light of the world. A city on a hill cannot be hidden. 15Neither do people light a lamp and put it under a bowl. Instead they put it on its stand, and it gives light to everyone in the house. 16In the same way, let your light shine before men, that they may see your good deeds and praise your Father in heaven."

John 3 21"But whoever lives by the truth comes into the light, so that it may be seen plainly that what he has done has been done through God."

John 7 17"If anyone chooses to do God's will, he will find out whether my teaching comes from God or whether I speak on my own."

Rom 8 13For if you live according to the sinful nature, you will die; but if by the Spirit you put to death the misdeeds of the body, you will live, 14because those who are led by the Spirit of God are sons of God. 15For you did not receive a spirit that makes you a slave again to fear, but you received the Spirit of sonship. And by him we cry, "*Abba,* Father." 16The Spirit himself testifies with our spirit that we are God's children. 17Now if we are children, then we are heirs—heirs of God and co-heirs with Christ, if indeed we share in his sufferings in order that we may also share in his glory.

1 Cor 2 9However, as it is written: "No eye has seen, no ear has heard, no mind has conceived what God has prepared for those who love him"—10but God has revealed it to us by his Spirit.

The Spirit searches all things, even the deep things of God. 11For who among men knows the thoughts of a man except the man's spirit within him? In the same way no one knows the thoughts of God except the Spirit of God. 12We have not received the spirit of the world but the Spirit who is from God, that we may understand what God has freely given us. 13This is what we speak, not in words taught us by human wisdom but in words taught by the Spirit, expressing spiritual truths in spiritual words. 14The man without the Spirit does not accept the things that come from the Spirit of God, for they are foolishness to him, and he cannot understand them, because they are spiritually discerned. 15The spiritual man makes judgments about all things, but he himself is not subject to any man's

judgment: 16“For who has known the mind of the Lord that he may instruct him?” But we have the mind of Christ.
2 Cor 4 4The god of this age has blinded the minds of unbelievers, so that they cannot see the light of the gospel of the glory of Christ, who is the image of God. 5For we do not preach ourselves, but Jesus Christ as Lord, and ourselves as your servants for Jesus' sake. 6For God, who said, “Let light shine out of darkness,” made his light shine in our hearts to give us the light of the knowledge of the glory of God in the face of Christ. . . . 10We always carry around in our body the death of Jesus, so that the life of Jesus may also be revealed in our body. 11For we who are alive are always being given over to death for Jesus' sake, so that his life may be revealed in our mortal body.
Gal 4 4But when the time had fully come, God sent his Son, born of a woman, born under law, 5to redeem those under law, that we might receive the full rights of sons. 6Because you are sons, God sent the Spirit of his Son into our hearts, the Spirit who calls out, “*Abba,* Father.”
Eph 1 17I keep asking that the God of our Lord Jesus Christ, the glorious Father, may give you the Spirit of wisdom and revelation, so that you may know him better.
Phil 3 15All of us who are mature should take such a view of things. And if on some point you think differently, that too God will make clear to you.
Heb 11 6And without faith it is impossible to please God, because anyone who comes to him must believe that he exists and that he rewards those who earnestly seek him.
2 Pet 1 16We did not follow cleverly invented stories when we told you about the power and coming of our Lord Jesus Christ, but we were eyewitnesses of his majesty. 17For he received honor and glory from God the Father when the voice came to him from the Majestic Glory, saying, “This is my Son, whom I love; with him I am well pleased.” 18We ourselves heard this voice that came from heaven when we were with him on the sacred mountain.

19And we have the word of the prophets made more certain, and you will do well to pay attention to it, as to a light shining in a dark place, until the day dawns and the morning star rises in your hearts.
1 John 2 23No one who denies the Son has the Father; whoever acknowledges the Son has the Father also. . . .

26I am writing these things to you about those who are trying to lead you astray. 27As for you, the anointing you received from him remains in you, and you do not need anyone to teach you. But as his anointing teaches you about all things and as that anointing is real, not counterfeit—just as it has taught you, remain in him.
1 John 5 10Anyone who believes in the Son of God has this testimony in his heart. Anyone who does not believe God has made him out to be a liar, because he has not believed the testimony God has given about his Son. 11And this is the testimony: God has given us eternal life, and this life is in his Son. 12He who has the Son has life; he who does not have the Son of God does not have life. . . .

18We know that anyone born of God does not continue to sin; the one who was born of God keeps him safe, and the evil one cannot harm him. 19We know that we are children of God, and that the whole world is under the control of the evil one. 20We know also that the Son of God has come and has given us understanding, so that we may know him who is true. And we are in him who is true—even in his Son Jesus Christ. He is the true God and eternal life.

C. Revelation through Deep Sleep

Gen 15 12As the sun was setting, Abram fell into a deep sleep, and a thick and dreadful darkness came over him. 13Then the LORD said to him, “Know for certain that your descendants will be strangers in a country not their own, and they will be enslaved and mistreated four hundred years. 14But I will punish the nation they serve as slaves, and afterward they will come out with great possessions. 15You, however, will go to your fathers in peace and be buried at a good old age. 16In the fourth generation your descendants will come back here, for the sin of the Amorites has not yet reached its full measure.”
Job 4 12“A word was secretly brought to me, my ears caught a whisper of it. 13Amid disquieting dreams in the night, when deep sleep falls on men, 14fear and trembling seized me and made all my bones shake. 15A spirit glided past my face, and the hair on my body stood on end. 16It stopped, but I could not tell what it was. A form stood before my eyes, and I heard a hushed voice. . . .”
Job 33 14“For God does speak—now one way, now another—though man may not perceive it. 15In a dream, in a vision of the night, when deep sleep falls on men as they slumber in their beds, 16he may speak in their ears and terrify them with warnings, 17to turn man from wrongdoing and keep him from pride, 18to preserve his soul from the pit, his life from perishing by the sword.”
Dan 8 18While he was speaking to me, I was in a deep sleep, with my face to the ground. Then he touched me and raised me to my feet.

19He said: “I am going to tell you what will happen later in the time of wrath, because the vision concerns the appointed time of the end.”
Dan 10 9Then I heard him speaking, and as I listened to him, I fell into a deep sleep, my face to the ground.

10A hand touched me and set me trembling on my hands and knees. 11He said, “Daniel, you who are highly esteemed, consider carefully the words I am about to speak to you, and stand up, for I have now been sent to you.” And when he said this to me, I stood up trembling.

D. Revelation through Direct Speech

Gen 3 8Then the man and his wife heard the sound of the LORD God as he was walking in the garden in the cool of the day, and they hid from the LORD God among the trees of the garden. 9But the LORD God called to the man, “Where are you?”

10He answered, “I heard you in the garden, and I was afraid because I was naked; so I hid.”

11And he said, “Who told you that you were naked? Have you eaten from the tree that I commanded you not to eat from?”

12The man said, “The woman you put here with me—she gave me some fruit from the tree, and I ate it.”

13Then the LORD God said to the woman, “What is this you have done?”

The woman said, “The serpent deceived me, and I ate.”
Gen 6 13So God said to Noah, “I am going to put an end to all people, for the earth is filled with violence because of them. I am surely going to destroy both them and the earth.”
Gen 12 1The LORD had said to Abram, “Leave your country, your people and your father's household and go to the land I will show you.

2“I will make you into a great nation and I will bless you; I will make your name great, and you will be a blessing. 3I will bless those who bless you, and whoever curses you I will curse; and all peoples on earth will be blessed through you.”

4So Abram left, as the LORD had told him; and Lot went with him. Abram was seventy-five years old when he set out from Haran.
Gen 22 1Some time later God tested Abraham. He said to him, “Abraham!”

“Here I am,” he replied.

2Then God said, “Take your son, your only son, Isaac, whom you love, and go to the region of Moriah. Sacrifice him there as a burnt offering on one of the mountains I will tell you about.” . . .

9When they reached the place God had told him about, Abraham built an altar there and arranged the wood on it. He bound his son Isaac and laid him on the altar, on top of the wood. . . . 11But the angel of the LORD called out to him from heaven, “Abraham! Abraham!”

“Here I am,” he replied.

12“Do not lay a hand on the boy,” he said. “Do not do anything to him. Now I know that you fear God, because you have not withheld from me your son, your only son.” . . .

15The angel of the LORD called to Abraham from heaven a second time 16and said, “I swear by myself, declares the LORD, that because you have done this and have not withheld your son, your only son, 17I will surely bless you and make your descendants as numerous as the stars in the sky and as the sand on the seashore. Your descendants will take possession of the cities of their enemies, 18and through your offspring all nations on earth will be blessed, because you have obeyed me."

Gen 35 9After Jacob returned from Paddan Aram, God appeared to him again and blessed him. 10God said to him, "Your name is Jacob, but you will no longer be called Jacob; your name will be Israel." So he named him Israel.

11And God said to him, "I am God Almighty; be fruitful and increase in number. A nation and a community of nations will come from you, and kings will come from your body."

Num 7 89When Moses entered the Tent of Meeting to speak with the LORD, he heard the voice speaking to him from between the two cherubim above the atonement cover on the ark of the Testimony. And he spoke with him.

Num 12 5Then the LORD came down in a pillar of cloud; he stood at the entrance to the Tent and summoned Aaron and Miriam. When both of them stepped forward, 6he said, "Listen to my words: When a prophet of the LORD is among you, I reveal myself to him in visions, I speak to him in dreams. 7But this is not true of my servant Moses; he is faithful in all my house. 8With him I speak face to face, clearly and not in riddles; he sees the form of the LORD. Why then were you not afraid to speak against my servant Moses?"

Num 22 4The Moabites said to the elders of Midian, "This horde is going to lick up everything around us, as an ox licks up the grass of the field."

So Balak son of Zippor, who was king of Moab at that time, 5sent messengers to summon Balaam son of Beor, who was at Pethor, near the River, in his native land. Balak said: "A people has come out of Egypt; they cover the face of the land and have settled next to me. 6Now come and put a curse on these people, because they are too powerful for me. Perhaps then I will be able to defeat them and drive them out of the country. For I know that those you bless are blessed, and those you curse are cursed."

7The elders of Moab and Midian left, taking with them the fee for divination. When they came to Balaam, they told him what Balak had said.

8"Spend the night here," Balaam said to them, "and I will bring you back the answer the LORD gives me." So the Moabite princes stayed with him.

9God came to Balaam and asked, "Who are these men with you?"

10Balaam said to God, "Balak son of Zippor, king of Moab, sent me this message: 11'A people that has come out of Egypt covers the face of the land. Now come and put a curse on them for me. Perhaps then I will be able to fight them and drive them away.'"

12But God said to Balaam, "Do not go with them. You must not put a curse on those people, because they are blessed."

1 Sam 3 2One night Eli, whose eyes were becoming so weak that he could barely see, was lying down in his usual place. 3The lamp of God had not yet gone out, and Samuel was lying down in the temple of the LORD, where the ark of God was. 4Then the LORD called Samuel.

Samuel answered, "Here I am." 5And he ran to Eli and said, "Here I am; you called me."

But Eli said, "I did not call; go back and lie down." So he went and lay down.

6Again the LORD called, "Samuel!" And Samuel got up and went to Eli and said, "Here I am; you called me."

"My son," Eli said, "I did not call; go back and lie down."

7Now Samuel did not yet know the LORD: The word of the LORD had not yet been revealed to him.

8The LORD called Samuel a third time, and Samuel got up and went to Eli and said, "Here I am; you called me."

Then Eli realized that the LORD was calling the boy. 9So Eli told Samuel, "Go and lie down, and if he calls you, say, 'Speak, LORD, for your servant is listening.'" So Samuel went and lay down in his place.

10The LORD came and stood there, calling as at the other times, "Samuel! Samuel!"

Then Samuel said, "Speak, for your servant is listening."

11And the LORD said to Samuel: "See, I am about to do something in Israel that will make the ears of everyone who hears of it tingle. 12At that time I will carry out against Eli everything I spoke against his family—from beginning to end. 13For I told him that I would judge his family forever because of the sin he knew about; his sons made themselves contemptible, and he failed to restrain them. 14Therefore, I swore to the house of Eli, 'The guilt of Eli's house will never be atoned for by sacrifice or offering.'" . . . 21The LORD continued to appear at Shiloh, and there he revealed himself to Samuel through his word.

Job 33 14"For God does speak—now one way, now another—though man may not perceive it."

Isa 7 3Then the LORD said to Isaiah, "Go out, you and your son Shear-Jashub, to meet Ahaz at the end of the aqueduct of the Upper Pool, on the road to the Washerman's Field. 4Say to him, 'Be careful, keep calm and don't be afraid. Do not lose heart because of these two smoldering stubs of firewood—because of the fierce anger of Rezin and Aram and of the son of Remaliah. . . .'"

10Again the LORD spoke to Ahaz. . . .

Isa 8 1The LORD said to me, "Take a large scroll and write on it with an ordinary pen: Maher-Shalal-Hash-Baz. 2And I will call in Uriah the priest and Zechariah son of Jeberekiah as reliable witnesses for me."

Isa 8 11The LORD spoke to me with his strong hand upon me, warning me not to follow the way of this people. He said: 12"Do not call conspiracy everything that these people call conspiracy; do not fear what they fear, and do not dread it."

Isa 22 14The LORD Almighty has revealed this in my hearing: "Till your dying day this sin will not be atoned for," says the Lord, the LORD Almighty.

Jer 1 4The word of the LORD came to me, saying, 5"Before I formed you in the womb I knew you, before you were born I set you apart; I appointed you as a prophet to the nations."

6"Ah, Sovereign LORD," I said, "I do not know how to speak; I am only a child."

7But the LORD said to me, "Do not say, 'I am only a child.' You must go to everyone I send you to and say whatever I command you. 8Do not be afraid of them, for I am with you and will rescue you," declares the LORD.

9Then the LORD reached out his hand and touched my mouth and said to me, "Now, I have put my words in your mouth. 10See, today I appoint you over nations and kingdoms to uproot and tear down, to destroy and overthrow, to build and to plant."

11The word of the LORD came to me: "What do you see, Jeremiah?"

"I see the branch of an almond tree," I replied.

12The LORD said to me, "You have seen correctly, for I am watching to see that my word is fulfilled."

13The word of the LORD came to me again: "What do you see?"

"I see a boiling pot, tilting away from the north," I answered.

14The LORD said to me, "From the north disaster will be poured out on all who live in the land. 15I am about to summon all the peoples of the northern kingdoms," declares the LORD.

"Their kings will come and set up their thrones in the entrance of the gates of Jerusalem; they will come against all her surrounding walls and against all the towns of Judah."

Ezek 6 1The word of the LORD came to me: 2"Son of man, set your face against the mountains of Israel; prophesy against them 3and say: 'O mountains of Israel, hear the word of the Sovereign LORD. This is what the Sovereign LORD says to the mountains and hills, to the ravines and valleys: I am about to bring a sword against you, and I will destroy your high places.'"

Matt 3 16As soon as Jesus was baptized, he went up out of the water. At that moment heaven was opened, and he saw the Spirit of God descending like a dove and lighting on him. 17And a voice from heaven said, "This is my Son, whom I love; with him I am well pleased."

Matt 17 5While he was still speaking, a bright cloud enveloped them, and a voice from the cloud said, "This is my Son, whom I love; with him I am well pleased. Listen to him!"

Acts 9 3As he neared Damascus on his journey, suddenly a light from heaven flashed around him. 4He fell to the ground and heard a voice say to him, "Saul, Saul, why do you persecute me?"

[5]"Who are you, Lord?" Saul asked.

"I am Jesus, whom you are persecuting," he replied. [6]"Now get up and go into the city, and you will be told what you must do."

Acts 10 [19]While Peter was still thinking about the vision, the Spirit said to him, "Simon, three men are looking for you. [20]So get up and go downstairs. Do not hesitate to go with them, for I have sent them."

E. Revelation through Divine Confrontation

Gen 3 [8]Then the man and his wife heard the sound of the LORD God as he was walking in the garden in the cool of the day, and they hid from the LORD God among the trees of the garden.

Gen 18 [1]The LORD appeared to Abraham near the great trees of Mamre while he was sitting at the entrance to his tent in the heat of the day.

Gen 32 [22]That night Jacob got up and took his two wives, his two maidservants and his eleven sons and crossed the ford of the Jabbok. [23]After he had sent them across the stream, he sent over all his possessions. [24]So Jacob was left alone, and a man wrestled with him till daybreak. [25]When the man saw that he could not overpower him, he touched the socket of Jacob's hip so that his hip was wrenched as he wrestled with the man. [26]Then the man said, "Let me go, for it is daybreak."

But Jacob replied, "I will not let you go unless you bless me."

[27]The man asked him, "What is your name?"

"Jacob," he answered.

[28]Then the man said, "Your name will no longer be Jacob, but Israel, because you have struggled with God and with men and have overcome."

[29]Jacob said, "Please tell me your name."

But he replied, "Why do you ask my name?" Then he blessed him there.

[30]So Jacob called the place Peniel, saying, "It is because I saw God face to face, and yet my life was spared."

Gen 35 [7]There he built an altar, and he called the place El Bethel, because it was there that God revealed himself to him when he was fleeing from his brother.

Exod 24 [9]Moses and Aaron, Nadab and Abihu, and the seventy elders of Israel went up [10]and saw the God of Israel. Under his feet was something like a pavement made of sapphire, clear as the sky itself. [11]But God did not raise his hand against these leaders of the Israelites; they saw God, and they ate and drank.

1 Sam 3 [21]The LORD continued to appear at Shiloh, and there he revealed himself to Samuel through his word.

2 Kings 8 [10]Elisha answered, "Go and say to him, 'You will certainly recover'; but the LORD has revealed to me that he will in fact die."

Ps 98 [2]The LORD has made his salvation known and revealed his righteousness to the nations.

Dan 2 [27]Daniel replied, "No wise man, enchanter, magician or diviner can explain to the king the mystery he has asked about, [28]but there is a God in heaven who reveals mysteries. He has shown King Nebuchadnezzar what will happen in days to come. Your dream and the visions that passed through your mind as you lay on your bed are these. . . . [30]As for me, this mystery has been revealed to me, not because I have greater wisdom than other living men, but so that you, O king, may know the interpretation and that you may understand what went through your mind."

Amos 4 [13]He who forms the mountains, creates the wind, and reveals his thoughts to man, he who turns dawn to darkness, and treads the high places of the earth—the LORD God Almighty is his name.

Matt 16 [16]Simon Peter answered, "You are the Christ, the Son of the living God."

[17]Jesus replied, "Blessed are you, Simon son of Jonah, for this was not revealed to you by man, but by my Father in heaven."

Luke 2 [26]It had been revealed to him by the Holy Spirit that he would not die before he had seen the Lord's Christ.

Acts 26 [15]"Then I asked, 'Who are you, Lord?'

"'I am Jesus, whom you are persecuting,' the Lord replied. [16]'Now get up and stand on your feet. I have appeared to you to appoint you as a servant and as a witness of what you have seen of me and what I will show you. [17]I will rescue you from your own people and from the Gentiles. I am sending you to them [18]to open their eyes and turn them from darkness to light, and from the power of Satan to God, so that they may receive forgiveness of sins and a place among those who are sanctified by faith in me.'"

Gal 1 [11]I want you to know, brothers, that the gospel I preached is not something that man made up. [12]I did not receive it from any man, nor was I taught it; rather, I received it by revelation from Jesus Christ.

Gal 2 [2]I went in response to a revelation and set before them the gospel that I preach among the Gentiles. But I did this privately to those who seemed to be leaders, for fear that I was running or had run my race in vain.

Eph 3 [2]Surely you have heard about the administration of God's grace that was given to me for you, [3]that is, the mystery made known to me by revelation, as I have already written briefly. [4]In reading this, then, you will be able to understand my insight into the mystery of Christ, [5]which was not made known to men in other generations as it has now been revealed by the Spirit to God's holy apostles and prophets.

F. Revelation through Dreams

Gen 20 [3]But God came to Abimelech in a dream one night and said to him, "You are as good as dead because of the woman you have taken; she is a married woman."

[4]Now Abimelech had not gone near her, so he said, "Lord, will you destroy an innocent nation? [5]Did he not say to me, 'She is my sister,' and didn't she also say, 'He is my brother'? I have done this with a clear conscience and clean hands."

[6]Then God said to him in the dream, "Yes, I know you did this with a clear conscience, and so I have kept you from sinning against me. That is why I did not let you touch her. [7]Now return the man's wife, for he is a prophet, and he will pray for you and you will live. But if you do not return her, you may be sure that you and all yours will die."

Gen 28 [10]Jacob left Beersheba and set out for Haran. [11]When he reached a certain place, he stopped for the night because the sun had set. Taking one of the stones there, he put it under his head and lay down to sleep. [12]He had a dream in which he saw a stairway resting on the earth, with its top reaching to heaven, and the angels of God were ascending and descending on it. [13]There above it stood the LORD, and he said: "I am the LORD, the God of your father Abraham and the God of Isaac. I will give you and your descendants the land on which you are lying. [14]Your descendants will be like the dust of the earth, and you will spread out to the west and to the east, to the north and to the south. All peoples on earth will be blessed through you and your offspring. [15]I am with you and will watch over you wherever you go, and I will bring you back to this land. I will not leave you until I have done what I have promised you."

[16]When Jacob awoke from his sleep, he thought, "Surely the LORD is in this place, and I was not aware of it." [17]He was afraid and said, "How awesome is this place! This is none other than the house of God; this is the gate of heaven."

Gen 31 [10]"In breeding season I once had a dream in which I looked up and saw that the male goats mating with the flock were streaked, speckled or spotted. [11]The angel of God said to me in the dream, 'Jacob.' I answered, 'Here I am.' [12]And he said, 'Look up and see that all the male goats mating with the flock are streaked, speckled or spotted, for I have seen all that Laban has been doing to you. [13]I am the God of Bethel, where you anointed a pillar and where you made a vow to me. Now leave this land at once and go back to your native land.'"

Gen 31 [24]Then God came to Laban the Aramean in a dream at night and said to him, "Be careful not to say anything to Jacob, either good or bad."

Gen 37 [5]Joseph had a dream, and when he told it to his brothers, they hated him all the more. [6]He said to them, "Listen to this dream I had: [7]We were binding sheaves of grain out in the

field when suddenly my sheaf rose and stood upright, while your sheaves gathered around mine and bowed down to it."
Gen 40 [4]The captain of the guard assigned them to Joseph, and he attended them.

After they had been in custody for some time, [5]each of the two men—the cupbearer and the baker of the king of Egypt, who were being held in prison—had a dream the same night, and each dream had a meaning of its own.

[6]When Joseph came to them the next morning, he saw that they were dejected. . . .

[8]"We both had dreams," they answered, "but there is no one to interpret them."

Then Joseph said to them, "Do not interpretations belong to God? Tell me your dreams."
Gen 41 [1]When two full years had passed, Pharaoh had a dream: He was standing by the Nile, [2]when out of the river there came up seven cows, sleek and fat, and they grazed among the reeds. [3]After them, seven other cows, ugly and gaunt, came up out of the Nile and stood beside those on the riverbank. [4]And the cows that were ugly and gaunt ate up the seven sleek, fat cows. Then Pharaoh woke up.

[5]He fell asleep again and had a second dream: Seven heads of grain, healthy and good, were growing on a single stalk. [6]After them, seven other heads of grain sprouted—thin and scorched by the east wind. [7]The thin heads of grain swallowed up the seven healthy, full heads. Then Pharaoh woke up; it had been a dream. . . .

[15]Pharaoh said to Joseph, "I had a dream, and no one can interpret it. But I have heard it said of you that when you hear a dream you can interpret it."

[16]"I cannot do it," Joseph replied to Pharaoh, "but God will give Pharaoh the answer he desires."
Num 12 [6]he said, "Listen to my words: When a prophet of the LORD is among you, I reveal myself to him in visions, I speak to him in dreams."
Judg 7 [13]Gideon arrived just as a man was telling a friend his dream. "I had a dream," he was saying. "A round loaf of barley bread came tumbling into the Midianite camp. It struck the tent with such force that the tent overturned and collapsed."

[14]His friend responded, "This can be nothing other than the sword of Gideon son of Joash, the Israelite. God has given the Midianites and the whole camp into his hands."

[15]When Gideon heard the dream and its interpretation, he worshiped God. He returned to the camp of Israel and called out, "Get up! The LORD has given the Midianite camp into your hands."
1 Sam 28 [6]He inquired of the LORD, but the LORD did not answer him by dreams or Urim or prophets.
1 Kings 3 [5]At Gibeon the LORD appeared to Solomon during the night in a dream, and God said, "Ask for whatever you want me to give you." . . .

[7]"Now, O LORD my God, you have made your servant king in place of my father David. But I am only a little child and do not know how to carry out my duties. [8]Your servant is here among the people you have chosen, a great people, too numerous to count or number. [9]So give your servant a discerning heart to govern your people and to distinguish between right and wrong. For who is able to govern this great people of yours?"

[10]The Lord was pleased that Solomon had asked for this. [11]So God said to him, "Since you have asked for this and not for long life or wealth for yourself, nor have asked for the death of your enemies but for discernment in administering justice, [12]I will do what you have asked. I will give you a wise and discerning heart, so that there will never have been anyone like you, nor will there ever be. [13]Moreover, I will give you what you have not asked for—both riches and honor—so that in your lifetime you will have no equal among kings. [14]And if you walk in my ways and obey my statutes and commands as David your father did, I will give you a long life." [15]Then Solomon awoke—and he realized it had been a dream.

He returned to Jerusalem, stood before the ark of the Lord's covenant and sacrificed burnt offerings and fellowship offerings. Then he gave a feast for all his court.
Jer 23 [28]"Let the prophet who has a dream tell his dream, but let the one who has my word speak it faithfully. For what has straw to do with grain?" declares the LORD.
Dan 1 [17]To these four young men God gave knowledge and understanding of all kinds of literature and learning. And Daniel could understand visions and dreams of all kinds.
Dan 2 [1]In the second year of his reign, Nebuchadnezzar had dreams; his mind was troubled and he could not sleep.
Dan 4 [4]I, Nebuchadnezzar, was at home in my palace, contented and prosperous. [5]I had a dream that made me afraid. As I was lying in my bed, the images and visions that passed through my mind terrified me.
Dan 7 [1]In the first year of Belshazzar king of Babylon, Daniel had a dream, and visions passed through his mind as he was lying on his bed. He wrote down the substance of his dream.
Joel 2 [28]"And afterward, I will pour out my Spirit on all people. Your sons and daughters will prophesy, your old men will dream dreams, your young men will see visions."
Matt 1 [20]But after he had considered this, an angel of the Lord appeared to him in a dream and said, "Joseph son of David, do not be afraid to take Mary home as your wife, because what is conceived in her is from the Holy Spirit. [21]She will give birth to a son, and you are to give him the name Jesus, because he will save his people from their sins."
Matt 2 [12]And having been warned in a dream not to go back to Herod, they returned to their country by another route.
Matt 2 [13]When they had gone, an angel of the Lord appeared to Joseph in a dream. "Get up," he said, "take the child and his mother and escape to Egypt. Stay there until I tell you, for Herod is going to search for the child to kill him."
Matt 2 [19]After Herod died, an angel of the Lord appeared in a dream to Joseph in Egypt [20]and said, "Get up, take the child and his mother and go to the land of Israel, for those who were trying to take the child's life are dead."
Matt 2 [22]But when he heard that Archelaus was reigning in Judea in place of his father Herod, he was afraid to go there. Having been warned in a dream, he withdrew to the district of Galilee. . . .
Matt 27 [19]While Pilate was sitting on the judge's seat, his wife sent him this message: "Don't have anything to do with that innocent man, for I have suffered a great deal today in a dream because of him."

G. Revelation through Historical Events

Exod 20 [1]And God spoke all these words: [2]"I am the LORD your God, who brought you out of Egypt, out of the land of slavery."
Deut 6 [5]Love the LORD your God with all your heart and with all your soul and with all your strength. [6]These commandments that I give you today are to be upon your hearts. [7]Impress them on your children. Talk about them when you sit at home and when you walk along the road, when you lie down and when you get up. [8]Tie them as symbols on your hands and bind them on your foreheads. [9]Write them on the doorframes of your houses and on your gates.

[10]When the LORD your God brings you into the land he swore to your fathers, to Abraham, Isaac and Jacob, to give you—a land with large, flourishing cities you did not build, . . . [12]be careful that you do not forget the LORD, who brought you out of Egypt, out of the land of slavery.
2 Kings 17 [36]"But the LORD, who brought you up out of Egypt with mighty power and outstretched arm, is the one you must worship. To him you shall bow down and to him offer sacrifices."
Ps 78 [1]O my people, hear my teaching; listen to the words of my mouth. [2]I will open my mouth in parables, I will utter hidden things, things from of old—[3]what we have heard and known, what our fathers have told us. [4]We will not hide them from their children; we will tell the next generation the praiseworthy deeds of the LORD, his power, and the wonders he has done. . . . [13]He divided the sea and led them through; he made the water stand firm like a wall. [14]He guided them with the cloud by day and with light from the fire all night. [15]He split the rocks in the desert and gave them water as abundant as the seas; [16]he brought streams out of a rocky crag and made water flow down like rivers. . . . [23]Yet he gave a command to the skies above and opened the doors of the heavens; [24]he rained down

manna for the people to eat, he gave them the grain of heaven. 25Men ate the bread of angels; he sent them all the food they could eat. 26He let loose the east wind from the heavens and led forth the south wind by his power. 27He rained meat down on them like dust, flying birds like sand on the seashore. 28He made them come down inside their camp, all around their tents. 29They ate till they had more than enough, for he had given them what they craved.

Ps 105 1Give thanks to the LORD, call on his name; make known among the nations what he has done. 2Sing to him, sing praise to him; tell of all his wonderful acts. . . .

5Remember the wonders he has done, his miracles, and the judgments he pronounced. . . .

8He remembers his covenant forever, the word he commanded, for a thousand generations, 9the covenant he made with Abraham, the oath he swore to Isaac. 10He confirmed it to Jacob as a decree, to Israel as an everlasting covenant: 11"To you I will give the land of Canaan as the portion you will inherit."

12When they were but few in number, few indeed, and strangers in it, 13they wandered from nation to nation, from one kingdom to another. 14He allowed no one to oppress them; for their sake he rebuked kings: 15"Do not touch my anointed ones; do my prophets no harm."

16He called down famine on the land and destroyed all their supplies of food; 17and he sent a man before them—Joseph, sold as a slave. 18They bruised his feet with shackles, his neck was put in irons, 19till what he foretold came to pass, till the word of the LORD proved him true. 20The king sent and released him, the ruler of peoples set him free. 21He made him master of his household, ruler over all he possessed, 22to instruct his princes as he pleased and teach his elders wisdom.

23Then Israel entered Egypt; Jacob lived as an alien in the land of Ham. 24The LORD made his people very fruitful; he made them too numerous for their foes, 25whose hearts he turned to hate his people, to conspire against his servants. 26He sent Moses his servant, and Aaron, whom he had chosen. 27They performed his miraculous signs among them, his wonders in the land of Ham. 28He sent darkness and made the land dark—for had they not rebelled against his words? 29He turned their waters into blood, causing their fish to die. 30Their land teemed with frogs, which went up into the bedrooms of their rulers. 31He spoke, and there came swarms of flies, and gnats throughout their country. 32He turned their rain into hail, with lightning throughout their land; 33he struck down their vines and fig trees and shattered the trees of their country. 34He spoke, and the locusts came, grasshoppers without number; 35they ate up every green thing in their land, ate up the produce of their soil. 36Then he struck down all the firstborn in their land, the firstfruits of all their manhood.

37He brought out Israel, laden with silver and gold, and from among their tribes no one faltered. 38Egypt was glad when they left, because dread of Israel had fallen on them. 39He spread out a cloud as a covering, and a fire to give light at night. 40They asked, and he brought them quail and satisfied them with the bread of heaven. 41He opened the rock, and water gushed out; like a river it flowed in the desert.

42For he remembered his holy promise given to his servant Abraham. 43He brought out his people with rejoicing, his chosen ones with shouts of joy; 44he gave them the lands of the nations, and they fell heir to what others had toiled for—45that they might keep his precepts and observe his laws.

Praise the LORD.

Mic 6 4"I brought you up out of Egypt and redeemed you from the land of slavery. I sent Moses to lead you, also Aaron and Miriam. 5My people, remember what Balak king of Moab counseled and what Balaam son of Beor answered. Remember your journey from Shittim to Gilgal, that you may know the righteous acts of the LORD."

Acts 7 2To this he replied: "Brothers and fathers, listen to me! The God of glory appeared to our father Abraham while he was still in Mesopotamia, before he lived in Haran. 3'Leave your country and your people,' God said, 'and go to the land I will show you.'

4"So he left the land of the Chaldeans and settled in Haran. After the death of his father, God sent him to this land where you are now living. 5He gave him no inheritance here, not even a foot of ground. But God promised him that he and his descendants after him would possess the land, even though at that time Abraham had no child. . . . 8Then he gave Abraham the covenant of circumcision. And Abraham became the father of Isaac and circumcised him eight days after his birth. Later Isaac became the father of Jacob, and Jacob became the father of the twelve patriarchs.

9"Because the patriarchs were jealous of Joseph, they sold him as a slave into Egypt. But God was with him 10and rescued him from all his troubles. He gave Joseph wisdom and enabled him to gain the goodwill of Pharaoh king of Egypt; so he made him ruler over Egypt and all his palace.

11"Then a famine struck all Egypt and Canaan, bringing great suffering, and our fathers could not find food. 12When Jacob heard that there was grain in Egypt, he sent our fathers on their first visit. 13On their second visit, Joseph told his brothers who he was, and Pharaoh learned about Joseph's family. 14After this, Joseph sent for his father Jacob and his whole family, seventy-five in all. 15Then Jacob went down to Egypt, where he and our fathers died. 16Their bodies were brought back to Shechem and placed in the tomb that Abraham had bought from the sons of Hamor at Shechem for a certain sum of money.

17"As the time drew near for God to fulfill his promise to Abraham, the number of our people in Egypt greatly increased. 18Then another king, who knew nothing about Joseph, became ruler of Egypt. 19He dealt treacherously with our people and oppressed our forefathers by forcing them to throw out their newborn babies so that they would die.

20"At that time Moses was born, and he was no ordinary child. For three months he was cared for in his father's house. 21When he was placed outside, Pharaoh's daughter took him and brought him up as her own son. 22Moses was educated in all the wisdom of the Egyptians and was powerful in speech and action.

23"When Moses was forty years old, he decided to visit his fellow Israelites. 24He saw one of them being mistreated by an Egyptian, so he went to his defense and avenged him by killing the Egyptian. 25Moses thought that his own people would realize that God was using him to rescue them, but they did not. 26The next day Moses came upon two Israelites who were fighting. He tried to reconcile them by saying, 'Men, you are brothers; why do you want to hurt each other?'

27"But the man who was mistreating the other pushed Moses aside and said, 'Who made you ruler and judge over us? 28Do you want to kill me as you killed the Egyptian yesterday?' 29When Moses heard this, he fled to Midian, where he settled as a foreigner and had two sons.

30"After forty years had passed, an angel appeared to Moses in the flames of a burning bush in the desert near Mount Sinai. 31When he saw this, he was amazed at the sight. As he went over to look more closely, he heard the Lord's voice: 32'I am the God of your fathers, the God of Abraham, Isaac and Jacob.' Moses trembled with fear and did not dare to look.

33"Then the Lord said to him, 'Take off your sandals; the place where you are standing is holy ground. 34I have indeed seen the oppression of my people in Egypt. I have heard their groaning and have come down to set them free. Now come, I will send you back to Egypt.'

35"This is the same Moses whom they had rejected with the words, 'Who made you ruler and judge?' He was sent to be their ruler and deliverer by God himself, through the angel who appeared to him in the bush. 36He led them out of Egypt and did wonders and miraculous signs in Egypt, at the Red Sea and for forty years in the desert. . . .

44"Our forefathers had the tabernacle of the Testimony with them in the desert. It had been made as God directed Moses, according to the pattern he had seen. 45Having received the tabernacle, our fathers under Joshua brought it with them when they took the land from the nations God drove out before them. It remained in the land until the time of David, 46who enjoyed God's favor and asked that he might provide a dwelling place for the God of Jacob. 47But it was Solomon who built the house for him. . . .

51"You stiff-necked people, with uncircumcised hearts and

ears! You are just like your fathers: You always resist the Holy Spirit! [52]Was there ever a prophet your fathers did not persecute? They even killed those who predicted the coming of the Righteous One. And now you have betrayed and murdered him—[53]you who have received the law that was put into effect through angels but have not obeyed it."

Acts 13 [16]Standing up, Paul motioned with his hand and said: "Men of Israel and you Gentiles who worship God, listen to me! [17]The God of the people of Israel chose our fathers; he made the people prosper during their stay in Egypt, with mighty power he led them out of that country, [18]he endured their conduct for about forty years in the desert, [19]he overthrew seven nations in Canaan and gave their land to his people as their inheritance. [20]All this took about 450 years.

"After this, God gave them judges until the time of Samuel the prophet. [21]Then the people asked for a king, and he gave them Saul son of Kish, of the tribe of Benjamin, who ruled forty years. [22]After removing Saul, he made David their king. He testified concerning him: 'I have found David son of Jesse a man after my own heart; he will do everything I want him to do.'

[23]"From this man's descendants God has brought to Israel the Savior Jesus, as he promised. [24]Before the coming of Jesus, John preached repentance and baptism to all the people of Israel. [25]As John was completing his work, he said: 'Who do you think I am? I am not that one. No, but he is coming after me, whose sandals I am not worthy to untie.'

[26]"Brothers, children of Abraham, and you God-fearing Gentiles, it is to us that this message of salvation has been sent. [27]The people of Jerusalem and their rulers did not recognize Jesus, yet in condemning him they fulfilled the words of the prophets that are read every Sabbath. [28]Though they found no proper ground for a death sentence, they asked Pilate to have him executed. [29]When they had carried out all that was written about him, they took him down from the tree and laid him in a tomb. [30]But God raised him from the dead, [31]and for many days he was seen by those who had traveled with him from Galilee to Jerusalem. They are now his witnesses to our people.

[32]"We tell you the good news: What God promised our fathers [33]he has fulfilled for us, their children, by raising up Jesus. As it is written in the second Psalm: 'You are my Son; today I have become your Father.' [34]The fact that God raised him from the dead, never to decay, is stated in these words: 'I will give you the holy and sure blessings promised to David.' [35]So it is stated elsewhere: 'You will not let your Holy One see decay.'

[36]"For when David had served God's purpose in his own generation, he fell asleep; he was buried with his fathers and his body decayed. [37]But the one whom God raised from the dead did not see decay.

[38]"Therefore, my brothers, I want you to know that through Jesus the forgiveness of sins is proclaimed to you. [39]Through him everyone who believes is justified from everything you could not be justified from by the law of Moses. [40]Take care that what the prophets have said does not happen to you: [41]'Look, you scoffers, wonder and perish, for I am going to do something in your days that you would never believe, even if someone told you.'"

1 Cor 10 [1]For I do not want you to be ignorant of the fact, brothers, that our forefathers were all under the cloud and that they all passed through the sea. [2]They were all baptized into Moses in the cloud and in the sea. [3]They all ate the same spiritual food [4]and drank the same spiritual drink; for they drank from the spiritual rock that accompanied them, and that rock was Christ. [5]Nevertheless, God was not pleased with most of them; their bodies were scattered over the desert.

[6]Now these things occurred as examples to keep us from setting our hearts on evil things as they did. [7]Do not be idolaters, as some of them were; as it is written: "The people sat down to eat and drink and got up to indulge in pagan revelry." [8]We should not commit sexual immorality, as some of them did—and in one day twenty-three thousand of them died. [9]We should not test the Lord, as some of them did—and were killed by snakes. [10]And do not grumble, as some of them did—and were killed by the destroying angel.

[11]These things happened to them as examples and were written down as warnings for us, on whom the fulfillment of the ages has come.

H. Revelation through Human Authority and Intuition

Gen 14 [18]Then Melchizedek king of Salem brought out bread and wine. He was priest of God Most High, [19]and he blessed Abram, saying, "Blessed be Abram by God Most High, Creator of heaven and earth. [20]And blessed be God Most High, who delivered your enemies into your hand." Then Abram gave him a tenth of everything.

Exod 18 [13]The next day Moses took his seat to serve as judge for the people, and they stood around him from morning till evening. [14]When his father-in-law saw all that Moses was doing for the people, he said, "What is this you are doing for the people? Why do you alone sit as judge, while all these people stand around you from morning till evening?"

[15]Moses answered him, "Because the people come to me to seek God's will. [16]Whenever they have a dispute, it is brought to me, and I decide between the parties and inform them of God's decrees and laws."

[17]Moses' father-in-law replied, "What you are doing is not good. [18]You and these people who come to you will only wear yourselves out. The work is too heavy for you; you cannot handle it alone. [19]Listen now to me and I will give you some advice, and may God be with you. You must be the people's representative before God and bring their disputes to him. [20]Teach them the decrees and laws, and show them the way to live and the duties they are to perform. [21]But select capable men from all the people—men who fear God, trustworthy men who hate dishonest gain—and appoint them as officials over thousands, hundreds, fifties and tens. [22]Have them serve as judges for the people at all times, but have them bring every difficult case to you; the simple cases they can decide themselves. That will make your load lighter, because they will share it with you. [23]If you do this and God so commands, you will be able to stand the strain, and all these people will go home satisfied."

[24]Moses listened to his father-in-law and did everything he said.

Ezek 16 [44]"'Everyone who quotes proverbs will quote this proverb about you: "Like mother, like daughter." [45]You are a true daughter of your mother, who despised her husband and her children; and you are a true sister of your sisters, who despised their husbands and their children. Your mother was a Hittite and your father an Amorite.'"

Luke 4 [23]Jesus said to them, "Surely you will quote this proverb to me: 'Physician, heal yourself! Do here in your hometown what we have heard that you did in Capernaum.'"

Acts 10 [34]Then Peter began to speak: "I now realize how true it is that God does not show favoritism [35]but accepts men from every nation who fear him and do what is right."

Acts 17 [28]"'For in him we live and move and have our being.' As some of your own poets have said, 'We are his offspring.'"

Rom 1 [20]For since the creation of the world God's invisible qualities—his eternal power and divine nature—have been clearly seen, being understood from what has been made, so that men are without excuse.

[21]For although they knew God, they neither glorified him as God nor gave thanks to him, but their thinking became futile and their foolish hearts were darkened. [22]Although they claimed to be wise, they became fools [23]and exchanged the glory of the immortal God for images made to look like mortal man and birds and animals and reptiles.

Rom 2 [14](Indeed, when Gentiles, who do not have the law, do by nature things required by the law, they are a law for themselves, even though they do not have the law, [15]since they show that the requirements of the law are written on their hearts, their consciences also bearing witness, and their thoughts now accusing, now even defending them.)

Eph 6 [4]Fathers, do not exasperate your children; instead, bring them up in the training and instruction of the Lord.

2 Pet 2 [22]Of them the proverbs are true: "A dog returns to its vomit," and, "A sow that is washed goes back to her wallowing in the mud."

I. Revelation through the Incarnation

Matt 11 [25]At that time Jesus said, "I praise you, Father, Lord of heaven and earth, because you have hidden these things from the wise and learned, and revealed them to little children. [26]Yes, Father, for this was your good pleasure.

[27]"All things have been committed to me by my Father. No one knows the Son except the Father, and no one knows the Father except the Son and those to whom the Son chooses to reveal him."

Matt 17 [1]After six days Jesus took with him Peter, James and John the brother of James, and led them up a high mountain by themselves. [2]There he was transfigured before them. His face shone like the sun, and his clothes became as white as the light.

Luke 2 [28]Simeon took him in his arms and praised God, saying: [29]"Sovereign Lord, as you have promised, you now dismiss your servant in peace. [30]For my eyes have seen your salvation, [31]which you have prepared in the sight of all people, [32]a light for revelation to the Gentiles and for glory to your people Israel."

Luke 5 [1]One day as Jesus was standing by the lake of Gennesaret, with the people crowding around him and listening to the word of God . . .

[4]When he had finished speaking, he said to Simon, "Put out into deep water, and let down the nets for a catch." . . .

[6]When they had done so, they caught such a large number of fish that their nets began to break. . . .

[8]When Simon Peter saw this, he fell at Jesus' knees and said, "Go away from me, Lord; I am a sinful man!"

John 1 [1]In the beginning was the Word, and the Word was with God, and the Word was God. . . .

[14]The Word became flesh and made his dwelling among us. We have seen his glory, the glory of the One and Only, who came from the Father, full of grace and truth.

[15]John testifies concerning him. He cries out, saying, "This was he of whom I said, 'He who comes after me has surpassed me because he was before me.'" [16]From the fullness of his grace we have all received one blessing after another. [17]For the law was given through Moses; grace and truth came through Jesus Christ. [18]No one has ever seen God, but God the One and Only, who is at the Father's side, has made him known.

John 3 [2]He came to Jesus at night and said, "Rabbi, we know you are a teacher who has come from God. For no one could perform the miraculous signs you are doing if God were not with him."

John 4 [25]The woman said, "I know that Messiah" (called Christ) "is coming. When he comes, he will explain everything to us."

[26]Then Jesus declared, "I who speak to you am he."

John 14 [8]Philip said, "Lord, show us the Father and that will be enough for us."

[9]Jesus answered: "Don't you know me, Philip, even after I have been among you such a long time? Anyone who has seen me has seen the Father. How can you say, 'Show us the Father'?"

John 17 [1]After Jesus said this, he looked toward heaven and prayed. . . .

[6]"I have revealed you to those whom you gave me out of the world. They were yours; you gave them to me and they have obeyed your word."

Rom 5 [8]But God demonstrates his own love for us in this: While we were still sinners, Christ died for us.

Rom 9 [5]Theirs are the patriarchs, and from them is traced the human ancestry of Christ, who is God over all, forever praised! Amen.

1 Cor 1 [24]but to those whom God has called, both Jews and Greeks, Christ the power of God and the wisdom of God.

Gal 3 [23]Before this faith came, we were held prisoners by the law, locked up until faith should be revealed. [24]So the law was put in charge to lead us to Christ that we might be justified by faith. [25]Now that faith has come, we are no longer under the supervision of the law.

Gal 4 [4]But when the time had fully come, God sent his Son, born of a woman, born under law. . . .

Col 1 [15]He is the image of the invisible God, the firstborn over all creation.

Col 2 [9]For in Christ all the fullness of the Deity lives in bodily form. . . .

1 Tim 3 [16]Beyond all question, the mystery of godliness is great: He appeared in a body, was vindicated by the Spirit, was seen by angels, was preached among the nations, was believed on in the world, was taken up in glory.

Heb 1 [1]In the past God spoke to our forefathers through the prophets at many times and in various ways, [2]but in these last days he has spoken to us by his Son, whom he appointed heir of all things, and through whom he made the universe. [3]The Son is the radiance of God's glory and the exact representation of his being, sustaining all things by his powerful word. After he had provided purification for sins, he sat down at the right hand of the Majesty in heaven.

1 John 1 [1]That which was from the beginning, which we have heard, which we have seen with our eyes, which we have looked at and our hands have touched—this we proclaim concerning the Word of life. [2]The life appeared; we have seen it and testify to it, and we proclaim to you the eternal life, which was with the Father and has appeared to us. [3]We proclaim to you what we have seen and heard, so that you also may have fellowship with us. And our fellowship is with the Father and with his Son, Jesus Christ.

1 John 3 [16]This is how we know what love is: Jesus Christ laid down his life for us. And we ought to lay down our lives for our brothers.

J. Revelation through the Lot

1 Sam 14 [41]Then Saul prayed to the LORD, the God of Israel, "Give me the right answer." And Jonathan and Saul were taken by lot, and the men were cleared. [42]Saul said, "Cast the lot between me and Jonathan my son." And Jonathan was taken.

Prov 16 [33]The lot is cast into the lap, but its every decision is from the LORD.

Jon 1 [7]Then the sailors said to each other, "Come, let us cast lots to find out who is responsible for this calamity." They cast lots and the lot fell on Jonah.

Acts 1 [24]Then they prayed, "Lord, you know everyone's heart. Show us which of these two you have chosen [25]to take over this apostolic ministry, which Judas left to go where he belongs." [26]Then they cast lots, and the lot fell to Matthias; so he was added to the eleven apostles.

K. Revelation through Man Himself

Gen 1 [26]Then God said, "Let us make man in our image, in our likeness, and let them rule over the fish of the sea and the birds of the air, over the livestock, over all the earth, and over all the creatures that move along the ground."

[27]So God created man in his own image, in the image of God he created him; male and female he created them.

Gen 5 [1]This is the written account of Adam's line.

When God created man, he made him in the likeness of God. [2]He created them male and female and blessed them. And when they were created, he called them "man."

[3]When Adam had lived 130 years, he had a son in his own likeness, in his own image; and he named him Seth.

Gen 9 [6]"Whoever sheds the blood of man, by man shall his blood be shed; for in the image of God has God made man."

1 Cor 11 [7]A man ought not to cover his head, since he is the image and glory of God; but the woman is the glory of man.

James 3 [9]With the tongue we praise our Lord and Father, and with it we curse men, who have been made in God's likeness.

L. Revelation through Miracles

Exod 4 [2]Then the LORD said to him, "What is that in your hand?"

"A staff," he replied.

[3]The LORD said, "Throw it on the ground."

Moses threw it on the ground and it became a snake, and he ran from it. 4Then the LORD said to him, "Reach out your hand and take it by the tail." So Moses reached out and took hold of the snake and it turned back into a staff in his hand. 5"This," said the LORD, "is so that they may believe that the LORD, the God of their fathers—the God of Abraham, the God of Isaac and the God of Jacob—has appeared to you."

6Then the LORD said, "Put your hand inside your cloak." So Moses put his hand into his cloak, and when he took it out, it was leprous, like snow.

7"Now put it back into your cloak," he said. So Moses put his hand back into his cloak, and when he took it out, it was restored, like the rest of his flesh.

8Then the LORD said, "If they do not believe you or pay attention to the first miraculous sign, they may believe the second. 9But if they do not believe these two signs or listen to you, take some water from the Nile and pour it on the dry ground. The water you take from the river will become blood on the ground."

1 Kings 18 21Elijah went before the people and said, "How long will you waver between two opinions? If the LORD is God, follow him; but if Baal is God, follow him."

But the people said nothing.

22Then Elijah said to them, "I am the only one of the LORD's prophets left, but Baal has four hundred and fifty prophets. 23Get two bulls for us. Let them choose one for themselves, and let them cut it into pieces and put it on the wood but not set fire to it. I will prepare the other bull and put it on the wood but not set fire to it. 24Then you call on the name of your god, and I will call on the name of the LORD. The god who answers by fire—he is God."

Then all the people said, "What you say is good."

25Elijah said to the prophets of Baal, "Choose one of the bulls and prepare it first, since there are so many of you. Call on the name of your god, but do not light the fire." 26So they took the bull given them and prepared it.

Then they called on the name of Baal from morning till noon. "O Baal, answer us!" they shouted. But there was no response; no one answered. And they danced around the altar they had made.

27At noon Elijah began to taunt them. "Shout louder!" he said. "Surely he is a god! Perhaps he is deep in thought, or busy, or traveling. Maybe he is sleeping and must be awakened." 28So they shouted louder and slashed themselves with swords and spears, as was their custom, until their blood flowed. 29Midday passed, and they continued their frantic prophesying until the time for the evening sacrifice. But there was no response, no one answered, no one paid attention.

30Then Elijah said to all the people, "Come here to me." They came to him, and he repaired the altar of the LORD, which was in ruins. 31Elijah took twelve stones, one for each of the tribes descended from Jacob, to whom the word of the LORD had come, saying, "Your name shall be Israel." 32With the stones he built an altar in the name of the LORD, and he dug a trench around it large enough to hold two seahs of seed. 33He arranged the wood, cut the bull into pieces and laid it on the wood. Then he said to them, "Fill four large jars with water and pour it on the offering and on the wood."

34"Do it again," he said, and they did it again.

"Do it a third time," he ordered, and they did it the third time. 35The water ran down around the altar and even filled the trench.

36At the time of sacrifice, the prophet Elijah stepped forward and prayed: "O LORD, God of Abraham, Isaac and Israel, let it be known today that you are God in Israel and that I am your servant and have done all these things at your command. 37Answer me, O LORD, answer me, so these people will know that you, O LORD, are God, and that you are turning their hearts back again."

38Then the fire of the LORD fell and burned up the sacrifice, the wood, the stones and the soil, and also licked up the water in the trench.

39When all the people saw this, they fell prostrate and cried, "The LORD—he is God! The LORD—he is God!"

Matt 11 2When John heard in prison what Christ was doing, he sent his disciples 3to ask him, "Are you the one who was to come, or should we expect someone else?"

4Jesus replied, "Go back and report to John what you hear and see: 5The blind receive sight, the lame walk, those who have leprosy are cured, the deaf hear, the dead are raised, and the good news is preached to the poor. 6Blessed is the man who does not fall away on account of me."

John 2 11This, the first of his miraculous signs, Jesus performed at Cana of Galilee. He thus revealed his glory, and his disciples put their faith in him.

John 5 36"I have testimony weightier than that of John. For the very work that the Father has given me to finish, and which I am doing, testifies that the Father has sent me."

John 10 25Jesus answered, "I did tell you, but you do not believe. The miracles I do in my Father's name speak for me, 26but you do not believe because you are not my sheep." . . . 37"Do not believe me unless I do what my Father does. 38But if I do it, even though you do not believe me, believe the miracles, that you may know and understand that the Father is in me, and I in the Father."

John 20 30Jesus did many other miraculous signs in the presence of his disciples, which are not recorded in this book. 31But these are written that you may believe that Jesus is the Christ, the Son of God, and that by believing you may have life in his name.

Acts 2 22"Men of Israel, listen to this: Jesus of Nazareth was a man accredited by God to you by miracles, wonders and signs, which God did among you through him, as you yourselves know."

M. Revelation through Physical Nature

Job 36 24"Remember to extol his work, which men have praised in song. 25All mankind has seen it; men gaze on it from afar. 26How great is God—beyond our understanding! The number of his years is past finding out.

27"He draws up the drops of water, which distill as rain to the streams; 28the clouds pour down their moisture and abundant showers fall on mankind. 29Who can understand how he spreads out the clouds, how he thunders from his pavilion? 30See how he scatters his lightning about him, bathing the depths of the sea. 31This is the way he governs the nations and provides food in abundance. 32He fills his hands with lightning and commands it to strike its mark. 33His thunder announces the coming storm; even the cattle make known its approach."

Job 37 1"At this my heart pounds and leaps from its place. 2Listen! Listen to the roar of his voice, to the rumbling that comes from his mouth. 3He unleashes his lightning beneath the whole heaven and sends it to the ends of the earth. 4After that comes the sound of his roar; he thunders with his majestic voice. When his voice resounds, he holds nothing back. 5God's voice thunders in marvelous ways; he does great things beyond our understanding. 6He says to the snow, 'Fall on the earth,' and to the rain shower, 'Be a mighty downpour.' 7So that all men he has made may know his work, he stops every man from his labor. 8The animals take cover; they remain in their dens. 9The tempest comes out from its chamber, the cold from the driving winds. 10The breath of God produces ice, and the broad waters become frozen. 11He loads the clouds with moisture; he scatters his lightning through them. 12At his direction they swirl around over the face of the whole earth to do whatever he commands them. 13He brings the clouds to punish men, or to water his earth and show his love."

Ps 8 1O LORD, our Lord, how majestic is your name in all the earth!

You have set your glory above the heavens. 2From the lips of children and infants you have ordained praise because of your enemies, to silence the foe and the avenger.

3When I consider your heavens, the work of your fingers, the moon and the stars, which you have set in place, 4what is man that you are mindful of him, the son of man that you care for him?

Ps 19 1The heavens declare the glory of God; the skies proclaim the work of his hands. 2Day after day they pour forth speech; night after night they display knowledge. 3There is no speech or language where their voice is not heard. [4]Their voice goes out into all the earth, their words to the ends of the world.

In the heavens he has pitched a tent for the sun, [5]which is like a bridegroom coming forth from his pavilion, like a champion rejoicing to run his course. [6]It rises at one end of the heavens and makes its circuit to the other; nothing is hidden from its heat.

Ps 29 [1]Ascribe to the LORD, O mighty ones, ascribe to the LORD glory and strength. [2]Ascribe to the LORD the glory due his name; worship the LORD in the splendor of his holiness.

[3]The voice of the LORD is over the waters; the God of glory thunders, the LORD thunders over the mighty waters. [4]The voice of the LORD is powerful; the voice of the LORD is majestic. [5]The voice of the LORD breaks the cedars; the LORD breaks in pieces the cedars of Lebanon. [6]He makes Lebanon skip like a calf, Sirion like a young wild ox. [7]The voice of the LORD strikes with flashes of lightning. [8]The voice of the LORD shakes the desert; the LORD shakes the Desert of Kadesh. [9]The voice of the LORD twists the oaks and strips the forests bare. And in his temple all cry, "Glory!"

[10]The LORD sits enthroned over the flood; the LORD is enthroned as King forever. [11]The LORD gives strength to his people; the LORD blesses his people with peace.

Acts 14 [15]"Men, why are you doing this? We too are only men, human like you. We are bringing you good news, telling you to turn from these worthless things to the living God, who made heaven and earth and sea and everything in them. [16]In the past, he let all nations go their own way. [17]Yet he has not left himself without testimony: He has shown kindness by giving you rain from heaven and crops in their seasons; he provides you with plenty of food and fills your hearts with joy."

Acts 17 [24]"The God who made the world and everything in it is the Lord of heaven and earth and does not live in temples built by hands. [25]And he is not served by human hands, as if he needed anything, because he himself gives all men life and breath and everything else. [26]From one man he made every nation of men, that they should inhabit the whole earth; and he determined the times set for them and the exact places where they should live. [27]God did this so that men would seek him and perhaps reach out for him and find him, though he is not far from each one of us. [28]'For in him we live and move and have our being.' As some of your own poets have said, 'We are his offspring.'"

Rom 1 [18]The wrath of God is being revealed from heaven against all the godlessness and wickedness of men who suppress the truth by their wickedness, [19]since what may be known about God is plain to them, because God has made it plain to them. [20]For since the creation of the world God's invisible qualities—his eternal power and divine nature—have been clearly seen, being understood from what has been made, so that men are without excuse.

[21]For although they knew God, they neither glorified him as God nor gave thanks to him, but their thinking became futile and their foolish hearts were darkened.

N. Revelation through Prophets

Exod 4 [11]The LORD said to him, "Who gave man his mouth? Who makes him deaf or mute? Who gives him sight or makes him blind? Is it not I, the LORD? [12]Now go; I will help you speak and will teach you what to say." . . . [15]"You shall speak to him and put words in his mouth; I will help both of you speak and will teach you what to do. [16]He will speak to the people for you, and it will be as if he were your mouth and as if you were God to him."

Deut 18 [15]The LORD your God will raise up for you a prophet like me from among your own brothers. You must listen to him. [16]For this is what you asked of the LORD your God at Horeb on the day of the assembly when you said, "Let us not hear the voice of the LORD our God nor see this great fire anymore, or we will die."

[17]The LORD said to me: "What they say is good. [18]I will raise up for them a prophet like you from among their brothers; I will put my words in his mouth, and he will tell them everything I command him. [19]If anyone does not listen to my words that the prophet speaks in my name, I myself will call him to account. [20]But a prophet who presumes to speak in my name anything I have not commanded him to say, or a prophet who speaks in the name of other gods, must be put to death."

[21]You may say to yourselves, "How can we know when a message has not been spoken by the LORD?" [22]If what a prophet proclaims in the name of the LORD does not take place or come true, that is a message the LORD has not spoken. That prophet has spoken presumptuously. Do not be afraid of him.

1 Sam 3 [19]The LORD was with Samuel as he grew up, and he let none of his words fall to the ground. [20]And all Israel from Dan to Beersheba recognized that Samuel was attested as a prophet of the LORD. [21]The LORD continued to appear at Shiloh, and there he revealed himself to Samuel through his word.

1 Sam 28 [6]He inquired of the LORD, but the LORD did not answer him by dreams or Urim or prophets.

2 Sam 23 [2]"The Spirit of the LORD spoke through me; his word was on my tongue."

1 Kings 13 [20]While they were sitting at the table, the word of the LORD came to the old prophet who had brought him back. [21]He cried out to the man of God who had come from Judah, "This is what the LORD says: 'You have defied the word of the LORD and have not kept the command the LORD your God gave you. [22]You came back and ate bread and drank water in the place where he told you not to eat or drink. Therefore your body will not be buried in the tomb of your fathers.'"

1 Kings 14 [11]"'Dogs will eat those belonging to Jeroboam who die in the city, and the birds of the air will feed on those who die in the country. The LORD has spoken!'

[12]"As for you, go back home. When you set foot in your city, the boy will die. . . ."

[17]Then Jeroboam's wife got up and left and went to Tirzah. As soon as she stepped over the threshold of the house, the boy died. [18]They buried him, and all Israel mourned for him, as the LORD had said through his servant the prophet Ahijah.

2 Kings 21 [10]The LORD said through his servants the prophets . . .

2 Chron 20 [20]Early in the morning they left for the Desert of Tekoa. As they set out, Jehoshaphat stood and said, "Listen to me, Judah and people of Jerusalem! Have faith in the LORD your God and you will be upheld; have faith in his prophets and you will be successful."

2 Chron 36 [12]He did evil in the eyes of the LORD his God and did not humble himself before Jeremiah the prophet, who spoke the word of the LORD.

2 Chron 36 [16]But they mocked God's messengers, despised his words and scoffed at his prophets until the wrath of the LORD was aroused against his people and there was no remedy.

Isa 6 [1]In the year that King Uzziah died, I saw the Lord seated on a throne, high and exalted, and the train of his robe filled the temple. . . .

[8]Then I heard the voice of the Lord saying, "Whom shall I send? And who will go for us?"

And I said, "Here am I. Send me!"

[9]He said, "Go and tell this people: 'Be ever hearing, but never understanding; be ever seeing, but never perceiving.'"

Jer 23 [21]"I did not send these prophets, yet they have run with their message; I did not speak to them, yet they have prophesied. [22]But if they had stood in my council, they would have proclaimed my words to my people and would have turned them from their evil ways and from their evil deeds."

Ezek 1 [3]the word of the LORD came to Ezekiel the priest, the son of Buzi, by the Kebar River in the land of the Babylonians. There the hand of the LORD was upon him.

Ezek 2 [3]He said: "Son of man, I am sending you to the Israelites, to a rebellious nation that has rebelled against me; they and their fathers have been in revolt against me to this very day. [4]The people to whom I am sending you are obstinate and stubborn. Say to them, 'This is what the Sovereign LORD says.' [5]And whether they listen or fail to listen—for they are a rebellious house—they will know that a prophet has been among them. . . . [7]You must speak my words to them, whether they listen or fail to listen, for they are rebellious."

Ezek 3 [1]Then he said to me, "Son of man, eat what is before you, eat this scroll; then go and speak to the house of Israel."

Ezek 3 [10]And he said to me, "Son of man, listen carefully and take to heart all the words I speak to you."

Hos 6 5“Therefore I cut you in pieces with my prophets, I killed you with the words of my mouth; my judgments flashed like lightning upon you.”

Joel 2 28“And afterward, I will pour out my Spirit on all people. Your sons and daughters will prophesy, your old men will dream dreams, your young men will see visions. 29Even on my servants, both men and women, I will pour out my Spirit in those days.”

Amos 3 7Surely the Sovereign LORD does nothing without revealing his plan to his servants the prophets.

8The lion has roared—who will not fear? The Sovereign LORD has spoken—who can but prophesy?

Zech 7 7“‘Are these not the words the LORD proclaimed through the earlier prophets when Jerusalem and its surrounding towns were at rest and prosperous, and the Negev and the western foothills were settled?’”

Acts 3 18“But this is how God fulfilled what he had foretold through all the prophets, saying that his Christ would suffer.”

Rom 1 1Paul, a servant of Christ Jesus, called to be an apostle and set apart for the gospel of God—2the gospel he promised beforehand through his prophets in the Holy Scriptures . . .

Heb 1 1In the past God spoke to our forefathers through the prophets at many times and in various ways. . . .

1 Pet 1 10Concerning this salvation, the prophets, who spoke of the grace that was to come to you, searched intently and with the greatest care, 11trying to find out the time and circumstances to which the Spirit of Christ in them was pointing when he predicted the sufferings of Christ and the glories that would follow. 12It was revealed to them that they were not serving themselves but you, when they spoke of the things that have now been told you by those who have preached the gospel to you by the Holy Spirit sent from heaven. Even angels long to look into these things.

2 Pet 1 21For prophecy never had its origin in the will of man, but men spoke from God as they were carried along by the Holy Spirit.

Rev 10 7“But in the days when the seventh angel is about to sound his trumpet, the mystery of God will be accomplished, just as he announced to his servants the prophets.”

O. Revelation through Religious Experience

Isa 45 14This is what the LORD says: “The products of Egypt and the merchandise of Cush, and those tall Sabeans—they will come over to you and will be yours; they will trudge behind you, coming over to you in chains. They will bow down before you and plead with you, saying, ‘Surely God is with you, and there is no other; there is no other god.’”

Dan 2 47The king said to Daniel, “Surely your God is the God of gods and the Lord of kings and a revealer of mysteries, for you were able to reveal this mystery.”

Jon 1 13Instead, the men did their best to row back to land. But they could not, for the sea grew even wilder than before. 14Then they cried to the LORD, “O LORD, please do not let us die for taking this man’s life. Do not hold us accountable for killing an innocent man, for you, O LORD, have done as you pleased.” 15Then they took Jonah and threw him overboard, and the raging sea grew calm. 16At this the men greatly feared the LORD, and they offered a sacrifice to the LORD and made vows to him.

Zech 8 23This is what the LORD Almighty says: “In those days ten men from all languages and nations will take firm hold of one Jew by the hem of his robe and say, ‘Let us go with you, because we have heard that God is with you.’”

John 1 4In him was life, and that life was the light of men. . . . 9The true light that gives light to every man was coming into the world.

John 4 15The woman said to him, “Sir, give me this water so that I won’t get thirsty and have to keep coming here to draw water.”

16He told her, “Go, call your husband and come back.”

17“I have no husband,” she replied.

Jesus said to her, “You are right when you say you have no husband. 18The fact is, you have had five husbands, and the man you now have is not your husband. What you have just said is quite true.”

19“Sir,” the woman said, “I can see that you are a prophet.”

John 16 7“But I tell you the truth: It is for your good that I am going away. Unless I go away, the Counselor will not come to you; but if I go, I will send him to you. 8When he comes, he will convict the world of guilt in regard to sin and righteousness and judgment: 9in regard to sin, because men do not believe in me; 10in regard to righteousness, because I am going to the Father, where you can see me no longer; 11and in regard to judgment, because the prince of this world now stands condemned.”

Acts 2 2Suddenly a sound like the blowing of a violent wind came from heaven and filled the whole house where they were sitting. . . .

5Now there were staying in Jerusalem God-fearing Jews from every nation under heaven. 6When they heard this sound, a crowd came together in bewilderment, because each one heard them speaking in his own language. . . .

37When the people heard this, they were cut to the heart and said to Peter and the other apostles, “Brothers, what shall we do?”

Rom 2 14(Indeed, when Gentiles, who do not have the law, do by nature things required by the law, they are a law for themselves, even though they do not have the law, 15since they show that the requirements of the law are written on their hearts, their consciences also bearing witness, and their thoughts now accusing, now even defending them.)

1 Cor 14 24But if an unbeliever or someone who does not understand comes in while everybody is prophesying, he will be convinced by all that he is a sinner and will be judged by all, 25and the secrets of his heart will be laid bare. So he will fall down and worship God, exclaiming, “God is really among you!”

P. Revelation through Scripture

Ps 1 1Blessed is the man who does not walk in the counsel of the wicked or stand in the way of sinners or sit in the seat of mockers. 2But his delight is in the law of the LORD, and on his law he meditates day and night. 3He is like a tree planted by streams of water, which yields its fruit in season and whose leaf does not wither. Whatever he does prospers.

Ps 19 7The law of the LORD is perfect, reviving the soul. The statutes of the LORD are trustworthy, making wise the simple. 8The precepts of the LORD are right, giving joy to the heart. The commands of the LORD are radiant, giving light to the eyes. 9The fear of the LORD is pure, enduring forever. The ordinances of the LORD are sure and altogether righteous. 10They are more precious than gold, than much pure gold; they are sweeter than honey, than honey from the comb. 11By them is your servant warned; in keeping them there is great reward.

Ps 119 1Blessed are they whose ways are blameless, who walk according to the law of the LORD. 2Blessed are they who keep his statutes and seek him with all their heart. 3They do nothing wrong; they walk in his ways. 4You have laid down precepts that are to be fully obeyed.

Ps 119 13With my lips I recount all the laws that come from your mouth. 14I rejoice in following your statutes as one rejoices in great riches. 15I meditate on your precepts and consider your ways. 16I delight in your decrees; I will not neglect your word.

Ps 119 27Let me understand the teaching of your precepts; then I will meditate on your wonders. . . . 29Keep me from deceitful ways; be gracious to me through your law. 30I have chosen the way of truth; I have set my heart on your laws. 31I hold fast to your statutes, O LORD; do not let me be put to shame. 32I run in the path of your commands, for you have set my heart free.

Ps 119 57You are my portion, O LORD; I have promised to obey your words.

Ps 119 75I know, O LORD, that your laws are righteous, and in faithfulness you have afflicted me.

Ps 119 89Your word, O LORD, is eternal; it stands firm in the heavens. 90Your faithfulness continues through all generations; you established the earth, and it endures. 91Your laws endure to this day, for all things serve you. 92If your law had not been my delight, I would have perished in my affliction. 93I will never

forget your precepts, for by them you have preserved my life. . . . 96To all perfection I see a limit; but your commands are boundless.
Ps 119 105Your word is a lamp to my feet and a light for my path.
Ps 119 137Righteous are you, O LORD, and your laws are right. 138The statutes you have laid down are righteous; they are fully trustworthy.
Ps 119 151Yet you are near, O LORD, and all your commands are true. 152Long ago I learned from your statutes that you established them to last forever.
Ps 119 160All your words are true; all your righteous laws are eternal.
Ps 119 161Rulers persecute me without cause, but my heart trembles at your word. 162I rejoice in your promise like one who finds great spoil. 163I hate and abhor falsehood but I love your law. 164Seven times a day I praise you for your righteous laws. 165Great peace have they who love your law, and nothing can make them stumble. 166I wait for your salvation, O LORD, and I follow your commands. 167I obey your statutes, for I love them greatly. 168I obey your precepts and your statutes, for all my ways are known to you.
Isa 30 8Go now, write it on a tablet for them, inscribe it on a scroll, that for the days to come it may be an everlasting witness.
Dan 9 2in the first year of his reign, I, Daniel, understood from the Scriptures, according to the word of the LORD given to Jeremiah the prophet, that the desolation of Jerusalem would last seventy years.
Matt 22 43He said to them, "How is it then that David, speaking by the Spirit, calls him 'Lord'? For he says, 44'The Lord said to my Lord: "Sit at my right hand until I put your enemies under your feet."'" (Ps 110:1)
Luke 24 27And beginning with Moses and all the Prophets, he explained to them what was said in all the Scriptures concerning himself.
Luke 24 44He said to them, "This is what I told you while I was still with you: Everything must be fulfilled that is written about me in the Law of Moses, the Prophets and the Psalms."

45Then he opened their minds so they could understand the Scriptures.
John 5 39"You diligently study the Scriptures because you think that by them you possess eternal life. These are the Scriptures that testify about me, 40yet you refuse to come to me to have life. . . . 46If you believed Moses, you would believe me, for he wrote about me."
John 10 34Jesus answered them, "Is it not written in your Law, 'I have said you are gods'? 35If he called them 'gods,' to whom the word of God came—and the Scripture cannot be broken . . ."
Acts 1 16and said, "Brothers, the Scripture had to be fulfilled which the Holy Spirit spoke long ago through the mouth of David concerning Judas, who served as guide for those who arrested Jesus. . . ."
Acts 17 2As his custom was, Paul went into the synagogue, and on three Sabbath days he reasoned with them from the Scriptures, 3explaining and proving that the Christ had to suffer and rise from the dead. "This Jesus I am proclaiming to you is the Christ," he said.
Acts 18 28For he vigorously refuted the Jews in public debate, proving from the Scriptures that Jesus was the Christ.
Acts 28 23They arranged to meet Paul on a certain day, and came in even larger numbers to the place where he was staying. From morning till evening he explained and declared to them the kingdom of God and tried to convince them about Jesus from the Law of Moses and from the Prophets. . . . 25They disagreed among themselves and began to leave after Paul had made this final statement: "The Holy Spirit spoke the truth to your forefathers when he said through Isaiah the prophet: 26'Go to this people and say, "You will be ever hearing but never understanding; you will be ever seeing but never perceiving." 27For this people's heart has become calloused; they hardly hear with their ears, and they have closed their eyes. Otherwise they might see with their eyes, hear with their ears, understand with their hearts and turn, and I would heal them.'" (Isa 6:9–10)
Rom 1 1Paul, a servant of Christ Jesus, called to be an apostle and set apart for the gospel of God—2the gospel he promised beforehand through his prophets in the Holy Scriptures 3regarding his Son, who as to his human nature was a descendant of David . . .
Rom 15 4For everything that was written in the past was written to teach us, so that through endurance and the encouragement of the Scriptures we might have hope.
1 Cor 15 1Now, brothers, I want to remind you of the gospel I preached to you, which you received and on which you have taken your stand. 2By this gospel you are saved, if you hold firmly to the word I preached to you. Otherwise, you have believed in vain.

3For what I received I passed on to you as of first importance: that Christ died for our sins according to the Scriptures, 4that he was buried, that he was raised on the third day according to the Scriptures. . . .
Gal 3 22But the Scripture declares that the whole world is a prisoner of sin, so that what was promised, being given through faith in Jesus Christ, might be given to those who believe.
2 Tim 3 15and how from infancy you have known the holy Scriptures, which are able to make you wise for salvation through faith in Christ Jesus. 16All Scripture is God-breathed and is useful for teaching, rebuking, correcting and training in righteousness, 17so that the man of God may be thoroughly equipped for every good work.
Heb 3 7So, as the Holy Spirit says: "Today, if you hear his voice, 8do not harden your hearts as you did in the rebellion, during the time of testing in the desert, 9where your fathers tested and tried me and for forty years saw what I did. 10That is why I was angry with that generation, and I said, 'Their hearts are always going astray, and they have not known my ways.' 11So I declared on oath in my anger, 'They shall never enter my rest.'" (Ps 95:7–11)
Heb 10 15The Holy Spirit also testifies to us about this. First he says: 16"This is the covenant I will make with them after that time, says the Lord. I will put my laws in their hearts, and I will write them on their minds." 17Then he adds: "Their sins and lawless acts I will remember no more." (Jer 31:33–34)
James 2 8If you really keep the royal law found in Scripture, "Love your neighbor as yourself," you are doing right.
2 Pet 1 19And we have the word of the prophets made more certain, and you will do well to pay attention to it, as to a light shining in a dark place, until the day dawns and the morning star rises in your hearts. 20Above all, you must understand that no prophecy of Scripture came about by the prophet's own interpretation. 21For prophecy never had its origin in the will of man, but men spoke from God as they were carried along by the Holy Spirit.

Q. Revelation through Theophanies

Gen 16 7The angel of the LORD found Hagar near a spring in the desert; it was the spring that is beside the road to Shur. 8And he said, "Hagar, servant of Sarai, where have you come from, and where are you going?"

"I'm running away from my mistress Sarai," she answered.

9Then the angel of the LORD told her, "Go back to your mistress and submit to her." 10The angel added, "I will so increase your descendants that they will be too numerous to count."

11The angel of the LORD also said to her: "You are now with child and you will have a son. You shall name him Ishmael, for the LORD has heard of your misery. 12He will be a wild donkey of a man; his hand will be against everyone and everyone's hand against him, and he will live in hostility toward all his brothers."

13She gave this name to the LORD who spoke to her: "You are the God who sees me," for she said, "I have now seen the One who sees me." 14That is why the well was called Beer Lahai Roi; it is still there, between Kadesh and Bered.
Gen 32 24So Jacob was left alone, and a man wrestled with him till daybreak. 25When the man saw that he could not overpower him, he touched the socket of Jacob's hip so that his hip was wrenched as he wrestled with the man. 26Then the man said, "Let me go, for it is daybreak."

But Jacob replied, "I will not let you go unless you bless me."

27The man asked him, "What is your name?"

"Jacob," he answered.

28Then the man said, "Your name will no longer be Jacob, but Israel, because you have struggled with God and with men and have overcome."

29Jacob said, "Please tell me your name."

But he replied, "Why do you ask my name?" Then he blessed him there.

30So Jacob called the place Peniel, saying, "It is because I saw God face to face, and yet my life was spared."

Exod 3 2There the angel of the LORD appeared to him in flames of fire from within a bush. Moses saw that though the bush was on fire it did not burn up. 3So Moses thought, "I will go over and see this strange sight—why the bush does not burn up."

4When the LORD saw that he had gone over to look, God called to him from within the bush, "Moses! Moses!"

And Moses said, "Here I am."

5"Do not come any closer," God said. "Take off your sandals, for the place where you are standing is holy ground." 6Then he said, "I am the God of your father, the God of Abraham, the God of Isaac and the God of Jacob." At this, Moses hid his face, because he was afraid to look at God.

Exod 23 20"See, I am sending an angel ahead of you to guard you along the way and to bring you to the place I have prepared. 21Pay attention to him and listen to what he says. Do not rebel against him; he will not forgive your rebellion, since my Name is in him."

Exod 33 9As Moses went into the tent, the pillar of cloud would come down and stay at the entrance, while the LORD spoke with Moses. 10Whenever the people saw the pillar of cloud standing at the entrance to the tent, they all stood and worshiped, each at the entrance to his tent. 11The LORD would speak to Moses face to face, as a man speaks with his friend. Then Moses would return to the camp, but his young aide Joshua son of Nun did not leave the tent.

Num 22 21Balaam got up in the morning, saddled his donkey and went with the princes of Moab. 22But God was very angry when he went, and the angel of the LORD stood in the road to oppose him. Balaam was riding on his donkey, and his two servants were with him. 23When the donkey saw the angel of the LORD standing in the road with a drawn sword in his hand, she turned off the road into a field. Balaam beat her to get her back on the road.

24Then the angel of the LORD stood in a narrow path between two vineyards, with walls on both sides. 25When the donkey saw the angel of the LORD, she pressed close to the wall, crushing Balaam's foot against it. So he beat her again.

26Then the angel of the LORD moved on ahead and stood in a narrow place where there was no room to turn, either to the right or to the left. 27When the donkey saw the angel of the LORD, she lay down under Balaam, and he was angry and beat her with his staff. . . .

31Then the LORD opened Balaam's eyes, and he saw the angel of the LORD standing in the road with his sword drawn. So he bowed low and fell facedown.

32The angel of the LORD asked him, "Why have you beaten your donkey these three times? I have come here to oppose you because your path is a reckless one before me. 33The donkey saw me and turned away from me these three times. If she had not turned away, I would certainly have killed you by now, but I would have spared her."

34Balaam said to the angel of the LORD, "I have sinned. I did not realize you were standing in the road to oppose me. Now if you are displeased, I will go back."

35The angel of the LORD said to Balaam, "Go with the men, but speak only what I tell you." So Balaam went with the princes of Balak.

36When Balak heard that Balaam was coming, he went out to meet him at the Moabite town on the Arnon border, at the edge of his territory. 37Balak said to Balaam, "Did I not send you an urgent summons? Why didn't you come to me? Am I really not able to reward you?"

38"Well, I have come to you now," Balaam replied. "But can I say just anything? I must speak only what God puts in my mouth."

Deut 4 11You came near and stood at the foot of the mountain while it blazed with fire to the very heavens, with black clouds and deep darkness. 12Then the LORD spoke to you out of the fire. You heard the sound of words but saw no form; there was only a voice. 13He declared to you his covenant, the Ten Commandments, which he commanded you to follow and then wrote them on two stone tablets. 14And the LORD directed me at that time to teach you the decrees and laws you are to follow in the land that you are crossing the Jordan to possess.

Deut 5 4The LORD spoke to you face to face out of the fire on the mountain. 5(At that time I stood between the LORD and you to declare to you the word of the LORD, because you were afraid of the fire and did not go up the mountain.) And he said . . .

Josh 5 13Now when Joshua was near Jericho, he looked up and saw a man standing in front of him with a drawn sword in his hand. Joshua went up to him and asked, "Are you for us or for our enemies?"

14"Neither," he replied, "but as commander of the army of the LORD I have now come." Then Joshua fell facedown to the ground in reverence, and asked him, "What message does my Lord have for his servant?"

15The commander of the LORD's army replied, "Take off your sandals, for the place where you are standing is holy." And Joshua did so.

Judg 2 1The angel of the LORD went up from Gilgal to Bokim and said, "I brought you up out of Egypt and led you into the land that I swore to give to your forefathers. I said, 'I will never break my covenant with you, 2and you shall not make a covenant with the people of this land, but you shall break down their altars.' Yet you have disobeyed me. Why have you done this? 3Now therefore I tell you that I will not drive them out before you; they will be thorns in your sides and their gods will be a snare to you."

4When the angel of the LORD had spoken these things to all the Israelites, the people wept aloud, 5and they called that place Bokim. There they offered sacrifices to the LORD.

Judg 6 11The angel of the LORD came and sat down under the oak in Ophrah that belonged to Joash the Abiezrite, where his son Gideon was threshing wheat in a winepress to keep it from the Midianites. 12When the angel of the LORD appeared to Gideon, he said, "The LORD is with you, mighty warrior."

13"But sir," Gideon replied, "if the LORD is with us, why has all this happened to us? Where are all his wonders that our fathers told us about when they said, 'Did not the LORD bring us up out of Egypt?' But now the LORD has abandoned us and put us into the hand of Midian."

14The LORD turned to him and said, "Go in the strength you have and save Israel out of Midian's hand. Am I not sending you?"

15"But Lord," Gideon asked, "how can I save Israel? My clan is the weakest in Manasseh, and I am the least in my family."

16The LORD answered, "I will be with you, and you will strike down all the Midianites together."

17Gideon replied, "If now I have found favor in your eyes, give me a sign that it is really you talking to me. 18Please do not go away until I come back and bring my offering and set it before you."

And the LORD said, "I will wait until you return."

19Gideon went in, prepared a young goat, and from an ephah of flour he made bread without yeast. Putting the meat in a basket and its broth in a pot, he brought them out and offered them to him under the oak.

20The angel of God said to him, "Take the meat and the unleavened bread, place them on this rock, and pour out the broth." And Gideon did so. 21With the tip of the staff that was in his hand, the angel of the LORD touched the meat and the unleavened bread. Fire flared from the rock, consuming the meat and the bread. And the angel of the LORD disappeared. 22When Gideon realized that it was the angel of the LORD, he exclaimed, "Ah, Sovereign LORD! I have seen the angel of the LORD face to face!"

23But the LORD said to him, "Peace! Do not be afraid. You are not going to die."

[24]So Gideon built an altar to the LORD there and called it The LORD is Peace. To this day it stands in Ophrah of the Abiezrites.

Judg 13 [2]A certain man of Zorah, named Manoah, from the clan of the Danites, had a wife who was sterile and remained childless. [3]The angel of the LORD appeared to her and said, "You are sterile and childless, but you are going to conceive and have a son. [4]Now see to it that you drink no wine or other fermented drink and that you do not eat anything unclean, [5]because you will conceive and give birth to a son. No razor may be used on his head, because the boy is to be a Nazirite, set apart to God from birth, and he will begin the deliverance of Israel from the hands of the Philistines."

[6]Then the woman went to her husband and told him, "A man of God came to me. He looked like an angel of God, very awesome. I didn't ask him where he came from, and he didn't tell me his name. [7]But he said to me, 'You will conceive and give birth to a son. Now then, drink no wine or other fermented drink and do not eat anything unclean, because the boy will be a Nazirite of God from birth until the day of his death.'"

[8]Then Manoah prayed to the LORD: "O Lord, I beg you, let the man of God you sent to us come again to teach us how to bring up the boy who is to be born."

[9]God heard Manoah, and the angel of God came again to the woman while she was out in the field; but her husband Manoah was not with her. [10]The woman hurried to tell her husband, "He's here! The man who appeared to me the other day!"

[11]Manoah got up and followed his wife. When he came to the man, he said, "Are you the one who talked to my wife?"

"I am," he said.

[12]So Manoah asked him, "When your words are fulfilled, what is to be the rule for the boy's life and work?"

[13]The angel of the LORD answered, "Your wife must do all that I have told her. [14]She must not eat anything that comes from the grapevine, nor drink any wine or other fermented drink nor eat anything unclean. She must do everything I have commanded her."

[15]Manoah said to the angel of the LORD, "We would like you to stay until we prepare a young goat for you."

[16]The angel of the LORD replied, "Even though you detain me, I will not eat any of your food. But if you prepare a burnt offering, offer it to the LORD." (Manoah did not realize that it was the angel of the LORD.)

[17]Then Manoah inquired of the angel of the LORD, "What is your name, so that we may honor you when your word comes true?"

[18]He replied, "Why do you ask my name? It is beyond understanding." [19]Then Manoah took a young goat, together with the grain offering, and sacrificed it on a rock to the LORD. And the LORD did an amazing thing while Manoah and his wife watched: [20]As the flame blazed up from the altar toward heaven, the angel of the LORD ascended in the flame. Seeing this, Manoah and his wife fell with their faces to the ground. [21]When the angel of the LORD did not show himself again to Manoah and his wife, Manoah realized that it was the angel of the LORD.

[22]"We are doomed to die!" he said to his wife. "We have seen God!"

[23]But his wife answered, "If the LORD had meant to kill us, he would not have accepted a burnt offering and grain offering from our hands, nor shown us all these things or now told us this."

1 Kings 19 [5]Then he lay down under the tree and fell asleep.

All at once an angel touched him and said, "Get up and eat." [6]He looked around, and there by his head was a cake of bread baked over hot coals, and a jar of water. He ate and drank and then lay down again.

[7]The angel of the LORD came back a second time and touched him and said, "Get up and eat, for the journey is too much for you."

2 Kings 1 [15]The angel of the LORD said to Elijah, "Go down with him; do not be afraid of him." So Elijah got up and went down with him to the king.

R. Revelation through Urim and Thummim

Exod 28 [30]"Also put the Urim and the Thummim in the breastpiece, so they may be over Aaron's heart whenever he enters the presence of the LORD. Thus Aaron will always bear the means of making decisions for the Israelites over his heart before the LORD."

Num 27 [21]"He is to stand before Eleazar the priest, who will obtain decisions for him by inquiring of the Urim before the LORD. At his command he and the entire community of the Israelites will go out, and at his command they will come in."

1 Sam 28 [6]He inquired of the LORD, but the LORD did not answer him by dreams or Urim or prophets.

S. Revelation through Visions

Gen 15 [1]After this, the word of the LORD came to Abram in a vision: "Do not be afraid, Abram. I am your shield, your very great reward."

[2]But Abram said, "O Sovereign LORD, what can you give me since I remain childless and the one who will inherit my estate is Eliezer of Damascus?"

Num 12 [6]he said, "Listen to my words: When a prophet of the LORD is among you, I reveal myself to him in visions, I speak to him in dreams."

1 Sam 3 [1]The boy Samuel ministered before the LORD under Eli. In those days the word of the LORD was rare; there were not many visions.

Isa 30 [9]These are rebellious people, deceitful children, children unwilling to listen to the LORD's instruction. [10]They say to the seers, "See no more visions!" and to the prophets, "Give us no more visions of what is right! Tell us pleasant things, prophesy illusions."

Lam 2 [9]Her gates have sunk into the ground; their bars he has broken and destroyed. Her king and her princes are exiled among the nations, the law is no more, and her prophets no longer find visions from the LORD.

Ezek 1 [1]In the thirtieth year, in the fourth month on the fifth day, while I was among the exiles by the Kebar River, the heavens were opened and I saw visions of God.

Ezek 12 [21]The word of the LORD came to me: [22]"Son of man, what is this proverb you have in the land of Israel: 'The days go by and every vision comes to nothing'? [23]Say to them, 'This is what the Sovereign LORD says: I am going to put an end to this proverb, and they will no longer quote it in Israel.' Say to them, 'The days are near when every vision will be fulfilled. [24]For there will be no more false visions or flattering divinations among the people of Israel. [25]But I the LORD will speak what I will, and it shall be fulfilled without delay. For in your days, you rebellious house, I will fulfill whatever I say, declares the Sovereign LORD.'"

Dan 2 [19]During the night the mystery was revealed to Daniel in a vision. Then Daniel praised the God of heaven. . . .

Dan 8 [1]In the third year of King Belshazzar's reign, I, Daniel, had a vision, after the one that had already appeared to me. [2]In my vision I saw myself in the citadel of Susa in the province of Elam; in the vision I was beside the Ulai Canal. . . .

[15]While I, Daniel, was watching the vision and trying to understand it, there before me stood one who looked like a man. [16]And I heard a man's voice from the Ulai calling, "Gabriel, tell this man the meaning of the vision."

Hos 12 [9]"I am the LORD your God, who brought you out of Egypt; I will make you live in tents again, as in the days of your appointed feasts. [10]I spoke to the prophets, gave them many visions and told parables through them."

Zech 1 [8]During the night I had a vision—and there before me was a man riding a red horse! He was standing among the myrtle trees in a ravine. Behind him were red, brown and white horses.

Luke 1 [22]When he came out, he could not speak to them. They realized he had seen a vision in the temple, for he kept making signs to them but remained unable to speak.

Acts 9 [10]In Damascus there was a disciple named Ananias. The Lord called to him in a vision, "Ananias!"

"Yes, Lord," he answered.

[11]The Lord told him, "Go to the house of Judas on Straight Street and ask for a man from Tarsus named Saul, for he is praying. [12]In a vision he has seen a man named Ananias come and place his hands on him to restore his sight."

Acts 10 [9]About noon the following day as they were on their journey and approaching the city, Peter went up on the roof to pray. [10]He became hungry and wanted something to eat, and while the meal was being prepared, he fell into a trance. [11]He saw heaven opened and something like a large sheet being let down to earth by its four corners. [12]It contained all kinds of four-footed animals, as well as reptiles of the earth and birds of the air. [13]Then a voice told him, "Get up, Peter. Kill and eat."

[14]"Surely not, Lord!" Peter replied. "I have never eaten anything impure or unclean."

[15]The voice spoke to him a second time, "Do not call anything impure that God has made clean."

[16]This happened three times, and immediately the sheet was taken back to heaven.

[17]While Peter was wondering about the meaning of the vision, the men sent by Cornelius found out where Simon's house was and stopped at the gate. [18]They called out, asking if Simon who was known as Peter was staying there.

[19]While Peter was still thinking about the vision, the Spirit said to him, "Simon, three men are looking for you. [20]So get up and go downstairs. Do not hesitate to go with them, for I have sent them."

Acts 11 [5]"I was in the city of Joppa praying, and in a trance I saw a vision. I saw something like a large sheet being let down from heaven by its four corners, and it came down to where I was."

Acts 16 [9]During the night Paul had a vision of a man of Macedonia standing and begging him, "Come over to Macedonia and help us." [10]After Paul had seen the vision, we got ready at once to leave for Macedonia, concluding that God had called us to preach the gospel to them.

Acts 18 [9]One night the Lord spoke to Paul in a vision: "Do not be afraid; keep on speaking, do not be silent. [10]For I am with you, and no one is going to attack and harm you, because I have many people in this city."

Acts 22 [17]"When I returned to Jerusalem and was praying at the temple, I fell into a trance [18]and saw the Lord speaking. 'Quick!' he said to me. 'Leave Jerusalem immediately, because they will not accept your testimony about me.'

[19]"'Lord,' I replied, 'these men know that I went from one synagogue to another to imprison and beat those who believe in you. [20]And when the blood of your martyr Stephen was shed, I stood there giving my approval and guarding the clothes of those who were killing him.'

[21]"Then the Lord said to me, 'Go; I will send you far away to the Gentiles.'"

Acts 26 [19]"So then, King Agrippa, I was not disobedient to the vision from heaven."

2 Cor 12 [1]I must go on boasting. Although there is nothing to be gained, I will go on to visions and revelations from the Lord.

II
General Revelation

A. Knowledge of God Is Revealed

Ps 19 [1]The heavens declare the glory of God; the skies proclaim the work of his hands. [2]Day after day they pour forth speech; night after night they display knowledge. [3]There is no speech or language where their voice is not heard. [4]Their voice goes out into all the earth, their words to the ends of the world.

In the heavens he has pitched a tent for the sun. . . .

Ps 22 [27]All the ends of the earth will remember and turn to the LORD, and all the families of the nations will bow down before him, [28]for dominion belongs to the LORD and he rules over the nations.

Ps 48 [10]Like your name, O God, your praise reaches to the ends of the earth; your right hand is filled with righteousness.

John 1 [1]In the beginning was the Word, and the Word was with God, and the Word was God. [2]He was with God in the beginning.

[3]Through him all things were made; without him nothing was made that has been made. [4]In him was life, and that life was the light of men. [5]The light shines in the darkness, but the darkness has not understood it. . . . [9]The true light that gives light to every man was coming into the world.

Rom 1 [18]The wrath of God is being revealed from heaven against all the godlessness and wickedness of men who suppress the truth by their wickedness, [19]since what may be known about God is plain to them, because God has made it plain to them. [20]For since the creation of the world God's invisible qualities—his eternal power and divine nature—have been clearly seen, being understood from what has been made, so that men are without excuse. . . .

[28]Furthermore, since they did not think it worthwhile to retain the knowledge of God, he gave them over to a depraved mind, to do what ought not to be done.

B. The Nature of God Is Revealed

1. God as Living Creator Is Revealed

Acts 14 [15]"Men, why are you doing this? We too are only men, human like you. We are bringing you good news, telling you to turn from these worthless things to the living God, who made heaven and earth and sea and everything in them. [16]In the past, he let all nations go their own way. [17]Yet he has not left himself without testimony: He has shown kindness by giving you rain from heaven and crops in their seasons; he provides you with plenty of food and fills your hearts with joy."

2. God's Divine Nature Is Revealed

Rom 1 [20]For since the creation of the world God's invisible qualities—his eternal power and divine nature—have been clearly seen, being understood from what has been made, so that men are without excuse.

3. God's Immanence and Transcendence Are Revealed

Acts 17 [24]"The God who made the world and everything in it is the Lord of heaven and earth and does not live in temples built by hands. [25]And he is not served by human hands, as if he needed anything, because he himself gives all men life and breath and everything else. [26]From one man he made every nation of men, that they should inhabit the whole earth; and he determined the times set for them and the exact places where they should live. [27]God did this so that men would seek him and perhaps reach out for him and find him, though he is not far from each one of us. [28]'For in him we live and move and have our being.' As some of your own poets have said, 'We are his offspring.'"

4. God's Kindness Is Revealed

Matt 5 [45]". . . that you may be sons of your Father in heaven. He causes his sun to rise on the evil and the good, and sends rain on the righteous and the unrighteous."

Acts 14 [17]"Yet he has not left himself without testimony: He has shown kindness by giving you rain from heaven and crops in their seasons; he provides you with plenty of food and fills your hearts with joy."

5. God's Majesty and Glory Are Revealed

Ps 8 [1]O LORD, our Lord, how majestic is your name in all the earth!

You have set your glory above the heavens. [2]From the lips of children and infants you have ordained praise because of your enemies, to silence the foe and the avenger.

[3]When I consider your heavens, the work of your fingers, the moon and the stars, which you have set in place, [4]what is man that you are mindful of him, the son of man that you care for him?

Ps 19 [1]The heavens declare the glory of God; the skies proclaim the work of his hands.

6. God's Power Is Revealed

Ps 29 [3]The voice of the LORD is over the waters; the God of glory thunders, the LORD thunders over the mighty waters. [4]The voice of the LORD is powerful; the voice of the LORD is majestic. [5]The voice of the LORD breaks the cedars; the LORD breaks in pieces the cedars of Lebanon. [6]He makes Lebanon skip like a calf, Sirion like a young wild ox. [7]The voice of the LORD strikes with flashes of lightning. [8]The voice of the LORD shakes the desert; the LORD shakes the Desert of Kadesh. [9]The voice of the LORD twists the oaks and strips the forests bare. And in his temple all cry, "Glory!"

[10]The LORD sits enthroned over the flood; the LORD is enthroned as King forever.

Rom 1 [20]For since the creation of the world God's invisible qualities—his eternal power and divine nature—have been clearly seen, being understood from what has been made, so that men are without excuse.

7. God's Righteousness Is Revealed

Rom 1 [20]For since the creation of the world God's invisible qualities—his eternal power and divine nature—have been clearly seen, being understood from what has been made, so that men are without excuse. . . . [32]Although they know God's righteous decree that those who do such things deserve death, they not only continue to do these very things but also approve of those who practice them.

8. God's Truth Is Revealed

Rom 1 [21]For although they knew God, they neither glorified him as God nor gave thanks to him, but their thinking became futile and their foolish hearts were darkened. . . . [25]They exchanged the truth of God for a lie, and worshiped and served created things rather than the Creator—who is forever praised. Amen.

C. The Moral Requirements of God Are Revealed

1. Basic Moral Principles Are Revealed

Matt 5 [46]"If you love those who love you, what reward will you get? Are not even the tax collectors doing that? [47]And if you greet only your brothers, what are you doing more than others? Do not even pagans do that?"

Rom 2 [13]For it is not those who hear the law who are righteous in God's sight, but it is those who obey the law who will be declared righteous. [14](Indeed, when Gentiles, who do not have the law, do by nature things required by the law, they are a law for themselves, even though they do not have the law, [15]since they show that the requirements of the law are written on their hearts, their consciences also bearing witness, and their thoughts now accusing, now even defending them.) [16]This will take place on the day when God will judge men's secrets through Jesus Christ, as my gospel declares.

2. The Fact of Judgment Is Revealed

Rom 1 [21]For although they knew God, they neither glorified him as God nor gave thanks to him, but their thinking became futile and their foolish hearts were darkened. [22]Although they claimed to be wise, they became fools [23]and exchanged the glory of the immortal God for images made to look like mortal man and birds and animals and reptiles.

[24]Therefore God gave them over in the sinful desires of their hearts to sexual impurity for the degrading of their bodies with one another. [25]They exchanged the truth of God for a lie, and worshiped and served created things rather than the Creator—who is forever praised. Amen. . . . [32]Although they know God's righteous decree that those who do such things deserve death, they not only continue to do these very things but also approve of those who practice them.

3. The Need to Seek God Is Revealed

Acts 17 [27]"God did this so that men would seek him and perhaps reach out for him and find him, though he is not far from each one of us."

4. The Need to Worship Is Revealed

Acts 17 [22]Paul then stood up in the meeting of the Areopagus and said: "Men of Athens! I see that in every way you are very religious. [23]For as I walked around and looked carefully at your objects of worship, I even found an altar with this inscription: TO AN UNKNOWN GOD. Now what you worship as something unknown I am going to proclaim to you."

D. The Will of God to Save Is Revealed

Acts 17 [27]"God did this so that men would seek him and perhaps reach out for him and find him, though he is not far from each one of us."

Rom 2 [5]But because of your stubbornness and your unrepentant heart, you are storing up wrath against yourself for the day of God's wrath, when his righteous judgment will be revealed. [6]God "will give to each person according to what he has done." [7]To those who by persistence in doing good seek glory, honor and immortality, he will give eternal life. [8]But for those who are self-seeking and who reject the truth and follow evil, there will be wrath and anger. [9]There will be trouble and distress for every human being who does evil: first for the Jew, then for the Gentile; [10]but glory, honor and peace for everyone who does good: first for the Jew, then for the Gentile. [11]For God does not show favoritism.

Titus 2 [11]For the grace of God that brings salvation has appeared to all men.

2 Pet 3 [3]First of all, you must understand that in the last days scoffers will come, scoffing and following their own evil desires. [4]They will say, "Where is this 'coming' he promised? Ever since our fathers died, everything goes on as it has since the beginning of creation." . . .

[8]But do not forget this one thing, dear friends: With the Lord a day is like a thousand years, and a thousand years are like a day. [9]The Lord is not slow in keeping his promise, as some understand slowness. He is patient with you, not wanting anyone to perish, but everyone to come to repentance.

See also p. 1b, The Existence of God; p. 39a, God Is Known by Various Ways

III
Special Revelation

A. The Divine Authority of Scripture

1. The Source of the Bible

a) Scripture Is God's Word

Matt 15 [4]"For God said, 'Honor your father and mother' and 'Anyone who curses his father or mother must be put to death.' [5]But you say that if a man says to his father or mother, 'Whatever help you might otherwise have received from me is a gift devoted to God,' [6]he is not to 'honor his father' with it. Thus you nullify the word of God for the sake of your tradition."

Luke 8 [19]Now Jesus' mother and brothers came to see him, but they were not able to get near him because of the crowd. [20]Someone told him, "Your mother and brothers are standing outside, wanting to see you."

[21]He replied, "My mother and brothers are those who hear God's word and put it into practice."

Acts 4 [31]After they prayed, the place where they were meeting was shaken. And they were all filled with the Holy Spirit and spoke the word of God boldly.

Acts 13 [32]"We tell you the good news: What God promised our fathers [33]he has fulfilled for us, their children, by raising up Jesus. As it is written in the second Psalm: 'You are my Son; today I have become your Father.'"

Acts 13 [46]Then Paul and Barnabas answered them boldly: "We had to speak the word of God to you first. Since you reject it and do not consider yourselves worthy of eternal life, we now turn to the Gentiles. [47]For this is what the Lord has commanded us: 'I have made you a light for the Gentiles, that you may bring salvation to the ends of the earth.'"

2 Tim 3 [16]All Scripture is God-breathed and is useful for teaching, rebuking, correcting and training in righteousness. . . .

b) Scripture Was Written at God's Command

Exod 17 [14]Then the LORD said to Moses, "Write this on a scroll as something to be remembered and make sure that Joshua hears it, because I will completely blot out the memory of Amalek from under heaven."

Exod 32 [15]Moses turned and went down the mountain with the two tablets of the Testimony in his hands. They were inscribed on both sides, front and back. [16]The tablets were the work of God; the writing was the writing of God, engraved on the tablets.

Exod 34 [1]The LORD said to Moses, "Chisel out two stone tablets like the first ones, and I will write on them the words that were on the first tablets, which you broke." . . .

[27]Then the LORD said to Moses, "Write down these words, for in accordance with these words I have made a covenant with you and with Israel."

Deut 10 [1]At that time the LORD said to me, "Chisel out two stone tablets like the first ones and come up to me on the mountain. Also make a wooden chest. [2]I will write on the tablets the words that were on the first tablets, which you broke. Then you are to put them in the chest."

Jer 30 [2]"This is what the LORD, the God of Israel, says: 'Write in a book all the words I have spoken to you.'"

Jer 36 [2]"Take a scroll and write on it all the words I have spoken to you concerning Israel, Judah and all the other nations from the time I began speaking to you in the reign of Josiah till now."

Hab 2 [2]Then the LORD replied: "Write down the revelation and make it plain on tablets so that a herald may run with it."

Acts 4 [24]When they heard this, they raised their voices together in prayer to God. "Sovereign Lord," they said, "you made the heaven and the earth and the sea, and everything in them. [25]You spoke by the Holy Spirit through the mouth of your servant, our father David: 'Why do the nations rage and the peoples plot in vain? [26]The kings of the earth take their stand and the rulers gather together against the Lord and against his Anointed One.'"

Rev 1 [11]which said: "Write on a scroll what you see and send it to the seven churches: to Ephesus, Smyrna, Pergamum, Thyatira, Sardis, Philadelphia and Laodicea."

[12]I turned around to see the voice that was speaking to me. And when I turned I saw seven golden lampstands, [13]and among the lampstands was someone "like a son of man," dressed in a robe reaching down to his feet and with a golden sash around his chest. [14]His head and hair were white like wool, as white as snow, and his eyes were like blazing fire. [15]His feet were like bronze glowing in a furnace, and his voice was like the sound of rushing waters. [16]In his right hand he held seven stars, and out of his mouth came a sharp double-edged sword. His face was like the sun shining in all its brilliance.

[17]When I saw him, I fell at his feet as though dead. Then he placed his right hand on me and said: "Do not be afraid. I am the First and the Last. [18]I am the Living One; I was dead, and behold I am alive for ever and ever! And I hold the keys of death and Hades.

[19]"Write, therefore, what you have seen, what is now and what will take place later."

c) Scripture Cannot Be Broken

Ps 119 [160]All your words are true; all your righteous laws are eternal.

Matt 5 [17]"Do not think that I have come to abolish the Law or the Prophets; I have not come to abolish them but to fulfill them. [18]I tell you the truth, until heaven and earth disappear, not the smallest letter, not the least stroke of a pen, will by any means disappear from the Law until everything is accomplished."

John 10 [35]"If he called them 'gods,' to whom the word of God came—and the Scripture cannot be broken . . ."

Acts 1 [15]In those days Peter stood up among the believers (a group numbering about a hundred and twenty) [16]and said, "Brothers, the Scripture had to be fulfilled which the Holy Spirit spoke long ago through the mouth of David concerning Judas, who served as guide for those who arrested Jesus—[17]he was one of our number and shared in this ministry."

d) Scripture Has God's Final Authority

Acts 24 [14]"However, I admit that I worship the God of our fathers as a follower of the Way, which they call a sect. I believe everything that agrees with the Law and that is written in the Prophets. . . ."

Rom 3 [4]Not at all! Let God be true, and every man a liar. As it is written: "So that you may be proved right when you speak and prevail when you judge."

Rom 4 [16]Therefore, the promise comes by faith, so that it may be by grace and may be guaranteed to all Abraham's offspring—not only to those who are of the law but also to those who are of the faith of Abraham. He is the father of us all. [17]As it is written: "I have made you a father of many nations." He is our father in the sight of God, in whom he believed—the God who gives life to the dead and calls things that are not as though they were. . . . [22]This is why "it was credited to him as righteousness." [23]The words "it was credited to him" were written not for him alone, [24]but also for us, to whom God will credit righteousness—for us who believe in him who raised Jesus our Lord from the dead.

Rom 10 [10]For it is with your heart that you believe and are justified, and it is with your mouth that you confess and are saved. [11]As the Scripture says, "Anyone who trusts in him will never be put to shame." . . .

[16]But not all the Israelites accepted the good news. For Isaiah says, "Lord, who has believed our message?"

Rom 15 [3]For even Christ did not please himself but, as it is written: "The insults of those who insult you have fallen on me." [4]For everything that was written in the past was written to teach us, so that through endurance and the encouragement of the Scriptures we might have hope.

[5]May the God who gives endurance and encouragement give you a spirit of unity among yourselves as you follow Christ Jesus, [6]so that with one heart and mouth you may glorify the God and Father of our Lord Jesus Christ.

1 Cor 2 [9]However, as it is written: "No eye has seen, no ear has heard, no mind has conceived what God has prepared for those who love him"—[10]but God has revealed it to us by his Spirit.

The Spirit searches all things, even the deep things of God.

Gal 3 [10]All who rely on observing the law are under a curse, for it is written: "Cursed is everyone who does not continue to do everything written in the Book of the Law."

See also p. 258a, Christ Considered the OT Inspired; p. 259b, Christ Used the OT Authoritatively

e) Scripture Possesses God's Qualities

Ps 18 [30]As for God, his way is perfect; the word of the LORD is flawless. He is a shield for all who take refuge in him.

Ps 33 [4]For the word of the LORD is right and true; he is faithful in all he does.

Ps 119 [89]Your word, O LORD, is eternal; it stands firm in the heavens.

Prov 30 [5]"Every word of God is flawless; he is a shield to those who take refuge in him."

Gal 3 [8]The Scripture foresaw that God would justify the Gentiles by faith, and announced the gospel in advance to Abraham: "All nations will be blessed through you."

Heb 4 [12]For the word of God is living and active. Sharper than any double-edged sword, it penetrates even to dividing soul and spirit, joints and marrow; it judges the thoughts and attitudes of the heart. [13]Nothing in all creation is hidden from God's sight. Everything is uncovered and laid bare before the eyes of him to whom we must give account.

[14]Therefore, since we have a great high priest who has gone through the heavens, Jesus the Son of God, let us hold firmly to the faith we profess.

1 Pet 1 [23]For you have been born again, not of perishable seed, but of imperishable, through the living and enduring word of God. [24]For, "All men are like grass, and all their glory is like the flowers of the field; the grass withers and the flowers fall, [25]but the word of the Lord stands forever." And this is the word that was preached to you.

2. Names for the Bible (or for Parts of It)

1) Ancient Laws

Ps 119 [52]I remember your ancient laws, O LORD, and I find comfort in them.

2) Book of Moses

2 Chron 25 [4]Yet he did not put their sons to death, but acted in accordance with what is written in the Law, in the Book of Moses, where the LORD commanded: "Fathers shall not be put to death for their children, nor children put to death for their fathers; each is to die for his own sins."
Neh 13 [1]On that day the Book of Moses was read aloud in the hearing of the people and there it was found written that no Ammonite or Moabite should ever be admitted into the assembly of God. . . .

3) Book of Prophecy

Rev 22 [18]I warn everyone who hears the words of the prophecy of this book: If anyone adds anything to them, God will add to him the plagues described in this book. [19]And if anyone takes words away from this book of prophecy, God will take away from him his share in the tree of life and in the holy city, which are described in this book.

4) Book of the Covenant

Exod 24 [7]Then he took the Book of the Covenant and read it to the people. They responded, "We will do everything the LORD has said; we will obey."
2 Chron 34 [30]He went up to the temple of the LORD with the men of Judah, the people of Jerusalem, the priests and the Levites—all the people from the least to the greatest. He read in their hearing all the words of the Book of the Covenant, which had been found in the temple of the LORD.

5) Book of the Law

Deut 28 [61]The LORD will also bring on you every kind of sickness and disaster not recorded in this Book of the Law, until you are destroyed.
Josh 1 [8]"Do not let this Book of the Law depart from your mouth; meditate on it day and night, so that you may be careful to do everything written in it. Then you will be prosperous and successful."
2 Kings 22 [8]Hilkiah the high priest said to Shaphan the secretary, "I have found the Book of the Law in the temple of the LORD." He gave it to Shaphan, who read it. [9]Then Shaphan the secretary went to the king and reported to him: "Your officials have paid out the money that was in the temple of the LORD and have entrusted it to the workers and supervisors at the temple." [10]Then Shaphan the secretary informed the king, "Hilkiah the priest has given me a book." And Shaphan read from it in the presence of the king.

[11]When the king heard the words of the Book of the Law, he tore his robes. [12]He gave these orders to Hilkiah the priest, Ahikam son of Shaphan, Acbor son of Micaiah, Shaphan the secretary and Asaiah the king's attendant: [13]"Go and inquire of the LORD for me and for the people and for all Judah about what is written in this book that has been found. Great is the LORD's anger that burns against us because our fathers have not obeyed the words of this book; they have not acted in accordance with all that is written there concerning us."
Neh 8 [3]He read it aloud from daybreak till noon as he faced the square before the Water Gate in the presence of the men, women and others who could understand. And all the people listened attentively to the Book of the Law.
Gal 3 [10]All who rely on observing the law are under a curse, for it is written: "Cursed is everyone who does not continue to do everything written in the Book of the Law."

6) Book of the Law of God

Josh 24 [26]And Joshua recorded these things in the Book of the Law of God. Then he took a large stone and set it up there under the oak near the holy place of the LORD.
Neh 8 [8]They read from the Book of the Law of God, making it clear and giving the meaning so that the people could understand what was being read.

7) Book of the Law of Moses

Josh 8 [30]Then Joshua built on Mount Ebal an altar to the LORD, the God of Israel, [31]as Moses the servant of the LORD had commanded the Israelites. He built it according to what is written in the Book of the Law of Moses—an altar of uncut stones, on which no iron tool had been used. On it they offered to the LORD burnt offerings and sacrificed fellowship offerings.
Josh 23 [6]"Be very strong; be careful to obey all that is written in the Book of the Law of Moses, without turning aside to the right or to the left."
2 Kings 14 [6]Yet he did not put the sons of the assassins to death, in accordance with what is written in the Book of the Law of Moses where the LORD commanded: "Fathers shall not be put to death for their children, nor children put to death for their fathers; each is to die for his own sins."

8) Book of the Law of the Lord

2 Chron 17 [9]They taught throughout Judah, taking with them the Book of the Law of the LORD; they went around to all the towns of Judah and taught the people.

9) Book of the Prophets

Acts 7 [42]"But God turned away and gave them over to the worship of the heavenly bodies. This agrees with what is written in the book of the prophets: 'Did you bring me sacrifices and offerings forty years in the desert, O house of Israel? [43]You have lifted up the shrine of Molech and the star of your god Rephan, the idols you made to worship. Therefore I will send you into exile' beyond Babylon."

10) Book of Truth

Dan 10 [21]". . . but first I will tell you what is written in the Book of Truth. (No one supports me against them except Michael, your prince.)"

11) Commands

1 Kings 3 [14]"And if you walk in my ways and obey my statutes and commands as David your father did, I will give you a long life."
1 Kings 11 [38]"'If you do whatever I command you and walk in my ways and do what is right in my eyes by keeping my statutes and commands, as David my servant did, I will be with you. I will build you a dynasty as enduring as the one I built for David and will give Israel to you.'"
Ps 19 [8]The precepts of the LORD are right, giving joy to the heart. The commands of the LORD are radiant, giving light to the eyes.
Ps 119 [73]Your hands made me and formed me; give me understanding to learn your commands.
Ps 119 [86]All your commands are trustworthy; help me, for men persecute me without cause.
Ps 119 ^{131}I open my mouth and pant, longing for your commands.
Ps 119 [151]Yet you are near, O LORD, and all your commands are true.
Ps 119 [172]May my tongue sing of your word, for all your commands are righteous.

12) Covenants

Rom 9 [3]For I could wish that I myself were cursed and cut off from Christ for the sake of my brothers, those of my own race, [4]the people of Israel. Theirs is the adoption as sons; theirs the divine glory, the covenants, the receiving of the law, the temple worship and the promises.

13) Covenants of the Promise

Eph 2 [12]remember that at that time you were separate from Christ, excluded from citizenship in Israel and foreigners to the covenants of the promise, without hope and without God in the world.

14) Decrees

1 Kings 9 [4]"As for you, if you walk before me in integrity of heart and uprightness, as David your father did, and do all I command and observe my decrees and laws . . ."

Neh 1 [7]"We have acted very wickedly toward you. We have not obeyed the commands, decrees and laws you gave your servant Moses."
Ps 119 [16]I delight in your decrees; I will not neglect your word.
Ps 119 [48]I lift up my hands to your commands, which I love, and I meditate on your decrees.
Ps 119 [54]Your decrees are the theme of my song wherever I lodge.
Ps 119 [64]The earth is filled with your love, O LORD; teach me your decrees.
Ps 119 [112]My heart is set on keeping your decrees to the very end.
Ezek 18 [17]"He withholds his hand from sin and takes no usury or excessive interest. He keeps my laws and follows my decrees. He will not die for his father's sin; he will surely live."

15) Holy Scriptures

Rom 1 [2]the gospel he promised beforehand through his prophets in the Holy Scriptures . . .
2 Tim 3 [15]and how from infancy you have known the holy Scriptures, which are able to make you wise for salvation through faith in Christ Jesus.

16) Law

2 Chron 25 [4]Yet he did not put their sons to death, but acted in accordance with what is written in the Law, in the Book of Moses, where the LORD commanded: "Fathers shall not be put to death for their children, nor children put to death for their fathers; each is to die for his own sins."
2 Chron 34 [19]When the king heard the words of the Law, he tore his robes.
Ezra 10 [3]"Now let us make a covenant before our God to send away all these women and their children, in accordance with the counsel of my lord and of those who fear the commands of our God. Let it be done according to the Law."
Neh 8 [7]The Levites—Jeshua, Bani, Sherebiah, Jamin, Akkub, Shabbethai, Hodiah, Maaseiah, Kelita, Azariah, Jozabad, Hanan and Pelaiah—instructed the people in the Law while the people were standing there. . . .

[9]Then Nehemiah the governor, Ezra the priest and scribe, and the Levites who were instructing the people said to them all, "This day is sacred to the LORD your God. Do not mourn or weep." For all the people had been weeping as they listened to the words of the Law.
Neh 10 [34]"We—the priests, the Levites and the people—have cast lots to determine when each of our families is to bring to the house of our God at set times each year a contribution of wood to burn on the altar of the LORD our God, as it is written in the Law."
Ps 19 [7]The law of the LORD is perfect, reviving the soul. The statutes of the LORD are trustworthy, making wise the simple.
Ps 119 [72]The law from your mouth is more precious to me than thousands of pieces of silver and gold.
Ps 119 [97]Oh, how I love your law! I meditate on it all day long.
Ps 119 [142]Your righteousness is everlasting and your law is true.
Ps 119 [174]I long for your salvation, O LORD, and your law is my delight.
Matt 5 [18]"I tell you the truth, until heaven and earth disappear, not the smallest letter, not the least stroke of a pen, will by any means disappear from the Law until everything is accomplished."
Matt 12 [5]"Or haven't you read in the Law that on the Sabbath the priests in the temple desecrate the day and yet are innocent?"
Luke 10 [26]"What is written in the Law?" he replied. "How do you read it?"

[27]He answered: "'Love the Lord your God with all your heart and with all your soul and with all your strength and with all your mind'; and, 'Love your neighbor as yourself.'"

[28]"You have answered correctly," Jesus replied. "Do this and you will live."
Luke 16 [17]"It is easier for heaven and earth to disappear than for the least stroke of a pen to drop out of the Law."
John 7 [19]"Has not Moses given you the law? Yet not one of you keeps the law. Why are you trying to kill me?"
John 10 [34]Jesus answered them, "Is it not written in your Law, 'I have said you are gods'?"
1 Cor 14 [21]In the Law it is written: "Through men of strange tongues and through the lips of foreigners I will speak to this people, but even then they will not listen to me," says the Lord.

17) Law and the Prophets

Matt 5 [17]"Do not think that I have come to abolish the Law or the Prophets; I have not come to abolish them but to fulfill them."
Matt 11 [13]"For all the Prophets and the Law prophesied until John."
Luke 16 [16]"The Law and the Prophets were proclaimed until John. Since that time, the good news of the kingdom of God is being preached, and everyone is forcing his way into it."
John 1 [45]Philip found Nathanael and told him, "We have found the one Moses wrote about in the Law, and about whom the prophets also wrote—Jesus of Nazareth, the son of Joseph."
Acts 13 [15]After the reading from the Law and the Prophets, the synagogue rulers sent word to them, saying, "Brothers, if you have a message of encouragement for the people, please speak."
Acts 28 [23]They arranged to meet Paul on a certain day, and came in even larger numbers to the place where he was staying. From morning till evening he explained and declared to them the kingdom of God and tried to convince them about Jesus from the Law of Moses and from the Prophets.
Rom 3 [21]But now a righteousness from God, apart from law, has been made known, to which the Law and the Prophets testify.

18) Law of God

Neh 10 [28]"The rest of the people—priests, Levites, gatekeepers, singers, temple servants and all who separated themselves from the neighboring peoples for the sake of the Law of God, together with their wives and all their sons and daughters who are able to understand—[29]all these now join their brothers the nobles, and bind themselves with a curse and an oath to follow the Law of God given through Moses the servant of God and to obey carefully all the commands, regulations and decrees of the LORD our Lord."
Ps 37 [31]The law of his God is in his heart; his feet do not slip.
Isa 1 [10]Hear the word of the LORD, you rulers of Sodom; listen to the law of our God, you people of Gomorrah!
Hos 4 [6]". . . my people are destroyed from lack of knowledge.

"Because you have rejected knowledge, I also reject you as my priests; because you have ignored the law of your God, I also will ignore your children."

19) Law of Moses

1 Kings 2 [3]". . . and observe what the LORD your God requires: Walk in his ways, and keep his decrees and commands, his laws and requirements, as written in the Law of Moses, so that you may prosper in all you do and wherever you go. . . ."
2 Chron 23 [18]Then Jehoiada placed the oversight of the temple of the LORD in the hands of the priests, who were Levites, to whom David had made assignments in the temple, to present the burnt offerings of the LORD as written in the Law of Moses, with rejoicing and singing, as David had ordered.
Dan 9 [11]"All Israel has transgressed your law and turned away, refusing to obey you.

"Therefore the curses and sworn judgments written in the Law of Moses, the servant of God, have been poured out on us, because we have sinned against you."
Luke 2 [22]When the time of their purification according to the Law of Moses had been completed, Joseph and Mary took him to Jerusalem to present him to the Lord. . . .
Acts 13 [39]"Through him everyone who believes is justified from everything you could not be justified from by the law of Moses."
1 Cor 9 [9]For it is written in the Law of Moses: "Do not muzzle an ox while it is treading out the grain." Is it about oxen that God is concerned?
Heb 10 [28]Anyone who rejected the law of Moses died without mercy on the testimony of two or three witnesses.

20) Law of Moses, the Prophets, and the Psalms

Luke 24 [44]He said to them, "This is what I told you while I was still with you: Everything must be fulfilled that is written about me in the Law of Moses, the Prophets and the Psalms."

21) *Law of the God of Heaven*

Ezra 7 [12]Artaxerxes, king of kings,

To Ezra the priest, a teacher of the Law of the God of heaven: Greetings.

Ezra 7 [21]Now I, King Artaxerxes, order all the treasurers of Trans-Euphrates to provide with diligence whatever Ezra the priest, a teacher of the Law of the God of heaven, may ask of you. . . .

22) *Law of the Lord*

1 Chron 16 [40]to present burnt offerings to the LORD on the altar of burnt offering regularly, morning and evening, in accordance with everything written in the Law of the LORD, which he had given Israel.

2 Chron 31 [3]The king contributed from his own possessions for the morning and evening burnt offerings and for the burnt offerings on the Sabbaths, New Moons and appointed feasts as written in the Law of the LORD. [4]He ordered the people living in Jerusalem to give the portion due the priests and Levites so they could devote themselves to the Law of the LORD.

Ps 1 [2]But his delight is in the law of the LORD, and on his law he meditates day and night.

Ps 19 [7]The law of the LORD is perfect, reviving the soul. The statutes of the LORD are trustworthy, making wise the simple.

Ps 119 [1]Blessed are they whose ways are blameless, who walk according to the law of the LORD.

Jer 8 [8]"'How can you say, "We are wise, for we have the law of the LORD," when actually the lying pen of the scribes has handled it falsely?'"

Luke 2 [39]When Joseph and Mary had done everything required by the Law of the Lord, they returned to Galilee to their own town of Nazareth.

23) *Living Words*

Acts 7 [38]"He was in the assembly in the desert, with the angel who spoke to him on Mount Sinai, and with our fathers; and he received living words to pass on to us."

24) *Moses*

Acts 15 [21]"For Moses has been preached in every city from the earliest times and is read in the synagogues on every Sabbath."

2 Cor 3 [15]Even to this day when Moses is read, a veil covers their hearts.

25) *Moses and the Prophets*

Luke 16 [29]"Abraham replied, 'They have Moses and the Prophets; let them listen to them.'"

Luke 24 [27]And beginning with Moses and all the Prophets, he explained to them what was said in all the Scriptures concerning himself.

26) *Perfect Law*

James 1 [25]But the man who looks intently into the perfect law that gives freedom, and continues to do this, not forgetting what he has heard, but doing it—he will be blessed in what he does.

27) *Precepts*

Ps 19 [8]The precepts of the LORD are right, giving joy to the heart. The commands of the LORD are radiant, giving light to the eyes.

Ps 103 [17]But from everlasting to everlasting the LORD's love is with those who fear him, and his righteousness with their children's children—[18]with those who keep his covenant and remember to obey his precepts.

Ps 119 [4]You have laid down precepts that are to be fully obeyed.

Ps 119 [15]I meditate on your precepts and consider your ways.

Ps 119 [56]This has been my practice: I obey your precepts.

Ps 119 [69]Though the arrogant have smeared me with lies, I keep your precepts with all my heart.

Ps 119 [104]I gain understanding from your precepts; therefore I hate every wrong path.

Ps 119 [128]and because I consider all your precepts right, I hate every wrong path.

Ps 119 [173]May your hand be ready to help me, for I have chosen your precepts.

28) *Prophetic Writings*

Rom 16 [25]Now to him who is able to establish you by my gospel and the proclamation of Jesus Christ, according to the revelation of the mystery hidden for long ages past, [26]but now revealed and made known through the prophetic writings by the command of the eternal God, so that all nations might believe and obey him . . .

29) *Righteous Laws*

Ps 119 [7]I will praise you with an upright heart as I learn your righteous laws.

Ps 119 [106]I have taken an oath and confirmed it, that I will follow your righteous laws.

Ps 119 [160]All your words are true; all your righteous laws are eternal.

Ps 119 [164]Seven times a day I praise you for your righteous laws.

30) *Scripture*

Matt 21 [42]Jesus said to them, "Have you never read in the Scriptures: 'The stone the builders rejected has become the capstone; the Lord has done this, and it is marvelous in our eyes'?"

Matt 22 [29]Jesus replied, "You are in error because you do not know the Scriptures or the power of God."

Mark 12 [10]"Haven't you read this scripture: 'The stone the builders rejected has become the capstone . . .'?"

Luke 4 [21]and he began by saying to them, "Today this scripture is fulfilled in your hearing."

Luke 24 [27]And beginning with Moses and all the Prophets, he explained to them what was said in all the Scriptures concerning himself.

John 2 [22]After he was raised from the dead, his disciples recalled what he had said. Then they believed the Scripture and the words that Jesus had spoken.

John 5 [39]"You diligently study the Scriptures because you think that by them you possess eternal life. These are the Scriptures that testify about me, [40]yet you refuse to come to me to have life."

John 7 [42]"Does not the Scripture say that the Christ will come from David's family and from Bethlehem, the town where David lived?"

John 10 [35]"If he called them 'gods,' to whom the word of God came—and the Scripture cannot be broken . . ."

John 20 [9](They still did not understand from Scripture that Jesus had to rise from the dead.)

Acts 17 [11]Now the Bereans were of more noble character than the Thessalonians, for they received the message with great eagerness and examined the Scriptures every day to see if what Paul said was true.

Acts 18 [28]For he vigorously refuted the Jews in public debate, proving from the Scriptures that Jesus was the Christ.

Rom 10 [11]As the Scripture says, "Anyone who trusts in him will never be put to shame."

Rom 15 [4]For everything that was written in the past was written to teach us, so that through endurance and the encouragement of the Scriptures we might have hope.

1 Cor 15 [3]For what I received I passed on to you as of first importance: that Christ died for our sins according to the Scriptures, [4]that he was buried, that he was raised on the third day according to the Scriptures. . . .

Gal 3 [8]The Scripture foresaw that God would justify the Gentiles by faith, and announced the gospel in advance to Abraham: "All nations will be blessed through you."

Gal 3 [22]But the Scripture declares that the whole world is a prisoner of sin, so that what was promised, being given through faith in Jesus Christ, might be given to those who believe.

1 Tim 4 [13]Until I come, devote yourself to the public reading of Scripture, to preaching and to teaching.

2 Tim 3 [16]All Scripture is God-breathed and is useful for teaching, rebuking, correcting and training in righteousness, [17]so that the man of God may be thoroughly equipped for every good work.

2 Pet 1 [20]Above all, you must understand that no prophecy of Scripture came about by the prophet's own interpretation.

2 Pet 3 [16]He writes the same way in all his letters, speaking in them of these matters. His letters contain some things that are hard to understand, which ignorant and unstable people distort, as they do the other Scriptures, to their own destruction.

31) Scroll

Ps 40 [7]Then I said, "Here I am, I have come—it is written about me in the scroll."

32) Scroll of the Lord

Isa 34 [16]Look in the scroll of the LORD and read: None of these will be missing, not one will lack her mate. For it is his mouth that has given the order, and his Spirit will gather them together.

33) Statutes

1 Kings 3 [14]"And if you walk in my ways and obey my statutes and commands as David your father did, I will give you a long life."
1 Kings 11 [38]"'If you do whatever I command you and walk in my ways and do what is right in my eyes by keeping my statutes and commands, as David my servant did, I will be with you. I will build you a dynasty as enduring as the one I built for David and will give Israel to you.'"
Ps 19 [7]The law of the LORD is perfect, reviving the soul. The statutes of the LORD are trustworthy, making wise the simple.
Ps 93 [5]Your statutes stand firm; holiness adorns your house for endless days, O LORD.
Ps 119 [2]Blessed are they who keep his statutes and seek him with all their heart.
Ps 119 [24]Your statutes are my delight; they are my counselors.
Ps 119 [46]I will speak of your statutes before kings and will not be put to shame. . . .
Ps 119 [88]Preserve my life according to your love, and I will obey the statutes of your mouth.
Ps 119 [99]I have more insight than all my teachers, for I meditate on your statutes.
Ps 119 [111]Your statutes are my heritage forever; they are the joy of my heart.
Ps 119 [129]Your statutes are wonderful; therefore I obey them.
Ps 119 [138]The statutes you have laid down are righteous; they are fully trustworthy.
Ps 119 [144]Your statutes are forever right; give me understanding that I may live.
Ps 119 [152]Long ago I learned from your statutes that you established them to last forever.

34) Sword of the Spirit

Eph 6 [17]Take the helmet of salvation and the sword of the Spirit, which is the word of God.

35) The Very Words of God

Rom 3 [2]Much in every way! First of all, they have been entrusted with the very words of God.
1 Pet 4 [11]If anyone speaks, he should do it as one speaking the very words of God. If anyone serves, he should do it with the strength God provides, so that in all things God may be praised through Jesus Christ. To him be the glory and the power for ever and ever. Amen.

36) Word

Ps 119 [9]How can a young man keep his way pure? By living according to your word.
Ps 119 [11]I have hidden your word in my heart that I might not sin against you.
Ps 119 [89]Your word, O LORD, is eternal; it stands firm in the heavens.
Ps 119 [105]Your word is a lamp to my feet and a light for my path.
Ps 119 [114]You are my refuge and my shield; I have put my hope in your word.
Ps 119 [133]Direct my footsteps according to your word; let no sin rule over me.
Ps 119 [169]May my cry come before you, O LORD; give me understanding according to your word.
Gal 6 [6]Anyone who receives instruction in the word must share all good things with his instructor.
2 Tim 4 [2]Preach the Word; be prepared in season and out of season; correct, rebuke and encourage—with great patience and careful instruction.
James 1 [21]Therefore, get rid of all moral filth and the evil that is so prevalent and humbly accept the word planted in you, which can save you.

[22]Do not merely listen to the word, and so deceive yourselves. Do what it says. [23]Anyone who listens to the word but does not do what it says is like a man who looks at his face in a mirror [24]and, after looking at himself, goes away and immediately forgets what he looks like.
1 Pet 1 [25]". . . but the word of the Lord stands forever." And this is the word that was preached to you.
1 Pet 3 [1]Wives, in the same way be submissive to your husbands so that, if any of them do not believe the word, they may be won over without words by the behavior of their wives. . . .

37) Word of Christ

Rom 10 [17]Consequently, faith comes from hearing the message, and the message is heard through the word of Christ.
Eph 5 [25]Husbands, love your wives, just as Christ loved the church and gave himself up for her [26]to make her holy, cleansing her by the washing with water through the word, [27]and to present her to himself as a radiant church, without stain or wrinkle or any other blemish, but holy and blameless.
Col 3 [16]Let the word of Christ dwell in you richly as you teach and admonish one another with all wisdom, and as you sing psalms, hymns and spiritual songs with gratitude in your hearts to God.

38) Word of Encouragement

Heb 12 [5]And you have forgotten that word of encouragement that addresses you as sons: "My son, do not make light of the Lord's discipline, and do not lose heart when he rebukes you, [6]because the Lord disciplines those he loves, and he punishes everyone he accepts as a son." (Prov 3:11–12).

39) Word of Faith

Rom 10 [8]But what does it say? "The word is near you; it is in your mouth and in your heart," that is, the word of faith we are proclaiming. . . .

40) Word of God

Mark 7 [13]"Thus you nullify the word of God by your tradition that you have handed down. And you do many things like that."
Luke 11 [28]He replied, "Blessed rather are those who hear the word of God and obey it."
John 10 [35]"If he called them 'gods,' to whom the word of God came—and the Scripture cannot be broken . . ."
Acts 4 [31]After they prayed, the place where they were meeting was shaken. And they were all filled with the Holy Spirit and spoke the word of God boldly.
Acts 13 [5]When they arrived at Salamis, they proclaimed the word of God in the Jewish synagogues. John was with them as their helper.
Rom 9 [6]It is not as though God's word had failed. For not all who are descended from Israel are Israel.
2 Cor 2 [17]Unlike so many, we do not peddle the word of God for profit. On the contrary, in Christ we speak before God with sincerity, like men sent from God.
2 Cor 4 [2]Rather, we have renounced secret and shameful ways; we do not use deception, nor do we distort the word of God. On the contrary, by setting forth the truth plainly we commend ourselves to every man's conscience in the sight of God.
Eph 6 [17]Take the helmet of salvation and the sword of the Spirit, which is the word of God.
Phil 1 [14]Because of my chains, most of the brothers in the Lord have been encouraged to speak the word of God more courageously and fearlessly.
Col 1 [25]I have become its servant by the commission God gave me to present to you the word of God in its fullness. . . .
1 Thess 2 [13]And we also thank God continually because, when you received the word of God, which you heard from us, you accepted it not as the word of men, but as it actually is, the word of God, which is at work in you who believe.

1 Tim 4 [5]because it is consecrated by the word of God and prayer.
2 Tim 2 [8]Remember Jesus Christ, raised from the dead, descended from David. This is my gospel, [9]for which I am suffering even to the point of being chained like a criminal. But God's word is not chained.
Heb 4 [12]For the word of God is living and active. Sharper than any double-edged sword, it penetrates even to dividing soul and spirit, joints and marrow; it judges the thoughts and attitudes of the heart.
Heb 5 [12]In fact, though by this time you ought to be teachers, you need someone to teach you the elementary truths of God's word all over again. You need milk, not solid food!
Heb 13 [7]Remember your leaders, who spoke the word of God to you. Consider the outcome of their way of life and imitate their faith.
1 Pet 1 [22]Now that you have purified yourselves by obeying the truth so that you have sincere love for your brothers, love one another deeply, from the heart. [23]For you have been born again, not of perishable seed, but of imperishable, through the living and enduring word of God.
1 John 2 [14]I write to you, fathers, because you have known him who is from the beginning. I write to you, young men, because you are strong, and the word of God lives in you, and you have overcome the evil one.

41) Word of His Grace

Acts 20 [32]"Now I commit you to God and to the word of his grace, which can build you up and give you an inheritance among all those who are sanctified."

42) Word of Life

Phil 2 [14]Do everything without complaining or arguing, [15]so that you may become blameless and pure, children of God without fault in a crooked and depraved generation, in which you shine like stars in the universe [16]as you hold out the word of life—in order that I may boast on the day of Christ that I did not run or labor for nothing.

43) Word of the Lord

Isa 1 [10]Hear the word of the LORD, you rulers of Sodom; listen to the law of our God, you people of Gomorrah!
Acts 8 [25]When they had testified and proclaimed the word of the Lord, Peter and John returned to Jerusalem, preaching the gospel in many Samaritan villages.
1 Thess 4 [15]According to the Lord's own word, we tell you that we who are still alive, who are left till the coming of the Lord, will certainly not precede those who have fallen asleep.
1 Pet 1 [25]". . . but the word of the Lord stands forever." And this is the word that was preached to you.

44) Word of the Prophets

2 Pet 1 [19]And we have the word of the prophets made more certain, and you will do well to pay attention to it, as to a light shining in a dark place, until the day dawns and the morning star rises in your hearts.

45) Word of Truth

Ps 119 [43]Do not snatch the word of truth from my mouth, for I have put my hope in your laws.
Eph 1 [13]And you also were included in Christ when you heard the word of truth, the gospel of your salvation. Having believed, you were marked in him with a seal, the promised Holy Spirit. . . .
Col 1 [4]because we have heard of your faith in Christ Jesus and of the love you have for all the saints—[5]the faith and love that spring from the hope that is stored up for you in heaven and that you have already heard about in the word of truth, the gospel [6]that has come to you. All over the world this gospel is bearing fruit and growing, just as it has been doing among you since the day you heard it and understood God's grace in all its truth.
2 Tim 2 [15]Do your best to present yourself to God as one approved, a workman who does not need to be ashamed and who correctly handles the word of truth.
James 1 [18]He chose to give us birth through the word of truth, that we might be a kind of firstfruits of all he created.

46) Writings of the Prophets

Matt 26 [56]"But this has all taken place that the writings of the prophets might be fulfilled." Then all the disciples deserted him and fled.

3. Metaphors for the Bible and the Words of God

a) Scripture Is like a Counselor

Ps 119 [24]Your statutes are my delight; they are my counselors.

b) Scripture Is like Fire

Jer 5 [14]Therefore this is what the LORD God Almighty says: "Because the people have spoken these words, I will make my words in your mouth a fire and these people the wood it consumes."
Jer 23 [29]"Is not my word like fire," declares the LORD, "and like a hammer that breaks a rock in pieces?"

c) Scripture Is like Gold

Ps 19 [9]The fear of the LORD is pure, enduring forever. The ordinances of the LORD are sure and altogether righteous. [10]They are more precious than gold, than much pure gold; they are sweeter than honey, than honey from the comb.

d) Scripture Is like a Hammer

Jer 23 [29]"Is not my word like fire," declares the LORD, "and like a hammer that breaks a rock in pieces?"

e) Scripture Is like a Heritage

Ps 119 [111]Your statutes are my heritage forever; they are the joy of my heart.

f) Scripture Is like Honey

Ps 19 [9]The fear of the LORD is pure, enduring forever. The ordinances of the LORD are sure and altogether righteous. [10]They are more precious than gold, than much pure gold; they are sweeter than honey, than honey from the comb.
Ps 119 [103]How sweet are your words to my taste, sweeter than honey to my mouth!

g) Scripture Is like a Lamp

Ps 119 [105]Your word is a lamp to my feet and a light for my path.

h) Scripture Is like a Light

Ps 119 [105]Your word is a lamp to my feet and a light for my path.
Ps 119 [130]The unfolding of your words gives light; it gives understanding to the simple.
2 Pet 1 [19]And we have the word of the prophets made more certain, and you will do well to pay attention to it, as to a light shining in a dark place, until the day dawns and the morning star rises in your hearts.

i) Scripture Is like Milk

1 Cor 3 [1]Brothers, I could not address you as spiritual but as worldly—mere infants in Christ. [2]I gave you milk, not solid food, for you were not yet ready for it. Indeed, you are still not ready. [3]You are still worldly. For since there is jealousy and quarreling among you, are you not worldly? Are you not acting like mere men?
Heb 5 [11]We have much to say about this, but it is hard to explain because you are slow to learn. [12]In fact, though by this time you ought to be teachers, you need someone to teach you the elementary truths of God's word all over again. You need milk, not solid food! [13]Anyone who lives on milk, being still an infant, is not acquainted with the teaching about righteousness.
1 Pet 2 [2]Like newborn babies, crave pure spiritual milk, so that by it you may grow up in your salvation. . . .

j) Scripture Is like a Mirror

James 1 [23]Anyone who listens to the word but does not do what it says is like a man who looks at his face in a mirror [24]and, after looking at himself, goes away and immediately forgets what he looks like. [25]But the man who looks intently into the perfect law that gives freedom, and continues to do this, not forgetting what he has heard, but doing it—he will be blessed in what he does.

k) Scripture Is like Rain

Isa 55 [10]"As the rain and the snow come down from heaven, and do not return to it without watering the earth and making it bud and flourish, so that it yields seed for the sower and bread for the eater, [11]so is my word that goes out from my mouth: It will not return to me empty, but will accomplish what I desire and achieve the purpose for which I sent it."

l) Scripture Is like a Seed

1 Pet 1 [23]For you have been born again, not of perishable seed, but of imperishable, through the living and enduring word of God.

m) Scripture Is like Snow

Isa 55 [10]"As the rain and the snow come down from heaven, and do not return to it without watering the earth and making it bud and flourish, so that it yields seed for the sower and bread for the eater, [11]so is my word that goes out from my mouth: It will not return to me empty, but will accomplish what I desire and achieve the purpose for which I sent it."

n) Scripture Is like Solid Food

Heb 5 [11]We have much to say about this, but it is hard to explain because you are slow to learn. [12]In fact, though by this time you ought to be teachers, you need someone to teach you the elementary truths of God's word all over again. You need milk, not solid food! . . . [14]But solid food is for the mature, who by constant use have trained themselves to distinguish good from evil.

o) Scripture Is like a Sword

Eph 6 [17]Take the helmet of salvation and the sword of the Spirit, which is the word of God.
Heb 4 [12]For the word of God is living and active. Sharper than any double-edged sword, it penetrates even to dividing soul and spirit, joints and marrow; it judges the thoughts and attitudes of the heart.

p) Scripture Is like Water

Eph 5 [25]Husbands, love your wives, just as Christ loved the church and gave himself up for her [26]to make her holy, cleansing her by the washing with water through the word. . . .

4. The Purpose of the Bible

a) Scripture Is for Admonishment

Ps 17 [4]As for the deeds of men—by the word of your lips I have kept myself from the ways of the violent.
Ps 19 [9]The fear of the LORD is pure, enduring forever. The ordinances of the LORD are sure and altogether righteous. . . . [11]By them is your servant warned; in keeping them there is great reward.
1 Cor 10 [11]These things happened to them as examples and were written down as warnings for us, on whom the fulfillment of the ages has come.

b) Scripture Is for Assurance

1 John 5 [13]I write these things to you who believe in the name of the Son of God so that you may know that you have eternal life.

c) Scripture Is for Blessing

Deut 11 [22]If you carefully observe all these commands I am giving you to follow—to love the LORD your God, to walk in all his ways and to hold fast to him—[23]then the LORD will drive out all these nations before you, and you will dispossess nations larger and stronger than you. [24]Every place where you set your foot will be yours: Your territory will extend from the desert to Lebanon, and from the Euphrates River to the western sea. [25]No man will be able to stand against you. The LORD your God, as he promised you, will put the terror and fear of you on the whole land, wherever you go.

[26]See, I am setting before you today a blessing and a curse—[27]the blessing if you obey the commands of the LORD your God that I am giving you today; [28]the curse if you disobey the commands of the LORD your God and turn from the way that I command you today by following other gods, which you have not known.
Josh 1 [8]"Do not let this Book of the Law depart from your mouth; meditate on it day and night, so that you may be careful to do everything written in it. Then you will be prosperous and successful. [9]Have I not commanded you? Be strong and courageous. Do not be terrified; do not be discouraged, for the LORD your God will be with you wherever you go."
Ps 1 [1]Blessed is the man who does not walk in the counsel of the wicked or stand in the way of sinners or sit in the seat of mockers. [2]But his delight is in the law of the LORD, and on his law he meditates day and night. [3]He is like a tree planted by streams of water, which yields its fruit in season and whose leaf does not wither. Whatever he does prospers.
Ps 119 [1]Blessed are they whose ways are blameless, who walk according to the law of the LORD. [2]Blessed are they who keep his statutes and seek him with all their heart.
Luke 11 [28]He replied, "Blessed rather are those who hear the word of God and obey it."
James 1 [25]But the man who looks intently into the perfect law that gives freedom, and continues to do this, not forgetting what he has heard, but doing it—he will be blessed in what he does.
Rev 1 [3]Blessed is the one who reads the words of this prophecy, and blessed are those who hear it and take to heart what is written in it, because the time is near.

d) Scripture Is for Comfort

Ps 119 [50]My comfort in my suffering is this: Your promise preserves my life. [51]The arrogant mock me without restraint, but I do not turn from your law. [52]I remember your ancient laws, O LORD, and I find comfort in them.
Ps 119 [76]May your unfailing love be my comfort, according to your promise to your servant.

e) Scripture Is for Discipline

2 Tim 3 [16]All Scripture is God-breathed and is useful for teaching, rebuking, correcting and training in righteousness, [17]so that the man of God may be thoroughly equipped for every good work.

f) Scripture Is for Edification

Ps 19 [7]The law of the LORD is perfect, reviving the soul. The statutes of the LORD are trustworthy, making wise the simple. [8]The precepts of the LORD are right, giving joy to the heart. The commands of the LORD are radiant, giving light to the eyes.
Ps 119 [28]My soul is weary with sorrow; strengthen me according to your word.
Acts 20 [32]"Now I commit you to God and to the word of his grace, which can build you up and give you an inheritance among all those who are sanctified."
1 Tim 4 [6]If you point these things out to the brothers, you will be a good minister of Christ Jesus, brought up in the truths of the faith and of the good teaching that you have followed.

g) Scripture Is for Encouragement

Rom 15 [4]For everything that was written in the past was written to teach us, so that through endurance and the encouragement of the Scriptures we might have hope.
1 Thess 4 [18]Therefore encourage each other with these words.
Heb 12 [5]And you have forgotten that word of encouragement that addresses you as sons: "My son, do not make light of the Lord's discipline, and do not lose heart when he rebukes you, [6]because the Lord disciplines those he loves, and he punishes everyone he accepts as a son."

h) Scripture Is for Giving Life

John 6 [63]"The Spirit gives life; the flesh counts for nothing. The words I have spoken to you are spirit and they are life."
John 6 [68]Simon Peter answered him, "Lord, to whom shall we go? You have the words of eternal life."

i) Scripture Is for Guidance

Ps 19 [8]The precepts of the LORD are right, giving joy to the heart. The commands of the LORD are radiant, giving light to the eyes.
Ps 119 [35]Direct me in the path of your commands, for there I find delight.

Ps 119 [105]Your word is a lamp to my feet and a light for my path.
Ps 119 [130]The unfolding of your words gives light; it gives understanding to the simple.
Ps 119 [133]Direct my footsteps according to your word; let no sin rule over me.
Isa 8 [19]When men tell you to consult mediums and spiritists, who whisper and mutter, should not a people inquire of their God? Why consult the dead on behalf of the living? [20]To the law and to the testimony! If they do not speak according to this word, they have no light of dawn.
Acts 17 [11]Now the Bereans were of more noble character than the Thessalonians, for they received the message with great eagerness and examined the Scriptures every day to see if what Paul said was true.
2 Pet 1 [19]And we have the word of the prophets made more certain, and you will do well to pay attention to it, as to a light shining in a dark place, until the day dawns and the morning star rises in your hearts.

j) Scripture Is for Hearing

Exod 19 [7]So Moses went back and summoned the elders of the people and set before them all the words the LORD had commanded him to speak. . . .

[9]The LORD said to Moses, "I am going to come to you in a dense cloud, so that the people will hear me speaking with you and will always put their trust in you." Then Moses told the LORD what the people had said.
Deut 4 [1]Hear now, O Israel, the decrees and laws I am about to teach you. Follow them so that you may live and may go in and take possession of the land that the LORD, the God of your fathers, is giving you. [2]Do not add to what I command you and do not subtract from it, but keep the commands of the LORD your God that I give you.
Deut 4 [9]Only be careful, and watch yourselves closely so that you do not forget the things your eyes have seen or let them slip from your heart as long as you live. Teach them to your children and to their children after them. [10]Remember the day you stood before the LORD your God at Horeb, when he said to me, "Assemble the people before me to hear my words so that they may learn to revere me as long as they live in the land and may teach them to their children." [11]You came near and stood at the foot of the mountain while it blazed with fire to the very heavens, with black clouds and deep darkness. [12]Then the LORD spoke to you out of the fire. You heard the sound of words but saw no form; there was only a voice. [13]He declared to you his covenant, the Ten Commandments, which he commanded you to follow and then wrote them on two stone tablets.
Deut 31 [10]Then Moses commanded them: "At the end of every seven years, in the year for canceling debts, during the Feast of Tabernacles, [11]when all Israel comes to appear before the LORD your God at the place he will choose, you shall read this law before them in their hearing. [12]Assemble the people—men, women and children, and the aliens living in your towns—so they can listen and learn to fear the LORD your God and follow carefully all the words of this law. [13]Their children, who do not know this law, must hear it and learn to fear the LORD your God as long as you live in the land you are crossing the Jordan to possess."
Josh 3 [9]Joshua said to the Israelites, "Come here and listen to the words of the LORD your God."
Ps 85 [8]I will listen to what God the LORD will say; he promises peace to his people, his saints—but let them not return to folly.
Ezek 20 [47]"Say to the southern forest: 'Hear the word of the LORD. This is what the Sovereign LORD says: I am about to set fire to you, and it will consume all your trees, both green and dry. The blazing flame will not be quenched, and every face from south to north will be scorched by it.'"
Acts 2 [22]"Men of Israel, listen to this: Jesus of Nazareth was a man accredited by God to you by miracles, wonders and signs, which God did among you through him, as you yourselves know."
Acts 13 [7]who was an attendant of the proconsul, Sergius Paulus. The proconsul, an intelligent man, sent for Barnabas and Saul because he wanted to hear the word of God.
Acts 13 [44]On the next Sabbath almost the whole city gathered to hear the word of the Lord.
Rev 1 [3]Blessed is the one who reads the words of this prophecy, and blessed are those who hear it and take to heart what is written in it, because the time is near.
Rev 22 [18]I warn everyone who hears the words of the prophecy of this book: If anyone adds anything to them, God will add to him the plagues described in this book. [19]And if anyone takes words away from this book of prophecy, God will take away from him his share in the tree of life and in the holy city, which are described in this book.

k) Scripture Is for Hope

Ps 119 [49]Remember your word to your servant, for you have given me hope.
Rom 15 [4]For everything that was written in the past was written to teach us, so that through endurance and the encouragement of the Scriptures we might have hope.

l) Scripture Is for Learning

Deut 5 [1]Moses summoned all Israel and said: Hear, O Israel, the decrees and laws I declare in your hearing today. Learn them and be sure to follow them.
Ps 119 [7]I will praise you with an upright heart as I learn your righteous laws.
Ps 119 [71]It was good for me to be afflicted so that I might learn your decrees.
Ps 119 [73]Your hands made me and formed me; give me understanding to learn your commands.
Ps 119 [98]Your commands make me wiser than my enemies, for they are ever with me. [99]I have more insight than all my teachers, for I meditate on your statutes. [100]I have more understanding than the elders, for I obey your precepts. . . . [102]I have not departed from your laws, for you yourself have taught me. . . . [104]I gain understanding from your precepts; therefore I hate every wrong path.
Ps 119 [130]The unfolding of your words gives light; it gives understanding to the simple.
Luke 24 [45]Then he opened their minds so they could understand the Scriptures.
1 Cor 2 [10]but God has revealed it to us by his Spirit.

The Spirit searches all things, even the deep things of God. [11]For who among men knows the thoughts of a man except the man's spirit within him? In the same way no one knows the thoughts of God except the Spirit of God. [12]We have not received the spirit of the world but the Spirit who is from God, that we may understand what God has freely given us. [13]This is what we speak, not in words taught us by human wisdom but in words taught by the Spirit, expressing spiritual truths in spiritual words.

m) Scripture Is for Preaching

Acts 8 [4]Those who had been scattered preached the word wherever they went.
Acts 8 [25]When they had testified and proclaimed the word of the Lord, Peter and John returned to Jerusalem, preaching the gospel in many Samaritan villages.
Acts 14 [25]and when they had preached the word in Perga, they went down to Attalia.
Acts 17 [13]When the Jews in Thessalonica learned that Paul was preaching the word of God at Berea, they went there too, agitating the crowds and stirring them up.
1 Cor 15 [2]By this gospel you are saved, if you hold firmly to the word I preached to you. Otherwise, you have believed in vain.
2 Tim 4 [2]Preach the Word; be prepared in season and out of season; correct, rebuke and encourage—with great patience and careful instruction.

n) Scripture Is for Preservation

Ps 119 [25]I am laid low in the dust; preserve my life according to your word.
Ps 119 [37]Turn my eyes away from worthless things; preserve my life according to your word.
Ps 119 [50]My comfort in my suffering is this: Your promise preserves my life.
Ps 119 [93]I will never forget your precepts, for by them you have preserved my life.

Ps 119 [107]I have suffered much; preserve my life, O LORD, according to your word.
Ps 119 [116]Sustain me according to your promise, and I will live; do not let my hopes be dashed.
Ps 119 [175]Let me live that I may praise you, and may your laws sustain me.
Eph 6 [13]Therefore put on the full armor of God, so that when the day of evil comes, you may be able to stand your ground, and after you have done everything, to stand. . . . [17]Take the helmet of salvation and the sword of the Spirit, which is the word of God.
1 John 2 [1]My dear children, I write this to you so that you will not sin. But if anybody does sin, we have one who speaks to the Father in our defense—Jesus Christ, the Righteous One.

o) Scripture Is for Reading

Deut 17 [18]When he takes the throne of his kingdom, he is to write for himself on a scroll a copy of this law, taken from that of the priests, who are Levites. [19]It is to be with him, and he is to read it all the days of his life so that he may learn to revere the LORD his God and follow carefully all the words of this law and these decrees [20]and not consider himself better than his brothers and turn from the law to the right or to the left. Then he and his descendants will reign a long time over his kingdom in Israel.
Deut 31 [11]". . . when all Israel comes to appear before the LORD your God at the place he will choose, you shall read this law before them in their hearing."
Neh 8 [2]So on the first day of the seventh month Ezra the priest brought the Law before the assembly, which was made up of men and women and all who were able to understand. [3]He read it aloud from daybreak till noon as he faced the square before the Water Gate in the presence of the men, women and others who could understand. And all the people listened attentively to the Book of the Law.
Jer 36 [6]"So you go to the house of the LORD on a day of fasting and read to the people from the scroll the words of the LORD that you wrote as I dictated. Read them to all the people of Judah who come in from their towns."
Matt 21 [42]Jesus said to them, "Have you never read in the Scriptures: 'The stone the builders rejected has become the capstone; the Lord has done this, and it is marvelous in our eyes'?"
Acts 8 [27]So he started out, and on his way he met an Ethiopian eunuch, an important official in charge of all the treasury of Candace, queen of the Ethiopians. This man had gone to Jerusalem to worship, [28]and on his way home was sitting in his chariot reading the book of Isaiah the prophet.
Acts 13 [15]After the reading from the Law and the Prophets, the synagogue rulers sent word to them, saying, "Brothers, if you have a message of encouragement for the people, please speak."
Eph 3 [2]Surely you have heard about the administration of God's grace that was given to me for you, [3]that is, the mystery made known to me by revelation, as I have already written briefly. [4]In reading this, then, you will be able to understand my insight into the mystery of Christ. . . .
Col 4 [16]After this letter has been read to you, see that it is also read in the church of the Laodiceans and that you in turn read the letter from Laodicea.
1 Thess 5 [27]I charge you before the Lord to have this letter read to all the brothers.
1 Tim 4 [13]Until I come, devote yourself to the public reading of Scripture, to preaching and to teaching.
Rev 1 [3]Blessed is the one who reads the words of this prophecy, and blessed are those who hear it and take to heart what is written in it, because the time is near.

p) Scripture Is for Revealing Christ

Matt 5 [17]"Do not think that I have come to abolish the Law or the Prophets; I have not come to abolish them but to fulfill them."
Matt 26 [24]"The Son of Man will go just as it is written about him. But woe to that man who betrays the Son of Man! It would be better for him if he had not been born."
John 5 [39]"You diligently study the Scriptures because you think that by them you possess eternal life. These are the Scriptures that testify about me, [40]yet you refuse to come to me to have life."
Acts 10 [43]"All the prophets testify about him that everyone who believes in him receives forgiveness of sins through his name."
Acts 18 [28]For he vigorously refuted the Jews in public debate, proving from the Scriptures that Jesus was the Christ.
Acts 28 [23]They arranged to meet Paul on a certain day, and came in even larger numbers to the place where he was staying. From morning till evening he explained and declared to them the kingdom of God and tried to convince them about Jesus from the Law of Moses and from the Prophets.
1 Cor 15 [3]For what I received I passed on to you as of first importance: that Christ died for our sins according to the Scriptures, [4]that he was buried, that he was raised on the third day according to the Scriptures. . . .
1 Pet 1 [10]Concerning this salvation, the prophets, who spoke of the grace that was to come to you, searched intently and with the greatest care, [11]trying to find out the time and circumstances to which the Spirit of Christ in them was pointing when he predicted the sufferings of Christ and the glories that would follow. [12]It was revealed to them that they were not serving themselves but you, when they spoke of the things that have now been told you by those who have preached the gospel to you by the Holy Spirit sent from heaven. Even angels long to look into these things.
Rev 19 [10]At this I fell at his feet to worship him. But he said to me, "Do not do it! I am a fellow servant with you and with your brothers who hold to the testimony of Jesus. Worship God! For the testimony of Jesus is the spirit of prophecy."

q) Scripture Is for Salvation

Ps 119 [41]May your unfailing love come to me, O LORD, your salvation according to your promise; [42]then I will answer the one who taunts me, for I trust in your word.
John 5 [24]"I tell you the truth, whoever hears my word and believes him who sent me has eternal life and will not be condemned; he has crossed over from death to life. . . . [46]If you believed Moses, you would believe me, for he wrote about me. [47]But since you do not believe what he wrote, how are you going to believe what I say?"
John 20 [31]But these are written that you may believe that Jesus is the Christ, the Son of God, and that by believing you may have life in his name.
Rom 1 [2]the gospel he promised beforehand through his prophets in the Holy Scriptures . . .

[16]I am not ashamed of the gospel, because it is the power of God for the salvation of everyone who believes: first for the Jew, then for the Gentile. [17]For in the gospel a righteousness from God is revealed, a righteousness that is by faith from first to last, just as it is written: "The righteous will live by faith."
Rom 10 [13]for, "Everyone who calls on the name of the Lord will be saved."

[14]How, then, can they call on the one they have not believed in? And how can they believe in the one of whom they have not heard? And how can they hear without someone preaching to them? . . . [17]Consequently, faith comes from hearing the message, and the message is heard through the word of Christ.
Rom 16 [25]Now to him who is able to establish you by my gospel and the proclamation of Jesus Christ, according to the revelation of the mystery hidden for long ages past, [26]but now revealed and made known through the prophetic writings by the command of the eternal God, so that all nations might believe and obey him—[27]to the only wise God be glory forever through Jesus Christ! Amen.
2 Thess 1 [8]He will punish those who do not know God and do not obey the gospel of our Lord Jesus. [9]They will be punished with everlasting destruction and shut out from the presence of the Lord and from the majesty of his power [10]on the day he comes to be glorified in his holy people and to be marveled at among all those who have believed. This includes you, because you believed our testimony to you.
2 Tim 3 [15]and how from infancy you have known the holy Scriptures, which are able to make you wise for salvation through faith in Christ Jesus.
James 1 [18]He chose to give us birth through the word of truth,

that we might be a kind of firstfruits of all he created. . . . [21]Therefore, get rid of all moral filth and the evil that is so prevalent and humbly accept the word planted in you, which can save you.

1 Pet 1 [23]For you have been born again, not of perishable seed, but of imperishable, through the living and enduring word of God.

r) Scripture Is for Sanctification and Spiritual Growth

Deut 6 [6]These commandments that I give you today are to be upon your hearts. [7]Impress them on your children. Talk about them when you sit at home and when you walk along the road, when you lie down and when you get up.

Deut 8 [3]He humbled you, causing you to hunger and then feeding you with manna, which neither you nor your fathers had known, to teach you that man does not live on bread alone but on every word that comes from the mouth of the LORD.

Ps 119 [9]How can a young man keep his way pure? By living according to your word. [10]I seek you with all my heart; do not let me stray from your commands. [11]I have hidden your word in my heart that I might not sin against you.

Ps 119 [175]Let me live that I may praise you, and may your laws sustain me.

John 15 [3]"You are already clean because of the word I have spoken to you."

John 17 [17]"Sanctify them by the truth; your word is truth."

Eph 5 [25]Husbands, love your wives, just as Christ loved the church and gave himself up for her [26]to make her holy, cleansing her by the washing with water through the word, [27]and to present her to himself as a radiant church, without stain or wrinkle or any other blemish, but holy and blameless.

Col 3 [16]Let the word of Christ dwell in you richly as you teach and admonish one another with all wisdom, and as you sing psalms, hymns and spiritual songs with gratitude in your hearts to God.

1 Thess 2 [13]And we also thank God continually because, when you received the word of God, which you heard from us, you accepted it not as the word of men, but as it actually is, the word of God, which is at work in you who believe.

2 Tim 3 [16]All Scripture is God-breathed and is useful for teaching, rebuking, correcting and training in righteousness, [17]so that the man of God may be thoroughly equipped for every good work.

1 Pet 1 [22]Now that you have purified yourselves by obeying the truth so that you have sincere love for your brothers, love one another deeply, from the heart. [23]For you have been born again, not of perishable seed, but of imperishable, through the living and enduring word of God.

1 Pet 2 [2]Like newborn babies, crave pure spiritual milk, so that by it you may grow up in your salvation. . . .

s) Scripture Is for Study

Ezra 7 [10]For Ezra had devoted himself to the study and observance of the Law of the LORD, and to teaching its decrees and laws in Israel.

Neh 8 [13]On the second day of the month, the heads of all the families, along with the priests and the Levites, gathered around Ezra the scribe to give attention to the words of the Law. . . .

[18]Day after day, from the first day to the last, Ezra read from the Book of the Law of God. They celebrated the feast for seven days, and on the eighth day, in accordance with the regulation, there was an assembly.

Ps 1 [1]Blessed is the man who does not walk in the counsel of the wicked or stand in the way of sinners or sit in the seat of mockers. [2]But his delight is in the law of the LORD, and on his law he meditates day and night.

Ps 119 [48]I lift up my hands to your commands, which I love, and I meditate on your decrees.

Ps 119 [148]My eyes stay open through the watches of the night, that I may meditate on your promises.

John 5 [39]"You diligently study the Scriptures because you think that by them you possess eternal life. These are the Scriptures that testify about me. . . ."

2 Tim 2 [14]Keep reminding them of these things. Warn them before God against quarreling about words; it is of no value, and only ruins those who listen. [15]Do your best to present yourself to God as one approved, a workman who does not need to be ashamed and who correctly handles the word of truth.

t) Scripture Is for Teaching

Deut 4 [5]See, I have taught you decrees and laws as the LORD my God commanded me, so that you may follow them in the land you are entering to take possession of it.

Deut 6 [6]These commandments that I give you today are to be upon your hearts. [7]Impress them on your children. Talk about them when you sit at home and when you walk along the road, when you lie down and when you get up. [8]Tie them as symbols on your hands and bind them on your foreheads. [9]Write them on the doorframes of your houses and on your gates.

Deut 11 [8]Observe therefore all the commands I am giving you today, so that you may have the strength to go in and take over the land that you are crossing the Jordan to possess. . . . [19]Teach them to your children, talking about them when you sit at home and when you walk along the road, when you lie down and when you get up. [20]Write them on the doorframes of your houses and on your gates, [21]so that your days and the days of your children may be many in the land that the LORD swore to give your forefathers, as many as the days that the heavens are above the earth.

2 Chron 17 [9]They taught throughout Judah, taking with them the Book of the Law of the LORD; they went around to all the towns of Judah and taught the people.

Ezra 7 [10]For Ezra had devoted himself to the study and observance of the Law of the LORD, and to teaching its decrees and laws in Israel.

Neh 8 [9]Then Nehemiah the governor, Ezra the priest and scribe, and the Levites who were instructing the people said to them all, "This day is sacred to the LORD your God. Do not mourn or weep." For all the people had been weeping as they listened to the words of the Law.

Ps 119 [12]Praise be to you, O LORD; teach me your decrees. [13]With my lips I recount all the laws that come from your mouth.

Ps 119 [64]The earth is filled with your love, O LORD; teach me your decrees.

Acts 8 [30]Then Philip ran up to the chariot and heard the man reading Isaiah the prophet. "Do you understand what you are reading?" Philip asked.

[31]"How can I," he said, "unless someone explains it to me?" So he invited Philip to come up and sit with him.

[32]The eunuch was reading this passage of Scripture: "He was led like a sheep to the slaughter, and as a lamb before the shearer is silent, so he did not open his mouth. [33]In his humiliation he was deprived of justice. Who can speak of his descendants? For his life was taken from the earth."

[34]The eunuch asked Philip, "Tell me, please, who is the prophet talking about, himself or someone else?" [35]Then Philip began with that very passage of Scripture and told him the good news about Jesus.

Rom 15 [4]For everything that was written in the past was written to teach us, so that through endurance and the encouragement of the Scriptures we might have hope.

2 Cor 4 [2]Rather, we have renounced secret and shameful ways; we do not use deception, nor do we distort the word of God. On the contrary, by setting forth the truth plainly we commend ourselves to every man's conscience in the sight of God.

2 Tim 3 [16]All Scripture is God-breathed and is useful for teaching, rebuking, correcting and training in righteousness, [17]so that the man of God may be thoroughly equipped for every good work.

1 Pet 4 [11]If anyone speaks, he should do it as one speaking the very words of God. If anyone serves, he should do it with the strength God provides, so that in all things God may be praised through Jesus Christ. To him be the glory and the power for ever and ever. Amen.

5. Right Responses to the Bible

a) The Scriptures Are Awe Inspiring

Ps 119 [120]My flesh trembles in fear of you; I stand in awe of your laws.

Ps 119 161Rulers persecute me without cause, but my heart trembles at your word.
Isa 66 2"Has not my hand made all these things, and so they came into being?" declares the LORD.

"This is the one I esteem: he who is humble and contrite in spirit, and trembles at my word."

b) The Scriptures Are Cherished

Ps 119 53Indignation grips me because of the wicked, who have forsaken your law. 54Your decrees are the theme of my song wherever I lodge.
Ps 119 126It is time for you to act, O LORD; your law is being broken. 127Because I love your commands more than gold, more than pure gold, 128and because I consider all your precepts right, I hate every wrong path.
Ps 119 136Streams of tears flow from my eyes, for your law is not obeyed.
Ps 119 139My zeal wears me out, for my enemies ignore your words.
Ps 119 158I look on the faithless with loathing, for they do not obey your word.

c) The Scriptures Are Delighted In

Ps 1 2But his delight is in the law of the LORD, and on his law he meditates day and night.
Ps 119 16I delight in your decrees; I will not neglect your word.
Ps 119 24Your statutes are my delight; they are my counselors.
Ps 119 35Direct me in the path of your commands, for there I find delight.
Ps 119 70Their hearts are callous and unfeeling, but I delight in your law.
Ps 119 77Let your compassion come to me that I may live, for your law is my delight.
Ps 119 92If your law had not been my delight, I would have perished in my affliction.
Ps 119 143Trouble and distress have come upon me, but your commands are my delight.
Ps 119 174I long for your salvation, O LORD, and your law is my delight.

d) The Scriptures Are Given Thanks For

Ps 119 62At midnight I rise to give you thanks for your righteous laws.

e) The Scriptures Are Hoped In

Ps 119 43Do not snatch the word of truth from my mouth, for I have put my hope in your laws.
Ps 119 49Remember your word to your servant, for you have given me hope.
Ps 119 74May those who fear you rejoice when they see me, for I have put my hope in your word.
Ps 119 81My soul faints with longing for your salvation, but I have put my hope in your word.
Ps 119 114You are my refuge and my shield; I have put my hope in your word.
Ps 119 147I rise before dawn and cry for help; I have put my hope in your word.

f) The Scriptures Are Lived According To

Ps 119 87They almost wiped me from the earth, but I have not forsaken your precepts.
Ps 119 102I have not departed from your laws, for you yourself have taught me.
Ps 119 105Your word is a lamp to my feet and a light for my path.
Ps 119 133Direct my footsteps according to your word; let no sin rule over me.

g) The Scriptures Are Longed For

Ps 119 20My soul is consumed with longing for your laws at all times.
Ps 119 33Teach me, O LORD, to follow your decrees; then I will keep them to the end. 34Give me understanding, and I will keep your law and obey it with all my heart.
Ps 119 131I open my mouth and pant, longing for your commands.

h) The Scriptures Are Loved

Ps 119 47for I delight in your commands because I love them. 48I lift up my hands to your commands, which I love, and I meditate on your decrees.
Ps 119 97Oh, how I love your law! I meditate on it all day long.
Ps 119 113I hate double-minded men, but I love your law.
Ps 119 119All the wicked of the earth you discard like dross; therefore I love your statutes.
Ps 119 127Because I love your commands more than gold, more than pure gold, 128and because I consider all your precepts right, I hate every wrong path.
Ps 119 140Your promises have been thoroughly tested, and your servant loves them.
Ps 119 159See how I love your precepts; preserve my life, O LORD, according to your love.
Ps 119 163I hate and abhor falsehood but I love your law.
Ps 119 165Great peace have they who love your law, and nothing can make them stumble.
Ps 119 167I obey your statutes, for I love them greatly.

i) The Scriptures Are Meditated On

Ps 1 2But his delight is in the law of the LORD, and on his law he meditates day and night.
Ps 119 15I meditate on your precepts and consider your ways.
Ps 119 48I lift up my hands to your commands, which I love, and I meditate on your decrees.
Ps 119 95The wicked are waiting to destroy me, but I will ponder your statutes.
Ps 119 97Oh, how I love your law! I meditate on it all day long.
Ps 119 148My eyes stay open through the watches of the night, that I may meditate on your promises.

j) The Scriptures Are Obeyed

Deut 4 1Hear now, O Israel, the decrees and laws I am about to teach you. Follow them so that you may live and may go in and take possession of the land that the LORD, the God of your fathers, is giving you. . . .

9Only be careful, and watch yourselves closely so that you do not forget the things your eyes have seen or let them slip from your heart as long as you live. Teach them to your children and to their children after them. . . . 12Then the LORD spoke to you out of the fire. You heard the sound of words but saw no form; there was only a voice. 13He declared to you his covenant, the Ten Commandments, which he commanded you to follow and then wrote them on two stone tablets. 14And the LORD directed me at that time to teach you the decrees and laws you are to follow in the land that you are crossing the Jordan to possess. . . . 29But if from there you seek the LORD your God, you will find him if you look for him with all your heart and with all your soul. 30When you are in distress and all these things have happened to you, then in later days you will return to the LORD your God and obey him. 31For the LORD your God is a merciful God; he will not abandon or destroy you or forget the covenant with your forefathers, which he confirmed to them by oath.
Deut 5 29"Oh, that their hearts would be inclined to fear me and keep all my commands always, so that it might go well with them and their children forever! . . ."

32So be careful to do what the LORD your God has commanded you; do not turn aside to the right or to the left. 33Walk in all the way that the LORD your God has commanded you, so that you may live and prosper and prolong your days in the land that you will possess.
Deut 11 13So if you faithfully obey the commands I am giving you today—to love the LORD your God and to serve him with all your heart and with all your soul—14then I will send rain on your land in its season, both autumn and spring rains, so that you may gather in your grain, new wine and oil. 15I will provide grass in the fields for your cattle, and you will eat and be satisfied.
Josh 22 5"But be very careful to keep the commandment and the law that Moses the servant of the LORD gave you: to love the LORD your God, to walk in all his ways, to obey his commands, to hold fast to him and to serve him with all your heart and all your soul."
1 Kings 6 12"As for this temple you are building, if you follow

my decrees, carry out my regulations and keep all my commands and obey them, I will fulfill through you the promise I gave to David your father."
Ps 119 [4]You have laid down precepts that are to be fully obeyed. [5]Oh, that my ways were steadfast in obeying your decrees! [6]Then I would not be put to shame when I consider all your commands.
Ps 119 [34]Give me understanding, and I will keep your law and obey it with all my heart.
Ps 119 [44]I will always obey your law, for ever and ever.
Ps 119 [56]This has been my practice: I obey your precepts.
Ps 119 [60]I will hasten and not delay to obey your commands.
Ps 119 [67]Before I was afflicted I went astray, but now I obey your word.
Ps 119 [112]My heart is set on keeping your decrees to the very end.
Ps 119 [134]Redeem me from the oppression of men, that I may obey your precepts.
Jer 7 [23]"'. . . but I gave them this command: Obey me, and I will be your God and you will be my people. Walk in all the ways I command you, that it may go well with you.'"
Ezek 11 [20]"Then they will follow my decrees and be careful to keep my laws. They will be my people, and I will be their God."
Matt 7 [24]"Therefore everyone who hears these words of mine and puts them into practice is like a wise man who built his house on the rock. [25]The rain came down, the streams rose, and the winds blew and beat against that house; yet it did not fall, because it had its foundation on the rock."
Luke 8 [21]He replied, "My mother and brothers are those who hear God's word and put it into practice."
John 14 [15]"If you love me, you will obey what I command."
John 17 [6]"I have revealed you to those whom you gave me out of the world. They were yours; you gave them to me and they have obeyed your word."
2 Thess 1 [8]He will punish those who do not know God and do not obey the gospel of our Lord Jesus.
2 Thess 3 [14]If anyone does not obey our instruction in this letter, take special note of him. Do not associate with him, in order that he may feel ashamed.
James 1 [22]Do not merely listen to the word, and so deceive yourselves. Do what it says. [23]Anyone who listens to the word but does not do what it says is like a man who looks at his face in a mirror [24]and, after looking at himself, goes away and immediately forgets what he looks like. [25]But the man who looks intently into the perfect law that gives freedom, and continues to do this, not forgetting what he has heard, but doing it—he will be blessed in what he does.
1 Pet 4 [17]For it is time for judgment to begin with the family of God; and if it begins with us, what will the outcome be for those who do not obey the gospel of God?
1 John 5 [2]This is how we know that we love the children of God: by loving God and carrying out his commands. [3]This is love for God: to obey his commands. And his commands are not burdensome. . . .

k) The Scriptures Are Praised

Ps 56 [4]In God, whose word I praise, in God I trust; I will not be afraid. What can mortal man do to me?
Ps 119 [164]Seven times a day I praise you for your righteous laws.
Ps 119 [171]May my lips overflow with praise, for you teach me your decrees. [172]May my tongue sing of your word, for all your commands are righteous.

l) The Scriptures Are Rejoiced Over

Ps 119 [14]I rejoice in following your statutes as one rejoices in great riches.
Ps 119 [111]Your statutes are my heritage forever; they are the joy of my heart.
Ps 119 [162]I rejoice in your promise like one who finds great spoil.
Jer 15 [16]When your words came, I ate them; they were my joy and my heart's delight, for I bear your name, O Lord God Almighty.

m) The Scriptures Are Remembered

Ps 119 [11]I have hidden your word in my heart that I might not sin against you.
Ps 119 [16]I delight in your decrees; I will not neglect your word.
Ps 119 [61]Though the wicked bind me with ropes, I will not forget your law.
Ps 119 [83]Though I am like a wineskin in the smoke, I do not forget your decrees.
Ps 119 [109]Though I constantly take my life in my hands, I will not forget your law.
Ps 119 [141]Though I am lowly and despised, I do not forget your precepts.
Ps 119 [153]Look upon my suffering and deliver me, for I have not forgotten your law.
Ps 119 [176]I have strayed like a lost sheep. Seek your servant, for I have not forgotten your commands.

n) The Scriptures Are Shared

Acts 4 [29]"Now, Lord, consider their threats and enable your servants to speak your word with great boldness. . . ."
[31]After they prayed, the place where they were meeting was shaken. And they were all filled with the Holy Spirit and spoke the word of God boldly.
Acts 8 [4]Those who had been scattered preached the word wherever they went.
Acts 8 [25]When they had testified and proclaimed the word of the Lord, Peter and John returned to Jerusalem, preaching the gospel in many Samaritan villages.
2 Cor 2 [17]Unlike so many, we do not peddle the word of God for profit. On the contrary, in Christ we speak before God with sincerity, like men sent from God.
Phil 1 [14]Because of my chains, most of the brothers in the Lord have been encouraged to speak the word of God more courageously and fearlessly.
1 Thess 1 [8]The Lord's message rang out from you not only in Macedonia and Achaia—your faith in God has become known everywhere. Therefore we do not need to say anything about it. . . .

o) The Scriptures Are Sought Out

Ps 119 [94]Save me, for I am yours; I have sought out your precepts.

p) The Scriptures Are Sung About

Ps 119 [172]May my tongue sing of your word, for all your commands are righteous.

q) The Scriptures Are Sweet Tasting

Ps 119 [103]How sweet are your words to my taste, sweeter than honey to my mouth!

r) The Scriptures Are Treasured

Job 23 [12]"I have not departed from the commands of his lips; I have treasured the words of his mouth more than my daily bread."
Ps 119 [72]The law from your mouth is more precious to me than thousands of pieces of silver and gold.
Ps 119 [127]Because I love your commands more than gold, more than pure gold, [128]and because I consider all your precepts right, I hate every wrong path.
Ps 119 [162]I rejoice in your promise like one who finds great spoil.

s) The Scriptures Are Trembled At

Ps 119 [161]Rulers persecute me without cause, but my heart trembles at your word.

t) The Scriptures Are Trusted In

Ps 119 [30]I have chosen the way of truth; I have set my heart on your laws. [31]I hold fast to your statutes, O Lord; do not let me be put to shame. [32]I run in the path of your commands, for you have set my heart free.
Ps 119 [42]then I will answer the one who taunts me, for I trust in your word.
Ps 119 [66]Teach me knowledge and good judgment, for I believe in your commands.

B. The Inspiration of Scripture

1. The OT's Inspiration

a) OT Claims to Its Inspiration

Exod 4 [11]The LORD said to him, "Who gave man his mouth? Who makes him deaf or mute? Who gives him sight or makes him blind? Is it not I, the LORD? [12]Now go; I will help you speak and will teach you what to say."

[13]But Moses said, "O Lord, please send someone else to do it."

[14]Then the LORD's anger burned against Moses and he said, "What about your brother, Aaron the Levite? I know he can speak well. He is already on his way to meet you, and his heart will be glad when he sees you. [15]You shall speak to him and put words in his mouth; I will help both of you speak and will teach you what to do. [16]He will speak to the people for you, and it will be as if he were your mouth and as if you were God to him." . . .

[29]Moses and Aaron brought together all the elders of the Israelites, [30]and Aaron told them everything the LORD had said to Moses. He also performed the signs before the people, [31]and they believed. And when they heard that the LORD was concerned about them and had seen their misery, they bowed down and worshiped.

Exod 7 [1]Then the LORD said to Moses, "See, I have made you like God to Pharaoh, and your brother Aaron will be your prophet. [2]You are to say everything I command you, and your brother Aaron is to tell Pharaoh to let the Israelites go out of his country."

Exod 19 [7]So Moses went back and summoned the elders of the people and set before them all the words the LORD had commanded him to speak. [8]The people all responded together, "We will do everything the LORD has said." So Moses brought their answer back to the LORD.

[9]The LORD said to Moses, "I am going to come to you in a dense cloud, so that the people will hear me speaking with you and will always put their trust in you." Then Moses told the LORD what the people had said.

Exod 20 [1]And God spoke all these words: [2]"I am the LORD your God, who brought you out of Egypt, out of the land of slavery."

Exod 24 [4]Moses then wrote down everything the LORD had said.

He got up early the next morning and built an altar at the foot of the mountain and set up twelve stone pillars representing the twelve tribes of Israel.

Exod 24 [12]The LORD said to Moses, "Come up to me on the mountain and stay here, and I will give you the tablets of stone, with the law and commands I have written for their instruction."

Exod 25 [21]"Place the cover on top of the ark and put in the ark the Testimony, which I will give you. [22]There, above the cover between the two cherubim that are over the ark of the Testimony, I will meet with you and give you all my commands for the Israelites."

Exod 31 [18]When the LORD finished speaking to Moses on Mount Sinai, he gave him the two tablets of the Testimony, the tablets of stone inscribed by the finger of God.

Exod 32 [15]Moses turned and went down the mountain with the two tablets of the Testimony in his hands. They were inscribed on both sides, front and back. [16]The tablets were the work of God; the writing was the writing of God, engraved on the tablets.

Exod 34 [27]Then the LORD said to Moses, "Write down these words, for in accordance with these words I have made a covenant with you and with Israel." [28]Moses was there with the LORD forty days and forty nights without eating bread or drinking water. And he wrote on the tablets the words of the covenant—the Ten Commandments.

Lev 26 [46]These are the decrees, the laws and the regulations that the LORD established on Mount Sinai between himself and the Israelites through Moses.

Deut 4 [5]See, I have taught you decrees and laws as the LORD my God commanded me, so that you may follow them in the land you are entering to take possession of it.

Deut 5 [5](At that time I stood between the LORD and you to declare to you the word of the LORD, because you were afraid of the fire and did not go up the mountain.) And he said: [6]"I am the LORD your God, who brought you out of Egypt, out of the land of slavery."

Deut 6 [1]These are the commands, decrees and laws the LORD your God directed me to teach you to observe in the land that you are crossing the Jordan to possess, [2]so that you, your children and their children after them may fear the LORD your God as long as you live by keeping all his decrees and commands that I give you, and so that you may enjoy long life. . . . [6]These commandments that I give you today are to be upon your hearts. [7]Impress them on your children. Talk about them when you sit at home and when you walk along the road, when you lie down and when you get up. [8]Tie them as symbols on your hands and bind them on your foreheads. [9]Write them on the doorframes of your houses and on your gates.

Deut 18 [17]The LORD said to me: "What they say is good. [18]I will raise up for them a prophet like you from among their brothers; I will put my words in his mouth, and he will tell them everything I command him. [19]If anyone does not listen to my words that the prophet speaks in my name, I myself will call him to account. [20]But a prophet who presumes to speak in my name anything I have not commanded him to say, or a prophet who speaks in the name of other gods, must be put to death."

[21]You may say to yourselves, "How can we know when a message has not been spoken by the LORD?" [22]If what a prophet proclaims in the name of the LORD does not take place or come true, that is a message the LORD has not spoken. That prophet has spoken presumptuously. Do not be afraid of him.

Deut 31 [19]"Now write down for yourselves this song and teach it to the Israelites and have them sing it, so that it may be a witness for me against them. . . ." [22]So Moses wrote down this song that day and taught it to the Israelites.

2 Sam 23 [1]These are the last words of David: "The oracle of David son of Jesse, the oracle of the man exalted by the Most High, the man anointed by the God of Jacob, Israel's singer of songs: [2]The Spirit of the LORD spoke through me; his word was on my tongue."

2 Kings 17 [13]The LORD warned Israel and Judah through all his prophets and seers: "Turn from your evil ways. Observe my commands and decrees, in accordance with the entire Law that I commanded your fathers to obey and that I delivered to you through my servants the prophets."

Neh 9 [13]"You came down on Mount Sinai; you spoke to them from heaven. You gave them regulations and laws that are just and right, and decrees and commands that are good. [14]You made known to them your holy Sabbath and gave them commands, decrees and laws through your servant Moses."

Job 23 [12]"I have not departed from the commands of his lips; I have treasured the words of his mouth more than my daily bread."

Ps 19 [7]The law of the LORD is perfect, reviving the soul. The statutes of the LORD are trustworthy, making wise the simple. [8]The precepts of the LORD are right, giving joy to the heart. The commands of the LORD are radiant, giving light to the eyes. [9]The fear of the LORD is pure, enduring forever. The ordinances of the LORD are sure and altogether righteous. [10]They are more precious than gold, than much pure gold; they are sweeter than honey, than honey from the comb. [11]By them is your servant warned; in keeping them there is great reward.

Ps 78 [5]He decreed statutes for Jacob and established the law in Israel, which he commanded our forefathers to teach their children. . . .

Ps 99 [7]He spoke to them from the pillar of cloud; they kept his statutes and the decrees he gave them.

Ps 119 [160]All your words are true; all your righteous laws are eternal.

Ps 147 [19]He has revealed his word to Jacob, his laws and decrees to Israel.

Isa 34 [16]Look in the scroll of the LORD and read: None of these will be missing, not one will lack her mate. For it is his mouth that has given the order, and his Spirit will gather them together.

Isa 51 [16]"I have put my words in your mouth and covered you with the shadow of my hand—I who set the heavens in place, who laid the foundations of the earth, and who say to Zion, 'You are my people.'"

Isa 59 21"As for me, this is my covenant with them," says the LORD. "My Spirit, who is on you, and my words that I have put in your mouth will not depart from your mouth, or from the mouths of your children, or from the mouths of their descendants from this time on and forever," says the LORD.

Jer 1 9Then the LORD reached out his hand and touched my mouth and said to me, "Now, I have put my words in your mouth."

Jer 1 17"Get yourself ready! Stand up and say to them whatever I command you. Do not be terrified by them, or I will terrify you before them."

Jer 30 2"This is what the LORD, the God of Israel, says: 'Write in a book all the words I have spoken to you.'"

Jer 36 1In the fourth year of Jehoiakim son of Josiah king of Judah, this word came to Jeremiah from the LORD: 2"Take a scroll and write on it all the words I have spoken to you concerning Israel, Judah and all the other nations from the time I began speaking to you in the reign of Josiah till now. . . ."

4So Jeremiah called Baruch son of Neriah, and while Jeremiah dictated all the words the LORD had spoken to him, Baruch wrote them on the scroll. . . .

27After the king burned the scroll containing the words that Baruch had written at Jeremiah's dictation, the word of the LORD came to Jeremiah: 28"Take another scroll and write on it all the words that were on the first scroll, which Jehoiakim king of Judah burned up. . . ."

32So Jeremiah took another scroll and gave it to the scribe Baruch son of Neriah, and as Jeremiah dictated, Baruch wrote on it all the words of the scroll that Jehoiakim king of Judah had burned in the fire. And many similar words were added to them.

Ezek 2 7"You must speak my words to them, whether they listen or fail to listen, for they are rebellious."

Ezek 3 10And he said to me, "Son of man, listen carefully and take to heart all the words I speak to you. 11Go now to your countrymen in exile and speak to them. Say to them, 'This is what the Sovereign LORD says,' whether they listen or fail to listen."

Ezek 3 16At the end of seven days the word of the LORD came to me: 17"Son of man, I have made you a watchman for the house of Israel; so hear the word I speak and give them warning from me."

Ezek 11 24The Spirit lifted me up and brought me to the exiles in Babylonia in the vision given by the Spirit of God.

Then the vision I had seen went up from me, 25and I told the exiles everything the LORD had shown me.

Dan 10 18Again the one who looked like a man touched me and gave me strength. . . .

20So he said, "Do you know why I have come to you? Soon I will return to fight against the prince of Persia, and when I go, the prince of Greece will come; 21but first I will tell you what is written in the Book of Truth. (No one supports me against them except Michael, your prince.)"

Hos 8 12"I wrote for them the many things of my law, but they regarded them as something alien."

Amos 3 8The lion has roared—who will not fear? The Sovereign LORD has spoken—who can but prophesy?

Mic 3 8But as for me, I am filled with power, with the Spirit of the LORD, and with justice and might, to declare to Jacob his transgression, to Israel his sin.

Zech 7 12"They made their hearts as hard as flint and would not listen to the law or to the words that the LORD Almighty had sent by his Spirit through the earlier prophets. So the LORD Almighty was very angry."

b) NT Claims to the OT's Inspiration: OT Quotations

Matt 4 4Jesus answered, "It is written: 'Man does not live on bread alone, but on every word that comes from the mouth of God.'" (Deut 8:3)

Matt 4 7Jesus answered him, "It is also written: 'Do not put the Lord your God to the test.'" (Deut 6:16)

Matt 4 10Jesus said to him, "Away from me, Satan! For it is written: 'Worship the Lord your God, and serve him only.'" (Deut 6:13)

Luke 4 14Jesus returned to Galilee in the power of the Spirit, and news about him spread through the whole countryside. 15He taught in their synagogues, and everyone praised him.

16He went to Nazareth, where he had been brought up, and on the Sabbath day he went into the synagogue, as was his custom. And he stood up to read. 17The scroll of the prophet Isaiah was handed to him. Unrolling it, he found the place where it is written: 18"The Spirit of the Lord is on me, because he has anointed me to preach good news to the poor. He has sent me to proclaim freedom for the prisoners and recovery of sight for the blind, to release the oppressed, 19to proclaim the year of the Lord's favor."

20Then he rolled up the scroll, gave it back to the attendant and sat down. The eyes of everyone in the synagogue were fastened on him, 21and he began by saying to them, "Today this scripture is fulfilled in your hearing." (Isa 61:1–2)

Acts 1 16and said, "Brothers, the Scripture had to be fulfilled which the Holy Spirit spoke long ago through the mouth of David concerning Judas, who served as guide for those who arrested Jesus. . . ."

20"For," said Peter, "it is written in the book of Psalms, 'May his place be deserted; let there be no one to dwell in it,' and, 'May another take his place of leadership.'" (Pss 69:25; 109:8)

Acts 13 32"We tell you the good news: What God promised our fathers 33he has fulfilled for us, their children, by raising up Jesus. As it is written in the second Psalm: 'You are my Son; today I have become your Father.' 34The fact that God raised him from the dead, never to decay, is stated in these words: 'I will give you the holy and sure blessings promised to David.' 35So it is stated elsewhere: 'You will not let your Holy One see decay.'" (Ps 2:7; Isa 55:3; Ps 16:10)

Acts 28 23They arranged to meet Paul on a certain day, and came in even larger numbers to the place where he was staying. From morning till evening he explained and declared to them the kingdom of God and tried to convince them about Jesus from the Law of Moses and from the Prophets. 24Some were convinced by what he said, but others would not believe. 25They disagreed among themselves and began to leave after Paul had made this final statement: "The Holy Spirit spoke the truth to your forefathers when he said through Isaiah the prophet: 26'Go to this people and say, "You will be ever hearing but never understanding; you will be ever seeing but never perceiving." 27For this people's heart has become calloused; they hardly hear with their ears, and they have closed their eyes. Otherwise they might see with their eyes, hear with their ears, understand with their hearts and turn, and I would heal them.'

28"Therefore I want you to know that God's salvation has been sent to the Gentiles, and they will listen!" (Isa 6:9–10)

Rom 9 17For the Scripture says to Pharaoh: "I raised you up for this very purpose, that I might display my power in you and that my name might be proclaimed in all the earth." (Exod 9:16)

Gal 3 8The Scripture foresaw that God would justify the Gentiles by faith, and announced the gospel in advance to Abraham: "All nations will be blessed through you." (Gen 12:3; 18:18; 22:18)

Eph 4 8This is why it says: "When he ascended on high, he led captives in his train and gave gifts to men." (Ps 68:18)

Heb 1 8But about the Son he says, "Your throne, O God, will last for ever and ever, and righteousness will be the scepter of your kingdom. 9You have loved righteousness and hated wickedness; therefore God, your God, has set you above your companions by anointing you with the oil of joy." (Ps 45:6–7)

Heb 2 6But there is a place where someone has testified: "What is man that you are mindful of him, the son of man that you care for him? 7You made him a little lower than the angels; you crowned him with glory and honor 8and put everything under his feet." In putting everything under him, God left nothing that is not subject to him. Yet at present we do not see everything subject to him. (Ps 8:4–6)

Heb 3 7So, as the Holy Spirit says: "Today, if you hear his voice, 8do not harden your hearts as you did in the rebellion, during the time of testing in the desert, 9where your fathers tested and tried me and for forty years saw what I did. 10That is

why I was angry with that generation, and I said, 'Their hearts are always going astray, and they have not known my ways.' [11]So I declared on oath in my anger, 'They shall never enter my rest.'" (Ps 95:7–11)
Heb 4 [3]Now we who have believed enter that rest, just as God has said, "So I declared on oath in my anger, 'They shall never enter my rest.'" And yet his work has been finished since the creation of the world. (Ps 95:11)
Heb 5 [5]So Christ also did not take upon himself the glory of becoming a high priest. But God said to him, "You are my Son; today I have become your Father." [6]And he says in another place, "You are a priest forever, in the order of Melchizedek." (Pss 2:7; 110:4)
Heb 7 [21]but he became a priest with an oath when God said to him: "The Lord has sworn and will not change his mind: 'You are a priest forever.'" (Ps 110:4)
Heb 10 [15]The Holy Spirit also testifies to us about this. First he says: [16]"This is the covenant I will make with them after that time, says the Lord. I will put my laws in their hearts, and I will write them on their minds." [17]Then he adds: "Their sins and lawless acts I will remember no more." (Jer 31:33–34)
Heb 12 [5]And you have forgotten that word of encouragement that addresses you as sons: "My son, do not make light of the Lord's discipline, and do not lose heart when he rebukes you, [6]because the Lord disciplines those he loves, and he punishes everyone he accepts as a son." (Prov 3:11–12)
Heb 13 [5]Keep your lives free from the love of money and be content with what you have, because God has said, "Never will I leave you; never will I forsake you." (Deut 31:6)
1 Pet 1 [23]For you have been born again, not of perishable seed, but of imperishable, through the living and enduring word of God. [24]For, "All men are like grass, and all their glory is like the flowers of the field; the grass withers and the flowers fall, [25]but the word of the Lord stands forever." And this is the word that was preached to you. (Isa 40:6–8)

c) NT Claims to the OT's Inspiration: Jesus' Teachings

Matt 5 [17]"Do not think that I have come to abolish the Law or the Prophets; I have not come to abolish them but to fulfill them. [18]I tell you the truth, until heaven and earth disappear, not the smallest letter, not the least stroke of a pen, will by any means disappear from the Law until everything is accomplished. [19]Anyone who breaks one of the least of these commandments and teaches others to do the same will be called least in the kingdom of heaven, but whoever practices and teaches these commands will be called great in the kingdom of heaven."
Matt 19 [3]Some Pharisees came to him to test him. They asked, "Is it lawful for a man to divorce his wife for any and every reason?"

[4]"Haven't you read," he replied, "that at the beginning the Creator 'made them male and female,' [5]and said, 'For this reason a man will leave his father and mother and be united to his wife, and the two will become one flesh'? [6]So they are no longer two, but one. Therefore what God has joined together, let man not separate."

[7]"Why then," they asked, "did Moses command that a man give his wife a certificate of divorce and send her away?"

[8]Jesus replied, "Moses permitted you to divorce your wives because your hearts were hard. But it was not this way from the beginning. [9]I tell you that anyone who divorces his wife, except for marital unfaithfulness, and marries another woman commits adultery."
Matt 22 [29]Jesus replied, "You are in error because you do not know the Scriptures or the power of God. [30]At the resurrection people will neither marry nor be given in marriage; they will be like the angels in heaven. [31]But about the resurrection of the dead—have you not read what God said to you, [32]'I am the God of Abraham, the God of Isaac, and the God of Jacob'? He is not the God of the dead but of the living."
Matt 22 [41]While the Pharisees were gathered together, Jesus asked them, [42]"What do you think about the Christ? Whose son is he?"

"The son of David," they replied.

[43]He said to them, "How is it then that David, speaking by the Spirit, calls him 'Lord'? For he says, [44]'The Lord said to my Lord: "Sit at my right hand until I put your enemies under your feet."' [45]If then David calls him 'Lord,' how can he be his son?"
Mark 7 [5]So the Pharisees and teachers of the law asked Jesus, "Why don't your disciples live according to the tradition of the elders instead of eating their food with 'unclean' hands?"

[6]He replied, "Isaiah was right when he prophesied about you hypocrites; as it is written: 'These people honor me with their lips, but their hearts are far from me. [7]They worship me in vain; their teachings are but rules taught by men.' [8]You have let go of the commands of God and are holding on to the traditions of men."

[9]And he said to them: "You have a fine way of setting aside the commands of God in order to observe your own traditions! [10]For Moses said, 'Honor your father and your mother,' and, 'Anyone who curses his father or mother must be put to death.' [11]But you say that if a man says to his father or mother: 'Whatever help you might otherwise have received from me is Corban' (that is, a gift devoted to God), [12]then you no longer let him do anything for his father or mother. [13]Thus you nullify the word of God by your tradition that you have handed down. And you do many things like that."
Luke 16 [16]"The Law and the Prophets were proclaimed until John. Since that time, the good news of the kingdom of God is being preached, and everyone is forcing his way into it. [17]It is easier for heaven and earth to disappear than for the least stroke of a pen to drop out of the Law."
Luke 16 [27]"He answered, 'Then I beg you, father, send Lazarus to my father's house, [28]for I have five brothers. Let him warn them, so that they will not also come to this place of torment.'

[29]"Abraham replied, 'They have Moses and the Prophets; let them listen to them.'

[30]"'No, father Abraham,' he said, 'but if someone from the dead goes to them, they will repent.'

[31]"He said to him, 'If they do not listen to Moses and the Prophets, they will not be convinced even if someone rises from the dead.'"
Luke 22 [36]He said to them, "But now if you have a purse, take it, and also a bag; and if you don't have a sword, sell your cloak and buy one. [37]It is written: 'And he was numbered with the transgressors'; and I tell you that this must be fulfilled in me. Yes, what is written about me is reaching its fulfillment."
Luke 24 [25]He said to them, "How foolish you are, and how slow of heart to believe all that the prophets have spoken! [26]Did not the Christ have to suffer these things and then enter his glory?" [27]And beginning with Moses and all the Prophets, he explained to them what was said in all the Scriptures concerning himself.
Luke 24 [44]He said to them, "This is what I told you while I was still with you: Everything must be fulfilled that is written about me in the Law of Moses, the Prophets and the Psalms."

[45]Then he opened their minds so they could understand the Scriptures.
John 10 [34]Jesus answered them, "Is it not written in your Law, 'I have said you are gods'? [35]If he called them 'gods,' to whom the word of God came—and the Scripture cannot be broken—[36]what about the one whom the Father set apart as his very own and sent into the world? Why then do you accuse me of blasphemy because I said, 'I am God's Son'?"

d) Other NT Claims to the OT's Inspiration

Acts 3 [18]"But this is how God fulfilled what he had foretold through all the prophets, saying that his Christ would suffer."
Acts 18 [28]For he vigorously refuted the Jews in public debate, proving from the Scriptures that Jesus was the Christ.
Rom 3 [1]What advantage, then, is there in being a Jew, or what value is there in circumcision? [2]Much in every way! First of all, they have been entrusted with the very words of God.
2 Tim 3 [16]All Scripture is God-breathed and is useful for teaching, rebuking, correcting and training in righteousness, [17]so that the man of God may be thoroughly equipped for every good work.
Heb 1 [1]In the past God spoke to our forefathers through the prophets at many times and in various ways, [2]but in these last days he has spoken to us by his Son, whom he appointed heir of all things, and through whom he made the universe.

James 2 8If you really keep the royal law found in Scripture, "Love your neighbor as yourself," you are doing right.

1 Pet 1 10Concerning this salvation, the prophets, who spoke of the grace that was to come to you, searched intently and with the greatest care, 11trying to find out the time and circumstances to which the Spirit of Christ in them was pointing when he predicted the sufferings of Christ and the glories that would follow. 12It was revealed to them that they were not serving themselves but you, when they spoke of the things that have now been told you by those who have preached the gospel to you by the Holy Spirit sent from heaven. Even angels long to look into these things.

2 Pet 1 19And we have the word of the prophets made more certain, and you will do well to pay attention to it, as to a light shining in a dark place, until the day dawns and the morning star rises in your hearts. 20Above all, you must understand that no prophecy of Scripture came about by the prophet's own interpretation. 21For prophecy never had its origin in the will of man, but men spoke from God as they were carried along by the Holy Spirit.

2 Pet 3 2I want you to recall the words spoken in the past by the holy prophets and the command given by our Lord and Savior through your apostles.

2 Pet 3 15Bear in mind that our Lord's patience means salvation, just as our dear brother Paul also wrote you with the wisdom that God gave him. 16He writes the same way in all his letters, speaking in them of these matters. His letters contain some things that are hard to understand, which ignorant and unstable people distort, as they do the other Scriptures, to their own destruction.

2. The NT's Inspiration

a) Jesus' View of the Inspiration of the NT

(1) Christ's Teaching and the NT's Inspiration

Matt 7 24"Therefore everyone who hears these words of mine and puts them into practice is like a wise man who built his house on the rock. 25The rain came down, the streams rose, and the winds blew and beat against that house; yet it did not fall, because it had its foundation on the rock."

Matt 24 35"Heaven and earth will pass away, but my words will never pass away."

John 4 25The woman said, "I know that Messiah" (called Christ) "is coming. When he comes, he will explain everything to us."

26Then Jesus declared, "I who speak to you am he."

John 5 36"I have testimony weightier than that of John. For the very work that the Father has given me to finish, and which I am doing, testifies that the Father has sent me. 37And the Father who sent me has himself testified concerning me. You have never heard his voice nor seen his form, 38nor does his word dwell in you, for you do not believe the one he sent. 39You diligently study the Scriptures because you think that by them you possess eternal life. These are the Scriptures that testify about me, 40yet you refuse to come to me to have life.

41"I do not accept praise from men, 42but I know you. I know that you do not have the love of God in your hearts. 43I have come in my Father's name, and you do not accept me; but if someone else comes in his own name, you will accept him. 44How can you believe if you accept praise from one another, yet make no effort to obtain the praise that comes from the only God?

45"But do not think I will accuse you before the Father. Your accuser is Moses, on whom your hopes are set. 46If you believed Moses, you would believe me, for he wrote about me. 47But since you do not believe what he wrote, how are you going to believe what I say?"

John 6 68Simon Peter answered him, "Lord, to whom shall we go? You have the words of eternal life."

John 7 16Jesus answered, "My teaching is not my own. It comes from him who sent me."

John 8 26"I have much to say in judgment of you. But he who sent me is reliable, and what I have heard from him I tell the world." . . .

28So Jesus said, "When you have lifted up the Son of Man, then you will know that I am the one I claim to be and that I do nothing on my own but speak just what the Father has taught me."

John 12 48"There is a judge for the one who rejects me and does not accept my words; that very word which I spoke will condemn him at the last day. 49For I did not speak of my own accord, but the Father who sent me commanded me what to say and how to say it. 50I know that his command leads to eternal life. So whatever I say is just what the Father has told me to say."

John 14 10"Don't you believe that I am in the Father, and that the Father is in me? The words I say to you are not just my own. Rather, it is the Father, living in me, who is doing his work."

John 17 1After Jesus said this, he looked toward heaven and prayed: "Father, the time has come. Glorify your Son, that your Son may glorify you. . . . 8For I gave them the words you gave me and they accepted them. They knew with certainty that I came from you, and they believed that you sent me. . . . 14I have given them your word and the world has hated them, for they are not of the world any more than I am of the world. . . . 17Sanctify them by the truth; your word is truth."

(2) Christ's Promise of the NT's Inspiration

Luke 21 15"For I will give you words and wisdom that none of your adversaries will be able to resist or contradict."

John 14 26"But the Counselor, the Holy Spirit, whom the Father will send in my name, will teach you all things and will remind you of everything I have said to you."

John 15 26"When the Counselor comes, whom I will send to you from the Father, the Spirit of truth who goes out from the Father, he will testify about me. 27And you also must testify, for you have been with me from the beginning."

John 16 12"I have much more to say to you, more than you can now bear. 13But when he, the Spirit of truth, comes, he will guide you into all truth. He will not speak on his own; he will speak only what he hears, and he will tell you what is yet to come. 14He will bring glory to me by taking from what is mine and making it known to you. 15All that belongs to the Father is mine. That is why I said the Spirit will take from what is mine and make it known to you."

b) The Apostles' Views of the Inspiration of the NT

(1) Paul and the NT's Inspiration

Acts 22 13"He stood beside me and said, 'Brother Saul, receive your sight!' And at that very moment I was able to see him.

14"Then he said: 'The God of our fathers has chosen you to know his will and to see the Righteous One and to hear words from his mouth. 15You will be his witness to all men of what you have seen and heard.'"

Rom 16 25Now to him who is able to establish you by my gospel and the proclamation of Jesus Christ, according to the revelation of the mystery hidden for long ages past, 26but now revealed and made known through the prophetic writings by the command of the eternal God, so that all nations might believe and obey him—27to the only wise God be glory forever through Jesus Christ! Amen.

1 Cor 2 12We have not received the spirit of the world but the Spirit who is from God, that we may understand what God has freely given us. 13This is what we speak, not in words taught us by human wisdom but in words taught by the Spirit, expressing spiritual truths in spiritual words.

1 Cor 7 10To the married I give this command (not I, but the Lord): A wife must not separate from her husband.

1 Cor 14 37If anybody thinks he is a prophet or spiritually gifted, let him acknowledge that what I am writing to you is the Lord's command.

Eph 3 2Surely you have heard about the administration of God's grace that was given to me for you, 3that is, the mystery made known to me by revelation, as I have already written briefly. 4In reading this, then, you will be able to understand my insight into the mystery of Christ, 5which was not made known to men in other generations as it has now been revealed by the Spirit to God's holy apostles and prophets.

Eph 6 17Take the helmet of salvation and the sword of the Spirit, which is the word of God.

Col 3 16Let the word of Christ dwell in you richly as you teach and admonish one another with all wisdom, and as you sing psalms, hymns and spiritual songs with gratitude in your hearts to God.

1 Thess 2 [13]And we also thank God continually because, when you received the word of God, which you heard from us, you accepted it not as the word of men, but as it actually is, the word of God, which is at work in you who believe.

Titus 1 [2]a faith and knowledge resting on the hope of eternal life, which God, who does not lie, promised before the beginning of time, [3]and at his appointed season he brought his word to light through the preaching entrusted to me by the command of God our Savior. . . .

(2) Peter and the NT's Inspiration

1 Pet 1 [23]For you have been born again, not of perishable seed, but of imperishable, through the living and enduring word of God. [24]For, "All men are like grass, and all their glory is like the flowers of the field; the grass withers and the flowers fall, [25]but the word of the Lord stands forever." And this is the word that was preached to you.

2 Pet 3 [15]Bear in mind that our Lord's patience means salvation, just as our dear brother Paul also wrote you with the wisdom that God gave him. [16]He writes the same way in all his letters, speaking in them of these matters. His letters contain some things that are hard to understand, which ignorant and unstable people distort, as they do the other Scriptures, to their own destruction.

(3) John and the NT's Inspiration

1 John 1 [1]That which was from the beginning, which we have heard, which we have seen with our eyes, which we have looked at and our hands have touched—this we proclaim concerning the Word of life. [2]The life appeared; we have seen it and testify to it, and we proclaim to you the eternal life, which was with the Father and has appeared to us. [3]We proclaim to you what we have seen and heard, so that you also may have fellowship with us. And our fellowship is with the Father and with his Son, Jesus Christ. [4]We write this to make our joy complete.

[5]This is the message we have heard from him and declare to you: God is light; in him there is no darkness at all.

Rev 1 [1]The revelation of Jesus Christ, which God gave him to show his servants what must soon take place. He made it known by sending his angel to his servant John, [2]who testifies to everything he saw—that is, the word of God and the testimony of Jesus Christ. [3]Blessed is the one who reads the words of this prophecy, and blessed are those who hear it and take to heart what is written in it, because the time is near.

Rev 1 [10]On the Lord's Day I was in the Spirit, and I heard behind me a loud voice like a trumpet, [11]which said: "Write on a scroll what you see and send it to the seven churches: to Ephesus, Smyrna, Pergamum, Thyatira, Sardis, Philadelphia and Laodicea."

Rev 1 [17]When I saw him, I fell at his feet as though dead. Then he placed his right hand on me and said: "Do not be afraid. I am the First and the Last. [18]I am the Living One; I was dead, and behold I am alive for ever and ever! And I hold the keys of death and Hades.

[19]"Write, therefore, what you have seen, what is now and what will take place later. [20]The mystery of the seven stars that you saw in my right hand and of the seven golden lampstands is this: The seven stars are the angels of the seven churches, and the seven lampstands are the seven churches."

Rev 19 [9]Then the angel said to me, "Write: 'Blessed are those who are invited to the wedding supper of the Lamb!'" And he added, "These are the true words of God."

[10]At this I fell at his feet to worship him. But he said to me, "Do not do it! I am a fellow servant with you and with your brothers who hold to the testimony of Jesus. Worship God! For the testimony of Jesus is the spirit of prophecy."

Rev 22 [6]The angel said to me, "These words are trustworthy and true. The Lord, the God of the spirits of the prophets, sent his angel to show his servants the things that must soon take place."

[7]"Behold, I am coming soon! Blessed is he who keeps the words of the prophecy in this book."

[8]I, John, am the one who heard and saw these things. And when I had heard and seen them, I fell down to worship at the feet of the angel who had been showing them to me. . . .

[18]I warn everyone who hears the words of the prophecy of this book: If anyone adds anything to them, God will add to him the plagues described in this book. [19]And if anyone takes words away from this book of prophecy, God will take away from him his share in the tree of life and in the holy city, which are described in this book.

C. Jesus' View of the OT

1. Christ Affirmed the OT's Historicity

a) The Historicity of OT Persons

(1) Abel

Matt 23 [35]"And so upon you will come all the righteous blood that has been shed on earth, from the blood of righteous Abel to the blood of Zechariah son of Berekiah, whom you murdered between the temple and the altar."

(2) Abraham

Matt 8 [11]"I say to you that many will come from the east and the west, and will take their places at the feast with Abraham, Isaac and Jacob in the kingdom of heaven."

Luke 13 [28]"There will be weeping there, and gnashing of teeth, when you see Abraham, Isaac and Jacob and all the prophets in the kingdom of God, but you yourselves thrown out."

John 8 [37]"I know you are Abraham's descendants. Yet you are ready to kill me, because you have no room for my word. . . ."

[39]"Abraham is our father," they answered.

"If you were Abraham's children," said Jesus, "then you would do the things Abraham did. [40]As it is, you are determined to kill me, a man who has told you the truth that I heard from God. Abraham did not do such things. . . . [56]Your father Abraham rejoiced at the thought of seeing my day; he saw it and was glad." . . .

[58]"I tell you the truth," Jesus answered, "before Abraham was born, I am!"

(3) Daniel

Matt 24 [15]"So when you see standing in the holy place 'the abomination that causes desolation,' spoken of through the prophet Daniel—let the reader understand—[16]then let those who are in Judea flee to the mountains."

(4) David

Luke 6 [3]Jesus answered them, "Have you never read what David did when he and his companions were hungry? [4]He entered the house of God, and taking the consecrated bread, he ate what is lawful only for priests to eat. And he also gave some to his companions."

(5) Elijah

Matt 11 [13]"For all the Prophets and the Law prophesied until John. [14]And if you are willing to accept it, he is the Elijah who was to come."

Luke 4 [25]"I assure you that there were many widows in Israel in Elijah's time, when the sky was shut for three and a half years and there was a severe famine throughout the land. [26]Yet Elijah was not sent to any of them, but to a widow in Zarephath in the region of Sidon."

(6) Elisha

Luke 4 [27]"And there were many in Israel with leprosy in the time of Elisha the prophet, yet not one of them was cleansed—only Naaman the Syrian."

(7) Isaac

Matt 8 [11]"I say to you that many will come from the east and the west, and will take their places at the feast with Abraham, Isaac and Jacob in the kingdom of heaven."

Luke 13 [28]"There will be weeping there, and gnashing of teeth, when you see Abraham, Isaac and Jacob and all the prophets in the kingdom of God, but you yourselves thrown out."

(8) Jacob

Matt 8 [11]"I say to you that many will come from the east and the west, and will take their places at the feast with Abraham, Isaac and Jacob in the kingdom of heaven."

Luke 13 [28]"There will be weeping there, and gnashing of teeth, when you see Abraham, Isaac and Jacob and all the prophets in the kingdom of God, but you yourselves thrown out."

(9) Jonah

Matt 12 39He answered, "A wicked and adulterous generation asks for a miraculous sign! But none will be given it except the sign of the prophet Jonah. 40For as Jonah was three days and three nights in the belly of a huge fish, so the Son of Man will be three days and three nights in the heart of the earth. 41The men of Nineveh will stand up at the judgment with this generation and condemn it; for they repented at the preaching of Jonah, and now one greater than Jonah is here."

Matt 16 4"A wicked and adulterous generation looks for a miraculous sign, but none will be given it except the sign of Jonah." Jesus then left them and went away.

(10) Lot

Luke 17 28"It was the same in the days of Lot. People were eating and drinking, buying and selling, planting and building. 29But the day Lot left Sodom, fire and sulfur rained down from heaven and destroyed them all.

30"It will be just like this on the day the Son of Man is revealed. 31On that day no one who is on the roof of his house, with his goods inside, should go down to get them. Likewise, no one in the field should go back for anything. 32Remember Lot's wife!"

(11) Moses

Mark 1 44"See that you don't tell this to anyone. But go, show yourself to the priest and offer the sacrifices that Moses commanded for your cleansing, as a testimony to them."

Mark 10 2Some Pharisees came and tested him by asking, "Is it lawful for a man to divorce his wife?"

3"What did Moses command you?" he replied.

4They said, "Moses permitted a man to write a certificate of divorce and send her away."

5"It was because your hearts were hard that Moses wrote you this law," Jesus replied.

Mark 12 26"Now about the dead rising—have you not read in the book of Moses, in the account of the bush, how God said to him, 'I am the God of Abraham, the God of Isaac, and the God of Jacob'?"

John 3 14"Just as Moses lifted up the snake in the desert, so the Son of Man must be lifted up. . . ."

John 5 45"But do not think I will accuse you before the Father. Your accuser is Moses, on whom your hopes are set. 46If you believed Moses, you would believe me, for he wrote about me."

John 6 32Jesus said to them, "I tell you the truth, it is not Moses who has given you the bread from heaven, but it is my Father who gives you the true bread from heaven."

(12) Noah

Matt 24 37"As it was in the days of Noah, so it will be at the coming of the Son of Man. 38For in the days before the flood, people were eating and drinking, marrying and giving in marriage, up to the day Noah entered the ark; 39and they knew nothing about what would happen until the flood came and took them all away. That is how it will be at the coming of the Son of Man."

(13) The Queen of the South

Matt 12 42"The Queen of the South will rise at the judgment with this generation and condemn it; for she came from the ends of the earth to listen to Solomon's wisdom, and now one greater than Solomon is here."

(14) Solomon

Matt 6 29"Yet I tell you that not even Solomon in all his splendor was dressed like one of these."

Matt 12 42"The Queen of the South will rise at the judgment with this generation and condemn it; for she came from the ends of the earth to listen to Solomon's wisdom, and now one greater than Solomon is here."

Luke 12 27"Consider how the lilies grow. They do not labor or spin. Yet I tell you, not even Solomon in all his splendor was dressed like one of these."

(15) Zechariah

Matt 23 35"And so upon you will come all the righteous blood that has been shed on earth, from the blood of righteous Abel to the blood of Zechariah son of Berekiah, whom you murdered between the temple and the altar."

b) The Historicity of OT Practices

(1) Circumcision

John 7 22"Yet, because Moses gave you circumcision (though actually it did not come from Moses, but from the patriarchs), you circumcise a child on the Sabbath. 23Now if a child can be circumcised on the Sabbath so that the law of Moses may not be broken, why are you angry with me for healing the whole man on the Sabbath?"

(2) Priestly Work on the Sabbath

Matt 12 5"Or haven't you read in the Law that on the Sabbath the priests in the temple desecrate the day and yet are innocent? 6I tell you that one greater than the temple is here."

c) The Historicity of OT Places

(1) Nineveh

Luke 11 30"For as Jonah was a sign to the Ninevites, so also will the Son of Man be to this generation. . . . 32The men of Nineveh will stand up at the judgment with this generation and condemn it; for they repented at the preaching of Jonah, and now one greater than Jonah is here."

(2) Sodom and Gomorrah

Matt 10 15"I tell you the truth, it will be more bearable for Sodom and Gomorrah on the day of judgment than for that town."

Matt 11 23"And you, Capernaum, will you be lifted up to the skies? No, you will go down to the depths. If the miracles that were performed in you had been performed in Sodom, it would have remained to this day. 24But I tell you that it will be more bearable for Sodom on the day of judgment than for you."

Luke 17 29"But the day Lot left Sodom, fire and sulfur rained down from heaven and destroyed them all."

(3) Tyre and Sidon

Matt 11 21"Woe to you, Korazin! Woe to you, Bethsaida! If the miracles that were performed in you had been performed in Tyre and Sidon, they would have repented long ago in sackcloth and ashes. 22But I tell you, it will be more bearable for Tyre and Sidon on the day of judgment than for you."

d) The Historicity of OT Objects

(1) The Bronze Snake

John 3 14"Just as Moses lifted up the snake in the desert, so the Son of Man must be lifted up. . . ."

(2) Manna

John 6 30So they asked him, "What miraculous sign then will you give that we may see it and believe you? What will you do? 31Our forefathers ate the manna in the desert; as it is written: 'He gave them bread from heaven to eat.'"

32Jesus said to them, "I tell you the truth, it is not Moses who has given you the bread from heaven, but it is my Father who gives you the true bread from heaven. . . . 49Your forefathers ate the manna in the desert, yet they died. 50But here is the bread that comes down from heaven, which a man may eat and not die. . . . 58This is the bread that came down from heaven. Your forefathers ate manna and died, but he who feeds on this bread will live forever."

e) The Historicity of OT Events

(1) Creation

Mark 10 6"But at the beginning of creation God 'made them male and female.' 7'For this reason a man will leave his father and mother and be united to his wife, 8and the two will become one flesh.' So they are no longer two, but one. 9Therefore what God has joined together, let man not separate."

(2) The Flood

Matt 24 37"As it was in the days of Noah, so it will be at the coming of the Son of Man. 38For in the days before the flood, people were eating and drinking, marrying and giving in marriage, up to the day Noah entered the ark; 39and they knew nothing about what would happen until the flood came and took them all away. That is how it will be at the coming of the Son of Man."

Luke 17 26"Just as it was in the days of Noah, so also will it be in the days of the Son of Man. [27]People were eating, drinking, marrying and being given in marriage up to the day Noah entered the ark. Then the flood came and destroyed them all."

(3) The Burning Bush

Luke 20 [34]Jesus replied, "The people of this age marry and are given in marriage. [35]But those who are considered worthy of taking part in that age and in the resurrection from the dead will neither marry nor be given in marriage, [36]and they can no longer die; for they are like the angels. They are God's children, since they are children of the resurrection. [37]But in the account of the bush, even Moses showed that the dead rise, for he calls the Lord 'the God of Abraham, and the God of Isaac, and the God of Jacob.' [38]He is not the God of the dead, but of the living, for to him all are alive."

(4) The Giving of the Law

Matt 8 [4]Then Jesus said to him, "See that you don't tell anyone. But go, show yourself to the priest and offer the gift Moses commanded, as a testimony to them."
Matt 19 [8]Jesus replied, "Moses permitted you to divorce your wives because your hearts were hard. But it was not this way from the beginning."
John 7 [19]"Has not Moses given you the law? Yet not one of you keeps the law. Why are you trying to kill me?"

(5) Eating the Consecrated Bread

Mark 2 [25]He answered, "Have you never read what David did when he and his companions were hungry and in need? [26]In the days of Abiathar the high priest, he entered the house of God and ate the consecrated bread, which is lawful only for priests to eat. And he also gave some to his companions."

(6) The Suffering of the Prophets

Matt 5 [11]"Blessed are you when people insult you, persecute you and falsely say all kinds of evil against you because of me. [12]Rejoice and be glad, because great is your reward in heaven, for in the same way they persecuted the prophets who were before you."
Matt 23 [29]"Woe to you, teachers of the law and Pharisees, you hypocrites! You build tombs for the prophets and decorate the graves of the righteous. [30]And you say, 'If we had lived in the days of our forefathers, we would not have taken part with them in shedding the blood of the prophets.' [31]So you testify against yourselves that you are the descendants of those who murdered the prophets. [32]Fill up, then, the measure of the sin of your forefathers!"
Luke 11 [47]"Woe to you, because you build tombs for the prophets, and it was your forefathers who killed them. [48]So you testify that you approve of what your forefathers did; they killed the prophets, and you build their tombs. . . . [50]Therefore this generation will be held responsible for the blood of all the prophets that has been shed since the beginning of the world, [51]from the blood of Abel to the blood of Zechariah, who was killed between the altar and the sanctuary. Yes, I tell you, this generation will be held responsible for it all."

f) The Historicity of Moses' Authorship of the Pentateuch

Mark 10 [5]"It was because your hearts were hard that Moses wrote you this law," Jesus replied.
John 5 [46]"If you believed Moses, you would believe me, for he wrote about me. [47]But since you do not believe what he wrote, how are you going to believe what I say?"

g) The Historicity of Isaiah as Author

Mark 7 [6]He replied, "Isaiah was right when he prophesied about you hypocrites; as it is written: 'These people honor me with their lips, but their hearts are far from me. [7]They worship me in vain; their teachings are but rules taught by men.'"

2. Christ Considered the OT Inspired

a) The OT Is God's Word

Matt 15 [6]". . . he is not to 'honor his father' with it. Thus you nullify the word of God for the sake of your tradition."
Matt 22 [43]He said to them, "How is it then that David, speaking by the Spirit, calls him 'Lord'? For he says, [44]'The Lord said to my Lord: "Sit at my right hand until I put your enemies under your feet."' [45]If then David calls him 'Lord,' how can he be his son?"
Matt 24 [15]"So when you see standing in the holy place 'the abomination that causes desolation,' spoken of through the prophet Daniel—let the reader understand—[16]then let those who are in Judea flee to the mountains."
Mark 7 [6]He replied, "Isaiah was right when he prophesied about you hypocrites; as it is written: 'These people honor me with their lips, but their hearts are far from me. [7]They worship me in vain; their teachings are but rules taught by men.' [8]You have let go of the commands of God and are holding on to the traditions of men."

[9]And he said to them: "You have a fine way of setting aside the commands of God in order to observe your own traditions! [10]For Moses said, 'Honor your father and your mother,' and, 'Anyone who curses his father or mother must be put to death.'"
Luke 11 [28]He replied, "Blessed rather are those who hear the word of God and obey it."
John 10 [34]Jesus answered them, "Is it not written in your Law, 'I have said you are gods'? [35]If he called them 'gods,' to whom the word of God came—and the Scripture cannot be broken . . ."

b) OT Prophecies Have Been Fulfilled

Matt 11 [10]"This is the one about whom it is written: 'I will send my messenger ahead of you, who will prepare your way before you.'" (Mal 3:1)
Matt 26 [23]Jesus replied, "The one who has dipped his hand into the bowl with me will betray me. [24]The Son of Man will go just as it is written about him. But woe to that man who betrays the Son of Man! It would be better for him if he had not been born."
Matt 26 [31]Then Jesus told them, "This very night you will all fall away on account of me, for it is written: 'I will strike the shepherd, and the sheep of the flock will be scattered.'" (Zech 13:7)
Matt 26 [53]"Do you think I cannot call on my Father, and he will at once put at my disposal more than twelve legions of angels? [54]But how then would the Scriptures be fulfilled that say it must happen in this way?"

[55]At that time Jesus said to the crowd, "Am I leading a rebellion, that you have come out with swords and clubs to capture me? Every day I sat in the temple courts teaching, and you did not arrest me. [56]But this has all taken place that the writings of the prophets might be fulfilled." Then all the disciples deserted him and fled.
Mark 9 [12]Jesus replied, "To be sure, Elijah does come first, and restores all things. Why then is it written that the Son of Man must suffer much and be rejected? [13]But I tell you, Elijah has come, and they have done to him everything they wished, just as it is written about him."
Luke 4 [16]He went to Nazareth, where he had been brought up, and on the Sabbath day he went into the synagogue, as was his custom. And he stood up to read. [17]The scroll of the prophet Isaiah was handed to him. Unrolling it, he found the place where it is written: [18]"The Spirit of the Lord is on me, because he has anointed me to preach good news to the poor. He has sent me to proclaim freedom for the prisoners and recovery of sight for the blind, to release the oppressed, [19]to proclaim the year of the Lord's favor."

[20]Then he rolled up the scroll, gave it back to the attendant and sat down. The eyes of everyone in the synagogue were fastened on him, [21]and he began by saying to them, "Today this scripture is fulfilled in your hearing." (Isa 61:1–2)
Luke 18 [31]Jesus took the Twelve aside and told them, "We are going up to Jerusalem, and everything that is written by the prophets about the Son of Man will be fulfilled. [32]He will be handed over to the Gentiles. They will mock him, insult him, spit on him, flog him and kill him. [33]On the third day he will rise again."
Luke 21 [20]"When you see Jerusalem being surrounded by armies, you will know that its desolation is near. [21]Then let those who are in Judea flee to the mountains, let those in the city get out, and let those in the country not enter the city. [22]For this is the time of punishment in fulfillment of all that has been

written. [23]How dreadful it will be in those days for pregnant women and nursing mothers! There will be great distress in the land and wrath against this people. [24]They will fall by the sword and will be taken as prisoners to all the nations. Jerusalem will be trampled on by the Gentiles until the times of the Gentiles are fulfilled."

Luke 22 [37]"It is written: 'And he was numbered with the transgressors'; and I tell you that this must be fulfilled in me. Yes, what is written about me is reaching its fulfillment." (Isa 53:12)

Luke 24 [25]He said to them, "How foolish you are, and how slow of heart to believe all that the prophets have spoken! [26]Did not the Christ have to suffer these things and then enter his glory?" [27]And beginning with Moses and all the Prophets, he explained to them what was said in all the Scriptures concerning himself.

Luke 24 [44]He said to them, "This is what I told you while I was still with you: Everything must be fulfilled that is written about me in the Law of Moses, the Prophets and the Psalms."

[45]Then he opened their minds so they could understand the Scriptures. [46]He told them, "This is what is written: The Christ will suffer and rise from the dead on the third day, [47]and repentance and forgiveness of sins will be preached in his name to all nations, beginning at Jerusalem."

John 5 [39]"You diligently study the Scriptures because you think that by them you possess eternal life. These are the Scriptures that testify about me, [40]yet you refuse to come to me to have life.

[41]"I do not accept praise from men, [42]but I know you. I know that you do not have the love of God in your hearts. [43]I have come in my Father's name, and you do not accept me; but if someone else comes in his own name, you will accept him. [44]How can you believe if you accept praise from one another, yet make no effort to obtain the praise that comes from the only God?

[45]"But do not think I will accuse you before the Father. Your accuser is Moses, on whom your hopes are set. [46]If you believed Moses, you would believe me, for he wrote about me. [47]But since you do not believe what he wrote, how are you going to believe what I say?"

John 13 [18]"I am not referring to all of you; I know those I have chosen. But this is to fulfill the scripture: 'He who shares my bread has lifted up his heel against me.'" (Ps 41:9)

John 15 [25]"But this is to fulfill what is written in their Law: 'They hated me without reason.'" (Pss 35:19; 69:4)

John 17 [12]"While I was with them, I protected them and kept them safe by that name you gave me. None has been lost except the one doomed to destruction so that Scripture would be fulfilled."

See also p. 78b, Prophecies concerning Christ

c) The OT Possesses Authority

Matt 4 [4]Jesus answered, "It is written: 'Man does not live on bread alone, but on every word that comes from the mouth of God.'" (Deut 8:3)

Matt 4 [7]Jesus answered him, "It is also written: 'Do not put the Lord your God to the test.'" (Deut 6:16)

Matt 4 [10]Jesus said to him, "Away from me, Satan! For it is written: 'Worship the Lord your God, and serve him only.'" (Deut 6:13)

Matt 5 [18]"I tell you the truth, until heaven and earth disappear, not the smallest letter, not the least stroke of a pen, will by any means disappear from the Law until everything is accomplished."

Matt 12 [3]He answered, "Haven't you read what David did when he and his companions were hungry? [4]He entered the house of God, and he and his companions ate the consecrated bread—which was not lawful for them to do, but only for the priests. [5]Or haven't you read in the Law that on the Sabbath the priests in the temple desecrate the day and yet are innocent?"

Matt 19 [4]"Haven't you read," he replied, "that at the beginning the Creator 'made them male and female,' [5]and said, 'For this reason a man will leave his father and mother and be united to his wife, and the two will become one flesh'? [6]So they are no longer two, but one. Therefore what God has joined together, let man not separate." (Gen 1:27; 2:24)

Matt 21 [16]"Do you hear what these children are saying?" they asked him.

"Yes," replied Jesus, "have you never read, 'From the lips of children and infants you have ordained praise'?" (Ps 8:2)

Matt 21 [42]Jesus said to them, "Have you never read in the Scriptures: 'The stone the builders rejected has become the capstone; the Lord has done this, and it is marvelous in our eyes'?" (Ps 118:22-23)

Matt 22 [29]Jesus replied, "You are in error because you do not know the Scriptures or the power of God. . . . [31]But about the resurrection of the dead—have you not read what God said to you, [32]'I am the God of Abraham, the God of Isaac, and the God of Jacob'? He is not the God of the dead but of the living." (Exod 3:6)

Matt 26 [50]Jesus replied, "Friend, do what you came for."

Then the men stepped forward, seized Jesus and arrested him. . . .

[53]"Do you think I cannot call on my Father, and he will at once put at my disposal more than twelve legions of angels? [54]But how then would the Scriptures be fulfilled that say it must happen in this way?"

Mark 11 [17]And as he taught them, he said, "Is it not written: 'My house will be called a house of prayer for all nations'? But you have made it 'a den of robbers.'" (Isa 56:7; Jer 7:11)

Luke 4 [21]and he began by saying to them, "Today this scripture is fulfilled in your hearing."

Luke 16 [16]"The Law and the Prophets were proclaimed until John. Since that time, the good news of the kingdom of God is being preached, and everyone is forcing his way into it. [17]It is easier for heaven and earth to disappear than for the least stroke of a pen to drop out of the Law."

Luke 16 [29]"Abraham replied, 'They have Moses and the Prophets; let them listen to them.'

[30]"'No, father Abraham,' he said, 'but if someone from the dead goes to them, they will repent.'

[31]"He said to him, 'If they do not listen to Moses and the Prophets, they will not be convinced even if someone rises from the dead.'"

John 5 [39]"You diligently study the Scriptures because you think that by them you possess eternal life. These are the Scriptures that testify about me, [40]yet you refuse to come to me to have life. . . .

[45]"But do not think I will accuse you before the Father. Your accuser is Moses, on whom your hopes are set. [46]If you believed Moses, you would believe me, for he wrote about me. [47]But since you do not believe what he wrote, how are you going to believe what I say?"

John 7 [38]"Whoever believes in me, as the Scripture has said, streams of living water will flow from within him."

John 13 [18]"I am not referring to all of you; I know those I have chosen. But this is to fulfill the scripture: 'He who shares my bread has lifted up his heel against me.'" (Ps 41:9)

3. Christ Used the OT Authoritatively

a) Jesus Used the OT in Ethical Discussion

Matt 7 [12]"So in everything, do to others what you would have them do to you, for this sums up the Law and the Prophets."

Matt 19 [17]"Why do you ask me about what is good?" Jesus replied. "There is only One who is good. If you want to enter life, obey the commandments."

[18]"Which ones?" the man inquired.

Jesus replied, "'Do not murder, do not commit adultery, do not steal, do not give false testimony, [19]honor your father and mother,' and 'love your neighbor as yourself.'" (Exod 20:12–16; Deut 5:16–20; Lev 19:18)

Matt 22 [37]Jesus replied: "'Love the Lord your God with all your heart and with all your soul and with all your mind.' [38]This is the first and greatest commandment. [39]And the second is like it: 'Love your neighbor as yourself.' [40]All the Law and the Prophets hang on these two commandments." (Deut 6:5; Lev 19:18)

b) Jesus Used the OT in Refutation

(1) Christ Refuted Satan with the OT

Matt 4 [4]Jesus answered, "It is written: 'Man does not live on bread alone, but on every word that comes from the mouth of God.'" (Deut 8:3)

Matt 4 [7]Jesus answered him, "It is also written: 'Do not put the Lord your God to the test.'" (Deut 6:16)
Matt 4 [10]Jesus said to him, "Away from me, Satan! For it is written: 'Worship the Lord your God, and serve him only.'" (Deut 6:13)

(2) Christ Refuted Jewish Leaders with the OT

Matt 9 [12]On hearing this, Jesus said, "It is not the healthy who need a doctor, but the sick. [13]But go and learn what this means: 'I desire mercy, not sacrifice.' For I have not come to call the righteous, but sinners." (Hos 6:6)
Matt 12 [7]"If you had known what these words mean, 'I desire mercy, not sacrifice,' you would not have condemned the innocent. [8]For the Son of Man is Lord of the Sabbath." (Hos 6:6)
Matt 15 [3]Jesus replied, "And why do you break the command of God for the sake of your tradition? [4]For God said, 'Honor your father and mother' and 'Anyone who curses his father or mother must be put to death.' [5]But you say that if a man says to his father or mother, 'Whatever help you might otherwise have received from me is a gift devoted to God,' [6]he is not to 'honor his father' with it. Thus you nullify the word of God for the sake of your tradition." (Exod 20:12; 21:17; Lev 20:9; Deut 5:16)
Matt 21 [15]But when the chief priests and the teachers of the law saw the wonderful things he did and the children shouting in the temple area, "Hosanna to the Son of David," they were indignant.

[16]"Do you hear what these children are saying?" they asked him.

"Yes," replied Jesus, "have you never read, 'From the lips of children and infants you have ordained praise'?" (Ps 8:2)
Matt 21 [42]Jesus said to them, "Have you never read in the Scriptures: 'The stone the builders rejected has become the capstone; the Lord has done this, and it is marvelous in our eyes'?

[43]"Therefore I tell you that the kingdom of God will be taken away from you and given to a people who will produce its fruit." (Ps 118:22–23)
Matt 22 [29]Jesus replied, "You are in error because you do not know the Scriptures or the power of God. [30]At the resurrection people will neither marry nor be given in marriage; they will be like the angels in heaven. [31]But about the resurrection of the dead—have you not read what God said to you, [32]'I am the God of Abraham, the God of Isaac, and the God of Jacob'? He is not the God of the dead but of the living." (Exod 3:6)
Matt 22 [41]While the Pharisees were gathered together, Jesus asked them, [42]"What do you think about the Christ? Whose son is he?"

"The son of David," they replied.

[43]He said to them, "How is it then that David, speaking by the Spirit, calls him 'Lord'? For he says, [44]'The Lord said to my Lord: "Sit at my right hand until I put your enemies under your feet."' [45]If then David calls him 'Lord,' how can he be his son?" (Ps 110:1)
Mark 7 [5]So the Pharisees and teachers of the law asked Jesus, "Why don't your disciples live according to the tradition of the elders instead of eating their food with 'unclean' hands?"

[6]He replied, "Isaiah was right when he prophesied about you hypocrites; as it is written: 'These people honor me with their lips, but their hearts are far from me. [7]They worship me in vain; their teachings are but rules taught by men.' [8]You have let go of the commands of God and are holding on to the traditions of men."

[9]And he said to them: "You have a fine way of setting aside the commands of God in order to observe your own traditions! [10]For Moses said, 'Honor your father and your mother,' and, 'Anyone who curses his father or mother must be put to death.' [11]But you say that if a man says to his father or mother: 'Whatever help you might otherwise have received from me is Corban' (that is, a gift devoted to God), [12]then you no longer let him do anything for his father or mother. [13]Thus you nullify the word of God by your tradition that you have handed down. And you do many things like that."
Mark 12 [28]One of the teachers of the law came and heard them debating. Noticing that Jesus had given them a good answer, he asked him, "Of all the commandments, which is the most important?"

[29]"The most important one," answered Jesus, "is this: 'Hear, O Israel, the Lord our God, the Lord is one. [30]Love the Lord your God with all your heart and with all your soul and with all your mind and with all your strength.' [31]The second is this: 'Love your neighbor as yourself.' There is no commandment greater than these." (Deut 6:4-5; Lev 19:18)

(3) Christ Refuted the Crowds with the OT

John 7 [21]Jesus said to them, "I did one miracle, and you are all astonished. [22]Yet, because Moses gave you circumcision (though actually it did not come from Moses, but from the patriarchs), you circumcise a child on the Sabbath. [23]Now if a child can be circumcised on the Sabbath so that the law of Moses may not be broken, why are you angry with me for healing the whole man on the Sabbath? [24]Stop judging by mere appearances, and make a right judgment."

(4) Christ Refuted Temple Merchants with the OT

Matt 21 [13]"It is written," he said to them, "'My house will be called a house of prayer,' but you are making it a 'den of robbers.'" (Isa 56:7; Jer 7:11)

c) Jesus Used the OT in Teaching

(1) Christ Used the OT to Describe His Mission

Matt 10 [34]"Do not suppose that I have come to bring peace to the earth. I did not come to bring peace, but a sword. [35]For I have come to turn 'a man against his father, a daughter against her mother, a daughter-in-law against her mother-in-law—[36]a man's enemies will be the members of his own household.'

[37]"Anyone who loves his father or mother more than me is not worthy of me; anyone who loves his son or daughter more than me is not worthy of me; [38]and anyone who does not take his cross and follow me is not worthy of me. [39]Whoever finds his life will lose it, and whoever loses his life for my sake will find it." (Mic 7:6)
John 6 [44]"No one can come to me unless the Father who sent me draws him, and I will raise him up at the last day. [45]It is written in the Prophets: 'They will all be taught by God.' Everyone who listens to the Father and learns from him comes to me. [46]No one has seen the Father except the one who is from God; only he has seen the Father. [47]I tell you the truth, he who believes has everlasting life. [48]I am the bread of life." (Isa 54:13)

(2) Christ Pronounced Fulfillments of the OT: John the Baptist

Matt 11 [9]"Then what did you go out to see? A prophet? Yes, I tell you, and more than a prophet. [10]This is the one about whom it is written: 'I will send my messenger ahead of you, who will prepare your way before you.' [11]I tell you the truth: Among those born of women there has not risen anyone greater than John the Baptist; yet he who is least in the kingdom of heaven is greater than he. . . . [13]For all the Prophets and the Law prophesied until John. [14]And if you are willing to accept it, he is the Elijah who was to come." (Mal 3:1)

(3) Christ Pronounced Fulfillments of the OT: Israel's Hardness of Heart

Matt 13 [10]The disciples came to him and asked, "Why do you speak to the people in parables?"

[11]He replied, "The knowledge of the secrets of the kingdom of heaven has been given to you, but not to them. [12]Whoever has will be given more, and he will have an abundance. Whoever does not have, even what he has will be taken from him. [13]This is why I speak to them in parables: Though seeing, they do not see; though hearing, they do not hear or understand. [14]In them is fulfilled the prophecy of Isaiah: 'You will be ever hearing but never understanding; you will be ever seeing but never perceiving. [15]For this people's heart has become calloused; they hardly hear with their ears, and they have closed their eyes. Otherwise they might see with their eyes, hear with their ears, understand with their hearts and turn, and I would heal them.' [16]But blessed are your eyes because they see, and your ears because they hear." (Isa 6:9–10)
Matt 15 [7]"You hypocrites! Isaiah was right when he prophesied about you: [8]'These people honor me with their lips, but their hearts are far from me. [9]They worship me in vain; their teachings are but rules taught by men.'" (Isa 29:13)

(4) Christ Reinterpreted the OT

Matt 5 [21]"You have heard that it was said to the people long ago, 'Do not murder, and anyone who murders will be subject to judgment.' [22]But I tell you that anyone who is angry with his brother will be subject to judgment. Again, anyone who says to his brother, 'Raca,' is answerable to the Sanhedrin. But anyone who says, 'You fool!' will be in danger of the fire of hell." (Exod 20:13)

Matt 5 [27]"You have heard that it was said, 'Do not commit adultery.' [28]But I tell you that anyone who looks at a woman lustfully has already committed adultery with her in his heart. [29]If your right eye causes you to sin, gouge it out and throw it away. It is better for you to lose one part of your body than for your whole body to be thrown into hell. [30]And if your right hand causes you to sin, cut it off and throw it away. It is better for you to lose one part of your body than for your whole body to go into hell." (Exod 20:14)

Matt 5 [31]"It has been said, 'Anyone who divorces his wife must give her a certificate of divorce.' [32]But I tell you that anyone who divorces his wife, except for marital unfaithfulness, causes her to become an adulteress, and anyone who marries the divorced woman commits adultery." (Deut 24:1)

Matt 5 [33]"Again, you have heard that it was said to the people long ago, 'Do not break your oath, but keep the oaths you have made to the Lord.' [34]But I tell you, Do not swear at all: either by heaven, for it is God's throne; [35]or by the earth, for it is his footstool; or by Jerusalem, for it is the city of the Great King. [36]And do not swear by your head, for you cannot make even one hair white or black. [37]Simply let your 'Yes' be 'Yes,' and your 'No,' 'No'; anything beyond this comes from the evil one." (Num 30:2)

Matt 5 [38]"You have heard that it was said, 'Eye for eye, and tooth for tooth.' [39]But I tell you, Do not resist an evil person. If someone strikes you on the right cheek, turn to him the other also. [40]And if someone wants to sue you and take your tunic, let him have your cloak as well. [41]If someone forces you to go one mile, go with him two miles. [42]Give to the one who asks you, and do not turn away from the one who wants to borrow from you." (Exod 21:24; Lev 24:20; Deut 19:21)

Matt 5 [43]"You have heard that it was said, 'Love your neighbor and hate your enemy.' [44]But I tell you: Love your enemies and pray for those who persecute you, [45]that you may be sons of your Father in heaven. He causes his sun to rise on the evil and the good, and sends rain on the righteous and the unrighteous." (Lev 19:18)

Matt 12 [11]He said to them, "If any of you has a sheep and it falls into a pit on the Sabbath, will you not take hold of it and lift it out? [12]How much more valuable is a man than a sheep! Therefore it is lawful to do good on the Sabbath." (Exod 20:8–11)

Matt 19 [8]Jesus replied, "Moses permitted you to divorce your wives because your hearts were hard. But it was not this way from the beginning. [9]I tell you that anyone who divorces his wife, except for marital unfaithfulness, and marries another woman commits adultery." (Deut 24:1)

John 7 [37]On the last and greatest day of the Feast, Jesus stood and said in a loud voice, "If anyone is thirsty, let him come to me and drink. [38]Whoever believes in me, as the Scripture has said, streams of living water will flow from within him." (Isa 58:11; Jer 2:13; 17:13)

(5) Christ Illustrated His Teaching with the OT

Matt 11 [2]When John heard in prison what Christ was doing, he sent his disciples [3]to ask him, "Are you the one who was to come, or should we expect someone else?"

[4]Jesus replied, "Go back and report to John what you hear and see: [5]The blind receive sight, the lame walk, those who have leprosy are cured, the deaf hear, the dead are raised, and the good news is preached to the poor."

Matt 11 [9]"Then what did you go out to see? A prophet? Yes, I tell you, and more than a prophet. [10]This is the one about whom it is written: 'I will send my messenger ahead of you, who will prepare your way before you.' [11]I tell you the truth: Among those born of women there has not risen anyone greater than John the Baptist; yet he who is least in the kingdom of heaven is greater than he. [12]From the days of John the Baptist until now, the kingdom of heaven has been forcefully advancing, and forceful men lay hold of it. [13]For all the Prophets and the Law prophesied until John. [14]And if you are willing to accept it, he is the Elijah who was to come. [15]He who has ears, let him hear."

Matt 11 [20]Then Jesus began to denounce the cities in which most of his miracles had been performed, because they did not repent. [21]"Woe to you, Korazin! Woe to you, Bethsaida! If the miracles that were performed in you had been performed in Tyre and Sidon, they would have repented long ago in sackcloth and ashes. [22]But I tell you, it will be more bearable for Tyre and Sidon on the day of judgment than for you. [23]And you, Capernaum, will you be lifted up to the skies? No, you will go down to the depths. If the miracles that were performed in you had been performed in Sodom, it would have remained to this day. [24]But I tell you that it will be more bearable for Sodom on the day of judgment than for you."

Matt 12 [3]He answered, "Haven't you read what David did when he and his companions were hungry? [4]He entered the house of God, and he and his companions ate the consecrated bread—which was not lawful for them to do, but only for the priests. [5]Or haven't you read in the Law that on the Sabbath the priests in the temple desecrate the day and yet are innocent? [6]I tell you that one greater than the temple is here. [7]If you had known what these words mean, 'I desire mercy, not sacrifice,' you would not have condemned the innocent. [8]For the Son of Man is Lord of the Sabbath."

Matt 12 [39]He answered, "A wicked and adulterous generation asks for a miraculous sign! But none will be given it except the sign of the prophet Jonah. [40]For as Jonah was three days and three nights in the belly of a huge fish, so the Son of Man will be three days and three nights in the heart of the earth. [41]The men of Nineveh will stand up at the judgment with this generation and condemn it; for they repented at the preaching of Jonah, and now one greater than Jonah is here. [42]The Queen of the South will rise at the judgment with this generation and condemn it; for she came from the ends of the earth to listen to Solomon's wisdom, and now one greater than Solomon is here."

Matt 19 [17]"Why do you ask me about what is good?" Jesus replied. "There is only One who is good. If you want to enter life, obey the commandments."

[18]"Which ones?" the man inquired.

Jesus replied, "'Do not murder, do not commit adultery, do not steal, do not give false testimony, [19]honor your father and mother,' and 'love your neighbor as yourself.'" (Exod 20:12–16; Deut 5:16–20; Lev 19:18)

Matt 24 [37]"As it was in the days of Noah, so it will be at the coming of the Son of Man. [38]For in the days before the flood, people were eating and drinking, marrying and giving in marriage, up to the day Noah entered the ark; [39]and they knew nothing about what would happen until the flood came and took them all away. That is how it will be at the coming of the Son of Man."

Mark 9 [47]"And if your eye causes you to sin, pluck it out. It is better for you to enter the kingdom of God with one eye than to have two eyes and be thrown into hell, [48]where 'their worm does not die, and the fire is not quenched.'" (Isa 66:24)

Luke 10 [25]On one occasion an expert in the law stood up to test Jesus. "Teacher," he asked, "what must I do to inherit eternal life?"

[26]"What is written in the Law?" he replied. "How do you read it?"

[27]He answered: "'Love the Lord your God with all your heart and with all your soul and with all your strength and with all your mind'; and, 'Love your neighbor as yourself.'"

[28]"You have answered correctly," Jesus replied. "Do this and you will live."

d) Jesus Used the OT in Prophecy

Matt 24 [15]"So when you see standing in the holy place 'the abomination that causes desolation,' spoken of through the prophet Daniel—let the reader understand—[16]then let those who are in Judea flee to the mountains." (Dan 9:27; 11:31; 12:11)

Matt 24 [29]"Immediately after the distress of those days 'the sun will be darkened, and the moon will not give its light; the stars will fall from the sky, and the heavenly bodies will be shaken.'" (Isa 13:10; 34:4)

Luke 21 20“When you see Jerusalem being surrounded by armies, you will know that its desolation is near. 21Then let those who are in Judea flee to the mountains, let those in the city get out, and let those in the country not enter the city. 22For this is the time of punishment in fulfillment of all that has been written.”

Luke 23 28Jesus turned and said to them, “Daughters of Jerusalem, do not weep for me; weep for yourselves and for your children. 29For the time will come when you will say, ‘Blessed are the barren women, the wombs that never bore and the breasts that never nursed!’ 30Then ‘they will say to the mountains, “Fall on us!” and to the hills, “Cover us!”’” (Hos 10:8)

4. Christ Saw Himself as the OT’s Fulfillment

a) Jesus Fulfilled OT Predictions

(1) He Fulfilled Them as the Promised Messiah

Matt 23 10“Nor are you to be called ‘teacher,’ for you have one Teacher, the Christ.”

Mark 8 27Jesus and his disciples went on to the villages around Caesarea Philippi. On the way he asked them, “Who do people say I am?”

28They replied, “Some say John the Baptist; others say Elijah; and still others, one of the prophets.”

29“But what about you?” he asked. “Who do you say I am?”

Peter answered, “You are the Christ.”

30Jesus warned them not to tell anyone about him.

Mark 14 61But Jesus remained silent and gave no answer.

Again the high priest asked him, “Are you the Christ, the Son of the Blessed One?”

62“I am,” said Jesus. “And you will see the Son of Man sitting at the right hand of the Mighty One and coming on the clouds of heaven.”

John 4 25The woman said, “I know that Messiah” (called Christ) “is coming. When he comes, he will explain everything to us.”

26Then Jesus declared, “I who speak to you am he.”

(2) He Fulfilled Them in His Public Ministry

Luke 4 16He went to Nazareth, where he had been brought up, and on the Sabbath day he went into the synagogue, as was his custom. And he stood up to read. 17The scroll of the prophet Isaiah was handed to him. Unrolling it, he found the place where it is written: 18“The Spirit of the Lord is on me, because he has anointed me to preach good news to the poor. He has sent me to proclaim freedom for the prisoners and recovery of sight for the blind, to release the oppressed, 19to proclaim the year of the Lord’s favor.”

20Then he rolled up the scroll, gave it back to the attendant and sat down. The eyes of everyone in the synagogue were fastened on him, 21and he began by saying to them, “Today this scripture is fulfilled in your hearing.” (Isa 61:1–2)

John 15 25“But this is to fulfill what is written in their Law: ‘They hated me without reason.’” (Ps 35:19; 69:4)

(3) He Fulfilled Them in His Passion

Matt 26 23Jesus replied, “The one who has dipped his hand into the bowl with me will betray me. 24The Son of Man will go just as it is written about him. But woe to that man who betrays the Son of Man! It would be better for him if he had not been born.”

Matt 26 54“But how then would the Scriptures be fulfilled that say it must happen in this way?”

55At that time Jesus said to the crowd, “Am I leading a rebellion, that you have come out with swords and clubs to capture me? Every day I sat in the temple courts teaching, and you did not arrest me. 56But this has all taken place that the writings of the prophets might be fulfilled.” Then all the disciples deserted him and fled.

Luke 18 31Jesus took the Twelve aside and told them, “We are going up to Jerusalem, and everything that is written by the prophets about the Son of Man will be fulfilled. 32He will be handed over to the Gentiles. They will mock him, insult him, spit on him, flog him and kill him. 33On the third day he will rise again.”

Luke 22 36He said to them, “But now if you have a purse, take it, and also a bag; and if you don’t have a sword, sell your cloak and buy one. 37It is written: ‘And he was numbered with the transgressors’; and I tell you that this must be fulfilled in me. Yes, what is written about me is reaching its fulfillment.” (Isa 53:12)

Luke 24 44He said to them, “This is what I told you while I was still with you: Everything must be fulfilled that is written about me in the Law of Moses, the Prophets and the Psalms.”

45Then he opened their minds so they could understand the Scriptures. 46He told them, “This is what is written: The Christ will suffer and rise from the dead on the third day, 47and repentance and forgiveness of sins will be preached in his name to all nations, beginning at Jerusalem. 48You are witnesses of these things. 49I am going to send you what my Father has promised; but stay in the city until you have been clothed with power from on high.”

John 13 18“I am not referring to all of you; I know those I have chosen. But this is to fulfill the scripture: ‘He who shares my bread has lifted up his heel against me.’

19“I am telling you now before it happens, so that when it does happen you will believe that I am He. 20I tell you the truth, whoever accepts anyone I send accepts me; and whoever accepts me accepts the one who sent me.”

21After he had said this, Jesus was troubled in spirit and testified, “I tell you the truth, one of you is going to betray me.” (Ps 41:9)

See also p. 78b, Christological Prophecies and Fulfillments

b) Jesus Fulfilled OT Types

(1) The Bronze Snake as a Type of Christ

John 3 14“Just as Moses lifted up the snake in the desert, so the Son of Man must be lifted up, 15that everyone who believes in him may have eternal life.”

(2) Jonah as a Type of Christ

Matt 12 40“For as Jonah was three days and three nights in the belly of a huge fish, so the Son of Man will be three days and three nights in the heart of the earth.”

(3) Manna as a Type of Christ

John 6 32Jesus said to them, “I tell you the truth, it is not Moses who has given you the bread from heaven, but it is my Father who gives you the true bread from heaven. 33For the bread of God is he who comes down from heaven and gives life to the world.” . . .

41At this the Jews began to grumble about him because he said, “I am the bread that came down from heaven.” . . .

48“I am the bread of life. 49Your forefathers ate the manna in the desert, yet they died. 50But here is the bread that comes down from heaven, which a man may eat and not die. 51I am the living bread that came down from heaven. If anyone eats of this bread, he will live forever. This bread is my flesh, which I will give for the life of the world.” . . . 58“This is the bread that came down from heaven. Your forefathers ate manna and died, but he who feeds on this bread will live forever.”

(4) Solomon as a Type of Christ

Matt 12 42“The Queen of the South will rise at the judgment with this generation and condemn it; for she came from the ends of the earth to listen to Solomon’s wisdom, and now one greater than Solomon is here.”

See also p. 72b, Christ in Type

c) Jesus Fulfilled OT Parallels

(1) Elijah as a Parallel of Christ

Luke 4 24“I tell you the truth,” he continued, “no prophet is accepted in his hometown. 25I assure you that there were many widows in Israel in Elijah’s time, when the sky was shut for three and a half years and there was a severe famine throughout the land. 26Yet Elijah was not sent to any of them, but to a widow in Zarephath in the region of Sidon.”

(2) Elisha as a Parallel of Christ

Luke 4 24“I tell you the truth,” he continued, “no prophet is accepted in his hometown. . . . 27And there were many in Israel with leprosy in the time of Elisha the prophet, yet not one of them was cleansed—only Naaman the Syrian.”

(3) The Temple as a Parallel of Christ

Matt 12 [5]"Or haven't you read in the Law that on the Sabbath the priests in the temple desecrate the day and yet are innocent? [6]I tell you that one greater than the temple is here."
John 2 [19]Jesus answered them, "Destroy this temple, and I will raise it again in three days." . . . [21]But the temple he had spoken of was his body.

D. The Characteristics of Scripture

1. The Bible Is Active

Heb 4 [12]For the word of God is living and active. Sharper than any double-edged sword, it penetrates even to dividing soul and spirit, joints and marrow; it judges the thoughts and attitudes of the heart.

2. The Bible Is Alive

Acts 7 [38]"He was in the assembly in the desert, with the angel who spoke to him on Mount Sinai, and with our fathers; and he received living words to pass on to us."
Heb 4 [12]For the word of God is living and active. Sharper than any double-edged sword, it penetrates even to dividing soul and spirit, joints and marrow; it judges the thoughts and attitudes of the heart.
1 Pet 1 [23]For you have been born again, not of perishable seed, but of imperishable, through the living and enduring word of God.

3. The Bible Is All-Sufficient

Deut 8 [3]He humbled you, causing you to hunger and then feeding you with manna, which neither you nor your fathers had known, to teach you that man does not live on bread alone but on every word that comes from the mouth of the LORD.
Deut 30 [14]No, the word is very near you; it is in your mouth and in your heart so you may obey it.
Luke 16 [29]"Abraham replied, 'They have Moses and the Prophets; let them listen to them.'

[30]"'No, father Abraham,' he said, 'but if someone from the dead goes to them, they will repent.'

[31]"He said to him, 'If they do not listen to Moses and the Prophets, they will not be convinced even if someone rises from the dead.'"

4. The Bible Is Boundless

Ps 119 [96]To all perfection I see a limit; but your commands are boundless.

5. The Bible Is Difficult to Comprehend

2 Pet 3 [15]Bear in mind that our Lord's patience means salvation, just as our dear brother Paul also wrote you with the wisdom that God gave him. [16]He writes the same way in all his letters, speaking in them of these matters. His letters contain some things that are hard to understand, which ignorant and unstable people distort, as they do the other Scriptures, to their own destruction.

6. The Bible Is Efficacious

Deut 32 [1]Listen, O heavens, and I will speak; hear, O earth, the words of my mouth. [2]Let my teaching fall like rain and my words descend like dew, like showers on new grass, like abundant rain on tender plants.
Isa 55 [10]"As the rain and the snow come down from heaven, and do not return to it without watering the earth and making it bud and flourish, so that it yields seed for the sower and bread for the eater, [11]so is my word that goes out from my mouth: It will not return to me empty, but will accomplish what I desire and achieve the purpose for which I sent it."
2 Cor 7 [8]Even if I caused you sorrow by my letter, I do not regret it. Though I did regret it—I see that my letter hurt you, but only for a little while—[9]yet now I am happy, not because you were made sorry, but because your sorrow led you to repentance. For you became sorrowful as God intended and so were not harmed in any way by us.
2 Cor 10 [9]I do not want to seem to be trying to frighten you with my letters. [10]For some say, "His letters are weighty and forceful, but in person he is unimpressive and his speaking amounts to nothing." [11]Such people should realize that what we are in our letters when we are absent, we will be in our actions when we are present.

7. The Bible Is Enduring

Ps 93 [5]Your statutes stand firm; holiness adorns your house for endless days, O LORD.
Ps 119 [89]Your word, O LORD, is eternal; it stands firm in the heavens. . . . [91]Your laws endure to this day, for all things serve you.
Matt 5 [17]"Do not think that I have come to abolish the Law or the Prophets; I have not come to abolish them but to fulfill them. [18]I tell you the truth, until heaven and earth disappear, not the smallest letter, not the least stroke of a pen, will by any means disappear from the Law until everything is accomplished."
Luke 16 [16]"The Law and the Prophets were proclaimed until John. Since that time, the good news of the kingdom of God is being preached, and everyone is forcing his way into it. [17]It is easier for heaven and earth to disappear than for the least stroke of a pen to drop out of the Law."
Luke 21 [33]"Heaven and earth will pass away, but my words will never pass away."
John 10 [35]"If he called them 'gods,' to whom the word of God came—and the Scripture cannot be broken . . ."
1 Pet 1 [23]For you have been born again, not of perishable seed, but of imperishable, through the living and enduring word of God.

8. The Bible Is Eternal

Ps 19 [9]The fear of the LORD is pure, enduring forever. The ordinances of the LORD are sure and altogether righteous.
Ps 119 [89]Your word, O LORD, is eternal; it stands firm in the heavens.
Ps 119 [152]Long ago I learned from your statutes that you established them to last forever.
Ps 119 [160]All your words are true; all your righteous laws are eternal.
Isa 40 [6]A voice says, "Cry out."

And I said, "What shall I cry?"

"All men are like grass, and all their glory is like the flowers of the field. [7]The grass withers and the flowers fall, because the breath of the LORD blows on them. Surely the people are grass. [8]The grass withers and the flowers fall, but the word of our God stands forever."
Matt 24 [35]"Heaven and earth will pass away, but my words will never pass away."

9. The Bible Is Exalted

Ps 138 [2]I will bow down toward your holy temple and will praise your name for your love and your faithfulness, for you have exalted above all things your name and your word.

10. The Bible Is for All Believers

Deut 29 [29]The secret things belong to the LORD our God, but the things revealed belong to us and to our children forever, that we may follow all the words of this law.
Deut 30 [11]Now what I am commanding you today is not too difficult for you or beyond your reach. [12]It is not up in heaven, so that you have to ask, "Who will ascend into heaven to get it and proclaim it to us so we may obey it?" [13]Nor is it beyond the sea, so that you have to ask, "Who will cross the sea to get it and proclaim it to us so we may obey it?" [14]No, the word is very near you; it is in your mouth and in your heart so you may obey it.
1 John 2 [12]I write to you, dear children, because your sins have been forgiven on account of his name. [13]I write to you, fathers, because you have known him who is from the beginning. I write to you, young men, because you have overcome the evil one. I write to you, dear children, because you have known the Father. [14]I write to you, fathers, because you have known him

who is from the beginning. I write to you, young men, because you are strong, and the word of God lives in you, and you have overcome the evil one.

11. The Bible Is Good

Ps 119 [39]Take away the disgrace I dread, for your laws are good.
Isa 39 [8]"The word of the LORD you have spoken is good," Hezekiah replied. For he thought, "There will be peace and security in my lifetime."
Rom 7 [12]So then, the law is holy, and the commandment is holy, righteous and good.

12. The Bible Is Holy

Rom 1 [2]the gospel he promised beforehand through his prophets in the Holy Scriptures . . .
Rom 7 [12]So then, the law is holy, and the commandment is holy, righteous and good.
2 Tim 3 [15]and how from infancy you have known the holy Scriptures, which are able to make you wise for salvation through faith in Christ Jesus.

13. The Bible Is Illuminating

Ps 119 [105]Your word is a lamp to my feet and a light for my path.
Ps 119 [130]The unfolding of your words gives light; it gives understanding to the simple.
Ps 119 [133]Direct my footsteps according to your word; let no sin rule over me.
2 Pet 1 [19]And we have the word of the prophets made more certain, and you will do well to pay attention to it, as to a light shining in a dark place, until the day dawns and the morning star rises in your hearts.
1 John 2 [8]Yet I am writing you a new command; its truth is seen in him and you, because the darkness is passing and the true light is already shining.

14. The Bible Is Inspired

2 Sam 23 [1]These are the last words of David: "The oracle of David son of Jesse, the oracle of the man exalted by the Most High, the man anointed by the God of Jacob, Israel's singer of songs: [2]The Spirit of the LORD spoke through me; his word was on my tongue."
Neh 9 [13]"You came down on Mount Sinai; you spoke to them from heaven. You gave them regulations and laws that are just and right, and decrees and commands that are good. [14]You made known to them your holy Sabbath and gave them commands, decrees and laws through your servant Moses."
Acts 1 [15]In those days Peter stood up among the believers (a group numbering about a hundred and twenty) [16]and said, "Brothers, the Scripture had to be fulfilled which the Holy Spirit spoke long ago through the mouth of David concerning Judas, who served as guide for those who arrested Jesus. . . ."
Rom 1 [2]the gospel he promised beforehand through his prophets in the Holy Scriptures . . .
1 Cor 14 [36]Did the word of God originate with you? Or are you the only people it has reached? [37]If anybody thinks he is a prophet or spiritually gifted, let him acknowledge that what I am writing to you is the Lord's command.
Gal 1 [11]I want you to know, brothers, that the gospel I preached is not something that man made up. [12]I did not receive it from any man, nor was I taught it; rather, I received it by revelation from Jesus Christ.
1 Thess 2 [13]And we also thank God continually because, when you received the word of God, which you heard from us, you accepted it not as the word of men, but as it actually is, the word of God, which is at work in you who believe.
2 Tim 3 [16]All Scripture is God-breathed and is useful for teaching, rebuking, correcting and training in righteousness. . . .
1 Pet 1 [10]Concerning this salvation, the prophets, who spoke of the grace that was to come to you, searched intently and with the greatest care, [11]trying to find out the time and circumstances to which the Spirit of Christ in them was pointing when he predicted the sufferings of Christ and the glories that would follow. [12]It was revealed to them that they were not serving themselves but you, when they spoke of the things that have now been told you by those who have preached the gospel to you by the Holy Spirit sent from heaven. Even angels long to look into these things.
2 Pet 1 [20]Above all, you must understand that no prophecy of Scripture came about by the prophet's own interpretation. [21]For prophecy never had its origin in the will of man, but men spoke from God as they were carried along by the Holy Spirit.
1 John 5 [9]We accept man's testimony, but God's testimony is greater because it is the testimony of God, which he has given about his Son.

15. The Bible Is Instructive

Ps 119 [24]Your statutes are my delight; they are my counselors.
Ps 119 [169]May my cry come before you, O LORD; give me understanding according to your word.
Rom 15 [4]For everything that was written in the past was written to teach us, so that through endurance and the encouragement of the Scriptures we might have hope.
2 Tim 3 [14]But as for you, continue in what you have learned and have become convinced of, because you know those from whom you learned it, [15]and how from infancy you have known the holy Scriptures, which are able to make you wise for salvation through faith in Christ Jesus. [16]All Scripture is God-breathed and is useful for teaching, rebuking, correcting and training in righteousness, [17]so that the man of God may be thoroughly equipped for every good work.

16. The Bible Is Perfect

Ps 19 [7]The law of the LORD is perfect, reviving the soul. The statutes of the LORD are trustworthy, making wise the simple.
James 1 [25]But the man who looks intently into the perfect law that gives freedom, and continues to do this, not forgetting what he has heard, but doing it—he will be blessed in what he does.

17. The Bible Is Powerful

Jer 23 [29]"Is not my word like fire," declares the LORD, "and like a hammer that breaks a rock in pieces?"
Eph 6 [17]Take the helmet of salvation and the sword of the Spirit, which is the word of God.
2 Tim 2 [8]Remember Jesus Christ, raised from the dead, descended from David. This is my gospel, [9]for which I am suffering even to the point of being chained like a criminal. But God's word is not chained.
Heb 4 [12]For the word of God is living and active. Sharper than any double-edged sword, it penetrates even to dividing soul and spirit, joints and marrow; it judges the thoughts and attitudes of the heart.

18. The Bible Is Precious

Ps 19 [9]The fear of the LORD is pure, enduring forever. The ordinances of the LORD are sure and altogether righteous. [10]They are more precious than gold, than much pure gold; they are sweeter than honey, than honey from the comb.

19. The Bible Is Pure

2 Sam 22 [31]"As for God, his way is perfect; the word of the LORD is flawless. He is a shield for all who take refuge in him."
Ps 12 [6]And the words of the LORD are flawless, like silver refined in a furnace of clay, purified seven times.
Ps 18 [30]As for God, his way is perfect; the word of the LORD is flawless. He is a shield for all who take refuge in him.
Ps 19 [9]The fear of the LORD is pure, enduring forever. The ordinances of the LORD are sure and altogether righteous.
Prov 30 [5]"Every word of God is flawless; he is a shield to those who take refuge in him."
John 15 [3]"You are already clean because of the word I have spoken to you."

20. The Bible Is Radiant

Ps 19 [8]The precepts of the LORD are right, giving joy to the heart. The commands of the LORD are radiant, giving light to the eyes.

21. The Bible Is a Record of Revelation

Exod 17 [14]Then the LORD said to Moses, "Write this on a scroll as something to be remembered and make sure that Joshua hears it, because I will completely blot out the memory of Amalek from under heaven."

Exod 24 [4]Moses then wrote down everything the LORD had said.

He got up early the next morning and built an altar at the foot of the mountain and set up twelve stone pillars representing the twelve tribes of Israel.

Josh 8 [32]There, in the presence of the Israelites, Joshua copied on stones the law of Moses, which he had written.

Josh 24 [26]And Joshua recorded these things in the Book of the Law of God. Then he took a large stone and set it up there under the oak near the holy place of the LORD.

2 Chron 26 [22]The other events of Uzziah's reign, from beginning to end, are recorded by the prophet Isaiah son of Amoz.

Jer 30 [2]"This is what the LORD, the God of Israel, says: 'Write in a book all the words I have spoken to you.'"

Jer 45 [1]This is what Jeremiah the prophet told Baruch son of Neriah in the fourth year of Jehoiakim son of Josiah king of Judah, after Baruch had written on a scroll the words Jeremiah was then dictating: [2]"This is what the LORD, the God of Israel, says to you, Baruch. . . ."

Hab 2 [2]Then the LORD replied: "Write down the revelation and make it plain on tablets so that a herald may run with it."

John 20 [30]Jesus did many other miraculous signs in the presence of his disciples, which are not recorded in this book. [31]But these are written that you may believe that Jesus is the Christ, the Son of God, and that by believing you may have life in his name.

Rev 1 [10]On the Lord's Day I was in the Spirit, and I heard behind me a loud voice like a trumpet, [11]which said: "Write on a scroll what you see and send it to the seven churches: to Ephesus, Smyrna, Pergamum, Thyatira, Sardis, Philadelphia and Laodicea."

Rev 1 [17]When I saw him, I fell at his feet as though dead. Then he placed his right hand on me and said: "Do not be afraid. I am the First and the Last. [18]I am the Living One; I was dead, and behold I am alive for ever and ever! And I hold the keys of death and Hades.

[19]"Write, therefore, what you have seen, what is now and what will take place later."

Rev 22 [18]I warn everyone who hears the words of the prophecy of this book: If anyone adds anything to them, God will add to him the plagues described in this book. [19]And if anyone takes words away from this book of prophecy, God will take away from him his share in the tree of life and in the holy city, which are described in this book.

22. The Bible Is Reliable

1 Kings 8 [56]"Praise be to the LORD, who has given rest to his people Israel just as he promised. Not one word has failed of all the good promises he gave through his servant Moses."

Ps 19 [9]The fear of the LORD is pure, enduring forever. The ordinances of the LORD are sure and altogether righteous.

Ps 105 [19]till what he foretold came to pass, till the word of the LORD proved him true.

Ps 111 [5]He provides food for those who fear him; he remembers his covenant forever.

Ps 119 [140]Your promises have been thoroughly tested, and your servant loves them.

Prov 22 [19]So that your trust may be in the LORD, I teach you today, even you. [20]Have I not written thirty sayings for you, sayings of counsel and knowledge, [21]teaching you true and reliable words, so that you can give sound answers to him who sent you?

Ezek 12 [25]"'But I the LORD will speak what I will, and it shall be fulfilled without delay. For in your days, you rebellious house, I will fulfill whatever I say, declares the Sovereign LORD.'"

Luke 24 [44]He said to them, "This is what I told you while I was still with you: Everything must be fulfilled that is written about me in the Law of Moses, the Prophets and the Psalms."

23. The Bible Is Right

Ps 19 [8]The precepts of the LORD are right, giving joy to the heart. The commands of the LORD are radiant, giving light to the eyes.

Ps 33 [4]For the word of the LORD is right and true; he is faithful in all he does.

Ps 119 [128]and because I consider all your precepts right, I hate every wrong path.

Ps 119 [137]Righteous are you, O LORD, and your laws are right.

Ps 119 [144]Your statutes are forever right; give me understanding that I may live.

24. The Bible Is Righteous

Deut 4 [8]And what other nation is so great as to have such righteous decrees and laws as this body of laws I am setting before you today?

Ps 19 [9]The fear of the LORD is pure, enduring forever. The ordinances of the LORD are sure and altogether righteous.

Ps 119 [7]I will praise you with an upright heart as I learn your righteous laws.

Ps 119 [75]I know, O LORD, that your laws are righteous, and in faithfulness you have afflicted me.

Ps 119 [106]I have taken an oath and confirmed it, that I will follow your righteous laws.

Ps 119 [138]The statutes you have laid down are righteous; they are fully trustworthy.

Ps 119 [160]All your words are true; all your righteous laws are eternal.

Ps 119 [164]Seven times a day I praise you for your righteous laws.

Eccles 12 [10]The Teacher searched to find just the right words, and what he wrote was upright and true.

Rom 7 [12]So then, the law is holy, and the commandment is holy, righteous and good.

25. The Bible Is a Safeguard

Ps 17 [4]As for the deeds of men—by the word of your lips I have kept myself from the ways of the violent. [5]My steps have held to your paths; my feet have not slipped.

Ps 19 [9]The fear of the LORD is pure, enduring forever. The ordinances of the LORD are sure and altogether righteous. . . . [11]By them is your servant warned; in keeping them there is great reward.

Ps 119 [9]How can a young man keep his way pure? By living according to your word. . . . [11]I have hidden your word in my heart that I might not sin against you.

Ps 119 [25]I am laid low in the dust; preserve my life according to your word.

Ps 119 [116]Sustain me according to your promise, and I will live; do not let my hopes be dashed.

26. The Bible Is the Standard of Truth

Matt 15 [1]Then some Pharisees and teachers of the law came to Jesus from Jerusalem and asked, [2]"Why do your disciples break the tradition of the elders? They don't wash their hands before they eat!"

[3]Jesus replied, "And why do you break the command of God for the sake of your tradition?"

Mark 7 [7]"'They worship me in vain; their teachings are but rules taught by men.' [8]You have let go of the commands of God and are holding on to the traditions of men."

[9]And he said to them: "You have a fine way of setting aside the commands of God in order to observe your own traditions! . . . [13]Thus you nullify the word of God by your tradition that you have handed down. And you do many things like that."

John 5 [46]"If you believed Moses, you would believe me, for he wrote about me. [47]But since you do not believe what he wrote, how are you going to believe what I say?"

Acts 18 [28]For he vigorously refuted the Jews in public debate, proving from the Scriptures that Jesus was the Christ.

Acts 28 [23]They arranged to meet Paul on a certain day, and came in even larger numbers to the place where he was staying. From morning till evening he explained and declared to them the kingdom of God and tried to convince them about Jesus from the Law of Moses and from the Prophets.

27. The Bible Is Sure

Ps 19 [9]The fear of the LORD is pure, enduring forever. The ordinances of the LORD are sure and altogether righteous.

28. The Bible Is True

1 Kings 17 [24]Then the woman said to Elijah, "Now I know that you are a man of God and that the word of the LORD from your mouth is the truth."
Ps 33 [4]For the word of the LORD is right and true; he is faithful in all he does.
Ps 119 [43]Do not snatch the word of truth from my mouth, for I have put my hope in your laws.
Ps 119 [142]Your righteousness is everlasting and your law is true.
Ps 119 [151]Yet you are near, O LORD, and all your commands are true.
Ps 119 [160]All your words are true; all your righteous laws are eternal.
Prov 22 [20]Have I not written thirty sayings for you, sayings of counsel and knowledge, [21]teaching you true and reliable words, so that you can give sound answers to him who sent you?
Eccles 12 [10]The Teacher searched to find just the right words, and what he wrote was upright and true.
Dan 10 [21]". . . but first I will tell you what is written in the Book of Truth. (No one supports me against them except Michael, your prince.)"
John 17 [17]"Sanctify them by the truth; your word is truth."
John 21 [24]This is the disciple who testifies to these things and who wrote them down. We know that his testimony is true.
Eph 1 [13]And you also were included in Christ when you heard the word of truth, the gospel of your salvation. Having believed, you were marked in him with a seal, the promised Holy Spirit. . . .
Col 1 [3]We always thank God, the Father of our Lord Jesus Christ, when we pray for you, [4]because we have heard of your faith in Christ Jesus and of the love you have for all the saints—[5]the faith and love that spring from the hope that is stored up for you in heaven and that you have already heard about in the word of truth, the gospel [6]that has come to you. All over the world this gospel is bearing fruit and growing, just as it has been doing among you since the day you heard it and understood God's grace in all its truth.
2 Tim 2 [15]Do your best to present yourself to God as one approved, a workman who does not need to be ashamed and who correctly handles the word of truth.
James 1 [18]He chose to give us birth through the word of truth, that we might be a kind of firstfruits of all he created.
Rev 19 [9]Then the angel said to me, "Write: 'Blessed are those who are invited to the wedding supper of the Lamb!'" And he added, "These are the true words of God."
Rev 21 [5]He who was seated on the throne said, "I am making everything new!" Then he said, "Write this down, for these words are trustworthy and true."

29. The Bible Is Trustworthy

2 Sam 7 [28]"O Sovereign LORD, you are God! Your words are trustworthy, and you have promised these good things to your servant."
Ps 19 [7]The law of the LORD is perfect, reviving the soul. The statutes of the LORD are trustworthy, making wise the simple.
Ps 111 [7]The works of his hands are faithful and just; all his precepts are trustworthy.
Ps 119 [42]then I will answer the one who taunts me, for I trust in your word.
Ps 119 [86]All your commands are trustworthy; help me, for men persecute me without cause.
Ps 119 [138]The statutes you have laid down are righteous; they are fully trustworthy.
Rev 22 [6]The angel said to me, "These words are trustworthy and true. The Lord, the God of the spirits of the prophets, sent his angel to show his servants the things that must soon take place."

30. The Bible Is Wonderful

Ps 119 [129]Your statutes are wonderful; therefore I obey them.

E. The Spirit and Scripture

1. The Spirit in the Revelation and Inspiration of Scripture

2 Sam 23 [1]These are the last words of David: "The oracle of David son of Jesse, the oracle of the man exalted by the Most High, the man anointed by the God of Jacob, Israel's singer of songs: [2]The Spirit of the LORD spoke through me; his word was on my tongue. [3]The God of Israel spoke, the Rock of Israel said to me: 'When one rules over men in righteousness, when he rules in the fear of God . . .'"
Ezek 2 [2]As he spoke, the Spirit came into me and raised me to my feet, and I heard him speaking to me.

[3]He said: "Son of man, I am sending you to the Israelites, to a rebellious nation that has rebelled against me; they and their fathers have been in revolt against me to this very day."
Ezek 8 [3]He stretched out what looked like a hand and took me by the hair of my head. The Spirit lifted me up between earth and heaven and in visions of God he took me to Jerusalem, to the entrance to the north gate of the inner court, where the idol that provokes to jealousy stood.
Ezek 11 [1]Then the Spirit lifted me up and brought me to the gate of the house of the LORD that faces east. There at the entrance to the gate were twenty-five men, and I saw among them Jaazaniah son of Azzur and Pelatiah son of Benaiah, leaders of the people. . . .

[5]Then the Spirit of the LORD came upon me, and he told me to say: "This is what the LORD says: That is what you are saying, O house of Israel, but I know what is going through your mind." . . . [24]The Spirit lifted me up and brought me to the exiles in Babylonia in the vision given by the Spirit of God.

Then the vision I had seen went up from me. . . .
Mic 3 [8]But as for me, I am filled with power, with the Spirit of the LORD, and with justice and might, to declare to Jacob his transgression, to Israel his sin.
Matt 22 [43]He said to them, "How is it then that David, speaking by the Spirit, calls him 'Lord'? For he says, [44]'The Lord said to my Lord: "Sit at my right hand until I put your enemies under your feet."'"
Mark 12 [36]"David himself, speaking by the Holy Spirit, declared: 'The Lord said to my Lord: "Sit at my right hand until I put your enemies under your feet."'"
John 14 [26]"But the Counselor, the Holy Spirit, whom the Father will send in my name, will teach you all things and will remind you of everything I have said to you."
John 16 [12]"I have much more to say to you, more than you can now bear. [13]But when he, the Spirit of truth, comes, he will guide you into all truth. He will not speak on his own; he will speak only what he hears, and he will tell you what is yet to come. [14]He will bring glory to me by taking from what is mine and making it known to you. [15]All that belongs to the Father is mine. That is why I said the Spirit will take from what is mine and make it known to you."
Acts 1 [15]In those days Peter stood up among the believers (a group numbering about a hundred and twenty) [16]and said, "Brothers, the Scripture had to be fulfilled which the Holy Spirit spoke long ago through the mouth of David concerning Judas, who served as guide for those who arrested Jesus. . . ."
Acts 4 [25]"You spoke by the Holy Spirit through the mouth of your servant, our father David: 'Why do the nations rage and the peoples plot in vain?'"
Acts 28 [25]They disagreed among themselves and began to leave after Paul had made this final statement: "The Holy Spirit spoke the truth to your forefathers when he said through Isaiah the prophet . . ."
1 Cor 2 [9]However, as it is written: "No eye has seen, no ear has heard, no mind has conceived what God has prepared for those who love him"—[10]but God has revealed it to us by his Spirit.

The Spirit searches all things, even the deep things of God.

Heb 3 [7]So, as the Holy Spirit says: "Today, if you hear his voice . . ."
Heb 9 [7]But only the high priest entered the inner room, and that only once a year, and never without blood, which he offered for himself and for the sins the people had committed in ignorance. [8]The Holy Spirit was showing by this that the way into the Most Holy Place had not yet been disclosed as long as the first tabernacle was still standing.
Heb 10 [15]The Holy Spirit also testifies to us about this. First he says: [16]"This is the covenant I will make with them after that time, says the Lord. I will put my laws in their hearts, and I will write them on their minds." [17]Then he adds: "Their sins and lawless acts I will remember no more."
1 Pet 1 [10]Concerning this salvation, the prophets, who spoke of the grace that was to come to you, searched intently and with the greatest care, [11]trying to find out the time and circumstances to which the Spirit of Christ in them was pointing when he predicted the sufferings of Christ and the glories that would follow.
2 Pet 1 [21]For prophecy never had its origin in the will of man, but men spoke from God as they were carried along by the Holy Spirit.
Rev 2 [7]"He who has an ear, let him hear what the Spirit says to the churches. To him who overcomes, I will give the right to eat from the tree of life, which is in the paradise of God."

2. The Spirit in the Illumination of Scripture

Isa 11 [2]The Spirit of the LORD will rest on him—the Spirit of wisdom and of understanding, the Spirit of counsel and of power, the Spirit of knowledge and of the fear of the LORD. . . .
John 14 [26]"But the Counselor, the Holy Spirit, whom the Father will send in my name, will teach you all things and will remind you of everything I have said to you."
Rom 8 [5]Those who live according to the sinful nature have their minds set on what that nature desires; but those who live in accordance with the Spirit have their minds set on what the Spirit desires. [6]The mind of sinful man is death, but the mind controlled by the Spirit is life and peace; [7]the sinful mind is hostile to God. It does not submit to God's law, nor can it do so.
1 Cor 2 [12]We have not received the spirit of the world but the Spirit who is from God, that we may understand what God has freely given us. [13]This is what we speak, not in words taught us by human wisdom but in words taught by the Spirit, expressing spiritual truths in spiritual words. [14]The man without the Spirit does not accept the things that come from the Spirit of God, for they are foolishness to him, and he cannot understand them, because they are spiritually discerned. [15]The spiritual man makes judgments about all things, but he himself is not subject to any man's judgment: [16]"For who has known the mind of the Lord that he may instruct him?" But we have the mind of Christ.
Eph 1 [17]I keep asking that the God of our Lord Jesus Christ, the glorious Father, may give you the Spirit of wisdom and revelation, so that you may know him better.
1 John 2 [20]But you have an anointing from the Holy One, and all of you know the truth. . . . [27]As for you, the anointing you received from him remains in you, and you do not need anyone to teach you. But as his anointing teaches you about all things and as that anointing is real, not counterfeit—just as it has taught you, remain in him.

3. The Spirit in the Message of Scripture

Eph 6 [17]Take the helmet of salvation and the sword of the Spirit, which is the word of God.

Supernatural Beings

I
Good Angels

A. Descriptive Titles of Good Angels

1. Angel

Gen 19 [1]The two angels arrived at Sodom in the evening, and Lot was sitting in the gateway of the city. When he saw them, he got up to meet them and bowed down with his face to the ground.

2 Sam 24 [16]When the angel stretched out his hand to destroy Jerusalem, the LORD was grieved because of the calamity and said to the angel who was afflicting the people, "Enough! Withdraw your hand." The angel of the LORD was then at the threshing floor of Araunah the Jebusite.

[17]When David saw the angel who was striking down the people, he said to the LORD, "I am the one who has sinned and done wrong. These are but sheep. What have they done? Let your hand fall upon me and my family."

1 Kings 13 [18]The old prophet answered, "I too am a prophet, as you are. And an angel said to me by the word of the LORD: 'Bring him back with you to your house so that he may eat bread and drink water.'" (But he was lying to him.)

1 Chron 21 [15]And God sent an angel to destroy Jerusalem. But as the angel was doing so, the LORD saw it and was grieved because of the calamity and said to the angel who was destroying the people, "Enough! Withdraw your hand." The angel of the LORD was then standing at the threshing floor of Araunah the Jebusite.

2 Chron 32 [21]And the LORD sent an angel, who annihilated all the fighting men and the leaders and officers in the camp of the Assyrian king. So he withdrew to his own land in disgrace. And when he went into the temple of his god, some of his sons cut him down with the sword.

Ps 148 [2]Praise him, all his angels, praise him, all his heavenly hosts.

Dan 6 [22]"My God sent his angel, and he shut the mouths of the lions. They have not hurt me, because I was found innocent in his sight. Nor have I ever done any wrong before you, O king."

Hos 12 [4]He struggled with the angel and overcame him; he wept and begged for his favor. He found him at Bethel and talked with him there. . . .

Zech 4 [1]Then the angel who talked with me returned and wakened me, as a man is wakened from his sleep.

Matt 22 [30]"At the resurrection people will neither marry nor be given in marriage; they will be like the angels in heaven."

Mark 13 [27]"And he will send his angels and gather his elect from the four winds, from the ends of the earth to the ends of the heavens."

Luke 22 [43]An angel from heaven appeared to him and strengthened him.
Acts 27 [23]"Last night an angel of the God whose I am and whom I serve stood beside me. . . ."
1 Cor 6 [3]Do you not know that we will judge angels? How much more the things of this life!
Heb 12 [22]But you have come to Mount Zion, to the heavenly Jerusalem, the city of the living God. You have come to thousands upon thousands of angels in joyful assembly. . . .
Rev 7 [11]All the angels were standing around the throne and around the elders and the four living creatures. They fell down on their faces before the throne and worshiped God. . . .

2. Angel of God

Gen 28 [12]He had a dream in which he saw a stairway resting on the earth, with its top reaching to heaven, and the angels of God were ascending and descending on it.
Gen 32 [1]Jacob also went on his way, and the angels of God met him.
1 Sam 29 [9]Achish answered, "I know that you have been as pleasing in my eyes as an angel of God; nevertheless, the Philistine commanders have said, 'He must not go up with us into battle.'"
2 Sam 19 [27]"And he has slandered your servant to my lord the king. My lord the king is like an angel of God; so do whatever pleases you."
Acts 10 [3]One day at about three in the afternoon he had a vision. He distinctly saw an angel of God, who came to him and said, "Cornelius!"
Gal 4 [14]Even though my illness was a trial to you, you did not treat me with contempt or scorn. Instead, you welcomed me as if I were an angel of God, as if I were Christ Jesus himself.

3. Angel of His Presence

Isa 63 [9]In all their distress he too was distressed, and the angel of his presence saved them. In his love and mercy he redeemed them; he lifted them up and carried them all the days of old.

4. Angel of Light

2 Cor 11 [14]And no wonder, for Satan himself masquerades as an angel of light.

5. Angel of the Lord

2 Sam 24 [16]When the angel stretched out his hand to destroy Jerusalem, the LORD was grieved because of the calamity and said to the angel who was afflicting the people, "Enough! Withdraw your hand." The angel of the LORD was then at the threshing floor of Araunah the Jebusite.
1 Chron 21 [16]David looked up and saw the angel of the LORD standing between heaven and earth, with a drawn sword in his hand extended over Jerusalem. Then David and the elders, clothed in sackcloth, fell facedown. . . .

[18]Then the angel of the LORD ordered Gad to tell David to go up and build an altar to the LORD on the threshing floor of Araunah the Jebusite.
Matt 28 [2]There was a violent earthquake, for an angel of the Lord came down from heaven and, going to the tomb, rolled back the stone and sat on it.
Luke 1 [11]Then an angel of the Lord appeared to him, standing at the right side of the altar of incense.
Luke 2 [9]An angel of the Lord appeared to them, and the glory of the Lord shone around them, and they were terrified.
Acts 5 [19]But during the night an angel of the Lord opened the doors of the jail and brought them out.
Acts 8 [26]Now an angel of the Lord said to Philip, "Go south to the road—the desert road—that goes down from Jerusalem to Gaza."
Acts 12 [7]Suddenly an angel of the Lord appeared and a light shone in the cell. He struck Peter on the side and woke him up. "Quick, get up!" he said, and the chains fell off Peter's wrists.

[8]Then the angel said to him, "Put on your clothes and sandals." And Peter did so. "Wrap your cloak around you and follow me," the angel told him. [9]Peter followed him out of the prison, but he had no idea that what the angel was doing was really happening; he thought he was seeing a vision. [10]They passed the first and second guards and came to the iron gate leading to the city. It opened for them by itself, and they went through it. When they had walked the length of one street, suddenly the angel left him.

[11]Then Peter came to himself and said, "Now I know without a doubt that the Lord sent his angel and rescued me from Herod's clutches and from everything the Jewish people were anticipating."

6. Archangel

1 Thess 4 [16]For the Lord himself will come down from heaven, with a loud command, with the voice of the archangel and with the trumpet call of God, and the dead in Christ will rise first.
Jude [9]But even the archangel Michael, when he was disputing with the devil about the body of Moses, did not dare to bring a slanderous accusation against him, but said, "The Lord rebuke you!"

7. Cherubim

Gen 3 [24]After he drove the man out, he placed on the east side of the Garden of Eden cherubim and a flaming sword flashing back and forth to guard the way to the tree of life.
Ps 18 [10]He mounted the cherubim and flew; he soared on the wings of the wind.
Ps 99 [1]The LORD reigns, let the nations tremble; he sits enthroned between the cherubim, let the earth shake.
Ezek 10 [1]I looked, and I saw the likeness of a throne of sapphire above the expanse that was over the heads of the cherubim. [2]The LORD said to the man clothed in linen, "Go in among the wheels beneath the cherubim. Fill your hands with burning coals from among the cherubim and scatter them over the city." And as I watched, he went in.

[3]Now the cherubim were standing on the south side of the temple when the man went in, and a cloud filled the inner court. [4]Then the glory of the LORD rose from above the cherubim and moved to the threshold of the temple. The cloud filled the temple, and the court was full of the radiance of the glory of the LORD. [5]The sound of the wings of the cherubim could be heard as far away as the outer court, like the voice of God Almighty when he speaks.

[6]When the LORD commanded the man in linen, "Take fire from among the wheels, from among the cherubim," the man went in and stood beside a wheel. [7]Then one of the cherubim reached out his hand to the fire that was among them. He took up some of it and put it into the hands of the man in linen, who took it and went out. [8](Under the wings of the cherubim could be seen what looked like the hands of a man.)

[9]I looked, and I saw beside the cherubim four wheels, one beside each of the cherubim; the wheels sparkled like chrysolite. [10]As for their appearance, the four of them looked alike; each was like a wheel intersecting a wheel. [11]As they moved, they would go in any one of the four directions the cherubim faced; the wheels did not turn about as the cherubim went. The cherubim went in whatever direction the head faced, without turning as they went. [12]Their entire bodies, including their backs, their hands and their wings, were completely full of eyes, as were their four wheels. [13]I heard the wheels being called "the whirling wheels." [14]Each of the cherubim had four faces: One face was that of a cherub, the second the face of a man, the third the face of a lion, and the fourth the face of an eagle.

[15]Then the cherubim rose upward. These were the living creatures I had seen by the Kebar River. [16]When the cherubim moved, the wheels beside them moved; and when the cherubim spread their wings to rise from the ground, the wheels did not leave their side. [17]When the cherubim stood still, they also stood still; and when the cherubim rose, they rose with them, because the spirit of the living creatures was in them.

[18]Then the glory of the LORD departed from over the threshold of the temple and stopped above the cherubim. [19]While I watched, the cherubim spread their wings and rose from the ground, and as they went, the wheels went with them. They stopped at the entrance to the east gate of the LORD's house, and the glory of the God of Israel was above them.

8. Chief Princes

Dan 10 [13]"But the prince of the Persian kingdom resisted me twenty-one days. Then Michael, one of the chief princes, came to help me, because I was detained there with the king of Persia."

9. Great Prince

Dan 12 [1]"At that time Michael, the great prince who protects your people, will arise. There will be a time of distress such as has not happened from the beginning of nations until then. But at that time your people—everyone whose name is found written in the book—will be delivered."

10. Heavenly Host

2 Chron 18 [18]Micaiah continued, "Therefore hear the word of the Lord: I saw the Lord sitting on his throne with all the host of heaven standing on his right and on his left."
Ps 89 [6]For who in the skies above can compare with the Lord? Who is like the Lord among the heavenly beings?
Luke 2 [13]Suddenly a great company of the heavenly host appeared with the angel, praising God and saying . . .

11. Holy One

Job 5 [1]"Call if you will, but who will answer you? To which of the holy ones will you turn?"
Ps 89 [7]In the council of the holy ones God is greatly feared; he is more awesome than all who surround him.
Dan 4 [13]"In the visions I saw while lying in my bed, I looked, and there before me was a messenger, a holy one, coming down from heaven."
Dan 4 [17]"'The decision is announced by messengers, the holy ones declare the verdict, so that the living may know that the Most High is sovereign over the kingdoms of men and gives them to anyone he wishes and sets over them the lowliest of men.'"
Dan 4 [23]"You, O king, saw a messenger, a holy one, coming down from heaven and saying, 'Cut down the tree and destroy it, but leave the stump, bound with iron and bronze, in the grass of the field, while its roots remain in the ground. Let him be drenched with the dew of heaven; let him live like the wild animals, until seven times pass by for him.'"
Dan 8 [13]Then I heard a holy one speaking, and another holy one said to him, "How long will it take for the vision to be fulfilled—the vision concerning the daily sacrifice, the rebellion that causes desolation, and the surrender of the sanctuary and of the host that will be trampled underfoot?"

12. Living Creatures

Ezek 1 [2]On the fifth of the month—it was the fifth year of the exile of King Jehoiachin—[3]the word of the Lord came to Ezekiel the priest, the son of Buzi, by the Kebar River in the land of the Babylonians. There the hand of the Lord was upon him.

[4]I looked, and I saw a windstorm coming out of the north—an immense cloud with flashing lightning and surrounded by brilliant light. The center of the fire looked like glowing metal, [5]and in the fire was what looked like four living creatures. In appearance their form was that of a man, [6]but each of them had four faces and four wings. [7]Their legs were straight; their feet were like those of a calf and gleamed like burnished bronze. [8]Under their wings on their four sides they had the hands of a man. All four of them had faces and wings, [9]and their wings touched one another. Each one went straight ahead; they did not turn as they moved.

[10]Their faces looked like this: Each of the four had the face of a man, and on the right side each had the face of a lion, and on the left the face of an ox; each also had the face of an eagle. [11]Such were their faces. Their wings were spread out upward; each had two wings, one touching the wing of another creature on either side, and two wings covering its body. [12]Each one went straight ahead. Wherever the spirit would go, they would go, without turning as they went. [13]The appearance of the living creatures was like burning coals of fire or like torches. Fire moved back and forth among the creatures; it was bright, and lightning flashed out of it. [14]The creatures sped back and forth like flashes of lightning.

[15]As I looked at the living creatures, I saw a wheel on the ground beside each creature with its four faces. [16]This was the appearance and structure of the wheels: They sparkled like chrysolite, and all four looked alike. Each appeared to be made like a wheel intersecting a wheel. [17]As they moved, they would go in any one of the four directions the creatures faced; the wheels did not turn about as the creatures went. [18]Their rims were high and awesome, and all four rims were full of eyes all around.

[19]When the living creatures moved, the wheels beside them moved; and when the living creatures rose from the ground, the wheels also rose. [20]Wherever the spirit would go, they would go, and the wheels would rise along with them, because the spirit of the living creatures was in the wheels. [21]When the creatures moved, they also moved; when the creatures stood still, they also stood still; and when the creatures rose from the ground, the wheels rose along with them, because the spirit of the living creatures was in the wheels.

[22]Spread out above the heads of the living creatures was what looked like an expanse, sparkling like ice, and awesome. [23]Under the expanse their wings were stretched out one toward the other, and each had two wings covering its body. [24]When the creatures moved, I heard the sound of their wings, like the roar of rushing waters, like the voice of the Almighty, like the tumult of an army. When they stood still, they lowered their wings.
Ezek 10 [20]These were the living creatures I had seen beneath the God of Israel by the Kebar River, and I realized that they were cherubim. [21]Each had four faces and four wings, and under their wings was what looked like the hands of a man. [22]Their faces had the same appearance as those I had seen by the Kebar River. Each one went straight ahead.
Rev 4 [6]Also before the throne there was what looked like a sea of glass, clear as crystal.

In the center, around the throne, were four living creatures, and they were covered with eyes, in front and in back. [7]The first living creature was like a lion, the second was like an ox, the third had a face like a man, the fourth was like a flying eagle. [8]Each of the four living creatures had six wings and was covered with eyes all around, even under his wings. Day and night they never stop saying: "Holy, holy, holy is the Lord God Almighty, who was, and is, and is to come." [9]Whenever the living creatures give glory, honor and thanks to him who sits on the throne and who lives for ever and ever . . .
Rev 5 [14]The four living creatures said, "Amen," and the elders fell down and worshiped.
Rev 6 [1]I watched as the Lamb opened the first of the seven seals. Then I heard one of the four living creatures say in a voice like thunder, "Come!" [2]I looked, and there before me was a white horse! Its rider held a bow, and he was given a crown, and he rode out as a conqueror bent on conquest.

[3]When the Lamb opened the second seal, I heard the second living creature say, "Come!" [4]Then another horse came out, a fiery red one. Its rider was given power to take peace from the earth and to make men slay each other. To him was given a large sword.

[5]When the Lamb opened the third seal, I heard the third living creature say, "Come!" I looked, and there before me was a black horse! Its rider was holding a pair of scales in his hand. [6]Then I heard what sounded like a voice among the four living creatures, saying, "A quart of wheat for a day's wages, and three quarts of barley for a day's wages, and do not damage the oil and the wine!"

[7]When the Lamb opened the fourth seal, I heard the voice of the fourth living creature say, "Come!" [8]I looked, and there before me was a pale horse! Its rider was named Death, and Hades was following close behind him. They were given power over a fourth of the earth to kill by sword, famine and plague, and by the wild beasts of the earth.
Rev 15 [7]Then one of the four living creatures gave to the seven angels seven golden bowls filled with the wrath of God, who lives for ever and ever.

13. Lord

Gen 19 [2]"My lords," he said, "please turn aside to your servant's house. You can wash your feet and spend the night and then go on your way early in the morning."

"No," they answered, "we will spend the night in the square."

Gen 19 [18]But Lot said to them, "No, my lords, please!"

Dan 10 [16]Then one who looked like a man touched my lips, and I opened my mouth and began to speak. I said to the one standing before me, "I am overcome with anguish because of the vision, my lord, and I am helpless. [17]How can I, your servant, talk with you, my lord? My strength is gone and I can hardly breathe." . . .

[19]"Do not be afraid, O man highly esteemed," he said. "Peace! Be strong now; be strong."

When he spoke to me, I was strengthened and said, "Speak, my lord, since you have given me strength."

Dan 12 [8]I heard, but I did not understand. So I asked, "My lord, what will the outcome of all this be?"

Zech 1 [9]I asked, "What are these, my lord?"

The angel who was talking with me answered, "I will show you what they are."

Zech 6 [4]I asked the angel who was speaking to me, "What are these, my lord?"

14. Man

Gen 18 [2]Abraham looked up and saw three men standing nearby. When he saw them, he hurried from the entrance of his tent to meet them and bowed low to the ground.

Gen 18 [16]When the men got up to leave, they looked down toward Sodom, and Abraham walked along with them to see them on their way.

Gen 19 [1]The two angels arrived at Sodom in the evening, and Lot was sitting in the gateway of the city. When he saw them, he got up to meet them and bowed down with his face to the ground. [2]"My lords," he said, "please turn aside to your servant's house. You can wash your feet and spend the night and then go on your way early in the morning."

"No," they answered, "we will spend the night in the square."

[3]But he insisted so strongly that they did go with him and entered his house. He prepared a meal for them, baking bread without yeast, and they ate. [4]Before they had gone to bed, all the men from every part of the city of Sodom—both young and old—surrounded the house. [5]They called to Lot, "Where are the men who came to you tonight? Bring them out to us so that we can have sex with them."

[6]Lot went outside to meet them and shut the door behind him [7]and said, "No, my friends. Don't do this wicked thing. [8]Look, I have two daughters who have never slept with a man. Let me bring them out to you, and you can do what you like with them. But don't do anything to these men, for they have come under the protection of my roof."

[9]"Get out of our way," they replied. And they said, "This fellow came here as an alien, and now he wants to play the judge! We'll treat you worse than them." They kept bringing pressure on Lot and moved forward to break down the door.

[10]But the men inside reached out and pulled Lot back into the house and shut the door. [11]Then they struck the men who were at the door of the house, young and old, with blindness so that they could not find the door.

[12]The two men said to Lot, "Do you have anyone else here—sons-in-law, sons or daughters, or anyone else in the city who belongs to you? Get them out of here, [13]because we are going to destroy this place. The outcry to the LORD against its people is so great that he has sent us to destroy it."

[14]So Lot went out and spoke to his sons-in-law, who were pledged to marry his daughters. He said, "Hurry and get out of this place, because the LORD is about to destroy the city!" But his sons-in-law thought he was joking.

[15]With the coming of dawn, the angels urged Lot, saying, "Hurry! Take your wife and your two daughters who are here, or you will be swept away when the city is punished."

[16]When he hesitated, the men grasped his hand and the hands of his wife and of his two daughters and led them safely out of the city, for the LORD was merciful to them. [17]As soon as they had brought them out, one of them said, "Flee for your lives! Don't look back, and don't stop anywhere in the plain! Flee to the mountains or you will be swept away!"

Dan 10 [5]I looked up and there before me was a man dressed in linen, with a belt of the finest gold around his waist. [6]His body was like chrysolite, his face like lightning, his eyes like flaming torches, his arms and legs like the gleam of burnished bronze, and his voice like the sound of a multitude. . . . [16]Then one who looked like a man touched my lips, and I opened my mouth and began to speak. I said to the one standing before me, "I am overcome with anguish because of the vision, my lord, and I am helpless. . . ."

[18]Again the one who looked like a man touched me and gave me strength.

Dan 12 [5]Then I, Daniel, looked, and there before me stood two others, one on this bank of the river and one on the opposite bank. [6]One of them said to the man clothed in linen, who was above the waters of the river, "How long will it be before these astonishing things are fulfilled?"

[7]The man clothed in linen, who was above the waters of the river, lifted his right hand and his left hand toward heaven, and I heard him swear by him who lives forever, saying, "It will be for a time, times and half a time. When the power of the holy people has been finally broken, all these things will be completed."

Zech 1 [8]During the night I had a vision—and there before me was a man riding a red horse! He was standing among the myrtle trees in a ravine. Behind him were red, brown and white horses. . . .

[10]Then the man standing among the myrtle trees explained, "They are the ones the LORD has sent to go throughout the earth."

Mark 16 [5]As they entered the tomb, they saw a young man dressed in a white robe sitting on the right side, and they were alarmed.

Luke 24 [4]While they were wondering about this, suddenly two men in clothes that gleamed like lightning stood beside them. [5]In their fright the women bowed down with their faces to the ground, but the men said to them, "Why do you look for the living among the dead?"

Acts 1 [10]They were looking intently up into the sky as he was going, when suddenly two men dressed in white stood beside them.

Acts 10 [30]Cornelius answered: "Four days ago I was in my house praying at this hour, at three in the afternoon. Suddenly a man in shining clothes stood before me. . . ."

15. Messenger

Dan 4 [13]"In the visions I saw while lying in my bed, I looked, and there before me was a messenger, a holy one, coming down from heaven."

Dan 4 [17]"'The decision is announced by messengers, the holy ones declare the verdict, so that the living may know that the Most High is sovereign over the kingdoms of men and gives them to anyone he wishes and sets over them the lowliest of men.'"

Dan 4 [23]"You, O king, saw a messenger, a holy one, coming down from heaven and saying, 'Cut down the tree and destroy it, but leave the stump, bound with iron and bronze, in the grass of the field, while its roots remain in the ground. Let him be drenched with the dew of heaven; let him live like the wild animals, until seven times pass by for him.'"

16. Mighty One

Ps 29 [1]Ascribe to the LORD, O mighty ones, ascribe to the LORD glory and strength. [2]Ascribe to the LORD the glory due his name; worship the LORD in the splendor of his holiness.

17. Ministering Spirits

Heb 1 [14]Are not all angels ministering spirits sent to serve those who will inherit salvation?

18. Morning Stars

Job 38 [7]". . . while the morning stars sang together and all the angels shouted for joy?"

19. Multitudes of Heaven

Neh 9 [6]"You alone are the LORD. You made the heavens, even the highest heavens, and all their starry host, the earth and all that is on it, the seas and all that is in them. You give life to everything, and the multitudes of heaven worship you."

20. Prince

Dan 10 [21]". . . but first I will tell you what is written in the Book of Truth. (No one supports me against them except Michael, your prince.)"

21. Seraphs

Isa 6 [1]In the year that King Uzziah died, I saw the Lord seated on a throne, high and exalted, and the train of his robe filled the temple. [2]Above him were seraphs, each with six wings: With two wings they covered their faces, with two they covered their feet, and with two they were flying. [3]And they were calling to one another: "Holy, holy, holy is the LORD Almighty; the whole earth is full of his glory." [4]At the sound of their voices the doorposts and thresholds shook and the temple was filled with smoke.

[5]"Woe to me!" I cried. "I am ruined! For I am a man of unclean lips, and I live among a people of unclean lips, and my eyes have seen the King, the LORD Almighty."

[6]Then one of the seraphs flew to me with a live coal in his hand, which he had taken with tongs from the altar. [7]With it he touched my mouth and said, "See, this has touched your lips; your guilt is taken away and your sin atoned for."

22. Servants

Job 4 [18]"'If God places no trust in his servants, if he charges his angels with error, [19]how much more those who live in houses of clay, whose foundations are in the dust, who are crushed more readily than a moth!'"

23. Sons of God

Gen 6 [1]When men began to increase in number on the earth and daughters were born to them, [2]the sons of God saw that the daughters of men were beautiful, and they married any of them they chose. [3]Then the LORD said, "My Spirit will not contend with man forever, for he is mortal; his days will be a hundred and twenty years."

[4]The Nephilim were on the earth in those days—and also afterward—when the sons of God went to the daughters of men and had children by them. They were the heroes of old, men of renown.

24. Spirit

Job 4 [15]"A spirit glided past my face, and the hair on my body stood on end. [16]It stopped, but I could not tell what it was. A form stood before my eyes, and I heard a hushed voice: [17]'Can a mortal be more righteous than God? Can a man be more pure than his Maker?'"

B. The Names of Some Good Angels

1. Gabriel

Dan 8 [16]And I heard a man's voice from the Ulai calling, "Gabriel, tell this man the meaning of the vision."
Dan 9 [21]while I was still in prayer, Gabriel, the man I had seen in the earlier vision, came to me in swift flight about the time of the evening sacrifice.
Luke 1 [19]The angel answered, "I am Gabriel. I stand in the presence of God, and I have been sent to speak to you and to tell you this good news."
Luke 1 [26]In the sixth month, God sent the angel Gabriel to Nazareth, a town in Galilee. . . .

2. Michael

Dan 10 [13]"But the prince of the Persian kingdom resisted me twenty-one days. Then Michael, one of the chief princes, came to help me, because I was detained there with the king of Persia."
Dan 10 [21]". . . but first I will tell you what is written in the Book of Truth. (No one supports me against them except Michael, your prince.)"
Dan 12 [1]"At that time Michael, the great prince who protects your people, will arise. There will be a time of distress such as has not happened from the beginning of nations until then. But at that time your people—everyone whose name is found written in the book—will be delivered."
Jude [9]But even the archangel Michael, when he was disputing with the devil about the body of Moses, did not dare to bring a slanderous accusation against him, but said, "The Lord rebuke you!"
Rev 12 [7]And there was war in heaven. Michael and his angels fought against the dragon, and the dragon and his angels fought back.

C. The Nature of Good Angels

1. The Being of Good Angels

a) Good Angels Are Created

Neh 9 [6]"You alone are the LORD. You made the heavens, even the highest heavens, and all their starry host, the earth and all that is on it, the seas and all that is in them. You give life to everything, and the multitudes of heaven worship you."
Ps 148 [2]Praise him, all his angels, praise him, all his heavenly hosts. . . . [5]Let them praise the name of the LORD, for he commanded and they were created.
Col 1 [15]He is the image of the invisible God, the firstborn over all creation. [16]For by him all things were created: things in heaven and on earth, visible and invisible, whether thrones or powers or rulers or authorities; all things were created by him and for him.

b) Good Angels Are Personal

(1) Angels Have Intelligence

2 Sam 14 [17]"And now your servant says, 'May the word of my lord the king bring me rest, for my lord the king is like an angel of God in discerning good and evil. May the LORD your God be with you.'" . . . [20]"Your servant Joab did this to change the present situation. My lord has wisdom like that of an angel of God—he knows everything that happens in the land."
Matt 24 [36]"No one knows about that day or hour, not even the angels in heaven, nor the Son, but only the Father."
1 Cor 13 [1]If I speak in the tongues of men and of angels, but have not love, I am only a resounding gong or a clanging cymbal.
Eph 3 [10]His intent was that now, through the church, the manifold wisdom of God should be made known to the rulers and authorities in the heavenly realms. . . .

(2) Angels Have Emotion

Job 38 [7]". . . while the morning stars sang together and all the angels shouted for joy?"
Luke 2 [13]Suddenly a great company of the heavenly host appeared with the angel, praising God and saying, [14]"Glory to God in the highest, and on earth peace to men on whom his favor rests."
Luke 15 [7]"I tell you that in the same way there will be more rejoicing in heaven over one sinner who repents than over ninety-nine righteous persons who do not need to repent. . . .
[10]In the same way, I tell you, there is rejoicing in the presence of the angels of God over one sinner who repents."
Heb 12 [22]But you have come to Mount Zion, to the heavenly Jerusalem, the city of the living God. You have come to thousands upon thousands of angels in joyful assembly. . . .
Rev 5 [11]Then I looked and heard the voice of many angels, numbering thousands upon thousands, and ten thousand times ten thousand. They encircled the throne and the living creatures and the elders. [12]In a loud voice they sang: "Worthy is the

Lamb, who was slain, to receive power and wealth and wisdom and strength and honor and glory and praise!"

(3) Angels Have a Will

1 Pet 1 12It was revealed to them that they were not serving themselves but you, when they spoke of the things that have now been told you by those who have preached the gospel to you by the Holy Spirit sent from heaven. Even angels long to look into these things.

Rev 22 8I, John, am the one who heard and saw these things. And when I had heard and seen them, I fell down to worship at the feet of the angel who had been showing them to me. 9But he said to me, "Do not do it! I am a fellow servant with you and with your brothers the prophets and of all who keep the words of this book. Worship God!"

c) Good Angels Do Not Marry

Mark 12 25"When the dead rise, they will neither marry nor be given in marriage; they will be like the angels in heaven."

d) Good Angels Are Immaterial

Ps 104 4He makes winds his messengers, flames of fire his servants.

Heb 1 7In speaking of the angels he says, "He makes his angels winds, his servants flames of fire."

Heb 1 14Are not all angels ministering spirits sent to serve those who will inherit salvation?

e) Good Angels Are Immortal

Luke 20 36". . . and they can no longer die; for they are like the angels. They are God's children, since they are children of the resurrection."

2. The Qualities of Good Angels

a) Good Angels Are Holy

Job 5 1"Call if you will, but who will answer you? To which of the holy ones will you turn?"

Job 15 15"If God places no trust in his holy ones, if even the heavens are not pure in his eyes . . ."

Ps 89 7In the council of the holy ones God is greatly feared; he is more awesome than all who surround him.

Dan 4 13"In the visions I saw while lying in my bed, I looked, and there before me was a messenger, a holy one, coming down from heaven."

Dan 4 17"'The decision is announced by messengers, the holy ones declare the verdict, so that the living may know that the Most High is sovereign over the kingdoms of men and gives them to anyone he wishes and sets over them the lowliest of men.'"

Dan 4 23"You, O king, saw a messenger, a holy one, coming down from heaven and saying, 'Cut down the tree and destroy it, but leave the stump, bound with iron and bronze, in the grass of the field, while its roots remain in the ground. Let him be drenched with the dew of heaven; let him live like the wild animals, until seven times pass by for him.'"

Dan 8 13Then I heard a holy one speaking, and another holy one said to him, "How long will it take for the vision to be fulfilled—the vision concerning the daily sacrifice, the rebellion that causes desolation, and the surrender of the sanctuary and of the host that will be trampled underfoot?"

Mark 8 38"If anyone is ashamed of me and my words in this adulterous and sinful generation, the Son of Man will be ashamed of him when he comes in his Father's glory with the holy angels."

Jude 14Enoch, the seventh from Adam, prophesied about these men: "See, the Lord is coming with thousands upon thousands of his holy ones. . . ."

Rev 14 10". . . he, too, will drink of the wine of God's fury, which has been poured full strength into the cup of his wrath. He will be tormented with burning sulfur in the presence of the holy angels and of the Lamb."

b) Good Angels Are Imperfect

Job 4 18"'If God places no trust in his servants, if he charges his angels with error . . .'"

Job 15 15"If God places no trust in his holy ones, if even the heavens are not pure in his eyes . . ."

c) Good Angels Are Meek

2 Pet 2 11yet even angels, although they are stronger and more powerful, do not bring slanderous accusations against such beings in the presence of the Lord.

Jude 9But even the archangel Michael, when he was disputing with the devil about the body of Moses, did not dare to bring a slanderous accusation against him, but said, "The Lord rebuke you!"

d) Good Angels Are Mighty and Powerful

Gen 19 10But the men inside reached out and pulled Lot back into the house and shut the door. 11Then they struck the men who were at the door of the house, young and old, with blindness so that they could not find the door.

Ps 29 1Ascribe to the LORD, O mighty ones, ascribe to the LORD glory and strength.

Ps 103 20Praise the LORD, you his angels, you mighty ones who do his bidding, who obey his word.

Dan 9 21while I was still in prayer, Gabriel, the man I had seen in the earlier vision, came to me in swift flight about the time of the evening sacrifice.

Dan 10 13"But the prince of the Persian kingdom resisted me twenty-one days. Then Michael, one of the chief princes, came to help me, because I was detained there with the king of Persia."

Matt 24 31"And he will send his angels with a loud trumpet call, and they will gather his elect from the four winds, from one end of the heavens to the other."

Matt 28 2There was a violent earthquake, for an angel of the Lord came down from heaven and, going to the tomb, rolled back the stone and sat on it.

Mark 16 3and they asked each other, "Who will roll the stone away from the entrance of the tomb?"

4But when they looked up, they saw that the stone, which was very large, had been rolled away. 5As they entered the tomb, they saw a young man dressed in a white robe sitting on the right side, and they were alarmed.

Luke 2 13Suddenly a great company of the heavenly host appeared with the angel, praising God and saying, 14"Glory to God in the highest, and on earth peace to men on whom his favor rests."

15When the angels had left them and gone into heaven, the shepherds said to one another, "Let's go to Bethlehem and see this thing that has happened, which the Lord has told us about."

Acts 5 19But during the night an angel of the Lord opened the doors of the jail and brought them out.

Acts 12 7Suddenly an angel of the Lord appeared and a light shone in the cell. He struck Peter on the side and woke him up. "Quick, get up!" he said, and the chains fell off Peter's wrists.

8Then the angel said to him, "Put on your clothes and sandals." And Peter did so. "Wrap your cloak around you and follow me," the angel told him. 9Peter followed him out of the prison, but he had no idea that what the angel was doing was really happening; he thought he was seeing a vision. 10They passed the first and second guards and came to the iron gate leading to the city. It opened for them by itself, and they went through it. When they had walked the length of one street, suddenly the angel left him.

11Then Peter came to himself and said, "Now I know without a doubt that the Lord sent his angel and rescued me from Herod's clutches and from everything the Jewish people were anticipating."

Acts 12 23Immediately, because Herod did not give praise to God, an angel of the Lord struck him down, and he was eaten by worms and died.

2 Thess 1 7and give relief to you who are troubled, and to us as well. This will happen when the Lord Jesus is revealed from heaven in blazing fire with his powerful angels.

2 Pet 2 11yet even angels, although they are stronger and more powerful, do not bring slanderous accusations against such beings in the presence of the Lord.

Rev 7 1After this I saw four angels standing at the four corners of the earth, holding back the four winds of the earth to prevent any wind from blowing on the land or on the sea or on any tree.

Rev 12 [7]And there was war in heaven. Michael and his angels fought against the dragon, and the dragon and his angels fought back. [8]But he was not strong enough, and they lost their place in heaven.
Rev 14 [17]Another angel came out of the temple in heaven, and he too had a sharp sickle. [18]Still another angel, who had charge of the fire, came from the altar and called in a loud voice to him who had the sharp sickle, "Take your sharp sickle and gather the clusters of grapes from the earth's vine, because its grapes are ripe." [19]The angel swung his sickle on the earth, gathered its grapes and threw them into the great winepress of God's wrath.
Rev 15 [5]After this I looked and in heaven the temple, that is, the tabernacle of the Testimony, was opened. [6]Out of the temple came the seven angels with the seven plagues. They were dressed in clean, shining linen and wore golden sashes around their chests. [7]Then one of the four living creatures gave to the seven angels seven golden bowls filled with the wrath of God, who lives for ever and ever. [8]And the temple was filled with smoke from the glory of God and from his power, and no one could enter the temple until the seven plagues of the seven angels were completed.
Rev 18 [1]After this I saw another angel coming down from heaven. He had great authority, and the earth was illuminated by his splendor.

e) Good Angels Are Obedient

Ps 103 [20]Praise the LORD, you his angels, you mighty ones who do his bidding, who obey his word.
Matt 6 [10]"'. . . your kingdom come, your will be done on earth as it is in heaven.'"

f) Good Angels Are Wise

2 Sam 14 [20]"Your servant Joab did this to change the present situation. My lord has wisdom like that of an angel of God—he knows everything that happens in the land."

3. The Organization of Good Angels

a) The Innumerability of Good Angels

Deut 33 [2]He said: "The LORD came from Sinai and dawned over them from Seir; he shone forth from Mount Paran. He came with myriads of holy ones from the south, from his mountain slopes."
1 Kings 22 [19]Micaiah continued, "Therefore hear the word of the LORD: I saw the LORD sitting on his throne with all the host of heaven standing around him on his right and on his left."
Job 25 [2]"Dominion and awe belong to God; he establishes order in the heights of heaven. [3]Can his forces be numbered? Upon whom does his light not rise?"
Job 33 [23]"Yet if there is an angel on his side as a mediator, one out of a thousand, to tell a man what is right for him . . ."
Ps 68 [17]The chariots of God are tens of thousands and thousands of thousands; the Lord has come from Sinai into his sanctuary.
Dan 7 [10]"A river of fire was flowing, coming out from before him. Thousands upon thousands attended him; ten thousand times ten thousand stood before him. The court was seated, and the books were opened."
Matt 26 [53]"Do you think I cannot call on my Father, and he will at once put at my disposal more than twelve legions of angels?"
Luke 2 [13]Suddenly a great company of the heavenly host appeared with the angel, praising God and saying . . .
Heb 12 [22]But you have come to Mount Zion, to the heavenly Jerusalem, the city of the living God. You have come to thousands upon thousands of angels in joyful assembly. . . .
Jude [14]Enoch, the seventh from Adam, prophesied about these men: "See, the Lord is coming with thousands upon thousands of his holy ones. . . ."
Rev 5 [11]Then I looked and heard the voice of many angels, numbering thousands upon thousands, and ten thousand times ten thousand. They encircled the throne and the living creatures and the elders.

b) The Assembly of Good Angels

Ps 89 [5]The heavens praise your wonders, O LORD, your faithfulness too, in the assembly of the holy ones. [6]For who in the skies above can compare with the LORD? Who is like the LORD among the heavenly beings? [7]In the council of the holy ones God is greatly feared; he is more awesome than all who surround him.
Heb 12 [22]But you have come to Mount Zion, to the heavenly Jerusalem, the city of the living God. You have come to thousands upon thousands of angels in joyful assembly. . . .

c) The Ranks and Titles of Good Angels

(1) Various Seats of Power

Eph 1 [20]which he exerted in Christ when he raised him from the dead and seated him at his right hand in the heavenly realms, [21]far above all rule and authority, power and dominion, and every title that can be given, not only in the present age but also in the one to come.
Col 1 [16]For by him all things were created: things in heaven and on earth, visible and invisible, whether thrones or powers or rulers or authorities; all things were created by him and for him.
Col 2 [10]and you have been given fullness in Christ, who is the head over every power and authority.
1 Pet 3 [22]who has gone into heaven and is at God's right hand—with angels, authorities and powers in submission to him.

(2) Archangel

1 Thess 4 [16]For the Lord himself will come down from heaven, with a loud command, with the voice of the archangel and with the trumpet call of God, and the dead in Christ will rise first.
Jude [9]But even the archangel Michael, when he was disputing with the devil about the body of Moses, did not dare to bring a slanderous accusation against him, but said, "The Lord rebuke you!"

(3) Cherubim

Gen 3 [24]After he drove the man out, he placed on the east side of the Garden of Eden cherubim and a flaming sword flashing back and forth to guard the way to the tree of life.

(4) Prince

Dan 10 [13]"But the prince of the Persian kingdom resisted me twenty-one days. Then Michael, one of the chief princes, came to help me, because I was detained there with the king of Persia."
Dan 10 [21]". . . but first I will tell you what is written in the Book of Truth. (No one supports me against them except Michael, your prince.)"

(5) Seraphs

Isa 6 [1]In the year that King Uzziah died, I saw the Lord seated on a throne, high and exalted, and the train of his robe filled the temple. [2]Above him were seraphs, each with six wings: With two wings they covered their faces, with two they covered their feet, and with two they were flying. [3]And they were calling to one another: "Holy, holy, holy is the LORD Almighty; the whole earth is full of his glory." [4]At the sound of their voices the doorposts and thresholds shook and the temple was filled with smoke.

[5]"Woe to me!" I cried. "I am ruined! For I am a man of unclean lips, and I live among a people of unclean lips, and my eyes have seen the King, the LORD Almighty."

[6]Then one of the seraphs flew to me with a live coal in his hand, which he had taken with tongs from the altar. [7]With it he touched my mouth and said, "See, this has touched your lips; your guilt is taken away and your sin atoned for."

4. The Election of Good Angels

Matt 18 [10]"See that you do not look down on one of these little ones. For I tell you that their angels in heaven always see the face of my Father in heaven."
1 Tim 5 [21]I charge you, in the sight of God and Christ Jesus and the elect angels, to keep these instructions without partiality, and to do nothing out of favoritism.

5. The Status of Good Angels

a) Angels and God

Ps 89 [6]For who in the skies above can compare with the LORD? Who is like the LORD among the heavenly beings?

b) Angels and Christ

(1) Angels Are Subject to Christ

Eph 1 [19]and his incomparably great power for us who believe. That power is like the working of his mighty strength, [20]which he exerted in Christ when he raised him from the dead and seated him at his right hand in the heavenly realms, [21]far above all rule and authority, power and dominion, and every title that can be given, not only in the present age but also in the one to come.

Phil 2 [9]Therefore God exalted him to the highest place and gave him the name that is above every name, [10]that at the name of Jesus every knee should bow, in heaven and on earth and under the earth, [11]and every tongue confess that Jesus Christ is Lord, to the glory of God the Father.

Col 1 [15]He is the image of the invisible God, the firstborn over all creation. [16]For by him all things were created: things in heaven and on earth, visible and invisible, whether thrones or powers or rulers or authorities; all things were created by him and for him.

Col 2 [10]and you have been given fullness in Christ, who is the head over every power and authority.

1 Pet 3 [21]and this water symbolizes baptism that now saves you also—not the removal of dirt from the body but the pledge of a good conscience toward God. It saves you by the resurrection of Jesus Christ, [22]who has gone into heaven and is at God's right hand—with angels, authorities and powers in submission to him.

(2) Angels Are Inferior to Christ

Heb 1 [3]The Son is the radiance of God's glory and the exact representation of his being, sustaining all things by his powerful word. After he had provided purification for sins, he sat down at the right hand of the Majesty in heaven. [4]So he became as much superior to the angels as the name he has inherited is superior to theirs.

[5]For to which of the angels did God ever say, "You are my Son; today I have become your Father"? Or again, "I will be his Father, and he will be my Son"? [6]And again, when God brings his firstborn into the world, he says, "Let all God's angels worship him." [7]In speaking of the angels he says, "He makes his angels winds, his servants flames of fire." [8]But about the Son he says, "Your throne, O God, will last for ever and ever, and righteousness will be the scepter of your kingdom. [9]You have loved righteousness and hated wickedness; therefore God, your God, has set you above your companions by anointing you with the oil of joy." [10]He also says, "In the beginning, O Lord, you laid the foundations of the earth, and the heavens are the work of your hands. [11]They will perish, but you remain; they will all wear out like a garment. [12]You will roll them up like a robe; like a garment they will be changed. But you remain the same, and your years will never end." [13]To which of the angels did God ever say, "Sit at my right hand until I make your enemies a footstool for your feet"?

(3) Angels Are Not Inferior during the Incarnation

Heb 2 [5]It is not to angels that he has subjected the world to come, about which we are speaking. [6]But there is a place where someone has testified: "What is man that you are mindful of him, the son of man that you care for him? [7]You made him a little lower than the angels; you crowned him with glory and honor [8]and put everything under his feet." In putting everything under him, God left nothing that is not subject to him. Yet at present we do not see everything subject to him. [9]But we see Jesus, who was made a little lower than the angels, now crowned with glory and honor because he suffered death, so that by the grace of God he might taste death for everyone.

c) Angels and Humans

(1) Angels Are Distinct from Humans

Job 38 [6]"On what were its footings set, or who laid its cornerstone—[7]while the morning stars sang together and all the angels shouted for joy?"

Ps 8 [4]what is man that you are mindful of him, the son of man that you care for him? [5]You made him a little lower than the heavenly beings and crowned him with glory and honor.

Acts 23 [8](The Sadducees say that there is no resurrection, and that there are neither angels nor spirits, but the Pharisees acknowledge them all.)

1 Cor 11 [10]For this reason, and because of the angels, the woman ought to have a sign of authority on her head.

1 Cor 13 [1]If I speak in the tongues of men and of angels, but have not love, I am only a resounding gong or a clanging cymbal.

Gal 1 [8]But even if we or an angel from heaven should preach a gospel other than the one we preached to you, let him be eternally condemned!

Heb 13 [2]Do not forget to entertain strangers, for by so doing some people have entertained angels without knowing it.

(2) Angels Are Examples for Humans

1 Sam 29 [9]Achish answered, "I know that you have been as pleasing in my eyes as an angel of God; nevertheless, the Philistine commanders have said, 'He must not go up with us into battle.'"

2 Sam 14 [17]"And now your servant says, 'May the word of my lord the king bring me rest, for my lord the king is like an angel of God in discerning good and evil. May the LORD your God be with you.'". . . [20]"Your servant Joab did this to change the present situation. My lord has wisdom like that of an angel of God—he knows everything that happens in the land."

2 Sam 19 [27]"And he has slandered your servant to my lord the king. My lord the king is like an angel of God; so do whatever pleases you."

Matt 22 [30]"At the resurrection people will neither marry nor be given in marriage; they will be like the angels in heaven."

Acts 6 [15]All who were sitting in the Sanhedrin looked intently at Stephen, and they saw that his face was like the face of an angel.

Gal 4 [14]Even though my illness was a trial to you, you did not treat me with contempt or scorn. Instead, you welcomed me as if I were an angel of God, as if I were Christ Jesus himself.

(3) Angels Are Not to Be Worshiped by Humans

Col 2 [18]Do not let anyone who delights in false humility and the worship of angels disqualify you for the prize. Such a person goes into great detail about what he has seen, and his unspiritual mind puffs him up with idle notions.

Rev 19 [9]Then the angel said to me, "Write: 'Blessed are those who are invited to the wedding supper of the Lamb!'" And he added, "These are the true words of God."

[10]At this I fell at his feet to worship him. But he said to me, "Do not do it! I am a fellow servant with you and with your brothers who hold to the testimony of Jesus. Worship God! For the testimony of Jesus is the spirit of prophecy."

Rev 22 [8]I, John, am the one who heard and saw these things. And when I had heard and seen them, I fell down to worship at the feet of the angel who had been showing them to me. [9]But he said to me, "Do not do it! I am a fellow servant with you and with your brothers the prophets and of all who keep the words of this book. Worship God!"

(4) Angels Are Now More Powerful Than Humans

Ps 8 [4]what is man that you are mindful of him, the son of man that you care for him? [5]You made him a little lower than the heavenly beings and crowned him with glory and honor.

2 Pet 2 [10]This is especially true of those who follow the corrupt desire of the sinful nature and despise authority.

Bold and arrogant, these men are not afraid to slander celestial beings, [11]yet even angels, although they are stronger and more powerful, do not bring slanderous accusations against such beings in the presence of the Lord.

(5) Angels' Final Destiny Is Lower Than That of Humans

1 Cor 6 [3]Do you not know that we will judge angels? How much more the things of this life!

D. The Work of Good Angels

1. Angels before God

a) Angels Attend God

2 Chron 18 [18]Micaiah continued, "Therefore hear the word of the LORD: I saw the LORD sitting on his throne with all the host of heaven standing on his right and on his left."

Ps 103 [20]Praise the LORD, you his angels, you mighty ones who do his bidding, who obey his word.
Dan 7 [10]"A river of fire was flowing, coming out from before him. Thousands upon thousands attended him; ten thousand times ten thousand stood before him. The court was seated, and the books were opened."
Matt 18 [10]"See that you do not look down on one of these little ones. For I tell you that their angels in heaven always see the face of my Father in heaven."
Heb 12 [22]But you have come to Mount Zion, to the heavenly Jerusalem, the city of the living God. You have come to thousands upon thousands of angels in joyful assembly. . . .

b) Angels Meet with God

Job 1 [6]One day the angels came to present themselves before the LORD, and Satan also came with them.
Job 2 [1]On another day the angels came to present themselves before the LORD, and Satan also came with them to present himself before him.

c) Angels Rejoice Over God

Job 38 [6]"On what were its footings set, or who laid its cornerstone—[7]while the morning stars sang together and all the angels shouted for joy?"

d) Angels Serve God

Ps 103 [21]Praise the LORD, all his heavenly hosts, you his servants who do his will.

e) Angels Worship God

Ps 29 [1]Ascribe to the LORD, mighty ones, ascribe to the LORD glory and strength. [2]Ascribe to the LORD the glory due his name; worship the LORD in the splendor of his holiness.
Ps 89 [7]In the council of the holy ones God is greatly feared; he is more awesome than all who surround him.
Ps 103 [20]Praise the LORD, you his angels, you mighty ones who do his bidding, who obey his word. [21]Praise the LORD, all his heavenly hosts, you his servants who do his will.
Ps 148 [1]Praise the LORD. Praise the LORD from the heavens, praise him in the heights above. [2]Praise him, all his angels, praise him, all his heavenly hosts.
Isa 6 [1]In the year that King Uzziah died, I saw the Lord seated on a throne, high and exalted, and the train of his robe filled the temple. [2]Above him were seraphs, each with six wings: With two wings they covered their faces, with two they covered their feet, and with two they were flying. [3]And they were calling to one another: "Holy, holy, holy is the LORD Almighty; the whole earth is full of his glory." [4]At the sound of their voices the doorposts and thresholds shook and the temple was filled with smoke.
Ezek 10 [1]I looked, and I saw the likeness of a throne of sapphire above the expanse that was over the heads of the cherubim. [2]The LORD said to the man clothed in linen, "Go in among the wheels beneath the cherubim. Fill your hands with burning coals from among the cherubim and scatter them over the city." And as I watched, he went in.

[3]Now the cherubim were standing on the south side of the temple when the man went in, and a cloud filled the inner court. [4]Then the glory of the LORD rose from above the cherubim and moved to the threshold of the temple. The cloud filled the temple, and the court was full of the radiance of the glory of the LORD. [5]The sound of the wings of the cherubim could be heard as far away as the outer court, like the voice of God Almighty when he speaks.

[6]When the LORD commanded the man in linen, "Take fire from among the wheels, from among the cherubim," the man went in and stood beside a wheel. [7]Then one of the cherubim reached out his hand to the fire that was among them. He took up some of it and put it into the hands of the man in linen, who took it and went out. [8](Under the wings of the cherubim could be seen what looked like the hands of a man.)

[9]I looked, and I saw beside the cherubim four wheels, one beside each of the cherubim; the wheels sparkled like chrysolite. [10]As for their appearance, the four of them looked alike; each was like a wheel intersecting a wheel. [11]As they moved, they would go in any one of the four directions the cherubim faced; the wheels did not turn about as the cherubim went. The cherubim went in whatever direction the head faced, without turning as they went. [12]Their entire bodies, including their backs, their hands and their wings, were completely full of eyes, as were their four wheels. [13]I heard the wheels being called "the whirling wheels." [14]Each of the cherubim had four faces: One face was that of a cherub, the second the face of a man, the third the face of a lion, and the fourth the face of an eagle.

[15]Then the cherubim rose upward. These were the living creatures I had seen by the Kebar River. [16]When the cherubim moved, the wheels beside them moved; and when the cherubim spread their wings to rise from the ground, the wheels did not leave their side. [17]When the cherubim stood still, they also stood still; and when the cherubim rose, they rose with them, because the spirit of the living creatures was in them.

[18]Then the glory of the LORD departed from over the threshold of the temple and stopped above the cherubim. [19]While I watched, the cherubim spread their wings and rose from the ground, and as they went, the wheels went with them. They stopped at the entrance to the east gate of the LORD's house, and the glory of the God of Israel was above them.
Rev 4 [6]Also before the throne there was what looked like a sea of glass, clear as crystal.

In the center, around the throne, were four living creatures, and they were covered with eyes, in front and in back. [7]The first living creature was like a lion, the second was like an ox, the third had a face like a man, the fourth was like a flying eagle. [8]Each of the four living creatures had six wings and was covered with eyes all around, even under his wings. Day and night they never stop saying: "Holy, holy, holy is the Lord God Almighty, who was, and is, and is to come." [9]Whenever the living creatures give glory, honor and thanks to him who sits on the throne and who lives for ever and ever . . .

2. Angels in Nature

a) Angels and Fire

Dan 3 [25]He said, "Look! I see four men walking around in the fire, unbound and unharmed, and the fourth looks like a son of the gods."

[26]Nebuchadnezzar then approached the opening of the blazing furnace and shouted, "Shadrach, Meshach and Abednego, servants of the Most High God, come out! Come here!"

So Shadrach, Meshach and Abednego came out of the fire, [27]and the satraps, prefects, governors and royal advisers crowded around them. They saw that the fire had not harmed their bodies, nor was a hair of their heads singed; their robes were not scorched, and there was no smell of fire on them.

[28]Then Nebuchadnezzar said, "Praise be to the God of Shadrach, Meshach and Abednego, who has sent his angel and rescued his servants! They trusted in him and defied the king's command and were willing to give up their lives rather than serve or worship any god except their own God."
Rev 14 [18]Still another angel, who had charge of the fire, came from the altar and called in a loud voice to him who had the sharp sickle, "Take your sharp sickle and gather the clusters of grapes from the earth's vine, because its grapes are ripe."

b) Angels and Matter

Matt 28 [2]There was a violent earthquake, for an angel of the Lord came down from heaven and, going to the tomb, rolled back the stone and sat on it.
Mark 16 [3]and they asked each other, "Who will roll the stone away from the entrance of the tomb?"

[4]But when they looked up, they saw that the stone, which was very large, had been rolled away. [5]As they entered the tomb, they saw a young man dressed in a white robe sitting on the right side, and they were alarmed.
Rev 16 [12]The sixth angel poured out his bowl on the great river Euphrates, and its water was dried up to prepare the way for the kings from the East.

c) Angels and Space

Luke 2 [13]Suddenly a great company of the heavenly host appeared with the angel, praising God and saying, [14]"Glory to

God in the highest, and on earth peace to men on whom his favor rests."

15When the angels had left them and gone into heaven, the shepherds said to one another, "Let's go to Bethlehem and see this thing that has happened, which the Lord has told us about."

d) Angels and Wild Animals

Dan 6 22"My God sent his angel, and he shut the mouths of the lions. They have not hurt me, because I was found innocent in his sight. Nor have I ever done any wrong before you, O king."

3. Angels in OT History

a) Angels and the Garden of Eden

Gen 3 24After he drove the man out, he placed on the east side of the Garden of Eden cherubim and a flaming sword flashing back and forth to guard the way to the tree of life.

b) Angels during the Patriarchal Period

Gen 18 2Abraham looked up and saw three men standing nearby. When he saw them, he hurried from the entrance of his tent to meet them and bowed low to the ground. . . .

7Then he ran to the herd and selected a choice, tender calf and gave it to a servant, who hurried to prepare it. 8He then brought some curds and milk and the calf that had been prepared, and set these before them. While they ate, he stood near them under a tree. . . .

16When the men got up to leave, they looked down toward Sodom, and Abraham walked along with them to see them on their way. . . .

22The men turned away and went toward Sodom, but Abraham remained standing before the LORD.

Gen 19 1The two angels arrived at Sodom in the evening, and Lot was sitting in the gateway of the city. When he saw them, he got up to meet them and bowed down with his face to the ground. 2"My lords," he said, "please turn aside to your servant's house. You can wash your feet and spend the night and then go on your way early in the morning."

"No," they answered, "we will spend the night in the square."

3But he insisted so strongly that they did go with him and entered his house. He prepared a meal for them, baking bread without yeast, and they ate.

Gen 19 15With the coming of dawn, the angels urged Lot, saying, "Hurry! Take your wife and your two daughters who are here, or you will be swept away when the city is punished."

Gen 24 7"The LORD, the God of heaven, who brought me out of my father's household and my native land and who spoke to me and promised me on oath, saying, 'To your offspring I will give this land'—he will send his angel before you so that you can get a wife for my son from there."

Gen 28 12He had a dream in which he saw a stairway resting on the earth, with its top reaching to heaven, and the angels of God were ascending and descending on it.

Gen 32 1Jacob also went on his way, and the angels of God met him. 2When Jacob saw them, he said, "This is the camp of God!" So he named that place Mahanaim.

Hos 12 2The LORD has a charge to bring against Judah; he will punish Jacob according to his ways and repay him according to his deeds. 3In the womb he grasped his brother's heel; as a man he struggled with God. 4He struggled with the angel and overcame him; he wept and begged for his favor. He found him at Bethel and talked with him there. . . .

c) Angels and the Nation of Israel

(1) Angels Acted as God's Spokesmen

Num 22 21Balaam got up in the morning, saddled his donkey and went with the princes of Moab. 22But God was very angry when he went, and the angel of the LORD stood in the road to oppose him. Balaam was riding on his donkey, and his two servants were with him. 23When the donkey saw the angel of the LORD standing in the road with a drawn sword in his hand, she turned off the road into a field. Balaam beat her to get her back on the road.

24Then the angel of the LORD stood in a narrow path between two vineyards, with walls on both sides. 25When the donkey saw the angel of the LORD, she pressed close to the wall, crushing Balaam's foot against it. So he beat her again.

26Then the angel of the LORD moved on ahead and stood in a narrow place where there was no room to turn, either to the right or to the left. 27When the donkey saw the angel of the LORD, she lay down under Balaam, and he was angry and beat her with his staff. 28Then the LORD opened the donkey's mouth, and she said to Balaam, "What have I done to you to make you beat me these three times?"

29Balaam answered the donkey, "You have made a fool of me! If I had a sword in my hand, I would kill you right now."

30The donkey said to Balaam, "Am I not your own donkey, which you have always ridden, to this day? Have I been in the habit of doing this to you?"

"No," he said.

31Then the LORD opened Balaam's eyes, and he saw the angel of the LORD standing in the road with his sword drawn. So he bowed low and fell facedown.

32The angel of the LORD asked him, "Why have you beaten your donkey these three times? I have come here to oppose you because your path is a reckless one before me. 33The donkey saw me and turned away from me these three times. If she had not turned away, I would certainly have killed you by now, but I would have spared her."

34Balaam said to the angel of the LORD, "I have sinned. I did not realize you were standing in the road to oppose me. Now if you are displeased, I will go back."

35The angel of the LORD said to Balaam, "Go with the men, but speak only what I tell you." So Balaam went with the princes of Balak. . . .

38"Well, I have come to you now," Balaam replied. "But can I say just anything? I must speak only what God puts in my mouth."

1 Kings 13 18The old prophet answered, "I too am a prophet, as you are. And an angel said to me by the word of the LORD: 'Bring him back with you to your house so that he may eat bread and drink water.'" (But he was lying to him.)

2 Kings 1 3But the angel of the LORD said to Elijah the Tishbite, "Go up and meet the messengers of the king of Samaria and ask them, 'Is it because there is no God in Israel that you are going off to consult Baal-Zebub, the god of Ekron?' 4Therefore this is what the LORD says: 'You will not leave the bed you are lying on. You will certainly die!'" So Elijah went.

2 Kings 1 15The angel of the LORD said to Elijah, "Go down with him; do not be afraid of him." So Elijah got up and went down with him to the king.

1 Chron 21 18Then the angel of the LORD ordered Gad to tell David to go up and build an altar to the LORD on the threshing floor of Araunah the Jebusite.

Dan 8 16And I heard a man's voice from the Ulai calling, "Gabriel, tell this man the meaning of the vision."

Dan 9 21while I was still in prayer, Gabriel, the man I had seen in the earlier vision, came to me in swift flight about the time of the evening sacrifice. 22He instructed me and said to me, "Daniel, I have now come to give you insight and understanding."

Dan 10 5I looked up and there before me was a man dressed in linen, with a belt of the finest gold around his waist. 6His body was like chrysolite, his face like lightning, his eyes like flaming torches, his arms and legs like the gleam of burnished bronze, and his voice like the sound of a multitude. . . .

10A hand touched me and set me trembling on my hands and knees. 11He said, "Daniel, you who are highly esteemed, consider carefully the words I am about to speak to you, and stand up, for I have now been sent to you." And when he said this to me, I stood up trembling.

Zech 1 9I asked, "What are these, my lord?"

The angel who was talking with me answered, "I will show you what they are."

Zech 2 3Then the angel who was speaking to me left, and another angel came to meet him. . . .

Zech 4 1Then the angel who talked with me returned and wakened me, as a man is wakened from his sleep.

(2) Angels Brought Deliverance

Exod 14 19Then the angel of God, who had been traveling in front of Israel's army, withdrew and went behind them. The pillar of cloud also moved from in front and stood behind them, [20]coming between the armies of Egypt and Israel. Throughout the night the cloud brought darkness to the one side and light to the other side; so neither went near the other all night long.

Exod 32 [34]"Now go, lead the people to the place I spoke of, and my angel will go before you. However, when the time comes for me to punish, I will punish them for their sin."

Num 20 [16]". . . but when we cried out to the LORD, he heard our cry and sent an angel and brought us out of Egypt.

"Now we are here at Kadesh, a town on the edge of your territory."

2 Chron 32 [21]And the LORD sent an angel, who annihilated all the fighting men and the leaders and officers in the camp of the Assyrian king. So he withdrew to his own land in disgrace. And when he went into the temple of his god, some of his sons cut him down with the sword.

[22]So the LORD saved Hezekiah and the people of Jerusalem from the hand of Sennacherib king of Assyria and from the hand of all others. He took care of them on every side.

Ps 78 [25]Men ate the bread of angels; he sent them all the food they could eat.

Isa 63 [9]In all their distress he too was distressed, and the angel of his presence saved them. In his love and mercy he redeemed them; he lifted them up and carried them all the days of old.

(3) Angels Executed Punishment

2 Kings 19 [35]That night the angel of the LORD went out and put to death a hundred and eighty-five thousand men in the Assyrian camp. When the people got up the next morning—there were all the dead bodies!

1 Chron 21 [11]So Gad went to David and said to him, "This is what the LORD says: 'Take your choice: [12]three years of famine, three months of being swept away before your enemies, with their swords overtaking you, or three days of the sword of the LORD—days of plague in the land, with the angel of the LORD ravaging every part of Israel.' Now then, decide how I should answer the one who sent me."

[13]David said to Gad, "I am in deep distress. Let me fall into the hands of the LORD, for his mercy is very great; but do not let me fall into the hands of men."

[14]So the LORD sent a plague on Israel, and seventy thousand men of Israel fell dead. [15]And God sent an angel to destroy Jerusalem. But as the angel was doing so, the LORD saw it and was grieved because of the calamity and said to the angel who was destroying the people, "Enough! Withdraw your hand." The angel of the LORD was then standing at the threshing floor of Araunah the Jebusite.

[16]David looked up and saw the angel of the LORD standing between heaven and earth, with a drawn sword in his hand extended over Jerusalem. Then David and the elders, clothed in sackcloth, fell facedown. . . .

[27]Then the LORD spoke to the angel, and he put his sword back into its sheath. [28]At that time, when David saw that the LORD had answered him on the threshing floor of Araunah the Jebusite, he offered sacrifices there. [29]The tabernacle of the LORD, which Moses had made in the desert, and the altar of burnt offering were at that time on the high place at Gibeon. [30]But David could not go before it to inquire of God, because he was afraid of the sword of the angel of the LORD.

Ps 78 [49]He unleashed against them his hot anger, his wrath, indignation and hostility—a band of destroying angels.

1 Cor 10 [10]And do not grumble, as some of them did—and were killed by the destroying angel.

(4) Angels Gave Protection

Exod 23 [20]"See, I am sending an angel ahead of you to guard you along the way and to bring you to the place I have prepared. [21]Pay attention to him and listen to what he says. Do not rebel against him; he will not forgive your rebellion, since my Name is in him. [22]If you listen carefully to what he says and do all that I say, I will be an enemy to your enemies and will oppose those who oppose you. [23]My angel will go ahead of you and bring you into the land of the Amorites, Hittites, Perizzites, Canaanites, Hivites and Jebusites, and I will wipe them out."

Dan 3 [25]He said, "Look! I see four men walking around in the fire, unbound and unharmed, and the fourth looks like a son of the gods."

[26]Nebuchadnezzar then approached the opening of the blazing furnace and shouted, "Shadrach, Meshach and Abednego, servants of the Most High God, come out! Come here!"

So Shadrach, Meshach and Abednego came out of the fire, [27]and the satraps, prefects, governors and royal advisers crowded around them. They saw that the fire had not harmed their bodies, nor was a hair of their heads singed; their robes were not scorched, and there was no smell of fire on them.

[28]Then Nebuchadnezzar said, "Praise be to the God of Shadrach, Meshach and Abednego, who has sent his angel and rescued his servants! They trusted in him and defied the king's command and were willing to give up their lives rather than serve or worship any god except their own God."

Dan 6 [22]"My God sent his angel, and he shut the mouths of the lions. They have not hurt me, because I was found innocent in his sight. Nor have I ever done any wrong before you, O king."

Jude [9]But even the archangel Michael, when he was disputing with the devil about the body of Moses, did not dare to bring a slanderous accusation against him, but said, "The Lord rebuke you!"

(5) Angels Mediated God's Law

Acts 7 [38]"He was in the assembly in the desert, with the angel who spoke to him on Mount Sinai, and with our fathers; and he received living words to pass on to us."

Acts 7 [53]". . . you who have received the law that was put into effect through angels but have not obeyed it."

Gal 3 [19]What, then, was the purpose of the law? It was added because of transgressions until the Seed to whom the promise referred had come. The law was put into effect through angels by a mediator.

Heb 2 [2]For if the message spoken by angels was binding, and every violation and disobedience received its just punishment . . .

(6) Angels Strengthened Prophets

1 Kings 19 [5]Then he lay down under the tree and fell asleep.

All at once an angel touched him and said, "Get up and eat." [6]He looked around, and there by his head was a cake of bread baked over hot coals, and a jar of water. He ate and drank and then lay down again.

[7]The angel of the LORD came back a second time and touched him and said, "Get up and eat, for the journey is too much for you." [8]So he got up and ate and drank. Strengthened by that food, he traveled forty days and forty nights until he reached Horeb, the mountain of God.

4. Angels among the Nations

Dan 4 [17]"'The decision is announced by messengers, the holy ones declare the verdict, so that the living may know that the Most High is sovereign over the kingdoms of men and gives them to anyone he wishes and sets over them the lowliest of men.'"

Dan 10 [13]"But the prince of the Persian kingdom resisted me twenty-one days. Then Michael, one of the chief princes, came to help me, because I was detained there with the king of Persia."

Dan 10 [20]So he said, "Do you know why I have come to you? Soon I will return to fight against the prince of Persia, and when I go, the prince of Greece will come; [21]but first I will tell you what is written in the Book of Truth. (No one supports me against them except Michael, your prince. **11** [1]And in the first year of Darius the Mede, I took my stand to support and protect him.

Dan 12 [1]"At that time Michael, the great prince who protects your people, will arise. There will be a time of distress such as has not happened from the beginning of nations until then. But at that time your people—everyone whose name is found written in the book—will be delivered."

5. Angels in Christ's Ministry

a) Angels in Christ's Incarnation

(1) Angels and Christ's Childhood

Matt 1 [20]But after he had considered this, an angel of the Lord appeared to him in a dream and said, "Joseph son of David, do not be afraid to take Mary home as your wife, because what is conceived in her is from the Holy Spirit. 21She will give birth to a son, and you are to give him the name Jesus, because he will save his people from their sins." . . .

24When Joseph woke up, he did what the angel of the Lord had commanded him and took Mary home as his wife. 25But he had no union with her until she gave birth to a son. And he gave him the name Jesus.

Matt 2 13When they had gone, an angel of the Lord appeared to Joseph in a dream. "Get up," he said, "take the child and his mother and escape to Egypt. Stay there until I tell you, for Herod is going to search for the child to kill him."

Matt 2 19After Herod died, an angel of the Lord appeared in a dream to Joseph in Egypt 20and said, "Get up, take the child and his mother and go to the land of Israel, for those who were trying to take the child's life are dead."

Luke 1 11Then an angel of the Lord appeared to him, standing at the right side of the altar of incense. 12When Zechariah saw him, he was startled and was gripped with fear. 13But the angel said to him: "Do not be afraid, Zechariah; your prayer has been heard. Your wife Elizabeth will bear you a son, and you are to give him the name John. 14He will be a joy and delight to you, and many will rejoice because of his birth, 15for he will be great in the sight of the Lord. He is never to take wine or other fermented drink, and he will be filled with the Holy Spirit even from birth. 16Many of the people of Israel will he bring back to the Lord their God. 17And he will go on before the Lord, in the spirit and power of Elijah, to turn the hearts of the fathers to their children and the disobedient to the wisdom of the righteous—to make ready a people prepared for the Lord."

Luke 1 26In the sixth month, God sent the angel Gabriel to Nazareth, a town in Galilee, 27to a virgin pledged to be married to a man named Joseph, a descendant of David. The virgin's name was Mary. 28The angel went to her and said, "Greetings, you who are highly favored! The Lord is with you."

29Mary was greatly troubled at his words and wondered what kind of greeting this might be. 30But the angel said to her, "Do not be afraid, Mary, you have found favor with God. 31You will be with child and give birth to a son, and you are to give him the name Jesus. 32He will be great and will be called the Son of the Most High. The Lord God will give him the throne of his father David, 33and he will reign over the house of Jacob forever; his kingdom will never end."

34"How will this be," Mary asked the angel, "since I am a virgin?"

35The angel answered, "The Holy Spirit will come upon you, and the power of the Most High will overshadow you. So the holy one to be born will be called the Son of God. 36Even Elizabeth your relative is going to have a child in her old age, and she who was said to be barren is in her sixth month. 37For nothing is impossible with God."

38"I am the Lord's servant," Mary answered. "May it be to me as you have said." Then the angel left her.

Luke 2 8And there were shepherds living out in the fields nearby, keeping watch over their flocks at night. 9An angel of the Lord appeared to them, and the glory of the Lord shone around them, and they were terrified. 10But the angel said to them, "Do not be afraid. I bring you good news of great joy that will be for all the people. 11Today in the town of David a Savior has been born to you; he is Christ the Lord. 12This will be a sign to you: You will find a baby wrapped in cloths and lying in a manger."

13Suddenly a great company of the heavenly host appeared with the angel, praising God and saying, 14"Glory to God in the highest, and on earth peace to men on whom his favor rests."

15When the angels had left them and gone into heaven, the shepherds said to one another, "Let's go to Bethlehem and see this thing that has happened, which the Lord has told us about."

(2) Angels and Christ's Earthly Ministry

Matt 4 11Then the devil left him, and angels came and attended him.

(3) Angels and the Week of Christ's Passion

Matt 26 53"Do you think I cannot call on my Father, and he will at once put at my disposal more than twelve legions of angels?"

Luke 22 39Jesus went out as usual to the Mount of Olives, and his disciples followed him. 40On reaching the place, he said to them, "Pray that you will not fall into temptation." 41He withdrew about a stone's throw beyond them, knelt down and prayed, 42"Father, if you are willing, take this cup from me; yet not my will, but yours be done." 43An angel from heaven appeared to him and strengthened him.

(4) Angels and Christ's Resurrection and Ascension

Matt 28 1After the Sabbath, at dawn on the first day of the week, Mary Magdalene and the other Mary went to look at the tomb.

2There was a violent earthquake, for an angel of the Lord came down from heaven and, going to the tomb, rolled back the stone and sat on it. 3His appearance was like lightning, and his clothes were white as snow. 4The guards were so afraid of him that they shook and became like dead men.

5The angel said to the women, "Do not be afraid, for I know that you are looking for Jesus, who was crucified. 6He is not here; he has risen, just as he said. Come and see the place where he lay. 7Then go quickly and tell his disciples: 'He has risen from the dead and is going ahead of you into Galilee. There you will see him.' Now I have told you."

Mark 16 2Very early on the first day of the week, just after sunrise, they were on their way to the tomb 3and they asked each other, "Who will roll the stone away from the entrance of the tomb?"

4But when they looked up, they saw that the stone, which was very large, had been rolled away. 5As they entered the tomb, they saw a young man dressed in a white robe sitting on the right side, and they were alarmed.

6"Don't be alarmed," he said. "You are looking for Jesus the Nazarene, who was crucified. He has risen! He is not here. See the place where they laid him. 7But go, tell his disciples and Peter, 'He is going ahead of you into Galilee. There you will see him, just as he told you.'"

Luke 24 1On the first day of the week, very early in the morning, the women took the spices they had prepared and went to the tomb. 2They found the stone rolled away from the tomb, 3but when they entered, they did not find the body of the Lord Jesus. 4While they were wondering about this, suddenly two men in clothes that gleamed like lightning stood beside them. 5In their fright the women bowed down with their faces to the ground, but the men said to them, "Why do you look for the living among the dead? 6He is not here; he has risen! Remember how he told you, while he was still with you in Galilee: 7'The Son of Man must be delivered into the hands of sinful men, be crucified and on the third day be raised again.'"

John 20 10Then the disciples went back to their homes, 11but Mary stood outside the tomb crying. As she wept, she bent over to look into the tomb 12and saw two angels in white, seated where Jesus' body had been, one at the head and the other at the foot.

Acts 1 10They were looking intently up into the sky as he was going, when suddenly two men dressed in white stood beside them. 11"Men of Galilee," they said, "why do you stand here looking into the sky? This same Jesus, who has been taken from you into heaven, will come back in the same way you have seen him go into heaven."

b) Angels in Christ's Exaltation

(1) Angels Attest to Christ's Exaltation

Luke 12 8"I tell you, whoever acknowledges me before men, the Son of Man will also acknowledge him before the angels of God. 9But he who disowns me before men will be disowned before the angels of God."

1 Tim 3 16Beyond all question, the mystery of godliness is great: He appeared in a body, was vindicated by the Spirit, was seen by angels, was preached among the nations, was believed on in the world, was taken up in glory.

(2) Angels Worship and Praise the Exalted Christ

Heb 1 4So he became as much superior to the angels as the name he has inherited is superior to theirs. . . . 6And again,

when God brings his firstborn into the world, he says, "Let all
God's angels worship him."
Rev 5 11Then I looked and heard the voice of many angels,
numbering thousands upon thousands, and ten thousand times
ten thousand. They encircled the throne and the living creatures and the elders. 12In a loud voice they sang: "Worthy is the
Lamb, who was slain, to receive power and wealth and wisdom
and strength and honor and glory and praise!"

13Then I heard every creature in heaven and on earth and
under the earth and on the sea, and all that is in them, singing:
"To him who sits on the throne and to the Lamb be praise and
honor and glory and power, for ever and ever!" 14The four living
creatures said, "Amen," and the elders fell down and worshiped.

c) Angels in Christ's Gospel

1 Pet 1 12It was revealed to them that they were not serving
themselves but you, when they spoke of the things that have
now been told you by those who have preached the gospel to
you by the Holy Spirit sent from heaven. Even angels long to
look into these things.
Rev 14 6Then I saw another angel flying in midair, and he had
the eternal gospel to proclaim to those who live on the
earth—to every nation, tribe, language and people.

d) Angels in Christ's Second Coming

(1) Angels Will Attend Christ

Matt 16 27"For the Son of Man is going to come in his Father's
glory with his angels, and then he will reward each person
according to what he has done."
Matt 25 31"When the Son of Man comes in his glory, and all
the angels with him, he will sit on his throne in heavenly glory."
Mark 8 38"If anyone is ashamed of me and my words in this
adulterous and sinful generation, the Son of Man will be
ashamed of him when he comes in his Father's glory with the
holy angels."
2 Thess 1 7and give relief to you who are troubled, and to us as
well. This will happen when the Lord Jesus is revealed from
heaven in blazing fire with his powerful angels.

(2) Angels Will Execute Judgment

Rev 8 5Then the angel took the censer, filled it with fire from
the altar, and hurled it on the earth; and there came peals of
thunder, rumblings, flashes of lightning and an earthquake.

6Then the seven angels who had the seven trumpets prepared to sound them.

7The first angel sounded his trumpet, and there came hail
and fire mixed with blood, and it was hurled down upon the
earth. A third of the earth was burned up, a third of the trees
were burned up, and all the green grass was burned up.

8The second angel sounded his trumpet, and something like
a huge mountain, all ablaze, was thrown into the sea. A third of
the sea turned into blood, 9a third of the living creatures in the
sea died, and a third of the ships were destroyed.

10The third angel sounded his trumpet, and a great star,
blazing like a torch, fell from the sky on a third of the rivers
and on the springs of water. . . .

12The fourth angel sounded his trumpet, and a third of the
sun was struck, a third of the moon, and a third of the stars, so
that a third of them turned dark. A third of the day was without
light, and also a third of the night.

13As I watched, I heard an eagle that was flying in midair
call out in a loud voice: "Woe! Woe! Woe to the inhabitants of
the earth, because of the trumpet blasts about to be sounded by
the other three angels!"
Rev 14 8A second angel followed and said, "Fallen! Fallen is
Babylon the Great, which made all the nations drink the maddening wine of her adulteries."

9A third angel followed them and said in a loud voice: "If
anyone worships the beast and his image and receives his mark
on the forehead or on the hand, 10he, too, will drink of the wine
of God's fury, which has been poured full strength into the cup
of his wrath. He will be tormented with burning sulfur in the
presence of the holy angels and of the Lamb."
Rev 14 17Another angel came out of the temple in heaven, and
he too had a sharp sickle. 18Still another angel, who had charge
of the fire, came from the altar and called in a loud voice to
him who had the sharp sickle, "Take your sharp sickle and
gather the clusters of grapes from the earth's vine, because its
grapes are ripe." 19The angel swung his sickle on the earth,
gathered its grapes and threw them into the great winepress of
God's wrath.
Rev 16 1Then I heard a loud voice from the temple saying to
the seven angels, "Go, pour out the seven bowls of God's wrath
on the earth."

2The first angel went and poured out his bowl on the land,
and ugly and painful sores broke out on the people who had
the mark of the beast and worshiped his image.

3The second angel poured out his bowl on the sea, and it
turned into blood like that of a dead man, and every living
thing in the sea died.

4The third angel poured out his bowl on the rivers and
springs of water, and they became blood. . . .

8The fourth angel poured out his bowl on the sun, and the
sun was given power to scorch people with fire. . . .

10The fifth angel poured out his bowl on the throne of the
beast, and his kingdom was plunged into darkness. Men
gnawed their tongues in agony. . . .

12The sixth angel poured out his bowl on the great river
Euphrates, and its water was dried up to prepare the way for
the kings from the East. . . .

17The seventh angel poured out his bowl into the air, and
out of the temple came a loud voice from the throne, saying, "It
is done!" 18Then there came flashes of lightning, rumblings,
peals of thunder and a severe earthquake. No earthquake like it
has ever occurred since man has been on earth, so tremendous
was the quake.
Rev 18 21Then a mighty angel picked up a boulder the size of a
large millstone and threw it into the sea, and said: "With such
violence the great city of Babylon will be thrown down, never
to be found again."

(3) Angels Will Gather the Elect

Matt 24 31"And he will send his angels with a loud trumpet
call, and they will gather his elect from the four winds, from
one end of the heavens to the other."
1 Thess 4 16For the Lord himself will come down from heaven,
with a loud command, with the voice of the archangel and with
the trumpet call of God, and the dead in Christ will rise first.

(4) Angels Will Purge Evil

Matt 13 37He answered, "The one who sowed the good seed is
the Son of Man. 38The field is the world, and the good seed
stands for the sons of the kingdom. The weeds are the sons of
the evil one, 39and the enemy who sows them is the devil. The
harvest is the end of the age, and the harvesters are angels.

40"As the weeds are pulled up and burned in the fire, so it
will be at the end of the age. 41The Son of Man will send out his
angels, and they will weed out of his kingdom everything that
causes sin and all who do evil. 42They will throw them into the
fiery furnace, where there will be weeping and gnashing of
teeth. . . . 49This is how it will be at the end of the age. The
angels will come and separate the wicked from the righteous
50and throw them into the fiery furnace, where there will be
weeping and gnashing of teeth."

6. Angels among Believers

a) Angels Bear Witness to Believers

Luke 12 8"I tell you, whoever acknowledges me before men,
the Son of Man will also acknowledge him before the angels of
God. 9But he who disowns me before men will be disowned
before the angels of God."
1 Cor 4 9For it seems to me that God has put us apostles on
display at the end of the procession, like men condemned to
die in the arena. We have been made a spectacle to the whole
universe, to angels as well as to men.
1 Tim 5 21I charge you, in the sight of God and Christ Jesus
and the elect angels, to keep these instructions without partiality, and to do nothing out of favoritism.

b) Angels Deliver Believers

Matt 24 31"And he will send his angels with a loud trumpet
call, and they will gather his elect from the four winds, from
one end of the heavens to the other."

Luke 16 [22]"The time came when the beggar died and the angels carried him to Abraham's side. The rich man also died and was buried."
Acts 5 [19]But during the night an angel of the Lord opened the doors of the jail and brought them out.
Acts 12 [5]So Peter was kept in prison, but the church was earnestly praying to God for him.
[6]The night before Herod was to bring him to trial, Peter was sleeping between two soldiers, bound with two chains, and sentries stood guard at the entrance. [7]Suddenly an angel of the Lord appeared and a light shone in the cell. He struck Peter on the side and woke him up. "Quick, get up!" he said, and the chains fell off Peter's wrists.
[8]Then the angel said to him, "Put on your clothes and sandals." And Peter did so. "Wrap your cloak around you and follow me," the angel told him. [9]Peter followed him out of the prison, but he had no idea that what the angel was doing was really happening; he thought he was seeing a vision. [10]They passed the first and second guards and came to the iron gate leading to the city. It opened for them by itself, and they went through it. When they had walked the length of one street, suddenly the angel left him.
[11]Then Peter came to himself and said, "Now I know without a doubt that the Lord sent his angel and rescued me from Herod's clutches and from everything the Jewish people were anticipating."

c) Angels Give Divine Messages to Believers

Acts 10 [3]One day at about three in the afternoon he had a vision. He distinctly saw an angel of God, who came to him and said, "Cornelius!"
[4]Cornelius stared at him in fear. "What is it, Lord?" he asked.
The angel answered, "Your prayers and gifts to the poor have come up as a memorial offering before God. [5]Now send men to Joppa to bring back a man named Simon who is called Peter. [6]He is staying with Simon the tanner, whose house is by the sea."
[7]When the angel who spoke to him had gone, Cornelius called two of his servants and a devout soldier who was one of his attendants. [8]He told them everything that had happened and sent them to Joppa. . . .
[21]Peter went down and said to the men, "I'm the one you're looking for. Why have you come?"
[22]The men replied, "We have come from Cornelius the centurion. He is a righteous and God-fearing man, who is respected by all the Jewish people. A holy angel told him to have you come to his house so that he could hear what you have to say." . . .
[30]Cornelius answered: "Four days ago I was in my house praying at this hour, at three in the afternoon. Suddenly a man in shining clothes stood before me [31]and said, 'Cornelius, God has heard your prayer and remembered your gifts to the poor. [32]Send to Joppa for Simon who is called Peter. He is a guest in the home of Simon the tanner, who lives by the sea.'"
Acts 23 [9]There was a great uproar, and some of the teachers of the law who were Pharisees stood up and argued vigorously. "We find nothing wrong with this man," they said. "What if a spirit or an angel has spoken to him?"
Acts 27 [23]"Last night an angel of the God whose I am and whom I serve stood beside me [24]and said, 'Do not be afraid, Paul. You must stand trial before Caesar; and God has graciously given you the lives of all who sail with you.'"
Rev 1 [1]The revelation of Jesus Christ, which God gave him to show his servants what must soon take place. He made it known by sending his angel to his servant John. . . .
[20]"The mystery of the seven stars that you saw in my right hand and of the seven golden lampstands is this: The seven stars are the angels of the seven churches, and the seven lampstands are the seven churches."

d) Angels Guide Believers

Acts 8 [26]Now an angel of the Lord said to Philip, "Go south to the road—the desert road—that goes down from Jerusalem to Gaza."

e) Angels Protect Believers

Ps 34 [7]The angel of the LORD encamps around those who fear him, and he delivers them.
Ps 91 [9]If you make the Most High your dwelling—even the LORD, who is my refuge—[10]then no harm will befall you, no disaster will come near your tent. [11]For he will command his angels concerning you to guard you in all your ways. . . .

f) Angels Serve Believers

Heb 1 [14]Are not all angels ministering spirits sent to serve those who will inherit salvation?

7. Angels among Unbelievers

a) Angels Carry Out Judgment

Gen 19 [12]The two men said to Lot, "Do you have anyone else here—sons-in-law, sons or daughters, or anyone else in the city who belongs to you? Get them out of here, [13]because we are going to destroy this place. The outcry to the LORD against its people is so great that he has sent us to destroy it."
Acts 12 [23]Immediately, because Herod did not give praise to God, an angel of the Lord struck him down, and he was eaten by worms and died.
Rev 16 [1]Then I heard a loud voice from the temple saying to the seven angels, "Go, pour out the seven bowls of God's wrath on the earth."
Rev 19 [17]And I saw an angel standing in the sun, who cried in a loud voice to all the birds flying in midair, "Come, gather together for the great supper of God, [18]so that you may eat the flesh of kings, generals, and mighty men, of horses and their riders, and the flesh of all people, free and slave, small and great."
See also p. 281a, Angels Will Execute Judgment

b) Angels Subdue Evil

Ps 35 [5]May they be like chaff before the wind, with the angel of the LORD driving them away; [6]may their path be dark and slippery, with the angel of the LORD pursuing them.
Matt 13 [37]He answered, "The one who sowed the good seed is the Son of Man. [38]The field is the world, and the good seed stands for the sons of the kingdom. The weeds are the sons of the evil one, [39]and the enemy who sows them is the devil. The harvest is the end of the age, and the harvesters are angels.
[40]"As the weeds are pulled up and burned in the fire, so it will be at the end of the age. [41]The Son of Man will send out his angels, and they will weed out of his kingdom everything that causes sin and all who do evil. [42]They will throw them into the fiery furnace, where there will be weeping and gnashing of teeth."
Rev 10 [1]Then I saw another mighty angel coming down from heaven. He was robed in a cloud, with a rainbow above his head; his face was like the sun, and his legs were like fiery pillars. [2]He was holding a little scroll, which lay open in his hand. He planted his right foot on the sea and his left foot on the land. . . .
[5]Then the angel I had seen standing on the sea and on the land raised his right hand to heaven. [6]And he swore by him who lives for ever and ever, who created the heavens and all that is in them, the earth and all that is in it, and the sea and all that is in it, and said, "There will be no more delay! [7]But in the days when the seventh angel is about to sound his trumpet, the mystery of God will be accomplished, just as he announced to his servants the prophets."

E. The Abode of Good Angels

1. Angels Live in God's Presence

2 Chron 18 [18]Micaiah continued, "Therefore hear the word of the LORD: I saw the LORD sitting on his throne with all the host of heaven standing on his right and on his left."
Ps 89 [7]In the council of the holy ones God is greatly feared; he is more awesome than all who surround him.
Isa 6 [1]In the year that King Uzziah died, I saw the Lord seated on a throne, high and exalted, and the train of his robe filled the temple. [2]Above him were seraphs, each with six wings: With two wings they covered their faces, with two they covered

their feet, and with two they were flying. [3]And they were calling to one another: "Holy, holy, holy is the LORD Almighty; the whole earth is full of his glory." [4]At the sound of their voices the doorposts and thresholds shook and the temple was filled with smoke.

[5]"Woe to me!" I cried. "I am ruined! For I am a man of unclean lips, and I live among a people of unclean lips, and my eyes have seen the King, the LORD Almighty."

[6]Then one of the seraphs flew to me with a live coal in his hand, which he had taken with tongs from the altar. [7]With it he touched my mouth and said, "See, this has touched your lips; your guilt is taken away and your sin atoned for."

Isa 63 [9]In all their distress he too was distressed, and the angel of his presence saved them. In his love and mercy he redeemed them; he lifted them up and carried them all the days of old.

Dan 7 [10]"A river of fire was flowing, coming out from before him. Thousands upon thousands attended him; ten thousand times ten thousand stood before him. The court was seated, and the books were opened."

Matt 18 [10]"See that you do not look down on one of these little ones. For I tell you that their angels in heaven always see the face of my Father in heaven."

Luke 1 [19]The angel answered, "I am Gabriel. I stand in the presence of God, and I have been sent to speak to you and to tell you this good news."

Rev 4 [6]Also before the throne there was what looked like a sea of glass, clear as crystal.

In the center, around the throne, were four living creatures, and they were covered with eyes, in front and in back. [7]The first living creature was like a lion, the second was like an ox, the third had a face like a man, the fourth was like a flying eagle. [8]Each of the four living creatures had six wings and was covered with eyes all around, even under his wings. Day and night they never stop saying: "Holy, holy, holy is the Lord God Almighty, who was, and is, and is to come." [9]Whenever the living creatures give glory, honor and thanks to him who sits on the throne and who lives for ever and ever, [10]the twenty-four elders fall down before him who sits on the throne, and worship him who lives for ever and ever. They lay their crowns before the throne and say: [11]"You are worthy, our Lord and God, to receive glory and honor and power, for you created all things, and by your will they were created and have their being."

2. Angels Live in Heaven

2 Chron 18 [18]Micaiah continued, "Therefore hear the word of the LORD: I saw the LORD sitting on his throne with all the host of heaven standing on his right and on his left."

Ps 148 [1]Praise the LORD. Praise the LORD from the heavens, praise him in the heights above. [2]Praise him, all his angels, praise him, all his heavenly hosts.

Dan 7 [10]"A river of fire was flowing, coming out from before him. Thousands upon thousands attended him; ten thousand times ten thousand stood before him. The court was seated, and the books were opened."

Matt 24 [36]"No one knows about that day or hour, not even the angels in heaven, nor the Son, but only the Father."

Matt 28 [2]There was a violent earthquake, for an angel of the Lord came down from heaven and, going to the tomb, rolled back the stone and sat on it.

Mark 12 [25]"When the dead rise, they will neither marry nor be given in marriage; they will be like the angels in heaven."

Luke 2 [15]When the angels had left them and gone into heaven, the shepherds said to one another, "Let's go to Bethlehem and see this thing that has happened, which the Lord has told us about."

Luke 12 [8]"I tell you, whoever acknowledges me before men, the Son of Man will also acknowledge him before the angels of God."

John 1 [51]He then added, "I tell you the truth, you shall see heaven open, and the angels of God ascending and descending on the Son of Man."

Gal 1 [8]But even if we or an angel from heaven should preach a gospel other than the one we preached to you, let him be eternally condemned!

2 Thess 1 [7]and give relief to you who are troubled, and to us as well. This will happen when the Lord Jesus is revealed from heaven in blazing fire with his powerful angels.

Heb 12 [22]But you have come to Mount Zion, to the heavenly Jerusalem, the city of the living God. You have come to thousands upon thousands of angels in joyful assembly. . . .

Rev 5 [11]Then I looked and heard the voice of many angels, numbering thousands upon thousands, and ten thousand times ten thousand. They encircled the throne and the living creatures and the elders.

Rev 12 [7]And there was war in heaven. Michael and his angels fought against the dragon, and the dragon and his angels fought back. [8]But he was not strong enough, and they lost their place in heaven. [9]The great dragon was hurled down—that ancient serpent called the devil, or Satan, who leads the whole world astray. He was hurled to the earth, and his angels with him.

F. Some Humans to Whom Good Angels Appeared

1. Abraham

Gen 18 [2]Abraham looked up and saw three men standing nearby. When he saw them, he hurried from the entrance of his tent to meet them and bowed low to the ground. . . .

[7]Then he ran to the herd and selected a choice, tender calf and gave it to a servant, who hurried to prepare it. [8]He then brought some curds and milk and the calf that had been prepared, and set these before them. While they ate, he stood near them under a tree. . . .

[16]When the men got up to leave, they looked down toward Sodom, and Abraham walked along with them to see them on their way. . . .

[22]The men turned away and went toward Sodom, but Abraham remained standing before the LORD.

2. Lot

Gen 19 [1]The two angels arrived at Sodom in the evening, and Lot was sitting in the gateway of the city. When he saw them, he got up to meet them and bowed down with his face to the ground. [2]"My lords," he said, "please turn aside to your servant's house. You can wash your feet and spend the night and then go on your way early in the morning."

"No," they answered, "we will spend the night in the square."

[3]But he insisted so strongly that they did go with him and entered his house. He prepared a meal for them, baking bread without yeast, and they ate. [4]Before they had gone to bed, all the men from every part of the city of Sodom—both young and old—surrounded the house. [5]They called to Lot, "Where are the men who came to you tonight? Bring them out to us so that we can have sex with them."

[6]Lot went outside to meet them and shut the door behind him [7]and said, "No, my friends. Don't do this wicked thing. [8]Look, I have two daughters who have never slept with a man. Let me bring them out to you, and you can do what you like with them. But don't do anything to these men, for they have come under the protection of my roof."

[9]"Get out of our way," they replied. And they said, "This fellow came here as an alien, and now he wants to play the judge! We'll treat you worse than them." They kept bringing pressure on Lot and moved forward to break down the door.

[10]But the men inside reached out and pulled Lot back into the house and shut the door. [11]Then they struck the men who were at the door of the house, young and old, with blindness so that they could not find the door.

[12]The two men said to Lot, "Do you have anyone else here—sons-in-law, sons or daughters, or anyone else in the city who belongs to you? Get them out of here, [13]because we are going to destroy this place. The outcry to the LORD against its people is so great that he has sent us to destroy it."

[14]So Lot went out and spoke to his sons-in-law, who were pledged to marry his daughters. He said, "Hurry and get out of

this place, because the LORD is about to destroy the city!" But his sons-in-law thought he was joking.

[15]With the coming of dawn, the angels urged Lot, saying, "Hurry! Take your wife and your two daughters who are here, or you will be swept away when the city is punished."

[16]When he hesitated, the men grasped his hand and the hands of his wife and of his two daughters and led them safely out of the city, for the LORD was merciful to them. [17]As soon as they had brought them out, one of them said, "Flee for your lives! Don't look back, and don't stop anywhere in the plain! Flee to the mountains or you will be swept away!"

[18]But Lot said to them, "No, my lords, please! [19]Your servant has found favor in your eyes, and you have shown great kindness to me in sparing my life. But I can't flee to the mountains; this disaster will overtake me, and I'll die. [20]Look, here is a town near enough to run to, and it is small. Let me flee to it—it is very small, isn't it? Then my life will be spared."

[21]He said to him, "Very well, I will grant this request too; I will not overthrow the town you speak of. [22]But flee there quickly, because I cannot do anything until you reach it." (That is why the town was called Zoar.)

3. Jacob

Gen 28 [12]He had a dream in which he saw a stairway resting on the earth, with its top reaching to heaven, and the angels of God were ascending and descending on it.

Gen 32 [1]Jacob also went on his way, and the angels of God met him. [2]When Jacob saw them, he said, "This is the camp of God!" So he named that place Mahanaim.

Hos 12 [4]He struggled with the angel and overcame him; he wept and begged for his favor. He found him at Bethel and talked with him there. . . .

4. Moses

Acts 7 [30]"After forty years had passed, an angel appeared to Moses in the flames of a burning bush in the desert near Mount Sinai. . . .

[35]"This is the same Moses whom they had rejected with the words, 'Who made you ruler and judge?' He was sent to be their ruler and deliverer by God himself, through the angel who appeared to him in the bush. . . . [38]He was in the assembly in the desert, with the angel who spoke to him on Mount Sinai, and with our fathers; and he received living words to pass on to us."

5. Israelites

Exod 14 [19]Then the angel of God, who had been traveling in front of Israel's army, withdrew and went behind them. The pillar of cloud also moved from in front and stood behind them. . . .

Judg 2 [1]The angel of the LORD went up from Gilgal to Bokim and said, "I brought you up out of Egypt and led you into the land that I swore to give to your forefathers. I said, 'I will never break my covenant with you, [2]and you shall not make a covenant with the people of this land, but you shall break down their altars.' Yet you have disobeyed me. Why have you done this? [3]Now therefore I tell you that I will not drive them out before you; they will be thorns in your sides and their gods will be a snare to you."

[4]When the angel of the LORD had spoken these things to all the Israelites, the people wept aloud. . . .

6. Balaam

Num 22 [31]Then the LORD opened Balaam's eyes, and he saw the angel of the LORD standing in the road with his sword drawn. So he bowed low and fell facedown.

[32]The angel of the LORD asked him, "Why have you beaten your donkey these three times? I have come here to oppose you because your path is a reckless one before me. [33]The donkey saw me and turned away from me these three times. If she had not turned away, I would certainly have killed you by now, but I would have spared her."

[34]Balaam said to the angel of the LORD, "I have sinned. I did not realize you were standing in the road to oppose me. Now if you are displeased, I will go back."

[35]The angel of the LORD said to Balaam, "Go with the men, but speak only what I tell you." So Balaam went with the princes of Balak.

7. David

2 Sam 24 [16]When the angel stretched out his hand to destroy Jerusalem, the LORD was grieved because of the calamity and said to the angel who was afflicting the people, "Enough! Withdraw your hand." The angel of the LORD was then at the threshing floor of Araunah the Jebusite.

[17]When David saw the angel who was striking down the people, he said to the LORD, "I am the one who has sinned and done wrong. These are but sheep. What have they done? Let your hand fall upon me and my family."

8. Araunah

1 Chron 21 [20]While Araunah was threshing wheat, he turned and saw the angel; his four sons who were with him hid themselves.

9. Elijah

1 Kings 19 [3]Elijah was afraid and ran for his life. When he came to Beersheba in Judah, he left his servant there, [4]while he himself went a day's journey into the desert. He came to a broom tree, sat down under it and prayed that he might die. "I have had enough, LORD," he said. "Take my life; I am no better than my ancestors." [5]Then he lay down under the tree and fell asleep.

All at once an angel touched him and said, "Get up and eat." . . .

[7]The angel of the LORD came back a second time and touched him and said, "Get up and eat, for the journey is too much for you."

10. Elisha

2 Kings 6 [16]"Don't be afraid," the prophet answered. "Those who are with us are more than those who are with them."

[17]And Elisha prayed, "O LORD, open his eyes so he may see." Then the LORD opened the servant's eyes, and he looked and saw the hills full of horses and chariots of fire all around Elisha.

11. Shadrach, Meshach, and Abednego

Dan 3 [25]He said, "Look! I see four men walking around in the fire, unbound and unharmed, and the fourth looks like a son of the gods."

[26]Nebuchadnezzar then approached the opening of the blazing furnace and shouted, "Shadrach, Meshach and Abednego, servants of the Most High God, come out! Come here!"

So Shadrach, Meshach and Abednego came out of the fire, [27]and the satraps, prefects, governors and royal advisers crowded around them. They saw that the fire had not harmed their bodies, nor was a hair of their heads singed; their robes were not scorched, and there was no smell of fire on them.

[28]Then Nebuchadnezzar said, "Praise be to the God of Shadrach, Meshach and Abednego, who has sent his angel and rescued his servants! They trusted in him and defied the king's command and were willing to give up their lives rather than serve or worship any god except their own God."

12. Nebuchadnezzar

Dan 4 [4]I, Nebuchadnezzar, was at home in my palace, contented and prosperous. . . .

[13]"In the visions I saw while lying in my bed, I looked, and there before me was a messenger, a holy one, coming down from heaven."

Dan 4 [17]"'The decision is announced by messengers, the holy ones declare the verdict, so that the living may know that the Most High is sovereign over the kingdoms of men and gives them to anyone he wishes and sets over them the lowliest of men.'"

Dan 4 [23]"You, O king, saw a messenger, a holy one, coming down from heaven and saying, 'Cut down the tree and destroy it, but leave the stump, bound with iron and bronze, in the grass of the field, while its roots remain in the ground. Let him be drenched with the dew of heaven; let him live like the wild animals, until seven times pass by for him.'"

13. Daniel

Dan 6 [22]"My God sent his angel, and he shut the mouths of the lions. They have not hurt me, because I was found innocent in his sight. Nor have I ever done any wrong before you, O king."

Dan 8 [13]Then I heard a holy one speaking, and another holy one said to him, "How long will it take for the vision to be fulfilled—the vision concerning the daily sacrifice, the rebellion that causes desolation, and the surrender of the sanctuary and of the host that will be trampled underfoot?"

Dan 8 [15]While I, Daniel, was watching the vision and trying to understand it, there before me stood one who looked like a man. [16]And I heard a man's voice from the Ulai calling, "Gabriel, tell this man the meaning of the vision."

Dan 9 [21]while I was still in prayer, Gabriel, the man I had seen in the earlier vision, came to me in swift flight about the time of the evening sacrifice. [22]He instructed me and said to me, "Daniel, I have now come to give you insight and understanding."

Dan 10 [5]I looked up and there before me was a man dressed in linen, with a belt of the finest gold around his waist. [6]His body was like chrysolite, his face like lightning, his eyes like flaming torches, his arms and legs like the gleam of burnished bronze, and his voice like the sound of a multitude.

[7]I, Daniel, was the only one who saw the vision; the men with me did not see it, but such terror overwhelmed them that they fled and hid themselves. [8]So I was left alone, gazing at this great vision; I had no strength left, my face turned deathly pale and I was helpless. [9]Then I heard him speaking, and as I listened to him, I fell into a deep sleep, my face to the ground.

[10]A hand touched me and set me trembling on my hands and knees. [11]He said, "Daniel, you who are highly esteemed, consider carefully the words I am about to speak to you, and stand up, for I have now been sent to you." And when he said this to me, I stood up trembling.

[12]Then he continued, "Do not be afraid, Daniel. Since the first day that you set your mind to gain understanding and to humble yourself before your God, your words were heard, and I have come in response to them. [13]But the prince of the Persian kingdom resisted me twenty-one days. Then Michael, one of the chief princes, came to help me, because I was detained there with the king of Persia. [14]Now I have come to explain to you what will happen to your people in the future, for the vision concerns a time yet to come."

[15]While he was saying this to me, I bowed with my face toward the ground and was speechless. [16]Then one who looked like a man touched my lips, and I opened my mouth and began to speak. I said to the one standing before me, "I am overcome with anguish because of the vision, my lord, and I am helpless. [17]How can I, your servant, talk with you, my lord? My strength is gone and I can hardly breathe."

[18]Again the one who looked like a man touched me and gave me strength. [19]"Do not be afraid, O man highly esteemed," he said. "Peace! Be strong now; be strong."

When he spoke to me, I was strengthened and said, "Speak, my lord, since you have given me strength."

[20]So he said, "Do you know why I have come to you? Soon I will return to fight against the prince of Persia, and when I go, the prince of Greece will come; [21]but first I will tell you what is written in the Book of Truth. (No one supports me against them except Michael, your prince. **11** [1]And in the first year of Darius the Mede, I took my stand to support and protect him.)"

Dan 12 [5]Then I, Daniel, looked, and there before me stood two others, one on this bank of the river and one on the opposite bank. [6]One of them said to the man clothed in linen, who was above the waters of the river, "How long will it be before these astonishing things are fulfilled?"

[7]The man clothed in linen, who was above the waters of the river, lifted his right hand and his left hand toward heaven, and I heard him swear by him who lives forever, saying, "It will be for a time, times and half a time. When the power of the holy people has been finally broken, all these things will be completed."

14. Zechariah the Prophet

Zech 2 [3]Then the angel who was speaking to me left, and another angel came to meet him. . . .

Zech 3 [1]Then he showed me Joshua the high priest standing before the angel of the LORD, and Satan standing at his right side to accuse him. [2]The LORD said to Satan, "The LORD rebuke you, Satan! The LORD, who has chosen Jerusalem, rebuke you! Is not this man a burning stick snatched from the fire?"

Zech 4 [1]Then the angel who talked with me returned and wakened me, as a man is wakened from his sleep.

Zech 5 [5]Then the angel who was speaking to me came forward and said to me, "Look up and see what this is that is appearing."

15. Zechariah the Priest

Luke 1 [11]Then an angel of the Lord appeared to him, standing at the right side of the altar of incense. [12]When Zechariah saw him, he was startled and was gripped with fear. [13]But the angel said to him: "Do not be afraid, Zechariah; your prayer has been heard. Your wife Elizabeth will bear you a son, and you are to give him the name John. [14]He will be a joy and delight to you, and many will rejoice because of his birth, [15]for he will be great in the sight of the Lord. He is never to take wine or other fermented drink, and he will be filled with the Holy Spirit even from birth. [16]Many of the people of Israel will he bring back to the Lord their God. [17]And he will go on before the Lord, in the spirit and power of Elijah, to turn the hearts of the fathers to their children and the disobedient to the wisdom of the righteous—to make ready a people prepared for the Lord."

[18]Zechariah asked the angel, "How can I be sure of this? I am an old man and my wife is well along in years."

[19]The angel answered, "I am Gabriel. I stand in the presence of God, and I have been sent to speak to you and to tell you this good news. [20]And now you will be silent and not able to speak until the day this happens, because you did not believe my words, which will come true at their proper time."

16. Mary

Luke 1 [26]In the sixth month, God sent the angel Gabriel to Nazareth, a town in Galilee, [27]to a virgin pledged to be married to a man named Joseph, a descendant of David. The virgin's name was Mary. [28]The angel went to her and said, "Greetings, you who are highly favored! The Lord is with you."

[29]Mary was greatly troubled at his words and wondered what kind of greeting this might be. [30]But the angel said to her, "Do not be afraid, Mary, you have found favor with God. [31]You will be with child and give birth to a son, and you are to give him the name Jesus. [32]He will be great and will be called the Son of the Most High. The Lord God will give him the throne of his father David, [33]and he will reign over the house of Jacob forever; his kingdom will never end."

[34]"How will this be," Mary asked the angel, "since I am a virgin?"

[35]The angel answered, "The Holy Spirit will come upon you, and the power of the Most High will overshadow you. So the holy one to be born will be called the Son of God. [36]Even Elizabeth your relative is going to have a child in her old age, and she who was said to be barren is in her sixth month. [37]For nothing is impossible with God."

[38]"I am the Lord's servant," Mary answered. "May it be to me as you have said." Then the angel left her.

17. Joseph

Matt 1 [20]But after he had considered this, an angel of the Lord appeared to him in a dream and said, "Joseph son of David, do not be afraid to take Mary home as your wife, because what is conceived in her is from the Holy Spirit."

Matt 2 [13]When they had gone, an angel of the Lord appeared to Joseph in a dream. "Get up," he said, "take the child and his mother and escape to Egypt. Stay there until I tell you, for Herod is going to search for the child to kill him."

Matt 2 [19]After Herod died, an angel of the Lord appeared in a dream to Joseph in Egypt. . . .

18. Shepherds

Luke 2 [8]And there were shepherds living out in the fields nearby, keeping watch over their flocks at night. [9]An angel of the Lord appeared to them, and the glory of the Lord shone around them, and they were terrified. [10]But the angel said to them, "Do not be afraid. I bring you good news of great joy that will be for all the people. [11]Today in the town of David a Savior has been born to you; he is Christ the Lord. [12]This will be a sign to you: You will find a baby wrapped in cloths and lying in a manger."

[13]Suddenly a great company of the heavenly host appeared with the angel, praising God and saying, [14]"Glory to God in the highest, and on earth peace to men on whom his favor rests."

[15]When the angels had left them and gone into heaven, the shepherds said to one another, "Let's go to Bethlehem and see this thing that has happened, which the Lord has told us about."

19. Jesus

Matt 4 [11]Then the devil left him, and angels came and attended him.

Luke 22 [43]An angel from heaven appeared to him and strengthened him.

20. Women at the Tomb

Matt 28 [2]There was a violent earthquake, for an angel of the Lord came down from heaven and, going to the tomb, rolled back the stone and sat on it. [3]His appearance was like lightning, and his clothes were white as snow. [4]The guards were so afraid of him that they shook and became like dead men.

[5]The angel said to the women, "Do not be afraid, for I know that you are looking for Jesus, who was crucified. [6]He is not here; he has risen, just as he said. Come and see the place where he lay."

Mark 16 [1]When the Sabbath was over, Mary Magdalene, Mary the mother of James, and Salome bought spices so that they might go to anoint Jesus' body. . . . [5]As they entered the tomb, they saw a young man dressed in a white robe sitting on the right side, and they were alarmed.

[6]"Don't be alarmed," he said. "You are looking for Jesus the Nazarene, who was crucified. He has risen! He is not here. See the place where they laid him. [7]But go, tell his disciples and Peter, 'He is going ahead of you into Galilee. There you will see him, just as he told you.'"

Luke 24 [4]While they were wondering about this, suddenly two men in clothes that gleamed like lightning stood beside them. [5]In their fright the women bowed down with their faces to the ground, but the men said to them, "Why do you look for the living among the dead? [6]He is not here; he has risen! Remember how he told you, while he was still with you in Galilee . . ."

Luke 24 [22]"In addition, some of our women amazed us. They went to the tomb early this morning [23]but didn't find his body. They came and told us that they had seen a vision of angels, who said he was alive."

John 20 [11]but Mary stood outside the tomb crying. As she wept, she bent over to look into the tomb [12]and saw two angels in white, seated where Jesus' body had been, one at the head and the other at the foot.

21. Disciples

Acts 1 [10]They were looking intently up into the sky as he was going, when suddenly two men dressed in white stood beside them. [11]"Men of Galilee," they said, "why do you stand here looking into the sky? This same Jesus, who has been taken from you into heaven, will come back in the same way you have seen him go into heaven."

Acts 5 [19]But during the night an angel of the Lord opened the doors of the jail and brought them out. [20]"Go, stand in the temple courts," he said, "and tell the people the full message of this new life."

22. Peter

Acts 12 [7]Suddenly an angel of the Lord appeared and a light shone in the cell. He struck Peter on the side and woke him up. "Quick, get up!" he said, and the chains fell off Peter's wrists.

[8]Then the angel said to him, "Put on your clothes and sandals." And Peter did so. "Wrap your cloak around you and follow me," the angel told him. [9]Peter followed him out of the prison, but he had no idea that what the angel was doing was really happening; he thought he was seeing a vision. [10]They passed the first and second guards and came to the iron gate leading to the city. It opened for them by itself, and they went through it. When they had walked the length of one street, suddenly the angel left him.

[11]Then Peter came to himself and said, "Now I know without a doubt that the Lord sent his angel and rescued me from Herod's clutches and from everything the Jewish people were anticipating."

23. John

Acts 5 [19]But during the night an angel of the Lord opened the doors of the jail and brought them out.

Rev 1 [1]The revelation of Jesus Christ, which God gave him to show his servants what must soon take place. He made it known by sending his angel to his servant John. . . .

Rev 5 [2]And I saw a mighty angel proclaiming in a loud voice, "Who is worthy to break the seals and open the scroll?"

Rev 7 [11]All the angels were standing around the throne and around the elders and the four living creatures. They fell down on their faces before the throne and worshiped God. . . .

Rev 10 [9]So I went to the angel and asked him to give me the little scroll. He said to me, "Take it and eat it. It will turn your stomach sour, but in your mouth it will be as sweet as honey."

Rev 11 [1]I was given a reed like a measuring rod and was told, "Go and measure the temple of God and the altar, and count the worshipers there."

Rev 17 [7]Then the angel said to me: "Why are you astonished? I will explain to you the mystery of the woman and of the beast she rides, which has the seven heads and ten horns."

Rev 18 [1]After this I saw another angel coming down from heaven. He had great authority, and the earth was illuminated by his splendor.

Rev 19 [9]Then the angel said to me, "Write: 'Blessed are those who are invited to the wedding supper of the Lamb!'" And he added, "These are the true words of God."

[10]At this I fell at his feet to worship him. But he said to me, "Do not do it! I am a fellow servant with you and with your brothers who hold to the testimony of Jesus. Worship God! For the testimony of Jesus is the spirit of prophecy."

Rev 22 [8]I, John, am the one who heard and saw these things. And when I had heard and seen them, I fell down to worship at the feet of the angel who had been showing them to me.

24. Philip

Acts 8 [26]Now an angel of the Lord said to Philip, "Go south to the road—the desert road—that goes down from Jerusalem to Gaza."

25. Cornelius

Acts 10 [3]One day at about three in the afternoon he had a vision. He distinctly saw an angel of God, who came to him and said, "Cornelius!" . . .

[22]The men replied, "We have come from Cornelius the centurion. He is a righteous and God-fearing man, who is respected by all the Jewish people. A holy angel told him to have you come to his house so that he could hear what you have to say." . . .

[30]Cornelius answered: "Four days ago I was in my house

praying at this hour, at three in the afternoon. Suddenly a man in shining clothes stood before me [31]and said, 'Cornelius, God has heard your prayer and remembered your gifts to the poor. [32]Send to Joppa for Simon who is called Peter. He is a guest in the home of Simon the tanner, who lives by the sea.'"
Acts 11 [13]"He told us how he had seen an angel appear in his house and say, 'Send to Joppa for Simon who is called Peter.'"

26. Paul

Acts 27 [23]"Last night an angel of the God whose I am and whom I serve stood beside me [24]and said, 'Do not be afraid, Paul. You must stand trial before Caesar; and God has graciously given you the lives of all who sail with you.'"

II Evil Angels

A. The Fallenness of Evil Angels

2 Pet 2 [4]For if God did not spare angels when they sinned, but sent them to hell, putting them into gloomy dungeons to be held for judgment . . .
Jude [6]And the angels who did not keep their positions of authority but abandoned their own home—these he has kept in darkness, bound with everlasting chains for judgment on the great Day.
Rev 12 [7]And there was war in heaven. Michael and his angels fought against the dragon, and the dragon and his angels fought back. [8]But he was not strong enough, and they lost their place in heaven. [9]The great dragon was hurled down—that ancient serpent called the devil, or Satan, who leads the whole world astray. He was hurled to the earth, and his angels with him.

B. The Work of Evil Angels

1. Evil Angels Hinder Good Angels

Dan 10 [13]"But the prince of the Persian kingdom resisted me twenty-one days. Then Michael, one of the chief princes, came to help me, because I was detained there with the king of Persia."

2. Evil Angels Oppose the People of God

Eph 6 [12]For our struggle is not against flesh and blood, but against the rulers, against the authorities, against the powers of this dark world and against the spiritual forces of evil in the heavenly realms.

3. Evil Angels Support Satan

Rev 12 [7]And there was war in heaven. Michael and his angels fought against the dragon, and the dragon and his angels fought back. [8]But he was not strong enough, and they lost their place in heaven. [9]The great dragon was hurled down—that ancient serpent called the devil, or Satan, who leads the whole world astray. He was hurled to the earth, and his angels with him.

C. The Abode of Evil Angels

1. Evil Angels Inhabit Heavenly Realms

Eph 3 [10]His intent was that now, through the church, the manifold wisdom of God should be made known to the rulers and authorities in the heavenly realms. . . .
Eph 6 [12]For our struggle is not against flesh and blood, but against the rulers, against the authorities, against the powers of this dark world and against the spiritual forces of evil in the heavenly realms.

2. Evil Angels Inhabit the Earth

Rev 9 [14]It said to the sixth angel who had the trumpet, "Release the four angels who are bound at the great river Euphrates." [15]And the four angels who had been kept ready for this very hour and day and month and year were released to kill a third of mankind. [16]The number of the mounted troops was two hundred million. I heard their number.

3. Evil Angels Inhabit the Abyss

Luke 8 [31]And they begged him repeatedly not to order them to go into the Abyss.
Rev 9 [11]They had as king over them the angel of the Abyss, whose name in Hebrew is Abaddon, and in Greek, Apollyon.

D. The Future Judgment of Evil Angels

1. Some Evil Angels Are Confined

1 Pet 3 [19]through whom also he went and preached to the spirits in prison [20]who disobeyed long ago when God waited patiently in the days of Noah while the ark was being built. In it only a few people, eight in all, were saved through water. . . .
2 Pet 2 [4]For if God did not spare angels when they sinned, but sent them to hell, putting them into gloomy dungeons to be held for judgment . . .
Jude [6]And the angels who did not keep their positions of authority but abandoned their own home—these he has kept in darkness, bound with everlasting chains for judgment on the great Day.

2. Evil Angels Are Bound during the Millennium

Isa 24 [21]In that day the LORD will punish the powers in the heavens above and the kings on the earth below. [22]They will be herded together like prisoners bound in a dungeon; they will be shut up in prison and be punished after many days. [23]The moon will be abashed, the sun ashamed; for the LORD Almighty will reign on Mount Zion and in Jerusalem, and before its elders, gloriously.
Rev 20 [1]And I saw an angel coming down out of heaven, having the key to the Abyss and holding in his hand a great chain. [2]He seized the dragon, that ancient serpent, who is the devil, or Satan, and bound him for a thousand years. [3]He threw him into the Abyss, and locked and sealed it over him, to keep him from deceiving the nations anymore until the thousand years were ended. After that, he must be set free for a short time.

3. All Evil Angels Are Condemned to the Place of Final Judgment

Matt 25 [41]"Then he will say to those on his left, 'Depart from me, you who are cursed, into the eternal fire prepared for the devil and his angels.'"
Rev 20 [7]When the thousand years are over, Satan will be released from his prison [8]and will go out to deceive the nations in the four corners of the earth—Gog and Magog—to gather them for battle. In number they are like the sand on the seashore. [9]They marched across the breadth of the earth and surrounded the camp of God's people, the city he loves. But fire came down from heaven and devoured them. [10]And the devil, who deceived them, was thrown into the lake of burning sulfur, where the beast and the false prophet had been thrown. They will be tormented day and night for ever and ever. . . . [14]Then death and Hades were thrown into the lake of fire. The lake of fire is the second death. [15]If anyone's name was not found written in the book of life, he was thrown into the lake of fire.

III Demons

A. The Nature of Demons

1. Terms Describing Demons

a) Deceiving Spirits

2 Cor 11 [13]For such men are false apostles, deceitful workmen, masquerading as apostles of Christ. [14]And no wonder, for Satan himself masquerades as an angel of light. [15]It is not surprising, then, if his servants masquerade as servants of righteousness. Their end will be what their actions deserve.

1 Tim 4 [1]The Spirit clearly says that in later times some will abandon the faith and follow deceiving spirits and things taught by demons.

b) Demons

Deut 32 [17]They sacrificed to demons, which are not God—gods they had not known, gods that recently appeared, gods your fathers did not fear.

Ps 106 [37]They sacrificed their sons and their daughters to demons.

Mark 1 [34]and Jesus healed many who had various diseases. He also drove out many demons, but he would not let the demons speak because they knew who he was.

Mark 7 [26]The woman was a Greek, born in Syrian Phoenicia. She begged Jesus to drive the demon out of her daughter. . . .

[29]Then he told her, "For such a reply, you may go; the demon has left your daughter."

[30]She went home and found her child lying on the bed, and the demon gone.

Luke 10 [17]The seventy-two returned with joy and said, "Lord, even the demons submit to us in your name."

John 10 [21]But others said, "These are not the sayings of a man possessed by a demon. Can a demon open the eyes of the blind?"

Rom 8 [38]For I am convinced that neither death nor life, neither angels nor demons, neither the present nor the future, nor any powers . . .

1 Cor 10 [20]No, but the sacrifices of pagans are offered to demons, not to God, and I do not want you to be participants with demons. [21]You cannot drink the cup of the Lord and the cup of demons too; you cannot have a part in both the Lord's table and the table of demons.

James 2 [19]You believe that there is one God. Good! Even the demons believe that—and shudder.

Rev 9 [20]The rest of mankind that were not killed by these plagues still did not repent of the work of their hands; they did not stop worshiping demons, and idols of gold, silver, bronze, stone and wood—idols that cannot see or hear or walk.

c) Evil Spirits

Matt 10 [1]He called his twelve disciples to him and gave them authority to drive out evil spirits and to heal every disease and sickness.

Matt 12 [43]"When an evil spirit comes out of a man, it goes through arid places seeking rest and does not find it. [44]Then it says, 'I will return to the house I left.' When it arrives, it finds the house unoccupied, swept clean and put in order. [45]Then it goes and takes with it seven other spirits more wicked than itself, and they go in and live there. And the final condition of that man is worse than the first. That is how it will be with this wicked generation."

Mark 1 [23]Just then a man in their synagogue who was possessed by an evil spirit cried out, [24]"What do you want with us, Jesus of Nazareth? Have you come to destroy us? I know who you are—the Holy One of God!"

[25]"Be quiet!" said Jesus sternly. "Come out of him!" [26]The evil spirit shook the man violently and came out of him with a shriek.

[27]The people were all so amazed that they asked each other, "What is this? A new teaching—and with authority! He even gives orders to evil spirits and they obey him."

Mark 3 [11]Whenever the evil spirits saw him, they fell down before him and cried out, "You are the Son of God."

Mark 7 [25]In fact, as soon as she heard about him, a woman whose little daughter was possessed by an evil spirit came and fell at his feet.

Luke 7 [21]At that very time Jesus cured many who had diseases, sicknesses and evil spirits, and gave sight to many who were blind.

Acts 5 [16]Crowds gathered also from the towns around Jerusalem, bringing their sick and those tormented by evil spirits, and all of them were healed.

Acts 8 [7]With shrieks, evil spirits came out of many, and many paralytics and cripples were healed.

Acts 19 [11]God did extraordinary miracles through Paul, [12]so that even handkerchiefs and aprons that had touched him were taken to the sick, and their illnesses were cured and the evil spirits left them.

[13]Some Jews who went around driving out evil spirits tried to invoke the name of the Lord Jesus over those who were demon-possessed. They would say, "In the name of Jesus, whom Paul preaches, I command you to come out." [14]Seven sons of Sceva, a Jewish chief priest, were doing this. [15]One day the evil spirit answered them, "Jesus I know, and I know about Paul, but who are you?" [16]Then the man who had the evil spirit jumped on them and overpowered them all. He gave them such a beating that they ran out of the house naked and bleeding.

Rev 16 [13]Then I saw three evil spirits that looked like frogs; they came out of the mouth of the dragon, out of the mouth of the beast and out of the mouth of the false prophet. [14]They are spirits of demons performing miraculous signs, and they go out to the kings of the whole world, to gather them for the battle on the great day of God Almighty.

Rev 18 [2]With a mighty voice he shouted: "Fallen! Fallen is Babylon the Great! She has become a home for demons and a haunt for every evil spirit, a haunt for every unclean and detestable bird."

d) Spirits

Matt 8 [16]When evening came, many who were demon-possessed were brought to him, and he drove out the spirits with a word and healed all the sick.

Mark 9 [17]A man in the crowd answered, "Teacher, I brought you my son, who is possessed by a spirit that has robbed him of speech. [18]Whenever it seizes him, it throws him to the ground. He foams at the mouth, gnashes his teeth and becomes rigid. I asked your disciples to drive out the spirit, but they could not." . . .

[20]So they brought him. When the spirit saw Jesus, it immediately threw the boy into a convulsion. He fell to the ground and rolled around, foaming at the mouth. . . .

[25]When Jesus saw that a crowd was running to the scene, he rebuked the evil spirit. "You deaf and mute spirit," he said, "I command you, come out of him and never enter him again."

Luke 10 [20]"However, do not rejoice that the spirits submit to you, but rejoice that your names are written in heaven."

Luke 13 [11]and a woman was there who had been crippled by a spirit for eighteen years. She was bent over and could not straighten up at all.

Acts 16 [16]Once when we were going to the place of prayer, we were met by a slave girl who had a spirit by which she predicted the future. She earned a great deal of money for her owners by fortune-telling. [17]This girl followed Paul and the rest of us, shouting, "These men are servants of the Most High God, who are telling you the way to be saved." [18]She kept this up for many days. Finally Paul became so troubled that he turned around and said to the spirit, "In the name of Jesus Christ I command you to come out of her!" At that moment the spirit left her.

2. The Qualities of Demons

a) Demons Are Immaterial

Matt 8 [16]When evening came, many who were demon-possessed were brought to him, and he drove out the spirits with a word and healed all the sick.

Matt 9 [32]While they were going out, a man who was demon-possessed and could not talk was brought to Jesus. [33]And when the demon was driven out, the man who had been mute spoke. The crowd was amazed and said, "Nothing like this has ever been seen in Israel."

Matt 12 [22]Then they brought him a demon-possessed man who was blind and mute, and Jesus healed him, so that he could both talk and see.

Mark 5 [2]When Jesus got out of the boat, a man with an evil spirit came from the tombs to meet him. . . .

[6]When he saw Jesus from a distance, he ran and fell on his knees in front of him. [7]He shouted at the top of his voice, "What do you want with me, Jesus, Son of the Most High God?

Swear to God that you won't torture me!" [8]For Jesus had said to him, "Come out of this man, you evil spirit!"

[9]Then Jesus asked him, "What is your name?"

"My name is Legion," he replied, "for we are many." [10]And he begged Jesus again and again not to send them out of the area.

[11]A large herd of pigs was feeding on the nearby hillside. [12]The demons begged Jesus, "Send us among the pigs; allow us to go into them." [13]He gave them permission, and the evil spirits came out and went into the pigs. The herd, about two thousand in number, rushed down the steep bank into the lake and were drowned.

Mark 7 [29]Then he told her, "For such a reply, you may go; the demon has left your daughter."

[30]She went home and found her child lying on the bed, and the demon gone.

Mark 9 [25]When Jesus saw that a crowd was running to the scene, he rebuked the evil spirit. "You deaf and mute spirit," he said, "I command you, come out of him and never enter him again."

Luke 10 [17]The seventy-two returned with joy and said, "Lord, even the demons submit to us in your name."

[18]He replied, "I saw Satan fall like lightning from heaven. . . . [20]However, do not rejoice that the spirits submit to you, but rejoice that your names are written in heaven."

Luke 11 [24]"When an evil spirit comes out of a man, it goes through arid places seeking rest and does not find it. Then it says, 'I will return to the house I left.' [25]When it arrives, it finds the house swept clean and put in order. [26]Then it goes and takes seven other spirits more wicked than itself, and they go in and live there. And the final condition of that man is worse than the first."

Eph 6 [12]For our struggle is not against flesh and blood, but against the rulers, against the authorities, against the powers of this dark world and against the spiritual forces of evil in the heavenly realms.

b) Demons Are Personal

(1) Demons Have Intelligence

Matt 8 [29]"What do you want with us, Son of God?" they shouted. "Have you come here to torture us before the appointed time?"

Mark 1 [24]"What do you want with us, Jesus of Nazareth? Have you come to destroy us? I know who you are—the Holy One of God!"

Mark 1 [34]and Jesus healed many who had various diseases. He also drove out many demons, but he would not let the demons speak because they knew who he was.

Mark 5 [6]When he saw Jesus from a distance, he ran and fell on his knees in front of him. [7]He shouted at the top of his voice, "What do you want with me, Jesus, Son of the Most High God? Swear to God that you won't torture me!"

Luke 4 [41]Moreover, demons came out of many people, shouting, "You are the Son of God!" But he rebuked them and would not allow them to speak, because they knew he was the Christ.

Acts 16 [16]Once when we were going to the place of prayer, we were met by a slave girl who had a spirit by which she predicted the future. She earned a great deal of money for her owners by fortune-telling.

Acts 19 [15]One day the evil spirit answered them, "Jesus I know, and I know about Paul, but who are you?"

1 Tim 4 [1]The Spirit clearly says that in later times some will abandon the faith and follow deceiving spirits and things taught by demons.

(2) Demons Have Emotion

Luke 8 [28]When he saw Jesus, he cried out and fell at his feet, shouting at the top of his voice, "What do you want with me, Jesus, Son of the Most High God? I beg you, don't torture me!"

James 2 [19]You believe that there is one God. Good! Even the demons believe that—and shudder.

(3) Demons Have a Will

Mark 1 [27]The people were all so amazed that they asked each other, "What is this? A new teaching—and with authority! He even gives orders to evil spirits and they obey him."

Luke 8 [31]And they begged him repeatedly not to order them to go into the Abyss.

[32]A large herd of pigs was feeding there on the hillside. The demons begged Jesus to let them go into them, and he gave them permission.

Luke 10 [17]The seventy-two returned with joy and said, "Lord, even the demons submit to us in your name."

c) Demons Are Powerful

Matt 8 [28]When he arrived at the other side in the region of the Gadarenes, two demon-possessed men coming from the tombs met him. They were so violent that no one could pass that way.

Mark 5 [3]This man lived in the tombs, and no one could bind him any more, not even with a chain. [4]For he had often been chained hand and foot, but he tore the chains apart and broke the irons on his feet. No one was strong enough to subdue him. . . .

[11]A large herd of pigs was feeding on the nearby hillside. [12]The demons begged Jesus, "Send us among the pigs; allow us to go into them." [13]He gave them permission, and the evil spirits came out and went into the pigs. The herd, about two thousand in number, rushed down the steep bank into the lake and were drowned.

Mark 9 [20]So they brought him. When the spirit saw Jesus, it immediately threw the boy into a convulsion. He fell to the ground and rolled around, foaming at the mouth.

[21]Jesus asked the boy's father, "How long has he been like this?"

"From childhood," he answered. [22]"It has often thrown him into fire or water to kill him. But if you can do anything, take pity on us and help us."

[23]"'If you can'?" said Jesus. "Everything is possible for him who believes."

[24]Immediately the boy's father exclaimed, "I do believe; help me overcome my unbelief!"

[25]When Jesus saw that a crowd was running to the scene, he rebuked the evil spirit. "You deaf and mute spirit," he said, "I command you, come out of him and never enter him again."

[26]The spirit shrieked, convulsed him violently and came out. The boy looked so much like a corpse that many said, "He's dead." [27]But Jesus took him by the hand and lifted him to his feet, and he stood up.

[28]After Jesus had gone indoors, his disciples asked him privately, "Why couldn't we drive it out?"

[29]He replied, "This kind can come out only by prayer."

Acts 19 [16]Then the man who had the evil spirit jumped on them and overpowered them all. He gave them such a beating that they ran out of the house naked and bleeding.

d) Demons Are Morally Depraved

Luke 7 [21]At that very time Jesus cured many who had diseases, sicknesses and evil spirits, and gave sight to many who were blind.

Luke 11 [24]"When an evil spirit comes out of a man, it goes through arid places seeking rest and does not find it. Then it says, 'I will return to the house I left.' [25]When it arrives, it finds the house swept clean and put in order. [26]Then it goes and takes seven other spirits more wicked than itself, and they go in and live there. And the final condition of that man is worse than the first."

2 Cor 11 [13]For such men are false apostles, deceitful workmen, masquerading as apostles of Christ. [14]And no wonder, for Satan himself masquerades as an angel of light. [15]It is not surprising, then, if his servants masquerade as servants of righteousness. Their end will be what their actions deserve.

1 Tim 4 [1]The Spirit clearly says that in later times some will abandon the faith and follow deceiving spirits and things taught by demons. [2]Such teachings come through hypocritical liars, whose consciences have been seared as with a hot iron. [3]They forbid people to marry and order them to abstain from certain foods, which God created to be received with thanksgiving by those who believe and who know the truth.

Rev 18 [2]With a mighty voice he shouted: "Fallen! Fallen is Babylon the Great! She has become a home for demons and a haunt for every evil spirit, a haunt for every unclean and detestable bird."

3. The Activities of Demons

a) Demons Communicate with Mankind

Acts 16 [16]Once when we were going to the place of prayer, we were met by a slave girl who had a spirit by which she predicted the future. She earned a great deal of money for her owners by fortune-telling.

b) Demons Desire to Hurt People

See Possession by Demons

c) Demons Lead People to Evil

1 Sam 18 [10]The next day an evil spirit from God came forcefully upon Saul. He was prophesying in his house, while David was playing the harp, as he usually did. Saul had a spear in his hand [11]and he hurled it, saying to himself, "I'll pin David to the wall." But David eluded him twice.
Ps 106 [37]They sacrificed their sons and their daughters to demons.
1 Cor 10 [20]No, but the sacrifices of pagans are offered to demons, not to God, and I do not want you to be participants with demons. [21]You cannot drink the cup of the Lord and the cup of demons too; you cannot have a part in both the Lord's table and the table of demons.
1 Tim 4 [1]The Spirit clearly says that in later times some will abandon the faith and follow deceiving spirits and things taught by demons. [2]Such teachings come through hypocritical liars, whose consciences have been seared as with a hot iron.
James 3 [14]But if you harbor bitter envy and selfish ambition in your hearts, do not boast about it or deny the truth. [15]Such "wisdom" does not come down from heaven but is earthly, unspiritual, of the devil.
Rev 9 [20]The rest of mankind that were not killed by these plagues still did not repent of the work of their hands; they did not stop worshiping demons, and idols of gold, silver, bronze, stone and wood—idols that cannot see or hear or walk. [21]Nor did they repent of their murders, their magic arts, their sexual immorality or their thefts.

d) Demons Work Miracles

Rev 16 [13]Then I saw three evil spirits that looked like frogs; they came out of the mouth of the dragon, out of the mouth of the beast and out of the mouth of the false prophet. [14]They are spirits of demons performing miraculous signs, and they go out to the kings of the whole world, to gather them for the battle on the great day of God Almighty.

4. The Relation of Demons to Christ

a) Demons Fear Christ

Mark 5 [7]He shouted at the top of his voice, "What do you want with me, Jesus, Son of the Most High God? Swear to God that you won't torture me!"
Luke 8 [31]And they begged him repeatedly not to order them to go into the Abyss.

b) Demons Obey Christ

Mark 1 [23]Just then a man in their synagogue who was possessed by an evil spirit cried out, [24]"What do you want with us, Jesus of Nazareth? Have you come to destroy us? I know who you are—the Holy One of God!"

[25]"Be quiet!" said Jesus sternly. "Come out of him!" [26]The evil spirit shook the man violently and came out of him with a shriek.

[27]The people were all so amazed that they asked each other, "What is this? A new teaching—and with authority! He even gives orders to evil spirits and they obey him."
Mark 1 [32]That evening after sunset the people brought to Jesus all the sick and demon-possessed. [33]The whole town gathered at the door, [34]and Jesus healed many who had various diseases. He also drove out many demons, but he would not let the demons speak because they knew who he was.
Mark 7 [25]In fact, as soon as she heard about him, a woman whose little daughter was possessed by an evil spirit came and fell at his feet. [26]The woman was a Greek, born in Syrian Phoenicia. She begged Jesus to drive the demon out of her daughter.

[27]"First let the children eat all they want," he told her, "for it is not right to take the children's bread and toss it to their dogs."

[28]"Yes, Lord," she replied, "but even the dogs under the table eat the children's crumbs."

[29]Then he told her, "For such a reply, you may go; the demon has left your daughter."

[30]She went home and found her child lying on the bed, and the demon gone.
Mark 9 [25]When Jesus saw that a crowd was running to the scene, he rebuked the evil spirit. "You deaf and mute spirit," he said, "I command you, come out of him and never enter him again."

[26]The spirit shrieked, convulsed him violently and came out. The boy looked so much like a corpse that many said, "He's dead."
Acts 16 [18]She kept this up for many days. Finally Paul became so troubled that he turned around and said to the spirit, "In the name of Jesus Christ I command you to come out of her!" At that moment the spirit left her.

c) Demons Testify to Christ

Matt 8 [29]"What do you want with us, Son of God?" they shouted. "Have you come here to torture us before the appointed time?"
Mark 1 [23]Just then a man in their synagogue who was possessed by an evil spirit cried out, [24]"What do you want with us, Jesus of Nazareth? Have you come to destroy us? I know who you are—the Holy One of God!"
Mark 3 [11]Whenever the evil spirits saw him, they fell down before him and cried out, "You are the Son of God."
Acts 16 [16]Once when we were going to the place of prayer, we were met by a slave girl who had a spirit by which she predicted the future. She earned a great deal of money for her owners by fortune-telling. [17]This girl followed Paul and the rest of us, shouting, "These men are servants of the Most High God, who are telling you the way to be saved."
Acts 19 [15]One day the evil spirit answered them, "Jesus I know, and I know about Paul, but who are you?"

B. Possession by Demons

1. Description of Demon Possession

a) Indwelling and Control by Spiritual Beings

1 Sam 16 [14]Now the Spirit of the LORD had departed from Saul, and an evil spirit from the LORD tormented him.

[15]Saul's attendants said to him, "See, an evil spirit from God is tormenting you. [16]Let our lord command his servants here to search for someone who can play the harp. He will play when the evil spirit from God comes upon you, and you will feel better." . . .

[23]Whenever the spirit from God came upon Saul, David would take his harp and play. Then relief would come to Saul; he would feel better, and the evil spirit would leave him.
1 Sam 18 [10]The next day an evil spirit from God came forcefully upon Saul. He was prophesying in his house, while David was playing the harp, as he usually did. Saul had a spear in his hand [11]and he hurled it, saying to himself, "I'll pin David to the wall." But David eluded him twice.
Matt 9 [32]While they were going out, a man who was demon-possessed and could not talk was brought to Jesus.
Matt 12 [43]"When an evil spirit comes out of a man, it goes through arid places seeking rest and does not find it. [44]Then it says, 'I will return to the house I left.' When it arrives, it finds the house unoccupied, swept clean and put in order. [45]Then it goes and takes with it seven other spirits more wicked than itself, and they go in and live there. And the final condition of that man is worse than the first. That is how it will be with this wicked generation."
Mark 7 [25]In fact, as soon as she heard about him, a woman whose little daughter was possessed by an evil spirit came and fell at his feet. [26]The woman was a Greek, born in Syrian Phoenicia. She begged Jesus to drive the demon out of her daughter.
Mark 9 [17]A man in the crowd answered, "Teacher, I brought

you my son, who is possessed by a spirit that has robbed him of speech. 18Whenever it seizes him, it throws him to the ground. He foams at the mouth, gnashes his teeth and becomes rigid. I asked your disciples to drive out the spirit, but they could not."

19"O unbelieving generation," Jesus replied, "how long shall I stay with you? How long shall I put up with you? Bring the boy to me."

20So they brought him. When the spirit saw Jesus, it immediately threw the boy into a convulsion. He fell to the ground and rolled around, foaming at the mouth.

21Jesus asked the boy's father, "How long has he been like this?"

"From childhood," he answered. 22"It has often thrown him into fire or water to kill him. But if you can do anything, take pity on us and help us."

23"'If you can'?" said Jesus. "Everything is possible for him who believes."

24Immediately the boy's father exclaimed, "I do believe; help me overcome my unbelief!"

25When Jesus saw that a crowd was running to the scene, he rebuked the evil spirit. "You deaf and mute spirit," he said, "I command you, come out of him and never enter him again."

26The spirit shrieked, convulsed him violently and came out. The boy looked so much like a corpse that many said, "He's dead." 27But Jesus took him by the hand and lifted him to his feet, and he stood up.

28After Jesus had gone indoors, his disciples asked him privately, "Why couldn't we drive it out?"

29He replied, "This kind can come out only by prayer."

Luke 4 33In the synagogue there was a man possessed by a demon, an evil spirit. He cried out at the top of his voice, 34"Ha! What do you want with us, Jesus of Nazareth? Have you come to destroy us? I know who you are—the Holy One of God!"

Luke 8 27When Jesus stepped ashore, he was met by a demon-possessed man from the town. For a long time this man had not worn clothes or lived in a house, but had lived in the tombs. 28When he saw Jesus, he cried out and fell at his feet, shouting at the top of his voice, "What do you want with me, Jesus, Son of the Most High God? I beg you, don't torture me!" 29For Jesus had commanded the evil spirit to come out of the man. Many times it had seized him, and though he was chained hand and foot and kept under guard, he had broken his chains and had been driven by the demon into solitary places.

30Jesus asked him, "What is your name?"

"Legion," he replied, because many demons had gone into him. 31And they begged him repeatedly not to order them to go into the Abyss.

32A large herd of pigs was feeding there on the hillside. The demons begged Jesus to let them go into them, and he gave them permission. 33When the demons came out of the man, they went into the pigs, and the herd rushed down the steep bank into the lake and was drowned.

Acts 16 16Once when we were going to the place of prayer, we were met by a slave girl who had a spirit by which she predicted the future. She earned a great deal of money for her owners by fortune-telling. . . . 18She kept this up for many days. Finally Paul became so troubled that he turned around and said to the spirit, "In the name of Jesus Christ I command you to come out of her!" At that moment the spirit left her.

Acts 19 13Some Jews who went around driving out evil spirits tried to invoke the name of the Lord Jesus over those who were demon-possessed. They would say, "In the name of Jesus, whom Paul preaches, I command you to come out." 14Seven sons of Sceva, a Jewish chief priest, were doing this. 15One day the evil spirit answered them, "Jesus I know, and I know about Paul, but who are you?" 16Then the man who had the evil spirit jumped on them and overpowered them all. He gave them such a beating that they ran out of the house naked and bleeding.

b) Never Complete in the Believer

Col 1 13For he has rescued us from the dominion of darkness and brought us into the kingdom of the Son he loves, 14in whom we have redemption, the forgiveness of sins.

1 John 5 18We know that anyone born of God does not continue to sin; the one who was born of God keeps him safe, and the evil one cannot harm him.

2. Results of Demon Possession

a) Destructive Presence

Mark 5 5Night and day among the tombs and in the hills he would cry out and cut himself with stones.

Mark 9 17A man in the crowd answered, "Teacher, I brought you my son, who is possessed by a spirit that has robbed him of speech. 18Whenever it seizes him, it throws him to the ground. He foams at the mouth, gnashes his teeth and becomes rigid. I asked your disciples to drive out the spirit, but they could not. . . . 22It has often thrown him into fire or water to kill him. But if you can do anything, take pity on us and help us." . . .

26The spirit shrieked, convulsed him violently and came out. The boy looked so much like a corpse that many said, "He's dead."

Luke 4 35"Be quiet!" Jesus said sternly. "Come out of him!" Then the demon threw the man down before them all and came out without injuring him.

b) Increased Strength

Mark 5 2When Jesus got out of the boat, a man with an evil spirit came from the tombs to meet him. 3This man lived in the tombs, and no one could bind him any more, not even with a chain. 4For he had often been chained hand and foot, but he tore the chains apart and broke the irons on his feet. No one was strong enough to subdue him.

Acts 19 16Then the man who had the evil spirit jumped on them and overpowered them all. He gave them such a beating that they ran out of the house naked and bleeding.

c) Mental Disturbance

1 Sam 16 14Now the Spirit of the LORD had departed from Saul, and an evil spirit from the LORD tormented him.

Luke 8 27When Jesus stepped ashore, he was met by a demon-possessed man from the town. For a long time this man had not worn clothes or lived in a house, but had lived in the tombs. . . . 29For Jesus had commanded the evil spirit to come out of the man. Many times it had seized him, and though he was chained hand and foot and kept under guard, he had broken his chains and had been driven by the demon into solitary places.

d) Physical Harm

Matt 9 32While they were going out, a man who was demon-possessed and could not talk was brought to Jesus. 33And when the demon was driven out, the man who had been mute spoke. The crowd was amazed and said, "Nothing like this has ever been seen in Israel."

Matt 12 22Then they brought him a demon-possessed man who was blind and mute, and Jesus healed him, so that he could both talk and see.

Matt 15 22A Canaanite woman from that vicinity came to him, crying out, "Lord, Son of David, have mercy on me! My daughter is suffering terribly from demon-possession."

Matt 17 15"Lord, have mercy on my son," he said. "He has seizures and is suffering greatly. He often falls into the fire or into the water." . . . 18Jesus rebuked the demon, and it came out of the boy, and he was healed from that moment.

Mark 9 17A man in the crowd answered, "Teacher, I brought you my son, who is possessed by a spirit that has robbed him of speech." . . .

20So they brought him. When the spirit saw Jesus, it immediately threw the boy into a convulsion. He fell to the ground and rolled around, foaming at the mouth.

Luke 11 14Jesus was driving out a demon that was mute. When the demon left, the man who had been mute spoke, and the crowd was amazed.

e) Violence

1 Sam 18 10The next day an evil spirit from God came forcefully upon Saul. He was prophesying in his house, while David was playing the harp, as he usually did. Saul had a spear in his

hand [11]and he hurled it, saying to himself, "I'll pin David to the wall." But David eluded him twice.
Matt 8 [28]When he arrived at the other side in the region of the Gadarenes, two demon-possessed men coming from the tombs met him. They were so violent that no one could pass that way.
Acts 19 [16]Then the man who had the evil spirit jumped on them and overpowered them all. He gave them such a beating that they ran out of the house naked and bleeding.

f) Recognition as Such by Others

Matt 9 [33]And when the demon was driven out, the man who had been mute spoke. The crowd was amazed and said, "Nothing like this has ever been seen in Israel."

[34]But the Pharisees said, "It is by the prince of demons that he drives out demons."
Mark 7 [25]In fact, as soon as she heard about him, a woman whose little daughter was possessed by an evil spirit came and fell at his feet. [26]The woman was a Greek, born in Syrian Phoenicia. She begged Jesus to drive the demon out of her daughter.
Mark 9 [17]A man in the crowd answered, "Teacher, I brought you my son, who is possessed by a spirit that has robbed him of speech." . . .

[21]Jesus asked the boy's father, "How long has he been like this?"

"From childhood," he answered.
Luke 8 [34]When those tending the pigs saw what had happened, they ran off and reported this in the town and countryside, [35]and the people went out to see what had happened. When they came to Jesus, they found the man from whom the demons had gone out, sitting at Jesus' feet, dressed and in his right mind; and they were afraid. [36]Those who had seen it told the people how the demon-possessed man had been cured.
Acts 16 [16]Once when we were going to the place of prayer, we were met by a slave girl who had a spirit by which she predicted the future. She earned a great deal of money for her owners by fortune-telling. . . . [18]She kept this up for many days. Finally Paul became so troubled that he turned around and said to the spirit, "In the name of Jesus Christ I command you to come out of her!" At that moment the spirit left her.

[19]When the owners of the slave girl realized that their hope of making money was gone, they seized Paul and Silas and dragged them into the marketplace to face the authorities.
Acts 19 [15]One day the evil spirit answered them, "Jesus I know, and I know about Paul, but who are you?" [16]Then the man who had the evil spirit jumped on them and overpowered them all. He gave them such a beating that they ran out of the house naked and bleeding.

[17]When this became known to the Jews and Greeks living in Ephesus, they were all seized with fear, and the name of the Lord Jesus was held in high honor.

C. The Exorcism of Demons

1. The Expulsion of Demons

a) Jesus Expelled Demons

(1) He Expelled Them by Direct Command

Matt 8 [16]When evening came, many who were demon-possessed were brought to him, and he drove out the spirits with a word and healed all the sick.
Mark 1 [34]and Jesus healed many who had various diseases. He also drove out many demons, but he would not let the demons speak because they knew who he was.
Mark 9 [25]When Jesus saw that a crowd was running to the scene, he rebuked the evil spirit. "You deaf and mute spirit," he said, "I command you, come out of him and never enter him again."
Luke 4 [33]In the synagogue there was a man possessed by a demon, an evil spirit. He cried out at the top of his voice, [34]"Ha! What do you want with us, Jesus of Nazareth? Have you come to destroy us? I know who you are—the Holy One of God!"

[35]"Be quiet!" Jesus said sternly. "Come out of him!" Then the demon threw the man down before them all and came out without injuring him.

(2) He Expelled Them by Pronouncement

Matt 15 [22]A Canaanite woman from that vicinity came to him, crying out, "Lord, Son of David, have mercy on me! My daughter is suffering terribly from demon-possession."

[23]Jesus did not answer a word. So his disciples came to him and urged him, "Send her away, for she keeps crying out after us."

[24]He answered, "I was sent only to the lost sheep of Israel."

[25]The woman came and knelt before him. "Lord, help me!" she said.

[26]He replied, "It is not right to take the children's bread and toss it to their dogs."

[27]"Yes, Lord," she said, "but even the dogs eat the crumbs that fall from their masters' table."

[28]Then Jesus answered, "Woman, you have great faith! Your request is granted." And her daughter was healed from that very hour.

(3) He Expelled Them by Concession

Mark 5 [6]When he saw Jesus from a distance, he ran and fell on his knees in front of him. [7]He shouted at the top of his voice, "What do you want with me, Jesus, Son of the Most High God? Swear to God that you won't torture me!" [8]For Jesus had said to him, "Come out of this man, you evil spirit!"

[9]Then Jesus asked him, "What is your name?"

"My name is Legion," he replied, "for we are many." [10]And he begged Jesus again and again not to send them out of the area.

[11]A large herd of pigs was feeding on the nearby hillside. [12]The demons begged Jesus, "Send us among the pigs; allow us to go into them." [13]He gave them permission, and the evil spirits came out and went into the pigs. The herd, about two thousand in number, rushed down the steep bank into the lake and were drowned.

b) Jesus' Followers Expelled Demons

(1) They Had Been Given Jesus' Authority

Mark 3 [14]He appointed twelve—designating them apostles—that they might be with him and that he might send them out to preach [15]and to have authority to drive out demons.
Mark 6 [7]Calling the Twelve to him, he sent them out two by two and gave them authority over evil spirits. . . . [13]They drove out many demons and anointed many sick people with oil and healed them.
Luke 9 [1]When Jesus had called the Twelve together, he gave them power and authority to drive out all demons and to cure diseases. . . .

(2) They Exorcised Demons in Jesus' Name

Matt 7 [22]"Many will say to me on that day, 'Lord, Lord, did we not prophesy in your name, and in your name drive out demons and perform many miracles?'"
Mark 9 [38]"Teacher," said John, "we saw a man driving out demons in your name and we told him to stop, because he was not one of us."

[39]"Do not stop him," Jesus said. "No one who does a miracle in my name can in the next moment say anything bad about me, [40]for whoever is not against us is for us."
Mark 16 [17]"And these signs will accompany those who believe: In my name they will drive out demons; they will speak in new tongues. . . ."
Luke 10 [17]The seventy-two returned with joy and said, "Lord, even the demons submit to us in your name."

[18]He replied, "I saw Satan fall like lightning from heaven. [19]I have given you authority to trample on snakes and scorpions and to overcome all the power of the enemy; nothing will harm you. [20]However, do not rejoice that the spirits submit to you, but rejoice that your names are written in heaven."
Acts 5 [15]As a result, people brought the sick into the streets and laid them on beds and mats so that at least Peter's shadow might fall on some of them as he passed by. [16]Crowds gathered also from the towns around Jerusalem, bringing their sick and those tormented by evil spirits, and all of them were healed.
Acts 8 [5]Philip went down to a city in Samaria and proclaimed the Christ there. . . . [7]With shrieks, evil spirits came out of many, and many paralytics and cripples were healed.

Acts 16 [16]Once when we were going to the place of prayer, we were met by a slave girl who had a spirit by which she predicted the future. She earned a great deal of money for her owners by fortune-telling. [17]This girl followed Paul and the rest of us, shouting, "These men are servants of the Most High God, who are telling you the way to be saved." [18]She kept this up for many days. Finally Paul became so troubled that he turned around and said to the spirit, "In the name of Jesus Christ I command you to come out of her!" At that moment the spirit left her.
Acts 19 [11]God did extraordinary miracles through Paul, [12]so that even handkerchiefs and aprons that had touched him were taken to the sick, and their illnesses were cured and the evil spirits left them.

[13]Some Jews who went around driving out evil spirits tried to invoke the name of the Lord Jesus over those who were demon-possessed. They would say, "In the name of Jesus, whom Paul preaches, I command you to come out."

2. The Results of Exorcism

a) Complete Healing

Matt 9 [33]And when the demon was driven out, the man who had been mute spoke. The crowd was amazed and said, "Nothing like this has ever been seen in Israel."
Matt 12 [22]Then they brought him a demon-possessed man who was blind and mute, and Jesus healed him, so that he could both talk and see.
Matt 15 [22]A Canaanite woman from that vicinity came to him, crying out, "Lord, Son of David, have mercy on me! My daughter is suffering terribly from demon-possession." . . .

[28]Then Jesus answered, "Woman, you have great faith! Your request is granted." And her daughter was healed from that very hour.
Matt 17 [18]Jesus rebuked the demon, and it came out of the boy, and he was healed from that moment.
Luke 6 [18]who had come to hear him and to be healed of their diseases. Those troubled by evil spirits were cured. . . .
Luke 8 [35]and the people went out to see what had happened. When they came to Jesus, they found the man from whom the demons had gone out, sitting at Jesus' feet, dressed and in his right mind; and they were afraid.
Luke 11 [14]Jesus was driving out a demon that was mute. When the demon left, the man who had been mute spoke, and the crowd was amazed.

b) Departure of Demons

Mark 7 [30]She went home and found her child lying on the bed, and the demon gone.
Mark 9 [26]The spirit shrieked, convulsed him violently and came out. The boy looked so much like a corpse that many said, "He's dead."
Luke 8 [2]and also some women who had been cured of evil spirits and diseases: Mary (called Magdalene) from whom seven demons had come out . . .
Acts 16 [18]She kept this up for many days. Finally Paul became so troubled that he turned around and said to the spirit, "In the name of Jesus Christ I command you to come out of her!" At that moment the spirit left her.

c) Spiritual Consciousness

Luke 8 [38]The man from whom the demons had gone out begged to go with him, but Jesus sent him away, saying, [39]"Return home and tell how much God has done for you." So the man went away and told all over town how much Jesus had done for him.

3. The Reactions to Exorcism

a) Amazement

Matt 9 [33]And when the demon was driven out, the man who had been mute spoke. The crowd was amazed and said, "Nothing like this has ever been seen in Israel."
Matt 12 [22]Then they brought him a demon-possessed man who was blind and mute, and Jesus healed him, so that he could both talk and see. [23]All the people were astonished and said, "Could this be the Son of David?"
Luke 4 [36]All the people were amazed and said to each other, "What is this teaching? With authority and power he gives orders to evil spirits and they come out!"
Luke 9 [42]Even while the boy was coming, the demon threw him to the ground in a convulsion. But Jesus rebuked the evil spirit, healed the boy and gave him back to his father. [43]And they were all amazed at the greatness of God.

While everyone was marveling at all that Jesus did, he said to his disciples . . .

b) Anger

Acts 16 [16]Once when we were going to the place of prayer, we were met by a slave girl who had a spirit by which she predicted the future. She earned a great deal of money for her owners by fortune-telling. . . . [18]She kept this up for many days. Finally Paul became so troubled that he turned around and said to the spirit, "In the name of Jesus Christ I command you to come out of her!" At that moment the spirit left her.

[19]When the owners of the slave girl realized that their hope of making money was gone, they seized Paul and Silas and dragged them into the marketplace to face the authorities. [20]They brought them before the magistrates and said, "These men are Jews, and are throwing our city into an uproar [21]by advocating customs unlawful for us Romans to accept or practice."

[22]The crowd joined in the attack against Paul and Silas, and the magistrates ordered them to be stripped and beaten. [23]After they had been severely flogged, they were thrown into prison, and the jailer was commanded to guard them carefully. [24]Upon receiving such orders, he put them in the inner cell and fastened their feet in the stocks.

c) Fear and Respect toward God

Luke 8 [36]Those who had seen it told the people how the demon-possessed man had been cured. [37]Then all the people of the region of the Gerasenes asked Jesus to leave them, because they were overcome with fear. So he got into the boat and left.

D. The Proper Attitude toward Demons

1. Believers Must Keep God Foremost

1 Cor 10 [20]No, but the sacrifices of pagans are offered to demons, not to God, and I do not want you to be participants with demons. [21]You cannot drink the cup of the Lord and the cup of demons too; you cannot have a part in both the Lord's table and the table of demons.

2. Believers Must Depend on Christ

Rom 8 [37]No, in all these things we are more than conquerors through him who loved us. [38]For I am convinced that neither death nor life, neither angels nor demons, neither the present nor the future, nor any powers, [39]neither height nor depth, nor anything else in all creation, will be able to separate us from the love of God that is in Christ Jesus our Lord.

3. Believers Must Not Hold the Demonic Realm in Contempt

Jude [8]In the very same way, these dreamers pollute their own bodies, reject authority and slander celestial beings. [9]But even the archangel Michael, when he was disputing with the devil about the body of Moses, did not dare to bring a slanderous accusation against him, but said, "The Lord rebuke you!"

4. Believers Must Beware of the Empty Soul

Matt 12 [43]"When an evil spirit comes out of a man, it goes through arid places seeking rest and does not find it. [44]Then it says, 'I will return to the house I left.' When it arrives, it finds the house unoccupied, swept clean and put in order. [45]Then it goes and takes with it seven other spirits more wicked than itself, and they go in and live there. And the final condition of that man is worse than the first. That is how it will be with this wicked generation."

5. Believers Must Not Participate in Spiritism (Even to Refute It)

Lev 20 [25]"'You must therefore make a distinction between clean and unclean animals and between unclean and clean birds. Do not defile yourselves by any animal or bird or anything that moves along the ground—those which I have set apart as unclean for you. [26]You are to be holy to me because I, the LORD, am holy, and I have set you apart from the nations to be my own.

[27]"'A man or woman who is a medium or spiritist among you must be put to death. You are to stone them; their blood will be on their own heads.'"

Deut 18 [10]Let no one be found among you who sacrifices his son or daughter in the fire, who practices divination or sorcery, interprets omens, engages in witchcraft, [11]or casts spells, or who is a medium or spiritist or who consults the dead. [12]Anyone who does these things is detestable to the LORD, and because of these detestable practices the LORD your God will drive out those nations before you. [13]You must be blameless before the LORD your God.

1 Chron 10 [13]Saul died because he was unfaithful to the LORD; he did not keep the word of the LORD and even consulted a medium for guidance, [14]and did not inquire of the LORD. So the LORD put him to death and turned the kingdom over to David son of Jesse.

Isa 8 [19]When men tell you to consult mediums and spiritists, who whisper and mutter, should not a people inquire of their God? Why consult the dead on behalf of the living? [20]To the law and to the testimony! If they do not speak according to this word, they have no light of dawn.

6. Believers Must Avail Themselves of Spiritual Provisions

Eph 6 [10]Finally, be strong in the Lord and in his mighty power. [11]Put on the full armor of God so that you can take your stand against the devil's schemes. [12]For our struggle is not against flesh and blood, but against the rulers, against the authorities, against the powers of this dark world and against the spiritual forces of evil in the heavenly realms. [13]Therefore put on the full armor of God, so that when the day of evil comes, you may be able to stand your ground, and after you have done everything, to stand. [14]Stand firm then, with the belt of truth buckled around your waist, with the breastplate of righteousness in place, [15]and with your feet fitted with the readiness that comes from the gospel of peace. [16]In addition to all this, take up the shield of faith, with which you can extinguish all the flaming arrows of the evil one. [17]Take the helmet of salvation and the sword of the Spirit, which is the word of God. [18]And pray in the Spirit on all occasions with all kinds of prayers and requests. With this in mind, be alert and always keep on praying for all the saints.

IV
Other Supernatural Beings

A. Authorities

1 Cor 15 [24]Then the end will come, when he hands over the kingdom to God the Father after he has destroyed all dominion, authority and power.

Eph 6 [12]For our struggle is not against flesh and blood, but against the rulers, against the authorities, against the powers of this dark world and against the spiritual forces of evil in the heavenly realms.

Col 2 [15]And having disarmed the powers and authorities, he made a public spectacle of them, triumphing over them by the cross.

1 Pet 3 [22]who has gone into heaven and is at God's right hand—with angels, authorities and powers in submission to him.

B. Dominion

1 Cor 15 [24]Then the end will come, when he hands over the kingdom to God the Father after he has destroyed all dominion, authority and power.

C. Kings

Dan 10 [13]"But the prince of the Persian kingdom resisted me twenty-one days. Then Michael, one of the chief princes, came to help me, because I was detained there with the king of Persia."

D. Powers

Rom 8 [38]For I am convinced that neither death nor life, neither angels nor demons, neither the present nor the future, nor any powers . . .

1 Cor 15 [24]Then the end will come, when he hands over the kingdom to God the Father after he has destroyed all dominion, authority and power.

Col 2 [15]And having disarmed the powers and authorities, he made a public spectacle of them, triumphing over them by the cross.

1 Pet 3 [22]who has gone into heaven and is at God's right hand—with angels, authorities and powers in submission to him.

E. Powers of This Dark World

Eph 6 [12]For our struggle is not against flesh and blood, but against the rulers, against the authorities, against the powers of this dark world and against the spiritual forces of evil in the heavenly realms.

F. Princes

Dan 10 [13]"But the prince of the Persian kingdom resisted me twenty-one days. Then Michael, one of the chief princes, came to help me, because I was detained there with the king of Persia."

Dan 10 [20]So he said, "Do you know why I have come to you? Soon I will return to fight against the prince of Persia, and when I go, the prince of Greece will come. . . ."

G. Rulers

Eph 6 [12]For our struggle is not against flesh and blood, but against the rulers, against the authorities, against the powers of this dark world and against the spiritual forces of evil in the heavenly realms.

H. Spiritual Forces of Evil

Eph 6 [12]For our struggle is not against flesh and blood, but against the rulers, against the authorities, against the powers of this dark world and against the spiritual forces of evil in the heavenly realms.

V
Satan

A. Names of Satan

1. Abaddon

Rev 9 [11]They had as king over them the angel of the Abyss, whose name in Hebrew is Abaddon, and in Greek, Apollyon.

2. Accuser of Our Brothers

Rev 12 [10]Then I heard a loud voice in heaven say: "Now have come the salvation and the power and the kingdom of our God, and the authority of his Christ. For the accuser of our brothers, who accuses them before our God day and night, has been hurled down."

3. Angel of the Abyss

Rev 9 [11]They had as king over them the angel of the Abyss, whose name in Hebrew is Abaddon, and in Greek, Apollyon.

4. Apollyon

Rev 9 [11]They had as king over them the angel of the Abyss, whose name in Hebrew is Abaddon, and in Greek, Apollyon.

5. Beelzebub

Matt 12 [24]But when the Pharisees heard this, they said, "It is only by Beelzebub, the prince of demons, that this fellow drives out demons."
Mark 3 [22]And the teachers of the law who came down from Jerusalem said, "He is possessed by Beelzebub! By the prince of demons he is driving out demons."
Luke 11 [18]"If Satan is divided against himself, how can his kingdom stand? I say this because you claim that I drive out demons by Beelzebub. [19]Now if I drive out demons by Beelzebub, by whom do your followers drive them out? So then, they will be your judges."

6. Belial

2 Cor 6 [15]What harmony is there between Christ and Belial? What does a believer have in common with an unbeliever?

7. Devil

Matt 4 [1]Then Jesus was led by the Spirit into the desert to be tempted by the devil. . . .

[5]Then the devil took him to the holy city and had him stand on the highest point of the temple. . . .

[8]Again, the devil took him to a very high mountain and showed him all the kingdoms of the world and their splendor. . . .

[11]Then the devil left him, and angels came and attended him.
Matt 25 [41]"Then he will say to those on his left, 'Depart from me, you who are cursed, into the eternal fire prepared for the devil and his angels.'"
Luke 8 [12]"Those along the path are the ones who hear, and then the devil comes and takes away the word from their hearts, so that they may not believe and be saved."
John 13 [2]The evening meal was being served, and the devil had already prompted Judas Iscariot, son of Simon, to betray Jesus.
Acts 10 [38]". . . how God anointed Jesus of Nazareth with the Holy Spirit and power, and how he went around doing good and healing all who were under the power of the devil, because God was with him."
Acts 13 [10]"You are a child of the devil and an enemy of everything that is right! You are full of all kinds of deceit and trickery. Will you never stop perverting the right ways of the Lord?"
Eph 4 [27]and do not give the devil a foothold.
Eph 6 [11]Put on the full armor of God so that you can take your stand against the devil's schemes.
1 Tim 3 [6]He must not be a recent convert, or he may become conceited and fall under the same judgment as the devil. [7]He must also have a good reputation with outsiders, so that he will not fall into disgrace and into the devil's trap.
2 Tim 2 [26]and that they will come to their senses and escape from the trap of the devil, who has taken them captive to do his will.
Heb 2 [14]Since the children have flesh and blood, he too shared in their humanity so that by his death he might destroy him who holds the power of death—that is, the devil. . . .
James 4 [7]Submit yourselves, then, to God. Resist the devil, and he will flee from you.
1 Pet 5 [8]Be self-controlled and alert. Your enemy the devil prowls around like a roaring lion looking for someone to devour.
1 John 3 [8]He who does what is sinful is of the devil, because the devil has been sinning from the beginning. The reason the Son of God appeared was to destroy the devil's work. . . . [10]This is how we know who the children of God are and who the children of the devil are: Anyone who does not do what is right is not a child of God; nor is anyone who does not love his brother.
Jude [9]But even the archangel Michael, when he was disputing with the devil about the body of Moses, did not dare to bring a slanderous accusation against him, but said, "The Lord rebuke you!"
Rev 2 [10]"Do not be afraid of what you are about to suffer. I tell you, the devil will put some of you in prison to test you, and you will suffer persecution for ten days. Be faithful, even to the point of death, and I will give you the crown of life."
Rev 12 [12]"Therefore rejoice, you heavens and you who dwell in them! But woe to the earth and the sea, because the devil has gone down to you! He is filled with fury, because he knows that his time is short."
Rev 20 [2]He seized the dragon, that ancient serpent, who is the devil, or Satan, and bound him for a thousand years.
Rev 20 [10]And the devil, who deceived them, was thrown into the lake of burning sulfur, where the beast and the false prophet had been thrown. They will be tormented day and night for ever and ever.

8. Dragon

Rev 12 [3]Then another sign appeared in heaven: an enormous red dragon with seven heads and ten horns and seven crowns on his heads. [4]His tail swept a third of the stars out of the sky and flung them to the earth. The dragon stood in front of the woman who was about to give birth, so that he might devour her child the moment it was born. [5]She gave birth to a son, a male child, who will rule all the nations with an iron scepter. And her child was snatched up to God and to his throne. [6]The woman fled into the desert to a place prepared for her by God, where she might be taken care of for 1,260 days.

[7]And there was war in heaven. Michael and his angels fought against the dragon, and the dragon and his angels fought back. [8]But he was not strong enough, and they lost their place in heaven. [9]The great dragon was hurled down—that ancient serpent called the devil, or Satan, who leads the whole world astray. He was hurled to the earth, and his angels with him.
Rev 20 [2]He seized the dragon, that ancient serpent, who is the devil, or Satan, and bound him for a thousand years.

9. Enemy

Matt 13 [25]"But while everyone was sleeping, his enemy came and sowed weeds among the wheat, and went away [39]. . . and the enemy who sows them is the devil. The harvest is the end of the age, and the harvesters are angels."
1 Pet 5 [8]Be self-controlled and alert. Your enemy the devil prowls around like a roaring lion looking for someone to devour.

10. Evil One

Matt 6 [13]"'And lead us not into temptation, but deliver us from the evil one.'"
Matt 13 [19]"When anyone hears the message about the kingdom and does not understand it, the evil one comes and snatches away what was sown in his heart. This is the seed sown along the path."
Matt 13 [38]"The field is the world, and the good seed stands for the sons of the kingdom. The weeds are the sons of the evil one. . . ."
Eph 6 [16]In addition to all this, take up the shield of faith, with which you can extinguish all the flaming arrows of the evil one.
2 Thess 3 [3]But the Lord is faithful, and he will strengthen and protect you from the evil one.
1 John 2 [13]I write to you, fathers, because you have known him who is from the beginning. I write to you, young men, because you have overcome the evil one. I write to you, dear children, because you have known the Father. [14]I write to you, fathers, because you have known him who is from the beginning. I

write to you, young men, because you are strong, and the word of God lives in you, and you have overcome the evil one.
1 John 3 [12]Do not be like Cain, who belonged to the evil one and murdered his brother. And why did he murder him? Because his own actions were evil and his brother's were righteous.
1 John 5 [18]We know that anyone born of God does not continue to sin; the one who was born of God keeps him safe, and the evil one cannot harm him. [19]We know that we are children of God, and that the whole world is under the control of the evil one.

11. Father of Lies

John 8 [44]"You belong to your father, the devil, and you want to carry out your father's desire. He was a murderer from the beginning, not holding to the truth, for there is no truth in him. When he lies, he speaks his native language, for he is a liar and the father of lies."

12. God of This Age

2 Cor 4 [4]The god of this age has blinded the minds of unbelievers, so that they cannot see the light of the gospel of the glory of Christ, who is the image of God.

13. Guardian Cherub

Ezek 28 [14]"'You were anointed as a guardian cherub, for so I ordained you. You were on the holy mount of God; you walked among the fiery stones. [15]You were blameless in your ways from the day you were created till wickedness was found in you. [16]Through your widespread trade you were filled with violence, and you sinned. So I drove you in disgrace from the mount of God, and I expelled you, O guardian cherub, from among the fiery stones.'"

14. King of Tyre

Ezek 28 [12]"Son of man, take up a lament concerning the king of Tyre and say to him: 'This is what the Sovereign LORD says: You were the model of perfection, full of wisdom and perfect in beauty. [13]You were in Eden, the garden of God; every precious stone adorned you: ruby, topaz and emerald, chrysolite, onyx and jasper, sapphire, turquoise and beryl. Your settings and mountings were made of gold; on the day you were created they were prepared.'"

15. Liar

John 8 [44]"You belong to your father, the devil, and you want to carry out your father's desire. He was a murderer from the beginning, not holding to the truth, for there is no truth in him. When he lies, he speaks his native language, for he is a liar and the father of lies."

16. Morning Star

Isa 14 [12]How you have fallen from heaven, O morning star, son of the dawn! You have been cast down to the earth, you who once laid low the nations!

17. Murderer

John 8 [44]"You belong to your father, the devil, and you want to carry out your father's desire. He was a murderer from the beginning, not holding to the truth, for there is no truth in him. When he lies, he speaks his native language, for he is a liar and the father of lies."

18. Prince of Demons

Mark 3 [22]And the teachers of the law who came down from Jerusalem said, "He is possessed by Beelzebub! By the prince of demons he is driving out demons."

19. Prince of This World

John 12 [31]"Now is the time for judgment on this world; now the prince of this world will be driven out."
John 14 [30]"I will not speak with you much longer, for the prince of this world is coming. He has no hold on me. . . ."
John 16 [11]". . . and in regard to judgment, because the prince of this world now stands condemned."

20. Roaring Lion

1 Pet 5 [8]Be self-controlled and alert. Your enemy the devil prowls around like a roaring lion looking for someone to devour.

21. Ruler of the Kingdom of the Air

Eph 2 [2]in which you used to live when you followed the ways of this world and of the ruler of the kingdom of the air, the spirit who is now at work in those who are disobedient.

22. Satan

1 Chron 21 [1]Satan rose up against Israel and incited David to take a census of Israel.
Job 1 [6]One day the angels came to present themselves before the LORD, and Satan also came with them. [7]The LORD said to Satan, "Where have you come from?"

Satan answered the LORD, "From roaming through the earth and going back and forth in it."

[8]Then the LORD said to Satan, "Have you considered my servant Job? There is no one on earth like him; he is blameless and upright, a man who fears God and shuns evil."

[9]"Does Job fear God for nothing?" Satan replied. [10]"Have you not put a hedge around him and his household and everything he has? You have blessed the work of his hands, so that his flocks and herds are spread throughout the land. [11]But stretch out your hand and strike everything he has, and he will surely curse you to your face."

[12]The LORD said to Satan, "Very well, then, everything he has is in your hands, but on the man himself do not lay a finger."

Then Satan went out from the presence of the LORD.
Job 2 [1]On another day the angels came to present themselves before the LORD, and Satan also came with them to present himself before him. [2]And the LORD said to Satan, "Where have you come from?"

Satan answered the LORD, "From roaming through the earth and going back and forth in it."

[3]Then the LORD said to Satan, "Have you considered my servant Job? There is no one on earth like him; he is blameless and upright, a man who fears God and shuns evil. And he still maintains his integrity, though you incited me against him to ruin him without any reason."

[4]"Skin for skin!" Satan replied. "A man will give all he has for his own life. [5]But stretch out your hand and strike his flesh and bones, and he will surely curse you to your face."

[6]The LORD said to Satan, "Very well, then, he is in your hands; but you must spare his life."

[7]So Satan went out from the presence of the LORD and afflicted Job with painful sores from the soles of his feet to the top of his head.
Zech 3 [1]Then he showed me Joshua the high priest standing before the angel of the LORD, and Satan standing at his right side to accuse him. [2]The LORD said to Satan, "The LORD rebuke you, Satan! The LORD, who has chosen Jerusalem, rebuke you! Is not this man a burning stick snatched from the fire?"
Matt 4 [10]Jesus said to him, "Away from me, Satan! For it is written: 'Worship the Lord your God, and serve him only.'"
Mark 1 [13]and he was in the desert forty days, being tempted by Satan. He was with the wild animals, and angels attended him.
Luke 10 [18]He replied, "I saw Satan fall like lightning from heaven."
Luke 13 [16]"Then should not this woman, a daughter of Abraham, whom Satan has kept bound for eighteen long years, be set free on the Sabbath day from what bound her?"
John 13 [27]As soon as Judas took the bread, Satan entered into him.

"What you are about to do, do quickly," Jesus told him. . . .
Acts 5 [3]Then Peter said, "Ananias, how is it that Satan has so

filled your heart that you have lied to the Holy Spirit and have kept for yourself some of the money you received for the land?"
Acts 26 [17]"'I will rescue you from your own people and from the Gentiles. I am sending you to them [18]to open their eyes and turn them from darkness to light, and from the power of Satan to God, so that they may receive forgiveness of sins and a place among those who are sanctified by faith in me.'"
Rom 16 [20]The God of peace will soon crush Satan under your feet. The grace of our Lord Jesus be with you.
1 Cor 7 [5]Do not deprive each other except by mutual consent and for a time, so that you may devote yourselves to prayer. Then come together again so that Satan will not tempt you because of your lack of self-control.
2 Cor 2 [11]in order that Satan might not outwit us. For we are not unaware of his schemes.
1 Thess 2 [18]For we wanted to come to you—certainly I, Paul, did, again and again—but Satan stopped us.
2 Thess 2 [9]The coming of the lawless one will be in accordance with the work of Satan displayed in all kinds of counterfeit miracles, signs and wonders. . . .
1 Tim 5 [15]Some have in fact already turned away to follow Satan.
Rev 2 [9]"I know your afflictions and your poverty—yet you are rich! I know the slander of those who say they are Jews and are not, but are a synagogue of Satan."
Rev 12 [9]The great dragon was hurled down—that ancient serpent called the devil, or Satan, who leads the whole world astray. He was hurled to the earth, and his angels with him.
Rev 20 [2]He seized the dragon, that ancient serpent, who is the devil, or Satan, and bound him for a thousand years.
Rev 20 [7]When the thousand years are over, Satan will be released from his prison [8]and will go out to deceive the nations in the four corners of the earth—Gog and Magog—to gather them for battle. In number they are like the sand on the seashore.

23. Serpent

Gen 3 [1]Now the serpent was more crafty than any of the wild animals the LORD God had made. He said to the woman, "Did God really say, 'You must not eat from any tree in the garden'?"

[2]The woman said to the serpent, "We may eat fruit from the trees in the garden, [3]but God did say, 'You must not eat fruit from the tree that is in the middle of the garden, and you must not touch it, or you will die.'"

[4]"You will not surely die," the serpent said to the woman. . . .

[13]Then the LORD God said to the woman, "What is this you have done?"

The woman said, "The serpent deceived me, and I ate."

[14]So the LORD God said to the serpent, "Because you have done this, cursed are you above all the livestock and all the wild animals! You will crawl on your belly and you will eat dust all the days of your life. [15]And I will put enmity between you and the woman, and between your offspring and hers; he will crush your head, and you will strike his heel."
Rev 12 [9]The great dragon was hurled down—that ancient serpent called the devil, or Satan, who leads the whole world astray. He was hurled to the earth, and his angels with him.
Rev 20 [2]He seized the dragon, that ancient serpent, who is the devil, or Satan, and bound him for a thousand years.

24. Son of the Dawn

Isa 14 [12]How you have fallen from heaven, O morning star, son of the dawn! You have been cast down to the earth, you who once laid low the nations!

25. Spirit Who Works in Those Who Are Disobedient

Eph 2 [2]in which you used to live when you followed the ways of this world and of the ruler of the kingdom of the air, the spirit who is now at work in those who are disobedient.

26. Strong Man

Luke 11 [21]"When a strong man, fully armed, guards his own house, his possessions are safe."

27. Tempter

Matt 4 [3]The tempter came to him and said, "If you are the Son of God, tell these stones to become bread."
1 Thess 3 [5]For this reason, when I could stand it no longer, I sent to find out about your faith. I was afraid that in some way the tempter might have tempted you and our efforts might have been useless.

B. The Origin of Satan

1. Satan's Original State

Ezek 28 [12]"Son of man, take up a lament concerning the king of Tyre and say to him: 'This is what the Sovereign LORD says: You were the model of perfection, full of wisdom and perfect in beauty. [13]You were in Eden, the garden of God; every precious stone adorned you: ruby, topaz and emerald, chrysolite, onyx and jasper, sapphire, turquoise and beryl. Your settings and mountings were made of gold; on the day you were created they were prepared. [14]You were anointed as a guardian cherub, for so I ordained you. You were on the holy mount of God; you walked among the fiery stones. [15]You were blameless in your ways from the day you were created till wickedness was found in you.'"

2. Satan's Fall

Isa 14 [12]How you have fallen from heaven, O morning star, son of the dawn! You have been cast down to the earth, you who once laid low the nations! [13]You said in your heart, "I will ascend to heaven; I will raise my throne above the stars of God; I will sit enthroned on the mount of assembly, on the utmost heights of the sacred mountain. [14]I will ascend above the tops of the clouds; I will make myself like the Most High." [15]But you are brought down to the grave, to the depths of the pit.
Ezek 28 [15]"'You were blameless in your ways from the day you were created till wickedness was found in you. [16]Through your widespread trade you were filled with violence, and you sinned. So I drove you in disgrace from the mount of God, and I expelled you, O guardian cherub, from among the fiery stones. [17]Your heart became proud on account of your beauty, and you corrupted your wisdom because of your splendor. So I threw you to the earth; I made a spectacle of you before kings.'"
Luke 10 [18]He replied, "I saw Satan fall like lightning from heaven."
1 Tim 3 [6]He must not be a recent convert, or he may become conceited and fall under the same judgment as the devil.
Rev 12 [7]And there was war in heaven. Michael and his angels fought against the dragon, and the dragon and his angels fought back. [8]But he was not strong enough, and they lost their place in heaven. [9]The great dragon was hurled down—that ancient serpent called the devil, or Satan, who leads the whole world astray. He was hurled to the earth, and his angels with him.

C. The Present Abode of Satan

1. Satan Lives in Heavenly Places

Eph 6 [11]Put on the full armor of God so that you can take your stand against the devil's schemes. [12]For our struggle is not against flesh and blood, but against the rulers, against the authorities, against the powers of this dark world and against the spiritual forces of evil in the heavenly realms.

2. Satan Has Limited Access to God's Presence

Job 1 [6]One day the angels came to present themselves before the LORD, and Satan also came with them.
Job 2 [1]On another day the angels came to present themselves

before the LORD, and Satan also came with them to present himself before him.

Zech 3 [1]Then he showed me Joshua the high priest standing before the angel of the LORD, and Satan standing at his right side to accuse him. [2]The LORD said to Satan, "The LORD rebuke you, Satan! The LORD, who has chosen Jerusalem, rebuke you! Is not this man a burning stick snatched from the fire?"

3. Satan Roams the Earth

Job 1 [7]The LORD said to Satan, "Where have you come from?"

Satan answered the LORD, "From roaming through the earth and going back and forth in it."

1 Pet 5 [8]Be self-controlled and alert. Your enemy the devil prowls around like a roaring lion looking for someone to devour.

Rev 2 [12]"To the angel of the church in Pergamum write: These are the words of him who has the sharp, double-edged sword. [13]I know where you live—where Satan has his throne. Yet you remain true to my name. You did not renounce your faith in me, even in the days of Antipas, my faithful witness, who was put to death in your city—where Satan lives."

D. The Purpose and Work of Satan

1. The Intentions of Satan

a) Satan Intends to Oppose God

John 14 [30]"I will not speak with you much longer, for the prince of this world is coming. He has no hold on me. . . ."

Acts 13 [10]"You are a child of the devil and an enemy of everything that is right! You are full of all kinds of deceit and trickery. Will you never stop perverting the right ways of the Lord?"

Acts 26 [17]"'I will rescue you from your own people and from the Gentiles. I am sending you to them [18]to open their eyes and turn them from darkness to light, and from the power of Satan to God, so that they may receive forgiveness of sins and a place among those who are sanctified by faith in me.'"

Rom 16 [20]The God of peace will soon crush Satan under your feet. The grace of our Lord Jesus be with you.

2 Cor 6 [15]What harmony is there between Christ and Belial? What does a believer have in common with an unbeliever?

1 John 3 [7]Dear children, do not let anyone lead you astray. He who does what is right is righteous, just as he is righteous. [8]He who does what is sinful is of the devil, because the devil has been sinning from the beginning. The reason the Son of God appeared was to destroy the devil's work. [9]No one who is born of God will continue to sin, because God's seed remains in him; he cannot go on sinning, because he has been born of God. [10]This is how we know who the children of God are and who the children of the devil are: Anyone who does not do what is right is not a child of God; nor is anyone who does not love his brother.

Rev 12 [12]"Therefore rejoice, you heavens and you who dwell in them! But woe to the earth and the sea, because the devil has gone down to you! He is filled with fury, because he knows that his time is short."

[13]When the dragon saw that he had been hurled to the earth, he pursued the woman who had given birth to the male child.

b) Satan Intends to Ruin Believers

Luke 22 [31]"Simon, Simon, Satan has asked to sift you as wheat. [32]But I have prayed for you, Simon, that your faith may not fail. And when you have turned back, strengthen your brothers."

1 Cor 7 [5]Do not deprive each other except by mutual consent and for a time, so that you may devote yourselves to prayer. Then come together again so that Satan will not tempt you because of your lack of self-control.

1 John 3 [12]Do not be like Cain, who belonged to the evil one and murdered his brother. And why did he murder him? Because his own actions were evil and his brother's were righteous.

1 John 5 [18]We know that anyone born of God does not continue to sin; the one who was born of God keeps him safe, and the evil one cannot harm him.

Rev 12 [17]Then the dragon was enraged at the woman and went off to make war against the rest of her offspring—those who obey God's commandments and hold to the testimony of Jesus.

c) Satan Intends to Hinder True Faith

Matt 13 [38]"The field is the world, and the good seed stands for the sons of the kingdom. The weeds are the sons of the evil one, [39]and the enemy who sows them is the devil. The harvest is the end of the age, and the harvesters are angels. . . . [41]The Son of Man will send out his angels, and they will weed out of his kingdom everything that causes sin and all who do evil."

John 8 [44]"You belong to your father, the devil, and you want to carry out your father's desire. He was a murderer from the beginning, not holding to the truth, for there is no truth in him. When he lies, he speaks his native language, for he is a liar and the father of lies."

Acts 5 [3]Then Peter said, "Ananias, how is it that Satan has so filled your heart that you have lied to the Holy Spirit and have kept for yourself some of the money you received for the land?"

1 Tim 5 [15]Some have in fact already turned away to follow Satan.

Rev 12 [9]The great dragon was hurled down—that ancient serpent called the devil, or Satan, who leads the whole world astray. He was hurled to the earth, and his angels with him.

d) Satan Intends to Establish His Own Kingdom

Isa 14 [13]You said in your heart, "I will ascend to heaven; I will raise my throne above the stars of God; I will sit enthroned on the mount of assembly, on the utmost heights of the sacred mountain. [14]I will ascend above the tops of the clouds; I will make myself like the Most High."

Matt 12 [25]Jesus knew their thoughts and said to them, "Every kingdom divided against itself will be ruined, and every city or household divided against itself will not stand. [26]If Satan drives out Satan, he is divided against himself. How then can his kingdom stand? [27]And if I drive out demons by Beelzebub, by whom do your people drive them out? So then, they will be your judges."

Luke 4 [5]The devil led him up to a high place and showed him in an instant all the kingdoms of the world. [6]And he said to him, "I will give you all their authority and splendor, for it has been given to me, and I can give it to anyone I want to. [7]So if you worship me, it will all be yours."

Luke 11 [18]"If Satan is divided against himself, how can his kingdom stand? I say this because you claim that I drive out demons by Beelzebub."

2 Cor 4 [3]And even if our gospel is veiled, it is veiled to those who are perishing. [4]The god of this age has blinded the minds of unbelievers, so that they cannot see the light of the gospel of the glory of Christ, who is the image of God.

2 Cor 11 [11]Why? Because I do not love you? God knows I do! [12]And I will keep on doing what I am doing in order to cut the ground from under those who want an opportunity to be considered equal with us in the things they boast about.

[13]For such men are false apostles, deceitful workmen, masquerading as apostles of Christ. [14]And no wonder, for Satan himself masquerades as an angel of light. [15]It is not surprising, then, if his servants masquerade as servants of righteousness. Their end will be what their actions deserve.

Eph 2 [2]in which you used to live when you followed the ways of this world and of the ruler of the kingdom of the air, the spirit who is now at work in those who are disobedient.

Col 1 [13]For he has rescued us from the dominion of darkness and brought us into the kingdom of the Son he loves. . . .

1 John 5 [19]We know that we are children of God, and that the whole world is under the control of the evil one.

2. The Methods of Satan

a) Satan Accuses

Job 1 [6]One day the angels came to present themselves before the LORD, and Satan also came with them. [7]The LORD said to Satan, "Where have you come from?"

Satan answered the LORD, "From roaming through the earth and going back and forth in it."

[8]Then the LORD said to Satan, "Have you considered my

servant Job? There is no one on earth like him; he is blameless and upright, a man who fears God and shuns evil."

[9]"Does Job fear God for nothing?" Satan replied. [10]"Have you not put a hedge around him and his household and everything he has? You have blessed the work of his hands, so that his flocks and herds are spread throughout the land. [11]But stretch out your hand and strike everything he has, and he will surely curse you to your face."

Job 2 [1]On another day the angels came to present themselves before the LORD, and Satan also came with them to present himself before him. [2]And the LORD said to Satan, "Where have you come from?"

Satan answered the LORD, "From roaming through the earth and going back and forth in it."

[3]Then the LORD said to Satan, "Have you considered my servant Job? There is no one on earth like him; he is blameless and upright, a man who fears God and shuns evil. And he still maintains his integrity, though you incited me against him to ruin him without any reason."

[4]"Skin for skin!" Satan replied. "A man will give all he has for his own life. [5]But stretch out your hand and strike his flesh and bones, and he will surely curse you to your face."

Zech 3 [1]Then he showed me Joshua the high priest standing before the angel of the LORD, and Satan standing at his right side to accuse him.

Rev 12 [10]Then I heard a loud voice in heaven say: "Now have come the salvation and the power and the kingdom of our God, and the authority of his Christ. For the accuser of our brothers, who accuses them before our God day and night, has been hurled down."

b) Satan Afflicts

Job 1 [12]The LORD said to Satan, "Very well, then, everything he has is in your hands, but on the man himself do not lay a finger."

Then Satan went out from the presence of the LORD.

[13]One day when Job's sons and daughters were feasting and drinking wine at the oldest brother's house, [14]a messenger came to Job and said, "The oxen were plowing and the donkeys were grazing nearby, [15]and the Sabeans attacked and carried them off. They put the servants to the sword, and I am the only one who has escaped to tell you!"

[16]While he was still speaking, another messenger came and said, "The fire of God fell from the sky and burned up the sheep and the servants, and I am the only one who has escaped to tell you!"

[17]While he was still speaking, another messenger came and said, "The Chaldeans formed three raiding parties and swept down on your camels and carried them off. They put the servants to the sword, and I am the only one who has escaped to tell you!"

[18]While he was still speaking, yet another messenger came and said, "Your sons and daughters were feasting and drinking wine at the oldest brother's house, [19]when suddenly a mighty wind swept in from the desert and struck the four corners of the house. It collapsed on them and they are dead, and I am the only one who has escaped to tell you!"

Job 2 [6]The LORD said to Satan, "Very well, then, he is in your hands; but you must spare his life."

[7]So Satan went out from the presence of the LORD and afflicted Job with painful sores from the soles of his feet to the top of his head.

Luke 13 [16]"Then should not this woman, a daughter of Abraham, whom Satan has kept bound for eighteen long years, be set free on the Sabbath day from what bound her?"

Rev 2 [10]"Do not be afraid of what you are about to suffer. I tell you, the devil will put some of you in prison to test you, and you will suffer persecution for ten days. Be faithful, even to the point of death, and I will give you the crown of life."

c) Satan Conquers

Acts 10 [38]". . . how God anointed Jesus of Nazareth with the Holy Spirit and power, and how he went around doing good and healing all who were under the power of the devil, because God was with him."

Eph 6 [16]In addition to all this, take up the shield of faith, with which you can extinguish all the flaming arrows of the evil one.

2 Tim 2 [26]and that they will come to their senses and escape from the trap of the devil, who has taken them captive to do his will.

d) Satan Deceives

Gen 3 [1]Now the serpent was more crafty than any of the wild animals the LORD God had made. He said to the woman, "Did God really say, 'You must not eat from any tree in the garden'?"

[2]The woman said to the serpent, "We may eat fruit from the trees in the garden, [3]but God did say, 'You must not eat fruit from the tree that is in the middle of the garden, and you must not touch it, or you will die.'"

[4]"You will not surely die," the serpent said to the woman. [5]"For God knows that when you eat of it your eyes will be opened, and you will be like God, knowing good and evil."

[6]When the woman saw that the fruit of the tree was good for food and pleasing to the eye, and also desirable for gaining wisdom, she took some and ate it. She also gave some to her husband, who was with her, and he ate it. . . .

[13]Then the LORD God said to the woman, "What is this you have done?"

The woman said, "The serpent deceived me, and I ate."

John 8 [44]"You belong to your father, the devil, and you want to carry out your father's desire. He was a murderer from the beginning, not holding to the truth, for there is no truth in him. When he lies, he speaks his native language, for he is a liar and the father of lies."

Acts 13 [10]"You are a child of the devil and an enemy of everything that is right! You are full of all kinds of deceit and trickery. Will you never stop perverting the right ways of the Lord?"

2 Cor 4 [4]The god of this age has blinded the minds of unbelievers, so that they cannot see the light of the gospel of the glory of Christ, who is the image of God.

2 Cor 11 [13]For such men are false apostles, deceitful workmen, masquerading as apostles of Christ. [14]And no wonder, for Satan himself masquerades as an angel of light. [15]It is not surprising, then, if his servants masquerade as servants of righteousness. Their end will be what their actions deserve.

2 Thess 2 [9]The coming of the lawless one will be in accordance with the work of Satan displayed in all kinds of counterfeit miracles, signs and wonders, [10]and in every sort of evil that deceives those who are perishing. They perish because they refused to love the truth and so be saved.

Rev 2 [9]"I know your afflictions and your poverty—yet you are rich! I know the slander of those who say they are Jews and are not, but are a synagogue of Satan."

Rev 3 [9]"I will make those who are of the synagogue of Satan, who claim to be Jews though they are not, but are liars—I will make them come and fall down at your feet and acknowledge that I have loved you."

e) Satan Hinders

1 Thess 2 [18]For we wanted to come to you—certainly I, Paul, did, again and again—but Satan stopped us.

f) Satan Murders

John 8 [44]"You belong to your father, the devil, and you want to carry out your father's desire. He was a murderer from the beginning, not holding to the truth, for there is no truth in him. When he lies, he speaks his native language, for he is a liar and the father of lies."

g) Satan Perverts

Acts 13 [10]"You are a child of the devil and an enemy of everything that is right! You are full of all kinds of deceit and trickery. Will you never stop perverting the right ways of the Lord?"

2 Thess 2 [9]The coming of the lawless one will be in accordance with the work of Satan displayed in all kinds of counterfeit miracles, signs and wonders, [10]and in every sort of evil that deceives those who are perishing. They perish because they refused to love the truth and so be saved.

h) Satan Prompts

1 Chron 21 [1]Satan rose up against Israel and incited David to take a census of Israel.

John 13 [2]The evening meal was being served, and the devil had already prompted Judas Iscariot, son of Simon, to betray Jesus. . . .

[27]As soon as Judas took the bread, Satan entered into him. "What you are about to do, do quickly," Jesus told him. . . .

Acts 5 [3]Then Peter said, "Ananias, how is it that Satan has so filled your heart that you have lied to the Holy Spirit and have kept for yourself some of the money you received for the land?"

i) Satan Schemes

2 Cor 2 [11]in order that Satan might not outwit us. For we are not unaware of his schemes.

Eph 6 [11]Put on the full armor of God so that you can take your stand against the devil's schemes.

1 Tim 3 [7]He must also have a good reputation with outsiders, so that he will not fall into disgrace and into the devil's trap.

j) Satan Stalks

1 Pet 5 [8]Be self-controlled and alert. Your enemy the devil prowls around like a roaring lion looking for someone to devour.

k) Satan Steals

Matt 13 [19]"When anyone hears the message about the kingdom and does not understand it, the evil one comes and snatches away what was sown in his heart. This is the seed sown along the path."

Luke 8 [12]"Those along the path are the ones who hear, and then the devil comes and takes away the word from their hearts, so that they may not believe and be saved."

l) Satan Tempts

Matt 6 [13]"'And lead us not into temptation, but deliver us from the evil one.'"

Mark 1 [12]At once the Spirit sent him out into the desert, [13]and he was in the desert forty days, being tempted by Satan. He was with the wild animals, and angels attended him.

Luke 4 [1]Jesus, full of the Holy Spirit, returned from the Jordan and was led by the Spirit in the desert, [2]where for forty days he was tempted by the devil. He ate nothing during those days, and at the end of them he was hungry.

[3]The devil said to him, "If you are the Son of God, tell this stone to become bread."

[4]Jesus answered, "It is written: 'Man does not live on bread alone.'"

[5]The devil led him up to a high place and showed him in an instant all the kingdoms of the world. [6]And he said to him, "I will give you all their authority and splendor, for it has been given to me, and I can give it to anyone I want to. [7]So if you worship me, it will all be yours."

[8]Jesus answered, "It is written: 'Worship the Lord your God and serve him only.'"

[9]The devil led him to Jerusalem and had him stand on the highest point of the temple. "If you are the Son of God," he said, "throw yourself down from here. [10]For it is written: 'He will command his angels concerning you to guard you carefully; [11]they will lift you up in their hands, so that you will not strike your foot against a stone.'"

[12]Jesus answered, "It says: 'Do not put the Lord your God to the test.'"

[13]When the devil had finished all this tempting, he left him until an opportune time.

1 Cor 7 [5]Do not deprive each other except by mutual consent and for a time, so that you may devote yourselves to prayer. Then come together again so that Satan will not tempt you because of your lack of self-control.

1 Thess 3 [5]For this reason, when I could stand it no longer, I sent to find out about your faith. I was afraid that in some way the tempter might have tempted you and our efforts might have been useless.

m) Satan Threatens

Heb 2 [14]Since the children have flesh and blood, he too shared in their humanity so that by his death he might destroy him who holds the power of death—that is, the devil—[15]and free those who all their lives were held in slavery by their fear of death.

E. The Destiny of Satan

1. Satan Is Destined to Be Defeated

Gen 3 [14]So the LORD God said to the serpent, "Because you have done this, cursed are you above all the livestock and all the wild animals! You will crawl on your belly and you will eat dust all the days of your life. [15]And I will put enmity between you and the woman, and between your offspring and hers; he will crush your head, and you will strike his heel."

Isa 14 [12]How you have fallen from heaven, O morning star, son of the dawn! You have been cast down to the earth, you who once laid low the nations! [13]You said in your heart, "I will ascend to heaven; I will raise my throne above the stars of God; I will sit enthroned on the mount of assembly, on the utmost heights of the sacred mountain. [14]I will ascend above the tops of the clouds; I will make myself like the Most High." [15]But you are brought down to the grave, to the depths of the pit.

[16]Those who see you stare at you, they ponder your fate: "Is this the man who shook the earth and made kingdoms tremble, [17]the man who made the world a desert, who overthrew its cities and would not let his captives go home?"

Luke 10 [18]He replied, "I saw Satan fall like lightning from heaven."

John 12 [31]"Now is the time for judgment on this world; now the prince of this world will be driven out. [32]But I, when I am lifted up from the earth, will draw all men to myself."

John 14 [30]"I will not speak with you much longer, for the prince of this world is coming. He has no hold on me. . . ."

Rom 16 [20]The God of peace will soon crush Satan under your feet. The grace of our Lord Jesus be with you.

Col 2 [15]And having disarmed the powers and authorities, he made a public spectacle of them, triumphing over them by the cross.

2. Satan Is Destined to Be Condemned

John 16 [11]". . . and in regard to judgment, because the prince of this world now stands condemned."

1 Tim 3 [6]He must not be a recent convert, or he may become conceited and fall under the same judgment as the devil.

3. Satan Is Destined to Be Expelled from Heaven

Rev 12 [7]And there was war in heaven. Michael and his angels fought against the dragon, and the dragon and his angels fought back. [8]But he was not strong enough, and they lost their place in heaven. [9]The great dragon was hurled down—that ancient serpent called the devil, or Satan, who leads the whole world astray. He was hurled to the earth, and his angels with him.

[10]Then I heard a loud voice in heaven say: "Now have come the salvation and the power and the kingdom of our God, and the authority of his Christ. For the accuser of our brothers, who accuses them before our God day and night, has been hurled down. [11]They overcame him by the blood of the Lamb and by the word of their testimony; they did not love their lives so much as to shrink from death. [12]Therefore rejoice, you heavens and you who dwell in them! But woe to the earth and the sea, because the devil has gone down to you! He is filled with fury, because he knows that his time is short."

4. Satan Is Destined to Be Bound

Rev 20 [1]And I saw an angel coming down out of heaven, having the key to the Abyss and holding in his hand a great chain. [2]He seized the dragon, that ancient serpent, who is the devil, or Satan, and bound him for a thousand years. [3]He threw him into the Abyss, and locked and sealed it over him, to keep him from deceiving the nations anymore until the thousand years were ended. After that, he must be set free for a short time.

5. Satan Is Destined to Be Thrown into the Lake of Fire

Matt 25 [41]"Then he will say to those on his left, 'Depart from me, you who are cursed, into the eternal fire prepared for the devil and his angels.'"

Rev 20 [10]And the devil, who deceived them, was thrown into the lake of burning sulfur, where the beast and the false prophet had been thrown. They will be tormented day and night for ever and ever.

F. The Proper Attitude toward Satan

1. Believers Should Never Speak of Him Contemptuously

Jude [8]In the very same way, these dreamers pollute their own bodies, reject authority and slander celestial beings. [9]But even the archangel Michael, when he was disputing with the devil about the body of Moses, did not dare to bring a slanderous accusation against him, but said, "The Lord rebuke you!"

2. Believers Should Regard His Power as Limited

Job 1 [12]The LORD said to Satan, "Very well, then, everything he has is in your hands, but on the man himself do not lay a finger."

Then Satan went out from the presence of the LORD. . . .

[20]At this, Job got up and tore his robe and shaved his head. Then he fell to the ground in worship [21]and said: "Naked I came from my mother's womb, and naked I will depart. The LORD gave and the LORD has taken away; may the name of the LORD be praised."

[22]In all this, Job did not sin by charging God with wrongdoing.

Job 2 [6]The LORD said to Satan, "Very well, then, he is in your hands; but you must spare his life."

[7]So Satan went out from the presence of the LORD and afflicted Job with painful sores from the soles of his feet to the top of his head. . . .

[10]He replied, "You are talking like a foolish woman. Shall we accept good from God, and not trouble?"

In all this, Job did not sin in what he said.

Zech 3 [1]Then he showed me Joshua the high priest standing before the angel of the LORD, and Satan standing at his right side to accuse him. [2]The LORD said to Satan, "The LORD rebuke you, Satan! The LORD, who has chosen Jerusalem, rebuke you! Is not this man a burning stick snatched from the fire?"

3. Believers Should Remember That Christ's Work and Word Protect Them

John 17 [15]"My prayer is not that you take them out of the world but that you protect them from the evil one."

Heb 2 [14]Since the children have flesh and blood, he too shared in their humanity so that by his death he might destroy him who holds the power of death—that is, the devil. . . .

1 John 2 [14]I write to you, fathers, because you have known him who is from the beginning. I write to you, young men, because you are strong, and the word of God lives in you, and you have overcome the evil one.

Rev 12 [11]"They overcame him by the blood of the Lamb and by the word of their testimony; they did not love their lives so much as to shrink from death."

4. Believers Should Remember That God Providentially Uses Satan for Disciplining

Luke 22 [31]"Simon, Simon, Satan has asked to sift you as wheat. [32]But I have prayed for you, Simon, that your faith may not fail. And when you have turned back, strengthen your brothers."

1 Cor 5 [5]hand this man over to Satan, so that the sinful nature may be destroyed and his spirit saved on the day of the Lord.

2 Cor 12 [7]To keep me from becoming conceited because of these surpassingly great revelations, there was given me a thorn in my flesh, a messenger of Satan, to torment me.

1 Tim 1 [20]Among them are Hymenaeus and Alexander, whom I have handed over to Satan to be taught not to blaspheme.

5. Believers Should Remember That Satan Is a Judged and Defeated Foe

Matt 25 [41]"Then he will say to those on his left, 'Depart from me, you who are cursed, into the eternal fire prepared for the devil and his angels.'"

John 12 [31]"Now is the time for judgment on this world; now the prince of this world will be driven out."

John 16 [11]". . . and in regard to judgment, because the prince of this world now stands condemned."

Col 2 [15]And having disarmed the powers and authorities, he made a public spectacle of them, triumphing over them by the cross.

Rev 20 [10]And the devil, who deceived them, was thrown into the lake of burning sulfur, where the beast and the false prophet had been thrown. They will be tormented day and night for ever and ever.

6. Believers Should Resist Satan

Eph 4 [27]and do not give the devil a foothold.

Eph 6 [11]Put on the full armor of God so that you can take your stand against the devil's schemes. [12]For our struggle is not against flesh and blood, but against the rulers, against the authorities, against the powers of this dark world and against the spiritual forces of evil in the heavenly realms. [13]Therefore put on the full armor of God, so that when the day of evil comes, you may be able to stand your ground, and after you have done everything, to stand. [14]Stand firm then, with the belt of truth buckled around your waist, with the breastplate of righteousness in place, [15]and with your feet fitted with the readiness that comes from the gospel of peace. [16]In addition to all this, take up the shield of faith, with which you can extinguish all the flaming arrows of the evil one. [17]Take the helmet of salvation and the sword of the Spirit, which is the word of God. [18]And pray in the Spirit on all occasions with all kinds of prayers and requests. With this in mind, be alert and always keep on praying for all the saints.

James 4 [7]Submit yourselves, then, to God. Resist the devil, and he will flee from you.

1 Pet 5 [8]Be self-controlled and alert. Your enemy the devil prowls around like a roaring lion looking for someone to devour. [9]Resist him, standing firm in the faith, because you know that your brothers throughout the world are undergoing the same kind of sufferings.

7. Believers Should Turn to God for Deliverance from Satan

Matt 6 [13]"'And lead us not into temptation, but deliver us from the evil one.'"

Rom 16 [20]The God of peace will soon crush Satan under your feet. The grace of our Lord Jesus be with you.

2 Thess 3 [3]But the Lord is faithful, and he will strengthen and protect you from the evil one.

1 John 3 [8]He who does what is sinful is of the devil, because the devil has been sinning from the beginning. The reason the Son of God appeared was to destroy the devil's work. [9]No one who is born of God will continue to sin, because God's seed remains in him; he cannot go on sinning, because he has been born of God. [10]This is how we know who the children of God are and who the children of the devil are: Anyone who does not do what is right is not a child of God; nor is anyone who does not love his brother.

7

Human Beings: *General*

I. The Creation of the Human Race
- A. God Created Humankind
- B. God Created Humankind in His Own Image
- C. God Created Humankind for Immortality

II. Humans Are Created as Moral Beings
- A. People Possess Moral Consciousness
- B. People Make Moral Decisions
- C. People Express Moral Affections
- D. People Experience Moral Indignation

III. Humans Are Created as Religious Beings
- A. The Proper Response of Human Beings to God
- B. The Improper Response of Human Beings to God

IV. Humans Are Created with Power of Choice
- A. They Make Choices according to Personal Preference
- B. They Make Choices for the Sake of Others
- C. They Make Choices at the Request of Others
- D. The Place of the Human Will

V. The Place of Humankind in the Created Order
- A. Human Beings in Relation to God
- B. Human Beings in Relation to Other Created Beings

VI. Constituent Elements of Human Individuality
- A. The Human Soul
- B. The Human Spirit
- C. Human Flesh
- D. The Human Body
- E. Parts of the Human Body as Moral Aspects of Humanity
- F. The Inner Person
- G. The Outer Person
- H. The Old Self
- I. The New Self
- J. The Human Mind
- K. The Human Conscience
- L. The Human Will

VII. The Human Being as a Living Unity
- A. The Whole Person Represented by the Arm
- B. The Whole Person Represented by the Blood
- C. The Whole Person Represented by the Ear
- D. The Whole Person Represented by the Eyes
- E. The Whole Person Represented by the Face
- F. The Whole Person Represented by the Flesh
- G. The Whole Person Represented by the Foot
- H. The Whole Person Represented by the Hand
- I. The Whole Person Represented by the Heart
- J. The Whole Person Represented by the Knees
- K. The Whole Person Represented by the Mouth
- L. The Whole Person Represented by the Soul
- M. The Whole Person Represented by the Tongue

VIII. The Corporate Nature of the Human Race
- A. The Human Race Is United in Adam
- B. Israel as a Corporate Entity
- C. The Unity of Believers in Christ

I
The Creation of the Human Race

A. *God Created Humankind*

1. Humans Were a Special Work of God

See p. 184a, Humans Were a Special Work of God

2. Humans Were Created as Male and Female

See p. 184b, Humans Were Created as Male and Female

3. Humans Were Given Bodily Form

See p. 184b, Humans Were Given Bodily Form

4. Humans Were Made Living Beings

See p. 185a, Humans Were Made Living Beings

B. *God Created Humankind in His Own Image*

1. Human Beings Were Originally Created in God's Image

See p. 184b, Humans Were Fashioned in God's Image

2. The People of God Are Recreated in God's Image

Ps 17 15And I—in righteousness I will see your face; when I awake, I will be satisfied with seeing your likeness.
Rom 8 29For those God foreknew he also predestined to be conformed to the likeness of his Son, that he might be the firstborn among many brothers.
1 Cor 15 48As was the earthly man, so are those who are of the earth; and as is the man from heaven, so also are those who are of heaven. 49And just as we have borne the likeness of the earthly man, so shall we bear the likeness of the man from heaven.
2 Cor 3 18And we, who with unveiled faces all reflect the Lord's glory, are being transformed into his likeness with ever-increasing glory, which comes from the Lord, who is the Spirit.
Eph 4 22You were taught, with regard to your former way of life, to put off your old self, which is being corrupted by its deceitful desires; 23to be made new in the attitude of your minds; 24and to put on the new self, created to be like God in true righteousness and holiness.
Col 3 9Do not lie to each other, since you have taken off your old self with its practices 10and have put on the new self, which is being renewed in knowledge in the image of its Creator.
1 John 3 1How great is the love the Father has lavished on us, that we should be called children of God! And that is what we are! The reason the world does not know us is that it did not know him. 2Dear friends, now we are children of God, and what we will be has not yet been made known. But we know that when he appears, we shall be like him, for we shall see him as he is. 3Everyone who has this hope in him purifies himself, just as he is pure.

C. *God Created Humankind for Immortality*

1. The Presence of Death

See p. 737b, The Fact of Death; p. 740b, The Nature of Death

2. The Reality of Life after Death

See p. 742b, The Believer and Death; p. 744b, Intermediate State

II
Humans Are Created as Moral Beings

A. *People Possess Moral Consciousness*

1. They Feel Legitimate Guilt

Gen 3 6When the woman saw that the fruit of the tree was good for food and pleasing to the eye, and also desirable for gaining wisdom, she took some and ate it. She also gave some to her husband, who was with her, and he ate it. 7Then the eyes of both of them were opened, and they realized they were naked; so they sewed fig leaves together and made coverings for themselves.

8Then the man and his wife heard the sound of the LORD God as he was walking in the garden in the cool of the day, and they hid from the LORD God among the trees of the garden. 9But the LORD God called to the man, "Where are you?"

10He answered, "I heard you in the garden, and I was afraid because I was naked; so I hid."

11And he said, "Who told you that you were naked? Have you eaten from the tree that I commanded you not to eat from?"
Gen 4 8Now Cain said to his brother Abel, "Let's go out to the field." And while they were in the field, Cain attacked his brother Abel and killed him.

9Then the LORD said to Cain, "Where is your brother Abel?"

"I don't know," he replied. "Am I my brother's keeper?"

10The LORD said, "What have you done? Listen! Your brother's blood cries out to me from the ground. 11Now you are under a curse and driven from the ground, which opened its mouth to receive your brother's blood from your hand. 12When you work the ground, it will no longer yield its crops for you. You will be a restless wanderer on the earth."
Gen 42 21They said to one another, "Surely we are being punished because of our brother. We saw how distressed he was when he pleaded with us for his life, but we would not listen; that's why this distress has come upon us."
1 Sam 24 5Afterward, David was conscience-stricken for having cut off a corner of his robe.
2 Sam 24 10David was conscience-stricken after he had counted the fighting men, and he said to the LORD, "I have sinned greatly in what I have done. Now, O LORD, I beg you, take away the guilt of your servant. I have done a very foolish thing."
Ps 32 1Blessed is he whose transgressions are forgiven, whose sins are covered. 2Blessed is the man whose sin the LORD does not count against him and in whose spirit is no deceit.

3When I kept silent, my bones wasted away through my groaning all day long. 4For day and night your hand was heavy upon me; my strength was sapped as in the heat of summer. 5Then I acknowledged my sin to you and did not cover up my iniquity. I said, "I will confess my transgressions to the LORD"—and you forgave the guilt of my sin.
Ps 51 1Have mercy on me, O God, according to your unfailing love; according to your great compassion blot out my transgressions. 2Wash away all my iniquity and cleanse me from my sin.

3For I know my transgressions, and my sin is always before me. 4Against you, you only, have I sinned and done what is evil in your sight, so that you are proved right when you speak and justified when you judge. 5Surely I was sinful at birth, sinful from the time my mother conceived me. 6Surely you desire truth in the inner parts; you teach me wisdom in the inmost place.

7Cleanse me with hyssop, and I will be clean; wash me, and I will be whiter than snow. 8Let me hear joy and gladness; let the bones you have crushed rejoice. 9Hide your face from my sins and blot out all my iniquity.

10Create in me a pure heart, O God, and renew a steadfast spirit within me. 11Do not cast me from your presence or take your Holy Spirit from me. 12Restore to me the joy of your salvation and grant me a willing spirit, to sustain me.
Matt 27 1Early in the morning, all the chief priests and the

elders of the people came to the decision to put Jesus to death. [2]They bound him, led him away and handed him over to Pilate, the governor.

[3]When Judas, who had betrayed him, saw that Jesus was condemned, he was seized with remorse and returned the thirty silver coins to the chief priests and the elders. [4]"I have sinned," he said, "for I have betrayed innocent blood."

"What is that to us?" they replied. "That's your responsibility."

[5]So Judas threw the money into the temple and left. Then he went away and hanged himself.

Luke 22 [54]Then seizing him, they led him away and took him into the house of the high priest. Peter followed at a distance. [55]But when they had kindled a fire in the middle of the courtyard and had sat down together, Peter sat down with them. [56]A servant girl saw him seated there in the firelight. She looked closely at him and said, "This man was with him."

[57]But he denied it. "Woman, I don't know him," he said.

[58]A little later someone else saw him and said, "You also are one of them."

"Man, I am not!" Peter replied.

[59]About an hour later another asserted, "Certainly this fellow was with him, for he is a Galilean."

[60]Peter replied, "Man, I don't know what you're talking about!" Just as he was speaking, the rooster crowed. [61]The Lord turned and looked straight at Peter. Then Peter remembered the word the Lord had spoken to him: "Before the rooster crows today, you will disown me three times." [62]And he went outside and wept bitterly.

Luke 23 [32]Two other men, both criminals, were also led out with him to be executed. . . .

[39]One of the criminals who hung there hurled insults at him: "Aren't you the Christ? Save yourself and us!"

[40]But the other criminal rebuked him. "Don't you fear God," he said, "since you are under the same sentence? [41]We are punished justly, for we are getting what our deeds deserve. But this man has done nothing wrong."

[42]Then he said, "Jesus, remember me when you come into your kingdom."

John 8 [7]When they kept on questioning him, he straightened up and said to them, "If any one of you is without sin, let him be the first to throw a stone at her." . . .

[9]At this, those who heard began to go away one at a time, the older ones first, until only Jesus was left, with the woman still standing there.

Heb 9 [9]This is an illustration for the present time, indicating that the gifts and sacrifices being offered were not able to clear the conscience of the worshiper. . . . [14]How much more, then, will the blood of Christ, who through the eternal Spirit offered himself unblemished to God, cleanse our consciences from acts that lead to death, so that we may serve the living God!

Heb 10 [1]The law is only a shadow of the good things that are coming—not the realities themselves. For this reason it can never, by the same sacrifices repeated endlessly year after year, make perfect those who draw near to worship. [2]If it could, would they not have stopped being offered? For the worshipers would have been cleansed once for all, and would no longer have felt guilty for their sins. [22]. . . let us draw near to God with a sincere heart in full assurance of faith, having our hearts sprinkled to cleanse us from a guilty conscience and having our bodies washed with pure water.

1 John 3 [19]This then is how we know that we belong to the truth, and how we set our hearts at rest in his presence [20]whenever our hearts condemn us. For God is greater than our hearts, and he knows everything.

[21]Dear friends, if our hearts do not condemn us, we have confidence before God. . . .

2. They Have Self-Restraint

Rom 2 [14](Indeed, when Gentiles, who do not have the law, do by nature things required by the law, they are a law for themselves, even though they do not have the law, [15]since they show that the requirements of the law are written on their hearts, their consciences also bearing witness, and their thoughts now accusing, now even defending them.)

Rom 14 [5]One man considers one day more sacred than another; another man considers every day alike. Each one should be fully convinced in his own mind. . . . [20]Do not destroy the work of God for the sake of food. All food is clean, but it is wrong for a man to eat anything that causes someone else to stumble. . . . [23]But the man who has doubts is condemned if he eats, because his eating is not from faith; and everything that does not come from faith is sin.

1 Cor 8 [4]So then, about eating food sacrificed to idols: We know that an idol is nothing at all in the world and that there is no God but one. [5]For even if there are so-called gods, whether in heaven or on earth (as indeed there are many "gods" and many "lords"), [6]yet for us there is but one God, the Father, from whom all things came and for whom we live; and there is but one Lord, Jesus Christ, through whom all things came and through whom we live.

[7]But not everyone knows this. Some people are still so accustomed to idols that when they eat such food they think of it as having been sacrificed to an idol, and since their conscience is weak, it is defiled. [8]But food does not bring us near to God; we are no worse if we do not eat, and no better if we do.

[9]Be careful, however, that the exercise of your freedom does not become a stumbling block to the weak. [10]For if anyone with a weak conscience sees you who have this knowledge eating in an idol's temple, won't he be emboldened to eat what has been sacrificed to idols? [11]So this weak brother, for whom Christ died, is destroyed by your knowledge. [12]When you sin against your brothers in this way and wound their weak conscience, you sin against Christ. [13]Therefore, if what I eat causes my brother to fall into sin, I will never eat meat again, so that I will not cause him to fall.

1 Cor 10 [23]"Everything is permissible"—but not everything is beneficial. "Everything is permissible"—but not everything is constructive. [24]Nobody should seek his own good, but the good of others.

[25]Eat anything sold in the meat market without raising questions of conscience, [26]for, "The earth is the Lord's, and everything in it."

[27]If some unbeliever invites you to a meal and you want to go, eat whatever is put before you without raising questions of conscience. [28]But if anyone says to you, "This has been offered in sacrifice," then do not eat it, both for the sake of the man who told you and for conscience' sake—[29]the other man's conscience, I mean, not yours. For why should my freedom be judged by another's conscience? [30]If I take part in the meal with thankfulness, why am I denounced because of something I thank God for?

1 Tim 4 [7]Have nothing to do with godless myths and old wives' tales; rather, train yourself to be godly. [8]For physical training is of some value, but godliness has value for all things, holding promise for both the present life and the life to come.

2 Tim 4 [2]Preach the Word; be prepared in season and out of season; correct, rebuke and encourage—with great patience and careful instruction.

Titus 2 [2]Teach the older men to be temperate, worthy of respect, self-controlled, and sound in faith, in love and in endurance.

[3]Likewise, teach the older women to be reverent in the way they live, not to be slanderers or addicted to much wine, but to teach what is good. [4]Then they can train the younger women to love their husbands and children, [5]to be self-controlled and pure, to be busy at home, to be kind, and to be subject to their husbands, so that no one will malign the word of God.

[6]Similarly, encourage the young men to be self-controlled. [7]In everything set them an example by doing what is good. In your teaching show integrity, seriousness [8]and soundness of speech that cannot be condemned, so that those who oppose you may be ashamed because they have nothing bad to say about us.

3. They Have Self-Perception

Rom 9 [1]I speak the truth in Christ—I am not lying, my conscience confirms it in the Holy Spirit. . . .

2 Cor 1 [12]Now this is our boast: Our conscience testifies that

we have conducted ourselves in the world, and especially in our relations with you, in the holiness and sincerity that are from God. We have done so not according to worldly wisdom but according to God's grace.
2 Cor 4 2Rather, we have renounced secret and shameful ways; we do not use deception, nor do we distort the word of God. On the contrary, by setting forth the truth plainly we commend ourselves to every man's conscience in the sight of God.
2 Cor 5 11Since, then, we know what it is to fear the Lord, we try to persuade men. What we are is plain to God, and I hope it is also plain to your conscience.
Titus 1 13This testimony is true. Therefore, rebuke them sharply, so that they will be sound in the faith 14and will pay no attention to Jewish myths or to the commands of those who reject the truth. 15To the pure, all things are pure, but to those who are corrupted and do not believe, nothing is pure. In fact, both their minds and consciences are corrupted. 16They claim to know God, but by their actions they deny him. They are detestable, disobedient and unfit for doing anything good.
1 Pet 2 19For it is commendable if a man bears up under the pain of unjust suffering because he is conscious of God.

4. They Can Live Wholesome Lives

Gen 6 9This is the account of Noah.

Noah was a righteous man, blameless among the people of his time, and he walked with God.
Gen 20 5"Did he not say to me, 'She is my sister,' and didn't she also say, 'He is my brother'? I have done this with a clear conscience and clean hands."

6Then God said to him in the dream, "Yes, I know you did this with a clear conscience, and so I have kept you from sinning against me. That is why I did not let you touch her."
1 Sam 25 30"When the LORD has done for my master every good thing he promised concerning him and has appointed him leader over Israel, 31my master will not have on his conscience the staggering burden of needless bloodshed or of having avenged himself. And when the LORD has brought my master success, remember your servant."
1 Kings 9 4"As for you, if you walk before me in integrity of heart and uprightness, as David your father did, and do all I command and observe my decrees and laws . . ."
Job 27 6"I will maintain my righteousness and never let go of it; my conscience will not reproach me as long as I live."
Ps 24 3Who may ascend the hill of the LORD? Who may stand in his holy place? 4He who has clean hands and a pure heart, who does not lift up his soul to an idol or swear by what is false. 5He will receive blessing from the LORD and vindication from God his Savior.
Ps 73 1Surely God is good to Israel, to those who are pure in heart.
Prov 22 11He who loves a pure heart and whose speech is gracious will have the king for his friend.
Acts 23 1Paul looked straight at the Sanhedrin and said, "My brothers, I have fulfilled my duty to God in all good conscience to this day."
Acts 24 16"So I strive always to keep my conscience clear before God and man."
Rom 13 5Therefore, it is necessary to submit to the authorities, not only because of possible punishment but also because of conscience.
1 Cor 4 4My conscience is clear, but that does not make me innocent. It is the Lord who judges me.
1 Tim 1 5The goal of this command is love, which comes from a pure heart and a good conscience and a sincere faith. . . .

18Timothy, my son, I give you this instruction in keeping with the prophecies once made about you, so that by following them you may fight the good fight, 19holding on to faith and a good conscience. Some have rejected these and so have shipwrecked their faith.
1 Tim 3 8Deacons, likewise, are to be men worthy of respect, sincere, not indulging in much wine, and not pursuing dishonest gain. 9They must keep hold of the deep truths of the faith with a clear conscience.
2 Tim 1 3I thank God, whom I serve, as my forefathers did, with a clear conscience, as night and day I constantly remember you in my prayers.
Heb 13 18Pray for us. We are sure that we have a clear conscience and desire to live honorably in every way.
1 Pet 3 15But in your hearts set apart Christ as Lord. Always be prepared to give an answer to everyone who asks you to give the reason for the hope that you have. But do this with gentleness and respect, 16keeping a clear conscience, so that those who speak maliciously against your good behavior in Christ may be ashamed of their slander.

B. People Make Moral Decisions

1. The Existence of Moral Decisions

Gen 3 1Now the serpent was more crafty than any of the wild animals the LORD God had made. He said to the woman, "Did God really say, 'You must not eat from any tree in the garden'?"

2The woman said to the serpent, "We may eat fruit from the trees in the garden, 3but God did say, 'You must not eat fruit from the tree that is in the middle of the garden, and you must not touch it, or you will die.'"

4"You will not surely die," the serpent said to the woman. 5"For God knows that when you eat of it your eyes will be opened, and you will be like God, knowing good and evil."
Exod 19 5"'Now if you obey me fully and keep my covenant, then out of all nations you will be my treasured possession. Although the whole earth is mine . . .'"
Lev 26 3"'If you follow my decrees and are careful to obey my commands, 4I will send you rain in its season, and the ground will yield its crops and the trees of the field their fruit. 5Your threshing will continue until grape harvest and the grape harvest will continue until planting, and you will eat all the food you want and live in safety in your land.

6"'I will grant peace in the land, and you will lie down and no one will make you afraid. I will remove savage beasts from the land, and the sword will not pass through your country. . . .

9"'I will look on you with favor and make you fruitful and increase your numbers, and I will keep my covenant with you. 10You will still be eating last year's harvest when you will have to move it out to make room for the new. 11I will put my dwelling place among you, and I will not abhor you. 12I will walk among you and be your God, and you will be my people. . . .

14"'But if you will not listen to me and carry out all these commands, 15and if you reject my decrees and abhor my laws and fail to carry out all my commands and so violate my covenant, 16then I will do this to you: I will bring upon you sudden terror, wasting diseases and fever that will destroy your sight and drain away your life. You will plant seed in vain, because your enemies will eat it. 17I will set my face against you so that you will be defeated by your enemies; those who hate you will rule over you, and you will flee even when no one is pursuing you.'"
Deut 30 15See, I set before you today life and prosperity, death and destruction. 16For I command you today to love the LORD your God, to walk in his ways, and to keep his commands, decrees and laws; then you will live and increase, and the LORD your God will bless you in the land you are entering to possess.

17But if your heart turns away and you are not obedient, and if you are drawn away to bow down to other gods and worship them, 18I declare to you this day that you will certainly be destroyed. You will not live long in the land you are crossing the Jordan to enter and possess.

19This day I call heaven and earth as witnesses against you that I have set before you life and death, blessings and curses. Now choose life, so that you and your children may live 20and that you may love the LORD your God, listen to his voice, and hold fast to him. For the LORD is your life, and he will give you many years in the land he swore to give to your fathers, Abraham, Isaac and Jacob.
Josh 24 14"Now fear the LORD and serve him with all faithfulness. Throw away the gods your forefathers worshiped beyond the River and in Egypt, and serve the LORD. 15But if serving the LORD seems undesirable to you, then choose for yourselves this day whom you will serve, whether the gods your forefathers

served beyond the River, or the gods of the Amorites, in whose land you are living. But as for me and my household, we will serve the LORD."

2 Sam 24 12"Go and tell David, 'This is what the LORD says: I am giving you three options. Choose one of them for me to carry out against you.'"

13So Gad went to David and said to him, "Shall there come upon you three years of famine in your land? Or three months of fleeing from your enemies while they pursue you? Or three days of plague in your land? Now then, think it over and decide how I should answer the one who sent me."

1 Kings 3 14"And if you walk in my ways and obey my statutes and commands as David your father did, I will give you a long life."

1 Kings 18 21Elijah went before the people and said, "How long will you waver between two opinions? If the LORD is God, follow him; but if Baal is God, follow him."

But the people said nothing.

Job 36 11"If they obey and serve him, they will spend the rest of their days in prosperity and their years in contentment. 12But if they do not listen, they will perish by the sword and die without knowledge."

Ps 1 1Blessed is the man who does not walk in the counsel of the wicked or stand in the way of sinners or sit in the seat of mockers. 2But his delight is in the law of the LORD, and on his law he meditates day and night.

Ps 103 17But from everlasting to everlasting the LORD's love is with those who fear him, and his righteousness with their children's children—18with those who keep his covenant and remember to obey his precepts.

Ps 112 1Praise the LORD.

Blessed is the man who fears the LORD, who finds great delight in his commands.

Prov 1 29"Since they hated knowledge and did not choose to fear the LORD, 30since they would not accept my advice and spurned my rebuke, 31they will eat the fruit of their ways and be filled with the fruit of their schemes. 32For the waywardness of the simple will kill them, and the complacency of fools will destroy them; 33but whoever listens to me will live in safety and be at ease, without fear of harm."

Prov 19 16He who obeys instructions guards his life, but he who is contemptuous of his ways will die.

Prov 28 14Blessed is the man who always fears the LORD, but he who hardens his heart falls into trouble.

Isa 1 18"Come now, let us reason together," says the LORD. "Though your sins are like scarlet, they shall be as white as snow; though they are red as crimson, they shall be like wool. 19If you are willing and obedient, you will eat the best from the land; 20but if you resist and rebel, you will be devoured by the sword." For the mouth of the LORD has spoken.

Jer 21 8"Furthermore, tell the people, 'This is what the LORD says: See, I am setting before you the way of life and the way of death. 9Whoever stays in this city will die by the sword, famine or plague. But whoever goes out and surrenders to the Babylonians who are besieging you will live; he will escape with his life.'"

Jer 22 3"'This is what the LORD says: Do what is just and right. Rescue from the hand of his oppressor the one who has been robbed. Do no wrong or violence to the alien, the fatherless or the widow, and do not shed innocent blood in this place. 4For if you are careful to carry out these commands, then kings who sit on David's throne will come through the gates of this palace, riding in chariots and on horses, accompanied by their officials and their people. 5But if you do not obey these commands, declares the LORD, I swear by myself that this palace will become a ruin.'"

Ezek 33 14"And if I say to the wicked man, 'You will surely die,' but he then turns away from his sin and does what is just and right—15if he gives back what he took in pledge for a loan, returns what he has stolen, follows the decrees that give life, and does no evil, he will surely live; he will not die. 16None of the sins he has committed will be remembered against him. He has done what is just and right; he will surely live."

Matt 5 19"Anyone who breaks one of the least of these commandments and teaches others to do the same will be called least in the kingdom of heaven, but whoever practices and teaches these commands will be called great in the kingdom of heaven."

Matt 5 44"But I tell you: Love your enemies and pray for those who persecute you, 45that you may be sons of your Father in heaven. He causes his sun to rise on the evil and the good, and sends rain on the righteous and the unrighteous."

Matt 6 14"For if you forgive men when they sin against you, your heavenly Father will also forgive you. 15But if you do not forgive men their sins, your Father will not forgive your sins."

Matt 6 24"No one can serve two masters. Either he will hate the one and love the other, or he will be devoted to the one and despise the other. You cannot serve both God and Money."

Matt 7 1"Do not judge, or you too will be judged. 2For in the same way you judge others, you will be judged, and with the measure you use, it will be measured to you."

Mark 3 35"Whoever does God's will is my brother and sister and mother."

John 7 17"If anyone chooses to do God's will, he will find out whether my teaching comes from God or whether I speak on my own."

John 14 15"If you love me, you will obey what I command."

James 2 10For whoever keeps the whole law and yet stumbles at just one point is guilty of breaking all of it. 11For he who said, "Do not commit adultery," also said, "Do not murder." If you do not commit adultery but do commit murder, you have become a lawbreaker.

12Speak and act as those who are going to be judged by the law that gives freedom, 13because judgment without mercy will be shown to anyone who has not been merciful. Mercy triumphs over judgment!

2. Instances of Moral Decisions

a) Human Decisions for Good

Gen 6 9This is the account of Noah.

Noah was a righteous man, blameless among the people of his time, and he walked with God.

Gen 18 19"For I have chosen him, so that he will direct his children and his household after him to keep the way of the LORD by doing what is right and just, so that the LORD will bring about for Abraham what he has promised him."

Exod 24 7Then he took the Book of the Covenant and read it to the people. They responded, "We will do everything the LORD has said; we will obey."

Num 14 24"But because my servant Caleb has a different spirit and follows me wholeheartedly, I will bring him into the land he went to, and his descendants will inherit it."

Deut 1 35"Not a man of this evil generation shall see the good land I swore to give your forefathers, 36except Caleb son of Jephunneh. He will see it, and I will give him and his descendants the land he set his feet on, because he followed the LORD wholeheartedly."

Josh 11 15As the LORD commanded his servant Moses, so Moses commanded Joshua, and Joshua did it; he left nothing undone of all that the LORD commanded Moses.

Josh 22 1Then Joshua summoned the Reubenites, the Gadites and the half-tribe of Manasseh 2and said to them, "You have done all that Moses the servant of the LORD commanded, and you have obeyed me in everything I commanded."

Judg 6 25That same night the LORD said to him, "Take the second bull from your father's herd, the one seven years old. Tear down your father's altar to Baal and cut down the Asherah pole beside it. 26Then build a proper kind of altar to the LORD your God on the top of this height. Using the wood of the Asherah pole that you cut down, offer the second bull as a burnt offering."

27So Gideon took ten of his servants and did as the LORD told him. But because he was afraid of his family and the men of the town, he did it at night rather than in the daytime.

2 Kings 18 5Hezekiah trusted in the LORD, the God of Israel. There was no one like him among all the kings of Judah, either before him or after him. 6He held fast to the LORD and did not cease to follow him; he kept the commands the LORD had given Moses.

Neh 9 7"You are the LORD God, who chose Abram and brought him out of Ur of the Chaldeans and named him Abraham. 8You found his heart faithful to you, and you made a covenant with him to give to his descendants the land of the Canaanites, Hittites, Amorites, Perizzites, Jebusites and Girgashites. You have kept your promise because you are righteous."

Job 1 [8]Then the LORD said to Satan, "Have you considered my servant Job? There is no one on earth like him; he is blameless and upright, a man who fears God and shuns evil."

Ps 99 [7]He spoke to them from the pillar of cloud; they kept his statutes and the decrees he gave them.

Dan 3 [8]At this time some astrologers came forward and denounced the Jews. [9]They said to King Nebuchadnezzar, "O king, live forever! [10]You have issued a decree, O king, that everyone who hears the sound of the horn, flute, zither, lyre, harp, pipes and all kinds of music must fall down and worship the image of gold, [11]and that whoever does not fall down and worship will be thrown into a blazing furnace. [12]But there are some Jews whom you have set over the affairs of the province of Babylon—Shadrach, Meshach and Abednego—who pay no attention to you, O king. They neither serve your gods nor worship the image of gold you have set up."

Dan 6 [6]So the administrators and the satraps went as a group to the king and said: "O King Darius, live forever! [7]The royal administrators, prefects, satraps, advisers and governors have all agreed that the king should issue an edict and enforce the decree that anyone who prays to any god or man during the next thirty days, except to you, O king, shall be thrown into the lions' den. [8]Now, O king, issue the decree and put it in writing so that it cannot be altered—in accordance with the laws of the Medes and Persians, which cannot be repealed." [9]So King Darius put the decree in writing.

[10]Now when Daniel learned that the decree had been published, he went home to his upstairs room where the windows opened toward Jerusalem. Three times a day he got down on his knees and prayed, giving thanks to his God, just as he had done before.

Jon 3 [3]Jonah obeyed the word of the LORD and went to Nineveh. Now Nineveh was a very important city—a visit required three days.

Matt 1 [24]When Joseph woke up, he did what the angel of the Lord had commanded him and took Mary home as his wife.

Matt 2 [13]When they had gone, an angel of the Lord appeared to Joseph in a dream. "Get up," he said, "take the child and his mother and escape to Egypt. Stay there until I tell you, for Herod is going to search for the child to kill him."

[14]So he got up, took the child and his mother during the night and left for Egypt. . . .

Luke 1 [5]In the time of Herod king of Judea there was a priest named Zechariah, who belonged to the priestly division of Abijah; his wife Elizabeth was also a descendant of Aaron. [6]Both of them were upright in the sight of God, observing all the Lord's commandments and regulations blamelessly.

Luke 6 [46]"Why do you call me, 'Lord, Lord,' and do not do what I say? [47]I will show you what he is like who comes to me and hears my words and puts them into practice. [48]He is like a man building a house, who dug down deep and laid the foundation on rock. When a flood came, the torrent struck that house but could not shake it, because it was well built. [49]But the one who hears my words and does not put them into practice is like a man who built a house on the ground without a foundation. The moment the torrent struck that house, it collapsed and its destruction was complete."

Acts 4 [18]Then they called them in again and commanded them not to speak or teach at all in the name of Jesus. [19]But Peter and John replied, "Judge for yourselves whether it is right in God's sight to obey you rather than God. [20]For we cannot help speaking about what we have seen and heard."

Acts 5 [29]Peter and the other apostles replied: "We must obey God rather than men!"

Acts 23 [1]Paul looked straight at the Sanhedrin and said, "My brothers, I have fulfilled my duty to God in all good conscience to this day."

Acts 24 [16]"So I strive always to keep my conscience clear before God and man."

Heb 11 [4]By faith Abel offered God a better sacrifice than Cain did. By faith he was commended as a righteous man, when God spoke well of his offerings. And by faith he still speaks, even though he is dead.

[5]By faith Enoch was taken from this life, so that he did not experience death; he could not be found, because God had taken him away. For before he was taken, he was commended as one who pleased God. [6]And without faith it is impossible to please God, because anyone who comes to him must believe that he exists and that he rewards those who earnestly seek him.

[7]By faith Noah, when warned about things not yet seen, in holy fear built an ark to save his family. By his faith he condemned the world and became heir of the righteousness that comes by faith.

[8]By faith Abraham, when called to go to a place he would later receive as his inheritance, obeyed and went, even though he did not know where he was going. [9]By faith he made his home in the promised land like a stranger in a foreign country; he lived in tents, as did Isaac and Jacob, who were heirs with him of the same promise. [10]For he was looking forward to the city with foundations, whose architect and builder is God.

[11]By faith Abraham, even though he was past age—and Sarah herself was barren—was enabled to become a father because he considered him faithful who had made the promise. [12]And so from this one man, and he as good as dead, came descendants as numerous as the stars in the sky and as countless as the sand on the seashore.

[13]All these people were still living by faith when they died. They did not receive the things promised; they only saw them and welcomed them from a distance. And they admitted that they were aliens and strangers on earth. [14]People who say such things show that they are looking for a country of their own. [15]If they had been thinking of the country they had left, they would have had opportunity to return. [16]Instead, they were longing for a better country—a heavenly one. Therefore God is not ashamed to be called their God, for he has prepared a city for them.

[17]By faith Abraham, when God tested him, offered Isaac as a sacrifice. He who had received the promises was about to sacrifice his one and only son, [18]even though God had said to him, "It is through Isaac that your offspring will be reckoned." [19]Abraham reasoned that God could raise the dead, and figuratively speaking, he did receive Isaac back from death.

[20]By faith Isaac blessed Jacob and Esau in regard to their future.

[21]By faith Jacob, when he was dying, blessed each of Joseph's sons, and worshiped as he leaned on the top of his staff.

[22]By faith Joseph, when his end was near, spoke about the exodus of the Israelites from Egypt and gave instructions about his bones.

[23]By faith Moses' parents hid him for three months after he was born, because they saw he was no ordinary child, and they were not afraid of the king's edict.

[24]By faith Moses, when he had grown up, refused to be known as the son of Pharaoh's daughter. [25]He chose to be mistreated along with the people of God rather than to enjoy the pleasures of sin for a short time. [26]He regarded disgrace for the sake of Christ as of greater value than the treasures of Egypt, because he was looking ahead to his reward. [27]By faith he left Egypt, not fearing the king's anger; he persevered because he saw him who is invisible. [28]By faith he kept the Passover and the sprinkling of blood, so that the destroyer of the firstborn would not touch the firstborn of Israel.

[29]By faith the people passed through the Red Sea as on dry land; but when the Egyptians tried to do so, they were drowned.

[30]By faith the walls of Jericho fell, after the people had marched around them for seven days.

[31]By faith the prostitute Rahab, because she welcomed the spies, was not killed with those who were disobedient.

b) Human Decisions for Evil

Gen 3 [2]The woman said to the serpent, "We may eat fruit from the trees in the garden, [3]but God did say, 'You must not eat fruit from the tree that is in the middle of the garden, and you must not touch it, or you will die.'" . . .

6When the woman saw that the fruit of the tree was good for food and pleasing to the eye, and also desirable for gaining wisdom, she took some and ate it. She also gave some to her husband, who was with her, and he ate it.

Gen 4 6Then the LORD said to Cain, "Why are you angry? Why is your face downcast? 7If you do what is right, will you not be accepted? But if you do not do what is right, sin is crouching at your door; it desires to have you, but you must master it."

8Now Cain said to his brother Abel, "Let's go out to the field." And while they were in the field, Cain attacked his brother Abel and killed him.

9Then the LORD said to Cain, "Where is your brother Abel?"

"I don't know," he replied. "Am I my brother's keeper?"

10The LORD said, "What have you done? Listen! Your brother's blood cries out to me from the ground."

Gen 6 2the sons of God saw that the daughters of men were beautiful, and they married any of them they chose. . . .

5The LORD saw how great man's wickedness on the earth had become, and that every inclination of the thoughts of his heart was only evil all the time.

Gen 12 10Now there was a famine in the land, and Abram went down to Egypt to live there for a while because the famine was severe. 11As he was about to enter Egypt, he said to his wife Sarai, "I know what a beautiful woman you are. 12When the Egyptians see you, they will say, 'This is his wife.' Then they will kill me but will let you live. 13Say you are my sister, so that I will be treated well for your sake and my life will be spared because of you.". . .

17But the LORD inflicted serious diseases on Pharaoh and his household because of Abram's wife Sarai. 18So Pharaoh summoned Abram. "What have you done to me?" he said. "Why didn't you tell me she was your wife? 19Why did you say, 'She is my sister,' so that I took her to be my wife? Now then, here is your wife. Take her and go!"

Gen 19 15With the coming of dawn, the angels urged Lot, saying, "Hurry! Take your wife and your two daughters who are here, or you will be swept away when the city is punished." . . . 17As soon as they had brought them out, one of them said, "Flee for your lives! Don't look back, and don't stop anywhere in the plain! Flee to the mountains or you will be swept away!" . . . 26But Lot's wife looked back, and she became a pillar of salt.

Exod 9 33Then Moses left Pharaoh and went out of the city. He spread out his hands toward the LORD; the thunder and hail stopped, and the rain no longer poured down on the land. 34When Pharaoh saw that the rain and hail and thunder had stopped, he sinned again: He and his officials hardened their hearts. 35So Pharaoh's heart was hard and he would not let the Israelites go, just as the LORD had said through Moses.

Josh 5 6The Israelites had moved about in the desert forty years until all the men who were of military age when they left Egypt had died, since they had not obeyed the LORD. For the LORD had sworn to them that they would not see the land that he had solemnly promised their fathers to give us, a land flowing with milk and honey.

Josh 7 1But the Israelites acted unfaithfully in regard to the devoted things; Achan son of Carmi, the son of Zimri, the son of Zerah, of the tribe of Judah, took some of them. So the LORD's anger burned against Israel. . . .

19Then Joshua said to Achan, "My son, give glory to the LORD, the God of Israel, and give him the praise. Tell me what you have done; do not hide it from me."

20Achan replied, "It is true! I have sinned against the LORD, the God of Israel. This is what I have done: 21When I saw in the plunder a beautiful robe from Babylonia, two hundred shekels of silver and a wedge of gold weighing fifty shekels, I coveted them and took them. They are hidden in the ground inside my tent, with the silver underneath."

1 Sam 13 13"You acted foolishly," Samuel said. "You have not kept the command the LORD your God gave you; if you had, he would have established your kingdom over Israel for all time. 14But now your kingdom will not endure; the LORD has sought out a man after his own heart and appointed him leader of his people, because you have not kept the LORD's command."

1 Sam 28 16Samuel said, "Why do you consult me, now that the LORD has turned away from you and become your enemy? 17The LORD has done what he predicted through me. The LORD has torn the kingdom out of your hands and given it to one of your neighbors—to David. 18Because you did not obey the LORD or carry out his fierce wrath against the Amalekites, the LORD has done this to you today. 19The LORD will hand over both Israel and you to the Philistines, and tomorrow you and your sons will be with me. The LORD will also hand over the army of Israel to the Philistines."

2 Sam 12 9"'Why did you despise the word of the LORD by doing what is evil in his eyes? You struck down Uriah the Hittite with the sword and took his wife to be your own. You killed him with the sword of the Ammonites.'"

1 Kings 11 7On a hill east of Jerusalem, Solomon built a high place for Chemosh the detestable god of Moab, and for Molech the detestable god of the Ammonites. 8He did the same for all his foreign wives, who burned incense and offered sacrifices to their gods.

9The LORD became angry with Solomon because his heart had turned away from the LORD, the God of Israel, who had appeared to him twice. 10Although he had forbidden Solomon to follow other gods, Solomon did not keep the LORD's command.

1 Kings 20 35By the word of the LORD one of the sons of the prophets said to his companion, "Strike me with your weapon," but the man refused.

36So the prophet said, "Because you have not obeyed the LORD, as soon as you leave me a lion will kill you." And after the man went away, a lion found him and killed him.

1 Kings 20 42He said to the king, "This is what the LORD says: 'You have set free a man I had determined should die. Therefore it is your life for his life, your people for his people.'"

Ps 106 24Then they despised the pleasant land; they did not believe his promise. 25They grumbled in their tents and did not obey the LORD.

Eccles 7 29"This only have I found: God made mankind upright, but men have gone in search of many schemes."

Isa 1 12"When you come to appear before me, who has asked this of you, this trampling of my courts? 13Stop bringing meaningless offerings! Your incense is detestable to me. New Moons, Sabbaths and convocations—I cannot bear your evil assemblies. 14Your New Moon festivals and your appointed feasts my soul hates. They have become a burden to me; I am weary of bearing them. 15When you spread out your hands in prayer, I will hide my eyes from you; even if you offer many prayers, I will not listen. Your hands are full of blood; 16wash and make yourselves clean. Take your evil deeds out of my sight! Stop doing wrong, 17learn to do right! Seek justice, encourage the oppressed. Defend the cause of the fatherless, plead the case of the widow."

Jer 43 7So they entered Egypt in disobedience to the LORD and went as far as Tahpanhes.

Jer 44 8"Why provoke me to anger with what your hands have made, burning incense to other gods in Egypt, where you have come to live? You will destroy yourselves and make yourselves an object of cursing and reproach among all the nations on earth. 9Have you forgotten the wickedness committed by your fathers and by the kings and queens of Judah and the wickedness committed by you and your wives in the land of Judah and the streets of Jerusalem? 10To this day they have not humbled themselves or shown reverence, nor have they followed my law and the decrees I set before you and your fathers.

11"Therefore, this is what the LORD Almighty, the God of Israel, says: I am determined to bring disaster on you and to destroy all Judah. 12I will take away the remnant of Judah who were determined to go to Egypt to settle there. They will all perish in Egypt; they will fall by the sword or die from famine. From the least to the greatest, they will die by sword or famine. They will become an object of cursing and horror, of condemnation and reproach. . . ."

15Then all the men who knew that their wives were burning incense to other gods, along with all the women who were present—a large assembly—and all the people living in Lower and Upper Egypt, said to Jeremiah, 16"We will not listen to the message you have spoken to us in the name of the LORD!"

Dan 5 20"But when his heart became arrogant and hardened with pride, he was deposed from his royal throne and stripped of his glory. . . .

[22]"But you his son, O Belshazzar, have not humbled yourself, though you knew all this. [23]Instead, you have set yourself up against the Lord of heaven. You had the goblets from his temple brought to you, and you and your nobles, your wives and your concubines drank wine from them. You praised the gods of silver and gold, of bronze, iron, wood and stone, which cannot see or hear or understand. But you did not honor the God who holds in his hand your life and all your ways."

Matt 23 [37]"O Jerusalem, Jerusalem, you who kill the prophets and stone those sent to you, how often I have longed to gather your children together, as a hen gathers her chicks under her wings, but you were not willing."

1 Pet 4 [3]For you have spent enough time in the past doing what pagans choose to do—living in debauchery, lust, drunkenness, orgies, carousing and detestable idolatry.

C. People Express Moral Affections

1. They Express Altruism

Prov 3 [27]Do not withhold good from those who deserve it, when it is in your power to act.

Matt 25 [34]"Then the King will say to those on his right, 'Come, you who are blessed by my Father; take your inheritance, the kingdom prepared for you since the creation of the world. [35]For I was hungry and you gave me something to eat, I was thirsty and you gave me something to drink, I was a stranger and you invited me in, [36]I needed clothes and you clothed me, I was sick and you looked after me, I was in prison and you came to visit me.'"

Rom 12 [13]Share with God's people who are in need. Practice hospitality.

Rom 15 [1]We who are strong ought to bear with the failings of the weak and not to please ourselves. [2]Each of us should please his neighbor for his good, to build him up.

1 Cor 10 [24]Nobody should seek his own good, but the good of others.

Gal 6 [1]Brothers, if someone is caught in a sin, you who are spiritual should restore him gently. But watch yourself, or you also may be tempted. [2]Carry each other's burdens, and in this way you will fulfill the law of Christ.

Phil 2 [4]Each of you should look not only to your own interests, but also to the interests of others.

2. They Express Compassion

1 Kings 3 [26]The woman whose son was alive was filled with compassion for her son and said to the king, "Please, my lord, give her the living baby! Don't kill him!"

But the other said, "Neither I nor you shall have him. Cut him in two!"

Ps 103 [13]As a father has compassion on his children, so the LORD has compassion on those who fear him. . . .

Zech 7 [9]"This is what the LORD Almighty says: 'Administer true justice; show mercy and compassion to one another. [10]Do not oppress the widow or the fatherless, the alien or the poor. In your hearts do not think evil of each other.'"

Mal 3 [17]"They will be mine," says the LORD Almighty, "in the day when I make up my treasured possession. I will spare them, just as in compassion a man spares his son who serves him."

Matt 18 [27]"The servant's master took pity on him, canceled the debt and let him go."

Eph 4 [32]Be kind and compassionate to one another, forgiving each other, just as in Christ God forgave you.

Phil 2 [1]If you have any encouragement from being united with Christ, if any comfort from his love, if any fellowship with the Spirit, if any tenderness and compassion, [2]then make my joy complete by being like-minded, having the same love, being one in spirit and purpose.

Col 3 [12]Therefore, as God's chosen people, holy and dearly loved, clothe yourselves with compassion, kindness, humility, gentleness and patience.

1 Pet 3 [8]Finally, all of you, live in harmony with one another; be sympathetic, love as brothers, be compassionate and humble.

1 John 3 [17]If anyone has material possessions and sees his brother in need but has no pity on him, how can the love of God be in him? [18]Dear children, let us not love with words or tongue but with actions and in truth.

3. They Express Forgiveness

Gen 50 [15]When Joseph's brothers saw that their father was dead, they said, "What if Joseph holds a grudge against us and pays us back for all the wrongs we did to him?" [16]So they sent word to Joseph, saying, "Your father left these instructions before he died: [17]'This is what you are to say to Joseph: I ask you to forgive your brothers the sins and the wrongs they committed in treating you so badly.' Now please forgive the sins of the servants of the God of your father." When their message came to him, Joseph wept.

[18]His brothers then came and threw themselves down before him. "We are your slaves," they said.

[19]But Joseph said to them, "Don't be afraid. Am I in the place of God? [20]You intended to harm me, but God intended it for good to accomplish what is now being done, the saving of many lives. [21]So then, don't be afraid. I will provide for you and your children." And he reassured them and spoke kindly to them.

Matt 18 [21]Then Peter came to Jesus and asked, "Lord, how many times shall I forgive my brother when he sins against me? Up to seven times?"

[22]Jesus answered, "I tell you, not seven times, but seventy-seven times."

Mark 11 [25]"And when you stand praying, if you hold anything against anyone, forgive him, so that your Father in heaven may forgive you your sins."

Luke 6 [37]"Do not judge, and you will not be judged. Do not condemn, and you will not be condemned. Forgive, and you will be forgiven."

Luke 17 [3]"So watch yourselves.

"If your brother sins, rebuke him, and if he repents, forgive him. [4]If he sins against you seven times in a day, and seven times comes back to you and says, 'I repent,' forgive him."

2 Cor 2 [6]The punishment inflicted on him by the majority is sufficient for him. [7]Now instead, you ought to forgive and comfort him, so that he will not be overwhelmed by excessive sorrow. [8]I urge you, therefore, to reaffirm your love for him. [9]The reason I wrote you was to see if you would stand the test and be obedient in everything. [10]If you forgive anyone, I also forgive him. And what I have forgiven—if there was anything to forgive—I have forgiven in the sight of Christ for your sake, [11]in order that Satan might not outwit us. For we are not unaware of his schemes.

Eph 4 [32]Be kind and compassionate to one another, forgiving each other, just as in Christ God forgave you.

Col 3 [13]Bear with each other and forgive whatever grievances you may have against one another. Forgive as the Lord forgave you.

4. They Express Generosity

2 Sam 24 [22]Araunah said to David, "Let my lord the king take whatever pleases him and offer it up. Here are oxen for the burnt offering, and here are threshing sledges and ox yokes for the wood. [23]O king, Araunah gives all this to the king." Araunah also said to him, "May the LORD your God accept you."

[24]But the king replied to Araunah, "No, I insist on paying you for it. I will not sacrifice to the LORD my God burnt offerings that cost me nothing."

So David bought the threshing floor and the oxen and paid fifty shekels of silver for them.

Ps 37 [26]They are always generous and lend freely; their children will be blessed.

Ps 41 [1]Blessed is he who has regard for the weak; the LORD delivers him in times of trouble.

Ps 112 [5]Good will come to him who is generous and lends freely, who conducts his affairs with justice.

Prov 3 [27]Do not withhold good from those who deserve it, when it is in your power to act. [28]Do not say to your neighbor,

"Come back later; I'll give it tomorrow"—when you now have it with you.

Prov 11 [24]One man gives freely, yet gains even more; another withholds unduly, but comes to poverty.

[25]A generous man will prosper; he who refreshes others will himself be refreshed.

Prov 21 [25]The sluggard's craving will be the death of him, because his hands refuse to work. [26]All day long he craves for more, but the righteous give without sparing.

Eccles 11 [1]Cast your bread upon the waters, for after many days you will find it again.

Matt 5 [38]"You have heard that it was said, 'Eye for eye, and tooth for tooth.' [39]But I tell you, Do not resist an evil person. If someone strikes you on the right cheek, turn to him the other also. [40]And if someone wants to sue you and take your tunic, let him have your cloak as well. [41]If someone forces you to go one mile, go with him two miles. [42]Give to the one who asks you, and do not turn away from the one who wants to borrow from you."

Mark 14 [6]"Leave her alone," said Jesus. "Why are you bothering her? She has done a beautiful thing to me. [7]The poor you will always have with you, and you can help them any time you want. But you will not always have me. [8]She did what she could. She poured perfume on my body beforehand to prepare for my burial. [9]I tell you the truth, wherever the gospel is preached throughout the world, what she has done will also be told, in memory of her."

Luke 6 [35]"But love your enemies, do good to them, and lend to them without expecting to get anything back. Then your reward will be great, and you will be sons of the Most High, because he is kind to the ungrateful and wicked."

Acts 20 [35]"In everything I did, I showed you that by this kind of hard work we must help the weak, remembering the words the Lord Jesus himself said: 'It is more blessed to give than to receive.'"

2 Cor 8 [1]And now, brothers, we want you to know about the grace that God has given the Macedonian churches. [2]Out of the most severe trial, their overflowing joy and their extreme poverty welled up in rich generosity. [3]For I testify that they gave as much as they were able, and even beyond their ability. Entirely on their own, [4]they urgently pleaded with us for the privilege of sharing in this service to the saints.

2 Cor 9 [2]For I know your eagerness to help, and I have been boasting about it to the Macedonians, telling them that since last year you in Achaia were ready to give; and your enthusiasm has stirred most of them to action. . . . [5]So I thought it necessary to urge the brothers to visit you in advance and finish the arrangements for the generous gift you had promised. Then it will be ready as a generous gift, not as one grudgingly given. . . . [11]You will be made rich in every way so that you can be generous on every occasion, and through us your generosity will result in thanksgiving to God. . . . [13]Because of the service by which you have proved yourselves, men will praise God for the obedience that accompanies your confession of the gospel of Christ, and for your generosity in sharing with them and with everyone else.

Eph 4 [28]He who has been stealing must steal no longer, but must work, doing something useful with his own hands, that he may have something to share with those in need.

1 Tim 6 [18]Command them to do good, to be rich in good deeds, and to be generous and willing to share.

1 John 3 [17]If anyone has material possessions and sees his brother in need but has no pity on him, how can the love of God be in him?

5. They Express Goodness

Prov 11 [27]He who seeks good finds goodwill, but evil comes to him who searches for it.

Amos 5 [14]Seek good, not evil, that you may live. Then the LORD God Almighty will be with you, just as you say he is. [15]Hate evil, love good; maintain justice in the courts. Perhaps the LORD God Almighty will have mercy on the remnant of Joseph.

Mic 6 [8]He has showed you, O man, what is good. And what does the LORD require of you? To act justly and to love mercy and to walk humbly with your God.

Matt 5 [16]"In the same way, let your light shine before men, that they may see your good deeds and praise your Father in heaven."

Matt 5 [44]"But I tell you: Love your enemies and pray for those who persecute you, [45]that you may be sons of your Father in heaven. He causes his sun to rise on the evil and the good, and sends rain on the righteous and the unrighteous."

Luke 6 [35]"But love your enemies, do good to them, and lend to them without expecting to get anything back. Then your reward will be great, and you will be sons of the Most High, because he is kind to the ungrateful and wicked."

Rom 12 [9]Love must be sincere. Hate what is evil; cling to what is good. . . . [21]Do not be overcome by evil, but overcome evil with good.

2 Cor 9 [8]And God is able to make all grace abound to you, so that in all things at all times, having all that you need, you will abound in every good work.

1 Thess 5 [21]Test everything. Hold on to the good. [22]Avoid every kind of evil.

2 Tim 2 [20]In a large house there are articles not only of gold and silver, but also of wood and clay; some are for noble purposes and some for ignoble. [21]If a man cleanses himself from the latter, he will be an instrument for noble purposes, made holy, useful to the Master and prepared to do any good work.

2 Tim 3 [16]All Scripture is God-breathed and is useful for teaching, rebuking, correcting and training in righteousness, [17]so that the man of God may be thoroughly equipped for every good work.

Titus 2 [13]while we wait for the blessed hope—the glorious appearing of our great God and Savior, Jesus Christ, [14]who gave himself for us to redeem us from all wickedness and to purify for himself a people that are his very own, eager to do what is good.

Heb 10 [34]You sympathized with those in prison and joyfully accepted the confiscation of your property, because you knew that you yourselves had better and lasting possessions.

3 John [11]Dear friend, do not imitate what is evil but what is good. Anyone who does what is good is from God. Anyone who does what is evil has not seen God.

6. They Express Kindness

1 Sam 20 [5]So David said, "Look, tomorrow is the New Moon festival, and I am supposed to dine with the king; but let me go and hide in the field until the evening of the day after tomorrow. . . . [8]As for you, show kindness to your servant, for you have brought him into a covenant with you before the LORD. If I am guilty, then kill me yourself! Why hand me over to your father?"

[9]"Never!" Jonathan said. "If I had the least inkling that my father was determined to harm you, wouldn't I tell you?"

[10]David asked, "Who will tell me if your father answers you harshly?"

[11]"Come," Jonathan said, "let's go out into the field." So they went there together.

[12]Then Jonathan said to David: "By the LORD, the God of Israel, I will surely sound out my father by this time the day after tomorrow! If he is favorably disposed toward you, will I not send you word and let you know? [13]But if my father is inclined to harm you, may the LORD deal with me, be it ever so severely, if I do not let you know and send you away safely. May the LORD be with you as he has been with my father. [14]But show me unfailing kindness like that of the LORD as long as I live, so that I may not be killed, [15]and do not ever cut off your kindness from my family—not even when the LORD has cut off every one of David's enemies from the face of the earth."

[16]So Jonathan made a covenant with the house of David, saying, "May the LORD call David's enemies to account." [17]And Jonathan had David reaffirm his oath out of love for him, because he loved him as he loved himself.

1 Chron 19 [2]David thought, "I will show kindness to Hanun son of Nahash, because his father showed kindness to me." So David sent a delegation to express his sympathy to Hanun concerning his father.

When David's men came to Hanun in the land of the Ammonites to express sympathy to him . . .

Prov 11 16A kindhearted woman gains respect, but ruthless men gain only wealth.

17A kind man benefits himself, but a cruel man brings trouble on himself.

Prov 14 21He who despises his neighbor sins, but blessed is he who is kind to the needy.

Acts 28 2The islanders showed us unusual kindness. They built a fire and welcomed us all because it was raining and cold.

Eph 4 32Be kind and compassionate to one another, forgiving each other, just as in Christ God forgave you.

1 Thess 5 15Make sure that nobody pays back wrong for wrong, but always try to be kind to each other and to everyone else.

2 Pet 1 5For this very reason, make every effort to add to your faith goodness; and to goodness, knowledge; 6and to knowledge, self-control; and to self-control, perseverance; and to perseverance, godliness; 7and to godliness, brotherly kindness; and to brotherly kindness, love.

7. They Express Love

Lev 19 18"'Do not seek revenge or bear a grudge against one of your people, but love your neighbor as yourself. I am the LORD.'"

1 Sam 20 17And Jonathan had David reaffirm his oath out of love for him, because he loved him as he loved himself.

Prov 10 12Hatred stirs up dissension, but love covers over all wrongs.

Prov 21 21He who pursues righteousness and love finds life, prosperity and honor.

Song of Songs 8 6Place me like a seal over your heart, like a seal on your arm; for love is as strong as death, its jealousy unyielding as the grave. It burns like blazing fire, like a mighty flame. 7Many waters cannot quench love; rivers cannot wash it away. If one were to give all the wealth of his house for love, it would be utterly scorned.

Hos 12 6But you must return to your God; maintain love and justice, and wait for your God always.

John 13 34"A new command I give you: Love one another. As I have loved you, so you must love one another. 35By this all men will know that you are my disciples, if you love one another."

Rom 12 9Love must be sincere. Hate what is evil; cling to what is good. 10Be devoted to one another in brotherly love. Honor one another above yourselves.

1 Cor 13 1If I speak in the tongues of men and of angels, but have not love, I am only a resounding gong or a clanging cymbal. 2If I have the gift of prophecy and can fathom all mysteries and all knowledge, and if I have a faith that can move mountains, but have not love, I am nothing. 3If I give all I possess to the poor and surrender my body to the flames, but have not love, I gain nothing.

4Love is patient, love is kind. It does not envy, it does not boast, it is not proud. 5It is not rude, it is not self-seeking, it is not easily angered, it keeps no record of wrongs. 6Love does not delight in evil but rejoices with the truth. 7It always protects, always trusts, always hopes, always perseveres.

8Love never fails. But where there are prophecies, they will cease; where there are tongues, they will be stilled; where there is knowledge, it will pass away. . . .

13And now these three remain: faith, hope and love. But the greatest of these is love.

1 Cor 16 14Do everything in love.

Gal 5 13You, my brothers, were called to be free. But do not use your freedom to indulge the sinful nature; rather, serve one another in love. 14The entire law is summed up in a single command: "Love your neighbor as yourself."

Col 2 2My purpose is that they may be encouraged in heart and united in love, so that they may have the full riches of complete understanding, in order that they may know the mystery of God, namely, Christ. . . .

Col 3 14And over all these virtues put on love, which binds them all together in perfect unity.

1 Thess 1 3We continually remember before our God and Father your work produced by faith, your labor prompted by love, and your endurance inspired by hope in our Lord Jesus Christ.

1 Tim 1 5The goal of this command is love, which comes from a pure heart and a good conscience and a sincere faith.

2 Tim 2 22Flee the evil desires of youth, and pursue righteousness, faith, love and peace, along with those who call on the Lord out of a pure heart.

1 Pet 4 8Above all, love each other deeply, because love covers over a multitude of sins.

1 John 2 10Whoever loves his brother lives in the light, and there is nothing in him to make him stumble.

1 John 3 18Dear children, let us not love with words or tongue but with actions and in truth.

1 John 4 7Dear friends, let us love one another, for love comes from God. Everyone who loves has been born of God and knows God.

8. They Express Meekness

Ps 37 11But the meek will inherit the land and enjoy great peace.

Ps 149 4For the LORD takes delight in his people; he crowns the humble with salvation.

Prov 15 1A gentle answer turns away wrath, but a harsh word stirs up anger.

Prov 25 15Through patience a ruler can be persuaded, and a gentle tongue can break a bone.

Eccles 7 8The end of a matter is better than its beginning, and patience is better than pride.

Zeph 2 3Seek the LORD, all you humble of the land, you who do what he commands. Seek righteousness, seek humility; perhaps you will be sheltered on the day of the LORD's anger.

Matt 5 5"Blessed are the meek, for they will inherit the earth."

Matt 11 29"Take my yoke upon you and learn from me, for I am gentle and humble in heart, and you will find rest for your souls."

Eph 4 1As a prisoner for the Lord, then, I urge you to live a life worthy of the calling you have received. 2Be completely humble and gentle; be patient, bearing with one another in love.

Phil 2 14Do everything without complaining or arguing, 15so that you may become blameless and pure, children of God without fault in a crooked and depraved generation, in which you shine like stars in the universe. . . .

2 Tim 2 24And the Lord's servant must not quarrel; instead, he must be kind to everyone, able to teach, not resentful. 25Those who oppose him he must gently instruct, in the hope that God will grant them repentance leading them to a knowledge of the truth. . . .

Titus 3 1Remind the people to be subject to rulers and authorities, to be obedient, to be ready to do whatever is good, 2to slander no one, to be peaceable and considerate, and to show true humility toward all men.

James 3 13Who is wise and understanding among you? Let him show it by his good life, by deeds done in the humility that comes from wisdom. . . .

17But the wisdom that comes from heaven is first of all pure; then peace-loving, considerate, submissive, full of mercy and good fruit, impartial and sincere.

1 Pet 3 3Your beauty should not come from outward adornment, such as braided hair and the wearing of gold jewelry and fine clothes. 4Instead, it should be that of your inner self, the unfading beauty of a gentle and quiet spirit, which is of great worth in God's sight.

9. They Express Mercy

Mic 6 8He has showed you, O man, what is good. And what does the LORD require of you? To act justly and to love mercy and to walk humbly with your God.

Zech 7 9"This is what the LORD Almighty says: 'Administer true justice; show mercy and compassion to one another.'"

Matt 5 7"Blessed are the merciful, for they will be shown mercy."

Matt 23 23"Woe to you, teachers of the law and Pharisees, you hypocrites! You give a tenth of your spices—mint, dill and cummin. But you have neglected the more important matters of the law—justice, mercy and faithfulness. You should have practiced the latter, without neglecting the former."

Luke 6 36"Be merciful, just as your Father is merciful."

Rom 12 6We have different gifts, according to the grace given us. If a man's gift is prophesying, let him use it in proportion to his faith. 8. . . if it is encouraging, let him encourage; if it is contributing to the needs of others, let him give generously; if it is leadership, let him govern diligently; if it is showing mercy, let him do it cheerfully.
James 2 13because judgment without mercy will be shown to anyone who has not been merciful. Mercy triumphs over judgment!
Jude 22Be merciful to those who doubt; 23snatch others from the fire and save them; to others show mercy, mixed with fear—hating even the clothing stained by corrupted flesh.

D. People Experience Moral Indignation

1. They Can Be Indignant toward Evil

Gen 19 6Lot went outside to meet them and shut the door behind him 7and said, "No, my friends. Don't do this wicked thing."
Gen 44 4They had not gone far from the city when Joseph said to his steward, "Go after those men at once, and when you catch up with them, say to them, 'Why have you repaid good with evil? 5Isn't this the cup my master drinks from and also uses for divination? This is a wicked thing you have done.'"
Judg 11 27"I have not wronged you, but you are doing me wrong by waging war against me. Let the LORD, the Judge, decide the dispute this day between the Israelites and the Ammonites."
Judg 19 23The owner of the house went outside and said to them, "No, my friends, don't be so vile. Since this man is my guest, don't do this disgraceful thing."
1 Sam 25 21David had just said, "It's been useless—all my watching over this fellow's property in the desert so that nothing of his was missing. He has paid me back evil for good."
Job 1 1In the land of Uz there lived a man whose name was Job. This man was blameless and upright; he feared God and shunned evil.
Job 8 3"Does God pervert justice? Does the Almighty pervert what is right? 4When your children sinned against him, he gave them over to the penalty of their sin. . . .

20"Surely God does not reject a blameless man or strengthen the hands of evildoers."
Job 20 12"Though evil is sweet in his mouth and he hides it under his tongue, 13though he cannot bear to let it go and keeps it in his mouth, 14yet his food will turn sour in his stomach; it will become the venom of serpents within him. 15He will spit out the riches he swallowed; God will make his stomach vomit them up. 16He will suck the poison of serpents; the fangs of an adder will kill him."
Ps 1 1Blessed is the man who does not walk in the counsel of the wicked or stand in the way of sinners or sit in the seat of mockers.
Ps 7 14He who is pregnant with evil and conceives trouble gives birth to disillusionment. 15He who digs a hole and scoops it out falls into the pit he has made. 16The trouble he causes recoils on himself; his violence comes down on his own head.
Ps 26 5I abhor the assembly of evildoers and refuse to sit with the wicked.
Ps 35 12They repay me evil for good and leave my soul forlorn.
Ps 97 10Let those who love the LORD hate evil, for he guards the lives of his faithful ones and delivers them from the hand of the wicked.
Ps 141 9Keep me from the snares they have laid for me, from the traps set by evildoers. 10Let the wicked fall into their own nets, while I pass by in safety.
Prov 5 22The evil deeds of a wicked man ensnare him; the cords of his sin hold him fast.
Prov 8 13"To fear the LORD is to hate evil; I hate pride and arrogance, evil behavior and perverse speech."
Prov 11 7When a wicked man dies, his hope perishes; all he expected from his power comes to nothing.
Prov 17 4A wicked man listens to evil lips; a liar pays attention to a malicious tongue. . . .

11An evil man is bent only on rebellion; a merciless official will be sent against him. . . .

13If a man pays back evil for good, evil will never leave his house.
Prov 29 27The righteous detest the dishonest; the wicked detest the upright.
Isa 1 4Ah, sinful nation, a people loaded with guilt, a brood of evildoers, children given to corruption! They have forsaken the LORD; they have spurned the Holy One of Israel and turned their backs on him.
Isa 26 10Though grace is shown to the wicked, they do not learn righteousness; even in a land of uprightness they go on doing evil and regard not the majesty of the LORD.
Amos 5 14Seek good, not evil, that you may live. Then the LORD God Almighty will be with you, just as you say he is. 15Hate evil, love good; maintain justice in the courts. Perhaps the LORD God Almighty will have mercy on the remnant of Joseph.
Rom 12 9Love must be sincere. Hate what is evil; cling to what is good.
1 Cor 13 6Love does not delight in evil but rejoices with the truth.
1 Thess 5 22Avoid every kind of evil.
2 Tim 2 22Flee the evil desires of youth, and pursue righteousness, faith, love and peace, along with those who call on the Lord out of a pure heart.
James 1 13When tempted, no one should say, "God is tempting me." For God cannot be tempted by evil, nor does he tempt anyone; 14but each one is tempted when, by his own evil desire, he is dragged away and enticed. 15Then, after desire has conceived, it gives birth to sin; and sin, when it is full-grown, gives birth to death.
1 Pet 3 9Do not repay evil with evil or insult with insult, but with blessing, because to this you were called so that you may inherit a blessing.
3 John 11Dear friend, do not imitate what is evil but what is good. Anyone who does what is good is from God. Anyone who does what is evil has not seen God.

2. They Can Be Indignant toward Injustice

Exod 23 6"Do not deny justice to your poor people in their lawsuits. 7Have nothing to do with a false charge and do not put an innocent or honest person to death, for I will not acquit the guilty."
Lev 19 15"'Do not pervert justice; do not show partiality to the poor or favoritism to the great, but judge your neighbor fairly.'"
Deut 24 17Do not deprive the alien or the fatherless of justice, or take the cloak of the widow as a pledge.
1 Sam 8 1When Samuel grew old, he appointed his sons as judges for Israel. . . . 3But his sons did not walk in his ways. They turned aside after dishonest gain and accepted bribes and perverted justice.

4So all the elders of Israel gathered together and came to Samuel at Ramah. 5They said to him, "You are old, and your sons do not walk in your ways; now appoint a king to lead us, such as all the other nations have."
Job 16 12"All was well with me, but he shattered me; he seized me by the neck and crushed me. He has made me his target. . . . 16My face is red with weeping, deep shadows ring my eyes; 17yet my hands have been free of violence and my prayer is pure.

18"O earth, do not cover my blood; may my cry never be laid to rest! 19Even now my witness is in heaven; my advocate is on high."
Job 19 7"Though I cry, 'I've been wronged!' I get no response; though I call for help, there is no justice."
Job 24 2"Men move boundary stones; they pasture flocks they have stolen. 3They drive away the orphan's donkey and take the widow's ox in pledge. 4They thrust the needy from the path and force all the poor of the land into hiding."
Ps 37 21The wicked borrow and do not repay, but the righteous give generously. . . .
Ps 58 1Do you rulers indeed speak justly? Do you judge uprightly among men? 2No, in your heart you devise injustice, and your hands mete out violence on the earth. 3Even from birth the wicked go astray; from the womb they are wayward and speak lies. 4Their venom is like the venom of a snake, like

that of a cobra that has stopped its ears, [5]that will not heed the tune of the charmer, however skillful the enchanter may be.
Ps 64 [1]Hear me, O God, as I voice my complaint; protect my life from the threat of the enemy. [2]Hide me from the conspiracy of the wicked, from that noisy crowd of evildoers.

[3]They sharpen their tongues like swords and aim their words like deadly arrows. [4]They shoot from ambush at the innocent man; they shoot at him suddenly, without fear.

[5]They encourage each other in evil plans, they talk about hiding their snares; they say, "Who will see them?" [6]They plot injustice and say, "We have devised a perfect plan!" Surely the mind and heart of man are cunning.
Prov 16 [8]Better a little with righteousness than much gain with injustice.
Prov 17 [23]A wicked man accepts a bribe in secret to pervert the course of justice.
Prov 19 [28]A corrupt witness mocks at justice, and the mouth of the wicked gulps down evil.
Prov 20 [17]Food gained by fraud tastes sweet to a man, but he ends up with a mouth full of gravel.
Prov 28 [16]A tyrannical ruler lacks judgment, but he who hates ill-gotten gain will enjoy a long life.
Eccles 3 [16]And I saw something else under the sun: In the place of judgment—wickedness was there, in the place of justice—wickedness was there.
Eccles 5 [8]If you see the poor oppressed in a district, and justice and rights denied, do not be surprised at such things; for one official is eyed by a higher one, and over them both are others higher still.
Isa 5 [22]Woe to those who are heroes at drinking wine and champions at mixing drinks, [23]who acquit the guilty for a bribe, but deny justice to the innocent.
Isa 29 [20]The ruthless will vanish, the mockers will disappear, and all who have an eye for evil will be cut down—[21]those who with a word make a man out to be guilty, who ensnare the defender in court and with false testimony deprive the innocent of justice.
Jer 22 [13]"Woe to him who builds his palace by unrighteousness, his upper rooms by injustice, making his countrymen work for nothing, not paying them for their labor."
Hos 12 [7]The merchant uses dishonest scales; he loves to defraud.
Hab 1 [4]Therefore the law is paralyzed, and justice never prevails. The wicked hem in the righteous, so that justice is perverted.
Zeph 3 [5]The LORD within her is righteous; he does no wrong. Morning by morning he dispenses his justice, and every new day he does not fail, yet the unrighteous know no shame.

3. They Can Be Indignant toward Oppression

Neh 5 [1]Now the men and their wives raised a great outcry against their Jewish brothers. [2]Some were saying, "We and our sons and daughters are numerous; in order for us to eat and stay alive, we must get grain."

[3]Others were saying, "We are mortgaging our fields, our vineyards and our homes to get grain during the famine."

[4]Still others were saying, "We have had to borrow money to pay the king's tax on our fields and vineyards. [5]Although we are of the same flesh and blood as our countrymen and though our sons are as good as theirs, yet we have to subject our sons and daughters to slavery. Some of our daughters have already been enslaved, but we are powerless, because our fields and our vineyards belong to others."

[6]When I heard their outcry and these charges, I was very angry. [7]I pondered them in my mind and then accused the nobles and officials. I told them, "You are exacting usury from your own countrymen!" So I called together a large meeting to deal with them [8]and said: "As far as possible, we have bought back our Jewish brothers who were sold to the Gentiles. Now you are selling your brothers, only for them to be sold back to us!" They kept quiet, because they could find nothing to say.

[9]So I continued, "What you are doing is not right. Shouldn't you walk in the fear of our God to avoid the reproach of our Gentile enemies? [10]I and my brothers and my men are also lending the people money and grain. But let the exacting of usury stop! [11]Give back to them immediately their fields, vineyards, olive groves and houses, and also the usury you are charging them—the hundredth part of the money, grain, new wine and oil."
Job 20 [18]"What he toiled for he must give back uneaten; he will not enjoy the profit from his trading. [19]For he has oppressed the poor and left them destitute; he has seized houses he did not build.

[20]"Surely he will have no respite from his craving; he cannot save himself by his treasure. [21]Nothing is left for him to devour; his prosperity will not endure."
Job 22 [6]"You demanded security from your brothers for no reason; you stripped men of their clothing, leaving them naked. [7]You gave no water to the weary and you withheld food from the hungry. . . . [9]And you sent widows away empty-handed and broke the strength of the fatherless."
Job 24 [3]"They drive away the orphan's donkey and take the widow's ox in pledge. [4]They thrust the needy from the path and force all the poor of the land into hiding. [5]Like wild donkeys in the desert, the poor go about their labor of foraging food; the wasteland provides food for their children. [6]They gather fodder in the fields and glean in the vineyards of the wicked. [7]Lacking clothes, they spend the night naked; they have nothing to cover themselves in the cold. [8]They are drenched by mountain rains and hug the rocks for lack of shelter. [9]The fatherless child is snatched from the breast; the infant of the poor is seized for a debt. [10]Lacking clothes, they go about naked; they carry the sheaves, but still go hungry. [11]They crush olives among the terraces; they tread the winepresses, yet suffer thirst. [12]The groans of the dying rise from the city, and the souls of the wounded cry out for help. But God charges no one with wrongdoing."
Ps 10 [2]In his arrogance the wicked man hunts down the weak, who are caught in the schemes he devises. . . . [8]He lies in wait near the villages; from ambush he murders the innocent, watching in secret for his victims. [9]He lies in wait like a lion in cover; he lies in wait to catch the helpless; he catches the helpless and drags them off in his net. [10]His victims are crushed, they collapse; they fall under his strength.
Ps 37 [14]The wicked draw the sword and bend the bow to bring down the poor and needy, to slay those whose ways are upright.
Ps 62 [10]Do not trust in extortion or take pride in stolen goods; though your riches increase, do not set your heart on them.
Prov 13 [23]A poor man's field may produce abundant food, but injustice sweeps it away.
Prov 14 [20]The poor are shunned even by their neighbors, but the rich have many friends.
Prov 17 [5]He who mocks the poor shows contempt for their Maker; whoever gloats over disaster will not go unpunished.
Prov 19 [7]A poor man is shunned by all his relatives—how much more do his friends avoid him! Though he pursues them with pleading, they are nowhere to be found.
Prov 21 [13]If a man shuts his ears to the cry of the poor, he too will cry out and not be answered.
Prov 22 [16]He who oppresses the poor to increase his wealth and he who gives gifts to the rich—both come to poverty.
Prov 28 [15]Like a roaring lion or a charging bear is a wicked man ruling over a helpless people.
Prov 30 [14]". . . those whose teeth are swords and whose jaws are set with knives to devour the poor from the earth, the needy from among mankind."
Prov 31 [4]"It is not for kings, O Lemuel—not for kings to drink wine, not for rulers to crave beer, [5]lest they drink and forget what the law decrees, and deprive all the oppressed of their rights."
Isa 3 [14]The LORD enters into judgment against the elders and leaders of his people: "It is you who have ruined my vineyard; the plunder from the poor is in your houses. [15]What do you mean by crushing my people and grinding the faces of the poor?" declares the Lord, the LORD Almighty.
Isa 10 [1]Woe to those who make unjust laws, to those who issue oppressive decrees, [2]to deprive the poor of their rights and withhold justice from the oppressed of my people, making widows their prey and robbing the fatherless.
Isa 32 [6]For the fool speaks folly, his mind is busy with evil: He

practices ungodliness and spreads error concerning the LORD; the hungry he leaves empty and from the thirsty he withholds water. [7]The scoundrel's methods are wicked, he makes up evil schemes to destroy the poor with lies, even when the plea of the needy is just.
Jer 20 [13]Sing to the LORD! Give praise to the LORD! He rescues the life of the needy from the hands of the wicked.
Jer 22 [3]"'This is what the LORD says: Do what is just and right. Rescue from the hand of his oppressor the one who has been robbed. Do no wrong or violence to the alien, the fatherless or the widow, and do not shed innocent blood in this place.'"
Ezek 18 [12]"He oppresses the poor and needy. He commits robbery. He does not return what he took in pledge. He looks to the idols. He does detestable things."
Ezek 22 [29]"The people of the land practice extortion and commit robbery; they oppress the poor and needy and mistreat the alien, denying them justice."
Amos 5 [12]For I know how many are your offenses and how great your sins.

You oppress the righteous and take bribes and you deprive the poor of justice in the courts.

Amos 8 [4]Hear this, you who trample the needy and do away with the poor of the land, [5]saying, "When will the New Moon be over that we may sell grain, and the Sabbath be ended that we may market wheat?"—skimping the measure, boosting the price and cheating with dishonest scales, [6]buying the poor with silver and the needy for a pair of sandals, selling even the sweepings with the wheat.
Mic 3 [1]Then I said, "Listen, you leaders of Jacob, you rulers of the house of Israel. Should you not know justice, [2]you who hate good and love evil; who tear the skin from my people and the flesh from their bones; [3]who eat my people's flesh, strip off their skin and break their bones in pieces; who chop them up like meat for the pan, like flesh for the pot?"
Zech 7 [10]"'Do not oppress the widow or the fatherless, the alien or the poor. In your hearts do not think evil of each other.'"
James 2 [6]But you have insulted the poor. Is it not the rich who are exploiting you? Are they not the ones who are dragging you into court?

III
Humans Are Created as Religious Beings

A. The Proper Response of Human Beings to God

See chap. 12, Christian Living: *Responsibilities toward God*

B. The Improper Response of Human Beings to God

See p. 401a, Sins against God

IV
Humans Are Created with Power of Choice

A. They Make Choices according to Personal Preference

Gen 2 [16]And the LORD God commanded the man, "You are free to eat from any tree in the garden. . . ."
Gen 2 [19]Now the LORD God had formed out of the ground all the beasts of the field and all the birds of the air. He brought them to the man to see what he would name them; and whatever the man called each living creature, that was its name.
Gen 13 [5]Now Lot, who was moving about with Abram, also had flocks and herds and tents. [6]But the land could not support them while they stayed together, for their possessions were so great that they were not able to stay together. [7]And quarreling arose between Abram's herdsmen and the herdsmen of Lot. The Canaanites and Perizzites were also living in the land at that time.

[8]So Abram said to Lot, "Let's not have any quarreling between you and me, or between your herdsmen and mine, for we are brothers. [9]Is not the whole land before you? Let's part company. If you go to the left, I'll go to the right; if you go to the right, I'll go to the left."

[10]Lot looked up and saw that the whole plain of the Jordan was well watered, like the garden of the LORD, like the land of Egypt, toward Zoar. (This was before the LORD destroyed Sodom and Gomorrah.) [11]So Lot chose for himself the whole plain of the Jordan and set out toward the east. The two men parted company: [12]Abram lived in the land of Canaan, while Lot lived among the cities of the plain and pitched his tents near Sodom.
Gen 27 [5]Now Rebekah was listening as Isaac spoke to his son Esau. When Esau left for the open country to hunt game and bring it back, [6]Rebekah said to her son Jacob, "Look, I overheard your father say to your brother Esau, [7]'Bring me some game and prepare me some tasty food to eat, so that I may give you my blessing in the presence of the LORD before I die.' [8]Now, my son, listen carefully and do what I tell you: [9]Go out to the flock and bring me two choice young goats, so I can prepare some tasty food for your father, just the way he likes it. [10]Then take it to your father to eat, so that he may give you his blessing before he dies."
Gen 37 [25]As they sat down to eat their meal, they looked up and saw a caravan of Ishmaelites coming from Gilead. Their camels were loaded with spices, balm and myrrh, and they were on their way to take them down to Egypt.

[26]Judah said to his brothers, "What will we gain if we kill our brother and cover up his blood? [27]Come, let's sell him to the Ishmaelites and not lay our hands on him; after all, he is our brother, our own flesh and blood." His brothers agreed.
Num 32 [1]The Reubenites and Gadites, who had very large herds and flocks, saw that the lands of Jazer and Gilead were suitable for livestock. [2]So they came to Moses and Eleazar the priest and to the leaders of the community, and said, [3]"Ataroth, Dibon, Jazer, Nimrah, Heshbon, Elealeh, Sebam, Nebo and Beon—[4]the land the LORD subdued before the people of Israel—are suitable for livestock, and your servants have livestock. [5]If we have found favor in your eyes," they said, "let this land be given to your servants as our possession. Do not make us cross the Jordan." . . .

[20]Then Moses said to them, "If you will do this—if you will arm yourselves before the LORD for battle, [21]and if all of you will go armed over the Jordan before the LORD until he has driven his enemies out before him—[22]then when the land is subdued before the LORD, you may return and be free from your obligation to the LORD and to Israel. And this land will be your possession before the LORD.

[23]"But if you fail to do this, you will be sinning against the LORD; and you may be sure that your sin will find you out. [24]Build cities for your women and children, and pens for your flocks, but do what you have promised."

[25]The Gadites and Reubenites said to Moses, "We your servants will do as our lord commands. [26]Our children and wives, our flocks and herds will remain here in the cities of Gilead. [27]But your servants, every man armed for battle, will cross over to fight before the LORD, just as our lord says."
Deut 33 [20]About Gad he said: "Blessed is he who enlarges Gad's domain! Gad lives there like a lion, tearing at arm or head. [21]He chose the best land for himself; the leader's portion was kept for him. When the heads of the people assembled, he carried out the LORD's righteous will, and his judgments concerning Israel."
Josh 8 [3]So Joshua and the whole army moved out to attack Ai. He chose thirty thousand of his best fighting men and sent them out at night. . . .
Ezra 7 [10]For Ezra had devoted himself to the study and obser-

vance of the Law of the LORD, and to teaching its decrees and laws in Israel.
Prov 16 [9]In his heart a man plans his course, but the LORD determines his steps.
John 5 [35]"John was a lamp that burned and gave light, and you chose for a time to enjoy his light."
Acts 15 [39]They had such a sharp disagreement that they parted company. Barnabas took Mark and sailed for Cyprus, [40]but Paul chose Silas and left, commended by the brothers to the grace of the Lord.
Acts 19 [21]After all this had happened, Paul decided to go to Jerusalem, passing through Macedonia and Achaia. "After I have been there," he said, "I must visit Rome also."
Rom 7 [18]I know that nothing good lives in me, that is, in my sinful nature. For I have the desire to do what is good, but I cannot carry it out.
1 Cor 9 [17]If I preach voluntarily, I have a reward; if not voluntarily, I am simply discharging the trust committed to me.
2 Cor 9 [7]Each man should give what he has decided in his heart to give, not reluctantly or under compulsion, for God loves a cheerful giver.
2 Cor 12 [6]Even if I should choose to boast, I would not be a fool, because I would be speaking the truth. But I refrain, so no one will think more of me than is warranted by what I do or say.
Phil 1 [20]I eagerly expect and hope that I will in no way be ashamed, but will have sufficient courage so that now as always Christ will be exalted in my body, whether by life or by death. [21]For to me, to live is Christ and to die is gain. [22]If I am to go on living in the body, this will mean fruitful labor for me. Yet what shall I choose? I do not know! [23]I am torn between the two: I desire to depart and be with Christ, which is better by far; [24]but it is more necessary for you that I remain in the body.
Phil 3 [7]But whatever was to my profit I now consider loss for the sake of Christ. [8]What is more, I consider everything a loss compared to the surpassing greatness of knowing Christ Jesus my Lord, for whose sake I have lost all things. I consider them rubbish, that I may gain Christ [9]and be found in him, not having a righteousness of my own that comes from the law, but that which is through faith in Christ—the righteousness that comes from God and is by faith. [10]I want to know Christ and the power of his resurrection and the fellowship of sharing in his sufferings, becoming like him in his death, [11]and so, somehow, to attain to the resurrection from the dead.

B. They Make Choices for the Sake of Others

Rom 9 [2]I have great sorrow and unceasing anguish in my heart. [3]For I could wish that I myself were cursed and cut off from Christ for the sake of my brothers, those of my own race, [4]the people of Israel. Theirs is the adoption as sons; theirs the divine glory, the covenants, the receiving of the law, the temple worship and the promises.
2 Cor 1 [12]Now this is our boast: Our conscience testifies that we have conducted ourselves in the world, and especially in our relations with you, in the holiness and sincerity that are from God. We have done so not according to worldly wisdom but according to God's grace. [13]For we do not write you anything you cannot read or understand. And I hope that, [14]as you have understood us in part, you will come to understand fully that you can boast of us just as we will boast of you in the day of the Lord Jesus.

[15]Because I was confident of this, I planned to visit you first so that you might benefit twice. . . .

[23]I call God as my witness that it was in order to spare you that I did not return to Corinth.
1 Thess 2 [10]You are witnesses, and so is God, of how holy, righteous and blameless we were among you who believed. [11]For you know that we dealt with each of you as a father deals with his own children. . . .
Philem [12]I am sending him—who is my very heart—back to you. [13]I would have liked to keep him with me so that he could take your place in helping me while I am in chains for the gospel. [14]But I did not want to do anything without your consent, so that any favor you do will be spontaneous and not forced.

C. They Make Choices at the Request of Others

Gen 6 [22]Noah did everything just as God commanded him.
Gen 12 [4]So Abram left, as the LORD had told him; and Lot went with him. Abram was seventy-five years old when he set out from Haran.
Gen 17 [23]On that very day Abraham took his son Ishmael and all those born in his household or bought with his money, every male in his household, and circumcised them, as God told him.
Gen 22 [1]Some time later God tested Abraham. He said to him, "Abraham!"

"Here I am," he replied.

[2]Then God said, "Take your son, your only son, Isaac, whom you love, and go to the region of Moriah. Sacrifice him there as a burnt offering on one of the mountains I will tell you about."

[3]Early the next morning Abraham got up and saddled his donkey. He took with him two of his servants and his son Isaac. When he had cut enough wood for the burnt offering, he set out for the place God had told him about.
Exod 18 [24]Moses listened to his father-in-law and did everything he said. [25]He chose capable men from all Israel and made them leaders of the people, officials over thousands, hundreds, fifties and tens. [26]They served as judges for the people at all times. The difficult cases they brought to Moses, but the simple ones they decided themselves.
Deut 1 [13]"Choose some wise, understanding and respected men from each of your tribes, and I will set them over you."

[14]You answered me, "What you propose to do is good."

[15]So I took the leading men of your tribes, wise and respected men, and appointed them to have authority over you—as commanders of thousands, of hundreds, of fifties and of tens and as tribal officials.
2 Kings 10 [3]". . . choose the best and most worthy of your master's sons and set him on his father's throne. Then fight for your master's house."

[4]But they were terrified and said, "If two kings could not resist him, how can we?"

[5]So the palace administrator, the city governor, the elders and the guardians sent this message to Jehu: "We are your servants and we will do anything you say. We will not appoint anyone as king; you do whatever you think best."
Matt 3 [13]Then Jesus came from Galilee to the Jordan to be baptized by John. [14]But John tried to deter him, saying, "I need to be baptized by you, and do you come to me?"

[15]Jesus replied, "Let it be so now; it is proper for us to do this to fulfill all righteousness." Then John consented.
Matt 9 [9]As Jesus went on from there, he saw a man named Matthew sitting at the tax collector's booth. "Follow me," he told him, and Matthew got up and followed him.
Mark 1 [19]When he had gone a little farther, he saw James son of Zebedee and his brother John in a boat, preparing their nets. [20]Without delay he called them, and they left their father Zebedee in the boat with the hired men and followed him.
Acts 6 [1]In those days when the number of disciples was increasing, the Grecian Jews among them complained against the Hebraic Jews because their widows were being overlooked in the daily distribution of food. [2]So the Twelve gathered all the disciples together and said, "It would not be right for us to neglect the ministry of the word of God in order to wait on tables. [3]Brothers, choose seven men from among you who are known to be full of the Spirit and wisdom. We will turn this responsibility over to them [4]and will give our attention to prayer and the ministry of the word."

[5]This proposal pleased the whole group. They chose Stephen, a man full of faith and of the Holy Spirit; also Philip, Procorus, Nicanor, Timon, Parmenas, and Nicolas from Antioch, a convert to Judaism.
Acts 15 [22]Then the apostles and elders, with the whole church, decided to choose some of their own men and send them to

Antioch with Paul and Barnabas. They chose Judas (called Barsabbas) and Silas, two men who were leaders among the brothers.
1 Pet 5 [2]Be shepherds of God's flock that is under your care, serving as overseers—not because you must, but because you are willing, as God wants you to be; not greedy for money, but eager to serve; [3]not lording it over those entrusted to you, but being examples to the flock.

D. The Place of the Human Will

See p. 335b, The Human Will

V
The Place of Humankind in the Created Order

A. Human Beings in Relation to God

1. People Are Accountable to God

Ezek 18 [20]"The soul who sins is the one who will die. The son will not share the guilt of the father, nor will the father share the guilt of the son. The righteousness of the righteous man will be credited to him, and the wickedness of the wicked will be charged against him. . . .

[30]"Therefore, O house of Israel, I will judge you, each one according to his ways, declares the Sovereign LORD. Repent! Turn away from all your offenses; then sin will not be your downfall."
Matt 12 [36]"But I tell you that men will have to give account on the day of judgment for every careless word they have spoken. [37]For by your words you will be acquitted, and by your words you will be condemned."
John 3 [18]"Whoever believes in him is not condemned, but whoever does not believe stands condemned already because he has not believed in the name of God's one and only Son. [19]This is the verdict: Light has come into the world, but men loved darkness instead of light because their deeds were evil."
John 9 [41]Jesus said, "If you were blind, you would not be guilty of sin; but now that you claim you can see, your guilt remains."
John 15 [22]"If I had not come and spoken to them, they would not be guilty of sin. Now, however, they have no excuse for their sin. [23]He who hates me hates my Father as well. [24]If I had not done among them what no one else did, they would not be guilty of sin. But now they have seen these miracles, and yet they have hated both me and my Father."
Acts 3 [19]"Repent, then, and turn to God, so that your sins may be wiped out, that times of refreshing may come from the Lord. . . ."
Rom 2 [14](Indeed, when Gentiles, who do not have the law, do by nature things required by the law, they are a law for themselves, even though they do not have the law, [15]since they show that the requirements of the law are written on their hearts, their consciences also bearing witness, and their thoughts now accusing, now even defending them.)
Rom 5 [12]Therefore, just as sin entered the world through one man, and death through sin, and in this way death came to all men, because all sinned . . .
Rom 7 [7]What shall we say, then? Is the law sin? Certainly not! Indeed I would not have known what sin was except through the law. For I would not have known what coveting really was if the law had not said, "Do not covet."
1 Cor 3 [8]The man who plants and the man who waters have one purpose, and each will be rewarded according to his own labor. . . .

[10]By the grace God has given me, I laid a foundation as an expert builder, and someone else is building on it. But each one should be careful how he builds. [11]For no one can lay any foundation other than the one already laid, which is Jesus Christ. [12]If any man builds on this foundation using gold, silver, costly stones, wood, hay or straw, [13]his work will be shown for what it is, because the Day will bring it to light. It will be revealed with fire, and the fire will test the quality of each man's work. [14]If what he has built survives, he will receive his reward. [15]If it is burned up, he will suffer loss; he himself will be saved, but only as one escaping through the flames.
Rev 2 [23]"I will strike her children dead. Then all the churches will know that I am he who searches hearts and minds, and I will repay each of you according to your deeds."

2. People Are Dependent on God

2 Chron 20 [12]"O our God, will you not judge them? For we have no power to face this vast army that is attacking us. We do not know what to do, but our eyes are upon you."
Ps 16 [2]I said to the LORD, "You are my Lord; apart from you I have no good thing."
Ps 104 [14]He makes grass grow for the cattle, and plants for man to cultivate—bringing forth food from the earth: [15]wine that gladdens the heart of man, oil to make his face shine, and bread that sustains his heart. . . .

[27]These all look to you to give them their food at the proper time. [28]When you give it to them, they gather it up; when you open your hand, they are satisfied with good things. [29]When you hide your face, they are terrified; when you take away their breath, they die and return to the dust. [30]When you send your Spirit, they are created, and you renew the face of the earth.
Prov 20 [24]A man's steps are directed by the LORD. How then can anyone understand his own way?
Jer 10 [23]I know, O LORD, that a man's life is not his own; it is not for man to direct his steps.
Amos 4 [13]He who forms the mountains, creates the wind, and reveals his thoughts to man, he who turns dawn to darkness, and treads the high places of the earth—the LORD God Almighty is his name.
Matt 4 [4]Jesus answered, "It is written: 'Man does not live on bread alone, but on every word that comes from the mouth of God.'"
Matt 6 [9]"This, then, is how you should pray: 'Our Father in heaven, hallowed be your name. . . . [11]Give us today our daily bread.'"
Luke 12 [15]Then he said to them, "Watch out! Be on your guard against all kinds of greed; a man's life does not consist in the abundance of his possessions."

[16]And he told them this parable: "The ground of a certain rich man produced a good crop. . . .

[18]"Then he said, 'This is what I'll do. I will tear down my barns and build bigger ones, and there I will store all my grain and my goods. . . .'

[20]"But God said to him, 'You fool! This very night your life will be demanded from you. Then who will get what you have prepared for yourself?'

[21]"This is how it will be with anyone who stores up things for himself but is not rich toward God."
Acts 1 [7]He said to them: "It is not for you to know the times or dates the Father has set by his own authority."
2 Cor 3 [5]Not that we are competent in ourselves to claim anything for ourselves, but our competence comes from God.
James 1 [5]If any of you lacks wisdom, he should ask God, who gives generously to all without finding fault, and it will be given to him. [6]But when he asks, he must believe and not doubt, because he who doubts is like a wave of the sea, blown and tossed by the wind.
James 4 [13]Now listen, you who say, "Today or tomorrow we will go to this or that city, spend a year there, carry on business and make money." [14]Why, you do not even know what will happen tomorrow. What is your life? You are a mist that appears for a little while and then vanishes. [15]Instead, you ought to say, "If it is the Lord's will, we will live and do this or that."

3. People Are Frail, Weak, and Finite

Gen 3 [8]Then the man and his wife heard the sound of the LORD God as he was walking in the garden in the cool of the day, and they hid from the LORD God among the trees of the garden. [9]But the LORD God called to the man, "Where are you?"

[10]He answered, "I heard you in the garden, and I was afraid because I was naked; so I hid." . . .

[13]Then the LORD God said to the woman, "What is this you have done?"

The woman said, "The serpent deceived me, and I ate."

Gen 3 [16]To the woman he said, "I will greatly increase your pains in childbearing; with pain you will give birth to children. Your desire will be for your husband, and he will rule over you."

[17]To Adam he said, "Because you listened to your wife and ate from the tree about which I commanded you, 'You must not eat of it,' cursed is the ground because of you; through painful toil you will eat of it all the days of your life. [18]It will produce thorns and thistles for you, and you will eat the plants of the field. [19]By the sweat of your brow you will eat your food until you return to the ground, since from it you were taken; for dust you are and to dust you will return."

Gen 6 [3]Then the LORD said, "My Spirit will not contend with man forever, for he is mortal; his days will be a hundred and twenty years."

Gen 18 [27]Then Abraham spoke up again: "Now that I have been so bold as to speak to the Lord, though I am nothing but dust and ashes . . ."

1 Chron 29 [14]"But who am I, and who are my people, that we should be able to give as generously as this? Everything comes from you, and we have given you only what comes from your hand. [15]We are aliens and strangers in your sight, as were all our forefathers. Our days on earth are like a shadow, without hope."

2 Chron 32 [8]"With him is only the arm of flesh, but with us is the LORD our God to help us and to fight our battles." And the people gained confidence from what Hezekiah the king of Judah said.

Job 5 [7]"Yet man is born to trouble as surely as sparks fly upward."

Job 7 [1]"Does not man have hard service on earth? Are not his days like those of a hired man? [2]Like a slave longing for the evening shadows, or a hired man waiting eagerly for his wages, [3]so I have been allotted months of futility, and nights of misery have been assigned to me."

Ps 39 [4]"Show me, O LORD, my life's end and the number of my days; let me know how fleeting is my life. [5]You have made my days a mere handbreadth; the span of my years is as nothing before you. Each man's life is but a breath. [6]Man is a mere phantom as he goes to and fro: He bustles about, but only in vain; he heaps up wealth, not knowing who will get it."

Ps 49 [12]But man, despite his riches, does not endure; he is like the beasts that perish.

Ps 56 [4]In God, whose word I praise, in God I trust; I will not be afraid. What can mortal man do to me?

Ps 78 [38]Yet he was merciful; he forgave their iniquities and did not destroy them. Time after time he restrained his anger and did not stir up his full wrath. [39]He remembered that they were but flesh, a passing breeze that does not return.

Ps 90 [3]You turn men back to dust, saying, "Return to dust, O sons of men." . . . [5]You sweep men away in the sleep of death; they are like the new grass of the morning—[6]though in the morning it springs up new, by evening it is dry and withered. . . . [10]The length of our days is seventy years—or eighty, if we have the strength; yet their span is but trouble and sorrow, for they quickly pass, and we fly away.

Ps 103 [13]As a father has compassion on his children, so the LORD has compassion on those who fear him; [14]for he knows how we are formed, he remembers that we are dust. [15]As for man, his days are like grass, he flourishes like a flower of the field; [16]the wind blows over it and it is gone, and its place remembers it no more.

Prov 14 [1]The wise woman builds her house, but with her own hands the foolish one tears hers down.

[2]He whose walk is upright fears the LORD, but he whose ways are devious despises him.

Eccles 3 [18]I also thought, "As for men, God tests them so that they may see that they are like the animals. [19]Man's fate is like that of the animals; the same fate awaits them both: As one dies, so dies the other. All have the same breath; man has no advantage over the animal. Everything is meaningless. [20]All go to the same place; all come from dust, and to dust all return."

Isa 2 [22]Stop trusting in man, who has but a breath in his nostrils. Of what account is he?

Isa 31 [3]But the Egyptians are men and not God; their horses are flesh and not spirit. When the LORD stretches out his hand, he who helps will stumble, he who is helped will fall; both will perish together.

Isa 40 [6]A voice says, "Cry out." And I said, "What shall I cry?"

"All men are like grass, and all their glory is like the flowers of the field. [7]The grass withers and the flowers fall, because the breath of the LORD blows on them. Surely the people are grass. [8]The grass withers and the flowers fall, but the word of our God stands forever."

Jer 17 [5]This is what the LORD says: "Cursed is the one who trusts in man, who depends on flesh for his strength and whose heart turns away from the LORD."

4. People Are Ignorant

Job 8 [9]". . . for we were born only yesterday and know nothing, and our days on earth are but a shadow."

Job 11 [7]"Can you fathom the mysteries of God? Can you probe the limits of the Almighty? [8]They are higher than the heavens—what can you do? They are deeper than the depths of the grave—what can you know? [9]Their measure is longer than the earth and wider than the sea."

Job 28 [12]"But where can wisdom be found? Where does understanding dwell? [13]Man does not comprehend its worth; it cannot be found in the land of the living."

Job 36 [26]"How great is God—beyond our understanding! The number of his years is past finding out."

Ps 139 [6]Such knowledge is too wonderful for me, too lofty for me to attain.

Prov 16 [25]There is a way that seems right to a man, but in the end it leads to death.

Prov 27 [1]Do not boast about tomorrow, for you do not know what a day may bring forth.

Prov 30 [4]"Who has gone up to heaven and come down? Who has gathered up the wind in the hollow of his hands? Who has wrapped up the waters in his cloak? Who has established all the ends of the earth? What is his name, and the name of his son? Tell me if you know!"

Eccles 3 [11]He has made everything beautiful in its time. He has also set eternity in the hearts of men; yet they cannot fathom what God has done from beginning to end.

Eccles 6 [12]For who knows what is good for a man in life, during the few and meaningless days he passes through like a shadow? Who can tell him what will happen under the sun after he is gone?

Eccles 7 [23]All this I tested by wisdom and I said, "I am determined to be wise"—but this was beyond me. [24]Whatever wisdom may be, it is far off and most profound—who can discover it?

Eccles 8 [17]then I saw all that God has done. No one can comprehend what goes on under the sun. Despite all his efforts to search it out, man cannot discover its meaning. Even if a wise man claims he knows, he cannot really comprehend it.

Eccles 9 [12]Moreover, no man knows when his hour will come: As fish are caught in a cruel net, or birds are taken in a snare, so men are trapped by evil times that fall unexpectedly upon them.

Eccles 10 [14]and the fool multiplies words.

No one knows what is coming—who can tell him what will happen after him?

Eccles 11 [5]As you do not know the path of the wind, or how the body is formed in a mother's womb, so you cannot understand the work of God, the Maker of all things.

Isa 59 [10]Like the blind we grope along the wall, feeling our way like men without eyes. At midday we stumble as if it were twilight; among the strong, we are like the dead.

Acts 17 [23]"For as I walked around and looked carefully at your objects of worship, I even found an altar with this inscription: TO AN UNKNOWN GOD. Now what you worship as something unknown I am going to proclaim to you. . . . [30]In the past God overlooked such ignorance, but now he commands all people everywhere to repent."

Rom 8 [26]In the same way, the Spirit helps us in our weakness.

We do not know what we ought to pray for, but the Spirit himself intercedes for us with groans that words cannot express.
1 Cor 1 [20]Where is the wise man? Where is the scholar? Where is the philosopher of this age? Has not God made foolish the wisdom of the world?
1 Cor 3 [18]Do not deceive yourselves. If any one of you thinks he is wise by the standards of this age, he should become a "fool" so that he may become wise. [19]For the wisdom of this world is foolishness in God's sight. As it is written: "He catches the wise in their craftiness"; [20]and again, "The Lord knows that the thoughts of the wise are futile."
1 Cor 8 [2]The man who thinks he knows something does not yet know as he ought to know.

5. People Are Inferior to God

Num 23 [19]"God is not a man, that he should lie, nor a son of man, that he should change his mind. Does he speak and then not act? Does he promise and not fulfill?"
Job 4 [17]"'Can a mortal be more righteous than God? Can a man be more pure than his Maker? [18]If God places no trust in his servants, if he charges his angels with error, [19]how much more those who live in houses of clay, whose foundations are in the dust, who are crushed more readily than a moth!'"
Job 15 [14]"What is man, that he could be pure, or one born of woman, that he could be righteous? [15]If God places no trust in his holy ones, if even the heavens are not pure in his eyes, [16]how much less man, who is vile and corrupt, who drinks up evil like water!"
Job 22 [2]"Can a man be of benefit to God? Can even a wise man benefit him?"
Job 25 [4]"How then can a man be righteous before God? How can one born of woman be pure? [5]If even the moon is not bright and the stars are not pure in his eyes, [6]how much less man, who is but a maggot—a son of man, who is only a worm!"
Job 33 [12]"But I tell you, in this you are not right, for God is greater than man."
Job 35 [2]"Do you think this is just? You say, 'I will be cleared by God.' [3]Yet you ask him, 'What profit is it to me, and what do I gain by not sinning?'

[4]"I would like to reply to you and to your friends with you. [5]Look up at the heavens and see; gaze at the clouds so high above you. [6]If you sin, how does that affect him? If your sins are many, what does that do to him? [7]If you are righteous, what do you give to him, or what does he receive from your hand? [8]Your wickedness affects only a man like yourself, and your righteousness only the sons of men."
Job 38 [1]Then the LORD answered Job out of the storm. He said: . . . [4]"Where were you when I laid the earth's foundation? Tell me, if you understand. . . .

[12]"Have you ever given orders to the morning, or shown the dawn its place, [13]that it might take the earth by the edges and shake the wicked out of it?"
Ps 8 [3]When I consider your heavens, the work of your fingers, the moon and the stars, which you have set in place, [4]what is man that you are mindful of him, the son of man that you care for him?
Ps 60 [11]Give us aid against the enemy, for the help of man is worthless. [12]With God we will gain the victory, and he will trample down our enemies.
Ps 144 [3]O LORD, what is man that you care for him, the son of man that you think of him? [4]Man is like a breath; his days are like a fleeting shadow.
Hos 11 [9]"I will not carry out my fierce anger, nor will I turn and devastate Ephraim. For I am God, and not man—the Holy One among you. I will not come in wrath."
Acts 5 [38]"Therefore, in the present case I advise you: Leave these men alone! Let them go! For if their purpose or activity is of human origin, it will fail. [39]But if it is from God, you will not be able to stop these men; you will only find yourselves fighting against God."
Rom 9 [16]It does not, therefore, depend on man's desire or effort, but on God's mercy.
1 Cor 2 [7]No, we speak of God's secret wisdom, a wisdom that has been hidden and that God destined for our glory before time began. [8]None of the rulers of this age understood it, for if they had, they would not have crucified the Lord of glory. [9]However, as it is written: "No eye has seen, no ear has heard, no mind has conceived what God has prepared for those who love him"—[10]but God has revealed it to us by his Spirit.

The Spirit searches all things, even the deep things of God.
1 Cor 3 [7]So neither he who plants nor he who waters is anything, but only God, who makes things grow.

6. People Are Loved by God

Deut 4 [37]Because he loved your forefathers and chose their descendants after them, he brought you out of Egypt by his Presence and his great strength. . . .
Deut 7 [7]The LORD did not set his affection on you and choose you because you were more numerous than other peoples, for you were the fewest of all peoples. [8]But it was because the LORD loved you and kept the oath he swore to your forefathers that he brought you out with a mighty hand and redeemed you from the land of slavery, from the power of Pharaoh king of Egypt.
Ps 42 [8]By day the LORD directs his love, at night his song is with me—a prayer to the God of my life.
Ps 63 [3]Because your love is better than life, my lips will glorify you.
Ps 103 [13]As a father has compassion on his children, so the LORD has compassion on those who fear him; [14]for he knows how we are formed, he remembers that we are dust.
Prov 15 [9]The LORD detests the way of the wicked but he loves those who pursue righteousness.
Isa 38 [17]Surely it was for my benefit that I suffered such anguish. In your love you kept me from the pit of destruction; you have put all my sins behind your back.
Jer 31 [3]The LORD appeared to us in the past, saying: "I have loved you with an everlasting love; I have drawn you with loving-kindness."
Hos 11 [1]"When Israel was a child, I loved him, and out of Egypt I called my son."
Mal 1 [2]"I have loved you," says the LORD.

"But you ask, 'How have you loved us?'

"Was not Esau Jacob's brother?" the LORD says. "Yet I have loved Jacob. . . ."
John 3 [16]"For God so loved the world that he gave his one and only Son, that whoever believes in him shall not perish but have eternal life."
John 14 [21]"Whoever has my commands and obeys them, he is the one who loves me. He who loves me will be loved by my Father, and I too will love him and show myself to him. . . ."

[23]Jesus replied, "If anyone loves me, he will obey my teaching. My Father will love him, and we will come to him and make our home with him."
John 16 [27]"No, the Father himself loves you because you have loved me and have believed that I came from God."
John 17 [22]"I have given them the glory that you gave me, that they may be one as we are one: [23]I in them and you in me. May they be brought to complete unity to let the world know that you sent me and have loved them even as you have loved me."
Rom 5 [8]But God demonstrates his own love for us in this: While we were still sinners, Christ died for us.
2 Cor 13 [11]Finally, brothers, good-by. Aim for perfection, listen to my appeal, be of one mind, live in peace. And the God of love and peace will be with you.
Eph 2 [4]But because of his great love for us, God, who is rich in mercy, [5]made us alive with Christ even when we were dead in transgressions—it is by grace you have been saved.
2 Thess 2 [16]May our Lord Jesus Christ himself and God our Father, who loved us and by his grace gave us eternal encouragement and good hope, [17]encourage your hearts and strengthen you in every good deed and word.
1 John 4 [7]Dear friends, let us love one another, for love comes from God. Everyone who loves has been born of God and knows God. [8]Whoever does not love does not know God, because God is love. [9]This is how God showed his love among us: He sent his one and only Son into the world that we might live through him. [10]This is love: not that we loved God, but that he loved us and sent his Son as an atoning sacrifice for our

sins. [11]Dear friends, since God so loved us, we also ought to love one another. [12]No one has ever seen God; but if we love one another, God lives in us and his love is made complete in us.

See also p. 58b, God Is Love

7. People Have Value

Matt 6 [26]"Look at the birds of the air; they do not sow or reap or store away in barns, and yet your heavenly Father feeds them. Are you not much more valuable than they? . . .

[28]"And why do you worry about clothes? See how the lilies of the field grow. They do not labor or spin. [29]Yet I tell you that not even Solomon in all his splendor was dressed like one of these. [30]If that is how God clothes the grass of the field, which is here today and tomorrow is thrown into the fire, will he not much more clothe you, O you of little faith?"

Matt 10 [29]"Are not two sparrows sold for a penny? Yet not one of them will fall to the ground apart from the will of your Father. [30]And even the very hairs of your head are all numbered. [31]So don't be afraid; you are worth more than many sparrows."

Matt 12 [11]He said to them, "If any of you has a sheep and it falls into a pit on the Sabbath, will you not take hold of it and lift it out? [12]How much more valuable is a man than a sheep! Therefore it is lawful to do good on the Sabbath."

Mark 8 [35]"For whoever wants to save his life will lose it, but whoever loses his life for me and for the gospel will save it. [36]What good is it for a man to gain the whole world, yet forfeit his soul? [37]Or what can a man give in exchange for his soul?"

Mark 9 [42]"And if anyone causes one of these little ones who believe in me to sin, it would be better for him to be thrown into the sea with a large millstone tied around his neck. [43]If your hand causes you to sin, cut it off. It is better for you to enter life maimed than with two hands to go into hell, where the fire never goes out. [45]And if your foot causes you to sin, cut it off. It is better for you to enter life crippled than to have two feet and be thrown into hell. [47]And if your eye causes you to sin, pluck it out. It is better for you to enter the kingdom of God with one eye than to have two eyes and be thrown into hell. . . ."

8. People Live on Earth

Gen 1 [28]God blessed them and said to them, "Be fruitful and increase in number; fill the earth and subdue it. Rule over the fish of the sea and the birds of the air and over every living creature that moves on the ground."

Gen 6 [1]When men began to increase in number on the earth and daughters were born to them, [2]the sons of God saw that the daughters of men were beautiful, and they married any of them they chose. . . .

[5]The LORD saw how great man's wickedness on the earth had become, and that every inclination of the thoughts of his heart was only evil all the time. [6]The LORD was grieved that he had made man on the earth, and his heart was filled with pain. [7]So the LORD said, "I will wipe mankind, whom I have created, from the face of the earth—men and animals, and creatures that move along the ground, and birds of the air—for I am grieved that I have made them."

Deut 4 [32]Ask now about the former days, long before your time, from the day God created man on the earth; ask from one end of the heavens to the other. Has anything so great as this ever happened, or has anything like it ever been heard of?

Job 37 [13]"He brings the clouds to punish men, or to water his earth and show his love."

Ps 33 [8]Let all the earth fear the LORD; let all the people of the world revere him. . . . [13]From heaven the LORD looks down and sees all mankind; [14]from his dwelling place he watches all who live on earth. . . .

Ps 66 [4]"All the earth bows down to you; they sing praise to you, they sing praise to your name."

Ps 98 [9]let them sing before the LORD, for he comes to judge the earth. He will judge the world in righteousness and the peoples with equity.

Prov 8 [30]"Then I was the craftsman at his side. I was filled with delight day after day, rejoicing always in his presence, [31]rejoicing in his whole world and delighting in mankind."

Jer 27 [5]"'"With my great power and outstretched arm I made the earth and its people and the animals that are on it, and I give it to anyone I please."'"

Luke 21 [35]"For it will come upon all those who live on the face of the whole earth."

Acts 17 [26]"From one man he made every nation of men, that they should inhabit the whole earth; and he determined the times set for them and the exact places where they should live."

1 Cor 15 [45]So it is written: "The first man Adam became a living being"; the last Adam, a life-giving spirit. [46]The spiritual did not come first, but the natural, and after that the spiritual. [47]The first man was of the dust of the earth, the second man from heaven. [48]As was the earthly man, so are those who are of the earth; and as is the man from heaven, so also are those who are of heaven. [49]And just as we have borne the likeness of the earthly man, so shall we bear the likeness of the man from heaven.

Rev 3 [10]"Since you have kept my command to endure patiently, I will also keep you from the hour of trial that is going to come upon the whole world to test those who live on the earth."

B. Human Beings in Relation to Other Created Beings

1. People Are Superior to Animals

Gen 1 [28]God blessed them and said to them, "Be fruitful and increase in number; fill the earth and subdue it. Rule over the fish of the sea and the birds of the air and over every living creature that moves on the ground."

Gen 2 [19]Now the LORD God had formed out of the ground all the beasts of the field and all the birds of the air. He brought them to the man to see what he would name them; and whatever the man called each living creature, that was its name. [20]So the man gave names to all the livestock, the birds of the air and all the beasts of the field.

But for Adam no suitable helper was found.

Gen 9 [1]Then God blessed Noah and his sons, saying to them, "Be fruitful and increase in number and fill the earth. [2]The fear and dread of you will fall upon all the beasts of the earth and all the birds of the air, upon every creature that moves along the ground, and upon all the fish of the sea; they are given into your hands. [3]Everything that lives and moves will be food for you. Just as I gave you the green plants, I now give you everything."

Job 35 [10]"But no one says, 'Where is God my Maker, who gives songs in the night, [11]who teaches more to us than to the beasts of the earth and makes us wiser than the birds of the air?'"

Ps 8 [6]You made him ruler over the works of your hands; you put everything under his feet: [7]all flocks and herds, and the beasts of the field, [8]the birds of the air, and the fish of the sea, all that swim the paths of the seas.

Jer 27 [6]"'"Now I will hand all your countries over to my servant Nebuchadnezzar king of Babylon; I will make even the wild animals subject to him."'"

Dan 2 [37]"You, O king, are the king of kings. The God of heaven has given you dominion and power and might and glory; [38]in your hands he has placed mankind and the beasts of the field and the birds of the air. Wherever they live, he has made you ruler over them all. You are that head of gold."

Matt 12 [11]He said to them, "If any of you has a sheep and it falls into a pit on the Sabbath, will you not take hold of it and lift it out? [12]How much more valuable is a man than a sheep! Therefore it is lawful to do good on the Sabbath."

2. People Are Lower Than Angels

Job 4 [18]"'If God places no trust in his servants, if he charges his angels with error, [19]how much more those who live in houses of clay, whose foundations are in the dust, who are crushed more readily than a moth!'"

Ps 8 [4]what is man that you are mindful of him, the son of man that you care for him? [5]You made him a little lower than the heavenly beings and crowned him with glory and honor.

3. People Are Equal before God

Deut 10 [17]For the LORD your God is God of gods and Lord of lords, the great God, mighty and awesome, who shows no partiality and accepts no bribes.
Job 31 [13]"If I have denied justice to my menservants and maidservants when they had a grievance against me, [14]what will I do when God confronts me? What will I answer when called to account? [15]Did not he who made me in the womb make them? Did not the same one form us both within our mothers?"
Ps 33 [13]From heaven the LORD looks down and sees all mankind; [14]from his dwelling place he watches all who live on earth—[15]he who forms the hearts of all, who considers everything they do.
Prov 22 [2]Rich and poor have this in common: The LORD is the Maker of them all.
Matt 20 [25]Jesus called them together and said, "You know that the rulers of the Gentiles lord it over them, and their high officials exercise authority over them. [26]Not so with you. Instead, whoever wants to become great among you must be your servant, [27]and whoever wants to be first must be your slave—[28]just as the Son of Man did not come to be served, but to serve, and to give his life as a ransom for many."
Matt 23 [8]"But you are not to be called 'Rabbi,' for you have only one Master and you are all brothers."
Acts 10 [27]Talking with him, Peter went inside and found a large gathering of people. [28]He said to them: "You are well aware that it is against our law for a Jew to associate with a Gentile or visit him. But God has shown me that I should not call any man impure or unclean." . . .

[34]Then Peter began to speak: "I now realize how true it is that God does not show favoritism [35]but accepts men from every nation who fear him and do what is right."
Acts 17 [26]"From one man he made every nation of men, that they should inhabit the whole earth; and he determined the times set for them and the exact places where they should live."
Rom 2 [11]For God does not show favoritism.
Rom 3 [10]As it is written: "There is no one righteous, not even one; [11]there is no one who understands, no one who seeks God. . . ." [22]This righteousness from God comes through faith in Jesus Christ to all who believe. There is no difference, [23]for all have sinned and fall short of the glory of God, [24]and are justified freely by his grace through the redemption that came by Christ Jesus.
Gal 3 [28]There is neither Jew nor Greek, slave nor free, male nor female, for you are all one in Christ Jesus.
Eph 6 [8]because you know that the Lord will reward everyone for whatever good he does, whether he is slave or free.

[9]And masters, treat your slaves in the same way. Do not threaten them, since you know that he who is both their Master and yours is in heaven, and there is no favoritism with him.
Col 3 [25]Anyone who does wrong will be repaid for his wrong, and there is no favoritism.
1 Pet 1 [17]Since you call on a Father who judges each man's work impartially, live your lives as strangers here in reverent fear.

VI
Constituent Elements of Human Individuality

A. The Human Soul

1. The Soul as the Principle of Life (ET: breath, life, lifeblood)

Gen 37 [21]When Reuben heard this, he tried to rescue him from their hands. "Let's not take his life," he said.
Deut 19 [6]Otherwise, the avenger of blood might pursue him in a rage, overtake him if the distance is too great, and kill him even though he is not deserving of death, since he did it to his neighbor without malice aforethought.
Deut 19 [11]But if a man hates his neighbor and lies in wait for him, assaults and kills him, and then flees to one of these cities . . .
2 Sam 14 [14]"Like water spilled on the ground, which cannot be recovered, so we must die. But God does not take away life; instead, he devises ways so that a banished person may not remain estranged from him."
1 Kings 17 [21]Then he stretched himself out on the boy three times and cried to the LORD, "O LORD my God, let this boy's life return to him!"

[22]The LORD heard Elijah's cry, and the boy's life returned to him, and he lived. [23]Elijah picked up the child and carried him down from the room into the house. He gave him to his mother and said, "Look, your son is alive!"
Job 24 [12]"The groans of the dying rise from the city, and the souls of the wounded cry out for help. But God charges no one with wrongdoing."
Job 30 [16]"And now my life ebbs away; days of suffering grip me."
Ps 35 [4]May those who seek my life be disgraced and put to shame; may those who plot my ruin be turned back in dismay.
Ps 94 [21]They band together against the righteous and condemn the innocent to death.
Prov 7 [23]till an arrow pierces his liver, like a bird darting into a snare, little knowing it will cost him his life.
Jer 2 [34]"On your clothes men find the lifeblood of the innocent poor, though you did not catch them breaking in. Yet in spite of all this . . ."
Jer 38 [16]But King Zedekiah swore this oath secretly to Jeremiah: "As surely as the LORD lives, who has given us breath, I will neither kill you nor hand you over to those who are seeking your life."
Jer 40 [14]and said to him, "Don't you know that Baalis king of the Ammonites has sent Ishmael son of Nethaniah to take your life?" But Gedaliah son of Ahikam did not believe them.

[15]Then Johanan son of Kareah said privately to Gedaliah in Mizpah, "Let me go and kill Ishmael son of Nethaniah, and no one will know it. Why should he take your life and cause all the Jews who are gathered around you to be scattered and the remnant of Judah to perish?"
Ezek 22 [27]"Her officials within her are like wolves tearing their prey; they shed blood and kill people to make unjust gain."
Jon 1 [14]Then they cried to the LORD, "O LORD, please do not let us die for taking this man's life. Do not hold us accountable for killing an innocent man, for you, O LORD, have done as you pleased."
Matt 6 [25]"Therefore I tell you, do not worry about your life, what you will eat or drink; or about your body, what you will wear. Is not life more important than food, and the body more important than clothes?"
Acts 20 [9]Seated in a window was a young man named Eutychus, who was sinking into a deep sleep as Paul talked on and on. When he was sound asleep, he fell to the ground from the third story and was picked up dead. [10]Paul went down, threw himself on the young man and put his arms around him. "Don't be alarmed," he said. "He's alive!"
Acts 27 [22]"But now I urge you to keep up your courage, because not one of you will be lost; only the ship will be destroyed."
Rom 16 [4]They risked their lives for me. Not only I but all the churches of the Gentiles are grateful to them.
2 Cor 12 [15]So I will very gladly spend for you everything I have and expend myself as well. If I love you more, will you love me less?
Phil 2 [30]because he almost died for the work of Christ, risking his life to make up for the help you could not give me.
1 Thess 2 [8]We loved you so much that we were delighted to share with you not only the gospel of God but our lives as well, because you had become so dear to us.
Rev 12 [11]"They overcame him by the blood of the Lamb and by the word of their testimony; they did not love their lives so much as to shrink from death."

2. The Soul as the States of Mind

a) Human Appetite

Num 11 [6]"But now we have lost our appetite; we never see anything but this manna!"

Deut 24 [15]Pay him his wages each day before sunset, because he is poor and is counting on it. Otherwise he may cry to the LORD against you, and you will be guilty of sin.
Ps 10 [3]He boasts of the cravings of his heart; he blesses the greedy and reviles the LORD.
Ps 107 [5]They were hungry and thirsty, and their lives ebbed away. [9]. . . for he satisfies the thirsty and fills the hungry with good things.
Ps 143 [6]I spread out my hands to you; my soul thirsts for you like a parched land. . . . [8]Let the morning bring me word of your unfailing love, for I have put my trust in you. Show me the way I should go, for to you I lift up my soul.
Prov 6 [30]Men do not despise a thief if he steals to satisfy his hunger when he is starving.
Prov 25 [25]Like cold water to a weary soul is good news from a distant land.
Prov 27 [7]He who is full loathes honey, but to the hungry even what is bitter tastes sweet.
Eccles 7 [28]". . . while I was still searching but not finding—I found one upright man among a thousand, but not one upright woman among them all."
Isa 29 [8]as when a hungry man dreams that he is eating, but he awakens, and his hunger remains; as when a thirsty man dreams that he is drinking, but he awakens faint, with his thirst unquenched. So will it be with the hordes of all the nations that fight against Mount Zion.
Isa 58 [10]". . . and if you spend yourselves in behalf of the hungry and satisfy the needs of the oppressed, then your light will rise in the darkness, and your night will become like the noonday."
Jer 31 [25]"I will refresh the weary and satisfy the faint."
Lam 2 [12]They say to their mothers, "Where is bread and wine?" as they faint like wounded men in the streets of the city, as their lives ebb away in their mothers' arms.
Ezek 7 [19]"They will throw their silver into the streets, and their gold will be an unclean thing. Their silver and gold will not be able to save them in the day of the LORD's wrath. They will not satisfy their hunger or fill their stomachs with it, for it has made them stumble into sin."

b) Human Emotion

Gen 42 [21]They said to one another, "Surely we are being punished because of our brother. We saw how distressed he was when he pleaded with us for his life, but we would not listen; that's why this distress has come upon us."
1 Sam 1 [10]In bitterness of soul Hannah wept much and prayed to the LORD.
Job 3 [20]"Why is light given to those in misery, and life to the bitter of soul? . . ."
Job 10 [1]"I loathe my very life; therefore I will give free rein to my complaint and speak out in the bitterness of my soul."
Job 30 [25]"Have I not wept for those in trouble? Has not my soul grieved for the poor?"
Job 33 [20]". . . so that his very being finds food repulsive and his soul loathes the choicest meal."
Ps 6 [3]My soul is in anguish. How long, O LORD, how long?
Ps 35 [9]Then my soul will rejoice in the LORD and delight in his salvation.
Ps 43 [5]Why are you downcast, O my soul? Why so disturbed within me? Put your hope in God, for I will yet praise him, my Savior and my God.
Ps 84 [2]My soul yearns, even faints, for the courts of the LORD; my heart and my flesh cry out for the living God.
Ps 119 [81]My soul faints with longing for your salvation, but I have put my hope in your word.
Isa 38 [15]But what can I say? He has spoken to me, and he himself has done this. I will walk humbly all my years because of this anguish of my soul.
Isa 61 [10]I delight greatly in the LORD; my soul rejoices in my God. For he has clothed me with garments of salvation and arrayed me in a robe of righteousness, as a bridegroom adorns his head like a priest, and as a bride adorns herself with her jewels.
Lam 3 [20]I well remember them, and my soul is downcast within me.
Ezek 27 [31]"'They will shave their heads because of you and will put on sackcloth. They will weep over you with anguish of soul and with bitter mourning.'"
Zech 11 [8]In one month I got rid of the three shepherds.
The flock detested me, and I grew weary of them. . . .
Luke 12 [19]"'And I'll say to myself, "You have plenty of good things laid up for many years. Take life easy; eat, drink and be merry."'"
John 12 [27]"Now my heart is troubled, and what shall I say? 'Father, save me from this hour'? No, it was for this very reason I came to this hour."
1 Thess 5 [23]May God himself, the God of peace, sanctify you through and through. May your whole spirit, soul and body be kept blameless at the coming of our Lord Jesus Christ.

c) Human Intellect

Prov 2 [10]For wisdom will enter your heart, and knowledge will be pleasant to your soul.
Acts 14 [2]But the Jews who refused to believe stirred up the Gentiles and poisoned their minds against the brothers.
Acts 15 [24]We have heard that some went out from us without our authorization and disturbed you, troubling your minds by what they said.

d) Human Volition

Gen 23 [8]He said to them, "If you are willing to let me bury my dead, then listen to me and intercede with Ephron son of Zohar on my behalf. . . ."
Deut 21 [14]If you are not pleased with her, let her go wherever she wishes. You must not sell her or treat her as a slave, since you have dishonored her.
Ps 105 [22]to instruct his princes as he pleased and teach his elders wisdom.
Phil 1 [27]Whatever happens, conduct yourselves in a manner worthy of the gospel of Christ. Then, whether I come and see you or only hear about you in my absence, I will know that you stand firm in one spirit, contending as one man for the faith of the gospel. . . .

3. The Soul as the God-related Part of the Person

Ps 19 [7]The law of the LORD is perfect, reviving the soul. The statutes of the LORD are trustworthy, making wise the simple.
Ps 103 [1]Praise the LORD, O my soul; all my inmost being, praise his holy name. [2]Praise the LORD, O my soul, and forget not all his benefits. . . .
[22]Praise the LORD, all his works everywhere in his dominion.
Praise the LORD, O my soul.
Ps 116 [7]Be at rest once more, O my soul, for the LORD has been good to you.
Isa 26 [9]My soul yearns for you in the night; in the morning my spirit longs for you. When your judgments come upon the earth, the people of the world learn righteousness.
Matt 10 [28]"Do not be afraid of those who kill the body but cannot kill the soul. Rather, be afraid of the One who can destroy both soul and body in hell."
Mark 8 [36]"What good is it for a man to gain the whole world, yet forfeit his soul? [37]Or what can a man give in exchange for his soul?"
Luke 1 [46]And Mary said: "My soul glorifies the Lord. . . ."
Eph 6 [6]Obey them not only to win their favor when their eye is on you, but like slaves of Christ, doing the will of God from your heart.
Col 3 [23]Whatever you do, work at it with all your heart, as working for the Lord, not for men. . . .
Heb 6 [19]We have this hope as an anchor for the soul, firm and secure. It enters the inner sanctuary behind the curtain. . . .
James 5 [20]remember this: Whoever turns a sinner from the error of his way will save him from death and cover over a multitude of sins.
1 Pet 1 [9]for you are receiving the goal of your faith, the salvation of your souls.
1 Pet 2 [11]Dear friends, I urge you, as aliens and strangers in the world, to abstain from sinful desires, which war against your soul.
2 Pet 2 [8](for that righteous man, living among them day after

day, was tormented in his righteous soul by the lawless deeds he saw and heard) . . .
Rev 6 [9]When he opened the fifth seal, I saw under the altar the souls of those who had been slain because of the word of God and the testimony they had maintained.
Rev 20 [4]I saw thrones on which were seated those who had been given authority to judge. And I saw the souls of those who had been beheaded because of their testimony for Jesus and because of the word of God. They had not worshiped the beast or his image and had not received his mark on their foreheads or their hands. They came to life and reigned with Christ a thousand years.

B. The Human Spirit (ET: breath, heart, mind, resentment, strength)

1. The Spirit as Conscious Existence

Job 9 [18]"He would not let me regain my breath but would overwhelm me with misery."
Job 27 [3]". . . as long as I have life within me, the breath of God in my nostrils . . ."
Job 33 [4]"The Spirit of God has made me; the breath of the Almighty gives me life."
Job 34 [14]"If it were his intention and he withdrew his spirit and breath, [15]all mankind would perish together and man would return to the dust."
Ps 104 [30]When you send your Spirit, they are created, and you renew the face of the earth.
Ps 146 [4]When their spirit departs, they return to the ground; on that very day their plans come to nothing.
Eccles 12 [7]and the dust returns to the ground it came from, and the spirit returns to God who gave it.
Isa 24 [4]The earth dries up and withers, the world languishes and withers, the exalted of the earth languish.
Isa 33 [11]"You conceive chaff, you give birth to straw; your breath is a fire that consumes you."
Lam 4 [20]The LORD's anointed, our very life breath, was caught in their traps. We thought that under his shadow we would live among the nations.
Luke 8 [55]Her spirit returned, and at once she stood up. Then Jesus told them to give her something to eat.
Heb 4 [12]For the word of God is living and active. Sharper than any double-edged sword, it penetrates even to dividing soul and spirit, joints and marrow; it judges the thoughts and attitudes of the heart.
James 2 [26]As the body without the spirit is dead, so faith without deeds is dead.

2. The Spirit as Conscious Energy

Gen 41 [8]In the morning his mind was troubled, so he sent for all the magicians and wise men of Egypt. Pharaoh told them his dreams, but no one could interpret them for him.
Gen 45 [27]But when they told him everything Joseph had said to them, and when he saw the carts Joseph had sent to carry him back, the spirit of their father Jacob revived.
Josh 2 [11]"When we heard of it, our hearts melted and everyone's courage failed because of you, for the LORD your God is God in heaven above and on the earth below."
Josh 5 [1]Now when all the Amorite kings west of the Jordan and all the Canaanite kings along the coast heard how the LORD had dried up the Jordan before the Israelites until we had crossed over, their hearts melted and they no longer had the courage to face the Israelites.
Judg 8 [3]"God gave Oreb and Zeeb, the Midianite leaders, into your hands. What was I able to do compared to you?" At this, their resentment against him subsided.
Judg 15 [19]Then God opened up the hollow place in Lehi, and water came out of it. When Samson drank, his strength returned and he revived. So the spring was called En Hakkore, and it is still there in Lehi.
1 Sam 1 [15]"Not so, my lord," Hannah replied, "I am a woman who is deeply troubled. I have not been drinking wine or beer; I was pouring out my soul to the LORD."
1 Sam 30 [12]part of a cake of pressed figs and two cakes of raisins. He ate and was revived, for he had not eaten any food or drunk any water for three days and three nights.
1 Kings 10 [5]the food on his table, the seating of his officials, the attending servants in their robes, his cupbearers, and the burnt offerings he made at the temple of the LORD, she was overwhelmed.
Job 7 [11]"Therefore I will not keep silent; I will speak out in the anguish of my spirit, I will complain in the bitterness of my soul."
Job 32 [18]"For I am full of words, and the spirit within me compels me. . . ."
Ps 77 [3]I remembered you, O God, and I groaned; I mused, and my spirit grew faint.
Ps 142 [3]When my spirit grows faint within me, it is you who know my way. In the path where I walk men have hidden a snare for me.
Ps 143 [4]So my spirit grows faint within me; my heart within me is dismayed. . . .
[7]Answer me quickly, O LORD; my spirit fails. Do not hide your face from me or I will be like those who go down to the pit.
Prov 15 [4]The tongue that brings healing is a tree of life, but a deceitful tongue crushes the spirit.
Prov 17 [22]A cheerful heart is good medicine, but a crushed spirit dries up the bones.
Prov 18 [14]A man's spirit sustains him in sickness, but a crushed spirit who can bear?
Prov 25 [28]Like a city whose walls are broken down is a man who lacks self-control.
Eccles 7 [9]Do not be quickly provoked in your spirit, for anger resides in the lap of fools.
Eccles 10 [4]If a ruler's anger rises against you, do not leave your post; calmness can lay great errors to rest.
Isa 54 [6]"The LORD will call you back as if you were a wife deserted and distressed in spirit—a wife who married young, only to be rejected," says your God.
Isa 57 [16]"I will not accuse forever, nor will I always be angry, for then the spirit of man would grow faint before me—the breath of man that I have created."
Isa 61 [3]and provide for those who grieve in Zion—to bestow on them a crown of beauty instead of ashes, the oil of gladness instead of mourning, and a garment of praise instead of a spirit of despair. They will be called oaks of righteousness, a planting of the LORD for the display of his splendor.
Ezek 3 [14]The Spirit then lifted me up and took me away, and I went in bitterness and in the anger of my spirit, with the strong hand of the LORD upon me.
Dan 2 [3]he said to them, "I have had a dream that troubles me and I want to know what it means."
Matt 26 [41]"Watch and pray so that you will not fall into temptation. The spirit is willing, but the body is weak."
John 13 [21]After he had said this, Jesus was troubled in spirit and testified, "I tell you the truth, one of you is going to betray me."
1 Cor 2 [11]For who among men knows the thoughts of a man except the man's spirit within him? In the same way no one knows the thoughts of God except the Spirit of God.
1 Cor 7 [34]and his interests are divided. An unmarried woman or virgin is concerned about the Lord's affairs: Her aim is to be devoted to the Lord in both body and spirit. But a married woman is concerned about the affairs of this world—how she can please her husband.
1 Cor 16 [18]For they refreshed my spirit and yours also. Such men deserve recognition.
2 Cor 2 [13]I still had no peace of mind, because I did not find my brother Titus there. So I said good-by to them and went on to Macedonia.
Eph 4 [22]You were taught, with regard to your former way of life, to put off your old self, which is being corrupted by its deceitful desires; [23]to be made new in the attitude of your minds. . . .
Col 2 [5]For though I am absent from you in body, I am present with you in spirit and delight to see how orderly you are and how firm your faith in Christ is.

3. The Spirit as the God-related Part of the Person

Isa 26 [9]My soul yearns for you in the night; in the morning my spirit longs for you. When your judgments come upon the earth, the people of the world learn righteousness.
Mark 2 [8]Immediately Jesus knew in his spirit that this was what they were thinking in their hearts, and he said to them, "Why are you thinking these things?"
Acts 7 [59]While they were stoning him, Stephen prayed, "Lord Jesus, receive my spirit."
Rom 1 [9]God, whom I serve with my whole heart in preaching the gospel of his Son, is my witness how constantly I remember you. . . .
Rom 8 [16]The Spirit himself testifies with our spirit that we are God's children.
Rom 12 [11]Never be lacking in zeal, but keep your spiritual fervor, serving the Lord.
1 Cor 2 [13]This is what we speak, not in words taught us by human wisdom but in words taught by the Spirit, expressing spiritual truths in spiritual words. [14]The man without the Spirit does not accept the things that come from the Spirit of God, for they are foolishness to him, and he cannot understand them, because they are spiritually discerned. [15]The spiritual man makes judgments about all things, but he himself is not subject to any man's judgment. . . .
1 Cor 5 [3]Even though I am not physically present, I am with you in spirit. And I have already passed judgment on the one who did this, just as if I were present. [4]When you are assembled in the name of our Lord Jesus and I am with you in spirit, and the power of our Lord Jesus is present, [5]hand this man over to Satan, so that the sinful nature may be destroyed and his spirit saved on the day of the Lord.
1 Cor 14 [14]For if I pray in a tongue, my spirit prays, but my mind is unfruitful. [15]So what shall I do? I will pray with my spirit, but I will also pray with my mind; I will sing with my spirit, but I will also sing with my mind. [16]If you are praising God with your spirit, how can one who finds himself among those who do not understand say "Amen" to your thanksgiving, since he does not know what you are saying?
2 Cor 7 [1]Since we have these promises, dear friends, let us purify ourselves from everything that contaminates body and spirit, perfecting holiness out of reverence for God.
1 Thess 5 [23]May God himself, the God of peace, sanctify you through and through. May your whole spirit, soul and body be kept blameless at the coming of our Lord Jesus Christ.
2 Tim 4 [22]The Lord be with your spirit. Grace be with you.
Heb 4 [12]For the word of God is living and active. Sharper than any double-edged sword, it penetrates even to dividing soul and spirit, joints and marrow; it judges the thoughts and attitudes of the heart.
Heb 12 [23]to the church of the firstborn, whose names are written in heaven. You have come to God, the judge of all men, to the spirits of righteous men made perfect. . . .

C. Human Flesh

1. Flesh as Bodily Substance

Lev 13 [38]"When a man or woman has white spots on the skin . . ."
Lev 17 [15]"'Anyone, whether native-born or alien, who eats anything found dead or torn by wild animals must wash his clothes and bathe with water, and he will be ceremonially unclean till evening; then he will be clean. [16]But if he does not wash his clothes and bathe himself, he will be held responsible.'"
Num 8 [7]"To purify them, do this: Sprinkle the water of cleansing on them; then have them shave their whole bodies and wash their clothes, and so purify themselves."
2 Kings 6 [30]When the king heard the woman's words, he tore his robes. As he went along the wall, the people looked, and there, underneath, he had sackcloth on his body.
Job 4 [15]"A spirit glided past my face, and the hair on my body stood on end."
Job 14 [22]"He feels but the pain of his own body and mourns only for himself."
Job 21 [6]"When I think about this, I am terrified; trembling seizes my body."
Ps 16 [9]Therefore my heart is glad and my tongue rejoices; my body also will rest secure. . . .
Ps 63 [1]O God, you are my God, earnestly I seek you; my soul thirsts for you, my body longs for you, in a dry and weary land where there is no water.
Ps 84 [2]My soul yearns, even faints, for the courts of the LORD; my heart and my flesh cry out for the living God.
Ps 119 [120]My flesh trembles in fear of you; I stand in awe of your laws.
Prov 4 [22]for they are life to those who find them and health to a man's whole body.
Prov 14 [30]A heart at peace gives life to the body, but envy rots the bones.
Eccles 12 [12]Be warned, my son, of anything in addition to them.
Of making many books there is no end, and much study wearies the body.
Luke 24 [39]"Look at my hands and my feet. It is I myself! Touch me and see; a ghost does not have flesh and bones, as you see I have."
John 3 [6]"Flesh gives birth to flesh, but the Spirit gives birth to spirit."
Rom 2 [28]A man is not a Jew if he is only one outwardly, nor is circumcision merely outward and physical.
1 Cor 15 [39]All flesh is not the same: Men have one kind of flesh, animals have another, birds another and fish another.
Gal 2 [20]"I have been crucified with Christ and I no longer live, but Christ lives in me. The life I live in the body, I live by faith in the Son of God, who loved me and gave himself for me."
1 Tim 3 [16]Beyond all question, the mystery of godliness is great: He appeared in a body, was vindicated by the Spirit, was seen by angels, was preached among the nations, was believed on in the world, was taken up in glory.
Jude [8]In the very same way, these dreamers pollute their own bodies, reject authority and slander celestial beings.

2. Flesh as Finite Nature (ET: body, creature, mankind, mortal)

Gen 6 [3]Then the LORD said, "My Spirit will not contend with man forever, for he is mortal; his days will be a hundred and twenty years."
2 Chron 32 [8]"With him is only the arm of flesh, but with us is the LORD our God to help us and to fight our battles." And the people gained confidence from what Hezekiah the king of Judah said.
Job 10 [4]"Do you have eyes of flesh? Do you see as a mortal sees?"
Job 12 [10]"In his hand is the life of every creature and the breath of all mankind."
Job 34 [14]"If it were his intention and he withdrew his spirit and breath, [15]all mankind would perish together and man would return to the dust."
Ps 56 [4]In God, whose word I praise, in God I trust; I will not be afraid. What can mortal man do to me?
Ps 65 [2]O you who hear prayer, to you all men will come.
Ps 78 [39]He remembered that they were but flesh, a passing breeze that does not return.
Ps 145 [21]My mouth will speak in praise of the LORD. Let every creature praise his holy name for ever and ever.
Isa 40 [6]A voice says, "Cry out." And I said, "What shall I cry?"
"All men are like grass, and all their glory is like the flowers of the field. [7]The grass withers and the flowers fall, because the breath of the LORD blows on them. Surely the people are grass. [8]The grass withers and the flowers fall, but the word of our God stands forever."
Isa 66 [16]For with fire and with his sword the LORD will execute judgment upon all men, and many will be those slain by the LORD.
Jer 17 [5]This is what the LORD says: "Cursed is the one who trusts in man, who depends on flesh for his strength and whose heart turns away from the LORD."

Jer 25 [31]"'The tumult will resound to the ends of the earth, for the LORD will bring charges against the nations; he will bring judgment on all mankind and put the wicked to the sword,'" declares the LORD.
Jer 45 [5]"'Should you then seek great things for yourself? Seek them not. For I will bring disaster on all people, declares the LORD, but wherever you go I will let you escape with your life.'"
Joel 2 [28]"And afterward, I will pour out my Spirit on all people. Your sons and daughters will prophesy, your old men will dream dreams, your young men will see visions. . . . [32]And everyone who calls on the name of the LORD will be saved; for on Mount Zion and in Jerusalem there will be deliverance, as the LORD has said, among the survivors whom the LORD calls."
Zech 2 [13]"Be still before the LORD, all mankind, because he has roused himself from his holy dwelling."
Matt 16 [17]Jesus replied, "Blessed are you, Simon son of Jonah, for this was not revealed to you by man, but by my Father in heaven."
Matt 26 [41]"Watch and pray so that you will not fall into temptation. The spirit is willing, but the body is weak."
John 1 [13]children born not of natural descent, nor of human decision or a husband's will, but born of God.
John 8 [15]"You judge by human standards; I pass judgment on no one."
John 17 [2]"For you granted him authority over all people that he might give eternal life to all those you have given him."
Rom 6 [19]I put this in human terms because you are weak in your natural selves. Just as you used to offer the parts of your body in slavery to impurity and to ever-increasing wickedness, so now offer them in slavery to righteousness leading to holiness.
Phil 3 [3]For it is we who are the circumcision, we who worship by the Spirit of God, who glory in Christ Jesus, and who put no confidence in the flesh—[4]though I myself have reasons for such confidence.

If anyone else thinks he has reasons to put confidence in the flesh, I have more: [5]circumcised on the eighth day, of the people of Israel, of the tribe of Benjamin, a Hebrew of Hebrews; in regard to the law, a Pharisee. . . .
Heb 12 [9]Moreover, we have all had human fathers who disciplined us and we respected them for it. How much more should we submit to the Father of our spirits and live!
1 Pet 4 [6]For this is the reason the gospel was preached even to those who are now dead, so that they might be judged according to men in regard to the body, but live according to God in regard to the spirit.

3. Flesh as Fallen Nature

Rom 7 [5]For when we were controlled by the sinful nature, the sinful passions aroused by the law were at work in our bodies, so that we bore fruit for death.
Rom 8 [3]For what the law was powerless to do in that it was weakened by the sinful nature, God did by sending his own Son in the likeness of sinful man to be a sin offering. And so he condemned sin in sinful man, [4]in order that the righteous requirements of the law might be fully met in us, who do not live according to the sinful nature but according to the Spirit.

[5]Those who live according to the sinful nature have their minds set on what that nature desires; but those who live in accordance with the Spirit have their minds set on what the Spirit desires. [6]The mind of sinful man is death, but the mind controlled by the Spirit is life and peace; [7]the sinful mind is hostile to God. It does not submit to God's law, nor can it do so. [8]Those controlled by the sinful nature cannot please God.

[9]You, however, are controlled not by the sinful nature but by the Spirit, if the Spirit of God lives in you. And if anyone does not have the Spirit of Christ, he does not belong to Christ. . . .

[12]Therefore, brothers, we have an obligation—but it is not to the sinful nature, to live according to it. [13]For if you live according to the sinful nature, you will die; but if by the Spirit you put to death the misdeeds of the body, you will live. . . .
Gal 5 [13]You, my brothers, were called to be free. But do not use your freedom to indulge the sinful nature; rather, serve one another in love. . . . [17]For the sinful nature desires what is contrary to the Spirit, and the Spirit what is contrary to the sinful nature. They are in conflict with each other, so that you do not do what you want. . . .

[19]The acts of the sinful nature are obvious: sexual immorality, impurity and debauchery; [20]idolatry and witchcraft; hatred, discord, jealousy, fits of rage, selfish ambition, dissensions, factions [21]and envy; drunkenness, orgies, and the like. I warn you, as I did before, that those who live like this will not inherit the kingdom of God.
Eph 2 [3]All of us also lived among them at one time, gratifying the cravings of our sinful nature and following its desires and thoughts. Like the rest, we were by nature objects of wrath.
Col 2 [11]In him you were also circumcised, in the putting off of the sinful nature, not with a circumcision done by the hands of men but with the circumcision done by Christ. . . .
1 Pet 4 [2]As a result, he does not live the rest of his earthly life for evil human desires, but rather for the will of God.
2 Pet 2 [10]This is especially true of those who follow the corrupt desire of the sinful nature and despise authority.

Bold and arrogant, these men are not afraid to slander celestial beings. . . . [18]For they mouth empty, boastful words and, by appealing to the lustful desires of sinful human nature, they entice people who are just escaping from those who live in error.
1 John 2 [16]For everything in the world—the cravings of sinful man, the lust of his eyes and the boasting of what he has and does—comes not from the Father but from the world.

D. The Human Body

1. The Body as Material Substance

Matt 10 [28]"Do not be afraid of those who kill the body but cannot kill the soul. Rather, be afraid of the One who can destroy both soul and body in hell."
1 Cor 7 [34]and his interests are divided. An unmarried woman or virgin is concerned about the Lord's affairs: Her aim is to be devoted to the Lord in both body and spirit. But a married woman is concerned about the affairs of this world—how she can please her husband.
1 Thess 5 [23]May God himself, the God of peace, sanctify you through and through. May your whole spirit, soul and body be kept blameless at the coming of our Lord Jesus Christ.
James 2 [26]As the body without the spirit is dead, so faith without deeds is dead.

2. The Body as Morally Influenced

Matt 6 [22]"The eye is the lamp of the body. If your eyes are good, your whole body will be full of light. [23]But if your eyes are bad, your whole body will be full of darkness. If then the light within you is darkness, how great is that darkness!

[24]"No one can serve two masters. Either he will hate the one and love the other, or he will be devoted to the one and despise the other. You cannot serve both God and Money."
Luke 11 [33]"No one lights a lamp and puts it in a place where it will be hidden, or under a bowl. Instead he puts it on its stand, so that those who come in may see the light. [34]Your eye is the lamp of your body. When your eyes are good, your whole body also is full of light. But when they are bad, your body also is full of darkness. [35]See to it, then, that the light within you is not darkness. [36]Therefore, if your whole body is full of light, and no part of it dark, it will be completely lighted, as when the light of a lamp shines on you."
Rom 6 [6]For we know that our old self was crucified with him so that the body of sin might be done away with, that we should no longer be slaves to sin. . . . [12]Therefore do not let sin reign in your mortal body so that you obey its evil desires.
Rom 8 [10]But if Christ is in you, your body is dead because of sin, yet your spirit is alive because of righteousness. [11]And if the Spirit of him who raised Jesus from the dead is living in you, he who raised Christ from the dead will also give life to your mortal bodies through his Spirit, who lives in you. . . . [13]For if you live according to the sinful nature, you will die; but if by the Spirit you put to death the misdeeds of the body, you will live. . . .
1 Cor 6 [13]"Food for the stomach and the stomach for

food"—but God will destroy them both. The body is not meant for sexual immorality, but for the Lord, and the Lord for the body. . . .

[18]Flee from sexual immorality. All other sins a man commits are outside his body, but he who sins sexually sins against his own body. [19]Do you not know that your body is a temple of the Holy Spirit, who is in you, whom you have received from God? You are not your own; [20]you were bought at a price. Therefore honor God with your body.

1 Cor 9 [24]Do you not know that in a race all the runners run, but only one gets the prize? Run in such a way as to get the prize. [25]Everyone who competes in the games goes into strict training. They do it to get a crown that will not last; but we do it to get a crown that will last forever. [26]Therefore I do not run like a man running aimlessly; I do not fight like a man beating the air. [27]No, I beat my body and make it my slave so that after I have preached to others, I myself will not be disqualified for the prize.

Phil 3 [21]who, by the power that enables him to bring everything under his control, will transform our lowly bodies so that they will be like his glorious body.

Heb 10 [22]let us draw near to God with a sincere heart in full assurance of faith, having our hearts sprinkled to cleanse us from a guilty conscience and having our bodies washed with pure water.

James 3 [2]We all stumble in many ways. If anyone is never at fault in what he says, he is a perfect man, able to keep his whole body in check. . . . [6]The tongue also is a fire, a world of evil among the parts of the body. It corrupts the whole person, sets the whole course of his life on fire, and is itself set on fire by hell.

3. The Body as Representing the Person

Rom 12 [1]Therefore, I urge you, brothers, in view of God's mercy, to offer your bodies as living sacrifices, holy and pleasing to God—this is your spiritual act of worship.

E. Parts of the Human Body as Moral Aspects of Humanity

1. Human Facial Features

a) The Ears

1 Sam 3 [11]And the LORD said to Samuel: "See, I am about to do something in Israel that will make the ears of everyone who hears of it tingle."

Job 12 [11]"Does not the ear test words as the tongue tastes food?"

Job 13 [1]"My eyes have seen all this, my ears have heard and understood it."

Job 34 [3]"For the ear tests words as the tongue tastes food."

Prov 18 [15]The heart of the discerning acquires knowledge; the ears of the wise seek it out.

Prov 23 [12]Apply your heart to instruction and your ears to words of knowledge.

Isa 32 [3]Then the eyes of those who see will no longer be closed, and the ears of those who hear will listen.

Matt 13 [15]"'For this people's heart has become calloused; they hardly hear with their ears, and they have closed their eyes. Otherwise they might see with their eyes, hear with their ears, understand with their hearts and turn, and I would heal them.'"

Acts 7 [51]"You stiff-necked people, with uncircumcised hearts and ears! You are just like your fathers: You always resist the Holy Spirit!"

Acts 17 [20]"You are bringing some strange ideas to our ears, and we want to know what they mean."

2 Tim 4 [3]For the time will come when men will not put up with sound doctrine. Instead, to suit their own desires, they will gather around them a great number of teachers to say what their itching ears want to hear. [4]They will turn their ears away from the truth and turn aside to myths.

b) The Eyes

Gen 3 [6]When the woman saw that the fruit of the tree was good for food and pleasing to the eye, and also desirable for gaining wisdom, she took some and ate it. She also gave some to her husband, who was with her, and he ate it.

Num 15 [39]"'You will have these tassels to look at and so you will remember all the commands of the LORD, that you may obey them and not prostitute yourselves by going after the lusts of your own hearts and eyes.'"

Deut 28 [65]Among those nations you will find no repose, no resting place for the sole of your foot. There the LORD will give you an anxious mind, eyes weary with longing, and a despairing heart.

2 Chron 20 [12]"O our God, will you not judge them? For we have no power to face this vast army that is attacking us. We do not know what to do, but our eyes are upon you."

Ezra 9 [8]"But now, for a brief moment, the LORD our God has been gracious in leaving us a remnant and giving us a firm place in his sanctuary, and so our God gives light to our eyes and a little relief in our bondage."

Job 11 [20]"But the eyes of the wicked will fail, and escape will elude them; their hope will become a dying gasp."

Job 31 [16]"If I have denied the desires of the poor or let the eyes of the widow grow weary . . ."

Ps 25 [15]My eyes are ever on the LORD, for only he will release my feet from the snare.

Ps 31 [9]Be merciful to me, O LORD, for I am in distress; my eyes grow weak with sorrow, my soul and my body with grief.

Ps 54 [7]For he has delivered me from all my troubles, and my eyes have looked in triumph on my foes.

Ps 69 [3]I am worn out calling for help; my throat is parched. My eyes fail, looking for my God.

Ps 88 [9]my eyes are dim with grief. I call to you, O LORD, every day; I spread out my hands to you.

Ps 101 [5]Whoever slanders his neighbor in secret, him will I put to silence; whoever has haughty eyes and a proud heart, him will I not endure.

[6]My eyes will be on the faithful in the land, that they may dwell with me; he whose walk is blameless will minister to me.

Ps 123 [1]I lift up my eyes to you, to you whose throne is in heaven. [2]As the eyes of slaves look to the hand of their master, as the eyes of a maid look to the hand of her mistress, so our eyes look to the LORD our God, till he shows us his mercy.

Prov 21 [4]Haughty eyes and a proud heart, the lamp of the wicked, are sin!

Eccles 2 [10]I denied myself nothing my eyes desired; I refused my heart no pleasure. My heart took delight in all my work, and this was the reward for all my labor.

Isa 2 [11]The eyes of the arrogant man will be humbled and the pride of men brought low; the LORD alone will be exalted in that day.

Jer 22 [17]"But your eyes and your heart are set only on dishonest gain, on shedding innocent blood and on oppression and extortion."

Lam 4 [17]Moreover, our eyes failed, looking in vain for help; from our towers we watched for a nation that could not save us.

Ezek 24 [16]"Son of man, with one blow I am about to take away from you the delight of your eyes. Yet do not lament or weep or shed any tears."

Matt 18 [9]"And if your eye causes you to sin, gouge it out and throw it away. It is better for you to enter life with one eye than to have two eyes and be thrown into the fire of hell."

Luke 11 [34]"Your eye is the lamp of your body. When your eyes are good, your whole body also is full of light. But when they are bad, your body also is full of darkness."

Acts 26 [17]"'I will rescue you from your own people and from the Gentiles. I am sending you to them [18]to open their eyes and turn them from darkness to light, and from the power of Satan to God, so that they may receive forgiveness of sins and a place among those who are sanctified by faith in me.'"

Acts 28 [27]"'For this people's heart has become calloused; they hardly hear with their ears, and they have closed their eyes. Otherwise they might see with their eyes, hear with their ears, understand with their hearts and turn, and I would heal them.'"

Eph 1 [18]I pray also that the eyes of your heart may be enlightened in order that you may know the hope to which he has called you, the riches of his glorious inheritance in the saints. . . .

2 Pet 2 [14]With eyes full of adultery, they never stop sinning; they seduce the unstable; they are experts in greed—an accursed brood!
1 John 2 [16]For everything in the world—the cravings of sinful man, the lust of his eyes and the boasting of what he has and does—comes not from the Father but from the world.

c) The Forehead

Isa 48 [4]"For I knew how stubborn you were; the sinews of your neck were iron, your forehead was bronze."
Jer 3 [3]"Therefore the showers have been withheld, and no spring rains have fallen. Yet you have the brazen look of a prostitute; you refuse to blush with shame."
Ezek 3 [7]"But the house of Israel is not willing to listen to you because they are not willing to listen to me, for the whole house of Israel is hardened and obstinate. [8]But I will make you as unyielding and hardened as they are. [9]I will make your forehead like the hardest stone, harder than flint. Do not be afraid of them or terrified by them, though they are a rebellious house."

d) The Lips

Job 13 [6]"Hear now my argument; listen to the plea of my lips."
Job 15 [6]"Your own mouth condemns you, not mine; your own lips testify against you."
Job 33 [3]"My words come from an upright heart; my lips sincerely speak what I know."
Ps 12 [2]Everyone lies to his neighbor; their flattering lips speak with deception.
[3]May the LORD cut off all flattering lips and every boastful tongue. . . .
Ps 31 [18]Let their lying lips be silenced, for with pride and contempt they speak arrogantly against the righteous.
Ps 63 [3]Because your love is better than life, my lips will glorify you.
Ps 119 [171]May my lips overflow with praise, for you teach me your decrees.
Ps 140 [9]Let the heads of those who surround me be covered with the trouble their lips have caused.
Prov 5 [1]My son, pay attention to my wisdom, listen well to my words of insight, [2]that you may maintain discretion and your lips may preserve knowledge. [3]For the lips of an adulteress drip honey, and her speech is smoother than oil; [4]but in the end she is bitter as gall, sharp as a double-edged sword.
Prov 10 [13]Wisdom is found on the lips of the discerning, but a rod is for the back of him who lacks judgment.
Prov 10 [21]The lips of the righteous nourish many, but fools die for lack of judgment.
Prov 12 [19]Truthful lips endure forever, but a lying tongue lasts only a moment.
Prov 14 [3]A fool's talk brings a rod to his back, but the lips of the wise protect them.
Prov 15 [7]The lips of the wise spread knowledge; not so the hearts of fools.
Prov 16 [13]Kings take pleasure in honest lips; they value a man who speaks the truth.
Prov 16 [23]A wise man's heart guides his mouth, and his lips promote instruction.
Prov 17 [4]A wicked man listens to evil lips; a liar pays attention to a malicious tongue.
Prov 20 [15]Gold there is, and rubies in abundance, but lips that speak knowledge are a rare jewel.
Prov 23 [16]my inmost being will rejoice when your lips speak what is right.
Prov 26 [23]Like a coating of glaze over earthenware are fervent lips with an evil heart.
Isa 59 [3]For your hands are stained with blood, your fingers with guilt. Your lips have spoken lies, and your tongue mutters wicked things.
Mal 2 [7]"For the lips of a priest ought to preserve knowledge, and from his mouth men should seek instruction—because he is the messenger of the LORD Almighty."
Matt 15 [8]"'These people honor me with their lips, but their hearts are far from me.'"
Rom 3 [13]"Their throats are open graves; their tongues practice deceit."
"The poison of vipers is on their lips."
Col 3 [8]But now you must rid yourselves of all such things as these: anger, rage, malice, slander, and filthy language from your lips.
Heb 13 [15]Through Jesus, therefore, let us continually offer to God a sacrifice of praise—the fruit of lips that confess his name.

e) The Mouth

2 Sam 1 [16]For David had said to him, "Your blood be on your own head. Your own mouth testified against you when you said, 'I killed the LORD's anointed.'"
Job 6 [30]"Is there any wickedness on my lips? Can my mouth not discern malice?"
Job 9 [20]"Even if I were innocent, my mouth would condemn me; if I were blameless, it would pronounce me guilty."
Job 31 [30]"I have not allowed my mouth to sin by invoking a curse against his life. . . ."
Ps 17 [3]Though you probe my heart and examine me at night, though you test me, you will find nothing; I have resolved that my mouth will not sin.
Ps 37 [30]The mouth of the righteous man utters wisdom, and his tongue speaks what is just.
Ps 49 [3]My mouth will speak words of wisdom; the utterance from my heart will give understanding.
Ps 59 [12]For the sins of their mouths, for the words of their lips, let them be caught in their pride. For the curses and lies they utter . . .
Ps 119 [103]How sweet are your words to my taste, sweeter than honey to my mouth!
Ps 144 [11]Deliver me and rescue me from the hands of foreigners whose mouths are full of lies, whose right hands are deceitful.
Prov 4 [24]Put away perversity from your mouth; keep corrupt talk far from your lips.
Prov 8 [7]"My mouth speaks what is true, for my lips detest wickedness."
Prov 10 [31]The mouth of the righteous brings forth wisdom, but a perverse tongue will be cut out.
Prov 15 [2]The tongue of the wise commends knowledge, but the mouth of the fool gushes folly.
Prov 16 [23]A wise man's heart guides his mouth, and his lips promote instruction.
Prov 18 [6]A fool's lips bring him strife, and his mouth invites a beating.
Prov 26 [28]A lying tongue hates those it hurts, and a flattering mouth works ruin.
Prov 27 [2]Let another praise you, and not your own mouth; someone else, and not your own lips.
Eccles 5 [6]Do not let your mouth lead you into sin. And do not protest to the temple messenger, "My vow was a mistake." Why should God be angry at what you say and destroy the work of your hands?
Zeph 3 [13]"The remnant of Israel will do no wrong; they will speak no lies, nor will deceit be found in their mouths. They will eat and lie down and no one will make them afraid."
Mal 2 [6]"True instruction was in his mouth and nothing false was found on his lips. He walked with me in peace and uprightness, and turned many from sin."
Matt 12 [34]"You brood of vipers, how can you who are evil say anything good? For out of the overflow of the heart the mouth speaks."
Matt 15 [11]"What goes into a man's mouth does not make him 'unclean,' but what comes out of his mouth, that is what makes him 'unclean.'"
Rom 10 [8]But what does it say? "The word is near you; it is in your mouth and in your heart," that is, the word of faith we are proclaiming: [9]That if you confess with your mouth, "Jesus is Lord," and believe in your heart that God raised him from the dead, you will be saved. [10]For it is with your heart that you believe and are justified, and it is with your mouth that you confess and are saved.
James 3 [10]Out of the same mouth come praise and cursing. My brothers, this should not be.

f) The Tongue

Job 27 [4]". . . my lips will not speak wickedness, and my tongue will utter no deceit."

Ps 50 [19]"You use your mouth for evil and harness your tongue to deceit."

Ps 52 [2]Your tongue plots destruction; it is like a sharpened razor, you who practice deceit.

Ps 73 [9]Their mouths lay claim to heaven, and their tongues take possession of the earth.

Ps 120 [2]Save me, O LORD, from lying lips and from deceitful tongues.

[3]What will he do to you, and what more besides, O deceitful tongue? [4]He will punish you with a warrior's sharp arrows, with burning coals of the broom tree.

Prov 6 [24]keeping you from the immoral woman, from the smooth tongue of the wayward wife.

Prov 15 [2]The tongue of the wise commends knowledge, but the mouth of the fool gushes folly. . . .

[4]The tongue that brings healing is a tree of life, but a deceitful tongue crushes the spirit.

Prov 21 [6]A fortune made by a lying tongue is a fleeting vapor and a deadly snare.

Prov 25 [23]As a north wind brings rain, so a sly tongue brings angry looks.

Isa 54 [17]". . . no weapon forged against you will prevail, and you will refute every tongue that accuses you. This is the heritage of the servants of the LORD, and this is their vindication from me," declares the LORD.

Jer 9 [5]"Friend deceives friend, and no one speaks the truth. They have taught their tongues to lie; they weary themselves with sinning. . . . [8]Their tongue is a deadly arrow; it speaks with deceit. With his mouth each speaks cordially to his neighbor, but in his heart he sets a trap for him."

Mic 6 [12]"Her rich men are violent; her people are liars and their tongues speak deceitfully."

Acts 2 [26]"'Therefore my heart is glad and my tongue rejoices; my body also will live in hope. . . .'"

James 1 [26]If anyone considers himself religious and yet does not keep a tight rein on his tongue, he deceives himself and his religion is worthless.

James 3 [2]We all stumble in many ways. If anyone is never at fault in what he says, he is a perfect man, able to keep his whole body in check.

[3]When we put bits into the mouths of horses to make them obey us, we can turn the whole animal. [4]Or take ships as an example. Although they are so large and are driven by strong winds, they are steered by a very small rudder wherever the pilot wants to go. [5]Likewise the tongue is a small part of the body, but it makes great boasts. Consider what a great forest is set on fire by a small spark. [6]The tongue also is a fire, a world of evil among the parts of the body. It corrupts the whole person, sets the whole course of his life on fire, and is itself set on fire by hell.

[7]All kinds of animals, birds, reptiles and creatures of the sea are being tamed and have been tamed by man, [8]but no man can tame the tongue. It is a restless evil, full of deadly poison.

[9]With the tongue we praise our Lord and Father, and with it we curse men, who have been made in God's likeness.

1 Pet 3 [10]For, "Whoever would love life and see good days must keep his tongue from evil and his lips from deceitful speech."

1 John 3 [18]Dear children, let us not love with words or tongue but with actions and in truth.

2. Human Extremities

a) The Arm

2 Chron 32 [8]"With him is only the arm of flesh, but with us is the LORD our God to help us and to fight our battles." And the people gained confidence from what Hezekiah the king of Judah said.

Job 35 [9]"Men cry out under a load of oppression; they plead for relief from the arm of the powerful."

Ps 10 [15]Break the arm of the wicked and evil man; call him to account for his wickedness that would not be found out.

Prov 31 [17]She sets about her work vigorously; her arms are strong for her tasks.

Jer 48 [25]"Moab's horn is cut off; her arm is broken," declares the LORD.

Ezek 17 [9]"Say to them, 'This is what the Sovereign LORD says: Will it thrive? Will it not be uprooted and stripped of its fruit so that it withers? All its new growth will wither. It will not take a strong arm or many people to pull it up by the roots.'"

Ezek 30 [21]"Son of man, I have broken the arm of Pharaoh king of Egypt. It has not been bound up for healing or put in a splint so as to become strong enough to hold a sword. [22]Therefore this is what the Sovereign LORD says: I am against Pharaoh king of Egypt. I will break both his arms, the good arm as well as the broken one, and make the sword fall from his hand. . . . [24]I will strengthen the arms of the king of Babylon and put my sword in his hand, but I will break the arms of Pharaoh, and he will groan before him like a mortally wounded man. [25]I will strengthen the arms of the king of Babylon, but the arms of Pharaoh will fall limp. Then they will know that I am the LORD, when I put my sword into the hand of the king of Babylon and he brandishes it against Egypt."

b) The Fingers

Prov 6 [12]A scoundrel and villain, who goes about with a corrupt mouth, [13]who winks with his eye, signals with his feet and motions with his fingers, [14]who plots evil with deceit in his heart—he always stirs up dissension.

c) The Foot

(1) The Foot as Ill Will

Prov 6 [12]A scoundrel and villain, who goes about with a corrupt mouth, [13]who winks with his eye, signals with his feet and motions with his fingers . . .

Ezek 6 [11]"'This is what the Sovereign LORD says: Strike your hands together and stamp your feet and cry out "Alas!" because of all the wicked and detestable practices of the house of Israel, for they will fall by the sword, famine and plague.'"

Ezek 25 [6]"'For this is what the Sovereign LORD says: Because you have clapped your hands and stamped your feet, rejoicing with all the malice of your heart against the land of Israel . . .'"

Heb 10 [29]How much more severely do you think a man deserves to be punished who has trampled the Son of God under foot, who has treated as an unholy thing the blood of the covenant that sanctified him, and who has insulted the Spirit of grace?

(2) The Foot as Triumph and Sovereignty

Josh 10 [24]When they had brought these kings to Joshua, he summoned all the men of Israel and said to the army commanders who had come with him, "Come here and put your feet on the necks of these kings." So they came forward and placed their feet on their necks.

2 Sam 22 [39]"I crushed them completely, and they could not rise; they fell beneath my feet."

1 Kings 5 [3]"You know that because of the wars waged against my father David from all sides, he could not build a temple for the Name of the LORD his God until the LORD put his enemies under his feet."

Ps 8 [6]You made him ruler over the works of your hands; you put everything under his feet. . . .

Ps 47 [3]He subdued nations under us, peoples under our feet.

Ps 110 [1]The LORD says to my Lord: "Sit at my right hand until I make your enemies a footstool for your feet."

Lam 3 [34]To crush underfoot all prisoners in the land . . .

Mal 4 [3]"Then you will trample down the wicked; they will be ashes under the soles of your feet on the day when I do these things," says the LORD Almighty.

Rom 16 [20]The God of peace will soon crush Satan under your feet.

The grace of our Lord Jesus be with you.

d) The Hand

(1) The Hand as Aggression

Num 20 [10]He and Aaron gathered the assembly together in front of the rock and Moses said to them, "Listen, you rebels, must we bring you water out of this rock?" [11]Then Moses raised his arm and struck the rock twice with his staff. Water gushed out, and the community and their livestock drank.

Deut 32 [27]". . . but I dreaded the taunt of the enemy, lest the

adversary misunderstand and say, 'Our hand has triumphed; the LORD has not done all this.'"
2 Sam 18 [28]Then Ahimaaz called out to the king, "All is well!" He bowed down before the king with his face to the ground and said, "Praise be to the LORD your God! He has delivered up the men who lifted their hands against my lord the king."
2 Sam 20 [21]"That is not the case. A man named Sheba son of Bicri, from the hill country of Ephraim, has lifted up his hand against the king, against David. Hand over this one man, and I'll withdraw from the city."

The woman said to Joab, "His head will be thrown to you from the wall."
Job 31 [21]". . . if I have raised my hand against the fatherless, knowing that I had influence in court . . ."
Isa 10 [32]This day they will halt at Nob; they will shake their fist at the mount of the Daughter of Zion, at the hill of Jerusalem.
Jer 6 [9]This is what the LORD Almighty says: "Let them glean the remnant of Israel as thoroughly as a vine; pass your hand over the branches again, like one gathering grapes."
Ezek 38 [12]"'"I will plunder and loot and turn my hand against the resettled ruins and the people gathered from the nations, rich in livestock and goods, living at the center of the land."'"

(2) The Hand as Ethical Stature

1 Sam 24 [11]"See, my father, look at this piece of your robe in my hand! I cut off the corner of your robe but did not kill you. Now understand and recognize that I am not guilty of wrongdoing or rebellion. I have not wronged you, but you are hunting me down to take my life."
2 Sam 22 [21]"The LORD has dealt with me according to my righteousness; according to the cleanness of my hands he has rewarded me."
1 Chron 12 [17]David went out to meet them and said to them, "If you have come to me in peace, to help me, I am ready to have you unite with me. But if you have come to betray me to my enemies when my hands are free from violence, may the God of our fathers see it and judge you."
Job 11 [14]". . . if you put away the sin that is in your hand and allow no evil to dwell in your tent . . ."
Job 16 [17]". . . yet my hands have been free of violence and my prayer is pure."
Job 17 [9]"Nevertheless, the righteous will hold to their ways, and those with clean hands will grow stronger."
Job 31 [7]". . . if my steps have turned from the path, if my heart has been led by my eyes, or if my hands have been defiled . . ."
Ps 7 [3]O LORD my God, if I have done this and there is guilt on my hands . . .
Ps 18 [24]The LORD has rewarded me according to my righteousness, according to the cleanness of my hands in his sight.
Ps 26 [10]in whose hands are wicked schemes, whose right hands are full of bribes.
Isa 1 [15]"When you spread out your hands in prayer, I will hide my eyes from you; even if you offer many prayers, I will not listen. Your hands are full of blood. . . ."
Isa 31 [7]For in that day every one of you will reject the idols of silver and gold your sinful hands have made.
Ezek 18 [8]"He does not lend at usury or take excessive interest. He withholds his hand from doing wrong and judges fairly between man and man."
Ezek 23 [37]". . . for they have committed adultery and blood is on their hands. They committed adultery with their idols; they even sacrificed their children, whom they bore to me, as food for them. . . . [45]But righteous men will sentence them to the punishment of women who commit adultery and shed blood, because they are adulterous and blood is on their hands."
Mic 7 [3]Both hands are skilled in doing evil; the ruler demands gifts, the judge accepts bribes, the powerful dictate what they desire—they all conspire together.
Matt 18 [8]"If your hand or your foot causes you to sin, cut it off and throw it away. It is better for you to enter life maimed or crippled than to have two hands or two feet and be thrown into eternal fire."
1 Tim 2 [8]I want men everywhere to lift up holy hands in prayer, without anger or disputing.
James 4 [8]Come near to God and he will come near to you. Wash your hands, you sinners, and purify your hearts, you double-minded.

(3) The Hand as an Expression of a State of Mind

Num 24 [10]Then Balak's anger burned against Balaam. He struck his hands together and said to him, "I summoned you to curse my enemies, but you have blessed them these three times."
2 Sam 13 [19]Tamar put ashes on her head and tore the ornamented robe she was wearing. She put her hand on her head and went away, weeping aloud as she went.
Neh 8 [6]Ezra praised the LORD, the great God; and all the people lifted their hands and responded, "Amen! Amen!" Then they bowed down and worshiped the LORD with their faces to the ground.
Ps 28 [2]Hear my cry for mercy as I call to you for help, as I lift up my hands toward your Most Holy Place.
Ps 77 [2]When I was in distress, I sought the Lord; at night I stretched out untiring hands and my soul refused to be comforted.
Ps 134 [2]Lift up your hands in the sanctuary and praise the LORD.
Prov 1 [24]"But since you rejected me when I called and no one gave heed when I stretched out my hand . . ."
Jer 2 [37]"You will also leave that place with your hands on your head, for the LORD has rejected those you trust; you will not be helped by them."
Lam 1 [17]Zion stretches out her hands, but there is no one to comfort her. The LORD has decreed for Jacob that his neighbors become his foes; Jerusalem has become an unclean thing among them.
Ezek 25 [6]"'For this is what the Sovereign LORD says: Because you have clapped your hands and stamped your feet, rejoicing with all the malice of your heart against the land of Israel . . .'"
Nah 3 [19]Nothing can heal your wound; your injury is fatal. Everyone who hears the news about you claps his hands at your fall, for who has not felt your endless cruelty?
Zeph 2 [15]This is the carefree city that lived in safety. She said to herself, "I am, and there is none besides me." What a ruin she has become, a lair for wild beasts! All who pass by her scoff and shake their fists.

(4) The Hand as Honor

1 Kings 2 [19]When Bathsheba went to King Solomon to speak to him for Adonijah, the king stood up to meet her, bowed down to her and sat down on his throne. He had a throne brought for the king's mother, and she sat down at his right hand.
Ps 45 [9]Daughters of kings are among your honored women; at your right hand is the royal bride in gold of Ophir.
Gal 2 [9]James, Peter and John, those reputed to be pillars, gave me and Barnabas the right hand of fellowship when they recognized the grace given to me. They agreed that we should go to the Gentiles, and they to the Jews.

(5) The Hand as Intention

Deut 15 [8]Rather be openhanded and freely lend him whatever he needs. . . . [11]There will always be poor people in the land. Therefore I command you to be openhanded toward your brothers and toward the poor and needy in your land.
Josh 8 [26]For Joshua did not draw back the hand that held out his javelin until he had destroyed all who lived in Ai.
1 Kings 13 [4]When King Jeroboam heard what the man of God cried out against the altar at Bethel, he stretched out his hand from the altar and said, "Seize him!" But the hand he stretched out toward the man shriveled up, so that he could not pull it back.
Neh 6 [9]They were all trying to frighten us, thinking, "Their hands will get too weak for the work, and it will not be completed." But I prayed, "Now strengthen my hands."
Job 4 [3]"Think how you have instructed many, how you have strengthened feeble hands."
Isa 13 [7]Because of this, all hands will go limp, every man's heart will melt.
Jer 6 [24]We have heard reports about them, and our hands hang limp. Anguish has gripped us, pain like that of a woman in labor.
Jer 23 [14]"And among the prophets of Jerusalem I have seen something horrible: They commit adultery and live a lie. They

strengthen the hands of evildoers, so that no one turns from his wickedness. They are all like Sodom to me; the people of Jerusalem are like Gomorrah."

Jer 47 [3]". . . at the sound of the hoofs of galloping steeds, at the noise of enemy chariots and the rumble of their wheels. Fathers will not turn to help their children; their hands will hang limp."

Jer 50 [43]"The king of Babylon has heard reports about them, and his hands hang limp. Anguish has gripped him, pain like that of a woman in labor."

Ezek 7 [17]"Every hand will go limp, and every knee will become as weak as water."

Ezek 18 [8]"He does not lend at usury or take excessive interest. He withholds his hand from doing wrong and judges fairly between man and man. . . . [17]He withholds his hand from sin and takes no usury or excessive interest. He keeps my laws and follows my decrees. He will not die for his father's sin; he will surely live."

Zeph 3 [16]On that day they will say to Jerusalem, "Do not fear, O Zion; do not let your hands hang limp."

Matt 6 [3]"But when you give to the needy, do not let your left hand know what your right hand is doing. . . ."

Luke 22 [21]"But the hand of him who is going to betray me is with mine on the table."

(6) The Hand as Judgment

Deut 17 [7]The hands of the witnesses must be the first in putting him to death, and then the hands of all the people. You must purge the evil from among you.

1 Sam 18 [17]Saul said to David, "Here is my older daughter Merab. I will give her to you in marriage; only serve me bravely and fight the battles of the LORD." For Saul said to himself, "I will not raise a hand against him. Let the Philistines do that!"

1 Sam 24 [12]"May the LORD judge between you and me. And may the LORD avenge the wrongs you have done to me, but my hand will not touch you. [13]As the old saying goes, 'From evildoers come evil deeds,' so my hand will not touch you."

Job 9 [33]"If only there were someone to arbitrate between us, to lay his hand upon us both. . . ."

Ps 89 [25]"I will set his hand over the sea, his right hand over the rivers."

(7) The Hand as Power

Deut 8 [17]You may say to yourself, "My power and the strength of my hands have produced this wealth for me."

Deut 28 [32]Your sons and daughters will be given to another nation, and you will wear out your eyes watching for them day after day, powerless to lift a hand.

Judg 3 [10]The Spirit of the LORD came upon him, so that he became Israel's judge and went to war. The LORD gave Cushan-Rishathaim king of Aram into the hands of Othniel, who overpowered him.

Judg 4 [24]And the hand of the Israelites grew stronger and stronger against Jabin, the Canaanite king, until they destroyed him.

Job 30 [2]"Of what use was the strength of their hands to me, since their vigor had gone from them?"

Ps 76 [5]Valiant men lie plundered, they sleep their last sleep; not one of the warriors can lift his hands.

Isa 10 [13]"For he says: 'By the strength of my hand I have done this, and by my wisdom, because I have understanding. I removed the boundaries of nations, I plundered their treasures; like a mighty one I subdued their kings.'"

Isa 45 [9]"Woe to him who quarrels with his Maker, to him who is but a potsherd among the potsherds on the ground. Does the clay say to the potter, 'What are you making?' Does your work say, 'He has no hands'?"

Lam 3 [3]indeed, he has turned his hand against me again and again, all day long.

(8) The Hand as Protection

Ps 16 [8]I have set the LORD always before me. Because he is at my right hand, I will not be shaken.

Ps 73 [23]Yet I am always with you; you hold me by my right hand.

Ps 109 [31]For he stands at the right hand of the needy one, to save his life from those who condemn him.

Ps 110 [5]The Lord is at your right hand; he will crush kings on the day of his wrath.

Ps 121 [5]The LORD watches over you—the LORD is your shade at your right hand. . . .

Isa 41 [13]"For I am the LORD, your God, who takes hold of your right hand and says to you, Do not fear; I will help you."

Isa 45 [1]"This is what the LORD says to his anointed, to Cyrus, whose right hand I take hold of to subdue nations before him and to strip kings of their armor, to open doors before him so that gates will not be shut. . . ."

2 Cor 6 [7]in truthful speech and in the power of God; with weapons of righteousness in the right hand and in the left . . .

e) The Knee

Job 4 [4]"Your words have supported those who stumbled; you have strengthened faltering knees."

Isa 35 [3]Strengthen the feeble hands, steady the knees that give way. . . .

Ezek 7 [17]"Every hand will go limp, and every knee will become as weak as water."

Ezek 21 [7]"And when they ask you, 'Why are you groaning?' you shall say, 'Because of the news that is coming. Every heart will melt and every hand go limp; every spirit will become faint and every knee become as weak as water.' It is coming! It will surely take place, declares the Sovereign LORD."

Nah 2 [10]She is pillaged, plundered, stripped! Hearts melt, knees give way, bodies tremble, every face grows pale.

Heb 12 [12]Therefore, strengthen your feeble arms and weak knees.

f) The Neck

Exod 32 [9]"I have seen these people," the LORD said to Moses, "and they are a stiff-necked people."

Exod 34 [9]"O Lord, if I have found favor in your eyes," he said, "then let the Lord go with us. Although this is a stiff-necked people, forgive our wickedness and our sin, and take us as your inheritance."

Deut 9 [6]Understand, then, that it is not because of your righteousness that the LORD your God is giving you this good land to possess, for you are a stiff-necked people.

Deut 31 [27]"For I know how rebellious and stiff-necked you are. If you have been rebellious against the LORD while I am still alive and with you, how much more will you rebel after I die!"

2 Kings 17 [14]But they would not listen and were as stiff-necked as their fathers, who did not trust in the LORD their God.

2 Chron 30 [8]"Do not be stiff-necked, as your fathers were; submit to the LORD. Come to the sanctuary, which he has consecrated forever. Serve the LORD your God, so that his fierce anger will turn away from you."

Neh 9 [16]"But they, our forefathers, became arrogant and stiff-necked, and did not obey your commands. [17]They refused to listen and failed to remember the miracles you performed among them. They became stiff-necked and in their rebellion appointed a leader in order to return to their slavery. But you are a forgiving God, gracious and compassionate, slow to anger and abounding in love. Therefore you did not desert them. . . .

[29]"You warned them to return to your law, but they became arrogant and disobeyed your commands. They sinned against your ordinances, by which a man will live if he obeys them. Stubbornly they turned their backs on you, became stiff-necked and refused to listen."

Ps 75 [5]"'Do not lift your horns against heaven; do not speak with outstretched neck.'"

Prov 29 [1]A man who remains stiff-necked after many rebukes will suddenly be destroyed—without remedy.

Isa 3 [16]The LORD says, "The women of Zion are haughty, walking along with outstretched necks, flirting with their eyes, tripping along with mincing steps, with ornaments jingling on their ankles."

Jer 19 [15]"This is what the LORD Almighty, the God of Israel, says: 'Listen! I am going to bring on this city and the villages around it every disaster I pronounced against them, because they were stiff-necked and would not listen to my words.'"

Acts 7 [51]"You stiff-necked people, with uncircumcised hearts and ears! You are just like your fathers: You always resist the Holy Spirit!"

g) *The Shoulder*

Zeph 3 [9]"Then will I purify the lips of the peoples, that all of them may call on the name of the LORD and serve him shoulder to shoulder."

3. Human Internal Organs

a) *Human Blood as the Life Principle*

Gen 9 [4]"But you must not eat meat that has its lifeblood still in it. [5]And for your lifeblood I will surely demand an accounting. I will demand an accounting from every animal. And from each man, too, I will demand an accounting for the life of his fellow man.

[6]"Whoever sheds the blood of man, by man shall his blood be shed; for in the image of God has God made man."

Lev 17 [10]"'Any Israelite or any alien living among them who eats any blood—I will set my face against that person who eats blood and will cut him off from his people. [11]For the life of a creature is in the blood, and I have given it to you to make atonement for yourselves on the altar; it is the blood that makes atonement for one's life. [12]Therefore I say to the Israelites, "None of you may eat blood, nor may an alien living among you eat blood."

[13]"'Any Israelite or any alien living among you who hunts any animal or bird that may be eaten must drain out the blood and cover it with earth, [14]because the life of every creature is its blood. That is why I have said to the Israelites, "You must not eat the blood of any creature, because the life of every creature is its blood; anyone who eats it must be cut off."'"

Ps 72 [14]He will rescue them from oppression and violence, for precious is their blood in his sight.

Prov 1 [18]These men lie in wait for their own blood; they waylay only themselves!

b) *Human Bones*

Job 4 [14]". . . fear and trembling seized me and made all my bones shake."

Ps 31 [10]My life is consumed by anguish and my years by groaning; my strength fails because of my affliction, and my bones grow weak.

Ps 32 [3]When I kept silent, my bones wasted away through my groaning all day long.

Ps 38 [3]Because of your wrath there is no health in my body; my bones have no soundness because of my sin.

Ps 42 [10]My bones suffer mortal agony as my foes taunt me, saying to me all day long, "Where is your God?"

Ps 51 [8]Let me hear joy and gladness; let the bones you have crushed rejoice.

Ps 102 [3]For my days vanish like smoke; my bones burn like glowing embers. . . . [5]Because of my loud groaning I am reduced to skin and bones.

Ps 109 [18]He wore cursing as his garment; it entered into his body like water, into his bones like oil.

Prov 14 [30]A heart at peace gives life to the body, but envy rots the bones.

Prov 15 [30]A cheerful look brings joy to the heart, and good news gives health to the bones.

Prov 16 [24]Pleasant words are a honeycomb, sweet to the soul and healing to the bones.

Prov 17 [22]A cheerful heart is good medicine, but a crushed spirit dries up the bones.

Prov 25 [15]Through patience a ruler can be persuaded, and a gentle tongue can break a bone.

Jer 20 [9]But if I say, "I will not mention him or speak any more in his name," his word is in my heart like a fire, a fire shut up in my bones. I am weary of holding it in; indeed, I cannot.

Jer 23 [9]Concerning the prophets: My heart is broken within me; all my bones tremble. I am like a drunken man, like a man overcome by wine, because of the LORD and his holy words.

Lam 1 [13]"From on high he sent fire, sent it down into my bones. He spread a net for my feet and turned me back. He made me desolate, faint all the day long."

Ezek 37 [11]Then he said to me: "Son of man, these bones are the whole house of Israel. They say, 'Our bones are dried up and our hope is gone; we are cut off.'"

Hab 3 [16]I heard and my heart pounded, my lips quivered at the sound; decay crept into my bones, and my legs trembled. Yet I will wait patiently for the day of calamity to come on the nation invading us.

c) *Human Bowels (ET: affection, compassion, heart, inmost being)*

Job 30 [27]"The churning inside me never stops; days of suffering confront me."

Ps 22 [14]I am poured out like water, and all my bones are out of joint. My heart has turned to wax; it has melted away within me.

Ps 40 [8]"I desire to do your will, O my God; your law is within my heart."

Song of Songs 5 [4]My lover thrust his hand through the latch-opening; my heart began to pound for him.

Isa 16 [11]My heart laments for Moab like a harp, my inmost being for Kir Hareseth.

Jer 4 [19]Oh, my anguish, my anguish! I writhe in pain. Oh, the agony of my heart! My heart pounds within me, I cannot keep silent. For I have heard the sound of the trumpet; I have heard the battle cry.

Lam 1 [20]"See, O LORD, how distressed I am! I am in torment within, and in my heart I am disturbed, for I have been most rebellious. Outside, the sword bereaves; inside, there is only death."

Lam 2 [11]My eyes fail from weeping, I am in torment within, my heart is poured out on the ground because my people are destroyed, because children and infants faint in the streets of the city.

2 Cor 7 [15]And his affection for you is all the greater when he remembers that you were all obedient, receiving him with fear and trembling.

Phil 1 [8]God can testify how I long for all of you with the affection of Christ Jesus.

Col 3 [12]Therefore, as God's chosen people, holy and dearly loved, clothe yourselves with compassion, kindness, humility, gentleness and patience.

Philem [7]Your love has given me great joy and encouragement, because you, brother, have refreshed the hearts of the saints.

Philem [12]I am sending him—who is my very heart—back to you.

Philem [20]I do wish, brother, that I may have some benefit from you in the Lord; refresh my heart in Christ.

1 John 3 [17]If anyone has material possessions and sees his brother in need but has no pity on him, how can the love of God be in him?

d) *The Human Heart (ET: inmost thoughts, mind, thoughts, understanding)*

(1) The Heart as the Seat of Emotion

Lev 19 [17]"'Do not hate your brother in your heart. Rebuke your neighbor frankly so you will not share in his guilt.'"

Deut 20 [3]He shall say: "Hear, O Israel, today you are going into battle against your enemies. Do not be fainthearted or afraid; do not be terrified or give way to panic before them."

Deut 28 [67]In the morning you will say, "If only it were evening!" and in the evening, "If only it were morning!"—because of the terror that will fill your hearts and the sights that your eyes will see.

Josh 7 [5]who killed about thirty-six of them. They chased the Israelites from the city gate as far as the stone quarries and struck them down on the slopes. At this the hearts of the people melted and became like water.

1 Sam 2 [1]Then Hannah prayed and said: "My heart rejoices in the LORD; in the LORD my horn is lifted high. My mouth boasts over my enemies, for I delight in your deliverance."

1 Sam 4 [13]When he arrived, there was Eli sitting on his chair by the side of the road, watching, because his heart feared for the ark of God. When the man entered the town and told what had happened, the whole town sent up a cry.

Job 15 [12]"Why has your heart carried you away, and why do your eyes flash? . . ."

Ps 25 [17]The troubles of my heart have multiplied; free me from my anguish.

Ps 27 [3]Though an army besiege me, my heart will not fear; though war break out against me, even then will I be confident.

Ps 28 [7]The LORD is my strength and my shield; my heart trusts in him, and I am helped. My heart leaps for joy and I will give thanks to him in song.
Ps 31 [24]Be strong and take heart, all you who hope in the LORD.
Ps 39 [3]My heart grew hot within me, and as I meditated, the fire burned; then I spoke with my tongue. . . .
Ps 84 [2]My soul yearns, even faints, for the courts of the LORD; my heart and my flesh cry out for the living God.
Ps 102 [4]My heart is blighted and withered like grass; I forget to eat my food.
Prov 12 [25]An anxious heart weighs a man down, but a kind word cheers him up.
Prov 14 [10]Each heart knows its own bitterness, and no one else can share its joy.
Prov 15 [13]A happy heart makes the face cheerful, but heartache crushes the spirit.
Prov 23 [17]Do not let your heart envy sinners, but always be zealous for the fear of the LORD.
Eccles 2 [20]So my heart began to despair over all my toilsome labor under the sun.
Eccles 11 [10]So then, banish anxiety from your heart and cast off the troubles of your body, for youth and vigor are meaningless.
Isa 66 [14]When you see this, your heart will rejoice and you will flourish like grass; the hand of the LORD will be made known to his servants, but his fury will be shown to his foes.
Jer 8 [18]O my Comforter in sorrow, my heart is faint within me.
Lam 1 [20]"See, O LORD, how distressed I am! I am in torment within, and in my heart I am disturbed, for I have been most rebellious. Outside, the sword bereaves; inside, there is only death."
John 14 [1]"Do not let your hearts be troubled. Trust in God; trust also in me. . . ."
[27]"Peace I leave with you; my peace I give you. I do not give to you as the world gives. Do not let your hearts be troubled and do not be afraid."
Acts 2 [46]Every day they continued to meet together in the temple courts. They broke bread in their homes and ate together with glad and sincere hearts. . . .
Rom 9 [2]I have great sorrow and unceasing anguish in my heart.
2 Cor 2 [4]For I wrote you out of great distress and anguish of heart and with many tears, not to grieve you but to let you know the depth of my love for you.
2 Cor 7 [3]I do not say this to condemn you; I have said before that you have such a place in our hearts that we would live or die with you.
Phil 1 [7]It is right for me to feel this way about all of you, since I have you in my heart; for whether I am in chains or defending and confirming the gospel, all of you share in God's grace with me.

(2) The Heart as the Seat of Ethical Decision

Exod 14 [5]When the king of Egypt was told that the people had fled, Pharaoh and his officials changed their minds about them and said, "What have we done? We have let the Israelites go and have lost their services!"
Deut 30 [17]But if your heart turns away and you are not obedient, and if you are drawn away to bow down to other gods and worship them . . .
Josh 24 [23]"Now then," said Joshua, "throw away the foreign gods that are among you and yield your hearts to the LORD, the God of Israel."
2 Sam 15 [6]Absalom behaved in this way toward all the Israelites who came to the king asking for justice, and so he stole the hearts of the men of Israel.
1 Kings 8 [58]"May he turn our hearts to him, to walk in all his ways and to keep the commands, decrees and regulations he gave our fathers."
1 Kings 18 [37]"Answer me, O LORD, answer me, so these people will know that you, O LORD, are God, and that you are turning their hearts back again."
2 Chron 29 [31]Then Hezekiah said, "You have now dedicated yourselves to the LORD. Come and bring sacrifices and thank offerings to the temple of the LORD." So the assembly brought sacrifices and thank offerings, and all whose hearts were willing brought burnt offerings.
Neh 4 [6]So we rebuilt the wall till all of it reached half its height, for the people worked with all their heart.
Job 31 [7]". . . if my steps have turned from the path, if my heart has been led by my eyes, or if my hands have been defiled . . .
[9]"If my heart has been enticed by a woman, or if I have lurked at my neighbor's door . . ."
Job 31 [27]". . . so that my heart was secretly enticed and my hand offered them a kiss of homage . . ."
Ps 44 [18]Our hearts had not turned back; our feet had not strayed from your path.
Ps 58 [2]No, in your heart you devise injustice, and your hands mete out violence on the earth.
Ps 105 [25]whose hearts he turned to hate his people, to conspire against his servants.
Ps 141 [4]Let not my heart be drawn to what is evil, to take part in wicked deeds with men who are evildoers; let me not eat of their delicacies.
Prov 5 [12]You will say, "How I hated discipline! How my heart spurned correction!"
Prov 7 [25]Do not let your heart turn to her ways or stray into her paths.
Prov 21 [1]The king's heart is in the hand of the LORD; he directs it like a watercourse wherever he pleases.
Isa 44 [20]He feeds on ashes, a deluded heart misleads him; he cannot save himself, or say, "Is not this thing in my right hand a lie?"
Jer 17 [5]This is what the LORD says: "Cursed is the one who trusts in man, who depends on flesh for his strength and whose heart turns away from the LORD."
Ezek 6 [9]"'Then in the nations where they have been carried captive, those who escape will remember me—how I have been grieved by their adulterous hearts, which have turned away from me, and by their eyes, which have lusted after their idols. They will loathe themselves for the evil they have done and for all their detestable practices.'"
Ezek 33 [31]"My people come to you, as they usually do, and sit before you to listen to your words, but they do not put them into practice. With their mouths they express devotion, but their hearts are greedy for unjust gain."
Mal 4 [6]"He will turn the hearts of the fathers to their children, and the hearts of the children to their fathers; or else I will come and strike the land with a curse."
Matt 5 [8]"Blessed are the pure in heart, for they will see God."
Matt 5 [28]"But I tell you that anyone who looks at a woman lustfully has already committed adultery with her in his heart."
Matt 6 [21]"For where your treasure is, there your heart will be also."
Rom 1 [24]Therefore God gave them over in the sinful desires of their hearts to sexual impurity for the degrading of their bodies with one another.
James 3 [14]But if you harbor bitter envy and selfish ambition in your hearts, do not boast about it or deny the truth.

(3) The Heart as the Seat of Intelligence

Deut 30 [14]No, the word is very near you; it is in your mouth and in your heart so you may obey it.
Judg 5 [15]"The princes of Issachar were with Deborah; yes, Issachar was with Barak, rushing after him into the valley. In the districts of Reuben there was much searching of heart. [16]Why did you stay among the campfires to hear the whistling for the flocks? In the districts of Reuben there was much searching of heart."
1 Kings 3 [9]"So give your servant a discerning heart to govern your people and to distinguish between right and wrong. For who is able to govern this great people of yours?"
Neh 5 [7]I pondered them in my mind and then accused the nobles and officials. I told them, "You are exacting usury from your own countrymen!" So I called together a large meeting to deal with them. . . .
Job 8 [10]"Will they not instruct you and tell you? Will they not bring forth words from their understanding?"
Job 17 [11]"My days have passed, my plans are shattered, and so are the desires of my heart."
Ps 27 [8]My heart says of you, "Seek his face!" Your face, LORD, I will seek.
Ps 41 [6]Whenever one comes to see me, he speaks falsely, while

his heart gathers slander; then he goes out and spreads it abroad.

Ps 66 [18]If I had cherished sin in my heart, the Lord would not have listened. . . .

Prov 4 [4]he taught me and said, "Lay hold of my words with all your heart; keep my commands and you will live. . . ."

[20]My son, pay attention to what I say; listen closely to my words. [21]Do not let them out of your sight, keep them within your heart. . . .

Prov 15 [32]He who ignores discipline despises himself, but whoever heeds correction gains understanding.

Prov 16 [1]To man belong the plans of the heart, but from the LORD comes the reply of the tongue.

Prov 23 [33]Your eyes will see strange sights and your mind imagine confusing things.

Eccles 2 [1]I thought in my heart, "Come now, I will test you with pleasure to find out what is good." But that also proved to be meaningless. . . . [3]I tried cheering myself with wine, and embracing folly—my mind still guiding me with wisdom. I wanted to see what was worthwhile for men to do under heaven during the few days of their lives.

Eccles 3 [11]He has made everything beautiful in its time. He has also set eternity in the hearts of men; yet they cannot fathom what God has done from beginning to end.

Song of Songs 5 [2]I slept but my heart was awake. Listen! My lover is knocking: "Open to me, my sister, my darling, my dove, my flawless one. My head is drenched with dew, my hair with the dampness of the night."

Isa 51 [7]"Hear me, you who know what is right, you people who have my law in your hearts: Do not fear the reproach of men or be terrified by their insults."

Lam 3 [41]Let us lift up our hearts and our hands to God in heaven, and say . . .

Matt 12 [34]"You brood of vipers, how can you who are evil say anything good? For out of the overflow of the heart the mouth speaks."

Mark 7 [21]"For from within, out of men's hearts, come evil thoughts, sexual immorality, theft, murder, adultery, [22]greed, malice, deceit, lewdness, envy, slander, arrogance and folly. [23]All these evils come from inside and make a man 'unclean.'"

Mark 11 [23]"I tell you the truth, if anyone says to this mountain, 'Go, throw yourself into the sea,' and does not doubt in his heart but believes that what he says will happen, it will be done for him."

Luke 1 [51]"He has performed mighty deeds with his arm; he has scattered those who are proud in their inmost thoughts."

Luke 9 [47]Jesus, knowing their thoughts, took a little child and had him stand beside him.

Luke 24 [38]He said to them, "Why are you troubled, and why do doubts rise in your minds?"

Acts 8 [22]"Repent of this wickedness and pray to the Lord. Perhaps he will forgive you for having such a thought in your heart."

Rom 1 [21]For although they knew God, they neither glorified him as God nor gave thanks to him, but their thinking became futile and their foolish hearts were darkened.

Rom 10 [6]But the righteousness that is by faith says: "Do not say in your heart, 'Who will ascend into heaven?'" (that is, to bring Christ down). . . .

(4) The Heart as the Seat of Religious Life

Deut 6 [5]Love the LORD your God with all your heart and with all your soul and with all your strength.

1 Chron 28 [9]"And you, my son Solomon, acknowledge the God of your father, and serve him with wholehearted devotion and with a willing mind, for the LORD searches every heart and understands every motive behind the thoughts. If you seek him, he will be found by you; but if you forsake him, he will reject you forever."

Prov 7 [1]My son, keep my words and store up my commands within you. [2]Keep my commands and you will live; guard my teachings as the apple of your eye. [3]Bind them on your fingers; write them on the tablet of your heart.

Jer 31 [33]"This is the covenant I will make with the house of Israel after that time," declares the LORD. "I will put my law in their minds and write it on their hearts. I will be their God, and they will be my people."

Matt 11 [29]"Take my yoke upon you and learn from me, for I am gentle and humble in heart, and you will find rest for your souls."

Matt 13 [19]"When anyone hears the message about the kingdom and does not understand it, the evil one comes and snatches away what was sown in his heart. This is the seed sown along the path."

Luke 6 [45]"The good man brings good things out of the good stored up in his heart, and the evil man brings evil things out of the evil stored up in his heart. For out of the overflow of his heart his mouth speaks."

Luke 8 [15]"But the seed on good soil stands for those with a noble and good heart, who hear the word, retain it, and by persevering produce a crop."

Luke 16 [15]He said to them, "You are the ones who justify yourselves in the eyes of men, but God knows your hearts. What is highly valued among men is detestable in God's sight."

Acts 16 [14]One of those listening was a woman named Lydia, a dealer in purple cloth from the city of Thyatira, who was a worshiper of God. The Lord opened her heart to respond to Paul's message.

Rom 2 [15](. . . since they show that the requirements of the law are written on their hearts, their consciences also bearing witness, and their thoughts now accusing, now even defending them.)

Rom 5 [5]And hope does not disappoint us, because God has poured out his love into our hearts by the Holy Spirit, whom he has given us.

Rom 8 [27]And he who searches our hearts knows the mind of the Spirit, because the Spirit intercedes for the saints in accordance with God's will.

2 Cor 1 [21]Now it is God who makes both us and you stand firm in Christ. He anointed us, [22]set his seal of ownership on us, and put his Spirit in our hearts as a deposit, guaranteeing what is to come.

Gal 4 [6]Because you are sons, God sent the Spirit of his Son into our hearts, the Spirit who calls out, "*Abba*, Father."

Eph 3 [17]so that Christ may dwell in your hearts through faith. And I pray that you, being rooted and established in love . . .

Eph 6 [5]Slaves, obey your earthly masters with respect and fear, and with sincerity of heart, just as you would obey Christ.

Phil 4 [7]And the peace of God, which transcends all understanding, will guard your hearts and your minds in Christ Jesus.

Col 3 [15]Let the peace of Christ rule in your hearts, since as members of one body you were called to peace. And be thankful.

1 Thess 2 [4]On the contrary, we speak as men approved by God to be entrusted with the gospel. We are not trying to please men but God, who tests our hearts.

1 Thess 3 [13]May he strengthen your hearts so that you will be blameless and holy in the presence of our God and Father when our Lord Jesus comes with all his holy ones.

2 Thess 3 [5]May the Lord direct your hearts into God's love and Christ's perseverance.

1 Tim 1 [5]The goal of this command is love, which comes from a pure heart and a good conscience and a sincere faith.

Heb 13 [9]Do not be carried away by all kinds of strange teachings. It is good for our hearts to be strengthened by grace, not by ceremonial foods, which are of no value to those who eat them.

James 4 [8]Come near to God and he will come near to you. Wash your hands, you sinners, and purify your hearts, you double-minded.

1 Pet 1 [22]Now that you have purified yourselves by obeying the truth so that you have sincere love for your brothers, love one another deeply, from the heart.

1 Pet 3 [15]But in your hearts set apart Christ as Lord. Always be prepared to give an answer to everyone who asks you to give the reason for the hope that you have. But do this with gentleness and respect. . . .

2 Pet 1 [19]And we have the word of the prophets made more certain, and you will do well to pay attention to it, as to a light shining in a dark place, until the day dawns and the morning star rises in your hearts.

(5) The Heart as the Seat of Volition

Deut 8 [2]Remember how the LORD your God led you all the way

in the desert these forty years, to humble you and to test you in order to know what was in your heart, whether or not you would keep his commands.
2 Sam 7 [3]Nathan replied to the king, "Whatever you have in mind, go ahead and do it, for the LORD is with you."
1 Kings 8 [39]". . . then hear from heaven, your dwelling place. Forgive and act; deal with each man according to all he does, since you know his heart (for you alone know the hearts of all men). [47]. . . and if they have a change of heart in the land where they are held captive, and repent and plead with you in the land of their conquerors and say, 'We have sinned, we have done wrong, we have acted wickedly' . . ."
2 Chron 32 [31]But when envoys were sent by the rulers of Babylon to ask him about the miraculous sign that had occurred in the land, God left him to test him and to know everything that was in his heart.
Ps 20 [4]May he give you the desire of your heart and make all your plans succeed.
Ps 55 [21]His speech is smooth as butter, yet war is in his heart; his words are more soothing than oil, yet they are drawn swords.
Ps 139 [23]Search me, O God, and know my heart; test me and know my anxious thoughts.
Prov 10 [20]The tongue of the righteous is choice silver, but the heart of the wicked is of little value.
Eccles 7 [2]It is better to go to a house of mourning than to go to a house of feasting, for death is the destiny of every man; the living should take this to heart.
Isa 65 [17]"Behold, I will create new heavens and a new earth. The former things will not be remembered, nor will they come to mind."
Lam 2 [19]Arise, cry out in the night, as the watches of the night begin; pour out your heart like water in the presence of the Lord. Lift up your hands to him for the lives of your children, who faint from hunger at the head of every street.
Ezek 14 [5]"'I will do this to recapture the hearts of the people of Israel, who have all deserted me for their idols.'"
Dan 11 [27]"The two kings, with their hearts bent on evil, will sit at the same table and lie to each other, but to no avail, because an end will still come at the appointed time. [28]The king of the North will return to his own country with great wealth, but his heart will be set against the holy covenant. He will take action against it and then return to his own country."
Mal 2 [2]"If you do not listen, and if you do not set your heart to honor my name," says the LORD Almighty, "I will send a curse upon you, and I will curse your blessings. Yes, I have already cursed them, because you have not set your heart to honor me."
Luke 21 [14]"But make up your mind not to worry beforehand how you will defend yourselves."
Acts 11 [23]When he arrived and saw the evidence of the grace of God, he was glad and encouraged them all to remain true to the Lord with all their hearts.
Rom 10 [1]Brothers, my heart's desire and prayer to God for the Israelites is that they may be saved.
1 Cor 4 [4]My conscience is clear, but that does not make me innocent. It is the Lord who judges me. [5]Therefore judge nothing before the appointed time; wait till the Lord comes. He will bring to light what is hidden in darkness and will expose the motives of men's hearts. At that time each will receive his praise from God.
2 Cor 9 [7]Each man should give what he has decided in his heart to give, not reluctantly or under compulsion, for God loves a cheerful giver.
Eph 6 [22]I am sending him to you for this very purpose, that you may know how we are, and that he may encourage you. (ET: your hearts)
Col 4 [8]I am sending him to you for the express purpose that you may know about our circumstances and that he may encourage your hearts.

e) Human Kidneys (ET: heart, mind)

Job 19 [27]"I myself will see him with my own eyes—I, and not another. How my heart yearns within me!"
Ps 7 [9]O righteous God, who searches minds and hearts, bring to an end the violence of the wicked and make the righteous secure.
Ps 16 [7]I will praise the LORD, who counsels me; even at night my heart instructs me.
Ps 26 [2]Test me, O LORD, and try me, examine my heart and my mind. . . .
Ps 73 [21]When my heart was grieved and my spirit embittered . . .
Prov 23 [15]My son, if your heart is wise, then my heart will be glad; [16]my inmost being will rejoice when your lips speak what is right.
Jer 11 [20]But, O LORD Almighty, you who judge righteously and test the heart and mind, let me see your vengeance upon them, for to you I have committed my cause.
Jer 17 [10]"I the LORD search the heart and examine the mind, to reward a man according to his conduct, according to what his deeds deserve."
Jer 20 [12]O LORD Almighty, you who examine the righteous and probe the heart and mind, let me see your vengeance upon them, for to you I have committed my cause.
Rev 2 [23]"I will strike her children dead. Then all the churches will know that I am he who searches hearts and minds, and I will repay each of you according to your deeds."

f) The Human Stomach (ET: inmost being, inmost parts)

Job 20 [15]"He will spit out the riches he swallowed; God will make his stomach vomit them up. . . .
[20]"Surely he will have no respite from his craving; he cannot save himself by his treasure. . . . [23]When he has filled his belly, God will vent his burning anger against him and rain down his blows upon him."
Ps 103 [1]Praise the LORD, O my soul; all my inmost being, praise his holy name.
Prov 18 [8]The words of a gossip are like choice morsels; they go down to a man's inmost parts.
Prov 20 [27]The lamp of the LORD searches the spirit of a man; it searches out his inmost being. . . .
[30]Blows and wounds cleanse away evil, and beatings purge the inmost being.
Isa 16 [11]My heart laments for Moab like a harp, my inmost being for Kir Hareseth.
Phil 3 [19]Their destiny is destruction, their god is their stomach, and their glory is in their shame. Their mind is on earthly things.

g) The Human Womb

Job 15 [35]"They conceive trouble and give birth to evil; their womb fashions deceit."

F. The Inner Person

Rom 7 [22]For in my inner being I delight in God's law. . . .
2 Cor 4 [16]Therefore we do not lose heart. Though outwardly we are wasting away, yet inwardly we are being renewed day by day.
Eph 3 [16]I pray that out of his glorious riches he may strengthen you with power through his Spirit in your inner being. . . .

G. The Outer Person

2 Cor 4 [16]Therefore we do not lose heart. Though outwardly we are wasting away, yet inwardly we are being renewed day by day.

H. The Old Self

Rom 6 [6]For we know that our old self was crucified with him so that the body of sin might be done away with, that we should no longer be slaves to sin. . . .
Eph 4 [22]You were taught, with regard to your former way of life, to put off your old self, which is being corrupted by its deceitful desires. . . .
Col 3 [9]Do not lie to each other, since you have taken off your old self with its practices. . . .

I. The New Self

Eph 2 [15]by abolishing in his flesh the law with its commandments and regulations. His purpose was to create in himself one new man out of the two, thus making peace. . . .
Eph 4 [24]and to put on the new self, created to be like God in true righteousness and holiness.
Col 3 [10]and have put on the new self, which is being renewed in knowledge in the image of its Creator.

J. The Human Mind

Luke 24 [45]Then he opened their minds so they could understand the Scriptures.
Rom 1 [28]Furthermore, since they did not think it worthwhile to retain the knowledge of God, he gave them over to a depraved mind, to do what ought not to be done.
Rom 7 [23]but I see another law at work in the members of my body, waging war against the law of my mind and making me a prisoner of the law of sin at work within my members. . . .
[25]Thanks be to God—through Jesus Christ our Lord!

So then, I myself in my mind am a slave to God's law, but in the sinful nature a slave to the law of sin.
Rom 12 [2]Do not conform any longer to the pattern of this world, but be transformed by the renewing of your mind. Then you will be able to test and approve what God's will is—his good, pleasing and perfect will.
Rom 14 [5]One man considers one day more sacred than another; another man considers every day alike. Each one should be fully convinced in his own mind.
1 Cor 1 [10]I appeal to you, brothers, in the name of our Lord Jesus Christ, that all of you agree with one another so that there may be no divisions among you and that you may be perfectly united in mind and thought.
1 Cor 14 [14]For if I pray in a tongue, my spirit prays, but my mind is unfruitful.
Eph 4 [17]So I tell you this, and insist on it in the Lord, that you must no longer live as the Gentiles do, in the futility of their thinking.
Phil 4 [7]And the peace of God, which transcends all understanding, will guard your hearts and your minds in Christ Jesus.
Col 2 [18]Do not let anyone who delights in false humility and the worship of angels disqualify you for the prize. Such a person goes into great detail about what he has seen, and his unspiritual mind puffs him up with idle notions.
1 Tim 6 [5]and constant friction between men of corrupt mind, who have been robbed of the truth and who think that godliness is a means to financial gain.
2 Tim 3 [8]Just as Jannes and Jambres opposed Moses, so also these men oppose the truth—men of depraved minds, who, as far as the faith is concerned, are rejected.
Titus 1 [15]To the pure, all things are pure, but to those who are corrupted and do not believe, nothing is pure. In fact, both their minds and consciences are corrupted.

K. The Human Conscience

Acts 24 [16]"So I strive always to keep my conscience clear before God and man."
Rom 2 [15](. . . since they show that the requirements of the law are written on their hearts, their consciences also bearing witness, and their thoughts now accusing, now even defending them.)
Rom 9 [1]I speak the truth in Christ—I am not lying, my conscience confirms it in the Holy Spirit. . . .
1 Cor 8 [7]But not everyone knows this. Some people are still so accustomed to idols that when they eat such food they think of it as having been sacrificed to an idol, and since their conscience is weak, it is defiled. [8]But food does not bring us near to God; we are no worse if we do not eat, and no better if we do.

[9]Be careful, however, that the exercise of your freedom does not become a stumbling block to the weak. [10]For if anyone with a weak conscience sees you who have this knowledge eating in an idol's temple, won't he be emboldened to eat what has been sacrificed to idols? [11]So this weak brother, for whom Christ died, is destroyed by your knowledge. [12]When you sin against your brothers in this way and wound their weak conscience, you sin against Christ. [13]Therefore, if what I eat causes my brother to fall into sin, I will never eat meat again, so that I will not cause him to fall.
1 Cor 10 [25]Eat anything sold in the meat market without raising questions of conscience, [26]for, "The earth is the Lord's, and everything in it."

[27]If some unbeliever invites you to a meal and you want to go, eat whatever is put before you without raising questions of conscience. [28]But if anyone says to you, "This has been offered in sacrifice," then do not eat it, both for the sake of the man who told you and for conscience' sake—[29]the other man's conscience, I mean, not yours. For why should my freedom be judged by another's conscience?
2 Cor 4 [2]Rather, we have renounced secret and shameful ways; we do not use deception, nor do we distort the word of God. On the contrary, by setting forth the truth plainly we commend ourselves to every man's conscience in the sight of God.
1 Tim 1 [5]The goal of this command is love, which comes from a pure heart and a good conscience and a sincere faith.
1 Tim 3 [9]They must keep hold of the deep truths of the faith with a clear conscience.
1 Tim 4 [2]Such teachings come through hypocritical liars, whose consciences have been seared as with a hot iron.
Heb 9 [9]This is an illustration for the present time, indicating that the gifts and sacrifices being offered were not able to clear the conscience of the worshiper.
Heb 9 [14]How much more, then, will the blood of Christ, who through the eternal Spirit offered himself unblemished to God, cleanse our consciences from acts that lead to death, so that we may serve the living God!
1 Pet 3 [16]keeping a clear conscience, so that those who speak maliciously against your good behavior in Christ may be ashamed of their slander.

L. The Human Will

John 1 [13]children born not of natural descent, nor of human decision or a husband's will, but born of God.
1 Cor 7 [37]But the man who has settled the matter in his own mind, who is under no compulsion but has control over his own will, and who has made up his mind not to marry the virgin—this man also does the right thing.
2 Pet 1 [21]For prophecy never had its origin in the will of man, but men spoke from God as they were carried along by the Holy Spirit.

VII
The Human Being as a Living Unity

A. The Whole Person Represented by the Arm

Gen 49 [24]"But his bow remained steady, his strong arms stayed limber, because of the hand of the Mighty One of Jacob, because of the Shepherd, the Rock of Israel. . . ."
Job 26 [2]"How you have helped the powerless! How you have saved the arm that is feeble!"
Ps 44 [3]It was not by their sword that they won the land, nor did their arm bring them victory; it was your right hand, your arm, and the light of your face, for you loved them.
Isa 17 [5]"It will be as when a reaper gathers the standing grain and harvests the grain with his arm—as when a man gleans heads of grain in the Valley of Rephaim."

B. The Whole Person Represented by the Blood

Deut 21 [8]"Accept this atonement for your people Israel, whom

you have redeemed, O LORD, and do not hold your people guilty of the blood of an innocent man." And the bloodshed will be atoned for. [9]So you will purge from yourselves the guilt of shedding innocent blood, since you have done what is right in the eyes of the LORD.
2 Kings 21 [16]Moreover, Manasseh also shed so much innocent blood that he filled Jerusalem from end to end—besides the sin that he had caused Judah to commit, so that they did evil in the eyes of the LORD.
Ps 106 [38]They shed innocent blood, the blood of their sons and daughters, whom they sacrificed to the idols of Canaan, and the land was desecrated by their blood.
Prov 1 [11]If they say, "Come along with us; let's lie in wait for someone's blood, let's waylay some harmless soul . . ."
Prov 6 [16]There are six things the LORD hates, seven that are detestable to him: [17]haughty eyes, a lying tongue, hands that shed innocent blood. . . .
Isa 59 [7]Their feet rush into sin; they are swift to shed innocent blood. Their thoughts are evil thoughts; ruin and destruction mark their ways.
Jer 19 [4]"'For they have forsaken me and made this a place of foreign gods; they have burned sacrifices in it to gods that neither they nor their fathers nor the kings of Judah ever knew, and they have filled this place with the blood of the innocent.'"
Jer 22 [3]"'This is what the LORD says: Do what is just and right. Rescue from the hand of his oppressor the one who has been robbed. Do no wrong or violence to the alien, the fatherless or the widow, and do not shed innocent blood in this place.'"
Jer 22 [17]"But your eyes and your heart are set only on dishonest gain, on shedding innocent blood and on oppression and extortion."
Lam 4 [13]But it happened because of the sins of her prophets and the iniquities of her priests, who shed within her the blood of the righteous.
Joel 3 [19]"But Egypt will be desolate, Edom a desert waste, because of violence done to the people of Judah, in whose land they shed innocent blood."
Matt 23 [35]"And so upon you will come all the righteous blood that has been shed on earth, from the blood of righteous Abel to the blood of Zechariah son of Berekiah, whom you murdered between the temple and the altar."
Acts 20 [26]"Therefore, I declare to you today that I am innocent of the blood of all men."

C. The Whole Person Represented by the Ear

Isa 64 [4]Since ancient times no one has heard, no ear has perceived, no eye has seen any God besides you, who acts on behalf of those who wait for him.

D. The Whole Person Represented by the Eyes

Job 7 [8]"The eye that now sees me will see me no longer; you will look for me, but I will be no more."
Job 24 [15]"The eye of the adulterer watches for dusk; he thinks, 'No eye will see me,' and he keeps his face concealed."
Ps 119 [82]My eyes fail, looking for your promise; I say, "When will you comfort me?"
Ps 119 [148]My eyes stay open through the watches of the night, that I may meditate on your promises.
Prov 30 [17]"The eye that mocks a father, that scorns obedience to a mother, will be pecked out by the ravens of the valley, will be eaten by the vultures."
Isa 64 [4]Since ancient times no one has heard, no ear has perceived, no eye has seen any God besides you, who acts on behalf of those who wait for him.
Jer 32 [5]"'He will take Zedekiah to Babylon, where he will remain until I deal with him, declares the LORD. If you fight against the Babylonians, you will not succeed.'"
Mal 1 [5]"You will see it with your own eyes and say, 'Great is the LORD—even beyond the borders of Israel!'"
Luke 10 [23]Then he turned to his disciples and said privately, "Blessed are the eyes that see what you see."
Acts 1 [9]After he said this, he was taken up before their very eyes, and a cloud hid him from their sight.
2 Cor 4 [18]So we fix our eyes not on what is seen, but on what is unseen. For what is seen is temporary, but what is unseen is eternal.
Heb 12 [2]Let us fix our eyes on Jesus, the author and perfecter of our faith, who for the joy set before him endured the cross, scorning its shame, and sat down at the right hand of the throne of God.
Rev 1 [7]Look, he is coming with the clouds, and every eye will see him, even those who pierced him; and all the peoples of the earth will mourn because of him. So shall it be! Amen.

E. The Whole Person Represented by the Face

Gen 32 [30]So Jacob called the place Peniel, saying, "It is because I saw God face to face, and yet my life was spared."
Gen 33 [10]"No, please!" said Jacob. "If I have found favor in your eyes, accept this gift from me. For to see your face is like seeing the face of God, now that you have received me favorably."
Gen 43 [3]But Judah said to him, "The man warned us solemnly, 'You will not see my face again unless your brother is with you.' [4]If you will send our brother along with us, we will go down and buy food for you. [5]But if you will not send him, we will not go down, because the man said to us, 'You will not see my face again unless your brother is with you.'"
Gen 44 [23]"But you told your servants, 'Unless your youngest brother comes down with you, you will not see my face again.' . . ."

[26]"But we said, 'We cannot go down. Only if our youngest brother is with us will we go. We cannot see the man's face unless our youngest brother is with us.'"
Gen 48 [11]Israel said to Joseph, "I never expected to see your face again, and now God has allowed me to see your children too."
Exod 10 [28]Pharaoh said to Moses, "Get out of my sight! Make sure you do not appear before me again! The day you see my face you will die."

[29]"Just as you say," Moses replied, "I will never appear before you again."
Deut 7 [10]But those who hate him he will repay to their face by destruction; he will not be slow to repay to their face those who hate him.
Deut 34 [10]Since then, no prophet has risen in Israel like Moses, whom the LORD knew face to face. . . .
Judg 6 [22]When Gideon realized that it was the angel of the LORD, he exclaimed, "Ah, Sovereign LORD! I have seen the angel of the LORD face to face!"
2 Sam 14 [24]But the king said, "He must go to his own house; he must not see my face." So Absalom went to his own house and did not see the face of the king. . . .

[28]Absalom lived two years in Jerusalem without seeing the king's face. . . .

[32]Absalom said to Joab, "Look, I sent word to you and said, 'Come here so I can send you to the king to ask, "Why have I come from Geshur? It would be better for me if I were still there!"' Now then, I want to see the king's face, and if I am guilty of anything, let him put me to death."
2 Kings 14 [8]Then Amaziah sent messengers to Jehoash son of Jehoahaz, the son of Jehu, king of Israel, with the challenge: "Come, meet me face to face."
2 Chron 25 [17]After Amaziah king of Judah consulted his advisers, he sent this challenge to Jehoash son of Jehoahaz, the son of Jehu, king of Israel: "Come, meet me face to face." . . .

[21]So Jehoash king of Israel attacked. He and Amaziah king of Judah faced each other at Beth Shemesh in Judah.
Jer 34 [3]"'You will not escape from his grasp but will surely be captured and handed over to him. You will see the king of Babylon with your own eyes, and he will speak with you face to face. And you will go to Babylon.'"
Acts 20 [38]What grieved them most was his statement that they would never see his face again. Then they accompanied him to the ship.

1 Cor 13 [12]Now we see but a poor reflection as in a mirror; then we shall see face to face. Now I know in part; then I shall know fully, even as I am fully known.
2 Cor 10 [1]By the meekness and gentleness of Christ, I appeal to you—I, Paul, who am "timid" when face to face with you, but "bold" when away!
Gal 2 [11]When Peter came to Antioch, I opposed him to his face, because he was clearly in the wrong.

F. The Whole Person Represented by the Flesh (ET: body, man, people)

Job 4 [15]"A spirit glided past my face, and the hair on my body stood on end."
Job 13 [14]"Why do I put myself in jeopardy and take my life in my hands?"
Job 14 [22]"He feels but the pain of his own body and mourns only for himself."
Job 21 [6]"When I think about this, I am terrified; trembling seizes my body."
Ps 16 [9]Therefore my heart is glad and my tongue rejoices; my body also will rest secure. . . .
Ps 27 [2]When evil men advance against me to devour my flesh, when my enemies and my foes attack me, they will stumble and fall.
Ps 63 [1]O God, you are my God, earnestly I seek you; my soul thirsts for you, my body longs for you, in a dry and weary land where there is no water.
Ps 84 [2]My soul yearns, even faints, for the courts of the LORD; my heart and my flesh cry out for the living God.
Ps 119 [120]My flesh trembles in fear of you; I stand in awe of your laws.
Prov 4 [22]for they are life to those who find them and health to a man's whole body.
Prov 14 [30]A heart at peace gives life to the body, but envy rots the bones.
Eccles 2 [3]I tried cheering myself with wine, and embracing folly—my mind still guiding me with wisdom. I wanted to see what was worthwhile for men to do under heaven during the few days of their lives.
Eccles 11 [10]So then, banish anxiety from your heart and cast off the troubles of your body, for youth and vigor are meaningless.
Matt 16 [17]Jesus replied, "Blessed are you, Simon son of Jonah, for this was not revealed to you by man, but by my Father in heaven."
Matt 19 [5]". . . and said, 'For this reason a man will leave his father and mother and be united to his wife, and the two will become one flesh'? [6]So they are no longer two, but one. Therefore what God has joined together, let man not separate."
John 17 [2]"For you granted him authority over all people that he might give eternal life to all those you have given him."
Acts 2 [17]"'In the last days, God says, I will pour out my Spirit on all people. Your sons and daughters will prophesy, your young men will see visions, your old men will dream dreams.'"
Rom 11 [14]in the hope that I may somehow arouse my own people to envy and save some of them.
1 Cor 1 [29]so that no one may boast before him.
Gal 1 [16]to reveal his Son in me so that I might preach him among the Gentiles, I did not consult any man. . . .

G. The Whole Person Represented by the Foot

Job 28 [4]"Far from where people dwell he cuts a shaft, in places forgotten by the foot of man; far from men he dangles and sways."
Ps 36 [11]May the foot of the proud not come against me, nor the hand of the wicked drive me away.
Ps 44 [18]Our hearts had not turned back; our feet had not strayed from your path.
Prov 1 [15]my son, do not go along with them, do not set foot on their paths. . . .
Prov 4 [14]Do not set foot on the path of the wicked or walk in the way of evil men.
Prov 6 [16]There are six things the LORD hates, seven that are detestable to him . . . [18]a heart that devises wicked schemes, feet that are quick to rush into evil. . . .
Isa 59 [7]Their feet rush into sin; they are swift to shed innocent blood. Their thoughts are evil thoughts; ruin and destruction mark their ways.
Rom 10 [15]And how can they preach unless they are sent? As it is written, "How beautiful are the feet of those who bring good news!"

H. The Whole Person Represented by the Hand

Gen 31 [42]"If the God of my father, the God of Abraham and the Fear of Isaac, had not been with me, you would surely have sent me away empty-handed. But God has seen my hardship and the toil of my hands, and last night he rebuked you."
Deut 33 [7]And this he said about Judah: "Hear, O LORD, the cry of Judah; bring him to his people. With his own hands he defends his cause. Oh, be his help against his foes!"
2 Sam 4 [11]"How much more—when wicked men have killed an innocent man in his own house and on his own bed—should I not now demand his blood from your hand and rid the earth of you!"
Ps 9 [16]The LORD is known by his justice; the wicked are ensnared by the work of their hands.
Ps 78 [72]And David shepherded them with integrity of heart; with skillful hands he led them.
Prov 10 [4]Lazy hands make a man poor, but diligent hands bring wealth.
Prov 31 [13]She selects wool and flax and works with eager hands.
Mal 1 [9]"Now implore God to be gracious to us. With such offerings from your hands, will he accept you?"—says the LORD Almighty.

[10]"Oh, that one of you would shut the temple doors, so that you would not light useless fires on my altar! I am not pleased with you," says the LORD Almighty, "and I will accept no offering from your hands. . . . [13]And you say, 'What a burden!' and you sniff at it contemptuously," says the LORD Almighty.

"When you bring injured, crippled or diseased animals and offer them as sacrifices, should I accept them from your hands?" says the LORD.

Mal 2 [13]Another thing you do: You flood the LORD's altar with tears. You weep and wail because he no longer pays attention to your offerings or accepts them with pleasure from your hands.
Acts 17 [24]"The God who made the world and everything in it is the Lord of heaven and earth and does not live in temples built by hands. [25]And he is not served by human hands, as if he needed anything, because he himself gives all men life and breath and everything else."

I. The Whole Person Represented by the Heart

Lev 26 [41]"'. . . which made me hostile toward them so that I sent them into the land of their enemies—then when their uncircumcised hearts are humbled and they pay for their sin . . .'"
Deut 17 [17]He must not take many wives, or his heart will be led astray. He must not accumulate large amounts of silver and gold.
Deut 30 [17]But if your heart turns away and you are not obedient, and if you are drawn away to bow down to other gods and worship them . . .
1 Kings 2 [44]The king also said to Shimei, "You know in your heart all the wrong you did to my father David. Now the LORD will repay you for your wrongdoing."
Job 15 [12]"Why has your heart carried you away, and why do your eyes flash? . . ."
Job 31 [9]"If my heart has been enticed by a woman, or if I have lurked at my neighbor's door . . ."
Job 31 [27]". . . so that my heart was secretly enticed and my hand offered them a kiss of homage . . ."

Ps 25 [17]The troubles of my heart have multiplied; free me from my anguish.
Ps 27 [8]My heart says of you, "Seek his face!" Your face, LORD, I will seek.
Ps 28 [7]The LORD is my strength and my shield; my heart trusts in him, and I am helped. My heart leaps for joy and I will give thanks to him in song.
Ps 41 [6]Whenever one comes to see me, he speaks falsely, while his heart gathers slander; then he goes out and spreads it abroad.
Ps 45 [1]My heart is stirred by a noble theme as I recite my verses for the king; my tongue is the pen of a skillful writer.
Ps 73 [21]When my heart was grieved and my spirit embittered . . .
Ps 112 [7]He will have no fear of bad news; his heart is steadfast, trusting in the LORD.
Prov 4 [4]he taught me and said, "Lay hold of my words with all your heart; keep my commands and you will live."
Prov 5 [12]You will say, "How I hated discipline! How my heart spurned correction!"
Prov 6 [18]a heart that devises wicked schemes, feet that are quick to rush into evil . . .
Prov 7 [25]Do not let your heart turn to her ways or stray into her paths.
Prov 15 [14]The discerning heart seeks knowledge, but the mouth of a fool feeds on folly.
Prov 20 [9]Who can say, "I have kept my heart pure; I am clean and without sin"?
Prov 24 [17]Do not gloat when your enemy falls; when he stumbles, do not let your heart rejoice. . . .
Eccles 5 [2]Do not be quick with your mouth, do not be hasty in your heart to utter anything before God. God is in heaven and you are on earth, so let your words be few.
Eccles 7 [26]I find more bitter than death the woman who is a snare, whose heart is a trap and whose hands are chains. The man who pleases God will escape her, but the sinner she will ensnare.
Eccles 8 [5]Whoever obeys his command will come to no harm, and the wise heart will know the proper time and procedure.
Isa 44 [20]He feeds on ashes, a deluded heart misleads him; he cannot save himself, or say, "Is not this thing in my right hand a lie?"
Jer 17 [5]This is what the LORD says: "Cursed is the one who trusts in man, who depends on flesh for his strength and whose heart turns away from the LORD."
Ezek 6 [9]"'Then in the nations where they have been carried captive, those who escape will remember me—how I have been grieved by their adulterous hearts, which have turned away from me, and by their eyes, which have lusted after their idols. They will loathe themselves for the evil they have done and for all their detestable practices.'"
Ezek 20 [16]"'. . . because they rejected my laws and did not follow my decrees and desecrated my Sabbaths. For their hearts were devoted to their idols.'"
Matt 24 [48]"But suppose that servant is wicked and says to himself, 'My master is staying away a long time.' . . ."
Acts 1 [24]Then they prayed, "Lord, you know everyone's heart. Show us which of these two you have chosen. . . ."
1 Cor 14 [25]and the secrets of his heart will be laid bare. So he will fall down and worship God, exclaiming, "God is really among you!"

J. The Whole Person Represented by the Knees

1 Kings 19 [18]"Yet I reserve seven thousand in Israel—all whose knees have not bowed down to Baal and all whose mouths have not kissed him."
Isa 45 [23]"By myself I have sworn, my mouth has uttered in all integrity a word that will not be revoked: Before me every knee will bow; by me every tongue will swear."
Rom 14 [11]It is written: "'As surely as I live,' says the Lord, 'every knee will bow before me; every tongue will confess to God.'"
Phil 2 [10]that at the name of Jesus every knee should bow, in heaven and on earth and under the earth . . .

K. The Whole Person Represented by the Mouth

1 Kings 19 [18]"Yet I reserve seven thousand in Israel—all whose knees have not bowed down to Baal and all whose mouths have not kissed him."

L. The Whole Person Represented by the Soul (ET: being, human being, life, people, self, spirit)

Gen 2 [7]the LORD God formed the man from the dust of the ground and breathed into his nostrils the breath of life, and the man became a living being.
Gen 12 [5]He took his wife Sarai, his nephew Lot, all the possessions they had accumulated and the people they had acquired in Haran, and they set out for the land of Canaan, and they arrived there.
Gen 17 [14]"Any uncircumcised male, who has not been circumcised in the flesh, will be cut off from his people; he has broken my covenant."
Lev 11 [43]"'Do not defile yourselves by any of these creatures. Do not make yourselves unclean by means of them or be made unclean by them. [44]I am the LORD your God; consecrate yourselves and be holy, because I am holy. Do not make yourselves unclean by any creature that moves about on the ground.'"
Num 30 [3]"When a young woman still living in her father's house makes a vow to the LORD or obligates herself by a pledge [4]and her father hears about her vow or pledge but says nothing to her, then all her vows and every pledge by which she obligated herself will stand. [5]But if her father forbids her when he hears about it, none of her vows or the pledges by which she obligated herself will stand; the LORD will release her because her father has forbidden her.

[6]"If she marries after she makes a vow or after her lips utter a rash promise by which she obligates herself [7]and her husband hears about it but says nothing to her, then her vows or the pledges by which she obligated herself will stand. [8]But if her husband forbids her when he hears about it, he nullifies the vow that obligates her or the rash promise by which she obligates herself, and the LORD will release her.

[9]"Any vow or obligation taken by a widow or divorced woman will be binding on her.

[10]"If a woman living with her husband makes a vow or obligates herself by a pledge under oath [11]and her husband hears about it but says nothing to her and does not forbid her, then all her vows or the pledges by which she obligated herself will stand. [12]But if her husband nullifies them when he hears about them, then none of the vows or pledges that came from her lips will stand. Her husband has nullified them, and the LORD will release her. [13]Her husband may confirm or nullify any vow she makes or any sworn pledge to deny herself."
Deut 10 [22]Your forefathers who went down into Egypt were seventy in all, and now the LORD your God has made you as numerous as the stars in the sky.
Deut 24 [7]If a man is caught kidnapping one of his brother Israelites and treats him as a slave or sells him, the kidnapper must die. You must purge the evil from among you.
Judg 5 [21]"The river Kishon swept them away, the age-old river, the river Kishon. March on, my soul; be strong!"
Judg 16 [30]Samson said, "Let me die with the Philistines!" Then he pushed with all his might, and down came the temple on the rulers and all the people in it. Thus he killed many more when he died than while he lived.
1 Sam 18 [1]After David had finished talking with Saul, Jonathan became one in spirit with David, and he loved him as himself. . . . [3]And Jonathan made a covenant with David because he loved him as himself.
1 Kings 20 [32]Wearing sackcloth around their waists and ropes around their heads, they went to the king of Israel and said, "Your servant Ben-Hadad says: 'Please let me live.'"

The king answered, "Is he still alive? He is my brother."

Job 16 [4]"I also could speak like you, if you were in my place; I could make fine speeches against you and shake my head at you."
Job 30 [25]"Have I not wept for those in trouble? Has not my soul grieved for the poor?"
Ps 35 [12]They repay me evil for good and leave my soul forlorn. [13]Yet when they were ill, I put on sackcloth and humbled myself with fasting. When my prayers returned to me unanswered . . .
Ps 43 [5]Why are you downcast, O my soul? Why so disturbed within me? Put your hope in God, for I will yet praise him, my Savior and my God.
Ps 49 [18]Though while he lived he counted himself blessed—and men praise you when you prosper . . .
Ps 63 [1]O God, you are my God, earnestly I seek you; my soul thirsts for you, my body longs for you, in a dry and weary land where there is no water.
Ps 69 [18]Come near and rescue me; redeem me because of my foes.
Ps 84 [2]My soul yearns, even faints, for the courts of the LORD; my heart and my flesh cry out for the living God.
Ps 103 [1]Praise the LORD, O my soul; all my inmost being, praise his holy name. [2]Praise the LORD, O my soul, and forget not all his benefits. . . . [22]Praise the LORD, all his works everywhere in his dominion.
Praise the LORD, O my soul.
Ps 116 [7]Be at rest once more, O my soul, for the LORD has been good to you.
Ps 146 [1]Praise the LORD.
Praise the LORD, O my soul. [2]I will praise the LORD all my life; I will sing praise to my God as long as I live.
Prov 18 [7]A fool's mouth is his undoing, and his lips are a snare to his soul.
Prov 23 [14]Punish him with the rod and save his soul from death.
Isa 55 [3]"Give ear and come to me; hear me, that your soul may live. I will make an everlasting covenant with you, my faithful love promised to David."
Isa 61 [10]I delight greatly in the LORD; my soul rejoices in my God. For he has clothed me with garments of salvation and arrayed me in a robe of righteousness, as a bridegroom adorns his head like a priest, and as a bride adorns herself with her jewels.
Jer 37 [9]"This is what the LORD says: Do not deceive yourselves, thinking, 'The Babylonians will surely leave us.' They will not!"
Jer 38 [17]Then Jeremiah said to Zedekiah, "This is what the LORD God Almighty, the God of Israel, says: 'If you surrender to the officers of the king of Babylon, your life will be spared and this city will not be burned down; you and your family will live.' . . .
[20]"They will not hand you over," Jeremiah replied. "Obey the LORD by doing what I tell you. Then it will go well with you, and your life will be spared."
Lam 3 [25]The LORD is good to those whose hope is in him, to the one who seeks him. . . .
Mark 8 [35]"For whoever wants to save his life will lose it, but whoever loses his life for me and for the gospel will save it. [36]What good is it for a man to gain the whole world, yet forfeit his soul?"
Luke 9 [25]"What good is it for a man to gain the whole world, and yet lose or forfeit his very self?"
John 12 [25]"The man who loves his life will lose it, while the man who hates his life in this world will keep it for eternal life."
Acts 2 [43]Everyone was filled with awe, and many wonders and miraculous signs were done by the apostles.
Acts 7 [14]"After this, Joseph sent for his father Jacob and his whole family, seventy-five in all."
Acts 27 [37]Altogether there were 276 of us on board.
Rom 2 [9]There will be trouble and distress for every human being who does evil: first for the Jew, then for the Gentile. . . .
Rom 11 [3]"Lord, they have killed your prophets and torn down your altars; I am the only one left, and they are trying to kill me"?
Rom 13 [1]Everyone must submit himself to the governing authorities, for there is no authority except that which God has established. The authorities that exist have been established by God.
2 Cor 12 [15]So I will very gladly spend for you everything I have and expend myself as well. If I love you more, will you love me less?
1 Pet 3 [20]who disobeyed long ago when God waited patiently in the days of Noah while the ark was being built. In it only a few people, eight in all, were saved through water. . . .

M. The Whole Person Represented by the Tongue

Isa 45 [23]"By myself I have sworn, my mouth has uttered in all integrity a word that will not be revoked: Before me every knee will bow; by me every tongue will swear."
Phil 2 [11]and every tongue confess that Jesus Christ is Lord, to the glory of God the Father.

VIII
The Corporate Nature of the Human Race

A. The Human Race Is United in Adam

1. People Are United in Creation

Acts 17 [26]"From one man he made every nation of men, that they should inhabit the whole earth; and he determined the times set for them and the exact places where they should live."
1 Cor 15 [38]But God gives it a body as he has determined, and to each kind of seed he gives its own body. [39]All flesh is not the same: Men have one kind of flesh, animals have another, birds another and fish another. . . .
[47]The first man was of the dust of the earth, the second man from heaven. [48]As was the earthly man, so are those who are of the earth; and as is the man from heaven, so also are those who are of heaven. [49]And just as we have borne the likeness of the earthly man, so shall we bear the likeness of the man from heaven.

2. People Are United in Sin and Death

Gen 3 [6]When the woman saw that the fruit of the tree was good for food and pleasing to the eye, and also desirable for gaining wisdom, she took some and ate it. She also gave some to her husband, who was with her, and he ate it. [7]Then the eyes of both of them were opened, and they realized they were naked; so they sewed fig leaves together and made coverings for themselves.
[8]Then the man and his wife heard the sound of the LORD God as he was walking in the garden in the cool of the day, and they hid from the LORD God among the trees of the garden. [9]But the LORD God called to the man, "Where are you?"
[10]He answered, "I heard you in the garden, and I was afraid because I was naked; so I hid."
[11]And he said, "Who told you that you were naked? Have you eaten from the tree that I commanded you not to eat from?"
[12]The man said, "The woman you put here with me—she gave me some fruit from the tree, and I ate it."
[13]Then the LORD God said to the woman, "What is this you have done?"
The woman said, "The serpent deceived me, and I ate."
[14]So the LORD God said to the serpent, "Because you have done this,
"Cursed are you above all the livestock and all the wild animals! You will crawl on your belly and you will eat dust all the days of your life. [15]And I will put enmity between you and the woman, and between your offspring and hers; he will crush your head, and you will strike his heel."
[16]To the woman he said, "I will greatly increase your pains in childbearing; with pain you will give birth to children. Your desire will be for your husband, and he will rule over you."

17To Adam he said, "Because you listened to your wife and ate from the tree about which I commanded you, 'You must not eat of it,'

"Cursed is the ground because of you; through painful toil you will eat of it all the days of your life. 18It will produce thorns and thistles for you, and you will eat the plants of the field. 19By the sweat of your brow you will eat your food until you return to the ground, since from it you were taken; for dust you are and to dust you will return."

Rom 5 12Therefore, just as sin entered the world through one man, and death through sin, and in this way death came to all men, because all sinned—13for before the law was given, sin was in the world. But sin is not taken into account when there is no law. 14Nevertheless, death reigned from the time of Adam to the time of Moses, even over those who did not sin by breaking a command, as did Adam, who was a pattern of the one to come.

15But the gift is not like the trespass. For if the many died by the trespass of the one man, how much more did God's grace and the gift that came by the grace of the one man, Jesus Christ, overflow to the many! 16Again, the gift of God is not like the result of the one man's sin: The judgment followed one sin and brought condemnation, but the gift followed many trespasses and brought justification. 17For if, by the trespass of the one man, death reigned through that one man, how much more will those who receive God's abundant provision of grace and of the gift of righteousness reign in life through the one man, Jesus Christ.

18Consequently, just as the result of one trespass was condemnation for all men, so also the result of one act of righteousness was justification that brings life for all men. 19For just as through the disobedience of the one man the many were made sinners, so also through the obedience of the one man the many will be made righteous.

20The law was added so that the trespass might increase. But where sin increased, grace increased all the more, 21so that, just as sin reigned in death, so also grace might reign through righteousness to bring eternal life through Jesus Christ our Lord.

1 Cor 15 21For since death came through a man, the resurrection of the dead comes also through a man. 22For as in Adam all die, so in Christ all will be made alive.

B. Israel as a Corporate Entity

1. The Identification of Israel as a Group

a) Israel Identified by Ancestral Name

2 Chron 20 7"O our God, did you not drive out the inhabitants of this land before your people Israel and give it forever to the descendants of Abraham your friend?"

Ps 14 7Oh, that salvation for Israel would come out of Zion! When the LORD restores the fortunes of his people, let Jacob rejoice and Israel be glad!

Ps 105 6O descendants of Abraham his servant, O sons of Jacob, his chosen ones.

Isa 41 8"But you, O Israel, my servant, Jacob, whom I have chosen, you descendants of Abraham my friend . . .

21"Present your case," says the LORD. "Set forth your arguments," says Jacob's King.

Jer 33 23The word of the LORD came to Jeremiah: 24"Have you not noticed that these people are saying, 'The LORD has rejected the two kingdoms he chose'? So they despise my people and no longer regard them as a nation. 25This is what the LORD says: 'If I have not established my covenant with day and night and the fixed laws of heaven and earth, 26then I will reject the descendants of Jacob and David my servant and will not choose one of his sons to rule over the descendants of Abraham, Isaac and Jacob. For I will restore their fortunes and have compassion on them.'"

Lam 2 3In fierce anger he has cut off every horn of Israel. He has withdrawn his right hand at the approach of the enemy. He has burned in Jacob like a flaming fire that consumes everything around it.

Amos 5 15Hate evil, love good; maintain justice in the courts. Perhaps the LORD God Almighty will have mercy on the remnant of Joseph.

Amos 7 9"The high places of Isaac will be destroyed and the sanctuaries of Israel will be ruined; with my sword I will rise against the house of Jeroboam." . . .

16"Now then, hear the word of the LORD. You say, 'Do not prophesy against Israel, and stop preaching against the house of Isaac.'"

Mal 2 12As for the man who does this, whoever he may be, may the LORD cut him off from the tents of Jacob—even though he brings offerings to the LORD Almighty.

b) Israel Identified as God's Family

Exod 4 22"Then say to Pharaoh, 'This is what the LORD says: Israel is my firstborn son, 23and I told you, "Let my son go, so he may worship me." But you refused to let him go; so I will kill your firstborn son.'"

Deut 14 1You are the children of the LORD your God. Do not cut yourselves or shave the front of your heads for the dead. . . .

Deut 32 6Is this the way you repay the LORD, O foolish and unwise people? Is he not your Father, your Creator, who made you and formed you? . . .

18You deserted the Rock, who fathered you; you forgot the God who gave you birth.

19The LORD saw this and rejected them because he was angered by his sons and daughters.

Isa 1 2Hear, O heavens! Listen, O earth! For the LORD has spoken: "I reared children and brought them up, but they have rebelled against me. 3The ox knows his master, the donkey his owner's manger, but Israel does not know, my people do not understand."

Isa 43 1But now, this is what the LORD says—he who created you, O Jacob, he who formed you, O Israel: "Fear not, for I have redeemed you; I have summoned you by name; you are mine. . . . 6I will say to the north, 'Give them up!' and to the south, 'Do not hold them back.' Bring my sons from afar and my daughters from the ends of the earth. . . ."

Isa 45 11"This is what the LORD says—the Holy One of Israel, and its Maker: Concerning things to come, do you question me about my children, or give me orders about the work of my hands?"

Isa 63 7I will tell of the kindnesses of the LORD, the deeds for which he is to be praised, according to all the LORD has done for us—yes, the many good things he has done for the house of Israel, according to his compassion and many kindnesses. 8He said, "Surely they are my people, sons who will not be false to me"; and so he became their Savior. . . .

16But you are our Father, though Abraham does not know us or Israel acknowledge us; you, O LORD, are our Father, our Redeemer from of old is your name.

Jer 3 4"Have you not just called to me: 'My Father, my friend from my youth? . . .'

20"But like a woman unfaithful to her husband, so you have been unfaithful to me, O house of Israel," declares the LORD.

Jer 31 9"They will come with weeping; they will pray as I bring them back. I will lead them beside streams of water on a level path where they will not stumble, because I am Israel's father, and Ephraim is my firstborn son. . . .

20"Is not Ephraim my dear son, the child in whom I delight? Though I often speak against him, I still remember him. Therefore my heart yearns for him; I have great compassion for him," declares the LORD.

Hos 2 2"Rebuke your mother, rebuke her, for she is not my wife, and I am not her husband. Let her remove the adulterous look from her face and the unfaithfulness from between her breasts. 3Otherwise I will strip her naked and make her as bare as on the day she was born; I will make her like a desert, turn her into a parched land, and slay her with thirst. 4I will not show my love to her children, because they are the children of adultery. 5Their mother has been unfaithful and has conceived them in disgrace. She said, 'I will go after my lovers, who give me my food and my water, my wool and my linen, my oil and my drink.' 6Therefore I will block her path with thornbushes; I will wall her in so that she cannot find her way. 7She will chase after her lovers but not catch them; she will look for them but not find them. Then she will say, 'I will go back to my husband as at first, for then I was better off than now.' . . .

[16]"In that day," declares the LORD, "you will call me 'my husband'; you will no longer call me 'my master.' . . . [19]I will betroth you to me forever; I will betroth you in righteousness and justice, in love and compassion. [20]I will betroth you in faithfulness, and you will acknowledge the LORD."

Hos 11 [1]"When Israel was a child, I loved him, and out of Egypt I called my son."

Amos 3 [1]Hear this word the LORD has spoken against you, O people of Israel—against the whole family I brought up out of Egypt: [2]"You only have I chosen of all the families of the earth; therefore I will punish you for all your sins."

Mal 1 [6]"A son honors his father, and a servant his master. If I am a father, where is the honor due me? If I am a master, where is the respect due me?" says the LORD Almighty. "It is you, O priests, who show contempt for my name.

"But you ask, 'How have we shown contempt for your name?'"

Mal 3 [17]"They will be mine," says the LORD Almighty, "in the day when I make up my treasured possession. I will spare them, just as in compassion a man spares his son who serves him."

c) Israel Identified as God's Personal Possession

Exod 19 [5]"'Now if you obey me fully and keep my covenant, then out of all nations you will be my treasured possession. Although the whole earth is mine, [6]you will be for me a kingdom of priests and a holy nation.' These are the words you are to speak to the Israelites."

Deut 7 [6]For you are a people holy to the LORD your God. The LORD your God has chosen you out of all the peoples on the face of the earth to be his people, his treasured possession.

Deut 14 [2]for you are a people holy to the LORD your God. Out of all the peoples on the face of the earth, the LORD has chosen you to be his treasured possession.

Deut 26 [18]And the LORD has declared this day that you are his people, his treasured possession as he promised, and that you are to keep all his commands.

Deut 32 [9]For the LORD's portion is his people, Jacob his allotted inheritance.

Ps 135 [4]For the LORD has chosen Jacob to be his own, Israel to be his treasured possession.

Jer 2 [20]"Long ago you broke off your yoke and tore off your bonds; you said, 'I will not serve you!' Indeed, on every high hill and under every spreading tree you lay down as a prostitute."

Zech 9 [16]The LORD their God will save them on that day as the flock of his people. They will sparkle in his land like jewels in a crown.

d) Israel Identified by Implication

Deut 5 [3]It was not with our fathers that the LORD made this covenant, but with us, with all of us who are alive here today.

Deut 6 [12]be careful that you do not forget the LORD, who brought you out of Egypt, out of the land of slavery.

Deut 8 [2]Remember how the LORD your God led you all the way in the desert these forty years, to humble you and to test you in order to know what was in your heart, whether or not you would keep his commands. [3]He humbled you, causing you to hunger and then feeding you with manna, which neither you nor your fathers had known, to teach you that man does not live on bread alone but on every word that comes from the mouth of the LORD. [4]Your clothes did not wear out and your feet did not swell during these forty years. [5]Know then in your heart that as a man disciplines his son, so the LORD your God disciplines you.

[6]Observe the commands of the LORD your God, walking in his ways and revering him. [7]For the LORD your God is bringing you into a good land—a land with streams and pools of water, with springs flowing in the valleys and hills; [8]a land with wheat and barley, vines and fig trees, pomegranates, olive oil and honey; [9]a land where bread will not be scarce and you will lack nothing; a land where the rocks are iron and you can dig copper out of the hills.

[10]When you have eaten and are satisfied, praise the LORD your God for the good land he has given you. [11]Be careful that you do not forget the LORD your God, failing to observe his commands, his laws and his decrees that I am giving you this day. [12]Otherwise, when you eat and are satisfied, when you build fine houses and settle down, [13]and when your herds and flocks grow large and your silver and gold increase and all you have is multiplied, [14]then your heart will become proud and you will forget the LORD your God, who brought you out of Egypt, out of the land of slavery. [15]He led you through the vast and dreadful desert, that thirsty and waterless land, with its venomous snakes and scorpions. He brought you water out of hard rock. [16]He gave you manna to eat in the desert, something your fathers had never known, to humble and to test you so that in the end it might go well with you. [17]You may say to yourself, "My power and the strength of my hands have produced this wealth for me." [18]But remember the LORD your God, for it is he who gives you the ability to produce wealth, and so confirms his covenant, which he swore to your forefathers, as it is today.

[19]If you ever forget the LORD your God and follow other gods and worship and bow down to them, I testify against you today that you will surely be destroyed. [20]Like the nations the LORD destroyed before you, so you will be destroyed for not obeying the LORD your God.

Josh 24 [6]"'When I brought your fathers out of Egypt, you came to the sea, and the Egyptians pursued them with chariots and horsemen as far as the Red Sea. [7]But they cried to the LORD for help, and he put darkness between you and the Egyptians; he brought the sea over them and covered them. You saw with your own eyes what I did to the Egyptians. Then you lived in the desert for a long time.'"

2. The Importance of the Family Name in Israel

a) For Blessing: Continuation

Gen 12 [1]The LORD had said to Abram, "Leave your country, your people and your father's household and go to the land I will show you.

[2]"I will make you into a great nation and I will bless you; I will make your name great, and you will be a blessing. [3]I will bless those who bless you, and whoever curses you I will curse; and all peoples on earth will be blessed through you."

2 Sam 7 [9]"'I have been with you wherever you have gone, and I have cut off all your enemies from before you. Now I will make your name great, like the names of the greatest men of the earth.'"

1 Kings 1 [47]"Also, the royal officials have come to congratulate our lord King David, saying, 'May your God make Solomon's name more famous than yours and his throne greater than yours!' And the king bowed in worship on his bed. . . ."

1 Chron 28 [4]"Yet the LORD, the God of Israel, chose me from my whole family to be king over Israel forever. He chose Judah as leader, and from the house of Judah he chose my family, and from my father's sons he was pleased to make me king over all Israel. [5]Of all my sons—and the LORD has given me many—he has chosen my son Solomon to sit on the throne of the kingdom of the LORD over Israel. [6]He said to me: 'Solomon your son is the one who will build my house and my courts, for I have chosen him to be my son, and I will be his father. [7]I will establish his kingdom forever if he is unswerving in carrying out my commands and laws, as is being done at this time.'"

Ps 89 [19]Once you spoke in a vision, to your faithful people you said: "I have bestowed strength on a warrior; I have exalted a young man from among the people. . . . [27]I will also appoint him my firstborn, the most exalted of the kings of the earth. . . . [29]I will establish his line forever, his throne as long as the heavens endure."

Isa 66 [22]"As the new heavens and the new earth that I make will endure before me," declares the LORD, "so will your name and descendants endure."

b) For Judgment: Extermination

Exod 17 [14]Then the LORD said to Moses, "Write this on a scroll as something to be remembered and make sure that Joshua hears it, because I will completely blot out the memory of Amalek from under heaven."

Deut 9 [13]And the LORD said to me, "I have seen this people, and they are a stiff-necked people indeed! [14]Let me alone, so that I may destroy them and blot out their name from under heaven. And I will make you into a nation stronger and more numerous than they."

Deut 25 [19]When the LORD your God gives you rest from all the enemies around you in the land he is giving you to possess as an inheritance, you shall blot out the memory of Amalek from under heaven. Do not forget!

Deut 29 [20]The LORD will never be willing to forgive him; his wrath and zeal will burn against that man. All the curses written in this book will fall upon him, and the LORD will blot out his name from under heaven.

Josh 7 [9]"The Canaanites and the other people of the country will hear about this and they will surround us and wipe out our name from the earth. What then will you do for your own great name?"

1 Sam 24 [21]"Now swear to me by the LORD that you will not cut off my descendants or wipe out my name from my father's family."

[22]So David gave his oath to Saul. Then Saul returned home, but David and his men went up to the stronghold.

2 Sam 14 [5]The king asked her, "What is troubling you?"

She said, "I am indeed a widow; my husband is dead. [6]I your servant had two sons. They got into a fight with each other in the field, and no one was there to separate them. One struck the other and killed him. [7]Now the whole clan has risen up against your servant; they say, 'Hand over the one who struck his brother down, so that we may put him to death for the life of his brother whom he killed; then we will get rid of the heir as well.' They would put out the only burning coal I have left, leaving my husband neither name nor descendant on the face of the earth."

2 Kings 14 [27]And since the LORD had not said he would blot out the name of Israel from under heaven, he saved them by the hand of Jeroboam son of Jehoash.

Job 18 [17]"The memory of him perishes from the earth; he has no name in the land. [18]He is driven from light into darkness and is banished from the world. [19]He has no offspring or descendants among his people, no survivor where once he lived."

Ps 9 [5]You have rebuked the nations and destroyed the wicked; you have blotted out their name for ever and ever.

Ps 83 [4]"Come," they say, "let us destroy them as a nation, that the name of Israel be remembered no more."

Ps 109 [13]May his descendants be cut off, their names blotted out from the next generation. [14]May the iniquity of his fathers be remembered before the LORD; may the sin of his mother never be blotted out.

Jer 11 [19]I had been like a gentle lamb led to the slaughter; I did not realize that they had plotted against me, saying, "Let us destroy the tree and its fruit; let us cut him off from the land of the living, that his name be remembered no more."

3. The Preservation of Family Line in Israel

a) Through Bloodline Marriage

Gen 24 [1]Abraham was now old and well advanced in years, and the LORD had blessed him in every way. [2]He said to the chief servant in his household, the one in charge of all that he had, "Put your hand under my thigh. [3]I want you to swear by the LORD, the God of heaven and the God of earth, that you will not get a wife for my son from the daughters of the Canaanites, among whom I am living, [4]but will go to my country and my own relatives and get a wife for my son Isaac."

Gen 31 [43]Laban answered Jacob, "The women are my daughters, the children are my children, and the flocks are my flocks. All you see is mine. Yet what can I do today about these daughters of mine, or about the children they have borne?"

Num 36 [1]The family heads of the clan of Gilead son of Makir, the son of Manasseh, who were from the clans of the descendants of Joseph, came and spoke before Moses and the leaders, the heads of the Israelite families. [2]They said, "When the LORD commanded my lord to give the land as an inheritance to the Israelites by lot, he ordered you to give the inheritance of our brother Zelophehad to his daughters. [3]Now suppose they marry men from other Israelite tribes; then their inheritance will be taken from our ancestral inheritance and added to that of the tribe they marry into. And so part of the inheritance allotted to us will be taken away. [4]When the Year of Jubilee for the Israelites comes, their inheritance will be added to that of the tribe into which they marry, and their property will be taken from the tribal inheritance of our forefathers."

[5]Then at the LORD's command Moses gave this order to the Israelites: "What the tribe of the descendants of Joseph is saying is right. [6]This is what the LORD commands for Zelophehad's daughters: They may marry anyone they please as long as they marry within the tribal clan of their father. [7]No inheritance in Israel is to pass from tribe to tribe, for every Israelite shall keep the tribal land inherited from his forefathers. [8]Every daughter who inherits land in any Israelite tribe must marry someone in her father's tribal clan, so that every Israelite will possess the inheritance of his fathers. [9]No inheritance may pass from tribe to tribe, for each Israelite tribe is to keep the land it inherits."

[10]So Zelophehad's daughters did as the LORD commanded Moses. [11]Zelophehad's daughters—Mahlah, Tirzah, Hoglah, Milcah and Noah—married their cousins on their father's side. [12]They married within the clans of the descendants of Manasseh son of Joseph, and their inheritance remained in their father's clan and tribe.

Deut 7 [1]When the LORD your God brings you into the land you are entering to possess and drives out before you many nations—the Hittites, Girgashites, Amorites, Canaanites, Perizzites, Hivites and Jebusites, seven nations larger and stronger than you . . . [3]Do not intermarry with them. Do not give your daughters to their sons or take their daughters for your sons, [4]for they will turn your sons away from following me to serve other gods, and the LORD's anger will burn against you and will quickly destroy you.

Ezra 9 [1]After these things had been done, the leaders came to me and said, "The people of Israel, including the priests and the Levites, have not kept themselves separate from the neighboring peoples with their detestable practices, like those of the Canaanites, Hittites, Perizzites, Jebusites, Ammonites, Moabites, Egyptians and Amorites. [2]They have taken some of their daughters as wives for themselves and their sons, and have mingled the holy race with the peoples around them. And the leaders and officials have led the way in this unfaithfulness." . . .

[12]"'Therefore, do not give your daughters in marriage to their sons or take their daughters for your sons. Do not seek a treaty of friendship with them at any time, that you may be strong and eat the good things of the land and leave it to your children as an everlasting inheritance.'"

Neh 10 [30]"We promise not to give our daughters in marriage to the peoples around us or take their daughters for our sons."

Neh 13 [25]I rebuked them and called curses down on them. I beat some of the men and pulled out their hair. I made them take an oath in God's name and said: "You are not to give your daughters in marriage to their sons, nor are you to take their daughters in marriage for your sons or for yourselves. [26]Was it not because of marriages like these that Solomon king of Israel sinned? Among the many nations there was no king like him. He was loved by his God, and God made him king over all Israel, but even he was led into sin by foreign women. [27]Must we hear now that you too are doing all this terrible wickedness and are being unfaithful to our God by marrying foreign women?"

Mal 2 [11]Judah has broken faith. A detestable thing has been committed in Israel and in Jerusalem: Judah has desecrated the sanctuary the LORD loves, by marrying the daughter of a foreign god. [12]As for the man who does this, whoever he may be, may the LORD cut him off from the tents of Jacob—even though he brings offerings to the LORD Almighty.

b) Through Levirate Marriage

Gen 38 [8]Then Judah said to Onan, "Lie with your brother's wife and fulfill your duty to her as a brother-in-law to produce offspring for your brother." [9]But Onan knew that the offspring would not be his; so whenever he lay with his brother's wife, he spilled his semen on the ground to keep from producing offspring for his brother. . . .

[11]Judah then said to his daughter-in-law Tamar, "Live as a widow in your father's house until my son Shelah grows up." For he thought, "He may die too, just like his brothers." So Tamar went to live in her father's house.

Deut 25 [5]If brothers are living together and one of them dies without a son, his widow must not marry outside the family. Her husband's brother shall take her and marry her and fulfill the duty of a brother-in-law to her. [6]The first son she bears shall carry on the name of the dead brother so that his name will not be blotted out from Israel.

[7]However, if a man does not want to marry his brother's wife, she shall go to the elders at the town gate and say, "My husband's brother refuses to carry on his brother's name in Israel. He will not fulfill the duty of a brother-in-law to me." [8]Then the elders of his town shall summon him and talk to him. If he persists in saying, "I do not want to marry her," [9]his brother's widow shall go up to him in the presence of the elders, take off one of his sandals, spit in his face and say, "This is what is done to the man who will not build up his brother's family line." [10]That man's line shall be known in Israel as The Family of the Unsandaled.

Ruth 4 [5]Then Boaz said, "On the day you buy the land from Naomi and from Ruth the Moabitess, you acquire the dead man's widow, in order to maintain the name of the dead with his property."

1 Chron 23 [22]Eleazar died without having sons: he had only daughters. Their cousins, the sons of Kish, married them.

Matt 22 [24]"Teacher," they said, "Moses told us that if a man dies without having children, his brother must marry the widow and have children for him."

c) Through a Kinsman-Redeemer

Lev 25 [25]"'If one of your countrymen becomes poor and sells some of his property, his nearest relative is to come and redeem what his countryman has sold. [26]If, however, a man has no one to redeem it for him but he himself prospers and acquires sufficient means to redeem it, [27]he is to determine the value for the years since he sold it and refund the balance to the man to whom he sold it; he can then go back to his own property. [28]But if he does not acquire the means to repay him, what he sold will remain in the possession of the buyer until the Year of Jubilee. It will be returned in the Jubilee, and he can then go back to his property.

[29]"'If a man sells a house in a walled city, he retains the right of redemption a full year after its sale. During that time he may redeem it. [30]If it is not redeemed before a full year has passed, the house in the walled city shall belong permanently to the buyer and his descendants. It is not to be returned in the Jubilee. [31]But houses in villages without walls around them are to be considered as open country. They can be redeemed, and they are to be returned in the Jubilee.

[32]"'The Levites always have the right to redeem their houses in the Levitical towns, which they possess. [33]So the property of the Levites is redeemable—that is, a house sold in any town they hold—and is to be returned in the Jubilee, because the houses in the towns of the Levites are their property among the Israelites. [34]But the pastureland belonging to their towns must not be sold; it is their permanent possession.'"

Ruth 2 [20]"The LORD bless him!" Naomi said to her daughter-in-law. "He has not stopped showing his kindness to the living and the dead." She added, "That man is our close relative; he is one of our kinsman-redeemers."

Ruth 3 [9]"Who are you?" he asked.

"I am your servant Ruth," she said. "Spread the corner of your garment over me, since you are a kinsman-redeemer." . . .

[12]"Although it is true that I am near of kin, there is a kinsman-redeemer nearer than I. [13]Stay here for the night, and in the morning if he wants to redeem, good; let him redeem. But if he is not willing, as surely as the LORD lives I will do it. Lie here until morning."

Ruth 4 [1]Meanwhile Boaz went up to the town gate and sat there. When the kinsman-redeemer he had mentioned came along, Boaz said, "Come over here, my friend, and sit down." So he went over and sat down.

[2]Boaz took ten of the elders of the town and said, "Sit here," and they did so. [3]Then he said to the kinsman-redeemer, "Naomi, who has come back from Moab, is selling the piece of land that belonged to our brother Elimelech. [4]I thought I should bring the matter to your attention and suggest that you buy it in the presence of these seated here and in the presence of the elders of my people. If you will redeem it, do so. But if you will not, tell me, so I will know. For no one has the right to do it except you, and I am next in line."

"I will redeem it," he said.

[5]Then Boaz said, "On the day you buy the land from Naomi and from Ruth the Moabitess, you acquire the dead man's widow, in order to maintain the name of the dead with his property."

[6]At this, the kinsman-redeemer said, "Then I cannot redeem it because I might endanger my own estate. You redeem it yourself. I cannot do it."

[7](Now in earlier times in Israel, for the redemption and transfer of property to become final, one party took off his sandal and gave it to the other. This was the method of legalizing transactions in Israel.)

[8]So the kinsman-redeemer said to Boaz, "Buy it yourself." And he removed his sandal. . . .

[14]The women said to Naomi: "Praise be to the LORD, who this day has not left you without a kinsman-redeemer. May he become famous throughout Israel!"

4. Individuals Representing Israel as a Group

a) Representation in Blessings and Cursings

(1) Extended Corporal Blessing

Gen 12 [1]The LORD had said to Abram, "Leave your country, your people and your father's household and go to the land I will show you.

[2]"I will make you into a great nation and I will bless you; I will make your name great, and you will be a blessing. [3]I will bless those who bless you, and whoever curses you I will curse; and all peoples on earth will be blessed through you."

[4]So Abram left, as the LORD had told him; and Lot went with him. Abram was seventy-five years old when he set out from Haran. [5]He took his wife Sarai, his nephew Lot, all the possessions they had accumulated and the people they had acquired in Haran, and they set out for the land of Canaan, and they arrived there.

[6]Abram traveled through the land as far as the site of the great tree of Moreh at Shechem. At that time the Canaanites were in the land. [7]The LORD appeared to Abram and said, "To your offspring I will give this land." So he built an altar there to the LORD, who had appeared to him.

Gen 18 [23]Then Abraham approached him and said: "Will you sweep away the righteous with the wicked? [24]What if there are fifty righteous people in the city? Will you really sweep it away and not spare the place for the sake of the fifty righteous people in it? [25]Far be it from you to do such a thing—to kill the righteous with the wicked, treating the righteous and the wicked alike. Far be it from you! Will not the Judge of all the earth do right?"

[26]The LORD said, "If I find fifty righteous people in the city of Sodom, I will spare the whole place for their sake."

[27]Then Abraham spoke up again: "Now that I have been so bold as to speak to the Lord, though I am nothing but dust and ashes, [28]what if the number of the righteous is five less than fifty? Will you destroy the whole city because of five people?"

"If I find forty-five there," he said, "I will not destroy it."

[29]Once again he spoke to him, "What if only forty are found there?"

He said, "For the sake of forty, I will not do it."

[30]Then he said, "May the Lord not be angry, but let me speak. What if only thirty can be found there?"

He answered, "I will not do it if I find thirty there."

[31]Abraham said, "Now that I have been so bold as to speak to the Lord, what if only twenty can be found there?"

He said, "For the sake of twenty, I will not destroy it."

[32]Then he said, "May the Lord not be angry, but let me speak just once more. What if only ten can be found there?"

He answered, "For the sake of ten, I will not destroy it."

Exod 20 [5]"You shall not bow down to them or worship them; for I, the LORD your God, am a jealous God, punishing the children for the sin of the fathers to the third and fourth generation of those who hate me, [6]but showing love to a thousand generations of those who love me and keep my commandments."

Exod 32 [13]"Remember your servants Abraham, Isaac and Israel, to whom you swore by your own self: 'I will make your descendants as numerous as the stars in the sky and I will give your descendants all this land I promised them, and it will be their inheritance forever.'" [14]Then the LORD relented and did not bring on his people the disaster he had threatened.

Exod 32 [26]So he stood at the entrance to the camp and said, "Whoever is for the LORD, come to me." And all the Levites rallied to him.

[27]Then he said to them, "This is what the LORD, the God of Israel, says: 'Each man strap a sword to his side. Go back and forth through the camp from one end to the other, each killing his brother and friend and neighbor.'" [28]The Levites did as Moses commanded, and that day about three thousand of the people died. [29]Then Moses said, "You have been set apart to the LORD today, for you were against your own sons and brothers, and he has blessed you this day."

Deut 28 [1]If you fully obey the LORD your God and carefully follow all his commands I give you today, the LORD your God will set you high above all the nations on earth.

1 Kings 11 [11]So the LORD said to Solomon, "Since this is your attitude and you have not kept my covenant and my decrees, which I commanded you, I will most certainly tear the kingdom away from you and give it to one of your subordinates. [12]Nevertheless, for the sake of David your father, I will not do it during your lifetime. I will tear it out of the hand of your son. [13]Yet I will not tear the whole kingdom from him, but will give him one tribe for the sake of David my servant and for the sake of Jerusalem, which I have chosen."

1 Kings 15 [4]Nevertheless, for David's sake the LORD his God gave him a lamp in Jerusalem by raising up a son to succeed him and by making Jerusalem strong.

2 Kings 19 [34]"I will defend this city and save it, for my sake and for the sake of David my servant."

Ps 18 [50]He gives his king great victories; he shows unfailing kindness to his anointed, to David and his descendants forever.

Ps 28 [8]The LORD is the strength of his people, a fortress of salvation for his anointed one.

Ps 128 [1]Blessed are all who fear the LORD, who walk in his ways. [2]You will eat the fruit of your labor; blessings and prosperity will be yours. [3]Your wife will be like a fruitful vine within your house; your sons will be like olive shoots around your table. [4]Thus is the man blessed who fears the LORD.

[5]May the LORD bless you from Zion all the days of your life; may you see the prosperity of Jerusalem, [6]and may you live to see your children's children.

Peace be upon Israel.

Prov 3 [9]Honor the LORD with your wealth, with the firstfruits of all your crops; [10]then your barns will be filled to overflowing, and your vats will brim over with new wine.

Prov 3 [13]Blessed is the man who finds wisdom, the man who gains understanding. . . . [16]Long life is in her right hand; in her left hand are riches and honor.

(2) Extended Corporal Punishment

Gen 9 [20]Noah, a man of the soil, proceeded to plant a vineyard. [21]When he drank some of its wine, he became drunk and lay uncovered inside his tent. [22]Ham, the father of Canaan, saw his father's nakedness and told his two brothers outside. [23]But Shem and Japheth took a garment and laid it across their shoulders; then they walked in backward and covered their father's nakedness. Their faces were turned the other way so that they would not see their father's nakedness.

[24]When Noah awoke from his wine and found out what his youngest son had done to him, [25]he said, "Cursed be Canaan! The lowest of slaves will he be to his brothers."

[26]He also said, "Blessed be the LORD, the God of Shem! May Canaan be the slave of Shem. [27]May God extend the territory of Japheth; may Japheth live in the tents of Shem, and may Canaan be his slave."

Gen 26 [10]Then Abimelech said, "What is this you have done to us? One of the men might well have slept with your wife, and you would have brought guilt upon us."

Gen 49 [3]"Reuben, you are my firstborn, my might, the first sign of my strength, excelling in honor, excelling in power. [4]Turbulent as the waters, you will no longer excel, for you went up onto your father's bed, onto my couch and defiled it.

[5]"Simeon and Levi are brothers—their swords are weapons of violence. [6]Let me not enter their council, let me not join their assembly, for they have killed men in their anger and hamstrung oxen as they pleased. [7]Cursed be their anger, so fierce, and their fury, so cruel! I will scatter them in Jacob and disperse them in Israel."

Exod 20 [5]"You shall not bow down to them or worship them; for I, the LORD your God, am a jealous God, punishing the children for the sin of the fathers to the third and fourth generation of those who hate me. . . ."

Num 16 [19]When Korah had gathered all his followers in opposition to them at the entrance to the Tent of Meeting, the glory of the LORD appeared to the entire assembly. [20]The LORD said to Moses and Aaron, [21]"Separate yourselves from this assembly so I can put an end to them at once."

[22]But Moses and Aaron fell facedown and cried out, "O God, God of the spirits of all mankind, will you be angry with the entire assembly when only one man sins?"

[23]Then the LORD said to Moses, [24]"Say to the assembly, 'Move away from the tents of Korah, Dathan and Abiram.'"

[25]Moses got up and went to Dathan and Abiram, and the elders of Israel followed him. [26]He warned the assembly, "Move back from the tents of these wicked men! Do not touch anything belonging to them, or you will be swept away because of all their sins." [27]So they moved away from the tents of Korah, Dathan and Abiram. Dathan and Abiram had come out and were standing with their wives, children and little ones at the entrances to their tents.

[28]Then Moses said, "This is how you will know that the LORD has sent me to do all these things and that it was not my idea: [29]If these men die a natural death and experience only what usually happens to men, then the LORD has not sent me. [30]But if the LORD brings about something totally new, and the earth opens its mouth and swallows them, with everything that belongs to them, and they go down alive into the grave, then you will know that these men have treated the LORD with contempt."

[31]As soon as he finished saying all this, the ground under them split apart [32]and the earth opened its mouth and swallowed them, with their households and all Korah's men and all their possessions. [33]They went down alive into the grave, with everything they owned; the earth closed over them, and they perished and were gone from the community. [34]At their cries, all the Israelites around them fled, shouting, "The earth is going to swallow us, too!"

[35]And fire came out from the LORD and consumed the 250 men who were offering the incense.

Josh 7 [24]Then Joshua, together with all Israel, took Achan son of Zerah, the silver, the robe, the gold wedge, his sons and daughters, his cattle, donkeys and sheep, his tent and all that he had, to the Valley of Achor. [25]Joshua said, "Why have you brought this trouble on us? The LORD will bring trouble on you today."

Then all Israel stoned him, and after they had stoned the rest, they burned them. [26]Over Achan they heaped up a large pile of rocks, which remains to this day. Then the LORD turned from his fierce anger. Therefore that place has been called the Valley of Achor ever since.

1 Sam 15 [2]"This is what the LORD Almighty says: 'I will punish the Amalekites for what they did to Israel when they waylaid them as they came up from Egypt. [3]Now go, attack the Amalekites and totally destroy everything that belongs to them. Do not spare them; put to death men and women, children and infants, cattle and sheep, camels and donkeys.'"

[4]So Saul summoned the men and mustered them at Telaim—two hundred thousand foot soldiers and ten thousand

men from Judah. [5]Saul went to the city of Amalek and set an ambush in the ravine. . . .

[7]Then Saul attacked the Amalekites all the way from Havilah to Shur, to the east of Egypt. [8]He took Agag king of the Amalekites alive, and all his people he totally destroyed with the sword. . . .

[32]Then Samuel said, "Bring me Agag king of the Amalekites."

Agag came to him confidently, thinking, "Surely the bitterness of death is past."

[33]But Samuel said, "As your sword has made women childless, so will your mother be childless among women." And Samuel put Agag to death before the LORD at Gilgal.

2 Sam 21 [1]During the reign of David, there was a famine for three successive years; so David sought the face of the LORD. The LORD said, "It is on account of Saul and his blood-stained house; it is because he put the Gibeonites to death."

[2]The king summoned the Gibeonites and spoke to them. (Now the Gibeonites were not a part of Israel but were survivors of the Amorites; the Israelites had sworn to spare them, but Saul in his zeal for Israel and Judah had tried to annihilate them.) [3]David asked the Gibeonites, "What shall I do for you? How shall I make amends so that you will bless the LORD's inheritance?"

[4]The Gibeonites answered him, "We have no right to demand silver or gold from Saul or his family, nor do we have the right to put anyone in Israel to death."

"What do you want me to do for you?" David asked.

[5]They answered the king, "As for the man who destroyed us and plotted against us so that we have been decimated and have no place anywhere in Israel, [6]let seven of his male descendants be given to us to be killed and exposed before the LORD at Gibeah of Saul—the Lord's chosen one."

So the king said, "I will give them to you."

[7]The king spared Mephibosheth son of Jonathan, the son of Saul, because of the oath before the LORD between David and Jonathan son of Saul. [8]But the king took Armoni and Mephibosheth, the two sons of Aiah's daughter Rizpah, whom she had borne to Saul, together with the five sons of Saul's daughter Merab, whom she had borne to Adriel son of Barzillai the Meholathite. [9]He handed them over to the Gibeonites, who killed and exposed them on a hill before the LORD. All seven of them fell together; they were put to death during the first days of the harvest, just as the barley harvest was beginning.

[10]Rizpah daughter of Aiah took sackcloth and spread it out for herself on a rock. From the beginning of the harvest till the rain poured down from the heavens on the bodies, she did not let the birds of the air touch them by day or the wild animals by night. [11]When David was told what Aiah's daughter Rizpah, Saul's concubine, had done, [12]he went and took the bones of Saul and his son Jonathan from the citizens of Jabesh Gilead. (They had taken them secretly from the public square at Beth Shan, where the Philistines had hung them after they struck Saul down on Gilboa.) [13]David brought the bones of Saul and his son Jonathan from there, and the bones of those who had been killed and exposed were gathered up.

[14]They buried the bones of Saul and his son Jonathan in the tomb of Saul's father Kish, at Zela in Benjamin, and did everything the king commanded. After that. God answered prayer in behalf of the land.

1 Kings 21 [17]Then the word of the LORD came to Elijah the Tishbite: [18]"Go down to meet Ahab king of Israel, who rules in Samaria. He is now in Naboth's vineyard, where he has gone to take possession of it. [19]Say to him, 'This is what the LORD says: Have you not murdered a man and seized his property?' Then say to him, 'This is what the LORD says: In the place where dogs licked up Naboth's blood, dogs will lick up your blood—yes, yours!'"

[20]Ahab said to Elijah, "So you have found me, my enemy!"

"I have found you," he answered, "because you have sold yourself to do evil in the eyes of the LORD. [21]'I am going to bring disaster on you. I will consume your descendants and cut off from Ahab every last male in Israel—slave or free. [22]I will make your house like that of Jeroboam son of Nebat and that of Baasha son of Ahijah, because you have provoked me to anger and have caused Israel to sin.'

[23]"And also concerning Jezebel the LORD says: 'Dogs will devour Jezebel by the wall of Jezreel.'

[24]"Dogs will eat those belonging to Ahab who die in the city, and the birds of the air will feed on those who die in the country."

[25](There was never a man like Ahab, who sold himself to do evil in the eyes of the LORD, urged on by Jezebel his wife. [26]He behaved in the vilest manner by going after idols, like the Amorites the LORD drove out before Israel.)

[27]When Ahab heard these words, he tore his clothes, put on sackcloth and fasted. He lay in sackcloth and went around meekly.

[28]Then the word of the LORD came to Elijah the Tishbite: [29]"Have you noticed how Ahab has humbled himself before me? Because he has humbled himself, I will not bring this disaster in his day, but I will bring it on his house in the days of his son."

2 Kings 5 [27]"Naaman's leprosy will cling to you and to your descendants forever." Then Gehazi went from Elisha's presence and he was leprous, as white as snow.

2 Kings 9 [24]Then Jehu drew his bow and shot Joram between the shoulders. The arrow pierced his heart and he slumped down in his chariot. [25]Jehu said to Bidkar, his chariot officer, "Pick him up and throw him on the field that belonged to Naboth the Jezreelite. Remember how you and I were riding together in chariots behind Ahab his father when the LORD made this prophecy about him: [26]'Yesterday I saw the blood of Naboth and the blood of his sons, declares the LORD, and I will surely make you pay for it on this plot of ground, declares the LORD.' Now then, pick him up and throw him on that plot, in accordance with the word of the LORD."

Ezek 35 [5]"'Because you harbored an ancient hostility and delivered the Israelites over to the sword at the time of their calamity, the time their punishment reached its climax, [6]therefore as surely as I live, declares the Sovereign LORD, I will give you over to bloodshed and it will pursue you. Since you did not hate bloodshed, bloodshed will pursue you.'"

Dan 6 [24]At the king's command, the men who had falsely accused Daniel were brought in and thrown into the lions' den, along with their wives and children. And before they reached the floor of the den, the lions overpowered them and crushed all their bones.

Matt 11 [20]Then Jesus began to denounce the cities in which most of his miracles had been performed, because they did not repent. [21]"Woe to you, Korazin! Woe to you, Bethsaida! If the miracles that were performed in you had been performed in Tyre and Sidon, they would have repented long ago in sackcloth and ashes. [22]But I tell you, it will be more bearable for Tyre and Sidon on the day of judgment than for you. [23]And you, Capernaum, will you be lifted up to the skies? No, you will go down to the depths. If the miracles that were performed in you had been performed in Sodom, it would have remained to this day. [24]But I tell you that it will be more bearable for Sodom on the day of judgment than for you."

b) Representation in Leadership

(1) Patriarchal Authority

Gen 19 [6]Lot went outside to meet them and shut the door behind him [7]and said, "No, my friends. Don't do this wicked thing. [8]Look, I have two daughters who have never slept with a man. Let me bring them out to you, and you can do what you like with them. But don't do anything to these men, for they have come under the protection of my roof."

Gen 22 [1]Some time later God tested Abraham. He said to him, "Abraham!"

"Here I am," he replied.

[2]Then God said, "Take your son, your only son, Isaac, whom you love, and go to the region of Moriah. Sacrifice him there as a burnt offering on one of the mountains I will tell you about."

[3]Early the next morning Abraham got up and saddled his donkey. He took with him two of his servants and his son Isaac. When he had cut enough wood for the burnt offering, he set out for the place God had told him about. [4]On the third day Abraham looked up and saw the place in the distance. [5]He said to his servants, "Stay here with the donkey while I and the boy

go over there. We will worship and then we will come back to you."

Gen 42 37Then Reuben said to his father, "You may put both of my sons to death if I do not bring him back to you. Entrust him to my care, and I will bring him back."

Judg 11 29Then the Spirit of the LORD came upon Jephthah. He crossed Gilead and Manasseh, passed through Mizpah of Gilead, and from there he advanced against the Ammonites. 30And Jephthah made a vow to the LORD: "If you give the Ammonites into my hands, 31whatever comes out of the door of my house to meet me when I return in triumph from the Ammonites will be the LORD's, and I will sacrifice it as a burnt offering." . . .

34When Jephthah returned to his home in Mizpah, who should come out to meet him but his daughter, dancing to the sound of tambourines! She was an only child. Except for her he had neither son nor daughter. 35When he saw her, he tore his clothes and cried, "Oh! My daughter! You have made me miserable and wretched, because I have made a vow to the LORD that I cannot break."

36"My father," she replied, "you have given your word to the LORD. Do to me just as you promised, now that the LORD has avenged you of your enemies, the Ammonites. 37But grant me this one request," she said. "Give me two months to roam the hills and weep with my friends, because I will never marry."

38"You may go," he said. And he let her go for two months. She and the girls went into the hills and wept because she would never marry. 39After the two months, she returned to her father and he did to her as he had vowed. And she was a virgin.

From this comes the Israelite custom 40that each year the young women of Israel go out for four days to commemorate the daughter of Jephthah the Gileadite.

Judg 19 23The owner of the house went outside and said to them, "No, my friends, don't be so vile. Since this man is my guest, don't do this disgraceful thing. 24Look, here is my virgin daughter, and his concubine. I will bring them out to you now, and you can use them and do to them whatever you wish. But to this man, don't do such a disgraceful thing."

(2) Priestly Service

Exod 19 5"'Now if you obey me fully and keep my covenant, then out of all nations you will be my treasured possession. Although the whole earth is mine, 6you will be for me a kingdom of priests and a holy nation.' These are the words you are to speak to the Israelites."

Lev 4 3"'If the anointed priest sins, bringing guilt on the people, he must bring to the LORD a young bull without defect as a sin offering for the sin he has committed.'"

Lev 16 1The LORD spoke to Moses after the death of the two sons of Aaron who died when they approached the LORD. 2The LORD said to Moses: "Tell your brother Aaron not to come whenever he chooses into the Most Holy Place behind the curtain in front of the atonement cover on the ark, or else he will die, because I appear in the cloud over the atonement cover.

3"This is how Aaron is to enter the sanctuary area: with a young bull for a sin offering and a ram for a burnt offering. 4He is to put on the sacred linen tunic, with linen undergarments next to his body; he is to tie the linen sash around him and put on the linen turban. These are sacred garments; so he must bathe himself with water before he puts them on. 5From the Israelite community he is to take two male goats for a sin offering and a ram for a burnt offering.

6"Aaron is to offer the bull for his own sin offering to make atonement for himself and his household. 7Then he is to take the two goats and present them before the LORD at the entrance to the Tent of Meeting. 8He is to cast lots for the two goats—one lot for the LORD and the other for the scapegoat. 9Aaron shall bring the goat whose lot falls to the LORD and sacrifice it for a sin offering. 10But the goat chosen by lot as the scapegoat shall be presented alive before the LORD to be used for making atonement by sending it into the desert as a scapegoat.

11"Aaron shall bring the bull for his own sin offering to make atonement for himself and his household, and he is to slaughter the bull for his own sin offering. 12He is to take a censer full of burning coals from the altar before the LORD and two handfuls of finely ground fragrant incense and take them behind the curtain. 13He is to put the incense on the fire before the LORD, and the smoke of the incense will conceal the atonement cover above the Testimony, so that he will not die. 14He is to take some of the bull's blood and with his finger sprinkle it on the front of the atonement cover; then he shall sprinkle some of it with his finger seven times before the atonement cover.

15"He shall then slaughter the goat for the sin offering for the people and take its blood behind the curtain and do with it as he did with the bull's blood: He shall sprinkle it on the atonement cover and in front of it. 16In this way he will make atonement for the Most Holy Place because of the uncleanness and rebellion of the Israelites, whatever their sins have been. He is to do the same for the Tent of Meeting, which is among them in the midst of their uncleanness. 17No one is to be in the Tent of Meeting from the time Aaron goes in to make atonement in the Most Holy Place until he comes out, having made atonement for himself, his household and the whole community of Israel.

18"Then he shall come out to the altar that is before the LORD and make atonement for it. He shall take some of the bull's blood and some of the goat's blood and put it on all the horns of the altar. 19He shall sprinkle some of the blood on it with his finger seven times to cleanse it and to consecrate it from the uncleanness of the Israelites.

20"When Aaron has finished making atonement for the Most Holy Place, the Tent of Meeting and the altar, he shall bring forward the live goat. 21He is to lay both hands on the head of the live goat and confess over it all the wickedness and rebellion of the Israelites—all their sins—and put them on the goat's head. He shall send the goat away into the desert in the care of a man appointed for the task. 22The goat will carry on itself all their sins to a solitary place; and the man shall release it in the desert.

23"Then Aaron is to go into the Tent of Meeting and take off the linen garments he put on before he entered the Most Holy Place, and he is to leave them there."

Num 3 11The LORD also said to Moses, 12"I have taken the Levites from among the Israelites in place of the first male offspring of every Israelite woman. The Levites are mine, 13for all the firstborn are mine. When I struck down all the firstborn in Egypt, I set apart for myself every firstborn in Israel, whether man or animal. They are to be mine. I am the LORD." . . .

41"Take the Levites for me in place of all the firstborn of the Israelites, and the livestock of the Levites in place of all the firstborn of the livestock of the Israelites. I am the LORD." . . .

45"Take the Levites in place of all the firstborn of Israel, and the livestock of the Levites in place of their livestock. The Levites are to be mine. I am the LORD. 46To redeem the 273 firstborn Israelites who exceed the number of the Levites, 47collect five shekels for each one, according to the sanctuary shekel, which weighs twenty gerahs. 48Give the money for the redemption of the additional Israelites to Aaron and his sons."

49So Moses collected the redemption money from those who exceeded the number redeemed by the Levites. 50From the firstborn of the Israelites he collected silver weighing 1,365 shekels, according to the sanctuary shekel. 51Moses gave the redemption money to Aaron and his sons, as he was commanded by the word of the LORD.

Num 8 14"In this way you are to set the Levites apart from the other Israelites, and the Levites will be mine.

15"After you have purified the Levites and presented them as a wave offering, they are to come to do their work at the Tent of Meeting. 16They are the Israelites who are to be given wholly to me. I have taken them as my own in place of the firstborn, the first male offspring from every Israelite woman. 17Every firstborn male in Israel, whether man or animal, is mine. When I struck down all the firstborn in Egypt, I set them apart for myself. 18And I have taken the Levites in place of all the firstborn sons in Israel."

(3) Prophetic Intercession

Exod 32 31So Moses went back to the LORD and said, "Oh, what a great sin these people have committed! They have made themselves gods of gold. 32But now, please forgive their sin—but if not, then blot me out of the book you have written."

33The LORD replied to Moses, "Whoever has sinned against

me I will blot out of my book. 34Now go, lead the people to the place I spoke of, and my angel will go before you. However, when the time comes for me to punish, I will punish them for their sin."

35And the LORD struck the people with a plague because of what they did with the calf Aaron had made.

Neh 9 5And the Levites—Jeshua, Kadmiel, Bani, Hashabneiah, Sherebiah, Hodiah, Shebaniah and Pethahiah—said: "Stand up and praise the LORD your God, who is from everlasting to everlasting."

"Blessed be your glorious name, and may it be exalted above all blessing and praise. . . . 33In all that has happened to us, you have been just; you have acted faithfully, while we did wrong."

Jer 15 1Then the LORD said to me: "Even if Moses and Samuel were to stand before me, my heart would not go out to this people. Send them away from my presence! Let them go!"

Dan 9 2in the first year of his reign, I, Daniel, understood from the Scriptures, according to the word of the LORD given to Jeremiah the prophet, that the desolation of Jerusalem would last seventy years. 3So I turned to the Lord God and pleaded with him in prayer and petition, in fasting, and in sackcloth and ashes.

4I prayed to the LORD my God and confessed: "O Lord, the great and awesome God, who keeps his covenant of love with all who love him and obey his commands, 5we have sinned and done wrong. We have been wicked and have rebelled; we have turned away from your commands and laws. 6We have not listened to your servants the prophets, who spoke in your name to our kings, our princes and our fathers, and to all the people of the land.

7"Lord, you are righteous, but this day we are covered with shame—the men of Judah and people of Jerusalem and all Israel, both near and far, in all the countries where you have scattered us because of our unfaithfulness to you. 8O LORD, we and our kings, our princes and our fathers are covered with shame because we have sinned against you. 9The Lord our God is merciful and forgiving, even though we have rebelled against him; 10we have not obeyed the LORD our God or kept the laws he gave us through his servants the prophets. 11All Israel has transgressed your law and turned away, refusing to obey you.

"Therefore the curses and sworn judgments written in the Law of Moses, the servant of God, have been poured out on us, because we have sinned against you. 12You have fulfilled the words spoken against us and against our rulers by bringing upon us great disaster. Under the whole heaven nothing has ever been done like what has been done to Jerusalem. 13Just as it is written in the Law of Moses, all this disaster has come upon us, yet we have not sought the favor of the LORD our God by turning from our sins and giving attention to your truth. 14The LORD did not hesitate to bring the disaster upon us, for the LORD our God is righteous in everything he does; yet we have not obeyed him.

15"Now, O Lord our God, who brought your people out of Egypt with a mighty hand and who made for yourself a name that endures to this day, we have sinned, we have done wrong. 16O Lord, in keeping with all your righteous acts, turn away your anger and your wrath from Jerusalem, your city, your holy hill. Our sins and the iniquities of our fathers have made Jerusalem and your people an object of scorn to all those around us.

17"Now, our God, hear the prayers and petitions of your servant. For your sake, O Lord, look with favor on your desolate sanctuary. 18Give ear, O God, and hear; open your eyes and see the desolation of the city that bears your Name. We do not make requests of you because we are righteous, but because of your great mercy. 19O Lord, listen! O Lord, forgive! O Lord, hear and act! For your sake, O my God, do not delay, because your city and your people bear your Name."

(4) Kingly Rule

Gen 20 7"Now return the man's wife, for he is a prophet, and he will pray for you and you will live. But if you do not return her, you may be sure that you and all yours will die."

8Early the next morning Abimelech summoned all his officials, and when he told them all that had happened, they were very much afraid. 9Then Abimelech called Abraham in and said, "What have you done to us? How have I wronged you that you have brought such great guilt upon me and my kingdom? You have done things to me that should not be done."

2 Sam 18 2David sent the troops out—a third under the command of Joab, a third under Joab's brother Abishai son of Zeruiah, and a third under Ittai the Gittite. The king told the troops, "I myself will surely march out with you."

3But the men said, "You must not go out; if we are forced to flee, they won't care about us. Even if half of us die, they won't care; but you are worth ten thousand of us. It would be better now for you to give us support from the city."

2 Sam 21 17But Abishai son of Zeruiah came to David's rescue; he struck the Philistine down and killed him. Then David's men swore to him, saying, "Never again will you go out with us to battle, so that the lamp of Israel will not be extinguished."

1 Kings 22 51Ahaziah son of Ahab became king of Israel in Samaria in the seventeenth year of Jehoshaphat king of Judah, and he reigned over Israel two years. 52He did evil in the eyes of the LORD, because he walked in the ways of his father and mother and in the ways of Jeroboam son of Nebat, who caused Israel to sin.

1 Chron 21 3But Joab replied, "May the LORD multiply his troops a hundred times over. My lord the king, are they not all my lord's subjects? Why does my lord want to do this? Why should he bring guilt on Israel?"

Jer 15 4"I will make them abhorrent to all the kingdoms of the earth because of what Manasseh son of Hezekiah king of Judah did in Jerusalem."

Lam 4 20The LORD's anointed, our very life breath, was caught in their traps. We thought that under his shadow we would live among the nations.

c) Representation in Sacrificial Offering

Exod 12 1The LORD said to Moses and Aaron in Egypt, 2"This month is to be for you the first month, the first month of your year. 3Tell the whole community of Israel that on the tenth day of this month each man is to take a lamb for his family, one for each household. 4If any household is too small for a whole lamb, they must share one with their nearest neighbor, having taken into account the number of people there are. You are to determine the amount of lamb needed in accordance with what each person will eat. 5The animals you choose must be year-old males without defect, and you may take them from the sheep or the goats. 6Take care of them until the fourteenth day of the month, when all the people of the community of Israel must slaughter them at twilight. 7Then they are to take some of the blood and put it on the sides and tops of the doorframes of the houses where they eat the lambs. 8That same night they are to eat the meat roasted over the fire, along with bitter herbs, and bread made without yeast. 9Do not eat the meat raw or cooked in water, but roast it over the fire—head, legs and inner parts. 10Do not leave any of it till morning; if some is left till morning, you must burn it. 11This is how you are to eat it: with your cloak tucked into your belt, your sandals on your feet and your staff in your hand. Eat it in haste; it is the LORD's Passover.

12"On that same night I will pass through Egypt and strike down every firstborn—both men and animals—and I will bring judgment on all the gods of Egypt. I am the LORD. 13The blood will be a sign for you on the houses where you are; and when I see the blood, I will pass over you. No destructive plague will touch you when I strike Egypt."

Isa 53 4Surely he took up our infirmities and carried our sorrows, yet we considered him stricken by God, smitten by him, and afflicted. 5But he was pierced for our transgressions, he was crushed for our iniquities; the punishment that brought us peace was upon him, and by his wounds we are healed. 6We all, like sheep, have gone astray, each of us has turned to his own way; and the LORD has laid on him the iniquity of us all.

7He was oppressed and afflicted, yet he did not open his mouth; he was led like a lamb to the slaughter, and as a sheep before her shearers is silent, so he did not open his mouth. 8By oppression and judgment he was taken away. And who can speak of his descendants? For he was cut off from the land of the living; for the transgression of my people he was stricken. 9He was assigned a grave with the wicked, and with the rich in his death, though he had done no violence, nor was any deceit in his mouth.

[10]Yet it was the LORD's will to crush him and cause him to suffer, and though the LORD makes his life a guilt offering, he will see his offspring and prolong his days, and the will of the LORD will prosper in his hand.

d) Representation in Surviving Remnant

1 Kings 19 [18]"Yet I reserve seven thousand in Israel—all whose knees have not bowed down to Baal and all whose mouths have not kissed him."
Isa 1 [9]Unless the LORD Almighty had left us some survivors, we would have become like Sodom, we would have been like Gomorrah.
Isa 4 [3]Those who are left in Zion, who remain in Jerusalem, will be called holy, all who are recorded among the living in Jerusalem.
Isa 28 [5]In that day the LORD Almighty will be a glorious crown, a beautiful wreath for the remnant of his people.
Isa 37 [31]"Once more a remnant of the house of Judah will take root below and bear fruit above. [32]For out of Jerusalem will come a remnant, and out of Mount Zion a band of survivors. The zeal of the LORD Almighty will accomplish this."
Jer 23 [3]"I myself will gather the remnant of my flock out of all the countries where I have driven them and will bring them back to their pasture, where they will be fruitful and increase in number. [4]I will place shepherds over them who will tend them, and they will no longer be afraid or terrified, nor will any be missing," declares the LORD.
Ezek 11 [17]"Therefore say: 'This is what the Sovereign LORD says: I will gather you from the nations and bring you back from the countries where you have been scattered, and I will give you back the land of Israel again.'

[18]"They will return to it and remove all its vile images and detestable idols. [19]I will give them an undivided heart and put a new spirit in them; I will remove from them their heart of stone and give them a heart of flesh. [20]Then they will follow my decrees and be careful to keep my laws. They will be my people, and I will be their God."
Amos 3 [12]This is what the LORD says: "As a shepherd saves from the lion's mouth only two leg bones or a piece of an ear, so will the Israelites be saved, those who sit in Samaria on the edge of their beds and in Damascus on their couches."
Amos 4 [11]"I overthrew some of you as I overthrew Sodom and Gomorrah. You were like a burning stick snatched from the fire, yet you have not returned to me," declares the LORD.
Amos 5 [15]Hate evil, love good; maintain justice in the courts. Perhaps the LORD God Almighty will have mercy on the remnant of Joseph.
Mic 2 [12]"I will surely gather all of you, O Jacob; I will surely bring together the remnant of Israel. I will bring them together like sheep in a pen, like a flock in its pasture; the place will throng with people."
Mic 5 [7]The remnant of Jacob will be in the midst of many peoples like dew from the LORD, like showers on the grass, which do not wait for man or linger for mankind. [8]The remnant of Jacob will be among the nations, in the midst of many peoples, like a lion among the beasts of the forest, like a young lion among flocks of sheep, which mauls and mangles as it goes, and no one can rescue.

C. The Unity of Believers in Christ

See also p. 686a, The Head and Ruler of the Church: *Christ*; p. 687b, Metaphors and Names for the People of God, the Church

1. Believers as the Body of Christ

Rom 12 [3]For by the grace given me I say to every one of you: Do not think of yourself more highly than you ought, but rather think of yourself with sober judgment, in accordance with the measure of faith God has given you. [4]Just as each of us has one body with many members, and these members do not all have the same function, [5]so in Christ we who are many form one body, and each member belongs to all the others.
1 Cor 6 [15]Do you not know that your bodies are members of Christ himself? Shall I then take the members of Christ and unite them with a prostitute? Never! [16]Do you not know that he who unites himself with a prostitute is one with her in body? For it is said, "The two will become one flesh." [17]But he who unites himself with the Lord is one with him in spirit.
1 Cor 10 [16]Is not the cup of thanksgiving for which we give thanks a participation in the blood of Christ? And is not the bread that we break a participation in the body of Christ? [17]Because there is one loaf, we, who are many, are one body, for we all partake of the one loaf.
1 Cor 11 [29]For anyone who eats and drinks without recognizing the body of the Lord eats and drinks judgment on himself.
1 Cor 12 [27]Now you are the body of Christ, and each one of you is a part of it.
Gal 3 [28]There is neither Jew nor Greek, slave nor free, male nor female, for you are all one in Christ Jesus.
Eph 1 [22]And God placed all things under his feet and appointed him to be head over everything for the church, [23]which is his body, the fullness of him who fills everything in every way.
Eph 4 [11]It was he who gave some to be apostles, some to be prophets, some to be evangelists, and some to be pastors and teachers, [12]to prepare God's people for works of service, so that the body of Christ may be built up [13]until we all reach unity in the faith and in the knowledge of the Son of God and become mature, attaining to the whole measure of the fullness of Christ.
Eph 4 [22]You were taught, with regard to your former way of life, to put off your old self, which is being corrupted by its deceitful desires; [23]to be made new in the attitude of your minds; [24]and to put on the new self, created to be like God in true righteousness and holiness.

[25]Therefore each of you must put off falsehood and speak truthfully to his neighbor, for we are all members of one body.
Col 1 [24]Now I rejoice in what was suffered for you, and I fill up in my flesh what is still lacking in regard to Christ's afflictions, for the sake of his body, which is the church.
Col 2 [19]He has lost connection with the Head, from whom the whole body, supported and held together by its ligaments and sinews, grows as God causes it to grow.

2. Believers as the Bride of Christ

2 Cor 11 [2]I am jealous for you with a godly jealousy. I promised you to one husband, to Christ, so that I might present you as a pure virgin to him. [3]But I am afraid that just as Eve was deceived by the serpent's cunning, your minds may somehow be led astray from your sincere and pure devotion to Christ.
Eph 5 [22]Wives, submit to your husbands as to the Lord. [23]For the husband is the head of the wife as Christ is the head of the church, his body, of which he is the Savior. [24]Now as the church submits to Christ, so also wives should submit to their husbands in everything.

[25]Husbands, love your wives, just as Christ loved the church and gave himself up for her [26]to make her holy, cleansing her by the washing with water through the word, [27]and to present her to himself as a radiant church, without stain or wrinkle or any other blemish, but holy and blameless. [28]In this same way, husbands ought to love their wives as their own bodies. He who loves his wife loves himself. [29]After all, no one ever hated his own body, but he feeds and cares for it, just as Christ does the church—[30]for we are members of his body. [31]"For this reason a man will leave his father and mother and be united to his wife, and the two will become one flesh." [32]This is a profound mystery—but I am talking about Christ and the church. [33]However, each one of you also must love his wife as he loves himself, and the wife must respect her husband.

3. Believers as the New Israel

John 10 [16]"I have other sheep that are not of this sheep pen. I must bring them also. They too will listen to my voice, and there shall be one flock and one shepherd."
Rom 2 [28]A man is not a Jew if he is only one outwardly, nor is circumcision merely outward and physical. [29]No, a man is a Jew if he is one inwardly; and circumcision is circumcision of

the heart, by the Spirit, not by the written code. Such a man's praise is not from men, but from God.

Rom 4 [11]And he received the sign of circumcision, a seal of the righteousness that he had by faith while he was still uncircumcised. So then, he is the father of all who believe but have not been circumcised, in order that righteousness might be credited to them. . . .

[16]Therefore, the promise comes by faith, so that it may be by grace and may be guaranteed to all Abraham's offspring—not only to those who are of the law but also to those who are of the faith of Abraham. He is the father of us all.

Rom 9 [6]It is not as though God's word had failed. For not all who are descended from Israel are Israel. . . . [8]In other words, it is not the natural children who are God's children, but it is the children of the promise who are regarded as Abraham's offspring.

Rom 11 [17]If some of the branches have been broken off, and you, though a wild olive shoot, have been grafted in among the others and now share in the nourishing sap from the olive root, [18]do not boast over those branches. If you do, consider this: You do not support the root, but the root supports you. [19]You will say then, "Branches were broken off so that I could be grafted in." [20]Granted. But they were broken off because of unbelief, and you stand by faith. Do not be arrogant, but be afraid. [21]For if God did not spare the natural branches, he will not spare you either.

[22]Consider therefore the kindness and sternness of God: sternness to those who fell, but kindness to you, provided that you continue in his kindness. Otherwise, you also will be cut off. [23]And if they do not persist in unbelief, they will be grafted in, for God is able to graft them in again. [24]After all, if you were cut out of an olive tree that is wild by nature, and contrary to nature were grafted into a cultivated olive tree, how much more readily will these, the natural branches, be grafted into their own olive tree!

Rom 15 [27]They were pleased to do it, and indeed they owe it to them. For if the Gentiles have shared in the Jews' spiritual blessings, they owe it to the Jews to share with them their material blessings.

Gal 3 [7]Understand, then, that those who believe are children of Abraham.

Gal 6 [15]Neither circumcision nor uncircumcision means anything; what counts is a new creation. [16]Peace and mercy to all who follow this rule, even to the Israel of God.

Eph 2 [12]remember that at that time you were separate from Christ, excluded from citizenship in Israel and foreigners to the covenants of the promise, without hope and without God in the world. [13]But now in Christ Jesus you who once were far away have been brought near through the blood of Christ. . . .

[19]Consequently, you are no longer foreigners and aliens, but fellow citizens with God's people and members of God's household, [20]built on the foundation of the apostles and prophets, with Christ Jesus himself as the chief cornerstone.

Phil 3 [3]For it is we who are the circumcision, we who worship by the Spirit of God, who glory in Christ Jesus, and who put no confidence in the flesh. . . .

James 1 [1]James, a servant of God and of the Lord Jesus Christ,

To the twelve tribes scattered among the nations: Greetings.

1 Pet 2 [9]But you are a chosen people, a royal priesthood, a holy nation, a people belonging to God, that you may declare the praises of him who called you out of darkness into his wonderful light.

4. Believers as One New Man

Eph 2 [14]For he himself is our peace, who has made the two one and has destroyed the barrier, the dividing wall of hostility, [15]by abolishing in his flesh the law with its commandments and regulations. His purpose was to create in himself one new man out of the two, thus making peace, [16]and in this one body to reconcile both of them to God through the cross, by which he put to death their hostility.

5. Believers as the Temple of God

1 Cor 3 [16]Don't you know that you yourselves are God's temple and that God's Spirit lives in you? [17]If anyone destroys God's temple, God will destroy him; for God's temple is sacred, and you are that temple.

1 Cor 6 [19]Do you not know that your body is a temple of the Holy Spirit, who is in you, whom you have received from God? You are not your own. . . .

Eph 2 [19]Consequently, you are no longer foreigners and aliens, but fellow citizens with God's people and members of God's household, [20]built on the foundation of the apostles and prophets, with Christ Jesus himself as the chief cornerstone. [21]In him the whole building is joined together and rises to become a holy temple in the Lord. [22]And in him you too are being built together to become a dwelling in which God lives by his Spirit.

1 Pet 2 [5]you also, like living stones, are being built into a spiritual house to be a holy priesthood, offering spiritual sacrifices acceptable to God through Jesus Christ.

Human Beings: *Women*

I
Women as Creations of God

A. *Women Are a Special Creation of God*

Gen 2 21So the LORD God caused the man to fall into a deep sleep; and while he was sleeping, he took one of the man's ribs and closed up the place with flesh. 22Then the LORD God made a woman from the rib he had taken out of the man, and he brought her to the man.

23The man said, "This is now bone of my bones and flesh of my flesh; she shall be called 'woman,' for she was taken out of man." 24For this reason a man will leave his father and mother and be united to his wife, and they will become one flesh.

25The man and his wife were both naked, and they felt no shame.
Matt 19 4"Haven't you read," he replied, "that at the beginning the Creator 'made them male and female'? . . ."
Mark 10 6"But at the beginning of creation God 'made them male and female.'"

B. *Women Are Made in the Image of God*

Gen 1 26Then God said, "Let us make man in our image, in our likeness, and let them rule over the fish of the sea and the birds of the air, over the livestock, over all the earth, and over all the creatures that move along the ground."

27So God created man in his own image, in the image of God he created him; male and female he created them.
Gen 5 1This is the written account of Adam's line.

When God created man, he made him in the likeness of God. 2He created them male and female and blessed them. And when they were created, he called them "man."

C. *Women Are Interdependent with Men, Dependent on God*

1 Cor 11 11In the Lord, however, woman is not independent of man, nor is man independent of woman. 12For as woman came from man, so also man is born of woman. But everything comes from God.

D. *Women Are Men's Helpers*

Gen 2 18The LORD God said, "It is not good for the man to be alone. I will make a helper suitable for him." . . . 20So the man gave names to all the livestock, the birds of the air and all the beasts of the field.

But for Adam no suitable helper was found. 21So the LORD God caused the man to fall into a deep sleep; and while he was sleeping, he took one of the man's ribs and closed up the place with flesh. 22Then the LORD God made a woman from the rib he had taken out of the man, and he brought her to the man.
1 Cor 11 7A man ought not to cover his head, since he is the image and glory of God; but the woman is the glory of man. 8For man did not come from woman, but woman from man; 9neither was man created for woman, but woman for man.

E. *Women Rule Creation*

Gen 1 26Then God said, "Let us make man in our image, in our likeness, and let them rule over the fish of the sea and the birds of the air, over the livestock, over all the earth, and over all the creatures that move along the ground."

[27]So God created man in his own image, in the image of God he created him; male and female he created them.

[28]God blessed them and said to them, "Be fruitful and increase in number; fill the earth and subdue it. Rule over the fish of the sea and the birds of the air and over every living creature that moves on the ground."

F. Women Bear Children

Gen 1 [28]God blessed them and said to them, "Be fruitful and increase in number; fill the earth and subdue it. Rule over the fish of the sea and the birds of the air and over every living creature that moves on the ground."
Gen 3 [16]To the woman he said, "I will greatly increase your pains in childbearing; with pain you will give birth to children. Your desire will be for your husband, and he will rule over you."
Gen 3 [20]Adam named his wife Eve, because she would become the mother of all the living.
Gen 4 [1]Adam lay with his wife Eve, and she became pregnant and gave birth to Cain. She said, "With the help of the LORD I have brought forth a man."

G. Women Are Blessed by God

Gen 1 [27]So God created man in his own image, in the image of God he created him; male and female he created them.

[28]God blessed them and said to them, "Be fruitful and increase in number; fill the earth and subdue it. Rule over the fish of the sea and the birds of the air and over every living creature that moves on the ground."

H. Women Are Declared Very Good

Gen 1 [27]So God created man in his own image, in the image of God he created him; male and female he created them. . . . [31]God saw all that he had made, and it was very good. And there was evening, and there was morning—the sixth day.

I. Women Are a Great Work of God

Deut 4 [32]Ask now about the former days, long before your time, from the day God created man on the earth; ask from one end of the heavens to the other. Has anything so great as this ever happened, or has anything like it ever been heard of?

J. Women Are under the Curse of the Fall

See p. 372b, Sin Originated on Earth with Adam and Eve

II
Women as Members of Society

A. Women in Marriage

1. The Wife Is of One Flesh with Her Husband

Gen 2 [22]Then the LORD God made a woman from the rib he had taken out of the man, and he brought her to the man.

[23]The man said, "This is now bone of my bones and flesh of my flesh; she shall be called 'woman,' for she was taken out of man." [24]For this reason a man will leave his father and mother and be united to his wife, and they will become one flesh.
Matt 19 [5]". . . and said, 'For this reason a man will leave his father and mother and be united to his wife, and the two will become one flesh'? [6]So they are no longer two, but one. Therefore what God has joined together, let man not separate."

2. The Wife and Husband Are Responsible to Each Other

1 Cor 7 [2]But since there is so much immorality, each man should have his own wife, and each woman her own husband. [3]The husband should fulfill his marital duty to his wife, and likewise the wife to her husband. [4]The wife's body does not belong to her alone but also to her husband. In the same way, the husband's body does not belong to him alone but also to his wife. [5]Do not deprive each other except by mutual consent and for a time, so that you may devote yourselves to prayer. Then come together again so that Satan will not tempt you because of your lack of self-control.
1 Cor 7 [33]But a married man is concerned about the affairs of this world—how he can please his wife—[34]and his interests are divided. An unmarried woman or virgin is concerned about the Lord's affairs. Her aim is to be devoted to the Lord in both body and spirit. But a married woman is concerned about the affairs of this world—how she can please her husband.

3. The Wife Is to Respect and Honor Her Husband

1 Cor 11 [3]Now I want you to realize that the head of every man is Christ, and the head of the woman is man, and the head of Christ is God.
Eph 5 [22]Wives, submit to your husbands as to the Lord. [23]For the husband is the head of the wife as Christ is the head of the church, his body, of which he is the Savior. [24]Now as the church submits to Christ, so also wives should submit to their husbands in everything.
Eph 5 [33]However, each one of you also must love his wife as he loves himself, and the wife must respect her husband.
Col 3 [18]Wives, submit to your husbands, as is fitting in the Lord.
Titus 2 [3]Likewise, teach the older women to be reverent in the way they live, not to be slanderers or addicted to much wine, but to teach what is good. [4]Then they can train the younger women to love their husbands and children, [5]to be self-controlled and pure, to be busy at home, to be kind, and to be subject to their husbands, so that no one will malign the word of God.
1 Pet 3 [1]Wives, in the same way be submissive to your husbands so that, if any of them do not believe the word, they may be won over without words by the behavior of their wives, [2]when they see the purity and reverence of your lives. [3]Your beauty should not come from outward adornment, such as braided hair and the wearing of gold jewelry and fine clothes. [4]Instead, it should be that of your inner self, the unfading beauty of a gentle and quiet spirit, which is of great worth in God's sight. [5]For this is the way the holy women of the past who put their hope in God used to make themselves beautiful. They were submissive to their own husbands, [6]like Sarah, who obeyed Abraham and called him her master. You are her daughters if you do what is right and do not give way to fear.

4. The Wife Is to Be Loved by Her Husband

Eph 5 [25]Husbands, love your wives, just as Christ loved the church and gave himself up for her [26]to make her holy, cleansing her by the washing with water through the word, [27]and to present her to himself as a radiant church, without stain or wrinkle or any other blemish, but holy and blameless. [28]In this same way, husbands ought to love their wives as their own bodies. He who loves his wife loves himself. [29]After all, no one ever hated his own body, but he feeds and cares for it, just as Christ does the church—[30]for we are members of his body.
Col 3 [19]Husbands, love your wives and do not be harsh with them.
1 Pet 3 [7]Husbands, in the same way be considerate as you live with your wives, and treat them with respect as the weaker partner and as heirs with you of the gracious gift of life, so that nothing will hinder your prayers.

5. The Believing Wife Sanctifies Her Unbelieving Husband

1 Cor 7 [12]To the rest I say this (I, not the Lord): If any brother

has a wife who is not a believer and she is willing to live with him, he must not divorce her. [13]And if a woman has a husband who is not a believer and he is willing to live with her, she must not divorce him.[14]For the unbelieving husband has been sanctified through his wife, and the unbelieving wife has been sanctified through her believing husband. Otherwise your children would be unclean, but as it is, they are holy.
1 Pet 3 [1]Wives, in the same way be submissive to your husbands so that, if any of them do not believe the word, they may be won over without words by the behavior of their wives, [2]when they see the purity and reverence of your lives. [3]Your beauty should not come from outward adornment, such as braided hair and the wearing of gold jewelry and fine clothes. [4]Instead, it should be that of your inner self, the unfading beauty of a gentle and quiet spirit, which is of great worth in God's sight.

6. The Older Women Instruct Younger Wives

Titus 2 [3]Likewise, teach the older women to be reverent in the way they live, not to be slanderers or addicted to much wine, but to teach what is good. [4]Then they can train the younger women to love their husbands and children, [5]to be self-controlled and pure, to be busy at home, to be kind, and to be subject to their husbands, so that no one will malign the word of God.

7. Wives Are Called Holy

1 Pet 3 [5]For this is the way the holy women of the past who put their hope in God used to make themselves beautiful. They were submissive to their own husbands, [6]like Sarah, who obeyed Abraham and called him her master. You are her daughters if you do what is right and do not give way to fear.

8. Wives Are Heirs to God's Promises

1 Pet 3 [7]Husbands, in the same way be considerate as you live with your wives, and treat them with respect as the weaker partner and as heirs with you of the gracious gift of life, so that nothing will hinder your prayers.

9. The Godly Wife Is Praised, the Ungodly Wife Is Rebuked

Prov 12 [4]A wife of noble character is her husband's crown, but a disgraceful wife is like decay in his bones.
Prov 14 [1]The wise woman builds her house, but with her own hands the foolish one tears hers down.
Prov 18 [22]He who finds a wife finds what is good and receives favor from the LORD.
Prov 19 [13]A foolish son is his father's ruin, and a quarrelsome wife is like a constant dripping.

[14]Houses and wealth are inherited from parents, but a prudent wife is from the LORD.
Prov 23 [27]for a prostitute is a deep pit and a wayward wife is a narrow well. [28]Like a bandit she lies in wait, and multiplies the unfaithful among men.
Prov 25 [24]Better to live on a corner of the roof than share a house with a quarrelsome wife.
Prov 27 [15]A quarrelsome wife is like a constant dripping on a rainy day; [16]restraining her is like restraining the wind or grasping oil with the hand.
Prov 31 [10]A wife of noble character who can find? She is worth far more than rubies. . . . [28]Her children arise and call her blessed; her husband also, and he praises her: [29]"Many women do noble things, but you surpass them all." [30]Charm is deceptive, and beauty is fleeting; but a woman who fears the LORD is to be praised. [31]Give her the reward she has earned, and let her works bring her praise at the city gate.

B. Women in the Family

1. The Woman Bears Children

Gen 3 [16]To the woman he said, "I will greatly increase your pains in childbearing; with pain you will give birth to children. Your desire will be for your husband, and he will rule over you."
Prov 23 [25]May your father and mother be glad; may she who gave you birth rejoice!
John 16 [21]"A woman giving birth to a child has pain because her time has come; but when her baby is born she forgets the anguish because of her joy that a child is born into the world."
1 Tim 2 [15]But women will be saved through childbearing—if they continue in faith, love and holiness with propriety.

2. The Mother Trains and Disciplines Her Children

Prov 1 [8]Listen, my son, to your father's instruction and do not forsake your mother's teaching.
Prov 6 [20]My son, keep your father's commands and do not forsake your mother's teaching. [21]Bind them upon your heart forever; fasten them around your neck. [22]When you walk, they will guide you; when you sleep, they will watch over you; when you awake, they will speak to you. [23]For these commands are a lamp, this teaching is a light, and the corrections of discipline are the way to life. . . .
Prov 19 [18]Discipline your son, for in that there is hope; do not be a willing party to his death.
Prov 22 [6]Train a child in the way he should go, and when he is old he will not turn from it.
Prov 23 [13]Do not withhold discipline from a child; if you punish him with the rod, he will not die. [14]Punish him with the rod and save his soul from death.
Prov 29 [15]The rod of correction imparts wisdom, but a child left to himself disgraces his mother. . . .

[17]Discipline your son, and he will give you peace; he will bring delight to your soul.

3. The Mother Provides for Her Children

2 Cor 12 [14]Now I am ready to visit you for the third time, and I will not be a burden to you, because what I want is not your possessions but you. After all, children should not have to save up for their parents, but parents for their children.

4. The Mother Loves Her Children

Isa 49 [15]"Can a mother forget the baby at her breast and have no compassion on the child she has borne? Though she may forget, I will not forget you!"
Isa 66 [13]"As a mother comforts her child, so will I comfort you; and you will be comforted over Jerusalem."
Titus 2 [4]Then they can train the younger women to love their husbands and children. . . .

5. The Mother Is to Be Honored by Her Children

Exod 20 [12]"Honor your father and your mother, so that you may live long in the land the LORD your God is giving you."
Exod 21 [15]"Anyone who attacks his father or his mother must be put to death. . . .

[17]"Anyone who curses his father or mother must be put to death."
Lev 19 [3]"'Each of you must respect his mother and father, and you must observe my Sabbaths. I am the LORD your God.'"
Lev 20 [9]"'If anyone curses his father or mother, he must be put to death. He has cursed his father or his mother, and his blood will be on his own head.'"
Prov 15 [20]A wise son brings joy to his father, but a foolish man despises his mother.
Prov 19 [26]He who robs his father and drives out his mother is a son who brings shame and disgrace.
Prov 20 [20]If a man curses his father or mother, his lamp will be snuffed out in pitch darkness.
Prov 23 [22]Listen to your father, who gave you life, and do not despise your mother when she is old.
Prov 31 [28]Her children arise and call her blessed; her husband also, and he praises her. . . .

Matt 15 [3]Jesus replied, "And why do you break the command of God for the sake of your tradition? [4]For God said, 'Honor your father and mother' and 'Anyone who curses his father or mother must be put to death.' [5]But you say that if a man says to his father or mother, 'Whatever help you might otherwise have received from me is a gift devoted to God,' [6]he is not to 'honor his father' with it. Thus you nullify the word of God for the sake of your tradition."

6. The Mother Is to Be Obeyed by Her Children

Eph 6 [1]Children, obey your parents in the Lord, for this is right.
Col 3 [20]Children, obey your parents in everything, for this pleases the Lord.

7. The Mother Is Blessed as Childbearer

Gen 1 [28]God blessed them and said to them, "Be fruitful and increase in number; fill the earth and subdue it. Rule over the fish of the sea and the birds of the air and over every living creature that moves on the ground."
Gen 17 [15]God also said to Abraham, "As for Sarai your wife, you are no longer to call her Sarai; her name will be Sarah. [16]I will bless her and will surely give you a son by her. I will bless her so that she will be the mother of nations; kings of peoples will come from her."
1 Sam 2 [21]And the LORD was gracious to Hannah; she conceived and gave birth to three sons and two daughters. Meanwhile, the boy Samuel grew up in the presence of the LORD.
Ps 128 [3]Your wife will be like a fruitful vine within your house; your sons will be like olive shoots around your table.
Ezek 19 [10]"'Your mother was like a vine in your vineyard planted by the water; it was fruitful and full of branches because of abundant water.'"
Luke 1 [13]But the angel said to him: "Do not be afraid, Zechariah; your prayer has been heard. Your wife Elizabeth will bear you a son, and you are to give him the name John." . . . [24]After this his wife Elizabeth became pregnant and for five months remained in seclusion. [25]"The Lord has done this for me," she said. "In these days he has shown his favor and taken away my disgrace among the people."

8. Motherly Love Is Modeled by Many

a) Hagar

Gen 21 [14]Early the next morning Abraham took some food and a skin of water and gave them to Hagar. He set them on her shoulders and then sent her off with the boy. She went on her way and wandered in the desert of Beersheba.

[15]When the water in the skin was gone, she put the boy under one of the bushes. [16]Then she went off and sat down nearby, about a bowshot away, for she thought, "I cannot watch the boy die." And as she sat there nearby, she began to sob.

b) Hannah

1 Sam 2 [18]But Samuel was ministering before the LORD—a boy wearing a linen ephod. [19]Each year his mother made him a little robe and took it to him when she went up with her husband to offer the annual sacrifice. [20]Eli would bless Elkanah and his wife, saying, "May the LORD give you children by this woman to take the place of the one she prayed for and gave to the LORD." Then they would go home. [21]And the LORD was gracious to Hannah; she conceived and gave birth to three sons and two daughters. Meanwhile, the boy Samuel grew up in the presence of the LORD.

c) An Infant's Mother

1 Kings 3 [16]Now two prostitutes came to the king and stood before him. [17]One of them said, "My lord, this woman and I live in the same house. I had a baby while she was there with me. [18]The third day after my child was born, this woman also had a baby. We were alone; there was no one in the house but the two of us.

[19]"During the night this woman's son died because she lay on him. [20]So she got up in the middle of the night and took my son from my side while I your servant was asleep. She put him by her breast and put her dead son by my breast. [21]The next morning, I got up to nurse my son—and he was dead! But when I looked at him closely in the morning light, I saw that it wasn't the son I had borne."

[22]The other woman said, "No! The living one is my son; the dead one is yours."

But the first one insisted, "No! The dead one is yours; the living one is mine." And so they argued before the king.

[23]The king said, "This one says, 'My son is alive and your son is dead,' while that one says, 'No! Your son is dead and mine is alive.'"

[24]Then the king said, "Bring me a sword." So they brought a sword for the king. [25]He then gave an order: "Cut the living child in two and give half to one and half to the other."

[26]The woman whose son was alive was filled with compassion for her son and said to the king, "Please, my lord, give her the living baby! Don't kill him!"

But the other said, "Neither I nor you shall have him. Cut him in two!"

[27]Then the king gave his ruling: "Give the living baby to the first woman. Do not kill him; she is his mother."

d) Mary

Luke 2 [48]When his parents saw him, they were astonished. His mother said to him, "Son, why have you treated us like this? Your father and I have been anxiously searching for you.". . .

[51]Then he went down to Nazareth with them and was obedient to them. But his mother treasured all these things in her heart.
John 19 [25]Near the cross of Jesus stood his mother, his mother's sister, Mary the wife of Clopas, and Mary Magdalene. [26]When Jesus saw his mother there, and the disciple whom he loved standing nearby, he said to his mother, "Dear woman, here is your son," [27]and to the disciple, "Here is your mother." From that time on, this disciple took her into his home.

e) Moses' Mother

Exod 2 [1]Now a man of the house of Levi married a Levite woman, [2]and she became pregnant and gave birth to a son. When she saw that he was a fine child, she hid him for three months. [3]But when she could hide him no longer, she got a papyrus basket for him and coated it with tar and pitch. Then she placed the child in it and put it among the reeds along the bank of the Nile. [4]His sister stood at a distance to see what would happen to him.

[5]Then Pharaoh's daughter went down to the Nile to bathe, and her attendants were walking along the river bank. She saw the basket among the reeds and sent her slave girl to get it. [6]She opened it and saw the baby. He was crying, and she felt sorry for him. "This is one of the Hebrew babies," she said.

[7]Then his sister asked Pharaoh's daughter, "Shall I go and get one of the Hebrew women to nurse the baby for you?"

[8]"Yes, go," she answered. And the girl went and got the baby's mother. [9]Pharaoh's daughter said to her, "Take this baby and nurse him for me, and I will pay you." So the woman took the baby and nursed him. [10]When the child grew older, she took him to Pharaoh's daughter and he became her son. She named him Moses, saying, "I drew him out of the water."

f) Naomi

Ruth 1 [8]Then Naomi said to her two daughters-in-law, "Go back, each of you, to your mother's home. May the LORD show kindness to you, as you have shown to your dead and to me. [9]May the LORD grant that each of you will find rest in the home of another husband."

Then she kissed them and they wept aloud [10]and said to her, "We will go back with you to your people."

[11]But Naomi said, "Return home, my daughters. Why would you come with me? Am I going to have any more sons, who could become your husbands? [12]Return home, my daughters; I am too old to have another husband. Even if I thought there was still hope for me—even if I had a husband tonight and then gave birth to sons—[13]would you wait until they grew up? Would you remain unmarried for them? No, my daughters.

It is more bitter for me than for you, because the LORD's hand has gone out against me!"

14At this they wept again. Then Orpah kissed her mother-in-law good-by, but Ruth clung to her.

15"Look," said Naomi, "your sister-in-law is going back to her people and her gods. Go back with her."

16But Ruth replied, "Don't urge me to leave you or to turn back from you. Where you go I will go, and where you stay I will stay. Your people will be my people and your God my God. 17Where you die I will die, and there I will be buried. May the LORD deal with me, be it ever so severely, if anything but death separates you and me." 18When Naomi realized that Ruth was determined to go with her, she stopped urging her.

g) Rebekah

Gen 25 28Isaac, who had a taste for wild game, loved Esau, but Rebekah loved Jacob.

h) Rebekah's Mother

Gen 24 52When Abraham's servant heard what they said, he bowed down to the ground before the LORD. 53Then the servant brought out gold and silver jewelry and articles of clothing and gave them to Rebekah; he also gave costly gifts to her brother and to her mother. 54Then he and the men who were with him ate and drank and spent the night there.

When they got up the next morning, he said, "Send me on my way to my master."

55But her brother and her mother replied, "Let the girl remain with us ten days or so; then you may go."

i) Rizpah

2 Sam 21 8But the king took Armoni and Mephibosheth, the two sons of Aiah's daughter Rizpah, whom she had borne to Saul, together with the five sons of Saul's daughter Merab, whom she had borne to Adriel son of Barzillai the Meholathite. 9He handed them over to the Gibeonites, who killed and exposed them on a hill before the LORD. All seven of them fell together; they were put to death during the first days of the harvest, just as the barley harvest was beginning.

10Rizpah daughter of Aiah took sackcloth and spread it out for herself on a rock. From the beginning of the harvest till the rain poured down from the heavens on the bodies, she did not let the birds of the air touch them by day or the wild animals by night. 11When David was told what Aiah's daughter Rizpah, Saul's concubine, had done, 12he went and took the bones of Saul and his son Jonathan from the citizens of Jabesh Gilead. (They had taken them secretly from the public square at Beth Shan, where the Philistines had hung them after they struck Saul down on Gilboa.) 13David brought the bones of Saul and his son Jonathan from there, and the bones of those who had been killed and exposed were gathered up.

j) Widow of Nain

Luke 7 11Soon afterward, Jesus went to a town called Nain, and his disciples and a large crowd went along with him. 12As he approached the town gate, a dead person was being carried out—the only son of his mother, and she was a widow. And a large crowd from the town was with her. 13When the Lord saw her, his heart went out to her and he said, "Don't cry."

14Then he went up and touched the coffin, and those carrying it stood still. He said, "Young man, I say to you, get up!" 15The dead man sat up and began to talk, and Jesus gave him back to his mother.

k) Widow of Zarephath

1 Kings 17 7Some time later the brook dried up because there had been no rain in the land. 8Then the word of the LORD came to him: 9"Go at once to Zarephath of Sidon and stay there. I have commanded a widow in that place to supply you with food." 10So he went to Zarephath. When he came to the town gate, a widow was there gathering sticks. He called to her and asked, "Would you bring me a little water in a jar so I may have a drink?" 11As she was going to get it, he called, "And bring me, please, a piece of bread."

12"As surely as the LORD your God lives," she replied, "I don't have any bread—only a handful of flour in a jar and a little oil in a jug. I am gathering a few sticks to take home and make a meal for myself and my son, that we may eat it—and die."

13Elijah said to her, "Don't be afraid. Go home and do as you have said. But first make a small cake of bread for me from what you have and bring it to me, and then make something for yourself and your son. 14For this is what the LORD, the God of Israel, says: 'The jar of flour will not be used up and the jug of oil will not run dry until the day the LORD gives rain on the land.'"

15She went away and did as Elijah had told her. So there was food every day for Elijah and for the woman and her family. 16For the jar of flour was not used up and the jug of oil did not run dry, in keeping with the word of the LORD spoken by Elijah.

17Some time later the son of the woman who owned the house became ill. He grew worse and worse, and finally stopped breathing. 18She said to Elijah, "What do you have against me, man of God? Did you come to remind me of my sin and kill my son?"

19"Give me your son," Elijah replied. He took him from her arms, carried him to the upper room where he was staying, and laid him on his bed. 20Then he cried out to the LORD, "O LORD my God, have you brought tragedy also upon this widow I am staying with, by causing her son to die?" 21Then he stretched himself out on the boy three times and cried to the LORD, "O LORD my God, let this boy's life return to him!"

22The LORD heard Elijah's cry, and the boy's life returned to him, and he lived. 23Elijah picked up the child and carried him down from the room into the house. He gave him to his mother and said, "Look, your son is alive!"

24Then the woman said to Elijah, "Now I know that you are a man of God and that the word of the LORD from your mouth is the truth."

C. Women in Leadership

1. A Woman as Judge: Deborah

Judg 4 4Deborah, a prophetess, the wife of Lappidoth, was leading Israel at that time. 5She held court under the Palm of Deborah between Ramah and Bethel in the hill country of Ephraim, and the Israelites came to her to have their disputes decided. 6She sent for Barak son of Abinoam from Kedesh in Naphtali and said to him, "The LORD, the God of Israel, commands you: 'Go, take with you ten thousand men of Naphtali and Zebulun and lead the way to Mount Tabor. 7I will lure Sisera, the commander of Jabin's army, with his chariots and his troops to the Kishon River and give him into your hands.'"

8Barak said to her, "If you go with me, I will go; but if you don't go with me, I won't go."

9"Very well," Deborah said, "I will go with you. But because of the way you are going about this, the honor will not be yours, for the LORD will hand Sisera over to a woman." So Deborah went with Barak to Kedesh, 10where he summoned Zebulun and Naphtali. Ten thousand men followed him, and Deborah also went with him.

11Now Heber the Kenite had left the other Kenites, the descendants of Hobab, Moses' brother-in-law, and pitched his tent by the great tree in Zaanannim near Kedesh.

12When they told Sisera that Barak son of Abinoam had gone up to Mount Tabor, 13Sisera gathered together his nine hundred iron chariots and all the men with him, from Harosheth Haggoyim to the Kishon River.

14Then Deborah said to Barak, "Go! This is the day the LORD has given Sisera into your hands. Has not the LORD gone ahead of you?" So Barak went down Mount Tabor, followed by ten thousand men.

2. Women as Prophetesses

a) Anna

Luke 2 36There was also a prophetess, Anna, the daughter of Phanuel, of the tribe of Asher. She was very old; she had lived with her husband seven years after her marriage, 37and then was a widow until she was eighty-four. She never left the temple but worshiped night and day, fasting and praying. 38Coming up to them at that very moment, she gave thanks to God and spoke about the child to all who were looking forward to the redemption of Jerusalem.

b) Elizabeth

Luke 1 41When Elizabeth heard Mary's greeting, the baby leaped in her womb, and Elizabeth was filled with the Holy Spirit. 42In a loud voice she exclaimed: "Blessed are you among women, and blessed is the child you will bear! 43But why am I so favored, that the mother of my Lord should come to me? 44As soon as the sound of your greeting reached my ears, the baby in my womb leaped for joy. 45Blessed is she who has believed that what the Lord has said to her will be accomplished!"

c) Huldah

2 Kings 22 14Hilkiah the priest, Ahikam, Acbor, Shaphan and Asaiah went to speak to the prophetess Huldah, who was the wife of Shallum son of Tikvah, the son of Harhas, keeper of the wardrobe. She lived in Jerusalem, in the Second District.

15She said to them, "This is what the LORD, the God of Israel, says: Tell the man who sent you to me, 16'This is what the LORD says: I am going to bring disaster on this place and its people, according to everything written in the book the king of Judah has read. 17Because they have forsaken me and burned incense to other gods and provoked me to anger by all the idols their hands have made, my anger will burn against this place and will not be quenched.' 18Tell the king of Judah, who sent you to inquire of the LORD, 'This is what the LORD, the God of Israel, says concerning the words you heard: 19Because your heart was responsive and you humbled yourself before the LORD when you heard what I have spoken against this place and its people, that they would become accursed and laid waste, and because you tore your robes and wept in my presence, I have heard you, declares the LORD. 20Therefore I will gather you to your fathers, and you will be buried in peace. Your eyes will not see all the disaster I am going to bring on this place.'"

So they took her answer back to the king.

d) Isaiah's Wife

Isa 8 3Then I went to the prophetess, and she conceived and gave birth to a son. And the LORD said to me, "Name him Maher-Shalal-Hash-Baz."

e) Miriam

Exod 15 20Then Miriam the prophetess, Aaron's sister, took a tambourine in her hand, and all the women followed her, with tambourines and dancing.
Mic 6 4"I brought you up out of Egypt and redeemed you from the land of slavery. I sent Moses to lead you, also Aaron and Miriam."

f) Noadiah

Neh 6 14Remember Tobiah and Sanballat, O my God, because of what they have done; remember also the prophetess Noadiah and the rest of the prophets who have been trying to intimidate me.

g) Philip's Daughters

Acts 21 8Leaving the next day, we reached Caesarea and stayed at the house of Philip the evangelist, one of the Seven. 9He had four unmarried daughters who prophesied.

3. Women as Rulers

a) Athaliah

2 Kings 11 1When Athaliah the mother of Ahaziah saw that her son was dead, she proceeded to destroy the whole royal family. 2But Jehosheba, the daughter of King Jehoram and sister of Ahaziah, took Joash son of Ahaziah and stole him away from among the royal princes, who were about to be murdered. She put him and his nurse in a bedroom to hide him from Athaliah; so he was not killed. 3He remained hidden with his nurse at the temple of the LORD for six years while Athaliah ruled the land.

4In the seventh year Jehoiada sent for the commanders of units of a hundred, the Carites and the guards and had them brought to him at the temple of the LORD. He made a covenant with them and put them under oath at the temple of the LORD. Then he showed them the king's son. 5He commanded them, saying, "This is what you are to do: You who are in the three companies that are going on duty on the Sabbath—a third of you guarding the royal palace, 6a third at the Sur Gate, and a third at the gate behind the guard, who take turns guarding the temple—7and you who are in the other two companies that normally go off Sabbath duty are all to guard the temple for the king. 8Station yourselves around the king, each man with his weapon in his hand. Anyone who approaches your ranks must be put to death. Stay close to the king wherever he goes."

9The commanders of units of a hundred did just as Jehoiada the priest ordered. Each one took his men—those who were going on duty on the Sabbath and those who were going off duty—and came to Jehoiada the priest. 10Then he gave the commanders the spears and shields that had belonged to King David and that were in the temple of the LORD. 11The guards, each with his weapon in his hand, stationed themselves around the king—near the altar and the temple, from the south side to the north side of the temple.

12Jehoiada brought out the king's son and put the crown on him; he presented him with a copy of the covenant and proclaimed him king. They anointed him, and the people clapped their hands and shouted, "Long live the king!"

13When Athaliah heard the noise made by the guards and the people, she went to the people at the temple of the LORD. 14She looked and there was the king, standing by the pillar, as the custom was. The officers and the trumpeters were beside the king, and all the people of the land were rejoicing and blowing trumpets. Then Athaliah tore her robes and called out, "Treason! Treason!"

15Jehoiada the priest ordered the commanders of units of a hundred, who were in charge of the troops: "Bring her out between the ranks and put to the sword anyone who follows her." For the priest had said, "She must not be put to death in the temple of the LORD." 16So they seized her as she reached the place where the horses enter the palace grounds, and there she was put to death.

b) Candace

Acts 8 27So he started out, and on his way he met an Ethiopian eunuch, an important official in charge of all the treasury of Candace, queen of the Ethiopians. This man had gone to Jerusalem to worship. . . .

c) Esther

Esther 2 17Now the king was attracted to Esther more than to any of the other women, and she won his favor and approval more than any of the other virgins. So he set a royal crown on her head and made her queen instead of Vashti.

d) Queen of Babylonia

Dan 5 10The queen, hearing the voices of the king and his nobles, came into the banquet hall. "O king, live forever!" she said. "Don't be alarmed! Don't look so pale! 11There is a man in your kingdom who has the spirit of the holy gods in him. In the time of your father he was found to have insight and intelligence and wisdom like that of the gods. King Nebuchadnezzar your father—your father the king, I say—appointed him chief of the magicians, enchanters, astrologers and diviners. 12This man Daniel, whom the king called Belteshazzar, was found to have a keen mind and knowledge and understanding, and also the ability to interpret dreams, explain riddles and solve difficult problems. Call for Daniel, and he will tell you what the writing means."

e) Queen of Persia

Neh 2 6Then the king, with the queen sitting beside him, asked me, "How long will your journey take, and when will you get back?" It pleased the king to send me; so I set a time.

f) Queen of Sheba

1 Kings 10 1When the queen of Sheba heard about the fame of Solomon and his relation to the name of the LORD, she came to test him with hard questions. 2Arriving at Jerusalem with a very great caravan—with camels carrying spices, large quantities of gold, and precious stones—she came to Solomon and talked with him about all that she had on her mind. 3Solomon answered all her questions; nothing was too hard for the king to explain to her. 4When the queen of Sheba saw all the wisdom of Solomon and the palace he had built, 5the food on his table, the seating of his officials, the attending servants in their robes, his cupbearers, and the burnt offerings he made at the temple of the LORD, she was overwhelmed.

6She said to the king, "The report I heard in my own country about your achievements and your wisdom is true. 7But I did not believe these things until I came and saw with my own eyes. Indeed, not even half was told me; in wisdom and wealth you have far exceeded the report I heard. 8How happy your men must be! How happy your officials, who continually stand before you and hear your wisdom! 9Praise be to the LORD your God, who has delighted in you and placed you on the throne of Israel. Because of the LORD's eternal love for Israel, he has made you king, to maintain justice and righteousness."

10And she gave the king 120 talents of gold, large quantities of spices, and precious stones. Never again were so many spices brought in as those the queen of Sheba gave to King Solomon. . . .

13King Solomon gave the queen of Sheba all she desired and asked for, besides what he had given her out of his royal bounty. Then she left and returned with her retinue to her own country.

g) Tahpenes

1 Kings 11 19Pharaoh was so pleased with Hadad that he gave him a sister of his own wife, Queen Tahpenes, in marriage. 20The sister of Tahpenes bore him a son named Genubath, whom Tahpenes brought up in the royal palace. There Genubath lived with Pharaoh's own children.

h) Vashti

Esther 1 9Queen Vashti also gave a banquet for the women in the royal palace of King Xerxes.

D. The Exemplary Behavior of Women

1. Abigail

1 Sam 25 1Now Samuel died, and all Israel assembled and mourned for him; and they buried him at his home in Ramah.

Then David moved down into the Desert of Maon. 2A certain man in Maon, who had property there at Carmel, was very wealthy. He had a thousand goats and three thousand sheep, which he was shearing in Carmel. 3His name was Nabal and his wife's name was Abigail. She was an intelligent and beautiful woman, but her husband, a Calebite, was surly and mean in his dealings.

4While David was in the desert, he heard that Nabal was shearing sheep. . . .

14One of the servants told Nabal's wife Abigail: "David sent messengers from the desert to give our master his greetings, but he hurled insults at them. 15Yet these men were very good to us. They did not mistreat us, and the whole time we were out in the fields near them nothing was missing. 16Night and day they were a wall around us all the time we were herding our sheep near them. 17Now think it over and see what you can do, because disaster is hanging over our master and his whole household. He is such a wicked man that no one can talk to him."

18Abigail lost no time. She took two hundred loaves of bread, two skins of wine, five dressed sheep, five seahs of roasted grain, a hundred cakes of raisins and two hundred cakes of pressed figs, and loaded them on donkeys. 19Then she told her servants, "Go on ahead; I'll follow you." But she did not tell her husband Nabal.

20As she came riding her donkey into a mountain ravine, there were David and his men descending toward her, and she met them. 21David had just said, "It's been useless—all my watching over this fellow's property in the desert so that nothing of his was missing. He has paid me back evil for good. 22May God deal with David, be it ever so severely, if by morning I leave alive one male of all who belong to him!"

23When Abigail saw David, she quickly got off her donkey and bowed down before David with her face to the ground. 24She fell at his feet and said: "My lord, let the blame be on me alone. Please let your servant speak to you; hear what your servant has to say. 25May my lord pay no attention to that wicked man Nabal. He is just like his name—his name is Fool, and folly goes with him. But as for me, your servant, I did not see the men my master sent.

26"Now since the LORD has kept you, my master, from bloodshed and from avenging yourself with your own hands, as surely as the LORD lives and as you live, may your enemies and all who intend to harm my master be like Nabal. 27And let this gift, which your servant has brought to my master, be given to the men who follow you. 28Please forgive your servant's offense, for the LORD will certainly make a lasting dynasty for my master, because he fights the LORD's battles. Let no wrongdoing be found in you as long as you live. 29Even though someone is pursuing you to take your life, the life of my master will be bound securely in the bundle of the living by the LORD your God. But the lives of your enemies he will hurl away as from the pocket of a sling. 30When the LORD has done for my master every good thing he promised concerning him and has appointed him leader over Israel, 31my master will not have on his conscience the staggering burden of needless bloodshed or of having avenged himself. And when the LORD has brought my master success, remember your servant."

32David said to Abigail, "Praise be to the LORD, the God of Israel, who has sent you today to meet me. 33May you be blessed for your good judgment and for keeping me from bloodshed this day and from avenging myself with my own hands. 34Otherwise, as surely as the LORD, the God of Israel, lives, who has kept me from harming you, if you had not come quickly to meet me, not one male belonging to Nabal would have been left alive by daybreak."

35Then David accepted from her hand what she had brought him and said, "Go home in peace. I have heard your words and granted your request."

36When Abigail went to Nabal, he was in the house holding a banquet like that of a king. He was in high spirits and very drunk. So she told him nothing until daybreak. 37Then in the morning, when Nabal was sober, his wife told him all these things, and his heart failed him and he became like a stone. 38About ten days later, the LORD struck Nabal and he died.

39When David heard that Nabal was dead, he said, "Praise be to the LORD, who has upheld my cause against Nabal for treating me with contempt. He has kept his servant from doing wrong and has brought Nabal's wrongdoing down on his own head."

Then David sent word to Abigail, asking her to become his wife. 40His servants went to Carmel and said to Abigail, "David has sent us to you to take you to become his wife."

41She bowed down with her face to the ground and said, "Here is your maidservant, ready to serve you and wash the feet of my master's servants." 42Abigail quickly got on a donkey and, attended by her five maids, went with David's messengers and became his wife.

2. Jael

Judg 4 8Barak said to her, "If you go with me, I will go; but if you don't go with me, I won't go."

9"Very well," Deborah said, "I will go with you. But because of the way you are going about this, the honor will not be yours, for the LORD will hand Sisera over to a woman." So Deborah went with Barak to Kedesh. . . . 15At Barak's advance, the LORD routed Sisera and all his chariots and army by the sword, and Sisera abandoned his chariot and fled on foot. 16But Barak pursued the chariots and army as far as Harosheth Haggoyim. All the troops of Sisera fell by the sword; not a man was left.

17Sisera, however, fled on foot to the tent of Jael, the wife of Heber the Kenite, because there were friendly relations between Jabin king of Hazor and the clan of Heber the Kenite.

18Jael went out to meet Sisera and said to him, "Come, my lord, come right in. Don't be afraid." So he entered her tent, and she put a covering over him.

[19]"I'm thirsty," he said. "Please give me some water." She opened a skin of milk, gave him a drink, and covered him up.

[20]"Stand in the doorway of the tent," he told her. "If someone comes by and asks you, 'Is anyone here?' say 'No.'"

[21]But Jael, Heber's wife, picked up a tent peg and a hammer and went quietly to him while he lay fast asleep, exhausted. She drove the peg through his temple into the ground, and he died.

[22]Barak came by in pursuit of Sisera, and Jael went out to meet him. "Come," she said, "I will show you the man you're looking for." So he went in with her, and there lay Sisera with the tent peg through his temple—dead.

Judg 5 [24]"Most blessed of women be Jael, the wife of Heber the Kenite, most blessed of tent-dwelling women. [25]He asked for water, and she gave him milk; in a bowl fit for nobles she brought him curdled milk. [26]Her hand reached for the tent peg, her right hand for the workman's hammer. She struck Sisera, she crushed his head, she shattered and pierced his temple. [27]At her feet he sank, he fell; there he lay. At her feet he sank, he fell; where he sank, there he fell—dead."

3. Rahab

Josh 2 [1]Then Joshua son of Nun secretly sent two spies from Shittim. "Go, look over the land," he said, "especially Jericho." So they went and entered the house of a prostitute named Rahab and stayed there.

[2]The king of Jericho was told, "Look! Some of the Israelites have come here tonight to spy out the land." [3]So the king of Jericho sent this message to Rahab: "Bring out the men who came to you and entered your house, because they have come to spy out the whole land."

[4]But the woman had taken the two men and hidden them. She said, "Yes, the men came to me, but I did not know where they had come from. [5]At dusk, when it was time to close the city gate, the men left. I don't know which way they went. Go after them quickly. You may catch up with them." [6](But she had taken them up to the roof and hidden them under the stalks of flax she had laid out on the roof.) [7]So the men set out in pursuit of the spies on the road that leads to the fords of the Jordan, and as soon as the pursuers had gone out, the gate was shut.

[8]Before the spies lay down for the night, she went up on the roof [9]and said to them, "I know that the LORD has given this land to you and that a great fear of you has fallen on us, so that all who live in this country are melting in fear because of you. [10]We have heard how the LORD dried up the water of the Red Sea for you when you came out of Egypt, and what you did to Sihon and Og, the two kings of the Amorites east of the Jordan, whom you completely destroyed. [11]When we heard of it, our hearts melted and everyone's courage failed because of you, for the LORD your God is God in heaven above and on the earth below. [12]Now then, please swear to me by the LORD that you will show kindness to my family, because I have shown kindness to you. Give me a sure sign [13]that you will spare the lives of my father and mother, my brothers and sisters, and all who belong to them, and that you will save us from death."

[14]"Our lives for your lives!" the men assured her. "If you don't tell what we are doing, we will treat you kindly and faithfully when the LORD gives us the land."

[15]So she let them down by a rope through the window, for the house she lived in was part of the city wall. [16]Now she had said to them, "Go to the hills so the pursuers will not find you. Hide yourselves there three days until they return, and then go on your way."

Josh 6 [23]So the young men who had done the spying went in and brought out Rahab, her father and mother and brothers and all who belonged to her. They brought out her entire family and put them in a place outside the camp of Israel. . . . [25]But Joshua spared Rahab the prostitute, with her family and all who belonged to her, because she hid the men Joshua had sent as spies to Jericho—and she lives among the Israelites to this day.

Heb 11 [31]By faith the prostitute Rahab, because she welcomed the spies, was not killed with those who were disobedient.

James 2 [25]In the same way, was not even Rahab the prostitute considered righteous for what she did when she gave lodging to the spies and sent them off in a different direction?

4. Tabitha

Acts 9 [36]In Joppa there was a disciple named Tabitha (which, when translated, is Dorcas), who was always doing good and helping the poor.

5. Wise Woman

2 Sam 20 [14]Sheba passed through all the tribes of Israel to Abel Beth Maacah and through the entire region of the Berites, who gathered together and followed him. [15]All the troops with Joab came and besieged Sheba in Abel Beth Maacah. They built a siege ramp up to the city, and it stood against the outer fortifications. While they were battering the wall to bring it down, [16]a wise woman called from the city, "Listen! Listen! Tell Joab to come here so I can speak to him." [17]He went toward her, and she asked, "Are you Joab?"

"I am," he answered.

She said, "Listen to what your servant has to say."

"I'm listening," he said.

[18]She continued, "Long ago they used to say, 'Get your answer at Abel,' and that settled it. [19]We are the peaceful and faithful in Israel. You are trying to destroy a city that is a mother in Israel. Why do you want to swallow up the LORD's inheritance?"

[20]"Far be it from me!" Joab replied, "Far be it from me to swallow up or destroy! [21]That is not the case. A man named Sheba son of Bicri, from the hill country of Ephraim, has lifted up his hand against the king, against David. Hand over this one man, and I'll withdraw from the city."

The woman said to Joab, "His head will be thrown to you from the wall."

[22]Then the woman went to all the people with her wise advice, and they cut off the head of Sheba son of Bicri and threw it to Joab. So he sounded the trumpet, and his men dispersed from the city, each returning to his home. And Joab went back to the king in Jerusalem.

6. Zipporah

Exod 4 [24]At a lodging place on the way, the LORD met Moses and was about to kill him. [25]But Zipporah took a flint knife, cut off her son's foreskin and touched Moses' feet with it. "Surely you are a bridegroom of blood to me," she said. [26]So the LORD let him alone. (At that time she said "bridegroom of blood," referring to circumcision.)

E. Poetic Response in Women

1. Deborah's Song

Judg 5 [1]On that day Deborah and Barak son of Abinoam sang this song: [2]"When the princes in Israel take the lead, when the people willingly offer themselves—praise the LORD!

[3]"Hear this, you kings! Listen, you rulers! I will sing to the LORD, I will sing; I will make music to the LORD, the God of Israel.

[4]"O LORD, when you went out from Seir, when you marched from the land of Edom, the earth shook, the heavens poured, the clouds poured down water. [5]The mountains quaked before the LORD, the One of Sinai, before the LORD, the God of Israel.

[6]"In the days of Shamgar son of Anath, in the days of Jael, the roads were abandoned; travelers took to winding paths. [7]Village life in Israel ceased, ceased until I, Deborah, arose, arose a mother in Israel. [8]When they chose new gods, war came to the city gates, and not a shield or spear was seen among forty thousand in Israel. [9]My heart is with Israel's princes, with the willing volunteers among the people. Praise the LORD!

[10]"You who ride on white donkeys, sitting on your saddle blankets, and you who walk along the road, consider [11]the voice of the singers at the watering places. They recite the righteous acts of the LORD, the righteous acts of his warriors in Israel.

"Then the people of the LORD went down to the city gates. [12]'Wake up, wake up, Deborah! Wake up, wake up, break out in song! Arise, O Barak! Take captive your captives, O son of Abinoam.'

13"Then the men who were left came down to the nobles; the people of the LORD came to me with the mighty. 14Some came from Ephraim, whose roots were in Amalek; Benjamin was with the people who followed you. From Makir captains came down, from Zebulun those who bear a commander's staff. 15The princes of Issachar were with Deborah; yes, Issachar was with Barak, rushing after him into the valley. In the districts of Reuben there was much searching of heart. 16Why did you stay among the campfires to hear the whistling for the flocks? In the districts of Reuben there was much searching of heart. 17Gilead stayed beyond the Jordan. And Dan, why did he linger by the ships? Asher remained on the coast and stayed in his coves. 18The people of Zebulun risked their very lives; so did Naphtali on the heights of the field.

19"Kings came, they fought; the kings of Canaan fought at Taanach by the waters of Megiddo, but they carried off no silver, no plunder. 20From the heavens the stars fought, from their courses they fought against Sisera. 21The river Kishon swept them away, the age-old river, the river Kishon. March on, my soul; be strong! 22Then thundered the horses' hoofs—galloping, galloping go his mighty steeds. 23'Curse Meroz,' said the angel of the LORD. 'Curse its people bitterly, because they did not come to help the LORD, to help the LORD against the mighty.'

24"Most blessed of women be Jael, the wife of Heber the Kenite, most blessed of tent-dwelling women. 25He asked for water, and she gave him milk; in a bowl fit for nobles she brought him curdled milk. 26Her hand reached for the tent peg, her right hand for the workman's hammer. She struck Sisera, she crushed his head, she shattered and pierced his temple. 27At her feet he sank, he fell; there he lay. At her feet he sank, he fell; where he sank, there he fell—dead.

28"Through the window peered Sisera's mother; behind the lattice she cried out, 'Why is his chariot so long in coming? Why is the clatter of his chariots delayed?' 29The wisest of her ladies answer her; indeed, she keeps saying to herself, 30'Are they not finding and dividing the spoils: a girl or two for each man, colorful garments as plunder for Sisera, colorful garments embroidered, highly embroidered garments for my neck—all this as plunder?'

31"So may all your enemies perish, O LORD! But may they who love you be like the sun when it rises in its strength."

Then the land had peace forty years.

2. Hannah's Prayer

1 Sam 2 1Then Hannah prayed and said: "My heart rejoices in the LORD; in the LORD my horn is lifted high. My mouth boasts over my enemies, for I delight in your deliverance.

2"There is no one holy like the LORD; there is no one besides you; there is no Rock like our God.

3"Do not keep talking so proudly or let your mouth speak such arrogance, for the LORD is a God who knows, and by him deeds are weighed.

4"The bows of the warriors are broken, but those who stumbled are armed with strength. 5Those who were full hire themselves out for food, but those who were hungry hunger no more. She who was barren has borne seven children, but she who has had many sons pines away.

6"The LORD brings death and makes alive; he brings down to the grave and raises up. 7The LORD sends poverty and wealth; he humbles and he exalts. 8He raises the poor from the dust and lifts the needy from the ash heap; he seats them with princes and has them inherit a throne of honor.

"For the foundations of the earth are the LORD's; upon them he has set the world. 9He will guard the feet of his saints, but the wicked will be silenced in darkness.

"It is not by strength that one prevails; 10those who oppose the LORD will be shattered. He will thunder against them from heaven; the LORD will judge the ends of the earth.

"He will give strength to his king and exalt the horn of his anointed."

3. Mary's Song

Luke 1 46And Mary said: "My soul glorifies the Lord 47and my spirit rejoices in God my Savior, 48for he has been mindful of the humble state of his servant. From now on all generations will call me blessed, 49for the Mighty One has done great things for me—holy is his name. 50His mercy extends to those who fear him, from generation to generation. 51He has performed mighty deeds with his arm; he has scattered those who are proud in their inmost thoughts. 52He has brought down rulers from their thrones but has lifted up the humble. 53He has filled the hungry with good things but has sent the rich away empty. 54He has helped his servant Israel, remembering to be merciful 55to Abraham and his descendants forever, even as he said to our fathers."

4. Miriam's Song

Exod 15 21Miriam sang to them: "Sing to the LORD, for he is highly exalted. The horse and its rider he has hurled into the sea."

F. The Virtuous Woman

Ruth 3 11"And now, my daughter, don't be afraid. I will do for you all you ask. All my fellow townsmen know that you are a woman of noble character."

Prov 31 10A wife of noble character who can find? She is worth far more than rubies. 11Her husband has full confidence in her and lacks nothing of value. 12She brings him good, not harm, all the days of her life. 13She selects wool and flax and works with eager hands. 14She is like the merchant ships, bringing her food from afar. 15She gets up while it is still dark; she provides food for her family and portions for her servant girls. 16She considers a field and buys it; out of her earnings she plants a vineyard. 17She sets about her work vigorously; her arms are strong for her tasks. 18She sees that her trading is profitable, and her lamp does not go out at night. 19In her hand she holds the distaff and grasps the spindle with her fingers. 20She opens her arms to the poor and extends her hands to the needy. 21When it snows, she has no fear for her household; for all of them are clothed in scarlet. 22She makes coverings for her bed; she is clothed in fine linen and purple. 23Her husband is respected at the city gate, where he takes his seat among the elders of the land. 24She makes linen garments and sells them, and supplies the merchants with sashes. 25She is clothed with strength and dignity; she can laugh at the days to come. 26She speaks with wisdom, and faithful instruction is on her tongue. 27She watches over the affairs of her household and does not eat the bread of idleness. 28Her children arise and call her blessed; her husband also, and he praises her: 29"Many women do noble things, but you surpass them all." 30Charm is deceptive, and beauty is fleeting; but a woman who fears the LORD is to be praised. 31Give her the reward she has earned, and let her works bring her praise at the city gate.

III
Women as Participants in Religion

A. Women in OT Worship

1. Women Prayed and Were Answered by God

a) Hannah

1 Sam 1 10In bitterness of soul Hannah wept much and prayed to the LORD. 11And she made a vow, saying, "O LORD Almighty, if you will only look upon your servant's misery and remember me, and not forget your servant but give her a son, then I will give him to the LORD for all the days of his life, and no razor will ever be used on his head."

12As she kept on praying to the LORD, Eli observed her mouth. 13Hannah was praying in her heart, and her lips were moving but her voice was not heard. Eli thought she was drunk 14and said to her, "How long will you keep on getting drunk? Get rid of your wine."

15"Not so, my lord," Hannah replied, "I am a woman who is

deeply troubled. I have not been drinking wine or beer; I was pouring out my soul to the LORD. [16]Do not take your servant for a wicked woman; I have been praying here out of my great anguish and grief."

[17]Eli answered, "Go in peace, and may the God of Israel grant you what you have asked of him."

[18]She said, "May your servant find favor in your eyes." Then she went her way and ate something, and her face was no longer downcast.

[19]Early the next morning they arose and worshiped before the LORD and then went back to their home at Ramah. Elkanah lay with Hannah his wife, and the LORD remembered her. [20]So in the course of time Hannah conceived and gave birth to a son. She named him Samuel, saying, "Because I asked the LORD for him."

b) Rachel

Gen 30 [6]Then Rachel said, "God has vindicated me; he has listened to my plea and given me a son." Because of this she named him Dan.

Gen 30 [22]Then God remembered Rachel; he listened to her and opened her womb.

c) Rebekah

Gen 25 [21]Isaac prayed to the LORD on behalf of his wife, because she was barren. The LORD answered his prayer, and his wife Rebekah became pregnant. [22]The babies jostled each other within her, and she said, "Why is this happening to me?" So she went to inquire of the LORD.

[23]The LORD said to her, "Two nations are in your womb, and two peoples from within you will be separated; one people will be stronger than the other, and the older will serve the younger."

2. Women Were Met by God

a) Hagar

Gen 16 [7]The angel of the LORD found Hagar near a spring in the desert; it was the spring that is beside the road to Shur. [8]And he said, "Hagar, servant of Sarai, where have you come from, and where are you going?"

"I'm running away from my mistress Sarai," she answered.

[9]Then the angel of the LORD told her, "Go back to your mistress and submit to her." [10]The angel added, "I will so increase your descendants that they will be too numerous to count."

[11]The angel of the LORD also said to her: "You are now with child and you will have a son. You shall name him Ishmael, for the LORD has heard of your misery. [12]He will be a wild donkey of a man; his hand will be against everyone and everyone's hand against him, and he will live in hostility toward all his brothers."

[13]She gave this name to the LORD who spoke to her: "You are the God who sees me," for she said, "I have now seen the One who sees me." [14]That is why the well was called Beer Lahai Roi; it is still there, between Kadesh and Bered.

b) Manoah's Wife

Judg 13 [2]A certain man of Zorah, named Manoah, from the clan of the Danites, had a wife who was sterile and remained childless. [3]The angel of the LORD appeared to her and said, "You are sterile and childless, but you are going to conceive and have a son. [4]Now see to it that you drink no wine or other fermented drink and that you do not eat anything unclean, [5]because you will conceive and give birth to a son. No razor may be used on his head, because the boy is to be a Nazirite, set apart to God from birth, and he will begin the deliverance of Israel from the hands of the Philistines."

[6]Then the woman went to her husband and told him, "A man of God came to me. He looked like an angel of God, very awesome. I didn't ask him where he came from, and he didn't tell me his name. [7]But he said to me, 'You will conceive and give birth to a son. Now then, drink no wine or other fermented drink and do not eat anything unclean, because the boy will be a Nazirite of God from birth until the day of his death.'"

[8]Then Manoah prayed to the LORD: "O Lord, I beg you, let the man of God you sent to us come again to teach us how to bring up the boy who is to be born."

[9]God heard Manoah, and the angel of God came again to the woman while she was out in the field; but her husband Manoah was not with her. [10]The woman hurried to tell her husband, "He's here! The man who appeared to me the other day!"

[11]Manoah got up and followed his wife. When he came to the man, he said, "Are you the one who talked to my wife?"

"I am," he said.

[12]So Manoah asked him, "When your words are fulfilled, what is to be the rule for the boy's life and work?"

[13]The angel of the LORD answered, "Your wife must do all that I have told her."

3. Women Praised God's Work

Exod 15 [20]Then Miriam the prophetess, Aaron's sister, took a tambourine in her hand, and all the women followed her, with tambourines and dancing. [21]Miriam sang to them: "Sing to the LORD, for he is highly exalted. The horse and its rider he has hurled into the sea."

Judg 11 [34]When Jephthah returned to his home in Mizpah, who should come out to meet him but his daughter, dancing to the sound of tambourines! She was an only child. Except for her he had neither son nor daughter.

1 Sam 18 [6]When the men were returning home after David had killed the Philistine, the women came out from all the towns of Israel to meet King Saul with singing and dancing, with joyful songs and with tambourines and lutes. [7]As they danced, they sang: "Saul has slain his thousands, and David his tens of thousands."

4. Women Were Required to Attend the Reading of the Law

Deut 31 [12]"Assemble the people—men, women and children, and the aliens living in your towns—so they can listen and learn to fear the LORD your God and follow carefully all the words of this law."

Josh 8 [35]There was not a word of all that Moses had commanded that Joshua did not read to the whole assembly of Israel, including the women and children, and the aliens who lived among them.

5. Women Brought Sacrifices for Purification

Lev 12 [6]"'When the days of her purification for a son or daughter are over, she is to bring to the priest at the entrance to the Tent of Meeting a year-old lamb for a burnt offering and a young pigeon or a dove for a sin offering. [7]He shall offer them before the LORD to make atonement for her, and then she will be ceremonially clean from her flow of blood.

"'These are the regulations for the woman who gives birth to a boy or a girl.'"

Lev 15 [28]"'When she is cleansed from her discharge, she must count off seven days, and after that she will be ceremonially clean. [29]On the eighth day she must take two doves or two young pigeons and bring them to the priest at the entrance to the Tent of Meeting. [30]The priest is to sacrifice one for a sin offering and the other for a burnt offering. In this way he will make atonement for her before the LORD for the uncleanness of her discharge.'"

6. Women Were Eligible for the Nazirite Vow

Num 6 [1]The LORD said to Moses, [2]"Speak to the Israelites and say to them: 'If a man or woman wants to make a special vow, a vow of separation to the LORD as a Nazirite, [3]he must abstain from wine and other fermented drink and must not drink vinegar made from wine or from other fermented drink. He must not drink grape juice or eat grapes or raisins. [4]As long as he is a Nazirite, he must not eat anything that comes from the grapevine, not even the seeds or skins.

[5]"'During the entire period of his vow of separation no razor may be used on his head. He must be holy until the period of his separation to the LORD is over; he must let the hair of his head grow long. [6]Throughout the period of his sepa-

ration to the LORD he must not go near a dead body. [7]Even if his own father or mother or brother or sister dies, he must not make himself ceremonially unclean on account of them, because the symbol of his separation to God is on his head. [8]Throughout the period of his separation he is consecrated to the LORD.'"

7. Women Served at the Tabernacle

Exod 38 [8]They made the bronze basin and its bronze stand from the mirrors of the women who served at the entrance to the Tent of Meeting.

8. Women Sang in Choirs

Ezra 2 [65]besides their 7,337 menservants and maidservants; and they also had 200 men and women singers.

B. Women in the Ministry of Jesus

1. Women in Jesus' Life

a) Women in Jesus' Genealogy

(1) Tamar

Matt 1 [3]Judah the father of Perez and Zerah, whose mother was Tamar, Perez the father of Hezron, Hezron the father of Ram . . .

(2) Rahab

Matt 1 [5]Salmon the father of Boaz, whose mother was Rahab, Boaz the father of Obed, whose mother was Ruth, Obed the father of Jesse . . .

(3) Ruth

Matt 1 [5]Salmon the father of Boaz, whose mother was Rahab, Boaz the father of Obed, whose mother was Ruth, Obed the father of Jesse . . .

(4) Bathsheba

Matt 1 [6]and Jesse the father of King David. David was the father of Solomon, whose mother had been Uriah's wife. . . .

(5) Mary

Matt 1 [16]and Jacob the father of Joseph, the husband of Mary, of whom was born Jesus, who is called Christ.

b) Women in Jesus' Public Career

(1) Women Cared for Jesus' Personal Needs

Matt 8 [14]When Jesus came into Peter's house, he saw Peter's mother-in-law lying in bed with a fever. [15]He touched her hand and the fever left her, and she got up and began to wait on him.
Matt 27 [55]Many women were there, watching from a distance. They had followed Jesus from Galilee to care for his needs. [56]Among them were Mary Magdalene, Mary the mother of James and Joses, and the mother of Zebedee's sons.
Mark 15 [41]In Galilee these women had followed him and cared for his needs. Many other women who had come up with him to Jerusalem were also there.
Luke 8 [1]After this, Jesus traveled about from one town and village to another, proclaiming the good news of the kingdom of God. The Twelve were with him, [2]and also some women who had been cured of evil spirits and diseases: Mary (called Magdalene) from whom seven demons had come out; [3]Joanna the wife of Cuza, the manager of Herod's household; Susanna; and many others. These women were helping to support them out of their own means.

(2) Women Listened to Jesus' Teaching

Luke 10 [38]As Jesus and his disciples were on their way, he came to a village where a woman named Martha opened her home to him. [39]She had a sister called Mary, who sat at the Lord's feet listening to what he said. [40]But Martha was distracted by all the preparations that had to be made. She came to him and asked, "Lord, don't you care that my sister has left me to do the work by myself? Tell her to help me!"

[41]"Martha, Martha," the Lord answered, "you are worried and upset about many things, [42]but only one thing is needed. Mary has chosen what is better, and it will not be taken away from her."

(3) Women Remained at the Cross

Mark 15 [40]Some women were watching from a distance. Among them were Mary Magdalene, Mary the mother of James the younger and of Joses, and Salome. [41]In Galilee these women had followed him and cared for his needs. Many other women who had come up with him to Jerusalem were also there.
Luke 23 [27]A large number of people followed him, including women who mourned and wailed for him.
Luke 23 [49]But all those who knew him, including the women who had followed him from Galilee, stood at a distance, watching these things.
John 19 [25]Near the cross of Jesus stood his mother, his mother's sister, Mary the wife of Clopas, and Mary Magdalene.

(4) Women Went to the Tomb to Embalm Jesus' Body

Mark 15 [46]So Joseph bought some linen cloth, took down the body, wrapped it in the linen, and placed it in a tomb cut out of rock. Then he rolled a stone against the entrance of the tomb. [47]Mary Magdalene and Mary the mother of Joses saw where he was laid.
Mark 16 [1]When the Sabbath was over, Mary Magdalene, Mary the mother of James, and Salome bought spices so that they might go to anoint Jesus' body. [2]Very early on the first day of the week, just after sunrise, they were on their way to the tomb [3]and they asked each other, "Who will roll the stone away from the entrance of the tomb?"

[4]But when they looked up, they saw that the stone, which was very large, had been rolled away. [5]As they entered the tomb, they saw a young man dressed in a white robe sitting on the right side, and they were alarmed.

[6]"Don't be alarmed," he said. "You are looking for Jesus the Nazarene, who was crucified. He has risen! He is not here. See the place where they laid him. [7]But go, tell his disciples and Peter, 'He is going ahead of you into Galilee. There you will see him, just as he told you.'"

[8]Trembling and bewildered, the women went out and fled from the tomb. They said nothing to anyone, because they were afraid.
Luke 23 [55]The women who had come with Jesus from Galilee followed Joseph and saw the tomb and how his body was laid in it. [56]Then they went home and prepared spices and perfumes. But they rested on the Sabbath in obedience to the commandment.
Luke 24 [1]On the first day of the week, very early in the morning, the women took the spices they had prepared and went to the tomb. [2]They found the stone rolled away from the tomb, [3]but when they entered, they did not find the body of the Lord Jesus. [4]While they were wondering about this, suddenly two men in clothes that gleamed like lightning stood beside them. [5]In their fright the women bowed down with their faces to the ground, but the men said to them, "Why do you look for the living among the dead? [6]He is not here; he has risen! Remember how he told you, while he was still with you in Galilee: [7]'The Son of Man must be delivered into the hands of sinful men, be crucified and on the third day be raised again.'" [8]Then they remembered his words.

[9]When they came back from the tomb, they told all these things to the Eleven and to all the others. [10]It was Mary Magdalene, Joanna, Mary the mother of James, and the others with them who told this to the apostles. [11]But they did not believe the women, because their words seemed to them like nonsense. [12]Peter, however, got up and ran to the tomb. Bending over, he saw the strips of linen lying by themselves, and he went away, wondering to himself what had happened.

(5) Women Witnessed First the Resurrected Christ

Matt 28 [1]After the Sabbath, at dawn on the first day of the week, Mary Magdalene and the other Mary went to look at the tomb.

[2]There was a violent earthquake, for an angel of the Lord came down from heaven and, going to the tomb, rolled back

the stone and sat on it. 3His appearance was like lightning, and his clothes were white as snow. 4The guards were so afraid of him that they shook and became like dead men.

5The angel said to the women, "Do not be afraid, for I know that you are looking for Jesus, who was crucified. 6He is not here; he has risen, just as he said. Come and see the place where he lay. 7Then go quickly and tell his disciples: 'He has risen from the dead and is going ahead of you into Galilee. There you will see him.' Now I have told you."

8So the women hurried away from the tomb, afraid yet filled with joy, and ran to tell his disciples. 9Suddenly Jesus met them. "Greetings," he said. They came to him, clasped his feet and worshiped him. 10Then Jesus said to them, "Do not be afraid. Go and tell my brothers to go to Galilee; there they will see me."

John 20 1Early on the first day of the week, while it was still dark, Mary Magdalene went to the tomb and saw that the stone had been removed from the entrance. 2So she came running to Simon Peter and the other disciple, the one Jesus loved, and said, "They have taken the Lord out of the tomb, and we don't know where they have put him!" . . .

10Then the disciples went back to their homes, 11but Mary stood outside the tomb crying. As she wept, she bent over to look into the tomb 12and saw two angels in white, seated where Jesus' body had been, one at the head and the other at the foot.

13They asked her, "Woman, why are you crying?"

"They have taken my Lord away," she said, "and I don't know where they have put him." 14At this, she turned around and saw Jesus standing there, but she did not realize that it was Jesus.

15"Woman," he said, "why are you crying? Who is it you are looking for?"

Thinking he was the gardener, she said, "Sir, if you have carried him away, tell me where you have put him, and I will get him."

16Jesus said to her, "Mary."

She turned toward him and cried out in Aramaic, "Rabboni!" (which means Teacher).

17Jesus said, "Do not hold on to me, for I have not yet returned to the Father. Go instead to my brothers and tell them, 'I am returning to my Father and your Father, to my God and your God.'"

18Mary Magdalene went to the disciples with the news: "I have seen the Lord!" And she told them that he had said these things to her.

2. Women in Jesus' Teaching

a) Women Are the Central Characters in Some Parables

(1) The Parable of the Lost Coin

Luke 15 8"Or suppose a woman has ten silver coins and loses one. Does she not light a lamp, sweep the house and search carefully until she finds it? 9And when she finds it, she calls her friends and neighbors together and says, 'Rejoice with me; I have found my lost coin.' 10In the same way, I tell you, there is rejoicing in the presence of the angels of God over one sinner who repents."

(2) The Parable of the Persistent Widow

Luke 18 1Then Jesus told his disciples a parable to show them that they should always pray and not give up. 2He said: "In a certain town there was a judge who neither feared God nor cared about men. 3And there was a widow in that town who kept coming to him with the plea, 'Grant me justice against my adversary.'

4"For some time he refused. But finally he said to himself, 'Even though I don't fear God or care about men, 5yet because this widow keeps bothering me, I will see that she gets justice, so that she won't eventually wear me out with her coming!'"

6And the Lord said, "Listen to what the unjust judge says. 7And will not God bring about justice for his chosen ones, who cry out to him day and night? Will he keep putting them off? 8I tell you, he will see that they get justice, and quickly. However, when the Son of Man comes, will he find faith on the earth?"

(3) The Parable of the Ten Virgins

Matt 25 1"At that time the kingdom of heaven will be like ten virgins who took their lamps and went out to meet the bridegroom. 2Five of them were foolish and five were wise. 3The foolish ones took their lamps but did not take any oil with them. 4The wise, however, took oil in jars along with their lamps. 5The bridegroom was a long time in coming, and they all became drowsy and fell asleep.

6"At midnight the cry rang out: 'Here's the bridegroom! Come out to meet him!'

7"Then all the virgins woke up and trimmed their lamps. 8The foolish ones said to the wise, 'Give us some of your oil; our lamps are going out.'

9"'No,' they replied, 'there may not be enough for both us and you. Instead, go to those who sell oil and buy some for yourselves.'

10"But while they were on their way to buy the oil, the bridegroom arrived. The virgins who were ready went in with him to the wedding banquet. And the door was shut.

11"Later the others also came. 'Sir! Sir!' they said. 'Open the door for us!'

12"But he replied, 'I tell you the truth, I don't know you.'

13"Therefore keep watch, because you do not know the day or the hour."

(4) The Parable of Yeast and Flour

Matt 13 33He told them still another parable: "The kingdom of heaven is like yeast that a woman took and mixed into a large amount of flour until it worked all through the dough."

b) Women Are Members of the Kingdom of God

Matt 12 49Pointing to his disciples, he said, "Here are my mother and my brothers. 50For whoever does the will of my Father in heaven is my brother and sister and mother."

Mark 3 34Then he looked at those seated in a circle around him and said, "Here are my mother and my brothers! 35Whoever does God's will is my brother and sister and mother."

Luke 8 21He replied, "My mother and brothers are those who hear God's word and put it into practice."

c) The Family Is Important

(1) The Sanctity of Marriage

Mark 10 2Some Pharisees came and tested him by asking, "Is it lawful for a man to divorce his wife?"

3"What did Moses command you?" he replied.

4They said, "Moses permitted a man to write a certificate of divorce and send her away."

5"It was because your hearts were hard that Moses wrote you this law," Jesus replied. 6"But at the beginning of creation God 'made them male and female.' 7'For this reason a man will leave his father and mother and be united to his wife, 8and the two will become one flesh.' So they are no longer two, but one. 9Therefore what God has joined together, let man not separate."

10When they were in the house again, the disciples asked Jesus about this. 11He answered, "Anyone who divorces his wife and marries another woman commits adultery against her. 12And if she divorces her husband and marries another man, she commits adultery."

(2) The Honoring of Parents

Mark 7 9And he said to them: "You have a fine way of setting aside the commands of God in order to observe your own traditions! 10For Moses said, 'Honor your father and your mother,' and, 'Anyone who curses his father or mother must be put to death.' 11But you say that if a man says to his father or mother 'Whatever help you might otherwise have received from me is Corban' (that is, a gift devoted to God), 12then you no longer let him do anything for his father or mother. 13Thus you nullify the word of God by your tradition that you have handed down. And you do many things like that."

3. Women as Examples of Faith

a) A Canaanite Woman

Matt 15 22A Canaanite woman from that vicinity came to him, crying out, "Lord, Son of David, have mercy on me! My daughter is suffering terribly from demon-possession."

[23]Jesus did not answer a word. So his disciples came to him and urged him, "Send her away, for she keeps crying out after us."

[24]He answered, "I was sent only to the lost sheep of Israel."

[25]The woman came and knelt before him. "Lord, help me!" she said.

[26]He replied, "It is not right to take the children's bread and toss it to their dogs."

[27]"Yes, Lord," she said, "but even the dogs eat the crumbs that fall from their masters' table."

[28]Then Jesus answered, "Woman, you have great faith! Your request is granted." And her daughter was healed from that very hour.

b) A Crippled Woman

Luke 13 [10]On a Sabbath Jesus was teaching in one of the synagogues, [11]and a woman was there who had been crippled by a spirit for eighteen years. She was bent over and could not straighten up at all. [12]When Jesus saw her, he called her forward and said to her, "Woman, you are set free from your infirmity." [13]Then he put his hands on her, and immediately she straightened up and praised God.

[14]Indignant because Jesus had healed on the Sabbath, the synagogue ruler said to the people, "There are six days for work. So come and be healed on those days, not on the Sabbath."

[15]The Lord answered him, "You hypocrites! Doesn't each of you on the Sabbath untie his ox or donkey from the stall and lead it out to give it water? [16]Then should not this woman, a daughter of Abraham, whom Satan has kept bound for eighteen long years, be set free on the Sabbath day from what bound her?"

[17]When he said this, all his opponents were humiliated, but the people were delighted with all the wonderful things he was doing.

c) A Generous Widow

Mark 12 [41]Jesus sat down opposite the place where the offerings were put and watched the crowd putting their money into the temple treasury. Many rich people threw in large amounts. [42]But a poor widow came and put in two very small copper coins, worth only a fraction of a penny.

[43]Calling his disciples to him, Jesus said, "I tell you the truth, this poor widow has put more into the treasury than all the others. [44]They all gave out of their wealth; but she, out of her poverty, put in everything—all she had to live on."

d) Martha

John 11 [21]"Lord," Martha said to Jesus, "if you had been here, my brother would not have died. [22]But I know that even now God will give you whatever you ask."

[23]Jesus said to her, "Your brother will rise again."

[24]Martha answered, "I know he will rise again in the resurrection at the last day."

[25]Jesus said to her, "I am the resurrection and the life. He who believes in me will live, even though he dies; [26]and whoever lives and believes in me will never die. Do you believe this?"

[27]"Yes, Lord," she told him, "I believe that you are the Christ, the Son of God, who was to come into the world."

e) Mary, Mother of Jesus

John 2 [1]On the third day a wedding took place at Cana in Galilee. Jesus' mother was there, [2]and Jesus and his disciples had also been invited to the wedding. [3]When the wine was gone, Jesus' mother said to him, "They have no more wine."

[4]"Dear woman, why do you involve me?" Jesus replied, "My time has not yet come."

[5]His mother said to the servants, "Do whatever he tells you."

f) The Queen of the South

Luke 11 [31]"The Queen of the South will rise at the judgment with the men of this generation and condemn them; for she came from the ends of the earth to listen to Solomon's wisdom, and now one greater than Solomon is here."

g) A Samaritan Woman

John 4 [4]Now he had to go through Samaria. [5]So he came to a town in Samaria called Sychar, near the plot of ground Jacob had given to his son Joseph. [6]Jacob's well was there, and Jesus, tired as he was from the journey, sat down by the well. It was about the sixth hour.

[7]When a Samaritan woman came to draw water, Jesus said to her, "Will you give me a drink?" [8](His disciples had gone into the town to buy food.)

[9]The Samaritan woman said to him, "You are a Jew and I am a Samaritan woman. How can you ask me for a drink?" (For Jews do not associate with Samaritans.)

[10]Jesus answered her, "If you knew the gift of God and who it is that asks you for a drink, you would have asked him and he would have given you living water."

[11]"Sir," the woman said, "you have nothing to draw with and the well is deep. Where can you get this living water? [12]Are you greater than our father Jacob, who gave us the well and drank from it himself, as did also his sons and his flocks and herds?"

[13]Jesus answered, "Everyone who drinks this water will be thirsty again, [14]but whoever drinks the water I give him will never thirst. Indeed, the water I give him will become in him a spring of water welling up to eternal life."

[15]The woman said to him, "Sir, give me this water so that I won't get thirsty and have to keep coming here to draw water."

[16]He told her, "Go, call your husband and come back."

[17]"I have no husband," she replied.

Jesus said to her, "You are right when you say you have no husband. [18]The fact is, you have had five husbands, and the man you now have is not your husband. What you have just said is quite true."

[19]"Sir," the woman said, "I can see that you are a prophet. [20]Our fathers worshiped on this mountain, but you Jews claim that the place where we must worship is in Jerusalem."

[21]Jesus declared, "Believe me, woman, a time is coming when you will worship the Father neither on this mountain nor in Jerusalem. [22]You Samaritans worship what you do not know; we worship what we do know, for salvation is from the Jews. [23]Yet a time is coming and has now come when the true worshipers will worship the Father in spirit and truth, for they are the kind of worshipers the Father seeks. [24]God is spirit, and his worshipers must worship in spirit and in truth."

[25]The woman said, "I know that Messiah" (called Christ) "is coming. When he comes, he will explain everything to us."

[26]Then Jesus declared, "I who speak to you am he."

[27]Just then his disciples returned and were surprised to find him talking with a woman. But no one asked, "What do you want?" or "Why are you talking with her?"

[28]Then, leaving her water jar, the woman went back to the town and said to the people, [29]"Come, see a man who told me everything I ever did. Could this be the Christ?" [30]They came out of the town and made their way toward him.

h) A Sick Woman

Mark 5 [25]And a woman was there who had been subject to bleeding for twelve years. [26]She had suffered a great deal under the care of many doctors and had spent all she had, yet instead of getting better she grew worse. [27]When she heard about Jesus, she came up behind him in the crowd and touched his cloak, [28]because she thought, "If I just touch his clothes, I will be healed." [29]Immediately her bleeding stopped and she felt in her body that she was freed from her suffering.

[30]At once Jesus realized that power had gone out from him. He turned around in the crowd and asked, "Who touched my clothes?"

[31]"You see the people crowding against you," his disciples answered, "and yet you can ask, 'Who touched me?'"

[32]But Jesus kept looking around to see who had done it. [33]Then the woman, knowing what had happened to her, came and fell at his feet and, trembling with fear, told him the whole truth. [34]He said to her, "Daughter, your faith has healed you. Go in peace and be freed from your suffering."

i) The Woman Who Anointed Jesus

Mark 14 [3]While he was in Bethany, reclining at the table in the home of a man known as Simon the Leper, a woman came with an alabaster jar of very expensive perfume, made of pure nard. She broke the jar and poured the perfume on his head.

[4]Some of those present were saying indignantly to one another, "Why this waste of perfume? [5]It could have been sold for more than a year's wages and the money given to the poor." And they rebuked her harshly.

[6]"Leave her alone," said Jesus. "Why are you bothering her? She has done a beautiful thing to me. [7]The poor you will always have with you, and you can help them any time you want. But you will not always have me. [8]She did what she could. She poured perfume on my body beforehand to prepare for my burial. [9]I tell you the truth, wherever the gospel is preached throughout the world, what she has done will also be told, in memory of her."

Luke 7 [36]Now one of the Pharisees invited Jesus to have dinner with him, so he went to the Pharisee's house and reclined at the table. [37]When a woman who had lived a sinful life in that town learned that Jesus was eating at the Pharisee's house, she brought an alabaster jar of perfume, [38]and as she stood behind him at his feet weeping, she began to wet his feet with her tears. Then she wiped them with her hair, kissed them and poured perfume on them.

[39]When the Pharisee who had invited him saw this, he said to himself, "If this man were a prophet, he would know who is touching him and what kind of woman she is—that she is a sinner."

[40]Jesus answered him, "Simon, I have something to tell you."

"Tell me, teacher," he said.

[41]"Two men owed money to a certain moneylender. One owed him five hundred denarii, and the other fifty. [42]Neither of them had the money to pay him back, so he canceled the debts of both. Now which of them will love him more?"

[43]Simon replied, "I suppose the one who had the bigger debt canceled."

"You have judged correctly," Jesus said.

[44]Then he turned toward the woman and said to Simon, "Do you see this woman? I came into your house. You did not give me any water for my feet, but she wet my feet with her tears and wiped them with her hair. [45]You did not give me a kiss, but this woman, from the time I entered, has not stopped kissing my feet. [46]You did not put oil on my head, but she has poured perfume on my feet. [47]Therefore, I tell you, her many sins have been forgiven—for she loved much. But he who has been forgiven little loves little."

[48]Then Jesus said to her, "Your sins are forgiven."

[49]The other guests began to say among themselves, "Who is this who even forgives sins?"

[50]Jesus said to the woman, "Your faith has saved you; go in peace."

C. Women in the Early Church

1. Women Received the Promised Spirit of God

Acts 2 [17]"'In the last days, God says, I will pour out my Spirit on all people. Your sons and daughters will prophesy, your young men will see visions, your old men will dream dreams. [18]Even on my servants, both men and women, I will pour out my Spirit in those days, and they will prophesy.'"

2. Women Were Invited to Believe

Acts 2 [21]"'And everyone who calls on the name of the Lord will be saved.'"

3. Women Were Part of the Believing Community

a) Women Became Members of the Church

Acts 1 [12]Then they returned to Jerusalem from the hill called the Mount of Olives, a Sabbath day's walk from the city. [13]When they arrived, they went upstairs to the room where they were staying. Those present were Peter, John, James and Andrew; Philip and Thomas, Bartholomew and Matthew; James son of Alphaeus and Simon the Zealot, and Judas son of James. [14]They all joined together constantly in prayer, along with the women and Mary the mother of Jesus, and with his brothers.

Acts 5 [14]Nevertheless, more and more men and women believed in the Lord and were added to their number.

Acts 8 [5]Philip went down to a city in Samaria and proclaimed the Christ there. . . .

[12]But when they believed Philip as he preached the good news of the kingdom of God and the name of Jesus Christ, they were baptized, both men and women.

Acts 17 [1]When they had passed through Amphipolis and Apollonia, they came to Thessalonica, where there was a Jewish synagogue. . . . [4]Some of the Jews were persuaded and joined Paul and Silas, as did a large number of God-fearing Greeks and not a few prominent women.

Acts 17 [10]As soon as it was night, the brothers sent Paul and Silas away to Berea. On arriving there, they went to the Jewish synagogue. . . . [12]Many of the Jews believed, as did also a number of prominent Greek women and many Greek men.

b) Women Were Recognized as Part of the Church

(1) Claudia (Rome)

2 Tim 4 [21]Do your best to get here before winter. Eubulus greets you, and so do Pudens, Linus, Claudia and all the brothers.

(2) Damaris (Athens)

Acts 17 [34]A few men became followers of Paul and believed. Among them was Dionysius, a member of the Areopagus, also a woman named Damaris, and a number of others.

(3) Eunice (Lystra)

Acts 16 [1]He came to Derbe and then to Lystra, where a disciple named Timothy lived, whose mother was a Jewess and a believer, but whose father was a Greek.

2 Tim 1 [5]I have been reminded of your sincere faith, which first lived in your grandmother Lois and in your mother Eunice and, I am persuaded, now lives in you also.

(4) Euodia (Philippi)

Phil 4 [2]I plead with Euodia and I plead with Syntyche to agree with each other in the Lord. [3]Yes, and I ask you, loyal yokefellow, help these women who have contended at my side in the cause of the gospel, along with Clement and the rest of my fellow workers, whose names are in the book of life.

(5) Julia (Rome)

Rom 16 [15]Greet Philologus, Julia, Nereus and his sister, and Olympas and all the saints with them.

(6) Lois (Lystra)

2 Tim 1 [5]I have been reminded of your sincere faith, which first lived in your grandmother Lois and in your mother Eunice and, I am persuaded, now lives in you also.

(7) Lydia (Philippi)

Acts 16 [14]One of those listening was a woman named Lydia, a dealer in purple cloth from the city of Thyatira, who was a worshiper of God. The Lord opened her heart to respond to Paul's message. [15]When she and the members of her household were baptized, she invited us to her home. "If you consider me a believer in the Lord," she said, "come and stay at my house." And she persuaded us.

(8) Mary (Rome)

Rom 16 [6]Greet Mary, who worked very hard for you.

(9) Mother of Rufus (Rome)

Rom 16 [13]Greet Rufus, chosen in the Lord, and his mother, who has been a mother to me, too.

(10) Persis (Rome)

Rom 16 [12]Greet Tryphena and Tryphosa, those women who work hard in the Lord. Greet my dear friend Persis, another woman who has worked very hard in the Lord.

(11) Phoebe (Cenchrea)

Rom 16 [1]I commend to you our sister Phoebe, a servant of the church in Cenchrea. [2]I ask you to receive her in the Lord in a way worthy of the saints and to give her any help she may need from you, for she has been a great help to many people, including me.

(12) Priscilla (Rome)

Acts 18 [1]After this, Paul left Athens and went to Corinth. [2]There he met a Jew named Aquila, a native of Pontus, who had recently come from Italy with his wife Priscilla, because Claudius had ordered all the Jews to leave Rome. Paul went to see them, [3]and because he was a tentmaker as they were, he stayed and worked with them. . . .

[18]Paul stayed on in Corinth for some time. Then he left the brothers and sailed for Syria, accompanied by Priscilla and Aquila. Before he sailed, he had his hair cut off at Cenchrea because of a vow he had taken. [19]They arrived at Ephesus, where Paul left Priscilla and Aquila. He himself went into the synagogue and reasoned with the Jews. . . . [26][Apollos] began to speak boldly in the synagogue. When Priscilla and Aquila heard him, they invited him to their home and explained to him the way of God more adequately.

Rom 16 [3]Greet Priscilla and Aquila, my fellow workers in Christ Jesus. [4]They risked their lives for me. Not only I but all the churches of the Gentiles are grateful to them.

[5]Greet also the church that meets at their house.

1 Cor 16 [19]The churches in the province of Asia send you greetings. Aquila and Priscilla greet you warmly in the Lord, and so does the church that meets at their house.

2 Tim 4 [19]Greet Priscilla and Aquila and the household of Onesiphorus.

(13) Sister of Nereus (Rome)

Rom 16 [15]Greet Philologus, Julia, Nereus and his sister, and Olympas and all the saints with them.

(14) Syntyche (Philippi)

Phil 4 [2]I plead with Euodia and I plead with Syntyche to agree with each other in the Lord. [3]Yes, and I ask you, loyal yokefellow, help these women who have contended at my side in the cause of the gospel, along with Clement and the rest of my fellow workers, whose names are in the book of life.

(15) Tabitha (Joppa)

Acts 9 [36]In Joppa there was a disciple named Tabitha (which, when translated, is Dorcas), who was always doing good and helping the poor.

(16) Tryphena (Rome)

Rom 16 [12]Greet Tryphena and Tryphosa, those women who work hard in the Lord. Greet my dear friend Persis, another woman who has worked very hard in the Lord.

(17) Tryphosa (Rome)

Rom 16 [12]Greet Tryphena and Tryphosa, those women who work hard in the Lord. Greet my dear friend Persis, another woman who has worked very hard in the Lord.

4. Women Were Workers in the Church of God

a) Women Were Administrators

Rom 16 [1]I commend to you our sister Phoebe, a servant of the church in Cenchrea. [2]I ask you to receive her in the Lord in a way worthy of the saints and to give her any help she may need from you, for she has been a great help to many people, including me.

b) Women Cared for the Poor

Acts 9 [36]In Joppa there was a disciple named Tabitha (which, when translated, is Dorcas), who was always doing good and helping the poor.

c) Women Cared for Widows and Others

Acts 9 [39]Peter went with them, and when he arrived he was taken upstairs to the room. All the widows stood around him, crying and showing him the robes and other clothing that Dorcas had made while she was still with them.

1 Tim 5 [3]Give proper recognition to those widows who are really in need. [4]But if a widow has children or grandchildren, these should learn first of all to put their religion into practice by caring for their own family and so repaying their parents and grandparents, for this is pleasing to God. . . . [8]If anyone does not provide for his relatives, and especially for his immediate family, he has denied the faith and is worse than an unbeliever.

[9]No widow may be put on the list of widows unless she is over sixty, has been faithful to her husband, [10]and is well known for her good deeds, such as bringing up children, showing hospitality, washing the feet of the saints, helping those in trouble and devoting herself to all kinds of good deeds. . . .

[16]If any woman who is a believer has widows in her family, she should help them and not let the church be burdened with them, so that the church can help those widows who are really in need.

d) Women Played Host to Believers

Acts 12 [12]When this had dawned on him, he went to the house of Mary the mother of John, also called Mark, where many people had gathered and were praying.

Acts 16 [15]When she and the members of her household were baptized, she invited us to her home. "If you consider me a believer in the Lord," she said, "come and stay at my house." And she persuaded us.

Rom 16 [3]Greet Priscilla and Aquila, my fellow workers in Christ Jesus. . . . [5]Greet also the church that meets at their house. Greet my dear friend Epenetus, who was the first convert to Christ in the province of Asia.

1 Cor 16 [19]The churches in the province of Asia send you greetings. Aquila and Priscilla greet you warmly in the Lord, and so does the church that meets at their house.

Col 4 [15]Give my greetings to the brothers at Laodicea, and to Nympha and the church in her house.

e) Women Instructed Believers

Acts 18 [24]Meanwhile a Jew named Apollos, a native of Alexandria, came to Ephesus. He was a learned man, with a thorough knowledge of the Scriptures. [25]He had been instructed in the way of the Lord, and he spoke with great fervor and taught about Jesus accurately, though he knew only the baptism of John. [26]He began to speak boldly in the synagogue. When Priscilla and Aquila heard him, they invited him to their home and explained to him the way of God more adequately.

f) Women Prophesied

Acts 21 [9]He had four unmarried daughters who prophesied.

1 Cor 11 [5]And every woman who prays or prophesies with her head uncovered dishonors her head—it is just as though her head were shaved.

g) Women Served as Fellow Workers

Rom 16 [3]Greet Priscilla and Aquila, my fellow workers in Christ Jesus. [4]They risked their lives for me. Not only I but all the churches of the Gentiles are grateful to them.

Phil 4 [2]I plead with Euodia and I plead with Syntyche to agree with each other in the Lord. [3]Yes, and I ask you, loyal yokefellow, help these women who have contended at my side in the cause of the gospel, along with Clement and the rest of my fellow workers, whose names are in the book of life.

5. Women Worshiped God

1 Tim 2 [9]I also want women to dress modestly, with decency and propriety, not with braided hair or gold or pearls or expensive clothes, [10]but with good deeds, appropriate for women who profess to worship God.

6. Women Were Equal with Men before God

Gal 3 [28]There is neither Jew nor Greek, slave nor free, male nor female, for you are all one in Christ Jesus.

9

Sin

I
The Nature of Sin

A. Sin Contradicts All That Is God

Gen 39 [9]"No one is greater in this house than I am. My master has withheld nothing from me except you, because you are his wife. How then could I do such a wicked thing and sin against God?"
Lev 19 [2]"Speak to the entire assembly of Israel and say to them: 'Be holy because I, the LORD your God, am holy.'"
Deut 32 [4]He is the Rock, his works are perfect, and all his ways are just. A faithful God who does no wrong, upright and just is he.

Job 25 4"How then can a man be righteous before God? How can one born of woman be pure? 5If even the moon is not bright and the stars are not pure in his eyes, 6how much less man, who is but a maggot—a son of man, who is only a worm!"

Job 34 10"So listen to me, you men of understanding. Far be it from God to do evil, from the Almighty to do wrong."

Job 42 1Then Job replied to the LORD: 2"I know that you can do all things; no plan of yours can be thwarted. 3You asked, 'Who is this that obscures my counsel without knowledge?' Surely I spoke of things I did not understand, things too wonderful for me to know.

4"You said, 'Listen now, and I will speak; I will question you, and you shall answer me.' 5My ears had heard of you but now my eyes have seen you. 6Therefore I despise myself and repent in dust and ashes."

Ps 18 30As for God, his way is perfect; the word of the LORD is flawless. He is a shield for all who take refuge in him.

Ps 33 4For the word of the LORD is right and true; he is faithful in all he does. 5The LORD loves righteousness and justice; the earth is full of his unfailing love.

Ps 47 8God reigns over the nations; God is seated on his holy throne.

Ps 48 10Like your name, O God, your praise reaches to the ends of the earth; your right hand is filled with righteousness.

Ps 51 4Against you, you only, have I sinned and done what is evil in your sight, so that you are proved right when you speak and justified when you judge.

Ps 92 15proclaiming, "The LORD is upright; he is my Rock, and there is no wickedness in him."

Ps 145 17The LORD is righteous in all his ways and loving toward all he has made.

Isa 6 1In the year that King Uzziah died, I saw the Lord seated on a throne, high and exalted, and the train of his robe filled the temple. 2Above him were seraphs, each with six wings: With two wings they covered their faces, with two they covered their feet, and with two they were flying. 3And they were calling to one another: "Holy, holy, holy is the LORD Almighty; the whole earth is full of his glory." 4At the sound of their voices the doorposts and thresholds shook and the temple was filled with smoke.

5"Woe to me!" I cried. "I am ruined! For I am a man of unclean lips, and I live among a people of unclean lips, and my eyes have seen the King, the LORD Almighty."

6Then one of the seraphs flew to me with a live coal in his hand, which he had taken with tongs from the altar.

Isa 57 15For this is what the high and lofty One says—he who lives forever, whose name is holy: "I live in a high and holy place, but also with him who is contrite and lowly in spirit, to revive the spirit of the lowly and to revive the heart of the contrite."

Isa 59 1Surely the arm of the LORD is not too short to save, nor his ear too dull to hear. 2But your iniquities have separated you from your God; your sins have hidden his face from you, so that he will not hear.

Isa 64 5You come to the help of those who gladly do right, who remember your ways. But when we continued to sin against them, you were angry. How then can we be saved? . . . 7No one calls on your name or strives to lay hold of you; for you have hidden your face from us and made us waste away because of our sins. . . . 9Do not be angry beyond measure, O LORD; do not remember our sins forever. Oh, look upon us, we pray, for we are all your people.

Jer 2 5This is what the LORD says: "What fault did your fathers find in me, that they strayed so far from me? They followed worthless idols and became worthless themselves."

Jer 2 29"Why do you bring charges against me? You have all rebelled against me," declares the LORD.

Ezek 39 7"'I will make known my holy name among my people Israel. I will no longer let my holy name be profaned, and the nations will know that I the LORD am the Holy One in Israel.'"

Hos 11 9"I will not carry out my fierce anger, nor will I turn and devastate Ephraim. For I am God, and not man—the Holy One among you. I will not come in wrath."

Amos 3 2"You only have I chosen of all the families of the earth; therefore I will punish you for all your sins."

3Do two walk together unless they have agreed to do so?

Mic 3 4Then they will cry out to the LORD, but he will not answer them. At that time he will hide his face from them because of the evil they have done.

Hab 1 12O LORD, are you not from everlasting? My God, my Holy One, we will not die. O LORD, you have appointed them to execute judgment; O Rock, you have ordained them to punish. 13Your eyes are too pure to look on evil; you cannot tolerate wrong. Why then do you tolerate the treacherous? Why are you silent while the wicked swallow up those more righteous than themselves?

Matt 5 48"Be perfect, therefore, as your heavenly Father is perfect."

Mark 10 18"Why do you call me good?" Jesus answered. "No one is good—except God alone."

Luke 5 8When Simon Peter saw this, he fell at Jesus' knees and said, "Go away from me, Lord; I am a sinful man!"

Luke 13 27"But he will reply, 'I don't know you or where you come from. Away from me, all you evildoers!'"

Rom 1 22Although they claimed to be wise, they became fools 23and exchanged the glory of the immortal God for images made to look like mortal man and birds and animals and reptiles.

Rom 9 14What then shall we say? Is God unjust? Not at all!

Heb 1 8But about the Son he says, "Your throne, O God, will last for ever and ever, and righteousness will be the scepter of your kingdom."

Heb 12 14Make every effort to live in peace with all men and to be holy; without holiness no one will see the Lord.

James 1 13When tempted, no one should say, "God is tempting me." For God cannot be tempted by evil, nor does he tempt anyone. . . .

1 Pet 1 15But just as he who called you is holy, so be holy in all you do; 16for it is written: "Be holy, because I am holy."

1 John 1 5This is the message we have heard from him and declare to you: God is light; in him there is no darkness at all.

Rev 4 8Each of the four living creatures had six wings and was covered with eyes all around, even under his wings. Day and night they never stop saying: "Holy, holy, holy is the Lord God Almighty, who was, and is, and is to come."

Rev 15 4"Who will not fear you, O Lord, and bring glory to your name? For you alone are holy. All nations will come and worship before you, for your righteous acts have been revealed."

B. Sin Is a Moral Inclination to Evil

Gen 6 5The LORD saw how great man's wickedness on the earth had become, and that every inclination of the thoughts of his heart was only evil all the time.

Gen 8 21The LORD smelled the pleasing aroma and said in his heart: "Never again will I curse the ground because of man, even though every inclination of his heart is evil from childhood. And never again will I destroy all living creatures, as I have done."

Job 14 4"Who can bring what is pure from the impure? No one!"

Job 15 14"What is man, that he could be pure, or one born of woman, that he could be righteous? 15If God places no trust in his holy ones, if even the heavens are not pure in his eyes, 16how much less man, who is vile and corrupt, who drinks up evil like water!"

Ps 5 9Not a word from their mouth can be trusted; their heart is filled with destruction. Their throat is an open grave; with their tongue they speak deceit.

Ps 14 1The fool says in his heart, "There is no God." They are corrupt, their deeds are vile; there is no one who does good.

2The LORD looks down from heaven on the sons of men to see if there are any who understand, any who seek God. 3All have turned aside, they have together become corrupt; there is no one who does good, not even one.

Ps 51 5Surely I have been a sinner from birth, sinful from the time my mother conceived me. . . .

7Cleanse me with hyssop, and I will be clean; wash me, and I will be whiter than snow. 8Let me hear joy and gladness; let the bones you have crushed rejoice. . . .

[10]Create in me a pure heart, O God, and renew a steadfast spirit within me.

Ps 94 [11]The LORD knows the thoughts of man; he knows that they are futile.

Ps 143 [2]Do not bring your servant into judgment, for no one living is righteous before you.

Eccles 7 [20]There is not a righteous man on earth who does what is right and never sins. . . .

[29]"This only have I found: God made mankind upright, but men have gone in search of many schemes."

Eccles 9 [3]This is the evil in everything that happens under the sun: The same destiny overtakes all. The hearts of men, moreover, are full of evil and there is madness in their hearts while they live, and afterward they join the dead.

Isa 1 [5]Why should you be beaten anymore? Why do you persist in rebellion? Your whole head is injured, your whole heart afflicted. [6]From the sole of your foot to the top of your head there is no soundness—only wounds and welts and open sores, not cleansed or bandaged or soothed with oil.

Isa 64 [6]All of us have become like one who is unclean, and all our righteous acts are like filthy rags; we all shrivel up like a leaf, and like the wind our sins sweep us away.

Jer 13 [23]"Can the Ethiopian change his skin or the leopard its spots? Neither can you do good who are accustomed to doing evil."

Jer 17 [9]The heart is deceitful above all things and beyond cure. Who can understand it?

Ezek 36 [25]"'I will sprinkle clean water on you, and you will be clean; I will cleanse you from all your impurities and from all your idols. [26]I will give you a new heart and put a new spirit in you; I will remove from you your heart of stone and give you a heart of flesh. [27]And I will put my Spirit in you and move you to follow my decrees and be careful to keep my laws.'"

Mic 7 [2]The godly have been swept from the land; not one upright man remains. All men lie in wait to shed blood; each hunts his brother with a net. [3]Both hands are skilled in doing evil; the ruler demands gifts, the judge accepts bribes, the powerful dictate what they desire—they all conspire together. [4]The best of them is like a brier, the most upright worse than a thorn hedge. The day of your watchmen has come, the day God visits you. Now is the time of their confusion.

Matt 7 [17]"Likewise every good tree bears good fruit, but a bad tree bears bad fruit. [18]A good tree cannot bear bad fruit, and a bad tree cannot bear good fruit. [19]Every tree that does not bear good fruit is cut down and thrown into the fire."

Matt 15 [17]"Don't you see that whatever enters the mouth goes into the stomach and then out of the body? [18]But the things that come out of the mouth come from the heart, and these make a man 'unclean.' [19]For out of the heart come evil thoughts, murder, adultery, sexual immorality, theft, false testimony, slander."

Luke 6 [45]"The good man brings good things out of the good stored up in his heart, and the evil man brings evil things out of the evil stored up in his heart. For out of the overflow of his heart his mouth speaks."

John 3 [19]"This is the verdict: Light has come into the world, but men loved darkness instead of light because their deeds were evil."

Rom 1 [21]For although they knew God, they neither glorified him as God nor gave thanks to him, but their thinking became futile and their foolish hearts were darkened. [22]Although they claimed to be wise, they became fools [23]and exchanged the glory of the immortal God for images made to look like mortal man and birds and animals and reptiles.

[24]Therefore God gave them over in the sinful desires of their hearts to sexual impurity for the degrading of their bodies with one another. [25]They exchanged the truth of God for a lie, and worshiped and served created things rather than the Creator—who is forever praised. Amen.

[26]Because of this, God gave them over to shameful lusts. Even their women exchanged natural relations for unnatural ones. [27]In the same way the men also abandoned natural relations with women and were inflamed with lust for one another. Men committed indecent acts with other men, and received in themselves the due penalty for their perversion.

[28]Furthermore, since they did not think it worthwhile to retain the knowledge of God, he gave them over to a depraved mind, to do what ought not to be done. [29]They have become filled with every kind of wickedness, evil, greed and depravity. They are full of envy, murder, strife, deceit and malice. They are gossips, [30]slanderers, God-haters, insolent, arrogant and boastful; they invent ways of doing evil; they disobey their parents; [31]they are senseless, faithless, heartless, ruthless. [32]Although they know God's righteous decree that those who do such things deserve death, they not only continue to do these very things but also approve of those who practice them.

Rom 5 [12]Therefore, just as sin entered the world through one man, and death through sin, and in this way death came to all men, because all sinned—[13]for before the law was given, sin was in the world. But sin is not taken into account when there is no law. [14]Nevertheless, death reigned from the time of Adam to the time of Moses, even over those who did not sin by breaking a command, as did Adam, who was a pattern of the one to come.

Rom 6 [12]Therefore do not let sin reign in your mortal body so that you obey its evil desires. [13]Do not offer the parts of your body to sin, as instruments of wickedness, but rather offer yourselves to God, as those who have been brought from death to life; and offer the parts of your body to him as instruments of righteousness. [14]For sin shall not be your master, because you are not under law, but under grace.

Rom 7 [14]We know that the law is spiritual; but I am unspiritual, sold as a slave to sin. [15]I do not understand what I do. For what I want to do I do not do, but what I hate I do. [16]And if I do what I do not want to do, I agree that the law is good. [17]As it is, it is no longer I myself who do it, but it is sin living in me. [18]I know that nothing good lives in me, that is, in my sinful nature. For I have the desire to do what is good, but I cannot carry it out. [19]For what I do is not the good I want to do; no, the evil I do not want to do—this I keep on doing. [20]Now if I do what I do not want to do, it is no longer I who do it, but it is sin living in me that does it.

[21]So I find this law at work: When I want to do good, evil is right there with me. [22]For in my inner being I delight in God's law; [23]but I see another law at work in the members of my body, waging war against the law of my mind and making me a prisoner of the law of sin at work within my members. [24]What a wretched man I am! Who will rescue me from this body of death? [25]Thanks be to God—through Jesus Christ our Lord!

So then, I myself in my mind am a slave to God's law, but in the sinful nature a slave to the law of sin.

Rom 8 [5]Those who live according to the sinful nature have their minds set on what that nature desires; but those who live in accordance with the Spirit have their minds set on what the Spirit desires. [6]The mind of sinful man is death, but the mind controlled by the Spirit is life and peace; [7]the sinful mind is hostile to God. It does not submit to God's law, nor can it do so. [8]Those controlled by the sinful nature cannot please God.

1 Cor 2 [14]The man without the Spirit does not accept the things that come from the Spirit of God, for they are foolishness to him, and he cannot understand them, because they are spiritually discerned.

Gal 3 [10]All who rely on observing the law are under a curse, for it is written: "Cursed is everyone who does not continue to do everything written in the Book of the Law."

Eph 2 [1]As for you, you were dead in your transgressions and sins, [2]in which you used to live when you followed the ways of this world and of the ruler of the kingdom of the air, the spirit who is now at work in those who are disobedient.

Eph 4 [17]So I tell you this, and insist on it in the Lord, that you must no longer live as the Gentiles do, in the futility of their thinking. [18]They are darkened in their understanding and separated from the life of God because of the ignorance that is in them due to the hardening of their hearts. [19]Having lost all sensitivity, they have given themselves over to sensuality so as to indulge in every kind of impurity, with a continual lust for more.

[20]You, however, did not come to know Christ that way. [21]Surely you heard of him and were taught in him in accordance with the truth that is in Jesus. [22]You were taught, with regard to your former way of life, to put off your old self, which is being corrupted by its deceitful desires; [23]to be made new in

the attitude of your minds; [24]and to put on the new self, created to be like God in true righteousness and holiness.
Eph 5 [8]For you were once darkness, but now you are light in the Lord. Live as children of light. . . .
Col 2 [13]When you were dead in your sins and in the uncircumcision of your sinful nature, God made you alive with Christ. He forgave us all our sins. . . .
Titus 1 [15]To the pure, all things are pure, but to those who are corrupted and do not believe, nothing is pure. In fact, both their minds and consciences are corrupted. [16]They claim to know God, but by their actions they deny him. They are detestable, disobedient and unfit for doing anything good.
James 1 [14]but each one is tempted when, by his own evil desire, he is dragged away and enticed. [15]Then, after desire has conceived, it gives birth to sin; and sin, when it is full-grown, gives birth to death.
James 2 [10]For whoever keeps the whole law and yet stumbles at just one point is guilty of breaking all of it.
1 Pet 2 [9]But you are a chosen people, a royal priesthood, a holy nation, a people belonging to God, that you may declare the praises of him who called you out of darkness into his wonderful light.
1 John 1 [8]If we claim to be without sin, we deceive ourselves and the truth is not in us.
1 John 5 [19]We know that we are children of God, and that the whole world is under the control of the evil one.

C. Sin Is an Active Violation of God's Law

1. Being Ignorant of the Law

Ezek 45 [20]"'You are to do the same on the seventh day of the month for anyone who sins unintentionally or through ignorance; so you are to make atonement for the temple.'"
Acts 3 [17]"Now, brothers, I know that you acted in ignorance, as did your leaders."
Rom 5 [14]Nevertheless, death reigned from the time of Adam to the time of Moses, even over those who did not sin by breaking a command, as did Adam, who was a pattern of the one to come.
Eph 4 [18]They are darkened in their understanding and separated from the life of God because of the ignorance that is in them due to the hardening of their hearts.
1 Tim 1 [13]Even though I was once a blasphemer and a persecutor and a violent man, I was shown mercy because I acted in ignorance and unbelief.
Heb 9 [7]But only the high priest entered the inner room, and that only once a year, and never without blood, which he offered for himself and for the sins the people had committed in ignorance.
1 Pet 1 [14]As obedient children, do not conform to the evil desires you had when you lived in ignorance.

2. Disobeying or Rejecting the Law

Exod 23 [21]"Pay attention to him and listen to what he says. Do not rebel against him; he will not forgive your rebellion, since my Name is in him."
Lev 26 [40]"'But if they will confess their sins and the sins of their fathers—their treachery against me and their hostility toward me . . .'"
Num 14 [41]But Moses said, "Why are you disobeying the LORD's command? This will not succeed! [42]Do not go up, because the LORD is not with you. You will be defeated by your enemies. . . ."
Deut 21 [18]If a man has a stubborn and rebellious son who does not obey his father and mother and will not listen to them when they discipline him . . .
Ps 78 [8]They would not be like their forefathers—a stubborn and rebellious generation, whose hearts were not loyal to God, whose spirits were not faithful to him. . . .
[57]Like their fathers they were disloyal and faithless, as unreliable as a faulty bow.
Isa 1 [2]Hear, O heavens! Listen, O earth! For the LORD has spoken: "I reared children and brought them up, but they have rebelled against me."
Jer 2 [29]"Why do you bring charges against me? You have all rebelled against me," declares the LORD.
Ezek 2 [3]He said: "Son of man, I am sending you to the Israelites, to a rebellious nation that has rebelled against me; they and their fathers have been in revolt against me to this very day."
Ezek 15 [8]"I will make the land desolate because they have been unfaithful, declares the Sovereign LORD."
Mal 2 [11]Judah has broken faith. A detestable thing has been committed in Israel and in Jerusalem: Judah has desecrated the sanctuary the LORD loves, by marrying the daughter of a foreign god.
Matt 18 [17]"If he refuses to listen to them, tell it to the church; and if he refuses to listen even to the church, treat him as you would a pagan or a tax collector."
Luke 1 [17]"And he will go on before the Lord, in the spirit and power of Elijah, to turn the hearts of the fathers to their children and the disobedient to the wisdom of the righteous—to make ready a people prepared for the Lord."
John 3 [36]"Whoever believes in the Son has eternal life, but whoever rejects the Son will not see life, for God's wrath remains on him."
Acts 14 [2]But the Jews who refused to believe stirred up the Gentiles and poisoned their minds against the brothers.
Rom 5 [19]For just as through the disobedience of the one man the many were made sinners, so also through the obedience of the one man the many will be made righteous.
2 Cor 10 [6]And we will be ready to punish every act of disobedience, once your obedience is complete.
Eph 5 [6]Let no one deceive you with empty words, for because of such things God's wrath comes on those who are disobedient.
2 Thess 2 [3]Don't let anyone deceive you in any way, for that day will not come until the rebellion occurs and the man of lawlessness is revealed, the man doomed to destruction.
1 Tim 4 [1]The Spirit clearly says that in later times some will abandon the faith and follow deceiving spirits and things taught by demons.
Heb 2 [2]For if the message spoken by angels was binding, and every violation and disobedience received its just punishment, [3]how shall we escape if we ignore such a great salvation? This salvation, which was first announced by the Lord, was confirmed to us by those who heard him.
Heb 3 [18]And to whom did God swear that they would never enter his rest if not to those who disobeyed?
Heb 11 [31]By faith the prostitute Rahab, because she welcomed the spies, was not killed with those who were disobedient.
1 Pet 2 [8]and, "A stone that causes men to stumble and a rock that makes them fall." They stumble because they disobey the message—which is also what they were destined for.
1 Pet 4 [17]For it is time for judgment to begin with the family of God; and if it begins with us, what will the outcome be for those who do not obey the gospel of God?

3. Failing to Live Up to the Law

Gen 18 [20]Then the LORD said, "The outcry against Sodom and Gomorrah is so great and their sin so grievous. . . ."
Lev 16 [30]". . . because on this day atonement will be made for you, to cleanse you. Then, before the LORD, you will be clean from all your sins."
1 Sam 12 [23]"As for me, far be it from me that I should sin against the LORD by failing to pray for you. And I will teach you the way that is good and right."
Neh 9 [2]Those of Israelite descent had separated themselves from all foreigners. They stood in their places and confessed their sins and the wickedness of their fathers.
Ps 25 [7]Remember not the sins of my youth and my rebellious ways; according to your love remember me, for you are good, O LORD.
Ps 51 [2]Wash away all my iniquity and cleanse me from my sin.
[3]For I know my transgressions, and my sin is always before me.

Prov 13 [6]Righteousness guards the man of integrity, but wickedness overthrows the sinner.
Isa 59 [12]For our offenses are many in your sight, and our sins testify against us. Our offenses are ever with us, and we acknowledge our iniquities. . . .
Lam 5 [7]Our fathers sinned and are no more, and we bear their punishment.
Dan 9 [20]While I was speaking and praying, confessing my sin and the sin of my people Israel and making my request to the LORD my God for his holy hill . . .
Mic 6 [7]Will the LORD be pleased with thousands of rams, with ten thousand rivers of oil? Shall I offer my firstborn for my transgression, the fruit of my body for the sin of my soul?
Matt 27 [4]"I have sinned," he said, "for I have betrayed innocent blood."

"What is that to us?" they replied. "That's your responsibility."
John 9 [2]His disciples asked him, "Rabbi, who sinned, this man or his parents, that he was born blind?"
Acts 25 [8]Then Paul made his defense: "I have done nothing wrong against the law of the Jews or against the temple or against Caesar."
Rom 3 [23]for all have sinned and fall short of the glory of God. . . .
Rom 5 [12]Therefore, just as sin entered the world through one man, and death through sin, and in this way death came to all men, because all sinned . . .
Gal 3 [22]But the Scripture declares that the whole world is a prisoner of sin, so that what was promised, being given through faith in Jesus Christ, might be given to those who believe.
Heb 12 [1]Therefore, since we are surrounded by such a great cloud of witnesses, let us throw off everything that hinders and the sin that so easily entangles, and let us run with perseverance the race marked out for us.
James 5 [15]And the prayer offered in faith will make the sick person well; the Lord will raise him up. If he has sinned, he will be forgiven.
1 John 1 [8]If we claim to be without sin, we deceive ourselves and the truth is not in us. [9]If we confess our sins, he is faithful and just and will forgive us our sins and purify us from all unrighteousness. [10]If we claim we have not sinned, we make him out to be a liar and his word has no place in our lives.
1 John 2 [1]My dear children, I write this to you so that you will not sin. But if anybody does sin, we have one who speaks to the Father in our defense—Jesus Christ, the Righteous One. [2]He is the atoning sacrifice for our sins, and not only for ours but also for the sins of the whole world.
Rev 1 [5]and from Jesus Christ, who is the faithful witness, the firstborn from the dead, and the ruler of the kings of the earth.

To him who loves us and has freed us from our sins by his blood . . .

4. Misunderstanding the Law, Intentionally or Unintentionally

Lev 4 [13]"'If the whole Israelite community sins unintentionally and does what is forbidden in any of the LORD's commands, even though the community is unaware of the matter, they are guilty.'"
Lev 22 [14]"'If anyone eats a sacred offering by mistake, he must make restitution to the priest for the offering and add a fifth of the value to it.'"
Job 6 [24]"Teach me, and I will be quiet; show me where I have been wrong."
Job 12 [16]"To him belong strength and victory; both deceived and deceiver are his."
Job 19 [4]"If it is true that I have gone astray, my error remains my concern alone."
Ps 119 [67]Before I was afflicted I went astray, but now I obey your word.
Isa 29 [24]"Those who are wayward in spirit will gain understanding; those who complain will accept instruction."
Ezek 44 [10]"'The Levites who went far from me when Israel went astray and who wandered from me after their idols must bear the consequences of their sin.'"
Mark 13 [5]Jesus said to them: "Watch out that no one deceives you. [6]Many will come in my name, claiming, 'I am he,' and will deceive many."
1 Cor 6 [9]Do you not know that the wicked will not inherit the kingdom of God? Do not be deceived: Neither the sexually immoral nor idolaters nor adulterers nor male prostitutes nor homosexual offenders [10]nor thieves nor the greedy nor drunkards nor slanderers nor swindlers will inherit the kingdom of God.
Gal 6 [7]Do not be deceived: God cannot be mocked. A man reaps what he sows.
2 Thess 2 [9]The coming of the lawless one will be in accordance with the work of Satan displayed in all kinds of counterfeit miracles, signs and wonders, [10]and in every sort of evil that deceives those who are perishing. They perish because they refused to love the truth and so be saved. [11]For this reason God sends them a powerful delusion so that they will believe the lie [12]and so that all will be condemned who have not believed the truth but have delighted in wickedness.
1 Tim 2 [14]And Adam was not the one deceived; it was the woman who was deceived and became a sinner.
Heb 3 [10]"That is why I was angry with that generation, and I said, 'Their hearts are always going astray, and they have not known my ways.'"
1 John 3 [7]Dear children, do not let anyone lead you astray. He who does what is right is righteous, just as he is righteous.
2 John [7]Many deceivers, who do not acknowledge Jesus Christ as coming in the flesh, have gone out into the world. Any such person is the deceiver and the antichrist.

5. Offending God

Rom 1 [18]The wrath of God is being revealed from heaven against all the godlessness and wickedness of men who suppress the truth by their wickedness. . . .
Rom 6 [13]Do not offer the parts of your body to sin, as instruments of wickedness, but rather offer yourselves to God, as those who have been brought from death to life; and offer the parts of your body to him as instruments of righteousness.
1 Cor 6 [9]Do you not know that the wicked will not inherit the kingdom of God? Do not be deceived: Neither the sexually immoral nor idolaters nor adulterers nor male prostitutes nor homosexual offenders [10]nor thieves nor the greedy nor drunkards nor slanderers nor swindlers will inherit the kingdom of God.
Col 3 [25]Anyone who does wrong will be repaid for his wrong, and there is no favoritism.
1 Tim 1 [9]We also know that law is made not for the righteous but for lawbreakers and rebels, the ungodly and sinful, the unholy and irreligious; for those who kill their fathers or mothers, for murderers . . .
2 Tim 2 [16]Avoid godless chatter, because those who indulge in it will become more and more ungodly.
Titus 2 [12]It teaches us to say "No" to ungodliness and worldly passions, and to live self-controlled, upright and godly lives in this present age. . . .
1 Pet 3 [18]For Christ died for sins once for all, the righteous for the unrighteous, to bring you to God. He was put to death in the body but made alive by the Spirit. . . .
2 Pet 3 [7]By the same word the present heavens and earth are reserved for fire, being kept for the day of judgment and destruction of ungodly men.
1 John 1 [9]If we confess our sins, he is faithful and just and will forgive us our sins and purify us from all unrighteousness.
Jude [14]Enoch, the seventh from Adam, prophesied about these men: "See, the Lord is coming with thousands upon thousands of his holy ones [15]to judge everyone, and to convict all the ungodly of all the ungodly acts they have done in the ungodly way, and of all the harsh words ungodly sinners have spoken against him."

6. Perverting the Law

Job 33 [27]"Then he comes to men and says, 'I sinned, and perverted what was right, but I did not get what I deserved.'"
Prov 12 [8]A man is praised according to his wisdom, but men with warped minds are despised.
Jer 3 [21]A cry is heard on the barren heights, the weeping and pleading of the people of Israel, because they have perverted their ways and have forgotten the LORD their God.

Ezek 18 [24]"But if a righteous man turns from his righteousness and commits sin and does the same detestable things the wicked man does, will he live? None of the righteous things he has done will be remembered. Because of the unfaithfulness he is guilty of and because of the sins he has committed, he will die."

7. Transgressing or Violating the Law

Deut 17 [2]If a man or woman living among you in one of the towns the LORD gives you is found doing evil in the eyes of the LORD your God in violation of his covenant . . .
Josh 23 [16]"If you violate the covenant of the LORD your God, which he commanded you, and go and serve other gods and bow down to them, the LORD's anger will burn against you, and you will quickly perish from the good land he has given you."
2 Chron 24 [20]Then the Spirit of God came upon Zechariah son of Jehoiada the priest. He stood before the people and said, "This is what God says: 'Why do you disobey the LORD's commands? You will not prosper. Because you have forsaken the LORD, he has forsaken you.'"
Jer 34 [18]"The men who have violated my covenant and have not fulfilled the terms of the covenant they made before me, I will treat like the calf they cut in two and then walked between its pieces."
Dan 9 [11]"All Israel has transgressed your law and turned away, refusing to obey you.
"Therefore the curses and sworn judgments written in the Law of Moses, the servant of God, have been poured out on us, because we have sinned against you."
Hos 6 [7]"Like Adam, they have broken the covenant—they were unfaithful to me there."
Hos 8 [1]"Put the trumpet to your lips! An eagle is over the house of the LORD because the people have broken my covenant and rebelled against my law."
Rom 3 [20]Therefore no one will be declared righteous in his sight by observing the law; rather, through the law we become conscious of sin.
Rom 4 [15]because law brings wrath. And where there is no law there is no transgression.
Rom 7 [7]What shall we say, then? Is the law sin? Certainly not! Indeed I would not have known what sin was except through the law. For I would not have known what coveting really was if the law had not said, "Do not covet." [8]But sin, seizing the opportunity afforded by the commandment, produced in me every kind of covetous desire. For apart from law, sin is dead. [9]Once I was alive apart from law; but when the commandment came, sin sprang to life and I died. [10]I found that the very commandment that was intended to bring life actually brought death. [11]For sin, seizing the opportunity afforded by the commandment, deceived me, and through the commandment put me to death. [12]So then, the law is holy, and the commandment is holy, righteous and good.
[13]Did that which is good, then, become death to me? By no means! But in order that sin might be recognized as sin, it produced death in me through what was good, so that through the commandment sin might become utterly sinful.
Gal 3 [10]All who rely on observing the law are under a curse, for it is written: "Cursed is everyone who does not continue to do everything written in the Book of the Law." . . . [12]The law is not based on faith; on the contrary, "The man who does these things will live by them."
1 Tim 2 [14]And Adam was not the one deceived; it was the woman who was deceived and became a sinner.
James 2 [8]If you really keep the royal law found in Scripture, "Love your neighbor as yourself," you are doing right. [9]But if you show favoritism, you sin and are convicted by the law as lawbreakers. [10]For whoever keeps the whole law and yet stumbles at just one point is guilty of breaking all of it. [11]For he who said, "Do not commit adultery," also said, "Do not murder." If you do not commit adultery but do commit murder, you have become a lawbreaker.
1 John 3 [4]Everyone who sins breaks the law; in fact, sin is lawlessness.

D. Sin Is Selfishness

Isa 53 [6]We all, like sheep, have gone astray, each of us has turned to his own way; and the LORD has laid on him the iniquity of us all.
Jer 16 [12]"'But you have behaved more wickedly than your fathers. See how each of you is following the stubbornness of his evil heart instead of obeying me.'"
Luke 6 [32]"If you love those who love you, what credit is that to you? Even 'sinners' love those who love them. [33]And if you do good to those who are good to you, what credit is that to you? Even 'sinners' do that. [34]And if you lend to those from whom you expect repayment, what credit is that to you? Even 'sinners' lend to 'sinners,' expecting to be repaid in full."
2 Thess 2 [3]Don't let anyone deceive you in any way, for that day will not come until the rebellion occurs and the man of lawlessness is revealed, the man doomed to destruction. [4]He will oppose and will exalt himself over everything that is called God or is worshiped, so that he sets himself up in God's temple, proclaiming himself to be God.
2 Tim 3 [1]But mark this: There will be terrible times in the last days. [2]People will be lovers of themselves, lovers of money, boastful, proud, abusive, disobedient to their parents, ungrateful, unholy, [3]without love, unforgiving, slanderous, without self-control, brutal, not lovers of the good, [4]treacherous, rash, conceited, lovers of pleasure rather than lovers of God. . . .
1 John 3 [17]If anyone has material possessions and sees his brother in need but has no pity on him, how can the love of God be in him?

II
The Origin of Sin

A. Sin Originated in Heaven with Satan and His Angels

Isa 14 [12]How you have fallen from heaven, O morning star, son of the dawn! You have been cast down to the earth, you who once laid low the nations!
[13]You said in your heart, "I will ascend to heaven; I will raise my throne above the stars of God; I will sit enthroned on the mount of assembly, on the utmost heights of the sacred mountain. [14]I will ascend above the tops of the clouds; I will make myself like the Most High." [15]But you are brought down to the grave, to the depths of the pit.
Ezek 28 [15]"'You were blameless in your ways from the day you were created till wickedness was found in you. [16]Through your widespread trade you were filled with violence, and you sinned. So I drove you in disgrace from the mount of God, and I expelled you, O guardian cherub, from among the fiery stones. [17]Your heart became proud on account of your beauty, and you corrupted your wisdom because of your splendor. So I threw you to earth; I made a spectacle of you before kings.'"
John 8 [44]"You belong to your father, the devil, and you want to carry out your father's desire. He was a murderer from the beginning, not holding to the truth, for there is no truth in him. When he lies, he speaks his native language, for he is a liar and the father of lies."
2 Pet 2 [4]For if God did not spare angels when they sinned, but sent them to hell, putting them into gloomy dungeons to be held for judgment . . .
1 John 3 [8]He who does what is sinful is of the devil, because the devil has been sinning from the beginning. The reason the Son of God appeared was to destroy the devil's work.
Jude [6]And the angels who did not keep their positions of authority but abandoned their own home—these he has kept in darkness, bound with everlasting chains for judgment on the great Day.

B. Sin Originated on Earth with Adam and Eve

1. The Test of Adam and Eve

Gen 2 [16]And the LORD God commanded the man, "You are free to eat from any tree in the garden; [17]but you must not eat from the tree of the knowledge of good and evil, for when you eat of it you will surely die."

2. The Temptation of Adam and Eve

Gen 3 1Now the serpent was more crafty than any of the wild animals the LORD God had made. He said to the woman, "Did God really say, 'You must not eat from any tree in the garden'?"

2The woman said to the serpent, "We may eat fruit from the trees in the garden, 3but God did say, 'You must not eat fruit from the tree that is in the middle of the garden, and you must not touch it, or you will die.'"

4"You will not surely die," the serpent said to the woman. 5"For God knows that when you eat of it your eyes will be opened, and you will be like God, knowing good and evil."

James 1 13When tempted, no one should say, "God is tempting me." For God cannot be tempted by evil, nor does he tempt anyone; 14but each one is tempted when, by his own evil desire, he is dragged away and enticed. 15Then, after desire has conceived, it gives birth to sin; and sin, when it is full-grown, gives birth to death.

3. The Disobedience of Adam and Eve

Gen 3 6When the woman saw that the fruit of the tree was good for food and pleasing to the eye, and also desirable for gaining wisdom, she took some and ate it. She also gave some to her husband, who was with her, and he ate it.

2 Cor 11 3But I am afraid that just as Eve was deceived by the serpent's cunning, your minds may somehow be led astray from your sincere and pure devotion to Christ.

1 Tim 2 14And Adam was not the one deceived; it was the woman who was deceived and became a sinner.

4. The Consequences of Adam's and Eve's Disobedience

a) Shame and Guilt

Gen 3 7Then the eyes of both of them were opened, and they realized they were naked; so they sewed fig leaves together and made coverings for themselves.

8Then the man and his wife heard the sound of the LORD God as he was walking in the garden in the cool of the day, and they hid from the LORD God among the trees of the garden. 9But the LORD God called to the man, "Where are you?"

10He answered, "I heard you in the garden, and I was afraid because I was naked; so I hid."

11And he said, "Who told you that you were naked? Have you eaten from the tree that I commanded you not to eat from?"

12The man said, "The woman you put here with me—she gave me some fruit from the tree, and I ate it."

13Then the LORD God said to the woman, "What is this you have done?"

The woman said, "The serpent deceived me, and I ate."

b) Judgment

Gen 3 14So the LORD God said to the serpent, "Because you have done this, Cursed are you above all the livestock and all the wild animals! You will crawl on your belly and you will eat dust all the days of your life. 15And I will put enmity between you and the woman, and between your offspring and hers; he will crush your head, and you will strike his heel."

16To the woman he said, "I will greatly increase your pains in childbearing; with pain you will give birth to children. Your desire will be for your husband, and he will rule over you."

17To Adam he said, "Because you listened to your wife and ate from the tree about which I commanded you, 'You must not eat of it,' Cursed is the ground because of you; through painful toil you will eat of it all the days of your life. 18It will produce thorns and thistles for you, and you will eat the plants of the field. 19By the sweat of your brow you will eat your food until you return to the ground, since from it you were taken; for dust you are and to dust you will return."

Rom 8 19The creation waits in eager expectation for the sons of God to be revealed. 20For the creation was subjected to frustration, not by its own choice, but by the will of the one who subjected it, in hope 21that the creation itself will be liberated from its bondage to decay and brought into the glorious freedom of the children of God.

c) Gracious Discipline

Gen 3 21The LORD God made garments of skin for Adam and his wife and clothed them. 22And the LORD God said, "The man has now become like one of us, knowing good and evil. He must not be allowed to reach out his hand and take also from the tree of life and eat, and live forever." 23So the LORD God banished him from the Garden of Eden to work the ground from which he had been taken. 24After he drove the man out, he placed on the east side of the Garden of Eden cherubim and a flaming sword flashing back and forth to guard the way to the tree of life.

III
The Universality of Sin

A. Universal Depravity

1. Corrupt in Nature

Job 14 4"Who can bring what is pure from the impure? No one!"

Job 15 14"What is man, that he could be pure, or one born of woman, that he could be righteous? 15If God places no trust in his holy ones, if even the heavens are not pure in his eyes, 16how much less man, who is vile and corrupt, who drinks up evil like water!"

Job 25 4"How then can a man be righteous before God? How can one born of woman be pure? 5If even the moon is not bright and the stars are not pure in his eyes, 6how much less man, who is but a maggot—a son of man, who is only a worm!"

Ps 19 12Who can discern his errors? Forgive my hidden faults.

Ps 51 5Surely I have been a sinner from birth, sinful from the time my mother conceived me. 6Surely you desire truth in the inner parts; you teach me wisdom in the inmost place.

7Cleanse me with hyssop, and I will be clean; wash me, and I will be whiter than snow.

Ps 58 3Even from birth the wicked go astray; from the womb they are wayward and speak lies.

Jer 13 23Can the Ethiopian change his skin or the leopard its spots? Neither can you do good who are accustomed to doing evil.

Jer 17 9The heart is deceitful above all things and beyond cure. Who can understand it?

Matt 12 34"You brood of vipers, how can you who are evil say anything good? For out of the overflow of the heart the mouth speaks."

Luke 6 43"No good tree bears bad fruit, nor does a bad tree bear good fruit. 44Each tree is recognized by its own fruit. People do not pick figs from thornbushes, or grapes from briers. 45The good man brings good things out of the good stored up in his heart, and the evil man brings evil things out of the evil stored up in his heart. For out of the overflow of his heart his mouth speaks."

Luke 11 13"If you then, though you are evil, know how to give good gifts to your children, how much more will your Father in heaven give the Holy Spirit to those who ask him!"

Rom 5 12Therefore, just as sin entered the world through one man, and death through sin, and in this way death came to all men, because all sinned—13for before the law was given, sin was in the world. But sin is not taken into account when there is no law. 14Nevertheless, death reigned from the time of Adam to the time of Moses, even over those who did not sin by breaking a command, as did Adam, who was a pattern of the one to come.

15But the gift is not like the trespass. For if the many died by the trespass of the one man, how much more did God's grace and the gift that came by the grace of the one man, Jesus Christ, overflow to the many! 16Again, the gift of God is not like the result of the one man's sin: The judgment followed one sin and brought condemnation, but the gift followed many trespasses and brought justification. 17For if, by the trespass of the one man, death reigned through that one man, how much more will those who receive God's abundant provision of grace and of the gift of righteousness reign in life through the one man, Jesus Christ.

[18]Consequently, just as the result of one trespass was condemnation for all men, so also the result of one act of righteousness was justification that brings life for all men. [19]For just as through the disobedience of the one man the many were made sinners, so also through the obedience of the one man the many will be made righteous.
Rom 7 [24]What a wretched man I am! Who will rescue me from this body of death?
Eph 2 [3]All of us also lived among them at one time, gratifying the cravings of our sinful nature and following its desires and thoughts. Like the rest, we were by nature objects of wrath.

2. Evil in Desire

Gen 6 [5]The LORD saw how great man's wickedness on the earth had become, and that every inclination of the thoughts of his heart was only evil all the time.
Job 20 [12]"Though evil is sweet in his mouth and he hides it under his tongue, [13]though he cannot bear to let it go and keeps it in his mouth . . ."
Ps 36 [1]An oracle is within my heart concerning the sinfulness of the wicked: There is no fear of God before his eyes. [2]For in his own eyes he flatters himself too much to detect or hate his sin. [3]The words of his mouth are wicked and deceitful; he has ceased to be wise and to do good. [4]Even on his bed he plots evil; he commits himself to a sinful course and does not reject what is wrong.
Prov 4 [16]For they cannot sleep till they do evil; they are robbed of slumber till they make someone fall. [17]They eat the bread of wickedness and drink the wine of violence.
Jer 16 [12]"'But you have behaved more wickedly than your fathers. See how each of you is following the stubbornness of his evil heart instead of obeying me.'"
John 3 [19]"This is the verdict: Light has come into the world, but men loved darkness instead of light because their deeds were evil. [20]Everyone who does evil hates the light, and will not come into the light for fear that his deeds will be exposed."

3. Sinful in Deed

1 Kings 8 [46]"When they sin against you—for there is no one who does not sin—and you become angry with them and give them over to the enemy, who takes them captive to his own land, far away or near . . ."
Ps 14 [1]The fool says in his heart, "There is no God." They are corrupt, their deeds are vile; there is no one who does good.

[2]The LORD looks down from heaven on the sons of men to see if there are any who understand, any who seek God. [3]All have turned aside, they have together become corrupt; there is no one who does good, not even one.
Ps 143 [2]Do not bring your servant into judgment, for no one living is righteous before you.
Prov 20 [9]Who can say, "I have kept my heart pure; I am clean and without sin"?
Eccles 7 [20]There is not a righteous man on earth who does what is right and never sins.
Isa 64 [6]All of us have become like one who is unclean, and all our righteous acts are like filthy rags; we all shrivel up like a leaf, and like the wind our sins sweep us away.
Rom 3 [9]What shall we conclude then? Are we any better? Not at all! We have already made the charge that Jews and Gentiles alike are all under sin. [10]As it is written: "There is no one righteous, not even one; [11]there is no one who understands, no one who seeks God. [12]All have turned away, they have together become worthless; there is no one who does good, not even one." [13]"Their throats are open graves; their tongues practice deceit." "The poison of vipers is on their lips." [14]"Their mouths are full of cursing and bitterness." [15]"Their feet are swift to shed blood; [16]ruin and misery mark their ways, [17]and the way of peace they do not know." [18]"There is no fear of God before their eyes."

[19]Now we know that whatever the law says, it says to those who are under the law, so that every mouth may be silenced and the whole world held accountable to God. [20]Therefore no one will be declared righteous in his sight by observing the law; rather, through the law we become conscious of sin. [23]. . . for all have sinned and fall short of the glory of God. . . .
Gal 3 [22]But the Scripture declares that the whole world is a prisoner of sin, so that what was promised, being given through faith in Jesus Christ, might be given to those who believe.
James 3 [2]We all stumble in many ways. If anyone is never at fault in what he says, he is a perfect man, able to keep his whole body in check.
1 John 1 [8]If we claim to be without sin, we deceive ourselves and the truth is not in us. . . . [10]If we claim we have not sinned, we make him out to be a liar and his word has no place in our lives.

B. Universal Guilt

Lev 5 [17]"If a person sins and does what is forbidden in any of the LORD's commands, even though he does not know it, he is guilty and will be held responsible."
Isa 64 [6]All of us have become like one who is unclean, and all our righteous acts are like filthy rags; we all shrivel up like a leaf, and like the wind our sins sweep us away.
Rom 3 [19]Now we know that whatever the law says, it says to those who are under the law, so that every mouth may be silenced and the whole world held accountable to God. [20]Therefore no one will be declared righteous in his sight by observing the law; rather, through the law we become conscious of sin. [23]. . . for all have sinned and fall short of the glory of God. . . .
Rom 5 [12]Therefore, just as sin entered the world through one man, and death through sin, and in this way death came to all men, because all sinned . . .

C. Universal Need for Repentance

1 Kings 8 [46]"When they sin against you—for there is no one who does not sin—and you become angry with them and give them over to the enemy, who takes them captive to his own land, far away or near; [47]and if they have a change of heart in the land where they are held captive, and repent and plead with you in the land of their conquerors and say, 'We have sinned, we have done wrong, we have acted wickedly'; [48]and if they turn back to you with all their heart and soul in the land of their enemies who took them captive, and pray to you toward the land you gave their fathers, toward the city you have chosen and the temple I have built for your Name . . ."
Ezek 14 [6]"Therefore say to the house of Israel, 'This is what the Sovereign LORD says: Repent! Turn from your idols and renounce all your detestable practices!

[7]"'When any Israelite or any alien living in Israel separates himself from me and sets up idols in his heart and puts a wicked stumbling block before his face and then goes to a prophet to inquire of me, I the LORD will answer him myself. [8]I will set my face against that man and make him an example and a byword. I will cut him off from my people. Then you will know that I am the LORD.'"
Mark 1 [15]"The time has come," he said. "The kingdom of God is near. Repent and believe the good news!"
Luke 24 [47]". . . and repentance and forgiveness of sins will be preached in his name to all nations, beginning at Jerusalem."
John 3 [3]In reply Jesus declared, "I tell you the truth, no one can see the kingdom of God unless he is born again."

[4]"How can a man be born when he is old?" Nicodemus asked. "Surely he cannot enter a second time into his mother's womb to be born!"

[5]Jesus answered, "I tell you the truth, no one can enter the kingdom of God unless he is born of water and the Spirit."
Acts 17 [30]"In the past God overlooked such ignorance, but now he commands all people everywhere to repent."
2 Cor 5 [14]For Christ's love compels us, because we are convinced that one died for all, and therefore all died. [15]And he died for all, that those who live should no longer live for themselves but for him who died for them and was raised again. . . . [20]We are therefore Christ's ambassadors, as though God were

making his appeal through us. We implore you on Christ's behalf: Be reconciled to God. 21God made him who had no sin to be sin for us, so that in him we might become the righteousness of God.

D. Universal Punishment for Rejection of God

John 3 18"Whoever believes in him is not condemned, but whoever does not believe stands condemned already because he has not believed in the name of God's one and only Son."
John 3 36"Whoever believes in the Son has eternal life, but whoever rejects the Son will not see life, for God's wrath remains on him."
1 John 5 18We know that anyone born of God does not continue to sin; the one who was born of God keeps him safe; and the evil one does not touch him. 19We know that we are children of God, and that the whole world is under the control of the evil one.
Rev 9 15And the four angels who had been kept ready for this very hour and day and month and year were released to kill a third of mankind. 16The number of the mounted troops was two hundred million. I heard their number. . . .

20The rest of mankind that were not killed by these plagues still did not repent of the work of their hands; they did not stop worshiping demons, and idols of gold, silver, bronze, stone and wood—idols that cannot see or hear or walk. 21Nor did they repent of their murders, their magic arts, their sexual immorality or their thefts.

IV The Consequences of Sin

A. Sin Results in Alienation from God

Gen 3 22And the LORD God said, "The man has now become like one of us, knowing good and evil. He must not be allowed to reach out his hand and take also from the tree of life and eat, and live forever." 23So the LORD God banished him from the Garden of Eden to work the ground from which he had been taken. 24After he drove the man out, he placed on the east side of the Garden of Eden cherubim and a flaming sword flashing back and forth to guard the way to the tree of life.
Deut 25 16For the LORD your God detests anyone who does these things, anyone who deals dishonestly.
Deut 31 16And the LORD said to Moses: "You are going to rest with your fathers, and these people will soon prostitute themselves to the foreign gods of the land they are entering. They will forsake me and break the covenant I made with them. 17On that day I will become angry with them and forsake them; I will hide my face from them, and they will be destroyed. Many disasters and difficulties will come upon them, and on that day they will ask, 'Have not these disasters come upon us because our God is not with us?' 18And I will certainly hide my face on that day because of all their wickedness in turning to other gods."
2 Chron 24 20Then the Spirit of God came upon Zechariah son of Jehoiada the priest. He stood before the people and said, "This is what God says: 'Why do you disobey the LORD's commands? You will not prosper. Because you have forsaken the LORD, he has forsaken you.'"
Job 35 12"He does not answer when men cry out because of the arrogance of the wicked. 13Indeed, God does not listen to their empty plea; the Almighty pays no attention to it."
Ps 5 4You are not a God who takes pleasure in evil; with you the wicked cannot dwell. 5The arrogant cannot stand in your presence; you hate all who do wrong. 6You destroy those who tell lies; bloodthirsty and deceitful men the LORD abhors.
Ps 11 5The LORD examines the righteous, but the wicked and those who love violence his soul hates.
Ps 66 18If I had cherished sin in my heart, the Lord would not have listened. . . .
Ps 78 58They angered him with their high places; they aroused his jealousy with their idols. 59When God heard them, he was very angry; he rejected Israel completely. 60He abandoned the tabernacle of Shiloh, the tent he had set up among men. 61He sent the ark of his might into captivity, his splendor into the hands of the enemy.
Prov 1 28"Then they will call to me but I will not answer; they will look for me but will not find me. 29Since they hated knowledge and did not choose to fear the LORD . . ."
Prov 10 29The way of the LORD is a refuge for the righteous, but it is the ruin of those who do evil.

30The righteous will never be uprooted, but the wicked will not remain in the land.
Prov 15 8The LORD detests the sacrifice of the wicked, but the prayer of the upright pleases him.

9The LORD detests the way of the wicked but he loves those who pursue righteousness. . . .

29The LORD is far from the wicked but he hears the prayer of the righteous.
Isa 1 15"When you spread out your hands in prayer, I will hide my eyes from you; even if you offer many prayers, I will not listen. Your hands are full of blood. . . ."
Isa 43 24"You have not bought any fragrant calamus for me, or lavished on me the fat of your sacrifices. But you have burdened me with your sins and wearied me with your offenses."
Isa 59 1Surely the arm of the LORD is not too short to save, nor his ear too dull to hear. 2But your iniquities have separated you from your God; your sins have hidden his face from you, so that he will not hear.
Isa 64 7No one calls on your name or strives to lay hold of you; for you have hidden your face from us and made us waste away because of our sins.
Hos 9 10"When I found Israel, it was like finding grapes in the desert; when I saw your fathers, it was like seeing the early fruit on the fig tree. But when they came to Baal Peor, they consecrated themselves to that shameful idol and became as vile as the thing they loved. . . . 12Even if they rear children, I will bereave them of every one. Woe to them when I turn away from them!"
Amos 3 2"You only have I chosen of all the families of the earth; therefore I will punish you for all your sins."
Mic 3 4Then they will cry out to the LORD, but he will not answer them. At that time he will hide his face from them because of the evil they have done.
Hab 1 13Your eyes are too pure to look on evil; you cannot tolerate wrong. Why then do you tolerate the treacherous? Why are you silent while the wicked swallow up those more righteous than themselves?
Zech 8 17". . . do not plot evil against your neighbor, and do not love to swear falsely. I hate all this," declares the LORD.
Matt 7 23"Then I will tell them plainly, 'I never knew you. Away from me, you evildoers!'"
Luke 16 15He said to them, "You are the ones who justify yourselves in the eyes of men, but God knows your hearts. What is highly valued among men is detestable in God's sight."
John 9 31"We know that God does not listen to sinners. He listens to the godly man who does his will."
Rom 8 7the sinful mind is hostile to God. It does not submit to God's law, nor can it do so.
1 Cor 6 9Do you not know that the wicked will not inherit the kingdom of God? Do not be deceived: Neither the sexually immoral nor idolaters nor adulterers nor male prostitutes nor homosexual offenders 10nor thieves nor the greedy nor drunkards nor slanderers nor swindlers will inherit the kingdom of God.
Eph 2 1As for you, you were dead in your transgressions and sins. . . . 3All of us also lived among them at one time, gratifying the cravings of our sinful nature and following its desires and thoughts. Like the rest, we were by nature objects of wrath. 4But because of his great love for us, God, who is rich in mercy, 5made us alive with Christ even when we were dead in transgressions—it is by grace you have been saved.

12. . . remember that at that time you were separate from Christ, excluded from citizenship in Israel and foreigners to the covenants of the promise, without hope and without God in the world.

Eph 4 [18]They are darkened in their understanding and separated from the life of God because of the ignorance that is in them due to the hardening of their hearts.
Eph 5 [5]For of this you can be sure: No immoral, impure or greedy person—such a man is an idolater—has any inheritance in the kingdom of Christ and of God.
Heb 12 [14]Make every effort to live in peace with all men and to be holy; without holiness no one will see the Lord.
James 4 [3]When you ask, you do not receive, because you ask with wrong motives, that you may spend what you get on your pleasures.

[4]You adulterous people, don't you know that friendship with the world is hatred toward God? Anyone who chooses to be a friend of the world becomes an enemy of God.
Rev 21 [23]The city does not need the sun or the moon to shine on it, for the glory of God gives it light, and the Lamb is its lamp. . . . [27]Nothing impure will ever enter it, nor will anyone who does what is shameful or deceitful, but only those whose names are written in the Lamb's book of life.

B. Sin Results in an Aversion to Righteousness

2 Chron 36 [15]The LORD, the God of their fathers, sent word to them through his messengers again and again, because he had pity on his people and on his dwelling place. [16]But they mocked God's messengers, despised his words and scoffed at his prophets until the wrath of the LORD was aroused against his people and there was no remedy.
Job 15 [25]". . . because he shakes his fist at God and vaunts himself against the Almighty, [26]defiantly charging against him with a thick, strong shield."
Job 15 [35]"They conceive trouble and give birth to evil; their womb fashions deceit."
Job 24 [13]"There are those who rebel against the light, who do not know its ways or stay in its paths. [14]When daylight is gone, the murderer rises up and kills the poor and needy; in the night he steals forth like a thief. [15]The eye of the adulterer watches for dusk; he thinks, 'No eye will see me,' and he keeps his face concealed. [16]In the dark, men break into houses, but by day they shut themselves in; they want nothing to do with the light. [17]For all of them, deep darkness is their morning; they make friends with the terrors of darkness."
Ps 10 [2]In his arrogance the wicked man hunts down the weak, who are caught in the schemes he devises. [3]He boasts of the cravings of his heart; he blesses the greedy and reviles the LORD. [4]In his pride the wicked does not seek him; in all his thoughts there is no room for God. [5]His ways are always prosperous; he is haughty and your laws are far from him; he sneers at all his enemies. [6]He says to himself, "Nothing will shake me; I'll always be happy and never have trouble." [7]His mouth is full of curses and lies and threats; trouble and evil are under his tongue. [8]He lies in wait near the villages; from ambush he murders the innocent, watching in secret for his victims. [9]He lies in wait like a lion in cover; he lies in wait to catch the helpless; he catches the helpless and drags them off in his net. [10]His victims are crushed, they collapse; they fall under his strength. [11]He says to himself, "God has forgotten; he covers his face and never sees."
Ps 50 [16]But to the wicked, God says: "What right have you to recite my laws or take my covenant on your lips? [17]You hate my instruction and cast my words behind you."
Ps 52 [7]"Here now is the man who did not make God his stronghold but trusted in his great wealth and grew strong by destroying others!"
Ps 58 [3]Even from birth the wicked go astray; from the womb they are wayward and speak lies. [4]Their venom is like the venom of a snake, like that of a cobra that has stopped its ears, [5]that will not heed the tune of the charmer, however skillful the enchanter may be.
Ps 64 [5]They encourage each other in evil plans, they talk about hiding their snares; they say, "Who will see them?"
Ps 73 [1]Surely God is good to Israel, to those who are pure in heart.

[2]But as for me, my feet had almost slipped; I had nearly lost my foothold. [3]For I envied the arrogant when I saw the prosperity of the wicked.

[4]They have no struggles; their bodies are healthy and strong. [5]They are free from the burdens common to man; they are not plagued by human ills. [6]Therefore pride is their necklace; they clothe themselves with violence. [7]From their callous hearts comes iniquity; the evil conceits of their minds know no limits. [8]They scoff, and speak with malice; in their arrogance they threaten oppression. [9]Their mouths lay claim to heaven, and their tongues take possession of the earth. [10]Therefore their people turn to them and drink up waters in abundance. [11]They say, "How can God know? Does the Most High have knowledge?"

[12]This is what the wicked are like—always carefree, they increase in wealth.

[13]Surely in vain have I kept my heart pure; in vain have I washed my hands in innocence. [14]All day long I have been plagued; I have been punished every morning. [15]If I had said, "I will speak thus," I would have betrayed your children. [16]When I tried to understand all this, it was oppressive to me [17]till I entered the sanctuary of God; then I understood their final destiny.
Prov 10 [23]A fool finds pleasure in evil conduct, but a man of understanding delights in wisdom.
Isa 3 [9]The look on their faces testifies against them; they parade their sin like Sodom; they do not hide it. Woe to them! They have brought disaster upon themselves.
Isa 32 [6]For the fool speaks folly, his mind is busy with evil: He practices ungodliness and spreads error concerning the LORD; the hungry he leaves empty and from the thirsty he withholds water. [7]The scoundrel's methods are wicked, he makes up evil schemes to destroy the poor with lies, even when the plea of the needy is just.
Isa 48 [4]"For I knew how stubborn you were; the sinews of your neck were iron, your forehead was bronze. . . . [8]You have neither heard nor understood; from of old your ear has not been open. Well do I know how treacherous you are; you were called a rebel from birth."
Isa 65 [11]"But as for you who forsake the LORD and forget my holy mountain, who spread a table for fortune and fill bowls of mixed wine for Destiny, [12]I will destine you for the sword, and you will all bend down for the slaughter; for I called but you did not answer, I spoke but you did not listen. You did evil in my sight and chose what displeases me."
Jer 16 [12]"'But you have behaved more wickedly than your fathers. See how each of you is following the stubbornness of his evil heart instead of obeying me.'"
Jer 18 [12]"'But they will reply, 'It's no use. We will continue with our own plans; each of us will follow the stubbornness of his evil heart.'"
Jer 44 [16]"We will not listen to the message you have spoken to us in the name of the LORD! [17]We will certainly do everything we said we would: We will burn incense to the Queen of Heaven and will pour out drink offerings to her just as we and our fathers, our kings and our officials did in the towns of Judah and in the streets of Jerusalem. At that time we had plenty of food and were well off and suffered no harm. [18]But ever since we stopped burning incense to the Queen of Heaven and pouring out drink offerings to her, we have had nothing and have been perishing by sword and famine."
Dan 9 [13]"Just as it is written in the Law of Moses, all this disaster has come upon us, yet we have not sought the favor of the LORD our God by turning from our sins and giving attention to your truth."
Hos 5 [4]"Their deeds do not permit them to return to their God. A spirit of prostitution is in their heart; they do not acknowledge the LORD."
Zech 7 [11]"But they refused to pay attention; stubbornly they turned their backs and stopped up their ears. [12]They made their hearts as hard as flint and would not listen to the law or to the words that the LORD Almighty had sent by his Spirit through the earlier prophets. So the LORD Almighty was very angry."
Matt 5 [11]"Blessed are you when people insult you, persecute you and falsely say all kinds of evil against you because of me. [12]Rejoice and be glad, because great is your reward in heaven,

for in the same way they persecuted the prophets who were before you."

Matt 13 [14]"In them is fulfilled the prophecy of Isaiah: 'You will be ever hearing but never understanding; you will be ever seeing but never perceiving. [15]For this people's heart has become calloused; they hardly hear with their ears, and they have closed their eyes. Otherwise they might see with their eyes, hear with their ears, understand with their hearts and turn, and I would heal them.'"

Acts 7 [51]"You stiff-necked people, with uncircumcised hearts and ears! You are just like your fathers: You always resist the Holy Spirit!"

Rom 2 [4]Or do you show contempt for the riches of his kindness, tolerance and patience, not realizing that God's kindness leads you toward repentance?

[5]But because of your stubbornness and your unrepentant heart, you are storing up wrath against yourself for the day of God's wrath, when his righteous judgment will be revealed.

C. Sin Results in Enslavement to Evil

Jer 2 [25]"Do not run until your feet are bare and your throat is dry. But you said, 'It's no use! I love foreign gods, and I must go after them.'"

Jer 13 [23]Can the Ethiopian change his skin or the leopard its spots? Neither can you do good who are accustomed to doing evil.

John 8 [34]Jesus replied, "I tell you the truth, everyone who sins is a slave to sin. [35]Now a slave has no permanent place in the family, but a son belongs to it forever. [36]So if the Son sets you free, you will be free indeed."

Rom 6 [16]Don't you know that when you offer yourselves to someone to obey him as slaves, you are slaves to the one whom you obey—whether you are slaves to sin, which leads to death, or to obedience, which leads to righteousness? [17]But thanks be to God that, though you used to be slaves to sin, you wholeheartedly obeyed the form of teaching to which you were entrusted. [18]You have been set free from sin and have become slaves to righteousness.

Rom 7 [14]We know that the law is spiritual; but I am unspiritual, sold as a slave to sin. [15]I do not understand what I do. For what I want to do I do not do, but what I hate I do. [16]And if I do what I do not want to do, I agree that the law is good. [17]As it is, it is no longer I myself who do it, but it is sin living in me. [18]I know that nothing good lives in me, that is, in my sinful nature. For I have the desire to do what is good, but I cannot carry it out. [19]For what I do is not the good I want to do; no, the evil I do not want to do—this I keep on doing. [20]Now if I do what I do not want to do, it is no longer I who do it, but it is sin living in me that does it.

2 Pet 2 [13]They will be paid back with harm for the harm they have done. Their idea of pleasure is to carouse in broad daylight. They are blots and blemishes, reveling in their pleasures while they feast with you. [14]With eyes full of adultery, they never stop sinning; they seduce the unstable; they are experts in greed—an accursed brood! . . .

[17]These men are springs without water and mists driven by a storm. Blackest darkness is reserved for them. [18]For they mouth empty, boastful words and, by appealing to the lustful desires of sinful human nature, they entice people who are just escaping from those who live in error. [19]They promise them freedom, while they themselves are slaves of depravity—for a man is a slave to whatever has mastered him.

D. Sin Results in Eternal Damnation

Ezek 18 [4]"For every living soul belongs to me, the father as well as the son—both alike belong to me. The soul who sins is the one who will die. . . . [20]The soul who sins is the one who will die. The son will not share the guilt of the father, nor will the father share the guilt of the son. The righteousness of the righteous man will be credited to him, and the wickedness of the wicked will be charged against him."

Dan 12 [2]"Multitudes who sleep in the dust of the earth will awake: some to everlasting life, others to shame and everlasting contempt."

Mal 4 [1]"Surely the day is coming; it will burn like a furnace. All the arrogant and every evildoer will be stubble, and that day that is coming will set them on fire," says the LORD Almighty. "Not a root or a branch will be left to them."

Matt 10 [28]"Do not be afraid of those who kill the body but cannot kill the soul. Rather, be afraid of the One who can destroy both soul and body in hell."

Matt 18 [8]"If your hand or your foot causes you to sin, cut it off and throw it away. It is better for you to enter life maimed or crippled than to have two hands or two feet and be thrown into eternal fire. [9]And if your eye causes you to sin, gouge it out and throw it away. It is better for you to enter life with one eye than to have two eyes and be thrown into the fire of hell."

Matt 25 [41]"Then he will say to those on his left, 'Depart from me, you who are cursed, into the eternal fire prepared for the devil and his angels.'"

Mark 3 [29]"But whoever blasphemes against the Holy Spirit will never be forgiven; he is guilty of an eternal sin."

Luke 3 [17]"His winnowing fork is in his hand to clear his threshing floor and to gather the wheat into his barn, but he will burn up the chaff with unquenchable fire."

2 Thess 1 [8]He will punish those who do not know God and do not obey the gospel of our Lord Jesus. [9]They will be punished with everlasting destruction and shut out from the presence of the Lord and from the majesty of his power. . . .

Heb 10 [28]Anyone who rejected the law of Moses died without mercy on the testimony of two or three witnesses. [29]How much more severely do you think a man deserves to be punished who has trampled the Son of God under foot, who has treated as an unholy thing the blood of the covenant that sanctified him, and who has insulted the Spirit of grace? [30]For we know him who said, "It is mine to avenge; I will repay," and again, "The Lord will judge his people." [31]It is a dreadful thing to fall into the hands of the living God.

Rev 14 [9]A third angel followed them and said in a loud voice: "If anyone worships the beast and his image and receives his mark on the forehead or on the hand, [10]he, too, will drink of the wine of God's fury, which has been poured full strength into the cup of his wrath. He will be tormented with burning sulfur in the presence of the holy angels and of the Lamb. [11]And the smoke of their torment rises for ever and ever. There is no rest day or night for those who worship the beast and his image, or for anyone who receives the mark of his name."

Rev 20 [10]And the devil, who deceived them, was thrown into the lake of burning sulfur, where the beast and the false prophet had been thrown. They will be tormented day and night for ever and ever.

[11]Then I saw a great white throne and him who was seated on it. Earth and sky fled from his presence, and there was no place for them. [12]And I saw the dead, great and small, standing before the throne, and books were opened. Another book was opened, which is the book of life. The dead were judged according to what they had done as recorded in the books. [13]The sea gave up the dead that were in it, and death and Hades gave up the dead that were in them, and each person was judged according to what he had done. [14]Then death and Hades were thrown into the lake of fire. The lake of fire is the second death. [15]If anyone's name was not found written in the book of life, he was thrown into the lake of fire.

E. Sin Results in Injustice and Innocent Suffering

Job 24 [2]"Men move boundary stones; they pasture flocks they have stolen. [3]They drive away the orphan's donkey and take the widow's ox in pledge. [4]They thrust the needy from the path and force all the poor of the land into hiding."

Ps 10 [2]In his arrogance the wicked man hunts down the weak, who are caught in the schemes he devises.

Prov 30 [11]"There are those who curse their fathers and do not bless their mothers; . . . [14]those whose teeth are swords and whose jaws are set with knives to devour the poor from the earth, the needy from among mankind."

Eccles 3 16And I saw something else under the sun: In the place of judgment—wickedness was there, in the place of justice—wickedness was there.
Eccles 4 1Again I looked and saw all the oppression that was taking place under the sun: I saw the tears of the oppressed—and they have no comforter; power was on the side of their oppressors—and they have no comforter.
Eccles 5 8If you see the poor oppressed in a district, and justice and rights denied, do not be surprised at such things; for one official is eyed by a higher one, and over them both are others higher still. 9The increase from the land is taken by all; the king himself profits from the fields.
Jer 22 13"Woe to him who builds his palace by unrighteousness, his upper rooms by injustice, making his countrymen work for nothing, not paying them for their labor."
Ezek 22 29"The people of the land practice extortion and commit robbery; they oppress the poor and needy and mistreat the alien, denying them justice."
Amos 5 11You trample on the poor and force him to give you grain. Therefore, though you have built stone mansions, you will not live in them; though you have planted lush vineyards, you will not drink their wine. 12For I know how many are your offenses and how great your sins.

You oppress the righteous and take bribes and you deprive the poor of justice in the courts.
Amos 8 4Hear this, you who trample the needy and do away with the poor of the land, 5saying, "When will the New Moon be over that we may sell grain, and the Sabbath be ended that we may market wheat?"—skimping the measure, boosting the price and cheating with dishonest scales, 6buying the poor with silver and the needy for a pair of sandals, selling even the sweepings with the wheat.
Mic 2 1Woe to those who plan iniquity, to those who plot evil on their beds! At morning's light they carry it out because it is in their power to do it. 2They covet fields and seize them, and houses, and take them. They defraud a man of his home, a fellowman of his inheritance.
Matt 23 2"The teachers of the law and the Pharisees sit in Moses' seat. 3So you must obey them and do everything they tell you. But do not do what they do, for they do not practice what they preach. 4They tie up heavy loads and put them on men's shoulders, but they themselves are not willing to lift a finger to move them."
James 5 4Look! The wages you failed to pay the workmen who mowed your fields are crying out against you. The cries of the harvesters have reached the ears of the Lord Almighty.

F. Sin Results in Judgment on Future Generations

Exod 20 5"You shall not bow down to them or worship them; for I, the LORD your God, am a jealous God, punishing the children for the sin of the fathers to the third and fourth generation of those who hate me. . . ."
Exod 34 6And he passed in front of Moses, proclaiming, "The LORD, the LORD, the compassionate and gracious God, slow to anger, abounding in love and faithfulness, 7maintaining love to thousands, and forgiving wickedness, rebellion and sin. Yet he does not leave the guilty unpunished; he punishes the children and their children for the sin of the fathers to the third and fourth generation."
Lev 26 39"'Those of you who are left will waste away in the lands of their enemies because of their sins; also because of their fathers' sins they will waste away.'"
Num 14 33"'Your children will be shepherds here for forty years, suffering for your unfaithfulness, until the last of your bodies lies in the desert.'"
Job 5 3"I myself have seen a fool taking root, but suddenly his house was cursed. 4His children are far from safety, crushed in court without a defender."
Job 18 19"He has no offspring or descendants among his people, no survivor where once he lived. . . . 21Surely such is the dwelling of an evil man; such is the place of one who knows not God."
Job 21 19"It is said, 'God stores up a man's punishment for his sons.' Let him repay the man himself, so that he will know it!"
Ps 21 10You will destroy their descendants from the earth, their posterity from mankind. 11Though they plot evil against you and devise wicked schemes, they cannot succeed. . . .
Ps 37 28For the LORD loves the just and will not forsake his faithful ones.

They will be protected forever, but the offspring of the wicked will be cut off. . . .
Ps 109 9May his children be fatherless and his wife a widow. 10May his children be wandering beggars; may they be driven from their ruined homes. 11May a creditor seize all he has; may strangers plunder the fruits of his labor. 12May no one extend kindness to him or take pity on his fatherless children. 13May his descendants be cut off, their names blotted out from the next generation. 14May the iniquity of his fathers be remembered before the LORD; may the sin of his mother never be blotted out. 15May their sins always remain before the LORD, that he may cut off the memory of them from the earth.
Prov 14 11The house of the wicked will be destroyed, but the tent of the upright will flourish.
Isa 14 20you will not join them in burial, for you have destroyed your land and killed your people.

The offspring of the wicked will never be mentioned again. 21Prepare a place to slaughter his sons for the sins of their forefathers; they are not to rise to inherit the land and cover the earth with their cities.

22"I will rise up against them," declares the LORD Almighty. "I will cut off from Babylon her name and survivors, her offspring and descendants," declares the LORD.
Jer 32 18"You show love to thousands but bring the punishment for the fathers' sins into the laps of their children after them. O great and powerful God, whose name is the LORD Almighty . . ."
Lam 5 7Our fathers sinned and are no more, and we bear their punishment.
Rom 5 12Therefore, just as sin entered the world through one man, and death through sin, and in this way death came to all men, because all sinned . . .

G. Sin Results in Moral and Spiritual Blindness

Job 21 14"Yet they say to God, 'Leave us alone! We have no desire to know your ways.'"
Ps 82 5"They know nothing, they understand nothing. They walk about in darkness; all the foundations of the earth are shaken."
Prov 4 19But the way of the wicked is like deep darkness; they do not know what makes them stumble.
Prov 14 12There is a way that seems right to a man, but in the end it leads to death.
Prov 30 20"This is the way of an adulteress: She eats and wipes her mouth and says, 'I've done nothing wrong.'"
Isa 6 9He said, "Go and tell this people: 'Be ever hearing, but never understanding; be ever seeing, but never perceiving.' 10Make the heart of this people calloused; make their ears dull and close their eyes. Otherwise they might see with their eyes, hear with their ears, understand with their hearts, and turn and be healed."
Isa 44 18They know nothing, they understand nothing; their eyes are plastered over so they cannot see, and their minds closed so they cannot understand. 19No one stops to think, no one has the knowledge or understanding to say, "Half of it I used for fuel; I even baked bread over its coals, I roasted meat and I ate. Shall I make a detestable thing from what is left? Shall I bow down to a block of wood?" 20He feeds on ashes, a deluded heart misleads him; he cannot save himself, or say, "Is not this thing in my right hand a lie?"
Jer 9 3"They make ready their tongue like a bow, to shoot lies; it is not by truth that they triumph in the land. They go from one sin to another; they do not acknowledge me," declares the LORD. 4"Beware of your friends; do not trust your brothers. For every brother is a deceiver, and every friend a slanderer. 5Friend deceives friend, and no one speaks the truth. They have taught

their tongues to lie; they weary themselves with sinning. [6]You live in the midst of deception; in their deceit they refuse to acknowledge me," declares the LORD.

Ezek 12 [2]"Son of man, you are living among a rebellious people. They have eyes to see but do not see and ears to hear but do not hear, for they are a rebellious people."

Dan 12 [10]"Many will be purified, made spotless and refined, but the wicked will continue to be wicked. None of the wicked will understand, but those who are wise will understand."

Amos 9 [10]"All the sinners among my people will die by the sword, all those who say, 'Disaster will not overtake or meet us.'"

Mic 4 [12]But they do not know the thoughts of the LORD; they do not understand his plan, he who gathers them like sheaves to the threshing floor.

Zeph 3 [5]The LORD within her is righteous; he does no wrong. Morning by morning he dispenses his justice, and every new day he does not fail, yet the unrighteous know no shame.

Matt 13 [22]"The one who received the seed that fell among the thorns is the man who hears the word, but the worries of this life and the deceitfulness of wealth choke it, making it unfruitful."

John 1 [5]The light shines in the darkness, but the darkness has not understood it. . . .

[10]He was in the world, and though the world was made through him, the world did not recognize him.

John 8 [12]When Jesus spoke again to the people, he said, "I am the light of the world. Whoever follows me will never walk in darkness, but will have the light of life."

Acts 26 [17]"'I will rescue you from your own people and from the Gentiles. I am sending you to them [18]to open their eyes and turn them from darkness to light, and from the power of Satan to God, so that they may receive forgiveness of sins and a place among those who are sanctified by faith in me.'"

Rom 1 [21]For although they knew God, they neither glorified him as God nor gave thanks to him, but their thinking became futile and their foolish hearts were darkened. [22]Although they claimed to be wise, they became fools [23]and exchanged the glory of the immortal God for images made to look like mortal man and birds and animals and reptiles.

[24]Therefore God gave them over in the sinful desires of their hearts to sexual impurity for the degrading of their bodies with one another. [25]They exchanged the truth of God for a lie, and worshiped and served created things rather than the Creator—who is forever praised. Amen.

[26]Because of this, God gave them over to shameful lusts. Even their women exchanged natural relations for unnatural ones. [27]In the same way the men also abandoned natural relations with women and were inflamed with lust for one another. Men committed indecent acts with other men, and received in themselves the due penalty for their perversion.

[28]Furthermore, since they did not think it worthwhile to retain the knowledge of God, he gave them over to a depraved mind, to do what ought not to be done. [29]They have become filled with every kind of wickedness, evil, greed and depravity. They are full of envy, murder, strife, deceit and malice. They are gossips, [30]slanderers, God-haters, insolent, arrogant and boastful; they invent ways of doing evil; they disobey their parents; [31]they are senseless, faithless, heartless, ruthless. [32]Although they know God's righteous decree that those who do such things deserve death, they not only continue to do these very things but also approve of those who practice them.

2 Cor 3 [14]But their minds were made dull, for to this day the same veil remains when the old covenant is read. It has not been removed, because only in Christ is it taken away. [15]Even to this day when Moses is read, a veil covers their hearts.

Eph 4 [18]They are darkened in their understanding and separated from the life of God because of the ignorance that is in them due to the hardening of their hearts. [19]Having lost all sensitivity, they have given themselves over to sensuality so as to indulge in every kind of impurity, with a continual lust for more.

2 Thess 2 [9]The coming of the lawless one will be in accordance with the work of Satan displayed in all kinds of counterfeit miracles, signs and wonders, [10]and in every sort of evil that deceives those who are perishing. They perish because they refused to love the truth and so be saved.

1 Tim 4 [2]Such teachings come through hypocritical liars, whose consciences have been seared as with a hot iron.

2 Tim 3 [13]while evil men and impostors will go from bad to worse, deceiving and being deceived.

Titus 1 [15]To the pure, all things are pure, but to those who are corrupted and do not believe, nothing is pure. In fact, both their minds and consciences are corrupted.

Heb 11 [25]He chose to be mistreated along with the people of God rather than to enjoy the pleasures of sin for a short time.

2 Pet 1 [5]For this very reason, make every effort to add to your faith goodness; and to goodness, knowledge. . . . [8]For if you possess these qualities in increasing measure, they will keep you from being ineffective and unproductive in your knowledge of our Lord Jesus Christ. [9]But if anyone does not have them, he is nearsighted and blind, and has forgotten that he has been cleansed from his past sins.

2 Pet 2 [19]They promise them freedom, while they themselves are slaves of depravity—for a man is a slave to whatever has mastered him.

1 John 1 [6]If we claim to have fellowship with him yet walk in the darkness, we lie and do not live by the truth. . . .

[8]If we claim to be without sin, we deceive ourselves and the truth is not in us.

1 John 2 [11]But whoever hates his brother is in the darkness and walks around in the darkness; he does not know where he is going, because the darkness has blinded him.

1 John 3 [6]No one who lives in him keeps on sinning. No one who continues to sin has either seen him or known him.

[7]Dear children, do not let anyone lead you astray. He who does what is right is righteous, just as he is righteous.

H. Sin Results in Moral Guilt

Exod 32 [33]The LORD replied to Moses, "Whoever has sinned against me I will blot out of my book. [34]Now go, lead the people to the place I spoke of, and my angel will go before you. However, when the time comes for me to punish, I will punish them for their sin."

Lev 5 [17]"If a person sins and does what is forbidden in any of the LORD's commands, even though he does not know it, he is guilty and will be held responsible."

Num 32 [23]"But if you fail to do this, you will be sinning against the LORD; and you may be sure that your sin will find you out."

Ps 5 [10]Declare them guilty, O God! Let their intrigues be their downfall. Banish them for their many sins, for they have rebelled against you.

Ps 19 [12]Who can discern his errors? Forgive my hidden faults.

Ps 38 [4]My guilt has overwhelmed me like a burden too heavy to bear.

Prov 10 [9]The man of integrity walks securely, but he who takes crooked paths will be found out.

Jer 14 [16]"And the people they are prophesying to will be thrown out into the streets of Jerusalem because of the famine and sword. There will be no one to bury them or their wives, their sons or their daughters. I will pour out on them the calamity they deserve."

Ezek 11 [21]"But as for those whose hearts are devoted to their vile images and detestable idols, I will bring down on their own heads what they have done, declares the Sovereign LORD."

Ezek 21 [24]"Therefore this is what the Sovereign LORD says: 'Because you people have brought to mind your guilt by your open rebellion, revealing your sins in all that you do—because you have done this, you will be taken captive.'"

Hos 12 [14]But Ephraim has bitterly provoked him to anger; his Lord will leave upon him the guilt of his bloodshed and will repay him for his contempt.

Matt 5 [21]"You have heard that it was said to the people long ago, 'Do not murder, and anyone who murders will be subject to judgment.' [22]But I tell you that anyone who is angry with his brother will be subject to judgment. Again, anyone who says to his brother, 'Raca,' is answerable to the Sanhedrin. But anyone who says, 'You fool!' will be in danger of the fire of hell."

Matt 5 [27]"You have heard that it was said, 'Do not commit adultery.' [28]But I tell you that anyone who looks at a woman lustfully has already committed adultery with her in his heart. [29]If your right eye causes you to sin, gouge it out and throw it away. It is better for you to lose one part of your body than for your whole body to be thrown into hell. [30]And if your right hand causes you to sin, cut it off and throw it away. It is better for you to lose one part of your body than for your whole body to go into hell."

Matt 11 [20]Then Jesus began to denounce the cities in which most of his miracles had been performed, because they did not repent. [21]"Woe to you, Korazin! Woe to you, Bethsaida! If the miracles that were performed in you had been performed in Tyre and Sidon, they would have repented long ago in sackcloth and ashes. [22]But I tell you, it will be more bearable for Tyre and Sidon on the day of judgment than for you. [23]And you, Capernaum, will you be lifted up to the skies? No, you will go down to the depths. If the miracles that were performed in you had been performed in Sodom, it would have remained to this day. [24]But I tell you that it will be more bearable for Sodom on the day of judgment than for you."

Matt 23 [33]"You snakes! You brood of vipers! How will you escape being condemned to hell?"

Luke 12 [47]"That servant who knows his master's will and does not get ready or does not do what his master wants will be beaten with many blows. [48]But the one who does not know and does things deserving punishment will be beaten with few blows. From everyone who has been given much, much will be demanded; and from the one who has been entrusted with much, much more will be asked."

Luke 20 [46]"Beware of the teachers of the law. They like to walk around in flowing robes and love to be greeted in the marketplaces and have the most important seats in the synagogues and the places of honor at banquets. [47]They devour widows' houses and for a show make lengthy prayers. Such men will be punished most severely."

John 19 [11]Jesus answered, "You would have no power over me if it were not given to you from above. Therefore the one who handed me over to you is guilty of a greater sin."

1 Cor 11 [27]Therefore, whoever eats the bread or drinks the cup of the Lord in an unworthy manner will be guilty of sinning against the body and blood of the Lord.

James 2 [10]For whoever keeps the whole law and yet stumbles at just one point is guilty of breaking all of it.

1 John 3 [19]This then is how we know that we belong to the truth, and how we set our hearts at rest in his presence [20]whenever our hearts condemn us. For God is greater than our hearts, and he knows everything.

I. Sin Results in National Destruction

Exod 32 [9]"I have seen these people," the LORD said to Moses, "and they are a stiff-necked people. [10]Now leave me alone so that my anger may burn against them and that I may destroy them. Then I will make you into a great nation."

Deut 9 [8]At Horeb you aroused the LORD's wrath so that he was angry enough to destroy you. . . .

[13]And the LORD said to me, "I have seen this people, and they are a stiff-necked people indeed! [14]Let me alone, so that I may destroy them and blot out their name from under heaven. And I will make you into a nation stronger and more numerous than they." . . .

[22]You also made the LORD angry at Taberah, at Massah and at Kibroth Hattaavah.

2 Chron 30 [8]"Do not be stiff-necked, as your fathers were; submit to the LORD. Come to the sanctuary, which he has consecrated forever. Serve the LORD your God, so that his fierce anger will turn away from you."

Neh 9 [36]"But see, we are slaves today, slaves in the land you gave our forefathers so they could eat its fruit and the other good things it produces. [37]Because of our sins, its abundant harvest goes to the kings you have placed over us. They rule over our bodies and our cattle as they please. We are in great distress."

Ps 9 [17]The wicked return to the grave, all the nations that forget God.

Isa 28 [18]"Your covenant with death will be annulled; your agreement with the grave will not stand. When the overwhelming scourge sweeps by, you will be beaten down by it. [19]As often as it comes it will carry you away; morning after morning, by day and by night, it will sweep through."

The understanding of this message will bring sheer terror. [20]The bed is too short to stretch out on, the blanket too narrow to wrap around you. [21]The LORD will rise up as he did at Mount Perazim, he will rouse himself as in the Valley of Gibeon—to do his work, his strange work, and perform his task, his alien task. [22]Now stop your mocking, or your chains will become heavier; the Lord, the LORD Almighty, has told me of the destruction decreed against the whole land.

Isa 32 [9]You women who are so complacent, rise up and listen to me; you daughters who feel secure, hear what I have to say! [10]In little more than a year you who feel secure will tremble; the grape harvest will fail, and the harvest of fruit will not come. [11]Tremble, you complacent women; shudder, you daughters who feel secure! Strip off your clothes, put sackcloth around your waists. [12]Beat your breasts for the pleasant fields, for the fruitful vines [13]and for the land of my people, a land overgrown with thorns and briers—yes, mourn for all houses of merriment and for this city of revelry. [14]The fortress will be abandoned, the noisy city deserted; citadel and watchtower will become a wasteland forever, the delight of donkeys, a pasture for flocks. . . .

Isa 43 [27]"Your first father sinned; your spokesmen rebelled against me. [28]So I will disgrace the dignitaries of your temple, and I will consign Jacob to destruction and Israel to scorn."

Isa 60 [12]"For the nation or kingdom that will not serve you will perish; it will be utterly ruined."

Jer 5 [28]". . . and have grown fat and sleek. Their evil deeds have no limit; they do not plead the case of the fatherless to win it, they do not defend the rights of the poor. [29]Should I not punish them for this?" declares the LORD. "Should I not avenge myself on such a nation as this?"

Jer 6 [6]This is what the LORD Almighty says: "Cut down the trees and build siege ramps against Jerusalem. This city must be punished; it is filled with oppression. [7]As a well pours out its water, so she pours out her wickedness. Violence and destruction resound in her; her sickness and wounds are ever before me. [8]Take warning, O Jerusalem, or I will turn away from you and make your land desolate so no one can live in it."

Jer 8 [14]"Why are we sitting here? Gather together! Let us flee to the fortified cities and perish there! For the LORD our God has doomed us to perish and given us poisoned water to drink, because we have sinned against him."

Jer 12 [17]"But if any nation does not listen, I will completely uproot and destroy it," declares the LORD.

Jer 15 [13]"Your wealth and your treasures I will give as plunder, without charge, because of all your sins throughout your country."

Jer 25 [15]This is what the LORD, the God of Israel, said to me: "Take from my hand this cup filled with the wine of my wrath and make all the nations to whom I send you drink it. [16]When they drink it, they will stagger and go mad because of the sword I will send among them."

[17]So I took the cup from the LORD's hand and made all the nations to whom he sent me drink it: [18]Jerusalem and the towns of Judah, its kings and officials, to make them a ruin and an object of horror and scorn and cursing, as they are today; [19]Pharaoh king of Egypt, his attendants, his officials and all his people, [20]and all the foreign people there; all the kings of Uz; all the kings of the Philistines (those of Ashkelon, Gaza, Ekron, and the people left at Ashdod); [21]Edom, Moab and Ammon; [22]all the kings of Tyre and Sidon; the kings of the coastlands across the sea; [23]Dedan, Tema, Buz and all who are in distant places; [24]all the kings of Arabia and all the kings of the foreign people who live in the desert; [25]all the kings of Zimri, Elam and Media; [26]and all the kings of the north, near and far, one after the other—all the kingdoms on the face of the earth. And after all of them, the king of Sheshach will drink it too.

[27]"Then tell them, 'This is what the LORD Almighty, the God of Israel, says: Drink, get drunk and vomit, and fall to rise no more because of the sword I will send among you.' [28]But if they refuse to take the cup from your hand and drink, tell them, 'This is what the LORD Almighty says: You must drink it! [29]See, I am beginning to bring disaster on the city that bears my

Name, and will you indeed go unpunished? You will not go unpunished, for I am calling down a sword upon all who live on the earth, declares the LORD Almighty.'"

Jer 36 [31]"'I will punish him and his children and his attendants for their wickedness; I will bring on them and those living in Jerusalem and the people of Judah every disaster I pronounced against them, because they have not listened.'"

Jer 50 [29]"Summon archers against Babylon, all those who draw the bow. Encamp all around her; let no one escape. Repay her for her deeds; do to her as she has done. For she has defied the LORD, the Holy One of Israel. . . ." [45]Therefore, hear what the LORD has planned against Babylon, what he has purposed against the land of the Babylonians: The young of the flock will be dragged away; he will completely destroy their pasture because of them. [46]At the sound of Babylon's capture the earth will tremble; its cry will resound among the nations.

Lam 1 [8]Jerusalem has sinned greatly and so has become unclean. All who honored her despise her, for they have seen her nakedness; she herself groans and turns away.

[9]Her filthiness clung to her skirts; she did not consider her future. Her fall was astounding; there was none to comfort her. "Look, O LORD, on my affliction, for the enemy has triumphed."

Ezek 29 [8]"'Therefore this is what the Sovereign LORD says: I will bring a sword against you and kill your men and their animals. [9]Egypt will become a desolate wasteland. Then they will know that I am the LORD.

"'Because you said, "The Nile is mine; I made it," [10]therefore I am against you and against your streams, and I will make the land of Egypt a ruin and a desolate waste from Migdol to Aswan, as far as the border of Cush. [11]No foot of man or animal will pass through it; no one will live there for forty years. [12]I will make the land of Egypt desolate among devastated lands, and her cities will lie desolate forty years among ruined cities. And I will disperse the Egyptians among the nations and scatter them through the countries.'"

Hos 5 [5]"Israel's arrogance testifies against them; the Israelites, even Ephraim, stumble in their sin; Judah also stumbles with them. . . . [7]They are unfaithful to the LORD; they give birth to illegitimate children. Now their New Moon festivals will devour them and their fields."

Amos 1 [3]This is what the LORD says: "For three sins of Damascus, even for four, I will not turn back my wrath. Because she threshed Gilead with sledges having iron teeth . . ."

Amos 1 [6]This is what the LORD says: "For three sins of Gaza, even for four, I will not turn back my wrath. Because she took captive whole communities and sold them to Edom . . ."

Amos 1 [9]This is what the LORD says: "For three sins of Tyre, even for four, I will not turn back my wrath. Because she sold whole communities of captives to Edom, disregarding a treaty of brotherhood . . ."

Amos 1 [13]This is what the LORD says: "For three sins of Ammon, even for four, I will not turn back my wrath. Because he ripped open the pregnant women of Gilead in order to extend his borders . . ."

Amos 2 [1]This is what the LORD says: "For three sins of Moab, even for four, I will not turn back my wrath. Because he burned, as if to lime, the bones of Edom's king . . ."

Amos 2 [4]This is what the LORD says: "For three sins of Judah, even for four, I will not turn back my wrath. Because they have rejected the law of the LORD and have not kept his decrees, because they have been led astray by false gods, the gods their ancestors followed . . ."

Amos 2 [6]This is what the LORD says: "For three sins of Israel, even for four, I will not turn back my wrath. They sell the righteous for silver, and the needy for a pair of sandals."

Amos 3 [13]"Hear this and testify against the house of Jacob," declares the Lord, the LORD God Almighty. [14]"On the day I punish Israel for her sins, I will destroy the altars of Bethel; the horns of the altar will be cut off and fall to the ground. [15]I will tear down the winter house along with the summer house; the houses adorned with ivory will be destroyed and the mansions will be demolished," declares the LORD.

Amos 6 [8]The Sovereign LORD has sworn by himself—the LORD God Almighty declares: "I abhor the pride of Jacob and detest his fortresses; I will deliver up the city and everything in it."

Amos 9 [1]I saw the Lord standing by the altar, and he said: "Strike the tops of the pillars so that the thresholds shake. Bring them down on the heads of all the people; those who are left I will kill with the sword. Not one will get away, none will escape. [2]Though they dig down to the depths of the grave, from there my hand will take them. Though they climb up to the heavens, from there I will bring them down. [3]Though they hide themselves on the top of Carmel, there I will hunt them down and seize them. Though they hide from me at the bottom of the sea, there I will command the serpent to bite them. [4]Though they are driven into exile by their enemies, there I will command the sword to slay them. I will fix my eyes upon them for evil and not for good."

Zeph 2 [13]He will stretch out his hand against the north and destroy Assyria, leaving Nineveh utterly desolate and dry as the desert. [14]Flocks and herds will lie down there, creatures of every kind. The desert owl and the screech owl will roost on her columns. Their calls will echo through the windows, rubble will be in the doorways, the beams of cedar will be exposed. [15]This is the carefree city that lived in safety. She said to herself, "I am, and there is none besides me." What a ruin she has become, a lair for wild beasts! All who pass by her scoff and shake their fists.

Rev 18 [2]With a mighty voice he shouted: "Fallen! Fallen is Babylon the Great! She has become a home for demons and a haunt for every evil spirit, a haunt for every unclean and detestable bird. . . ."

[4]Then I heard another voice from heaven say: "Come out of her, my people, so that you will not share in her sins, so that you will not receive any of her plagues; [5]for her sins are piled up to heaven, and God has remembered her crimes. [6]Give back to her as she has given; pay her back double for what she has done. Mix her a double portion from her own cup. [7]Give her as much torture and grief as the glory and luxury she gave herself. In her heart she boasts, 'I sit as queen; I am not a widow, and I will never mourn.' [8]Therefore in one day her plagues will overtake her: death, mourning and famine. She will be consumed by fire, for mighty is the Lord God who judges her."

J. Sin Results in Personal Distress and Anxiety

Job 4 [8]"As I have observed, those who plow evil and those who sow trouble reap it."

Job 5 [2]"Resentment kills a fool, and envy slays the simple."

Job 15 [20]"All his days the wicked man suffers torment, the ruthless through all the years stored up for him. [21]Terrifying sounds fill his ears; when all seems well, marauders attack him. [22]He despairs of escaping the darkness; he is marked for the sword. [23]He wanders about—food for vultures; he knows the day of darkness is at hand. [24]Distress and anguish fill him with terror; they overwhelm him, like a king poised to attack, [25]because he shakes his fist at God and vaunts himself against the Almighty, [26]defiantly charging against him with a thick, strong shield."

Job 18 [5]"The lamp of the wicked is snuffed out; the flame of his fire stops burning. . . . [7]The vigor of his step is weakened; his own schemes throw him down. [8]His feet thrust him into a net and he wanders into its mesh. [9]A trap seizes him by the heel; a snare holds him fast. [10]A noose is hidden for him on the ground; a trap lies in his path. [11]Terrors startle him on every side and dog his every step. [12]Calamity is hungry for him; disaster is ready for him when he falls. [13]It eats away parts of his skin; death's firstborn devours his limbs. [14]He is torn from the security of his tent and marched off to the king of terrors."

Ps 38 [3]Because of your wrath there is no health in my body; my bones have no soundness because of my sin. [4]My guilt has overwhelmed me like a burden too heavy to bear.

Ps 141 [10]Let the wicked fall into their own nets, while I pass by in safety.

Prov 1 [29]"Since they hated knowledge and did not choose to fear the LORD, [30]since they would not accept my advice and spurned my rebuke, [31]they will eat the fruit of their ways and be filled with the fruit of their schemes. [32]For the waywardness

of the simple will kill them, and the complacency of fools will destroy them. . . ."
Prov 5 [22]The evil deeds of a wicked man ensnare him; the cords of his sin hold him fast. [23]He will die for lack of discipline, led astray by his own great folly.
Prov 8 [35]"For whoever finds me finds life and receives favor from the LORD. [36]But whoever fails to find me harms himself; all who hate me love death."
Prov 11 [5]The righteousness of the blameless makes a straight way for them, but the wicked are brought down by their own wickedness.

[6]The righteousness of the upright delivers them, but the unfaithful are trapped by evil desires. . . .

[27]He who seeks good finds goodwill, but evil comes to him who searches for it.
Prov 12 [13]An evil man is trapped by his sinful talk, but a righteous man escapes trouble.
Prov 12 [21]No harm befalls the righteous, but the wicked have their fill of trouble.
Prov 13 [6]Righteousness guards the man of integrity, but wickedness overthrows the sinner.
Prov 13 [15]Good understanding wins favor, but the way of the unfaithful is hard.
Prov 22 [8]He who sows wickedness reaps trouble, and the rod of his fury will be destroyed.
Prov 28 [1]The wicked man flees though no one pursues, but the righteous are as bold as a lion.
Isa 3 [11]Woe to the wicked! Disaster is upon them! They will be paid back for what their hands have done.
Isa 57 [20]But the wicked are like the tossing sea, which cannot rest, whose waves cast up mire and mud. [21]"There is no peace," says my God, "for the wicked."
Jer 2 [19]"Your wickedness will punish you; your backsliding will rebuke you. Consider then and realize how evil and bitter it is for you when you forsake the LORD your God and have no awe of me," declares the LORD, the LORD Almighty.
Rom 2 [8]But for those who are self-seeking and who reject the truth and follow evil, there will be wrath and anger. [9]There will be trouble and distress for every human being who does evil: first for the Jew, then for the Gentile. . . .

K. Sin Results in Physical Death

Gen 3 [19]"By the sweat of your brow you will eat your food until you return to the ground, since from it you were taken; for dust you are and to dust you will return."
Gen 6 [5]The LORD saw how great man's wickedness on the earth had become, and that every inclination of the thoughts of his heart was only evil all the time. [6]The LORD was grieved that he had made man on the earth, and his heart was filled with pain. [7]So the LORD said, "I will wipe mankind, whom I have created, from the face of the earth—men and animals, and creatures that move along the ground, and birds of the air—for I am grieved that I have made them."
Num 27 [3]"Our father died in the desert. He was not among Korah's followers, who banded together against the LORD, but he died for his own sin and left no sons."
Job 14 [1]"Man born of woman is of few days and full of trouble. [2]He springs up like a flower and withers away; like a fleeting shadow, he does not endure. [3]Do you fix your eye on such a one? Will you bring him before you for judgment? [4]Who can bring what is pure from the impure? No one! [5]Man's days are determined; you have decreed the number of his months and have set limits he cannot exceed. [6]So look away from him and let him alone, till he has put in his time like a hired man."
Ps 90 [7]We are consumed by your anger and terrified by your indignation. [8]You have set our iniquities before you, our secret sins in the light of your presence. [9]All our days pass away under your wrath; we finish our years with a moan. [10]The length of our days is seventy years—or eighty, if we have the strength; yet their span is but trouble and sorrow, for they quickly pass, and we fly away.
Ps 94 [23]He will repay them for their sins and destroy them for their wickedness; the LORD our God will destroy them.
Rom 5 [12]Therefore, just as sin entered the world through one man, and death through sin, and in this way death came to all men, because all sinned . . .
Rom 8 [10]But if Christ is in you, your body is dead because of sin, yet your spirit is alive because of righteousness.
1 Cor 15 [22]For as in Adam all die, so in Christ all will be made alive.
2 Cor 5 [1]Now we know that if the earthly tent we live in is destroyed, we have a building from God, an eternal house in heaven, not built by human hands.
2 Tim 1 [10]but it has now been revealed through the appearing of our Savior, Christ Jesus, who has destroyed death and has brought life and immortality to light through the gospel.

L. Sin Results in the Pollution of Creation

Gen 3 [17]To Adam he said, "Because you listened to your wife and ate from the tree about which I commanded you, 'You must not eat of it,' Cursed is the ground because of you; through painful toil you will eat of it all the days of your life. [18]It will produce thorns and thistles for you, and you will eat the plants of the field. [19]By the sweat of your brow you will eat your food until you return to the ground, since from it you were taken; for dust you are and to dust you will return."
Rom 8 [19]The creation waits in eager expectation for the sons of God to be revealed. [20]For the creation was subjected to frustration, not by its own choice, but by the will of the one who subjected it, in hope [21]that the creation itself will be liberated from its bondage to decay and brought into the glorious freedom of the children of God. [22]We know that the whole creation has been groaning as in the pains of childbirth right up to the present time.

M. Sin Results in Spiritual Condemnation

Prov 11 [19]The truly righteous man attains life, but he who pursues evil goes to his death.
John 3 [36]"Whoever believes in the Son has eternal life, but whoever rejects the Son will not see life, for God's wrath remains on him."
John 5 [28]"Do not be amazed at this, for a time is coming when all who are in their graves will hear his voice [29]and come out—those who have done good will rise to live, and those who have done evil will rise to be condemned."
Rom 2 [5]But because of your stubbornness and your unrepentant heart, you are storing up wrath against yourself for the day of God's wrath, when his righteous judgment will be revealed. [6]God "will give to each person according to what he has done." [7]To those who by persistence in doing good seek glory, honor and immortality, he will give eternal life. [8]But for those who are self-seeking and who reject the truth and follow evil, there will be wrath and anger.
Rom 5 [12]Therefore, just as sin entered the world through one man, and death through sin, and in this way death came to all men, because all sinned . . .

[16]Again, the gift of God is not like the result of the one man's sin: The judgment followed one sin and brought condemnation, but the gift followed many trespasses and brought justification. [17]For if, by the trespass of the one man, death reigned through that one man, how much more will those who receive God's abundant provision of grace and of the gift of righteousness reign in life through the one man, Jesus Christ.

[18]Consequently, just as the result of one trespass was condemnation for all men, so also the result of one act of righteousness was justification that brings life for all men. [19]For just as through the disobedience of the one man the many were made sinners, so also through the obedience of the one man the many will be made righteous.

[20]The law was added so that the trespass might increase. But where sin increased, grace increased all the more, [21]so that, just as sin reigned in death, so also grace might reign through

righteousness to bring eternal life through Jesus Christ our Lord.
Rom 6 [23]For the wages of sin is death, but the gift of God is eternal life in Christ Jesus our Lord.
Rom 7 [11]For sin, seizing the opportunity afforded by the commandment, deceived me, and through the commandment put me to death.
Rom 8 [1]Therefore, there is now no condemnation for those who are in Christ Jesus. . . .
Rom 8 [5]Those who live according to the sinful nature have their minds set on what that nature desires; but those who live in accordance with the Spirit have their minds set on what the Spirit desires. [6]The mind of sinful man is death, but the mind controlled by the Spirit is life and peace; [7]the sinful mind is hostile to God. It does not submit to God's law, nor can it do so. [8]Those controlled by the sinful nature cannot please God.
Rom 11 [21]For if God did not spare the natural branches, he will not spare you either.

[22]Consider therefore the kindness and sternness of God: sternness to those who fell, but kindness to you, provided that you continue in his kindness. Otherwise, you also will be cut off.
Eph 2 [1]As for you, you were dead in your transgressions and sins. . . .
2 Thess 2 [9]The coming of the lawless one will be in accordance with the work of Satan displayed in all kinds of counterfeit miracles, signs and wonders, [10]and in every sort of evil that deceives those who are perishing. They perish because they refused to love the truth and so be saved. [11]For this reason God sends them a powerful delusion so that they will believe the lie [12]and so that all will be condemned who have not believed the truth but have delighted in wickedness.
James 1 [15]Then, after desire has conceived, it gives birth to sin; and sin, when it is full-grown, gives birth to death.
James 5 [19]My brothers, if one of you should wander from the truth and someone should bring him back, [20]remember this: Whoever turns a sinner from the error of his way will save him from death and cover over a multitude of sins.
1 John 3 [14]We know that we have passed from death to life, because we love our brothers. Anyone who does not love remains in death.

N. Sin Results in Temporal Calamity

Lev 26 [23]"'If in spite of these things you do not accept my correction but continue to be hostile toward me, [24]I myself will be hostile toward you and will afflict you for your sins seven times over. [25]And I will bring the sword upon you to avenge the breaking of the covenant. When you withdraw into your cities, I will send a plague among you, and you will be given into enemy hands.'"
Deut 28 [15]However, if you do not obey the LORD your God and do not carefully follow all his commands and decrees I am giving you today, all these curses will come upon you and overtake you. . . .
1 Sam 12 [25]"Yet if you persist in doing evil, both you and your king will be swept away."
Job 5 [12]"He thwarts the plans of the crafty, so that their hands achieve no success. [13]He catches the wise in their craftiness, and the schemes of the wily are swept away."
Job 15 [20]"All his days the wicked man suffers torment, the ruthless through all the years stored up for him. . . .

[27]"Though his face is covered with fat and his waist bulges with flesh, [28]he will inhabit ruined towns and houses where no one lives, houses crumbling to rubble. [29]He will no longer be rich and his wealth will not endure, nor will his possessions spread over the land."
Job 27 [13]"Here is the fate God allots to the wicked, the heritage a ruthless man receives from the Almighty: . . . [16]Though he heaps up silver like dust and clothes like piles of clay, [17]what he lays up the righteous will wear, and the innocent will divide his silver."
Ps 9 [15]The nations have fallen into the pit they have dug; their feet are caught in the net they have hidden. [16]The LORD is known by his justice; the wicked are ensnared by the work of their hands.
Ps 73 [18]Surely you place them on slippery ground; you cast them down to ruin. [19]How suddenly are they destroyed, completely swept away by terrors!
Ps 107 [10]Some sat in darkness and the deepest gloom, prisoners suffering in iron chains, [11]for they had rebelled against the words of God and despised the counsel of the Most High. [12]So he subjected them to bitter labor; they stumbled, and there was no one to help. . . .

[39]Then their numbers decreased, and they were humbled by oppression, calamity and sorrow; [40]he who pours contempt on nobles made them wander in a trackless waste.
Prov 1 [16]for their feet rush into sin, they are swift to shed blood. . . . [18]These men lie in wait for their own blood; they waylay only themselves! [19]Such is the end of all who go after ill-gotten gain; it takes away the lives of those who get it.
Prov 1 [24]"But since you rejected me when I called and no one gave heed when I stretched out my hand, [25]since you ignored all my advice and would not accept my rebuke, [26]I in turn will laugh at your disaster; I will mock when calamity overtakes you—[27]when calamity overtakes you like a storm, when disaster sweeps over you like a whirlwind, when distress and trouble overwhelm you."
Prov 3 [33]The LORD's curse is on the house of the wicked, but he blesses the home of the righteous.
Prov 10 [6]Blessings crown the head of the righteous, but violence overwhelms the mouth of the wicked.
Prov 10 [7]The memory of the righteous will be a blessing, but the name of the wicked will rot.
Prov 11 [3]The integrity of the upright guides them, but the unfaithful are destroyed by their duplicity.
Prov 11 [5]The righteousness of the blameless makes a straight way for them, but the wicked are brought down by their own wickedness.
Prov 13 [25]The righteous eat to their hearts' content, but the stomach of the wicked goes hungry.
Prov 23 [21]for drunkards and gluttons become poor, and drowsiness clothes them in rags.
Eccles 2 [26]To the man who pleases him, God gives wisdom, knowledge and happiness, but to the sinner he gives the task of gathering and storing up wealth to hand it over to the one who pleases God. This too is meaningless, a chasing after the wind.
Isa 1 [28]But rebels and sinners will both be broken, and those who forsake the LORD will perish.

[29]"You will be ashamed because of the sacred oaks in which you have delighted; you will be disgraced because of the gardens that you have chosen. [30]You will be like an oak with fading leaves, like a garden without water. [31]The mighty man will become tinder and his work a spark; both will burn together, with no one to quench the fire."
Isa 5 [18]Woe to those who draw sin along with cords of deceit, and wickedness as with cart ropes, [19]to those who say, "Let God hurry, let him hasten his work so we may see it. Let it approach, let the plan of the Holy One of Israel come, so we may know it."

[20]Woe to those who call evil good and good evil, who put darkness for light and light for darkness, who put bitter for sweet and sweet for bitter.

[21]Woe to those who are wise in their own eyes and clever in their own sight.

[22]Woe to those who are heroes at drinking wine and champions at mixing drinks, [23]who acquit the guilty for a bribe, but deny justice to the innocent. [24]Therefore, as tongues of fire lick up straw and as dry grass sinks down in the flames, so their roots will decay and their flowers blow away like dust; for they have rejected the law of the LORD Almighty and spurned the word of the Holy One of Israel.
Isa 9 [16]Those who guide this people mislead them, and those who are guided are led astray. [17]Therefore the Lord will take no pleasure in the young men, nor will he pity the fatherless and widows, for everyone is ungodly and wicked, every mouth speaks vileness.

Yet for all this, his anger is not turned away, his hand is still upraised.

Jer 14 [15]"Therefore, this is what the LORD says about the prophets who are prophesying in my name: I did not send them, yet they are saying, 'No sword or famine will touch this land.' Those same prophets will perish by sword and famine. [16]And the people they are prophesying to will be thrown out into the streets of Jerusalem because of the famine and sword. There will be no one to bury them or their wives, their sons or their daughters. I will pour out on them the calamity they deserve."

Jer 18 [16]"Their land will be laid waste, an object of lasting scorn; all who pass by will be appalled and will shake their heads. [17]Like a wind from the east, I will scatter them before their enemies; I will show them my back and not my face in the day of their disaster."

Rom 2 [9]There will be trouble and distress for every human being who does evil: first for the Jew, then for the Gentile. . . .

Phil 3 [19]Their destiny is destruction, their god is their stomach, and their glory is in their shame. Their mind is on earthly things.

O. Sin Results in Tempting Others to Sin

Gen 3 [1]Now the serpent was more crafty than any of the wild animals the LORD God had made. He said to the woman, "Did God really say, 'You must not eat from any tree in the garden'?"

[2]The woman said to the serpent, "We may eat fruit from the trees in the garden, [3]but God did say, 'You must not eat fruit from the tree that is in the middle of the garden, and you must not touch it, or you will die.'"

[4]"You will not surely die," the serpent said to the woman. [5]"For God knows that when you eat of it your eyes will be opened, and you will be like God, knowing good and evil."

[6]When the woman saw that the fruit of the tree was good for food and pleasing to the eye, and also desirable for gaining wisdom, she took some and ate it. She also gave some to her husband, who was with her, and he ate it.

1 Kings 16 [2]"I lifted you up from the dust and made you leader of my people Israel, but you walked in the ways of Jeroboam and caused my people Israel to sin and to provoke me to anger by their sins."

1 Kings 21 [25](There was never a man like Ahab, who sold himself to do evil in the eyes of the LORD, urged on by Jezebel his wife. . . .)

Prov 1 [10]My son, if sinners entice you, do not give in to them. [11]If they say, "Come along with us; let's lie in wait for someone's blood, let's waylay some harmless soul; [12]let's swallow them alive, like the grave, and whole, like those who go down to the pit; [13]we will get all sorts of valuable things and fill our houses with plunder; [14]throw in your lot with us, and we will share a common purse" . . .

Prov 16 [29]A violent man entices his neighbor and leads him down a path that is not good.

Prov 28 [10]He who leads the upright along an evil path will fall into his own trap, but the blameless will receive a good inheritance.

Eccles 7 [26]I find more bitter than death the woman who is a snare, whose heart is a trap and whose hands are chains. The man who pleases God will escape her, but the sinner she will ensnare.

Matt 5 [19]"Anyone who breaks one of the least of these commandments and teaches others to do the same will be called least in the kingdom of heaven, but whoever practices and teaches these commands will be called great in the kingdom of heaven."

Matt 18 [6]"But if anyone causes one of these little ones who believe in me to sin, it would be better for him to have a large millstone hung around his neck and to be drowned in the depths of the sea.

[7]"Woe to the world because of the things that cause people to sin! Such things must come, but woe to the man through whom they come!"

Mark 13 [21]"At that time if anyone says to you, 'Look, here is the Christ!' or, 'Look, there he is!' do not believe it. [22]For false Christs and false prophets will appear and perform signs and miracles to deceive the elect—if that were possible."

Luke 4 [1]Jesus, full of the Holy Spirit, returned from the Jordan and was led by the Spirit in the desert, [2]where for forty days he was tempted by the devil. He ate nothing during those days, and at the end of them he was hungry.

[3]The devil said to him, "If you are the Son of God, tell this stone to become bread."

[4]Jesus answered, "It is written: 'Man does not live on bread alone.'"

[5]The devil led him up to a high place and showed him in an instant all the kingdoms of the world. [6]And he said to him, "I will give you all their authority and splendor, for it has been given to me, and I can give it to anyone I want to. [7]So if you worship me, it will all be yours."

[8]Jesus answered, "It is written: 'Worship the Lord your God and serve him only.'"

[9]The devil led him to Jerusalem and had him stand on the highest point of the temple. "If you are the Son of God," he said, "throw yourself down from here. [10]For it is written: 'He will command his angels concerning you to guard you carefully; [11]they will lift you up in their hands, so that you will not strike your foot against a stone.'"

[12]Jesus answered, "It says: 'Do not put the Lord your God to the test.'"

[13]When the devil had finished all this tempting, he left him until an opportune time.

Rom 14 [13]Therefore let us stop passing judgment on one another. Instead, make up your mind not to put any stumbling block or obstacle in your brother's way.

1 Cor 8 [9]Be careful, however, that the exercise of your freedom does not become a stumbling block to the weak. [10]For if anyone with a weak conscience sees you who have this knowledge eating in an idol's temple, won't he be emboldened to eat what has been sacrificed to idols? [11]So this weak brother, for whom Christ died, is destroyed by your knowledge. [12]When you sin against your brothers in this way and wound their weak conscience, you sin against Christ. [13]Therefore, if what I eat causes my brother to fall into sin, I will never eat meat again, so that I will not cause him to fall.

Eph 6 [11]Put on the full armor of God so that you can take your stand against the devil's schemes.

1 Thess 3 [5]For this reason, when I could stand it no longer, I sent to find out about your faith. I was afraid that in some way the tempter might have tempted you and our efforts might have been useless.

2 Tim 3 [6]They are the kind who worm their way into homes and gain control over weak-willed women, who are loaded down with sins and are swayed by all kinds of evil desires, [7]always learning but never able to acknowledge the truth. [8]Just as Jannes and Jambres opposed Moses, so also these men oppose the truth—men of depraved minds, who, as far as the faith is concerned, are rejected. [9]But they will not get very far because, as in the case of those men, their folly will be clear to everyone.

James 4 [7]Submit yourselves, then, to God. Resist the devil, and he will flee from you.

1 Pet 5 [8]Be self-controlled and alert. Your enemy the devil prowls around like a roaring lion looking for someone to devour. [9]Resist him, standing firm in the faith, because you know that your brothers throughout the world are undergoing the same kind of sufferings.

2 Pet 2 [18]For they mouth empty, boastful words and, by appealing to the lustful desires of sinful human nature, they entice people who are just escaping from those who live in error.

2 Pet 3 [17]Therefore, dear friends, since you already know this, be on your guard so that you may not be carried away by the error of lawless men and fall from your secure position.

1 John 2 [16]For everything in the world—the cravings of sinful man, the lust of his eyes and the boasting of what he has and does—comes not from the Father but from the world. . . .

[26]I am writing these things to you about those who are trying to lead you astray.

P. Sin Results in the Wrath of God

See p. 443a, Negatively, God's Attitude Is One of Wrath

V
Descriptions of Sins and the Sinner

A. Descriptive Titles of Sinners

1. Sinful People Are Sinners

Ps 1 [1]Blessed is the man who does not walk in the counsel of the wicked or stand in the way of sinners or sit in the seat of mockers. . . .

[5]Therefore the wicked will not stand in the judgment, nor sinners in the assembly of the righteous.

Ps 26 [9]Do not take away my soul along with sinners, my life with bloodthirsty men, [10]in whose hands are wicked schemes, whose right hands are full of bribes.

Ps 37 [38]But all sinners will be destroyed; the future of the wicked will be cut off.

Prov 1 [10]My son, if sinners entice you, do not give in to them.

Prov 11 [31]If the righteous receive their due on earth, how much more the ungodly and the sinner!

Prov 13 [21]Misfortune pursues the sinner, but prosperity is the reward of the righteous.

Eccles 9 [18]Wisdom is better than weapons of war, but one sinner destroys much good.

Isa 1 [28]But rebels and sinners will both be broken, and those who forsake the LORD will perish.

Isa 33 [14]The sinners in Zion are terrified; trembling grips the godless: "Who of us can dwell with the consuming fire? Who of us can dwell with everlasting burning?"

Amos 9 [10]"All the sinners among my people will die by the sword, all those who say, 'Disaster will not overtake or meet us.'"

Matt 26 [45]Then he returned to the disciples and said to them, "Are you still sleeping and resting? Look, the hour is near, and the Son of Man is betrayed into the hands of sinners."

John 9 [31]"We know that God does not listen to sinners. He listens to the godly man who does his will."

Rom 5 [8]But God demonstrates his own love for us in this: While we were still sinners, Christ died for us.

Rom 5 [19]For just as through the disobedience of the one man the many were made sinners, so also through the obedience of the one man the many will be made righteous.

1 Tim 1 [15]Here is a trustworthy saying that deserves full acceptance: Christ Jesus came into the world to save sinners—of whom I am the worst.

Jude [15]". . . to judge everyone, and to convict all the ungodly of all the ungodly acts they have done in the ungodly way, and of all the harsh words ungodly sinners have spoken against him."

2. Sinners Are an Accursed Brood

2 Pet 2 [14]With eyes full of adultery, they never stop sinning; they seduce the unstable; they are experts in greed—an accursed brood!

3. Sinners Are an Adulterous and Sinful Generation

Mark 8 [38]"If anyone is ashamed of me and my words in this adulterous and sinful generation, the Son of Man will be ashamed of him when he comes in his Father's glory with the holy angels."

4. Sinners Are Adversaries of the Lord

1 Sam 2 [10]". . . those who oppose the LORD will be shattered. He will thunder against them from heaven; the LORD will judge the ends of the earth.

"He will give strength to his king and exalt the horn of his anointed."

Jer 50 [24]"I set a trap for you, O Babylon, and you were caught before you knew it; you were found and captured because you opposed the LORD."

5. Sinners Are a Base and Nameless Brood

Job 30 [8]"A base and nameless brood, they were driven out of the land."

6. Sinners Are a Brood of Evildoers

Isa 1 [4]Ah, sinful nation, a people loaded with guilt, a brood of evildoers, children given to corruption! They have forsaken the LORD; they have spurned the Holy One of Israel and turned their backs on him.

7. Sinners Are a Brood of Rebels

Isa 57 [4]"Whom are you mocking? At whom do you sneer and stick out your tongue? Are you not a brood of rebels, the offspring of liars?"

8. Sinners Are a Brood of Sinners

Num 32 [14]"And here you are, a brood of sinners, standing in the place of your fathers and making the LORD even more angry with Israel."

9. Sinners Are Children Given to Corruption

Isa 1 [4]Ah, sinful nation, a people loaded with guilt, a brood of evildoers, children given to corruption! They have forsaken the LORD; they have spurned the Holy One of Israel and turned their backs on him.

10. Sinners Are Children of the Devil

John 8 [44]"You belong to your father, the devil, and you want to carry out your father's desire. He was a murderer from the beginning, not holding to the truth, for there is no truth in him. When he lies, he speaks his native language, for he is a liar and the father of lies."

Acts 13 [10]"You are a child of the devil and an enemy of everything that is right! You are full of all kinds of deceit and trickery. Will you never stop perverting the right ways of the Lord?"

1 John 3 [8]He who does what is sinful is of the devil, because the devil has been sinning from the beginning. The reason the Son of God appeared was to destroy the devil's work. . . . [10]This is how we know who the children of God are and who the children of the devil are: Anyone who does not do what is right is not a child of God; nor is anyone who does not love his brother.

11. Sinners Are Children Unwilling to Listen to the Lord's Instruction

Isa 30 [9]These are rebellious people, deceitful children, children unwilling to listen to the LORD's instruction.

12. Sinners Are Children Who Are Unfaithful

Deut 32 [20]"I will hide my face from them," he said, "and see what their end will be; for they are a perverse generation, children who are unfaithful."

13. Sinners Are a Corrupt Generation

Acts 2 [40]With many other words he warned them; and he pleaded with them, "Save yourselves from this corrupt generation."

14. Sinners Are a Crooked and Depraved Generation

Phil 2 [15]so that you may become blameless and pure, children of God without fault in a crooked and depraved generation, in which you shine like stars in the universe . . .

15. Sinners Are Deceitful Children

Isa 30 [9]These are rebellious people, deceitful children, children unwilling to listen to the LORD's instruction.

16. Sinners Are Deceitful Men

Job 11 [11]"Surely he recognizes deceitful men; and when he sees evil, does he not take note?"
Ps 5 [6]You destroy those who tell lies; bloodthirsty and deceitful men the LORD abhors.
Ps 26 [4]I do not sit with deceitful men, nor do I consort with hypocrites. . . .
Ps 43 [1]Vindicate me, O God, and plead my cause against an ungodly nation; rescue me from deceitful and wicked men.
Ps 55 [23]But you, O God, will bring down the wicked into the pit of corruption; bloodthirsty and deceitful men will not live out half their days.
But as for me, I trust in you.
Ps 109 [2]for wicked and deceitful men have opened their mouths against me; they have spoken against me with lying tongues.

17. Sinners Are Deceitful Workmen

2 Cor 11 [13]For such men are false apostles, deceitful workmen, masquerading as apostles of Christ.

18. Sinners Are Enemies of All That Is Right

Acts 13 [10]"You are a child of the devil and an enemy of everything that is right! You are full of all kinds of deceit and trickery. Will you never stop perverting the right ways of the Lord?"

19. Sinners Are Enemies of the Cross of Christ

Phil 3 [18]For, as I have often told you before and now say again even with tears, many live as enemies of the cross of Christ.

20. Sinners Are Enemies of God

Ps 37 [20]But the wicked will perish: The LORD's enemies will be like the beauty of the fields, they will vanish—vanish like smoke.
Rom 5 [10]For if, when we were God's enemies, we were reconciled to him through the death of his Son, how much more, having been reconciled, shall we be saved through his life!
Col 1 [21]Once you were alienated from God and were enemies in your minds because of your evil behavior.
James 4 [4]You adulterous people, don't you know that friendship with the world is hatred toward God? Anyone who chooses to be a friend of the world becomes an enemy of God.

21. Sinners Are Evildoers

1 Sam 24 [13]"As the old saying goes, 'From evildoers come evil deeds,' so my hand will not touch you."
Ps 26 [5]I abhor the assembly of evildoers and refuse to sit with the wicked.
Ps 28 [3]Do not drag me away with the wicked, with those who do evil, who speak cordially with their neighbors but harbor malice in their hearts.
Ps 36 [12]See how the evildoers lie fallen—thrown down, not able to rise!
Ps 92 [9]For surely your enemies, O LORD, surely your enemies will perish; all evildoers will be scattered.
Ps 94 [4]They pour out arrogant words; all the evildoers are full of boasting.
Ps 101 [8]Every morning I will put to silence all the wicked in the land; I will cut off every evildoer from the city of the LORD.
Prov 21 [15]When justice is done, it brings joy to the righteous but terror to evildoers.
Isa 31 [2]Yet he too is wise and can bring disaster; he does not take back his words. He will rise up against the house of the wicked, against those who help evildoers.
Hos 10 [9]"Since the days of Gibeah, you have sinned, O Israel, and there you have remained. Did not war overtake the evildoers in Gibeah?"
Luke 13 [27]"But he will reply, 'I don't know you or where you come from. Away from me, all you evildoers!'"

22. Sinners Are an Evil Generation

Deut 1 [35]"Not a man of this evil generation shall see the good land I swore to give your forefathers. . . ."

23. Sinners Are Evil Men

Job 16 [11]"God has turned me over to evil men and thrown me into the clutches of the wicked."
Job 18 [21]"Surely such is the dwelling of an evil man; such is the place of one who knows not God."
Job 24 [20]"The womb forgets them, the worm feasts on them; evil men are no longer remembered but are broken like a tree."
Ps 37 [1]Do not fret because of evil men or be envious of those who do wrong; [2]for like the grass they will soon wither, like green plants they will soon die away.
Ps 37 [7]Be still before the LORD and wait patiently for him; do not fret when men succeed in their ways, when they carry out their wicked schemes. [8]Refrain from anger and turn from wrath; do not fret—it leads only to evil. [9]For evil men will be cut off, but those who hope in the LORD will inherit the land.
Ps 71 [4]Deliver me, O my God, from the hand of the wicked, from the grasp of evil and cruel men.
Prov 4 [14]Do not set foot on the path of the wicked or walk in the way of evil men.
Prov 12 [13]An evil man is trapped by his sinful talk, but a righteous man escapes trouble.
Prov 14 [19]Evil men will bow down in the presence of the good, and the wicked at the gates of the righteous.
Prov 17 [11]An evil man is bent only on rebellion; a merciless official will be sent against him.
Prov 24 [19]Do not fret because of evil men or be envious of the wicked, [20]for the evil man has no future hope, and the lamp of the wicked will be snuffed out.
Prov 28 [5]Evil men do not understand justice, but those who seek the LORD understand it fully.
Prov 29 [6]An evil man is snared by his own sin, but a righteous one can sing and be glad.
Matt 12 [35]"The good man brings good things out of the good stored up in him, and the evil man brings evil things out of the evil stored up in him."
2 Thess 3 [2]And pray that we may be delivered from wicked and evil men, for not everyone has faith.
2 Tim 3 [13]while evil men and impostors will go from bad to worse, deceiving and being deceived.

24. Sinners Are False Apostles

2 Cor 11 [13]For such men are false apostles, deceitful workmen, masquerading as apostles of Christ. [14]And no wonder, for Satan himself masquerades as an angel of light. [15]It is not surprising, then, if his servants masquerade as servants of righteousness. Their end will be what their actions deserve.

25. Sinners Are False Brothers

2 Cor 11 [26]I have been constantly on the move. I have been in danger from rivers, in danger from bandits, in danger from my own countrymen, in danger from Gentiles; in danger in the city, in danger in the country, in danger at sea; and in danger from false brothers.
Gal 2 [4]This matter arose because some false brothers had infiltrated our ranks to spy on the freedom we have in Christ Jesus and to make us slaves.

26. Sinners Are False Prophets

Isa 44 [24]"This is what the LORD says—your Redeemer, who formed you in the womb: I am the LORD, who has made all things, who alone stretched out the heavens, who spread out the earth by myself, [25]who foils the signs of false prophets and makes fools of diviners, who overthrows the learning of the wise and turns it into nonsense. . . ."
Jer 50 [36]"A sword against her false prophets! They will become fools. A sword against her warriors! They will be filled with terror."
Matt 7 [15]"Watch out for false prophets. They come to you in sheep's clothing, but inwardly they are ferocious wolves."

Matt 24 [11]". . . and many false prophets will appear and deceive many people. . . . [24]For false Christs and false prophets will appear and perform great signs and miracles to deceive even the elect—if that were possible."
1 John 4 [1]Dear friends, do not believe every spirit, but test the spirits to see whether they are from God, because many false prophets have gone out into the world.

27. Sinners Are False Teachers

2 Pet 2 [1]But there were also false prophets among the people, just as there will be false teachers among you. They will secretly introduce destructive heresies, even denying the sovereign Lord who bought them—bringing swift destruction on themselves. [2]Many will follow their shameful ways and will bring the way of truth into disrepute. [3]In their greed these teachers will exploit you with stories they have made up. Their condemnation has long been hanging over them, and their destruction has not been sleeping.

28. Sinners Are Fools

Ps 74 [22]Rise up, O God, and defend your cause; remember how fools mock you all day long.
Prov 1 [7]The fear of the LORD is the beginning of knowledge, but fools despise wisdom and discipline.
Prov 10 [23]A fool finds pleasure in evil conduct, but a man of understanding delights in wisdom.
Prov 13 [19]A longing fulfilled is sweet to the soul, but fools detest turning from evil.
Prov 14 [9]Fools mock at making amends for sin, but goodwill is found among the upright.
Rom 1 [22]Although they claimed to be wise, they became fools. . . .

29. Sinners Are Foreigners

Ps 144 [7]Reach down your hand from on high; deliver me and rescue me from the mighty waters, from the hands of foreigners. . . .
Eph 2 [12]remember that at that time you were separate from Christ, excluded from citizenship in Israel and foreigners to the covenants of the promise, without hope and without God in the world. . . .

[19]Consequently, you are no longer foreigners and aliens, but fellow citizens with God's people and members of God's household. . . .

30. Sinners Are Godless Men

Job 13 [16]"Indeed, this will turn out for my deliverance, for no godless man would dare come before him!"
Job 20 [5]". . . that the mirth of the wicked is brief, the joy of the godless lasts but a moment."
Job 27 [8]"For what hope has the godless when he is cut off, when God takes away his life?"
Jude [4]For certain men whose condemnation was written about long ago have secretly slipped in among you. They are godless men, who change the grace of our God into a license for immorality and deny Jesus Christ our only Sovereign and Lord.

31. Sinners Are Hardened Rebels

Jer 6 [28]"They are all hardened rebels, going about to slander. They are bronze and iron; they all act corruptly."

32. Sinners Are Haters of God

Ps 81 [15]"Those who hate the LORD would cringe before him, and their punishment would last forever."
Rom 1 [30]slanderers, God-haters, insolent, arrogant and boastful; they invent ways of doing evil; they disobey their parents. . . .

33. Sinners Are Illegitimate Children

Hos 5 [7]"They are unfaithful to the LORD; they give birth to illegitimate children. Now their New Moon festivals will devour them and their fields."
Heb 12 [8]If you are not disciplined (and everyone undergoes discipline), then you are illegitimate children and not true sons.

34. Sinners Are Men of Corrupt Mind

1 Tim 6 [5]and constant friction between men of corrupt mind, who have been robbed of the truth and who think that godliness is a means to financial gain.

35. Sinners Are Men of This World

Ps 17 [14]O LORD, by your hand save me from such men, from men of this world whose reward is in this life.

You still the hunger of those you cherish; their sons have plenty, and they store up wealth for their children.

36. Sinners Are Natural Children

Rom 9 [8]In other words, it is not the natural children who are God's children, but it is the children of the promise who are regarded as Abraham's offspring.

37. Sinners Are Objects of Wrath

Rom 9 [22]What if God, choosing to show his wrath and make his power known, bore with great patience the objects of his wrath—prepared for destruction?
Eph 2 [3]All of us also lived among them at one time, gratifying the cravings of our sinful nature and following its desires and thoughts. Like the rest, we were by nature objects of wrath.

38. Sinners Are Obstinate

Isa 30 [1]"Woe to the obstinate children," declares the LORD, "to those who carry out plans that are not mine, forming an alliance, but not by my Spirit, heaping sin upon sin. . . ."
Isa 65 [2]"All day long I have held out my hands to an obstinate people, who walk in ways not good, pursuing their own imaginations—[3]a people who continually provoke me to my very face, offering sacrifices in gardens and burning incense on altars of brick; [4]who sit among the graves and spend their nights keeping secret vigil; who eat the flesh of pigs, and whose pots hold broth of unclean meat; [5]who say, 'Keep away; don't come near me, for I am too sacred for you!' Such people are smoke in my nostrils, a fire that keeps burning all day."
Ezek 2 [4]"The people to whom I am sending you are obstinate and stubborn. Say to them, 'This is what the Sovereign LORD says.'"

39. Sinners Are the Offspring of Liars

Isa 57 [4]"Whom are you mocking? At whom do you sneer and stick out your tongue? Are you not a brood of rebels, the offspring of liars?"

40. Sinners Are the Offspring of the Wicked

Ps 37 [28]For the LORD loves the just and will not forsake his faithful ones.

They will be protected forever, but the offspring of the wicked will be cut off. . . .
Isa 14 [20]you will not join them in burial, for you have destroyed your land and killed your people.

The offspring of the wicked will never be mentioned again.

41. Sinners Are Pagans

2 Kings 23 [5]He did away with the pagan priests appointed by the kings of Judah to burn incense on the high places of the towns of Judah and on those around Jerusalem—those who burned incense to Baal, to the sun and moon, to the constellations and to all the starry hosts.
Isa 2 [6]You have abandoned your people, the house of Jacob. They are full of superstitions from the East; they practice divination like the Philistines and clasp hands with pagans.
Zeph 1 [4]"I will stretch out my hand against Judah and against all who live in Jerusalem. I will cut off from this place every remnant of Baal, the names of the pagan and the idolatrous priests. . . ."

1 Cor 12 [2]You know that when you were pagans, somehow or other you were influenced and led astray to mute idols.
1 Pet 4 [3]For you have spent enough time in the past doing what pagans choose to do—living in debauchery, lust, drunkenness, orgies, carousing and detestable idolatry. [4]They think it strange that you do not plunge with them into the same flood of dissipation, and they heap abuse on you. [5]But they will have to give account to him who is ready to judge the living and the dead.

42. Sinners Are People Loaded with Guilt

Isa 1 [4]Ah, sinful nation, a people loaded with guilt, a brood of evildoers, children given to corruption! They have forsaken the LORD; they have spurned the Holy One of Israel and turned their backs on him.

43. Sinners Are People of This World

Luke 16 [8]"The master commended the dishonest manager because he had acted shrewdly. For the people of this world are more shrewd in dealing with their own kind than are the people of the light."

44. Sinners Are a Perverse Generation

Deut 32 [20]"I will hide my face from them," he said, "and see what their end will be; for they are a perverse generation, children who are unfaithful."

45. Sinners Are Rebellious People

Isa 1 [2]Hear, O heavens! Listen, O earth! For the LORD has spoken: "I reared children and brought them up, but they have rebelled against me."
Isa 30 [9]These are rebellious people, deceitful children, children unwilling to listen to the LORD's instruction.
Ezek 12 [2]"Son of man, you are living among a rebellious people. They have eyes to see but do not see and ears to hear but do not hear, for they are a rebellious people."
Titus 1 [10]For there are many rebellious people, mere talkers and deceivers, especially those of the circumcision group.

46. Sinners Are Senseless Children

Jer 4 [22]"My people are fools; they do not know me. They are senseless children; they have no understanding. They are skilled in doing evil; they know not how to do good."

47. Sinners Are Slaves of Depravity

2 Pet 2 [19]They promise them freedom, while they themselves are slaves of depravity—for a man is a slave to whatever has mastered him.

48. Sinners Are Slaves to Sin

John 8 [34]Jesus replied, "I tell you the truth, everyone who sins is a slave to sin."
Rom 6 [6]For we know that our old self was crucified with him so that the body of sin might be done away with, that we should no longer be slaves to sin. . . .

[16]Don't you know that when you offer yourselves to someone to obey him as slaves, you are slaves to the one whom you obey—whether you are slaves to sin, which leads to death, or to obedience, which leads to righteousness? [17]But thanks be to God that, though you used to be slaves to sin, you wholeheartedly obeyed the form of teaching to which you were entrusted. . . .

[20]When you were slaves to sin, you were free from the control of righteousness.

49. Sinners Are Sons of the Evil One

Matt 13 [38]"The field is the world, and the good seed stands for the sons of the kingdom. The weeds are the sons of the evil one. . . ."

50. Sinners Are Sons of Hell

Matt 23 [15]"Woe to you, teachers of the law and Pharisees, you hypocrites! You travel over land and sea to win a single convert, and when he becomes one, you make him twice as much a son of hell as you are."

51. Sinners Are a Stubborn and Rebellious Generation

Ps 78 [8]They would not be like their forefathers—a stubborn and rebellious generation, whose hearts were not loyal to God, whose spirits were not faithful to him.

52. Sinners Are a Synagogue of Satan

Rev 2 [9]"I know your afflictions and your poverty—yet you are rich! I know the slander of those who say they are Jews and are not, but are a synagogue of Satan."
Rev 3 [9]"I will make those who are of the synagogue of Satan, who claim to be Jews though they are not, but are liars—I will make them come and fall down at your feet and acknowledge that I have loved you."

53. Sinners Are Those Who Are Disobedient

Eph 2 [2]in which you used to live when you followed the ways of this world and of the ruler of the kingdom of the air, the spirit who is now at work in those who are disobedient.
Eph 5 [6]Let no one deceive you with empty words, for because of such things God's wrath comes on those who are disobedient.

54. Sinners Are Those Who Do Wrong

Ps 37 [1]Do not fret because of evil men or be envious of those who do wrong; [2]for like the grass they will soon wither, like green plants they will soon die away.

55. Sinners Are Transgressors

Ps 51 [13]Then I will teach transgressors your ways, and sinners will turn back to you.
Isa 53 [12]Therefore I will give him a portion among the great, and he will divide the spoils with the strong, because he poured out his life unto death, and was numbered with the transgressors. For he bore the sin of many, and made intercession for the transgressors.

56. Sinners Are Unbelievers

Luke 12 [46]"The master of that servant will come on a day when he does not expect him and at an hour he is not aware of. He will cut him to pieces and assign him a place with the unbelievers."
2 Cor 4 [4]The god of this age has blinded the minds of unbelievers, so that they cannot see the light of the gospel of the glory of Christ, who is the image of God.
2 Cor 6 [15]What harmony is there between Christ and Belial? What does a believer have in common with an unbeliever?
1 Tim 5 [8]If anyone does not provide for his relatives, and especially for his immediate family, he has denied the faith and is worse than an unbeliever.

57. Sinners Are an Unbelieving and Perverse Generation

Matt 17 [17]"O unbelieving and perverse generation," Jesus replied, "how long shall I stay with you? How long shall I put up with you? Bring the boy here to me."

58. Sinners Are Villains

Prov 6 [12]A scoundrel and villain, who goes about with a corrupt mouth, [13]who winks with his eye, signals with his feet and motions with his fingers, [14]who plots evil with deceit in his heart—he always stirs up dissension. [15]Therefore disaster will overtake him in an instant; he will suddenly be destroyed—without remedy.

59. Sinners Are a Warped and Crooked Generation

Deut 32 [5]They have acted corruptly toward him; to their shame they are no longer his children, but a warped and crooked generation.

60. Sinners Are a Wicked and Adulterous Generation

Matt 12 [39]He answered, "A wicked and adulterous generation asks for a miraculous sign! But none will be given it except the sign of the prophet Jonah. [40]For as Jonah was three days and three nights in the belly of a huge fish, so the Son of Man will be three days and three nights in the heart of the earth. [41]The men of Nineveh will stand up at the judgment with this generation and condemn it; for they repented at the preaching of Jonah, and now one greater than Jonah is here. [42]The Queen of the South will rise at the judgment with this generation and condemn it; for she came from the ends of the earth to listen to Solomon's wisdom, and now one greater than Solomon is here."

Matt 16 [4]"A wicked and adulterous generation looks for a miraculous sign, but none will be given it except the sign of Jonah." Jesus then left them and went away.

61. Sinners Are a Wicked Generation

Matt 12 [45]"Then it goes and takes with it seven other spirits more wicked than itself, and they go in and live there. And the final condition of that man is worse than the first. That is how it will be with this wicked generation."

62. Sinners Are the Wicked of the Earth

Ps 75 [8]In the hand of the LORD is a cup full of foaming wine mixed with spices; he pours it out, and all the wicked of the earth drink it down to its very dregs.

63. Sinners Are Wicked Traitors

Ps 59 [5]O LORD God Almighty, the God of Israel, rouse yourself to punish all the nations; show no mercy to wicked traitors.

64. Sinners Are Worthless Scoundrels

2 Chron 13 [7]"Some worthless scoundrels gathered around him and opposed Rehoboam son of Solomon when he was young and indecisive and not strong enough to resist them."

Prov 16 [27]A scoundrel plots evil, and his speech is like a scorching fire.

Isa 32 [7]The scoundrel's methods are wicked, he makes up evil schemes to destroy the poor with lies, even when the plea of the needy is just.

65. Sinners Are Worthless Servants

Matt 25 [24]"Then the man who had received the one talent came. 'Master,' he said, 'I knew that you are a hard man, harvesting where you have not sown and gathering where you have not scattered seed. [25]So I was afraid and went out and hid your talent in the ground. See, here is what belongs to you.'

[26]"His master replied, 'You wicked, lazy servant! So you knew that I harvest where I have not sown and gather where I have not scattered seed? [27]Well then, you should have put my money on deposit with the bankers, so that when I returned I would have received it back with interest.

[28]"'Take the talent from him and give it to the one who has the ten talents. [29]For everyone who has will be given more, and he will have an abundance. Whoever does not have, even what he has will be taken from him. [30]And throw that worthless servant outside, into the darkness, where there will be weeping and gnashing of teeth.'"

B. Metaphors for Sinners

1. Sinners Are like Ashes under the Feet

Mal 4 [3]"Then you will trample down the wicked; they will be ashes under the soles of your feet on the day when I do these things," says the LORD Almighty.

2. Sinners Are like Autumn Trees without Fruit

Jude [12]These men are blemishes at your love feasts, eating with you without the slightest qualm—shepherds who feed only themselves. They are clouds without rain, blown along by the wind; autumn trees, without fruit and uprooted—twice dead.

3. Sinners Are like Bad Fish

Matt 13 [47]"Once again, the kingdom of heaven is like a net that was let down into the lake and caught all kinds of fish. [48]When it was full, the fishermen pulled it up on the shore. Then they sat down and collected the good fish in baskets, but threw the bad away. [49]This is how it will be at the end of the age. The angels will come and separate the wicked from the righteous [50]and throw them into the fiery furnace, where there will be weeping and gnashing of teeth."

4. Sinners Are like Bad Trees

Luke 6 [43]"No good tree bears bad fruit, nor does a bad tree bear good fruit. . . . [45]The good man brings good things out of the good stored up in his heart, and the evil man brings evil things out of the evil stored up in his heart. For out of the overflow of his heart his mouth speaks."

5. Sinners Are like Beasts

Ps 49 [12]But man, despite his riches, does not endure; he is like the beasts that perish.

Ps 49 [20]A man who has riches without understanding is like the beasts that perish.

2 Pet 2 [12]But these men blaspheme in matters they do not understand. They are like brute beasts, creatures of instinct, born only to be caught and destroyed, and like beasts they too will perish.

6. Sinners Are like Blind Guides

Matt 15 [14]"Leave them; they are blind guides. If a blind man leads a blind man, both will fall into a pit."

7. Sinners Are like Blind Men

Deut 28 [15]However, if you do not obey the LORD your God and do not carefully follow all his commands and decrees I am giving you today, all these curses will come upon you and overtake you. . . . [29]At midday you will grope about like a blind man in the dark. You will be unsuccessful in everything you do; day after day you will be oppressed and robbed, with no one to rescue you.

Lam 4 [13]But it happened because of the sins of her prophets and the iniquities of her priests, who shed within her the blood of the righteous. [14]Now they grope through the streets like men who are blind. They are so defiled with blood that no one dares to touch their garments.

Zeph 1 [17]"I will bring distress on the people and they will walk like blind men, because they have sinned against the LORD. Their blood will be poured out like dust and their entrails like filth."

Luke 6 [39]He also told them this parable: "Can a blind man lead a blind man? Will they not both fall into a pit?"

8. Sinners Are like Blots and Blemishes

2 Pet 2 [13]They will be paid back with harm for the harm they have done. Their idea of pleasure is to carouse in broad daylight. They are blots and blemishes, reveling in their pleasures while they feast with you.

Jude [12]These men are blemishes at your love feasts, eating with you without the slightest qualm—shepherds who feed only themselves. They are clouds without rain, blown along by the wind; autumn trees, without fruit and uprooted—twice dead.

9. Sinners Are like Briers and Thorns

Ezek 2 [6]"And you, son of man, do not be afraid of them or their words. Do not be afraid, though briers and thorns are all around you and you live among scorpions. Do not be afraid of what they say or terrified by them, though they are a rebellious house."
Mic 7 [1]What misery is mine! I am like one who gathers summer fruit at the gleaning of the vineyard; there is no cluster of grapes to eat, none of the early figs that I crave. [2]The godly have been swept from the land; not one upright man remains. All men lie in wait to shed blood; each hunts his brother with a net. [3]Both hands are skilled in doing evil; the ruler demands gifts, the judge accepts bribes, the powerful dictate what they desire—they all conspire together. [4]The best of them is like a brier, the most upright worse than a thorn hedge. The day of your watchmen has come, the day God visits you. Now is the time of their confusion.
Luke 6 [44]"Each tree is recognized by its own fruit. People do not pick figs from thornbushes, or grapes from briers. [45]The good man brings good things out of the good stored up in his heart, and the evil man brings evil things out of the evil stored up in his heart. For out of the overflow of his heart his mouth speaks."

10. Sinners Are like Bronze and Iron

Jer 6 [28]"They are all hardened rebels, going about to slander. They are bronze and iron; they all act corruptly. [29]The bellows blow fiercely to burn away the lead with fire, but the refining goes on in vain; the wicked are not purged out."

11. Sinners Are like a Brood of Vipers

Matt 3 [7]But when he saw many of the Pharisees and Sadducees coming to where he was baptizing, he said to them: "You brood of vipers! Who warned you to flee from the coming wrath?"
Matt 12 [34]"You brood of vipers, how can you who are evil say anything good? For out of the overflow of the heart the mouth speaks."
Matt 23 [33]"You snakes! You brood of vipers! How will you escape being condemned to hell?"

12. Sinners Are like the Bulls of Bashan

Ps 22 [12]Many bulls surround me; strong bulls of Bashan encircle me.

13. Sinners Are like Burning Lime

Isa 33 [12]"The peoples will be burned as if to lime; like cut thornbushes they will be set ablaze."

14. Sinners Are like Burning Thorns

Ps 118 [12]They swarmed around me like bees, but they died out as quickly as burning thorns; in the name of the LORD I cut them off.

15. Sinners Are like a Bush in the Wastelands

Jer 17 [6]"He will be like a bush in the wastelands; he will not see prosperity when it comes. He will dwell in the parched places of the desert, in a salt land where no one lives."
Jer 48 [6]"Flee! Run for your lives; become like a bush in the desert."

16. Sinners Are like Chaff

Job 21 [18]"How often are they like straw before the wind, like chaff swept away by a gale?"
Ps 1 [4]Not so the wicked! They are like chaff that the wind blows away.
Ps 35 [5]May they be like chaff before the wind, with the angel of the LORD driving them away. . . .
Isa 40 [24]No sooner are they planted, no sooner are they sown, no sooner do they take root in the ground, than he blows on them and they wither, and a whirlwind sweeps them away like chaff.
Jer 13 [24]"I will scatter you like chaff driven by the desert wind. [25]This is your lot, the portion I have decreed for you," declares the LORD, "because you have forgotten me and trusted in false gods."
Hos 13 [2]Now they sin more and more; they make idols for themselves from their silver, cleverly fashioned images, all of them the work of craftsmen. It is said of these people, "They offer human sacrifice and kiss the calf-idols." [3]Therefore they will be like the morning mist, like the early dew that disappears, like chaff swirling from a threshing floor, like smoke escaping through a window.
Matt 3 [12]"His winnowing fork is in his hand, and he will clear his threshing floor, gathering his wheat into the barn and burning up the chaff with unquenchable fire."

17. Sinners Are like Clouds without Rain

Prov 25 [14]Like clouds and wind without rain is a man who boasts of gifts he does not give.
Jude [12]These men are blemishes at your love feasts, eating with you without the slightest qualm—shepherds who feed only themselves. They are clouds without rain, blown along by the wind; autumn trees, without fruit and uprooted—twice dead.

18. Sinners Are like a Coating of Glaze over Earthenware

Prov 26 [23]Like a coating of glaze over earthenware are fervent lips with an evil heart.

19. Sinners Are like Corpses Trampled Underfoot

Isa 14 [19]But you are cast out of your tomb like a rejected branch; you are covered with the slain, with those pierced by the sword, those who descend to the stones of the pit. Like a corpse trampled underfoot, [20]you will not join them in burial, for you have destroyed your land and killed your people.
The offspring of the wicked will never be mentioned again.

20. Sinners Are like the Cows of Bashan

Amos 4 [1]Hear this word, you cows of Bashan on Mount Samaria, you women who oppress the poor and crush the needy and say to your husbands, "Bring us some drinks!" [2]The Sovereign LORD has sworn by his holiness: "The time will surely come when you will be taken away with hooks, the last of you with fishhooks."

21. Sinners Are like Darkness

Prov 4 [19]But the way of the wicked is like deep darkness; they do not know what makes them stumble.
Acts 26 [17]"'I will rescue you from your own people and from the Gentiles. I am sending you to them [18]to open their eyes and turn them from darkness to light, and from the power of Satan to God, so that they may receive forgiveness of sins and a place among those who are sanctified by faith in me.'"
Eph 5 [8]For you were once darkness, but now you are light in the Lord. Live as children of light. . . .
Col 1 [13]For he has rescued us from the dominion of darkness and brought us into the kingdom of the Son he loves. . . .

22. Sinners Are like a Deaf Cobra

Ps 58 [3]Even from birth the wicked go astray; from the womb they are wayward and speak lies. [4]Their venom is like the venom of a snake, like that of a cobra that has stopped its ears, [5]that will not heed the tune of the charmer, however skillful the enchanter may be.

23. Sinners Are like Dogs

Ps 22 [16]Dogs have surrounded me; a band of evil men has encircled me, they have pierced my hands and my feet. . . . [20]Deliver my life from the sword, my precious life from the power of the dogs.

Prov 26 [11]As a dog returns to its vomit, so a fool repeats his folly.
Isa 56 [10]Israel's watchmen are blind, they all lack knowledge; they are all mute dogs, they cannot bark; they lie around and dream, they love to sleep. [11]They are dogs with mighty appetites; they never have enough. They are shepherds who lack understanding; they all turn to their own way, each seeks his own gain.
Matt 7 [6]"Do not give dogs what is sacred; do not throw your pearls to pigs. If you do, they may trample them under their feet, and then turn and tear you to pieces."
Phil 3 [2]Watch out for those dogs, those men who do evil, those mutilators of the flesh.
Rev 22 [15]"Outside are the dogs, those who practice magic arts, the sexually immoral, the murderers, the idolaters and everyone who loves and practices falsehood."

24. Sinners Are like a Dream

Job 20 [6]"Though his pride reaches to the heavens and his head touches the clouds, [7]he will perish forever, like his own dung; those who have seen him will say, 'Where is he?' [8]Like a dream he flies away, no more to be found, banished like a vision of the night. [9]The eye that saw him will not see him again; his place will look on him no more."

25. Sinners Are like Dross

Ps 119 [119]All the wicked of the earth you discard like dross; therefore I love your statutes.
Prov 25 [4]Remove the dross from the silver, and out comes material for the silversmith; [5]remove the wicked from the king's presence, and his throne will be established through righteousness.
Isa 1 [25]"I will turn my hand against you; I will thoroughly purge away your dross and remove all your impurities."
Ezek 22 [17]Then the word of the LORD came to me: [18]"Son of man, the house of Israel has become dross to me; all of them are the copper, tin, iron and lead left inside a furnace. They are but the dross of silver. [19]Therefore this is what the Sovereign LORD says: 'Because you have all become dross, I will gather you into Jerusalem. [20]As men gather silver, copper, iron, lead and tin into a furnace to melt it with a fiery blast, so will I gather you in my anger and my wrath and put you inside the city and melt you. [21]I will gather you and I will blow on you with my fiery wrath, and you will be melted inside her. [22]As silver is melted in a furnace, so you will be melted inside her, and you will know that I the LORD have poured out my wrath upon you.'"

26. Sinners Are like Early Dew That Disappears

Hos 13 [2]Now they sin more and more; they make idols for themselves from their silver, cleverly fashioned images, all of them the work of craftsmen. It is said of these people, "They offer human sacrifice and kiss the calf-idols." [3]Therefore they will be like the morning mist, like the early dew that disappears, like chaff swirling from a threshing floor, like smoke escaping through a window.

27. Sinners Are like Fading Oaks

Isa 1 [29]"You will be ashamed because of the sacred oaks in which you have delighted; you will be disgraced because of the gardens that you have chosen. [30]You will be like an oak with fading leaves, like a garden without water."

28. Sinners Are like Fattened Animals

Jer 46 [21]"The mercenaries in her ranks are like fattened calves. They too will turn and flee together, they will not stand their ground, for the day of disaster is coming upon them, the time for them to be punished."
Ezek 39 [17]"Son of man, this is what the Sovereign LORD says: Call out to every kind of bird and all the wild animals: 'Assemble and come together from all around to the sacrifice I am preparing for you, the great sacrifice on the mountains of Israel. There you will eat flesh and drink blood. [18]You will eat the flesh of mighty men and drink the blood of the princes of the earth as if they were rams and lambs, goats and bulls—all of them fattened animals from Bashan. [19]At the sacrifice I am preparing for you, you will eat fat till you are glutted and drink blood till you are drunk. [20]At my table you will eat your fill of horses and riders, mighty men and soldiers of every kind,' declares the Sovereign LORD. . . . [23]And the nations will know that the people of Israel went into exile for their sin, because they were unfaithful to me. So I hid my face from them and handed them over to their enemies, and they all fell by the sword. [24]I dealt with them according to their uncleanness and their offenses, and I hid my face from them."

29. Sinners Are like a Fiery Furnace

Ps 21 [9]At the time of your appearing you will make them like a fiery furnace. In his wrath the LORD will swallow them up, and his fire will consume them.
Hos 7 [4]"They are all adulterers, burning like an oven whose fire the baker need not stir from the kneading of the dough till it rises."

30. Sinners Are like Fools Building on Sand

Matt 7 [24]"Therefore everyone who hears these words of mine and puts them into practice is like a wise man who built his house on the rock. [25]The rain came down, the streams rose, and the winds blew and beat against that house; yet it did not fall, because it had its foundation on the rock. [26]But everyone who hears these words of mine and does not put them into practice is like a foolish man who built his house on sand. [27]The rain came down, the streams rose, and the winds blew and beat against that house, and it fell with a great crash."

31. Sinners Are like Fuel for Fire

Isa 9 [19]By the wrath of the LORD Almighty the land will be scorched and the people will be fuel for the fire; no one will spare his brother.
Ezek 21 [32]"'You will be fuel for the fire, your blood will be shed in your land, you will be remembered no more; for I the LORD have spoken.'"

32. Sinners Are like a Garden without Water

Isa 1 [29]"You will be ashamed because of the sacred oaks in which you have delighted; you will be disgraced because of the gardens that you have chosen. [30]You will be like an oak with fading leaves, like a garden without water."

33. Sinners Are like Goats

Matt 25 [31]"When the Son of Man comes in his glory, and all the angels with him, he will sit on his throne in heavenly glory. [32]All the nations will be gathered before him, and he will separate the people one from another as a shepherd separates the sheep from the goats. [33]He will put the sheep on his right and the goats on his left. . . .

[41]"Then he will say to those on his left, 'Depart from me, you who are cursed, into the eternal fire prepared for the devil and his angels. [42]For I was hungry and you gave me nothing to eat, I was thirsty and you gave me nothing to drink, [43]I was a stranger and you did not invite me in, I needed clothes and you did not clothe me, I was sick and in prison and you did not look after me.'

[44]"They also will answer, 'Lord, when did we see you hungry or thirsty or a stranger or needing clothes or sick or in prison, and did not help you?'

[45]"He will reply, 'I tell you the truth, whatever you did not do for one of the least of these, you did not do for me.'

[46]"Then they will go away to eternal punishment, but the righteous to eternal life."

34. Sinners Are like Grass

2 Kings 19 [26]"'Their people, drained of power, are dismayed and put to shame. They are like plants in the field, like tender green shoots, like grass sprouting on the roof, scorched before it grows up.'"

Job 8 [12]"While still growing and uncut, they wither more quickly than grass. [13]Such is the destiny of all who forget God; so perishes the hope of the godless."

Ps 37 [1]Do not fret because of evil men or be envious of those who do wrong; [2]for like the grass they will soon wither, like green plants they will soon die away.

Ps 92 [7]that though the wicked spring up like grass and all evildoers flourish, they will be forever destroyed.

Ps 129 [5]May all who hate Zion be turned back in shame. [6]May they be like grass on the roof, which withers before it can grow. . . .

35. Sinners Are like Green Plants

Ps 37 [1]Do not fret because of evil men or be envious of those who do wrong; [2]for like the grass they will soon wither, like green plants they will soon die away.

36. Sinners Are like Green Trees

Ps 37 [35]I have seen a wicked and ruthless man flourishing like a green tree in its native soil, [36]but he soon passed away and was no more; though I looked for him, he could not be found.

37. Sinners Are like Horses Charging into Battle

Jer 8 [6]"'I have listened attentively, but they do not say what is right. No one repents of his wickedness, saying, "What have I done?" Each pursues his own course like a horse charging into battle.'"

38. Sinners Are like Idols

Ps 115 [2]Why do the nations say, "Where is their God?" [3]Our God is in heaven; he does whatever pleases him. [4]But their idols are silver and gold, made by the hands of men. [5]They have mouths, but cannot speak, eyes, but they cannot see; [6]they have ears, but cannot hear, noses, but they cannot smell; [7]they have hands, but cannot feel, feet, but they cannot walk; nor can they utter a sound with their throats. [8]Those who make them will be like them, and so will all who trust in them.

39. Sinners Are like Lions Hungry for Prey

Ps 17 [10]They close up their callous hearts, and their mouths speak with arrogance. [11]They have tracked me down, they now surround me, with eyes alert, to throw me to the ground. [12]They are like a lion hungry for prey, like a great lion crouching in cover.

Ps 22 [13]Roaring lions tearing their prey open their mouths wide against me. . . . [21]Rescue me from the mouth of the lions; save me from the horns of the wild oxen.

Ezek 22 [25]"There is a conspiracy of her princes within her like a roaring lion tearing its prey; they devour people, take treasures and precious things and make many widows within her."

40. Sinners Are like Maggots

Job 25 [4]"How then can a man be righteous before God? How can one born of woman be pure? [5]If even the moon is not bright and the stars are not pure in his eyes, [6]how much less man, who is but a maggot—a son of man, who is only a worm!"

41. Sinners Are like Melting Wax

Ps 68 [2]As smoke is blown away by the wind, may you blow them away; as wax melts before the fire, may the wicked perish before God.

42. Sinners Are like Morning Mist

Hos 13 [2]Now they sin more and more; they make idols for themselves from their silver, cleverly fashioned images, all of them the work of craftsmen. It is said of these people, "They offer human sacrifice and kiss the calf-idols." [3]Therefore they will be like the morning mist, like the early dew that disappears, like chaff swirling from a threshing floor, like smoke escaping through a window.

43. Sinners Are like Moth-eaten Garments

Isa 50 [9]It is the Sovereign LORD who helps me. Who is he that will condemn me? They will all wear out like a garment; the moths will eat them up.

Isa 51 [7]"Hear me, you who know what is right, you people who have my law in your hearts: Do not fear the reproach of men or be terrified by their insults. [8]For the moth will eat them up like a garment; the worm will devour them like wool. But my righteousness will last forever, my salvation through all generations."

44. Sinners Are like Plants in the Field

2 Kings 19 [26]"'Their people, drained of power, are dismayed and put to shame. They are like plants in the field, like tender green shoots, like grass sprouting on the roof, scorched before it grows up.'"

45. Sinners Are like Poor Figs

Jer 24 [8]"'But like the poor figs, which are so bad they cannot be eaten,' says the LORD, 'so will I deal with Zedekiah king of Judah, his officials and the survivors from Jerusalem, whether they remain in this land or live in Egypt. [9]I will make them abhorrent and an offense to all the kingdoms of the earth, a reproach and a byword, an object of ridicule and cursing, wherever I banish them. [10]I will send the sword, famine and plague against them until they are destroyed from the land I gave to them and their fathers.'"

46. Sinners Are like Rejected Branches

Isa 14 [19]But you are cast out of your tomb like a rejected branch; you are covered with the slain, with those pierced by the sword, those who descend to the stones of the pit. Like a corpse trampled underfoot . . .

47. Sinners Are like Rejected Silver

Jer 6 [30]"They are called rejected silver, because the LORD has rejected them."

48. Sinners Are like Rocky Places

Matt 13 [5]"Some fell on rocky places, where it did not have much soil. It sprang up quickly, because the soil was shallow. [6]But when the sun came up, the plants were scorched, and they withered because they had no root."

49. Sinners Are like Scorpions

Ezek 2 [6]"And you, son of man, do not be afraid of them or their words. Do not be afraid, though briers and thorns are all around you and you live among scorpions. Do not be afraid of what they say or terrified by them, though they are a rebellious house."

50. Sinners Are like Selfish Shepherds

Isa 56 [10]Israel's watchmen are blind, they all lack knowledge; they are all mute dogs, they cannot bark; they lie around and dream, they love to sleep. [11]They are dogs with mighty appetites; they never have enough. They are shepherds who lack understanding; they all turn to their own way, each seeks his own gain. [12]"Come," each one cries, "let me get wine! Let us drink our fill of beer! And tomorrow will be like today, or even far better."

Jude [12]These men are blemishes at your love feasts, eating with you without the slightest qualm—shepherds who feed only themselves. They are clouds without rain, blown along by the wind; autumn trees, without fruit and uprooted—twice dead.

51. Sinners Are like Shattered Pottery

Ps 2 [9]"You will rule them with an iron scepter; you will dash them to pieces like pottery."

52. Sinners Are like Smoke

Ps 37 [20]But the wicked will perish: The LORD's enemies will be like the beauty of the fields, they will vanish—vanish like smoke.
Ps 68 [1]May God arise, may his enemies be scattered; may his foes flee before him. [2]As smoke is blown away by the wind, may you blow them away; as wax melts before the fire, may the wicked perish before God.
Hos 13 [2]Now they sin more and more; they make idols for themselves from their silver, cleverly fashioned images, all of them the work of craftsmen. It is said of these people, "They offer human sacrifice and kiss the calf-idols." [3]Therefore they will be like the morning mist, like the early dew that disappears, like chaff swirling from a threshing floor, like smoke escaping through a window.

53. Sinners Are like Snakes

Mic 7 [17]They will lick dust like a snake, like creatures that crawl on the ground. They will come trembling out of their dens; they will turn in fear to the LORD our God and will be afraid of you.
Matt 23 [33]"You snakes! You brood of vipers! How will you escape being condemned to hell?"

54. Sinners Are like Springs without Water

2 Pet 2 [17]These men are springs without water and mists driven by a storm. Blackest darkness is reserved for them.

55. Sinners Are like Straw

Job 21 [18]"How often are they like straw before the wind, like chaff swept away by a gale?"
Isa 33 [11]"You conceive chaff, you give birth to straw; your breath is a fire that consumes you."

56. Sinners Are like Stubble

Isa 47 [14]"Surely they are like stubble; the fire will burn them up. They cannot even save themselves from the power of the flame. Here are no coals to warm anyone; here is no fire to sit by."
Nah 1 [10]They will be entangled among thorns and drunk from their wine; they will be consumed like dry stubble.
Mal 4 [1]"Surely the day is coming; it will burn like a furnace. All the arrogant and every evildoer will be stubble, and that day that is coming will set them on fire," says the LORD Almighty. "Not a root or a branch will be left to them."

57. Sinners Are like Swarming Bees

Ps 118 [12]They swarmed around me like bees, but they died out as quickly as burning thorns; in the name of the LORD I cut them off.

58. Sinners Are like Swine

Matt 7 [6]"Do not give dogs what is sacred; do not throw your pearls to pigs. If you do, they may trample them under their feet, and then turn and tear you to pieces."
2 Pet 2 [21]It would have been better for them not to have known the way of righteousness, than to have known it and then to turn their backs on the sacred command that was passed on to them. [22]Of them the proverbs are true: "A dog returns to its vomit," and, "A sow that is washed goes back to her wallowing in the mud."

59. Sinners Are like Tender Green Shoots

2 Kings 19 [26]"'Their people, drained of power, are dismayed and put to shame. They are like plants in the field, like tender green shoots, like grass sprouting on the roof, scorched before it grows up.'"

60. Sinners Are like Tinder

Isa 1 [31]"The mighty man will become tinder and his work a spark; both will burn together, with no one to quench the fire."

61. Sinners Are like a Tossing Sea

Isa 57 [20]But the wicked are like the tossing sea, which cannot rest, whose waves cast up mire and mud. [21]"There is no peace," says my God, "for the wicked."

62. Sinners Are like Tumbleweed

Ps 83 [13]Make them like tumbleweed, O my God, like chaff before the wind. [14]As fire consumes the forest or a flame sets the mountains ablaze, [15]so pursue them with your tempest and terrify them with your storm.
Isa 17 [13]Although the peoples roar like the roar of surging waters, when he rebukes them they flee far away, driven before the wind like chaff on the hills, like tumbleweed before a gale. [14]In the evening, sudden terror! Before the morning, they are gone! This is the portion of those who loot us, the lot of those who plunder us.

63. Sinners Are like a Vision of the Night

Job 20 [6]"Though his pride reaches to the heavens and his head touches the clouds, [7]he will perish forever, like his own dung; those who have seen him will say, 'Where is he?' [8]Like a dream he flies away, no more to be found, banished like a vision of the night. [9]The eye that saw him will not see him again; his place will look on him no more."

64. Sinners Are like Wandering Stars

Jude [13]They are wild waves of the sea, foaming up their shame; wandering stars, for whom blackest darkness has been reserved forever.

65. Sinners Are like Wayward Children

Matt 11 [16]"To what can I compare this generation? They are like children sitting in the marketplaces and calling out to others: [17]'We played the flute for you, and you did not dance; we sang a dirge, and you did not mourn.' [18]For John came neither eating nor drinking, and they say, 'He has a demon.' [19]The Son of Man came eating and drinking, and they say, 'Here is a glutton and a drunkard, a friend of tax collectors and "sinners."' But wisdom is proved right by her actions."

66. Sinners Are like Weeds

Matt 13 [37]He answered, "The one who sowed the good seed is the Son of Man. [38]The field is the world, and the good seed stands for the sons of the kingdom. The weeds are the sons of the evil one, [39]and the enemy who sows them is the devil. The harvest is the end of the age, and the harvesters are angels.

[40]"As the weeds are pulled up and burned in the fire, so it will be at the end of the age. [41]The Son of Man will send out his angels, and they will weed out of his kingdom everything that causes sin and all who do evil. [42]They will throw them into the fiery furnace, where there will be weeping and gnashing of teeth."

67. Sinners Are like Whitewashed Tombs

Matt 23 [27]"Woe to you, teachers of the law and Pharisees, you hypocrites! You are like whitewashed tombs, which look beautiful on the outside but on the inside are full of dead men's bones and everything unclean. [28]In the same way, on the outside you appear to people as righteous but on the inside you are full of hypocrisy and wickedness."
Acts 23 [3]Then Paul said to him, "God will strike you, you whitewashed wall! You sit there to judge me according to the law, yet you yourself violate the law by commanding that I be struck!"

68. Sinners Are like Wild Oxen

Ps 22 [21]Rescue me from the mouth of the lions; save me from the horns of the wild oxen.

69. Sinners Are like Wild Waves of the Sea

Jude [13]They are wild waves of the sea, foaming up their shame; wandering stars, for whom blackest darkness has been reserved forever.

70. Sinners Are like Wine Left on Its Dregs

Zeph 1 [12]"At that time I will search Jerusalem with lamps and punish those who are complacent, who are like wine left on its dregs, who think, 'The LORD will do nothing, either good or bad.'"

71. Sinners Are like Wolves

Ezek 22 [27]"Her officials within her are like wolves tearing their prey; they shed blood and kill people to make unjust gain."
Matt 10 [16]"I am sending you out like sheep among wolves. Therefore be as shrewd as snakes and as innocent as doves."

72. Sinners Are like Worm-devoured Wool

Isa 51 [7]"Hear me, you who know what is right, you people who have my law in your hearts: Do not fear the reproach of men or be terrified by their insults. [8]For the moth will eat them up like a garment; the worm will devour them like wool. But my righteousness will last forever, my salvation through all generations."

73. Sinners Are like Worms

Job 25 [4]"How then can a man be righteous before God? How can one born of woman be pure? [5]If even the moon is not bright and the stars are not pure in his eyes, [6]how much less man, who is but a maggot—a son of man, who is only a worm!"

C. The Character of Sinners

1. Sinners Are Abusive

2 Kings 19 [16]"Give ear, O LORD, and hear; open your eyes, O LORD, and see; listen to the words Sennacherib has sent to insult the living God."
2 Chron 36 [16]But they mocked God's messengers, despised his words and scoffed at his prophets until the wrath of the LORD was aroused against his people and there was no remedy.
Neh 4 [1]When Sanballat heard that we were rebuilding the wall, he became angry and was greatly incensed. He ridiculed the Jews, [2]and in the presence of his associates and the army of Samaria, he said, "What are those feeble Jews doing? Will they restore their wall? Will they offer sacrifices? Will they finish in a day? Can they bring the stones back to life from those heaps of rubble—burned as they are?"

[3]Tobiah the Ammonite, who was at his side, said, "What they are building—if even a fox climbed up on it, he would break down their wall of stones!"

[4]Hear us, O our God, for we are despised. Turn their insults back on their own heads. Give them over as plunder in a land of captivity. [5]Do not cover up their guilt or blot out their sins from your sight, for they have thrown insults in the face of the builders.
Ps 1 [1]Blessed is the man who does not walk in the counsel of the wicked or stand in the way of sinners or sit in the seat of mockers.
Ps 10 [3]He boasts of the cravings of his heart; he blesses the greedy and reviles the LORD.
Ps 22 [6]But I am a worm and not a man, scorned by men and despised by the people. [7]All who see me mock me; they hurl insults, shaking their heads: [8]"He trusts in the LORD; let the LORD rescue him. Let him deliver him, since he delights in him."
Ps 69 [7]For I endure scorn for your sake, and shame covers my face. [8]I am a stranger to my brothers, an alien to my own mother's sons; [9]for zeal for your house consumes me, and the insults of those who insult you fall on me. [10]When I weep and fast, I must endure scorn; [11]when I put on sackcloth, people make sport of me. [12]Those who sit at the gate mock me, and I am the song of the drunkards.
Ps 123 [3]Have mercy on us, O LORD, have mercy on us, for we have endured much contempt. [4]We have endured much ridicule from the proud, much contempt from the arrogant.
Prov 22 [10]Drive out the mocker, and out goes strife; quarrels and insults are ended.
Isa 37 [23]"Who is it you have insulted and blasphemed? Against whom have you raised your voice and lifted your eyes in pride? Against the Holy One of Israel! [24]By your messengers you have heaped insults on the Lord. And you have said, 'With my many chariots I have ascended the heights of the mountains, the utmost heights of Lebanon. I have cut down its tallest cedars, the choicest of its pines. I have reached its remotest heights, the finest of its forests.'"
Isa 57 [4]"Whom are you mocking? At whom do you sneer and stick out your tongue? Are you not a brood of rebels, the offspring of liars?"
Jer 20 [7]O LORD, you deceived me, and I was deceived; you overpowered me and prevailed. I am ridiculed all day long; everyone mocks me.
Luke 16 [14]The Pharisees, who loved money, heard all this and were sneering at Jesus.
Luke 23 [11]Then Herod and his soldiers ridiculed and mocked him. Dressing him in an elegant robe, they sent him back to Pilate.
Acts 2 [13]Some, however, made fun of them and said, "They have had too much wine."
Acts 17 [32]When they heard about the resurrection of the dead, some of them sneered, but others said, "We want to hear you again on this subject."
Heb 10 [29]How much more severely do you think a man deserves to be punished who has trampled the Son of God under foot, who has treated as an unholy thing the blood of the covenant that sanctified him, and who has insulted the Spirit of grace?
2 Pet 3 [3]First of all, you must understand that in the last days scoffers will come, scoffing and following their own evil desires. [4]They will say, "Where is this 'coming' he promised? Ever since our fathers died, everything goes on as it has since the beginning of creation."

2. Sinners Are Apostate

Deut 32 [15]Jeshurun grew fat and kicked; filled with food, he became heavy and sleek. He abandoned the God who made him and rejected the Rock his Savior.
Jer 17 [5]This is what the LORD says: "Cursed is the one who trusts in man, who depends on flesh for his strength and whose heart turns away from the LORD. [6]He will be like a bush in the wastelands; he will not see prosperity when it comes. He will dwell in the parched places of the desert, in a salt land where no one lives."
Ezek 18 [24]"But if a righteous man turns from his righteousness and commits sin and does the same detestable things the wicked man does, will he live? None of the righteous things he has done will be remembered. Because of the unfaithfulness he is guilty of and because of the sins he has committed, he will die."
Matt 13 [20]"The one who received the seed that fell on rocky places is the man who hears the word and at once receives it with joy. [21]But since he has no root, he lasts only a short time. When trouble or persecution comes because of the word, he quickly falls away."
John 15 [6]"If anyone does not remain in me, he is like a branch that is thrown away and withers; such branches are picked up, thrown into the fire and burned."
Acts 7 [39]"But our fathers refused to obey him. Instead, they rejected him and in their hearts turned back to Egypt. [40]They

told Aaron, 'Make us gods who will go before us. As for this fellow Moses who led us out of Egypt—we don't know what has happened to him!' 41That was the time they made an idol in the form of a calf. They brought sacrifices to it and held a celebration in honor of what their hands had made. 42But God turned away and gave them over to the worship of the heavenly bodies. This agrees with what is written in the book of the prophets: 'Did you bring me sacrifices and offerings forty years in the desert, O house of Israel? 43You have lifted up the shrine of Molech and the star of your god Rephan, the idols you made to worship. Therefore I will send you into exile' beyond Babylon."

1 Tim 4 1The Spirit clearly says that in later times some will abandon the faith and follow deceiving spirits and things taught by demons.

1 Tim 5 15Some have in fact already turned away to follow Satan.

2 Tim 4 3For the time will come when men will not put up with sound doctrine. Instead, to suit their own desires, they will gather around them a great number of teachers to say what their itching ears want to hear. 4They will turn their ears away from the truth and turn aside to myths.

Heb 10 26If we deliberately keep on sinning after we have received the knowledge of the truth, no sacrifice for sins is left, 27but only a fearful expectation of judgment and of raging fire that will consume the enemies of God. 28Anyone who rejected the law of Moses died without mercy on the testimony of two or three witnesses. 29How much more severely do you think a man deserves to be punished who has trampled the Son of God under foot, who has treated as an unholy thing the blood of the covenant that sanctified him, and who has insulted the Spirit of grace?

2 Pet 3 17Therefore, dear friends, since you already know this, be on your guard so that you may not be carried away by the error of lawless men and fall from your secure position.

Jude 4For certain men whose condemnation was written about long ago have secretly slipped in among you. They are godless men, who change the grace of our God into a license for immorality and deny Jesus Christ our only Sovereign and Lord.

5Though you already know all this, I want to remind you that the Lord delivered his people out of Egypt, but later destroyed those who did not believe. 6And the angels who did not keep their positions of authority but abandoned their own home—these he has kept in darkness, bound with everlasting chains for judgment on the great Day.

3. Sinners Are Arrogant

Job 35 12"He does not answer when men cry out because of the arrogance of the wicked."

Job 41 34"He looks down on all that are haughty; he is king over all that are proud."

Ps 5 5The arrogant cannot stand in your presence; you hate all who do wrong.

Ps 10 2In his arrogance the wicked man hunts down the weak, who are caught in the schemes he devises. . . . 5His ways are always prosperous; he is haughty and your laws are far from him; he sneers at all his enemies.

Ps 17 10They close up their callous hearts, and their mouths speak with arrogance.

Ps 73 8They scoff, and speak with malice; in their arrogance they threaten oppression.

Ps 75 4"To the arrogant I say, 'Boast no more,' and to the wicked, 'Do not lift up your horns.'"

Ps 101 5Whoever slanders his neighbor in secret, him will I put to silence; whoever has haughty eyes and a proud heart, him will I not endure.

Ps 119 21You rebuke the arrogant, who are cursed and who stray from your commands.

Ps 119 51The arrogant mock me without restraint, but I do not turn from your law.

Ps 119 69Though the arrogant have smeared me with lies, I keep your precepts with all my heart.

Ps 119 78May the arrogant be put to shame for wronging me without cause; but I will meditate on your precepts.

Ps 119 85The arrogant dig pitfalls for me, contrary to your law.

Ps 119 122Ensure your servant's well-being; let not the arrogant oppress me.

Isa 2 17The arrogance of man will be brought low and the pride of men humbled; the LORD alone will be exalted in that day. . . .

Isa 13 11I will punish the world for its evil, the wicked for their sins. I will put an end to the arrogance of the haughty and will humble the pride of the ruthless.

Mal 4 1"Surely the day is coming; it will burn like a furnace. All the arrogant and every evildoer will be stubble, and that day that is coming will set them on fire," says the LORD Almighty. "Not a root or a branch will be left to them."

2 Pet 2 10This is especially true of those who follow the corrupt desire of the sinful nature and despise authority.

Bold and arrogant, these men are not afraid to slander celestial beings. . . .

4. Sinners Are Blasphemous

2 Chron 32 19They spoke about the God of Jerusalem as they did about the gods of the other peoples of the world—the work of men's hands.

Ps 73 9Their mouths lay claim to heaven, and their tongues take possession of the earth. . . . 11They say, "How can God know? Does the Most High have knowledge?"

Ps 139 20They speak of you with evil intent; your adversaries misuse your name.

Isa 45 9"Woe to him who quarrels with his Maker, to him who is but a potsherd among the potsherds on the ground. Does the clay say to the potter, 'What are you making?' Does your work say, 'He has no hands'?"

Dan 11 36"The king will do as he pleases. He will exalt and magnify himself above every god and will say unheard-of things against the God of gods. He will be successful until the time of wrath is completed, for what has been determined must take place. 37He will show no regard for the gods of his fathers or for the one desired by women, nor will he regard any god, but will exalt himself above them all. 38Instead of them, he will honor a god of fortresses; a god unknown to his fathers he will honor with gold and silver, with precious stones and costly gifts. 39He will attack the mightiest fortresses with the help of a foreign god and will greatly honor those who acknowledge him. He will make them rulers over many people and will distribute the land at a price.

40"At the time of the end the king of the South will engage him in battle, and the king of the North will storm out against him with chariots and cavalry and a great fleet of ships. He will invade many countries and sweep through them like a flood."

Matt 27 39Those who passed by hurled insults at him, shaking their heads 40and saying, "You who are going to destroy the temple and build it in three days, save yourself! Come down from the cross, if you are the Son of God!"

2 Thess 2 4He will oppose and will exalt himself over everything that is called God or is worshiped, so that he sets himself up in God's temple, proclaiming himself to be God.

Rev 16 9They were seared by the intense heat and they cursed the name of God, who had control over these plagues, but they refused to repent and glorify him.

10The fifth angel poured out his bowl on the throne of the beast, and his kingdom was plunged into darkness. Men gnawed their tongues in agony 11and cursed the God of heaven because of their pains and their sores, but they refused to repent of what they had done. . . .

21From the sky huge hailstones of about a hundred pounds each fell upon men. And they cursed God on account of the plague of hail, because the plague was so terrible.

5. Sinners Are Blind

Exod 5 2Pharaoh said, "Who is the LORD, that I should obey him and let Israel go? I do not know the LORD and I will not let Israel go."

Isa 5 20Woe to those who call evil good and good evil, who put darkness for light and light for darkness, who put bitter for sweet and sweet for bitter.

Jer 4 22"My people are fools; they do not know me. They are senseless children; they have no understanding. They are skilled in doing evil; they know not how to do good."

Mark 7 [18]"Are you so dull?" he asked. "Don't you see that nothing that enters a man from the outside can make him 'unclean'?"
Luke 11 [52]"Woe to you experts in the law, because you have taken away the key to knowledge. You yourselves have not entered, and you have hindered those who were entering."
2 Cor 3 [14]But their minds were made dull, for to this day the same veil remains when the old covenant is read. It has not been removed, because only in Christ is it taken away.
2 Cor 4 [3]And even if our gospel is veiled, it is veiled to those who are perishing. [4]The god of this age has blinded the minds of unbelievers, so that they cannot see the light of the gospel of the glory of Christ, who is the image of God.
1 John 2 [11]But whoever hates his brother is in the darkness and walks around in the darkness; he does not know where he is going, because the darkness has blinded him.
Rev 3 [17]"You say, 'I am rich; I have acquired wealth and do not need a thing.' But you do not realize that you are wretched, pitiful, poor, blind and naked."

6. Sinners Are Conceited

Ps 73 [7]From their callous hearts comes iniquity; the evil conceits of their minds know no limits.
1 Tim 6 [3]If anyone teaches false doctrines and does not agree to the sound instruction of our Lord Jesus Christ and to godly teaching, [4]he is conceited and understands nothing. He has an unhealthy interest in controversies and quarrels about words that result in envy, strife, malicious talk, evil suspicions. . . .
2 Tim 3 [4]treacherous, rash, conceited, lovers of pleasure rather than lovers of God . . .

7. Sinners Are Corrupt

Deut 31 [29]"For I know that after my death you are sure to become utterly corrupt and to turn from the way I have commanded you. In days to come, disaster will fall upon you because you will do evil in the sight of the LORD and provoke him to anger by what your hands have made."
Deut 32 [5]They have acted corruptly toward him; to their shame they are no longer his children, but a warped and crooked generation.
Judg 2 [19]But when the judge died, the people returned to ways even more corrupt than those of their fathers, following other gods and serving and worshiping them. They refused to give up their evil practices and stubborn ways.
Ezra 9 [11]". . . you gave through your servants the prophets when you said: 'The land you are entering to possess is a land polluted by the corruption of its peoples. By their detestable practices they have filled it with their impurity from one end to the other.'"
Job 15 [16]". . . how much less man, who is vile and corrupt, who drinks up evil like water!"
Ps 53 [1]The fool says in his heart, "There is no God." They are corrupt, and their ways are vile; there is no one who does good. . . . [3]Everyone has turned away, they have together become corrupt; there is no one who does good, not even one.
Ps 143 [2]Do not bring your servant into judgment, for no one living is righteous before you.
Hos 9 [9]They have sunk deep into corruption, as in the days of Gibeah. God will remember their wickedness and punish them for their sins.
1 Tim 6 [5]and constant friction between men of corrupt mind, who have been robbed of the truth and who think that godliness is a means to financial gain.
Titus 1 [15]To the pure, all things are pure, but to those who are corrupted and do not believe, nothing is pure. In fact, both their minds and consciences are corrupted.
Jude [23]snatch others from the fire and save them; to others show mercy, mixed with fear—hating even the clothing stained by corrupted flesh.

8. Sinners Are Darkened in Understanding

Rom 1 [21]For although they knew God, they neither glorified him as God nor gave thanks to him, but their thinking became futile and their foolish hearts were darkened.
Eph 4 [18]They are darkened in their understanding and separated from the life of God because of the ignorance that is in them due to the hardening of their hearts.

9. Sinners Are Destructive

Ps 5 [9]Not a word from their mouth can be trusted; their heart is filled with destruction. Their throat is an open grave; with their tongue they speak deceit.
Ps 14 [4]Will evildoers never learn—those who devour my people as men eat bread and who do not call on the LORD?
Ps 52 [2]Your tongue plots destruction; it is like a sharpened razor, you who practice deceit.
Ps 69 [4]Those who hate me without reason outnumber the hairs of my head; many are my enemies without cause, those who seek to destroy me. I am forced to restore what I did not steal.
Prov 11 [9]With his mouth the godless destroys his neighbor, but through knowledge the righteous escape.
Prov 11 [11]Through the blessing of the upright a city is exalted, but by the mouth of the wicked it is destroyed.
Prov 28 [24]He who robs his father or mother and says, "It's not wrong"—he is partner to him who destroys.
Isa 32 [7]The scoundrel's methods are wicked, he makes up evil schemes to destroy the poor with lies, even when the plea of the needy is just.
Isa 59 [7]Their feet rush into sin; they are swift to shed innocent blood. Their thoughts are evil thoughts; ruin and destruction mark their ways.
Acts 8 [3]But Saul began to destroy the church. Going from house to house, he dragged off men and women and put them in prison.
Gal 1 [13]For you have heard of my previous way of life in Judaism, how intensely I persecuted the church of God and tried to destroy it.
1 Tim 6 [9]People who want to get rich fall into temptation and a trap and into many foolish and harmful desires that plunge men into ruin and destruction.
2 Pet 2 [1]But there were also false prophets among the people, just as there will be false teachers among you. They will secretly introduce destructive heresies, even denying the sovereign Lord who bought them—bringing swift destruction on themselves.
Rev 11 [18]"The nations were angry; and your wrath has come. The time has come for judging the dead, and for rewarding your servants the prophets and your saints and those who reverence your name, both small and great—and for destroying those who destroy the earth."

10. Sinners Are Detestable

Lev 18 [24]"'Do not defile yourselves in any of these ways, because this is how the nations that I am going to drive out before you became defiled. [25]Even the land was defiled; so I punished it for its sin, and the land vomited out its inhabitants. [26]But you must keep my decrees and my laws. The native-born and the aliens living among you must not do any of these detestable things, [27]for all these things were done by the people who lived in the land before you, and the land became defiled. [28]And if you defile the land, it will vomit you out as it vomited out the nations that were before you.

[29]"'Everyone who does any of these detestable things—such persons must be cut off from their people. [30]Keep my requirements and do not follow any of the detestable customs that were practiced before you came and do not defile yourselves with them. I am the LORD your God.'"
Ps 26 [5]I abhor the assembly of evildoers and refuse to sit with the wicked.
Prov 6 [16]There are six things the LORD hates, seven that are detestable to him: [17]haughty eyes, a lying tongue, hands that shed innocent blood, [18]a heart that devises wicked schemes, feet that are quick to rush into evil, [19]a false witness who pours out lies and a man who stirs up dissension among brothers.
Prov 21 [27]The sacrifice of the wicked is detestable—how much more so when brought with evil intent!
Titus 1 [16]They claim to know God, but by their actions they

deny him. They are detestable, disobedient and unfit for doing anything good.
Rev 21 [8]"But the cowardly, the unbelieving, the vile, the murderers, the sexually immoral, those who practice magic arts, the idolaters and all liars—their place will be in the fiery lake of burning sulfur. This is the second death."

11. Sinners Are Devious

Prov 2 [12]Wisdom will save you from the ways of wicked men, from men whose words are perverse . . . [15]whose paths are crooked and who are devious in their ways.
Prov 14 [2]He whose walk is upright fears the LORD, but he whose ways are devious despises him.
Prov 21 [8]The way of the guilty is devious, but the conduct of the innocent is upright.

12. Sinners Are Disobedient

Neh 9 [26]"But they were disobedient and rebelled against you; they put your law behind their backs. They killed your prophets, who had admonished them in order to turn them back to you; they committed awful blasphemies."
Ps 119 [158]I look on the faithless with loathing, for they do not obey your word.
Isa 30 [9]These are rebellious people, deceitful children, children unwilling to listen to the LORD's instruction.
Jer 22 [21]"I warned you when you felt secure, but you said, 'I will not listen!' This has been your way from your youth; you have not obeyed me."
Jer 35 [14]"'Jonadab son of Recab ordered his sons not to drink wine and this command has been kept. To this day they do not drink wine, because they obey their forefather's command. But I have spoken to you again and again, yet you have not obeyed me.'"
Acts 7 [39]"But our fathers refused to obey him. Instead, they rejected him and in their hearts turned back to Egypt."
Eph 2 [1]As for you, you were dead in your transgressions and sins, [2]in which you used to live when you followed the ways of this world and of the ruler of the kingdom of the air, the spirit who is now at work in those who are disobedient.
Titus 3 [3]At one time we too were foolish, disobedient, deceived and enslaved by all kinds of passions and pleasures. We lived in malice and envy, being hated and hating one another.
Heb 4 [6]It still remains that some will enter that rest, and those who formerly had the gospel preached to them did not go in, because of their disobedience. . . . [11]Let us, therefore, make every effort to enter that rest, so that no one will fall by following their example of disobedience.
1 Pet 2 [7]Now to you who believe, this stone is precious. But to those who do not believe, "The stone the builders rejected has become the capstone," [8]and, "A stone that causes men to stumble and a rock that makes them fall." They stumble because they disobey the message—which is also what they were destined for.
2 Pet 2 [14]With eyes full of adultery, they never stop sinning; they seduce the unstable; they are experts in greed—an accursed brood!

13. Sinners Are Fearful

Job 15 [20]"All his days the wicked man suffers torment, the ruthless through all the years stored up for him. [21]Terrifying sounds fill his ears; when all seems well, marauders attack him. [22]He despairs of escaping the darkness; he is marked for the sword. [23]He wanders about—food for vultures; he knows the day of darkness is at hand. [24]Distress and anguish fill him with terror; they overwhelm him, like a king poised to attack, [25]because he shakes his fist at God and vaunts himself against the Almighty, [26]defiantly charging against him with a thick, strong shield."
Job 18 [5]"The lamp of the wicked is snuffed out; the flame of his fire stops burning. . . . [11]Terrors startle him on every side and dog his every step."
Job 27 [20]"Terrors overtake him like a flood; a tempest snatches him away in the night."
Ps 53 [5]There they were, overwhelmed with dread, where there was nothing to dread. God scattered the bones of those who attacked you; you put them to shame, for God despised them.
Prov 10 [24]What the wicked dreads will overtake him; what the righteous desire will be granted.
Prov 28 [1]The wicked man flees though no one pursues, but the righteous are as bold as a lion.
Isa 66 [4]". . . so I also will choose harsh treatment for them and will bring upon them what they dread. For when I called, no one answered, when I spoke, no one listened. They did evil in my sight and chose what displeases me."
Rom 8 [15]For you did not receive a spirit that makes you a slave again to fear, but you received the Spirit of sonship. And by him we cry, "*Abba*, Father."
Heb 2 [15]and free those who all their lives were held in slavery by their fear of death.

14. Sinners Are Futile in Thinking

Ps 94 [11]The LORD knows the thoughts of man; he knows that they are futile.
Rom 1 [21]For although they knew God, they neither glorified him as God nor gave thanks to him, but their thinking became futile and their foolish hearts were darkened.
1 Cor 3 [19]For the wisdom of this world is foolishness in God's sight. As it is written: "He catches the wise in their craftiness"; [20]and again, "The Lord knows that the thoughts of the wise are futile."
Eph 4 [17]So I tell you this, and insist on it in the Lord, that you must no longer live as the Gentiles do, in the futility of their thinking.

15. Sinners Are Godless

Ps 10 [4]In his pride the wicked does not seek him; in all his thoughts there is no room for God.
Ps 14 [1]The fool says in his heart, "There is no God." They are corrupt, their deeds are vile; there is no one who does good.
Ps 36 [1]An oracle is within my heart concerning the sinfulness of the wicked: There is no fear of God before his eyes.
Ps 53 [1]The fool says in his heart, "There is no God." They are corrupt, and their ways are vile; there is no one who does good.
Ps 54 [3]Strangers are attacking me; ruthless men seek my life—men without regard for God.
Ps 55 [19]God, who is enthroned forever, will hear them and afflict them—men who never change their ways and have no fear of God.
Rom 1 [28]Furthermore, since they did not think it worthwhile to retain the knowledge of God, he gave them over to a depraved mind, to do what ought not to be done.
Eph 2 [12]remember that at that time you were separate from Christ, excluded from citizenship in Israel and foreigners to the covenants of the promise, without hope and without God in the world.

16. Sinners Are Hostile to God

Job 21 [14]"Yet they say to God, 'Leave us alone! We have no desire to know your ways.'"
Ps 2 [1]Why do the nations conspire and the peoples plot in vain? [2]The kings of the earth take their stand and the rulers gather together against the LORD and against his Anointed One.
Jer 10 [25]Pour out your wrath on the nations that do not acknowledge you, on the peoples who do not call on your name. For they have devoured Jacob; they have devoured him completely and destroyed his homeland.
Hos 7 [15]"I trained them and strengthened them, but they plot evil against me."
Nah 1 [9]Whatever they plot against the LORD he will bring to an end; trouble will not come a second time.
Rom 8 [7]the sinful mind is hostile to God. It does not submit to God's law, nor can it do so.
Col 1 [21]Once you were alienated from God and were enemies in your minds because of your evil behavior.

17. Sinners Are Hypocritical

Ps 5 [9]Not a word from their mouth can be trusted; their heart

is filled with destruction. Their throat is an open grave; with their tongue they speak deceit.
Ps 52 [3]You love evil rather than good, falsehood rather than speaking the truth. [4]You love every harmful word, O you deceitful tongue!
Isa 29 [13]The Lord says: "These people come near to me with their mouth and honor me with their lips, but their hearts are far from me. Their worship of me is made up only of rules taught by men."
Jer 3 [10]"In spite of all this, her unfaithful sister Judah did not return to me with all her heart, but only in pretense," declares the LORD.
Ezek 33 [30]"As for you, son of man, your countrymen are talking together about you by the walls and at the doors of the houses, saying to each other, 'Come and hear the message that has come from the LORD.' [31]My people come to you, as they usually do, and sit before you to listen to your words, but they do not put them into practice. With their mouths they express devotion, but their hearts are greedy for unjust gain. [32]Indeed, to them you are nothing more than one who sings love songs with a beautiful voice and plays an instrument well, for they hear your words but do not put them into practice."
Mic 3 [11]Her leaders judge for a bribe, her priests teach for a price, and her prophets tell fortunes for money. Yet they lean upon the LORD and say, "Is not the LORD among us? No disaster will come upon us."
Mal 1 [6]"A son honors his father, and a servant his master. If I am a father, where is the honor due me? If I am a master, where is the respect due me?" says the LORD Almighty. "It is you, O priests, who show contempt for my name.

"But you ask, 'How have we shown contempt for your name?'

[7]"You place defiled food on my altar.

"But you ask, 'How have we defiled you?'

"By saying that the LORD's table is contemptible. [8]When you bring blind animals for sacrifice, is that not wrong? When you sacrifice crippled or diseased animals, is that not wrong? Try offering them to your governor! Would he be pleased with you? Would he accept you?" says the LORD Almighty.

[9]"Now implore God to be gracious to us. With such offerings from your hands, will he accept you?"—says the LORD Almighty.

[10]"Oh, that one of you would shut the temple doors, so that you would not light useless fires on my altar! I am not pleased with you," says the LORD Almighty, "and I will accept no offering from your hands. [11]My name will be great among the nations, from the rising to the setting of the sun. In every place incense and pure offerings will be brought to my name, because my name will be great among the nations," says the LORD Almighty.

[12]"But you profane it by saying of the Lord's table, 'It is defiled,' and of its food, 'It is contemptible.' [13]And you say, 'What a burden!' and you sniff at it contemptuously," says the LORD Almighty.

"When you bring injured, crippled or diseased animals and offer them as sacrifices, should I accept them from your hands?" says the LORD. [14]"Cursed is the cheat who has an acceptable male in his flock and vows to give it, but then sacrifices a blemished animal to the Lord. For I am a great king," says the LORD Almighty, "and my name is to be feared among the nations."
Luke 12 [1]Meanwhile, when a crowd of many thousands had gathered, so that they were trampling on one another, Jesus began to speak first to his disciples, saying: "Be on your guard against the yeast of the Pharisees, which is hypocrisy. [2]There is nothing concealed that will not be disclosed, or hidden that will not be made known."
Luke 18 [11]"The Pharisee stood up and prayed about himself: 'God, I thank you that I am not like other men—robbers, evildoers, adulterers—or even like this tax collector. [12]I fast twice a week and give a tenth of all I get.'"
Luke 20 [46]"Beware of the teachers of the law. They like to walk around in flowing robes and love to be greeted in the marketplaces and have the most important seats in the synagogues and the places of honor at banquets. [47]They devour widows' houses and for a show make lengthy prayers. Such men will be punished most severely."
2 Tim 3 [2]People will be lovers of themselves, lovers of money, boastful, proud, abusive, disobedient to their parents, ungrateful, unholy . . . [5]having a form of godliness but denying its power. Have nothing to do with them.
Titus 1 [16]They claim to know God, but by their actions they deny him. They are detestable, disobedient and unfit for doing anything good.
Rev 3 [1]"To the angel of the church in Sardis write: These are the words of him who holds the seven spirits of God and the seven stars. I know your deeds; you have a reputation of being alive, but you are dead."

18. Sinners Are Ignorant of God

Matt 22 [29]Jesus replied, "You are in error because you do not know the Scriptures or the power of God."
John 14 [17]". . . the Spirit of truth. The world cannot accept him, because it neither sees him nor knows him. But you know him, for he lives with you and will be in you."
Gal 4 [8]Formerly, when you did not know God, you were slaves to those who by nature are not gods.
Eph 4 [18]They are darkened in their understanding and separated from the life of God because of the ignorance that is in them due to the hardening of their hearts.
1 Thess 4 [5]not in passionate lust like the heathen, who do not know God . . .
2 Thess 1 [8]He will punish those who do not know God and do not obey the gospel of our Lord Jesus.

19. Sinners Are Prompted by Evil Desires

Prov 11 [6]The righteousness of the upright delivers them, but the unfaithful are trapped by evil desires.
Rom 1 [24]Therefore God gave them over in the sinful desires of their hearts to sexual impurity for the degrading of their bodies with one another. . . .

[26]Because of this, God gave them over to shameful lusts. Even their women exchanged natural relations for unnatural ones. . . .

[28]Furthermore, since they did not think it worthwhile to retain the knowledge of God, he gave them over to a depraved mind, to do what ought not to be done.
Rom 6 [12]Therefore do not let sin reign in your mortal body so that you obey its evil desires.
Rom 13 [14]Rather, clothe yourselves with the Lord Jesus Christ, and do not think about how to gratify the desires of the sinful nature.
Gal 5 [16]So I say, live by the Spirit, and you will not gratify the desires of the sinful nature. [17]For the sinful nature desires what is contrary to the Spirit, and the Spirit what is contrary to the sinful nature. They are in conflict with each other, so that you do not do what you want.
Eph 2 [3]All of us also lived among them at one time, gratifying the cravings of our sinful nature and following its desires and thoughts. Like the rest, we were by nature objects of wrath.
Eph 4 [22]You were taught, with regard to your former way of life, to put off your old self, which is being corrupted by its deceitful desires. . . .
1 Tim 6 [9]People who want to get rich fall into temptation and a trap and into many foolish and harmful desires that plunge men into ruin and destruction.
2 Tim 3 [6]They are the kind who worm their way into homes and gain control over weak-willed women, who are loaded down with sins and are swayed by all kinds of evil desires. . . .
James 1 [14]but each one is tempted when, by his own evil desire, he is dragged away and enticed. [15]Then, after desire has conceived, it gives birth to sin; and sin, when it is full-grown, gives birth to death.
1 Pet 1 [14]As obedient children, do not conform to the evil desires you had when you lived in ignorance.
1 Pet 4 [2]As a result, he does not live the rest of his earthly life for evil human desires, but rather for the will of God.
2 Pet 2 [10]This is especially true of those who follow the corrupt desire of the sinful nature and despise authority.

Bold and arrogant, these men are not afraid to slander celestial beings. . . .
2 Pet 3 [3]First of all, you must understand that in the last days scoffers will come, scoffing and following their own evil desires.
Jude [16]These men are grumblers and faultfinders; they follow their own evil desires; they boast about themselves and flatter others for their own advantage.

20. Sinners Are Seared in Conscience

Jer 6 [15]"Are they ashamed of their loathsome conduct? No, they have no shame at all; they do not even know how to blush. So they will fall among the fallen; they will be brought down when I punish them," says the LORD.
Amos 6 [1]Woe to you who are complacent in Zion, and to you who feel secure on Mount Samaria, you notable men of the foremost nation, to whom the people of Israel come! . . . [4]You lie on beds inlaid with ivory and lounge on your couches. You dine on choice lambs and fattened calves. [5]You strum away on your harps like David and improvise on musical instruments. [6]You drink wine by the bowlful and use the finest lotions, but you do not grieve over the ruin of Joseph.
Eph 4 [19]Having lost all sensitivity, they have given themselves over to sensuality so as to indulge in every kind of impurity, with a continual lust for more.
1 Tim 4 [2]Such teachings come through hypocritical liars, whose consciences have been seared as with a hot iron.
Titus 1 [15]To the pure, all things are pure, but to those who are corrupted and do not believe, nothing is pure. In fact, both their minds and consciences are corrupted.

21. Sinners Are Self-Deceived

Job 22 [13]"Yet you say, 'What does God know? Does he judge through such darkness? [14]Thick clouds veil him, so he does not see us as he goes about in the vaulted heavens.' . . . [17]They said to God, 'Leave us alone! What can the Almighty do to us?'"
Ps 10 [6]He says to himself, "Nothing will shake me; I'll always be happy and never have trouble." . . . [11]He says to himself, "God has forgotten; he covers his face and never sees." . . . [13]Why does the wicked man revile God? Why does he say to himself, "He won't call me to account"?
Ps 94 [7]They say, "The LORD does not see; the God of Jacob pays no heed."
Prov 14 [12]There is a way that seems right to a man, but in the end it leads to death.
Isa 29 [15]Woe to those who go to great depths to hide their plans from the LORD, who do their work in darkness and think, "Who sees us? Who will know?"
Ezek 8 [12]He said to me, "Son of man, have you seen what the elders of the house of Israel are doing in the darkness, each at the shrine of his own idol? They say, 'The LORD does not see us; the LORD has forsaken the land.'"
Ezek 9 [9]He answered me, "The sin of the house of Israel and Judah is exceedingly great; the land is full of bloodshed and the city is full of injustice. They say, 'The LORD has forsaken the land; the LORD does not see.'"
Amos 9 [10]"All the sinners among my people will die by the sword, all those who say, 'Disaster will not overtake or meet us.'"
Zeph 1 [12]"At that time I will search Jerusalem with lamps and punish those who are complacent, who are like wine left on its dregs, who think, 'The LORD will do nothing, either good or bad.'"
Rev 18 [7]"Give her as much torture and grief as the glory and luxury she gave herself. In her heart she boasts, 'I sit as queen; I am not a widow, and I will never mourn.'"

22. Sinners Are Spiritually Undiscerning

Deut 32 [28]They are a nation without sense, there is no discernment in them. [29]If only they were wise and would understand this and discern what their end will be!
John 14 [17]". . . the Spirit of truth. The world cannot accept him, because it neither sees him nor knows him. But you know him, for he lives with you and will be in you."
1 Cor 2 [14]The man without the Spirit does not accept the things that come from the Spirit of God, for they are foolishness to him, and he cannot understand them, because they are spiritually discerned.
Jude [19]These are the men who divide you, who follow mere natural instincts and do not have the Spirit.

23. Sinners Are Treacherous

Ps 25 [3]No one whose hope is in you will ever be put to shame, but they will be put to shame who are treacherous without excuse.
Isa 24 [16]From the ends of the earth we hear singing: "Glory to the Righteous One."

But I said, "I waste away, I waste away! Woe to me! The treacherous betray! With treachery the treacherous betray!"
Isa 48 [8]"You have neither heard nor understood; from of old your ear has not been open. Well do I know how treacherous you are; you were called a rebel from birth."
Isa 59 [12]For our offenses are many in your sight, and our sins testify against us. Our offenses are ever with us, and we acknowledge our iniquities: [13]rebellion and treachery against the LORD, turning our backs on our God, fomenting oppression and revolt, uttering lies our hearts have conceived.
Zeph 3 [4]Her prophets are arrogant; they are treacherous men. Her priests profane the sanctuary and do violence to the law.
2 Tim 3 [4]treacherous, rash, conceited, lovers of pleasure rather than lovers of God . . .

24. Sinners Are Unable to Acknowledge the Truth

Hos 5 [4]"Their deeds do not permit them to return to their God. A spirit of prostitution is in their heart; they do not acknowledge the LORD."
2 Tim 3 [6]They are the kind who worm their way into homes and gain control over weak-willed women, who are loaded down with sins and are swayed by all kinds of evil desires, [7]always learning but never able to acknowledge the truth. . . .

[12]In fact, everyone who wants to live a godly life in Christ Jesus will be persecuted, [13]while evil men and impostors will go from bad to worse, deceiving and being deceived.

25. Sinners Are Untrustworthy

Ps 5 [9]Not a word from their mouth can be trusted; their heart is filled with destruction. Their throat is an open grave; with their tongue they speak deceit.
Ps 28 [3]Do not drag me away with the wicked, with those who do evil, who speak cordially with their neighbors but harbor malice in their hearts.
Ps 55 [21]His speech is smooth as butter, yet war is in his heart; his words are more soothing than oil, yet they are drawn swords.
Ps 62 [4]They fully intend to topple him from his lofty place; they take delight in lies. With their mouths they bless, but in their hearts they curse.
Prov 5 [3]For the lips of an adulteress drip honey, and her speech is smoother than oil; [4]but in the end she is bitter as gall, sharp as a double-edged sword.
Jer 9 [8]"Their tongue is a deadly arrow; it speaks with deceit. With his mouth each speaks cordially to his neighbor, but in his heart he sets a trap for him."
Rom 3 [13]"Their throats are open graves; their tongues practice deceit." "The poison of vipers is on their lips."

26. Sinners Are Vile

Job 15 [14]"What is man, that he could be pure, or one born of woman, that he could be righteous? [15]If God places no trust in his holy ones, if even the heavens are not pure in his eyes, [16]how much less man, who is vile and corrupt, who drinks up evil like water!"
Ps 14 [1]The fool says in his heart, "There is no God." They are corrupt, their deeds are vile; there is no one who does good.
Ezek 16 [52]"Bear your disgrace, for you have furnished some justification for your sisters. Because your sins were more vile than theirs, they appear more righteous than you. So then, be

ashamed and bear your disgrace, for you have made your sisters appear righteous.'"
Hos 9 [10]"When I found Israel, it was like finding grapes in the desert; when I saw your fathers, it was like seeing the early fruit on the fig tree. But when they came to Baal Peor, they consecrated themselves to that shameful idol and became as vile as the thing they loved."
Nah 1 [14]The LORD has given a command concerning you, Nineveh: "You will have no descendants to bear your name. I will destroy the carved images and cast idols that are in the temple of your gods. I will prepare your grave, for you are vile."
Rev 21 [8]"But the cowardly, the unbelieving, the vile, the murderers, the sexually immoral, those who practice magic arts, the idolaters and all liars—their place will be in the fiery lake of burning sulfur. This is the second death."

27. Sinners Are Violent

Ps 17 [11]They have tracked me down, they now surround me, with eyes alert, to throw me to the ground.
Ps 37 [14]The wicked draw the sword and bend the bow to bring down the poor and needy, to slay those whose ways are upright.
Ps 59 [3]See how they lie in wait for me! Fierce men conspire against me for no offense or sin of mine, O LORD. [4]I have done no wrong, yet they are ready to attack me. Arise to help me; look on my plight!
Ps 140 [1]Rescue me, O LORD, from evil men; protect me from men of violence, [2]who devise evil plans in their hearts and stir up war every day.
Prov 4 [17]They eat the bread of wickedness and drink the wine of violence.
Mic 3 [1]Then I said, "Listen, you leaders of Jacob, you rulers of the house of Israel. Should you not know justice, [2]you who hate good and love evil; who tear the skin from my people and the flesh from their bones; [3]who eat my people's flesh, strip off their skin and break their bones in pieces; who chop them up like meat for the pan, like flesh for the pot?"

28. Sinners Are Willfully Obstinate

Isa 1 [4]Ah, sinful nation, a people loaded with guilt, a brood of evildoers, children given to corruption! They have forsaken the LORD; they have spurned the Holy One of Israel and turned their backs on him.
Isa 26 [10]Though grace is shown to the wicked, they do not learn righteousness; even in a land of uprightness they go on doing evil and regard not the majesty of the LORD.
Isa 57 [17]"I was enraged by his sinful greed; I punished him, and hid my face in anger, yet he kept on in his willful ways."
Isa 63 [10]Yet they rebelled and grieved his Holy Spirit. So he turned and became their enemy and he himself fought against them.
Jer 6 [10]To whom can I speak and give warning? Who will listen to me? Their ears are closed so they cannot hear. The word of the LORD is offensive to them; they find no pleasure in it.
Ezek 2 [4]"The people to whom I am sending you are obstinate and stubborn. Say to them, 'This is what the Sovereign LORD says.'"
Ezek 3 [7]"But the house of Israel is not willing to listen to you because they are not willing to listen to me, for the whole house of Israel is hardened and obstinate."
Acts 7 [51]"You stiff-necked people, with uncircumcised hearts and ears! You are just like your fathers: You always resist the Holy Spirit!"

29. Sinners Are without Hope

Job 8 [13]"Such is the destiny of all who forget God; so perishes the hope of the godless."
Job 11 [20]"But the eyes of the wicked will fail, and escape will elude them; their hope will become a dying gasp."
Job 15 [34]"For the company of the godless will be barren, and fire will consume the tents of those who love bribes."
Job 27 [8]"For what hope has the godless when he is cut off, when God takes away his life?"
Eph 2 [12]remember that at that time you were separate from Christ, excluded from citizenship in Israel and foreigners to the covenants of the promise, without hope and without God in the world.
1 Thess 4 [13]Brothers, we do not want you to be ignorant about those who fall asleep, or to grieve like the rest of men, who have no hope.

30. Sinners Are Worthless

2 Kings 17 [15]They rejected his decrees and the covenant he had made with their fathers and the warnings he had given them. They followed worthless idols and themselves became worthless. They imitated the nations around them although the LORD had ordered them, "Do not do as they do," and they did the things the LORD had forbidden them to do.
Jer 2 [5]This is what the LORD says: "What fault did your fathers find in me, that they strayed so far from me? They followed worthless idols and became worthless themselves."
Jer 51 [18]"They are worthless, the objects of mockery; when their judgment comes, they will perish."
Hos 12 [11]Is Gilead wicked? Its people are worthless! Do they sacrifice bulls in Gilgal? Their altars will be like piles of stones on a plowed field.
Rom 3 [12]"All have turned away, they have together become worthless; there is no one who does good, not even one."

31. Sinners Conspire against God and His People

Neh 4 [8]They all plotted together to come and fight against Jerusalem and stir up trouble against it.
Neh 6 [2]Sanballat and Geshem sent me this message: "Come, let us meet together in one of the villages on the plain of Ono."
But they were scheming to harm me. . . .
Ps 38 [12]Those who seek my life set their traps, those who would harm me talk of my ruin; all day long they plot deception.
Ps 56 [6]They conspire, they lurk, they watch my steps, eager to take my life.
Ps 64 [2]Hide me from the conspiracy of the wicked, from that noisy crowd of evildoers.
Ps 71 [10]For my enemies speak against me; those who wait to kill me conspire together.
Ps 83 [3]With cunning they conspire against your people; they plot against those you cherish.
Ps 88 [17]All day long they surround me like a flood; they have completely engulfed me.
Acts 4 [27]"Indeed Herod and Pontius Pilate met together with the Gentiles and the people of Israel in this city to conspire against your holy servant Jesus, whom you anointed."
Acts 9 [23]After many days had gone by, the Jews conspired to kill him. . . .
1 Thess 2 [14]For you, brothers, became imitators of God's churches in Judea, which are in Christ Jesus: You suffered from your own countrymen the same things those churches suffered from the Jews, [15]who killed the Lord Jesus and the prophets and also drove us out. They displease God and are hostile to all men [16]in their effort to keep us from speaking to the Gentiles so that they may be saved. In this way they always heap up their sins to the limit. The wrath of God has come upon them at last.

32. Sinners Delight in the Sins of Others

Prov 2 [14]who delight in doing wrong and rejoice in the perverseness of evil . . .
Prov 10 [23]A fool finds pleasure in evil conduct, but a man of understanding delights in wisdom.
Jer 11 [15]"What is my beloved doing in my temple as she works out her evil schemes with many? Can consecrated meat avert your punishment? When you engage in your wickedness, then you rejoice."
Luke 11 [48]"So you testify that you approve of what your forefathers did; they killed the prophets, and you build their tombs."
Acts 22 [20]"'And when the blood of your martyr Stephen was shed, I stood there giving my approval and guarding the clothes of those who were killing him.'"

Rom 1 [32]Although they know God's righteous decree that those who do such things deserve death, they not only continue to do these very things but also approve of those who practice them.

33. Sinners Entice to Evil

Prov 12 [26]A righteous man is cautious in friendship, but the way of the wicked leads them astray.
Prov 16 [29]A violent man entices his neighbor and leads him down a path that is not good.
Gal 2 [4]This matter arose because some false brothers had infiltrated our ranks to spy on the freedom we have in Christ Jesus and to make us slaves.
2 Tim 3 [6]They are the kind who worm their way into homes and gain control over weak-willed women, who are loaded down with sins and are swayed by all kinds of evil desires. . . .
2 Pet 2 [18]For they mouth empty, boastful words and, by appealing to the lustful desires of sinful human nature, they entice people who are just escaping from those who live in error.
Jude [4]For certain men whose condemnation was written about long ago have secretly slipped in among you. They are godless men, who change the grace of our God into a license for immorality and deny Jesus Christ our only Sovereign and Lord.

34. Sinners Glory in Their Shame

Phil 3 [19]Their destiny is destruction, their god is their stomach, and their glory is in their shame. Their mind is on earthly things.

35. Sinners Hate the Light

Job 24 [13]"There are those who rebel against the light, who do not know its ways or stay in its paths. [14]When daylight is gone, the murderer rises up and kills the poor and needy; in the night he steals forth like a thief. [15]The eye of the adulterer watches for dusk; he thinks, 'No eye will see me,' and he keeps his face concealed. [16]In the dark, men break into houses, but by day they shut themselves in; they want nothing to do with the light. [17]For all of them, deep darkness is their morning; they make friends with the terrors of darkness."
John 1 [5]The light shines in the darkness, but the darkness has not understood it.
John 3 [20]"Everyone who does evil hates the light, and will not come into the light for fear that his deeds will be exposed."

36. Sinners Love Pleasure More Than God

Phil 3 [19]Their destiny is destruction, their god is their stomach, and their glory is in their shame. Their mind is on earthly things.
2 Tim 3 [4]treacherous, rash, conceited, lovers of pleasure rather than lovers of God . . .

37. Sinners Oppose Truth

Rom 1 [18]The wrath of God is being revealed from heaven against all the godlessness and wickedness of men who suppress the truth by their wickedness. . . .
Rom 1 [25]They exchanged the truth of God for a lie, and worshiped and served created things rather than the Creator—who is forever praised. Amen.
2 Thess 2 [10]and in every sort of evil that deceives those who are perishing. They perish because they refused to love the truth and so be saved. [11]For this reason God sends them a powerful delusion so that they will believe the lie [12]and so that all will be condemned who have not believed the truth but have delighted in wickedness.
2 Tim 3 [8]Just as Jannes and Jambres opposed Moses, so also these men oppose the truth—men of depraved minds, who, as far as the faith is concerned, are rejected.
2 Pet 3 [3]First of all, you must understand that in the last days scoffers will come, scoffing and following their own evil desires. [4]They will say, "Where is this 'coming' he promised? Ever since our fathers died, everything goes on as it has since the beginning of creation."

38. Sinners Rejoice in the Suffering of God's People

Ps 35 [15]But when I stumbled, they gathered in glee; attackers gathered against me when I was unaware. They slandered me without ceasing.
Ps 42 [3]My tears have been my food day and night, while men say to me all day long, "Where is your God?" . . . [10]My bones suffer mortal agony as my foes taunt me, saying to me all day long, "Where is your God?"
Ps 79 [10]Why should the nations say, "Where is their God?" Before our eyes, make known among the nations that you avenge the outpoured blood of your servants.
Joel 2 [17]Let the priests, who minister before the LORD, weep between the temple porch and the altar. Let them say, "Spare your people, O LORD. Do not make your inheritance an object of scorn, a byword among the nations. Why should they say among the peoples, 'Where is their God?'"
Obad [12]"You should not look down on your brother in the day of his misfortune, nor rejoice over the people of Judah in the day of their destruction, nor boast so much in the day of their trouble."
Mic 4 [11]But now many nations are gathered against you. They say, "Let her be defiled, let our eyes gloat over Zion!"

39. Sinners Scheme Evil

Job 15 [35]"They conceive trouble and give birth to evil; their womb fashions deceit."
Ps 7 [14]He who is pregnant with evil and conceives trouble gives birth to disillusionment.
Ps 36 [4]Even on his bed he plots evil; he commits himself to a sinful course and does not reject what is wrong.
Ps 64 [6]They plot injustice and say, "We have devised a perfect plan!" Surely the mind and heart of man are cunning.
Ps 83 [3]With cunning they conspire against your people; they plot against those you cherish.
Prov 4 [16]For they cannot sleep till they do evil; they are robbed of slumber till they make someone fall.
Prov 16 [27]A scoundrel plots evil, and his speech is like a scorching fire.
Eccles 8 [11]When the sentence for a crime is not quickly carried out, the hearts of the people are filled with schemes to do wrong.
Isa 59 [4]No one calls for justice; no one pleads his case with integrity. They rely on empty arguments and speak lies; they conceive trouble and give birth to evil.
Hos 7 [15]"I trained them and strengthened them, but they plot evil against me."
Mic 2 [1]Woe to those who plan iniquity, to those who plot evil on their beds! At morning's light they carry it out because it is in their power to do it.
Mic 7 [3]Both hands are skilled in doing evil; the ruler demands gifts, the judge accepts bribes, the powerful dictate what they desire—they all conspire together.
Nah 1 [11]From you, O Nineveh, has one come forth who plots evil against the LORD and counsels wickedness.
Eph 4 [14]Then we will no longer be infants, tossed back and forth by the waves, and blown here and there by every wind of teaching and by the cunning and craftiness of men in their deceitful scheming.

VI Sins against God

A. Sins of Sacrilege

1. Worshiping Idols

a) Idol Worship Is Vain

Judg 6 [31]But Joash replied to the hostile crowd around him, "Are you going to plead Baal's cause? Are you trying to save him? Whoever fights for him shall be put to death by morning!

If Baal really is a god, he can defend himself when someone breaks down his altar."

1 Kings 18 [21]Elijah went before the people and said, "How long will you waver between two opinions? If the LORD is God, follow him; but if Baal is God, follow him."

But the people said nothing. . . .

[27]At noon Elijah began to taunt them. "Shout louder!" he said. "Surely he is a god! Perhaps he is deep in thought, or busy, or traveling. Maybe he is sleeping and must be awakened." [28]So they shouted louder and slashed themselves with swords and spears, as was their custom, until their blood flowed. [29]Midday passed, and they continued their frantic prophesying until the time for the evening sacrifice. But there was no response, no one answered, no one paid attention.

2 Kings 19 [18]"They have thrown their gods into the fire and destroyed them, for they were not gods but only wood and stone, fashioned by men's hands."

1 Chron 16 [26]For all the gods of the nations are idols, but the LORD made the heavens.

Isa 40 [18]To whom, then, will you compare God? What image will you compare him to? [19]As for an idol, a craftsman casts it, and a goldsmith overlays it with gold and fashions silver chains for it. [20]A man too poor to present such an offering selects wood that will not rot. He looks for a skilled craftsman to set up an idol that will not topple.

[21]Do you not know? Have you not heard? Has it not been told you from the beginning? Have you not understood since the earth was founded? [22]He sits enthroned above the circle of the earth, and its people are like grasshoppers. He stretches out the heavens like a canopy, and spreads them out like a tent to live in. [23]He brings princes to naught and reduces the rulers of this world to nothing. [24]No sooner are they planted, no sooner are they sown, no sooner do they take root in the ground, than he blows on them and they wither, and a whirlwind sweeps them away like chaff.

[25]"To whom will you compare me? Or who is my equal?" says the Holy One.

Isa 41 [21]"Present your case," says the LORD. "Set forth your arguments," says Jacob's King. [22]"Bring in your idols to tell us what is going to happen. Tell us what the former things were, so that we may consider them and know their final outcome. Or declare to us the things to come, [23]tell us what the future holds, so we may know that you are gods. Do something, whether good or bad, so that we will be dismayed and filled with fear. [24]But you are less than nothing and your works are utterly worthless; he who chooses you is detestable."

Isa 44 [6]"This is what the LORD says—Israel's King and Redeemer, the LORD Almighty: I am the first and I am the last; apart from me there is no God. [7]Who then is like me? Let him proclaim it. Let him declare and lay out before me what has happened since I established my ancient people, and what is yet to come—yes, let him foretell what will come. [8]Do not tremble, do not be afraid. Did I not proclaim this and foretell it long ago? You are my witnesses. Is there any God besides me? No, there is no other Rock; I know not one."

[9]All who make idols are nothing, and the things they treasure are worthless. Those who would speak up for them are blind; they are ignorant, to their own shame. [10]Who shapes a god and casts an idol, which can profit him nothing? [11]He and his kind will be put to shame; craftsmen are nothing but men. Let them all come together and take their stand; they will be brought down to terror and infamy.

[12]The blacksmith takes a tool and works with it in the coals; he shapes an idol with hammers, he forges it with the might of his arm. He gets hungry and loses his strength; he drinks no water and grows faint. [13]The carpenter measures with a line and makes an outline with a marker; he roughs it out with chisels and marks it with compasses. He shapes it in the form of man, of man in all his glory, that it may dwell in a shrine. [14]He cut down cedars, or perhaps took a cypress or oak. He let it grow among the trees of the forest, or planted a pine, and the rain made it grow. [15]It is man's fuel for burning; some of it he takes and warms himself, he kindles a fire and bakes bread. But he also fashions a god and worships it; he makes an idol and bows down to it. [16]Half of the wood he burns in the fire; over it he prepares his meal, he roasts his meat and eats his fill. He also warms himself and says, "Ah! I am warm; I see the fire." [17]From the rest he makes a god, his idol; he bows down to it and worships. He prays to it and says, "Save me; you are my god." [18]They know nothing, they understand nothing; their eyes are plastered over so they cannot see, and their minds closed so they cannot understand. [19]No one stops to think, no one has the knowledge or understanding to say, "Half of it I used for fuel; I even baked bread over its coals, I roasted meat and I ate. Shall I make a detestable thing from what is left? Shall I bow down to a block of wood?" [20]He feeds on ashes, a deluded heart misleads him; he cannot save himself, or say, "Is not this thing in my right hand a lie?"

[21]"Remember these things, O Jacob, for you are my servant, O Israel. I have made you, you are my servant; O Israel, I will not forget you. [22]I have swept away your offenses like a cloud, your sins like the morning mist. Return to me, for I have redeemed you."

Isa 45 [20]"Gather together and come; assemble, you fugitives from the nations. Ignorant are those who carry about idols of wood, who pray to gods that cannot save."

Isa 46 [5]"To whom will you compare me or count me equal? To whom will you liken me that we may be compared? [6]Some pour out gold from their bags and weigh out silver on the scales; they hire a goldsmith to make it into a god, and they bow down and worship it. [7]They lift it to their shoulders and carry it; they set it up in its place, and there it stands. From that spot it cannot move. Though one cries out to it, it does not answer; it cannot save him from his troubles.

[8]"Remember this, fix it in mind, take it to heart, you rebels. [9]Remember the former things, those of long ago; I am God, and there is no other; I am God, and there is none like me."

Jer 10 [3]"For the customs of the peoples are worthless; they cut a tree out of the forest, and a craftsman shapes it with his chisel. [4]They adorn it with silver and gold; they fasten it with hammer and nails so it will not totter. [5]Like a scarecrow in a melon patch, their idols cannot speak; they must be carried because they cannot walk. Do not fear them; they can do no harm nor can they do any good."

[6]No one is like you, O LORD; you are great, and your name is mighty in power. [7]Who should not revere you, O King of the nations? This is your due. Among all the wise men of the nations and in all their kingdoms, there is no one like you. [8]They are all senseless and foolish; they are taught by worthless wooden idols. [9]Hammered silver is brought from Tarshish and gold from Uphaz. What the craftsman and goldsmith have made is then dressed in blue and purple—all made by skilled workers. [10]But the LORD is the true God; he is the living God, the eternal King. When he is angry, the earth trembles; the nations cannot endure his wrath.

Hab 2 [18]"Of what value is an idol, since a man has carved it? Or an image that teaches lies? For he who makes it trusts in his own creation; he makes idols that cannot speak. [19]Woe to him who says to wood, 'Come to life!' Or to lifeless stone, 'Wake up!' Can it give guidance? It is covered with gold and silver; there is no breath in it. [20]But the LORD is in his holy temple; let all the earth be silent before him."

Acts 17 [29]"Therefore since we are God's offspring, we should not think that the divine being is like gold or silver or stone—an image made by man's design and skill."

Acts 19 [26]"And you see and hear how this fellow Paul has convinced and led astray large numbers of people here in Ephesus and in practically the whole province of Asia. He says that man-made gods are no gods at all."

Rom 1 [25]They exchanged the truth of God for a lie, and worshiped and served created things rather than the Creator—who is forever praised. Amen.

1 Cor 8 [4]So then, about eating food sacrificed to idols: We know that an idol is nothing at all in the world and that there is no God but one. [5]For even if there are so-called gods, whether in heaven or on earth (as indeed there are many "gods" and many "lords") . . .

Gal 4 [8]Formerly, when you did not know God, you were slaves to those who by nature are not gods.

b) Idol Worship Is Abhorrent to God

Deut 9 [12]Then the LORD told me, "Go down from here at once, because your people whom you brought out of Egypt have become corrupt. They have turned away quickly from what I commanded them and have made a cast idol for themselves." . . . [16]When I looked, I saw that you had sinned against the LORD your God; you had made for yourselves an idol cast in the shape of a calf. You had turned aside quickly from the way that the LORD had commanded you.

Deut 16 [21]Do not set up any wooden Asherah pole beside the altar you build to the LORD your God, [22]and do not erect a sacred stone, for these the LORD your God hates.

1 Kings 14 [22]Judah did evil in the eyes of the LORD. By the sins they committed they stirred up his jealous anger more than their fathers had done. [23]They also set up for themselves high places, sacred stones and Asherah poles on every high hill and under every spreading tree. [24]There were even male shrine prostitutes in the land; the people engaged in all the detestable practices of the nations the LORD had driven out before the Israelites.

1 Kings 19 [18]"Yet I reserve seven thousand in Israel—all whose knees have not bowed down to Baal and all whose mouths have not kissed him."

Neh 9 [17]"They refused to listen and failed to remember the miracles you performed among them. They became stiff-necked and in their rebellion appointed a leader in order to return to their slavery. But you are a forgiving God, gracious and compassionate, slow to anger and abounding in love. Therefore you did not desert them, [18]even when they cast for themselves an image of a calf and said, 'This is your god, who brought you up out of Egypt,' or when they committed awful blasphemies."

Ps 106 [19]At Horeb they made a calf and worshiped an idol cast from metal. [20]They exchanged their Glory for an image of a bull, which eats grass. [21]They forgot the God who saved them, who had done great things in Egypt, [22]miracles in the land of Ham and awesome deeds by the Red Sea. [23]So he said he would destroy them—had not Moses, his chosen one, stood in the breach before him to keep his wrath from destroying them.

Isa 42 [8]"I am the LORD; that is my name! I will not give my glory to another or my praise to idols."

2 Cor 6 [16]What agreement is there between the temple of God and idols? For we are the temple of the living God. As God has said: "I will live with them and walk among them, and I will be their God, and they will be my people."

c) Idol Worship Is Forbidden

Gen 35 [2]So Jacob said to his household and to all who were with him, "Get rid of the foreign gods you have with you, and purify yourselves and change your clothes. . . ." [4]So they gave Jacob all the foreign gods they had and the rings in their ears, and Jacob buried them under the oak at Shechem.

Exod 20 [3]"You shall have no other gods before me.

[4]"You shall not make for yourself an idol in the form of anything in heaven above or on the earth beneath or in the waters below. [5]You shall not bow down to them or worship them; for I, the LORD your God, am a jealous God, punishing the children for the sin of the fathers to the third and fourth generation of those who hate me. . . ."

Exod 23 [24]"Do not bow down before their gods or worship them or follow their practices. You must demolish them and break their sacred stones to pieces."

Exod 23 [32]"Do not make a covenant with them or with their gods. [33]Do not let them live in your land, or they will cause you to sin against me, because the worship of their gods will certainly be a snare to you."

Exod 34 [12]"Be careful not to make a treaty with those who live in the land where you are going, or they will be a snare among you. [13]Break down their altars, smash their sacred stones and cut down their Asherah poles. [14]Do not worship any other god, for the LORD, whose name is Jealous, is a jealous God.

[15]"Be careful not to make a treaty with those who live in the land; for when they prostitute themselves to their gods and sacrifice to them, they will invite you and you will eat their sacrifices. [16]And when you choose some of their daughters as wives for your sons and those daughters prostitute themselves to their gods, they will lead your sons to do the same.

[17]"Do not make cast idols."

Lev 19 [4]"'Do not turn to idols or make gods of cast metal for yourselves. I am the LORD your God.'"

Lev 26 [1]"'Do not make idols or set up an image or a sacred stone for yourselves, and do not place a carved stone in your land to bow down before it. I am the LORD your God.'"

Deut 4 [12]Then the LORD spoke to you out of the fire. You heard the sound of words but saw no form; there was only a voice. [13]He declared to you his covenant, the Ten Commandments, which he commanded you to follow and then wrote them on two stone tablets. [14]And the LORD directed me at that time to teach you the decrees and laws you are to follow in the land that you are crossing the Jordan to possess.

[15]You saw no form of any kind the day the LORD spoke to you at Horeb out of the fire. Therefore watch yourselves very carefully, [16]so that you do not become corrupt and make for yourselves an idol, an image of any shape, whether formed like a man or a woman, [17]or like any animal on earth or any bird that flies in the air, [18]or like any creature that moves along the ground or any fish in the waters below.

Deut 4 [23]Be careful not to forget the covenant of the LORD your God that he made with you; do not make for yourselves an idol in the form of anything the LORD your God has forbidden. [24]For the LORD your God is a consuming fire, a jealous God.

Deut 7 [2]and when the LORD your God has delivered them over to you and you have defeated them, then you must destroy them totally. Make no treaty with them, and show them no mercy. [3]Do not intermarry with them. Do not give your daughters to their sons or take their daughters for your sons, [4]for they will turn your sons away from following me to serve other gods, and the LORD's anger will burn against you and will quickly destroy you. [5]This is what you are to do to them: Break down their altars, smash their sacred stones, cut down their Asherah poles and burn their idols in the fire. [6]For you are a people holy to the LORD your God. The LORD your God has chosen you out of all the peoples on the face of the earth to be his people, his treasured possession.

Deut 20 [17]Completely destroy them—the Hittites, Amorites, Canaanites, Perizzites, Hivites and Jebusites—as the LORD your God has commanded you. [18]Otherwise, they will teach you to follow all the detestable things they do in worshiping their gods, and you will sin against the LORD your God.

Josh 24 [14]"Now fear the LORD and serve him with all faithfulness. Throw away the gods your forefathers worshiped beyond the River and in Egypt, and serve the LORD. . . .

[23]"Now then," said Joshua, "throw away the foreign gods that are among you and yield your hearts to the LORD, the God of Israel."

Judg 10 [13]"But you have forsaken me and served other gods, so I will no longer save you. [14]Go and cry out to the gods you have chosen. Let them save you when you are in trouble!"

[15]But the Israelites said to the LORD, "We have sinned. Do with us whatever you think best, but please rescue us now." [16]Then they got rid of the foreign gods among them and served the LORD. And he could bear Israel's misery no longer.

1 Sam 7 [3]And Samuel said to the whole house of Israel, "If you are returning to the LORD with all your hearts, then rid yourselves of the foreign gods and the Ashtoreths and commit yourselves to the LORD and serve him only, and he will deliver you out of the hand of the Philistines." [4]So the Israelites put away their Baals and Ashtoreths, and served the LORD only.

2 Kings 23 [4]The king ordered Hilkiah the high priest, the priests next in rank and the doorkeepers to remove from the temple of the LORD all the articles made for Baal and Asherah and all the starry hosts. He burned them outside Jerusalem in the fields of the Kidron Valley and took the ashes to Bethel. [5]He did away with the pagan priests appointed by the kings of Judah to burn incense on the high places of the towns of Judah and on those around Jerusalem—those who burned incense to Baal, to the sun and moon, to the constellations and to all the starry hosts. [6]He took the Asherah pole from the temple of the LORD to the Kidron Valley outside Jerusalem and burned it there. He ground it to powder and scattered the dust over the graves of the common people. [7]He also tore down the quarters of the male shrine prostitutes, which were in the temple of the LORD and where women did weaving for Asherah.

2 Chron 33 [15]He got rid of the foreign gods and removed the image from the temple of the LORD, as well as all the altars he had built on the temple hill and in Jerusalem; and he threw them out of the city. [16]Then he restored the altar of the LORD and sacrificed fellowship offerings and thank offerings on it, and told Judah to serve the LORD, the God of Israel.

Ps 81 [9]"You shall have no foreign god among you; you shall not bow down to an alien god."

Dan 3 [12]"But there are some Jews whom you have set over the affairs of the province of Babylon—Shadrach, Meshach and Abednego—who pay no attention to you, O king. They neither serve your gods nor worship the image of gold you have set up." . . .

[16]Shadrach, Meshach and Abednego replied to the king, "O Nebuchadnezzar, we do not need to defend ourselves before you in this matter. [17]If we are thrown into the blazing furnace, the God we serve is able to save us from it, and he will rescue us from your hand, O king. [18]But even if he does not, we want you to know, O king, that we will not serve your gods or worship the image of gold you have set up."

Hos 13 [4]"But I am the LORD your God, who brought you out of Egypt. You shall acknowledge no God but me, no Savior except me."

Hos 14 [3]"Assyria cannot save us; we will not mount warhorses. We will never again say 'Our gods' to what our own hands have made, for in you the fatherless find compassion."

1 Cor 10 [7]Do not be idolaters, as some of them were; as it is written: "The people sat down to eat and drink and got up to indulge in pagan revelry."

1 John 5 [21]Dear children, keep yourselves from idols.

d) Idols Are to Be Destroyed

Exod 32 [19]When Moses approached the camp and saw the calf and the dancing, his anger burned and he threw the tablets out of his hands, breaking them to pieces at the foot of the mountain. [20]And he took the calf they had made and burned it in the fire; then he ground it to powder, scattered it on the water and made the Israelites drink it.

Num 33 [52]"' . . . drive out all the inhabitants of the land before you. Destroy all their carved images and their cast idols, and demolish all their high places.'"

2 Kings 3 [1]Joram son of Ahab became king of Israel in Samaria in the eighteenth year of Jehoshaphat king of Judah, and he reigned twelve years. [2]He did evil in the eyes of the LORD, but not as his father and mother had done. He got rid of the sacred stone of Baal that his father had made.

2 Kings 10 [25]As soon as Jehu had finished making the burnt offering, he ordered the guards and officers: "Go in and kill them; let no one escape." So they cut them down with the sword. The guards and officers threw the bodies out and then entered the inner shrine of the temple of Baal. [26]They brought the sacred stone out of the temple of Baal and burned it. [27]They demolished the sacred stone of Baal and tore down the temple of Baal, and people have used it for a latrine to this day.

[28]So Jehu destroyed Baal worship in Israel.

2 Kings 11 [17]Jehoiada then made a covenant between the LORD and the king and people that they would be the LORD's people. He also made a covenant between the king and the people. [18]All the people of the land went to the temple of Baal and tore it down. They smashed the altars and idols to pieces and killed Mattan the priest of Baal in front of the altars.

Then Jehoiada the priest posted guards at the temple of the LORD.

2 Kings 18 [1]In the third year of Hoshea son of Elah king of Israel, Hezekiah son of Ahaz king of Judah began to reign. . . . [3]He did what was right in the eyes of the LORD, just as his father David had done. [4]He removed the high places, smashed the sacred stones and cut down the Asherah poles. He broke into pieces the bronze snake Moses had made, for up to that time the Israelites had been burning incense to it. (It was called Nehushtan.)

2 Kings 23 [13]The king also desecrated the high places that were east of Jerusalem on the south of the Hill of Corruption—the ones Solomon king of Israel had built for Ashtoreth the vile goddess of the Sidonians, for Chemosh the vile god of Moab, and for Molech the detestable god of the people of Ammon. [14]Josiah smashed the sacred stones and cut down the Asherah poles and covered the sites with human bones.

2 Chron 14 [2]Asa did what was good and right in the eyes of the LORD his God. [3]He removed the foreign altars and the high places, smashed the sacred stones and cut down the Asherah poles. [4]He commanded Judah to seek the LORD, the God of their fathers, and to obey his laws and commands. [5]He removed the high places and incense altars in every town in Judah, and the kingdom was at peace under him.

Isa 30 [22]Then you will defile your idols overlaid with silver and your images covered with gold; you will throw them away like a menstrual cloth and say to them, "Away with you!"

e) Idolaters Will Be Judged

Exod 12 [12]"On that same night I will pass through Egypt and strike down every firstborn—both men and animals—and I will bring judgment on all the gods of Egypt. I am the LORD."

Exod 22 [20]"Whoever sacrifices to any god other than the LORD must be destroyed."

Lev 20 [5]"'I will set my face against that man and his family and will cut off from their people both him and all who follow him in prostituting themselves to Molech.'"

Num 33 [3]The Israelites set out from Rameses on the fifteenth day of the first month, the day after the Passover. They marched out boldly in full view of all the Egyptians, [4]who were burying all their firstborn, whom the LORD had struck down among them; for the LORD had brought judgment on their gods.

Deut 4 [25]After you have had children and grandchildren and have lived in the land a long time—if you then become corrupt and make any kind of idol, doing evil in the eyes of the LORD your God and provoking him to anger, [26]I call heaven and earth as witnesses against you this day that you will quickly perish from the land that you are crossing the Jordan to possess. You will not live there long but will certainly be destroyed. [27]The LORD will scatter you among the peoples, and only a few of you will survive among the nations to which the LORD will drive you. [28]There you will worship man-made gods of wood and stone, which cannot see or hear or eat or smell.

Deut 8 [19]If you ever forget the LORD your God and follow other gods and worship and bow down to them, I testify against you today that you will surely be destroyed. [20]Like the nations the LORD destroyed before you, so you will be destroyed for not obeying the LORD your God.

Deut 27 [15]"Cursed is the man who carves an image or casts an idol—a thing detestable to the LORD, the work of the craftsman's hands—and sets it up in secret." Then all the people shall say, "Amen!"

Josh 23 [16]"If you violate the covenant of the LORD your God, which he commanded you, and go and serve other gods and bow down to them, the LORD's anger will burn against you, and you will quickly perish from the good land he has given you."

Josh 24 [20]"If you forsake the LORD and serve foreign gods, he will turn and bring disaster on you and make an end of you, after he has been good to you."

1 Kings 9 [6]"But if you or your sons turn away from me and do not observe the commands and decrees I have given you and go off to serve other gods and worship them, [7]then I will cut off Israel from the land I have given them and will reject this temple I have consecrated for my Name. Israel will then become a byword and an object of ridicule among all peoples."

1 Kings 14 [9]"'You have done more evil than all who lived before you. You have made for yourself other gods, idols made of metal; you have provoked me to anger and thrust me behind your back.

[10]"'Because of this, I am going to bring disaster on the house of Jeroboam. I will cut off from Jeroboam every last male in Israel—slave or free. I will burn up the house of Jeroboam as one burns dung, until it is all gone.'"

Ps 16 [4]The sorrows of those will increase who run after other gods. I will not pour out their libations of blood or take up their names on my lips.

Jer 1 [16]"I will pronounce my judgments on my people because of their wickedness in forsaking me, in burning incense to other gods and in worshiping what their hands have made."

Jer 16 [13]"'So I will throw you out of this land into a land neither you nor your fathers have known, and there you will serve other gods day and night, for I will show you no favor.'"

Jer 22 [8]"People from many nations will pass by this city and will ask one another, 'Why has the LORD done such a thing to this great city?' [9]And the answer will be: 'Because they have forsaken the covenant of the LORD their God and have worshiped and served other gods.'"

Jer 50 [37]"A sword against her horses and chariots and all the foreigners in her ranks! They will become women. A sword against her treasures! They will be plundered. [38]A drought on her waters! They will dry up. For it is a land of idols, idols that will go mad with terror."

Ezek 7 [20]"They were proud of their beautiful jewelry and used it to make their detestable idols and vile images. Therefore I will turn these into an unclean thing for them. [21]I will hand it all over as plunder to foreigners and as loot to the wicked of the earth, and they will defile it. [22]I will turn my face away from them, and they will desecrate my treasured place; robbers will enter it and desecrate it."

Ezek 8 [12]He said to me, "Son of man, have you seen what the elders of the house of Israel are doing in the darkness, each at the shrine of his own idol? They say, 'The LORD does not see us; the LORD has forsaken the land.'" . . . [18]"Therefore I will deal with them in anger; I will not look on them with pity or spare them. Although they shout in my ears, I will not listen to them."

Ezek 14 [3]"Son of man, these men have set up idols in their hearts and put wicked stumbling blocks before their faces. Should I let them inquire of me at all? [4]Therefore speak to them and tell them, 'This is what the Sovereign LORD says: When any Israelite sets up idols in his heart and puts a wicked stumbling block before his face and then goes to a prophet, I the LORD will answer him myself in keeping with his great idolatry. [5]I will do this to recapture the hearts of the people of Israel, who have all deserted me for their idols.'

[6]"Therefore say to the house of Israel, 'This is what the Sovereign LORD says: Repent! Turn from your idols and renounce all your detestable practices!

[7]"'When any Israelite or any alien living in Israel separates himself from me and sets up idols in his heart and puts a wicked stumbling block before his face and then goes to a prophet to inquire of me, I the LORD will answer him myself. [8]I will set my face against that man and make him an example and a byword. I will cut him off from my people. Then you will know that I am the LORD.'"

Ezek 22 [3]". . . and say: 'This is what the Sovereign LORD says: O city that brings on herself doom by shedding blood in her midst and defiles herself by making idols, [4]you have become guilty because of the blood you have shed and have become defiled by the idols you have made. You have brought your days to a close, and the end of your years has come. Therefore I will make you an object of scorn to the nations and a laughingstock to all the countries.'"

Hos 10 [1]Israel was a spreading vine; he brought forth fruit for himself. As his fruit increased, he built more altars; as his land prospered, he adorned his sacred stones. [2]Their heart is deceitful, and now they must bear their guilt. The LORD will demolish their altars and destroy their sacred stones.

Hos 13 [2]Now they sin more and more; they make idols for themselves from their silver, cleverly fashioned images, all of them the work of craftsmen. It is said of these people, "They offer human sacrifice and kiss the calf-idols." [3]Therefore they will be like the morning mist, like the early dew that disappears, like chaff swirling from a threshing floor, like smoke escaping through a window.

Amos 5 [26]"You have lifted up the shrine of your king, the pedestal of your idols, the star of your god—which you made for yourselves. [27]Therefore I will send you into exile beyond Damascus," says the LORD, whose name is God Almighty.

Zeph 2 [11]The LORD will be awesome to them when he destroys all the gods of the land. The nations on every shore will worship him, every one in its own land.

Rev 14 [9]A third angel followed them and said in a loud voice: "If anyone worships the beast and his image and receives his mark on the forehead or on the hand, [10]he, too, will drink of the wine of God's fury, which has been poured full strength into the cup of his wrath. He will be tormented with burning sulfur in the presence of the holy angels and of the Lamb."

f) Idolaters Will Be Punished

Num 25 [3]So Israel joined in worshiping the Baal of Peor. And the LORD's anger burned against them.

[4]The LORD said to Moses, "Take all the leaders of these people, kill them and expose them in broad daylight before the LORD, so that the LORD's fierce anger may turn away from Israel."

[5]So Moses said to Israel's judges, "Each of you must put to death those of your men who have joined in worshiping the Baal of Peor."

Deut 32 [15]Jeshurun grew fat and kicked; filled with food, he became heavy and sleek. He abandoned the God who made him and rejected the Rock his Savior. [16]They made him jealous with their foreign gods and angered him with their detestable idols. [17]They sacrificed to demons, which are not God—gods they had not known, gods that recently appeared, gods your fathers did not fear. [18]You deserted the Rock, who fathered you; you forgot the God who gave you birth.

[19]The LORD saw this and rejected them because he was angered by his sons and daughters. [20]"I will hide my face from them," he said, "and see what their end will be; for they are a perverse generation, children who are unfaithful. [21]They made me jealous by what is no god and angered me with their worthless idols. I will make them envious by those who are not a people; I will make them angry by a nation that has no understanding. . . .

[23]"I will heap calamities upon them and spend my arrows against them. [24]I will send wasting famine against them, consuming pestilence and deadly plague; I will send against them the fangs of wild beasts, the venom of vipers that glide in the dust. [25]In the street the sword will make them childless; in their homes terror will reign. Young men and young women will perish, infants and gray-haired men. . . . [35]It is mine to avenge; I will repay. In due time their foot will slip; their day of disaster is near and their doom rushes upon them."

Judg 2 [1]The angel of the LORD went up from Gilgal to Bokim and said, "I brought you up out of Egypt and led you into the land that I swore to give to your forefathers. I said, 'I will never break my covenant with you, [2]and you shall not make a covenant with the people of this land, but you shall break down their altars.' Yet you have disobeyed me. Why have you done this? [3]Now therefore I tell you that I will not drive them out before you; they will be thorns in your sides and their gods will be a snare to you."

Judg 2 [10]After that whole generation had been gathered to their fathers, another generation grew up, who knew neither the LORD nor what he had done for Israel. [11]Then the Israelites did evil in the eyes of the LORD and served the Baals. [12]They forsook the LORD, the God of their fathers, who had brought them out of Egypt. They followed and worshiped various gods of the peoples around them. They provoked the LORD to anger [13]because they forsook him and served Baal and the Ashtoreths. [14]In his anger against Israel the LORD handed them over to raiders who plundered them. He sold them to their enemies all around, whom they were no longer able to resist. [15]Whenever Israel went out to fight, the hand of the LORD was against them to defeat them, just as he had sworn to them. They were in great distress.

[16]Then the LORD raised up judges, who saved them out of the hands of these raiders. [17]Yet they would not listen to their judges but prostituted themselves to other gods and worshiped them. Unlike their fathers, they quickly turned from the way in which their fathers had walked, the way of obedience to the LORD's commands. [18]Whenever the LORD raised up a judge for them, he was with the judge and saved them out of the hands of their enemies as long as the judge lived; for the LORD had compassion on them as they groaned under those who oppressed and afflicted them. [19]But when the judge died, the people returned to ways even more corrupt than those of their fathers, following other gods and serving and worshiping them. They refused to give up their evil practices and stubborn ways.

Judg 5 [8]"When they chose new gods, war came to the city gates, and not a shield or spear was seen among forty thousand in Israel."

1 Kings 11 1King Solomon, however, loved many foreign women besides Pharaoh's daughter—Moabites, Ammonites, Edomites, Sidonians and Hittites. 2They were from nations about which the LORD had told the Israelites, "You must not intermarry with them, because they will surely turn your hearts after their gods." Nevertheless, Solomon held fast to them in love. . . . 4As Solomon grew old, his wives turned his heart after other gods, and his heart was not fully devoted to the LORD his God, as the heart of David his father had been. . . . 6So Solomon did evil in the eyes of the LORD; he did not follow the LORD completely, as David his father had done. . . .

9The LORD became angry with Solomon because his heart had turned away from the LORD, the God of Israel, who had appeared to him twice. 10Although he had forbidden Solomon to follow other gods, Solomon did not keep the LORD's command. 11So the LORD said to Solomon, "Since this is your attitude and you have not kept my covenant and my decrees, which I commanded you, I will most certainly tear the kingdom away from you and give it to one of your subordinates. 12Nevertheless, for the sake of David your father, I will not do it during your lifetime. I will tear it out of the hand of your son. 13Yet I will not tear the whole kingdom from him, but will give him one tribe for the sake of David my servant and for the sake of Jerusalem, which I have chosen."

1 Kings 16 31He not only considered it trivial to commit the sins of Jeroboam son of Nebat, but he also married Jezebel daughter of Ethbaal king of the Sidonians, and began to serve Baal and worship him. . . . 33Ahab also made an Asherah pole and did more to provoke the LORD, the God of Israel, to anger than did all the kings of Israel before him. . . .

17 1Now Elijah the Tishbite, from Tishbe in Gilead, said to Ahab, "As the LORD, the God of Israel, lives, whom I serve, there will be neither dew nor rain in the next few years except at my word." . . .

7Some time later the brook dried up because there had been no rain in the land.

1 Kings 21 20Ahab said to Elijah, "So you have found me, my enemy!"

"I have found you," he answered, "because you have sold yourself to do evil in the eyes of the LORD. 21'I am going to bring disaster on you. I will consume your descendants and cut off from Ahab every last male in Israel—slave or free. . . .'

23"And also concerning Jezebel the LORD says: 'Dogs will devour Jezebel by the wall of Jezreel.' . . ."

25(There was never a man like Ahab, who sold himself to do evil in the eyes of the LORD, urged on by Jezebel his wife. 26He behaved in the vilest manner by going after idols, like the Amorites the LORD drove out before Israel.)

2 Kings 17 7All this took place because the Israelites had sinned against the LORD their God, who had brought them up out of Egypt from under the power of Pharaoh king of Egypt. They worshiped other gods 8and followed the practices of the nations the LORD had driven out before them, as well as the practices that the kings of Israel had introduced. . . .

16They forsook all the commands of the LORD their God and made for themselves two idols cast in the shape of calves, and an Asherah pole. They bowed down to all the starry hosts, and they worshiped Baal. 17They sacrificed their sons and daughters in the fire. They practiced divination and sorcery and sold themselves to do evil in the eyes of the LORD, provoking him to anger.

18So the LORD was very angry with Israel and removed them from his presence. Only the tribe of Judah was left, 19and even Judah did not keep the commands of the LORD their God. They followed the practices Israel had introduced. 20Therefore the LORD rejected all the people of Israel; he afflicted them and gave them into the hands of plunderers, until he thrust them from his presence.

2 Kings 22 16"'This is what the LORD says: I am going to bring disaster on this place and its people, according to everything written in the book the king of Judah has read. 17Because they have forsaken me and burned incense to other gods and provoked me to anger by all the idols their hands have made, my anger will burn against this place and will not be quenched.'"

2 Chron 28 1Ahaz was twenty years old when he became king, and he reigned in Jerusalem sixteen years. Unlike David his father, he did not do what was right in the eyes of the LORD. 2He walked in the ways of the kings of Israel and also made cast idols for worshiping the Baals. 3He burned sacrifices in the Valley of Ben Hinnom and sacrificed his sons in the fire, following the detestable ways of the nations the LORD had driven out before the Israelites. 4He offered sacrifices and burned incense at the high places, on the hilltops and under every spreading tree.

5Therefore the LORD his God handed him over to the king of Aram. The Arameans defeated him and took many of his people as prisoners and brought them to Damascus.

He was also given into the hands of the king of Israel, who inflicted heavy casualties on him. 6In one day Pekah son of Remaliah killed a hundred and twenty thousand soldiers in Judah—because Judah had forsaken the LORD, the God of their fathers.

2 Chron 33 1Manasseh was twelve years old when he became king, and he reigned in Jerusalem fifty-five years. 2He did evil in the eyes of the LORD, following the detestable practices of the nations the LORD had driven out before the Israelites. 3He rebuilt the high places his father Hezekiah had demolished; he also erected altars to the Baals and made Asherah poles. He bowed down to all the starry hosts and worshiped them. 4He built altars in the temple of the LORD, of which the LORD had said, "My Name will remain in Jerusalem forever." 5In both courts of the temple of the LORD, he built altars to all the starry hosts. 6He sacrificed his sons in the fire in the Valley of Ben Hinnom, practiced sorcery, divination and witchcraft, and consulted mediums and spiritists. He did much evil in the eyes of the LORD, provoking him to anger.

7He took the carved image he had made and put it in God's temple, of which God had said to David and to his son Solomon, "In this temple and in Jerusalem, which I have chosen out of all the tribes of Israel, I will put my Name forever. 8I will not again make the feet of the Israelites leave the land I assigned to your forefathers, if only they will be careful to do everything I commanded them concerning all the laws, decrees and ordinances given through Moses." 9But Manasseh led Judah and the people of Jerusalem astray, so that they did more evil than the nations the LORD had destroyed before the Israelites.

10The LORD spoke to Manasseh and his people, but they paid no attention. 11So the LORD brought against them the army commanders of the king of Assyria, who took Manasseh prisoner, put a hook in his nose, bound him with bronze shackles and took him to Babylon.

Ps 78 58They angered him with their high places; they aroused his jealousy with their idols. 59When God heard them, he was very angry; he rejected Israel completely. 60He abandoned the tabernacle of Shiloh, the tent he had set up among men. 61He sent the ark of his might into captivity, his splendor into the hands of the enemy. 62He gave his people over to the sword; he was very angry with his inheritance. 63Fire consumed their young men, and their maidens had no wedding songs; 64their priests were put to the sword, and their widows could not weep.

Ps 97 7All who worship images are put to shame, those who boast in idols—worship him, all you gods!

Ps 106 28They yoked themselves to the Baal of Peor and ate sacrifices offered to lifeless gods; 29they provoked the LORD to anger by their wicked deeds, and a plague broke out among them. . . .

34They did not destroy the peoples as the LORD had commanded them, 35but they mingled with the nations and adopted their customs. 36They worshiped their idols, which became a snare to them. 37They sacrificed their sons and their daughters to demons. 38They shed innocent blood, the blood of their sons and daughters, whom they sacrificed to the idols of Canaan, and the land was desecrated by their blood. 39They defiled themselves by what they did; by their deeds they prostituted themselves.

40Therefore the LORD was angry with his people and abhorred his inheritance. 41He handed them over to the nations, and their foes ruled over them. 42Their enemies oppressed them and subjected them to their power. [43]Many times he delivered them, but they were bent on rebellion and they wasted away in their sin.

Isa 57 [3]"But you—come here, you sons of a sorceress, you offspring of adulterers and prostitutes! . . . [5]You burn with lust among the oaks and under every spreading tree; you sacrifice your children in the ravines and under the overhanging crags. [6]The idols among the smooth stones of the ravines are your portion; they, they are your lot. Yes, to them you have poured out drink offerings and offered grain offerings. In the light of these things, should I relent? . . . [13]When you cry out for help, let your collection of idols save you! The wind will carry all of them off, a mere breath will blow them away. But the man who makes me his refuge will inherit the land and possess my holy mountain."

Jer 5 [19]"And when the people ask, 'Why has the LORD our God done all this to us?' you will tell them, 'As you have forsaken me and served foreign gods in your own land, so now you will serve foreigners in a land not your own.'"

Jer 11 [10]"They have returned to the sins of their forefathers, who refused to listen to my words. They have followed other gods to serve them. Both the house of Israel and the house of Judah have broken the covenant I made with their forefathers. [11]Therefore this is what the LORD says: 'I will bring on them a disaster they cannot escape. Although they cry out to me, I will not listen to them.'"

Jer 13 [9]"This is what the LORD says: 'In the same way I will ruin the pride of Judah and the great pride of Jerusalem. [10]These wicked people, who refuse to listen to my words, who follow the stubbornness of their hearts and go after other gods to serve and worship them, will be like this belt—completely useless!'"

Ezek 16 [17]"'You also took the fine jewelry I gave you, the jewelry made of my gold and silver, and you made for yourself male idols and engaged in prostitution with them. [18]And you took your embroidered clothes to put on them, and you offered my oil and incense before them. [19]Also the food I provided for you—the fine flour, olive oil and honey I gave you to eat—you offered as fragrant incense before them. That is what happened, declares the Sovereign LORD.

[20]"'And you took your sons and daughters whom you bore to me and sacrificed them as food to the idols. Was your prostitution not enough? [21]You slaughtered my children and sacrificed them to the idols. [22]In all your detestable practices and your prostitution you did not remember the days of your youth, when you were naked and bare, kicking about in your blood.

[23]"'Woe! Woe to you, declares the Sovereign LORD. In addition to all your other wickedness, [24]you built a mound for yourself and made a lofty shrine in every public square. [25]At the head of every street you built your lofty shrines and degraded your beauty, offering your body with increasing promiscuity to anyone who passed by. [26]You engaged in prostitution with the Egyptians, your lustful neighbors, and provoked me to anger with your increasing promiscuity. [27]So I stretched out my hand against you and reduced your territory; I gave you over to the greed of your enemies, the daughters of the Philistines, who were shocked by your lewd conduct.'"

Ezek 20 [32]"'You say, "We want to be like the nations, like the peoples of the world, who serve wood and stone." But what you have in mind will never happen. [33]As surely as I live, declares the Sovereign LORD, I will rule over you with a mighty hand and an outstretched arm and with outpoured wrath.'"

Zeph 1 [4]"I will stretch out my hand against Judah and against all who live in Jerusalem. I will cut off from this place every remnant of Baal, the names of the pagan and the idolatrous priests—[5]those who bow down on the roofs to worship the starry host, those who bow down and swear by the LORD and who also swear by Molech. . . ."

Rom 1 [22]Although they claimed to be wise, they became fools [23]and exchanged the glory of the immortal God for images made to look like mortal man and birds and animals and reptiles.

[24]Therefore God gave them over in the sinful desires of their hearts to sexual impurity for the degrading of their bodies with one another. [25]They exchanged the truth of God for a lie, and worshiped and served created things rather than the Creator—who is forever praised. Amen.

2. Profaning God's Name

a) Misusing God's Name

Exod 20 [7]"You shall not misuse the name of the LORD your God, for the LORD will not hold anyone guiltless who misuses his name."

Lev 18 [21]"'Do not give any of your children to be sacrificed to Molech, for you must not profane the name of your God. I am the LORD.'"

Lev 20 [3]"'I will set my face against that man and I will cut him off from his people; for by giving his children to Molech, he has defiled my sanctuary and profaned my holy name.'"

Lev 21 [6]"'They must be holy to their God and must not profane the name of their God. Because they present the offerings made to the LORD by fire, the food of their God, they are to be holy.'"

Lev 22 [2]"Tell Aaron and his sons to treat with respect the sacred offerings the Israelites consecrate to me, so they will not profane my holy name. I am the LORD. . . .

[32]"Do not profane my holy name. I must be acknowledged as holy by the Israelites. I am the LORD, who makes you holy. . . ."

Ps 139 [19]If only you would slay the wicked, O God! Away from me, you bloodthirsty men! [20]They speak of you with evil intent; your adversaries misuse your name.

Ezek 36 [20]"And wherever they went among the nations they profaned my holy name, for it was said of them, 'These are the LORD's people, and yet they had to leave his land.'"

b) Swearing Falsely by God's Name

Lev 6 [2]"If anyone sins and is unfaithful to the LORD by deceiving his neighbor about something entrusted to him or left in his care or stolen, or if he cheats him, [3]or if he finds lost property and lies about it, or if he swears falsely, or if he commits any such sin that people may do—[4]when he thus sins and becomes guilty, he must return what he has stolen or taken by extortion, or what was entrusted to him, or the lost property he found, [5]or whatever it was he swore falsely about. He must make restitution in full, add a fifth of the value to it and give it all to the owner on the day he presents his guilt offering."

Lev 19 [12]"'Do not swear falsely by my name and so profane the name of your God. I am the LORD.'"

Hos 4 [15]"Though you commit adultery, O Israel, let not Judah become guilty.

"Do not go to Gilgal; do not go up to Beth Aven. And do not swear, 'As surely as the LORD lives!'"

Zech 5 [3]And he said to me, "This is the curse that is going out over the whole land; for according to what it says on one side, every thief will be banished, and according to what it says on the other, everyone who swears falsely will be banished. [4]The LORD Almighty declares, 'I will send it out, and it will enter the house of the thief and the house of him who swears falsely by my name. It will remain in his house and destroy it, both its timbers and its stones.'"

Zech 8 [17]". . . do not plot evil against your neighbor, and do not love to swear falsely. I hate all this," declares the LORD.

c) Swearing by Other Beings

Josh 23 [7]"Do not associate with these nations that remain among you; do not invoke the names of their gods or swear by them. You must not serve them or bow down to them."

Jer 5 [7]"Why should I forgive you? Your children have forsaken me and sworn by gods that are not gods. I supplied all their needs, yet they committed adultery and thronged to the houses of prostitutes."

Amos 8 [14]"They who swear by the shame of Samaria, or say, 'As surely as your god lives, O Dan,' or, 'As surely as the god of Beersheba lives'—they will fall, never to rise again."

Zeph 1 [4]"I will stretch out my hand against Judah and against all who live in Jerusalem. I will cut off from this place every remnant of Baal, the names of the pagan and the idolatrous priests—[5]those who bow down on the roofs to worship the starry host, those who bow down and swear by the LORD and who also swear by Molech. . . ."

Matt 5 [34]"But I tell you, Do not swear at all: either by heaven, for it is God's throne; [35]or by the earth, for it is his footstool; or by Jerusalem, for it is the city of the Great King. [36]And do not swear by your head, for you cannot make even one hair white or black."
Matt 23 [16]"Woe to you, blind guides! You say, 'If anyone swears by the temple, it means nothing; but if anyone swears by the gold of the temple, he is bound by his oath.' [17]You blind fools! Which is greater: the gold, or the temple that makes the gold sacred? [18]You also say, 'If anyone swears by the altar, it means nothing; but if anyone swears by the gift on it, he is bound by his oath.' [19]You blind men! Which is greater: the gift, or the altar that makes the gift sacred? [20]Therefore, he who swears by the altar swears by it and by everything on it. [21]And he who swears by the temple swears by it and by the one who dwells in it. [22]And he who swears by heaven swears by God's throne and by the one who sits on it."
James 5 [12]Above all, my brothers, do not swear—not by heaven or by earth or by anything else. Let your "Yes" be yes, and your "No," no, or you will be condemned.

d) Blaspheming, Cursing, and Slandering God

Lev 24 [10]Now the son of an Israelite mother and an Egyptian father went out among the Israelites, and a fight broke out in the camp between him and an Israelite. [11]The son of the Israelite woman blasphemed the Name with a curse; so they brought him to Moses. (His mother's name was Shelomith, the daughter of Dibri the Danite.) [12]They put him in custody until the will of the LORD should be made clear to them.

[13]Then the LORD said to Moses: [14]"Take the blasphemer outside the camp. All those who heard him are to lay their hands on his head, and the entire assembly is to stone him. [15]Say to the Israelites: 'If anyone curses his God, he will be held responsible; [16]anyone who blasphemes the name of the LORD must be put to death. The entire assembly must stone him. Whether an alien or native-born, when he blasphemes the Name, he must be put to death.'"
2 Sam 12 [14]"But because by doing this you have made the enemies of the LORD show utter contempt, the son born to you will die."
Job 2 [9]His wife said to him, "Are you still holding on to your integrity? Curse God and die!"
Ps 74 [10]How long will the enemy mock you, O God? Will the foe revile your name forever? . . .

[18]Remember how the enemy has mocked you, O LORD, how foolish people have reviled your name.
Isa 52 [5]"And now what do I have here?" declares the LORD. "For my people have been taken away for nothing, and those who rule them mock," declares the LORD. "And all day long my name is constantly blasphemed."
Ezek 20 [27]"Therefore, son of man, speak to the people of Israel and say to them, 'This is what the Sovereign LORD says: In this also your fathers blasphemed me by forsaking me. . . .'"
Luke 22 [63]The men who were guarding Jesus began mocking and beating him. [64]They blindfolded him and demanded, "Prophesy! Who hit you?" [65]And they said many other insulting things to him.
Acts 26 [11]"Many a time I went from one synagogue to another to have them punished, and I tried to force them to blaspheme. In my obsession against them, I even went to foreign cities to persecute them."
Rom 2 [24]As it is written: "God's name is blasphemed among the Gentiles because of you."
1 Tim 1 [20]Among them are Hymenaeus and Alexander, whom I have handed over to Satan to be taught not to blaspheme.
1 Tim 6 [1]All who are under the yoke of slavery should consider their masters worthy of full respect, so that God's name and our teaching may not be slandered.
Titus 2 [5]to be self-controlled and pure, to be busy at home, to be kind, and to be subject to their husbands, so that no one will malign the word of God.
James 2 [7]Are they not the ones who are slandering the noble name of him to whom you belong?
Rev 13 [1]And the dragon stood on the shore of the sea.

And I saw a beast coming out of the sea. He had ten horns and seven heads, with ten crowns on his horns, and on each head a blasphemous name. . . .

[5]The beast was given a mouth to utter proud words and blasphemies and to exercise his authority for forty-two months. [6]He opened his mouth to blaspheme God, and to slander his name and his dwelling place and those who live in heaven.
Rev 16 [9]They were seared by the intense heat and they cursed the name of God, who had control over these plagues, but they refused to repent and glorify him.

[10]The fifth angel poured out his bowl on the throne of the beast, and his kingdom was plunged into darkness. Men gnawed their tongues in agony [11]and cursed the God of heaven because of their pains and their sores, but they refused to repent of what they had done.

3. Engaging in Occult Practices

a) Occultism Is Forbidden

Exod 22 [18]"Do not allow a sorceress to live."
Lev 17 [7]"'They must no longer offer any of their sacrifices to the goat idols to whom they prostitute themselves. This is to be a lasting ordinance for them and for the generations to come.'"
Lev 19 [26]"'Do not eat any meat with the blood still in it.

"'Do not practice divination or sorcery. . . .

[31]"'Do not turn to mediums or seek out spiritists, for you will be defiled by them. I am the LORD your God.'"
Deut 18 [10]Let no one be found among you who sacrifices his son or daughter in the fire, who practices divination or sorcery, interprets omens, engages in witchcraft, [11]or casts spells, or who is a medium or spiritist or who consults the dead. . . .

[14]The nations you will dispossess listen to those who practice sorcery or divination. But as for you, the LORD your God has not permitted you to do so.
Ezek 12 [24]"'For there will be no more false visions or flattering divinations among the people of Israel.'"
1 Cor 10 [19]Do I mean then that a sacrifice offered to an idol is anything, or that an idol is anything? [20]No, but the sacrifices of pagans are offered to demons, not to God, and I do not want you to be participants with demons.
Col 2 [18]Do not let anyone who delights in false humility and the worship of angels disqualify you for the prize. Such a person goes into great detail about what he has seen, and his unspiritual mind puffs him up with idle notions.

b) The Occult Is Powerless before God

Num 23 [23]"There is no sorcery against Jacob, no divination against Israel. It will now be said of Jacob and of Israel, 'See what God has done!'"
Isa 8 [19]When men tell you to consult mediums and spiritists, who whisper and mutter, should not a people inquire of their God? Why consult the dead on behalf of the living? [20]To the law and to the testimony! If they do not speak according to this word, they have no light of dawn.
Isa 19 [3]"The Egyptians will lose heart, and I will bring their plans to nothing; they will consult the idols and the spirits of the dead, the mediums and the spiritists."
Isa 44 [24]"This is what the LORD says—your Redeemer, who formed you in the womb: I am the LORD, who has made all things, who alone stretched out the heavens, who spread out the earth by myself, [25]who foils the signs of false prophets and makes fools of diviners, who overthrows the learning of the wise and turns it into nonsense, [26]who carries out the words of his servants and fulfills the predictions of his messengers, who says of Jerusalem, 'It shall be inhabited,' of the towns of Judah, 'They shall be built,' and of their ruins, 'I will restore them.' . . ."
Isa 47 [9]"Both of these will overtake you in a moment, on a single day: loss of children and widowhood. They will come upon you in full measure, in spite of your many sorceries and all your potent spells."
Jer 27 [9]"'"So do not listen to your prophets, your diviners, your interpreters of dreams, your mediums or your sorcerers who tell you, 'You will not serve the king of Babylon.' [10]They prophesy lies to you that will only serve to remove you far from your lands; I will banish you and you will perish."'"
Mic 3 [7]"The seers will be ashamed and the diviners disgraced.

They will all cover their faces because there is no answer from God."

c) Occultism Is a Reproach before God

Lev 20 6"'I will set my face against the person who turns to mediums and spiritists to prostitute himself by following them, and I will cut him off from his people.'"
Deut 18 10Let no one be found among you who sacrifices his son or daughter in the fire, who practices divination or sorcery, interprets omens, engages in witchcraft, 11or casts spells, or who is a medium or spiritist or who consults the dead. 12Anyone who does these things is detestable to the LORD, and because of these detestable practices the LORD your God will drive out those nations before you.
2 Kings 9 22When Joram saw Jehu he asked, "Have you come in peace, Jehu?"
"How can there be peace," Jehu replied, "as long as all the idolatry and witchcraft of your mother Jezebel abound?"
2 Chron 33 6He sacrificed his sons in the fire in the Valley of Ben Hinnom, practiced sorcery, divination and witchcraft, and consulted mediums and spiritists. He did much evil in the eyes of the LORD, provoking him to anger.
Jer 14 14Then the LORD said to me, "The prophets are prophesying lies in my name. I have not sent them or appointed them or spoken to them. They are prophesying to you false visions, divinations, idolatries and the delusions of their own minds."
Jer 29 8Yes, this is what the LORD Almighty, the God of Israel, says: "Do not let the prophets and diviners among you deceive you. Do not listen to the dreams you encourage them to have. 9They are prophesying lies to you in my name. I have not sent them," declares the LORD.
Zech 10 2The idols speak deceit, diviners see visions that lie; they tell dreams that are false, they give comfort in vain. Therefore the people wander like sheep oppressed for lack of a shepherd.
3"My anger burns against the shepherds, and I will punish the leaders; for the LORD Almighty will care for his flock, the house of Judah, and make them like a proud horse in battle."

d) Practitioners of the Occult Are Judged

Lev 20 27"'A man or woman who is a medium or spiritist among you must be put to death. You are to stone them; their blood will be on their own heads.'"
Josh 13 22In addition to those slain in battle, the Israelites had put to the sword Balaam son of Beor, who practiced divination.
1 Sam 15 23"For rebellion is like the sin of divination, and arrogance like the evil of idolatry. Because you have rejected the word of the LORD, he has rejected you as king."
2 Kings 17 16They forsook all the commands of the LORD their God and made for themselves two idols cast in the shape of calves, and an Asherah pole. They bowed down to all the starry hosts, and they worshiped Baal. 17They sacrificed their sons and daughters in the fire. They practiced divination and sorcery and sold themselves to do evil in the eyes of the LORD, provoking him to anger.
18So the LORD was very angry with Israel and removed them from his presence. Only the tribe of Judah was left, 19and even Judah did not keep the commands of the LORD their God. They followed the practices Israel had introduced. 20Therefore the LORD rejected all the people of Israel; he afflicted them and gave them into the hands of plunderers, until he thrust them from his presence.
2 Kings 21 1Manasseh was twelve years old when he became king, and he reigned in Jerusalem fifty-five years. His mother's name was Hephzibah. 2He did evil in the eyes of the LORD, following the detestable practices of the nations the LORD had driven out before the Israelites. . . . 5In both courts of the temple of the LORD, he built altars to all the starry hosts. 6He sacrificed his own son in the fire, practiced sorcery and divination, and consulted mediums and spiritists. He did much evil in the eyes of the LORD, provoking him to anger.
Isa 2 6You have abandoned your people, the house of Jacob. They are full of superstitions from the East; they practice divination like the Philistines and clasp hands with pagans. . . . 9So man will be brought low and mankind humbled—do not forgive them.
Ezek 13 9"'My hand will be against the prophets who see false visions and utter lying divinations. They will not belong to the council of my people or be listed in the records of the house of Israel, nor will they enter the land of Israel. Then you will know that I am the Sovereign LORD.'"
Ezek 21 29"'Despite false visions concerning you and lying divinations about you, it will be laid on the necks of the wicked who are to be slain, whose day has come, whose time of punishment has reached its climax.'"
Mic 3 11Her leaders judge for a bribe, her priests teach for a price, and her prophets tell fortunes for money. Yet they lean upon the LORD and say, "Is not the LORD among us? No disaster will come upon us." 12Therefore because of you, Zion will be plowed like a field, Jerusalem will become a heap of rubble, the temple hill a mound overgrown with thickets.
Mic 5 12"I will destroy your witchcraft and you will no longer cast spells."
Nah 3 4all because of the wanton lust of a harlot, alluring, the mistress of sorceries, who enslaved nations by her prostitution and peoples by her witchcraft.
5"I am against you," declares the LORD Almighty. "I will lift your skirts over your face. I will show the nations your nakedness and the kingdoms your shame."
Mal 3 5"So I will come near to you for judgment. I will be quick to testify against sorcerers, adulterers and perjurers, against those who defraud laborers of their wages, who oppress the widows and the fatherless, and deprive aliens of justice, but do not fear me," says the LORD Almighty.
Gal 5 19The acts of the sinful nature are obvious: sexual immorality, impurity and debauchery; 20idolatry and witchcraft; hatred, discord, jealousy, fits of rage, selfish ambition, dissensions, factions 21and envy; drunkenness, orgies, and the like. I warn you, as I did before, that those who live like this will not inherit the kingdom of God.
Rev 9 20The rest of mankind that were not killed by these plagues still did not repent of the work of their hands; they did not stop worshiping demons, and idols of gold, silver, bronze, stone and wood—idols that cannot see or hear or walk. 21Nor did they repent of their murders, their magic arts, their sexual immorality or their thefts.
Rev 18 2With a mighty voice he shouted: "Fallen! Fallen is Babylon the Great! She has become a home for demons and a haunt for every evil spirit, a haunt for every unclean and detestable bird."
Rev 21 8"But the cowardly, the unbelieving, the vile, the murderers, the sexually immoral, those who practice magic arts, the idolaters and all liars—their place will be in the fiery lake of burning sulfur. This is the second death."
Rev 22 14"Blessed are those who wash their robes, that they may have the right to the tree of life and may go through the gates into the city. 15Outside are the dogs, those who practice magic arts, the sexually immoral, the murderers, the idolaters and everyone who loves and practices falsehood."

4. Sinning against the Holy Spirit

See p. 160a, Sins against the Holy Spirit

B. Sins of Disregard

1. Being Unthankful to God

Rom 1 21For although they knew God, they neither glorified him as God nor gave thanks to him, but their thinking became futile and their foolish hearts were darkened.
2 Tim 3 2People will be lovers of themselves, lovers of money, boastful, proud, abusive, disobedient to their parents, ungrateful, unholy. . . .

2. Boasting

Ps 10 3He boasts of the cravings of his heart; he blesses the greedy and reviles the LORD. 4In his pride the wicked does not seek him; in all his thoughts there is no room for God.
Ps 49 5Why should I fear when evil days come, when wicked deceivers surround me—6those who trust in their wealth and boast of their great riches? 7No man can redeem the life of

another or give to God a ransom for him—[8]the ransom for a life is costly, no payment is ever enough—[9]that he should live on forever and not see decay.

Ps 94 [4]They pour out arrogant words; all the evildoers are full of boasting. . . . [7]They say, "The LORD does not see; the God of Jacob pays no heed."

Isa 10 [15]Does the ax raise itself above him who swings it, or the saw boast against him who uses it? As if a rod were to wield him who lifts it up, or a club brandish him who is not wood! [16]Therefore, the Lord, the LORD Almighty, will send a wasting disease upon his sturdy warriors; under his pomp a fire will be kindled like a blazing flame.

Ezek 35 [13]"'You boasted against me and spoke against me without restraint, and I heard it. [14]This is what the Sovereign LORD says: While the whole earth rejoices, I will make you desolate.'"

Rom 1 [29]They have become filled with every kind of wickedness, evil, greed and depravity. They are full of envy, murder, strife, deceit and malice. They are gossips, [30]slanderers, God-haters, insolent, arrogant and boastful; they invent ways of doing evil; they disobey their parents. . . .

Rom 2 [23]You who brag about the law, do you dishonor God by breaking the law? [24]As it is written: "God's name is blasphemed among the Gentiles because of you."

Rom 3 [27]Where, then, is boasting? It is excluded. On what principle? On that of observing the law? No, but on that of faith.

Eph 2 [8]For it is by grace you have been saved, through faith—and this not from yourselves, it is the gift of God—[9]not by works, so that no one can boast. [10]For we are God's workmanship, created in Christ Jesus to do good works, which God prepared in advance for us to do.

James 4 [13]Now listen, you who say, "Today or tomorrow we will go to this or that city, spend a year there, carry on business and make money." [14]Why, you do not even know what will happen tomorrow. What is your life? You are a mist that appears for a little while and then vanishes. [15]Instead, you ought to say, "If it is the Lord's will, we will live and do this or that." [16]As it is, you boast and brag. All such boasting is evil. [17]Anyone, then, who knows the good he ought to do and doesn't do it, sins.

3. Dishonoring God

Num 20 [12]But the LORD said to Moses and Aaron, "Because you did not trust in me enough to honor me as holy in the sight of the Israelites, you will not bring this community into the land I give them."

1 Sam 2 [29]"'Why do you scorn my sacrifice and offering that I prescribed for my dwelling? Why do you honor your sons more than me by fattening yourselves on the choice parts of every offering made by my people Israel?'

[30]"Therefore the LORD, the God of Israel, declares: 'I promised that your house and your father's house would minister before me forever.' But now the LORD declares: 'Far be it from me! Those who honor me I will honor, but those who despise me will be disdained.'"

Isa 29 [13]The Lord says: "These people come near to me with their mouth and honor me with their lips, but their hearts are far from me. Their worship of me is made up only of rules taught by men. [14]Therefore once more I will astound these people with wonder upon wonder; the wisdom of the wise will perish, the intelligence of the intelligent will vanish."

Isa 58 [1]"Shout it aloud, do not hold back. Raise your voice like a trumpet. Declare to my people their rebellion and the house of Jacob their sins. [2]For day after day they seek me out; they seem eager to know my ways, as if they were a nation that does what is right and has not forsaken the commands of its God. They ask me for just decisions and seem eager for God to come near them."

Dan 5 [18]"O king, the Most High God gave your father Nebuchadnezzar sovereignty and greatness and glory and splendor. . . . [20]But when his heart became arrogant and hardened with pride, he was deposed from his royal throne and stripped of his glory. [21]He was driven away from people and given the mind of an animal; he lived with the wild donkeys and ate grass like cattle; and his body was drenched with the dew of heaven, until he acknowledged that the Most High God is sovereign over the kingdoms of men and sets over them anyone he wishes.

[22]"But you his son, O Belshazzar, have not humbled yourself, though you knew all this. [23]Instead, you have set yourself up against the Lord of heaven. You had the goblets from his temple brought to you, and you and your nobles, your wives and your concubines drank wine from them. You praised the gods of silver and gold, of bronze, iron, wood and stone, which cannot see or hear or understand. But you did not honor the God who holds in his hand your life and all your ways. . . ."

Mal 2 [2]"If you do not listen, and if you do not set your heart to honor my name," says the LORD Almighty, "I will send a curse upon you, and I will curse your blessings. Yes, I have already cursed them, because you have not set your heart to honor me."

Rom 2 [23]You who brag about the law, do you dishonor God by breaking the law?

4. Not Glorifying God

Acts 12 [23]Immediately, because Herod did not give praise to God, an angel of the Lord struck him down, and he was eaten by worms and died.

Rom 1 [21]For although they knew God, they neither glorified him as God nor gave thanks to him, but their thinking became futile and their foolish hearts were darkened. . . .

[24]Therefore God gave them over in the sinful desires of their hearts to sexual impurity for the degrading of their bodies with one another.

Rom 3 [23]for all have sinned and fall short of the glory of God. . . .

Rev 16 [9]They were seared by the intense heat and they cursed the name of God, who had control over these plagues, but they refused to repent and glorify him.

5. Not Serving God

Deut 28 [47]Because you did not serve the LORD your God joyfully and gladly in the time of prosperity, [48]therefore in hunger and thirst, in nakedness and dire poverty, you will serve the enemies the LORD sends against you. He will put an iron yoke on your neck until he has destroyed you.

Neh 9 [35]"Even while they were in their kingdom, enjoying your great goodness to them in the spacious and fertile land you gave them, they did not serve you or turn from their evil ways.

[36]"But see, we are slaves today, slaves in the land you gave our forefathers so they could eat its fruit and the other good things it produces."

Job 21 [14]"Yet they say to God, 'Leave us alone! We have no desire to know your ways. [15]Who is the Almighty, that we should serve him? What would we gain by praying to him?' [16]But their prosperity is not in their own hands, so I stand aloof from the counsel of the wicked."

Jer 2 [20]"Long ago you broke off your yoke and tore off your bonds; you said, 'I will not serve you!' Indeed, on every high hill and under every spreading tree you lay down as a prostitute."

Jer 17 [1]"Judah's sin is engraved with an iron tool, inscribed with a flint point, on the tablets of their hearts and on the horns of their altars. [2]Even their children remember their altars and Asherah poles beside the spreading trees and on the high hills. [3]My mountain in the land and your wealth and all your treasures I will give away as plunder, together with your high places, because of sin throughout your country. [4]Through your own fault you will lose the inheritance I gave you. I will enslave you to your enemies in a land you do not know, for you have kindled my anger, and it will burn forever."

[5]This is what the LORD says: "Cursed is the one who trusts in man, who depends on flesh for his strength and whose heart turns away from the LORD."

Mal 3 [14]"You have said, 'It is futile to serve God. What did we gain by carrying out his requirements and going about like mourners before the LORD Almighty? [15]But now we call the arrogant blessed. Certainly the evildoers prosper, and even those who challenge God escape.' . . . [18]And you will again see the distinction between the righteous and the wicked, between those who serve God and those who do not."

Matt 24 [48]"But suppose that servant is wicked and says to him-

self, 'My master is staying away a long time,' [49]and he then begins to beat his fellow servants and to eat and drink with drunkards. [50]The master of that servant will come on a day when he does not expect him and at an hour he is not aware of. [51]He will cut him to pieces and assign him a place with the hypocrites, where there will be weeping and gnashing of teeth."
Matt 25 [22]"The man with the two talents also came. 'Master,' he said, 'you entrusted me with two talents; see, I have gained two more.'

[23]"His master replied, 'Well done, good and faithful servant! You have been faithful with a few things; I will put you in charge of many things. Come and share your master's happiness!'

[24]"Then the man who had received the one talent came. 'Master,' he said, 'I knew that you are a hard man, harvesting where you have not sown and gathering where you have not scattered seed. [25]So I was afraid and went out and hid your talent in the ground. See, here is what belongs to you.'

[26]"His master replied, 'You wicked, lazy servant! So you knew that I harvest where I have not sown and gather where I have not scattered seed? [27]Well then, you should have put my money on deposit with the bankers, so that when I returned I would have received it back with interest.

[28]"'Take the talent from him and give it to the one who has the ten talents. [29]For everyone who has will be given more, and he will have an abundance. Whoever does not have, even what he has will be taken from him. [30]And throw that worthless servant outside, into the darkness, where there will be weeping and gnashing of teeth.'

[31]"When the Son of Man comes in his glory, and all the angels with him, he will sit on his throne in heavenly glory."
Luke 12 [47]"That servant who knows his master's will and does not get ready or does not do what his master wants will be beaten with many blows. [48]But the one who does not know and does things deserving punishment will be beaten with few blows. From everyone who has been given much, much will be demanded; and from the one who has been entrusted with much, much more will be asked."
Rom 1 [25]They exchanged the truth of God for a lie, and worshiped and served created things rather than the Creator—who is forever praised. Amen.

[26]Because of this, God gave them over to shameful lusts. Even their women exchanged natural relations for unnatural ones.

C. Sins of Rejection

1. Falling Away from God

Ps 14 [3]All have turned aside, they have together become corrupt; there is no one who does good, not even one.
Ps 58 [3]Even from birth the wicked go astray; from the womb they are wayward and speak lies.
Ps 78 [57]Like their fathers they were disloyal and faithless, as unreliable as a faulty bow.
Ps 95 [10]For forty years I was angry with that generation; I said, "They are a people whose hearts go astray, and they have not known my ways."
Ps 119 [21]You rebuke the arrogant, who are cursed and who stray from your commands. . . .

[118]You reject all who stray from your decrees, for their deceitfulness is in vain.
Prov 5 [23]He will die for lack of discipline, led astray by his own great folly.
Prov 14 [14]The faithless will be fully repaid for their ways, and the good man rewarded for his. . . . [22]Do not those who plot evil go astray? But those who plan what is good find love and faithfulness.
Isa 44 [20]He feeds on ashes, a deluded heart misleads him; he cannot save himself, or say, "Is not this thing in my right hand a lie?"
Jer 2 [19]"Your wickedness will punish you; your backsliding will rebuke you. Consider then and realize how evil and bitter it is for you when you forsake the LORD your God and have no awe of me," declares the Lord, the LORD Almighty. . . .

[27]"They say to wood, 'You are my father,' and to stone, 'You gave me birth.' They have turned their backs to me and not their faces; yet when they are in trouble, they say, 'Come and save us!'"
Jer 3 [22]"Return, faithless people; I will cure you of backsliding."

"Yes, we will come to you, for you are the LORD our God."
Jer 5 [6]Therefore a lion from the forest will attack them, a wolf from the desert will ravage them, a leopard will lie in wait near their towns to tear to pieces any who venture out, for their rebellion is great and their backslidings many.

[7]"Why should I forgive you? Your children have forsaken me and sworn by gods that are not gods. I supplied all their needs, yet they committed adultery and thronged to the houses of prostitutes."
Jer 7 [24]"'But they did not listen or pay attention; instead, they followed the stubborn inclinations of their evil hearts. They went backward and not forward.'"
Jer 14 [2]"Judah mourns, her cities languish; they wail for the land, and a cry goes up from Jerusalem. [3]The nobles send their servants for water; they go to the cisterns but find no water. They return with their jars unfilled; dismayed and despairing, they cover their heads. [4]The ground is cracked because there is no rain in the land; the farmers are dismayed and cover their heads. [5]Even the doe in the field deserts her newborn fawn because there is no grass. [6]Wild donkeys stand on the barren heights and pant like jackals; their eyesight fails for lack of pasture."

[7]Although our sins testify against us, O LORD, do something for the sake of your name. For our backsliding is great; we have sinned against you.
Jer 15 [6]"You have rejected me," declares the LORD. "You keep on backsliding. So I will lay hands on you and destroy you; I can no longer show compassion."
Hos 11 [6]"Swords will flash in their cities, will destroy the bars of their gates and put an end to their plans. [7]My people are determined to turn from me. Even if they call to the Most High, he will by no means exalt them."
Hos 14 [1]Return, O Israel, to the LORD your God. Your sins have been your downfall! . . .

[4]"I will heal their waywardness and love them freely, for my anger has turned away from them."
Rom 1 [27]In the same way the men also abandoned natural relations with women and were inflamed with lust for one another. Men committed indecent acts with other men, and received in themselves the due penalty for their perversion.
Heb 10 [38]"But my righteous one will live by faith. And if he shrinks back, I will not be pleased with him." [39]But we are not of those who shrink back and are destroyed, but of those who believe and are saved.
2 Pet 3 [17]Therefore, dear friends, since you already know this, be on your guard so that you may not be carried away by the error of lawless men and fall from your secure position.

2. Forsaking God

Deut 31 [16]And the LORD said to Moses: "You are going to rest with your fathers, and these people will soon prostitute themselves to the foreign gods of the land they are entering. They will forsake me and break the covenant I made with them. [17]On that day I will become angry with them and forsake them; I will hide my face from them, and they will be destroyed. Many disasters and difficulties will come upon them, and on that day they will ask, 'Have not these disasters come upon us because our God is not with us?'"
Josh 24 [20]"If you forsake the LORD and serve foreign gods, he will turn and bring disaster on you and make an end of you, after he has been good to you."
Judg 10 [13]"But you have forsaken me and served other gods, so I will no longer save you. [14]Go and cry out to the gods you have chosen. Let them save you when you are in trouble!"
1 Sam 12 [10]"They cried out to the LORD and said, 'We have sinned; we have forsaken the LORD and served the Baals and the Ashtoreths. But now deliver us from the hands of our enemies, and we will serve you.'"
1 Chron 28 [9]"And you, my son Solomon, acknowledge the God of your father, and serve him with wholehearted devotion and with a willing mind, for the LORD searches every heart and

understands every motive behind the thoughts. If you seek him, he will be found by you; but if you forsake him, he will reject you forever."

2 Chron 7 19"But if you turn away and forsake the decrees and commands I have given you and go off to serve other gods and worship them, 20then I will uproot Israel from my land, which I have given them, and will reject this temple I have consecrated for my Name. I will make it a byword and an object of ridicule among all peoples."

2 Chron 15 2He went out to meet Asa and said to him, "Listen to me, Asa and all Judah and Benjamin. The LORD is with you when you are with him. If you seek him, he will be found by you, but if you forsake him, he will forsake you."

2 Chron 24 20Then the Spirit of God came upon Zechariah son of Jehoiada the priest. He stood before the people and said, "This is what God says: 'Why do you disobey the LORD's commands? You will not prosper. Because you have forsaken the LORD, he has forsaken you.'"

Ezra 8 22I was ashamed to ask the king for soldiers and horsemen to protect us from enemies on the road, because we had told the king, "The gracious hand of our God is on everyone who looks to him, but his great anger is against all who forsake him."

Ps 89 30"If his sons forsake my law and do not follow my statutes, 31if they violate my decrees and fail to keep my commands, 32I will punish their sin with the rod, their iniquity with flogging; 33but I will not take my love from him, nor will I ever betray my faithfulness."

Ps 119 53Indignation grips me because of the wicked, who have forsaken your law.

Isa 1 4Ah, sinful nation, a people loaded with guilt, a brood of evildoers, children gi en to corruption! They have forsaken the LORD; they have spurned the Holy One of Israel and turned their backs on him. . . . 28But rebels and sinners will both be broken, and those who forsake the LORD will perish.

Isa 65 11"But as for you who forsake the LORD and forget my holy mountain, who spread a table for Fortune and fill bowls of mixed wine for Destiny, 12I will destine you for the sword, and you will all bend down for the slaughter; for I called but you did not answer, I spoke but you did not listen. You did evil in my sight and chose what displeases me."

Jer 2 13"My people have committed two sins: They have forsaken me, the spring of living water, and have dug their own cisterns, broken cisterns that cannot hold water. 14Is Israel a servant, a slave by birth? Why then has he become plunder? 15Lions have roared; they have growled at him. They have laid waste his land; his towns are burned and deserted. 16Also, the men of Memphis and Tahpanhes have shaved the crown of your head. 17Have you not brought this on yourselves by forsaking the LORD your God when he led you in the way? 18Now why go to Egypt to drink water from the Shihor? And why go to Assyria to drink water from the River? 19Your wickedness will punish you; your backsliding will rebuke you. Consider then and realize how evil and bitter it is for you when you forsake the LORD your God and have no awe of me," declares the Lord, the LORD Almighty.

Jer 8 5"'Why then have these people turned away? Why does Jerusalem always turn away? They cling to deceit; they refuse to return.'"

Jer 17 5This is what the LORD says: "Cursed is the one who trusts in man, who depends on flesh for his strength and whose heart turns away from the LORD." . . .

13O LORD, the hope of Israel, all who forsake you will be put to shame. Those who turn away from you will be written in the dust because they have forsaken the LORD, the spring of living water.

Ezek 18 24"But if a righteous man turns from his righteousness and commits sin and does the same detestable things the wicked man does, will he live? None of the righteous things he has done will be remembered. Because of the unfaithfulness he is guilty of and because of the sins he has committed, he will die."

Ezek 33 12"Therefore, son of man, say to your countrymen, 'The righteousness of the righteous man will not save him when he disobeys, and the wickedness of the wicked man will not cause him to fall when he turns from it. The righteous man, if he sins, will not be allowed to live because of his former righteousness.'"

Rev 2 4"Yet I hold this against you: You have forsaken your first love."

3. Not Seeking God

2 Chron 12 14He did evil because he had not set his heart on seeking the LORD.

2 Chron 16 12In the thirty-ninth year of his reign Asa was afflicted with a disease in his feet. Though his disease was severe, even in his illness he did not seek help from the LORD, but only from the physicians.

Job 31 24"If I have put my trust in gold or said to pure gold, 'You are my security,' 25if I have rejoiced over my great wealth, the fortune my hands had gained, . . . 28then these also would be sins to be judged, for I would have been unfaithful to God on high."

Ps 10 13Why does the wicked man revile God? Why does he say to himself, "He won't call me to account"?

Ps 14 1The fool says in his heart, "There is no God." They are corrupt, their deeds are vile; there is no one who does good.

2The LORD looks down from heaven on the sons of men to see if there are any who understand, any who seek God. 3All have turned aside, they have together become corrupt; there is no one who does good, not even one.

Ps 83 16Cover their faces with shame so that men will seek your name, O LORD.

Ps 118 8It is better to take refuge in the LORD than to trust in man. 9It is better to take refuge in the LORD than to trust in princes.

Ps 119 155Salvation is far from the wicked, for they do not seek out your decrees.

Prov 1 28"Then they will call to me but I will not answer; they will look for me but will not find me. 29Since they hated knowledge and did not choose to fear the LORD, 30since they would not accept my advice and spurned my rebuke, 31they will eat the fruit of their ways and be filled with the fruit of their schemes."

Isa 9 13But the people have not returned to him who struck them, nor have they sought the LORD Almighty. 14So the LORD will cut off from Israel both head and tail, both palm branch and reed in a single day. . . .

Isa 31 1Woe to those who go down to Egypt for help, who rely on horses, who trust in the multitude of their chariots and in the great strength of their horsemen, but do not look to the Holy One of Israel, or seek help from the LORD.

Jer 2 31"You of this generation, consider the word of the LORD: Have I been a desert to Israel or a land of great darkness? Why do my people say, 'We are free to roam; we will come to you no more'?"

Jer 10 25Pour out your wrath on the nations that do not acknowledge you, on the peoples who do not call on your name. For they have devoured Jacob; they have devoured him completely and destroyed his homeland.

Ezek 29 16"'Egypt will no longer be a source of confidence for the people of Israel but will be a reminder of their sin in turning to her for help. Then they will know that I am the Sovereign LORD.'"

Hos 5 4"Their deeds do not permit them to return to their God. A spirit of prostitution is in their heart; they do not acknowledge the LORD. 5Israel's arrogance testifies against them; the Israelites, even Ephraim, stumble in their sin; Judah also stumbles with them. 6When they go with their flocks and herds to seek the LORD, they will not find him; he has withdrawn himself from them. . . . 15Then I will go back to my place until they admit their guilt. And they will seek my face; in their misery they will earnestly seek me."

Hos 7 10"Israel's arrogance testifies against him, but despite all this he does not return to the LORD his God or search for him. . . . 13Woe to them, because they have strayed from me! Destruction to them, because they have rebelled against me! I long to redeem them but they speak lies against me. 14They do not cry out to me from their hearts but wail upon their beds. They gather together for grain and new wine but turn away from me. . . . 16They do not turn to the Most High; they are like a faulty bow. Their leaders will fall by the sword because of their insolent words. For this they will be ridiculed in the land of Egypt."

Zeph 1 [4]"I will stretch out my hand against Judah and against all who live in Jerusalem. I will cut off from this place every remnant of Baal, the names of the pagan and the idolatrous priests . . . [6]those who turn back from following the LORD and neither seek the LORD nor inquire of him."

4. Obstinacy against God

Exod 32 [9]"I have seen these people," the LORD said to Moses, "and they are a stiff-necked people. [10]Now leave me alone so that my anger may burn against them and that I may destroy them. Then I will make you into a great nation."

Exod 33 [3]"Go up to the land flowing with milk and honey. But I will not go with you, because you are a stiff-necked people and I might destroy you on the way." . . . [5]For the LORD had said to Moses, "Tell the Israelites, 'You are a stiff-necked people. If I were to go with you even for a moment, I might destroy you. Now take off your ornaments and I will decide what to do with you.'"

Deut 9 [6]Understand, then, that it is not because of your righteousness that the LORD your God is giving you this good land to possess, for you are a stiff-necked people. . . .

[13]And the LORD said to me, "I have seen this people, and they are a stiff-necked people indeed!"

Deut 29 [19]When such a person hears the words of this oath, he invokes a blessing on himself and therefore thinks, "I will be safe, even though I persist in going my own way." This will bring disaster on the watered land as well as the dry. [20]The LORD will never be willing to forgive him; his wrath and zeal will burn against that man. All the curses written in this book will fall upon him, and the LORD will blot out his name from under heaven.

2 Chron 24 [19]Although the LORD sent prophets to the people to bring them back to him, and though they testified against them, they would not listen.

Ps 78 [17]But they continued to sin against him, rebelling in the desert against the Most High.

Prov 28 [14]Blessed is the man who always fears the LORD, but he who hardens his heart falls into trouble.

Isa 26 [10]Though grace is shown to the wicked, they do not learn righteousness; even in a land of uprightness they go on doing evil and regard not the majesty of the LORD. [11]O LORD, your hand is lifted high, but they do not see it. Let them see your zeal for your people and be put to shame; let the fire reserved for your enemies consume them.

Isa 30 [1]"Woe to the obstinate children," declares the LORD, "to those who carry out plans that are not mine, forming an alliance, but not by my Spirit, heaping sin upon sin. . . ."

Isa 48 [4]"For I knew how stubborn you were; the sinews of your neck were iron, your forehead was bronze. . . . [8]You have neither heard nor understood; from of old your ear has not been open. Well do I know how treacherous you are; you were called a rebel from birth."

Isa 65 [2]"All day long I have held out my hands to an obstinate people, who walk in ways not good, pursuing their own imaginations—[3]a people who continually provoke me to my very face, offering sacrifices in gardens and burning incense on altars of brick. . . .

[6]"See, it stands written before me: I will not keep silent but will pay back in full; I will pay it back into their laps. . . ."

Jer 3 [17]"At that time they will call Jerusalem The Throne of the LORD, and all nations will gather in Jerusalem to honor the name of the LORD. No longer will they follow the stubbornness of their evil hearts."

Jer 5 [3]O LORD, do not your eyes look for truth? You struck them, but they felt no pain; you crushed them, but they refused correction. They made their faces harder than stone and refused to repent.

Jer 6 [16]This is what the LORD says: "Stand at the crossroads and look; ask for the ancient paths, ask where the good way is, and walk in it, and you will find rest for your souls. But you said, 'We will not walk in it.'"

Jer 7 [23]"'. . . but I gave them this command: Obey me, and I will be your God and you will be my people. Walk in all the ways I command you, that it may go well with you. [24]But they did not listen or pay attention; instead, they followed the stubborn inclinations of their evil hearts. They went backward and not forward. [25]From the time your forefathers left Egypt until now, day after day, again and again I sent you my servants the prophets. [26]But they did not listen to me or pay attention. They were stiff-necked and did more evil than their forefathers.'"

Jer 8 [6]"'I have listened attentively, but they do not say what is right. No one repents of his wickedness, saying, "What have I done?" Each pursues his own course like a horse charging into battle. . . . [12]Are they ashamed of their loathsome conduct? No, they have no shame at all; they do not even know how to blush. So they will fall among the fallen; they will be brought down when they are punished, says the LORD.'"

Jer 19 [15]"This is what the LORD Almighty, the God of Israel, says: 'Listen! I am going to bring on this city and the villages around it every disaster I pronounced against them, because they were stiff-necked and would not listen to my words.'"

Jer 31 [18]"I have surely heard Ephraim's moaning: 'You disciplined me like an unruly calf, and I have been disciplined. Restore me, and I will return, because you are the LORD my God.'"

Hos 4 [16]"The Israelites are stubborn, like a stubborn heifer. How then can the LORD pasture them like lambs in a meadow?"

Mark 8 [17]Aware of their discussion, Jesus asked them: "Why are you talking about having no bread? Do you still not see or understand? Are your hearts hardened? [18]Do you have eyes but fail to see, and ears but fail to hear? And don't you remember? [19]When I broke the five loaves for the five thousand, how many basketfuls of pieces did you pick up?"

"Twelve," they replied.

[20]"And when I broke the seven loaves for the four thousand, how many basketfuls of pieces did you pick up?"

They answered, "Seven."

[21]He said to them, "Do you still not understand?"

Acts 7 [51]"You stiff-necked people, with uncircumcised hearts and ears! You are just like your fathers: You always resist the Holy Spirit!"

Rom 10 [21]But concerning Israel he says, "All day long I have held out my hands to a disobedient and obstinate people."

Heb 5 [11]We have much to say about this, but it is hard to explain because you are slow to learn. [12]In fact, though by this time you ought to be teachers, you need someone to teach you the elementary truths of God's word all over again. You need milk, not solid food! [13]Anyone who lives on milk, being still an infant, is not acquainted with the teaching about righteousness. [14]But solid food is for the mature, who by constant use have trained themselves to distinguish good from evil.

5. Rebelling against God

Num 14 [9]"Only do not rebel against the LORD. And do not be afraid of the people of the land, because we will swallow them up. Their protection is gone, but the LORD is with us. Do not be afraid of them."

Num 20 [24]"Aaron will be gathered to his people. He will not enter the land I give the Israelites, because both of you rebelled against my command at the waters of Meribah."

Deut 1 [26]But you were unwilling to go up; you rebelled against the command of the LORD your God. [27]You grumbled in your tents and said, "The LORD hates us; so he brought us out of Egypt to deliver us into the hands of the Amorites to destroy us." . . .

[43]So I told you, but you would not listen. You rebelled against the LORD's command and in your arrogance you marched up into the hill country.

Deut 9 [7]Remember this and never forget how you provoked the LORD your God to anger in the desert. From the day you left Egypt until you arrived here, you have been rebellious against the LORD. . . .

[23]And when the LORD sent you out from Kadesh Barnea, he said, "Go up and take possession of the land I have given you." But you rebelled against the command of the LORD your God. You did not trust him or obey him. [24]You have been rebellious against the LORD ever since I have known you.

Deut 31 27"For I know how rebellious and stiff-necked you are. If you have been rebellious against the LORD while I am still alive and with you, how much more will you rebel after I die!"
Josh 22 29"Far be it from us to rebel against the LORD and turn away from him today by building an altar for burnt offerings, grain offerings and sacrifices, other than the altar of the LORD our God that stands before his tabernacle."
1 Sam 12 15"But if you do not obey the LORD, and if you rebel against his commands, his hand will be against you, as it was against your fathers."
1 Sam 15 23"For rebellion is like the sin of divination, and arrogance like the evil of idolatry. Because you have rejected the word of the LORD, he has rejected you as king."
Neh 9 26"But they were disobedient and rebelled against you; they put your law behind their backs. They killed your prophets, who had admonished them in order to turn them back to you; they committed awful blasphemies. 27So you handed them over to their enemies, who oppressed them. But when they were oppressed they cried out to you. From heaven you heard them, and in your great compassion you gave them deliverers, who rescued them from the hand of their enemies."
Job 15 24"Distress and anguish fill him with terror; they overwhelm him, like a king poised to attack, 25because he shakes his fist at God and vaunts himself against the Almighty, 26defiantly charging against him with a thick, strong shield."
Ps 68 6God sets the lonely in families, he leads forth the prisoners with singing; but the rebellious live in a sun-scorched land.
Ps 73 8They scoff, and speak with malice; in their arrogance they threaten oppression. 9Their mouths lay claim to heaven, and their tongues take possession of the earth. 10Therefore their people turn to them and drink up waters in abundance. 11They say, "How can God know? Does the Most High have knowledge?"
Ps 78 8They would not be like their forefathers—a stubborn and rebellious generation, whose hearts were not loyal to God, whose spirits were not faithful to him. . . .

40How often they rebelled against him in the desert and grieved him in the wasteland!
Ps 107 11for they had rebelled against the words of God and despised the counsel of the Most High. 12So he subjected them to bitter labor; they stumbled, and there was no one to help.
Isa 1 2Hear, O heavens! Listen, O earth! For the LORD has spoken: "I reared children and brought them up, but they have rebelled against me." . . .

5Why should you be beaten anymore? Why do you persist in rebellion? Your whole head is injured, your whole heart afflicted. . . . 19"If you are willing and obedient, you will eat the best from the land; 20but if you resist and rebel, you will be devoured by the sword." For the mouth of the LORD has spoken.
Isa 30 9These are rebellious people, deceitful children, children unwilling to listen to the LORD's instruction.
Isa 31 6Return to him you have so greatly revolted against, O Israelites.
Isa 45 9"Woe to him who quarrels with his Maker, to him who is but a potsherd among the potsherds on the ground. Does the clay say to the potter, 'What are you making?' Does your work say, 'He has no hands'?"
Isa 63 10Yet they rebelled and grieved his Holy Spirit. So he turned and became their enemy and he himself fought against them.
Jer 4 17"'They surround her like men guarding a field, because she has rebelled against me,'" declares the LORD. 18"Your own conduct and actions have brought this upon you. This is your punishment. How bitter it is! How it pierces to the heart!"
Jer 5 23"But these people have stubborn and rebellious hearts; they have turned aside and gone away."
Jer 6 28"They are all hardened rebels, going about to slander. They are bronze and iron; they all act corruptly."
Lam 3 42"We have sinned and rebelled and you have not forgiven.

43"You have covered yourself with anger and pursued us; you have slain without pity."
Ezek 20 8"But they rebelled against me and would not listen to me; they did not get rid of the vile images they had set their eyes on, nor did they forsake the idols of Egypt. So I said I would pour out my wrath on them and spend my anger against them in Egypt. . . .

13"'Yet the people of Israel rebelled against me in the desert. They did not follow my decrees but rejected my laws—although the man who obeys them will live by them—and they utterly desecrated my Sabbaths. So I said I would pour out my wrath on them and destroy them in the desert. . . .

38"'I will purge you of those who revolt and rebel against me. Although I will bring them out of the land where they are living, yet they will not enter the land of Israel. Then you will know that I am the LORD.'"
Dan 9 5". . . we have sinned and done wrong. We have been wicked and have rebelled; we have turned away from your commands and laws."
Hos 7 13"Woe to them, because they have strayed from me! Destruction to them, because they have rebelled against me! I long to redeem them but they speak lies against me."
Hos 9 15"Because of all their wickedness in Gilgal, I hated them there. Because of their sinful deeds, I will drive them out of my house. I will no longer love them; all their leaders are rebellious."
Hos 13 16"The people of Samaria must bear their guilt, because they have rebelled against their God. They will fall by the sword; their little ones will be dashed to the ground, their pregnant women ripped open."

6. Testing God

Num 14 22". . . not one of the men who saw my glory and the miraculous signs I performed in Egypt and in the desert but who disobeyed me and tested me ten times—23not one of them will ever see the land I promised on oath to their forefathers. No one who has treated me with contempt will ever see it."
Deut 6 16Do not test the LORD your God as you did at Massah.
Ps 78 18They willfully put God to the test by demanding the food they craved. 19They spoke against God, saying, "Can God spread a table in the desert?" . . . 41Again and again they put God to the test; they vexed the Holy One of Israel. 42They did not remember his power—the day he redeemed them from the oppressor. . . .

56But they put God to the test and rebelled against the Most High; they did not keep his statutes. 57Like their fathers they were disloyal and faithless, as unreliable as a faulty bow. 58They angered him with their high places; they aroused his jealousy with their idols.
Ps 95 8do not harden your hearts as you did at Meribah, as you did that day at Massah in the desert, 9where your fathers tested and tried me, though they had seen what I did.
Ps 106 14In the desert they gave in to their craving; in the wasteland they put God to the test.
Isa 7 10Again the LORD spoke to Ahaz, 11"Ask the LORD your God for a sign, whether in the deepest depths or in the highest heights."

12But Ahaz said, "I will not ask; I will not put the LORD to the test."

13Then Isaiah said, "Hear now, you house of David! Is it not enough to try the patience of men? Will you try the patience of my God also?"
Matt 16 1The Pharisees and Sadducees came to Jesus and tested him by asking him to show them a sign from heaven.
Matt 22 35One of them, an expert in the law, tested him with this question. . . .
Mark 8 11The Pharisees came and began to question Jesus. To test him, they asked him for a sign from heaven.
John 6 30So they asked him, "What miraculous sign then will you give that we may see it and believe you? What will you do?"
Acts 15 10"Now then, why do you try to test God by putting on the necks of the disciples a yoke that neither we nor our fathers have been able to bear?"
1 Cor 10 9We should not test the Lord, as some of them did—and were killed by snakes.

D. Sins of Unbelief

1. Denying God and His Power

Exod 5 2Pharaoh said, "Who is the LORD, that I should obey him and let Israel go? I do not know the LORD and I will not let Israel go."

Job 21 14“Yet they say to God, ‘Leave us alone! We have no desire to know your ways. 15Who is the Almighty, that we should serve him? What would we gain by praying to him?’”

Job 22 12“Is not God in the heights of heaven? And see how lofty are the highest stars! 13Yet you say, ‘What does God know? Does he judge through such darkness? 14Thick clouds veil him, so he does not see us as he goes about in the vaulted heavens.’ . . . 17They said to God, ‘Leave us alone! What can the Almighty do to us?’”

Job 34 9“For he says, ‘It profits a man nothing when he tries to please God.’”

Ps 10 4In his pride the wicked does not seek him; in all his thoughts there is no room for God. . . . 11He says to himself, “God has forgotten; he covers his face and never sees.” . . . 13Why does the wicked man revile God? Why does he say to himself, “He won’t call me to account”?

Ps 14 1The fool says in his heart, “There is no God.” They are corrupt, their deeds are vile; there is no one who does good. . . .

4Will evildoers never learn—those who devour my people as men eat bread and who do not call on the LORD?

Ps 73 11They say, “How can God know? Does the Most High have knowledge?”

Ps 79 6Pour out your wrath on the nations that do not acknowledge you, on the kingdoms that do not call on your name. . . .

Isa 1 3“The ox knows his master, the donkey his owner’s manger, but Israel does not know, my people do not understand.”

4Ah, sinful nation, a people loaded with guilt, a brood of evildoers, children given to corruption! They have forsaken the LORD; they have spurned the Holy One of Israel and turned their backs on him.

Isa 29 15Woe to those who go to great depths to hide their plans from the LORD, who do their work in darkness and think, “Who sees us? Who will know?” 16You turn things upside down, as if the potter were thought to be like the clay! Shall what is formed say to him who formed it, “He did not make me”? Can the pot say of the potter, “He knows nothing”?

Jer 4 22“My people are fools; they do not know me. They are senseless children; they have no understanding. They are skilled in doing evil; they know not how to do good.”

Jer 5 4I thought, “These are only the poor; they are foolish, for they do not know the way of the LORD, the requirements of their God. 5So I will go to the leaders and speak to them; surely they know the way of the LORD, the requirements of their God.” But with one accord they too had broken off the yoke and torn off the bonds.

Jer 9 3“They make ready their tongue like a bow, to shoot lies; it is not by truth that they triumph in the land. They go from one sin to another; they do not acknowledge me,” declares the LORD.

Ezek 8 12He said to me, “Son of man, have you seen what the elders of the house of Israel are doing in the darkness, each at the shrine of his own idol? They say, ‘The LORD does not see us; the LORD has forsaken the land.’”

Hos 4 1Hear the word of the LORD, you Israelites, because the LORD has a charge to bring against you who live in the land: “There is no faithfulness, no love, no acknowledgment of God in the land.”

Hos 5 4“Their deeds do not permit them to return to their God. A spirit of prostitution is in their heart; they do not acknowledge the LORD.”

John 8 19Then they asked him, “Where is your father?”

“You do not know me or my Father,” Jesus replied. “If you knew me, you would know my Father also.”

John 16 3“They will do such things because they have not known the Father or me.”

John 17 25“Righteous Father, though the world does not know you, I know you, and they know that you have sent me.”

1 Cor 15 34Come back to your senses as you ought, and stop sinning; for there are some who are ignorant of God—I say this to your shame.

Titus 1 16They claim to know God, but by their actions they deny him. They are detestable, disobedient and unfit for doing anything good.

2 Pet 2 1But there were also false prophets among the people, just as there will be false teachers among you. They will secretly introduce destructive heresies, even denying the sovereign Lord who bought them—bringing swift destruction on themselves.

2 Pet 3 3First of all, you must understand that in the last days scoffers will come, scoffing and following their own evil desires. 4They will say, “Where is this ‘coming’ he promised? Ever since our fathers died, everything goes on as it has since the beginning of creation.”

1 John 4 8Whoever does not love does not know God, because God is love.

Jude 4For certain men whose condemnation was written about long ago have secretly slipped in among you. They are godless men, who change the grace of our God into a license for immorality and deny Jesus Christ our only Sovereign and Lord.

2. Forgetting God

Deut 8 11Be careful that you do not forget the LORD your God, failing to observe his commands, his laws and his decrees that I am giving you this day. 12Otherwise, when you eat and are satisfied, when you build fine houses and settle down, 13and when your herds and flocks grow large and your silver and gold increase and all you have is multiplied, 14then your heart will become proud and you will forget the LORD your God, who brought you out of Egypt, out of the land of slavery.

Deut 32 18You deserted the Rock, who fathered you; you forgot the God who gave you birth.

Judg 3 7The Israelites did evil in the eyes of the LORD; they forgot the LORD their God and served the Baals and the Asherahs. 8The anger of the LORD burned against Israel so that he sold them into the hands of Cushan-Rishathaim king of Aram Naharaim, to whom the Israelites were subject for eight years.

Judg 8 33No sooner had Gideon died than the Israelites again prostituted themselves to the Baals. They set up Baal-Berith as their god and 34did not remember the LORD their God, who had rescued them from the hands of all their enemies on every side.

1 Sam 12 9“But they forgot the LORD their God; so he sold them into the hand of Sisera, the commander of the army of Hazor, and into the hands of the Philistines and the king of Moab, who fought against them.”

Job 8 11“Can papyrus grow tall where there is no marsh? Can reeds thrive without water? 12While still growing and uncut, they wither more quickly than grass. 13Such is the destiny of all who forget God; so perishes the hope of the godless.”

Ps 9 17The wicked return to the grave, all the nations that forget God.

Ps 44 17All this happened to us, though we had not forgotten you or been false to your covenant. 18Our hearts had not turned back; our feet had not strayed from your path. 19But you crushed us and made us a haunt for jackals and covered us over with deep darkness.

20If we had forgotten the name of our God or spread out our hands to a foreign god, 21would not God have discovered it, since he knows the secrets of the heart? 22Yet for your sake we face death all day long; we are considered as sheep to be slaughtered.

Ps 50 21“These things you have done and I kept silent; you thought I was altogether like you. But I will rebuke you and accuse you to your face.

22“Consider this, you who forget God, or I will tear you to pieces, with none to rescue. . . .”

Ps 78 10they did not keep God’s covenant and refused to live by his law. 11They forgot what he had done, the wonders he had shown them. . . . 42They did not remember his power—the day he redeemed them from the oppressor. . . .

Ps 106 21They forgot the God who saved them, who had done great things in Egypt. . . .

Isa 17 10You have forgotten God your Savior; you have not remembered the Rock, your fortress. Therefore, though you set out the finest plants and plant imported vines, 11though on the day you set them out, you make them grow, and on the morning when you plant them, you bring them to bud, yet the harvest will be as nothing in the day of disease and incurable pain.

Isa 51 12“I, even I, am he who comforts you. Who are you that you fear mortal men, the sons of men, who are but grass, 13that you forget the LORD your Maker, who stretched out the heavens

and laid the foundations of the earth, that you live in constant terror every day because of the wrath of the oppressor, who is bent on destruction? For where is the wrath of the oppressor?"
Isa 57 [11]"Whom have you so dreaded and feared that you have been false to me, and have neither remembered me nor pondered this in your hearts? Is it not because I have long been silent that you do not fear me?"
Jer 2 [32]"Does a maiden forget her jewelry, a bride her wedding ornaments? Yet my people have forgotten me, days without number."
Jer 3 [21]A cry is heard on the barren heights, the weeping and pleading of the people of Israel, because they have perverted their ways and have forgotten the LORD their God.
Jer 13 [25]"This is your lot, the portion I have decreed for you," declares the LORD, "because you have forgotten me and trusted in false gods."
Ezek 22 [12]"'In you men accept bribes to shed blood; you take usury and excessive interest and make unjust gain from your neighbors by extortion. And you have forgotten me, declares the Sovereign LORD.'"
Ezek 23 [35]"Therefore this is what the Sovereign LORD says: Since you have forgotten me and thrust me behind your back, you must bear the consequences of your lewdness and prostitution."
Hos 8 [14]"Israel has forgotten his Maker and built palaces; Judah has fortified many towns. But I will send fire upon their cities that will consume their fortresses."
Hos 13 [6]"When I fed them, they were satisfied; when they were satisfied, they became proud; then they forgot me."

3. Hating God

Deut 7 [10]But those who hate him he will repay to their face by destruction; he will not be slow to repay to their face those who hate him.
2 Chron 19 [2]Jehu the seer, the son of Hanani, went out to meet him and said to the king, "Should you help the wicked and love those who hate the LORD? Because of this, the wrath of the LORD is upon you."
Ps 21 [8]Your hand will lay hold on all your enemies; your right hand will seize your foes.
Ps 68 [1]May God arise, may his enemies be scattered; may his foes flee before him.
Ps 139 [21]Do I not hate those who hate you, O LORD, and abhor those who rise up against you? [22]I have nothing but hatred for them; I count them my enemies.
Prov 8 [36]"But whoever fails to find me harms himself; all who hate me love death."
John 15 [23]"He who hates me hates my Father as well. [24]If I had not done among them what no one else did, they would not be guilty of sin. But now they have seen these miracles, and yet they have hated both me and my Father. [25]But this is to fulfill what is written in their Law: 'They hated me without reason.'"
Rom 1 [28]Furthermore, since they did not think it worthwhile to retain the knowledge of God, he gave them over to a depraved mind, to do what ought not to be done. [29]They have become filled with every kind of wickedness, evil, greed and depravity. They are full of envy, murder, strife, deceit and malice. They are gossips, [30]slanderers, God-haters, insolent, arrogant and boastful; they invent ways of doing evil; they disobey their parents; [31]they are senseless, faithless, heartless, ruthless. [32]Although they know God's righteous decree that those who do such things deserve death, they not only continue to do these very things but also approve of those who practice them.

4. Not Fearing God

Gen 20 [11]Abraham replied, "I said to myself, 'There is surely no fear of God in this place, and they will kill me because of my wife.'"
Exod 9 [30]"But I know that you and your officials still do not fear the LORD God."
Deut 25 [18]When you were weary and worn out, they met you on your journey and cut off all who were lagging behind; they had no fear of God.
Job 6 [14]"A despairing man should have the devotion of his friends, even though he forsakes the fear of the Almighty."
Job 15 [4]"But you even undermine piety and hinder devotion to God."
Ps 36 [1]An oracle is within my heart concerning the sinfulness of the wicked: There is no fear of God before his eyes.
Ps 55 [19]God, who is enthroned forever, will hear them and afflict them—men who never change their ways and have no fear of God.
Ps 64 [4]They shoot from ambush at the innocent man; they shoot at him suddenly, without fear.
Jer 3 [8]"I gave faithless Israel her certificate of divorce and sent her away because of all her adulteries. Yet I saw that her unfaithful sister Judah had no fear; she also went out and committed adultery."
Jer 5 [22]"Should you not fear me?" declares the LORD. "Should you not tremble in my presence? I made the sand a boundary for the sea, an everlasting barrier it cannot cross. The waves may roll, but they cannot prevail; they may roar, but they cannot cross it. [23]But these people have stubborn and rebellious hearts; they have turned aside and gone away. [24]They do not say to themselves, 'Let us fear the LORD our God, who gives autumn and spring rains in season, who assures us of the regular weeks of harvest.'"
Hos 10 [3]Then they will say, "We have no king because we did not revere the LORD. But even if we had a king, what could he do for us?"
Luke 23 [40]But the other criminal rebuked him. "Don't you fear God," he said, "since you are under the same sentence?"
Jude [12]These men are blemishes at your love feasts, eating with you without the slightest qualm—shepherds who feed only themselves. They are clouds without rain, blown along by the wind; autumn trees, without fruit and uprooted—twice dead.

VIII
Sins against Neighbor

A. Sins of Dislike

1. Anger

Gen 49 [5]"Simeon and Levi are brothers—their swords are weapons of violence. [6]Let me not enter their council, let me not join their assembly, for they have killed men in their anger and hamstrung oxen as they pleased. [7]Cursed be their anger, so fierce, and their fury, so cruel! I will scatter them in Jacob and disperse them in Israel."
Ps 37 [8]Refrain from anger and turn from wrath; do not fret—it leads only to evil.
Ps 106 [33]for they rebelled against the Spirit of God, and rash words came from Moses' lips.
Prov 12 [16]A fool shows his annoyance at once, but a prudent man overlooks an insult.
Prov 14 [17]A quick-tempered man does foolish things, and a crafty man is hated.
Prov 15 [1]A gentle answer turns away wrath, but a harsh word stirs up anger.
Prov 16 [32]Better a patient man than a warrior, a man who controls his temper than one who takes a city.
Prov 19 [11]A man's wisdom gives him patience; it is to his glory to overlook an offense. . . .
[19]A hot-tempered man must pay the penalty; if you rescue him, you will have to do it again.
Prov 21 [14]A gift given in secret soothes anger, and a bribe concealed in the cloak pacifies great wrath.
Prov 22 [8]He who sows wickedness reaps trouble, and the rod of his fury will be destroyed.
Prov 22 [24]Do not make friends with a hot-tempered man, do not associate with one easily angered, [25]or you may learn his ways and get yourself ensnared.
Prov 27 [4]Anger is cruel and fury overwhelming, but who can stand before jealousy?
Prov 29 [22]An angry man stirs up dissension, and a hot-tempered one commits many sins.

Eccles 7 [9]Do not be quickly provoked in your spirit, for anger resides in the lap of fools.
Isa 14 [5]The LORD has broken the rod of the wicked, the scepter of the rulers, [6]which in anger struck down peoples with unceasing blows, and in fury subdued nations with relentless aggression.
Amos 1 [11]This is what the LORD says: "For three sins of Edom, even for four, I will not turn back my wrath. Because he pursued his brother with a sword, stifling all compassion, because his anger raged continually and his fury flamed unchecked. . . ."
Matt 5 [22]"But I tell you that anyone who is angry with his brother will be subject to judgment. Again, anyone who says to his brother, 'Raca,' is answerable to the Sanhedrin. But anyone who says, 'You fool!' will be in danger of the fire of hell."
John 7 [23]"Now if a child can be circumcised on the Sabbath so that the law of Moses may not be broken, why are you angry with me for healing the whole man on the Sabbath?"
2 Cor 12 [20]For I am afraid that when I come I may not find you as I want you to be, and you may not find me as you want me to be. I fear that there may be quarreling, jealousy, outbursts of anger, factions, slander, gossip, arrogance and disorder.
Gal 5 [19]The acts of the sinful nature are obvious: sexual immorality, impurity and debauchery; [20]idolatry and witchcraft; hatred, discord, jealousy, fits of rage, selfish ambition, dissensions, factions. . . .
Eph 4 [26]"In your anger do not sin": Do not let the sun go down while you are still angry, [27]and do not give the devil a foothold. . . . [31]Get rid of all bitterness, rage and anger, brawling and slander, along with every form of malice.
Eph 6 [4]Fathers, do not exasperate your children; instead, bring them up in the training and instruction of the Lord.
Col 3 [8]But now you must rid yourselves of all such things as these: anger, rage, malice, slander, and filthy language from your lips.
1 Tim 2 [8]I want men everywhere to lift up holy hands in prayer, without anger or disputing.
Titus 1 [7]Since an overseer is entrusted with God's work, he must be blameless—not overbearing, not quick-tempered, not given to drunkenness, not violent, not pursuing dishonest gain.
James 1 [19]My dear brothers, take note of this: Everyone should be quick to listen, slow to speak and slow to become angry, [20]for man's anger does not bring about the righteous life that God desires.

2. Gossip

Prov 11 [13]A gossip betrays a confidence, but a trustworthy man keeps a secret.
Prov 16 [28]A perverse man stirs up dissension, and a gossip separates close friends.
Prov 20 [19]A gossip betrays a confidence; so avoid a man who talks too much.
Prov 26 [20]Without wood a fire goes out; without gossip a quarrel dies down.
Rom 1 [29]They have become filled with every kind of wickedness, evil, greed and depravity. They are full of envy, murder, strife, deceit and malice. They are gossips. . . .
2 Cor 12 [20]For I am afraid that when I come I may not find you as I want you to be, and you may not find me as you want me to be. I fear that there may be quarreling, jealousy, outbursts of anger, factions, slander, gossip, arrogance and disorder.
1 Tim 5 [13]Besides, they get into the habit of being idle and going about from house to house. And not only do they become idlers, but also gossips and busybodies, saying things they ought not to.
3 John [10]So if I come, I will call attention to what he is doing, gossiping maliciously about us. Not satisfied with that, he refuses to welcome the brothers. He also stops those who want to do so and puts them out of the church.

3. Hatred

Exod 23 [5]"If you see the donkey of someone who hates you fallen down under its load, do not leave it there; be sure you help him with it."
Lev 19 [17]"'Do not hate your brother in your heart. Rebuke your neighbor frankly so you will not share in his guilt.'"
Deut 7 [15]The LORD will keep you free from every disease. He will not inflict on you the horrible diseases you knew in Egypt, but he will inflict them on all who hate you.
Deut 30 [7]The LORD your God will put all these curses on your enemies who hate and persecute you.
Deut 33 [11]"Bless all his skills, O LORD, and be pleased with the work of his hands. Smite the loins of those who rise up against him; strike his foes till they rise no more."
Job 8 [22]"Your enemies will be clothed in shame, and the tents of the wicked will be no more."
Ps 25 [19]See how my enemies have increased and how fiercely they hate me!
Ps 35 [19]Let not those gloat over me who are my enemies without cause; let not those who hate me without reason maliciously wink the eye.
Ps 38 [19]Many are those who are my vigorous enemies; those who hate me without reason are numerous.
Ps 41 [7]All my enemies whisper together against me; they imagine the worst for me, saying, [8]"A vile disease has beset him; he will never get up from the place where he lies." [9]Even my close friend, whom I trusted, he who shared my bread, has lifted up his heel against me.
Ps 69 [14]Rescue me from the mire, do not let me sink; deliver me from those who hate me, from the deep waters.
Prov 10 [12]Hatred stirs up dissension, but love covers over all wrongs.
Prov 29 [10]Bloodthirsty men hate a man of integrity and seek to kill the upright.
Ezek 35 [5]"'Because you harbored an ancient hostility and delivered the Israelites over to the sword at the time of their calamity, the time their punishment reached its climax, [6]therefore as surely as I live, declares the Sovereign LORD, I will give you over to bloodshed and it will pursue you. Since you did not hate bloodshed, bloodshed will pursue you.'"
Amos 5 [10]you hate the one who reproves in court and despise him who tells the truth.
Mic 3 [2]". . . you who hate good and love evil; who tear the skin from my people and the flesh from their bones . . ."
Matt 10 [22]"All men will hate you because of me, but he who stands firm to the end will be saved."
Luke 6 [22]"Blessed are you when men hate you, when they exclude you and insult you and reject your name as evil, because of the Son of Man.

[23]"Rejoice in that day and leap for joy, because great is your reward in heaven. For that is how their fathers treated the prophets."
John 7 [7]"The world cannot hate you, but it hates me because I testify that what it does is evil."
John 17 [14]"I have given them your word and the world has hated them, for they are not of the world any more than I am of the world."
Titus 3 [3]At one time we too were foolish, disobedient, deceived and enslaved by all kinds of passions and pleasures. We lived in malice and envy, being hated and hating one another.
1 John 2 [9]Anyone who claims to be in the light but hates his brother is still in the darkness. . . . [11]But whoever hates his brother is in the darkness and walks around in the darkness; he does not know where he is going, because the darkness has blinded him.
1 John 3 [13]Do not be surprised, my brothers, if the world hates you. [14]We know that we have passed from death to life, because we love our brothers. Anyone who does not love remains in death. [15]Anyone who hates his brother is a murderer, and you know that no murderer has eternal life in him.
1 John 4 [20]If anyone says, "I love God," yet hates his brother, he is a liar. For anyone who does not love his brother, whom he has seen, cannot love God, whom he has not seen.

4. Malice

Num 35 [20]"'If anyone with malice aforethought shoves another or throws something at him intentionally so that he dies [21]or if in hostility he hits him with his fist so that he dies, that person

shall be put to death; he is a murderer. The avenger of blood shall put the murderer to death when he meets him.'"
Job 6 30"Is there any wickedness on my lips? Can my mouth not discern malice?"
Ps 10 7His mouth is full of curses and lies and threats; trouble and evil are under his tongue.
Ps 12 5"Because of the oppression of the weak and the groaning of the needy, I will now arise," says the LORD. "I will protect them from those who malign them."
Ps 28 3Do not drag me away with the wicked, with those who do evil, who speak cordially with their neighbors but harbor malice in their hearts.
Ps 41 5My enemies say of me in malice, "When will he die and his name perish?"
Ps 52 4You love every harmful word, O you deceitful tongue!
5Surely God will bring you down to everlasting ruin: He will snatch you up and tear you from your tent; he will uproot you from the land of the living.
Ps 55 10Day and night they prowl about on its walls; malice and abuse are within it.
Ps 56 5All day long they twist my words; they are always plotting to harm me.
Ps 64 6They plot injustice and say, "We have devised a perfect plan!" Surely the mind and heart of man are cunning.
Prov 4 24Put away perversity from your mouth; keep corrupt talk far from your lips.
Prov 6 12A scoundrel and villain, who goes about with a corrupt mouth . . .
Prov 10 31The mouth of the righteous brings forth wisdom, but a perverse tongue will be cut out. 32The lips of the righteous know what is fitting, but the mouth of the wicked only what is perverse.
Prov 16 27A scoundrel plots evil, and his speech is like a scorching fire.
28A perverse man stirs up dissension, and a gossip separates close friends.
Prov 17 20A man of perverse heart does not prosper; he whose tongue is deceitful falls into trouble.
Prov 26 26His malice may be concealed by deception, but his wickedness will be exposed in the assembly.
Ezek 25 6"'For this is what the Sovereign LORD says: Because you have clapped your hands and stamped your feet, rejoicing with all the malice of your heart against the land of Israel,
7therefore I will stretch out my hand against you and give you as plunder to the nations. I will cut you off from the nations and exterminate you from the countries. I will destroy you, and you will know that I am the LORD.'"
Ezek 36 5"'. . . this is what the Sovereign LORD says: In my burning zeal I have spoken against the rest of the nations, and against all Edom, for with glee and with malice in their hearts they made my land their own possession so that they might plunder its pastureland.'"
Rom 1 28Furthermore, since they did not think it worthwhile to retain the knowledge of God, he gave them over to a depraved mind, to do what ought not to be done. 29They have become filled with every kind of wickedness, evil, greed and depravity. They are full of envy, murder, strife, deceit and malice. They are gossips. . . .
1 Cor 5 8Therefore let us keep the Festival, not with the old yeast, the yeast of malice and wickedness, but with bread without yeast, the bread of sincerity and truth.
1 Cor 14 20Brothers, stop thinking like children. In regard to evil be infants, but in your thinking be adults.
Eph 4 31Get rid of all bitterness, rage and anger, brawling and slander, along with every form of malice.
Col 3 8But now you must rid yourselves of all such things as these: anger, rage, malice, slander, and filthy language from your lips.
Titus 3 3At one time we too were foolish, disobedient, deceived and enslaved by all kinds of passions and pleasures. We lived in malice and envy, being hated and hating one another.
1 Pet 2 1Therefore, rid yourselves of all malice and all deceit, hypocrisy, envy, and slander of every kind.
3 John 9I wrote to the church, but Diotrephes, who loves to be first, will have nothing to do with us. 10So if I come, I will call attention to what he is doing, gossiping maliciously about us. Not satisfied with that, he refuses to welcome the brothers. He also stops those who want to do so and puts them out of the church.

5. Neglect or Unconcern

Ezek 16 49"'Now this was the sin of your sister Sodom: She and her daughters were arrogant, overfed and unconcerned; they did not help the poor and needy.'"

6. Passing Judgment

Matt 7 1"Do not judge, or you too will be judged. 2For in the same way you judge others, you will be judged, and with the measure you use, it will be measured to you.
3"Why do you look at the speck of sawdust in your brother's eye and pay no attention to the plank in your own eye? 4How can you say to your brother, 'Let me take the speck out of your eye,' when all the time there is a plank in your own eye? 5You hypocrite, first take the plank out of your own eye, and then you will see clearly to remove the speck from your brother's eye."
John 7 24"Stop judging by mere appearances, and make a right judgment."
John 8 7When they kept on questioning him, he straightened up and said to them, "If any one of you is without sin, let him be the first to throw a stone at her."
Rom 2 1You, therefore, have no excuse, you who pass judgment on someone else, for at whatever point you judge the other, you are condemning yourself, because you who pass judgment do the same things. 2Now we know that God's judgment against those who do such things is based on truth. 3So when you, a mere man, pass judgment on them and yet do the same things, do you think you will escape God's judgment?
Rom 14 2One man's faith allows him to eat everything, but another man, whose faith is weak, eats only vegetables. 3The man who eats everything must not look down on him who does not, and the man who does not eat everything must not condemn the man who does, for God has accepted him. 4Who are you to judge someone else's servant? To his own master he stands or falls. And he will stand, for the Lord is able to make him stand.
5One man considers one day more sacred than another; another man considers every day alike. Each one should be fully convinced in his own mind. . . . 10You, then, why do you judge your brother? Or why do you look down on your brother? For we will all stand before God's judgment seat. 11It is written: "'As surely as I live,' says the Lord, 'every knee will bow before me; every tongue will confess to God.'" 12So then, each of us will give an account of himself to God.
13Therefore let us stop passing judgment on one another. Instead, make up your mind not to put any stumbling block or obstacle in your brother's way.
1 Cor 4 3I care very little if I am judged by you or by any human court; indeed, I do not even judge myself. 4My conscience is clear, but that does not make me innocent. It is the Lord who judges me. 5Therefore judge nothing before the appointed time; wait till the Lord comes. He will bring to light what is hidden in darkness and will expose the motives of men's hearts. At that time each will receive his praise from God.
Col 2 16Therefore do not let anyone judge you by what you eat or drink, or with regard to a religious festival, a New Moon celebration or a Sabbath day.
James 2 12Speak and act as those who are going to be judged by the law that gives freedom, 13because judgment without mercy will be shown to anyone who has not been merciful. Mercy triumphs over judgment!
James 4 12There is only one Lawgiver and Judge, the one who is able to save and destroy. But you—who are you to judge your neighbor?

7. Returning Evil for Good or Evil

Judg 8 35They also failed to show kindness to the family of Jerub-Baal (that is, Gideon) for all the good things he had done for them.

1 Sam 23 5So David and his men went to Keilah, fought the Philistines and carried off their livestock. He inflicted heavy losses on the Philistines and saved the people of Keilah. . . .

9When David learned that Saul was plotting against him, he said to Abiathar the priest, "Bring the ephod." 10David said, "O LORD, God of Israel, your servant has heard definitely that Saul plans to come to Keilah and destroy the town on account of me. 11Will the citizens of Keilah surrender me to him? Will Saul come down, as your servant has heard? O LORD, God of Israel, tell your servant."

And the LORD said, "He will."

12Again David asked, "Will the citizens of Keilah surrender me and my men to Saul?"

And the LORD said, "They will."

1 Sam 25 21David had just said, "It's been useless—all my watching over this fellow's property in the desert so that nothing of his was missing. He has paid me back evil for good. 22May God deal with David, be it ever so severely, if by morning I leave alive one male of all who belong to him!"

Ps 35 12They repay me evil for good and leave my soul forlorn. 13Yet when they were ill, I put on sackcloth and humbled myself with fasting. When my prayers returned to me unanswered, 14I went about mourning as though for my friend or brother. I bowed my head in grief as though weeping for my mother. 15But when I stumbled, they gathered in glee; attackers gathered against me when I was unaware. They slandered me without ceasing.

Ps 38 20Those who repay my good with evil slander me when I pursue what is good.

Ps 109 4In return for my friendship they accuse me, but I am a man of prayer. 5They repay me evil for good, and hatred for my friendship.

Prov 17 13If a man pays back evil for good, evil will never leave his house.

Prov 20 22Do not say, "I'll pay you back for this wrong!" Wait for the LORD, and he will deliver you.

Prov 24 29Do not say, "I'll do to him as he has done to me; I'll pay that man back for what he did."

Eccles 9 14There was once a small city with only a few people in it. And a powerful king came against it, surrounded it and built huge siegeworks against it. 15Now there lived in that city a man poor but wise, and he saved the city by his wisdom. But nobody remembered that poor man.

Jer 18 20Should good be repaid with evil? Yet they have dug a pit for me. Remember that I stood before you and spoke in their behalf to turn your wrath away from them.

Luke 9 53but the people there did not welcome him, because he was heading for Jerusalem. 54When the disciples James and John saw this, they asked, "Lord, do you want us to call fire down from heaven to destroy them?" 55But Jesus turned and rebuked them. . . .

Rom 12 17Do not repay anyone evil for evil. Be careful to do what is right in the eyes of everybody. . . . 19Do not take revenge, my friends, but leave room for God's wrath, for it is written: "It is mine to avenge; I will repay," says the Lord.

1 Thess 5 15Make sure that nobody pays back wrong for wrong, but always try to be kind to each other and to everyone else.

8. Scorn

2 Chron 36 16But they mocked God's messengers, despised his words and scoffed at his prophets until the wrath of the LORD was aroused against his people and there was no remedy.

Job 34 7"What man is like Job, who drinks scorn like water?"

Ps 1 1Blessed is the man who does not walk in the counsel of the wicked or stand in the way of sinners or sit in the seat of mockers.

Ps 22 6But I am a worm and not a man, scorned by men and despised by the people.

Ps 39 8"Save me from all my transgressions; do not make me the scorn of fools."

Ps 73 8They scoff, and speak with malice; in their arrogance they threaten oppression.

Ps 123 4We have endured much ridicule from the proud, much contempt from the arrogant.

Prov 1 22"How long will you simple ones love your simple ways? How long will mockers delight in mockery and fools hate knowledge?"

Prov 3 34He mocks proud mockers but gives grace to the humble.

Prov 9 7"Whoever corrects a mocker invites insult; whoever rebukes a wicked man incurs abuse. 8Do not rebuke a mocker or he will hate you; rebuke a wise man and he will love you. . . . 12If you are wise, your wisdom will reward you; if you are a mocker, you alone will suffer."

Prov 13 1A wise son heeds his father's instruction, but a mocker does not listen to rebuke.

Prov 14 6The mocker seeks wisdom and finds none, but knowledge comes easily to the discerning.

Prov 15 12A mocker resents correction; he will not consult the wise.

Prov 19 29Penalties are prepared for mockers, and beatings for the backs of fools.

Prov 21 11When a mocker is punished, the simple gain wisdom; when a wise man is instructed, he gets knowledge.

Prov 21 24The proud and arrogant man—"Mocker" is his name; he behaves with overweening pride.

Prov 22 10Drive out the mocker, and out goes strife; quarrels and insults are ended.

Prov 24 9The schemes of folly are sin, and men detest a mocker.

Prov 29 8Mockers stir up a city, but wise men turn away anger.

Isa 28 14Therefore hear the word of the LORD, you scoffers who rule this people in Jerusalem. 15You boast, "We have entered into a covenant with death, with the grave we have made an agreement. When an overwhelming scourge sweeps by, it cannot touch us, for we have made a lie our refuge and falsehood our hiding place."

16So this is what the Sovereign LORD says: "See, I lay a stone in Zion, a tested stone, a precious cornerstone for a sure foundation; the one who trusts will never be dismayed. 17I will make justice the measuring line and righteousness the plumb line; hail will sweep away your refuge, the lie, and water will overflow your hiding place. 18Your covenant with death will be annulled; your agreement with the grave will not stand. When the overwhelming scourge sweeps by, you will be beaten down by it. 19As often as it comes it will carry you away; morning after morning, by day and by night, it will sweep through."

The understanding of this message will bring sheer terror.

Isa 29 20The ruthless will vanish, the mockers will disappear, and all who have an eye for evil will be cut down. . . .

Isa 57 4"Whom are you mocking? At whom do you sneer and stick out your tongue? Are you not a brood of rebels, the offspring of liars?"

Hos 7 5"On the day of the festival of our king the princes become inflamed with wine, and he joins hands with the mockers."

Acts 2 13Some, however, made fun of them and said, "They have had too much wine."

Acts 17 18A group of Epicurean and Stoic philosophers began to dispute with him. Some of them asked, "What is this babbler trying to say?" Others remarked, "He seems to be advocating foreign gods." They said this because Paul was preaching the good news about Jesus and the resurrection. . . .

32When they heard about the resurrection of the dead, some of them sneered, but others said, "We want to hear you again on this subject."

Gal 4 14Even though my illness was a trial to you, you did not treat me with contempt or scorn. Instead, you welcomed me as if I were an angel of God, as if I were Christ Jesus himself.

Heb 10 29How much more severely do you think a man deserves to be punished who has trampled the Son of God under foot, who has treated as an unholy thing the blood of the covenant that sanctified him, and who has insulted the Spirit of grace?

2 Pet 3 3First of all, you must understand that in the last days scoffers will come, scoffing and following their own evil desires. 4They will say, "Where is this 'coming' he promised? Ever since our fathers died, everything goes on as it has since the beginning of creation."

Jude [18]They said to you, "In the last times there will be scoffers who will follow their own ungodly desires."

9. Slander

Deut 19 [16]If a malicious witness takes the stand to accuse a man of a crime, [17]the two men involved in the dispute must stand in the presence of the LORD before the priests and the judges who are in office at the time. [18]The judges must make a thorough investigation, and if the witness proves to be a liar, giving false testimony against his brother, [19]then do to him as he intended to do to his brother. You must purge the evil from among you.
Ps 41 [5]My enemies say of me in malice, "When will he die and his name perish?"
Ps 41 [6]Whenever one comes to see me, he speaks falsely, while his heart gathers slander; then he goes out and spreads it abroad.
Prov 10 [18]He who conceals his hatred has lying lips, and whoever spreads slander is a fool.
Jer 6 [27]"I have made you a tester of metals and my people the ore, that you may observe and test their ways. [28]They are all hardened rebels, going about to slander. They are bronze and iron; they all act corruptly."
Matt 15 [19]"For out of the heart come evil thoughts, murder, adultery, sexual immorality, theft, false testimony, slander. [20]These are what make a man 'unclean'; but eating with unwashed hands does not make him 'unclean.'"
Rom 1 [28]Furthermore, since they did not think it worthwhile to retain the knowledge of God, he gave them over to a depraved mind, to do what ought not to be done. [30]. . . slanderers, God-haters, insolent, arrogant and boastful; they invent ways of doing evil; they disobey their parents. . . .
2 Cor 12 [20]For I am afraid that when I come I may not find you as I want you to be, and you may not find me as you want me to be. I fear that there may be quarreling, jealousy, outbursts of anger, factions, slander, gossip, arrogance and disorder.
Eph 4 [31]Get rid of all bitterness, rage and anger, brawling and slander, along with every form of malice.
Col 3 [8]But now you must rid yourselves of all such things as these: anger, rage, malice, slander, and filthy language from your lips.
Titus 3 [1]Remind the people to be subject to rulers and authorities, to be obedient, to be ready to do whatever is good, [2]to slander no one, to be peaceable and considerate, and to show true humility toward all men.
James 4 [11]Brothers, do not slander one another. Anyone who speaks against his brother or judges him speaks against the law and judges it. When you judge the law, you are not keeping it, but sitting in judgment on it.

10. Strife and Quarreling

Gen 13 [5]Now Lot, who was moving about with Abram, also had flocks and herds and tents. [6]But the land could not support them while they stayed together, for their possessions were so great that they were not able to stay together. [7]And quarreling arose between Abram's herdsmen and the herdsmen of Lot. The Canaanites and Perizzites were also living in the land at that time.

[8]So Abram said to Lot, "Let's not have any quarreling between you and me, or between your herdsmen and mine, for we are brothers. [9]Is not the whole land before you? Let's part company. If you go to the left, I'll go to the right; if you go to the right, I'll go to the left."
Prov 3 [29]Do not plot harm against your neighbor, who lives trustfully near you. [30]Do not accuse a man for no reason—when he has done you no harm.
Prov 15 [18]A hot-tempered man stirs up dissension, but a patient man calms a quarrel.
Prov 17 [1]Better a dry crust with peace and quiet than a house full of feasting, with strife.
Prov 17 [14]Starting a quarrel is like breaching a dam; so drop the matter before a dispute breaks out.
Prov 17 [19]He who loves a quarrel loves sin; he who builds a high gate invites destruction.
Prov 18 [6]A fool's lips bring him strife, and his mouth invites a beating.
Prov 18 [19]An offended brother is more unyielding than a fortified city, and disputes are like the barred gates of a citadel.
Prov 20 [3]It is to a man's honor to avoid strife, but every fool is quick to quarrel.
Prov 22 [10]Drive out the mocker, and out goes strife; quarrels and insults are ended.
Prov 23 [29]Who has woe? Who has sorrow? Who has strife? Who has complaints? Who has needless bruises? Who has bloodshot eyes? [30]Those who linger over wine, who go to sample bowls of mixed wine.
Prov 26 [20]Without wood a fire goes out; without gossip a quarrel dies down.

[21]As charcoal to embers and as wood to fire, so is a quarrelsome man for kindling strife.
Prov 29 [9]If a wise man goes to court with a fool, the fool rages and scoffs, and there is no peace.
Isa 49 [25]But this is what the LORD says: "Yes, captives will be taken from warriors, and plunder retrieved from the fierce; I will contend with those who contend with you, and your children I will save."
Hab 1 [3]Why do you make me look at injustice? Why do you tolerate wrong? Destruction and violence are before me; there is strife, and conflict abounds.
Matt 12 [19]"He will not quarrel or cry out; no one will hear his voice in the streets."
Mark 3 [24]"If a kingdom is divided against itself, that kingdom cannot stand. [25]If a house is divided against itself, that house cannot stand."
Rom 13 [13]Let us behave decently, as in the daytime, not in orgies and drunkenness, not in sexual immorality and debauchery, not in dissension and jealousy.
1 Cor 3 [3]You are still worldly. For since there is jealousy and quarreling among you, are you not worldly? Are you not acting like mere men? [4]For when one says, "I follow Paul," and another, "I follow Apollos," are you not mere men?
1 Cor 11 [16]If anyone wants to be contentious about this, we have no other practice—nor do the churches of God.
2 Cor 12 [20]For I am afraid that when I come I may not find you as I want you to be, and you may not find me as you want me to be. I fear that there may be quarreling, jealousy, outbursts of anger, factions, slander, gossip, arrogance and disorder.
Gal 5 [15]If you keep on biting and devouring each other, watch out or you will be destroyed by each other.
1 Tim 6 [3]If anyone teaches false doctrines and does not agree to the sound instruction of our Lord Jesus Christ and to godly teaching, [4]he is conceited and understands nothing. He has an unhealthy interest in controversies and quarrels about words that result in envy, strife, malicious talk, evil suspicions. . . .
2 Tim 2 [23]Don't have anything to do with foolish and stupid arguments, because you know they produce quarrels. [24]And the Lord's servant must not quarrel; instead, he must be kind to everyone, able to teach, not resentful.
Titus 3 [9]But avoid foolish controversies and genealogies and arguments and quarrels about the law, because these are unprofitable and useless.

B. Sins of Injury

1. Injustice and Favoritism

Lev 19 [15]"'Do not pervert justice; do not show partiality to the poor or favoritism to the great, but judge your neighbor fairly.'"
Deut 1 [17]Do not show partiality in judging; hear both small and great alike. Do not be afraid of any man, for judgment belongs to God. Bring me any case too hard for you, and I will hear it.
Ps 58 [1]Do you rulers indeed speak justly? Do you judge uprightly among men? [2]No, in your heart you devise injustice, and your hands mete out violence on the earth.
Ps 64 [6]They plot injustice and say, "We have devised a perfect plan!" Surely the mind and heart of man are cunning.
Isa 58 [6]"Is not this the kind of fasting I have chosen: to loose the chains of injustice and untie the cords of the yoke, to set

the oppressed free and break every yoke? [7]Is it not to share your food with the hungry and to provide the poor wanderer with shelter—when you see the naked, to clothe him, and not to turn away from your own flesh and blood?"
Ezek 9 [9]He answered me, "The sin of the house of Israel and Judah is exceedingly great; the land is full of bloodshed and the city is full of injustice. They say, 'The LORD has forsaken the land; the LORD does not see.'"
Hab 1 [3]Why do you make me look at injustice? Why do you tolerate wrong? Destruction and violence are before me; there is strife, and conflict abounds.
Mal 3 [5]"So I will come near to you for judgment. I will be quick to testify against sorcerers, adulterers and perjurers, against those who defraud laborers of their wages, who oppress the widows and the fatherless, and deprive aliens of justice, but do not fear me," says the LORD Almighty.
Acts 10 [34]Then Peter began to speak: "I now realize how true it is that God does not show favoritism [35]but accepts men from every nation who fear him and do what is right."
Eph 6 [9]And masters, treat your slaves in the same way. Do not threaten them, since you know that he who is both their Master and yours is in heaven, and there is no favoritism with him.
Col 3 [25]Anyone who does wrong will be repaid for his wrong, and there is no favoritism.
1 Tim 5 [21]I charge you, in the sight of God and Christ Jesus and the elect angels, to keep these instructions without partiality, and to do nothing out of favoritism.
James 2 [1]My brothers, as believers in our glorious Lord Jesus Christ, don't show favoritism. . . . [9]But if you show favoritism, you sin and are convicted by the law as lawbreakers.

2. Murder

Gen 9 [5]"And for your lifeblood I will surely demand an accounting. I will demand an accounting from every animal. And from each man, too, I will demand an accounting for the life of his fellow man.

[6]"Whoever sheds the blood of man, by man shall his blood be shed; for in the image of God has God made man."
Exod 20 [13]"You shall not murder."
Exod 21 [12]"Anyone who strikes a man and kills him shall surely be put to death. [13]However, if he does not do it intentionally, but God lets it happen, he is to flee to a place I will designate. [14]But if a man schemes and kills another man deliberately, take him away from my altar and put him to death."
Lev 24 [17]"'If anyone takes the life of a human being, he must be put to death.'"
Num 35 [16]"'If a man strikes someone with an iron object so that he dies, he is a murderer; the murderer shall be put to death. [17]Or if anyone has a stone in his hand that could kill, and he strikes someone so that he dies, he is a murderer; the murderer shall be put to death. [18]Or if anyone has a wooden object in his hand that could kill, and he hits someone so that he dies, he is a murderer; the murderer shall be put to death. [21]. . . or if in hostility he hits him with his fist so that he dies, that person shall be put to death; he is a murderer. The avenger of blood shall put the murderer to death when he meets him. . . .

[30]"'Anyone who kills a person is to be put to death as a murderer only on the testimony of witnesses. But no one is to be put to death on the testimony of only one witness.

[31]"'Do not accept a ransom for the life of a murderer, who deserves to die. He must surely be put to death.'"
Deut 19 [11]But if a man hates his neighbor and lies in wait for him, assaults and kills him, and then flees to one of these cities, [12]the elders of his town shall send for him, bring him back from the city, and hand him over to the avenger of blood to die. [13]Show him no pity. You must purge from Israel the guilt of shedding innocent blood, so that it may go well with you.
Ps 55 [23]But you, O God, will bring down the wicked into the pit of corruption; bloodthirsty and deceitful men will not live out half their days.

But as for me, I trust in you.
Ps 106 [38]They shed innocent blood, the blood of their sons and daughters, whom they sacrificed to the idols of Canaan, and the land was desecrated by their blood. . . .

[40]Therefore the LORD was angry with his people and abhorred his inheritance.
Prov 28 [17]A man tormented by the guilt of murder will be a fugitive till death; let no one support him.
Isa 59 [3]For your hands are stained with blood, your fingers with guilt. Your lips have spoken lies, and your tongue mutters wicked things. . . . [7]Their feet rush into sin; they are swift to shed innocent blood. Their thoughts are evil thoughts; ruin and destruction mark their ways.
Jer 7 [9]"'Will you steal and murder, commit adultery and perjury, burn incense to Baal and follow other gods you have not known, [10]and then come and stand before me in this house, which bears my Name, and say, "We are safe"—safe to do all these detestable things?'"
Jer 19 [3]". . . and say, 'Hear the word of the LORD, O kings of Judah and people of Jerusalem. This is what the LORD Almighty, the God of Israel, says: Listen! I am going to bring a disaster on this place that will make the ears of everyone who hears of it tingle. [4]For they have forsaken me and made this a place of foreign gods; they have burned sacrifices in it to gods that neither they nor their fathers nor the kings of Judah ever knew, and they have filled this place with the blood of the innocent.'"
Lam 4 [13]But it happened because of the sins of her prophets and the iniquities of her priests, who shed within her the blood of the righteous.

[14]Now they grope through the streets like men who are blind. They are so defiled with blood that no one dares to touch their garments.
Ezek 24 [6]"'For this is what the Sovereign LORD says: Woe to the city of bloodshed, to the pot now encrusted, whose deposit will not go away! Empty it piece by piece without casting lots for them. . . .

[9]"'Therefore this is what the Sovereign LORD says: Woe to the city of bloodshed! I, too, will pile the wood high.'"
Ezek 35 [6]"'. . . therefore as surely as I live, declares the Sovereign LORD, I will give you over to bloodshed and it will pursue you. Since you did not hate bloodshed, bloodshed will pursue you.'"
Hos 4 [2]"There is only cursing, lying and murder, stealing and adultery; they break all bounds, and bloodshed follows bloodshed. [3]Because of this the land mourns, and all who live in it waste away; the beasts of the field and the birds of the air and the fish of the sea are dying."
Jon 1 [14]Then they cried to the LORD, "O LORD, please do not let us die for taking this man's life. Do not hold us accountable for killing an innocent man, for you, O LORD, have done as you pleased."
Nah 3 [1]Woe to the city of blood, full of lies, full of plunder, never without victims!
Hab 2 [10]"You have plotted the ruin of many peoples, shaming your own house and forfeiting your life. [11]The stones of the wall will cry out, and the beams of the woodwork will echo it.

[12]"Woe to him who builds a city with bloodshed and establishes a town by crime!"
Matt 23 [35]"And so upon you will come all the righteous blood that has been shed on earth, from the blood of righteous Abel to the blood of Zechariah son of Berekiah, whom you murdered between the temple and the altar."
John 8 [44]"You belong to your father, the devil, and you want to carry out your father's desire. He was a murderer from the beginning, not holding to the truth, for there is no truth in him. When he lies, he speaks his native language, for he is a liar and the father of lies."
1 Tim 1 [9]We also know that law is made not for the righteous but for lawbreakers and rebels, the ungodly and sinful, the unholy and irreligious; for those who kill their fathers or mothers, for murderers . . .
James 4 [1]What causes fights and quarrels among you? Don't they come from your desires that battle within you? [2]You want something but don't get it. You kill and covet, but you cannot have what you want. You quarrel and fight. You do not have, because you do not ask God.
James 5 [6]You have condemned and murdered innocent men, who were not opposing you.

1 John 3 [15]Anyone who hates his brother is a murderer, and you know that no murderer has eternal life in him.
Rev 21 [8]"But the cowardly, the unbelieving, the vile, the murderers, the sexually immoral, those who practice magic arts, the idolaters and all liars—their place will be in the fiery lake of burning sulfur. This is the second death."
Rev 22 [15]"Outside are the dogs, those who practice magic arts, the sexually immoral, the murderers, the idolaters and everyone who loves and practices falsehood."

3. Oppression

Job 6 [27]"You would even cast lots for the fatherless and barter away your friend."
Job 20 [19]"For he has oppressed the poor and left them destitute; he has seized houses he did not build.

[20]"Surely he will have no respite from his craving; he cannot save himself by his treasure. [21]Nothing is left for him to devour; his prosperity will not endure. [22]In the midst of his plenty, distress will overtake him; the full force of misery will come upon him."
Job 22 [5]"Is not your wickedness great? Are not your sins endless? [6]You demanded security from your brothers for no reason; you stripped men of their clothing, leaving them naked. [7]You gave no water to the weary and you withheld food from the hungry, [8]though you were a powerful man, owning land—an honored man, living on it. [9]And you sent widows away empty-handed and broke the strength of the fatherless."
Job 24 [21]"They prey on the barren and childless woman, and to the widow show no kindness."
Job 34 [26]"He punishes them for their wickedness where everyone can see them. . . . [28]They caused the cry of the poor to come before him, so that he heard the cry of the needy."
Job 35 [9]"Men cry out under a load of oppression; they plead for relief from the arm of the powerful."
Ps 42 [9]I say to God my Rock, "Why have you forgotten me? Why must I go about mourning, oppressed by the enemy?" [10]My bones suffer mortal agony as my foes taunt me, saying to me all day long, "Where is your God?"
Ps 62 [10]Do not trust in extortion or take pride in stolen goods; though your riches increase, do not set your heart on them.
Ps 73 [8]They scoff, and speak with malice; in their arrogance they threaten oppression.
Ps 103 [6]The LORD works righteousness and justice for all the oppressed.
Prov 14 [31]He who oppresses the poor shows contempt for their Maker, but whoever is kind to the needy honors God.
Prov 22 [16]He who oppresses the poor to increase his wealth and he who gives gifts to the rich—both come to poverty. . . .

[22]Do not exploit the poor because they are poor and do not crush the needy in court, [23]for the LORD will take up their case and will plunder those who plunder them.
Prov 28 [3]A ruler who oppresses the poor is like a driving rain that leaves no crops. . . .

[8]He who increases his wealth by exorbitant interest amasses it for another, who will be kind to the poor. . . .

[15]Like a roaring lion or a charging bear is a wicked man ruling over a helpless people.

[16]A tyrannical ruler lacks judgment, but he who hates ill-gotten gain will enjoy a long life.
Eccles 5 [8]If you see the poor oppressed in a district, and justice and rights denied, do not be surprised at such things; for one official is eyed by a higher one, and over them both are others higher still.
Isa 1 [17]". . . learn to do right! Seek justice, encourage the oppressed. Defend the cause of the fatherless, plead the case of the widow."
Isa 5 [8]Woe to you who add house to house and join field to field till no space is left and you live alone in the land.
Isa 29 [20]The ruthless will vanish, the mockers will disappear, and all who have an eye for evil will be cut down—[21]those who with a word make a man out to be guilty, who ensnare the defender in court and with false testimony deprive the innocent of justice.
Isa 30 [12]Therefore, this is what the Holy One of Israel says: "Because you have rejected this message, relied on oppression and depended on deceit, [13]this sin will become for you like a high wall, cracked and bulging, that collapses suddenly, in an instant. [14]It will break in pieces like pottery, shattered so mercilessly that among its pieces not a fragment will be found for taking coals from a hearth or scooping water out of a cistern."
Isa 32 [7]The scoundrel's methods are wicked, he makes up evil schemes to destroy the poor with lies, even when the plea of the needy is just.
Isa 49 [26]"I will make your oppressors eat their own flesh; they will be drunk on their own blood, as with wine. Then all mankind will know that I, the LORD, am your Savior, your Redeemer, the Mighty One of Jacob."
Isa 59 [12]For our offenses are many in your sight, and our sins testify against us. Our offenses are ever with us, and we acknowledge our iniquities: [13]rebellion and treachery against the LORD, turning our backs on our God, fomenting oppression and revolt, uttering lies our hearts have conceived. [14]So justice is driven back, and righteousness stands at a distance; truth has stumbled in the streets, honesty cannot enter. [15]Truth is nowhere to be found, and whoever shuns evil becomes a prey.

The LORD looked and was displeased that there was no justice.
Jer 6 [6]This is what the LORD Almighty says: "Cut down the trees and build siege ramps against Jerusalem. This city must be punished; it is filled with oppression."
Jer 17 [11]Like a partridge that hatches eggs it did not lay is the man who gains riches by unjust means. When his life is half gone, they will desert him, and in the end he will prove to be a fool.
Jer 21 [12]"'O house of David, this is what the LORD says: Administer justice every morning; rescue from the hand of his oppressor the one who has been robbed, or my wrath will break out and burn like fire because of the evil you have done—burn with no one to quench it.'"
Jer 22 [13]"Woe to him who builds his palace by unrighteousness, his upper rooms by injustice, making his countrymen work for nothing, not paying them for their labor. . . .

[17]"But your eyes and your heart are set only on dishonest gain, on shedding innocent blood and on oppression and extortion."
Ezek 18 [12]"He oppresses the poor and needy. He commits robbery. He does not return what he took in pledge. He looks to the idols. He does detestable things. [13]He lends at usury and takes excessive interest. Will such a man live? He will not! Because he has done all these detestable things, he will surely be put to death and his blood will be on his own head. . . . [18]But his father will die for his own sin, because he practiced extortion, robbed his brother and did what was wrong among his people."
Ezek 45 [9]"'This is what the Sovereign LORD says: You have gone far enough, O princes of Israel! Give up your violence and oppression and do what is just and right. Stop dispossessing my people, declares the Sovereign LORD. [10]You are to use accurate scales, an accurate ephah and an accurate bath.'"
Hos 12 [7]The merchant uses dishonest scales; he loves to defraud.
Amos 4 [1]Hear this word, you cows of Bashan on Mount Samaria, you women who oppress the poor and crush the needy and say to your husbands, "Bring us some drinks!" [2]The Sovereign LORD has sworn by his holiness: "The time will surely come when you will be taken away with hooks, the last of you with fishhooks."
Mic 2 [1]Woe to those who plan iniquity, to those who plot evil on their beds! At morning's light they carry it out because it is in their power to do it. [2]They covet fields and seize them, and houses, and take them. They defraud a man of his home, a fellowman of his inheritance.

[3]Therefore, the LORD says: "I am planning disaster against this people, from which you cannot save yourselves. You will no longer walk proudly, for it will be a time of calamity."
Hab 2 [6]"Will not all of them taunt him with ridicule and scorn, saying, 'Woe to him who piles up stolen goods and makes himself wealthy by extortion! How long must this go on?'"
Luke 3 [12]Tax collectors also came to be baptized. "Teacher," they asked, "what should we do?"

[13]"Don't collect any more than you are required to," he told them.

[14]Then some soldiers asked him, "And what should we do?"

He replied, "Don't extort money and don't accuse people falsely—be content with your pay."

4. Violence

Gen 6 [11]Now the earth was corrupt in God's sight and was full of violence. . . . [13]So God said to Noah, "I am going to put an end to all people, for the earth is filled with violence because of them. I am surely going to destroy both them and the earth."
Ps 7 [9]O righteous God, who searches minds and hearts, bring to an end the violence of the wicked and make the righteous secure.
Ps 11 [5]The LORD examines the righteous, but the wicked and those who love violence his soul hates.
Ps 73 [3]For I envied the arrogant when I saw the prosperity of the wicked. . . . [6]Therefore pride is their necklace; they clothe themselves with violence.
Ps 74 [20]Have regard for your covenant, because haunts of violence fill the dark places of the land.
Prov 13 [2]From the fruit of his lips a man enjoys good things, but the unfaithful have a craving for violence.
Prov 24 [1]Do not envy wicked men, do not desire their company; [2]for their hearts plot violence, and their lips talk about making trouble.
Isa 59 [1]Surely the arm of the LORD is not too short to save, nor his ear too dull to hear. [2]But your iniquities have separated you from your God; your sins have hidden his face from you, so that he will not hear. . . . [6]Their cobwebs are useless for clothing; they cannot cover themselves with what they make. Their deeds are evil deeds, and acts of violence are in their hands.
Ezek 7 [23]"Prepare chains, because the land is full of bloodshed and the city is full of violence. [24]I will bring the most wicked of the nations to take possession of their houses; I will put an end to the pride of the mighty, and their sanctuaries will be desecrated."
Ezek 8 [17]He said to me, "Have you seen this, son of man? Is it a trivial matter for the house of Judah to do the detestable things they are doing here? Must they also fill the land with violence and continually provoke me to anger? Look at them putting the branch to their nose!"
Jon 3 [8]"But let man and beast be covered with sackcloth. Let everyone call urgently on God. Let them give up their evil ways and their violence."
Hab 1 [2]How long, O LORD, must I call for help, but you do not listen? Or cry out to you, "Violence!" but you do not save? [3]Why do you make me look at injustice? Why do you tolerate wrong? Destruction and violence are before me; there is strife, and conflict abounds. [9]". . . they all come bent on violence. Their hordes advance like a desert wind and gather prisoners like sand."
Zeph 1 [9]"On that day I will punish all who avoid stepping on the threshold, who fill the temple of their gods with violence and deceit."

C. Sins of Deception

1. Flattery

Job 32 [20]"I must speak and find relief; I must open my lips and reply. [21]I will show partiality to no one, nor will I flatter any man; [22]for if I were skilled in flattery, my Maker would soon take me away."
Ps 12 [2]Everyone lies to his neighbor; their flattering lips speak with deception.

[3]May the LORD cut off all flattering lips and every boastful tongue. . . .

Ps 36 [2]For in his own eyes he flatters himself too much to detect or hate his sin.
Ps 78 [36]But then they would flatter him with their mouths, lying to him with their tongues. . . .
Prov 24 [24]Whoever says to the guilty, "You are innocent"—peoples will curse him and nations denounce him.
Prov 26 [28]A lying tongue hates those it hurts, and a flattering mouth works ruin.
Prov 28 [23]He who rebukes a man will in the end gain more favor than he who has a flattering tongue.
Prov 29 [5]Whoever flatters his neighbor is spreading a net for his feet.
Ezek 12 [24]"'For there will be no more false visions or flattering divinations among the people of Israel.'"
Dan 11 [32]"With flattery he will corrupt those who have violated the covenant, but the people who know their God will firmly resist him."
Rom 16 [18]For such people are not serving our Lord Christ, but their own appetites. By smooth talk and flattery they deceive the minds of naive people.
1 Thess 2 [5]You know we never used flattery, nor did we put on a mask to cover up greed—God is our witness.
Jude [16]These men are grumblers and faultfinders; they follow their own evil desires; they boast about themselves and flatter others for their own advantage.

2. Fraud and Dishonesty

Lev 19 [11]"'Do not steal.

"'Do not lie.

"'Do not deceive one another.'"

Lev 19 [35]"'Do not use dishonest standards when measuring length, weight or quantity. [36]Use honest scales and honest weights, an honest ephah and an honest hin. I am the LORD your God, who brought you out of Egypt.'"
Lev 25 [14]"'If you sell land to one of your countrymen or buy any from him, do not take advantage of each other.'"
Deut 19 [14]Do not move your neighbor's boundary stone set up by your predecessors in the inheritance you receive in the land the LORD your God is giving you to possess.
Deut 25 [13]Do not have two differing weights in your bag—one heavy, one light. [14]Do not have two differing measures in your house—one large, one small. [15]You must have accurate and honest weights and measures, so that you may live long in the land the LORD your God is giving you. [16]For the LORD your God detests anyone who does these things, anyone who deals dishonestly.
Deut 27 [17]"Cursed is the man who moves his neighbor's boundary stone." Then all the people shall say, "Amen!"
Job 24 [2]"Men move boundary stones; they pasture flocks they have stolen."
Ps 37 [21]The wicked borrow and do not repay, but the righteous give generously. . . .
Prov 11 [1]The LORD abhors dishonest scales, but accurate weights are his delight.
Prov 11 [26]People curse the man who hoards grain, but blessing crowns him who is willing to sell.
Prov 16 [11]Honest scales and balances are from the LORD; all the weights in the bag are of his making.
Prov 20 [14]"It's no good, it's no good!" says the buyer; then off he goes and boasts about his purchase. . . .

[17]Food gained by fraud tastes sweet to a man, but he ends up with a mouth full of gravel. . . .

[23]The LORD detests differing weights, and dishonest scales do not please him.

Prov 22 [28]Do not move an ancient boundary stone set up by your forefathers.
Prov 23 [10]Do not move an ancient boundary stone or encroach on the fields of the fatherless, [11]for their Defender is strong; he will take up their case against you.
Hos 12 [7]The merchant uses dishonest scales; he loves to defraud. [8]Ephraim boasts, "I am very rich; I have become wealthy. With all my wealth they will not find in me any iniquity or sin." . . . [14]But Ephraim has bitterly provoked him to anger; his Lord will leave upon him the guilt of his bloodshed and will repay him for his contempt.
Amos 8 [5]saying, "When will the New Moon be over that we may sell grain, and the Sabbath be ended that we may market wheat?"—skimping the measure, boosting the price and cheating with dishonest scales, [6]buying the poor with silver and the needy for a pair of sandals, selling even the sweepings with the wheat.

Mic 6 10"Am I still to forget, O wicked house, your ill-gotten treasures and the short ephah, which is accursed? 11Shall I acquit a man with dishonest scales, with a bag of false weights? 12Her rich men are violent; her people are liars and their tongues speak deceitfully. 13Therefore, I have begun to destroy you, to ruin you because of your sins."
Hab 2 6"Will not all of them taunt him with ridicule and scorn, saying, 'Woe to him who piles up stolen goods and makes himself wealthy by extortion! How long must this go on?'"
1 Cor 6 8Instead, you yourselves cheat and do wrong, and you do this to your brothers.
1 Thess 4 6and that in this matter no one should wrong his brother or take advantage of him. The Lord will punish men for all such sins, as we have already told you and warned you.
James 5 4Look! The wages you failed to pay the workmen who mowed your fields are crying out against you. The cries of the harvesters have reached the ears of the Lord Almighty.

3. Hypocrisy

Job 17 1"My spirit is broken, my days are cut short, the grave awaits me. 2Surely mockers surround me; my eyes must dwell on their hostility.

3"Give me, O God, the pledge you demand. Who else will put up security for me? 4You have closed their minds to understanding; therefore you will not let them triumph. 5If a man denounces his friends for reward, the eyes of his children will fail.

6"God has made me a byword to everyone, a man in whose face people spit. 7My eyes have grown dim with grief; my whole frame is but a shadow. 8Upright men are appalled at this; the innocent are aroused against the ungodly. 9Nevertheless, the righteous will hold to their ways, and those with clean hands will grow stronger."
Ps 5 9Not a word from their mouth can be trusted; their heart is filled with destruction. Their throat is an open grave; with their tongue they speak deceit.
Ps 26 4I do not sit with deceitful men, nor do I consort with hypocrites. . . .
Ps 50 16But to the wicked, God says: "What right have you to recite my laws or take my covenant on your lips? 17You hate my instruction and cast my words behind you. 18When you see a thief, you join with him; you throw in your lot with adulterers. 19You use your mouth for evil and harness your tongue to deceit. 20You speak continually against your brother and slander your own mother's son. 21These things you have done and I kept silent; you thought I was altogether like you. But I will rebuke you and accuse you to your face.

22"Consider this, you who forget God, or I will tear you to pieces, with none to rescue: 23He who sacrifices thank offerings honors me, and he prepares the way so that I may show him the salvation of God."
Isa 29 13The Lord says: "These people come near to me with their mouth and honor me with their lips, but their hearts are far from me. Their worship of me is made up only of rules taught by men."
Isa 32 5No longer will the fool be called noble nor the scoundrel be highly respected. 6For the fool speaks folly, his mind is busy with evil: He practices ungodliness and spreads error concerning the LORD; the hungry he leaves empty and from the thirsty he withholds water. 7The scoundrel's methods are wicked, he makes up evil schemes to destroy the poor with lies, even when the plea of the needy is just. 8But the noble man makes noble plans, and by noble deeds he stands.
Isa 48 1"Listen to this, O house of Jacob, you who are called by the name of Israel and come from the line of Judah, you who take oaths in the name of the LORD and invoke the God of Israel—but not in truth or righteousness. . . ."
Isa 58 1"Shout it aloud, do not hold back. Raise your voice like a trumpet. Declare to my people their rebellion and to the house of Jacob their sins. 2For day after day they seek me out; they seem eager to know my ways, as if they were a nation that does what is right and has not forsaken the commands of its God. They ask me for just decisions and seem eager for God to come near them."
Ezek 33 31"My people come to you, as they usually do, and sit before you to listen to your words, but they do not put them into practice. With their mouths they express devotion, but their hearts are greedy for unjust gain. 32Indeed, to them you are nothing more than one who sings love songs with a beautiful voice and plays an instrument well, for they hear your words but do not put them into practice."
Matt 6 24"No one can serve two masters. Either he will hate the one and love the other, or he will be devoted to the one and despise the other. You cannot serve both God and Money."
Matt 15 7"You hypocrites! Isaiah was right when he prophesied about you: 8'These people honor me with their lips, but their hearts are far from me. 9They worship me in vain; their teachings are but rules taught by men.'"
Matt 16 5When they went across the lake, the disciples forgot to take bread. 6"Be careful," Jesus said to them. "Be on your guard against the yeast of the Pharisees and Sadducees."

7They discussed this among themselves and said, "It is because we didn't bring any bread."

8Aware of their discussion, Jesus asked, "You of little faith, why are you talking among yourselves about having no bread? 9Do you still not understand? Don't you remember the five loaves for the five thousand, and how many basketfuls you gathered? 10Or the seven loaves for the four thousand, and how many basketfuls you gathered? 11How is it you don't understand that I was not talking to you about bread? But be on your guard against the yeast of the Pharisees and Sadducees." 12Then they understood that he was not telling them to guard against the yeast used in bread, but against the teaching of the Pharisees and Sadducees.
Matt 23 1Then Jesus said to the crowds and to his disciples: 2"The teachers of the law and the Pharisees sit in Moses' seat. 3So you must obey them and do everything they tell you. But do not do what they do, for they do not practice what they preach. 4They tie up heavy loads and put them on men's shoulders, but they themselves are not willing to lift a finger to move them.

5"Everything they do is done for men to see: They make their phylacteries wide and the tassels on their garments long; 6they love the place of honor at banquets and the most important seats in the synagogues; 7they love to be greeted in the marketplaces and to have men call them 'Rabbi.'

8"But you are not to be called 'Rabbi,' for you have only one Master and you are all brothers. 9And do not call anyone on earth 'father,' for you have one Father, and he is in heaven. 10Nor are you to be called 'teacher,' for you have one Teacher, the Christ. 11The greatest among you will be your servant. 12For whoever exalts himself will be humbled, and whoever humbles himself will be exalted.

13"Woe to you, teachers of the law and Pharisees, you hypocrites! You shut the kingdom of heaven in men's faces. You yourselves do not enter, nor will you let those enter who are trying to.

15"Woe to you, teachers of the law and Pharisees, you hypocrites! You travel over land and sea to win a single convert, and when he becomes one, you make him twice as much a son of hell as you are.

16"Woe to you, blind guides! You say, 'If anyone swears by the temple, it means nothing; but if anyone swears by the gold of the temple, he is bound by his oath.' 17You blind fools! Which is greater: the gold, or the temple that makes the gold sacred? 18You also say, 'If anyone swears by the altar, it means nothing; but if anyone swears by the gift on it, he is bound by his oath.' 19You blind men! Which is greater: the gift, or the altar that makes the gift sacred? 20Therefore, he who swears by the altar swears by it and by everything on it. 21And he who swears by the temple swears by it and by the one who dwells in it. 22And he who swears by heaven swears by God's throne and by the one who sits on it.

23"Woe to you, teachers of the law and Pharisees, you hypocrites! You give a tenth of your spices—mint, dill and cummin. But you have neglected the more important matters of the law—justice, mercy and faithfulness. You should have practiced the latter, without neglecting the former. 24You blind guides! You strain out a gnat but swallow a camel.

25"Woe to you, teachers of the law and Pharisees, you hypocrites! You clean the outside of the cup and dish, but inside they are full of greed and self-indulgence. 26Blind Pharisee! First clean the inside of the cup and dish, and then the outside also will be clean.

27"Woe to you, teachers of the law and Pharisees, you hypocrites! You are like whitewashed tombs, which look beautiful on the outside but on the inside are full of dead men's bones and everything unclean. 28In the same way, on the outside you appear to people as righteous but on the inside you are full of hypocrisy and wickedness.

29"Woe to you, teachers of the law and Pharisees, you hypocrites! You build tombs for the prophets and decorate the graves of the righteous. 30And you say, 'If we had lived in the days of our forefathers, we would not have taken part with them in shedding the blood of the prophets.' 31So you testify against yourselves that you are the descendants of those who murdered the prophets. 32Fill up, then, the measure of the sin of your forefathers!

33"You snakes! You brood of vipers! How will you escape being condemned to hell? 34Therefore I am sending you prophets and wise men and teachers. Some of them you will kill and crucify; others you will flog in your synagogues and pursue from town to town. 35And so upon you will come all the righteous blood that has been shed on earth, from the blood of righteous Abel to the blood of Zechariah son of Berekiah, whom you murdered between the temple and the altar."

Rom 2 17Now you, if you call yourself a Jew; if you rely on the law and brag about your relationship to God; 18if you know his will and approve of what is superior because you are instructed by the law; 19if you are convinced that you are a guide for the blind, a light for those who are in the dark, 20an instructor of the foolish, a teacher of infants, because you have in the law the embodiment of knowledge and truth—21you, then, who teach others, do you not teach yourself? You who preach against stealing, do you steal? 22You who say that people should not commit adultery, do you commit adultery? You who abhor idols, do you rob temples? 23You who brag about the law, do you dishonor God by breaking the law? 24As it is written: "God's name is blasphemed among the Gentiles because of you."

Gal 2 13The other Jews joined him in his hypocrisy, so that by their hypocrisy even Barnabas was led astray.

1 Tim 4 2Such teachings come through hypocritical liars, whose consciences have been seared as with a hot iron.

Titus 1 16They claim to know God, but by their actions they deny him. They are detestable, disobedient and unfit for doing anything good.

1 Pet 2 1Therefore, rid yourselves of all malice and all deceit, hypocrisy, envy, and slander of every kind.

4. Lying and Falsity

Exod 20 16"You shall not give false testimony against your neighbor."

Job 15 35"They conceive trouble and give birth to evil; their womb fashions deceit."

Job 21 34"So how can you console me with your nonsense? Nothing is left of your answers but falsehood!"

Job 24 25"If this is not so, who can prove me false and reduce my words to nothing?"

Job 31 33". . . if I have concealed my sin as men do, by hiding my guilt in my heart . . ."

Ps 5 6You destroy those who tell lies; bloodthirsty and deceitful men the Lord abhors.

Ps 31 18Let their lying lips be silenced, for with pride and contempt they speak arrogantly against the righteous.

Ps 50 19"You use your mouth for evil and harness your tongue to deceit."

Ps 52 2Your tongue plots destruction; it is like a sharpened razor, you who practice deceit. 3You love evil rather than good, falsehood rather than speaking the truth. 4You love every harmful word, O you deceitful tongue!

Ps 55 20My companion attacks his friends; he violates his covenant. 21His speech is smooth as butter, yet war is in his heart; his words are more soothing than oil, yet they are drawn swords.

Ps 62 4They fully intend to topple him from his lofty place; they take delight in lies. With their mouths they bless, but in their hearts they curse.

Ps 63 11But the king will rejoice in God; all who swear by God's name will praise him, while the mouths of liars will be silenced.

Ps 116 11And in my dismay I said, "All men are liars."

Ps 119 69Though the arrogant have smeared me with lies, I keep your precepts with all my heart.

Ps 120 3What will he do to you, and what more besides, O deceitful tongue? 4He will punish you with a warrior's sharp arrows, with burning coals of the broom tree.

Prov 2 12Wisdom will save you from the ways of wicked men, from men whose words are perverse, 13who leave the straight paths to walk in dark ways, 14who delight in doing wrong and rejoice in the perverseness of evil, 15whose paths are crooked and who are devious in their ways.

Prov 6 16There are six things the Lord hates, seven that are detestable to him: 17haughty eyes, a lying tongue, hands that shed innocent blood . . . 19a false witness who pours out lies and a man who stirs up dissension among brothers.

Prov 10 18He who conceals his hatred has lying lips, and whoever spreads slander is a fool.

Prov 12 22The Lord detests lying lips, but he delights in men who are truthful.

Prov 17 4A wicked man listens to evil lips; a liar pays attention to a malicious tongue.

Prov 19 22What a man desires is unfailing love; better to be poor than a liar.

Prov 21 6A fortune made by a lying tongue is a fleeting vapor and a deadly snare.

Prov 26 23Like a coating of glaze over earthenware are fervent lips with an evil heart.

24A malicious man disguises himself with his lips, but in his heart he harbors deceit. 25Though his speech is charming, do not believe him, for seven abominations fill his heart. 26His malice may be concealed by deception, but his wickedness will be exposed in the assembly.

Isa 59 2But your iniquities have separated you from your God; your sins have hidden his face from you, so that he will not hear. 3For your hands are stained with blood, your fingers with guilt. Your lips have spoken lies, and your tongue mutters wicked things.

Jer 5 2"Although they say, 'As surely as the Lord lives,' still they are swearing falsely."

Jer 7 8"'But look, you are trusting in deceptive words that are worthless.'"

Jer 9 3"They make ready their tongue like a bow, to shoot lies; it is not by truth that they triumph in the land. They go from one sin to another; they do not acknowledge me," declares the Lord. 4"Beware of your friends; do not trust your brothers. For every brother is a deceiver, and every friend a slanderer. 5Friend deceives friend, and no one speaks the truth. They have taught their tongues to lie; they weary themselves with sinning. 6You live in the midst of deception; in their deceit they refuse to acknowledge me," declares the Lord.

Hos 4 1Hear the word of the Lord, you Israelites, because the Lord has a charge to bring against you who live in the land: "There is no faithfulness, no love, no acknowledgment of God in the land. 2There is only cursing, lying and murder, stealing and adultery; they break all bounds, and bloodshed follows bloodshed."

Hos 11 12Ephraim has surrounded me with lies, the house of Israel with deceit. And Judah is unruly against God, even against the faithful Holy One.

Zech 8 16"These are the things you are to do: Speak the truth to each other, and render true and sound judgment in your courts; 17do not plot evil against your neighbor, and do not love to swear falsely. I hate all this," declares the Lord.

Acts 5 7About three hours later his wife came in, not knowing what had happened. 8Peter asked her, "Tell me, is this the price you and Ananias got for the land?"

"Yes," she said, "that is the price."

9Peter said to her, "How could you agree to test the Spirit of the Lord? Look! The feet of the men who buried your husband are at the door, and they will carry you out also."

Eph 4 25Therefore each of you must put off falsehood and

speak truthfully to his neighbor, for we are all members of one body.
Col 3 [9]Do not lie to each other, since you have taken off your old self with its practices. . . .
Rev 21 [8]"But the cowardly, the unbelieving, the vile, the murderers, the sexually immoral, those who practice magic arts, the idolaters and all liars—their place will be in the fiery lake of burning sulfur. This is the second death."
Rev 22 [15]"Outside are the dogs, those who practice magic arts, the sexually immoral, the murderers, the idolaters and everyone who loves and practices falsehood."

5. Tempting Others to Sin

Num 25 [1]While Israel was staying in Shittim, the men began to indulge in sexual immorality with Moabite women, [2]who invited them to the sacrifices to their gods. The people ate and bowed down before these gods.
Neh 6 [13]He had been hired to intimidate me so that I would commit a sin by doing this, and then they would give me a bad name to discredit me.
Prov 1 [10]My son, if sinners entice you, do not give in to them. [11]If they say, "Come along with us; let's lie in wait for someone's blood, let's waylay some harmless soul; [12]let's swallow them alive, like the grave, and whole, like those who go down to the pit; [13]we will get all sorts of valuable things and fill our houses with plunder; [14]throw in your lot with us, and we will share a common purse"—[15]my son, do not go along with them, do not set foot on their paths; [16]for their feet rush into sin, they are swift to shed blood.
Prov 4 [14]Do not set foot on the path of the wicked or walk in the way of evil men. [15]Avoid it, do not travel on it; turn from it and go on your way. . . . [25]Let your eyes look straight ahead, fix your gaze directly before you. [26]Make level paths for your feet and take only ways that are firm. [27]Do not swerve to the right or the left; keep your foot from evil.
Prov 16 [29]A violent man entices his neighbor and leads him down a path that is not good.
Prov 28 [10]He who leads the upright along an evil path will fall into his own trap, but the blameless will receive a good inheritance.
Isa 33 [15]He who walks righteously and speaks what is right, who rejects gain from extortion and keeps his hand from accepting bribes, who stops his ears against plots of murder and shuts his eyes against contemplating evil—[16]this is the man who will dwell on the heights, whose refuge will be the mountain fortress. His bread will be supplied, and water will not fail him.
Jer 20 [10]I hear many whispering, "Terror on every side! Report him! Let's report him!" All my friends are waiting for me to slip, saying, "Perhaps he will be deceived; then we will prevail over him and take our revenge on him."
Hab 2 [15]"Woe to him who gives drink to his neighbors, pouring it from the wineskin till they are drunk, so that he can gaze on their naked bodies."
Matt 18 [6]"But if anyone causes one of these little ones who believe in me to sin, it would be better for him to have a large millstone hung around his neck and to be drowned in the depths of the sea.

[7]"Woe to the world because of the things that cause people to sin! Such things must come, but woe to the man through whom they come! [8]If your hand or your foot causes you to sin, cut it off and throw it away. It is better for you to enter life maimed or crippled than to have two hands or two feet and be thrown into eternal fire. [9]And if your eye causes you to sin, gouge it out and throw it away. It is better for you to enter life with one eye than to have two eyes and be thrown into the fire of hell."
Luke 17 [1]Jesus said to his disciples: "Things that cause people to sin are bound to come, but woe to that person through whom they come. [2]It would be better for him to be thrown into the sea with a millstone tied around his neck than for him to cause one of these little ones to sin."
Rom 14 [13]Therefore let us stop passing judgment on one another. Instead, make up your mind not to put any stumbling block or obstacle in your brother's way. . . . [20]Do not destroy the work of God for the sake of food. All food is clean, but it is wrong for a man to eat anything that causes someone else to stumble. [21]It is better not to eat meat or drink wine or to do anything else that will cause your brother to fall.
1 Cor 8 [9]Be careful, however, that the exercise of your freedom does not become a stumbling block to the weak. . . . [12]When you sin against your brothers in this way and wound their weak conscience, you sin against Christ. [13]Therefore, if what I eat causes my brother to fall into sin, I will never eat meat again, so that I will not cause him to fall.
1 Tim 5 [22]Do not be hasty in the laying on of hands, and do not share in the sins of others. Keep yourself pure.
1 John 2 [26]I am writing these things to you about those who are trying to lead you astray.
Rev 2 [14]"Nevertheless, I have a few things against you: You have people there who hold to the teaching of Balaam, who taught Balak to entice the Israelites to sin by eating food sacrificed to idols and by committing sexual immorality."

D. Sins of Desire

1. Covetousness and Greed

Exod 20 [17]"You shall not covet your neighbor's house. You shall not covet your neighbor's wife, or his manservant or maidservant, his ox or donkey, or anything that belongs to your neighbor."
Deut 5 [21]"You shall not covet your neighbor's wife. You shall not set your desire on your neighbor's house or land, his manservant or maidservant, his ox or donkey, or anything that belongs to your neighbor."
Ps 10 [3]He boasts of the cravings of his heart; he blesses the greedy and reviles the LORD.
Ps 119 [36]Turn my heart toward your statutes and not toward selfish gain.
Prov 1 [18]These men lie in wait for their own blood; they waylay only themselves! [19]Such is the end of all who go after ill-gotten gain; it takes away the lives of those who get it.
Prov 15 [27]A greedy man brings trouble to his family, but he who hates bribes will live.
Prov 27 [20]Death and Destruction are never satisfied, and neither are the eyes of man.
Eccles 4 [8]There was a man all alone; he had neither son nor brother. There was no end to his toil, yet his eyes were not content with his wealth. "For whom am I toiling," he asked, "and why am I depriving myself of enjoyment?" This too is meaningless—a miserable business!
Eccles 5 [10]Whoever loves money never has money enough; whoever loves wealth is never satisfied with his income. This too is meaningless.
Isa 5 [8]Woe to you who add house to house and join field to field till no space is left and you live alone in the land. [9]The LORD Almighty has declared in my hearing: "Surely the great houses will become desolate, the fine mansions left without occupants. [10]A ten-acre vineyard will produce only a bath of wine, a homer of seed only an ephah of grain."
Isa 57 [17]"I was enraged by his sinful greed; I punished him, and hid my face in anger, yet he kept on in his willful ways."
Jer 8 [10]"'Therefore I will give their wives to other men and their fields to new owners. From the least to the greatest, all are greedy for gain; prophets and priests alike, all practice deceit.'"
Jer 22 [17]"But your eyes and your heart are set only on dishonest gain, on shedding innocent blood and on oppression and extortion."
Mic 2 [1]Woe to those who plan iniquity, to those who plot evil on their beds! At morning's light they carry it out because it is in their power to do it. [2]They covet fields and seize them, and houses, and take them. They defraud a man of his home, a fellowman of his inheritance.
Hab 2 [9]"Woe to him who builds his realm by unjust gain to set his nest on high, to escape the clutches of ruin! [10]You have plotted the ruin of many peoples, shaming your own house and forfeiting your life."
Matt 16 [26]"What good will it be for a man if he gains the whole world, yet forfeits his soul? Or what can a man give in exchange for his soul?"

Mark 7 [22]". . . greed, malice, deceit, lewdness, envy, slander, arrogance and folly. [23]All these evils come from inside and make a man 'unclean.'"
Luke 12 [15]Then he said to them, "Watch out! Be on your guard against all kinds of greed; a man's life does not consist in the abundance of his possessions."
Luke 16 [13]"No servant can serve two masters. Either he will hate the one and love the other, or he will be devoted to the one and despise the other. You cannot serve both God and Money."

[14]The Pharisees, who loved money, heard all this and were sneering at Jesus. [15]He said to them, "You are the ones who justify yourselves in the eyes of men, but God knows your hearts. What is highly valued among men is detestable in God's sight."
Rom 7 [7]What shall we say, then? Is the law sin? Certainly not! Indeed I would not have known what sin was except through the law. For I would not have known what coveting really was if the law had not said, "Do not covet."
Rom 13 [9]The commandments, "Do not commit adultery," "Do not murder," "Do not steal," "Do not covet," and whatever other commandment there may be, are summed up in this one rule: "Love your neighbor as yourself."
1 Cor 5 [11]But now I am writing you that you must not associate with anyone who calls himself a brother but is sexually immoral or greedy, an idolater or a slanderer, a drunkard or a swindler. With such a man do not even eat.
1 Cor 6 [9]Do you not know that the wicked will not inherit the kingdom of God? Do not be deceived: Neither the sexually immoral nor idolaters nor adulterers nor male prostitutes nor homosexual offenders [10]nor thieves nor the greedy nor drunkards nor slanderers nor swindlers will inherit the kingdom of God.
Eph 5 [3]But among you there must not be even a hint of sexual immorality, or of any kind of impurity, or of greed, because these are improper for God's holy people. . . . [5]For of this you can be sure: No immoral, impure or greedy person—such a man is an idolater—has any inheritance in the kingdom of Christ and of God.
Phil 2 [4]Each of you should look not only to your own interests, but also to the interests of others.
Col 3 [5]Put to death, therefore, whatever belongs to your earthly nature: sexual immorality, impurity, lust, evil desires and greed, which is idolatry.
1 Tim 6 [9]People who want to get rich fall into temptation and a trap and into many foolish and harmful desires that plunge men into ruin and destruction. [10]For the love of money is a root of all kinds of evil. Some people, eager for money, have wandered from the faith and pierced themselves with many griefs.
Heb 13 [5]Keep your lives free from the love of money and be content with what you have, because God has said, "Never will I leave you; never will I forsake you."
2 Pet 2 [14]With eyes full of adultery, they never stop sinning; they seduce the unstable; they are experts in greed—an accursed brood! [15]They have left the straight way and wandered off to follow the way of Balaam son of Beor, who loved the wages of wickedness.
Jude [11]Woe to them! They have taken the way of Cain; they have rushed for profit into Balaam's error; they have been destroyed in Korah's rebellion.

2. Envy and Jealousy

Num 11 [28]Joshua son of Nun, who had been Moses' aide since youth, spoke up and said, "Moses, my lord, stop them!"

[29]But Moses replied, "Are you jealous for my sake? I wish that all the LORD's people were prophets and that the LORD would put his Spirit on them!" [30]Then Moses and the elders of Israel returned to the camp.
Num 12 [2]"Has the LORD spoken only through Moses?" they asked. "Hasn't he also spoken through us?" And the LORD heard this.
Job 5 [2]"Resentment kills a fool, and envy slays the simple."
Ps 37 [1]Do not fret because of evil men or be envious of those who do wrong. . . .
Ps 73 [2]But as for me, my feet had almost slipped; I had nearly lost my foothold. [3]For I envied the arrogant when I saw the prosperity of the wicked.
Ps 106 [16]In the camp they grew envious of Moses and of Aaron, who was consecrated to the LORD.
Prov 3 [31]Do not envy a violent man or choose any of his ways. . . .
Prov 14 [30]A heart at peace gives life to the body, but envy rots the bones.
Prov 23 [17]Do not let your heart envy sinners, but always be zealous for the fear of the LORD.
Prov 24 [1]Do not envy wicked men, do not desire their company. . . .

[19]Do not fret because of evil men or be envious of the wicked. . . .
Prov 27 [4]Anger is cruel and fury overwhelming, but who can stand before jealousy?
Eccles 4 [4]And I saw that all labor and all achievement spring from man's envy of his neighbor. This too is meaningless, a chasing after the wind.
Isa 11 [13]Ephraim's jealousy will vanish, and Judah's enemies will be cut off; Ephraim will not be jealous of Judah, nor Judah hostile toward Ephraim.
Mark 15 [9]"Do you want me to release to you the king of the Jews?" asked Pilate, [10]knowing it was out of envy that the chief priests had handed Jesus over to him.
Acts 5 [17]Then the high priest and all his associates, who were members of the party of the Sadducees, were filled with jealousy. [18]They arrested the apostles and put them in the public jail.
Acts 7 [9]"Because the patriarchs were jealous of Joseph, they sold him as a slave into Egypt. But God was with him. . . ."
Acts 13 [45]When the Jews saw the crowds, they were filled with jealousy and talked abusively against what Paul was saying.
Acts 17 [5]But the Jews were jealous; so they rounded up some bad characters from the marketplace, formed a mob and started a riot in the city. They rushed to Jason's house in search of Paul and Silas in order to bring them out to the crowd.
Rom 1 [29]They have become filled with every kind of wickedness, evil, greed and depravity. They are full of envy, murder, strife, deceit and malice. They are gossips. . . .
Rom 13 [13]Let us behave decently, as in the daytime, not in orgies and drunkenness, not in sexual immorality and debauchery, not in dissension and jealousy.
1 Cor 3 [3]You are still worldly. For since there is jealousy and quarreling among you, are you not worldly? Are you not acting like mere men?
2 Cor 12 [20]For I am afraid that when I come I may not find you as I want you to be, and you may not find me as you want me to be. I fear that there may be quarreling, jealousy, outbursts of anger, factions, slander, gossip, arrogance and disorder.
Gal 5 [26]Let us not become conceited, provoking and envying each other.
Phil 1 [15]It is true that some preach Christ out of envy and rivalry, but others out of goodwill.
1 Tim 6 [3]If anyone teaches false doctrines and does not agree to the sound instruction of our Lord Jesus Christ and to godly teaching, [4]he is conceited and understands nothing. He has an unhealthy interest in controversies and quarrels about words that result in envy, strife, malicious talk, evil suspicions. . . .
Titus 3 [3]At one time we too were foolish, disobedient, deceived and enslaved by all kinds of passions and pleasures. We lived in malice and envy, being hated and hating one another.
James 3 [14]But if you harbor bitter envy and selfish ambition in your hearts, do not boast about it or deny the truth. [15]Such "wisdom" does not come down from heaven but is earthly, unspiritual, of the devil. [16]For where you have envy and selfish ambition, there you find disorder and every evil practice.
1 Pet 2 [1]Therefore, rid yourselves of all malice and all deceit, hypocrisy, envy, and slander of every kind.

3. Theft and Kidnapping

Exod 20 [15]"You shall not steal."
Exod 21 [16]"Anyone who kidnaps another and either sells him or still has him when he is caught must be put to death."

Exod 22 [1]"If a man steals an ox or a sheep and slaughters it or sells it, he must pay back five head of cattle for the ox and four sheep for the sheep.

[2]"If a thief is caught breaking in and is struck so that he dies, the defender is not guilty of bloodshed. . . .

[7]"If a man gives his neighbor silver or goods for safekeeping and they are stolen from the neighbor's house, the thief, if he is caught, must pay back double."

Lev 19 [13]"'Do not defraud your neighbor or rob him.

"'Do not hold back the wages of a hired man overnight.'"

Deut 24 [7]If a man is caught kidnapping one of his brother Israelites and treats him as a slave or sells him, the kidnapper must die. You must purge the evil from among you.

Josh 7 [11]"Israel has sinned; they have violated my covenant, which I commanded them to keep. They have taken some of the devoted things; they have stolen, they have lied, they have put them with their own possessions. [12]That is why the Israelites cannot stand against their enemies; they turn their backs and run because they have been made liable to destruction. I will not be with you anymore unless you destroy whatever among you is devoted to destruction."

Job 5 [5]"The hungry consume his harvest, taking it even from among thorns, and the thirsty pant after his wealth."

Ps 50 [18]"When you see a thief, you join with him; you throw in your lot with adulterers."

Ps 62 [10]Do not trust in extortion or take pride in stolen goods; though your riches increase, do not set your heart on them.

Prov 6 [30]Men do not despise a thief if he steals to satisfy his hunger when he is starving.

Prov 29 [24]The accomplice of a thief is his own enemy; he is put under oath and dare not testify.

Prov 30 [8]"Keep falsehood and lies far from me; give me neither poverty nor riches, but give me only my daily bread. [9]Otherwise, I may have too much and disown you and say, 'Who is the LORD?' Or I may become poor and steal, and so dishonor the name of my God."

Isa 10 [1]Woe to those who make unjust laws, to those who issue oppressive decrees, [2]to deprive the poor of their rights and withhold justice from the oppressed of my people, making widows their prey and robbing the fatherless.

Isa 17 [14]In the evening, sudden terror! Before the morning, they are gone! This is the portion of those who loot us, the lot of those who plunder us.

Isa 61 [8]"For I, the LORD, love justice; I hate robbery and iniquity. In my faithfulness I will reward them and make an everlasting covenant with them."

Jer 7 [9]"'Will you steal and murder, commit adultery and perjury, burn incense to Baal and follow other gods you have not known, [10]and then come and stand before me in this house, which bears my Name, and say, "We are safe"—safe to do all these detestable things?'"

Ezek 18 [10]"Suppose he has a violent son, who sheds blood or does any of these other things. . . . [12]He oppresses the poor and needy. He commits robbery. He does not return what he took in pledge. He looks to the idols. He does detestable things. [13]He lends at usury and takes excessive interest. Will such a man live? He will not! Because he has done all these detestable things, he will surely be put to death and his blood will be on his own head."

Ezek 22 [29]"The people of the land practice extortion and commit robbery; they oppress the poor and needy and mistreat the alien, denying them justice."

Hos 4 [2]"There is only cursing, lying and murder, stealing and adultery; they break all bounds, and bloodshed follows bloodshed."

Amos 3 [10]"They do not know how to do right," declares the LORD, "who hoard plunder and loot in their fortresses."

[11]Therefore this is what the Sovereign LORD says: "An enemy will overrun the land; he will pull down your strongholds and plunder your fortresses."

Nah 3 [1]Woe to the city of blood, full of lies, full of plunder, never without victims!

Zech 5 [3]And he said to me, "This is the curse that is going out over the whole land; for according to what it says on one side, every thief will be banished, and according to what it says on the other, everyone who swears falsely will be banished. [4]The LORD Almighty declares, 'I will send it out, and it will enter the house of the thief and the house of him who swears falsely by my name. It will remain in his house and destroy it, both its timbers and its stones.'"

Luke 19 [8]But Zacchaeus stood up and said to the Lord, "Look, Lord! Here and now I give half of my possessions to the poor, and if I have cheated anybody out of anything, I will pay back four times the amount."

1 Cor 6 [9]Do you not know that the wicked will not inherit the kingdom of God? Do not be deceived: Neither the sexually immoral nor idolaters nor adulterers nor male prostitutes nor homosexual offenders [10]nor thieves nor the greedy nor drunkards nor slanderers nor swindlers will inherit the kingdom of God.

1 Tim 1 [9]We also know that law is made not for the righteous but for lawbreakers and rebels, the ungodly and sinful, the unholy and irreligious; for those who kill their fathers or mothers, for murderers, [10]for adulterers and perverts, for slave traders and liars and perjurers—and for whatever else is contrary to the sound doctrine. . . .

VIII
Sins of the Flesh

A. Sins of the Flesh Are Defined

1. Adultery

Lev 18 [20]"'Do not have sexual relations with your neighbor's wife and defile yourself with her.'"

Lev 20 [10]"'If a man commits adultery with another man's wife—with the wife of his neighbor—both the adulterer and the adulteress must be put to death.'"

Deut 5 [18]"You shall not commit adultery."

Jer 7 [9]"'Will you steal and murder, commit adultery and perjury, burn incense to Baal and follow other gods you have not known, [10]and then come and stand before me in this house, which bears my Name, and say, "We are safe"—safe to do all these detestable things?'"

Ezek 16 [32]"'You adulterous wife! You prefer strangers to your own husband! [33]Every prostitute receives a fee, but you give gifts to all your lovers, bribing them to come to you from everywhere for your illicit favors.'"

Matt 5 [27]"You have heard that it was said, 'Do not commit adultery.' [28]But I tell you that anyone who looks at a woman lustfully has already committed adultery with her in his heart."

Mark 10 [11]He answered, "Anyone who divorces his wife and marries another woman commits adultery against her. [12]And if she divorces her husband and marries another man, she commits adultery."

Rom 2 [22]You who say that people should not commit adultery, do you commit adultery? You who abhor idols, do you rob temples?

2. Bestiality

Exod 22 [19]"Anyone who has sexual relations with an animal must be put to death."

Lev 18 [23]"'Do not have sexual relations with an animal and defile yourself with it. A woman must not present herself to an animal to have sexual relations with it; that is a perversion.'"

Lev 20 [15]"'If a man has sexual relations with an animal, he must be put to death, and you must kill the animal.

[16]"'If a woman approaches an animal to have sexual relations with it, kill both the woman and the animal. They must be put to death; their blood will be on their own heads.'"

Deut 27 [21]"Cursed is the man who has sexual relations with any animal."

Then all the people shall say, "Amen!"

3. Homosexuality

Lev 18 [22]"'Do not lie with a man as one lies with a woman; that is detestable.'"

Lev 20 [13]"'If a man lies with a man as one lies with a woman, both of them have done what is detestable. They must be put to death; their blood will be on their own heads.'"
Judg 19 [22]While they were enjoying themselves, some of the wicked men of the city surrounded the house. Pounding on the door, they shouted to the old man who owned the house, "Bring out the man who came to your house so we can have sex with him."

[23]The owner of the house went outside and said to them, "No, my friends, don't be so vile. Since this man is my guest, don't do this disgraceful thing."
Rom 1 [24]Therefore God gave them over in the sinful desires of their hearts to sexual impurity for the degrading of their bodies with one another. . . .

[26]Because of this, God gave them over to shameful lusts. Even their women exchanged natural relations for unnatural ones. [27]In the same way the men also abandoned natural relations with women and were inflamed with lust for one another. Men committed indecent acts with other men, and received in themselves the due penalty for their perversion.
1 Cor 6 [9]Do you not know that the wicked will not inherit the kingdom of God? Do not be deceived: Neither the sexually immoral nor idolaters nor adulterers nor male prostitutes nor homosexual offenders [10]nor theives nor the greedy nor drunkards nor slanderers nor swindlers will inherit the kingdom of God.
1 Tim 1 [9]We also know that law is made not for the righteous but for lawbreakers and rebels, the ungodly and sinful, the unholy and irreligious; for those who kill their fathers or mothers, for murderers, [10]for adulterers and perverts, for slave traders and liars and perjurers—and for whatever else is contrary to the sound doctrine. . . .

4. Incest

Lev 18 [6]"'No one is to approach any close relative to have sexual relations. I am the LORD.

[7]"'Do not dishonor your father by having sexual relations with your mother. She is your mother; do not have relations with her.

[8]"'Do not have sexual relations with your father's wife; that would dishonor your father.

[9]"'Do not have sexual relations with your sister, either your father's daughter or your mother's daughter, whether she was born in the same home or elsewhere.

[10]"'Do not have sexual relations with your son's daughter or your daughter's daughter; that would dishonor you.

[11]"'Do not have sexual relations with the daughter of your father's wife, born to your father; she is your sister.

[12]"'Do not have sexual relations with your father's sister; she is your father's close relative.

[13]"'Do not have sexual relations with you mother's sister, because she is your mother's close relative.

[14]"'Do not dishonor your father's brother by approaching his wife to have sexual relations; she is your aunt.

[15]"'Do not have sexual relations with your daughter-in-law. She is your son's wife; do not have relations with her.'"
Lev 20 [11]"'If a man sleeps with his father's wife, he has dishonored his father. Both the man and the woman must be put to death; their blood will be on their own heads.

[12]"'If a man sleeps with his daughter-in-law, both of them must be put to death. What they have done is a perversion; their blood will be on their own heads.'"
Deut 27 [20]"Cursed is the man who sleeps with his father's wife, for he dishonors his father's bed."

Then all the people shall say, "Amen!" . . .

[22]"Cursed is the man who sleeps with his sister, the daughter of his father or the daughter of his mother."

Then all the people shall say, "Amen!"

[23]"Cursed is the man who sleeps with his mother-in-law."

Then all the people shall say, "Amen!"
1 Cor 5 [1]It is actually reported that there is sexual immorality among you, and of a kind that does not occur even among pagans: A man has his father's wife. . . . [4]When you are assembled in the name of our Lord Jesus and I am with you in spirit, and the power of our Lord Jesus is present, [5]hand this man over to Satan, so that the sinful nature may be destroyed and his spirit saved on the day of the Lord.

5. Lust

Matt 5 [28]"But I tell you that anyone who looks at a woman lustfully has already committed adultery with her in his heart."
Rom 1 [26]Because of this, God gave them over to shameful lusts. Even their women exchanged natural relations for unnatural ones.
1 Thess 4 [3]It is God's will that you should be sanctified: that you should avoid sexual immorality; [4]that each of you should learn to control his own body in a way that is holy and honorable, [5]not in passionate lust like the heathen, who do not know God. . . .
1 Pet 4 [3]For you have spent enough time in the past doing what pagans choose to do—living in debauchery, lust, drunkenness, orgies, carousing and detestable idolatry.
2 Pet 2 [18]For they mouth empty, boastful words and, by appealing to the lustful desires of sinful human nature, they entice people who are just escaping from those who live in error.

6. Prostitution

Lev 19 [29]"'Do not degrade your daughter by making her a prostitute, or the land will turn to prostitution and be filled with wickedness.'"
Deut 23 [17]No Israelite man or woman is to become a shrine prostitute. [18]You must not bring the earnings of a female prostitute or of a male prostitute into the house of the LORD your God to pay any vow, because the LORD your God detests them both.
1 Kings 14 [22]Judah did evil in the eyes of the LORD. By the sins they committed they stirred up his jealous anger more than their fathers had done. . . . [24]There were even male shrine prostitutes in the land; the people engaged in all the detestable practices of the nations the LORD had driven out before the Israelites.
Job 36 [13]"The godless in heart harbor resentment; even when he fetters them, they do not cry for help. [14]They die in their youth, among male prostitutes of the shrines."
Ezek 16 [15]"'But you trusted in your beauty and used your fame to become a prostitute. You lavished your favors on anyone who passed by and your beauty became his. [16]You took some of your garments to make gaudy high places, where you carried on your prostitution. Such things should not happen, nor should they ever occur. [17]You also took the fine jewelry I gave you, the jewelry made of my gold and silver, and you made for yourself male idols and engaged in prostitution with them. [18]And you took your embroidered clothes to put on them, and you offered my oil and incense before them. [19]Also the food I provided for you—the fine flour, olive oil and honey I gave you to eat—you offered as fragrant incense before them. That is what happened, declares the Sovereign LORD.'"

7. Rape

Deut 22 [25]But if out in the country a man happens to meet a girl pledged to be married and rapes her, only the man who has done this shall die. [26]Do nothing to the girl; she has committed no sin deserving death.
Judg 19 [25]But the men would not listen to him. So the man took his concubine and sent her outside to them, and they raped her and abused her throughout the night, and at dawn they let her go. [26]At daybreak the woman went back to the house where her master was staying, fell down at the door and lay there until daylight.
Judg 20 [3]. . . Then the Israelites said, "Tell us how this awful thing happened."

[4]So the Levite, the husband of the murdered woman, said, "I and my concubine came to Gibeah in Benjamin to spend the night. [5]During the night the men of Gibeah came after me and surrounded the house, intending to kill me. They raped my concubine, and she died. . . .

[12]The tribes of Israel sent men throughout the tribe of

Benjamin, saying, "What about this awful crime that was committed among you?"
2 Sam 13 [12]"Don't, my brother!" she said to him. "Don't force me. Such a thing should not be done in Israel! Don't do this wicked thing. [13]What about me? Where could I get rid of my disgrace? And what about you? You would be like one of the wicked fools in Israel. Please speak to the king; he will not keep me from being married to you." [14]But he refused to listen to her, and since he was stronger than she, he raped her.

8. Sexual Immorality

Ezek 16 [26]"'You engaged in prostitution with the Egyptians, your lustful neighbors, and provoked me to anger with your increasing promiscuity. [27]So I stretched out my hand against you and reduced your territory; I gave you over to the greed of your enemies, the daughters of the Philistines, who were shocked by your lewd conduct. . . . [34]So in your prostitution you are the opposite of others; no one runs after you for your favors. You are the very opposite, for you give payment and none is given to you.'"
2 Cor 12 [21]I am afraid that when I come again my God will humble me before you, and I will be grieved over many who have sinned earlier and have not repented of the impurity, sexual sin and debauchery in which they have indulged.
Gal 5 [19]The acts of the sinful nature are obvious: Sexual immorality, impurity and debauchery. . . .
Eph 4 [17]So I tell you this, and insist on it in the Lord, that you must no longer live as the Gentiles do, in the futility of their thinking. [18]They are darkened in their understanding and separated from the life of God because of the ignorance that is in them due to the hardening of their hearts. [19]Having lost all sensitivity, they have given themselves over to sensuality so as to indulge in every kind of impurity, with a continual lust for more.
2 Tim 3 [6]They are the kind who worm their way into homes and gain control over weak-willed women, who are loaded down with sins and are swayed by all kinds of evil desires, [7]always learning but never able to acknowledge the truth.
1 Pet 4 [1]Therefore, since Christ suffered in his body, arm yourselves also with the same attitude, because he who has suffered in his own body is done with sin. [2]As a result, he does not live the rest of his earthly life for evil human desires, but rather for the will of God. [3]For you have spent enough time in the past doing what pagans choose to do—living in debauchery, lust, drunkenness, orgies, carousing and detestable idolatry.
Jude [4]For certain men whose condemnation was written about long ago have secretly slipped in among you. They are godless men, who change the grace of our God into a license for immorality and deny Jesus Christ our only Sovereign and Lord. . . . [18]They [the apostles] said to you, "In the last times there will be scoffers who will follow their own ungodly desires." [19]These are the men who divide you, who follow mere natural instincts and do not have the Spirit.

B. Sexual Sins Are Forbidden

Exod 20 [14]"You shall not commit adultery."
Lev 18 [20]"'Do not have sexual relations with your neighbor's wife and defile yourself with her. . . .
[24]"'Do not defile yourselves in any of these ways, because this is how the nations that I am going to drive out before you became defiled.'"
Lev 19 [29]"'Do not degrade your daughter by making her a prostitute, or the land will turn to prostitution and be filled with wickedness.'"
Lev 21 [7]"'They must not marry women defiled by prostitution or divorced from their husbands, because priests are holy to their God.'"
Deut 23 [17]No Israelite man or woman is to become a shrine prostitute.
Prov 6 [23]For these commands are a lamp, this teaching is a light, and the corrections of discipline are the way to life, [24]keeping you from the immoral woman, from the smooth tongue of the wayward wife. [25]Do not lust in your heart after her beauty or let her captivate you with her eyes, [26]for the prostitute reduces you to a loaf of bread, and the adulteress preys upon your very life.
Prov 7 [4]Say to wisdom, "You are my sister," and call understanding your kinsman; [5]they will keep you from the adulteress, from the wayward wife with her seductive words.
Prov 23 [26]My son, give me your heart and let your eyes keep to my ways, [27]for a prostitute is a deep pit and a wayward wife is a narrow well. [28]Like a bandit she lies in wait, and multiplies the unfaithful among men.
Ezek 18 [5]"Suppose there is a righteous man who does what is just and right. [6]He does not eat at the mountain shrines or look to the idols of the house of Israel. He does not defile his neighbor's wife or lie with a woman during her period. . . . [9]He follows my decrees and faithfully keeps my laws. That man is righteous; he will surely live, declares the Sovereign LORD."
Mark 10 [19]"You know the commandments: 'Do not murder, do not commit adultery, do not steal, do not give false testimony, do not defraud, honor your father and mother.'"
Acts 15 [19]"It is my judgment, therefore, that we should not make it difficult for the Gentiles who are turning to God. [20]Instead we should write to them, telling them to abstain from food polluted by idols, from sexual immorality, from the meat of strangled animals and from blood."
Acts 15 [28]It seemed good to the Holy Spirit and to us not to burden you with anything beyond the following requirements: [29]You are to abstain from food sacrificed to idols, from blood, from the meat of strangled animals and from sexual immorality. You will do well to avoid these things. Farewell.
Rom 13 [13]Let us behave decently, as in the daytime, not in orgies and drunkenness, not in sexual immorality and debauchery, not in dissension and jealousy. [14]Rather, clothe yourselves with the Lord Jesus Christ, and do not think about how to gratify the desires of the sinful nature.
1 Cor 3 [16]Don't you know that you yourselves are God's temple and that God's Spirit lives in you? [17]If anyone destroys God's temple, God will destroy him; for God's temple is sacred, and you are that temple.
1 Cor 6 [13]"Food for the stomach and the stomach for food"—but God will destroy them both. The body is not meant for sexual immorality, but for the Lord, and the Lord for the body. . . . [15]Do you not know that your bodies are members of Christ himself? Shall I then take the members of Christ and unite them with a prostitute? Never! [16]Do you not know that he who unites himself with a prostitute is one with her in body? For it is said, "The two will become one flesh." [17]But he who unites himself with the Lord is one with him in spirit.
[18]Flee from sexual immorality. All other sins a man commits are outside his body, but he who sins sexually sins against his own body. [19]Do you not know that your body is a temple of the Holy Spirit, who is in you, whom you have received from God? You are not your own; [20]you were bought at a price. Therefore honor God with your body.
1 Cor 7 [9]But if they cannot control themselves, they should marry, for it is better to marry than to burn with passion.
1 Cor 10 [8]We should not commit sexual immorality, as some of them did—and in one day twenty-three thousand of them died.
Eph 5 [3]But among you there must not be even a hint of sexual immorality, or of any kind of impurity, or of greed, because these are improper for God's holy people.
Col 3 [5]Put to death, therefore, whatever belongs to your earthly nature: sexual immorality, impurity, lust, evil desires and greed, which is idolatry.
1 Thess 4 [3]It is God's will that you should be sanctified: that you should avoid sexual immorality; [4]that each of you should learn to control his own body in a way that is holy and honorable, [5]not in passionate lust like the heathen, who do not know God. . . . [7]For God did not call us to be impure, but to live a holy life.
2 Tim 2 [22]Flee the evil desires of youth, and pursue righteousness, faith, love and peace, along with those who call on the Lord out of a pure heart.
James 2 [11]For he who said, "Do not commit adultery," also said, "Do not murder." If you do not commit adultery but do commit murder, you have become a lawbreaker.
1 Pet 2 [11]Dear friends, I urge you, as aliens and strangers in

the world, to abstain from sinful desires, which war against your soul.

C. Sexual Sins Are Punished

Gen 12 [15]And when Pharaoh's officials saw her, they praised her to Pharaoh, and she was taken into his palace. . . .

[17]But the LORD inflicted serious diseases on Pharaoh and his household because of Abram's wife Sarai. [18]So Pharaoh summoned Abram. "What have you done to me?" he said. "Why didn't you tell me she was your wife? [19]Why did you say, 'She is my sister,' so that I took her to be my wife? Now then, here is your wife. Take her and go!"

Gen 20 [2]and there Abraham said of his wife Sarah, "She is my sister." Then Abimelech king of Gerar sent for Sarah and took her.

[3]But God came to Abimelech in a dream one night and said to him, "You are as good as dead because of the woman you have taken; she is a married woman." . . .

[6]Then God said to him in the dream, "Yes, I know you did this with a clear conscience, and so I have kept you from sinning against me. That is why I did not let you touch her. [7]Now return the man's wife, for he is a prophet, and he will pray for you and you will live. But if you do not return her, you may be sure that you and all yours will die." . . .

[9]Then Abimelech called Abraham in and said, "What have you done to us? How have I wronged you that you have brought such great guilt upon me and my kingdom? You have done things to me that should not be done."

Gen 49 [4]"Turbulent as the waters, you will no longer excel, for you went up onto your father's bed, onto my couch and defiled it."

Lev 18 [24]"'Do not defile yourselves in any of these ways [see vv. 6–23], because this is how the nations that I am going to drive out before you became defiled. [25]Even the land was defiled; so I punished it for its sin, and the land vomited out its inhabitants. [26]But you must keep my decrees and my laws. The native-born and the aliens living among you must not do any of these detestable things, [27]for all these things were done by the people who lived in the land before you, and the land became defiled. [28]And if you defile the land, it will vomit you out as it vomited out the nations that were before you.

[29]"'Everyone who does any of these detestable things—such persons must be cut off from their people.'"

Lev 20 [10]"'If a man commits adultery with another man's wife—with the wife of his neighbor—both the adulterer and the adulteress must be put to death.

[11]"'If a man sleeps with his father's wife, he has dishonored his father. Both the man and the woman must be put to death; their blood will be on their own heads.

[12]"'If a man sleeps with his daughter-in-law, both of them must be put to death. What they have done is a perversion; their blood will be on their own heads.

[13]"'If a man lies with a man as one lies with a woman, both of them have done what is detestable. They must be put to death; their blood will be on their own heads.

[14]"'If a man marries both a woman and her mother, it is wicked. Both he and they must be burned in the fire, so that no wickedness will be among you.

[15]"'If a man has sexual relations with an animal, he must be put to death, and you must kill the animal.

[16]"'If a woman approaches an animal to have sexual relations with it, kill both the woman and the animal. They must be put to death; their blood will be on their own heads.

[17]"'If a man marries his sister, the daughter of either his father or his mother, and they have sexual relations, it is a disgrace. They must be cut off before the eyes of their people. He has dishonored his sister and will be held responsible.

[18]"'If a man lies with a woman during her monthly period and has sexual relations with her, he has exposed the source of her flow, and she has also uncovered it. Both of them must be cut off from their people.

[19]"'Do not have sexual relations with the sister of either your mother or your father, for that would dishonor a close relative; both of you would be held responsible.

[20]"'If a man sleeps with his aunt, he has dishonored his uncle. They will be held responsible; they will die childless.

[21]"'If a man marries his brother's wife, it is an act of impurity; he has dishonored his brother. They will be childless.

[22]"'Keep all my decrees and laws and follow them, so that the land where I am bringing you to live may not vomit you out.'"

Num 5 [12]"Speak to the Israelites and say to them: 'If a man's wife goes astray and is unfaithful to him [13]by sleeping with another man, and this is hidden from her husband and her impurity is undetected (since there is no witness against her and she has not been caught in the act) . . . [15]then he is to take his wife to the priest. He must also take an offering of a tenth of an ephah of barley flour on her behalf. He must not pour oil on it or put incense on it, because it is a grain offering for jealousy, a reminder offering to draw attention to guilt. . . . [19]Then the priest shall put the woman under oath and say to her, "If no other man has slept with you and you have not gone astray and become impure while married to your husband, may this bitter water that brings a curse not harm you." . . . [27]If she has defiled herself and been unfaithful to her husband, then when she is made to drink the water that brings a curse, it will go into her and cause bitter suffering; her abdomen will swell and her thigh waste away, and she will become accursed among her people.'"

Deut 22 [22]If a man is found sleeping with another man's wife, both the man who slept with her and the woman must die. You must purge the evil from Israel. [23]If a man happens to meet in a town a virgin pledged to be married and he sleeps with her, [24]you shall take both of them to the gate of that town and stone them to death—the girl because she was in a town and did not scream for help, and the man because he violated another man's wife. You must purge the evil from among you.

[25]But if out in the country a man happens to meet a girl pledged to be married and rapes her, only the man who has done this shall die. [26]Do nothing to the girl; she has committed no sin deserving death. This case is like that of someone who attacks and murders his neighbor, [27]for the man found the girl out in the country, and though the betrothed girl screamed, there was no one to rescue her.

[28]If a man happens to meet a virgin who is not pledged to be married and rapes her and they are discovered, [29]he shall pay the girl's father fifty shekels of silver. He must marry the girl, for he has violated her. He can never divorce her as long as he lives.

Deut 23 [2]No one born of a forbidden marriage nor any of his descendants may enter the assembly of the LORD, even down to the tenth generation.

Deut 23 [18]You must not bring the earnings of a female prostitute or of a male prostitute into the house of the LORD your God to pay any vow, because the LORD your God detests them both.

2 Sam 12 [4]"Now a traveler came to the rich man, but the rich man refrained from taking one of his own sheep or cattle to prepare a meal for the traveler who had come to him. Instead, he took the ewe lamb that belonged to the poor man and prepared it for the one who had come to him."

[5]David burned with anger against the man and said to Nathan, "As surely as the LORD lives, the man who did this deserves to die! [6]He must pay for that lamb four times over, because he did such a thing and had no pity."

[7]Then Nathan said to David, "You are the man! This is what the LORD, the God of Israel, says: 'I anointed you king over Israel, and I delivered you from the hand of Saul. [8]I gave your master's house to you, and your master's wives into your arms. I gave you the house of Israel and Judah. And if all this had been too little, I would have given you even more. [9]Why did you despise the word of the LORD by doing what is evil in his eyes? You struck down Uriah the Hittite with the sword and took his wife to be your own. You killed him with the sword of the Ammonites. [10]Now, therefore, the sword will never depart from your house, because you despised me and took the wife of Uriah the Hittite to be your own.'"

Job 24 [15]"The eye of the adulterer watches for dusk; he thinks, 'No eye will see me,' and he keeps his face concealed. . . . [17]For all of them, deep darkness is their morning; they make friends with the terrors of darkness. . . . 19As heat and drought snatch away the melted snow, so the grave snatches away those who have sinned."

Job 31 9"If my heart nas been enticed by a woman, or if I have lurked at my neighbor's door, 10then may my wife grind another man's grain, and may other men sleep with her. 11For that would have been shameful, a sin to be judged. 12It is a fire that burns to Destruction; it would have uprooted my harvest."

Prov 5 3For the lips of an adulteress drip honey, and her speech is smoother than oil; 4but in the end she is bitter as gall, sharp as a double-edged sword. 5Her feet go down to death; her steps lead straight to the grave. 6She gives no thought to the way of life; her paths are crooked, but she knows it not. . . . 8Keep to a path far from her, do not go near the door of her house, 9lest you give your best strength to others and your years to one who is cruel, 10lest strangers feast on your wealth and your toil enrich another man's house. 11At the end of your life you will groan, when your flesh and body are spent. . . . 20Why be captivated, my son, by an adulteress? Why embrace the bosom of another man's wife?

21For a man's ways are in full view of the LORD, and he examines all his paths. 22The evil deeds of a wicked man ensnare him; the cords of his sin hold him fast. 23He will die for lack of discipline, led astray by his own great folly.

Prov 6 24keeping you from the immoral woman, from the smooth tongue of the wayward wife. 25Do not lust in your heart after her beauty or let her captivate you with her eyes, 26for the prostitute reduces you to a loaf of bread, and the adulteress preys upon your very life. 27Can a man scoop fire into his lap without his clothes being burned? 28Can a man walk on hot coals without his feet being scorched? 29So is he who sleeps with another man's wife; no one who touches her will go unpunished.

Prov 6 32But a man who commits adultery lacks judgment; whoever does so destroys himself. 33Blows and disgrace are his lot, and his shame will never be wiped away; 34for jealousy arouses a husband's fury, and he will show no mercy when he takes revenge. 35He will not accept any compensation; he will refuse the bribe, however great it is.

Prov 7 6At the window of my house I looked out through the lattice. 7I saw among the simple, I noticed among the young men, a youth who lacked judgment. 8He was going down the street near her corner, walking along in the direction of her house 9at twilight, as the day was fading, as the dark of night set in.

10Then out came a woman to meet him, dressed like a prostitute and with crafty intent. 11(She is loud and defiant, her feet never stay at home; 12now in the street, now in the squares, at every corner she lurks.) 13She took hold of him and kissed him and with a brazen face she said: 14"I have fellowship offerings at home; today I fulfilled my vows. 15So I came out to meet you; I looked for you and have found you! 16I have covered my bed with colored linens from Egypt. 17I have perfumed my bed with myrrh, aloes and cinnamon. 18Come, let's drink deep of love till morning; let's enjoy ourselves with love! 19My husband is not at home; he has gone on a long journey. 20He took his purse filled with money and will not be home till full moon."

21With persuasive words she led him astray; she seduced him with her smooth talk. 22All at once he followed her like an ox going to the slaughter, like a deer stepping into a noose 23till an arrow pierces his liver, like a bird darting into a snare, little knowing it will cost him his life.

24Now then, my sons, listen to me; pay attention to what I say. 25Do not let your heart turn to her ways or stray into her paths. 26Many are the victims she has brought down; her slain are a mighty throng. 27Her house is a highway to the grave, leading down to the chambers of death.

Prov 22 14The mouth of an adulteress is a deep pit; he who is under the LORD's wrath will fall into it.

Prov 31 3". . . do not spend your strength on women, your vigor on those who ruin kings."

Eccles 7 26I find more bitter than death the woman who is a snare, whose heart is a trap and whose hands are chains. The man who pleases God will escape her, but the sinner she will ensnare.

Jer 5 7"Why should I forgive you? Your children have forsaken me and sworn by gods that are not gods. I supplied all their needs, yet they committed adultery and thronged to the houses of prostitutes. 8They are well-fed, lusty stallions, each neighing for another man's wife. 9Should I not punish them for this?" declares the LORD. "Should I not avenge myself on such a nation as this?"

Jer 7 9"'Will you steal and murder, commit adultery and perjury, burn incense to Baal and follow other gods you have not known, 10and then come and stand before me in this house, which bears my Name, and say, "We are safe"—safe to do all these detestable things? 11Has this house, which bears my Name, become a den of robbers to you? But I have been watching! declares the LORD. . . . 15I will thrust you from my presence, just as I did all your brothers, the people of Ephraim.'"

Jer 8 16"The snorting of the enemy's horses is heard from Dan; at the neighing of their stallions the whole land trembles. They have come to devour the land and everything in it, the city and all who live there."

17"See, I will send venomous snakes among you, vipers that cannot be charmed, and they will bite you," declares the LORD. . . . 21Since my people are crushed, I am crushed; I mourn, and horror grips me. . . . **9** 2Oh, that I had in the desert a lodging place for travelers, so that I might leave my people and go away from them; for they are all adulterers, a crowd of unfaithful people.

Jer 13 26"I will pull up your skirts over your face that your shame may be seen—27your adulteries and lustful neighings, your shameless prostitution! I have seen your detestable acts on the hills and in the fields. Woe to you, O Jerusalem! How long will you be unclean?"

Jer 23 10The land is full of adulterers; because of the curse the land lies parched and the pastures in the desert are withered. The prophets follow an evil course and use their power unjustly.

Jer 29 21This is what the LORD Almighty, the God of Israel, says about Ahab son of Kolaiah and Zedekiah son of Maaseiah, who are prophesying lies to you in my name: "I will hand them over to Nebuchadnezzar king of Babylon, and he will put them to death before your very eyes. 22Because of them, all the exiles from Judah who are in Babylon will use this curse: 'The LORD treat you like Zedekiah and Ahab, whom the king of Babylon burned in the fire.' 23For they have done outrageous things in Israel; they have committed adultery with their neighbors' wives and in my name have spoken lies, which I did not tell them to do. I know it and am a witness to it," declares the LORD.

Ezek 22 11"'In you one man commits a detestable offense with his neighbor's wife, another shamefully defiles his daughter-in-law, and another violates his sister, his own father's daughter. . . . 15I will disperse you among the nations and scatter you through the countries; and I will put an end to your uncleanness.'"

Ezek 23 11"Her sister Oholibah saw this, yet in her lust and prostitution she was more depraved than her sister. . . .

14"But she carried her prostitution still further. She saw men portrayed on a wall, figures of Chaldeans portrayed in red, 15with belts around their waists and flowing turbans on their heads; all of them looked like Babylonian chariot officers, natives of Chaldea. 16As soon as she saw them, she lusted after them and sent messengers to them in Chaldea. 17Then the Babylonians came to her, to the bed of love, and in their lust they defiled her. After she had been defiled by them, she turned away from them in disgust. 18When she carried on her prostitution openly and exposed her nakedness, I turned away from her in disgust, just as I had turned away from her sister. 19Yet she became more and more promiscuous as she recalled the days of her youth, when she was a prostitute in Egypt. 20There she lusted after her lovers, whose genitals were like those of donkeys and whose emission was like that of horses. 21So you longed for the lewdness of your youth, when in Egypt your bosom was caressed and your young breasts fondled. . . . 27So I will put a stop to the lewdness and prostitution you began in Egypt. You will not look on these things with longing or remember Egypt anymore.

28"For this is what the Sovereign LORD says: I am about to hand you over to those you hate, to those you turned away from in disgust. [29]They will deal with you in hatred and take away everything you have worked for. They will leave you naked and bare, and the shame of your prostitution will be exposed. Your lewdness and promiscuity [30]have brought this upon you, because you lusted after the nations and defiled yourself with their idols."

Hos 4 [2]"There is only cursing, lying and murder, stealing and adultery; they break all bounds, and bloodshed follows bloodshed. [3]Because of this the land mourns, and all who live in it waste away; the beasts of the field and the birds of the air and the fish of the sea are dying. . . . [13]They sacrifice on the mountaintops and burn offerings on the hills, under oak, poplar and terebinth, where the shade is pleasant. Therefore your daughters turn to prostitution and your daughters-in-law to adultery.

[14]"I will not punish your daughters when they turn to prostitution, nor your daughters-in-law when they commit adultery, because the men themselves consort with harlots and sacrifice with shrine prostitutes—a people without understanding will come to ruin!"

Hos 7 [4]"They are all adulterers, burning like an oven whose fire the baker need not stir from the kneading of the dough till it rises. [5]On the day of the festival of our king the princes become inflamed with wine, and he joins hands with the mockers. [6]Their hearts are like an oven; they approach him with intrigue. Their passion smolders all night; in the morning it blazes like a flaming fire. [7]All of them are hot as an oven; they devour their rulers. All their kings fall, and none of them calls on me."

Mal 3 [5]"So I will come near to you for judgment. I will be quick to testify against sorcerers, adulterers and perjurers, against those who defraud laborers of their wages, who oppress the widows and the fatherless, and deprive aliens of justice, but do not fear me," says the LORD Almighty.

Matt 5 [17]"Do not think that I have come to abolish the Law or the Prophets; I have not come to abolish them but to fulfill them. [18]I tell you the truth, until heaven and earth disappear, not the smallest letter, not the least stroke of a pen, will by any means disappear from the Law until everything is accomplished. . . .

[27]"You have heard that it was said, 'Do not commit adultery.' [28]But I tell you that anyone who looks at a woman lustfully has already committed adultery with her in his heart. [29]If your right eye causes you to sin, gouge it out and throw it away. It is better for you to lose one part of your body than for your whole body to be thrown into hell."

Rom 1 [21]For although they knew God, they neither glorified him as God nor gave thanks to him, but their thinking became futile and their foolish hearts were darkened. . . .

[24]Therefore God gave them over in the sinful desires of their hearts to sexual impurity for the degrading of their bodies with one another. . . .

[26]Because of this, God gave them over to shameful lusts. Even their women exchanged natural relations for unnatural ones. [27]In the same way the men also abandoned natural relations with women and were inflamed with lust for one another. Men committed indecent acts with other men, and received in themselves the due penalty for their perversion.

[28]Furthermore, since they did not think it worthwhile to retain the knowledge of God, he gave them over to a depraved mind, to do what ought not to be done.

1 Cor 5 [1]It is actually reported that there is sexual immorality among you, and of a kind that does not occur even among pagans: A man has his father's wife. . . .

[9]I have written you in my letter not to associate with sexually immoral people—[10]not at all meaning the people of this world who are immoral, or the greedy and swindlers, or idolaters. In that case you would have to leave this world. [11]But now I am writing you that you must not associate with anyone who calls himself a brother but is sexually immoral or greedy, an idolater or a slanderer, a drunkard or a swindler. With such a man do not even eat.

1 Cor 6 [9]Do you not know that the wicked will not inherit the kingdom of God? Do not be deceived: Neither the sexually immoral nor idolaters nor adulterers nor male prostitutes nor homosexual offenders [10]nor thieves nor the greedy nor drunkards nor slanderers nor swindlers will inherit the kingdom of God.

Eph 5 [5]For of this you can be sure: No immoral, impure or greedy person—such a man is an idolater—has any inheritance in the kingdom of Christ and of God.

Col 3 [5]Put to death, therefore, whatever belongs to your earthly nature: sexual immorality, impurity, lust, evil desires and greed, which is idolatry. [6]Because of these, the wrath of God is coming.

1 Tim 1 [9]We also know that law is made not for the righteous but for lawbreakers and rebels, the ungodly and sinful, the unholy and irreligious; for those who kill their fathers or mothers, for murderers, [10]for adulterers and perverts, for slave traders and liars and perjurers—and for whatever else is contrary to the sound doctrine. . . .

Heb 13 [4]Marriage should be honored by all, and the marriage bed kept pure, for God will judge the adulterer and all the sexually immoral.

2 Pet 2 [13]They will be paid back with harm for the harm they have done. Their idea of pleasure is to carouse in broad daylight. They are blots and blemishes, reveling in their pleasures while they feast with you. [14]With eyes full of adultery, they never stop sinning; they seduce the unstable; they are experts in greed—an accursed brood!

Jude [7]In a similar way, Sodom and Gomorrah and the surrounding towns gave themselves up to sexual immorality and perversion. They serve as an example of those who suffer the punishment of eternal fire.

[8]In the very same way, these dreamers pollute their own bodies, reject authority and slander celestial beings.

Rev 21 [8]"But the cowardly, the unbelieving, the vile, the murderers, the sexually immoral, those who practice magic arts, the idolaters and all liars—their place will be in the fiery lake of burning sulfur. This is the second death."

Rev 22 [14]"Blessed are those who wash their robes, that they may have the right to the tree of life and may go through the gates into the city. [15]Outside are the dogs, those who practice magic arts, the sexually immoral, the murderers, the idolaters and everyone who loves and practices falsehood."

IX
Sins of the Spirit

A. Sins of Self-Worship

1. Boasting

1 Kings 20 [11]The king of Israel answered, "Tell him: 'One who puts on his armor should not boast like one who takes it off.'"

Ps 10 [3]He boasts of the cravings of his heart; he blesses the greedy and reviles the LORD.

Ps 12 [3]May the LORD cut off all flattering lips and every boastful tongue. . . .

Ps 49 [5]Why should I fear when evil days come, when wicked deceivers surround me—[6]those who trust in their wealth and boast of their great riches? [7]No man can redeem the life of another or give to God a ransom for him—[8]the ransom for a life is costly, no payment is ever enough—[9]that he should live on forever and not see decay.

Ps 52 [1]Why do you boast of evil, you mighty man? Why do you boast all day long, you who are a disgrace in the eyes of God? [2]Your tongue plots destruction; it is like a sharpened razor, you who practice deceit. [3]You love evil rather than good, falsehood rather than speaking the truth. [4]You love every harmful word, O you deceitful tongue!

Ps 94 [4]They pour out arrogant words; all the evildoers are full of boasting.

Prov 25 [6]Do not exalt yourself in the king's presence, and do not claim a place among great men. . . .

[14]Like clouds and wind without rain is a man who boasts of gifts he does not give. . . .

[27]It is not good to eat too much honey, nor is it honorable to seek one's own honor.

Prov 27 [1]Do not boast about tomorrow, for you do not know what a day may bring forth.

[2]Let another praise you, and not your own mouth; someone else, and not your own lips.

Jer 9 [23]This is what the LORD says: "Let not the wise man boast of his wisdom or the strong man boast of his strength or the rich man boast of his riches, [24]but let him who boasts boast about this: that he understands and knows me, that I am the LORD, who exercises kindness, justice and righteousness on earth, for in these I delight," declares the LORD.

Jer 49 [4]"Why do you boast of your valleys, boast of your valleys so fruitful? O unfaithful daughter, you trust in your riches and say, 'Who will attack me?' [5]I will bring terror on you from all those around you," declares the Lord, the LORD Almighty. "Every one of you will be driven away, and no one will gather the fugitives."

Luke 12 [16]And he told them this parable: "The ground of a certain rich man produced a good crop. [17]He thought to himself, 'What shall I do? I have no place to store my crops.'

[18]"Then he said, 'This is what I'll do. I will tear down my barns and build bigger ones, and there I will store all my grain and my goods. [19]And I'll say to myself, "You have plenty of good things laid up for many years. Take life easy; eat, drink and be merry."'

[20]"But God said to him, 'You fool! This very night your life will be demanded from you. Then who will get what you have prepared for yourself?'"

Rom 1 [28]Furthermore, since they did not think it worthwhile to retain the knowledge of God, he gave them over to a depraved mind, to do what ought not to be done. [29]They have become filled with every kind of wickedness, evil, greed and depravity. They are full of envy, murder, strife, deceit and malice. They are gossips, [30]slanderers, God-haters, insolent, arrogant and boastful; they invent ways of doing evil; they disobey their parents. . . .

Rom 3 [27]Where, then, is boasting? It is excluded. On what principle? On that of observing the law? No, but on that of faith.

Rom 11 [17]If some of the branches have been broken off, and you, though a wild olive shoot, have been grafted in among the others and now share in the nourishing sap from the olive root, [18]do not boast over those branches. If you do, consider this: You do not support the root, but the root supports you. [19]You will say then, "Branches were broken off so that I could be grafted in." [20]Granted. But they were broken off because of unbelief, and you stand by faith. Do not be arrogant, but be afraid. [21]For if God did not spare the natural branches, he will not spare you either.

1 Cor 1 [28]He chose the lowly things of this world and the despised things—and the things that are not—to nullify the things that are, [29]so that no one may boast before him.

1 Cor 3 [21]So then, no more boasting about men! All things are yours, [22]whether Paul or Apollos or Cephas or the world or life or death or the present or the future—all are yours, [23]and you are of Christ, and Christ is of God.

1 Cor 4 [7]For who makes you different from anyone else? What do you have that you did not receive? And if you did receive it, why do you boast as though you did not?

1 Cor 5 [2]And you are proud! Shouldn't you rather have been filled with grief and have put out of your fellowship the man who did this? . . .

[6]Your boasting is not good. Don't you know that a little yeast works through the whole batch of dough?

2 Cor 5 [12]We are not trying to commend ourselves to you again, but are giving you an opportunity to take pride in us, so that you can answer those who take pride in what is seen rather than in what is in the heart.

2 Cor 10 [12]We do not dare to classify or compare ourselves with some who commend themselves. When they measure themselves by themselves and compare themselves with themselves, they are not wise. [13]We, however, will not boast beyond proper limits, but will confine our boasting to the field God has assigned to us, a field that reaches even to you.

2 Cor 11 [16]I repeat: Let no one take me for a fool. But if you do, then receive me just as you would a fool, so that I may do a little boasting. [17]In this self-confident boasting I am not talking as the Lord would, but as a fool. [18]Since many are boasting in the way the world does, I too will boast. . . .

[30]If I must boast, I will boast of the things that show my weakness.

2 Cor 12 [5]I will boast about a man like that, but I will not boast about myself, except about my weaknesses.

Eph 2 [8]For it is by grace you have been saved, through faith—and this not from yourselves, it is the gift of God—[9]not by works, so that no one can boast.

James 3 [5]Likewise the tongue is a small part of the body, but it makes great boasts. Consider what a great forest is set on fire by a small spark. [6]The tongue also is a fire, a world of evil among the parts of the body. It corrupts the whole person, sets the whole course of his life on fire, and is itself set on fire by hell.

James 4 [13]Now listen, you who say, "Today or tomorrow we will go to this or that city, spend a year there, carry on business and make money." [14]Why, you do not even know what will happen tomorrow. What is your life? You are a mist that appears for a little while and then vanishes. [15]Instead, you ought to say, "If it is the Lord's will, we will live and do this or that." [16]As it is, you boast and brag. All such boasting is evil.

Rev 3 [17]"You say, 'I am rich; I have acquired wealth and do not need a thing.' But you do not realize that you are wretched, pitiful, poor, blind and naked."

2. Pride

a) Pride Is the Great Sin

Deut 8 [11]Be careful that you do not forget the LORD your God, failing to observe his commands, his laws and his decrees that I am giving you this day. [12]Otherwise, when you eat and are satisfied, when you build fine houses and settle down, [13]and when your herds and flocks grow large and your silver and gold increase and all you have is multiplied, [14]then your heart will become proud and you will forget the LORD your God, who brought you out of Egypt, out of the land of slavery. . . . [17]You may say to yourself, "My power and the strength of my hands have produced this wealth for me."

Deut 17 [18]When he takes the throne of his kingdom, he is to write for himself on a scroll a copy of this law, taken from that of the priests, who are Levites. [19]It is to be with him, and he is to read it all the days of his life so that he may learn to revere the LORD his God and follow carefully all the words of this law and these decrees [20]and not consider himself better than his brothers and turn from the law to the right or to the left. Then he and his descendants will reign a long time over his kingdom in Israel.

Ps 10 [2]In his arrogance the wicked man hunts down the weak, who are caught in the schemes he devises. [3]He boasts of the cravings of his heart; he blesses the greedy and reviles the LORD. [4]In his pride the wicked does not seek him; in all his thoughts there is no room for God.

Ps 17 [10]They close up their callous hearts, and their mouths speak with arrogance. [11]They have tracked me down, they now surround me, with eyes alert, to throw me to the ground.

Ps 36 [11]May the foot of the proud not come against me, nor the hand of the wicked drive me away.

Ps 38 [16]For I said, "Do not let them gloat or exalt themselves over me when my foot slips."

Ps 40 [4]Blessed is the man who makes the LORD his trust, who does not look to the proud, to those who turn aside to false gods.

Ps 73 [6]Therefore pride is their necklace; they clothe themselves with violence. [7]From their callous hearts comes iniquity; the evil conceits of their minds know no limits. [8]They scoff, and speak with malice; in their arrogance they threaten oppression. [9]Their mouths lay claim to heaven, and their tongues take possession of the earth. . . . [11]They say, "How can God know? Does the Most High have knowledge?"

Ps 119 [51]The arrogant mock me without restraint, but I do not turn from your law. . . . [69]Though the arrogant have smeared me with lies, I keep your precepts with all my heart. . . . [78]May the arrogant be put to shame for wronging me without cause; but I will meditate on your precepts. . . . [85]The arrogant dig pit-

falls for me, contrary to your law. . . . [122]Ensure your servant's well-being; let not the arrogant oppress me.
Ps 123 [4]We have endured much ridicule from the proud, much contempt from the arrogant.
Ps 131 [1]My heart is not proud, O LORD, my eyes are not haughty; I do not concern myself with great matters or things too wonderful for me.
Ps 140 [5]Proud men have hidden a snare for me; they have spread out the cords of their net and have set traps for me along my path.
Prov 13 [10]Pride only breeds quarrels, but wisdom is found in those who take advice.
Prov 18 [12]Before his downfall a man's heart is proud, but humility comes before honor.
Prov 21 [24]The proud and arrogant man—"Mocker" is his name; he behaves with overweening pride.
Prov 30 [13]". . . those whose eyes are ever so haughty, whose glances are so disdainful . . ."
Prov 30 [32]"If you have played the fool and exalted yourself, or if you have planned evil, clap your hand over your mouth!"
Isa 65 [2]"All day long I have held out my hands to an obstinate people, who walk in ways not good, pursuing their own imaginations—[3]a people who continually provoke me to my very face, offering sacrifices in gardens and burning incense on altars of brick . . . [5]who say, 'Keep away; don't come near me, for I am too sacred for you!' Such people are smoke in my nostrils, a fire that keeps burning all day."
Ezek 16 [49]"'Now this was the sin of your sister Sodom: She and her daughters were arrogant, overfed and unconcerned; they did not help the poor and needy.'"
1 Cor 8 [1]Now about food sacrificed to idols: We know that we all possess knowledge. Knowledge puffs up, but love builds up. [2]The man who thinks he knows something does not yet know as he ought to know.
1 Cor 10 [12]So, if you think you are standing firm, be careful that you don't fall!
2 Thess 2 [4]He will oppose and will exalt himself over everything that is called God or is worshiped, so that he sets himself up in God's temple, proclaiming himself to be God.
2 Tim 3 [2]People will be lovers of themselves, lovers of money, boastful, proud, abusive, disobedient to their parents, ungrateful, unholy. . . .

b) We Are Warned against Pride

1 Sam 2 [3]"Do not keep talking so proudly or let your mouth speak such arrogance, for the LORD is a God who knows, and by him deeds are weighed."
2 Sam 22 [28]"You save the humble, but your eyes are on the haughty to bring them low."
2 Chron 25 [19]"You say to yourself that you have defeated Edom, and now you are arrogant and proud. But stay at home! Why ask for trouble and cause your own downfall and that of Judah also?"
Job 40 [12]". . . look at every proud man and humble him, crush the wicked where they stand. [13]Bury them all in the dust together; shroud their faces in the grave."
Ps 31 [18]Let their lying lips be silenced, for with pride and contempt they speak arrogantly against the righteous.
Ps 35 [26]May all who gloat over my distress be put to shame and confusion; may all who exalt themselves over me be clothed with shame and disgrace.
Ps 59 [12]For the sins of their mouths, for the words of their lips, let them be caught in their pride. For the curses and lies they utter, [13]consume them in wrath, consume them till they are no more. Then it will be known to the ends of the earth that God rules over Jacob.
Ps 94 [2]Rise up, O Judge of the earth; pay back to the proud what they deserve.
Ps 119 [21]You rebuke the arrogant, who are cursed and who stray from your commands.
Ps 138 [6]Though the LORD is on high, he looks upon the lowly, but the proud he knows from afar.
Prov 6 [16]There are six things the LORD hates, seven that are detestable to him: [17]haughty eyes, a lying tongue, hands that shed innocent blood . . .
Prov 8 [13]"To fear the LORD is to hate evil; I hate pride and arrogance, evil behavior and perverse speech."
Prov 11 [2]When pride comes, then comes disgrace, but with humility comes wisdom.
Prov 16 [5]The LORD detests all the proud of heart. Be sure of this: They will not go unpunished. . . .
[18]Pride goes before destruction, a haughty spirit before a fall.
Prov 21 [4]Haughty eyes and a proud heart, the lamp of the wicked, are sin!
Prov 29 [23]A man's pride brings him low, but a man of lowly spirit gains honor.
Isa 2 [11]The eyes of the arrogant man will be humbled and the pride of men brought low; the LORD alone will be exalted in that day.
[12]The LORD Almighty has a day in store for all the proud and lofty, for all that is exalted (and they will be humbled). . . .
Isa 3 [16]The LORD says, "The women of Zion are haughty, walking along with outstretched necks, flirting with their eyes, tripping along with mincing steps, with ornaments jingling on their ankles. [17]Therefore the Lord will bring sores on the heads of the women of Zion; the LORD will make their scalps bald."
Isa 13 [11]I will punish the world for its evil, the wicked for their sins. I will put an end to the arrogance of the haughty and will humble the pride of the ruthless.
Isa 23 [9]The LORD Almighty planned it, to bring low the pride of all glory and to humble all who are renowned on the earth.
Isa 25 [11]They will spread out their hands in it, as a swimmer spreads out his hands to swim. God will bring down their pride despite the cleverness of their hands.
Isa 26 [5]He humbles those who dwell on high, he lays the lofty city low; he levels it to the ground and casts it down to the dust.
Jer 13 [15]Hear and pay attention, do not be arrogant, for the LORD has spoken. [16]Give glory to the LORD your God before he brings the darkness, before your feet stumble on the darkening hills. You hope for light, but he will turn it to thick darkness and change it to deep gloom.
Ezek 16 [50]"'They were haughty and did detestable things before me. Therefore I did away with them as you have seen.'"
Dan 4 [37]Now I, Nebuchadnezzar, praise and exalt and glorify the King of heaven, because everything he does is right and all his ways are just. And those who walk in pride he is able to humble.
Mic 2 [3]Therefore, the LORD says: "I am planning disaster against this people, from which you cannot save yourselves. You will no longer walk proudly, for it will be a time of calamity."
Zeph 2 [10]This is what they will get in return for their pride, for insulting and mocking the people of the LORD Almighty. [11]The LORD will be awesome to them when he destroys all the gods of the land. The nations on every shore will worship him, every one in its own land.
Zeph 3 [11]"On that day you will not be put to shame for all the wrongs you have done to me, because I will remove from this city those who rejoice in their pride. Never again will you be haughty on my holy hill."
Matt 23 [12]"For whoever exalts himself will be humbled, and whoever humbles himself will be exalted."
Mark 7 [21]"For from within, out of men's hearts, come evil thoughts, sexual immorality, theft, murder, adultery, [22]greed, malice, deceit, lewdness, envy, slander, arrogance and folly. [23]All these evils come from inside and make a man 'unclean.'"
Luke 1 [51]"He has performed mighty deeds with his arm; he has scattered those who are proud in their inmost thoughts."

B. Sins of Self-Deception

1. Folly

a) Folly as Lack of Discernment

Job 5 [2]"Resentment kills a fool, and envy slays the simple."
Job 11 [12]"But a witless man can no more become wise than a wild donkey's colt can be born a man."
Prov 1 [7]The fear of the LORD is the beginning of knowledge, but fools despise wisdom and discipline.
Prov 1 [22]"How long will you simple ones love your simple

ways? How long will mockers delight in mockery and fools hate knowledge?"
Prov 10 [14]Wise men store up knowledge, but the mouth of a fool invites ruin.
Prov 10 [23]A fool finds pleasure in evil conduct, but a man of understanding delights in wisdom.
Prov 11 [12]A man who lacks judgment derides his neighbor, but a man of understanding holds his tongue.
Prov 12 [16]A fool shows his annoyance at once, but a prudent man overlooks an insult.
Prov 12 [23]A prudent man keeps his knowledge to himself, but the heart of fools blurts out folly.
Prov 13 [3]He who guards his lips guards his life, but he who speaks rashly will come to ruin.
Prov 13 [16]Every prudent man acts out of knowledge, but a fool exposes his folly.
Prov 14 [7]Stay away from a foolish man, for you will not find knowledge on his lips.

[8]The wisdom of the prudent is to give thought to their ways, but the folly of fools is deception.

[9]Fools mock at making amends for sin, but goodwill is found among the upright.
Prov 14 [15]A simple man believes anything, but a prudent man gives thought to his steps.

[16]A wise man fears the LORD and shuns evil, but a fool is hotheaded and reckless.

[17]A quick-tempered man does foolish things, and a crafty man is hated.

[18]The simple inherit folly, but the prudent are crowned with knowledge.
Prov 15 [2]The tongue of the wise commends knowledge, but the mouth of the fool gushes folly.
Prov 15 [5]A fool spurns his father's discipline, but whoever heeds correction shows prudence.
Prov 15 [7]The lips of the wise spread knowledge; not so the hearts of fools. . . .

[14]The discerning heart seeks knowledge, but the mouth of a fool feeds on folly.
Prov 15 [21]Folly delights a man who lacks judgment, but a man of understanding keeps a straight course.
Prov 16 [22]Understanding is a fountain of life to those who have it, but folly brings punishment to fools.
Prov 17 [7]Arrogant lips are unsuited to a fool—how much worse lying lips to a ruler!
Prov 17 [10]A rebuke impresses a man of discernment more than a hundred lashes a fool.
Prov 17 [12]Better to meet a bear robbed of her cubs than a fool in his folly.
Prov 17 [16]Of what use is money in the hand of a fool, since he has no desire to get wisdom?
Prov 17 [21]To have a fool for a son brings grief; there is no joy for the father of a fool.
Prov 17 [24]A discerning man keeps wisdom in view, but a fool's eyes wander to the ends of the earth.
Prov 18 [2]A fool finds no pleasure in understanding but delights in airing his own opinions.
Prov 18 [6]A fool's lips bring him strife, and his mouth invites a beating.

[7]A fool's mouth is his undoing, and his lips are a snare to his soul.
Prov 19 [13]A foolish son is his father's ruin, and a quarrelsome wife is like a constant dripping.
Prov 19 [29]Penalties are prepared for mockers, and beatings for the backs of fools.
Prov 20 [3]It is to a man's honor to avoid strife, but every fool is quick to quarrel.
Prov 23 [9]Do not speak to a fool, for he will scorn the wisdom of your words.
Prov 24 [7]Wisdom is too high for a fool; in the assembly at the gate he has nothing to say.
Prov 26 [1]Like snow in summer or rain in harvest, honor is not fitting for a fool.
Prov 26 [3]A whip for the horse, a halter for the donkey, and a rod for the backs of fools!

[4]Do not answer a fool according to his folly, or you will be like him yourself.
Prov 26 [7]Like a lame man's legs that hang limp is a proverb in the mouth of a fool.

[8]Like tying a stone in a sling is the giving of honor to a fool. . . .

[10]Like an archer who wounds at random is he who hires a fool or any passer-by.

[11]As a dog returns to its vomit, so a fool repeats his folly.
Prov 27 [3]Stone is heavy and sand a burden, but provocation by a fool is heavier than both.
Prov 27 [12]The prudent see danger and take refuge, but the simple keep going and suffer for it.
Prov 27 [22]Though you grind a fool in a mortar, grinding him like grain with a pestle, you will not remove his folly from him.
Prov 29 [9]If a wise man goes to court with a fool, the fool rages and scoffs, and there is no peace.
Prov 29 [11]A fool gives full vent to his anger, but a wise man keeps himself under control.
Eccles 4 [5]The fool folds his hands and ruins himself.
Eccles 5 [3]As a dream comes when there are many cares, so the speech of a fool when there are many words.
Eccles 7 [4]The heart of the wise is in the house of mourning, but the heart of fools is in the house of pleasure. [5]It is better to heed a wise man's rebuke than to listen to the song of fools. [6]Like the crackling of thorns under the pot, so is the laughter of fools. This too is meaningless. . . .

[9]Do not be quickly provoked in your spirit, for anger resides in the lap of fools.
Eccles 9 [17]The quiet words of the wise are more to be heeded than the shouts of a ruler of fools.
Eccles 10 [2]The heart of the wise inclines to the right, but the heart of the fool to the left. [3]Even as he walks along the road, the fool lacks sense and shows everyone how stupid he is. . . .

[5]There is an evil I have seen under the sun, the sort of error that arises from a ruler: [6]Fools are put in many high positions, while the rich occupy the low ones. [7]I have seen slaves on horseback, while princes go on foot like slaves. . . .

[12]Words from a wise man's mouth are gracious, but a fool is consumed by his own lips. [13]At the beginning his words are folly; at the end they are wicked madness—[14]and the fool multiplies words.

No one knows what is coming—who can tell him what will happen after him?

[15]A fool's work wearies him; he does not know the way to town.

b) Folly as Wickedness

Num 12 [11]and he said to Moses, "Please, my lord, do not hold against us the sin we have so foolishly committed."
Deut 32 [6]Is this the way you repay the LORD, O foolish and unwise people? Is he not your Father, your Creator, who made you and formed you?
1 Sam 13 [13]"You acted foolishly," Samuel said. "You have not kept the command the LORD your God gave you; if you had, he would have established your kingdom over Israel for all time."
2 Sam 24 [10]David was conscience-stricken after he had counted the fighting men, and he said to the LORD, "I have sinned greatly in what I have done. Now, O LORD, I beg you, take away the guilt of your servant. I have done a very foolish thing."
Job 5 [3]"I myself have seen a fool taking root, but suddenly his house was cursed."
Ps 14 [1]The fool says in his heart, "There is no God." They are corrupt, their deeds are vile; there is no one who does good.
Ps 36 [1]An oracle is within my heart concerning the sinfulness of the wicked: There is no fear of God before his eyes. [2]For in his own eyes he flatters himself too much to detect or hate his sin. [3]The words of his mouth are wicked and deceitful; he has ceased to be wise and to do good. [4]Even on his bed he plots evil; he commits himself to a sinful course and does not reject what is wrong.
Ps 38 [5]My wounds fester and are loathsome because of my sinful folly.
Ps 69 [5]You know my folly, O God; my guilt is not hidden from you.
Ps 74 [18]Remember how the enemy has mocked you, O LORD, how foolish people have reviled your name. . . .

22Rise up, O God, and defend your cause; remember how fools mock you all day long.

Ps 85 8I will listen to what God the LORD will say; he promises peace to his people, his saints—but let them not return to folly.

Ps 94 7They say, "The LORD does not see; the God of Jacob pays no heed."

8Take heed, you senseless ones among the people; you fools, when will you become wise? 9Does he who implanted the ear not hear? Does he who formed the eye not see? 10Does he who disciplines nations not punish? Does he who teaches man lack knowledge? 11The LORD knows the thoughts of man; he knows that they are futile.

Ps 107 17Some became fools through their rebellious ways and suffered affliction because of their iniquities.

Prov 1 32For the waywardness of the simple will kill them, and the complacency of fools will destroy them. . . .

Prov 9 6"Leave your simple ways and you will live; walk in the way of understanding. . . ."

13The woman Folly is loud; she is undisciplined and without knowledge. . . . 16"Let all who are simple come in here!" she says to those who lack judgment. 17"Stolen water is sweet; food eaten in secret is delicious!" 18But little do they know that the dead are there, that her guests are in the depths of the grave.

Prov 10 8The wise in heart accept commands, but a chattering fool comes to ruin.

Prov 10 21The lips of the righteous nourish many, but fools die for lack of judgment.

Prov 13 19A longing fulfilled is sweet to the soul, but fools detest turning from evil.

Prov 14 9Fools mock at making amends for sin, but goodwill is found among the upright.

Prov 21 30There is no wisdom, no insight, no plan that can succeed against the LORD.

Prov 24 9The schemes of folly are sin, and men detest a mocker.

Eccles 5 1Guard your steps when you go to the house of God. Go near to listen rather than to offer the sacrifice of fools, who do not know that they do wrong. . . .

4When you make a vow to God, do not delay in fulfilling it. He has no pleasure in fools; fulfill your vow.

Eccles 7 7Extortion turns a wise man into a fool, and a bribe corrupts the heart.

Jer 4 22"My people are fools; they do not know me. They are senseless children; they have no understanding. They are skilled in doing evil; they know not how to do good."

Jer 5 4I thought, "These are only the poor; they are foolish, for they do not know the way of the LORD, the requirements of their God."

Jer 8 9"'The wise will be put to shame; they will be dismayed and trapped. Since they have rejected the word of the LORD, what kind of wisdom do they have?'"

Jer 10 8They are all senseless and foolish; they are taught by worthless wooden idols.

Matt 7 26"But everyone who hears these words of mine and does not put them into practice is like a foolish man who built his house on sand. 27The rain came down, the streams rose, and the winds blew and beat against that house, and it fell with a great crash."

Matt 23 17"You blind fools! Which is greater: the gold, or the temple that makes the gold sacred? 18You also say, 'If anyone swears by the altar, it means nothing; but if anyone swears by the gift on it, he is bound by his oath.'"

Matt 25 1"At that time the kingdom of heaven will be like ten virgins who took their lamps and went out to meet the bridegroom. 2Five of them were foolish and five were wise. 3The foolish ones took their lamps but did not take any oil with them. 4The wise, however, took oil in jars along with their lamps. 5The bridegroom was a long time in coming, and they all became drowsy and fell asleep.

6"At midnight the cry rang out: 'Here's the bridegroom! Come out to meet him!'

7"Then all the virgins woke up and trimmed their lamps. 8The foolish ones said to the wise, 'Give us some of your oil; our lamps are going out.'

9"'No,' they replied, 'there may not be enough for both us and you. Instead, go to those who sell oil and buy some for yourselves.'

10"But while they were on their way to buy the oil, the bridegroom arrived. The virgins who were ready went in with him to the wedding banquet. And the door was shut.

11"Later the others also came. 'Sir! Sir!' they said. 'Open the door for us!'

12"But he replied, 'I tell you the truth, I don't know you.'

13"Therefore keep watch, because you do not know the day or the hour."

Mark 7 20He went on: "What comes out of a man is what makes him 'unclean.' 21For from within, out of men's hearts, come evil thoughts, sexual immorality, theft, murder, adultery, 22greed, malice, deceit, lewdness, envy, slander, arrogance and folly. 23All these evils come from inside and make a man 'unclean.'"

Luke 11 39Then the Lord said to him, "Now then, you Pharisees clean the outside of the cup and dish, but inside you are full of greed and wickedness. 40You foolish people! Did not the one who made the outside make the inside also?"

Luke 12 16And he told them this parable: "The ground of a certain rich man produced a good crop. 17He thought to himself, 'What shall I do? I have no place to store my crops.'

18"Then he said, 'This is what I'll do. I will tear down my barns and build bigger ones, and there I will store all my grain and my goods. 19And I'll say to myself, "You have plenty of good things laid up for many years. Take life easy; eat, drink and be merry."'

20"But God said to him, 'You fool! This very night your life will be demanded from you. Then who will get what you have prepared for yourself?'

21"This is how it will be with anyone who stores up things for himself but is not rich toward God."

Rom 1 21For although they knew God, they neither glorified him as God nor gave thanks to him, but their thinking became futile and their foolish hearts were darkened. 22Although they claimed to be wise, they became fools 23and exchanged the glory of the immortal God for images made to look like mortal man and birds and animals and reptiles.

1 Cor 1 19For it is written: "I will destroy the wisdom of the wise; the intelligence of the intelligent I will frustrate."

20Where is the wise man? Where is the scholar? Where is the philosopher of this age? Has not God made foolish the wisdom of the world? 21For since in the wisdom of God the world through its wisdom did not know him, God was pleased through the foolishness of what was preached to save those who believe. 22Jews demand miraculous signs and Greeks look for wisdom, 23but we preach Christ crucified: a stumbling block to Jews and foolishness to Gentiles, 24but to those whom God has called, both Jews and Greeks, Christ the power of God and the wisdom of God. 25For the foolishness of God is wiser than man's wisdom, and the weakness of God is stronger than man's strength.

1 Cor 2 6We do, however, speak a message of wisdom among the mature, but not the wisdom of this age or of the rulers of this age, who are coming to nothing. 7No, we speak of God's secret wisdom, a wisdom that has been hidden and that God destined for our glory before time began. 8None of the rulers of this age understood it, for if they had, they would not have crucified the Lord of glory. . . . 14The man without the Spirit does not accept the things that come from the Spirit of God, for they are foolishness to him, and he cannot understand them, because they are spiritually discerned.

1 Cor 3 18Do not deceive yourselves. If any one of you thinks he is wise by the standards of this age, he should become a "fool" so that he may become wise. 19For the wisdom of this world is foolishness in God's sight. As it is written: "He catches the wise in their craftiness"; 20and again, "The Lord knows that the thoughts of the wise are futile."

Gal 3 1You foolish Galatians! Who has bewitched you? Before your very eyes Jesus Christ was clearly portrayed as crucified. . . . 3Are you so foolish? After beginning with the Spirit, are you now trying to attain your goal by human effort?

1 Pet 2 15For it is God's will that by doing good you should silence the ignorant talk of foolish men.

2. Self-Righteousness and Conceit

Deut 9 [4]After the LORD your God has driven them out before you, do not say to yourself, "The LORD has brought me here to take possession of this land because of my righteousness." No, it is on account of the wickedness of these nations that the LORD is going to drive them out before you. [5]It is not because of your righteousness or your integrity that you are going in to take possession of their land; but on account of the wickedness of these nations, the LORD your God will drive them out before you, to accomplish what he swore to your fathers, to Abraham, Isaac and Jacob. [6]Understand, then, that it is not because of your righteousness that the LORD your God is giving you this good land to possess, for you are a stiff-necked people.
1 Sam 17 [28]When Eliab, David's oldest brother, heard him speaking with the men, he burned with anger at him and asked, "Why have you come down here? And with whom did you leave those few sheep in the desert? I know how conceited you are and how wicked your heart is; you came down only to watch the battle."
Job 11 [4]"You say to God, 'My beliefs are flawless and I am pure in your sight.' [5]Oh, how I wish that God would speak, that he would open his lips against you [6]and disclose to you the secrets of wisdom, for true wisdom has two sides. Know this: God has even forgotten some of your sin."
Job 12 [2]"Doubtless you are the people, and wisdom will die with you! [3]But I have a mind as well as you; I am not inferior to you. Who does not know all these things?"
Job 15 [8]"Do you listen in on God's council? Do you limit wisdom to yourself?"
Job 18 [2]"When will you end these speeches? Be sensible, and then we can talk. [3]Why are we regarded as cattle and considered stupid in your sight? [4]You who tear yourself to pieces in your anger, is the earth to be abandoned for your sake? Or must the rocks be moved from their place?"
Job 32 [1]So these three men stopped answering Job, because he was righteous in his own eyes. [2]But Elihu son of Barakel the Buzite, of the family of Ram, became very angry with Job for justifying himself rather than God. [3]He was also angry with the three friends, because they had found no way to refute Job, and yet had condemned him. [4]Now Elihu had waited before speaking to Job because they were older than he. [5]But when he saw that the three men had nothing more to say, his anger was aroused.
Ps 73 [7]From their callous hearts comes iniquity; the evil conceits of their minds know no limits.
Prov 3 [7]Do not be wise in your own eyes; fear the LORD and shun evil.
Prov 12 [15]The way of a fool seems right to him, but a wise man listens to advice.
Prov 14 [12]There is a way that seems right to a man, but in the end it leads to death.
Prov 26 [12]Do you see a man wise in his own eyes? There is more hope for a fool than for him.
Prov 26 [16]The sluggard is wiser in his own eyes than seven men who answer discreetly.
Prov 28 [11]A rich man may be wise in his own eyes, but a poor man who has discernment sees through him.
Prov 28 [26]He who trusts in himself is a fool, but he who walks in wisdom is kept safe.
Isa 5 [21]Woe to those who are wise in their own eyes and clever in their own sight.
Isa 10 [12]When the Lord has finished all his work against Mount Zion and Jerusalem, he will say, "I will punish the king of Assyria for the willful pride of his heart and the haughty look in his eyes. [13]For he says: 'By the strength of my hand I have done this, and by my wisdom, because I have understanding. I removed the boundaries of nations, I plundered their treasures; like a mighty one I subdued their kings. [14]As one reaches into a nest, so my hand reached for the wealth of the nations; as men gather abandoned eggs, so I gathered all the countries; not one flapped a wing, or opened its mouth to chirp.'"
Isa 16 [6]We have heard of Moab's pride—her overweening pride and conceit, her pride and her insolence—but her boasts are empty.
Isa 65 [2]"All day long I have held out my hands to an obstinate people, who walk in ways not good, pursuing their own imaginations . . . [4]who sit among the graves and spend their nights keeping secret vigil; who eat the flesh of pigs, and whose pots hold broth of unclean meat; [5]who say, 'Keep away; don't come near me, for I am too sacred for you!' Such people are smoke in my nostrils, a fire that keeps burning all day."
Jer 8 [8]"'How can you say, "We are wise, for we have the law of the LORD," when actually the lying pen of the scribes has handled it falsely? [9]The wise will be put to shame; they will be dismayed and trapped. Since they have rejected the word of the LORD, what kind of wisdom do they have?'"
Jer 48 [29]"We have heard of Moab's pride—her overweening pride and conceit, her pride and arrogance and the haughtiness of her heart. [30]I know her insolence but it is futile," declares the LORD, "and her boasts accomplish nothing."
Luke 16 [15]He said to them, "You are the ones who justify yourselves in the eyes of men, but God knows your hearts. What is highly valued among men is detestable in God's sight."
Luke 18 [9]To some who were confident of their own righteousness and looked down on everybody else, Jesus told this parable: . . . [11]"The Pharisee stood up and prayed about himself: 'God, I thank you that I am not like other men—robbers, evildoers, adulterers—or even like this tax collector. [12]I fast twice a week and give a tenth of all I get.'

[13]"But the tax collector stood at a distance. He would not even look up to heaven, but beat his breast and said, 'God have mercy on me, a sinner.'

[14]"I tell you that this man, rather than the other, went home justified before God. For everyone who exalts himself will be humbled, and he who humbles himself will be exalted."
John 9 [41]Jesus said, "If you were blind, you would not be guilty of sin; but now that you claim you can see, your guilt remains."
Rom 1 [22]Although they claimed to be wise, they became fools [23]and exchanged the glory of the immortal God for images made to look like mortal man and birds and animals and reptiles.
Rom 10 [3]Since they did not know the righteousness that comes from God and sought to establish their own, they did not submit to God's righteousness.
Rom 11 [25]I do not want you to be ignorant of this mystery, brothers, so that you may not be conceited: Israel has experienced a hardening in part until the full number of the Gentiles has come in.
Rom 12 [16]Live in harmony with one another. Do not be proud, but be willing to associate with people of low position. Do not be conceited.
1 Cor 3 [18]Do not deceive yourselves. If any one of you thinks he is wise by the standards of this age, he should become a "fool" so that he may become wise.
2 Cor 10 [12]We do not dare to classify or compare ourselves with some who commend themselves. When they measure themselves by themselves and compare themselves with themselves, they are not wise. . . . [17]But, "Let him who boasts boast in the Lord." [18]For it is not the one who commends himself who is approved, but the one whom the Lord commends.
2 Cor 12 [7]To keep me from becoming conceited because of these surpassingly great revelations, there was given me a thorn in my flesh, a messenger of Satan, to torment me.
Gal 5 [26]Let us not become conceited, provoking and envying each other.
Gal 6 [3]If anyone thinks he is something when he is nothing, he deceives himself.
Phil 2 [3]Do nothing out of selfish ambition or vain conceit, but in humility consider others better than yourselves.
Col 2 [23]Such regulations indeed have an appearance of wisdom, with their self-imposed worship, their false humility and their harsh treatment of the body, but they lack any value in restraining sensual indulgence.
1 Tim 6 [3]If anyone teaches false doctrines and does not agree to the sound instruction of our Lord Jesus Christ and to godly teaching, [4]he is conceited and understands nothing. He has an unhealthy interest in controversies and quarrels about words that result in envy, strife, malicious talk, evil suspicions [5]and constant friction between men of corrupt mind, who have been robbed of the truth and who think that godliness is a means to financial gain.

3. Spiritual Blindness

Job 17 [10]"But come on, all of you, try again! I will not find a wise man among you."
Job 38 [2]"Who is this that darkens my counsel with words without knowledge?"
Prov 12 [8]A man is praised according to his wisdom, but men with warped minds are despised.
Prov 14 [7]Stay away from a foolish man, for you will not find knowledge on his lips.
Prov 19 [2]It is not good to have zeal without knowledge, nor to be hasty and miss the way. [3]A man's own folly ruins his life, yet his heart rages against the LORD.
Matt 13 [13]"This is why I speak to them in parables: Though seeing, they do not see; though hearing, they do not hear or understand. [14]In them is fulfilled the prophecy of Isaiah: 'You will be ever hearing but never understanding; you will be ever seeing but never perceiving. [15]For this people's heart has become calloused; they hardly hear with their ears, and they have closed their eyes. Otherwise they might see with their eyes, hear with their ears, understand with their hearts and turn, and I would heal them.'"
1 Cor 15 [34]Come back to your senses as you ought, and stop sinning; for there are some who are ignorant of God—I say this to your shame.
Eph 4 [18]They are darkened in their understanding and separated from the life of God because of the ignorance that is in them due to the hardening of their hearts. [19]Having lost all sensitivity, they have given themselves over to sensuality so as to indulge in every kind of impurity, with a continual lust for more.
2 Tim 3 [6]They are the kind who worm their way into homes and gain control over weak-willed women, who are loaded down with sins and are swayed by all kinds of evil desires, [7]always learning but never able to acknowledge the truth.
2 Pet 2 [12]But these men blaspheme in matters they do not understand. They are like brute beasts, creatures of instinct, born only to be caught and destroyed, and like beasts they too will perish.
Jude [10]Yet these men speak abusively against whatever they do not understand; and what things they do understand by instinct, like unreasoning animals—these are the very things that destroy them.

C. Sins of Self-Indulgence

1. Ambition

2 Kings 14 [8]Then Amaziah sent messengers to Jehoash son of Jehoahaz, the son of Jehu, king of Israel, with the challenge: "Come, meet me face to face."

[9]But Jehoash king of Israel replied to Amaziah king of Judah: "A thistle in Lebanon sent a message to a cedar in Lebanon, 'Give your daughter to my son in marriage.' Then a wild beast in Lebanon came along and trampled the thistle underfoot. [10]You have indeed defeated Edom and now you are arrogant. Glory in your victory, but stay at home! Why ask for trouble and cause your own downfall and that of Judah also?"
Ps 49 [11]Their tombs will remain their houses forever, their dwellings for endless generations, though they had named lands after themselves.

[12]But man, despite his riches, does not endure; he is like the beasts that perish.

[13]This is the fate of those who trust in themselves, and of their followers, who approve their sayings.
Isa 5 [8]Woe to you who add house to house and join field to field till no space is left and you live alone in the land.
Hab 2 [5]". . . indeed, wine betrays him; he is arrogant and never at rest. Because he is as greedy as the grave and like death is never satisfied, he gathers to himself all the nations and takes captive all the peoples.

[6]"Will not all of them taunt him with ridicule and scorn, saying, 'Woe to him who piles up stolen goods and makes himself wealthy by extortion! How long must this go on?'"
Matt 4 [8]Again, the devil took him to a very high mountain and showed him all the kingdoms of the world and their splendor. [9]"All this I will give you," he said, "if you will bow down and worship me."

[10]Jesus said to him, "Away from me, Satan! For it is written: 'Worship the Lord your God, and serve him only.'"
Matt 23 [11]"The greatest among you will be your servant. [12]For whoever exalts himself will be humbled, and whoever humbles himself will be exalted."
Mark 9 [33]They came to Capernaum. When he was in the house, he asked them, "What were you arguing about on the road?" [34]But they kept quiet because on the way they had argued about who was the greatest.

[35]Sitting down, Jesus called the Twelve and said, "If anyone wants to be first, he must be the very last, and the servant of all."

[36]He took a little child and had him stand among them. Taking him in his arms, he said to them, [37]"Whoever welcomes one of these little children in my name welcomes me; and whoever welcomes me does not welcome me but the one who sent me."
Mark 10 [35]Then James and John, the sons of Zebedee, came to him. "Teacher," they said, "we want you to do for us whatever we ask."

[36]"What do you want me to do for you?" he asked.

[37]They replied, "Let one of us sit at your right and the other at your left in your glory."

[38]"You don't know what you are asking," Jesus said. "Can you drink the cup I drink or be baptized with the baptism I am baptized with?"

[39]"We can," they answered.

Jesus said to them, "You will drink the cup I drink and be baptized with the baptism I am baptized with, [40]but to sit at my right or left is not for me to grant. These places belong to those for whom they have been prepared."

[41]When the ten heard about this, they became indignant with James and John. [42]Jesus called them together and said, "You know that those who are regarded as rulers of the Gentiles lord it over them, and their high officials exercise authority over them. [43]Not so with you. Instead, whoever wants to become great among you must be your servant, [44]and whoever wants to be first must be slave of all. [45]For even the Son of Man did not come to be served, but to serve, and to give his life as a ransom for many."
Luke 9 [25]"What good is it for a man to gain the whole world, and yet lose or forfeit his very self?"
Luke 20 [45]While all the people were listening, Jesus said to his disciples, [46]"Beware of the teachers of the law. They like to walk around in flowing robes and love to be greeted in the marketplaces and have the most important seats in the synagogues and the places of honor at banquets. [47]They devour widows' houses and for a show make lengthy prayers. Such men will be punished most severely."
Gal 5 [19]The acts of the sinful nature are obvious: sexual immorality, impurity and debauchery; [20]idolatry and witchcraft; hatred, discord, jealousy, fits of rage, selfish ambition, dissensions, factions. . . .
Phil 2 [3]Do nothing out of selfish ambition or vain conceit, but in humility consider others better than yourselves.
James 3 [14]But if you harbor bitter envy and selfish ambition in your hearts, do not boast about it or deny the truth. [15]Such "wisdom" does not come down from heaven but is earthly, unspiritual, of the devil. [16]For where you have envy and selfish ambition, there you find disorder and every evil practice.
James 4 [1]What causes fights and quarrels among you? Don't they come from your desires that battle within you? [2]You want something but don't get it. You kill and covet, but you cannot have what you want. You quarrel and fight. You do not have, because you do not ask God.
1 John 2 [16]For everything in the world—the cravings of sinful man, the lust of his eyes and the boasting of what he has and does—comes not from the Father but from the world.

2. Discontent

Exod 15 [24]So the people grumbled against Moses, saying, "What are we to drink?"
Exod 16 [2]In the desert the whole community grumbled against

Moses and Aaron. [3]The Israelites said to them, "If only we had died by the LORD's hand in Egypt! There we sat around pots of meat and ate all the food we wanted, but you have brought us out into this desert to starve this entire assembly to death."

[4]Then the LORD said to Moses, "I will rain down bread from heaven for you. The people are to go out each day and gather enough for that day. In this way I will test them and see whether they will follow my instructions. [5]On the sixth day they are to prepare what they bring in, and that is to be twice as much as they gather on the other days."

[6]So Moses and Aaron said to all the Israelites, "In the evening you will know that it was the LORD who brought you out of Egypt, [7]and in the morning you will see the glory of the LORD, because he has heard your grumbling against him. Who are we, that you should grumble against us?" [8]Moses also said, "You will know that it was the LORD when he gives you meat to eat in the evening and all the bread you want in the morning, because he has heard your grumbling against him. Who are we? You are not grumbling against us, but against the LORD."

[9]Then Moses told Aaron, "Say to the entire Israelite community, 'Come before the LORD, for he has heard your grumbling.'"

[10]While Aaron was speaking to the whole Israelite community, they looked toward the desert, and there was the glory of the LORD appearing in the cloud.

[11]The LORD said to Moses, [12]"I have heard the grumbling of the Israelites. Tell them, 'At twilight you will eat meat, and in the morning you will be filled with bread. Then you will know that I am the LORD your God.'"

Lev 19 [18]"'Do not seek revenge or bear a grudge against one of your people, but love your neighbor as yourself. I am the LORD.'"

Num 14 [2]All the Israelites grumbled against Moses and Aaron, and the whole assembly said to them, "If only we had died in Egypt! Or in this desert!" . . .

[26]The LORD said to Moses and Aaron: [27]"How long will this wicked community grumble against me? I have heard the complaints of these grumbling Israelites. . . . [29]In this desert your bodies will fall—every one of you twenty years old or more who was counted in the census and who has grumbled against me. . . ."

[36]So the men Moses had sent to explore the land, who returned and made the whole community grumble against him by spreading a bad report about it—[37]these men responsible for spreading the bad report about the land were struck down and died of a plague before the LORD.

Num 16 [11]"It is against the LORD that you and all your followers have banded together. Who is Aaron that you should grumble against him?" . . .

[41]The next day the whole Israelite community grumbled against Moses and Aaron. "You have killed the LORD's people," they said.

Job 15 [11]"Are God's consolations not enough for you, words spoken gently to you? [12]Why has your heart carried you away, and why do your eyes flash, [13]so that you vent your rage against God and pour out such words from your mouth?"

Job 33 [12]"But I tell you, in this you are not right, for God is greater than man. [13]Why do you complain to him that he answers none of man's words?"

Job 34 [37]"To his sin he adds rebellion; scornfully he claps his hands among us and multiplies his words against God."

Ps 37 [1]Do not fret because of evil men or be envious of those who do wrong. . . .

[7]Be still before the LORD and wait patiently for him; do not fret when men succeed in their ways, when they carry out their wicked schemes.

Ps 78 [17]But they continued to sin against him, rebelling in the desert against the Most High. [18]They willfully put God to the test by demanding the food they craved. [19]They spoke against God, saying, "Can God spread a table in the desert? [20]When he struck the rock, water gushed out, and streams flowed abundantly. But can he also give us food? Can he supply meat for his people?" [21]When the LORD heard them, he was very angry; his fire broke out against Jacob, and his wrath rose against Israel, [22]for they did not believe in God or trust in his deliverance.

Prov 19 [3]A man's own folly ruins his life, yet his heart rages against the LORD.

Eccles 4 [6]Better one handful with tranquillity than two handfuls with toil and chasing after the wind.

Eccles 7 [10]Do not say, "Why were the old days better than these?" For it is not wise to ask such questions.

Lam 3 [39]Why should any living man complain when punished for his sins?

Luke 3 [14]Then some soldiers asked him, "And what should we do?"

He replied, "Don't extort money and don't accuse people falsely—be content with your pay."

Rom 9 [19]One of you will say to me: "Then why does God still blame us? For who resists his will?" [20]But who are you, O man, to talk back to God? "Shall what is formed say to him who formed it, 'Why did you make me like this?'"

1 Cor 10 [10]And do not grumble, as some of them did—and were killed by the destroying angel.

2 Cor 9 [7]Each man should give what he has decided in his heart to give, not reluctantly or under compulsion, for God loves a cheerful giver.

Gal 5 [26]Let us not become conceited, provoking and envying each other.

Phil 2 [14]Do everything without complaining or arguing. . . .

Phil 4 [11]I am not saying this because I am in need, for I have learned to be content whatever the circumstances. [12]I know what it is to be in need, and I know what it is to have plenty. I have learned the secret of being content in any and every situation, whether well fed or hungry, whether living in plenty or in want.

1 Tim 6 [6]But godliness with contentment is great gain. [7]For we brought nothing into the world, and we can take nothing out of it. [8]But if we have food and clothing, we will be content with that. [9]People who want to get rich fall into temptation and a trap and into many foolish and harmful desires that plunge men into ruin and destruction. [10]For the love of money is a root of all kinds of evil. Some people, eager for money, have wandered from the faith and pierced themselves with many griefs.

Heb 13 [5]Keep your lives free from the love of money and be content with what you have, because God has said, "Never will I leave you; never will I forsake you."

James 5 [9]Don't grumble against each other, brothers, or you will be judged. The Judge is standing at the door!

1 Pet 4 [9]Offer hospitality to one another without grumbling.

Jude [16]These men are grumblers and faultfinders; they follow their own evil desires; they boast about themselves and flatter others for their own advantage.

3. Drunkenness and Excessiveness

Deut 21 [20]They shall say to the elders, "This son of ours is stubborn and rebellious. He will not obey us. He is a profligate and a drunkard." [21]Then all the men of his town shall stone him to death. You must purge the evil from among you. All Israel will hear of it and be afraid.

Prov 20 [1]Wine is a mocker and beer a brawler; whoever is led astray by them is not wise.

Prov 21 [17]He who loves pleasure will become poor; whoever loves wine and oil will never be rich.

Prov 23 [1]When you sit to dine with a ruler, note well what is before you, [2]and put a knife to your throat if you are given to gluttony. [3]Do not crave his delicacies, for that food is deceptive. . . . [20]Do not join those who drink too much wine or gorge themselves on meat, [21]for drunkards and gluttons become poor, and drowsiness clothes them in rags. . . .

[29]Who has woe? Who has sorrow? Who has strife? Who has complaints? Who has needless bruises? Who has bloodshot eyes? [30]Those who linger over wine, who go to sample bowls of mixed wine. [31]Do not gaze at wine when it is red, when it sparkles in the cup, when it goes down smoothly! [32]In the end it bites like a snake and poisons like a viper. [33]Your eyes will see strange sights and your mind imagine confusing things. [34]You will be like one sleeping on the high seas, lying on top of the rigging. [35]"They hit me," you will say, "but I'm not hurt! They

beat me, but I don't feel it! When will I wake up so I can find another drink?"

Prov 28 [7]He who keeps the law is a discerning son, but a companion of gluttons disgraces his father.

Isa 5 [11]Woe to those who rise early in the morning to run after their drinks, who stay up late at night till they are inflamed with wine. . . .

[22]Woe to those who are heroes at drinking wine and champions at mixing drinks. . . .

Isa 56 [11]They are dogs with mighty appetites; they never have enough. They are shepherds who lack understanding; they all turn to their own way, each seeks his own gain. [12]"Come," each one cries, "let me get wine! Let us drink our fill of beer! And tomorrow will be like today, or even far better."

Amos 6 [6]You drink wine by the bowlful and use the finest lotions, but you do not grieve over the ruin of Joseph.

Hab 2 [15]"Woe to him who gives drink to his neighbors, pouring it from the wineskin till they are drunk, so that he can gaze on their naked bodies. [16]You will be filled with shame instead of glory. Now it is your turn! Drink and be exposed! The cup from the LORD's right hand is coming around to you, and disgrace will cover your glory."

Matt 24 [48]"But suppose that servant is wicked and says to himself, 'My master is staying away a long time,' [49]and he then begins to beat his fellow servants and to eat and drink with drunkards. [50]The master of that servant will come on a day when he does not expect him and at an hour he is not aware of. [51]He will cut him to pieces and assign him a place with the hypocrites, where there will be weeping and gnashing of teeth."

Luke 21 [34]"Be careful, or your hearts will be weighed down with dissipation, drunkenness and the anxieties of life, and that day will close on you unexpectedly like a trap."

Rom 13 [13]Let us behave decently, as in the daytime, not in orgies and drunkenness, not in sexual immorality and debauchery, not in dissension and jealousy. [14]Rather, clothe yourselves with the Lord Jesus Christ, and do not think about how to gratify the desires of the sinful nature.

1 Cor 5 [11]But now I am writing you that you must not associate with anyone who calls himself a brother but is sexually immoral or greedy, an idolater or a slanderer, a drunkard or a swindler. With such a man do not even eat.

1 Cor 9 [25]Everyone who competes in the games goes into strict training. They do it to get a crown that will not last; but we do it to get a crown that will last forever. . . . [27]No, I beat my body and make it my slave so that after I have preached to others, I myself will not be disqualified for the prize.

Gal 5 [19]The acts of the sinful nature are obvious: sexual immorality, impurity and debauchery . . . [21]and envy; drunkenness, orgies, and the like. I warn you, as I did before, that those who live like this will not inherit the kingdom of God.

Eph 5 [18]Do not get drunk on wine, which leads to debauchery. Instead, be filled with the Spirit.

Phil 3 [19]Their destiny is destruction, their god is their stomach, and their glory is in their shame. Their mind is on earthly things.

1 Thess 5 [7]For those who sleep, sleep at night, and those who get drunk, get drunk at night. [8]But since we belong to the day, let us be self-controlled, putting on faith and love as a breastplate, and the hope of salvation as a helmet.

1 Pet 4 [3]For you have spent enough time in the past doing what pagans choose to do—living in debauchery, lust, drunkenness, orgies, carousing and detestable idolatry. [4]They think it strange that you do not plunge with them into the same flood of dissipation, and they heap abuse on you. [5]But they will have to give account to him who is ready to judge the living and the dead.

2 Pet 2 [13]They will be paid back with harm for the harm they have done. Their idea of pleasure is to carouse in broad daylight. They are blots and blemishes, reveling in their pleasures while they feast with you.

Jude [12]These men are blemishes at your love feasts, eating with you without the slightest qualm—shepherds who feed only themselves. They are clouds without rain, blown along by the wind; autumn trees, without fruit and uprooted—twice dead.

4. Extravagance

Isa 13 [19]Babylon, the jewel of kingdoms, the glory of the Babylonians' pride, will be overthrown by God like Sodom and Gomorrah. . . . [21]But desert creatures will lie there, jackals will fill her houses; there the owls will dwell, and there the wild goats will leap about. [22]Hyenas will howl in her strongholds, jackals in her luxurious palaces. Her time is at hand, and her days will not be prolonged.

Ezek 27 [1]The word of the LORD came to me: [2]"Son of man, take up a lament concerning Tyre. [3]Say to Tyre, situated at the gateway to the sea, merchant of peoples on many coasts, 'This is what the Sovereign LORD says: You say, O Tyre, "I am perfect in beauty." [4]Your domain was on the high seas; your builders brought your beauty to perfection. [5]They made all your timbers of pine trees from Senir; they took a cedar from Lebanon to make a mast for you. [6]Of oaks from Bashan they made your oars; of cypress wood from the coasts of Cyprus they made your deck, inlaid with ivory. [7]Fine embroidered linen from Egypt was your sail and served as your banner; your awnings were of blue and purple from the coasts of Elishah. [8]Men of Sidon and Arvad were your oarsmen; your skilled men, O Tyre, were aboard as your seamen. [9]Veteran craftsmen of Gebal were on board as shipwrights to caulk your seams. All the ships of the sea and their sailors came alongside to trade for your wares.

[10]"'Men of Persia, Lydia and Put served as soldiers in your army. They hung their shields and helmets on your walls, bringing you splendor. [11]Men of Arvad and Helech manned your walls on every side; men of Gammad were in your towers. They hung their shields around your walls; they brought your beauty to perfection.

[12]"'Tarshish did business with you because of your great wealth of goods; they exchanged silver, iron, tin and lead for your merchandise.

[13]"'Greece, Tubal and Meshech traded with you; they exchanged slaves and articles of bronze for your wares.

[14]"'Men of Beth Togarmah exchanged work horses, war horses and mules for your merchandise.

[15]"'The men of Rhodes traded with you, and many coastlands were your customers; they paid you with ivory tusks and ebony.

[16]"'Aram did business with you because of your many products; they exchanged turquoise, purple fabric, embroidered work, fine linen, coral and rubies for your merchandise.

[17]"'Judah and Israel traded with you; they exchanged wheat from Minnith and confections, honey, oil and balm for your wares.

[18]"'Damascus, because of your many products and great wealth of goods, did business with you in wine from Helbon and wool from Zahar.

[19]"'Danites and Greeks from Uzal bought your merchandise; they exchanged wrought iron, cassia and calamus for your wares.

[20]"'Dedan traded in saddle blankets with you.

[21]"'Arabia and all the princes of Kedar were your customers; they did business with you in lambs, rams and goats.

[22]"'The merchants of Sheba and Raamah traded with you; for your merchandise they exchanged the finest of all kinds of spices and precious stones, and gold.

[23]"'Haran, Canneh and Eden and merchants of Sheba, Asshur and Kilmad traded with you. [24]In your marketplace they traded with you beautiful garments, blue fabric, embroidered work and multicolored rugs with cords twisted and tightly knotted.

[25]"'The ships of Tarshish serve as carriers for your wares. You are filled with heavy cargo in the heart of the sea. [26]Your oarsmen take you out to the high seas. But the east wind will break you to pieces in the heart of the sea. [27]Your wealth, merchandise and wares, your mariners, seamen and shipwrights, your merchants and all your soldiers, and everyone else on board will sink into the heart of the sea on the day of your shipwreck. [28]The shorelands will quake when your seamen cry out. [29]All who handle the oars will abandon their ships; the mariners and all the seamen will stand on the shore. [30]They will raise their voice and cry bitterly over you; they will sprinkle

dust on their heads and roll in ashes. [31]They will shave their heads because of you and will put on sackcloth. They will weep over you with anguish of soul and with bitter mourning. [32]As they wail and mourn over you, they will take up a lament concerning you: "Who was ever silenced like Tyre, surrounded by the sea?" [33]When your merchandise went out on the seas, you satisfied many nations; with your great wealth and your wares you enriched the kings of the earth. [34]Now you are shattered by the sea in the depths of the waters; your wares and all your company have gone down with you. [35]All who live in the coastlands are appalled at you; their kings shudder with horror and their faces are distorted with fear. [36]The merchants among the nations hiss at you; you have come to a horrible end and will be no more.'"

Matt 11 [7]As John's disciples were leaving, Jesus began to speak to the crowd about John: "What did you go out into the desert to see? A reed swayed by the wind? [8]If not, what did you go out to see? A man dressed in fine clothes? No, those who wear fine clothes are in kings' palaces. [9]Then what did you go out to see? A prophet? Yes, I tell you, and more than a prophet."

Luke 7 [24]After John's messengers left, Jesus began to speak to the crowd about John: "What did you go out into the desert to see? A reed swayed by the wind? [25]If not, what did you go out to see? A man dressed in fine clothes? No, those who wear expensive clothes and indulge in luxury are in palaces. [26]But what did you go out to see? A prophet? Yes, I tell you, and more than a prophet."

Luke 16 [19]"There was a rich man who was dressed in purple and fine linen and lived in luxury every day. [20]At his gate was laid a beggar named Lazarus, covered with sores [21]and longing to eat what fell from the rich man's table. Even the dogs came and licked his sores.

[22]"The time came when the beggar died and the angels carried him to Abraham's side. The rich man also died and was buried. [23]In hell, where he was in torment, he looked up and saw Abraham far away, with Lazarus by his side. [24]So he called to him, 'Father Abraham, have pity on me and send Lazarus to dip the tip of his finger in water and cool my tongue, because I am in agony in this fire.'

[25]"But Abraham replied, 'Son, remember that in your lifetime you received your good things, while Lazarus received bad things, but now he is comforted here and you are in agony.'"

James 5 [5]You have lived on earth in luxury and self-indulgence. You have fattened yourselves in the day of slaughter.

1 Pet 3 [1]Wives, in the same way be submissive to your husbands so that, if any of them do not believe the word, they may be won over without words by the behavior of their wives, [2]when they see the purity and reverence of your lives. [3]Your beauty should not come from outward adornment, such as braided hair and the wearing of gold jewelry and fine clothes. [4]Instead, it should be that of your inner self, the unfading beauty of a gentle and quiet spirit, which is of great worth in God's sight. [5]For this is the way the holy women of the past who put their hope in God used to make themselves beautiful. They were submissive to their own husbands. . . .

Rev 18 [2]With a mighty voice he shouted: "Fallen! Fallen is Babylon the Great! She has become a home for demons and a haunt for every evil spirit, a haunt for every unclean and detestable bird. [3]For all the nations have drunk the maddening wine of her adulteries. The kings of the earth committed adultery with her, and the merchants of the earth grew rich from her excessive luxuries." . . . [7]"Give her as much torture and grief as the glory and luxury she gave herself. In her heart she boasts, 'I sit as queen; I am not a widow, and I will never mourn.' . . .

[9]"When the kings of the earth who committed adultery with her and shared her luxury see the smoke of her burning, they will weep and mourn over her. [10]Terrified at her torment, they will stand far off and cry: 'Woe! Woe, O great city, O Babylon, city of power! In one hour your doom has come!'

[11]"The merchants of the earth will weep and mourn over her because no one buys their cargoes any more—[12]cargoes of gold, silver, precious stones and pearls; fine linen, purple, silk and scarlet cloth; every sort of citron wood, and articles of every kind made of ivory, costly wood, bronze, iron and marble; [13]cargoes of cinnamon and spice, of incense, myrrh and frankincense, of wine and olive oil, of fine flour and wheat; cattle and sheep; horses and carriages; and bodies and souls of men.

[14]"They will say, 'The fruit you longed for is gone from you. All your riches and splendor have vanished, never to be recovered.' [15]The merchants who sold these things and gained their wealth from her will stand far off, terrified at her torment. They will weep and mourn [16]and cry out: 'Woe! Woe, O great city, dressed in fine linen, purple and scarlet, and glittering with gold, precious stones and pearls! [17]In one hour such great wealth has been brought to ruin!'

"Every sea captain, and all who travel by ship, the sailors, and all who earn their living from the sea, will stand far off. . . . [19]They will throw dust on their heads, and with weeping and mourning cry out: 'Woe! Woe, O great city, where all who had ships on the sea became rich through her wealth! In one hour she has been brought to ruin! [20]Rejoice over her, O heaven! Rejoice, saints and apostles and prophets! God has judged her for the way she treated you.'"

5. Filthy Language

Col 3 [8]But now you must rid yourselves of all such things as these: anger, rage, malice, slander, and filthy language from your lips.

6. Laziness

Prov 6 [6]Go to the ant, you sluggard; consider its ways and be wise! [7]It has no commander, no overseer or ruler, [8]yet it stores its provisions in summer and gathers its food at harvest.

Prov 10 [4]Lazy hands make a man poor, but diligent hands bring wealth.

[5]He who gathers crops in summer is a wise son, but he who sleeps during harvest is a disgraceful son.

Prov 10 [26]As vinegar to the teeth and smoke to the eyes, so is a sluggard to those who send him.

Prov 12 [24]Diligent hands will rule, but laziness ends in slave labor.

Prov 12 [27]The lazy man does not roast his game, but the diligent man prizes his possessions.

Prov 13 [4]The sluggard craves and gets nothing, but the desires of the diligent are fully satisfied.

Prov 14 [23]All hard work brings a profit, but mere talk leads only to poverty.

Prov 15 [19]The way of the sluggard is blocked with thorns, but the path of the upright is a highway.

Prov 18 [9]One who is slack in his work is brother to one who destroys.

Prov 19 [15]Laziness brings on deep sleep, and the shiftless man goes hungry.

Prov 20 [4]A sluggard does not plow in season; so at harvest time he looks but finds nothing.

Prov 20 [13]Do not love sleep or you will grow poor; stay awake and you will have food to spare.

Prov 21 [25]The sluggard's craving will be the death of him, because his hands refuse to work.

Prov 22 [13]The sluggard says, "There is a lion outside!" or, "I will be murdered in the streets!"

Prov 23 [21]for drunkards and gluttons become poor, and drowsiness clothes them in rags.

Prov 24 [30]I went past the field of the sluggard, past the vineyard of the man who lacks judgment; [31]thorns had come up everywhere, the ground was covered with weeds, and the stone wall was in ruins. [32]I applied my heart to what I observed and learned a lesson from what I saw: [33]A little sleep, a little slumber, a little folding of the hands to rest—[34]and poverty will come on you like a bandit and scarcity like an armed man.

Prov 26 [14]As a door turns on its hinges, so a sluggard turns on his bed.

[15]The sluggard buries his hand in the dish; he is too lazy to bring it back to his mouth.

[16]The sluggard is wiser in his own eyes than seven men who answer discreetly.

Eccles 4 [5]The fool folds his hands and ruins himself.

Eccles 10 [18]If a man is lazy, the rafters sag; if his hands are idle, the house leaks.

Isa 56 [10]Israel's watchmen are blind, they all lack knowledge;

they are all mute dogs, they cannot bark; they lie around and dream, they love to sleep.
Matt 25 [26]"His master replied, 'You wicked, lazy servant! So you knew that I harvest where I have not sown and gather where I have not scattered seed? [27]Well then, you should have put my money on deposit with the bankers, so that when I returned I would have received it back with interest.'"
2 Thess 3 [10]For even when we were with you, we gave you this rule: "If a man will not work, he shall not eat."

[11]We hear that some among you are idle. They are not busy; they are busybodies. [12]Such people we command and urge in the Lord Jesus Christ to settle down and earn the bread they eat.
1 Tim 5 [13]Besides, they get into the habit of being idle and going about from house to house. And not only do they become idlers, but also gossips and busybodies, saying things they ought not to.
Heb 6 [12]We do not want you to become lazy, but to imitate those who through faith and patience inherit what has been promised.

7. Miserliness

Deut 15 [9]Be careful not to harbor this wicked thought: "The seventh year, the year for canceling debts, is near," so that you do not show ill will toward your needy brother and give him nothing. He may then appeal to the LORD against you, and you will be found guilty of sin.
Prov 11 [26]People curse the man who hoards grain, but blessing crowns him who is willing to sell.
Prov 17 [5]He who mocks the poor shows contempt for their Maker; whoever gloats over disaster will not go unpunished.
Prov 21 [26]All day long he craves for more, but the righteous give without sparing.
Prov 23 [6]Do not eat the food of a stingy man, do not crave his delicacies; [7]for he is the kind of man who is always thinking about the cost. "Eat and drink," he says to you, but his heart is not with you. [8]You will vomit up the little you have eaten and will have wasted your compliments.
Prov 28 [22]A stingy man is eager to get rich and is unaware that poverty awaits him.
Prov 28 [27]He who gives to the poor will lack nothing, but he who closes his eyes to them receives many curses.
Eccles 4 [7]Again I saw something meaningless under the sun: [8]There was a man all alone; he had neither son nor brother. There was no end to his toil, yet his eyes were not content with his wealth. "For whom am I toiling," he asked, "and why am I depriving myself of enjoyment?" This too is meaningless—a miserable business!
Eccles 5 [13]I have seen a grievous evil under the sun: wealth hoarded to the harm of its owner. . . .
Amos 3 [10]"They do not know how to do right," declares the LORD, "who hoard plunder and loot in their fortresses."
James 2 [15]Suppose a brother or sister is without clothes and daily food. [16]If one of you says to him, "Go, I wish you well; keep warm and well fed," but does nothing about his physical needs, what good is it?
James 5 [3]Your gold and silver are corroded. Their corrosion will testify against you and eat your flesh like fire. You have hoarded wealth in the last days.
1 John 3 [17]If anyone has material possessions and sees his brother in need but has no pity on him, how can the love of God be in him?

X
God's Attitude toward Sin

A. Negatively, God's Attitude Is One of Wrath

Exod 22 [22]"Do not take advantage of a widow or an orphan. [23]If you do and they cry out to me, I will certainly hear their cry. [24]My anger will be aroused, and I will kill you with the sword; your wives will become widows and your children fatherless."
Exod 32 [9]"I have seen these people," the LORD said to Moses, "and they are a stiff-necked people. [10]Now leave me alone so that my anger may burn against them and that I may destroy them. Then I will make you into a great nation."
Num 12 [9]The anger of the LORD burned against them, and he left them.
Deut 9 [8]At Horeb you aroused the LORD's wrath so that he was angry enough to destroy you. . . .

[22]You also made the LORD angry at Taberah, at Massah and at Kibroth Hattaavah.
Josh 7 [1]But the Israelites acted unfaithfully in regard to the devoted things; Achan son of Carmi, the son of Zimri, the son of Zerah, of the tribe of Judah, took some of them. So the LORD's anger burned against Israel.
Josh 23 [16]"If you violate the covenant of the LORD your God, which he commanded you, and go and serve other gods and bow down to them, the LORD's anger will burn against you, and you will quickly perish from the good land he has given you."
Judg 2 [12]They forsook the LORD, the God of their fathers, who had brought them out of Egypt. They followed and worshiped various gods of the peoples around them. They provoked the LORD to anger [13]because they forsook him and served Baal and the Ashtoreths. [14]In his anger against Israel the LORD handed them over to raiders who plundered them. He sold them to their enemies all around, whom they were no longer able to resist. [15]Whenever Israel went out to fight, the hand of the LORD was against them to defeat them, just as he had sworn to them. They were in great distress.
1 Sam 28 [18]"Because you did not obey the LORD or carry out his fierce wrath against the Amalekites, the LORD has done this to you today."
2 Sam 22 [1]David sang to the LORD the words of this song when the LORD delivered him from the hand of all his enemies and from the hand of Saul. . . .

[8]"The earth trembled and quaked, the foundations of the heavens shook; they trembled because he was angry. [9]Smoke rose from his nostrils; consuming fire came from his mouth, burning coals blazed out of it. [10]He parted the heavens and came down; dark clouds were under his feet. [11]He mounted the cherubim and flew; he soared on the wings of the wind. [12]He made darkness his canopy around him—the dark rain clouds of the sky. [13]Out of the brightness of his presence bolts of lightning blazed forth. [14]The LORD thundered from heaven; the voice of the Most High resounded. [15]He shot arrows and scattered the enemies, bolts of lightning and routed them. [16]The valleys of the sea were exposed and the foundations of the earth laid bare at the rebuke of the LORD, at the blast of breath from his nostrils."
1 Kings 11 [9]The LORD became angry with Solomon because his heart had turned away from the LORD, the God of Israel, who had appeared to him twice.
2 Kings 22 [13]"Go and inquire of the LORD for me and for the people and for all Judah about what is written in this book that has been found. Great is the LORD's anger that burns against us because our fathers have not obeyed the words of this book; they have not acted in accordance with all that is written there concerning us."
2 Chron 30 [8]"Do not be stiff-necked, as your fathers were; submit to the LORD. Come to the sanctuary, which he has consecrated forever. Serve the LORD your God, so that his fierce anger will turn away from you."
Job 20 [23]"When he has filled his belly, God will vent his burning anger against him and rain down his blows upon him."
Ps 7 [11]God is a righteous judge, a God who expresses his wrath every day.
Ps 69 [24]Pour out your wrath on them; let your fierce anger overtake them.
Ps 74 [1]Why have you rejected us forever, O God? Why does your anger smolder against the sheep of your pasture?
Ps 76 [7]You alone are to be feared. Who can stand before you when you are angry?
Ps 90 [11]Who knows the power of your anger? For your wrath is as great as the fear that is due you.
Ps 106 [23]So he said he would destroy them—had not Moses,

his chosen one, stood in the breach before him to keep his wrath from destroying them.

[29]. . . they provoked the LORD to anger by their wicked deeds, and a plague broke out among them. . . .

[32]By the waters of Meribah they angered the LORD, and trouble came to Moses because of them. . . .

[40]Therefore the LORD was angry with his people and abhorred his inheritance.

Ps 110 [5]The Lord is at your right hand; he will crush kings on the day of his wrath.

Prov 6 [16]There are six things the LORD hates, seven that are detestable to him: [17]haughty eyes, a lying tongue, hands that shed innocent blood, [18]a heart that devises wicked schemes, feet that are quick to rush into evil, [19]a false witness who pours out lies and a man who stirs up dissension among brothers.

Prov 17 [15]Acquitting the guilty and condemning the innocent—the LORD detests them both.

Isa 5 [24]Therefore, as tongues of fire lick up straw and as dry grass sinks down in the flames, so their roots will decay and their flowers blow away like dust; for they have rejected the law of the LORD Almighty and spurned the word of the Holy One of Israel. [25]Therefore the LORD's anger burns against his people; his hand is raised and he strikes them down. The mountains shake, and the dead bodies are like refuse in the streets.

Yet for all this, his anger is not turned away, his hand is still upraised.

Isa 30 [27]See, the Name of the LORD comes from afar, with burning anger and dense clouds of smoke; his lips are full of wrath, and his tongue is a consuming fire. [28]His breath is like a rushing torrent, rising up to the neck. He shakes the nations in the sieve of destruction; he places in the jaws of the peoples a bit that leads them astray.

Isa 57 [16]"I will not accuse forever, nor will I always be angry, for then the spirit of man would grow faint before me—the breath of man that I have created. [17]I was enraged by his sinful greed; I punished him, and hid my face in anger, yet he kept on in his willful ways."

Isa 63 [3]"I have trodden the winepress alone; from the nations no one was with me. I trampled them in my anger and trod them down in my wrath; their blood spattered my garments, and I stained all my clothing. [4]For the day of vengeance was in my heart, and the year of my redemption has come. [5]I looked, but there was no one to help, I was appalled that no one gave support; so my own arm worked salvation for me, and my own wrath sustained me. [6]I trampled the nations in my anger; in my wrath I made them drunk and poured their blood on the ground."

Isa 66 [15]See, the LORD is coming with fire, and his chariots are like a whirlwind; he will bring down his anger with fury, and his rebuke with flames of fire. [16]For with fire and with his sword the LORD will execute judgment upon all men, and many will be those slain by the LORD.

Jer 4 [4]"Circumcise yourselves to the LORD, circumcise your hearts, you men of Judah and people of Jerusalem, or my wrath will break out and burn like fire because of the evil you have done—burn with no one to quench it."

Jer 10 [10]But the LORD is the true God; he is the living God, the eternal King. When he is angry, the earth trembles; the nations cannot endure his wrath.

Jer 21 [12]"'O house of David, this is what the LORD says: Administer justice every morning; rescue from the hand of his oppressor the one who has been robbed, or my wrath will break out and burn like fire because of the evil you have done—burn with no one to quench it. [13]I am against you, Jerusalem, you who live above this valley on the rocky plateau, declares the LORD—you who say, "Who can come against us? Who can enter our refuge?"'"

Lam 4 [11]The LORD has given full vent to his wrath; he has poured out his fierce anger. He kindled a fire in Zion that consumed her foundations.

Ezek 5 [13]"Then my anger will cease and my wrath against them will subside, and I will be avenged. And when I have spent my wrath upon them, they will know that I the LORD have spoken in my zeal.

[14]"I will make you a ruin and a reproach among the nations around you, in the sight of all who pass by. [15]You will be a reproach and a taunt, a warning and an object of horror to the nations around you when I inflict punishment on you in anger and in wrath and with stinging rebuke. I the LORD have spoken."

Dan 9 [16]"O Lord, in keeping with all your righteous acts, turn away your anger and your wrath from Jerusalem, your city, your holy hill. Our sins and the iniquities of our fathers have made Jerusalem and your people an object of scorn to all those around us."

Hos 13 [11]"So in my anger I gave you a king, and in my wrath I took him away."

Nah 1 [2]The LORD is a jealous and avenging God; the LORD takes vengeance and is filled with wrath. The LORD takes vengeance on his foes and maintains his wrath against his enemies. [3]The LORD is slow to anger and great in power; the LORD will not leave the guilty unpunished. His way is in the whirlwind and the storm, and clouds are the dust of his feet. . . . [6]Who can withstand his indignation? Who can endure his fierce anger? His wrath is poured out like fire; the rocks are shattered before him.

Matt 22 [2]"The kingdom of heaven is like a king who prepared a wedding banquet for his son. . . .

[7]"The king was enraged. He sent his army and destroyed those murderers and burned their city. . . .

[13]"Then the king told the attendants, 'Tie him hand and foot, and throw him outside, into the darkness, where there will be weeping and gnashing of teeth.'

[14]"For many are invited, but few are chosen."

Rom 1 [18]The wrath of God is being revealed from heaven against all the godlessness and wickedness of men who suppress the truth by their wickedness. . . .

Rom 2 [5]But because of your stubbornness and your unrepentant heart, you are storing up wrath against yourself for the day of God's wrath, when his righteous judgment will be revealed.

Eph 5 [6]Let no one deceive you with empty words, for because of such things God's wrath comes on those who are disobedient.

Col 3 [6]Because of these, the wrath of God is coming.

Heb 3 [7]So, as the Holy Spirit says: "Today, if you hear his voice, [8]do not harden your hearts as you did in the rebellion, during the time of testing in the desert, [9]where your fathers tested and tried me and for forty years saw what I did. [10]That is why I was angry with that generation, and I said, 'Their hearts are always going astray, and they have not known my ways.' [11]So I declared on oath in my anger, 'They shall never enter my rest.'"

James 4 [4]You adulterous people, don't you know that friendship with the world is hatred toward God? Anyone who chooses to be a friend of the world becomes an enemy of God.

Rev 6 [16]They called to the mountains and the rocks, "Fall on us and hide us from the face of him who sits on the throne and from the wrath of the Lamb! [17]For the great day of their wrath has come, and who can stand?"

Rev 14 [9]A third angel followed them and said in a loud voice: "If anyone worships the beast and his image and receives his mark on the forehead or on the hand, [10]he, too, will drink of the wine of God's fury, which has been poured full strength into the cup of his wrath. He will be tormented with burning sulfur in the presence of the holy angels and of the Lamb. [11]And the smoke of their torment rises for ever and ever. There is no rest day or night for those who worship the beast and his image, or for anyone who receives the mark of his name."

Rev 16 [19]The great city split into three parts, and the cities of the nations collapsed. God remembered Babylon the Great and gave her the cup filled with the wine of the fury of his wrath.

Rev 19 [15]Out of his mouth comes a sharp sword with which to strike down the nations. "He will rule them with an iron scepter." He treads the winepress of the fury of the wrath of God Almighty.

See also p. 375a, The Consequences of Sin

B. Positively, God's Attitude Is One of Redemption

Exod 15 [2]"The LORD is my strength and my song; he has

become my salvation. He is my God, and I will praise him, my father's God, and I will exalt him."

Ps 19 [14]May the words of my mouth and the meditation of my heart be pleasing in your sight, O LORD, my Rock and my Redeemer.

Ps 27 [1]The LORD is my light and my salvation—whom shall I fear? The LORD is the stronghold of my life—of whom shall I be afraid?

Ps 31 [5]Into your hands I commit my spirit; redeem me, O LORD, the God of truth.

Ps 34 [22]The LORD redeems his servants; no one will be condemned who takes refuge in him.

Ps 62 [1]My soul finds rest in God alone; my salvation comes from him.

Ps 98 [2]The LORD has made his salvation known and revealed his righteousness to the nations. [3]He has remembered his love and his faithfulness to the house of Israel; all the ends of the earth have seen the salvation of our God.

Ps 111 [9]He provided redemption for his people; he ordained his covenant forever—holy and awesome is his name.

Ps 130 [7]O Israel, put your hope in the LORD, for with the LORD is unfailing love and with him is full redemption.

Isa 12 [2]"Surely God is my salvation; I will trust and not be afraid. The LORD, the LORD, is my strength and my song; he has become my salvation."

Isa 41 [14]"Do not be afraid, O worm Jacob, O little Israel, for I myself will help you," declares the LORD, your Redeemer, the Holy One of Israel.

Isa 63 [16]But you are our Father, though Abraham does not know us or Israel acknowledge us; you, O LORD, are our Father, our Redeemer from of old is your name.

Jer 30 [17]"'But I will restore you to health and heal your wounds,' declares the LORD, 'because you are called an outcast, Zion for whom no one cares.'"

Ezek 37 [23]"'They will no longer defile themselves with their idols and vile images or with any of their offenses, for I will save them from all their sinful backsliding, and I will cleanse them. They will be my people, and I will be their God.'"

Luke 2 [38]Coming up to them at that very moment, she gave thanks to God and spoke about the child to all who were looking forward to the redemption of Jerusalem.

John 3 [16]"For God so loved the world that he gave his one and only Son, that whoever believes in him shall not perish but have eternal life. [17]For God did not send his Son into the world to condemn the world, but to save the world through him."

John 6 [39]"And this is the will of him who sent me, that I shall lose none of all that he has given me, but raise them up at the last day."

Acts 20 [28]"Keep watch over yourselves and all the flock of which the Holy Spirit has made you overseers. Be shepherds of the church of God, which he bought with his own blood."

Rom 1 [16]I am not ashamed of the gospel, because it is the power of God for the salvation of everyone who believes: first for the Jew, then for the Gentile.

Rom 3 [22]This righteousness from God comes through faith in Jesus Christ to all who believe. There is no difference, [23]for all have sinned and fall short of the glory of God, [24]and are justified freely by his grace through the redemption that came by Christ Jesus. [25]God presented him as a sacrifice of atonement, through faith in his blood. He did this to demonstrate his justice, because in his forbearance he had left the sins committed beforehand unpunished—[26]he did it to demonstrate his justice at the present time, so as to be just and the one who justifies those who have faith in Jesus.

Rom 6 [23]For the wages of sin is death, but the gift of God is eternal life in Christ Jesus our Lord.

1 Cor 1 [30]It is because of him that you are in Christ Jesus, who has become for us wisdom from God—that is, our righteousness, holiness and redemption.

1 Cor 7 [23]You were bought at a price; do not become slaves of men.

2 Cor 5 [18]All this is from God, who reconciled us to himself through Christ and gave us the ministry of reconciliation. . . .

Gal 1 [3]Grace and peace to you from God our Father and the Lord Jesus Christ, [4]who gave himself for our sins to rescue us from the present evil age, according to the will of our God and Father. . . .

Gal 2 [20]"I have been crucified with Christ and I no longer live, but Christ lives in me. The life I live in the body, I live by faith in the Son of God, who loved me and gave himself for me."

Gal 4 [4]But when the time had fully come, God sent his Son, born of a woman, born under law, [5]to redeem those under law, that we might receive the full rights of sons.

Eph 1 [3]Praise be to the God and Father of our Lord Jesus Christ, who has blessed us in the heavenly realms with every spiritual blessing in Christ. [4]For he chose us in him before the creation of the world to be holy and blameless in his sight. In love [5]he predestined us to be adopted as his sons through Jesus Christ, in accordance with his pleasure and will—[6]to the praise of his glorious grace, which he has freely given us in the One he loves. [7]In him we have redemption through his blood, the forgiveness of sins, in accordance with the riches of God's grace. . . .

Eph 4 [30]And do not grieve the Holy Spirit of God, with whom you were sealed for the day of redemption.

Eph 5 [1]Be imitators of God, therefore, as dearly loved children [2]and live a life of love, just as Christ loved us and gave himself up for us as a fragrant offering and sacrifice to God.

Col 1 [19]For God was pleased to have all his fullness dwell in him, [20]and through him to reconcile to himself all things, whether things on earth or things in heaven, by making peace through his blood, shed on the cross.

[21]Once you were alienated from God and were enemies in your minds because of your evil behavior. [22]But now he has reconciled you by Christ's physical body through death to present you holy in his sight, without blemish and free from accusation. . . .

1 Thess 5 [9]For God did not appoint us to suffer wrath but to receive salvation through our Lord Jesus Christ.

2 Thess 2 [13]But we ought always to thank God for you, brothers loved by the Lord, because from the beginning God chose you to be saved through the sanctifying work of the Spirit and through belief in the truth. . . .

[16]May our Lord Jesus Christ himself and God our Father, who loved us and by his grace gave us eternal encouragement and good hope . . .

1 Tim 2 [3]This is good, and pleases God our Savior, [4]who wants all men to be saved and to come to a knowledge of the truth. [5]For there is one God and one mediator between God and men, the man Christ Jesus, [6]who gave himself as a ransom for all men—the testimony given in its proper time.

2 Tim 1 [8]So do not be ashamed to testify about our Lord, or ashamed of me his prisoner. But join with me in suffering for the gospel, by the power of God, [9]who has saved us and called us to a holy life—not because of anything we have done but because of his own purpose and grace. This grace was given us in Christ Jesus before the beginning of time. . . .

Titus 1 [2]a faith and knowledge resting on the hope of eternal life, which God, who does not lie, promised before the beginning of time, [3]and at his appointed season he brought his word to light through the preaching entrusted to me by the command of God our Savior . . .

Titus 2 [11]For the grace of God that brings salvation has appeared to all men. [13]. . . while we wait for the blessed hope—the glorious appearing of our great God and Savior, Jesus Christ, [14]who gave himself for us to redeem us from all wickedness and to purify for himself a people that are his very own, eager to do what is good.

Heb 9 [11]When Christ came as high priest of the good things that are already here, he went through the greater and more perfect tabernacle that is not man-made, that is to say, not a part of this creation. [12]He did not enter by means of the blood of goats and calves; but he entered the Most Holy Place once for all by his own blood, having obtained eternal redemption. [13]The blood of goats and bulls and the ashes of a heifer sprinkled on those who are ceremonially unclean sanctify them so that they are outwardly clean. [14]How much more, then, will the blood of Christ, who through the eternal Spirit offered himself unblemished to God, cleanse our consciences from acts that lead to death, so that we may serve the living God!

[15]For this reason Christ is the mediator of a new covenant, that those who are called may receive the promised eternal inheritance—now that he has died as a ransom to set them free from the sins committed under the first covenant.

1 Pet 1 [18]For you know that it was not with perishable things such as silver or gold that you were redeemed from the empty way of life handed down to you from your forefathers, [19]but with the precious blood of Christ, a lamb without blemish or defect. [20]He was chosen before the creation of the world, but was revealed in these last times for your sake. [21]Through him you believe in God, who raised him from the dead and glorified him, and so your faith and hope are in God.

1 John 4 [9]This is how God showed his love among us: He sent his one and only Son into the world that we might live through him. [10]This is love: not that we loved God, but that he loved us and sent his Son as an atoning sacrifice for our sins.

1 John 5 [11]And this is the testimony: God has given us eternal life, and this life is in his Son.

Rev 5 [9]And they sang a new song: "You are worthy to take the scroll and to open its seals, because you were slain, and with your blood you purchased men for God from every tribe and language and people and nation. [10]You have made them to be a kingdom and priests to serve our God, and they will reign on the earth."

Rev 7 [10]And they cried out in a loud voice: "Salvation belongs to our God, who sits on the throne, and to the Lamb."

Rev 19 [1]After this I heard what sounded like the roar of a great multitude in heaven shouting: "Hallelujah! Salvation and glory and power belong to our God. . . ."

10

Salvation

I
Salvation in General

A. Faith Is the Means of Salvation

See p. 488b, Saving Faith

B. Salvation Is an Act of Grace

John 1 [16]From the fullness of his grace we have all received one blessing after another.
Acts 15 [11]"No! We believe it is through the grace of our Lord Jesus that we are saved, just as they are."
Acts 20 [24]"However, I consider my life worth nothing to me, if only I may finish the race and complete the task the Lord Jesus has given me—the task of testifying to the gospel of God's grace."
Rom 3 [22]This righteousness from God comes through faith in Jesus Christ to all who believe. There is no difference, [23]for all have sinned and fall short of the glory of God, [24]and are justified freely by his grace through the redemption that came by Christ Jesus.
Rom 5 [15]But the gift is not like the trespass. For if the many died by the trespass of the one man, how much more did God's grace and the gift that came by the grace of the one man, Jesus Christ, overflow to the many! [16]Again, the gift of God is not like the result of the one man's sin: The judgment followed one sin and brought condemnation, but the gift followed many trespasses and brought justification. [17]For if, by the trespass of the one man, death reigned through that one man, how much more will those who receive God's abundant provision of grace and of the gift of righteousness reign in life through the one man, Jesus Christ.
Rom 11 [5]So too, at the present time there is a remnant chosen by grace. [6]And if by grace, then it is no longer by works; if it were, grace would no longer be grace.
1 Cor 15 [2]By this gospel you are saved, if you hold firmly to the word I preached to you. Otherwise, you have believed in vain.

[3]For what I received I passed on to you as of first importance: that Christ died for our sins according to the Scriptures, [4]that he was buried, that he was raised on the third day according to the Scriptures, [5]and that he appeared to Peter, and then to the Twelve. . . .

[9]For I am the least of the apostles and do not even deserve to be called an apostle, because I persecuted the church of God. [10]But by the grace of God I am what I am, and his grace to me was not without effect. No, I worked harder than all of them—yet not I, but the grace of God that was with me.
2 Cor 6 [1]As God's fellow workers we urge you not to receive God's grace in vain. [2]For he says, "In the time of my favor I heard you, and in the day of salvation I helped you." I tell you, now is the time of God's favor, now is the day of salvation.
Eph 1 [5]he predestined us to be adopted as his sons through Jesus Christ, in accordance with his pleasure and will—[6]to the praise of his glorious grace, which he has freely given us in the One he loves. [7]In him we have redemption through his blood, the forgiveness of sins, in accordance with the riches of God's grace [8]that he lavished on us with all wisdom and understanding.
Eph 2 [4]But because of his great love for us, God, who is rich in mercy, [5]made us alive with Christ even when we were dead in transgressions—it is by grace you have been saved. [6]And God raised us up with Christ and seated us with him in the heavenly realms in Christ Jesus, [7]in order that in the coming ages he might show the incomparable riches of his grace, expressed in his kindness to us in Christ Jesus. [8]For it is by grace you have been saved, through faith—and this not from yourselves, it is the gift of God—[9]not by works, so that no one can boast. [10]For we are God's workmanship, created in Christ Jesus to do good works, which God prepared in advance for us to do.
1 Tim 1 [14]The grace of our Lord was poured out on me abundantly, along with the faith and love that are in Christ Jesus.

[15]Here is a trustworthy saying that deserves full acceptance: Christ Jesus came into the world to save sinners—of whom I am the worst.
2 Tim 1 [9]who has saved us and called us to a holy life—not because of anything we have done but because of his own purpose and grace. This grace was given us in Christ Jesus before the beginning of time. . . .
Titus 2 [11]For the grace of God that brings salvation has appeared to all men.
Titus 3 [4]But when the kindness and love of God our Savior appeared, [5]he saved us, not because of righteous things we had done, but because of his mercy. He saved us through the washing of rebirth and renewal by the Holy Spirit, [6]whom he poured out on us generously through Jesus Christ our Savior, [7]so that, having been justified by his grace, we might become heirs having the hope of eternal life.
Heb 2 [9]But we see Jesus, who was made a little lower than the angels, now crowned with glory and honor because he suffered death, so that by the grace of God he might taste death for everyone.
1 Pet 1 [3]Praise be to the God and Father of our Lord Jesus Christ! In his great mercy he has given us new birth into a living hope through the resurrection of Jesus Christ from the dead. . . .

[10]Concerning this salvation, the prophets, who spoke of the grace that was to come to you, searched intently and with the greatest care. . . .
2 Pet 3 [18]But grow in the grace and knowledge of our Lord and Savior Jesus Christ. To him be glory both now and forever! Amen.

C. Salvation Is an Act of Mercy

Ps 51 [1]Have mercy on me, O God, according to your unfailing love; according to your great compassion blot out my transgressions. [2]Wash away all my iniquity and cleanse me from my sin.
Luke 1 [77]". . . to give his people the knowledge of salvation through the forgiveness of their sins, [78]because of the tender mercy of our God, by which the rising sun will come to us from heaven. . . ."
Rom 9 [14]What then shall we say? Is God unjust? Not at all! [15]For he says to Moses, "I will have mercy on whom I have mercy, and I will have compassion on whom I have compassion." [16]It does not, therefore, depend on man's desire or effort, but on God's mercy. [17]For the Scripture says to Pharaoh: "I raised you up for this very purpose, that I might display my power in you and that my name might be proclaimed in all the earth." [18]Therefore God has mercy on whom he wants to have mercy, and he hardens whom he wants to harden. . . .

[22]What if God, choosing to show his wrath and make his power known, bore with great patience the objects of his wrath—prepared for destruction? [23]What if he did this to make the riches of his glory known to the objects of his mercy, whom he prepared in advance for glory—[24]even us, whom he also called, not only from the Jews but also from the Gentiles?
Rom 11 [30]Just as you who were at one time disobedient to God have now received mercy as a result of their disobedience, [31]so they too have now become disobedient in order that they too may now receive mercy as a result of God's mercy to you. [32]For God has bound all men over to disobedience so that he may have mercy on them all.
Eph 2 [4]But because of his great love for us, God, who is rich in mercy, [5]made us alive with Christ even when we were dead in transgressions—it is by grace you have been saved.
1 Tim 1 [13]Even though I was once a blasphemer and a persecutor and a violent man, I was shown mercy because I acted in ignorance and unbelief. . . .

[15]Here is a trustworthy saying that deserves full acceptance: Christ Jesus came into the world to save sinners—of whom I am the worst. [16]But for that very reason I was shown mercy so that in me, the worst of sinners, Christ Jesus might display his unlimited patience as an example for those who would believe on him and receive eternal life.
Titus 3 [5]he saved us, not because of righteous things we had done, but because of his mercy. He saved us through the washing of rebirth and renewal by the Holy Spirit. . . .

1 Pet 1 [3]Praise be to the God and Father of our Lord Jesus Christ! In his great mercy he has given us new birth into a living hope through the resurrection of Jesus Christ from the dead. . . .
1 Pet 2 [10]Once you were not a people, but now you are the people of God; once you had not received mercy, but now you have received mercy.
Jude [21]Keep yourselves in God's love as you wait for the mercy of our Lord Jesus Christ to bring you to eternal life.

D. Salvation Is Expressed Nationally

Ps 69 [35]for God will save Zion and rebuild the cities of Judah. Then people will settle there and possess it. . . .
Ps 85 [9]Surely his salvation is near those who fear him, that his glory may dwell in our land.
Ps 98 [2]The LORD has made his salvation known and revealed his righteousness to the nations. [3]He has remembered his love and his faithfulness to the house of Israel; all the ends of the earth have seen the salvation of our God.
Isa 25 [7]On this mountain he will destroy the shroud that enfolds all peoples, the sheet that covers all nations; [8]he will swallow up death forever. The Sovereign LORD will wipe away the tears from all faces; he will remove the disgrace of his people from all the earth. The LORD has spoken. [9]In that day they will say, "Surely this is our God; we trusted in him, and he saved us. This is the LORD, we trusted in him; let us rejoice and be glad in his salvation."
Isa 43 [1]But now, this is what the LORD says—he who created you, O Jacob, he who formed you, O Israel: "Fear not, for I have redeemed you; I have summoned you by name; you are mine. [2]When you pass through the waters, I will be with you; and when you pass through the rivers, they will not sweep over you. When you walk through the fire, you will not be burned; the flames will not set you ablaze. [3]For I am the LORD, your God, the Holy One of Israel, your Savior; I give Egypt for your ransom, Cush and Seba in your stead."
Isa 45 [17]But Israel will be saved by the LORD with an everlasting salvation; you will never be put to shame or disgraced, to ages everlasting.
Isa 46 [13]"I am bringing my righteousness near, it is not far away; and my salvation will not be delayed. I will grant salvation to Zion, my splendor to Israel."
Isa 49 [6]he says: "It is too small a thing for you to be my servant to restore the tribes of Jacob and bring back those of Israel I have kept. I will also make you a light for the Gentiles, that you may bring my salvation to the ends of the earth." . . .

[25]But this is what the LORD says: "Yes, captives will be taken from warriors, and plunder retrieved from the fierce; I will contend with those who contend with you, and your children I will save. [26]I will make your oppressors eat their own flesh; they will be drunk on their own blood, as with wine. Then all mankind will know that I, the LORD, am your Savior, your Redeemer, the Mighty One of Jacob."
Isa 52 [10]The LORD will lay bare his holy arm in the sight of all the nations, and all the ends of the earth will see the salvation of our God.
Jer 3 [23]"Surely the idolatrous commotion on the hills and mountains is a deception; surely in the LORD our God is the salvation of Israel."
Jer 14 [8]O Hope of Israel, its Savior in times of distress, why are you like a stranger in the land, like a traveler who stays only a night?
Jer 31 [31]"The time is coming," declares the LORD, "when I will make a new covenant with the house of Israel and with the house of Judah. [32]It will not be like the covenant I made with their forefathers when I took them by the hand to lead them out of Egypt, because they broke my covenant, though I was a husband to them," declares the LORD. [33]"This is the covenant I will make with the house of Israel after that time," declares the LORD. "I will put my law in their minds and write it on their hearts. I will be their God, and they will be my people. [34]No longer will a man teach his neighbor, or a man his brother, saying, 'Know the LORD,' because they will all know me, from the least of them to the greatest," declares the LORD. "For I will forgive their wickedness and will remember their sins no more."
Jer 46 [27]"Do not fear, O Jacob my servant; do not be dismayed, O Israel. I will surely save you out of a distant place, your descendants from the land of their exile. Jacob will again have peace and security, and no one will make him afraid."
Ezek 36 [24]"'For I will take you out of the nations; I will gather you from all the countries and bring you back into your own land. . . . [26]I will give you a new heart and put a new spirit in you; I will remove from you your heart of stone and give you a heart of flesh.'"
Ezek 37 [21]". . . and say to them, 'This is what the Sovereign LORD says: I will take the Israelites out of the nations where they have gone. I will gather them from all around and bring them back into their own land. [22]I will make them one nation in the land, on the mountains of Israel. There will be one king over all of them and they will never again be two nations or be divided into two kingdoms. [23]They will no longer defile themselves with their idols and vile images or with any of their offenses, for I will save them from all their sinful backsliding, and I will cleanse them. They will be my people, and I will be their God.'"
Hos 1 [7]"Yet I will show love to the house of Judah; and I will save them—not by bow, sword or battle, or by horses and horsemen, but by the LORD their God."
Hos 13 [4]"But I am the LORD your God, who brought you out of Egypt. You shall acknowledge no God but me, no Savior except me."
Zech 9 [10]I will take away the chariots from Ephraim and the war-horses from Jerusalem, and the battle bow will be broken. He will proclaim peace to the nations. His rule will extend from sea to sea and from the River to the ends of the earth. . . . [16]The LORD their God will save them on that day as the flock of his people. They will sparkle in his land like jewels in a crown.
Rom 11 [26]And so all Israel will be saved, as it is written: "The deliverer will come from Zion; he will turn godlessness away from Jacob."

E. Salvation Is Expressed Personally

Exod 14 [13]Moses answered the people, "Do not be afraid. Stand firm and you will see the deliverance the LORD will bring you today. The Egyptians you see today you will never see again."
Exod 15 [2]"The LORD is my strength and my song; he has become my salvation. He is my God, and I will praise him, my father's God, and I will exalt him."
2 Sam 22 [3]". . . my God is my rock, in whom I take refuge, my shield and the horn of my salvation. He is my stronghold, my refuge and my savior—from violent men you save me."
Ps 13 [5]But I trust in your unfailing love; my heart rejoices in your salvation.
Ps 27 [1]The LORD is my light and my salvation—whom shall I fear? The LORD is the stronghold of my life—of whom shall I be afraid?
Ps 62 [1]My soul finds rest in God alone; my salvation comes from him.
Ps 86 [13]For great is your love toward me; you have delivered me from the depths of the grave.
Ps 118 [14]The LORD is my strength and my song; he has become my salvation.
Ps 121 [1]I lift up my eyes to the hills—where does my help come from? [2]My help comes from the LORD, the Maker of heaven and earth.
Isa 12 [2]"Surely God is my salvation; I will trust and not be afraid. The LORD, the LORD, is my strength and my song; he has become my salvation."
Isa 35 [4]say to those with fearful hearts, "Be strong, do not fear; your God will come, he will come with vengeance; with divine retribution he will come to save you."
Isa 45 [22]"Turn to me and be saved, all you ends of the earth; for I am God, and there is no other."
Mic 7 [7]But as for me, I watch in hope for the LORD, I wait for God my Savior; my God will hear me.
Hab 3 [18]yet I will rejoice in the LORD, I will be joyful in God my Savior.
Luke 1 [46]And Mary said: "My soul glorifies the Lord [47]and my spirit rejoices in God my Savior. . . ."

John 10 9"I am the gate; whoever enters through me will be saved. He will come in and go out, and find pasture."
Acts 2 21"'And everyone who calls on the name of the Lord will be saved.'"
Acts 16 31They replied, "Believe in the Lord Jesus, and you will be saved—you and your household."
Rom 10 9That if you confess with your mouth, "Jesus is Lord," and believe in your heart that God raised him from the dead, you will be saved.
1 Tim 2 3This is good, and pleases God our Savior, 4who wants all men to be saved and to come to a knowledge of the truth.
1 Tim 4 10(and for this we labor and strive), that we have put our hope in the living God, who is the Savior of all men, and especially of those who believe.
Heb 7 25Therefore he is able to save completely those who come to God through him, because he always lives to intercede for them.
Heb 10 10And by that will, we have been made holy through the sacrifice of the body of Jesus Christ once for all. 14. . . because by one sacrifice he has made perfect forever those who are being made holy.
Jude 24To him who is able to keep you from falling and to present you before his glorious presence without fault and with great joy—25to the only God our Savior be glory, majesty, power and authority, through Jesus Christ our Lord, before all ages, now and forevermore! Amen.

F. Salvation Is God's Ultimate Act and Humankind's Ultimate Decision

John 3 17"For God did not send his Son into the world to condemn the world, but to save the world through him. 18Whoever believes in him is not condemned, but whoever does not believe stands condemned already because he has not believed in the name of God's one and only Son." . . . 36"Whoever believes in the Son has eternal life, but whoever rejects the Son will not see life, for God's wrath remains on him."
John 5 37"And the Father who sent me has himself testified concerning me. You have never heard his voice nor seen his form, 38nor does his word dwell in you, for you do not believe the one he sent. 39You diligently study the Scriptures because you think that by them you possess eternal life. These are the Scriptures that testify about me, 40yet you refuse to come to me to have life."
John 8 12When Jesus spoke again to the people, he said, "I am the light of the world. Whoever follows me will never walk in darkness, but will have the light of life." . . . 24"I told you that you would die in your sins; if you do not believe that I am the one I claim to be, you will indeed die in your sins."
John 10 14"I am the good shepherd; I know my sheep and my sheep know me—15just as the Father knows me and I know the Father—and I lay down my life for the sheep. 16I have other sheep that are not of this sheep pen. I must bring them also. They too will listen to my voice, and there shall be one flock and one shepherd. 17The reason my Father loves me is that I lay down my life—only to take it up again. 18No one takes it from me, but I lay it down of my own accord. I have authority to lay it down and authority to take it up again. This command I received from my Father."
John 16 5"Now I am going to him who sent me, yet none of you asks me, 'Where are you going?' . . . 7But I tell you the truth: It is for your good that I am going away. Unless I go away, the Counselor will not come to you; but if I go, I will send him to you. 8When he comes, he will convict the world of guilt in regard to sin and righteousness and judgment: 9in regard to sin, because men do not believe in me. . . ."
Acts 3 18"But this is how God fulfilled what he had foretold through all the prophets, saying that his Christ would suffer. 19Repent, then, and turn to God, so that your sins may be wiped out, that times of refreshing may come from the Lord. . . . 23'Anyone who does not listen to him will be completely cut off from among his people.'"
Rom 1 18The wrath of God is being revealed from heaven against all the godlessness and wickedness of men who suppress the truth by their wickedness, 19since what may be known about God is plain to them, because God has made it plain to them.
1 Cor 1 18For the message of the cross is foolishness to those who are perishing, but to us who are being saved it is the power of God.
Heb 10 26If we deliberately keep on sinning after we have received the knowledge of the truth, no sacrifice for sins is left, 27but only a fearful expectation of judgment and of raging fire that will consume the enemies of God. 28Anyone who rejected the law of Moses died without mercy on the testimony of two or three witnesses. 29How much more severely do you think a man deserves to be punished who has trampled the Son of God under foot, who has treated as an unholy thing the blood of the covenant that sanctified him, and who has insulted the Spirit of grace? 30For we know him who said, "It is mine to avenge; I will repay," and again, "The Lord will judge his people." 31It is a dreadful thing to fall into the hands of the living God.
Heb 12 2Let us fix our eyes on Jesus, the author and perfecter of our faith, who for the joy set before him endured the cross, scorning its shame, and sat down at the right hand of the throne of God. . . .

25See to it that you do not refuse him who speaks. If they did not escape when they refused him who warned them on earth, how much less will we, if we turn away from him who warns us from heaven?
1 Pet 2 4As you come to him, the living Stone—rejected by men but chosen by God and precious to him—5you also, like living stones, are being built into a spiritual house to be a holy priesthood, offering spiritual sacrifices acceptable to God through Jesus Christ. 6For in Scripture it says: "See, I lay a stone in Zion, a chosen and precious cornerstone, and the one who trusts in him will never be put to shame." 7Now to you who believe, this stone is precious. But to those who do not believe, "The stone the builders rejected has become the capstone," 8and, "A stone that causes men to stumble and a rock that makes them fall." They stumble because they disobey the message—which is also what they were destined for.
1 John 5 10Anyone who believes in the Son of God has this testimony in his heart. Anyone who does not believe God has made him out to be a liar, because he has not believed the testimony God has given about his Son. . . . 12He who has the Son has life; he who does not have the Son of God does not have life.

G. Salvation Is Grounded in God's Love

Deut 7 7The LORD did not set his affection on you and choose you because you were more numerous than other peoples, for you were the fewest of all peoples. 8But it was because the LORD loved you and kept the oath he swore to your forefathers that he brought you out with a mighty hand and redeemed you from the land of slavery, from the power of Pharaoh king of Egypt.
Ps 6 4Turn, O LORD, and deliver me; save me because of your unfailing love.
John 3 16"For God so loved the world that he gave his one and only Son, that whoever believes in him shall not perish but have eternal life."
John 14 21"Whoever has my commands and obeys them, he is the one who loves me. He who loves me will be loved by my Father, and I too will love him and show myself to him."

22Then Judas (not Judas Iscariot) said, "But, Lord, why do you intend to show yourself to us and not to the world?"

23Jesus replied, "If anyone loves me, he will obey my teaching. My Father will love him, and we will come to him and make our home with him. 24He who does not love me will not obey my teaching. These words you hear are not my own; they belong to the Father who sent me."
John 15 12"My command is this: Love each other as I have loved you. 13Greater love has no one than this, that he lay down his life for his friends."
John 16 27"No, the Father himself loves you because you have loved me and have believed that I came from God."
John 17 23"I in them and you in me. May they be brought to complete unity to let the world know that you sent me and have loved them even as you have loved me. . . . 26I have made

you known to them, and will continue to make you known in order that the love you have for me may be in them and that I myself may be in them."
Rom 5 8But God demonstrates his own love for us in this: While we were still sinners, Christ died for us.
Eph 2 4But because of his great love for us, God, who is rich in mercy, 5made us alive with Christ even when we were dead in transgressions—it is by grace you have been saved.
2 Thess 2 16May our Lord Jesus Christ himself and God our Father, who loved us and by his grace gave us eternal encouragement and good hope . . .
Titus 3 4But when the kindness and love of God our Savior appeared, 5he saved us, not because of righteous things we had done, but because of his mercy. He saved us through the washing of rebirth and renewal by the Holy Spirit. . . .
1 John 3 1How great is the love the Father has lavished on us, that we should be called children of God! And that is what we are! The reason the world does not know us is that it did not know him.
1 John 4 7Dear friends, let us love one another, for love comes from God. Everyone who loves has been born of God and knows God. 8Whoever does not love does not know God, because God is love. 9This is how God showed his love among us: He sent his one and only Son into the world that we might live through him. 10This is love: not that we loved God, but that he loved us and sent his Son as an atoning sacrifice for our sins. 11Dear friends, since God so loved us, we also ought to love one another. 12No one has ever seen God; but if we love one another, God lives in us and his love is made complete in us.

13We know that we live in him and he in us, because he has given us of his Spirit. 14And we have seen and testify that the Father has sent his Son to be the Savior of the world. 15If anyone acknowledges that Jesus is the Son of God, God lives in him and he in God. 16And so we know and rely on the love God has for us.

God is love. Whoever lives in love lives in God, and God in him. 17In this way, love is made complete among us so that we will have confidence on the day of judgment, because in this world we are like him. 18There is no fear in love. But perfect love drives out fear, because fear has to do with punishment. The one who fears is not made perfect in love.

19We love because he first loved us.
Rev 1 5and from Jesus Christ, who is the faithful witness, the firstborn from the dead, and the ruler of the kings of the earth.

To him who loves us and has freed us from our sins by his blood . . .

H. Salvation Is Not according to Our Works

Acts 15 7After much discussion, Peter got up and addressed them: "Brothers, you know that some time ago God made a choice among you that the Gentiles might hear from my lips the message of the gospel and believe. 8God, who knows the heart, showed that he accepted them by giving the Holy Spirit to them, just as he did to us. 9He made no distinction between us and them, for he purified their hearts by faith. 10Now then, why do you try to test God by putting on the necks of the disciples a yoke that neither we nor our fathers have been able to bear? 11No! We believe it is through the grace of our Lord Jesus that we are saved, just as they are."
Rom 3 28For we maintain that a man is justified by faith apart from observing the law.
Rom 4 1What then shall we say that Abraham, our forefather, discovered in this matter? 2If, in fact, Abraham was justified by works, he had something to boast about—but not before God. 3What does the Scripture say? "Abraham believed God, and it was credited to him as righteousness."

4Now when a man works, his wages are not credited to him as a gift, but as an obligation. 5However, to the man who does not work but trusts God who justifies the wicked, his faith is credited as righteousness. 6David says the same thing when he speaks of the blessedness of the man to whom God credits righteousness apart from works: 7"Blessed are they whose transgressions are forgiven, whose sins are covered. 8Blessed is the man whose sin the Lord will never count against him."

9Is this blessedness only for the circumcised, or also for the uncircumcised? We have been saying that Abraham's faith was credited to him as righteousness. 10Under what circumstances was it credited? Was it after he was circumcised, or before? It was not after, but before! 11And he received the sign of circumcision, a seal of the righteousness that he had by faith while he was still uncircumcised. So then, he is the father of all who believe but have not been circumcised, in order that righteousness might be credited to them. 12And he is also the father of the circumcised who not only are circumcised but who also walk in the footsteps of the faith that our father Abraham had before he was circumcised.

13It was not through law that Abraham and his offspring received the promise that he would be heir of the world, but through the righteousness that comes by faith. 14For if those who live by law are heirs, faith has no value and the promise is worthless, 15because law brings wrath. And where there is no law there is no transgression.

16Therefore, the promise comes by faith, so that it may be by grace and may be guaranteed to all Abraham's offspring—not only to those who are of the law but also to those who are of the faith of Abraham. He is the father of us all. . . . 25He was delivered over to death for our sins and was raised to life for our justification.
Rom 9 30What then shall we say? That the Gentiles, who did not pursue righteousness, have obtained it, a righteousness that is by faith; 31but Israel, who pursued a law of righteousness, has not attained it. 32Why not? Because they pursued it not by faith but as if it were by works. They stumbled over the "stumbling stone." 33As it is written: "See, I lay in Zion a stone that causes men to stumble and a rock that makes them fall, and the one who trusts in him will never be put to shame."
Rom 11 2God did not reject his people, whom he foreknew. . . . 5So too, at the present time there is a remnant chosen by grace. 6And if by grace, then it is no longer by works; if it were, grace would no longer be grace.
Gal 2 16". . . know that a man is not justified by observing the law, but by faith in Jesus Christ. So we, too, have put our faith in Christ Jesus that we may be justified by faith in Christ and not by observing the law, because by observing the law no one will be justified."
Gal 2 21"I do not set aside the grace of God, for if righteousness could be gained through the law, Christ died for nothing!"
Eph 2 8For it is by grace you have been saved, through faith—and this not from yourselves, it is the gift of God—9not by works, so that no one can boast.
Phil 3 7But whatever was to my profit I now consider loss for the sake of Christ. 8What is more, I consider everything a loss compared to the surpassing greatness of knowing Christ Jesus my Lord, for whose sake I have lost all things. I consider them rubbish, that I may gain Christ 9and be found in him, not having a righteousness of my own that comes from the law, but that which is through faith in Christ—the righteousness that comes from God and is by faith. 10I want to know Christ and the power of his resurrection and the fellowship of sharing in his sufferings, becoming like him in his death, 11and so, somehow, to attain to the resurrection from the dead.
2 Tim 1 9who has saved us and called us to a holy life—not because of anything we have done but because of his own purpose and grace. This grace was given us in Christ Jesus before the beginning of time. . . .

I. Salvation Is Open to All

Isa 55 1"Come, all you who are thirsty, come to the waters; and you who have no money, come, buy and eat! Come, buy wine and milk without money and without cost. 2Why spend money on what is not bread, and your labor on what does not satisfy? Listen, listen to me, and eat what is good, and your soul will delight in the richest of fare. 3Give ear and come to me; hear me, that your soul may live. I will make an everlasting covenant with you, my faithful love promised to David. 4See, I have made him a witness to the peoples, a leader and commander of the peoples. 5Surely you will summon nations you know not, and nations that do not know you will hasten to you, because of the LORD your God, the Holy One of Israel, for he has endowed you with splendor."

[6]Seek the LORD while he may be found; call on him while he is near. [7]Let the wicked forsake his way and the evil man his thoughts. Let him turn to the LORD, and he will have mercy on him, and to our God, for he will freely pardon.

John 3 [16]"For God so loved the world that he gave his one and only Son, that whoever believes in him shall not perish but have eternal life."

John 5 [24]"I tell you the truth, whoever hears my word and believes him who sent me has eternal life and will not be condemned; he has crossed over from death to life."

John 11 [51]He did not say this on his own, but as high priest that year he prophesied that Jesus would die for the Jewish nation, [52]and not only for that nation but also for the scattered children of God, to bring them together and make them one.

John 12 [30]Jesus said, "This voice was for your benefit, not mine. . . . [32]But I, when I am lifted up from the earth, will draw all men to myself."

Acts 11 [17]"So if God gave them the same gift as he gave us, who believed in the Lord Jesus Christ, who was I to think that I could oppose God?"

[18]When they heard this, they had no further objections and praised God, saying, "So then, God has granted even the Gentiles repentance unto life."

Acts 13 [26]"Brothers, children of Abraham, and you God-fearing Gentiles, it is to us that this message of salvation has been sent. . . .

[38]"Therefore, my brothers, I want you to know that through Jesus the forgiveness of sins is proclaimed to you. [39]Through him everyone who believes is justified from everything you could not be justified from by the law of Moses. . . ."

[47]"For this is what the Lord has commanded us: 'I have made you a light for the Gentiles, that you may bring salvation to the ends of the earth.'"

Acts 20 [21]"I have declared to both Jews and Greeks that they must turn to God in repentance and have faith in our Lord Jesus."

Acts 28 [28]"Therefore I want you to know that God's salvation has been sent to the Gentiles, and they will listen!"

Rom 1 [5]Through him and for his name's sake, we received grace and apostleship to call people from among all the Gentiles to the obedience that comes from faith. . . .

[14]I am obligated both to Greeks and non-Greeks, both to the wise and the foolish. . . .

[16]I am not ashamed of the gospel, because it is the power of God for the salvation of everyone who believes: first for the Jew, then for the Gentile.

Rom 3 [21]But now a righteousness from God, apart from law, has been made known, to which the Law and the Prophets testify. [22]This righteousness from God comes through faith in Jesus Christ to all who believe. There is no difference, [23]for all have sinned and fall short of the glory of God, [24]and are justified freely by his grace through the redemption that came by Christ Jesus. . . . [29]Is God the God of Jews only? Is he not the God of Gentiles too? Yes, of Gentiles too. . . .

Rom 10 [10]For it is with your heart that you believe and are justified, and it is with your mouth that you confess and are saved. [11]As the Scripture says, "Anyone who trusts in him will never be put to shame." [12]For there is no difference between Jew and Gentile—the same Lord is Lord of all and richly blesses all who call on him, [13]for, "Everyone who calls on the name of the Lord will be saved."

1 Cor 1 [21]For since in the wisdom of God the world through its wisdom did not know him, God was pleased through the foolishness of what was preached to save those who believe. [23]. . . but we preach Christ crucified: a stumbling block to Jews and foolishness to Gentiles, [24]but to those whom God has called, both Jews and Greeks, Christ the power of God and the wisdom of God.

Gal 3 [26]You are all sons of God through faith in Christ Jesus, [27]for all of you who were baptized into Christ have clothed yourselves with Christ. [28]There is neither Jew nor Greek, slave nor free, male nor female, for you are all one in Christ Jesus.

Eph 2 [11]Therefore, remember that formerly you who are Gentiles by birth and called "uncircumcised" by those who call themselves "the circumcision" (that done in the body by the hands of men)—[12]remember that at that time you were separate from Christ, excluded from citizenship in Israel and foreigners to the covenants of the promise, without hope and without God in the world. [13]But now in Christ Jesus you who once were far away have been brought near through the blood of Christ. . . . [17]He came and preached peace to you who were far away and peace to those who were near.

Eph 3 [6]This mystery is that through the gospel the Gentiles are heirs together with Israel, members together of one body, and sharers together in the promise in Christ Jesus.

Col 1 [26]the mystery that has been kept hidden for ages and generations, but is now disclosed to the saints. [27]To them God has chosen to make known among the Gentiles the glorious riches of this mystery, which is Christ in you, the hope of glory.

[28]We proclaim him, admonishing and teaching everyone with all wisdom, so that we may present everyone perfect in Christ.

Col 3 [11]Here there is no Greek or Jew, circumcised or uncircumcised, barbarian, Scythian, slave or free, but Christ is all, and is in all.

1 Tim 2 [3]This is good, and pleases God our Savior, [4]who wants all men to be saved and to come to a knowledge of the truth.

1 Tim 4 [10](and for this we labor and strive), that we have put our hope in the living God, who is the Savior of all men, and especially of those who believe.

Titus 2 [11]For the grace of God that brings salvation has appeared to all men.

Heb 5 [7]During the days of Jesus' life on earth, he offered up prayers and petitions with loud cries and tears to the one who could save him from death, and he was heard because of his reverent submission. [9]. . . and, once made perfect, he became the source of eternal salvation for all who obey him. . . .

2 Pet 3 [9]The Lord is not slow in keeping his promise, as some understand slowness. He is patient with you, not wanting anyone to perish, but everyone to come to repentance.

Rev 5 [9]And they sang a new song: "You are worthy to take the scroll and to open its seals, because you were slain, and with your blood you purchased men for God from every tribe and language and people and nation."

Rev 14 [6]Then I saw another angel flying in midair, and he had the eternal gospel to proclaim to those who live on the earth—to every nation, tribe, language and people.

Rev 22 [17]The Spirit and the bride say, "Come!" And let him who hears say, "Come!" Whoever is thirsty, let him come; and whoever wishes, let him take the free gift of the water of life.

J. Salvation Is a Trinitarian Act

1. God and Salvation

1 Chron 16 [23]Sing to the LORD, all the earth; proclaim his salvation day after day.

Ps 3 [8]From the LORD comes deliverance. May your blessing be on your people.

Ps 37 [39]The salvation of the righteous comes from the LORD; he is their stronghold in time of trouble.

Ps 68 [19]Praise be to the Lord, to God our Savior, who daily bears our burdens. [20]Our God is a God who saves; from the Sovereign LORD comes escape from death.

Ps 74 [12]But you, O God, are my king from of old; you bring salvation upon the earth.

Ps 96 [2]Sing to the LORD, praise his name; proclaim his salvation day after day.

Isa 43 [11]"I, even I, am the LORD, and apart from me there is no savior."

Isa 45 [8]"You heavens above, rain down righteousness; let the clouds shower it down. Let the earth open wide, let salvation spring up, let righteousness grow with it; I, the LORD, have created it. . . .

[20]"Gather together and come; assemble, you fugitives from the nations. Ignorant are those who carry about idols of wood, who pray to gods that cannot save. [21]Declare what is to be, present it—let them take counsel together. Who foretold this long ago, who declared it from the distant past? Was it not I, the

LORD? And there is no God apart from me, a righteous God and a Savior; there is none but me.

[22]"Turn to me and be saved, all you ends of the earth; for I am God, and there is no other."

Isa 49 [1]Listen to me, you islands; hear this, you distant nations: Before I was born the LORD called me; from my birth he has made mention of my name.

Isa 59 [15]Truth is nowhere to be found, and whoever shuns evil becomes a prey.

The LORD looked and was displeased that there was no justice. [16]He saw that there was no one, he was appalled that there was no one to intervene; so his own arm worked salvation for him, and his own righteousness sustained him. [17]He put on righteousness as his breastplate, and the helmet of salvation on his head; he put on the garments of vengeance and wrapped himself in zeal as in a cloak.

Ezek 34 [11]"'For this is what the Sovereign LORD says: I myself will search for my sheep and look after them. . . . [22]I will save my flock, and they will no longer be plundered. I will judge between one sheep and another.'"

Jon 2 [9]"But I, with a song of thanksgiving, will sacrifice to you. What I have vowed I will make good. Salvation comes from the LORD."

Luke 1 [68]"Praise be to the Lord, the God of Israel, because he has come and has redeemed his people. [69]He has raised up a horn of salvation for us in the house of his servant David. . . ."

Luke 3 [6]"'And all mankind will see God's salvation.'"

John 3 [17]"For God did not send his Son into the world to condemn the world, but to save the world through him."

Acts 5 [31]"God exalted him to his own right hand as Prince and Savior that he might give repentance and forgiveness of sins to Israel."

Acts 13 [23]"From this man's descendants God has brought to Israel the Savior Jesus, as he promised."

Rom 1 [16]I am not ashamed of the gospel, because it is the power of God for the salvation of everyone who believes: first for the Jew, then for the Gentile.

1 Thess 5 [9]For God did not appoint us to suffer wrath but to receive salvation through our Lord Jesus Christ.

Titus 3 [4]But when the kindness and love of God our Savior appeared, [5]he saved us, not because of righteous things we had done, but because of his mercy. He saved us through the washing of rebirth and renewal by the Holy Spirit, [6]whom he poured out on us generously through Jesus Christ our Savior, [7]so that, having been justified by his grace, we might become heirs having the hope of eternal life.

Heb 2 [3]how shall we escape if we ignore such a great salvation? This salvation, which was first announced by the Lord, was confirmed to us by those who heard him. [4]God also testified to it by signs, wonders and various miracles, and gifts of the Holy Spirit distributed according to his will.

1 John 4 [14]And we have seen and testify that the Father has sent his Son to be the Savior of the world.

1 John 5 [11]And this is the testimony: God has given us eternal life, and this life is in his Son.

Rev 19 [1]After this I heard what sounded like the roar of a great multitude in heaven shouting: "Hallelujah! Salvation and glory and power belong to our God. . . ."

2. Christ and Salvation

Isa 63 [8]He said, "Surely they are my people, sons who will not be false to me"; and so he became their Savior. [9]In all their distress he too was distressed, and the angel of his presence saved them. In his love and mercy he redeemed them; he lifted them up and carried them all the days of old.

Jer 23 [5]"The days are coming," declares the LORD, "when I will raise up to David a righteous Branch, a King who will reign wisely and do what is just and right in the land. [6]In his days Judah will be saved and Israel will live in safety. This is the name by which he will be called: The LORD Our Righteousness."

Matt 1 [21]"She will give birth to a son, and you are to give him the name Jesus, because he will save his people from their sins."

Luke 1 [76]"And you, my child, will be called a prophet of the Most High; for you will go on before the Lord to prepare the way for him, [77]to give his people the knowledge of salvation through the forgiveness of their sins. . . ."

Luke 2 [11]"Today in the town of David a Savior has been born to you; he is Christ the Lord."

Luke 4 [14]Jesus returned to Galilee in the power of the Spirit, and news about him spread through the whole countryside. [15]He taught in their synagogues, and everyone praised him.

[16]He went to Nazareth, where he had been brought up, and on the Sabbath day he went into the synagogue, as was his custom. And he stood up to read. [17]The scroll of the prophet Isaiah was handed to him. Unrolling it, he found the place where it is written: [18]"The Spirit of the Lord is on me, because he has anointed me to preach good news to the poor. He has sent me to proclaim freedom for the prisoners and recovery of sight for the blind, to release the oppressed, [19]to proclaim the year of the Lord's favor."

[20]Then he rolled up the scroll, gave it back to the attendant and sat down. The eyes of everyone in the synagogue were fastened on him, [21]and he began by saying to them, "Today this scripture is fulfilled in your hearing."

Luke 19 [10]"For the Son of Man came to seek and to save what was lost."

John 4 [42]They said to the woman, "We no longer believe just because of what you said; now we have heard for ourselves, and we know that this man really is the Savior of the world."

John 12 [44]Then Jesus cried out, "When a man believes in me, he does not believe in me only, but in the one who sent me. . . .

[47]"As for the person who hears my words but does not keep them, I do not judge him. For I did not come to judge the world, but to save it."

Acts 4 [10]". . . then know this, you and all the people of Israel: It is by the name of Jesus Christ of Nazareth, whom you crucified but whom God raised from the dead, that this man stands before you healed. . . . [12]Salvation is found in no one else, for there is no other name under heaven given to men by which we must be saved."

Acts 5 [30]"The God of our fathers raised Jesus from the dead—whom you had killed by hanging him on a tree. [31]God exalted him to his own right hand as Prince and Savior that he might give repentance and forgiveness of sins to Israel."

Rom 5 [1]Therefore, since we have been justified through faith, we have peace with God through our Lord Jesus Christ, [2]through whom we have gained access by faith into this grace in which we now stand. And we rejoice in the hope of the glory of God.

Rom 5 [9]Since we have now been justified by his blood, how much more shall we be saved from God's wrath through him! [10]For if, when we were God's enemies, we were reconciled to him through the death of his Son, how much more, having been reconciled, shall we be saved through his life!

Eph 5 [23]For the husband is the head of the wife as Christ is the head of the church, his body, of which he is the Savior.

Phil 3 [20]But our citizenship is in heaven. And we eagerly await a Savior from there, the Lord Jesus Christ, [21]who, by the power that enables him to bring everything under his control, will transform our lowly bodies so that they will be like his glorious body.

1 Tim 1 [15]Here is a trustworthy saying that deserves full acceptance: Christ Jesus came into the world to save sinners—of whom I am the worst.

2 Tim 1 [9]who has saved us and called us to a holy life—not because of anything we have done but because of his own purpose and grace. This grace was given us in Christ Jesus before the beginning of time, [10]but it has now been revealed through the appearing of our Savior, Christ Jesus, who has destroyed death and has brought life and immortality to light through the gospel.

Titus 3 [6]whom he poured out on us generously through Jesus Christ our Savior . . .

Heb 2 [3]how shall we escape if we ignore such a great salvation? This salvation, which was first announced by the Lord, was confirmed to us by those who heard him.

Heb 2 [9]But we see Jesus, who was made a little lower than the angels, now crowned with glory and honor because he suffered death, so that by the grace of God he might taste death for everyone.

[10]In bringing many sons to glory, it was fitting that God, for whom and through whom everything exists, should make the author of their salvation perfect through suffering.

Heb 5 [7]During the days of Jesus' life on earth, he offered up prayers and petitions with loud cries and tears to the one who could save him from death, and he was heard because of his reverent submission. [8]Although he was a son, he learned obedience from what he suffered [9]and, once made perfect, he became the source of eternal salvation for all who obey him. . . .

Heb 7 [24]but because Jesus lives forever, he has a permanent priesthood. [25]Therefore he is able to save completely those who come to God through him, because he always lives to intercede for them.

Heb 9 [28]so Christ was sacrificed once to take away the sins of many people; and he will appear a second time, not to bear sin, but to bring salvation to those who are waiting for him.

1 John 4 [14]And we have seen and testify that the Father has sent his Son to be the Savior of the world.

3. The Spirit and Salvation

John 3 [5]Jesus answered, "I tell you the truth, no one can enter the kingdom of God unless he is born of water and the Spirit. [6]Flesh gives birth to flesh, but the Spirit gives birth to spirit. . . . [8]The wind blows wherever it pleases. You hear its sound, but you cannot tell where it comes from or where it is going. So it is with everyone born of the Spirit."

John 6 [63]"The Spirit gives life; the flesh counts for nothing. The words I have spoken to you are spirit and they are life."

Rom 1 [4]and who through the Spirit of holiness was declared with power to be the Son of God by his resurrection from the dead: Jesus Christ our Lord.

Gal 3 [3]Are you so foolish? After beginning with the Spirit, are you now trying to attain your goal by human effort?

1 Thess 1 [5]because our gospel came to you not simply with words, but also with power, with the Holy Spirit and with deep conviction. You know how we lived among you for your sake.

2 Thess 2 [13]But we ought always to thank God for you, brothers loved by the Lord, because from the beginning God chose you to be saved through the sanctifying work of the Spirit and through belief in the truth.

Titus 3 [5]he saved us, not because of righteous things we had done, but because of his mercy. He saved us through the washing of rebirth and renewal by the Holy Spirit, [6]whom he poured out on us generously through Jesus Christ our Savior. . . .

1 Pet 1 [2]who have been chosen according to the foreknowledge of God the Father, through the sanctifying work of the Spirit, for obedience to Jesus Christ and sprinkling by his blood: Grace and peace be yours in abundance.

1 Pet 3 [18]For Christ died for sins once for all, the righteous for the unrighteous, to bring you to God. He was put to death in the body but made alive by the Spirit. . . .

K. Salvation Provides Benefits for Believers

1. Adoption into the Family of God

John 1 [12]Yet to all who received him, to those who believed in his name, he gave the right to become children of God. . . .

Gal 4 [4]But when the time had fully come, God sent his Son, born of a woman, born under law, [5]to redeem those under law, that we might receive the full rights of sons. [6]Because you are sons, God sent the Spirit of his Son into our hearts, the Spirit who calls out, "*Abba,* Father." [7]So you are no longer a slave, but a son; and since you are a son, God has made you also an heir.

2. Christ Dwelling Within

Rom 8 [10]But if Christ is in you, your body is dead because of sin, yet your spirit is alive because of righteousness. [11]And if the Spirit of him who raised Jesus from the dead is living in you, he who raised Christ from the dead will also give life to your mortal bodies through his Spirit, who lives in you.

Col 1 [27]To them God has chosen to make known among the Gentiles the glorious riches of this mystery, which is Christ in you, the hope of glory.

3. Citizenship in Heaven

Eph 2 [13]But now in Christ Jesus you who once were far away have been brought near through the blood of Christ. . . .

[19]Consequently, you are no longer foreigners and aliens, but fellow citizens with God's people and members of God's household. . . .

Phil 3 [20]But our citizenship is in heaven. And we eagerly await a Savior from there, the Lord Jesus Christ. . . .

Col 3 [1]Since, then, you have been raised with Christ, set your hearts on things above, where Christ is seated at the right hand of God. [2]Set your minds on things above, not on earthly things. [3]For you died, and your life is now hidden with Christ in God.

Heb 12 [22]But you have come to Mount Zion, to the heavenly Jerusalem, the city of the living God. You have come to thousands upon thousands of angels in joyful assembly, [23]to the church of the firstborn, whose names are written in heaven. You have come to God, the judge of all men, to the spirits of righteous men made perfect, [24]to Jesus the mediator of a new covenant, and to the sprinkled blood that speaks a better word than the blood of Abel.

4. Completion

Phil 1 [6]being confident of this, that he who began a good work in you will carry it on to completion until the day of Christ Jesus.

5. A Divine Inheritance

Col 1 [12]giving thanks to the Father, who has qualified you to share in the inheritance of the saints in the kingdom of light.

6. Eternal Life

See p. 500b, Eternal Life

7. Forgiveness of Sin

Ps 32 [1]Blessed is he whose transgressions are forgiven, whose sins are covered. [2]Blessed is the man whose sin the LORD does not count against him and in whose spirit is no deceit.

Matt 26 [28]"This is my blood of the covenant, which is poured out for many for the forgiveness of sins."

Luke 1 [76]"And you, my child, will be called a prophet of the Most High; for you will go on before the Lord to prepare the way for him, [77]to give his people the knowledge of salvation through the forgiveness of their sins. . . ."

Luke 24 [46]He told them, "This is what is written: The Christ will suffer and rise from the dead on the third day, [47]and repentance and forgiveness of sins will be preached in his name to all nations, beginning at Jerusalem."

Acts 5 [30]"The God of our fathers raised Jesus from the dead—whom you had killed by hanging him on a tree. [31]God exalted him to his own right hand as Prince and Savior that he might give repentance and forgiveness of sins to Israel."

Acts 10 [36]"You know the message God sent to the people of Israel, telling the good news of peace through Jesus Christ, who is Lord of all. . . .

[39]"We are witnesses of everything he did in the country of the Jews and in Jerusalem. They killed him by hanging him on a tree. . . . [43]All the prophets testify about him that everyone who believes in him receives forgiveness of sins through his name."

Acts 13 [38]"Therefore, my brothers, I want you to know that through Jesus the forgiveness of sins is proclaimed to you."

2 Cor 5 [19]that God was reconciling the world to himself in Christ, not counting men's sins against them. And he has committed to us the message of reconciliation.

Eph 1 [3]Praise be to the God and Father of our Lord Jesus Christ, who has blessed us in the heavenly realms with every spiritual blessing in Christ. . . . [7]In him we have redemption through his blood, the forgiveness of sins, in accordance with the riches of God's grace. . . .

Col 1 [13]For he has rescued us from the dominion of darkness and brought us into the kingdom of the Son he loves, [14]in whom we have redemption, the forgiveness of sins.
Col 2 [13]When you were dead in your sins and in the uncircumcision of your sinful nature, God made you alive with Christ. He forgave us all our sins. . . .

8. Freedom from Condemnation and Judgment

Isa 50 [8]He who vindicates me is near. Who then will bring charges against me? Let us face each other! Who is my accuser? Let him confront me! [9]It is the Sovereign LORD who helps me. Who is he that will condemn me? They will all wear out like a garment; the moths will eat them up.
Rom 8 [1]Therefore, there is now no condemnation for those who are in Christ Jesus, [2]because through Christ Jesus the law of the Spirit of life set me free from the law of sin and death.
Rom 8 [33]Who will bring any charge against those whom God has chosen? It is God who justifies. [34]Who is he that condemns? Christ Jesus, who died—more than that, who was raised to life—is at the right hand of God and is also interceding for us. [35]Who shall separate us from the love of Christ? Shall trouble or hardship or persecution or famine or nakedness or danger or sword? [36]As it is written: "For your sake we face death all day long; we are considered as sheep to be slaughtered." [37]No, in all these things we are more than conquerors through him who loved us. [38]For I am convinced that neither death nor life, neither angels nor demons, neither the present nor the future, nor any powers, [39]neither height nor depth, nor anything else in all creation, will be able to separate us from the love of God that is in Christ Jesus our Lord.
Col 1 [22]But now he has reconciled you by Christ's physical body through death to present you holy in his sight, without blemish and free from accusation. . . .

9. Freedom from the Power of Sin

Rom 6 [14]For sin shall not be your master, because you are not under law, but under grace.
Rom 8 [2]because through Christ Jesus the law of the Spirit of life set me free from the law of sin and death. [3]For what the law was powerless to do in that it was weakened by the sinful nature, God did by sending his own Son in the likeness of sinful man to be a sin offering. And so he condemned sin in sinful man, [4]in order that the righteous requirements of the law might be fully met in us, who do not live according to the sinful nature but according to the Spirit.
Gal 1 [3]Grace and peace to you from God our Father and the Lord Jesus Christ, [4]who gave himself for our sins to rescue us from the present evil age, according to the will of our God and Father. . . .
1 Pet 2 [21]To this you were called, because Christ suffered for you, leaving you an example, that you should follow in his steps. . . . [24]He himself bore our sins in his body on the tree, so that we might die to sins and live for righteousness; by his wounds you have been healed.
Rev 1 [5]and from Jesus Christ, who is the faithful witness, the firstborn from the dead, and the ruler of the kings of the earth.

To him who loves us and has freed us from our sins by his blood . . .

10. God's Will Being Worked Within

Phil 2 [13]for it is God who works in you to will and to act according to his good purpose.

11. The Holy Spirit and His Fruit

Gal 5 [22]But the fruit of the Spirit is love, joy, peace, patience, kindness, goodness, faithfulness, [23]gentleness and self-control. Against such things there is no law. [24]Those who belong to Christ Jesus have crucified the sinful nature with its passions and desires. [25]Since we live by the Spirit, let us keep in step with the Spirit.

12. Hope for Tomorrow

Rom 8 [28]And we know that in all things God works for the good of those who love him, who have been called according to his purpose.
See also p. 43a, Saving Faith Is a Personal Relationship of Trust in Christ as Lord and Savior

13. Inner Cleansing

Heb 1 [3]The Son is the radiance of God's glory and the exact representation of his being, sustaining all things by his powerful word. After he had provided purification for sins, he sat down at the right hand of the Majesty in heaven.
Heb 9 [14]How much more, then, will the blood of Christ, who through the eternal Spirit offered himself unblemished to God, cleanse our consciences from acts that lead to death, so that we may serve the living God!
Heb 10 [19]Therefore, brothers, since we have confidence to enter the Most Holy Place by the blood of Jesus, [20]by a new and living way opened for us through the curtain, that is, his body, [21]and since we have a great priest over the house of God, [22]let us draw near to God with a sincere heart in full assurance of faith, having our hearts sprinkled to cleanse us from a guilty conscience and having our bodies washed with pure water.
1 John 1 [7]But if we walk in the light, as he is in the light, we have fellowship with one another, and the blood of Jesus, his Son, purifies us from all sin.

14. Justification in God's Sight

Rom 5 [8]But God demonstrates his own love for us in this: While we were still sinners, Christ died for us.

[9]Since we have now been justified by his blood, how much more shall we be saved from God's wrath through him!

15. Lightness in the Lord

Eph 5 [1]Be imitators of God, therefore, as dearly loved children [2]and live a life of love, just as Christ loved us and gave himself up for us as a fragrant offering and sacrifice to God. . . .

[8]For you were once darkness, but now you are light in the Lord. Live as children of light. . . .

16. The Mind of Christ

John 15 [15]"I no longer call you servants, because a servant does not know his master's business. Instead, I have called you friends, for everything that I learned from my Father I have made known to you."
1 Cor 2 [16]"For who has known the mind of the Lord that he may instruct him?" But we have the mind of Christ.
Phil 2 [5]Your attitude should be the same as that of Christ Jesus. . . .

17. Nearness to God

Acts 2 [36]"Therefore let all Israel be assured of this: God has made this Jesus, whom you crucified, both Lord and Christ." . . .

[38]Peter replied, "Repent and be baptized, every one of you, in the name of Jesus Christ for the forgiveness of your sins. And you will receive the gift of the Holy Spirit. [39]The promise is for you and your children and for all who are far off—for all whom the Lord our God will call."
Eph 2 [13]But now in Christ Jesus you who once were far away have been brought near through the blood of Christ.

18. A New Creation in Christ

Rom 6 [4]We were therefore buried with him through baptism into death in order that, just as Christ was raised from the dead through the glory of the Father, we too may live a new life.
2 Cor 5 [14]For Christ's love compels us, because we are convinced that one died for all, and therefore all died. [15]And he died for all, that those who live should no longer live for themselves but for him who died for them and was raised again. . . . [17]Therefore, if anyone is in Christ, he is a new creation; the old has gone, the new has come!
Gal 6 [14]May I never boast except in the cross of our Lord Jesus

Christ, through which the world has been crucified to me, and I to the world. [15]Neither circumcision nor uncircumcision means anything; what counts is a new creation.

Eph 2 [10]For we are God's workmanship, created in Christ Jesus to do good works, which God prepared in advance for us to do. [15]. . . by abolishing in his flesh the law with its commandments and regulations. His purpose was to create in himself one new man out of the two, thus making peace. . . .

19. A New Self and Governing Disposition

Jer 31 [33]"This is the covenant I will make with the house of Israel after that time," declares the LORD. "I will put my law in their minds and write it on their hearts. I will be their God, and they will be my people."

Ezek 11 [19]"I will give them an undivided heart and put a new spirit in them; I will remove from them their heart of stone and give them a heart of flesh."

Rom 6 [17]But thanks be to God that, though you used to be slaves to sin, you wholeheartedly obeyed the form of teaching to which you were entrusted. [22]But now that you have been set free from sin and have become slaves to God, the benefit you reap leads to holiness, and the result is eternal life. . . .

Rom 8 [1]Therefore, there is now no condemnation for those who are in Christ Jesus, [2]because through Christ Jesus the law of the Spirit of life set me free from the law of sin and death. [3]For what the law was powerless to do in that it was weakened by the sinful nature, God did by sending his own Son in the likeness of sinful man to be a sin offering. And so he condemned sin in sinful man, [4]in order that the righteous requirements of the law might be fully met in us, who do not live according to the sinful nature but according to the Spirit.

[5]Those who live according to the sinful nature have their minds set on what that nature desires; but those who live in accordance with the Spirit have their minds set on what the Spirit desires. [6]The mind of sinful man is death, but the mind controlled by the Spirit is life and peace; [7]the sinful mind is hostile to God. It does not submit to God's law, nor can it do so. [8]Those controlled by the sinful nature cannot please God.

[9]You, however, are controlled not by the sinful nature but by the Spirit, if the Spirit of God lives in you. And if anyone does not have the Spirit of Christ, he does not belong to Christ. [10]But if Christ is in you, your body is dead because of sin, yet your spirit is alive because of righteousness. [11]And if the Spirit of him who raised Jesus from the dead is living in you, he who raised Christ from the dead will also give life to your mortal bodies through his Spirit, who lives in you.

Eph 4 [22]You were taught, with regard to your former way of life, to put off your old self, which is being corrupted by its deceitful desires; [23]to be made new in the attitude of your minds; [24]and to put on the new self, created to be like God in true righteousness and holiness.

Col 3 [9]Do not lie to each other, since you have taken off your old self with its practices [10]and have put on the new self, which is being renewed in knowledge in the image of its Creator.

1 John 2 [29]If you know that he is righteous, you know that everyone who does what is right has been born of him.

20. One's Name in the Book of Life

Phil 4 [3]Yes, and I ask you, loyal yokefellow, help these women who have contended at my side in the cause of the gospel, along with Clement and the rest of my fellow workers, whose names are in the book of life.

21. Peace with God

Isa 9 [6]For to us a child is born, to us a son is given, and the government will be on his shoulders. And he will be called Wonderful Counselor, Mighty God, Everlasting Father, Prince of Peace.

Isa 53 [5]But he was pierced for our transgressions, he was crushed for our iniquities; the punishment that brought us peace was upon him, and by his wounds we are healed.

Isa 54 [10]"Though the mountains be shaken and the hills be removed, yet my unfailing love for you will not be shaken nor my covenant of peace be removed," says the LORD, who has compassion on you.

Ezek 34 [25]"'I will make a covenant of peace with them and rid the land of wild beasts so that they may live in the desert and sleep in the forests in safety.'"

Zech 6 [13]"'It is he who will build the temple of the LORD, and he will be clothed with majesty and will sit and rule on his throne. And he will be a priest on his throne. And there will be harmony between the two.'"

Zech 9 [10]I will take away the chariots from Ephraim and the war-horses from Jerusalem, and the battle bow will be broken. He will proclaim peace to the nations. His rule will extend from sea to sea and from the River to the ends of the earth.

Luke 1 [76]"And you, my child, will be called a prophet of the Most High; for you will go on before the Lord to prepare the way for him, [77]to give his people the knowledge of salvation through the forgiveness of their sins, [78]because of the tender mercy of our God, by which the rising sun will come to us from heaven [79]to shine on those living in darkness and in the shadow of death, to guide our feet into the path of peace."

Luke 2 [14]"Glory to God in the highest, and on earth peace to men on whom his favor rests."

Luke 19 [38]"Blessed is the king who comes in the name of the Lord!"

"Peace in heaven and glory in the highest!"

John 16 [33]"I have told you these things, so that in me you may have peace. In this world you will have trouble. But take heart! I have overcome the world."

Acts 10 [36]"You know the message God sent to the people of Israel, telling the good news of peace through Jesus Christ, who is Lord of all. . . .

[39]"We are witnesses of everything he did in the country of the Jews and in Jerusalem. They killed him by hanging him on a tree, [40]but God raised him from the dead on the third day and caused him to be seen."

Rom 5 [1]Therefore, since we have been justified through faith, we have peace with God through our Lord Jesus Christ. . . .

Eph 2 [13]But now in Christ Jesus you who once were far away have been brought near through the blood of Christ.

[14]For he himself is our peace, who has made the two one and has destroyed the barrier, the dividing wall of hostility, [15]by abolishing in his flesh the law with its commandments and regulations. His purpose was to create in himself one new man out of the two, thus making peace, [16]and in this one body to reconcile both of them to God through the cross, by which he put to death their hostility. [17]He came and preached peace to you who were far away and peace to those who were near. [18]For through him we both have access to the Father by one Spirit.

Eph 6 [10]Finally, be strong in the Lord and in his mighty power. . . . [14]Stand firm then, with the belt of truth buckled around your waist, with the breastplate of righteousness in place, [15]and with your feet fitted with the readiness that comes from the gospel of peace.

Phil 4 [7]And the peace of God, which transcends all understanding, will guard your hearts and your minds in Christ Jesus.

Col 1 [13]For he has rescued us from the dominion of darkness and brought us into the kingdom of the Son he loves, [14]in whom we have redemption, the forgiveness of sins. . . . [19]For God was pleased to have all his fullness dwell in him, [20]and through him to reconcile to himself all things, whether things on earth or things in heaven, by making peace through his blood, shed on the cross.

Col 3 [15]Let the peace of Christ rule in your hearts, since as members of one body you were called to peace. And be thankful.

Heb 13 [20]May the God of peace, who through the blood of the eternal covenant brought back from the dead our Lord Jesus, that great Shepherd of the sheep, [21]equip you with everything good for doing his will, and may he work in us what is pleasing to him, through Jesus Christ, to whom be glory for ever and ever. Amen.

22. Power to Overcome the World

1 John 4 [4]You, dear children, are from God and have overcome them, because the one who is in you is greater than the one who is in the world.
1 John 5 [4]for everyone born of God overcomes the world. This is the victory that has overcome the world, even our faith. [5]Who is it that overcomes the world? Only he who believes that Jesus is the Son of God.

23. Rebirth

John 1 [12]Yet to all who received him, to those who believed in his name, he gave the right to become children of God—[13]children born not of natural descent, nor of human decision or a husband's will, but born of God.
John 3 [3]In reply Jesus declared, "I tell you the truth, no one can see the kingdom of God unless he is born again."

[4]"How can a man be born when he is old?" Nicodemus asked. "Surely he cannot enter a second time into his mother's womb to be born!"

[5]Jesus answered, "I tell you the truth, no one can enter the kingdom of God unless he is born of water and the Spirit. [6]Flesh gives birth to flesh, but the Spirit gives birth to spirit. [7]You should not be surprised at my saying, 'You must be born again.'"
James 1 [18]He chose to give us birth through the word of truth, that we might be a kind of firstfruits of all he created.
1 Pet 1 [18]For you know that it was not with perishable things such as silver or gold that you were redeemed from the empty way of life handed down to you from your forefathers, [19]but with the precious blood of Christ, a lamb without blemish or defect. . . . [23]For you have been born again, not of perishable seed, but of imperishable, through the living and enduring word of God.
1 John 3 [9]No one who is born of God will continue to sin, because God's seed remains in him; he cannot go on sinning, because he has been born of God.

24. The Righteousness of God

Isa 61 [10]I delight greatly in the LORD; my soul rejoices in my God. For he has clothed me with garments of salvation and arrayed me in a robe of righteousness, as a bridegroom adorns his head like a priest, and as a bride adorns herself with her jewels.
Rom 1 [17]For in the gospel a righteousness from God is revealed, a righteousness that is by faith from first to last, just as it is written: "The righteous will live by faith."
Rom 3 [22]This righteousness from God comes through faith in Jesus Christ to all who believe. There is no difference. . . .
Rom 4 [5]However, to the man who does not work but trusts God who justifies the wicked, his faith is credited as righteousness. [6]David says the same thing when he speaks of the blessedness of the man to whom God credits righteousness apart from works: [7]"Blessed are they whose transgressions are forgiven, whose sins are covered. [8]Blessed is the man whose sin the Lord will never count against him."
1 Cor 1 [30]It is because of him that you are in Christ Jesus, who has become for us wisdom from God—that is, our righteousness, holiness and redemption.
2 Cor 5 [14]For Christ's love compels us, because we are convinced that one died for all, and therefore all died. . . . [21]God made him who had no sin to be sin for us, so that in him we might become the righteousness of God.
Gal 3 [6]Consider Abraham: "He believed God, and it was credited to him as righteousness."
Phil 3 [9]and be found in him, not having a righteousness of my own that comes from the law, but that which is through faith in Christ—the righteousness that comes from God and is by faith. [10]I want to know Christ and the power of his resurrection and the fellowship of sharing in his sufferings, becoming like him in his death. . . .
James 2 [23]And the scripture was fulfilled that says, "Abraham believed God, and it was credited to him as righteousness," and he was called God's friend.

25. Salvation from God's Wrath

Rom 5 [8]But God demonstrates his own love for us in this: While we were still sinners, Christ died for us.

[9]Since we have now been justified by his blood, how much more shall we be saved from God's wrath through him!
1 Thess 1 [10]and to wait for his Son from heaven, whom he raised from the dead—Jesus, who rescues us from the coming wrath.

26. The Security of Being Christ's

John 16 [33]"I have told you these things, so that in me you may have peace. In this world you will have trouble. But take heart! I have overcome the world."
Rom 8 [31]What, then, shall we say in response to this? If God is for us, who can be against us? . . . [37]No, in all these things we are more than conquerors through him who loved us. [38]For I am convinced that neither death nor life, neither angels nor demons, neither the present nor the future, nor any powers, [39]neither height nor depth, nor anything else in all creation, will be able to separate us from the love of God that is in Christ Jesus our Lord.
2 Cor 2 [14]But thanks be to God, who always leads us in triumphal procession in Christ and through us spreads everywhere the fragrance of the knowledge of him.
Phil 4 [6]Do not be anxious about anything, but in everything, by prayer and petition, with thanksgiving, present your requests to God. [7]And the peace of God, which transcends all understanding, will guard your hearts and your minds in Christ Jesus. . . . [12]I know what it is to be in need, and I know what it is to have plenty. I have learned the secret of being content in any and every situation, whether well fed or hungry, whether living in plenty or in want. [13]I can do everything through him who gives me strength.
Heb 10 [19]Therefore, brothers, since we have confidence to enter the Most Holy Place by the blood of Jesus, [20]by a new and living way opened for us through the curtain, that is, his body, [21]and since we have a great priest over the house of God, [22]let us draw near to God with a sincere heart in full assurance of faith, having our hearts sprinkled to cleanse us from a guilty conscience and having our bodies washed with pure water.

27. Transfer to the Kingdom of Christ from Satan's Dominion

Col 1 [13]For he has rescued us from the dominion of darkness and brought us into the kingdom of the Son he loves. . . .

28. Ultimate Glorification

Rom 8 [29]For those God foreknew he also predestined to be conformed to the likeness of his Son, that he might be the firstborn among many brothers. [30]And those he predestined, he also called; those he called, he also justified; those he justified, he also glorified.

29. Unity with Other Believers

John 11 [51]He did not say this on his own, but as high priest that year he prophesied that Jesus would die for the Jewish nation, [52]and not only for that nation but also for the scattered children of God, to bring them together and make them one.
Gal 3 [26]You are all sons of God through faith in Christ Jesus, [27]for all of you who were baptized into Christ have clothed yourselves with Christ. [28]There is neither Jew nor Greek, slave nor free, male nor female, for you are all one in Christ Jesus.
Eph 3 [6]This mystery is that through the gospel the Gentiles are heirs together with Israel, members together of one body, and sharers together in the promise in Christ Jesus.
Col 3 [11]Here there is no Greek or Jew, circumcised or uncircumcised, barbarian, Scythian, slave or free, but Christ is all, and is in all.

II
Christ's Death as Saving Act

A. Christ's Death Is the Only Means of Salvation

1. Jesus' Death Was Sufficient and Lacked Nothing

John 1 [7]He came as a witness to testify concerning that light, so that through him all men might believe. . . . [9]The true light that gives light to every man was coming into the world.
John 3 [14]"Just as Moses lifted up the snake in the desert, so the Son of Man must be lifted up, [15]that everyone who believes in him may have eternal life.

[16]"For God so loved the world that he gave his one and only Son, that whoever believes in him shall not perish but have eternal life. [17]For God did not send his Son into the world to condemn the world, but to save the world through him."
John 4 [13]Jesus answered, "Everyone who drinks this water will be thirsty again, [14]but whoever drinks the water I give him will never thirst. Indeed, the water I give him will become in him a spring of water welling up to eternal life."
John 6 [35]Then Jesus declared, "I am the bread of life. He who comes to me will never go hungry, and he who believes in me will never be thirsty."
John 7 [37]On the last and greatest day of the Feast, Jesus stood and said in a loud voice, "If anyone is thirsty, let him come to me and drink. [38]Whoever believes in me, as the Scripture has said, streams of living water will flow from within him."
John 11 [25]Jesus said to her, "I am the resurrection and the life. He who believes in me will live, even though he dies; [26]and whoever lives and believes in me will never die. Do you believe this?"
John 15 [1]"I am the true vine, and my Father is the gardener . . .

[5]"I am the vine; you are the branches. If a man remains in me and I in him, he will bear much fruit; apart from me you can do nothing. [6]If anyone does not remain in me, he is like a branch that is thrown away and withers; such branches are picked up, thrown into the fire and burned."
Rom 7 [24]What a wretched man I am! Who will rescue me from this body of death? [25]Thanks be to God—through Jesus Christ our Lord!

So then, I myself in my mind am a slave to God's law, but in the sinful nature a slave to the law of sin.
1 Cor 1 [18]For the message of the cross is foolishness to those who are perishing, but to us who are being saved it is the power of God.
1 Cor 6 [11]And that is what some of you were. But you were washed, you were sanctified, you were justified in the name of the Lord Jesus Christ and by the Spirit of our God.
Eph 5 [1]Be imitators of God, therefore, as dearly loved children [2]and live a life of love, just as Christ loved us and gave himself up for us as a fragrant offering and sacrifice to God. [14]. . . for it is light that makes everything visible. This is why it is said: "Wake up, O sleeper, rise from the dead, and Christ will shine on you."
Col 1 [20]and through him to reconcile to himself all things, whether things on earth or things in heaven, by making peace through his blood, shed on the cross.

[21]Once you were alienated from God and were enemies in your minds because of your evil behavior. [22]But now he has reconciled you by Christ's physical body through death to present you holy in his sight, without blemish and free from accusation. . . .
1 Thess 5 [8]But since we belong to the day, let us be self-controlled, putting on faith and love as a breastplate, and the hope of salvation as a helmet. [9]For God did not appoint us to suffer wrath but to receive salvation through our Lord Jesus Christ. [10]He died for us so that, whether we are awake or asleep, we may live together with him.
1 Tim 1 [13]Even though I was once a blasphemer and a persecutor and a violent man, I was shown mercy because I acted in ignorance and unbelief. [14]The grace of our Lord was poured out on me abundantly, along with the faith and love that are in Christ Jesus.

[15]Here is a trustworthy saying that deserves full acceptance: Christ Jesus came into the world to save sinners—of whom I am the worst. [16]But for that very reason I was shown mercy so that in me, the worst of sinners, Christ Jesus might display his unlimited patience as an example for those who would believe on him and receive eternal life.
Titus 3 [3]At one time we too were foolish, disobedient, deceived and enslaved by all kinds of passions and pleasures. We lived in malice and envy, being hated and hating one another. [4]But when the kindness and love of God our Savior appeared, [5]he saved us, not because of righteous things we had done, but because of his mercy. He saved us through the washing of rebirth and renewal by the Holy Spirit, [6]whom he poured out on us generously through Jesus Christ our Savior, [7]so that, having been justified by his grace, we might become heirs having the hope of eternal life.
Heb 7 [24]but because Jesus lives forever, he has a permanent priesthood. [25]Therefore he is able to save completely those who come to God through him, because he always lives to intercede for them.
Rev 21 [6]He said to me: "It is done. I am the Alpha and the Omega, the Beginning and the End. To him who is thirsty I will give to drink without cost from the spring of the water of life."

2. Jesus' Death Was Once-for-All

John 17 [1]After Jesus said this, he looked toward heaven and prayed: "Father, the time has come. Glorify your Son, that your Son may glorify you. [2]For you granted him authority over all people that he might give eternal life to all those you have given him. [3]Now this is eternal life: that they may know you, the only true God, and Jesus Christ, whom you have sent. [4]I have brought you glory on earth by completing the work you gave me to do."
Acts 3 [18]"But this is how God fulfilled what he had foretold through all the prophets, saying that his Christ would suffer. [19]Repent, then, and turn to God, so that your sins may be wiped out, that times of refreshing may come from the Lord. . . ."
Acts 4 [10]". . . then know this, you and all the people of Israel: It is by the name of Jesus Christ of Nazareth, whom you crucified but whom God raised from the dead, that this man stands before you healed. . . . [12]Salvation is found in no one else, for there is no other name under heaven given to men by which we must be saved."
Rom 6 [8]Now if we died with Christ, we believe that we will also live with him. . . . [10]The death he died, he died to sin once for all; but the life he lives, he lives to God.
Gal 1 [3]Grace and peace to you from God our Father and the Lord Jesus Christ, [4]who gave himself for our sins to rescue us from the present evil age, according to the will of our God and Father. . . .
Gal 4 [4]But when the time had fully come, God sent his Son, born of a woman, born under law, [5]to redeem those under law, that we might receive the full rights of sons.
Eph 1 [5]he predestined us to be adopted as his sons through Jesus Christ, in accordance with his pleasure and will. . . . [7]In him we have redemption through his blood, the forgiveness of sins, in accordance with the riches of God's grace. . . . [9]And he made known to us the mystery of his will according to his good pleasure, which he purposed in Christ, [10]to be put into effect when the times will have reached their fulfillment—to bring all things in heaven and on earth together under one head, even Christ.
1 Tim 2 [5]For there is one God and one mediator between God and men, the man Christ Jesus, [6]who gave himself as a ransom for all men—the testimony given in its proper time.
2 Tim 1 [9]who has saved us and called us to a holy life—not because of anything we have done but because of his own purpose and grace. This grace was given us in Christ Jesus before the beginning of time, [10]but it has now been revealed through the appearing of our Savior, Christ Jesus, who has destroyed death and has brought life and immortality to light through the gospel.

Heb 7 [24]but because Jesus lives forever, he has a permanent priesthood. . . .

[26]Such a high priest meets our need—one who is holy, blameless, pure, set apart from sinners, exalted above the heavens. [27]Unlike the other high priests, he does not need to offer sacrifices day after day, first for his own sins, and then for the sins of the people. He sacrificed for their sins once for all when he offered himself.

Heb 9 [11]When Christ came as high priest of the good things that are already here, he went through the greater and more perfect tabernacle that is not man-made, that is to say, not a part of this creation. [12]He did not enter by means of the blood of goats and calves; but he entered the Most Holy Place once for all by his own blood, having obtained eternal redemption.

Heb 10 [10]And by that will, we have been made holy through the sacrifice of the body of Jesus Christ once for all.

1 Pet 1 [9]for you are receiving the goal of your faith, the salvation of your souls.

[10]Concerning this salvation, the prophets, who spoke of the grace that was to come to you, searched intently and with the greatest care, [11]trying to find out the time and circumstances to which the Spirit of Christ in them was pointing when he predicted the sufferings of Christ and the glories that would follow.

1 Pet 3 [18]For Christ died for sins once for all, the righteous for the unrighteous, to bring you to God. He was put to death in the body but made alive by the Spirit. . . .

1 John 4 [9]This is how God showed his love among us: He sent his one and only Son into the world that we might live through him. [10]This is love: not that we loved God, but that he loved us and sent his Son as an atoning sacrifice for our sins.

1 John 5 [11]And this is the testimony: God has given us eternal life, and this life is in his Son.

Rev 7 [9]After this I looked and there before me was a great multitude that no one could count, from every nation, tribe, people and language, standing before the throne and in front of the Lamb. They were wearing white robes and were holding palm branches in their hands. [10]And they cried out in a loud voice: "Salvation belongs to our God, who sits on the throne, and to the Lamb."

B. Those for Whom Christ Died

1. Jesus Died for All

2 Cor 5 [14]For Christ's love compels us, because we are convinced that one died for all, and therefore all died. [15]And he died for all, that those who live should no longer live for themselves but for him who died for them and was raised again.

1 Tim 2 [3]This is good, and pleases God our Savior, [4]who wants all men to be saved and to come to a knowledge of the truth.

1 Tim 2 [5]For there is one God and one mediator between God and men, the man Christ Jesus, [6]who gave himself as a ransom for all men—the testimony given in its proper time.

1 Tim 4 [10](and for this we labor and strive), that we have put our hope in the living God, who is the Savior of all men, and especially of those who believe.

Heb 2 [9]But we see Jesus, who was made a little lower than the angels, now crowned with glory and honor because he suffered death, so that by the grace of God he might taste death for everyone.

2. Jesus Died for a Brother

Rom 14 [15]If your brother is distressed because of what you eat, you are no longer acting in love. Do not by your eating destroy your brother for whom Christ died.

3. Jesus Died for the Children of God

John 11 [51]He did not say this on his own, but as high priest that year he prophesied that Jesus would die for the Jewish nation, [52]and not only for that nation but also for the scattered children of God, to bring them together and make them one.

4. Jesus Died for the Church

Acts 20 [28]"Keep watch over yourselves and all the flock of which the Holy Spirit has made you overseers. Be shepherds of the church of God, which he bought with his own blood."

Eph 5 [25]Husbands, love your wives, just as Christ loved the church and gave himself up for her. . . .

5. Jesus Died for the Elect

2 Tim 2 [10]Therefore I endure everything for the sake of the elect, that they too may obtain the salvation that is in Christ Jesus, with eternal glory.

6. Jesus Died for the Gentiles

Acts 13 [47]"For this is what the Lord has commanded us: 'I have made you a light for the Gentiles, that you may bring salvation to the ends of the earth.'"

Acts 28 [28]"Therefore I want you to know that God's salvation has been sent to the Gentiles, and they will listen!"

Rom 11 [11]Again I ask: Did they stumble so as to fall beyond recovery? Not at all! Rather, because of their transgression, salvation has come to the Gentiles to make Israel envious.

7. Jesus Died for His People

Matt 1 [21]"She will give birth to a son, and you are to give him the name Jesus, because he will save his people from their sins."

8. Jesus Died for His Sheep

John 10 [11]"I am the good shepherd. The good shepherd lays down his life for the sheep. [12]The hired hand is not the shepherd who owns the sheep. So when he sees the wolf coming, he abandons the sheep and runs away. Then the wolf attacks the flock and scatters it. [13]The man runs away because he is a hired hand and cares nothing for the sheep.

[14]"I am the good shepherd; I know my sheep and my sheep know me—[15]just as the Father knows me and I know the Father—and I lay down my life for the sheep. [16]I have other sheep that are not of this sheep pen. I must bring them also. They too will listen to my voice, and there shall be one flock and one shepherd. [17]The reason my Father loves me is that I lay down my life—only to take it up again. [18]No one takes it from me, but I lay it down of my own accord. I have authority to lay it down and authority to take it up again. This command I received from my Father."

9. Jesus Died for Israel

Acts 5 [31]"God exalted him to his own right hand as Prince and Savior that he might give repentance and forgiveness of sins to Israel."

Acts 13 [23]"From this man's descendants God has brought to Israel the Savior Jesus, as he promised."

10. Jesus Died for the Jewish Nation

John 11 [51]He did not say this on his own, but as high priest that year he prophesied that Jesus would die for the Jewish nation, [52]and not only for that nation but also for the scattered children of God, to bring them together and make them one.

11. Jesus Died for the Lost

Luke 19 [10]"For the Son of Man came to seek and to save what was lost."

12. Jesus Died for Many

Isa 53 [12]Therefore I will give him a portion among the great, and he will divide the spoils with the strong, because he poured out his life unto death, and was numbered with the transgressors. For he bore the sin of many, and made intercession for the transgressors.

Matt 20 [28]". . . just as the Son of Man did not come to be served, but to serve, and to give his life as a ransom for many."

Matt 26 [28]"This is my blood of the covenant, which is poured out for many for the forgiveness of sins."

Heb 9 [28]so Christ was sacrificed once to take away the sins of many people; and he will appear a second time, not to bear sin, but to bring salvation to those who are waiting for him.

13. Jesus Died for People as Individuals

Rom 5 [6]You see, at just the right time, when we were still powerless, Christ died for the ungodly. . . . [8]But God demonstrates his own love for us in this: While we were still sinners, Christ died for us.
Gal 2 [20]"I have been crucified with Christ and I no longer live, but Christ lives in me. The life I live in the body, I live by faith in the Son of God, who loved me and gave himself for me."
Eph 5 [2]and live a life of love, just as Christ loved us and gave himself up for us as a fragrant offering and sacrifice to God.
1 Thess 5 [10]He died for us so that, whether we are awake or asleep, we may live together with him.
Titus 2 [13]while we wait for the blessed hope—the glorious appearing of our great God and Savior, Jesus Christ, [14]who gave himself for us to redeem us from all wickedness and to purify for himself a people that are his very own, eager to do what is good.
Heb 2 [14]Since the children have flesh and blood, he too shared in their humanity so that by his death he might destroy him who holds the power of death—that is, the devil—[15]and free those who all their lives were held in slavery by their fear of death.
Heb 13 [12]And so Jesus also suffered outside the city gate to make the people holy through his own blood.
1 Pet 2 [21]To this you were called, because Christ suffered for you, leaving you an example, that you should follow in his steps.

14. Jesus Died for Sinners

Rom 5 [8]But God demonstrates his own love for us in this: While we were still sinners, Christ died for us.
Rom 8 [3]For what the law was powerless to do in that it was weakened by the sinful nature, God did by sending his own Son in the likeness of sinful man to be a sin offering. And so he condemned sin in sinful man. . . .
1 Tim 1 [15]Here is a trustworthy saying that deserves full acceptance: Christ Jesus came into the world to save sinners—of whom I am the worst.

15. Jesus Died for Sons

Heb 2 [10]In bringing many sons to glory, it was fitting that God, for whom and through whom everything exists, should make the author of their salvation perfect through suffering.

16. Jesus Died for Those Living in Darkness

Luke 1 [77]". . . to give his people the knowledge of salvation through the forgiveness of their sins, [78]because of the tender mercy of our God, by which the rising sun will come to us from heaven [79]to shine on those living in darkness and in the shadow of death, to guide our feet into the path of peace."

17. Jesus Died for Those Living in the Shadow of Death

Luke 1 [77]". . . to give his people the knowledge of salvation through the forgiveness of their sins, [78]because of the tender mercy of our God, by which the rising sun will come to us from heaven [79]to shine on those living in darkness and in the shadow of death, to guide our feet into the path of peace."

18. Jesus Died for Those Who Are Called

Heb 9 [15]For this reason Christ is the mediator of a new covenant, that those who are called may receive the promised eternal inheritance—now that he has died as a ransom to set them free from the sins committed under the first covenant.

19. Jesus Died for Transgressors

Isa 53 [12]Therefore I will give him a portion among the great, and he will divide the spoils with the strong, because he poured out his life unto death, and was numbered with the transgressors. For he bore the sin of many, and made intercession for the transgressors.

20. Jesus Died for the Ungodly

Rom 5 [6]You see, at just the right time, when we were still powerless, Christ died for the ungodly.

21. Jesus Died for the Unrighteous

1 Pet 3 [18]For Christ died for sins once for all, the righteous for the unrighteous, to bring you to God. He was put to death in the body but made alive by the Spirit. . . .

22. Jesus Died for the World

John 1 [29]The next day John saw Jesus coming toward him and said, "Look, the Lamb of God, who takes away the sin of the world!"
John 3 [16]"For God so loved the world that he gave his one and only Son, that whoever believes in him shall not perish but have eternal life. [17]For God did not send his Son into the world to condemn the world, but to save the world through him."
John 4 [42]They said to the woman, "We no longer believe just because of what you said; now we have heard for ourselves, and we know that this man really is the Savior of the world."
John 12 [44]Then Jesus cried out, "When a man believes in me, he does not believe in me only, but in the one who sent me. . . .
[47]"As for the person who hears my words but does not keep them, I do not judge him. For I did not come to judge the world, but to save it."
2 Cor 5 [19]that God was reconciling the world to himself in Christ, not counting men's sins against them. And he has committed to us the message of reconciliation.
1 John 2 [1]My dear children, I write this to you so that you will not sin. But if anybody does sin, we have one who speaks to the Father in our defense—Jesus Christ, the Righteous One. [2]He is the atoning sacrifice for our sins, and not only for ours but also for the sins of the whole world.
1 John 4 [14]And we have seen and testify that the Father has sent his Son to be the Savior of the world.

C. Reasons for Christ's Death

1. Jesus Died to Destroy the Enemy's Power

a) Christ's Death Destroyed the Power of Death

Rom 6 [9]For we know that since Christ was raised from the dead, he cannot die again; death no longer has mastery over him.
2 Cor 7 [10]Godly sorrow brings repentance that leads to salvation and leaves no regret, but worldly sorrow brings death.
2 Tim 1 [10]but it has now been revealed through the appearing of our Savior, Christ Jesus, who has destroyed death and has brought life and immortality to light through the gospel.
Rev 1 [17]When I saw him, I fell at his feet as though dead. Then he placed his right hand on me and said: "Do not be afraid. I am the First and the Last. [18]I am the Living One; I was dead, and behold I am alive for ever and ever! And I hold the keys of death and Hades."

b) Christ's Death Destroyed the Power of Demonic Forces

Col 2 [13]When you were dead in your sins and in the uncircumcision of your sinful nature, God made you alive with Christ. He forgave us all our sins, [14]having canceled the written code, with its regulations, that was against us and that stood opposed to us; he took it away, nailing it to the cross. [15]And having disarmed the powers and authorities, he made a public spectacle of them, triumphing over them by the cross.

c) Christ's Death Destroyed the Power of Satan

Heb 2 [14]Since the children have flesh and blood, he too shared

in their humanity so that by his death he might destroy him who holds the power of death—that is, the devil. . . .
1 John 3 [8]He who does what is sinful is of the devil, because the devil has been sinning from the beginning. The reason the Son of God appeared was to destroy the devil's work.

2. Jesus Died to Do Away with Evil

a) Christ's Death Did Away with Guilt

Isa 53 [10]Yet it was the LORD's will to crush him and cause him to suffer, and though the LORD makes his life a guilt offering, he will see his offspring and prolong his days, and the will of the LORD will prosper in his hand.

b) Christ's Death Did Away with Impurity

Zech 13 [1]"On that day a fountain will be opened to the house of David and the inhabitants of Jerusalem, to cleanse them from sin and impurity."

c) Christ's Death Did Away with Infirmity

Isa 53 [4]Surely he took up our infirmities and carried our sorrows, yet we considered him stricken by God, smitten by him, and afflicted.

d) Christ's Death Did Away with Iniquity

Isa 53 [5]But he was pierced for our transgressions, he was crushed for our iniquities; the punishment that brought us peace was upon him, and by his wounds we are healed. [6]We all, like sheep, have gone astray, each of us has turned to his own way; and the LORD has laid on him the iniquity of us all. . . . [11]After the suffering of his soul, he will see the light of life and be satisfied; by his knowledge my righteous servant will justify many, and he will bear their iniquities.

e) Christ's Death Did Away with Sin

Isa 53 [12]Therefore I will give him a portion among the great, and he will divide the spoils with the strong, because he poured out his life unto death, and was numbered with the transgressors. For he bore the sin of many, and made intercession for the transgressors.
Matt 1 [21]"She will give birth to a son, and you are to give him the name Jesus, because he will save his people from their sins."
John 1 [29]The next day John saw Jesus coming toward him and said, "Look, the Lamb of God, who takes away the sin of the world!"
Rom 6 [9]For we know that since Christ was raised from the dead, he cannot die again; death no longer has mastery over him. [10]The death he died, he died to sin once for all; but the life he lives, he lives to God.
Rom 8 [3]For what the law was powerless to do in that it was weakened by the sinful nature, God did by sending his own Son in the likeness of sinful man to be a sin offering. And so he condemned sin in sinful man. . . .
1 Cor 15 [3]For what I received I passed on to you as of first importance: that Christ died for our sins according to the Scriptures. . . .
2 Cor 5 [21]God made him who had no sin to be sin for us, so that in him we might become the righteousness of God.
Gal 1 [3]Grace and peace to you from God our Father and the Lord Jesus Christ, [4]who gave himself for our sins to rescue us from the present evil age, according to the will of our God and Father. . . .
Heb 1 [3]The Son is the radiance of God's glory and the exact representation of his being, sustaining all things by his powerful word. After he had provided purification for sins, he sat down at the right hand of the Majesty in heaven.
Heb 9 [26]Then Christ would have had to suffer many times since the creation of the world. But now he has appeared once for all at the end of the ages to do away with sin by the sacrifice of himself. [28]. . . so Christ was sacrificed once to take away the sins of many people; and he will appear a second time, not to bear sin, but to bring salvation to those who are waiting for him.
1 Pet 3 [18]For Christ died for sins once for all, the righteous for the unrighteous, to bring you to God. He was put to death in the body but made alive by the Spirit. . . .
1 John 2 [1]My dear children, I write this to you so that you will not sin. But if anybody does sin, we have one who speaks to the Father in our defense—Jesus Christ, the Righteous One. [2]He is the atoning sacrifice for our sins, and not only for ours but also for the sins of the whole world.
1 John 3 [5]But you know that he appeared so that he might take away our sins. And in him is no sin.
Rev 1 [5]and from Jesus Christ, who is the faithful witness, the firstborn from the dead, and the ruler of the kings of the earth.
To him who loves us and has freed us from our sins by his blood. . . .

f) Christ's Death Did Away with Sorrow

Isa 53 [4]Surely he took up our infirmities and carried our sorrows, yet we considered him stricken by God, smitten by him, and afflicted.

g) Christ's Death Did Away with Transgression

Isa 53 [5]But he was pierced for our transgressions, he was crushed for our iniquities; the punishment that brought us peace was upon him, and by his wounds we are healed. . . . [8]By oppression and judgment he was taken away. And who can speak of his descendants? For he was cut off from the land of the living; for the transgression of my people he was stricken.

h) Christ's Death Did Away with Wicked Ways

Acts 3 [26]"When God raised up his servant, he sent him first to you to bless you by turning each of you from your wicked ways."

3. Jesus Died to Free Us from God's Wrath

Rom 5 [9]Since we have now been justified by his blood, how much more shall we be saved from God's wrath through him!
1 Thess 1 [10]and to wait for his Son from heaven, whom he raised from the dead—Jesus, who rescues us from the coming wrath.
1 Thess 5 [9]For God did not appoint us to suffer wrath but to receive salvation through our Lord Jesus Christ.

4. Jesus Died to Satisfy God's Justice

Rom 3 [23]for all have sinned and fall short of the glory of God, [24]and are justified freely by his grace through the redemption that came by Christ Jesus. [25]God presented him as a sacrifice of atonement, through faith in his blood. He did this to demonstrate his justice, because in his forbearance he had left the sins committed beforehand unpunished—[26]he did it to demonstrate his justice at the present time, so as to be just and the one who justifies those who have faith in Jesus.
Gal 3 [11]Clearly no one is justified before God by the law, because, "The righteous will live by faith." . . . [13]Christ redeemed us from the curse of the law by becoming a curse for us, for it is written: "Cursed is everyone who is hung on a tree."

5. Jesus Died to Save Mankind

See p. 459a, Those for Whom Christ Died

D. Christ's Death Was the Perfect Atonement

1. OT Antecedents for Christ's Atoning Death

Exod 12 [1]The LORD said to Moses and Aaron in Egypt, [2]"This month is to be for you the first month, the first month of your year. [3]Tell the whole community of Israel that on the tenth day of this month each man is to take a lamb for his family, one for each household. [4]If any household is too small for a whole lamb, they must share one with their nearest neighbor, having taken into account the number of people there are. You are to determine the amount of lamb needed in accordance with what each person will eat. [5]The animals you choose must be year-old males without defect, and you may take them from the sheep or the goats. 6Take care of them until the fourteenth day of the month, when all the people of the community of Israel must slaughter them at twilight. 7Then they are to take some of the blood and put it on the sides and tops of the doorframes of the houses where they eat the lambs. 8That same night they are to eat the meat roasted over the fire, along with bitter herbs, and bread made without yeast. 9Do not eat the meat raw or cooked in water, but roast it over the fire—head, legs and inner parts. 10Do not leave any of it till morning; if some is left till morning, you must burn it. 11This is how you are to eat it: with your cloak tucked into your belt, your sandals on your feet and your staff in your hand. Eat it in haste; it is the LORD's Passover.

12"On that same night I will pass through Egypt and strike down every firstborn—both men and animals—and I will bring judgment on all the gods of Egypt. I am the LORD. 13The blood will be a sign for you on the houses where you are; and when I see the blood, I will pass over you. No destructive plague will touch you when I strike Egypt."

Exod 29 36"Sacrifice a bull each day as a sin offering to make atonement. Purify the altar by making atonement for it, and anoint it to consecrate it."

Exod 30 12"When you take a census of the Israelites to count them, each one must pay the LORD a ransom for his life at the time he is counted. Then no plague will come on them when you number them. 13Each one who crosses over to those already counted is to give a half shekel, according to the sanctuary shekel, which weighs twenty gerahs. This half shekel is an offering to the LORD. 14All who cross over, those twenty years old or more, are to give an offering to the LORD. 15The rich are not to give more than a half shekel and the poor are not to give less when you make the offering to the LORD to atone for your lives. 16Receive the atonement money from the Israelites and use it for the service of the Tent of Meeting. It will be a memorial for the Israelites before the LORD, making atonement for your lives."

Lev 1 4"'He is to lay his hand on the head of the burnt offering, and it will be accepted on his behalf to make atonement for him.'"

Lev 4 20"'. . . and do with this bull just as he did with the bull for the sin offering. In this way the priest will make atonement for them, and they will be forgiven. 21Then he shall take the bull outside the camp and burn it as he burned the first bull. This is the sin offering for the community.

22"'When a leader sins unintentionally and does what is forbidden in any of the commands of the LORD his God, he is guilty. 23When he is made aware of the sin he committed, he must bring as his offering a male goat without defect. 24He is to lay his hand on the goat's head and slaughter it at the place where the burnt offering is slaughtered before the LORD. It is a sin offering. 25Then the priest shall take some of the blood of the sin offering with his finger and put it on the horns of the altar of burnt offering and pour out the rest of the blood at the base of the altar. 26He shall burn all the fat on the altar as he burned the fat of the fellowship offering. In this way the priest will make atonement for the man's sin, and he will be forgiven.

27"'If a member of the community sins unintentionally and does what is forbidden in any of the LORD's commands, he is guilty. 28When he is made aware of the sin he committed, he must bring as his offering for the sin he committed a female goat without defect. 29He is to lay his hand on the head of the sin offering and slaughter it at the place of the burnt offering. 30Then the priest is to take some of the blood with his finger and put it on the horns of the altar of burnt offering and pour out the rest of the blood at the base of the altar. 31He shall remove all the fat, just as the fat is removed from the fellowship offering, and the priest shall burn it on the altar as an aroma pleasing to the LORD. In this way the priest will make atonement for him, and he will be forgiven.

32"'If he brings a lamb as his sin offering, he is to bring a female without defect. 33He is to lay his hand on its head and slaughter it for a sin offering at the place where the burnt offering is slaughtered. 34Then the priest shall take some of the blood of the sin offering with his finger and put it on the horns of the altar of burnt offering and pour out the rest of the blood at the base of the altar. 35He shall remove all the fat, just as the fat is removed from the lamb of the fellowship offering, and the priest shall burn it on the altar on top of the offerings made to the LORD by fire. In this way the priest will make atonement for him for the sin he has committed, and he will be forgiven.'"

Lev 5 5"'When anyone is guilty in any of these ways, he must confess in what way he has sinned 6and, as a penalty for the sin he has committed, he must bring to the LORD a female lamb or goat from the flock as a sin offering; and the priest shall make atonement for him for his sin.

7"'If he cannot afford a lamb, he is to bring two doves or two young pigeons to the LORD as a penalty for his sin—one for a sin offering and the other for a burnt offering. 8He is to bring them to the priest, who shall first offer the one for the sin offering. He is to wring its head from its neck, not severing it completely, 9and is to sprinkle some of the blood of the sin offering against the side of the altar; the rest of the blood must be drained out at the base of the altar. It is a sin offering. 10The priest shall then offer the other as a burnt offering in the prescribed way and make atonement for him for the sin he has committed, and he will be forgiven.'"

Lev 6 7"In this way the priest will make atonement for him before the LORD, and he will be forgiven for any of these things he did that made him guilty."

Lev 7 7"'The same law applies to both the sin offering and the guilt offering: They belong to the priest who makes atonement with them.'"

Lev 9 7Moses said to Aaron, "Come to the altar and sacrifice your sin offering and your burnt offering and make atonement for yourself and the people; sacrifice the offering that is for the people and make atonement for them, as the LORD has commanded."

Lev 10 17"Why didn't you eat the sin offering in the sanctuary area? It is most holy; it was given to you to take away the guilt of the community by making atonement for them before the LORD."

Lev 12 6"'When the days of her purification for a son or daughter are over, she is to bring to the priest at the entrance to the Tent of Meeting a year-old lamb for a burnt offering and a young pigeon or a dove for a sin offering. 7He shall offer them before the LORD to make atonement for her, and then she will be ceremonially clean from her flow of blood.

"'These are the regulations for the woman who gives birth to a boy or a girl. 8If she cannot afford a lamb, she is to bring two doves or two young pigeons, one for a burnt offering and the other for a sin offering. In this way the priest will make atonement for her, and she will be clean.'"

Lev 14 12"Then the priest is to take one of the male lambs and offer it as a guilt offering, along with the log of oil; he shall wave them before the LORD as a wave offering. 13He is to slaughter the lamb in the holy place where the sin offering and the burnt offering are slaughtered. Like the sin offering, the guilt offering belongs to the priest; it is most holy. 14The priest is to take some of the blood of the guilt offering and put it on the lobe of the right ear of the one to be cleansed, on the thumb of his right hand and on the big toe of his right foot. 15The priest shall then take some of the log of oil, pour it in the palm of his own left hand, 16dip his right forefinger into the oil in his palm, and with his finger sprinkle some of it before the LORD seven times. 17The priest is to put some of the oil remaining in his palm on the lobe of the right ear of the one to be cleansed, on the thumb of his right hand and on the big toe of his right foot, on top of the blood of the guilt offering. 18The rest of the oil in his palm the priest shall put on the head of the one to be cleansed and make atonement for him before the LORD.

19"Then the priest is to sacrifice the sin offering and make atonement for the one to be cleansed from his uncleanness. After that, the priest shall slaughter the burnt offering 20and offer it on the altar, together with the grain offering, and make atonement for him, and he will be clean."

Lev 16 6"Aaron is to offer the bull for his own sin offering to make atonement for himself and his household. . . . 10But the goat chosen by lot as the scapegoat shall be presented alive before the LORD to be used for making atonement by sending it into the desert as a scapegoat.

11"Aaron shall bring the bull for his own sin offering to

make atonement for himself and his household, and he is to slaughter the bull for his own sin offering. . . .

[15]"He shall then slaughter the goat for the sin offering for the people and take its blood behind the curtain and do with it as he did with the bull's blood: He shall sprinkle it on the atonement cover and in front of it. [16]In this way he will make atonement for the Most Holy Place because of the uncleanness and rebellion of the Israelites, whatever their sins have been. He is to do the same for the Tent of Meeting, which is among them in the midst of their uncleanness. [17]No one is to be in the Tent of Meeting from the time Aaron goes in to make atonement in the Most Holy Place until he comes out, having made atonement for himself, his household and the whole community of Israel.

[18]"Then he shall come out to the altar that is before the LORD and make atonement for it. He shall take some of the bull's blood and some of the goat's blood and put it on all the horns of the altar. [19]He shall sprinkle some of the blood on it with his finger seven times to cleanse it and to consecrate it from the uncleanness of the Israelites. . . .

[23]"Then Aaron is to go into the Tent of Meeting and take off the linen garments he put on before he entered the Most Holy Place, and he is to leave them there. [24]He shall bathe himself with water in a holy place and put on his regular garments. Then he shall come out and sacrifice the burnt offering for himself and the burnt offering for the people, to make atonement for himself and for the people. [25]He shall also burn the fat of the sin offering on the altar.

[26]"The man who releases the goat as a scapegoat must wash his clothes and bathe himself with water; afterward he may come into the camp. [27]The bull and the goat for the sin offerings, whose blood was brought into the Most Holy Place to make atonement, must be taken outside the camp; their hides, flesh and offal are to be burned up. [28]The man who burns them must wash his clothes and bathe himself with water; afterward he may come into the camp.

[29]"This is to be a lasting ordinance for you: On the tenth day of the seventh month you must deny yourselves and not do any work—whether native-born or an alien living among you—[30]because on this day atonement will be made for you, to cleanse you. Then, before the LORD, you will be clean from all your sins. [31]It is a sabbath of rest, and you must deny yourselves; it is a lasting ordinance. [32]The priest who is anointed and ordained to succeed his father as high priest is to make atonement. He is to put on the sacred linen garments [33]and make atonement for the Most Holy Place, for the Tent of Meeting and the altar, and for the priests and all the people of the community.

[34]"This is to be a lasting ordinance for you: Atonement is to be made once a year for all the sins of the Israelites."

And it was done, as the LORD commanded Moses.

Lev 17 [11]"'For the life of a creature is in the blood, and I have given it to you to make atonement for yourselves on the altar; it is the blood that makes atonement for one's life.'"

Lev 19 [22]"'With the ram of the guilt offering the priest is to make atonement for him before the LORD for the sin he has committed, and his sin will be forgiven.'"

Num 15 [22]"'Now if you unintentionally fail to keep any of these commands the LORD gave Moses—[23]any of the LORD's commands to you through him, from the day the LORD gave them and continuing through the generations to come—[24]and if this is done unintentionally without the community being aware of it, then the whole community is to offer a young bull for a burnt offering as an aroma pleasing to the LORD, along with its prescribed grain offering and drink offering, and a male goat for a sin offering. [25]The priest is to make atonement for the whole Israelite community, and they will be forgiven, for it was not intentional and they have brought to the LORD for their wrong an offering made by fire and a sin offering. [26]The whole Israelite community and the aliens living among them will be forgiven, because all the people were involved in the unintentional wrong.

[27]"'But if just one person sins unintentionally, he must bring a year-old female goat for a sin offering. [28]The priest is to make atonement before the LORD for the one who erred by sinning unintentionally, and when atonement has been made for him, he will be forgiven.'"

Num 28 [26]"'On the day of firstfruits, when you present to the LORD an offering of new grain during the Feast of Weeks, hold a sacred assembly and do no regular work. . . . [30]Include one male goat to make atonement for you.'"

Num 29 [1]"'On the first day of the seventh month hold a sacred assembly and do no regular work. It is a day for you to sound the trumpets. . . . [5]Include one male goat as a sin offering to make atonement for you.'"

Num 29 [7]"'On the tenth day of this seventh month hold a sacred assembly. You must deny yourselves and do no work. . . . [11]Include one male goat as a sin offering, in addition to the sin offering for atonement and the regular burnt offering with its grain offering, and their drink offerings.'"

Zech 9 [11]As for you, because of the blood of my covenant with you, I will free your prisoners from the waterless pit.

Heb 9 [22]In fact, the law requires that nearly everything be cleansed with blood, and without the shedding of blood there is no forgiveness.

2. NT Teaching concerning Christ's Atoning Death

a) The Blood of Jesus Was Shed

Matt 26 [28]"This is my blood of the covenant, which is poured out for many for the forgiveness of sins."

Acts 20 [28]"Keep watch over yourselves and all the flock of which the Holy Spirit has made you overseers. Be shepherds of the church of God, which he bought with his own blood."

Rom 3 [24]and are justified freely by his grace through the redemption that came by Christ Jesus. [25]God presented him as a sacrifice of atonement, through faith in his blood. He did this to demonstrate his justice, because in his forbearance he had left the sins committed beforehand unpunished. . . .

Rom 5 [8]But God demonstrates his own love for us in this: While we were still sinners, Christ died for us.

[9]Since we have now been justified by his blood, how much more shall we be saved from God's wrath through him!

Eph 1 [5]he predestined us to be adopted as his sons through Jesus Christ, in accordance with his pleasure and will. . . . [7]In him we have redemption through his blood, the forgiveness of sins, in accordance with the riches of God's grace. . . .

Eph 2 [13]But now in Christ Jesus you who once were far away have been brought near through the blood of Christ.

Col 1 [20]and through him to reconcile to himself all things, whether things on earth or things in heaven, by making peace through his blood, shed on the cross.

Heb 9 [12]He did not enter by means of the blood of goats and calves; but he entered the Most Holy Place once for all by his own blood, having obtained eternal redemption. . . . [14]How much more, then, will the blood of Christ, who through the eternal Spirit offered himself unblemished to God, cleanse our consciences from acts that lead to death, so that we may serve the living God! . . . [22]In fact, the law requires that nearly everything be cleansed with blood, and without the shedding of blood there is no forgiveness.

Heb 10 [19]Therefore, brothers, since we have confidence to enter the Most Holy Place by the blood of Jesus, [20]by a new and living way opened for us through the curtain, that is, his body . . .

Heb 12 [24]to Jesus the mediator of a new covenant, and to the sprinkled blood that speaks a better word than the blood of Abel.

Heb 13 [12]And so Jesus also suffered outside the city gate to make the people holy through his own blood.

Heb 13 [20]May the God of peace, who through the blood of the eternal covenant brought back from the dead our Lord Jesus, that great Shepherd of the sheep . . .

1 Pet 1 [2]who have been chosen according to the foreknowledge of God the Father, through the sanctifying work of the Spirit, for obedience to Jesus Christ and sprinkling by his blood: Grace and peace be yours in abundance.

1 Pet 1 [18]For you know that it was not with perishable things such as silver or gold that you were redeemed from the empty way of life handed down to you from your forefathers, [19]but with the precious blood of Christ, a lamb without blemish or defect.

1 John 1 [7]But if we walk in the light, as he is in the light, we have fellowship with one another, and the blood of Jesus, his Son, purifies us from all sin.

1 John 5 [6]This is the one who came by water and blood—Jesus Christ. He did not come by water only, but by water and blood. And it is the Spirit who testifies, because the Spirit is the truth.

Rev 1 [5]and from Jesus Christ, who is the faithful witness, the firstborn from the dead, and the ruler of the kings of the earth.

To him who loves us and has freed us from our sins by his blood. . . .

Rev 5 [9]And they sang a new song: "You are worthy to take the scroll and to open its seals, because you were slain, and with your blood you purchased men for God from every tribe and language and people and nation."

Rev 7 [14]I answered, "Sir, you know."

And he said, "These are they who have come out of the great tribulation; they have washed their robes and made them white in the blood of the Lamb."

Rev 12 [11]"They overcame him by the blood of the Lamb and by the word of their testimony; they did not love their lives so much as to shrink from death."

Rev 13 [8]All inhabitants of the earth will worship the beast—all whose names have not been written in the book of life belonging to the Lamb that was slain from the creation of the world.

b) Jesus Died for Our Sins

John 1 [29]The next day John saw Jesus coming toward him and said, "Look, the Lamb of God, who takes away the sin of the world!"

Rom 6 [9]For we know that since Christ was raised from the dead, he cannot die again; death no longer has mastery over him. [10]The death he died, he died to sin once for all; but the life he lives, he lives to God.

1 Cor 15 [3]For what I received I passed on to you as of first importance: that Christ died for our sins according to the Scriptures. . . .

2 Cor 5 [14]For Christ's love compels us, because we are convinced that one died for all, and therefore all died. . . . [21]God made him who had no sin to be sin for us, so that in him we might become the righteousness of God.

Gal 1 [3]Grace and peace to you from God our Father and the Lord Jesus Christ, [4]who gave himself for our sins to rescue us from the present evil age, according to the will of our God and Father. . . .

1 Pet 3 [18]For Christ died for sins once for all, the righteous for the unrighteous, to bring you to God. He was put to death in the body but made alive by the Spirit. . . .

c) Jesus Freely Gave His Life

John 3 [16]"For God so loved the world that he gave his one and only Son, that whoever believes in him shall not perish but have eternal life."

John 6 [51]"I am the living bread that came down from heaven. If anyone eats of this bread, he will live forever. This bread is my flesh, which I will give for the life of the world."

John 10 [11]"I am the good shepherd. The good shepherd lays down his life for the sheep.

[15]". . . just as the Father knows me and I know the Father—and I lay down my life for the sheep. . . . [17]The reason my Father loves me is that I lay down my life—only to take it up again. [18]No one takes it from me, but I lay it down of my own accord. I have authority to lay it down and authority to take it up again. This command I received from my Father."

Acts 2 [23]"This man was handed over to you by God's set purpose and foreknowledge; and you, with the help of wicked men, put him to death by nailing him to the cross."

Rom 5 [8]But God demonstrates his own love for us in this: While we were still sinners, Christ died for us.

Rom 8 [32]He who did not spare his own Son, but gave him up for us all—how will he not also, along with him, graciously give us all things?

Gal 1 [3]Grace and peace to you from God our Father and the Lord Jesus Christ, [4]who gave himself for our sins to rescue us from the present evil age, according to the will of our God and Father. . . .

Gal 2 [20]"I have been crucified with Christ and I no longer live, but Christ lives in me. The life I live in the body, I live by faith in the Son of God, who loved me and gave himself for me."

Eph 5 [25]Husbands, love your wives, just as Christ loved the church and gave himself up for her. . . .

Titus 2 [13]while we wait for the blessed hope—the glorious appearing of our great God and Savior, Jesus Christ, [14]who gave himself for us to redeem us from all wickedness and to purify for himself a people that are his very own, eager to do what is good.

1 John 3 [16]This is how we know what love is: Jesus Christ laid down his life for us. And we ought to lay down our lives for our brothers.

1 John 4 [9]This is how God showed his love among us: He sent his one and only Son into the world that we might live through him. [10]This is love: not that we loved God, but that he loved us and sent his Son as an atoning sacrifice for our sins.

1 John 5 [11]And this is the testimony: God has given us eternal life, and this life is in his Son.

d) Jesus' Death Delivers, Redeems, and Rescues

Job 19 [25]"I know that my Redeemer lives, and that in the end he will stand upon the earth."

Ps 111 [9]He provided redemption for his people; he ordained his covenant forever—holy and awesome is his name.

Isa 59 [20]"The Redeemer will come to Zion, to those in Jacob who repent of their sins," declares the LORD.

Luke 2 [38]Coming up to them at that very moment, she gave thanks to God and spoke about the child to all who were looking forward to the redemption of Jerusalem.

Luke 4 [18]"The Spirit of the Lord is on me, because he has anointed me to preach good news to the poor. He has sent me to proclaim freedom for the prisoners and recovery of sight for the blind, to release the oppressed, [19]to proclaim the year of the Lord's favor."

Rom 3 [23]for all have sinned and fall short of the glory of God, [24]and are justified freely by his grace through the redemption that came by Christ Jesus.

Rom 8 [2]because through Christ Jesus the law of the Spirit of life set me free from the law of sin and death.

1 Cor 1 [30]It is because of him that you are in Christ Jesus, who has become for us wisdom from God—that is, our righteousness, holiness and redemption.

Gal 1 [3]Grace and peace to you from God our Father and the Lord Jesus Christ, [4]who gave himself for our sins to rescue us from the present evil age, according to the will of our God and Father. . . .

Gal 3 [13]Christ redeemed us from the curse of the law by becoming a curse for us, for it is written: "Cursed is everyone who is hung on a tree." [14]He redeemed us in order that the blessing given to Abraham might come to the Gentiles through Christ Jesus, so that by faith we might receive the promise of the Spirit.

Gal 4 [4]But when the time had fully come, God sent his Son, born of a woman, born under law, [5]to redeem those under law, that we might receive the full rights of sons.

Gal 5 [1]It is for freedom that Christ has set us free. Stand firm, then, and do not let yourselves be burdened again by a yoke of slavery.

Eph 1 [7]In him we have redemption through his blood, the forgiveness of sins, in accordance with the riches of God's grace. . . .

Col 1 [13]For he has rescued us from the dominion of darkness and brought us into the kingdom of the Son he loves, [14]in whom we have redemption, the forgiveness of sins.

1 Thess 1 [10]and to wait for his Son from heaven, whom he raised from the dead—Jesus, who rescues us from the coming wrath.

Titus 2 [13]while we wait for the blessed hope—the glorious appearing of our great God and Savior, Jesus Christ, [14]who gave himself for us to redeem us from all wickedness and to purify for himself a people that are his very own, eager to do what is good.

Heb 9 [11]When Christ came as high priest of the good things that are already here, he went through the greater and more perfect tabernacle that is not man-made, that is to say, not a part of this creation. [12]He did not enter by means of the blood of goats and calves; but he entered the Most Holy Place once for all by his own blood, having obtained eternal redemption.
1 Pet 1 [18]For you know that it was not with perishable things such as silver or gold that you were redeemed from the empty way of life handed down to you from your forefathers, [19]but with the precious blood of Christ, a lamb without blemish or defect.
Rev 14 [3]And they sang a new song before the throne and before the four living creatures and the elders. No one could learn the song except the 144,000 who had been redeemed from the earth.

e) Jesus' Death Was a Means of Reconciliation

Rom 5 [6]You see, at just the right time, when we were still powerless, Christ died for the ungodly. [7]Very rarely will anyone die for a righteous man, though for a good man someone might possibly dare to die. [8]But God demonstrates his own love for us in this: While we were still sinners, Christ died for us.

[9]Since we have now been justified by his blood, how much more shall we be saved from God's wrath through him! [10]For if, when we were God's enemies, we were reconciled to him through the death of his Son, how much more, having been reconciled, shall we be saved through his life! [11]Not only is this so, but we also rejoice in God through our Lord Jesus Christ, through whom we have now received reconciliation.
2 Cor 5 [18]All this is from God, who reconciled us to himself through Christ and gave us the ministry of reconciliation: [19]that God was reconciling the world to himself in Christ, not counting men's sins against them. And he has committed to us the message of reconciliation.
Eph 1 [10]to be put into effect when the times will have reached their fulfillment—to bring all things in heaven and on earth together under one head, even Christ.
Eph 2 [13]But now in Christ Jesus you who once were far away have been brought near through the blood of Christ.

[14]For he himself is our peace, who has made the two one and has destroyed the barrier, the dividing wall of hostility, [15]by abolishing in his flesh the law with its commandments and regulations. His purpose was to create in himself one new man out of the two, thus making peace, [16]and in this one body to reconcile both of them to God through the cross, by which he put to death their hostility.
Col 1 [19]For God was pleased to have all his fullness dwell in him, [20]and through him to reconcile to himself all things, whether things on earth or things in heaven, by making peace through his blood, shed on the cross.

[21]Once you were alienated from God and were enemies in your minds because of your evil behavior. [22]But now he has reconciled you by Christ's physical body through death to present you holy in his sight, without blemish and free from accusation. . . .

f) Jesus' Death Was an Offering

Isa 53 [7]He was oppressed and afflicted, yet he did not open his mouth; he was led like a lamb to the slaughter, and as a sheep before her shearers is silent, so he did not open his mouth. . . .

[10]Yet it was the LORD's will to crush him and cause him to suffer, and though the LORD makes his life a guilt offering, he will see his offspring and prolong his days, and the will of the LORD will prosper in his hand. . . . [12]Therefore I will give him a portion among the great, and he will divide the spoils with the strong, because he poured out his life unto death, and was numbered with the transgressors. For he bore the sin of many, and made intercession for the transgressors.
Rom 8 [3]For what the law was powerless to do in that it was weakened by the sinful nature, God did by sending his own Son in the likeness of sinful man to be a sin offering. And so he condemned sin in sinful man. . . .
Eph 5 [2]and live a life of love, just as Christ loved us and gave himself up for us as a fragrant offering and sacrifice to God.
Heb 8 [1]The point of what we are saying is this: We do have such a high priest, who sat down at the right hand of the throne of the Majesty in heaven. . . .

[3]Every high priest is appointed to offer both gifts and sacrifices, and so it was necessary for this one also to have something to offer.
Heb 9 [14]How much more, then, will the blood of Christ, who through the eternal Spirit offered himself unblemished to God, cleanse our consciences from acts that lead to death, so that we may serve the living God!
Heb 13 [11]The high priest carries the blood of animals into the Most Holy Place as a sin offering, but the bodies are burned outside the camp. [12]And so Jesus also suffered outside the city gate to make the people holy through his own blood.

g) Jesus' Death Was a Passover Sacrifice

1 Cor 5 [7]Get rid of the old yeast that you may be a new batch without yeast—as you really are. For Christ, our Passover lamb, has been sacrificed.

h) Jesus' Death Was a Payment or Purchase

Acts 20 [28]"Keep watch over yourselves and all the flock of which the Holy Spirit has made you overseers. Be shepherds of the church of God, which he bought with his own blood."
1 Cor 6 [19]Do you not know that your body is a temple of the Holy Spirit, who is in you, whom you have received from God? You are not your own; [20]you were bought at a price. Therefore honor God with your body.
1 Cor 7 [23]You were bought at a price; do not become slaves of men.
Rev 5 [9]And they sang a new song: "You are worthy to take the scroll and to open its seals, because you were slain, and with your blood you purchased men for God from every tribe and language and people and nation."
Rev 14 [4]These are those who did not defile themselves with women, for they kept themselves pure. They follow the Lamb wherever he goes. They were purchased from among men and offered as firstfruits to God and the Lamb.

i) Jesus' Death Was a Propitiation, an Atonement

Isa 53 [5]But he was pierced for our transgressions, he was crushed for our iniquities; the punishment that brought us peace was upon him, and by his wounds we are healed.
Rom 3 [25]God presented him as a sacrifice of atonement, through faith in his blood. He did this to demonstrate his justice, because in his forbearance he had left the sins committed beforehand unpunished. . . .
Rom 5 [1]Therefore, since we have been justified through faith, we have peace with God through our Lord Jesus Christ. . . .
Heb 2 [17]For this reason he had to be made like his brothers in every way, in order that he might become a merciful and faithful high priest in service to God, and that he might make atonement for the sins of the people.
1 John 2 [2]He is the atoning sacrifice for our sins, and not only for ours but also for the sins of the whole world.
1 John 4 [10]This is love: not that we loved God, but that he loved us and sent his Son as an atoning sacrifice for our sins.

j) Jesus' Death Was a Ransom

Job 33 [24]". . . to be gracious to him and say, 'Spare him from going down to the pit; I have found a ransom for him'. . . ."
Isa 35 [10]and the ransomed of the LORD will return. They will enter Zion with singing; everlasting joy will crown their heads. Gladness and joy will overtake them, and sorrow and sighing will flee away.
Hos 13 [14]"I will ransom them from the power of the grave; I will redeem them from death. Where, O death, are your plagues? Where, O grave, is your destruction?

"I will have no compassion. . . ."
Mark 10 [45]"For even the Son of Man did not come to be served, but to serve, and to give his life as a ransom for many."
1 Tim 2 [5]For there is one God and one mediator between God and men, the man Christ Jesus, [6]who gave himself as a ransom for all men—the testimony given in its proper time.
Heb 9 [15]For this reason Christ is the mediator of a new covenant, that those who are called may receive the promised eter-

nal inheritance—now that he has died as a ransom to set them free from the sins committed under the first covenant.

k) Jesus' Death Was a Sacrifice

Rom 3 [25]God presented him as a sacrifice of atonement, through faith in his blood. He did this to demonstrate his justice, because in his forbearance he had left the sins committed beforehand unpunished. . . .

Eph 5 [2]and live a life of love, just as Christ loved us and gave himself up for us as a fragrant offering and sacrifice to God.

Heb 7 [24]but because Jesus lives forever, he has a permanent priesthood. . . . [27]Unlike the other high priests, he does not need to offer sacrifices day after day, first for his own sins, and then for the sins of the people. He sacrificed for their sins once for all when he offered himself.

Heb 9 [26]Then Christ would have had to suffer many times since the creation of the world. But now he has appeared once for all at the end of the ages to do away with sin by the sacrifice of himself. [27]Just as man is destined to die once, and after that to face judgment, [28]so Christ was sacrificed once to take away the sins of many people; and he will appear a second time, not to bear sin, but to bring salvation to those who are waiting for him.

Heb 10 [5]Therefore, when Christ came into the world, he said: "Sacrifice and offering you did not desire, but a body you prepared for me; [6]with burnt offerings and sin offerings you were not pleased. [7]Then I said, 'Here I am—it is written about me in the scroll—I have come to do your will, O God.'" [8]First he said, "Sacrifices and offerings, burnt offerings and sin offerings you did not desire, nor were you pleased with them" (although the law required them to be made). [9]Then he said, "Here I am, I have come to do your will." He sets aside the first to establish the second. [10]And by that will, we have been made holy through the sacrifice of the body of Jesus Christ once for all.

[11]Day after day every priest stands and performs his religious duties; again and again he offers the same sacrifices, which can never take away sins. [12]But when this priest had offered for all time one sacrifice for sins, he sat down at the right hand of God. [13]Since that time he waits for his enemies to be made his footstool, [14]because by one sacrifice he has made perfect forever those who are being made holy.

1 John 2 [1]My dear children, I write this to you so that you will not sin. But if anybody does sin, we have one who speaks to the Father in our defense—Jesus Christ, the Righteous One. [2]He is the atoning sacrifice for our sins, and not only for ours but also for the sins of the whole world.

1 John 4 [10]This is love: not that we loved God, but that he loved us and sent his Son as an atoning sacrifice for our sins.

l) Jesus' Death Was Substitutionary

Isa 53 [3]He was despised and rejected by men, a man of sorrows, and familiar with suffering. Like one from whom men hide their faces he was despised, and we esteemed him not.

[4]Surely he took up our infirmities and carried our sorrows, yet we considered him stricken by God, smitten by him, and afflicted. [5]But he was pierced for our transgressions, he was crushed for our iniquities; the punishment that brought us peace was upon him, and by his wounds we are healed. [6]We all, like sheep, have gone astray, each of us has turned to his own way; and the LORD has laid on him the iniquity of us all.

[7]He was oppressed and afflicted, yet he did not open his mouth; he was led like a lamb to the slaughter, and as a sheep before her shearers is silent, so he did not open his mouth. [8]By oppression and judgment he was taken away. And who can speak of his descendants? For he was cut off from the land of the living; for the transgression of my people he was stricken. [9]He was assigned a grave with the wicked, and with the rich in his death, though he had done no violence, nor was any deceit in his mouth.

[10]Yet it was the LORD's will to crush him and cause him to suffer, and though the LORD makes his life a guilt offering, he will see his offspring and prolong his days, and the will of the LORD will prosper in his hand. [11]After the suffering of his soul, he will see the light of life and be satisfied; by his knowledge my righteous servant will justify many, and he will bear their iniquities. [12]Therefore I will give him a portion among the great, and he will divide the spoils with the strong, because he poured out his life unto death, and was numbered with the transgressors. For he bore the sin of many, and made intercession for the transgressors.

Matt 20 [28]". . . just as the Son of Man did not come to be served, but to serve, and to give his life as a ransom for many."

Matt 26 [28]"This is my blood of the covenant, which is poured out for many for the forgiveness of sins."

Mark 10 [45]"For even the Son of Man did not come to be served, but to serve, and to give his life as a ransom for many."

Rom 5 [6]You see, at just the right time, when we were still powerless, Christ died for the ungodly. . . . [8]But God demonstrates his own love for us in this: While we were still sinners, Christ died for us.

Rom 14 [15]If your brother is distressed because of what you eat, you are no longer acting in love. Do not by your eating destroy your brother for whom Christ died.

2 Cor 5 [14]For Christ's love compels us, because we are convinced that one died for all, and therefore all died. [15]And he died for all, that those who live should no longer live for themselves but for him who died for them and was raised again.

1 Thess 5 [9]For God did not appoint us to suffer wrath but to receive salvation through our Lord Jesus Christ. [10]He died for us so that, whether we are awake or asleep, we may live together with him.

Heb 2 [9]But we see Jesus, who was made a little lower than the angels, now crowned with glory and honor because he suffered death, so that by the grace of God he might taste death for everyone.

1 Pet 2 [21]To this you were called, because Christ suffered for you, leaving you an example, that you should follow in his steps. . . . [24]He himself bore our sins in his body on the tree, so that we might die to sins and live for righteousness; by his wounds you have been healed.

1 Pet 3 [18]For Christ died for sins once for all, the righteous for the unrighteous, to bring you to God. He was put to death in the body but made alive by the Spirit. . . .

III
Christ's Resurrection as Saving Event

A. The Fact of the Resurrection of Christ

1. Jesus Foretold His Resurrection

Matt 12 [40]"For as Jonah was three days and three nights in the belly of a huge fish, so the Son of Man will be three days and three nights in the heart of the earth."

Matt 16 [21]From that time on Jesus began to explain to his disciples that he must go to Jerusalem and suffer many things at the hands of the elders, chief priests and teachers of the law, and that he must be killed and on the third day be raised to life.

Matt 17 [22]When they came together in Galilee, he said to them, "The Son of Man is going to be betrayed into the hands of men. [23]They will kill him, and on the third day he will be raised to life." And the disciples were filled with grief.

Mark 9 [9]As they were coming down the mountain, Jesus gave them orders not to tell anyone what they had seen until the Son of Man had risen from the dead. [10]They kept the matter to themselves, discussing what "rising from the dead" meant.

Mark 10 [32]They were on their way up to Jerusalem, with Jesus leading the way, and the disciples were astonished, while those who followed were afraid. Again he took the Twelve aside and told them what was going to happen to him. [33]"We are going up to Jerusalem," he said, "and the Son of Man will be betrayed to the chief priests and teachers of the law. They will condemn him to death and will hand him over to the Gentiles, [34]who will mock him and spit on him, flog him and kill him. Three days later he will rise."

Mark 14 [27]"You will all fall away," Jesus told them, "for it is written: 'I will strike the shepherd, and the sheep will be scattered.' [28]But after I have risen, I will go ahead of you into Galilee."

Luke 9 [30]Two men, Moses and Elijah, [31]appeared in glorious splendor, talking with Jesus. They spoke about his departure, which he was about to bring to fulfillment at Jerusalem.

John 2 [19]Jesus answered them, "Destroy this temple, and I will raise it again in three days."

[20]The Jews replied, "It has taken forty-six years to build this temple, and you are going to raise it in three days?" [21]But the temple he had spoken of was his body. [22]After he was raised from the dead, his disciples recalled what he had said. Then they believed the Scripture and the words that Jesus had spoken.

John 10 [14]"I am the good shepherd; I know my sheep and my sheep know me—[15]just as the Father knows me and I know the Father—and I lay down my life for the sheep. [16]I have other sheep that are not of this sheep pen. I must bring them also. They too will listen to my voice, and there shall be one flock and one shepherd. [17]The reason my Father loves me is that I lay down my life—only to take it up again. [18]No one takes it from me, but I lay it down of my own accord. I have authority to lay it down and authority to take it up again. This command I received from my Father."

John 16 [16]"In a little while you will see me no more, and then after a little while you will see me."

[17]Some of his disciples said to one another, "What does he mean by saying, 'In a little while you will see me no more, and then after a little while you will see me,' and 'Because I am going to the Father'?" [18]They kept asking, "What does he mean by 'a little while'? We don't understand what he is saying."

[19]Jesus saw that they wanted to ask him about this, so he said to them, "Are you asking one another what I meant when I said, 'In a little while you will see me no more, and then after a little while you will see me'? [20]I tell you the truth, you will weep and mourn while the world rejoices. You will grieve, but your grief will turn to joy. [21]A woman giving birth to a child has pain because her time has come; but when her baby is born she forgets the anguish because of her joy that a child is born into the world. [22]So with you: Now is your time of grief, but I will see you again and you will rejoice, and no one will take away your joy."

2. Jesus Was Raised from the Dead by God

Acts 2 [22]"Men of Israel, listen to this: Jesus of Nazareth was a man accredited by God to you by miracles, wonders and signs, which God did among you through him, as you yourselves know. [23]This man was handed over to you by God's set purpose and foreknowledge; and you, with the help of wicked men, put him to death by nailing him to the cross. [24]But God raised him from the dead, freeing him from the agony of death, because it was impossible for death to keep its hold on him."

Acts 3 [15]"You killed the author of life, but God raised him from the dead. We are witnesses of this."

Acts 3 [26]"When God raised up his servant, he sent him first to you to bless you by turning each of you from your wicked ways."

Acts 4 [10]". . . then know this, you and all the people of Israel: It is by the name of Jesus Christ of Nazareth, whom you crucified but whom God raised from the dead, that this man stands before you healed."

Acts 5 [30]"The God of our fathers raised Jesus from the dead—whom you had killed by hanging him on a tree."

Acts 13 [30]"But God raised him from the dead. . . .

[32]"We tell you the good news: What God promised our fathers [33]he has fulfilled for us, their children, by raising up Jesus. As it is written in the second Psalm: 'You are my Son; today I have become your Father.' [34]The fact that God raised him from the dead, never to decay, is stated in these words: 'I will give you the holy and sure blessings promised to David.'"

Rom 1 [4]and who through the Spirit of holiness was declared with power to be the Son of God by his resurrection from the dead: Jesus Christ our Lord.

Rom 4 [24]but also for us, to whom God will credit righteousness—for us who believe in him who raised Jesus our Lord from the dead. [25]He was delivered over to death for our sins and was raised to life for our justification.

Rom 6 [4]We were therefore buried with him through baptism into death in order that, just as Christ was raised from the dead through the glory of the Father, we too may live a new life.

Rom 7 [4]So, my brothers, you also died to the law through the body of Christ, that you might belong to another, to him who was raised from the dead, in order that we might bear fruit to God.

Rom 8 [11]And if the Spirit of him who raised Jesus from the dead is living in you, he who raised Christ from the dead will also give life to your mortal bodies through his Spirit, who lives in you.

Rom 10 [9]That if you confess with your mouth, "Jesus is Lord," and believe in your heart that God raised him from the dead, you will be saved.

1 Cor 6 [14]By his power God raised the Lord from the dead, and he will raise us also.

1 Cor 15 [12]But if it is preached that Christ has been raised from the dead, how can some of you say that there is no resurrection of the dead? [13]If there is no resurrection of the dead, then not even Christ has been raised. [14]And if Christ has not been raised, our preaching is useless and so is your faith. [15]More than that, we are then found to be false witnesses about God, for we have testified about God that he raised Christ from the dead. But he did not raise him if in fact the dead are not raised. [16]For if the dead are not raised, then Christ has not been raised either. [17]And if Christ has not been raised, your faith is futile; you are still in your sins. [18]Then those also who have fallen asleep in Christ are lost. [19]If only for this life we have hope in Christ, we are to be pitied more than all men.

[20]But Christ has indeed been raised from the dead, the firstfruits of those who have fallen asleep.

2 Cor 4 [14]because we know that the one who raised the Lord Jesus from the dead will also raise us with Jesus and present us with you in his presence.

Gal 1 [1]Paul, an apostle—sent not from men nor by man, but by Jesus Christ and God the Father, who raised him from the dead. . . .

Eph 1 [17]I keep asking that the God of our Lord Jesus Christ, the glorious Father, may give you the Spirit of wisdom and revelation, so that you may know him better. [18]I pray also that the eyes of your heart may be enlightened in order that you may know the hope to which he has called you, the riches of his glorious inheritance in the saints, [19]and his incomparably great power for us who believe. That power is like the working of his mighty strength, [20]which he exerted in Christ when he raised him from the dead and seated him at his right hand in the heavenly realms. . . .

Col 2 [11]In him you were also circumcised, in the putting off of the sinful nature, not with a circumcision done by the hands of men but with the circumcision done by Christ, [12]having been buried with him in baptism and raised with him through your faith in the power of God, who raised him from the dead.

1 Thess 1 [9]for they themselves report what kind of reception you gave us. They tell how you turned to God from idols to serve the living and true God, [10]and to wait for his Son from heaven, whom he raised from the dead—Jesus, who rescues us from the coming wrath.

2 Tim 2 [8]Remember Jesus Christ, raised from the dead, descended from David. This is my gospel. . . .

Heb 13 [20]May the God of peace, who through the blood of the eternal covenant brought back from the dead our Lord Jesus, that great Shepherd of the sheep . . .

1 Pet 1 [18]For you know that it was not with perishable things such as silver or gold that you were redeemed from the empty way of life handed down to you from your forefathers, [19]but with the precious blood of Christ, a lamb without blemish or defect. . . . [21]Through him you believe in God, who raised him from the dead and glorified him, and so your faith and hope are in God.

Rev 1 [5]and from Jesus Christ, who is the faithful witness, the firstborn from the dead, and the ruler of the kings of the earth.

To him who loves us and has freed us from our sins by his blood. . . .

3. The Empty Tomb Testified to His Resurrection

Matt 28 1After the Sabbath, at dawn on the first day of the week, Mary Magdalene and the other Mary went to look at the tomb.

2There was a violent earthquake, for an angel of the Lord came down from heaven and, going to the tomb, rolled back the stone and sat on it. 3His appearance was like lightning, and his clothes were white as snow. 4The guards were so afraid of him that they shook and became like dead men.

5The angel said to the women, "Do not be afraid, for I know that you are looking for Jesus, who was crucified. 6He is not here; he has risen, just as he said. Come and see the place where he lay. 7Then go quickly and tell his disciples: 'He has risen from the dead and is going ahead of you into Galilee. There you will see him.' Now I have told you."

8So the women hurried away from the tomb, afraid yet filled with joy, and ran to tell his disciples. 9Suddenly Jesus met them. "Greetings," he said. They came to him, clasped his feet and worshiped him. 10Then Jesus said to them, "Do not be afraid. Go and tell my brothers to go to Galilee; there they will see me."

Mark 16 1When the Sabbath was over, Mary Magdalene, Mary the mother of James, and Salome bought spices so that they might go to anoint Jesus' body. 2Very early on the first day of the week, just after sunrise, they were on their way to the tomb 3and they asked each other, "Who will roll the stone away from the entrance of the tomb?"

4But when they looked up, they saw that the stone, which was very large, had been rolled away. 5As they entered the tomb, they saw a young man dressed in a white robe sitting on the right side, and they were alarmed.

6"Don't be alarmed," he said. "You are looking for Jesus the Nazarene, who was crucified. He has risen! He is not here. See the place where they laid him. 7But go, tell his disciples and Peter, 'He is going ahead of you into Galilee. There you will see him, just as he told you.'"

8Trembling and bewildered, the women went out and fled from the tomb. They said nothing to anyone, because they were afraid.

Luke 24 1On the first day of the week, very early in the morning, the women took the spices they had prepared and went to the tomb. 2They found the stone rolled away from the tomb, 3but when they entered, they did not find the body of the Lord Jesus. 4While they were wondering about this, suddenly two men in clothes that gleamed like lightning stood beside them. 5In their fright the women bowed down with their faces to the ground, but the men said to them, "Why do you look for the living among the dead? 6He is not here; he has risen! Remember how he told you, while he was still with you in Galilee: 7'The Son of Man must be delivered into the hands of sinful men, be crucified and on the third day be raised again.'" 8Then they remembered his words.

9When they came back from the tomb, they told all these things to the Eleven and to all the others. 10It was Mary Magdalene, Joanna, Mary the mother of James, and the others with them who told this to the apostles. 11But they did not believe the women, because their words seemed to them like nonsense. 12Peter, however, got up and ran to the tomb. Bending over, he saw the strips of linen lying by themselves, and he went away, wondering to himself what had happened.

John 20 1Early on the first day of the week, while it was still dark, Mary Magdalene went to the tomb and saw that the stone had been removed from the entrance. 2So she came running to Simon Peter and the other disciple, the one Jesus loved, and said, "They have taken the Lord out of the tomb, and we don't know where they have put him!"

3So Peter and the other disciple started for the tomb. 4Both were running, but the other disciple outran Peter and reached the tomb first. 5He bent over and looked in at the strips of linen lying there but did not go in. 6Then Simon Peter, who was behind him, arrived and went into the tomb. He saw the strips of linen lying there, 7as well as the burial cloth that had been around Jesus' head. The cloth was folded up by itself, separate from the linen. 8Finally the other disciple, who had reached the tomb first, also went inside. He saw and believed. 9(They still did not understand from Scripture that Jesus had to rise from the dead.)

10Then the disciples went back to their homes, 11but Mary stood outside the tomb crying. As she wept, she bent over to look into the tomb 12and saw two angels in white, seated where Jesus' body had been, one at the head and the other at the foot.

13They asked her, "Woman, why are you crying?"

"They have taken my Lord away," she said, "and I don't know where they have put him." 14At this, she turned around and saw Jesus standing there, but she did not realize that it was Jesus.

15"Woman," he said, "why are you crying? Who is it you are looking for?"

Thinking he was the gardener, she said, "Sir, if you have carried him away, tell me where you have put him, and I will get him."

16Jesus said to her, "Mary."

She turned toward him and cried out in Aramaic, "Rabboni!" (which means Teacher).

17Jesus said, "Do not hold on to me, for I have not yet returned to the Father. Go instead to my brothers and tell them, 'I am returning to my Father and your Father, to my God and your God.'"

18Mary Magdalene went to the disciples with the news: "I have seen the Lord!" And she told them that he had said these things to her.

4. Jesus Appeared to Many after His Resurrection

Matt 28 16Then the eleven disciples went to Galilee, to the mountain where Jesus had told them to go. 17When they saw him, they worshiped him; but some doubted.

Luke 24 13Now that same day two of them were going to a village called Emmaus, about seven miles from Jerusalem. 14They were talking with each other about everything that had happened. 15As they talked and discussed these things with each other, Jesus himself came up and walked along with them; 16but they were kept from recognizing him. . . .

33They got up and returned at once to Jerusalem. There they found the Eleven and those with them, assembled together 34and saying, "It is true! The Lord has risen and has appeared to Simon." 35Then the two told what had happened on the way, and how Jesus was recognized by them when he broke the bread.

36While they were still talking about this, Jesus himself stood among them and said to them, "Peace be with you."

37They were startled and frightened, thinking they saw a ghost. 38He said to them, "Why are you troubled, and why do doubts rise in your minds? 39Look at my hands and my feet. It is I myself! Touch me and see; a ghost does not have flesh and bones, as you see I have."

40When he had said this, he showed them his hands and feet. 41And while they still did not believe it because of joy and amazement, he asked them, "Do you have anything here to eat?" 42They gave him a piece of broiled fish, 43and he took it and ate it in their presence.

John 20 19On the evening of that first day of the week, when the disciples were together, with the doors locked for fear of the Jews, Jesus came and stood among them and said, "Peace be with you!" 20After he said this, he showed them his hands and side. The disciples were overjoyed when they saw the Lord. . . .

26A week later his disciples were in the house again, and Thomas was with them. Though the doors were locked, Jesus came and stood among them and said, "Peace be with you!" 27Then he said to Thomas, "Put your finger here; see my hands. Reach out your hand and put it into my side. Stop doubting and believe."

28Thomas said to him, "My Lord and my God!"

29Then Jesus told him, "Because you have seen me, you have believed; blessed are those who have not seen and yet have believed."

John 21 1Afterward Jesus appeared again to his disciples, by the Sea of Tiberias. It happened this way: 2Simon Peter, Thomas (called Didymus), Nathanael from Cana in Galilee, the sons of Zebedee, and two other disciples were together. 3"I'm going out to fish," Simon Peter told them, and they said, "We'll go with you." So they went out and got into the boat, but that night they caught nothing.

4Early in the morning, Jesus stood on the shore, but the disciples did not realize that it was Jesus.

5He called out to them, "Friends, haven't you any fish?"

"No," they answered.

6He said, "Throw your net on the right side of the boat and you will find some." When they did, they were unable to haul the net in because of the large number of fish.

7Then the disciple whom Jesus loved said to Peter, "It is the Lord!" As soon as Simon Peter heard him say, "It is the Lord," he wrapped his outer garment around him (for he had taken it off) and jumped into the water. 8The other disciples followed in the boat, towing the net full of fish, for they were not far from shore, about a hundred yards.

Acts 1 1In my former book, Theophilus, I wrote about all that Jesus began to do and to teach 2until the day he was taken up to heaven, after giving instructions through the Holy Spirit to the apostles he had chosen. 3After his suffering, he showed himself to these men and gave many convincing proofs that he was alive. He appeared to them over a period of forty days and spoke about the kingdom of God.

Acts 1 21"Therefore it is necessary to choose one of the men who have been with us the whole time the Lord Jesus went in and out among us, 22beginning from John's baptism to the time when Jesus was taken up from us. For one of these must become a witness with us of his resurrection."

Acts 2 31"Seeing what was ahead, he spoke of the resurrection of the Christ, that he was not abandoned to the grave, nor did his body see decay. 32God has raised this Jesus to life, and we are all witnesses of the fact."

Acts 3 15"You killed the author of life, but God raised him from the dead. We are witnesses of this."

Acts 5 30"The God of our fathers raised Jesus from the dead—whom you had killed by hanging him on a tree. 31God exalted him to his own right hand as Prince and Savior that he might give repentance and forgiveness of sins to Israel. 32We are witnesses of these things, and so is the Holy Spirit, whom God has given to those who obey him."

Acts 10 39"We are witnesses of everything he did in the country of the Jews and in Jerusalem. They killed him by hanging him on a tree, 40but God raised him from the dead on the third day and caused him to be seen. 41He was not seen by all the people, but by witnesses whom God had already chosen—by us who ate and drank with him after he rose from the dead. 42He commanded us to preach to the people and to testify that he is the one whom God appointed as judge of the living and the dead. 43All the prophets testify about him that everyone who believes in him receives forgiveness of sins through his name."

Acts 13 27"The people of Jerusalem and their rulers did not recognize Jesus, yet in condemning him they fulfilled the words of the prophets that are read every Sabbath. . . . 30But God raised him from the dead, 31and for many days he was seen by those who had traveled with him from Galilee to Jerusalem. They are now his witnesses to our people."

1 Cor 15 3For what I received I passed on to you as of first importance that Christ died for our sins according to the Scriptures, 4that he was buried, that he was raised on the third day according to the Scriptures, 5and that he appeared to Peter, and then to the Twelve. 6After that, he appeared to more than five hundred of the brothers at the same time, most of whom are still living, though some have fallen asleep. 7Then he appeared to James, then to all the apostles, 8and last of all he appeared to me also, as to one abnormally born.

1 John 1 1That which was from the beginning, which we have heard, which we have seen with our eyes, which we have looked at and our hands have touched—this we proclaim concerning the Word of life. 2The life appeared; we have seen it and testify to it, and we proclaim to you the eternal life, which was with the Father and has appeared to us. 3We proclaim to you what we have seen and heard, so that you also may have fellowship with us. And our fellowship is with the Father and with his Son, Jesus Christ.

B. The Meaning of the Resurrection of Christ

1. Believers Are Justified by Jesus' Resurrection

Acts 2 22"Men of Israel, listen to this: Jesus of Nazareth was a man accredited by God to you by miracles, wonders and signs, which God did among you through him, as you yourselves know. 23This man was handed over to you by God's set purpose and foreknowledge; and you, with the help of wicked men, put him to death by nailing him to the cross. 24But God raised him from the dead, freeing him from the agony of death, because it was impossible for death to keep its hold on him. . . . 32God has raised this Jesus to life, and we are all witnesses of the fact. 33Exalted to the right hand of God, he has received from the Father the promised Holy Spirit and has poured out what you now see and hear. 34For David did not ascend to heaven, and yet he said, 'The Lord said to my Lord: "Sit at my right hand 35until I make your enemies a footstool for your feet."'

36"Therefore let all Israel be assured of this: God has made this Jesus, whom you crucified, both Lord and Christ."

37When the people heard this, they were cut to the heart and said to Peter and the other apostles, "Brothers, what shall we do?"

38Peter replied, "Repent and be baptized, every one of you, in the name of Jesus Christ for the forgiveness of your sins. And you will receive the gift of the Holy Spirit. 39The promise is for you and your children and for all who are far off—for all whom the Lord our God will call."

Acts 4 10". . . then know this, you and all the people of Israel: It is by the name of Jesus Christ of Nazareth, whom you crucified but whom God raised from the dead, that this man stands before you healed. 11He is 'the stone you builders rejected, which has become the capstone.' 12Salvation is found in no one else, for there is no other name under heaven given to men by which we must be saved."

Acts 13 29"When they had carried out all that was written about him, they took him down from the tree and laid him in a tomb. 30But God raised him from the dead, 31and for many days he was seen by those who had traveled with him from Galilee to Jerusalem. They are now his witnesses to our people.

32"We tell you the good news: What God promised our fathers 33he has fulfilled for us, their children, by raising up Jesus. As it is written in the second Psalm: 'You are my Son; today I have become your Father.' 34The fact that God raised him from the dead, never to decay, is stated in these words: 'I will give you the holy and sure blessings promised to David.' 35So it is stated elsewhere: 'You will not let your Holy One see decay.'

36"For when David had served God's purpose in his own generation, he fell asleep; he was buried with his fathers and his body decayed. 37But the one whom God raised from the dead did not see decay.

38"Therefore, my brothers, I want you to know that through Jesus the forgiveness of sins is proclaimed to you. 39Through him everyone who believes is justified from everything you could not be justified from by the law of Moses."

Acts 17 30"In the past God overlooked such ignorance, but now he commands all people everywhere to repent. 31For he has set a day when he will judge the world with justice by the man he has appointed. He has given proof of this to all men by raising him from the dead."

Rom 4 23The words "it was credited to him" were written not for him alone, 24but also for us, to whom God will credit righteousness—for us who believe in him who raised Jesus our Lord from the dead. 25He was delivered over to death for our sins and was raised to life for our justification.

Rom 5 9Since we have now been justified by his blood, how much more shall we be saved from God's wrath through him! 10For if, when we were God's enemies, we were reconciled to him through the death of his Son, how much more, having been reconciled, shall we be saved through his life! . . .

18Consequently, just as the result of one trespass was condemnation for all men, so also the result of one act of righteousness was justification that brings life for all men. 21. . . so that, just as sin reigned in death, so also grace might reign through righteousness to bring eternal life through Jesus Christ our Lord.

Rom 10 [9]That if you confess with your mouth, "Jesus is Lord," and believe in your heart that God raised him from the dead, you will be saved. [10]For it is with your heart that you believe and are justified, and it is with your mouth that you confess and are saved.

1 Cor 15 [3]For what I received I passed on to you as of first importance: that Christ died for our sins according to the Scriptures, [4]that he was buried, that he was raised on the third day according to the Scriptures. . . .

[12]But if it is preached that Christ has been raised from the dead, how can some of you say that there is no resurrection of the dead? [13]If there is no resurrection of the dead, then not even Christ has been raised. [14]And if Christ has not been raised, our preaching is useless and so is your faith. [15]More than that, we are then found to be false witnesses about God, for we have testified about God that he raised Christ from the dead. But he did not raise him if in fact the dead are not raised. [16]For if the dead are not raised, then Christ has not been raised either. [17]And if Christ has not been raised, your faith is futile; you are still in your sins. [18]Then those also who have fallen asleep in Christ are lost. [19]If only for this life we have hope in Christ, we are to be pitied more than all men.

[20]But Christ has indeed been raised from the dead, the firstfruits of those who have fallen asleep. [21]For since death came through a man, the resurrection of the dead comes also through a man. [22]For as in Adam all die, so in Christ all will be made alive. [23]But each in his own turn: Christ, the firstfruits; then, when he comes, those who belong to him.

2 Cor 5 [14]For Christ's love compels us, because we are convinced that one died for all, and therefore all died. [15]And he died for all, that those who live should no longer live for themselves but for him who died for them and was raised again.

1 Pet 3 [18]For Christ died for sins once for all, the righteous for the unrighteous, to bring you to God. He was put to death in the body but made alive by the Spirit. . . . [21]and this water symbolizes baptism that now saves you also—not the removal of dirt from the body but the pledge of a good conscience toward God. It saves you by the resurrection of Jesus Christ. . . .

2. Believers Are Identified with Jesus' Resurrection

Rom 6 [1]What shall we say, then? Shall we go on sinning so that grace may increase? [2]By no means! We died to sin; how can we live in it any longer? [3]Or don't you know that all of us who were baptized into Christ Jesus were baptized into his death? [4]We were therefore buried with him through baptism into death in order that, just as Christ was raised from the dead through the glory of the Father, we too may live a new life.

[5]If we have been united with him like this in his death, we will certainly also be united with him in his resurrection. [6]For we know that our old self was crucified with him so that the body of sin might be done away with, that we should no longer be slaves to sin—[7]because anyone who has died has been freed from sin.

[8]Now if we died with Christ, we believe that we will also live with him. [9]For we know that since Christ was raised from the dead, he cannot die again; death no longer has mastery over him. [10]The death he died, he died to sin once for all; but the life he lives, he lives to God.

[11]In the same way, count yourselves dead to sin but alive to God in Christ Jesus.

Rom 8 [10]But if Christ is in you, your body is dead because of sin, yet your spirit is alive because of righteousness. [11]And if the Spirit of him who raised Jesus from the dead is living in you, he who raised Christ from the dead will also give life to your mortal bodies through his Spirit, who lives in you.

2 Cor 5 [14]For Christ's love compels us, because we are convinced that one died for all, and therefore all died. [15]And he died for all, that those who live should no longer live for themselves but for him who died for them and was raised again.

2 Cor 13 [4]For to be sure, he was crucified in weakness, yet he lives by God's power. Likewise, we are weak in him, yet by God's power we will live with him to serve you.

Gal 2 [20]"I have been crucified with Christ and I no longer live, but Christ lives in me. The life I live in the body, I live by faith in the Son of God, who loved me and gave himself for me."

Eph 2 [1]As for you, you were dead in your transgressions and sins, [2]in which you used to live when you followed the ways of this world and of the ruler of the kingdom of the air, the spirit who is now at work in those who are disobedient. [3]All of us also lived among them at one time, gratifying the cravings of our sinful nature and following its desires and thoughts. Like the rest, we were by nature objects of wrath. [4]But because of his great love for us, God, who is rich in mercy, [5]made us alive with Christ even when we were dead in transgressions—it is by grace you have been saved. [6]And God raised us up with Christ and seated us with him in the heavenly realms in Christ Jesus. . . .

Phil 3 [10]I want to know Christ and the power of his resurrection and the fellowship of sharing in his sufferings, becoming like him in his death, [11]and so, somehow, to attain to the resurrection from the dead.

Col 2 [9]For in Christ all the fullness of the Deity lives in bodily form, [10]and you have been given fullness in Christ, who is the head over every power and authority. [11]In him you were also circumcised, in the putting off of the sinful nature, not with a circumcision done by the hands of men but with the circumcision done by Christ, [12]having been buried with him in baptism and raised with him through your faith in the power of God, who raised him from the dead.

2 Tim 2 [8]Remember Jesus Christ, raised from the dead, descended from David. This is my gospel, [9]for which I am suffering even to the point of being chained like a criminal. But God's word is not chained. [10]Therefore I endure everything for the sake of the elect, that they too may obtain the salvation that is in Christ Jesus, with eternal glory.

[11]Here is a trustworthy saying: If we died with him, we will also live with him. . . .

3. Believers' Hope Is Grounded in Jesus' Resurrection

Acts 26 [23]". . . that the Christ would suffer and, as the first to rise from the dead, would proclaim light to his own people and to the Gentiles."

1 Cor 6 [14]By his power God raised the Lord from the dead, and he will raise us also.

2 Cor 4 [10]We always carry around in our body the death of Jesus, so that the life of Jesus may also be revealed in our body. [11]For we who are alive are always being given over to death for Jesus' sake, so that his life may be revealed in our mortal body. [14]. . . because we know that the one who raised the Lord Jesus from the dead will also raise us with Jesus and present us with you in his presence.

1 Thess 1 [10]and to wait for his Son from heaven, whom he raised from the dead—Jesus, who rescues us from the coming wrath.

1 Thess 4 [14]We believe that Jesus died and rose again and so we believe that God will bring with Jesus those who have fallen asleep in him. [15]According to the Lord's own word, we tell you that we who are still alive, who are left till the coming of the Lord, will certainly not precede those who have fallen asleep. [16]For the Lord himself will come down from heaven, with a loud command, with the voice of the archangel and with the trumpet call of God, and the dead in Christ will rise first.

1 Pet 1 [3]Praise be to the God and Father of our Lord Jesus Christ! In his great mercy he has given us new birth into a living hope through the resurrection of Jesus Christ from the dead, [4]and into an inheritance that can never perish, spoil or fade—kept in heaven for you, [5]who through faith are shielded by God's power until the coming of the salvation that is ready to be revealed in the last time.

Rev 1 [5]and from Jesus Christ, who is the faithful witness, the firstborn from the dead, and the ruler of the kings of the earth.

To him who loves us and has freed us from our sins by his blood, [6]and has made us to be a kingdom and priests to serve

his God and Father—to him be glory and power for ever and ever! Amen.
Rev 1 [17]When I saw him, I fell at his feet as though dead. Then he placed his right hand on me and said: "Do not be afraid. I am the First and the Last. [18]I am the Living One; I was dead, and behold I am alive for ever and ever! And I hold the keys of death and Hades."

4. Believers' Living High Priest Is Now the Resurrected Jesus

a) Jesus Is an Advocate

Heb 9 [24]For Christ did not enter a man-made sanctuary that was only a copy of the true one; he entered heaven itself, now to appear for us in God's presence.
1 John 2 [1]My dear children, I write this to you so that you will not sin. But if anybody does sin, we have one who speaks to the Father in our defense—Jesus Christ, the Righteous One.

b) Jesus Is the High Priest

Heb 2 [17]For this reason he had to be made like his brothers in every way, in order that he might become a merciful and faithful high priest in service to God, and that he might make atonement for the sins of the people. [18]Because he himself suffered when he was tempted, he is able to help those who are being tempted.
Heb 3 [1]Therefore, holy brothers, who share in the heavenly calling, fix your thoughts on Jesus, the apostle and high priest whom we confess. [2]He was faithful to the one who appointed him, just as Moses was faithful in all God's house. [3]Jesus has been found worthy of greater honor than Moses, just as the builder of a house has greater honor than the house itself. [4]For every house is built by someone, but God is the builder of everything. [5]Moses was faithful as a servant in all God's house, testifying to what would be said in the future. [6]But Christ is faithful as a son over God's house. And we are his house, if we hold on to our courage and the hope of which we boast.
Heb 4 [14]Therefore, since we have a great high priest who has gone through the heavens, Jesus the Son of God, let us hold firmly to the faith we profess. [15]For we do not have a high priest who is unable to sympathize with our weaknesses, but we have one who has been tempted in every way, just as we are—yet was without sin. [16]Let us then approach the throne of grace with confidence, so that we may receive mercy and find grace to help us in our time of need.
Heb 5 [4]No one takes this honor upon himself; he must be called by God, just as Aaron was. [5]So Christ also did not take upon himself the glory of becoming a high priest. But God said to him, "You are my Son; today I have become your Father." [6]And he says in another place, "You are a priest forever, in the order of Melchizedek."

[7]During the days of Jesus' life on earth, he offered up prayers and petitions with loud cries and tears to the one who could save him from death, and he was heard because of his reverent submission. [8]Although he was a son, he learned obedience from what he suffered [9]and, once made perfect, he became the source of eternal salvation for all who obey him [10]and was designated by God to be high priest in the order of Melchizedek.
Heb 6 [19]We have this hope as an anchor for the soul, firm and secure. It enters the inner sanctuary behind the curtain, [20]where Jesus, who went before us, has entered on our behalf. He has become a high priest forever, in the order of Melchizedek.
Heb 7 [11]If perfection could have been attained through the Levitical priesthood (for on the basis of it the law was given to the people), why was there still need for another priest to come—one in the order of Melchizedek, not in the order of Aaron? [12]For when there is a change of the priesthood, there must also be a change of the law. [13]He of whom these things are said belonged to a different tribe, and no one from that tribe has ever served at the altar. [14]For it is clear that our Lord descended from Judah, and in regard to that tribe Moses said nothing about priests. [15]And what we have said is even more clear if another priest like Melchizedek appears, [16]one who has become a priest not on the basis of a regulation as to his ancestry but on the basis of the power of an indestructible life. [17]For it is declared: "You are a priest forever, in the order of Melchizedek."

[18]The former regulation is set aside because it was weak and useless [19](for the law made nothing perfect), and a better hope is introduced, by which we draw near to God.

[20]And it was not without an oath! Others became priests without any oath, [21]but he became a priest with an oath when God said to him: "The Lord has sworn and will not change his mind: 'You are a priest forever.'" [22]Because of this oath, Jesus has become the guarantee of a better covenant.

[23]Now there have been many of those priests, since death prevented them from continuing in office; [24]but because Jesus lives forever, he has a permanent priesthood. [25]Therefore he is able to save completely those who come to God through him, because he always lives to intercede for them.

[26]Such a high priest meets our need—one who is holy, blameless, pure, set apart from sinners, exalted above the heavens. [27]Unlike the other high priests, he does not need to offer sacrifices day after day, first for his own sins, and then for the sins of the people. He sacrificed for their sins once for all when he offered himself. [28]For the law appoints as high priests men who are weak; but the oath, which came after the law, appointed the Son, who has been made perfect forever.
Heb 8 [1]The point of what we are saying is this: We do have such a high priest, who sat down at the right hand of the throne of the Majesty in heaven, [2]and who serves in the sanctuary, the true tabernacle set up by the Lord, not by man.
Heb 9 [11]When Christ came as high priest of the good things that are already here, he went through the greater and more perfect tabernacle that is not man-made, that is to say, not a part of this creation. [12]He did not enter by means of the blood of goats and calves; but he entered the Most Holy Place once for all by his own blood, having obtained eternal redemption. [13]The blood of goats and bulls and the ashes of a heifer sprinkled on those who are ceremonially unclean sanctify them so that they are outwardly clean. [14]How much more, then, will the blood of Christ, who through the eternal Spirit offered himself unblemished to God, cleanse our consciences from acts that lead to death, so that we may serve the living God!
Heb 10 [19]Therefore, brothers, since we have confidence to enter the Most Holy Place by the blood of Jesus, [20]by a new and living way opened for us through the curtain, that is, his body, [21]and since we have a great priest over the house of God, [22]let us draw near to God with a sincere heart in full assurance of faith, having our hearts sprinkled to cleanse us from a guilty conscience and having our bodies washed with pure water.

c) Jesus Is an Intercessor

Isa 53 [12]Therefore I will give him a portion among the great, and he will divide the spoils with the strong, because he poured out his life unto death, and was numbered with the transgressors. For he bore the sin of many, and made intercession for the transgressors.
Luke 22 [31]"Simon, Simon, Satan has asked to sift you as wheat. [32]But I have prayed for you, Simon, that your faith may not fail. And when you have turned back, strengthen your brothers."
Luke 23 [34]Jesus said, "Father, forgive them, for they do not know what they are doing." And they divided up his clothes by casting lots.
John 17 [9]"I pray for them. I am not praying for the world, but for those you have given me, for they are yours. . . . [11]I will remain in the world no longer, but they are still in the world, and I am coming to you. Holy Father, protect them by the power of your name—the name you gave me—so that they may be one as we are one. . . .

[20]"My prayer is not for them alone. I pray also for those who will believe in me through their message, [21]that all of them may be one, Father, just as you are in me and I am in you. May they also be in us so that the world may believe that you have sent me."
Rom 8 [34]Who is he that condemns? Christ Jesus, who died—more than that, who was raised to life—is at the right hand of God and is also interceding for us.
Heb 7 [24]but because Jesus lives forever, he has a permanent

priesthood. [25]Therefore he is able to save completely those who come to God through him, because he always lives to intercede for them.

d) Jesus Is the Mediator

Matt 18 [19]"Again, I tell you that if two of you on earth agree about anything you ask for, it will be done for you by my Father in heaven. [20]For where two or three come together in my name, there am I with them."
John 14 [6]Jesus answered, "I am the way and the truth and the life. No one comes to the Father except through me."
John 14 [26]"But the Counselor, the Holy Spirit, whom the Father will send in my name, will teach you all things and will remind you of everything I have said to you."
John 16 [23]"In that day you will no longer ask me anything. I tell you the truth, my Father will give you whatever you ask in my name. [24]Until now you have not asked for anything in my name. Ask and you will receive, and your joy will be complete.

[25]"Though I have been speaking figuratively, a time is coming when I will no longer use this kind of language but will tell you plainly about my Father. [26]In that day you will ask in my name. I am not saying that I will ask the Father on your behalf. [27]No, the Father himself loves you because you have loved me and have believed that I came from God."
Acts 2 [22]"Men of Israel, listen to this: Jesus of Nazareth was a man accredited by God to you by miracles, wonders and signs, which God did among you through him, as you yourselves know. [23]This man was handed over to you by God's set purpose and foreknowledge; and you, with the help of wicked men, put him to death by nailing him to the cross."
Eph 1 [5]he predestined us to be adopted as his sons through Jesus Christ, in accordance with his pleasure and will—[6]to the praise of his glorious grace, which he has freely given us in the One he loves.
Eph 2 [13]But now in Christ Jesus you who once were far away have been brought near through the blood of Christ. . . . [18]For through him we both have access to the Father by one Spirit.
Eph 3 [12]In him and through faith in him we may approach God with freedom and confidence.
Col 3 [17]And whatever you do, whether in word or deed, do it all in the name of the Lord Jesus, giving thanks to God the Father through him.
1 Tim 2 [5]For there is one God and one mediator between God and men, the man Christ Jesus. . . .
Heb 8 [6]But the ministry Jesus has received is as superior to theirs as the covenant of which he is mediator is superior to the old one, and it is founded on better promises.
Heb 9 [15]For this reason Christ is the mediator of a new covenant, that those who are called may receive the promised eternal inheritance—now that he has died as a ransom to set them free from the sins committed under the first covenant.
Heb 12 [24]to Jesus the mediator of a new covenant, and to the sprinkled blood that speaks a better word than the blood of Abel.
1 Pet 2 [4]As you come to him, the living Stone—rejected by men but chosen by God and precious to him—[5]you also, like living stones, are being built into a spiritual house to be a holy priesthood, offering spiritual sacrifices acceptable to God through Jesus Christ.

e) Jesus Is a Shepherd

John 10 [2]"The man who enters by the gate is the shepherd of his sheep. [3]The watchman opens the gate for him, and the sheep listen to his voice. He calls his own sheep by name and leads them out. [4]When he has brought out all his own, he goes on ahead of them, and his sheep follow him because they know his voice. . . .

[11]"I am the good shepherd. The good shepherd lays down his life for the sheep. . . .

[14]"I am the good shepherd; I know my sheep and my sheep know me—[15]just as the Father knows me and I know the Father—and I lay down my life for the sheep. [16]I have other sheep that are not of this sheep pen. I must bring them also. They too will listen to my voice, and there shall be one flock and one shepherd. [17]The reason my Father loves me is that I lay down my life—only to take it up again. [18]No one takes it from me, but I lay it down of my own accord. I have authority to lay it down and authority to take it up again. This command I received from my Father."
Heb 13 [20]May the God of peace, who through the blood of the eternal covenant brought back from the dead our Lord Jesus, that great Shepherd of the sheep . . .
1 Pet 2 [25]For you were like sheep going astray, but now you have returned to the Shepherd and Overseer of your souls.
1 Pet 5 [4]And when the Chief Shepherd appears, you will receive the crown of glory that will never fade away.
Rev 7 [16]"Never again will they hunger; never again will they thirst. The sun will not beat upon them, nor any scorching heat. [17]For the Lamb at the center of the throne will be their shepherd; he will lead them to springs of living water. And God will wipe away every tear from their eyes."

IV
Election

***See* p. 176a, God's Election to Salvation of Believers and the Believing Community**

V
Calling

A. The Nature of the Call

1. Those Whom God Calls

a) God Calls All People

Ps 19 [1]The heavens declare the glory of God; the skies proclaim the work of his hands. [2]Day after day they pour forth speech; night after night they display knowledge. [3]There is no speech or language where their voice is not heard. [4]Their voice goes out into all the earth, their words to the ends of the world.

In the heavens he has pitched a tent for the sun. . . .
Isa 45 [22]"Turn to me and be saved, all you ends of the earth; for I am God, and there is no other."
Isa 49 [5]And now the LORD says—he who formed me in the womb to be his servant to bring Jacob back to him and gather Israel to himself, for I am honored in the eyes of the LORD and my God has been my strength—[6]he says: "It is too small a thing for you to be my servant to restore the tribes of Jacob and bring back those of Israel I have kept. I will also make you a light for the Gentiles, that you may bring my salvation to the ends of the earth."
Isa 55 [1]"Come, all you who are thirsty, come to the waters; and you who have no money, come, buy and eat! Come, buy wine and milk without money and without cost. [2]Why spend money on what is not bread, and your labor on what does not satisfy? Listen, listen to me, and eat what is good, and your soul will delight in the richest of fare. [3]Give ear and come to me; hear me, that your soul may live. I will make an everlasting covenant with you, my faithful love promised to David. [4]See, I have made him a witness to the peoples, a leader and commander of the peoples. [5]Surely you will summon nations you know not, and nations that do not know you will hasten to you, because of the LORD your God, the Holy One of Israel, for he has endowed you with splendor."
Matt 11 [28]"Come to me, all you who are weary and burdened, and I will give you rest."
Matt 28 [18]Then Jesus came to them and said, "All authority in heaven and on earth has been given to me. [19]Therefore go and make disciples of all nations, baptizing them in the name of the Father and of the Son and of the Holy Spirit. . . ."
John 3 [14]"Just as Moses lifted up the snake in the desert, so the Son of Man must be lifted up, [15]that everyone who believes in him may have eternal life.

[16]"For God so loved the world that he gave his one and only

Son, that whoever believes in him shall not perish but have eternal life. [17]For God did not send his Son into the world to condemn the world, but to save the world through him."
John 4 [13]Jesus answered, "Everyone who drinks this water will be thirsty again, [14]but whoever drinks the water I give him will never thirst. Indeed, the water I give him will become in him a spring of water welling up to eternal life."
John 6 [51]"I am the living bread that came down from heaven. If anyone eats of this bread, he will live forever. This bread is my flesh, which I will give for the life of the world."
John 7 [37]On the last and greatest day of the Feast, Jesus stood and said in a loud voice, "If anyone is thirsty, let him come to me and drink. [38]Whoever believes in me, as the Scripture has said, streams of living water will flow from within him."
John 11 [25]Jesus said to her, "I am the resurrection and the life. He who believes in me will live, even though he dies; [26]and whoever lives and believes in me will never die. Do you believe this?"
John 12 [32]"But I, when I am lifted up from the earth, will draw all men to myself."
Acts 2 [39]"The promise is for you and your children and for all who are far off—for all whom the Lord our God will call."
Rom 1 [20]For since the creation of the world God's invisible qualities—his eternal power and divine nature—have been clearly seen, being understood from what has been made, so that men are without excuse.
1 Cor 1 [26]Brothers, think of what you were when you were called. Not many of you were wise by human standards; not many were influential; not many were of noble birth. [27]But God chose the foolish things of the world to shame the wise; God chose the weak things of the world to shame the strong. [28]He chose the lowly things of this world and the despised things—and the things that are not—to nullify the things that are, [29]so that no one may boast before him.
Eph 3 [6]This mystery is that through the gospel the Gentiles are heirs together with Israel, members together of one body, and sharers together in the promise in Christ Jesus.

[7]I became a servant of this gospel by the gift of God's grace given me through the working of his power. [8]Although I am less than the least of all God's people, this grace was given me: to preach to the Gentiles the unsearchable riches of Christ, [9]and to make plain to everyone the administration of this mystery, which for ages past was kept hidden in God, who created all things.
Col 1 [22]But now he has reconciled you by Christ's physical body through death to present you holy in his sight, without blemish and free from accusation—[23]if you continue in your faith, established and firm, not moved from the hope held out in the gospel. This is the gospel that you heard and that has been proclaimed to every creature under heaven, and of which I, Paul, have become a servant.
1 Tim 2 [3]This is good, and pleases God our Savior, [4]who wants all men to be saved and to come to a knowledge of the truth. [5]For there is one God and one mediator between God and men, the man Christ Jesus, [6]who gave himself as a ransom for all men—the testimony given in its proper time.
1 Tim 4 [10](and for this we labor and strive), that we have put our hope in the living God, who is the Savior of all men, and especially of those who believe.
2 Tim 4 [17]But the Lord stood at my side and gave me strength, so that through me the message might be fully proclaimed and all the Gentiles might hear it. And I was delivered from the lion's mouth.
Titus 2 [11]For the grace of God that brings salvation has appeared to all men.
2 Pet 3 [9]The Lord is not slow in keeping his promise, as some understand slowness. He is patient with you, not wanting anyone to perish, but everyone to come to repentance.
Rev 22 [17]The Spirit and the bride say, "Come!" And let him who hears say, "Come!" Whoever is thirsty, let him come; and whoever wishes, let him take the free gift of the water of life.

b) God Calls Christ's Sheep

John 10 [2]"The man who enters by the gate is the shepherd of his sheep. [3]The watchman opens the gate for him, and the sheep listen to his voice. He calls his own sheep by name and leads them out. [4]When he has brought out all his own, he goes on ahead of them, and his sheep follow him because they know his voice."
John 10 [11]"I am the good shepherd. The good shepherd lays down his life for the sheep. [12]The hired hand is not the shepherd who owns the sheep. So when he sees the wolf coming, he abandons the sheep and runs away. Then the wolf attacks the flock and scatters it. [13]The man runs away because he is a hired hand and cares nothing for the sheep.

[14]"I am the good shepherd, I know my sheep and my sheep know me—[15]just as the Father knows me and I know the Father—and I lay down my life for the sheep. [16]I have other sheep that are not of this sheep pen. I must bring them also. They too will listen to my voice, and there shall be one flock and one shepherd."

c) God Calls Jew and Gentile

John 10 [16]"I have other sheep that are not of this sheep pen. I must bring them also. They too will listen to my voice, and there shall be one flock and one shepherd."
Acts 13 [47]"For this is what the Lord has commanded us: 'I have made you a light for the Gentiles, that you may bring salvation to the ends of the earth.'"

[48]When the Gentiles heard this, they were glad and honored the word of the Lord; and all who were appointed for eternal life believed.
Rom 9 [24]even us, whom he also called, not only from the Jews but also from the Gentiles? [25]As he says in Hosea: "I will call them 'my people' who are not my people; and I will call her 'my loved one' who is not my loved one," [26]and, "It will happen that in the very place where it was said to them, 'You are not my people,' they will be called 'sons of the living God.'"
1 Cor 1 [24]but to those whom God has called, both Jews and Greeks, Christ the power of God and the wisdom of God. [25]For the foolishness of God is wiser than man's wisdom, and the weakness of God is stronger than man's strength.
2 Tim 4 [17]But the Lord stood at my side and gave me strength, so that through me the message might be fully proclaimed and all the Gentiles might hear it. And I was delivered from the lion's mouth.

d) God Calls the People of God

1 Pet 2 [9]But you are a chosen people, a royal priesthood, a holy nation, a people belonging to God, that you may declare the praises of him who called you out of darkness into his wonderful light.

e) God Calls the Predestined

Rom 8 [30]And those he predestined, he also called; those he called, he also justified; those he justified, he also glorified.

f) God Calls Sinners

Matt 9 [13]"But go and learn what this means: 'I desire mercy, not sacrifice.' For I have not come to call the righteous, but sinners."
Mark 2 [17]On hearing this, Jesus said to them, "It is not the healthy who need a doctor, but the sick. I have not come to call the righteous, but sinners."

g) God Calls Those Loved by God the Father

Jude [1]Jude, a servant of Jesus Christ and a brother of James,

To those who have been called, who are loved by God the Father and kept by Jesus Christ. . . .

h) God Calls the Weary and Burdened

Matt 11 [28]"Come to me, all you who are weary and burdened, and I will give you rest."

2. What God Calls People To

a) God Calls People to Do Good

1 Pet 2 [20]But how is it to your credit if you receive a beating for doing wrong and endure it? But if you suffer for doing good and you endure it, this is commendable before God. [21]To this you were called, because Christ suffered for you, leaving you an example, that you should follow in his steps.
1 Pet 3 [8]Finally, all of you, live in harmony with one another;

be sympathetic, love as brothers, be compassionate and humble. [9]Do not repay evil with evil or insult with insult, but with blessing, because to this you were called so that you may inherit a blessing.

b) God Calls People to an Eternal Inheritance

Heb 9 [15]For this reason Christ is the mediator of a new covenant, that those who are called may receive the promised eternal inheritance—now that he has died as a ransom to set them free from the sins committed under the first covenant.

c) God Calls People to Eternal Life

1 Tim 6 [12]Fight the good fight of the faith. Take hold of the eternal life to which you were called when you made your good confession in the presence of many witnesses.

d) God Calls People to Faith

Mark 1 [14]After John was put in prison, Jesus went into Galilee, proclaiming the good news of God. [15]"The time has come," he said. "The kingdom of God is near. Repent and believe the good news!"
John 6 [29]Jesus answered, "The work of God is this: to believe in the one he has sent."
John 20 [30]Jesus did many other miraculous signs in the presence of his disciples, which are not recorded in this book. [31]But these are written that you may believe that Jesus is the Christ, the Son of God, and that by believing you may have life in his name.
Acts 16 [31]They replied, "Believe in the Lord Jesus, and you will be saved—you and your household."
Acts 20 [21]"I have declared to both Jews and Greeks that they must turn to God in repentance and have faith in our Lord Jesus."
Rom 10 [9]That if you confess with your mouth, "Jesus is Lord," and believe in your heart that God raised him from the dead, you will be saved.
2 Tim 3 [15]and how from infancy you have known the holy Scriptures, which are able to make you wise for salvation through faith in Christ Jesus.
1 John 3 [23]And this is his command: to believe in the name of his Son, Jesus Christ, and to love one another as he commanded us.

e) God Calls People to Fellowship with Christ

Rom 1 [6]And you also are among those who are called to belong to Jesus Christ.
1 Cor 1 [9]God, who has called you into fellowship with his Son Jesus Christ our Lord, is faithful.
Rev 17 [14]"They will make war against the Lamb, but the Lamb will overcome them because he is Lord of lords and King of kings—and with him will be his called, chosen and faithful followers."

f) God Calls People to Freedom

Gal 5 [2]Mark my words! I, Paul, tell you that if you let yourselves be circumcised, Christ will be of no value to you at all. [3]Again I declare to every man who lets himself be circumcised that he is obligated to obey the whole law. [4]You who are trying to be justified by law have been alienated from Christ; you have fallen away from grace. . . . [8]That kind of persuasion does not come from the one who calls you. . . .

[13]You, my brothers, were called to be free. But do not use your freedom to indulge the sinful nature; rather, serve one another in love.

g) God Calls People to Glory

John 17 [22]"I have given them the glory that you gave me, that they may be one as we are one. . . ."
Rom 9 [22]What if God, choosing to show his wrath and make his power known, bore with great patience the objects of his wrath—prepared for destruction? [23]What if he did this to make the riches of his glory known to the objects of his mercy, whom he prepared in advance for glory—[24]even us, whom he also called, not only from the Jews but also from the Gentiles?
Col 3 [4]When Christ, who is your life, appears, then you also will appear with him in glory.
1 Thess 2 [12]encouraging, comforting and urging you to live lives worthy of God, who calls you into his kingdom and glory.
2 Thess 2 [14]He called you to this through our gospel, that you might share in the glory of our Lord Jesus Christ.
1 Pet 5 [10]And the God of all grace, who called you to his eternal glory in Christ, after you have suffered a little while, will himself restore you and make you strong, firm and steadfast.

h) God Calls People to a Heavenly Reward

Phil 3 [14]I press on toward the goal to win the prize for which God has called me heavenward in Christ Jesus.

i) God Calls People to His Kingdom

1 Thess 2 [11]For you know that we dealt with each of you as a father deals with his own children, [12]encouraging, comforting and urging you to live lives worthy of God, who calls you into his kingdom and glory.

j) God Calls People to Holiness

1 Thess 4 [7]For God did not call us to be impure, but to live a holy life.
2 Tim 1 [8]So do not be ashamed to testify about our Lord, or ashamed of me his prisoner. But join with me in suffering for the gospel, by the power of God, [9]who has saved us and called us to a holy life—not because of anything we have done but because of his own purpose and grace. This grace was given us in Christ Jesus before the beginning of time. . . .
1 Pet 1 [15]But just as he who called you is holy, so be holy in all you do; [16]for it is written: "Be holy, because I am holy."

k) God Calls People to Holy Service

Heb 5 [1]Every high priest is selected from among men and is appointed to represent them in matters related to God, to offer gifts and sacrifices for sins. [2]He is able to deal gently with those who are ignorant and are going astray, since he himself is subject to weakness. [3]This is why he has to offer sacrifices for his own sins, as well as for the sins of the people.

[4]No one takes this honor upon himself; he must be called by God, just as Aaron was.

l) God Calls People to Hope

Eph 1 [17]I keep asking that the God of our Lord Jesus Christ, the glorious Father, may give you the Spirit of wisdom and revelation, so that you may know him better. [18]I pray also that the eyes of your heart may be enlightened in order that you may know the hope to which he has called you, the riches of his glorious inheritance in the saints. . . .
Eph 4 [4]There is one body and one Spirit—just as you were called to one hope when you were called. . . .

m) God Calls People to the Light

1 Pet 2 [9]But you are a chosen people, a royal priesthood, a holy nation, a people belonging to God, that you may declare the praises of him who called you out of darkness into his wonderful light.

n) God Calls People to Peace

1 Cor 7 [15]But if the unbeliever leaves, let him do so. A believing man or woman is not bound in such circumstances; God has called us to live in peace.
Col 3 [15]Let the peace of Christ rule in your hearts, since as members of one body you were called to peace. And be thankful.

o) God Calls People to Repentance

Matt 3 [2]and saying, "Repent, for the kingdom of heaven is near."
Matt 4 [17]From that time on Jesus began to preach, "Repent, for the kingdom of heaven is near."
Luke 5 [31]Jesus answered them, "It is not the healthy who need a doctor, but the sick. [32]I have not come to call the righteous, but sinners to repentance."
Acts 2 [38]Peter replied, "Repent and be baptized, every one of you, in the name of Jesus Christ for the forgiveness of your sins. And you will receive the gift of the Holy Spirit."

Acts 17 [30]"In the past God overlooked such ignorance, but now he commands all people everywhere to repent."
Rom 2 [4]Or do you show contempt for the riches of his kindness, tolerance and patience, not realizing that God's kindness leads you toward repentance?
2 Tim 2 [25]Those who oppose him he must gently instruct, in the hope that God will grant them repentance leading them to a knowledge of the truth. . . .
James 4 [8]Come near to God and he will come near to you. Wash your hands, you sinners, and purify your hearts, you double-minded. [9]Grieve, mourn and wail. Change your laughter to mourning and your joy to gloom. [10]Humble yourselves before the Lord, and he will lift you up.
2 Pet 3 [9]The Lord is not slow in keeping his promise, as some understand slowness. He is patient with you, not wanting anyone to perish, but everyone to come to repentance.

p) God Calls People to Sonship

1 John 3 [1]How great is the love the Father has lavished on us, that we should be called children of God! And that is what we are! The reason the world does not know us is that it did not know him.

q) God Calls People to Ultimate Victory

Rev 17 [14]"They will make war against the Lamb, but the Lamb will overcome them because he is Lord of lords and King of kings—and with him will be his called, chosen and faithful followers."

B. The Origin and Means of the Call

1. God's Creation and His Call

Acts 17 [26]"From one man he made every nation of men, that they should inhabit the whole earth; and he determined the times set for them and the exact places where they should live. [27]God did this so that men would seek him and perhaps reach out for him and find him, though he is not far from each one of us. [28]'For in him we live and move and have our being.' As some of your own poets have said, 'We are his offspring.'"
Rom 1 [20]For since the creation of the world God's invisible qualities—his eternal power and divine nature—have been clearly seen, being understood from what has been made, so that men are without excuse.

2. God's Glory and Goodness and His Call

2 Pet 1 [3]His divine power has given us everything we need for life and godliness through our knowledge of him who called us by his own glory and goodness.

3. God's Grace and His Call

Gal 1 [6]I am astonished that you are so quickly deserting the one who called you by the grace of Christ and are turning to a different gospel. . . . [15]But when God, who set me apart from birth and called me by his grace, was pleased . . .
2 Tim 1 [8]So do not be ashamed to testify about our Lord, or ashamed of me his prisoner. But join with me in suffering for the gospel, by the power of God, [9]who has saved us and called us to a holy life—not because of anything we have done but because of his own purpose and grace. This grace was given us in Christ Jesus before the beginning of time. . . .

4. God's Purpose and His Call

Rom 8 [28]And we know that in all things God works for the good of those who love him, who have been called according to his purpose.
Rom 9 [23]What if he did this to make the riches of his glory known to the objects of his mercy, whom he prepared in advance for glory—[24]even us, whom he also called, not only from the Jews but also from the Gentiles?
2 Tim 1 [8]So do not be ashamed to testify about our Lord, or ashamed of me his prisoner. But join with me in suffering for the gospel, by the power of God, [9]who has saved us and called us to a holy life—not because of anything we have done but because of his own purpose and grace. This grace was given us in Christ Jesus before the beginning of time. . . .

5. God's Word and His Call

Rom 10 [16]But not all the Israelites accepted the good news. For Isaiah says, "Lord, who has believed our message?" [17]Consequently, faith comes from hearing the message, and the message is heard through the word of Christ.
1 Thess 2 [13]And we also thank God continually because, when you received the word of God, which you heard from us, you accepted it not as the word of men, but as it actually is, the word of God, which is at work in you who believe.

6. The Gospel of Christ and God's Call

2 Thess 2 [13]But we ought always to thank God for you, brothers loved by the Lord, because from the beginning God chose you to be saved through the sanctifying work of the Spirit and through belief in the truth. [14]He called you to this through our gospel, that you might share in the glory of our Lord Jesus Christ.
1 Tim 6 [12]Fight the good fight of the faith. Take hold of the eternal life to which you were called when you made your good confession in the presence of many witnesses.

7. The Holy Spirit and God's Call

John 16 [7]"But I tell you the truth: It is for your good that I am going away. Unless I go away, the Counselor will not come to you; but if I go, I will send him to you. [8]When he comes, he will convict the world of guilt in regard to sin and righteousness and judgment: [9]in regard to sin, because men do not believe in me; [10]in regard to righteousness, because I am going to the Father, where you can see me no longer; [11]and in regard to judgment, because the prince of this world now stands condemned."
1 Thess 1 [4]For we know, brothers loved by God, that he has chosen you, [5]because our gospel came to you not simply with words, but also with power, with the Holy Spirit and with deep conviction. You know how we lived among you for your sake.
2 Thess 2 [13]But we ought always to thank God for you, brothers loved by the Lord, because from the beginning God chose you to be saved through the sanctifying work of the Spirit and through belief in the truth. [14]He called you to this through our gospel, that you might share in the glory of our Lord Jesus Christ.

8. The People of God and His Call

2 Chron 36 [15]The LORD, the God of their fathers, sent word to them through his messengers again and again, because he had pity on his people and on his dwelling place.
Jer 25 [4]And though the LORD has sent all his servants the prophets to you again and again, you have not listened or paid any attention.
Matt 22 [2]"The kingdom of heaven is like a king who prepared a wedding banquet for his son. [3]He sent his servants to those who had been invited to the banquet to tell them to come, but they refused to come.

[4]"Then he sent some more servants and said, 'Tell those who have been invited that I have prepared my dinner: My oxen and fattened cattle have been butchered, and everything is ready. Come to the wedding banquet.'

[5]"But they paid no attention and went off—one to his field, another to his business. [6]The rest seized his servants, mistreated them and killed them. [7]The king was enraged. He sent his army and destroyed those murderers and burned their city.

[8]"Then he said to his servants, 'The wedding banquet is ready, but those I invited did not deserve to come. [9]Go to the street corners and invite to the banquet anyone you find.' [10]So the servants went out into the streets and gathered all the people they could find, both good and bad, and the wedding hall was filled with guests."
Rom 10 [14]How, then, can they call on the one they have not believed in? And how can they believe in the one of whom they have not heard? And how can they hear without someone preaching to them? [15]And how can they preach unless they are

sent? As it is written, "How beautiful are the feet of those who bring good news!"

2 Cor 5 [20]We are therefore Christ's ambassadors, as though God were making his appeal through us. We implore you on Christ's behalf: Be reconciled to God.

1 Thess 1 [4]For we know, brothers loved by God, that he has chosen you, [5]because our gospel came to you not simply with words, but also with power, with the Holy Spirit and with deep conviction. You know how we lived among you for your sake.

C. Responses to the Call

1. Results of a Positive Response to God's Call

a) Certainty

Rom 11 [29]for God's gifts and his call are irrevocable.

1 Thess 5 [24]The one who calls you is faithful and he will do it.

Jude [1]Jude, a servant of Jesus Christ and a brother of James,

To those who have been called, who are loved by God the Father and kept by Jesus Christ. . . .

b) Obedience to God

Heb 11 [8]By faith Abraham, when called to go to a place he would later receive as his inheritance, obeyed and went, even though he did not know where he was going.

c) Perseverance

2 Pet 1 [10]Therefore, my brothers, be all the more eager to make your calling and election sure. For if you do these things, you will never fall. . . .

d) Praise to God

1 Pet 2 [9]But you are a chosen people, a royal priesthood, a holy nation, a people belonging to God, that you may declare the praises of him who called you out of darkness into his wonderful light.

e) Right Living

Eph 4 [1]As a prisoner for the Lord, then, I urge you to live a life worthy of the calling you have received. [2]Be completely humble and gentle; be patient, bearing with one another in love. [3]Make every effort to keep the unity of the Spirit through the bond of peace.

1 Thess 2 [12]encouraging, comforting and urging you to live lives worthy of God, who calls you into his kingdom and glory.

2 Thess 1 [11]With this in mind, we constantly pray for you, that our God may count you worthy of his calling, and that by his power he may fulfill every good purpose of yours and every act prompted by your faith.

2 Pet 1 [5]For this very reason, make every effort to add to your faith goodness; and to goodness, knowledge; [6]and to knowledge, self-control; and to self-control, perseverance; and to perseverance, godliness; [7]and to godliness, brotherly kindness; and to brotherly kindness, love. . . .

[10]Therefore, my brothers, be all the more eager to make your calling and election sure. For if you do these things, you will never fall, [11]and you will receive a rich welcome into the eternal kingdom of our Lord and Savior Jesus Christ.

2. Results of a Negative Response to God's Call

a) Alienation from God

Acts 13 [46]Then Paul and Barnabas answered them boldly: "We had to speak the word of God to you first. Since you reject it and do not consider yourselves worthy of eternal life, we now turn to the Gentiles."

Acts 18 [6]But when the Jews opposed Paul and became abusive, he shook out his clothes in protest and said to them, "Your blood be on your own heads! I am clear of my responsibility. From now on I will go to the Gentiles."

Acts 28 [24]Some were convinced by what he said, but others would not believe. [25]They disagreed among themselves and began to leave after Paul had made this final statement: "The Holy Spirit spoke the truth to your forefathers when he said through Isaiah the prophet: [26]'Go to this people and say, "You will be ever hearing but never understanding; you will be ever seeing but never perceiving." [27]For this people's heart has become calloused; they hardly hear with their ears, and they have closed their eyes. Otherwise they might see with their eyes, hear with their ears, understand with their hearts and turn, and I would heal them.'

[28]"Therefore I want you to know that God's salvation has been sent to the Gentiles, and they will listen!"

Rom 11 [7]What then? What Israel sought so earnestly it did not obtain, but the elect did. The others were hardened, [8]as it is written: "God gave them a spirit of stupor, eyes so that they could not see and ears so that they could not hear, to this very day." [9]And David says: "May their table become a snare and a trap, a stumbling block and a retribution for them. [10]May their eyes be darkened so they cannot see, and their backs be bent forever."

b) Condemnation by God

John 12 [48]"There is a judge for the one who rejects me and does not accept my words; that very word which I spoke will condemn him at the last day. [49]For I did not speak of my own accord, but the Father who sent me commanded me what to say and how to say it."

2 Thess 2 [10]and in every sort of evil that deceives those who are perishing. They perish because they refused to love the truth and so be saved. [11]For this reason God sends them a powerful delusion so that they will believe the lie [12]and so that all will be condemned who have not believed the truth but have delighted in wickedness.

c) Judgment from God

Prov 1 [24]"But since you rejected me when I called and no one gave heed when I stretched out my hand, [25]since you ignored all my advice and would not accept my rebuke, [26]I in turn will laugh at your disaster; I will mock when calamity overtakes you—[27]when calamity overtakes you like a storm, when disaster sweeps over you like a whirlwind, when distress and trouble overwhelm you.

[28]"Then they will call to me but I will not answer; they will look for me but will not find me. [29]Since they hated knowledge and did not choose to fear the LORD, [30]since they would not accept my advice and spurned my rebuke, [31]they will eat the fruit of their ways and be filled with the fruit of their schemes. [32]For the waywardness of the simple will kill them, and the complacency of fools will destroy them. . . ."

Matt 22 [2]"The kingdom of heaven is like a king who prepared a wedding banquet for his son. [3]He sent his servants to those who had been invited to the banquet to tell them to come, but they refused to come.

[4]"Then he sent some more servants and said, 'Tell those who have been invited that I have prepared my dinner: My oxen and fattened cattle have been butchered, and everything is ready. Come to the wedding banquet.'

[5]"But they paid no attention and went off—one to his field, another to his business. [6]The rest seized his servants, mistreated them and killed them. [7]The king was enraged. He sent his army and destroyed those murderers and burned their city."

Luke 14 [15]When one of those at the table with him heard this, he said to Jesus, "Blessed is the man who will eat at the feast in the kingdom of God."

[16]Jesus replied: "A certain man was preparing a great banquet and invited many guests. [17]At the time of the banquet he sent his servant to tell those who had been invited, 'Come, for everything is now ready.'

[18]"But they all alike began to make excuses. The first said, 'I have just bought a field, and I must go and see it. Please excuse me.'

[19]"Another said, 'I have just bought five yoke of oxen, and I'm on my way to try them out. Please excuse me.'

[20]"Still another said, 'I just got married, so I can't come.'

[21]"The servant came back and reported this to his master. Then the owner of the house became angry and ordered his servant, 'Go out quickly into the streets and alleys of the town and bring in the poor, the crippled, the blind and the lame.'

[22]"'Sir,' the servant said, 'what you ordered has been done, but there is still room.'

[23]"Then the master told his servant, 'Go out to the roads and country lanes and make them come in, so that my house will be full. [24]I tell you, not one of those men who were invited will get a taste of my banquet.'"

VI
Conversion

See Repentance; p. 488b, Saving Faith; and p. 494b, Regeneration.

VII
Repentance

A. The Nature of Repentance

1. Repentance Is Not a Mere Recognition of Sin

a) Pharaoh and Repentance

Exod 9 [27]Then Pharaoh summoned Moses and Aaron. "This time I have sinned," he said to them. "The LORD is in the right, and I and my people are in the wrong. [28]Pray to the LORD, for we have had enough thunder and hail. I will let you go; you don't have to stay any longer."

b) Israel and Repentance

Num 14 [39]When Moses reported this to all the Israelites, they mourned bitterly. [40]Early the next morning they went up toward the high hill country. "We have sinned," they said. "We will go up to the place the LORD promised."

[41]But Moses said, "Why are you disobeying the LORD's command? This will not succeed! [42]Do not go up, because the LORD is not with you. You will be defeated by your enemies, [43]for the Amalekites and Canaanites will face you there. Because you have turned away from the LORD, he will not be with you and you will fall by the sword."

[44]Nevertheless, in their presumption they went up toward the high hill country, though neither Moses nor the ark of the LORD's covenant moved from the camp. [45]Then the Amalekites and Canaanites who lived in that hill country came down and attacked them and beat them down all the way to Hormah.
Ps 78 [34]Whenever God slew them, they would seek him; they eagerly turned to him again. [35]They remembered that God was their Rock, that God Most High was their Redeemer. [36]But then they would flatter him with their mouths, lying to him with their tongues; [37]their hearts were not loyal to him, they were not faithful to his covenant.

c) Balaam and Repentance

Num 22 [34]Balaam said to the angel of the LORD, "I have sinned. I did not realize you were standing in the road to oppose me. Now if you are displeased, I will go back."

d) Achan and Repentance

Josh 7 [20]Achan replied, "It is true! I have sinned against the LORD, the God of Israel. This is what I have done. . . ."

e) Saul and Repentance

1 Sam 15 [24]Then Saul said to Samuel, "I have sinned. I violated the LORD's command and your instructions. I was afraid of the people and so I gave in to them. [25]Now I beg you, forgive my sin and come back with me, so that I may worship the LORD."

[26]But Samuel said to him, "I will not go back with you. You have rejected the word of the LORD, and the LORD has rejected you as king over Israel!"

[27]As Samuel turned to leave, Saul caught hold of the hem of his robe, and it tore. [28]Samuel said to him, "The LORD has torn the kingdom of Israel from you today and has given it to one of your neighbors—to one better than you. [29]He who is the Glory of Israel does not lie or change his mind; for he is not a man, that he should change his mind."

[30]Saul replied, "I have sinned. But please honor me before the elders of my people and before Israel; come back with me, so that I may worship the LORD your God."

f) Ahab and Repentance

1 Kings 21 [27]When Ahab heard these words, he tore his clothes, put on sackcloth and fasted. He lay in sackcloth and went around meekly.

[28]Then the word of the LORD came to Elijah the Tishbite: [29]"Have you noticed how Ahab has humbled himself before me? Because he has humbled himself, I will not bring this disaster in his day, but I will bring it on his house in the days of his son."

g) Judas and Repentance

Matt 27 [3]When Judas, who had betrayed him, saw that Jesus was condemned, he was seized with remorse and returned the thirty silver coins to the chief priests and the elders. [4]"I have sinned," he said, "for I have betrayed innocent blood."

"What is that to us?" they replied. "That's your responsibility."

[5]So Judas threw the money into the temple and left. Then he went away and hanged himself.

h) The Ungodly and Repentance

Rom 1 [32]Although they know God's righteous decree that those who do such things deserve death, they not only continue to do these very things but also approve of those who practice them.

2. Repentance Is an Inward Turning from Sin to God

a) Repentance Involves the Whole Person

(1) The Emotions and Repentance

Ps 38 [18]I confess my iniquity; I am troubled by my sin.
Ps 51 [1]Have mercy on me, O God, according to your unfailing love; according to your great compassion blot out my transgressions. [2]Wash away all my iniquity and cleanse me from my sin. . . . [10]Create in me a pure heart, O God, and renew a steadfast spirit within me. . . .

[14]Save me from bloodguilt, O God, the God who saves me, and my tongue will sing of your righteousness.
2 Cor 7 [9]yet now I am happy, not because you were made sorry, but because your sorrow led you to repentance. For you became sorrowful as God intended and so were not harmed in any way by us. [10]Godly sorrow brings repentance that leads to salvation and leaves no regret, but worldly sorrow brings death.

(2) The Intellect and Repentance

2 Chron 6 [29]". . . and when a prayer or plea is made by any of your people Israel—each one aware of his afflictions and pains, and spreading out his hands toward this temple—[30]then hear from heaven, your dwelling place. Forgive, and deal with each man according to all he does, since you know his heart (for you alone know the hearts of men), [31]so that they will fear you and walk in your ways all the time they live in the land you gave our fathers."
Job 42 [5]"My ears had heard of you but now my eyes have seen you. [6]Therefore I despise myself and repent in dust and ashes."
Ps 51 [3]For I know my transgressions, and my sin is always before me. . . . [11]Do not cast me from your presence or take your Holy Spirit from me.
Lam 3 [40]Let us examine our ways and test them, and let us return to the LORD.
Rom 3 [20]Therefore no one will be declared righteous in his sight by observing the law; rather, through the law we become conscious of sin.

(3) The Will and Repentance

Ps 51 [5]Surely I was sinful at birth, sinful from the time my mother conceived me. . . .

[7]Cleanse me with hyssop, and I will be clean; wash me, and I will be whiter than snow. . . .

[10]Create in me a pure heart, O God, and renew a steadfast spirit within me.

Jer 25 [5]They said, "Turn now, each of you, from your evil ways and your evil practices, and you can stay in the land the LORD gave to you and your fathers for ever and ever."
Luke 15 [18]"I will set out and go back to my father and say to him: Father, I have sinned against heaven and against you. . . .'
[21]"The son said to him, 'Father, I have sinned against heaven and against you. I am no longer worthy to be called your son.'"
Luke 23 [42]Then he said, "Jesus, remember me when you come into your kingdom."
John 7 [17]"If anyone chooses to do God's will, he will find out whether my teaching comes from God or whether I speak on my own."
Acts 2 [38]Peter replied, "Repent and be baptized, every one of you, in the name of Jesus Christ for the forgiveness of your sins. And you will receive the gift of the Holy Spirit."
Rom 2 [4]Or do you show contempt for the riches of his kindness, tolerance and patience, not realizing that God's kindness leads you toward repentance?
Rom 11 [23]And if they do not persist in unbelief, they will be grafted in, for God is able to graft them in again.

b) Repentance Is Realized through Several Things

(1) Repentance Is Realized through Considering God's Works and Ways

Deut 4 [39]Acknowledge and take to heart this day that the LORD is God in heaven above and on the earth below. There is no other.
1 Sam 12 [24]"But be sure to fear the LORD and serve him faithfully with all your heart; consider what great things he has done for you."
Job 23 [13]"But he stands alone, and who can oppose him? He does whatever he pleases. [14]He carries out his decree against me, and many such plans he still has in store. [15]That is why I am terrified before him; when I think of all this, I fear him."
Job 37 [14]"Listen to this, Job; stop and consider God's wonders."
Job 42 [5]"My ears had heard of you but now my eyes have seen you. [6]Therefore I despise myself and repent in dust and ashes."
Ps 8 [1]O LORD, our Lord, how majestic is your name in all the earth!
You have set your glory above the heavens. . . . [3]When I consider your heavens, the work of your fingers, the moon and the stars, which you have set in place . . .
Ps 64 [9]All mankind will fear; they will proclaim the works of God and ponder what he has done.
Ps 119 [94]Save me, for I am yours; I have sought out your precepts. [95]The wicked are waiting to destroy me, but I will ponder your statutes.
Eccles 7 [13]Consider what God has done: Who can straighten what he has made crooked?
Isa 41 [19]"I will put in the desert the cedar and the acacia, the myrtle and the olive. I will set pines in the wasteland, the fir and the cypress together, [20]so that people may see and know, may consider and understand, that the hand of the LORD has done this, that the Holy One of Israel has created it."
Jer 30 [24]The fierce anger of the LORD will not turn back until he fully accomplishes the purposes of his heart. In days to come you will understand this.
Ezek 12 [2]"Son of man, you are living among a rebellious people. They have eyes to see but do not see and ears to hear but do not hear, for they are a rebellious people.
[3]"Therefore, son of man, pack your belongings for exile and in the daytime, as they watch, set out and go from where you are to another place. Perhaps they will understand, though they are a rebellious house."

(2) Repentance Is Realized through Distress

2 Kings 22 [19]"'Because your heart was responsive and you humbled yourself before the LORD when you heard what I have spoken against this place and its people, that they would become accursed and laid waste, and because you tore your robes and wept in my presence, I have heard you, declares the LORD.'"
Neh 9 [34]"Our kings, our leaders, our priests and our fathers did not follow your law; they did not pay attention to your commands or the warnings you gave them. [35]Even while they were in their kingdom, enjoying your great goodness to them in the spacious and fertile land you gave them, they did not serve you or turn from their evil ways.
[36]"But see, we are slaves today, slaves in the land you gave our forefathers so they could eat its fruit and the other good things it produces. [37]Because of our sins, its abundant harvest goes to the kings you have placed over us. They rule over our bodies and our cattle as they please. We are in great distress.
[38]"In view of all this, we are making a binding agreement, putting it in writing, and our leaders, our Levites and our priests are affixing their seals to it."
Job 16 [20]"My intercessor is my friend as my eyes pour out tears to God; [21]on behalf of a man he pleads with God as a man pleads for his friend."
Ps 6 [8]Away from me, all you who do evil, for the LORD has heard my weeping. [9]The LORD has heard my cry for mercy; the LORD accepts my prayer.
Ps 39 [12]"Hear my prayer, O LORD, listen to my cry for help; be not deaf to my weeping. For I dwell with you as an alien, a stranger, as all my fathers were."
Ps 42 [3]My tears have been my food day and night, while men say to me all day long, "Where is your God?" [4]These things I remember as I pour out my soul: how I used to go with the multitude, leading the procession to the house of God, with shouts of joy and thanksgiving among the festive throng. [5]Why are you downcast, O my soul? Why so disturbed within me? Put your hope in God, for I will yet praise him, my Savior and [6]my God.
My soul is downcast within me; therefore I will remember you from the land of the Jordan, the heights of Hermon—from Mount Mizar.
Ps 102 [9]For I eat ashes as my food and mingle my drink with tears [10]because of your great wrath, for you have taken me up and thrown me aside. [11]My days are like the evening shadow; I wither away like grass. . . .
[19]"The LORD looked down from his sanctuary on high, from heaven he viewed the earth, [20]to hear the groans of the prisoners and release those condemned to death."
Ps 126 [5]Those who sow in tears will reap with songs of joy. [6]He who goes out weeping, carrying seed to sow, will return with songs of joy, carrying sheaves with him.
Jer 31 [9]"They will come with weeping; they will pray as I bring them back. I will lead them beside streams of water on a level path where they will not stumble, because I am Israel's father, and Ephraim is my firstborn son."
Jer 50 [4]"In those days, at that time," declares the LORD, "the people of Israel and the people of Judah together will go in tears to seek the LORD their God. [5]They will ask the way to Zion and turn their faces toward it. They will come and bind themselves to the LORD in an everlasting covenant that will not be forgotten."
Lam 2 [11]My eyes fail from weeping, I am in torment within, my heart is poured out on the ground because my people are destroyed, because children and infants faint in the streets of the city. . . .
[18]The hearts of the people cry out to the Lord. O wall of the Daughter of Zion, let your tears flow like a river day and night; give yourself no relief, your eyes no rest.
Hos 5 [15]"Then I will go back to my place until they admit their guilt. And they will seek my face; in their misery they will earnestly seek me."
Joel 2 [17]Let the priests, who minister before the LORD, weep between the temple porch and the altar. Let them say, "Spare your people, O LORD. Do not make your inheritance an object of scorn, a byword among the nations. Why should they say among the peoples, 'Where is their God?'"
James 4 [8]Come near to God and he will come near to you. Wash your hands, you sinners, and purify your hearts, you double-minded. [9]Grieve, mourn and wail. Change your laughter to mourning and your joy to gloom.

(3) Repentance Is Realized through Divine Prompting

Isa 22 [12]The Lord, the LORD Almighty, called you on that day to weep and to wail, to tear out your hair and put on sackcloth.
Isa 45 [22]"Turn to me and be saved, all you ends of the earth; for I am God, and there is no other."

Isa 57 [15]For this is what the high and lofty One says—he who lives forever, whose name is holy: "I live in a high and holy place, but also with him who is contrite and lowly in spirit, to revive the spirit of the lowly and to revive the heart of the contrite."
Jer 24 [7]"'I will give them a heart to know me, that I am the LORD. They will be my people, and I will be their God, for they will return to me with all their heart.'"
Ezek 14 [6]"Therefore say to the house of Israel, 'This is what the Sovereign LORD says: Repent! Turn from your idols and renounce all your detestable practices!'"
Ezek 18 [30]"Therefore, O house of Israel, I will judge you, each one according to his ways, declares the Sovereign LORD. Repent! Turn away from all your offenses; then sin will not be your downfall."
Hag 1 [7]This is what the LORD Almighty says: "Give careful thought to your ways."
Zech 12 [10]"And I will pour out on the house of David and the inhabitants of Jerusalem a spirit of grace and supplication. They will look on me, the one they have pierced, and they will mourn for him as one mourns for an only child, and grieve bitterly for him as one grieves for a firstborn son."
Mal 3 [7]"Ever since the time of your forefathers you have turned away from my decrees and have not kept them. Return to me, and I will return to you," says the LORD Almighty.

"But you ask, 'How are we to return?'"
Acts 3 [26]"When God raised up his servant, he sent him first to you to bless you by turning each of you from your wicked ways."
Acts 5 [31]"God exalted him to his own right hand as Prince and Savior that he might give repentance and forgiveness of sins to Israel."
Acts 11 [18]When they heard this, they had no further objections and praised God, saying, "So then, God has granted even the Gentiles repentance unto life."
Acts 11 [21]The Lord's hand was with them, and a great number of people believed and turned to the Lord.
Rom 2 [4]Or do you show contempt for the riches of his kindness, tolerance and patience, not realizing that God's kindness leads you toward repentance?
2 Tim 2 [25]Those who oppose him he must gently instruct, in the hope that God will grant them repentance leading them to a knowledge of the truth. . . .
Heb 12 [10]Our fathers disciplined us for a little while as they thought best; but God disciplines us for our good, that we may share in his holiness.
Rev 2 [5]"Remember the height from which you have fallen! Repent and do the things you did at first. If you do not repent, I will come to you and remove your lampstand from its place."
Rev 2 [16]"Repent therefore! Otherwise, I will soon come to you and will fight against them with the sword of my mouth."
Rev 3 [3]"Remember, therefore, what you have received and heard; obey it, and repent. But if you do not wake up, I will come like a thief, and you will not know at what time I will come to you."
Rev 3 [19]"Those whom I love I rebuke and discipline. So be earnest, and repent. [20]Here I am! I stand at the door and knock. If anyone hears my voice and opens the door, I will come in and eat with him, and he with me."

(4) Repentance Is Realized through Guilt

1 Sam 24 [5]Afterward, David was conscience-stricken for having cut off a corner of his robe. [6]He said to his men, "The LORD forbid that I should do such a thing to my master, the LORD's anointed, or lift my hand against him; for he is the anointed of the LORD."
2 Sam 24 [10]David was conscience-stricken after he had counted the fighting men, and he said to the LORD, "I have sinned greatly in what I have done. Now, O LORD, I beg you, take away the guilt of your servant. I have done a very foolish thing." . . .

[17]When David saw the angel who was striking down the people, he said to the LORD, "I am the one who has sinned and done wrong. These are but sheep. What have they done? Let your hand fall upon me and my family."
Ezra 9 [5]Then, at the evening sacrifice, I rose from my self-abasement, with my tunic and cloak torn, and fell on my knees with my hands spread out to the LORD my God [6]and prayed: "O my God, I am too ashamed and disgraced to lift up my face to you, my God, because our sins are higher than our heads and our guilt has reached to the heavens."
Ps 38 [1]O LORD, do not rebuke me in your anger or discipline me in your wrath. [2]For your arrows have pierced me, and your hand has come down upon me. [3]Because of your wrath there is no health in my body; my bones have no soundness because of my sin. [4]My guilt has overwhelmed me like a burden too heavy to bear.

[5]My wounds fester and are loathsome because of my sinful folly. [6]I am bowed down and brought very low; all day long I go about mourning. [7]My back is filled with searing pain; there is no health in my body. [8]I am feeble and utterly crushed; I groan in anguish of heart.

[9]All my longings lie open before you, O Lord; my sighing is not hidden from you. [10]My heart pounds, my strength fails me; even the light has gone from my eyes. [11]My friends and companions avoid me because of my wounds; my neighbors stay far away. [12]Those who seek my life set their traps, those who would harm me talk of my ruin; all day long they plot deception.

[13]I am like a deaf man, who cannot hear, like a mute, who cannot open his mouth; [14]I have become like a man who does not hear, whose mouth can offer no reply. [15]I wait for you, O LORD; you will answer, O Lord my God. . . .

[17]For I am about to fall, and my pain is ever with me. [18]I confess my iniquity; I am troubled by my sin. . . .

[21]O LORD, do not forsake me; be not far from me, O my God. [22]Come quickly to help me, O Lord my Savior.
Ps 40 [12]For troubles without number surround me; my sins have overtaken me, and I cannot see. They are more than the hairs of my head, and my heart fails within me.
Ps 51 [3]For I know my transgressions, and my sin is always before me. . . .[17]The sacrifices of God are a broken spirit; a broken and contrite heart, O God, you will not despise.
Dan 9 [5]". . . we have sinned and done wrong. We have been wicked and have rebelled; we have turned away from your commands and laws. . . .

[15]"Now, O Lord our God, who brought your people out of Egypt with a mighty hand and who made for yourself a name that endures to this day, we have sinned, we have done wrong. [16]O Lord, in keeping with all your righteous acts, turn away your anger and your wrath from Jerusalem, your city, your holy hill. Our sins and the iniquities of our fathers have made Jerusalem and your people an object of scorn to all those around us.

[17]"Now, our God, hear the prayers and petitions of your servant. For your sake, O Lord, look with favor on your desolate sanctuary. [18]Give ear, O God, and hear; open your eyes and see the desolation of the city that bears your Name. We do not make requests of you because we are righteous, but because of your great mercy. [19]O Lord, listen! O Lord, forgive! O Lord, hear and act! For your sake, O my God, do not delay, because your city and your people bear your Name."
Acts 2 [37]When the people heard this, they were cut to the heart and said to Peter and the other apostles, "Brothers, what shall we do?"

[38]Peter replied, "Repent and be baptized, every one of you, in the name of Jesus Christ for the forgiveness of your sins. And you will receive the gift of the Holy Spirit."

(5) Repentance Is Realized through Mourning

Exod 33 [4]When the people heard these distressing words, they began to mourn and no one put on any ornaments.
Ezra 10 [6]Then Ezra withdrew from before the house of God and went to the room of Jehohanan son of Eliashib. While he was there, he ate no food and drank no water, because he continued to mourn over the unfaithfulness of the exiles.
Job 5 [8]"But if it were I, I would appeal to God; I would lay my cause before him. . . . [11]The lowly he sets on high, and those who mourn are lifted to safety."
Ps 38 [6]I am bowed down and brought very low; all day long I go about mourning. . . . [18]I confess my iniquity; I am troubled by my sin.
Isa 61 [1]The Spirit of the Sovereign LORD is on me, because the LORD has anointed me to preach good news to the poor. He has

sent me to bind up the brokenhearted, to proclaim freedom for the captives and release from darkness for the prisoners, 2to proclaim the year of the LORD's favor and the day of vengeance of our God, to comfort all who mourn, 3and provide for those who grieve in Zion—to bestow on them a crown of beauty instead of ashes, the oil of gladness instead of mourning, and a garment of praise instead of a spirit of despair. They will be called oaks of righteousness, a planting of the LORD for the display of his splendor.

Ezek 7 16"All who survive and escape will be in the mountains, moaning like doves of the valleys, each because of his sins. . . . 27The king will mourn, the prince will be clothed with despair, and the hands of the people of the land will tremble. I will deal with them according to their conduct, and by their own standards I will judge them. Then they will know that I am the LORD."

Dan 10 2At that time I, Daniel, mourned for three weeks. 3I ate no choice food; no meat or wine touched my lips; and I used no lotions at all until the three weeks were over.

Joel 1 9Grain offerings and drink offerings are cut off from the house of the LORD. The priests are in mourning, those who minister before the LORD.

Joel 2 12"Even now," declares the LORD, "return to me with all your heart, with fasting and weeping and mourning."

13Rend your heart and not your garments. Return to the LORD your God, for he is gracious and compassionate, slow to anger and abounding in love, and he relents from sending calamity.

Zech 12 10"And I will pour out on the house of David and the inhabitants of Jerusalem a spirit of grace and supplication. They will look on me, the one they have pierced, and they will mourn for him as one mourns for an only child, and grieve bitterly for him as one grieves for a firstborn son. . . . 12The land will mourn, each clan by itself, with their wives by themselves: the clan of the house of David and their wives, the clan of the house of Nathan and their wives. . . ."

(6) Repentance Is Realized through Personal Reflection

1 Kings 8 38". . . and when a prayer or plea is made by any of your people Israel—each one aware of the afflictions of his own heart, and spreading out his hands toward this temple . . ."

Ps 4 4In your anger do not sin; when you are on your beds, search your hearts and be silent.

Ps 119 59I have considered my ways and have turned my steps to your statutes.

Lam 3 40Let us examine our ways and test them, and let us return to the LORD.

1 Cor 11 28A man ought to examine himself before he eats of the bread and drinks of the cup.

2 Cor 13 5Examine yourselves to see whether you are in the faith; test yourselves. Do you not realize that Christ Jesus is in you—unless, of course, you fail the test?

Gal 6 4Each one should test his own actions. Then he can take pride in himself, without comparing himself to somebody else. . . .

2 Tim 2 7Reflect on what I am saying, for the Lord will give you insight into all this.

(7) Repentance Is Realized through Preaching

Isa 31 6Return to him you have so greatly revolted against, O Israelites.

Jer 25 5They said, "Turn now, each of you, from your evil ways and your evil practices, and you can stay in the land the LORD gave to you and your fathers for ever and ever."

Hos 10 12"Sow for yourselves righteousness, reap the fruit of unfailing love, and break up your unplowed ground; for it is time to seek the LORD, until he comes and showers righteousness on you."

Joel 1 14Declare a holy fast; call a sacred assembly. Summon the elders and all who live in the land to the house of the LORD your God, and cry out to the LORD.

Matt 3 1In those days John the Baptist came, preaching in the Desert of Judea 2and saying, "Repent, for the kingdom of heaven is near."

Matt 4 17From that time on Jesus began to preach, "Repent, for the kingdom of heaven is near."

Matt 9 13"But go and learn what this means: 'I desire mercy, not sacrifice.' For I have not come to call the righteous, but sinners."

Mark 6 12They went out and preached that people should repent.

Luke 24 47". . . and repentance and forgiveness of sins will be preached in his name to all nations, beginning at Jerusalem."

Acts 2 38Peter replied, "Repent and be baptized, every one of you, in the name of Jesus Christ for the forgiveness of your sins. And you will receive the gift of the Holy Spirit. . . ."

40With many other words he warned them; and he pleaded with them, "Save yourselves from this corrupt generation."

Acts 3 19"Repent, then, and turn to God, so that your sins may be wiped out, that times of refreshing may come from the Lord, 20and that he may send the Christ, who has been appointed for you—even Jesus."

Acts 8 22"Repent of this wickedness and pray to the Lord. Perhaps he will forgive you for having such a thought in your heart."

Acts 13 24"Before the coming of Jesus, John preached repentance and baptism to all the people of Israel."

Acts 14 15"Men, why are you doing this? We too are only men, human like you. We are bringing you good news, telling you to turn from these worthless things to the living God, who made heaven and earth and sea and everything in them."

Acts 19 4Paul said, "John's baptism was a baptism of repentance. He told the people to believe in the one coming after him, that is, in Jesus."

Acts 20 21"I have declared to both Jews and Greeks that they must turn to God in repentance and have faith in our Lord Jesus."

Acts 26 20"First to those in Damascus, then to those in Jerusalem and in all Judea, and to the Gentiles also, I preached that they should repent and turn to God and prove their repentance by their deeds."

(8) Repentance Is Realized through Shame

Job 42 2"I know that you can do all things; no plan of yours can be thwarted. 3You asked, 'Who is this that obscures my counsel without knowledge?' Surely I spoke of things I did not understand, things too wonderful for me to know.

4"You said, 'Listen now, and I will speak; I will question you, and you shall answer me.' 5My ears had heard of you but now my eyes have seen you. 6Therefore I despise myself and repent in dust and ashes."

Ps 34 5Those who look to him are radiant; their faces are never covered with shame.

Jer 3 25"Let us lie down in our shame, and let our disgrace cover us. We have sinned against the LORD our God, both we and our fathers; from our youth till this day we have not obeyed the LORD our God."

Jer 22 22"The wind will drive all your shepherds away, and your allies will go into exile. Then you will be ashamed and disgraced because of all your wickedness."

Jer 31 19"'After I strayed, I repented; after I came to understand, I beat my breast. I was ashamed and humiliated because I bore the disgrace of my youth.'"

Ezek 6 9"'Then in the nations where they have been carried captive, those who escape will remember me—how I have been grieved by their adulterous hearts, which have turned away from me, and by their eyes, which have lusted after their idols. They will loathe themselves for the evil they have done and for all their detestable practices.'"

Ezek 20 43"'There you will remember your conduct and all the actions by which you have defiled yourselves, and you will loathe yourselves for all the evil you have done.'"

Ezek 43 10"Son of man, describe the temple to the people of Israel, that they may be ashamed of their sins. Let them consider the plan, 11and if they are ashamed of all they have done, make known to them the design of the temple—its arrangement, its exits and entrances—its whole design and all its regulations and laws. Write these down before them so that they may be faithful to its design and follow all its regulations."

Rom 6 21What benefit did you reap at that time from the things you are now ashamed of? Those things result in death!

(9) Repentance Is Realized through Sorrow

Ps 13 [2]How long must I wrestle with my thoughts and every day have sorrow in my heart? How long will my enemy triumph over me?

[3]Look on me and answer, O LORD my God. Give light to my eyes, or I will sleep in death. . . .

Ps 38 [17]For I am about to fall, and my pain is ever with me. [18]I confess my iniquity; I am troubled by my sin.

Ps 116 [3]The cords of death entangled me, the anguish of the grave came upon me; I was overcome by trouble and sorrow. [4]Then I called on the name of the LORD: "O LORD, save me!"

Ps 119 [28]My soul is weary with sorrow; strengthen me according to your word.

Jer 31 [9]"They will come with weeping; they will pray as I bring them back. I will lead them beside streams of water on a level path where they will not stumble, because I am Israel's father, and Ephraim is my firstborn son. . . . [13]Then maidens will dance and be glad, young men and old as well. I will turn their mourning into gladness; I will give them comfort and joy instead of sorrow."

2 Cor 7 [9]yet now I am happy, not because you were made sorry, but because your sorrow led you to repentance. For you became sorrowful as God intended and so were not harmed in any way by us. [10]Godly sorrow brings repentance that leads to salvation and leaves no regret, but worldly sorrow brings death.

3. Repentance Leads to Salvation

a) Repentance and the Conviction of Sin

1 Kings 8 [38]". . . and when a prayer or plea is made by any of your people Israel—each one aware of the afflictions of his own heart, and spreading out his hands toward this temple—[39]then hear from heaven, your dwelling place. Forgive and act; deal with each man according to all he does, since you know his heart (for you alone know the hearts of all men), [40]so that they will fear you all the time they live in the land you gave our fathers."

Prov 28 [13]He who conceals his sins does not prosper, but whoever confesses and renounces them finds mercy.

Isa 6 [5]"Woe to me!" I cried. "I am ruined! For I am a man of unclean lips, and I live among a people of unclean lips, and my eyes have seen the King, the LORD Almighty."

Lam 1 [20]"See, O LORD, how distressed I am! I am in torment within, and in my heart I am disturbed, for I have been most rebellious. Outside, the sword bereaves; inside, there is only death."

Ezek 33 [10]"Son of man, say to the house of Israel, 'This is what you are saying: "Our offenses and sins weigh us down, and we are wasting away because of them. How then can we live?"' [11]Say to them, 'As surely as I live, declares the Sovereign LORD, I take no pleasure in the death of the wicked, but rather that they turn from their ways and live. Turn! Turn from your evil ways! Why will you die, O house of Israel?'"

Acts 2 [37]When the people heard this, they were cut to the heart and said to Peter and the other apostles, "Brothers, what shall we do?"

Acts 9 [3]As he neared Damascus on his journey, suddenly a light from heaven flashed around him. [4]He fell to the ground and heard a voice say to him, "Saul, Saul, why do you persecute me?"

[5]"Who are you, Lord?" Saul asked.

"I am Jesus, whom you are persecuting," he replied. [6]"Now get up and go into the city, and you will be told what you must do."

Acts 16 [29]The jailer called for lights, rushed in and fell trembling before Paul and Silas. [30]He then brought them out and asked, "Sirs, what must I do to be saved?"

b) Repentance and the Confession of Sin

Lev 26 [40]"'But if they will confess their sins and the sins of their fathers—their treachery against me and their hostility toward me, . . . [42]I will remember my covenant with Jacob and my covenant with Isaac and my covenant with Abraham, and I will remember the land.'"

Ezra 9 [5]Then, at the evening sacrifice, I rose from my self-abasement, with my tunic and cloak torn, and fell on my knees with my hands spread out to the LORD my God [6]and prayed: "O my God, I am too ashamed and disgraced to lift up my face to you, my God, because our sins are higher than our heads and our guilt has reached to the heavens. [7]From the days of our forefathers until now, our guilt has been great. Because of our sins, we and our kings and our priests have been subjected to the sword and captivity, to pillage and humiliation at the hand of foreign kings, as it is today. . . .

[13]"What has happened to us is a result of our evil deeds and our great guilt, and yet, our God, you have punished us less than our sins have deserved and have given us a remnant like this. . . . [15]O LORD, God of Israel, you are righteous! We are left this day as a remnant. Here we are before you in our guilt, though because of it not one of us can stand in your presence."

Ezra 10 [1]While Ezra was praying and confessing, weeping and throwing himself down before the house of God, a large crowd of Israelites—men, women and children—gathered around him. They too wept bitterly.

Neh 1 [5]Then I said: "O LORD, God of heaven, the great and awesome God, who keeps his covenant of love with those who love him and obey his commands, [6]let your ear be attentive and your eyes open to hear the prayer your servant is praying before you day and night for your servants, the people of Israel. I confess the sins we Israelites, including myself and my father's house, have committed against you. [7]We have acted very wickedly toward you. We have not obeyed the commands, decrees and laws you gave your servant Moses."

Job 9 [20]"Even if I were innocent, my mouth would condemn me; if I were blameless, it would pronounce me guilty."

Job 13 [23]"How many wrongs and sins have I committed? Show me my offense and my sin."

Ps 32 [5]Then I acknowledged my sin to you and did not cover up my iniquity. I said, "I will confess my transgressions to the LORD"—and you forgave the guilt of my sin.

Ps 38 [18]I confess my iniquity; I am troubled by my sin.

Ps 40 [12]For troubles without number surround me; my sins have overtaken me, and I cannot see. They are more than the hairs of my head, and my heart fails within me.

Ps 41 [4]I said, "O LORD, have mercy on me; heal me, for I have sinned against you."

Ps 51 [2]Wash away all my iniquity and cleanse me from my sin.

[3]For I know my transgressions, and my sin is always before me. [4]Against you, you only, have I sinned and done what is evil in your sight, so that you are proved right when you speak and justified when you judge. [5]Surely I was sinful at birth, sinful from the time my mother conceived me. [6]Surely you desire truth in the inner parts; you teach me wisdom in the inmost place.

[7]Cleanse me with hyssop, and I will be clean; wash me, and I will be whiter than snow.

Ps 69 [5]You know my folly, O God; my guilt is not hidden from you.

Prov 28 [13]He who conceals his sins does not prosper, but whoever confesses and renounces them finds mercy.

Isa 59 [12]For our offenses are many in your sight, and our sins testify against us. Our offenses are ever with us, and we acknowledge our iniquities: [13]rebellion and treachery against the LORD, turning our backs on our God, fomenting oppression and revolt, uttering lies our hearts have conceived.

Isa 64 [6]All of us have become like one who is unclean, and all our righteous acts are like filthy rags; we all shrivel up like a leaf, and like the wind our sins sweep us away.

Jer 14 [7]Although our sins testify against us, O LORD, do something for the sake of your name. For our backsliding is great; we have sinned against you. . . . [20]O LORD, we acknowledge our wickedness and the guilt of our fathers; we have indeed sinned against you.

Lam 3 [40]Let us examine our ways and test them, and let us return to the LORD. [41]Let us lift up our hearts and our hands to God in heaven, and say: [42]"We have sinned and rebelled and you have not forgiven."

Dan 9 [4]I prayed to the LORD my God and confessed: "O Lord, the great and awesome God, who keeps his covenant of love with all who love him and obey his commands, [5]we have sinned and done wrong. We have been wicked and have rebelled; we have turned away from your commands and laws.

[6]We have not listened to your servants the prophets, who spoke in your name to our kings, our princes and our fathers, and to all the people of the land. . . . [8]O LORD, we and our kings, our princes and our fathers are covered with shame because we have sinned against you."
Acts 19 [18]Many of those who believed now came and openly confessed their evil deeds.

c) Repentance and the Pardoning of Sin

1 Kings 8 [33]"When your people Israel have been defeated by an enemy because they have sinned against you, and when they turn back to you and confess your name, praying and making supplication to you in this temple, [34]then hear from heaven and forgive the sin of your people Israel and bring them back to the land you gave to their fathers."
Ps 51 [9]Hide your face from my sins and blot out all my iniquity.
Ps 130 [1]Out of the depths I cry to you, O LORD; [2]O Lord, hear my voice. Let your ears be attentive to my cry for mercy.
[3]If you, O LORD, kept a record of sins, O Lord, who could stand? [4]But with you there is forgiveness; therefore you are feared.
Prov 28 [13]He who conceals his sins does not prosper, but whoever confesses and renounces them finds mercy.
Isa 1 [16]". . . wash and make yourselves clean. Take your evil deeds out of my sight! Stop doing wrong, [17]learn to do right! Seek justice, encourage the oppressed. Defend the cause of the fatherless, plead the case of the widow.
[18]"Come now, let us reason together," says the LORD. "Though your sins are like scarlet, they shall be as white as snow; though they are red as crimson, they shall be like wool."
Isa 55 [7]Let the wicked forsake his way and the evil man his thoughts. Let him turn to the LORD, and he will have mercy on him, and to our God, for he will freely pardon.
Ezek 33 [14]"And if I say to the wicked man, 'You will surely die,' but he then turns away from his sin and does what is just and right—[15]if he gives back what he took in pledge for a loan, returns what he has stolen, follows the decrees that give life, and does no evil, he will surely live; he will not die. [16]None of the sins he has committed will be remembered against him. He has done what is just and right; he will surely live."
Luke 3 [3]He went into all the country around the Jordan, preaching a baptism of repentance for the forgiveness of sins.
Luke 24 [47]". . . and repentance and forgiveness of sins will be preached in his name to all nations, beginning at Jerusalem."
Acts 2 [38]Peter replied, "Repent and be baptized, every one of you, in the name of Jesus Christ for the forgiveness of your sins. And you will receive the gift of the Holy Spirit."
Acts 3 [19]"Repent, then, and turn to God, so that your sins may be wiped out, that times of refreshing may come from the Lord. . . ."
Acts 8 [22]"Repent of this wickedness and pray to the Lord. Perhaps he will forgive you for having such a thought in your heart."

d) Repentance and Life

Ezek 18 [32]"For I take no pleasure in the death of anyone, declares the Sovereign LORD. Repent and live!"
Ezek 33 [11]"Say to them, 'As surely as I live, declares the Sovereign LORD, I take no pleasure in the death of the wicked, but rather that they turn from their ways and live. Turn! Turn from your evil ways! Why will you die, O house of Israel?'"
Acts 11 [18]When they heard this, they had no further objections and praised God, saying, "So then, God has granted even the Gentiles repentance unto life."

e) Repentance and Salvation

Ps 80 [3]Restore us, O God; make your face shine upon us, that we may be saved.
Ps 85 [4]Restore us again, O God our Savior, and put away your displeasure toward us. [5]Will you be angry with us forever? Will you prolong your anger through all generations? [6]Will you not revive us again, that your people may rejoice in you? [7]Show us your unfailing love, O LORD, and grant us your salvation.
Isa 45 [22]"Turn to me and be saved, all you ends of the earth; for I am God, and there is no other."
Luke 13 [2]Jesus answered, "Do you think that these Galileans were worse sinners than all the other Galileans because they suffered this way? [3]I tell you, no! But unless you repent, you too will all perish. [4]Or those eighteen who died when the tower in Siloam fell on them—do you think they were more guilty than all the others living in Jerusalem? [5]I tell you, no! But unless you repent, you too will all perish."
2 Cor 7 [10]Godly sorrow brings repentance that leads to salvation and leaves no regret, but worldly sorrow brings death.

f) Repentance and Redemption

Isa 1 [27]Zion will be redeemed with justice, her penitent ones with righteousness.
Isa 44 [22]"I have swept away your offenses like a cloud, your sins like the morning mist. Return to me, for I have redeemed you."
Isa 59 [20]"The Redeemer will come to Zion, to those in Jacob who repent of their sins," declares the LORD.

4. Repentance Is Illustrated in Scripture

a) Illustrations of Repentance in Parables

(1) The Lost Sheep and Repentance

Luke 15 [4]"Suppose one of you has a hundred sheep and loses one of them. Does he not leave the ninety-nine in the open country and go after the lost sheep until he finds it? [5]And when he finds it, he joyfully puts it on his shoulders [6]and goes home. Then he calls his friends and neighbors together and says, 'Rejoice with me; I have found my lost sheep.' [7]I tell you that in the same way there will be more rejoicing in heaven over one sinner who repents than over ninety-nine righteous persons who do not need to repent."

(2) The Prodigal Son and Repentance

Luke 15 [11]Jesus continued: "There was a man who had two sons. [12]The younger one said to his father, 'Father, give me my share of the estate.' So he divided his property between them.
[13]"Not long after that, the younger son got together all he had, set off for a distant country and there squandered his wealth in wild living. [14]After he had spent everything, there was a severe famine in that whole country, and he began to be in need. [15]So he went and hired himself out to a citizen of that country, who sent him to his fields to feed pigs. [16]He longed to fill his stomach with the pods that the pigs were eating, but no one gave him anything.
[17]"When he came to his senses, he said, 'How many of my father's hired men have food to spare, and here I am starving to death! [18]I will set out and go back to my father and say to him: Father, I have sinned against heaven and against you. [19]I am no longer worthy to be called your son; make me like one of your hired men.' [20]So he got up and went to his father.
"But while he was still a long way off, his father saw him and was filled with compassion for him; he ran to his son, threw his arms around him and kissed him.
[21]"The son said to him, 'Father, I have sinned against heaven and against you. I am no longer worthy to be called your son.'
[22]"But the father said to his servants, 'Quick! Bring the best robe and put it on him. Put a ring on his finger and sandals on his feet. [23]Bring the fattened calf and kill it. Let's have a feast and celebrate. [24]For this son of mine was dead and is alive again; he was lost and is found.' So they began to celebrate.
[25]"Meanwhile, the older son was in the field. When he came near the house, he heard music and dancing. [26]So he called one of the servants and asked him what was going on. [27]'Your brother has come,' he replied, 'and your father has killed the fattened calf because he has him back safe and sound.'
[28]"The older brother became angry and refused to go in. So his father went out and pleaded with him. [29]But he answered his father, 'Look! All these years I've been slaving for you and never disobeyed your orders. Yet you never gave me even a young goat so I could celebrate with my friends. [30]But when this son of yours who has squandered your property with prostitutes comes home, you kill the fattened calf for him!'
[31]"'My son,' the father said, 'you are always with me, and everything I have is yours. [32]But we had to celebrate and be glad, because this brother of yours was dead and is alive again; he was lost and is found.'"

(3) The Humble Tax Collector and Repentance

Luke 18 [10]"Two men went up to the temple to pray, one a Pharisee and the other a tax collector. [11]The Pharisee stood up and prayed about himself: 'God, I thank you that I am not like other men—robbers, evildoers, adulterers—or even like this tax collector. [12]I fast twice a week and give a tenth of all I get.'

[13]"But the tax collector stood at a distance. He would not even look up to heaven, but beat his breast and said, 'God, have mercy on me, a sinner.'

[14]"I tell you that this man, rather than the other, went home justified before God. For everyone who exalts himself will be humbled, and he who humbles himself will be exalted."

(4) The Repentant Son

Matt 21 [28]"What do you think? There was a man who had two sons. He went to the first and said, 'Son, go and work today in the vineyard.'

[29]"'I will not,' he answered, but later he changed his mind and went.

[30]"Then the father went to the other son and said the same thing. He answered, 'I will, sir,' but he did not go.

[31]"Which of the two did what his father wanted?"

"The first," they answered.

Jesus said to them, "I tell you the truth, the tax collectors and the prostitutes are entering the kingdom of God ahead of you."

b) Personal Illustrations of Repentance

(1) Israel's Repentance

Judg 10 [15]But the Israelites said to the LORD, "We have sinned. Do with us whatever you think best, but please rescue us now." [16]Then they got rid of the foreign gods among them and served the LORD. And he could bear Israel's misery no longer.

2 Chron 15 [4]"But in their distress they turned to the LORD, the God of Israel, and sought him, and he was found by them."

Ezra 6 [21]So the Israelites who had returned from the exile ate it, together with all who had separated themselves from the unclean practices of their Gentile neighbors in order to seek the LORD, the God of Israel.

(2) Ezra's Repentance

Ezra 9 [1]After these things had been done, the leaders came to me and said, "The people of Israel, including the priests and the Levites, have not kept themselves separate from the neighboring peoples with their detestable practices, like those of the Canaanites, Hittites, Perizzites, Jebusites, Ammonites, Moabites, Egyptians and Amorites. [2]They have taken some of their daughters as wives for themselves and their sons, and have mingled the holy race with the peoples around them. And the leaders and officials have led the way in this unfaithfulness."

[3]When I heard this, I tore my tunic and cloak, pulled hair from my head and beard and sat down appalled. . . .

[5]Then, at the evening sacrifice, I rose from my self-abasement, with my tunic and cloak torn, and fell on my knees with my hands spread out to the LORD my God [6]and prayed: "O my God, I am too ashamed and disgraced to lift up my face to you, my God, because our sins are higher than our heads and our guilt has reached to the heavens."

Ezra 10 [1]While Ezra was praying and confessing, weeping and throwing himself down before the house of God, a large crowd of Israelites—men, women and children—gathered around him. They too wept bitterly.

(3) David's Repentance

2 Sam 12 [13]Then David said to Nathan, "I have sinned against the LORD."

Nathan replied, "The LORD has taken away your sin. You are not going to die."

(4) Manasseh's Repentance

2 Chron 33 [12]In his distress he sought the favor of the LORD his God and humbled himself greatly before the God of his fathers. [13]And when he prayed to him, the LORD was moved by his entreaty and listened to his plea; so he brought him back to Jerusalem and to his kingdom. Then Manasseh knew that the LORD is God.

(5) Job's Repentance

Job 42 [6]"Therefore I despise myself and repent in dust and ashes."

(6) Nineveh's Repentance

Jon 3 [5]The Ninevites believed God. They declared a fast, and all of them, from the greatest to the least, put on sackcloth.

[6]When the news reached the king of Nineveh, he rose from his throne, took off his royal robes, covered himself with sackcloth and sat down in the dust. [7]Then he issued a proclamation in Nineveh: "By the decree of the king and his nobles: Do not let any man or beast, herd or flock, taste anything; do not let them eat or drink. [8]But let man and beast be covered with sackcloth. Let everyone call urgently on God. Let them give up their evil ways and their violence. [9]Who knows? God may yet relent and with compassion turn from his fierce anger so that we will not perish."

[10]When God saw what they did and how they turned from their evil ways, he had compassion and did not bring upon them the destruction he had threatened.

Matt 12 [41]"The men of Nineveh will stand up at the judgment with this generation and condemn it; for they repented at the preaching of Jonah, and now one greater than Jonah is here."

(7) Zacchaeus's Repentance

Luke 19 [8]But Zacchaeus stood up and said to the Lord, "Look, Lord! Here and now I give half of my possessions to the poor, and if I have cheated anybody out of anything, I will pay back four times the amount."

(8) Peter's Repentance

Luke 22 [61]The Lord turned and looked straight at Peter. Then Peter remembered the word the Lord had spoken to him: "Before the rooster crows today, you will disown me three times." [62]And he went outside and wept bitterly.

(9) The Repentance of the Thief on the Cross

Luke 23 [39]One of the criminals who hung there hurled insults at him: "Aren't you the Christ? Save yourself and us!"

[40]But the other criminal rebuked him. "Don't you fear God," he said, "since you are under the same sentence? [41]We are punished justly, for we are getting what our deeds deserve. But this man has done nothing wrong."

[42]Then he said, "Jesus, remember me when you come into your kingdom."

[43]Jesus answered him, "I tell you the truth, today you will be with me in paradise."

(10) Paul's Repentance

Gal 1 [23]They only heard the report: "The man who formerly persecuted us is now preaching the faith he once tried to destroy."

(11) The Ephesians' Repentance

Acts 19 [17]When this became known to the Jews and Greeks living in Ephesus, they were all seized with fear, and the name of the Lord Jesus was held in high honor. [18]Many of those who believed now came and openly confessed their evil deeds.

(12) The Corinthians' Repentance

2 Cor 7 [9]yet now I am happy, not because you were made sorry, but because your sorrow led you to repentance. For you became sorrowful as God intended and so were not harmed in any way by us. [10]Godly sorrow brings repentance that leads to salvation and leaves no regret, but worldly sorrow brings death.

B. Exhortation to Repentance

1. A Promise to the Penitent

Deut 4 [29]But if from there you seek the LORD your God, you will find him if you look for him with all your heart and with all your soul. [30]When you are in distress and all these things have happened to you, then in later days you will return to the LORD your God and obey him. [31]For the LORD your God is a merciful God; he will not abandon or destroy you or forget the covenant with your forefathers, which he confirmed to them by oath.

Deut 30 [1]When all these blessings and curses I have set before you come upon you and you take them to heart wherever the

LORD your God disperses you among the nations, [2]and when you and your children return to the LORD your God and obey him with all your heart and with all your soul according to everything I command you today, [3]then the LORD your God will restore your fortunes and have compassion on you and gather you again from all the nations where he scattered you. [4]Even if you have been banished to the most distant land under the heavens, from there the LORD your God will gather you and bring you back. [5]He will bring you to the land that belonged to your fathers, and you will take possession of it. He will make you more prosperous and numerous than your fathers. [6]The LORD your God will circumcise your hearts and the hearts of your descendants, so that you may love him with all your heart and with all your soul, and live. [7]The LORD your God will put all these curses on your enemies who hate and persecute you. [8]You will again obey the LORD and follow all his commands I am giving you today. [9]Then the LORD your God will make you most prosperous in all the work of your hands and in the fruit of your womb, the young of your livestock and the crops of your land. The LORD will again delight in you and make you prosperous, just as he delighted in your fathers, [10]if you obey the LORD your God and keep his commands and decrees that are written in this Book of the Law and turn to the LORD your God with all your heart and with all your soul.

1 Sam 7 [3]And Samuel said to the whole house of Israel, "If you are returning to the LORD with all your hearts, then rid yourselves of the foreign gods and the Ashtoreths and commit yourselves to the LORD and serve him only, and he will deliver you out of the hand of the Philistines."

1 Kings 8 [33]"When your people Israel have been defeated by an enemy because they have sinned against you, and when they turn back to you and confess your name, praying and making supplication to you in this temple, [34]then hear from heaven and forgive the sin of your people Israel and bring them back to the land you gave to their fathers.

[35]"When the heavens are shut up and there is no rain because your people have sinned against you, and when they pray toward this place and confess your name and turn from their sin because you have afflicted them, [36]then hear from heaven and forgive the sin of your servants, your people Israel. Teach them the right way to live, and send rain on the land you gave your people for an inheritance.

[37]"When famine or plague comes to the land, or blight or mildew, locusts or grasshoppers, or when an enemy besieges them in any of their cities, whatever disaster or disease may come, [38]and when a prayer or plea is made by any of your people Israel—each one aware of the afflictions of his own heart, and spreading out his hands toward this temple—[39]then hear from heaven, your dwelling place. Forgive and act; deal with each man according to all he does, since you know his heart (for you alone know the hearts of all men), [40]so that they will fear you all the time they live in the land you gave our fathers. . . .

[46]"When they sin against you—for there is no one who does not sin—and you become angry with them and give them over to the enemy, who takes them captive to his own land, far away or near; [47]and if they have a change of heart in the land where they are held captive, and repent and plead with you in the land of their conquerors and say, 'We have sinned, we have done wrong, we have acted wickedly'; [48]and if they turn back to you with all their heart and soul in the land of their enemies who took them captive, and pray to you toward the land you gave their fathers, toward the city you have chosen and the temple I have built for your Name; [49]then from heaven, your dwelling place, hear their prayer and their plea, and uphold their cause. [50]And forgive your people, who have sinned against you; forgive all the offenses they have committed against you, and cause their conquerors to show them mercy. . . ."

2 Chron 30 [6]At the king's command, couriers went throughout Israel and Judah with letters from the king and from his officials, which read: "People of Israel, return to the LORD, the God of Abraham, Isaac and Israel, that he may return to you who are left, who have escaped from the hand of the kings of Assyria. [7]Do not be like your fathers and brothers, who were unfaithful to the LORD, the God of their fathers, so that he made them an object of horror, as you see. [8]Do not be stiff-necked, as your fathers were; submit to the LORD. Come to the sanctuary, which he has consecrated forever. Serve the LORD your God, so that his fierce anger will turn away from you. [9]If you return to the LORD, then your brothers and your children will be shown compassion by their captors and will come back to this land, for the LORD your God is gracious and compassionate. He will not turn his face from you if you return to him."

Neh 1 [8]"Remember the instruction you gave your servant Moses, saying, 'If you are unfaithful, I will scatter you among the nations, [9]but if you return to me and obey my commands, then even if your exiled people are at the farthest horizon, I will gather them from there and bring them to the place I have chosen as a dwelling for my Name.'"

Job 22 [23]"If you return to the Almighty, you will be restored: If you remove wickedness far from your tent [24]and assign your nuggets to the dust, your gold of Ophir to the rocks in the ravines, [25]then the Almighty will be your gold, the choicest silver for you."

Isa 55 [7]Let the wicked forsake his way and the evil man his thoughts. Let him turn to the LORD, and he will have mercy on him, and to our God, for he will freely pardon.

Jer 3 [12]"Go, proclaim this message toward the north: 'Return, faithless Israel,' declares the LORD, 'I will frown on you no longer, for I am merciful,' declares the LORD, 'I will not be angry forever. . . .'"

[14]"Return, faithless people," declares the LORD, "for I am your husband. I will choose you—one from a town and two from a clan—and bring you to Zion." . . .

[22]"Return, faithless people; I will cure you of backsliding."

"Yes, we will come to you, for you are the LORD our God."

Jer 4 [1]"If you will return, O Israel, return to me," declares the LORD. "If you put your detestable idols out of my sight and no longer go astray, [2]and if in a truthful, just and righteous way you swear, 'As surely as the LORD lives,' then the nations will be blessed by him and in him they will glory."

Jer 7 [3]"'This is what the LORD Almighty, the God of Israel, says: Reform your ways and your actions, and I will let you live in this place.'"

Jer 15 [19]Therefore this is what the LORD says: "If you repent, I will restore you that you may serve me; if you utter worthy, not worthless, words, you will be my spokesman. Let this people turn to you, but you must not turn to them. [20]I will make you a wall to this people, a fortified wall of bronze; they will fight against you but will not overcome you, for I am with you to rescue and save you," declares the LORD. [21]"I will save you from the hands of the wicked and redeem you from the grasp of the cruel."

Jer 18 [7]"If at any time I announce that a nation or kingdom is to be uprooted, torn down and destroyed, [8]and if that nation I warned repents of its evil, then I will relent and not inflict on it the disaster I had planned."

Jer 26 [2]"This is what the LORD says: Stand in the courtyard of the LORD's house and speak to all the people of the towns of Judah who come to worship in the house of the LORD. Tell them everything I command you; do not omit a word. [3]Perhaps they will listen and each will turn from his evil way. Then I will relent and not bring on them the disaster I was planning because of the evil they have done."

Jer 36 [3]"Perhaps when the people of Judah hear about every disaster I plan to inflict on them, each of them will turn from his wicked way; then I will forgive their wickedness and their sin."

Ezek 18 [21]"But if a wicked man turns away from all the sins he has committed and keeps all my decrees and does what is just and right, he will surely live; he will not die. [22]None of the offenses he has committed will be remembered against him. Because of the righteous things he has done, he will live. [23]Do I take any pleasure in the death of the wicked? declares the Sovereign LORD. Rather, am I not pleased when they turn from their ways and live? . . . [27]But if a wicked man turns away from the wickedness he has committed and does what is just and right, he will save his life. [28]Because he considers all the offenses he has committed and turns away from them, he will surely live; he will not die. . . .

[30]"Therefore, O house of Israel, I will judge you, each one

according to his ways, declares the Sovereign LORD. Repent! Turn away from all your offenses; then sin will not be your downfall. [31]Rid yourselves of all the offenses you have committed, and get a new heart and a new spirit. Why will you die, O house of Israel? [32]For I take no pleasure in the death of anyone, declares the Sovereign LORD. Repent and live!"

Ezek 33 [11]"Say to them, 'As surely as I live, declares the Sovereign LORD, I take no pleasure in the death of the wicked, but rather that they turn from their ways and live. Turn! Turn from your evil ways! Why will you die, O house of Israel?' . . . [14]And if I say to the wicked man, 'You will surely die,' but he then turns away from his sin and does what is just and right—[15]if he gives back what he took in pledge for a loan, returns what he has stolen, follows the decrees that give life, and does no evil, he will surely live; he will not die. [16]None of the sins he has committed will be remembered against him. He has done what is just and right; he will surely live. . . . [19]And if a wicked man turns away from his wickedness and does what is just and right, he will live by doing so."

Hos 6 [1]"Come, let us return to the LORD. He has torn us to pieces but he will heal us; he has injured us but he will bind up our wounds."

Hos 14 [1]Return, O Israel, to the LORD your God. Your sins have been your downfall! [2]Take words with you and return to the LORD. Say to him: "Forgive all our sins and receive us graciously, that we may offer the fruit of our lips. . . .

[7]"Men will dwell again in his shade. He will flourish like the grain. He will blossom like a vine, and his fame will be like the wine from Lebanon."

Joel 2 [12]"Even now," declares the LORD, "return to me with all your heart, with fasting and weeping and mourning."

[13]Rend your heart and not your garments. Return to the LORD your God, for he is gracious and compassionate, slow to anger and abounding in love, and he relents from sending calamity.

Zech 1 [3]"Therefore tell the people: This is what the LORD Almighty says: 'Return to me,' declares the LORD Almighty, 'and I will return to you,' says the LORD Almighty."

Mal 3 [7]"Ever since the time of your forefathers you have turned away from my decrees and have not kept them. Return to me, and I will return to you," says the LORD Almighty.

"But you ask, 'How are we to return?'"

2. A Warning to the Impenitent

2 Kings 17 [13]The LORD warned Israel and Judah through all his prophets and seers: "Turn from your evil ways. Observe my commands and decrees, in accordance with the entire Law that I commanded your fathers to obey and that I delivered to you through my servants the prophets."

[14]But they would not listen and were as stiff-necked as their fathers, who did not trust in the LORD their God. . . .

[20]Therefore the LORD rejected all the people of Israel; he afflicted them and gave them into the hands of plunderers, until he thrust them from his presence.

Ps 7 [12]If he does not relent, he will sharpen his sword; he will bend and string his bow. [13]He has prepared his deadly weapons; he makes ready his flaming arrows.

Ps 50 [22]"Consider this, you who forget God, or I will tear you to pieces, with none to rescue. . . ."

Prov 1 [22]"How long will you simple ones love your simple ways? How long will mockers delight in mockery and fools hate knowledge? [23]If you had responded to my rebuke, I would have poured out my heart to you and made my thoughts known to you. [24]But since you rejected me when I called and no one gave heed when I stretched out my hand, [25]since you ignored all my advice and would not accept my rebuke, [26]I in turn will laugh at your disaster; I will mock when calamity overtakes you—[27]when calamity overtakes you like a storm, when disaster sweeps over you like a whirlwind, when distress and trouble overwhelm you.

[28]"Then they will call to me but I will not answer; they will look for me but will not find me. [29]Since they hated knowledge and did not choose to fear the LORD, [30]since they would not accept my advice and spurned my rebuke, [31]they will eat the fruit of their ways and be filled with the fruit of their schemes. [32]For the waywardness of the simple will kill them, and the complacency of fools will destroy them. . . ."

Jer 4 [3]This is what the LORD says to the men of Judah and to Jerusalem: "Break up your unplowed ground and do not sow among thorns. [4]Circumcise yourselves to the LORD, circumcise your hearts, you men of Judah and people of Jerusalem, or my wrath will break out and burn like fire because of the evil you have done—burn with no one to quench it."

Jer 5 [3]O LORD, do not your eyes look for truth? You struck them, but they felt no pain; you crushed them, but they refused correction. They made their faces harder than stone and refused to repent. [4]I thought, "These are only the poor; they are foolish, for they do not know the way of the LORD, the requirements of their God. [5]So I will go to the leaders and speak to them; surely they know the way of the LORD, the requirements of their God." But with one accord they too had broken off the yoke and torn off the bonds. [6]Therefore a lion from the forest will attack them, a wolf from the desert will ravage them, a leopard will lie in wait near their towns to tear to pieces any who venture out, for their rebellion is great and their backslidings many.

Jer 8 [5]"'Why then have these people turned away? Why does Jerusalem always turn away? They cling to deceit; they refuse to return. [6]I have listened attentively, but they do not say what is right. No one repents of his wickedness, saying, "What have I done?" Each pursues his own course like a horse charging into battle. [7]Even the stork in the sky knows her appointed seasons, and the dove, the swift and the thrush observe the time of their migration. But my people do not know the requirements of the LORD. . . . [10]Therefore I will give their wives to other men and their fields to new owners. From the least to the greatest, all are greedy for gain; prophets and priests alike, all practice deceit.'"

Jer 15 [7]"I will winnow them with a winnowing fork at the city gates of the land. I will bring bereavement and destruction on my people, for they have not changed their ways."

Jer 18 [11]"Now therefore say to the people of Judah and those living in Jerusalem, 'This is what the LORD says: Look! I am preparing a disaster for you and devising a plan against you. So turn from your evil ways, each one of you, and reform your ways and your actions.' [12]But they will reply, 'It's no use. We will continue with our own plans; each of us will follow the stubbornness of his evil heart.'"

Jer 23 [14]"And among the prophets of Jerusalem I have seen something horrible: They commit adultery and live a lie. They strengthen the hands of evildoers, so that no one turns from his wickedness. They are all like Sodom to me; the people of Jerusalem are like Gomorrah."

[15]Therefore, this is what the LORD Almighty says concerning the prophets: "I will make them eat bitter food and drink poisoned water, because from the prophets of Jerusalem ungodliness has spread throughout the land."

Jer 25 [4]And though the LORD has sent all his servants the prophets to you again and again, you have not listened or paid any attention. [5]They said, "Turn now, each of you, from your evil ways and your evil practices, and you can stay in the land the LORD gave to you and your fathers for ever and ever. [6]Do not follow other gods to serve and worship them; do not provoke me to anger with what your hands have made. Then I will not harm you."

[7]"But you did not listen to me," declares the LORD, "and you have provoked me with what your hands have made, and you have brought harm to yourselves."

[8]Therefore the LORD Almighty says this: "Because you have not listened to my words, [9]I will summon all the peoples of the north and my servant Nebuchadnezzar king of Babylon," declares the LORD, "and I will bring them against this land and its inhabitants and against all the surrounding nations. I will completely destroy them and make them an object of horror and scorn, and an everlasting ruin. [10]I will banish from them the sounds of joy and gladness, the voices of bride and bridegroom, the sound of millstones and the light of the lamp. [11]This whole country will become a desolate wasteland, and these nations will serve the king of Babylon seventy years."

Jer 35 [15]"'Again and again I sent all my servants the prophets to you. They said, "Each of you must turn from your wicked ways and reform your actions; do not follow other gods to serve them. Then you will live in the land I have given to you and your fathers." But you have not paid attention or listened to me.'"

Jer 44 [4]"Again and again I sent my servants the prophets, who said, 'Do not do this detestable thing that I hate!' [5]But they did not listen or pay attention; they did not turn from their wickedness or stop burning incense to other gods. [6]Therefore, my fierce anger was poured out; it raged against the towns of Judah and the streets of Jerusalem and made them the desolate ruins they are today."

Ezek 3 [18]"When I say to a wicked man, 'You will surely die,' and you do not warn him or speak out to dissuade him from his evil ways in order to save his life, that wicked man will die for his sin, and I will hold you accountable for his blood. [19]But if you do warn the wicked man and he does not turn from his wickedness or from his evil ways, he will die for his sin; but you will have saved yourself."

Ezek 13 [22]"'Because you disheartened the righteous with your lies, when I had brought them no grief, and because you encouraged the wicked not to turn from their evil ways and so save their lives, [23]therefore you will no longer see false visions or practice divination. I will save my people from your hands. And then you will know that I am the LORD.'"

Dan 9 [13]"Just as it is written in the Law of Moses, all this disaster has come upon us, yet we have not sought the favor of the LORD our God by turning from our sins and giving attention to your truth. [14]The LORD did not hesitate to bring the disaster upon us, for the LORD our God is righteous in everything he does; yet we have not obeyed him."

Hos 7 [10]"Israel's arrogance testifies against him, but despite all this he does not return to the LORD his God or search for him.

[11]"Ephraim is like a dove, easily deceived and senseless—now calling to Egypt, now turning to Assyria. [12]When they go, I will throw my net over them; I will pull them down like birds of the air. When I hear them flocking together, I will catch them. [13]Woe to them, because they have strayed from me! Destruction to them, because they have rebelled against me! I long to redeem them but they speak lies against me. [14]They do not cry out to me from their hearts but wail upon their beds. They gather together for grain and new wine but turn away from me. [15]I trained them and strengthened them, but they plot evil against me. [16]They do not turn to the Most High; they are like a faulty bow. Their leaders will fall by the sword because of their insolent words. For this they will be ridiculed in the land of Egypt."

Hos 11 [5]"Will they not return to Egypt and will not Assyria rule over them because they refuse to repent?"

Amos 4 [6]"I gave you empty stomachs in every city and lack of bread in every town, yet you have not returned to me," declares the LORD.

[7]"I also withheld rain from you when the harvest was still three months away. I sent rain on one town, but withheld it from another. One field had rain; another had none and dried up. [8]People staggered from town to town for water but did not get enough to drink, yet you have not returned to me," declares the LORD.

[9]"Many times I struck your gardens and vineyards, I struck them with blight and mildew. Locusts devoured your fig and olive trees, yet you have not returned to me," declares the LORD.

[10]"I sent plagues among you as I did to Egypt. I killed your young men with the sword, along with your captured horses. I filled your nostrils with the stench of your camps, yet you have not returned to me," declares the LORD.

[11]"I overthrew some of you as I overthrew Sodom and Gomorrah. You were like a burning stick snatched from the fire, yet you have not returned to me," declares the LORD.

[12]"Therefore this is what I will do to you, Israel, and because I will do this to you, prepare to meet your God, O Israel."

Zech 1 [4]"Do not be like your forefathers, to whom the earlier prophets proclaimed: This is what the LORD Almighty says: 'Turn from your evil ways and your evil practices.' But they would not listen or pay attention to me, declares the LORD. [5]Where are your forefathers now? And the prophets, do they live forever? [6]But did not my words and my decrees, which I commanded my servants the prophets, overtake your forefathers?

"Then they repented and said, 'The LORD Almighty has done to us what our ways and practices deserve, just as he determined to do.'"

Matt 11 [20]Then Jesus began to denounce the cities in which most of his miracles had been performed, because they did not repent. [21]"Woe to you, Korazin! Woe to you, Bethsaida! If the miracles that were performed in you had been performed in Tyre and Sidon, they would have repented long ago in sackcloth and ashes. [22]But I tell you, it will be more bearable for Tyre and Sidon on the day of judgment than for you. [23]And you, Capernaum, will you be lifted up to the skies? No, you will go down to the depths. If the miracles that were performed in you had been performed in Sodom, it would have remained to this day. [24]But I tell you that it will be more bearable for Sodom on the day of judgment than for you."

Matt 18 [3]And he said: "I tell you the truth, unless you change and become like little children, you will never enter the kingdom of heaven."

Matt 21 [31]"Which of the two did what his father wanted?"

"The first," they answered.

Jesus said to them, "I tell you the truth, the tax collectors and the prostitutes are entering the kingdom of God ahead of you. [32]For John came to you to show you the way of righteousness, and you did not believe him, but the tax collectors and the prostitutes did. And even after you saw this, you did not repent and believe him."

Luke 11 [32]"The men of Nineveh will stand up at the judgment with this generation and condemn it; for they repented at the preaching of Jonah, and now one greater than Jonah is here."

Luke 16 [30]"'No, father Abraham,' he said, 'but if someone from the dead goes to them, they will repent.'

[31]"He said to him, 'If they do not listen to Moses and the Prophets, they will not be convinced even if someone rises from the dead.'"

Rev 2 [5]"Remember the height from which you have fallen! Repent and do the things you did at first. If you do not repent, I will come to you and remove your lampstand from its place."

Rev 2 [16]"Repent therefore! Otherwise, I will soon come to you and will fight against them with the sword of my mouth."

Rev 2 [21]"I have given her time to repent of her immorality, but she is unwilling. [22]So I will cast her on a bed of suffering, and I will make those who commit adultery with her suffer intensely, unless they repent of her ways."

Rev 3 [3]"Remember, therefore, what you have received and heard; obey it, and repent. But if you do not wake up, I will come like a thief, and you will not know at what time I will come to you."

Rev 9 [20]The rest of mankind that were not killed by these plagues still did not repent of the work of their hands; they did not stop worshiping demons, and idols of gold, silver, bronze, stone and wood—idols that cannot see or hear or walk. [21]Nor did they repent of their murders, their magic arts, their sexual immorality or their thefts.

Rev 16 [9]They were seared by the intense heat and they cursed the name of God, who had control over these plagues, but they refused to repent and glorify him.

3. The Obligation to God for Repentance

Deut 10 [16]Circumcise your hearts, therefore, and do not be stiff-necked any longer.

Job 11 [13]"Yet if you devote your heart to him and stretch out your hands to him, [14]if you put away the sin that is in your hand and allow no evil to dwell in your tent, [15]then you will lift up your face without shame; you will stand firm and without fear."

Ps 4 [4]In your anger do not sin; when you are on your beds, search your hearts and be silent.

Ps 34 [14]Turn from evil and do good; seek peace and pursue it.

Prov 9 [6]"Leave your simple ways and you will live; walk in the way of understanding."

Isa 1 [16]". . . wash and make yourselves clean. Take your evil deeds out of my sight! Stop doing wrong. . . ."

Jer 4 [4]"Circumcise yourselves to the LORD, circumcise your hearts, you men of Judah and people of Jerusalem, or my wrath will break out and burn like fire because of the evil you have done—burn with no one to quench it."
Jer 13 [15]Hear and pay attention, do not be arrogant, for the LORD has spoken. [16]Give glory to the LORD your God before he brings the darkness, before your feet stumble on the darkening hills. You hope for light, but he will turn it to thick darkness and change it to deep gloom.
Ezek 14 [6]"Therefore say to the house of Israel, 'This is what the Sovereign LORD says: Repent! Turn from your idols and renounce all your detestable practices!'"
Hos 2 [7]"She will chase after her lovers but not catch them; she will look for them but not find them. Then she will say, 'I will go back to my husband as at first, for then I was better off than now.'"
Matt 6 [19]"Do not store up for yourselves treasures on earth, where moth and rust destroy, and where thieves break in and steal. [20]But store up for yourselves treasures in heaven, where moth and rust do not destroy, and where thieves do not break in and steal. [21]For where your treasure is, there your heart will be also."
Luke 3 [8]"Produce fruit in keeping with repentance. And do not begin to say to yourselves, 'We have Abraham as our father.' For I tell you that out of these stones God can raise up children for Abraham."
John 5 [14]Later Jesus found him at the temple and said to him, "See, you are well again. Stop sinning or something worse may happen to you."
John 8 [11]"No one, sir," she said.
"Then neither do I condemn you," Jesus declared. "Go now and leave your life of sin."
Acts 2 [38]Peter replied, "Repent and be baptized, every one of you, in the name of Jesus Christ for the forgiveness of your sins. And you will receive the gift of the Holy Spirit."
Acts 3 [19]"Repent, then, and turn to God, so that your sins may be wiped out, that times of refreshing may come from the Lord. . . ."
Acts 8 [22]"Repent of this wickedness and pray to the Lord. Perhaps he will forgive you for having such a thought in your heart."
Acts 17 [30]"In the past God overlooked such ignorance, but now he commands all people everywhere to repent."
Rom 6 [1]What shall we say, then? Shall we go on sinning so that grace may increase? [2]By no means! We died to sin; how can we live in it any longer?
Eph 5 [14]for it is light that makes everything visible. This is why it is said: "Wake up, O sleeper, rise from the dead, and Christ will shine on you."
James 4 [7]Submit yourselves, then, to God. Resist the devil, and he will flee from you. [8]Come near to God and he will come near to you. Wash your hands, you sinners, and purify your hearts, you double-minded.

4. The Desire of God for Repentance

Ps 34 [18]The LORD is close to the brokenhearted and saves those who are crushed in spirit.
Isa 45 [22]"Turn to me and be saved, all you ends of the earth; for I am God, and there is no other."
Jer 24 [7]"'I will give them a heart to know me, that I am the LORD. They will be my people, and I will be their God, for they will return to me with all their heart.'"
Luke 15 [7]"I tell you that in the same way there will be more rejoicing in heaven over one sinner who repents than over ninety-nine righteous persons who do not need to repent."
Rom 14 [11]It is written: "'As surely as I live,' says the Lord, 'every knee will bow before me; every tongue will confess to God.'"
2 Pet 3 [9]The Lord is not slow in keeping his promise, as some understand slowness. He is patient with you, not wanting anyone to perish, but everyone to come to repentance.

5. The Best Time for Repentance: Now

Ps 95 [7]for he is our God and we are the people of his pasture, the flock under his care.
Today, if you hear his voice, [8]do not harden your hearts as you did at Meribah, as you did that day at Massah in the desert. . . .
Prov 27 [1]Do not boast about tomorrow, for you do not know what a day may bring forth.
Isa 55 [6]Seek the LORD while he may be found; call on him while he is near. [7]Let the wicked forsake his way and the evil man his thoughts. Let him turn to the LORD, and he will have mercy on him, and to our God, for he will freely pardon.
2 Cor 6 [2]For he says, "In the time of my favor I heard you, and in the day of salvation I helped you." I tell you, now is the time of God's favor, now is the day of salvation.
Heb 4 [7]Therefore God again set a certain day, calling it Today, when a long time later he spoke through David, as was said before: "Today, if you hear his voice, do not harden your hearts."

C. The Results of Repentance

1. Results of Repenting

a) The Penitent Are Fruitful

Matt 3 [8]"Produce fruit in keeping with repentance."

b) The Penitent Are Humble

2 Chron 7 [14]". . . if my people, who are called by my name, will humble themselves and pray and seek my face and turn from their wicked ways, then will I hear from heaven and will forgive their sin and will heal their land."
James 4 [9]Grieve, mourn and wail. Change your laughter to mourning and your joy to gloom. [10]Humble yourselves before the Lord, and he will lift you up.

c) The Penitent Do Good Works

Dan 4 [27]"Therefore, O king, be pleased to accept my advice: Renounce your sins by doing what is right, and your wickedness by being kind to the oppressed. It may be that then your prosperity will continue."
Acts 26 [20]"First to those in Damascus, then to those in Jerusalem and in all Judea, and to the Gentiles also, I preached that they should repent and turn to God and prove their repentance by their deeds."

d) The Penitent Experience Salvation

See p. 481a, Repentance Leads to Salvation

e) The Penitent Preach Repentance to Others

Luke 24 [46]He told them, "This is what is written: The Christ will suffer and rise from the dead on the third day, [47]and repentance and forgiveness of sins will be preached in his name to all nations, beginning at Jerusalem."
Acts 26 [17]"'I will rescue you from your own people and from the Gentiles. I am sending you to them [18]to open their eyes and turn them from darkness to light, and from the power of Satan to God, so that they may receive forgiveness of sins and a place among those who are sanctified by faith in me.'"

f) The Penitent Render Service to God

1 Thess 1 [9]for they themselves report what kind of reception you gave us. They tell how you turned to God from idols to serve the living and true God. . . .

2. Results of Failure to Repent

a) The Impenitent Are Condemned

Matt 11 [20]Then Jesus began to denounce the cities in which most of his miracles had been performed, because they did not repent.

b) The Impenitent Are Forsaken by God

2 Kings 17 [13]The LORD warned Israel and Judah through all his prophets and seers: "Turn from your evil ways. Observe my commands and decrees, in accordance with the entire Law that I commanded your fathers to obey and that I delivered to you through my servants the prophets."
[14]But they would not listen and were as stiff-necked as their fathers, who did not trust in the LORD their God. . . .

[18]So the LORD was very angry with Israel and removed them from his presence. Only the tribe of Judah was left, [19]and even Judah did not keep the commands of the LORD their God. They followed the practices Israel had introduced. [20]Therefore the LORD rejected all the people of Israel; he afflicted them and gave them into the hands of plunderers, until he thrust them from his presence.

2 Chron 29 [6]"Our fathers were unfaithful; they did evil in the eyes of the LORD our God and forsook him. They turned their faces away from the LORD's dwelling place and turned their backs on him. [7]They also shut the doors of the portico and put out the lamps. They did not burn incense or present any burnt offerings at the sanctuary to the God of Israel. [8]Therefore, the anger of the LORD has fallen on Judah and Jerusalem; he has made them an object of dread and horror and scorn, as you can see with your own eyes. [9]This is why our fathers have fallen by the sword and why our sons and daughters and our wives are in captivity."

c) The Impenitent Are Hard of Heart

Jer 6 [16]This is what the LORD says: "Stand at the crossroads and look; ask for the ancient paths, ask where the good way is, and walk in it, and you will find rest for your souls. But you said, 'We will not walk in it.'"

Jer 8 [6]"I have listened attentively, but they do not say what is right. No one repents of his wickedness, saying, "What have I done?" Each pursues his own course like a horse charging into battle.'"

Matt 13 [13]"This is why I speak to them in parables: Though seeing, they do not see; though hearing, they do not hear or understand. [14]In them is fulfilled the prophecy of Isaiah: 'You will be ever hearing but never understanding; you will be ever seeing but never perceiving. [15]For this people's heart has become calloused; they hardly hear with their ears, and they have closed their eyes. Otherwise they might see with their eyes, hear with their ears, understand with their hearts and turn, and I would heal them.'"

Matt 21 [31]"Which of the two did what his father wanted?"

"The first," they answered.

Jesus said to them, "I tell you the truth, the tax collectors and the prostitutes are entering the kingdom of God ahead of you. [32]For John came to you to show you the way of righteousness, and you did not believe him, but the tax collectors and the prostitutes did. And even after you saw this, you did not repent and believe him."

Luke 16 [30]"'No, father Abraham,' he said, 'but if someone from the dead goes to them, they will repent.'

[31]"He said to him, 'If they do not listen to Moses and the Prophets, they will not be convinced even if someone rises from the dead.'"

Rom 2 [5]But because of your stubbornness and your unrepentant heart, you are storing up wrath against yourself for the day of God's wrath, when his righteous judgment will be revealed.

Heb 3 [7]So, as the Holy Spirit says: "Today, if you hear his voice, [8]do not harden your hearts as you did in the rebellion, during the time of testing in the desert, [9]where your fathers tested and tried me and for forty years saw what I did. [10]That is why I was angry with that generation, and I said, 'Their hearts are always going astray, and they have not known my ways.' [11]So I declared on oath in my anger, 'They shall never enter my rest.'"

Heb 6 [4]It is impossible for those who have once been enlightened, who have tasted the heavenly gift, who have shared in the Holy Spirit, [5]who have tasted the goodness of the word of God and the powers of the coming age, [6]if they fall away, to be brought back to repentance, because to their loss they are crucifying the Son of God all over again and subjecting him to public disgrace.

Rev 2 [21]"I have given her time to repent of her immorality, but she is unwilling."

Rev 9 [20]The rest of mankind that were not killed by these plagues still did not repent of the work of their hands; they did not stop worshiping demons, and idols of gold, silver, bronze, stone and wood—idols that cannot see or hear or walk. [21]Nor did they repent of their murders, their magic arts, their sexual immorality or their thefts.

Rev 16 [9]They were seared by the intense heat and they cursed the name of God, who had control over these plagues, but they refused to repent and glorify him.

d) The Impenitent Are Irreverent

Isa 5 [12]They have harps and lyres at their banquets, tambourines and flutes and wine, but they have no regard for the deeds of the LORD, no respect for the work of his hands.

e) The Impenitent Are Spiritually and Morally Blind

Deut 32 [29]If only they were wise and would understand this and discern what their end will be!

Ps 82 [5]"They know nothing, they understand nothing. They walk about in darkness; all the foundations of the earth are shaken."

Ps 94 [8]Take heed, you senseless ones among the people; you fools, when will you become wise?

Eccles 5 [1]Guard your steps when you go to the house of God. Go near to listen rather than to offer the sacrifice of fools, who do not know that they do wrong.

Isa 1 [3]"The ox knows his master, the donkey his owner's manger, but Israel does not know, my people do not understand."

Jer 10 [8]They are all senseless and foolish; they are taught by worthless wooden idols.

Hos 7 [2]". . . but they do not realize that I remember all their evil deeds. Their sins engulf them; they are always before me."

Matt 7 [3]"Why do you look at the speck of sawdust in your brother's eye and pay no attention to the plank in your own eye? [4]How can you say to your brother, 'Let me take the speck out of your eye,' when all the time there is a plank in your own eye? [5]You hypocrite, first take the plank out of your own eye, and then you will see clearly to remove the speck from your brother's eye."

Luke 19 [42]and said, "If you, even you, had only known on this day what would bring you peace—but now it is hidden from your eyes."

Luke 23 [28]Jesus turned and said to them, "Daughters of Jerusalem, do not weep for me; weep for yourselves and for your children. [29]For the time will come when you will say, 'Blessed are the barren women, the wombs that never bore and the breasts that never nursed!' [30]Then 'they will say to the mountains, "Fall on us!" and to the hills, "Cover us!"' [31]For if men do these things when the tree is green, what will happen when it is dry?"

John 12 [40]"He has blinded their eyes and deadened their hearts, so they can neither see with their eyes, nor understand with their hearts, nor turn—and I would heal them."

Rom 11 [8]as it is written: "God gave them a spirit of stupor, eyes so that they could not see and ears so that they could not hear, to this very day."

Rev 3 [17]"You say, 'I am rich; I have acquired wealth and do not need a thing.' But you do not realize that you are wretched, pitiful, poor, blind and naked."

VIII Saving Faith

A. The Nature of Saving Faith

1. Saving Faith Is More Than Intellectual Acknowledgment

John 2 [23]Now while he was in Jerusalem at the Passover Feast, many people saw the miraculous signs he was doing and believed in his name. [24]But Jesus would not entrust himself to them, for he knew all men. [25]He did not need man's testimony about man, for he knew what was in a man.

John 3 [1]Now there was a man of the Pharisees named Nicodemus, a member of the Jewish ruling council. [2]He came to Jesus at night and said, "Rabbi, we know you are a teacher who has come from God. For no one could perform the miraculous signs you are doing if God were not with him."

[3]In reply Jesus declared, "I tell you the truth, no one can see the kingdom of God unless he is born again."

[4]"How can a man be born when he is old?" Nicodemus asked. "Surely he cannot enter a second time into his mother's womb to be born!"

[5]Jesus answered, "I tell you the truth, no one can enter the kingdom of God unless he is born of water and the Spirit."

Acts 8 [13]Simon himself believed and was baptized. And he followed Philip everywhere, astonished by the great signs and miracles he saw.

[14]When the apostles in Jerusalem heard that Samaria had accepted the word of God, they sent Peter and John to them. [15]When they arrived, they prayed for them that they might receive the Holy Spirit, [16]because the Holy Spirit had not yet come upon any of them; they had simply been baptized into the name of the Lord Jesus. [17]Then Peter and John placed their hands on them, and they received the Holy Spirit.

[18]When Simon saw that the Spirit was given at the laying on of the apostles' hands, he offered them money [19]and said, "Give me also this ability so that everyone on whom I lay my hands may receive the Holy Spirit."

[20]Peter answered: "May your money perish with you, because you thought you could buy the gift of God with money! [21]You have no part or share in this ministry, because your heart is not right before God. [22]Repent of this wickedness and pray to the Lord. Perhaps he will forgive you for having such a thought in your heart. [23]For I see that you are full of bitterness and captive to sin."

[24]Then Simon answered, "Pray to the Lord for me so that nothing you have said may happen to me."

James 2 [19]You believe that there is one God. Good! Even the demons believe that—and shudder.

2. Saving Faith Is More Than Emotional Assent

Ps 106 [12]Then they believed his promises and sang his praise.

[13]But they soon forgot what he had done and did not wait for his counsel.

Ezek 33 [31]"My people come to you, as they usually do, and sit before you to listen to your words, but they do not put them into practice. With their mouths they express devotion, but their hearts are greedy for unjust gain. [32]Indeed, to them you are nothing more than one who sings love songs with a beautiful voice and plays an instrument well, for they hear your words but do not put them into practice."

Matt 13 [20]"The one who received the seed that fell on rocky places is the man who hears the word and at once receives it with joy. [21]But since he has no root, he lasts only a short time. When trouble or persecution comes because of the word, he quickly falls away."

John 8 [29]"The one who sent me is with me; he has not left me alone, for I always do what pleases him." [30]Even as he spoke, many put their faith in him.

[31]To the Jews who had believed him, Jesus said, "If you hold to my teaching, you are really my disciples."

3. Saving Faith Is a Personal Relationship of Trust in Christ as Lord and Savior

Matt 11 [28]"Come to me, all you who are weary and burdened, and I will give you rest. [29]Take my yoke upon you and learn from me, for I am gentle and humble in heart, and you will find rest for your souls. [30]For my yoke is easy and my burden is light."

John 1 [12]Yet to all who received him, to those who believed in his name, he gave the right to become children of God. . . .

John 4 [13]Jesus answered, "Everyone who drinks this water will be thirsty again, [14]but whoever drinks the water I give him will never thirst. Indeed, the water I give him will become in him a spring of water welling up to eternal life."

John 6 [53]Jesus said to them, "I tell you the truth, unless you eat the flesh of the Son of Man and drink his blood, you have no life in you. [54]Whoever eats my flesh and drinks my blood has eternal life, and I will raise him up at the last day. [55]For my flesh is real food and my blood is real drink. [56]Whoever eats my flesh and drinks my blood remains in me, and I in him. [57]Just as the living Father sent me and I live because of the Father, so the one who feeds on me will live because of me. [58]This is the bread that came down from heaven. Your forefathers ate manna and died, but he who feeds on this bread will live forever."

John 8 [12]When Jesus spoke again to the people, he said, "I am the light of the world. Whoever follows me will never walk in darkness, but will have the light of life."

John 14 [1]"Do not let your hearts be troubled. Trust in God; trust also in me."

John 20 [31]But these are written that you may believe that Jesus is the Christ, the Son of God, and that by believing you may have life in his name.

Acts 16 [31]They replied, "Believe in the Lord Jesus, and you will be saved—you and your household."

Rom 10 [9]That if you confess with your mouth, "Jesus is Lord," and believe in your heart that God raised him from the dead, you will be saved. [10]For it is with your heart that you believe and are justified, and it is with your mouth that you confess and are saved.

1 John 3 [23]And this is his command: to believe in the name of his Son, Jesus Christ, and to love one another as he commanded us.

1 John 5 [5]Who is it that overcomes the world? Only he who believes that Jesus is the Son of God.

Rev 3 [20]"Here I am! I stand at the door and knock. If anyone hears my voice and opens the door, I will come in and eat with him, and he with me."

B. The Object of Saving Faith

1. God Is the Object of Saving Faith

2 Chron 20 [20]Early in the morning they left for the Desert of Tekoa. As they set out, Jehoshaphat stood and said, "Listen to me, Judah and people of Jerusalem! Have faith in the LORD your God and you will be upheld; have faith in his prophets and you will be successful."

Ps 4 [5]Offer right sacrifices and trust in the LORD.

Ps 9 [10]Those who know your name will trust in you, for you, LORD, have never forsaken those who seek you.

Ps 31 [6]I hate those who cling to worthless idols; I trust in the LORD.

Ps 37 [3]Trust in the LORD and do good; dwell in the land and enjoy safe pasture.

Ps 119 [65]Do good to your servant according to your word, O LORD. [66]Teach me knowledge and good judgment, for I believe in your commands.

Isa 26 [4]Trust in the LORD forever, for the LORD, the LORD, is the Rock eternal.

Isa 43 [10]"You are my witnesses," declares the LORD, "and my servant whom I have chosen, so that you may know and believe me and understand that I am he. Before me no god was formed, nor will there be one after me."

Isa 50 [10]Who among you fears the LORD and obeys the word of his servant? Let him who walks in the dark, who has no light, trust in the name of the LORD and rely on his God.

Mark 11 [22]"Have faith in God," Jesus answered.

John 12 [44]Then Jesus cried out, "When a man believes in me, he does not believe in me only, but in the one who sent me."

Heb 6 [1]Therefore let us leave the elementary teachings about Christ and go on to maturity, not laying again the foundation of repentance from acts that lead to death, and of faith in God. . . .

Heb 11 [1]Now faith is being sure of what we hope for and certain of what we do not see. . . . [6]And without faith it is impossible to please God, because anyone who comes to him must believe that he exists and that he rewards those who earnestly seek him.

1 Pet 1 [21]Through him you believe in God, who raised him from the dead and glorified him, and so your faith and hope are in God.

2. Christ Is the Object of Saving Faith

John 1 [12]Yet to all who received him, to those who believed in his name, he gave the right to become children of God. . . .
John 3 [16]"For God so loved the world that he gave his one and only Son, that whoever believes in him shall not perish but have eternal life."
John 6 [29]Jesus answered, "The work of God is this: to believe in the one he has sent."
John 9 [35]Jesus heard that they had thrown him out, and when he found him, he said, "Do you believe in the Son of Man?"

[36]"Who is he, sir?" the man asked. "Tell me so that I may believe in him."

[37]Jesus said, "You have now seen him; in fact, he is the one speaking with you."

[38]Then the man said, "Lord, I believe," and he worshiped him.
John 11 [27]"Yes, Lord," she told him, "I believe that you are the Christ, the Son of God, who was to come into the world."
John 12 [36]"Put your trust in the light while you have it, so that you may become sons of light." When he had finished speaking, Jesus left and hid himself from them.
John 14 [1]"Do not let your hearts be troubled. Trust in God; trust also in me." . . .

[6]Jesus answered, "I am the way and the truth and the life. No one comes to the Father except through me."
John 20 [27]Then he said to Thomas, "Put your finger here; see my hands. Reach out your hand and put it into my side. Stop doubting and believe." . . .

[31]But these are written that you may believe that Jesus is the Christ, the Son of God, and that by believing you may have life in his name.
Acts 8 [37]Philip said, "If you believe with all your heart, you may." The eunuch answered, "I believe that Jesus Christ is the Son of God." [38]And he gave orders to stop the chariot. Then both Philip and the eunuch went down into the water and Philip baptized him.
Acts 16 [31]They replied, "Believe in the Lord Jesus, and you will be saved—you and your household."
Acts 20 [21]"I have declared to both Jews and Greeks that they must turn to God in repentance and have faith in our Lord Jesus."
Rom 10 [9]That if you confess with your mouth, "Jesus is Lord," and believe in your heart that God raised him from the dead, you will be saved. [10]For it is with your heart that you believe and are justified, and it is with your mouth that you confess and are saved.
Gal 2 [20]"I have been crucified with Christ and I no longer live, but Christ lives in me. The life I live in the body, I live by faith in the Son of God, who loved me and gave himself for me."
Eph 1 [13]And you also were included in Christ when you heard the word of truth, the gospel of your salvation. Having believed, you were marked in him with a seal, the promised Holy Spirit. . . .
1 Thess 4 [14]We believe that Jesus died and rose again and so we believe that God will bring with Jesus those who have fallen asleep in him.
1 Tim 1 [16]But for that very reason I was shown mercy so that in me, the worst of sinners, Christ Jesus might display his unlimited patience as an example for those who would believe on him and receive eternal life.
1 Tim 4 [10](and for this we labor and strive), that we have put our hope in the living God, who is the Savior of all men, and especially of those who believe.
2 Tim 1 [13]What you heard from me, keep as the pattern of sound teaching, with faith and love in Christ Jesus.
Heb 10 [39]But we are not of those who shrink back and are destroyed, but of those who believe and are saved.
1 John 3 [23]And this is his command: to believe in the name of his Son, Jesus Christ, and to love one another as he commanded us.
1 John 5 [10]Anyone who believes in the Son of God has this testimony in his heart. Anyone who does not believe God has made him out to be a liar, because he has not believed the testimony God has given about his Son. [11]And this is the testimony: God has given us eternal life, and this life is in his Son. [12]He who has the Son has life; he who does not have the Son of God does not have life.

[13]I write these things to you who believe in the name of the Son of God so that you may know that you have eternal life.

C. The Source of Saving Faith

1. God Is the Source of Saving Faith

Ps 52 [8]But I am like an olive tree flourishing in the house of God; I trust in God's unfailing love for ever and ever.
Matt 16 [16]Simon Peter answered, "You are the Christ, the Son of the living God."

[17]Jesus replied, "Blessed are you, Simon son of Jonah, for this was not revealed to you by man, but by my Father in heaven."
John 1 [12]Yet to all who received him, to those who believed in his name, he gave the right to become children of God—[13]children born not of natural descent, nor of human decision or a husband's will, but born of God.
Acts 11 [21]The Lord's hand was with them, and a great number of people believed and turned to the Lord.
Acts 13 [48]When the Gentiles heard this, they were glad and honored the word of the Lord; and all who were appointed for eternal life believed.
Acts 14 [27]On arriving there, they gathered the church together and reported all that God had done through them and how he had opened the door of faith to the Gentiles.
Rom 12 [3]For by the grace given me I say to every one of you: Do not think of yourself more highly than you ought, but rather think of yourself with sober judgment, in accordance with the measure of faith God has given you.
1 Cor 2 [4]My message and my preaching were not with wise and persuasive words, but with a demonstration of the Spirit's power, [5]so that your faith might not rest on men's wisdom, but on God's power.
1 Cor 3 [5]What, after all, is Apollos? And what is Paul? Only servants, through whom you came to believe—as the Lord has assigned to each his task. [6]I planted the seed, Apollos watered it, but God made it grow. [7]So neither he who plants nor he who waters is anything, but only God, who makes things grow.
Eph 2 [8]For it is by grace you have been saved, through faith—and this not from yourselves, it is the gift of God. . . .
Phil 1 [29]For it has been granted to you on behalf of Christ not only to believe on him, but also to suffer for him. . . .
2 Thess 2 [13]But we ought always to thank God for you, brothers loved by the Lord, because from the beginning God chose you to be saved through the sanctifying work of the Spirit and through belief in the truth.
1 John 4 [14]And we have seen and testify that the Father has sent his Son to be the Savior of the world. [15]If anyone acknowledges that Jesus is the Son of God, God lives in him and he in God.
1 John 5 [1]Everyone who believes that Jesus is the Christ is born of God, and everyone who loves the father loves his child as well.
1 John 5 [6]This is the one who came by water and blood—Jesus Christ. He did not come by water only, but by water and blood. And it is the Spirit who testifies, because the Spirit is the truth. [7]For there are three that testify: [8]the Spirit, the water and the blood; and the three are in agreement. [9]We accept man's testimony, but God's testimony is greater because it is the testimony of God, which he has given about his Son.

2. Christ Is the Source of Saving Faith

Luke 17 [5]The apostles said to the Lord, "Increase our faith!"
Eph 6 [23]Peace to the brothers, and love with faith from God the Father and the Lord Jesus Christ.
1 Tim 1 [14]The grace of our Lord was poured out on me abundantly, along with the faith and love that are in Christ Jesus.
Heb 12 [2]Let us fix our eyes on Jesus, the author and perfecter of our faith, who for the joy set before him endured the cross, scorning its shame, and sat down at the right hand of the throne of God.
1 Pet 1 [21]Through him you believe in God, who raised him from the dead and glorified him, and so your faith and hope are in God.

2 Pet 1 [1]Simon Peter, a servant and apostle of Jesus Christ,
To those who through the righteousness of our God and Savior Jesus Christ have received a faith as precious as ours. . . .

3. The Spirit Is the Source of Saving Faith

1 Cor 12 [8]To one there is given through the Spirit the message of wisdom, to another the message of knowledge by means of the same Spirit, [9]to another faith by the same Spirit, to another gifts of healing by that one Spirit. . . .
Gal 5 [22]But the fruit of the Spirit is love, joy, peace, patience, kindness, goodness, faithfulness. . . .

D. The Means of Saving Faith

1. The Gospel Message Preached Is a Means of Saving Faith

John 1 [6]There came a man who was sent from God; his name was John. [7]He came as a witness to testify concerning that light, so that through him all men might believe.
John 17 [20]"My prayer is not for them alone. I pray also for those who will believe in me through their message. . . ."
John 19 [34]Instead, one of the soldiers pierced Jesus' side with a spear, bringing a sudden flow of blood and water. [35]The man who saw it has given testimony, and his testimony is true. He knows that he tells the truth, and he testifies so that you also may believe.
Acts 2 [38]Peter replied, "Repent and be baptized, every one of you, in the name of Jesus Christ for the forgiveness of your sins. And you will receive the gift of the Holy Spirit. . . ."
[41]Those who accepted his message were baptized, and about three thousand were added to their number that day.
Acts 4 [2]They were greatly disturbed because the apostles were teaching the people and proclaiming in Jesus the resurrection of the dead. . . . [4]But many who heard the message believed, and the number of men grew to about five thousand.
Acts 8 [12]But when they believed Philip as he preached the good news of the kingdom of God and the name of Jesus Christ, they were baptized, both men and women.
Acts 11 [21]The Lord's hand was with them, and a great number of people believed and turned to the Lord.
Acts 14 [1]At Iconium Paul and Barnabas went as usual into the Jewish synagogue. There they spoke so effectively that a great number of Jews and Gentiles believed.
Acts 15 [7]After much discussion, Peter got up and addressed them: "Brothers, you know that some time ago God made a choice among you that the Gentiles might hear from my lips the message of the gospel and believe."
Acts 17 [32]When they heard about the resurrection of the dead, some of them sneered, but others said, "We want to hear you again on this subject." . . . [34]A few men became followers of Paul and believed. Among them was Dionysius, a member of the Areopagus, also a woman named Damaris, and a number of others.
Acts 26 [17]"'I will rescue you from your own people and from the Gentiles. I am sending you to them [18]to open their eyes and turn them from darkness to light, and from the power of Satan to God, so that they may receive forgiveness of sins and a place among those who are sanctified by faith in me.'"
Rom 1 [5]Through him and for his name's sake, we received grace and apostleship to call people from among all the Gentiles to the obedience that comes from faith.
Rom 1 [16]I am not ashamed of the gospel, because it is the power of God for the salvation of everyone who believes: first for the Jew, then for the Gentile.
Rom 10 [8]But what does it say? "The word is near you; it is in your mouth and in your heart," that is, the word of faith we are proclaiming: [9]That if you confess with your mouth, "Jesus is Lord," and believe in your heart that God raised him from the dead, you will be saved.
Rom 10 [14]How, then, can they call on the one they have not believed in? And how can they believe in the one of whom they have not heard? And how can they hear without someone preaching to them? [15]And how can they preach unless they are sent? As it is written, "How beautiful are the feet of those who bring good news!" . . . [17]Consequently, faith comes from hearing the message, and the message is heard through the word of Christ.
Rom 16 [25]Now to him who is able to establish you by my gospel and the proclamation of Jesus Christ, according to the revelation of the mystery hidden for long ages past, [26]but now revealed and made known through the prophetic writings by the command of the eternal God, so that all nations might believe and obey him . . .
1 Cor 1 [21]For since in the wisdom of God the world through its wisdom did not know him, God was pleased through the foolishness of what was preached to save those who believe.
1 Cor 15 [1]Now, brothers, I want to remind you of the gospel I preached to you, which you received and on which you have taken your stand. [2]By this gospel you are saved, if you hold firmly to the word I preached to you. Otherwise, you have believed in vain. . . . [11]Whether, then, it was I or they, this is what we preach, and this is what you believed.
Gal 1 [23]They only heard the report: "The man who formerly persecuted us is now preaching the faith he once tried to destroy."
Eph 2 [20]built on the foundation of the apostles and prophets, with Christ Jesus himself as the chief cornerstone.
Phil 2 [17]But even if I am being poured out like a drink offering on the sacrifice and service coming from your faith, I am glad and rejoice with all of you.
Heb 13 [7]Remember your leaders, who spoke the word of God to you. Consider the outcome of their way of life and imitate their faith.

2. God's Written Word Is a Means of Saving Faith

Luke 1 [3]Therefore, since I myself have carefully investigated everything from the beginning, it seemed good also to me to write an orderly account for you, most excellent Theophilus, [4]so that you may know the certainty of the things you have been taught.
John 20 [31]But these are written that you may believe that Jesus is the Christ, the Son of God, and that by believing you may have life in his name.
Acts 17 [2]As his custom was, Paul went into the synagogue, and on three Sabbath days he reasoned with them from the Scriptures, [3]explaining and proving that the Christ had to suffer and rise from the dead. "This Jesus I am proclaiming to you is the Christ," he said. [4]Some of the Jews were persuaded and joined Paul and Silas, as did a large number of God-fearing Greeks and not a few prominent women.
Gal 3 [8]The Scripture foresaw that God would justify the Gentiles by faith, and announced the gospel in advance to Abraham: "All nations will be blessed through you."
2 Tim 3 [15]and how from infancy you have known the holy Scriptures, which are able to make you wise for salvation through faith in Christ Jesus.
1 John 5 [13]I write these things to you who believe in the name of the Son of God so that you may know that you have eternal life.
Jude [3]Dear friends, although I was very eager to write to you about the salvation we share, I felt I had to write and urge you to contend for the faith that was once for all entrusted to the saints.

E. Evidences of Saving Faith

See p. 550b, Evidences of True Faith

F. The Relation of Saving Faith to Works

1. Salvation Is by Faith Alone, Not by Works

John 5 [24]"I tell you the truth, whoever hears my word and believes him who sent me has eternal life and will not be condemned; he has crossed over from death to life."
Acts 13 [38]"Therefore, my brothers, I want you to know that

through Jesus the forgiveness of sins is proclaimed to you. 39Through him everyone who believes is justified from everything you could not be justified from by the law of Moses."
Rom 3 21But now a righteousness from God, apart from law, has been made known, to which the Law and the Prophets testify. 22This righteousness from God comes through faith in Jesus Christ to all who believe. There is no difference, 23for all have sinned and fall short of the glory of God, 24and are justified freely by his grace through the redemption that came by Christ Jesus. 25God presented him as a sacrifice of atonement, through faith in his blood. He did this to demonstrate his justice, because in his forbearance he had left the sins committed beforehand unpunished—26he did it to demonstrate his justice at the present time, so as to be just and the one who justifies those who have faith in Jesus. . . . 28For we maintain that a man is justified by faith apart from observing the law. 30. . . since there is only one God, who will justify the circumcised by faith and the uncircumcised through that same faith.
Rom 5 1Therefore, since we have been justified through faith, we have peace with God through our Lord Jesus Christ. . . .
Rom 8 3For what the law was powerless to do in that it was weakened by the sinful nature, God did by sending his own Son in the likeness of sinful man to be a sin offering. And so he condemned sin in sinful man. . . .
Rom 10 3Since they did not know the righteousness that comes from God and sought to establish their own, they did not submit to God's righteousness. 4Christ is the end of the law so that there may be righteousness for everyone who believes.
Gal 2 14When I saw that they were not acting in line with the truth of the gospel, I said to Peter in front of them all, "You are a Jew, yet you live like a Gentile and not like a Jew. How is it, then, that you force Gentiles to follow Jewish customs?

15"We who are Jews by birth and not 'Gentile sinners' 16know that a man is not justified by observing the law, but by faith in Jesus Christ. So we, too, have put our faith in Christ Jesus that we may be justified by faith in Christ and not by observing the law, because by observing the law no one will be justified.

17"If, while we seek to be justified in Christ, it becomes evident that we ourselves are sinners, does that mean that Christ promotes sin? Absolutely not! 18If I rebuild what I destroyed, I prove that I am a lawbreaker. 19For through the law I died to the law so that I might live for God. 20I have been crucified with Christ and I no longer live, but Christ lives in me. The life I live in the body, I live by faith in the Son of God, who loved me and gave himself for me. 21I do not set aside the grace of God, for if righteousness could be gained through the law, Christ died for nothing!"
Gal 3 1You foolish Galatians! Who has bewitched you? Before your very eyes Jesus Christ was clearly portrayed as crucified. 2I would like to learn just one thing from you: Did you receive the Spirit by observing the law, or by believing what you heard? 3Are you so foolish? After beginning with the Spirit, are you now trying to attain your goal by human effort? 4Have you suffered so much for nothing—if it really was for nothing? 5Does God give you his Spirit and work miracles among you because you observe the law, or because you believe what you heard?

6Consider Abraham: "He believed God, and it was credited to him as righteousness." 7Understand, then, that those who believe are children of Abraham. 8The Scripture foresaw that God would justify the Gentiles by faith, and announced the gospel in advance to Abraham: "All nations will be blessed through you." 9So those who have faith are blessed along with Abraham, the man of faith.

10All who rely on observing the law are under a curse, for it is written: "Cursed is everyone who does not continue to do everything written in the Book of the Law." 11Clearly no one is justified before God by the law, because, "The righteous will live by faith." 12The law is not based on faith; on the contrary, "The man who does these things will live by them." 13Christ redeemed us from the curse of the law by becoming a curse for us, for it is written: "Cursed is everyone who is hung on a tree." 14He redeemed us in order that the blessing given to Abraham might come to the Gentiles through Christ Jesus, so that by faith we might receive the promise of the Spirit.

15Brothers, let me take an example from everyday life. Just as no one can set aside or add to a human covenant that has been duly established, so it is in this case. 16The promises were spoken to Abraham and to his seed. The Scripture does not say "and to seeds," meaning many people, but "and to your seed," meaning one person, who is Christ. 17What I mean is this: The law, introduced 430 years later, does not set aside the covenant previously established by God and thus do away with the promise. 18For if the inheritance depends on the law, then it no longer depends on a promise; but God in his grace gave it to Abraham through a promise.

19What, then, was the purpose of the law? It was added because of transgressions until the Seed to whom the promise referred had come. The law was put into effect through angels by a mediator. 20A mediator, however, does not represent just one party; but God is one.

21Is the law, therefore, opposed to the promises of God? Absolutely not! For if a law had been given that could impart life, then righteousness would certainly have come by the law. 22But the Scripture declares that the whole world is a prisoner of sin, so that what was promised, being given through faith in Jesus Christ, might be given to those who believe.

23Before this faith came, we were held prisoners by the law, locked up until faith should be revealed. 24So the law was put in charge to lead us to Christ that we might be justified by faith. 25Now that faith has come, we are no longer under the supervision of the law.

26You are all sons of God through faith in Christ Jesus, 27for all of you who were baptized into Christ have clothed yourselves with Christ. 28There is neither Jew nor Greek, slave nor free, male nor female, for you are all one in Christ Jesus. 29If you belong to Christ, then you are Abraham's seed, and heirs according to the promise.
Gal 5 4You who are trying to be justified by law have been alienated from Christ; you have fallen away from grace. 5But by faith we eagerly await through the Spirit the righteousness for which we hope. 6For in Christ Jesus neither circumcision nor uncircumcision has any value. The only thing that counts is faith expressing itself through love.
Phil 3 8What is more, I consider everything a loss compared to the surpassing greatness of knowing Christ Jesus my Lord, for whose sake I have lost all things. I consider them rubbish, that I may gain Christ 9and be found in him, not having a righteousness of my own that comes from the law, but that which is through faith in Christ—the righteousness that comes from God and is by faith.

2. Saving Faith Results in Works

Matt 7 16"By their fruit you will recognize them. Do people pick grapes from thornbushes, or figs from thistles? 17Likewise every good tree bears good fruit, but a bad tree bears bad fruit. 18A good tree cannot bear bad fruit, and a bad tree cannot bear good fruit. 19Every tree that does not bear good fruit is cut down and thrown into the fire. 20Thus, by their fruit you will recognize them."
Matt 12 33"Make a tree good and its fruit will be good, or make a tree bad and its fruit will be bad, for a tree is recognized by its fruit."
Luke 3 8"Produce fruit in keeping with repentance. And do not begin to say to yourselves, 'We have Abraham as our father.' For I tell you that out of these stones God can raise up children for Abraham. 9The ax is already at the root of the trees, and every tree that does not produce good fruit will be cut down and thrown into the fire."
Luke 6 43"No good tree bears bad fruit, nor does a bad tree bear good fruit. 44Each tree is recognized by its own fruit. People do not pick figs from thornbushes, or grapes from briers. 45The good man brings good things out of the good stored up in his heart, and the evil man brings evil things out of the evil stored up in his heart. For out of the overflow of his heart his mouth speaks."
Rom 2 11For God does not show favoritism. . . . 13For it is not those who hear the law who are righteous in God's sight, but it is those who obey the law who will be declared righteous. . . . 16This will take place on the day when God will judge men's secrets through Jesus Christ, as my gospel declares.

Rom 3 [30]since there is only one God, who will justify the circumcised by faith and the uncircumcised through that same faith. [31]Do we, then, nullify the law by this faith? Not at all! Rather, we uphold the law.
Titus 3 [8]This is a trustworthy saying. And I want you to stress these things, so that those who have trusted in God may be careful to devote themselves to doing what is good. These things are excellent and profitable for everyone. . . . [14]Our people must learn to devote themselves to doing what is good, in order that they may provide for daily necessities and not live unproductive lives.
Heb 6 [9]Even though we speak like this, dear friends, we are confident of better things in your case—things that accompany salvation. [10]God is not unjust; he will not forget your work and the love you have shown him as you have helped his people and continue to help them. [11]We want each of you to show this same diligence to the very end, in order to make your hope sure. [12]We do not want you to become lazy, but to imitate those who through faith and patience inherit what has been promised.
James 2 [14]What good is it, my brothers, if a man claims to have faith but has no deeds? Can such faith save him? [15]Suppose a brother or sister is without clothes and daily food. [16]If one of you says to him, "Go, I wish you well; keep warm and well fed," but does nothing about his physical needs, what good is it? [17]In the same way, faith by itself, if it is not accompanied by action, is dead.

[18]But someone will say, "You have faith; I have deeds."

Show me your faith without deeds, and I will show you my faith by what I do. [19]You believe that there is one God. Good! Even the demons believe that—and shudder.

[20]You foolish man, do you want evidence that faith without deeds is useless? [21]Was not our ancestor Abraham considered righteous for what he did when he offered his son Isaac on the altar? [22]You see that his faith and his actions were working together, and his faith was made complete by what he did. [23]And the scripture was fulfilled that says, "Abraham believed God, and it was credited to him as righteousness," and he was called God's friend. [24]You see that a person is justified by what he does and not by faith alone.

[25]In the same way, was not even Rahab the prostitute considered righteous for what she did when she gave lodging to the spies and sent them off in a different direction? [26]As the body without the spirit is dead, so faith without deeds is dead.
Rev 22 [12]"Behold, I am coming soon! My reward is with me, and I will give to everyone according to what he has done. [13]I am the Alpha and the Omega, the First and the Last, the Beginning and the End.

[14]"Blessed are those who wash their robes, that they may have the right to the tree of life and may go through the gates into the city."

G. Eternal Benefits of Saving Faith

1. A Benefit of Faith Is Adoption into God's Family

John 1 [12]Yet to all who received him, to those who believed in his name, he gave the right to become children of God. . . .
Gal 3 [26]You are all sons of God through faith in Christ Jesus. . . .

2. A Benefit of Faith Is Assurance

John 6 [69]"We believe and know that you are the Holy One of God."
2 Tim 1 [12]That is why I am suffering as I am. Yet I am not ashamed, because I know whom I have believed, and am convinced that he is able to guard what I have entrusted to him for that day.
Heb 10 [22]let us draw near to God with a sincere heart in full assurance of faith, having our hearts sprinkled to cleanse us from a guilty conscience and having our bodies washed with pure water.
1 John 5 [10]Anyone who believes in the Son of God has this testimony in his heart. Anyone who does not believe God has made him out to be a liar, because he has not believed the testimony God has given about his Son. [11]And this is the testimony: God has given us eternal life, and this life is in his Son. [12]He who has the Son has life; he who does not have the Son of God does not have life.

3. A Benefit of Faith Is Confidence

1 Pet 2 [6]For in Scripture it says: "See, I lay a stone in Zion, a chosen and precious cornerstone, and the one who trusts in him will never be put to shame."

4. A Benefit of Faith Is Eternal Life

John 3 [15]". . . that everyone who believes in him may have eternal life.

[16]"For God so loved the world that he gave his one and only Son, that whoever believes in him shall not perish but have eternal life."
John 3 [36]"Whoever believes in the Son has eternal life, but whoever rejects the Son will not see life, for God's wrath remains on him."
John 6 [40]"For my Father's will is that everyone who looks to the Son and believes in him shall have eternal life, and I will raise him up at the last day."
John 6 [47]"I tell you the truth, he who believes has everlasting life."
1 John 2 [24]See that what you have heard from the beginning remains in you. If it does, you also will remain in the Son and in the Father. [25]And this is what he promised us—even eternal life.
1 John 5 [11]And this is the testimony: God has given us eternal life, and this life is in his Son. [12]He who has the Son has life; he who does not have the Son of God does not have life.

[13]I write these things to you who believe in the name of the Son of God so that you may know that you have eternal life.
Jude [21]Keep yourselves in God's love as you wait for the mercy of our Lord Jesus Christ to bring you to eternal life.

5. A Benefit of Faith Is Forgiveness of Sins

Acts 10 [43]"All the prophets testify about him that everyone who believes in him receives forgiveness of sins through his name."
Rom 3 [25]God presented him as a sacrifice of atonement, through faith in his blood. He did this to demonstrate his justice, because in his forbearance he had left the sins committed beforehand unpunished. . . .

6. A Benefit of Faith Is Inheriting God's Promises

Gal 3 [22]But the Scripture declares that the whole world is a prisoner of sin, so that what was promised, being given through faith in Jesus Christ, might be given to those who believe.
Heb 6 [12]We do not want you to become lazy, but to imitate those who through faith and patience inherit what has been promised.

7. A Benefit of Faith Is Justification

Acts 13 [39]"Through him everyone who believes is justified from everything you could not be justified from by the law of Moses."
Rom 3 [21]But now a righteousness from God, apart from law, has been made known, to which the Law and the Prophets testify. [22]This righteousness from God comes through faith in Jesus Christ to all who believe. There is no difference, [23]for all have sinned and fall short of the glory of God, [24]and are justified freely by his grace through the redemption that came by Christ Jesus. [25]God presented him as a sacrifice of atonement, through faith in his blood. He did this to demonstrate his justice, because in his forbearance he had left the sins committed beforehand unpunished—[26]he did it to demonstrate his justice at the present time, so as to be just and the one who justifies those who have faith in Jesus. . . . [28]For we maintain that a man is justified by faith apart from observing the law.

[30]. . . since there is only one God, who will justify the circumcised by faith and the uncircumcised through that same faith.
Rom 4 [5]However, to the man who does not work but trusts God who justifies the wicked, his faith is credited as righteousness.
Rom 5 [1]Therefore, since we have been justified through faith, we have peace with God through our Lord Jesus Christ. . . .
Gal 2 [16]". . . know that a man is not justified by observing the law, but by faith in Jesus Christ. So we, too, have put our faith in Christ Jesus that we may be justified by faith in Christ and not by observing the law, because by observing the law no one will be justified."
Gal 3 [8]The Scripture foresaw that God would justify the Gentiles by faith, and announced the gospel in advance to Abraham: "All nations will be blessed through you." [9]So those who have faith are blessed along with Abraham, the man of faith.

8. A Benefit of Faith Is Not Being Condemned

Ps 34 [22]The LORD redeems his servants; no one will be condemned who takes refuge in him.
John 3 [18]"Whoever believes in him is not condemned, but whoever does not believe stands condemned already because he has not believed in the name of God's one and only Son."
John 5 [24]"I tell you the truth, whoever hears my word and believes him who sent me has eternal life and will not be condemned; he has crossed over from death to life."

9. A Benefit of Faith Is Preservation

1 Pet 1 [3]Praise be to the God and Father of our Lord Jesus Christ! In his great mercy he has given us new birth into a living hope through the resurrection of Jesus Christ from the dead, [4]and into an inheritance that can never perish, spoil or fade—kept in heaven for you, [5]who through faith are shielded by God's power until the coming of the salvation that is ready to be revealed in the last time.

10. A Benefit of Faith Is Reward

2 Tim 4 [7]I have fought the good fight, I have finished the race, I have kept the faith. [8]Now there is in store for me the crown of righteousness, which the Lord, the righteous Judge, will award to me on that day—and not only to me, but also to all who have longed for his appearing.

11. A Benefit of Faith Is Righteousness from God

Rom 3 [21]But now a righteousness from God, apart from law, has been made known, to which the Law and the Prophets testify. [22]This righteousness from God comes through faith in Jesus Christ to all who believe. There is no difference. . . .

12. A Benefit of Faith Is Salvation

Ps 149 [4]For the LORD takes delight in his people; he crowns the humble with salvation.
Acts 15 [11]"No! We believe it is through the grace of our Lord Jesus that we are saved, just as they are."
Acts 16 [31]They replied, "Believe in the Lord Jesus, and you will be saved—you and your household."
Rom 10 [9]That if you confess with your mouth, "Jesus is Lord," and believe in your heart that God raised him from the dead, you will be saved.
Eph 2 [8]For it is by grace you have been saved, through faith—and this not from yourselves, it is the gift of God. . . .
2 Thess 2 [13]But we ought always to thank God for you, brothers loved by the Lord, because from the beginning God chose you to be saved through the sanctifying work of the Spirit and through belief in the truth.
2 Tim 3 [15]and how from infancy you have known the holy Scriptures, which are able to make you wise for salvation through faith in Christ Jesus.
Heb 10 [39]But we are not of those who shrink back and are destroyed, but of those who believe and are saved.
1 Pet 1 [5]who through faith are shielded by God's power until the coming of the salvation that is ready to be revealed in the last time.

13. A Benefit of Faith Is Sanctification

Acts 15 [9]"He made no distinction between us and them, for he purified their hearts by faith."
Acts 26 [18]"'. . . to open their eyes and turn them from darkness to light, and from the power of Satan to God, so that they may receive forgiveness of sins and a place among those who are sanctified by faith in me.'"

H. Present, Temporal Benefits of Saving Faith

See p. 552a, Benefits of Faith

IX Regeneration

A. The Need for Regeneration

1. Jesus Said People Need Regeneration

John 3 [3]In reply Jesus declared, "I tell you the truth, no one can see the kingdom of God unless he is born again."

[4]"How can a man be born when he is old?" Nicodemus asked. "Surely he cannot enter a second time into his mother's womb to be born!"

[5]Jesus answered, "I tell you the truth, no one can enter the kingdom of God unless he is born of water and the Spirit. [6]Flesh gives birth to flesh, but the Spirit gives birth to spirit. [7]You should not be surprised at my saying, 'You must be born again.' [8]The wind blows wherever it pleases. You hear its sound, but you cannot tell where it comes from or where it is going. So it is with everyone born of the Spirit."

2. People Are Slaves to Sin

1 Kings 8 [46]"When they sin against you—for there is no one who does not sin—and you become angry with them and give them over to the enemy, who takes them captive to his own land, far away or near . . ."
Ps 14 [3]All have turned aside, they have together become corrupt; there is no one who does good, not even one.
Ps 130 [3]If you, O LORD, kept a record of sins, O Lord, who could stand?
Ps 143 [2]Do not bring your servant into judgment, for no one living is righteous before you.
Prov 20 [9]Who can say, "I have kept my heart pure; I am clean and without sin"?
Eccles 7 [20]There is not a righteous man on earth who does what is right and never sins.
Jer 13 [23]Can the Ethiopian change his skin or the leopard its spots? Neither can you do good who are accustomed to doing evil.
Rom 3 [9]What shall we conclude then? Are we any better? Not at all! We have already made the charge that Jews and Gentiles alike are all under sin. [10]As it is written: "There is no one righteous, not even one; [11]there is no one who understands, no one who seeks God. [12]All have turned away, they have together become worthless; there is no one who does good, not even one."[13]"Their throats are open graves; their tongues practice deceit." "The poison of vipers is on their lips." [14]"Their mouths are full of cursing and bitterness." [15]"Their feet are swift to shed blood; [16]ruin and misery mark their ways, [17]and the way of peace they do not know." [18]"There is no fear of God before their eyes."

[23]. . . for all have sinned and fall short of the glory of God. . . .
Rom 11 [32]For God has bound all men over to disobedience so that he may have mercy on them all.
Gal 3 [22]But the Scripture declares that the whole world is a

prisoner of sin, so that what was promised, being given through faith in Jesus Christ, might be given to those who believe.

Eph 2 [3]All of us also lived among them at one time, gratifying the cravings of our sinful nature and following its desires and thoughts. Like the rest, we were by nature objects of wrath.

3. People Cannot Initiate Regeneration

John 3 [16]"For God so loved the world that he gave his one and only Son, that whoever believes in him shall not perish but have eternal life. [17]For God did not send his Son into the world to condemn the world, but to save the world through him. [18]Whoever believes in him is not condemned, but whoever does not believe stands condemned already because he has not believed in the name of God's one and only Son. [19]This is the verdict: Light has come into the world, but men loved darkness instead of light because their deeds were evil. [20]Everyone who does evil hates the light, and will not come into the light for fear that his deeds will be exposed. [21]But whoever lives by the truth comes into the light, so that it may be seen plainly that what he has done has been done through God."

John 6 [44]"No one can come to me unless the Father who sent me draws him, and I will raise him up at the last day."

John 6 [65]He went on to say, "This is why I told you that no one can come to me unless the Father has enabled him."

John 12 [35]Then Jesus told them, "You are going to have the light just a little while longer. Walk while you have the light, before darkness overtakes you. The man who walks in the dark does not know where he is going. [36]Put your trust in the light while you have it, so that you may become sons of light." When he had finished speaking, Jesus left and hid himself from them. . . .

[46]"I have come into the world as a light, so that no one who believes in me should stay in darkness."

Acts 16 [14]One of those listening was a woman named Lydia, a dealer in purple cloth from the city of Thyatira, who was a worshiper of God. The Lord opened her heart to respond to Paul's message.

B. The Nature of Regeneration

1. Regeneration Is an Act of God the Father

Deut 30 [6]The LORD your God will circumcise your hearts and the hearts of your descendants, so that you may love him with all your heart and with all your soul, and live.

Jer 24 [7]"'I will give them a heart to know me, that I am the LORD. They will be my people, and I will be their God, for they will return to me with all their heart.'"

Jer 31 [31]"The time is coming," declares the LORD, "when I will make a new covenant with the house of Israel and with the house of Judah. [32]It will not be like the covenant I made with their forefathers when I took them by the hand to lead them out of Egypt, because they broke my covenant, though I was a husband to them," declares the LORD. [33]"This is the covenant I will make with the house of Israel after that time," declares the LORD. "I will put my law in their minds and write it on their hearts. I will be their God, and they will be my people. [34]No longer will a man teach his neighbor, or a man his brother, saying, 'Know the LORD,' because they will all know me, from the least of them to the greatest," declares the LORD. "For I will forgive their wickedness and will remember their sins no more."

Jer 32 [39]"I will give them singleness of heart and action, so that they will always fear me for their own good and the good of their children after them. [40]I will make an everlasting covenant with them: I will never stop doing good to them, and I will inspire them to fear me, so that they will never turn away from me. [41]I will rejoice in doing them good and will assuredly plant them in this land with all my heart and soul."

Ezek 11 [19]"I will give them an undivided heart and put a new spirit in them; I will remove from them their heart of stone and give them a heart of flesh. [20]Then they will follow my decrees and be careful to keep my laws. They will be my people, and I will be their God."

Ezek 36 [25]"'I will sprinkle clean water on you, and you will be clean; I will cleanse you from all your impurities and from all your idols. [26]I will give you a new heart and put a new spirit in you; I will remove from you your heart of stone and give you a heart of flesh. [27]And I will put my Spirit in you and move you to follow my decrees and be careful to keep my laws.'"

Ezek 37 [1]The hand of the LORD was upon me, and he brought me out by the Spirit of the LORD and set me in the middle of a valley; it was full of bones. [2]He led me back and forth among them, and I saw a great many bones on the floor of the valley, bones that were very dry. [3]He asked me, "Son of man, can these bones live?"

I said, "O Sovereign LORD, you alone know."

[4]Then he said to me, "Prophesy to these bones and say to them, 'Dry bones, hear the word of the LORD! [5]This is what the Sovereign LORD says to these bones: I will make breath enter you, and you will come to life. [6]I will attach tendons to you and make flesh come upon you and cover you with skin; I will put breath in you, and you will come to life. Then you will know that I am the LORD.'"

[7]So I prophesied as I was commanded. And as I was prophesying, there was a noise, a rattling sound, and the bones came together, bone to bone. [8]I looked, and tendons and flesh appeared on them and skin covered them, but there was no breath in them.

[9]Then he said to me, "Prophesy to the breath; prophesy, son of man, and say to it, 'This is what the Sovereign LORD says: Come from the four winds, O breath, and breathe into these slain, that they may live.'" [10]So I prophesied as he commanded me, and breath entered them; they came to life and stood up on their feet—a vast army.

[11]Then he said to me: "Son of man, these bones are the whole house of Israel. They say, 'Our bones are dried up and our hope is gone; we are cut off.' [12]Therefore prophesy and say to them: 'This is what the Sovereign LORD says: O my people, I am going to open your graves and bring you up from them; I will bring you back to the land of Israel. [13]Then you, my people, will know that I am the LORD, when I open your graves and bring you up from them. [14]I will put my Spirit in you and you will live, and I will settle you in your own land. Then you will know that I the LORD have spoken, and I have done it, declares the LORD.'"

1 Pet 1 [3]Praise be to the God and Father of our Lord Jesus Christ! In his great mercy he has given us new birth into a living hope through the resurrection of Jesus Christ from the dead. . . .

2. Regeneration Is an Act of Christ the Son

John 5 [21]"For just as the Father raises the dead and gives them life, even so the Son gives life to whom he is pleased to give it."

3. Regeneration Is the Work of the Holy Spirit

John 3 [5]Jesus answered, "I tell you the truth, no one can enter the kingdom of God unless he is born of water and the Spirit. [6]Flesh gives birth to flesh, but the Spirit gives birth to spirit. [7]You should not be surprised at my saying, 'You must be born again.'"

4. Regeneration Is Effected by God's Word

1 Cor 4 [15]Even though you have ten thousand guardians in Christ, you do not have many fathers, for in Christ Jesus I became your father through the gospel.

James 1 [17]Every good and perfect gift is from above, coming down from the Father of the heavenly lights, who does not change like shifting shadows. [18]He chose to give us birth through the word of truth, that we might be a kind of firstfruits of all he created.

1 Pet 1 [23]For you have been born again, not of perishable seed, but of imperishable, through the living and enduring word of God.

5. Regeneration Is Not a Human Work

John 1 [12]Yet to all who received him, to those who believed in his name, he gave the right to become children of God—[13]children born not of natural descent, nor of human decision or a husband's will, but born of God.
Titus 3 [4]But when the kindness and love of God our Savior appeared, [5]he saved us, not because of righteous things we had done, but because of his mercy. He saved us through the washing of rebirth and renewal by the Holy Spirit, [6]whom he poured out on us generously through Jesus Christ our Savior. . . .

C. The Results of Regeneration

See p. 454a, Salvation Provides Benefits for Believers; 510b, We Are Renewed in Christ

X
Justification

A. The Source of Justification: God

Isa 45 [25]But in the LORD all the descendants of Israel will be found righteous and will exult.
Isa 50 [8]He who vindicates me is near. Who then will bring charges against me? Let us face each other! Who is my accuser? Let him confront me! [9]It is the Sovereign LORD who helps me. Who is he that will condemn me? They will all wear out like a garment; the moths will eat them up.
Rom 3 [19]Now we know that whatever the law says, it says to those who are under the law, so that every mouth may be silenced and the whole world held accountable to God. [20]Therefore no one will be declared righteous in his sight by observing the law; rather, through the law we become conscious of sin.

[21]But now a righteousness from God, apart from law, has been made known, to which the Law and the Prophets testify. [22]This righteousness from God comes through faith in Jesus Christ to all who believe. There is no difference, [23]for all have sinned and fall short of the glory of God, [24]and are justified freely by his grace through the redemption that came by Christ Jesus. [25]God presented him as a sacrifice of atonement, through faith in his blood. He did this to demonstrate his justice, because in his forbearance he had left the sins committed beforehand unpunished—[26]he did it to demonstrate his justice at the present time, so as to be just and the one who justifies those who have faith in Jesus.

[27]Where, then, is boasting? It is excluded. On what principle? On that of observing the law? No, but on that of faith. [28]For we maintain that a man is justified by faith apart from observing the law. [29]Is God the God of Jews only? Is he not the God of Gentiles too? Yes, of Gentiles too, [30]since there is only one God, who will justify the circumcised by faith and the uncircumcised through that same faith.
Rom 4 [5]However, to the man who does not work but trusts God who justifies the wicked, his faith is credited as righteousness. . . . [17]As it is written: "I have made you a father of many nations." He is our father in the sight of God, in whom he believed—the God who gives life to the dead and calls things that are not as though they were. . . . [23]The words "it was credited to him" were written not for him alone, [24]but also for us, to whom God will credit righteousness—for us who believe in him who raised Jesus our Lord from the dead. [25]He was delivered over to death for our sins and was raised to life for our justification.
Rom 8 [30]And those he predestined, he also called; those he called, he also justified; those he justified, he also glorified.

[31]What, then, shall we say in response to this? If God is for us, who can be against us? [32]He who did not spare his own Son, but gave him up for us all—how will he not also, along with him, graciously give us all things? [33]Who will bring any charge against those whom God has chosen? It is God who justifies. [34]Who is he that condemns? Christ Jesus, who died—more than that, who was raised to life—is at the right hand of God and is also interceding for us.
1 Cor 6 [11]And that is what some of you were. But you were washed, you were sanctified, you were justified in the name of the Lord Jesus Christ and by the Spirit of our God.

B. The Means of Justification

1. Justification Is Not by Human Effort

a) Justification Is Not by Circumcision

Rom 2 [25]Circumcision has value if you observe the law, but if you break the law, you have become as though you had not been circumcised. [26]If those who are not circumcised keep the law's requirements, will they not be regarded as though they were circumcised? [27]The one who is not circumcised physically and yet obeys the law will condemn you who, even though you have the written code and circumcision, are a lawbreaker.

[28]A man is not a Jew if he is only one outwardly, nor is circumcision merely outward and physical. [29]No, a man is a Jew if he is one inwardly; and circumcision is circumcision of the heart, by the Spirit, not by the written code. Such a man's praise is not from men, but from God.
Rom 3 [29]Is God the God of Jews only? Is he not the God of Gentiles too? Yes, of Gentiles too, [30]since there is only one God, who will justify the circumcised by faith and the uncircumcised through that same faith.
Rom 4 [9]Is this blessedness only for the circumcised, or also for the uncircumcised? We have been saying that Abraham's faith was credited to him as righteousness. [10]Under what circumstances was it credited? Was it after he was circumcised, or before? It was not after, but before! [11]And he received the sign of circumcision, a seal of the righteousness that he had by faith while he was still uncircumcised. So then, he is the father of all who believe but have not been circumcised, in order that righteousness might be credited to them. [12]And he is also the father of the circumcised who not only are circumcised but who also walk in the footsteps of the faith that our father Abraham had before he was circumcised.
Gal 5 [2]Mark my words! I, Paul, tell you that if you let yourselves be circumcised, Christ will be of no value to you at all. [3]Again I declare to every man who lets himself be circumcised that he is obligated to obey the whole law. . . . [6]For in Christ Jesus neither circumcision nor uncircumcision has any value. The only thing that counts is faith expressing itself through love.
Gal 6 [12]Those who want to make a good impression outwardly are trying to compel you to be circumcised. The only reason they do this is to avoid being persecuted for the cross of Christ. [13]Not even those who are circumcised obey the law, yet they want you to be circumcised that they may boast about your flesh. [14]May I never boast except in the cross of our Lord Jesus Christ, through which the world has been crucified to me, and I to the world. [15]Neither circumcision nor uncircumcision means anything; what counts is a new creation. [16]Peace and mercy to all who follow this rule, even to the Israel of God.

b) Justification Is Not by the Law

Job 9 [2]"Indeed, I know that this is true. But how can a mortal be righteous before God? [3]Though one wished to dispute with him, he could not answer him one time out of a thousand. . . . [20]Even if I were innocent, my mouth would condemn me; if I were blameless, it would pronounce me guilty."
Ps 130 [3]If you, O LORD, kept a record of sins, O Lord, who could stand?
Ps 143 [2]Do not bring your servant into judgment, for no one living is righteous before you.
Acts 13 [39]"Through him everyone who believes is justified from everything you could not be justified from by the law of Moses."
Rom 3 [10]As it is written: "There is no one righteous, not even one. . . ."

[19]Now we know that whatever the law says, it says to those who are under the law, so that every mouth may be silenced and the whole world held accountable to God. [20]Therefore no one will be declared righteous in his sight by observing the law;

rather, through the law we become conscious of sin. . . . [28]For we maintain that a man is justified by faith apart from observing the law.
Rom 4 [14]For if those who live by law are heirs, faith has no value and the promise is worthless, [15]because law brings wrath. And where there is no law there is no transgression.
Rom 8 [3]For what the law was powerless to do in that it was weakened by the sinful nature, God did by sending his own Son in the likeness of sinful man to be a sin offering. And so he condemned sin in sinful man. . . .
Gal 2 [16]". . . know that a man is not justified by observing the law, but by faith in Jesus Christ. So we, too, have put our faith in Christ Jesus that we may be justified by faith in Christ and not by observing the law, because by observing the law no one will be justified."
Gal 3 [10]All who rely on observing the law are under a curse, for it is written: "Cursed is everyone who does not continue to do everything written in the Book of the Law." [11]Clearly no one is justified before God by the law, because, "The righteous will live by faith." [12]The law is not based on faith; on the contrary, "The man who does these things will live by them."
Gal 5 [4]You who are trying to be justified by law have been alienated from Christ; you have fallen away from grace.
James 2 [10]For whoever keeps the whole law and yet stumbles at just one point is guilty of breaking all of it.

c) Justification Is Not by Works

Isa 64 [6]All of us have become like one who is unclean, and all our righteous acts are like filthy rags; we all shrivel up like a leaf, and like the wind our sins sweep us away.
Rom 4 [4]Now when a man works, his wages are not credited to him as a gift, but as an obligation. [5]However, to the man who does not work but trusts God who justifies the wicked, his faith is credited as righteousness. [6]David says the same thing when he speaks of the blessedness of the man to whom God credits righteousness apart from works: [7]"Blessed are they whose transgressions are forgiven, whose sins are covered. [8]Blessed is the man whose sin the Lord will never count against him."
Rom 9 [31]but Israel, who pursued a law of righteousness, has not attained it. [32]Why not? Because they pursued it not by faith but as if it were by works. They stumbled over the "stumbling stone."
Rom 11 [1]I ask then: Did God reject his people? By no means! I am an Israelite myself, a descendant of Abraham, from the tribe of Benjamin. [2]God did not reject his people, whom he foreknew. Don't you know what the Scripture says in the passage about Elijah—how he appealed to God against Israel: [3]"Lord, they have killed your prophets and torn down your altars; I am the only one left, and they are trying to kill me"? [4]And what was God's answer to him? "I have reserved for myself seven thousand who have not bowed the knee to Baal." [5]So too, at the present time there is a remnant chosen by grace. [6]And if by grace, then it is no longer by works; if it were, grace would no longer be grace.
Eph 2 [8]For it is by grace you have been saved, through faith—and this not from yourselves, it is the gift of God—[9]not by works, so that no one can boast.
Titus 3 [4]But when the kindness and love of God our Savior appeared, [5]he saved us, not because of righteous things we had done, but because of his mercy. He saved us through the washing of rebirth and renewal by the Holy Spirit. . . .

2. Justification Is by Faith

a) Justification Is in God

Gen 15 [6]Abram believed the Lord, and he credited it to him as righteousness.
Rom 4 [5]However, to the man who does not work but trusts God who justifies the wicked, his faith is credited as righteousness.

b) Justification Is in Christ

Isa 53 [11]After the suffering of his soul, he will see the light of life and be satisfied; by his knowledge my righteous servant will justify many, and he will bear their iniquities.
Acts 13 [38]"Therefore, my brothers, I want you to know that through Jesus the forgiveness of sins is proclaimed to you. [39]Through him everyone who believes is justified from everything you could not be justified from by the law of Moses."
Rom 3 [21]But now a righteousness from God, apart from law, has been made known, to which the Law and the Prophets testify. [22]This righteousness from God comes through faith in Jesus Christ to all who believe. There is no difference, [23]for all have sinned and fall short of the glory of God, [24]and are justified freely by his grace through the redemption that came by Christ Jesus. [25]God presented him as a sacrifice of atonement, through faith in his blood. He did this to demonstrate his justice, because in his forbearance he had left the sins committed beforehand unpunished—[26]he did it to demonstrate his justice at the present time, so as to be just and the one who justifies those who have faith in Jesus.
Rom 4 [24]but also for us, to whom God will credit righteousness—for us who believe in him who raised Jesus our Lord from the dead. [25]He was delivered over to death for our sins and was raised to life for our justification.
Rom 5 [1]Therefore, since we have been justified through faith, we have peace with God through our Lord Jesus Christ, [2]through whom we have gained access by faith into this grace in which we now stand. And we rejoice in the hope of the glory of God. . . . [9]Since we have now been justified by his blood, how much more shall we be saved from God's wrath through him! . . .

[16]Again, the gift of God is not like the result of the one man's sin: The judgment followed one sin and brought condemnation, but the gift followed many trespasses and brought justification. [17]For if, by the trespass of the one man, death reigned through that one man, how much more will those who receive God's abundant provision of grace and of the gift of righteousness reign in life through the one man, Jesus Christ.

[18]Consequently, just as the result of one trespass was condemnation for all men, so also the result of one act of righteousness was justification that brings life for all men. [19]For just as through the disobedience of the one man the many were made sinners, so also through the obedience of the one man the many will be made righteous.

[20]The law was added so that the trespass might increase. But where sin increased, grace increased all the more, [21]so that, just as sin reigned in death, so also grace might reign through righteousness to bring eternal life through Jesus Christ our Lord.
Rom 8 [1]Therefore, there is now no condemnation for those who are in Christ Jesus, [2]because through Christ Jesus the law of the Spirit of life set me free from the law of sin and death.
Rom 10 [3]Since they did not know the righteousness that comes from God and sought to establish their own, they did not submit to God's righteousness. [4]Christ is the end of the law so that there may be righteousness for everyone who believes.
1 Cor 6 [11]And that is what some of you were. But you were washed, you were sanctified, you were justified in the name of the Lord Jesus Christ and by the Spirit of our God.
1 Cor 15 [17]And if Christ has not been raised, your faith is futile; you are still in your sins.
2 Cor 1 [21]Now it is God who makes both us and you stand firm in Christ. He anointed us. . . . [24]Not that we lord it over your faith, but we work with you for your joy, because it is by faith you stand firm.
Gal 2 [16]". . . know that a man is not justified by observing the law, but by faith in Jesus Christ. So we, too, have put our faith in Christ Jesus that we may be justified by faith in Christ and not by observing the law, because by observing the law no one will be justified.

[17]"If, while we seek to be justified in Christ, it becomes evident that we ourselves are sinners, does that mean that Christ promotes sin? Absolutely not! [18]If I rebuild what I destroyed, I prove that I am a lawbreaker. [19]For through the law I died to the law so that I might live for God. [20]I have been crucified with Christ and I no longer live, but Christ lives in me. The life I live in the body, I live by faith in the Son of God, who loved me and gave himself for me. [21]I do not set aside the grace of God, for if righteousness could be gained through the law, Christ died for nothing!"
Gal 3 [8]The Scripture foresaw that God would justify the Gentiles by faith, and announced the gospel in advance to

Abraham: "All nations will be blessed through you." . . . 11Clearly no one is justified before God by the law, because, "The righteous will live by faith." 12The law is not based on faith; on the contrary, "The man who does these things will live by them." 13Christ redeemed us from the curse of the law by becoming a curse for us, for it is written: "Cursed is everyone who is hung on a tree." 14He redeemed us in order that the blessing given to Abraham might come to the Gentiles through Christ Jesus, so that by faith we might receive the promise of the Spirit. . . .

21Is the law, therefore, opposed to the promises of God? Absolutely not! For if a law had been given that could impart life, then righteousness would certainly have come by the law. 22But the Scripture declares that the whole world is a prisoner of sin, so that what was promised, being given through faith in Jesus Christ, might be given to those who believe.

23Before this faith came, we were held prisoners by the law, locked up until faith should be revealed. 24So the law was put in charge to lead us to Christ that we might be justified by faith. 25Now that faith has come, we are no longer under the supervision of the law.

Gal 5 4You who are trying to be justified by law have been alienated from Christ; you have fallen away from grace. 5But by faith we eagerly await through the Spirit the righteousness for which we hope. 6For in Christ Jesus neither circumcision nor uncircumcision has any value. The only thing that counts is faith expressing itself through love.

Phil 3 7But whatever was to my profit I now consider loss for the sake of Christ. 8What is more, I consider everything a loss compared to the surpassing greatness of knowing Christ Jesus my Lord, for whose sake I have lost all things. I consider them rubbish, that I may gain Christ 9and be found in him, not having a righteousness of my own that comes from the law, but that which is through faith in Christ—the righteousness that comes from God and is by faith. 10I want to know Christ and the power of his resurrection and the fellowship of sharing in his sufferings, becoming like him in his death. . . .

c) Justification Is by Grace

Rom 3 23for all have sinned and fall short of the glory of God, 24and are justified freely by his grace through the redemption that came by Christ Jesus.

Rom 4 16Therefore, the promise comes by faith, so that it may be by grace and may be guaranteed to all Abraham's offspring—not only to those who are of the law but also to those who are of the faith of Abraham. He is the father of us all.

Rom 5 15But the gift is not like the trespass. For if the many died by the trespass of the one man, how much more did God's grace and the gift that came by the grace of the one man, Jesus Christ, overflow to the many! 16Again, the gift of God is not like the result of the one man's sin: The judgment followed one sin and brought condemnation, but the gift followed many trespasses and brought justification. 17For if, by the trespass of the one man, death reigned through that one man, how much more will those who receive God's abundant provision of grace and of the gift of righteousness reign in life through the one man, Jesus Christ. . . .

20The law was added so that the trespass might increase. But where sin increased, grace increased all the more, 21so that, just as sin reigned in death, so also grace might reign through righteousness to bring eternal life through Jesus Christ our Lord.

Gal 2 21"I do not set aside the grace of God, for if righteousness could be gained through the law, Christ died for nothing!"

Gal 5 4You who are trying to be justified by law have been alienated from Christ; you have fallen away from grace.

Titus 3 5he saved us, not because of righteous things we had done, but because of his mercy. He saved us through the washing of rebirth and renewal by the Holy Spirit, 6whom he poured out on us generously through Jesus Christ our Savior, 7so that, having been justified by his grace, we might become heirs having the hope of eternal life.

d) Justification Is Freely Given

Isa 53 11After the suffering of his soul, he will see the light of life and be satisfied; by his knowledge my righteous servant will justify many, and he will bear their iniquities.

Rom 3 23for all have sinned and fall short of the glory of God, 24and are justified freely by his grace through the redemption that came by Christ Jesus.

e) Justification Excludes Boasting

Rom 3 26he did it to demonstrate his justice at the present time, so as to be just and the one who justifies those who have faith in Jesus.

27Where, then, is boasting? It is excluded. On what principle? On that of observing the law? No, but on that of faith.

Rom 4 2If, in fact, Abraham was justified by works, he had something to boast about—but not before God.

1 Cor 1 28He chose the lowly things of this world and the despised things—and the things that are not—to nullify the things that are, 29so that no one may boast before him. 30It is because of him that you are in Christ Jesus, who has become for us wisdom from God—that is, our righteousness, holiness and redemption. 31Therefore, as it is written: "Let him who boasts boast in the Lord."

Eph 2 8For it is by grace you have been saved, through faith—and this not from yourselves, it is the gift of God—9not by works, so that no one can boast.

C. The Results of Justification

See p. 454a, Salvation Provides Benefits for Believers

XI
Union with Christ

***See* chap. 11, Sanctification**

XII
Adoption

A. Adoption and God

1. God Is Our Father

1 Chron 22 9"'But you will have a son who will be a man of peace and rest, and I will give him rest from all his enemies on every side. His name will be Solomon, and I will grant Israel peace and quiet during his reign. 10He is the one who will build a house for my Name. He will be my son, and I will be his father. And I will establish the throne of his kingdom over Israel forever.'"

Isa 63 16But you are our Father, though Abraham does not know us or Israel acknowledge us; you, O LORD, are our Father, our Redeemer from of old is your name.

Matt 6 9"This, then, is how you should pray: 'Our Father in heaven, hallowed be your name. . . .'"

Matt 23 9"And do not call anyone on earth 'father,' for you have one Father, and he is in heaven."

John 20 17Jesus said, "Do not hold on to me, for I have not yet returned to the Father. Go instead to my brothers and tell them, 'I am returning to my Father and your Father, to my God and your God.'"

Rom 8 15For you did not receive a spirit that makes you a slave again to fear, but you received the Spirit of sonship. And by him we cry, "*Abba*, Father."

Gal 4 6Because you are sons, God sent the Spirit of his Son into our hearts, the Spirit who calls out, "*Abba*, Father."

Eph 3 14For this reason I kneel before the Father, 15from whom his whole family in heaven and on earth derives its name.

Heb 12 9Moreover, we have all had human fathers who disciplined us and we respected them for it. How much more should we submit to the Father of our spirits and live!

2. We Are Preserved and Disciplined by God

Deut 8 [5]Know then in your heart that as a man disciplines his son, so the LORD your God disciplines you.
2 Sam 7 [14]"'I will be his father, and he will be my son. When he does wrong, I will punish him with the rod of men, with floggings inflicted by men.'"
Prov 3 [11]My son, do not despise the LORD's discipline and do not resent his rebuke, [12]because the LORD disciplines those he loves, as a father the son he delights in.
Prov 14 [26]He who fears the LORD has a secure fortress, and for his children it will be a refuge.
Heb 12 [5]And you have forgotten that word of encouragement that addresses you as sons: "My son, do not make light of the Lord's discipline, and do not lose heart when he rebukes you, [6]because the Lord disciplines those he loves, and he punishes everyone he accepts as a son."

[7]Endure hardship as discipline; God is treating you as sons. For what son is not disciplined by his father? [8]If you are not disciplined (and everyone undergoes discipline), then you are illegitimate children and not true sons. [9]Moreover, we have all had human fathers who disciplined us and we respected them for it. How much more should we submit to the Father of our spirits and live! [10]Our fathers disciplined us for a little while as they thought best; but God disciplines us for our good, that we may share in his holiness. [11]No discipline seems pleasant at the time, but painful. Later on, however, it produces a harvest of righteousness and peace for those who have been trained by it.

3. We Were Chosen by God in Eternity Past

Rom 8 [29]For those God foreknew he also predestined to be conformed to the likeness of his Son, that he might be the firstborn among many brothers.
Eph 1 [4]For he chose us in him before the creation of the world to be holy and blameless in his sight. In love [5]he predestined us to be adopted as his sons through Jesus Christ, in accordance with his pleasure and will. . . .

B. Adoption and Christ

1. Christ Is Our Brother

John 20 [17]Jesus said, "Do not hold on to me, for I have not yet returned to the Father. Go instead to my brothers and tell them, 'I am returning to my Father and your Father, to my God and your God.'"
Rom 8 [29]For those God foreknew he also predestined to be conformed to the likeness of his Son, that he might be the firstborn among many brothers.
Heb 2 [11]Both the one who makes men holy and those who are made holy are of the same family. So Jesus is not ashamed to call them brothers. [12]He says, "I will declare your name to my brothers; in the presence of the congregation I will sing your praises."

2. We Are Heirs of God and Co-Heirs with Christ

Rom 8 [16]The Spirit himself testifies with our spirit that we are God's children. [17]Now if we are children, then we are heirs—heirs of God and co-heirs with Christ, if indeed we share in his sufferings in order that we may also share in his glory.
Gal 3 [29]If you belong to Christ, then you are Abraham's seed, and heirs according to the promise.
Gal 4 [7]So you are no longer a slave, but a son; and since you are a son, God has made you also an heir.
Eph 3 [6]This mystery is that through the gospel the Gentiles are heirs together with Israel, members together of one body, and sharers together in the promise in Christ Jesus.

3. We Are Redeemed by Christ

John 11 [51]He did not say this on his own, but as high priest that year he prophesized that Jesus would die for the Jewish nation, [52]and not only for that nation but also for the scattered children of God, to bring them together and make them one.
Gal 4 [4]But when the time had fully come, God sent his Son, born of a woman, born under law, [5]to redeem those under law, that we might receive the full rights of sons.
Eph 1 [5]he predestined us to be adopted as his sons through Jesus Christ, in accordance with his pleasure and will. . . .
Heb 2 [9]But we see Jesus, who was made a little lower than the angels, now crowned with glory and honor because he suffered death, so that by the grace of God he might taste death for everyone. [10]In bringing many sons to glory, it was fitting that God, for whom and through whom everything exists, should make the author of their salvation perfect through suffering.

C. Adoption and the Holy Spirit

1. We Are Given the Spirit

Rom 8 [15]For you did not receive a spirit that makes you a slave again to fear, but you received the Spirit of sonship. And by him we cry, "*Abba,* Father."
Gal 4 [6]Because you are sons, God sent the Spirit of his Son into our hearts, the Spirit who calls out, "*Abba,* Father."
Eph 1 [11]In him we were also chosen, having been predestined according to the plan of him who works out everything in conformity with the purpose of his will, [12]in order that we, who were the first to hope in Christ, might be for the praise of his glory. [13]And you also were included in Christ when you heard the word of truth, the gospel of your salvation. Having believed, you were marked in him with a seal, the promised Holy Spirit, [14]who is a deposit guaranteeing our inheritance until the redemption of those who are God's possession—to the praise of his glory.

2. We Are Led by the Spirit

Rom 8 [14]because those who are led by the Spirit of God are sons of God.

D. The Believer as God's Child

1. We Are God's Children

Isa 43 [6]"I will say to the north, 'Give them up!' and to the south, 'Do not hold them back.' Bring my sons from afar and my daughters from the ends of the earth—[7]everyone who is called by my name, whom I created for my glory, whom I formed and made."
Isa 63 [8]He said, "Surely they are my people, sons who will not be false to me"; and so he became their Savior.
Rom 8 [14]because those who are led by the Spirit of God are sons of God. [15]For you did not receive a spirit that makes you a slave again to fear, but you received the Spirit of sonship. And by him we cry, "*Abba,* Father." [16]The Spirit himself testifies with our spirit that we are God's children.
2 Cor 6 [17]"Therefore come out from them and be separate, says the Lord. Touch no unclean thing, and I will receive you." [18]"I will be a Father to you, and you will be my sons and daughters, says the Lord Almighty."
Gal 3 [26]You are all sons of God through faith in Christ Jesus, [27]for all of you who were baptized into Christ have clothed yourselves with Christ. [28]There is neither Jew nor Greek, slave nor free, male nor female, for you are all one in Christ Jesus. [29]If you belong to Christ, then you are Abraham's seed, and heirs according to the promise.
Gal 4 [4]But when the time had fully come, God sent his Son, born of a woman, born under law, [5]to redeem those under law, that we might receive the full rights of sons. [6]Because you are sons, God sent the Spirit of his Son into our hearts, the Spirit who calls out, "*Abba,* Father." [7]So you are no longer a slave, but a son; and since you are a son, God has made you also an heir.
Eph 2 [19]Consequently, you are no longer foreigners and aliens, but fellow citizens with God's people and members of God's household, [20]built on the foundation of the apostles and prophets, with Christ Jesus himself as the chief cornerstone.
Eph 5 [1]Be imitators of God, therefore, as dearly loved children. . . .

1 Pet 1 [14]As obedient children, do not conform to the evil desires you had when you lived in ignorance.
1 John 3 [1]How great is the love the Father has lavished on us, that we should be called children of God! And that is what we are! The reason the world does not know us is that it did not know him.

2. Our Adoption Is Realized by Faith in Christ

John 1 [12]Yet to all who received him, to those who believed in his name, he gave the right to become children of God—[13]children born not of natural descent, nor of human decision or a husband's will, but born of God.
Rom 4 [16]Therefore, the promise comes by faith, so that it may be by grace and may be guaranteed to all Abraham's offspring—not only to those who are of the law but also to those who are of the faith of Abraham. He is the father of us all. [17]As it is written: "I have made you a father of many nations." He is our father in the sight of God, in whom he believed—the God who gives life to the dead and calls things that are not as though they were.
Gal 3 [7]Understand, then, that those who believe are children of Abraham. . . .
[26]You are all sons of God through faith in Christ Jesus. . . .

3. Our Adoption Is Finalized at Christ's Return

Rom 8 [19]The creation waits in eager expectation for the sons of God to be revealed. . . . [23]Not only so, but we ourselves, who have the firstfruits of the Spirit, groan inwardly as we wait eagerly for our adoption as sons, the redemption of our bodies.
Phil 3 [20]But our citizenship is in heaven. And we eagerly await a Savior from there, the Lord Jesus Christ, [21]who, by the power that enables him to bring everything under his control, will transform our lowly bodies so that they will be like his glorious body.

E. Exhortations to God's Children

1. We Are to Be Peacemakers

Matt 5 [9]"Blessed are the peacemakers, for they will be called sons of God."

2. We Are to Bear Witness of God

Matt 5 [44]"But I tell you: Love your enemies and pray for those who persecute you, [45]that you may be sons of your Father in heaven. He causes his sun to rise on the evil and the good, and sends rain on the righteous and the unrighteous. . . . [48]Be perfect, therefore, as your heavenly Father is perfect."
Luke 6 [35]"But love your enemies, do good to them, and lend to them without expecting to get anything back. Then your reward will be great, and you will be sons of the Most High, because he is kind to the ungrateful and wicked."
Eph 5 [1]Be imitators of God, therefore, as dearly loved children [2]and live a life of love, just as Christ loved us and gave himself up for us as a fragrant offering and sacrifice to God.

3. We Are to Live Holy Lives before God

2 Cor 6 [17]"Therefore come out from them and be separate, says the Lord. Touch no unclean thing, and I will receive you." [18]"I will be a Father to you, and you will be my sons and daughters, says the Lord Almighty."
2 Cor 7 [1]Since we have these promises, dear friends, let us purify ourselves from everything that contaminates body and spirit, perfecting holiness out of reverence for God.
Phil 2 [14]Do everything without complaining or arguing, [15]so that you may become blameless and pure, children of God without fault in a crooked and depraved generation, in which you shine like stars in the universe. . . .
1 John 3 [10]This is how we know who the children of God are and who the children of the devil are: Anyone who does not do what is right is not a child of God; nor is anyone who does not love his brother.
Rev 21 [7]"He who overcomes will inherit all this, and I will be his God and he will be my son."

4. We Are to Obey God

Deut 26 [18]And the Lord has declared this day that you are his people, his treasured possession as he promised, and that you are to keep all his commands.
Deut 27 [9]Then Moses and the priests, who are Levites, said to all Israel, "Be silent, O Israel, and listen! You have now become the people of the LORD your God. [10]Obey the LORD your God and follow his commands and decrees that I give you today."
Jer 3 [19]"I myself said, "'How gladly would I treat you like sons and give you a desirable land, the most beautiful inheritance of any nation.' I thought you would call me 'Father' and not turn away from following me."

5. We Are to Worship God

Exod 4 [22]"Then say to Pharaoh, 'This is what the LORD says: Israel is my firstborn son, [23]and I told you, "Let my son go, so he may worship me." But you refused to let him go; so I will kill your firstborn son.'"
John 4 [23]"Yet a time is coming and has now come when the true worshipers will worship the Father in spirit and truth, for they are the kind of worshipers the Father seeks. [24]God is spirit, and his worshipers must worship in spirit and in truth."
Rom 12 [1]Therefore, I urge you, brothers, in view of God's mercy, to offer your bodies as living sacrifices, holy and pleasing to God—this is your spiritual act of worship.
Phil 3 [3]For it is we who are the circumcision, we who worship by the Spirit of God, who glory in Christ Jesus, and who put no confidence in the flesh. . . .
Rev 14 [7]He said in a loud voice, "Fear God and give him glory, because the hour of his judgment has come. Worship him who made the heavens, the earth, the sea and the springs of water."

XIII Glorification

See **Eternal Life**

XIV Bodily Resurrection

See **p. 754b, The Resurrection of the Dead**

XV Eternal Life

A. The Nature of Eternal Life

1. Eternal Life Is the Believer's Eternal Dwelling

2 Cor 5 [1]Now we know that if the earthly tent we live in is destroyed, we have a building from God, an eternal house in heaven, not built by human hands.
Phil 3 [20]But our citizenship is in heaven. And we eagerly await a Savior from there, the Lord Jesus Christ. . . .
Col 3 [1]Since, then, you have been raised with Christ, set your hearts on things above, where Christ is seated at the right hand of God. [2]Set your minds on things above, not on earthly things. [3]For you died, and your life is now hidden with Christ in God.

[4]When Christ, who is your life, appears, then you also will appear with him in glory.
Heb 12 [22]But you have come to Mount Zion, to the heavenly Jerusalem, the city of the living God. You have come to thousands upon thousands of angels in joyful assembly, [23]to the church of the firstborn, whose names are written in heaven. You have come to God, the judge of all men, to the spirits of righteous men made perfect, [24]to Jesus the mediator of a new covenant, and to the sprinkled blood that speaks a better word than the blood of Abel.

2. Eternal Life Is the Believer's Hope

Acts 2 [26]"'Therefore my heart is glad and my tongue rejoices; my body also will live in hope, [27]because you will not abandon me to the grave, nor will you let your Holy One see decay.'"
Rom 8 [23]Not only so, but we ourselves, who have the firstfruits of the Spirit, groan inwardly as we wait eagerly for our adoption as sons, the redemption of our bodies. [24]For in this hope we were saved. But hope that is seen is no hope at all. Who hopes for what he already has? [25]But if we hope for what we do not yet have, we wait for it patiently.
Gal 5 [5]But by faith we eagerly await through the Spirit the righteousness for which we hope.
Gal 6 [8]The one who sows to please his sinful nature, from that nature will reap destruction; the one who sows to please the Spirit, from the Spirit will reap eternal life. [9]Let us not become weary in doing good, for at the proper time we will reap a harvest if we do not give up.
Eph 1 [18]I pray also that the eyes of your heart may be enlightened in order that you may know the hope to which he has called you, the riches of his glorious inheritance in the saints. . . .
Col 1 [27]To them God has chosen to make known among the Gentiles the glorious riches of this mystery, which is Christ in you, the hope of glory.
2 Thess 2 [16]May our Lord Jesus Christ himself and God our Father, who loved us and by his grace gave us eternal encouragement and good hope . . .
Titus 1 [1]Paul, a servant of God and an apostle of Jesus Christ for the faith of God's elect and the knowledge of the truth that leads to godliness—[2]a faith and knowledge resting on the hope of eternal life, which God, who does not lie, promised before the beginning of time . . .
Titus 3 [7]so that, having been justified by his grace, we might become heirs having the hope of eternal life.
1 Pet 1 [3]Praise be to the God and Father of our Lord Jesus Christ! In his great mercy he has given us new birth into a living hope through the resurrection of Jesus Christ from the dead. . . .

3. Eternal Life Is the Believer's Inheritance

Matt 19 [28]Jesus said to them, "I tell you the truth, at the renewal of all things, when the Son of Man sits on his glorious throne, you who have followed me will also sit on twelve thrones, judging the twelve tribes of Israel. [29]And everyone who has left houses or brothers or sisters or father or mother or children or fields for my sake will receive a hundred times as much and will inherit eternal life."
Eph 1 [13]And you also were included in Christ when you heard the word of truth, the gospel of your salvation. Having believed, you were marked in him with a seal, the promised Holy Spirit, [14]who is a deposit guaranteeing our inheritance until the redemption of those who are God's possession—to the praise of his glory.
Eph 1 [18]I pray also that the eyes of your heart may be enlightened in order that you may know the hope to which he has called you, the riches of his glorious inheritance in the saints, [19]and his incomparably great power for us who believe. That power is like the working of his mighty strength. . . .
Heb 9 [15]For this reason Christ is the mediator of a new covenant, that those who are called may receive the promised eternal inheritance—now that he has died as a ransom to set them free from the sins committed under the first covenant.
1 Pet 1 [3]Praise be to the God and Father of our Lord Jesus Christ! In his great mercy he has given us new birth into a living hope through the resurrection of Jesus Christ from the dead, [4]and into an inheritance that can never perish, spoil or fade—kept in heaven for you. . . .

4. Eternal Life Is the Believer's Present Possession

John 3 [36]"Whoever believes in the Son has eternal life, but whoever rejects the Son will not see life, for God's wrath remains on him."
John 5 [21]"For just as the Father raises the dead and gives them life, even so the Son gives life to whom he is pleased to give it. . . .

[24]"I tell you the truth, whoever hears my word and believes him who sent me has eternal life and will not be condemned; he has crossed over from death to life."
John 6 [27]"Do not work for food that spoils, but for food that endures to eternal life, which the Son of Man will give you. On him God the Father has placed his seal of approval."

[28]Then they asked him, "What must we do to do the works God requires?"

[29]Jesus answered, "The work of God is this: to believe in the one he has sent."
John 10 [27]"My sheep listen to my voice; I know them, and they follow me. [28]I give them eternal life, and they shall never perish; no one can snatch them out of my hand. [29]My Father, who has given them to me, is greater than all; no one can snatch them out of my Father's hand."
John 11 [25]Jesus said to her, "I am the resurrection and the life. He who believes in me will live, even though he dies; [26]and whoever lives and believes in me will never die. Do you believe this?"
John 17 [2]"For you granted him authority over all people that he might give eternal life to all those you have given him. [3]Now this is eternal life: that they may know you, the only true God, and Jesus Christ, whom you have sent."

5. Eternal Life Is Christ

1 John 1 [2]The life appeared; we have seen it and testify to it, and we proclaim to you the eternal life, which was with the Father and has appeared to us. [3]We proclaim to you what we have seen and heard, so that you also may have fellowship with us. And our fellowship is with the Father and with his Son, Jesus Christ.
1 John 5 [11]And this is the testimony: God has given us eternal life, and this life is in his Son. [12]He who has the Son has life; he who does not have the Son of God does not have life.
1 John 5 [20]We know also that the Son of God has come and has given us understanding, so that we may know him who is true. And we are in him who is true—even in his Son Jesus Christ. He is the true God and eternal life.

6. Eternal Life Is a Gift from God

Ps 133 [3]It is as if the dew of Hermon were falling on Mount Zion. For there the LORD bestows his blessing, even life forevermore.
Rom 6 [23]For the wages of sin is death, but the gift of God is eternal life in Christ Jesus our Lord.

7. Eternal Life Is Granted through Christ

Rom 5 [21]so that, just as sin reigned in death, so also grace might reign through righteousness to bring eternal life through Jesus Christ our Lord.
Rom 6 [23]For the wages of sin is death, but the gift of God is eternal life in Christ Jesus our Lord.

8. Eternal Life Is Guaranteed by the Spirit

2 Cor 1 [21]Now it is God who makes both us and you stand firm in Christ. He anointed us, [22]set his seal of ownership on us, and put his Spirit in our hearts as a deposit, guaranteeing what is to come.

2 Cor 5 [1]Now we know that if the earthly tent we live in is destroyed, we have a building from God, an eternal house in heaven, not built by human hands. . . . [5]Now it is God who has made us for this very purpose and has given us the Spirit as a deposit, guaranteeing what is to come.
Eph 1 [13]And you also were included in Christ when you heard the word of truth, the gospel of your salvation. Having believed, you were marked in him with a seal, the promised Holy Spirit, [14]who is a deposit guaranteeing our inheritance until the redemption of those who are God's possession—to the praise of his glory.
Eph 4 [30]And do not grieve the Holy Spirit of God, with whom you were sealed for the day of redemption.

9. Eternal Life Is Knowledge of God and Christ

John 17 [3]"Now this is eternal life: that they may know you, the only true God, and Jesus Christ, whom you have sent."

10. Eternal Life Is the Mercy of Christ

Jude [21]Keep yourselves in God's love as you wait for the mercy of our Lord Jesus Christ to bring you to eternal life.

11. Eternal Life Is Promised by God

1 Tim 4 [8]For physical training is of some value, but godliness has value for all things, holding promise for both the present life and the life to come.
2 Tim 1 [1]Paul, an apostle of Christ Jesus by the will of God, according to the promise of life that is in Christ Jesus . . .
Heb 9 [15]For this reason Christ is the mediator of a new covenant, that those who are called may receive the promised eternal inheritance—now that he has died as a ransom to set them free from the sins committed under the first covenant.
2 Pet 1 [4]Through these he has given us his very great and precious promises, so that through them you may participate in the divine nature and escape the corruption in the world caused by evil desires.
1 John 2 [24]See that what you have heard from the beginning remains in you. If it does, you also will remain in the Son and in the Father. [25]And this is what he promised us—even eternal life.

12. Eternal Life Is Revealed by Christ

John 6 [68]Simon Peter answered him, "Lord, to whom shall we go? You have the words of eternal life."
2 Tim 1 [9]who has saved us and called us to a holy life—not because of anything we have done but because of his own purpose and grace. This grace was given us in Christ Jesus before the beginning of time, [10]but it has now been revealed through the appearing of our Savior, Christ Jesus, who has destroyed death and has brought life and immortality to light through the gospel.

B. The Possessors of Eternal Life

1. Those Appointed for Eternal Life Have It

Acts 13 [48]When the Gentiles heard this, they were glad and honored the word of the Lord; and all who were appointed for eternal life believed.

2. Those God Has Given Christ Have Eternal Life

John 6 [39]"And this is the will of him who sent me, that I shall lose none of all that he has given me, but raise them up at the last day."
John 10 [28]"I give them eternal life, and they shall never perish; no one can snatch them out of my hand. [29]My Father, who has given them to me, is greater than all; no one can snatch them out of my Father's hand."
John 17 [2]"For you granted him authority over all people that he might give eternal life to all those you have given him."

3. Those Who Believe in Christ Have Eternal Life

John 3 [15]". . . that everyone who believes in him may have eternal life.

[16]"For God so loved the world that he gave his one and only Son, that whoever believes in him shall not perish but have eternal life."
John 3 [36]"Whoever believes in the Son has eternal life, but whoever rejects the Son will not see life, for God's wrath remains on him."
John 6 [40]"For my Father's will is that everyone who looks to the Son and believes in him shall have eternal life, and I will raise him up at the last day."
John 6 [47]"I tell you the truth, he who believes has everlasting life."

4. Those Who Believe in God Have Eternal Life

Ps 21 [4]He asked you for life, and you gave it to him—length of days, for ever and ever.
John 5 [24]"I tell you the truth, whoever hears my word and believes him who sent me has eternal life and will not be condemned; he has crossed over from death to life."
John 12 [25]"The man who loves his life will lose it, while the man who hates his life in this world will keep it for eternal life."

5. Those Who Drink the Water of Life Have Eternal Life

John 4 [14]". . . but whoever drinks the water I give him will never thirst. Indeed, the water I give him will become in him a spring of water welling up to eternal life."

6. Those Who Eat the Bread of Life Have Eternal Life

John 6 [48]"I am the bread of life. [49]Your forefathers ate the manna in the desert, yet they died. [50]But here is the bread that comes down from heaven, which a man may eat and not die. [51]I am the living bread that came down from heaven. If anyone eats of this bread, he will live forever. This bread is my flesh, which I will give for the life of the world."

[52]Then the Jews began to argue sharply among themselves, "How can this man give us his flesh to eat?"

[53]Jesus said to them, "I tell you the truth, unless you eat the flesh of the Son of Man and drink his blood, you have no life in you. [54]Whoever eats my flesh and drinks my blood has eternal life, and I will raise him up at the last day. [55]For my flesh is real food and my blood is real drink. [56]Whoever eats my flesh and drinks my blood remains in me, and I in him. [57]Just as the living Father sent me and I live because of the Father, so the one who feeds on me will live because of me. [58]This is the bread that came down from heaven. Your forefathers ate manna and died, but he who feeds on this bread will live forever."

7. Those Who Eat from the Tree of Life Have Eternal Life

Rev 2 [7]"He who has an ear, let him hear what the Spirit says to the churches. To him who overcomes, I will give the right to eat from the tree of life, which is in the paradise of God."

C. Exhortations and Assurances concerning Eternal Life

1. Exhortations and Assurances to the Believer

a) The Believer Is Assured of Eternal Life

1 John 5 [13]I write these things to you who believe in the name of the Son of God so that you may know that you have eternal life.

b) The Believer Is Preserved unto Eternal Life

John 10 [27]"My sheep listen to my voice; I know them, and they follow me. [28]I give them eternal life, and they shall never perish; no one can snatch them out of my hand. [29]My Father, who has given them to me, is greater than all; no one can snatch them out of my Father's hand."

c) The Believer Is to Live Accordingly

Rom 2 [6]God "will give to each person according to what he has done." [7]To those who by persistence in doing good seek glory, honor and immortality, he will give eternal life.
Rom 6 [13]Do not offer the parts of your body to sin, as instruments of wickedness, but rather offer yourselves to God, as those who have been brought from death to life; and offer the parts of your body to him as instruments of righteousness.

d) The Believer Is to Seek Eternal Life

John 6 [27]"Do not work for food that spoils, but for food that endures to eternal life, which the Son of Man will give you. On him God the Father has placed his seal of approval."

e) The Believer Is to Take Hold of Eternal Life

1 Tim 6 [12]Fight the good fight of the faith. Take hold of the eternal life to which you were called when you made your good confession in the presence of many witnesses.
1 Tim 6 [19]In this way they will lay up treasure for themselves as a firm foundation for the coming age, so that they may take hold of the life that is truly life.

f) The Believer Will Be Raised to Eternal Life

Dan 12 [1]"At that time Michael, the great prince who protects your people, will arise. There will be a time of distress such as has not happened from the beginning of nations until then. But at that time your people—everyone whose name is found written in the book—will be delivered. [2]Multitudes who sleep in the dust of the earth will awake: some to everlasting life, others to shame and everlasting contempt."
John 5 [28]"Do not be amazed at this, for a time is coming when all who are in their graves will hear his voice [29]and come out—those who have done good will rise to live, and those who have done evil will rise to be condemned."

g) The Believer Will Enter into Eternal Life

Matt 25 [34]"Then the King will say to those on his right, 'Come, you who are blessed by my Father; take your inheritance, the kingdom prepared for you since the creation of the world.'"

h) The Believer Will Not Be Condemned

John 3 [18]"Whoever believes in him is not condemned, but whoever does not believe stands condemned already because he has not believed in the name of God's one and only Son."
John 3 [36]"Whoever believes in the Son has eternal life, but whoever rejects the Son will not see life, for God's wrath remains on him."
John 5 [24]"I tell you the truth, whoever hears my word and believes him who sent me has eternal life and will not be condemned; he has crossed over from death to life."

i) The Believer Will Not Perish

John 3 [16]"For God so loved the world that he gave his one and only Son, that whoever believes in him shall not perish but have eternal life."

j) The Believer Will Reign in Eternity

Dan 7 [18]"'But the saints of the Most High will receive the kingdom and will possess it forever—yes, for ever and ever.'"
Rom 5 [17]For if, by the trespass of the one man, death reigned through that one man, how much more will those who receive God's abundant provision of grace and of the gift of righteousness reign in life through the one man, Jesus Christ.

2. Exhortations to the Unbeliever

a) Eternal Life Is Not Inherited by Works

Rom 3 [9]What shall we conclude then? Are we any better? Not at all! We have already made the charge that Jews and Gentiles alike are all under sin. [10]As it is written: "There is no one righteous, not even one; [11]there is no one who understands, no one who seeks God. [12]All have turned away, they have together become worthless; there is no one who does good, not even one." [13]"Their throats are open graves; their tongues practice deceit." "The poison of vipers is on their lips." [14]"Their mouths are full of cursing and bitterness." [15]"Their feet are swift to shed blood; [16]ruin and misery mark their ways, [17]and the way of peace they do not know." [18]"There is no fear of God before their eyes."

[19]Now we know that whatever the law says, it says to those who are under the law, so that every mouth may be silenced and the whole world held accountable to God. [20]Therefore no one will be declared righteous in his sight by observing the law; rather, through the law we become conscious of sin.

b) The Unbeliever Will Be Separated from Eternal Life

Matt 25 [41]"Then he will say to those on his left, 'Depart from me, you who are cursed, into the eternal fire prepared for the devil and his angels.'"
Acts 13 [46]Then Paul and Barnabas answered them boldly: "We had to speak the word of God to you first. Since you reject it and do not consider yourselves worthy of eternal life, we now turn to the Gentiles."
1 John 3 [14]We know that we have passed from death to life, because we love our brothers. Anyone who does not love remains in death. [15]Anyone who hates his brother is a murderer, and you know that no murderer has eternal life in him.

D. The Future Blessings of Eternal Life

See p. 771a, Heaven

XVI Perseverance

A. The Assurance of Eternal Security

Ps 37 [23]If the LORD delights in a man's way, he makes his steps firm; [24]though he stumble, he will not fall, for the LORD upholds him with his hand.
Ps 138 [8]The LORD will fulfill his purpose for me; your love, O LORD, endures forever—do not abandon the works of your hands.
Jer 32 [40]"I will make an everlasting covenant with them: I will never stop doing good to them, and I will inspire them to fear me, so that they will never turn away from me."
John 5 [24]"I tell you the truth, whoever hears my word and believes him who sent me has eternal life and will not be condemned; he has crossed over from death to life."
John 6 [37]"All that the Father gives me will come to me, and whoever comes to me I will never drive away. . . . [39]And this is the will of him who sent me, that I shall lose none of all that he has given me, but raise them up at the last day. [40]For my Father's will is that everyone who looks to the Son and believes in him shall have eternal life, and I will raise him up at the last day."
John 6 [68]Simon Peter answered him, "Lord, to whom shall we go? You have the words of eternal life. [69]We believe and know that you are the Holy One of God."
John 10 [27]"My sheep listen to my voice; I know them, and they follow me. [28]I give them eternal life, and they shall never perish; no one can snatch them out of my hand. [29]My Father, who has given them to me, is greater than all; no one can snatch them out of my Father's hand. [30]I and the Father are one."
John 16 [27]"No, the Father himself loves you because you have loved me and have believed that I came from God. . . ."

[29]Then Jesus' disciples said, "Now you are speaking clearly and without figures of speech. [30]Now we can see that you know all things and that you do not even need to have anyone ask you questions. This makes us believe that you came from God."

[31]"You believe at last!" Jesus answered. [32]"But a time is

coming, and has come, when you will be scattered, each to his own home. You will leave me all alone. Yet I am not alone, for my Father is with me.

[33]"I have told you these things, so that in me you may have peace. In this world you will have trouble. But take heart! I have overcome the world."

John 17 [8]"For I gave them the words you gave me and they accepted them. They knew with certainty that I came from you, and they believed that you sent me. . . . [11]I will remain in the world no longer, but they are still in the world, and I am coming to you. Holy Father, protect them by the power of your name—the name you gave me—so that they may be one as we are one."

Acts 1 [3]After his suffering, he showed himself to these men and gave many convincing proofs that he was alive. He appeared to them over a period of forty days and spoke about the kingdom of God.

Rom 4 [9]Is this blessedness only for the circumcised, or also for the uncircumcised? We have been saying that Abraham's faith was credited to him as righteousness. . . . [20]Yet he did not waver through unbelief regarding the promise of God, but was strengthened in his faith and gave glory to God, [21]being fully persuaded that God had power to do what he had promised. [22]This is why "it was credited to him as righteousness."

Rom 5 [1]Therefore, since we have been justified through faith, we have peace with God through our Lord Jesus Christ, [2]through whom we have gained access by faith into this grace in which we now stand. And we rejoice in the hope of the glory of God. [3]Not only so, but we also rejoice in our sufferings, because we know that suffering produces perseverance; [4]perseverance, character; and character, hope. [5]And hope does not disappoint us, because God has poured out his love into our hearts by the Holy Spirit, whom he has given us.

Rom 8 [15]For you did not receive a spirit that makes you a slave again to fear, but you received the Spirit of sonship. And by him we cry, "*Abba,* Father." [16]The Spirit himself testifies with our spirit that we are God's children. [17]Now if we are children, then we are heirs—heirs of God and co-heirs with Christ, if indeed we share in his sufferings in order that we may also share in his glory. . . .

[28]And we know that in all things God works for the good of those who love him, who have been called according to his purpose. [29]For those God foreknew he also predestined to be conformed to the likeness of his Son, that he might be the firstborn among many brothers. [30]And those he predestined, he also called; those he called, he also justified; those he justified, he also glorified. . . . [33]Who will bring any charge against those whom God has chosen? It is God who justifies. [34]Who is he that condemns? Christ Jesus, who died—more than that, who was raised to life—is at the right hand of God and is also interceding for us. [35]Who shall separate us from the love of Christ? Shall trouble or hardship or persecution or famine or nakedness or danger or sword? . . . [37]No, in all these things we are more than conquerors through him who loved us. [38]For I am convinced that neither death nor life, neither angels nor demons, neither the present nor the future, nor any powers, [39]neither height nor depth, nor anything else in all creation, will be able to separate us from the love of God that is in Christ Jesus our Lord.

Rom 11 [29]for God's gifts and his call are irrevocable.

1 Cor 1 [8]He will keep you strong to the end, so that you will be blameless on the day of our Lord Jesus Christ. [9]God, who has called you into fellowship with his Son Jesus Christ our Lord, is faithful.

2 Cor 1 [21]Now it is God who makes both us and you stand firm in Christ. He anointed us, [22]set his seal of ownership on us, and put his Spirit in our hearts as a deposit, guaranteeing what is to come.

Gal 4 [6]Because you are sons, God sent the Spirit of his Son into our hearts, the Spirit who calls out, "*Abba,* Father."

Eph 1 [4]For he chose us in him before the creation of the world to be holy and blameless in his sight. In love [5]he predestined us to be adopted as his sons through Jesus Christ, in accordance with his pleasure and will. . . .

Eph 4 [30]And do not grieve the Holy Spirit of God, with whom you were sealed for the day of redemption.

Phil 1 [6]being confident of this, that he who began a good work in you will carry it on to completion until the day of Christ Jesus.

Phil 2 [12]Therefore, my dear friends, as you have always obeyed—not only in my presence, but now much more in my absence—continue to work out your salvation with fear and trembling, [13]for it is God who works in you to will and to act according to his good purpose.

Col 2 [2]My purpose is that they may be encouraged in heart and united in love, so that they may have the full riches of complete understanding, in order that they may know the mystery of God, namely, Christ. . . .

1 Thess 5 [23]May God himself, the God of peace, sanctify you through and through. May your whole spirit, soul and body be kept blameless at the coming of our Lord Jesus Christ. [24]The one who calls you is faithful and he will do it.

2 Tim 1 [12]That is why I am suffering as I am. Yet I am not ashamed, because I know whom I have believed, and am convinced that he is able to guard what I have entrusted to him for that day.

2 Tim 4 [18]The Lord will rescue me from every evil attack and will bring me safely to his heavenly kingdom. To him be glory for ever and ever. Amen.

Heb 6 [11]We want each of you to show this same diligence to the very end, in order to make your hope sure.

Heb 7 [24]but because Jesus lives forever, he has a permanent priesthood. [25]Therefore he is able to save completely those who come to God through him, because he always lives to intercede for them.

Heb 10 [14]because by one sacrifice he has made perfect forever those who are being made holy.

Heb 10 [22]let us draw near to God with a sincere heart in full assurance of faith, having our hearts sprinkled to cleanse us from a guilty conscience and having our bodies washed with pure water. [23]Let us hold unswervingly to the hope we profess, for he who promised is faithful.

Heb 11 [1]Now faith is being sure of what we hope for and certain of what we do not see.

1 Pet 1 [3]Praise be to the God and Father of our Lord Jesus Christ! In his great mercy he has given us new birth into a living hope through the resurrection of Jesus Christ from the dead, [4]and into an inheritance that can never perish, spoil or fade—kept in heaven for you, [5]who through faith are shielded by God's power until the coming of the salvation that is ready to be revealed in the last time.

1 Pet 5 [10]And the God of all grace, who called you to his eternal glory in Christ, after you have suffered a little while, will himself restore you and make you strong, firm and steadfast.

1 John 2 [1]My dear children, I write this to you so that you will not sin. But if anybody does sin, we have one who speaks to the Father in our defense—Jesus Christ, the Righteous One. [2]He is the atoning sacrifice for our sins, and not only for ours but also for the sins of the whole world.

1 John 3 [9]No one who is born of God will continue to sin, because God's seed remains in him; he cannot go on sinning, because he has been born of God. . . . [14]We know that we have passed from death to life, because we love our brothers. Anyone who does not love remains in death. . . . [18]Dear children, let us not love with words or tongue but with actions and in truth. [19]This then is how we know that we belong to the truth, and how we set our hearts at rest in his presence [20]whenever our hearts condemn us. For God is greater than our hearts, and he knows everything.

1 John 4 [13]We know that we live in him and he in us, because he has given us of his Spirit.

1 John 5 [10]Anyone who believes in the Son of God has this testimony in his heart. Anyone who does not believe God has made him out to be a liar, because he has not believed the testimony God has given about his Son. [11]And this is the testimony: God has given us eternal life, and this life is in his Son. . . .

[13]I write these things to you who believe in the name of the Son of God so that you may know that you have eternal life. . . .

[18]We know that anyone born of God does not continue to sin; the one who was born of God keeps him safe, and the evil one cannot harm him.

Jude [1]Jude, a servant of Jesus Christ and a brother of James,

To those who have been called, who are loved by God the Father and kept by Jesus Christ. . . .
Jude [24]To him who is able to keep you from falling and to present you before his glorious presence without fault and with great joy . . .

B. Exhortations to Persevere

1 Chron 16 [11]Look to the LORD and his strength; seek his face always.
Job 17 [9]"Nevertheless, the righteous will hold to their ways, and those with clean hands will grow stronger."
Ezek 18 [24]"But if a righteous man turns from his righteousness and commits sin and does the same detestable things the wicked man does, will he live? None of the righteous things he has done will be remembered. Because of the unfaithfulness he is guilty of and because of the sins he has committed, he will die."
Hos 12 [6]But you must return to your God; maintain love and justice, and wait for your God always.
Mic 6 [8]He has showed you, O man, what is good. And what does the LORD require of you? To act justly and to love mercy and to walk humbly with your God.
Matt 10 [22]"All men will hate you because of me, but he who stands firm to the end will be saved."
Mark 4 [3]"Listen! A farmer went out to sow his seed. [4]As he was scattering the seed, some fell along the path, and the birds came and ate it up. [5]Some fell on rocky places, where it did not have much soil. It sprang up quickly, because the soil was shallow. [6]But when the sun came up, the plants were scorched, and they withered because they had no root. [7]Other seed fell among thorns, which grew up and choked the plants, so that they did not bear grain. [8]Still other seed fell on good soil. It came up, grew and produced a crop, multiplying thirty, sixty, or even a hundred times."
Luke 22 [31]"Simon, Simon, Satan has asked to sift you as wheat. [32]But I have prayed for you, Simon, that your faith may not fail. And when you have turned back, strengthen your brothers."
John 8 [31]To the Jews who had believed him, Jesus said, "If you hold to my teaching, you are really my disciples. [32]Then you will know the truth, and the truth will set you free."
John 15 [4]"Remain in me, and I will remain in you. No branch can bear fruit by itself; it must remain in the vine. Neither can you bear fruit unless you remain in me.

[5]"I am the vine; you are the branches. If a man remains in me and I in him, he will bear much fruit; apart from me you can do nothing. [6]If anyone does not remain in me, he is like a branch that is thrown away and withers; such branches are picked up, thrown into the fire and burned. [7]If you remain in me and my words remain in you, ask whatever you wish, and it will be given you. [8]This is to my Father's glory, that you bear much fruit, showing yourselves to be my disciples.

[9]"As the Father has loved me, so have I loved you. Now remain in my love. [10]If you obey my commands, you will remain in my love, just as I have obeyed my Father's commands and remain in his love. . . . [14]You are my friends if you do what I command."
Acts 11 [23]When he arrived and saw the evidence of the grace of God, he was glad and encouraged them all to remain true to the Lord with all their hearts.
Acts 13 [43]When the congregation was dismissed, many of the Jews and devout converts to Judaism followed Paul and Barnabas, who talked with them and urged them to continue in the grace of God.
Acts 14 [21]They preached the good news in that city and won a large number of disciples. Then they returned to Lystra, Iconium and Antioch, [22]strengthening the disciples and encouraging them to remain true to the faith. "We must go through many hardships to enter the kingdom of God," they said.
Rom 2 [6]God "will give to each person according to what he has done." [7]To those who by persistence in doing good seek glory, honor and immortality, he will give eternal life. [8]But for those who are self-seeking and who reject the truth and follow evil, there will be wrath and anger.
1 Cor 10 [12]So, if you think you are standing firm, be careful that you don't fall! [13]No temptation has seized you except what is common to man. And God is faithful; he will not let you be tempted beyond what you can bear. But when you are tempted, he will also provide a way out so that you can stand up under it.
1 Cor 15 [1]Now, brothers, I want to remind you of the gospel I preached to you, which you received and on which you have taken your stand. [2]By this gospel you are saved, if you hold firmly to the word I preached to you. Otherwise, you have believed in vain. . . .

[58]Therefore, my dear brothers, stand firm. Let nothing move you. Always give yourselves fully to the work of the Lord, because you know that your labor in the Lord is not in vain.
1 Cor 16 [13]Be on your guard; stand firm in the faith; be men of courage; be strong.
2 Cor 13 [5]Examine yourselves to see whether you are in the faith; test yourselves. Do you not realize that Christ Jesus is in you—unless, of course, you fail the test?
Gal 5 [1]It is for freedom that Christ has set us free. Stand firm, then, and do not let yourselves be burdened again by a yoke of slavery.

[2]Mark my words! I, Paul, tell you that if you let yourselves be circumcised, Christ will be of no value to you at all. [3]Again I declare to every man who lets himself be circumcised that he is obligated to obey the whole law. [4]You who are trying to be justified by law have been alienated from Christ; you have fallen away from grace.
Gal 6 [9]Let us not become weary in doing good, for at the proper time we will reap a harvest if we do not give up.
Eph 6 [13]Therefore put on the full armor of God, so that when the day of evil comes, you may be able to stand your ground, and after you have done everything, to stand. . . . [16]In addition to all this, take up the shield of faith, with which you can extinguish all the flaming arrows of the evil one. . . . [18]And pray in the Spirit on all occasions with all kinds of prayers and requests. With this in mind, be alert and always keep on praying for all the saints.
Phil 1 [27]Whatever happens, conduct yourselves in a manner worthy of the gospel of Christ. Then, whether I come and see you or only hear about you in my absence, I will know that you stand firm in one spirit, contending as one man for the faith of the gospel. . . .
Phil 3 [12]Not that I have already obtained all this, or have already been made perfect, but I press on to take hold of that for which Christ Jesus took hold of me. [13]Brothers, I do not consider myself yet to have taken hold of it. But one thing I do: Forgetting what is behind and straining toward what is ahead, [14]I press on toward the goal to win the prize for which God has called me heavenward in Christ Jesus.

[15]All of us who are mature should take such a view of things. And if on some point you think differently, that too God will make clear to you. [16]Only let us live up to what we have already attained.
Phil 4 [1]Therefore, my brothers, you whom I love and long for, my joy and crown, that is how you should stand firm in the Lord, dear friends!
Col 1 [22]But now he has reconciled you by Christ's physical body through death to present you holy in his sight, without blemish and free from accusation—[23]if you continue in your faith, established and firm, not moved from the hope held out in the gospel. This is the gospel that you heard and that has been proclaimed to every creature under heaven, and of which I, Paul, have become a servant.
Col 2 [5]For though I am absent from you in body, I am present with you in spirit and delight to see how orderly you are and how firm your faith in Christ is.

[6]So then, just as you received Christ Jesus as Lord, continue to live in him, [7]rooted and built up in him, strengthened in the faith as you were taught, and overflowing with thankfulness.
1 Thess 5 [21]Test everything. Hold on to the good.
2 Thess 2 [15]So then, brothers, stand firm and hold to the teachings we passed on to you, whether by word of mouth or by letter.

[16]May our Lord Jesus Christ himself and God our Father, who loved us and by his grace gave us eternal encouragement

and good hope, [17]encourage your hearts and strengthen you in every good deed and word.
1 Tim 6 [11]But you, man of God, flee from all this, and pursue righteousness, godliness, faith, love, endurance and gentleness. [12]Fight the good fight of the faith. Take hold of the eternal life to which you were called when you made your good confession in the presence of many witnesses.
2 Tim 2 [12]if we endure, we will also reign with him. If we disown him, he will also disown us. . . .
2 Tim 3 [14]But as for you, continue in what you have learned and have become convinced of, because you know those from whom you learned it. . . .
2 Tim 4 [7]I have fought the good fight, I have finished the race, I have kept the faith. [8]Now there is in store for me the crown of righteousness, which the Lord, the righteous Judge, will award to me on that day—and not only to me, but also to all who have longed for his appearing.
Heb 2 [1]We must pay more careful attention, therefore, to what we have heard, so that we do not drift away.
Heb 3 [14]We have come to share in Christ if we hold firmly till the end the confidence we had at first.
Heb 4 [14]Therefore, since we have a great high priest who has gone through the heavens, Jesus the Son of God, let us hold firmly to the faith we profess.
Heb 6 [4]It is impossible for those who have once been enlightened, who have tasted the heavenly gift, who have shared in the Holy Spirit, [5]who have tasted the goodness of the word of God and the powers of the coming age, [6]if they fall away, to be brought back to repentance, because to their loss they are crucifying the Son of God all over again and subjecting him to public disgrace. . . . [11]We want each of you to show this same diligence to the very end, in order to make your hope sure. [12]We do not want you to become lazy, but to imitate those who through faith and patience inherit what has been promised.
Heb 10 [23]Let us hold unswervingly to the hope we profess, for he who promised is faithful. . . .

[35]So do not throw away your confidence; it will be richly rewarded. [36]You need to persevere so that when you have done the will of God, you will receive what he has promised.
Heb 11 [27]By faith he left Egypt, not fearing the king's anger; he persevered because he saw him who is invisible.
Heb 12 [1]Therefore, since we are surrounded by such a great cloud of witnesses, let us throw off everything that hinders and the sin that so easily entangles, and let us run with perseverance the race marked out for us. [2]Let us fix our eyes on Jesus, the author and perfecter of our faith, who for the joy set before him endured the cross, scorning its shame, and sat down at the right hand of the throne of God. [3]Consider him who endured such opposition from sinful men, so that you will not grow weary and lose heart.

[4]In your struggle against sin, you have not yet resisted to the point of shedding your blood. [5]And you have forgotten that word of encouragement that addresses you as sons: "My son, do not make light of the Lord's discipline, and do not lose heart when he rebukes you, [6]because the Lord disciplines those he loves, and he punishes everyone he accepts as a son."

[7]Endure hardship as discipline; God is treating you as sons. For what son is not disciplined by his father? [8]If you are not disciplined (and everyone undergoes discipline), then you are illegitimate children and not true sons. [9]Moreover, we have all had human fathers who disciplined us and we respected them for it. How much more should we submit to the Father of our spirits and live! [10]Our fathers disciplined us for a little while as they thought best; but God disciplines us for our good, that we may share in his holiness. [11]No discipline seems pleasant at the time, but painful. Later on, however, it produces a harvest of righteousness and peace for those who have been trained by it.

[12]Therefore, strengthen your feeble arms and weak knees. [13]"Make level paths for your feet," so that the lame may not be disabled, but rather healed.
James 1 [2]Consider it pure joy, my brothers, whenever you face trials of many kinds, [3]because you know that the testing of your faith develops perseverance. [4]Perseverance must finish its work so that you may be mature and complete, not lacking anything.
James 1 [12]Blessed is the man who perseveres under trial, because when he has stood the test, he will receive the crown of life that God has promised to those who love him.
James 5 [10]Brothers, as an example of patience in the face of suffering, take the prophets who spoke in the name of the Lord. [11]As you know, we consider blessed those who have persevered. You have heard of Job's perseverance and have seen what the Lord finally brought about. The Lord is full of compassion and mercy.
1 Pet 1 [5]who through faith are shielded by God's power until the coming of the salvation that is ready to be revealed in the last time. [6]In this you greatly rejoice, though now for a little while you may have had to suffer grief in all kinds of trials. [7]These have come so that your faith—of greater worth than gold, which perishes even though refined by fire—may be proved genuine and may result in praise, glory and honor when Jesus Christ is revealed.
2 Pet 1 [10]Therefore, my brothers, be all the more eager to make your calling and election sure. For if you do these things, you will never fall, [11]and you will receive a rich welcome into the eternal kingdom of our Lord and Savior Jesus Christ.
2 Pet 3 [17]Therefore, dear friends, since you already know this, be on your guard so that you may not be carried away by the error of lawless men and fall from your secure position.
Jude [21]Keep yourselves in God's love as you wait for the mercy of our Lord Jesus Christ to bring you to eternal life.
Rev 2 [10]"Do not be afraid of what you are about to suffer. I tell you, the devil will put some of you in prison to test you, and you will suffer persecution for ten days. Be faithful, even to the point of death, and I will give you the crown of life."
Rev 2 [17]"He who has an ear, let him hear what the Spirit says to the churches. To him who overcomes, I will give some of the hidden manna. I will also give him a white stone with a new name written on it, known only to him who receives it."
Rev 3 [5]"He who overcomes will, like them, be dressed in white. I will never blot out his name from the book of life, but will acknowledge his name before my Father and his angels."
Rev 3 [11]"I am coming soon. Hold on to what you have, so that no one will take your crown. [12]Him who overcomes I will make a pillar in the temple of my God. Never again will he leave it. I will write on him the name of my God and the name of the city of my God, the new Jerusalem, which is coming down out of heaven from my God; and I will also write on him my new name."
Rev 3 [21]"To him who overcomes, I will give the right to sit with me on my throne, just as I overcame and sat down with my Father on his throne."
Rev 14 [12]This calls for patient endurance on the part of the saints who obey God's commandments and remain faithful to Jesus.
Rev 16 [15]"Behold, I come like a thief! Blessed is he who stays awake and keeps his clothes with him, so that he may not go naked and be shamefully exposed."
Rev 21 [7]"He who overcomes will inherit all this, and I will be his God and he will be my son."
Rev 22 [11]"Let him who does wrong continue to do wrong; let him who is vile continue to be vile; let him who does right continue to do right; and let him who is holy continue to be holy."

11

Sanctification

I
God's Work in Our Sanctification

A. Sanctification and the Father

1. Sanctification as God's Will

Eph 1 4For he chose us in him before the creation of the world to be holy and blameless in his sight. In love. . .
Eph 2 10For we are God's workmanship, created in Christ Jesus to do good works, which God prepared in advance for us to do.
Phil 1 3I thank my God every time I remember you. 4In all my prayers for all of you, I always pray with joy 5because of your partnership in the gospel from the first day until now, 6being confident of this, that he who began a good work in you will carry it on to completion until the day of Christ Jesus.

7It is right for me to feel this way about all of you, since I have you in my heart; for whether I am in chains or defending and confirming the gospel, all of you share in God's grace with me.
Phil 2 13for it is God who works in you to will and to act according to his good purpose.
2 Thess 2 13But we ought always to thank God for you, brothers loved by the Lord, because from the beginning God chose you to be saved through the sanctifying work of the Spirit and through belief in the truth. 14He called you to this through our gospel, that you might share in the glory of our Lord Jesus Christ.
2 Tim 1 8So do not be ashamed to testify about our Lord, or ashamed of me his prisoner. But join with me in suffering for the gospel, by the power of God, 9who has saved us and called us to a holy life—not because of anything we have done but because of his own purpose and grace. This grace was given us in Christ Jesus before the beginning of time. . . .
1 Pet 1 1Peter, an apostle of Jesus Christ,

To God's elect, strangers in the world, scattered throughout Pontus, Galatia, Cappadocia, Asia and Bithynia, 2who have been chosen according to the foreknowledge of God the Father, through the sanctifying work of the Spirit, for obedience to Jesus Christ and sprinkling by his blood: Grace and peace be yours in abundance.

2. God's Provisions for Holy Living

a) God Blesses the Righteous

Job 10 8"Your hands shaped me and made me. Will you now turn and destroy me? 9Remember that you molded me like clay. Will you now turn me to dust again? 10Did you not pour me out like milk and curdle me like cheese, 11clothe me with skin and flesh and knit me together with bones and sinews? 12You gave me life and showed me kindness, and in your providence watched over my spirit."
Ps 5 12For surely, O LORD, you bless the righteous; you surround them with your favor as with a shield.
Ps 24 4He who has clean hands and a pure heart, who does not lift up his soul to an idol or swear by what is false. 5He will receive blessing from the LORD and vindication from God his Savior.
Ps 84 11For the LORD God is a sun and shield; the LORD bestows favor and honor; no good thing does he withhold from those whose walk is blameless.
Ps 115 12The LORD remembers us and will bless us: He will bless the house of Israel, he will bless the house of Aaron, 13he will bless those who fear the LORD—small and great alike.
Ps 147 11the LORD delights in those who fear him, who put their hope in his unfailing love.
Acts 4 33With great power the apostles continued to testify to the resurrection of the Lord Jesus, and much grace was upon them all.
2 Cor 8 1And now, brothers, we want you to know about the grace that God has given the Macedonian churches.
2 Cor 9 14And in their prayers for you their hearts will go out to you, because of the surpassing grace God has given you.

b) God Delivers from Evil

Ps 23 [1]The LORD is my shepherd, I shall not be in want. [3]. . . he restores my soul. He guides me in paths of righteousness for his name's sake. [4]Even though I walk through the valley of the shadow of death, I will fear no evil, for you are with me; your rod and your staff, they comfort me.
Ps 41 [10]But you, O LORD, have mercy on me; raise me up, that I may repay them. [11]I know that you are pleased with me, for my enemy does not triumph over me. [12]In my integrity you uphold me and set me in your presence forever.
Ps 143 [11]For your name's sake, O LORD, preserve my life; in your righteousness, bring me out of trouble. [12]In your unfailing love, silence my enemies; destroy all my foes, for I am your servant.
Prov 16 [7]When a man's ways are pleasing to the LORD, he makes even his enemies live at peace with him.
Jer 15 [20]"I will make you a wall to this people, a fortified wall of bronze; they will fight against you but will not overcome you, for I am with you to rescue and save you," declares the LORD.

c) God Equips His People for Good Works

Acts 26 [22]"But I have had God's help to this very day, and so I stand here and testify to small and great alike. I am saying nothing beyond what the prophets and Moses said would happen. . . ."
1 Cor 1 [4]I always thank God for you because of his grace given you in Christ Jesus. [5]For in him you have been enriched in every way—in all your speaking and in all your knowledge— [6]because our testimony about Christ was confirmed in you. [7]Therefore you do not lack any spiritual gift as you eagerly wait for our Lord Jesus Christ to be revealed.
2 Cor 1 [12]Now this is our boast: Our conscience testifies that we have conducted ourselves in the world, and especially in our relations with you, in the holiness and sincerity that are from God. We have done so not according to worldly wisdom but according to God's grace.
2 Cor 9 [8]And God is able to make all grace abound to you, so that in all things at all times, having all that you need, you will abound in every good work.
Titus 2 [11]For the grace of God that brings salvation has appeared to all men. [12]It teaches us to say "No" to ungodliness and worldly passions, and to live self-controlled, upright and godly lives in this present age, [13]while we wait for the blessed hope—the glorious appearing of our great God and Savior, Jesus Christ. . . .
Heb 13 [20]May the God of peace, who through the blood of the eternal covenant brought back from the dead our Lord Jesus, that great Shepherd of the sheep, [21]equip you with everything good for doing his will, and may he work in us what is pleasing to him, through Jesus Christ, to whom be glory for ever and ever. Amen.
1 Pet 4 [10]Each one should use whatever gift he has received to serve others, faithfully administering God's grace in its various forms.

d) God Protects His People

Ps 94 [16]Who will rise up for me against the wicked? Who will take a stand for me against evildoers? [17]Unless the LORD had given me help, I would soon have dwelt in the silence of death. [18]When I said, "My foot is slipping," your love, O LORD, supported me. [19]When anxiety was great within me, your consolation brought joy to my soul.
Joel 3 [16]The LORD will roar from Zion and thunder from Jerusalem; the earth and the sky will tremble. But the LORD will be a refuge for his people, a stronghold for the people of Israel.

[17]"Then you will know that I, the LORD your God, dwell in Zion, my holy hill. Jerusalem will be holy; never again will foreigners invade her."
Zeph 3 [15]The LORD has taken away your punishment, he has turned back your enemy. The LORD, the King of Israel, is with you; never again will you fear any harm.
John 17 [11]"I will remain in the world no longer, but they are still in the world, and I am coming to you. Holy Father, protect them by the power of your name—the name you gave me—so that they may be one as we are one. [12]While I was with them, I protected them and kept them safe by that name you gave me. None has been lost except the one doomed to destruction so that Scripture would be fulfilled.

[13]"I am coming to you now, but I say these things while I am still in the world, so that they may have the full measure of my joy within them. [14]I have given them your word and the world has hated them, for they are not of the world any more than I am of the world. [15]My prayer is not that you take them out of the world but that you protect them from the evil one. [16]They are not of the world, even as I am not of it. [17]Sanctify them by the truth; your word is truth. [18]As you sent me into the world, I have sent them into the world. [19]For them I sanctify myself, that they too may be truly sanctified."
Rev 3 [10]"Since you have kept my command to endure patiently, I will also keep you from the hour of trial that is going to come upon the whole world to test those who live on the earth."

e) God Strengthens His People

Ps 30 [7]O LORD, when you favored me, you made my mountain stand firm; but when you hid your face, I was dismayed.
Ps 84 [5]Blessed are those whose strength is in you, who have set their hearts on pilgrimage. [6]As they pass through the Valley of Baca, they make it a place of springs; the autumn rains also cover it with pools. [7]They go from strength to strength, till each appears before God in Zion.
Ps 138 [3]When I called, you answered me; you made me bold and stouthearted.
Isa 40 [31]but those who hope in the LORD will renew their strength. They will soar on wings like eagles; they will run and not grow weary, they will walk and not be faint.
Dan 10 [18]Again the one who looked like a man touched me and gave me strength. [19]"Do not be afraid, O man highly esteemed," he said. "Peace! Be strong now; be strong."

When he spoke to me, I was strengthened and said, "Speak, my lord, since you have given me strength."
1 Cor 1 [8]He will keep you strong to the end, so that you will be blameless on the day of our Lord Jesus Christ. [9]God, who has called you into fellowship with his Son Jesus Christ our Lord, is faithful.
1 Cor 10 [13]No temptation has seized you except what is common to man. And God is faithful; he will not let you be tempted beyond what you can bear. But when you are tempted, he will also provide a way out so that you can stand up under it.
Eph 3 [16]I pray that out of his glorious riches he may strengthen you with power through his Spirit in your inner being, [17]so that Christ may dwell in your hearts through faith. And I pray that you, being rooted and established in love, [18]may have power, together with all the saints, to grasp how wide and long and high and deep is the love of Christ, [19]and to know this love that surpasses knowledge—that you may be filled to the measure of all the fullness of God.
Eph 6 [10]Finally, be strong in the Lord and in his mighty power.
Col 1 [10]And we pray this in order that you may live a life worthy of the Lord and may please him in every way: bearing fruit in every good work, growing in the knowledge of God, [11]being strengthened with all power according to his glorious might so that you may have great endurance and patience, and joyfully [12]giving thanks to the Father, who has qualified you to share in the inheritance of the saints in the kingdom of light. [13]For he has rescued us from the dominion of darkness and brought us into the kingdom of the Son he loves, [14]in whom we have redemption, the forgiveness of sins.
1 Thess 3 [10]Night and day we pray most earnestly that we may see you again and supply what is lacking in your faith.

[11]Now may our God and Father himself and our Lord Jesus clear the way for us to come to you. [12]May the Lord make your love increase and overflow for each other and for everyone else, just as ours does for you. [13]May he strengthen your hearts so that you will be blameless and holy in the presence of our God and Father when our Lord Jesus comes with all his holy ones.

B. Sanctification and the Son

1. Our Salvation Is in Christ

1) The Veil Is Removed in Christ

2 Cor 3 [14]But their minds were made dull, for to this day the same veil remains when the old covenant is read. It has not been removed, because only in Christ is it taken away.

2) We Achieve Holiness in Christ

1 Cor 1 [30]It is because of him that you are in Christ Jesus, who has become for us wisdom from God—that is, our righteousness, holiness and redemption.

3) We Are Brought Near in Christ

Eph 2 [13]But now in Christ Jesus you who once were far away have been brought near through the blood of Christ.

4) We Are Called in Christ

1 Cor 7 [22]For he who was a slave when he was called by the Lord is the Lord's freedman; similarly, he who was a free man when he was called is Christ's slave.

5) We Are Chosen by God in Christ

Eph 1 [4]For he chose us in him before the creation of the world to be holy and blameless in his sight. In love [5]he predestined us to be adopted as his sons through Jesus Christ, in accordance with his pleasure and will. . . .

[11]In him we were also chosen, having been predestined according to the plan of him who works out everything in conformity with the purpose of his will. . . .

6) We Are Established in Christ

2 Cor 1 [21]Now it is God who makes both us and you stand firm in Christ. He anointed us. . . .

7) We Are Forgiven in Christ

Eph 1 [6]to the praise of his glorious grace, which he has freely given us in the One he loves. [7]In him we have redemption through his blood, the forgiveness of sins, in accordance with the riches of God's grace. . . .
Eph 4 [32]Be kind and compassionate to one another, forgiving each other, just as in Christ God forgave you.
Col 1 [13]For he has rescued us from the dominion of darkness and brought us into the kingdom of the Son he loves, [14]in whom we have redemption, the forgiveness of sins.

8) We Are Found in Christ

Phil 3 [8]What is more, I consider everything a loss compared to the surpassing greatness of knowing Christ Jesus my Lord, for whose sake I have lost all things. I consider them rubbish, that I may gain Christ [9]and be found in him, not having a righteousness of my own that comes from the law, but that which is through faith in Christ—the righteousness that comes from God and is by faith.

9) We Are Freed from the Law in Christ

Rom 7 [4]So, my brothers, you also died to the law through the body of Christ, that you might belong to another, to him who was raised from the dead, in order that we might bear fruit to God.
Rom 8 [2]because through Christ Jesus the law of the Spirit of life set me free from the law of sin and death.

10) We Are Given Grace in Christ

1 Cor 1 [4]I always thank God for you because of his grace given you in Christ Jesus.
Eph 1 [6]to the praise of his glorious grace, which he has freely given us in the One he loves.
2 Tim 1 [9]who has saved us and called us to a holy life—not because of anything we have done but because of his own purpose and grace. This grace was given us in Christ Jesus before the beginning of time. . . .

11) We Are Glorified in Christ

2 Thess 1 [12]We pray this so that the name of our Lord Jesus may be glorified in you, and you in him, according to the grace of our God and the Lord Jesus Christ.

12) We Are Interceded for by Christ

Rom 8 [34]Who is he that condemns? Christ Jesus, who died—more than that, who was raised to life—is at the right hand of God and is also interceding for us.

13) We Are Justified in Christ

1 Cor 6 [11]And that is what some of you were. But you were washed, you were sanctified, you were justified in the name of the Lord Jesus Christ and by the Spirit of our God.
Gal 2 [16]". . . know that a man is not justified by observing the law, but by faith in Jesus Christ. So we, too, have put our faith in Christ Jesus that we may be justified by faith in Christ and not by observing the law, because by observing the law no one will be justified.

[17]"If, while we seek to be justified in Christ, it becomes evident that we ourselves are sinners, does that mean that Christ promotes sin? Absolutely not!"

14) We Are Made Acceptable to God in Christ

1 Pet 2 [5]you also, like living stones, are being built into a spiritual house to be a holy priesthood, offering spiritual sacrifices acceptable to God through Jesus Christ.

15) We Are Made Alive to God in Christ

Rom 6 [11]In the same way, count yourselves dead to sin but alive to God in Christ Jesus.

16) We Are Made the Righteousness of God in Christ

Rom 1 [9]God, whom I serve with my whole heart in preaching the gospel of his Son, is my witness how constantly I remember you. . . . [17]For in the gospel a righteousness from God is revealed, a righteousness that is by faith from first to last, just as it is written: "The righteous will live by faith."
Rom 3 [21]But now a righteousness from God, apart from law, has been made known, to which the Law and the Prophets testify. [22]This righteousness from God comes through faith in Jesus Christ to all who believe. There is no difference. . . . [25]God presented him as a sacrifice of atonement, through faith in his blood. He did this to demonstrate his justice, because in his forbearance he had left the sins committed beforehand unpunished—[26]he did it to demonstrate his justice at the present time, so as to be just and the one who justifies those who have faith in Jesus.
Rom 5 [17]For if, by the trespass of the one man, death reigned through that one man, how much more will those who receive God's abundant provision of grace and of the gift of righteousness reign in life through the one man, Jesus Christ. . . . [19]For just as through the disobedience of the one man the many were made sinners, so also through the obedience of the one man the many will be made righteous.
Rom 10 [3]Since they did not know the righteousness that comes from God and sought to establish their own, they did not submit to God's righteousness. [4]Christ is the end of the law so that there may be righteousness for everyone who believes.
1 Cor 1 [30]It is because of him that you are in Christ Jesus, who has become for us wisdom from God—that is, our righteousness, holiness and redemption.
2 Cor 5 [21]God made him who had no sin to be sin for us, so that in him we might become the righteousness of God.
Phil 3 [9]and be found in him, not having a righteousness of my own that comes from the law, but that which is through faith in Christ—the righteousness that comes from God and is by faith.

17) We Are Predestined in Christ

Eph 1 [5]he predestined us to be adopted as his sons through Jesus Christ, in accordance with his pleasure and will. . . .
1 Thess 5 [9]For God did not appoint us to suffer wrath but to receive salvation through our Lord Jesus Christ.

18) We Are Reconciled in Christ

Rom 5 [11]Not only is this so, but we also rejoice in God through our Lord Jesus Christ, through whom we have now received reconciliation.
Eph 2 [16]and in this one body to reconcile both of them to God through the cross, by which he put to death their hostility.
Col 1 [20]and through him to reconcile to himself all things, whether things on earth or things in heaven, by making peace through his blood, shed on the cross.

[21]Once you were alienated from God and were enemies in your minds because of your evil behavior. [22]But now he has

reconciled you by Christ's physical body through death to present you holy in his sight, without blemish and free from accusation. . . .

19) We Are Redeemed in Christ

Rom 3 [23]for all have sinned and fall short of the glory of God, [24]and are justified freely by his grace through the redemption that came by Christ Jesus.
1 Cor 1 [30]It is because of him that you are in Christ Jesus, who has become for us wisdom from God—that is, our righteousness, holiness and redemption.
Eph 1 [7]In him we have redemption through his blood, the forgiveness of sins, in accordance with the riches of God's grace. . . .
Col 1 [13]For he has rescued us from the dominion of darkness and brought us into the kingdom of the Son he loves, [14]in whom we have redemption, the forgiveness of sins.

20) We Are Rescued from Sin in Christ

Rom 7 [21]So I find this law at work: When I want to do good, evil is right there with me. [22]For in my inner being I delight in God's law; [23]but I see another law at work in the members of my body, waging war against the law of my mind and making me a prisoner of the law of sin at work within my members. [24]What a wretched man I am! Who will rescue me from this body of death? [25]Thanks be to God—through Jesus Christ our Lord!

So then, I myself in my mind am a slave to God's law, but in the sinful nature a slave to the law of sin.

21) We Are Sanctified in Christ

1 Cor 1 [2]To the church of God in Corinth, to those sanctified in Christ Jesus and called to be holy, together with all those everywhere who call on the name of our Lord Jesus Christ—their Lord and ours . . .
1 Cor 6 [11]And that is what some of you were. But you were washed, you were sanctified, you were justified in the name of the Lord Jesus Christ and by the Spirit of our God.

22) We Are Saved in Christ

2 Tim 2 [10]Therefore I endure everything for the sake of the elect, that they too may obtain the salvation that is in Christ Jesus, with eternal glory.
Heb 7 [25]Therefore he is able to save completely those who come to God through him, because he always lives to intercede for them.

23) We Are Sealed in Christ

Eph 1 [13]And you also were included in Christ when you heard the word of truth, the gospel of your salvation. Having believed, you were marked in him with a seal, the promised Holy Spirit. . . .

24) We Are Seated in the Heavenlies in Christ

Eph 2 [6]And God raised us up with Christ and seated us with him in the heavenly realms in Christ Jesus. . . .

25) We Have Eternal Life in Christ

Rom 5 [21]so that, just as sin reigned in death, so also grace might reign through righteousness to bring eternal life through Jesus Christ our Lord.
Rom 6 [23]For the wages of sin is death, but the gift of God is eternal life in Christ Jesus our Lord.
1 Pet 5 [10]And the God of all grace, who called you to his eternal glory in Christ, after you have suffered a little while, will himself restore you and make you strong, firm and steadfast.

26) We Put Off the Sinful Nature in Christ

Col 2 [11]In him you were also circumcised, in the putting off of the sinful nature, not with a circumcision done by the hands of men but with the circumcision done by Christ. . . .

27) We Receive the Blessing of Abraham in Christ

Gal 3 [14]He redeemed us in order that the blessing given to Abraham might come to the Gentiles through Christ Jesus, so that by faith we might receive the promise of the Spirit.

28) We Receive Victory over Death in Christ

1 Cor 15 [56]The sting of death is sin, and the power of sin is the law. [57]But thanks be to God! He gives us the victory through our Lord Jesus Christ.
1 Thess 4 [16]For the Lord himself will come down from heaven, with a loud command, with the voice of the archangel and with the trumpet call of God, and the dead in Christ will rise first.

2. We Are Renewed in Christ

1) Our Hearts and Minds Are Guarded in Christ

Phil 4 [7]And the peace of God, which transcends all understanding, will guard your hearts and your minds in Christ Jesus.

2) We Are Able to Do All Things in Christ

Phil 4 [13]I can do everything through him who gives me strength.

3) We Are Chosen in Christ

Rom 16 [13]Greet Rufus, chosen in the Lord, and his mother, who has been a mother to me, too.

4) We Are Circumcised in Christ

Col 2 [11]In him you were also circumcised, in the putting off of the sinful nature, not with a circumcision done by the hands of men but with the circumcision done by Christ. . . .

5) We Are Created unto Good Works in Christ

Eph 2 [10]For we are God's workmanship, created in Christ Jesus to do good works, which God prepared in advance for us to do.

6) We Are Enriched in Speech and Knowledge in Christ

1 Cor 1 [5]For in him you have been enriched in every way—in all your speaking and in all your knowledge. . . .

7) We Are Faithful in Christ

Eph 1 [1]Paul, an apostle of Christ Jesus by the will of God,
To the saints in Ephesus, the faithful in Christ Jesus. . . .
Col 1 [2]To the holy and faithful brothers in Christ at Colosse: Grace and peace to you from God our Father.

8) We Are Holy in Christ

Col 1 [2]To the holy and faithful brothers in Christ at Colosse: Grace and peace to you from God our Father.

9) We Are New Creations in Christ

2 Cor 5 [17]Therefore, if anyone is in Christ, he is a new creation; the old has gone, the new has come!

10) We Are Perfect in Christ

Col 1 [28]We proclaim him, admonishing and teaching everyone with all wisdom, so that we may present everyone perfect in Christ.

11) We Are Rooted and Built Up in Christ

Col 2 [6]So then, just as you received Christ Jesus as Lord, continue to live in him, [7]rooted and built up in him, strengthened in the faith as you were taught, and overflowing with thankfulness.

12) We Are Strong in Christ

Eph 6 [10]Finally, be strong in the Lord and in his mighty power.

13) We Are Tested and Approved in Christ

Rom 16 [10]Greet Apelles, tested and approved in Christ. Greet those who belong to the household of Aristobulus.

14) We Are Transformed in Christ

2 Cor 3 [18]And we, who with unveiled faces all reflect the Lord's glory, are being transformed into his likeness with ever-increasing glory, which comes from the Lord, who is the Spirit.
Gal 4 [19]My dear children, for whom I am again in the pains of childbirth until Christ is formed in you . . .

15) We Are United with Christ

Rom 16 [7]Greet Andronicus and Junias, my relatives who have been in prison with me. They are outstanding among the apostles, and they were in Christ before I was.
Rom 16 [11]Greet Herodion, my relative.
Greet those in the household of Narcissus who are in the Lord.
1 Cor 16 [24]My love to all of you in Christ Jesus. Amen.
2 Cor 12 [2]I know a man in Christ who fourteen years ago was caught up to the third heaven. Whether it was in the body or out of the body I do not know—God knows.
Gal 1 [22]I was personally unknown to the churches of Judea that are in Christ.
Gal 5 [6]For in Christ Jesus neither circumcision nor uncircumcision has any value. The only thing that counts is faith expressing itself through love.
Phil 1 [1]Paul and Timothy, servants of Christ Jesus,
To all the saints in Christ Jesus at Philippi, together with the overseers and deacons. . . .
Philem [16]no longer as a slave, but better than a slave, as a dear brother. He is very dear to me but even dearer to you, both as a man and as a brother in the Lord.
1 John 5 [20]We know also that the Son of God has come and has given us understanding, so that we may know him who is true. And we are in him who is true—even in his Son Jesus Christ. He is the true God and eternal life.

16) We Are Weak in Christ

2 Cor 13 [4]For to be sure, he was crucified in weakness, yet he lives by God's power. Likewise, we are weak in him, yet by God's power we will live with him to serve you.

17) We Believe in Christ

Gal 3 [22]But the Scripture declares that the whole world is a prisoner of sin, so that what was promised, being given through faith in Jesus Christ, might be given to those who believe. . . .
[26]You are all sons of God through faith in Christ Jesus. . . .
Eph 1 [13]And you also were included in Christ when you heard the word of truth, the gospel of your salvation. Having believed, you were marked in him with a seal, the promised Holy Spirit. . . .
Col 1 [4]because we have heard of your faith in Christ Jesus and of the love you have for all the saints . . .
2 Tim 3 [15]and how from infancy you have known the holy Scriptures, which are able to make you wise for salvation through faith in Christ Jesus.

18) We Have Boldness and Access to God in Christ

Rom 5 [1]Therefore, since we have been justified through faith, we have peace with God through our Lord Jesus Christ, [2]through whom we have gained access by faith into this grace in which we now stand. And we rejoice in the hope of the glory of God.
Eph 2 [18]For through him we both have access to the Father by one Spirit.
Eph 3 [12]In him and through faith in him we may approach God with freedom and confidence.

19) We Have Confidence in Christ

2 Cor 3 [4]Such confidence as this is ours through Christ before God.
Gal 5 [10]I am confident in the Lord that you will take no other view. The one who is throwing you into confusion will pay the penalty, whoever he may be.
2 Thess 3 [4]We have confidence in the Lord that you are doing and will continue to do the things we command.
Philem [8]Therefore, although in Christ I could be bold and order you to do what you ought to do . . .

20) We Have Fullness in Christ

Col 2 [10]and you have been given fullness in Christ, who is the head over every power and authority.

21) We Have Hope in Christ

Eph 1 [12]in order that we, who were the first to hope in Christ, might be for the praise of his glory.

22) We Have Liberty in Christ

John 8 [36]"So if the Son sets you free, you will be free indeed."
Gal 2 [4]This matter arose because some false brothers had infiltrated our ranks to spy on the freedom we have in Christ Jesus and to make us slaves.
Gal 5 [1]It is for freedom that Christ has set us free. Stand firm, then, and do not let yourselves be burdened again by a yoke of slavery.

23) We Have Light in Christ

2 Cor 4 [6]For God, who said, "Let light shine out of darkness," made his light shine in our hearts to give us the light of the knowledge of the glory of God in the face of Christ.
Eph 5 [8]For you were once darkness, but now you are light in the Lord. Live as children of light. . . .

24) We Have Love in Christ

John 15 [9]"As the Father has loved me, so have I loved you. Now remain in my love. . . . [12]My command is this: Love each other as I have loved you. [13]Greater love has no one than this, that he lay down his life for his friends."
Gal 5 [6]For in Christ Jesus neither circumcision nor uncircumcision has any value. The only thing that counts is faith expressing itself through love.

25) We Have a New Self in Christ

Col 3 [9]Do not lie to each other, since you have taken off your old self with its practices [10]and have put on the new self, which is being renewed in knowledge in the image of its Creator.

26) We Have No Condemnation in Christ

Rom 8 [1]Therefore, there is now no condemnation for those who are in Christ Jesus. . . .

27) We Have Unity in Christ

Rom 12 [5]so in Christ we who are many form one body, and each member belongs to all the others.
Gal 3 [28]There is neither Jew nor Greek, slave nor free, male nor female, for you are all one in Christ Jesus.

3. We Are Granted Blessings in Christ

1) The Blessing of Access to God

Rom 1 [8]First, I thank my God through Jesus Christ for all of you, because your faith is being reported all over the world.
Rom 5 [1]Therefore, since we have been justified through faith, we have peace with God through our Lord Jesus Christ, [2]through whom we have gained access by faith into this grace in which we now stand. And we rejoice in the hope of the glory of God.
Eph 2 [18]For through him we both have access to the Father by one Spirit.
Eph 3 [12]In him and through faith in him we may approach God with freedom and confidence.

2) The Blessing of All Things Created

Col 1 [13]For he has rescued us from the dominion of darkness and brought us into the kingdom of the Son he loves. . . .
[15]He is the image of the invisible God, the firstborn over all creation. [16]For by him all things were created: things in heaven and on earth, visible and invisible, whether thrones or powers or rulers or authorities; all things were created by him and for him.

3) The Blessing of All Things Held Together

Col 1 [17]He is before all things, and in him all things hold together.

4) The Blessing of All Things Summed Up in Christ

Eph 1 [9]And he made known to us the mystery of his will according to his good pleasure, which he purposed in Christ, [10]to be put into effect when the times will have reached their fulfillment—to bring all things in heaven and on earth together under one head, even Christ.

5) The Blessing of All the Treasures of Wisdom and Knowledge

Col 2 [2]My purpose is that they may be encouraged in heart and united in love, so that they may have the full riches of complete understanding, in order that they may know the mystery of God, namely, Christ, [3]in whom are hidden all the treasures of wisdom and knowledge.

6) The Blessing of Apostleship

Rom 1 [5]Through him and for his name's sake, we received grace and apostleship to call people from among all the Gentiles to the obedience that comes from faith.
1 Cor 9 [2]Even though I may not be an apostle to others, surely I am to you! For you are the seal of my apostleship in the Lord.

7) The Blessing of Becoming Equipped for Service

Heb 13 [20]May the God of peace, who through the blood of the eternal covenant brought back from the dead our Lord Jesus, that great Shepherd of the sheep, [21]equip you with everything good for doing his will, and may he work in us what is pleasing to him, through Jesus Christ, to whom be glory for ever and ever. Amen.

8) The Blessing of Christ's Affection

Phil 1 [8]God can testify how I long for all of you with the affection of Christ Jesus.

9) The Blessing of Christ's Indwelling

Rom 8 [10]But if Christ is in you, your body is dead because of sin, yet your spirit is alive because of righteousness.
2 Cor 13 [5]Examine yourselves to see whether you are in the faith; test yourselves. Do you not realize that Christ Jesus is in you—unless, of course, you fail the test?
Gal 2 [20]I have been crucified with Christ and I no longer live, but Christ lives in me. The life I live in the body, I live by faith in the Son of God, who loved me and gave himself for me.
Eph 3 [16]I pray that out of his glorious riches he may strengthen you with power through his Spirit in your inner being, [17]so that Christ may dwell in your hearts through faith. And I pray that you, being rooted and established in love . . .
Col 1 [27]To them God has chosen to make known among the Gentiles the glorious riches of this mystery, which is Christ in you, the hope of glory.
Col 3 [11]Here there is no Greek or Jew, circumcised or uncircumcised, barbarian, Scythian, slave or free, but Christ is all, and is in all.

10) The Blessing of Christ's Love

Rom 8 [35]Who shall separate us from the love of Christ? Shall trouble or hardship or persecution or famine or nakedness or danger or sword? [36]As it is written: "For your sake we face death all day long; we are considered as sheep to be slaughtered."

[37]No, in all these things we are more than conquerors through him who loved us.
2 Cor 5 [14]For Christ's love compels us, because we are convinced that one died for all, and therefore all died.
Eph 3 [17]so that Christ may dwell in your hearts through faith. And I pray that you, being rooted and established in love, [18]may have power, together with all the saints, to grasp how wide and long and high and deep is the love of Christ, [19]and to know this love that surpasses knowledge—that you may be filled to the measure of all the fullness of God.

11) The Blessing of Christ's Meekness and Gentleness

2 Cor 10 [1]By the meekness and gentleness of Christ, I appeal to you—I, Paul, who am "timid" when face to face with you, but "bold" when away!

12) The Blessing of Christ's Peace

Eph 2 [13]But now in Christ Jesus you who once were far away have been brought near through the blood of Christ.

[14]For he himself is our peace, who has made the two one and has destroyed the barrier, the dividing wall of hostility. . . .
Col 3 [15]Let the peace of Christ rule in your hearts, since as members of one body you were called to peace. And be thankful.
1 Pet 5 [14]Greet one another with a kiss of love.

Peace to all of you who are in Christ.

13) The Blessing of Christ's Perseverance

1 Cor 1 [7]Therefore you do not lack any spiritual gift as you eagerly wait for our Lord Jesus Christ to be revealed. [8]He will keep you strong to the end, so that you will be blameless on the day of our Lord Jesus Christ.
2 Thess 3 [5]May the Lord direct your hearts into God's love and Christ's perseverance.

14) The Blessing of Christ's Power

1 Cor 1 [24]but to those whom God has called, both Jews and Greeks, Christ the power of God and the wisdom of God.
1 Cor 5 [4]When you are assembled in the name of our Lord Jesus and I am with you in spirit, and the power of our Lord Jesus is present . . .
2 Cor 12 [9]But he said to me, "My grace is sufficient for you, for my power is made perfect in weakness." Therefore I will boast all the more gladly about my weaknesses, so that Christ's power may rest on me.
Phil 3 [20]But our citizenship is in heaven. And we eagerly await a Savior from there, the Lord Jesus Christ, [21]who, by the power that enables him to bring everything under his control, will transform our lowly bodies so that they will be like his glorious body.
Col 1 [28]We proclaim him, admonishing and teaching everyone with all wisdom, so that we may present everyone perfect in Christ. [29]To this end I labor, struggling with all his energy, which so powerfully works in me.

15) The Blessing of Christ's Riches

Eph 2 [7]in order that in the coming ages he might show the incomparable riches of his grace, expressed in his kindness to us in Christ Jesus.
Eph 3 [8]Although I am less than the least of all God's people, this grace was given me: to preach to the Gentiles the unsearchable riches of Christ. . . .
Phil 4 [19]And my God will meet all your needs according to his glorious riches in Christ Jesus.

16) The Blessing of Christ's Truth

2 Cor 11 [10]As surely as the truth of Christ is in me, nobody in the regions of Achaia will stop this boasting of mine.
Eph 4 [21]Surely you heard of him and were taught in him in accordance with the truth that is in Jesus.

17) The Blessing of Encouragement, Comfort, Fellowship, Tenderness, and Compassion

Phil 2 [1]If you have any encouragement from being united with Christ, if any comfort from his love, if any fellowship with the Spirit, if any tenderness and compassion . . .

18) The Blessing of the Faith

1 Tim 3 [13]Those who have served well gain an excellent standing and great assurance in their faith in Christ Jesus.

19) The Blessing of Faith and Love

1 Tim 1 [14]The grace of our Lord was poured out on me abundantly, along with the faith and love that are in Christ Jesus.
2 Tim 1 [13]What you heard from me, keep as the pattern of sound teaching, with faith and love in Christ Jesus.

20) The Blessing of the Fear of Christ

2 Cor 5 [11]Since, then, we know what it is to fear the Lord, we try to persuade men. What we are is plain to God, and I hope it is also plain to your conscience.
Eph 5 [21]Submit to one another out of reverence for Christ.

21) The Blessing of the Fruit of Righteousness

Phil 1 [11]filled with the fruit of righteousness that comes through Jesus Christ—to the glory and praise of God.

22) *The Blessing of the Fullness of Christ's Favor*

Rom 15 [29]I know that when I come to you, I will come in the full measure of the blessing of Christ.

23) *The Blessing of the Fullness of the Godhead*

Eph 3 [17]so that Christ may dwell in your hearts through faith. And I pray that you, being rooted and established in love, [18]may have power, together with all the saints, to grasp how wide and long and high and deep is the love of Christ, [19]and to know this love that surpasses knowledge—that you may be filled to the measure of all the fullness of God.
Eph 4 [13]until we all reach unity in the faith and in the knowledge of the Son of God and become mature, attaining to the whole measure of the fullness of Christ.
Col 1 [19]For God was pleased to have all his fullness dwell in him, [20]and through him to reconcile to himself all things, whether things on earth or things in heaven, by making peace through his blood, shed on the cross.
Col 2 [9]For in Christ all the fullness of the Deity lives in bodily form. . . .

24) *The Blessing of Glory*

Eph 3 [21]to him be glory in the church and in Christ Jesus throughout all generations, for ever and ever! Amen.

25) *The Blessing of God Himself*

2 Cor 5 [18]All this is from God, who reconciled us to himself through Christ and gave us the ministry of reconciliation: [19]that God was reconciling the world to himself in Christ, not counting men's sins against them. And he has committed to us the message of reconciliation.

26) *The Blessing of God's Calling*

Phil 3 [14]I press on toward the goal to win the prize for which God has called me heavenward in Christ Jesus.

27) *The Blessing of God's Love*

Rom 8 [38]For I am convinced that neither death nor life, neither angels nor demons, neither the present nor the future, nor any powers, [39]neither height nor depth, nor anything else in all creation, will be able to separate us from the love of God that is in Christ Jesus our Lord.

28) *The Blessing of God's Peace*

Rom 5 [1]Therefore, since we have been justified through faith, we have peace with God through our Lord Jesus Christ. . . .
Phil 4 [7]And the peace of God, which transcends all understanding, will guard your hearts and your minds in Christ Jesus.

29) *The Blessing of God's Purpose*

Eph 1 [9]And he made known to us the mystery of his will according to his good pleasure, which he purposed in Christ. . . .
Eph 3 [10]His intent was that now, through the church, the manifold wisdom of God should be made known to the rulers and authorities in the heavenly realms, [11]according to his eternal purpose which he accomplished in Christ Jesus our Lord.

30) *The Blessing of God's Will*

1 Thess 5 [16]Be joyful always; [17]pray continually; [18]give thanks in all circumstances, for this is God's will for you in Christ Jesus.

31) *The Blessing of God's Wisdom*

1 Cor 1 [24]but to those whom God has called, both Jews and Greeks, Christ the power of God and the wisdom of God.

32) *The Blessing of God's Work*

Eph 1 [19]and his incomparably great power for us who believe. That power is like the working of his mighty strength, [20]which he exerted in Christ when he raised him from the dead and seated him at his right hand in the heavenly realms. . . .

33) *The Blessing of God's Yes*

2 Cor 1 [19]For the Son of God, Jesus Christ, who was preached among you by me and Silas and Timothy, was not "Yes" and "No," but in him it has always been "Yes." [20]For no matter how many promises God has made, they are "Yes" in Christ. And so through him the "Amen" is spoken by us to the glory of God.

34) *The Blessing of Good Things*

Philem [6]I pray that you may be active in sharing your faith, so that you will have a full understanding of every good thing we have in Christ.

35) *The Blessing of Grace*

Rom 1 [4]and who through the Spirit of holiness was declared with power to be the Son of God by his resurrection from the dead: Jesus Christ our Lord. [5]Through him and for his name's sake, we received grace and apostleship to call people from among all the Gentiles to the obedience that comes from faith.
2 Tim 2 [1]You then, my son, be strong in the grace that is in Christ Jesus.

36) *The Blessing of a New Union with Christ*

John 15 [5]"I am the vine; you are the branches. If a man remains in me and I in him, he will bear much fruit; apart from me you can do nothing."
1 Cor 3 [23]and you are of Christ, and Christ is of God.
1 Cor 15 [23]But each in his own turn: Christ, the firstfruits; then, when he comes, those who belong to him.
2 Cor 10 [7]You are looking only on the surface of things. If anyone is confident that he belongs to Christ, he should consider again that we belong to Christ just as much as he.
Gal 3 [29]If you belong to Christ, then you are Abraham's seed, and heirs according to the promise.
Gal 5 [24]Those who belong to Christ Jesus have crucified the sinful nature with its passions and desires.
Phil 2 [1]If you have any encouragement from being united with Christ, if any comfort from his love, if any fellowship with the Spirit, if any tenderness and compassion . . .

37) *The Blessing of the Promise of Life*

2 Tim 1 [1]Paul, an apostle of Christ Jesus by the will of God, according to the promise of life that is in Christ Jesus . . .

38) *The Blessing of the Reality of Religious Observance*

Col 2 [16]Therefore do not let anyone judge you by what you eat or drink, or with regard to a religious festival, a New Moon celebration or a Sabbath day. [17]These are a shadow of the things that were to come; the reality, however, is found in Christ.

39) *The Blessing of the Spirit's Indwelling*

Titus 3 [5]he saved us, not because of righteous things we had done, but because of his mercy. He saved us through the washing of rebirth and renewal by the Holy Spirit, [6]whom he poured out on us generously through Jesus Christ our Savior. . . .

40) *Spiritual Blessings*

Eph 1 [3]Praise be to the God and Father of our Lord Jesus Christ, who has blessed us in the heavenly realms with every spiritual blessing in Christ.

4. We Live Life in Christ

1) *Christ Took Hold of Us*

Phil 3 [12]Not that I have already obtained all this, or have already been made perfect, but I press on to take hold of that for which Christ Jesus took hold of me.

2) *Our Imprisonments Are in Christ*

Phil 1 [13]As a result, it has become clear throughout the whole palace guard and to everyone else that I am in chains for Christ.
Philem [23]Epaphras, my fellow prisoner in Christ Jesus, sends you greetings.

3) *We Are Benefited by a Brother in Christ*

Philem [20]I do wish, brother, that I may have some benefit from you in the Lord; refresh my heart in Christ.

4) *We Are Led in Triumph by Christ*

2 Cor 2 [14]But thanks be to God, who always leads us in triumphal procession in Christ and through us spreads everywhere the fragrance of the knowledge of him.

5) We Are Refreshed in Heart in Christ

Philem [20]I do wish, brother, that I may have some benefit from you in the Lord; refresh my heart in Christ.

6) We Are Taught in Christ

Eph 4 [21]Surely you heard of him and were taught in him in accordance with the truth that is in Jesus.

7) We Are to Be Spiritual Fathers in Christ

1 Cor 4 [15]Even though you have ten thousand guardians in Christ, you do not have many fathers, for in Christ Jesus I became your father through the gospel.

8) We Boast and Glory in Christ

Rom 15 [17]Therefore I glory in Christ Jesus in my service to God.

1 Cor 1 [31]Therefore, as it is written: "Let him who boasts boast in the Lord."

1 Cor 15 [31]I die every day—I mean that, brothers—just as surely as I glory over you in Christ Jesus our Lord.

2 Cor 10 [17]But, "Let him who boasts boast in the Lord."

Phil 3 [3]For it is we who are the circumcision, we who worship by the Spirit of God, who glory in Christ Jesus, and who put no confidence in the flesh. . . .

9) We Clothe Ourselves in Christ

Rom 13 [14]Rather, clothe yourselves with the Lord Jesus Christ, and do not think about how to gratify the desires of the sinful nature.

Gal 3 [27]for all of you who were baptized into Christ have clothed yourselves with Christ.

10) We Command and Urge Others in Christ

2 Thess 3 [12]Such people we command and urge in the Lord Jesus Christ to settle down and earn the bread they eat.

11) We Do Things Fittingly in Christ

Col 3 [18]Wives, submit to your husbands, as is fitting in the Lord. . . .

[20]Children, obey your parents in everything, for this pleases the Lord.

12) We Fall Asleep in Christ

1 Cor 15 [17]And if Christ has not been raised, your faith is futile; you are still in your sins. [18]Then those also who have fallen asleep in Christ are lost. [19]If only for this life we have hope in Christ, we are to be pitied more than all men.

[20]But Christ has indeed been raised from the dead, the firstfruits of those who have fallen asleep.

13) We Greet Others in Christ

Rom 16 [22]I, Tertius, who wrote down this letter, greet you in the Lord.

1 Cor 16 [19]The churches in the province of Asia send you greetings. Aquila and Priscilla greet you warmly in the Lord, and so does the church that meets at their house.

Phil 4 [21]Greet all the saints in Christ Jesus. The brothers who are with me send greetings.

14) We Have Charge over Others in Christ

1 Thess 5 [12]Now we ask you, brothers, to respect those who work hard among you, who are over you in the Lord and who admonish you.

15) We Have Christ's Way of Life

1 Cor 4 [17]For this reason I am sending to you Timothy, my son whom I love, who is faithful in the Lord. He will remind you of my way of life in Christ Jesus, which agrees with what I teach everywhere in every church.

16) We Have Guardians in Christ

1 Cor 4 [15]Even though you have ten thousand guardians in Christ, you do not have many fathers, for in Christ Jesus I became your father through the gospel.

17) We Have Joy in Christ

Phil 1 [26]so that through my being with you again your joy in Christ Jesus will overflow on account of me.

18) We Hope in Christ

1 Cor 15 [19]If only for this life we have hope in Christ, we are to be pitied more than all men.

Phil 2 [19]I hope in the Lord Jesus to send Timothy to you soon, that I also may be cheered when I receive news about you.

1 Thess 1 [3]We continually remember before our God and Father your work produced by faith, your labor prompted by love, and your endurance inspired by hope in our Lord Jesus Christ.

19) We Know and Are Convinced in Christ

Rom 14 [14]As one who is in the Lord Jesus, I am fully convinced that no food is unclean in itself. But if anyone regards something as unclean, then for him it is unclean.

20) We Labor in Christ

Rom 16 [3]Greet Priscilla and Aquila, my fellow workers in Christ Jesus.

Rom 16 [9]Greet Urbanus, our fellow worker in Christ, and my dear friend Stachys.

Rom 16 [12]Greet Tryphena and Tryphosa, those women who work hard in the Lord.

Greet my dear friend Persis, another woman who has worked very hard in the Lord.

1 Cor 9 [1]Am I not free? Am I not an apostle? Have I not seen Jesus our Lord? Are you not the result of my work in the Lord?

1 Cor 15 [58]Therefore, my dear brothers, stand firm. Let nothing move you. Always give yourselves fully to the work of the Lord, because you know that your labor in the Lord is not in vain.

Eph 6 [21]Tychicus, the dear brother and faithful servant in the Lord, will tell you everything, so that you also may know how I am and what I am doing.

Col 4 [7]Tychicus will tell you all the news about me. He is a dear brother, a faithful minister and fellow servant in the Lord.

21) We Live Godly Lives in Christ

2 Tim 3 [12]In fact, everyone who wants to live a godly life in Christ Jesus will be persecuted. . . .

22) We Live in Harmony in Christ

Phil 4 [2]I plead with Euodia and I plead with Syntyche to agree with each other in the Lord.

23) We Love in Christ

Rom 16 [8]Greet Ampliatus, whom I love in the Lord.

24) We Make Requests and Exhortations in Christ

1 Thess 4 [1]Finally, brothers, we instructed you how to live in order to please God, as in fact you are living. Now we ask you and urge you in the Lord Jesus to do this more and more.

25) We Marry in Christ

1 Cor 7 [39]A woman is bound to her husband as long as he lives. But if her husband dies, she is free to marry anyone she wishes, but he must belong to the Lord.

26) We Mature in Christ

Eph 4 [15]Instead, speaking the truth in love, we will in all things grow up into him who is the Head, that is, Christ.

27) We Obey Our Parents in Christ

Eph 6 [1]Children, obey your parents in the Lord, for this is right.

28) We Receive Ministries in Christ

Col 4 [17]Tell Archippus: "See to it that you complete the work you have received in the Lord."

29) We Receive People in Christ

Rom 16 [2]I ask you to receive her in the Lord in a way worthy of the saints and to give her any help she may need from you, for she has been a great help to many people, including me.

Phil 2 [29]Welcome him in the Lord with great joy, and honor men like him. . . .

30) We Rejoice in Christ

Phil 3 [1]Finally, my brothers, rejoice in the Lord! It is no trouble for me to write the same things to you again, and it is a safeguard for you.
Phil 4 [4]Rejoice in the Lord always. I will say it again: Rejoice!
Phil 4 [10]I rejoice greatly in the Lord that at last you have renewed your concern for me. Indeed, you have been concerned, but you had no opportunity to show it.

31) We Speak and Testify in Christ

2 Cor 2 [17]Unlike so many, we do not peddle the word of God for profit. On the contrary, in Christ we speak before God with sincerity, like men sent from God.
2 Cor 12 [19]Have you been thinking all along that we have been defending ourselves to you? We have been speaking in the sight of God as those in Christ; and everything we do, dear friends, is for your strengthening.
2 Cor 13 [3]since you are demanding proof that Christ is speaking through me. He is not weak in dealing with you, but is powerful among you.
Eph 4 [17]So I tell you this, and insist on it in the Lord, that you must no longer live as the Gentiles do, in the futility of their thinking.

32) We Speak the Truth in Christ

Rom 9 [1]I speak the truth in Christ—I am not lying, my conscience confirms it in the Holy Spirit. . . .

33) We Stand Firm in Christ

Phil 4 [1]Therefore, my brothers, you whom I love and long for, my joy and crown, that is how you should stand firm in the Lord, dear friends!
1 Thess 3 [8]For now we really live, since you are standing firm in the Lord.

34) We Trust in Christ

Phil 2 [24]And I am confident in the Lord that I myself will come soon.

35) We Walk in Christ

Col 2 [6]So then, just as you received Christ Jesus as Lord, continue to live in him. . . .

36) Woman Is Not Independent of Man, Nor Man of Woman, in Christ

1 Cor 11 [11]In the Lord, however, woman is not independent of man, nor is man independent of woman. [12]For as woman came from man, so also man is born of woman. But everything comes from God.

5. We Identify with Christ

1) Our Lives Have Been Hidden with Christ

Col 3 [3]For you died, and your life is now hidden with Christ in God.

2) We Are Baptized into Christ

Rom 6 [3]Or don't you know that all of us who were baptized into Christ Jesus were baptized into his death? [4]We were therefore buried with him through baptism into death in order that, just as Christ was raised from the dead through the glory of the Father, we too may live a new life.
Gal 3 [27]for all of you who were baptized into Christ have clothed yourselves with Christ.
Col 2 [12]having been buried with him in baptism and raised with him through your faith in the power of God, who raised him from the dead.

3) We Are Buried with Christ

Rom 6 [4]We were therefore buried with him through baptism into death in order that, just as Christ was raised from the dead through the glory of the Father, we too may live a new life.
Col 2 [11]In him you also were circumcised, in the putting off of the sinful nature, not with a circumcision done by the hands of men but with the circumcision done by Christ, [12]having been buried with him in baptism and raised with him through your faith in the power of God, who raised him from the dead.

4) We Are Crucified with Christ

Rom 6 [6]For we know that our old self was crucified with him so that the body of sin might be done away with, that we should no longer be slaves to sin—[7]because anyone who has died has been freed from sin.
Gal 2 [20]I have been crucified with Christ and I no longer live, but Christ lives in me. The life I live in the body, I live by faith in the Son of God, who loved me and gave himself for me.

5) We Have Been Built Together with Christ

Eph 2 [19]Consequently, you are no longer foreigners and aliens, but fellow citizens with God's people and members of God's household, [20]built on the foundation of the apostles and prophets, with Christ Jesus himself as the chief cornerstone. . . . [22]And in him you too are being built together to become a dwelling in which God lives by his Spirit.

6) We Have Been Conformed to the Image of Christ

Rom 8 [29]For those God foreknew he also predestined to be conformed to the likeness of his Son, that he might be the firstborn among many brothers.
Phil 3 [10]I want to know Christ and the power of his resurrection and the fellowship of sharing in his sufferings, becoming like him in his death. . . . [20]But our citizenship is in heaven. And we eagerly await a Savior from there, the Lord Jesus Christ, [21]who, by the power that enables him to bring everything under his control, will transform our lowly bodies so that they will be like his glorious body.

7) We Have Been Delivered from Wrath through Christ

Rom 5 [9]Since we have now been justified by his blood, how much more shall we be saved from God's wrath through him!

8) We Have Been Freely Given All Things with Christ

Rom 8 [32]He who did not spare his own Son, but gave him up for us all—how will he not also, along with him, graciously give us all things?

9) We Have Been Glorified with Christ

Rom 8 [17]Now if we are children, then we are heirs—heirs of God and co-heirs with Christ, if indeed we share in his sufferings in order that we may also share in his glory.

10) We Have Been Made Alive with Christ

Rom 5 [17]For if, by the trespass of the one man, death reigned through that one man, how much more will those who receive God's abundant provision of grace and of the gift of righteousness reign in life through the one man, Jesus Christ.
1 Cor 15 [22]For as in Adam all die, so in Christ all will be made alive.
Eph 2 [4]But because of his great love for us, God, who is rich in mercy, [5]made us alive with Christ even when we were dead in transgressions—it is by grace you have been saved.
Col 2 [13]When you were dead in your sins and in the uncircumcision of your sinful nature, God made you alive with Christ. He forgave us all our sins. . . .

11) We Have Been Made Fellow-heirs with Christ

Rom 8 [17]Now if we are children, then we are heirs—heirs of God and co-heirs with Christ, if indeed we share in his sufferings in order that we may also share in his glory.
Eph 3 [6]This mystery is that through the gospel the Gentiles are heirs together with Israel, members together of one body, and sharers together in the promise in Christ Jesus.
Heb 3 [14]We have come to share in Christ if we hold firmly till the end the confidence we had at first.

12) We Have Been Made Members of One Body

Eph 3 [6]This mystery is that through the gospel the Gentiles are heirs together with Israel, members together of one body, and sharers together in the promise in Christ Jesus.

13) We Have Been Made Workers Together with Christ

2 Cor 6 [1]As God's fellow workers we urge you not to receive God's grace in vain.

14) We Have Been Raised with Christ

2 Cor 4 [14]because we know that the one who raised the Lord Jesus from the dead will also raise us with Jesus and present us with you in his presence.
Eph 2 [6]And God raised us up with Christ and seated us with him in the heavenly realms in Christ Jesus. . . .
Col 2 [12]having been buried with him in baptism and raised with him through your faith in the power of God, who raised him from the dead.
Col 3 [1]Since, then, you have been raised with Christ, set your hearts on things above, where Christ is seated at the right hand of God.

15) We Have Been Reconciled by Christ

Rom 5 [10]For if, when we were God's enemies, we were reconciled to him through the death of his Son, how much more, having been reconciled, shall we be saved through his life!
2 Cor 5 [18]All this is from God, who reconciled us to himself through Christ and gave us the ministry of reconciliation:
[19]that God was reconciling the world to himself in Christ, not counting men's sins against them. And he has committed to us the message of reconciliation. [20]We are therefore Christ's ambassadors, as though God were making his appeal through us. We implore you on Christ's behalf: Be reconciled to God.

16) We Have Been Seated with Christ

Eph 2 [6]And God raised us up with Christ and seated us with him in the heavenly realms in Christ Jesus. . . .

17) We Have Communion with Christ

1 Cor 1 [9]God, who has called you into fellowship with his Son Jesus Christ our Lord, is faithful.
1 Cor 10 [16]Is not the cup of thanksgiving for which we give thanks a participation in the blood of Christ? And is not the bread that we break a participation in the body of Christ?

18) We Have Died and Been Resurrected with Christ

Rom 6 [5]If we have been united with him like this in his death, we will certainly also be united with him in his resurrection.

19) We Have Died and Now Live with Christ

Rom 6 [8]Now if we died with Christ, we believe that we will also live with him. [9]For we know that since Christ was raised from the dead, he cannot die again; death no longer has mastery over him. [10]The death he died, he died to sin once for all; but the life he lives, he lives to God.
[11]In the same way, count yourselves dead to sin but alive to God in Christ Jesus.
Col 2 [20]Since you died with Christ to the basic principles of this world, why, as though you still belonged to it, do you submit to its rules? . . .
2 Tim 2 [11]Here is a trustworthy saying: If we died with him, we will also live with him. . . .

20) We Reign with Christ

2 Tim 2 [12]if we endure, we will also reign with him. If we disown him, he will also disown us. . . .

21) We Suffer with Christ

Rom 8 [17]Now if we are children, then we are heirs—heirs of God and co-heirs with Christ, if indeed we share in his sufferings in order that we may also share in his glory.
1 Cor 12 [26]If one part suffers, every part suffers with it; if one part is honored, every part rejoices with it.
[27]Now you are the body of Christ, and each one of you is a part of it.
2 Cor 1 [5]For just as the sufferings of Christ flow over into our lives, so also through Christ our comfort overflows.
Phil 3 [10]I want to know Christ and the power of his resurrection and the fellowship of sharing in his sufferings, becoming like him in his death. . . .
Col 1 [24]Now I rejoice in what was suffered for you, and I fill up in my flesh what is still lacking in regard to Christ's afflictions, for the sake of his body, which is the church.

22) We Will Be Revealed in Glory with Christ

Col 3 [4]When Christ, who is your life, appears, then you also will appear with him in glory.

23) We Will Live with Christ

2 Cor 13 [4]For to be sure, he was crucified in weakness, yet he lives by God's power. Likewise, we are weak in him, yet by God's power we will live with him to serve you.
1 Thess 5 [10]He died for us so that, whether we are awake or asleep, we may live together with him.

24) The Whole Body Has Been Fitted Together with Christ

Eph 2 [21]In him the whole building is joined together and rises to become a holy temple in the Lord.
Eph 4 [15]Instead, speaking the truth in love, we will in all things grow up into him who is the Head, that is, Christ. [16]From him the whole body, joined and held together by every supporting ligament, grows and builds itself up in love, as each part does its work.

C. Sanctification and the Spirit

See als p. 158a, Ministry of the Spirit

1. The Spirit Works Sanctification in the Believer

Rom 15 [16]to be a minister of Christ Jesus to the Gentiles with the priestly duty of proclaiming the gospel of God, so that the Gentiles might become an offering acceptable to God, sanctified by the Holy Spirit.
1 Cor 6 [11]And that is what some of you were. But you were washed, you were sanctified, you were justified in the name of the Lord Jesus Christ and by the Spirit of our God.
1 Cor 12 [12]The body is a unit, though it is made up of many parts; and though all its parts are many, they form one body. So it is with Christ. [13]For we were all baptized by one Spirit into one body—whether Jews or Greeks, slave or free—and we were all given the one Spirit to drink.
2 Thess 2 [13]But we ought always to thank God for you, brothers loved by the Lord, because from the beginning God chose you to be saved through the sanctifying work of the Spirit and through belief in the truth.
1 Pet 1 [2]who have been chosen according to the foreknowledge of God the Father, through the sanctifying work of the Spirit, for obedience to Jesus Christ and sprinkling by his blood: Grace and peace be yours in abundance.

2. The Spirit Frees the Believer from the Domination of Sin

Rom 8 [1]Therefore, there is now no condemnation for those who are in Christ Jesus, [2]because through Christ Jesus the law of the Spirit of life set me free from the law of sin and death.
[3]For what the law was powerless to do in that it was weakened by the sinful nature, God did by sending his own Son in the likeness of sinful man to be a sin offering. And so he condemned sin in sinful man, [4]in order that the righteous requirements of the law might be fully met in us, who do not live according to the sinful nature but according to the Spirit.
Gal 5 [16]So I say, live by the Spirit, and you will not gratify the desires of the sinful nature. [17]For the sinful nature desires what is contrary to the Spirit, and the Spirit what is contrary to the sinful nature. They are in conflict with each other, so that you do not do what you want. [18]But if you are led by the Spirit, you are not under law.

3. The Spirit Gives the Believer Life

Rom 8 [10]But if Christ is in you, your body is dead because of sin, yet your spirit is alive because of righteousness. [11]And if the Spirit of him who raised Jesus from the dead is living in you, he who raised Christ from the dead will also give life to your mortal bodies through his Spirit, who lives in you.

[12]Therefore, brothers, we have an obligation—but it is not to the sinful nature, to live according to it. [13]For if you live according to the sinful nature, you will die; but if by the Spirit you put to death the misdeeds of the body, you will live, [14]because those who are led by the Spirit of God are sons of God.

4. The Spirit Conforms the Believer to Christ's Image

Rom 8 [5]Those who live according to the sinful nature have their minds set on what that nature desires; but those who live in accordance with the Spirit have their minds set on what the Spirit desires. [6]The mind of sinful man is death, but the mind controlled by the Spirit is life and peace; [7]the sinful mind is hostile to God. It does not submit to God's law, nor can it do so. [8]Those controlled by the sinful nature cannot please God.

[9]You, however, are controlled not by the sinful nature but by the Spirit, if the Spirit of God lives in you. And if anyone does not have the Spirit of Christ, he does not belong to Christ. . . . [16]The Spirit himself testifies with our spirit that we are God's children. [17]Now if we are children, then we are heirs—heirs of God and co-heirs with Christ, if indeed we share in his sufferings in order that we may also share in his glory. . . . [29]For those God foreknew he also predestined to be conformed to the likeness of his Son, that he might be the firstborn among many brothers.

2 Cor 3 [18]And we, who with unveiled faces all reflect the Lord's glory, are being transformed into his likeness with ever-increasing glory, which comes from the Lord, who is the Spirit.

Gal 5 [22]But the fruit of the Spirit is love, joy, peace, patience, kindness, goodness, faithfulness, [23]gentleness and self-control. Against such things there is no law. [24]Those who belong to Christ Jesus have crucified the sinful nature with its passions and desires. [25]Since we live by the Spirit, let us keep in step with the Spirit.

5. The Spirit Produces Fruit in the Believer

Gal 5 [22]But the fruit of the Spirit is love, joy, peace, patience, kindness, goodness, faithfulness, [23]gentleness and self-control. Against such things there is no law.

6. The Spirit Produces Holiness in the Believer

1 Thess 4 [7]For God did not call us to be impure, but to live a holy life. [8]Therefore, he who rejects this instruction does not reject man but God, who gives you his Holy Spirit.

7. The Spirit Preserves the Believer until the Time of Complete Sanctification

Eph 4 [30]And do not grieve the Holy Spirit of God, with whom you were sealed for the day of redemption.

8. The Spirit Bestows Gifts for Service

See p. 156a, Gifts of the Spirit

II
Sanctification: *Accomplished Fact and Growth Process*

A. Sanctification as Accomplished Fact

1 Cor 1 [2]To the church of God in Corinth, to those sanctified in Christ Jesus and called to be holy, together with all those everywhere who call on the name of our Lord Jesus Christ—their Lord and ours. . . .

1 Cor 6 [9]Do you not know that the wicked will not inherit the kingdom of God? Do not be deceived: Neither the sexually immoral nor idolaters nor adulterers nor male prostitutes nor homosexual offenders [10]nor thieves nor the greedy nor drunkards nor slanderers nor swindlers will inherit the kingdom of God. [11]And that is what some of you were. But you were washed, you were sanctified, you were justified in the name of the Lord Jesus Christ and by the Spirit of our God.

Eph 5 [25]Husbands, love your wives, just as Christ loved the church and gave himself up for her [26]to make her holy, cleansing her by the washing with water through the word, [27]and to present her to himself as a radiant church, without stain or wrinkle or any other blemish, but holy and blameless.

Heb 2 [11]Both the one who makes men holy and those who are made holy are of the same family. So Jesus is not ashamed to call them brothers.

Heb 10 [10]And by that will, we have been made holy through the sacrifice of the body of Jesus Christ once for all.

[11]Day after day every priest stands and performs his religious duties; again and again he offers the same sacrifices, which can never take away sins. [12]But when this priest had offered for all time one sacrifice for sins, he sat down at the right hand of God. [13]Since that time he waits for his enemies to be made his footstool, [14]because by one sacrifice he has made perfect forever those who are being made holy.

Heb 10 [29]How much more severely do you think a man deserves to be punished who has trampled the Son of God under foot, who has treated as an unholy thing the blood of the covenant that sanctified him, and who has insulted the Spirit of grace?

Heb 13 [12]And so Jesus also suffered outside the city gate to make the people holy through his own blood.

B. Sanctification as Growth in Grace

1. The Fact and Need of Growth

Rom 12 [1]Therefore, I urge you, brothers, in view of God's mercy, to offer your bodies as living sacrifices, holy and pleasing to God—this is your spiritual act of worship. [2]Do not conform any longer to the pattern of this world, but be transformed by the renewing of your mind. Then you will be able to test and approve what God's will is—his good, pleasing and perfect will.

2 Cor 3 [18]And we, who with unveiled faces all reflect the Lord's glory, are being transformed into his likeness with ever-increasing glory, which comes from the Lord, who is the Spirit.

Eph 4 [11]It was he who gave some to be apostles, some to be prophets, some to be evangelists, and some to be pastors and teachers, [12]to prepare God's people for works of service, so that the body of Christ may be built up [13]until we all reach unity in the faith and in the knowledge of the Son of God and become mature, attaining to the whole measure of the fullness of Christ.

[14]Then we will no longer be infants, tossed back and forth by the waves, and blown here and there by every wind of teaching and by the cunning and craftiness of men in their deceitful scheming. [15]Instead, speaking the truth in love, we will in all things grow up into him who is the Head, that is, Christ.

Phil 3 [12]Not that I have already obtained all this, or have already been made perfect, but I press on to take hold of that for which Christ Jesus took hold of me.

Col 1 [6]that has come to you. All over the world this gospel is bearing fruit and growing, just as it has been doing among you since the day you heard it and understood God's grace in all its truth.

Col 1 [10]And we pray this in order that you may live a life worthy of the Lord and may please him in every way: bearing fruit in every good work, growing in the knowledge of God. . . .

Col 2 [18]Do not let anyone who delights in false humility and the worship of angels disqualify you for the prize. Such a person goes into great detail about what he has seen, and his unspiritual mind puffs him up with idle notions. [19]He has lost connection with the Head, from whom the whole body, supported and held together by its ligaments and sinews, grows as God causes it to grow.

1 Thess 4 [3]It is God's will that you should be sanctified: that you should avoid sexual immorality; [4]that each of you should learn to control his own body in a way that is holy and honorable, [5]not in passionate lust like the heathen, who do not know God; [6]and that in this matter no one should wrong his brother or take advantage of him. The Lord will punish men for all such sins, as we have already told you and warned you. [7]For God did not call us to be impure, but to live a holy life.

1 Thess 5 [23]May God himself, the God of peace, sanctify you through and through. May your whole spirit, soul and body be kept blameless at the coming of our Lord Jesus Christ. [24]The one who calls you is faithful and he will do it.

Heb 6 [1]Therefore let us leave the elementary teachings about Christ and go on to maturity, not laying again the foundation of repentance from acts that lead to death, and of faith in God, [2]instruction about baptisms, the laying on of hands, the resurrection of the dead, and eternal judgment. [3]And God permitting, we will do so.

Heb 12 [14]Make every effort to live in peace with all men and to be holy; without holiness no one will see the Lord.

1 Pet 2 [1]Therefore, rid yourselves of all malice and all deceit, hypocrisy, envy, and slander of every kind. [2]Like newborn babies, crave pure spiritual milk, so that by it you may grow up in your salvation, [3]now that you have tasted that the Lord is good.

2 Pet 3 [18]But grow in the grace and knowledge of our Lord and Savior Jesus Christ. To him be glory both now and forever! Amen.

2. The Means of Growth

a) Growth in Grace through the Armor of God

Rom 13 [12]The night is nearly over; the day is almost here. So let us put aside the deeds of darkness and put on the armor of light.

2 Cor 6 [4]Rather, as servants of God we commend ourselves in every way: in great endurance; in troubles, hardships and distresses; . . . [7]in truthful speech and in the power of God; with weapons of righteousness in the right hand and in the left. . . .

2 Cor 10 [3]For though we live in the world, we do not wage war as the world does. [4]The weapons we fight with are not the weapons of the world. On the contrary, they have divine power to demolish strongholds. [5]We demolish arguments and every pretension that sets itself up against the knowledge of God, and we take captive every thought to make it obedient to Christ. [6]And we will be ready to punish every act of disobedience, once your obedience is complete.

Eph 6 [10]Finally, be strong in the Lord and in his mighty power. [11]Put on the full armor of God so that you can take your stand against the devil's schemes. [12]For our struggle is not against flesh and blood, but against the rulers, against the authorities, against the powers of this dark world and against the spiritual forces of evil in the heavenly realms. [13]Therefore put on the full armor of God, so that when the day of evil comes, you may be able to stand your ground, and after you have done everything, to stand. [14]Stand firm then, with the belt of truth buckled around your waist, with the breastplate of righteousness in place, [15]and with your feet fitted with the readiness that comes from the gospel of peace. [16]In addition to all this, take up the shield of faith, with which you can extinguish all the flaming arrows of the evil one. [17]Take the helmet of salvation and the sword of the Spirit, which is the word of God.

1 Thess 5 [8]But since we belong to the day, let us be self-controlled, putting on faith and love as a breastplate, and the hope of salvation as a helmet.

1 Tim 1 [18]Timothy, my son, I give you this instruction in keeping with the prophecies once made about you, so that by following them you may fight the good fight, [19]holding on to faith and a good conscience. Some have rejected these and so have shipwrecked their faith.

1 Tim 6 [12]Fight the good fight of the faith. Take hold of the eternal life to which you were called when you made your good confession in the presence of many witnesses.

2 Tim 2 [3]Endure hardship with us like a good soldier of Christ Jesus.

2 Tim 4 [7]I have fought the good fight, I have finished the race, I have kept the faith.

Heb 4 [12]For the word of God is living and active. Sharper than any double-edged sword, it penetrates even to dividing soul and spirit, joints and marrow; it judges the thoughts and attitudes of the heart.

b) Growth in Grace through Confession of Sin

Ezra 9 [4]Then everyone who trembled at the words of the God of Israel gathered around me because of this unfaithfulness of the exiles. And I sat there appalled until the evening sacrifice.

[5]Then, at the evening sacrifice, I rose from my self-abasement, with my tunic and cloak torn, and fell on my knees with my hands spread out to the LORD my God [6]and prayed: "O my God, I am too ashamed and disgraced to lift up my face to you, my God, because our sins are higher than our heads and our guilt has reached to the heavens. [7]From the days of our forefathers until now, our guilt has been great. Because of our sins, we and our kings and our priests have been subjected to the sword and captivity, to pillage and humiliation at the hand of foreign kings, as it is today.

[8]"But now, for a brief moment, the LORD our God has been gracious in leaving us a remnant and giving us a firm place in his sanctuary, and so our God gives light to our eyes and a little relief in our bondage. [9]Though we are slaves, our God has not deserted us in our bondage. He has shown us kindness in the sight of the kings of Persia: He has granted us new life to rebuild the house of our God and repair its ruins, and he has given us a wall of protection in Judah and Jerusalem.

[10]"But now, O our God, what can we say after this? For we have disregarded the commands [11]you gave through your servants the prophets when you said: 'The land you are entering to possess is a land polluted by the corruption of its peoples. By their detestable practices they have filled it with their impurity from one end to the other. [12]Therefore, do not give your daughters in marriage to their sons or take their daughters for your sons. Do not seek a treaty of friendship with them at any time, that you may be strong and eat the good things of the land and leave it to your children as an everlasting inheritance.'

[13]"What has happened to us is a result of our evil deeds and our great guilt, and yet, our God, you have punished us less than our sins have deserved and have given us a remnant like this. [14]Shall we again break your commands and intermarry with the peoples who commit such detestable practices? Would you not be angry enough with us to destroy us, leaving us no remnant or survivor? [15]O LORD, God of Israel, you are righteous! We are left this day as a remnant. Here we are before you in our guilt, though because of it not one of us can stand in your presence."

Neh 1 [6]". . . let your ear be attentive and your eyes open to hear the prayer your servant is praying before you day and night for your servants, the people of Israel. I confess the sins we Israelites, including myself and my father's house, have committed against you. [7]We have acted very wickedly toward you. We have not obeyed the commands, decrees and laws you gave your servant Moses.

[8]"Remember the instruction you gave your servant Moses, saying, 'If you are unfaithful, I will scatter you among the nations, [9]but if you return to me and obey my commands, then even if your exiled people are at the farthest horizon, I will gather them from there and bring them to the place I have chosen as a dwelling for my Name.'"

Neh 9 [2]Those of Israelite descent had separated themselves from all foreigners. They stood in their places and confessed their sins and the wickedness of their fathers. [3]They stood where they were and read from the Book of the Law of the LORD their God for a quarter of the day, and spent another quarter in confession and in worshiping the LORD their God.

Job 9 [20]"Even if I were innocent, my mouth would condemn me; if I were blameless, it would pronounce me guilty."

Job 13 [23]"How many wrongs and sins have I committed? Show me my offense and my sin."

Job 40 4"I am unworthy—how can I reply to you? I put my hand over my mouth."
Job 42 5"My ears had heard of you but now my eyes have seen you. 6Therefore I despise myself and repent in dust and ashes."
Ps 19 12Who can discern his errors? Forgive my hidden faults.
Ps 32 5Then I acknowledged my sin to you and did not cover up my iniquity. I said, "I will confess my transgressions to the LORD"—and you forgave the guilt of my sin.
Ps 38 3Because of your wrath there is no health in my body; my bones have no soundness because of my sin. 4My guilt has overwhelmed me like a burden too heavy to bear. . . . 18I confess my iniquity; I am troubled by my sin.
Ps 40 11Do not withhold your mercy from me, O LORD; may your love and your truth always protect me. 12For troubles without number surround me; my sins have overtaken me, and I cannot see. They are more than the hairs of my head, and my heart fails within me.

13Be pleased, O LORD, to save me; O LORD, come quickly to help me.
Ps 41 4I said, "O LORD, have mercy on me; heal me, for I have sinned against you."
Ps 51 1Have mercy on me, O God, according to your unfailing love; according to your great compassion blot out my transgressions. 2Wash away all my iniquity and cleanse me from my sin.

3For I know my transgressions, and my sin is always before me. 4Against you, you only, have I sinned and done what is evil in your sight, so that you are proved right when you speak and justified when you judge. 5Surely I was sinful at birth, sinful from the time my mother conceived me.
Ps 69 5You know my folly, O God; my guilt is not hidden from you.
Ps 106 6We have sinned, even as our fathers did; we have done wrong and acted wickedly.
Ps 119 59I have considered my ways and have turned my steps to your statutes. 60I will hasten and not delay to obey your commands.
Ps 119 176I have strayed like a lost sheep. Seek your servant, for I have not forgotten your commands.
Ps 130 1Out of the depths I cry to you, O LORD; 2O Lord, hear my voice. Let your ears be attentive to my cry for mercy.

3If you, O LORD, kept a record of sins, O Lord, who could stand? 4But with you there is forgiveness; therefore you are feared.
Prov 28 13He who conceals his sins does not prosper, but whoever confesses and renounces them finds mercy.
Isa 6 5"Woe to me!" I cried. "I am ruined! For I am a man of unclean lips, and I live among a people of unclean lips, and my eyes have seen the King, the LORD Almighty."
Isa 59 12For our offenses are many in your sight, and our sins testify against us. Our offenses are ever with us, and we acknowledge our iniquities: 13rebellion and treachery against the LORD, turning our backs on our God, fomenting oppression and revolt, uttering lies our hearts have conceived. 14So justice is driven back, and righteousness stands at a distance; truth has stumbled in the streets, honesty cannot enter. 15Truth is nowhere to be found, and whoever shuns evil becomes a prey.

The LORD looked and was displeased that there was no justice.
Isa 64 5You come to the help of those who gladly do right, who remember your ways. But when we continued to sin against them, you were angry. How then can we be saved? 6All of us have become like one who is unclean, and all our righteous acts are like filthy rags; we all shrivel up like a leaf, and like the wind our sins sweep us away. 7No one calls on your name or strives to lay hold of you; for you have hidden your face from us and made us waste away because of our sins.
Jer 3 13"'Only acknowledge your guilt—you have rebelled against the LORD your God, you have scattered your favors to foreign gods under every spreading tree, and have not obeyed me,'" declares the LORD. . . .

21A cry is heard on the barren heights, the weeping and pleading of the people of Israel, because they have perverted their ways and have forgotten the LORD their God.

22"Return, faithless people; I will cure you of backsliding."

"Yes, we will come to you, for you are the LORD our God. . . . 25Let us lie down in our shame, and let our disgrace cover us. We have sinned against the LORD our God, both we and our fathers; from our youth till this day we have not obeyed the LORD our God."
Jer 14 7Although our sins testify against us, O LORD, do something for the sake of your name. For our backsliding is great; we have sinned against you. . . . 20O LORD, we acknowledge our wickedness and the guilt of our fathers; we have indeed sinned against you. 21For the sake of your name do not despise us; do not dishonor your glorious throne. Remember your covenant with us and do not break it. 22Do any of the worthless idols of the nations bring rain? Do the skies themselves send down showers? No, it is you, O LORD our God. Therefore our hope is in you, for you are the one who does all this.
Jer 31 18"I have surely heard Ephraim's moaning: 'You disciplined me like an unruly calf, and I have been disciplined. Restore me, and I will return, because you are the LORD my God. 19After I strayed, I repented; after I came to understand, I beat my breast. I was ashamed and humiliated because I bore the disgrace of my youth.'"
Lam 3 40Let us examine our ways and test them, and let us return to the LORD. 41Let us lift up our hearts and our hands to God in heaven, and say: 42"We have sinned and rebelled and you have not forgiven."
Dan 9 4I prayed to the LORD my God and confessed: "O Lord, the great and awesome God, who keeps his covenant of love with all who love him and obey his commands, 5we have sinned and done wrong. We have been wicked and have rebelled; we have turned away from your commands and laws. 6We have not listened to your servants the prophets, who spoke in your name to our kings, our princes and our fathers, and to all the people of the land.

7"Lord, you are righteous, but this day we are covered with shame—the men of Judah and people of Jerusalem and all Israel, both near and far, in all the countries where you have scattered us because of our unfaithfulness to you. 8O LORD, we and our kings, our princes and our fathers are covered with shame because we have sinned against you. 9The Lord our God is merciful and forgiving, even though we have rebelled against him; 10we have not obeyed the LORD our God or kept the laws he gave us through his servants the prophets. 11All Israel has transgressed your law and turned away, refusing to obey you.

"Therefore the curses and sworn judgments written in the Law of Moses, the servant of God, have been poured out on us, because we have sinned against you. 12You have fulfilled the words spoken against us and against our rulers by bringing upon us great disaster. Under the whole heaven nothing has ever been done like what has been done to Jerusalem. 13Just as it is written in the Law of Moses, all this disaster has come upon us, yet we have not sought the favor of the LORD our God by turning from our sins and giving attention to your truth. 14The LORD did not hesitate to bring the disaster upon us, for the LORD our God is righteous in everything he does; yet we have not obeyed him.

15"Now, O Lord our God, who brought your people out of Egypt with a mighty hand and who made for yourself a name that endures to this day, we have sinned, we have done wrong. 16O Lord, in keeping with all your righteous acts, turn away your anger and your wrath from Jerusalem, your city, your holy hill. Our sins and the iniquities of our fathers have made Jerusalem and your people an object of scorn to all those around us.

17"Now, our God, hear the prayers and petitions of your servant. For your sake, O Lord, look with favor on your desolate sanctuary. 18Give ear, O God, and hear; open your eyes and see the desolation of the city that bears your Name. We do not make requests of you because we are righteous, but because of your great mercy. 19O Lord, listen! O Lord, forgive! O Lord, hear and act! For your sake, O my God, do not delay, because your city and your people bear your Name."
Luke 15 17"When he came to his senses, he said, 'How many of my father's hired men have food to spare, and here I am starving to death! 18I will set out and go back to my father and say to him: Father, I have sinned against heaven and against you. 19I am no longer worthy to be called your son; make me like one of your hired men.' 20So he got up and went to his father.

"But while he was still a long way off, his father saw him and was filled with compassion for him; he ran to his son, threw his arms around him and kissed him.

[21]"The son said to him, 'Father, I have sinned against heaven and against you. I am no longer worthy to be called your son.'"

James 5 [16]Therefore confess your sins to each other and pray for each other so that you may be healed. The prayer of a righteous man is powerful and effective.

1 John 1 [9]If we confess our sins, he is faithful and just and will forgive us our sins and purify us from all unrighteousness.

c) Growth in Grace through Discipline

Deut 8 [5]Know then in your heart that as a man disciplines his son, so the LORD your God disciplines you.

Job 5 [17]"Blessed is the man whom God corrects; so do not despise the discipline of the Almighty."

Job 33 [14]"For God does speak—now one way, now another —though man may not perceive it. [15]In a dream, in a vision of the night, when deep sleep falls on men as they slumber in their beds, [16]he may speak in their ears and terrify them with warnings, [17]to turn man from wrongdoing and keep him from pride, [18]to preserve his soul from the pit, his life from perishing by the sword. [19]Or a man may be chastened on a bed of pain with constant distress in his bones, [20]so that his very being finds food repulsive and his soul loathes the choicest meal. [21]His flesh wastes away to nothing, and his bones, once hidden, now stick out. [22]His soul draws near to the pit, and his life to the messengers of death.

[23]"Yet if there is an angel on his side as a mediator, one out of a thousand, to tell a man what is right for him, [24]to be gracious to him and say, 'Spare him from going down to the pit; I have found a ransom for him'—[25]then his flesh is renewed like a child's; it is restored as in the days of his youth. [26]He prays to God and finds favor with him, he sees God's face and shouts for joy; he is restored by God to his righteous state. [27]Then he comes to men and says, 'I sinned, and perverted what was right, but I did not get what I deserved. [28]He redeemed my soul from going down to the pit, and I will live to enjoy the light.'

[29]"God does all these things to a man—twice, even three times—[30]to turn back his soul from the pit, that the light of life may shine on him."

Ps 6 [1]O LORD, do not rebuke me in your anger or discipline me in your wrath.

Ps 94 [12]Blessed is the man you discipline, O LORD, the man you teach from your law; [13]you grant him relief from days of trouble, till a pit is dug for the wicked.

Ps 118 [18]The LORD has chastened me severely, but he has not given me over to death.

Ps 119 [67]Before I was afflicted I went astray, but now I obey your word. . . . [71]It was good for me to be afflicted so that I might learn your decrees.

Prov 3 [11]My son, do not despise the LORD's discipline and do not resent his rebuke, [12]because the LORD disciplines those he loves, as a father the son he delights in.

1 Cor 11 [32]When we are judged by the Lord, we are being disciplined so that we will not be condemned with the world.

Heb 12 [3]Consider him who endured such opposition from sinful men, so that you will not grow weary and lose heart.

[4]In your struggle against sin, you have not yet resisted to the point of shedding your blood. [5]And you have forgotten that word of encouragement that addresses you as sons: "My son, do not make light of the Lord's discipline, and do not lose heart when he rebukes you, [6]because the Lord disciplines those he loves, and he punishes everyone he accepts as a son."

[7]Endure hardship as discipline; God is treating you as sons. For what son is not disciplined by his father? [8]If you are not disciplined (and everyone undergoes discipline), then you are illegitimate children and not true sons. [9]Moreover, we have all had human fathers who disciplined us and we respected them for it. How much more should we submit to the Father of our spirits and live! [10]Our fathers disciplined us for a little while as they thought best; but God disciplines us for our good, that we may share in his holiness. [11]No discipline seems pleasant at the time, but painful. Later on, however, it produces a harvest of righteousness and peace for those who have been trained by it.

[12]Therefore, strengthen your feeble arms and weak knees.

1 Pet 4 [1]Therefore, since Christ suffered in his body, arm yourselves also with the same attitude, because he who has suffered in his body is done with sin. [2]As a result, he does not live the rest of his earthly life for evil human desires, but rather for the will of God.

Rev 3 [19]"Those whom I love I rebuke and discipline. So be earnest, and repent."

d) Growth in Grace through Fasting

1 Sam 7 [6]When they had assembled at Mizpah, they drew water and poured it out before the LORD. On that day they fasted and there they confessed, "We have sinned against the LORD." And Samuel was leader of Israel at Mizpah.

2 Sam 12 [15]After Nathan had gone home, the LORD struck the child that Uriah's wife had borne to David, and he became ill. [16]David pleaded with God for the child. He fasted and went into his house and spent the nights lying on the ground. [17]The elders of his household stood beside him to get him up from the ground, but he refused, and he would not eat any food with them.

[18]On the seventh day the child died. David's servants were afraid to tell him that the child was dead, for they thought, "While the child was still living, we spoke to David but he would not listen to us. How can we tell him the child is dead? He may do something desperate."

[19]David noticed that his servants were whispering among themselves and he realized the child was dead. "Is the child dead?" he asked.

"Yes," they replied, "he is dead."

[20]Then David got up from the ground. After he had washed, put on lotions and changed his clothes, he went into the house of the LORD and worshiped. Then he went to his own house, and at his request they served him food, and he ate.

[21]His servants asked him, "Why are you acting this way? While the child was alive, you fasted and wept, but now that the child is dead, you get up and eat!"

[22]He answered, "While the child was still alive, I fasted and wept. I thought, 'Who knows? The LORD may be gracious to me and let the child live.' [23]But now that he is dead, why should I fast? Can I bring him back again? I will go to him, but he will not return to me."

1 Kings 21 [27]When Ahab heard these words, he tore his clothes, put on sackcloth and fasted. He lay in sackcloth and went around meekly.

[28]Then the word of the LORD came to Elijah the Tishbite: [29]"Have you noticed how Ahab has humbled himself before me? Because he has humbled himself, I will not bring this disaster in his day, but I will bring it on his house in the days of his son."

Neh 9 [1]On the twenty-fourth day of the same month, the Israelites gathered together, fasting and wearing sackcloth and having dust on their heads. [2]Those of Israelite descent had separated themselves from all foreigners. They stood in their places and confessed their sins and the wickedness of their fathers.

Ps 35 [13]Yet when they were ill, I put on sackcloth and humbled myself with fasting. When my prayers returned to me unanswered . . .

Dan 9 [3]So I turned to the Lord God and pleaded with him in prayer and petition, in fasting, and in sackcloth and ashes.

Joel 1 [14]Declare a holy fast; call a sacred assembly. Summon the elders and all who live in the land to the house of the LORD your God, and cry out to the LORD.

Joel 2 [12]"Even now," declares the LORD, "return to me with all your heart, with fasting and weeping and mourning."

[13]Rend your heart and not your garments. Return to the LORD your God, for he is gracious and compassionate, slow to anger and abounding in love, and he relents from sending calamity.

Jon 3 [4]On the first day, Jonah started into the city. He proclaimed: "Forty more days and Nineveh will be overturned." [5]The Ninevites believed God. They declared a fast, and all of them, from the greatest to the least, put on sackcloth.

[6]When the news reached the king of Nineveh, he rose from his throne, took off his royal robes, covered himself with sack-

cloth and sat down in the dust. 7Then he issued a proclamation in Nineveh: "By the decree of the king and his nobles: Do not let any man or beast, herd or flock, taste anything; do not let them eat or drink. 8But let man and beast be covered with sackcloth. Let everyone call urgently on God. Let them give up their evil ways and their violence. 9Who knows? God may yet relent and with compassion turn from his fierce anger so that we will not perish."

10When God saw what they did and how they turned from their evil ways, he had compassion and did not bring upon them the destruction he had threatened.

Matt 6 16"When you fast, do not look somber as the hypocrites do, for they disfigure their faces to show men they are fasting. I tell you the truth, they have received their reward in full. 17But when you fast, put oil on your head and wash your face, 18so that it will not be obvious to men that you are fasting, but only to your Father, who is unseen; and your Father, who sees what is done in secret, will reward you."

Matt 9 14Then John's disciples came and asked him, "How is it that we and the Pharisees fast, but your disciples do not fast?"

15Jesus answered, "How can the guests of the bridegroom mourn while he is with them? The time will come when the bridegroom will be taken from them; then they will fast."

Luke 2 37and then was a widow until she was eighty-four. She never left the temple but worshiped night and day, fasting and praying.

Acts 13 2While they were worshiping the Lord and fasting, the Holy Spirit said, "Set apart for me Barnabas and Saul for the work to which I have called them." 3So after they had fasted and prayed, they placed their hands on them and sent them off.

Acts 14 23Paul and Barnabas appointed elders for them in each church and, with prayer and fasting, committed them to the Lord, in whom they had put their trust.

e) Growth in Grace through Love

Rom 5 5And hope does not disappoint us, because God has poured out his love into our hearts by the Holy Spirit, whom he has given us.

Rom 8 28And we know that in all things God works for the good of those who love him, who have been called according to his purpose.

1 Cor 8 1Now about food sacrificed to idols: We know that we all possess knowledge. Knowledge puffs up, but love builds up.

1 Cor 14 1Follow the way of love and eagerly desire spiritual gifts, especially the gift of prophecy.

Gal 5 6For in Christ Jesus neither circumcision nor uncircumcision has any value. The only thing that counts is faith expressing itself through love.

Gal 5 13You, my brothers, were called to be free. But do not use your freedom to indulge the sinful nature; rather, serve one another in love.

Gal 5 22But the fruit of the Spirit is love, joy, peace, patience, kindness, goodness, faithfulness. . . .

Eph 4 15Instead, speaking the truth in love, we will in all things grow up into him who is the Head, that is, Christ.

Eph 5 1Be imitators of God, therefore, as dearly loved children 2and live a life of love, just as Christ loved us and gave himself up for us as a fragrant offering and sacrifice to God.

Phil 1 9And this is my prayer: that your love may abound more and more in knowledge and depth of insight. . . .

Col 3 12Therefore, as God's chosen people, holy and dearly loved, clothe yourselves with compassion, kindness, humility, gentleness and patience. 13Bear with each other and forgive whatever grievances you may have against one another. Forgive as the Lord forgave you. 14And over all these virtues put on love, which binds them all together in perfect unity.

1 Thess 3 12May the Lord make your love increase and overflow for each other and for everyone else, just as ours does for you.

1 Thess 4 9Now about brotherly love we do not need to write to you, for you yourselves have been taught by God to love each other.

1 Tim 1 5The goal of this command is love, which comes from a pure heart and a good conscience and a sincere faith.

Heb 10 24And let us consider how we may spur one another on toward love and good deeds.

1 Pet 1 22Now that you have purified yourselves by obeying the truth so that you have sincere love for your brothers, love one another deeply, from the heart.

1 Pet 4 8Above all, love each other deeply, because love covers over a multitude of sins.

1 John 2 10Whoever loves his brother lives in the light, and there is nothing in him to make him stumble.

1 John 3 11This is the message you heard from the beginning: We should love one another. 12Do not be like Cain, who belonged to the evil one and murdered his brother. And why did he murder him? Because his own actions were evil and his brother's were righteous. 13Do not be surprised, my brothers, if the world hates you. 14We know that we have passed from death to life, because we love our brothers. Anyone who does not love remains in death. 15Anyone who hates his brother is a murderer, and you know that no murderer has eternal life in him.

16This is how we know what love is: Jesus Christ laid down his life for us. And we ought to lay down our lives for our brothers. 17If anyone has material possessions and sees his brother in need but has no pity on him, how can the love of God be in him? 18Dear children, let us not love with words or tongue but with actions and in truth. 19This then is how we know that we belong to the truth, and how we set our hearts at rest in his presence 20whenever our hearts condemn us. For God is greater than our hearts, and he knows everything.

21Dear friends, if our hearts do not condemn us, we have confidence before God 22and receive from him anything we ask, because we obey his commands and do what pleases him. 23And this is his command: to believe in the name of his Son, Jesus Christ, and to love one another as he commanded us.

1 John 4 7Dear friends, let us love one another, for love comes from God. Everyone who loves has been born of God and knows God. 8Whoever does not love does not know God, because God is love. 9This is how God showed his love among us: He sent his one and only Son into the world that we might live through him. 10This is love: not that we loved God, but that he loved us and sent his Son as an atoning sacrifice for our sins. 11Dear friends, since God so loved us, we also ought to love one another. 12No one has ever seen God; but if we love one another, God lives in us and his love is made complete in us.

13We know that we live in him and he in us, because he has given us of his Spirit. 14And we have seen and testify that the Father has sent his Son to be the Savior of the world. 15If anyone acknowledges that Jesus is the Son of God, God lives in him and he in God. 16And so we know and rely on the love God has for us.

God is love. Whoever lives in love lives in God, and God in him. 17In this way, love is made complete among us so that we will have confidence on the day of judgment, because in this world we are like him. 18There is no fear in love. But perfect love drives out fear, because fear has to do with punishment. The one who fears is not made perfect in love.

19We love because he first loved us. 20If anyone says, "I love God," yet hates his brother, he is a liar. For anyone who does not love his brother, whom he has seen, cannot love God, whom he has not seen. 21And he has given us this command: Whoever loves God must also love his brother.

1 John 5 1Everyone who believes that Jesus is the Christ is born of God, and everyone who loves the father loves his child as well. 2This is how we know that we love the children of God: by loving God and carrying out his commands. 3This is love for God: to obey his commands. And his commands are not burdensome. . . .

See also p. 154a, Love

f) Growth in Grace through Meditation

Deut 6 6These commandments that I give you today are to be upon your hearts.

Deut 11 18Fix these words of mine in your hearts and minds; tie them as symbols on your hands and bind them on your foreheads.

Deut 32 46he said to them, "Take to heart all the words I have solemnly declared to you this day, so that you may command your children to obey carefully all the words of this law."

Josh 1 8“Do not let this Book of the Law depart from your mouth; meditate on it day and night, so that you may be careful to do everything written in it. Then you will be prosperous and successful.”
Job 22 22“Accept instruction from his mouth and lay up his words in your heart.”
Ps 1 2But his delight is in the law of the LORD, and on his law he meditates day and night.
Ps 4 4In your anger do not sin; when you are on your beds, search your hearts and be silent.
Ps 16 8I have set the LORD always before me. Because he is at my right hand, I will not be shaken.
Ps 19 14May the words of my mouth and the meditation of my heart be pleasing in your sight, O LORD, my Rock and my Redeemer.
Ps 37 31The law of his God is in his heart; his feet do not slip.
Ps 40 8“I desire to do your will, O my God; your law is within my heart.”
Ps 46 10“Be still, and know that I am God; I will be exalted among the nations, I will be exalted in the earth.”
Ps 48 9Within your temple, O God, we meditate on your unfailing love.
Ps 63 5My soul will be satisfied as with the richest of foods; with singing lips my mouth will praise you.

6On my bed I remember you; I think of you through the watches of the night.
Ps 77 10Then I thought, “To this I will appeal: the years of the right hand of the Most High.” 11I will remember the deeds of the LORD; yes, I will remember your miracles of long ago. 12I will meditate on all your works and consider all your mighty deeds.
Ps 104 33I will sing to the LORD all my life; I will sing praise to my God as long as I live. 34May my meditation be pleasing to him, as I rejoice in the LORD.
Ps 119 11I have hidden your word in my heart that I might not sin against you.
Ps 119 15I meditate on your precepts and consider your ways. 16I delight in your decrees; I will not neglect your word.
Ps 119 27Let me understand the teaching of your precepts; then I will meditate on your wonders.
Ps 119 48I lift up my hands to your commands, which I love, and I meditate on your decrees.
Ps 119 55In the night I remember your name, O LORD, and I will keep your law.
Ps 119 59I have considered my ways and have turned my steps to your statutes.
Ps 119 78May the arrogant be put to shame for wronging me without cause; but I will meditate on your precepts.
Ps 119 95The wicked are waiting to destroy me, but I will ponder your statutes.
Ps 119 97Oh, how I love your law! I meditate on it all day long. 98Your commands make me wiser than my enemies, for they are ever with me. 99I have more insight than all my teachers, for I meditate on your statutes.
Ps 119 148My eyes stay open through the watches of the night, that I may meditate on your promises.
Ps 139 17How precious to me are your thoughts, O God! How vast is the sum of them! 18Were I to count them, they would outnumber the grains of sand. When I awake, I am still with you.
Ps 143 5I remember the days of long ago; I meditate on all your works and consider what your hands have done. 6I spread out my hands to you; my soul thirsts for you like a parched land.
Ps 145 5They will speak of the glorious splendor of your majesty, and I will meditate on your wonderful works.

g) Growth in Grace through Overcoming Sin

Luke 10 19“I have given you authority to trample on snakes and scorpions and to overcome all the power of the enemy; nothing will harm you.”
Rom 12 21Do not be overcome by evil, but overcome evil with good.
1 John 2 13I write to you, fathers, because you have known him who is from the beginning. I write to you, young men, because you have overcome the evil one. I write to you, dear children, because you have known the Father.
1 John 4 3but every spirit that does not acknowledge Jesus is not from God. This is the spirit of the antichrist, which you have heard is coming and even now is already in the world.

4You, dear children, are from God and have overcome them, because the one who is in you is greater than the one who is in the world.
1 John 5 4for everyone born of God overcomes the world. This is the victory that has overcome the world, even our faith. 5Who is it that overcomes the world? Only he who believes that Jesus is the Son of God.
Rev 2 7“He who has an ear, let him hear what the Spirit says to the churches. To him who overcomes, I will give the right to eat from the tree of life, which is in the paradise of God.”
Rev 2 11“He who has an ear, let him hear what the Spirit says to the churches. He who overcomes will not be hurt at all by the second death.”
Rev 2 17“He who has an ear, let him hear what the Spirit says to the churches. To him who overcomes, I will give some of the hidden manna. I will also give him a white stone with a new name written on it, known only to him who receives it.”
Rev 2 26“To him who overcomes and does my will to the end, I will give authority over the nations—27‘He will rule them with an iron scepter; he will dash them to pieces like pottery’—just as I have received authority from my Father. 28I will also give him the morning star.”
Rev 3 4“Yet you have a few people in Sardis who have not soiled their clothes. They will walk with me, dressed in white, for they are worthy. 5He who overcomes will, like them, be dressed in white. I will never blot out his name from the book of life, but will acknowledge his name before my Father and his angels.”
Rev 3 12“Him who overcomes I will make a pillar in the temple of my God. Never again will he leave it. I will write on him the name of my God and the name of the city of my God, the new Jerusalem, which is coming down out of heaven from my God; and I will also write on him my new name.”
Rev 3 21“To him who overcomes, I will give the right to sit with me on my throne, just as I overcame and sat down with my Father on his throne.”
Rev 12 11“They overcame him by the blood of the Lamb and by the word of their testimony; they did not love their lives so much as to shrink from death.”

h) Growth in Grace through Positive Actions

Matt 5 3“Blessed are the poor in spirit, for theirs is the kingdom of heaven. 4Blessed are those who mourn, for they will be comforted. 5Blessed are the meek, for they will inherit the earth. 6Blessed are those who hunger and thirst for righteousness, for they will be filled. 7Blessed are the merciful, for they will be shown mercy. 8Blessed are the pure in heart, for they will see God. 9Blessed are the peacemakers, for they will be called sons of God. 10Blessed are those who are persecuted because of righteousness, for theirs is the kingdom of heaven.”
Matt 5 38“You have heard that it was said, ‘Eye for eye, and tooth for tooth.’ 39But I tell you, Do not resist an evil person. If someone strikes you on the right cheek, turn to him the other also. 40And if someone wants to sue you and take your tunic, let him have your cloak as well. 41If someone forces you to go one mile, go with him two miles. 42Give to the one who asks you, and do not turn away from the one who wants to borrow from you.

43“You have heard that it was said, ‘Love your neighbor and hate your enemy.’ 44But I tell you: Love your enemies and pray for those who persecute you, 45that you may be sons of your Father in heaven. He causes his sun to rise on the evil and the good, and sends rain on the righteous and the unrighteous. 46If you love those who love you, what reward will you get? Are not even the tax collectors doing that? 47And if you greet only your brothers, what are you doing more than others? Do not even pagans do that? 48Be perfect, therefore, as your heavenly Father is perfect.”
Matt 6 14“For if you forgive men when they sin against you,

your heavenly Father will also forgive you. 15But if you do not forgive men their sins, your Father will not forgive your sins."
Matt 18 21Then Peter came to Jesus and asked, "Lord, how many times shall I forgive my brother when he sins against me? Up to seven times?"

22Jesus answered, "I tell you, not seven times, but seventy-seven times.

23"Therefore, the kingdom of heaven is like a king who wanted to settle accounts with his servants. 24As he began the settlement, a man who owed him ten thousand talents was brought to him. 25Since he was not able to pay, the master ordered that he and his wife and his children and all that he had be sold to repay the debt.

26"The servant fell on his knees before him. 'Be patient with me,' he begged, 'and I will pay back everything.' 27The servant's master took pity on him, canceled the debt and let him go.

28"But when that servant went out, he found one of his fellow servants who owed him a hundred denarii. He grabbed him and began to choke him. 'Pay back what you owe me!' he demanded.

29"His fellow servant fell to his knees and begged him, 'Be patient with me, and I will pay you back.'

30"But he refused. Instead, he went off and had the man thrown into prison until he could pay the debt. 31When the other servants saw what had happened, they were greatly distressed and went and told their master everything that had happened.

32"Then the master called the servant in. 'You wicked servant,' he said, 'I canceled all that debt of yours because you begged me to. 33Shouldn't you have had mercy on your fellow servant just as I had on you?' 34In anger his master turned him over to the jailers to be tortured, until he should pay back all he owed.

35"This is how my heavenly Father will treat each of you unless you forgive your brother from your heart."
Mark 11 25"And when you stand praying, if you hold anything against anyone, forgive him, so that your Father in heaven may forgive you your sins."
Luke 6 35"But love your enemies, do good to them, and lend to them without expecting to get anything back. Then your reward will be great, and you will be sons of the Most High, because he is kind to the ungrateful and wicked. 36Be merciful, just as your Father is merciful.

37"Do not judge, and you will not be judged. Do not condemn, and you will not be condemned. Forgive, and you will be forgiven. 38Give, and it will be given to you. A good measure, pressed down, shaken together and running over, will be poured into your lap. For with the measure you use, it will be measured to you."
Luke 17 3"So watch yourselves.

"If your brother sins, rebuke him, and if he repents, forgive him. 4If he sins against you seven times in a day, and seven times comes back to you and says, 'I repent,' forgive him."
Luke 22 24Also a dispute arose among them as to which of them was considered to be greatest. 25Jesus said to them, "The kings of the Gentiles lord it over them; and those who exercise authority over them call themselves Benefactors. 26But you are not to be like that. Instead, the greatest among you should be like the youngest, and the one who rules like the one who serves. 27For who is greater, the one who is at the table or the one who serves? Is it not the one who is at the table? But I am among you as one who serves."
John 13 14"Now that I, your Lord and Teacher, have washed your feet, you also should wash one another's feet. 15I have set you an example that you should do as I have done for you. 16I tell you the truth, no servant is greater than his master, nor is a messenger greater than the one who sent him. 17Now that you know these things, you will be blessed if you do them."
Rom 12 10Be devoted to one another in brotherly love. Honor one another above yourselves. 11Never be lacking in zeal, but keep your spiritual fervor, serving the Lord. 12Be joyful in hope, patient in affliction, faithful in prayer. 13Share with God's people who are in need. Practice hospitality.

14Bless those who persecute you; bless and do not curse. 15Rejoice with those who rejoice; mourn with those who mourn. 16Live in harmony with one another. Do not be proud, but be willing to associate with people of low position. Do not be conceited.

17Do not repay anyone evil for evil. Be careful to do what is right in the eyes of everybody. 18If it is possible, as far as it depends on you, live at peace with everyone. 19Do not take revenge, my friends, but leave room for God's wrath, for it is written: "It is mine to avenge; I will repay," says the Lord. 20On the contrary: "If your enemy is hungry, feed him; if he is thirsty, give him something to drink. In doing this, you will heap burning coals on his head." 21Do not be overcome by evil, but overcome evil with good.
1 Cor 4 12We work hard with our own hands. When we are cursed, we bless; when we are persecuted, we endure it; 13when we are slandered, we answer kindly. Up to this moment we have become the scum of the earth, the refuse of the world.
2 Cor 1 2Grace and peace to you from God our Father and the Lord Jesus Christ.

3Praise be to the God and Father of our Lord Jesus Christ, the Father of compassion and the God of all comfort, 4who comforts us in all our troubles, so that we can comfort those in any trouble with the comfort we ourselves have received from God.
Gal 6 1Brothers, if someone is caught in a sin, you who are spiritual should restore him gently. But watch yourself, or you also may be tempted.
Eph 4 2Be completely humble and gentle; be patient, bearing with one another in love. . . . 32Be kind and compassionate to one another, forgiving each other, just as in Christ God forgave you.
Eph 5 21Submit to one another out of reverence for Christ.
Phil 2 3Do nothing out of selfish ambition or vain conceit, but in humility consider others better than yourselves.
Col 3 12Therefore, as God's chosen people, holy and dearly loved, clothe yourselves with compassion, kindness, humility, gentleness and patience. 13Bear with each other and forgive whatever grievances you may have against one another. Forgive as the Lord forgave you. . . . 16Let the word of Christ dwell in you richly as you teach and admonish one another with all wisdom, and as you sing psalms, hymns and spiritual songs with gratitude in your hearts to God.
Heb 3 13But encourage one another daily, as long as it is called Today, so that none of you may be hardened by sin's deceitfulness.
Heb 10 25Let us not give up meeting together, as some are in the habit of doing, but let us encourage one another—and all the more as you see the Day approaching.
Heb 13 16And do not forget to do good and to share with others, for with such sacrifices God is pleased.
1 Pet 3 8Finally, all of you, live in harmony with one another; be sympathetic, love as brothers, be compassionate and humble. 9Do not repay evil with evil or insult with insult, but with blessing, because to this you were called so that you may inherit a blessing.
1 John 3 17If anyone has material possessions and sees his brother in need but has no pity on him, how can the love of God be in him? 18Dear children, let us not love with words or tongue but with actions and in truth.

i) Growth in Grace through Prayer

2 Chron 7 14". . . if my people, who are called by my name, will humble themselves and pray and seek my face and turn from their wicked ways, then will I hear from heaven and will forgive their sin and will heal their land."
Ps 32 6Therefore let everyone who is godly pray to you while you may be found; surely when the mighty waters rise, they will not reach him.
Ps 145 18The LORD is near to all who call on him, to all who call on him in truth. 19He fulfills the desires of those who fear him; he hears their cry and saves them.
Matt 6 5"And when you pray, do not be like the hypocrites, for they love to pray standing in the synagogues and on the street corners to be seen by men. I tell you the truth, they have received their reward in full. 6But when you pray, go into your room, close the door and pray to your Father, who is unseen. Then your Father, who sees what is done in secret, will reward you. 7And when you pray, do not keep on babbling like pagans,

for they think they will be heard because of their many words. [8]Do not be like them, for your Father knows what you need before you ask him.

[9]"This, then, is how you should pray: 'Our Father in heaven, hallowed be your name, [10]your kingdom come, your will be done on earth as it is in heaven. [11]Give us today our daily bread. [12]Forgive us our debts, as we also have forgiven our debtors. [13]And lead us not into temptation, but deliver us from the evil one.'"

Matt 7 [7]"Ask and it will be given to you; seek and you will find; knock and the door will be opened to you. [8]For everyone who asks receives; he who seeks finds; and to him who knocks, the door will be opened.

[9]"Which of you, if his son asks for bread, will give him a stone? [10]Or if he asks for a fish, will give him a snake? [11]If you, then, though you are evil, know how to give good gifts to your children, how much more will your Father in heaven give good gifts to those who ask him!"

Luke 2 [37]and then was a widow until she was eighty-four. She never left the temple but worshiped night and day, fasting and praying.

Acts 4 [31]After they prayed, the place where they were meeting was shaken. And they were all filled with the Holy Spirit and spoke the word of God boldly.

Rom 8 [26]In the same way, the Spirit helps us in our weakness. We do not know what we ought to pray for, but the Spirit himself intercedes for us with groans that words cannot express.

Eph 6 [18]And pray in the Spirit on all occasions with all kinds of prayers and requests. With this in mind, be alert and always keep on praying for all the saints.

Phil 4 [6]Do not be anxious about anything, but in everything, by prayer and petition, with thanksgiving, present your requests to God.

Col 4 [2]Devote yourselves to prayer, being watchful and thankful.

1 Thess 5 [17]pray continually. . . .

1 Tim 2 [8]I want men everywhere to lift up holy hands in prayer, without anger or disputing.

1 Tim 4 [4]For everything God created is good, and nothing is to be rejected if it is received with thanksgiving, [5]because it is consecrated by the word of God and prayer.

Heb 4 [16]Let us then approach the throne of grace with confidence, so that we may receive mercy and find grace to help us in our time of need.

James 5 [16]Therefore confess your sins to each other and pray for each other so that you may be healed. The prayer of a righteous man is powerful and effective.

Jude [20]But you, dear friends, build yourselves up in your most holy faith and pray in the Holy Spirit.

j) Growth in Grace through the Proper Use of Scripture

Neh 8 [13]On the second day of the month, the heads of all the families, along with the priests and the Levites, gathered around Ezra the scribe to give attention to the words of the Law.

Ps 119 [12]Praise be to you, O LORD; teach me your decrees. [13]With my lips I recount all the laws that come from your mouth. [14]I rejoice in following your statutes as one rejoices in great riches. [15]I meditate on your precepts and consider your ways. [16]I delight in your decrees; I will not neglect your word. . . . [18]Open my eyes that I may see wonderful things in your law.

John 15 [3]"You are already clean because of the word I have spoken to you. . . . [7]If you remain in me and my words remain in you, ask whatever you wish, and it will be given you.'

John 17 [17]"Sanctify them by the truth; your word is truth. . . . [19]For them I sanctify myself, that they too may be truly sanctified."

Acts 17 [11]Now the Bereans were of more noble character than the Thessalonians, for they received the message with great eagerness and examined the Scriptures every day to see if what Paul said was true.

Eph 5 [25]Husbands, love your wives, just as Christ loved the church and gave himself up for her [26]to make her holy, cleansing her by the washing with water through the word. . . .

1 Tim 4 [4]For everything God created is good, and nothing is to be rejected if it is received with thanksgiving, [5]because it is consecrated by the word of God and prayer.

2 Tim 2 [15]Do your best to present yourself to God as one approved, a workman who does not need to be ashamed and who correctly handles the word of truth.

2 Tim 3 [16]All Scripture is God-breathed and is useful for teaching, rebuking, correcting and training in righteousness, [17]so that the man of God may be thoroughly equipped for every good work.

James 1 [25]But the man who looks intently into the perfect law that gives freedom, and continues to do this, not forgetting what he has heard, but doing it—he will be blessed in what he does.

k) Growth in Grace through the Pursuit of Holiness

Job 28 [28]"And he said to man, 'The fear of the Lord—that is wisdom, and to shun evil is understanding.'"

Ps 19 [13]Keep your servant also from willful sins; may they not rule over me. Then will I be blameless, innocent of great transgression.

Ps 24 [3]Who may ascend the hill of the LORD? Who may stand in his holy place? [4]He who has clean hands and a pure heart, who does not lift up his soul to an idol or swear by what is false. [5]He will receive blessing from the LORD and vindication from God his Savior. [6]Such is the generation of those who seek him, who seek your face, O God of Jacob.

Ps 37 [27]Turn from evil and do good; then you will dwell in the land forever. [28]For the LORD loves the just and will not forsake his faithful ones.

They will be protected forever, but the offspring of the wicked will be cut off. . . .

Ps 97 [10]Let those who love the LORD hate evil, for he guards the lives of his faithful ones and delivers them from the hand of the wicked.

Ps 119 [1]Blessed are they whose ways are blameless, who walk according to the law of the LORD. [2]Blessed are they who keep his statutes and seek him with all their heart. [3]They do nothing wrong; they walk in his ways.

Prov 16 [17]The highway of the upright avoids evil; he who guards his way guards his life.

Isa 51 [1]"Listen to me, you who pursue righteousness and who seek the LORD: Look to the rock from which you were cut and to the quarry from which you were hewn. . . ."

Matt 5 [6]"Blessed are those who hunger and thirst for righteousness, for they will be filled. . . . [8]Blessed are the pure in heart, for they will see God."

Acts 24 [16]"So I strive always to keep my conscience clear before God and man."

Rom 6 [1]What shall we say, then? Shall we go on sinning so that grace may increase? [2]By no means! We died to sin; how can we live in it any longer? [3]Or don't you know that all of us who were baptized into Christ Jesus were baptized into his death? [4]We were therefore buried with him through baptism into death in order that, just as Christ was raised from the dead through the glory of the Father, we too may live a new life.

[5]If we have been united with him like this in his death, we will certainly also be united with him in his resurrection. [6]For we know that our old self was crucified with him so that the body of sin might be done away with, that we should no longer be slaves to sin—[7]because anyone who has died has been freed from sin.

[8]Now if we died with Christ, we believe that we will also live with him. [9]For we know that since Christ was raised from the dead, he cannot die again; death no longer has mastery over him. [10]The death he died, he died to sin once for all; but the life he lives, he lives to God.

[11]In the same way, count yourselves dead to sin but alive to God in Christ Jesus. [12]Therefore do not let sin reign in your mortal body so that you obey its evil desires. [13]Do not offer the parts of your body to sin, as instruments of wickedness, but rather offer yourselves to God, as those who have been brought from death to life; and offer the parts of your body to him as instruments of righteousness. [14]For sin shall not be your master, because you are not under law, but under grace.

15What then? Shall we sin because we are not under law but under grace? By no means! 16Don't you know that when you offer yourselves to someone to obey him as slaves, you are slaves to the one whom you obey—whether you are slaves to sin, which leads to death, or to obedience, which leads to righteousness? 17But thanks be to God that, though you used to be slaves to sin, you wholeheartedly obeyed the form of teaching to which you were entrusted. 18You have been set free from sin and have become slaves to righteousness.

19I put this in human terms because you are weak in your natural selves. Just as you used to offer the parts of your body in slavery to impurity and to ever-increasing wickedness, so now offer them in slavery to righteousness leading to holiness. 20When you were slaves to sin, you were free from the control of righteousness. 21What benefit did you reap at that time from the things you are now ashamed of? Those things result in death! 22But now that you have been set free from sin and have become slaves to God, the benefit you reap leads to holiness, and the result is eternal life. 23For the wages of sin is death, but the gift of God is eternal life in Christ Jesus our Lord.

Rom 13 12The night is nearly over; the day is almost here. So let us put aside the deeds of darkness and put on the armor of light. 13Let us behave decently, as in the daytime, not in orgies and drunkenness, not in sexual immorality and debauchery, not in dissension and jealousy. 14Rather, clothe yourselves with the Lord Jesus Christ, and do not think about how to gratify the desires of the sinful nature.

Rom 16 19Everyone has heard about your obedience, so I am full of joy over you; but I want you to be wise about what is good, and innocent about what is evil.

1 Cor 3 16Don't you know that you yourselves are God's temple and that God's Spirit lives in you? 17If anyone destroys God's temple, God will destroy him; for God's temple is sacred, and you are that temple.

1 Cor 5 6Your boasting is not good. Don't you know that a little yeast works through the whole batch of dough? 7Get rid of the old yeast that you may be a new batch without yeast—as you really are. For Christ, our Passover lamb, has been sacrificed. 8Therefore let us keep the Festival, not with the old yeast, the yeast of malice and wickedness, but with bread without yeast, the bread of sincerity and truth.

1 Cor 9 24Do you not know that in a race all the runners run, but only one gets the prize? Run in such a way as to get the prize. 25Everyone who competes in the games goes into strict training. They do it to get a crown that will not last; but we do it to get a crown that will last forever. 26Therefore I do not run like a man running aimlessly; I do not fight like a man beating the air. 27No, I beat my body and make it my slave so that after I have preached to others, I myself will not be disqualified for the prize.

2 Cor 7 1Since we have these promises, dear friends, let us purify ourselves from everything that contaminates body and spirit, perfecting holiness out of reverence for God.

2 Cor 11 2I am jealous for you with a godly jealousy. I promised you to one husband, to Christ, so that I might present you as a pure virgin to him.

Gal 5 22But the fruit of the Spirit is love, joy, peace, patience, kindness, goodness, faithfulness, 23gentleness and self-control. Against such things there is no law. 24Those who belong to Christ Jesus have crucified the sinful nature with its passions and desires. 25Since we live by the Spirit, let us keep in step with the Spirit.

Eph 4 1As a prisoner for the Lord, then, I urge you to live a life worthy of the calling you have received.

Eph 5 8For you were once darkness, but now you are light in the Lord. Live as children of light 9(for the fruit of the light consists in all goodness, righteousness and truth) 10and find out what pleases the Lord. 11Have nothing to do with the fruitless deeds of darkness, but rather expose them.

Phil 2 14Do everything without complaining or arguing, 15so that you may become blameless and pure, children of God without fault in a crooked and depraved generation, in which you shine like stars in the universe 16as you hold out the word of life—in order that I may boast on the day of Christ that I did not run or labor for nothing.

Phil 3 12Not that I have already obtained all this, or have already been made perfect, but I press on to take hold of that for which Christ Jesus took hold of me. 13Brothers, I do not consider myself yet to have taken hold of it. But one thing I do: Forgetting what is behind and straining toward what is ahead, 14I press on toward the goal to win the prize for which God has called me heavenward in Christ Jesus.

Phil 4 8Finally, brothers, whatever is true, whatever is noble, whatever is right, whatever is pure, whatever is lovely, whatever is admirable—if anything is excellent or praiseworthy—think about such things.

1 Thess 4 3It is God's will that you should be sanctified: that you should avoid sexual immorality; 4that each of you should learn to control his own body in a way that is holy and honorable. . . . 7For God did not call us to be impure, but to live a holy life.

1 Thess 5 22Avoid every kind of evil.

1 Tim 5 22Do not be hasty in the laying on of hands, and do not share in the sins of others. Keep yourself pure.

1 Tim 6 11But you, man of God, flee from all this, and pursue righteousness, godliness, faith, love, endurance and gentleness. 12Fight the good fight of the faith. Take hold of the eternal life to which you were called when you made your good confession in the presence of many witnesses.

2 Tim 2 19Nevertheless, God's solid foundation stands firm, sealed with this inscription: "The Lord knows those who are his," and, "Everyone who confesses the name of the Lord must turn away from wickedness."

20In a large house there are articles not only of gold and silver, but also of wood and clay; some are for noble purposes and some for ignoble. 21If a man cleanses himself from the latter, he will be an instrument for noble purposes, made holy, useful to the Master and prepared to do any good work.

22Flee the evil desires of youth, and pursue righteousness, faith, love and peace, along with those who call on the Lord out of a pure heart.

Heb 12 1Therefore, since we are surrounded by such a great cloud of witnesses, let us throw off everything that hinders and the sin that so easily entangles, and let us run with perseverance the race marked out for us. 2Let us fix our eyes on Jesus, the author and perfecter of our faith, who for the joy set before him endured the cross, scorning its shame, and sat down at the right hand of the throne of God.

Heb 12 14Make every effort to live in peace with all men and to be holy; without holiness no one will see the Lord. 15See to it that no one misses the grace of God and that no bitter root grows up to cause trouble and defile many.

James 1 21Therefore, get rid of all moral filth and the evil that is so prevalent and humbly accept the word planted in you, which can save you. . . . 27Religion that God our Father accepts as pure and faultless is this: to look after orphans and widows in their distress and to keep oneself from being polluted by the world.

1 Pet 1 14As obedient children, do not conform to the evil desires you had when you lived in ignorance. 15But just as he who called you is holy, so be holy in all you do; 16for it is written: "Be holy, because I am holy."

1 Pet 2 9But you are a chosen people, a royal priesthood, a holy nation, a people belonging to God, that you may declare the praises of him who called you out of darkness into his wonderful light. 10Once you were not a people, but now you are the people of God; once you had not received mercy, but now you have received mercy.

11Dear friends, I urge you, as aliens and strangers in the world, to abstain from sinful desires, which war against your soul. 12Live such good lives among the pagans that, though they accuse you of doing wrong, they may see your good deeds and glorify God on the day he visits us.

1 Pet 3 10For, "Whoever would love life and see good days must keep his tongue from evil and his lips from deceitful speech. 11He must turn from evil and do good; he must seek peace and pursue it."

1 Pet 4 1Therefore, since Christ suffered in his body, arm yourselves also with the same attitude, because he who has suffered in his body is done with sin. 2As a result, he does not live the rest of his earthly life for evil human desires, but rather for the will of God.

2 Pet 3 11Since everything will be destroyed in this way, what kind of people ought you to be? You ought to live holy and godly lives 12as you look forward to the day of God and speed its coming. That day will bring about the destruction of the heavens by fire, and the elements will melt in the heat. 13But in keeping with his promise we are looking forward to a new heaven and a new earth, the home of righteousness. . . .
1 John 2 1My dear children, I write this to you so that you will not sin. But if anybody does sin, we have one who speaks to the Father in our defense—Jesus Christ, the Righteous One.

29If you know that he is righteous, you know that everyone who does what is right has been born of him.
1 John 3 2Dear friends, now we are children of God, and what we will be has not yet been made known. But we know that when he appears, we shall be like him, for we shall see him as he is. 3Everyone who has this hope in him purifies himself, just as he is pure.
1 John 5 21Dear children, keep yourselves from idols.
3 John 11Dear friend, do not imitate what is evil but what is good. Anyone who does what is good is from God. Anyone who does what is evil has not seen God.
Rev 14 4These are those who did not defile themselves with women, for they kept themselves pure. They follow the Lamb wherever he goes. They were purchased from among men and offered as firstfruits to God and the Lamb. 5No lie was found in their mouths; they are blameless.

l) Growth in Grace through Repentance

Deut 4 29But if from there you seek the LORD your God, you will find him if you look for him with all your heart and with all your soul. 30When you are in distress and all these things have happened to you, then in later days you will return to the LORD your God and obey him. 31For the LORD your God is a merciful God; he will not abandon or destroy you or forget the covenant with your forefathers, which he confirmed to them by oath.
2 Kings 22 19"'Because your heart was responsive and you humbled yourself before the LORD when you heard what I have spoken against this place and its people, that they would become accursed and laid waste, and because you tore your robes and wept in my presence, I have heard you, declares the LORD.'"
2 Chron 7 14". . . if my people, who are called by my name, will humble themselves and pray and seek my face and turn from their wicked ways, then will I hear from heaven and will forgive their sin and will heal their land."
Neh 1 9"'. . . but if you return to me and obey my commands, then even if your exiled people are at the farthest horizon, I will gather them from there and bring them to the place I have chosen as a dwelling for my Name.'"
Job 33 26"He prays to God and finds favor with him, he sees God's face and shouts for joy; he is restored by God to his righteous state. 27Then he comes to men and says, 'I sinned, and perverted what was right, but I did not get what I deserved. 28He redeemed my soul from going down to the pit, and I will live to enjoy the light.'"
Ps 6 8Away from me, all you who do evil, for the LORD has heard my weeping. 9The LORD has heard my cry for mercy; the LORD accepts my prayer.
Ps 51 17The sacrifices of God are a broken spirit; a broken and contrite heart, O God, you will not despise.
Isa 55 6Seek the LORD while he may be found; call on him while he is near. 7Let the wicked forsake his way and the evil man his thoughts. Let him turn to the LORD, and he will have mercy on him, and to our God, for he will freely pardon.
Isa 57 15For this is what the high and lofty One says—he who lives forever, whose name is holy: "I live in a high and holy place, but also with him who is contrite and lowly in spirit, to revive the spirit of the lowly and to revive the heart of the contrite."
Isa 66 2"Has not my hand made all these things, and so they came into being?" declares the LORD.

"This is the one I esteem: he who is humble and contrite in spirit, and trembles at my word."
Jer 24 7"'I will give them a heart to know me, that I am the LORD. They will be my people, and I will be their God, for they will return to me with all their heart.'"
Jer 31 9"They will come with weeping; they will pray as I bring them back. I will lead them beside streams of water on a level path where they will not stumble, because I am Israel's father, and Ephraim is my firstborn son."
Ezek 18 21"But if a wicked man turns away from all the sins he has committed and keeps all my decrees and does what is just and right, he will surely live; he will not die. 22None of the offenses he has committed will be remembered against him. Because of the righteous things he has done, he will live. 23Do I take any pleasure in the death of the wicked? declares the Sovereign LORD. Rather, am I not pleased when they turn from their ways and live?"
Hos 10 12"Sow for yourselves righteousness, reap the fruit of unfailing love, and break up your unplowed ground; for it is time to seek the LORD, until he comes and showers righteousness on you."
Luke 18 10"Two men went up to the temple to pray, one a Pharisee and the other a tax collector. 11The Pharisee stood up and prayed about himself: 'God, I thank you that I am not like other men—robbers, evildoers, adulterers—or even like this tax collector. 12I fast twice a week and give a tenth of all I get.'

13"But the tax collector stood at a distance. He would not even look up to heaven, but beat his breast and said, 'God, have mercy on me, a sinner.'

14"I tell you that this man, rather than the other, went home justified before God. For everyone who exalts himself will be humbled, and he who humbles himself will be exalted."
2 Cor 7 8Even if I caused you sorrow by my letter, I do not regret it. Though I did regret it—I see that my letter hurt you, but only for a little while—9yet now I am happy, not because you were made sorry, but because your sorrow led you to repentance. For you became sorrowful as God intended and so were not harmed in any way by us. 10Godly sorrow brings repentance that leads to salvation and leaves no regret, but worldly sorrow brings death. 11See what this godly sorrow has produced in you: what earnestness, what eagerness to clear yourselves, what indignation, what alarm, what longing, what concern, what readiness to see justice done. At every point you have proved yourselves to be innocent in this matter.
James 4 8Come near to God and he will come near to you. Wash your hands, you sinners, and purify your hearts, you double-minded. 9Grieve, mourn and wail. Change your laughter to mourning and your joy to gloom. 10Humble yourselves before the Lord, and he will lift you up.
1 Pet 2 25For you were like sheep going astray, but now you have returned to the Shepherd and Overseer of your souls.
Rev 2 5"Remember the height from which you have fallen! Repent and do the things you did at first. If you do not repent, I will come to you and remove your lampstand from its place."
Rev 2 16"Repent therefore! Otherwise, I will soon come to you and will fight against them with the sword of my mouth."
Rev 3 2"Wake up! Strengthen what remains and is about to die, for I have not found your deeds complete in the sight of my God. 3Remember, therefore, what you have received and heard; obey it, and repent. But if you do not wake up, I will come like a thief, and you will not know at what time I will come to you."
Rev 3 19"Those whom I love I rebuke and discipline. So be earnest, and repent. 20Here I am! I stand at the door and knock. If anyone hears my voice and opens the door, I will come in and eat with him, and he with me."

m) Growth in Grace through Seeking and Submitting to God

Deut 4 29But if from there you seek the LORD your God, you will find him if you look for him with all your heart and with all your soul.
1 Chron 16 11Look to the LORD and his strength; seek his face always.
1 Chron 22 19"Now devote your heart and soul to seeking the LORD your God. Begin to build the sanctuary of the LORD God, so that you may bring the ark of the covenant of the LORD and the sacred articles belonging to God into the temple that will be built for the Name of the LORD."
Ps 25 4Show me your ways, O LORD, teach me your paths; 5guide me in your truth and teach me, for you are God my

Savior, and my hope is in you all day long. . . . [20]Guard my life and rescue me; let me not be put to shame, for I take refuge in you. [21]May integrity and uprightness protect me, because my hope is in you.

Ps 27 [4]One thing I ask of the LORD, this is what I seek: that I may dwell in the house of the LORD all the days of my life, to gaze upon the beauty of the LORD and to seek him in his temple. . . . [8]My heart says of you, "Seek his face!" Your face, LORD, I will seek. . . .

[13]I am still confident of this: I will see the goodness of the LORD in the land of the living. [14]Wait for the LORD; be strong and take heart and wait for the LORD.

Ps 42 [1]As the deer pants for streams of water, so my soul pants for you, O God. [2]My soul thirsts for God, for the living God. When can I go and meet with God?

Ps 63 [1]O God, you are my God, earnestly I seek you; my soul thirsts for you, my body longs for you, in a dry and weary land where there is no water.

[2]I have seen you in the sanctuary and beheld your power and your glory. [3]Because your love is better than life, my lips will glorify you. [4]I will praise you as long as I live, and in your name I will lift up my hands. [5]My soul will be satisfied as with the richest of foods; with singing lips my mouth will praise you.

[6]On my bed I remember you; I think of you through the watches of the night. [7]Because you are my help, I sing in the shadow of your wings. [8]My soul clings to you; your right hand upholds me.

Ps 84 [1]How lovely is your dwelling place, O LORD Almighty! [2]My soul yearns, even faints, for the courts of the LORD; my heart and my flesh cry out for the living God.

[3]Even the sparrow has found a home, and the swallow a nest for herself, where she may have her young—a place near your altar, O LORD Almighty, my King and my God. [4]Blessed are those who dwell in your house; they are ever praising you.

Ps 105 [4]Look to the LORD and his strength; seek his face always.

Ps 130 [5]I wait for the LORD, my soul waits, and in his word I put my hope. [6]My soul waits for the Lord more than watchmen wait for the morning, more than watchmen wait for the morning.

Ps 143 [6]I spread out my hands to you; my soul thirsts for you like a parched land.

Ps 145 [18]The LORD is near to all who call on him, to all who call on him in truth. [19]He fulfills the desires of those who fear him; he hears their cry and saves them.

Jer 29 [13]"You will seek me and find me when you seek me with all your heart."

Lam 3 [25]The LORD is good to those whose hope is in him, to the one who seeks him; [26]it is good to wait quietly for the salvation of the LORD.

Matt 6 [33]"But seek first his kingdom and his righteousness, and all these things will be given to you as well."

Matt 11 [28]"Come to me, all you who are weary and burdened, and I will give you rest. [29]Take my yoke upon you and learn from me, for I am gentle and humble in heart, and you will find rest for your souls. [30]For my yoke is easy and my burden is light."

Luke 13 [23]Someone asked him, "Lord, are only a few people going to be saved?"

He said to them, [24]"Make every effort to enter through the narrow door, because many, I tell you, will try to enter and will not be able to."

Rom 6 [13]Do not offer the parts of your body to sin, as instruments of wickedness, but rather offer yourselves to God, as those who have been brought from death to life; and offer the parts of your body to him as instruments of righteousness. [14]For sin shall not be your master, because you are not under law, but under grace.

[15]What then? Shall we sin because we are not under law but under grace? By no means! [16]Don't you know that when you offer yourselves to someone to obey him as slaves, you are slaves to the one whom you obey—whether you are slaves to sin, which leads to death, or to obedience, which leads to righteousness? [17]But thanks be to God that, though you used to be slaves to sin, you wholeheartedly obeyed the form of teaching to which you were entrusted. [18]You have been set free from sin and have become slaves to righteousness.

[19]I put this in human terms because you are weak in your natural selves. Just as you used to offer the parts of your body in slavery to impurity and to ever-increasing wickedness, so now offer them in slavery to righteousness leading to holiness. [20]When you were slaves to sin, you were free from the control of righteousness. [21]What benefit did you reap at that time from the things you are now ashamed of? Those things result in death!

Rom 12 [1]Therefore, I urge you, brothers, in view of God's mercy, to offer your bodies as living sacrifices, holy and pleasing to God—this is your spiritual act of worship. [2]Do not conform any longer to the pattern of this world, but be transformed by the renewing of your mind. Then you will be able to test and approve what God's will is—his good, pleasing and perfect will.

2 Cor 5 [14]For Christ's love compels us, because we are convinced that one died for all, and therefore all died. [15]And he died for all, that those who live should no longer live for themselves but for him who died for them and was raised again.

Phil 2 [12]Therefore, my dear friends, as you have always obeyed—not only in my presence, but now much more in my absence—continue to work out your salvation with fear and trembling, [13]for it is God who works in you to will and to act according to his good purpose.

James 4 [8]Come near to God and he will come near to you. Wash your hands, you sinners, and purify your hearts, you double-minded.

n) Growth in Grace through Subduing the Flesh

Rom 6 [19]I put this in human terms because you are weak in your natural selves. Just as you used to offer the parts of your body in slavery to impurity and to ever-increasing wickedness, so now offer them in slavery to righteousness leading to holiness. [20]When you were slaves to sin, you were free from the control of righteousness. [21]What benefit did you reap at that time from the things you are now ashamed of? Those things result in death! [22]But now that you have been set free from sin and have become slaves to God, the benefit you reap leads to holiness, and the result is eternal life.

Rom 8 [1]Therefore, there is now no condemnation for those who are in Christ Jesus, [2]because through Christ Jesus the law of the Spirit of life set me free from the law of sin and death. [3]For what the law was powerless to do in that it was weakened by the sinful nature, God did by sending his own Son in the likeness of sinful man to be a sin offering. And so he condemned sin in sinful man, [4]in order that the righteous requirements of the law might be fully met in us, who do not live according to the sinful nature but according to the Spirit.

[5]Those who live according to the sinful nature have their minds set on what that nature desires; but those who live in accordance with the Spirit have their minds set on what the Spirit desires. [6]The mind of sinful man is death, but the mind controlled by the Spirit is life and peace; [7]the sinful mind is hostile to God. It does not submit to God's law, nor can it do so. [8]Those controlled by the sinful nature cannot please God.

[9]You, however, are controlled not by the sinful nature but by the Spirit, if the Spirit of God lives in you. And if anyone does not have the Spirit of Christ, he does not belong to Christ. [10]But if Christ is in you, your body is dead because of sin, yet your spirit is alive because of righteousness. [11]And if the Spirit of him who raised Jesus from the dead is living in you, he who raised Christ from the dead will also give life to your mortal bodies through his Spirit, who lives in you.

[12]Therefore, brothers, we have an obligation—but it is not to the sinful nature, to live according to it. [13]For if you live according to the sinful nature, you will die; but if by the Spirit you put to death the misdeeds of the body, you will live, [14]because those who are led by the Spirit of God are sons of God.

Rom 13 [14]Rather, clothe yourselves with the Lord Jesus Christ, and do not think about how to gratify the desires of the sinful nature.

Gal 2 [20]I have been crucified with Christ and I no longer live, but Christ lives in me. The life I live in the body, I live by faith in the Son of God, who loved me and gave himself for me.

Gal 3 [3]Are you so foolish? After beginning with the Spirit, are you now trying to attain your goal by human effort?
Gal 5 [13]You, my brothers, were called to be free. But do not use your freedom to indulge the sinful nature; rather, serve one another in love. . . .

[16]So I say, live by the Spirit, and you will not gratify the desires of the sinful nature. [17]For the sinful nature desires what is contrary to the Spirit, and the Spirit what is contrary to the sinful nature. They are in conflict with each other, so that you do not do what you want. [18]But if you are led by the Spirit, you are not under law.

[19]The acts of the sinful nature are obvious: sexual immorality, impurity and debauchery; [20]idolatry and witchcraft; hatred, discord, jealousy, fits of rage, selfish ambition, dissensions, factions [21]and envy; drunkenness, orgies, and the like. I warn you, as I did before, that those who live like this will not inherit the kingdom of God.

[22]But the fruit of the Spirit is love, joy, peace, patience, kindness, goodness, faithfulness, [23]gentleness and self-control. Against such things there is no law. [24]Those who belong to Christ Jesus have crucified the sinful nature with its passions and desires.
1 Pet 2 [11]Dear friends, I urge you, as aliens and strangers in the world, to abstain from sinful desires, which war against your soul.
Jude [23]snatch others from the fire and save them; to others show mercy, mixed with fear—hating even the clothing stained by corrupted flesh.

III
Sanctification: *Goals and Hindrances*

A. Goals of Sanctification

1. Total Moral Perfection

John 17 [19]"For them I sanctify myself, that they too may be truly sanctified."
2 Cor 7 [1]Since we have these promises, dear friends, let us purify ourselves from everything that contaminates body and spirit, perfecting holiness out of reverence for God.
2 Cor 13 [9]We are glad whenever we are weak but you are strong; and our prayer is for your perfection. . . .

[11]Finally, brothers, good-by. Aim for perfection, listen to my appeal, be of one mind, live in peace. And the God of love and peace will be with you.
Eph 1 [4]For he chose us in him before the creation of the world to be holy and blameless in his sight. In love . . .
Eph 5 [25]Husbands, love your wives, just as Christ loved the church and gave himself up for her [26]to make her holy, cleansing her by the washing with water through the word, [27]and to present her to himself as a radiant church, without stain or wrinkle or any other blemish, but holy and blameless.
Phil 1 [9]And this is my prayer: that your love may abound more and more in knowledge and depth of insight, [10]so that you may be able to discern what is best and may be pure and blameless until the day of Christ, [11]filled with the fruit of righteousness that comes through Jesus Christ—to the glory and praise of God.
Phil 2 [14]Do everything without complaining or arguing, [15]so that you may become blameless and pure, children of God without fault in a crooked and depraved generation, in which you shine like stars in the universe. . . .
Col 1 [21]Once you were alienated from God and were enemies in your minds because of your evil behavior. [22]But now he has reconciled you by Christ's physical body through death to present you holy in his sight, without blemish and free from accusation. . . .
Col 1 [28]We proclaim him, admonishing and teaching everyone with all wisdom, so that we may present everyone perfect in Christ. [29]To this end I labor, struggling with all his energy, which so powerfully works in me.
Col 3 [14]And over all these virtues put on love, which binds them all together in perfect unity.
1 Thess 3 [13]May he strengthen your hearts so that you will be blameless and holy in the presence of our God and Father when our Lord Jesus comes with all his holy ones.
1 Thess 5 [23]May God himself, the God of peace, sanctify you through and through. May your whole spirit, soul and body be kept blameless at the coming of our Lord Jesus Christ. [24]The one who calls you is faithful and he will do it.
2 Tim 3 [16]All Scripture is God-breathed and is useful for teaching, rebuking, correcting and training in righteousness, [17]so that the man of God may be thoroughly equipped for every good work.
James 1 [2]Consider it pure joy, my brothers, whenever you face trials of many kinds, [3]because you know that the testing of your faith develops perseverance. [4]Perseverance must finish its work so that you may be mature and complete, not lacking anything.
2 Pet 3 [13]But in keeping with his promise we are looking forward to a new heaven and a new earth, the home of righteousness.

[14]So then, dear friends, since you are looking forward to this, make every effort to be found spotless, blameless and at peace with him.
1 John 3 [2]Dear friends, now we are children of God, and what we will be has not yet been made known. But we know that when he appears, we shall be like him, for we shall see him as he is. [3]Everyone who has this hope in him purifies himself, just as he is pure. . . . [6]No one who lives in him keeps on sinning. No one who continues to sin has either seen him or known him. . . . [9]No one who is born of God will continue to sin, because God's seed remains in him; he cannot go on sinning, because he has been born of God.
1 John 4 [12]No one has ever seen God; but if we love one another, God lives in us and his love is made complete in us.

2. Moral Identification with God the Father

a) We Are to Be like the Father

Matt 5 [48]"Be perfect, therefore, as your heavenly Father is perfect."
Eph 4 [20]You, however, did not come to know Christ that way. [21]Surely you heard of him and were taught in him in accordance with the truth that is in Jesus. [22]You were taught, with regard to your former way of life, to put off your old self, which is being corrupted by its deceitful desires; [23]to be made new in the attitude of your minds; [24]and to put on the new self, created to be like God in true righteousness and holiness.

b) We Are to Imitate God Now

Lev 11 [44]"'I am the LORD your God; consecrate yourselves and be holy, because I am holy. Do not make yourselves unclean by any creature that moves about on the ground. [45]I am the LORD who brought you up out of Egypt to be your God; therefore be holy, because I am holy.'"
Luke 6 [36]"Be merciful, just as your Father is merciful."
Eph 4 [32]Be kind and compassionate to one another, forgiving each other, just as in Christ God forgave you.
Eph 5 [1]Be imitators of God, therefore, as dearly loved children [2]and live a life of love, just as Christ loved us and gave himself up for us as a fragrant offering and sacrifice to God.
1 Pet 1 [13]Therefore, prepare your minds for action; be self-controlled; set your hope fully on the grace to be given you when Jesus Christ is revealed. [14]As obedient children, do not conform to the evil desires you had when you lived in ignorance. [15]But just as he who called you is holy, so be holy in all you do; [16]for it is written: "Be holy, because I am holy."

3. Conformity to Christ the Son

a) We Are to Be like Christ

Rom 8 [28]And we know that in all things God works for the good of those who love him, who have been called according to his purpose. [29]For those God foreknew he also predestined to be conformed to the likeness of his Son, that he might be the firstborn among many brothers. [30]And those he predestined, he

also called; those he called, he also justified; those he justified, he also glorified.
1 Cor 2 [16]"For who has known the mind of the Lord that he may instruct him?" But we have the mind of Christ.
2 Cor 3 [18]And we, who with unveiled faces all reflect the Lord's glory, are being transformed into his likeness with ever-increasing glory, which comes from the Lord, who is the Spirit.
Eph 4 [11]It was he who gave some to be apostles, some to be prophets, some to be evangelists, and some to be pastors and teachers, [12]to prepare God's people for works of service, so that the body of Christ may be built up [13]until we all reach unity in the faith and in the knowledge of the Son of God and become mature, attaining to the whole measure of the fullness of Christ.
Phil 2 [5]Your attitude should be the same as that of Christ Jesus. . . .

b) We Are to Imitate Christ Now

John 13 [15]"I have set you an example that you should do as I have done for you."
Rom 13 [14]Rather, clothe yourselves with the Lord Jesus Christ, and do not think about how to gratify the desires of the sinful nature.
1 Cor 11 [1]Follow my example, as I follow the example of Christ.
Gal 3 [27]for all of you who were baptized into Christ have clothed yourselves with Christ.
Phil 3 [10]I want to know Christ and the power of his resurrection and the fellowship of sharing in his sufferings, becoming like him in his death. . . .
1 Thess 1 [6]You became imitators of us and of the Lord; in spite of severe suffering, you welcomed the message with the joy given by the Holy Spirit.
1 Pet 2 [21]To this you were called, because Christ suffered for you, leaving you an example, that you should follow in his steps.
2 Pet 1 [4]Through these he has given us his very great and precious promises, so that through them you may participate in the divine nature and escape the corruption in the world caused by evil desires.
1 John 2 [6]Whoever claims to live in him must walk as Jesus did.
1 John 3 [1]How great is the love the Father has lavished on us, that we should be called children of God! And that is what we are! The reason the world does not know us is that it did not know him. [2]Dear friends, now we are children of God, and what we will be has not yet been made known. But we know that when he appears, we shall be like him, for we shall see him as he is. [3]Everyone who has this hope in him purifies himself, just as he is pure.

4. A Life of Good Works

a) A Life of Good Works Has Been Commanded

(1) Jesus Commanded a Life of Good Works

Matt 5 [13]"You are the salt of the earth. But if the salt loses its saltiness, how can it be made salty again? It is no longer good for anything, except to be thrown out and trampled by men.

[14]"You are the light of the world. A city on a hill cannot be hidden. [15]Neither do people light a lamp and put it under a bowl. Instead they put it on its stand, and it gives light to everyone in the house. [16]In the same way, let your light shine before men, that they may see your good deeds and praise your Father in heaven."
Matt 6 [1]"Be careful not to do your 'acts of righteousness' before men, to be seen by them. If you do, you will have no reward from your Father in heaven.

[2]"So when you give to the needy, do not announce it with trumpets, as the hypocrites do in the synagogues and on the streets, to be honored by men. I tell you the truth, they have received their reward in full. [3]But when you give to the needy, do not let your left hand know what your right hand is doing, [4]so that your giving may be in secret. Then your Father, who sees what is done in secret, will reward you.

[5]"And when you pray, do not be like the hypocrites, for they love to pray standing in the synagogues and on the street corners to be seen by men. I tell you the truth, they have received their reward in full. [6]But when you pray, go into your room, close the door and pray to your Father, who is unseen. Then your Father, who sees what is done in secret, will reward you. [7]And when you pray, do not keep on babbling like pagans, for they think they will be heard because of their many words. [8]Do not be like them, for your Father knows what you need before you ask him.

[9]"This, then, is how you should pray: 'Our Father in heaven, hallowed be your name, [10]your kingdom come, your will be done on earth as it is in heaven. [11]Give us today our daily bread. [12]Forgive us our debts, as we also have forgiven our debtors. [13]And lead us not into temptation, but deliver us from the evil one.' [14]For if you forgive men when they sin against you, your heavenly Father will also forgive you. [15]But if you do not forgive men their sins, your Father will not forgive your sins.

[16]"When you fast, do not look somber as the hypocrites do, for they disfigure their faces to show men they are fasting. I tell you the truth, they have received their reward in full. [17]But when you fast, put oil on your head and wash your face, [18]so that it will not be obvious to men that you are fasting, but only to your Father, who is unseen; and your Father, who sees what is done in secret, will reward you.

[19]"Do not store up for yourselves treasures on earth, where moth and rust destroy, and where thieves break in and steal. [20]But store up for yourselves treasures in heaven, where moth and rust do not destroy, and where thieves do not break in and steal. [21]For where your treasure is, there your heart will be also.

[22]"The eye is the lamp of the body. If your eyes are good, your whole body will be full of light. [23]But if your eyes are bad, your whole body will be full of darkness. If then the light within you is darkness, how great is that darkness!

[24]"No one can serve two masters. Either he will hate the one and love the other, or he will be devoted to the one and despise the other. You cannot serve both God and Money."
John 3 [21]"But whoever lives by the truth comes into the light, so that it may be seen plainly that what he has done has been done through God."

(2) Paul Commanded a Life of Good Works

Rom 2 [9]There will be trouble and distress for every human being who does evil: first for the Jew, then for the Gentile; [10]but glory, honor and peace for everyone who does good: first for the Jew, then for the Gentile.
2 Cor 9 [8]And God is able to make all grace abound to you, so that in all things at all times, having all that you need, you will abound in every good work.
Eph 2 [10]For we are God's workmanship, created in Christ Jesus to do good works, which God prepared in advance for us to do.
Col 3 [12]Therefore, as God's chosen people, holy and dearly loved, clothe yourselves with compassion, kindness, humility, gentleness and patience. [13]Bear with each other and forgive whatever grievances you may have against one another. Forgive as the Lord forgave you. [14]And over all these virtues put on love, which binds them all together in perfect unity.

[15]Let the peace of Christ rule in your hearts, since as members of one body you were called to peace. And be thankful. [16]Let the word of Christ dwell in you richly as you teach and admonish one another with all wisdom, and as you sing psalms, hymns and spiritual songs with gratitude in your hearts to God. [17]And whatever you do, whether in word or deed, do it all in the name of the Lord Jesus, giving thanks to God the Father through him.
2 Thess 2 [16]May our Lord Jesus Christ himself and God our Father, who loved us and by his grace gave us eternal encouragement and good hope, [17]encourage your hearts and strengthen you in every good deed and word.
1 Tim 2 [9]I also want women to dress modestly, with decency and propriety, not with braided hair or gold or pearls or expensive clothes, [10]but with good deeds, appropriate for women who profess to worship God.
1 Tim 5 [9]No widow may be put on the list of widows unless she is over sixty, has been faithful to her husband, [10]and is well known for her good deeds, such as bringing up children, show-

ing hospitality, washing the feet of the saints, helping those in trouble and devoting herself to all kinds of good deeds.

1 Tim 6 [17]Command those who are rich in this present world not to be arrogant nor to put their hope in wealth, which is so uncertain, but to put their hope in God, who richly provides us with everything for our enjoyment. [18]Command them to do good, to be rich in good deeds, and to be generous and willing to share. [19]In this way they will lay up treasure for themselves as a firm foundation for the coming age, so that they may take hold of the life that is truly life.

2 Tim 2 [20]In a large house there are articles not only of gold and silver, but also of wood and clay; some are for noble purposes and some for ignoble. [21]If a man cleanses himself from the latter, he will be an instrument for noble purposes, made holy, useful to the Master and prepared to do any good work.

2 Tim 3 [16]All Scripture is God-breathed and is useful for teaching, rebuking, correcting and training in righteousness, [17]so that the man of God may be thoroughly equipped for every good work.

Titus 2 [11]For the grace of God that brings salvation has appeared to all men. [12]It teaches us to say "No" to ungodliness and worldly passions, and to live self-controlled, upright and godly lives in this present age, [13]while we wait for the blessed hope—the glorious appearing of our great God and Savior, Jesus Christ, [14]who gave himself for us to redeem us from all wickedness and to purify for himself a people that are his very own, eager to do what is good.

Titus 3 [1]Remind the people to be subject to rulers and authorities, to be obedient, to be ready to do whatever is good, [2]to slander no one, to be peaceable and considerate, and to show true humility toward all men.

Titus 3 [8]This is a trustworthy saying. And I want you to stress these things, so that those who have trusted in God may be careful to devote themselves to doing what is good. These things are excellent and profitable for everyone.

Titus 3 [14]Our people must learn to devote themselves to doing what is good, in order that they may provide for daily necessities and not live unproductive lives.

(3) The Author of Hebrews Commanded a Life of Good Works

Heb 10 [24]And let us consider how we may spur one another on toward love and good deeds. [25]Let us not give up meeting together, as some are in the habit of doing, but let us encourage one another—and all the more as you see the Day approaching.

Heb 13 [20]May the God of peace, who through the blood of the eternal covenant brought back from the dead our Lord Jesus, that great Shepherd of the sheep, [21]equip you with everything good for doing his will, and may he work in us what is pleasing to him, through Jesus Christ, to whom be glory for ever and ever. Amen.

(4) James Commanded a Life of Good Works

James 1 [19]My dear brothers, take note of this: Everyone should be quick to listen, slow to speak and slow to become angry, [20]for man's anger does not bring about the righteous life that God desires. [21]Therefore, get rid of all moral filth and the evil that is so prevalent and humbly accept the word planted in you, which can save you.

[22]Do not merely listen to the word, and so deceive yourselves. Do what it says. [23]Anyone who listens to the word but does not do what it says is like a man who looks at his face in a mirror [24]and, after looking at himself, goes away and immediately forgets what he looks like. [25]But the man who looks intently into the perfect law that gives freedom, and continues to do this, not forgetting what he has heard, but doing it—he will be blessed in what he does.

[26]If anyone considers himself religious and yet does not keep a tight rein on his tongue, he deceives himself and his religion is worthless. [27]Religion that God our Father accepts as pure and faultless is this: to look after orphans and widows in their distress and to keep oneself from being polluted by the world.

James 2 [14]What good is it, my brothers, if a man claims to have faith but has no deeds? Can such faith save him? [15]Suppose a brother or sister is without clothes and daily food. [16]If one of you says to him, "Go, I wish you well; keep warm and well fed," but does nothing about his physical needs, what good is it? [17]In the same way, faith by itself, if it is not accompanied by action, is dead.

[18]But someone will say, "You have faith; I have deeds."

Show me your faith without deeds, and I will show you my faith by what I do. [19]You believe that there is one God. Good! Even the demons believe that—and shudder.

[20]You foolish man, do you want evidence that faith without deeds is useless? [21]Was not our ancestor Abraham considered righteous for what he did when he offered his son Isaac on the altar? [22]You see that his faith and his actions were working together, and his faith was made complete by what he did. [23]And the scripture was fulfilled that says, "Abraham believed God, and it was credited to him as righteousness," and he was called God's friend. [24]You see that a person is justified by what he does and not by faith alone.

[25]In the same way, was not even Rahab the prostitute considered righteous for what she did when she gave lodging to the spies and sent them off in a different direction? [26]As the body without the spirit is dead, so faith without deeds is dead.

James 3 [13]Who is wise and understanding among you? Let him show it by his good life, by deeds done in the humility that comes from wisdom. [14]But if you harbor bitter envy and selfish ambition in your hearts, do not boast about it or deny the truth. [15]Such "wisdom" does not come down from heaven but is earthly, unspiritual, of the devil. [16]For where you have envy and selfish ambition, there you find disorder and every evil practice.

[17]But the wisdom that comes from heaven is first of all pure; then peace-loving, considerate, submissive, full of mercy and good fruit, impartial and sincere. [18]Peacemakers who sow in peace raise a harvest of righteousness.

(5) Peter Commanded a Life of Good Works

1 Pet 1 [14]As obedient children, do not conform to the evil desires you had when you lived in ignorance. [15]But just as he who called you is holy, so be holy in all you do; [16]for it is written: "Be holy, because I am holy."

1 Pet 2 [12]Live such good lives among the pagans that, though they accuse you of doing wrong, they may see your good deeds and glorify God on the day he visits us. . . . [15]For it is God's will that by doing good you should silence the ignorant talk of foolish men. [16]Live as free men, but do not use your freedom as a cover-up for evil; live as servants of God. [17]Show proper respect to everyone: Love the brotherhood of believers, fear God, honor the king.

(6) John Commanded a Life of Good Works

Rev 14 [13]Then I heard a voice from heaven say, "Write: Blessed are the dead who die in the Lord from now on."

"Yes," says the Spirit, "they will rest from their labor, for their deeds will follow them."

Rev 22 [14]"Blessed are those who wash their robes, that they may have the right to the tree of life and may go through the gates into the city."

b) A Life of Good Works Has Been Prayed For

Phil 1 [9]And this is my prayer: that your love may abound more and more in knowledge and depth of insight, [10]so that you may be able to discern what is best and may be pure and blameless until the day of Christ, [11]filled with the fruit of righteousness that comes through Jesus Christ—to the glory and praise of God.

Col 1 [10]And we pray this in order that you may live a life worthy of the Lord and may please him in every way: bearing fruit in every good work, growing in the knowledge of God. . . .

c) A Life of Good Works Has Been Exemplified

(1) Jesus Exemplified a Life of Good Works

John 10 [32]but Jesus said to them, "I have shown you many great miracles from the Father. For which of these do you stone me?"

Acts 10 [38]". . . how God anointed Jesus of Nazareth with the Holy Spirit and power, and how he went around doing good and healing all who were under the power of the devil, because God was with him."

(2) Dorcas Exemplified a Life of Good Works

Acts 9 [36]In Joppa there was a disciple named Tabitha (which, when translated, is Dorcas), who was always doing good and helping the poor.

(3) The Philippian Church Exemplified a Life of Good Works

Phil 2 [12]Therefore, my dear friends, as you have always obeyed—not only in my presence, but now much more in my absence—continue to work out your salvation with fear and trembling, [13]for it is God who works in you to will and to act according to his good purpose.

(4) The Thessalonian Church Exemplified a Life of Good Works

1 Thess 1 [3]We continually remember before our God and Father your work produced by faith, your labor prompted by love, and your endurance inspired by hope in our Lord Jesus Christ.

(5) The Recipients of Hebrews Exemplified a Life of Good Works

Heb 6 [9]Even though we speak like this, dear friends, we are confident of better things in your case—things that accompany salvation. [10]God is not unjust; he will not forget your work and the love you have shown him as you have helped his people and continue to help them. [11]We want each of you to show this same diligence to the very end, in order to make your hope sure. [12]We do not want you to become lazy, but to imitate those who through faith and patience inherit what has been promised.

(6) The Ephesian Church Exemplified a Life of Good Works

Rev 2 [1]"To the angel of the church in Ephesus write: These are the words of him who holds the seven stars in his right hand and walks among the seven golden lampstands: [2]I know your deeds, your hard work and your perseverance. I know that you cannot tolerate wicked men, that you have tested those who claim to be apostles but are not, and have found them false. [3]You have persevered and have endured hardships for my name, and have not grown weary."

(7) The Thyatiran Church Exemplified a Life of Good Works

Rev 2 [18]"To the church in Thyatira write: These are the words of the Son of God, whose eyes are like blazing fire and whose feet are like burnished bronze. [19]I know your deeds, your love and faith, your service and perseverance, and that you are now doing more than you did at first."

(8) The Philadelphian Church Exemplified a Life of Good Works

Rev 3 [7]"To the angel of the church in Philadelphia write: These are the words of him who is holy and true, who holds the key of David. What he opens no one can shut, and what he shuts no one can open. [8]I know your deeds. See, I have placed before you an open door that no one can shut. I know that you have little strength, yet you have kept my word and have not denied my name."

d) A Life of Good Works Has Been Illustrated

(1) A Life of Good Works in the Parable of the Talents

Matt 25 [14]"Again, it will be like a man going on a journey, who called his servants and entrusted his property to them. [15]To one he gave five talents of money, to another two talents, and to another one talent, each according to his ability. Then he went on his journey. [16]The man who had received the five talents went at once and put his money to work and gained five more. [17]So also, the one with the two talents gained two more. [18]But the man who had received the one talent went off, dug a hole in the ground and hid his master's money.

[19]"After a long time the master of those servants returned and settled accounts with them. [20]The man who had received the five talents brought the other five. 'Master,' he said, 'you entrusted me with five talents. See, I have gained five more.'

[21]"His master replied, 'Well done, good and faithful servant! You have been faithful with a few things; I will put you in charge of many things. Come and share your master's happiness!'

[22]"The man with the two talents also came. 'Master,' he said, 'you entrusted me with two talents; see, I have gained two more.'

[23]"His master replied, 'Well done, good and faithful servant! You have been faithful with a few things; I will put you in charge of many things. Come and share your master's happiness!'

[24]"Then the man who had received the one talent came. 'Master,' he said, 'I knew that you are a hard man, harvesting where you have not sown and gathering where you have not scattered seed. [25]So I was afraid and went out and hid your talent in the ground. See, here is what belongs to you.'

[26]"His master replied, 'You wicked, lazy servant! So you knew that I harvest where I have not sown and gather where I have not scattered seed? [27]Well then, you should have put my money on deposit with the bankers, so that when I returned I would have received it back with interest.

[28]"'Take the talent from him and give it to the one who has the ten talents. [29]For everyone who has will be given more, and he will have an abundance. Whoever does not have, even what he has will be taken from him.'"

(2) A Life of Good Works in the Parable of the Fig Tree

Luke 13 [6]Then he told this parable: "A man had a fig tree, planted in his vineyard, and he went to look for fruit on it, but did not find any. [7]So he said to the man who took care of the vineyard, 'For three years now I've been coming to look for fruit on this fig tree and haven't found any. Cut it down! Why should it use up the soil?'

[8]"'Sir,' the man replied, 'leave it alone for one more year, and I'll dig around it and fertilize it. [9]If it bears fruit next year, fine! If not, then cut it down.'"

(3) A Life of Good Works in the Metaphor of the Vine and the Branches

John 15 [4]"Remain in me, and I will remain in you. No branch can bear fruit by itself; it must remain in the vine. Neither can you bear fruit unless you remain in me.

[5]"I am the vine; you are the branches. If a man remains in me and I in him, he will bear much fruit; apart from me you can do nothing. [6]If anyone does not remain in me, he is like a branch that is thrown away and withers; such branches are picked up, thrown into the fire and burned. [7]If you remain in me and my words remain in you, ask whatever you wish, and it will be given you. [8]This is to my Father's glory, that you bear much fruit, showing yourselves to be my disciples."

5. A Full Christian Life

See chap. 12, Christian Living: *Responsibilities toward God*

B. Hindrances to Sanctification

1. Apostasy Cancels Sanctification

Deut 32 [15]Jeshurun grew fat and kicked; filled with food, he became heavy and sleek. He abandoned the God who made him and rejected the Rock his Savior. [16]They made him jealous with their foreign gods and angered him with their detestable idols. [17]They sacrificed to demons, which are not God—gods they had not known, gods that recently appeared, gods your fathers did not fear. [18]You deserted the Rock, who fathered you; you forgot the God who gave you birth.

1 Chron 28 [9]"And you, my son Solomon, acknowledge the God of your father, and serve him with wholehearted devotion and with a willing mind, for the LORD searches every heart and understands every motive behind the thoughts. If you seek him, he will be found by you; but if you forsake him, he will reject you forever."

Isa 65 [11]"But as for you who forsake the LORD and forget my holy mountain, who spread a table for Fortune and fill bowls of mixed wine for Destiny, [12]I will destine you for the sword, and you will all bend down for the slaughter; for I called but you did not answer, I spoke but you did not listen. You did evil in my sight and chose what displeases me."

[13]Therefore this is what the Sovereign LORD says: "My servants will eat, but you will go hungry; my servants will drink, but you will go thirsty; my servants will rejoice, but you will be put to shame. [14]My servants will sing out of the joy of their hearts, but you will cry out from anguish of heart and wail in brokenness of spirit. [15]You will leave your name to my chosen ones as a curse; the Sovereign LORD will put you to death, but to his servants he will give another name."

Jer 2 [21]"I had planted you like a choice vine of sound and reliable stock. How then did you turn against me into a corrupt, wild vine?"

Jer 18 [9]"And if at another time I announce that a nation or kingdom is to be built up and planted, [10]and if it does evil in my sight and does not obey me, then I will reconsider the good I had intended to do for it."

Zeph 1 [4]"I will stretch out my hand against Judah and against all who live in Jerusalem. I will cut off from this place every remnant of Baal, the names of the pagan and the idolatrous priests—[5]those who bow down on the roofs to worship the starry host, those who bow down and swear by the LORD and who also swear by Molech, [6]those who turn back from following the LORD and neither seek the LORD nor inquire of him."

Matt 3 [10]"The ax is already at the root of the trees, and every tree that does not produce good fruit will be cut down and thrown into the fire."

Matt 13 [3]Then he told them many things in parables, saying: "A farmer went out to sow his seed. [4]As he was scattering the seed, some fell along the path, and the birds came and ate it up. [5]Some fell on rocky places, where it did not have much soil. It sprang up quickly, because the soil was shallow. [6]But when the sun came up, the plants were scorched, and they withered because they had no root. [7]Other seed fell among thorns, which grew up and choked the plants. [8]Still other seed fell on good soil, where it produced a crop—a hundred, sixty or thirty times what was sown. . . .

[18]"Listen then to what the parable of the sower means. . . . [20]The one who received the seed that fell on rocky places is the man who hears the word and at once receives it with joy. [21]But since he has no root, he lasts only a short time. When trouble or persecution comes because of the word, he quickly falls away. [22]The one who received the seed that fell among the thorns is the man who hears the word, but the worries of this life and the deceitfulness of wealth choke it, making it unfruitful."

Matt 24 [9]"Then you will be handed over to be persecuted and put to death, and you will be hated by all nations because of me. [10]At that time many will turn away from the faith and will betray and hate each other, [11]and many false prophets will appear and deceive many people. [12]Because of the increase of wickedness, the love of most will grow cold. . . ."

Luke 8 [11]"This is the meaning of the parable: The seed is the word of God. . . . [13]Those on the rock are the ones who receive the word with joy when they hear it, but they have no root. They believe for a while, but in the time of testing they fall away."

Luke 9 [57]As they were walking along the road, a man said to him, "I will follow you wherever you go."

[58]Jesus replied, "Foxes have holes and birds of the air have nests, but the Son of Man has no place to lay his head."

[59]He said to another man, "Follow me."

But the man replied, "Lord, first let me go and bury my father."

[60]Jesus said to him, "Let the dead bury their own dead, but you go and proclaim the kingdom of God."

[61]Still another said, "I will follow you, Lord; but first let me go back and say good-by to my family."

[62]Jesus replied, "No one who puts his hand to the plow and looks back is fit for service in the kingdom of God."

Luke 11 [24]"When an evil spirit comes out of a man, it goes through arid places seeking rest and does not find it. Then it says, 'I will return to the house I left.' [25]When it arrives, it finds the house swept clean and put in order. [26]Then it goes and takes seven other spirits more wicked than itself, and they go in and live there. And the final condition of that man is worse than the first."

Luke 13 [6]Then he told this parable: "A man had a fig tree, planted in his vineyard, and he went to look for fruit on it, but did not find any. [7]So he said to the man who took care of the vineyard, 'For three years now I've been coming to look for fruit on this fig tree and haven't found any. Cut it down! Why should it use up the soil?'

[8]"'Sir,' the man replied, 'leave it alone for one more year, and I'll dig around it and fertilize it. [9]If it bears fruit next year, fine! If not, then cut it down.'"

John 15 [6]"If anyone does not remain in me, he is like a branch that is thrown away and withers; such branches are picked up, thrown into the fire and burned."

Acts 7 [39]"But our fathers refused to obey him. Instead, they rejected him and in their hearts turned back to Egypt. [40]They told Aaron, 'Make us gods who will go before us. As for this fellow Moses who led us out of Egypt—we don't know what has happened to him!' [41]That was the time they made an idol in the form of a calf. They brought sacrifices to it and held a celebration in honor of what their hands had made. [42]But God turned away and gave them over to the worship of the heavenly bodies. This agrees with what is written in the book of the prophets: 'Did you bring me sacrifices and offerings forty years in the desert, O house of Israel? [43]You have lifted up the shrine of Molech and the star of your god Rephan, the idols you made to worship. Therefore I will send you into exile' beyond Babylon."

1 Tim 1 [18]Timothy, my son, I give you this instruction in keeping with the prophecies once made about you, so that by following them you may fight the good fight, [19]holding on to faith and a good conscience. Some have rejected these and so have shipwrecked their faith. [20]Among them are Hymenaeus and Alexander, whom I have handed over to Satan to be taught not to blaspheme.

1 Tim 4 [1]The Spirit clearly says that in later times some will abandon the faith and follow deceiving spirits and things taught by demons. [2]Such teachings come through hypocritical liars, whose consciences have been seared as with a hot iron. [3]They forbid people to marry and order them to abstain from certain foods, which God created to be received with thanksgiving by those who believe and who know the truth.

2 Tim 3 [1]But mark this: There will be terrible times in the last days. [2]People will be lovers of themselves, lovers of money, boastful, proud, abusive, disobedient to their parents, ungrateful, unholy, [3]without love, unforgiving, slanderous, without self-control, brutal, not lovers of the good, [4]treacherous, rash, conceited, lovers of pleasure rather than lovers of God—[5]having a form of godliness but denying its power. Have nothing to do with them.

[6]They are the kind who worm their way into homes and gain control over weak-willed women, who are loaded down with sins and are swayed by all kinds of evil desires, [7]always learning but never able to acknowledge the truth. [8]Just as Jannes and Jambres opposed Moses, so also these men oppose the truth—men of depraved minds, who, as far as the faith is concerned, are rejected. [9]But they will not get very far because, as in the case of those men, their folly will be clear to everyone.

2 Tim 4 [3]For the time will come when men will not put up with sound doctrine. Instead, to suit their own desires, they will gather around them a great number of teachers to say what their itching ears want to hear. [4]They will turn their ears away from the truth and turn aside to myths.

2 Tim 4 [10]for Demas, because he loved this world, has deserted me and has gone to Thessalonica. Crescens has gone to Galatia, and Titus to Dalmatia.

Heb 3 [12]See to it, brothers, that none of you has a sinful, unbelieving heart that turns away from the living God. [13]But encourage one another daily, as long as it is called Today, so that none of you may be hardened by sin's deceitfulness.

Heb 4 [1]Therefore, since the promise of entering his rest still stands, let us be careful that none of you be found to have fallen short of it. [2]For we also have had the gospel preached to us, just as they did; but the message they heard was of no value to them, because those who heard did not combine it with faith. [3]Now we who have believed enter that rest, just as God has said, "So I declared on oath in my anger, 'They shall never enter my rest.'" And yet his work has been finished since the creation of the world. 4For somewhere he has spoken about the seventh day in these words: "And on the seventh day God rested from all his work." 5And again in the passage above he says, "They shall never enter my rest."

6It still remains that some will enter that rest, and those who formerly had the gospel preached to them did not go in, because of their disobedience. 7Therefore God again set a certain day, calling it Today, when a long time later he spoke through David, as was said before: "Today, if you hear his voice, do not harden your hearts." 8For if Joshua had given them rest, God would not have spoken later about another day. 9There remains, then, a Sabbath-rest for the people of God; 10for anyone who enters God's rest also rests from his own work, just as God did from his. 11Let us, therefore, make every effort to enter that rest, so that no one will fall by following their example of disobedience.

Heb 6 4It is impossible for those who have once been enlightened, who have tasted the heavenly gift, who have shared in the Holy Spirit, 5who have tasted the goodness of the word of God and the powers of the coming age, 6if they fall away, to be brought back to repentance, because to their loss they are crucifying the Son of God all over again and subjecting him to public disgrace.

7Land that drinks in the rain often falling on it and that produces a crop useful to those for whom it is farmed receives the blessing of God. 8But land that produces thorns and thistles is worthless and is in danger of being cursed. In the end it will be burned.

Heb 10 25Let us not give up meeting together, as some are in the habit of doing, but let us encourage one another—and all the more as you see the Day approaching.

26If we deliberately keep on sinning after we have received the knowledge of the truth, no sacrifice for sins is left, 27but only a fearful expectation of judgment and of raging fire that will consume the enemies of God. 28Anyone who rejected the law of Moses died without mercy on the testimony of two or three witnesses. 29How much more severely do you think a man deserves to be punished who has trampled the Son of God under foot, who has treated as an unholy thing the blood of the covenant that sanctified him, and who has insulted the Spirit of grace? 30For we know him who said, "It is mine to avenge; I will repay," and again, "The Lord will judge his people." 31It is a dreadful thing to fall into the hands of the living God. . . . 39But we are not of those who shrink back and are destroyed, but of those who believe and are saved.

2 Pet 2 1But there were also false prophets among the people, just as there will be false teachers among you. They will secretly introduce destructive heresies, even denying the sovereign Lord who bought them—bringing swift destruction on themselves. 2Many will follow their shameful ways and will bring the way of truth into disrepute. 3In their greed these teachers will exploit you with stories they have made up. Their condemnation has long been hanging over them, and their destruction has not been sleeping.

4For if God did not spare angels when they sinned, but sent them to hell, putting them into gloomy dungeons to be held for judgment; 5if he did not spare the ancient world when he brought the flood on its ungodly people, but protected Noah, a preacher of righteousness, and seven others; 6if he condemned the cities of Sodom and Gomorrah by burning them to ashes, and made them an example of what is going to happen to the ungodly; 7and if he rescued Lot, a righteous man, who was distressed by the filthy lives of lawless men 8(for that righteous man, living among them day after day, was tormented in his righteous soul by the lawless deeds he saw and heard)—9if this is so, then the Lord knows how to rescue godly men from trials and to hold the unrighteous for the day of judgment, while continuing their punishment. 10This is especially true of those who follow the corrupt desire of the sinful nature and despise authority.

Bold and arrogant, these men are not afraid to slander celestial beings; 11yet even angels, although they are stronger and more powerful, do not bring slanderous accusations against such beings in the presence of the Lord. 12But these men blaspheme in matters they do not understand. They are like brute beasts, creatures of instinct, born only to be caught and destroyed, and like beasts they too will perish.

13They will be paid back with harm for the harm they have done. Their idea of pleasure is to carouse in broad daylight. They are blots and blemishes, reveling in their pleasures while they feast with you. 14With eyes full of adultery, they never stop sinning; they seduce the unstable; they are experts in greed—an accursed brood! 15They have left the straight way and wandered off to follow the way of Balaam son of Beor, who loved the wages of wickedness. 16But he was rebuked for his wrongdoing by a donkey—a beast without speech—who spoke with a man's voice and restrained the prophet's madness.

17These men are springs without water and mists driven by a storm. Blackest darkness is reserved for them. 18For they mouth empty, boastful words and, by appealing to the lustful desires of sinful human nature, they entice people who are just escaping from those who live in error. 19They promise them freedom, while they themselves are slaves of depravity—for a man is a slave to whatever has mastered him. 20If they have escaped the corruption of the world by knowing our Lord and Savior Jesus Christ and are again entangled in it and overcome, they are worse off at the end than they were at the beginning. 21It would have been better for them not to have known the way of righteousness, than to have known it and then to turn their backs on the sacred command that was passed on to them. 22Of them the proverbs are true: "A dog returns to its vomit," and, "A sow that is washed goes back to her wallowing in the mud."

2 Pet 3 17Therefore, dear friends, since you already know this, be on your guard so that you may not be carried away by the error of lawless men and fall from your secure position.

Jude 4For certain men whose condemnation was written about long ago have secretly slipped in among you. They are godless men, who change the grace of our God into a license for immorality and deny Jesus Christ our only Sovereign and Lord.

2. Backsliding Hinders Sanctification

Job 34 26"He punishes them for their wickedness where everyone can see them, 27because they turned from following him and had no regard for any of his ways."

Ps 12 1Help, LORD, for the godly are no more; the faithful have vanished from among men.

Ps 36 3The words of his mouth are wicked and deceitful; he has ceased to be wise and to do good.

Ps 78 56But they put God to the test and rebelled against the Most High; they did not keep his statutes. 57Like their fathers they were disloyal and faithless, as unreliable as a faulty bow. 58They angered him with their high places; they aroused his jealousy with their idols.

Jer 17 5This is what the LORD says: "Cursed is the one who trusts in man, who depends on flesh for his strength and whose heart turns away from the LORD."

Ezek 18 24"But if a righteous man turns from his righteousness and commits sin and does the same detestable things the wicked man does, will he live? None of the righteous things he has done will be remembered. Because of the unfaithfulness he is guilty of and because of the sins he has committed, he will die.

25"Yet you say, 'The way of the Lord is not just.' Hear, O house of Israel: Is my way unjust? Is it not your ways that are unjust? 26If a righteous man turns from his righteousness and commits sin, he will die for it; because of the sin he has committed he will die."

Ezek 33 12"Therefore, son of man, say to your countrymen, 'The righteousness of the righteous man will not save him when he disobeys, and the wickedness of the wicked man will not cause him to fall when he turns from it. The righteous man, if he sins, will not be allowed to live because of his former righteousness.' 13If I tell the righteous man that he will surely live, but then he trusts in his righteousness and does evil, none of the righteous things he has done will be remembered; he will die for the evil he has done. . . . 18If a righteous man turns from his righteousness and does evil, he will die for it."

Matt 5 13"You are the salt of the earth. But if the salt loses its saltiness, how can it be made salty again? It is no longer good for anything, except to be thrown out and trampled by men."

2 Cor 12 20For I am afraid that when I come I may not find you as I want you to be, and you may not find me as you want me to be. I fear that there may be quarreling, jealousy, outbursts of anger, factions, slander, gossip, arrogance and disorder. 21I am afraid that when I come again my God will humble me before you, and I will be grieved over many who have sinned earlier and have not repented of the impurity, sexual sin and debauchery in which they have indulged.

Gal 1 6I am astonished that you are so quickly deserting the one who called you by the grace of Christ and are turning to a different gospel—7which is really no gospel at all. Evidently some people are throwing you into confusion and are trying to pervert the gospel of Christ.

Gal 3 1You foolish Galatians! Who has bewitched you? Before your very eyes Jesus Christ was clearly portrayed as crucified. 2I would like to learn just one thing from you: Did you receive the Spirit by observing the law, or by believing what you heard? 3Are you so foolish? After beginning with the Spirit, are you now trying to attain your goal by human effort? 4Have you suffered so much for nothing—if it really was for nothing? 5Does God give you his Spirit and work miracles among you because you observe the law, or because you believe what you heard?

Gal 4 9But now that you know God—or rather are known by God—how is it that you are turning back to those weak and miserable principles? Do you wish to be enslaved by them all over again? 10You are observing special days and months and seasons and years! 11I fear for you, that somehow I have wasted my efforts on you.

Gal 5 7You were running a good race. Who cut in on you and kept you from obeying the truth? 8That kind of persuasion does not come from the one who calls you. 9"A little yeast works through the whole batch of dough."

1 Tim 1 19holding on to faith and a good conscience. Some have rejected these and so have shipwrecked their faith. 20Among them are Hymenaeus and Alexander, whom I have handed over to Satan to be taught not to blaspheme.

1 Tim 6 20Timothy, guard what has been entrusted to your care. Turn away from godless chatter and the opposing ideas of what is falsely called knowledge, 21which some have professed and in so doing have wandered from the faith.

Grace be with you.

Heb 5 11We have much to say about this, but it is hard to explain because you are slow to learn. 12In fact, though by this time you ought to be teachers, you need someone to teach you the elementary truths of God's word all over again. You need milk, not solid food! 13Anyone who lives on milk, being still an infant, is not acquainted with the teaching about righteousness.

Heb 12 15See to it that no one misses the grace of God and that no bitter root grows up to cause trouble and defile many.

2 Pet 1 8For if you possess these qualities in increasing measure, they will keep you from being ineffective and unproductive in your knowledge of our Lord Jesus Christ. 9But if anyone does not have them, he is nearsighted and blind, and has forgotten that he has been cleansed from his past sins.

Rev 2 2"I know your deeds, your hard work and your perseverance. I know that you cannot tolerate wicked men, that you have tested those who claim to be apostles but are not, and have found them false. 3You have persevered and have endured hardships for my name, and have not grown weary.

4"Yet I hold this against you: You have forsaken your first love. 5Remember the height from which you have fallen! Repent and do the things you did at first. If you do not repent, I will come to you and remove your lampstand from its place."

Rev 3 1"To the angel of the church in Sardis write: These are the words of him who holds the seven spirits of God and the seven stars. I know your deeds; you have a reputation of being alive, but you are dead. 2Wake up! Strengthen what remains and is about to die, for I have not found your deeds complete in the sight of my God. 3Remember, therefore, what you have received and heard; obey it, and repent. But if you do not wake up, I will come like a thief, and you will not know at what time I will come to you."

3. The Devil Hinders Sanctification

Matt 13 18"Listen then to what the parable of the sower means: 19When anyone hears the message about the kingdom and does not understand it, the evil one comes and snatches away what was sown in his heart. This is the seed sown along the path."

Luke 8 12"Those along the path are the ones who hear, and then the devil comes and takes away the word from their hearts, so that they may not believe and be saved."

Acts 5 3Then Peter said, "Ananias, how is it that Satan has so filled your heart that you have lied to the Holy Spirit and have kept for yourself some of the money you received for the land?"

1 Cor 7 5Do not deprive each other except by mutual consent and for a time, so that you may devote yourselves to prayer. Then come together again so that Satan will not tempt you because of your lack of self-control.

2 Cor 2 5If anyone has caused grief, he has not so much grieved me as he has grieved all of you, to some extent—not to put it too severely. 6The punishment inflicted on him by the majority is sufficient for him. 7Now instead, you ought to forgive and comfort him, so that he will not be overwhelmed by excessive sorrow. 8I urge you, therefore, to reaffirm your love for him. 9The reason I wrote you was to see if you would stand the test and be obedient in everything. 10If you forgive anyone, I also forgive him. And what I have forgiven—if there was anything to forgive—I have forgiven in the sight of Christ for your sake, 11in order that Satan might not outwit us. For we are not unaware of his schemes.

2 Cor 11 3But I am afraid that just as Eve was deceived by the serpent's cunning, your minds may somehow be led astray from your sincere and pure devotion to Christ.

Eph 4 27and do not give the devil a foothold.

Eph 6 11Put on the full armor of God so that you can take your stand against the devil's schemes. 12For our struggle is not against flesh and blood, but against the rulers, against the authorities, against the powers of this dark world and against the spiritual forces of evil in the heavenly realms.

1 Thess 3 5For this reason, when I could stand it no longer, I sent to find out about your faith. I was afraid that in some way the tempter might have tempted you and our efforts might have been useless.

2 Thess 2 9The coming of the lawless one will be in accordance with the work of Satan displayed in all kinds of counterfeit miracles, signs and wonders, 10and in every sort of evil that deceives those who are perishing. They perish because they refused to love the truth and so be saved. 11For this reason God sends them a powerful delusion so that they will believe the lie 12and so that all will be condemned who have not believed the truth but have delighted in wickedness.

1 Tim 5 15Some have in fact already turned away to follow Satan.

James 4 7Submit yourselves, then, to God. Resist the devil, and he will flee from you.

1 Pet 5 8Be self-controlled and alert. Your enemy the devil prowls around like a roaring lion looking for someone to devour. 9Resist him, standing firm in the faith, because you know that your brothers throughout the world are undergoing the same kind of sufferings.

1 John 2 13I write to you, fathers, because you have known him who is from the beginning. I write to you, young men, because you have overcome the evil one. I write to you, dear children, because you have known the Father.

1 John 5 18We know that anyone born of God does not continue to sin; the one who was born of God keeps him safe, and the evil one cannot harm him.

Rev 2 9"I know your afflictions and your poverty—yet you are rich! I know the slander of those who say they are Jews and are not, but are a synagogue of Satan. 10Do not be afraid of what you are about to suffer. I tell you, the devil will put some of you in prison to test you, and you will suffer persecution for ten days. Be faithful, even to the point of death, and I will give you the crown of life."

Rev 2 13"I know where you live—where Satan has his throne.

Yet you remain true to my name. You did not renounce your faith in me, even in the days of Antipas, my faithful witness, who was put to death in your city—where Satan lives."
Rev 2 24"Now I say to the rest of you in Thyatira, to you who do not hold to her teaching and have not learned Satan's so-called deep secrets (I will not impose any other burden on you): 25Only hold on to what you have until I come."

4. Lust Hinders Sanctification

Prov 6 23For these commands are a lamp, this teaching is a light, and the corrections of discipline are the way to life, 24keeping you from the immoral woman, from the smooth tongue of the wayward wife. 25Do not lust in your heart after her beauty or let her captivate you with her eyes, 26for the prostitute reduces you to a loaf of bread, and the adulteress preys upon your very life.
Matt 5 28"But I tell you that anyone who looks at a woman lustfully has already committed adultery with her in his heart."
Mark 4 18"Still others, like seed sown among thorns, hear the word; 19but the worries of this life, the deceitfulness of wealth and the desires for other things come in and choke the word, making it unfruitful."
1 Cor 10 6Now these things occurred as examples to keep us from setting our hearts on evil things as they did. 7Do not be idolaters, as some of them were; as it is written: "The people sat down to eat and drink and got up to indulge in pagan revelry." 8We should not commit sexual immorality, as some of them did—and in one day twenty-three thousand of them died.
Eph 4 22You were taught, with regard to your former way of life, to put off your old self, which is being corrupted by its deceitful desires. . . .
Col 3 5Put to death, therefore, whatever belongs to your earthly nature: sexual immorality, impurity, lust, evil desires and greed, which is idolatry.
1 Tim 6 9People who want to get rich fall into temptation and a trap and into many foolish and harmful desires that plunge men into ruin and destruction. 10For the love of money is a root of all kinds of evil. Some people, eager for money, have wandered from the faith and pierced themselves with many griefs.
Titus 2 12It teaches us to say "No" to ungodliness and worldly passions, and to live self-controlled, upright and godly lives in this present age. . . .
1 Pet 1 14As obedient children, do not conform to the evil desires you had when you lived in ignorance.
1 Pet 2 11Dear friends, I urge you, as aliens and strangers in the world, to abstain from sinful desires, which war against your soul.
1 Pet 4 1Therefore, since Christ suffered in his body, arm yourselves also with the same attitude, because he who has suffered in his body is done with sin. 2As a result, he does not live the rest of his earthly life for evil human desires, but rather for the will of God.
2 Pet 1 4Through these he has given us his very great and precious promises, so that through them you may participate in the divine nature and escape the corruption in the world caused by evil desires.
2 Pet 2 14With eyes full of adultery, they never stop sinning; they seduce the unstable; they are experts in greed—an accursed brood! . . . 18For they mouth empty, boastful words and, by appealing to the lustful desires of sinful human nature, they entice people who are just escaping from those who live in error.
1 John 2 16For everything in the world—the cravings of sinful man, the lust of his eyes and the boasting of what he has and does—comes not from the Father but from the world. 17The world and its desires pass away, but the man who does the will of God lives forever.
Jude 16These men are grumblers and faultfinders; they follow their own evil desires; they boast about themselves and flatter others for their own advantage.

17But, dear friends, remember what the apostles of our Lord Jesus Christ foretold. 18They said to you, "In the last times there will be scoffers who will follow their own ungodly desires." 19These are the men who divide you, who follow mere natural instincts and do not have the Spirit.

5. Self-Indulgence Hinders Sanctification

Luke 8 14"The seed that fell among thorns stands for those who hear, but as they go on their way they are choked by life's worries, riches and pleasures, and they do not mature."
Luke 12 15Then he said to them, "Watch out! Be on your guard against all kinds of greed; a man's life does not consist in the abundance of his possessions."

16And he told them this parable: "The ground of a certain rich man produced a good crop. 17He thought to himself, 'What shall I do? I have no place to store my crops.'

18"Then he said, 'This is what I'll do. I will tear down my barns and build bigger ones, and there I will store all my grain and my goods. 19And I'll say to myself, "You have plenty of good things laid up for many years. Take life easy; eat, drink and be merry."'

20"But God said to him, 'You fool! This very night your life will be demanded from you. Then who will get what you have prepared for yourself?'

21"This is how it will be with anyone who stores up things for himself but is not rich toward God."
Luke 16 19"There was a rich man who was dressed in purple and fine linen and lived in luxury every day. 20At his gate was laid a beggar named Lazarus, covered with sores 21and longing to eat what fell from the rich man's table. Even the dogs came and licked his sores.

22"The time came when the beggar died and the angels carried him to Abraham's side. The rich man also died and was buried. 23In hell, where he was in torment, he looked up and saw Abraham far away, with Lazarus by his side. 24So he called to him, 'Father Abraham, have pity on me and send Lazarus to dip the tip of his finger in water and cool my tongue, because I am in agony in this fire.'

25"But Abraham replied, 'Son, remember that in your lifetime you received your good things, while Lazarus received bad things, but now he is comforted here and you are in agony. 26And besides all this, between us and you a great chasm has been fixed, so that those who want to go from here to you cannot, nor can anyone cross over from there to us.'

27"He answered, 'Then I beg you, father, send Lazarus to my father's house, 28for I have five brothers. Let him warn them, so that they will not also come to this place of torment.'

29"Abraham replied, 'They have Moses and the Prophets; let them listen to them.'

30"'No, father Abraham,' he said, 'but if someone from the dead goes to them, they will repent.'

31"He said to him, 'If they do not listen to Moses and the Prophets, they will not be convinced even if someone rises from the dead.'"
Luke 21 34"Be careful, or your hearts will be weighed down with dissipation, drunkenness and the anxieties of life, and that day will close on you unexpectedly like a trap."
Rom 13 13Let us behave decently, as in the daytime, not in orgies and drunkenness, not in sexual immorality and debauchery, not in dissension and jealousy.
1 Cor 5 11But now I am writing you that you must not associate with anyone who calls himself a brother but is sexually immoral or greedy, an idolater or a slanderer, a drunkard or a swindler. With such a man do not even eat.
1 Cor 6 9Do you not know that the wicked will not inherit the kingdom of God? Do not be deceived: Neither the sexually immoral nor idolaters nor adulterers nor male prostitutes nor homosexual offenders 10nor thieves nor the greedy nor drunkards nor slanderers nor swindlers will inherit the kingdom of God.
2 Cor 12 21I am afraid that when I come again my God will humble me before you, and I will be grieved over many who have sinned earlier and have not repented of the impurity, sexual sin and debauchery in which they have indulged.
Eph 4 19Having lost all sensitivity, they have given themselves over to sensuality so as to indulge in every kind of impurity, with a continual lust for more.

20You, however, did not come to know Christ that way. . . . 22You were taught, with regard to your former way of life, to put off your old self, which is being corrupted by its deceitful desires. . . .

Eph 5 18Do not get drunk on wine, which leads to debauchery. Instead, be filled with the Spirit.

Phil 3 18For, as I have often told you before and now say again even with tears, many live as enemies of the cross of Christ. 19Their destiny is destruction, their god is their stomach, and their glory is in their shame. Their mind is on earthly things.

Col 2 23Such regulations indeed have an appearance of wisdom, with their self-imposed worship, their false humility and their harsh treatment of the body, but they lack any value in restraining sensual indulgence.

1 Thess 5 7For those who sleep, sleep at night, and those who get drunk, get drunk at night. 8But since we belong to the day, let us be self-controlled, putting on faith and love as a breastplate, and the hope of salvation as a helmet.

2 Thess 3 10For even when we were with you, we gave you this rule: "If a man will not work, he shall not eat."

11We hear that some among you are idle. They are not busy; they are busybodies. 12Such people we command and urge in the Lord Jesus Christ to settle down and earn the bread they eat.

1 Tim 3 2Now the overseer must be above reproach, the husband of but one wife, temperate, self-controlled, respectable, hospitable, able to teach, 3not given to drunkenness, not violent but gentle, not quarrelsome, not a lover of money. . . .

8Deacons, likewise, are to be men worthy of respect, sincere, not indulging in much wine, and not pursuing dishonest gain.

James 4 1What causes fights and quarrels among you? Don't they come from your desires that battle within you? 2You want something but don't get it. You kill and covet, but you cannot have what you want. You quarrel and fight. You do not have, because you do not ask God. 3When you ask, you do not receive, because you ask with wrong motives, that you may spend what you get on your pleasures.

James 5 1Now listen, you rich people, weep and wail because of the misery that is coming upon you. 2Your wealth has rotted, and moths have eaten your clothes. 3Your gold and silver are corroded. Their corrosion will testify against you and eat your flesh like fire. You have hoarded wealth in the last days. 4Look! The wages you failed to pay the workmen who mowed your fields are crying out against you. The cries of the harvesters have reached the ears of the Lord Almighty. 5You have lived on earth in luxury and self-indulgence. You have fattened yourselves in the day of slaughter. 6You have condemned and murdered innocent men, who were not opposing you.

1 Pet 4 3For you have spent enough time in the past doing what pagans choose to do—living in debauchery, lust, drunkenness, orgies, carousing and detestable idolatry. 4They think it strange that you do not plunge with them into the same flood of dissipation, and they heap abuse on you.

2 Pet 2 13They will be paid back with harm for the harm they have done. Their idea of pleasure is to carouse in broad daylight. They are blots and blemishes, reveling in their pleasures while they feast with you.

Jude 12These men are blemishes at your love feasts, eating with you without the slightest qualm—shepherds who feed only themselves. They are clouds without rain, blown along by the wind; autumn trees, without fruit and uprooted—twice dead.

6. Sin Hinders Sanctification

Rom 6 12Therefore do not let sin reign in your mortal body so that you obey its evil desires. 13Do not offer the parts of your body to sin, as instruments of wickedness, but rather offer yourselves to God, as those who have been brought from death to life; and offer the parts of your body to him as instruments of righteousness. 14For sin shall not be your master, because you are not under law, but under grace. . . .

19I put this in human terms because you are weak in your natural selves. Just as you used to offer the parts of your body in slavery to impurity and to ever-increasing wickedness, so now offer them in slavery to righteousness leading to holiness.

Rom 8 6The mind of sinful man is death, but the mind controlled by the Spirit is life and peace; 7the sinful mind is hostile to God. It does not submit to God's law, nor can it do so.

Rom 14 20Do not destroy the work of God for the sake of food. All food is clean, but it is wrong for a man to eat anything that causes someone else to stumble. . . .

22So whatever you believe about these things keep between yourself and God. Blessed is the man who does not condemn himself by what he approves. 23But the man who has doubts is condemned if he eats, because his eating is not from faith; and everything that does not come from faith is sin.

1 Cor 8 12When you sin against your brothers in this way and wound their weak conscience, you sin against Christ. 13Therefore, if what I eat causes my brother to fall into sin, I will never eat meat again, so that I will not cause him to fall.

1 Cor 9 24Do you not know that in a race all the runners run, but only one gets the prize? Run in such a way as to get the prize. 25Everyone who competes in the games goes into strict training. They do it to get a crown that will not last; but we do it to get a crown that will last forever. 26Therefore I do not run like a man running aimlessly; I do not fight like a man beating the air. 27No, I beat my body and make it my slave so that after I have preached to others, I myself will not be disqualified for the prize.

1 Cor 10 12So, if you think you are standing firm, be careful that you don't fall!

James 1 13When tempted, no one should say, "God is tempting me." For God cannot be tempted by evil, nor does he tempt anyone; 14but each one is tempted when, by his own evil desire, he is dragged away and enticed. 15Then, after desire has conceived, it gives birth to sin; and sin, when it is full-grown, gives birth to death.

James 4 17Anyone, then, who knows the good he ought to do and doesn't do it, sins.

1 John 3 4Everyone who sins breaks the law; in fact, sin is lawlessness. 5But you know that he appeared so that he might take away our sins. And in him is no sin. 6No one who lives in him keeps on sinning. No one who continues to sin has either seen him or known him.

1 John 5 17All wrongdoing is sin, and there is sin that does not lead to death.

7. The Sinful Nature Hinders Sanctification

Rom 7 5For when we were controlled by the sinful nature, the sinful passions aroused by the law were at work in our bodies, so that we bore fruit for death. 6But now, by dying to what once bound us, we have been released from the law so that we serve in the new way of the Spirit, and not in the old way of the written code. . . .

14We know that the law is spiritual; but I am unspiritual, sold as a slave to sin. 15I do not understand what I do. For what I want to do I do not do, but what I hate I do. 16And if I do what I do not want to do, I agree that the law is good. 17As it is, it is no longer I myself who do it, but it is sin living in me. 18I know that nothing good lives in me, that is, in my sinful nature. For I have the desire to do what is good, but I cannot carry it out. 19For what I do is not the good I want to do; no, the evil I do not want to do—this I keep on doing. 20Now if I do what I do not want to do, it is no longer I who do it, but it is sin living in me that does it.

21So I find this law at work: When I want to do good, evil is right there with me. 22For in my inner being I delight in God's law; 23but I see another law at work in the members of my body, waging war against the law of my mind and making me a prisoner of the law of sin at work within my members. 24What a wretched man I am! Who will rescue me from this body of death? 25Thanks be to God—through Jesus Christ our Lord!

So then, I myself in my mind am a slave to God's law, but in the sinful nature a slave to the law of sin.

Rom 8 5Those who live according to the sinful nature have their minds set on what that nature desires; but those who live in accordance with the Spirit have their minds set on what the Spirit desires. 6The mind of sinful man is death, but the mind controlled by the Spirit is life and peace; 7the sinful mind is hostile to God. It does not submit to God's law, nor can it do so. [8]Those controlled by the sinful nature cannot please God.

[9]You, however, are controlled not by the sinful nature but by the Spirit, if the Spirit of God lives in you. And if anyone does not have the Spirit of Christ, he does not belong to Christ. [10]But if Christ is in you, your body is dead because of sin, yet your spirit is alive because of righteousness. [11]And if the Spirit of him who raised Jesus from the dead is living in you, he who raised Christ from the dead will also give life to your mortal bodies through his Spirit, who lives in you.

[12]Therefore, brothers, we have an obligation—but it is not to the sinful nature, to live according to it.

Rom 13 [14]Rather, clothe yourselves with the Lord Jesus Christ, and do not think about how to gratify the desires of the sinful nature.

Gal 5 [13]You, my brothers, were called to be free. But do not use your freedom to indulge the sinful nature; rather, serve one another in love. . . .

[16]So I say, live by the Spirit, and you will not gratify the desires of the sinful nature. [17]For the sinful nature desires what is contrary to the Spirit, and the Spirit what is contrary to the sinful nature. They are in conflict with each other, so that you do not do what you want. . . .

[19]The acts of the sinful nature are obvious: sexual immorality, impurity and debauchery; [20]idolatry and witchcraft; hatred, discord, jealousy, fits of rage, selfish ambition, dissensions, factions [21]and envy; drunkenness, orgies, and the like. I warn you, as I did before, that those who live like this will not inherit the kingdom of God. . . . [24]Those who belong to Christ Jesus have crucified the sinful nature with its passions and desires.

Gal 6 [7]Do not be deceived: God cannot be mocked. A man reaps what he sows. [8]The one who sows to please his sinful nature, from that nature will reap destruction; the one who sows to please the Spirit, from the Spirit will reap eternal life.

Eph 2 [3]All of us also lived among them at one time, gratifying the cravings of our sinful nature and following its desires and thoughts. Like the rest, we were by nature objects of wrath.

Col 2 [11]In him you were also circumcised, in the putting off of the sinful nature, not with a circumcision done by the hands of men but with the circumcision done by Christ. . . .

8. Unbelief Hinders Sanctification

See p. 558a, Exhortations against Faithlessness

IV
Names and Metaphors for Sanctified People

A. Names of Christians

1. Christians Are the Called

Rev 17 [14]"They will make war against the Lamb, but the Lamb will overcome them because he is Lord of lords and King of kings—and with him will be his called, chosen and faithful followers."

2. Christians Are Called Ambassadors of Christ

2 Cor 5 [20]We are therefore Christ's ambassadors, as though God were making his appeal through us. We implore you on Christ's behalf: Be reconciled to God.

3. Christians Are Called Believers

Acts 1 [15]In those days Peter stood up among the believers (a group numbering about a hundred and twenty). . . .

Acts 4 [32]All the believers were one in heart and mind. No one claimed that any of his possessions was his own, but they shared everything they had.

Acts 5 [12]The apostles performed many miraculous signs and wonders among the people. And all the believers used to meet together in Solomon's Colonnade. [13]No one else dared join them, even though they were highly regarded by the people. [14]Nevertheless, more and more men and women believed in the Lord and were added to their number.

Acts 16 [1]He came to Derbe and then to Lystra, where a disciple named Timothy lived, whose mother was a Jewess and a believer, but whose father was a Greek.

Acts 16 [15]When she and the members of her household were baptized, she invited us to her home. "If you consider me a believer in the Lord," she said, "come and stay at my house." And she persuaded us.

Acts 21 [25]"As for the Gentile believers, we have written to them our decision that they should abstain from food sacrificed to idols, from blood, from the meat of strangled animals and from sexual immorality."

2 Cor 6 [15]What harmony is there between Christ and Belial? What does a believer have in common with an unbeliever?

Gal 6 [10]Therefore, as we have opportunity, let us do good to all people, especially to those who belong to the family of believers.

1 Thess 1 [7]And so you became a model to all the believers in Macedonia and Achaia.

1 Tim 4 [10](and for this we labor and strive), that we have put our hope in the living God, who is the Savior of all men, and especially of those who believe.

1 Tim 4 [12]Don't let anyone look down on you because you are young, but set an example for the believers in speech, in life, in love, in faith and in purity.

1 Pet 2 [17]Show proper respect to everyone: Love the brotherhood of believers, fear God, honor the king.

4. Christians Are Called Brothers

Matt 28 [10]Then Jesus said to them, "Do not be afraid. Go and tell my brothers to go to Galilee; there they will see me."

John 20 [17]Jesus said, "Do not hold on to me, for I have not yet returned to the Father. Go instead to my brothers and tell them, 'I am returning to my Father and your Father, to my God and your God.'"

Acts 9 [17]Then Ananias went to the house and entered it. Placing his hands on Saul, he said, "Brother Saul, the Lord—Jesus, who appeared to you on the road as you were coming here—has sent me so that you may see again and be filled with the Holy Spirit."

Acts 14 [2]But the Jews who refused to believe stirred up the Gentiles and poisoned their minds against the brothers.

Acts 15 [36]Some time later Paul said to Barnabas, "Let us go back and visit the brothers in all the towns where we preached the word of the Lord and see how they are doing."

Acts 16 [2]The brothers at Lystra and Iconium spoke well of him.

Rom 8 [29]For those God foreknew he also predestined to be conformed to the likeness of his Son, that he might be the firstborn among many brothers.

Rom 12 [1]Therefore, I urge you, brothers, in view of God's mercy, to offer your bodies as living sacrifices, holy and pleasing to God—this is your spiritual act of worship.

1 Cor 15 [58]Therefore, my dear brothers, stand firm. Let nothing move you. Always give yourselves fully to the work of the Lord, because you know that your labor in the Lord is not in vain.

Col 1 [2]To the holy and faithful brothers in Christ at Colosse: Grace and peace to you from God our Father.

1 Thess 1 [4]For we know, brothers loved by God, that he has chosen you. . . .

2 Thess 2 [13]But we ought always to thank God for you, brothers loved by the Lord, because from the beginning God chose you to be saved through the sanctifying work of the Spirit and through belief in the truth.

Philem [15]Perhaps the reason he was separated from you for a little while was that you might have him back for good—[16]no longer as a slave, but better than a slave, as a dear brother. He is very dear to me but even dearer to you, both as a man and as a brother in the Lord.

Heb 2 [11]Both the one who makes men holy and those who are made holy are of the same family. So Jesus is not ashamed to call them brothers. [12]He says, "I will declare your name to my

brothers; in the presence of the congregation I will sing your praises." . . . [17]For this reason he had to be made like his brothers in every way, in order that he might become a merciful and faithful high priest in service to God, and that he might make atonement for the sins of the people.
James 1 [2]Consider it pure joy, my brothers, whenever you face trials of many kinds. . . .
James 2 [1]My brothers, as believers in our glorious Lord Jesus Christ, don't show favoritism.
1 John 3 [16]This is how we know what love is: Jesus Christ laid down his life for us. And we ought to lay down our lives for our brothers.
Rev 6 [11]Then each of them was given a white robe, and they were told to wait a little longer, until the number of their fellow servants and brothers who were to be killed as they had been was completed.
Rev 12 [10]Then I heard a loud voice in heaven say: "Now have come the salvation and the power and the kingdom of our God, and the authority of his Christ. For the accuser of our brothers, who accuses them before our God day and night, has been hurled down."

5. Christians Are Called Children

1 Cor 4 [14]I am not writing this to shame you, but to warn you, as my dear children.
2 Cor 6 [13]As a fair exchange—I speak as to my children—open wide your hearts also.
1 John 5 [21]Dear children, keep yourselves from idols.

6. Christians Are Called Children of Abraham

Gal 3 [7]Understand, then, that those who believe are children of Abraham.

7. Christians Are Called Children of the Free Woman

Gal 4 [31]Therefore, brothers, we are not children of the slave woman, but of the free woman.

8. Christians Are Called Children of God

Luke 20 [35]"But those who are considered worthy of taking part in that age and in the resurrection from the dead will neither marry nor be given in marriage, [36]and they can no longer die; for they are like the angels. They are God's children, since they are children of the resurrection."
Rom 8 [16]The Spirit himself testifies with our spirit that we are God's children.
Rom 8 [20]For the creation was subjected to frustration, not by its own choice, but by the will of the one who subjected it, in hope [21]that the creation itself will be liberated from its bondage to decay and brought into the glorious freedom of the children of God.
Eph 5 [1]Be imitators of God, therefore, as dearly loved children. . . .
Phil 2 [15]so that you may become blameless and pure, children of God without fault in a crooked and depraved generation, in which you shine like stars in the universe . . .
1 John 3 [1]How great is the love the Father has lavished on us, that we should be called children of God! And that is what we are! The reason the world does not know us is that it did not know him. [2]Dear friends, now we are children of God, and what we will be has not yet been made known. But we know that when he appears, we shall be like him, for we shall see him as he is.
1 John 5 [19]We know that we are children of God, and that the whole world is under the control of the evil one.

9. Christians Are Called Children of Light

Eph 5 [8]For you were once darkness, but now you are light in the Lord. Live as children of light. . . .

10. Christians Are Called Children of the Promise

Rom 9 [8]In other words, it is not the natural children who are God's children, but it is the children of the promise who are regarded as Abraham's offspring.
Gal 4 [28]Now you, brothers, like Isaac, are children of promise.

11. Christians Are Called Children of the Resurrection

Luke 20 [35]"But those who are considered worthy of taking part in that age and in the resurrection from the dead will neither marry nor be given in marriage, [36]and they can no longer die; for they are like the angels. They are God's children, since they are children of the resurrection."

12. Christians Are Called the Chosen

Rev 17 [14]"They will make war against the Lamb, but the Lamb will overcome them because he is Lord of lords and King of kings—and with him will be his called, chosen and faithful followers."

13. Christians Are Called Chosen People

Col 3 [12]Therefore, as God's chosen people, holy and dearly loved, clothe yourselves with compassion, kindness, humility, gentleness and patience.
1 Pet 2 [9]But you are a chosen people, a royal priesthood, a holy nation, a people belonging to God, that you may declare the praises of him who called you out of darkness into his wonderful light.

14. Christians Are Called Christians

Acts 11 [26]and when he found him, he brought him to Antioch. So for a whole year Barnabas and Saul met with the church and taught great numbers of people. The disciples were called Christians first at Antioch.
Acts 26 [28]Then Agrippa said to Paul, "Do you think that in such a short time you can persuade me to be a Christian?"
1 Pet 4 [16]However, if you suffer as a Christian, do not be ashamed, but praise God that you bear that name.

15. Christians Are Called the Church

See p. 690b, Church

16. Christians Are Called the Church of Christ

See p. 691a, Church in God the Father and the Lord Jesus Christ

17. Christians Are Called the Church of the Firstborn

See p. 691a

18. Christians Are Called the Church of God

See p. 691a

19. Christians Are Called the Church of the Living God

See p. 691a

20. Christians Are Called the Circumcision

Phil 3 [3]For it is we who are the circumcision, we who worship by the Spirit of God, who glory in Christ Jesus, and who put no confidence in the flesh. . . .

21. Christians Are Called Disciples

John 13 [35]"By this all men will know that you are my disciples, if you love one another."
Acts 6 [1]In those days when the number of disciples was

increasing, the Grecian Jews among them complained against the Hebraic Jews because their widows were being overlooked in the daily distribution of food. [2]So the Twelve gathered all the disciples together and said, "It would not be right for us to neglect the ministry of the word of God in order to wait on tables."
Acts 11 [26]and when he found him, he brought him to Antioch. So for a whole year Barnabas and Saul met with the church and taught great numbers of people. The disciples were called Christians first at Antioch.
Acts 14 [21]They preached the good news in that city and won a large number of disciples. Then they returned to Lystra, Iconium and Antioch, [22]strengthening the disciples and encouraging them to remain true to the faith. "We must go through many hardships to enter the kingdom of God," they said.
Acts 18 [27]When Apollos wanted to go to Achaia, the brothers encouraged him and wrote to the disciples there to welcome him. On arriving, he was a great help to those who by grace had believed.

22. Christians Are Called the Elect

Rom 11 [7]What then? What Israel sought so earnestly it did not obtain, but the elect did. The others were hardened. . . .
Titus 1 [1]Paul, a servant of God and an apostle of Jesus Christ for the faith of God's elect and the knowledge of the truth that leads to godliness . . .
1 Pet 1 [1]Peter, an apostle of Jesus Christ,
To God's elect, strangers in the world, scattered throughout Pontus, Galatia, Cappadocia, Asia and Bithynia. . . .

23. Christians Are Called Faithful Followers

Rev 17 [14]"They will make war against the Lamb, but the Lamb will overcome them because he is Lord of lords and King of kings—and with him will be his called, chosen and faithful followers."

24. Christians Are Called Fellow Citizens

Eph 2 [19]Consequently, you are no longer foreigners and aliens, but fellow citizens with God's people and members of God's household, [20]built on the foundation of the apostles and prophets, with Christ Jesus himself as the chief cornerstone.

25. Christians Are Called Fellow Servants

Rev 6 [11]Then each of them was given a white robe, and they were told to wait a little longer, until the number of their fellow servants and brothers who were to be killed as they had been was completed.

26. Christians Are Called Fellow Soldiers

Phil 2 [25]But I think it is necessary to send back to you Epaphroditus, my brother, fellow worker and fellow soldier, who is also your messenger, whom you sent to take care of my needs.

27. Christians Are Called Fellow Workers

1 Cor 3 [9]For we are God's fellow workers; you are God's field, God's building.
2 Cor 6 [1]As God's fellow workers we urge you not to receive God's grace in vain.
Phil 2 [25]But I think it is necessary to send back to you Epaphroditus, my brother, fellow worker and fellow soldier, who is also your messenger, whom you sent to take care of my needs.

28. Christians Are Called Followers of the Way

Acts 9 [1]Meanwhile, Saul was still breathing out murderous threats against the Lord's disciples. He went to the high priest [2]and asked him for letters to the synagogues in Damascus, so that if he found any there who belonged to the Way, whether men or women, he might take them as prisoners to Jerusalem.
Acts 19 [9]But some of them became obstinate; they refused to believe and publicly maligned the Way. So Paul left them. He took the disciples with him and had discussions daily in the lecture hall of Tyrannus.
Acts 19 [23]About that time there arose a great disturbance about the Way.
Acts 22 [4]"I persecuted the followers of this Way to their death, arresting both men and women and throwing them into prison. . . ."
Acts 24 [14]"However, I admit that I worship the God of our fathers as a follower of the Way, which they call a sect. I believe everything that agrees with the Law and that is written in the Prophets. . . ."
[22]Then Felix, who was well acquainted with the Way, adjourned the proceedings. "When Lysias the commander comes," he said, "I will decide your case."

29. Christians Are Called Fools for Christ

1 Cor 4 [10]We are fools for Christ, but you are so wise in Christ! We are weak, but you are strong! You are honored, we are dishonored!

30. Christians Are Called Freedmen of the Lord

1 Cor 7 [22]For he who was a slave when he was called by the Lord is the Lord's freedman; similarly, he who was a free man when he was called is Christ's slave.

31. Christians Are Called Friends

John 15 [13]"Greater love has no one than this, that he lay down his life for his friends. [14]You are my friends if you do what I command. [15]I no longer call you servants, because a servant does not know his master's business. Instead, I have called you friends, for everything that I learned from my Father I have made known to you."
Acts 27 [3]The next day we landed at Sidon; and Julius, in kindness to Paul, allowed him to go to his friends so they might provide for his needs.
James 2 [23]And the scripture was fulfilled that says, "Abraham believed God, and it was credited to him as righteousness," and he was called God's friend.
3 John [14]I hope to see you soon, and we will talk face to face.
Peace to you. The friends here send their greetings. Greet the friends there by name.

32. Christians Are Called Good Soldiers of Christ

2 Tim 2 [3]Endure hardship with us like a good soldier of Christ Jesus.

33. Christians Are Called Heirs

Rom 8 [17]Now if we are children, then we are heirs—heirs of God and co-heirs with Christ, if indeed we share in his sufferings in order that we may also share in his glory.
Gal 3 [29]If you belong to Christ, then you are Abraham's seed, and heirs according to the promise.
Gal 4 [7]So you are no longer a slave, but a son; and since you are a son, God has made you also an heir.
Eph 3 [6]This mystery is that through the gospel the Gentiles are heirs together with Israel, members together of one body, and sharers together in the promise in Christ Jesus.
Titus 3 [7]so that, having been justified by his grace, we might become heirs having the hope of eternal life.
1 Pet 3 [7]Husbands, in the same way be considerate as you live with your wives, and treat them with respect as the weaker partner and as heirs with you of the gracious gift of life, so that nothing will hinder your prayers.

34. Christians Are Called a Holy Nation

1 Pet 2 [9]But you are a chosen people, a royal priesthood, a holy nation, a people belonging to God, that you may declare the praises of him who called you out of darkness into his wonderful light.

35. Christians Are Called Holy Ones

1 Thess 3 13May he strengthen your hearts so that you will be blameless and holy in the presence of our God and Father when our Lord Jesus comes with all his holy ones.
Jude 14Enoch, the seventh from Adam, prophesied about these men: "See, the Lord is coming with thousands upon thousands of his holy ones. . . ."

36. Christians Are Called the Holy People of God

Eph 5 3But among you there must not be even a hint of sexual immorality, or of any kind of impurity, or of greed, because these are improper for God's holy people.
2 Thess 1 10on the day he comes to be glorified in his holy people and to be marveled at among all those who have believed. This includes you, because you believed our testimony to you.

37. Christians Are Called a Holy Priesthood

1 Pet 2 5you also, like living stones, are being built into a spiritual house to be a holy priesthood, offering spiritual sacrifices acceptable to God through Jesus Christ.

38. Christians Are Called Imitators of God

Eph 5 1Be imitators of God, therefore, as dearly loved children. . . .

39. Christians Are Called Israel

Gal 6 16Peace and mercy to all who follow this rule, even to the Israel of God.
Heb 8 8But God found fault with the people and said: "The time is coming, declares the Lord, when I will make a new covenant with the house of Israel and with the house of Judah. 9It will not be like the covenant I made with their forefathers when I took them by the hand to lead them out of Egypt, because they did not remain faithful to my covenant, and I turned away from them, declares the Lord. 10This is the covenant I will make with the house of Israel after that time, declares the Lord. I will put my laws in their minds and write them on their hearts. I will be their God, and they will be my people. 11No longer will a man teach his neighbor, or a man his brother, saying, 'Know the Lord,' because they will all know me, from the least of them to the greatest. 12For I will forgive their wickedness and will remember their sins no more."

40. Christians Are Called Loyal Yokefellows

Phil 4 3Yes, and I ask you, loyal yokefellow, help these women who have contended at my side in the cause of the gospel, along with Clement and the rest of my fellow workers, whose names are in the book of life.

41. Christians Are Called Members of God's Household

Eph 2 19Consequently, you are no longer foreigners and aliens, but fellow citizens with God's people and members of God's household, 20built on the foundation of the apostles and prophets, with Christ Jesus himself as the chief cornerstone.

42. Christians Are Called Ministers of a New Covenant

2 Cor 3 6He has made us competent as ministers of a new covenant—not of the letter but of the Spirit; for the letter kills, but the Spirit gives life.

43. Christians Are Called the Nazarenes

Acts 24 5"We have found this man to be a troublemaker, stirring up riots among the Jews all over the world. He is a ringleader of the Nazarene sect. . . ."

44. Christians Are Called the People of God

Rom 9 25As he says in Hosea: "I will call them 'my people' who are not my people; and I will call her 'my loved one' who is not my loved one." . . .
Eph 2 19Consequently, you are no longer foreigners and aliens, but fellow citizens with God's people and members of God's household. . . .
1 Pet 2 10Once you were not a people, but now you are the people of God; once you had not received mercy, but now you have received mercy.

45. Christians Are Called Priests

Rev 1 5and from Jesus Christ, who is the faithful witness, the firstborn from the dead, and the ruler of the kings of the earth.
To him who loves us and has freed us from our sins by his blood, 6and has made us to be a kingdom and priests to serve his God and Father—to him be glory and power for ever and ever! Amen.
Rev 5 10"You have made them to be a kingdom and priests to serve our God, and they will reign on the earth."

46. Christians Are Called Priests of God and Christ

Rev 20 6Blessed and holy are those who have part in the first resurrection. The second death has no power over them, but they will be priests of God and of Christ and will reign with him for a thousand years.

47. Christians Are Called Prisoners of Christ

Eph 3 1For this reason I, Paul, the prisoner of Christ Jesus for the sake of you Gentiles . . .
Eph 4 1As a prisoner for the Lord, then, I urge you to live a life worthy of the calling you have received.
Philem 1Paul, a prisoner of Christ Jesus, and Timothy our brother,
To Philemon our dear friend and fellow worker. . . .
Philem 9yet I appeal to you on the basis of love. I then, as Paul—an old man and now also a prisoner of Christ Jesus . . .
Philem 23Epaphras, my fellow prisoner in Christ Jesus, sends you greetings.

48. Christians Are Called the Righteous

1 Pet 3 12"For the eyes of the Lord are on the righteous and his ears are attentive to their prayer, but the face of the Lord is against those who do evil."
1 Pet 4 18And, "If it is hard for the righteous to be saved, what will become of the ungodly and the sinner?"

49. Christians Are Called the Righteousness of God

2 Cor 5 21God made him who had no sin to be sin for us, so that in him we might become the righteousness of God.

50. Christians Are Called a Royal Priesthood

1 Pet 2 9But you are a chosen people, a royal priesthood, a holy nation, a people belonging to God, that you may declare the praises of him who called you out of darkness into his wonderful light.

51. Christians Are Called Saints

Acts 26 10"And that is just what I did in Jerusalem. On the authority of the chief priests I put many of the saints in prison, and when they were put to death, I cast my vote against them."
Rom 8 27And he who searches our hearts knows the mind of the Spirit, because the Spirit intercedes for the saints in accordance with God's will.
1 Cor 6 1If any of you has a dispute with another, dare he take it before the ungodly for judgment instead of before the saints?

[2]Do you not know that the saints will judge the world? And if you are to judge the world, are you not competent to judge trivial cases?
2 Cor 13 [13]All the saints send their greetings.
Eph 1 [18]I pray also that the eyes of your heart may be enlightened in order that you may know the hope to which he has called you, the riches of his glorious inheritance in the saints. . . .
Eph 6 [18]And pray in the Spirit on all occasions with all kinds of prayers and requests. With this in mind, be alert and always keep on praying for all the saints.
Phil 1 [1]Paul and Timothy, servants of Christ Jesus,
To all the saints in Christ Jesus at Philippi, together with the overseers and deacons. . . .
Col 1 [26]the mystery that has been kept hidden for ages and generations, but is now disclosed to the saints.
Rev 8 [3]Another angel, who had a golden censer, came and stood at the altar. He was given much incense to offer, with the prayers of all the saints, on the golden altar before the throne. [4]The smoke of the incense, together with the prayers of the saints, went up before God from the angel's hand.
Rev 16 [6]". . . for they have shed the blood of your saints and prophets, and you have given them blood to drink as they deserve."
Rev 17 [6]I saw that the woman was drunk with the blood of the saints, the blood of those who bore testimony to Jesus.
When I saw her, I was greatly astonished.

52. Christians Are Called the Seed of Abraham

Gal 3 [29]If you belong to Christ, then you are Abraham's seed, and heirs according to the promise.

53. Christians Are Called Servants

Acts 4 [29]"Now, Lord, consider their threats and enable your servants to speak your word with great boldness."
Acts 16 [17]This girl followed Paul and the rest of us, shouting, "These men are servants of the Most High God, who are telling you the way to be saved."
2 Cor 6 [4]Rather, as servants of God we commend ourselves in every way: in great endurance; in troubles, hardships and distresses. . . .
1 Pet 2 [16]Live as free men, but do not use your freedom as a cover-up for evil; live as servants of God.
Rev 1 [1]The revelation of Jesus Christ, which God gave him to show his servants what must soon take place. He made it known by sending his angel to his servant John. . . .
Rev 2 [20]"Nevertheless, I have this against you: You tolerate that woman Jezebel, who calls herself a prophetess. By her teaching she misleads my servants into sexual immorality and the eating of food sacrificed to idols."

54. Christians Are Called Servants of Christ

Rom 1 [1]Paul, a servant of Christ Jesus, called to be an apostle and set apart for the gospel of God. . . .
1 Cor 4 [1]So then, men ought to regard us as servants of Christ and as those entrusted with the secret things of God.
2 Cor 11 [23]Are they servants of Christ? (I am out of my mind to talk like this.) I am more. I have worked much harder, been in prison more frequently, been flogged more severely, and been exposed to death again and again.
Gal 1 [10]Am I now trying to win the approval of men, or of God? Or am I trying to please men? If I were still trying to please men, I would not be a servant of Christ.
Eph 6 [21]Tychicus, the dear brother and faithful servant in the Lord, will tell you everything, so that you also may know how I am and what I am doing.
Phil 1 [1]Paul and Timothy, servants of Christ Jesus,
To all the saints in Christ Jesus at Philippi, together with the overseers and deacons. . . .
2 Tim 2 [24]And the Lord's servant must not quarrel; instead, he must be kind to everyone, able to teach, not resentful.

55. Christians Are Called Servants of God

2 Cor 6 [4]Rather, as servants of God we commend ourselves in every way: in great endurance; in troubles, hardships and distresses. . . .
James 1 [1]James, a servant of God and of the Lord Jesus Christ,
To the twelve tribes scattered among the nations: Greetings.
1 Pet 2 [16]Live as free men, but do not use your freedom as a cover-up for evil; live as servants of God.
Rev 7 [3]"Do not harm the land or the sea or the trees until we put a seal on the foreheads of the servants of our God."

56. Christians Are Called Servants of the Gospel

Eph 3 [7]I became a servant of this gospel by the gift of God's grace given me through the working of his power.

57. Christians Are Called Slaves of Christ

1 Cor 7 [22]For he who was a slave when he was called by the Lord is the Lord's freedman; similarly, he who was a free man when he was called is Christ's slave.
Eph 6 [6]Obey them not only to win their favor when their eye is on you, but like slaves of Christ, doing the will of God from your heart.

58. Christians Are Called Slaves of God

Rom 6 [22]But now that you have been set free from sin and have become slaves to God, the benefit you reap leads to holiness, and the result is eternal life.

59. Christians Are Called Sons

Rom 8 [15]For you did not receive a spirit that makes you a slave again to fear, but you received the Spirit of sonship. And by him we cry, "*Abba*, Father."
Rom 8 [23]Not only so, but we ourselves, who have the firstfruits of the Spirit, groan inwardly as we wait eagerly for our adoption as sons, the redemption of our bodies.
Gal 4 [7]So you are no longer a slave, but a son; and since you are a son, God has made you also an heir.
Eph 1 [5]he predestined us to be adopted as his sons through Jesus Christ, in accordance with his pleasure and will. . . .
Heb 12 [7]Endure hardship as discipline; God is treating you as sons. For what son is not disciplined by his father?

60. Christians Are Called Sons of the Day

1 Thess 5 [5]You are all sons of the light and sons of the day. We do not belong to the night or to the darkness.

61. Christians Are Called Sons of God

Matt 5 [9]"Blessed are the peacemakers, for they will be called sons of God."
Rom 8 [14]because those who are led by the Spirit of God are sons of God. . . . [19]The creation waits in eager expectation for the sons of God to be revealed.
Gal 3 [26]You are all sons of God through faith in Christ Jesus. . . .

62. Christians Are Called Sons of the Kingdom

Matt 13 [38]"The field is the world, and the good seed stands for the sons of the kingdom. The weeds are the sons of the evil one. . . ."

63. Christians Are Called Sons of the Light

1 Thess 5 [5]You are all sons of the light and sons of the day. We do not belong to the night or to the darkness.

64. Christians Are Called Sons of the Living God

Rom 9 [26]and, "It will happen that in the very place where it was said to them, 'You are not my people,' they will be called 'sons of the living God.'"

65. Christians Are Called Sons of the Most High

Luke 6 [35]"But love your enemies, do good to them, and lend to them without expecting to get anything back. Then your reward will be great, and you will be sons of the Most High, because he is kind to the ungrateful and wicked."

66. Christians Are Called Sons of Your Father in Heaven

Matt 5 [44]"But I tell you: Love your enemies and pray for those who persecute you, [45]that you may be sons of your Father in heaven. He causes his sun to rise on the evil and the good, and sends rain on the righteous and the unrighteous."

67. Christians Are Called Those Bearing Testimony to Jesus

Rev 17 [6]I saw that the woman was drunk with the blood of the saints, the blood of those who bore testimony to Jesus.

When I saw her, I was greatly astonished.

68. Christians Are Called Those Entrusted with the Secret Things of God

1 Cor 4 [1]So then, men ought to regard us as servants of Christ and as those entrusted with the secret things of God.

69. Christians Are Called Those Who Call on the Name of the Lord

Acts 9 [13]"Lord," Ananias answered, "I have heard many reports about this man and all the harm he has done to your saints in Jerusalem. [14]And he has come here with authority from the chief priests to arrest all who call on your name."

Rom 10 [12]For there is no difference between Jew and Gentile—the same Lord is Lord of all and richly blesses all who call on him, [13]for, "Everyone who calls on the name of the Lord will be saved."

1 Cor 1 [2]To the church of God in Corinth, to those sanctified in Christ Jesus and called to be holy, together with all those everywhere who call on the name of our Lord Jesus Christ—their Lord and ours. . . .

70. Christians Are Called Those Who Obey God's Commandments and Hold to the Testimony of Jesus

Rev 12 [17]Then the dragon was enraged at the woman and went off to make war against the rest of her offspring—those who obey God's commandments and hold to the testimony of Jesus.

71. Christians Are Called Those Who Reverence Your Name

Rev 11 [18]"The nations were angry; and your wrath has come. The time has come for judging the dead, and for rewarding your servants the prophets and your saints and those who reverence your name, both small and great—and for destroying those who destroy the earth."

72. Christians Are Called the Work of God's Hands

Eph 2 [10]For we are God's workmanship, created in Christ Jesus to do good works, which God prepared in advance for us to do.

73. Christians Are Called Worshipers

John 4 [23]"Yet a time is coming and has now come when the true worshipers will worship the Father in spirit and truth, for they are the kind of worshipers the Father seeks. [24]God is spirit, and his worshipers must worship in spirit and in truth."

Rev 11 [1]I was given a reed like a measuring rod and was told, "Go and measure the temple of God and the altar, and count the worshipers there."

B. Descriptions of and Metaphors for the Righteous (God's People)

1. The Righteous Are Called the Aroma of Christ

2 Cor 2 [15]For we are to God the aroma of Christ among those who are being saved and those who are perishing.

2. The Righteous Are Called a Bride

Isa 61 [10]I delight greatly in the LORD; my soul rejoices in my God. For he has clothed me with garments of salvation and arrayed me in a robe of righteousness, as a bridegroom adorns his head like a priest, and as a bride adorns herself with her jewels.

3. The Righteous Are Called a Bridegroom

Isa 61 [10]I delight greatly in the LORD; my soul rejoices in my God. For he has clothed me with garments of salvation and arrayed me in a robe of righteousness, as a bridegroom adorns his head like a priest, and as a bride adorns herself with her jewels.

4. The Righteous Are Called the Body of Christ

Rom 12 [4]Just as each of us has one body with many members, and these members do not all have the same function, [5]so in Christ we who are many form one body, and each member belongs to all the others.

1 Cor 10 [16]Is not the cup of thanksgiving for which we give thanks a participation in the blood of Christ? And is not the bread that we break a participation in the body of Christ? [17]Because there is one loaf, we, who are many, are one body, for we all partake of the one loaf.

1 Cor 12 [12]The body is a unit, though it is made up of many parts; and though all its parts are many, they form one body. So it is with Christ. [13]For we were all baptized by one Spirit into one body—whether Jews or Greeks, slave or free—and we were all given the one Spirit to drink.

[14]Now the body is not made up of one part but of many. [15]If the foot should say, "Because I am not a hand, I do not belong to the body," it would not for that reason cease to be part of the body. [16]And if the ear should say, "Because I am not an eye, I do not belong to the body," it would not for that reason cease to be part of the body. [17]If the whole body were an eye, where would the sense of hearing be? If the whole body were an ear, where would the sense of smell be? [18]But in fact God has arranged the parts in the body, every one of them, just as he wanted them to be. [19]If they were all one part, where would the body be? [20]As it is, there are many parts, but one body.

[21]The eye cannot say to the hand, "I don't need you!" And the head cannot say to the feet, "I don't need you!" [22]On the contrary, those parts of the body that seem to be weaker are indispensable, [23]and the parts that we think are less honorable we treat with special honor. And the parts that are unpresentable are treated with special modesty, [24]while our presentable parts need no special treatment. But God has combined the members of the body and has given greater honor to the parts that lacked it, [25]so that there should be no division in the body, but that its parts should have equal concern for each other. [26]If one part suffers, every part suffers with it; if one part is honored, every part rejoices with it.

[27]Now you are the body of Christ, and each one of you is a part of it.

Eph 4 [15]Instead, speaking the truth in love, we will in all things grow up into him who is the Head, that is, Christ. [16]From him the whole body, joined and held together by every supporting ligament, grows and builds itself up in love, as each part does its work.

Col 1 [18]And he is the head of the body, the church; he is the

beginning and the firstborn from among the dead, so that in everything he might have the supremacy.
Col 3 [15]Let the peace of Christ rule in your hearts, since as members of one body you were called to peace. And be thankful.

5. The Righteous Are Called Brothers

Ps 22 [22]I will declare your name to my brothers; in the congregation I will praise you.

6. The Righteous Are Called the Building of God

1 Cor 3 [9]For we are God's fellow workers; you are God's field, God's building.
[10]By the grace God has given me, I laid a foundation as an expert builder, and someone else is building on it. But each one should be careful how he builds. [11]For no one can lay any foundation other than the one already laid, which is Jesus Christ.

7. The Righteous Are Called Chosen Instruments

Acts 9 [15]But the Lord said to Ananias, "Go! This man is my chosen instrument to carry my name before the Gentiles and their kings and before the people of Israel."

8. The Righteous Are Called Clay

Isa 64 [8]Yet, O LORD, you are our Father. We are the clay, you are the potter; we are all the work of your hand.

9. The Righteous Are Called a Crown

Isa 62 [3]You will be a crown of splendor in the LORD's hand, a royal diadem in the hand of your God.
1 Thess 2 [19]For what is our hope, our joy, or the crown in which we will glory in the presence of our Lord Jesus when he comes? Is it not you? [20]Indeed, you are our glory and joy.

10. The Righteous Are Called a Field

1 Cor 3 [9]For we are God's fellow workers; you are God's field, God's building.

11. The Righteous Are Called Saints

Ps 34 [9]Fear the LORD, you his saints, for those who fear him lack nothing.
Ps 85 [8]I will listen to what God the LORD will say; he promises peace to his people, his saints—but let them not return to folly.

12. The Righteous Are Called Servants

Neh 1 [11]"O Lord, let your ear be attentive to the prayer of this your servant and to the prayer of your servants who delight in revering your name. Give your servant success today by granting him favor in the presence of this man."
I was cupbearer to the king.
Dan 3 [26]Nebuchadnezzar then approached the opening of the blazing furnace and shouted, "Shadrach, Meshach and Abednego, servants of the Most High God, come out! Come here!"
So Shadrach, Meshach and Abednego came out of the fire. . . .

13. The Righteous Are Called a Treasured Possession

Exod 19 [5]"'Now if you obey me fully and keep my covenant, then out of all nations you will be my treasured possession. Although the whole earth is mine, [6]you will be for me a kingdom of priests and a holy nation.' These are the words you are to speak to the Israelites."
Deut 14 [2]for you are a people holy to the LORD your God. Out of all the peoples on the face of the earth, the LORD has chosen you to be his treasured possession.
Ps 135 [4]For the LORD has chosen Jacob to be his own, Israel to be his treasured possession.
Mal 3 [17]"They will be mine," says the LORD Almighty, "in the day when I make up my treasured possession. I will spare them, just as in compassion a man spares his son who serves him."

14. The Righteous Are Called the Work of God's Hands

Isa 64 [8]Yet, O LORD, you are our Father. We are the clay, you are the potter; we are all the work of your hand.

15. The Righteous Are Called Worshipers

Zeph 3 [10]"From beyond the rivers of Cush my worshipers, my scattered people, will bring me offerings."

16. The Righteous Are like Aliens

1 Pet 2 [11]Dear friends, I urge you, as aliens and strangers in the world, to abstain from sinful desires, which war against your soul.

17. The Righteous Are like Articles of Gold and Silver

2 Tim 2 [20]In a large house there are articles not only of gold and silver, but also of wood and clay; some are for noble purposes and some for ignoble. [21]If a man cleanses himself from the latter, he will be an instrument for noble purposes, made holy, useful to the Master and prepared to do any good work.

18. The Righteous Are like Athletes

2 Tim 2 [5]Similarly, if anyone competes as an athlete, he does not receive the victor's crown unless he competes according to the rules.

19. The Righteous Are like the Brightness of the Heavens

Dan 12 [2]"Multitudes who sleep in the dust of the earth will awake: some to everlasting life, others to shame and everlasting contempt. [3]Those who are wise will shine like the brightness of the heavens, and those who lead many to righteousness, like the stars for ever and ever."

20. The Righteous Are like Calves

Mal 4 [2]"But for you who revere my name, the sun of righteousness will rise with healing in its wings. And you will go out and leap like calves released from the stall."

21. The Righteous Are like Cedars of Lebanon

Ps 92 [12]The righteous will flourish like a palm tree, they will grow like a cedar of Lebanon; [13]planted in the house of the LORD, they will flourish in the courts of our God. [14]They will still bear fruit in old age, they will stay fresh and green, [15]proclaiming, "The LORD is upright; he is my Rock, and there is no wickedness in him."
Hos 14 [5]"I will be like the dew to Israel; he will blossom like a lily. Like a cedar of Lebanon he will send down his roots; [6]his young shoots will grow. His splendor will be like an olive tree, his fragrance like a cedar of Lebanon. [7]Men will dwell again in his shade. He will flourish like the grain. He will blossom like a vine, and his fame will be like the wine from Lebanon."

22. The Righteous Are like Children

Ps 103 [13]As a father has compassion on his children, so the LORD has compassion on those who fear him. . . .

23. The Righteous Are like Dew

Mic 5 [7]The remnant of Jacob will be in the midst of many peoples like dew from the LORD, like showers on the grass, which do not wait for man or linger for mankind.

24. The Righteous Are like Doves

Ps 68 [13]“Even while you sleep among the campfires, the wings of my dove are sheathed with silver, its feathers with shining gold.”

Isa 60 [8]“Who are these that fly along like clouds, like doves to their nests? [9]Surely the islands look to me; in the lead are the ships of Tarshish, bringing your sons from afar, with their silver and gold, to the honor of the LORD your God, the Holy One of Israel, for he has endowed you with splendor.”

25. The Righteous Are like Eagles

Ps 103 [5]who satisfies your desires with good things so that your youth is renewed like the eagle’s.

Isa 40 [31]but those who hope in the LORD will renew their strength. They will soar on wings like eagles; they will run and not grow weary, they will walk and not be faint.

26. The Righteous Are like Farmers

1 Cor 9 [7]Who serves as a soldier at his own expense? Who plants a vineyard and does not eat of its grapes? Who tends a flock and does not drink of the milk? [8]Do I say this merely from a human point of view? Doesn’t the Law say the same thing? [9]For it is written in the Law of Moses: “Do not muzzle an ox while it is treading out the grain.” Is it about oxen that God is concerned? [10]Surely he says this for us, doesn’t he? Yes, this was written for us, because when the plowman plows and the thresher threshes, they ought to do so in the hope of sharing in the harvest. [11]If we have sown spiritual seed among you, is it too much if we reap a material harvest from you?

2 Tim 2 [6]The hardworking farmer should be the first to receive a share of the crops.

27. The Righteous Are like Firstfruits

Rev 14 [4]These are those who did not defile themselves with women, for they kept themselves pure. They follow the Lamb wherever he goes. They were purchased from among men and offered as firstfruits to God and the Lamb.

28. The Righteous Are like a Flock

Ps 77 [20]You led your people like a flock by the hand of Moses and Aaron.

Ps 78 [52]But he brought his people out like a flock; he led them like sheep through the desert.

Isa 40 [10]See, the Sovereign LORD comes with power, and his arm rules for him. See, his reward is with him, and his recompense accompanies him. [11]He tends his flock like a shepherd: He gathers the lambs in his arms and carries them close to his heart; he gently leads those that have young.

Jer 31 [10]“Hear the word of the LORD, O nations; proclaim it in distant coastlands: ‘He who scattered Israel will gather them and will watch over his flock like a shepherd.’”

Mic 5 [4]He will stand and shepherd his flock in the strength of the LORD, in the majesty of the name of the LORD his God. And they will live securely, for then his greatness will reach to the ends of the earth. [5]And he will be their peace.

When the Assyrian invades our land and marches through our fortresses, we will raise against him seven shepherds, even eight leaders of men.

Zech 9 [16]The LORD their God will save them on that day as the flock of his people. They will sparkle in his land like jewels in a crown.

Luke 12 [32]“Do not be afraid, little flock, for your Father has been pleased to give you the kingdom.”

29. The Righteous Are like the Fragrance of Life

2 Cor 2 [15]For we are to God the aroma of Christ among those who are being saved and those who are perishing. [16]To the one we are the smell of death; to the other, the fragrance of life. And who is equal to such a task?

30. The Righteous Are like Gold

Job 23 [10]“But he knows the way that I take; when he has tested me, I will come forth as gold.”

31. The Righteous Are like Good Figs

Jer 24 [1]After Jehoiachin son of Jehoiakim king of Judah and the officials, the craftsmen and the artisans of Judah were carried into exile from Jerusalem to Babylon by Nebuchadnezzar king of Babylon, the LORD showed me two baskets of figs placed in front of the temple of the LORD. [2]One basket had very good figs, like those that ripen early; the other basket had very poor figs, so bad they could not be eaten.

[3]Then the LORD asked me, “What do you see, Jeremiah?”

“Figs,” I answered. “The good ones are very good, but the poor ones are so bad they cannot be eaten.”

[4]Then the word of the LORD came to me: [5]“This is what the LORD, the God of Israel, says: ‘Like these good figs, I regard as good the exiles from Judah, whom I sent away from this place to the land of the Babylonians. [6]My eyes will watch over them for their good, and I will bring them back to this land. I will build them up and not tear them down; I will plant them and not uproot them. [7]I will give them a heart to know me, that I am the LORD. They will be my people, and I will be their God, for they will return to me with all their heart.’”

32. The Righteous Are like Good Fish

Matt 13 [47]“Once again, the kingdom of heaven is like a net that was let down into the lake and caught all kinds of fish. [48]When it was full, the fishermen pulled it up on the shore. Then they sat down and collected the good fish in baskets, but threw the bad away. [49]This is how it will be at the end of the age. The angels will come and separate the wicked from the righteous. . . . ”

33. The Righteous Are like Good Servants

Matt 24 [45]“Who then is the faithful and wise servant, whom the master has put in charge of the servants in his household to give them their food at the proper time? [46]It will be good for that servant whose master finds him doing so when he returns. [47]I tell you the truth, he will put him in charge of all his possessions.”

Matt 25 [21]“His master replied, ‘Well done, good and faithful servant! You have been faithful with a few things; I will put you in charge of many things. Come and share your master’s happiness!’”

34. The Righteous Are like Grain

Hos 14 [7]“Men will dwell again in his shade. He will flourish like the grain. He will blossom like a vine, and his fame will be like the wine from Lebanon.”

35. The Righteous Are like Grass in a Meadow

Isa 44 [3]“For I will pour water on the thirsty land, and streams on the dry ground; I will pour out my Spirit on your offspring, and my blessing on your descendants. [4]They will spring up like grass in a meadow, like poplar trees by flowing streams. [5]One will say ‘I belong to the LORD’; another will call himself by the name of Jacob; still another will write on his hand, ‘The LORD’s,’ and will take the name Israel.”

36. The Righteous Are like Infants

1 Cor 14 [20]Brothers, stop thinking like children. In regard to evil be infants, but in your thinking be adults.

37. The Righteous Are like Jerusalem

Ps 125 [2]As the mountains surround Jerusalem, so the LORD surrounds his people both now and forevermore.

38. The Righteous Are like the Jewels of a Crown

Zech 9 [16]The LORD their God will save them on that day as the flock of his people. They will sparkle in his land like jewels in a crown.

39. The Righteous Are like a Kingdom

Rev 1 [6]and has made us to be a kingdom and priests to serve his God and Father—to him be glory and power for ever and ever! Amen.
Rev 5 [10]"You have made them to be a kingdom and priests to serve our God, and they will reign on the earth."

40. The Righteous Are like Lambs

Isa 40 [10]See, the Sovereign LORD comes with power, and his arm rules for him. See, his reward is with him, and his recompense accompanies him. [11]He tends his flock like a shepherd: He gathers the lambs in his arms and carries them close to his heart; he gently leads those that have young.
John 21 [15]When they had finished eating, Jesus said to Simon Peter, "Simon son of John, do you truly love me more than these?"

"Yes, Lord," he said, "you know that I love you."

Jesus said, "Feed my lambs."

41. The Righteous Are like Lamps

2 Sam 21 [17]But Abishai son of Zeruiah came to David's rescue; he struck the Philistine down and killed him. Then David's men swore to him, saying, "Never again will you go out with us to battle, so that the lamp of Israel will not be extinguished."
John 5 [35]"John was a lamp that burned and gave light, and you chose for a time to enjoy his light."

42. The Righteous Are like Letters from Christ

2 Cor 3 [1]Are we beginning to commend ourselves again? Or do we need, like some people, letters of recommendation to you or from you? [2]You yourselves are our letter, written on our hearts, known and read by everybody. [3]You show that you are a letter from Christ, the result of our ministry, written not with ink but with the Spirit of the living God, not on tablets of stone but on tablets of human hearts.

43. The Righteous Are like Light in the Lord

Eph 5 [8]For you were once darkness, but now you are light in the Lord. Live as children of light. . . .

44. The Righteous Are like the Light of the World

Matt 5 [14]"You are the light of the world. A city on a hill cannot be hidden. [15]Neither do people light a lamp and put it under a bowl. Instead they put it on its stand, and it gives light to everyone in the house. [16]In the same way, let your light shine before men, that they may see your good deeds and praise your Father in heaven."

45. The Righteous Are like Lilies

Song of Songs 2 [2]Like a lily among thorns is my darling among the maidens.
Hos 14 [5]"I will be like the dew to Israel; he will blossom like a lily. Like a cedar of Lebanon he will send down his roots. . . ."

46. The Righteous Are like Lions

Prov 28 [1]The wicked man flees though no one pursues, but the righteous are as bold as a lion.
Mic 5 [8]The remnant of Jacob will be among the nations, in the midst of many peoples, like a lion among the beasts of the forest, like a young lion among flocks of sheep, which mauls and mangles as it goes, and no one can rescue.

47. The Righteous Are like Little Children

Matt 11 [25]At that time Jesus said, "I praise you, Father, Lord of heaven and earth, because you have hidden these things from the wise and learned, and revealed them to little children."
Matt 19 [14]Jesus said, "Let the little children come to me, and do not hinder them, for the kingdom of heaven belongs to such as these."
Luke 18 [15]People were also bringing babies to Jesus to have him touch them. When the disciples saw this, they rebuked them. [16]But Jesus called the children to him and said, "Let the little children come to me, and do not hinder them, for the kingdom of God belongs to such as these. [17]I tell you the truth, anyone who will not receive the kingdom of God like a little child will never enter it."

48. The Righteous Are like Living Stones

1 Pet 2 [5]you also, like living stones, are being built into a spiritual house to be a holy priesthood, offering spiritual sacrifices acceptable to God through Jesus Christ.

49. The Righteous Are like Mount Zion

Ps 125 [1]Those who trust in the LORD are like Mount Zion, which cannot be shaken but endures forever.

50. The Righteous Are like Newborn Babies

1 Pet 2 [2]Like newborn babies, crave pure spiritual milk, so that by it you may grow up in your salvation. . . .

51. The Righteous Are like Oaks of Righteousness

Isa 61 [3]and provide for those who grieve in Zion—to bestow on them a crown of beauty instead of ashes, the oil of gladness instead of mourning, and a garment of praise instead of a spirit of despair. They will be called oaks of righteousness, a planting of the LORD for the display of his splendor.

52. The Righteous Are like Obedient Children

1 Pet 1 [14]As obedient children, do not conform to the evil desires you had when you lived in ignorance. [15]But just as he who called you is holy, so be holy in all you do; [16]for it is written: "Be holy, because I am holy."

53. The Righteous Are like Olive Trees

Ps 52 [8]But I am like an olive tree flourishing in the house of God; I trust in God's unfailing love for ever and ever.
Jer 11 [16]The LORD called you a thriving olive tree with fruit beautiful in form. But with the roar of a mighty storm he will set it on fire, and its branches will be broken.
Hos 14 [6]". . . his young shoots will grow. His splendor will be like an olive tree, his fragrance like a cedar of Lebanon."
Rom 11 [17]If some of the branches have been broken off, and you, though a wild olive shoot, have been grafted in among the others and now share in the nourishing sap from the olive root . . .

54. The Righteous Are like Palm Trees

Ps 92 [12]The righteous will flourish like a palm tree, they will grow like a cedar of Lebanon; [13]planted in the house of the LORD, they will flourish in the courts of our God. [14]They will still bear fruit in old age, they will stay fresh and green, [15]proclaiming, "The LORD is upright; he is my Rock, and there is no wickedness in him."

55. The Righteous Are like Pillars in the Temple of God

Rev 3 [12]"Him who overcomes I will make a pillar in the temple of my God. Never again will he leave it. I will write on him the name of my God and the name of the city of my God, the new Jerusalem, which is coming down out of heaven from my God; and I will also write on him my new name."

56. The Righteous Are like a Planting of the Lord

Isa 61 [3]and provide for those who grieve in Zion—to bestow on them a crown of beauty instead of ashes, the oil of gladness instead of mourning, and a garment of praise instead of a spirit of despair. They will be called oaks of righteousness, a planting of the LORD for the display of his splendor.

57. The Righteous Are like Plants

Matt 15 [13]He replied, "Every plant that my heavenly Father has not planted will be pulled up by the roots."

58. The Righteous Are like Poplar Trees by Streams

Isa 44 [3]"For I will pour water on the thirsty land, and streams on the dry ground; I will pour out my Spirit on your offspring, and my blessing on your descendants. [4]They will spring up like grass in a meadow, like poplar trees by flowing streams. [5]One will say, 'I belong to the LORD'; another will call himself by the name of Jacob; still another will write on his hand, 'The LORD's,' and will take the name Israel."

59. The Righteous Are like the Refuse of the World

1 Cor 4 [9]For it seems to me that God has put us apostles on display at the end of the procession, like men condemned to die in the arena. We have been made a spectacle to the whole universe, to angels as well as to men. . . . [12]We work hard with our own hands. When we are cursed, we bless; when we are persecuted, we endure it; [13]when we are slandered, we answer kindly. Up to this moment we have become the scum of the earth, the refuse of the world.

60. The Righteous Are like a Royal Diadem

Isa 62 [3]You will be a crown of splendor in the LORD's hand, a royal diadem in the hand of your God.

61. The Righteous Are like Runners in a Race

1 Cor 9 [24]Do you not know that in a race all the runners run, but only one gets the prize? Run in such a way as to get the prize. [25]Everyone who competes in the games goes into strict training. They do it to get a crown that will not last; but we do it to get a crown that will last forever. [26]Therefore I do not run like a man running aimlessly; I do not fight like a man beating the air. [27]No, I beat my body and make it my slave so that after I have preached to others, I myself will not be disqualified for the prize.
Heb 12 [1]Therefore, since we are surrounded by such a great cloud of witnesses, let us throw off everything that hinders and the sin that so easily entangles, and let us run with perseverance the race marked out for us.

62. The Righteous Are like the Salt of the Earth

Matt 5 [13]"You are the salt of the earth. But if the salt loses its saltiness, how can it be made salty again? It is no longer good for anything, except to be thrown out and trampled by men."

63. The Righteous Are like the Scum of the Earth

1 Cor 4 [9]For it seems to me that God has put us apostles on display at the end of the procession, like men condemned to die in the arena. We have been made a spectacle to the whole universe, to angels as well as to men. [13]. . . when we are slandered, we answer kindly. Up to this moment we have become the scum of the earth, the refuse of the world.

64. The Righteous Are like Sheep

Ps 78 [52]But he brought his people out like a flock; he led them like sheep through the desert.
Ezek 34 [11]"'For this is what the Sovereign LORD says: I myself will search for my sheep and look after them. [12]As a shepherd looks after his scattered flock when he is with them, so will I look after my sheep. I will rescue them from all the places where they were scattered on a day of clouds and darkness. [13]I will bring them out from the nations and gather them from the countries, and I will bring them into their own land. I will pasture them on the mountains of Israel, in the ravines and in all the settlements in the land. [14]I will tend them in a good pasture, and the mountain heights of Israel will be their grazing land. There they will lie down in good grazing land, and there they will feed in a rich pasture on the mountains of Israel. [15]I myself will tend my sheep and have them lie down, declares the Sovereign LORD. [16]I will search for the lost and bring back the strays. I will bind up the injured and strengthen the weak, but the sleek and the strong I will destroy. I will shepherd the flock with justice. . . . [23]I will place over them one shepherd, my servant David, and he will tend them; he will tend them and be their shepherd. . . . [31]You my sheep, the sheep of my pasture, are people, and I am your God, declares the Sovereign LORD.'"
Matt 25 [31]"When the Son of Man comes in his glory, and all the angels with him, he will sit on his throne in heavenly glory. [32]All the nations will be gathered before him, and he will separate the people one from another as a shepherd separates the sheep from the goats. [33]He will put the sheep on his right and the goats on his left.

[34]"Then the King will say to those on his right, 'Come, you who are blessed by my Father; take your inheritance, the kingdom prepared for you since the creation of the world. [35]For I was hungry and you gave me something to eat, I was thirsty and you gave me something to drink, I was a stranger and you invited me in, [36]I needed clothes and you clothed me, I was sick and you looked after me, I was in prison and you came to visit me.'

[37]"Then the righteous will answer him, 'Lord, when did we see you hungry and feed you, or thirsty and give you something to drink? [38]When did we see you a stranger and invite you in, or needing clothes and clothe you? [39]When did we see you sick or in prison and go to visit you?'

[40]"The King will reply, 'I tell you the truth, whatever you did for one of the least of these brothers of mine, you did for me.'"
John 10 [1]"I tell you the truth, the man who does not enter the sheep pen by the gate, but climbs in by some other way, is a thief and a robber. [2]The man who enters by the gate is the shepherd of his sheep. [3]The watchman opens the gate for him, and the sheep listen to his voice. He calls his own sheep by name and leads them out. [4]When he has brought out all his own, he goes on ahead of them, and his sheep follow him because they know his voice. [5]But they will never follow a stranger; in fact, they will run away from him because they do not recognize a stranger's voice." [6]Jesus used this figure of speech, but they did not understand what he was telling them.

[7]Therefore Jesus said again, "I tell you the truth, I am the gate for the sheep. [8]All who ever came before me were thieves and robbers, but the sheep did not listen to them. [9]I am the gate; whoever enters through me will be saved. He will come in and go out, and find pasture. [10]The thief comes only to steal and kill and destroy; I have come that they may have life, and have it to the full.

[11]"I am the good shepherd. The good shepherd lays down his life for the sheep. [12]The hired hand is not the shepherd who owns the sheep. So when he sees the wolf coming, he abandons the sheep and runs away. Then the wolf attacks the flock and scatters it. [13]The man runs away because he is a hired hand and cares nothing for the sheep.

[14]"I am the good shepherd; I know my sheep and my sheep know me—[15]just as the Father knows me and I know the Father—and I lay down my life for the sheep. [16]I have other sheep that are not of this sheep pen. I must bring them also. They too will listen to my voice, and there shall be one flock and one shepherd."
John 21 [16]Again Jesus said, "Simon son of John, do you truly love me?"

He answered, "Yes, Lord, you know that I love you."

Jesus said, "Take care of my sheep."

[17]The third time he said to him, "Simon son of John, do you love me?"

Peter was hurt because Jesus asked him the third time, "Do you love me?" He said, "Lord, you know all things; you know that I love you."

Jesus said, "Feed my sheep."

65. The Righteous Are like Showers on the Grass

Mic 5 [7]The remnant of Jacob will be in the midst of many peoples like dew from the LORD, like showers on the grass, which do not wait for man or linger for mankind.

66. The Righteous Are like the Smell of Death

2 Cor 2 [16]To the one we are the smell of death; to the other, the fragrance of life. And who is equal to such a task?

67. The Righteous Are like Soldiers

1 Tim 1 [18]Timothy, my son, I give you this instruction in keeping with the prophecies once made about you, so that by following them you may fight the good fight. . . .

2 Tim 2 [3]Endure hardship with us like a good soldier of Christ Jesus. [4]No one serving as a soldier gets involved in civilian affairs—he wants to please his commanding officer.

68. The Righteous Are like Sons

Mal 3 [17]"They will be mine," says the LORD Almighty, "in the day when I make up my treasured possession. I will spare them, just as in compassion a man spares his son who serves him."

69. The Righteous Are like Sons of Light

John 12 [35]Then Jesus told them, "You are going to have the light just a little while longer. Walk while you have the light, before darkness overtakes you. The man who walks in the dark does not know where he is going. [36]Put your trust in the light while you have it, so that you may become sons of light." When he had finished speaking, Jesus left and hid himself from them. . . .

[46]"I have come into the world as a light, so that no one who believes in me should stay in darkness."

70. The Righteous Are like the Stars

Dan 12 [3]"Those who are wise will shine like the brightness of the heavens, and those who lead many to righteousness, like the stars for ever and ever."

Phil 2 [15]so that you may become blameless and pure, children of God without fault in a crooked and depraved generation, in which you shine like stars in the universe . . .

71. The Righteous Are like Strangers in the World

1 Pet 2 [11]Dear friends, I urge you, as aliens and strangers in the world, to abstain from sinful desires, which war against your soul.

72. The Righteous Are like the Sun

Judg 5 [31]"So may all your enemies perish, O LORD! But may they who love you be like the sun when it rises in its strength."

Then the land had peace forty years.

Matt 13 [43]"Then the righteous will shine like the sun in the kingdom of their Father. He who has ears, let him hear."

73. The Righteous Are like Temples

1 Cor 6 [19]Do you not know that your body is a temple of the Holy Spirit, who is in you, whom you have received from God? You are not your own; [20]you were bought at a price. Therefore honor God with your body.

74. The Righteous Are like Thirsting Deer

Ps 42 [1]As the deer pants for streams of water, so my soul pants for you, O God. [2]My soul thirsts for God, for the living God. When can I go and meet with God?

75. The Righteous Are like Trees Planted by Streams of Water

Ps 1 [2]But his delight is in the law of the LORD, and on his law he meditates day and night. [3]He is like a tree planted by streams of water, which yields its fruit in season and whose leaf does not wither. Whatever he does prospers.

Jer 17 [7]"But blessed is the man who trusts in the LORD, whose confidence is in him. [8]He will be like a tree planted by the water that sends out its roots by the stream. It does not fear when heat comes; its leaves are always green. It has no worries in a year of drought and never fails to bear fruit."

76. The Righteous Are like Unfailing Springs

Isa 58 [9]"Then you will call, and the LORD will answer; you will cry for help, and he will say: Here am I.

"If you do away with the yoke of oppression, with the pointing finger and malicious talk . . . [11]The LORD will guide you always; he will satisfy your needs in a sun-scorched land and will strengthen your frame. You will be like a well-watered garden, like a spring whose waters never fail."

77. The Righteous Are like Vines

Ps 128 [1]Blessed are all who fear the LORD, who walk in his ways. [2]You will eat the fruit of your labor; blessings and prosperity will be yours. [3]Your wife will be like a fruitful vine within your house; your sons will be like olive shoots around your table. [4]Thus is the man blessed who fears the LORD.

Ezek 19 [10]"'Your mother was like a vine in your vineyard planted by the water; it was fruitful and full of branches because of abundant water. [11]Its branches were strong, fit for a ruler's scepter. It towered high above the thick foliage, conspicuous for its height and for its many branches.'"

Hos 14 [5]"I will be like the dew to Israel; he will blossom like a lily. Like a cedar of Lebanon he will send down his roots. . . . [7]Men will dwell again in his shade. He will flourish like the grain. He will blossom like a vine, and his fame will be like the wine from Lebanon."

78. The Righteous Are like Vine Branches

John 15 [1]"I am the true vine, and my Father is the gardener. [2]He cuts off every branch in me that bears no fruit, while every branch that does bear fruit he prunes so that it will be even more fruitful. [3]You are already clean because of the word I have spoken to you. [4]Remain in me, and I will remain in you. No branch can bear fruit by itself; it must remain in the vine. Neither can you bear fruit unless you remain in me.

[5]"I am the vine; you are the branches. If a man remains in me and I in him, he will bear much fruit; apart from me you can do nothing."

79. The Righteous Are like Weaned Children

Ps 131 [1]My heart is not proud, O LORD, my eyes are not haughty; I do not concern myself with great matters or things too wonderful for me. [2]But I have stilled and quieted my soul; like a weaned child with its mother, like a weaned child is my soul within me.

80. The Righteous Are like Well-watered Gardens

Isa 58 [11]"The LORD will guide you always; he will satisfy your needs in a sun-scorched land and will strengthen your frame. You will be like a well-watered garden, like a spring whose waters never fail."

Jer 31 [12]"They will come and shout for joy on the heights of Zion; they will rejoice in the bounty of the LORD—the grain, the new wine and the oil, the young of the flocks and herds. They will be like a well-watered garden, and they will sorrow no more."

81. The Righteous Are like Wheat

Matt 3 [12]"His winnowing fork is in his hand, and he will clear his threshing floor, gathering his wheat into the barn and burning up the chaff with unquenchable fire."
Matt 13 [27]"The owner's servants came to him and said, 'Sir, didn't you sow good seed in your field? Where then did the weeds come from?'

[28]"'An enemy did this,' he replied.

"The servants asked him, 'Do you want us to go and pull them up?'

[29]"'No,' he answered, 'because while you are pulling the weeds, you may root up the wheat with them. [30]Let both grow together until the harvest. At that time I will tell the harvesters: First collect the weeds and tie them in bundles to be burned; then gather the wheat and bring it into my barn.'"

82. The Righteous Are like Wine

Hos 14 [5]"I will be like the dew to Israel; he will blossom like a lily. Like a cedar of Lebanon he will send down his roots. . . .
[7]Men will dwell again in his shade. He will flourish like the grain. He will blossom like a vine, and his fame will be like the wine from Lebanon."

12

Christian Living: *Responsibilities toward God*

I
Having Faith in God

A. Believe in God and Trust Him

1. The Nature of Faith

a) A Definition of Faith

2 Cor 4 [16]Therefore we do not lose heart. Though outwardly we are wasting away, yet inwardly we are being renewed day by day. [17]For our light and momentary troubles are achieving for us an eternal glory that far outweighs them all. [18]So we fix our eyes not on what is seen, but on what is unseen. For what is seen is temporary, but what is unseen is eternal.

Heb 11 [1]Now faith is being sure of what we hope for and certain of what we do not see. . . .

[3]By faith we understand that the universe was formed at God's command, so that what is seen was not made out of what was visible. . . . [6]And without faith it is impossible to please God, because anyone who comes to him must believe that he exists and that he rewards those who earnestly seek him.

b) A Description of Faith

(1) Faith Is Accompanied by Love

Eph 3 [16]I pray that out of his glorious riches he may strengthen you with power through his Spirit in your inner being, [17]so that Christ may dwell in your hearts through faith. And I pray that you, being rooted and established in love, [18]may have power, together with all the saints, to grasp how wide and long and high and deep is the love of Christ. . . .

(2) Faith Is Commendable

Heb 11 [1]Now faith is being sure of what we hope for and certain of what we do not see. [2]This is what the ancients were commended for.

(3) Faith Is Complete Allegiance

Matt 13 [44]"The kingdom of heaven is like treasure hidden in a field. When a man found it, he hid it again, and then in his joy went and sold all he had and bought that field.

[45]"Again, the kingdom of heaven is like a merchant looking

for fine pearls. [46]When he found one of great value, he went away and sold everything he had and bought it."
Mark 10 [28]Peter said to him, "We have left everything to follow you!"
Luke 5 [27]After this, Jesus went out and saw a tax collector by the name of Levi sitting at his tax booth. "Follow me," Jesus said to him, [28]and Levi got up, left everything and followed him.
Luke 9 [57]As they were walking along the road, a man said to him, "I will follow you wherever you go."

[58]Jesus replied, "Foxes have holes and birds of the air have nests, but the Son of Man has no place to lay his head."

[59]He said to another man, "Follow me."

But the man replied, "Lord, first let me go and bury my father."

[60]Jesus said to him, "Let the dead bury their own dead, but you go and proclaim the kingdom of God."

[61]Still another said, "I will follow you, Lord; but first let me go back and say good-by to my family."

[62]Jesus replied, "No one who puts his hand to the plow and looks back is fit for service in the kingdom of God."
Luke 14 [26]"If anyone comes to me and does not hate his father and mother, his wife and children, his brothers and sisters—yes, even his own life—he cannot be my disciple. [27]And anyone who does not carry his cross and follow me cannot be my disciple.

[28]"Suppose one of you wants to build a tower. Will he not first sit down and estimate the cost to see if he has enough money to complete it? [29]For if he lays the foundation and is not able to finish it, everyone who sees it will ridicule him, [30]saying, 'This fellow began to build and was not able to finish.'

[31]"Or suppose a king is about to go to war against another king. Will he not first sit down and consider whether he is able with ten thousand men to oppose the one coming against him with twenty thousand? [32]If he is not able, he will send a delegation while the other is still a long way off and will ask for terms of peace. [33]In the same way, any of you who does not give up everything he has cannot be my disciple."

(4) Faith Is Fruitful

1 Thess 1 [3]We continually remember before our God and Father your work produced by faith, your labor prompted by love, and your endurance inspired by hope in our Lord Jesus Christ.

(5) Faith Is a Gift of God

Rom 12 [3]For by the grace given me I say to every one of you: Do not think of yourself more highly than you ought, but rather think of yourself with sober judgment, in accordance with the measure of faith God has given you.
Eph 2 [8]For it is by grace you have been saved, through faith—and this not from yourselves, it is the gift of God. . . .

(6) Faith Is Hope in Christ

Eph 1 [11]In him we were also chosen, having been predestined according to the plan of him who works out everything in conformity with the purpose of his will, [12]in order that we, who were the first to hope in Christ, might be for the praise of his glory.
Heb 6 [18]God did this so that, by two unchangeable things in which it is impossible for God to lie, we who have fled to take hold of the hope offered to us may be greatly encouraged. [19]We have this hope as an anchor for the soul, firm and secure. It enters the inner sanctuary behind the curtain, [20]where Jesus, who went before us, has entered on our behalf. He has become a high priest forever, in the order of Melchizedek.

(7) Faith Is like a Breastplate

1 Thess 5 [8]But since we belong to the day, let us be self-controlled, putting on faith and love as a breastplate, and the hope of salvation as a helmet.

(8) Faith Is like a Shield

Eph 6 [16]In addition to all this, take up the shield of faith, with which you can extinguish all the flaming arrows of the evil one.
1 Pet 1 [5]who through faith are shielded by God's power until the coming of the salvation that is ready to be revealed in the last time.

(9) Faith Is the Mercy of Christ unto Eternal Life

Jude [21]Keep yourselves in God's love as you wait for the mercy of our Lord Jesus Christ to bring you to eternal life.

(10) Faith Is Most Holy

Jude [20]But you, dear friends, build yourselves up in your most holy faith and pray in the Holy Spirit.

(11) Faith Is of Degrees

John 20 [29]Then Jesus told him, "Because you have seen me, you have believed; blessed are those who have not seen and yet have believed."

(12) Faith Is of the Heart

Rom 10 [9]That if you confess with your mouth, "Jesus is Lord," and believe in your heart that God raised him from the dead, you will be saved. [10]For it is with your heart that you believe and are justified, and it is with your mouth that you confess and are saved.

(13) Faith Is Precious

2 Pet 1 [1]Simon Peter, a servant and apostle of Jesus Christ,

To those who through the righteousness of our God and Savior Jesus Christ have received a faith as precious as ours. . . .

(14) Faith Is the Work of God

John 6 [28]Then they asked him, "What must we do to do the works God requires?"

[29]Jesus answered, "The work of God is this: to believe in the one he has sent."

(15) Faith Overcomes the World

1 John 5 [4]for everyone born of God overcomes the world. This is the victory that has overcome the world, even our faith. [5]Who is it that overcomes the world? Only he who believes that Jesus is the Son of God.

2. The Object of Faith

See p. 489b, The Object of Saving Faith

3. The Source of Faith

See p. 491a, The Means of Saving Faith

4. Evidences of True Faith

a) Demonstrating the Fruit of the Spirit Is Evidence of Faith

Gal 5 [22]But the fruit of the Spirit is love, joy, peace, patience, kindness, goodness, faithfulness, [23]gentleness and self-control. Against such things there is no law.

b) Doing Good Works Is Evidence of Faith

See p. 491a, The Relation of Saving Faith to Works; p. 517b, Sanctification as Growth in Grace

c) Encouraging Others in the Faith Is Evidence of Faith

Titus 1 [1]Paul, a servant of God and an apostle of Jesus Christ for the faith of God's elect and the knowledge of the truth that leads to godliness . . .
Jude [20]But you, dear friends, build yourselves up in your most holy faith and pray in the Holy Spirit. [21]Keep yourselves in God's love as you wait for the mercy of our Lord Jesus Christ to bring you to eternal life.

d) Fearing God Is Evidence of Faith

Exod 14 [31]And when the Israelites saw the great power the LORD displayed against the Egyptians, the people feared the LORD and put their trust in him and in Moses his servant.

e) Growing Spiritually Is Evidence of Faith

2 Thess 1 [3]We ought always to thank God for you, brothers, and rightly so, because your faith is growing more and more, and the love every one of you has for each other is increasing.
2 Pet 1 [5]For this very reason, make every effort to add to your

faith goodness; and to goodness, knowledge; 6and to knowledge, self-control; and to self-control, perseverance; and to perseverance, godliness; 7and to godliness, brotherly kindness; and to brotherly kindness, love.

f) Humbling Oneself before God Is Evidence of Faith

Jon 3 5The Ninevites believed God. They declared a fast, and all of them, from the greatest to the least, put on sackcloth.

g) Living according to Faith Is Evidence of Faith

Ps 26 1Vindicate me, O LORD, for I have led a blameless life; I have trusted in the LORD without wavering. 2Test me, O LORD, and try me, examine my heart and my mind; 3for your love is ever before me, and I walk continually in your truth. 4I do not sit with deceitful men, nor do I consort with hypocrites; 5I abhor the assembly of evildoers and refuse to sit with the wicked. 6I wash my hands in innocence, and go about your altar, O LORD, 7proclaiming aloud your praise and telling of all your wonderful deeds. 8I love the house where you live, O LORD, the place where your glory dwells.

9Do not take away my soul along with sinners, my life with bloodthirsty men, 10in whose hands are wicked schemes, whose right hands are full of bribes. 11But I lead a blameless life; redeem me and be merciful to me. 12My feet stand on level ground; in the great assembly I will praise the LORD.

1 Thess 1 3We continually remember before our God and Father your work produced by faith, your labor prompted by love, and your endurance inspired by hope in our Lord Jesus Christ. . . . 6You became imitators of us and of the Lord; in spite of severe suffering, you welcomed the message with the joy given by the Holy Spirit. 7And so you became a model to all the believers in Macedonia and Achaia.

2 Thess 1 11With this in mind, we constantly pray for you, that our God may count you worthy of his calling, and that by his power he may fulfill every good purpose of yours and every act prompted by your faith.

1 Tim 2 15But women will be saved through childbearing—if they continue in faith, love and holiness with propriety.

1 Tim 4 12Don't let anyone look down on you because you are young, but set an example for the believers in speech, in life, in love, in faith and in purity.

2 Tim 2 22Flee the evil desires of youth, and pursue righteousness, faith, love and peace, along with those who call on the Lord out of a pure heart.

2 Tim 3 10You, however, know all about my teaching, my way of life, my purpose, faith, patience, love, endurance. . . . 14But as for you, continue in what you have learned and have become convinced of, because you know those from whom you learned it. . . .

Titus 2 1You must teach what is in accord with sound doctrine. 2Teach the older men to be temperate, worthy of respect, self-controlled, and sound in faith, in love and in endurance.

Titus 3 8This is a trustworthy saying. And I want you to stress these things, so that those who have trusted in God may be careful to devote themselves to doing what is good. These things are excellent and profitable for everyone.

James 2 14What good is it, my brothers, if a man claims to have faith but has no deeds? Can such faith save him? 15Suppose a brother or sister is without clothes and daily food. 16If one of you says to him, "Go, I wish you well; keep warm and well fed," but does nothing about his physical needs, what good is it? 17In the same way, faith by itself, if it is not accompanied by action, is dead.

18But someone will say, "You have faith; I have deeds."

Show me your faith without deeds, and I will show you my faith by what I do. 19You believe that there is one God. Good! Even the demons believe that—and shudder.

20You foolish man, do you want evidence that faith without deeds is useless? 21Was not our ancestor Abraham considered righteous for what he did when he offered his son Isaac on the altar? 22You see that his faith and his actions were working together, and his faith was made complete by what he did. 23And the scripture was fulfilled that says, "Abraham believed God, and it was credited to him as righteousness," and he was called God's friend. 24You see that a person is justified by what he does and not by faith alone.

25In the same way, was not even Rahab the prostitute considered righteous for what she did when she gave lodging to the spies and sent them off in a different direction? 26As the body without the spirit is dead, so faith without deeds is dead.

Rev 2 19"I know your deeds, your love and faith, your service and perseverance, and that you are now doing more than you did at first."

h) Loving Others Is Evidence of Faith

Gal 5 6For in Christ Jesus neither circumcision nor uncircumcision has any value. The only thing that counts is faith expressing itself through love.

Eph 1 15For this reason, ever since I heard about your faith in the Lord Jesus and your love for all the saints . . .

Eph 6 23Peace to the brothers, and love with faith from God the Father and the Lord Jesus Christ.

Col 1 4because we have heard of your faith in Christ Jesus and of the love you have for all the saints—5the faith and love that spring from the hope that is stored up for you in heaven and that you have already heard about in the word of truth, the gospel . . .

1 Tim 1 5The goal of this command is love, which comes from a pure heart and a good conscience and a sincere faith.

1 John 3 23And this is his command: to believe in the name of his Son, Jesus Christ, and to love one another as he commanded us.

i) Persevering Is Evidence of Faith

1 Thess 5 8But since we belong to the day, let us be self-controlled, putting on faith and love as a breastplate, and the hope of salvation as a helmet.

Heb 6 12We do not want you to become lazy, but to imitate those who through faith and patience inherit what has been promised.

Rev 13 10If anyone is to go into captivity, into captivity he will go. If anyone is to be killed with the sword, with the sword he will be killed. This calls for patient endurance and faithfulness on the part of the saints.

Rev 14 12This calls for patient endurance on the part of the saints who obey God's commandments and remain faithful to Jesus.

j) Preserving the Truths of the Faith Is Evidence of Faith

1 Tim 3 9They must keep hold of the deep truths of the faith with a clear conscience.

2 Tim 1 13What you heard from me, keep as the pattern of sound teaching, with faith and love in Christ Jesus.

k) Proclaiming God's Message to Others Is Evidence of Faith

Acts 20 21"I have declared to both Jews and Greeks that they must turn to God in repentance and have faith in our Lord Jesus."

Acts 24 24Several days later Felix came with his wife Drusilla, who was a Jewess. He sent for Paul and listened to him as he spoke about faith in Christ Jesus. 25As Paul discoursed on righteousness, self-control and the judgment to come, Felix was afraid and said, "That's enough for now! You may leave. When I find it convenient, I will send for you."

2 Cor 4 13It is written: "I believed; therefore I have spoken." With that same spirit of faith we also believe and therefore speak. . . .

l) Rejoicing in God Is Evidence of Faith

Ps 5 11But let all who take refuge in you be glad; let them ever sing for joy. Spread your protection over them, that those who love your name may rejoice in you.

Ps 13 5But I trust in your unfailing love; my heart rejoices in your salvation. 6I will sing to the LORD, for he has been good to me.

Ps 33 21In him our hearts rejoice, for we trust in his holy name.

Acts 16 34The jailer brought them into his house and set a meal before them; he was filled with joy because he had come to believe in God—he and his whole family.

m) Trusting in God Is Evidence of Faith

Ps 20 [7]Some trust in chariots and some in horses, but we trust in the name of the LORD our God. [8]They are brought to their knees and fall, but we rise up and stand firm.
Ps 21 [7]For the king trusts in the LORD; through the unfailing love of the Most High he will not be shaken.
Ps 56 [3]When I am afraid, I will trust in you. [4]In God, whose word I praise, in God I trust; I will not be afraid. What can mortal man do to me?
Ps 118 [8]It is better to take refuge in the LORD than to trust in man. [9]It is better to take refuge in the LORD than to trust in princes.

n) Working Mighty Deeds Is Evidence of Faith

1 Cor 13 [2]If I have the gift of prophecy and can fathom all mysteries and all knowledge, and if I have a faith that can move mountains, but have not love, I am nothing.

o) Worshiping and Praising God Is Evidence of Faith

Exod 4 [29]Moses and Aaron brought together all the elders of the Israelites, [30]and Aaron told them everything the LORD had said to Moses. He also performed the signs before the people, [31]and they believed. And when they heard that the LORD was concerned about them and had seen their misery, they bowed down and worshiped.
Ps 28 [7]The LORD is my strength and my shield; my heart trusts in him, and I am helped. My heart leaps for joy and I will give thanks to him in song.
Ps 106 [11]The waters covered their adversaries; not one of them survived. [12]Then they believed his promises and sang his praise.

5. Benefits of Faith

a) Access to God Is a Benefit of Faith

Eph 3 [12]In him and through faith in him we may approach God with freedom and confidence.

b) Adoption into God's Family Is a Benefit of Faith

John 1 [12]Yet to all who received him, to those who believed in his name, he gave the right to become children of God—[13]children born not of natural descent, nor of human decision or a husband's will, but born of God.
Gal 3 [26]You are all sons of God through faith in Christ Jesus. . . .

c) Christ's Indwelling Is a Benefit of Faith

Eph 3 [16]I pray that out of his glorious riches he may strengthen you with power through his Spirit in your inner being, [17]so that Christ may dwell in your hearts through faith. And I pray that you, being rooted and established in love . . .

d) Divine Blessing Is a Benefit of Faith

Ps 40 [4]Blessed is the man who makes the LORD his trust, who does not look to the proud, to those who turn aside to false gods.
Ps 84 [12]O LORD Almighty, blessed is the man who trusts in you.
Prov 16 [20]Whoever gives heed to instruction prospers, and blessed is he who trusts in the LORD.
Prov 28 [25]A greedy man stirs up dissension, but he who trusts in the LORD will prosper.
Isa 57 [13]"When you cry out for help, let your collection of idols save you! The wind will carry all of them off, a mere breath will blow them away. But the man who makes me his refuge will inherit the land and possess my holy mountain."
Jer 17 [7]"But blessed is the man who trusts in the LORD, whose confidence is in him. [8]He will be like a tree planted by the water that sends out its roots by the stream. It does not fear when heat comes; its leaves are always green. It has no worries in a year of drought and never fails to bear fruit."
Luke 1 [45]"Blessed is she who has believed that what the Lord has said to her will be accomplished!"

e) Divine Empowering Is a Benefit of Faith

Matt 17 [20]He replied, "Because you have so little faith. I tell you the truth, if you have faith as small as a mustard seed, you can say to this mountain, 'Move from here to there' and it will move. Nothing will be impossible for you."
Matt 21 [21]Jesus replied, "I tell you the truth, if you have faith and do not doubt, not only can you do what was done to the fig tree, but also you can say to this mountain, 'Go, throw yourself into the sea,' and it will be done. [22]If you believe, you will receive whatever you ask for in prayer."
John 14 [12]"I tell you the truth, anyone who has faith in me will do what I have been doing. He will do even greater things than these, because I am going to the Father. [13]And I will do whatever you ask in my name, so that the Son may bring glory to the Father. [14]You may ask me for anything in my name, and I will do it."

f) Divine Guidance Is a Benefit of Faith

Ps 143 [8]Let the morning bring me word of your unfailing love, for I have put my trust in you. Show me the way I should go, for to you I lift up my soul.
Prov 3 [5]Trust in the LORD with all your heart and lean not on your own understanding; [6]in all your ways acknowledge him, and he will make your paths straight.
John 12 [36]"Put your trust in the light while you have it, so that you may become sons of light." When he had finished speaking, Jesus left and hid himself from them.
John 12 [46]"I have come into the world as a light, so that no one who believes in me should stay in darkness."

g) Divine Intercession Is a Benefit of Faith

John 17 [20]"My prayer is not for them alone. I pray also for those who will believe in me through their message. . . ."

h) Divine Protection Is a Benefit of Faith

Ps 36 [7]How priceless is your unfailing love! Both high and low among men find refuge in the shadow of your wings.
Ps 57 [1]Have mercy on me, O God, have mercy on me, for in you my soul takes refuge. I will take refuge in the shadow of your wings until the disaster has passed.
Ps 62 [8]Trust in him at all times, O people; pour out your hearts to him, for God is our refuge.
Ps 91 [2]I will say of the LORD, "He is my refuge and my fortress, my God, in whom I trust."
Ps 115 [9]O house of Israel, trust in the LORD—he is their help and shield. [10]O house of Aaron, trust in the LORD—he is their help and shield. [11]You who fear him, trust in the LORD—he is their help and shield.
Prov 29 [25]Fear of man will prove to be a snare, but whoever trusts in the LORD is kept safe.

i) God's Indwelling Is a Benefit of Faith

1 John 4 [15]If anyone acknowledges that Jesus is the Son of God, God lives in him and he in God.

j) God's Love Is a Benefit of Faith

Ps 32 [10]Many are the woes of the wicked, but the LORD's unfailing love surrounds the man who trusts in him.
John 16 [27]"No, the Father himself loves you because you have loved me and have believed that I came from God."

k) Grace Is a Benefit of Faith

Rom 5 [1]Therefore, since we have been justified through faith, we have peace with God through our Lord Jesus Christ, [2]through whom we have gained access by faith into this grace in which we now stand. And we rejoice in the hope of the glory of God.

l) Joy Is a Benefit of Faith

Acts 16 [34]The jailer brought them into his house and set a meal before them; he was filled with joy because he had come to believe in God—he and his whole family.
Rom 15 [13]May the God of hope fill you with all joy and peace as you trust in him, so that you may overflow with hope by the power of the Holy Spirit.
1 Pet 1 [8]Though you have not seen him, you love him; and

even though you do not see him now, you believe in him and are filled with an inexpressible and glorious joy, [9]for you are receiving the goal of your faith, the salvation of your souls.

m) Justification Is a Benefit of Faith

Gen 15 [6]Abram believed the LORD, and he credited it to him as righteousness.

Ps 34 [22]The LORD redeems his servants; no one will be condemned who takes refuge in him.

John 5 [24]"I tell you the truth, whoever hears my word and believes him who sent me has eternal life and will not be condemned; he has crossed over from death to life."

Acts 13 [38]"Therefore, my brothers, I want you to know that through Jesus the forgiveness of sins is proclaimed to you. [39]Through him everyone who believes is justified from everything you could not be justified from by the law of Moses."

Rom 3 [21]But now a righteousness from God, apart from law, has been made known, to which the Law and the Prophets testify. [22]This righteousness from God comes through faith in Jesus Christ to all who believe. There is no difference, [23]for all have sinned and fall short of the glory of God, [24]and are justified freely by his grace through the redemption that came by Christ Jesus. [25]God presented him as a sacrifice of atonement, through faith in his blood. He did this to demonstrate his justice, because in his forbearance he had left the sins committed beforehand unpunished—[26]he did it to demonstrate his justice at the present time, so as to be just and the one who justifies those who have faith in Jesus. . . . [28]For we maintain that a man is justified by faith apart from observing the law. [30]. . . since there is only one God, who will justify the circumcised by faith and the uncircumcised through that same faith.

Rom 4 [5]However, to the man who does not work but trusts God who justifies the wicked, his faith is credited as righteousness.

Rom 5 [1]Therefore, since we have been justified through faith, we have peace with God through our Lord Jesus Christ. . . .

Rom 10 [4]Christ is the end of the law so that there may be righteousness for everyone who believes.

Gal 2 [15]"We who are Jews by birth and not 'Gentile sinners' [16]know that a man is not justified by observing the law, but by faith in Jesus Christ. So we, too, have put our faith in Christ Jesus that we may be justified by faith in Christ and not by observing the law, because by observing the law no one will be justified."

Gal 3 [8]The Scripture foresaw that God would justify the Gentiles by faith, and announced the gospel in advance to Abraham: "All nations will be blessed through you." [9]So those who have faith are blessed along with Abraham, the man of faith.

[10]All who rely on observing the law are under a curse, for it is written: "Cursed is everyone who does not continue to do everything written in the Book of the Law." [11]Clearly no one is justified before God by the law, because, "The righteous will live by faith." [12]The law is not based on faith; on the contrary, "The man who does these things will live by them." . . . [22]But the Scripture declares that the whole world is a prisoner of sin, so that what was promised, being given through faith in Jesus Christ, might be given to those who believe.

[23]Before this faith came, we were held prisoners by the law, locked up until faith should be revealed. [24]So the law was put in charge to lead us to Christ that we might be justified by faith.

Phil 3 [8]What is more, I consider everything a loss compared to the surpassing greatness of knowing Christ Jesus my Lord, for whose sake I have lost all things. I consider them rubbish, that I may gain Christ [9]and be found in him, not having a righteousness of my own that comes from the law, but that which is through faith in Christ—the righteousness that comes from God and is by faith.

n) Pardon of Sin Is a Benefit of Faith

Acts 10 [42]"He commanded us to preach to the people and to testify that he is the one whom God appointed as judge of the living and the dead. [43]All the prophets testify about him that everyone who believes in him receives forgiveness of sins through his name."

Acts 13 [38]"Therefore, my brothers, I want you to know that through Jesus the forgiveness of sins is proclaimed to you. [39]Through him everyone who believes is justified from everything you could not be justified from by the law of Moses."

Rom 3 [25]God presented him as a sacrifice of atonement, through faith in his blood. He did this to demonstrate his justice, because in his forbearance he had left the sins committed beforehand unpunished. . . .

o) Peace Is a Benefit of Faith

John 14 [1]"Do not let your hearts be troubled. Trust in God; trust also in me."

Rom 15 [13]May the God of hope fill you with all joy and peace as you trust in him, so that you may overflow with hope by the power of the Holy Spirit.

p) Regeneration Is a Benefit of Faith

John 3 [3]In reply Jesus declared, "I tell you the truth, no one can see the kingdom of God unless he is born again."

[4]"How can a man be born when he is old?" Nicodemus asked. "Surely he cannot enter a second time into his mother's womb to be born!"

[5]Jesus answered, "I tell you the truth, no one can enter the kingdom of God unless he is born of water and the Spirit. . . . [11]I tell you the truth, we speak of what we know, and we testify to what we have seen, but still you people do not accept our testimony. [12]I have spoken to you of earthly things and you do not believe; how then will you believe if I speak of heavenly things?"

1 John 5 [1]Everyone who believes that Jesus is the Christ is born of God, and everyone who loves the father loves his child as well.

q) Sanctification Is a Benefit of Faith

Acts 15 [9]"He made no distinction between us and them, for he purified their hearts by faith."

Acts 26 [17]"'I will rescue you from your own people and from the Gentiles. I am sending you to them [18]to open their eyes and turn them from darkness to light, and from the power of Satan to God, so that they may receive forgiveness of sins and a place among those who are sanctified by faith in me.'"

r) The Spirit's Indwelling Is a Benefit of Faith

John 7 [38]"Whoever believes in me, as the Scripture has said, streams of living water will flow from within him." [39]By this he meant the Spirit, whom those who believed in him were later to receive. Up to that time the Spirit had not been given, since Jesus had not yet been glorified.

Acts 11 [15]"As I began to speak, the Holy Spirit came on them as he had come on us at the beginning. [16]Then I remembered what the Lord had said: 'John baptized with water, but you will be baptized with the Holy Spirit.' [17]So if God gave them the same gift as he gave us, who believed in the Lord Jesus Christ, who was I to think that I could oppose God?"

Gal 3 [13]Christ redeemed us from the curse of the law by becoming a curse for us, for it is written: "Cursed is everyone who is hung on a tree." [14]He redeemed us in order that the blessing given to Abraham might come to the Gentiles through Christ Jesus, so that by faith we might receive the promise of the Spirit.

Eph 1 [13]And you also were included in Christ when you heard the word of truth, the gospel of your salvation. Having believed, you were marked in him with a seal, the promised Holy Spirit, [14]who is a deposit guaranteeing our inheritance until the redemption of those who are God's possession—to the praise of his glory.

s) Spiritual Salvation Is a Benefit of Faith

Isa 28 [16]So this is what the Sovereign LORD says: "See, I lay a stone in Zion, a tested stone, a precious cornerstone for a sure foundation; the one who trusts will never be dismayed."

John 3 [14]"Just as Moses lifted up the snake in the desert, so the Son of Man must be lifted up, [15]that everyone who believes in him may have eternal life.

[16]"For God so loved the world that he gave his one and only Son, that whoever believes in him shall not perish but have eternal life. [17]For God did not send his Son into the world to condemn the world, but to save the world through him. [18]Whoever believes in him is not condemned, but whoever does not believe stands condemned already because he has not believed in the name of God's one and only Son."

John 3 [36]"Whoever believes in the Son has eternal life, but whoever rejects the Son will not see life, for God's wrath remains on him."

John 6 [35]Then Jesus declared, "I am the bread of life. He who comes to me will never go hungry, and he who believes in me will never be thirsty. . . . [40]For my Father's will is that everyone who looks to the Son and believes in him shall have eternal life, and I will raise him up at the last day." . . .

[47]"I tell you the truth, he who believes has everlasting life."

John 11 [25]Jesus said to her, "I am the resurrection and the life. He who believes in me will live, even though he dies; [26]and whoever lives and believes in me will never die. Do you believe this?"

John 20 [31]But these are written that you may believe that Jesus is the Christ, the Son of God, and that by believing you may have life in his name.

Acts 16 [31]They replied, "Believe in the Lord Jesus, and you will be saved—you and your household."

Rom 10 [8]But what does it say? "The word is near you; it is in your mouth and in your heart," that is, the word of faith we are proclaiming: [9]That if you confess with your mouth, "Jesus is Lord," and believe in your heart that God raised him from the dead, you will be saved. [10]For it is with your heart that you believe and are justified, and it is with your mouth that you confess and are saved. [11]As the Scripture says, "Anyone who trusts in him will never be put to shame."

Eph 2 [8]For it is by grace you have been saved, through faith—and this not from yourselves, it is the gift of God. . . .

2 Thess 2 [13]But we ought always to thank God for you, brothers loved by the Lord, because from the beginning God chose you to be saved through the sanctifying work of the Spirit and through belief in the truth.

1 Tim 1 [16]But for that very reason I was shown mercy so that in me, the worst of sinners, Christ Jesus might display his unlimited patience as an example for those who would believe on him and receive eternal life.

1 Tim 6 [12]Fight the good fight of the faith. Take hold of the eternal life to which you were called when you made your good confession in the presence of many witnesses.

2 Tim 3 [15]and how from infancy you have known the holy Scriptures, which are able to make you wise for salvation through faith in Christ Jesus.

Heb 4 [2]For we also have had the gospel preached to us, just as they did; but the message they heard was of no value to them, because those who heard did not combine it with faith. [3]Now we who have believed enter that rest, just as God has said, "So I declared on oath in my anger, 'They shall never enter my rest.'" And yet his work has been finished since the creation of the world.

Heb 10 [39]But we are not of those who shrink back and are destroyed, but of those who believe and are saved.

1 Pet 1 [3]Praise be to the God and Father of our Lord Jesus Christ! In his great mercy he has given us new birth into a living hope through the resurrection of Jesus Christ from the dead, [4]and into an inheritance that can never perish, spoil or fade—kept in heaven for you, [5]who through faith are shielded by God's power until the coming of the salvation that is ready to be revealed in the last time. [9]. . . for you are receiving the goal of your faith, the salvation of your souls.

1 John 5 [13]I write these things to you who believe in the name of the Son of God so that you may know that you have eternal life.

t) Strength for Christian Living Is a Benefit of Faith

(1) Strength in Boldness of Preaching

2 Cor 4 [13]It is written: "I believed; therefore I have spoken." With that same spirit of faith we also believe and therefore speak. . . .

(2) Strength in Christian Warfare

Phil 1 [27]Whatever happens, conduct yourselves in a manner worthy of the gospel of Christ. Then, whether I come and see you or only hear about you in my absence, I will know that you stand firm in one spirit, contending as one man for the faith of the gospel [28]without being frightened in any way by those who oppose you. This is a sign to them that they will be destroyed, but that you will be saved—and that by God.

1 Tim 1 [18]Timothy, my son, I give you this instruction in keeping with the prophecies once made about you, so that by following them you may fight the good fight, [19]holding on to faith and a good conscience. Some have rejected these and so have shipwrecked their faith.

1 Tim 6 [12]Fight the good fight of the faith. Take hold of the eternal life to which you were called when you made your good confession in the presence of many witnesses.

2 Tim 4 [7]I have fought the good fight, I have finished the race, I have kept the faith. [8]Now there is in store for me the crown of righteousness, which the Lord, the righteous Judge, will award to me on that day—and not only to me, but also to all who have longed for his appearing.

(3) Strength in Life

2 Cor 5 [7]We live by faith, not by sight.

Gal 2 [20]"I have been crucified with Christ and I no longer live, but Christ lives in me. The life I live in the body, I live by faith in the Son of God, who loved me and gave himself for me."

(4) Strength in One's Stand

Rom 11 [20]Granted. But they were broken off because of unbelief, and you stand by faith. Do not be arrogant, but be afraid.

1 Cor 16 [13]Be on your guard; stand firm in the faith; be men of courage; be strong.

2 Cor 1 [24]Not that we lord it over your faith, but we work with you for your joy, because it is by faith you stand firm.

Phil 1 [27]Whatever happens, conduct yourselves in a manner worthy of the gospel of Christ. Then, whether I come and see you or only hear about you in my absence, I will know that you stand firm in one spirit, contending as one man for the faith of the gospel. . . .

(5) Strength in One's Walk

Rom 4 [12]And he is also the father of the circumcised who not only are circumcised but who also walk in the footsteps of the faith that our father Abraham had before he was circumcised.

(6) Strength in Overcoming the World

1 John 5 [3]This is love for God: to obey his commands. And his commands are not burdensome, [4]for everyone born of God overcomes the world. This is the victory that has overcome the world, even our faith. [5]Who is it that overcomes the world? Only he who believes that Jesus is the Son of God.

(7) Strength in Prayer

Matt 21 [21]Jesus replied, "I tell you the truth, if you have faith and do not doubt, not only can you do what was done to the fig tree, but also you can say to this mountain, 'Go, throw yourself into the sea,' and it will be done. [22]If you believe, you will receive whatever you ask for in prayer."

James 1 [5]If any of you lacks wisdom, he should ask God, who gives generously to all without finding fault, and it will be given to him. [6]But when he asks, he must believe and not doubt, because he who doubts is like a wave of the sea, blown and tossed by the wind.

(8) Strength in Resisting the Devil

Eph 6 [10]Finally, be strong in the Lord and in his mighty power. [11]Put on the full armor of God so that you can take your stand against the devil's schemes. [12]For our struggle is not against flesh and blood, but against the rulers, against the authorities, against the powers of this dark world and against the spiritual forces of evil in the heavenly realms. [13]Therefore put on the full armor of God, so that when the day of evil comes, you may be able to stand your ground, and after you have done everything, to stand. [14]Stand firm then, with the belt of truth buckled around your waist, with the breastplate of righteousness in place, [15]and with your feet fitted with the readiness that comes from the gospel of peace. [16]In addition to all this, take up the shield of faith, with which you can extinguish all the flaming arrows of the evil one.

1 Pet 5 8Be self-controlled and alert. Your enemy the devil prowls around like a roaring lion looking for someone to devour. 9Resist him, standing firm in the faith, because you know that your brothers throughout the world are undergoing the same kind of sufferings.

(9) Strength in Trial

James 1 2Consider it pure joy, my brothers, whenever you face trials of many kinds, 3because you know that the testing of your faith develops perseverance. 4Perseverance must finish its work so that you may be mature and complete, not lacking anything.
1 Pet 1 6In this you greatly rejoice, though now for a little while you may have had to suffer grief in all kinds of trials. 7These have come so that your faith—of greater worth than gold, which perishes even though refined by fire—may be proved genuine and may result in praise, glory and honor when Jesus Christ is revealed.

u) *Temporal Deliverance Is a Benefit of Faith*

Ps 22 4In you our fathers put their trust; they trusted and you delivered them. 5They cried to you and were saved; in you they trusted and were not disappointed.
Ps 112 7He will have no fear of bad news; his heart is steadfast, trusting in the LORD. 8His heart is secure, he will have no fear; in the end he will look in triumph on his foes.
Ps 119 41May your unfailing love come to me, O LORD, your salvation according to your promise; 42then I will answer the one who taunts me, for I trust in your word.
Ps 141 8But my eyes are fixed on you, O Sovereign LORD; in you I take refuge—do not give me over to death. 9Keep me from the snares they have laid for me, from the traps set by evildoers. 10Let the wicked fall into their own nets, while I pass by in safety.

6. Responsibilities of Faith

a) *One Must Continue in Faith*

Acts 14 21They preached the good news in that city and won a large number of disciples. Then they returned to Lystra, Iconium and Antioch, 22strengthening the disciples and encouraging them to remain true to the faith. "We must go through many hardships to enter the kingdom of God," they said.
2 Cor 13 5Examine yourselves to see whether you are in the faith; test yourselves. Do you not realize that Christ Jesus is in you—unless, of course, you fail the test?
Col 1 22But now he has reconciled you by Christ's physical body through death to present you holy in his sight, without blemish and free from accusation—23if you continue in your faith, established and firm, not moved from the hope held out in the gospel. This is the gospel that you heard and that has been proclaimed to every creature under heaven, and of which I, Paul, have become a servant.
Heb 11 27By faith he left Egypt, not fearing the king's anger; he persevered because he saw him who is invisible.

b) *One Must Excel in Faith*

2 Cor 8 7But just as you excel in everything—in faith, in speech, in knowledge, in complete earnestness and in your love for us—see that you also excel in this grace of giving.

c) *One Must Hold Fast to Faith*

1 Tim 1 18Timothy, my son, I give you this instruction in keeping with the prophecies once made about you, so that by following them you may fight the good fight, 19holding on to faith and a good conscience. Some have rejected these and so have shipwrecked their faith.
Heb 10 23Let us hold unswervingly to the hope we profess, for he who promised is faithful.

d) *One Must Remain Sincere in Faith*

1 Tim 1 5The goal of this command is love, which comes from a pure heart and a good conscience and a sincere faith.
2 Tim 1 5I have been reminded of your sincere faith, which first lived in your grandmother Lois and in your mother Eunice and, I am persuaded, now lives in you also.

e) *One Must Remain Sound in Faith*

Titus 1 13This testimony is true. Therefore, rebuke them sharply, so that they will be sound in the faith. . . .
2 Pet 3 17Therefore, dear friends, since you already know this, be on your guard so that you may not be carried away by the error of lawless men and fall from your secure position.

f) *One Must Remain Strong in Faith*

Rom 4 20Yet he did not waver through unbelief regarding the promise of God, but was strengthened in his faith and gave glory to God, 21being fully persuaded that God had power to do what he had promised. 22This is why "it was credited to him as righteousness." 23The words "it was credited to him" were written not for him alone, 24but also for us, to whom God will credit righteousness—for us who believe in him who raised Jesus our Lord from the dead.
1 Cor 16 13Be on your guard; stand firm in the faith; be men of courage; be strong.
Col 2 5For though I am absent from you in body, I am present with you in spirit and delight to see how orderly you are and how firm your faith in Christ is.

6So then, just as you received Christ Jesus as Lord, continue to live in him, 7rooted and built up in him, strengthened in the faith as you were taught, and overflowing with thankfulness.

7. Examples of Faith

1) *Abel Is an Example of Faith*

Heb 11 4By faith Abel offered God a better sacrifice than Cain did. By faith he was commended as a righteous man, when God spoke well of his offerings. And by faith he still speaks, even though he is dead.

2) *Enoch Is an Example of Faith*

Heb 11 5By faith Enoch was taken from this life, so that he did not experience death; he could not be found, because God had taken him away. For before he was taken, he was commended as one who pleased God.

3) *Noah Is an Example of Faith*

Heb 11 7By faith Noah, when warned about things not yet seen, in holy fear built an ark to save his family. By his faith he condemned the world and became heir of the righteousness that comes by faith.

4) *Abraham Is an Example of Faith*

Rom 4 18Against all hope, Abraham in hope believed and so became the father of many nations, just as it had been said to him, "So shall your offspring be." 19Without weakening in his faith, he faced the fact that his body was as good as dead—since he was about a hundred years old—and that Sarah's womb was also dead. 20Yet he did not waver through unbelief regarding the promise of God, but was strengthened in his faith and gave glory to God, 21being fully persuaded that God had power to do what he had promised.
Heb 11 8By faith Abraham, when called to go to a place he would later receive as his inheritance, obeyed and went, even though he did not know where he was going. 9By faith he made his home in the promised land like a stranger in a foreign country; he lived in tents, as did Isaac and Jacob, who were heirs with him of the same promise. 10For he was looking forward to the city with foundations, whose architect and builder is God.

11By faith Abraham, even though he was past age—and Sarah herself was barren—was enabled to become a father because he considered him faithful who had made the promise. 12And so from this one man, and he as good as dead, came descendants as numerous as the stars in the sky and as countless as the sand on the seashore. . . .

17By faith Abraham, when God tested him, offered Isaac as a sacrifice. He who had received the promises was about to sacrifice his one and only son, 18even though God had said to him, "It is through Isaac that your offspring will be reckoned." 19Abraham reasoned that God could raise the dead, and figuratively speaking, he did receive Isaac back from death.

5) Isaac Is an Example of Faith

Heb 11 [20]By faith Isaac blessed Jacob and Esau in regard to their future.

6) Jacob Is an Example of Faith

Heb 11 [21]By faith Jacob, when he was dying, blessed each of Joseph's sons, and worshiped as he leaned on the top of his staff.

7) Joseph Is an Example of Faith

Heb 11 [22]By faith Joseph, when his end was near, spoke about the exodus of the Israelites from Egypt and gave instructions about his bones.

8) Moses Is an Example of Faith

Heb 11 [24]By faith Moses, when he had grown up, refused to be known as the son of Pharaoh's daughter. [25]He chose to be mistreated along with the people of God rather than to enjoy the pleasures of sin for a short time. [26]He regarded disgrace for the sake of Christ as of greater value than the treasures of Egypt, because he was looking ahead to his reward. [27]By faith he left Egypt, not fearing the king's anger; he persevered because he saw him who is invisible. [28]By faith he kept the Passover and the sprinkling of blood, so that the destroyer of the firstborn would not touch the firstborn of Israel.

9) Rahab Is an Example of Faith

Heb 11 [31]By faith the prostitute Rahab, because she welcomed the spies, was not killed with those who were disobedient.

10) Caleb Is an Example of Faith

Num 13 [1]The LORD said to Moses, [2]"Send some men to explore the land of Canaan, which I am giving to the Israelites. From each ancestral tribe send one of its leaders." . . .

[27]They gave Moses this account: "We went into the land to which you sent us, and it does flow with milk and honey! Here is its fruit. [28]But the people who live there are powerful, and the cities are fortified and very large. We even saw descendants of Anak there. . . ."

[30]Then Caleb silenced the people before Moses and said, "We should go up and take possession of the land, for we can certainly do it."

Num 14 [24]"But because my servant Caleb has a different spirit and follows me wholeheartedly, I will bring him into the land he went to, and his descendants will inherit it."

11) Job Is an Example of Faith

Job 13 [15]"Though he slay me, yet will I hope in him; I will surely defend my ways to his face."

Job 19 [25]"I know that my Redeemer lives, and that in the end he will stand upon the earth."

12) The Psalmist (David) Is an Example of Faith

Ps 13 [5]But I trust in your unfailing love; my heart rejoices in your salvation.

Ps 22 [4]In you our fathers put their trust; they trusted and you delivered them. [5]They cried to you and were saved; in you they trusted and were not disappointed.

Ps 31 [14]But I trust in you, O LORD; I say, "You are my God."

Ps 40 [3]He put a new song in my mouth, a hymn of praise to our God. Many will see and fear and put their trust in the LORD.

[4]Blessed is the man who makes the LORD his trust, who does not look to the proud, to those who turn aside to false gods.

Ps 52 [8]But I am like an olive tree flourishing in the house of God; I trust in God's unfailing love for ever and ever. [9]I will praise you forever for what you have done; in your name I will hope, for your name is good. I will praise you in the presence of your saints.

13) Shadrach, Meshach, and Abednego Are Examples of Faith

Dan 3 [16]Shadrach, Meshach and Abednego replied to the king, "O Nebuchadnezzar, we do not need to defend ourselves before you in this matter. [17]If we are thrown into the blazing furnace, the God we serve is able to save us from it, and he will rescue us from your hand, O king. [18]But even if he does not, we want you to know, O king, that we will not serve your gods or worship the image of gold you have set up."

14) Daniel Is an Example of Faith

Dan 6 [7]"The royal administrators, prefects, satraps, advisers and governors have all agreed that the king should issue an edict and enforce the decree that anyone who prays to any god or man during the next thirty days, except to you, O king, shall be thrown into the lions' den. . . ."

[10]Now when Daniel learned that the decree had been published, he went home to his upstairs room where the windows opened toward Jerusalem. Three times a day he got down on his knees and prayed, giving thanks to his God, just as he had done before. . . .

[23]The king was overjoyed and gave orders to lift Daniel out of the den. And when Daniel was lifted from the den, no wound was found on him, because he had trusted in his God.

15) Peter Is an Example of Faith

Matt 16 [16]Simon Peter answered, "You are the Christ, the Son of the living God."

[17]Jesus replied, "Blessed are you, Simon son of Jonah, for this was not revealed to you by man, but by my Father in heaven. [18]And I tell you that you are Peter, and on this rock I will build my church, and the gates of Hades will not overcome it. [19]I will give you the keys of the kingdom of heaven; whatever you bind on earth will be bound in heaven, and whatever you loose on earth will be loosed in heaven."

16) The Righteous (Named and Unnamed) Are Examples of Faith

Heb 11 [13]All these people were still living by faith when they died. They did not receive the things promised; they only saw them and welcomed them from a distance. And they admitted that they were aliens and strangers on earth. [14]People who say such things show that they are looking for a country of their own. [15]If they had been thinking of the country they had left, they would have had opportunity to return. [16]Instead, they were longing for a better country—a heavenly one. Therefore God is not ashamed to be called their God, for he has prepared a city for them. . . .

[32]And what more shall I say? I do not have time to tell about Gideon, Barak, Samson, Jephthah, David, Samuel and the prophets, [33]who through faith conquered kingdoms, administered justice, and gained what was promised; who shut the mouths of lions, [34]quenched the fury of the flames, and escaped the edge of the sword; whose weakness was turned to strength; and who became powerful in battle and routed foreign armies. [35]Women received back their dead, raised to life again. Others were tortured and refused to be released, so that they might gain a better resurrection. [36]Some faced jeers and flogging, while still others were chained and put in prison. [37]They were stoned; they were sawed in two; they were put to death by the sword. They went about in sheepskins and goatskins, destitute, persecuted and mistreated—[38]the world was not worthy of them. They wandered in deserts and mountains, and in caves and holes in the ground.

[39]These were all commended for their faith, yet none of them received what had been promised. [40]God had planned something better for us so that only together with us would they be made perfect.

17) The Sinful Woman Is an Example of Faith

Luke 7 [36]Now one of the Pharisees invited Jesus to have dinner with him, so he went to the Pharisee's house and reclined at the table. [37]When a woman who had lived a sinful life in that town learned that Jesus was eating at the Pharisee's house, she brought an alabaster jar of perfume, [38]and as she stood behind him at his feet weeping, she began to wet his feet with her tears. Then she wiped them with her hair, kissed them and poured perfume on them.

[39]When the Pharisee who had invited him saw this, he said to himself, "If this man were a prophet, he would know who is touching him and what kind of woman she is—that she is a sinner."

[40]Jesus answered him, "Simon, I have something to tell you."

"Tell me, teacher," he said.

[41]"Two men owed money to a certain moneylender. One owed him five hundred denarii, and the other fifty. [42]Neither of them had the money to pay him back, so he canceled the debts of both. Now which of them will love him more?"

[43]Simon replied, "I suppose the one who had the bigger debt canceled."

"You have judged correctly," Jesus said.

[44]Then he turned toward the woman and said to Simon, "Do you see this woman? I came into your house. You did not give me any water for my feet, but she wet my feet with her tears and wiped them with her hair. [45]You did not give me a kiss, but this woman, from the time I entered, has not stopped kissing my feet. [46]You did not put oil on my head, but she has poured perfume on my feet. [47]Therefore, I tell you, her many sins have been forgiven—for she loved much. But he who has been forgiven little loves little."

[48]Then Jesus said to her, "Your sins are forgiven."

[49]The other guests began to say among themselves, "Who is this who even forgives sins?"

[50]Jesus said to the woman, "Your faith has saved you; go in peace."

18) Nathanael Is an Example of Faith

John 1 [49]Then Nathanael declared, "Rabbi, you are the Son of God; you are the King of Israel."

19) The Samaritans Are Examples of Faith

John 4 [39]Many of the Samaritans from that town believed in him because of the woman's testimony, "He told me everything I ever did." [40]So when the Samaritans came to him, they urged him to stay with them, and he stayed two days. [41]And because of his words many more became believers.

[42]They said to the woman, "We no longer believe just because of what you said; now we have heard for ourselves, and we know that this man really is the Savior of the world."

20) Martha Is an Example of Faith

John 11 [25]Jesus said to her, "I am the resurrection and the life. He who believes in me will live, even though he dies; [26]and whoever lives and believes in me will never die. Do you believe this?"

[27]"Yes, Lord," she told him, "I believe that you are the Christ, the Son of God, who was to come into the world."

21) Jesus' Disciples Are Examples of Faith

John 6 [67]"You do not want to leave too, do you?" Jesus asked the Twelve.

[68]Simon Peter answered him, "Lord, to whom shall we go? You have the words of eternal life. [69]We believe and know that you are the Holy One of God."

John 16 [29]Then Jesus' disciples said, "Now you are speaking clearly and without figures of speech. [30]Now we can see that you know all things and that you do not even need to have anyone ask you questions. This makes us believe that you came from God."

22) Thomas Is an Example of Faith

John 20 [24]Now Thomas (called Didymus), one of the Twelve, was not with the disciples when Jesus came. [25]So the other disciples told him, "We have seen the Lord!"

But he said to them, "Unless I see the nail marks in his hands and put my finger where the nails were, and put my hand into his side, I will not believe it."

[26]A week later his disciples were in the house again, and Thomas was with them. Though the doors were locked, Jesus came and stood among them and said, "Peace be with you!" [27]Then he said to Thomas, "Put your finger here; see my hands. Reach out your hand and put it into my side. Stop doubting and believe."

[28]Thomas said to him, "My Lord and my God!"

[29]Then Jesus told him, "Because you have seen me, you have believed; blessed are those who have not seen and yet have believed."

23) Stephen Is an Example of Faith

Acts 6 [5]This proposal pleased the whole group. They chose Stephen, a man full of faith and of the Holy Spirit; also Philip, Procorus, Nicanor, Timon, Parmenas, and Nicolas from Antioch, a convert to Judaism.

24) Jewish Priests Are Examples of Faith

Acts 6 [7]So the word of God spread. The number of disciples in Jerusalem increased rapidly, and a large number of priests became obedient to the faith.

25) Barnabas Is an Example of Faith

Acts 11 [22]News of this reached the ears of the church at Jerusalem, and they sent Barnabas to Antioch. . . . [24]He was a good man, full of the Holy Spirit and faith, and a great number of people were brought to the Lord.

26) Sergius Paulus Is an Example of Faith

Acts 13 [6]They traveled through the whole island until they came to Paphos. There they met a Jewish sorcerer and false prophet named Bar-Jesus, [7]who was an attendant of the proconsul, Sergius Paulus. The proconsul, an intelligent man, sent for Barnabas and Saul because he wanted to hear the word of God. [8]But Elymas the sorcerer (for that is what his name means) opposed them and tried to turn the proconsul from the faith. [9]Then Saul, who was also called Paul, filled with the Holy Spirit, looked straight at Elymas and said, [10]"You are a child of the devil and an enemy of everything that is right! You are full of all kinds of deceit and trickery. Will you never stop perverting the right ways of the Lord? [11]Now the hand of the Lord is against you. You are going to be blind, and for a time you will be unable to see the light of the sun."

Immediately mist and darkness came over him, and he groped about, seeking someone to lead him by the hand. [12]When the proconsul saw what had happened, he believed, for he was amazed at the teaching about the Lord.

27) The Philippian Jailer Is an Example of Faith

Acts 16 [29]The jailer called for lights, rushed in and fell trembling before Paul and Silas. [30]He then brought them out and asked, "Sirs, what must I do to be saved?"

[31]They replied, "Believe in the Lord Jesus, and you will be saved—you and your household." [32]Then they spoke the word of the Lord to him and to all the others in his house. [33]At that hour of the night the jailer took them and washed their wounds; then immediately he and all his family were baptized. [34]The jailer brought them into his house and set a meal before them; he was filled with joy because he had come to believe in God—he and his whole family.

28) Roman Believers Are Examples of Faith

Rom 1 [7]To all in Rome who are loved by God and called to be saints: Grace and peace to you from God our Father and from the Lord Jesus Christ.

[8]First, I thank my God through Jesus Christ for all of you, because your faith is being reported all over the world.

29) Colossian Believers Are Examples of Faith

Col 1 [2]To the holy and faithful brothers in Christ at Colosse: Grace and peace to you from God our Father.

[3]We always thank God, the Father of our Lord Jesus Christ, when we pray for you, [4]because we have heard of your faith in Christ Jesus and of the love you have for all the saints—[5]the faith and love that spring from the hope that is stored up for you in heaven and that you have already heard about in the word of truth, the gospel. . . .

30) Thessalonian Believers Are Examples of Faith

1 Thess 1 [1]Paul, Silas and Timothy,

To the church of the Thessalonians in God the Father and the Lord Jesus Christ: Grace and peace to you. . . . [3]We continually remember before our God and Father your work produced by faith, your labor prompted by love, and your endurance inspired by hope in our Lord Jesus Christ.

31) Lois Is an Example of Faith

2 Tim 1 [5]I have been reminded of your sincere faith, which first lived in your grandmother Lois and in your mother Eunice and, I am persuaded, now lives in you also.

32) Eunice Is an Example of Faith

2 Tim 1 [5]I have been reminded of your sincere faith, which first lived in your grandmother Lois and in your mother Eunice and, I am persuaded, now lives in you also.

33) Timothy Is an Example of Faith

2 Tim 1 [5]I have been reminded of your sincere faith, which first lived in your grandmother Lois and in your mother Eunice and, I am persuaded, now lives in you also.

34) Paul Is an Example of Faith

1 Tim 1 [1]Paul, an apostle of Christ Jesus by the command of God our Savior and of Christ Jesus our hope,

[2]To Timothy my true son in the faith: Grace, mercy and peace from God the Father and Christ Jesus our Lord. . . .

[16]But for that very reason I was shown mercy so that in me, the worst of sinners, Christ Jesus might display his unlimited patience as an example for those who would believe on him and receive eternal life.

2 Tim 4 [7]I have fought the good fight, I have finished the race, I have kept the faith.

8. Exhortations against Faithlessness

a) Unbelief Is Contrasted with Belief

John 3 [18]"Whoever believes in him is not condemned, but whoever does not believe stands condemned already because he has not believed in the name of God's one and only Son."

John 3 [36]"Whoever believes in the Son has eternal life, but whoever rejects the Son will not see life, for God's wrath remains on him."

Titus 1 [15]To the pure, all things are pure, but to those who are corrupted and do not believe, nothing is pure. In fact, both their minds and consciences are corrupted.

1 John 2 [22]Who is the liar? It is the man who denies that Jesus is the Christ. Such a man is the antichrist—he denies the Father and the Son. [23]No one who denies the Son has the Father; whoever acknowledges the Son has the Father also.

1 John 5 [10]Anyone who believes in the Son of God has this testimony in his heart. Anyone who does not believe God has made him out to be a liar, because he has not believed the testimony God has given about his Son. [11]And this is the testimony: God has given us eternal life, and this life is in his Son. [12]He who has the Son has life; he who does not have the Son of God does not have life.

b) Doubting Is Reproved

Matt 6 [30]"If that is how God clothes the grass of the field, which is here today and tomorrow is thrown into the fire, will he not much more clothe you, O you of little faith?"

Matt 7 [26]"But everyone who hears these words of mine and does not put them into practice is like a foolish man who built his house on sand. [27]The rain came down, the streams rose, and the winds blew and beat against that house, and it fell with a great crash."

Matt 14 [31]Immediately Jesus reached out his hand and caught him. "You of little faith," he said, "why did you doubt?"

Matt 16 [8]Aware of their discussion, Jesus asked, "You of little faith, why are you talking among yourselves about having no bread? [9]Do you still not understand? Don't you remember the five loaves for the five thousand, and how many basketfuls you gathered? [10]Or the seven loaves for the four thousand, and how many basketfuls you gathered?"

Matt 17 [17]"O unbelieving and perverse generation," Jesus replied, "how long shall I stay with you? How long shall I put up with you? Bring the boy here to me." [18]Jesus rebuked the demon, and it came out of the boy, and he was healed from that moment.

[19]Then the disciples came to Jesus in private and asked, "Why couldn't we drive it out?"

[20]He replied, "Because you have so little faith. I tell you the truth, if you have faith as small as a mustard seed, you can say to this mountain, 'Move from here to there' and it will move. Nothing will be impossible for you."

John 20 [27]Then he said to Thomas, "Put your finger here; see my hands. Reach out your hand and put it into my side. Stop doubting and believe."

Heb 3 [12]See to it, brothers, that none of you has a sinful, unbelieving heart that turns away from the living God. [13]But encourage one another daily, as long as it is called Today, so that none of you may be hardened by sin's deceitfulness.

Heb 5 [11]We have much to say about this, but it is hard to explain because you are slow to learn. [12]In fact, though by this time you ought to be teachers, you need someone to teach you the elementary truths of God's word all over again. You need milk, not solid food! [13]Anyone who lives on milk, being still an infant, is not acquainted with the teaching about righteousness.

c) Warnings Are Given against Unbelief

(1) Unbelief toward God

Num 14 [11]The LORD said to Moses, "How long will these people treat me with contempt? How long will they refuse to believe in me, in spite of all the miraculous signs I have performed among them? [12]I will strike them down with a plague and destroy them, but I will make you into a nation greater and stronger than they."

Num 20 [12]But the LORD said to Moses and Aaron, "Because you did not trust in me enough to honor me as holy in the sight of the Israelites, you will not bring this community into the land I give them."

Deut 1 [32]In spite of this, you did not trust in the LORD your God. . . .

[34]When the LORD heard what you said, he was angry and solemnly swore: [35]"Not a man of this evil generation shall see the good land I swore to give your forefathers. . . ."

2 Kings 17 [14]But they would not listen and were as stiff-necked as their fathers, who did not trust in the LORD their God. . . .

[18]So the LORD was very angry with Israel and removed them from his presence. Only the tribe of Judah was left, [19]and even Judah did not keep the commands of the LORD their God. They followed the practices Israel had introduced. [20]Therefore the LORD rejected all the people of Israel; he afflicted them and gave them into the hands of plunderers, until he thrust them from his presence.

Ps 78 [21]When the LORD heard them, he was very angry; his fire broke out against Jacob, and his wrath rose against Israel, [22]for they did not believe in God or trust in his deliverance. . . .

[32]In spite of all this, they kept on sinning; in spite of his wonders, they did not believe. [33]So he ended their days in futility and their years in terror.

Ps 106 [24]Then they despised the pleasant land; they did not believe his promise. [25]They grumbled in their tents and did not obey the LORD. [26]So he swore to them with uplifted hand that he would make them fall in the desert, [27]make their descendants fall among the nations and scatter them throughout the lands.

Isa 7 [9]"'The head of Ephraim is Samaria, and the head of Samaria is only Remaliah's son. If you do not stand firm in your faith, you will not stand at all.'"

Rom 11 [19]You will say then, "Branches were broken off so that I could be grafted in." [20]Granted. But they were broken off because of unbelief, and you stand by faith. Do not be arrogant, but be afraid. [21]For if God did not spare the natural branches, he will not spare you either.

Heb 3 [15]As has just been said: "Today, if you hear his voice, do not harden your hearts as you did in the rebellion."

[16]Who were they who heard and rebelled? Were they not all those Moses led out of Egypt? [17]And with whom was he angry for forty years? Was it not with those who sinned, whose bodies fell in the desert? [18]And to whom did God swear that they would never enter his rest if not to those who disobeyed? [19]So we see that they were not able to enter, because of their unbelief.

Heb 4 [2]For we also have had the gospel preached to us, just as they did; but the message they heard was of no value to them, because those who heard did not combine it with faith. [3]Now we who have believed enter that rest, just as God has said, "So I declared on oath in my anger, 'They shall never enter my rest.'"

And yet his work has been finished since the creation of the world. . . .

[6]It still remains that some will enter that rest, and those who formerly had the gospel preached to them did not go in, because of their disobedience. . . . [11]Let us, therefore, make every effort to enter that rest, so that no one will fall by following their example of disobedience.

Heb 10 [22]let us draw near to God with a sincere heart in full assurance of faith, having our hearts sprinkled to cleanse us from a guilty conscience and having our bodies washed with pure water. . . . [37]For in just a very little while, "He who is coming will come and will not delay. [38]But my righteous one will live by faith. And if he shrinks back, I will not be pleased with him."

Heb 11 [31]By faith the prostitute Rahab, because she welcomed the spies, was not killed with those who were disobedient.

Jude [5]Though you already know all this, I want to remind you that the Lord delivered his people out of Egypt, but later destroyed those who did not believe.

(2) Unbelief toward Christ

Matt 10 [33]"But whoever disowns me before men, I will disown him before my Father in heaven."

Matt 21 [31]"Which of the two did what his father wanted?"

"The first," they answered.

Jesus said to them, "I tell you the truth, the tax collectors and the prostitutes are entering the kingdom of God ahead of you. [32]For John came to you to show you the way of righteousness, and you did not believe him, but the tax collectors and the prostitutes did. And even after you saw this, you did not repent and believe him."

Luke 12 [8]"I tell you, whoever acknowledges me before men, the Son of Man will also acknowledge him before the angels of God. [9]But he who disowns me before men will be disowned before the angels of God."

Luke 12 [41]Peter asked, "Lord, are you telling this parable to us, or to everyone?"

[42]The Lord answered, "Who then is the faithful and wise manager, whom the master puts in charge of his servants to give them their food allowance at the proper time? [43]It will be good for that servant whom the master finds doing so when he returns. [44]I tell you the truth, he will put him in charge of all his possessions. [45]But suppose the servant says to himself, 'My master is taking a long time in coming,' and he then begins to beat the menservants and maidservants and to eat and drink and get drunk. [46]The master of that servant will come on a day when he does not expect him and at an hour he is not aware of. He will cut him to pieces and assign him a place with the unbelievers."

John 3 [18]"Whoever believes in him is not condemned, but whoever does not believe stands condemned already because he has not believed in the name of God's one and only Son."

John 3 [36]"Whoever believes in the Son has eternal life, but whoever rejects the Son will not see life, for God's wrath remains on him."

John 8 [21]Once more Jesus said to them, "I am going away, and you will look for me, and you will die in your sin. Where I go, you cannot come." . . . [24]"I told you that you would die in your sins; if you do not believe that I am the one I claim to be, you will indeed die in your sins."

Rom 9 [30]What then shall we say? That the Gentiles, who did not pursue righteousness, have obtained it, a righteousness that is by faith; [31]but Israel, who pursued a law of righteousness, has not attained it. [32]Why not? Because they pursued it not by faith but as if it were by works. They stumbled over the "stumbling stone."

2 Tim 2 [11]Here is a trustworthy saying: If we died with him, we will also live with him; [12]if we endure, we will also reign with him. If we disown him, he will also disown us. . . .

Heb 4 [2]For we also have had the gospel preached to us, just as they did; but the message they heard was of no value to them, because those who heard did not combine it with faith.

2 Pet 2 [1]But there were also false prophets among the people, just as there will be false teachers among you. They will secretly introduce destructive heresies, even denying the sovereign Lord who bought them—bringing swift destruction on themselves.

1 John 2 [22]Who is the liar? It is the man who denies that Jesus is the Christ. Such a man is the antichrist—he denies the Father and the Son. [23]No one who denies the Son has the Father; whoever acknowledges the Son has the Father also.

Jude [4]For certain men whose condemnation was written about long ago have secretly slipped in among you. They are godless men, who change the grace of our God into a license for immorality and deny Jesus Christ our only Sovereign and Lord.

Rev 21 [8]"But the cowardly, the unbelieving, the vile, the murderers, the sexually immoral, those who practice magic arts, the idolaters and all liars—their place will be in the fiery lake of burning sulfur. This is the second death."

B. Hope in God

1. The Objects of Hope

a) God Is an Object of Hope

Job 13 [15]"Though he slay me, yet will I hope in him; I will surely defend my ways to his face."

Ps 25 [5]guide me in your truth and teach me, for you are God my Savior, and my hope is in you all day long.

Ps 33 [20]We wait in hope for the LORD; he is our help and our shield. [21]In him our hearts rejoice, for we trust in his holy name. [22]May your unfailing love rest upon us, O LORD, even as we put our hope in you.

Ps 39 [7]"But now, Lord, what do I look for? My hope is in you."

Ps 42 [5]Why are you downcast, O my soul? Why so disturbed within me? Put your hope in God, for I will yet praise him, my Savior and [6]my God.

My soul is downcast within me; therefore I will remember you from the land of the Jordan, the heights of Hermon—from Mount Mizar. . . .

[11]Why are you downcast, O my soul? Why so disturbed within me? Put your hope in God, for I will yet praise him, my Savior and my God.

Ps 43 [5]Why are you downcast, O my soul? Why so disturbed within me? Put your hope in God, for I will yet praise him, my Savior and my God.

Ps 65 [5]You answer us with awesome deeds of righteousness, O God our Savior, the hope of all the ends of the earth and of the farthest seas. . . .

Ps 131 [3]O Israel, put your hope in the LORD both now and forevermore.

Ps 146 [5]Blessed is he whose help is the God of Jacob, whose hope is in the LORD his God. . . .

Jer 14 [22]Do any of the worthless idols of the nations bring rain? Do the skies themselves send down showers? No, it is you, O LORD our God. Therefore our hope is in you, for you are the one who does all this.

Jer 50 [7]"Whoever found them devoured them; their enemies said, 'We are not guilty, for they sinned against the LORD, their true pasture, the LORD, the hope of their fathers.'"

Rom 4 [17]As it is written: "I have made you a father of many nations." He is our father in the sight of God, in whom he believed—the God who gives life to the dead and calls things that are not as though they were.

[18]Against all hope, Abraham in hope believed and so became the father of many nations, just as it had been said to him, "So shall your offspring be."

1 Tim 5 [5]The widow who is really in need and left all alone puts her hope in God and continues night and day to pray and to ask God for help.

1 Tim 6 [17]Command those who are rich in this present world not to be arrogant nor to put their hope in wealth, which is so uncertain, but to put their hope in God, who richly provides us with everything for our enjoyment.

1 Pet 1 [21]Through him you believe in God, who raised him from the dead and glorified him, and so your faith and hope are in God.

b) God's Laws Are Objects of Hope

Ps 119 [43]Do not snatch the word of truth from my mouth, for I have put my hope in your laws.

Isa 42 [4]". . . he will not falter or be discouraged till he establishes justice on earth. In his law the islands will put their hope."

c) God's Word Is an Object of Hope

Ps 119 [74]May those who fear you rejoice when they see me, for I have put my hope in your word.
Ps 119 [81]My soul faints with longing for your salvation, but I have put my hope in your word.
Ps 119 [114]You are my refuge and my shield; I have put my hope in your word.
Ps 119 [147]I rise before dawn and cry for help; I have put my hope in your word.
Ps 130 [5]I wait for the LORD, my soul waits, and in his word I put my hope.

d) The Name of God Is an Object of Hope

Ps 52 [9]I will praise you forever for what you have done; in your name I will hope, for your name is good. I will praise you in the presence of your saints.

e) Christ Is an Object of Hope

Acts 28 [20]"For this reason I have asked to see you and talk with you. It is because of the hope of Israel that I am bound with this chain." . . .

[23]They arranged to meet Paul on a certain day, and came in even larger numbers to the place where he was staying. From morning till evening he explained and declared to them the kingdom of God and tried to convince them about Jesus from the Law of Moses and from the Prophets.
Rom 15 [12]And again, Isaiah says, "The Root of Jesse will spring up, one who will arise to rule over the nations; the Gentiles will hope in him."
1 Cor 15 [19]If only for this life we have hope in Christ, we are to be pitied more than all men.
Eph 1 [12]in order that we, who were the first to hope in Christ, might be for the praise of his glory.
Col 1 [23]if you continue in your faith, established and firm, not moved from the hope held out in the gospel. This is the gospel that you heard and that has been proclaimed to every creature under heaven, and of which I, Paul, have become a servant. . . .

[27]To them God has chosen to make known among the Gentiles the glorious riches of this mystery, which is Christ in you, the hope of glory.
1 Tim 1 [1]Paul, an apostle of Christ Jesus by the command of God our Savior and of Christ Jesus our hope . . .
1 Tim 4 [9]This is a trustworthy saying that deserves full acceptance [10](and for this we labor and strive), that we have put our hope in the living God, who is the Savior of all men, and especially of those who believe.
Heb 3 [6]But Christ is faithful as a son over God's house. And we are his house, if we hold on to our courage and the hope of which we boast.
Heb 7 [18]The former regulation is set aside because it was weak and useless [19](for the law made nothing perfect), and a better hope is introduced, by which we draw near to God.

[20]And it was not without an oath! Others became priests without any oath, [21]but he became a priest with an oath when God said to him: "The Lord has sworn and will not change his mind: 'You are a priest forever.'" [22]Because of this oath, Jesus has become the guarantee of a better covenant.

f) The Name of Christ Is an Object of Hope

Matt 12 [15]Aware of this, Jesus withdrew from that place. Many followed him, and he healed all their sick. . . . [17]This was to fulfill what was spoken through the prophet Isaiah: [18]"Here is my servant whom I have chosen, the one I love, in whom I delight; I will put my Spirit on him, and he will proclaim justice to the nations. . . . [21]In his name the nations will put their hope."

2. The Source of Our Hope

a) God's Calling and Salvation

Ps 62 [5]Find rest, O my soul, in God alone; my hope comes from him. [6]He alone is my rock and my salvation; he is my fortress, I will not be shaken.
Eph 1 [18]I pray also that the eyes of your heart may be enlightened in order that you may know the hope to which he has called you, the riches of his glorious inheritance in the saints. . . .
Eph 4 [4]There is one body and one Spirit—just as you were called to one hope when you were called. . . .
2 Thess 2 [16]May our Lord Jesus Christ himself and God our Father, who loved us and by his grace gave us eternal encouragement and good hope . . .
1 Pet 1 [3]Praise be to the God and Father of our Lord Jesus Christ! In his great mercy he has given us new birth into a living hope through the resurrection of Jesus Christ from the dead. . . .

b) The Holy Spirit

Rom 15 [13]May the God of hope fill you with all joy and peace as you trust in him, so that you may overflow with hope by the power of the Holy Spirit.

c) Love

1 Cor 13 [6]Love does not delight in evil but rejoices with the truth. [7]It always protects, always trusts, always hopes, always perseveres.

3. The Substance of Things Hoped For

a) Believers Hope for Deliverance from Death

Ps 16 [9]Therefore my heart is glad and my tongue rejoices; my body also will rest secure, [10]because you will not abandon me to the grave, nor will you let your Holy One see decay.
Ps 33 [18]But the eyes of the LORD are on those who fear him, on those whose hope is in his unfailing love, [19]to deliver them from death and keep them alive in famine.

b) Believers Hope for Deliverance from Enemies

Ps 71 [4]Deliver me, O my God, from the hand of the wicked, from the grasp of evil and cruel men.

[5]For you have been my hope, O Sovereign LORD, my confidence since my youth. . . .

[14]But as for me, I will always have hope; I will praise you more and more.

c) Believers Hope for Eternal Life

Titus 1 [2]a faith and knowledge resting on the hope of eternal life, which God, who does not lie, promised before the beginning of time . . .
Titus 3 [7]so that, having been justified by his grace, we might become heirs having the hope of eternal life.

d) Believers Hope for Freedom from Oppression

Job 5 [15]"He saves the needy from the sword in their mouth; he saves them from the clutches of the powerful. [16]So the poor have hope, and injustice shuts its mouth."

e) Believers Hope for Fruit from Their Spiritual Labors

1 Cor 9 [10]Surely he says this for us, doesn't he? Yes, this was written for us, because when the plowman plows and the thresher threshes, they ought to do so in the hope of sharing in the harvest.
1 Thess 2 [18]For we wanted to come to you—certainly I, Paul, did, again and again—but Satan stopped us. [19]For what is our hope, our joy, or the crown in which we will glory in the presence of our Lord Jesus when he comes? Is it not you?

f) Believers Hope for God's Abiding Presence

Ps 42 [1]As the deer pants for streams of water, so my soul pants for you, O God. [2]My soul thirsts for God, for the living God. When can I go and meet with God? [3]My tears have been my food day and night, while men say to me all day long, "Where is your God?" [4]These things I remember as I pour out my soul: how I used to go with the multitude, leading the procession to the house of God, with shouts of joy and thanksgiving among the festive throng. [5]Why are you downcast, O my soul? Why so disturbed within me? Put your hope in God, for I will yet praise him, my Savior and [6]my God.

My soul is downcast within me; therefore I will remember you from the land of the Jordan, the heights of Hermon—from

Mount Mizar. [7]Deep calls to deep in the roar of your waterfalls; all your waves and breakers have swept over me.

[8]By day the LORD directs his love, at night his song is with me—a prayer to the God of my life.

[9]I say to God my Rock, "Why have you forgotten me? Why must I go about mourning, oppressed by the enemy?" [10]My bones suffer mortal agony as my foes taunt me, saying to me all day long, "Where is your God?"

[11]Why are you downcast, O my soul? Why so disturbed within me? Put your hope in God, for I will yet praise him, my Savior and my God.

g) Believers Hope for God's Unfailing Love

Ps 33 [22]May your unfailing love rest upon us, O LORD, even as we put our hope in you.
Ps 147 [11]the LORD delights in those who fear him, who put their hope in his unfailing love.

h) Believers Hope for the Grace to Be Given

1 Pet 1 [13]Therefore, prepare your minds for action; be self-controlled; set your hope fully on the grace to be given you when Jesus Christ is revealed.

i) Believers Hope for the Redemption of Their Bodies

Rom 8 [23]Not only so, but we ourselves, who have the firstfruits of the Spirit, groan inwardly as we wait eagerly for our adoption as sons, the redemption of our bodies. [24]For in this hope we were saved. But hope that is seen is no hope at all. Who hopes for what he already has?

j) Believers Hope for the Resurrection of the Dead

Acts 23 [6]Then Paul, knowing that some of them were Sadducees and the others Pharisees, called out in the Sanhedrin, "My brothers, I am a Pharisee, the son of a Pharisee. I stand on trial because of my hope in the resurrection of the dead."
Acts 24 [15]". . . and I have the same hope in God as these men, that there will be a resurrection of both the righteous and the wicked."
Acts 26 [6]"And now it is because of my hope in what God has promised our fathers that I am on trial today. [7]This is the promise our twelve tribes are hoping to see fulfilled as they earnestly serve God day and night. O king, it is because of this hope that the Jews are accusing me. [8]Why should any of you consider it incredible that God raises the dead?"
1 Cor 15 [15]More than that, we are then found to be false witnesses about God, for we have testified about God that he raised Christ from the dead. But he did not raise him if in fact the dead are not raised. [16]For if the dead are not raised, then Christ has not been raised either. [17]And if Christ has not been raised, your faith is futile; you are still in your sins. [18]Then those also who have fallen asleep in Christ are lost. [19]If only for this life we have hope in Christ, we are to be pitied more than all men.

[20]But Christ has indeed been raised from the dead, the firstfruits of those who have fallen asleep. [21]For since death came through a man, the resurrection of the dead comes also through a man. [22]For as in Adam all die, so in Christ all will be made alive. [23]But each in his own turn: Christ, the firstfruits; then, when he comes, those who belong to him.
1 Thess 4 [13]Brothers, we do not want you to be ignorant about those who fall asleep, or to grieve like the rest of men, who have no hope. [14]We believe that Jesus died and rose again and so we believe that God will bring with Jesus those who have fallen asleep in him. [15]According to the Lord's own word, we tell you that we who are still alive, who are left till the coming of the Lord, will certainly not precede those who have fallen asleep. [16]For the Lord himself will come down from heaven, with a loud command, with the voice of the archangel and with the trumpet call of God, and the dead in Christ will rise first. [17]After that, we who are still alive and are left will be caught up together with them in the clouds to meet the Lord in the air. And so we will be with the Lord forever. [18]Therefore encourage each other with these words.

k) Believers Hope for the Return of Christ

Titus 2 [13]while we wait for the blessed hope—the glorious appearing of our great God and Savior, Jesus Christ . . .

l) Believers Hope for Righteousness

Gal 5 [5]But by faith we eagerly await through the Spirit the righteousness for which we hope.

m) Believers Hope for Security

Job 11 [13]"Yet if you devote your heart to him and stretch out your hands to him, [14]if you put away the sin that is in your hand and allow no evil to dwell in your tent, [15]then you will lift up your face without shame; you will stand firm and without fear. [16]You will surely forget your trouble, recalling it only as waters gone by. [17]Life will be brighter than noonday, and darkness will become like morning. [18]You will be secure, because there is hope; you will look about you and take your rest in safety."

n) Believers Hope for the Sharing of God's Glory

Rom 5 [1]Therefore, since we have been justified through faith, we have peace with God through our Lord Jesus Christ, [2]through whom we have gained access by faith into this grace in which we now stand. And we rejoice in the hope of the glory of God.

o) Believers Hope for Temporal and Spiritual Restoration

Ezra 10 [2]Then Shecaniah son of Jehiel, one of the descendants of Elam, said to Ezra, "We have been unfaithful to our God by marrying foreign women from the peoples around us. But in spite of this, there is still hope for Israel."
Ps 37 [9]For evil men will be cut off, but those who hope in the LORD will inherit the land.
Jer 14 [8]O Hope of Israel, its Savior in times of distress, why are you like a stranger in the land, like a traveler who stays only a night?
Jer 31 [17]"So there is hope for your future," declares the LORD. "Your children will return to their own land."
Lam 3 [29]Let him bury his face in the dust—there may yet be hope. . . .

[31]For men are not cast off by the Lord forever.
Hos 2 [15]"There I will give her back her vineyards, and will make the Valley of Achor a door of hope. There she will sing as in the days of her youth, as in the day she came up out of Egypt."
Zech 9 [12]Return to your fortress, O prisoners of hope; even now I announce that I will restore twice as much to you.

4. The Value of Hope

a) Hope Epitomizes Christian Faith

1 Cor 13 [13]And now these three remain: faith, hope and love. But the greatest of these is love.
Col 1 [3]We always thank God, the Father of our Lord Jesus Christ, when we pray for you, [4]because we have heard of your faith in Christ Jesus and of the love you have for all the saints—[5]the faith and love that spring from the hope that is stored up for you in heaven and that you have already heard about in the word of truth, the gospel. . . .
Heb 11 [1]Now faith is being sure of what we hope for and certain of what we do not see.

b) Hope Equips for Spiritual Warfare

1 Thess 5 [8]But since we belong to the day, let us be self-controlled, putting on faith and love as a breastplate, and the hope of salvation as a helmet.

c) Hope Gives Assurance

Ps 25 [3]No one whose hope is in you will ever be put to shame, but they will be put to shame who are treacherous without excuse.
Rom 8 [25]But if we hope for what we do not yet have, we wait for it patiently.
Heb 6 [16]Men swear by someone greater than themselves, and the oath confirms what is said and puts an end to all argument.

17Because God wanted to make the unchanging nature of his purpose very clear to the heirs of what was promised, he confirmed it with an oath. 18God did this so that, by two unchangeable things in which it is impossible for God to lie, we who have fled to take hold of the hope offered to us may be greatly encouraged. 19We have this hope as an anchor for the soul, firm and secure. It enters the inner sanctuary behind the curtain, 20where Jesus, who went before us, has entered on our behalf. He has become a high priest forever, in the order of Melchizedek.

d) Hope Invokes Divine Help

Ps 146 5Blessed is he whose help is the God of Jacob, whose hope is in the LORD his God, 6the Maker of heaven and earth, the sea, and everything in them—the LORD, who remains faithful forever. 7He upholds the cause of the oppressed and gives food to the hungry. The LORD sets prisoners free, 8the LORD gives sight to the blind, the LORD lifts up those who are bowed down, the LORD loves the righteous. 9The LORD watches over the alien and sustains the fatherless and the widow, but he frustrates the ways of the wicked.

10The LORD reigns forever, your God, O Zion, for all generations.

Praise the LORD.

e) Hope Is Alive

1 Pet 1 3Praise be to the God and Father of our Lord Jesus Christ! In his great mercy he has given us new birth into a living hope through the resurrection of Jesus Christ from the dead, 4and into an inheritance that can never perish, spoil or fade—kept in heaven for you, 5who through faith are shielded by God's power until the coming of the salvation that is ready to be revealed in the last time.

f) Hope Is Intelligible

Heb 10 23Let us hold unswervingly to the hope we profess, for he who promised is faithful.
1 Pet 3 15But in your hearts set apart Christ as Lord. Always be prepared to give an answer to everyone who asks you to give the reason for the hope that you have. But do this with gentleness and respect. . . .

g) Hope Leads to Rejoicing

Rom 5 1Therefore, since we have been justified through faith, we have peace with God through our Lord Jesus Christ, 2through whom we have gained access by faith into this grace in which we now stand. And we rejoice in the hope of the glory of God.
Rom 12 12Be joyful in hope, patient in affliction, faithful in prayer.

h) Hope Produces Boldness

2 Cor 3 12Therefore, since we have such a hope, we are very bold.

i) Hope Produces Godly Living

Ps 25 21May integrity and uprightness protect me, because my hope is in you.
Heb 6 10God is not unjust; he will not forget your work and the love you have shown him as you have helped his people and continue to help them. 11We want each of you to show this same diligence to the very end, in order to make your hope sure. 12We do not want you to become lazy, but to imitate those who through faith and patience inherit what has been promised.
1 John 3 2Dear friends, now we are children of God, and what we will be has not yet been made known. But we know that when he appears, we shall be like him, for we shall see him as he is. 3Everyone who has this hope in him purifies himself, just as he is pure.

j) Hope Receives Divine Goodness

Lam 3 25The LORD is good to those whose hope is in him, to the one who seeks him. . . .

k) Hope Strengthens and Encourages

Ps 31 24Be strong and take heart, all you who hope in the LORD.
Isa 40 31but those who hope in the LORD will renew their strength. They will soar on wings like eagles; they will run and not grow weary, they will walk and not be faint.
Isa 49 23"Kings will be your foster fathers, and their queens your nursing mothers. They will bow down before you with their faces to the ground; they will lick the dust at your feet. Then you will know that I am the LORD; those who hope in me will not be disappointed."
Rom 5 3Not only so, but we also rejoice in our sufferings, because we know that suffering produces perseverance; 4perseverance, character; and character, hope. 5And hope does not disappoint us, because God has poured out his love into our hearts by the Holy Spirit, whom he has given us.
Eph 1 18I pray also that the eyes of your heart may be enlightened in order that you may know the hope to which he has called you, the riches of his glorious inheritance in the saints, 19and his incomparably great power for us who believe. That power is like the working of his mighty strength. . . .
Phil 1 20I eagerly expect and hope that I will in no way be ashamed, but will have sufficient courage so that now as always Christ will be exalted in my body, whether by life or by death.

C. Be Confident in God

1. God and Christ as Our Confidence

Ps 71 5For you have been my hope, O Sovereign LORD, my confidence since my youth.
Jer 17 7"But blessed is the man who trusts in the LORD, whose confidence is in him."
2 Cor 3 1Are we beginning to commend ourselves again? Or do we need, like some people, letters of recommendation to you or from you? 2You yourselves are our letter, written on our hearts, known and read by everybody. 3You show that you are a letter from Christ, the result of our ministry, written not with ink but with the Spirit of the living God, not on tablets of stone but on tablets of human hearts.

4Such confidence as this is ours through Christ before God. 5Not that we are competent in ourselves to claim anything for ourselves, but our competence comes from God. 6He has made us competent as ministers of a new covenant—not of the letter but of the Spirit; for the letter kills, but the Spirit gives life.
Gal 5 10I am confident in the Lord that you will take no other view. The one who is throwing you into confusion will pay the penalty, whoever he may be.
Eph 3 12In him and through faith in him we may approach God with freedom and confidence.

2. The Value of Our Confidence in God

a) Confidence in God Assures Us of His Safekeeping Power

Phil 1 3I thank my God every time I remember you. 4In all my prayers for all of you, I always pray with joy 5because of your partnership in the gospel from the first day until now, 6being confident of this, that he who began a good work in you will carry it on to completion until the day of Christ Jesus.

b) Confidence in God Motivates Us for Christian Living

2 Cor 5 5Now it is God who has made us for this very purpose and has given us the Spirit as a deposit, guaranteeing what is to come.

6Therefore we are always confident and know that as long as we are at home in the body we are away from the Lord. 7We live by faith, not by sight. 8We are confident, I say, and would prefer to be away from the body and at home with the Lord. 9So we make it our goal to please him, whether we are at home in the body or away from it.
2 Thess 3 4We have confidence in the Lord that you are doing and will continue to do the things we command.
Heb 3 12See to it, brothers, that none of you has a sinful, unbelieving heart that turns away from the living God. 13But encourage one another daily, as long as it is called Today, so that none of you may be hardened by sin's deceitfulness. 14We have come to share in Christ if we hold firmly till the end the confidence we had at first.

1 John 2 [28]And now, dear children, continue in him, so that when he appears we may be confident and unashamed before him at his coming.
1 John 3 [21]Dear friends, if our hearts do not condemn us, we have confidence before God [22]and receive from him anything we ask, because we obey his commands and do what pleases him.

c) *Confidence in God Protects Us from Fear*

Gen 15 [1]After this, the word of the LORD came to Abram in a vision: "Do not be afraid, Abram. I am your shield, your very great reward."
Ps 3 [5]I lie down and sleep; I wake again, because the LORD sustains me. [6]I will not fear the tens of thousands drawn up against me on every side.
Ps 23 [1]The LORD is my shepherd, I shall not be in want. . . . [4]Even though I walk through the valley of the shadow of death, I will fear no evil, for you are with me; your rod and your staff, they comfort me.

[5]You prepare a table before me in the presence of my enemies. You anoint my head with oil; my cup overflows.
Ps 27 [1]The LORD is my light and my salvation—whom shall I fear? The LORD is the stronghold of my life—of whom shall I be afraid? [2]When evil men advance against me to devour my flesh, when my enemies and my foes attack me, they will stumble and fall. [3]Though an army besiege me, my heart will not fear; though war break out against me, even then will I be confident. . . .

[13]I am still confident of this: I will see the goodness of the LORD in the land of the living.
Ps 34 [4]I sought the LORD, and he answered me; he delivered me from all my fears.
Ps 46 [1]God is our refuge and strength, an ever-present help in trouble. [2]Therefore we will not fear, though the earth give way and the mountains fall into the heart of the sea. . . .

[7]The LORD Almighty is with us; the God of Jacob is our fortress.
Ps 91 [4]He will cover you with his feathers, and under his wings you will find refuge; his faithfulness will be your shield and rampart. [5]You will not fear the terror of night, nor the arrow that flies by day, [6]nor the pestilence that stalks in the darkness, nor the plague that destroys at midday. [7]A thousand may fall at your side, ten thousand at your right hand, but it will not come near you. [8]You will only observe with your eyes and see the punishment of the wicked.
Ps 112 [7]He will have no fear of bad news; his heart is steadfast, trusting in the LORD. [8]His heart is secure, he will have no fear; in the end he will look in triumph on his foes.
Ps 118 [6]The LORD is with me; I will not be afraid. What can man do to me? [7]The LORD is with me; he is my helper. I will look in triumph on my enemies.
Prov 1 [33]". . . but whoever listens to me will live in safety and be at ease, without fear of harm."
Prov 3 [25]Have no fear of sudden disaster or of the ruin that overtakes the wicked, [26]for the LORD will be your confidence and will keep your foot from being snared.
Rom 8 [15]For you did not receive a spirit that makes you a slave again to fear, but you received the Spirit of sonship. And by him we cry, "*Abba*, Father." [16]The Spirit himself testifies with our spirit that we are God's children.
Heb 2 [14]Since the children have flesh and blood, he too shared in their humanity so that by his death he might destroy him who holds the power of death—that is, the devil—[15]and free those who all their lives were held in slavery by their fear of death.
Heb 13 [6]So we say with confidence, "The Lord is my helper; I will not be afraid. What can man do to me?"
1 Pet 3 [12]"For the eyes of the Lord are on the righteous and his ears are attentive to their prayer, but the face of the Lord is against those who do evil."

[13]Who is going to harm you if you are eager to do good? [14]But even if you should suffer for what is right, you are blessed. "Do not fear what they fear; do not be frightened."
1 John 4 [16]And so we know and rely on the love God has for us.

God is love. Whoever lives in love lives in God, and God in him. [17]In this way, love is made complete among us so that we will have confidence on the day of judgment, because in this world we are like him. [18]There is no fear in love. But perfect love drives out fear, because fear has to do with punishment. The one who fears is not made perfect in love.

d) *Confidence in God Results in Answered Prayer*

1 John 5 [13]I write these things to you who believe in the name of the Son of God so that you may know that you have eternal life. [14]This is the confidence we have in approaching God: that if we ask anything according to his will, he hears us. [15]And if we know that he hears us—whatever we ask—we know that we have what we asked of him.

e) *Confidence in God Results in Blessing*

Jer 17 [7]"But blessed is the man who trusts in the LORD, whose confidence is in him."
Heb 6 [9]Even though we speak like this, dear friends, we are confident of better things in your case—things that accompany salvation. [10]God is not unjust; he will not forget your work and the love you have shown him as you have helped his people and continue to help them.
Heb 10 [35]So do not throw away your confidence; it will be richly rewarded. [36]You need to persevere so that when you have done the will of God, you will receive what he has promised.

f) *Confidence in God Results in Divine Help*

Heb 4 [14]Therefore, since we have a great high priest who has gone through the heavens, Jesus the Son of God, let us hold firmly to the faith we profess. [15]For we do not have a high priest who is unable to sympathize with our weaknesses, but we have one who has been tempted in every way, just as we are—yet was without sin. [16]Let us then approach the throne of grace with confidence, so that we may receive mercy and find grace to help us in our time of need.

g) *Confidence in God Results in Entering into His Presence*

Heb 10 [19]Therefore, brothers, since we have confidence to enter the Most Holy Place by the blood of Jesus, [20]by a new and living way opened for us through the curtain, that is, his body, [21]and since we have a great priest over the house of God, [22]let us draw near to God with a sincere heart in full assurance of faith, having our hearts sprinkled to cleanse us from a guilty conscience and having our bodies washed with pure water.

D. Boast in God

Ps 34 [2]My soul will boast in the LORD; let the afflicted hear and rejoice.
Ps 44 [8]In God we make our boast all day long, and we will praise your name forever.
Jer 9 [23]This is what the LORD says: "Let not the wise man boast of his wisdom or the strong man boast of his strength or the rich man boast of his riches, [24]but let him who boasts boast about this: that he understands and knows me, that I am the LORD, who exercises kindness, justice and righteousness on earth, for in these I delight," declares the LORD.
1 Cor 1 [26]Brothers, think of what you were when you were called. Not many of you were wise by human standards; not many were influential; not many were of noble birth. [27]But God chose the foolish things of the world to shame the wise; God chose the weak things of the world to shame the strong. [28]He chose the lowly things of this world and the despised things—and the things that are not—to nullify the things that are, [29]so that no one may boast before him. [30]It is because of him that you are in Christ Jesus, who has become for us wisdom from God—that is, our righteousness, holiness and redemption. [31]Therefore, as it is written: "Let him who boasts boast in the Lord."
2 Cor 10 [12]We do not dare to classify or compare ourselves with some who commend themselves. When they measure themselves by themselves and compare themselves with themselves, they are not wise. [13]We, however, will not boast beyond

proper limits, but will confine our boasting to the field God has assigned to us, a field that reaches even to you. [14]We are not going too far in our boasting, as would be the case if we had not come to you, for we did get as far as you with the gospel of Christ. [15]Neither do we go beyond our limits by boasting of work done by others. Our hope is that, as your faith continues to grow, our area of activity among you will greatly expand, [16]so that we can preach the gospel in the regions beyond you. For we do not want to boast about work already done in another man's territory. [17]But, "Let him who boasts boast in the Lord." [18]For it is not the one who commends himself who is approved, but the one whom the Lord commends.
Gal 6 [14]May I never boast except in the cross of our Lord Jesus Christ, through which the world has been crucified to me, and I to the world.
Heb 3 [6]But Christ is faithful as a son over God's house. And we are his house, if we hold on to our courage and the hope of which we boast.

II
Knowing God and Remembering Him

A. *Know God*

1. The Objects of Our Knowledge

a) We Know God

Col 1 [10]And we pray this in order that you may live a life worthy of the Lord and may please him in every way: bearing fruit in every good work, growing in the knowledge of God. . . .
2 Pet 1 [2]Grace and peace be yours in abundance through the knowledge of God and of Jesus our Lord.

b) We Know God's Glory

Hab 2 [14]"For the earth will be filled with the knowledge of the glory of the LORD, as the waters cover the sea."
2 Cor 4 [6]For God, who said, "Let light shine out of darkness," made his light shine in our hearts to give us the light of the knowledge of the glory of God in the face of Christ.

c) We Know God's Love

1 John 4 [16]And so we know and rely on the love God has for us.
God is love. Whoever lives in love lives in God, and God in him.

d) We Know God's Salvation

Luke 1 [76]"And you, my child, will be called a prophet of the Most High; for you will go on before the Lord to prepare the way for him, [77]to give his people the knowledge of salvation through the forgiveness of their sins. . . ."

e) We Know God's Truth

1 Tim 2 [3]This is good, and pleases God our Savior, [4]who wants all men to be saved and to come to a knowledge of the truth.
2 Tim 2 [25]Those who oppose him he must gently instruct, in the hope that God will grant them repentance leading them to a knowledge of the truth. . . .
Heb 10 [26]If we deliberately keep on sinning after we have received the knowledge of the truth, no sacrifice for sins is left. . . .

f) We Know God's Will

Col 1 [9]For this reason, since the day we heard about you, we have not stopped praying for you and asking God to fill you with the knowledge of his will through all spiritual wisdom and understanding.

g) We Know Christ

Eph 4 [13]until we all reach unity in the faith and in the knowledge of the Son of God and become mature, attaining to the whole measure of the fullness of Christ.
Phil 3 [10]I want to know Christ and the power of his resurrection and the fellowship of sharing in his sufferings, becoming like him in his death, [11]and so, somehow, to attain to the resurrection from the dead.
2 Pet 1 [8]For if you possess these qualities in increasing measure, they will keep you from being ineffective and unproductive in your knowledge of our Lord Jesus Christ.

h) We Know Scripture

Acts 18 [24]Meanwhile a Jew named Apollos, a native of Alexandria, came to Ephesus. He was a learned man, with a thorough knowledge of the Scriptures.

i) We Know the Secrets of God's Kingdom

Matt 13 [11]He replied, "The knowledge of the secrets of the kingdom of heaven has been given to you, but not to them."
Luke 8 [10]He said, "The knowledge of the secrets of the kingdom of God has been given to you, but to others I speak in parables, so that, 'though seeing, they may not see; though hearing, they may not understand.'"

2. The Commandment to Know God

Lev 22 [32]"Do not profane my holy name. I must be acknowledged as holy by the Israelites. I am the LORD, who makes you holy. . . ."
Deut 4 [39]Acknowledge and take to heart this day that the LORD is God in heaven above and on the earth below. There is no other.
Deut 7 [9]Know therefore that the LORD your God is God; he is the faithful God, keeping his covenant of love to a thousand generations of those who love him and keep his commands.
1 Chron 28 [9]"And you, my son Solomon, acknowledge the God of your father, and serve him with wholehearted devotion and with a willing mind, for the LORD searches every heart and understands every motive behind the thoughts. If you seek him, he will be found by you; but if you forsake him, he will reject you forever."
Ps 4 [3]Know that the LORD has set apart the godly for himself; the LORD will hear when I call to him.
Ps 46 [10]"Be still, and know that I am God; I will be exalted among the nations, I will be exalted in the earth."
Ps 100 [3]Know that the LORD is God. It is he who made us, and we are his; we are his people, the sheep of his pasture.
Prov 3 [5]Trust in the LORD with all your heart and lean not on your own understanding; [6]in all your ways acknowledge him, and he will make your paths straight.
Jer 9 [24]". . . but let him who boasts boast about this: that he understands and knows me, that I am the LORD, who exercises kindness, justice and righteousness on earth, for in these I delight," declares the LORD.
Hos 6 [6]"For I desire mercy, not sacrifice, and acknowledgment of God rather than burnt offerings."
Hos 13 [4]"But I am the LORD your God, who brought you out of Egypt. You shall acknowledge no God but me, no Savior except me."
2 Pet 3 [18]But grow in the grace and knowledge of our Lord and Savior Jesus Christ. To him be glory both now and forever! Amen.

3. The Promise of a Knowledge of God

Isa 19 [21]So the LORD will make himself known to the Egyptians, and in that day they will acknowledge the LORD. They will worship with sacrifices and grain offerings; they will make vows to the LORD and keep them.
Isa 54 [13]"All your sons will be taught by the LORD, and great will be your children's peace."
Isa 60 [2]"See, darkness covers the earth and thick darkness is over the peoples, but the LORD rises upon you and his glory appears over you. [3]Nations will come to your light, and kings to the brightness of your dawn."
Jer 24 [7]"'I will give them a heart to know me, that I am the LORD. They will be my people, and I will be their God, for they will return to me with all their heart.'"
Jer 31 [33]"This is the covenant I will make with the house of Israel after that time," declares the LORD. "I will put my law in their minds and write it on their hearts. I will be their God, and they will be my people. [34]No longer will a man teach his neigh-

bor, or a man his brother, saying, 'Know the LORD,' because they will all know me, from the least of them to the greatest," declares the LORD. "For I will forgive their wickedness and will remember their sins no more."
Hos 2 19"I will betroth you to me forever; I will betroth you in righteousness and justice, in love and compassion. 20I will betroth you in faithfulness, and you will acknowledge the LORD."
Hos 6 2"After two days he will revive us; on the third day he will restore us, that we may live in his presence. 3Let us acknowledge the LORD; let us press on to acknowledge him. As surely as the sun rises, he will appear; he will come to us like the winter rains, like the spring rains that water the earth."
Hab 2 14"For the earth will be filled with the knowledge of the glory of the LORD, as the waters cover the sea."
Mal 1 11"My name will be great among the nations, from the rising to the setting of the sun. In every place incense and pure offerings will be brought to my name, because my name will be great among the nations," says the LORD Almighty.

4. The Means of Knowing God

a) We Know God through Answered Prayer

Ps 56 9Then my enemies will turn back when I call for help. By this I will know that God is for me.

b) We Know God through God Himself

2 Cor 2 14But thanks be to God, who always leads us in triumphal procession in Christ and through us spreads everywhere the fragrance of the knowledge of him.
2 Cor 4 6For God, who said, "Let light shine out of darkness," made his light shine in our hearts to give us the light of the knowledge of the glory of God in the face of Christ.
Col 1 9For this reason, since the day we heard about you, we have not stopped praying for you and asking God to fill you with the knowledge of his will through all spiritual wisdom and understanding. 10And we pray this in order that you may live a life worthy of the Lord and may please him in every way: bearing fruit in every good work, growing in the knowledge of God. . . .

c) We Know God through His Word

1 Kings 18 37"Answer me, O LORD, answer me, so these people will know that you, O LORD, are God, and that you are turning their hearts back again."
Ezra 7 25And you, Ezra, in accordance with the wisdom of your God, which you possess, appoint magistrates and judges to administer justice to all the people of Trans-Euphrates—all who know the laws of your God. And you are to teach any who do not know them.

d) We Know God through His Works

Exod 6 6"Therefore, say to the Israelites: 'I am the LORD, and I will bring you out from under the yoke of the Egyptians. I will free you from being slaves to them, and I will redeem you with an outstretched arm and with mighty acts of judgment. 7I will take you as my own people, and I will be your God. Then you will know that I am the LORD your God, who brought you out from under the yoke of the Egyptians.'"
Deut 4 32Ask now about the former days, long before your time, from the day God created man on the earth; ask from one end of the heavens to the other. Has anything so great as this ever happened, or has anything like it ever been heard of? 33Has any other people heard the voice of God speaking out of fire, as you have, and lived? 34Has any god ever tried to take for himself one nation out of another nation, by testings, by miraculous signs and wonders, by war, by a mighty hand and an outstretched arm, or by great and awesome deeds, like all the things the LORD your God did for you in Egypt before your very eyes?

35You were shown these things so that you might know that the LORD is God; besides him there is no other. 36From heaven he made you hear his voice to discipline you. On earth he showed you his great fire, and you heard his words from out of the fire. 37Because he loved your forefathers and chose their descendants after them, he brought you out of Egypt by his Presence and his great strength, 38to drive out before you nations greater and stronger than you and to bring you into their land to give it to you for your inheritance, as it is today.
Deut 29 2Moses summoned all the Israelites and said to them: Your eyes have seen all that the LORD did in Egypt to Pharaoh, to all his officials and to all his land. 3With your own eyes you saw those great trials, those miraculous signs and great wonders. 4But to this day the LORD has not given you a mind that understands or eyes that see or ears that hear. 5During the forty years that I led you through the desert, your clothes did not wear out, nor did the sandals on your feet. 6You ate no bread and drank no wine or other fermented drink. I did this so that you might know that I am the LORD your God.
Josh 3 10"This is how you will know that the living God is among you and that he will certainly drive out before you the Canaanites, Hittites, Hivites, Perizzites, Girgashites, Amorites and Jebusites."
1 Kings 20 13Meanwhile a prophet came to Ahab king of Israel and announced, "This is what the LORD says: 'Do you see this vast army? I will give it into your hand today, and then you will know that I am the LORD.'" . . .

28The man of God came up and told the king of Israel, "This is what the LORD says: 'Because the Arameans think the LORD is a god of the hills and not a god of the valleys, I will deliver this vast army into your hands, and you will know that I am the LORD.'"
Ps 9 16The LORD is known by his justice; the wicked are ensnared by the work of their hands.
Ps 19 1The heavens declare the glory of God; the skies proclaim the work of his hands. 2Day after day they pour forth speech; night after night they display knowledge.
Isa 29 23"When they see among them their children, the work of my hands, they will keep my name holy; they will acknowledge the holiness of the Holy One of Jacob, and will stand in awe of the God of Israel."
Rom 1 20For since the creation of the world God's invisible qualities—his eternal power and divine nature—have been clearly seen, being understood from what has been made, so that men are without excuse.

e) We Know God through Jesus Christ

John 8 12When Jesus spoke again to the people, he said, "I am the light of the world. Whoever follows me will never walk in darkness, but will have the light of life." . . .

19Then they asked him, "Where is your father?"

"You do not know me or my Father," Jesus replied. "If you knew me, you would know my Father also."
John 10 14"I am the good shepherd; I know my sheep and my sheep know me—15just as the Father knows me and I know the Father—and I lay down my life for the sheep."
John 15 15"I no longer call you servants, because a servant does not know his master's business. Instead, I have called you friends, for everything that I learned from my Father I have made known to you."
John 17 25"Righteous Father, though the world does not know you, I know you, and they know that you have sent me. 26I have made you known to them, and will continue to make you known in order that the love you have for me may be in them and that I myself may be in them."
Eph 4 20You, however, did not come to know Christ that way. 21Surely you heard of him and were taught in him in accordance with the truth that is in Jesus. 22You were taught, with regard to your former way of life, to put off your old self, which is being corrupted by its deceitful desires; 23to be made new in the attitude of your minds; 24and to put on the new self, created to be like God in true righteousness and holiness.
1 John 5 20We know also that the Son of God has come and has given us understanding, so that we may know him who is true. And we are in him who is true—even in his Son Jesus Christ. He is the true God and eternal life.

f) We Know God through the Spirit

John 16 14"He will bring glory to me by taking from what is mine and making it known to you. 15All that belongs to the Father is mine. That is why I said the Spirit will take from what is mine and make it known to you."
Eph 1 17I keep asking that the God of our Lord Jesus Christ,

the glorious Father, may give you the Spirit of wisdom and revelation, so that you may know him better.
1 Thess 1 [4]For we know, brothers loved by God, that he has chosen you, [5]because our gospel came to you not simply with words, but also with power, with the Holy Spirit and with deep conviction. You know how we lived among you for your sake.
1 John 3 [24]Those who obey his commands live in him, and he in them. And this is how we know that he lives in us: We know it by the Spirit he gave us.
1 John 4 [13]We know that we live in him and he in us, because he has given us of his Spirit.

g) We Know God through Temporal Affairs

Ps 46 [10]"Be still, and know that I am God; I will be exalted among the nations, I will be exalted in the earth." [11]The LORD Almighty is with us; the God of Jacob is our fortress.

5. Qualities of Those Knowing God

a) They Are Concerned with Godly Living

Ps 41 [11]I know that you are pleased with me, for my enemy does not triumph over me. [12]In my integrity you uphold me and set me in your presence forever.
1 John 2 [3]We know that we have come to know him if we obey his commands. [4]The man who says, "I know him," but does not do what he commands is a liar, and the truth is not in him. [5]But if anyone obeys his word, God's love is truly made complete in him. This is how we know we are in him: [6]Whoever claims to live in him must walk as Jesus did. . . .

[29]If you know that he is righteous, you know that everyone who does what is right has been born of him.

b) They Are Willing to Learn

Exod 33 [12]Moses said to the LORD, "You have been telling me, 'Lead these people,' but you have not let me know whom you will send with me. You have said, 'I know you by name and you have found favor with me.' [13]If you are pleased with me, teach me your ways so I may know you and continue to find favor with you. Remember that this nation is your people."
2 Kings 3 [7]He also sent this message to Jehoshaphat king of Judah: "The king of Moab has rebelled against me. Will you go with me to fight against Moab?"

"I will go with you," he replied. "I am as you are, my people as your people, my horses as your horses."

[8]"By what route shall we attack?" he asked.

"Through the Desert of Edom," he answered.

[9]So the king of Israel set out with the king of Judah and the king of Edom. After a roundabout march of seven days, the army had no more water for themselves or for the animals with them.

[10]"What!" exclaimed the king of Israel. "Has the LORD called us three kings together only to hand us over to Moab?"

[11]But Jehoshaphat asked, "Is there no prophet of the LORD here, that we may inquire of the LORD through him?"

c) They Defend What Is Known about God

Acts 6 [8]Now Stephen, a man full of God's grace and power, did great wonders and miraculous signs among the people. [9]Opposition arose, however, from members of the Synagogue of the Freedmen (as it was called)—Jews of Cyrene and Alexandria as well as the provinces of Cilicia and Asia. These men began to argue with Stephen, [10]but they could not stand up against his wisdom or the Spirit by whom he spoke.
2 Cor 10 [5]We demolish arguments and every pretension that sets itself up against the knowledge of God, and we take captive every thought to make it obedient to Christ.

d) They Desire More Knowledge of God

Hos 6 [3]"Let us acknowledge the LORD; let us press on to acknowledge him. As surely as the sun rises, he will appear; he will come to us like the winter rains, like the spring rains that water the earth."
John 17 [3]"Now this is eternal life: that they may know you, the only true God, and Jesus Christ, whom you have sent."
Eph 4 [11]It was he who gave some to be apostles, some to be prophets, some to be evangelists, and some to be pastors and teachers, [12]to prepare God's people for works of service, so that the body of Christ may be built up [13]until we all reach unity in the faith and in the knowledge of the Son of God and become mature, attaining to the whole measure of the fullness of Christ.
Phil 1 [9]And this is my prayer: that your love may abound more and more in knowledge and depth of insight, [10]so that you may be able to discern what is best and may be pure and blameless until the day of Christ, [11]filled with the fruit of righteousness that comes through Jesus Christ—to the glory and praise of God.
Phil 3 [8]What is more, I consider everything a loss compared to the surpassing greatness of knowing Christ Jesus my Lord, for whose sake I have lost all things. I consider them rubbish, that I may gain Christ. . . . [10]I want to know Christ and the power of his resurrection and the fellowship of sharing in his sufferings, becoming like him in his death, [11]and so, somehow, to attain to the resurrection from the dead.
2 Pet 1 [5]For this very reason, make every effort to add to your faith goodness; and to goodness, knowledge; [6]and to knowledge, self-control; and to self-control, perseverance; and to perseverance, godliness. . . . [8]For if you possess these qualities in increasing measure, they will keep you from being ineffective and unproductive in your knowledge of our Lord Jesus Christ.

e) They Exhibit Divine Love

1 John 4 [7]Dear friends, let us love one another, for love comes from God. Everyone who loves has been born of God and knows God. [8]Whoever does not love does not know God, because God is love. [9]This is how God showed his love among us: He sent his one and only Son into the world that we might live through him. [10]This is love: not that we loved God, but that he loved us and sent his Son as an atoning sacrifice for our sins. [11]Dear friends, since God so loved us, we also ought to love one another. [12]No one has ever seen God; but if we love one another, God lives in us and his love is made complete in us.

[13]We know that we live in him and he in us, because he has given us of his Spirit. [14]And we have seen and testify that the Father has sent his Son to be the Savior of the world. [15]If anyone acknowledges that Jesus is the Son of God, God lives in him and he in God. [16]And so we know and rely on the love God has for us.

God is love. Whoever lives in love lives in God, and God in him. [17]In this way, love is made complete among us so that we will have confidence on the day of judgment, because in this world we are like him. [18]There is no fear in love. But perfect love drives out fear, because fear has to do with punishment. The one who fears is not made perfect in love.

[19]We love because he first loved us. [20]If anyone says, "I love God," yet hates his brother, he is a liar. For anyone who does not love his brother, whom he has seen, cannot love God, whom he has not seen. [21]And he has given us this command: Whoever loves God must also love his brother.

f) They Recognize the Limitations of Their Knowledge

Ps 71 [15]My mouth will tell of your righteousness, of your salvation all day long, though I know not its measure.
1 Cor 13 [12]Now we see but a poor reflection as in a mirror; then we shall see face to face. Now I know in part; then I shall know fully, even as I am fully known.

g) They Rely on God

Ps 9 [10]Those who know your name will trust in you, for you, LORD, have never forsaken those who seek you.

6. The Value of Knowing God

a) A Knowledge of God Assures One of His Steadfast Love

Ps 36 [10]Continue your love to those who know you, your righteousness to the upright in heart.

b) A Knowledge of God Channels His Blessings to the Believer

2 Pet 1 [2]Grace and peace be yours in abundance through the knowledge of God and of Jesus our Lord.

[3]His divine power has given us everything we need for life and godliness through our knowledge of him who called us by his own glory and goodness.

c) A Knowledge of God Clarifies One's Spiritual Destiny

2 Cor 5 [6]Therefore we are always confident and know that as long as we are at home in the body we are away from the Lord. . . . [8]We are confident, I say, and would prefer to be away from the body and at home with the Lord. . . . [10]For we must all appear before the judgment seat of Christ, that each one may receive what is due him for the things done while in the body, whether good or bad.

d) A Knowledge of God Creates a Sense of Spiritual Security

Ps 20 [6]Now I know that the LORD saves his anointed; he answers him from his holy heaven with the saving power of his right hand.
Rom 6 [6]For we know that our old self was crucified with him so that the body of sin might be done away with, that we should no longer be slaves to sin—[7]because anyone who has died has been freed from sin.

[8]Now if we died with Christ, we believe that we will also live with him. [9]For we know that since Christ was raised from the dead, he cannot die again; death no longer has mastery over him. [10]The death he died, he died to sin once for all; but the life he lives, he lives to God.

[11]In the same way, count yourselves dead to sin but alive to God in Christ Jesus.
2 Cor 4 [14]because we know that the one who raised the Lord Jesus from the dead will also raise us with Jesus and present us with you in his presence.
2 Tim 1 [12]That is why I am suffering as I am. Yet I am not ashamed, because I know whom I have believed, and am convinced that he is able to guard what I have entrusted to him for that day.
1 John 5 [13]I write these things to you who believe in the name of the Son of God so that you may know that you have eternal life.

e) A Knowledge of God Elicits Praise and Worship of Him

Ps 135 [5]I know that the LORD is great, that our Lord is greater than all gods. [6]The LORD does whatever pleases him, in the heavens and on the earth, in the seas and all their depths. [7]He makes clouds rise from the ends of the earth; he sends lightning with the rain and brings out the wind from his storehouses. . . .

[13]Your name, O LORD, endures forever, your renown, O LORD, through all generations.
Ps 139 [14]I praise you because I am fearfully and wonderfully made; your works are wonderful, I know that full well.

f) A Knowledge of God Gives Personal Confidence in His Purposes

Ps 119 [75]I know, O LORD, that your laws are righteous, and in faithfulness you have afflicted me.
Ps 140 [12]I know that the LORD secures justice for the poor and upholds the cause of the needy.
Rom 8 [28]And we know that in all things God works for the good of those who love him, who have been called according to his purpose.

g) A Knowledge of God Helps One to Resist Evil

Dan 11 [31]"His armed forces will rise up to desecrate the temple fortress and will abolish the daily sacrifice. Then they will set up the abomination that causes desolation. [32]With flattery he will corrupt those who have violated the covenant, but the people who know their God will firmly resist him."

h) A Knowledge of God Produces Reverence for Him

Eccles 3 [12]I know that there is nothing better for men than to be happy and do good while they live. [13]That everyone may eat and drink, and find satisfaction in all his toil—this is the gift of God. [14]I know that everything God does will endure forever; nothing can be added to it and nothing taken from it. God does it so that men will revere him.

i) A Knowledge of God Promises His Constant Protection

Ps 9 [10]Those who know your name will trust in you, for you, LORD, have never forsaken those who seek you.
Ps 91 [14]"Because he loves me," says the LORD, "I will rescue him; I will protect him, for he acknowledges my name."

j) A Knowledge of God Results in an Intimate Relationship with Him

John 17 [1]After Jesus said this, he looked toward heaven and prayed: "Father, the time has come. Glorify your Son, that your Son may glorify you. . . .

[6]"I have revealed you to those whom you gave me out of the world. They were yours; you gave them to me and they have obeyed your word. [7]Now they know that everything you have given me comes from you. [8]For I gave them the words you gave me and they accepted them. They knew with certainty that I came from you, and they believed that you sent me. [9]I pray for them. I am not praying for the world, but for those you have given me, for they are yours."
Gal 4 [8]Formerly, when you did not know God, you were slaves to those who by nature are not gods. [9]But now that you know God—or rather are known by God—how is it that you are turning back to those weak and miserable principles? Do you wish to be enslaved by them all over again?
1 John 2 [23]No one who denies the Son has the Father; whoever acknowledges the Son has the Father also.
1 John 4 [15]If anyone acknowledges that Jesus is the Son of God, God lives in him and he in God.

k) A Knowledge of God Transforms the Believer

Eph 4 [13]until we all reach unity in the faith and in the knowledge of the Son of God and become mature, attaining to the whole measure of the fullness of Christ.
Col 3 [9]Do not lie to each other, since you have taken off your old self with its practices [10]and have put on the new self, which is being renewed in knowledge in the image of its Creator.
Titus 1 [1]Paul, a servant of God and an apostle of Jesus Christ for the faith of God's elect and the knowledge of the truth that leads to godliness—[2]a faith and knowledge resting on the hope of eternal life, which God, who does not lie, promised before the beginning of time . . .

B. Remember God

1. The Believer Should Remember God

Deut 8 [18]But remember the LORD your God, for it is he who gives you the ability to produce wealth, and so confirms his covenant, which he swore to your forefathers, as it is today.
Neh 4 [14]After I looked things over, I stood up and said to the nobles, the officials and the rest of the people, "Don't be afraid of them. Remember the Lord, who is great and awesome, and fight for your brothers, your sons and your daughters, your wives and your homes."
Ps 42 [5]Why are you downcast, O my soul? Why so disturbed within me? Put your hope in God, for I will yet praise him, my Savior and [6]my God.

My soul is downcast within me; therefore I will remember you from the land of the Jordan, the heights of Hermon—from Mount Mizar.
Ps 63 [6]On my bed I remember you; I think of you through the watches of the night. [7]Because you are my help, I sing in the shadow of your wings. [8]My soul clings to you; your right hand upholds me.
Ps 119 [55]In the night I remember your name, O LORD, and I will keep your law.
Eccles 12 [1]Remember your Creator in the days of your youth, before the days of trouble come and the years approach when you will say, "I find no pleasure in them." . . .

[6]Remember him—before the silver cord is severed, or the golden bowl is broken; before the pitcher is shattered at the

spring, or the wheel broken at the well, [7]and the dust returns to the ground it came from, and the spirit returns to God who gave it.

Jer 51 [50]"You who have escaped the sword, leave and do not linger! Remember the LORD in a distant land, and think on Jerusalem."

Jon 2 [7]"When my life was ebbing away, I remembered you, LORD, and my prayer rose to you, to your holy temple."

Zech 10 [9]"Though I scatter them among the peoples, yet in distant lands they will remember me. They and their children will survive, and they will return."

2. The Believer Should Remember God's Word

Num 15 [39]"'You will have these tassels to look at and so you will remember all the commands of the LORD, that you may obey them and not prostitute yourselves by going after the lusts of your own hearts and eyes. [40]Then you will remember to obey all my commands and will be consecrated to your God.'"

Ps 119 [52]I remember your ancient laws, O LORD, and I find comfort in them.

Mal 4 [4]"Remember the law of my servant Moses, the decrees and laws I gave him at Horeb for all Israel."

3. The Believer Should Remember God's Deeds

Deut 7 [18]But do not be afraid of them; remember well what the LORD your God did to Pharaoh and to all Egypt.

Deut 9 [4]After the LORD your God has driven them out before you, do not say to yourself, "The LORD has brought me here to take possession of this land because of my righteousness." No, it is on account of the wickedness of these nations that the LORD is going to drive them out before you. . . .

[7]Remember this and never forget how you provoked the LORD your God to anger in the desert. From the day you left Egypt until you arrived here, you have been rebellious against the LORD.

Deut 24 [9]Remember what the LORD your God did to Miriam along the way after you came out of Egypt.

Job 36 [24]"Remember to extol his work, which men have praised in song. [25]All mankind has seen it; men gaze on it from afar."

Ps 77 [3]I remembered you, O God, and I groaned; I mused, and my spirit grew faint.

[4]You kept my eyes from closing; I was too troubled to speak. [5]I thought about the former days, the years of long ago; [6]I remembered my songs in the night. My heart mused and my spirit inquired: [7]"Will the Lord reject forever? Will he never show his favor again? [8]Has his unfailing love vanished forever? Has his promise failed for all time? [9]Has God forgotten to be merciful? Has he in anger withheld his compassion?"

[10]Then I thought, "To this I will appeal: the years of the right hand of the Most High." [11]I will remember the deeds of the LORD; yes, I will remember your miracles of long ago. [12]I will meditate on all your works and consider all your mighty deeds.

Ps 105 [5]Remember the wonders he has done, his miracles, and the judgments he pronounced. . . .

4. The Believer Should Remember Christ

1 Cor 11 [23]For I received from the Lord what I also passed on to you: The Lord Jesus, on the night he was betrayed, took bread, [24]and when he had given thanks, he broke it and said, "This is my body, which is for you; do this in remembrance of me." [25]In the same way, after supper he took the cup, saying, "This cup is the new covenant in my blood; do this, whenever you drink it, in remembrance of me."

2 Tim 2 [8]Remember Jesus Christ, raised from the dead, descended from David. This is my gospel. . . .

5. The Believer Should Remember Christ's Words

Acts 20 [35]"In everything I did, I showed you that by this kind of hard work we must help the weak, remembering the words the Lord Jesus himself said: 'It is more blessed to give than to receive.'"

III
Magnifying God

A. Give Thanks to God

1. The Character of Thanksgiving

a) Thanksgiving Characterizes the Righteous

Eph 5 [3]But among you there must not be even a hint of sexual immorality, or of any kind of impurity, or of greed, because these are improper for God's holy people. [4]Nor should there be obscenity, foolish talk or coarse joking, which are out of place, but rather thanksgiving.

Col 2 [6]So then, just as you received Christ Jesus as Lord, continue to live in him, [7]rooted and built up in him, strengthened in the faith as you were taught, and overflowing with thankfulness.

b) Thanksgiving Glorifies God

Ps 69 [30]I will praise God's name in song and glorify him with thanksgiving.

c) Thanksgiving Honors God

Ps 50 [23]"He who sacrifices thank offerings honors me, and he prepares the way so that I may show him the salvation of God."

d) Thanksgiving Is a Desire of the Righteous

Ps 30 [11]You turned my wailing into dancing; you removed my sackcloth and clothed me with joy, [12]that my heart may sing to you and not be silent. O LORD my God, I will give you thanks forever.

Ps 106 [47]Save us, O LORD our God, and gather us from the nations, that we may give thanks to your holy name and glory in your praise.

e) Thanksgiving Is Meaningless When Offered Hypocritically

Amos 4 [4]"Go to Bethel and sin; go to Gilgal and sin yet more. Bring your sacrifices every morning, your tithes every three years. [5]Burn leavened bread as a thank offering and brag about your freewill offerings—boast about them, you Israelites, for this is what you love to do," declares the Sovereign LORD.

Luke 18 [9]To some who were confident of their own righteousness and looked down on everybody else, Jesus told this parable: [10]"Two men went up to the temple to pray, one a Pharisee and the other a tax collector. [11]The Pharisee stood up and prayed about himself: 'God, I thank you that I am not like other men—robbers, evildoers, adulterers—or even like this tax collector. . . .'

[13]"But the tax collector stood at a distance. He would not even look up to heaven, but beat his breast and said, 'God, have mercy on me, a sinner.'

[14]"I tell you that this man, rather than the other, went home justified before God. For everyone who exalts himself will be humbled, and he who humbles himself will be exalted."

f) Thanksgiving Is Offered to Christ

Luke 17 [15]One of them, when he saw he was healed, came back, praising God in a loud voice. [16]He threw himself at Jesus' feet and thanked him—and he was a Samaritan.

1 Tim 1 [12]I thank Christ Jesus our Lord, who has given me strength, that he considered me faithful, appointing me to his service.

g) Thanksgiving Is Offered to God

1 Chron 29 [13]"Now, our God, we give you thanks, and praise your glorious name."

Ps 75 [1]We give thanks to you, O God, we give thanks, for your Name is near; men tell of your wonderful deeds.
Ps 100 [4]Enter his gates with thanksgiving and his courts with praise; give thanks to him and praise his name. [5]For the LORD is good and his love endures forever; his faithfulness continues through all generations.
Ps 118 [28]You are my God, and I will give you thanks; you are my God, and I will exalt you.
Ps 136 [1]Give thanks to the LORD, for he is good. *His love endures forever.* [2]Give thanks to the God of gods. *His love endures forever.* [3]Give thanks to the Lord of lords: *His love endures forever. . . .*

[26]Give thanks to the God of heaven. *His love endures forever.*
Jer 33 [11]"'. . . the sounds of joy and gladness, the voices of bride and bridegroom, and the voices of those who bring thank offerings to the house of the LORD, saying, "Give thanks to the LORD Almighty, for the LORD is good; his love endures forever." For I will restore the fortunes of the land as they were before,' says the LORD."
Rom 14 [6]He who regards one day as special, does so to the Lord. He who eats meat, eats to the Lord, for he gives thanks to God; and he who abstains, does so to the Lord and gives thanks to God.
Eph 5 [19]Speak to one another with psalms, hymns and spiritual songs. Sing and make music in your heart to the Lord, [20]always giving thanks to God the Father for everything, in the name of our Lord Jesus Christ.
Col 3 [17]And whatever you do, whether in word or deed, do it all in the name of the Lord Jesus, giving thanks to God the Father through him.

h) Thanksgiving Is Required of God's People

1 Chron 16 [8]Give thanks to the LORD, call on his name; make known among the nations what he has done.
Col 3 [15]Let the peace of Christ rule in your hearts, since as members of one body you were called to peace. And be thankful.
Heb 12 [28]Therefore, since we are receiving a kingdom that cannot be shaken, let us be thankful, and so worship God acceptably with reverence and awe. . . .

i) Thanksgiving Is Scorned by the Wicked

Rom 1 [21]For although they knew God, they neither glorified him as God nor gave thanks to him, but their thinking became futile and their foolish hearts were darkened.

2. Reasons for Thanksgiving

a) Give Thanks for Answered Prayer

Ps 118 [19]Open for me the gates of righteousness; I will enter and give thanks to the LORD. [20]This is the gate of the LORD through which the righteous may enter. [21]I will give you thanks, for you answered me; you have become my salvation.
2 Cor 1 [10]He has delivered us from such a deadly peril, and he will deliver us. On him we have set our hope that he will continue to deliver us, [11]as you help us by your prayers. Then many will give thanks on our behalf for the gracious favor granted us in answer to the prayers of many.

b) Give Thanks for Appointment to Christian Service

1 Tim 1 [12]I thank Christ Jesus our Lord, who has given me strength, that he considered me faithful, appointing me to his service.

c) Give Thanks for Christian Concern for Others

2 Cor 8 [16]I thank God, who put into the heart of Titus the same concern I have for you. [17]For Titus not only welcomed our appeal, but he is coming to you with much enthusiasm and on his own initiative.

d) Give Thanks for Christian Giving

2 Cor 9 [11]You will be made rich in every way so that you can be generous on every occasion, and through us your generosity will result in thanksgiving to God.

e) Give Thanks for Civil Authorities

1 Tim 2 [1]I urge, then, first of all, that requests, prayers, intercession and thanksgiving be made for everyone—[2]for kings and all those in authority, that we may live peaceful and quiet lives in all godliness and holiness.

f) Give Thanks for Converts

Rom 6 [17]But thanks be to God that, though you used to be slaves to sin, you wholeheartedly obeyed the form of teaching to which you were entrusted. [18]You have been set free from sin and have become slaves to righteousness.
2 Cor 4 [15]All this is for your benefit, so that the grace that is reaching more and more people may cause thanksgiving to overflow to the glory of God.
1 Thess 2 [13]And we also thank God continually because, when you received the word of God, which you heard from us, you acccepted it not as the word of men, but as it actually is, the word of God, which is at work in you who believe.
1 Thess 3 [8]For now we really live, since you are standing firm in the Lord. [9]How can we thank God enough for you in return for all the joy we have in the presence of our God because of you?

g) Give Thanks for Everything

Eph 5 [20]always giving thanks to God the Father for everything, in the name of our Lord Jesus Christ.

h) Give Thanks for Faith and Love

Rom 1 [8]First, I thank my God through Jesus Christ for all of you, because your faith is being reported all over the world.
Col 1 [3]We always thank God, the Father of our Lord Jesus Christ, when we pray for you, [4]because we have heard of your faith in Christ Jesus and of the love you have for all the saints—[5]the faith and love that spring from the hope that is stored up for you in heaven and that you have already heard about in the word of truth, the gospel [6]that has come to you. All over the world this gospel is bearing fruit and growing, just as it has been doing among you since the day you heard it and understood God's grace in all its truth.
2 Thess 1 [3]We ought always to thank God for you, brothers, and rightly so, because your faith is growing more and more, and the love every one of you has for each other is increasing.

i) Give Thanks for Food

John 6 [11]Jesus then took the loaves, gave thanks, and distributed to those who were seated as much as they wanted. He did the same with the fish.
Acts 27 [35]After he said this, he took some bread and gave thanks to God in front of them all. Then he broke it and began to eat.
Rom 14 [6]He who regards one day as special, does so to the Lord. He who eats meat, eats to the Lord, for he gives thanks to God; and he who abstains, does so to the Lord and gives thanks to God. [7]For none of us lives to himself alone and none of us dies to himself alone.
1 Cor 10 [30]If I take part in the meal with thankfulness, why am I denounced because of something I thank God for?

[31]So whether you eat or drink or whatever you do, do it all for the glory of God.
1 Tim 4 [3]They forbid people to marry and order them to abstain from certain foods, which God created to be received with thanksgiving by those who believe and who know the truth. [4]For everything God created is good, and nothing is to be rejected if it is received with thanksgiving. . . .

j) Give Thanks for the Goodness of God

Ps 106 [1]Praise the LORD.

Give thanks to the LORD, for he is good; his love endures forever.
Ps 107 [1]Give thanks to the LORD, for he is good; his love endures forever.
Ps 118 [1]Give thanks to the LORD, for he is good; his love endures forever.
Ps 118 [29]Give thanks to the LORD, for he is good; his love endures forever.

k) Give Thanks for Grace in Christ

1 Cor 1 [4]I always thank God for you because of his grace given you in Christ Jesus.
2 Cor 8 [9]For you know the grace of our Lord Jesus Christ, that though he was rich, yet for your sakes he became poor, so that you through his poverty might become rich.
2 Cor 9 [13]Because of the service by which you have proved yourselves, men will praise God for the obedience that accompanies your confession of the gospel of Christ, and for your generosity in sharing with them and with everyone else. [14]And in their prayers for you their hearts will go out to you, because of the surpassing grace God has given you. [15]Thanks be to God for his indescribable gift!

l) Give Thanks for the Inheritance of God's Kingdom

Col 1 [10]And we pray this in order that you may live a life worthy of the Lord and may please him in every way: bearing fruit in every good work, growing in the knowledge of God, [11]being strengthened with all power according to his glorious might so that you may have great endurance and patience, and joyfully [12]giving thanks to the Father, who has qualified you to share in the inheritance of the saints in the kingdom of light. [13]For he has rescued us from the dominion of darkness and brought us into the kingdom of the Son he loves, [14]in whom we have redemption, the forgiveness of sins.
Heb 12 [28]Therefore, since we are receiving a kingdom that cannot be shaken, let us be thankful, and so worship God acceptably with reverence and awe. . . .

m) Give Thanks for the Lord's Supper

1 Cor 10 [16]Is not the cup of thanksgiving for which we give thanks a participation in the blood of Christ? And is not the bread that we break a participation in the body of Christ?

n) Give Thanks for Partnership in the Gospel

Phil 1 [3]I thank my God every time I remember you. [4]In all my prayers for all of you, I always pray with joy [5]because of your partnership in the gospel from the first day until now. . . .

o) Give Thanks for the Power and Reign of God

Rev 11 [17]saying: "We give thanks to you, Lord God Almighty, the One who is and who was, because you have taken your great power and have begun to reign."

p) Give Thanks for the Presence of God

Ps 75 [1]We give thanks to you, O God, we give thanks, for your Name is near; men tell of your wonderful deeds.

q) Give Thanks for the Reception of God's Word by Others

1 Thess 2 [13]And we also thank God continually because, when you received the word of God, which you heard from us, you accepted it not as the word of men, but as it actually is, the word of God, which is at work in you who believe.

r) Give Thanks for Rescue from Sin

Rom 7 [21]So I find this law at work: When I want to do good, evil is right there with me. [22]For in my inner being I delight in God's law; [23]but I see another law at work in the members of my body, waging war against the law of my mind and making me a prisoner of the law of sin at work within my members. [24]What a wretched man I am! Who will rescue me from this body of death? [25]Thanks be to God—through Jesus Christ our Lord!

So then, I myself in my mind am a slave to God's law, but in the sinful nature a slave to the law of sin.

s) Give Thanks for the Righteousness of God

Ps 7 [17]I will give thanks to the LORD because of his righteousness and will sing praise to the name of the LORD Most High.

t) Give Thanks for the Triumph of the Gospel

2 Cor 2 [14]But thanks be to God, who always leads us in triumphal procession in Christ and through us spreads everywhere the fragrance of the knowledge of him.

u) Give Thanks for Victory over Sin and Death

1 Cor 15 [54]When the perishable has been clothed with the imperishable, and the mortal with immortality, then the saying that is written will come true: "Death has been swallowed up in victory." [55]"Where, O death, is your victory? Where, O death, is your sting?" [56]The sting of death is sin, and the power of sin is the law. [57]But thanks be to God! He gives us the victory through our Lord Jesus Christ.

v) Give Thanks for Wisdom and Power

Dan 2 [23]"I thank and praise you, O God of my fathers: You have given me wisdom and power, you have made known to me what we asked of you, you have made known to us the dream of the king."

w) Give Thanks for the Word of God

Ps 119 [62]At midnight I rise to give you thanks for your righteous laws.

x) Give Thanks for the Works of God

Ps 107 [8]Let them give thanks to the LORD for his unfailing love and his wonderful deeds for men, [9]for he satisfies the thirsty and fills the hungry with good things.
Ps 136 [1]Give thanks to the LORD, for he is good. *His love endures forever.* [2]Give thanks to the God of gods. *His love endures forever.* [3]Give thanks to the Lord of lords: *His love endures forever.*

[4]to him who alone does great wonders, *His love endures forever.* [5]who by his understanding made the heavens, *His love endures forever.* [6]who spread out the earth upon the waters, *His love endures forever.* [7]who made the great lights—*His love endures forever.* [8]the sun to govern the day, *His love endures forever.* [9]the moon and stars to govern the night; *His love endures forever.*

[10]to him who struck down the firstborn of Egypt *His love endures forever.* [11]and brought Israel out from among them *His love endures forever.* [12]with a mighty hand and outstretched arm; *His love endures forever.*

[13]to him who divided the Red Sea asunder *His love endures forever.* [14]and brought Israel through the midst of it, *His love endures forever.* [15]but swept Pharaoh and his army into the Red Sea; *His love endures forever.*

[16]to him who led his people through the desert, *His love endures forever.* [17]who struck down great kings, *His love endures forever.* [18]and killed mighty kings—*His love endures forever.* [19]Sihon king of the Amorites *His love endures forever.* [20]and Og king of Bashan—*His love endures forever.* [21]and gave their land as an inheritance, *His love endures forever.* [22]an inheritance to his servant Israel; *His love endures forever.*

[23]to the One who remembered us in our low estate *His love endures forever.* [24]and freed us from our enemies, *His love endures forever.* [25]and who gives food to every creature. *His love endures forever.*

[26]Give thanks to the God of heaven. *His love endures forever.*
Isa 12 [4]In that day you will say: "Give thanks to the LORD, call on his name; make known among the nations what he has done, and proclaim that his name is exalted. [5]Sing to the LORD, for he has done glorious things; let this be known to all the world. [6]Shout aloud and sing for joy, people of Zion, for great is the Holy One of Israel among you."

3. The Manner of Thanksgiving

a) Give Thanks as a Sacrifice

Lev 7 [11]"'These are the regulations for the fellowship offering a person may present to the LORD:

[12]"'If he offers it as an expression of thankfulness, then along with this thank offering he is to offer cakes of bread made without yeast and mixed with oil, wafers made without yeast and spread with oil, and cakes of fine flour well-kneaded and mixed with oil.'"
2 Chron 29 [31]Then Hezekiah said, "You have now dedicated yourselves to the LORD. Come and bring sacrifices and thank

offerings to the temple of the LORD." So the assembly brought sacrifices and thank offerings, and all whose hearts were willing brought burnt offerings.
2 Chron 33 [16]Then he restored the altar of the LORD and sacrificed fellowship offerings and thank offerings on it, and told Judah to serve the LORD, the God of Israel.
Ps 50 [14]"Sacrifice thank offerings to God, fulfill your vows to the Most High. . . ."
Ps 116 [17]I will sacrifice a thank offering to you and call on the name of the LORD.

b) Give Thanks in All Circumstances

1 Thess 5 [18]give thanks in all circumstances, for this is God's will for you in Christ Jesus.

c) Give Thanks in Levitical Service

1 Chron 16 [4]He appointed some of the Levites to minister before the ark of the LORD, to make petition, to give thanks, and to praise the LORD, the God of Israel. . . .
1 Chron 23 [28]The duty of the Levites was to help Aaron's descendants in the service of the temple of the LORD: to be in charge of the courtyards, the side rooms, the purification of all sacred things and the performance of other duties at the house of God. . . . [30]They were also to stand every morning to thank and praise the LORD. They were to do the same in the evening. . . .
2 Chron 31 [2]Hezekiah assigned the priests and Levites to divisions—each of them according to their duties as priests or Levites—to offer burnt offerings and fellowship offerings, to minister, to give thanks and to sing praises at the gates of the LORD's dwelling.

d) Give Thanks in Music and Song

1 Chron 16 [7]That day David first committed to Asaph and his associates this psalm of thanks to the LORD. . . .
1 Chron 25 [3]As for Jeduthun, from his sons: Gedaliah, Zeri, Jeshaiah, Shimei, Hashabiah and Mattithiah, six in all, under the supervision of their father Jeduthun, who prophesied, using the harp in thanking and praising the LORD.
Neh 12 [27]At the dedication of the wall of Jerusalem, the Levites were sought out from where they lived and were brought to Jerusalem to celebrate joyfully the dedication with songs of thanksgiving and with the music of cymbals, harps and lyres. . . .

[31]I had the leaders of Judah go up on top of the wall. I also assigned two large choirs to give thanks. One was to proceed on top of the wall to the right, toward the Dung Gate.
Ps 28 [7]The LORD is my strength and my shield; my heart trusts in him, and I am helped. My heart leaps for joy and I will give thanks to him in song.
Ps 95 [2]Let us come before him with thanksgiving and extol him with music and song.
Ps 147 [7]Sing to the LORD with thanksgiving; make music to our God on the harp.
Isa 12 [4]In that day you will say: "Give thanks to the LORD, call on his name; make known among the nations what he has done, and proclaim that his name is exalted. [5]Sing to the LORD, for he has done glorious things; let this be known to all the world."
Isa 51 [3]"The LORD will surely comfort Zion and will look with compassion on all her ruins; he will make her deserts like Eden, her wastelands like the garden of the LORD. Joy and gladness will be found in her, thanksgiving and the sound of singing."
Jer 30 [19]"'From them will come songs of thanksgiving and the sound of rejoicing. I will add to their numbers, and they will not be decreased; I will bring them honor, and they will not be disdained.'"
Eph 5 [19]Speak to one another with psalms, hymns and spiritual songs. Sing and make music in your heart to the Lord, [20]always giving thanks to God the Father for everything, in the name of our Lord Jesus Christ.

e) Give Thanks in the Name of Christ

Eph 5 [20]always giving thanks to God the Father for everything, in the name of our Lord Jesus Christ.

f) Give Thanks in Worship

2 Chron 7 [3]When all the Israelites saw the fire coming down and the glory of the LORD above the temple, they knelt on the pavement with their faces to the ground, and they worshiped and gave thanks to the LORD, saying, "He is good; his love endures forever."
Ps 35 [18]I will give you thanks in the great assembly; among throngs of people I will praise you.
Ps 100 [1]Shout for joy to the LORD, all the earth. [2]Worship the LORD with gladness; come before him with joyful songs. [3]Know that the LORD is God. It is he who made us, and we are his; we are his people, the sheep of his pasture. [4]Enter his gates with thanksgiving and his courts with praise; give thanks to him and praise his name. [5]For the LORD is good and his love endures forever; his faithfulness continues through all generations.
Heb 12 [28]Therefore, since we are receiving a kingdom that cannot be shaken, let us be thankful, and so worship God acceptably with reverence and awe. . . .
Rev 4 [9]Whenever the living creatures give glory, honor and thanks to him who sits on the throne and who lives for ever and ever, [10]the twenty-four elders fall down before him who sits on the throne, and worship him who lives for ever and ever. They lay their crowns before the throne and say: [11]"You are worthy, our Lord and God, to receive glory and honor and power, for you created all things, and by your will they were created and have their being."
Rev 7 [11]All the angels were standing around the throne and around the elders and the four living creatures. They fell down on their faces before the throne and worshiped God, [12]saying: "Amen! Praise and glory and wisdom and thanks and honor and power and strength be to our God for ever and ever. Amen!"
Rev 11 [16]And the twenty-four elders, who were seated on their thrones before God, fell on their faces and worshiped God, [17]saying: "We give thanks to you, Lord God Almighty, the One who is and who was, because you have taken your great power and have begun to reign."

g) Give Thanks through Christ

Rom 1 [8]First, I thank my God through Jesus Christ for all of you, because your faith is being reported all over the world.
Col 3 [17]And whatever you do, whether in word or deed, do it all in the name of the Lord Jesus, giving thanks to God the Father through him.
Heb 13 [15]Through Jesus, therefore, let us continually offer to God a sacrifice of praise—the fruit of lips that confess his name.

h) Give Thanks with Frequency

Ps 30 [12]that my heart may sing to you and not be silent. O LORD my God, I will give you thanks forever.
Ps 119 [62]At midnight I rise to give you thanks for your righteous laws.
Eph 1 [16]I have not stopped giving thanks for you, remembering you in my prayers.
Eph 5 [20]always giving thanks to God the Father for everything, in the name of our Lord Jesus Christ.
1 Thess 1 [2]We always thank God for all of you, mentioning you in our prayers.

i) Give Thanks with Praise

2 Chron 5 [13]The trumpeters and singers joined in unison, as with one voice, to give praise and thanks to the LORD. Accompanied by trumpets, cymbals and other instruments, they raised their voices in praise to the LORD and sang: "He is good; his love endures forever."

Then the temple of the LORD was filled with a cloud, [14]and the priests could not perform their service because of the cloud, for the glory of the LORD filled the temple of God.
Neh 12 [46]For long ago, in the days of David and Asaph, there had been directors for the singers and for the songs of praise and thanksgiving to God.
Ps 42 [4]These things I remember as I pour out my soul: how I used to go with the multitude, leading the procession to the house of God, with shouts of joy and thanksgiving among the festive throng.

Ps 100 [1]Shout for joy to the LORD, all the earth. . . . [4]Enter his gates with thanksgiving and his courts with praise; give thanks to him and praise his name.

j) Give Thanks with Prayer

Neh 11 [17]Mattaniah son of Mica, the son of Zabdi, the son of Asaph, the director who led in thanksgiving and prayer; Bakbukiah, second among his associates; and Abda son of Shammua, the son of Galal, the son of Jeduthun.
Dan 6 [10]Now when Daniel learned that the decree had been published, he went home to his upstairs room where the windows opened toward Jerusalem. Three times a day he got down on his knees and prayed, giving thanks to his God, just as he had done before.
Phil 4 [6]Do not be anxious about anything, but in everything, by prayer and petition, with thanksgiving, present your requests to God.
Col 4 [2]Devote yourselves to prayer, being watchful and thankful.
1 Tim 2 [1]I urge, then, first of all, that requests, prayers, intercession and thanksgiving be made for everyone. . . .
2 Tim 1 [3]I thank God, whom I serve, as my forefathers did, with a clear conscience, as night and day I constantly remember you in my prayers.
Philem [4]I always thank my God as I remember you in my prayers. . . .

4. Examples of Thanksgiving

a) Gifts for Constructing Solomon's Temple

1 Chron 29 [6]Then the leaders of families, the officers of the tribes of Israel, the commanders of thousands and commanders of hundreds, and the officials in charge of the king's work gave willingly. [7]They gave toward the work on the temple of God five thousand talents and ten thousand darics of gold, ten thousand talents of silver, eighteen thousand talents of bronze and a hundred thousand talents of iron. [8]Any who had precious stones gave them to the treasury of the temple of the LORD in the custody of Jehiel the Gershonite. [9]The people rejoiced at the willing response of their leaders, for they had given freely and wholeheartedly to the LORD. David the king also rejoiced greatly.

[10]David praised the LORD in the presence of the whole assembly, saying, "Praise be to you, O LORD, God of our father Israel, from everlasting to everlasting. [11]Yours, O LORD, is the greatness and the power and the glory and the majesty and the splendor, for everything in heaven and earth is yours. Yours, O LORD, is the kingdom; you are exalted as head over all. [12]Wealth and honor come from you; you are the ruler of all things. In your hands are strength and power to exalt and give strength to all. [13]Now, our God, we give you thanks, and praise your glorious name."

b) The Dedication of Solomon's Temple

2 Chron 7 [1]When Solomon finished praying, fire came down from heaven and consumed the burnt offering and the sacrifices, and the glory of the LORD filled the temple. [2]The priests could not enter the temple of the LORD because the glory of the LORD filled it. [3]When all the Israelites saw the fire coming down and the glory of the LORD above the temple, they knelt on the pavement with their faces to the ground, and they worshiped and gave thanks to the LORD, saying, "He is good; his love endures forever." [4]Then the king and all the people offered sacrifices before the LORD. [5]And King Solomon offered a sacrifice of twenty-two thousand head of cattle and a hundred and twenty thousand sheep and goats. So the king and all the people dedicated the temple of God. [6]The priests took their positions, as did the Levites with the LORD's musical instruments, which King David had made for praising the LORD and which were used when he gave thanks, saying, "His love endures forever." Opposite the Levites, the priests blew their trumpets, and all the Israelites were standing.

c) Jonah's Thanks

Jon 2 [9]"But I, with a song of thanksgiving, will sacrifice to you. What I have vowed I will make good. Salvation comes from the LORD."

d) Jehoshaphat's Thanks

2 Chron 20 [21]After consulting the people, Jehoshaphat appointed men to sing to the LORD and to praise him for the splendor of his holiness as they went out at the head of the army, saying: "Give thanks to the LORD, for his love endures forever."

e) Thanks at the Laying of the Temple's Foundation

Ezra 3 [10]When the builders laid the foundation of the temple of the LORD, the priests in their vestments and with trumpets, and the Levites (the sons of Asaph) with cymbals, took their places to praise the LORD, as prescribed by David king of Israel. [11]With praise and thanksgiving they sang to the LORD: "He is good; his love to Israel endures forever." And all the people gave a great shout of praise to the LORD, because the foundation of the house of the LORD was laid. [12]But many of the older priests and Levites and family heads, who had seen the former temple, wept aloud when they saw the foundation of this temple being laid, while many others shouted for joy. [13]No one could distinguish the sound of the shouts of joy from the sound of weeping, because the people made so much noise. And the sound was heard far away.

f) Thanks at the Dedication of the Jerusalem Wall

Neh 12 [27]At the dedication of the wall of Jerusalem, the Levites were sought out from where they lived and were brought to Jerusalem to celebrate joyfully the dedication with songs of thanksgiving and with the music of cymbals, harps and lyres. [28]The singers also were brought together from the region around Jerusalem—from the villages of the Netophathites, [29]from Beth Gilgal, and from the area of Geba and Azmaveth, for the singers had built villages for themselves around Jerusalem. [30]When the priests and Levites had purified themselves ceremonially, they purified the people, the gates and the wall.

[31]I had the leaders of Judah go up on top of the wall. I also assigned two large choirs to give thanks. One was to proceed on top of the wall to the right, toward the Dung Gate. [32]Hoshaiah and half the leaders of Judah followed them, [33]along with Azariah, Ezra, Meshullam, [34]Judah, Benjamin, Shemaiah, Jeremiah, [35]as well as some priests with trumpets, and also Zechariah son of Jonathan, the son of Shemaiah, the son of Mattaniah, the son of Micaiah, the son of Zaccur, the son of Asaph, [36]and his associates—Shemaiah, Azarel, Milalai, Gilalai, Maai, Nethanel, Judah and Hanani—with musical instruments prescribed by David the man of God. Ezra the scribe led the procession. [37]At the Fountain Gate they continued directly up the steps of the City of David on the ascent to the wall and passed above the house of David to the Water Gate on the east.

[38]The second choir proceeded in the opposite direction. I followed them on top of the wall, together with half the people—past the Tower of the Ovens to the Broad Wall, [39]over the Gate of Ephraim, the Jeshanah Gate, the Fish Gate, the Tower of Hananel and the Tower of the Hundred, as far as the Sheep Gate. At the Gate of the Guard they stopped.

[40]The two choirs that gave thanks then took their places in the house of God; so did I, together with half the officials, [41]as well as the priests—Eliakim, Maaseiah, Miniamin, Micaiah, Elioenai, Zechariah and Hananiah with their trumpets—[42]and also Maaseiah, Shemaiah, Eleazar, Uzzi, Jehohanan, Malkijah, Elam and Ezer. The choirs sang under the direction of Jezrahiah. [43]And on that day they offered great sacrifices, rejoicing because God had given them great joy. The women and children also rejoiced. The sound of rejoicing in Jerusalem could be heard far away.

g) Anna's Thanks

Luke 2 [36]There was also a prophetess, Anna, the daughter of Phanuel, of the tribe of Asher. She was very old; she had lived with her husband seven years after her marriage, [37]and then was a widow until she was eighty-four. She never left the temple but worshiped night and day, fasting and praying. 38Coming up to them at that very moment, she gave thanks to God and spoke about the child to all who were looking forward to the redemption of Jerusalem.

h) The Samaritan's Thanks

Luke 17 11Now on his way to Jerusalem, Jesus traveled along the border between Samaria and Galilee. 12As he was going into a village, ten men who had leprosy met him. They stood at a distance 13and called out in a loud voice, "Jesus, Master, have pity on us!"

14When he saw them, he said, "Go, show yourselves to the priests." And as they went, they were cleansed.

15One of them, when he saw he was healed, came back, praising God in a loud voice. 16He threw himself at Jesus' feet and thanked him—and he was a Samaritan.

17Jesus asked, "Were not all ten cleansed? Where are the other nine? 18Was no one found to return and give praise to God except this foreigner?" 19Then he said to him, "Rise and go; your faith has made you well."

i) Jesus' Thanks

Mark 14 22While they were eating, Jesus took bread, gave thanks and broke it, and gave it to his disciples, saying, "Take it; this is my body."

23Then he took the cup, gave thanks and offered it to them, and they all drank from it.

Luke 24 28As they approached the village to which they were going, Jesus acted as if he were going farther. 29But they urged him strongly, "Stay with us, for it is nearly evening; the day is almost over." So he went in to stay with them.

30When he was at the table with them, he took bread, gave thanks, broke it and began to give it to them. 31Then their eyes were opened and they recognized him, and he disappeared from their sight.

John 6 23Then some boats from Tiberias landed near the place where the people had eaten the bread after the Lord had given thanks.

John 11 41So they took away the stone. Then Jesus looked up and said, "Father, I thank you that you have heard me."

j) Paul's Thanks

Acts 28 15The brothers there had heard that we were coming, and they traveled as far as the Forum of Appius and the Three Taverns to meet us. At the sight of these men Paul thanked God and was encouraged.

Rom 1 1Paul, a servant of Christ Jesus, called to be an apostle and set apart for the gospel of God . . .

8First, I thank my God through Jesus Christ for all of you, because your faith is being reported all over the world.

B. Praise God

1. The Nature and Results of Praising God

a) Praise Brings Blessing from God

Ps 84 4Blessed are those who dwell in your house; they are ever praising you.

b) Praise Depends on God

Ps 8 2From the lips of children and infants you have ordained praise because of your enemies, to silence the foe and the avenger.

Ps 30 11You turned my wailing into dancing; you removed my sackcloth and clothed me with joy, 12that my heart may sing to you and not be silent. O LORD my God, I will give you thanks forever.

Ps 51 15O Lord, open my lips, and my mouth will declare your praise.

Ps 61 1Hear my cry, O God; listen to my prayer.

2From the ends of the earth I call to you, I call as my heart grows faint; lead me to the rock that is higher than I. 3For you have been my refuge, a strong tower against the foe.

4I long to dwell in your tent forever and take refuge in the shelter of your wings. 5For you have heard my vows, O God; you have given me the heritage of those who fear your name.

6Increase the days of the king's life, his years for many generations. 7May he be enthroned in God's presence forever; appoint your love and faithfulness to protect him.

8Then will I ever sing praise to your name and fulfill my vows day after day.

Ps 79 9Help us, O God our Savior, for the glory of your name; deliver us and forgive our sins for your name's sake. . . .

12Pay back into the laps of our neighbors seven times the reproach they have hurled at you, O Lord. 13Then we your people, the sheep of your pasture, will praise you forever; from generation to generation we will recount your praise.

Ps 119 175Let me live that I may praise you, and may your laws sustain me.

Ps 142 7Set me free from my prison, that I may praise your name.

Then the righteous will gather about me because of your goodness to me.

Isa 61 11For as the soil makes the sprout come up and a garden causes seeds to grow, so the Sovereign LORD will make righteousness and praise spring up before all nations.

c) Praise Glorifies God

Ps 66 2Sing the glory of his name; make his praise glorious!

d) Praise Is Acceptable through Christ

Heb 13 15Through Jesus, therefore, let us continually offer to God a sacrifice of praise—the fruit of lips that confess his name.

1 Pet 4 11If anyone speaks, he should do it as one speaking the very words of God. If anyone serves, he should do it with the strength God provides, so that in all things God may be praised through Jesus Christ. To him be the glory and the power for ever and ever. Amen.

e) Praise Is Commanded

Ps 30 4Sing to the LORD, you saints of his; praise his holy name.

Ps 68 26Praise God in the great congregation; praise the LORD in the assembly of Israel.

Ps 68 32Sing to God, O kingdoms of the earth, sing praise to the Lord. . . .

Ps 104 35But may sinners vanish from the earth and the wicked be no more.

Praise the LORD, O my soul.

Praise the LORD.

Ps 106 48Praise be to the LORD, the God of Israel, from everlasting to everlasting. Let all the people say, "Amen!"

Praise the LORD.

Ps 107 31Let them give thanks to the LORD for his unfailing love and his wonderful deeds for men. 32Let them exalt him in the assembly of the people and praise him in the council of the elders.

Rev 19 5Then a voice came from the throne, saying: "Praise our God, all you his servants, you who fear him, both small and great!"

6Then I heard what sounded like a great multitude, like the roar of rushing waters and like loud peals of thunder, shouting: "Hallelujah! For our Lord God Almighty reigns. 7Let us rejoice and be glad and give him glory! For the wedding of the Lamb has come, and his bride has made herself ready. 8Fine linen, bright and clean, was given her to wear." (Fine linen stands for the righteous acts of the saints.)

f) Praise Is Desired by God

Isa 43 20"The wild animals honor me, the jackals and the owls, because I provide water in the desert and streams in the wasteland, to give drink to my people, my chosen, 21the people I formed for myself that they may proclaim my praise."

Isa 61 11For as the soil makes the sprout come up and a garden causes seeds to grow, so the Sovereign LORD will make righteousness and praise spring up before all nations.

Jer 13 11"'For as a belt is bound around a man's waist, so I bound the whole house of Israel and the whole house of Judah to me,' declares the LORD, 'to be my people for my renown and praise and honor. But they have not listened.'"

Jer 33 8"'I will cleanse them from all the sin they have committed against me and will forgive all their sins of rebellion against me. [9]Then this city will bring me renown, joy, praise and honor before all nations on earth that hear of all the good things I do for it; and they will be in awe and will tremble at the abundant prosperity and peace I provide for it.'"

Matt 21 [16]"Do you hear what these children are saying?" they asked him.

"Yes," replied Jesus, "have you never read, 'From the lips of children and infants you have ordained praise'?"

1 Pet 2 [9]But you are a chosen people, a royal priesthood, a holy nation, a people belonging to God, that you may declare the praises of him who called you out of darkness into his wonderful light.

g) Praise Is Due God Alone

Exod 15 [11]"Who among the gods is like you, O LORD? Who is like you—majestic in holiness, awesome in glory, working wonders?"

Deut 10 [21]He is your praise; he is your God, who performed for you those great and awesome wonders you saw with your own eyes.

1 Chron 16 [25]For great is the LORD and most worthy of praise; he is to be feared above all gods. [26]For all the gods of the nations are idols, but the LORD made the heavens.

Ps 47 [7]For God is the King of all the earth; sing to him a psalm of praise.

Ps 50 [14]"Sacrifice thank offerings to God, fulfill your vows to the Most High, [15]and call upon me in the day of trouble; I will deliver you, and you will honor me."

Ps 135 [15]The idols of the nations are silver and gold, made by the hands of men. [17]. . . they have ears, but cannot hear, nor is there breath in their mouths. [18]Those who make them will be like them, and so will all who trust in them. . . . [21]Praise be to the LORD from Zion, to him who dwells in Jerusalem.

Praise the LORD.

Ps 148 [13]Let them praise the name of the LORD, for his name alone is exalted; his splendor is above the earth and the heavens.

Isa 42 [8]"I am the LORD; that is my name! I will not give my glory to another or my praise to idols."

h) Praise Is Everlasting

Ps 72 [19]Praise be to his glorious name forever; may the whole earth be filled with his glory. Amen and Amen.

Ps 111 [10]The fear of the LORD is the beginning of wisdom; all who follow his precepts have good understanding. To him belongs eternal praise.

Rom 1 [25]They exchanged the truth of God for a lie, and worshiped and served created things rather than the Creator—who is forever praised. Amen.

Rom 9 [5]Theirs are the patriarchs, and from them is traced the human ancestry of Christ, who is God over all, forever praised! Amen.

2 Cor 11 [31]The God and Father of the Lord Jesus, who is to be praised forever, knows that I am not lying.

i) Praise Is Good

Ps 92 [1]It is good to praise the LORD and make music to your name, O Most High. . . .

Ps 147 [1]Praise the LORD.

How good it is to sing praises to our God, how pleasant and fitting to praise him!

j) Praise Is Offered to Christ

John 12 [12]The next day the great crowd that had come for the Feast heard that Jesus was on his way to Jerusalem. [13]They took palm branches and went out to meet him, shouting, "Hosanna!" "Blessed is he who comes in the name of the Lord!" "Blessed is the King of Israel!"

k) Praise Is Ordained by God

Ps 8 [1]O LORD, our Lord, how majestic is your name in all the earth!

You have set your glory above the heavens. [2]From the lips of children and infants you have ordained praise because of your enemies, to silence the foe and the avenger.

l) Praise Is Pleasant

Ps 135 [3]Praise the LORD, for the LORD is good; sing praise to his name, for that is pleasant.

Ps 147 [1]Praise the LORD.

How good it is to sing praises to our God, how pleasant and fitting to praise him!

m) Praise Pleases God

Ps 69 [30]I will praise God's name in song and glorify him with thanksgiving. [31]This will please the LORD more than an ox, more than a bull with its horns and hoofs.

2. Reasons for Praising God

1) Praise God for Answered Prayer

Ps 28 [6]Praise be to the LORD, for he has heard my cry for mercy.

Ps 66 [19]but God has surely listened and heard my voice in prayer. [20]Praise be to God, who has not rejected my prayer or withheld his love from me!

2) Praise God for Christ

Luke 1 [68]"Praise be to the Lord, the God of Israel, because he has come and has redeemed his people. [69]He has raised up a horn of salvation for us in the house of his servant David. . . ."

Luke 2 [10]But the angel said to them, "Do not be afraid. I bring you good news of great joy that will be for all the people. [11]Today in the town of David a Savior has been born to you; he is Christ the Lord. . . ."

[13]Suddenly a great company of the heavenly host appeared with the angel, praising God and saying, [14]"Glory to God in the highest, and on earth peace to men on whom his favor rests."

Luke 2 [25]Now there was a man in Jerusalem called Simeon, who was righteous and devout. He was waiting for the consolation of Israel, and the Holy Spirit was upon him. [26]It had been revealed to him by the Holy Spirit that he would not die before he had seen the Lord's Christ. [27]Moved by the Spirit, he went into the temple courts. When the parents brought in the child Jesus to do for him what the custom of the Law required, [28]Simeon took him in his arms and praised God, saying . . .

Luke 24 [36]While they were still talking about this, Jesus himself stood among them and said to them, "Peace be with you." . . . [52]Then they worshiped him and returned to Jerusalem with great joy. [53]And they stayed continually at the temple, praising God.

3) Praise God for Christ's Worthiness

Rev 5 [12]In a loud voice they sang: "Worthy is the Lamb, who was slain, to receive power and wealth and wisdom and strength and honor and glory and praise!"

4) Praise God for His Awesomeness

Ps 96 [4]For great is the LORD and most worthy of praise; he is to be feared above all gods.

5) Praise God for His Blessing

Deut 10 [21]He is your praise; he is your God, who performed for you those great and awesome wonders you saw with your own eyes. [22]Your forefathers who went down into Egypt were seventy in all, and now the LORD your God has made you as numerous as the stars in the sky.

6) Praise God for His Compassion

Isa 49 [13]Shout for joy, O heavens; rejoice, O earth; burst into song, O mountains! For the LORD comforts his people and will have compassion on his afflicted ones.

Isa 52 [9]Burst into songs of joy together, you ruins of Jerusalem, for the LORD has comforted his people, he has redeemed Jerusalem.

2 Cor 1 [3]Praise be to the God and Father of our Lord Jesus Christ, the Father of compassion and the God of all comfort, [4]who comforts us in all our troubles, so that we can comfort those in any trouble with the comfort we ourselves have received from God.

7) Praise God for His Consolation

Ps 42 [5]Why are you downcast, O my soul? Why so disturbed within me? Put your hope in God, for I will yet praise him, my Savior and [6]my God.

My soul is downcast within me; therefore I will remember you from the land of the Jordan, the heights of Hermon—from Mount Mizar. . . .

[8]By day the LORD directs his love, at night his song is with me—a prayer to the God of my life.

Isa 12 [1]In that day you will say: "I will praise you, O LORD. Although you were angry with me, your anger has turned away and you have comforted me."

8) Praise God for His Counsel

Ps 16 [7]I will praise the LORD, who counsels me; even at night my heart instructs me.

9) Praise God for His Deliverance from Enemies

Gen 14 [20]"And blessed be God Most High, who delivered your enemies into your hand." Then Abram gave him a tenth of everything.

Exod 18 [10]He said, "Praise be to the LORD, who rescued you from the hand of the Egyptians and of Pharaoh, and who rescued the people from the hand of the Egyptians."

Judg 16 [24]When the people saw him, they praised their god, saying, "Our god has delivered our enemy into our hands, the one who laid waste our land and multiplied our slain."

Ps 9 [1]I will praise you, O LORD, with all my heart; I will tell of all your wonders. [2]I will be glad and rejoice in you; I will sing praise to your name, O Most High.

[3]My enemies turn back; they stumble and perish before you.

Ps 18 [46]The LORD lives! Praise be to my Rock! Exalted be God my Savior! [47]He is the God who avenges me, who subdues nations under me, [48]who saves me from my enemies. You exalted me above my foes; from violent men you rescued me. [49]Therefore I will praise you among the nations, O LORD; I will sing praises to your name.

Ps 30 [1]I will exalt you, O LORD, for you lifted me out of the depths and did not let my enemies gloat over me.

Ps 41 [11]I know that you are pleased with me, for my enemy does not triumph over me. [12]In my integrity you uphold me and set me in your presence forever.

[13]Praise be to the LORD, the God of Israel, from everlasting to everlasting. Amen and Amen.

Ps 43 [1]Vindicate me, O God, and plead my cause against an ungodly nation; rescue me from deceitful and wicked men. . . . [4]Then will I go to the altar of God, to God, my joy and my delight. I will praise you with the harp, O God, my God.

Ps 44 [7]but you give us victory over our enemies, you put our adversaries to shame. [8]In God we make our boast all day long, and we will praise your name forever.

Ps 57 [3]He sends from heaven and saves me, rebuking those who hotly pursue me; God sends his love and his faithfulness.

[4]I am in the midst of lions; I lie among ravenous beasts—men whose teeth are spears and arrows, whose tongues are sharp swords. [5]Be exalted, O God, above the heavens; let your glory be over all the earth.

[6]They spread a net for my feet—I was bowed down in distress. They dug a pit in my path—but they have fallen into it themselves.

[7]My heart is steadfast, O God, my heart is steadfast; I will sing and make music. [8]Awake, my soul! Awake, harp and lyre! I will awaken the dawn.

Ps 71 [10]For my enemies speak against me; those who wait to kill me conspire together. [11]They say, "God has forsaken him; pursue him and seize him, for no one will rescue him." . . .

[14]But as for me, I will always have hope; I will praise you more and more. . . .

[22]I will praise you with the harp for your faithfulness, O my God; I will sing praise to you with the lyre, O Holy One of Israel. [23]My lips will shout for joy when I sing praise to you—I, whom you have redeemed. [24]My tongue will tell of your righteous acts all day long, for those who wanted to harm me have been put to shame and confusion.

Ps 124 [1]If the LORD had not been on our side—let Israel say—[2]if the LORD had not been on our side when men attacked us, [3]when their anger flared against us, they would have swallowed us alive; [4]the flood would have engulfed us, the torrent would have swept over us, [5]the raging waters would have swept us away. [6]Praise be to the LORD, who has not let us be torn by their teeth. [7]We have escaped like a bird out of the fowler's snare; the snare has been broken, and we have escaped. [8]Our help is in the name of the LORD, the Maker of heaven and earth.

Rev 19 [1]After this I heard what sounded like the roar of a great multitude in heaven shouting: "Hallelujah! Salvation and glory and power belong to our God, [2]for true and just are his judgments. He has condemned the great prostitute who corrupted the earth by her adulteries. He has avenged on her the blood of his servants."

[3]And again they shouted: "Hallelujah! The smoke from her goes up for ever and ever."

10) Praise God for His Deliverance in Times of Trouble

Ps 22 [23]You who fear the LORD, praise him! All you descendants of Jacob, honor him! Revere him, all you descendants of Israel! [24]For he has not despised or disdained the suffering of the afflicted one; he has not hidden his face from him but has listened to his cry for help.

Ps 30 [11]You turned my wailing into dancing; you removed my sackcloth and clothed me with joy, [12]that my heart may sing to you and not be silent. O LORD my God, I will give you thanks forever.

Ps 34 [1]I will extol the LORD at all times; his praise will always be on my lips. . . .

[4]I sought the LORD, and he answered me; he delivered me from all my fears.

Ps 40 [1]I waited patiently for the LORD; he turned to me and heard my cry. [2]He lifted me out of the slimy pit, out of the mud and mire; he set my feet on a rock and gave me a firm place to stand. [3]He put a new song in my mouth, a hymn of praise to our God. Many will see and fear and put their trust in the LORD.

Ps 54 [6]I will sacrifice a freewill offering to you; I will praise your name, O LORD, for it is good. [7]For he has delivered me from all my troubles, and my eyes have looked in triumph on my foes.

Ps 68 [19]Praise be to the Lord, to God our Savior, who daily bears our burdens.

Jer 20 [13]Sing to the LORD! Give praise to the LORD! He rescues the life of the needy from the hands of the wicked.

11) Praise God for His Forgiveness of Sins

Ps 103 [1]Praise the LORD, O my soul; all my inmost being, praise his holy name. [2]Praise the LORD, O my soul, and forget not all his benefits—[3]who forgives all your sins and heals all your diseases. . . .

Hos 14 [2]Take words with you and return to the LORD. Say to him: "Forgive all our sins and receive us graciously, that we may offer the fruit of our lips."

12) Praise God for His Glory

Ps 72 [18]Praise be to the LORD God, the God of Israel, who alone does marvelous deeds. [19]Praise be to his glorious name forever; may the whole earth be filled with his glory. Amen and Amen.

Ps 138 [5]May they sing of the ways of the LORD, for the glory of the LORD is great.

Ezek 3 [12]Then the Spirit lifted me up, and I heard behind me a loud rumbling sound—May the glory of the LORD be praised in his dwelling place!

13) Praise God for His Goodness

Ps 100 [4]Enter his gates with thanksgiving and his courts with praise; give thanks to him and praise his name. [5]For the LORD is good and his love endures forever; his faithfulness continues through all generations.

Ps 106 [1]Praise the LORD.

Give thanks to the LORD, for he is good; his love endures forever.

14) Praise God for His Grace through Christ

Eph 1 [3]Praise be to the God and Father of our Lord Jesus Christ, who has blessed us in the heavenly realms with every spiritual blessing in Christ. [4]For he chose us in him before the creation of the world to be holy and blameless in his sight. In love [5]he predestined us to be adopted as his sons through Jesus Christ, in accordance with his pleasure and will—[6]to the praise of his glorious grace, which he has freely given us in the One he loves.

1 Pet 1 [3]Praise be to the God and Father of our Lord Jesus Christ! In his great mercy he has given us new birth into a living hope through the resurrection of Jesus Christ from the dead, [4]and into an inheritance that can never perish, spoil or fade—kept in heaven for you, [5]who through faith are shielded by God's power until the coming of the salvation that is ready to be revealed in the last time. [6]In this you greatly rejoice, though now for a little while you may have had to suffer grief in all kinds of trials.

15) Praise God for His Greatness and Majesty

Deut 32 [3]I will proclaim the name of the LORD. Oh, praise the greatness of our God!

1 Chron 16 [25]For great is the LORD and most worthy of praise; he is to be feared above all gods.

Neh 8 [6]Ezra praised the LORD, the great God; and all the people lifted their hands and responded, "Amen! Amen!" Then they bowed down and worshiped the LORD with their faces to the ground.

Ps 95 [2]Let us come before him with thanksgiving and extol him with music and song.

[3]For the LORD is the great God, the great King above all gods.

Ps 96 [4]For great is the LORD and most worthy of praise; he is to be feared above all gods. . . . [6]Splendor and majesty are before him; strength and glory are in his sanctuary.

Ps 104 [1]Praise the LORD, O my soul.

O LORD my God, you are very great; you are clothed with splendor and majesty.

Ps 145 [3]Great is the LORD and most worthy of praise; his greatness no one can fathom.

Ps 150 [2]Praise him for his acts of power; praise him for his surpassing greatness.

Isa 24 [14]They raise their voices, they shout for joy; from the west they acclaim the LORD's majesty.

Matt 9 [4]Knowing their thoughts, Jesus said, "Why do you entertain evil thoughts in your hearts? . . . [6]But so that you may know that the Son of Man has authority on earth to forgive sins. . . ." Then he said to the paralytic, "Get up, take your mat and go home." [7]And the man got up and went home. [8]When the crowd saw this, they were filled with awe; and they praised God, who had given such authority to men.

16) Praise God for His Guidance

Gen 24 [48]". . . and I bowed down and worshiped the LORD. I praised the LORD, the God of my master Abraham, who had led me on the right road to get the granddaughter of my master's brother for his son."

17) Praise God for His Justice

Ps 67 [3]May the peoples praise you, O God; may all the peoples praise you. [4]May the nations be glad and sing for joy, for you rule the peoples justly and guide the nations of the earth.

[5]May the peoples praise you, O God; may all the peoples praise you.

Ps 98 [8]Let the rivers clap their hands, let the mountains sing together for joy; [9]let them sing before the LORD, for he comes to judge the earth. He will judge the world in righteousness and the peoples with equity.

Ps 101 [1]I will sing of your love and justice; to you, O LORD, I will sing praise.

Dan 4 [37]Now I, Nebuchadnezzar, praise and exalt and glorify the King of heaven, because everything he does is right and all his ways are just. And those who walk in pride he is able to humble.

18) Praise God for His Love and Faithfulness

Ps 31 [21]Praise be to the LORD, for he showed his wonderful love to me when I was in a besieged city.

Ps 57 [9]I will praise you, O Lord, among the nations; I will sing of you among the peoples. [10]For great is your love, reaching to the heavens; your faithfulness reaches to the skies.

Ps 59 [16]But I will sing of your strength, in the morning I will sing of your love; for you are my fortress, my refuge in times of trouble.

[17]O my Strength, I sing praise to you; you, O God, are my fortress, my loving God.

Ps 63 [3]Because your love is better than life, my lips will glorify you. [4]I will praise you as long as I live, and in your name I will lift up my hands.

Ps 86 [12]I will praise you, O Lord my God, with all my heart; I will glorify your name forever. [13]For great is your love toward me; you have delivered me from the depths of the grave.

Ps 89 [1]I will sing of the LORD's great love forever; with my mouth I will make your faithfulness known through all generations. [2]I will declare that your love stands firm forever, that you established your faithfulness in heaven itself.

Ps 100 [4]Enter his gates with thanksgiving and his courts with praise; give thanks to him and praise his name. [5]For the LORD is good and his love endures forever; his faithfulness continues through all generations.

Ps 101 [1]I will sing of your love and justice; to you, O LORD, I will sing praise.

Ps 108 [3]I will praise you, O LORD, among the nations; I will sing of you among the peoples. [4]For great is your love, higher than the heavens; your faithfulness reaches to the skies.

Ps 117 [1]Praise the LORD, all you nations; extol him, all you peoples. [2]For great is his love toward us, and the faithfulness of the LORD endures forever.

Praise the LORD.

Ps 138 [2]I will bow down toward your holy temple and will praise your name for your love and your faithfulness, for you have exalted above all things your name and your word.

19) Praise God for His Name

2 Sam 22 [50]"Therefore I will praise you, O LORD, among the nations; I will sing praises to your name."

1 Chron 29 [13]"Now, our God, we give you thanks, and praise your glorious name."

Ps 18 [49]Therefore I will praise you among the nations, O LORD; I will sing praises to your name.

Ps 30 [4]Sing to the LORD, you saints of his; praise his holy name.

Ps 48 [10]Like your name, O God, your praise reaches to the ends of the earth; your right hand is filled with righteousness.

Ps 68 [4]Sing to God, sing praise to his name, extol him who rides on the clouds—his name is the LORD—and rejoice before him.

Ps 72 [19]Praise be to his glorious name forever; may the whole earth be filled with his glory. Amen and Amen.

Ps 74 [21]Do not let the oppressed retreat in disgrace; may the poor and needy praise your name.

Ps 97 [12]Rejoice in the LORD, you who are righteous, and praise his holy name.

Ps 99 [3]Let them praise your great and awesome name—he is holy.

Ps 100 [4]Enter his gates with thanksgiving and his courts with praise; give thanks to him and praise his name.

Ps 113 [1]Praise the LORD.

Praise, O servants of the LORD, praise the name of the LORD. [2]Let the name of the LORD be praised, both now and forevermore. [3]From the rising of the sun to the place where it sets, the name of the LORD is to be praised.

Ps 135 [3]Praise the LORD, for the LORD is good; sing praise to his name, for that is pleasant.

Ps 145 [1]I will exalt you, my God the King; I will praise your name for ever and ever. [2]Every day I will praise you and extol your name for ever and ever.

Ps 148 [13]Let them praise the name of the LORD, for his name alone is exalted; his splendor is above the earth and the heavens.

Isa 25 [1]O LORD, you are my God; I will exalt you and praise your name, for in perfect faithfulness you have done marvelous things, things planned long ago.

20) Praise God for His Promise-keeping

1 Kings 8 [15]Then he said: "Praise be to the LORD, the God of Israel, who with his own hand has fulfilled what he promised with his own mouth to my father David. For he said, [16]'Since the day I brought my people Israel out of Egypt, I have not chosen a city in any tribe of Israel to have a temple built for my Name to be there, but I have chosen David to rule my people Israel.' . . .

[20]"The LORD has kept the promise he made: I have succeeded David my father and now I sit on the throne of Israel, just as the LORD promised, and I have built the temple for the Name of the LORD, the God of Israel."

1 Kings 8 [56]"Praise be to the LORD, who has given rest to his people Israel just as he promised. Not one word has failed of all the good promises he gave through his servant Moses."

21) Praise God for His Provision of Food

Deut 8 [10]When you have eaten and are satisfied, praise the LORD your God for the good land he has given you.

Ps 22 [26]The poor will eat and be satisfied; they who seek the LORD will praise him—may your hearts live forever!

Isa 62 [8]The LORD has sworn by his right hand and by his mighty arm: "Never again will I give your grain as food for your enemies, and never again will foreigners drink the new wine for which you have toiled; [9]but those who harvest it will eat it and praise the LORD, and those who gather the grapes will drink it in the courts of my sanctuary."

Joel 2 [26]"You will have plenty to eat, until you are full, and you will praise the name of the LORD your God, who has worked wonders for you; never again will my people be shamed."

22) Praise God for His Redemption

Ps 71 [23]My lips will shout for joy when I sing praise to you—I, whom you have redeemed.

Isa 29 [19]Once more the humble will rejoice in the LORD; the needy will rejoice in the Holy One of Israel. [20]The ruthless will vanish, the mockers will disappear, and all who have an eye for evil will be cut down—[21]those who with a word make a man out to be guilty, who ensnare the defender in court and with false testimony deprive the innocent of justice.

Isa 35 [4]say to those with fearful hearts, "Be strong, do not fear; your God will come, he will come with vengeance; with divine retribution he will come to save you." . . . [6]Then will the lame leap like a deer, and the mute tongue shout for joy. Water will gush forth in the wilderness and streams in the desert. . . . [9]No lion will be there, nor will any ferocious beast get up on it; they will not be found there. But only the redeemed will walk there, [10]and the ransomed of the LORD will return. They will enter Zion with singing; everlasting joy will crown their heads. Gladness and joy will overtake them, and sorrow and sighing will flee away.

Isa 48 [20]Leave Babylon, flee from the Babylonians! Announce this with shouts of joy and proclaim it. Send it out to the ends of the earth; say, "The LORD has redeemed his servant Jacob."

Isa 51 [11]The ransomed of the LORD will return. They will enter Zion with singing; everlasting joy will crown their heads. Gladness and joy will overtake them, and sorrow and sighing will flee away.

23) Praise God for His Revealed Will

Ps 138 [4]May all the kings of the earth praise you, O LORD, when they hear the words of your mouth. [5]May they sing of the ways of the LORD, for the glory of the LORD is great.

Matt 11 [25]At that time Jesus said, "I praise you, Father, Lord of heaven and earth, because you have hidden these things from the wise and learned, and revealed them to little children. [26]Yes, Father, for this was your good pleasure."

24) Praise God for His Righteous Law

Ps 119 [164]Seven times a day I praise you for your righteous laws.

Ps 119 [171]May my lips overflow with praise, for you teach me your decrees. [172]May my tongue sing of your word, for all your commands are righteous.

25) Praise God for His Righteousness

Ps 7 [17]I will give thanks to the LORD because of his righteousness and will sing praise to the name of the LORD Most High.

Ps 51 [14]Save me from bloodguilt, O God, the God who saves me, and my tongue will sing of your righteousness. [15]O Lord, open my lips, and my mouth will declare your praise.

Dan 4 [37]Now I, Nebuchadnezzar, praise and exalt and glorify the King of heaven, because everything he does is right and all his ways are just. And those who walk in pride he is able to humble.

26) Praise God for His Salvation

Ps 18 [46]The LORD lives! Praise be to my Rock! Exalted be God my Savior!

Isa 35 [10]and the ransomed of the LORD will return. They will enter Zion with singing; everlasting joy will crown their heads. Gladness and joy will overtake them, and sorrow and sighing will flee away.

Isa 61 [10]I delight greatly in the LORD; my soul rejoices in my God. For he has clothed me with garments of salvation and arrayed me in a robe of righteousness, as a bridegroom adorns his head like a priest, and as a bride adorns herself with her jewels.

Acts 11 [18]When they heard this, they had no further objections and praised God, saying, "So then, God has granted even the Gentiles repentance unto life."

1 Pet 2 [9]But you are a chosen people, a royal priesthood, a holy nation, a people belonging to God, that you may declare the praises of him who called you out of darkness into his wonderful light.

27) Praise God for His Strength

Ps 21 [13]Be exalted, O LORD, in your strength; we will sing and praise your might.

Ps 28 [7]The LORD is my strength and my shield; my heart trusts in him, and I am helped. My heart leaps for joy and I will give thanks to him in song.

Ps 59 [16]But I will sing of your strength, in the morning I will sing of your love; for you are my fortress, my refuge in times of trouble.

[17]O my Strength, I sing praise to you; you, O God, are my fortress, my loving God.

Ps 68 [35]You are awesome, O God, in your sanctuary; the God of Israel gives power and strength to his people.

Praise be to God!

Ps 81 [1]Sing for joy to God our strength; shout aloud to the God of Jacob!

Ps 144 [1]Praise be to the LORD my Rock, who trains my hands for war, my fingers for battle. [2]He is my loving God and my fortress, my stronghold and my deliverer, my shield, in whom I take refuge, who subdues peoples under me.

28) Praise God for His Sustenance

Ps 66 [8]Praise our God, O peoples, let the sound of his praise be heard; [9]he has preserved our lives and kept our feet from slipping.

Ps 68 [19]Praise be to the Lord, to God our Savior, who daily bears our burdens.

Ps 71 [6]From birth I have relied on you; you brought me forth from my mother's womb. I will ever praise you. [7]I have become like a portent to many, but you are my strong refuge. [8]My mouth is filled with your praise, declaring your splendor all day long.

29) Praise God for His Wisdom

Dan 2 [19]During the night the mystery was revealed to Daniel in a vision. Then Daniel praised the God of heaven [20]and said: "Praise be to the name of God for ever and ever; wisdom and power are his. [21]He changes times and seasons; he sets up kings and deposes them. He gives wisdom to the wise and knowledge to the discerning. [22]He reveals deep and hidden things; he knows what lies in darkness, and light dwells with him. [23]I thank and praise you, O God of my fathers: You have given me wisdom and power, you have made known to me what we asked of you, you have made known to us the dream of the king."

Luke 4 [14]Jesus returned to Galilee in the power of the Spirit, and news about him spread through the whole countryside. [15]He taught in their synagogues, and everyone praised him.

30) Praise God for His Word

Ps 56 [4]In God, whose word I praise, in God I trust; I will not be afraid. What can mortal man do to me? . . . [10]In God, whose word I praise, in the LORD, whose word I praise . . .

31) Praise God for His Works

Ps 9 [11]Sing praises to the LORD, enthroned in Zion; proclaim among the nations what he has done.
Ps 26 [6]I wash my hands in innocence, and go about your altar, O LORD, [7]proclaiming aloud your praise and telling of all your wonderful deeds.
Ps 52 [9]I will praise you forever for what you have done; in your name I will hope, for your name is good. I will praise you in the presence of your saints.
Ps 72 [18]Praise be to the LORD God, the God of Israel, who alone does marvelous deeds.
Ps 78 [4]We will not hide them from their children; we will tell the next generation the praiseworthy deeds of the LORD, his power, and the wonders he has done.
Ps 92 [4]For you make me glad by your deeds, O LORD; I sing for joy at the works of your hands. [5]How great are your works, O LORD, how profound your thoughts!
Ps 103 [2]Praise the LORD, O my soul, and forget not all his benefits—[3]who forgives all your sins and heals all your diseases, [4]who redeems your life from the pit and crowns you with love and compassion, [5]who satisfies your desires with good things so that your youth is renewed like the eagle's.
Ps 105 [2]Sing to him, sing praise to him; tell of all his wonderful acts.
Ps 107 [22]Let them sacrifice thank offerings and tell of his works with songs of joy.
Ps 139 [14]I praise you because I am fearfully and wonderfully made; your works are wonderful, I know that full well.
Ps 145 [4]One generation will commend your works to another; they will tell of your mighty acts. [5]They will speak of the glorious splendor of your majesty, and I will meditate on your wonderful works. [6]They will tell of the power of your awesome works, and I will proclaim your great deeds. [7]They will celebrate your abundant goodness and joyfully sing of your righteousness.
Ps 150 [2]Praise him for his acts of power; praise him for his surpassing greatness.
Isa 12 [5]"Sing to the LORD, for he has done glorious things; let this be known to all the world."
Isa 63 [7]I will tell of the kindnesses of the LORD, the deeds for which he is to be praised, according to all the LORD has done for us—yes, the many good things he has done for the house of Israel, according to his compassion and many kindnesses.
Matt 15 [30]Great crowds came to him, bringing the lame, the blind, the crippled, the mute and many others, and laid them at his feet; and he healed them. [31]The people were amazed when they saw the mute speaking, the crippled made well, the lame walking and the blind seeing. And they praised the God of Israel.
Mark 2 [8]Immediately Jesus knew in his spirit that this was what they were thinking in their hearts, and he said to them, "Why are you thinking these things? . . . [11]I tell you, get up, take your mat and go home." [12]He got up, took his mat and walked out in full view of them all. This amazed everyone and they praised God, saying, "We have never seen anything like this!"
Luke 7 [14]Then he went up and touched the coffin, and those carrying it stood still. He said, "Young man, I say to you, get up!" [15]The dead man sat up and began to talk, and Jesus gave him back to his mother.

[16]They were all filled with awe and praised God. "A great prophet has appeared among us," they said. "God has come to help his people."
Luke 18 [42]Jesus said to him, "Receive your sight; your faith has healed you." [43]Immediately he received his sight and followed Jesus, praising God. When all the people saw it, they also praised God.
Acts 3 [2]Now a man crippled from birth was being carried to the temple gate called Beautiful, where he was put every day to beg from those going into the temple courts. [3]When he saw Peter and John about to enter, he asked them for money. . . .

[6]Then Peter said, "Silver or gold I do not have, but what I have I give you. In the name of Jesus Christ of Nazareth, walk." . . . [8]He jumped to his feet and began to walk. Then he went with them into the temple courts, walking and jumping, and praising God. [9]When all the people saw him walking and praising God . . .

32) Praise God for His Worthiness

2 Sam 22 [4]"I call to the LORD, who is worthy of praise, and I am saved from my enemies."
1 Chron 16 [25]For great is the LORD and most worthy of praise; he is to be feared above all gods.
Ps 18 [3]I call to the LORD, who is worthy of praise, and I am saved from my enemies.
Ps 48 [1]Great is the LORD, and most worthy of praise, in the city of our God, his holy mountain.
Ps 96 [4]For great is the LORD and most worthy of praise; he is to be feared above all gods.
Ps 145 [3]Great is the LORD and most worthy of praise; his greatness no one can fathom.

33) Praise God for the Saints

Matt 5 [16]"In the same way, let your light shine before men, that they may see your good deeds and praise your Father in heaven."
Rom 15 [7]Accept one another, then, just as Christ accepted you, in order to bring praise to God.
2 Cor 9 [13]Because of the service by which you have proved yourselves, men will praise God for the obedience that accompanies your confession of the gospel of Christ, and for your generosity in sharing with them and with everyone else.
Gal 1 [22]I was personally unknown to the churches of Judea that are in Christ. [23]They only heard the report: "The man who formerly persecuted us is now preaching the faith he once tried to destroy." [24]And they praised God because of me.
Eph 1 [11]In him we were also chosen, having been predestined according to the plan of him who works out everything in conformity with the purpose of his will, [12]in order that we, who were the first to hope in Christ, might be for the praise of his glory. [13]And you also were included in Christ when you heard the word of truth, the gospel of your salvation. Having believed, you were marked in him with a seal, the promised Holy Spirit, [14]who is a deposit guaranteeing our inheritance until the redemption of those who are God's possession—to the praise of his glory.

34) Praise God That You Bear His Name

1 Pet 4 [16]However, if you suffer as a Christian, do not be ashamed, but praise God that you bear that name.

3. The Manner of Praising God

a) Praise God at All Times

Ps 34 [1]I will extol the LORD at all times; his praise will always be on my lips.
Ps 35 [28]My tongue will speak of your righteousness and of your praises all day long.
Ps 52 [9]I will praise you forever for what you have done; in your name I will hope, for your name is good. I will praise you in the presence of your saints.
Ps 63 [4]I will praise you as long as I live, and in your name I will lift up my hands.
Ps 71 [8]My mouth is filled with your praise, declaring your splendor all day long.
Ps 71 [14]But as for me, I will always have hope; I will praise you more and more.
Ps 75 [9]As for me, I will declare this forever; I will sing praise to the God of Jacob.
Ps 79 [13]Then we your people, the sheep of your pasture, will praise you forever; from generation to generation we will recount your praise.
Ps 84 [4]Blessed are those who dwell in your house; they are ever praising you.
Ps 104 [33]I will sing to the LORD all my life; I will sing praise to my God as long as I live.
Ps 119 [164]Seven times a day I praise you for your righteous laws.

Ps 145 [1]I will exalt you, my God the King; I will praise your name for ever and ever. [2]Every day I will praise you and extol your name for ever and ever.
Ps 146 [2]I will praise the LORD all my life; I will sing praise to my God as long as I live.
Isa 38 [20]The LORD will save me, and we will sing with stringed instruments all the days of our lives in the temple of the LORD.

b) Praise God Gloriously

Ps 66 [2]Sing the glory of his name; make his praise glorious!

c) Praise God through Christ

Phil 1 [9]And this is my prayer: that your love may abound more and more in knowledge and depth of insight, [10]so that you may be able to discern what is best and may be pure and blameless until the day of Christ, [11]filled with the fruit of righteousness that comes through Jesus Christ—to the glory and praise of God.
Heb 13 [15]Through Jesus, therefore, let us continually offer to God a sacrifice of praise—the fruit of lips that confess his name.

d) Praise God with Joy

2 Chron 29 [30]King Hezekiah and his officials ordered the Levites to praise the LORD with the words of David and of Asaph the seer. So they sang praises with gladness and bowed their heads and worshiped.
Ps 33 [1]Sing joyfully to the LORD, you righteous; it is fitting for the upright to praise him.
Ps 71 [23]My lips will shout for joy when I sing praise to you—I, whom you have redeemed.
Ps 98 [4]Shout for joy to the LORD, all the earth, burst into jubilant song with music. . . .

e) Praise God with a Sincere Heart

Ps 86 [12]I will praise you, O Lord my God, with all my heart; I will glorify your name forever.
Ps 103 [1]Praise the LORD, O my soul; all my inmost being, praise his holy name.
Ps 111 [1]Praise the LORD.
I will extol the LORD with all my heart in the council of the upright and in the assembly.
Ps 138 [1]I will praise you, O LORD, with all my heart; before the "gods" I will sing your praise.

f) Praise God with Supreme Satisfaction

Ps 63 [5]My soul will be satisfied as with the richest of foods; with singing lips my mouth will praise you.

g) Praise God with Thanksgiving

Ezra 3 [11]With praise and thanksgiving they sang to the LORD: "He is good; his love to Israel endures forever." And all the people gave a great shout of praise to the LORD, because the foundation of the house of the LORD was laid.
Neh 12 [24]And the leaders of the Levites were Hashabiah, Sherebiah, Jeshua son of Kadmiel, and their associates, who stood opposite them to give praise and thanksgiving, one section responding to the other, as prescribed by David the man of God.
Ps 69 [30]I will praise God's name in song and glorify him with thanksgiving.
Ps 147 [7]Sing to the LORD with thanksgiving; make music to our God on the harp. [8]He covers the sky with clouds; he supplies the earth with rain and makes grass grow on the hills. [9]He provides food for the cattle and for the young ravens when they call.

h) Praise God with Understanding

1 Cor 14 [15]So what shall I do? I will pray with my spirit, but I will also pray with my mind; I will sing with my spirit, but I will also sing with my mind.

i) Praise God with an Upright Heart

Ps 64 [10]Let the righteous rejoice in the LORD and take refuge in him; let all the upright in heart praise him!
Ps 119 [7]I will praise you with an upright heart as I learn your righteous laws.

j) Praise God with Your Lips

Ps 34 [1]I will extol the LORD at all times; his praise will always be on my lips.
Ps 63 [3]Because your love is better than life, my lips will glorify you. . . . [5]My soul will be satisfied as with the richest of foods; with singing lips my mouth will praise you.
Ps 71 [23]My lips will shout for joy when I sing praise to you—I, whom you have redeemed.
Ps 119 [171]May my lips overflow with praise, for you teach me your decrees.
Isa 57 [18]"I have seen his ways, but I will heal him; I will guide him and restore comfort to him, [19]creating praise on the lips of the mourners in Israel. Peace, peace, to those far and near," says the LORD. "And I will heal them."

k) Praise God with Your Mouth

Ps 40 [3]He put a new song in my mouth, a hymn of praise to our God. Many will see and fear and put their trust in the LORD.
Ps 51 [15]O Lord, open my lips, and my mouth will declare your praise.
Ps 71 [8]My mouth is filled with your praise, declaring your splendor all day long. . . .
[14]But as for me, I will always have hope; I will praise you more and more.
Ps 109 [30]With my mouth I will greatly extol the LORD; in the great throng I will praise him. [31]For he stands at the right hand of the needy one, to save his life from those who condemn him.
Ps 119 [108]Accept, O LORD, the willing praise of my mouth, and teach me your laws.
Ps 145 [21]My mouth will speak in praise of the LORD. Let every creature praise his holy name for ever and ever.
Ps 149 [6]May the praise of God be in their mouths and a double-edged sword in their hands. . . .

l) Praise God with Your Tongue

Ps 35 [28]My tongue will speak of your righteousness and of your praises all day long.
Ps 66 [17]I cried out to him with my mouth; his praise was on my tongue.
Ps 71 [24]My tongue will tell of your righteous acts all day long, for those who wanted to harm me have been put to shame and confusion.

4. Participants in Praising God

a) All the Earth Praises God

Ps 66 [4]"All the earth bows down to you; they sing praise to you, they sing praise to your name."
Ps 69 [34]Let heaven and earth praise him, the seas and all that move in them. . . .
Hab 3 [3]God came from Teman, the Holy One from Mount Paran.
His glory covered the heavens and his praise filled the earth.

b) All Human Authority Praises God

Ps 138 [4]May all the kings of the earth praise you, O LORD, when they hear the words of your mouth. [5]May they sing of the ways of the LORD, for the glory of the LORD is great.
Ps 148 [7]Praise the LORD from the earth, you great sea creatures and all ocean depths, . . . [11]kings of the earth and all nations, you princes and all rulers on earth. . . .
[13]Let them praise the name of the LORD, for his name alone is exalted; his splendor is above the earth and the heavens.

c) All Nations Praise God

Ps 45 [17]I will perpetuate your memory through all generations; therefore the nations will praise you for ever and ever.
Ps 67 [3]May the peoples praise you, O God; may all the peoples praise you. [4]May the nations be glad and sing for joy, for you rule the peoples justly and guide the nations of the earth.
[5]May the peoples praise you, O God; may all the peoples praise you.
Ps 68 [32]Sing to God, O kingdoms of the earth, sing praise to the Lord. . . .
Ps 99 [2]Great is the LORD in Zion; he is exalted over all the

nations. [3]Let them praise your great and awesome name—he is holy.

Ps 102 [21]So the name of the LORD will be declared in Zion and his praise in Jerusalem [22]when the peoples and the kingdoms assemble to worship the LORD.

Ps 117 [1]Praise the LORD, all you nations; extol him, all you peoples.

Ps 135 [19]O house of Israel, praise the LORD; O house of Aaron, praise the LORD; [20]O house of Levi, praise the LORD; you who fear him, praise the LORD. [21]Praise be to the LORD from Zion, to him who dwells in Jerusalem.

Praise the LORD.

Ps 138 [4]May all the kings of the earth praise you, O LORD, when they hear the words of your mouth.

Ps 148 [7]Praise the LORD from the earth, you great sea creatures and all ocean depths, . . . [11]kings of the earth and all nations, you princes and all rulers on earth. . . .

Isa 61 [11]For as the soil makes the sprout come up and a garden causes seeds to grow, so the Sovereign LORD will make righteousness and praise spring up before all nations.

Rom 15 [11]And again, "Praise the Lord, all you Gentiles, and sing praises to him, all you peoples."

d) All of Creation Praises God

Ps 98 [1]Sing to the LORD a new song, for he has done marvelous things; his right hand and his holy arm have worked salvation for him. [2]The LORD has made his salvation known and revealed his righteousness to the nations. [3]He has remembered his love and his faithfulness to the house of Israel; all the ends of the earth have seen the salvation of our God.

[4]Shout for joy to the LORD, all the earth, burst into jubilant song with music; [5]make music to the LORD with the harp, with the harp and the sound of singing, [6]with trumpets and the blast of the ram's horn—shout for joy before the LORD, the King.

[7]Let the sea resound, and everything in it, the world, and all who live in it. [8]Let the rivers clap their hands, let the mountains sing together for joy; [9]let them sing before the LORD, for he comes to judge the earth. He will judge the world in righteousness and the peoples with equity.

Ps 103 [22]Praise the LORD, all his works everywhere in his dominion.

Praise the LORD, O my soul.

Ps 145 [10]All you have made will praise you, O LORD; your saints will extol you.

Ps 148 [1]Praise the LORD.

Praise the LORD from the heavens, praise him in the heights above. [2]Praise him, all his angels, praise him, all his heavenly hosts. [3]Praise him, sun and moon, praise him, all you shining stars. [4]Praise him, you highest heavens and you waters above the skies. [5]Let them praise the name of the LORD, for he commanded and they were created. [6]He set them in place for ever and ever; he gave a decree that will never pass away.

[7]Praise the LORD from the earth, you great sea creatures and all ocean depths, [8]lightning and hail, snow and clouds, stormy winds that do his bidding, [9]you mountains and all hills, fruit trees and all cedars, [10]wild animals and all cattle, small creatures and flying birds, . . . [12]young men and maidens, old men and children.

Isa 42 [10]Sing to the LORD a new song, his praise from the ends of the earth, you who go down to the sea, and all that is in it, you islands, and all who live in them. [11]Let the desert and its towns raise their voices; let the settlements where Kedar lives rejoice. Let the people of Sela sing for joy; let them shout from the mountaintops. [12]Let them give glory to the LORD and proclaim his praise in the islands.

Isa 55 [12]"You will go out in joy and be led forth in peace; the mountains and hills will burst into song before you, and all the trees of the field will clap their hands."

e) Angels Praise God

Job 38 [4]"Where were you when I laid the earth's foundation? Tell me, if you understand. . . . [6]On what were its footings set, or who laid its cornerstone—[7]while the morning stars sang together and all the angels shouted for joy?"

Ps 103 [20]Praise the LORD, you his angels, you mighty ones who do his bidding, who obey his word.

Ps 148 [2]Praise him, all his angels, praise him, all his heavenly hosts.

Rev 7 [11]All the angels were standing around the throne and around the elders and the four living creatures. They fell down on their faces before the throne and worshiped God, [12]saying: "Amen! Praise and glory and wisdom and thanks and honor and power and strength be to our God for ever and ever. Amen!"

f) Children Praise God

Ps 8 [2]From the lips of children and infants you have ordained praise because of your enemies, to silence the foe and the avenger.

Ps 148 [12]young men and maidens, old men and children.

[13]Let them praise the name of the LORD, for his name alone is exalted; his splendor is above the earth and the heavens.

Matt 21 [15]But when the chief priests and the teachers of the law saw the wonderful things he did and the children shouting in the temple area, "Hosanna to the Son of David," they were indignant.

[16]"Do you hear what these children are saying?" they asked him.

"Yes," replied Jesus, "have you never read, 'From the lips of children and infants you have ordained praise'?"

g) Every Living Creature Praises God

Ps 145 [21]My mouth will speak in praise of the LORD. Let every creature praise his holy name for ever and ever.

Ps 150 [6]Let everything that has breath praise the LORD.

Praise the LORD.

h) Future Generations Will Praise God

Ps 102 [18]Let this be written for a future generation, that a people not yet created may praise the LORD. . . .

i) The Heavenly Hosts Praise God

Ps 103 [21]Praise the LORD, all his heavenly hosts, you his servants who do his will.

Ps 148 [2]Praise him, all his angels, praise him, all his heavenly hosts.

Luke 2 [13]Suddenly a great company of the heavenly host appeared with the angel, praising God and saying, [14]"Glory to God in the highest, and on earth peace to men on whom his favor rests."

j) The Heavens Praise God

Ps 89 [5]The heavens praise your wonders, O LORD, your faithfulness too, in the assembly of the holy ones.

k) Israel Praises God

Ps 135 [19]O house of Israel, praise the LORD; O house of Aaron, praise the LORD; [20]O house of Levi, praise the LORD; you who fear him, praise the LORD. [21]Praise be to the LORD from Zion, to him who dwells in Jerusalem.

Praise the LORD.

l) The Living Praise God

Ps 115 [17]It is not the dead who praise the LORD, those who go down to silence; [18]it is we who extol the LORD, both now and forevermore.

Praise the LORD.

Isa 38 [19]The living, the living—they praise you, as I am doing today; fathers tell their children about your faithfulness.

m) The Poor and Needy Praise God

Ps 74 [21]Do not let the oppressed retreat in disgrace; may the poor and needy praise your name.

n) The Righteous Praise God

Ps 33 [1]Sing joyfully to the LORD, you righteous; it is fitting for the upright to praise him.

Ps 97 [12]Rejoice in the LORD, you who are righteous, and praise his holy name.

Ps 140 [13]Surely the righteous will praise your name and the upright will live before you.

o) The Saints Praise God

Ps 30 [4]Sing to the LORD, you saints of his; praise his holy name.

Ps 148 [14]He has raised up for his people a horn, the praise of all his saints, of Israel, the people close to his heart.

Praise the LORD.

Ps 149 [1]Praise the LORD.

Sing to the LORD a new song, his praise in the assembly of the saints. . . . [5]Let the saints rejoice in this honor and sing for joy on their beds.

p) Servants of the Lord Praise God

2 Chron 29 [4]He brought in the priests and the Levites, assembled them in the square on the east side . . . [11]"My sons, do not be negligent now, for the LORD has chosen you to stand before him and serve him, to minister before him and to burn incense." . . . [30]King Hezekiah and his officials ordered the Levites to praise the LORD with the words of David and of Asaph the seer. So they sang praises with gladness and bowed their heads and worshiped.

Ps 134 [1]Praise the LORD, all you servants of the LORD who minister by night in the house of the LORD. [2]Lift up your hands in the sanctuary and praise the LORD.

Ps 135 [1]Praise the LORD.

Praise the name of the LORD; praise him, you servants of the LORD, [2]you who minister in the house of the LORD, in the courts of the house of our God.

q) The Small and the Great Praise God

Rev 19 [5]Then a voice came from the throne, saying: "Praise our God, all you his servants, you who fear him, both small and great!"

r) Those Who Fear God Praise Him

Ps 22 [23]You who fear the LORD, praise him! All you descendants of Jacob, honor him! Revere him, all you descendants of Israel!

Ps 135 [20]O house of Levi, praise the LORD; you who fear him, praise the LORD.

s) Those Who Seek God Praise Him

Ps 22 [26]The poor will eat and be satisfied; they who seek the LORD will praise him—may your hearts live forever!

t) Young and Old Praise God

Ps 148 [7]Praise the LORD from the earth, you great sea creatures and all ocean depths, . . . [12]young men and maidens, old men and children.

5. Methods of Praising God

a) Praise God by Confessing Christ

Heb 13 [15]Through Jesus, therefore, let us continually offer to God a sacrifice of praise—the fruit of lips that confess his name.

b) Praise God in Public Worship

2 Chron 31 [2]Hezekiah assigned the priests and Levites to divisions—each of them according to their duties as priests or Levites—to offer burnt offerings and fellowship offerings, to minister, to give thanks and to sing praises at the gates of the LORD's dwelling.

Neh 9 [5]And the Levites—Jeshua, Kadmiel, Bani, Hashabneiah, Sherebiah, Hodiah, Shebaniah and Pethahiah—said: "Stand up and praise the LORD your God, who is from everlasting to everlasting."

"Blessed be your glorious name, and may it be exalted above all blessing and praise. [6]You alone are the LORD. You made the heavens, even the highest heavens, and all their starry host, the earth and all that is on it, the seas and all that is in them. You give life to everything, and the multitudes of heaven worship you."

Ps 9 [13]O LORD, see how my enemies persecute me! Have mercy and lift me up from the gates of death, [14]that I may declare your praises in the gates of the Daughter of Zion and there rejoice in your salvation.

Ps 22 [22]I will declare your name to my brothers; in the congregation I will praise you. . . .

[25]From you comes the theme of my praise in the great assembly; before those who fear you will I fulfill my vows.

Ps 26 [6]I wash my hands in innocence, and go about your altar, O LORD, [7]proclaiming aloud your praise and telling of all your wonderful deeds. [8]I love the house where you live, O LORD, the place where your glory dwells.

Ps 26 [12]My feet stand on level ground; in the great assembly I will praise the LORD.

Ps 27 [4]One thing I ask of the LORD, this is what I seek: that I may dwell in the house of the LORD all the days of my life, to gaze upon the beauty of the LORD and to seek him in his temple. . . . [6]Then my head will be exalted above the enemies who surround me; at his tabernacle will I sacrifice with shouts of joy; I will sing and make music to the LORD.

Ps 35 [18]I will give you thanks in the great assembly; among throngs of people I will praise you.

Ps 52 [9]I will praise you forever for what you have done; in your name I will hope, for your name is good. I will praise you in the presence of your saints.

Ps 65 [1]Praise awaits you, O God, in Zion; to you our vows will be fulfilled.

Ps 84 [4]Blessed are those who dwell in your house; they are ever praising you.

Ps 100 [4]Enter his gates with thanksgiving and his courts with praise; give thanks to him and praise his name.

Ps 102 [21]So the name of the LORD will be declared in Zion and his praise in Jerusalem [22]when the peoples and the kingdoms assemble to worship the LORD.

Ps 107 [32]Let them exalt him in the assembly of the people and praise him in the council of the elders.

Ps 109 [30]With my mouth I will greatly extol the LORD; in the great throng I will praise him.

Ps 134 [2]Lift up your hands in the sanctuary and praise the LORD.

Ps 135 [21]Praise be to the LORD from Zion, to him who dwells in Jerusalem.

Praise the LORD.

Ps 149 [1]Praise the LORD.

Sing to the LORD a new song, his praise in the assembly of the saints.

Ps 150 [1]Praise the LORD.

Praise God in his sanctuary; praise him in his mighty heavens.

Isa 64 [11]Our holy and glorious temple, where our fathers praised you, has been burned with fire, and all that we treasured lies in ruins.

Heb 2 [12]He says, "I will declare your name to my brothers; in the presence of the congregation I will sing your praises."

Rev 7 [11]All the angels were standing around the throne and around the elders and the four living creatures. They fell down on their faces before the throne and worshiped God, [12]saying: "Amen! Praise and glory and wisdom and thanks and honor and power and strength be to our God for ever and ever. Amen!"

c) Praise God with Dance

Exod 15 [19]When Pharaoh's horses, chariots and horsemen went into the sea, the LORD brought the waters of the sea back over them, but the Israelites walked through the sea on dry ground. [20]Then Miriam the prophetess, Aaron's sister, took a tambourine in her hand, and all the women followed her, with tambourines and dancing. [21]Miriam sang to them: "Sing to the LORD, for he is highly exalted. The horse and its rider he has hurled into the sea."

Ps 30 [11]You turned my wailing into dancing; you removed my sackcloth and clothed me with joy, [12]that my heart may sing to you and not be silent. O LORD my God, I will give you thanks forever.

Ps 149 [3]Let them praise his name with dancing and make music to him with tambourine and harp.

d) Praise God with a Musical Instrument

1 Chron 25 [3]As for Jeduthun, from his sons: Gedaliah, Zeri, Jeshaiah, Shimei, Hashabiah and Mattithiah, six in all, under

the supervision of their father Jeduthun, who prophesied, using the harp in thanking and praising the LORD.
2 Chron 7 [6]The priests took their positions, as did the Levites with the LORD's musical instruments, which King David had made for praising the LORD and which were used when he gave thanks, saying, "His love endures forever." Opposite the Levites, the priests blew their trumpets, and all the Israelites were standing.
Ps 33 [2]Praise the LORD with the harp; make music to him on the ten-stringed lyre.
Ps 57 [7]My heart is steadfast, O God, my heart is steadfast; I will sing and make music. [8]Awake, my soul! Awake, harp and lyre! I will awaken the dawn.
[9]I will praise you, O Lord, among the nations; I will sing of you among the peoples.
Ps 71 [22]I will praise you with the harp for your faithfulness, O my God; I will sing praise to you with the lyre, O Holy One of Israel.
Ps 92 [1]It is good to praise the LORD and make music to your name, O Most High, [2]to proclaim your love in the morning and your faithfulness at night, [3]to the music of the ten-stringed lyre and the melody of the harp.
Ps 108 [1]My heart is steadfast, O God; I will sing and make music with all my soul. [2]Awake, harp and lyre! I will awaken the dawn. [3]I will praise you, O LORD, among the nations; I will sing of you among the peoples.
Ps 144 [1]Praise be to the LORD my Rock, who trains my hands for war, my fingers for battle. . . .
[9]I will sing a new song to you, O God; on the ten-stringed lyre I will make music to you. . . .
Ps 150 [3]Praise him with the sounding of the trumpet, praise him with the harp and lyre, [4]praise him with tambourine and dancing, praise him with the strings and flute, [5]praise him with the clash of cymbals, praise him with resounding cymbals.
Isa 38 [20]The LORD will save me, and we will sing with stringed instruments all the days of our lives in the temple of the LORD.

e) Praise God with Sacrifice

Lev 19 [24]"'In the fourth year all its fruit will be holy, an offering of praise to the LORD.'"

f) Praise God with a Shout

Ezra 3 [11]With praise and thanksgiving they sang to the LORD: "He is good; his love to Israel endures forever." And all the people gave a great shout of praise to the LORD, because the foundation of the house of the LORD was laid.
Ps 42 [4]These things I remember as I pour out my soul: how I used to go with the multitude, leading the procession to the house of God, with shouts of joy and thanksgiving among the festive throng.
Ps 66 [1]Shout with joy to God, all the earth!
Ps 71 [23]My lips will shout for joy when I sing praise to you—I, whom you have redeemed.
Isa 12 [6]"Shout aloud and sing for joy, people of Zion, for great is the Holy One of Israel among you."
Isa 24 [14]They raise their voices, they shout for joy; from the west they acclaim the LORD's majesty.
Isa 49 [13]Shout for joy, O heavens; rejoice, O earth; burst into song, O mountains! For the LORD comforts his people and will have compassion on his afflicted ones.

g) Praise God with Singing

Ps 7 [17]I will give thanks to the LORD because of his righteousness and will sing praise to the name of the LORD Most High.
Ps 9 [2]I will be glad and rejoice in you; I will sing praise to your name, O Most High.
Ps 13 [6]I will sing to the LORD, for he has been good to me.
Ps 18 [49]Therefore I will praise you among the nations, O LORD; I will sing praises to your name.
Ps 33 [1]Sing joyfully to the LORD, you righteous; it is fitting for the upright to praise him. . . . [3]Sing to him a new song; play skillfully, and shout for joy.
Ps 47 [5]God has ascended amid shouts of joy, the LORD amid the sounding of trumpets. [6]Sing praises to God, sing praises; sing praises to our King, sing praises.
[7]For God is the King of all the earth; sing to him a psalm of praise.
Ps 63 [5]My soul will be satisfied as with the richest of foods; with singing lips my mouth will praise you.
Ps 68 [4]Sing to God, sing praise to his name, extol him who rides on the clouds—his name is the LORD—and rejoice before him.
Ps 68 [24]Your procession has come into view, O God, the procession of my God and King into the sanctuary. [25]In front are the singers, after them the musicians; with them are the maidens playing tambourines. [26]Praise God in the great congregation; praise the LORD in the assembly of Israel.
Ps 69 [30]I will praise God's name in song and glorify him with thanksgiving.
Ps 95 [1]Come, let us sing for joy to the LORD; let us shout aloud to the Rock of our salvation. [2]Let us come before him with thanksgiving and extol him with music and song.
Ps 96 [1]Sing to the LORD a new song; sing to the LORD, all the earth. [2]Sing to the LORD, praise his name; proclaim his salvation day after day.
Ps 100 [2]Worship the LORD with gladness; come before him with joyful songs.
Ps 105 [2]Sing to him, sing praise to him; tell of all his wonderful acts.
Ps 126 [1]When the LORD brought back the captives to Zion, we were like men who dreamed. [2]Our mouths were filled with laughter, our tongues with songs of joy. Then it was said among the nations, "The LORD has done great things for them."
Ps 149 [1]Praise the LORD.
Sing to the LORD a new song, his praise in the assembly of the saints.
Isa 35 [10]and the ransomed of the LORD will return. They will enter Zion with singing; everlasting joy will crown their heads. Gladness and joy will overtake them, and sorrow and sighing will flee away.
Acts 16 [25]About midnight Paul and Silas were praying and singing hymns to God, and the other prisoners were listening to them.
Eph 5 [19]Speak to one another with psalms, hymns and spiritual songs. Sing and make music in your heart to the Lord. . . .
Col 3 [16]Let the word of Christ dwell in you richly as you teach and admonish one another with all wisdom, and as you sing psalms, hymns and spiritual songs with gratitude in your hearts to God.
James 5 [13]Is any one of you in trouble? He should pray. Is anyone happy? Let him sing songs of praise.

6. Examples of Praising God

a) Melchizedek Praised God

Gen 14 [18]Then Melchizedek king of Salem brought out bread and wine. He was priest of God Most High, [19]and he blessed Abram, saying, "Blessed be Abram by God Most High, Creator of heaven and earth. [20]And blessed be God Most High, who delivered your enemies into your hand." Then Abram gave him a tenth of everything.

b) Moses and Israel Praised God

Exod 15 [1]Then Moses and the Israelites sang this song to the LORD: "I will sing to the LORD, for he is highly exalted. The horse and its rider he has hurled into the sea. [2]The LORD is my strength and my song; he has become my salvation. He is my God, and I will praise him, my father's God, and I will exalt him."

c) Miriam Praised God

Exod 15 [20]Then Miriam the prophetess, Aaron's sister, took a tambourine in her hand, and all the women followed her, with tambourines and dancing. [21]Miriam sang to them: "Sing to the LORD, for he is highly exalted. The horse and its rider he has hurled into the sea."

d) Jethro Praised God

Exod 18 [9]Jethro was delighted to hear about all the good things the LORD had done for Israel in rescuing them from the hand of the Egyptians. [10]He said, "Praise be to the LORD, who rescued you from the hand of the Egyptians and of Pharaoh, and who rescued the people from the hand of the Egyptians. [11]Now I know that the LORD is greater than all other gods, for he did this to those who had treated Israel arrogantly." [12]Then Jethro, Moses' father-in-law, brought a burnt offering and other sacrifices to God, and Aaron came with all the elders of Israel to eat bread with Moses' father-in-law in the presence of God.

e) Deborah and Barak Praised God

Judg 5 [1]On that day Deborah and Barak son of Abinoam sang this song: [2]"When the princes in Israel take the lead, when the people willingly offer themselves—praise the LORD!

[3]"Hear this, you kings! Listen, you rulers! I will sing to the LORD, I will sing; I will make music to the LORD, the God of Israel. . . . [9]My heart is with Israel's princes, with the willing volunteers among the people. Praise the LORD!"

f) David Praised God

1 Chron 16 [7]That day David first committed to Asaph and his associates this psalm of thanks to the LORD: [8]Give thanks to the LORD, call on his name; make known among the nations what he has done. [9]Sing to him, sing praise to him; tell of all his wonderful acts. [10]Glory in his holy name; let the hearts of those who seek the LORD rejoice. . . . [35]Cry out, "Save us, O God our Savior; gather us and deliver us from the nations, that we may give thanks to your holy name, that we may glory in your praise." [36]Praise be to the LORD, the God of Israel, from everlasting to everlasting.

Then all the people said "Amen" and "Praise the LORD."

1 Chron 29 [10]David praised the LORD in the presence of the whole assembly, saying, "Praise be to you, O LORD, God of our father Israel, from everlasting to everlasting. [11]Yours, O LORD, is the greatness and the power and the glory and the majesty and the splendor, for everything in heaven and earth is yours. Yours, O LORD, is the kingdom; you are exalted as head over all. [12]Wealth and honor come from you; you are the ruler of all things. In your hands are strength and power to exalt and give strength to all. [13]Now, our God, we give you thanks, and praise your glorious name."

g) The Israelites Praised God

1 Chron 16 [36]Praise be to the LORD, the God of Israel, from everlasting to everlasting.

Then all the people said "Amen" and "Praise the LORD."

h) Jehoshaphat and His Army Praised God

2 Chron 20 [20]Early in the morning they left for the Desert of Tekoa. As they set out, Jehoshaphat stood and said, "Listen to me, Judah and people of Jerusalem! Have faith in the LORD your God and you will be upheld; have faith in his prophets and you will be successful." [21]After consulting the people, Jehoshaphat appointed men to sing to the LORD and to praise him for the splendor of his holiness as they went out at the head of the army, saying: "Give thanks to the LORD, for his love endures forever."

[22]As they began to sing and praise, the LORD set ambushes against the men of Ammon and Moab and Mount Seir who were invading Judah, and they were defeated. [23]The men of Ammon and Moab rose up against the men from Mount Seir to destroy and annihilate them. After they finished slaughtering the men from Seir, they helped to destroy one another.

[24]When the men of Judah came to the place that overlooks the desert and looked toward the vast army, they saw only dead bodies lying on the ground; no one had escaped. [25]So Jehoshaphat and his men went to carry off their plunder, and they found among them a great amount of equipment and clothing and also articles of value—more than they could take away. There was so much plunder that it took three days to collect it. [26]On the fourth day they assembled in the Valley of Beracah, where they praised the LORD. This is why it is called the Valley of Beracah to this day.

[27]Then, led by Jehoshaphat, all the men of Judah and Jerusalem returned joyfully to Jerusalem, for the LORD had given them cause to rejoice over their enemies. [28]They entered Jerusalem and went to the temple of the LORD with harps and lutes and trumpets.

i) Hezekiah Praised God

Isa 38 [9]A writing of Hezekiah king of Judah after his illness and recovery: . . . [19]The living, the living—they praise you, as I am doing today; fathers tell their children about your faithfulness.

j) Daniel Praised God

Dan 2 [19]During the night the mystery was revealed to Daniel in a vision. Then Daniel praised the God of heaven [20]and said: "Praise be to the name of God for ever and ever; wisdom and power are his. [21]He changes times and seasons; he sets up kings and deposes them. He gives wisdom to the wise and knowledge to the discerning. [22]He reveals deep and hidden things; he knows what lies in darkness, and light dwells with him. [23]I thank and praise you, O God of my fathers: You have given me wisdom and power, you have made known to me what we asked of you, you have made known to us the dream of the king."

k) Nebuchadnezzar Praised God

Dan 4 [34]At the end of that time, I, Nebuchadnezzar, raised my eyes toward heaven, and my sanity was restored. Then I praised the Most High; I honored and glorified him who lives forever. His dominion is an eternal dominion; his kingdom endures from generation to generation. [35]All the peoples of the earth are regarded as nothing. He does as he pleases with the powers of heaven and the peoples of the earth. No one can hold back his hand or say to him: "What have you done?"

[36]At the same time that my sanity was restored, my honor and splendor were returned to me for the glory of my kingdom. My advisers and nobles sought me out, and I was restored to my throne and became even greater than before. [37]Now I, Nebuchadnezzar, praise and exalt and glorify the King of heaven, because everything he does is right and all his ways are just. And those who walk in pride he is able to humble.

l) Priests and Levites Praised God

2 Chron 5 [11]The priests then withdrew from the Holy Place. All the priests who were there had consecrated themselves, regardless of their divisions. [12]All the Levites who were musicians—Asaph, Heman, Jeduthun and their sons and relatives—stood on the east side of the altar, dressed in fine linen and playing cymbals, harps and lyres. They were accompanied by 120 priests sounding trumpets. [13]The trumpeters and singers joined in unison, as with one voice, to give praise and thanks to the LORD. Accompanied by trumpets, cymbals and other instruments, they raised their voices in praise to the LORD and sang: "He is good; his love endures forever."

Then the temple of the LORD was filled with a cloud, [14]and the priests could not perform their service because of the cloud, for the glory of the LORD filled the temple of God.

Ezra 3 [10]When the builders laid the foundation of the temple of the LORD, the priests in their vestments and with trumpets, and the Levites (the sons of Asaph) with cymbals, took their places to praise the LORD, as prescribed by David king of Israel. [11]With praise and thanksgiving they sang to the LORD: "He is good; his love to Israel endures forever." And all the people gave a great shout of praise to the LORD, because the foundation of the house of the LORD was laid.

m) Ezra Praised God

Neh 8 [6]Ezra praised the LORD, the great God; and all the people lifted their hands and responded, "Amen! Amen!" Then they bowed down and worshiped the LORD with their faces to the ground.

n) Zechariah Praised God

Luke 1 [57]When it was time for Elizabeth to have her baby, she gave birth to a son. [58]Her neighbors and relatives heard that the Lord had shown her great mercy, and they shared her joy.

[59]On the eighth day they came to circumcise the child, and they were going to name him after his father Zechariah, [60]but his mother spoke up and said, "No! He is to be called John."

[61]They said to her, "There is no one among your relatives who has that name."

[62]Then they made signs to his father, to find out what he would like to name the child. [63]He asked for a writing tablet, and to everyone's astonishment he wrote, "His name is John." [64]Immediately his mouth was opened and his tongue was loosed, and he began to speak, praising God. [65]The neighbors

were all filled with awe, and throughout the hill country of Judea people were talking about all these things. [66]Everyone who heard this wondered about it, asking, "What then is this child going to be?" For the Lord's hand was with him.

[67]His father Zechariah was filled with the Holy Spirit and prophesied: [68]"Praise be to the Lord, the God of Israel, because he has come and has redeemed his people. [69]He has raised up a horn of salvation for us in the house of his servant David. . . ."

o) The Shepherds Praised God

Luke 2 [20]The shepherds returned, glorifying and praising God for all the things they had heard and seen, which were just as they had been told.

p) Simeon Praised God

Luke 2 [28]Simeon took him in his arms and praised God, saying: [29]"Sovereign Lord, as you have promised, you now dismiss your servant in peace. [30]For my eyes have seen your salvation, [31]which you have prepared in the sight of all people, [32]a light for revelation to the Gentiles and for glory to your people Israel."

[33]The child's father and mother marveled at what was said about him.

q) Jesus Praised God

Luke 10 [21]At that time Jesus, full of joy through the Holy Spirit, said, "I praise you, Father, Lord of heaven and earth, because you have hidden these things from the wise and learned, and revealed them to little children. Yes, Father, for this was your good pleasure."

r) The Blind Beggar Praised God

Luke 18 [35]As Jesus approached Jericho, a blind man was sitting by the roadside begging. [36]When he heard the crowd going by, he asked what was happening. [37]They told him, "Jesus of Nazareth is passing by."

[38]He called out, "Jesus, Son of David, have mercy on me!"

[39]Those who led the way rebuked him and told him to be quiet, but he shouted all the more, "Son of David, have mercy on me!"

[40]Jesus stopped and ordered the man to be brought to him. When he came near, Jesus asked him, [41]"What do you want me to do for you?"

"Lord, I want to see," he replied.

[42]Jesus said to him, "Receive your sight; your faith has healed you." [43]Immediately he received his sight and followed Jesus, praising God. When all the people saw it, they also praised God.

s) The Disciples of Jesus Praised God

Luke 19 [37]When he came near the place where the road goes down the Mount of Olives, the whole crowd of disciples began joyfully to praise God in loud voices for all the miracles they had seen: [38]"Blessed is the king who comes in the name of the Lord!" "Peace in heaven and glory in the highest!"

t) The Apostles Praised God

Luke 24 [33]They got up and returned at once to Jerusalem. There they found the Eleven and those with them, assembled together. . . .

[50]When he had led them out to the vicinity of Bethany, he lifted up his hands and blessed them. [51]While he was blessing them, he left them and was taken up into heaven. [52]Then they worshiped him and returned to Jerusalem with great joy. [53]And they stayed continually at the temple, praising God.

u) The Early Converts Praised God

Acts 2 [46]Every day they continued to meet together in the temple courts. They broke bread in their homes and ate together with glad and sincere hearts, [47]praising God and enjoying the favor of all the people. And the Lord added to their number daily those who were being saved.

v) The Crippled Beggar Praised God

Acts 3 [1]One day Peter and John were going up to the temple at the time of prayer—at three in the afternoon. [2]Now a man crippled from birth was being carried to the temple gate called Beautiful, where he was put every day to beg from those going into the temple courts. [3]When he saw Peter and John about to enter, he asked them for money. [4]Peter looked straight at him, as did John. Then Peter said, "Look at us!" [5]So the man gave them his attention, expecting to get something from them.

[6]Then Peter said, "Silver or gold I do not have, but what I have I give you. In the name of Jesus Christ of Nazareth, walk." [7]Taking him by the right hand, he helped him up, and instantly the man's feet and ankles became strong. [8]He jumped to his feet and began to walk. Then he went with them into the temple courts, walking and jumping, and praising God. [9]When all the people saw him walking and praising God, [10]they recognized him as the same man who used to sit begging at the temple gate called Beautiful, and they were filled with wonder and amazement at what had happened to him.

w) Paul and Silas Praised God

Acts 16 [25]About midnight Paul and Silas were praying and singing hymns to God, and the other prisoners were listening to them.

x) The People of God Praised Him

Rev 15 [2]And I saw what looked like a sea of glass mixed with fire and, standing beside the sea, those who had been victorious over the beast and his image and over the number of his name. They held harps given them by God [3]and sang the song of Moses the servant of God and the song of the Lamb: "Great and marvelous are your deeds, Lord God Almighty. Just and true are your ways, King of the ages. [4]Who will not fear you, O Lord, and bring glory to your name? For you alone are holy. All nations will come and worship before you, for your righteous acts have been revealed."

7. The Responsibility for Praising God

a) Believers Should Continually Praise God

Ps 44 [8]In God we make our boast all day long, and we will praise your name forever.

Ps 52 [9]I will praise you forever for what you have done; in your name I will hope, for your name is good. I will praise you in the presence of your saints.

Ps 61 [8]Then will I ever sing praise to your name and fulfill my vows day after day.

Ps 63 [4]I will praise you as long as I live, and in your name I will lift up my hands.

Ps 104 [33]I will sing to the LORD all my life; I will sing praise to my God as long as I live.

Ps 115 [17]It is not the dead who praise the LORD, those who go down to silence; [18]it is we who extol the LORD, both now and forevermore.

Praise the LORD.

Ps 146 [2]I will praise the LORD all my life; I will sing praise to my God as long as I live.

b) Believers Should Declare God's Praises

Ps 9 [11]Sing praises to the LORD, enthroned in Zion; proclaim among the nations what he has done. . . .

[13]O LORD, see how my enemies persecute me! Have mercy and lift me up from the gates of death, [14]that I may declare your praises in the gates of the Daughter of Zion and there rejoice in your salvation.

Ps 33 [1]Sing joyfully to the LORD, you righteous; it is fitting for the upright to praise him.

Ps 51 [15]O Lord, open my lips, and my mouth will declare your praise.

Ps 147 [1]Praise the LORD.

How good it is to sing praises to our God, how pleasant and fitting to praise him!

James 5 [13]Is any one of you in trouble? He should pray. Is anyone happy? Let him sing songs of praise.

c) Believers Should Desire to Praise God

Ps 51 [15]O Lord, open my lips, and my mouth will declare your praise.

Ps 119 [171]May my lips overflow with praise, for you teach me your decrees.

d) Believers Should Glory in God's Praises

1 Chron 16 [35]Cry out, "Save us, O God our Savior; gather us and deliver us from the nations, that we may give thanks to your holy name, that we may glory in your praise."

e) Believers Should Honor God with Praise

Josh 7 [19]Then Joshua said to Achan, "My son, give glory to the LORD, the God of Israel, and give him the praise. Tell me what you have done; do not hide it from me."

f) Believers Should Invite Others to Praise God

Ps 34 [3]Glorify the LORD with me; let us exalt his name together.
Ps 66 [8]Praise our God, O peoples, let the sound of his praise be heard. . . .
Ps 95 [1]Come, let us sing for joy to the LORD; let us shout aloud to the Rock of our salvation.

g) Believers Should Praise God Even in Affliction

Acts 16 [25]About midnight Paul and Silas were praying and singing hymns to God, and the other prisoners were listening to them.

h) Praise Should Characterize Believers

Isa 61 [1]The Spirit of the Sovereign LORD is on me, because the LORD has anointed me to preach good news to the poor. He has sent me to bind up the brokenhearted, to proclaim freedom for the captives and release from darkness for the prisoners, [2]to proclaim the year of the LORD's favor and the day of vengeance of our God, to comfort all who mourn, [3]and provide for those who grieve in Zion—to bestow on them a crown of beauty instead of ashes, the oil of gladness instead of mourning, and a garment of praise instead of a spirit of despair. They will be called oaks of righteousness, a planting of the LORD for the display of his splendor.

C. Worship God

1. The Uniqueness of Worship

a) The Worship of God

2 Kings 17 [35]When the LORD made a covenant with the Israelites, he commanded them: "Do not worship any other gods or bow down to them, serve them or sacrifice to them. [36]But the LORD, who brought you up out of Egypt with mighty power and outstretched arm, is the one you must worship. To him you shall bow down and to him offer sacrifices. . . . [39]Rather, worship the LORD your God; it is he who will deliver you from the hand of all your enemies."
Neh 9 [6]"You alone are the LORD. You made the heavens, even the highest heavens, and all their starry host, the earth and all that is on it, the seas and all that is in them. You give life to everything, and the multitudes of heaven worship you."
Ps 22 [29]All the rich of the earth will feast and worship; all who go down to the dust will kneel before him—those who cannot keep themselves alive.
Ps 86 [9]All the nations you have made will come and worship before you, O LORD; they will bring glory to your name. [10]For you are great and do marvelous deeds; you alone are God.
Ps 97 [7]All who worship images are put to shame, those who boast in idols—worship him, all you gods!
Ps 99 [5]Exalt the LORD our God and worship at his footstool; he is holy. . . . [9]Exalt the LORD our God and worship at his holy mountain, for the LORD our God is holy.
Isa 66 [23]"From one New Moon to another and from one Sabbath to another, all mankind will come and bow down before me," says the LORD.
Zeph 2 [11]The LORD will be awesome to them when he destroys all the gods of the land. The nations on every shore will worship him, every one in its own land.
Rev 7 [11]All the angels were standing around the throne and around the elders and the four living creatures. They fell down on their faces before the throne and worshiped God, [12]saying: "Amen! Praise and glory and wisdom and thanks and honor and power and strength be to our God for ever and ever. Amen!"
Rev 11 [16]And the twenty-four elders, who were seated on their thrones before God, fell on their faces and worshiped God. . . .
Rev 14 [6]Then I saw another angel flying in midair, and he had the eternal gospel to proclaim to those who live on the earth—to every nation, tribe, language and people. [7]He said in a loud voice, "Fear God and give him glory, because the hour of his judgment has come. Worship him who made the heavens, the earth, the sea and the springs of water."
Rev 22 [8]I, John, am the one who heard and saw these things. And when I had heard and seen them, I fell down to worship at the feet of the angel who had been showing them to me. [9]But he said to me, "Do not do it! I am a fellow servant with you and with your brothers the prophets and of all who keep the words of this book. Worship God!"

b) The Worship of Christ

Ps 72 [17]May his name endure forever; may it continue as long as the sun.

All nations will be blessed through him, and they will call him blessed.

Matt 2 [11]On coming to the house, they saw the child with his mother Mary, and they bowed down and worshiped him. Then they opened their treasures and presented him with gifts of gold and of incense and of myrrh.
Matt 14 [33]Then those who were in the boat worshiped him, saying, "Truly you are the Son of God."
Matt 18 [20]"For where two or three come together in my name, there am I with them."
Matt 28 [9]Suddenly Jesus met them. "Greetings," he said. They came to him, clasped his feet and worshiped him. . . . [17]When they saw him, they worshiped him; but some doubted.
John 9 [35]Jesus heard that they had thrown him out, and when he found him, he said, "Do you believe in the Son of Man?"

[36]"Who is he, sir?" the man asked. "Tell me so that I may believe in him."

[37]Jesus said, "You have now seen him; in fact, he is the one speaking with you."

[38]Then the man said, "Lord, I believe," and he worshiped him.

Acts 13 [2]While they were worshiping the Lord and fasting, the Holy Spirit said, "Set apart for me Barnabas and Saul for the work to which I have called them."
1 Cor 1 [2]To the church of God in Corinth, to those sanctified in Christ Jesus and called to be holy, together with all those everywhere who call on the name of our Lord Jesus Christ—their Lord and ours. . . .
Gal 1 [3]Grace and peace to you from God our Father and the Lord Jesus Christ, . . . [5]to whom be glory for ever and ever. Amen.
Phil 2 [9]Therefore God exalted him to the highest place and gave him the name that is above every name, [10]that at the name of Jesus every knee should bow, in heaven and on earth and under the earth, [11]and every tongue confess that Jesus Christ is Lord, to the glory of God the Father.
Heb 1 [6]And again, when God brings his firstborn into the world, he says, "Let all God's angels worship him."
2 Pet 3 [18]But grow in the grace and knowledge of our Lord and Savior Jesus Christ. To him be glory both now and forever! Amen.

2. Attitudes of Worship

a) Worship with Concern for the Spiritual

John 4 [23]"Yet a time is coming and has now come when the true worshipers will worship the Father in spirit and truth, for they are the kind of worshipers the Father seeks. [24]God is spirit, and his worshipers must worship in spirit and in truth."
Phil 3 [3]For it is we who are the circumcision, we who worship by the Spirit of God, who glory in Christ Jesus, and who put no confidence in the flesh. . . .

b) Worship with Concern for Truth

Ps 51 [6]Surely you desire truth in the inner parts; you teach me wisdom in the inmost place.

John 4 [23]"Yet a time is coming and has now come when the true worshipers will worship the Father in spirit and truth, for they are the kind of worshipers the Father seeks. [24]God is spirit, and his worshipers must worship in spirit and in truth."

c) Worship with Consideration for God's Character

1 Chron 16 [29]ascribe to the LORD the glory due his name. Bring an offering and come before him; worship the LORD in the splendor of his holiness.

d) Worship with Dependence on Christ

Heb 10 [1]The law is only a shadow of the good things that are coming—not the realities themselves. For this reason it can never, by the same sacrifices repeated endlessly year after year, make perfect those who draw near to worship. [2]If it could, would they not have stopped being offered? For the worshipers would have been cleansed once for all, and would no longer have felt guilty for their sins. [3]But those sacrifices are an annual reminder of sins, [4]because it is impossible for the blood of bulls and goats to take away sins.

[5]Therefore, when Christ came into the world, he said: "Sacrifice and offering you did not desire, but a body you prepared for me; [6]with burnt offerings and sin offerings you were not pleased. [7]Then I said, 'Here I am—it is written about me in the scroll—I have come to do your will, O God.'" [8]First he said, "Sacrifices and offerings, burnt offerings and sin offerings you did not desire, nor were you pleased with them" (although the law required them to be made). [9]Then he said, "Here I am, I have come to do your will." He sets aside the first to establish the second. [10]And by that will, we have been made holy through the sacrifice of the body of Jesus Christ once for all.

e) Worship with Eager Expectation

Ps 27 [4]One thing I ask of the LORD, this is what I seek: that I may dwell in the house of the LORD all the days of my life, to gaze upon the beauty of the LORD and to seek him in his temple.

Ps 84 [1]How lovely is your dwelling place, O LORD Almighty! [2]My soul yearns, even faints, for the courts of the LORD; my heart and my flesh cry out for the living God.

[3]Even the sparrow has found a home, and the swallow a nest for herself, where she may have her young—a place near your altar, O LORD Almighty, my King and my God.

f) Worship with Faith in the Scriptures

Acts 24 [14]"However, I admit that I worship the God of our fathers as a follower of the Way, which they call a sect. I believe everything that agrees with the Law and that is written in the Prophets. . . ."

g) Worship with Unrestrained and Complete Devotion

1 Chron 29 [9]The people rejoiced at the willing response of their leaders, for they had given freely and wholeheartedly to the LORD. David the king also rejoiced greatly.

Rom 12 [1]Therefore, I urge you, brothers, in view of God's mercy, to offer your bodies as living sacrifices, holy and pleasing to God—this is your spiritual act of worship.

3. Examples of Worship

a) Abraham Worshiped God

Gen 12 [7]The LORD appeared to Abram and said, "To your offspring I will give this land." So he built an altar there to the LORD, who had appeared to him.

[8]From there he went on toward the hills east of Bethel and pitched his tent, with Bethel on the west and Ai on the east. There he built an altar to the LORD and called on the name of the LORD.

b) Abraham's Servant Worshiped God

Gen 24 [47]"I asked her, 'Whose daughter are you?'

"She said, 'The daughter of Bethuel son of Nahor, whom Milcah bore to him.'

"Then I put the ring in her nose and the bracelets on her arms, [48]and I bowed down and worshiped the LORD. I praised the LORD, the God of my master Abraham, who had led me on the right road to get the granddaughter of my master's brother for his son."

c) Jacob Worshiped God

Gen 35 [2]So Jacob said to his household and to all who were with him, "Get rid of the foreign gods you have with you, and purify yourselves and change your clothes. [3]Then come, let us go up to Bethel, where I will build an altar to God, who answered me in the day of my distress and who has been with me wherever I have gone." . . .

[14]Jacob set up a stone pillar at the place where God had talked with him, and he poured out a drink offering on it; he also poured oil on it.

d) The People of Israel Worshiped God

Exod 4 [29]Moses and Aaron brought together all the elders of the Israelites, [30]and Aaron told them everything the LORD had said to Moses. He also performed the signs before the people, [31]and they believed. And when they heard that the LORD was concerned about them and had seen their misery, they bowed down and worshiped.

Exod 12 [26]"And when your children ask you, 'What does this ceremony mean to you?' [27]then tell them, 'It is the Passover sacrifice to the LORD, who passed over the houses of the Israelites in Egypt and spared our homes when he struck down the Egyptians.'" Then the people bowed down and worshiped.

e) Moses Worshiped God

Exod 34 [8]Moses bowed to the ground at once and worshiped.

f) Gideon Worshiped God

Judg 7 [15]When Gideon heard the dream and its interpretation, he worshiped God. He returned to the camp of Israel and called out, "Get up! The LORD has given the Midianite camp into your hands."

g) Elkanah, Hannah, and Samuel Worshiped God

1 Sam 1 [19]Early the next morning they arose and worshiped before the LORD and then went back to their home at Ramah. Elkanah lay with Hannah his wife, and the LORD remembered her. [20]So in the course of time Hannah conceived and gave birth to a son. She named him Samuel, saying, "Because I asked the LORD for him." . . .

[24]After he was weaned, she took the boy with her, young as he was, along with a three-year-old bull, an ephah of flour and a skin of wine, and brought him to the house of the LORD at Shiloh. [25]When they had slaughtered the bull, they brought the boy to Eli, [26]and she said to him, "As surely as you live, my lord, I am the woman who stood here beside you praying to the LORD. [27]I prayed for this child, and the LORD has granted me what I asked of him. [28]So now I give him to the LORD. For his whole life he will be given over to the LORD." And he worshiped the LORD there.

h) Job Worshiped God

Job 1 [5]When a period of feasting had run its course, Job would send and have them purified. Early in the morning he would sacrifice a burnt offering for each of them, thinking, "Perhaps my children have sinned and cursed God in their hearts." This was Job's regular custom.

Job 1 [20]At this, Job got up and tore his robe and shaved his head. Then he fell to the ground in worship [21]and said: "Naked I came from my mother's womb, and naked I will depart. The LORD gave and the LORD has taken away; may the name of the LORD be praised."

i) David Worshiped God

1 Kings 1 [47]"Also, the royal officials have come to congratulate our lord King David, saying, 'May your God make Solomon's name more famous than yours and his throne greater than yours!' And the king bowed in worship on his bed [48]and said, 'Praise be to the LORD, the God of Israel, who has allowed my eyes to see a successor on my throne today.'"

j) Jehoshaphat Worshiped God

2 Chron 20 [18]Jehoshaphat bowed with his face to the ground, and all the people of Judah and Jerusalem fell down in worship before the LORD.

k) Hezekiah Worshiped God

2 Chron 29 [27]Hezekiah gave the order to sacrifice the burnt offering on the altar. As the offering began, singing to the LORD began also, accompanied by trumpets and the instruments of David king of Israel. [28]The whole assembly bowed in worship, while the singers sang and the trumpeters played. All this continued until the sacrifice of the burnt offering was completed.

[29]When the offerings were finished, the king and everyone present with him knelt down and worshiped. [30]King Hezekiah and his officials ordered the Levites to praise the LORD with the words of David and of Asaph the seer. So they sang praises with gladness and bowed their heads and worshiped.

l) Jonah Worshiped God

Jon 1 [9]He answered, "I am a Hebrew and I worship the LORD, the God of heaven, who made the sea and the land."

m) The Disciples Worshiped God

Matt 14 [22]Immediately Jesus make the disciples get into the boat and go on ahead of him to the other side, while he dismissed the crowd. . . . [33]Then those who were in the boat worshiped him, saying, "Truly you are the Son of God."
Matt 28 [16]Then the eleven disciples went to Galilee, to the mountain where Jesus had told them to go. [17]When they saw him, they worshiped him; but some doubted.
Luke 24 [51]While he was blessing them, he left them and was taken up into heaven. [52]Then they worshiped him and returned to Jerusalem with great joy.

n) The Blind Man Worshiped God

John 9 [35]Jesus heard that they had thrown him out, and when he found him, he said, "Do you believe in the Son of Man?" . . .

[38]Then the man said, "Lord, I believe," and he worshiped him.

o) Mary and Mary Magdalene Worshiped God

Matt 28 [1]After the Sabbath, at dawn on the first day of the week, Mary Magdalene and the other Mary went to look at the tomb. . . .

[8]So the women hurried away from the tomb, afraid yet filled with joy, and ran to tell his disciples. [9]Suddenly Jesus met them. "Greetings," he said. They came to him, clasped his feet and worshiped him.

p) Stephen Worshiped God

Acts 7 [55]But Stephen, full of the Holy Spirit, looked up to heaven and saw the glory of God, and Jesus standing at the right hand of God. [56]"Look," he said, "I see heaven open and the Son of Man standing at the right hand of God." . . .

[59]While they were stoning him, Stephen prayed, "Lord Jesus, receive my spirit." [60]Then he fell on his knees and cried out, "Lord, do not hold this sin against them." When he had said this, he fell asleep.

q) Paul Worshiped God

Acts 24 [14]"However, I admit that I worship the God of our fathers as a follower of the Way, which they call a sect. I believe everything that agrees with the Law and that is written in the Prophets, [15]and I have the same hope in God as these men, that there will be a resurrection of both the righteous and the wicked."
Phil 3 [3]For it is we who are the circumcision, we who worship by the Spirit of God, who glory in Christ Jesus, and who put no confidence in the flesh. . . .

r) Those before God's Heavenly Throne Worshiped Him

Rev 4 [10]the twenty-four elders fall down before him who sits on the throne, and worship him who lives for ever and ever. They lay their crowns before the throne and say: [11]"You are worthy, our Lord and God, to receive glory and honor and power, for you created all things, and by your will they were created and have their being."
Rev 5 [9]And they sang a new song: "You are worthy to take the scroll and to open its seals, because you were slain, and with your blood you purchased men for God from every tribe and language and people and nation. [10]You have made them to be a kingdom and priests to serve our God, and they will reign on the earth."

[11]Then I looked and heard the voice of many angels, numbering thousands upon thousands, and ten thousand times ten thousand. They encircled the throne and the living creatures and the elders. [12]In a loud voice they sang: "Worthy is the Lamb, who was slain, to receive power and wealth and wisdom and strength and honor and glory and praise!"

[13]Then I heard every creature in heaven and on earth and under the earth and on the sea, and all that is in them, singing: "To him who sits on the throne and to the Lamb be praise and honor and glory and power, for ever and ever!" [14]The four living creatures said, "Amen," and the elders fell down and worshiped.
Rev 7 [9]After this I looked and there before me was a great multitude that no one could count, from every nation, tribe, people and language, standing before the throne and in front of the Lamb. They were wearing white robes and were holding palm branches in their hands. [10]And they cried out in a loud voice: "Salvation belongs to our God, who sits on the throne, and to the Lamb." [11]All the angels were standing around the throne and around the elders and the four living creatures. They fell down on their faces before the throne and worshiped God. . . .
Rev 11 [16]And the twenty-four elders, who were seated on their thrones before God, fell on their faces and worshiped God, [17]saying: "We give thanks to you, Lord God Almighty, the One who is and who was, because you have taken your great power and have begun to reign. [18]The nations were angry; and your wrath has come. The time has come for judging the dead, and for rewarding your servants the prophets and your saints and those who reverence your name, both small and great—and for destroying those who destroy the earth."
Rev 15 [2]And I saw what looked like a sea of glass mixed with fire and, standing beside the sea, those who had been victorious over the beast and his image and over the number of his name. They held harps given them by God [3]and sang the song of Moses the servant of God and the song of the Lamb: "Great and marvelous are your deeds, Lord God Almighty. Just and true are your ways, King of the ages. [4]Who will not fear you, O Lord, and bring glory to your name? For you alone are holy. All nations will come and worship before you, for your righteous acts have been revealed."
Rev 19 [4]The twenty-four elders and the four living creatures fell down and worshiped God, who was seated on the throne. And they cried: "Amen, Hallelujah!"

D. Glorify God

1. The Nature of Glorifying God

a) The Glorification of God Accompanies the Fear of Him

Ps 96 [3]Declare his glory among the nations, his marvelous deeds among all peoples.

[4]For great is the LORD and most worthy of praise; he is to be feared above all gods.
Rev 14 [7]He said in a loud voice, "Fear God and give him glory, because the hour of his judgment has come. Worship him who made the heavens, the earth, the sea and the springs of water."
Rev 15 [4]"Who will not fear you, O Lord, and bring glory to your name? For you alone are holy. All nations will come and worship before you, for your righteous acts have been revealed."

b) The Glorification of God Is Commanded

1 Chron 16 [23]Sing to the LORD, all the earth; proclaim his salvation day after day. [24]Declare his glory among the nations, his marvelous deeds among all peoples.

1 Chron 16 [28]Ascribe to the LORD, O families of nations, ascribe to the LORD glory and strength, [29]ascribe to the LORD the glory due his name. Bring an offering and come before him; worship the LORD in the splendor of his holiness.

Ps 96 [3]Declare his glory among the nations, his marvelous deeds among all peoples.

Isa 42 [12]Let them give glory to the LORD and proclaim his praise in the islands.

c) The Glorification of God Is Denied to Him by the Wicked

Acts 12 [23]Immediately, because Herod did not give praise to God, an angel of the Lord struck him down, and he was eaten by worms and died.

Rom 1 [21]For although they knew God, they neither glorified him as God nor gave thanks to him, but their thinking became futile and their foolish hearts were darkened.

Rev 16 [9]They were seared by the intense heat and they cursed the name of God, who had control over these plagues, but they refused to repent and glorify him.

d) The Glorification of God Is a Desire of the Righteous

Ps 34 [3]Glorify the LORD with me; let us exalt his name together.

Ps 69 [30]I will praise God's name in song and glorify him with thanksgiving.

Ps 86 [12]I will praise you, O Lord my God, with all my heart; I will glorify your name forever.

Ps 118 [28]You are my God, and I will give you thanks; you are my God, and I will exalt you.

e) The Glorification of God Is Desired by Him

Isa 43 [5]"Do not be afraid, for I am with you; I will bring your children from the east and gather you from the west. [6]I will say to the north, 'Give them up!' and to the south, 'Do not hold them back.' Bring my sons from afar and my daughters from the ends of the earth—[7]everyone who is called by my name, whom I created for my glory, whom I formed and made."

Isa 66 [18]"And I, because of their actions and their imaginations, am about to come and gather all nations and tongues, and they will come and see my glory.

[19]"I will set a sign among them, and I will send some of those who survive to the nations—to Tarshish, to the Libyans and Lydians (famous as archers), to Tubal and Greece, and to the distant islands that have not heard of my fame or seen my glory. They will proclaim my glory among the nations."

Hab 2 [14]"For the earth will be filled with the knowledge of the glory of the LORD, as the waters cover the sea."

f) The Glorification of God Is Due Him

1 Chron 16 [29]ascribe to the LORD the glory due his name. Bring an offering and come before him; worship the LORD in the splendor of his holiness.

Ps 29 [1]Ascribe to the LORD, O mighty ones, ascribe to the LORD glory and strength. [2]Ascribe to the LORD the glory due his name; worship the LORD in the splendor of his holiness. . . . [9]The voice of the LORD twists the oaks and strips the forests bare. And in his temple all cry, "Glory!"

Ps 72 [18]Praise be to the LORD God, the God of Israel, who alone does marvelous deeds. [19]Praise be to his glorious name forever; may the whole earth be filled with his glory. Amen and Amen.

Ps 96 [7]Ascribe to the LORD, O families of nations, ascribe to the LORD glory and strength. [8]Ascribe to the LORD the glory due his name; bring an offering and come into his courts.

Isa 24 [14]They raise their voices, they shout for joy; from the west they acclaim the LORD's majesty. [15]Therefore in the east give glory to the LORD; exalt the name of the LORD, the God of Israel, in the islands of the sea. [16]From the ends of the earth we hear singing: "Glory to the Righteous One."

But I said, "I waste away, I waste away! Woe to me! The treacherous betray! With treachery the treacherous betray!"

g) The Glorification of God Is Made Possible through Christ

Rom 3 [22]This righteousness from God comes through faith in Jesus Christ to all who believe. There is no difference, [23]for all have sinned and fall short of the glory of God, [24]and are justified freely by his grace through the redemption that came by Christ Jesus.

2 Cor 1 [20]For no matter how many promises God has made, they are "Yes" in Christ. And so through him the "Amen" is spoken by us to the glory of God.

Eph 1 [5]he predestined us to be adopted as his sons through Jesus Christ, in accordance with his pleasure and will—[6]to the praise of his glorious grace, which he has freely given us in the One he loves.

h) The Glorification of God Is Offered to God and Christ

Ps 57 [5]Be exalted, O God, above the heavens; let your glory be over all the earth.

Ps 115 [1]Not to us, O LORD, not to us but to your name be the glory, because of your love and faithfulness.

1 Pet 4 [11]If anyone speaks, he should do it as one speaking the very words of God. If anyone serves, he should do it with the strength God provides, so that in all things God may be praised through Jesus Christ. To him be the glory and the power for ever and ever. Amen.

Rev 5 [13]Then I heard every creature in heaven and on earth and under the earth and on the sea, and all that is in them, singing: "To him who sits on the throne and to the Lamb be praise and honor and glory and power, for ever and ever!"

i) The Glorification of God Results from Unity in Christ

Rom 15 [5]May the God who gives endurance and encouragement give you a spirit of unity among yourselves as you follow Christ Jesus, [6]so that with one heart and mouth you may glorify the God and Father of our Lord Jesus Christ.

2. Reasons for Glorifying God

a) Glorify God for His Grace Demonstrated in Christ

2 Cor 4 [13]It is written: "I believed; therefore I have spoken." With that same spirit of faith we also believe and therefore speak, [14]because we know that the one who raised the Lord Jesus from the dead will also raise us with Jesus and present us with you in his presence. [15]All this is for your benefit, so that the grace that is reaching more and more people may cause thanksgiving to overflow to the glory of God.

b) Glorify God for His Holiness

Ps 99 [9]Exalt the LORD our God and worship at his holy mountain, for the LORD our God is holy.

Rev 15 [4]"Who will not fear you, O Lord, and bring glory to your name? For you alone are holy. All nations will come and worship before you, for your righteous acts have been revealed."

c) Glorify God for His Judgment

Ezek 28 [22]". . . and say: 'This is what the Sovereign LORD says: I am against you, O Sidon, and I will gain glory within you. They will know that I am the LORD, when I inflict punishment on her and show myself holy within her. [23]I will send a plague upon her and make blood flow in her streets. The slain will fall within her, with the sword against her on every side. Then they will know that I am the LORD.'"

Rev 11 [13]At that very hour there was a severe earthquake and a tenth of the city collapsed. Seven thousand people were killed in the earthquake, and the survivors were terrified and gave glory to the God of heaven.

Rev 14 [7]He said in a loud voice, "Fear God and give him glory, because the hour of his judgment has come. Worship him who made the heavens, the earth, the sea and the springs of water."

d) Glorify God for His Love and Faithfulness

Ps 63 [3]Because your love is better than life, my lips will glorify you.

Ps 115 [1]Not to us, O LORD, not to us but to your name be the glory, because of your love and faithfulness.

e) *Glorify God for His Mercy*

Rom 15 [8]For I tell you that Christ has become a servant of the Jews on behalf of God's truth, to confirm the promises made to the patriarchs [9]so that the Gentiles may glorify God for his mercy, as it is written: "Therefore I will praise you among the Gentiles; I will sing hymns to your name."

f) *Glorify God for His Works*

Ps 86 [8]Among the gods there is none like you, O Lord; no deeds can compare with yours. [9]All the nations you have made will come and worship before you, O LORD; they will bring glory to your name. [10]For you are great and do marvelous deeds; you alone are God.
Isa 25 [1]O LORD, you are my God; I will exalt you and praise your name, for in perfect faithfulness you have done marvelous things, things planned long ago.

3. The Means of Glorifying God

a) *Glorify God by Bearing the Fruit of Righteousness*

John 15 [8]"This is to my Father's glory, that you bear much fruit, showing yourselves to be my disciples."
Phil 1 [9]And this is my prayer: that your love may abound more and more in knowledge and depth of insight, [10]so that you may be able to discern what is best and may be pure and blameless until the day of Christ, [11]filled with the fruit of righteousness that comes through Jesus Christ—to the glory and praise of God.

b) *Glorify God by Confessing Sin*

Josh 7 [19]Then Joshua said to Achan, "My son, give glory to the LORD, the God of Israel, and give him the praise. Tell me what you have done; do not hide it from me."

c) *Glorify God by Demonstrating Power in Christ*

Acts 19 [11]God did extraordinary miracles through Paul, [12]so that even handkerchiefs and aprons that had touched him were taken to the sick, and their illnesses were cured and the evil spirits left them.

[13]Some Jews who went around driving out evil spirits tried to invoke the name of the Lord Jesus over those who were demon-possessed. They would say, "In the name of Jesus, whom Paul preaches, I command you to come out." [14]Seven sons of Sceva, a Jewish chief priest, were doing this. [15]One day the evil spirit answered them, "Jesus I know, and I know about Paul, but who are you?" [16]Then the man who had the evil spirit jumped on them and overpowered them all. He gave them such a beating that they ran out of the house naked and bleeding.

[17]When this became known to the Jews and Greeks living in Ephesus, they were all seized with fear, and the name of the Lord Jesus was held in high honor. [18]Many of those who believed now came and openly confessed their evil deeds. [19]A number who had practiced sorcery brought their scrolls together and burned them publicly. When they calculated the value of the scrolls, the total came to fifty thousand drachmas. [20]In this way the word of the Lord spread widely and grew in power.

d) *Glorify God by Dying for Him*

John 21 [19]Jesus said this to indicate the kind of death by which Peter would glorify God. Then he said to him, "Follow me!"

e) *Glorify God by Living to Please Him*

1 Cor 10 [31]So whether you eat or drink or whatever you do, do it all for the glory of God.
2 Thess 1 [11]With this in mind, we constantly pray for you, that our God may count you worthy of his calling, and that by his power he may fulfill every good purpose of yours and every act prompted by your faith. [12]We pray this so that the name of our Lord Jesus may be glorified in you, and you in him, according to the grace of our God and the Lord Jesus Christ.
1 Pet 2 [12]Live such good lives among the pagans that, though they accuse you of doing wrong, they may see your good deeds and glorify God on the day he visits us.

f) *Glorify God by Praising Him in Doxology*

Luke 2 [13]Suddenly a great company of the heavenly host appeared with the angel, praising God and saying, [14]"Glory to God in the highest, and on earth peace to men on whom his favor rests."
Rom 11 [33]Oh, the depth of the riches of the wisdom and knowledge of God! How unsearchable his judgments, and his paths beyond tracing out! [34]"Who has known the mind of the Lord? Or who has been his counselor?" [35]"Who has ever given to God, that God should repay him?" [36]For from him and through him and to him are all things. To him be the glory forever! Amen.
Rom 16 [27]to the only wise God be glory forever through Jesus Christ! Amen.
Gal 1 [3]Grace and peace to you from God our Father and the Lord Jesus Christ, . . . [5]to whom be glory for ever and ever. Amen.
Eph 3 [20]Now to him who is able to do immeasurably more than all we ask or imagine, according to his power that is at work within us, [21]to him be glory in the church and in Christ Jesus throughout all generations, for ever and ever! Amen.
Phil 4 [20]To our God and Father be glory for ever and ever. Amen.
2 Tim 4 [18]The Lord will rescue me from every evil attack and will bring me safely to his heavenly kingdom. To him be glory for ever and ever. Amen.
Heb 13 [20]May the God of peace, who through the blood of the eternal covenant brought back from the dead our Lord Jesus, that great Shepherd of the sheep, [21]equip you with everything good for doing his will, and may he work in us what is pleasing to him, through Jesus Christ, to whom be glory for ever and ever. Amen.
1 Pet 5 [10]And the God of all grace, who called you to his eternal glory in Christ, after you have suffered a little while, will himself restore you and make you strong, firm and steadfast. [11]To him be the power for ever and ever. Amen.
2 Pet 3 [18]But grow in the grace and knowledge of our Lord and Savior Jesus Christ. To him be glory both now and forever! Amen.
Jude [25]to the only God our Savior be glory, majesty, power and authority, through Jesus Christ our Lord, before all ages, now and forevermore! Amen.
Rev 4 [11]"You are worthy, our Lord and God, to receive glory and honor and power, for you created all things, and by your will they were created and have their being."
Rev 7 [12]saying: "Amen! Praise and glory and wisdom and thanks and honor and power and strength be to our God for ever and ever. Amen!"

g) *Glorify God by Relying on His Promises*

Rom 4 [20]Yet he did not waver through unbelief regarding the promise of God, but was strengthened in his faith and gave glory to God. . . .

h) *Glorify God by Suffering for Christ*

1 Pet 4 [12]Dear friends, do not be surprised at the painful trial you are suffering, as though something strange were happening to you. [13]But rejoice that you participate in the sufferings of Christ, so that you may be overjoyed when his glory is revealed. [14]If you are insulted because of the name of Christ, you are blessed, for the Spirit of glory and of God rests on you. [15]If you suffer, it should not be as a murderer or thief or any other kind of criminal, or even as a meddler. [16]However, if you suffer as a Christian, do not be ashamed, but praise God that you bear that name.

i) *Glorify God by Trusting in Christ*

Eph 1 [11]In him we were also chosen, having been predestined according to the plan of him who works out everything in conformity with the purpose of his will, [12]in order that we, who were the first to hope in Christ, might be for the praise of his glory. [13]And you also were included in Christ when you heard the word of truth, the gospel of your salvation. Having believed, you were marked in him with a seal, the promised Holy Spirit. . . .

j) Glorify God by Turning Back to Him

Isa 44 [23]Sing for joy, O heavens, for the LORD has done this; shout aloud, O earth beneath. Burst into song, you mountains, you forests and all your trees, for the LORD has redeemed Jacob, he displays his glory in Israel.

Isa 49 [3]He said to me, "You are my servant, Israel, in whom I will display my splendor." . . .

[5]And now the LORD says—he who formed me in the womb to be his servant to bring Jacob back to him and gather Israel to himself, for I am honored in the eyes of the LORD and my God has been my strength—[6]he says: "It is too small a thing for you to be my servant to restore the tribes of Jacob and bring back those of Israel I have kept. I will also make you a light for the Gentiles, that you may bring my salvation to the ends of the earth."

Isa 60 [1]"Arise, shine, for your light has come, and the glory of the LORD rises upon you. [2]See, darkness covers the earth and thick darkness is over the peoples, but the LORD rises upon you and his glory appears over you. . . .

[15]"Although you have been forsaken and hated, with no one traveling through, I will make you the everlasting pride and the joy of all generations. [16]You will drink the milk of nations and be nursed at royal breasts. Then you will know that I, the LORD, am your Savior, your Redeemer, the Mighty One of Jacob. . . . [18]No longer will violence be heard in your land, nor ruin or destruction within your borders, but you will call your walls Salvation and your gates Praise. [19]The sun will no more be your light by day, nor will the brightness of the moon shine on you, for the LORD will be your everlasting light, and your God will be your glory. [20]Your sun will never set again, and your moon will wane no more; the LORD will be your everlasting light, and your days of sorrow will end. [21]Then will all your people be righteous and they will possess the land forever. They are the shoot I have planted, the work of my hands, for the display of my splendor."

Isa 61 [1]The Spirit of the Sovereign LORD is on me, because the LORD has anointed me to preach good news to the poor. He has sent me to bind up the brokenhearted, to proclaim freedom for the captives and release from darkness for the prisoners, [2]to proclaim the year of the LORD's favor and the day of vengeance of our God, to comfort all who mourn, [3]and provide for those who grieve in Zion—to bestow on them a crown of beauty instead of ashes, the oil of gladness instead of mourning, and a garment of praise instead of a spirit of despair. They will be called oaks of righteousness, a planting of the LORD for the display of his splendor.

4. Illustrations of Glorifying God

a) Christ Glorified God

(1) Christ Sought Not His Own Glory, but the Father's

John 8 [50]"I am not seeking glory for myself; but there is one who seeks it, and he is the judge. . . ."

[54]Jesus replied, "If I glorify myself, my glory means nothing. My Father, whom you claim as your God, is the one who glorifies me."

John 13 [31]When he was gone, Jesus said, "Now is the Son of Man glorified and God is glorified in him. [32]If God is glorified in him, God will glorify the Son in himself, and will glorify him at once."

John 17 [22]"I have given them the glory that you gave me, that they may be one as we are one. . . .

[24]"Father, I want those you have given me to be with me where I am, and to see my glory, the glory you have given me because you loved me before the creation of the world."

(2) Christ Glorified God by His Works

John 17 [1]After Jesus said this, he looked toward heaven and prayed: "Father, the time has come. Glorify your Son, that your Son may glorigy you. . . . [4]I have brought you glory on earth by completing the work you gave me to do."

(3) Christ Was Glorified by His Disciples

Luke 19 [37]When he came near the place where the road goes down the Mount of Olives, the whole crowd of disciples began joyfully to praise God in loud voices for all the miracles they had seen: [38]"Blessed is the king who comes in the name of the Lord!" "Peace in heaven and glory in the highest!"

John 17 [6]"I have revealed you to those whom you gave me out of the world. They were yours; you gave them to me and they have obeyed your word. . . . [10]All I have is yours, and all you have is mine. And glory has come to me through them."

b) Others Glorified God

(1) Nebuchadnezzar Glorified God

Dan 4 [34]At the end of that time, I, Nebuchadnezzar, raised my eyes toward heaven, and my sanity was restored. Then I praised the Most High; I honored and glorified him who lives forever.

His dominion is an eternal dominion; his kingdom endures from generation to generation. [35]All the peoples of the earth are regarded as nothing. He does as he pleases with the powers of heaven and the peoples of the earth. No one can hold back his hand or say to him: "What have you done?"

[36]At the same time that my sanity was restored, my honor and splendor were returned to me for the glory of my kingdom. My advisers and nobles sought me out, and I was restored to my throne and became even greater than before. [37]Now I, Nebuchadnezzar, praise and exalt and glorify the King of heaven, because everything he does is right and all his ways are just. And those who walk in pride he is able to humble.

(2) Mary Glorified God

Luke 1 [46]And Mary said: "My soul glorifies the Lord. . . ."

(3) The Heavenly Host Glorified God

Luke 2 [13]Suddenly a great company of the heavenly host appeared with the angel, praising God and saying, [14]"Glory to God in the highest, and on earth peace to men on whom his favor rests."

(4) The Shepherds Glorified God

Luke 2 [20]The shepherds returned, glorifying and praising God for all the things they had heard and seen, which were just as they had been told.

E. Revere God

1. The Necessity of Fearing God

a) Fear Is God's Due

Exod 15 [11]"Who among the gods is like you, O LORD? Who is like you—majestic in holiness, awesome in glory, working wonders?"

Ps 76 [7]You alone are to be feared. Who can stand before you when you are angry? . . .

[11]Make vows to the LORD your God and fulfill them; let all the neighboring lands bring gifts to the One to be feared.

Ps 89 [7]In the council of the holy ones God is greatly feared; he is more awesome than all who surround him.

Ps 96 [4]For great is the LORD and most worthy of praise; he is to be feared above all gods.

Jer 5 [22]"Should you not fear me?" declares the LORD. "Should you not tremble in my presence? I made the sand a boundary for the sea, an everlasting barrier it cannot cross. The waves may roll, but they cannot prevail; they may roar, but they cannot cross it."

Jer 10 [7]Who should not revere you, O King of the nations? This is your due. Among all the wise men of the nations and in all their kingdoms, there is no one like you.

Mal 1 [6]"A son honors his father, and a servant his master. If I am a father, where is the honor due me? If I am a master, where is the respect due me?" says the LORD Almighty. "It is you, O priests, who show contempt for my name.

"But you ask, 'How have we shown contempt for your name?'"

Rev 15 [4]"Who will not fear you, O Lord, and bring glory to your name? For you alone are holy. All nations will come and worship before you, for your righteous acts have been revealed."

b) The Fear of God Is Commanded

Exod 20 [4]"You shall not make for yourself an idol in the form of anything in heaven above or on the earth beneath or in the waters below. [5]You shall not bow down to them or worship them; for I, the LORD your God, am a jealous God, punishing the children for the sin of the fathers to the third and fourth generation of those who hate me, [6]but showing love to a thousand generations of those who love me and keep my commandments.

[7]"You shall not misuse the name of the LORD your God, for the LORD will not hold anyone guiltless who misuses his name." . . .

[20]Moses said to the people, "Do not be afraid. God has come to test you, so that the fear of God will be with you to keep you from sinning."

Deut 6 [24]"The LORD commanded us to obey all these decrees and to fear the LORD our God, so that we might always prosper and be kept alive, as is the case today."

Josh 24 [14]"Now fear the LORD and serve him with all faithfulness. Throw away the gods your forefathers worshiped beyond the River and in Egypt, and serve the LORD."

1 Chron 16 [30]Tremble before him, all the earth! The world is firmly established; it cannot be moved.

Ps 22 [23]You who fear the LORD, praise him! All you descendants of Jacob, honor him! Revere him, all you descendants of Israel!

Ps 33 [8]Let all the earth fear the LORD; let all the people of the world revere him.

Ps 96 [9]Worship the LORD in the splendor of his holiness; tremble before him, all the earth.

Prov 23 [17]Do not let your heart envy sinners, but always be zealous for the fear of the LORD.

Prov 24 [21]Fear the LORD and the king, my son, and do not join with the rebellious. . . .

Eccles 12 [13]Now all has been heard; here is the conclusion of the matter: Fear God and keep his commandments, for this is the whole duty of man.

Isa 8 [11]The LORD spoke to me with his strong hand upon me, warning me not to follow the way of this people. He said: . . . [13]"The LORD Almighty is the one you are to regard as holy, he is the one you are to fear, he is the one you are to dread. . . ."

1 Pet 2 [17]Show proper respect to everyone: Love the brotherhood of believers, fear God, honor the king.

Rev 14 [7]He said in a loud voice, "Fear God and give him glory, because the hour of his judgment has come. Worship him who made the heavens, the earth, the sea and the springs of water."

c) The Fear of God Is Most Excellent

Job 28 [28]"And he said to man, 'The fear of the Lord—that is wisdom, and to shun evil is understanding.'"

Ps 19 [9]The fear of the LORD is pure, enduring forever. The ordinances of the LORD are sure and altogether righteous.

Ps 111 [10]The fear of the LORD is the beginning of wisdom; all who follow his precepts have good understanding. To him belongs eternal praise.

Prov 1 [7]The fear of the LORD is the beginning of knowledge, but fools despise wisdom and discipline.

Prov 9 [10]"The fear of the LORD is the beginning of wisdom, and knowledge of the Holy One is understanding."

Prov 15 [33]The fear of the LORD teaches a man wisdom, and humility comes before honor.

2. Reasons for Fearing God

a) Fear God Because of His Nature

Job 13 [9]"Would it turn out well if he examined you? Could you deceive him as you might deceive men? . . . [11]Would not his splendor terrify you? Would not the dread of him fall on you?"

Job 25 [2]"Dominion and awe belong to God; he establishes order in the heights of heaven."

Job 31 [23]"For I dreaded destruction from God, and for fear of his splendor I could not do such things."

Job 37 [22]"Out of the north he comes in golden splendor; God comes in awesome majesty. [23]The Almighty is beyond our reach and exalted in power; in his justice and great righteousness, he does not oppress. [24]Therefore, men revere him, for does he not have regard for all the wise in heart?"

Ps 111 [9]He provided redemption for his people; he ordained his covenant forever—holy and awesome is his name.

Ps 119 [120]My flesh trembles in fear of you; I stand in awe of your laws.

Ps 130 [4]But with you there is forgiveness; therefore you are feared.

Rev 15 [4]"Who will not fear you, O Lord, and bring glory to your name? For you alone are holy. All nations will come and worship before you, for your righteous acts have been revealed."

b) Fear God Because of His Word

Deut 4 [10]Remember the day you stood before the LORD your God at Horeb, when he said to me, "Assemble the people before me to hear my words so that they may learn to revere me as long as they live in the land and may teach them to their children."

Deut 31 [12]"Assemble the people—men, women and children, and the aliens living in your towns—so they can listen and learn to fear the LORD your God and follow carefully all the words of this law. [13]Their children, who do not know this law, must hear it and learn to fear the LORD your God as long as you live in the land you are crossing the Jordan to possess."

Ezra 9 [4]Then everyone who trembled at the words of the God of Israel gathered around me because of this unfaithfulness of the exiles. And I sat there appalled until the evening sacrifice.

Ezra 10 [3]"Now let us make a covenant before our God to send away all these women and their children, in accordance with the counsel of my lord and of those who fear the commands of our God. Let it be done according to the Law."

Ps 119 [120]My flesh trembles in fear of you; I stand in awe of your laws.

Isa 66 [2]"Has not my hand made all these things, and so they came into being?" declares the LORD.

"This is the one I esteem: he who is humble and contrite in spirit, and trembles at my word. . . ."

[5]Hear the word of the LORD, you who tremble at his word: "Your brothers who hate you, and exclude you because of my name, have said, 'Let the LORD be glorified, that we may see your joy!' Yet they will be put to shame."

c) Fear God Because of His Works

Josh 4 [23]"For the LORD your God dried up the Jordan before you until you had crossed over. The LORD your God did to the Jordan just what he had done to the Red Sea when he dried it up before us until we had crossed over. [24]He did this so that all the peoples of the earth might know that the hand of the LORD is powerful and so that you might always fear the LORD your God."

1 Kings 8 [39]". . . then hear from heaven, your dwelling place. Forgive and act; deal with each man according to all he does, since you know his heart (for you alone know the hearts of all men), [40]so that they will fear you all the time they live in the land you gave our fathers."

Ps 64 [9]All mankind will fear; they will proclaim the works of God and ponder what he has done.

Ps 65 [8]Those living far away fear your wonders; where morning dawns and evening fades you call forth songs of joy.

Eccles 3 [14]I know that everything God does will endure forever; nothing can be added to it and nothing taken from it. God does it so that men will revere him.

Jer 33 [8]"'I will cleanse them from all the sin they have committed against me and will forgive all their sins of rebellion against me. [9]Then this city will bring me renown, joy, praise and honor before all nations on earth that hear of all the good things I do for it; and they will be in awe and will tremble at the abundant prosperity and peace I provide for it.'"

3. Responses of Those Fearing God

a) Those Who Fear God Have Social Concern

Lev 19 [14]"'Do not curse the deaf or put a stumbling block in front of the blind, but fear your God. I am the LORD.

[15]"'Do not pervert justice; do not show partiality to the poor or favoritism to the great, but judge your neighbor fairly. . . .

[32]"'Rise in the presence of the aged, show respect for the

elderly and revere your God. I am the LORD.'"
Lev 25 [17]"'Do not take advantage of each other, but fear your God. I am the LORD your God. . . .

[35]"'If one of your countrymen becomes poor and is unable to support himself among you, help him as you would an alien or a temporary resident, so he can continue to live among you. [36]Do not take interest of any kind from him, but fear your God, so that your countryman may continue to live among you. . . . [42]Because the Israelites are my servants, whom I brought out of Egypt, they must not be sold as slaves. [43]Do not rule over them ruthlessly, but fear your God.'"

b) Those Who Fear God Live Righteously

Exod 18 [21]"But select capable men from all the people—men who fear God, trustworthy men who hate dishonest gain—and appoint them as officials over thousands, hundreds, fifties and tens."
Exod 20 [20]Moses said to the people, "Do not be afraid. God has come to test you, so that the fear of God will be with you to keep you from sinning."
Deut 13 [10]Stone him to death, because he tried to turn you away from the LORD your God, who brought you out of Egypt, out of the land of slavery. [11]Then all Israel will hear and be afraid, and no one among you will do such an evil thing again.
Neh 5 [9]So I continued, "What you are doing is not right. Shouldn't you walk in the fear of our God to avoid the reproach of our Gentile enemies? [10]I and my brothers and my men are also lending the people money and grain. But let the exacting of usury stop!"
Prov 3 [7]Do not be wise in your own eyes; fear the LORD and shun evil.
Prov 8 [13]"To fear the LORD is to hate evil; I hate pride and arrogance, evil behavior and perverse speech."
Prov 14 [16]A wise man fears the LORD and shuns evil, but a fool is hotheaded and reckless.
Prov 16 [6]Through love and faithfulness sin is atoned for; through the fear of the LORD a man avoids evil.
Acts 9 [31]Then the church throughout Judea, Galilee and Samaria enjoyed a time of peace. It was strengthened; and encouraged by the Holy Spirit, it grew in numbers, living in the fear of the Lord.
Acts 10 [34]Then Peter began to speak: "I now realize how true it is that God does not show favoritism [35]but accepts men from every nation who fear him and do what is right."
2 Cor 7 [1]Since we have these promises, dear friends, let us purify ourselves from everything that contaminates body and spirit, perfecting holiness out of reverence for God.
Phil 2 [12]Therefore, my dear friends, as you have always obeyed—not only in my presence, but now much more in my absence—continue to work out your salvation with fear and trembling, [13]for it is God who works in you to will and to act according to his good purpose.
1 Pet 3 [1]Wives, in the same way be submissive to your husbands so that, if any of them do not believe the word, they may be won over without words by the behavior of their wives, [2]when they see the purity and reverence of your lives.

c) Those Who Fear God Obey Him

Gen 22 [12]"Do not lay a hand on the boy," he said. "Do not do anything to him. Now I know that you fear God, because you have not withheld from me your son, your only son."
Deut 6 [1]These are the commands, decrees and laws the LORD your God directed me to teach you to observe in the land that you are crossing the Jordan to possess, [2]so that you, your children and their children after them may fear the LORD your God as long as you live by keeping all his decrees and commands that I give you, and so that you may enjoy long life. [3]Hear, O Israel, and be careful to obey so that it may go well with you and that you may increase greatly in a land flowing with milk and honey, just as the LORD, the God of your fathers, promised you.
Deut 10 [12]And now, O Israel, what does the LORD your God ask of you but to fear the LORD your God, to walk in all his ways, to love him, to serve the LORD your God with all your heart and with all your soul? . . . [20]Fear the LORD your God and serve him. Hold fast to him and take your oaths in his name.
Deut 13 [4]It is the LORD your God you must follow, and him you must revere. Keep his commands and obey him; serve him and hold fast to him.
Eccles 12 [13]Now all has been heard; here is the conclusion of the matter: Fear God and keep his commandments, for this is the whole duty of man.
Isa 50 [10]Who among you fears the LORD and obeys the word of his servant? Let him who walks in the dark, who has no light, trust in the name of the LORD and rely on his God.
Jer 32 [40]"I will make an everlasting covenant with them: I will never stop doing good to them, and I will inspire them to fear me, so that they will never turn away from me."
Eph 6 [5]Slaves, obey your earthly masters with respect and fear, and with sincerity of heart, just as you would obey Christ.
Col 3 [22]Slaves, obey your earthly masters in everything; and do it, not only when their eye is on you and to win their favor, but with sincerity of heart and reverence for the Lord.

d) Those Who Fear God Pray to Him

Ps 86 [11]Teach me your way, O LORD, and I will walk in your truth; give me an undivided heart, that I may fear your name.

e) Those Who Fear God Serve Him

Deut 6 [13]Fear the LORD your God, serve him only and take your oaths in his name.
Josh 24 [14]"Now fear the LORD and serve him with all faithfulness. Throw away the gods your forefathers worshiped beyond the River and in Egypt, and serve the LORD."
1 Sam 12 [24]"But be sure to fear the LORD and serve him faithfully with all your heart; consider what great things he has done for you."
Eph 5 [21]Submit to one another out of reverence for Christ.

f) Those Who Fear God Teach Others to Fear Him

Ps 34 [11]Come, my children, listen to me; I will teach you the fear of the LORD.

g) Those Who Fear God Worship Him

Ps 2 [11]Serve the LORD with fear and rejoice with trembling.
Ps 5 [7]But I, by your great mercy, will come into your house; in reverence will I bow down toward your holy temple.
Ps 22 [23]You who fear the LORD, praise him! All you descendants of Jacob, honor him! Revere him, all you descendants of Israel! . . .

[25]From you comes the theme of my praise in the great assembly; before those who fear you will I fulfill my vows.
Ps 135 [20]O house of Levi, praise the LORD; you who fear him, praise the LORD.
Acts 10 [2]He and all his family were devout and God-fearing; he gave generously to those in need and prayed to God regularly.
Heb 12 [28]Therefore, since we are receiving a kingdom that cannot be shaken, let us be thankful, and so worship God acceptably with reverence and awe, [29]for our "God is a consuming fire."

4. Promises to Those Fearing God

a) God Will Bless Those Who Fear Him

Deut 6 [24]"The LORD commanded us to obey all these decrees and to fear the LORD our God, so that we might always prosper and be kept alive, as is the case today."
Ps 31 [19]How great is your goodness, which you have stored up for those who fear you, which you bestow in the sight of men on those who take refuge in you.
Ps 67 [4]May the nations be glad and sing for joy, for you rule the peoples justly and guide the nations of the earth. . . . [7]God will bless us, and all the ends of the earth will fear him.
Ps 112 [1]Praise the LORD.

Blessed is the man who fears the LORD, who finds great delight in his commands.
Ps 115 [13]he will bless those who fear the LORD—small and great alike.
Ps 128 [1]Blessed are all who fear the LORD, who walk in his ways. [2]You will eat the fruit of your labor; blessings and prosperity will be yours. [3]Your wife will be like a fruitful vine within

your house; your sons will be like olive shoots around your table. [4]Thus is the man blessed who fears the LORD.
Prov 10 [27]The fear of the LORD adds length to life, but the years of the wicked are cut short.
Prov 19 [23]The fear of the LORD leads to life: Then one rests content, untouched by trouble.
Prov 22 [4]Humility and the fear of the LORD bring wealth and honor and life.
Prov 28 [14]Blessed is the man who always fears the LORD, but he who hardens his heart falls into trouble.

b) God Will Deliver Those Who Fear Him

Ps 33 [18]But the eyes of the LORD are on those who fear him, on those whose hope is in his unfailing love, [19]to deliver them from death and keep them alive in famine.
Ps 34 [7]The angel of the LORD encamps around those who fear him, and he delivers them.
Ps 85 [9]Surely his salvation is near those who fear him, that his glory may dwell in our land.
Ps 145 [19]He fulfills the desires of those who fear him; he hears their cry and saves them.

c) God Will Favor Those Who Fear Him

Neh 1 [11]"O Lord, let your ear be attentive to the prayer of this your servant and to the prayer of your servants who delight in revering your name. Give your servant success today by granting him favor in the presence of this man."

I was cupbearer to the king.
Ps 147 [11]the LORD delights in those who fear him, who put their hope in his unfailing love.
Prov 15 [16]Better a little with the fear of the LORD than great wealth with turmoil.
Eccles 8 [12]Although a wicked man commits a hundred crimes and still lives a long time, I know that it will go better with God-fearing men, who are reverent before God. [13]Yet because the wicked do not fear God, it will not go well with them, and their days will not lengthen like a shadow.
Luke 1 [50]"His mercy extends to those who fear him, from generation to generation."

d) God Will Give Understanding to Those Who Fear Him

Ps 25 [12]Who, then, is the man that fears the LORD? He will instruct him in the way chosen for him. . . . [14]The LORD confides in those who fear him; he makes his covenant known to them.
Eccles 7 [18]It is good to grasp the one and not let go of the other. The man who fears God will avoid all extremes.
Isa 33 [6]He will be the sure foundation for your times, a rich store of salvation and wisdom and knowledge; the fear of the LORD is the key to this treasure.

e) God Will Love Those Who Fear Him

Ps 103 [11]For as high as the heavens are above the earth, so great is his love for those who fear him. . . . [13]As a father has compassion on his children, so the LORD has compassion on those who fear him. . . . [17]But from everlasting to everlasting the LORD's love is with those who fear him, and his righteousness with their children's children. . . .

f) God Will Protect Those Who Fear Him

Ps 60 [4]But for those who fear you, you have raised a banner to be unfurled against the bow.
Ps 115 [11]You who fear him, trust in the LORD—he is their help and shield.
Prov 14 [26]He who fears the LORD has a secure fortress, and for his children it will be a refuge.

[27]The fear of the LORD is a fountain of life, turning a man from the snares of death.
Mal 3 [16]Then those who feared the LORD talked with each other, and the LORD listened and heard. A scroll of remembrance was written in his presence concerning those who feared the LORD and honored his name.

[17]"They will be mine," says the LORD Almighty, "in the day when I make up my treasured possession. I will spare them, just as in compassion a man spares his son who serves him."

g) God Will Restore Those Who Fear Him

Zeph 3 [7]"I said to the city, 'Surely you will fear me and accept correction!' Then her dwelling would not be cut off, nor all my punishments come upon her. But they were still eager to act corruptly in all they did."
Mal 4 [2]"But for you who revere my name, the sun of righteousness will rise with healing in its wings. And you will go out and leap like calves released from the stall."

h) God Will Reward Those Who Fear Him

Rev 11 [18]"The nations were angry; and your wrath has come. The time has come for judging the dead, and for rewarding your servants the prophets and your saints and those who reverence your name, both small and great—and for destroying those who destroy the earth."

i) God Will Sustain Those Who Fear Him

Ps 34 [9]Fear the LORD, you his saints, for those who fear him lack nothing.
Ps 111 [5]He provides food for those who fear him; he remembers his covenant forever.

5. Examples of Those Fearing God

a) Noah Feared God

Heb 11 [7]By faith Noah, when warned about things not yet seen, in holy fear built an ark to save his family. By his faith he condemned the world and became heir of the righteousness that comes by faith.

b) Isaac Feared God

Gen 31 [42]"If the God of my father, the God of Abraham and the Fear of Isaac, had not been with me, you would surely have sent me away empty-handed. But God has seen my hardship and the toil of my hands, and last night he rebuked you." . . .

[53]"May the God of Abraham and the God of Nahor, the God of their father, judge between us."

So Jacob took an oath in the name of the Fear of his father Isaac.

c) Joseph Feared God

Gen 42 [18]On the third day, Joseph said to them, "Do this and you will live, for I fear God. . . ."

d) The Hebrew Midwives Feared God

Exod 1 [17]The midwives, however, feared God and did not do what the king of Egypt had told them to do; they let the boys live. . . . [21]And because the midwives feared God, he gave them families of their own.

e) Officials of Pharaoh Feared God

Exod 9 [20]Those officials of Pharaoh who feared the word of the LORD hurried to bring their slaves and their livestock inside.

f) Israel Feared God

Exod 14 [31]And when the Israelites saw the great power the LORD displayed against the Egyptians, the people feared the LORD and put their trust in him and in Moses his servant.
1 Sam 12 [18]Then Samuel called upon the LORD, and that same day the LORD sent thunder and rain. So all the people stood in awe of the LORD and of Samuel.

g) Job Feared God

Job 1 [1]In the land of Uz there lived a man whose name was Job. This man was blameless and upright; he feared God and shunned evil. . . .

[8]Then the LORD said to Satan, "Have you considered my servant Job? There is no one on earth like him; he is blameless and upright, a man who fears God and shuns evil."
Job 2 [3]Then the LORD said to Satan, "Have you considered my servant Job? There is no one on earth like him; he is blameless and upright, a man who fears God and shuns evil. And he still maintains his integrity, though you incited me against him to ruin him without any reason."

h) The Levitical Priesthood Feared God

Mal 2 [4]"And you will know that I have sent you this admonition so that my covenant with Levi may continue," says the

LORD Almighty. [5]"My covenant was with him, a covenant of life and peace, and I gave them to him; this called for reverence and he revered me and stood in awe of my name. [6]True instruction was in his mouth and nothing false was found on his lips. He walked with me in peace and uprightness, and turned many from sin."

i) The Widow's Husband Feared God

2 Kings 4 [1]The wife of a man from the company of the prophets cried out to Elisha, "Your servant my husband is dead, and you know that he revered the LORD. But now his creditor is coming to take my two boys as his slaves."

j) Hanani Feared God

Neh 7 [2]I put in charge of Jerusalem my brother Hanani, along with Hananiah the commander of the citadel, because he was a man of integrity and feared God more than most men do.

k) The Jerusalem Church Feared God

Acts 5 [11]Great fear seized the whole church and all who heard about these events.

F. Honor God

1. The Obligation to Honor God

a) We Owe Honor to God

Exod 12 [42]Because the LORD kept vigil that night to bring them out of Egypt, on this night all the Israelites are to keep vigil to honor the LORD for the generations to come.

1 Sam 2 [29]"'Why do you scorn my sacrifice and offering that I prescribed for my dwelling? Why do you honor your sons more than me by fattening yourselves on the choice parts of every offering made by my people Israel?'

[30]"Therefore the LORD, the God of Israel, declares: 'I promised that your house and your father's house would minister before me forever.' But now the LORD declares: 'Far be it from me! Those who honor me I will honor, but those who despise me will be disdained.'"

Isa 26 [12]LORD, you establish peace for us; all that we have accomplished you have done for us. [13]O LORD, our God, other lords besides you have ruled over us, but your name alone do we honor.

Mal 1 [6]"A son honors his father, and a servant his master. If I am a father, where is the honor due me? If I am a master, where is the respect due me?" says the LORD Almighty. "It is you, O priests, who show contempt for my name.

"But you ask, 'How have we shown contempt for your name?'"

John 8 [49]"I am not possessed by a demon," said Jesus, "but I honor my Father and you dishonor me."

1 Tim 1 [17]Now to the King eternal, immortal, invisible, the only God, be honor and glory for ever and ever. Amen.

1 Tim 6 [15]which God will bring about in his own time—God, the blessed and only Ruler, the King of kings and Lord of lords, [16]who alone is immortal and who lives in unapproachable light, whom no one has seen or can see. To him be honor and might forever. Amen.

b) We Owe Honor to Christ

Matt 17 [5]While he was still speaking, a bright cloud enveloped them, and a voice from the cloud said, "This is my Son, whom I love; with him I am well pleased. Listen to him!"

John 5 [22]"Moreover, the Father judges no one, but has entrusted all judgment to the Son, [23]that all may honor the Son just as they honor the Father. He who does not honor the Son does not honor the Father, who sent him."

Rev 5 [12]In a loud voice they sang: "Worthy is the Lamb, who was slain, to receive power and wealth and wisdom and strength and honor and glory and praise!"

[13]Then I heard every creature in heaven and on earth and under the earth and on the sea, and all that is in them, singing: "To him who sits on the throne and to the Lamb be praise and honor and glory and power, for ever and ever!"

2. The Means of Honoring God

a) Honor God by Keeping the Sabbath

Isa 58 [13]"If you keep your feet from breaking the Sabbath and from doing as you please on my holy day, if you call the Sabbath a delight and the LORD's holy day honorable, and if you honor it by not going your own way and not doing as you please or speaking idle words, [14]then you will find your joy in the LORD, and I will cause you to ride on the heights of the land and to feast on the inheritance of your father Jacob." The mouth of the LORD has spoken.

b) Honor God through Acts of Mercy

Prov 14 [31]He who oppresses the poor shows contempt for their Maker, but whoever is kind to the needy honors God.

c) Honor God with Holy Living

Num 27 [12]Then the LORD said to Moses, "Go up this mountain in the Abarim range and see the land I have given the Israelites. [13]After you have seen it, you too will be gathered to your people, as your brother Aaron was, [14]for when the community rebelled at the waters in the Desert of Zin, both of you disobeyed my command to honor me as holy before their eyes." (These were the waters of Meribah Kadesh, in the Desert of Zin.)

Jer 33 [8]"'I will cleanse them from all the sin they have committed against me and will forgive all their sins of rebellion against me. [9]Then this city will bring me renown, joy, praise and honor before all nations on earth that hear of all the good things I do for it; and they will be in awe and will tremble at the abundant prosperity and peace I provide for it.'"

1 Cor 6 [19]Do you not know that your body is a temple of the Holy Spirit, who is in you, whom you have received from God? You are not your own; [20]you were bought at a price. Therefore honor God with your body.

d) Honor God with Offerings

Prov 3 [9]Honor the LORD with your wealth, with the firstfruits of all your crops; [10]then your barns will be filled to overflowing, and your vats will brim over with new wine.

2 Cor 8 [19]What is more, he was chosen by the churches to accompany us as we carry the offering, which we administer in order to honor the Lord himself and to show our eagerness to help.

e) Honor God with Worship and Praise

Ps 22 [22]I will declare your name to my brothers; in the congregation I will praise you. [23]You who fear the LORD, praise him! All you descendants of Jacob, honor him! Revere him, all you descendants of Israel!

Isa 43 [20]"The wild animals honor me, the jackals and the owls, because I provide water in the desert and streams in the wasteland, to give drink to my people, my chosen, [21]the people I formed for myself that they may proclaim my praise.

[22]"Yet you have not called upon me, O Jacob, you have not wearied yourselves for me, O Israel. [23]You have not brought me sheep for burnt offerings, nor honored me with your sacrifices. I have not burdened you with grain offerings nor wearied you with demands for incense."

Dan 4 [34]At the end of that time, I, Nebuchadnezzar, raised my eyes toward heaven, and my sanity was restored. Then I praised the Most High; I honored and glorified him who lives forever.

His dominion is an eternal dominion; his kingdom endures from generation to generation. [35]All the peoples of the earth are regarded as nothing. He does as he pleases with the powers of heaven and the peoples of the earth. No one can hold back his hand or say to him: "What have you done?"

[36]At the same time that my sanity was restored, my honor and splendor were returned to me for the glory of my kingdom. My advisers and nobles sought me out, and I was restored to my throne and became even greater than before. [37]Now I, Nebuchadnezzar, praise and exalt and glorify the King of heaven, because everything he does is right and all his ways are just. And those who walk in pride he is able to humble.

Dan 5 [23]"Instead, you have set yourself up against the Lord of heaven. You had the goblets from his temple brought to you, and you and your nobles, your wives and your concubines drank wine from them. You praised the gods of silver and gold, of bronze, iron, wood and stone, which cannot see or hear or understand. But you did not honor the God who holds in his hand your life and all your ways."

1 Tim 1 [17]Now to the King eternal, immortal, invisible, the only God, be honor and glory for ever and ever. Amen.

1 Tim 6 [15]which God will bring about in his own time—God, the blessed and only Ruler, the King of kings and Lord of lords, [16]who alone is immortal and who lives in unapproachable light, whom no one has seen or can see. To him be honor and might forever. Amen.

Rev 4 [11]"You are worthy, our Lord and God, to receive glory and honor and power, for you created all things, and by your will they were created and have their being."

Rev 7 [11]All the angels were standing around the throne and around the elders and the four living creatures. They fell down on their faces before the throne and worshiped God, [12]saying: "Amen! Praise and glory and wisdom and thanks and honor and power and strength be to our God for ever and ever. Amen!"

f) Honor God with Zeal for His Honor

Num 25 [10]The LORD said to Moses, [11]"Phinehas son of Eleazar, the son of Aaron, the priest, has turned my anger away from the Israelites; for he was as zealous as I am for my honor among them, so that in my zeal I did not put an end to them. [12]Therefore tell him I am making my covenant of peace with him. [13]He and his descendants will have a covenant of a lasting priesthood, because he was zealous for the honor of his God and made atonement for the Israelites."

IV
Loving God

A. The Duty of Loving God

1. Love of God Is Commanded

Deut 10 [12]And now, O Israel, what does the LORD your God ask of you but to fear the LORD your God, to walk in all his ways, to love him, to serve the LORD your God with all your heart and with all your soul, [13]and to observe the LORD's commands and decrees that I am giving you today for your own good?

Deut 11 [13]So if you faithfully obey the commands I am giving you today—to love the LORD your God and to serve him with all your heart and with all your soul . . .

Deut 30 [19]This day I call heaven and earth as witnesses against you that I have set before you life and death, blessings and curses. Now choose life, so that you and your children may live [20]and that you may love the LORD your God, listen to his voice, and hold fast to him. For the LORD is your life, and he will give you many years in the land he swore to give to your fathers, Abraham, Isaac and Jacob.

Ps 31 [23]Love the LORD, all his saints! The LORD preserves the faithful, but the proud he pays back in full.

Matt 22 [36]"Teacher, which is the greatest commandment in the Law?"

[37]Jesus replied: "'Love the Lord your God with all your heart and with all your soul and with all your mind.' [38]This is the first and greatest commandment."

1 Thess 5 [8]But since we belong to the day, let us be self-controlled, putting on faith and love as a breastplate, and the hope of salvation as a helmet.

1 Tim 6 [11]But you, man of God, flee from all this, and pursue righteousness, godliness, faith, love, endurance and gentleness.

1 John 5 [2]This is how we know that we love the children of God: by loving God and carrying out his commands. [3]This is love for God: to obey his commands. And his commands are not burdensome. . . .

Jude [21]Keep yourselves in God's love as you wait for the mercy of our Lord Jesus Christ to bring you to eternal life.

2. Love of God Is Prayed For

Eph 3 [14]For this reason I kneel before the Father, [15]from whom his whole family in heaven and on earth derives its name. [16]I pray that out of his glorious riches he may strengthen you with power through his Spirit in your inner being, [17]so that Christ may dwell in your hearts through faith. And I pray that you, being rooted and established in love, [18]may have power, together with all the saints, to grasp how wide and long and high and deep is the love of Christ, [19]and to know this love that surpasses knowledge—that you may be filled to the measure of all the fullness of God.

Eph 6 [23]Peace to the brothers, and love with faith from God the Father and the Lord Jesus Christ. [24]Grace to all who love our Lord Jesus Christ with an undying love.

Phil 1 [9]And this is my prayer: that your love may abound more and more in knowledge and depth of insight. . . .

2 Thess 3 [5]May the Lord direct your hearts into God's love and Christ's perseverance.

3. Failure to Love God Is Warned Against

Josh 23 [10]"One of you routs a thousand, because the LORD your God fights for you, just as he promised. [11]So be very careful to love the LORD your God.

[12]"But if you turn away and ally yourselves with the survivors of these nations that remain among you and if you intermarry with them and associate with them, [13]then you may be sure that the LORD your God will no longer drive out these nations before you. Instead, they will become snares and traps for you, whips on your backs and thorns in your eyes, until you perish from this good land, which the LORD your God has given you."

Matt 10 [37]"Anyone who loves his father or mother more than me is not worthy of me; anyone who loves his son or daughter more than me is not worthy of me. . . ."

1 Cor 16 [22]If anyone does not love the Lord—a curse be on him. Come, O Lord!

Rev 2 [4]"Yet I hold this against you: You have forsaken your first love."

B. The Nature of Loving God

1. Love of God Becomes the Means through Which Faith Is Expressed

John 16 [27]"No, the Father himself loves you because you have loved me and have believed that I came from God."

Gal 5 [6]For in Christ Jesus neither circumcision nor uncircumcision has any value. The only thing that counts is faith expressing itself through love.

Eph 4 [15]Instead, speaking the truth in love, we will in all things grow up into him who is the Head, that is, Christ. [16]From him the whole body, joined and held together by every supporting ligament, grows and builds itself up in love, as each part does its work.

1 Thess 1 [3]We continually remember before our God and Father your work produced by faith, your labor prompted by love, and your endurance inspired by hope in our Lord Jesus Christ.

Heb 6 [10]God is not unjust; he will not forget your work and the love you have shown him as you have helped his people and continue to help them.

1 John 3 [17]If anyone has material possessions and sees his brother in need but has no pity on him, how can the love of God be in him? . . . [23]And this is his command: to believe in the name of his Son, Jesus Christ, and to love one another as he commanded us.

1 John 4 [20]If anyone says, "I love God," yet hates his brother, he is a liar. For anyone who does not love his brother, whom he has seen, cannot love God, whom he has not seen.

2. Love of God Casts Out Fear

1 John 4 [17]In this way, love is made complete among us so that we will have confidence on the day of judgment, because in this world we are like him. [18]There is no fear in love. But perfect love drives out fear, because fear has to do with punishment. The one who fears is not made perfect in love.

3. Love of God Involves the Whole Person

Deut 6 [5]Love the LORD your God with all your heart and with all your soul and with all your strength.
Luke 10 [25]On one occasion an expert in the law stood up to test Jesus. "Teacher," he asked, "what must I do to inherit eternal life?"

[26]"What is written in the Law?" he replied. "How do you read it?"

[27]He answered: "'Love the Lord your God with all your heart and with all your soul and with all your strength and with all your mind'; and, 'Love your neighbor as yourself.'"

[28]"You have answered correctly," Jesus replied. "Do this and you will live."

4. Love of God Is an Eternal Relationship

Rom 8 [38]For I am convinced that neither death nor life, neither angels nor demons, neither the present nor the future, nor any powers, [39]neither height nor depth, nor anything else in all creation, will be able to separate us from the love of God that is in Christ Jesus our Lord.

5. Love of God Is Given through the Holy Spirit

Rom 5 [5]And hope does not disappoint us, because God has poured out his love into our hearts by the Holy Spirit, whom he has given us.
Gal 5 [22]But the fruit of the Spirit is love, joy, peace, patience, kindness, goodness, faithfulness. . . .
Col 1 [8]and who also told us of your love in the Spirit.

6. Love of God Joins the Believer in Intimate Union with God

Prov 8 [17]"I love those who love me, and those who seek me find me."
John 14 [21]"Whoever has my commands and obeys them, he is the one who loves me. He who loves me will be loved by my Father, and I too will love him and show myself to him." . . .

[23]Jesus replied, "If anyone loves me, he will obey my teaching. My Father will love him, and we will come to him and make our home with him."
1 Cor 8 [3]But the man who loves God is known by God.
2 Cor 13 [14]May the grace of the Lord Jesus Christ, and the love of God, and the fellowship of the Holy Spirit be with you all.

7. Love of God Reflects His Inmost Being

Deut 30 [2]and when you and your children return to the LORD your God and obey him with all your heart and with all your soul according to everything I command you today, [3]then the LORD your God will restore your fortunes and have compassion on you and gather you again from all the nations where he scattered you. . . . [6]The LORD your God will circumcise your hearts and the hearts of your descendants, so that you may love him with all your heart and with all your soul, and live.
1 John 4 [8]Whoever does not love does not know God, because God is love. . . . [16]And so we know and rely on the love God has for us.

God is love. Whoever lives in love lives in God, and God in him. . . .

[19]We love because he first loved us.

8. Love of God Requires the Love of Other People

1 John 4 [20]If anyone says, "I love God," yet hates his brother, he is a liar. For anyone who does not love his brother, whom he has seen, cannot love God, whom he has not seen. [21]And he has given us this command: Whoever loves God must also love his brother.
1 John 5 [1]Everyone who believes that Jesus is the Christ is born of God, and everyone who loves the father loves his child as well. [2]This is how we know that we love the children of God: by loving God and carrying out his commands.

9. Love of God Requires Obedience

Deut 11 [1]Love the LORD your God and keep his requirements, his decrees, his laws and his commands always.
Deut 30 [15]See, I set before you today life and prosperity, death and destruction. [16]For I command you today to love the LORD your God, to walk in his ways, and to keep his commands, decrees and laws; then you will live and increase, and the LORD your God will bless you in the land you are entering to possess.
Josh 22 [5]"But be very careful to keep the commandment and the law that Moses the servant of the LORD gave you: to love the LORD your God, to walk in all his ways, to obey his commands, to hold fast to him and to serve him with all your heart and all your soul."
Mark 12 [33]"To love him with all your heart, with all your understanding and with all your strength, and to love your neighbor as yourself is more important than all burnt offerings and sacrifices."
John 14 [15]"If you love me, you will obey what I command. . . . [21]Whoever has my commands and obeys them, he is the one who loves me. He who loves me will be loved by my Father, and I too will love him and show myself to him." . . .

[23]Jesus replied, "If anyone loves me, he will obey my teaching. My Father will love him, and we will come to him and make our home with him."
John 15 [10]"If you obey my commands, you will remain in my love, just as I have obeyed my Father's commands and remain in his love."
John 21 [15]When they had finished eating, Jesus said to Simon Peter, "Simon son of John, do you truly love me more than these?"

"Yes, Lord," he said, "you know that I love you."

Jesus said, "Feed my lambs."

[16]Again Jesus said, "Simon son of John, do you truly love me?"

He answered, "Yes, Lord, you know that I love you."

Jesus said, "Take care of my sheep."

[17]The third time he said to him, "Simon son of John, do you love me?"

Peter was hurt because Jesus asked him the third time, "Do you love me?" He said, "Lord, you know all things; you know that I love you."

Jesus said, "Feed my sheep."
2 Cor 5 [14]For Christ's love compels us, because we are convinced that one died for all, and therefore all died. [15]And he died for all, that those who live should no longer live for themselves, but for him who died for them and was raised again.
1 John 2 [4]The man who says, "I know him," but does not do what he commands is a liar, and the truth is not in him. [5]But if anyone obeys his word, God's love is truly made complete in him. This is how we know we are in him. . . .
1 John 5 [3]This is love for God: to obey his commands. And his commands are not burdensome. . . .
2 John [6]And this is love: that we walk in obedience to his commands. As you have heard from the beginning, his command is that you walk in love.

C. Promises to Those Loving God

1. God Faithfully Cares for Those Who Love Him

Deut 7 [9]Know therefore that the LORD your God is God; he is the faithful God, keeping his covenant of love to a thousand generations of those who love him and keep his commands.
Neh 1 [5]Then I said: "O LORD, God of heaven, the great and awesome God, who keeps his covenant of love with those who love him and obey his commands . . ."

2. God Forgives the Sins of Those Who Love Him

Luke 7 [47]"Therefore, I tell you, her many sins have been forgiven—for she loved much. But he who has been forgiven little loves little."

3. God Gives Assurance to Those Who Love Him

Rom 8 [28]And we know that in all things God works for the good of those who love him, who have been called according to his purpose.

4. God Gives an Inheritance to Those Who Love Him

1 Cor 2 [9]However, as it is written: "No eye has seen, no ear has heard, no mind has conceived what God has prepared for those who love him." . . .
James 1 [12]Blessed is the man who perseveres under trial, because when he has stood the test, he will receive the crown of life that God has promised to those who love him.
James 2 [5]Listen, my dear brothers: Has not God chosen those who are poor in the eyes of the world to be rich in faith and to inherit the kingdom he promised those who love him?

5. God Protects Those Who Love Him

Ps 5 [11]But let all who take refuge in you be glad; let them ever sing for joy. Spread your protection over them, that those who love your name may rejoice in you.
Ps 91 [14]"Because he loves me," says the LORD, "I will rescue him; I will protect him, for he acknowledges my name. [15]He will call upon me, and I will answer him; I will be with him in trouble, I will deliver him and honor him."
Ps 145 [20]The LORD watches over all who love him, but all the wicked he will destroy.

6. God Saves Those Who Love Him

Ps 91 [14]"Because he loves me," says the LORD, "I will rescue him; I will protect him, for he acknowledges my name. [15]He will call upon me, and I will answer him; I will be with him in trouble, I will deliver him and honor him. [16]With long life will I satisfy him and show him my salvation."
1 Pet 1 [8]Though you have not seen him, you love him; and even though you do not see him now, you believe in him and are filled with an inexpressible and glorious joy, [9]for you are receiving the goal of your faith, the salvation of your souls.

7. God Shows Mercy to Those Who Love Him

Exod 20 [5]"You shall not bow down to them or worship them; for I, the LORD your God, am a jealous God, punishing the children for the sin of the fathers to the third and fourth generation of those who hate me, [6]but showing love to a thousand generations of those who love me and keep my commandments."
Ps 119 [132]Turn to me and have mercy on me, as you always do to those who love your name.

D. Illustrations of Love

1. Love within the Godhead

a) The Father's Love for the Son

Matt 3 [17]And a voice from heaven said, "This is my Son, whom I love; with him I am well pleased."
Matt 12 [17]This was to fulfill what was spoken through the prophet Isaiah: [18]"Here is my servant whom I have chosen, the one I love, in whom I delight; I will put my Spirit on him, and he will proclaim justice to the nations."
Matt 17 [5]While he was still speaking, a bright cloud enveloped them, and a voice from the cloud said, "This is my Son, whom I love; with him I am well pleased. Listen to him!"
John 3 [35]"The Father loves the Son and has placed everything in his hands."
John 8 [29]"The one who sent me is with me; he has not left me alone, for I always do what pleases him." . . .
[42]Jesus said to them, "If God were your Father, you would love me, for I came from God and now am here. I have not come on my own; but he sent me."
John 17 [24]"Father, I want those you have given me to be with me where I am, and to see my glory, the glory you have given me because you loved me before the creation of the world. . . . [26]I have made you known to them, and will continue to make you known in order that the love you have for me may be in them and that I myself may be in them."
2 Pet 1 [17]For he received honor and glory from God the Father when the voice came to him from the Majestic Glory, saying, "This is my Son, whom I love; with him I am well pleased."

b) The Son's Love for the Father

John 14 [31]". . . but the world must learn that I love the Father and that I do exactly what my Father has commanded me.
"Come now; let us leave."

c) Christ's Love for the Church

John 15 [9]"As the Father has loved me, so have I loved you. Now remain in my love. [10]If you obey my commands, you will remain in my love, just as I have obeyed my Father's commands and remain in his love. [11]I have told you this so that my joy may be in you and that your joy may be complete. [12]My command is this: Love each other as I have loved you. [13]Greater love has no one than this, that he lay down his life for his friends."
Eph 5 [25]Husbands, love your wives, just as Christ loved the church and gave himself up for her. . . .

2. Love for God

a) David Loved God

Ps 18 [1]I love you, O LORD, my strength.

b) Solomon Loved God

1 Kings 3 [3]Solomon showed his love for the LORD by walking according to the statutes of his father David, except that he offered sacrifices and burned incense on the high places.

c) Peter Loved God

John 21 [15]When they had finished eating, Jesus said to Simon Peter, "Simon son of John, do you truly love me more than these?"
"Yes, Lord," he said, "you know that I love you."
Jesus said, "Feed my lambs."
[16]Again Jesus said, "Simon son of John, do you truly love me?"
He answered, "Yes, Lord, you know that I love you."
Jesus said, "Take care of my sheep."
[17]The third time he said to him, "Simon son of John, do you love me?"
Peter was hurt because Jesus asked him the third time, "Do you love me?" He said, "Lord, you know all things; you know that I love you."
Jesus said, "Feed my sheep."

d) Paul Loved God

2 Cor 6 [3]We put no stumbling block in anyone's path, so that our ministry will not be discredited. [4]Rather, as servants of God we commend ourselves in every way: in great endurance; in troubles, hardships and distresses; [5]in beatings, imprisonments and riots; in hard work, sleepless nights and hunger; [6]in purity, understanding, patience and kindness; in the Holy Spirit and in sincere love. . . .

e) The Church at Colosse Loved God

Col 1 [7]You learned it from Epaphras, our dear fellow servant, who is a faithful minister of Christ on our behalf, [8]and who also told us of your love in the Spirit.

V
Obeying God

A. Obey God

1. Characteristics of Obedience

a) Obedience Accompanies Faith and God's Calling

Acts 6 [7]So the word of God spread. The number of disciples in Jerusalem increased rapidly, and a large number of priests became obedient to the faith.
Rom 1 [5]Through him and for his name's sake, we received grace and apostleship to call people from among all the Gentiles to the obedience that comes from faith.
Rom 6 [16]Don't you know that when you offer yourselves to someone to obey him as slaves, you are slaves to the one whom you obey—whether you are slaves to sin, which leads to death, or to obedience, which leads to righteousness? [17]But thanks be to God that, though you used to be slaves to sin, you wholeheartedly obeyed the form of teaching to which you were entrusted.
Rom 15 [18]I will not venture to speak of anything except what Christ has accomplished through me in leading the Gentiles to obey God by what I have said and done. . . .
Heb 11 [6]And without faith it is impossible to please God, because anyone who comes to him must believe that he exists and that he rewards those who earnestly seek him. . . .
[8]By faith Abraham, when called to go to a place he would later receive as his inheritance, obeyed and went, even though he did not know where he was going.
1 Pet 1 [2]who have been chosen according to the foreknowledge of God the Father, through the sanctifying work of the Spirit, for obedience to Jesus Christ and sprinkling by his blood: Grace and peace be yours in abundance.

b) Obedience Accompanies the Fear of God

Deut 6 [24]"The LORD commanded us to obey all these decrees and to fear the LORD our God, so that we might always prosper and be kept alive, as is the case today."
Josh 24 [14]"Now fear the LORD and serve him with all faithfulness. Throw away the gods your forefathers worshiped beyond the River and in Egypt, and serve the LORD."
1 Sam 12 [14]"If you fear the LORD and serve and obey him and do not rebel against his commands, and if both you and the king who reigns over you follow the LORD your God—good!"
Ps 111 [10]The fear of the LORD is the beginning of wisdom; all who follow his precepts have good understanding. To him belongs eternal praise.
Eccles 12 [13]Now all has been heard; here is the conclusion of the matter: Fear God and keep his commandments, for this is the whole duty of man.
Hag 1 [12]Then Zerubbabel son of Shealtiel, Joshua son of Jehozadak, the high priest, and the whole remnant of the people obeyed the voice of the LORD their God and the message of the prophet Haggai, because the LORD their God had sent him. And the people feared the LORD.
2 Cor 7 [15]And his affection for you is all the greater when he remembers that you were all obedient, receiving him with fear and trembling.
Phil 2 [12]Therefore, my dear friends, as you have always obeyed—not only in my presence, but now much more in my absence—continue to work out your salvation with fear and trembling. . . .

c) Obedience Accompanies Repentance

1 Sam 7 [3]And Samuel said to the whole house of Israel, "If you are returning to the LORD with all your hearts, then rid yourselves of the foreign gods and the Ashtoreths and commit yourselves to the LORD and serve him only, and he will deliver you out of the hand of the Philistines."
Isa 1 [18]"Come now, let us reason together," says the LORD. "Though your sins are like scarlet, they shall be as white as snow; though they are red as crimson, they shall be like wool. [19]If you are willing and obedient, you will eat the best from the land. . . ."
[27]Zion will be redeemed with justice, her penitent ones with righteousness.

d) Obedience Establishes a Pattern for Others to Follow

Eph 6 [1]Children, obey your parents in the Lord, for this is right. [2]"Honor your father and mother"—which is the first commandment with a promise—[3]"that it may go well with you and that you may enjoy long life on the earth." . . .
[5]Slaves, obey your earthly masters with respect and fear, and with sincerity of heart, just as you would obey Christ. [6]Obey them not only to win their favor when their eye is on you, but like slaves of Christ, doing the will of God from your heart. [7]Serve wholeheartedly, as if you were serving the Lord, not men, [8]because you know that the Lord will reward everyone for whatever good he does, whether he is slave or free.
[9]And masters, treat your slaves in the same way. Do not threaten them, since you know that he who is both their Master and yours is in heaven, and there is no favoritism with him.
Col 3 [20]Children, obey your parents in everything, for this pleases the Lord.
[21]Fathers, do not embitter your children, or they will become discouraged.
[22]Slaves, obey your earthly masters in everything; and do it, not only when their eye is on you and to win their favor, but with sincerity of heart and reverence for the Lord. [23]Whatever you do, work at it with all your heart, as working for the Lord, not for men, [24]since you know that you will receive an inheritance from the Lord as a reward. It is the Lord Christ you are serving.

e) Obedience Is Accomplished through Christ

Rom 5 [19]For just as through the disobedience of the one man the many were made sinners, so also through the obedience of the one man the many will be made righteous.
Heb 5 [8]Although he was a son, he learned obedience from what he suffered [9]and, once made perfect, he became the source of eternal salvation for all who obey him. . . .

f) Obedience Is Better Than Sacrifice

1 Sam 15 [22]But Samuel replied: "Does the LORD delight in burnt offerings and sacrifices as much as in obeying the voice of the LORD? To obey is better than sacrifice, and to heed is better than the fat of rams."

g) Obedience Is Brought About by Divine Assistance

Deut 30 [6]The LORD your God will circumcise your hearts and the hearts of your descendants, so that you may love him with all your heart and with all your soul, and live. . . . [8]You will again obey the LORD and follow all his commands I am giving you today.
Isa 2 [3]Many peoples will come and say, "Come, let us go up to the mountain of the LORD, to the house of the God of Jacob. He will teach us his ways, so that we may walk in his paths." The law will go out from Zion, the word of the LORD from Jerusalem.
Jer 24 [7]"'I will give them a heart to know me, that I am the LORD. They will be my people, and I will be their God, for they will return to me with all their heart.'"
Jer 31 [33]"This is the covenant I will make with the house of Israel after that time," declares the LORD. "I will put my law in their minds and write it on their hearts. I will be their God, and they will be my people."
Jer 32 [39]"I will give them singleness of heart and action, so that they will always fear me for their own good and the good of their children after them."
Ezek 11 [19]"I will give them an undivided heart and put a new spirit in them; I will remove from them their heart of stone and give them a heart of flesh. [20]Then they will follow my decrees and be careful to keep my laws. They will be my people, and I will be their God."
Zeph 3 [9]"Then will I purify the lips of the peoples, that all of

them may call on the name of the LORD and serve him shoulder to shoulder."

John 15 [5]"I am the vine; you are the branches. If a man remains in me and I in him, he will bear much fruit; apart from me you can do nothing."

Acts 5 [32]"We are witnesses of these things, and so is the Holy Spirit, whom God has given to those who obey him."

Eph 2 [10]For we are God's workmanship, created in Christ Jesus to do good works, which God prepared in advance for us to do.

Phil 2 [13]for it is God who works in you to will and to act according to his good purpose.

h) Obedience Is Commanded

Exod 34 [10]Then the LORD said: "I am making a covenant with you. Before all your people I will do wonders never before done in any nation in all the world. The people you live among will see how awesome is the work that I, the LORD, will do for you. [11]Obey what I command you today. I will drive out before you the Amorites, Canaanites, Hittites, Perizzites, Hivites and Jebusites."

Lev 18 [4]"'You must obey my laws and be careful to follow my decrees. I am the LORD your God. [5]Keep my decrees and laws, for the man who obeys them will live by them. I am the LORD.'"

Deut 6 [3]Hear, O Israel, and be careful to obey so that it may go well with you and that you may increase greatly in a land flowing with milk and honey, just as the LORD, the God of your fathers, promised you.

Deut 13 [4]It is the LORD your God you must follow, and him you must revere. Keep his commands and obey him; serve him and hold fast to him.

Deut 27 [10]"Obey the LORD your God and follow his commands and decrees that I give you today."

Josh 22 [5]"But be very careful to keep the commandment and the law that Moses the servant of the LORD gave you: to love the LORD your God, to walk in all his ways, to obey his commands, to hold fast to him and to serve him with all your heart and all your soul."

Josh 24 [14]"Now fear the LORD and serve him with all faithfulness. Throw away the gods your forefathers worshiped beyond the River and in Egypt, and serve the LORD. [15]But if serving the LORD seems undesirable to you, then choose for yourselves this day whom you will serve, whether the gods your forefathers served beyond the River, or the gods of the Amorites, in whose land you are living. But as for me and my household, we will serve the LORD."

[16]Then the people answered, "Far be it from us to forsake the LORD to serve other gods! [17]It was the LORD our God himself who brought us and our fathers up out of Egypt, from that land of slavery, and performed those great signs before our eyes. He protected us on our entire journey and among all the nations through which we traveled. [18]And the LORD drove out before us all the nations, including the Amorites, who lived in the land. We too will serve the LORD, because he is our God."

2 Kings 17 [37]"You must always be careful to keep the decrees and ordinances, the laws and commands he wrote for you. Do not worship other gods."

1 Chron 28 [8]"So now I charge you in the sight of all Israel and of the assembly of the LORD, and in the hearing of our God: Be careful to follow all the commands of the LORD your God, that you may possess this good land and pass it on as an inheritance to your descendants forever."

Ps 119 [4]You have laid down precepts that are to be fully obeyed.

Jer 11 [3]"'Tell them that this is what the LORD, the God of Israel, says: 'Cursed is the man who does not obey the terms of this covenant—[4]the terms I commanded your forefathers when I brought them out of Egypt, out of the iron-smelting furnace.' I said, 'Obey me and do everything I command you, and you will be my people, and I will be your God.'"

Ezek 20 [19]"'"I am the LORD your God; follow my decrees and be careful to keep my laws."'"

Mal 4 [4]"Remember the law of my servant Moses, the decrees and laws I gave him at Horeb for all Israel."

James 1 [22]Do not merely listen to the word, and so deceive yourselves. Do what it says.

i) Obedience Is Desired by God

Deut 5 [29]"Oh, that their hearts would be inclined to fear me and keep all my commands always, so that it might go well with them and their children forever!"

j) Obedience Is Good

1 Sam 12 [14]"If you fear the LORD and serve and obey him and do not rebel against his commands, and if both you and the king who reigns over you follow the LORD your God—good!"

k) Obedience Is Learned through Suffering

Heb 5 [8]Although he was a son, he learned obedience from what he suffered. . . .

l) Obedience Is Motivated by Christ's Love

2 Cor 5 [14]For Christ's love compels us, because we are convinced that one died for all, and therefore all died. [15]And he died for all, that those who live should no longer live for themselves but for him who died for them and was raised again.

m) Obedience Is Not Burdensome

1 John 5 [3]This is love for God: to obey his commands. And his commands are not burdensome. . . .

n) Obedience Is a Process

2 Cor 10 [5]We demolish arguments and every pretension that sets itself up against the knowledge of God, and we take captive every thought to make it obedient to Christ. [6]And we will be ready to punish every act of disobedience, once your obedience is complete.

o) Obedience Is the Whole Duty of Humankind

Eccles 12 [13]Now all has been heard; here is the conclusion of the matter: Fear God and keep his commandments, for this is the whole duty of man.

p) Obedience Provides a Standard for Living

Lev 18 [5]"'Keep my decrees and laws, for the man who obeys them will live by them. I am the LORD.'"

Neh 9 [29]"You warned them to return to your law, but they became arrogant and disobeyed your commands. They sinned against your ordinances, by which a man will live if he obeys them. Stubbornly they turned their backs on you, became stiff-necked and refused to listen."

Ezek 20 [11]"'I gave them my decrees and made known to them my laws, for the man who obeys them will live by them.'"

q) Obedience Shows Love for Christ

John 14 [15]"If you love me, you will obey what I command. . . . [21]Whoever has my commands and obeys them, he is the one who loves me. He who loves me will be loved by my Father, and I too will love him and show myself to him."

John 14 [23]Jesus replied, "If anyone loves me, he will obey my teaching. My Father will love him, and we will come to him and make our home with him."

John 15 [10]"If you obey my commands, you will remain in my love, just as I have obeyed my Father's commands and remain in his love."

John 21 [15]When they had finished eating, Jesus said to Simon Peter, "Simon son of John, do you truly love me more than these?"

"Yes, Lord," he said, "you know that I love you."

Jesus said, "Feed my lambs."

[16]Again Jesus said, "Simon son of John, do you truly love me?"

He answered, "Yes, Lord, you know that I love you."

Jesus said, "Take care of my sheep."

[17]The third time he said to him, "Simon son of John, do you love me?"

Peter was hurt because Jesus asked him the third time, "Do you love me?" He said, "Lord, you know all things; you know that I love you."

Jesus said, "Feed my sheep."

1 John 5 [1]Everyone who believes that Jesus is the Christ is born of God, and everyone who loves the father loves his child as well. [2]This is how we know that we love the children of God:

by loving God and carrying out his commands. [3]This is love for God: to obey his commands. And his commands are not burdensome. . . .

2 John [6]And this is love: that we walk in obedience to his commands. As you have heard from the beginning, his command is that you walk in love.

r) Obedience Will Be Shown by All People

Dan 7 [27]"'Then the sovereignty, power and greatness of the kingdoms under the whole heaven will be handed over to the saints, the people of the Most High. His kingdom will be an everlasting kingdom, and all rulers will worship and obey him.'"

Rom 16 [25]Now to him who is able to establish you by my gospel and the proclamation of Jesus Christ, according to the revelation of the mystery hidden for long ages past, [26]but now revealed and made known through the prophetic writings by the command of the eternal God, so that all nations might believe and obey him—[27]to the only wise God be glory forever through Jesus Christ! Amen.

2. Objects of Obedience

a) We Must Obey the Book of the Covenant

2 Chron 34 [29]Then the king called together all the elders of Judah and Jerusalem. [30]He went up to the temple of the LORD with the men of Judah, the people of Jerusalem, the priests and the Levites—all the people from the least to the greatest. He read in their hearing all the words of the Book of the Covenant, which had been found in the temple of the LORD. [31]The king stood by his pillar and renewed the covenant in the presence of the LORD—to follow the LORD and keep his commands, regulations and decrees with all his heart and all his soul, and to obey the words of the covenant written in this book.

b) We Must Obey the Book of the Law of Moses

Josh 23 [6]"Be very strong; be careful to obey all that is written in the Book of the Law of Moses, without turning aside to the right or to the left."

c) We Must Obey Christ

2 Cor 10 [5]We demolish arguments and every pretension that sets itself up against the knowledge of God, and we take captive every thought to make it obedient to Christ.

d) We Must Obey Christ's Teachings

John 14 [23]Jesus replied, "If anyone loves me, he will obey my teaching. My Father will love him, and we will come to him and make our home with him."

2 John [9]Anyone who runs ahead and does not continue in the teaching of Christ does not have God; whoever continues in the teaching has both the Father and the Son.

e) We Must Obey the Commandments of God and Christ

Deut 11 [26]See, I am setting before you today a blessing and a curse—[27]the blessing if you obey the commands of the LORD your God that I am giving you today; [28]the curse if you disobey the commands of the LORD your God and turn from the way that I command you today by following other gods, which you have not known.

Judg 2 [17]Yet they would not listen to their judges but prostituted themselves to other gods and worshiped them. Unlike their fathers, they quickly turned from the way in which their fathers had walked, the way of obedience to the LORD's commands.

John 15 [10]"If you obey my commands, you will remain in my love, just as I have obeyed my Father's commands and remain in his love."

Rev 12 [17]Then the dragon was enraged at the woman and went off to make war against the rest of her offspring—those who obey God's commandments and hold to the testimony of Jesus.

Rev 14 [12]This calls for patient endurance on the part of the saints who obey God's commandments and remain faithful to Jesus.

f) We Must Obey God

Jer 26 [13]"Now reform your ways and your actions and obey the LORD your God. Then the LORD will relent and not bring the disaster he has pronounced against you."

Acts 4 [19]But Peter and John replied, "Judge for yourselves whether it is right in God's sight to obey you rather than God. [20]For we cannot help speaking about what we have seen and heard."

Acts 5 [29]Peter and the other apostles replied: "We must obey God rather than men!"

g) We Must Obey God's Laws

Lev 18 [4]"'You must obey my laws and be careful to follow my decrees. I am the LORD your God. [5]Keep my decrees and laws, for the man who obeys them will live by them. I am the LORD.'"

Lev 25 [18]"'Follow my decrees and be careful to obey my laws, and you will live safely in the land. [19]Then the land will yield its fruit, and you will eat your fill and live there in safety.'"

Ezra 7 [26]Whoever does not obey the law of your God and the law of the king must surely be punished by death, banishment, confiscation of property, or imprisonment.

Ps 1 [1]Blessed is the man who does not walk in the counsel of the wicked or stand in the way of sinners or sit in the seat of mockers. [2]But his delight is in the law of the LORD, and on his law he meditates day and night.

Ps 119 [106]I have taken an oath and confirmed it, that I will follow your righteous laws.

James 1 [25]But the man who looks intently into the perfect law that gives freedom, and continues to do this, not forgetting what he has heard, but doing it—he will be blessed in what he does.

h) We Must Obey God's Ways

Ps 18 [21]For I have kept the ways of the LORD; I have not done evil by turning from my God.

Isa 42 [24]Who handed Jacob over to become loot, and Israel to the plunderers? Was it not the LORD, against whom we have sinned? For they would not follow his ways; they did not obey his law.

Jer 7 [23]"'. . . but I gave them this command: Obey me, and I will be your God and you will be my people. Walk in all the ways I command you, that it may go well with you.'"

i) We Must Obey God's Will

Ps 143 [10]Teach me to do your will, for you are my God; may your good Spirit lead me on level ground.

Matt 7 [21]"Not everyone who says to me, 'Lord, Lord,' will enter the kingdom of heaven, but only he who does the will of my Father who is in heaven."

Mark 3 [35]"Whoever does God's will is my brother and sister and mother."

Col 4 [12]Epaphras, who is one of you and a servant of Christ Jesus, sends greetings. He is always wrestling in prayer for you, that you may stand firm in all the will of God, mature and fully assured.

Rev 2 [26]"To him who overcomes and does my will to the end, I will give authority over the nations. . . ."

j) We Must Obey God's Word

Ps 103 [20]Praise the LORD, you his angels, you mighty ones who do his bidding, who obey his word.

Ps 119 [17]Do good to your servant, and I will live; I will obey your word.

Ps 119 [88]Preserve my life according to your love, and I will obey the statutes of your mouth.

Luke 11 [28]He replied, "Blessed rather are those who hear the word of God and obey it."

John 17 [6]"I have revealed you to those whom you gave me out of the world. They were yours; you gave them to me and they have obeyed your word."

James 1 [22]Do not merely listen to the word, and so deceive yourselves. Do what it says.

Rev 3 [8]"I know your deeds. See, I have placed before you an open door that no one can shut. I know that you have little strength, yet you have kept my word and have not denied my name."

k) We Must Obey the Gospel

Rom 1 [5]Through him and for his name's sake, we received

grace and apostleship to call people from among all the Gentiles to the obedience that comes from faith.
Rom 6 [17]But thanks be to God that, though you used to be slaves to sin, you wholeheartedly obeyed the form of teaching to which you were entrusted.
2 Thess 1 [8]He will punish those who do not know God and do not obey the gospel of our Lord Jesus.
1 Pet 4 [17]For it is time for judgment to begin with the family of God; and if it begins with us, what will the outcome be for those who do not obey the gospel of God?

l) We Must Obey the Lord's Voice

1 Sam 15 [22]But Samuel replied: "Does the LORD delight in burnt offerings and sacrifices as much as in obeying the voice of the LORD? To obey is better than sacrifice, and to heed is better than the fat of rams."

m) We Must Obey the Truth

Gal 5 [7]You were running a good race. Who cut in on you and kept you from obeying the truth?
1 Pet 1 [22]Now that you have purified yourselves by obeying the truth so that you have sincere love for your brothers, love one another deeply, from the heart.

3. Attitudes toward Obedience

a) Obedience Should Be Accomplished with Resolution of Mind

Exod 24 [7]Then he took the Book of the Covenant and read it to the people. They responded, "We will do everything the LORD has said; we will obey."
Josh 24 [15]"But if serving the LORD seems undesirable to you, then choose for yourselves this day whom you will serve, whether the gods your forefathers served beyond the River, or the gods of the Amorites, in whose land you are living. But as for me and my household, we will serve the LORD." . . .
[24]And the people said to Joshua, "We will serve the LORD our God and obey him."
Ps 17 [3]Though you probe my heart and examine me at night, though you test me, you will find nothing; I have resolved that my mouth will not sin.
Ps 40 [8]"I desire to do your will, O my God; your law is within my heart."
Ps 101 [1]I will sing of your love and justice; to you, O LORD, I will sing praise. [2]I will be careful to lead a blameless life—when will you come to me?
I will walk in my house with blameless heart. [3]I will set before my eyes no vile thing.
The deeds of faithless men I hate; they will not cling to me. [4]Men of perverse heart shall be far from me; I will have nothing to do with evil.
Ps 119 [112]My heart is set on keeping your decrees to the very end.
Ps 119 [145]I call with all my heart; answer me, O LORD, and I will obey your decrees.
Col 4 [12]Epaphras, who is one of you and a servant of Christ Jesus, sends greetings. He is always wrestling in prayer for you, that you may stand firm in all the will of God, mature and fully assured.

b) Obedience Should Be Continuous

Phil 2 [12]Therefore, my dear friends, as you have always obeyed—not only in my presence, but now much more in my absence—continue to work out your salvation with fear and trembling. . . .

c) Obedience Should Be Genuine and Sincere

Deut 11 [13]So if you faithfully obey the commands I am giving you today—to love the LORD your God and to serve him with all your heart and with all your soul—[14]then I will send rain on your land in its season, both autumn and spring rains, so that you may gather in your grain, new wine and oil.
1 Sam 15 [22]But Samuel replied: "Does the LORD delight in burnt offerings and sacrifices as much as in obeying the voice of the LORD? To obey is better than sacrifice, and to heed is better than the fat of rams."
Ps 119 [34]Give me understanding, and I will keep your law and obey it with all my heart.

d) Obedience Should Be of Utmost Importance

Ps 119 [4]You have laid down precepts that are to be fully obeyed.
1 Cor 7 [19]Circumcision is nothing and uncircumcision is nothing. Keeping God's commands is what counts.

e) Obedience Should Be Practiced to Become More like God

1 Pet 1 [14]As obedient children, do not conform to the evil desires you had when you lived in ignorance. [15]But just as he who called you is holy, so be holy in all you do; [16]for it is written: "Be holy, because I am holy."

f) Obedience Should Be Wholehearted

Deut 28 [14]Do not turn aside from any of the commands I give you today, to the right or to the left, following other gods and serving them.
Josh 1 [7]"Be strong and very courageous. Be careful to obey all the law my servant Moses gave you; do not turn from it to the right or to the left, that you may be successful wherever you go."
Josh 22 [2]and said to them, "You have done all that Moses the servant of the LORD commanded, and you have obeyed me in everything I commanded. [3]For a long time now—to this very day—you have not deserted your brothers but have carried out the mission the LORD your God gave you. . . . [5]But be very careful to keep the commandment and the law that Moses the servant of the LORD gave you: to love the LORD your God, to walk in all his ways, to obey his commands, to hold fast to him and to serve him with all your heart and all your soul."
Ezra 7 [10]For Ezra had devoted himself to the study and observance of the Law of the LORD, and to teaching its decrees and laws in Israel.
Ps 18 [21]For I have kept the ways of the LORD; I have not done evil by turning from my God. [22]All his laws are before me; I have not turned away from his decrees. [23]I have been blameless before him and have kept myself from sin.
Ps 119 [69]Though the arrogant have smeared me with lies, I keep your precepts with all my heart.
Matt 6 [24]"No one can serve two masters. Either he will hate the one and love the other, or he will be devoted to the one and despise the other. You cannot serve both God and Money."

g) Obedience Should Be Willing

Isa 1 [19]"If you are willing and obedient, you will eat the best from the land. . . ."

h) Obedience Should Be without Impure Motives

1 Pet 4 [1]Therefore, since Christ suffered in his body, arm yourselves also with the same attitude, because he who has suffered in his body is done with sin. [2]As a result, he does not live the rest of his earthly life for evil human desires, but rather for the will of God.

i) Obedience Should Be Worked Out through Christ

2 Cor 10 [5]We demolish arguments and every pretension that sets itself up against the knowledge of God, and we take captive every thought to make it obedient to Christ.
1 Pet 4 [1]Therefore, since Christ suffered in his body, arm yourselves also with the same attitude, because he who has suffered in his body is done with sin.

j) The Obedient Should Follow the Example of Christ

John 13 [15]"I have set you an example that you should do as I have done for you."
1 John 2 [6]Whoever claims to live in him must walk as Jesus did.

k) The Obedient Should Have High Regard for God and His Word

Ps 1 [1]Blessed is the man who does not walk in the counsel of the wicked or stand in the way of sinners or sit in the seat of mockers. [2]But his delight is in the law of the LORD, and on his law he meditates day and night.
Ps 119 [11]I have hidden your word in my heart that I might not sin against you. . . . [15]I meditate on your precepts and consider your ways.
Ps 119 [20]My soul is consumed with longing for your laws at all times.
Ps 119 [83]Though I am like a wineskin in the smoke, I do not forget your decrees.
Ps 119 [97]Oh, how I love your law! I meditate on it all day long.
Ps 119 [111]Your statutes are my heritage forever; they are the joy of my heart.
Ps 119 [128]and because I consider all your precepts right, I hate every wrong path.
Rom 7 [22]For in my inner being I delight in God's law. . . .

l) The Obedient Should Instruct Others to Obey God

Matt 28 [19]"Therefore go and make disciples of all nations, baptizing them in the name of the Father and of the Son and of the Holy Spirit, [20]and teaching them to obey everything I have commanded you. And surely I am with you always, to the very end of the age."

m) The Obedient Should Reflect Their Confession of Faith in Their Works

Josh 24 [24]And the people said to Joshua, "We will serve the LORD our God and obey him."
2 Cor 9 [13]Because of the service by which you have proved yourselves, men will praise God for the obedience that accompanies your confession of the gospel of Christ, and for your generosity in sharing with them and with everyone else.
Heb 13 [15]Through Jesus, therefore, let us continually offer to God a sacrifice of praise—the fruit of lips that confess his name. [16]And do not forget to do good and to share with others, for with such sacrifices God is pleased.
James 1 [22]Do not merely listen to the word, and so deceive yourselves. Do what it says. [23]Anyone who listens to the word but does not do what it says is like a man who looks at his face in a mirror [24]and, after looking at himself, goes away and immediately forgets what he looks like. [25]But the man who looks intently into the perfect law that gives freedom, and continues to do this, not forgetting what he has heard, but doing it—he will be blessed in what he does.
James 2 [14]What good is it, my brothers, if a man claims to have faith but has no deeds? Can such faith save him? [15]Suppose a brother or sister is without clothes and daily food. [16]If one of you says to him, "Go, I wish you well; keep warm and well fed," but does nothing about his physical needs, what good is it? [17]In the same way, faith by itself, if it is not accompanied by action, is dead.

[18]But someone will say, "You have faith; I have deeds."

Show me your faith without deeds, and I will show you my faith by what I do. [19]You believe that there is one God. Good! Even the demons believe that—and shudder.

[20]You foolish man, do you want evidence that faith without deeds is useless?

1 Pet 1 [22]Now that you have purified yourselves by obeying the truth so that you have sincere love for your brothers, love one another deeply, from the heart.

n) The Obedient Should Rely on God's Enabling Grace and Power

1 Cor 15 [10]But by the grace of God I am what I am, and his grace to me was not without effect. No, I worked harder than all of them—yet not I, but the grace of God that was with me.
2 Cor 3 [5]Not that we are competent in ourselves to claim anything for ourselves, but our competence comes from God.
2 Cor 12 [10]That is why, for Christ's sake, I delight in weaknesses, in insults, in hardships, in persecutions, in difficulties. For when I am weak, then I am strong.
Eph 6 [10]Finally, be strong in the Lord and in his mighty power.
Phil 4 [13]I can do everything through him who gives me strength.
2 Tim 2 [1]You then, my son, be strong in the grace that is in Christ Jesus.

o) The Obedient Should Seek God's Help

1 Kings 8 [57]"May the LORD our God be with us as he was with our fathers; may he never leave us nor forsake us. [58]May he turn our hearts to him, to walk in all his ways and to keep the commands, decrees and regulations he gave our fathers."
1 Chron 22 [11]"Now, my son, the LORD be with you, and may you have success and build the house of the LORD your God, as he said you would. [12]May the LORD give you discretion and understanding when he puts you in command over Israel, so that you may keep the law of the LORD your God."
Ps 119 [33]Teach me, O LORD, to follow your decrees; then I will keep them to the end. [34]Give me understanding, and I will keep your law and obey it with all my heart. [35]Direct me in the path of your commands, for there I find delight. [36]Turn my heart toward your statutes and not toward selfish gain. [37]Turn my eyes away from worthless things; preserve my life according to your word.
Ps 143 [10]Teach me to do your will, for you are my God; may your good Spirit lead me on level ground.
Col 1 [9]For this reason, since the day we heard about you, we have not stopped praying for you and asking God to fill you with the knowledge of his will through all spiritual wisdom and understanding. [10]And we pray this in order that you may live a life worthy of the Lord and may please him in every way: bearing fruit in every good work, growing in the knowledge of God. . . .
2 Thess 2 [16]May our Lord Jesus Christ himself and God our Father, who loved us and by his grace gave us eternal encouragement and good hope, [17]encourage your hearts and strengthen you in every good deed and word.
Heb 13 [20]May the God of peace, who through the blood of the eternal covenant brought back from the dead our Lord Jesus, that great Shepherd of the sheep, [21]equip you with everything good for doing his will, and may he work in us what is pleasing to him, through Jesus Christ, to whom be glory for ever and ever. Amen.

4. Promises to the Obedient

a) God Promises His Love and Faithfulness to the Obedient

Deut 7 [9]Know therefore that the LORD your God is God; he is the faithful God, keeping his covenant of love to a thousand generations of those who love him and keep his commands.
Neh 1 [5]Then I said: "O LORD, God of heaven, the great and awesome God, who keeps his covenant of love with those who love him and obey his commands . . ."
Ps 25 [10]All the ways of the LORD are loving and faithful for those who keep the demands of his covenant.
Ps 103 [17]But from everlasting to everlasting the LORD's love is with those who fear him, and his righteousness with their children's children—[18]with those who keep his covenant and remember to obey his precepts.
Dan 9 [4]I prayed to the LORD my God and confessed: "O Lord, the great and awesome God, who keeps his covenant of love with all who love him and obey his commands . . ."

b) God Promises His Peace and Guidance to the Obedient

Ps 19 [8]The precepts of the LORD are right, giving joy to the heart. The commands of the LORD are radiant, giving light to the eyes.
Isa 48 [18]"If only you had paid attention to my commands, your peace would have been like a river, your righteousness like the waves of the sea."

c) God Promises His Spirit to the Obedient

Acts 5 [32]"We are witnesses of these things, and so is the Holy Spirit, whom God has given to those who obey him."

d) God Promises the Obedient Communion with God and Christ

Isa 56 [6]"And foreigners who bind themselves to the LORD to serve him, to love the name of the LORD, and to worship him, all who keep the Sabbath without desecrating it and who hold fast to my covenant—[7]these I will bring to my holy mountain and give them joy in my house of prayer. Their burnt offerings and sacrifices will be accepted on my altar; for my house will be called a house of prayer for all nations."
Matt 12 [50]"For whoever does the will of my Father in heaven is my brother and sister and mother."
John 9 [31]"We know that God does not listen to sinners. He listens to the godly man who does his will."
John 14 [23]Jesus replied, "If anyone loves me, he will obey my teaching. My Father will love him, and we will come to him and make our home with him."
John 15 [14]"You are my friends if you do what I command."
1 John 2 [3]We know that we have come to know him if we obey his commands.
1 John 3 [24]Those who obey his commands live in him, and he in them. And this is how we know that he lives in us: We know it by the Spirit he gave us.
2 John [9]Anyone who runs ahead and does not continue in the teaching of Christ does not have God; whoever continues in the teaching has both the Father and the Son.
Rev 21 [7]"He who overcomes will inherit all this, and I will be his God and he will be my son."

e) God Promises the Obedient Entrance into His Kingdom

Matt 7 [21]"Not everyone who says to me, 'Lord, Lord,' will enter the kingdom of heaven, but only he who does the will of my Father who is in heaven."

f) God Promises the Obedient Eternal Life

Matt 19 [16]Now a man came up to Jesus and asked, "Teacher, what good thing must I do to get eternal life?"

[17]"Why do you ask me about what is good?" Jesus replied. "There is only One who is good. If you want to enter life, obey the commandments."
John 8 [51]"I tell you the truth, if anyone keeps my word, he will never see death."
Rom 2 [7]To those who by persistence in doing good seek glory, honor and immortality, he will give eternal life.
1 John 2 [17]The world and its desires pass away, but the man who does the will of God lives forever.
Rev 22 [14]"Blessed are those who wash their robes, that they may have the right to the tree of life and may go through the gates into the city."

g) God Promises the Obedient Future Prosperity

Deut 4 [40]Keep his decrees and commands, which I am giving you today, so that it may go well with you and your children after you and that you may live long in the land the LORD your God gives you for all time.
Deut 12 [28]Be careful to obey all these regulations I am giving you, so that it may always go well with you and your children after you, because you will be doing what is good and right in the eyes of the LORD your God.
Deut 13 [17]None of those condemned things shall be found in your hands, so that the LORD will turn from his fierce anger; he will show you mercy, have compassion on you, and increase your numbers, as he promised on oath to your forefathers, [18]because you obey the LORD your God, keeping all his commands that I am giving you today and doing what is right in his eyes.
Deut 29 [9]Carefully follow the terms of this covenant, so that you may prosper in everything you do.
Josh 1 [7]"Be strong and very courageous. Be careful to obey all the law my servant Moses gave you; do not turn from it to the right or to the left, that you may be successful wherever you go."

h) God Promises the Obedient Help in Time of Trouble

Exod 23 [22]"If you listen carefully to what he says and do all that I say, I will be an enemy to your enemies and will oppose those who oppose you."

i) God Promises to Preserve the Lives of the Obedient

1 Kings 3 [14]"And if you walk in my ways and obey my statutes and commands as David your father did, I will give you a long life."
Prov 8 [34]"Blessed is the man who listens to me, watching daily at my doors, waiting at my doorway. [35]For whoever finds me finds life and receives favor from the LORD."
Ezek 18 [5]"Suppose there is a righteous man who does what is just and right. . . . [9]He follows my decrees and faithfully keeps my laws. That man is righteous; he will surely live, declares the Sovereign LORD."
Ezek 33 [14]"And if I say to the wicked man, 'You will surely die,' but he then turns away from his sin and does what is just and right—[15]if he gives back what he took in pledge for a loan, returns what he has stolen, follows the decrees that give life, and does no evil, he will surely live; he will not die. [16]None of the sins he has committed will be remembered against him. He has done what is just and right; he will surely live."

j) God Promises the Obedient Rest

Jer 6 [16]This is what the LORD says: "Stand at the crossroads and look; ask for the ancient paths, ask where the good way is, and walk in it, and you will find rest for your souls. But you said, 'We will not walk in it.'"

k) God Promises the Obedient Salvation

Heb 5 [9]and, once made perfect, he became the source of eternal salvation for all who obey him. . . .

l) God Promises the Obedient Success in Various Ventures

1 Kings 2 [3]". . . and observe what the LORD your God requires: Walk in his ways, and keep his decrees and commands, his laws and requirements, as written in the Law of Moses, so that you may prosper in all you do and wherever you go, [4]and that the LORD may keep his promise to me: 'If your descendants watch how they live, and if they walk faithfully before me with all their heart and soul, you will never fail to have a man on the throne of Israel.'"

m) God Promises the Obedient Wisdom

Matt 7 [24]"Therefore everyone who hears these words of mine and puts them into practice is like a wise man who built his house on the rock. [25]The rain came down, the streams rose, and the winds blew and beat against that house; yet it did not fall, because it had its foundation on the rock."

n) God Promises to Answer the Prayers of the Obedient

1 John 3 [21]Dear friends, if our hearts do not condemn us, we have confidence before God [22]and receive from him anything we ask, because we obey his commands and do what pleases him.

o) God Promises to Bless the Obedient

Lev 26 [3]"'If you follow my decrees and are careful to obey my commands, [4]I will send you rain in its season, and the ground will yield its crops and the trees of the field their fruit. [5]Your threshing will continue until grape harvest and the grape harvest will continue until planting, and you will eat all the food you want and live in safety in your land.

[6]"'I will grant peace in the land, and you will lie down and no one will make you afraid. I will remove savage beasts from the land, and the sword will not pass through your country. [7]You will pursue your enemies, and they will fall by the sword before you. [8]Five of you will chase a hundred, and a hundred of you will chase ten thousand, and your enemies will fall by the sword before you.

[9]"'I will look on you with favor and make you fruitful and increase your numbers, and I will keep my covenant with you. [10]You will still be eating last year's harvest when you will have to move it out to make room for the new. [11]I will put my dwelling place among you, and I will not abhor you. [12]I will walk among you and be your God, and you will be my people.'"

Deut 28 2All these blessings will come upon you and accompany you if you obey the LORD your God. . . .
Ps 19 9The fear of the LORD is pure, enduring forever. The ordinances of the LORD are sure and altogether righteous. 10They are more precious than gold, than much pure gold; they are sweeter than honey, than honey from the comb. 11By them is your servant warned; in keeping them there is great reward.
John 13 16"I tell you the truth, no servant is greater than his master, nor is a messenger greater than the one who sent him. 17Now that you know these things, you will be blessed if you do them."
James 1 25But the man who looks intently into the perfect law that gives freedom, and continues to do this, not forgetting what he has heard, but doing it—he will be blessed in what he does.

p) God Promises to Deliver the Obedient from Judgment

Jer 26 13"Now reform your ways and your actions and obey the LORD your God. Then the LORD will relent and not bring the disaster he has pronounced against you."
Jer 38 20"They will not hand you over," Jeremiah replied. "Obey the LORD by doing what I tell you. Then it will go well with you, and your life will be spared."

q) God Promises to Fulfill His Covenant for the Obedient

Deut 7 12If you pay attention to these laws and are careful to follow them, then the LORD your God will keep his covenant of love with you, as he swore to your forefathers.
Deut 28 1If you fully obey the LORD your God and carefully follow all his commands I give you today, the LORD your God will set you high above all the nations on earth.
2 Kings 21 8"I will not again make the feet of the Israelites wander from the land I gave their forefathers, if only they will be careful to do everything I commanded them and will keep the whole Law that my servant Moses gave them."
Neh 1 5Then I said: "O LORD, God of heaven, the great and awesome God, who keeps his covenant of love with those who love him and obey his commands . . .

8"Remember the instruction you gave your servant Moses, saying, 'If you are unfaithful, I will scatter you among the nations, 9but if you return to me and obey my commands, then even if your exiled people are at the farthest horizon, I will gather them from there and bring them to the place I have chosen as a dwelling for my Name.'"

r) God Promises to Honor the Obedient

John 12 26"Whoever serves me must follow me; and where I am, my servant also will be. My Father will honor the one who serves me."

s) God Promises to Make His Love Complete in the Obedient

1 John 2 5But if anyone obeys his word, God's love is truly made complete in him. This is how we know we are in him. . . .

5. Descriptions of the Obedient

a) The Obedient Are Blameless

Job 1 8Then the LORD said to Satan, "Have you considered my servant Job? There is no one on earth like him; he is blameless and upright, a man who fears God and shuns evil."
Rev 14 4These are those who did not defile themselves with women, for they kept themselves pure. They follow the Lamb wherever he goes. They were purchased from among men and offered as firstfruits to God and the Lamb. 5No lie was found in their mouths; they are blameless.

b) The Obedient Are Blessed

Ps 112 1Praise the LORD.

Blessed is the man who fears the LORD, who finds great delight in his commands.

2His children will be mighty in the land; the generation of the upright will be blessed. 3Wealth and riches are in his house, and his righteousness endures forever. 4Even in darkness light dawns for the upright, for the gracious and compassionate and righteous man. 5Good will come to him who is generous and lends freely, who conducts his affairs with justice. 6Surely he will never be shaken; a righteous man will be remembered forever. 7He will have no fear of bad news; his heart is steadfast, trusting in the LORD. 8His heart is secure, he will have no fear; in the end he will look in triumph on his foes. 9He has scattered abroad his gifts to the poor, his righteousness endures forever; his horn will be lifted high in honor.
Ps 119 1Blessed are they whose ways are blameless, who walk according to the law of the LORD. 2Blessed are they who keep his statutes and seek him with all their heart. 3They do nothing wrong; they walk in his ways.
Prov 8 32"Now then, my sons, listen to me; blessed are those who keep my ways."
Prov 29 18Where there is no revelation, the people cast off restraint; but blessed is he who keeps the law.
Luke 11 28He replied, "Blessed rather are those who hear the word of God and obey it."
Rev 22 14"Blessed are those who wash their robes, that they may have the right to the tree of life and may go through the gates into the city."

c) The Obedient Are Discerning Sons

Prov 28 7He who keeps the law is a discerning son, but a companion of gluttons disgraces his father.

d) The Obedient Are Doers of the Word

James 1 22Do not merely listen to the word, and so deceive yourselves. Do what it says. 23Anyone who listens to the word but does not do what it says is like a man who looks at his face in a mirror 24and, after looking at himself, goes away and immediately forgets what he looks like. 25But the man who looks intently into the perfect law that gives freedom, and continues to do this, not forgetting what he has heard, but doing it—he will be blessed in what he does.

e) The Obedient Are Firstfruits to God and the Lamb

Rev 14 1Then I looked, and there before me was the Lamb, standing on Mount Zion, and with him 144,000 who had his name and his Father's name written on their foreheads. 2And I heard a sound from heaven like the roar of rushing waters and like a loud peal of thunder. The sound I heard was like that of harpists playing their harps. 3And they sang a new song before the throne and before the four living creatures and the elders. No one could learn the song except the 144,000 who had been redeemed from the earth. 4These are those who did not defile themselves with women, for they kept themselves pure. They follow the Lamb wherever he goes. They were purchased from among men and offered as firstfruits to God and the Lamb.

f) The Obedient Are Great in God's Kingdom

Matt 5 19"Anyone who breaks one of the least of these commandments and teaches others to do the same will be called least in the kingdom of heaven, but whoever practices and teaches these commands will be called great in the kingdom of heaven."

g) The Obedient Are like Children Who Obey

1 Pet 1 14As obedient children, do not conform to the evil desires you had when you lived in ignorance.

h) The Obedient Are like Wise Builders

Luke 6 46"Why do you call me, 'Lord, Lord,' and do not do what I say? 47I will show you what he is like who comes to me and hears my words and puts them into practice. 48He is like a man building a house, who dug down deep and laid the foundation on rock. When a flood came, the torrent struck that house but could not shake it, because it was well built. 49But the one who hears my words and does not put them into practice is like a man who built a house on the ground without a foundation. The moment the torrent struck that house, it collapsed and its destruction was complete."

i) The Obedient Are Mighty

Joel 2 11The LORD thunders at the head of his army; his forces are beyond number, and mighty are those who obey his command. The day of the LORD is great; it is dreadful. Who can endure it?

j) The Obedient Are Righteous

Job 1 [8]Then the LORD said to Satan, "Have you considered my servant Job? There is no one on earth like him; he is blameless and upright, a man who fears God and shuns evil."
Luke 1 [6]Both of them were upright in the sight of God, observing all the Lord's commandments and regulations blamelessly.
Rom 6 [16]Don't you know that when you offer yourselves to someone to obey him as slaves, you are slaves to the one whom you obey—whether you are slaves to sin, which leads to death, or to obedience, which leads to righteousness?

k) The Obedient Are Servants of Christ

John 12 [26]"Whoever serves me must follow me; and where I am, my servant also will be. My Father will honor the one who serves me."

l) The Obedient Are Treasured Possessions

Exod 19 [5]"'Now if you obey me fully and keep my covenant, then out of all nations you will be my treasured possession. Although the whole earth is mine . . .'"

m) The Obedient Are Worthy

Rev 3 [4]"Yet you have a few people in Sardis who have not soiled their clothes. They will walk with me, dressed in white, for they are worthy."

n) The Obedient Walk according to the Lord's Law

Ps 119 [1]Blessed are they whose ways are blameless, who walk according to the law of the LORD.

6. Illustrations of Obedience

a) Noah Obeyed God

Gen 7 [5]And Noah did all that the LORD commanded him.

b) Abraham Obeyed God

Gen 22 [15]The angel of the LORD called to Abraham from heaven a second time [16]and said, "I swear by myself, declares the LORD, that because you have done this and have not withheld your son, your only son, [17]I will surely bless you and make your descendants as numerous as the stars in the sky and as the sand on the seashore. Your descendants will take possession of the cities of their enemies, [18]and through your offspring all nations on earth will be blessed, because you have obeyed me."
Heb 11 [8]By faith Abraham, when called to go to a place he would later receive as his inheritance, obeyed and went, even though he did not know where he was going. [9]By faith he made his home in the promised land like a stranger in a foreign country; he lived in tents, as did Isaac and Jacob, who were heirs with him of the same promise. [10]For he was looking forward to the city with foundations, whose architect and builder is God.

c) Moses Obeyed God

Heb 3 [2]He was faithful to the one who appointed him, just as Moses was faithful in all God's house. [3]Jesus has been found worthy of greater honor than Moses, just as the builder of a house has greater honor than the house itself.

d) Caleb Obeyed God

Deut 1 [35]"Not a man of this evil generation shall see the good land I swore to give your forefathers, [36]except Caleb son of Jephunneh. He will see it, and I will give him and his descendants the land he set his feet on, because he followed the LORD wholeheartedly."

e) Joshua Obeyed God

Josh 10 [40]So Joshua subdued the whole region, including the hill country, the Negev, the western foothills and the mountain slopes, together with all their kings. He left no survivors. He totally destroyed all who breathed, just as the LORD, the God of Israel, had commanded.
Josh 11 [15]As the LORD commanded his servant Moses, so Moses commanded Joshua, and Joshua did it; he left nothing undone of all that the LORD commanded Moses.

f) Job Obeyed God

Job 1 [8]Then the LORD said to Satan, "Have you considered my servant Job? There is no one on earth like him; he is blameless and upright, a man who fears God and shuns evil."

g) David's Prayer Illustrates Obedience

1 Chron 29 [10]David praised the LORD in the presence of the whole assembly, saying, "Praise be to you, O LORD, God of our father Israel, from everlasting to everlasting. [11]Yours, O LORD, is the greatness and the power and the glory and the majesty and the splendor, for everything in heaven and earth is yours. Yours, O LORD, is the kingdom; you are exalted as head over all. [12]Wealth and honor come from you; you are the ruler of all things. In your hands are strength and power to exalt and give strength to all. [13]Now, our God, we give you thanks, and praise your glorious name.

[14]"But who am I, and who are my people, that we should be able to give as generously as this? Everything comes from you, and we have given you only what comes from your hand. [15]We are aliens and strangers in your sight, as were all our forefathers. Our days on earth are like a shadow, without hope. [16]O LORD our God, as for all this abundance that we have provided for building you a temple for your Holy Name, it comes from your hand, and all of it belongs to you. [17]I know, my God, that you test the heart and are pleased with integrity. All these things have I given willingly and with honest intent. And now I have seen with joy how willingly your people who are here have given to you. [18]O LORD, God of our fathers Abraham, Isaac and Israel, keep this desire in the hearts of your people forever, and keep their hearts loyal to you. [19]And give my son Solomon the wholehearted devotion to keep your commands, requirements and decrees and to do everything to build the palatial structure for which I have provided."

h) Asa Obeyed God

1 Kings 15 [11]Asa did what was right in the eyes of the LORD, as his father David had done.

i) Elijah Obeyed God

1 Kings 17 [1]Now Elijah the Tishbite, from Tishbe in Gilead, said to Ahab, "As the LORD, the God of Israel, lives, whom I serve, there will be neither dew nor rain in the next few years except at my word."

[2]Then the word of the LORD came to Elijah: [3]"Leave here, turn eastward and hide in the Kerith Ravine, east of the Jordan. [4]You will drink from the brook, and I have ordered the ravens to feed you there."

[5]So he did what the LORD had told him. He went to the Kerith Ravine, east of the Jordan, and stayed there. [6]The ravens brought him bread and meat in the morning and bread and meat in the evening, and he drank from the brook.

j) Jehoshaphat Obeyed God

1 Kings 22 [42]Jehoshaphat was thirty-five years old when he became king, and he reigned in Jerusalem twenty-five years. His mother's name was Azubah daughter of Shilhi. [43]In everything he walked in the ways of his father Asa and did not stray from them; he did what was right in the eyes of the LORD. The high places, however, were not removed, and the people continued to offer sacrifices and burn incense there.

k) Jonah Obeyed God

Jon 3 [1]Then the word of the LORD came to Jonah a second time: [2]"Go to the great city of Nineveh and proclaim to it the message I give you."

[3]Jonah obeyed the word of the LORD and went to Nineveh. Now Nineveh was a very important city—a visit required three days.

l) Hezekiah Obeyed God

2 Kings 18 [5]Hezekiah trusted in the LORD, the God of Israel. There was no one like him among all the kings of Judah, either before him or after him. [6]He held fast to the LORD and did not cease to follow him; he kept the commands the LORD had given

Moses.

m) Josiah Obeyed God

2 Kings 23 [3]The king stood by the pillar and renewed the covenant in the presence of the LORD—to follow the LORD and keep his commands, regulations and decrees with all his heart and all his soul, thus confirming the words of the covenant written in this book. Then all the people pledged themselves to the covenant. . . . [25]Neither before nor after Josiah was there a king like him who turned to the LORD as he did—with all his heart and with all his soul and with all his strength, in accordance with all the Law of Moses.

n) Shadrach, Meshach, and Abednego Obeyed God

Dan 3 [26]Nebuchadnezzar then approached the opening of the blazing furnace and shouted, "Shadrach, Meshach and Abednego, servants of the Most High God, come out! Come here!"

So Shadrach, Meshach and Abednego came out of the fire, [27]and the satraps, prefects, governors and royal advisers crowded around them. They saw that the fire had not harmed their bodies, nor was a hair of their heads singed; their robes were not scorched, and there was no smell of fire on them.

[28]Then Nebuchadnezzar said, "Praise be to the God of Shadrach, Meshach and Abednego, who has sent his angel and rescued his servants! They trusted in him and defied the king's command and were willing to give up their lives rather than serve or worship any god except their own God. [29]Therefore I decree that the people of any nation or language who say anything against the God of Shadrach, Meshach and Abednego be cut into pieces and their houses be turned into piles of rubble, for no other god can save in this way."

o) Zerubbabel Obeyed God

Hag 1 [12]Then Zerubbabel son of Shealtiel, Joshua son of Jehozadak, the high priest, and the whole remnant of the people obeyed the voice of the LORD their God and the message of the prophet Haggai, because the LORD their God had sent him. And the people feared the LORD.

p) Joseph Obeyed God

Matt 1 [24]When Joseph woke up, he did what the angel of the Lord had commanded him and took Mary home as his wife. [25]But he had no union with her until she gave birth to a son. And he gave him the name Jesus.

Matt 2 [13]When they had gone, an angel of the Lord appeared to Joseph in a dream. "Get up," he said, "take the child and his mother and escape to Egypt. Stay there until I tell you, for Herod is going to search for the child to kill him."

[14]So he got up, took the child and his mother during the night and left for Egypt, [15]where he stayed until the death of Herod. And so was fulfilled what the Lord had said through the prophet: "Out of Egypt I called my son."

q) Zechariah and Elizabeth Obeyed God

Luke 1 [5]In the time of Herod king of Judea there was a priest named Zechariah, who belonged to the priestly division of Abijah; his wife Elizabeth was also a descendant of Aaron. [6]Both of them were upright in the sight of God, observing all the Lord's commandments and regulations blamelessly.

r) Jesus Christ Obeyed God

Matt 3 [13]Then Jesus came from Galilee to the Jordan to be baptized by John. [14]But John tried to deter him, saying, "I need to be baptized by you, and do you come to me?"

[15]Jesus replied, "Let it be so now; it is proper for us to do this to fulfill all righteousness." Then John consented.

[16]As soon as Jesus was baptized, he went up out of the water. At that moment heaven was opened, and he saw the Spirit of God descending like a dove and lighting on him. [17]And a voice from heaven said, "This is my Son, whom I love; with him I am well pleased."

Luke 2 [41]Every year his parents went to Jerusalem for the Feast of the Passover. [42]When he was twelve years old, they went up to the Feast, according to the custom. [43]After the Feast was over, while his parents were returning home, the boy Jesus stayed behind in Jerusalem, but they were unaware of it. [44]Thinking he was in their company, they traveled on for a day. Then they began looking for him among their relatives and friends. [45]When they did not find him, they went back to Jerusalem to look for him. [46]After three days they found him in the temple courts, sitting among the teachers, listening to them and asking them questions. [47]Everyone who heard him was amazed at his understanding and his answers. [48]When his parents saw him, they were astonished. His mother said to him, "Son, why have you treated us like this? Your father and I have been anxiously searching for you."

[49]"Why were you searching for me?" he asked. "Didn't you know I had to be in my Father's house?" [50]But they did not understand what he was saying to them.

John 4 [34]"My food," said Jesus, "is to do the will of him who sent me and to finish his work."

John 8 [29]"The one who sent me is with me; he has not left me alone, for I always do what pleases him."

John 15 [10]"If you obey my commands, you will remain in my love, just as I have obeyed my Father's commands and remain in his love."

John 17 [4]"I have brought you glory on earth by completing the work you gave me to do."

Phil 2 [5]Your attitude should be the same as that of Christ Jesus: [6]Who, being in very nature God, did not consider equality with God something to be grasped, [7]but made himself nothing, taking the very nature of a servant, being made in human likeness. [8]And being found in appearance as a man, he humbled himself and became obedient to death—even death on a cross!

Heb 5 [7]During the days of Jesus' life on earth, he offered up prayers and petitions with loud cries and tears to the one who could save him from death, and he was heard because of his reverent submission. [8]Although he was a son, he learned obedience from what he suffered. . . .

Heb 10 [5]Therefore, when Christ came into the world, he said: "Sacrifice and offering you did not desire, but a body you prepared for me; [6]with burnt offerings and sin offerings you were not pleased. [7]Then I said, 'Here I am—it is written about me in the scroll—I have come to do your will, O God.'"

s) Paul Obeyed God

Acts 23 [1]Paul looked straight at the Sanhedrin and said, "My brothers, I have fulfilled my duty to God in all good conscience to this day."

Acts 26 [9]"I too was convinced that I ought to do all that was possible to oppose the name of Jesus of Nazareth. [10]And that is just what I did in Jerusalem. On the authority of the chief priests I put many of the saints in prison, and when they were put to death, I cast my vote against them. [11]Many a time I went from one synagogue to another to have them punished, and I tried to force them to blaspheme. In my obsession against them, I even went to foreign cities to persecute them.

[12]"On one of these journeys I was going to Damascus with the authority and commission of the chief priests. [13]About noon, O king, as I was on the road, I saw a light from heaven, brighter than the sun, blazing around me and my companions. [14]We all fell to the ground, and I heard a voice saying to me in Aramaic, 'Saul, Saul, why do you persecute me? It is hard for you to kick against the goads.'

[15]"Then I asked, 'Who are you, Lord?'

"'I am Jesus, whom you are persecuting,' the Lord replied. [16]'Now get up and stand on your feet. I have appeared to you to appoint you as a servant and as a witness of what you have seen of me and what I will show you. [17]I will rescue you from your own people and from the Gentiles. I am sending you to them [18]to open their eyes and turn them from darkness to light, and from the power of Satan to God, so that they may receive forgiveness of sins and a place among those who are sanctified by faith in me.'

[19]"So then, King Agrippa, I was not disobedient to the vision from heaven. [20]First to those in Damascus, then to those in Jerusalem and in all Judea, and to the Gentiles also, I preached that they should repent and turn to God and prove their repentance by their deeds."

2 Tim 1 [3]I thank God, whom I serve, as my forefathers did, with a clear conscience, as night and day I constantly remember you in my prayers.

t) The Roman Believers Obeyed God

Rom 16 [19]Everyone has heard about your obedience, so I am full of joy over you; but I want you to be wise about what is good, and innocent about what is evil.

B. Submit to God

2 Chron 30 [8]"Do not be stiff-necked, as your fathers were; submit to the LORD. Come to the sanctuary, which he has consecrated forever. Serve the LORD your God, so that his fierce anger will turn away from you."
Job 22 [21]"Submit to God and be at peace with him; in this way prosperity will come to you."
Heb 12 [9]Moreover, we have all had human fathers who disciplined us and we respected them for it. How much more should we submit to the Father of our spirits and live!
James 4 [7]Submit yourselves, then, to God. Resist the devil, and he will flee from you.

C. Follow God

1. Following God

Deut 13 [4]It is the LORD your God you must follow, and him you must revere. Keep his commands and obey him; serve him and hold fast to him.
1 Sam 12 [14]"If you fear the LORD and serve and obey him and do not rebel against his commands, and if both you and the king who reigns over you follow the LORD your God—good!"
Eph 5 [1]Be imitators of God, therefore, as dearly loved children. . . .

2. Following Christ

Matt 16 [24]Then Jesus said to his disciples, "If anyone would come after me, he must deny himself and take up his cross and follow me."
John 8 [12]When Jesus spoke again to the people, he said, "I am the light of the world. Whoever follows me will never walk in darkness, but will have the light of life."
John 10 [25]Jesus answered, "I did tell you, but you do not believe. The miracles I do in my Father's name speak for me, [26]but you do not believe because you are not my sheep. [27]My sheep listen to my voice; I know them, and they follow me."
John 12 [26]"Whoever serves me must follow me; and where I am, my servant also will be. My Father will honor the one who serves me."
Rom 15 [5]May the God who gives endurance and encouragement give you a spirit of unity among yourselves as you follow Christ Jesus. . . .

3. Illustrations of Following God

a) Caleb Followed God

Deut 1 [34]When the LORD heard what you said, he was angry and solemnly swore: [35]"Not a man of this evil generation shall see the good land I swore to give your forefathers, [36]except Caleb son of Jephunneh. He will see it, and I will give him and his descendants the land he set his feet on, because he followed the LORD wholeheartedly."
Josh 14 [6]Now the men of Judah approached Joshua at Gilgal, and Caleb son of Jephunneh the Kenizzite said to him, "You know what the LORD said to Moses the man of God at Kadesh Barnea about you and me. [7]I was forty years old when Moses the servant of the LORD sent me from Kadesh Barnea to explore the land. And I brought him back a report according to my convictions, [8]but my brothers who went up with me made the hearts of the people melt with fear. I, however, followed the LORD my God wholeheartedly. [9]So on that day Moses swore to me, 'The land on which your feet have walked will be your inheritance and that of your children forever, because you have followed the LORD my God wholeheartedly.' . . ."

[13]Then Joshua blessed Caleb son of Jephunneh and gave him Hebron as his inheritance. [14]So Hebron has belonged to Caleb son of Jephunneh the Kenizzite ever since, because he followed the LORD, the God of Israel, wholeheartedly.

b) Job Followed God

Job 23 [11]"My feet have closely followed his steps; I have kept to his way without turning aside."

c) Josiah Followed God

2 Chron 34 [31]The king stood by his pillar and renewed the covenant in the presence of the LORD—to follow the LORD and keep his commands, regulations and decrees with all his heart and all his soul, and to obey the words of the covenant written in this book.

[32]Then he had everyone in Jerusalem and Benjamin pledge themselves to it; the people of Jerusalem did this in accordance with the covenant of God, the God of their fathers.

[33]Josiah removed all the detestable idols from all the territory belonging to the Israelites, and he had all who were present in Israel serve the LORD their God. As long as he lived, they did not fail to follow the LORD, the God of their fathers.

4. Illustrations of Following Christ

a) Paul Followed Christ

1 Cor 11 [1]Follow my example, as I follow the example of Christ.

b) The Church Follows Christ

Rev 14 [3]And they sang a new song before the throne and before the four living creatures and the elders. No one could learn the song except the 144,000 who had been redeemed from the earth. [4]These are those who did not defile themselves with women, for they kept themselves pure. They follow the Lamb wherever he goes. They were purchased from among men and offered as firstfruits to God and the Lamb.
Rev 17 [14]"They will make war against the Lamb, but the Lamb will overcome them because he is Lord of lords and King of kings—and with him will be his called, chosen and faithful followers."

VI
Communicating with God

A. Pray to God

1. Elements of Prayer

a) Adoration and Communion

Ps 27 [4]One thing I ask of the LORD, this is what I seek: that I may dwell in the house of the LORD all the days of my life, to gaze upon the beauty of the LORD and to seek him in his temple.
Ps 63 [1]O God, you are my God, earnestly I seek you; my soul thirsts for you, my body longs for you, in a dry and weary land where there is no water.

[2]I have seen you in the sanctuary and beheld your power and your glory. [3]Because your love is better than life, my lips will glorify you. [4]I will praise you as long as I live, and in your name I will lift up my hands. [5]My soul will be satisfied as with the richest of foods; with singing lips my mouth will praise you.

[6]On my bed I remember you; I think of you through the watches of the night. [7]Because you are my help, I sing in the shadow of your wings. [8]My soul clings to you; your right hand upholds me.
Ps 73 [25]Whom have I in heaven but you? And earth has nothing I desire besides you. [26]My flesh and my heart may fail, but God is the strength of my heart and my portion forever.
Luke 6 [12]One of those days Jesus went out to a mountainside to pray, and spent the night praying to God.
1 John 1 [3]We proclaim to you what we have seen and heard, so that you also may have fellowship with us. And our fellowship is with the Father and with his Son, Jesus Christ.
Rev 3 [14]"To the angel of the church in Laodicea write: These

are the words of the Amen, the faithful and true witness, the ruler of God's creation. . . . [20]Here I am! I stand at the door and knock. If anyone hears my voice and opens the door, I will come in and eat with him, and he with me."

b) Confession

See p. 615b, Manner of Prayer

c) Intercession

(1) Intercession for the Afflicted

Ps 10 [12]Arise, LORD! Lift up your hand, O God. Do not forget the helpless. . . . [17]You hear, O LORD, the desire of the afflicted; you encourage them, and you listen to their cry. . . .
Ps 74 [21]Do not let the oppressed retreat in disgrace; may the poor and needy praise your name.

(2) Intercession for Believers by Christian Leaders

Num 6 [22]The LORD said to Moses, [23]"Tell Aaron and his sons, 'This is how you are to bless the Israelites. Say to them: [24]"The LORD bless you and keep you; [25]the LORD make his face shine upon you and be gracious to you; [26]the LORD turn his face toward you and give you peace."'"
1 Sam 12 [23]"As for me, far be it from me that I should sin against the LORD by failing to pray for you. And I will teach you the way that is good and right."
Joel 2 [17]Let the priests, who minister before the LORD, weep between the temple porch and the altar. Let them say, "Spare your people, O LORD. Do not make your inheritance an object of scorn, a byword among the nations. Why should they say among the peoples, 'Where is their God?'"
Rom 1 [9]God, whom I serve with my whole heart in preaching the gospel of his Son, is my witness how constantly I remember you [10]in my prayers at all times; and I pray that now at last by God's will the way may be opened for me to come to you.
Rom 15 [13]May the God of hope fill you with all joy and peace as you trust in him, so that you may overflow with hope by the power of the Holy Spirit.
2 Cor 13 [7]Now we pray to God that you will not do anything wrong. Not that people will see that we have stood the test but that you will do what is right even though we may seem to have failed.
Eph 1 [16]I have not stopped giving thanks for you, remembering you in my prayers.
Phil 1 [3]I thank my God every time I remember you. . . .
[9]And this is my prayer: that your love may abound more and more in knowledge and depth of insight, [10]so that you may be able to discern what is best and may be pure and blameless until the day of Christ, [11]filled with the fruit of righteousness that comes through Jesus Christ—to the glory and praise of God.
Col 1 [9]For this reason, since the day we heard about you, we have not stopped praying for you and asking God to fill you with the knowledge of his will through all spiritual wisdom and understanding.
Col 4 [12]Epaphras, who is one of you and a servant of Christ Jesus, sends greetings. He is always wrestling in prayer for you, that you may stand firm in all the will of God, mature and fully assured.
1 Thess 3 [12]May the Lord make your love increase and overflow for each other and for everyone else, just as ours does for you. [13]May he strengthen your hearts so that you will be blameless and holy in the presence of our God and Father when our Lord Jesus comes with all his holy ones.
1 Thess 5 [23]May God himself, the God of peace, sanctify you through and through. May your whole spirit, soul and body be kept blameless at the coming of our Lord Jesus Christ.
2 Thess 1 [11]With this in mind, we constantly pray for you, that our God may count you worthy of his calling, and that by his power he may fulfill every good purpose of yours and every act prompted by your faith. [12]We pray this so that the name of our Lord Jesus may be glorified in you, and you in him, according to the grace of our God and the Lord Jesus Christ.
2 Thess 2 [16]May our Lord Jesus Christ himself and God our Father, who loved us and by his grace gave us eternal encouragement and good hope, [17]encourage your hearts and strengthen you in every good deed and word.
Philem [4]I always thank my God as I remember you in my prayers. . . .
James 5 [14]Is any one of you sick? He should call the elders of the church to pray over him and anoint him with oil in the name of the Lord. [15]And the prayer offered in faith will make the sick person well; the Lord will raise him up. If he has sinned, he will be forgiven.

(3) Intercession for Believers in General

2 Chron 6 [41]"Now arise, O LORD God, and come to your resting place, you and the ark of your might. May your priests, O LORD God, be clothed with salvation, may your saints rejoice in your goodness."
Job 42 [8]"So now take seven bulls and seven rams and go to my servant Job and sacrifice a burnt offering for yourselves. My servant Job will pray for you, and I will accept his prayer and not deal with you according to your folly. You have not spoken of me what is right, as my servant Job has." [9]So Eliphaz the Temanite, Bildad the Shuhite and Zophar the Naamathite did what the LORD told them; and the LORD accepted Job's prayer.
Ps 36 [10]Continue your love to those who know you, your righteousness to the upright in heart.
Ps 40 [16]But may all who seek you rejoice and be glad in you; may those who love your salvation always say, "The LORD be exalted!"
Ps 67 [1]May God be gracious to us and bless us and make his face shine upon us, [2]that your ways may be known on earth, your salvation among all nations.
Ps 70 [4]But may all who seek you rejoice and be glad in you; may those who love your salvation always say, "Let God be exalted!"
Ps 90 [16]May your deeds be shown to your servants, your splendor to their children.
Ps 122 [6]Pray for the peace of Jerusalem: "May those who love you be secure."
Ps 125 [4]Do good, O LORD, to those who are good, to those who are upright in heart.
Isa 62 [6]I have posted watchmen on your walls, O Jerusalem; they will never be silent day or night. You who call on the LORD, give yourselves no rest, [7]and give him no rest till he establishes Jerusalem and makes her the praise of the earth.
Eph 6 [18]And pray in the Spirit on all occasions with all kinds of prayers and requests. With this in mind, be alert and always keep on praying for all the saints.
James 5 [16]Therefore confess your sins to each other and pray for each other so that you may be healed. The prayer of a righteous man is powerful and effective.
1 John 5 [16]If anyone sees his brother commit a sin that does not lead to death, he should pray and God will give him life. I refer to those whose sin does not lead to death. There is a sin that leads to death. I am not saying that he should pray about that.

(4) Intercession for Children by Parents

Gen 17 [18]And Abraham said to God, "If only Ishmael might live under your blessing!"
[19]Then God said, "Yes, but your wife Sarah will bear you a son, and you will call him Isaac. I will establish my covenant with him as an everlasting covenant for his descendants after him. [20]And as for Ishmael, I have heard you: I will surely bless him; I will make him fruitful and will greatly increase his numbers. He will be the father of twelve rulers, and I will make him into a great nation."
2 Sam 12 [16]David pleaded with God for the child. He fasted and went into his house and spent the nights lying on the ground.
Job 1 [5]When a period of feasting had run its course, Job would send and have them purified. Early in the morning he would sacrifice a burnt offering for each of them, thinking, "Perhaps my children have sinned and cursed God in their hearts." This was Job's regular custom.

(5) Intercession for Enemies

Jer 29 [7]"Also, seek the peace and prosperity of the city to which I have carried you into exile. Pray to the LORD for it, because if it prospers, you too will prosper."

Matt 5 [44]"But I tell you: Love your enemies and pray for those who persecute you. . . ."
Luke 23 [34]Jesus said, "Father, forgive them, for they do not know what they are doing." And they divided up his clothes by casting lots.
Acts 7 [60]Then he fell on his knees and cried out, "Lord, do not hold this sin against them." When he had said this, he fell asleep.
2 Tim 4 [16]At my first defense, no one came to my support, but everyone deserted me. May it not be held against them.

(6) Intercession for Everyone

1 Tim 2 [1]I urge, then, first of all, that requests, prayers, intercession and thanksgiving be made for everyone. . . .

(7) Intercession for Ministers

Rom 15 [30]I urge you, brothers, by our Lord Jesus Christ and by the love of the Spirit, to join me in my struggle by praying to God for me. [31]Pray that I may be rescued from the unbelievers in Judea and that my service in Jerusalem may be acceptable to the saints there, [32]so that by God's will I may come to you with joy and together with you be refreshed.
2 Cor 1 [11]as you help us by your prayers. Then many will give thanks on our behalf for the gracious favor granted us in answer to the prayers of many.
Eph 6 [19]Pray also for me, that whenever I open my mouth, words may be given me so that I will fearlessly make known the mystery of the gospel, [20]for which I am an ambassador in chains. Pray that I may declare it fearlessly, as I should.
Col 4 [3]And pray for us, too, that God may open a door for our message, so that we may proclaim the mystery of Christ, for which I am in chains. [4]Pray that I may proclaim it clearly, as I should.
1 Thess 5 [25]Brothers, pray for us.
2 Thess 3 [1]Finally, brothers, pray for us that the message of the Lord may spread rapidly and be honored, just as it was with you. [2]And pray that we may be delivered from wicked and evil men, for not everyone has faith.
Heb 13 [18]Pray for us. We are sure that we have a clear conscience and desire to live honorably in every way. [19]I particularly urge you to pray so that I may be restored to you soon.

(8) Intercession for Public Authorities

Ezra 6 [10]so that they may offer sacrifices pleasing to the God of heaven and pray for the well-being of the king and his sons.
1 Tim 2 [1]I urge, then, first of all, that requests, prayers, intercession and thanksgiving be made for everyone—[2]for kings and all those in authority, that we may live peaceful and quiet lives in all godliness and holiness. [3]This is good, and pleases God our Savior. . . .

(9) Intercession for the Unsaved

Rom 10 [1]Brothers, my heart's desire and prayer to God for the Israelites is that they may be saved.

d) Petition

(1) Petition for Conviction of Sin

Job 13 [23]"How many wrongs and sins have I committed? Show me my offense and my sin."
Ps 26 [2]Test me, O LORD, and try me, examine my heart and my mind. . . .
Ps 139 [23]Search me, O God, and know my heart; test me and know my anxious thoughts. [24]See if there is any offensive way in me, and lead me in the way everlasting.

(2) Petition for Daily Provision

Matt 6 [9]"This, then, is how you should pray: 'Our Father in heaven, hallowed be your name. . . . [11]Give us today our daily bread.'"

(3) Petition for Deliverance from Difficulty

Ps 4 [1]Answer me when I call to you, O my righteous God. Give me relief from my distress; be merciful to me and hear my prayer.
Ps 25 [17]The troubles of my heart have multiplied; free me from my anguish.
Ps 40 [1]I waited patiently for the LORD; he turned to me and heard my cry. [2]He lifted me out of the slimy pit, out of the mud and mire; he set my feet on a rock and gave me a firm place to stand. [3]He put a new song in my mouth, a hymn of praise to our God. Many will see and fear and put their trust in the LORD.
Ps 50 [15]". . . and call upon me in the day of trouble; I will deliver you, and you will honor me."
Ps 77 [1]I cried out to God for help; I cried out to God to hear me. [2]When I was in distress, I sought the Lord; at night I stretched out untiring hands and my soul refused to be comforted.

[3]I remembered you, O God, and I groaned; I mused, and my spirit grew faint.

[4]You kept my eyes from closing; I was too troubled to speak.

Ps 91 [15]"He will call upon me, and I will answer him; I will be with him in trouble, I will deliver him and honor him."
Ps 107 [6]Then they cried out to the LORD in their trouble, and he delivered them from their distress.
Ps 118 [5]In my anguish I cried to the LORD, and he answered by setting me free.
Jon 2 [1]From inside the fish Jonah prayed to the LORD his God. [2]He said: "In my distress I called to the LORD, and he answered me. From the depths of the grave I called for help, and you listened to my cry. [3]You hurled me into the deep, into the very heart of the seas, and the currents swirled about me; all your waves and breakers swept over me. [4]I said, 'I have been banished from your sight; yet I will look again toward your holy temple.' [5]The engulfing waters threatened me, the deep surrounded me; seaweed was wrapped around my head. [6]To the roots of the mountains I sank down; the earth beneath barred me in forever. But you brought my life up from the pit, O LORD my God.

[7]"When my life was ebbing away, I remembered you, LORD, and my prayer rose to you, to your holy temple.

[8]"Those who cling to worthless idols forfeit the grace that could be theirs. [9]But I, with a song of thanksgiving, will sacrifice to you. What I have vowed I will make good. Salvation comes from the LORD."

[10]And the LORD commanded the fish, and it vomited Jonah onto dry land.

Acts 12 [5]So Peter was kept in prison, but the church was earnestly praying to God for him.

(4) Petition for Deliverance from Enemies

Deut 33 [7]And this he said about Judah: "Hear, O LORD, the cry of Judah; bring him to his people. With his own hands he defends his cause. Oh, be his help against his foes!"
Judg 3 [7]The Israelites did evil in the eyes of the LORD; they forgot the LORD their God and served the Baals and the Asherahs. [8]The anger of the LORD burned against Israel so that he sold them into the hands of Cushan-Rishathaim king of Aram Naharaim, to whom the Israelites were subject for eight years. [9]But when they cried out to the LORD, he raised up for them a deliverer, Othniel son of Kenaz, Caleb's younger brother, who saved them.
1 Sam 7 [4]So the Israelites put away their Baals and Ashtoreths, and served the LORD only.

[5]Then Samuel said, "Assemble all Israel at Mizpah and I will intercede with the LORD for you." [6]When they had assembled at Mizpah, they drew water and poured it out before the LORD. On that day they fasted and there they confessed, "We have sinned against the LORD." And Samuel was leader of Israel at Mizpah.

[7]When the Philistines heard that Israel had assembled at Mizpah, the rulers of the Philistines came up to attack them. And when the Israelites heard of it, they were afraid because of the Philistines. [8]They said to Samuel, "Do not stop crying out to the LORD our God for us, that he may rescue us from the hand of the Philistines." [9]Then Samuel took a suckling lamb and offered it up as a whole burnt offering to the LORD. He cried out to the LORD on Israel's behalf, and the LORD answered him.

[10]While Samuel was sacrificing the burnt offering, the Philistines drew near to engage Israel in battle. But that day the LORD thundered with loud thunder against the Philistines and threw them into such a panic that they were routed before the Israelites. [11]The men of Israel rushed out of Mizpah and pursued the Philistines, slaughtering them along the way to a point below Beth Car.

2 Kings 19 [9]Now Sennacherib received a report that Tirhakah, the Cushite king of Egypt, was marching out to fight against him. So he again sent messengers to Hezekiah with this word: [10]"Say to Hezekiah king of Judah: Do not let the god you depend on deceive you when he says, 'Jerusalem will not be handed over to the king of Assyria.' [11]Surely you have heard what the kings of Assyria have done to all the countries, destroying them completely. And will you be delivered? . . ."

[14]Hezekiah received the letter from the messengers and read it. Then he went up to the temple of the LORD and spread it out before the LORD. [15]And Hezekiah prayed to the LORD: "O LORD, God of Israel, enthroned between the cherubim, you alone are God over all the kingdoms of the earth. You have made heaven and earth. [16]Give ear, O LORD, and hear; open your eyes, O LORD, and see; listen to the words Sennacherib has sent to insult the living God."

2 Chron 14 [11]Then Asa called to the LORD his God and said, "LORD, there is no one like you to help the powerless against the mighty. Help us, O LORD our God, for we rely on you, and in your name we have come against this vast army. O LORD, you are our God; do not let man prevail against you."

Neh 4 [9]But we prayed to our God and posted a guard day and night to meet this threat.

Ps 5 [8]Lead me, O LORD, in your righteousness because of my enemies—make straight your way before me.

Ps 7 [1]O LORD my God, I take refuge in you; save and deliver me from all who pursue me, [2]or they will tear me like a lion and rip me to pieces with no one to rescue me. . . .

[6]Arise, O LORD, in your anger; rise up against the rage of my enemies. Awake, my God; decree justice.

Ps 17 [8]Keep me as the apple of your eye; hide me in the shadow of your wings [9]from the wicked who assail me, from my mortal enemies who surround me.

Ps 18 [3]I call to the LORD, who is worthy of praise, and I am saved from my enemies.

Ps 27 [11]Teach me your way, O LORD; lead me in a straight path because of my oppressors. [12]Do not turn me over to the desire of my foes, for false witnesses rise up against me, breathing out violence.

Ps 30 [1]I will exalt you, O LORD, for you lifted me out of the depths and did not let my enemies gloat over me.

Ps 31 [15]My times are in your hands; deliver me from my enemies and from those who pursue me.

Ps 36 [11]May the foot of the proud not come against me, nor the hand of the wicked drive me away.

Ps 43 [1]Vindicate me, O God, and plead my cause against an ungodly nation; rescue me from deceitful and wicked men. [2]You are God my stronghold. Why have you rejected me? Why must I go about mourning, oppressed by the enemy? [3]Send forth your light and your truth, let them guide me; let them bring me to your holy mountain, to the place where you dwell.

Ps 55 [1]Listen to my prayer, O God, do not ignore my plea; [2]hear me and answer me. My thoughts trouble me and I am distraught [3]at the voice of the enemy, at the stares of the wicked; for they bring down suffering upon me and revile me in their anger.

[4]My heart is in anguish within me; the terrors of death assail me. [5]Fear and trembling have beset me; horror has overwhelmed me. [6]I said, "Oh, that I had the wings of a dove! I would fly away and be at rest—[7]I would flee far away and stay in the desert; [8]I would hurry to my place of shelter, far from the tempest and storm."

[9]Confuse the wicked, O Lord, confound their speech, for I see violence and strife in the city. [10]Day and night they prowl about on its walls; malice and abuse are within it. [11]Destructive forces are at work in the city; threats and lies never leave its streets.

[12]If an enemy were insulting me, I could endure it; if a foe were raising himself against me, I could hide from him. [13]But it is you, a man like myself, my companion, my close friend, [14]with whom I once enjoyed sweet fellowship as we walked with the throng at the house of God.

[15]Let death take my enemies by surprise; let them go down alive to the grave, for evil finds lodging among them.

[16]But I call to God, and the LORD saves me. [17]Evening, morning and noon I cry out in distress, and he hears my voice. [18]He ransoms me unharmed from the battle waged against me, even though many oppose me.

Ps 56 [9]Then my enemies will turn back when I call for help. By this I will know that God is for me.

Ps 59 [1]Deliver me from my enemies, O God; protect me from those who rise up against me. [2]Deliver me from evildoers and save me from bloodthirsty men.

Ps 60 [11]Give us aid against the enemy, for the help of man is worthless.

Ps 64 [1]Hear me, O God, as I voice my complaint; protect my life from the threat of the enemy. [2]Hide me from the conspiracy of the wicked, from that noisy crowd of evildoers.

Ps 69 [18]Come near and rescue me; redeem me because of my foes.

Ps 70 [1]Hasten, O God, to save me; O LORD, come quickly to help me.

Ps 71 [1]In you, O LORD, I have taken refuge; let me never be put to shame. [2]Rescue me and deliver me in your righteousness; turn your ear to me and save me. . . . [4]Deliver me, O my God, from the hand of the wicked, from the grasp of evil and cruel men.

Ps 120 [1]I call on the LORD in my distress, and he answers me. [2]Save me, O LORD, from lying lips and from deceitful tongues.

Ps 140 [1]Rescue me, O LORD, from evil men; protect me from men of violence, [2]who devise evil plans in their hearts and stir up war every day. [3]They make their tongues as sharp as a serpent's; the poison of vipers is on their lips.

[4]Keep me, O LORD, from the hands of the wicked; protect me from men of violence who plan to trip my feet.

Ps 141 [3]Set a guard over my mouth, O LORD; keep watch over the door of my lips. [4]Let not my heart be drawn to what is evil, to take part in wicked deeds with men who are evildoers; let me not eat of their delicacies.

Ps 143 [9]Rescue me from my enemies, O LORD, for I hide myself in you. . . .

[11]For your name's sake, O LORD, preserve my life; in your righteousness, bring me out of trouble.

(5) Petition for Deliverance from Oppression

Job 34 [26]"He punishes them for their wickedness where everyone can see them, [27]because they turned from following him and had no regard for any of his ways. [28]They caused the cry of the poor to come before him, so that he heard the cry of the needy."

Ps 34 [6]This poor man called, and the LORD heard him; he saved him out of all his troubles.

Ps 72 [12]For he will deliver the needy who cry out, the afflicted who have no one to help.

Ps 102 [17]He will respond to the prayer of the destitute; he will not despise their plea.

Ps 119 [134]Redeem me from the oppression of men, that I may obey your precepts.

(6) Petition for Favor in Old Age

Ps 71 [9]Do not cast me away when I am old; do not forsake me when my strength is gone.

(7) Petition for Help

Judg 6 [6]Midian so impoverished the Israelites that they cried out to the LORD for help.

1 Sam 12 [8]"After Jacob entered Egypt, they cried to the LORD for help, and the LORD sent Moses and Aaron, who brought your forefathers out of Egypt and settled them in this place."

Ps 18 [6]In my distress I called to the LORD; I cried to my God for help. From his temple he heard my voice; my cry came before him, into his ears.

Ps 40 [13]Be pleased, O LORD, to save me; O LORD, come quickly to help me.

Ps 56 [8]Record my lament; list my tears on your scroll—are they not in your record?

[9]Then my enemies will turn back when I call for help. By this I will know that God is for me.

Ps 70 [1]Hasten, O God, to save me; O LORD, come quickly to help me.

Ps 109 [26]Help me, O LORD my God; save me in accordance with your love.

Dan 6 [11]Then these men went as a group and found Daniel praying and asking God for help.

Matt 15 [25]The woman came and knelt before him. "Lord, help me!" she said.
1 Tim 5 [5]The widow who is really in need and left all alone puts her hope in God and continues night and day to pray and to ask God for help.

(8) Petition for the Holy Spirit

Luke 11 [13]"If you then, though you are evil, know how to give good gifts to your children, how much more will your Father in heaven give the Holy Spirit to those who ask him!"

(9) Petition for Instruction

Exod 33 [12]Moses said to the LORD, "You have been telling me, 'Lead these people,' but you have not let me know whom you will send with me. You have said, 'I know you by name and you have found favor with me.' [13]If you are pleased with me, teach me your ways so I may know you and continue to find favor with you. Remember that this nation is your people."
Ps 25 [4]Show me your ways, O LORD, teach me your paths; [5]guide me in your truth and teach me, for you are God my Savior, and my hope is in you all day long.
Ps 27 [11]Teach me your way, O LORD; lead me in a straight path because of my oppressors.
Ps 86 [11]Teach me your way, O LORD, and I will walk in your truth; give me an undivided heart, that I may fear your name.
Ps 119 [12]Praise be to you, O LORD; teach me your decrees.
Ps 119 [26]I recounted my ways and you answered me; teach me your decrees. [27]Let me understand the teaching of your precepts; then I will meditate on your wonders.
Ps 119 [33]Teach me, O LORD, to follow your decrees; then I will keep them to the end. [34]Give me understanding, and I will keep your law and obey it with all my heart.
Ps 119 [66]Teach me knowledge and good judgment, for I believe in your commands. . . . [68]You are good, and what you do is good; teach me your decrees.
Ps 119 [108]Accept, O LORD, the willing praise of my mouth, and teach me your laws.
Ps 119 [124]Deal with your servant according to your love and teach me your decrees. [125]I am your servant; give me discernment that I may understand your statutes.
Ps 143 [10]Teach me to do your will, for you are my God; may your good Spirit lead me on level ground.

(10) Petition for Judgment on Enemies

Deut 33 [11]"Bless all his skills, O LORD, and be pleased with the work of his hands. Smite the loins of those who rise up against him; strike his foes till they rise no more."
Judg 16 [28]Then Samson prayed to the LORD, "O Sovereign LORD, remember me. O God, please strengthen me just once more, and let me with one blow get revenge on the Philistines for my two eyes."
Neh 4 [4]Hear us, O our God, for we are despised. Turn their insults back on their own heads. Give them over as plunder in a land of captivity. [5]Do not cover up their guilt or blot out their sins from your sight, for they have thrown insults in the face of the builders.
Job 27 [7]"May my enemies be like the wicked, my adversaries like the unjust! [8]For what hope has the godless when he is cut off, when God takes away his life?"
Ps 35 [4]May those who seek my life be disgraced and put to shame; may those who plot my ruin be turned back in dismay. [8]. . . may ruin overtake them by surprise—may the net they hid entangle them, may they fall into the pit, to their ruin. . . .

[26]May all who gloat over my distress be put to shame and confusion; may all who exalt themselves over me be clothed with shame and disgrace.
Ps 54 [5]Let evil recoil on those who slander me; in your faithfulness destroy them.
Ps 55 [15]Let death take my enemies by surprise; let them go down alive to the grave, for evil finds lodging among them.
Ps 70 [1]Hasten, O God, to save me; O LORD, come quickly to help me. [2]May those who seek my life be put to shame and confusion; may all who desire my ruin be turned back in disgrace. [3]May those who say to me, "Aha! Aha!" turn back because of their shame.
Ps 71 [12]Be not far from me, O God; come quickly, O my God, to help me. [13]May my accusers perish in shame; may those who want to harm me be covered with scorn and disgrace.
Ps 119 [84]How long must your servant wait? When will you punish my persecutors?
Ps 140 [7]O Sovereign LORD, my strong deliverer, who shields my head in the day of battle—[8]do not grant the wicked their desires, O LORD; do not let their plans succeed, or they will become proud.

[9]Let the heads of those who surround me be covered with the trouble their lips have caused. [10]Let burning coals fall upon them; may they be thrown into the fire, into miry pits, never to rise.
Ps 143 [11]For your name's sake, O LORD, preserve my life; in your righteousness, bring me out of trouble. [12]In your unfailing love, silence my enemies; destroy all my foes, for I am your servant.

(11) Petition for Judgment on the Nations

Ps 9 [20]Strike them with terror, O LORD; let the nations know they are but men.
Ps 56 [7]On no account let them escape; in your anger, O God, bring down the nations.
Ps 59 [5]O LORD God Almighty, the God of Israel, rouse yourself to punish all the nations; show no mercy to wicked traitors. . . . [12]For the sins of their mouths, for the words of their lips, let them be caught in their pride. For the curses and lies they utter . . .
Ps 79 [10]Why should the nations say, "Where is their God?" Before our eyes, make known among the nations that you avenge the outpoured blood of your servants. [11]May the groans of the prisoners come before you; by the strength of your arm preserve those condemned to die.

[12]Pay back into the laps of our neighbors seven times the reproach they have hurled at you, O Lord.
Ps 83 [5]With one mind they plot together; they form an alliance against you—[6]the tents of Edom and the Ishmaelites, of Moab and the Hagrites, [7]Gebal, Ammon and Amalek, Philistia, with the people of Tyre. [8]Even Assyria has joined them to lend strength to the descendants of Lot. . . .

[13]Make them like tumbleweed, O my God, like chaff before the wind. [14]As fire consumes the forest or a flame sets the mountains ablaze, [15]so pursue them with your tempest and terrify them with your storm. [16]Cover their faces with shame so that men will seek your name, O LORD.

[17]May they ever be ashamed and dismayed; may they perish in disgrace. [18]Let them know that you, whose name is the LORD—that you alone are the Most High over all the earth.

(12) Petition for Judgment on Oneself

2 Sam 24 [17]When David saw the angel who was striking down the people, he said to the LORD, "I am the one who has sinned and done wrong. These are but sheep. What have they done? Let your hand fall upon me and my family."
Ps 7 [3]O LORD my God, if I have done this and there is guilt on my hands—[4]if I have done evil to him who is at peace with me or without cause have robbed my foe—[5]then let my enemy pursue and overtake me; let him trample my life to the ground and make me sleep in the dust.

(13) Petition for Judgment on Oppressors of the Poor

Ps 109 [7]When he is tried, let him be found guilty, and may his prayers condemn him. [8]May his days be few; may another take his place of leadership. [9]May his children be fatherless and his wife a widow. [10]May his children be wandering beggars; may they be driven from their ruined homes. [11]May a creditor seize all he has; may strangers plunder the fruits of his labor. [12]May no one extend kindness to him or take pity on his fatherless children. [13]May his descendants be cut off, their names blotted out from the next generation. [14]May the iniquity of his fathers be remembered before the LORD; may the sin of his mother never be blotted out. [15]May their sins always remain before the LORD, that he may cut off the memory of them from the earth.

[16]For he never thought of doing a kindness, but hounded to death the poor and the needy and the brokenhearted.

(14) Petition for Judgment on Preachers of Another Gospel

Gal 1 [8]But even if we or an angel from heaven should preach a gospel other than the one we preached to you, let him be eternally condemned! [9]As we have already said, so now I say again: If anybody is preaching to you a gospel other than what you accepted, let him be eternally condemned!

(15) Petition for Judgment on the Wicked

Ps 5 [10]Declare them guilty, O God! Let their intrigues be their downfall. Banish them for their many sins, for they have rebelled against you.
Ps 10 [15]Break the arm of the wicked and evil man; call him to account for his wickedness that would not be found out.
Ps 28 [4]Repay them for their deeds and for their evil work; repay them for what their hands have done and bring back upon them what they deserve.
Ps 31 [17]Let me not be put to shame, O LORD, for I have cried out to you; but let the wicked be put to shame and lie silent in the grave. [18]Let their lying lips be silenced, for with pride and contempt they speak arrogantly against the righteous.
Ps 55 [9]Confuse the wicked, O Lord, confound their speech, for I see violence and strife in the city.
Ps 69 [22]May the table set before them become a snare; may it become retribution and a trap. [23]May their eyes be darkened so they cannot see, and their backs be bent forever. [24]Pour out your wrath on them; let your fierce anger overtake them. [25]May their place be deserted; let there be no one to dwell in their tents. [26]For they persecute those you wound and talk about the pain of those you hurt. [27]Charge them with crime upon crime; do not let them share in your salvation. [28]May they be blotted out of the book of life and not be listed with the righteous.
Ps 94 [1]O LORD, the God who avenges, O God who avenges, shine forth. [2]Rise up, O Judge of the earth; pay back to the proud what they deserve. [3]How long will the wicked, O LORD, how long will the wicked be jubilant?
Ps 129 [5]May all who hate Zion be turned back in shame.
Jer 11 [18]Because the LORD revealed their plot to me, I knew it, for at that time he showed me what they were doing. [19]I had been like a gentle lamb led to the slaughter; I did not realize that they had plotted against me, saying, "Let us destroy the tree and its fruit; let us cut him off from the land of the living, that his name be remembered no more." [20]But, O LORD Almighty, you who judge righteously and test the heart and mind, let me see your vengeance upon them, for to you I have committed my cause.
Jer 12 [1]You are always righteous, O LORD, when I bring a case before you. Yet I would speak with you about your justice: Why does the way of the wicked prosper? Why do all the faithless live at ease? [2]You have planted them, and they have taken root; they grow and bear fruit. You are always on their lips but far from their hearts. [3]Yet you know me, O LORD; you see me and test my thoughts about you. Drag them off like sheep to be butchered! Set them apart for the day of slaughter! [4]How long will the land lie parched and the grass in every field be withered? Because those who live in it are wicked, the animals and birds have perished. Moreover, the people are saying, "He will not see what happens to us."
Jer 15 [15]You understand, O LORD; remember me and care for me. Avenge me on my persecutors. You are long-suffering—do not take me away; think of how I suffer reproach for your sake.
Jer 17 [18]Let my persecutors be put to shame, but keep me from shame; let them be terrified, but keep me from terror. Bring on them the day of disaster; destroy them with double destruction.
Jer 18 [19]Listen to me, O LORD; hear what my accusers are saying! [20]Should good be repaid with evil? Yet they have dug a pit for me. Remember that I stood before you and spoke in their behalf to turn your wrath away from them. [21]So give their children over to famine; hand them over to the power of the sword. Let their wives be made childless and widows; let their men be put to death, their young men slain by the sword in battle. [22]Let a cry be heard from their houses when you suddenly bring invaders against them, for they have dug a pit to capture me and have hidden snares for my feet. [23]But you know, O LORD, all their plots to kill me. Do not forgive their crimes or blot out their sins from your sight. Let them be overthrown before you; deal with them in the time of your anger.
Lam 1 [22]"Let all their wickedness come before you; deal with them as you have dealt with me because of all my sins. My groans are many and my heart is faint."
Lam 3 [64]Pay them back what they deserve, O LORD, for what their hands have done. [65]Put a veil over their hearts, and may your curse be on them! [66]Pursue them in anger and destroy them from under the heavens of the LORD.
Luke 18 [7]"And will not God bring about justice for his chosen ones, who cry out to him day and night? Will he keep putting them off? [8]I tell you, he will see that they get justice, and quickly. However, when the Son of Man comes, will he find faith on the earth?"
2 Tim 4 [14]Alexander the metalworker did me a great deal of harm. The Lord will repay him for what he has done. [15]You too should be on your guard against him, because he strongly opposed our message.
Rev 6 [9]When he opened the fifth seal, I saw under the altar the souls of those who had been slain because of the word of God and the testimony they had maintained. [10]They called out in a loud voice, "How long, Sovereign Lord, holy and true, until you judge the inhabitants of the earth and avenge our blood?"

(16) Petition for Mercy and Grace

2 Chron 6 [18]"But will God really dwell on earth with men? The heavens, even the highest heavens, cannot contain you. How much less this temple I have built! [19]Yet give attention to your servant's prayer and his plea for mercy, O LORD my God. Hear the cry and the prayer that your servant is praying in your presence."
Ps 25 [16]Turn to me and be gracious to me, for I am lonely and afflicted.
Ps 28 [2]Hear my cry for mercy as I call to you for help, as I lift up my hands toward your Most Holy Place.
Ps 30 [8]To you, O LORD, I called; to the Lord I cried for mercy. . . .
Ps 31 [9]Be merciful to me, O LORD, for I am in distress; my eyes grow weak with sorrow, my soul and my body with grief. [10]My life is consumed by anguish and my years by groaning; my strength fails because of my affliction, and my bones grow weak.
Ps 41 [10]But you, O LORD, have mercy on me; raise me up, that I may repay them.
Ps 86 [3]Have mercy on me, O Lord, for I call to you all day long. . . . [6]Hear my prayer, O LORD; listen to my cry for mercy.
Ps 116 [1]I love the LORD, for he heard my voice; he heard my cry for mercy. [2]Because he turned his ear to me, I will call on him as long as I live.
Ps 119 [132]Turn to me and have mercy on me, as you always do to those who love your name.
Ps 123 [2]As the eyes of slaves look to the hand of their master, as the eyes of a maid look to the hand of her mistress, so our eyes look to the LORD our God, till he shows us his mercy.

[3]Have mercy on us, O LORD, have mercy on us, for we have endured much contempt.
Ps 130 [1]Out of the depths I cry to you, O LORD; [2]O Lord, hear my voice. Let your ears be attentive to my cry for mercy.
Ps 140 [6]O LORD, I say to you, "You are my God." Hear, O LORD, my cry for mercy.
Ps 142 [1]I cry aloud to the LORD; I lift up my voice to the LORD for mercy. [2]I pour out my complaint before him; before him I tell my trouble.

[3]When my spirit grows faint within me, it is you who know my way. In the path where I walk men have hidden a snare for me. [4]Look to my right and see; no one is concerned for me. I have no refuge; no one cares for my life.

[5]I cry to you, O LORD; I say, "You are my refuge, my portion in the land of the living." [6]Listen to my cry, for I am in desperate need; rescue me from those who pursue me, for they are too strong for me. [7]Set me free from my prison, that I may praise your name.

Then the righteous will gather about me because of your goodness to me.
Ps 143 [1]O LORD, hear my prayer, listen to my cry for mercy; in your faithfulness and righteousness come to my relief.
Matt 9 [27]As Jesus went on from there, two blind men followed him, calling out, "Have mercy on us, Son of David!"
Matt 20 [30]Two blind men were sitting by the roadside, and when they heard that Jesus was going by, they shouted, "Lord, Son of David, have mercy on us!"

[31]The crowd rebuked them and told them to be quiet, but

they shouted all the louder, "Lord, Son of David, have mercy on us!"

Heb 4 [16]Let us then approach the throne of grace with confidence, so that we may receive mercy and find grace to help us in our time of need.

(17) Petition for Pardon of Sin

2 Chron 6 [21]"Hear the supplications of your servant and of your people Israel when they pray toward this place. Hear from heaven, your dwelling place; and when you hear, forgive."

2 Chron 6 [25]". . . then hear from heaven and forgive the sin of your people Israel and bring them back to the land you gave to them and their fathers."

2 Chron 6 [27]". . . then hear from heaven and forgive the sin of your servants, your people Israel. Teach them the right way to live, and send rain on the land you gave your people for an inheritance."

2 Chron 6 [39]". . . then from heaven, your dwelling place, hear their prayer and their pleas, and uphold their cause. And forgive your people, who have sinned against you."

Ps 25 [7]Remember not the sins of my youth and my rebellious ways; according to your love remember me, for you are good, O LORD. . . . [11]For the sake of your name, O LORD, forgive my iniquity, though it is great. . . . [18]Look upon my affliction and my distress and take away all my sins.

Ps 39 [8]"Save me from all my transgressions; do not make me the scorn of fools."

Ps 51 [1]Have mercy on me, O God, according to your unfailing love; according to your great compassion blot out my transgressions. . . . [8]Let me hear joy and gladness; let the bones you have crushed rejoice. [9]Hide your face from my sins and blot out all my iniquity. . . . [14]Save me from bloodguilt, O God, the God who saves me, and my tongue will sing of your righteousness.

Dan 9 [18]"Give ear, O God, and hear; open your eyes and see the desolation of the city that bears your Name. We do not make requests of you because we are righteous, but because of your great mercy. [19]O Lord, listen! O Lord, forgive! O Lord, hear and act! For your sake, O my God, do not delay, because your city and your people bear your Name."

Hos 14 [1]Return, O Israel, to the LORD your God. Your sins have been your downfall! [2]Take words with you and return to the LORD. Say to him: "Forgive all our sins and receive us graciously, that we may offer the fruit of our lips."

Matt 6 [12]"'Forgive us our debts, as we also have forgiven our debtors.'"

Luke 11 [4]"'Forgive us our sins, for we also forgive everyone who sins against us. And lead us not into temptation.'"

(18) Petition for Physical Well-Being

2 Kings 20 [1]In those days Hezekiah became ill and was at the point of death. The prophet Isaiah son of Amoz went to him and said, "This is what the LORD says: Put your house in order, because you are going to die; you will not recover."

[2]Hezekiah turned his face to the wall and prayed to the LORD, [3]"Remember, O LORD, how I have walked before you faithfully and with wholehearted devotion and have done what is good in your eyes." And Hezekiah wept bitterly.

[4]Before Isaiah had left the middle court, the word of the LORD came to him: [5]"Go back and tell Hezekiah, the leader of my people, 'This is what the LORD, the God of your father David, says: I have heard your prayer and seen your tears; I will heal you. On the third day from now you will go up to the temple of the LORD. [6]I will add fifteen years to your life. And I will deliver you and this city from the hand of the king of Assyria. I will defend this city for my sake and for the sake of my servant David.'"

[7]Then Isaiah said, "Prepare a poultice of figs." They did so and applied it to the boil, and he recovered.

Acts 9 [36]In Joppa there was a disciple named Tabitha (which, when translated, is Dorcas), who was always doing good and helping the poor. [37]About that time she became sick and died, and her body was washed and placed in an upstairs room. [38]Lydda was near Joppa; so when the disciples heard that Peter was in Lydda, they sent two men to him and urged him, "Please come at once!"

[39]Peter went with them, and when he arrived he was taken upstairs to the room. All the widows stood around him, crying and showing him the robes and other clothing that Dorcas had made while she was still with them.

[40]Peter sent them all out of the room; then he got down on his knees and prayed. Turning toward the dead woman, he said, "Tabitha, get up." She opened her eyes, and seeing Peter she sat up.

Acts 28 [7]There was an estate nearby that belonged to Publius, the chief official of the island. He welcomed us to his home and for three days entertained us hospitably. [8]His father was sick in bed, suffering from fever and dysentery. Paul went in to see him and, after prayer, placed his hands on him and healed him. [9]When this had happened, the rest of the sick on the island came and were cured.

James 5 [13]Is any one of you in trouble? He should pray. Is anyone happy? Let him sing songs of praise. [14]Is any one of you sick? He should call the elders of the church to pray over him and anoint him with oil in the name of the Lord. [15]And the prayer offered in faith will make the sick person well; the Lord will raise him up. If he has sinned, he will be forgiven.

(19) Petition for Spiritual Development

1 Kings 18 [36]At the time of sacrifice, the prophet Elijah stepped forward and prayed: "O LORD, God of Abraham, Isaac and Israel, let it be known today that you are God in Israel and that I am your servant and have done all these things at your command. [37]Answer me, O LORD, answer me, so these people will know that you, O LORD, are God, and that you are turning their hearts back again."

Ps 51 [2]Wash away all my iniquity and cleanse me from my sin. . . .

[7]Cleanse me with hyssop, and I will be clean; wash me, and I will be whiter than snow. . . .

[10]Create in me a pure heart, O God, and renew a steadfast spirit within me.

Eph 1 [16]I have not stopped giving thanks for you, remembering you in my prayers. [17]I keep asking that the God of our Lord Jesus Christ, the glorious Father, may give you the Spirit of wisdom and revelation, so that you may know him better. [18]I pray also that the eyes of your heart may be enlightened in order that you may know the hope to which he has called you, the riches of his glorious inheritance in the saints, [19]and his incomparably great power for us who believe. That power is like the working of his mighty strength. . . .

Phil 1 [3]I thank my God every time I remember you. [4]In all my prayers for all of you, I always pray with joy . . . [6]being confident of this, that he who began a good work in you will carry it on to completion until the day of Christ Jesus.

Col 1 [9]For this reason, since the day we heard about you, we have not stopped praying for you and asking God to fill you with the knowledge of his will through all spiritual wisdom and understanding.

Col 4 [12]Epaphras, who is one of you and a servant of Christ Jesus, sends greetings. He is always wrestling in prayer for you, that you may stand firm in all the will of God, mature and fully assured.

1 Thess 3 [10]Night and day we pray most earnestly that we may see you again and supply what is lacking in your faith. . . . [12]May the Lord make your love increase and overflow for each other and for everyone else, just as ours does for you.

2 Tim 1 [3]I thank God, whom I serve, as my forefathers did, with a clear conscience, as night and day I constantly remember you in my prayers. [4]Recalling your tears, I long to see you, so that I may be filled with joy. [5]I have been reminded of your sincere faith, which first lived in your grandmother Lois and in your mother Eunice and, I am persuaded, now lives in you also. [6]For this reason I remind you to fan into flame the gift of God, which is in you through the laying on of my hands.

Philem [4]I always thank my God as I remember you in my prayers, [5]because I hear about your faith in the Lord Jesus and your love for all the saints. [6]I pray that you may be active in sharing your faith, so that you will have a full understanding of every good thing we have in Christ.

(20) Petition for Strength amidst Trouble

Neh 9 [32]"Now therefore, O our God, the great, mighty and awesome God, who keeps his covenant of love, do not let all this hardship seem trifling in your eyes—the hardship that has come upon us, upon our kings and leaders, upon our priests and prophets, upon our fathers and all your people, from the days of the kings of Assyria until today."

Ps 20 [1]May the LORD answer you when you are in distress; may the name of the God of Jacob protect you.

Ps 22 [11]Do not be far from me, for trouble is near and there is no one to help.

Ps 61 [1]Hear my cry, O God; listen to my prayer.

[2]From the ends of the earth I call to you, I call as my heart grows faint; lead me to the rock that is higher than I.

Ps 69 [17]Do not hide your face from your servant; answer me quickly, for I am in trouble.

Ps 86 [7]In the day of my trouble I will call to you, for you will answer me.

Ps 88 [1]O LORD, the God who saves me, day and night I cry out before you. [2]May my prayer come before you; turn your ear to my cry.

[3]For my soul is full of trouble and my life draws near the grave. [4]I am counted among those who go down to the pit; I am like a man without strength. [5]I am set apart with the dead, like the slain who lie in the grave, whom you remember no more, who are cut off from your care.

[6]You have put me in the lowest pit, in the darkest depths. [7]Your wrath lies heavily upon me; you have overwhelmed me with all your waves. [8]You have taken from me my closest friends and have made me repulsive to them. I am confined and cannot escape; [9]my eyes are dim with grief.

I call to you, O LORD, every day; I spread out my hands to you.

Ps 102 [2]Do not hide your face from me when I am in distress. Turn your ear to me; when I call, answer me quickly.

Ps 116 [3]The cords of death entangled me, the anguish of the grave came upon me; I was overcome by trouble and sorrow. [4]Then I called on the name of the LORD: "O LORD, save me!"

[5]The LORD is gracious and righteous; our God is full of compassion. [6]The LORD protects the simplehearted; when I was in great need, he saved me.

[7]Be at rest once more, O my soul, for the LORD has been good to you.

[8]For you, O LORD, have delivered my soul from death, my eyes from tears, my feet from stumbling, [9]that I may walk before the LORD in the land of the living.

Ps 138 [3]When I called, you answered me; you made me bold and stouthearted. . . . [7]Though I walk in the midst of trouble, you preserve my life; you stretch out your hand against the anger of my foes, with your right hand you save me.

Ps 143 [11]For your name's sake, O LORD, preserve my life; in your righteousness, bring me out of trouble.

Isa 33 [2]O LORD, be gracious to us; we long for you. Be our strength every morning, our salvation in time of distress.

Lam 3 [55]I called on your name, O LORD, from the depths of the pit. [56]You heard my plea: "Do not close your ears to my cry for relief."

(21) Petition for Success

Gen 24 [12]Then he prayed, "O LORD, God of my master Abraham, give me success today, and show kindness to my master Abraham. [13]See, I am standing beside this spring, and the daughters of the townspeople are coming out to draw water. [14]May it be that when I say to a girl, 'Please let down your jar that I may have a drink,' and she says, 'Drink, and I'll water your camels too'—let her be the one you have chosen for your servant Isaac. By this I will know that you have shown kindness to my master."

[15]Before he had finished praying, Rebekah came out with her jar on her shoulder. She was the daughter of Bethuel son of Milcah, who was the wife of Abraham's brother Nahor.

1 Chron 4 [10]Jabez cried out to the God of Israel, "Oh, that you would bless me and enlarge my territory! Let your hand be with me, and keep me from harm so that I will be free from pain." And God granted his request.

Neh 1 [11]"O Lord, let your ear be attentive to the prayer of this your servant and to the prayer of your servants who delight in revering your name. Give your servant success today by granting him favor in the presence of this man."

I was cupbearer to the king.

(22) Petition for Wisdom

2 Chron 1 [7]That night God appeared to Solomon and said to him, "Ask for whatever you want me to give you."

[8]Solomon answered God, "You have shown great kindness to David my father and have made me king in his place. [9]Now, LORD God, let your promise to my father David be confirmed, for you have made me king over a people who are as numerous as the dust of the earth. [10]Give me wisdom and knowledge, that I may lead this people, for who is able to govern this great people of yours?"

[11]God said to Solomon, "Since this is your heart's desire and you have not asked for wealth, riches or honor, nor for the death of your enemies, and since you have not asked for a long life but for wisdom and knowledge to govern my people over whom I have made you king, [12]therefore wisdom and knowledge will be given you. And I will also give you wealth, riches and honor, such as no king who was before you ever had and none after you will have."

James 1 [5]If any of you lacks wisdom, he should ask God, who gives generously to all without finding fault, and it will be given to him.

(23) Petition for the Work of Ministry

Matt 9 [37]Then he said to his disciples, "The harvest is plentiful but the workers are few. [38]Ask the Lord of the harvest, therefore, to send out workers into his harvest field."

Acts 4 [18]Then they called them in again and commanded them not to speak or teach at all in the name of Jesus. . . .

[24]When they heard this, they raised their voices together in prayer to God. "Sovereign Lord," they said, "you made the heaven and the earth and the sea, and everything in them. . . . [29]Now, Lord, consider their threats and enable your servants to speak your word with great boldness. [30]Stretch out your hand to heal and perform miraculous signs and wonders through the name of your holy servant Jesus."

[31]After they prayed, the place where they were meeting was shaken. And they were all filled with the Holy Spirit and spoke the word of God boldly.

e) Submission

(1) Job Submitted to God in Prayer

Job 1 [20]At this, Job got up and tore his robe and shaved his head. Then he fell to the ground in worship [21]and said: "Naked I came from my mother's womb, and naked I will depart. The LORD gave and the LORD has taken away; may the name of the LORD be praised."

[22]In all this, Job did not sin by charging God with wrongdoing.

(2) David Submitted to God in Prayer

2 Sam 12 [15]After Nathan had gone home, the LORD struck the child that Uriah's wife had borne to David, and he became ill. [16]David pleaded with God for the child. He fasted and went into his house and spent the nights lying on the ground. . . .

[19]David noticed that his servants were whispering among themselves and he realized the child was dead. "Is the child dead?" he asked.

"Yes," they replied, "he is dead."

[20]Then David got up from the ground. After he had washed, put on lotions and changed his clothes, he went into the house of the LORD and worshiped. . . .

[22]He answered, "While the child was still alive, I fasted and wept. I thought, 'Who knows? The LORD may be gracious to me and let the child live.' [23]But now that he is dead, why should I fast? Can I bring him back again? I will go to him, but he will not return to me."

(3) Jesus Submitted to the Father in Prayer

Matt 26 [39]Going a little farther, he fell with his face to the ground and prayed, "My Father, if it is possible, may this cup be taken from me. Yet not as I will, but as you will."

Luke 22 [42]"Father, if you are willing, take this cup from me; yet not my will, but yours be done."

Heb 5 [7]During the days of Jesus' life on earth, he offered up prayers and petitions with loud cries and tears to the one who could save him from death, and he was heard because of his reverent submission.

(4) Paul Submitted to God in Prayer

2 Cor 12 [7]To keep me from becoming conceited because of these surpassingly great revelations, there was given me a thorn in my flesh, a messenger of Satan, to torment me. [8]Three times I pleaded with the Lord to take it away from me. [9]But he said to me, "My grace is sufficient for you, for my power is made perfect in weakness." Therefore I will boast all the more gladly about my weaknesses, so that Christ's power may rest on me.

f) Thanksgiving

(1) Thanks for Answered Prayer

John 11 [41]So they took away the stone. Then Jesus looked up and said, "Father, I thank you that you have heard me."

(2) Thanks for Food

Matt 14 [19]And he directed the people to sit down on the grass. Taking the five loaves and the two fish and looking up to heaven, he gave thanks and broke the loaves. Then he gave them to the disciples, and the disciples gave them to the people.
Acts 27 [35]After he said this, he took some bread and gave thanks to God in front of them all. Then he broke it and began to eat.
Rom 14 [6]He who regards one day as special, does so to the Lord. He who eats meat, eats to the Lord, for he gives thanks to God; and he who abstains, does so to the Lord and gives thanks to God.
1 Cor 10 [30]If I take part in the meal with thankfulness, why am I denounced because of something I thank God for?
1 Tim 4 [3]They forbid people to marry and order them to abstain from certain foods, which God created to be received with thanksgiving by those who believe and who know the truth. [4]For everything God created is good, and nothing is to be rejected if it is received with thanksgiving, [5]because it is consecrated by the word of God and prayer.

(3) Thanks for God's Blessings

Phil 4 [6]Do not be anxious about anything, but in everything, by prayer and petition, with thanksgiving, present your requests to God.
Col 1 [10]And we pray this in order that you may live a life worthy of the Lord and may please him in every way: bearing fruit in every good work, growing in the knowledge of God, [11]being strengthened with all power according to his glorious might so that you may have great endurance and patience, and joyfully [12]giving thanks to the Father, who has qualified you to share in the inheritance of the saints in the kingdom of light.

(4) Thanks for God's Wondrous Deeds

1 Chron 16 [7]That day David first committed to Asaph and his associates this psalm of thanks to the LORD: [8]Give thanks to the LORD, call on his name; make known among the nations what he has done. [9]Sing to him, sing praise to him; tell of all his wonderful acts. [10]Glory in his holy name; let the hearts of those who seek the LORD rejoice.
Ps 103 [1]Praise the LORD, O my soul; all my inmost being, praise his holy name. [2]Praise the LORD, O my soul, and forget not all his benefits—[3]who forgives all your sins and heals all your diseases, [4]who redeems your life from the pit and crowns you with love and compassion, [5]who satisfies your desires with good things so that your youth is renewed like the eagle's.

[6]The LORD works righteousness and justice for all the oppressed.

[7]He made known his ways to Moses, his deeds to the people of Israel: [8]The LORD is compassionate and gracious, slow to anger, abounding in love. [9]He will not always accuse, nor will he harbor his anger forever; [10]he does not treat us as our sins deserve or repay us according to our iniquities. [11]For as high as the heavens are above the earth, so great is his love for those who fear him; [12]as far as the east is from the west, so far has he removed our transgressions from us. [13]As a father has compassion on his children, so the LORD has compassion on those who fear him; [14]for he knows how we are formed, he remembers that we are dust. [15]As for man, his days are like grass, he flourishes like a flower of the field; [16]the wind blows over it and it is gone, and its place remembers it no more. [17]But from everlasting to everlasting the LORD's love is with those who fear him, and his righteousness with their children's children—[18]with those who keep his covenant and remember to obey his precepts.

[19]The LORD has established his throne in heaven, and his kingdom rules over all.

[20]Praise the LORD, you his angels, you mighty ones who do his bidding, who obey his word. [21]Praise the LORD, all his heavenly hosts, you his servants who do his will. [22]Praise the LORD, all his works everywhere in his dominion.

Praise the LORD, O my soul.

(5) Thanks for Other Believers

1 Cor 1 [4]I always thank God for you because of his grace given you in Christ Jesus.
Eph 1 [15]For this reason, ever since I heard about your faith in the Lord Jesus and your love for all the saints, [16]I have not stopped giving thanks for you, remembering you in my prayers.
Phil 1 [3]I thank my God every time I remember you. [4]In all my prayers for all of you, I always pray with joy [5]because of your partnership in the gospel from the first day until now. . . .
Col 1 [3]We always thank God, the Father of our Lord Jesus Christ, when we pray for you, [4]because we have heard of your faith in Christ Jesus and of the love you have for all the saints. . . .
1 Thess 1 [2]We always thank God for all of you, mentioning you in our prayers.
2 Tim 1 [3]I thank God, whom I serve, as my forefathers did, with a clear conscience, as night and day I constantly remember you in my prayers.
Philem [4]I always thank my God as I remember you in my prayers, [5]because I hear about your faith in the Lord Jesus and your love for all the saints.

g) The Elements of Prayer in the Lord's Prayer

Matt 6 [9]"This, then, is how you should pray: 'Our Father in heaven, hallowed be your name, [10]your kingdom come, your will be done on earth as it is in heaven. [11]Give us today our daily bread. [12]Forgive us our debts, as we also have forgiven our debtors. [13]And lead us not into temptation, but deliver us from the evil one.'"
Luke 11 [1]One day Jesus was praying in a certain place. When he finished, one of his disciples said to him, "Lord, teach us to pray, just as John taught his disciples."

[2]He said to them, "When you pray, say: 'Father, hallowed be your name, your kingdom come. [3]Give us each day our daily bread. [4]Forgive us our sins, for we also forgive everyone who sins against us. And lead us not into temptation.'"

2. The Manner of Prayer

a) Pray according to God's Will

1 John 5 [14]This is the confidence we have in approaching God: that if we ask anything according to his will, he hears us. [15]And if we know that he hears us—whatever we ask—we know that we have what we asked of him.

b) Pray in Corporate Worship

1 Kings 8 [22]Then Solomon stood before the altar of the LORD in front of the whole assembly of Israel, spread out his hands toward heaven [23]and said: "O LORD, God of Israel, there is no God like you in heaven above or on earth below—you who keep your covenant of love with your servants who continue wholeheartedly in your way. . . .

[27]"But will God really dwell on earth? The heavens, even the highest heaven, cannot contain you. How much less this temple I have built! [28]Yet give attention to your servant's prayer and his plea for mercy, O LORD my God. Hear the cry and the prayer that your servant is praying in your presence this day. [29]May your eyes be open toward this temple night and day, this place of which you said, 'My Name shall be there,' so that you will hear the prayer your servant prays toward this place. [30]Hear the supplication of your servant and of your people Israel when they pray toward this place. Hear from heaven, your dwelling place, and when you hear, forgive."
2 Chron 7 [12]the LORD appeared to him at night and said: "I have heard your prayer and have chosen this place for myself as a temple for sacrifices. [14]. . . if my people, who are called by

my name, will humble themselves and pray and seek my face and turn from their wicked ways, then will I hear from heaven and will forgive their sin and will heal their land. [15]Now my eyes will be open and my ears attentive to the prayers offered in this place. [16]I have chosen and consecrated this temple so that my Name may be there forever. My eyes and my heart will always be there."

Ps 116 [17]I will sacrifice a thank offering to you and call on the name of the LORD. [18]I will fulfill my vows to the LORD in the presence of all his people, [19]in the courts of the house of the LORD—in your midst, O Jerusalem.

Praise the LORD.

Isa 56 [7]". . . these I will bring to my holy mountain and give them joy in my house of prayer. Their burnt offerings and sacrifices will be accepted on my altar; for my house will be called a house of prayer for all nations."

Joel 2 [15]Blow the trumpet in Zion, declare a holy fast, call a sacred assembly. [16]Gather the people, consecrate the assembly; bring together the elders, gather the children, those nursing at the breast. Let the bridegroom leave his room and the bride her chamber. [17]Let the priests, who minister before the LORD, weep between the temple porch and the altar. Let them say, "Spare your people, O LORD. Do not make your inheritance an object of scorn, a byword among the nations. Why should they say among the peoples, 'Where is their God?'"

Zech 8 [21]". . . and the inhabitants of one city will go to another and say, 'Let us go at once to entreat the LORD and seek the LORD Almighty. I myself am going.' [22]And many peoples and powerful nations will come to Jerusalem to seek the LORD Almighty and to entreat him."

Matt 18 [19]"Again, I tell you that if two of you on earth agree about anything you ask for, it will be done for you by my Father in heaven. [20]For where two or three come together in my name, there am I with them."

Luke 1 [10]And when the time for the burning of incense came, all the assembled worshipers were praying outside.

c) Pray in Faith

Ps 62 [8]Trust in him at all times, O people; pour out your hearts to him, for God is our refuge.

Ps 121 [1]I lift up my eyes to the hills—where does my help come from? [2]My help comes from the LORD, the Maker of heaven and earth.

Matt 21 [22]"If you believe, you will receive whatever you ask for in prayer."

John 15 [7]"If you remain in me and my words remain in you, ask whatever you wish, and it will be given you."

Eph 3 [12]In him and through faith in him we may approach God with freedom and confidence.

Heb 10 [22]let us draw near to God with a sincere heart in full assurance of faith, having our hearts sprinkled to cleanse us from a guilty conscience and having our bodies washed with pure water.

Heb 11 [6]And without faith it is impossible to please God, because anyone who comes to him must believe that he exists and that he rewards those who earnestly seek him.

James 1 [6]But when he asks, he must believe and not doubt, because he who doubts is like a wave of the sea, blown and tossed by the wind.

James 5 [15]And the prayer offered in faith will make the sick person well; the Lord will raise him up. If he has sinned, he will be forgiven.

d) Pray in the Name of Christ

John 14 [13]"And I will do whatever you ask in my name, so that the Son may bring glory to the Father. [14]You may ask me for anything in my name, and I will do it."

John 16 [23]"In that day you will no longer ask me anything. I tell you the truth, my Father will give you whatever you ask in my name. [24]Until now you have not asked for anything in my name. Ask and you will receive, and your joy will be complete.

[25]"Though I have been speaking figuratively, a time is coming when I will no longer use this kind of language but will tell you plainly about my Father. [26]In that day you will ask in my name. I am not saying that I will ask the Father on your behalf. [27]No, the Father himself loves you because you have loved me and have believed that I came from God."

Col 3 [17]And whatever you do, whether in word or deed, do it all in the name of the Lord Jesus, giving thanks to God the Father through him.

e) Pray in Personal Meditation

Matt 6 [6]"But when you pray, go into your room, close the door and pray to your Father, who is unseen. Then your Father, who sees what is done in secret, will reward you."

Matt 14 [23]After he had dismissed them, he went up on a mountainside by himself to pray. When evening came, he was there alone. . . .

Mark 1 [35]Very early in the morning, while it was still dark, Jesus got up, left the house and went off to a solitary place, where he prayed.

Luke 5 [16]But Jesus often withdrew to lonely places and prayed.

Luke 9 [18]Once when Jesus was praying in private and his disciples were with him, he asked them, "Who do the crowds say I am?"

Acts 10 [9]About noon the following day as they were on their journey and approaching the city, Peter went up on the roof to pray.

Acts 10 [30]Cornelius answered: "Four days ago I was in my house praying at this hour, at three in the afternoon. Suddenly a man in shining clothes stood before me. . . ."

f) Pray in Righteousness

Ps 4 [3]Know that the LORD has set apart the godly for himself; the LORD will hear when I call to him.

Ps 34 [15]The eyes of the LORD are on the righteous and his ears are attentive to their cry. . . .

Prov 15 [29]The LORD is far from the wicked but he hears the prayer of the righteous.

1 Tim 2 [8]I want men everywhere to lift up holy hands in prayer, without anger or disputing.

g) Pray in Truth

Ps 145 [18]The LORD is near to all who call on him, to all who call on him in truth.

h) Pray through the Spirit's Intercession

Rom 8 [26]In the same way, the Spirit helps us in our weakness. We do not know what we ought to pray for, but the Spirit himself intercedes for us with groans that words cannot express. [27]And he who searches our hearts knows the mind of the Spirit, because the Spirit intercedes for the saints in accordance with God's will.

Gal 4 [6]Because you are sons, God sent the Spirit of his Son into our hearts, the Spirit who calls out, "*Abba,* Father."

Eph 6 [18]And pray in the Spirit on all occasions with all kinds of prayers and requests. With this in mind, be alert and always keep on praying for all the saints.

Jude [20]But you, dear friends, build yourselves up in your most holy faith and pray in the Holy Spirit.

i) Pray with a Clear Mind and Self-Control

1 Pet 4 [7]The end of all things is near. Therefore be clear minded and self-controlled so that you can pray.

j) Pray with Corresponding Good Works

Prov 21 [13]If a man shuts his ears to the cry of the poor, he too will cry out and not be answered.

Isa 58 [6]"Is not this the kind of fasting I have chosen: to loose the chains of injustice and untie the cords of the yoke, to set the oppressed free and break every yoke? [7]Is it not to share your food with the hungry and to provide the poor wanderer with shelter—when you see the naked, to clothe him, and not to turn away from your own flesh and blood? [8]Then your light will break forth like the dawn, and your healing will quickly appear; then your righteousness will go before you, and the glory of the LORD will be your rear guard. [9]Then you will call, and the LORD will answer; you will cry for help, and he will say: Here am I.

"If you do away with the yoke of oppression, with the pointing finger and malicious talk . . ."

Acts 10 [2]He and all his family were devout and God-fearing; he gave generously to those in need and prayed to God regularly. [3]One day at about three in the afternoon he had a vision. He distinctly saw an angel of God, who came to him and said, "Cornelius!"

[4]Cornelius stared at him in fear. "What is it, Lord?" he asked.

The angel answered, "Your prayers and gifts to the poor have come up as a memorial offering before God."

k) Pray with Fasting

Deut 9 [18]Then once again I fell prostrate before the LORD for forty days and forty nights; I ate no bread and drank no water, because of all the sin you had committed, doing what was evil in the LORD's sight and so provoking him to anger.
Neh 1 [4]When I heard these things, I sat down and wept. For some days I mourned and fasted and prayed before the God of heaven.
Ps 35 [13]Yet when they were ill, I put on sackcloth and humbled myself with fasting. When my prayers returned to me unanswered . . .
Dan 9 [3]So I turned to the Lord God and pleaded with him in prayer and petition, in fasting, and in sackcloth and ashes.
Acts 13 [2]While they were worshiping the Lord and fasting, the Holy Spirit said, "Set apart for me Barnabas and Saul for the work to which I have called them." [3]So after they had fasted and prayed, they placed their hands on them and sent them off.

l) Pray with the Fear of God

Ps 145 [19]He fulfills the desires of those who fear him; he hears their cry and saves them.

m) Pray with Fervency and Depth of Feeling

Exod 2 [23]During that long period, the king of Egypt died. The Israelites groaned in their slavery and cried out, and their cry for help because of their slavery went up to God. [24]God heard their groaning and he remembered his covenant with Abraham, with Isaac and with Jacob.
Judg 20 [26]Then the Israelites, all the people, went up to Bethel, and there they sat weeping before the LORD. They fasted that day until evening and presented burnt offerings and fellowship offerings to the LORD.
1 Sam 1 [9]Once when they had finished eating and drinking in Shiloh, Hannah stood up. Now Eli the priest was sitting on a chair by the doorpost of the LORD's temple. [10]In bitterness of soul Hannah wept much and prayed to the LORD.
2 Kings 20 [2]Hezekiah turned his face to the wall and prayed to the LORD, [3]"Remember, O LORD, how I have walked before you faithfully and with wholehearted devotion and have done what is good in your eyes." And Hezekiah wept bitterly.
Job 16 [20]"My intercessor is my friend as my eyes pour out tears to God. . . ."
Ps 6 [6]I am worn out from groaning; all night long I flood my bed with weeping and drench my couch with tears. [7]My eyes grow weak with sorrow; they fail because of all my foes.

[8]Away from me, all you who do evil, for the LORD has heard my weeping. [9]The LORD has heard my cry for mercy; the LORD accepts my prayer.
Ps 39 [12]"Hear my prayer, O LORD, listen to my cry for help; be not deaf to my weeping. For I dwell with you as an alien, a stranger, as all my fathers were."
Ps 42 [3]My tears have been my food day and night, while men say to me all day long, "Where is your God?" [4]These things I remember as I pour out my soul: how I used to go with the multitude, leading the procession to the house of God, with shouts of joy and thanksgiving among the festive throng.
Ps 62 [8]Trust in him at all times, O people; pour out your hearts to him, for God is our refuge.
Jer 31 [9]"They will come with weeping; they will pray as I bring them back. I will lead them beside streams of water on a level path where they will not stumble, because I am Israel's father, and Ephraim is my firstborn son."
Lam 2 [19]Arise, cry out in the night, as the watches of the night begin; pour out your heart like water in the presence of the Lord. Lift up your hands to him for the lives of your children, who faint from hunger at the head of every street.
Mark 7 [34]He looked up to heaven and with a deep sigh said to him, "*Ephphatha!*" (which means, "Be opened!").
Heb 5 [7]During the days of Jesus' life on earth, he offered up prayers and petitions with loud cries and tears to the one who could save him from death, and he was heard because of his reverent submission.

n) Pray with Forgiveness toward Others

Matt 6 [9]"This, then, is how you should pray: 'Our Father in heaven, hallowed be your name. . . . [12]Forgive us our debts, as we also have forgiven our debtors. . . .' [14]For if you forgive men when they sin against you, your heavenly Father will also forgive you. [15]But if you do not forgive men their sins, your Father will not forgive your sins."
Luke 6 [37]"Do not judge, and you will not be judged. Do not condemn, and you will not be condemned. Forgive, and you will be forgiven."
1 Tim 2 [8]I want men everywhere to lift up holy hands in prayer, without anger or disputing.

o) Pray with Humility, Confession of Sin, and Penitence

2 Sam 24 [17]When David saw the angel who was striking down the people, he said to the LORD, "I am the one who has sinned and done wrong. These are but sheep. What have they done? Let your hand fall upon me and my family." . . . [25]David built an altar to the LORD there and sacrificed burnt offerings and fellowship offerings. Then the LORD answered prayer in behalf of the land, and the plague on Israel was stopped.
1 Kings 8 [33]"When your people Israel have been defeated by an enemy because they have sinned against you, and when they turn back to you and confess your name, praying and making supplication to you in this temple, [34]then hear from heaven and forgive the sin of your people Israel and bring them back to the land you gave to their fathers.

[35]"When the heavens are shut up and there is no rain because your people have sinned against you, and when they pray toward this place and confess your name and turn from their sin because you have afflicted them, [36]then hear from heaven and forgive the sin of your servants, your people Israel. Teach them the right way to live, and send rain on the land you gave your people for an inheritance.

[37]"When famine or plague comes to the land, or blight or mildew, locusts or grasshoppers, or when an enemy besieges them in any of their cities, whatever disaster or disease may come, [38]and when a prayer or plea is made by any of your people Israel—each one aware of the afflictions of his own heart, and spreading out his hands toward this temple—[39]then hear from heaven, your dwelling place. Forgive and act; deal with each man according to all he does, since you know his heart (for you alone know the hearts of all men), [40]so that they will fear you all the time they live in the land you gave our fathers.

[41]"As for the foreigner who does not belong to your people Israel but has come from a distant land because of your name—[42]for men will hear of your great name and your mighty hand and your outstretched arm—when he comes and prays toward this temple, [43]then hear from heaven, your dwelling place, and do whatever the foreigner asks of you, so that all the peoples of the earth may know your name and fear you, as do your own people Israel, and may know that this house I have built bears your Name.

[44]"When your people go to war against their enemies, wherever you send them, and when they pray to the LORD toward the city you have chosen and the temple I have built for your Name, [45]then hear from heaven their prayer and their plea, and uphold their cause.

[46]"When they sin against you—for there is no one who does not sin—and you become angry with them and give them over to the enemy, who takes them captive to his own land, far away or near; [47]and if they have a change of heart in the land where they are held captive, and repent and plead with you in the land of their conquerors and say, 'We have sinned, we have done wrong, we have acted wickedly'; [48]and if they turn back to you with all their heart and soul in the land of their enemies who took them captive, and pray to you toward the land you gave their fathers, toward the city you have chosen and the

temple I have built for your Name; 49then from heaven, your dwelling place, hear their prayer and their plea, and uphold their cause. 50And forgive your people, who have sinned against you; forgive all the offenses they have committed against you, and cause their conquerors to show them mercy. . . ."

2 Chron 7 14". . . if my people, who are called by my name, will humble themselves and pray and seek my face and turn from their wicked ways, then will I hear from heaven and will forgive their sin and will heal their land."

2 Chron 33 10The LORD spoke to Manasseh and his people, but they paid no attention. 11So the LORD brought against them the army commanders of the king of Assyria, who took Manasseh prisoner, put a hook in his nose, bound him with bronze shackles and took him to Babylon. 12In his distress he sought the favor of the LORD his God and humbled himself greatly before the God of his fathers. 13And when he prayed to him, the LORD was moved by his entreaty and listened to his plea; so he brought him back to Jerusalem and to his kingdom. Then Manasseh knew that the LORD is God.

Neh 9 1On the twenty-fourth day of the same month, the Israelites gathered together, fasting and wearing sackcloth and having dust on their heads. 2Those of Israelite descent had separated themselves from all foreigners. They stood in their places and confessed their sins and the wickedness of their fathers. 3They stood where they were and read from the Book of the Law of the LORD their God for a quarter of the day, and spent another quarter in confession and in worshiping the LORD their God.

Ps 32 5Then I acknowledged my sin to you and did not cover up my iniquity. I said, "I will confess my transgressions to the LORD"—and you forgave the guilt of my sin.

Ps 35 13Yet when they were ill, I put on sackcloth and humbled myself with fasting. When my prayers returned to me unanswered . . .

Ps 51 1Have mercy on me, O God, according to your unfailing love; according to your great compassion blot out my transgressions. 2Wash away all my iniquity and cleanse me from my sin.

3For I know my transgressions, and my sin is always before me. 4Against you, you only, have I sinned and done what is evil in your sight, so that you are proved right when you speak and justified when you judge. 5Surely I was sinful at birth, sinful from the time my mother conceived me. 6Surely you desire truth in the inner parts; you teach me wisdom in the inmost place.

7Cleanse me with hyssop, and I will be clean; wash me, and I will be whiter than snow. 8Let me hear joy and gladness; let the bones you have crushed rejoice. 9Hide your face from my sins and blot out all my iniquity.

10Create in me a pure heart, O God, and renew a steadfast spirit within me. 11Do not cast me from your presence or take your Holy Spirit from me. 12Restore to me the joy of your salvation and grant me a willing spirit, to sustain me.

Jer 36 6"So you go to the house of the LORD on a day of fasting and read to the people from the scroll the words of the LORD that you wrote as I dictated. Read them to all the people of Judah who come in from their towns. 7Perhaps they will bring their petition before the LORD, and each will turn from his wicked ways, for the anger and wrath pronounced against this people by the LORD are great."

Jon 3 3Jonah obeyed the word of the LORD and went to Nineveh. Now Nineveh was a very important city—a visit required three days. 4On the first day, Jonah started into the city. He proclaimed: "Forty more days and Nineveh will be overturned." 5The Ninevites believed God. They declared a fast, and all of them, from the greatest to the least, put on sackcloth.

6When the news reached the king of Nineveh, he rose from his throne, took off his royal robes, covered himself with sackcloth and sat down in the dust. 7Then he issued a proclamation in Nineveh: "By the decree of the king and his nobles: Do not let any man or beast, herd or flock, taste anything; do not let them eat or drink. 8But let man and beast be covered with sackcloth. Let everyone call urgently on God. Let them give up their evil ways and their violence. 9Who knows? God may yet relent and with compassion turn from his fierce anger so that we will not perish."

Matt 5 23"Therefore, if you are offering your gift at the altar and there remember that your brother has something against you, 24leave your gift there in front of the altar. First go and be reconciled to your brother; then come and offer your gift."

Luke 18 9To some who were confident of their own righteousness and looked down on everybody else, Jesus told this parable: 10"Two men went up to the temple to pray, one a Pharisee and the other a tax collector. 11The Pharisee stood up and prayed about himself: 'God, I thank you that I am not like other men—robbers, evildoers, adulterers—or even like this tax collector. 12I fast twice a week and give a tenth of all I get.'

13"But the tax collector stood at a distance. He would not even look up to heaven, but beat his breast and said, 'God, have mercy on me, a sinner.'

14"I tell you that this man, rather than the other, went home justified before God. For everyone who exalts himself will be humbled, and he who humbles himself will be exalted."

p) Pray with Love for God

Ps 91 14"Because he loves me," says the LORD, "I will rescue him; I will protect him, for he acknowledges my name. 15He will call upon me, and I will answer him; I will be with him in trouble, I will deliver him and honor him."

q) Pray with Obedience to God

1 Kings 8 58"May he turn our hearts to him, to walk in all his ways and to keep the commands, decrees and regulations he gave our fathers. 59And may these words of mine, which I have prayed before the LORD, be near to the LORD our God day and night, that he may uphold the cause of his servant and the cause of his people Israel according to each day's need, 60so that all the peoples of the earth may know that the LORD is God and that there is no other. 61But your hearts must be fully committed to the LORD our God, to live by his decrees and obey his commands, as at this time."

Prov 28 9If anyone turns a deaf ear to the law, even his prayers are detestable.

Isa 56 6"And foreigners who bind themselves to the LORD to serve him, to love the name of the LORD, and to worship him, all who keep the Sabbath without desecrating it and who hold fast to my covenant—7these I will bring to my holy mountain and give them joy in my house of prayer. Their burnt offerings and sacrifices will be accepted on my altar; for my house will be called a house of prayer for all nations."

John 9 31"We know that God does not listen to sinners. He listens to the godly man who does his will."

1 John 3 21Dear friends, if our hearts do not condemn us, we have confidence before God 22and receive from him anything we ask, because we obey his commands and do what pleases him.

r) Pray with Patience

Ps 40 1I waited patiently for the LORD; he turned to me and heard my cry.

s) Pray with Perseverance

1 Chron 16 11Look to the LORD and his strength; seek his face always.

Ps 5 1Give ear to my words, O LORD, consider my sighing. 2Listen to my cry for help, my King and my God, for to you I pray. 3In the morning, O LORD, you hear my voice; in the morning I lay my requests before you and wait in expectation.

Ps 55 17Evening, morning and noon I cry out in distress, and he hears my voice.

Ps 86 3Have mercy on me, O Lord, for I call to you all day long.

Ps 88 1O LORD, the God who saves me, day and night I cry out before you.

Ps 109 4In return for my friendship they accuse me, but I am a man of prayer.

Ps 116 2Because he turned his ear to me, I will call on him as long as I live.

Luke 11 5Then he said to them, "Suppose one of you has a friend, and he goes to him at midnight and says, 'Friend, lend me three loaves of bread, 6because a friend of mine on a journey has come to me, and I have nothing to set before him.'

7"Then the one inside answers, 'Don't bother me. The door is already locked, and my children are with me in bed. I can't get up and give you anything.' [8]I tell you, though he will not get up and give him the bread because he is his friend, yet because of the man's boldness he will get up and give him as much as he needs.

[9]"So I say to you: Ask and it will be given to you; seek and you will find; knock and the door will be opened to you. [10]For everyone who asks receives; he who seeks finds; and to him who knocks, the door will be opened."

Luke 18 [1]Then Jesus told his disciples a parable to show them that they should always pray and not give up. [2]He said: "In a certain town there was a judge who neither feared God nor cared about men. [3]And there was a widow in that town who kept coming to him with the plea, 'Grant me justice against my adversary.'

[4]"For some time he refused. But finally he said to himself, 'Even though I don't fear God or care about men, [5]yet because this widow keeps bothering me, I will see that she gets justice, so that she won't eventually wear me out with her coming!'"

[6]And the Lord said, "Listen to what the unjust judge says. [7]And will not God bring about justice for his chosen ones, who cry out to him day and night? Will he keep putting them off? [8]I tell you, he will see that they get justice, and quickly. However, when the Son of Man comes, will he find faith on the earth?"

Rom 12 [12]Be joyful in hope, patient in affliction, faithful in prayer.

Eph 6 [18]And pray in the Spirit on all occasions with all kinds of prayers and requests. With this in mind, be alert and always keep on praying for all the saints.

1 Thess 5 [17]pray continually. . . .

t) Pray with Sincerity of Heart

Deut 4 [29]But if from there you seek the LORD your God, you will find him if you look for him with all your heart and with all your soul.

Ps 17 [1]Hear, O LORD, my righteous plea; listen to my cry. Give ear to my prayer—it does not rise from deceitful lips.

Ps 25 [1]To you, O LORD, I lift up my soul. . . .

Ps 145 [18]The LORD is near to all who call on him, to all who call on him in truth.

Jer 29 [13]"You will seek me and find me when you seek me with all your heart."

Lam 3 [41]Let us lift up our hearts and our hands to God in heaven, and say . . .

2 Tim 2 [22]Flee the evil desires of youth, and pursue righteousness, faith, love and peace, along with those who call on the Lord out of a pure heart.

Heb 10 [22]let us draw near to God with a sincere heart in full assurance of faith, having our hearts sprinkled to cleanse us from a guilty conscience and having our bodies washed with pure water.

u) Pray with Wise and Appropriate Words

Eccles 5 [1]Guard your steps when you go to the house of God. Go near to listen rather than to offer the sacrifice of fools, who do not know that they do wrong.

[2]Do not be quick with your mouth, do not be hasty in your heart to utter anything before God. God is in heaven and you are on earth, so let your words be few. [3]As a dream comes when there are many cares, so the speech of a fool when there are many words.

[4]When you make a vow to God, do not delay in fulfilling it. He has no pleasure in fools; fulfill your vow. [5]It is better not to vow than to make a vow and not fulfill it. [6]Do not let your mouth lead you into sin. And do not protest to the temple messenger, "My vow was a mistake." Why should God be angry at what you say and destroy the work of your hands? [7]Much dreaming and many words are meaningless. Therefore stand in awe of God.

Matt 6 [7]"And when you pray, do not keep on babbling like pagans, for they think they will be heard because of their many words."

1 Cor 14 [14]For if I pray in a tongue, my spirit prays, but my mind is unfruitful. [15]So what shall I do? I will pray with my spirit, but I will also pray with my mind; I will sing with my spirit, but I will also sing with my mind. [16]If you are praising God with your spirit, how can one who finds himself among those who do not understand say "Amen" to your thanksgiving, since he does not know what you are saying? [17]You may be giving thanks well enough, but the other man is not edified.

[18]I thank God that I speak in tongues more than all of you. [19]But in the church I would rather speak five intelligible words to instruct others than ten thousand words in a tongue.

3. Motives for Prayer

a) Pray Because God Hears Prayer

Deut 4 [7]What other nation is so great as to have their gods near them the way the LORD our God is near us whenever we pray to him?

1 Kings 9 [3]The LORD said to him: "I have heard the prayer and plea you have made before me; I have consecrated this temple, which you have built, by putting my Name there forever. My eyes and my heart will always be there."

2 Kings 19 [20]Then Isaiah son of Amoz sent a message to Hezekiah: "This is what the LORD, the God of Israel, says: I have heard your prayer concerning Sennacherib king of Assyria."

2 Kings 20 [5]"Go back and tell Hezekiah, the leader of my people, 'This is what the LORD, the God of your father David, says: I have heard your prayer and seen your tears; I will heal you. On the third day from now you will go up to the temple of the LORD. [6]I will add fifteen years to your life. And I will deliver you and this city from the hand of the king of Assyria. I will defend this city for my sake and for the sake of my servant David.'"

Ps 34 [15]The eyes of the LORD are on the righteous and his ears are attentive to their cry. . . .

[17]The righteous cry out, and the LORD hears them; he delivers them from all their troubles.

Ps 65 [2]O you who hear prayer, to you all men will come.

Ps 86 [5]You are forgiving and good, O Lord, abounding in love to all who call to you. . . . [7]In the day of my trouble I will call to you, for you will answer me.

Prov 15 [29]The LORD is far from the wicked but he hears the prayer of the righteous.

Isa 30 [19]O people of Zion, who live in Jerusalem, you will weep no more. How gracious he will be when you cry for help! As soon as he hears, he will answer you.

Isa 49 [8]This is what the LORD says: "In the time of my favor I will answer you, and in the day of salvation I will help you; I will keep you and will make you to be a covenant for the people, to restore the land and to reassign its desolate inheritances. . . ."

Isa 65 [24]"Before they call I will answer; while they are still speaking I will hear."

Jer 29 [12]"Then you will call upon me and come and pray to me, and I will listen to you."

Jer 33 [3]"'Call to me and I will answer you and tell you great and unsearchable things you do not know.'"

Joel 2 [32]"And everyone who calls on the name of the LORD will be saved; for on Mount Zion and in Jerusalem there will be deliverance, as the LORD has said, among the survivors whom the LORD calls."

Zech 13 [9]"This third I will bring into the fire; I will refine them like silver and test them like gold. They will call on my name and I will answer them; I will say, 'They are my people,' and they will say, 'The LORD is our God.'"

Matt 7 [8]"For everyone who asks receives; he who seeks finds; and to him who knocks, the door will be opened.

[9]"Which of you, if his son asks for bread, will give him a stone? [10]Or if he asks for a fish, will give him a snake? [11]If you, then, though you are evil, know how to give good gifts to your children, how much more will your Father in heaven give good gifts to those who ask him!"

Matt 18 [19]"Again, I tell you that if two of you on earth agree about anything you ask for, it will be done for you by my Father in heaven. [20]For where two or three come together in my name, there am I with them."

John 16 [24]"Until now you have not asked for anything in my name. Ask and you will receive, and your joy will be complete."

Rom 10 [12]For there is no difference between Jew and Gentile—the same Lord is Lord of all and richly blesses all who

call on him, [13]for, "Everyone who calls on the name of the Lord will be saved."
James 5 [16]Therefore confess your sins to each other and pray for each other so that you may be healed. The prayer of a righteous man is powerful and effective.

b) Pray Because It Is a Christian Duty

Matt 7 [7]"Ask and it will be given to you; seek and you will find; knock and the door will be opened to you."
Rom 12 [12]Be joyful in hope, patient in affliction, faithful in prayer.
Phil 4 [6]Do not be anxious about anything, but in everything, by prayer and petition, with thanksgiving, present your requests to God.
Col 4 [2]Devote yourselves to prayer, being watchful and thankful.
1 Thess 5 [17]pray continually. . . .
1 Tim 2 [8]I want men everywhere to lift up holy hands in prayer, without anger or disputing.
James 4 [8]Come near to God and he will come near to you. Wash your hands, you sinners, and purify your hearts, you double-minded.
1 Pet 4 [7]The end of all things is near. Therefore be clear minded and self-controlled so that you can pray.

c) Pray in Confidence That Prayers Are Heard

Deut 9 [19]I feared the anger and wrath of the LORD, for he was angry enough with you to destroy you. But again the LORD listened to me.
Deut 26 [7]"Then we cried out to the LORD, the God of our fathers, and the LORD heard our voice and saw our misery, toil and oppression."
2 Sam 22 [7]"In my distress I called to the LORD; I called out to my God. From his temple he heard my voice; my cry came to his ears."
Ps 3 [4]To the LORD I cry aloud, and he answers me from his holy hill.
Ps 4 [3]Know that the LORD has set apart the godly for himself; the LORD will hear when I call to him.
Ps 6 [9]The LORD has heard my cry for mercy; the LORD accepts my prayer.
Ps 10 [17]You hear, O LORD, the desire of the afflicted; you encourage them, and you listen to their cry. . . .
Ps 17 [6]I call on you, O God, for you will answer me; give ear to me and hear my prayer.
Ps 18 [6]In my distress I called to the LORD; I cried to my God for help. From his temple he heard my voice; my cry came before him, into his ears.
Ps 22 [24]For he has not despised or disdained the suffering of the afflicted one; he has not hidden his face from him but has listened to his cry for help.
Ps 34 [4]I sought the LORD, and he answered me; he delivered me from all my fears.
Ps 38 [15]I wait for you, O LORD; you will answer, O Lord my God.
Ps 55 [17]Evening, morning and noon I cry out in distress, and he hears my voice.
Ps 66 [19]but God has surely listened and heard my voice in prayer.
Ps 116 [1]I love the LORD, for he heard my voice; he heard my cry for mercy.
Ps 119 [26]I recounted my ways and you answered me; teach me your decrees.
Lam 3 [55]I called on your name, O LORD, from the depths of the pit. [56]You heard my plea: "Do not close your ears to my cry for relief." [57]You came near when I called you, and you said, "Do not fear."
Jon 2 [1]From inside the fish Jonah prayed to the LORD his God. [2]He said: "In my distress I called to the LORD, and he answered me. From the depths of the grave I called for help, and you listened to my cry."
John 11 [41]So they took away the stone. Then Jesus looked up and said, "Father, I thank you that you have heard me. [42]I knew that you always hear me, but I said this for the benefit of the people standing here, that they may believe that you sent me."

d) Pray out of a Desire for the Things of God

Matt 6 [33]"But seek first his kingdom and his righteousness, and all these things will be given to you as well."
Col 3 [1]Since, then, you have been raised with Christ, set your hearts on things above, where Christ is seated at the right hand of God. [2]Set your minds on things above, not on earthly things.

e) Pray with Certainty of Personal Access to God

Eph 3 [12]In him and through faith in him we may approach God with freedom and confidence.
Heb 4 [14]Therefore, since we have a great high priest who has gone through the heavens, Jesus the Son of God, let us hold firmly to the faith we profess. [15]For we do not have a high priest who is unable to sympathize with our weaknesses, but we have one who has been tempted in every way, just as we are—yet was without sin. [16]Let us then approach the throne of grace with confidence, so that we may receive mercy and find grace to help us in our time of need.

4. Times of Prayer

a) Pray Always, Constantly, Regularly

Ps 116 [2]Because he turned his ear to me, I will call on him as long as I live.
Ps 119 [164]Seven times a day I praise you for your righteous laws.
Dan 6 [10]Now when Daniel learned that the decree had been published, he went home to his upstairs room where the windows opened toward Jerusalem. Three times a day he got down on his knees and prayed, giving thanks to his God, just as he had done before.
Luke 18 [1]Then Jesus told his disciples a parable to show them that they should always pray and not give up.
Acts 1 [14]They all joined together constantly in prayer, along with the women and Mary the mother of Jesus, and with his brothers.
Acts 2 [42]They devoted themselves to the apostles' teaching and to the fellowship, to the breaking of bread and to prayer.
Acts 3 [1]One day Peter and John were going up to the temple at the time of prayer—at three in the afternoon.
Acts 6 [3]"Brothers, choose seven men from among you who are known to be full of the Spirit and wisdom. We will turn this responsibility over to them [4]and will give our attention to prayer and the ministry of the word."
Acts 10 [2]He and all his family were devout and God-fearing; he gave generously to those in need and prayed to God regularly.
Rom 1 [9]God, whom I serve with my whole heart in preaching the gospel of his Son, is my witness how constantly I remember you [10]in my prayers at all times; and I pray that now at last by God's will the way may be opened for me to come to you.
Eph 6 [18]And pray in the Spirit on all occasions with all kinds of prayers and requests. With this in mind, be alert and always keep on praying for all the saints.
1 Thess 1 [2]We always thank God for all of you, mentioning you in our prayers.
1 Thess 5 [17]pray continually. . . .
2 Thess 1 [11]With this in mind, we constantly pray for you, that our God may count you worthy of his calling, and that by his power he may fulfill every good purpose of yours and every act prompted by your faith.

b) Pray Anytime, Day or Night

1 Kings 18 [36]At the time of sacrifice, the prophet Elijah stepped forward and prayed: "O LORD, God of Abraham, Isaac and Israel, let it be known today that you are God in Israel and that I am your servant and have done all these things at your command."
1 Chron 23 [30]They were also to stand every morning to thank and praise the LORD. They were to do the same in the evening. . . .
Ps 4 [4]In your anger do not sin; when you are on your beds, search your hearts and be silent.
Ps 5 [3]In the morning, O LORD, you hear my voice; in the morning I lay my requests before you and wait in expectation.

Ps 55 [17]Evening, morning and noon I cry out in distress, and he hears my voice.
Ps 86 [3]Have mercy on me, O Lord, for I call to you all day long.
Ps 88 [1]O LORD, the God who saves me, day and night I cry out before you.
Ps 88 [13]But I cry to you for help, O LORD; in the morning my prayer comes before you.
Ps 119 [147]I rise before dawn and cry for help; I have put my hope in your word.
Mark 1 [35]Very early in the morning, while it was still dark, Jesus got up, left the house and went off to a solitary place, where he prayed.
Luke 2 [37]and then was a widow until she was eighty-four. She never left the temple but worshiped night and day, fasting and praying.
Luke 6 [12]One of those days Jesus went out to a mountainside to pray, and spent the night praying to God.
Acts 3 [1]One day Peter and John were going up to the temple at the time of prayer—at three in the afternoon.
Acts 10 [30]Cornelius answered: "Four days ago I was in my house praying at this hour, at three in the afternoon. Suddenly a man in shining clothes stood before me. . . ."
Acts 16 [25]About midnight Paul and Silas were praying and singing hymns to God, and the other prisoners were listening to them.
1 Thess 3 [10]Night and day we pray most earnestly that we may see you again and supply what is lacking in your faith.
1 Tim 5 [5]The widow who is really in need and left all alone puts her hope in God and continues night and day to pray and to ask God for help.
2 Tim 1 [3]I thank God, whom I serve, as my forefathers did, with a clear conscience, as night and day I constantly remember you in my prayers.

c) Pray at Mealtimes

Deut 8 [10]When you have eaten and are satisfied, praise the LORD your God for the good land he has given you.
John 6 [11]Jesus then took the loaves, gave thanks, and distributed to those who were seated as much as they wanted. He did the same with the fish.
John 6 [23]Then some boats from Tiberias landed near the place where the people had eaten the bread after the Lord had given thanks.
1 Tim 4 [3]They forbid people to marry and order them to abstain from certain foods, which God created to be received with thanksgiving by those who believe and who know the truth. [4]For everything God created is good, and nothing is to be rejected if it is received with thanksgiving, [5]because it is consecrated by the word of God and prayer.

d) Pray in Times of Need

See p. 609a, Petition

e) Pray in Times of Rejoicing

See p. 615a, Thanksgiving

f) Pray on Special Occasions

(1) David Prayed in Preparing to Build the Temple

1 Chron 29 [10]David praised the LORD in the presence of the whole assembly, saying, "Praise be to you, O LORD, God of our father Israel, from everlasting to everlasting. [11]Yours, O LORD, is the greatness and the power and the glory and the majesty and the splendor, for everything in heaven and earth is yours. Yours, O LORD, is the kingdom; you are exalted as head over all. [12]Wealth and honor come from you; you are the ruler of all things. In your hands are strength and power to exalt and give strength to all. [13]Now, our God, we give you thanks, and praise your glorious name.

[14]"But who am I, and who are my people, that we should be able to give as generously as this? Everything comes from you, and we have given you only what comes from your hand. [15]We are aliens and strangers in your sight, as were all our forefathers. Our days on earth are like a shadow, without hope. [16]O LORD our God, as for all this abundance that we have provided for building you a temple for your Holy Name, it comes from your hand, and all of it belongs to you. [17]I know, my God, that you test the heart and are pleased with integrity. All these things have I given willingly and with honest intent. And now I have seen with joy how willingly your people who are here have given to you. [18]O LORD, God of our fathers Abraham, Isaac and Israel, keep this desire in the hearts of your people forever, and keep their hearts loyal to you. [19]And give my son Solomon the wholehearted devotion to keep your commands, requirements and decrees and to do everything to build the palatial structure for which I have provided."

[20]Then David said to the whole assembly, "Praise the LORD your God." So they all praised the LORD, the God of their fathers; they bowed low and fell prostrate before the LORD and the king.

(2) Solomon Prayed in Dedicating the Temple

1 Kings 8 [22]Then Solomon stood before the altar of the LORD in front of the whole assembly of Israel, spread out his hands toward heaven [23]and said: "O LORD, God of Israel, there is no God like you in heaven above or on earth below—you who keep your covenant of love with your servants who continue wholeheartedly in your way. [24]You have kept your promise to your servant David my father; with your mouth you have promised and with your hand you have fulfilled it—as it is today.

[25]"Now LORD, God of Israel, keep for your servant David my father the promises you made to him when you said, 'You shall never fail to have a man to sit before me on the throne of Israel, if only your sons are careful in all they do to walk before me as you have done.' [26]And now, O God of Israel, let your word that you promised your servant David my father come true.

[27]"But will God really dwell on earth? The heavens, even the highest heaven, cannot contain you. How much less this temple I have built! [28]Yet give attention to your servant's prayer and his plea for mercy, O LORD my God. Hear the cry and the prayer that your servant is praying in your presence this day. [29]May your eyes be open toward this temple night and day, this place of which you said, 'My Name shall be there,' so that you will hear the prayer your servant prays toward this place. [30]Hear the supplication of your servant and of your people Israel when they pray toward this place. Hear from heaven, your dwelling place, and when you hear, forgive.

[31]"When a man wrongs his neighbor and is required to take an oath and he comes and swears the oath before your altar in this temple, [32]then hear from heaven and act. Judge between your servants, condemning the guilty and bringing down on his own head what he has done. Declare the innocent not guilty, and so establish his innocence.

[33]"When your people Israel have been defeated by an enemy because they have sinned against you, and when they turn back to you and confess your name, praying and making supplication to you in this temple, [34]then hear from heaven and forgive the sin of your people Israel and bring them back to the land you gave to their fathers.

[35]"When the heavens are shut up and there is no rain because your people have sinned against you, and when they pray toward this place and confess your name and turn from their sin because you have afflicted them, [36]then hear from heaven and forgive the sin of your servants, your people Israel. Teach them the right way to live, and send rain on the land you gave your people for an inheritance.

[37]"When famine or plague comes to the land, or blight or mildew, locusts or grasshoppers, or when an enemy besieges them in any of their cities, whatever disaster or disease may come, [38]and when a prayer or plea is made by any of your people Israel—each one aware of the afflictions of his own heart, and spreading out his hands toward this temple—[39]then hear from heaven, your dwelling place. Forgive and act; deal with each man according to all he does, since you know his heart (for you alone know the hearts of all men), [40]so that they will fear you all the time they live in the land you gave our fathers.

[41]"As for the foreigner who does not belong to your people Israel but has come from a distant land because of your name—[42]for men will hear of your great name and your mighty hand and your outstretched arm—when he comes and prays toward this temple, [43]then hear from heaven, your dwelling place, and do whatever the foreigner asks of you, so that all the peoples of the earth may know your name and fear you, as do your own people Israel, and may know that this house I have built bears your Name.

[44]"When your people go to war against their enemies, wherever you send them, and when they pray to the LORD toward the city you have chosen and the temple I have built for your Name, [45]then hear from heaven their prayer and their plea, and uphold their cause.

[46]"When they sin against you—for there is no one who does not sin—and you become angry with them and give them over to the enemy, who takes them captive to his own land, far away or near; [47]and if they have a change of heart in the land where they are held captive, and repent and plead with you in the land of their conquerors and say, 'We have sinned, we have done wrong, we have acted wickedly'; [48]and if they turn back to you with all their heart and soul in the land of their enemies who took them captive, and pray to you toward the land you gave their fathers, toward the city you have chosen and the temple I have built for your Name; [49]then from heaven, your dwelling place, hear their prayer and their plea, and uphold their cause. [50]And forgive your people, who have sinned against you; forgive all the offenses they have committed against you, and cause their conquerors to show them mercy; [51]for they are your people and your inheritance, whom you brought out of Egypt, out of that iron-smelting furnace.

[52]"May your eyes be open to your servant's plea and to the plea of your people Israel, and may you listen to them whenever they cry out to you. [53]For you singled them out from all the nations of the world to be your own inheritance, just as you declared through your servant Moses when you, O Sovereign LORD, brought our fathers out of Egypt."

(3) The Jews Prayed in Worshiping at the Temple

Luke 1 [8]Once when Zechariah's division was on duty and he was serving as priest before God, [9]he was chosen by lot, according to the custom of the priesthood, to go into the temple of the Lord and burn incense. [10]And when the time for the burning of incense came, all the assembled worshipers were praying outside.

5. Postures and Gestures of Prayer

a) The Arms and Hands during Prayer

Exod 9 [29]Moses replied, "When I have gone out of the city, I will spread out my hands in prayer to the LORD. The thunder will stop and there will be no more hail, so you may know that the earth is the LORD's."
1 Kings 8 [54]When Solomon had finished all these prayers and supplications to the LORD, he rose from before the altar of the LORD, where he had been kneeling with his hands spread out toward heaven.
2 Chron 6 [13]Now he had made a bronze platform, five cubits long, five cubits wide and three cubits high, and had placed it in the center of the outer court. He stood on the platform and then knelt down before the whole assembly of Israel and spread out his hands toward heaven.
Ps 63 [4]I will praise you as long as I live, and in your name I will lift up my hands.
Isa 1 [15]"When you spread out your hands in prayer, I will hide my eyes from you; even if you offer many prayers, I will not listen. Your hands are full of blood. . . ."
Luke 18 [13]"But the tax collector stood at a distance. He would not even look up to heaven, but beat his breast and said, 'God, have mercy on me, a sinner.'"
1 Tim 2 [8]I want men everywhere to lift up holy hands in prayer, without anger or disputing.

b) The Body during Prayer

(1) Bow to the Earth When Praying

Gen 24 [52]When Abraham's servant heard what they said, he bowed down to the ground before the LORD.
Exod 34 [8]Moses bowed to the ground at once and worshiped.

(2) Kneel When Praying

1 Kings 8 [54]When Solomon had finished all these prayers and supplications to the LORD, he rose from before the altar of the LORD, where he had been kneeling with his hands spread out toward heaven.
2 Chron 6 [13]Now he had made a bronze platform, five cubits long, five cubits wide and three cubits high, and had placed it in the center of the outer court. He stood on the platform and then knelt down before the whole assembly of Israel and spread out his hands toward heaven.
Dan 6 [10]Now when Daniel learned that the decree had been published, he went home to his upstairs room where the windows opened toward Jerusalem. Three times a day he got down on his knees and prayed, giving thanks to his God, just as he had done before.
Luke 22 [41]He withdrew about a stone's throw beyond them, knelt down and prayed. . . .
Acts 9 [40]Peter sent them all out of the room; then he got down on his knees and prayed. Turning toward the dead woman, he said, "Tabitha, get up." She opened her eyes, and seeing Peter she sat up.
Acts 20 [36]When he had said this, he knelt down with all of them and prayed.
Acts 21 [5]But when our time was up, we left and continued on our way. All the disciples and their wives and children accompanied us out of the city, and there on the beach we knelt to pray.

(3) Prostrate Yourself When Praying

Deut 9 [25]I lay prostrate before the LORD those forty days and forty nights because the LORD had said he would destroy you.
1 Chron 21 [16]David looked up and saw the angel of the LORD standing between heaven and earth, with a drawn sword in his hand extended over Jerusalem. Then David and the elders, clothed in sackcloth, fell facedown.
1 Chron 29 [20]Then David said to the whole assembly, "Praise the LORD your God." So they all praised the LORD, the God of their fathers; they bowed low and fell prostrate before the LORD and the king.
Ezra 10 [1]While Ezra was praying and confessing, weeping and throwing himself down before the house of God, a large crowd of Israelites—men, women and children—gathered around him. They too wept bitterly.
Job 1 [20]At this, Job got up and tore his robe and shaved his head. Then he fell to the ground in worship. . . .
Ezek 9 [8]While they were killing and I was left alone, I fell facedown, crying out, "Ah, Sovereign LORD! Are you going to destroy the entire remnant of Israel in this outpouring of your wrath on Jerusalem?"
Matt 26 [39]Going a little farther, he fell with his face to the ground and prayed, "My Father, if it is possible, may this cup be taken from me. Yet not as I will, but as you will."

(4) Sit When Praying

Judg 20 [26]Then the Israelites, all the people, went up to Bethel, and there they sat weeping before the LORD. They fasted that day until evening and presented burnt offerings and fellowship offerings to the LORD.
2 Sam 7 [18]Then King David went in and sat before the LORD, and he said: "Who am I, O Sovereign LORD, and what is my family, that you have brought me this far?"
Neh 1 [4]When I heard these things, I sat down and wept. For some days I mourned and fasted and prayed before the God of heaven.

(5) Stand When Praying

Gen 24 [12]Then he prayed, "O LORD, God of my master Abraham, give me success today, and show kindness to my master Abraham. [13]See, I am standing beside this spring, and the daughters of the townspeople are coming out to draw water. [14]May it be that when I say to a girl, 'Please let down your jar that I may have a drink,' and she says, 'Drink, and I'll water your camels too'—let her be the one you have chosen for your servant Isaac. By this I will know that you have shown kindness to my master."
Luke 18 [10]"Two men went up to the temple to pray, one a Pharisee and the other a tax collector. [11]The Pharisee stood up and prayed about himself: 'God, I thank you that I am not like other men—robbers, evildoers, adulterers—or even like this tax collector. [12]I fast twice a week and give a tenth of all I get.'

[13]"But the tax collector stood at a distance. He would not even look up to heaven, but beat his breast and said, 'God, have mercy on me, a sinner.'"

c) The Head during Prayer

2 Chron 29 [29]When the offerings were finished, the king and everyone present with him knelt down and worshiped. [30]King Hezekiah and his officials ordered the Levites to praise the LORD with the words of David and of Asaph the seer. So they sang praises with gladness and bowed their heads and worshiped.
Luke 18 [13]"But the tax collector stood at a distance. He would not even look up to heaven, but beat his breast and said, 'God, have mercy on me, a sinner.'"
John 17 [1]After Jesus said this, he looked toward heaven and prayed: "Father, the time has come. Glorify your Son, that your Son may glorify you."
1 Cor 11 [4]Every man who prays or prophesies with his head covered dishonors his head. [5]And every woman who prays or prophesies with her head uncovered dishonors her head—it is just as though her head were shaved. [6]If a woman does not cover her head, she should have her hair cut off; and if it is a disgrace for a woman to have her hair cut or shaved off, she should cover her head. [7]A man ought not to cover his head, since he is the image and glory of God; but the woman is the glory of man.

6. Places and Occasions for Prayer

a) Pray Everywhere

1 Tim 2 [8]I want men everywhere to lift up holy hands in prayer, without anger or disputing.

b) Pray in Normal Times

(1) Pray Inside

1 Kings 8 [27]"But will God really dwell on earth? The heavens, even the highest heaven, cannot contain you. How much less this temple I have built! [28]Yet give attention to your servant's prayer and his plea for mercy, O LORD my God. Hear the cry and the prayer that your servant is praying in your presence this day. [29]May your eyes be open toward this temple night and day, this place of which you said, 'My Name shall be there,' so that you will hear the prayer your servant prays toward this place. [30]Hear the supplication of your servant and of your people Israel when they pray toward this place. Hear from heaven, your dwelling place, and when you hear, forgive."
Dan 6 [10]Now when Daniel learned that the decree had been published, he went home to his upstairs room where the windows opened toward Jerusalem. Three times a day he got down on his knees and prayed, giving thanks to his God, just as he had done before.
Matt 6 [6]"But when you pray, go into your room, close the door and pray to your Father, who is unseen. Then your Father, who sees what is done in secret, will reward you."

(2) Pray Outside

Matt 26 [36]Then Jesus went with his disciples to a place called Gethsemane, and he said to them, "Sit here while I go over there and pray." [37]He took Peter and the two sons of Zebedee along with him, and he began to be sorrowful and troubled. [38]Then he said to them, "My soul is overwhelmed with sorrow to the point of death. Stay here and keep watch with me."

[39]Going a little farther, he fell with his face to the ground and prayed, "My Father, if it is possible, may this cup be taken from me. Yet not as I will, but as you will."

[40]Then he returned to his disciples and found them sleeping. "Could you men not keep watch with me for one hour?" he asked Peter. [41]"Watch and pray so that you will not fall into temptation. The spirit is willing, but the body is weak."

[42]He went away a second time and prayed, "My Father, if it is not possible for this cup to be taken away unless I drink it, may your will be done."

[43]When he came back, he again found them sleeping, because their eyes were heavy. [44]So he left them and went away once more and prayed the third time, saying the same thing.
Mark 1 [35]Very early in the morning, while it was still dark, Jesus got up, left the house and went off to a solitary place, where he prayed.
Luke 5 [16]But Jesus often withdrew to lonely places and prayed.
Luke 6 [12]One of those days Jesus went out to a mountainside to pray, and spent the night praying to God.
Acts 10 [9]About noon the following day as they were on their journey and approaching the city, Peter went up on the roof to pray.
Acts 16 [13]On the Sabbath we went outside the city gate to the river, where we expected to find a place of prayer. We sat down and began to speak to the women who had gathered there.
Acts 21 [5]But when our time was up, we left and continued on our way. All the disciples and their wives and children accompanied us out of the city, and there on the beach we knelt to pray.

c) Pray in Times of Crisis

2 Chron 13 [14]Judah turned and saw that they were being attacked at both front and rear. Then they cried out to the LORD. The priests blew their trumpets [15]and the men of Judah raised the battle cry. At the sound of their battle cry, God routed Jeroboam and all Israel before Abijah and Judah.
Jon 2 [1]From inside the fish Jonah prayed to the LORD his God.
Acts 16 [23]After they had been severely flogged, they were thrown into prison, and the jailer was commanded to guard them carefully. [24]Upon receiving such orders, he put them in the inner cell and fastened their feet in the stocks.

[25]About midnight Paul and Silas were praying and singing hymns to God, and the other prisoners were listening to them. [26]Suddenly there was such a violent earthquake that the foundations of the prison were shaken. At once all the prison doors flew open, and everybody's chains came loose.

7. The Value of Prayer

a) Prayer Assures One of the Lord's Presence

Ps 145 [18]The LORD is near to all who call on him, to all who call on him in truth.
James 4 [8]Come near to God and he will come near to you. Wash your hands, you sinners, and purify your hearts, you double-minded.

b) Prayer Brings Blessing from God

Ps 86 [5]You are forgiving and good, O Lord, abounding in love to all who call to you.
Matt 7 [11]"If you, then, though you are evil, know how to give good gifts to your children, how much more will your Father in heaven give good gifts to those who ask him!"
Luke 11 [9]"So I say to you: Ask and it will be given to you; seek and you will find; knock and the door will be opened to you. [10]For everyone who asks receives; he who seeks finds; and to him who knocks, the door will be opened."
Rom 10 [12]For there is no difference between Jew and Gentile—the same Lord is Lord of all and richly blesses all who call on him. . . .

c) Prayer Brings Help in Time of Need

Heb 4 [16]Let us then approach the throne of grace with confidence, so that we may receive mercy and find grace to help us in our time of need.

d) Prayer Brings Joy

John 16 [24]"Until now you have not asked for anything in my name. Ask and you will receive, and your joy will be complete."

e) Prayer Brings Physical and Spiritual Healing

James 5 [15]And the prayer offered in faith will make the sick person well; the Lord will raise him up. If he has sinned, he will be forgiven. [16]Therefore confess your sins to each other and pray for each other so that you may be healed. The prayer of a righteous man is powerful and effective.

f) Prayer Brings Understanding

Jer 33 [3]"'Call to me and I will answer you and tell you great and unsearchable things you do not know.'"

g) Prayer Consecrates All of God's Creation

1 Tim 4 [4]For everything God created is good, and nothing is to be rejected if it is received with thanksgiving, [5]because it is consecrated by the word of God and prayer.

h) Prayer Is Powerful and Effective

James 5 16Therefore confess your sins to each other and pray for each other so that you may be healed. The prayer of a righteous man is powerful and effective.

i) Prayer Pleases God

Prov 15 8The LORD detests the sacrifice of the wicked, but the prayer of the upright pleases him.

j) Prayer Strengthens against Temptation

Matt 26 41"Watch and pray so that you will not fall into temptation. The spirit is willing, but the body is weak."

8. Hindrances to Prayer

a) Anxiety Hinders Prayer

Phil 4 6Do not be anxious about anything, but in everything, by prayer and petition, with thanksgiving, present your requests to God.

b) Disobedience Hinders Prayer

Deut 1 43So I told you, but you would not listen. You rebelled against the LORD's command and in your arrogance you marched up into the hill country. 44The Amorites who lived in those hills came out against you; they chased you like a swarm of bees and beat you down from Seir all the way to Hormah. 45You came back and wept before the LORD, but he paid no attention to your weeping and turned a deaf ear to you.
Deut 3 26But because of you the LORD was angry with me and would not listen to me. "That is enough," the LORD said. "Do not speak to me anymore about this matter."
2 Sam 22 27". . . to the pure you show yourself pure, but to the crooked you show yourself shrewd. . . . 41You made my enemies turn their backs in flight, and I destroyed my foes. 42They cried for help, but there was no one to save them—to the LORD, but he did not answer."
Jer 11 10"They have returned to the sins of their forefathers, who refused to listen to my words. They have followed other gods to serve them. Both the house of Israel and the house of Judah have broken the covenant I made with their forefathers. 11Therefore this is what the LORD says: 'I will bring on them a disaster they cannot escape. Although they cry out to me, I will not listen to them.'"
Lam 3 8Even when I call out or cry for help, he shuts out my prayer. . . . 39Why should any living man complain when punished for his sins? . . . 41Let us lift up our hearts and our hands to God in heaven and say: 42"We have sinned and rebelled and you have not forgiven. . . . 44You have covered yourself with a cloud so that no prayer can get through."
Mic 3 4Then they will cry out to the LORD, but he will not answer them. At that time he will hide his face from them because of the evil they have done.

c) Doubt Hinders Prayer

James 1 5If any of you lacks wisdom, he should ask God, who gives generously to all without finding fault, and it will be given to him. 6But when he asks, he must believe and not doubt, because he who doubts is like a wave of the sea, blown and tossed by the wind. 7That man should not think he will receive anything from the Lord; 8he is a double-minded man, unstable in all he does.

d) Failure to Heed God's Law Hinders Prayer

Prov 28 9If anyone turns a deaf ear to the law, even his prayers are detestable.
Zech 7 12"They made their hearts as hard as flint and would not listen to the law or to the words that the LORD Almighty had sent by his Spirit through the earlier prophets. So the LORD Almighty was very angry.

13"'When I called, they did not listen; so when they called, I would not listen,' says the LORD Almighty."

e) Failure to Pray Hinders Prayer

1 Sam 12 23"As for me, far be it from me that I should sin against the LORD by failing to pray for you. And I will teach you the way that is good and right."
Hos 7 7"All of them are hot as an oven; they devour their rulers. All their kings fall, and none of them calls on me."
James 4 2You want something but don't get it. You kill and covet, but you cannot have what you want. You quarrel and fight. You do not have, because you do not ask God.

f) Failure to Remain in Christ Hinders Prayer

John 15 7"If you remain in me and my words remain in you, ask whatever you wish, and it will be given you."

g) Faithlessness Hinders Prayer

Heb 11 6And without faith it is impossible to please God, because anyone who comes to him must believe that he exists and that he rewards those who earnestly seek him.

h) Forsaking God Hinders Prayer

2 Chron 15 2He went out to meet Asa and said to him, "Listen to me, Asa and all Judah and Benjamin. The LORD is with you when you are with him. If you seek him, he will be found by you, but if you forsake him, he will forsake you."
Prov 1 24"But since you rejected me when I called and no one gave heed when I stretched out my hand, 25since you ignored all my advice and would not accept my rebuke, 26I in turn will laugh at your disaster; I will mock when calamity overtakes you—27when calamity overtakes you like a storm, when disaster sweeps over you like a whirlwind, when distress and trouble overwhelm you.

28"Then they will call to me but I will not answer; they will look for me but will not find me. 29Since they hated knowledge and did not choose to fear the LORD, 30since they would not accept my advice and spurned my rebuke, 31they will eat the fruit of their ways and be filled with the fruit of their schemes. 32For the waywardness of the simple will kill them, and the complacency of fools will destroy them. . . ."

i) Haughtiness Hinders Prayer

Job 35 12"He does not answer when men cry out because of the arrogance of the wicked. 13Indeed, God does not listen to their empty plea; the Almighty pays no attention to it."
James 4 6But he gives us more grace. That is why Scripture says: "God opposes the proud but gives grace to the humble." . . . 10Humble yourselves before the Lord, and he will lift you up.

j) Hypocrisy Hinders Prayer

Ps 78 36But then they would flatter him with their mouths, lying to him with their tongues; 37their hearts were not loyal to him, they were not faithful to his covenant.
Ezek 33 31"My people come to you, as they usually do, and sit before you to listen to your words, but they do not put them into practice. With their mouths they express devotion, but their hearts are greedy for unjust gain."
Matt 15 1Then some Pharisees and teachers of the law came to Jesus from Jerusalem and asked, 2"Why do your disciples break the tradition of the elders? They don't wash their hands before they eat!"

3Jesus replied, "And why do you break the command of God for the sake of your tradition? 4For God said, 'Honor your father and mother' and 'Anyone who curses his father or mother must be put to death.' 5But you say that if a man says to his father or mother, 'Whatever help you might otherwise have received from me is a gift devoted to God,' 6he is not to 'honor his father' with it. Thus you nullify the word of God for the sake of your tradition. 7You hypocrites! Isaiah was right when he prophesied about you: 8'These people honor me with their lips, but their hearts are far from me. 9They worship me in vain; their teachings are but rules taught by men.'"
Mark 12 38As he taught, Jesus said, "Watch out for the teachers of the law. They like to walk around in flowing robes and be greeted in the marketplaces, 39and have the most important seats in the synagogues and the places of honor at banquets. 40They devour widows' houses and for a show make lengthy prayers. Such men will be punished most severely."

k) Idolatry Hinders Prayer

Jer 11 10"They have returned to the sins of their forefathers, who refused to listen to my words. They have followed other gods to serve them. Both the house of Israel and the house of Judah have broken the covenant I made with their forefathers. 11Therefore this is what the LORD says: 'I will bring on them a disaster they cannot escape. Although they cry out to me, I will not listen to them. . . .'

14"Do not pray for this people nor offer any plea or petition for them, because I will not listen when they call to me in the time of their distress."

Ezek 14 1Some of the elders of Israel came to me and sat down in front of me. 2Then the word of the LORD came to me: 3"Son of man, these men have set up idols in their hearts and put wicked stumbling blocks before their faces. Should I let them inquire of me at all?"

Ezek 20 31"'When you offer your gifts—the sacrifice of your sons in the fire—you continue to defile yourselves with all your idols to this day. Am I to let you inquire of me, O house of Israel? As surely as I live, declares the Sovereign LORD, I will not let you inquire of me.'"

Zeph 1 4"I will stretch out my hand against Judah and against all who live in Jerusalem. I will cut off from this place every remnant of Baal, the names of the pagan and the idolatrous priests—5those who bow down on the roofs to worship the starry host, those who bow down and swear by the LORD and who also swear by Molech, 6those who turn back from following the LORD and neither seek the LORD nor inquire of him."

l) An Improper Husband-Wife Relationship Hinders Prayer

1 Pet 3 7Husbands, in the same way be considerate as you live with your wives, and treat them with respect as the weaker partner and as heirs with you of the gracious gift of life, so that nothing will hinder your prayers.

m) Insincerity Hinders Prayer

Deut 4 29But if from there you seek the LORD your God, you will find him if you look for him with all your heart and with all your soul.

n) Irreverence Hinders Prayer

Mal 1 7"You place defiled food on my altar.

"But you ask, 'How have we defiled you?'

"By saying that the LORD's table is contemptible. 8When you bring blind animals for sacrifice, is that not wrong? When you sacrifice crippled or diseased animals, is that not wrong? Try offering them to your governor! Would he be pleased with you? Would he accept you?" says the LORD Almighty.

9"Now implore God to be gracious to us. With such offerings from your hands, will he accept you?"—says the LORD Almighty.

10"Oh, that one of you would shut the temple doors, so that you would not light useless fires on my altar! I am not pleased with you," says the LORD Almighty, "and I will accept no offering from your hands."

o) Losing Heart Hinders Prayer

Luke 18 1Then Jesus told his disciples a parable to show them that they should always pray and not give up.

p) Meaningless Repetition Hinders Prayer

Matt 6 7"And when you pray, do not keep on babbling like pagans, for they think they will be heard because of their many words."

q) Praying Contrary to God's Will Hinders Prayer

1 John 5 14This is the confidence we have in approaching God: that if we ask anything according to his will, he hears us.

r) Pretentiousness Hinders Prayer

Matt 6 5"And when you pray, do not be like the hypocrites, for they love to pray standing in the synagogues and on the street corners to be seen by men. I tell you the truth, they have received their reward in full."

s) Refusal to Help the Poor Hinders Prayer

Prov 21 13If a man shuts his ears to the cry of the poor, he too will cry out and not be answered.

t) Selfishness Hinders Prayer

James 4 3When you ask, you do not receive, because you ask with wrong motives, that you may spend what you get on your pleasures.

u) Self-Righteousness Hinders Prayer

Luke 18 9To some who were confident of their own righteousness and looked down on everybody else, Jesus told this parable: 10"Two men went up to the temple to pray, one a Pharisee and the other a tax collector. 11The Pharisee stood up and prayed about himself: 'God, I thank you that I am not like other men—robbers, evildoers, adulterers—or even like this tax collector. 12I fast twice a week and give a tenth of all I get.'

13"But the tax collector stood at a distance. He would not even look up to heaven, but beat his breast and said, 'God, have mercy on me, a sinner.'

14"I tell you that this man, rather than the other, went home justified before God. For everyone who exalts himself will be humbled, and he who humbles himself will be exalted."

v) Sleepiness Hinders Prayer

Matt 26 40Then he returned to his disciples and found them sleeping. "Could you men not keep watch with me for one hour?" he asked Peter. 41"Watch and pray so that you will not fall into temptation. The spirit is willing, but the body is weak."

42He went away a second time and prayed, "My Father, if it is not possible for this cup to be taken away unless I drink it, may your will be done."

43When he came back, he again found them sleeping, because their eyes were heavy. 44So he left them and went away once more and prayed the third time, saying the same thing.

w) Unconfessed Sin Hinders Prayer

Ps 66 18If I had cherished sin in my heart, the Lord would not have listened. . . .

Isa 59 1Surely the arm of the LORD is not too short to save, nor his ear too dull to hear. 2But your iniquities have separated you from your God; your sins have hidden his face from you, so that he will not hear.

John 9 31"We know that God does not listen to sinners. He listens to the godly man who does his will."

James 4 8Come near to God and he will come near to you. Wash your hands, you sinners, and purify your hearts, you double-minded.

x) Unfaithfulness Hinders Prayer

Hos 5 6"When they go with their flocks and herds to seek the LORD, they will not find him; he has withdrawn himself from them. 7They are unfaithful to the LORD; they give birth to illegitimate children. Now their New Moon festivals will devour them and their fields."

Mal 2 11Judah has broken faith. A detestable thing has been committed in Israel and in Jerusalem: Judah has desecrated the sanctuary the LORD loves, by marrying the daughter of a foreign god. 12As for the man who does this, whoever he may be, may the LORD cut him off from the tents of Jacob—even though he brings offerings to the LORD Almighty.

13Another thing you do: You flood the LORD's altar with tears. You weep and wail because he no longer pays attention to your offerings or accepts them with pleasure from your hands. 14You ask, "Why?" It is because the LORD is acting as the witness between you and the wife of your youth, because you have broken faith with her, though she is your partner, the wife of your marriage covenant.

y) An Unforgiving Spirit Hinders Prayer

Matt 6 14"For if you forgive men when they sin against you, your heavenly Father will also forgive you. 15But if you do not forgive men their sins, your Father will not forgive your sins."

Mark 11 25"And when you stand praying, if you hold anything against anyone, forgive him, so that your Father in heaven may forgive you your sins."

z) Wickedness Hinders Prayer

Prov 1 24"But since you rejected me when I called and no one gave heed when I stretched out my hand, 25since you ignored all my advice and would not accept my rebuke, 26I in turn will laugh at your disaster; I will mock when calamity overtakes you—[27]when calamity overtakes you like a storm, when disaster sweeps over you like a whirlwind, when distress and trouble overwhelm you.

[28]"Then they will call to me but I will not answer; they will look for me but will not find me. [29]Since they hated knowledge and did not choose to fear the LORD, [30]since they would not accept my advice and spurned my rebuke, [31]they will eat the fruit of their ways and be filled with the fruit of their schemes."

Prov 15 [8]The LORD detests the sacrifice of the wicked, but the prayer of the upright pleases him.

Prov 15 [29]The LORD is far from the wicked but he hears the prayer of the righteous.

Isa 1 [15]"When you spread out your hands in prayer, I will hide my eyes from you; even if you offer many prayers, I will not listen. Your hands are full of blood; [16]wash and make yourselves clean. Take your evil deeds out of my sight! Stop doing wrong. . . ."

Isa 59 [1]Surely the arm of the LORD is not too short to save, nor his ear too dull to hear. [2]But your iniquities have separated you from your God; your sins have hidden his face from you, so that he will not hear.

9. Examples of Persevering Prayer

a) Anna Persevered in Prayer

Luke 2 [36]There was also a prophetess, Anna, the daughter of Phanuel, of the tribe of Asher. She was very old; she had lived with her husband seven years after her marriage, [37]and then was a widow until she was eighty-four. She never left the temple but worshiped night and day, fasting and praying.

b) The Apostles Persevered in Prayer

Acts 6 [2]So the Twelve gathered all the disciples together and said, "It would not be right for us to neglect the ministry of the word of God in order to wait on tables. [3]Brothers, choose seven men from among you who are known to be full of the Spirit and wisdom. We will turn this responsibility over to them [4]and will give our attention to prayer and the ministry of the word."

c) Cornelius Persevered in Prayer

Acts 10 [1]At Caesarea there was a man named Cornelius, a centurion in what was known as the Italian Regiment. [2]He and all his family were devout and God-fearing; he gave generously to those in need and prayed to God regularly.

d) Daniel Persevered in Prayer

Dan 6 [10]Now when Daniel learned that the decree had been published, he went home to his upstairs room where the windows opened toward Jerusalem. Three times a day he got down on his knees and prayed, giving thanks to his God, just as he had done before.

e) Epaphras Persevered in Prayer

Col 4 [12]Epaphras, who is one of you and a servant of Christ Jesus, sends greetings. He is always wrestling in prayer for you, that you may stand firm in all the will of God, mature and fully assured.

f) Jacob Persevered in Prayer

Gen 32 [24]So Jacob was left alone, and a man wrestled with him till daybreak. [25]When the man saw that he could not overpower him, he touched the socket of Jacob's hip so that his hip was wrenched as he wrestled with the man. [26]Then the man said, "Let me go, for it is daybreak."

But Jacob replied, "I will not let you go unless you bless me."

[27]The man asked him, "What is your name?"

"Jacob," he answered.

[28]Then the man said, "Your name will no longer be Jacob, but Israel, because you have struggled with God and with men and have overcome."

g) The Jerusalem Church Persevered in Prayer

Acts 12 [1]It was about this time that King Herod arrested some who belonged to the church, intending to persecute them. [2]He had James, the brother of John, put to death with the sword. [3]When he saw that this pleased the Jews, he proceeded to seize Peter also. This happened during the Feast of Unleavened Bread. [4]After arresting him, he put him in prison, handing him over to be guarded by four squads of four soldiers each. Herod intended to bring him out for public trial after the Passover.

[5]So Peter was kept in prison, but the church was earnestly praying to God for him.

[6]The night before Herod was to bring him to trial, Peter was sleeping between two soldiers, bound with two chains, and sentries stood guard at the entrance. [7]Suddenly an angel of the Lord appeared and a light shone in the cell. He struck Peter on the side and woke him up. "Quick, get up!" he said, and the chains fell off Peter's wrists.

[8]Then the angel said to him, "Put on your clothes and sandals." And Peter did so. "Wrap your cloak around you and follow me," the angel told him. [9]Peter followed him out of the prison, but he had no idea that what the angel was doing was really happening; he thought he was seeing a vision. [10]They passed the first and second guards and came to the iron gate leading to the city. It opened for them by itself, and they went through it. When they had walked the length of one street, suddenly the angel left him.

[11]Then Peter came to himself and said, "Now I know without a doubt that the Lord sent his angel and rescued me from Herod's clutches and from everything the Jewish people were anticipating."

[12]When this had dawned on him, he went to the house of Mary the mother of John, also called Mark, where many people had gathered and were praying. [13]Peter knocked at the outer entrance, and a servant girl named Rhoda came to answer the door. [14]When she recognized Peter's voice, she was so overjoyed she ran back without opening it and exclaimed, "Peter is at the door!"

[15]"You're out of your mind," they told her. When she kept insisting that it was so, they said, "It must be his angel."

[16]But Peter kept on knocking, and when they opened the door and saw him, they were astonished. [17]Peter motioned with his hand for them to be quiet and described how the Lord had brought him out of prison. "Tell James and the brothers about this," he said, and then he left for another place.

h) Moses Persevered in Prayer

Deut 9 [18]Then once again I fell prostrate before the LORD for forty days and forty nights; I ate no bread and drank no water, because of all the sin you had committed, doing what was evil in the LORD's sight and so provoking him to anger. [19]I feared the anger and wrath of the LORD, for he was angry enough with you to destroy you. But again the LORD listened to me.

i) Paul Persevered in Prayer

Acts 9 [11]The Lord told him, "Go to the house of Judas on Straight Street and ask for a man from Tarsus named Saul, for he is praying."

Rom 1 [9]God, whom I serve with my whole heart in preaching the gospel of his Son, is my witness how constantly I remember you [10]in my prayers at all times; and I pray that now at last by God's will the way may be opened for me to come to you.

Eph 1 [16]I have not stopped giving thanks for you, remembering you in my prayers.

Col 1 [9]For this reason, since the day we heard about you, we have not stopped praying for you and asking God to fill you with the knowledge of his will through all spiritual wisdom and understanding.

1 Thess 3 [10]Night and day we pray most earnestly that we may see you again and supply what is lacking in your faith.

2 Tim 1 [3]I thank God, whom I serve, as my forefathers did, with a clear conscience, as night and day I constantly remember you in my prayers.

j) Samuel Persevered in Prayer

1 Sam 7 [8]They said to Samuel, "Do not stop crying out to the LORD our God for us, that he may rescue us from the hand of the Philistines." [9]Then Samuel took a suckling lamb and offered it up as a whole burnt offering to the LORD. He cried out to the LORD on Israel's behalf, and the LORD answered him.

B. Confess to God

1. The Character of Confession

a) Confession Accompanies Faith

Acts 19 [18]Many of those who believed now came and openly confessed their evil deeds.

b) Confession Accompanies the Fear of God

Ps 130 [3]If you, O LORD, kept a record of sins, O Lord, who could stand? [4]But with you there is forgiveness; therefore you are feared.

Luke 23 [39]One of the criminals who hung there hurled insults at him: "Aren't you the Christ? Save yourself and us!"

[40]But the other criminal rebuked him. "Don't you fear God," he said, "since you are under the same sentence? [41]We are punished justly, for we are getting what our deeds deserve. But this man has done nothing wrong."

c) Confession Accompanies Prayer

Dan 9 [20]While I was speaking and praying, confessing my sin and the sin of my people Israel and making my request to the LORD my God for his holy hill—[21]while I was still in prayer, Gabriel, the man I had seen in the earlier vision, came to me in swift flight about the time of the evening sacrifice.

d) Confession Accompanies Worship

1 Sam 15 [24]Then Saul said to Samuel, "I have sinned. I violated the LORD's command and your instructions. I was afraid of the people and so I gave in to them. [25]Now I beg you, forgive my sin and come back with me, so that I may worship the LORD."

Neh 9 [3]They stood where they were and read from the Book of the Law of the LORD their God for a quarter of the day, and spent another quarter in confession and in worshiping the LORD their God.

e) Confession Honors God

Josh 7 [19]Then Joshua said to Achan, "My son, give glory to the LORD, the God of Israel, and give him the praise. Tell me what you have done; do not hide it from me."

f) Confession Involves the Acknowledgment of Sin

Lev 16 [21]"He is to lay both hands on the head of the live goat and confess over it all the wickedness and rebellion of the Israelites—all their sins—and put them on the goat's head. He shall send the goat away into the desert in the care of a man appointed for the task."

Neh 1 [6]". . . let your ear be attentive and your eyes open to hear the prayer your servant is praying before you day and night for your servants, the people of Israel. I confess the sins we Israelites, including myself and my father's house, have committed against you. [7]We have acted very wickedly toward you. We have not obeyed the commands, decrees and laws you gave your servant Moses."

Isa 59 [12]For our offenses are many in your sight, and our sins testify against us. Our offenses are ever with us, and we acknowledge our iniquities: [13]rebellion and treachery against the LORD, turning our backs on our God, fomenting oppression and revolt, uttering lies our hearts have conceived.

Jer 14 [20]O LORD, we acknowledge our wickedness and the guilt of our fathers; we have indeed sinned against you.

g) Confession Involves Cleansing

Ps 51 [2]Wash away all my iniquity and cleanse me from my sin.

[3]For I know my transgressions, and my sin is always before me. [4]Against you, you only, have I sinned and done what is evil in your sight, so that you are proved right when you speak and justified when you judge. . . .

[7]Cleanse me with hyssop, and I will be clean; wash me, and I will be whiter than snow.

Isa 1 [15]"When you spread out your hands in prayer, I will hide my eyes from you; even if you offer many prayers, I will not listen. Your hands are full of blood; [16]wash and make yourselves clean. Take your evil deeds out of my sight! Stop doing wrong. . . ."

James 4 [8]Come near to God and he will come near to you. Wash your hands, you sinners, and purify your hearts, you double-minded.

1 John 1 [9]If we confess our sins, he is faithful and just and will forgive us our sins and purify us from all unrighteousness.

h) Confession Involves Humility

Lev 26 [40]"'But if they will confess their sins and the sins of their fathers—their treachery against me and their hostility toward me, [41]which made me hostile toward them so that I sent them into the land of their enemies—then when their uncircumcised hearts are humbled and they pay for their sin, [42]I will remember my covenant with Jacob and my covenant with Isaac and my covenant with Abraham, and I will remember the land.'"

i) Confession Involves Introspection

Lam 3 [40]Let us examine our ways and test them, and let us return to the LORD. [41]Let us lift up our hearts and our hands to God in heaven, and say: [42]"We have sinned and rebelled and you have not forgiven."

j) Confession Involves Remorse

Ps 38 [17]For I am about to fall, and my pain is ever with me. [18]I confess my iniquity; I am troubled by my sin.

Jer 3 [21]A cry is heard on the barren heights, the weeping and pleading of the people of Israel, because they have perverted their ways and have forgotten the LORD their God. . . .

[25]"Let us lie down in our shame, and let our disgrace cover us. We have sinned against the LORD our God, both we and our fathers; from our youth till this day we have not obeyed the LORD our God."

Jer 31 [18]"I have surely heard Ephraim's moaning: 'You disciplined me like an unruly calf, and I have been disciplined. Restore me, and I will return, because you are the LORD my God. [19]After I strayed, I repented; after I came to understand, I beat my breast. I was ashamed and humiliated because I bore the disgrace of my youth.'"

Lam 1 [20]"See, O LORD, how distressed I am! I am in torment within, and in my heart I am disturbed, for I have been most rebellious. Outside, the sword bereaves; inside, there is only death."

k) Confession Involves Repentance

1 Kings 8 [33]"When your people Israel have been defeated by an enemy because they have sinned against you, and when they turn back to you and confess your name, praying and making supplication to you in this temple, [34]then hear from heaven and forgive the sin of your people Israel and bring them back to the land you gave to their fathers.

[35]"When the heavens are shut up and there is no rain because your people have sinned against you, and when they pray toward this place and confess your name and turn from their sin because you have afflicted them, [36]then hear from heaven and forgive the sin of your servants, your people Israel. Teach them the right way to live, and send rain on the land you gave your people for an inheritance."

Job 42 [5]"My ears had heard of you but now my eyes have seen you. [6]Therefore I despise myself and repent in dust and ashes."

l) Confession Involves Restitution

Num 5 [5]The LORD said to Moses, [6]"Say to the Israelites: 'When a man or woman wrongs another in any way and so is unfaithful to the LORD, that person is guilty [7]and must confess the sin he has committed. He must make full restitution for his wrong, add one fifth to it and give it all to the person he has wronged.'"

m) Confession Is Demanded by God

Lev 5 [5]"'When anyone is guilty in any of these ways, he must confess in what way he has sinned. . . .'"

Num 5 [5]The LORD said to Moses, [6]"Say to the Israelites: 'When a man or woman wrongs another in any way and so is unfaithful to the LORD, that person is guilty [7]and must confess the sin he has committed. He must make full restitution for his wrong, add one fifth to it and give it all to the person he has wronged.'"

Jer 3 [13]"'Only acknowledge your guilt—you have rebelled against the LORD your God, you have scattered your favors to foreign gods under every spreading tree, and have not obeyed me,'" declares the LORD.

Hos 5 [15]"Then I will go back to my place until they admit their guilt. And they will seek my face; in their misery they will earnestly seek me."

Rom 14 [11]It is written: "'As surely as I live,' says the Lord, 'every knee will bow before me; every tongue will confess to God.'"

2. Results of Confession

a) Confession Results in Communion with Christ

Luke 23 [40]But the other criminal rebuked him. "Don't you fear God," he said, "since you are under the same sentence? [41]We are punished justly, for we are getting what our deeds deserve. But this man has done nothing wrong."

[42]Then he said, "Jesus, remember me when you come into your kingdom."

[43]Jesus answered him, "I tell you the truth, today you will be with me in paradise."

b) Confession Results in Divine Blessing

Lev 26 [40]"'But if they will confess their sins and the sins of their fathers—their treachery against me and their hostility toward me, [41]which made me hostile toward them so that I sent them into the land of their enemies—then when their uncircumcised hearts are humbled and they pay for their sin, [42]I will remember my covenant with Jacob and my covenant with Isaac and my covenant with Abraham, and I will remember the land.'"

c) Confession Results in Divine Healing

Ps 41 [4]I said, "O LORD, have mercy on me; heal me, for I have sinned against you."

James 5 [16]Therefore confess your sins to each other and pray for each other so that you may be healed. The prayer of a righteous man is powerful and effective.

d) Confession Results in Divine Mercy

Job 33 [27]"Then he comes to men and says, 'I sinned, and perverted what was right, but I did not get what I deserved. [28]He redeemed my soul from going down to the pit, and I will live to enjoy the light.'

[29]"God does all these things to a man—twice, even three times—[30]to turn back his soul from the pit, that the light of life may shine on him."

Prov 28 [13]He who conceals his sins does not prosper, but whoever confesses and renounces them finds mercy.

e) Confession Results in Forgiveness of Sin

Ps 32 [5]Then I acknowledged my sin to you and did not cover up my iniquity. I said, "I will confess my transgressions to the LORD"—and you forgave the guilt of my sin.

1 John 1 [9]If we confess our sins, he is faithful and just and will forgive us our sins and purify us from all unrighteousness.

f) Confession Results in Godly Living

Ps 51 [3]For I know my transgressions, and my sin is always before me. [4]Against you, you only, have I sinned and done what is evil in your sight, so that you are proved right when you speak and justified when you judge. . . . [11]Do not cast me from your presence or take your Holy Spirit from me. [12]Restore to me the joy of your salvation and grant me a willing spirit, to sustain me.

[13]Then I will teach transgressors your ways, and sinners will turn back to you.

Matt 3 [5]People went out to him from Jerusalem and all Judea and the whole region of the Jordan. [6]Confessing their sins, they were baptized by him in the Jordan River.

[7]But when he saw many of the Pharisees and Sadducees coming to where he was baptizing, he said to them: "You brood of vipers! Who warned you to flee from the coming wrath? [8]Produce fruit in keeping with repentance."

g) Confession Results in Praise

Ps 51 [14]Save me from bloodguilt, O God, the God who saves me, and my tongue will sing of your righteousness. [15]O Lord, open my lips, and my mouth will declare your praise.

h) Confession Results in Separation from Evil

1 Sam 7 [2]It was a long time, twenty years in all, that the ark remained at Kiriath Jearim, and all the people of Israel mourned and sought after the LORD. [3]And Samuel said to the whole house of Israel, "If you are returning to the LORD with all your hearts, then rid yourselves of the foreign gods and the Ashtoreths and commit yourselves to the LORD and serve him only, and he will deliver you out of the hand of the Philistines." [4]So the Israelites put away their Baals and Ashtoreths, and served the LORD only.

[5]Then Samuel said, "Assemble all Israel at Mizpah and I will intercede with the LORD for you." [6]When they had assembled at Mizpah, they drew water and poured it out before the LORD. On that day they fasted and there they confessed, "We have sinned against the LORD." And Samuel was leader of Israel at Mizpah.

Ezra 10 [11]"Now make confession to the LORD, the God of your fathers, and do his will. Separate yourselves from the peoples around you and from your foreign wives."

Job 34 [31]"Suppose a man says to God, 'I am guilty but will offend no more. [32]Teach me what I cannot see; if I have done wrong, I will not do so again.'"

3. Expressions of Confession

a) Illustrations of Confession

(1) The Confession of the Prodigal Son

Luke 15 [17]"When he came to his senses, he said, 'How many of my father's hired men have food to spare, and here I am starving to death! [18]I will set out and go back to my father and say to him: Father, I have sinned against heaven and against you. [19]I am no longer worthy to be called your son; make me like one of your hired men.' [20]So he got up and went to his father.

"But while he was still a long way off, his father saw him and was filled with compassion for him; he ran to his son, threw his arms around him and kissed him.

[21]"The son said to him, 'Father, I have sinned against heaven and against you. I am no longer worthy to be called your son.'

[22]"But the father said to his servants, 'Quick! Bring the best robe and put it on him. Put a ring on his finger and sandals on his feet. [23]Bring the fattened calf and kill it. Let's have a feast and celebrate. [24]For this son of mine was dead and is alive again; he was lost and is found.' So they began to celebrate."

(2) The Confession of the Tax Collector

Luke 18 [13]"But the tax collector stood at a distance. He would not even look up to heaven, but beat his breast and said, 'God, have mercy on me, a sinner.'

[14]"I tell you that this man, rather than the other, went home justified before God. For everyone who exalts himself will be humbled, and he who humbles himself will be exalted."

b) Confession in the Lives of God's People

(1) Aaron's Confession

Num 12 [9]The anger of the LORD burned against them, and he left them.

[10]When the cloud lifted from above the Tent, there stood Miriam—leprous, like snow. Aaron turned toward her and saw that she had leprosy; [11]and he said to Moses, "Please, my lord, do not hold against us the sin we have so foolishly committed. [12]Do not let her be like a stillborn infant coming from its mother's womb with its flesh half eaten away."

[13]So Moses cried out to the LORD, "O God, please heal her!"

(2) Israel's Confession

Judg 10 [10]Then the Israelites cried out to the LORD, "We have sinned against you, forsaking our God and serving the Baals."

[11]The LORD replied, "When the Egyptians, the Amorites, the Ammonites, the Philistines, [12]the Sidonians, the Amalekites and the Maonites oppressed you and you cried to me for help, did I not save you from their hands? [13]But you have forsaken me and served other gods, so I will no longer save you. [14]Go

and cry out to the gods you have chosen. Let them save you when you are in trouble!"

[15]But the Israelites said to the LORD, "We have sinned. Do with us whatever you think best, but please rescue us now." [16]Then they got rid of the foreign gods among them and served the LORD. And he could bear Israel's misery no longer.

(3) Job's Confession

Job 14 [4]"Who can bring what is pure from the impure? No one! . . . [17]My offenses will be sealed up in a bag; you will cover over my sin."

Job 40 [1]The LORD said to Job: [2]"Will the one who contends with the Almighty correct him? Let him who accuses God answer him!"

[3]Then Job answered the LORD: [4]"I am unworthy—how can I reply to you? I put my hand over my mouth. [5]I spoke once, but I have no answer—twice, but I will say no more."

(4) David's Confession

1 Chron 21 [8]Then David said to God, "I have sinned greatly by doing this. Now, I beg you, take away the guilt of your servant. I have done a very foolish thing."

Ps 38 [3]Because of your wrath there is no health in my body; my bones have no soundness because of my sin. [4]My guilt has overwhelmed me like a burden too heavy to bear. . . . [18]I confess my iniquity; I am troubled by my sin.

Ps 40 [11]Do not withhold your mercy from me, O LORD; may your love and your truth always protect me. [12]For troubles without number surround me; my sins have overtaken me, and I cannot see. They are more than the hairs of my head, and my heart fails within me.

Ps 51 [1]Have mercy on me, O God, according to your unfailing love; according to your great compassion blot out my transgressions. [2]Wash away all my iniquity and cleanse me from my sin.

[3]For I know my transgressions, and my sin is always before me. [4]Against you, you only, have I sinned and done what is evil in your sight, so that you are proved right when you speak and justified when you judge. [5]Surely I was sinful at birth, sinful from the time my mother conceived me. [6]Surely you desire truth in the inner parts; you teach me wisdom in the inmost place.

[7]Cleanse me with hyssop, and I will be clean; wash me, and I will be whiter than snow. [8]Let me hear joy and gladness; let the bones you have crushed rejoice. [9]Hide your face from my sins and blot out all my iniquity.

[10]Create in me a pure heart, O God, and renew a steadfast spirit within me. [11]Do not cast me from your presence or take your Holy Spirit from me. [12]Restore to me the joy of your salvation and grant me a willing spirit, to sustain me.

Ps 69 [5]You know my folly, O God; my guilt is not hidden from you.

(5) Isaiah's Confession

Isa 6 [5]"Woe to me!" I cried. "I am ruined! For I am a man of unclean lips, and I live among a people of unclean lips, and my eyes have seen the King, the LORD Almighty."

Isa 64 [5]You come to the help of those who gladly do right, who remember your ways. But when we continued to sin against them, you were angry. How then can we be saved? [6]All of us have become like one who is unclean, and all our righteous acts are like filthy rags; we all shrivel up like a leaf, and like the wind our sins sweep us away. [7]No one calls on your name or strives to lay hold of you; for you have hidden your face from us and made us waste away because of our sins.

(6) Jeremiah's Confession

Jer 14 [7]Although our sins testify against us, O LORD, do something for the sake of your name. For our backsliding is great; we have sinned against you.

(7) Daniel's Confession

Dan 9 [4]I prayed to the LORD my God and confessed: "O Lord, the great and awesome God, who keeps his covenant of love with all who love him and obey his commands, [5]we have sinned and done wrong. We have been wicked and have rebelled; we have turned away from your commands and laws. [6]We have not listened to your servants the prophets, who spoke in your name to our kings, our princes and our fathers, and to all the people of the land.

[7]"Lord, you are righteous, but this day we are covered with shame—the men of Judah and people of Jerusalem and all Israel, both near and far, in all the countries where you have scattered us because of our unfaithfulness to you. [8]O LORD, we and our kings, our princes and our fathers are covered with shame because we have sinned against you."

(8) Ezra's Confession

Ezra 9 [5]Then, at the evening sacrifice, I rose from my self-abasement, with my tunic and cloak torn, and fell on my knees with my hands spread out to the LORD my God [6]and prayed: "O my God, I am too ashamed and disgraced to lift up my face to you, my God, because our sins are higher than our heads and our guilt has reached to the heavens. [7]From the days of our forefathers until now, our guilt has been great. Because of our sins, we and our kings and our priests have been subjected to the sword and captivity, to pillage and humiliation at the hand of foreign kings, as it is today. . . .

[13]"What has happened to us is a result of our evil deeds and our great guilt, and yet, our God, you have punished us less than our sins have deserved and have given us a remnant like this. . . . [15]O LORD, God of Israel, you are righteous! We are left this day as a remnant. Here we are before you in our guilt, though because of it not one of us can stand in your presence."

(9) Nehemiah's Confession

Neh 1 [4]When I heard these things, I sat down and wept. For some days I mourned and fasted and prayed before the God of heaven. [5]Then I said: "O LORD, God of heaven, the great and awesome God, who keeps his covenant of love with those who love him and obey his commands, [6]let your ear be attentive and your eyes open to hear the prayer your servant is praying before you day and night for your servants, the people of Israel. I confess the sins we Israelites, including myself and my father's house, have committed against you. [7]We have acted very wickedly toward you. We have not obeyed the commands, decrees and laws you gave your servant Moses."

(10) The Levites' Confession

Neh 9 [5]And the Levites—Jeshua, Kadmiel, Bani, Hashabneiah, Sherebiah, Hodiah, Shebaniah and Pethahiah—said: "Stand up and praise the LORD your God, who is from everlasting to everlasting."

"Blessed be your glorious name, and may it be exalted above all blessing and praise. . . . [33]In all that has happened to us, you have been just; you have acted faithfully, while we did wrong. [34]Our kings, our leaders, our priests and our fathers did not follow your law; they did not pay attention to your commands or the warnings you gave them. [35]Even while they were in their kingdom, enjoying your great goodness to them in the spacious and fertile land you gave them, they did not serve you or turn from their evil ways.

[36]"But see, we are slaves today, slaves in the land you gave our forefathers so they could eat its fruit and the other good things it produces. [37]Because of our sins, its abundant harvest goes to the kings you have placed over us. They rule over our bodies and our cattle as they please. We are in great distress."

(11) Peter's Confession

Luke 5 [8]When Simon Peter saw this, he fell at Jesus' knees and said, "Go away from me, Lord; I am a sinful man!"

(12) The Penitent Thief's Confession

Luke 23 [40]But the other criminal rebuked him. "Don't you fear God," he said, "since you are under the same sentence? [41]We are punished justly, for we are getting what our deeds deserve. But this man has done nothing wrong."

[42]Then he said, "Jesus, remember me when you come into your kingdom."

(13) Paul's Confession

Rom 7 [18]I know that nothing good lives in me, that is, in my sinful nature. For I have the desire to do what is good, but I cannot carry it out. [19]For what I do is not the good I want to do; no, the evil I do not want to do—this I keep on doing. . . .

[21]So I find this law at work: When I want to do good, evil is right there with me. [22]For in my inner being I delight in God's

law; [23]but I see another law at work in the members of my body, waging war against the law of my mind and making me a prisoner of the law of sin at work within my members.

C. Meditate on God

1. Meditation on God Himself

Ps 16 [8]I have set the LORD always before me. Because he is at my right hand, I will not be shaken.
Ps 19 [14]May the words of my mouth and the meditation of my heart be pleasing in your sight, O LORD, my Rock and my Redeemer.
Ps 48 [9]Within your temple, O God, we meditate on your unfailing love.
Ps 63 [6]On my bed I remember you; I think of you through the watches of the night.
Ps 104 [34]May my meditation be pleasing to him, as I rejoice in the LORD.

2. Meditation on God's Word

Josh 1 [8]"Do not let this Book of the Law depart from your mouth; meditate on it day and night, so that you may be careful to do everything written in it. Then you will be prosperous and successful."
Job 22 [22]"Accept instruction from his mouth and lay up his words in your heart."
Ps 1 [2]But his delight is in the law of the LORD, and on his law he meditates day and night.
Ps 37 [31]The law of his God is in his heart; his feet do not slip.
Ps 40 [8]"I desire to do your will, O my God; your law is within my heart."
Ps 119 [11]I have hidden your word in my heart that I might not sin against you.
Ps 119 [15]I meditate on your precepts and consider your ways.
Ps 119 [23]Though rulers sit together and slander me, your servant will meditate on your decrees.
Ps 119 [48]I lift up my hands to your commands, which I love, and I meditate on your decrees.
Ps 119 [78]May the arrogant be put to shame for wronging me without cause; but I will meditate on your precepts.
Ps 119 [97]Oh, how I love your law! I meditate on it all day long.
Ps 119 [99]I have more insight than all my teachers, for I meditate on your statutes.
Ps 119 [148]My eyes stay open through the watches of the night, that I may meditate on your promises.

3. Meditation on God's Work

Ps 77 [12]I will meditate on all your works and consider all your mighty deeds.
Ps 119 [15]I meditate on your precepts and consider your ways.
Ps 119 [27]Let me understand the teaching of your precepts; then I will meditate on your wonders.
Ps 143 [5]I remember the days of long ago; I meditate on all your works and consider what your hands have done.
Ps 145 [5]They will speak of the glorious splendor of your majesty, and I will meditate on your wonderful works.

D. Commune with God

1. Divine Participants in Communion

a) Communion with the Father

1 John 1 [3]We proclaim to you what we have seen and heard, so that you also may have fellowship with us. And our fellowship is with the Father and with his Son, Jesus Christ.

b) Communion with the Son

1 Cor 1 [9]God, who has called you into fellowship with his Son Jesus Christ our Lord, is faithful.
1 John 1 [3]We proclaim to you what we have seen and heard, so that you also may have fellowship with us. And our fellowship is with the Father and with his Son, Jesus Christ.
Rev 3 [20]"Here I am! I stand at the door and knock. If anyone hears my voice and opens the door, I will come in and eat with him, and he with me."

c) Communion with the Spirit

2 Cor 13 [14]May the grace of the Lord Jesus Christ, and the love of God, and the fellowship of the Holy Spirit be with you all.
Phil 2 [1]If you have any encouragement from being united with Christ, if any comfort from his love, if any fellowship with the Spirit, if any tenderness and compassion, [2]then make my joy complete by being like-minded, having the same love, being one in spirit and purpose.

2. Means of Communion

a) Communion through the Lord's Supper

1 Cor 10 [16]Is not the cup of thanksgiving for which we give thanks a participation in the blood of Christ? And is not the bread that we break a participation in the body of Christ? [17]Because there is one loaf, we, who are many, are one body, for we all partake of the one loaf.

b) Communion through Meditation

Ps 19 [14]May the words of my mouth and the meditation of my heart be pleasing in your sight, O LORD, my Rock and my Redeemer.
Ps 63 [6]On my bed I remember you; I think of you through the watches of the night. [7]Because you are my help, I sing in the shadow of your wings. [8]My soul clings to you; your right hand upholds me.
Ps 139 [17]How precious to me are your thoughts, O God! How vast is the sum of them! [18]Were I to count them, they would outnumber the grains of sand. When I awake, I am still with you.

c) Communion through Prayer

Ps 42 [8]By day the LORD directs his love, at night his song is with me—a prayer to the God of my life.
Phil 4 [6]Do not be anxious about anything, but in everything, by prayer and petition, with thanksgiving, present your requests to God. [7]And the peace of God, which transcends all understanding, will guard your hearts and your minds in Christ Jesus.
Heb 4 [14]Therefore, since we have a great high priest who has gone through the heavens, Jesus the Son of God, let us hold firmly to the faith we profess. [15]For we do not have a high priest who is unable to sympathize with our weaknesses, but we have one who has been tempted in every way, just as we are—yet was without sin. [16]Let us then approach the throne of grace with confidence, so that we may receive mercy and find grace to help us in our time of need.

d) Communion through Worship

Ps 63 [1]O God, you are my God, earnestly I seek you; my soul thirsts for you, my body longs for you, in a dry and weary land where there is no water.

[2]I have seen you in the sanctuary and beheld your power and your glory. [3]Because your love is better than life, my lips will glorify you. [4]I will praise you as long as I live, and in your name I will lift up my hands. [5]My soul will be satisfied as with the richest of foods; with singing lips my mouth will praise you.

3. Prerequisites of Communion

a) Holiness Is a Prerequisite of Communion

2 Cor 6 [14]Do not be yoked together with unbelievers. For what do righteousness and wickedness have in common? Or what fellowship can light have with darkness? [15]What harmony is there between Christ and Belial? What does a believer have in common with an unbeliever? [16]What agreement is there between the temple of God and idols? For we are the temple of the living God. As God has said: "I will live with them and walk among them, and I will be their God, and they will be my people."

[17]"Therefore come out from them and be separate, says the Lord. Touch no unclean thing, and I will receive you." [18]"I will be a Father to you, and you will be my sons and daughters, says the Lord Almighty."

7 1Since we have these promises, dear friends, let us purify ourselves from everything that contaminates body and spirit, perfecting holiness out of reverence for God.

b) Love and Obedience Are Prerequisites of Communion

John 14 6Jesus answered, "I am the way and the truth and the life. No one comes to the Father except through me." . . .

15"If you love me, you will obey what I command. 16And I will ask the Father, and he will give you another Counselor to be with you forever—17the Spirit of truth. The world cannot accept him, because it neither sees him nor knows him. But you know him, for he lives with you and will be in you. 18I will not leave you as orphans; I will come to you. 19Before long, the world will not see me anymore, but you will see me. Because I live, you also will live. 20On that day you will realize that I am in my Father, and you are in me, and I am in you. 21Whoever has my commands and obeys them, he is the one who loves me. He who loves me will be loved by my Father, and I too will love him and show myself to him." . . .

23Jesus replied, "If anyone loves me, he will obey my teaching. My Father will love him, and we will come to him and make our home with him."

1 John 3 24Those who obey his commands live in him, and he in them. And this is how we know that he lives in us: We know it by the Spirit he gave us.

c) Reconciliation Is a Prerequisite of Communion

Amos 3 3Do two walk together unless they have agreed to do so?

1 John 1 6If we claim to have fellowship with him yet walk in the darkness, we lie and do not live by the truth. 7But if we walk in the light, as he is in the light, we have fellowship with one another, and the blood of Jesus, his Son, purifies us from all sin.

4. Results of Communion

a) Communion Imparts the Peace of God

Phil 4 6Do not be anxious about anything, but in everything, by prayer and petition, with thanksgiving, present your requests to God. 7And the peace of God, which transcends all understanding, will guard your hearts and your minds in Christ Jesus.

b) Communion Produces Christ-likeness

Phil 3 10I want to know Christ and the power of his resurrection and the fellowship of sharing in his sufferings, becoming like him in his death, 11and so, somehow, to attain to the resurrection from the dead.

c) Communion Produces the Desire for More Communion

Ps 16 8I have set the LORD always before me. Because he is at my right hand, I will not be shaken.

Ps 42 1As the deer pants for streams of water, so my soul pants for you, O God. 2My soul thirsts for God, for the living God. When can I go and meet with God? 3My tears have been my food day and night, while men say to me all day long, "Where is your God?" 4These things I remember as I pour out my soul: how I used to go with the multitude, leading the procession to the house of God, with shouts of joy and thanksgiving among the festive throng. 5Why are you downcast, O my soul? Why so disturbed within me? Put your hope in God, for I will yet praise him, my Savior and 6my God.

My soul is downcast within me; therefore I will remember you from the land of the Jordan, the heights of Hermon—from Mount Mizar. 7Deep calls to deep in the roar of your waterfalls; all your waves and breakers have swept over me.

8By day the LORD directs his love, at night his song is with me—a prayer to the God of my life.

9I say to God my Rock, "Why have you forgotten me? Why must I go about mourning, oppressed by the enemy?" 10My bones suffer mortal agony as my foes taunt me, saying to me all day long, "Where is your God?"

11Why are you downcast, O my soul? Why so disturbed within me? Put your hope in God, for I will yet praise him, my Savior and my God.

Phil 1 23I am torn between the two: I desire to depart and be with Christ, which is better by far; 24but it is more necessary for you that I remain in the body.

d) Communion Provides Divine Assistance in Times of Need

Heb 4 16Let us then approach the throne of grace with confidence, so that we may receive mercy and find grace to help us in our time of need.

e) Communion Unites One with Other Believers

1 Cor 12 13For we were all baptized by one Spirit into one body—whether Jews or Greeks, slave or free—and we were all given the one Spirit to drink.

Phil 2 1If you have any encouragement from being united with Christ, if any comfort from his love, if any fellowship with the Spirit, if any tenderness and compassion, 2then make my joy complete by being like-minded, having the same love, being one in spirit and purpose.

5. Illustrations of Communion

a) Enoch Communed with God

Gen 5 22And after he became the father of Methuselah, Enoch walked with God 300 years and had other sons and daughters. 23Altogether, Enoch lived 365 years. 24Enoch walked with God; then he was no more, because God took him away.

b) Noah Communed with God

Gen 6 9This is the account of Noah.

Noah was a righteous man, blameless among the people of his time, and he walked with God.

c) Moses Communed with God

Exod 33 9As Moses went into the tent, the pillar of cloud would come down and stay at the entrance, while the LORD spoke with Moses. . . . 11The LORD would speak to Moses face to face, as a man speaks with his friend. Then Moses would return to the camp, but his young aide Joshua son of Nun did not leave the tent.

12Moses said to the LORD, "You have been telling me, 'Lead these people,' but you have not let me know whom you will send with me. You have said, 'I know you by name and you have found favor with me.' 13If you are pleased with me, teach me your ways so I may know you and continue to find favor with you. Remember that this nation is your people."

14The LORD replied, "My Presence will go with you, and I will give you rest."

15Then Moses said to him, "If your Presence does not go with us, do not send us up from here. 16How will anyone know that you are pleased with me and with your people unless you go with us? What else will distinguish me and your people from all the other people on the face of the earth?"

17And the LORD said to Moses, "I will do the very thing you have asked, because I am pleased with you and I know you by name."

18Then Moses said, "Now show me your glory."

19And the LORD said, "I will cause all my goodness to pass in front of you, and I will proclaim my name, the LORD, in your presence. I will have mercy on whom I will have mercy, and I will have compassion on whom I will have compassion. 20But," he said, "you cannot see my face, for no one may see me and live."

21Then the LORD said, "There is a place near me where you may stand on a rock. 22When my glory passes by, I will put you in a cleft in the rock and cover you with my hand until I have passed by. 23Then I will remove my hand and you will see my back; but my face must not be seen."

d) Jesus Communed with the Father

John 17 20"My prayer is not for them alone. I pray also for those who will believe in me through their message, 21that all of them may be one, Father, just as you are in me and I am in you. May they also be in us so that the world may believe that you have sent me. [22]I have given them the glory that you gave me, that they may be one as we are one: [23]I in them and you in me. May they be brought to complete unity to let the world know that you sent me and have loved them even as you have loved me.

[24]"Father, I want those you have given me to be with me where I am, and to see my glory, the glory you have given me because you loved me before the creation of the world.

[25]"Righteous Father, though the world does not know you, I know you, and they know that you have sent me. [26]I have made you known to them, and will continue to make you known in order that the love you have for me may be in them and that I myself may be in them."

VII
Pursuing God

A. Seek God

1. The Necessity of Seeking God

a) All People Are Commanded to Seek Him

Ps 27 [8]My heart says of you, "Seek his face!" Your face, LORD, I will seek.
Ps 83 [16]Cover their faces with shame so that men will seek your name, O LORD.
Ps 105 [4]Look to the LORD and his strength; seek his face always.
Isa 8 [19]When men tell you to consult mediums and spiritists, who whisper and mutter, should not a people inquire of their God? Why consult the dead on behalf of the living?
Isa 55 [6]Seek the LORD while he may be found; call on him while he is near.
Hos 10 [12]"Sow for yourselves righteousness, reap the fruit of unfailing love, and break up your unplowed ground; for it is time to seek the LORD, until he comes and showers righteousness on you."
Amos 5 [4]This is what the LORD says to the house of Israel: "Seek me and live. . . ."
Zeph 1 [4]"I will stretch out my hand against Judah and against all who live in Jerusalem. I will cut off from this place every remnant of Baal, the names of the pagan and the idolatrous priests—[5]those who bow down on the roofs to worship the starry host, those who bow down and swear by the LORD and who also swear by Molech, [6]those who turn back from following the LORD and neither seek the LORD nor inquire of him."
Zeph 2 [3]Seek the LORD, all you humble of the land, you who do what he commands. Seek righteousness, seek humility; perhaps you will be sheltered on the day of the LORD's anger.
Matt 6 [33]"But seek first his kingdom and his righteousness, and all these things will be given to you as well."

b) God Desires That People Seek Him

Ps 53 [2]God looks down from heaven on the sons of men to see if there are any who understand, any who seek God.
Acts 17 [27]"God did this so that men would seek him and perhaps reach out for him and find him, though he is not far from each one of us."

2. Attitudes of Those Seeking God

a) God-Seekers Are Committed to Pursuing Him

Deut 4 [29]But if from there you seek the LORD your God, you will find him if you look for him with all your heart and with all your soul.
1 Chron 16 [11]Look to the LORD and his strength; seek his face always.
2 Chron 15 [12]They entered into a covenant to seek the LORD, the God of their fathers, with all their heart and soul.
Ps 27 [4]One thing I ask of the LORD, this is what I seek: that I may dwell in the house of the LORD all the days of my life, to gaze upon the beauty of the LORD and to seek him in his temple.
Ps 63 [1]O God, you are my God, earnestly I seek you; my soul thirsts for you, my body longs for you, in a dry and weary land where there is no water. . . . [8]My soul clings to you; your right hand upholds me.
Ps 119 [2]Blessed are they who keep his statutes and seek him with all their heart.
Isa 26 [9]My soul yearns for you in the night; in the morning my spirit longs for you. When your judgments come upon the earth, the people of the world learn righteousness.
Isa 51 [1]"Listen to me, you who pursue righteousness and who seek the LORD: Look to the rock from which you were cut and to the quarry from which you were hewn. . . ."
Isa 58 [2]"For day after day they seek me out; they seem eager to know my ways, as if they were a nation that does what is right and has not forsaken the commands of its God. They ask me for just decisions and seem eager for God to come near them."
Jer 29 [13]"You will seek me and find me when you seek me with all your heart."
Hos 3 [5]Afterward the Israelites will return and seek the LORD their God and David their king. They will come trembling to the LORD and to his blessings in the last days.

b) God-Seekers Desire His Favor

Ps 45 [12]The Daughter of Tyre will come with a gift, men of wealth will seek your favor.
Jer 26 [19]"Did Hezekiah king of Judah or anyone else in Judah put him to death? Did not Hezekiah fear the LORD and seek his favor? And did not the LORD relent, so that he did not bring the disaster he pronounced against them? We are about to bring a terrible disaster on ourselves!"

c) God-Seekers Have a Sense of Brokenness

2 Chron 7 [14]". . . if my people, who are called by my name, will humble themselves and pray and seek my face and turn from their wicked ways, then will I hear from heaven and will forgive their sin and will heal their land."
Jer 50 [4]"In those days, at that time," declares the LORD, "the people of Israel and the people of Judah together will go in tears to seek the LORD their God."

d) God-Seekers Have a Sense of Urgency

Ps 34 [4]I sought the LORD, and he answered me; he delivered me from all my fears.
Ps 63 [1]O God, you are my God, earnestly I seek you; my soul thirsts for you, my body longs for you, in a dry and weary land where there is no water.
Ps 77 [1]I cried out to God for help; I cried out to God to hear me. [2]When I was in distress, I sought the Lord; at night I stretched out untiring hands and my soul refused to be comforted.
Hos 5 [15]"Then I will go back to my place until they admit their guilt. And they will seek my face; in their misery they will earnestly seek me."
Zech 8 [20]This is what the LORD Almighty says: "Many peoples and the inhabitants of many cities will yet come, [21]and the inhabitants of one city will go to another and say, 'Let us go at once to entreat the LORD and seek the LORD Almighty. I myself am going.' [22]And many peoples and powerful nations will come to Jerusalem to seek the LORD Almighty and to entreat him."

e) God-Seekers Have a Spirit of Thanksgiving

1 Chron 16 [8]Give thanks to the LORD, call on his name; make known among the nations what he has done. . . . [10]Glory in his holy name; let the hearts of those who seek the LORD rejoice.
Ps 22 [26]The poor will eat and be satisfied; they who seek the LORD will praise him—may your hearts live forever!
Ps 40 [16]But may all who seek you rejoice and be glad in you; may those who love your salvation always say, "The LORD be exalted!"
Ps 70 [4]But may all who seek you rejoice and be glad in you; may those who love your salvation always say, "Let God be exalted!"

Ps 105 [3]Glory in his holy name; let the hearts of those who seek the LORD rejoice.

f) God-Seekers Need His Guidance

Exod 18 [15]Moses answered him, "Because the people come to me to seek God's will."
1 Kings 22 [5]But Jehoshaphat also said to the king of Israel, "First seek the counsel of the LORD."

3. Promises to Those Seeking God

a) God-Seekers Are Guaranteed They Will Find God

Prov 8 [17]"I love those who love me, and those who seek me find me."
Isa 45 [19]"I have not spoken in secret, from somewhere in a land of darkness; I have not said to Jacob's descendants, 'Seek me in vain.' I, the LORD, speak the truth; I declare what is right."
Matt 7 [7]"Ask and it will be given to you; seek and you will find; knock and the door will be opened to you. [8]For everyone who asks receives; he who seeks finds; and to him who knocks, the door will be opened."

b) God-Seekers Are Promised Generous Blessing

Ps 24 [3]Who may ascend the hill of the LORD? Who may stand in his holy place? [4]He who has clean hands and a pure heart, who does not lift up his soul to an idol or swear by what is false. [5]He will receive blessing from the LORD and vindication from God his Savior. [6]Such is the generation of those who seek him, who seek your face, O God of Jacob.
Ps 34 [10]The lions may grow weak and hungry, but those who seek the LORD lack no good thing.
Ps 40 [14]May all who seek to take my life be put to shame and confusion; may all who desire my ruin be turned back in disgrace. . . . [16]But may all who seek you rejoice and be glad in you; may those who love your salvation always say, "The LORD be exalted!"
Isa 65 [10]"Sharon will become a pasture for flocks, and the Valley of Achor a resting place for herds, for my people who seek me."
Lam 3 [25]The LORD is good to those whose hope is in him, to the one who seeks him. . . .
Hos 10 [12]"Sow for yourselves righteousness, reap the fruit of unfailing love, and break up your unplowed ground; for it is time to seek the LORD, until he comes and showers righteousness on you."

c) God-Seekers Are Promised Life

Ps 69 [32]The poor will see and be glad—you who seek God, may your hearts live! [33]The LORD hears the needy and does not despise his captive people. [35]. . . for God will save Zion and rebuild the cities of Judah. Then people will settle there and possess it; [36]the children of his servants will inherit it, and those who love his name will dwell there.
Amos 5 [6]Seek the LORD and live, or he will sweep through the house of Joseph like a fire; it will devour, and Bethel will have no one to quench it.

d) God-Seekers Are Promised Moral Sensitivity

Prov 28 [5]Evil men do not understand justice, but those who seek the LORD understand it fully.

e) God-Seekers Are Promised Reward

Heb 11 [6]And without faith it is impossible to please God, because anyone who comes to him must believe that he exists and that he rewards those who earnestly seek him.

f) God-Seekers Are Promised Spiritual Security

Ps 9 [10]Those who know your name will trust in you, for you, LORD, have never forsaken those who seek you.
Zeph 2 [3]Seek the LORD, all you humble of the land, you who do what he commands. Seek righteousness, seek humility; perhaps you will be sheltered on the day of the LORD's anger. . . . [6]The land by the sea, where the Kerethites dwell, will be a place for shepherds and sheep pens. [7]It will belong to the remnant of the house of Judah; there they will find pasture. In the evening they will lie down in the houses of Ashkelon. The LORD their God will care for them; he will restore their fortunes.

4. Examples of Seeking God

a) David Sought God

Ps 34 [4]I sought the LORD, and he answered me; he delivered me from all my fears.

b) Solomon Sought God

1 Chron 28 [9]"And you, my son Solomon, acknowledge the God of your father, and serve him with wholehearted devotion and with a willing mind, for the LORD searches every heart and understands every motive behind the thoughts. If you seek him, he will be found by you; but if you forsake him, he will reject you forever."
2 Chron 6 [12]Then Solomon stood before the altar of the LORD in front of the whole assembly of Israel and spread out his hands. . . . [14]He said: "O LORD, God of Israel, there is no God like you in heaven or on earth—you who keep your covenant of love with your servants who continue wholeheartedly in your way. [15]You have kept your promise to your servant David my father; with your mouth you have promised and with your hand you have fulfilled it—as it is today. . . .

[18]"But will God really dwell on earth with men? The heavens, even the highest heavens, cannot contain you. How much less this temple I have built!"

c) The Builders of Solomon's Temple Were Commanded to Seek God

1 Chron 22 [19]"Now devote your heart and soul to seeking the LORD your God. Begin to build the sanctuary of the LORD God, so that you may bring the ark of the covenant of the LORD and the sacred articles belonging to God into the temple that will be built for the Name of the LORD."

d) Israel Sought God

2 Chron 11 [16]Those from every tribe of Israel who set their hearts on seeking the LORD, the God of Israel, followed the Levites to Jerusalem to offer sacrifices to the LORD, the God of their fathers.
2 Chron 20 [4]The people of Judah came together to seek help from the LORD; indeed, they came from every town in Judah to seek him.
2 Chron 30 [18]Although most of the many people who came from Ephraim, Manasseh, Issachar and Zebulun had not purified themselves, yet they ate the Passover, contrary to what was written. But Hezekiah prayed for them, saying, "May the LORD, who is good, pardon everyone [19]who sets his heart on seeking God—the LORD, the God of his fathers—even if he is not clean according to the rules of the sanctuary." [20]And the LORD heard Hezekiah and healed the people.
Ezra 6 [21]So the Israelites who had returned from the exile ate it, together with all who had separated themselves from the unclean practices of their Gentile neighbors in order to seek the LORD, the God of Israel.
Jer 50 [4]"In those days, at that time," declares the LORD, "the people of Israel and the people of Judah together will go in tears to seek the LORD their God."
Mal 3 [1]"See, I will send my messenger, who will prepare the way before me. Then suddenly the Lord you are seeking will come to his temple; the messenger of the covenant, whom you desire, will come," says the LORD Almighty.

e) Asa Sought God

2 Chron 14 [2]Asa did what was good and right in the eyes of the LORD his God. [3]He removed the foreign altars and the high places, smashed the sacred stones and cut down the Asherah poles. [4]He commanded Judah to seek the LORD, the God of their fathers, and to obey his laws and commands. . . .

[7]"Let us build up these towns," he said to Judah, "and put walls around them, with towers, gates and bars. The land is still ours, because we have sought the LORD our God; we sought him and he has given us rest on every side." So they built and prospered.

2 Chron 15 [2]He went out to meet Asa and said to him, "Listen to me, Asa and all Judah and Benjamin. The LORD is with you when you are with him. If you seek him, he will be found by you, but if you forsake him, he will forsake you."

f) Jehoshaphat Sought God

2 Chron 17 [3]The LORD was with Jehoshaphat because in his early years he walked in the ways his father David had followed. He did not consult the Baals [4]but sought the God of his father and followed his commands rather than the practices of Israel.
2 Chron 19 [1]When Jehoshaphat king of Judah returned safely to his palace in Jerusalem, [2]Jehu the seer, the son of Hanani, went out to meet him and said to the king, "Should you help the wicked and love those who hate the LORD? Because of this, the wrath of the LORD is upon you. [3]There is, however, some good in you, for you have rid the land of the Asherah poles and have set your heart on seeking God."
2 Chron 22 [9]He then went in search of Ahaziah, and his men captured him while he was hiding in Samaria. He was brought to Jehu and put to death. They buried him, for they said, "He was a son of Jehoshaphat, who sought the LORD with all his heart." So there was no one in the house of Ahaziah powerful enough to retain the kingdom.

g) Uzziah Sought God

2 Chron 26 [3]Uzziah was sixteen years old when he became king, and he reigned in Jerusalem fifty-two years. His mother's name was Jecoliah; she was from Jerusalem. [4]He did what was right in the eyes of the LORD, just as his father Amaziah had done. [5]He sought God during the days of Zechariah, who instructed him in the fear of God. As long as he sought the LORD, God gave him success.

h) Hezekiah Sought God

2 Chron 31 [20]This is what Hezekiah did throughout Judah, doing what was good and right and faithful before the LORD his God. [21]In everything that he undertook in the service of God's temple and in obedience to the law and the commands, he sought his God and worked wholeheartedly. And so he prospered.

i) Josiah Sought God

2 Chron 34 [1]Josiah was eight years old when he became king, and he reigned in Jerusalem thirty-one years. [2]He did what was right in the eyes of the LORD and walked in the ways of his father David, not turning aside to the right or to the left.

[3]In the eighth year of his reign, while he was still young, he began to seek the God of his father David. In his twelfth year he began to purge Judah and Jerusalem of high places, Asherah poles, carved idols and cast images.

j) Multitudes Will Seek God

Isa 11 [10]In that day the Root of Jesse will stand as a banner for the peoples; the nations will rally to him, and his place of rest will be glorious.
Zech 8 [21]". . . and the inhabitants of one city will go to another and say, 'Let us go at once to entreat the LORD and seek the LORD Almighty. I myself am going.' [22]And many peoples and powerful nations will come to Jerusalem to seek the LORD Almighty and to entreat him."

[23]This is what the LORD Almighty says: "In those days ten men from all languages and nations will take firm hold of one Jew by the hem of his robe and say, 'Let us go with you, because we have heard that God is with you.'"

5. The Hindrance to Seeking God: Sin

Prov 1 [24]"But since you rejected me when I called and no one gave heed when I stretched out my hand, . . . [26]I in turn will laugh at your disaster; I will mock when calamity overtakes you. . . .

[28]"Then they will call to me but I will not answer; they will look for me but will not find me."
Isa 9 [13]But the people have not returned to him who struck them, nor have they sought the LORD Almighty. [14]So the LORD will cut off from Israel both head and tail, both palm branch and reed in a single day. . . .
Hos 5 [4]"Their deeds do not permit them to return to their God. A spirit of prostitution is in their heart; they do not acknowledge the LORD. [5]Israel's arrogance testifies against them; the Israelites, even Ephraim, stumble in their sin; Judah also stumbles with them. [6]When they go with their flocks and herds to seek the LORD, they will not find him; he has withdrawn himself from them."
Hos 7 [10]"Israel's arrogance testifies against him, but despite all this he does not return to the LORD his God or search for him."

B. Draw Near to God

Lev 10 [3]Moses then said to Aaron, "This is what the LORD spoke of when he said: 'Among those who approach me I will show myself holy; in the sight of all the people I will be honored.'"

Aaron remained silent.
Ps 65 [2]O you who hear prayer, to you all men will come. . . . [4]Blessed are those you choose and bring near to live in your courts! We are filled with the good things of your house, of your holy temple.
Ps 73 [28]But as for me, it is good to be near God. I have made the Sovereign LORD my refuge; I will tell of all your deeds.
Isa 55 [3]"Give ear and come to me; hear me, that your soul may live. I will make an everlasting covenant with you, my faithful love promised to David."
Jer 3 [22]"Return, faithless people; I will cure you of backsliding."

"Yes, we will come to you, for you are the LORD our God."
Jer 30 [21]"'Their leader will be one of their own; their ruler will arise from among them. I will bring him near and he will come close to me, for who is he who will devote himself to be close to me?' declares the LORD.

[22]"'So you will be my people, and I will be your God.'"
Heb 7 [18]The former regulation is set aside because it was weak and useless [19](for the law made nothing perfect), and a better hope is introduced, by which we draw near to God.
Heb 10 [22]let us draw near to God with a sincere heart in full assurance of faith, having our hearts sprinkled to cleanse us from a guilty conscience and having our bodies washed with pure water.
James 4 [8]Come near to God and he will come near to you. Wash your hands, you sinners, and purify your hearts, you double-minded.

C. Wait upon God

1. Waiting on God

Ps 5 [3]In the morning, O LORD, you hear my voice; in the morning I lay my requests before you and wait in expectation.
Ps 27 [14]Wait for the LORD; be strong and take heart and wait for the LORD.
Ps 33 [20]We wait in hope for the LORD; he is our help and our shield.
Ps 37 [7]Be still before the LORD and wait patiently for him; do not fret when men succeed in their ways, when they carry out their wicked schemes. . . .

[34]Wait for the LORD and keep his way. He will exalt you to inherit the land; when the wicked are cut off, you will see it.
Ps 38 [15]I wait for you, O LORD; you will answer, O Lord my God.
Ps 40 [1]I waited patiently for the LORD; he turned to me and heard my cry.
Ps 59 [9]O my Strength, I watch for you; you, O God, are my fortress, [10]my loving God.

God will go before me and will let me gloat over those who slander me.
Ps 119 [166]I wait for your salvation, O LORD, and I follow your commands.
Ps 130 [5]I wait for the LORD, my soul waits, and in his word I put my hope. [6]My soul waits for the Lord more than watchmen wait for the morning, more than watchmen wait for the morning.
Prov 20 [22]Do not say, "I'll pay you back for this wrong!" Wait for the LORD, and he will deliver you.

Isa 8 17I will wait for the LORD, who is hiding his face from the house of Jacob. I will put my trust in him.
Isa 26 8Yes, LORD, walking in the way of your laws, we wait for you; your name and renown are the desire of our hearts.
Isa 30 18Yet the LORD longs to be gracious to you; he rises to show you compassion. For the LORD is a God of justice. Blessed are all who wait for him!
Isa 51 5"My righteousness draws near speedily, my salvation is on the way, and my arm will bring justice to the nations. The islands will look to me and wait in hope for my arm."
Isa 64 4Since ancient times no one has heard, no ear has perceived, no eye has seen any God besides you, who acts on behalf of those who wait for him.
Lam 3 24I say to myself, "The LORD is my portion; therefore I will wait for him." 26. . . it is good to wait quietly for the salvation of the LORD.
Hos 12 6But you must return to your God; maintain love and justice, and wait for your God always.
Mic 7 7But as for me, I watch in hope for the LORD, I wait for God my Savior; my God will hear me.
Zeph 3 8"Therefore wait for me," declares the LORD, "for the day I will stand up to testify. I have decided to assemble the nations, to gather the kingdoms and to pour out my wrath on them—all my fierce anger. The whole world will be consumed by the fire of my jealous anger."
Mark 15 43Joseph of Arimathea, a prominent member of the Council, who was himself waiting for the kingdom of God, went boldly to Pilate and asked for Jesus' body.
Rev 6 9When he opened the fifth seal, I saw under the altar the souls of those who had been slain because of the word of God and the testimony they had maintained. 10They called out in a loud voice, "How long, Sovereign Lord, holy and true, until you judge the inhabitants of the earth and avenge our blood?" 11Then each of them was given a white robe, and they were told to wait a little longer, until the number of their fellow servants and brothers who were to be killed as they had been was completed.

2. Waiting on Christ

Luke 2 25Now there was a man in Jerusalem called Simeon, who was righteous and devout. He was waiting for the consolation of Israel, and the Holy Spirit was upon him.
Luke 12 35"Be dressed ready for service and keep your lamps burning, 36like men waiting for their master to return from a wedding banquet, so that when he comes and knocks they can immediately open the door for him. 37It will be good for those servants whose master finds them watching when he comes. I tell you the truth, he will dress himself to serve, will have them recline at the table and will come and wait on them. 38It will be good for those servants whose master finds them ready, even if he comes in the second or third watch of the night. 39But understand this: If the owner of the house had known at what hour the thief was coming, he would not have let his house be broken into. 40You also must be ready, because the Son of Man will come at an hour when you do not expect him."
Rom 8 23Not only so, but we ourselves, who have the firstfruits of the Spirit, groan inwardly as we wait eagerly for our adoption as sons, the redemption of our bodies. 24For in this hope we were saved. But hope that is seen is no hope at all. Who hopes for what he already has? 25But if we hope for what we do not yet have, we wait for it patiently.
1 Cor 1 5For in him you have been enriched in every way—in all your speaking and in all your knowledge. . . . 7Therefore you do not lack any spiritual gift as you eagerly wait for our Lord Jesus Christ to be revealed.
1 Cor 4 5Therefore judge nothing before the appointed time; wait till the Lord comes. He will bring to light what is hidden in darkness and will expose the motives of men's hearts. At that time each will receive his praise from God.
Gal 5 5But by faith we eagerly await through the Spirit the righteousness for which we hope.
1 Thess 1 9for they themselves report what kind of reception you gave us. They tell how you turned to God from idols to serve the living and true God, 10and to wait for his Son from heaven, whom he raised from the dead—Jesus, who rescues us from the coming wrath.
Titus 2 13while we wait for the blessed hope—the glorious appearing of our great God and Savior, Jesus Christ . . .
Heb 9 28so Christ was sacrificed once to take away the sins of many people; and he will appear a second time, not to bear sin, but to bring salvation to those who are waiting for him.
James 5 7Be patient, then, brothers, until the Lord's coming. See how the farmer waits for the land to yield its valuable crop and how patient he is for the autumn and spring rains. 8You too, be patient and stand firm, because the Lord's coming is near.
Jude 21Keep yourselves in God's love as you wait for the mercy of our Lord Jesus Christ to bring you to eternal life.

D. Fast

1. Attitudes toward Fasting

a) Fasting Does Not Replace God-Given Responsibilities

Zech 7 1In the fourth year of King Darius, the word of the LORD came to Zechariah on the fourth day of the ninth month, the month of Kislev. 2The people of Bethel had sent Sharezer and Regem-Melech, together with their men, to entreat the LORD 3by asking the priests of the house of the LORD Almighty and the prophets, "Should I mourn and fast in the fifth month, as I have done for so many years?"

4Then the word of the LORD Almighty came to me: 5"Ask all the people of the land and the priests, 'When you fasted and mourned in the fifth and seventh months for the past seventy years, was it really for me that you fasted? 6And when you were eating and drinking, were you not just feasting for yourselves? 7Are these not the words the LORD proclaimed through the earlier prophets when Jerusalem and its surrounding towns were at rest and prosperous, and the Negev and the western foothills were settled?'"

8And the word of the LORD came again to Zechariah: 9"This is what the LORD Almighty says: 'Administer true justice; show mercy and compassion to one another. 10Do not oppress the widow or the fatherless, the alien or the poor. In your hearts do not think evil of each other.'

11"But they refused to pay attention; stubbornly they turned their backs and stopped up their ears. 12They made their hearts as hard as flint and would not listen to the law or to the words that the LORD Almighty had sent by his Spirit through the earlier prophets. So the LORD Almighty was very angry.

13"'When I called, they did not listen; so when they called, I would not listen,' says the LORD Almighty. 14'I scattered them with a whirlwind among all the nations, where they were strangers. The land was left so desolate behind them that no one could come or go. This is how they made the pleasant land desolate.'"

b) Fasting Is Accompanied by Humiliation and Prayer

Judg 20 26Then the Israelites, all the people, went up to Bethel, and there they sat weeping before the LORD. They fasted that day until evening and presented burnt offerings and fellowship offerings to the LORD. 27And the Israelites inquired of the LORD. (In those days the ark of the covenant of God was there, 28with Phinehas son of Eleazar, the son of Aaron, ministering before it.) They asked, "Shall we go up again to battle with Benjamin our brother, or not?"

The LORD responded, "Go, for tomorrow I will give them into your hands."
Ezra 8 21There, by the Ahava Canal, I proclaimed a fast, so that we might humble ourselves before our God and ask him for a safe journey for us and our children, with all our possessions. 22I was ashamed to ask the king for soldiers and horsemen to protect us from enemies on the road, because we had told the king, "The gracious hand of our God is on everyone who looks to him, but his great anger is against all who forsake him." 23So we fasted and petitioned our God about this, and he answered our prayer.
Neh 1 4When I heard these things, I sat down and wept. For

some days I mourned and fasted and prayed before the God of heaven.

Ps 35 [13]Yet when they were ill, I put on sackcloth and humbled myself with fasting. When my prayers returned to me unanswered . . .

Ps 69 [10]When I weep and fast, I must endure scorn. . . .

Ps 109 [22]For I am poor and needy, and my heart is wounded within me. [23]I fade away like an evening shadow; I am shaken off like a locust. [24]My knees give way from fasting; my body is thin and gaunt. [25]I am an object of scorn to my accusers; when they see me, they shake their heads.

Dan 9 [3]So I turned to the Lord God and pleaded with him in prayer and petition, in fasting, and in sackcloth and ashes.

Dan 10 [2]At that time I, Daniel, mourned for three weeks. [3]I ate no choice food; no meat or wine touched my lips; and I used no lotions at all until the three weeks were over.

Acts 9 [8]Saul got up from the ground, but when he opened his eyes he could see nothing. So they led him by the hand into Damascus. [9]For three days he was blind, and did not eat or drink anything.

[10]In Damascus there was a disciple named Ananias. The Lord called to him in a vision, "Ananias!"

"Yes, Lord," he answered.

[11]The Lord told him, "Go to the house of Judas on Straight Street and ask for a man from Tarsus named Saul, for he is praying."

c) Fasting Is an Act of Piety Directed toward God

Matt 6 [16]"When you fast, do not look somber as the hypocrites do, for they disfigure their faces to show men they are fasting. I tell you the truth, they have received their reward in full. [17]But when you fast, put oil on your head and wash your face, [18]so that it will not be obvious to men that you are fasting, but only to your Father, who is unseen; and your Father, who sees what is done in secret, will reward you."

Mark 2 [18]Now John's disciples and the Pharisees were fasting. Some people came and asked Jesus, "How is it that John's disciples and the disciples of the Pharisees are fasting, but yours are not?"

[19]Jesus answered, "How can the guests of the bridegroom fast while he is with them? They cannot, so long as they have him with them. [20]But the time will come when the bridegroom will be taken from them, and on that day they will fast."

d) Fasting Is an Act of Worship

Luke 2 [36]There was also a prophetess, Anna, the daughter of Phanuel, of the tribe of Asher. She was very old; she had lived with her husband seven years after her marriage, [37]and then was a widow until she was eighty-four. She never left the temple but worshiped night and day, fasting and praying.

e) Fasting Is Commanded by God

Lev 16 [29]"This is to be a lasting ordinance for you: On the tenth day of the seventh month you must deny yourselves and not do any work—whether native-born or an alien living among you—[30]because on this day atonement will be made for you, to cleanse you. Then, before the LORD, you will be clean from all your sins. [31]It is a sabbath of rest, and you must deny yourselves; it is a lasting ordinance."

Lev 23 [26]The LORD said to Moses, [27]"The tenth day of this seventh month is the Day of Atonement. Hold a sacred assembly and deny yourselves, and present an offering made to the LORD by fire. [28]Do no work on that day, because it is the Day of Atonement, when atonement is made for you before the LORD your God. [29]Anyone who does not deny himself on that day must be cut off from his people. [30]I will destroy from among his people anyone who does any work on that day. [31]You shall do no work at all. This is to be a lasting ordinance for the generations to come, wherever you live. [32]It is a sabbath of rest for you, and you must deny yourselves. From the evening of the ninth day of the month until the following evening you are to observe your sabbath."

f) Fasting Is Meaningless without Repentance

Isa 58 [1]"Shout it aloud, do not hold back. Raise your voice like a trumpet. Declare to my people their rebellion and to the house of Jacob their sins. [2]For day after day they seek me out; they seem eager to know my ways, as if they were a nation that does what is right and has not forsaken the commands of its God. They ask me for just decisions and seem eager for God to come near them. [3]'Why have we fasted,' they say, 'and you have not seen it? Why have we humbled ourselves, and you have not noticed?'

"Yet on the day of your fasting, you do as you please and exploit all your workers. [4]Your fasting ends in quarreling and strife, and in striking each other with wicked fists. You cannot fast as you do today and expect your voice to be heard on high. [5]Is this the kind of fast I have chosen, only a day for a man to humble himself? Is it only for bowing one's head like a reed and for lying on sackcloth and ashes? Is that what you call a fast, a day acceptable to the LORD?

[6]"Is not this the kind of fasting I have chosen: to loose the chains of injustice and untie the cords of the yoke, to set the oppressed free and break every yoke? [7]Is it not to share your food with the hungry and to provide the poor wanderer with shelter—when you see the naked, to clothe him, and not to turn away from your own flesh and blood? [8]Then your light will break forth like the dawn, and your healing will quickly appear; then your righteousness will go before you, and the glory of the LORD will be your rear guard. [9]Then you will call, and the LORD will answer; you will cry for help, and he will say: Here am I.

"If you do away with the yoke of oppression, with the pointing finger and malicious talk, [10]and if you spend yourselves in behalf of the hungry and satisfy the needs of the oppressed, then your light will rise in the darkness, and your night will become like the noonday."

Jer 14 [10]This is what the LORD says about this people: "They greatly love to wander; they do not restrain their feet. So the LORD does not accept them; he will now remember their wickedness and punish them for their sins."

[11]Then the LORD said to me, "Do not pray for the well-being of this people. [12]Although they fast, I will not listen to their cry; though they offer burnt offerings and grain offerings, I will not accept them. Instead, I will destroy them with the sword, famine and plague."

Luke 18 [9]To some who were confident of their own righteousness and looked down on everybody else, Jesus told this parable: [10]"Two men went up to the temple to pray, one a Pharisee and the other a tax collector. [11]The Pharisee stood up and prayed about himself: 'God, I thank you that I am not like other men—robbers, evildoers, adulterers—or even like this tax collector. [12]I fast twice a week and give a tenth of all I get.'

[13]"But the tax collector stood at a distance. He would not even look up to heaven, but beat his breast and said, 'God, have mercy on me, a sinner.'

[14]"I tell you that this man, rather than the other, went home justified before God. For everyone who exalts himself will be humbled, and he who humbles himself will be exalted."

g) Fasting Necessitates a Spirit of Repentance

Joel 1 [13]Put on sackcloth, O priests, and mourn; wail, you who minister before the altar. Come, spend the night in sackcloth, you who minister before my God; for the grain offerings and drink offerings are withheld from the house of your God. [14]Declare a holy fast; call a sacred assembly. Summon the elders and all who live in the land to the house of the LORD your God, and cry out to the LORD.

Joel 2 [12]"Even now," declares the LORD, "return to me with all your heart, with fasting and weeping and mourning."

[13]Rend your heart and not your garments. Return to the LORD your God, for he is gracious and compassionate, slow to anger and abounding in love, and he relents from sending calamity.

Jon 3 [1]Then the word of the LORD came to Jonah a second time: [2]"Go to the great city of Nineveh and proclaim to it the message I give you."

[3]Jonah obeyed the word of the LORD and went to Nineveh. Now Nineveh was a very important city—a visit required three days. [4]On the first day, Jonah started into the city. He proclaimed: "Forty more days and Nineveh will be overturned."

[5]The Ninevites believed God. They declared a fast, and all of them, from the greatest to the least, put on sackcloth.

[6]When the news reached the king of Nineveh, he rose from his throne, took off his royal robes, covered himself with sackcloth and sat down in the dust. [7]Then he issued a proclamation in Nineveh: "By the decree of the king and his nobles: Do not let any man or beast, herd or flock, taste anything; do not let them eat or drink. [8]But let man and beast be covered with sackcloth. Let everyone call urgently on God. Let them give up their evil ways and their violence. [9]Who knows? God may yet relent and with compassion turn from his fierce anger so that we will not perish."

[10]When God saw what they did and how they turned from their evil ways, he had compassion and did not bring upon them the destruction he had threatened.

h) Fasting Should Be Accompanied by Confession

1 Sam 7 [5]Then Samuel said, "Assemble all Israel at Mizpah and I will intercede with the LORD for you." [6]When they had assembled at Mizpah, they drew water and poured it out before the LORD. On that day they fasted and there they confessed, "We have sinned against the LORD." And Samuel was leader of Israel at Mizpah.

Neh 9 [1]On the twenty-fourth day of the same month, the Israelites gathered together, fasting and wearing sackcloth and having dust on their heads. [2]Those of Israelite descent had separated themselves from all foreigners. They stood in their places and confessed their sins and the wickedness of their fathers.

Dan 9 [3]So I turned to the Lord God and pleaded with him in prayer and petition, in fasting, and in sackcloth and ashes.

[4]I prayed to the LORD my God and confessed: "O Lord, the great and awesome God, who keeps his covenant of love with all who love him and obey his commands, [5]we have sinned and done wrong. We have been wicked and have rebelled; we have turned away from your commands and laws. [6]We have not listened to your servants the prophets, who spoke in your name to our kings, our princes and our fathers, and to all the people of the land."

2. Occasions for Fasting

a) Fasting When Commissioning Ministers

Acts 13 [1]In the church at Antioch there were prophets and teachers: Barnabas, Simeon called Niger, Lucius of Cyrene, Manaen (who had been brought up with Herod the tetrarch) and Saul. [2]While they were worshiping the Lord and fasting, the Holy Spirit said, "Set apart for me Barnabas and Saul for the work to which I have called them." [3]So after they had fasted and prayed, they placed their hands on them and sent them off.

Acts 14 [23]Paul and Barnabas appointed elders for them in each church and, with prayer and fasting, committed them to the Lord, in whom they had put their trust.

b) Fasting on Special Days and with Regularity

(1) Fasting in Israel

Lev 23 [14]"'You must not eat any bread, or roasted or new grain, until the very day you bring this offering to your God. This is to be a lasting ordinance for the generations to come, wherever you live.'"

Num 29 [7]"'On the tenth day of this seventh month hold a sacred assembly. You must deny yourselves and do no work.'"

Esther 9 [30]And Mordecai sent letters to all the Jews in the 127 provinces of the kingdom of Xerxes—words of goodwill and assurance—[31]to establish these days of Purim at their designated times, as Mordecai the Jew and Queen Esther had decreed for them, and as they had established for themselves and their descendants in regard to their times of fasting and lamentation.

Zech 7 [2]The people of Bethel had sent Sharezer and Regem-Melech, together with their men, to entreat the LORD [3]by asking the priests of the house of the LORD Almighty and the prophets, "Should I mourn and fast in the fifth month, as I have done for so many years?"

Zech 8 [19]This is what the LORD Almighty says: "The fasts of the fourth, fifth, seventh and tenth months will become joyful and glad occasions and happy festivals for Judah. Therefore love truth and peace."

(2) Anna and Fasting

Luke 2 [36]There was also a prophetess, Anna, the daughter of Phanuel, of the tribe of Asher. She was very old; she had lived with her husband seven years after her marriage, [37]and then was a widow until she was eighty-four. She never left the temple but worshiped night and day, fasting and praying.

(3) John the Baptist and Fasting

Matt 11 [18]"For John came neither eating nor drinking, and they say, 'He has a demon.'"

Luke 7 [33]"For John the Baptist came neither eating bread nor drinking wine, and you say, 'He has a demon.'"

(4) John the Baptist's Disciples and Fasting

Matt 9 [14]Then John's disciples came and asked him, "How is it that we and the Pharisees fast, but your disciples do not fast?"

Mark 2 [18]Now John's disciples and the Pharisees were fasting. Some people came and asked Jesus, "How is it that John's disciples and the disciples of the Pharisees are fasting, but yours are not?"

(5) The Pharisees and Fasting

Mark 2 [18]Now John's disciples and the Pharisees were fasting. Some people came and asked Jesus, "How is it that John's disciples and the disciples of the Pharisees are fasting, but yours are not?"

Luke 18 [11]"The Pharisee stood up and prayed about himself: 'God, I thank you that I am not like other men—robbers, evildoers, adulterers—or even like this tax collector. [12]I fast twice a week and give a tenth of all I get.'"

c) Fasting When Facing Dangerous Enemies

(1) Jehoshaphat Fasted in the Face of Danger

2 Chron 20 [1]After this, the Moabites and Ammonites with some of the Meunites came to make war on Jehoshaphat.

[2]Some men came and told Jehoshaphat, "A vast army is coming against you from Edom, from the other side of the Sea. It is already in Hazazon Tamar" (that is, En Gedi). [3]Alarmed, Jehoshaphat resolved to inquire of the LORD, and he proclaimed a fast for all Judah. [4]The people of Judah came together to seek help from the LORD; indeed, they came from every town in Judah to seek him.

(2) Saul and His Army Fasted in the Face of Danger

1 Sam 14 [24]Now the men of Israel were in distress that day, because Saul had bound the people under an oath, saying, "Cursed be any man who eats food before evening comes, before I have avenged myself on my enemies!" So none of the troops tasted food.

1 Sam 28 [15]Samuel said to Saul, "Why have you disturbed me by bringing me up?"

"I am in great distress," Saul said. "The Philistines are fighting against me, and God has turned away from me. He no longer answers me, either by prophets or by dreams. So I have called on you to tell me what to do." . . .

[20]Immediately Saul fell full length on the ground, filled with fear because of Samuel's words. His strength was gone, for he had eaten nothing all that day and night.

[21]When the woman came to Saul and saw that he was greatly shaken, she said, "Look, your maidservant has obeyed you. I took my life in my hands and did what you told me to do. [22]Now please listen to your servant and let me give you some food so you may eat and have the strength to go on your way."

[23]He refused and said, "I will not eat."

But his men joined the woman in urging him, and he listened to them. He got up from the ground and sat on the couch.

(3) Esther Fasted in the Face of Danger

Esther 4 [15]Then Esther sent this reply to Mordecai: [16]"Go, gather together all the Jews who are in Susa, and fast for me. Do not eat or drink for three days, night or day. I and my maids will fast as you do. When this is done, I will go to the king, even though it is against the law. And if I perish, I perish."

d) *Fasting When Facing Judgment from God*

(1) Moses Fasted in the Face of Judgment

Deut 9 [7]Remember this and never forget how you provoked the LORD your God to anger in the desert. From the day you left Egypt until you arrived here, you have been rebellious against the LORD. [8]At Horeb you aroused the LORD's wrath so that he was angry enough to destroy you. [9]When I went up on the mountain to receive the tablets of stone, the tablets of the covenant that the LORD had made with you, I stayed on the mountain forty days and forty nights; I ate no bread and drank no water. . . .

[18]Then once again I fell prostrate before the LORD for forty days and forty nights; I ate no bread and drank no water, because of all the sin you had committed, doing what was evil in the LORD's sight and so provoking him to anger. [19]I feared the anger and wrath of the LORD, for he was angry enough with you to destroy you. But again the LORD listened to me.

(2) Ahab Fasted in the Face of Judgment

1 Kings 21 [27]When Ahab heard these words, he tore his clothes, put on sackcloth and fasted. He lay in sackcloth and went around meekly.

[28]Then the word of the LORD came to Elijah the Tishbite: [29]"Have you noticed how Ahab has humbled himself before me? Because he has humbled himself, I will not bring this disaster in his day, but I will bring it on his house in the days of his son."

(3) Baruch Fasted in the Face of Judgment

Jer 36 [5]Then Jeremiah told Baruch, "I am restricted; I cannot go to the LORD's temple. [6]So you go to the house of the LORD on a day of fasting and read to the people from the scroll the words of the LORD that you wrote as I dictated. Read them to all the people of Judah who come in from their towns. [7]Perhaps they will bring their petition before the LORD, and each will turn from his wicked ways, for the anger and wrath pronounced against this people by the LORD are great."

[8]Baruch son of Neriah did everything Jeremiah the prophet told him to do; at the LORD's temple he read the words of the LORD from the scroll. [9]In the ninth month of the fifth year of Jehoiakim son of Josiah king of Judah, a time of fasting before the LORD was proclaimed for all the people in Jerusalem and those who had come from the towns of Judah.

(4) Joel Fasted in the Face of Judgment

Joel 1 [14]Declare a holy fast; call a sacred assembly. Summon the elders and all who live in the land to the house of the LORD your God, and cry out to the LORD.

[15]Alas for that day! For the day of the LORD is near; it will come like destruction from the Almighty.

Joel 2 [15]Blow the trumpet in Zion, declare a holy fast, call a sacred assembly. [16]Gather the people, consecrate the assembly; bring together the elders, gather the children, those nursing at the breast. Let the bridegroom leave his room and the bride her chamber. [17]Let the priests, who minister before the LORD, weep between the temple porch and the altar. Let them say, "Spare your people, O LORD. Do not make your inheritance an object of scorn, a byword among the nations. Why should they say among the peoples, 'Where is their God?'"

(5) The Ninevites Fasted in the Face of Judgment

Jon 3 [4]On the first day, Jonah started into the city. He proclaimed: "Forty more days and Nineveh will be overturned." [5]The Ninevites believed God. They declared a fast, and all of them, from the greatest to the least, put on sackcloth.

e) *Fasting in Times of Affliction and Spiritual Distress*

(1) David Fasted When Afflicted

2 Sam 12 [15]After Nathan had gone home, the LORD struck the child that Uriah's wife had borne to David, and he became ill. [16]David pleaded with God for the child. He fasted and went into his house and spent the nights lying on the ground. [17]The elders of his household stood beside him to get him up from the ground, but he refused, and he would not eat any food with them.

[18]On the seventh day the child died. David's servants were afraid to tell him that the child was dead, for they thought, "While the child was still living, we spoke to David but he would not listen to us. How can we tell him the child is dead? He may do something desperate."

[19]David noticed that his servants were whispering among themselves and he realized the child was dead. "Is the child dead?" he asked.

"Yes," they replied, "he is dead."

[20]Then David got up from the ground. After he had washed, put on lotions and changed his clothes, he went into the house of the LORD and worshiped. Then he went to his own house, and at his request they served him food, and he ate.

[21]His servants asked him, "Why are you acting this way? While the child was alive, you fasted and wept, but now that the child is dead, you get up and eat!"

[22]He answered, "While the child was still alive, I fasted and wept. I thought, 'Who knows? The LORD may be gracious to me and let the child live.' [23]But now that he is dead, why should I fast? Can I bring him back again? I will go to him, but he will not return to me."

Ps 69 [8]I am a stranger to my brothers, an alien to my own mother's sons; [9]for zeal for your house consumes me, and the insults of those who insult you fall on me. [10]When I weep and fast, I must endure scorn. . . .

Ps 109 [22]For I am poor and needy, and my heart is wounded within me. [23]I fade away like an evening shadow; I am shaken off like a locust. [24]My knees give way from fasting; my body is thin and gaunt.

(2) Jonathan Fasted When Afflicted

1 Sam 20 [34]Jonathan got up from the table in fierce anger; on that second day of the month he did not eat, because he was grieved at his father's shameful treatment of David.

(3) Ezra Fasted When Afflicted

Ezra 8 [21]There, by the Ahava Canal, I proclaimed a fast, so that we might humble ourselves before our God and ask him for a safe journey for us and our children, with all our possessions. [22]I was ashamed to ask the king for soldiers and horsemen to protect us from enemies on the road, because we had told the king, "The gracious hand of our God is on everyone who looks to him, but his great anger is against all who forsake him." [23]So we fasted and petitioned our God about this, and he answered our prayer.

(4) Darius Fasted When Afflicted

Dan 6 [17]A stone was brought and placed over the mouth of the den, and the king sealed it with his own signet ring and with the rings of his nobles, so that Daniel's situation might not be changed. [18]Then the king returned to his palace and spent the night without eating and without any entertainment being brought to him. And he could not sleep.

(5) Daniel Fasted When Afflicted

Dan 9 [2]in the first year of his reign, I, Daniel, understood from the Scriptures, according to the word of the LORD given to Jeremiah the prophet, that the desolation of Jerusalem would last seventy years. [3]So I turned to the Lord God and pleaded with him in prayer and petition, in fasting, and in sackcloth and ashes.

Dan 10 [2]At that time I, Daniel, mourned for three weeks. [3]I ate no choice food; no meat or wine touched my lips; and I used no lotions at all until the three weeks were over.

(6) Israel Fasted When Afflicted

Esther 4 [3]In every province to which the edict and order of the king came, there was great mourning among the Jews, with fasting, weeping and wailing. Many lay in sackcloth and ashes.

(7) Christ Fasted When Distressed

Matt 4 [1]Then Jesus was led by the Spirit into the desert to be tempted by the devil. [2]After fasting forty days and forty nights, he was hungry. [3]The tempter came to him and said, "If you are the Son of God, tell these stones to become bread."

[4]Jesus answered, "It is written: 'Man does not live on bread alone, but on every word that comes from the mouth of God.'"

[5]Then the devil took him to the holy city and had him stand on the highest point of the temple. [6]"If you are the Son of God," he said, "throw yourself down. For it is written: 'He will com-

mand his angels concerning you, and they will lift you up in their hands, so that you will not strike your foot against a stone.'"

[7]Jesus answered him, "It is also written: 'Do not put the Lord your God to the test.'"

[8]Again, the devil took him to a very high mountain and showed him all the kingdoms of the world and their splendor. [9]"All this I will give you," he said, "if you will bow down and worship me."

[10]Jesus said to him, "Away from me, Satan! For it is written: 'Worship the Lord your God, and serve him only.'"

[11]Then the devil left him, and angels came and attended him.

Luke 4 [1]Jesus, full of the Holy Spirit, returned from the Jordan and was led by the Spirit in the desert, [2]where for forty days he was tempted by the devil. He ate nothing during those days, and at the end of them he was hungry.

f) Fasting in Times of Bereavement

(1) David Fasted When Saul and Jonathan Died

2 Sam 1 [11]Then David and all the men with him took hold of their clothes and tore them. [12]They mourned and wept and fasted till evening for Saul and his son Jonathan, and for the army of the LORD and the house of Israel, because they had fallen by the sword.

(2) David Fasted When Abner Died

2 Sam 3 [31]Then David said to Joab and all the people with him, "Tear your clothes and put on sackcloth and walk in mourning in front of Abner." King David himself walked behind the bier. [32]They buried Abner in Hebron, and the king wept aloud at Abner's tomb. All the people wept also.

[33]The king sang this lament for Abner: "Should Abner have died as the lawless die? [34]Your hands were not bound, your feet were not fettered. You fell as one falls before wicked men."

And all the people wept over him again.

[35]Then they all came and urged David to eat something while it was still day; but David took an oath, saying, "May God deal with me, be it ever so severely, if I taste bread or anything else before the sun sets!"

[36]All the people took note and were pleased; indeed, everything the king did pleased them. [37]So on that day all the people and all Israel knew that the king had no part in the murder of Abner son of Ner.

(3) The People of Jabesh Gilead Fasted When Saul Died

1 Chron 10 [11]When all the inhabitants of Jabesh Gilead heard of everything the Philistines had done to Saul, [12]all their valiant men went and took the bodies of Saul and his sons and brought them to Jabesh. Then they buried their bones under the great tree in Jabesh, and they fasted seven days.

g) Fasting for the Sake of Others

Ezra 10 [6]Then Ezra withdrew from before the house of God and went to the room of Jehohanan son of Eliashib. While he was there, he ate no food and drank no water, because he continued to mourn over the unfaithfulness of the exiles.

Ps 35 [11]Ruthless witnesses come forward; they question me on things I know nothing about. . . . [13]Yet when they were ill, I put on sackcloth and humbled myself with fasting. When my prayers returned to me unanswered, [14]I went about mourning as though for my friend or brother. I bowed my head in grief as though weeping for my mother.

h) Fasting as a Personal Decision or Testimony

Gen 24 [33]Then food was set before him, but he said, "I will not eat until I have told you what I have to say."

"Then tell us," Laban said.

Dan 1 [12]"Please test your servants for ten days: Give us nothing but vegetables to eat and water to drink. [13]Then compare our appearance with that of the young men who eat the royal food, and treat your servants in accordance with what you see." [14]So he agreed to this and tested them for ten days.

[15]At the end of the ten days they looked healthier and better nourished than any of the young men who ate the royal food. [16]So the guard took away their choice food and the wine they were to drink and gave them vegetables instead.

Acts 9 [8]Saul got up from the ground, but when he opened his eyes he could see nothing. So they led him by the hand into Damascus. [9]For three days he was blind, and did not eat or drink anything.

E. Look to God

1 Chron 16 [11]Look to the LORD and his strength; seek his face always.

Ezra 8 [22]I was ashamed to ask the king for soldiers and horsemen to protect us from enemies on the road, because we had told the king, "The gracious hand of our God is on everyone who looks to him, but his great anger is against all who forsake him."

Ps 34 [5]Those who look to him are radiant; their faces are never covered with shame.

Ps 123 [1]I lift up my eyes to you, to you whose throne is in heaven. [2]As the eyes of slaves look to the hand of their master, as the eyes of a maid look to the hand of her mistress, so our eyes look to the LORD our God, till he shows us his mercy.

Isa 17 [7]In that day men will look to their Maker and turn their eyes to the Holy One of Israel.

VIII
Enjoying God

A. Delight in God

1. God as a Source of Delight

Neh 1 [11]"O Lord, let your ear be attentive to the prayer of this your servant and to the prayer of your servants who delight in revering your name. Give your servant success today by granting him favor in the presence of this man."

I was cupbearer to the king.

Job 22 [23]"If you return to the Almighty, you will be restored: If you remove wickedness far from your tent [24]and assign your nuggets to the dust, your gold of Ophir to the rocks in the ravines, [25]then the Almighty will be your gold, the choicest silver for you. [26]Surely then you will find delight in the Almighty and will lift up your face to God."

Ps 22 [8]"He trusts in the LORD; let the LORD rescue him. Let him deliver him, since he delights in him."

Ps 37 [4]Delight yourself in the LORD and he will give you the desires of your heart.

Ps 43 [3]Send forth your light and your truth, let them guide me; let them bring me to your holy mountain, to the place where you dwell. [4]Then will I go to the altar of God, to God, my joy and my delight. I will praise you with the harp, O God, my God.

Isa 61 [10]I delight greatly in the LORD; my soul rejoices in my God. For he has clothed me with garments of salvation and arrayed me in a robe of righteousness, as a bridegroom adorns his head like a priest, and as a bride adorns herself with her jewels.

2. His Word as a Source of Delight

Ps 1 [2]But his delight is in the law of the LORD, and on his law he meditates day and night.

Ps 112 [1]Praise the LORD.

Blessed is the man who fears the LORD, who finds great delight in his commands.

Ps 119 [16]I delight in your decrees; I will not neglect your word.

Ps 119 [24]Your statutes are my delight; they are my counselors.

Ps 119 [35]Direct me in the path of your commands, for there I find delight.

Ps 119 [47]for I delight in your commands because I love them.

Ps 119 [70]Their hearts are callous and unfeeling, but I delight in your law.

Ps 119 [77]Let your compassion come to me that I may live, for your law is my delight.
Ps 119 [92]If your law had not been my delight, I would have perished in my affliction.
Rom 7 [22]For in my inner being I delight in God's law. . . .

3. His Work as a Source of Delight

1 Sam 2 [1]Then Hannah prayed and said: "My heart rejoices in the LORD; in the LORD my horn is lifted high. My mouth boasts over my enemies, for I delight in your deliverance."
Ps 35 [4]May those who seek my life be disgraced and put to shame; may those who plot my ruin be turned back in dismay. [5]May they be like chaff before the wind, with the angel of the LORD driving them away; [6]may their path be dark and slippery, with the angel of the LORD pursuing them. [7]Since they hid their net for me without cause and without cause dug a pit for me, [8]may ruin overtake them by surprise—may the net they hid entangle them, may they fall into the pit, to their ruin. [9]Then my soul will rejoice in the LORD and delight in his salvation.

B. Rejoice in God

1. Encouragement of Believers to Have Joy

a) Everyone Is to Rejoice

Ps 66 [1]Shout with joy to God, all the earth!
Ps 67 [4]May the nations be glad and sing for joy, for you rule the peoples justly and guide the nations of the earth.
Ps 96 [1]Sing to the LORD a new song; sing to the LORD, all the earth. . . .

[10]Say among the nations, "The LORD reigns." The world is firmly established, it cannot be moved; he will judge the peoples with equity. [11]Let the heavens rejoice, let the earth be glad; let the sea resound, and all that is in it. . . .
Ps 100 [1]Shout for joy to the LORD, all the earth.

b) The Humble and the Needy Are to Rejoice

Isa 29 [19]Once more the humble will rejoice in the LORD; the needy will rejoice in the Holy One of Israel.

c) The Righteous Are to Rejoice

Job 8 [20]"Surely God does not reject a blameless man or strengthen the hands of evildoers. [21]He will yet fill your mouth with laughter and your lips with shouts of joy."
Job 33 [26]"He prays to God and finds favor with him, he sees God's face and shouts for joy; he is restored by God to his righteous state."
Ps 32 [11]Rejoice in the LORD and be glad, you righteous; sing, all you who are upright in heart!
Ps 33 [1]Sing joyfully to the LORD, you righteous; it is fitting for the upright to praise him.
Ps 64 [10]Let the righteous rejoice in the LORD and take refuge in him; let all the upright in heart praise him!
Ps 68 [3]But may the righteous be glad and rejoice before God; may they be happy and joyful.
Ps 97 [11]Light is shed upon the righteous and joy on the upright in heart. [12]Rejoice in the LORD, you who are righteous, and praise his holy name.
Ps 107 [42]The upright see and rejoice, but all the wicked shut their mouths.
Prov 10 [28]The prospect of the righteous is joy, but the hopes of the wicked come to nothing.
Matt 25 [21]"His master replied, 'Well done, good and faithful servant! You have been faithful with a few things; I will put you in charge of many things. Come and share your master's happiness!'"

d) Those Believing in God Are to Rejoice

Ps 33 [21]In him our hearts rejoice, for we trust in his holy name.
Acts 16 [34]The jailer brought them into his house and set a meal before them; he was filled with joy because he had come to believe in God—he and his whole family.
Rom 15 [13]May the God of hope fill you with all joy and peace as you trust in him, so that you may overflow with hope by the power of the Holy Spirit.
Phil 1 [25]Convinced of this, I know that I will remain, and I will continue with all of you for your progress and joy in the faith. . . .
1 Pet 1 [8]Though you have not seen him, you love him; and even though you do not see him now, you believe in him and are filled with an inexpressible and glorious joy. . . .

e) Those Hoping in God Are to Rejoice

Luke 10 [20]"However, do not rejoice that the spirits submit to you, but rejoice that your names are written in heaven."
Rom 5 [1]Therefore, since we have been justified through faith, we have peace with God through our Lord Jesus Christ, [2]through whom we have gained access by faith into this grace in which we now stand. And we rejoice in the hope of the glory of God.
Rom 12 [12]Be joyful in hope, patient in affliction, faithful in prayer.
1 Pet 1 [3]Praise be to the God and Father of our Lord Jesus Christ! In his great mercy he has given us new birth into a living hope through the resurrection of Jesus Christ from the dead. . . . [6]In this you greatly rejoice, though now for a little while you may have had to suffer grief in all kinds of trials.

f) Those Loving God Are to Rejoice

Ps 5 [11]But let all who take refuge in you be glad; let them ever sing for joy. Spread your protection over them, that those who love your name may rejoice in you.

g) Those Seeking God Are to Rejoice

1 Chron 16 [10]Glory in his holy name; let the hearts of those who seek the LORD rejoice.
Ps 40 [16]But may all who seek you rejoice and be glad in you; may those who love your salvation always say, "The LORD be exalted!"
Ps 70 [4]But may all who seek you rejoice and be glad in you; may those who love your salvation always say, "Let God be exalted!"
Ps 105 [3]Glory in his holy name; let the hearts of those who seek the LORD rejoice.

2. The Object of Believers' Joy

a) Believers Rejoice in God

1 Chron 16 [27]Splendor and majesty are before him; strength and joy in his dwelling place.
Ps 2 [11]Serve the LORD with fear and rejoice with trembling.
Ps 4 [3]Know that the LORD has set apart the godly for himself; the LORD will hear when I call to him. . . . [7]You have filled my heart with greater joy than when their grain and new wine abound.
Ps 27 [6]Then my head will be exalted above the enemies who surround me; at his tabernacle will I sacrifice with shouts of joy; I will sing and make music to the LORD.
Ps 42 [4]These things I remember as I pour out my soul: how I used to go with the multitude, leading the procession to the house of God, with shouts of joy and thanksgiving among the festive throng.
Ps 43 [4]Then will I go to the altar of God, to God, my joy and my delight. I will praise you with the harp, O God, my God.
Ps 68 [4]Sing to God, sing praise to his name, extol him who rides on the clouds—his name is the LORD—and rejoice before him.
Ps 81 [1]Sing for joy to God our strength; shout aloud to the God of Jacob! [2]Begin the music, strike the tambourine, play the melodious harp and lyre.
Ps 89 [15]Blessed are those who have learned to acclaim you, who walk in the light of your presence, O LORD. [16]They rejoice in your name all day long; they exult in your righteousness.
Ps 118 [24]This is the day the LORD has made; let us rejoice and be glad in it.
Ps 122 [1]I rejoiced with those who said to me, "Let us go to the house of the LORD."
Rom 5 [11]Not only is this so, but we also rejoice in God through our Lord Jesus Christ, through whom we have now received reconciliation.

Phil 4 [4]Rejoice in the Lord always. I will say it again: Rejoice!

b) Believers Rejoice in Christ

John 8 [56]"Your father Abraham rejoiced at the thought of seeing my day; he saw it and was glad."
John 15 [11]"I have told you this so that my joy may be in you and that your joy may be complete."
John 16 [22]"So with you: Now is your time of grief, but I will see you again and you will rejoice, and no one will take away your joy."
John 17 [13]"I am coming to you now, but I say these things while I am still in the world, so that they may have the full measure of my joy within them."
Phil 3 [1]Finally, my brothers, rejoice in the Lord! It is no trouble for me to write the same things to you again, and it is a safeguard for you. . . . [3]For it is we who are the circumcision, we who worship by the Spirit of God, who glory in Christ Jesus, and who put no confidence in the flesh. . . .
1 John 1 [1]That which was from the beginning, which we have heard, which we have seen with our eyes, which we have looked at and our hands have touched—this we proclaim concerning the Word of life. [2]The life appeared; we have seen it and testify to it, and we proclaim to you the eternal life, which was with the Father and has appeared to us. [3]We proclaim to you what we have seen and heard, so that you also may have fellowship with us. And our fellowship is with the Father and with his Son, Jesus Christ. [4]We write this to make our joy complete.
Rev 19 [7]Let us rejoice and be glad and give him glory! For the wedding of the Lamb has come, and his bride has made herself ready.

c) Believers Rejoice in the Spirit

Rom 14 [17]For the kingdom of God is not a matter of eating and drinking, but of righteousness, peace and joy in the Holy Spirit. . . .
Gal 5 [22]But the fruit of the Spirit is love, joy, peace, patience, kindness, goodness, faithfulness. . . .

3. Reasons for Believers' Joy

a) Believers Rejoice Because God Accepts Their Worship

1 Sam 6 [13]Now the people of Beth Shemesh were harvesting their wheat in the valley, and when they looked up and saw the ark, they rejoiced at the sight.
2 Sam 6 [12]Now King David was told, "The LORD has blessed the household of Obed-Edom and everything he has, because of the ark of God." So David went down and brought up the ark of God from the house of Obed-Edom to the City of David with rejoicing. [13]When those who were carrying the ark of the LORD had taken six steps, he sacrificed a bull and a fattened calf. [14]David, wearing a linen ephod, danced before the LORD with all his might, [15]while he and the entire house of Israel brought up the ark of the LORD with shouts and the sound of trumpets.
1 Kings 8 [65]So Solomon observed the festival at that time, and all Israel with him—a vast assembly, people from Lebo Hamath to the Wadi of Egypt. They celebrated it before the LORD our God for seven days and seven days more, fourteen days in all. [66]On the following day he sent the people away. They blessed the king and then went home, joyful and glad in heart for all the good things the LORD had done for his servant David and his people Israel.
1 Chron 15 [16]David told the leaders of the Levites to appoint their brothers as singers to sing joyful songs, accompanied by musical instruments: lyres, harps and cymbals.
1 Chron 29 [9]The people rejoiced at the willing response of their leaders, for they had given freely and wholeheartedly to the LORD. David the king also rejoiced greatly.
2 Chron 6 [41]"Now arise, O LORD God, and come to your resting place, you and the ark of your might. May your priests, O LORD God, be clothed with salvation, may your saints rejoice in your goodness."
2 Chron 23 [18]Then Jehoiada placed the oversight of the temple of the LORD in the hands of the priests, who were Levites, to whom David had made assignments in the temple, to present the burnt offerings of the LORD as written in the Law of Moses, with rejoicing and singing, as David had ordered.
2 Chron 24 [8]At the king's command, a chest was made and placed outside, at the gate of the temple of the LORD. . . .[10]All the officials and all the people brought their contributions gladly, dropping them into the chest until it was full.
2 Chron 29 [35]There were burnt offerings in abundance, together with the fat of the fellowship offerings and the drink offerings that accompanied the burnt offerings.

So the service of the temple of the LORD was reestablished. [36]Hezekiah and all the people rejoiced at what God had brought about for his people, because it was done so quickly.
2 Chron 30 [1]Hezekiah sent word to all Israel and Judah and also wrote letters to Ephraim and Manasseh, inviting them to come to the temple of the LORD in Jerusalem and celebrate the Passover to the LORD, the God of Israel. . . .

[21]The Israelites who were present in Jerusalem celebrated the Feast of Unleavened Bread for seven days with great rejoicing, while the Levites and priests sang to the LORD every day, accompanied by the LORD's instruments of praise. . . . [26]There was great joy in Jerusalem, for since the days of Solomon son of David king of Israel there had been nothing like this in Jerusalem.
Ezra 3 [12]But many of the older priests and Levites and family heads, who had seen the former temple, wept aloud when they saw the foundation of this temple being laid, while many others shouted for joy. [13]No one could distinguish the sound of the shouts of joy from the sound of weeping, because the people made so much noise. And the sound was heard far away.
Ezra 6 [16]Then the people of Israel—the priests, the Levites and the rest of the exiles—celebrated the dedication of the house of God with joy. . . . [22]For seven days they celebrated with joy the Feast of Unleavened Bread, because the LORD had filled them with joy by changing the attitude of the king of Assyria, so that he assisted them in the work on the house of God, the God of Israel.
Neh 8 [9]Then Nehemiah the governor, Ezra the priest and scribe, and the Levites who were instructing the people said to them all, "This day is sacred to the LORD your God. Do not mourn or weep." For all the people had been weeping as they listened to the words of the Law.

[10]Nehemiah said, "Go and enjoy choice food and sweet drinks, and send some to those who have nothing prepared. This day is sacred to our Lord. Do not grieve, for the joy of the LORD is your strength." . . .

[12]Then all the people went away to eat and drink, to send portions of food and to celebrate with great joy, because they now understood the words that had been made known to them.

b) Believers Rejoice Because God Blesses His People

Deut 12 [7]There, in the presence of the LORD your God, you and your families shall eat and shall rejoice in everything you have put your hand to, because the LORD your God has blessed you.
Isa 9 [3]You have enlarged the nation and increased their joy; they rejoice before you as people rejoice at the harvest, as men rejoice when dividing the plunder. [4]For as in the day of Midian's defeat, you have shattered the yoke that burdens them, the bar across their shoulders, the rod of their oppressor. [5]Every warrior's boot used in battle and every garment rolled in blood will be destined for burning, will be fuel for the fire. [6]For to us a child is born, to us a son is given, and the government will be on his shoulders. And he will be called Wonderful Counselor, Mighty God, Everlasting Father, Prince of Peace. [7]Of the increase of his government and peace there will be no end. He will reign on David's throne and over his kingdom, establishing and upholding it with justice and righteousness from that time on and forever. The zeal of the LORD Almighty will accomplish this.
Isa 35 [1]The desert and the parched land will be glad; the wilderness will rejoice and blossom. Like the crocus, [2]it will burst into bloom; it will rejoice greatly and shout for joy. The glory of Lebanon will be given to it, the splendor of Carmel and Sharon; they will see the glory of the LORD, the splendor of our God. . . .

[8]And a highway will be there; it will be called the Way of Holiness. The unclean will not journey on it; it will be for those

who walk in that Way; wicked fools will not go about on it. [9]No lion will be there, nor will any ferocious beast get up on it; they will not be found there. But only the redeemed will walk there, [10]and the ransomed of the LORD will return. They will enter Zion with singing; everlasting joy will crown their heads. Gladness and joy will overtake them, and sorrow and sighing will flee away.

Isa 49 [13]Shout for joy, O heavens; rejoice, O earth; burst into song, O mountains! For the LORD comforts his people and will have compassion on his afflicted ones.

Isa 60 [14]"The sons of your oppressors will come bowing before you; all who despise you will bow down at your feet and will call you the City of the LORD, Zion of the Holy One of Israel.

[15]"Although you have been forsaken and hated, with no one traveling through, I will make you the everlasting pride and the joy of all generations."

Isa 61 [10]I delight greatly in the LORD; my soul rejoices in my God. For he has clothed me with garments of salvation and arrayed me in a robe of righteousness, as a bridegroom adorns his head like a priest, and as a bride adorns herself with her jewels.

Jer 31 [13]"Then maidens will dance and be glad, young men and old as well. I will turn their mourning into gladness; I will give them comfort and joy instead of sorrow. [14]I will satisfy the priests with abundance, and my people will be filled with my bounty," declares the LORD.

Jer 33 [8]"'I will cleanse them from all the sin they have committed against me and will forgive all their sins of rebellion against me. [9]Then this city will bring me renown, joy, praise and honor before all nations on earth that hear of all the good things I do for it; and they will be in awe and will tremble at the abundant prosperity and peace I provide for it.'"

Luke 1 [46]And Mary said: "My soul glorifies the Lord [47]and my spirit rejoices in God my Savior, [48]for he has been mindful of the humble state of his servant. From now on all generations will call me blessed. . . ."

c) Believers Rejoice Because God Cares for Them Providentially

1 Chron 16 [31]Let the heavens rejoice, let the earth be glad; let them say among the nations, "The LORD reigns!" . . .

[34]Give thanks to the LORD, for he is good; his love endures forever.

Ps 9 [2]I will be glad and rejoice in you; I will sing praise to your name, O Most High.

[3]My enemies turn back; they stumble and perish before you. [4]For you have upheld my right and my cause; you have sat on your throne, judging righteously. [5]You have rebuked the nations and destroyed the wicked; you have blotted out their name for ever and ever.

Ps 67 [4]May the nations be glad and sing for joy, for you rule the peoples justly and guide the nations of the earth.

Ps 89 [3]You said, "I have made a covenant with my chosen one, I have sworn to David my servant, [4]'I will establish your line forever and make your throne firm through all generations.'" . . . [8]O LORD God Almighty, who is like you? You are mighty, O LORD, and your faithfulness surrounds you. . . . [12]You created the north and the south; Tabor and Hermon sing for joy at your name.

Ps 96 [10]Say among the nations, "The LORD reigns." The world is firmly established, it cannot be moved; he will judge the peoples with equity. [11]Let the heavens rejoice, let the earth be glad; let the sea resound, and all that is in it; [12]let the fields be jubilant, and everything in them. Then all the trees of the forest will sing for joy; [13]they will sing before the LORD, for he comes, he comes to judge the earth. He will judge the world in righteousness and the peoples in his truth.

Ps 97 [1]The LORD reigns, let the earth be glad; let the distant shores rejoice.

Ps 98 [4]Shout for joy to the LORD, all the earth, burst into jubilant song with music; [5]make music to the LORD with the harp, with the harp and the sound of singing, [6]with trumpets and the blast of the ram's horn—shout for joy before the LORD, the King. [7]Let the sea resound, and everything in it, the world, and all who live in it. [8]Let the rivers clap their hands, let the mountains sing together for joy; [9]let them sing before the LORD, for he comes to judge the earth. He will judge the world in righteousness and the peoples with equity.

Hab 3 [17]Though the fig tree does not bud and there are no grapes on the vines, though the olive crop fails and the fields produce no food, though there are no sheep in the pen and no cattle in the stalls, [18]yet I will rejoice in the LORD, I will be joyful in God my Savior.

[19]The Sovereign LORD is my strength; he makes my feet like the feet of a deer, he enables me to go on the heights.

Rev 19 [6]Then I heard what sounded like a great multitude, like the roar of rushing waters and like loud peals of thunder, shouting: "Hallelujah! For our Lord God Almighty reigns. [7]Let us rejoice and be glad and give him glory! For the wedding of the Lamb has come, and his bride has made herself ready."

d) Believers Rejoice Because God Delivers His People from Their Enemies

Deut 16 [11]And rejoice before the LORD your God at the place he will choose as a dwelling for his Name—you, your sons and daughters, your menservants and maidservants, the Levites in your towns, and the aliens, the fatherless and the widows living among you. [12]Remember that you were slaves in Egypt, and follow carefully these decrees.

1 Sam 2 [1]Then Hannah prayed and said: "My heart rejoices in the LORD; in the LORD my horn is lifted high. My mouth boasts over my enemies, for I delight in your deliverance."

Ps 13 [3]Look on me and answer, O LORD my God. Give light to my eyes, or I will sleep in death; [4]my enemy will say, "I have overcome him," and my foes will rejoice when I fall.

[5]But I trust in your unfailing love; my heart rejoices in your salvation. [6]I will sing to the LORD, for he has been good to me.

Ps 21 [1]O LORD, the king rejoices in your strength. How great is his joy in the victories you give!

Ps 35 [9]Then my soul will rejoice in the LORD and delight in his salvation. . . . [27]May those who delight in my vindication shout for joy and gladness; may they always say, "The LORD be exalted, who delights in the well-being of his servant."

Ps 118 [15]Shouts of joy and victory resound in the tents of the righteous: "The LORD's right hand has done mighty things! [16]The LORD's right hand is lifted high; the LORD's right hand has done mighty things!"

e) Believers Rejoice Because God Empowers His People

Ps 16 [8]I have set the LORD always before me. Because he is at my right hand, I will not be shaken.

[9]Therefore my heart is glad and my tongue rejoices; my body also will rest secure. . . .

Ps 28 [7]The LORD is my strength and my shield; my heart trusts in him, and I am helped. My heart leaps for joy and I will give thanks to him in song.

f) Believers Rejoice Because God Exacts Vengeance on the Wicked

Deut 32 [43]Rejoice, O nations, with his people, for he will avenge the blood of his servants; he will take vengeance on his enemies and make atonement for his land and people.

Ps 48 [11]Mount Zion rejoices, the villages of Judah are glad because of your judgments.

Ps 58 [10]The righteous will be glad when they are avenged, when they bathe their feet in the blood of the wicked.

g) Believers Rejoice Because God Has Done Marvelous Works

Ps 9 [1]I will praise you, O LORD, with all my heart; I will tell of all your wonders.

Ps 92 [4]For you make me glad by your deeds, O LORD; I sing for joy at the works of your hands.

Ps 107 [22]Let them sacrifice thank offerings and tell of his works with songs of joy.

Ps 126 [3]The LORD has done great things for us, and we are filled with joy.

h) Believers Rejoice Because God Has Given His Word

Ps 19 [8]The precepts of the LORD are right, giving joy to the

heart. The commands of the LORD are radiant, giving light to the eyes.
Ps 119 [14]I rejoice in following your statutes as one rejoices in great riches.
Ps 119 [92]If your law had not been my delight, I would have perished in my affliction.
Ps 119 [174]I long for your salvation, O LORD, and your law is my delight.
Jer 15 [16]When your words came, I ate them; they were my joy and my heart's delight, for I bear your name, O LORD God Almighty.
1 Thess 1 [6]You became imitators of us and of the Lord; in spite of severe suffering, you welcomed the message with the joy given by the Holy Spirit.
1 John 1 [4]We write this to make our joy complete.

i) Believers Rejoice Because God Is Present with His People

Ps 16 [11]You have made known to me the path of life; you will fill me with joy in your presence, with eternal pleasures at your right hand.
Ps 46 [1]God is our refuge and strength, an ever-present help in trouble. [2]Therefore we will not fear, though the earth give way and the mountains fall into the heart of the sea, [3]though its waters roar and foam and the mountains quake with their surging.

[4]There is a river whose streams make glad the city of God, the holy place where the Most High dwells. [5]God is within her, she will not fall; God will help her at break of day.
Ps 48 [1]Great is the LORD, and most worthy of praise, in the city of our God, his holy mountain. [2]It is beautiful in its loftiness, the joy of the whole earth. Like the utmost heights of Zaphon is Mount Zion, the city of the Great King. [3]God is in her citadels; he has shown himself to be her fortress.
Isa 12 [6]"Shout aloud and sing for joy, people of Zion, for great is the Holy One of Israel among you."
Zeph 3 [14]Sing, O Daughter of Zion; shout aloud, O Israel! Be glad and rejoice with all your heart, O Daughter of Jerusalem! [15]The LORD has taken away your punishment, he has turned back your enemy. The LORD, the King of Israel, is with you; never again will you fear any harm. [16]On that day they will say to Jerusalem, "Do not fear, O Zion; do not let your hands hang limp. [17]The LORD your God is with you, he is mighty to save. He will take great delight in you, he will quiet you with his love, he will rejoice over you with singing."

[18]"The sorrows for the appointed feasts I will remove from you; they are a burden and a reproach to you. [19]At that time I will deal with all who oppressed you; I will rescue the lame and gather those who have been scattered. I will give them praise and honor in every land where they were put to shame. [20]At that time I will gather you; at that time I will bring you home. I will give you honor and praise among all the peoples of the earth when I restore your fortunes before your very eyes," says the LORD.
Zech 2 [10]"Shout and be glad, O Daughter of Zion. For I am coming, and I will live among you," declares the LORD.
Zech 9 [9]Rejoice greatly, O Daughter of Zion! Shout, Daughter of Jerusalem! See, your king comes to you, righteous and having salvation, gentle and riding on a donkey, on a colt, the foal of a donkey.

j) Believers Rejoice Because God Loves Them

Ps 31 [7]I will be glad and rejoice in your love, for you saw my affliction and knew the anguish of my soul.
Ps 85 [6]Will you not revive us again, that your people may rejoice in you? [7]Show us your unfailing love, O LORD, and grant us your salvation.

4. The Promise of Joy to Believers

Ps 4 [3]Know that the LORD has set apart the godly for himself; the LORD will hear when I call to him. . . . [7]You have filled my heart with greater joy than when their grain and new wine abound.
Ps 16 [11]You have made known to me the path of life; you will fill me with joy in your presence, with eternal pleasures at your right hand.
Ps 126 [5]Those who sow in tears will reap with songs of joy. [6]He who goes out weeping, carrying seed to sow, will return with songs of joy, carrying sheaves with him.
Ps 132 [16]"I will clothe her priests with salvation, and her saints will ever sing for joy."
Eccles 2 [26]To the man who pleases him, God gives wisdom, knowledge and happiness, but to the sinner he gives the task of gathering and storing up wealth to hand it over to the one who pleases God. This too is meaningless, a chasing after the wind.
Isa 65 [14]"My servants will sing out of the joy of their hearts, but you will cry out from anguish of heart and wail in brokenness of spirit."
Isa 66 [14]When you see this, your heart will rejoice and you will flourish like grass; the hand of the LORD will be made known to his servants, but his fury will be shown to his foes.
John 16 [20]"I tell you the truth, you will weep and mourn while the world rejoices. You will grieve, but your grief will turn to joy. [21]A woman giving birth to a child has pain because her time has come; but when her baby is born she forgets the anguish because of her joy that a child is born into the world. [22]So with you: Now is your time of grief, but I will see you again and you will rejoice, and no one will take away your joy. [23]In that day you will no longer ask me anything. I tell you the truth, my Father will give you whatever you ask in my name. [24]Until now you have not asked for anything in my name. Ask and you will receive, and your joy will be complete."

C. Find Rest in God

Ps 55 [22]Cast your cares on the LORD and he will sustain you; he will never let the righteous fall.
Ps 62 [1]My soul finds rest in God alone; my salvation comes from him. [2]He alone is my rock and my salvation; he is my fortress, I will never be shaken. . . .

[5]Find rest, O my soul, in God alone; my hope comes from him.
Ps 91 [1]He who dwells in the shelter of the Most High will rest in the shadow of the Almighty.
Ps 116 [7]Be at rest once more, O my soul, for the LORD has been good to you.
Jer 6 [16]This is what the LORD says: "Stand at the crossroads and look; ask for the ancient paths, ask where the good way is, and walk in it, and you will find rest for your souls. But you said, 'We will not walk in it.'"
Matt 6 [25]"Therefore I tell you, do not worry about your life, what you will eat or drink; or about your body, what you will wear. Is not life more important than food, and the body more important than clothes? [26]Look at the birds of the air; they do not sow or reap or store away in barns, and yet your heavenly Father feeds them. Are you not much more valuable than they? [27]Who of you by worrying can add a single hour to his life?

[28]"And why do you worry about clothes? See how the lilies of the field grow. They do not labor or spin. [29]Yet I tell you that not even Solomon in all his splendor was dressed like one of these. [30]If that is how God clothes the grass of the field, which is here today and tomorrow is thrown into the fire, will he not much more clothe you, O you of little faith? [31]So do not worry, saying, 'What shall we eat?' or 'What shall we drink?' or 'What shall we wear?' [32]For the pagans run after all these things, and your heavenly Father knows that you need them. [33]But seek first his kingdom and his righteousness, and all these things will be given to you as well. [34]Therefore do not worry about tomorrow, for tomorrow will worry about itself. Each day has enough trouble of its own."
Heb 4 [9]There remains, then, a Sabbath-rest for the people of God; [10]for anyone who enters God's rest also rests from his own work, just as God did from his. [11]Let us, therefore, make every effort to enter that rest, so that no one will fall by following their example of disobedience.
1 Pet 5 [7]Cast all your anxiety on him because he cares for you.
1 John 3 [19]This then is how we know that we belong to the truth, and how we set our hearts at rest in his presence [20]whenever our hearts condemn us. For God is greater than our hearts, and he knows everything.

D. Find Satisfaction in God

Ps 17 15And I—in righteousness I will see your face; when I awake, I will be satisfied with seeing your likeness.
Ps 22 26The poor will eat and be satisfied; they who seek the LORD will praise him—may your hearts live forever!
Ps 36 8They feast on the abundance of your house; you give them drink from your river of delights. 9For with you is the fountain of life; in your light we see light.
Ps 63 5My soul will be satisfied as with the richest of foods; with singing lips my mouth will praise you.
Ps 65 4Blessed are those you choose and bring near to live in your courts! We are filled with the good things of your house, of your holy temple.
Ps 90 14Satisfy us in the morning with your unfailing love, that we may sing for joy and be glad all our days.
Ps 91 14"Because he loves me," says the LORD, "I will rescue him; I will protect him, for he acknowledges my name. 15He will call upon me, and I will answer him; I will be with him in trouble, I will deliver him and honor him. 16With long life will I satisfy him and show him my salvation."
Ps 103 2Praise the LORD, O my soul, and forget not all his benefits—3who forgives all your sins and heals all your diseases, 4who redeems your life from the pit and crowns you with love and compassion, 5who satisfies your desires with good things so that your youth is renewed like the eagle's.
Ps 107 8Let them give thanks to the LORD for his unfailing love and his wonderful deeds for men, 9for he satisfies the thirsty and fills the hungry with good things.
Ps 132 13For the LORD has chosen Zion, he has desired it for his dwelling: 14"This is my resting place for ever and ever; here I will sit enthroned, for I have desired it—15I will bless her with abundant provisions; her poor will I satisfy with food. 16I will clothe her priests with salvation, and her saints will ever sing for joy."
Ps 147 12Extol the LORD, O Jerusalem; praise your God, O Zion, 13for he strengthens the bars of your gates and blesses your people within you. 14He grants peace to your borders and satisfies you with the finest of wheat.
Isa 55 1"Come, all you who are thirsty, come to the waters; and you who have no money, come, buy and eat! Come, buy wine and milk without money and without cost. 2Why spend money on what is not bread, and your labor on what does not satisfy? Listen, listen to me, and eat what is good, and your soul will delight in the richest of fare."
Isa 58 11"The LORD will guide you always; he will satisfy your needs in a sun-scorched land and will strengthen your frame. You will be like a well-watered garden, like a spring whose waters never fail."
Jer 31 14"I will satisfy the priests with abundance, and my people will be filled with my bounty," declares the LORD. . . . 25"I will refresh the weary and satisfy the faint."

E. Find Comfort in God

1. Finding Comfort in General

Matt 5 4"Blessed are those who mourn, for they will be comforted."
Luke 16 25"But Abraham replied, 'Son, remember that in your lifetime you received your good things, while Lazarus received bad things, but now he is comforted here and you are in agony.'"

2. Finding Comfort in God

Job 15 11"Are God's consolations not enough for you, words spoken gently to you?"
Ps 23 1The LORD is my shepherd, I shall not be in want. 2He makes me lie down in green pastures, he leads me beside quiet waters, 3he restores my soul. He guides me in paths of righteousness for his name's sake. 4Even though I walk through the valley of the shadow of death, I will fear no evil, for you are with me; your rod and your staff, they comfort me.
Ps 71 19Your righteousness reaches to the skies, O God, you who have done great things. Who, O God, is like you? 20Though you have made me see troubles, many and bitter, you will restore my life again; from the depths of the earth you will again bring me up. 21You will increase my honor and comfort me once again.
Ps 86 17Give me a sign of your goodness, that my enemies may see it and be put to shame, for you, O LORD, have helped me and comforted me.
Ps 94 19When anxiety was great within me, your consolation brought joy to my soul.
Ps 119 50My comfort in my suffering is this: Your promise preserves my life. . . . 52I remember your ancient laws, O LORD, and I find comfort in them.
Ps 119 76May your unfailing love be my comfort, according to your promise to your servant. . . . 82My eyes fail, looking for your promise; I say, "When will you comfort me?"
Isa 12 1In that day you will say: "I will praise you, O LORD. Although you were angry with me, your anger has turned away and you have comforted me."
Isa 40 1Comfort, comfort my people, says your God. 2Speak tenderly to Jerusalem, and proclaim to her that her hard service has been completed, that her sin has been paid for, that she has received from the LORD's hand double for all her sins.
Isa 49 13Shout for joy, O heavens; rejoice, O earth; burst into song, O mountains! For the LORD comforts his people and will have compassion on his afflicted ones.
Isa 51 3"The LORD will surely comfort Zion and will look with compassion on all her ruins; he will make her deserts like Eden, her wastelands like the garden of the LORD. Joy and gladness will be found in her, thanksgiving and the sound of singing. . . .

12"I, even I, am he who comforts you. Who are you that you fear mortal men, the sons of men, who are but grass? . . ."
Isa 52 9Burst into songs of joy together, you ruins of Jerusalem, for the LORD has comforted his people, he has redeemed Jerusalem.
Isa 57 16"I will not accuse forever, nor will I always be angry, for then the spirit of man would grow faint before me—the breath of man that I have created. . . . 18I have seen his ways, but I will heal him; I will guide him and restore comfort to him. . . ."
Isa 61 1The Spirit of the Sovereign LORD is on me, because the LORD has anointed me to preach good news to the poor. He has sent me to bind up the brokenhearted, to proclaim freedom for the captives and release from darkness for the prisoners, 2to proclaim the year of the LORD's favor and the day of vengeance of our God, to comfort all who mourn, 3and provide for those who grieve in Zion—to bestow on them a crown of beauty instead of ashes, the oil of gladness instead of mourning, and a garment of praise instead of a spirit of despair. They will be called oaks of righteousness, a planting of the LORD for the display of his splendor.
Isa 66 13"As a mother comforts her child, so will I comfort you; and you will be comforted over Jerusalem."
Jer 31 13"Then maidens will dance and be glad, young men and old as well. I will turn their mourning into gladness; I will give them comfort and joy instead of sorrow."
Hos 2 14"Therefore I am now going to allure her; I will lead her into the desert and speak tenderly to her. 15There I will give her back her vineyards, and will make the Valley of Achor a door of hope. There she will sing as in the days of her youth, as in the day she came up out of Egypt."
Zech 1 13So the LORD spoke kind and comforting words to the angel who talked with me. . . .

17"Proclaim further: This is what the LORD Almighty says: 'My towns will again overflow with prosperity, and the LORD will again comfort Zion and choose Jerusalem.'"
Rom 15 5May the God who gives endurance and encouragement give you a spirit of unity among yourselves as you follow Christ Jesus. . . .
2 Cor 1 3Praise be to the God and Father of our Lord Jesus Christ, the Father of compassion and the God of all comfort, 4who comforts us in all our troubles, so that we can comfort those in any trouble with the comfort we ourselves have received from God.
2 Cor 7 6But God, who comforts the downcast, comforted us by the coming of Titus. . . .

Heb 6 [18]God did this so that, by two unchangeable things in which it is impossible for God to lie, we who have fled to take hold of the hope offered to us may be greatly encouraged.

3. Finding Comfort in Christ

John 14 [18]"I will not leave you as orphans; I will come to you."
John 14 [27]"Peace I leave with you; my peace I give you. I do not give to you as the world gives. Do not let your hearts be troubled and do not be afraid."
2 Cor 1 [5]For just as the sufferings of Christ flow over into our lives, so also through Christ our comfort overflows.
Phil 2 [1]If you have any encouragement from being united with Christ, if any comfort from his love, if any fellowship with the Spirit, if any tenderness and compassion, [2]then make my joy complete by being like-minded, having the same love, being one in spirit and purpose.
2 Thess 2 [16]May our Lord Jesus Christ himself and God our Father, who loved us and by his grace gave us eternal encouragement and good hope, [17]encourage your hearts and strengthen you in every good deed and word.

4. Finding Comfort in the Spirit

John 14 [16]"And I will ask the Father, and he will give you another Counselor to be with you forever—[17]the Spirit of truth. The world cannot accept him, because it neither sees him nor knows him. But you know him, for he lives with you and will be in you."
Acts 9 [31]Then the church throughout Judea, Galilee and Samaria enjoyed a time of peace. It was strengthened; and encouraged by the Holy Spirit, it grew in numbers, living in the fear of the Lord.

5. Finding Comfort in Scripture

Rom 15 [4]For everything that was written in the past was written to teach us, so that through endurance and the encouragement of the Scriptures we might have hope.

13

Christian Living: *Responsibilities to Others and to Nature*

I Responsibilities toward Nature

A. Praise God as Creator of Nature

Ps 33 [1]Sing joyfully to the LORD, you righteous; it is fitting for the upright to praise him. . . . [8]Let all the earth fear the LORD; let all the people of the world revere him. [9]For he spoke, and it came to be; he commanded, and it stood firm.

Prov 3 [19]By wisdom the LORD laid the earth's foundations, by understanding he set the heavens in place; [20]by his knowledge the deeps were divided, and the clouds let drop the dew.

Isa 40 [25]"To whom will you compare me? Or who is my equal?" says the Holy One. [26]Lift your eyes and look to the heavens: Who created all these? He who brings out the starry host one by one, and calls them each by name. Because of his great power and mighty strength, not one of them is missing.

[27]Why do you say, O Jacob, and complain, O Israel, "My way is hidden from the LORD; my cause is disregarded by my God"? [28]Do you not know? Have you not heard? The LORD is the everlasting God, the Creator of the ends of the earth. He will not grow tired or weary, and his understanding no one can fathom.

Isa 42 [5]This is what God the LORD says—he who created the heavens and stretched them out, who spread out the earth and all that comes out of it, who gives breath to its people, and life to those who walk on it. . . .

[10]Sing to the LORD a new song, his praises from the ends of the earth, you who go down to the sea, and all that is in it, you islands, and all who live in them. [11]Let the desert and its towns raise their voices; let the settlements where Kedar lives rejoice. Let the people of Sela sing for joy; let them shout from the mountaintops. [12]Let them give glory to the LORD and proclaim his praise in the islands.

Isa 45 [5]"I am the LORD, and there is no other; apart from me there is no God. I will strengthen you, though you have not acknowledged me, [6]so that from the rising of the sun to the place of its setting men may know there is none besides me. I am the LORD, and there is no other. [7]I form the light and create darkness, I bring prosperity and create disaster; I, the LORD, do all these things.

[8]"You heavens above, rain down righteousness; let the clouds shower it down. Let the earth open wide, let salvation spring up, let righteousness grow with it; I, the LORD, have created it.

[9]"Woe to him who quarrels with his Maker, to him who is but a potsherd among the potsherds on the ground. Does the clay say to the potter, 'What are you making?' Does your work say, 'He has no hands'? [10]Woe to him who says to his father, 'What have you begotten?' or to his mother, 'What have you brought to birth?'

[11]"This is what the LORD says—the Holy One of Israel, and its Maker: Concerning things to come, do you question me about my children, or give me orders about the work of my hands? [12]It is I who made the earth and created mankind upon it. My own hands stretched out the heavens; I marshaled their starry hosts. . . ."

[18]For this is what the LORD says—he who created the heavens, he is God; he who fashioned and made the earth, he founded it; he did not create it to be empty, but formed it to be inhabited—he says: "I am the LORD, and there is no other."

Jer 10 [11]"Tell them this: 'These gods, who did not make the heavens and the earth, will perish from the earth and from under the heavens.'"

[12]But God made the earth by his power; he founded the world by his wisdom and stretched out the heavens by his understanding. [13]When he thunders, the waters in the heavens roar; he makes clouds rise from the ends of the earth. He sends lightning with the rain and brings out the wind from his storehouses.

Rev 10 [6]And he swore by him who lives for ever and ever, who created the heavens and all that is in them, the earth and all that is in it, and the sea and all that is in it, and said, "There will be no more delay!"

B. Maintain a Sense of Wonder at Nature

1. The Beauty of Nature

Eccles 3 [11]He has made everything beautiful in its time. He has also set eternity in the hearts of men; yet they cannot fathom what God has done from beginning to end.
Eccles 11 [7]Light is sweet, and it pleases the eyes to see the sun.

2. The Complexity of Nature

Job 38 [1]Then the LORD answered Job out of the storm. He said: [2]"Who is this that darkens my counsel with words without knowledge? [3]Brace yourself like a man; I will question you, and you shall answer me.

[4]"Where were you when I laid the earth's foundation? Tell me, if you understand. [5]Who marked off its dimensions? Surely you know! Who stretched a measuring line across it? [6]On what were its footings set, or who laid its cornerstone—[7]while the morning stars sang together and all the angels shouted for joy?

[8]"Who shut up the sea behind doors when it burst forth from the womb, [9]when I made the clouds its garment and wrapped it in thick darkness, [10]when I fixed limits for it and set its doors and bars in place, [11]when I said, 'This far you may come and no farther; here is where your proud waves halt'?

[12]"Have you ever given orders to the morning, or shown the dawn its place, [13]that it might take the earth by the edges and shake the wicked out of it? [14]The earth takes shape like clay under a seal; its features stand out like those of a garment. [15]The wicked are denied their light, and their upraised arm is broken.

[16]"Have you journeyed to the springs of the sea or walked in the recesses of the deep? [17]Have the gates of death been shown to you? Have you seen the gates of the shadow of death? [18]Have you comprehended the vast expanses of the earth? Tell me, if you know all this.

[19]"What is the way to the abode of light? And where does darkness reside? [20]Can you take them to their places? Do you know the paths to their dwellings? [21]Surely you know, for you were already born! You have lived so many years!

[22]"Have you entered the storehouses of the snow or seen the storehouses of the hail, [23]which I reserve for times of trouble, for days of war and battle? [24]What is the way to the place where the lightning is dispersed, or the place where the east winds are scattered over the earth? [25]Who cuts a channel for the torrents of rain, and a path for the thunderstorm, [26]to water a land where no man lives, a desert with no one in it, [27]to satisfy a desolate wasteland and make it sprout with grass? [28]Does the rain have a father? Who fathers the drops of dew? [29]From whose womb comes the ice? Who gives birth to the frost from the heavens [30]when the waters become hard as stone, when the surface of the deep is frozen?

[31]"Can you bind the beautiful Pleiades? Can you loose the cords of Orion? [32]Can you bring forth the constellations in their seasons or lead out the Bear with its cubs? [33]Do you know the laws of the heavens? Can you set up God's dominion over the earth?

[34]"Can you raise your voice to the clouds and cover yourself with a flood of water? [35]Do you send the lightning bolts on their way? Do they report to you, 'Here we are'? [36]Who endowed the heart with wisdom or gave understanding to the mind? [37]Who has the wisdom to count the clouds? Who can tip over the water jars of the heavens [38]when the dust becomes hard and the clods of earth stick together?

[39]"Do you hunt the prey for the lioness and satisfy the hunger of the lions [40]when they crouch in their dens or lie in wait in a thicket? [41]Who provides food for the raven when its young cry out to God and wander about for lack of food?"
Job 39 [1]"Do you know when the mountain goats give birth? Do you watch when the doe bears her fawn? [2]Do you count the months till they bear? Do you know the time they give birth? [3]They crouch down and bring forth their young; their labor pains are ended. [4]Their young thrive and grow strong in the wilds; they leave and do not return.

[5]"Who let the wild donkey go free? Who untied his ropes? [6]I gave him the wasteland as his home, the salt flats as his habitat. [7]He laughs at the commotion in the town; he does not hear a driver's shout. [8]He ranges the hills for his pasture and searches for any green thing.

[9]"Will the wild ox consent to serve you? Will he stay by your manger at night? [10]Can you hold him to the furrow with a harness? Will he till the valleys behind you? [11]Will you rely on him for his great strength? Will you leave your heavy work to him? [12]Can you trust him to bring in your grain and gather it to your threshing floor?

[13]"The wings of the ostrich flap joyfully, but they cannot compare with the pinions and feathers of the stork. [14]She lays her eggs on the ground and lets them warm in the sand, [15]unmindful that a foot may crush them, that some wild animal may trample them. [16]She treats her young harshly, as if they were not hers; she cares not that her labor was in vain, [17]for God did not endow her with wisdom or give her a share of good sense. [18]Yet when she spreads her feathers to run, she laughs at horse and rider.

[19]"Do you give the horse his strength or clothe his neck with a flowing mane? [20]Do you make him leap like a locust, striking terror with his proud snorting? [21]He paws fiercely, rejoicing in his strength, and charges into the fray. [22]He laughs at fear, afraid of nothing; he does not shy away from the sword. [23]The quiver rattles against his side, along with the flashing spear and lance. [24]In frenzied excitement he eats up the ground; he cannot stand still when the trumpet sounds. [25]At the blast of the trumpet he snorts, 'Aha!' He catches the scent of battle from afar, the shout of commanders and the battle cry.

[26]"Does the hawk take flight by your wisdom and spread his wings toward the south? [27]Does the eagle soar at your command and build his nest on high? [28]He dwells on a cliff and stays there at night; a rocky crag is his stronghold. [29]From there he seeks out his food; his eyes detect it from afar. [30]His young ones feast on blood, and where the slain are, there is he."
Job 40 [6]Then the LORD spoke to Job out of the storm: [7]"Brace yourself like a man; I will question you, and you shall answer me. . . .

[15]"Look at the behemoth, which I made along with you and which feeds on grass like an ox. [16]What strength he has in his loins, what power in the muscles of his belly! [17]His tail sways like a cedar; the sinews of his thighs are close-knit. [18]His bones are tubes of bronze, his limbs like rods of iron. [19]He ranks first among the works of God, yet his Maker can approach him with his sword. [20]The hills bring him their produce, and all the wild animals play nearby. [21]Under the lotus plants he lies, hidden among the reeds in the marsh. [22]The lotuses conceal him in their shadow; the poplars by the stream surround him. [23]When the river rages, he is not alarmed; he is secure, though the Jordan should surge against his mouth. [24]Can anyone capture him by the eyes, or trap him and pierce his nose?"
Job 41 [1]"Can you pull in the leviathan with a fishhook or tie down his tongue with a rope? [2]Can you put a cord through his nose or pierce his jaw with a hook? [3]Will he keep begging you for mercy? Will he speak to you with gentle words? [4]Will he make an agreement with you for you to take him as your slave for life? [5]Can you make a pet of him like a bird or put him on a leash for your girls? [6]Will traders barter for him? Will they divide him up among the merchants? [7]Can you fill his hide with harpoons or his head with fishing spears? [8]If you lay a hand on him, you will remember the struggle and never do it again! [9]Any hope of subduing him is false; the mere sight of him is overpowering. [10]No one is fierce enough to rouse him. Who then is able to stand against me? [11]Who has a claim against me that I must pay? Everything under heaven belongs to me.

[12]"I will not fail to speak of his limbs, his strength and his graceful form. [13]Who can strip off his outer coat? Who would approach him with a bridle? [14]Who dares open the doors of his mouth, ringed about with his fearsome teeth? [15]His back has rows of shields tightly sealed together; [16]each is so close to the next that no air can pass between. [17]They are joined fast to one another; they cling together and cannot be parted. [18]His snorting throws out flashes of light; his eyes are like the rays of dawn. [19]Firebrands stream from his mouth; sparks of fire shoot out. [20]Smoke pours from his nostrils as from a boiling pot over

a fire of reeds. 21His breath sets coals ablaze, and flames dart from his mouth. 22Strength resides in his neck; dismay goes before him. 23The folds of his flesh are tightly joined; they are firm and immovable. 24His chest is hard as rock, hard as a lower millstone. 25When he rises up, the mighty are terrified; they retreat before his thrashing. 26The sword that reaches him has no effect, nor does the spear or the dart or the javelin. 27Iron he treats like straw and bronze like rotten wood. 28Arrows do not make him flee; slingstones are like chaff to him. 29A club seems to him but a piece of straw; he laughs at the rattling of the lance. 30His undersides are jagged potsherds, leaving a trail in the mud like a threshing sledge. 31He makes the depths churn like a boiling caldron and stirs up the sea like a pot of ointment. 32Behind him he leaves a glistening wake; one would think the deep had white hair. 33Nothing on earth is his equal—a creature without fear. 34He looks down on all that are haughty; he is king over all that are proud."

Ps 139 13For you created my inmost being; you knit me together in my mother's womb. 14I praise you because I am fearfully and wonderfully made; your works are wonderful, I know that full well. 15My frame was not hidden from you when I was made in the secret place. When I was woven together in the depths of the earth, 16your eyes saw my unformed body. All the days ordained for me were written in your book before one of them came to be.

3. The Orderliness of Nature

Job 36 22"God is exalted in his power. Who is a teacher like him? 23Who has prescribed his ways for him, or said to him, 'You have done wrong'? 24Remember to extol his work, which men have praised in song. 25All mankind has seen it; men gaze on it from afar. 26How great is God—beyond our understanding! The number of his years is past finding out.

27"He draws up the drops of water, which distill as rain to the streams; 28the clouds pour down their moisture and abundant showers fall on mankind. 29Who can understand how he spreads out the clouds, how he thunders from his pavilion? 30See how he scatters his lightning about him, bathing the depths of the sea. 31This is the way he governs the nations and provides food in abundance. 32He fills his hands with lightning and commands it to strike its mark. 33His thunder announces the coming storm; even the cattle make known its approach."

Ps 19 1The heavens declare the glory of God; the skies proclaim the work of his hands. 2Day after day they pour forth speech; night after night they display knowledge. 3There is no speech or language where their voice is not heard. 4Their voice goes out into all the earth, their words to the ends of the world.

In the heavens he has pitched a tent for the sun, 5which is like a bridegroom coming forth from his pavilion, like a champion rejoicing to run his course. 6It rises at one end of the heavens and makes its circuit to the other; nothing is hidden from its heat.

Ps 104 1Praise the LORD, O my soul.

O LORD my God, you are very great; you are clothed with splendor and majesty. 2He wraps himself in light as with a garment; he stretches out the heavens like a tent 3and lays the beams of his upper chambers on their waters. He makes the clouds his chariot and rides on the wings of the wind. 4He makes winds his messengers, flames of fire his servants.

5He set the earth on its foundations; it can never be moved. 6You covered it with the deep as with a garment; the waters stood above the mountains. 7But at your rebuke the waters fled, at the sound of your thunder they took to flight; 8they flowed over the mountains, they went down into the valleys, to the place you assigned for them. 9You set a boundary they cannot cross; never again will they cover the earth.

10He makes springs pour water into the ravines; it flows between the mountains. 11They give water to all the beasts of the field; the wild donkeys quench their thirst. 12The birds of the air nest by the waters; they sing among the branches. 13He waters the mountains from his upper chambers; the earth is satisfied by the fruit of his work. 14He makes grass grow for the cattle, and plants for man to cultivate—bringing forth food from the earth: 15wine that gladdens the heart of man, oil to make his face shine, and bread that sustains his heart. 16The trees of the LORD are well watered, the cedars of Lebanon that he planted. 17There the birds make their nests; the stork has its home in the pine trees. 18The high mountains belong to the wild goats; the crags are a refuge for the coneys.

19The moon marks off the seasons, and the sun knows when to go down. 20You bring darkness, it becomes night, and all the beasts of the forest prowl. 21The lions roar for their prey and seek their food from God. 22The sun rises, and they steal away; they return and lie down in their dens. 23Then man goes out to his work, to his labor until evening.

24How many are your works, O LORD! In wisdom you made them all; the earth is full of your creatures. 25There is the sea, vast and spacious, teeming with creatures beyond number—living things both large and small. 26There the ships go to and fro and the leviathan, which you formed to frolic there.

27These all look to you to give them their food at the proper time. 28When you give it to them, they gather it up; when you open your hand, they are satisfied with good things. 29When you hide your face, they are terrified; when you take away their breath, they die and return to the dust. 30When you send your Spirit, they are created, and you renew the face of the earth.

31May the glory of the LORD endure forever; may the LORD rejoice in his works—32he who looks at the earth, and it trembles, who touches the mountains, and they smoke.

4. The Sustaining of Nature by God

Ps 75 3"When the earth and all its people quake, it is I who hold its pillars firm."

Ps 147 1Praise the LORD. How good it is to sing praises to our God, how pleasant and fitting to praise him!

2The LORD builds up Jerusalem; he gathers the exiles of Israel. 3He heals the brokenhearted and binds up their wounds.

4He determines the number of the stars and calls them each by name. 5Great is our Lord and mighty in power; his understanding has no limit. 6The LORD sustains the humble but casts the wicked to the ground.

7Sing to the LORD with thanksgiving; make music to our God on the harp. 8He covers the sky with clouds; he supplies the earth with rain and makes grass grow on the hills. 9He provides food for the cattle and for the young ravens when they call.

10His pleasure is not in the strength of the horse, nor his delight in the legs of a man; 11the LORD delights in those who fear him, who put their hope in his unfailing love.

12Extol the LORD, O Jerusalem; praise your God, O Zion, 13for he strengthens the bars of your gates and blesses your people within you. 14He grants peace to your borders and satisfies you with the finest of wheat.

15He sends his command to the earth; his word runs swiftly. 16He spreads the snow like wool and scatters the frost like ashes. 17He hurls down his hail like pebbles. Who can withstand his icy blast? 18He sends his word and melts them; he stirs up his breezes, and the waters flow.

Matt 10 29"Are not two sparrows sold for a penny? Yet not one of them will fall to the ground apart from the will of your Father. 30And even the very hairs of your head are all numbered. 31So don't be afraid; you are worth more than many sparrows."

Acts 17 24"The God who made the world and everything in it is the Lord of heaven and earth and does not live in temples built by hands. 25And he is not served by human hands, as if he needed anything, because he himself gives all men life and breath and everything else. 26From one man he made every nation of men, that they should inhabit the whole earth; and he determined the times set for them and the exact places where they should live. 27God did this so that men would seek him and perhaps reach out for him and find him, though he is not far from each one of us. 28'For in him we live and move and have our being.' As some of your own poets have said, 'We are his offspring.'"

Col 1 17He is before all things, and in him all things hold together.

Heb 2 [10]In bringing many sons to glory, it was fitting that God, for whom and through whom everything exists, should make the author of their salvation perfect through suffering.

5. The Vastness of Nature

Gen 2 [1]Thus the heavens and the earth were completed in all their vast array.
Job 38 [4]"Where were you when I laid the earth's foundation? Tell me, if you understand. [7]. . . while the morning stars sang together and all the angels shouted for joy? . . .
[16]"Have you journeyed to the springs of the sea or walked in the recesses of the deep? . . . [18]Have you comprehended the vast expanses of the earth? Tell me, if you know all this. . . . [24]What is the way to the place where the lightning is dispersed, or the place where the east winds are scattered over the earth? . . .
[31]"Can you bind the beautiful Pleiades? Can you loose the cords of Orion?"
Ps 8 [3]When I consider your heavens, the work of your fingers, the moon and the stars, which you have set in place, [4]what is man that you are mindful of him, the son of man that you care for him?
Ps 103 [15]As for man, his days are like grass, he flourishes like a flower of the field; [16]the wind blows over it and it is gone, and its place remembers it no more.
Ps 139 [7]Where can I go from your Spirit? Where can I flee from your presence? [8]If I go up to the heavens, you are there; if I make my bed in the depths, you are there. [9]If I rise on the wings of the dawn, if I settle on the far side of the sea, [10]even there your hand will guide me, your right hand will hold me fast.
[11]If I say, "Surely the darkness will hide me and the light become night around me," [12]even the darkness will not be dark to you; the night will shine like the day, for darkness is as light to you.
Isa 40 [6]A voice says, "Cry out." And I said, "What shall I cry?"
"All men are like grass, and all their glory is like the flowers of the field. [7]The grass withers and the flowers fall, because the breath of the LORD blows on them. Surely the people are grass. [8]The grass withers and the flowers fall, but the word of our God stands forever."
Isa 40 [12]Who has measured the waters in the hollow of his hand, or with the breadth of his hand marked off the heavens? Who has held the dust of the earth in a basket, or weighed the mountains on the scales and the hills in a balance? [13]Who has understood the mind of the LORD, or instructed him as his counselor? [14]Whom did the LORD consult to enlighten him, and who taught him the right way? Who was it that taught him knowledge or showed him the path of understanding?
[15]Surely the nations are like a drop in a bucket; they are regarded as dust on the scales; he weighs the islands as though they were fine dust.
Isa 40 [21]Do you not know? Have you not heard? Has it not been told you from the beginning? Have you not understood since the earth was founded? [22]He sits enthroned above the circle of the earth, and its people are like grasshoppers. He stretches out the heavens like a canopy, and spreads them out like a tent to live in.

C. Recognize Humankind's Association with Nature

1. Humankind and Nature Were Both Created by God

Gen 1 [1]In the beginning God created the heavens and the earth. . . .
[11]Then God said, "Let the land produce vegetation: seed-bearing plants and trees on the land that bear fruit with seed in it, according to their various kinds." And it was so. . . . [21]So God created the great creatures of the sea and every living and moving thing with which the water teems, according to their kinds, and every winged bird according to its kind. And God saw that it was good. . . . [25]God made the wild animals according to their kinds, the livestock according to their kinds, and all the creatures that move along the ground according to their kinds. And God saw that it was good. . . .
[27]So God created man in his own image, in the image of God he created him; male and female he created them. . . .
[31]God saw all that he had made, and it was very good. And there was evening, and there was morning—the sixth day.
John 1 [1]In the beginning was the Word, and the Word was with God, and the Word was God. [2]He was with God in the beginning.
[3]Through him all things were made; without him nothing was made that has been made.
Acts 17 [24]"The God who made the world and everything in it is the Lord of heaven and earth and does not live in temples built by hands."
1 Cor 8 [6]yet for us there is but one God, the Father, from whom all things came and for whom we live; and there is but one Lord, Jesus Christ, through whom all things came and through whom we live.
1 Cor 15 [27]For he "has put everything under his feet." Now when it says that "everything" has been put under him, it is clear that this does not include God himself, who put everything under Christ. [28]When he has done this, then the Son himself will be made subject to him who put everything under him, so that God may be all in all.
Eph 3 [9]and to make plain to everyone the administration of this mystery, which for ages past was kept hidden in God, who created all things.
Col 1 [15]He is the image of the invisible God, the firstborn over all creation. [16]For by him all things were created: things in heaven and on earth, visible and invisible, whether thrones or powers or rulers or authorities; all things were created by him and for him.
Heb 11 [3]By faith we understand that the universe was formed at God's command, so that what is seen was not made out of what was visible.
Rev 4 [11]"You are worthy, our Lord and God, to receive glory and honor and power, for you created all things, and by your will they were created and have their being."

2. Humankind and Nature Have Things in Common

a) They Hope through Christ Together

Rom 8 [19]The creation waits in eager expectation for the sons of God to be revealed. [20]For the creation was subjected to frustration, not by its own choice, but by the will of the one who subjected it, in hope [21]that the creation itself will be liberated from its bondage to decay and brought into the glorious freedom of the children of God.
Eph 1 [9]And he made known to us the mystery of his will according to his good pleasure, which he purposed in Christ, [10]to be put into effect when the times will have reached their fulfillment—to bring all things in heaven and on earth together under one head, even Christ.
Col 1 [19]For God was pleased to have all his fullness dwell in him, [20]and through him to reconcile to himself all things, whether things on earth or things in heaven, by making peace through his blood, shed on the cross.

b) They Praise God Together

Ps 19 [1]The heavens declare the glory of God; the skies proclaim the work of his hands. [2]Day after day they pour forth speech; night after night they display knowledge. [3]There is no speech or language where their voice is not heard. [4]Their voice goes out into all the earth, their words to the ends of the world.
In the heavens he has pitched a tent for the sun, [5]which is like a bridegroom coming forth from his pavilion, like a champion rejoicing to run his course. [6]It rises at one end of the heavens and makes its circuit to the other; nothing is hidden from its heat.
Ps 96 [10]Say among the nations, "The LORD reigns." The world is firmly established, it cannot be moved; he will judge the peoples with equity. [11]Let the heavens rejoice, let the earth be glad; let the sea resound, and all that is in it; [12]let the fields be jubilant, and everything in them. Then all the trees of the forest

will sing for joy; [13]they will sing before the LORD, for he comes, he comes to judge the earth. He will judge the world in righteousness and the peoples in his truth.

Ps 148 [1]Praise the LORD.

Praise the LORD from the heavens, praise him in the heights above. [2]Praise him, all his angels, praise him, all his heavenly hosts. [3]Praise him, sun and moon, praise him, all you shining stars. [4]Praise him, you highest heavens and you waters above the skies. [5]Let them praise the name of the LORD, for he commanded and they were created. [6]He set them in place for ever and ever; he gave a decree that will never pass away.

[7]Praise the LORD from the earth, you great sea creatures and all ocean depths, [8]lightning and hail, snow and clouds, stormy winds that do his bidding, [9]you mountains and all hills, fruit trees and all cedars, [10]wild animals and all cattle, small creatures and flying birds, [11]kings of the earth and all nations, you princes and all rulers on earth, [12]young men and maidens, old men and children.

[13]Let them praise the name of the LORD, for his name alone is exalted; his splendor is above the earth and the heavens.

c) They Suffer Together

Lev 18 [25]"'Even the land was defiled; so I punished it for its sin, and the land vomited out its inhabitants.'"

Rom 8 [18]I consider that our present sufferings are not worth comparing with the glory that will be revealed in us. . . . [20]For the creation was subjected to frustration, not by its own choice, but by the will of the one who subjected it, in hope [21]that the creation itself will be liberated from its bondage to decay and brought into the glorious freedom of the children of God.

[22]We know that the whole creation has been groaning as in the pains of childbirth right up to the present time.

3. Humankind Is the Steward of Nature

Gen 1 [26]Then God said, "Let us make man in our image, in our likeness, and let them rule over the fish of the sea and the birds of the air, over the livestock, over all the earth, and over all the creatures that move along the ground."

[27]So God created man in his own image, in the image of God he created him; male and female he created them.

[28]God blessed them and said to them, "Be fruitful and increase in number; fill the earth and subdue it. Rule over the fish of the sea and the birds of the air and over every living creature that moves on the ground."

[29]Then God said, "I give you every seed-bearing plant on the face of the whole earth and every tree that has fruit with seed in it. They will be yours for food. [30]And to all the beasts of the earth and all the birds of the air and all the creatures that move on the ground—everything that has the breath of life in it—I give every green plant for food." And it was so.

Gen 2 [15]The LORD God took the man and put him in the Garden of Eden to work it and take care of it.

Ps 8 [5]You made him a little lower than the heavenly beings and crowned him with glory and honor.

[6]You made him ruler over the works of your hands; you put everything under his feet: [7]all flocks and herds, and the beasts of the field, [8]the birds of the air, and the fish of the sea, all that swim the paths of the seas.

Ps 115 [16]The highest heavens belong to the LORD, but the earth he has given to man.

D. Join with Creation in Anticipating God's Future Work in Nature

Isa 35 [1]The desert and the parched land will be glad; the wilderness will rejoice and blossom. Like the crocus, [2]it will burst into bloom; it will rejoice greatly and shout for joy. The glory of Lebanon will be given to it, the splendor of Carmel and Sharon; they will see the glory of the LORD, the splendor of our God.

[3]Strengthen the feeble hands, steady the knees that give way; [4]say to those with fearful hearts, "Be strong, do not fear; your God will come, he will come with vengeance; with divine retribution he will come to save you."

[5]Then will the eyes of the blind be opened and the ears of the deaf unstopped. [6]Then will the lame leap like a deer, and the mute tongue shout for joy. Water will gush forth in the wilderness and streams in the desert. [7]The burning sand will become a pool, the thirsty ground bubbling springs. In the haunts where jackals once lay, grass and reeds and papyrus will grow.

[8]And a highway will be there; it will be called the Way of Holiness. The unclean will not journey on it; it will be for those who walk in that Way; wicked fools will not go about on it. [9]No lion will be there, nor will any ferocious beast get up on it; they will not be found there. But only the redeemed will walk there, [10]and the ransomed of the LORD will return. They will enter Zion with singing; everlasting joy will crown their heads. Gladness and joy will overtake them, and sorrow and sighing will flee away.

Rom 8 [19]The creation waits in eager expectation for the sons of God to be revealed. [20]For the creation was subjected to frustration, not by its own choice, but by the will of the one who subjected it, in hope [21]that the creation itself will be liberated from its bondage to decay and brought into the glorious freedom of the children of God.

[22]We know that the whole creation has been groaning as in the pains of childbirth right up to the present time. [23]Not only so, but we ourselves, who have the firstfruits of the Spirit, groan inwardly as we wait eagerly for our adoption as sons, the redemption of our bodies. [24]For in this hope we were saved. But hope that is seen is no hope at all. Who hopes for what he already has? [25]But if we hope for what we do not yet have, we wait for it patiently.

E. Remember That God Will Recreate Nature

Isa 11 [6]The wolf will live with the lamb, the leopard will lie down with the goat, the calf and the lion and the yearling together; and a little child will lead them. [7]The cow will feed with the bear, their young will lie down together, and the lion will eat straw like the ox. [8]The infant will play near the hole of the cobra, and the young child put his hand into the viper's nest. [9]They will neither harm nor destroy on all my holy mountain, for the earth will be full of the knowledge of the LORD as the waters cover the sea.

Isa 65 [17]"Behold, I will create new heavens and a new earth. The former things will not be remembered, nor will they come to mind. [18]But be glad and rejoice forever in what I will create, for I will create Jerusalem to be a delight and its people a joy. [19]I will rejoice over Jerusalem and take delight in my people; the sound of weeping and of crying will be heard in it no more.

[20]"Never again will there be in it an infant who lives but a few days, or an old man who does not live out his years; he who dies at a hundred will be thought a mere youth; he who fails to reach a hundred will be considered accursed. [21]They will build houses and dwell in them; they will plant vineyards and eat their fruit. [22]No longer will they build houses and others live in them, or plant and others eat. For as the days of a tree, so will be the days of my people; my chosen ones will long enjoy the works of their hands. [23]They will not toil in vain or bear children doomed to misfortune; for they will be a people blessed by the LORD, they and their descendants with them. [24]Before they call I will answer; while they are still speaking I will hear. [25]The wolf and the lamb will feed together, and the lion will eat straw like the ox, but dust will be the serpent's food. They will neither harm nor destroy on all my holy mountain," says the LORD.

Isa 66 [22]"As the new heavens and the new earth that I make will endure before me," declares the LORD, "so will your name and descendants endure."

2 Pet 3 [13]But in keeping with his promise we are looking forward to a new heaven and a new earth, the home of righteousness.

Rev 21 [1]Then I saw a new heaven and a new earth, for the first heaven and the first earth had passed away, and there was no longer any sea.

II
Responsibilities toward Other People

A. Duties to Specific Groups of People

1. Responsibilities of Husbands toward Wives

a) Husbands Are to Be Intimate with Their Wives

1 Cor 7 3The husband should fulfill his marital duty to his wife, and likewise the wife to her husband. 4The wife's body does not belong to her alone but also to her husband. In the same way, the husband's body does not belong to him alone but also to his wife. 5Do not deprive each other except by mutual consent and for a time, so that you may devote yourselves to prayer. Then come together again so that Satan will not tempt you because of your lack of self-control.

b) Husbands Are to Comfort Their Wives

1 Sam 1 8Elkanah her husband would say to her, "Hannah, why are you weeping? Why don't you eat? Why are you downhearted? Don't I mean more to you than ten sons?"

c) Husbands Are to Enjoy Their Wives

Eccles 9 9Enjoy life with your wife, whom you love, all the days of this meaningless life that God has given you under the sun—all your meaningless days. For this is your lot in life and in your toilsome labor under the sun.

d) Husbands Are to Love Their Wives

Eph 5 25Husbands, love your wives, just as Christ loved the church and gave himself up for her 26to make her holy, cleansing her by the washing with water through the word, 27and to present her to himself as a radiant church, without stain or wrinkle or any other blemish, but holy and blameless. 28In this same way, husbands ought to love their wives as their own bodies. He who loves his wife loves himself. 29After all, no one ever hated his own body, but he feeds and cares for it, just as Christ does the church. . . . 33However, each one of you also must love his wife as he loves himself, and the wife must respect her husband.
Col 3 19Husbands, love your wives and do not be harsh with them.

e) Husbands Are to Please Their Wives

1 Cor 7 33But a married man is concerned about the affairs of this world—how he can please his wife. . . .

f) Husbands Are to Praise Their Wives

Prov 31 28Her children arise and call her blessed; her husband also, and he praises her: 29"Many women do noble things, but you surpass them all." 30Charm is deceptive, and beauty is fleeting; but a woman who fears the Lord is to be praised.

g) Husbands Are to Remain Faithful to Their Wives

Gen 2 23The man said, "This is now bone of my bones and flesh of my flesh; she shall be called 'woman,' for she was taken out of man." 24For this reason a man will leave his father and mother and be united to his wife, and they will become one flesh.
Exod 20 14"You shall not commit adultery."
Prov 5 15Drink water from your own cistern, running water from your own well. 16Should your springs overflow in the streets, your streams of water in the public squares? 17Let them be yours alone, never to be shared with strangers. 18May your fountain be blessed, and may you rejoice in the wife of your youth. 19A loving doe, a graceful deer—may her breasts satisfy you always, may you ever be captivated by her love.
Mal 2 14You ask, "Why?" It is because the Lord is acting as the witness between you and the wife of your youth, because you have broken faith with her, though she is your partner, the wife of your marriage covenant.

15Has not the Lord made them one? In flesh and spirit they are his. And why one? Because he was seeking godly offspring. So guard yourself in your spirit, and do not break faith with the wife of your youth.
Matt 19 3Some Pharisees came to him to test him. They asked, "Is it lawful for a man to divorce his wife for any and every reason?"

4"Haven't you read," he replied, "that at the beginning the Creator 'made them male and female,' 5and said, 'For this reason a man will leave his father and mother and be united to his wife, and the two will become one flesh'? 6So they are no longer two, but one. Therefore what God has joined together, let man not separate."

7"Why then," they asked, "did Moses command that a man give his wife a certificate of divorce and send her away?"

8Jesus replied, "Moses permitted you to divorce your wives because your hearts were hard. But it was not this way from the beginning. 9I tell you that anyone who divorces his wife, except for marital unfaithfulness, and marries another woman commits adultery."
1 Cor 7 2But since there is so much immorality, each man should have his own wife, and each woman her own husband.

h) Husbands Are to Respect Their Wives

Prov 31 11Her husband has full confidence in her and lacks nothing of value.
1 Pet 3 7Husbands, in the same way be considerate as you live with your wives, and treat them with respect as the weaker partner and as heirs with you of the gracious gift of life, so that nothing will hinder your prayers.

2. Responsibilities of Wives toward Husbands

a) Wives Are to Be Intimate with Their Husbands

1 Cor 7 3The husband should fulfill his marital duty to his wife, and likewise the wife to her husband. 4The wife's body does not belong to her alone but also to her husband. In the same way, the husband's body does not belong to him alone but also to his wife. 5Do not deprive each other except by mutual consent and for a time, so that you may devote yourselves to prayer. Then come together again so that Satan will not tempt you because of your lack of self-control.

b) Wives Are to Love Their Husbands

Titus 2 4Then they can train the younger women to love their husbands and children. . . .

c) Wives Are to Please Their Husbands

Prov 12 4A wife of noble character is her husband's crown, but a disgraceful wife is like decay in his bones.
1 Cor 7 33But a married man is concerned about the affairs of this world—how he can please his wife—34and his interests are divided. An unmarried woman or virgin is concerned about the Lord's affairs: Her aim is to be devoted to the Lord in both body and spirit. But a married woman is concerned about the affairs of this world—how she can please her husband.

d) Wives Are to Remain Faithful to Their Husbands

Exod 20 14"You shall not commit adultery."
Rom 7 2For example, by law a married woman is bound to her husband as long as he is alive, but if her husband dies, she is released from the law of marriage. 3So then, if she marries another man while her husband is still alive, she is called an adulteress. But if her husband dies, she is released from that law and is not an adulteress even though she marries another man.
1 Cor 7 2But since there is so much immorality, each man should have his own wife, and each woman her own husband.
1 Cor 7 10To the married I give this command (not I, but the Lord): A wife must not separate from her husband.
1 Cor 7 39A woman is bound to her husband as long as he lives. But if her husband dies, she is free to marry anyone she wishes, but he must belong to the Lord.

e) Wives Are to Respect Their Husbands

Eph 5 33However, each one of you also must love his wife as he loves himself, and the wife must respect her husband.

f) Wives Are to Submit to Their Husbands

Eph 5 22Wives, submit to your husbands as to the Lord. 23For the husband is the head of the wife as Christ is the head of the church, his body, of which he is the Savior. 24Now as the church submits to Christ, so also wives should submit to their husbands in everything.
Col 3 18Wives, submit to your husbands, as is fitting in the Lord.
Titus 2 4Then they can train the younger women to love their husbands and children, 5to be self-controlled and pure, to be busy at home, to be kind, and to be subject to their husbands, so that no one will malign the word of God.
1 Pet 3 1Wives, in the same way be submissive to your husbands so that, if any of them do not believe the word, they may be won over without words by the behavior of their wives, 2when they see the purity and reverence of your lives. 3Your beauty should not come from outward adornment, such as braided hair and the wearing of gold jewelry and fine clothes. 4Instead, it should be that of your inner self, the unfading beauty of a gentle and quiet spirit, which is of great worth in God's sight. 5For this is the way the holy women of the past who put their hope in God used to make themselves beautiful. They were submissive to their own husbands, 6like Sarah, who obeyed Abraham and called him her master. You are her daughters if you do what is right and do not give way to fear.

3. Responsibilities toward Aliens (Foreigners)

a) God's Attitude toward Aliens

(1) God Considers the Oppression of Aliens a Serious Offense

Jer 7 2"Stand at the gate of the LORD's house and there proclaim this message: 'Hear the word of the LORD, all you people of Judah who come through these gates to worship the LORD. 3This is what the LORD Almighty, the God of Israel, says: Reform your ways and your actions, and I will let you live in this place. 4Do not trust in deceptive words and say, "This is the temple of the LORD, the temple of the LORD, the temple of the LORD!" 5If you really change your ways and your actions and deal with each other justly, 6if you do not oppress the alien, the fatherless or the widow and do not shed innocent blood in this place, and if you do not follow other gods to your own harm, 7then I will let you live in this place, in the land I gave your forefathers for ever and ever.'"
Ezek 22 29"The people of the land practice extortion and commit robbery; they oppress the poor and needy and mistreat the alien, denying them justice. . . . 31So I will pour out my wrath on them and consume them with my fiery anger, bringing down on their own heads all they have done, declares the Sovereign LORD."

(2) God Forbids the Oppression of Aliens

Jer 22 3"'This is what the LORD says: Do what is just and right. Rescue from the hand of his oppressor the one who has been robbed. Do no wrong or violence to the alien, the fatherless or the widow, and do not shed innocent blood in this place.'"
Zech 7 8And the word of the LORD came again to Zechariah: 9"This is what the LORD Almighty says: 'Administer true justice; show mercy and compassion to one another. 10Do not oppress the widow or the fatherless, the alien or the poor. In your hearts do not think evil of each other.'"

(3) God Forgives Aliens

Num 15 22"'Now if you unintentionally fail to keep any of these commands the LORD gave Moses—23any of the LORD's commands to you through him, from the day the LORD gave them and continuing through the generations to come—24and if this is done unintentionally without the community being aware of it, then the whole community is to offer a young bull for a burnt offering as an aroma pleasing to the LORD, along with its prescribed grain offering and drink offering, and a male goat for a sin offering. 25The priest is to make atonement for the whole Israelite community, and they will be forgiven, for it was not intentional and they have brought to the LORD for their wrong an offering made by fire and a sin offering. 26The whole Israelite community and the aliens living among them will be forgiven, because all the people were involved in the unintentional wrong.'"

(4) God Loves Aliens

Deut 10 17For the LORD your God is God of gods and Lord of lords, the great God, mighty and awesome, who shows no partiality and accepts no bribes. 18He defends the cause of the fatherless and the widow, and loves the alien, giving him food and clothing.

(5) God Promises Salvation for Aliens

Isa 56 1This is what the LORD says: "Maintain justice and do what is right, for my salvation is close at hand and my righteousness will soon be revealed. 2Blessed is the man who does this, the man who holds it fast, who keeps the Sabbath without desecrating it, and keeps his hand from doing any evil."

3Let no foreigner who has bound himself to the LORD say, "The LORD will surely exclude me from his people." And let not any eunuch complain, "I am only a dry tree."

4For this is what the LORD says: "To the eunuchs who keep my Sabbaths, who choose what pleases me and hold fast to my covenant—5to them I will give within my temple and its walls a memorial and a name better than sons and daughters; I will give them an everlasting name that will not be cut off. 6And foreigners who bind themselves to the LORD to serve him, to love the name of the LORD, and to worship him, all who keep the Sabbath without desecrating it and who hold fast to my covenant—7these I will bring to my holy mountain and give them joy in my house of prayer. Their burnt offerings and sacrifices will be accepted on my altar; for my house will be called a house of prayer for all nations." 8The Sovereign LORD declares—he who gathers the exiles of Israel: "I will gather still others to them besides those already gathered."

(6) God Promises to Punish the Oppressors of Aliens

Ezek 22 7"'In you they have treated father and mother with contempt; in you they have oppressed the alien and mistreated the fatherless and the widow. . . .

13"'I will surely strike my hands together at the unjust gain you have made and at the blood you have shed in your midst.' . . . 29The people of the land practice extortion and commit robbery; they oppress the poor and needy and mistreat the alien, denying them justice. . . . 31So I will pour out my wrath on them and consume them with my fiery anger, bringing down on their own heads all they have done, declares the Sovereign LORD."
Mal 3 5"So I will come near to you for judgment. I will be quick to testify against sorcerers, adulterers and perjurers, against those who defraud laborers of their wages, who oppress the widows and the fatherless, and deprive aliens of justice, but do not fear me," says the LORD Almighty.

(7) God Protects Aliens

Ps 146 9The LORD watches over the alien and sustains the fatherless and the widow, but he frustrates the ways of the wicked.

(8) God Provides for Aliens

Deut 26 1When you have entered the land the LORD your God is giving you as an inheritance and have taken possession of it and settled in it, 2take some of the firstfruits of all that you produce from the soil of the land the LORD your God is giving you and put them in a basket. Then go to the place the LORD your God will choose as a dwelling for his Name 3and say to the priest in office at the time, "I declare today to the LORD your God that I have come to the land the LORD swore to our forefathers to give us." 4The priest shall take the basket from your hands and set it down in front of the altar of the LORD your God. 5Then you shall declare before the LORD your God: "My father was a wandering Aramean, and he went down into Egypt with a few people and lived there and became a great nation, powerful and numerous. 6But the Egyptians mistreated us and made us suffer, putting us to hard labor. 7Then we cried out to the LORD, the God of our fathers, and the LORD heard our voice and saw our misery, toil and oppression. [8]So the LORD brought us out of Egypt with a mighty hand and an outstretched arm, with great terror and with miraculous signs and wonders. [9]He brought us to this place and gave us this land, a land flowing with milk and honey; [10]and now I bring the firstfruits of the soil that you, O LORD, have given me." Place the basket before the LORD your God and bow down before him. [11]And you and the Levites and the aliens among you shall rejoice in all the good things the LORD your God has given to you and your household.

b) The Believer's Duty to Aliens

(1) Consider Aliens Equal in Status

Ezek 47 [21]"You are to distribute this land among yourselves according to the tribes of Israel. [22]You are to allot it as an inheritance for yourselves and for the aliens who have settled among you and who have children. You are to consider them as native-born Israelites; along with you they are to be allotted an inheritance among the tribes of Israel. [23]In whatever tribe the alien settles, there you are to give him his inheritance," declares the Sovereign LORD.

(2) Consider Aliens Part of God's Covenant People

Deut 29 [9]Carefully follow the terms of this covenant, so that you may prosper in everything you do. [10]All of you are standing today in the presence of the LORD your God—your leaders and chief men, your elders and officials, and all the other men of Israel, [11]together with your children and your wives, and the aliens living in your camps who chop your wood and carry your water. [12]You are standing here in order to enter into a covenant with the LORD your God, a covenant the LORD is making with you this day and sealing with an oath, [13]to confirm you this day as his people, that he may be your God as he promised you and as he swore to your fathers, Abraham, Isaac and Jacob. [14]I am making this covenant, with its oath, not only with you [15]who are standing here with us today in the presence of the LORD our God but also with those who are not here today.

Deut 31 [12]"Assemble the people—men, women and children, and the aliens living in your towns—so they can listen and learn to fear the LORD your God and follow carefully all the words of this law."

Josh 8 [33]All Israel, aliens and citizens alike, with their elders, officials and judges, were standing on both sides of the ark of the covenant of the LORD, facing those who carried it—the priests, who were Levites. Half of the people stood in front of Mount Gerizim and half of them in front of Mount Ebal, as Moses the servant of the LORD had formerly commanded when he gave instructions to bless the people of Israel.

[34]Afterward, Joshua read all the words of the law—the blessings and the curses—just as it is written in the Book of the Law. [35]There was not a word of all that Moses had commanded that Joshua did not read to the whole assembly of Israel, including the women and children, and the aliens who lived among them.

Isa 14 [1]The LORD will have compassion on Jacob; once again he will choose Israel and will settle them in their own land. Aliens will join them and unite with the house of Jacob.

(3) Demonstrate Hospitality to Aliens

Matt 25 [34]"Then the King will say to those on his right, 'Come, you who are blessed by my Father; take your inheritance, the kingdom prepared for you since the creation of the world. [35]For I was hungry and you gave me something to eat, I was thirsty and you gave me something to drink, I was a stranger and you invited me in. . . .'"

Heb 13 [2]Do not forget to entertain strangers, for by so doing some people have entertained angels without knowing it.

(4) Despise the Oppression of Aliens

Ps 94 [1]O LORD, the God who avenges, O God who avenges, shine forth. [2]Rise up, O Judge of the earth; pay back to the proud what they deserve. [3]How long will the wicked, O LORD, how long will the wicked be jubilant?

[4]They pour out arrogant words; all the evildoers are full of boasting. [5]They crush your people, O LORD; they oppress your inheritance. [6]They slay the widow and the alien; they murder the fatherless.

(5) Do Not Oppress Aliens

Exod 23 [9]"Do not oppress an alien; you yourselves know how it feels to be aliens, because you were aliens in Egypt."

(6) Give Liberally to Aliens

Lev 19 [9]"'When you reap the harvest of your land, do not reap to the very edges of your field or gather the gleanings of your harvest. [10]Do not go over your vineyard a second time or pick up the grapes that have fallen. Leave them for the poor and the alien. I am the LORD your God.'"

Lev 23 [22]"'When you reap the harvest of your land, do not reap to the very edges of your field or gather the gleanings of your harvest. Leave them for the poor and the alien. I am the LORD your God.'"

Lev 25 [35]"'If one of your countrymen becomes poor and is unable to support himself among you, help him as you would an alien or a temporary resident, so he can continue to live among you. [36]Do not take interest of any kind from him, but fear your God, so that your countryman may continue to live among you. [37]You must not lend him money at interest or sell him food at a profit.'"

Deut 14 [28]At the end of every three years, bring all the tithes of that year's produce and store it in your towns, [29]so that the Levites (who have no allotment or inheritance of their own) and the aliens, the fatherless and the widows who live in your towns may come and eat and be satisfied, and so that the LORD your God may bless you in all the work of your hands.

Deut 24 [19]When you are harvesting in your field and you overlook a sheaf, do not go back to get it. Leave it for the alien, the fatherless and the widow, so that the LORD your God may bless you in all the work of your hands. [20]When you beat the olives from your trees, do not go over the branches a second time. Leave what remains for the alien, the fatherless and the widow. [21]When you harvest the grapes in your vineyard, do not go over the vines again. Leave what remains for the alien, the fatherless and the widow.

(7) Involve Aliens in the Religious Community

Exod 12 [17]"Celebrate the Feast of Unleavened Bread, because it was on this very day that I brought your divisions out of Egypt. Celebrate this day as a lasting ordinance for the generations to come. [18]In the first month you are to eat bread made without yeast, from the evening of the fourteenth day until the evening of the twenty-first day. [19]For seven days no yeast is to be found in your houses. And whoever eats anything with yeast in it must be cut off from the community of Israel, whether he is an alien or native-born. [20]Eat nothing made with yeast. Wherever you live, you must eat unleavened bread."

Exod 12 [43]The LORD said to Moses and Aaron, "These are the regulations for the Passover: No foreigner is to eat of it. [44]Any slave you have bought may eat of it after you have circumcised him, [45]but a temporary resident and a hired worker may not eat of it.

[46]"It must be eaten inside one house; take none of the meat outside the house. Do not break any of the bones. [47]The whole community of Israel must celebrate it.

[48]"An alien living among you who wants to celebrate the LORD's Passover must have all the males in his household circumcised; then he may take part like one born in the land. No uncircumcised male may eat of it. [49]The same law applies to the native-born and to the alien living among you."

Exod 20 [8]"Remember the Sabbath day by keeping it holy. [9]Six days you shall labor and do all your work, [10]but the seventh day is a Sabbath to the LORD your God. On it you shall not do any work, neither you, nor your son or daughter, nor your manservant or maidservant, nor your animals, nor the alien within your gates. [11]For in six days the LORD made the heavens and the earth, the sea, and all that is in them, but he rested on the seventh day. Therefore the LORD blessed the Sabbath day and made it holy."

Exod 23 [12]"Six days do your work, but on the seventh day do not work, so that your ox and your donkey may rest and the slave born in your household, and the alien as well, may be refreshed."

Lev 22 [17]The LORD said to Moses, [18]"Speak to Aaron and his sons and to all the Israelites and say to them: 'If any of you—either an Israelite or an alien living in Israel—presents a gift for a burnt offering to the LORD, either to fulfill a vow or as a freewill offering, [19]you must present a male without defect from the cattle, sheep or goats in order that it may be accepted on your behalf.'"

Deut 16 [9]Count off seven weeks from the time you begin to put the sickle to the standing grain. [10]Then celebrate the Feast of Weeks to the LORD your God by giving a freewill offering in proportion to the blessings the LORD your God has given you. [11]And rejoice before the LORD your God at the place he will choose as a dwelling for his Name—you, your sons and daughters, your menservants and maidservants, the Levites in your towns, and the aliens, the fatherless and the widows living among you. [12]Remember that you were slaves in Egypt, and follow carefully these decrees.

Deut 16 [13]Celebrate the Feast of Tabernacles for seven days after you have gathered the produce of your threshing floor and your winepress. [14]Be joyful at your Feast—you, your sons and daughters, your menservants and maidservants, and the Levites, the aliens, the fatherless and the widows who live in your towns. [15]For seven days celebrate the Feast to the LORD your God at the place the LORD will choose. For the LORD your God will bless you in all your harvest and in all the work of your hands, and your joy will be complete.

(8) Love Aliens as One's Own People

Lev 19 [34]"'The alien living with you must be treated as one of your native-born. Love him as yourself, for you were aliens in Egypt. I am the LORD your God.'"

Deut 10 [19]And you are to love those who are aliens, for you yourselves were aliens in Egypt.

(9) Maintain Equal Justice for Aliens

Lev 24 [22]"'You are to have the same law for the alien and the native-born. I am the LORD your God.'"

Deut 1 [16]And I charged your judges at that time: Hear the disputes between your brothers and judge fairly, whether the case is between brother Israelites or between one of them and an alien. [17]Do not show partiality in judging; hear both small and great alike. Do not be afraid of any man, for judgment belongs to God. Bring me any case too hard for you, and I will hear it.

Deut 24 [17]Do not deprive the alien or the fatherless of justice, or take the cloak of the widow as a pledge.

Deut 27 [19]"Cursed is the man who withholds justice from the alien, the fatherless or the widow." Then all the people shall say, "Amen!"

Job 29 [16]"I was a father to the needy; I took up the case of the stranger."

(10) Show Respect for Aliens

Deut 23 [7]Do not abhor an Edomite, for he is your brother. Do not abhor an Egyptian, because you lived as an alien in his country. [8]The third generation of children born to them may enter the assembly of the LORD.

(11) Subject Aliens to the Same Legal Restrictions and Privileges as Israelites

Lev 17 [8]"Say to them: 'Any Israelite or any alien living among them who offers a burnt offering or sacrifice [9]and does not bring it to the entrance to the Tent of Meeting to sacrifice it to the LORD—that man must be cut off from his people.

[10]"'Any Israelite or any alien living among them who eats any blood—I will set my face against that person who eats blood and will cut him off from his people. [11]For the life of a creature is in the blood, and I have given it to you to make atonement for yourselves on the altar; it is the blood that makes atonement for one's life. [12]Therefore I say to the Israelites, "None of you may eat blood, nor may an alien living among you eat blood."

[13]"'Any Israelite or any alien living among you who hunts any animal or bird that may be eaten must drain out the blood and cover it with earth, [14]because the life of every creature is its blood. That is why I have said to the Israelites, "You must not eat the blood of any creature, because the life of every creature is its blood; anyone who eats it must be cut off."

[15]"'Anyone, whether native-born or alien, who eats anything found dead or torn by wild animals must wash his clothes and bathe with water, and he will be ceremonially unclean till evening; then he will be clean. [16]But if he does not wash his clothes and bathe himself, he will be held responsible.'"

Lev 18 [26]"'But you must keep my decrees and my laws. The native-born and the aliens living among you must not do any of these detestable things. . . .'"

Lev 20 [2]"Say to the Israelites: 'Any Israelite or any alien living in Israel who gives any of his children to Molech must be put to death. The people of the community are to stone him.'"

Lev 24 [15]"Say to the Israelites: 'If anyone curses his God, he will be held responsible; [16]anyone who blasphemes the name of the LORD must be put to death. The entire assembly must stone him. Whether an alien or native-born, when he blasphemes the Name, he must be put to death.'"

Num 9 [14]"'An alien living among you who wants to celebrate the LORD's Passover must do so in accordance with its rules and regulations. You must have the same regulations for the alien and the native-born.'"

Num 15 [14]"'For the generations to come, whenever an alien or anyone else living among you presents an offering made by fire as an aroma pleasing to the LORD, he must do exactly as you do. [15]The community is to have the same rules for you and for the alien living among you; this is a lasting ordinance for the generations to come. You and the alien shall be the same before the LORD: [16]The same laws and regulations will apply both to you and to the alien living among you. . . . [29]One and the same law applies to everyone who sins unintentionally, whether he is a native-born Israelite or an alien.

[30]"'But anyone who sins defiantly, whether native-born or alien, blasphemes the LORD, and that person must be cut off from his people.'"

Josh 20 [2]"Tell the Israelites to designate the cities of refuge, as I instructed you through Moses, [3]so that anyone who kills a person accidentally and unintentionally may flee there and find protection from the avenger of blood.". . . [9]Any of the Israelites or any alien living among them who killed someone accidentally could flee to these designated cities and not be killed by the avenger of blood prior to standing trial before the assembly.

Ezek 14 [7]"'When any Israelite or any alien living in Israel separates himself from me and sets up idols in his heart and puts a wicked stumbling block before his face and then goes to a prophet to inquire of me, I the LORD will answer him myself. [8]I will set my face against that man and make him an example and a byword. I will cut him off from my people. Then you will know that I am the LORD.'"

(12) Treat Aliens with Fairness

Exod 22 [21]"Do not mistreat an alien or oppress him, for you were aliens in Egypt."

Lev 19 [33]"'When an alien lives with you in your land, do not mistreat him.'"

Deut 24 [14]Do not take advantage of a hired man who is poor and needy, whether he is a brother Israelite or an alien living in one of your towns. [15]Pay him his wages each day before sunset, because he is poor and is counting on it. Otherwise he may cry to the LORD against you, and you will be guilty of sin.

4. Responsibilities toward Children

a) The Believer's Attitude toward Children

(1) Discipline Children

Prov 13 [24]He who spares the rod hates his son, but he who loves him is careful to discipline him.

Prov 19 [18]Discipline your son, for in that there is hope; do not be a willing party to his death.

Prov 23 [13]Do not withhold discipline from a child; if you punish him with the rod, he will not die.

Prov 29 [17]Discipline your son, and he will give you peace; he will bring delight to your soul.

Heb 12 [7]Endure hardship as discipline; God is treating you as sons. For what son is not disciplined by his father? [8]If you are not disciplined (and everyone undergoes discipline), then you are illegitimate children and not true sons. [9]Moreover, we have all had human fathers who disciplined us and we respected them for it. How much more should we submit to the Father of our spirits and live!

(2) Have Compassion for Children

Ps 103 [13]As a father has compassion on his children, so the LORD has compassion on those who fear him. . . .

(3) Love Children

Isa 49 [15]"Can a mother forget the baby at her breast and have no compassion on the child she has borne? Though she may forget, I will not forget you!"

Titus 2 [4]Then they can train the younger women to love their husbands and children. . . .

(4) Pray for Children

2 Sam 12 [15]After Nathan had gone home, the LORD struck the child that Uriah's wife had borne to David, and he became ill. [16]David pleaded with God for the child. He fasted and went into his house and spent the nights lying on the ground. [17]The elders of his household stood beside him to get him up from the ground, but he refused, and he would not eat any food with them.

1 Chron 29 [19]"And give my son Solomon the wholehearted devotion to keep your commands, requirements and decrees and to do everything to build the palatial structure for which I have provided."

Job 1 [5]When a period of feasting had run its course, Job would send and have them purified. Early in the morning he would sacrifice a burnt offering for each of them, thinking, "Perhaps my children have sinned and cursed God in their hearts." This was Job's regular custom.

(5) Provide for Children

Job 42 [15]Nowhere in all the land were there found women as beautiful as Job's daughters, and their father granted them an inheritance along with their brothers.

Prov 19 [14]Houses and wealth are inherited from parents, but a prudent wife is from the LORD.

2 Cor 12 [14]Now I am ready to visit you for the third time, and I will not be a burden to you, because what I want is not your possessions but you. After all, children should not have to save up for their parents, but parents for their children.

(6) Respect Children

Eph 6 [4]Fathers, do not exasperate your children; instead, bring them up in the training and instruction of the Lord.

Col 3 [21]Fathers, do not embitter your children, or they will become discouraged.

(7) Train Children in the Lord's Way

Deut 11 [18]Fix these words of mine in your hearts and minds; tie them as symbols on your hands and bind them on your foreheads. [19]Teach them to your children, talking about them when you sit at home and when you walk along the road, when you lie down and when you get up. [20]Write them on the doorframes of your houses and on your gates, [21]so that your days and the days of your children may be many in the land that the LORD swore to give your forefathers, as many as the days that the heavens are above the earth.

Deut 32 [46]he said to them, "Take to heart all the words I have solemnly declared to you this day, so that you may command your children to obey carefully all the words of this law."

Prov 22 [6]Train a child in the way he should go, and when he is old he will not turn from it.

Isa 38 [19]The living, the living—they praise you, as I am doing today; fathers tell their children about your faithfulness.

Eph 6 [4]Fathers, do not exasperate your children; instead, bring them up in the training and instruction of the Lord.

2 Tim 1 [5]I have been reminded of your sincere faith, which first lived in your grandmother Lois and in your mother Eunice and, I am persuaded, now lives in you also.

2 Tim 3 [14]But as for you, continue in what you have learned and have become convinced of, because you know those from whom you learned it, [15]and how from infancy you have known the holy Scriptures, which are able to make you wise for salvation through faith in Christ Jesus.

b) Examples of Love for Children

(1) Hagar Showed Love for a Child

Gen 21 [14]Early the next morning Abraham took some food and a skin of water and gave them to Hagar. He set them on her shoulders and then sent her off with the boy. She went on her way and wandered in the desert of Beersheba.

[15]When the water in the skin was gone, she put the boy under one of the bushes. [16]Then she went off and sat down nearby, about a bowshot away, for she thought, "I cannot watch the boy die." And as she sat there nearby, she began to sob.

[17]God heard the boy crying, and the angel of God called to Hagar from heaven and said to her, "What is the matter, Hagar? Do not be afraid; God has heard the boy crying as he lies there. [18]Lift the boy up and take him by the hand, for I will make him into a great nation."

[19]Then God opened her eyes and she saw a well of water. So she went and filled the skin with water and gave the boy a drink.

(2) Laban Showed Love for Children

Gen 31 [55]Early the next morning Laban kissed his grandchildren and his daughters and blessed them. Then he left and returned home.

(3) Jacob Showed Love for a Child

Gen 44 [20]"And we answered, 'We have an aged father, and there is a young son born to him in his old age. His brother is dead, and he is the only one of his mother's sons left, and his father loves him.' . . .

[30]"So now, if the boy is not with us when I go back to your servant my father and if my father, whose life is closely bound up with the boy's life, [31]sees that the boy isn't there, he will die. Your servants will bring the gray head of our father down to the grave in sorrow. [32]Your servant guaranteed the boy's safety to my father. I said, 'If I do not bring him back to you, I will bear the blame before you, my father, all my life!'

[33]"Now then, please let your servant remain here as my lord's slave in place of the boy, and let the boy return with his brothers. [34]How can I go back to my father if the boy is not with me? No! Do not let me see the misery that would come upon my father."

(4) David Showed Love for a Child

2 Sam 13 [37]Absalom fled and went to Talmai son of Ammihud, the king of Geshur. But King David mourned for his son every day.

[38]After Absalom fled and went to Geshur, he stayed there three years. [39]And the spirit of the king longed to go to Absalom, for he was consoled concerning Amnon's death.

(5) Mary and Joseph Showed Love for a Child

Luke 2 [41]Every year his parents went to Jerusalem for the Feast of the Passover. [42]When he was twelve years old, they went up to the Feast, according to the custom. [43]After the Feast was over, while his parents were returning home, the boy Jesus stayed behind in Jerusalem, but they were unaware of it. [44]Thinking he was in their company, they traveled on for a day. Then they began looking for him among their relatives and friends. [45]When they did not find him, they went back to Jerusalem to look for him. [46]After three days they found him in the temple courts, sitting among the teachers, listening to them and asking them questions. [47]Everyone who heard him was amazed at his understanding and his answers. [48]When his parents saw him, they were astonished. His mother said to him, "Son, why have you treated us like this? Your father and I have been anxiously searching for you."

[49]"Why were you searching for me?" he asked. "Didn't you know I had to be in my Father's house?" [50]But they did not understand what he was saying to them.

[51]Then he went down to Nazareth with them and was obedient to them. But his mother treasured all these things in her heart.

(6) Jairus Showed Love for a Child

Mark 5 [21]When Jesus had again crossed over by boat to the other side of the lake, a large crowd gathered around him while he was by the lake. [22]Then one of the synagogue rulers, named Jairus, came there. Seeing Jesus, he fell at his feet [23]and pleaded earnestly with him, "My little daughter is dying. Please come and put your hands on her so that she will be healed and live."

(7) A Royal Official Showed Love for a Child

John 4 [46]Once more he visited Cana in Galilee, where he had turned the water into wine. And there was a certain royal official whose son lay sick at Capernaum. [47]When this man heard that Jesus had arrived in Galilee from Judea, he went to him and begged him to come and heal his son, who was close to death. . . .

[49]The royal official said, "Sir, come down before my child dies."

5. Responsibilities toward Civil Authorities

a) Honor Civil Authorities

Rom 13 [7]Give everyone what you owe him: If you owe taxes, pay taxes; if revenue, then revenue; if respect, then respect; if honor, then honor.

1 Pet 2 [17]Show proper respect to everyone: Love the brotherhood of believers, fear God, honor the king.

b) Pray for Civil Authorities

1 Tim 2 [1]I urge, then, first of all, that requests, prayers, intercession and thanksgiving be made for everyone—[2]for kings and all those in authority, that we may live peaceful and quiet lives in all godliness and holiness.

c) Submit to Civil Authorities

Rom 13 [1]Everyone must submit himself to the governing authorities, for there is no authority except that which God has established. The authorities that exist have been established by God. [2]Consequently, he who rebels against the authority is rebelling against what God has instituted, and those who do so will bring judgment on themselves. [3]For rulers hold no terror for those who do right, but for those who do wrong. Do you want to be free from fear of the one in authority? Then do what is right and he will commend you. [4]For he is God's servant to do you good. But if you do wrong, be afraid, for he does not bear the sword for nothing. He is God's servant, an agent of wrath to bring punishment on the wrongdoer. [5]Therefore, it is necessary to submit to the authorities, not only because of possible punishment but also because of conscience.

[6]This is also why you pay taxes, for the authorities are God's servants, who give their full time to governing.

1 Pet 2 [13]Submit yourselves for the Lord's sake to every authority instituted among men: whether to the king, as the supreme authority, [14]or to governors, who are sent by him to punish those who do wrong and to commend those who do right. [15]For it is God's will that by doing good you should silence the ignorant talk of foolish men. [16]Live as free men, but do not use your freedom as a cover-up for evil; live as servants of God.

6. Responsibilities toward the Elderly

a) Care for the Elderly

1 Tim 5 [4]But if a widow has children or grandchildren, these should learn first of all to put their religion into practice by caring for their own family and so repaying their parents and grandparents, for this is pleasing to God. . . . [8]If anyone does not provide for his relatives, and especially for his immediate family, he has denied the faith and is worse than an unbeliever.

b) Encourage the Elderly

1 Tim 5 [1]Do not rebuke an older man harshly, but exhort him as if he were your father. Treat younger men as brothers, [2]older women as mothers, and younger women as sisters, with absolute purity.

Titus 2 [2]Teach the older men to be temperate, worthy of respect, self-controlled, and sound in faith, in love and in endurance.

[3]Likewise, teach the older women to be reverent in the way they live, not to be slanderers or addicted to much wine, but to teach what is good.

c) Respect the Elderly

Lev 19 [32]"'Rise in the presence of the aged, show respect for the elderly and revere your God. I am the LORD.'"

Job 32 [6]So Elihu son of Barakel the Buzite said: "I am young in years, and you are old; that is why I was fearful, not daring to tell you what I know. [7]I thought, 'Age should speak; advanced years should teach wisdom.'"

1 Pet 5 [5]Young men, in the same way be submissive to those who are older. All of you, clothe yourselves with humility toward one another, because, "God opposes the proud but gives grace to the humble."

7. Responsibilities toward Enemies

a) The Believer's Duty to Enemies

(1) Be Merciful to Enemies

Exod 23 [4]"If you come across your enemy's ox or donkey wandering off, be sure to take it back to him. [5]If you see the donkey of someone who hates you fallen down under its load, do not leave it there; be sure you help him with it."

Matt 5 [7]"Blessed are the merciful, for they will be shown mercy."

Luke 6 [36]"Be merciful, just as your Father is merciful."

Rom 12 [17]Do not repay anyone evil for evil. Be careful to do what is right in the eyes of everybody. . . . [19]Do not take revenge, my friends, but leave room for God's wrath, for it is written: "It is mine to avenge; I will repay," says the Lord. [20]On the contrary: "If your enemy is hungry, feed him; if he is thirsty, give him something to drink. In doing this, you will heap burning coals on his head." [21]Do not be overcome by evil, but overcome evil with good.

(2) Bless Enemies

Luke 6 [28]". . . bless those who curse you, pray for those who mistreat you."

Rom 12 [14]Bless those who persecute you; bless and do not curse.

1 Cor 4 [12]We work hard with our own hands. When we are cursed, we bless; when we are persecuted, we endure it. . . .

1 Pet 3 [9]Do not repay evil with evil or insult with insult, but with blessing, because to this you were called so that you may inherit a blessing.

(3) Do Good to Enemies

Prov 25 [21]If your enemy is hungry, give him food to eat; if he is thirsty, give him water to drink. [22]In doing this, you will heap burning coals on his head, and the LORD will reward you.

Luke 6 [27]"But I tell you who hear me: Love your enemies, do good to those who hate you, [28]bless those who curse you, pray for those who mistreat you. [29]If someone strikes you on one cheek, turn to him the other also. If someone takes your cloak, do not stop him from taking your tunic. [30]Give to everyone who asks you, and if anyone takes what belongs to you, do not demand it back. [31]Do to others as you would have them do to you. . . . [35]But love your enemies, do good to them, and lend to them without expecting to get anything back. Then your reward will be great, and you will be sons of the Most High, because he is kind to the ungrateful and wicked."

1 Cor 4 [13]when we are slandered, we answer kindly. Up to this moment we have become the scum of the earth, the refuse of the world.

(4) Forgive Enemies

Matt 6 [12]"'Forgive us our debts, as we also have forgiven our debtors. . . .' [14]For if you forgive men when they sin against you, your heavenly Father will also forgive you. [15]But if you do not forgive men their sins, your Father will not forgive your sins."

Matt 18 [21]Then Peter came to Jesus and asked, "Lord, how many times shall I forgive my brother when he sins against me? Up to seven times?"

[22]Jesus answered, "I tell you, not seven times, but seventy-seven times.

[23]"Therefore, the kingdom of heaven is like a king who wanted to settle accounts with his servants. [24]As he began the settlement, a man who owed him ten thousand talents was brought to him. [25]Since he was not able to pay, the master ordered that he and his wife and his children and all that he had be sold to repay the debt.

[26]"The servant fell on his knees before him. 'Be patient with me,' he begged, 'and I will pay back everything.' [27]The servant's master took pity on him, canceled the debt and let him go.

[28]"But when that servant went out, he found one of his fel-

low servants who owed him a hundred denarii. He grabbed him and began to choke him. 'Pay back what you owe me!' he demanded.

29"His fellow servant fell to his knees and begged him, 'Be patient with me, and I will pay you back.'

30"But he refused. Instead, he went off and had the man thrown into prison until he could pay the debt. 31When the other servants saw what had happened, they were greatly distressed and went and told their master everything that had happened.

32"Then the master called the servant in. 'You wicked servant,' he said, 'I canceled all that debt of yours because you begged me to. 33Shouldn't you have had mercy on your fellow servant just as I had on you?' 34In anger his master turned him over to the jailers to be tortured, until he should pay back all he owed.

35"This is how my heavenly Father will treat each of you unless you forgive your brother from your heart."

Luke 17 3"So watch yourselves.

"If your brother sins, rebuke him, and if he repents, forgive him. 4If he sins against you seven times in a day, and seven times comes back to you and says, 'I repent,' forgive him."

(5) Love Enemies

Matt 5 43"You have heard that it was said, 'Love your neighbor and hate your enemy.' 44But I tell you: Love your enemies and pray for those who persecute you, 45that you may be sons of your Father in heaven. He causes his sun to rise on the evil and the good, and sends rain on the righteous and the unrighteous. 46If you love those who love you, what reward will you get? Are not even the tax collectors doing that? 47And if you greet only your brothers, what are you doing more than others? Do not even pagans do that? 48Be perfect, therefore, as your heavenly Father is perfect."

Luke 6 27"But I tell you who hear me: Love your enemies, do good to those who hate you. . . .

32"If you love those who love you, what credit is that to you? Even 'sinners' love those who love them. 33And if you do good to those who are good to you, what credit is that to you? Even 'sinners' do that. 34And if you lend to those from whom you expect repayment, what credit is that to you? Even 'sinners' lend to 'sinners,' expecting to be repaid in full. 35But love your enemies, do good to them, and lend to them without expecting to get anything back. Then your reward will be great, and you will be sons of the Most High, because he is kind to the ungrateful and wicked."

(6) Pray for Enemies

Matt 5 44"But I tell you: Love your enemies and pray for those who persecute you. . . ."

Luke 6 28". . . bless those who curse you, pray for those who mistreat you."

(7) Withhold Judgment from Enemies

Job 31 29"If I have rejoiced at my enemy's misfortune or gloated over the trouble that came to him—30I have not allowed my mouth to sin by invoking a curse against his life. . . ."

Prov 24 17Do not gloat when your enemy falls; when he stumbles, do not let your heart rejoice, 18or the LORD will see and disapprove and turn his wrath away from him.

Rom 12 19Do not take revenge, my friends, but leave room for God's wrath, for it is written: "It is mine to avenge; I will repay," says the Lord.

b) Examples of Forgiving Enemies

(1) Esau Forgave an Enemy

Gen 33 1Jacob looked up and there was Esau, coming with his four hundred men; so he divided the children among Leah, Rachel and the two maidservants. 2He put the maidservants and their children in front, Leah and her children next, and Rachel and Joseph in the rear. 3He himself went on ahead and bowed down to the ground seven times as he approached his brother.

4But Esau ran to meet Jacob and embraced him; he threw his arms around his neck and kissed him. And they wept. 5Then Esau looked up and saw the women and children. "Who are these with you?" he asked.

Jacob answered, "They are the children God has graciously given your servant."

6Then the maidservants and their children approached and bowed down. 7Next, Leah and her children came and bowed down. Last of all came Joseph and Rachel, and they too bowed down.

8Esau asked, "What do you mean by all these droves I met?"

"To find favor in your eyes, my lord," he said.

9But Esau said, "I already have plenty, my brother. Keep what you have for yourself."

10"No, please!" said Jacob. "If I have found favor in your eyes, accept this gift from me. For to see your face is like seeing the face of God, now that you have received me favorably. 11Please accept the present that was brought to you, for God has been gracious to me and I have all I need." And because Jacob insisted, Esau accepted it.

(2) Joseph Forgave His Enemies

Gen 45 5"And now, do not be distressed and do not be angry with yourselves for selling me here, because it was to save lives that God sent me ahead of you. 6For two years now there has been famine in the land, and for the next five years there will not be plowing and reaping. 7But God sent me ahead of you to preserve for you a remnant on earth and to save your lives by a great deliverance.

8"So then, it was not you who sent me here, but God. He made me father to Pharaoh, lord of his entire household and ruler of all Egypt. 9Now hurry back to my father and say to him, 'This is what your son Joseph says: God has made me lord of all Egypt. Come down to me; don't delay. 10You shall live in the region of Goshen and be near me—you, your children and grandchildren, your flocks and herds, and all you have. 11I will provide for you there, because five years of famine are still to come. Otherwise you and your household and all who belong to you will become destitute.'

12"You can see for yourselves, and so can my brother Benjamin, that it is really I who am speaking to you. 13Tell my father about all the honor accorded me in Egypt and about everything you have seen. And bring my father down here quickly."

14Then he threw his arms around his brother Benjamin and wept, and Benjamin embraced him, weeping. 15And he kissed all his brothers and wept over them. Afterward his brothers talked with him.

Gen 50 15When Joseph's brothers saw that their father was dead, they said, "What if Joseph holds a grudge against us and pays us back for all the wrongs we did to him?" 16So they sent word to Joseph, saying, "Your father left these instructions before he died: 17'This is what you are to say to Joseph: I ask you to forgive your brothers the sins and the wrongs they committed in treating you so badly.' Now please forgive the sins of the servants of the God of your father." When their message came to him, Joseph wept.

18His brothers then came and threw themselves down before him. "We are your slaves," they said.

19But Joseph said to them, "Don't be afraid. Am I in the place of God? 20You intended to harm me, but God intended it for good to accomplish what is now being done, the saving of many lives. 21So then, don't be afraid. I will provide for you and your children." And he reassured them and spoke kindly to them.

(3) David Forgave an Enemy

1 Sam 24 8Then David went out of the cave and called out to Saul, "My lord the king!" When Saul looked behind him, David bowed down and prostrated himself with his face to the ground. 9He said to Saul, "Why do you listen when men say, 'David is bent on harming you'? 10This day you have seen with your own eyes how the LORD delivered you into my hands in the cave. Some urged me to kill you, but I spared you; I said, 'I will not lift my hand against my master, because he is the LORD's anointed.' 11See, my father, look at this piece of your robe in my hand! I cut off the corner of your robe but did not kill you. Now understand and recognize that I am not guilty of wrongdoing or rebellion. I have not wronged you, but you are hunting me down to take my life. 12May the LORD judge between you and me. And may the LORD avenge the wrongs you have done to me, but my hand will not touch you."

1 Sam 26 [21]Then Saul said, "I have sinned. Come back, David my son. Because you considered my life precious today, I will not try to harm you again. Surely I have acted like a fool and have erred greatly."

[22]"Here is the king's spear," David answered. "Let one of your young men come over and get it. [23]The LORD rewards every man for his righteousness and faithfulness. The LORD delivered you into my hands today, but I would not lay a hand on the LORD's anointed. [24]As surely as I valued your life today, so may the LORD value my life and deliver me from all trouble."

[25]Then Saul said to David, "May you be blessed, my son David; you will do great things and surely triumph."

So David went on his way, and Saul returned home.

(4) Jesus Forgave His Enemies

Luke 23 [33]When they came to the place called the Skull, there they crucified him, along with the criminals—one on his right, the other on his left. [34]Jesus said, "Father, forgive them, for they do not know what they are doing." And they divided up his clothes by casting lots.

(5) Stephen Forgave His Enemies

Acts 7 [59]While they were stoning him, Stephen prayed, "Lord Jesus, receive my spirit." [60]Then he fell on his knees and cried out, "Lord, do not hold this sin against them." When he had said this, he fell asleep.

(6) Paul Forgave His Enemies

2 Tim 4 [16]At my first defense, no one came to my support, but everyone deserted me. May it not be held against them.

8. Responsibilities toward the Fatherless (Orphans)

a) God's Attitude toward Orphans

(1) God Cares for Orphans

Ps 68 [5]A father to the fatherless, a defender of widows, is God in his holy dwelling.

Hos 14 [3]"Assyria cannot save us; we will not mount war-horses. We will never again say 'Our gods' to what our own hands have made, for in you the fatherless find compassion."

(2) God Considers the Oppression of Orphans a Serious Offense

Jer 7 [2]"Stand at the gate of the LORD's house and there proclaim this message: 'Hear the word of the LORD, all you people of Judah who come through these gates to worship the LORD. [3]This is what the LORD Almighty, the God of Israel, says: Reform your ways and your actions, and I will let you live in this place. [4]Do not trust in deceptive words and say, "This is the temple of the LORD, the temple of the LORD, the temple of the LORD!" [5]If you really change your ways and your actions and deal with each other justly, [6]if you do not oppress the alien, the fatherless or the widow and do not shed innocent blood in this place, and if you do not follow other gods to your own harm, [7]then I will let you live in this place, in the land I gave your forefathers for ever and ever.'"

(3) God Defends Orphans

Deut 10 [17]For the LORD your God is God of gods and Lord of lords, the great God, mighty and awesome, who shows no partiality and accepts no bribes. [18]He defends the cause of the fatherless and the widow, and loves the alien, giving him food and clothing.

Ps 10 [17]You hear, O LORD, the desire of the afflicted; you encourage them, and you listen to their cry, [18]defending the fatherless and the oppressed, in order that man, who is of the earth, may terrify no more.

(4) God Helps Orphans

Ps 10 [14]But you, O God, do see trouble and grief; you consider it to take it in hand. The victim commits himself to you; you are the helper of the fatherless.

(5) God Prohibits the Oppression of Orphans

Jer 22 [3]"'This is what the LORD says: Do what is just and right. Rescue from the hand of his oppressor the one who has been robbed. Do no wrong or violence to the alien, the fatherless or the widow, and do not shed innocent blood in this place.'"

Zech 7 [8]And the word of the LORD came again to Zechariah . . . [10]"'Do not oppress the widow or the fatherless, the alien or the poor. In your hearts do not think evil of each other.'"

(6) God Promises to Punish the Oppressors of Orphans

Exod 22 [22]"Do not take advantage of a widow or an orphan. [23]If you do and they cry out to me, I will certainly hear their cry. [24]My anger will be aroused, and I will kill you with the sword; your wives will become widows and your children fatherless."

Isa 1 [23]Your rulers are rebels, companions of thieves; they all love bribes and chase after gifts. They do not defend the cause of the fatherless; the widow's case does not come before them. [24]Therefore the Lord, the LORD Almighty, the Mighty One of Israel, declares: "Ah, I will get relief from my foes and avenge myself on my enemies. [25]I will turn my hand against you; I will thoroughly purge away your dross and remove all your impurities."

Isa 10 [1]Woe to those who make unjust laws, to those who issue oppressive decrees, [2]to deprive the poor of their rights and withhold justice from the oppressed of my people, making widows their prey and robbing the fatherless.

Jer 5 [27]"Like cages full of birds, their houses are full of deceit; they have become rich and powerful [28]and have grown fat and sleek. Their evil deeds have no limit; they do not plead the case of the fatherless to win it, they do not defend the rights of the poor. [29]Should I not punish them for this?" declares the LORD. "Should I not avenge myself on such a nation as this?"

Ezek 22 [7]"'In you they have treated father and mother with contempt; in you they have oppressed the alien and mistreated the fatherless and the widow. . . .

[13]"'I will surely strike my hands together at the unjust gain you have made and at the blood you have shed in your midst.'"

Mal 3 [5]"So I will come near to you for judgment. I will be quick to testify against sorcerers, adulterers and perjurers, against those who defraud laborers of their wages, who oppress the widows and the fatherless, and deprive aliens of justice, but do not fear me," says the LORD Almighty.

(7) God Protects Orphans

Jer 49 [11]"Leave your orphans; I will protect their lives. Your widows too can trust in me."

(8) God Provides for Orphans

Deut 14 [28]At the end of every three years, bring all the tithes of that year's produce and store it in your towns, [29]so that the Levites (who have no allotment or inheritance of their own) and the aliens, the fatherless and the widows who live in your towns may come and eat and be satisfied, and so that the LORD your God may bless you in all the work of your hands.

Deut 26 [12]When you have finished setting aside a tenth of all your produce in the third year, the year of the tithe, you shall give it to the Levite, the alien, the fatherless and the widow, so that they may eat in your towns and be satisfied. [13]Then say to the LORD your God: "I have removed from my house the sacred portion and have given it to the Levite, the alien, the fatherless and the widow, according to all you commanded. I have not turned aside from your commands nor have I forgotten any of them."

(9) God Sustains Orphans

Ps 146 [9]The LORD watches over the alien and sustains the fatherless and the widow, but he frustrates the ways of the wicked.

b) The Believer's Duty to Orphans

(1) Care for Orphans

Job 31 [16]"If I have denied the desires of the poor or let the eyes of the widow grow weary, [17]if I have kept my bread to myself, not sharing it with the fatherless—[18]but from my youth I reared him as would a father, and from my birth I guided the widow—[19]if I have seen anyone perishing for lack of clothing, or a needy man without a garment, . . . [21]if I have raised my hand against the fatherless, knowing that I had influence in court, [22]then let my arm fall from the shoulder, let it be broken off at the joint. 23For I dreaded destruction from God, and for fear of his splendor I could not do such things."

James 1 27Religion that God our Father accepts as pure and faultless is this: to look after orphans and widows in their distress and to keep oneself from being polluted by the world.

(2) Detest the Oppression of Orphans

Ps 94 1O LORD, the God who avenges, O God who avenges, shine forth. 2Rise up, O Judge of the earth; pay back to the proud what they deserve. 3How long will the wicked, O LORD, how long will the wicked be jubilant?

4They pour out arrogant words; all the evildoers are full of boasting. 5They crush your people, O LORD; they oppress your inheritance. 6They slay the widow and the alien; they murder the fatherless.

Prov 23 10Do not move an ancient boundary stone or encroach on the fields of the fatherless, 11for their Defender is strong; he will take up their case against you.

(3) Entreat God to Deliver Orphans

Job 24 1"Why does the Almighty not set times for judgment? Why must those who know him look in vain for such days? 2Men move boundary stones; they pasture flocks they have stolen. 3They drive away the orphan's donkey and take the widow's ox in pledge."

Ps 82 3"Defend the cause of the weak and fatherless; maintain the rights of the poor and oppressed."

(4) Give Generously to Orphans

Deut 24 19When you are harvesting in your field and you overlook a sheaf, do not go back to get it. Leave it for the alien, the fatherless and the widow, so that the LORD your God may bless you in all the work of your hands. 20When you beat the olives from your trees, do not go over the branches a second time. Leave what remains for the alien, the fatherless and the widow. 21When you harvest the grapes in your vineyard, do not go over the vines again. Leave what remains for the alien, the fatherless and the widow.

(5) Involve Orphans in the Religious Community

Deut 16 9Count off seven weeks from the time you begin to put the sickle to the standing grain. 10Then celebrate the Feast of Weeks to the LORD your God by giving a freewill offering in proportion to the blessings the LORD your God has given you. 11And rejoice before the LORD your God at the place he will choose as a dwelling for his Name—you, your sons and daughters, your menservants and maidservants, the Levites in your towns, and the aliens, the fatherless and the widows living among you.

Deut 16 13Celebrate the Feast of Tabernacles for seven days after you have gathered the produce of your threshing floor and your winepress. 14Be joyful at your Feast—you, your sons and daughters, your menservants and maidservants, and the Levites, the aliens, the fatherless and the widows who live in your towns. 15For seven days celebrate the Feast to the LORD your God at the place the LORD will choose. For the LORD your God will bless you in all your harvest and in all the work of your hands, and your joy will be complete.

(6) Treat Orphans Justly

Deut 24 17Do not deprive the alien or the fatherless of justice, or take the cloak of the widow as a pledge. 18Remember that you were slaves in Egypt and the LORD your God redeemed you from there. That is why I command you to do this.

Deut 27 19"Cursed is the man who withholds justice from the alien, the fatherless or the widow." Then all the people shall say, "Amen!"

Isa 1 17". . . learn to do right! Seek justice, encourage the oppressed. Defend the cause of the fatherless, plead the case of the widow."

9. Responsibilities toward Laborers

a) God's Attitude toward Laborers

(1) God Condemns Injustice toward Laborers

Jer 22 13"Woe to him who builds his palace by unrighteousness, his upper rooms by injustice, making his countrymen work for nothing, not paying them for their labor."

(2) God Hears the Cry of Laborers

Deut 24 14Do not take advantage of a hired man who is poor and needy, whether he is a brother Israelite or an alien living in one of your towns. 15Pay him his wages each day before sunset, because he is poor and is counting on it. Otherwise he may cry to the LORD against you, and you will be guilty of sin.

(3) God Punishes Those Who Oppress Laborers

Mal 3 5"So I will come near to you for judgment. I will be quick to testify against sorcerers, adulterers and perjurers, against those who defraud laborers of their wages, who oppress the widows and the fatherless, and deprive aliens of justice, but do not fear me," says the LORD Almighty.

b) The Believer's Duty to Laborers

(1) Be Merciful to Laborers

Lev 25 39"'If one of your countrymen becomes poor among you and sells himself to you, do not make him work as a slave. 40He is to be treated as a hired worker or a temporary resident among you; he is to work for you until the Year of Jubilee. 41Then he and his children are to be released, and he will go back to his own clan and to the property of his forefathers. 42Because the Israelites are my servants, whom I brought out of Egypt, they must not be sold as slaves. 43Do not rule over them ruthlessly, but fear your God.'"

(2) Require Fairness toward Laborers

Lev 19 13"'Do not defraud your neighbor or rob him.

"'Do not hold back the wages of a hired man overnight.'"

Deut 24 14Do not take advantage of a hired man who is poor and needy, whether he is a brother Israelite or an alien living in one of your towns. 15Pay him his wages each day before sunset, because he is poor and is counting on it. Otherwise he may cry to the LORD against you, and you will be guilty of sin.

Luke 10 1After this the Lord appointed seventy-two others and sent them two by two ahead of him to every town and place where he was about to go. . . . 7"Stay in that house, eating and drinking whatever they give you, for the worker deserves his wages. Do not move around from house to house."

Rom 4 4Now when a man works, his wages are not credited to him as a gift, but as an obligation.

1 Tim 5 18For the Scripture says, "Do not muzzle the ox while it is treading out the grain," and "The worker deserves his wages."

(3) Respect Laborers as Creations of God

Job 31 13"If I have denied justice to my menservants and maidservants when they had a grievance against me, 14what will I do when God confronts me? What will I answer when called to account? 15Did not he who made me in the womb make them? Did not the same one form us both within our mothers?"

Luke 7 2There a centurion's servant, whom his master valued highly, was sick and about to die.

Eph 6 9And masters, treat your slaves in the same way. Do not threaten them, since you know that he who is both their Master and yours is in heaven, and there is no favoritism with him.

Col 4 1Masters, provide your slaves with what is right and fair, because you know that you also have a Master in heaven.

10. Responsibilities toward Neighbors

a) God's Attitude toward Neighbors

(1) God Hears the Pleadings of Neighbors

Exod 22 26"If you take your neighbor's cloak as a pledge, return it to him by sunset, 27because his cloak is the only covering he has for his body. What else will he sleep in? When he cries out to me, I will hear, for I am compassionate."

(2) God Makes a Covenant-Promise to Save Neighbors

Jer 31 31"The time is coming," declares the LORD, "when I will make a new covenant with the house of Israel and with the house of Judah. 32It will not be like the covenant I made with their forefathers when I took them by the hand to lead them out of Egypt, because they broke my covenant, though I was a husband to them," declares the LORD. 33"This is the covenant I will make with the house of Israel after that time," declares the LORD. "I will put my law in their minds and write it on their hearts. I will be their God, and they will be my people. 34No longer will a man teach his neighbor, or a man his brother, saying, 'Know the LORD,' because they will all know me, from the least of them to the greatest," declares the LORD. "For I will forgive their wickedness and will remember their sins no more."

(3) God Promises to Punish the Oppressors of Neighbors

Jer 9 [8]"Their tongue is a deadly arrow; it speaks with deceit. With his mouth each speaks cordially to his neighbor, but in his heart he sets a trap for him. [9]Should I not punish them for this?" declares the LORD. "Should I not avenge myself on such a nation as this?"

Hab 2 [15]"Woe to him who gives drink to his neighbors, pouring it from the wineskin till they are drunk, so that he can gaze on their naked bodies. [16]You will be filled with shame instead of glory. Now it is your turn! Drink and be exposed! The cup from the LORD's right hand is coming around to you, and disgrace will cover your glory."

b) The Believer's Duty to Neighbors

(1) Administer Justice toward Your Neighbor

Lev 19 [17]"'Do not hate your brother in your heart. Rebuke your neighbor frankly so you will not share in his guilt.'"

Lev 20 [10]"'If a man commits adultery with another man's wife—with the wife of his neighbor—both the adulterer and the adulteress must be put to death.'"

Deut 19 [4]This is the rule concerning the man who kills another and flees there to save his life—one who kills his neighbor unintentionally, without malice aforethought. [5]For instance, a man may go into the forest with his neighbor to cut wood, and as he swings his ax to fell a tree, the head may fly off and hit his neighbor and kill him. That man may flee to one of these cities and save his life. [6]Otherwise, the avenger of blood might pursue him in a rage, overtake him if the distance is too great, and kill him even though he is not deserving of death, since he did it to his neighbor without malice aforethought. . . .

[11]But if a man hates his neighbor and lies in wait for him, assaults and kills him, and then flees to one of these cities, [12]the elders of his town shall send for him, bring him back from the city, and hand him over to the avenger of blood to die.

(2) Avoid Coveting the Belongings of Your Neighbor

Exod 20 [17]"You shall not covet your neighbor's house. You shall not covet your neighbor's wife, or his manservant or maidservant, his ox or donkey, or anything that belongs to your neighbor."

Eccles 4 [4]And I saw that all labor and all achievement spring from man's envy of his neighbor. This too is meaningless, a chasing after the wind.

(3) Avoid False Testimony against Your Neighbor

Exod 20 [16]"You shall not give false testimony against your neighbor."

Prov 3 [28]Do not say to your neighbor, "Come back later; I'll give it tomorrow"—when you now have it with you.

[29]Do not plot harm against your neighbor, who lives trustfully near you. [30]Do not accuse a man for no reason—when he has done you no harm.

Prov 24 [28]Do not testify against your neighbor without cause, or use your lips to deceive.

Prov 25 [18]Like a club or a sword or a sharp arrow is the man who gives false testimony against his neighbor.

(4) Avoid Immorality against Your Neighbor

Lev 18 [20]"'Do not have sexual relations with your neighbor's wife and defile yourself with her.'"

(5) Be Considerate of Your Neighbor

Exod 22 [26]"If you take your neighbor's cloak as a pledge, return it to him by sunset, [27]because his cloak is the only covering he has for his body. What else will he sleep in? When he cries out to me, I will hear, for I am compassionate."

Lev 19 [16]"'Do not go about spreading slander among your people.

"'Do not do anything that endangers your neighbor's life. I am the LORD.'"

Deut 24 [10]When you make a loan of any kind to your neighbor, do not go into his house to get what he is offering as a pledge. [11]Stay outside and let the man to whom you are making the loan bring the pledge out to you. [12]If the man is poor, do not go to sleep with his pledge in your possession. [13]Return his cloak to him by sunset so that he may sleep in it. Then he will thank you, and it will be regarded as a righteous act in the sight of the LORD your God.

Prov 14 [21]He who despises his neighbor sins, but blessed is he who is kind to the needy.

Prov 25 [17]Seldom set foot in your neighbor's house—too much of you, and he will hate you.

Prov 27 [14]If a man loudly blesses his neighbor early in the morning, it will be taken as a curse.

(6) Build Up Your Neighbor

Rom 15 [2]Each of us should please his neighbor for his good, to build him up.

(7) Hate Wickedness toward Neighbors

Ps 12 [1]Help, LORD, for the godly are no more; the faithful have vanished from among men. [2]Everyone lies to his neighbor; their flattering lips speak with deception.

Ps 28 [2]Hear my cry for mercy as I call to you for help, as I lift up my hands toward your Most Holy Place.

[3]Do not drag me away with the wicked, with those who do evil, who speak cordially with their neighbors but harbor malice in their hearts.

Ps 101 [3]I will set before my eyes no vile thing.

The deeds of faithless men I hate; they will not cling to me. [4]Men of perverse heart shall be far from me; I will have nothing to do with evil.

[5]Whoever slanders his neighbor in secret, him will I put to silence; whoever has haughty eyes and a proud heart, him will I not endure.

(8) Live Righteously before Your Neighbor

Ps 15 [2]He whose walk is blameless and who does what is righteous, who speaks the truth from his heart [3]and has no slander on his tongue, who does his neighbor no wrong and casts no slur on his fellowman . . . [5]who lends his money without usury and does not accept a bribe against the innocent.

He who does these things will never be shaken.

(9) Love Your Neighbor as Yourself

Lev 19 [18]"'Do not seek revenge or bear a grudge against one of your people, but love your neighbor as yourself. I am the LORD.'"

Mark 12 [28]One of the teachers of the law came and heard them debating. Noticing that Jesus had given them a good answer, he asked him, "Of all the commandments, which is the most important?"

[29]"The most important one," answered Jesus, "is this: 'Hear, O Israel, the Lord our God, the Lord is one. [30]Love the Lord your God with all your heart and with all your soul and with all your mind and with all your strength.' [31]The second is this: 'Love your neighbor as yourself.' There is no commandment greater than these."

[32]"Well said, teacher," the man replied. "You are right in saying that God is one and there is no other but him. [33]To love him with all your heart, with all your understanding and with all your strength, and to love your neighbor as yourself is more important than all burnt offerings and sacrifices."

[34]When Jesus saw that he had answered wisely, he said to him, "You are not far from the kingdom of God." And from then on no one dared ask him any more questions.

Luke 10 [25]On one occasion an expert in the law stood up to test Jesus. "Teacher," he asked, "what must I do to inherit eternal life?"

[26]"What is written in the Law?" he replied. "How do you read it?"

[27]He answered: "'Love the Lord your God with all your heart and with all your soul and with all your strength and with all your mind'; and, 'Love your neighbor as yourself.'"

[28]"You have answered correctly," Jesus replied. "Do this and you will live."

[29]But he wanted to justify himself, so he asked Jesus, "And who is my neighbor?"

[30]In reply Jesus said: "A man was going down from

Jerusalem to Jericho, when he fell into the hands of robbers. They stripped him of his clothes, beat him and went away, leaving him half dead. [31]A priest happened to be going down the same road, and when he saw the man, he passed by on the other side. [32]So too, a Levite, when he came to the place and saw him, passed by on the other side. [33]But a Samaritan, as he traveled, came where the man was; and when he saw him, he took pity on him. [34]He went to him and bandaged his wounds, pouring on oil and wine. Then he put the man on his own donkey, took him to an inn and took care of him. [35]The next day he took out two silver coins and gave them to the innkeeper. 'Look after him,' he said, 'and when I return, I will reimburse you for any extra expense you may have.'

[36]"Which of these three do you think was a neighbor to the man who fell into the hands of robbers?"

[37]The expert in the law replied, "The one who had mercy on him."

Jesus told him, "Go and do likewise."

Rom 13 [8]Let no debt remain outstanding, except the continuing debt to love one another, for he who loves his fellowman has fulfilled the law. [9]The commandments, "Do not commit adultery," "Do not murder," "Do not steal," "Do not covet," and whatever other commandment there may be, are summed up in this one rule: "Love your neighbor as yourself." [10]Love does no harm to its neighbor. Therefore love is the fulfillment of the law.

Gal 5 [13]You, my brothers, were called to be free. But do not use your freedom to indulge the sinful nature; rather, serve one another in love. [14]The entire law is summed up in a single command: "Love your neighbor as yourself." [15]If you keep on biting and devouring each other, watch out or you will be destroyed by each other.

James 2 [8]If you really keep the royal law found in Scripture, "Love your neighbor as yourself," you are doing right.

(10) Maintain the Integrity of Your Neighbor

Prov 11 [9]With his mouth the godless destroys his neighbor, but through knowledge the righteous escape.

Prov 11 [12]A man who lacks judgment derides his neighbor, but a man of understanding holds his tongue.

Prov 16 [29]A violent man entices his neighbor and leads him down a path that is not good.

Prov 26 [18]Like a madman shooting firebrands or deadly arrows [19]is a man who deceives his neighbor and says, "I was only joking!"

(11) Make Restitution for Wrongdoings against Your Neighbor

Lev 6 [1]The LORD said to Moses: [2]"If anyone sins and is unfaithful to the LORD by deceiving his neighbor about something entrusted to him or left in his care or stolen, or if he cheats him, [3]or if he finds lost property and lies about it, or if he swears falsely, or if he commits any such sin that people may do—[4] when he thus sins and becomes guilty, he must return what he has stolen or taken by extortion, or what was entrusted to him, or the lost property he found, [5]or whatever it was he swore falsely about. He must make restitution in full, add a fifth of the value to it and give it all to the owner on the day he presents his guilt offering."

(12) Preserve the Innocence of a Guiltless Neighbor

1 Kings 8 [22]Then Solomon stood before the altar of the LORD in front of the whole assembly of Israel, spread out his hands toward heaven [23]and said: "O LORD, God of Israel, there is no God like you in heaven above or on earth below—you who keep your covenant of love with your servants who continue wholeheartedly in your way. . . .

[31]"When a man wrongs his neighbor and is required to take an oath and he comes and swears the oath before your altar in this temple, [32]then hear from heaven and act. Judge between your servants, condemning the guilty and bringing down on his own head what he has done. Declare the innocent not guilty, and so establish his innocence."

(13) Speak Truthfully to Your Neighbor

Eph 4 [25]Therefore each of you must put off falsehood and speak truthfully to his neighbor, for we are all members of one body.

(14) Treat Your Neighbor with Fairness

Lev 19 [13]"'Do not defraud your neighbor or rob him.

"'Do not hold back the wages of a hired man overnight.'"

Lev 19 [15]"'Do not pervert justice; do not show partiality to the poor or favoritism to the great, but judge your neighbor fairly.'"

Deut 19 [14]Do not move your neighbor's boundary stone set up by your predecessors in the inheritance you receive in the land the LORD your God is giving you to possess.

Deut 27 [17]"Cursed is the man who moves his neighbor's boundary stone." Then all the people shall say, "Amen!"

James 4 [11]Brothers, do not slander one another. Anyone who speaks against his brother or judges him speaks against the law and judges it. When you judge the law, you are not keeping it, but sitting in judgment on it. [12]There is only one Lawgiver and Judge, the one who is able to save and destroy. But you—who are you to judge your neighbor?

11. Responsibilities toward the Oppressed

a) God's Attitude toward the Oppressed

(1) God Defends the Oppressed

Job 36 [6]"He does not keep the wicked alive but gives the afflicted their rights."

Ps 9 [9]The LORD is a refuge for the oppressed, a stronghold in times of trouble.

Ps 72 [2]He will judge your people in righteousness, your afflicted ones with justice. . . . [4]He will defend the afflicted among the people and save the children of the needy; he will crush the oppressor.

Ps 103 [6]The LORD works righteousness and justice for all the oppressed.

Ps 146 [7]He upholds the cause of the oppressed and gives food to the hungry. The LORD sets prisoners free. . . .

Isa 14 [32]What answer shall be given to the envoys of that nation? "The LORD has established Zion, and in her his afflicted people will find refuge."

Jer 50 [33]This is what the LORD Almighty says: "The people of Israel are oppressed, and the people of Judah as well. All their captors hold them fast, refusing to let them go. [34]Yet their Redeemer is strong; the LORD Almighty is his name. He will vigorously defend their cause so that he may bring rest to their land, but unrest to those who live in Babylon."

(2) God Delivers the Oppressed from Their Oppressors

Judg 10 [11]The LORD replied, "When the Egyptians, the Amorites, the Ammonites, the Philistines, [12]the Sidonians, the Amalekites and the Maonites oppressed you and you cried to me for help, did I not save you from their hands?"

1 Sam 10 [17]Samuel summoned the people of Israel to the LORD at Mizpah [18]and said to them, "This is what the LORD, the God of Israel, says: 'I brought Israel up out of Egypt, and I delivered you from the power of Egypt and all the kingdoms that oppressed you.'"

Ps 72 [12]For he will deliver the needy who cry out, the afflicted who have no one to help. . . . [14]He will rescue them from oppression and violence, for precious is their blood in his sight.

Ps 76 [8]From heaven you pronounced judgment, and the land feared and was quiet—[9]when you, O God, rose up to judge, to save all the afflicted of the land.

Ps 106 [42]Their enemies oppressed them and subjected them to their power. [43]Many times he delivered them, but they were bent on rebellion and they wasted away in their sin.

Isa 26 [5]He humbles those who dwell on high, he lays the lofty city low; he levels it to the ground and casts it down to the dust. [6]Feet trample it down—the feet of the oppressed, the footsteps of the poor.

(3) God Gives Hope to the Oppressed

Ps 9 [18]But the needy will not always be forgotten, nor the hope of the afflicted ever perish.

Isa 54 [11]"O afflicted city, lashed by storms and not comforted, I will build you with stones of turquoise, your foundations with sapphires."

Zeph 3 [19]"At that time I will deal with all who oppressed you; I will rescue the lame and gather those who have been scattered. I will give them praise and honor in every land where they were put to shame. [20]At that time I will gather you; at that time I will bring you home. I will give you honor and praise among all the peoples of the earth when I restore your fortunes before your very eyes," says the LORD.

(4) God Hears the Cry of the Oppressed

Ps 9 [12]For he who avenges blood remembers; he does not ignore the cry of the afflicted.
Ps 10 [17]You hear, O LORD, the desire of the afflicted; you encourage them, and you listen to their cry, [18]defending the fatherless and the oppressed, in order that man, who is of the earth, may terrify no more.
Ps 22 [24]For he has not despised or disdained the suffering of the afflicted one; he has not hidden his face from him but has listened to his cry for help.
Ps 106 [44]But he took note of their distress when he heard their cry; [45]for their sake he remembered his covenant and out of his great love he relented. [46]He caused them to be pitied by all who held them captive.

(5) God Is Compassionate to the Oppressed

Judg 2 [18]Whenever the LORD raised up a judge for them, he was with the judge and saved them out of the hands of their enemies as long as the judge lived; for the LORD had compassion on them as they groaned under those who oppressed and afflicted them.
Neh 9 [27]"So you handed them over to their enemies, who oppressed them. But when they were oppressed they cried out to you. From heaven you heard them, and in your great compassion you gave them deliverers, who rescued them from the hand of their enemies."
Isa 49 [13]Shout for joy, O heavens; rejoice, O earth; burst into song, O mountains! For the LORD comforts his people and will have compassion on his afflicted ones.

(6) God Promises to Punish Oppressors

Isa 10 [1]Woe to those who make unjust laws, to those who issue oppressive decrees, [2]to deprive the poor of their rights and withhold justice from the oppressed of my people, making widows their prey and robbing the fatherless. [3]What will you do on the day of reckoning, when disaster comes from afar? To whom will you run for help? Where will you leave your riches?
Amos 2 [6]This is what the LORD says: "For three sins of Israel, even for four, I will not turn back my wrath. They sell the righteous for silver, and the needy for a pair of sandals. [7]They trample on the heads of the poor as upon the dust of the ground and deny justice to the oppressed. Father and son use the same girl and so profane my holy name."

b) The Believer's Duty to the Oppressed

(1) Encourage the Oppressed

Job 6 [14]"A despairing man should have the devotion of his friends, even though he forsakes the fear of the Almighty."
Ps 34 [2]My soul will boast in the LORD; let the afflicted hear and rejoice.
Isa 1 [17]". . . learn to do right! Seek justice, encourage the oppressed. Defend the cause of the fatherless, plead the case of the widow."

(2) Help the Oppressed

Isa 58 [6]"Is not this the kind of fasting I have chosen: to loose the chains of injustice and untie the cords of the yoke, to set the oppressed free and break every yoke? [7]Is it not to share your food with the hungry and to provide the poor wanderer with shelter—when you see the naked, to clothe him, and not to turn away from your own flesh and blood? [8]Then your light will break forth like the dawn, and your healing will quickly appear; then your righteousness will go before you, and the glory of the LORD will be your rear guard. [9]Then you will call, and the LORD will answer; you will cry for help, and he will say: Here am I.

"If you do away with the yoke of oppression, with the pointing finger and malicious talk, [10]and if you spend yourselves in behalf of the hungry and satisfy the needs of the oppressed, then your light will rise in the darkness, and your night will become like the noonday. [11]The LORD will guide you always; he will satisfy your needs in a sun-scorched land and will strengthen your frame. You will be like a well-watered garden, like a spring whose waters never fail."
1 Tim 5 [9]No widow may be put on the list of widows unless she is over sixty, has been faithful to her husband, [10]and is well known for her good deeds, such as bringing up children, showing hospitality, washing the feet of the saints, helping those in trouble and devoting herself to all kinds of good deeds.

(3) Petition God on Behalf of the Oppressed

Ps 74 [18]Remember how the enemy has mocked you, O LORD, how foolish people have reviled your name. [19]Do not hand over the life of your dove to wild beasts; do not forget the lives of your afflicted people forever. [20]Have regard for your covenant, because haunts of violence fill the dark places of the land. [21]Do not let the oppressed retreat in disgrace; may the poor and needy praise your name.
Ps 82 [3]"Defend the cause of the weak and fatherless; maintain the rights of the poor and oppressed. [4]Rescue the weak and needy; deliver them from the hand of the wicked."

12. Responsibilities toward Parents

a) The Believer's Attitude toward Parents

(1) Be a Blessing to Your Parents

Prov 10 [1]The proverbs of Solomon: A wise son brings joy to his father, but a foolish son grief to his mother.
Prov 17 [6]Children's children are a crown to the aged, and parents are the pride of their children.
Prov 23 [22]Listen to your father, who gave you life, and do not despise your mother when she is old. [23]Buy the truth and do not sell it; get wisdom, discipline and understanding. [24]The father of a righteous man has great joy; he who has a wise son delights in him. [25]May your father and mother be glad; may she who gave you birth rejoice!
Prov 27 [11]Be wise, my son, and bring joy to my heart; then I can answer anyone who treats me with contempt.
Prov 29 [17]Discipline your son, and he will give you peace; he will bring delight to your soul.

(2) Care and Provide for Your Parents

Mark 7 [10]"For Moses said, 'Honor your father and your mother,' and, 'Anyone who curses his father or mother must be put to death.' [11]But you say that if a man says to his father or mother: 'Whatever help you might otherwise have received from me is Corban' (that is, a gift devoted to God), [12]then you no longer let him do anything for his father or mother. [13]Thus you nullify the word of God by your tradition that you have handed down. And you do many things like that."
1 Tim 5 [4]But if a widow has children or grandchildren, these should learn first of all to put their religion into practice by caring for their own family and so repaying their parents and grandparents, for this is pleasing to God. . . . [8]If anyone does not provide for his relatives, and especially for his immediate family, he has denied the faith and is worse than an unbeliever.

(3) Honor Your Parents

Exod 20 [12]"Honor your father and your mother, so that you may live long in the land the LORD your God is giving you."
Mal 1 [6]"A son honors his father, and a servant his master. If I am a father, where is the honor due me? If I am a master, where is the respect due me?" says the LORD Almighty. "It is you, O priests, who show contempt for my name.

"But you ask, 'How have we shown contempt for your name?'"
Matt 15 [1]Then some Pharisees and teachers of the law came to Jesus from Jerusalem and asked, [2]"Why do your disciples break the tradition of the elders? They don't wash their hands before they eat!"

[3]Jesus replied, "And why do you break the command of God for the sake of your tradition? [4]For God said, 'Honor your father and mother' and 'Anyone who curses his father or mother must be put to death.' [5]But you say that if a man says to his father or mother, 'Whatever help you might otherwise have received from me is a gift devoted to God,' [6]he is not to 'honor his father' with it. Thus you nullify the word of God for the sake of your tradition."
Luke 18 [19]"Why do you call me good?" Jesus answered. "No

one is good—except God alone. [20]You know the commandments: 'Do not commit adultery, do not murder, do not steal, do not give false testimony, honor your father and mother.'"
Eph 6 [2]"Honor your father and mother"—which is the first commandment with a promise—[3]"that it may go well with you and that you may enjoy long life on the earth."

(4) Love Your Parents

Gen 46 [29]Joseph had his chariot made ready and went to Goshen to meet his father Israel. As soon as Joseph appeared before him, he threw his arms around his father and wept for a long time.

(5) Obey Your Parents

Prov 1 [8]Listen, my son, to your father's instruction and do not forsake your mother's teaching. [9]They will be a garland to grace your head and a chain to adorn your neck.
Prov 3 [1]My son, do not forget my teaching, but keep my commands in your heart, [2]for they will prolong your life many years and bring you prosperity.
Prov 4 [1]Listen, my sons, to a father's instruction; pay attention and gain understanding. [2]I give you sound learning, so do not forsake my teaching. [3]When I was a boy in my father's house, still tender, and an only child of my mother, [4]he taught me and said, "Lay hold of my words with all your heart; keep my commands and you will live. . . ."

[10]Listen, my son, accept what I say, and the years of your life will be many. [11]I guide you in the way of wisdom and lead you along straight paths. . . .

[20]My son, pay attention to what I say; listen closely to my words. [21]Do not let them out of your sight, keep them within your heart; [22]for they are life to those who find them and health to a man's whole body.
Prov 5 [1]My son, pay attention to my wisdom, listen well to my words of insight. . . .
Prov 6 [20]My son, keep your father's commands and do not forsake your mother's teaching. [21]Bind them upon your heart forever; fasten them around your neck. [22]When you walk, they will guide you; when you sleep, they will watch over you; when you awake, they will speak to you. [23]For these commands are a lamp, this teaching is a light, and the corrections of discipline are the way to life. . . .
Prov 13 [1]A wise son heeds his father's instruction, but a mocker does not listen to rebuke.
Eph 6 [1]Children, obey your parents in the Lord, for this is right.
Col 3 [20]Children, obey your parents in everything, for this pleases the Lord.

(6) Praise Your Parents

Prov 31 [28]Her children arise and call her blessed; her husband also, and he praises her. . . .[30]Charm is deceptive, and beauty is fleeting; but a woman who fears the LORD is to be praised.

(7) Respect Your Parents

Lev 19 [3]"'Each of you must respect his mother and father, and you must observe my Sabbaths. I am the LORD your God.'"
1 Tim 3 [4]He must manage his own family well and see that his children obey him with proper respect.
Heb 12 [9]Moreover, we have all had human fathers who disciplined us and we respected them for it. How much more should we submit to the Father of our spirits and live!

b) *Examples of Honoring and Obeying Parents*

(1) Shem and Japheth Honored Their Parent(s)

Gen 9 [23]But Shem and Japheth took a garment and laid it across their shoulders; then they walked in backward and covered their father's nakedness. Their faces were turned the other way so that they would not see their father's nakedness.

(2) Isaac Honored His Parent(s)

Gen 22 [6]Abraham took the wood for the burnt offering and placed it on his son Isaac, and he himself carried the fire and the knife. As the two of them went on together, [7]Isaac spoke up and said to his father Abraham, "Father?"

"Yes, my son?" Abraham replied.

"The fire and wood are here," Isaac said, "but where is the lamb for the burnt offering?"

[8]Abraham answered, "God himself will provide the lamb for the burnt offering, my son." And the two of them went on together.

[9]When they reached the place God had told him about, Abraham built an altar there and arranged the wood on it. He bound his son Isaac and laid him on the altar, on top of the wood. [10]Then he reached out his hand and took the knife to slay his son. [11]But the angel of the LORD called out to him from heaven, "Abraham! Abraham!"

"Here I am," he replied.

[12]"Do not lay a hand on the boy," he said. "Do not do anything to him. Now I know that you fear God, because you have not withheld from me your son, your only son."

(3) Joseph Honored His Parent(s)

Gen 45 [8]"So then, it was not you who sent me here, but God. He made me father to Pharaoh, lord of his entire household and ruler of all Egypt. [9]Now hurry back to my father and say to him, 'This is what your son Joseph says: God has made me lord of all Egypt. Come down to me; don't delay. [10]You shall live in the region of Goshen and be near me—you, your children and grandchildren, your flocks and herds, and all you have. [11]I will provide for you there, because five years of famine are still to come. Otherwise you and your household and all who belong to you will become destitute.'"
Gen 47 [11]So Joseph settled his father and his brothers in Egypt and gave them property in the best part of the land, the district of Rameses, as Pharaoh directed. [12]Joseph also provided his father and his brothers and all his father's household with food, according to the number of their children.

(4) Jephthah's Daughter Honored Her Parent(s)

Judg 11 [34]When Jephthah returned to his home in Mizpah, who should come out to meet him but his daughter, dancing to the sound of tambourines! She was an only child. Except for her he had neither son nor daughter. . . .

[36]"My father," she replied, "you have given your word to the LORD. Do to me just as you promised, now that the LORD has avenged you of your enemies, the Ammonites."

(5) Ruth Honored Her Parent(s)

Ruth 1 [15]"Look," said Naomi, "your sister-in-law is going back to her people and her gods. Go back with her."

[16]But Ruth replied, "Don't urge me to leave you or to turn back from you. Where you go I will go, and where you stay I will stay. Your people will be my people and your God my God. [17]Where you die I will die, and there I will be buried. May the LORD deal with me, be it ever so severely, if anything but death separates you and me." [18]When Naomi realized that Ruth was determined to go with her, she stopped urging her.

(6) Timothy Honored His Parent(s)

2 Tim 1 [5]I have been reminded of your sincere faith, which first lived in your grandmother Lois and in your mother Eunice and, I am persuaded, now lives in you also.
2 Tim 3 [14]But as for you, continue in what you have learned and have become convinced of, because you know those from whom you learned it, [15]and how from infancy you have known the holy Scriptures, which are able to make you wise for salvation through faith in Christ Jesus.

13. Responsibilities toward the Poor

a) *God's Attitude toward the Poor*

(1) God Forbids the Oppression of the Poor

Zech 7 [10]"'Do not oppress the widow or the fatherless, the alien or the poor. In your hearts do not think evil of each other.'"

(2) God Gives Hope to the Poor

Ps 9 [18]But the needy will not always be forgotten, nor the hope of the afflicted ever perish.
Ps 14 [4]Will evildoers never learn—those who devour my people as men eat bread and who do not call on the LORD? [5]There they are, overwhelmed with dread, for God is present in the company of the righteous. [6]You evildoers frustrate the plans of the poor, but the LORD is their refuge.

[7]Oh, that salvation for Israel would come out of Zion! When the LORD restores the fortunes of his people, let Jacob rejoice and Israel be glad!

Ps 40 [17]Yet I am poor and needy; may the Lord think of me. You are my help and my deliverer; O my God, do not delay.

(3) God Has Compassion for the Poor

Ps 72 [13]He will take pity on the weak and the needy and save the needy from death.

(4) God Hears the Cry of the Poor

Job 34 [28]"They caused the cry of the poor to come before him, so that he heard the cry of the needy."

Ps 34 [6]This poor man called, and the LORD heard him; he saved him out of all his troubles.

Ps 69 [32]The poor will see and be glad—you who seek God, may your hearts live! [33]The LORD hears the needy and does not despise his captive people.

Ps 86 [1]Hear, O LORD, and answer me, for I am poor and needy.

Isa 41 [17]"The poor and needy search for water, but there is none; their tongues are parched with thirst. But I the LORD will answer them; I, the God of Israel, will not forsake them."

(5) God Intervenes on Behalf of the Poor

Ps 109 [30]With my mouth I will greatly extol the LORD; in the great throng I will praise him. [31]For he stands at the right hand of the needy one, to save his life from those who condemn him.

Ps 140 [12]I know that the LORD secures justice for the poor and upholds the cause of the needy.

Prov 22 [22]Do not exploit the poor because they are poor and do not crush the needy in court, [23]for the LORD will take up their case and will plunder those who plunder them.

Isa 11 [4]but with righteousness he will judge the needy, with justice he will give decisions for the poor of the earth. He will strike the earth with the rod of his mouth; with the breath of his lips he will slay the wicked.

(6) God Promises to Deliver the Poor

Ps 107 [41]But he lifted the needy out of their affliction and increased their families like flocks.

Isa 14 [29]Do not rejoice, all you Philistines, that the rod that struck you is broken; from the root of that snake will spring up a viper, its fruit will be a darting, venomous serpent. [30]The poorest of the poor will find pasture, and the needy will lie down in safety. But your root I will destroy by famine; it will slay your survivors.

Isa 29 [19]Once more the humble will rejoice in the LORD; the needy will rejoice in the Holy One of Israel.

(7) God Promises to Punish Those Who Oppress the Poor

Prov 17 [5]He who mocks the poor shows contempt for their Maker; whoever gloats over disaster will not go unpunished.

Isa 3 [14]The LORD enters into judgment against the elders and leaders of his people: "It is you who have ruined my vineyard; the plunder from the poor is in your houses. [15]What do you mean by crushing my people and grinding the faces of the poor?" declares the Lord, the LORD Almighty.

Isa 10 [1]Woe to those who make unjust laws, to those who issue oppressive decrees, [2]to deprive the poor of their rights and withhold justice from the oppressed of my people, making widows their prey and robbing the fatherless. [3]What will you do on the day of reckoning, when disaster comes from afar? To whom will you run for help? Where will you leave your riches?

Amos 2 [6]This is what the LORD says: "For three sins of Israel, even for four, I will not turn back my wrath. They sell the righteous for silver, and the needy for a pair of sandals. [7]They trample on the heads of the poor as upon the dust of the ground and deny justice to the oppressed. Father and son use the same girl and so profane my holy name."

Amos 5 [11]You trample on the poor and force him to give you grain. Therefore, though you have built stone mansions, you will not live in them; though you have planted lush vineyards, you will not drink their wine.

(8) God Protects the Poor

Ps 12 [5]"Because of the oppression of the weak and the groaning of the needy, I will now arise," says the LORD. "I will protect them from those who malign them."

Isa 25 [4]You have been a refuge for the poor, a refuge for the needy in his distress, a shelter from the storm and a shade from the heat. For the breath of the ruthless is like a storm driving against a wall. . . .

(9) God Provides for the Poor

Exod 23 [10]"For six years you are to sow your fields and harvest the crops, [11]but during the seventh year let the land lie unplowed and unused. Then the poor among your people may get food from it, and the wild animals may eat what they leave. Do the same with your vineyard and your olive grove."

Ps 22 [26]The poor will eat and be satisfied; they who seek the LORD will praise him—may your hearts live forever!

Ps 68 [10]Your people settled in it, and from your bounty, O God, you provided for the poor.

Ps 132 [15]"I will bless her with abundant provisions; her poor will I satisfy with food."

(10) God Rescues the Poor

1 Sam 2 [8]"He raises the poor from the dust and lifts the needy from the ash heap; he seats them with princes and has them inherit a throne of honor.

"For the foundations of the earth are the LORD's; upon them he has set the world."

Job 5 [15]"He saves the needy from the sword in their mouth; he saves them from the clutches of the powerful. [16]So the poor have hope, and injustice shuts its mouth."

Ps 35 [10]My whole being will exclaim, "Who is like you, O LORD? You rescue the poor from those too strong for them, the poor and needy from those who rob them."

Ps 70 [5]Yet I am poor and needy; come quickly to me, O God. You are my help and my deliverer; O LORD, do not delay.

Ps 113 [7]He raises the poor from the dust and lifts the needy from the ash heap. . . .

Jer 20 [13]Sing to the LORD! Give praise to the LORD! He rescues the life of the needy from the hands of the wicked.

(11) God Restores the Poor

Ps 68 [9]You gave abundant showers, O God; you refreshed your weary inheritance. [10]Your people settled in it, and from your bounty, O God, you provided for the poor.

Ps 145 [14]The LORD upholds all those who fall and lifts up all who are bowed down.

Ps 146 [5]Blessed is he whose help is the God of Jacob, whose hope is in the LORD his God, [6]the Maker of heaven and earth, the sea, and everything in them—the LORD, who remains faithful forever. [7]He upholds the cause of the oppressed and gives food to the hungry. The LORD sets prisoners free, [8]the LORD gives sight to the blind, the LORD lifts up those who are bowed down, the LORD loves the righteous.

Isa 29 [18]In that day the deaf will hear the words of the scroll, and out of gloom and darkness the eyes of the blind will see. [19]Once more the humble will rejoice in the LORD; the needy will rejoice in the Holy One of Israel.

Isa 40 [28]Do you not know? Have you not heard? The LORD is the everlasting God, the Creator of the ends of the earth. He will not grow tired or weary, and his understanding no one can fathom. [29]He gives strength to the weary and increases the power of the weak. [30]Even youths grow tired and weary, and young men stumble and fall; [31]but those who hope in the LORD will renew their strength. They will soar on wings like eagles; they will run and not grow weary, they will walk and not be faint.

b) The Believer's Duty to the Poor

(1) Administer Justice Equitably to the Poor

Exod 23 [3]". . . and do not show favoritism to a poor man in his lawsuit. . . .

[6]"Do not deny justice to your poor people in their lawsuits."

Lev 19 [15]"'Do not pervert justice; do not show partiality to the poor or favoritism to the great, but judge your neighbor fairly.'"

Prov 22 [22]Do not exploit the poor because they are poor and do not crush the needy in court, [23]for the LORD will take up their case and will plunder those who plunder them.

Prov 29 [7]The righteous care about justice for the poor, but the wicked have no such concern.

Jer 5 [28]". . . and have grown fat and sleek. Their evil deeds have no limit; they do not plead the case of the fatherless to win it, they do not defend the rights of the poor."

Jer 22 [15]"Does it make you a king to have more and more cedar? Did not your father have food and drink? He did what was right and just, so all went well with him. [16]He defended the cause of the poor and needy, and so all went well. Is that not what it means to know me?" declares the LORD.

(2) Be Kind to the Poor

Deut 24 10When you make a loan of any kind to your neighbor, do not go into his house to get what he is offering as a pledge. . . . 12If the man is poor, do not go to sleep with his pledge in your possession. 13Return his cloak to him by sunset so that he may sleep in it. Then he will thank you, and it will be regarded as a righteous act in the sight of the LORD your God.

Prov 14 21He who despises his neighbor sins, but blessed is he who is kind to the needy.

Prov 14 31He who oppresses the poor shows contempt for their Maker, but whoever is kind to the needy honors God.

Prov 19 17He who is kind to the poor lends to the LORD, and he will reward him for what he has done.

Prov 28 8He who increases his wealth by exorbitant interest amasses it for another, who will be kind to the poor.

(3) Give Liberally to the Poor

Lev 19 9"'When you reap the harvest of your land, do not reap to the very edges of your field or gather the gleanings of your harvest. 10Do not go over your vineyard a second time or pick up the grapes that have fallen. Leave them for the poor and the alien. I am the LORD your God.'"

Deut 15 7If there is a poor man among your brothers in any of the towns of the land that the LORD your God is giving you, do not be hardhearted or tightfisted toward your poor brother. 8Rather be openhanded and freely lend him whatever he needs. 9Be careful not to harbor this wicked thought: "The seventh year, the year for canceling debts, is near," so that you do not show ill will toward your needy brother and give him nothing. He may then appeal to the LORD against you, and you will be found guilty of sin. 10Give generously to him and do so without a grudging heart; then because of this the LORD your God will bless you in all your work and in everything you put your hand to. 11There will always be poor people in the land. Therefore I command you to be openhanded toward your brothers and toward the poor and needy in your land.

Ps 37 21The wicked borrow and do not repay, but the righteous give generously. . . . 26They are always generous and lend freely; their children will be blessed.

Ps 112 4Even in darkness light dawns for the upright, for the gracious and compassionate and righteous man. 5Good will come to him who is generous and lends freely, who conducts his affairs with justice. . . . 9He has scattered abroad his gifts to the poor, his righteousness endures forever; his horn will be lifted high in honor.

Prov 22 9A generous man will himself be blessed, for he shares his food with the poor.

Prov 28 27He who gives to the poor will lack nothing, but he who closes his eyes to them receives many curses.

Matt 6 2"So when you give to the needy, do not announce it with trumpets, as the hypocrites do in the synagogues and on the streets, to be honored by men. I tell you the truth, they have received their reward in full. 3But when you give to the needy, do not let your left hand know what your right hand is doing, 4so that your giving may be in secret. Then your Father, who sees what is done in secret, will reward you."

Matt 19 16Now a man came up to Jesus and asked, "Teacher, what good thing must I do to get eternal life?"

17"Why do you ask me about what is good?" Jesus replied. "There is only One who is good. If you want to enter life, obey the commandments."

18"Which ones?" the man inquired.

Jesus replied, "'Do not murder, do not commit adultery, do not steal, do not give false testimony, 19honor your father and mother,' and 'love your neighbor as yourself.'"

20"All these I have kept," the young man said. "What do I still lack?"

21Jesus answered, "If you want to be perfect, go, sell your possessions and give to the poor, and you will have treasure in heaven. Then come, follow me."

Gal 2 10All they asked was that we should continue to remember the poor, the very thing I was eager to do.

(4) Help Meet the Needs of the Poor

Prov 21 13If a man shuts his ears to the cry of the poor, he too will cry out and not be answered.

Prov 31 20She opens her arms to the poor and extends her hands to the needy.

(5) Love the Poor

1 Cor 13 3If I give all I possess to the poor and surrender my body to the flames, but have not love, I gain nothing.

(6) Make Provisions for the Poor

Exod 22 25"If you lend money to one of my people among you who is needy, do not be like a moneylender; charge him no interest."

Lev 14 21"If, however, he is poor and cannot afford these, he must take one male lamb as a guilt offering to be waved to make atonement for him, together with a tenth of an ephah of fine flour mixed with oil for a grain offering, a log of oil, 22and two doves or two young pigeons, which he can afford, one for a sin offering and the other for a burnt offering. . . ."

32These are the regulations for anyone who has an infectious skin disease and who cannot afford the regular offerings for his cleansing.

Lev 27 8"'If anyone making the vow is too poor to pay the specified amount, he is to present the person to the priest, who will set the value for him according to what the man making the vow can afford.'"

(7) Oppose the Oppression of the Poor

Job 24 1"Why does the Almighty not set times for judgment? Why must those who know him look in vain for such days? 2Men move boundary stones; they pasture flocks they have stolen. 3They drive away the orphan's donkey and take the widow's ox in pledge. 4They thrust the needy from the path and force all the poor of the land into hiding. 5Like wild donkeys in the desert, the poor go about their labor of foraging food; the wasteland provides food for their children. 6They gather fodder in the fields and glean in the vineyards of the wicked. 7Lacking clothes, they spend the night naked; they have nothing to cover themselves in the cold. 8They are drenched by mountain rains and hug the rocks for lack of shelter. 9The fatherless child is snatched from the breast; the infant of the poor is seized for a debt. 10Lacking clothes, they go about naked; they carry the sheaves, but still go hungry. 11They crush olives among the terraces; they tread the winepresses, yet suffer thirst. 12The groans of the dying rise from the city, and the souls of the wounded cry out for help. But God charges no one with wrongdoing."

Ps 37 14The wicked draw the sword and bend the bow to bring down the poor and needy, to slay those whose ways are upright. 15But their swords will pierce their own hearts, and their bows will be broken.

16Better the little that the righteous have than the wealth of many wicked; 17for the power of the wicked will be broken, but the LORD upholds the righteous.

Prov 31 9"Speak up and judge fairly; defend the rights of the poor and needy."

Isa 32 7The scoundrel's methods are wicked, he makes up evil schemes to destroy the poor with lies, even when the plea of the needy is just.

(8) Pray for the Deliverance of the Poor

Ps 74 18Remember how the enemy has mocked you, O LORD, how foolish people have reviled your name. . . . 21Do not let the oppressed retreat in disgrace; may the poor and needy praise your name.

Ps 82 2"How long will you defend the unjust and show partiality to the wicked? 3Defend the cause of the weak and fatherless; maintain the rights of the poor and oppressed. 4Rescue the weak and needy; deliver them from the hand of the wicked."

(9) Respect the Poor as Fellow Creatures

Prov 22 2Rich and poor have this in common: The LORD is the Maker of them all.

Prov 29 13The poor man and the oppressor have this in common: The LORD gives sight to the eyes of both.

(10) Show Compassion to the Poor

2 Sam 12 1The LORD sent Nathan to David. When he came to him, he said, "There were two men in a certain town, one rich and the other poor. 2The rich man had a very large number of sheep and cattle, 3but the poor man had nothing except one little ewe lamb he had bought. He raised it, and it grew up with him and his children. It shared his food, drank from his cup and even slept in his arms. It was like a daughter to him.

[4]"Now a traveler came to the rich man, but the rich man refrained from taking one of his own sheep or cattle to prepare a meal for the traveler who had come to him. Instead, he took the ewe lamb that belonged to the poor man and prepared it for the one who had come to him."

[5]David burned with anger against the man and said to Nathan, "As surely as the LORD lives, the man who did this deserves to die! [6]He must pay for that lamb four times over, because he did such a thing and had no pity."

Job 30 [25]"Have I not wept for those in trouble? Has not my soul grieved for the poor?"

(11) Treat the Poor Fairly

Deut 24 [14]Do not take advantage of a hired man who is poor and needy, whether he is a brother Israelite or an alien living in one of your towns. [15]Pay him his wages each day before sunset, because he is poor and is counting on it. Otherwise he may cry to the LORD against you, and you will be guilty of sin.

c) Examples of Giving Generously to the Poor

(1) Boaz Gave to the Poor

Ruth 2 [15]As she got up to glean, Boaz gave orders to his men, "Even if she gathers among the sheaves, don't embarrass her. [16]Rather, pull out some stalks for her from the bundles and leave them for her to pick up, and don't rebuke her."

[17]So Ruth gleaned in the field until evening. Then she threshed the barley she had gathered, and it amounted to about an ephah. [18]She carried it back to town, and her mother-in-law saw how much she had gathered. Ruth also brought out and gave her what she had left over after she had eaten enough.

[19]Her mother-in-law asked her, "Where did you glean today? Where did you work? Blessed be the man who took notice of you!"

Then Ruth told her mother-in-law about the one at whose place she had been working. "The name of the man I worked with today is Boaz," she said.

(2) Job Gave to the Poor

Job 29 [11]"Whoever heard me spoke well of me, and those who saw me commended me, [12]because I rescued the poor who cried for help, and the fatherless who had none to assist him. [13]The man who was dying blessed me; I made the widow's heart sing. [14]I put on righteousness as my clothing; justice was my robe and my turban. [15]I was eyes to the blind and feet to the lame. [16]I was a father to the needy; I took up the case of the stranger."

Job 31 [16]"If I have denied the desires of the poor or let the eyes of the widow grow weary, [17]if I have kept my bread to myself, not sharing it with the fatherless—[18]but from my youth I reared him as would a father, and from my birth I guided the widow—[19]if I have seen anyone perishing for lack of clothing, or a needy man without a garment, [20]and his heart did not bless me for warming him with the fleece from my sheep, [21]if I have raised my hand against the fatherless, knowing that I had influence in court, [22]then let my arm fall from the shoulder, let it be broken off at the joint. [23]For I dreaded destruction from God, and for fear of his splendor I could not do such things."

(3) The Jews Gave to the Poor

Esther 9 [20]Mordecai recorded these events, and he sent letters to all the Jews throughout the provinces of King Xerxes, near and far, [21]to have them celebrate annually the fourteenth and fifteenth days of the month of Adar [22]as the time when the Jews got relief from their enemies, and as the month when their sorrow was turned into joy and their mourning into a day of celebration. He wrote them to observe the days as days of feasting and joy and giving presents of food to one another and gifts to the poor.

(4) Nehemiah Gave to the Poor

Neh 8 [10]Nehemiah said, "Go and enjoy choice food and sweet drinks, and send some to those who have nothing prepared. This day is sacred to our Lord. Do not grieve, for the joy of the LORD is your strength." . . .

[12]Then all the people went away to eat and drink, to send portions of food and to celebrate with great joy, because they now understood the words that had been made known to them.

(5) Zacchaeus Gave to the Poor

Luke 19 [8]But Zacchaeus stood up and said to the Lord, "Look, Lord! Here and now I give half of my possessions to the poor, and if I have cheated anybody out of anything, I will pay back four times the amount."

(6) The Jerusalem Church Gave to the Poor

Acts 4 [34]There were no needy persons among them. For from time to time those who owned lands or houses sold them, brought the money from the sales [35]and put it at the apostles' feet, and it was distributed to anyone as he had need.

(7) Dorcas Gave to the Poor

Acts 9 [36]In Joppa there was a disciple named Tabitha (which, when translated, is Dorcas), who was always doing good and helping the poor.

(8) Cornelius Gave to the Poor

Acts 10 [2]He and all his family were devout and God-fearing; he gave generously to those in need and prayed to God regularly. [3]One day at about three in the afternoon he had a vision. He distinctly saw an angel of God, who came to him and said, "Cornelius!"

[4]Cornelius stared at him in fear. "What is it, Lord?" he asked.

The angel answered, "Your prayers and gifts to the poor have come up as a memorial offering before God."

(9) The Church at Antioch Gave to the Poor

Acts 11 [27]During this time some prophets came down from Jerusalem to Antioch. [28]One of them, named Agabus, stood up and through the Spirit predicted that a severe famine would spread over the entire Roman world. (This happened during the reign of Claudius.) [29]The disciples, each according to his ability, decided to provide help for the brothers living in Judea. [30]This they did, sending their gift to the elders by Barnabas and Saul.

(10) The Macedonian and Achaian Believers Gave to the Poor

Rom 15 [25]Now, however, I am on my way to Jerusalem in the service of the saints there. [26]For Macedonia and Achaia were pleased to make a contribution for the poor among the saints in Jerusalem. [27]They were pleased to do it, and indeed they owe it to them. For if the Gentiles have shared in the Jews' spiritual blessings, they owe it to the Jews to share with them their material blessings.

2 Cor 8 [1]And now, brothers, we want you to know about the grace that God has given the Macedonian churches. [2]Out of the most severe trial, their overflowing joy and their extreme poverty welled up in rich generosity. [3]For I testify that they gave as much as they were able, and even beyond their ability. Entirely on their own, [4]they urgently pleaded with us for the privilege of sharing in this service to the saints.

(11) Paul Gave to the Poor

Acts 20 [35]"In everything I did, I showed you that by this kind of hard work we must help the weak, remembering the words the Lord Jesus himself said: 'It is more blessed to give than to receive.'"

14. Responsibilities toward Widows

a) God's Attitude toward Widows

(1) God Condemns the Oppressors of Widows

Exod 22 [22]"Do not take advantage of a widow or an orphan. [23]If you do and they cry out to me, I will certainly hear their cry. [24]My anger will be aroused, and I will kill you with the sword; your wives will become widows and your children fatherless."

Isa 1 [23]Your rulers are rebels, companions of thieves; they all love bribes and chase after gifts. They do not defend the cause of the fatherless; the widow's case does not come before them. [24]Therefore the Lord, the LORD Almighty, the Mighty One of Israel, declares: "Ah, I will get relief from my foes and avenge myself on my enemies. [25]I will turn my hand against you; I will thoroughly purge away your dross and remove all your impurities."

Isa 10 [1]Woe to those who make unjust laws, to those who issue oppressive decrees, [2]to deprive the poor of their rights and withhold justice from the oppressed of my people, making widows their prey and robbing the fatherless.

Jer 7 [2]"Stand at the gate of the LORD's house and there proclaim this message: 'Hear the word of the LORD, all you people of Judah who come through these gates to worship the LORD. [3]This is what the LORD Almighty, the God of Israel, says: Reform your ways and your actions, and I will let you live in this place. [4]Do not trust in deceptive words and say, "This is the temple of the LORD, the temple of the LORD, the temple of the LORD!" [5]If you really change your ways and your actions and deal with each other justly, [6]if you do not oppress the alien, the fatherless or the widow and do not shed innocent blood in this place, and if you do not follow other gods to your own harm, [7]then I will let you live in this place, in the land I gave your forefathers for ever and ever.'"

Ezek 22 [7]"'In you they have treated father and mother with contempt; in you they have oppressed the alien and mistreated the fatherless and the widow. . . .

[13]"'I will surely strike my hands together at the unjust gain you have made and at the blood you have shed in your midst.'"

Mal 3 [5]"So I will come near to you for judgment. I will be quick to testify against sorcerers, adulterers and perjurers, against those who defraud laborers of their wages, who oppress the widows and the fatherless, and deprive aliens of justice, but do not fear me," says the LORD Almighty.

Luke 20 [45]While all the people were listening, Jesus said to his disciples, [46]"Beware of the teachers of the law. They like to walk around in flowing robes and love to be greeted in the marketplaces and have the most important seats in the synagogues and the places of honor at banquets. [47]They devour widows' houses and for a show make lengthy prayers. Such men will be punished most severely."

(2) God Defends Widows

Deut 10 [17]For the LORD your God is God of gods and Lord of lords, the great God, mighty and awesome, who shows no partiality and accepts no bribes. [18]He defends the cause of the fatherless and the widow, and loves the alien, giving him food and clothing.

Ps 68 [5]A father to the fatherless, a defender of widows, is God in his holy dwelling.

Luke 18 [2]He said: "In a certain town there was a judge who neither feared God nor cared about men. [3]And there was a widow in that town who kept coming to him with the plea, 'Grant me justice against my adversary.'

[4]"For some time he refused. But finally he said to himself, 'Even though I don't fear God or care about men, [5]yet because this widow keeps bothering me, I will see that she gets justice, so that she won't eventually wear me out with her coming!'"

[6]And the Lord said, "Listen to what the unjust judge says. [7]And will not God bring about justice for his chosen ones, who cry out to him day and night? Will he keep putting them off? [8]I tell you, he will see that they get justice, and quickly. However, when the Son of Man comes, will he find faith on the earth?"

(3) God Forbids the Oppression of Widows

Jer 22 [3]"'This is what the LORD says: Do what is just and right. Rescue from the hand of his oppressor the one who has been robbed. Do no wrong or violence to the alien, the fatherless or the widow, and do not shed innocent blood in this place.'"

Zech 7 [10]"'Do not oppress the widow or the fatherless, the alien or the poor. In your hearts do not think evil of each other.'"

(4) God Praises a Widow's Generosity

Mark 12 [41]Jesus sat down opposite the place where the offerings were put and watched the crowd putting their money into the temple treasury. Many rich people threw in large amounts. [42]But a poor widow came and put in two very small copper coins, worth only a fraction of a penny.

[43]Calling his disciples to him, Jesus said, "I tell you the truth, this poor widow has put more into the treasury than all the others. [44]They all gave out of their wealth; but she, out of her poverty, put in everything—all she had to live on."

(5) God Protects Widows

Jer 49 [11]"Leave your orphans; I will protect their lives. Your widows too can trust in me."

(6) God Provides for Widows

Deut 24 [17]Do not deprive the alien or the fatherless of justice, or take the cloak of the widow as a pledge. [18]Remember that you were slaves in Egypt and the LORD your God redeemed you from there. That is why I command you to do this.

[19]When you are harvesting in your field and you overlook a sheaf, do not go back to get it. Leave it for the alien, the fatherless and the widow, so that the LORD your God may bless you in all the work of your hands.

Deut 26 [12]When you have finished setting aside a tenth of all your produce in the third year, the year of the tithe, you shall give it to the Levite, the alien, the fatherless and the widow, so that they may eat in your towns and be satisfied. [13]Then say to the LORD your God: "I have removed from my house the sacred portion and have given it to the Levite, the alien, the fatherless and the widow, according to all you commanded. I have not turned aside from your commands nor have I forgotten any of them."

(7) God Sustains Widows

Ps 146 [9]The LORD watches over the alien and sustains the fatherless and the widow, but he frustrates the ways of the wicked.

Prov 15 [25]The LORD tears down the proud man's house but he keeps the widow's boundaries intact.

b) The Believer's Duty to Widows

(1) Abhor the Oppression of Widows

Job 24 [3]"They drive away the orphan's donkey and take the widow's ox in pledge. . . . [21]They prey on the barren and childless woman, and to the widow show no kindness. [22]But God drags away the mighty by his power; though they become established, they have no assurance of life. . . . [24]For a little while they are exalted, and then they are gone; they are brought low and gathered up like all others; they are cut off like heads of grain."

(2) Appeal to God for Deliverance of Widows

Job 24 [1]"Why does the Almighty not set times for judgment? Why must those who know him look in vain for such days? [2]Men move boundary stones; they pasture flocks they have stolen. [3]They drive away the orphan's donkey and take the widow's ox in pledge."

Ps 94 [1]O LORD, the God who avenges, O God who avenges, shine forth. [2]Rise up, O Judge of the earth; pay back to the proud what they deserve. [3]How long will the wicked, O LORD, how long will the wicked be jubilant?

[4]They pour out arrogant words; all the evildoers are full of boasting. [5]They crush your people, O LORD; they oppress your inheritance. [6]They slay the widow and the alien; they murder the fatherless.

(3) Be Considerate of Widows

Deut 24 [17]Do not deprive the alien or the fatherless of justice, or take the cloak of the widow as a pledge.

(4) Care for Widows

1 Tim 5 [3]Give proper recognition to those widows who are really in need. [4]But if a widow has children or grandchildren, these should learn first of all to put their religion into practice by caring for their own family and so repaying their parents and grandparents, for this is pleasing to God. [5]The widow who is really in need and left all alone puts her hope in God and continues night and day to pray and to ask God for help. . . . [7]Give the people these instructions, too, so that no one may be open to blame. [8]If anyone does not provide for his relatives, and especially for his immediate family, he has denied the faith and is worse than an unbeliever.

[9]No widow may be put on the list of widows unless she is over sixty, has been faithful to her husband, [10]and is well known for her good deeds, such as bringing up children, showing hospitality, washing the feet of the saints, helping those in trouble and devoting herself to all kinds of good deeds.

[11]As for younger widows, do not put them on such a list. For when their sensual desires overcome their dedication to

Christ, they want to marry. [12]Thus they bring judgment on themselves, because they have broken their first pledge. [13]Besides, they get into the habit of being idle and going about from house to house. And not only do they become idlers, but also gossips and busybodies, saying things they ought not to. [14]So I counsel younger widows to marry, to have children, to manage their homes and to give the enemy no opportunity for slander. . . .

[16]If any woman who is a believer has widows in her family, she should help them and not let the church be burdened with them, so that the church can help those widows who are really in need.

James 1 [27]Religion that God our Father accepts as pure and faultless is this: to look after orphans and widows in their distress and to keep oneself from being polluted by the world.

(5) Give Liberally to Widows

Deut 24 [19]When you are harvesting in your field and you overlook a sheaf, do not go back to get it. Leave it for the alien, the fatherless and the widow, so that the LORD your God may bless you in all the work of your hands. [20]When you beat the olives from your trees, do not go over the branches a second time. Leave what remains for the alien, the fatherless and the widow. [21]When you harvest the grapes in your vineyard, do not go over the vines again. Leave what remains for the alien, the fatherless and the widow.

(6) Grant Equal Justice to Widows

Deut 27 [19]"Cursed is the man who withholds justice from the alien, the fatherless or the widow." Then all the people shall say, "Amen!"

Isa 1 [17]". . . learn to do right! Seek justice, encourage the oppressed. Defend the cause of the fatherless, plead the case of the widow."

(7) Involve Widows in the Religious Community

Deut 16 [9]Count off seven weeks from the time you begin to put the sickle to the standing grain. [10]Then celebrate the Feast of Weeks to the LORD your God by giving a freewill offering in proportion to the blessings the LORD your God has given you. [11]And rejoice before the LORD your God at the place he will choose as a dwelling for his Name—you, your sons and daughters, your menservants and maidservants, the Levites in your towns, and the aliens, the fatherless and the widows living among you.

Deut 16 [13]Celebrate the Feast of Tabernacles for seven days after you have gathered the produce of your threshing floor and your winepress. [14]Be joyful at your Feast—you, your sons and daughters, your menservants and maidservants, and the Levites, the aliens, the fatherless and the widows who live in your towns. [15]For seven days celebrate the Feast to the LORD your God at the place the LORD will choose. For the LORD your God will bless you in all your harvest and in all the work of your hands, and your joy will be complete.

c) Examples of Ministering to Widows

(1) Job Ministered to Widows

Job 29 [11]"Whoever heard me spoke well of me, and those who saw me commended me. . . . [13]The man who was dying blessed me; I made the widow's heart sing. [14]I put on righteousness as my clothing; justice was my robe and my turban."

Job 31 [16]"If I have denied the desires of the poor or let the eyes of the widow grow weary, [17]if I have kept my bread to myself, not sharing it with the fatherless—[18]but from my youth I reared him as would a father, and from my birth I guided the widow—[19]if I have seen anyone perishing for lack of clothing, or a needy man without a garment . . . [22]then let my arm fall from the shoulder, let it be broken off at the joint. [23]For I dreaded destruction from God, and for fear of his splendor I could not do such things."

(2) The Jerusalem Church Ministered to Widows

Acts 6 [1]In those days when the number of disciples was increasing, the Grecian Jews among them complained against the Hebraic Jews because their widows were being overlooked in the daily distribution of food. [2]So the Twelve gathered all the disciples together and said, "It would not be right for us to neglect the ministry of the word of God in order to wait on tables. [3]Brothers, choose seven men from among you who are known to be full of the Spirit and wisdom. We will turn this responsibility over to them [4]and will give our attention to prayer and the ministry of the word."

[5]This proposal pleased the whole group. They chose Stephen, a man full of faith and of the Holy Spirit; also Philip, Procorus, Nicanor, Timon, Parmenas, and Nicolas from Antioch, a convert to Judaism. [6]They presented these men to the apostles, who prayed and laid their hands on them.

(3) Dorcas Ministered to Widows

Acts 9 [36]In Joppa there was a disciple named Tabitha (which, when translated, is Dorcas), who was always doing good and helping the poor. [37]About that time she became sick and died, and her body was washed and placed in an upstairs room. [38]Lydda was near Joppa; so when the disciples heard that Peter was in Lydda, they sent two men to him and urged him, "Please come at once!"

[39]Peter went with them, and when he arrived he was taken upstairs to the room. All the widows stood around him, crying and showing him the robes and other clothing that Dorcas had made while she was still with them.

[40]Peter sent them all out of the room; then he got down on his knees and prayed. Turning toward the dead woman, he said, "Tabitha, get up." She opened her eyes, and seeing Peter she sat up. [41]He took her by the hand and helped her to her feet. Then he called the believers and the widows and presented her to them alive. [42]This became known all over Joppa, and many people believed in the Lord.

B. Duties to Other People in General or Other Christians

1. Accept Mutual Accountability toward Others

Matt 18 [15]"If your brother sins against you, go and show him his fault, just between the two of you. If he listens to you, you have won your brother over. [16]But if he will not listen, take one or two others along, so that 'every matter may be established by the testimony of two or three witnesses.' [17]If he refuses to listen to them, tell it to the church; and if he refuses to listen even to the church, treat him as you would a pagan or a tax collector."

Luke 17 [3]"So watch yourselves.

"If your brother sins, rebuke him, and if he repents, forgive him. [4]If he sins against you seven times in a day, and seven times comes back to you and says, 'I repent,' forgive him."

Gal 6 [1]Brothers, if someone is caught in a sin, you who are spiritual should restore him gently. But watch yourself, or you also may be tempted. [2]Carry each other's burdens, and in this way you will fulfill the law of Christ.

James 5 [16]Therefore confess your sins to each other and pray for each other so that you may be healed. The prayer of a righteous man is powerful and effective.

2. Be at Peace with Others

Rom 12 [18]If it is possible, as far as it depends on you, live at peace with everyone.

Heb 12 [14]Make every effort to live in peace with all men and to be holy; without holiness no one will see the Lord.

3. Be Compassionate toward Others

Zech 7 [9]"This is what the LORD Almighty says: 'Administer true justice; show mercy and compassion to one another.'"

Eph 4 [32]Be kind and compassionate to one another, forgiving each other, just as in Christ God forgave you.

1 Pet 3 [8]Finally, all of you, live in harmony with one another; be sympathetic, love as brothers, be compassionate and humble.

1 John 3 [17]If anyone has material possessions and sees his brother in need but has no pity on him, how can the love of God be in him?

4. Be Generous toward Others

a) Our Duty to Be Generous

Prov 3 [9]Honor the LORD with your wealth, with the firstfruits of all your crops; [10]then your barns will be filled to overflowing, and your vats will brim over with new wine.
Eccles 11 [1]Cast your bread upon the waters, for after many days you will find it again. [2]Give portions to seven, yes to eight, for you do not know what disaster may come upon the land.
Luke 6 [38]"Give, and it will be given to you. A good measure, pressed down, shaken together and running over, will be poured into your lap. For with the measure you use, it will be measured to you."
2 Cor 8 [6]So we urged Titus, since he had earlier made a beginning, to bring also to completion this act of grace on your part. [7]But just as you excel in everything—in faith, in speech, in knowledge, in complete earnestness and in your love for us—see that you also excel in this grace of giving.

[8]I am not commanding you, but I want to test the sincerity of your love by comparing it with the earnestness of others. . . .

[10]And here is my advice about what is best for you in this matter: Last year you were the first not only to give but also to have the desire to do so. [11]Now finish the work, so that your eager willingness to do it may be matched by your completion of it, according to your means. [12]For if the willingness is there, the gift is acceptable according to what one has, not according to what he does not have.

[13]Our desire is not that others might be relieved while you are hard pressed, but that there might be equality. [14]At the present time your plenty will supply what they need, so that in turn their plenty will supply what you need. Then there will be equality, [15]as it is written: "He who gathered much did not have too much, and he who gathered little did not have too little." . . . [24]Therefore show these men the proof of your love and the reason for our pride in you, so that the churches can see it.
Gal 2 [10]All they asked was that we should continue to remember the poor, the very thing I was eager to do.
1 Tim 6 [18]Command them to do good, to be rich in good deeds, and to be generous and willing to share.
Heb 13 [16]And do not forget to do good and to share with others, for with such sacrifices God is pleased.

b) Examples of Generosity

(1) The Antiochian Believers Were Generous

Acts 11 [27]During this time some prophets came down from Jerusalem to Antioch. [28]One of them, named Agabus, stood up and through the Spirit predicted that a severe famine would spread over the entire Roman world. (This happened during the reign of Claudius.) [29]The disciples, each according to his ability, decided to provide help for the brothers living in Judea. [30]This they did, sending their gift to the elders by Barnabas and Saul.

(2) Barnabas Was Generous

Acts 4 [36]Joseph, a Levite from Cyprus, whom the apostles called Barnabas (which means Son of Encouragement), [37]sold a field he owned and brought the money and put it at the apostles' feet.

(3) The Corinthian Believers Were Generous

1 Cor 16 [3]Then, when I arrive, I will give letters of introduction to the men you approve and send them with your gift to Jerusalem.
2 Cor 8 [10]And here is my advice about what is best for you in this matter: Last year you were the first not only to give but also to have the desire to do so.

(4) The Jerusalem Believers Were Generous

Acts 2 [44]All the believers were together and had everything in common. [45]Selling their possessions and goods, they gave to anyone as he had need.
Acts 4 [32]All the believers were one in heart and mind. No one claimed that any of his possessions was his own, but they shared everything they had. . . . [34]There were no needy persons among them. For from time to time those who owned lands or houses sold them, brought the money from the sales [35]and put it at the apostles' feet, and it was distributed to anyone as he had need.

(5) The Macedonian and Achaian Believers Were Generous

Rom 15 [25]Now, however, I am on my way to Jerusalem in the service of the saints there. [26]For Macedonia and Achaia were pleased to make a contribution for the poor among the saints in Jerusalem. [27]They were pleased to do it, and indeed they owe it to them. For if the Gentiles have shared in the Jews' spiritual blessings, they owe it to the Jews to share with them their material blessings. [28]So after I have completed this task and have made sure that they have received this fruit, I will go to Spain and visit you on the way.
2 Cor 8 [1]And now, brothers, we want you to know about the grace that God has given the Macedonian churches. [2]Out of the most severe trial, their overflowing joy and their extreme poverty welled up in rich generosity. [3]For I testify that they gave as much as they were able, and even beyond their ability. Entirely on their own, [4]they urgently pleaded with us for the privilege of sharing in this service to the saints. [5]And they did not do as we expected, but they gave themselves first to the Lord and then to us in keeping with God's will.

(6) The Philippian Believers Were Generous

Phil 4 [10]I rejoice greatly in the Lord that at last you have renewed your concern for me. Indeed, you have been concerned, but you had no opportunity to show it. . . .

[14]Yet it was good of you to share in my troubles. [15]Moreover, as you Philippians know, in the early days of your acquaintance with the gospel, when I set out from Macedonia, not one church shared with me in the matter of giving and receiving, except you only; [16]for even when I was in Thessalonica, you sent me aid again and again when I was in need. [17]Not that I am looking for a gift, but I am looking for what may be credited to your account. [18]I have received full payment and even more; I am amply supplied, now that I have received from Epaphroditus the gifts you sent. They are a fragrant offering, an acceptable sacrifice, pleasing to God. [19]And my God will meet all your needs according to his glorious riches in Christ Jesus.

5. Be a Good Example for Others

Matt 5 [13]"You are the salt of the earth. But if the salt loses its saltiness, how can it be made salty again? It is no longer good for anything, except to be thrown out and trampled by men.

[14]"You are the light of the world. A city on a hill cannot be hidden. [15]Neither do people light a lamp and put it under a bowl. Instead they put it on its stand, and it gives light to everyone in the house. [16]In the same way, let your light shine before men, that they may see your good deeds and praise your Father in heaven."
Rom 13 [7]Give everyone what you owe him: If you owe taxes, pay taxes; if revenue, then revenue; if respect, then respect; if honor, then honor.
2 Cor 8 [21]For we are taking pains to do what is right, not only in the eyes of the Lord but also in the eyes of men.
1 Thess 4 [11]Make it your ambition to lead a quiet life, to mind your own business and to work with your hands, just as we told you, [12]so that your daily life may win the respect of outsiders and so that you will not be dependent on anybody.
1 Tim 4 [12]Don't let anyone look down on you because you are young, but set an example for the believers in speech, in life, in love, in faith and in purity.

6. Be Kind to Others

a) Our Duty to Be Kind

Eph 4 [32]Be kind and compassionate to one another, forgiving each other, just as in Christ God forgave you.
1 Thess 5 [15]Make sure that nobody pays back wrong for wrong, but always try to be kind to each other and to everyone else.
2 Tim 2 [24]And the Lord's servant must not quarrel; instead, he must be kind to everyone, able to teach, not resentful.
2 Pet 1 [5]For this very reason, make every effort to add to your faith goodness; and to goodness, knowledge; [6]and to knowledge, self-control; and to self-control, perseverance; and to per-

severance, godliness; [7]and to godliness, brotherly kindness; and to brotherly kindness, love.

b) An Example of Kindness: Peter

Acts 4 [8]Then Peter, filled with the Holy Spirit, said to them: "Rulers and elders of the people! [9]If we are being called to account today for an act of kindness shown to a cripple and are asked how he was healed, [10]then know this, you and all the people of Israel: It is by the name of Jesus Christ of Nazareth, whom you crucified but whom God raised from the dead, that this man stands before you healed."

7. Be Patient with Others

Matt 7 [1]"Do not judge, or you too will be judged. [2]For in the same way you judge others, you will be judged, and with the measure you use, it will be measured to you.

[3]"Why do you look at the speck of sawdust in your brother's eye and pay no attention to the plank in your own eye?"

Rom 14 [1]Accept him whose faith is weak, without passing judgment on disputable matters. [2]One man's faith allows him to eat everything, but another man, whose faith is weak, eats only vegetables. [3]The man who eats everything must not look down on him who does not, and the man who does not eat everything must not condemn the man who does, for God has accepted him. [4]Who are you to judge someone else's servant? To his own master he stands or falls. And he will stand, for the Lord is able to make him stand.

[5]One man considers one day more sacred than another; another man considers every day alike. Each one should be fully convinced in his own mind. . . . [10]You, then, why do you judge your brother? Or why do you look down on your brother? For we will all stand before God's judgment seat. [11]It is written: "'As surely as I live,' says the Lord, 'every knee will bow before me; every tongue will confess to God.'" [12]So then, each of us will give an account of himself to God.

[13]Therefore let us stop passing judgment on one another. Instead, make up your mind not to put any stumbling block or obstacle in your brother's way.

Eph 4 [2]Be completely humble and gentle; be patient, bearing with one another in love.

Col 3 [13]Bear with each other and forgive whatever grievances you may have against one another. Forgive as the Lord forgave you.

1 Thess 5 [14]And we urge you, brothers, warn those who are idle, encourage the timid, help the weak, be patient with everyone.

James 4 [11]Brothers, do not slander one another. Anyone who speaks against his brother or judges him speaks against the law and judges it. When you judge the law, you are not keeping it, but sitting in judgment on it. [12]There is only one Lawgiver and Judge, the one who is able to save and destroy. But you—who are you to judge your neighbor?

8. Be Wise toward Others

Col 4 [5]Be wise in the way you act toward outsiders; make the most of every opportunity. [6]Let your conversation be always full of grace, seasoned with salt, so that you may know how to answer everyone.

9. Defend the Faith before Others

1 Pet 3 [15]But in your hearts set apart Christ as Lord. Always be prepared to give an answer to everyone who asks you to give the reason for the hope that you have. But do this with gentleness and respect. . . .

10. Do Good to Others

Matt 7 [12]"So in everything, do to others what you would have them do to you, for this sums up the Law and the Prophets."

Matt 25 [31]"When the Son of Man comes in his glory, and all the angels with him, he will sit on his throne in heavenly glory. [32]All the nations will be gathered before him, and he will separate the people one from another as a shepherd separates the sheep from the goats. [33]He will put the sheep on his right and the goats on his left.

[34]"Then the King will say to those on his right, 'Come, you who are blessed by my Father; take your inheritance, the kingdom prepared for you since the creation of the world. [35]For I was hungry and you gave me something to eat, I was thirsty and you gave me something to drink, I was a stranger and you invited me in, [36]I needed clothes and you clothed me, I was sick and you looked after me, I was in prison and you came to visit me.'

[37]"Then the righteous will answer him, 'Lord, when did we see you hungry and feed you, or thirsty and give you something to drink? [38]When did we see you a stranger and invite you in, or needing clothes and clothe you? [39]When did we see you sick or in prison and go to visit you?'

[40]"The King will reply, 'I tell you the truth, whatever you did for one of the least of these brothers of mine, you did for me.'"

Gal 6 [9]Let us not become weary in doing good, for at the proper time we will reap a harvest if we do not give up. [10]Therefore, as we have opportunity, let us do good to all people, especially to those who belong to the family of believers.

1 Pet 2 [15]For it is God's will that by doing good you should silence the ignorant talk of foolish men. [16]Live as free men, but do not use your freedom as a cover-up for evil; live as servants of God.

11. Forgive Others

Matt 6 [14]"For if you forgive men when they sin against you, your heavenly Father will also forgive you. [15]But if you do not forgive men their sins, your Father will not forgive your sins."

Matt 18 [21]Then Peter came to Jesus and asked, "Lord, how many times shall I forgive my brother when he sins against me? Up to seven times?"

[22]Jesus answered, "I tell you, not seven times, but seventy-seven times."

Mark 11 [25]"And when you stand praying, if you hold anything against anyone, forgive him, so that your Father in heaven may forgive you your sins."

Luke 6 [37]"Do not judge, and you will not be judged. Do not condemn, and you will not be condemned. Forgive, and you will be forgiven."

Luke 17 [3]"So watch yourselves.

"If your brother sins, rebuke him, and if he repents, forgive him. [4]If he sins against you seven times in a day, and seven times comes back to you and says, 'I repent,' forgive him."

2 Cor 2 [6]The punishment inflicted on him by the majority is sufficient for him. [7]Now instead, you ought to forgive and comfort him, so that he will not be overwhelmed by excessive sorrow. . . . [10]If you forgive anyone, I also forgive him. And what I have forgiven—if there was anything to forgive—I have forgiven in the sight of Christ for your sake. . . .

Eph 4 [32]Be kind and compassionate to one another, forgiving each other, just as in Christ God forgave you.

Col 3 [13]Bear with each other and forgive whatever grievances you may have against one another. Forgive as the Lord forgave you.

12. Give Good Counsel to Others

a) Our Duty to Give Good Counsel

(1) We Are to Edify One Another

Rom 14 [19]Let us therefore make every effort to do what leads to peace and to mutual edification. [20]Do not destroy the work of God for the sake of food. All food is clean, but it is wrong for a man to eat anything that causes someone else to stumble. [21]It is better not to eat meat or drink wine or to do anything else that will cause your brother to fall.

Rom 15 [2]Each of us should please his neighbor for his good, to build him up.

1 Cor 8 [1]Now about food sacrificed to idols: We know that we all possess knowledge. Knowledge puffs up, but love builds up.

1 Cor 10 [23]"Everything is permissible"—but not everything is beneficial. "Everything is permissible"—but not everything is constructive. [24]Nobody should seek his own good, but the good of others.

1 Cor 14 [26]What then shall we say, brothers? When you come together, everyone has a hymn, or a word of instruction, a revelation, a tongue or an interpretation. All of these must be done for the strengthening of the church.

Eph 4 [29]Do not let any unwholesome talk come out of your

mouths, but only what is helpful for building others up according to their needs, that it may benefit those who listen.
1 Thess 5 [11]Therefore encourage one another and build each other up, just as in fact you are doing.

(2) We Are to Encourage One Another

Rom 1 [11]I long to see you so that I may impart to you some spiritual gift to make you strong—[12]that is, that you and I may be mutually encouraged by each other's faith.
1 Thess 4 [18]Therefore encourage each other with these words.
1 Thess 5 [11]Therefore encourage one another and build each other up, just as in fact you are doing.
1 Thess 5 [14]And we urge you, brothers, warn those who are idle, encourage the timid, help the weak, be patient with everyone.
Heb 3 [13]But encourage one another daily, as long as it is called Today, so that none of you may be hardened by sin's deceitfulness.
Heb 10 [24]And let us consider how we may spur one another on toward love and good deeds. [25]Let us not give up meeting together, as some are in the habit of doing, but let us encourage one another—and all the more as you see the Day approaching.

(3) We Are to Instruct One Another

Rom 15 [14]I myself am convinced, my brothers, that you yourselves are full of goodness, complete in knowledge and competent to instruct one another.
Col 3 [16]Let the word of Christ dwell in you richly as you teach and admonish one another with all wisdom, and as you sing psalms, hymns and spiritual songs with gratitude in your hearts to God.
1 Thess 5 [12]Now we ask you, brothers, to respect those who work hard among you, who are over you in the Lord and who admonish you.
2 Tim 2 [24]And the Lord's servant must not quarrel; instead, he must be kind to everyone, able to teach, not resentful. [25]Those who oppose him he must gently instruct, in the hope that God will grant them repentance leading them to a knowledge of the truth, [26]and that they will come to their senses and escape from the trap of the devil, who has taken them captive to do his will.

(4) We Are to Rebuke One Another

1 Tim 5 [20]Those who sin are to be rebuked publicly, so that the others may take warning.
2 Tim 4 [2]Preach the Word; be prepared in season and out of season; correct, rebuke and encourage—with great patience and careful instruction.
Titus 2 [15]These, then, are the things you should teach. Encourage and rebuke with all authority. Do not let anyone despise you.

(5) We Are to Warn One Another

1 Thess 5 [14]And we urge you, brothers, warn those who are idle, encourage the timid, help the weak, be patient with everyone.
2 Thess 3 [14]If anyone does not obey our instruction in this letter, take special note of him. Do not associate with him, in order that he may feel ashamed. [15]Yet do not regard him as an enemy, but warn him as a brother.
2 Tim 2 [14]Keep reminding them of these things. Warn them before God against quarreling about words; it is of no value, and only ruins those who listen.

b) Examples of Giving Good Counsel

(1) Barnabas Gave Good Counsel

Acts 11 [22]News of this reached the ears of the church at Jerusalem, and they sent Barnabas to Antioch. [23]When he arrived and saw the evidence of the grace of God, he was glad and encouraged them all to remain true to the Lord with all their hearts.

(2) The Ephesian Believers Gave Good Counsel

Acts 18 [24]Meanwhile a Jew named Apollos, a native of Alexandria, came to Ephesus. He was a learned man, with a thorough knowledge of the Scriptures. . . . [26]He began to speak boldly in the synagogue. When Priscilla and Aquila heard him, they invited him to their home and explained to him the way of God more adequately.
[27]When Apollos wanted to go to Achaia, the brothers encouraged him and wrote to the disciples there to welcome him. On arriving, he was a great help to those who by grace had believed.

(3) Judas and Silas Gave Good Counsel

Acts 15 [32]Judas and Silas, who themselves were prophets, said much to encourage and strengthen the brothers.

(4) Paul Gave Good Counsel

Acts 16 [40]After Paul and Silas came out of the prison, they went to Lydia's house, where they met with the brothers and encouraged them. Then they left.
Acts 20 [1]When the uproar had ended, Paul sent for the disciples and, after encouraging them, said good-by and set out for Macedonia. [2]He traveled through that area, speaking many words of encouragement to the people, and finally arrived in Greece. . . .
2 Cor 13 [2]I already gave you a warning when I was with you the second time. I now repeat it while absent: On my return I will not spare those who sinned earlier or any of the others. . . .
Col 1 [28]We proclaim him, admonishing and teaching everyone with all wisdom, so that we may present everyone perfect in Christ.
1 Thess 2 [11]For you know that we dealt with each of you as a father deals with his own children, [12]encouraging, comforting and urging you to live lives worthy of God, who calls you into his kingdom and glory.
1 Thess 4 [6]and that in this matter no one should wrong his brother or take advantage of him. The Lord will punish men for all such sins, as we have already told you and warned you.

(5) Timothy Gave Good Counsel

1 Thess 3 [2]We sent Timothy, who is our brother and God's fellow worker in spreading the gospel of Christ, to strengthen and encourage you in your faith, [3]so that no one would be unsettled by these trials. You know quite well that we were destined for them.

(6) Tychicus Gave Good Counsel

Eph 6 [21]Tychicus, the dear brother and faithful servant in the Lord, will tell you everything, so that you also may know how I am and what I am doing. [22]I am sending him to you for this very purpose, that you may know how we are, and that he may encourage you.
Col 4 [7]Tychicus will tell you all the news about me. He is a dear brother, a faithful minister and fellow servant in the Lord. [8]I am sending him to you for the express purpose that you may know about our circumstances and that he may encourage your hearts. [9]He is coming with Onesimus, our faithful and dear brother, who is one of you. They will tell you everything that is happening here.

13. Honor Others

Rom 12 [10]Be devoted to one another in brotherly love. Honor one another above yourselves.
Rom 13 [7]Give everyone what you owe him: If you owe taxes, pay taxes; if revenue, then revenue; if respect, then respect; if honor, then honor.
Phil 2 [29]Welcome him in the Lord with great joy, and honor men like him, [30]because he almost died for the work of Christ, risking his life to make up for the help you could not give me.
1 Tim 5 [17]The elders who direct the affairs of the church well are worthy of double honor, especially those whose work is preaching and teaching.

14. Live at Peace with Others

Ps 34 [14]Turn from evil and do good; seek peace and pursue it.
Rom 14 [19]Let us therefore make every effort to do what leads to peace and to mutual edification.
2 Cor 13 [11]Finally, brothers, good-by. Aim for perfection, listen to my appeal, be of one mind, live in peace. And the God of love and peace will be with you.
1 Thess 5 [13]Hold them in the highest regard in love because of their work. Live in peace with each other.
James 3 [17]But the wisdom that comes from heaven is first of all pure; then peace-loving, considerate, submissive, full of mercy and good fruit, impartial and sincere. [18]Peacemakers who sow in peace raise a harvest of righteousness.

15. Live in Harmony (Unity) with Others

a) Our Duty to Live in Harmony

Ps 133 [1]How good and pleasant it is when brothers live together in unity!

John 17 [20]"My prayer is not for them alone. I pray also for those who will believe in me through their message, [21]that all of them may be one, Father, just as you are in me and I am in you. May they also be in us so that the world may believe that you have sent me. [22]I have given them the glory that you gave me, that they may be one as we are one: [23]I in them and you in me. May they be brought to complete unity to let the world know that you sent me and have loved them even as you have loved me."

Rom 15 [5]May the God who gives endurance and encouragement give you a spirit of unity among yourselves as you follow Christ Jesus, [6]so that with one heart and mouth you may glorify the God and Father of our Lord Jesus Christ.

[7]Accept one another, then, just as Christ accepted you, in order to bring praise to God.

1 Cor 1 [10]I appeal to you, brothers, in the name of our Lord Jesus Christ, that all of you agree with one another so that there may be no divisions among you and that you may be perfectly united in mind and thought.

2 Cor 13 [11]Finally, brothers, good-by. Aim for perfection, listen to my appeal, be of one mind, live in peace. And the God of love and peace will be with you.

Gal 5 [15]If you keep on biting and devouring each other, watch out or you will be destroyed by each other.

Phil 1 [27]Whatever happens, conduct yourselves in a manner worthy of the gospel of Christ. Then, whether I come and see you or only hear about you in my absence, I will know that you stand firm in one spirit, contending as one man for the faith of the gospel. . . .

Phil 2 [1]If you have any encouragement from being united with Christ, if any comfort from his love, if any fellowship with the Spirit, if any tenderness and compassion, [2]then make my joy complete by being like-minded, having the same love, being one in spirit and purpose.

Phil 4 [2]I plead with Euodia and I plead with Syntyche to agree with each other in the Lord.

1 Pet 3 [8]Finally, all of you, live in harmony with one another; be sympathetic, love as brothers, be compassionate and humble.

b) An Example of Living in Harmony: The Jerusalem Church

Acts 4 [32]All the believers were one in heart and mind. No one claimed that any of his possessions was his own, but they shared everything they had.

16. Love Others

a) Our Duty to Love Others

Lev 19 [18]"'Do not seek revenge or bear a grudge against one of your people, but love your neighbor as yourself. I am the LORD.'"

Matt 5 [43]"You have heard that it was said, 'Love your neighbor and hate your enemy.' [44]But I tell you: Love your enemies and pray for those who persecute you, [45]that you may be sons of your Father in heaven. He causes his sun to rise on the evil and the good, and sends rain on the righteous and the unrighteous. [46]If you love those who love you, what reward will you get? Are not even the tax collectors doing that?"

Matt 22 [35]One of them, an expert in the law, tested him with this question: [36]"Teacher, which is the greatest commandment in the Law?"

[37]Jesus replied: "'Love the Lord your God with all your heart and with all your soul and with all your mind.' [38]This is the first and greatest commandment. [39]And the second is like it: 'Love your neighbor as yourself.' [40]All the Law and the Prophets hang on these two commandments."

John 15 [12]"My command is this: Love each other as I have loved you. [13]Greater love has no one than this, that he lay down his life for his friends. [14]You are my friends if you do what I command. [15]I no longer call you servants, because a servant does not know his master's business. Instead, I have called you friends, for everything that I learned from my Father I have made known to you. [16]You did not choose me, but I chose you and appointed you to go and bear fruit—fruit that will last. Then the Father will give you whatever you ask in my name. [17]This is my command: Love each other."

Rom 12 [9]Love must be sincere. Hate what is evil; cling to what is good. [10]Be devoted to one another in brotherly love. Honor one another above yourselves.

Rom 13 [8]Let no debt remain outstanding, except the continuing debt to love one another, for he who loves his fellowman has fulfilled the law. [9]The commandments, "Do not commit adultery," "Do not murder," "Do not steal," "Do not covet," and whatever other commandment there may be, are summed up in this one rule: "Love your neighbor as yourself." [10]Love does no harm to its neighbor. Therefore love is the fulfillment of the law.

1 Cor 16 [14]Do everything in love.

Gal 5 [13]You, my brothers, were called to be free. But do not use your freedom to indulge the sinful nature; rather, serve one another in love. [14]The entire law is summed up in a single command: "Love your neighbor as yourself."

Eph 5 [1]Be imitators of God, therefore, as dearly loved children [2]and live a life of love, just as Christ loved us and gave himself up for us as a fragrant offering and sacrifice to God.

1 Thess 3 [12]May the Lord make your love increase and overflow for each other and for everyone else, just as ours does for you.

1 Thess 4 [9]Now about brotherly love we do not need to write to you, for you yourselves have been taught by God to love each other. [10]And in fact, you do love all the brothers throughout Macedonia. Yet we urge you, brothers, to do so more and more.

Heb 10 [24]And let us consider how we may spur one another on toward love and good deeds.

1 Pet 1 [22]Now that you have purified yourselves by obeying the truth so that you have sincere love for your brothers, love one another deeply, from the heart.

1 Pet 2 [17]Show proper respect to everyone: Love the brotherhood of believers, fear God, honor the king.

1 Pet 3 [8]Finally, all of you, live in harmony with one another; be sympathetic, love as brothers, be compassionate and humble.

1 Pet 4 [8]Above all, love each other deeply, because love covers over a multitude of sins.

1 Pet 5 [14]Greet one another with a kiss of love.

Peace to all of you who are in Christ.

1 John 3 [11]This is the message you heard from the beginning: We should love one another.

1 John 4 [7]Dear friends, let us love one another, for love comes from God. Everyone who loves has been born of God and knows God. [8]Whoever does not love does not know God, because God is love. [9]This is how God showed his love among us: He sent his one and only Son into the world that we might live through him. [10]This is love: not that we loved God, but that he loved us and sent his Son as an atoning sacrifice for our sins. [11]Dear friends, since God so loved us, we also ought to love one another. [12]No one has ever seen God; but if we love one another, God lives in us and his love is made complete in us.

[13]We know that we live in him and he in us, because he has given us of his Spirit. [14]And we have seen and testify that the Father has sent his Son to be the Savior of the world. [15]If anyone acknowledges that Jesus is the Son of God, God lives in him and he in God. [16]And so we know and rely on the love God has for us.

God is love. Whoever lives in love lives in God, and God in him. [17]In this way, love is made complete among us so that we will have confidence on the day of judgment, because in this world we are like him. [18]There is no fear in love. But perfect love drives out fear, because fear has to do with punishment. The one who fears is not made perfect in love.

[19]We love because he first loved us. [20]If anyone says, "I love God," yet hates his brother, he is a liar. For anyone who does not love his brother, whom he has seen, cannot love God, whom he has not seen. [21]And he has given us this command: Whoever loves God must also love his brother.

b) A Description of Loving Others

1 Cor 13 [1]If I speak in the tongues of men and of angels, but have not love, I am only a resounding gong or a clanging cymbal. 2If I have the gift of prophecy and can fathom all mysteries and all knowledge, and if I have a faith that can move mountains, but have not love, I am nothing. 3If I give all I possess to the poor and surrender my body to the flames, but have not love, I gain nothing.

4Love is patient, love is kind. It does not envy, it does not boast, it is not proud. 5It is not rude, it is not self-seeking, it is not easily angered, it keeps no record of wrongs. 6Love does not delight in evil but rejoices with the truth. 7It always protects, always trusts, always hopes, always perseveres.

8Love never fails. But where there are prophecies, they will cease; where there are tongues, they will be stilled; where there is knowledge, it will pass away. 9For we know in part and we prophesy in part, 10but when perfection comes, the imperfect disappears. 11When I was a child, I talked like a child, I thought like a child, I reasoned like a child. When I became a man, I put childish ways behind me. 12Now we see but a poor reflection as in a mirror; then we shall see face to face. Now I know in part; then I shall know fully, even as I am fully known.

13And now these three remain: faith, hope and love. But the greatest of these is love.

c) Examples of Loving Others

(1) The Colossian Believers Showed Love

Col 1 3We always thank God, the Father of our Lord Jesus Christ, when we pray for you, 4because we have heard of your faith in Christ Jesus and of the love you have for all the saints—5the faith and love that spring from the hope that is stored up for you in heaven and that you have already heard about in the word of truth, the gospel 6that has come to you. All over the world this gospel is bearing fruit and growing, just as it has been doing among you since the day you heard it and understood God's grace in all its truth. 7You learned it from Epaphras, our dear fellow servant, who is a faithful minister of Christ on our behalf, 8and who also told us of your love in the Spirit.

(2) The Hebrew Believers Showed Love

Heb 6 10God is not unjust; he will not forget your work and the love you have shown him as you have helped his people and continue to help them.

(3) John Showed Love

2 John 1The elder,

To the chosen lady and her children, whom I love in the truth—and not I only, but also all who know the truth. . . .

3 John 1The elder,

To my dear friend Gaius, whom I love in the truth.

(4) Paul Showed Love

Rom 16 8Greet Ampliatus, whom I love in the Lord.

1 Cor 16 24My love to all of you in Christ Jesus. Amen.

2 Cor 2 4For I wrote you out of great distress and anguish of heart and with many tears, not to grieve you but to let you know the depth of my love for you.

Phil 4 1Therefore, my brothers, you whom I love and long for, my joy and crown, that is how you should stand firm in the Lord, dear friends!

(5) Philemon Showed Love

Philem 4I always thank my God as I remember you in my prayers, 5because I hear about your faith in the Lord Jesus and your love for all the saints. 6I pray that you may be active in sharing your faith, so that you will have a full understanding of every good thing we have in Christ. 7Your love has given me great joy and encouragement, because you, brother, have refreshed the hearts of the saints.

(6) The Thessalonian Believers Showed Love

1 Thess 1 3We continually remember before our God and Father your work produced by faith, your labor prompted by love, and your endurance inspired by hope in our Lord Jesus Christ.

2 Thess 1 3We ought always to thank God for you, brothers, and rightly so, because your faith is growing more and more, and the love every one of you has for each other is increasing.

17. Pray for Others

Eph 6 19Pray also for me, that whenever I open my mouth, words may be given me so that I will fearlessly make known the mystery of the gospel, 20for which I am an ambassador in chains. Pray that I may declare it fearlessly, as I should.

Col 4 3And pray for us, too, that God may open a door for our message, so that we may proclaim the mystery of Christ, for which I am in chains. 4Pray that I may proclaim it clearly, as I should.

1 Thess 5 25Brothers, pray for us.

2 Thess 3 1Finally, brothers, pray for us that the message of the Lord may spread rapidly and be honored, just as it was with you. 2And pray that we may be delivered from wicked and evil men, for not everyone has faith.

1 Tim 2 1I urge, then, first of all, that requests, prayers, intercession and thanksgiving be made for everyone. . . .

Heb 13 18Pray for us. We are sure that we have a clear conscience and desire to live honorably in every way. 19I particularly urge you to pray so that I may be restored to you soon.

James 5 16Therefore confess your sins to each other and pray for each other so that you may be healed. The prayer of a righteous man is powerful and effective.

18. Proclaim the Gospel by Word and Deed

a) The Content of the Proclamation

(1) Christ

Acts 5 42Day after day, in the temple courts and from house to house, they never stopped teaching and proclaiming the good news that Jesus is the Christ.

Acts 8 5Philip went down to a city in Samaria and proclaimed the Christ there.

Acts 17 2As his custom was, Paul went into the synagogue, and on three Sabbath days he reasoned with them from the Scriptures, 3explaining and proving that the Christ had to suffer and rise from the dead.

2 Cor 1 18But as surely as God is faithful, our message to you is not "Yes" and "No." 19For the Son of God, Jesus Christ, who was preached among you by me and Silas and Timothy, was not "Yes" and "No," but in him it has always been "Yes."

Gal 1 15But when God, who set me apart from birth and called me by his grace, was pleased 16to reveal his Son in me so that I might preach him among the Gentiles . . .

Phil 1 15It is true that some preach Christ out of envy and rivalry, but others out of goodwill. 16The latter do so in love, knowing that I am put here for the defense of the gospel. 17The former preach Christ out of selfish ambition, not sincerely, supposing that they can stir up trouble for me while I am in chains. 18But what does it matter? The important thing is that in every way, whether from false motives or true, Christ is preached. And because of this I rejoice.

Yes, and I will continue to rejoice. . . .

Col 1 28We proclaim him, admonishing and teaching everyone with all wisdom, so that we may present everyone perfect in Christ.

2 Tim 1 8So do not be ashamed to testify about our Lord, or ashamed of me his prisoner. But join with me in suffering for the gospel. . . .

1 John 1 1That which was from the beginning, which we have heard, which we have seen with our eyes, which we have looked at and our hands have touched—this we proclaim concerning the Word of life.

1 John 4 14And we have seen and testify that the Father has sent his Son to be the Savior of the world.

(2) Christ as Lord

2 Cor 4 5For we do not preach ourselves, but Jesus Christ as Lord, and ourselves as your servants for Jesus' sake.

(3) The Christian Message

Rom 10 8But what does it say? "The word is near you; it is in your mouth and in your heart," that is, the word of faith we are proclaiming: 9That if you confess with your mouth, "Jesus is Lord," and believe in your heart that God raised him from the dead, you will be saved.

2 Tim 4 17But the Lord stood at my side and gave me strength, so that through me the message might be fully proclaimed and all the Gentiles might hear it. And I was delivered from the lion's mouth.

1 Pet 1 [23]For you have been born again, not of perishable seed, but of imperishable, through the living and enduring word of God. [24]For, "All men are like grass, and all their glory is like the flowers of the field; the grass withers and the flowers fall, [25]but the word of the Lord stands forever." And this is the word that was preached to you.

(4) The Death and Resurrection of Christ

Acts 4 [33]With great power the apostles continued to testify to the resurrection of the Lord Jesus, and much grace was upon them all.

Acts 26 [22]"But I have had God's help to this very day, and so I stand here and testify to small and great alike. I am saying nothing beyond what the prophets and Moses said would happen—[23]that the Christ would suffer and, as the first to rise from the dead, would proclaim light to his own people and to the Gentiles."

(5) Eternal Life

1 John 1 [2] The life appeared; we have seen it and testify to it, and we proclaim to you the eternal life, which was with the Father and has appeared to us.

(6) Forgiveness of Sins

Acts 13 [38]"Therefore, my brothers, I want you to know that through Jesus the forgiveness of sins is proclaimed to you. [39]Through him everyone who believes is justified from everything you could not be justified from by the law of Moses."

(7) God

Acts 17 [23]"For as I walked around and looked carefully at your objects of worship, I even found an altar with this inscription: TO AN UNKNOWN GOD. Now what you worship as something unknown I am going to proclaim to you."

1 Cor 2 [1]When I came to you, brothers, I did not come with eloquence or superior wisdom as I proclaimed to you the testimony about God.

(8) The Good News (Gospel) of Christ

Acts 13 [30]"But God raised him from the dead, [31]and for many days he was seen by those who had traveled with him from Galilee to Jerusalem. They are now his witnesses to our people.

[32]"We tell you the good news: What God promised our fathers [33]he has fulfilled for us, their children, by raising up Jesus. As it is written in the second Psalm: 'You are my Son; today I have become your Father.'"

Acts 16 [10]After Paul had seen the vision, we got ready at once to leave for Macedonia, concluding that God had called us to preach the gospel to them.

Rom 15 [19]by the power of signs and miracles, through the power of the Spirit. So from Jerusalem all the way around to Illyricum, I have fully proclaimed the gospel of Christ.

1 Cor 15 [1]Now, brothers, I want to remind you of the gospel I preached to you, which you received and on which you have taken your stand. [2]By this gospel you are saved, if you hold firmly to the word I preached to you. Otherwise, you have believed in vain.

[3]For what I received I passed on to you as of first importance: that Christ died for our sins according to the Scriptures, [4]that he was buried, that he was raised on the third day according to the Scriptures, [5]and that he appeared to Peter, and then to the Twelve.

Gal 1 [11]I want you to know, brothers, that the gospel I preached is not something that man made up. [12]I did not receive it from any man, nor was I taught it; rather, I received it by revelation from Jesus Christ.

Col 1 [23]if you continue in your faith, established and firm, not moved from the hope held out in the gospel. This is the gospel that you heard and that has been proclaimed to every creature under heaven, and of which I, Paul, have become a servant.

(9) The Grace of God

Acts 20 [24]"However, I consider my life worth nothing to me, if only I may finish the race and complete the task the Lord Jesus has given me—the task of testifying to the gospel of God's grace."

1 Pet 5 [12]With the help of Silas, whom I regard as a faithful brother, I have written to you briefly, encouraging you and testifying that this is the true grace of God. Stand fast in it.

(10) The Kingdom of God

Luke 9 [60]Jesus said to him, "Let the dead bury their own dead, but you go and proclaim the kingdom of God."

Acts 8 [12]But when they believed Philip as he preached the good news of the kingdom of God and the name of Jesus Christ, they were baptized, both men and women.

Acts 28 [23]They arranged to meet Paul on a certain day, and came in even larger numbers to the place where he was staying. From morning till evening he explained and declared to them the kingdom of God and tried to convince them about Jesus from the Law of Moses and from the Prophets.

Acts 28 [31]Boldly and without hindrance he preached the kingdom of God and taught about the Lord Jesus Christ.

(11) The Mystery of Christ

Col 4 [3]And pray for us, too, that God may open a door for our message, so that we may proclaim the mystery of Christ, for which I am in chains. [4]Pray that I may proclaim it clearly, as I should.

(12) Repentance

Acts 26 [19]"So then, King Agrippa, I was not disobedient to the vision from heaven. [20]First to those in Damascus, then to those in Jerusalem and in all Judea, and to the Gentiles also, I preached that they should repent and turn to God and prove their repentance by their deeds."

(13) The Resurrection of the Dead

Acts 4 [1]The priests and the captain of the temple guard and the Sadducees came up to Peter and John while they were speaking to the people. [2]They were greatly disturbed because the apostles were teaching the people and proclaiming in Jesus the resurrection of the dead.

(14) The Testimony about God

1 Cor 2 [1]When I came to you, brothers, I did not come with eloquence or superior wisdom as I proclaimed to you the testimony about God.

(15) The Whole Will of God

Acts 20 [27]"For I have not hesitated to proclaim to you the whole will of God."

(16) The Word of God

Acts 8 [25]When they had testified and proclaimed the word of the Lord, Peter and John returned to Jerusalem, preaching the gospel in many Samaritan villages.

Acts 13 [5]When they arrived at Salamis, they proclaimed the word of God in the Jewish synagogues. John was with them as their helper.

2 Tim 4 [1]In the presence of God and of Christ Jesus, who will judge the living and the dead, and in view of his appearing and his kingdom, I give you this charge: [2]Preach the Word; be prepared in season and out of season; correct, rebuke and encourage—with great patience and careful instruction.

b) How the Gospel Should Be Proclaimed

(1) As Commissioned by God

Acts 10 [39]"We are witnesses of everything he did in the country of the Jews and in Jerusalem. They killed him by hanging him on a tree, [40]but God raised him from the dead on the third day and caused him to be seen. [41]He was not seen by all the people, but by witnesses whom God had already chosen—by us who ate and drank with him after he rose from the dead. [42]He commanded us to preach to the people and to testify that he is the one whom God appointed as judge of the living and the dead."

Rom 1 [14]I am obligated both to Greeks and non-Greeks, both to the wise and the foolish. [15]That is why I am so eager to preach the gospel also to you who are at Rome.

[16]I am not ashamed of the gospel, because it is the power of God for the salvation of everyone who believes: first for the Jew, then for the Gentile.

1 Cor 9 [16]Yet when I preach the gospel, I cannot boast, for I am compelled to preach. Woe to me if I do not preach the gospel! [17]If I preach voluntarily, I have a reward; if not voluntarily, I am simply discharging the trust committed to me. [18]What then is my reward? Just this: that in preaching the gospel I may offer it free of charge, and so not make use of my rights in preaching it.

2 Cor 5 [20]We are therefore Christ's ambassadors, as though God were making his appeal through us. We implore you on Christ's behalf: Be reconciled to God.

Gal 2 [7]On the contrary, they saw that I had been entrusted with the task of preaching the gospel to the Gentiles, just as Peter had been to the Jews. [8]For God, who was at work in the ministry of Peter as an apostle to the Jews, was also at work in my ministry as an apostle to the Gentiles. [9]James, Peter and John, those reputed to be pillars, gave me and Barnabas the right hand of fellowship when they recognized the grace given to me. They agreed that we should go to the Gentiles, and they to the Jews.

1 Thess 2 [3]For the appeal we make does not spring from error or impure motives, nor are we trying to trick you. [4]On the contrary, we speak as men approved by God to be entrusted with the gospel. We are not trying to please men but God, who tests our hearts. [5]You know we never used flattery, nor did we put on a mask to cover up greed—God is our witness.

(2) By the Grace of God

Rom 15 [15]I have written you quite boldly on some points, as if to remind you of them again, because of the grace God gave me [16]to be a minister of Christ Jesus to the Gentiles with the priestly duty of proclaiming the gospel of God, so that the Gentiles might become an offering acceptable to God, sanctified by the Holy Spirit.

1 Cor 15 [10]But by the grace of God I am what I am, and his grace to me was not without effect. No, I worked harder than all of them—yet not I, but the grace of God that was with me. [11]Whether, then, it was I or they, this is what we preach, and this is what you believed.

(3) In Reliance on God

2 Cor 1 [8]We do not want you to be uninformed, brothers, about the hardships we suffered in the province of Asia. We were under great pressure, far beyond our ability to endure, so that we despaired even of life. [9]Indeed, in our hearts we felt the sentence of death. But this happened that we might not rely on ourselves but on God, who raises the dead. [10]He has delivered us from such a deadly peril, and he will deliver us. On him we have set our hope that he will continue to deliver us. . . .

(4) Through the Holy Spirit

Luke 12 [11]"When you are brought before synagogues, rulers and authorities, do not worry about how you will defend yourselves or what you will say, [12]for the Holy Spirit will teach you at that time what you should say."

1 Pet 1 [10]Concerning this salvation, the prophets, who spoke of the grace that was to come to you, searched intently and with the greatest care, [11]trying to find out the time and circumstances to which the Spirit of Christ in them was pointing when he predicted the sufferings of Christ and the glories that would follow. [12]It was revealed to them that they were not serving themselves but you, when they spoke of the things that have now been told you by those who have preached the gospel to you by the Holy Spirit sent from heaven. Even angels long to look into these things.

(5) Through the Strength of God

2 Tim 4 [17]But the Lord stood at my side and gave me strength, so that through me the message might be fully proclaimed and all the Gentiles might hear it. And I was delivered from the lion's mouth.

(6) With Genuine Love

1 Thess 2 [8]We loved you so much that we were delighted to share with you not only the gospel of God but our lives as well, because you had become so dear to us. [9]Surely you remember, brothers, our toil and hardship; we worked night and day in order not to be a burden to anyone while we preached the gospel of God to you.

[10]You are witnesses, and so is God, of how holy, righteous and blameless we were among you who believed.

(7) With the Help of God

Acts 26 [22]"But I have had God's help to this very day, and so I stand here and testify to small and great alike. I am saying nothing beyond what the prophets and Moses said would happen. . . ."

1 Thess 2 [2]We had previously suffered and been insulted in Philippi, as you know, but with the help of our God we dared to tell you his gospel in spite of strong opposition.

(8) With Sincerity

Acts 20 [22]"And now, compelled by the Spirit, I am going to Jerusalem, not knowing what will happen to me there. [23]I only know that in every city the Holy Spirit warns me that prison and hardships are facing me. [24]However, I consider my life worth nothing to me, if only I may finish the race and complete the task the Lord Jesus has given me—the task of testifying to the gospel of God's grace."

Rom 1 [9]God, whom I serve with my whole heart in preaching the gospel of his Son, is my witness how constantly I remember you [10]in my prayers at all times; and I pray that now at last by God's will the way may be opened for me to come to you.

2 Cor 2 [15]For we are to God the aroma of Christ among those who are being saved and those who are perishing. [16]To the one we are the smell of death; to the other, the fragrance of life. And who is equal to such a task? [17]Unlike so many, we do not peddle the word of God for profit. On the contrary, in Christ we speak before God with sincerity, like men sent from God.

c) The Gospel Should Be Proclaimed Everywhere

Matt 28 [18]Then Jesus came to them and said, "All authority in heaven and on earth has been given to me. [19]Therefore go and make disciples of all nations, baptizing them in the name of the Father and of the Son and of the Holy Spirit, [20]and teaching them to obey everything I have commanded you. And surely I am with you always, to the very end of the age."

Acts 1 [8]"But you will receive power when the Holy Spirit comes on you; and you will be my witnesses in Jerusalem, and in all Judea and Samaria, and to the ends of the earth."

Acts 13 [46]Then Paul and Barnabas answered them boldly: "We had to speak the word of God to you first. Since you reject it and do not consider yourselves worthy of eternal life, we now turn to the Gentiles. [47]For this is what the Lord has commanded us: 'I have made you a light for the Gentiles, that you may bring salvation to the ends of the earth.'"

Rom 15 [20]It has always been my ambition to preach the gospel where Christ was not known, so that I would not be building on someone else's foundation.

2 Cor 2 [12]Now when I went to Troas to preach the gospel of Christ and found that the Lord had opened a door for me, [13]I still had no peace of mind, because I did not find my brother Titus there. So I said good-by to them and went on to Macedonia.

[14]But thanks be to God, who always leads us in triumphal procession in Christ and through us spreads everywhere the fragrance of the knowledge of him.

2 Cor 10 [15]Neither do we go beyond our limits by boasting of work done by others. Our hope is that, as your faith continues to grow, our area of activity among you will greatly expand, [16]so that we can preach the gospel in the regions beyond you. For we do not want to boast about work already done in another man's territory.

d) The Gospel Should Be Proclaimed to Everyone

Acts 16 [9]During the night Paul had a vision of a man of Macedonia standing and begging him, "Come over to Macedonia and help us." [10]After Paul had seen the vision, we got ready at once to leave for Macedonia, concluding that God had called us to preach the gospel to them.

Acts 22 [14]"Then he said: 'The God of our fathers has chosen you to know his will and to see the Righteous One and to hear words from his mouth. [15]You will be his witness to all men of what you have seen and heard.'"

Acts 26 [15]"Then I asked, 'Who are you, Lord?'

"'I am Jesus, whom you are persecuting,' the Lord replied. [16]'Now get up and stand on your feet. I have appeared to you to appoint you as a servant and as a witness of what you have seen of me and what I will show you. [17]I will rescue you from your own people and from the Gentiles. I am sending you to them [18]to open their eyes and turn them from darkness to light,

and from the power of Satan to God, so that they may receive forgiveness of sins and a place among those who are sanctified by faith in me.'"
Acts 28 [28]"Therefore I want you to know that God's salvation has been sent to the Gentiles, and they will listen!"

[30]For two whole years Paul stayed there in his own rented house and welcomed all who came to see him.

19. Provide Comfort for Others

a) Our Duty to Provide Comfort

2 Cor 2 [5]If anyone has caused grief, he has not so much grieved me as he has grieved all of you, to some extent—not to put it too severely. [6]The punishment inflicted on him by the majority is sufficient for him. [7]Now instead, you ought to forgive and comfort him, so that he will not be overwhelmed by excessive sorrow.
1 Thess 2 [11]For you know that we dealt with each of you as a father deals with his own children, [12]encouraging, comforting and urging you to live lives worthy of God, who calls you into his kingdom and glory.

b) The Source of Comfort: God

2 Cor 1 [3]Praise be to the God and Father of our Lord Jesus Christ, the Father of compassion and the God of all comfort, [4]who comforts us in all our troubles, so that we can comfort those in any trouble with the comfort we ourselves have received from God. [5]For just as the sufferings of Christ flow over into our lives, so also through Christ our comfort overflows. [6]If we are distressed, it is for your comfort and salvation; if we are comforted, it is for your comfort, which produces in you patient endurance of the same sufferings we suffer. [7]And our hope for you is firm, because we know that just as you share in our sufferings, so also you share in our comfort.

c) Examples of People Comforting Others

(1) Job's Friends Attempted to Provide Comfort

Job 2 [11]When Job's three friends, Eliphaz the Temanite, Bildad the Shuhite and Zophar the Naamathite, heard about all the troubles that had come upon him, they set out from their homes and met together by agreement to go and sympathize with him and comfort him. [12]When they saw him from a distance, they could hardly recognize him; they began to weep aloud, and they tore their robes and sprinkled dust on their heads. [13]Then they sat on the ground with him for seven days and seven nights. No one said a word to him, because they saw how great his suffering was.

(2) The Corinthian Believers Provided Comfort

2 Cor 7 [5]For when we came into Macedonia, this body of ours had no rest, but we were harassed at every turn—conflicts on the outside, fears within. [6]But God, who comforts the downcast, comforted us by the coming of Titus, [7]and not only by his coming but also by the comfort you had given him. He told us about your longing for me, your deep sorrow, your ardent concern for me, so that my joy was greater than ever.

(3) Paul's Jewish Comrades Provided Comfort

Col 4 [10]My fellow prisoner Aristarchus sends you his greetings, as does Mark, the cousin of Barnabas. (You have received instructions about him; if he comes to you, welcome him.) [11]Jesus, who is called Justus, also sends greetings. These are the only Jews among my fellow workers for the kingdom of God, and they have proved a comfort to me.

20. Recognize the Equality of Others

Job 31 [13]"If I have denied justice to my menservants and maidservants when they had a grievance against me, [14]what will I do when God confronts me? What will I answer when called to account? [15]Did not he who made me in the womb make them? Did not the same one form us both within our mothers?"
Ps 33 [13]From heaven the LORD looks down and sees all mankind; [14]from his dwelling place he watches all who live on earth—[15]he who forms the hearts of all, who considers everything they do. [16]No king is saved by the size of his army; no warrior escapes by his great strength. [17]A horse is a vain hope for deliverance; despite all its great strength it cannot save. [18]But the eyes of the LORD are on those who fear him, on those whose hope is in his unfailing love. . . .
Prov 22 [2]Rich and poor have this in common: The LORD is the Maker of them all.
Acts 10 [28]He said to them: "You are well aware that it is against our law for a Jew to associate with a Gentile or visit him. But God has shown me that I should not call any man impure or unclean."
Acts 17 [26]"From one man he made every nation of men, that they should inhabit the whole earth; and he determined the times set for them and the exact places where they should live."
Gal 3 [28]There is neither Jew nor Greek, slave nor free, male nor female, for you are all one in Christ Jesus.

21. Respect Others

Rom 13 [7]Give everyone what you owe him: If you owe taxes, pay taxes; if revenue, then revenue; if respect, then respect; if honor, then honor.
1 Pet 2 [17]Show proper respect to everyone: Love the brotherhood of believers, fear God, honor the king.

22. Serve Others

Matt 10 [37]"Anyone who loves his father or mother more than me is not worthy of me; anyone who loves his son or daughter more than me is not worthy of me; [38]and anyone who does not take his cross and follow me is not worthy of me. [39]Whoever finds his life will lose it, and whoever loses his life for my sake will find it.

[40]"He who receives you receives me, and he who receives me receives the one who sent me. [41]Anyone who receives a prophet because he is a prophet will receive a prophet's reward, and anyone who receives a righteous man because he is a righteous man will receive a righteous man's reward. [42]And if anyone gives even a cup of cold water to one of these little ones because he is my disciple, I tell you the truth, he will certainly not lose his reward."
Matt 25 [35]"'For I was hungry and you gave me something to eat, I was thirsty and you gave me something to drink, I was a stranger and you invited me in, [36]I needed clothes and you clothed me, I was sick and you looked after me, I was in prison and you came to visit me.'

[37]"Then the righteous will answer him, 'Lord, when did we see you hungry and feed you, or thirsty and give you something to drink? [38]When did we see you a stranger and invite you in, or needing clothes and clothe you? [39]When did we see you sick or in prison and go to visit you?'

[40]"The King will reply, 'I tell you the truth, whatever you did for one of the least of these brothers of mine, you did for me.'

[41]"Then he will say to those on his left, 'Depart from me, you who are cursed, into the eternal fire prepared for the devil and his angels. [42]For I was hungry and you gave me nothing to eat, I was thirsty and you gave me nothing to drink, [43]I was a stranger and you did not invite me in, I needed clothes and you did not clothe me, I was sick and in prison and you did not look after me.'

[44]"They also will answer, 'Lord, when did we see you hungry or thirsty or a stranger or needing clothes or sick or in prison, and did not help you?'

[45]"He will reply, 'I tell you the truth, whatever you did not do for one of the least of these, you did not do for me.'"

23. Show Hospitality to Others

a) Our Duty to Be Hospitable

Matt 25 [34]"Then the King will say to those on his right, 'Come, you who are blessed by my Father; take your inheritance, the kingdom prepared for you since the creation of the world. [35]For I was hungry and you gave me something to eat, I was thirsty and you gave me something to drink, I was a stranger and you invited me in. . . .'

[37]"Then the righteous will answer him, 'Lord, when did we see you hungry and feed you, or thirsty and give you something to drink? [38]When did we see you a stranger and invite you in, or needing clothes and clothe you? . . .'

[40]"The King will reply, 'I tell you the truth, whatever you did for one of the least of these brothers of mine, you did for me.'"
Mark 9 [41]"I tell you the truth, anyone who gives you a cup of water in my name because you belong to Christ will certainly not lose his reward."
Rom 12 [13]Share with God's people who are in need. Practice hospitality.
James 2 [15]Suppose a brother or sister is without clothes and daily food. [16]If one of you says to him, "Go, I wish you well; keep warm and well fed," but does nothing about his physical needs, what good is it?
1 Pet 4 [9]Offer hospitality to one another without grumbling. [10]Each one should use whatever gift he has received to serve others, faithfully administering God's grace in its various forms. [11]If anyone speaks, he should do it as one speaking the very words of God. If anyone serves, he should do it with the strength God provides, so that in all things God may be praised through Jesus Christ. To him be the glory and the power for ever and ever. Amen.
1 John 3 [17]If anyone has material possessions and sees his brother in need but has no pity on him, how can the love of God be in him?
3 John [5]Dear friend, you are faithful in what you are doing for the brothers, even though they are strangers to you. [6]They have told the church about your love. You will do well to send them on their way in a manner worthy of God. [7]It was for the sake of the Name that they went out, receiving no help from the pagans. [8]We ought therefore to show hospitality to such men so that we may work together for the truth.

b) Examples of Hospitality

(1) Gaius Showed Hospitality

Rom 16 [23]Gaius, whose hospitality I and the whole church here enjoy, sends you his greetings.

Erastus, who is the city's director of public works, and our brother Quartus send you their greetings.

(2) Onesiphorus Showed Hospitality

2 Tim 1 [16]May the Lord show mercy to the household of Onesiphorus, because he often refreshed me and was not ashamed of my chains. [17]On the contrary, when he was in Rome, he searched hard for me until he found me. [18]May the Lord grant that he will find mercy from the Lord on that day! You know very well in how many ways he helped me in Ephesus.

24. Show Mercy to Others

Mic 6 [8]He has showed you, O man, what is good. And what does the LORD require of you? To act justly and to love mercy and to walk humbly with your God.
Zech 7 [9]"This is what the LORD Almighty says: 'Administer true justice; show mercy and compassion to one another.'"
Matt 5 [7]"Blessed are the merciful, for they will be shown mercy."
James 2 [12]Speak and act as those who are going to be judged by the law that gives freedom, [13]because judgment without mercy will be shown to anyone who has not been merciful. Mercy triumphs over judgment!
Jude [22]Be merciful to those who doubt. . . .

25. Show Sympathy to Others

a) Our Duty to Be Sympathetic

1 Pet 3 [8]Finally, all of you, live in harmony with one another; be sympathetic, love as brothers, be compassionate and humble.

b) Examples of Showing Sympathy

(1) Job's Friends Attempted to Show Sympathy

Job 2 [11]When Job's three friends, Eliphaz the Temanite, Bildad the Shuhite and Zophar the Naamathite, heard about all the troubles that had come upon him, they set out from their homes and met together by agreement to go and sympathize with him and comfort him. [12]When they saw him from a distance, they could hardly recognize him; they began to weep aloud, and they tore their robes and sprinkled dust on their heads. [13]Then they sat on the ground with him for seven days and seven nights. No one said a word to him, because they saw how great his suffering was.

(2) The Hebrew Christians Showed Sympathy

Heb 10 [32]Remember those earlier days after you had received the light, when you stood your ground in a great contest in the face of suffering. [33]Sometimes you were publicly exposed to insult and persecution; at other times you stood side by side with those who were so treated. [34]You sympathized with those in prison and joyfully accepted the confiscation of your property, because you knew that you yourselves had better and lasting possessions.

26. Submit to Others

1 Cor 16 [15]You know that the household of Stephanas were the first converts in Achaia, and they have devoted themselves to the service of the saints. I urge you, brothers, [16]to submit to such as these and to everyone who joins in the work, and labors at it.
Eph 5 [21]Submit to one another out of reverence for Christ.
Heb 13 [17]Obey your leaders and submit to their authority. They keep watch over you as men who must give an account. Obey them so that their work will be a joy, not a burden, for that would be of no advantage to you.

III
The Responsibility to Seek Virtues and Certain Personal Qualities

1. Altruism

1 Cor 10 [24]Nobody should seek his own good, but the good of others.
Gal 2 [10]All they asked was that we should continue to remember the poor, the very thing I was eager to do.
Phil 2 [4]Each of you should look not only to your own interests, but also to the interests of others.
1 Tim 6 [18]Command them to do good, to be rich in good deeds, and to be generous and willing to share.
Heb 6 [10]God is not unjust; he will not forget your work and the love you have shown him as you have helped his people and continue to help them.
Heb 13 [16]And do not forget to do good and to share with others, for with such sacrifices God is pleased.
1 John 3 [17]If anyone has material possessions and sees his brother in need but has no pity on him, how can the love of God be in him?

2. Blamelessness and Purity

Ps 119 [1]Blessed are they whose ways are blameless, who walk according to the law of the LORD.
Matt 5 [8]"Blessed are the pure in heart, for they will see God."
Phil 2 [14]Do everything without complaining or arguing, [15]so that you may become blameless and pure, children of God without fault in a crooked and depraved generation, in which you shine like stars in the universe. . . .
1 John 3 [3]Everyone who has this hope in him purifies himself, just as he is pure.

3. Boldness

Prov 28 [1]The wicked man flees though no one pursues, but the righteous are as bold as a lion.
2 Cor 3 [12]Therefore, since we have such a hope, we are very bold.

4. Character

Rom 5 [3]Not only so, but we also rejoice in our sufferings, because we know that suffering produces perseverance; [4]perseverance, character; and character, hope.

5. Chastity

Rom 13 [13]Let us behave decently, as in the daytime, not in orgies and drunkenness, not in sexual immorality and debauchery, not in dissension and jealousy. [14]Rather, clothe yourselves with the Lord Jesus Christ, and do not think about how to gratify the desires of the sinful nature.
1 Thess 4 [3]It is God's will that you should be sanctified: that you should avoid sexual immorality; [4]that each of you should learn to control his own body in a way that is holy and honorable, [5]not in passionate lust like the heathen, who do not know God; [6]and that in this matter no one should wrong his brother or take advantage of him. The Lord will punish men for all such sins, as we have already told you and warned you.
Rev 14 [1]Then I looked, and there before me was the Lamb, standing on Mount Zion, and with him 144,000 who had his name and his Father's name written on their foreheads. [2]And I heard a sound from heaven like the roar of rushing waters and like a loud peal of thunder. The sound I heard was like that of harpists playing their harps. [3]And they sang a new song before the throne and before the four living creatures and the elders. No one could learn the song except the 144,000 who had been redeemed from the earth. [4]These are those who did not defile themselves with women, for they kept themselves pure. They follow the Lamb wherever he goes. They were purchased from among men and offered as firstfruits to God and the Lamb. [5]No lie was found in their mouths; they are blameless.

6. Compassion

Ps 112 [4]Even in darkness light dawns for the upright, for the gracious and compassionate and righteous man.
Col 3 [12]Therefore, as God's chosen people, holy and dearly loved, clothe yourselves with compassion, kindness, humility, gentleness and patience.
1 Pet 3 [8]Finally, all of you, live in harmony with one another; be sympathetic, love as brothers, be compassionate and humble.

7. Contentment

Phil 4 [11]I am not saying this because I am in need, for I have learned to be content whatever the circumstances. [12]I know what it is to be in need, and I know what it is to have plenty. I have learned the secret of being content in any and every situation, whether well fed or hungry, whether living in plenty or in want.
1 Tim 6 [6]But godliness with contentment is great gain. [7]For we brought nothing into the world, and we can take nothing out of it. [8]But if we have food and clothing, we will be content with that.
Heb 13 [5]Keep your lives free from the love of money and be content with what you have, because God has said, "Never will I leave you; never will I forsake you."

8. Contrition

Ps 51 [17]The sacrifices of God are a broken spirit; a broken and contrite heart, O God, you will not despise.
Isa 57 [15]For this is what the high and lofty One says—he who lives forever, whose name is holy: "I live in a high and holy place, but also with him who is contrite and lowly in spirit, to revive the spirit of the lowly and to revive the heart of the contrite."
Isa 66 [2]"Has not my hand made all these things, and so they came into being?" declares the LORD.
"This is the one I esteem: he who is humble and contrite in spirit, and trembles at my word."

9. Courage

Ps 112 [8]His heart is secure, he will have no fear; in the end he will look in triumph on his foes.
1 Cor 16 [13]Be on your guard; stand firm in the faith; be men of courage; be strong.
Eph 6 [19]Pray also for me, that whenever I open my mouth, words may be given me so that I will fearlessly make known the mystery of the gospel, [20]for which I am an ambassador in chains. Pray that I may declare it fearlessly, as I should.
Phil 1 [20]I eagerly expect and hope that I will in no way be ashamed, but will have sufficient courage so that now as always Christ will be exalted in my body, whether by life or by death.

10. Desire for the Spiritual

Ps 25 [4]Show me your ways, O LORD, teach me your paths; [5]guide me in your truth and teach me, for you are God my Savior, and my hope is in you all day long.
Ps 62 [1]My soul finds rest in God alone; my salvation comes from him.
Ps 84 [1]How lovely is your dwelling place, O LORD Almighty! [2]My soul yearns, even faints, for the courts of the LORD; my heart and my flesh cry out for the living God.
Ps 86 [11]Teach me your way, O LORD, and I will walk in your truth; give me an undivided heart, that I may fear your name. [12]I will praise you, O Lord my God, with all my heart; I will glorify your name forever.
Ps 118 [17]I will not die but live, and will proclaim what the LORD has done. [18]The LORD has chastened me severely, but he has not given me over to death.
[19]Open for me the gates of righteousness; I will enter and give thanks to the LORD.
Ps 123 [1]I lift up my eyes to you, to you whose throne is in heaven. [2]As the eyes of slaves look to the hand of their master, as the eyes of a maid look to the hand of her mistress, so our eyes look to the LORD our God, till he shows us his mercy.
Ps 130 [5]I wait for the LORD, my soul waits, and in his word I put my hope. [6]My soul waits for the Lord more than watchmen wait for the morning, more than watchmen wait for the morning.
Ps 143 [5]I remember the days of long ago; I meditate on all your works and consider what your hands have done. [6]I spread out my hands to you; my soul thirsts for you like a parched land.
Isa 40 [31]but those who hope in the LORD will renew their strength. They will soar on wings like eagles; they will run and not grow weary, they will walk and not be faint.
Phil 3 [12]Not that I have already obtained all this, or have already been made perfect, but I press on to take hold of that for which Christ Jesus took hold of me. [13]Brothers, I do not consider myself yet to have taken hold of it. But one thing I do: Forgetting what is behind and straining toward what is ahead, [14]I press on toward the goal to win the prize for which God has called me heavenward in Christ Jesus.
Heb 11 [6]And without faith it is impossible to please God, because anyone who comes to him must believe that he exists and that he rewards those who earnestly seek him.

11. Desire to Seek God

Ps 27 [8]My heart says of you, "Seek his face!" Your face, LORD, I will seek.
Ps 105 [3]Glory in his holy name; let the hearts of those who seek the LORD rejoice. [4]Look to the LORD and his strength; seek his face always.
Ps 119 [2]Blessed are they who keep his statutes and seek him with all their heart.

12. Devotion

1 Kings 18 [3]and Ahab had summoned Obadiah, who was in charge of his palace. (Obadiah was a devout believer in the LORD.)
Luke 2 [25]Now there was a man in Jerusalem called Simeon,

who was righteous and devout. He was waiting for the consolation of Israel, and the Holy Spirit was upon him.
Acts 10 [2]He and all his family were devout and God-fearing; he gave generously to those in need and prayed to God regularly.
Acts 22 [12]"A man named Ananias came to see me. He was a devout observer of the law and highly respected by all the Jews living there."

13. *Eagerness to Do Good Works*

Matt 7 [16]"By their fruit you will recognize them. Do people pick grapes from thornbushes, or figs from thistles? [17]Likewise every good tree bears good fruit, but a bad tree bears bad fruit. [18]A good tree cannot bear bad fruit, and a bad tree cannot bear good fruit."
Matt 13 [23]"But the one who received the seed that fell on good soil is the man who hears the word and understands it. He produces a crop, yielding a hundred, sixty or thirty times what was sown."
Titus 2 [13]while we wait for the blessed hope—the glorious appearing of our great God and Savior, Jesus Christ, [14]who gave himself for us to redeem us from all wickedness and to purify for himself a people that are his very own, eager to do what is good.
James 1 [25]But the man who looks intently into the perfect law that gives freedom, and continues to do this, not forgetting what he has heard, but doing it—he will be blessed in what he does.

14. *Faithfulness*

Gal 5 [22]But the fruit of the Spirit is love, joy, peace, patience, kindness, goodness, faithfulness. . . .
Eph 1 [1]Paul, an apostle of Christ Jesus by the will of God,
To the saints in Ephesus, the faithful in Christ Jesus. . . .
Rev 17 [14]"They will make war against the Lamb, but the Lamb will overcome them because he is Lord of lords and King of kings—and with him will be his called, chosen and faithful followers."

15. *Fear of God*

Mal 3 [16]Then those who feared the LORD talked with each other, and the LORD listened and heard. A scroll of remembrance was written in his presence concerning those who feared the LORD and honored his name.
Acts 10 [2]He and all his family were devout and God-fearing; he gave generously to those in need and prayed to God regularly.

16. *Generosity*

Ps 37 [21]The wicked borrow and do not repay, but the righteous give generously. . . .
[25]I was young and now I am old, yet I have never seen the righteous forsaken or their children begging bread. [26]They are always generous and lend freely; their children will be blessed.
Ps 112 [5]Good will come to him who is generous and lends freely, who conducts his affairs with justice. . . . [9]He has scattered abroad his gifts to the poor, his righteousness endures forever; his horn will be lifted high in honor.
1 Cor 9 [11]If we have sown spiritual seed among you, is it too much if we reap a material harvest from you? [12]If others have this right of support from you, shouldn't we have it all the more?
But we did not use this right. On the contrary, we put up with anything rather than hinder the gospel of Christ. [13]Don't you know that those who work in the temple get their food from the temple, and those who serve at the altar share in what is offered on the altar? [14]In the same way, the Lord has commanded that those who preach the gospel should receive their living from the gospel.

17. *Gentleness*

Gal 5 [22]But the fruit of the Spirit is love, joy, peace, patience, kindness, goodness, faithfulness, [23]gentleness and self-control. Against such things there is no law.
Eph 4 [2]Be completely humble and gentle; be patient, bearing with one another in love.
Phil 4 [5]Let your gentleness be evident to all. The Lord is near.
Col 3 [12]Therefore, as God's chosen people, holy and dearly loved, clothe yourselves with compassion, kindness, humility, gentleness and patience.

18. *Genuineness*

John 1 [47]When Jesus saw Nathanael approaching, he said of him, "Here is a true Israelite, in whom there is nothing false."
2 Cor 6 [4]Rather, as servants of God we commend ourselves in every way: in great endurance; in troubles, hardships and distresses; . . . [8]through glory and dishonor, bad report and good report; genuine, yet regarded as impostors. . . .

19. *Godliness*

Ps 4 [3]Know that the LORD has set apart the godly for himself; the LORD will hear when I call to him.
John 3 [21]"But whoever lives by the truth comes into the light, so that it may be seen plainly that what he has done has been done through God."
Acts 8 [2]Godly men buried Stephen and mourned deeply for him.
2 Pet 1 [5]For this very reason, make every effort to add to your faith goodness; and to goodness, knowledge; [6]and to knowledge, self-control; and to self-control, perseverance; and to perseverance, godliness; [7]and to godliness, brotherly kindness; and to brotherly kindness, love.
2 Pet 2 [9]if this is so, then the Lord knows how to rescue godly men from trials and to hold the unrighteous for the day of judgment, while continuing their punishment.

20. *Goodness*

Luke 6 [45]"The good man brings good things out of the good stored up in his heart, and the evil man brings evil things out of the evil stored up in his heart. For out of the overflow of his heart his mouth speaks."
Rom 15 [14]I myself am convinced, my brothers, that you yourselves are full of goodness, complete in knowledge and competent to instruct one another.
Gal 5 [22]But the fruit of the Spirit is love, joy, peace, patience, kindness, goodness, faithfulness. . . .
2 Pet 1 [5]For this very reason, make every effort to add to your faith goodness; and to goodness, knowledge. . . .

21. *Graciousness*

Ps 112 [4]Even in darkness light dawns for the upright, for the gracious and compassionate and righteous man.

22. *Hatred of Evil*

Ps 31 [6]I hate those who cling to worthless idols; I trust in the LORD.
Ps 45 [7]You love righteousness and hate wickedness; therefore God, your God, has set you above your companions by anointing you with the oil of joy.
Ps 97 [10]Let those who love the LORD hate evil, for he guards the lives of his faithful ones and delivers them from the hand of the wicked.
Ps 101 [3]I will set before my eyes no vile thing.
The deeds of faithless men I hate; they will not cling to me.
Ps 119 [104]I gain understanding from your precepts; therefore I hate every wrong path.
Ps 119 [128]and because I consider all your precepts right, I hate every wrong path.
Ps 119 [163]I hate and abhor falsehood but I love your law.

23. *Holiness*

Deut 7 [6]For you are a people holy to the LORD your God. The LORD your God has chosen you out of all the peoples on the face of the earth to be his people, his treasured possession.
Deut 14 [2]for you are a people holy to the LORD your God. Out of all the peoples on the face of the earth, the LORD has chosen you to be his treasured possession.
Rom 12 [1]Therefore, I urge you, brothers, in view of God's mercy, to offer your bodies as living sacrifices, holy and pleasing to God—this is your spiritual act of worship. [2]Do not conform any longer to the pattern of this world, but be transformed by the renewing of your mind. Then you will be able to test and approve what God's will is—his good, pleasing and perfect will.
1 Cor 5 [7]Get rid of the old yeast that you may be a new batch without yeast—as you really are. For Christ, our Passover lamb, has been sacrificed. [8]Therefore let us keep the Festival, not with the old yeast, the yeast of malice and wickedness, but with bread without yeast, the bread of sincerity and truth.
2 Cor 7 [1]Since we have these promises, dear friends, let us purify ourselves from everything that contaminates body and spirit, perfecting holiness out of reverence for God.
Col 3 [12]Therefore, as God's chosen people, holy and dearly loved, clothe yourselves with compassion, kindness, humility, gentleness and patience.
Heb 12 [14]Make every effort to live in peace with all men and to be holy; without holiness no one will see the Lord.
1 Pet 1 [15]But just as he who called you is holy, so be holy in all you do; [16]for it is written: "Be holy, because I am holy."

24. *Hope in Christ*

Rom 5 [1]Therefore, since we have been justified through faith, we have peace with God through our Lord Jesus Christ, [2]through whom we have gained access by faith into this grace in which we now stand. And we rejoice in the hope of the glory of God. [3]Not only so, but we also rejoice in our sufferings, because we know that suffering produces perseverance; [4]perseverance, character; and character, hope. [5]And hope does not disappoint us, because God has poured out his love into our hearts by the Holy Spirit, whom he has given us.
Rom 8 [17]Now if we are children, then we are heirs—heirs of God and co-heirs with Christ, if indeed we share in his sufferings in order that we may also share in his glory. . . .

[22]We know that the whole creation has been groaning as in the pains of childbirth right up to the present time. [23]Not only so, but we ourselves, who have the firstfruits of the Spirit, groan inwardly as we wait eagerly for our adoption as sons, the redemption of our bodies. [24]For in this hope we were saved. But hope that is seen is no hope at all. Who hopes for what he already has? [25]But if we hope for what we do not yet have, we wait for it patiently.
Heb 3 [6]But Christ is faithful as a son over God's house. And we are his house, if we hold on to our courage and the hope of which we boast.

25. *Humility*

Isa 29 [19]Once more the humble will rejoice in the LORD; the needy will rejoice in the Holy One of Israel.
Mic 6 [8]He has showed you, O man, what is good. And what does the LORD require of you? To act justly and to love mercy and to walk humbly with your God.
Rom 12 [3]For by the grace given me I say to every one of you: Do not think of yourself more highly than you ought, but rather think of yourself with sober judgment, in accordance with the measure of faith God has given you.
Phil 2 [3]Do nothing out of selfish ambition or vain conceit, but in humility consider others better than yourselves.
Col 3 [12]Therefore, as God's chosen people, holy and dearly loved, clothe yourselves with compassion, kindness, humility, gentleness and patience.
1 Pet 3 [8]Finally, all of you, live in harmony with one another; be sympathetic, love as brothers, be compassionate and humble.
1 Pet 5 [5]Young men, in the same way be submissive to those who are older. All of you, clothe yourselves with humility toward one another, because, "God opposes the proud but gives grace to the humble."

26. *Hunger and Thirst for Righteousness*

Matt 5 [6]"Blessed are those who hunger and thirst for righteousness, for they will be filled."

27. *Innocence*

Rom 16 [19]Everyone has heard about your obedience, so I am full of joy over you; but I want you to be wise about what is good, and innocent about what is evil.

28. *Introspectiveness*

Ps 4 [4]In your anger do not sin; when you are on your beds, search your hearts and be silent.
Ps 19 [12]Who can discern his errors? Forgive my hidden faults. . . . [14]May the words of my mouth and the meditation of my heart be pleasing in your sight, O LORD, my Rock and my Redeemer.
Ps 77 [6]I remembered my songs in the night. My heart mused and my spirit inquired. . . .
Ps 119 [59]I have considered my ways and have turned my steps to your statutes.
Ps 139 [23]Search me, O God, and know my heart; test me and know my anxious thoughts. [24]See if there is any offensive way in me, and lead me in the way everlasting.

29. *Joyfulness*

Rom 12 [15]Rejoice with those who rejoice; mourn with those who mourn.
Rom 15 [13]May the God of hope fill you with all joy and peace as you trust in him, so that you may overflow with hope by the power of the Holy Spirit.
Gal 5 [22]But the fruit of the Spirit is love, joy, peace, patience, kindness, goodness, faithfulness. . . .
Phil 4 [4]Rejoice in the Lord always. I will say it again: Rejoice!
1 Thess 5 [16]Be joyful always. . . .

30. *Kindness*

2 Cor 6 [4]Rather, as servants of God we commend ourselves in every way: in great endurance; in troubles, hardships and distresses; . . . [6]in purity, understanding, patience and kindness; in the Holy Spirit and in sincere love. . . .
Gal 5 [22]But the fruit of the Spirit is love, joy, peace, patience, kindness, goodness, faithfulness. . . .
Col 3 [12]Therefore, as God's chosen people, holy and dearly loved, clothe yourselves with compassion, kindness, humility, gentleness and patience.
2 Pet 1 [5]For this very reason, make every effort to add to your faith goodness; and to goodness, knowledge; . . . [7]and to godliness, brotherly kindness; and to brotherly kindness, love.

31. *Love*

Gal 5 [22]But the fruit of the Spirit is love, joy, peace, patience, kindness, goodness, faithfulness. . . .
Col 1 [4]because we have heard of your faith in Christ Jesus and of the love you have for all the saints . . .
Col 3 [14]And over all these virtues put on love, which binds them all together in perfect unity.
1 Thess 4 [9]Now about brotherly love we do not need to write to you, for you yourselves have been taught by God to love each other.
2 Pet 1 [5]For this very reason, make every effort to add to your faith goodness; and to goodness, knowledge; . . . [7]and to godliness, brotherly kindness; and to brotherly kindness, love.
1 John 4 [7]Dear friends, let us love one another, for love comes

from God. Everyone who loves has been born of God and knows God.

32. Lowliness in Spirit

Prov 16 [19]Better to be lowly in spirit and among the oppressed than to share plunder with the proud.
Isa 57 [15]For this is what the high and lofty One says—he who lives forever, whose name is holy: "I live in a high and holy place, but also with him who is contrite and lowly in spirit, to revive the spirit of the lowly and to revive the heart of the contrite."
1 Cor 1 [28]He chose the lowly things of this world and the despised things—and the things that are not—to nullify the things that are. . . .

33. Meekness

Ps 37 [10]A little while, and the wicked will be no more; though you look for them, they will not be found. [11]But the meek will inherit the land and enjoy great peace.
Zeph 3 [12]"But I will leave within you the meek and humble, who trust in the name of the LORD."
Matt 5 [5]"Blessed are the meek, for they will inherit the earth."

34. Mercy

Matt 5 [7]"Blessed are the merciful, for they will be shown mercy."
Luke 6 [36]"Be merciful, just as your Father is merciful."
1 Pet 3 [9]Do not repay evil with evil or insult with insult, but with blessing, because to this you were called so that you may inherit a blessing.

35. Mindfulness of Christ's Leading

John 10 [3]"The watchman opens the gate for him, and the sheep listen to his voice. He calls his own sheep by name and leads them out. [4]When he has brought out all his own, he goes on ahead of them, and his sheep follow him because they know his voice. . . .

[14]"I am the good shepherd; I know my sheep and my sheep know me—[15]just as the Father knows me and I know the Father—and I lay down my life for the sheep. [16]I have other sheep that are not of this sheep pen. I must bring them also. They too will listen to my voice, and there shall be one flock and one shepherd."

36. Obedience

Rom 16 [19]Everyone has heard about your obedience, so I am full of joy over you; but I want you to be wise about what is good, and innocent about what is evil.
1 Pet 1 [14]As obedient children, do not conform to the evil desires you had when you lived in ignorance.
1 John 2 [3]We know that we have come to know him if we obey his commands.

37. Patience

Gal 5 [22]But the fruit of the Spirit is love, joy, peace, patience, kindness, goodness, faithfulness. . . .
Col 1 [11]being strengthened with all power according to his glorious might so that you may have great endurance and patience, and joyfully . . .
Col 3 [12]Therefore, as God's chosen people, holy and dearly loved, clothe yourselves with compassion, kindness, humility, gentleness and patience.
Heb 6 [12]We do not want you to become lazy, but to imitate those who through faith and patience inherit what has been promised.
James 5 [7]Be patient, then, brothers, until the Lord's coming. See how the farmer waits for the land to yield its valuable crop and how patient he is for the autumn and spring rains. [8]You too, be patient and stand firm, because the Lord's coming is near.

38. Peacefulness

Matt 5 [9]"Blessed are the peacemakers, for they will be called sons of God."
Gal 5 [22]But the fruit of the Spirit is love, joy, peace, patience, kindness, goodness, faithfulness. . . .
James 3 [18]Peacemakers who sow in peace raise a harvest of righteousness.

39. Perseverance

Rom 5 [3]Not only so, but we also rejoice in our sufferings, because we know that suffering produces perseverance; [4]perseverance, character; and character, hope.
Col 1 [11]being strengthened with all power according to his glorious might so that you may have great endurance and patience, and joyfully . . .
2 Pet 1 [5]For this very reason, make every effort to add to your faith goodness; and to goodness, knowledge; [6]and to knowledge, self-control; and to self-control, perseverance; and to perseverance, godliness. . . .

40. Poverty in Spirit

Matt 5 [3]"Blessed are the poor in spirit, for theirs is the kingdom of heaven."

41. Prudence

Prov 16 [21]The wise in heart are called discerning, and pleasant words promote instruction.
1 Cor 6 [12]"Everything is permissible for me"—but not everything is beneficial. "Everything is permissible for me"—but I will not be mastered by anything.
Phil 4 [8]Finally, brothers, whatever is true, whatever is noble, whatever is right, whatever is pure, whatever is lovely, whatever is admirable—if anything is excellent or praiseworthy—think about such things.
Col 4 [5]Be wise in the way you act toward outsiders; make the most of every opportunity.
James 1 [19]My dear brothers, take note of this: Everyone should be quick to listen, slow to speak and slow to become angry. . . .

42. Righteousness

Gen 6 [9]This is the account of Noah.

Noah was a righteous man, blameless among the people of his time, and he walked with God.
Ps 97 [11]Light is shed upon the righteous and joy on the upright in heart. [12]Rejoice in the LORD, you who are righteous, and praise his holy name.
Ps 140 [13]Surely the righteous will praise your name and the upright will live before you.
Ps 146 [8]the LORD gives sight to the blind, the LORD lifts up those who are bowed down, the LORD loves the righteous.
Hab 2 [4]"See, he is puffed up; his desires are not upright—but the righteous will live by his faith. . . ."
Luke 1 [6]Both of them were upright in the sight of God, observing all the Lord's commandments and regulations blamelessly.
Luke 2 [25]Now there was a man in Jerusalem called Simeon, who was righteous and devout. He was waiting for the consolation of Israel, and the Holy Spirit was upon him.
1 John 3 [7]Dear children, do not let anyone lead you astray. He who does what is right is righteous, just as he is righteous.

43. Sanctification in Christ

1 Cor 1 [2]To the church of God in Corinth, to those sanctified in Christ Jesus and called to be holy, together with all those everywhere who call on the name of our Lord Jesus Christ—their Lord and ours . . .

1 Cor 6 [11]And that is what some of you were. But you were washed, you were sanctified, you were justified in the name of the Lord Jesus Christ and by the Spirit of our God.
1 Thess 5 [23]May God himself, the God of peace, sanctify you through and through. May your whole spirit, soul and body be kept blameless at the coming of our Lord Jesus Christ.

44. *Self-Control*

Gal 5 [22]But the fruit of the Spirit is love, joy, peace, patience, kindness, goodness, faithfulness, [23]gentleness and self-control. Against such things there is no law.
1 Thess 5 [6]So then, let us not be like others, who are asleep, but let us be alert and self-controlled. [7]For those who sleep, sleep at night, and those who get drunk, get drunk at night. [8]But since we belong to the day, let us be self-controlled, putting on faith and love as a breastplate, and the hope of salvation as a helmet.
1 Pet 5 [8]Be self-controlled and alert. Your enemy the devil prowls around like a roaring lion looking for someone to devour.
2 Pet 1 [5]For this very reason, make every effort to add to your faith goodness; and to goodness, knowledge; [6]and to knowledge, self-control; and to self-control, perseverance; and to perseverance, godliness. . . .

45. *Self-Denial*

Rom 6 [6]For we know that our old self was crucified with him so that the body of sin might be done away with, that we should no longer be slaves to sin. . . .
Rom 13 [14]Rather, clothe yourselves with the Lord Jesus Christ, and do not think about how to gratify the desires of the sinful nature.
1 Cor 10 [23]"Everything is permissible"—but not everything is beneficial. "Everything is permissible"—but not everything is constructive. [24]Nobody should seek his own good, but the good of others.
Gal 2 [20]"I have been crucified with Christ and I no longer live, but Christ lives in me. The life I live in the body, I live by faith in the Son of God, who loved me and gave himself for me."
2 Tim 2 [3]Endure hardship with us like a good soldier of Christ Jesus. [4]No one serving as a soldier gets involved in civilian affairs—he wants to please his commanding officer. . . . [10]Therefore I endure everything for the sake of the elect, that they too may obtain the salvation that is in Christ Jesus, with eternal glory.

[11]Here is a trustworthy saying: If we died with him, we will also live with him. . . .
Rev 12 [11]"They overcame him by the blood of the Lamb and by the word of their testimony; they did not love their lives so much as to shrink from death."

46. *Self-Discipline*

2 Tim 1 [7]For God did not give us a spirit of timidity, but a spirit of power, of love and of self-discipline.

47. *Sincerity*

Acts 2 [46]Every day they continued to meet together in the temple courts. They broke bread in their homes and ate together with glad and sincere hearts. . . .
2 Cor 1 [12]Now this is our boast: Our conscience testifies that we have conducted ourselves in the world, and especially in our relations with you, in the holiness and sincerity that are from God. We have done so not according to worldly wisdom but according to God's grace.
2 Cor 2 [17]Unlike so many, we do not peddle the word of God for profit. On the contrary, in Christ we speak before God with sincerity, like men sent from God.
Heb 10 [22]let us draw near to God with a sincere heart in full assurance of faith, having our hearts sprinkled to cleanse us from a guilty conscience and having our bodies washed with pure water.

48. *Steadfastness*

Ps 37 [31]The law of his God is in his heart; his feet do not slip.
Ps 112 [7]He will have no fear of bad news; his heart is steadfast, trusting in the LORD.
Col 2 [5]For though I am absent from you in body, I am present with you in spirit and delight to see how orderly you are and how firm your faith in Christ is.
2 Thess 2 [15]So then, brothers, stand firm and hold to the teachings we passed on to you, whether by word of mouth or by letter.
Heb 10 [23]Let us hold unswervingly to the hope we profess, for he who promised is faithful.

49. *Strength*

Ps 84 [7]They go from strength to strength, till each appears before God in Zion.
1 Cor 4 [10]We are fools for Christ, but you are so wise in Christ! We are weak, but you are strong! You are honored, we are dishonored!
1 Cor 16 [13]Be on your guard; stand firm in the faith; be men of courage; be strong.
2 Cor 12 [10]That is why, for Christ's sake, I delight in weaknesses, in insults, in hardships, in persecutions, in difficulties. For when I am weak, then I am strong.
Eph 6 [10]Finally, be strong in the Lord and in his mighty power.
1 John 2 [14]I write to you, fathers, because you have known him who is from the beginning. I write to you, young men, because you are strong, and the word of God lives in you, and you have overcome the evil one.

50. *Submissiveness*

Eph 5 [24]Now as the church submits to Christ, so also wives should submit to their husbands in everything.
Heb 12 [9]Moreover, we have all had human fathers who disciplined us and we respected them for it. How much more should we submit to the Father of our spirits and live!
James 4 [7]Submit yourselves, then, to God. Resist the devil, and he will flee from you.

51. *Temperance*

Rom 13 [14]Rather, clothe yourselves with the Lord Jesus Christ, and do not think about how to gratify the desires of the sinful nature.
1 Cor 9 [24]Do you not know that in a race all the runners run, but only one gets the prize? Run in such a way as to get the prize. [25]Everyone who competes in the games goes into strict training. They do it to get a crown that will not last; but we do it to get a crown that will last forever. [26]Therefore I do not run like a man running aimlessly; I do not fight like a man beating the air. [27]No, I beat my body and make it my slave so that after I have preached to others, I myself will not be disqualified for the prize.

52. *Thankfulness*

Col 2 [6]So then, just as you received Christ Jesus as Lord, continue to live in him, [7]rooted and built up in him, strengthened in the faith as you were taught, and overflowing with thankfulness.
Col 3 [15]Let the peace of Christ rule in your hearts, since as members of one body you were called to peace. And be thankful.
Heb 12 [28]Therefore, since we are receiving a kingdom that cannot be shaken, let us be thankful, and so worship God acceptably with reverence and awe. . . .

53. *Trustworthiness*

Ps 15 [1]LORD, who may dwell in your sanctuary? Who may live on your holy hill?

[2]He whose walk is blameless and who does what is righ-

teous, who speaks the truth from his heart [3]and has no slander on his tongue, who does his neighbor no wrong and casts no slur on his fellowman, [4]who despises a vile man but honors those who fear the LORD, who keeps his oath even when it hurts. . . .
1 Cor 4 [2]Now it is required that those who have been given a trust must prove faithful.

54. Truthfulness

Ps 15 [2]He whose walk is blameless and who does what is righteous, who speaks the truth from his heart . . .
Prov 13 [5]The righteous hate what is false, but the wicked bring shame and disgrace.
Isa 63 [8]He said, "Surely they are my people, sons who will not be false to me"; and so he became their Savior.
2 Cor 4 [1]Therefore, since through God's mercy we have this ministry, we do not lose heart. [2]Rather, we have renounced secret and shameful ways; we do not use deception, nor do we distort the word of God. On the contrary, by setting forth the truth plainly we commend ourselves to every man's conscience in the sight of God.

55. Watchfulness

Luke 12 [37]"It will be good for those servants whose master finds them watching when he comes. I tell you the truth, he will dress himself to serve, will have them recline at the table and will come and wait on them. [38]It will be good for those servants whose master finds them ready, even if he comes in the second or third watch of the night."
Col 4 [2]Devote yourselves to prayer, being watchful and thankful.
1 Thess 5 [6]So then, let us not be like others, who are asleep, but let us be alert and self-controlled. [7]For those who sleep, sleep at night, and those who get drunk, get drunk at night. [8]But since we belong to the day, let us be self-controlled, putting on faith and love as a breastplate, and the hope of salvation as a helmet.
1 Pet 5 [8]Be self-controlled and alert. Your enemy the devil prowls around like a roaring lion looking for someone to devour.

56. Willingness to Be Led by God's Spirit

Rom 8 [14]because those who are led by the Spirit of God are sons of God.

57. Willingness to Be Taught by God

Isa 54 [13]"All your sons will be taught by the LORD, and great will be your children's peace."
1 Cor 2 [12]We have not received the spirit of the world but the Spirit who is from God, that we may understand what God has freely given us. [13]This is what we speak, not in words taught us by human wisdom but in words taught by the Spirit, expressing spiritual truths in spiritual words.
1 John 2 [27]As for you, the anointing you received from him remains in you, and you do not need anyone to teach you. But as his anointing teaches you about all things and as that anointing is real, not counterfeit—just as it has taught you, remain in him.

58. Willingness to Follow Christ

John 10 [4]"When he has brought out all his own, he goes on ahead of them, and his sheep follow him because they know his voice." . . . [27]"My sheep listen to my voice; I know them, and they follow me."

59. Willingness to Suffer for Christ's Sake

Matt 5 [11]"Blessed are you when people insult you, persecute you and falsely say all kinds of evil against you because of me."

60. Willingness to Suffer Persecution Because of Righteousness

Matt 5 [10]"Blessed are those who are persecuted because of righteousness, for theirs is the kingdom of heaven.

[11]"Blessed are you when people insult you, persecute you and falsely say all kinds of evil against you because of me. [12]Rejoice and be glad, because great is your reward in heaven, for in the same way they persecuted the prophets who were before you."

61. Wisdom

Ps 37 [30]The mouth of the righteous man utters wisdom, and his tongue speaks what is just.
Rom 16 [19]Everyone has heard about your obedience, so I am full of joy over you; but I want you to be wise about what is good, and innocent about what is evil.
1 Cor 3 [18]Do not deceive yourselves. If any one of you thinks he is wise by the standards of this age, he should become a "fool" so that he may become wise.
Eph 5 [15]Be very careful, then, how you live—not as unwise but as wise. . . .
James 3 [13]Who is wise and understanding among you? Let him show it by his good life, by deeds done in the humility that comes from wisdom. [14]But if you harbor bitter envy and selfish ambition in your hearts, do not boast about it or deny the truth. [15]Such "wisdom" does not come down from heaven but is earthly, unspiritual, of the devil. [16]For where you have envy and selfish ambition, there you find disorder and every evil practice.

[17]But the wisdom that comes from heaven is first of all pure; then peace-loving, considerate, submissive, full of mercy and good fruit, impartial and sincere.

14

The Church

I The Head and Ruler of the Church: *Christ*

Ps 118 [22]The stone the builders rejected has become the capstone; [23]the LORD has done this, and it is marvelous in our eyes.
Matt 12 [6]"I tell you that one greater than the temple is here. . . . [8]For the Son of Man is Lord of the Sabbath."
Matt 16 [18]"And I tell you that you are Peter, and on this rock I will build my church, and the gates of Hades will not overcome it. [19]I will give you the keys of the kingdom of heaven; whatever you bind on earth will be bound in heaven, and whatever you loose on earth will be loosed in heaven."
Matt 18 [19]"Again, I tell you that if two of you on earth agree about anything you ask for, it will be done for you by my Father in heaven. [20]For where two or three come together in my name, there am I with them."
Matt 21 [42]Jesus said to them, "Have you never read in the Scriptures: 'The stone the builders rejected has become the capstone; the Lord has done this, and it is marvelous in our eyes'?

[43]"Therefore I tell you that the kingdom of God will be taken away from you and given to a people who will produce its fruit. [44]He who falls on this stone will be broken to pieces, but he on whom it falls will be crushed."
Matt 23 [8]"But you are not to be called 'Rabbi,' for you have only one Master and you are all brothers. . . . [10]Nor are you to be called 'teacher,' for you have one Teacher, the Christ."
John 13 [13]"You call me 'Teacher' and 'Lord,' and rightly so, for that is what I am. [14]Now that I, your Lord and Teacher, have washed your feet, you also should wash one another's feet. [15]I have set you an example that you should do as I have done for you. [16]I tell you the truth, no servant is greater than his master, nor is a messenger greater than the one who sent him."
John 15 [1]"I am the true vine, and my Father is the gardener. [2]He cuts off every branch in me that bears no fruit, while every branch that does bear fruit he prunes so that it will be even more fruitful. [3]You are already clean because of the word I have spoken to you. [4]Remain in me, and I will remain in you. No branch can bear fruit by itself; it must remain in the vine. Neither can you bear fruit unless you remain in me.

[5]"I am the vine; you are the branches. If a man remains in me and I in him, he will bear much fruit; apart from me you can do nothing. [6]If anyone does not remain in me, he is like a branch that is thrown away and withers; such branches are picked up, thrown into the fire and burned. [7]If you remain in me and my words remain in you, ask whatever you wish, and it will be given you. [8]This is to my Father's glory, that you bear much fruit, showing yourselves to be my disciples.

[9]"As the Father has loved me, so have I loved you. Now remain in my love. [10]If you obey my commands, you will remain in my love, just as I have obeyed my Father's commands and remain in his love. [11]I have told you this so that my joy may be in you and that your joy may be complete. [12]My command is this: Love each other as I have loved you. [13]Greater love has no one than this, that he lay down his life for his friends. [14]You are my friends if you do what I command. [15]I no longer call you servants, because a servant does not know his master's business. Instead, I have called you friends, for everything that I learned from my Father I have made known to you. [16]You did not choose me, but I chose you and appointed you to go and bear fruit—fruit that will last. Then the Father will give you whatever you ask in my name."
Acts 2 [36]"Therefore let all Israel be assured of this: God has made this Jesus, whom you crucified, both Lord and Christ."
Rom 8 [29]For those God foreknew he also predestined to be conformed to the likeness of his Son, that he might be the firstborn among many brothers.
Rom 9 [5]Theirs are the patriarchs, and from them is traced the human ancestry of Christ, who is God over all, forever praised! Amen.
1 Cor 3 [11]For no one can lay any foundation other than the one already laid, which is Jesus Christ.
1 Cor 11 [3]Now I want you to realize that the head of every man is Christ, and the head of the woman is man, and the head of Christ is God.
1 Cor 12 [5]There are different kinds of service, but the same Lord.
Eph 1 [9]And he made known to us the mystery of his will according to his good pleasure, which he purposed in Christ, [10]to be put into effect when the times will have reached their fulfillment—to bring all things in heaven and on earth together under one head, even Christ.

[20]. . . which he exerted in Christ when he raised him from the dead and seated him at his right hand in the heavenly realms, [21]far above all rule and authority, power and dominion, and every title that can be given, not only in the present age but also in the one to come. [22]And God placed all things under his feet and appointed him to be head over everything for the church, [23]which is his body, the fullness of him who fills everything in every way.
Eph 2 [19]Consequently, you are no longer foreigners and aliens, but fellow citizens with God's people and members of God's household, [20]built on the foundation of the apostles and prophets, with Christ Jesus himself as the chief cornerstone. [21]In him the whole building is joined together and rises to become a holy temple in the Lord. [22]And in him you too are being built together to become a dwelling in which God lives by his Spirit.
Eph 4 [15]Instead, speaking the truth in love, we will in all things grow up into him who is the Head, that is, Christ.
Eph 5 [22]Wives, submit to your husbands as to the Lord. [23]For the husband is the head of the wife as Christ is the head of the church, his body, of which he is the Savior. [24]Now as the church submits to Christ, so also wives should submit to their husbands in everything.

[25]Husbands, love your wives, just as Christ loved the church and gave himself up for her [26]to make her holy, cleansing her by the washing with water through the word, [27]and to present her to himself as a radiant church, without stain or wrinkle or any other blemish, but holy and blameless. [28]In this same way, husbands ought to love their wives as their own bodies. He who loves his wife loves himself. [29]After all, no one ever hated his own body, but he feeds and cares for it, just as Christ does the church—[30]for we are members of his body. [31]"For this reason a man will leave his father and mother and be united to his wife, and the two will become one flesh." [32]This is a profound mystery—but I am talking about Christ and the church.
Col 1 [18]And he is the head of the body, the church; he is the beginning and the firstborn from among the dead, so that in everything he might have the supremacy.
Col 2 [10]and you have been given fullness in Christ, who is the head over every power and authority.
Col 2 [19]He has lost connection with the Head, from whom the whole body, supported and held together by its ligaments and sinews, grows as God causes it to grow.
Col 3 [11]Here there is no Greek or Jew, circumcised or uncircumcised, barbarian, Scythian, slave or free, but Christ is all, and is in all.
Heb 3 [3]Jesus has been found worthy of greater honor than Moses, just as the builder of a house has greater honor than the house itself. [4]For every house is built by someone, but God is the builder of everything. [5]Moses was faithful as a servant in all God's house, testifying to what would be said in the future. [6]But Christ is faithful as a son over God's house. And we are his house, if we hold on to our courage and the hope of which we boast.

1 Pet 2 [4]As you come to him, the living stone—rejected by men but chosen by God and precious to him—[5]you also, like living stones, are being built into a spiritual house to be a holy priesthood, offering spiritual sacrifices acceptable to God through Jesus Christ. [6]For in Scripture it says: "See, I lay a stone in Zion, a chosen and precious cornerstone, and the one who trusts in him will never be put to shame." [7]Now to you who believe, this stone is precious. But to those who do not believe, "The stone the builders rejected has become the capstone," [8]and, "A stone that causes men to stumble and a rock that makes them fall." They stumble because they disobey the message—which is also what they were destined for.
Rev 1 [12]I turned around to see the voice that was speaking to me. And when I turned I saw seven golden lampstands, [13]and among the lampstands was someone "like a son of man," dressed in a robe reaching down to his feet and with a golden sash around his chest.
Rev 2 [1]"To the angel of the church in Ephesus write: These are the words of him who holds the seven stars in his right hand and walks among the seven golden lampstands: [2]I know your deeds, your hard work and your perseverance. I know that you cannot tolerate wicked men, that you have tested those who claim to be apostles but are not, and have found them false."
Rev 2 [8]"To the angel of the church in Smyrna write: These are the words of him who is the First and the Last, who died and came to life again. [9]I know your afflictions and your poverty—yet you are rich! I know the slander of those who say they are Jews and are not, but are a synagogue of Satan."
Rev 2 [12]"To the angel of the church in Pergamum write: These are the words of him who has the sharp, double-edged sword. [13]I know where you live—where Satan has his throne. Yet you remain true to my name. You did not renounce your faith in me, even in the days of Antipas, my faithful witness, who was put to death in your city—where Satan lives."
Rev 2 [18]"To the angel of the church in Thyatira write: These are the words of the Son of God, whose eyes are like blazing fire and whose feet are like burnished bronze. [19]I know your deeds, your love and faith, your service and perseverance, and that you are now doing more than you did at first."
Rev 3 [1]"To the angel of the church in Sardis write: These are the words of him who holds the seven spirits of God and the seven stars. I know your deeds; you have a reputation of being alive, but you are dead."
Rev 3 [7]"To the angel of the church in Philadelphia write: These are the words of him who is holy and true, who holds the key of David. What he opens no one can shut, and what he shuts no one can open. [8]I know your deeds. See, I have placed before you an open door that no one can shut. I know that you have little strength, yet you have kept my word and have not denied my name."
Rev 3 [14]"To the angel of the church in Laodicea write: These are the words of the Amen, the faithful and true witness, the ruler of God's creation. [15]I know your deeds, that you are neither cold nor hot. I wish you were either one or the other!"
Rev 5 [6]Then I saw a Lamb, looking as if it had been slain, standing in the center of the throne, encircled by the four living creatures and the elders. He had seven horns and seven eyes, which are the seven spirits of God sent out into all the earth. [7]He came and took the scroll from the right hand of him who sat on the throne. [8]And when he had taken it, the four living creatures and the twenty-four elders fell down before the Lamb. Each one had a harp and they were holding golden bowls full of incense, which are the prayers of the saints. [9]And they sang a new song: "You are worthy to take the scroll and to open its seals, because you were slain, and with your blood you purchased men for God from every tribe and language and people and nation. [10]You have made them to be a kingdom and priests to serve our God, and they will reign on the earth."
Rev 21 [22]I did not see a temple in the city, because the Lord God Almighty and the Lamb are its temple. [23]The city does not need the sun or the moon to shine on it, for the glory of God gives it light, and the Lamb is its lamp.
Rev 22 [16]"I, Jesus, have sent my angel to give you this testimony for the churches. I am the Root and the Offspring of David, and the bright Morning Star."

II Metaphors and Names for the People of God, the Church

A. OT Metaphors and Names

1. Assembly of Israel

Lev 19 [2]"Speak to the entire assembly of Israel and say to them: 'Be holy because I, the LORD your God, am holy.'"
Deut 31 [30]And Moses recited the words of this song from beginning to end in the hearing of the whole assembly of Israel. . . .
Josh 8 [35]There was not a word of all that Moses had commanded that Joshua did not read to the whole assembly of Israel, including the women and children, and the aliens who lived among them.
Josh 18 [1]The whole assembly of the Israelites gathered at Shiloh and set up the Tent of Meeting there. The country was brought under their control. . . .
1 Kings 8 [5]and King Solomon and the entire assembly of Israel that had gathered about him were before the ark, sacrificing so many sheep and cattle that they could not be recorded or counted.
Neh 5 [13]I also shook out the folds of my robe and said, "In this way may God shake out of his house and possessions every man who does not keep this promise. So may such a man be shaken out and emptied!"

At this the whole assembly said, "Amen," and praised the LORD. And the people did as they had promised.
Ps 68 [26]Praise God in the great congregation; praise the LORD in the assembly of Israel.

2. Assembly of Jacob

Deut 33 [4]". . . the law that Moses gave us, the possession of the assembly of Jacob."

3. Assembly of the Lord

Mic 2 [5]Therefore you will have no one in the assembly of the LORD to divide the land by lot.

4. Assembly of the People of God

Judg 20 [2]The leaders of all the people of the tribes of Israel took their places in the assembly of the people of God, four hundred thousand soldiers armed with swords.

5. Assembly of the Righteous

Ps 1 [5]Therefore the wicked will not stand in the judgment, nor sinners in the assembly of the righteous.

6. Assembly of the Saints

Ps 149 [1]Praise the LORD. Sing to the LORD a new song, his praise in the assembly of the saints.

7. Bride

Isa 49 [18]"Lift up your eyes and look around; all your sons gather and come to you. As surely as I live," declares the LORD, "you will wear them all as ornaments; you will put them on, like a bride."
Isa 62 [5]As a young man marries a maiden, so will your sons marry you; as a bridegroom rejoices over his bride, so will your God rejoice over you.
Jer 2 [2]"Go and proclaim in the hearing of Jerusalem: 'I remember the devotion of your youth, how as a bride you loved me and followed me through the desert, through a land not sown.'"

8. Chosen Ones

Ps 105 [6]O descendants of Abraham his servant, O sons of Jacob, his chosen ones. . . .

[43]He brought out his people with rejoicing, his chosen ones with shouts of joy. . . .

Ps 106 [5]that I may enjoy the prosperity of your chosen ones, that I may share in the joy of your nation and join your inheritance in giving praise.
Isa 65 [22]No longer will they build houses and others live in them, or plant and others eat. For as the days of a tree, so will be the days of my people; my chosen ones will long enjoy the works of their hands.

9. Chosen People

Isa 65 [9]"I will bring forth descendants from Jacob, and from Judah those who will possess my mountains; my chosen people will inherit them, and there will my servants live."

10. Community of Israel

Exod 12 [3]"Tell the whole community of Israel that on the tenth day of this month each man is to take a lamb for his family, one for each household. . . . [6]Take care of them until the fourteenth day of the month, when all the people of the community of Israel must slaughter them at twilight. . . .

[19]"For seven days no yeast is to be found in your houses. And whoever eats anything with yeast in it must be cut off from the community of Israel, whether he is an alien or native-born."
Exod 12 [47]"The whole community of Israel must celebrate it."
Exod 16 [1]The whole Israelite community set out from Elim and came to the Desert of Sin, which is between Elim and Sinai, on the fifteenth day of the second month after they had come out of Egypt. [2]In the desert the whole community grumbled against Moses and Aaron. . . .

[9]Then Moses told Aaron, "Say to the entire Israelite community, 'Come before the LORD, for he has heard your grumbling.'"

[10]While Aaron was speaking to the whole Israelite community, they looked toward the desert, and there was the glory of the LORD appearing in the cloud.
Lev 4 [13]"'If the whole Israelite community sins unintentionally and does what is forbidden in any of the LORD's commands, even though the community is unaware of the matter, they are guilty.'"
Lev 16 [5]"From the Israelite community he is to take two male goats for a sin offering and a ram for a burnt offering."
Num 1 [2]"Take a census of the whole Israelite community by their clans and families, listing every man by name, one by one."

11. Community of Peoples

Gen 28 [3]"May God Almighty bless you and make you fruitful and increase your numbers until you become a community of peoples."
Gen 48 [4]". . . and said to me, 'I am going to make you fruitful and will increase your numbers. I will make you a community of peoples, and I will give this land as an everlasting possession to your descendants after you.'"

12. Community of the Lord

Josh 22 [17]"'Was not the sin of Peor enough for us? Up to this very day we have not cleansed ourselves from that sin, even though a plague fell on the community of the LORD!'"

13. Congregation

Ps 22 [22]I will declare your name to my brothers; in the congregation I will praise you.

14. Council of the Upright

Ps 111 [1]Praise the LORD. I will extol the LORD with all my heart in the council of the upright and in the assembly.

15. Flock of God

Ps 78 [52]But he brought his people out like a flock; he led them like sheep through the desert.
Ps 95 [7]for he is our God and we are the people of his pasture, the flock under his care. . . .
Isa 40 [11]He tends his flock like a shepherd: He gathers the lambs in his arms and carries them close to his heart; he gently leads those that have young.
Jer 23 [3]"I myself will gather the remnant of my flock out of all the countries where I have driven them and will bring them back to their pasture, where they will be fruitful and increase in number."
Jer 31 [10]"Hear the word of the LORD, O nations; proclaim it in distant coastlands: 'He who scattered Israel will gather them and will watch over his flock like a shepherd.'"
Ezek 34 [15]"'I myself will tend my sheep and have them lie down, declares the Sovereign LORD. [16]I will search for the lost and bring back the strays. I will bind up the injured and strengthen the weak, but the sleek and the strong I will destroy. I will shepherd the flock with justice. . . . [22]I will save my flock, and they will no longer be plundered. I will judge between one sheep and another.'"
Mic 2 [12]"I will surely gather all of you, O Jacob; I will surely bring together the remnant of Israel. I will bring them together like sheep in a pen, like a flock in its pasture; the place will throng with people. [13]One who breaks open the way will go up before them; they will break through the gate and go out. Their king will pass through before them, the LORD at their head."

16. Flock of Inheritance

Mic 7 [14]Shepherd your people with your staff, the flock of your inheritance, which lives by itself in a forest, in fertile pasturelands. Let them feed in Bashan and Gilead as in days long ago.

17. Great Assembly

Ps 26 [12]My feet stand on level ground; in the great assembly I will praise the LORD.
Ps 35 [18]I will give you thanks in the great assembly; among throngs of people I will praise you.
Ps 40 [9]I proclaim righteousness in the great assembly; I do not seal my lips, as you know, O LORD. [10]I do not hide your righteousness in my heart; I speak of your faithfulness and salvation. I do not conceal your love and your truth from the great assembly.
Ps 82 [1]God presides in the great assembly; he gives judgment among the "gods." . . .

18. Great Congregation

Ps 68 [26]Praise God in the great congregation; praise the LORD in the assembly of Israel.

19. Holy Nation

Exod 19 [6]"'. . . you will be for me a kingdom of priests and a holy nation.' These are the words you are to speak to the Israelites."

20. Holy Ones

Deut 33 [2]He said: "The LORD came from Sinai and dawned over them from Seir; he shone forth from Mount Paran. He came with myriads of holy ones from the south, from his mountain slopes. [3]Surely it is you who love the people; all the holy ones are in your hand. At your feet they all bow down, and from you receive instruction. . . ."
Job 15 [15]"If God places no trust in his holy ones, if even the heavens are not pure in his eyes . . ."
Zech 14 [5]You will flee by my mountain valley, for it will extend to Azel. You will flee as you fled from the earthquake in the days of Uzziah king of Judah. Then the LORD my God will come, and all the holy ones with him.

21. Holy People

Exod 22 [31]"You are to be my holy people. So do not eat the meat of an animal torn by wild beasts; throw it to the dogs."
Deut 7 [6]For you are a people holy to the LORD your God. The LORD your God has chosen you out of all the peoples on the face of the earth to be his people, his treasured possession.
Deut 28 [9]The LORD will establish you as his holy people, as he

promised you on oath, if you keep the commands of the LORD your God and walk in his ways.
Isa 62 [12]They will be called the Holy People, the Redeemed of the LORD; and you will be called Sought After, the City No Longer Deserted.
Dan 8 [24]"He will become very strong, but not by his own power. He will cause astounding devastation and will succeed in whatever he does. He will destroy the mighty men and the holy people."

22. Inheritance

Deut 9 [29]"But they are your people, your inheritance that you brought out by your great power and your outstretched arm."
1 Sam 10 [1]Then Samuel took a flask of oil and poured it on Saul's head and kissed him, saying, "Has not the LORD anointed you leader over his inheritance?"
Ps 28 [9]Save your people and bless your inheritance; be their shepherd and carry them forever.
Ps 33 [12]Blessed is the nation whose God is the LORD, the people he chose for his inheritance.
Ps 106 [5]that I may enjoy the prosperity of your chosen ones, that I may share in the joy of your nation and join your inheritance in giving praise.
Isa 19 [25]The LORD Almighty will bless them, saying, "Blessed be Egypt my people, Assyria my handiwork, and Israel my inheritance."
Jer 51 [19]"He who is the Portion of Jacob is not like these, for he is the Maker of all things, including the tribe of his inheritance—the LORD Almighty is his name."
Joel 3 [2]"I will gather all nations and bring them down to the Valley of Jehoshaphat. There I will enter into judgment against them concerning my inheritance, my people Israel, for they scattered my people among the nations and divided up my land."

23. Kingdom of Priests

Exod 19 [6]"'. . . you will be for me a kingdom of priests and a holy nation.' These are the words you are to speak to the Israelites."

24. Lord's Portion

Deut 32 [9]For the LORD's portion is his people, Jacob his allotted inheritance.

25. Oaks of Righteousness

Isa 61 [3]and provide for those who grieve in Zion—to bestow on them a crown of beauty instead of ashes, the oil of gladness instead of mourning, and a garment of praise instead of a spirit of despair. They will be called oaks of righteousness, a planting of the LORD for the display of his splendor.

26. People of His Inheritance

Deut 4 [20]But as for you, the LORD took you and brought you out of the iron-smelting furnace, out of Egypt, to be the people of his inheritance, as you now are.

27. Planting of the Lord

Isa 61 [3]and provide for those who grieve in Zion—to bestow on them a crown of beauty instead of ashes, the oil of gladness instead of mourning, and a garment of praise instead of a spirit of despair. They will be called oaks of righteousness, a planting of the LORD for the display of his splendor.

28. Ransomed of the Lord

Isa 51 [11]The ransomed of the LORD will return. They will enter Zion with singing; everlasting joy will crown their heads. Gladness and joy will overtake them, and sorrow and sighing will flee away.

29. Redeemed of the Lord

Ps 107 [2]Let the redeemed of the LORD say this—those he redeemed from the hand of the foe. . . .
Isa 62 [12]They will be called the Holy People, the Redeemed of the LORD; and you will be called Sought After, the City No Longer Deserted.

30. Servants

Lev 25 [55]"'. . . for the Israelites belong to me as servants. They are my servants, whom I brought out of Egypt. I am the LORD your God.'"
1 Kings 8 [23]and said: "O LORD, God of Israel, there is no God like you in heaven above or on earth below—you who keep your covenant of love with your servants who continue wholeheartedly in your way."
Ezra 5 [11]This is the answer they gave us: "We are the servants of the God of heaven and earth, and we are rebuilding the temple that was built many years ago, one that a great king of Israel built and finished."
Neh 1 [10]"They are your servants and your people, whom you redeemed by your great strength and your mighty hand."
Ps 34 [22]The LORD redeems his servants; no one will be condemned who takes refuge in him.
Ps 113 [1]Praise the LORD. Praise, O servants of the LORD, praise the name of the LORD.
Ps 135 [14]For the LORD will vindicate his people and have compassion on his servants.
Isa 65 [9]"I will bring forth descendants from Jacob, and from Judah those who will possess my mountains; my chosen people will inherit them, and there will my servants live."

31. Sheep in a Pen

Mic 2 [12]"I will surely gather all of you, O Jacob; I will surely bring together the remnant of Israel. I will bring them together like sheep in a pen, like a flock in its pasture; the place will throng with people. [13]One who breaks open the way will go up before them; they will break through the gate and go out. Their king will pass through before them, the LORD at their head."

32. Sheep of God's Pasture

Ps 79 [13]Then we your people, the sheep of your pasture, will praise you forever; from generation to generation we will recount your praise.
Ps 100 [3]Know that the LORD is God. It is he who made us, and we are his; we are his people, the sheep of his pasture.
Jer 23 [1]"Woe to the shepherds who are destroying and scattering the sheep of my pasture!" declares the LORD.
Ezek 34 [31]"'You my sheep, the sheep of my pasture, are people, and I am your God, declares the Sovereign LORD.'"

33. Shoot of God's Planting

Isa 60 [21]"Then will all your people be righteous and they will possess the land forever. They are the shoot I have planted, the work of my hands, for the display of my splendor."

34. Treasured Possession

Deut 7 [6]For you are a people holy to the LORD your God. The LORD your God has chosen you out of all the peoples on the face of the earth to be his people, his treasured possession.

35. Work of God's Hands

Isa 29 [23]"When they see among them their children, the work of my hands, they will keep my name holy; they will acknowledge the holiness of the Holy One of Jacob, and will stand in awe of the God of Israel."
Isa 45 [11]"This is what the LORD says—the Holy One of Israel, and its Maker: Concerning things to come, do you question me about my children, or give me orders about the work of my hands?"
Isa 60 [21]"Then will all your people be righteous and they will possess the land forever. They are the shoot I have planted, the work of my hands, for the display of my splendor."

B. NT Metaphors and Names

1. Abraham's Offspring

Rom 4 [16]Therefore, the promise comes by faith, so that it may be by grace and may be guaranteed to all Abraham's offspring—not only to those who are of the law but also to those who are of the faith of Abraham. He is the father of us all.

2. Abraham's Seed

Gal 3 [29]If you belong to Christ, then you are Abraham's seed, and heirs according to the promise.

3. Body of Christ

Rom 12 [4]Just as each of us has one body with many members, and these members do not all have the same function, [5]so in Christ we who are many form one body, and each member belongs to all the others.
1 Cor 6 [15]Do you not know that your bodies are members of Christ himself? Shall I then take the members of Christ and unite them with a prostitute? Never! [16]Do you not know that he who unites himself with a prostitute is one with her in body? For it is said, "The two will become one flesh." [17]But he who unites himself with the Lord is one with him in spirit.
1 Cor 10 [16]Is not the cup of thanksgiving for which we give thanks a participation in the blood of Christ? And is not the bread that we break a participation in the body of Christ? [17]Because there is one loaf, we, who are many, are one body, for we all partake of the one loaf.
1 Cor 11 [29]For anyone who eats and drinks without recognizing the body of the Lord eats and drinks judgment on himself.
1 Cor 12 [12]The body is a unit, though it is made up of many parts; and though all its parts are many, they form one body. So it is with Christ. [13]For we were all baptized by one Spirit into one body—whether Jews or Greeks, slave or free—and we were all given the one Spirit to drink.

[14]Now the body is not made up of one part but of many. [15]If the foot should say, "Because I am not a hand, I do not belong to the body," it would not for that reason cease to be part of the body. [16]And if the ear should say, "Because I am not an eye, I do not belong to the body," it would not for that reason cease to be part of the body. [17]If the whole body were an eye, where would the sense of hearing be? If the whole body were an ear, where would the sense of smell be? [18]But in fact God has arranged the parts in the body, every one of them, just as he wanted them to be. [19]If they were all one part, where would the body be? [20]As it is, there are many parts, but one body.

[21]The eye cannot say to the hand, "I don't need you!" And the head cannot say to the feet, "I don't need you!" [22]On the contrary, those parts of the body that seem to be weaker are indispensable, [23]and the parts that we think are less honorable we treat with special honor. And the parts that are unpresentable are treated with special modesty, [24]while our presentable parts need no special treatment. But God has combined the members of the body and has given greater honor to the parts that lacked it, [25]so that there should be no division in the body, but that its parts should have equal concern for each other. [26]If one part suffers, every part suffers with it; if one part is honored, every part rejoices with it.

[27]Now you are the body of Christ, and each one of you is a part of it.
Eph 1 [22]And God placed all things under his feet and appointed him to be head over everything for the church, [23]which is his body, the fullness of him who fills everything in every way.
Eph 4 [12]to prepare God's people for works of service, so that the body of Christ may be built up . . .
Col 1 [24]Now I rejoice in what was suffered for you, and I fill up in my flesh what is still lacking in regard to Christ's afflictions, for the sake of his body, which is the church.

4. Branches of the Vine

John 15 [1]"I am the true vine, and my Father is the gardener. [2]He cuts off every branch in me that bears no fruit, while every branch that does bear fruit he prunes so that it will be even more fruitful. [3]You are already clean because of the word I have spoken to you. [4]Remain in me, and I will remain in you. No branch can bear fruit by itself; it must remain in the vine. Neither can you bear fruit unless you remain in me.

[5]"I am the vine; you are the branches. If a man remains in me and I in him, he will bear much fruit; apart from me you can do nothing."

5. Bride

Rev 19 [7]"Let us rejoice and be glad and give him glory! For the wedding of the Lamb has come, and his bride has made herself ready. [8]Fine linen, bright and clean, was given her to wear." (Fine linen stands for the righteous acts of the saints.)
Rev 21 [2]I saw the Holy City, the new Jerusalem, coming down out of heaven from God, prepared as a bride beautifully dressed for her husband. . . .

[9]One of the seven angels who had the seven bowls full of the seven last plagues came and said to me, "Come, I will show you the bride, the wife of the Lamb."
Rev 22 [17]The Spirit and the bride say, "Come!" And let him who hears say, "Come!" Whoever is thirsty, let him come; and whoever wishes, let him take the free gift of the water of life.

6. Building of God

1 Cor 3 [9]For we are God's fellow workers; you are God's field, God's building.

7. Children of God

1 John 3 [1]How great is the love the Father has lavished on us, that we should be called children of God! And that is what we are! The reason the world does not know us is that it did not know him. [2]Dear friends, now we are children of God, and what we will be has not yet been made known. But we know that when he appears, we shall be like him, for we shall see him as he is. . . .

[9]No one who is born of God will continue to sin, because God's seed remains in him; he cannot go on sinning, because he has been born of God. [10]This is how we know who the children of God are and who the children of the devil are: Anyone who does not do what is right is not a child of God; nor is anyone who does not love his brother.

8. Chosen Ones

Luke 18 [7]"And will not God bring about justice for his chosen ones, who cry out to him day and night? Will he keep putting them off?"

9. Chosen People

Col 3 [12]Therefore, as God's chosen people, holy and dearly loved, clothe yourselves with compassion, kindness, humility, gentleness and patience.
1 Pet 2 [9]But you are a chosen people, a royal priesthood, a holy nation, a people belonging to God, that you may declare the praises of him who called you out of darkness into his wonderful light.

10. Church

Matt 16 [18]"And I tell you that you are Peter, and on this rock I will build my church, and the gates of Hades will not overcome it."
Matt 18 [17]"If he refuses to listen to them, tell it to the church; and if he refuses to listen even to the church, treat him as you would a pagan or a tax collector."
Acts 5 [11]Great fear seized the whole church and all who heard about these events.
Eph 1 [22]And God placed all things under his feet and appointed him to be head over everything for the church. . . .
Eph 3 [10]His intent was that now, through the church, the manifold wisdom of God should be made known to the rulers and authorities in the heavenly realms. . . .
Eph 3 [21]to him be glory in the church and in Christ Jesus throughout all generations, for ever and ever! Amen.
Col 1 [24]Now I rejoice in what was suffered for you, and I fill up

in my flesh what is still lacking in regard to Christ's afflictions, for the sake of his body, which is the church.

11. Church in God the Father and the Lord Jesus Christ

1 Thess 1 [1]Paul, Silas and Timothy,

To the church of the Thessalonians in God the Father and the Lord Jesus Christ: Grace and peace to you.

12. Church of the Firstborn

Heb 12 [23]to the church of the firstborn, whose names are written in heaven. You have come to God, the judge of all men, to the spirits of righteous men made perfect. . . .

13. Church of God

Acts 20 [28]"Keep watch over yourselves and all the flock of which the Holy Spirit has made you overseers. Be shepherds of the church of God, which he bought with his own blood."
1 Cor 1 [2]To the church of God in Corinth, to those sanctified in Christ Jesus and called to be holy, together with all those everywhere who call on the name of our Lord Jesus Christ—their Lord and ours. . . .
1 Cor 10 [32]Do not cause anyone to stumble, whether Jews, Greeks or the church of God. . . .
1 Cor 11 [22]Don't you have homes to eat and drink in? Or do you despise the church of God and humiliate those who have nothing? What shall I say to you? Shall I praise you for this? Certainly not!
1 Cor 15 [9]For I am the least of the apostles and do not even deserve to be called an apostle, because I persecuted the church of God.
2 Cor 1 [1]Paul, an apostle of Christ Jesus by the will of God, and Timothy our brother,

To the church of God in Corinth, together with all the saints throughout Achaia. . . .
Gal 1 [13]For you have heard of my previous way of life in Judaism, how intensely I persecuted the church of God and tried to destroy it.

14. Church of the Living God

1 Tim 3 [15]if I am delayed, you will know how people ought to conduct themselves in God's household, which is the church of the living God, the pillar and foundation of the truth.

15. City of the Living God

Heb 12 [22]But you have come to Mount Zion, to the heavenly Jerusalem, the city of the living God. You have come to thousands upon thousands of angels in joyful assembly. . . .

16. City of My God

Rev 3 [12]Him who overcomes I will make a pillar in the temple of my God. Never again will he leave it. I will write on him the name of my God and the name of the city of my God, the new Jerusalem, which is coming down out of heaven from my God; and I will also write on him my new name.

17. Congregations of the Saints

1 Cor 14 [33]For God is not a God of disorder but of peace. As in all the congregations of the saints . . .

18. Cultivated Olive Tree

Rom 11 [24]After all, if you were cut out of an olive tree that is wild by nature, and contrary to nature were grafted into a cultivated olive tree, how much more readily will these, the natural branches, be grafted into their own olive tree!

19. Dwelling of God

Eph 2 [22]And in him you too are being built together to become a dwelling in which God lives by his Spirit.

20. Elect

Mark 13 [20]"If the Lord had not cut short those days, no one would survive. But for the sake of the elect, whom he has chosen, he has shortened them. . . . [22]For false Christs and false prophets will appear and perform signs and miracles to deceive the elect—if that were possible. . . .

[27]"And he will send his angels and gather his elect from the four winds, from the ends of the earth to the ends of the heavens."
Rom 11 [7]What then? What Israel sought so earnestly it did not obtain, but the elect did. The others were hardened. . . .
Titus 1 [1]Paul, a servant of God and an apostle of Jesus Christ for the faith of God's elect and the knowledge of the truth that leads to godliness. . . .

21. Family in Heaven and on Earth

Eph 3 [14]For this reason I kneel before the Father, [15]from whom his whole family in heaven and on earth derives its name.

22. Family of Believers

Gal 6 [10]Therefore, as we have opportunity, let us do good to all people, especially to those who belong to the family of believers.

23. Family of God

1 Pet 4 [17]For it is time for judgment to begin with the family of God; and if it begins with us, what will the outcome be for those who do not obey the gospel of God?

24. Fellow Citizens

Eph 2 [19]Consequently, you are no longer foreigners and aliens, but fellow citizens with God's people and members of God's household. . . .

25. Flock of God

John 10 [16]"I have other sheep that are not of this sheep pen. I must bring them also. They too will listen to my voice, and there shall be one flock and one shepherd."
1 Pet 5 [2]Be shepherds of God's flock that is under your care, serving as overseers—not because you must, but because you are willing, as God wants you to be; not greedy for money, but eager to serve; [3]not lording it over those entrusted to you, but being examples to the flock.

26. Foundation of the Truth

1 Tim 3 [15]if I am delayed, you will know how people ought to conduct themselves in God's household, which is the church of the living God, the pillar and foundation of the truth.

27. God's Church

1 Tim 3 [5](If anyone does not know how to manage his own family, how can he take care of God's church?)

28. God's Field

1 Cor 3 [9]For we are God's fellow workers; you are God's field, God's building.

29. God's Household

Eph 2 [19]Consequently, you are no longer foreigners and aliens, but fellow citizens with God's people and members of God's household. . . .
1 Tim 3 [15]if I am delayed, you will know how people ought to conduct themselves in God's household, which is the church of the living God, the pillar and foundation of the truth.

30. Golden Lampstand

Rev 1 [12]I turned around to see the voice that was speaking to me. And when I turned I saw seven golden lampstands, [13]and among the lampstands was someone "like a son of man," dressed in a robe reaching down to his feet and with a golden sash around his chest. . . .

[20]"The mystery of the seven stars that you saw in my right hand and of the seven golden lampstands is this: The seven stars are the angels of the seven churches, and the seven lampstands are the seven churches."

Rev 2 [1]"To the angel of the church in Ephesus write: These are the words of him who holds the seven stars in his right hand and walks among the seven golden lampstands. . . ."

31. Great Multitude

Rev 7 [9]After this I looked and there before me was a great multitude that no one could count, from every nation, tribe, people and language, standing before the throne and in front of the Lamb. They were wearing white robes and were holding palm branches in their hands. [10]And they cried out in a loud voice: "Salvation belongs to our God, who sits on the throne, and to the Lamb." [11]All the angels were standing around the throne and around the elders and the four living creatures. They fell down on their faces before the throne and worshiped God, [12]saying: "Amen! Praise and glory and wisdom and thanks and honor and power and strength be to our God for ever and ever. Amen!"

[13]Then one of the elders asked me, "These in white robes—who are they, and where did they come from?"

[14]I answered, "Sir, you know."

And he said, "These are they who have come out of the great tribulation; they have washed their robes and made them white in the blood of the Lamb. [15]Therefore, they are before the throne of God and serve him day and night in his temple; and he who sits on the throne will spread his tent over them. [16]Never again will they hunger; never again will they thirst. The sun will not beat upon them, nor any scorching heat. [17]For the Lamb at the center of the throne will be their shepherd; he will lead them to springs of living water. And God will wipe away every tear from their eyes."

32. Heavenly Jerusalem

Gal 4 [26]But the Jerusalem that is above is free, and she is our mother.

Heb 12 [22]But you have come to Mount Zion, to the heavenly Jerusalem, the city of the living God. You have come to thousands upon thousands of angels in joyful assembly. . . .

33. Holy City

Rev 21 [2]I saw the Holy City, the new Jerusalem, coming down out of heaven from God, prepared as a bride beautifully dressed for her husband. . . .

[10]And he carried me away in the Spirit to a mountain great and high, and showed me the Holy City, Jerusalem, coming down out of heaven from God.

Rev 22 [19]And if anyone takes words away from this book of prophecy, God will take away from him his share in the tree of life and in the holy city, which are described in this book.

34. Holy Nation

1 Pet 2 [9]But you are a chosen people, a royal priesthood, a holy nation, a people belonging to God, that you may declare the praises of him who called you out of darkness into his wonderful light.

35. Holy Ones

1 Thess 3 [13]May he strengthen your hearts so that you will be blameless and holy in the presence of our God and Father when our Lord Jesus comes with all his holy ones.

36. Holy People

Eph 5 [3]But among you there must not be even a hint of sexual immorality, or of any kind of impurity, or of greed, because these are improper for God's holy people.

2 Thess 1 [10]on the day he comes to be glorified in his holy people and to be marveled at among all those who have believed. This includes you, because you believed our testimony to you.

37. Holy Priesthood

1 Pet 2 [5]you also, like living stones, are being built into a spiritual house to be a holy priesthood, offering spiritual sacrifices acceptable to God through Jesus Christ.

38. Holy Temple

Eph 2 [19]Consequently, you are no longer foreigners and aliens, but fellow citizens with God's people and members of God's household, [20]built on the foundation of the apostles and prophets, with Christ Jesus himself as the chief cornerstone. [21]In him the whole building is joined together and rises to become a holy temple in the Lord.

39. House of God

Heb 3 [6]But Christ is faithful as a son over God's house. And we are his house, if we hold on to our courage and the hope of which we boast.

Heb 10 [21]and since we have a great priest over the house of God . . .

40. House of Israel

Heb 8 [8]But God found fault with the people and said: "The time is coming, declares the Lord, when I will make a new covenant with the house of Israel and with the house of Judah. [9]It will not be like the covenant I made with their forefathers when I took them by the hand to lead them out of Egypt, because they did not remain faithful to my covenant, and I turned away from them, declares the Lord. [10]This is the covenant I will make with the house of Israel after that time, declares the Lord. I will put my laws in their minds and write them on their hearts. I will be their God, and they will be my people.

41. Israel of God

Gal 6 [16]Peace and mercy to all who follow this rule, even to the Israel of God.

42. Kingdom

Rev 1 [6]and has made us to be a kingdom and priests to serve his God and Father—to him be glory and power for ever and ever! Amen.

Rev 5 [10]"You have made them to be a kingdom and priests to serve our God, and they will reign on the earth."

43. Letter from Christ

2 Cor 3 [2]You yourselves are our letter, written on our hearts, known and read by everybody. [3]You show that you are a letter from Christ, the result of our ministry, written not with ink but with the Spirit of the living God, not on tablets of stone but on tablets of human hearts.

44. Living Stones

1 Pet 2 [5]you also, like living stones, are being built into a spiritual house to be a holy priesthood, offering spiritual sacrifices acceptable to God through Jesus Christ.

45. Members of One Body

Eph 4 [25]Therefore each of you must put off falsehood and speak truthfully to his neighbor, for we are all members of one body.

Eph 5 [30]for we are members of his body.

Col 3 [15]Let the peace of Christ rule in your hearts, since as members of one body you were called to peace. And be thankful.

46. Mount Zion

Heb 12 [22]But you have come to Mount Zion, to the heavenly Jerusalem, the city of the living God. You have come to thousands upon thousands of angels in joyful assembly. . . .

47. My Loved One

Rom 9 [25]As he says in Hosea: "I will call them 'my people' who are not my people; and I will call her 'my loved one' who is not my loved one." . . .

48. My People Israel

Matt 2 [6]"'But you, Bethlehem, in the land of Judah, are by no means least among the rulers of Judah; for out of you will come a ruler who will be the shepherd of my people Israel.'"

49. New Jerusalem

Rev 3 [12]"Him who overcomes I will make a pillar in the temple of my God. Never again will he leave it. I will write on him the name of my God and the name of the city of my God, the new Jerusalem, which is coming down out of heaven from my God; and I will also write on him my new name."
Rev 21 [2]I saw the Holy City, the new Jerusalem, coming down out of heaven from God, prepared as a bride beautifully dressed for her husband.
Rev 21 [10]And he carried me away in the Spirit to a mountain great and high, and showed me the Holy City, Jerusalem, coming down out of heaven from God.

50. People Belonging to God

1 Pet 2 [9]But you are a chosen people, a royal priesthood, a holy nation, a people belonging to God, that you may declare the praises of him who called you out of darkness into his wonderful light.

51. People of God

Matt 1 [21]"She will give birth to a son, and you are to give him the name Jesus, because he will save his people from their sins."
Luke 1 [17]"And he will go on before the Lord, in the spirit and power of Elijah, to turn the hearts of the fathers to their children and the disobedient to the wisdom of the righteous—to make ready a people prepared for the Lord."
Acts 3 [23]"'Anyone who does not listen to him will be completely cut off from among his people.'"
Acts 15 [14]Simon has described to us how God at first showed his concern by taking from the Gentiles a people for himself.
Rom 9 [25]As he says in Hosea: "I will call them 'my people' who are not my people; and I will call her 'my loved one' who is not my loved one," [26]and, "It will happen that in the very place where it was said to them, 'You are not my people,' they will be called 'sons of the living God.'"
Rom 15 [10]Again, it says, "Rejoice, O Gentiles, with his people."
2 Cor 6 [16]What agreement is there between the temple of God and idols? For we are the temple of the living God. As God has said: "I will live with them and walk among them, and I will be their God, and they will be my people."
Eph 2 [19]Consequently, you are no longer foreigners and aliens, but fellow citizens with God's people and members of God's household. . . .
Eph 3 [8]Although I am less than the least of all God's people, this grace was given me: to preach to the Gentiles the unsearchable riches of Christ. . . .
Heb 2 [17]For this reason he had to be made like his brothers in every way, in order that he might become a merciful and faithful high priest in service to God, and that he might make atonement for the sins of the people.
Heb 4 [9]There remains, then, a Sabbath-rest for the people of God. . . .
Heb 8 [10]"This is the covenant I will make with the house of Israel after that time, declares the Lord. I will put my laws in their minds and write them on their hearts. I will be their God, and they will be my people."
Heb 10 [30]For we know him who said, "It is mine to avenge; I will repay," and again, "The Lord will judge his people."
Heb 11 [25]He chose to be mistreated along with the people of God rather than to enjoy the pleasures of sin for a short time.
Heb 13 [12]And so Jesus also suffered outside the city gate to make the people holy through his own blood.
1 Pet 2 [10]Once you were not a people, but now you are the people of God; once you had not received mercy, but now you have received mercy.
Rev 18 [4]Then I heard another voice from heaven say: "Come out of her, my people, so that you will not share in her sins, so that you will not receive any of her plagues. . . ."
Rev 21 [3]And I heard a loud voice from the throne saying, "Now the dwelling of God is with men, and he will live with them. They will be his people, and God himself will be with them and be their God."

52. People of His Very Own

Titus 2 [14]who gave himself for us to redeem us from all wickedness and to purify for himself a people that are his very own, eager to do what is good.

53. Pillar of the Truth

1 Tim 3 [15]if I am delayed, you will know how people ought to conduct themselves in God's household, which is the church of the living God, the pillar and foundation of the truth.

54. Priests

Rev 1 [6]and has made us to be a kingdom and priests to serve his God and Father—to him be glory and power for ever and ever! Amen.
Rev 5 [10]"You have made them to be a kingdom and priests to serve our God, and they will reign on the earth."

55. Pure Virgin

2 Cor 11 [2]I am jealous for you with a godly jealousy. I promised you to one husband, to Christ, so that I might present you as a pure virgin to him.

56. Royal Priesthood

1 Pet 2 [9]But you are a chosen people, a royal priesthood, a holy nation, a people belonging to God, that you may declare the praises of him who called you out of darkness into his wonderful light.

57. Salt of the Earth

Matt 5 [13]"You are the salt of the earth. But if the salt loses its saltiness, how can it be made salty again? It is no longer good for anything, except to be thrown out and trampled by men."

58. Sons of God

Rom 8 [14]because those who are led by the Spirit of God are sons of God. [15]For you did not receive a spirit that makes you a slave again to fear, but you received the Spirit of sonship. And by him we cry, "Abba, Father."
Gal 3 [26]You are all sons of God through faith in Christ Jesus, [27]for all of you who were baptized into Christ have clothed yourselves with Christ. [28]There is neither Jew nor Greek, slave nor free, male nor female, for you are all one in Christ Jesus. [29]If you belong to Christ, then you are Abraham's seed, and heirs according to the promise.
Gal 4 [1]What I am saying is that as long as the heir is a child, he is no different from a slave, although he owns the whole estate. [2]He is subject to guardians and trustees until the time set by his father. [3]So also, when we were children, we were in slavery under the basic principles of the world. [4]But when the time had fully come, God sent his Son, born of a woman, born under law, [5]to redeem those under law, that we might receive the full rights of sons. [6]Because you are sons, God sent the Spirit of his Son into our hearts, the Spirit who calls out, "Abba, Father." [7]So you are no longer a slave, but a son; and since you are a son, God has made you also an heir.

59. Sons of the Living God

Rom 9 [26]and, "It will happen that in the very place where it was said to them, 'You are not my people,' they will be called 'sons of the living God.'"

60. Spiritual House

1 Pet 2 [5]you also, like living stones, are being built into a spiritual house to be a holy priesthood, offering spiritual sacrifices acceptable to God through Jesus Christ.

61. Temple of God

1 Cor 3 [16]Don't you know that you yourselves are God's temple and that God's Spirit lives in you? [17]If anyone destroys God's temple, God will destroy him; for God's temple is sacred, and you are that temple.
Rev 3 [12]"Him who overcomes I will make a pillar in the temple of my God. Never again will he leave it. I will write on him the name of my God and the name of the city of my God, the new Jerusalem, which is coming down out of heaven from my God; and I will also write on him my new name."

62. Temple of the Living God

2 Cor 6 [16]What agreement is there between the temple of God and idols? For we are the temple of the living God. As God has said: "I will live with them and walk among them, and I will be their God, and they will be my people."

63. Those Who Belong to Christ

1 Cor 15 [23]But each in his own turn: Christ, the firstfruits; then, when he comes, those who belong to him.

64. Twelve Tribes

James 1 [1]James, a servant of God and of the Lord Jesus Christ,
To the twelve tribes scattered among the nations: Greetings.
Rev 7 [4]Then I heard the number of those who were sealed: 144,000 from all the tribes of Israel.

65. Virgins

Rev 14 [1]Then I looked, and there before me was the Lamb, standing on Mount Zion, and with him 144,000 who had his name and his Father's name written on their foreheads. [2]And I heard a sound from heaven like the roar of rushing waters and like a loud peal of thunder. The sound I heard was like that of harpists playing their harps. [3]And they sang a new song before the throne and before the four living creatures and the elders. No one could learn the song except the 144,000 who had been redeemed from the earth. [4]These are those who did not defile themselves with women, for they kept themselves pure. They follow the Lamb wherever he goes. They were purchased from among men and offered as firstfruits to God and the Lamb.

66. Wife of the Lamb

Rev 21 [9]One of the seven angels who had the seven bowls full of the seven last plagues came and said to me, "Come, I will show you the bride, the wife of the Lamb."

67. Woman Clothed with the Sun

Rev 12 [1]A great and wondrous sign appeared in heaven: a woman clothed with the sun, with the moon under her feet and a crown of twelve stars on her head. [2]She was pregnant and cried out in pain as she was about to give birth.

III
The Nature of the Church

A. The Church Is Universal

1. The Church Is a Work of God

Isa 60 [21]"Then will all your people be righteous and they will possess the land forever. They are the shoot I have planted, the work of my hands, for the display of my splendor."
Acts 20 [28]Keep watch over yourselves and all the flock of which the Holy Spirit has made you overseers. Be shepherds of the church of God, which he bought with his own blood.
1 Cor 3 [9]For we are God's fellow workers; you are God's field, God's building.
1 Cor 15 [9]For I am the least of the apostles and do not even deserve to be called an apostle, because I persecuted the church of God.
2 Cor 6 [16]What agreement is there between the temple of God and idols? For we are the temple of the living God. As God has said: "I will live with them and walk among them, and I will be their God, and they will be my people."
Eph 3 [10]His intent was that now, through the church, the manifold wisdom of God should be made known to the rulers and authorities in the heavenly realms. . . .

[20]Now to him who is able to do immeasurably more than all we ask or imagine, according to his power that is at work within us, [21]to him be glory in the church and in Christ Jesus throughout all generations, for ever and ever! Amen.
1 Tim 3 [15]if I am delayed, you will know how people ought to conduct themselves in God's household, which is the church of the living God, the pillar and foundation of the truth.
Heb 13 [20]May the God of peace, who through the blood of the eternal covenant brought back from the dead our Lord Jesus, that great Shepherd of the sheep . . .
Rev 3 [12]Him who overcomes I will make a pillar in the temple of my God. Never again will he leave it. I will write on him the name of my God and the name of the city of my God, the new Jerusalem, which is coming down out of heaven from my God; and I will also write on him my new name.

2. The Church Was Established in the Person and Work of Christ

Matt 16 [18]"And I tell you that you are Peter, and on this rock I will build my church, and the gates of Hades will not overcome it."
1 Cor 3 [10]By the grace God has given me, I laid a foundation as an expert builder, and someone else is building on it. But each one should be careful how he builds. [11]For no one can lay any foundation other than the one already laid, which is Jesus Christ.
1 Cor 6 [11]And that is what some of you were. But you were washed, you were sanctified, you were justified in the name of the Lord Jesus Christ and by the Spirit of our God.
Eph 1 [18]I pray also that the eyes of your heart may be enlightened in order that you may know the hope to which he has called you, the riches of his glorious inheritance in the saints, [19]and his incomparably great power for us who believe. That power is like the working of his mighty strength, [20]which he exerted in Christ when he raised him from the dead and seated him at his right hand in the heavenly realms, [21]far above all rule and authority, power and dominion, and every title that can be given, not only in the present age but also in the one to come. [22]And God placed all things under his feet and appointed him to be head over everything for the church, [23]which is his body, the fullness of him who fills everything in every way.
Eph 2 [19]Consequently, you are no longer foreigners and aliens, but fellow citizens with God's people and members of God's household, [20]built on the foundation of the apostles and prophets, with Christ Jesus himself as the chief cornerstone. [21]In him the whole building is joined together and rises to become a holy temple in the Lord.
Eph 5 [23]For the husband is the head of the wife as Christ is the head of the church, his body, of which he is the Savior.
Col 1 [18]And he is the head of the body, the church; he is the beginning and the firstborn from among the dead, so that in everything he might have the supremacy.
Col 1 [24]Now I rejoice in what was suffered for you, and I fill up in my flesh what is still lacking in regard to Christ's afflictions, for the sake of his body, which is the church.
Col 3 [11]Here there is no Greek or Jew, circumcised or uncircumcised, barbarian, Scythian, slave or free, but Christ is all, and is in all.
Heb 9 [12]He did not enter by means of the blood of goats and calves; but he entered the Most Holy Place once for all by his own blood, having obtained eternal redemption. . . . [14]How

much more, then, will the blood of Christ, who through the eternal Spirit offered himself unblemished to God, cleanse our consciences from acts that lead to death, so that we may serve the living God!

Heb 9 [26]Then Christ would have had to suffer many times since the creation of the world. But now he has appeared once for all at the end of the ages to do away with sin by the sacrifice of himself. [27]Just as man is destined to die once, and after that to face judgment, [28]so Christ was sacrificed once to take away the sins of many people; and he will appear a second time, not to bear sin, but to bring salvation to those who are waiting for him.

1 Pet 1 [3]Praise be to the God and Father of our Lord Jesus Christ! In his great mercy he has given us new birth into a living hope through the resurrection of Jesus Christ from the dead, [4]and into an inheritance that can never perish, spoil or fade—kept in heaven for you, [5]who through faith are shielded by God's power until the coming of the salvation that is ready to be revealed in the last time. [6]In this you greatly rejoice, though now for a little while you may have had to suffer grief in all kinds of trials. [7]These have come so that your faith—of greater worth than gold, which perishes even though refined by fire—may be proved genuine and may result in praise, glory and honor when Jesus Christ is revealed. [8]Though you have not seen him, you love him; and even though you do not see him now, you believe in him and are filled with an inexpressible and glorious joy, [9]for you are receiving the goal of your faith, the salvation of your souls.

1 Pet 1 [22]Now that you have purified yourselves by obeying the truth so that you have sincere love for your brothers, love one another deeply, from the heart. [23]For you have been born again, not of perishable seed, but of imperishable, through the living and enduring word of God.

[24]For, "All men are like grass, and all their glory is like the flowers of the field; the grass withers and the flowers fall, [25]but the word of the Lord stands forever."

And this is the word that was preached to you.

3. The Church Is Indwelt and Energized by the Holy Spirit

1 Cor 3 [16]Don't you know that you yourselves are God's temple and that God's Spirit lives in you?

1 Cor 12 [13]For we were all baptized by one Spirit into one body—whether Jews or Greeks, slave or free—and we were all given the one Spirit to drink.

Eph 2 [22]And in him you too are being built together to become a dwelling in which God lives by his Spirit.

1 John 2 [20]But you have an anointing from the Holy One, and all of you know the truth. . . .

[27]As for you, the anointing you received from him remains in you, and you do not need anyone to teach you. But as his anointing teaches you about all things and as that anointing is real, not counterfeit—just as it has taught you, remain in him.

4. The Church Is Composed of the People of God

John 15 [5]"I am the vine; you are the branches. If a man remains in me and I in him, he will bear much fruit; apart from me you can do nothing."

1 Cor 12 [27]Now you are the body of Christ, and each one of you is a part of it.

1 Cor 15 [23]But each in his own turn: Christ, the firstfruits; then, when he comes, those who belong to him.

Eph 3 [6]This mystery is that through the gospel the Gentiles are heirs together with Israel, members together of one body, and sharers together in the promise in Christ Jesus.

Eph 5 [29]After all, no one ever hated his own body, but he feeds and cares for it, just as Christ does the church—[30]for we are members of his body. . . . [32]This is a profound mystery—but I am talking about Christ and the church.

Col 1 [4]because we have heard of your faith in Christ Jesus and of the love you have for all the saints—[5]the faith and love that spring from the hope that is stored up for you in heaven and that you have already heard about in the word of truth, the gospel [6]that has come to you. All over the world this gospel is bearing fruit and growing, just as it has been doing among you since the day you heard it and understood God's grace in all its truth.

Heb 13 [15]Through Jesus, therefore, let us continually offer to God a sacrifice of praise—the fruit of lips that confess his name.

1 Pet 2 [9]But you are a chosen people, a royal priesthood, a holy nation, a people belonging to God, that you may declare the praises of him who called you out of darkness into his wonderful light.

Rev 1 [5]and from Jesus Christ, who is the faithful witness, the firstborn from the dead, and the ruler of the kings of the earth.

To him who loves us and has freed us from our sins by his blood, [6]and has made us to be a kingdom and priests to serve his God and Father—to him be glory and power for ever and ever! Amen.

B. The Church Is Local

1. General Designations for the Church

a) The Church of Antioch

Acts 13 [1]In the church at Antioch there were prophets and teachers: Barnabas, Simeon called Niger, Lucius of Cyrene, Manaen (who had been brought up with Herod the tetrarch) and Saul.

b) The Church of Asia

1 Cor 16 [19]The churches in the province of Asia send you greetings. Aquila and Priscilla greet you warmly in the Lord, and so does the church that meets at their house.

Rev 1 [4]John, To the seven churches in the province of Asia: Grace and peace to you from him who is, and who was, and who is to come, and from the seven spirits before his throne. . . .

c) The Church of Babylon

1 Pet 5 [13]She who is in Babylon, chosen together with you, sends you her greetings, and so does my son Mark.

d) The Church of Caesarea

Acts 18 [22]When he landed at Caesarea, he went up and greeted the church and then went down to Antioch.

e) The Church of Cenchrea

Rom 16 [1]I commend to you our sister Phoebe, a servant of the church in Cenchrea.

f) The Church of Cilicia

Acts 15 [41]He went through Syria and Cilicia, strengthening the churches.

g) The Church of Colosse

Col 1 [2]To the holy and faithful brothers in Christ at Colosse: Grace and peace to you from God our Father.

h) The Church of Corinth

1 Cor 1 [2]To the church of God in Corinth, to those sanctified in Christ Jesus and called to be holy, together with all those everywhere who call on the name of our Lord Jesus Christ—their Lord and ours. . . .

2 Cor 1 [1]Paul, an apostle of Christ Jesus by the will of God, and Timothy our brother,

To the church of God in Corinth, together with all the saints throughout Achaia. . . .

i) The Church of Ephesus

Acts 20 [17]From Miletus, Paul sent to Ephesus for the elders of the church.

Eph 1 [1]Paul, an apostle of Christ Jesus by the will of God,

To the saints in Ephesus, the faithful in Christ Jesus: [2]Grace and peace to you from God our Father and the Lord Jesus Christ.

Rev 2 [1]"To the angel of the church in Ephesus write: These are the words of him who holds the seven stars in his right hand and walks among the seven golden lampstands. . . ."

j) The Church of Galatia

Gal 1 [2]and all the brothers with me,
To the churches in Galatia. . . .
1 Cor 16 [1]Now about the collection for God's people: Do what I told the Galatian churches to do.

k) The Church of Galilee

Acts 9 [31]Then the church throughout Judea, Galilee and Samaria enjoyed a time of peace. It was strengthened; and encouraged by the Holy Spirit, it grew in numbers, living in the fear of the Lord.

l) The Church of Hierapolis

Col 4 [13]I vouch for him that he is working hard for you and for those at Laodicea and Hierapolis.

m) The Church of Jerusalem

Acts 8 [1]And Saul was there, giving approval to his death.
On that day a great persecution broke out against the church at Jerusalem, and all except the apostles were scattered throughout Judea and Samaria.
Acts 11 [22]News of this reached the ears of the church at Jerusalem, and they sent Barnabas to Antioch.
Acts 15 [4]When they came to Jerusalem, they were welcomed by the church and the apostles and elders, to whom they reported everything God had done through them.

n) The Church of Joppa

Acts 9 [42]This became known all over Joppa, and many people believed in the Lord.

o) The Church of Judea

Acts 9 [31]Then the church throughout Judea, Galilee and Samaria enjoyed a time of peace. It was strengthened; and encouraged by the Holy Spirit, it grew in numbers, living in the fear of the Lord.
Gal 1 [22]I was personally unknown to the churches of Judea that are in Christ.
1 Thess 2 [14]For you, brothers, became imitators of God's churches in Judea, which are in Christ Jesus: You suffered from your own countrymen the same things those churches suffered from the Jews. . . .

p) The Church of Laodicea

Col 4 [13]I vouch for him that he is working hard for you and for those at Laodicea and Hierapolis. . . . [15]Give my greetings to the brothers at Laodicea, and to Nympha and the church in her house.
[16]After this letter has been read to you, see that it is also read in the church of the Laodiceans and that you in turn read the letter from Laodicea.
Rev 3 [14]"To the angel of the church in Laodicea write: These are the words of the Amen, the faithful and true witness, the ruler of God's creation."

q) The Church of Macedonia

2 Cor 8 [1]And now, brothers, we want you to know about the grace that God has given the Macedonian churches.

r) The Church of Pergamum

Rev 2 [12]"To the angel of the church in Pergamum write: These are the words of him who has the sharp, double-edged sword."

s) The Church of Philadelphia

Rev 3 [7]"To the angel of the church in Philadelphia write: These are the words of him who is holy and true, who holds the key of David. What he opens no one can shut, and what he shuts no one can open."

t) The Church of Philippi

Phil 1 [1]Paul and Timothy, servants of Christ Jesus,
To all the saints in Christ Jesus at Philippi, together with the overseers and deacons. . . .

u) The Church of Samaria

Acts 9 [31]Then the church throughout Judea, Galilee and Samaria enjoyed a time of peace. It was strengthened; and encouraged by the Holy Spirit, it grew in numbers, living in the fear of the Lord.

v) The Church of Sardis

Rev 3 [1]"To the angel of the church in Sardis write: These are the words of him who holds the seven spirits of God and the seven stars. I know your deeds; you have a reputation of being alive, but you are dead."

w) The Church of Smyrna

Rev 2 [8]"To the angel of the church in Smyrna write: These are the words of him who is the First and the Last, who died and came to life again."

x) The Church of Syria

Acts 15 [41]He went through Syria and Cilicia, strengthening the churches.

y) The Church of Thessalonica

1 Thess 1 [1]Paul, Silas and Timothy,
To the church of the Thessalonians in God the Father and the Lord Jesus Christ: Grace and peace to you.
2 Thess 1 [1]Paul, Silas and Timothy,
To the church of the Thessalonians in God our Father and the Lord Jesus Christ. . . .

z) The Church of Thyatira

Rev 2 [18]"To the angel of the church in Thyatira write: These are the words of the Son of God, whose eyes are like blazing fire and whose feet are like burnished bronze."

2. Specific Designations of House Churches

a) Priscilla's and Aquila's House

Rom 16 [3]Greet Priscilla and Aquila, my fellow workers in Christ Jesus. [4]They risked their lives for me. Not only I but all the churches of the Gentiles are grateful to them.
[5]Greet also the church that meets at their house.
1 Cor 16 [19]The churches in the province of Asia send you greetings. Aquila and Priscilla greet you warmly in the Lord, and so does the church that meets at their house.

b) Jason's House

Acts 17 [5]But the Jews were jealous; so they rounded up some bad characters from the marketplace, formed a mob and started a riot in the city. They rushed to Jason's house in search of Paul and Silas in order to bring them out to the crowd. [6]But when they did not find them, they dragged Jason and some other brothers before the city officials, shouting: "These men who have caused trouble all over the world have now come here, [7]and Jason has welcomed them into his house. They are all defying Caesar's decrees, saying that there is another king, one called Jesus."

c) Nympha's House

Col 4 [15]Give my greetings to the brothers at Laodicea, and to Nympha and the church in her house.

d) Philemon's House

Philem [1]Paul, a prisoner of Christ Jesus, and Timothy our brother,
To Philemon our dear friend and fellow worker, [2]to Apphia our sister, to Archippus our fellow soldier and to the church that meets in your home. . . .

C. The Church Is United

Ps 133 [1]How good and pleasant it is when brothers live together in unity!
John 10 [16]"I have other sheep that are not of this sheep pen. I must bring them also. They too will listen to my voice, and there shall be one flock and one shepherd."
John 17 [11]"I will remain in the world no longer, but they are still in the world, and I am coming to you. Holy Father, protect them by the power of your name—the name you gave me—so that they may be one as we are one. . . .
[20]"My prayer is not for them alone. I pray also for those

who will believe in me through their message, [21]that all of them may be one, Father, just as you are in me and I am in you. May they also be in us so that the world may believe that you have sent me. [22]I have given them the glory that you gave me, that they may be one as we are one: [23]I in them and you in me. May they be brought to complete unity to let the world know that you sent me and have loved them even as you have loved me."

Acts 4 [32]All the believers were one in heart and mind. No one claimed that any of his possessions was his own, but they shared everything they had.

Rom 12 [4]Just as each of us has one body with many members, and these members do not all have the same function, [5]so in Christ we who are many form one body, and each member belongs to all the others.

Rom 15 [5]May the God who gives endurance and encouragement give you a spirit of unity among yourselves as you follow Christ Jesus, [6]so that with one heart and mouth you may glorify the God and Father of our Lord Jesus Christ.

1 Cor 1 [10]I appeal to you, brothers, in the name of our Lord Jesus Christ, that all of you agree with one another so that there may be no divisions among you and that you may be perfectly united in mind and thought.

1 Cor 10 [17]Because there is one loaf, we, who are many, are one body, for we all partake of the one loaf.

1 Cor 12 [4]There are different kinds of gifts, but the same Spirit. [5]There are different kinds of service, but the same Lord. [6]There are different kinds of working, but the same God works all of them in all men.

[7]Now to each one the manifestation of the Spirit is given for the common good.

Gal 3 [27]for all of you who were baptized into Christ have clothed yourselves with Christ. [28]There is neither Jew nor Greek, slave nor free, male nor female, for you are all one in Christ Jesus.

Eph 1 [9]And he made known to us the mystery of his will according to his good pleasure, which he purposed in Christ, [10]to be put into effect when the times will have reached their fulfillment—to bring all things in heaven and on earth together under one head, even Christ.

Eph 2 [14]For he himself is our peace, who has made the two one and has destroyed the barrier, the dividing wall of hostility, [15]by abolishing in his flesh the law with its commandments and regulations. His purpose was to create in himself one new man out of the two, thus making peace, [16]and in this one body to reconcile both of them to God through the cross, by which he put to death their hostility. [17]He came and preached peace to you who were far away and peace to those who were near. [18]For through him we both have access to the Father by one Spirit.

[19]Consequently, you are no longer foreigners and aliens, but fellow citizens with God's people and members of God's household, [20]built on the foundation of the apostles and prophets, with Christ Jesus himself as the chief cornerstone.

Eph 3 [6]This mystery is that through the gospel the Gentiles are heirs together with Israel, members together of one body, and sharers together in the promise in Christ Jesus.

Eph 4 [1]As a prisoner for the Lord, then, I urge you to live a life worthy of the calling you have received. [2]Be completely humble and gentle; be patient, bearing with one another in love. [3]Make every effort to keep the unity of the Spirit through the bond of peace. [4]There is one body and one Spirit—just as you were called to one hope when you were called—[5]one Lord, one faith, one baptism; [6]one God and Father of all, who is over all and through all and in all.

[7]But to each one of us grace has been given as Christ apportioned it. . . . [11]It was he who gave some to be apostles, some to be prophets, some to be evangelists, and some to be pastors and teachers, [12]to prepare God's people for works of service, so that the body of Christ may be built up [13]until we all reach unity in the faith and in the knowledge of the Son of God and become mature, attaining to the whole measure of the fullness of Christ. . . .

[16]From him the whole body, joined and held together by every supporting ligament, grows and builds itself up in love, as each part does its work.

Phil 2 [1]If you have any encouragement from being united with Christ, if any comfort from his love, if any fellowship with the Spirit, if any tenderness and compassion, [2]then make my joy complete by being like-minded, having the same love, being one in spirit and purpose.

Col 3 [11]Here there is no Greek or Jew, circumcised or uncircumcised, barbarian, Scythian, slave or free, but Christ is all, and is in all.

[12]Therefore, as God's chosen people, holy and dearly loved, clothe yourselves with compassion, kindness, humility, gentleness and patience. [13]Bear with each other and forgive whatever grievances you may have against one another. Forgive as the Lord forgave you. [14]And over all these virtues put on love, which binds them all together in perfect unity.

[15]Let the peace of Christ rule in your hearts, since as members of one body you were called to peace. And be thankful.

D. The Church Is Holy

Deut 14 [2]for you are a people holy to the LORD your God. Out of all the peoples on the face of the earth, the LORD has chosen you to be his treasured possession.

Isa 62 [12]They will be called the Holy People, the Redeemed of the LORD; and you will be called Sought After, the City No Longer Deserted.

Matt 5 [48]"Be perfect, therefore, as your heavenly Father is perfect."

John 17 [17]"Sanctify them by the truth; your word is truth. [18]As you sent me into the world, I have sent them into the world. [19]For them I sanctify myself, that they too may be truly sanctified."

Rom 12 [1]Therefore, I urge you, brothers, in view of God's mercy, to offer your bodies as living sacrifices, holy and pleasing to God—this is your spiritual act of worship.

1 Cor 1 [2]To the church of God in Corinth, to those sanctified in Christ Jesus and called to be holy, together with all those everywhere who call on the name of our Lord Jesus Christ—their Lord and ours. . . .

1 Cor 3 [10]By the grace God has given me, I laid a foundation as an expert builder, and someone else is building on it. But each one should be careful how he builds. [11]For no one can lay any foundation other than the one already laid, which is Jesus Christ. . . .

[16]Don't you know that you yourselves are God's temple and that God's Spirit lives in you? [17]If anyone destroys God's temple, God will destroy him; for God's temple is sacred, and you are that temple.

1 Cor 6 [19]Do you not know that your body is a temple of the Holy Spirit, who is in you, whom you have received from God? You are not your own. . . .

Eph 2 [19]Consequently, you are no longer foreigners and aliens, but fellow citizens with God's people and members of God's household, [20]built on the foundation of the apostles and prophets, with Christ Jesus himself as the chief cornerstone. [21]In him the whole building is joined together and rises to become a holy temple in the Lord.

Eph 5 [3]But among you there must not be even a hint of sexual immorality, or of any kind of impurity, or of greed, because these are improper for God's holy people.

Eph 5 [25]Husbands, love your wives, just as Christ loved the church and gave himself up for her [26]to make her holy, cleansing her by the washing with water through the word, [27]and to present her to himself as a radiant church, without stain or wrinkle or any other blemish, but holy and blameless.

1 Thess 3 [13]May he strengthen your hearts so that you will be blameless and holy in the presence of our God and Father when our Lord Jesus comes with all his holy ones.

2 Thess 1 [10]on the day he comes to be glorified in his holy people and to be marveled at among all those who have believed. This includes you, because you believed our testimony to you.

2 Thess 2 [13]But we ought always to thank God for you, brothers loved by the Lord, because from the beginning God chose you to be saved through the sanctifying work of the Spirit and through belief in the truth.

Heb 10 [10]And by that will, we have been made holy through the sacrifice of the body of Jesus Christ once for all.

[14]. . . because by one sacrifice he has made perfect forever those who are being made holy.
1 Pet 2 [4]As you come to him, the living Stone—rejected by men but chosen by God and precious to him—[5]you also, like living stones, are being built into a spiritual house to be a holy priesthood, offering spiritual sacrifices acceptable to God through Jesus Christ.
Rev 19 [7]"Let us rejoice and be glad and give him glory! For the wedding of the Lamb has come, and his bride has made herself ready. [8]Fine linen, bright and clean, was given her to wear." (Fine linen stands for the righteous acts of the saints.)
Rev 21 [9]One of the seven angels who had the seven bowls full of the seven last plagues came and said to me, "Come, I will show you the bride, the wife of the Lamb." [10]And he carried me away in the Spirit to a mountain great and high, and showed me the Holy City, Jerusalem, coming down out of heaven from God.

E. The Church Has Members

Isa 44 [5]"One will say, 'I belong to the LORD'; another will call himself by the name of Jacob; still another will write on his hand, 'The LORD's,' and will take the name Israel."
Matt 4 [18]As Jesus was walking beside the Sea of Galilee, he saw two brothers, Simon called Peter and his brother Andrew. They were casting a net into the lake, for they were fishermen. [19]"Come, follow me," Jesus said, "and I will make you fishers of men." [20]At once they left their nets and followed him.

[21]Going on from there, he saw two other brothers, James son of Zebedee and his brother John. They were in a boat with their father Zebedee, preparing their nets. Jesus called them, [22]and immediately they left the boat and their father and followed him.
Matt 9 [9]As Jesus went on from there, he saw a man named Matthew sitting at the tax collector's booth. "Follow me," he told him, and Matthew got up and followed him.
Matt 12 [50]"For whoever does the will of my Father in heaven is my brother and sister and mother."
Luke 5 [1]One day as Jesus was standing by the Lake of Gennesaret, with the people crowding around him and listening to the word of God, [2]he saw at the water's edge two boats, left there by the fishermen, who were washing their nets. [3]He got into one of the boats, the one belonging to Simon, and asked him to put out a little from shore. Then he sat down and taught the people from the boat.

[4]When he had finished speaking, he said to Simon, "Put out into deep water, and let down the nets for a catch."

[5]Simon answered, "Master, we've worked hard all night and haven't caught anything. But because you say so, I will let down the nets."

[6]When they had done so, they caught such a large number of fish that their nets began to break. [7]So they signaled their partners in the other boat to come and help them, and they came and filled both boats so full that they began to sink.

[8]When Simon Peter saw this, he fell at Jesus' knees and said, "Go away from me, Lord; I am a sinful man!" [9]For he and all his companions were astonished at the catch of fish they had taken, [10]and so were James and John, the sons of Zebedee, Simon's partners.

Then Jesus said to Simon, "Don't be afraid; from now on you will catch men." [11]So they pulled their boats up on shore, left everything and followed him.
Luke 18 [16]But Jesus called the children to him and said, "Let the little children come to me, and do not hinder them, for the kingdom of God belongs to such as these. [17]I tell you the truth, anyone who will not receive the kingdom of God like a little child will never enter it."
John 15 [5]"I am the vine; you are the branches. If a man remains in me and I in him, he will bear much fruit; apart from me you can do nothing."
Acts 2 [41]Those who accepted his message were baptized, and about three thousand were added to their number that day.
Acts 2 [46]Every day they continued to meet together in the temple courts. They broke bread in their homes and ate together with glad and sincere hearts, [47]praising God and enjoying the favor of all the people. And the Lord added to their number daily those who were being saved.
Acts 4 [4]But many who heard the message believed, and the number of men grew to about five thousand.
Acts 5 [14]Nevertheless, more and more men and women believed in the Lord and were added to their number.
Acts 6 [7]So the word of God spread. The number of disciples in Jerusalem increased rapidly, and a large number of priests became obedient to the faith.
Acts 9 [35]All those who lived in Lydda and Sharon saw him and turned to the Lord. [36]In Joppa there was a disciple named Tabitha (which, when translated, is Dorcas), who was always doing good and helping the poor. . . . [42]This became known all over Joppa, and many people believed in the Lord.
Acts 11 [21]The Lord's hand was with them, and a great number of people believed and turned to the Lord.
Acts 16 [5]So the churches were strengthened in the faith and grew daily in numbers.
Acts 17 [12]Many of the Jews believed, as did also a number of prominent Greek women and many Greek men.
Acts 17 [34]A few men became followers of Paul and believed. Among them was Dionysius, a member of the Areopagus, also a woman named Damaris, and a number of others.
Acts 26 [14]"We all fell to the ground, and I heard a voice saying to me in Aramaic, 'Saul, Saul, why do you persecute me? It is hard for you to kick against the goads.' . . .

[16]"'Now get up and stand on your feet. I have appeared to you to appoint you as a servant and as a witness of what you have seen of me and what I will show you. [17]I will rescue you from your own people and from the Gentiles. I am sending you to them [18]to open their eyes and turn them from darkness to light, and from the power of Satan to God, so that they may receive forgiveness of sins and a place among those who are sanctified by faith in me.'"
1 Cor 3 [11]For no one can lay any foundation other than the one already laid, which is Jesus Christ. [12]If any man builds on this foundation using gold, silver, costly stones, wood, hay or straw, [13]his work will be shown for what it is, because the Day will bring it to light. It will be revealed with fire, and the fire will test the quality of each man's work. [14]If what he has built survives, he will receive his reward. [15]If it is burned up, he will suffer loss; he himself will be saved, but only as one escaping through the flames.
1 Cor 12 [12]The body is a unit, though it is made up of many parts; and though all its parts are many, they form one body. So it is with Christ. [13]For we were all baptized by one Spirit into one body—whether Jews or Greeks, slave or free—and we were all given the one Spirit to drink.

[14]Now the body is not made up of one part but of many. [15]If the foot should say, "Because I am not a hand, I do not belong to the body," it would not for that reason cease to be part of the body. [16]And if the ear should say, "Because I am not an eye, I do not belong to the body," it would not for that reason cease to be part of the body. [17]If the whole body were an eye, where would the sense of hearing be? If the whole body were an ear, where would the sense of smell be? [18]But in fact God has arranged the parts in the body, every one of them, just as he wanted them to be. [19]If they were all one part, where would the body be? [20]As it is, there are many parts, but one body.

[21]The eye cannot say to the hand, "I don't need you!" And the head cannot say to the feet, "I don't need you!" [22]On the contrary, those parts of the body that seem to be weaker are indispensable, [23]and the parts that we think are less honorable we treat with special honor. And the parts that are unpresentable are treated with special modesty, [24]while our presentable parts need no special treatment. But God has combined the members of the body and has given greater honor to the parts that lacked it, [25]so that there should be no division in the body, but that its parts should have equal concern for each other. [26]If one part suffers, every part suffers with it; if one part is honored, every part rejoices with it.

[27]Now you are the body of Christ, and each one of you is a part of it. [28]And in the church God has appointed first of all apostles, second prophets, third teachers, then workers of miracles, also those having gifts of healing, those able to help oth-

ers, those with gifts of administration, and those speaking in different kinds of tongues.

Eph 4 [25]Therefore each of you must put off falsehood and speak truthfully to his neighbor, for we are all members of one body.

Phil 4 [3]Yes, and I ask you, loyal yokefellow, help these women who have contended at my side in the cause of the gospel, along with Clement and the rest of my fellow workers, whose names are in the book of life.

1 John 4 [2]This is how you can recognize the Spirit of God: Every spirit that acknowledges that Jesus Christ has come in the flesh is from God. . . .

Rev 21 [27]Nothing impure will ever enter it, nor will anyone who does what is shameful or deceitful, but only those whose names are written in the Lamb's book of life.

F. The Church Is Persecuted

See p. 700a, Problems in the Church Stemming from Unbelievers

G. The Church Is Triumphant

Deut 33 [2]He said: "The LORD came from Sinai and dawned over them from Seir; he shone forth from Mount Paran. He came with myriads of holy ones from the south, from his mountain slopes. [3]Surely it is you who love the people; all the holy ones are in your hand. At your feet they all bow down, and from you receive instruction. . . ."

Dan 7 [9]"As I looked, thrones were set in place, and the Ancient of Days took his seat. His clothing was as white as snow; the hair of his head was white like wool. His throne was flaming with fire, and its wheels were all ablaze. [10]A river of fire was flowing, coming out from before him. Thousands upon thousands attended him; ten thousand times ten thousand stood before him. The court was seated, and the books were opened."

Gal 4 [26]But the Jerusalem that is above is free, and she is our mother.

Heb 12 [22]But you have come to Mount Zion, to the heavenly Jerusalem, the city of the living God. You have come to thousands upon thousands of angels in joyful assembly, [23]to the church of the firstborn, whose names are written in heaven. You have come to God, the judge of all men, to the spirits of righteous men made perfect. . . .

Jude [14]Enoch, the seventh from Adam, prophesied about these men: "See, the Lord is coming with thousands upon thousands of his holy ones [15]to judge everyone, and to convict all the ungodly of all the ungodly acts they have done in the ungodly way, and of all the harsh words ungodly sinners have spoken against him."

Rev 3 [12]"Him who overcomes I will make a pillar in the temple of my God. Never again will he leave it. I will write on him the name of my God and the name of the city of my God, the new Jerusalem, which is coming down out of heaven from my God; and I will also write on him my new name."

Rev 19 [11]I saw heaven standing open and there before me was a white horse, whose rider is called Faithful and True. With justice he judges and makes war. [12]His eyes are like blazing fire, and on his head are many crowns. He has a name written on him that no one knows but he himself. [13]He is dressed in a robe dipped in blood, and his name is the Word of God. [14]The armies of heaven were following him, riding on white horses and dressed in fine linen, white and clean. [15]Out of his mouth comes a sharp sword with which to strike down the nations. "He will rule them with an iron scepter." He treads the winepress of the fury of the wrath of God Almighty. [16]On his robe and on his thigh he has this name written: KING OF KINGS AND LORD OF LORDS.

Rev 21 [2]I saw the Holy City, the new Jerusalem, coming down out of heaven from God, prepared as a bride beautifully dressed for her husband. [3]And I heard a loud voice from the throne saying, "Now the dwelling of God is with men, and he will live with them. They will be his people, and God himself will be with them and be their God."

IV
Problems Confronting the Church

A. General Problems Facing Everyone

1. Anxiety

Matt 6 [25]"Therefore I tell you, do not worry about your life, what you will eat or drink; or about your body, what you will wear. Is not life more important than food, and the body more important than clothes? [26]Look at the birds of the air; they do not sow or reap or store away in barns, and yet your heavenly Father feeds them. Are you not much more valuable than they? [27]Who of you by worrying can add a single hour to his life?

[28]"And why do you worry about clothes? See how the lilies of the field grow. They do not labor or spin. [29]Yet I tell you that not even Solomon in all his splendor was dressed like one of these. [30]If that is how God clothes the grass of the field, which is here today and tomorrow is thrown into the fire, will he not much more clothe you, O you of little faith? [31]So do not worry, saying, 'What shall we eat?' or 'What shall we drink?' or 'What shall we wear?' [32]For the pagans run after all these things, and your heavenly Father knows that you need them. [33]But seek first his kingdom and his righteousness, and all these things will be given to you as well. [34]Therefore do not worry about tomorrow, for tomorrow will worry about itself. Each day has enough trouble of its own."

Phil 2 [28]Therefore I am all the more eager to send him, so that when you see him again you may be glad and I may have less anxiety.

Phil 4 [6]Do not be anxious about anything, but in everything, by prayer and petition, with thanksgiving, present your requests to God.

1 Thess 3 [5]For this reason, when I could stand it no longer, I sent to find out about your faith. I was afraid that in some way the tempter might have tempted you and our efforts might have been useless.

1 Pet 5 [7]Cast all your anxiety on him because he cares for you.

2. Famine

Acts 11 [27]During this time some prophets came down from Jerusalem to Antioch. [28]One of them, named Agabus, stood up and through the Spirit predicted that a severe famine would spread over the entire Roman world. (This happened during the reign of Claudius.)

3. Hardships

Acts 20 [23]I only know that in every city the Holy Spirit warns me that prison and hardships are facing me.

2 Cor 4 [8]We are hard pressed on every side, but not crushed; perplexed, but not in despair; [9]persecuted, but not abandoned; struck down, but not destroyed. [10]We always carry around in our body the death of Jesus, so that the life of Jesus may also be revealed in our body. [11]For we who are alive are always being given over to death for Jesus' sake, so that his life may be revealed in our mortal body.

2 Cor 6 [3]We put no stumbling block in anyone's path, so that our ministry will not be discredited. [4]Rather, as servants of God we commend ourselves in every way: in great endurance; in troubles, hardships and distresses; [5]in beatings, imprisonments and riots; in hard work, sleepless nights and hunger; [6]in purity, understanding, patience and kindness; in the Holy Spirit and in sincere love; [7]in truthful speech and in the power of God; with weapons of righteousness in the right hand and in the left; [8]through glory and dishonor, bad report and good report; genuine, yet regarded as impostors; [9]known, yet regarded as unknown; dying, and yet we live on; beaten, and yet not killed; [10]sorrowful, yet always rejoicing; poor, yet making many rich; having nothing, and yet possessing everything.

2 Cor 11 [21]To my shame I admit that we were too weak for that! What anyone else dares to boast about—I am speaking as a fool—I also dare to boast about. [22]Are they Hebrews? So am I. Are they Israelites? So am I. Are they Abraham's descendants? So am I. [23]Are they servants of Christ? (I am out of my mind to talk like this.) I am more. I have worked much harder, been in prison more frequently, been flogged more severely, and been exposed to death again and again. [24]Five times I received from the Jews the forty lashes minus one. [25]Three times I was beaten with rods, once I was stoned, three times I was shipwrecked, I spent a night and a day in the open sea, [26]I have been constantly on the move. I have been in danger from rivers, in danger from bandits, in danger from my own countrymen, in danger from Gentiles; in danger in the city, in danger in the country, in danger at sea; and in danger from false brothers. [27]I have labored and toiled and have often gone without sleep; I have known hunger and thirst and have often gone without food; I have been cold and naked. [28]Besides everything else, I face daily the pressure of my concern for all the churches.

Heb 11 [35]Women received back their dead, raised to life again. Others were tortured and refused to be released, so that they might gain a better resurrection. [36]Some faced jeers and flogging, while still others were chained and put in prison. [37]They were stoned; they were sawed in two; they were put to death by the sword. They went about in sheepskins and goatskins, destitute, persecuted and mistreated—[38]the world was not worthy of them. They wandered in deserts and mountains, and in caves and holes in the ground.

Rev 2 [3]"You have persevered and have endured hardships for my name, and have not grown weary."

4. Illness

Gal 4 [13]As you know, it was because of an illness that I first preached the gospel to you. [14]Even though my illness was a trial to you, you did not treat me with contempt or scorn. Instead, you welcomed me as if I were an angel of God, as if I were Christ Jesus himself.

Phil 2 [26]For he longs for all of you and is distressed because you heard he was ill. [27]Indeed he was ill, and almost died. But God had mercy on him, and not on him only but also on me, to spare me sorrow upon sorrow.

5. Lack of the Necessities of Life

Phil 4 [12]I know what it is to be in need, and I know what it is to have plenty. I have learned the secret of being content in any and every situation, whether well fed or hungry, whether living in plenty or in want.

6. Poverty

Rom 15 [26]For Macedonia and Achaia were pleased to make a contribution for the poor among the saints in Jerusalem.

Rev 2 [9]"I know your afflictions and your poverty—yet you are rich! I know the slander of those who say they are Jews and are not, but are a synagogue of Satan."

B. Problems in the Church Stemming from Unbelievers

1. Confiscation of Believer's Property

Heb 10 [34]You sympathized with those in prison and joyfully accepted the confiscation of your property, because you knew that you yourselves had better and lasting possessions.

2. Deification of the Gospel Messenger

Acts 14 [8]In Lystra there sat a man crippled in his feet, who was lame from birth and had never walked. [9]He listened to Paul as he was speaking. Paul looked directly at him, saw that he had faith to be healed [10]and called out, "Stand up on your feet!" At that, the man jumped up and began to walk.

[11]When the crowd saw what Paul had done, they shouted in the Lycaonian language, "The gods have come down to us in human form!" [12]Barnabas they called Zeus, and Paul they called Hermes because he was the chief speaker. [13]The priest of Zeus, whose temple was just outside the city, brought bulls and wreaths to the city gates because he and the crowd wanted to offer sacrifices to them.

[14]But when the apostles Barnabas and Paul heard of this, they tore their clothes and rushed out into the crowd, shouting: [15]"Men, why are you doing this? We too are only men, human like you. We are bringing you good news, telling you to turn from these worthless things to the living God, who made heaven and earth and sea and everything in them. [16]In the past, he let all nations go their own way. [17]Yet he has not left himself without testimony: He has shown kindness by giving you rain from heaven and crops in their seasons; he provides you with plenty of food and fills your hearts with joy." [18]Even with these words, they had difficulty keeping the crowd from sacrificing to them.

Acts 28 [1]Once safely on shore, we found out that the island was called Malta. [2]The islanders showed us unusual kindness. They built a fire and welcomed us all because it was raining and cold. [3]Paul gathered a pile of brushwood and, as he put it on the fire, a viper, driven out by the heat, fastened itself on his hand. [4]When the islanders saw the snake hanging from his hand, they said to each other, "This man must be a murderer; for though he escaped from the sea, Justice has not allowed him to live." [5]But Paul shook the snake off into the fire and suffered no ill effects. [6]The people expected him to swell up or suddenly fall dead, but after waiting a long time and seeing nothing unusual happen to him, they changed their minds and said he was a god.

3. False Testimony against Believers

Acts 6 [8]Now Stephen, a man full of God's grace and power, did great wonders and miraculous signs among the people. [9]Opposition arose, however, from members of the Synagogue of the Freedmen (as it was called)—Jews of Cyrene and Alexandria as well as the provinces of Cilicia and Asia. These men began to argue with Stephen, [10]but they could not stand up against his wisdom or the Spirit by whom he spoke.

[11]Then they secretly persuaded some men to say, "We have heard Stephen speak words of blasphemy against Moses and against God." [12]So they stirred up the people and the elders and the teachers of the law. They seized Stephen and brought him before the Sanhedrin. [13]They produced false witnesses, who testified, "This fellow never stops speaking against this holy place and against the law. [14]For we have heard him say that this Jesus of Nazareth will destroy this place and change the customs Moses handed down to us."

4. Imprisonment of Believers

Acts 4 [1]The priests and the captain of the temple guard and the Sadducees came up to Peter and John while they were speaking to the people. [2]They were greatly disturbed because the apostles were teaching the people and proclaiming in Jesus the resurrection of the dead. [3]They seized Peter and John, and because it was evening, they put them in jail until the next day.

Acts 5 [17]Then the high priest and all his associates, who were members of the party of the Sadducees, were filled with jealousy. [18]They arrested the apostles and put them in the public jail.

Acts 9 [1]Meanwhile, Saul was still breathing out murderous threats against the Lord's disciples. He went to the high priest [2]and asked him for letters to the synagogues in Damascus, so that if he found any there who belonged to the Way, whether men or women, he might take them as prisoners to Jerusalem.

Acts 12 [1]It was about this time that King Herod arrested some who belonged to the church, intending to persecute them. . . . [3]When he saw that this pleased the Jews, he proceeded to seize Peter also. This happened during the Feast of Unleavened Bread. [4]After arresting him, he put him in prison, handing him over to be guarded by four squads of four soldiers each. Herod intended to bring him out for public trial after the Passover.

Acts 16 [23]After they had been severely flogged, they were thrown into prison, and the jailer was commanded to guard them carefully. [24]Upon receiving such orders, he put them in the inner cell and fastened their feet in the stocks.

Eph 3 [1]For this reason I, Paul, the prisoner of Christ Jesus for the sake of you Gentiles . . .

2 Tim 2 [8]Remember Jesus Christ, raised from the dead, descended from David. This is my gospel, [9]for which I am suffering even to the point of being chained like a criminal. But God's word is not chained.

Rev 2 [10]"Do not be afraid of what you are about to suffer. I tell you, the devil will put some of you in prison to test you, and you will suffer persecution for ten days. Be faithful, even to the point of death, and I will give you the crown of life."

5. Martyrdom of Believers

Acts 7 [54]When they heard this, they were furious and gnashed their teeth at him. [55]But Stephen, full of the Holy Spirit, looked up to heaven and saw the glory of God, and Jesus standing at the right hand of God. [56]"Look," he said, "I see heaven open and the Son of Man standing at the right hand of God."

[57]At this they covered their ears and, yelling at the top of their voices, they all rushed at him, [58]dragged him out of the city and began to stone him. Meanwhile, the witnesses laid their clothes at the feet of a young man named Saul.

[59]While they were stoning him, Stephen prayed, "Lord Jesus, receive my spirit." [60]Then he fell on his knees and cried out, "Lord, do not hold this sin against them." When he had said this, he fell asleep.

Acts 12 [2]He had James, the brother of John, put to death with the sword.

Rev 2 [13]"I know where you live—where Satan has his throne. Yet you remain true to my name. You did not renounce your faith in me, even in the days of Antipas, my faithful witness, who was put to death in your city—where Satan lives."

Rev 6 [9]When he opened the fifth seal, I saw under the altar the souls of those who had been slain because of the word of God and the testimony they had maintained. [10]They called out in a loud voice, "How long, Sovereign Lord, holy and true, until you judge the inhabitants of the earth and avenge our blood?" [11]Then each of them was given a white robe, and they were told to wait a little longer, until the number of their fellow servants and brothers who were to be killed as they had been was completed.

6. Opposition to the Gospel

Acts 13 [8]But Elymas the sorcerer (for that is what his name means) opposed them and tried to turn the proconsul from the faith.

Acts 14 [2]But the Jews who refused to believe stirred up the Gentiles and poisoned their minds against the brothers.

Acts 17 [5]But the Jews were jealous; so they rounded up some bad characters from the marketplace, formed a mob and started a riot in the city. They rushed to Jason's house in search of Paul and Silas in order to bring them out to the crowd. [6]But when they did not find them, they dragged Jason and some other brothers before the city officials, shouting: "These men who have caused trouble all over the world have now come here, [7]and Jason has welcomed them into his house. They are all defying Caesar's decrees, saying that there is another king, one called Jesus." [8]When they heard this, the crowd and the city officials were thrown into turmoil. [9]Then they made Jason and the others post bond and let them go.

Acts 17 [13]When the Jews in Thessalonica learned that Paul was preaching the word of God at Berea, they went there too, agitating the crowds and stirring them up.

1 Thess 2 [14]For you, brothers, became imitators of God's churches in Judea, which are in Christ Jesus: You suffered from your own countrymen the same things those churches suffered from the Jews, [15]who killed the Lord Jesus and the prophets and also drove us out. They displease God and are hostile to all men [16]in their effort to keep us from speaking to the Gentiles so that they may be saved. In this way they always heap up their sins to the limit. The wrath of God has come upon them at last.

2 Tim 4 [14]Alexander the metalworker did me a great deal of harm. The Lord will repay him for what he has done. [15]You too should be on your guard against him, because he strongly opposed our message.

7. Persecution of Believers

Acts 8 [1]And Saul was there, giving approval to his death. On that day a great persecution broke out against the church at Jerusalem, and all except the apostles were scattered throughout Judea and Samaria. [2]Godly men buried Stephen and mourned deeply for him. [3]But Saul began to destroy the church. Going from house to house, he dragged off men and women and put them in prison.

Acts 13 [49]The word of the Lord spread through the whole region. [50]But the Jews incited the God-fearing women of high standing and the leading men of the city. They stirred up persecution against Paul and Barnabas, and expelled them from their region.

1 Thess 3 [7]Therefore, brothers, in all our distress and persecution we were encouraged about you because of your faith.

2 Thess 1 [4]Therefore, among God's churches we boast about your perseverance and faith in all the persecutions and trials you are enduring.

Heb 10 [33]Sometimes you were publicly exposed to insult and persecution; at other times you stood side by side with those who were so treated.

Rev 12 [17]Then the dragon was enraged at the woman and went off to make war against the rest of her offspring—those who obey God's commandments and hold to the testimony of Jesus.

8. Physical Punishment of Believers

Acts 5 [40]His speech persuaded them. They called the apostles in and had them flogged. Then they ordered them not to speak in the name of Jesus, and let them go.

Acts 16 [19]When the owners of the slave girl realized that their hope of making money was gone, they seized Paul and Silas and dragged them into the marketplace to face the authorities. [20]They brought them before the magistrates and said, "These men are Jews, and are throwing our city into an uproar [21]by advocating customs unlawful for us Romans to accept or practice."

[22]The crowd joined in the attack against Paul and Silas, and the magistrates ordered them to be stripped and beaten.

9. Suffering of Believers

1 Thess 1 [6]You became imitators of us and of the Lord; in spite of severe suffering, you welcomed the message with the joy given by the Holy Spirit.

1 Thess 2 [2]We had previously suffered and been insulted in Philippi, as you know, but with the help of our God we dared to tell you his gospel in spite of strong opposition.

1 Thess 2 [14]For you, brothers, became imitators of God's churches in Judea, which are in Christ Jesus: You suffered from your own countrymen the same things those churches suffered from the Jews. . . .

2 Tim 1 [12]That is why I am suffering as I am. Yet I am not ashamed, because I know whom I have believed, and am convinced that he is able to guard what I have entrusted to him for that day.

Rev 2 [10]"Do not be afraid of what you are about to suffer. I tell you, the devil will put some of you in prison to test you, and you will suffer persecution for ten days. Be faithful, even to the point of death, and I will give you the crown of life."

10. Threats on the Lives of Believers

Acts 9 [23]After many days had gone by, the Jews conspired to kill him, [24]but Saul learned of their plan. Day and night they kept close watch on the city gates in order to kill him.

Acts 9 [28]So Saul stayed with them and moved about freely in Jerusalem, speaking boldly in the name of the Lord. [29]He talked and debated with the Grecian Jews, but they tried to kill him.

Acts 14 [19]Then some Jews came from Antioch and Iconium and won the crowd over. They stoned Paul and dragged him outside the city, thinking he was dead.

Acts 21 [27]When the seven days were nearly over, some Jews from the province of Asia saw Paul at the temple. They stirred up the whole crowd and seized him, [28]shouting, "Men of Israel, help us! This is the man who teaches all men everywhere against our people and our law and this place. And besides, he has brought Greeks into the temple area and defiled this holy place." 29(They had previously seen Trophimus the Ephesian in the city with Paul and assumed that Paul had brought him into the temple area.)

30The whole city was aroused, and the people came running from all directions. Seizing Paul, they dragged him from the temple, and immediately the gates were shut. 31While they were trying to kill him, news reached the commander of the Roman troops that the whole city of Jerusalem was in an uproar. 32He at once took some officers and soldiers and ran down to the crowd. When the rioters saw the commander and his soldiers, they stopped beating Paul.

Acts 23 12The next morning the Jews formed a conspiracy and bound themselves with an oath not to eat or drink until they had killed Paul. 13More than forty men were involved in this plot. 14They went to the chief priests and elders and said, "We have taken a solemn oath not to eat anything until we have killed Paul. 15Now then, you and the Sanhedrin petition the commander to bring him before you on the pretext of wanting more accurate information about his case. We are ready to kill him before he gets here."

11. Verbal Abuse of Believers

Acts 2 4All of them were filled with the Holy Spirit and began to speak in other tongues as the Spirit enabled them. . . .

13Some, however, made fun of them and said, "They have had too much wine."

Acts 17 32When they heard about the resurrection of the dead, some of them sneered, but others said, "We want to hear you again on this subject."

Acts 18 6But when the Jews opposed Paul and became abusive, he shook out his clothes in protest and said to them, "Your blood be on your own heads! I am clear of my responsibility. From now on I will go to the Gentiles."

Acts 19 8Paul entered the synagogue and spoke boldly there for three months, arguing persuasively about the kingdom of God. 9But some of them became obstinate; they refused to believe and publicly maligned the Way. So Paul left them. He took the disciples with him and had discussions daily in the lecture hall of Tyrannus.

Acts 19 23About that time there arose a great disturbance about the Way. 24A silversmith named Demetrius, who made silver shrines of Artemis, brought in no little business for the craftsmen. 25He called them together, along with the workmen in related trades, and said: "Men, you know we receive a good income from this business. 26And you see and hear how this fellow Paul has convinced and led astray large numbers of people here in Ephesus and in practically the whole province of Asia. He says that man-made gods are no gods at all. 27There is danger not only that our trade will lose its good name, but also that the temple of the great goddess Artemis will be discredited, and the goddess herself, who is worshiped throughout the province of Asia and the world, will be robbed of her divine majesty."

28When they heard this, they were furious and began shouting: "Great is Artemis of the Ephesians!" 29Soon the whole city was in an uproar. The people seized Gaius Aristarchus, Paul's traveling companions from Macedonia, and rushed as one man into the theater. 30Paul wanted to appear before the crowd, but the disciples would not let him. 31Even some of the officials of the province, friends of Paul, sent him a message begging him not to venture into the theater.

32The assembly was in confusion: Some were shouting one thing, some another. Most of the people did not even know why they were there. 33The Jews pushed Alexander to the front, and some of the crowd shouted instructions to him. He motioned for silence in order to make a defense before the people. 34But when they realized he was a Jew, they all shouted in unison for about two hours: "Great is Artemis of the Ephesians!"

1 Pet 4 4They think it strange that you do not plunge with them into the same flood of dissipation, and they heap abuse on you.

Rev 2 9"I know your afflictions and your poverty—yet you are rich! I know the slander of those who say they are Jews and are not, but are a synagogue of Satan."

C. Personal and Social Problems in the Church

1. Believers Boasting in Certain Men

1 Cor 3 18Do not deceive yourselves. If any one of you thinks he is wise by the standards of this age, he should become a "fool" so that he may become wise. 19For the wisdom of this world is foolishness in God's sight. As it is written: "He catches the wise in their craftiness"; 20and again, "The Lord knows that the thoughts of the wise are futile." 21So then, no more boasting about men! All things are yours, 22whether Paul or Apollos or Cephas or the world or life or death or the present or the future—all are yours. . . .

1 Cor 4 6Now, brothers, I have applied these things to myself and Apollos for your benefit, so that you may learn from us the meaning of the saying, "Do not go beyond what is written." Then you will not take pride in one man over against another. 7For who makes you different from anyone else? What do you have that you did not receive? And if you did receive it, why do you boast as though you did not? . . .

18Some of you have become arrogant, as if I were not coming to you. 19But I will come to you very soon, if the Lord is willing, and then I will find out not only how these arrogant people are talking, but what power they have. 20For the kingdom of God is not a matter of talk but of power. 21What do you prefer? Shall I come to you with a whip, or in love and with a gentle spirit?

2. Believers Judging One Another

Rom 14 13Therefore let us stop passing judgment on one another. Instead, make up your mind not to put any stumbling block or obstacle in your brother's way.

3. Believers' Family Cares

Eph 6 1Children, obey your parents in the Lord, for this is right. 2"Honor your father and mother"—which is the first commandment with a promise—3"that it may go well with you and that you may enjoy long life on the earth."

4Fathers, do not exasperate your children; instead, bring them up in the training and instruction of the Lord.

4. Believers' Marital Problems

a) Strong Desires of Unmarried Christians

1 Cor 7 8Now to the unmarried and the widows I say: It is good for them to stay unmarried, as I am. 9But if they cannot control themselves, they should marry, for it is better to marry than to burn with passion.

b) Engagement Concerns of Christians

1 Cor 7 36If anyone thinks he is acting improperly toward the virgin he is engaged to, and if she is getting along in years and he feels he ought to marry, he should do as he wants. He is not sinning. They should get married. 37But the man who has settled the matter in his own mind, who is under no compulsion but has control over his own will, and who has made up his mind not to marry the virgin—this man also does the right thing. 38So then, he who marries the virgin does right, but he who does not marry her does even better.

c) Sexual Needs of Married Christians

1 Cor 7 2But since there is so much immorality, each man should have his own wife, and each woman her own husband. 3The husband should fulfill his marital duty to his wife, and likewise the wife to her husband. 4The wife's body does not belong to her alone but also to her husband. In the same way, the husband's body does not belong to him alone but also to his wife. 5Do not deprive each other except by mutual consent and for a time, so that you may devote yourselves to prayer. Then come together again so that Satan will not tempt you because of your lack of self-control.

d) The Unbelieving Partner of a Christian

1 Cor 7 10To the married I give this command (not I, but the Lord): A wife must not separate from her husband. 11But if she does, she must remain unmarried or else be reconciled to her husband. And a husband must not divorce his wife.

12To the rest I say this (I, not the Lord): If any brother has a wife who is not a believer and she is willing to live with him, he must not divorce her. 13And if a woman has a husband who is not a believer and he is willing to live with her, she must not divorce him. 14For the unbelieving husband has been sanctified through his wife, and the unbelieving wife has been sanctified through her believing husband. Otherwise your children would be unclean, but as it is, they are holy.

15But if the unbeliever leaves, let him do so. A believing man or woman is not bound in such circumstances; God has called us to live in peace. 16How do you know, wife, whether you will save your husband? Or, how do you know, husband, whether you will save your wife?

1 Pet 3 1Wives, in the same way be submissive to your husbands so that, if any of them do not believe the word, they may be won over without words by the behavior of their wives, 2when they see the purity and reverence of your lives. 3Your beauty should not come from outward adornment, such as braided hair and the wearing of gold jewelry and fine clothes. 4Instead, it should be that of your inner self, the unfading beauty of a gentle and quiet spirit, which is of great worth in God's sight. 5For this is the way the holy women of the past who put their hope in God used to make themselves beautiful. They were submissive to their own husbands, 6like Sarah, who obeyed Abraham and called him her master. You are her daughters if you do what is right and do not give way to fear.

5. Class Problems among Believers

a) Masters and Slaves

Eph 6 5Slaves, obey your earthly masters with respect and fear, and with sincerity of heart, just as you would obey Christ. 6Obey them not only to win their favor when their eye is on you, but like slaves of Christ, doing the will of God from your heart. 7Serve wholeheartedly, as if you were serving the Lord, not men, 8because you know that the Lord will reward everyone for whatever good he does, whether he is slave or free.

9And masters, treat your slaves in the same way. Do not threaten them, since you know that he who is both their Master and yours is in heaven, and there is no favoritism with him.

1 Pet 2 18Slaves, submit yourselves to your masters with all respect, not only to those who are good and considerate, but also to those who are harsh. 19For it is commendable if a man bears up under the pain of unjust suffering because he is conscious of God. 20But how is it to your credit if you receive a beating for doing wrong and endure it? But if you suffer for doing good and you endure it, this is commendable before God. 21To this you were called, because Christ suffered for you, leaving you an example, that you should follow in his steps.

b) Civic Officials and Citizens

Rom 13 1Everyone must submit himself to the governing authorities, for there is no authority except that which God has established. The authorities that exist have been established by God. 2Consequently, he who rebels against the authority is rebelling against what God has instituted, and those who do so will bring judgment on themselves. 3For rulers hold no terror for those who do right, but for those who do wrong. Do you want to be free from fear of the one in authority? Then do what is right and he will commend you. 4For he is God's servant to do you good. But if you do wrong, be afraid, for he does not bear the sword for nothing. He is God's servant, an agent of wrath to bring punishment on the wrongdoer. 5Therefore, it is necessary to submit to the authorities, not only because of possible punishment but also because of conscience.

1 Pet 2 13Submit yourselves for the Lord's sake to every authority instituted among men: whether to the king, as the supreme authority, 14or to governors, who are sent by him to punish those who do wrong and to commend those who do right. 15For it is God's will that by doing good you should silence the ignorant talk of foolish men.

c) The Rich and the Poor

James 2 1My brothers, as believers in our glorious Lord Jesus Christ, don't show favoritism. 2Suppose a man comes into your meeting wearing a gold ring and fine clothes, and a poor man in shabby clothes also comes in. 3If you show special attention to the man wearing fine clothes and say, "Here's a good seat for you," but say to the poor man, "You stand there" or "Sit on the floor by my feet," 4have you not discriminated among yourselves and become judges with evil thoughts?

5Listen, my dear brothers: Has not God chosen those who are poor in the eyes of the world to be rich in faith and to inherit the kingdom he promised those who love him? 6But you have insulted the poor. Is it not the rich who are exploiting you? Are they not the ones who are dragging you into court? 7Are they not the ones who are slandering the noble name of him to whom you belong?

8If you really keep the royal law found in Scripture, "Love your neighbor as yourself," you are doing right. 9But if you show favoritism, you sin and are convicted by the law as lawbreakers.

James 5 1Now listen, you rich people, weep and wail because of the misery that is coming upon you. 2Your wealth has rotted, and moths have eaten your clothes. 3Your gold and silver are corroded. Their corrosion will testify against you and eat your flesh like fire. You have hoarded wealth in the last days. 4Look! The wages you failed to pay the workmen who mowed your fields are crying out against you. The cries of the harvesters have reached the ears of the Lord Almighty. 5You have lived on earth in luxury and self-indulgence. You have fattened yourselves in the day of slaughter. 6You have condemned and murdered innocent men, who were not opposing you.

6. Divisiveness among Believers

1 Cor 1 10I appeal to you, brothers, in the name of our Lord Jesus Christ, that all of you agree with one another so that there may be no divisions among you and that you may be perfectly united in mind and thought. 11My brothers, some from Chloe's household have informed me that there are quarrels among you. 12What I mean is this: One of you says, "I follow Paul"; another, "I follow Apollos"; another, "I follow Cephas"; still another, "I follow Christ."

1 Cor 3 1Brothers, I could not address you as spiritual but as worldly—mere infants in Christ. 2I gave you milk, not solid food, for you were not yet ready for it. Indeed, you are still not ready. 3You are still worldly. For since there is jealousy and quarreling among you, are you not worldly? Are you not acting like mere men? 4For when one says, "I follow Paul," and another, "I follow Apollos," are you not mere men?

1 Cor 11 18In the first place, I hear that when you come together as a church, there are divisions among you, and to some extent I believe it.

7. Idleness among Believers

2 Thess 3 11We hear that some among you are idle. They are not busy; they are busybodies.

1 Tim 5 13Besides, they get into the habit of being idle and going about from house to house. And not only do they become idlers, but also gossips and busybodies, saying things they ought not to.

8. Lawsuits between Believers

1 Cor 6 1If any of you has a dispute with another, dare he take it before the ungodly for judgment instead of before the saints? 2Do you not know that the saints will judge the world? And if you are to judge the world, are you not competent to judge trivial cases? 3Do you not know that we will judge angels? How much more the things of this life! 4Therefore, if you have disputes about such matters, appoint as judges even men of little account in the church! 5I say this to shame you. Is it possible that there is nobody among you wise enough to judge a dispute between believers? 6But instead, one brother goes to law against another—and this in front of unbelievers!

7The very fact that you have lawsuits among you means you have been completely defeated already. Why not rather be wronged? Why not rather be cheated? 8Instead, you yourselves cheat and do wrong, and you do this to your brothers.

9. Quarrelsomeness among Believers

Acts 15 [36]Some time later Paul said to Barnabas, "Let us go back and visit the brothers in all the towns where we preached the word of the Lord and see how they are doing." [37]Barnabas wanted to take John, also called Mark, with them, [38]but Paul did not think it wise to take him, because he had deserted them in Pamphylia and had not continued with them in the work. [39]They had such a sharp disagreement that they parted company. Barnabas took Mark and sailed for Cyprus, [40]but Paul chose Silas and left, commended by the brothers to the grace of the Lord.
Gal 5 [15]If you keep on biting and devouring each other, watch out or you will be destroyed by each other.
Phil 4 [2]I plead with Euodia and I plead with Syntyche to agree with each other in the Lord.
2 Tim 2 [14]Keep reminding them of these things. Warn them before God against quarreling about words; it is of no value, and only ruins those who listen.
2 Tim 2 [24]And the Lord's servant must not quarrel; instead, he must be kind to everyone, able to teach, not resentful. [25]Those who oppose him he must gently instruct, in the hope that God will grant them repentance leading them to a knowledge of the truth, [26]and that they will come to their senses and escape from the trap of the devil, who has taken them captive to do his will.

10. Race Conflict among Believers

Acts 11 [2]So when Peter went up to Jerusalem, the circumcised believers criticized him [3]and said, "You went into the house of uncircumcised men and ate with them."
Gal 2 [11]When Peter came to Antioch, I opposed him to his face, because he was clearly in the wrong. [12]Before certain men came from James, he used to eat with the Gentiles. But when they arrived, he began to draw back and separate himself from the Gentiles because he was afraid of those who belonged to the circumcision group. [13]The other Jews joined him in his hypocrisy, so that by their hypocrisy even Barnabas was led astray.

[14]When I saw that they were not acting in line with the truth of the gospel, I said to Peter in front of them all, "You are a Jew, yet you live like a Gentile and not like a Jew. How is it, then, that you force Gentiles to follow Jewish customs?"

11. Stubbornness in Believers' Interpersonal Relationships

Matt 18 [15]"If your brother sins against you, go and show him his fault, just between the two of you. If he listens to you, you have won your brother over. [16]But if he will not listen, take one or two others along, so that 'every matter may be established by the testimony of two or three witnesses.' [17]If he refuses to listen to them, tell it to the church; and if he refuses to listen even to the church, treat him as you would a pagan or a tax collector."

D. Moral Problems in the Church

1. Moral Problems Characterize Believers at Salvation

1 Cor 6 [9]Do you not know that the wicked will not inherit the kingdom of God? Do not be deceived: Neither the sexually immoral nor idolaters nor adulterers nor male prostitutes nor homosexual offenders [10]nor thieves nor the greedy nor drunkards nor slanderers nor swindlers will inherit the kingdom of God. [11]And that is what some of you were. But you were washed, you were sanctified, you were justified in the name of the Lord Jesus Christ and by the Spirit of our God.
Titus 3 [3]At one time we too were foolish, disobedient, deceived and enslaved by all kinds of passions and pleasures. We lived in malice and envy, being hated and hating one another.

2. Moral Problems Pollute Present Christian Experience

2 Cor 12 [20]For I am afraid that when I come I may not find you as I want you to be, and you may not find me as you want me to be. I fear that there may be quarreling, jealousy, outbursts of anger, factions, slander, gossip, arrogance and disorder. [21]I am afraid that when I come again my God will humble me before you, and I will be grieved over many who have sinned earlier and have not repented of the impurity, sexual sin and debauchery in which they have indulged.

3. Believers Are Exhorted to Put Off or Avoid Moral Problems

Rom 13 [13]Let us behave decently, as in the daytime, not in orgies and drunkenness, not in sexual immorality and debauchery, not in dissension and jealousy.
Gal 5 [16]So I say, live by the Spirit, and you will not gratify the desires of the sinful nature. [17]For the sinful nature desires what is contrary to the Spirit, and the Spirit what is contrary to the sinful nature. They are in conflict with each other, so that you do not do what you want. [18]But if you are led by the Spirit, you are not under law.

[19]The acts of the sinful nature are obvious: sexual immorality, impurity and debauchery; [20]idolatry and witchcraft; hatred, discord, jealousy, fits of rage, selfish ambition, dissensions, factions [21]and envy; drunkenness, orgies, and the like. I warn you, as I did before, that those who live like this will not inherit the kingdom of God.
Eph 4 [25]Therefore each of you must put off falsehood and speak truthfully to his neighbor, for we are all members of one body. [26]"In your anger do not sin": Do not let the sun go down while you are still angry, [27]and do not give the devil a foothold. [28]He who has been stealing must steal no longer, but must work, doing something useful with his own hands, that he may have something to share with those in need.

[29]Do not let any unwholesome talk come out of your mouths, but only what is helpful for building others up according to their needs, that it may benefit those who listen. [30]And do not grieve the Holy Spirit of God, with whom you were sealed for the day of redemption. [31]Get rid of all bitterness, rage and anger, brawling and slander, along with every form of malice.
Eph 5 [3]But among you there must not be even a hint of sexual immorality, or of any kind of impurity, or of greed, because these are improper for God's holy people. [4]Nor should there be obscenity, foolish talk or coarse joking, which are out of place, but rather thanksgiving.
Phil 2 [3]Do nothing out of selfish ambition or vain conceit, but in humility consider others better than yourselves.
Phil 2 [14]Do everything without complaining or arguing. . . .
Col 3 [5]Put to death, therefore, whatever belongs to your earthly nature: sexual immorality, impurity, lust, evil desires and greed, which is idolatry. [6]Because of these, the wrath of God is coming. [7]You used to walk in these ways, in the life you once lived. [8]But now you must rid yourselves of all such things as these: anger, rage, malice, slander, and filthy language from your lips. [9]Do not lie to each other, since you have taken off your old self with its practices. . . .
2 Tim 3 [1]But mark this: There will be terrible times in the last days. [2]People will be lovers of themselves, lovers of money, boastful, proud, abusive, disobedient to their parents, ungrateful, unholy, [3]without love, unforgiving, slanderous, without self-control, brutal, not lovers of the good, [4]treacherous, rash, conceited, lovers of pleasure rather than lovers of God—[5]having a form of godliness but denying its power. Have nothing to do with them.

[6]They are the kind who worm their way into homes and gain control over weak-willed women, who are loaded down with sins and are swayed by all kinds of evil desires, [7]always learning but never able to acknowledge the truth. [8]Just as Jannes and Jambres opposed Moses, so also these men oppose the truth—men of depraved minds, who, as far as the faith is concerned, are rejected. [9]But they will not get very far because, as in the case of those men, their folly will be clear to everyone.
1 Pet 2 [1]Therefore, rid yourselves of all malice and all deceit, hypocrisy, envy, and slander of every kind. . . .

[11]Dear friends, I urge you, as aliens and strangers in the world, to abstain from sinful desires, which war against your soul.
1 Pet 4 [1]Therefore, since Christ suffered in his body, arm your-

selves also with the same attitude, because he who has suffered in his body is done with sin. [2]As a result, he does not live the rest of his earthly life for evil human desires, but rather for the will of God. [3]For you have spent enough time in the past doing what pagans choose to do—living in debauchery, lust, drunkenness, orgies, carousing and detestable idolatry.
Rev 3 [1]"To the angel of the church in Sardis write: These are the words of him who holds the seven spirits of God and the seven stars. I know your deeds; you have a reputation of being alive, but you are dead. [2]Wake up! Strengthen what remains and is about to die, for I have not found your deeds complete in the sight of my God. [3]Remember, therefore, what you have received and heard; obey it, and repent. But if you do not wake up, I will come like a thief, and you will not know at what time I will come to you."
Rev 3 [15]"I know your deeds, that you are neither cold nor hot. I wish you were either one or the other! [16]So, because you are lukewarm—neither hot nor cold—I am about to spit you out of my mouth. [17]You say, 'I am rich; I have acquired wealth and do not need a thing.' But you do not realize that you are wretched, pitiful, poor, blind and naked. [18]I counsel you to buy from me gold refined in the fire, so you can become rich; and white clothes to wear, so you can cover your shameful nakedness; and salve to put on your eyes, so you can see."

E. Spiritual and Religious Problems in the Church

1. Personal and Subjective Spiritual Problems

a) Apostasy

Heb 3 [12]See to it, brothers, that none of you has a sinful, unbelieving heart that turns away from the living God.
Heb 6 [4]It is impossible for those who have once been enlightened, who have tasted the heavenly gift, who have shared in the Holy Spirit, [5]who have tasted the goodness of the word of God and the powers of the coming age, [6]if they fall away, to be brought back to repentance, because to their loss they are crucifying the Son of God all over again and subjecting him to public disgrace.

b) The Continuing Struggle with Sin

Rom 7 [14]We know that the law is spiritual; but I am unspiritual, sold as a slave to sin. [15]I do not understand what I do. For what I want to do I do not do, but what I hate I do. [16]And if I do what I do not want to do, I agree that the law is good. [17]As it is, it is no longer I myself who do it, but it is sin living in me. [18]I know that nothing good lives in me, that is, in my sinful nature. For I have the desire to do what is good, but I cannot carry it out. [19]For what I do is not the good I want to do; no, the evil I do not want to do—this I keep on doing. [20]Now if I do what I do not want to do, it is no longer I who do it, but it is sin living in me that does it.

[21]So I find this law at work: When I want to do good, evil is right there with me. [22]For in my inner being I delight in God's law; [23]but I see another law at work in the members of my body, waging war against the law of my mind and making me a prisoner of the law of sin at work within my members. [24]What a wretched man I am! Who will rescue me from this body of death? [25]Thanks be to God—through Jesus Christ our Lord!

So then, I myself in my mind am a slave to God's law, but in the sinful nature a slave to the law of sin.
Heb 3 [13]But encourage one another daily, as long as it is called Today, so that none of you may be hardened by sin's deceitfulness.

c) Desertion

Gal 1 [6]I am astonished that you are so quickly deserting the one who called you by the grace of Christ and are turning to a different gospel—[7]which is really no gospel at all. Evidently some people are throwing you into confusion and are trying to pervert the gospel of Christ. [8]But even if we or an angel from heaven should preach a gospel other than the one we preached to you, let him be eternally condemned! [9]As we have already said, so now I say again: If anybody is preaching to you a gospel other than what you accepted, let him be eternally condemned!
2 Tim 1 [15]You know that everyone in the province of Asia has deserted me, including Phygelus and Hermogenes.
2 Tim 4 [10]for Demas, because he loved this world, has deserted me and has gone to Thessalonica. Crescens has gone to Galatia, and Titus to Dalmatia.
2 Tim 4 [16]At my first defense, no one came to my support, but everyone deserted me. May it not be held against them.

d) A Faulty Prayer Life

James 4 [2]You want something but don't get it. You kill and covet, but you cannot have what you want. You quarrel and fight. You do not have, because you do not ask God. [3]When you ask, you do not receive, because you ask with wrong motives, that you may spend what you get on your pleasures.

e) Friendship with the World

James 4 [1]What causes fights and quarrels among you? Don't they come from your desires that battle within you? [2]You want something but don't get it. You kill and covet, but you cannot have what you want. You quarrel and fight. You do not have, because you do not ask God. [3]When you ask, you do not receive, because you ask with wrong motives, that you may spend what you get on your pleasures.

[4]You adulterous people, don't you know that friendship with the world is hatred toward God? Anyone who chooses to be a friend of the world becomes an enemy of God. [5]Or do you think Scripture says without reason that the spirit he caused to live in us envies intensely? [6]But he gives us more grace. That is why Scripture says: "God opposes the proud but gives grace to the humble."

f) A Lack of Faith

James 1 [6]But when he asks, he must believe and not doubt, because he who doubts is like a wave of the sea, blown and tossed by the wind. [7]That man should not think he will receive anything from the Lord; [8]he is a double-minded man, unstable in all he does.

g) The Lack of Spiritual Decisiveness

Rev 2 [20]"Nevertheless, I have this against you: You tolerate that woman Jezebel, who calls herself a prophetess. By her teaching she misleads my servants into sexual immorality and the eating of food sacrificed to idols."

h) The Lack of Spiritual Discernment

Rev 2 [14]"Nevertheless, I have a few things against you: You have people there who hold to the teaching of Balaam, who taught Balak to entice the Israelites to sin by eating food sacrificed to idols and by committing sexual immorality. [15]Likewise you also have those who hold to the teaching of the Nicolaitans."
Rev 3 [17]"You say, 'I am rich; I have acquired wealth and do not need a thing.' But you do not realize that you are wretched, pitiful, poor, blind and naked."

i) The Loss of Spiritual Fervency

Rev 2 [4]"Yet I hold this against you: You have forsaken your first love. [5]Remember the height from which you have fallen! Repent and do the things you did at first. If you do not repent, I will come to you and remove your lampstand from its place."
Rev 3 [15]"I know your deeds, that you are neither cold nor hot. I wish you were either one or the other! [16]So, because you are lukewarm—neither hot nor cold—I am about to spit you out of my mouth."

j) The Neglect of Corporate Worship

Heb 10 [25]Let us not give up meeting together, as some are in the habit of doing, but let us encourage one another—and all the more as you see the Day approaching.

k) The Neglect of Doing Right

Heb 13 [16]And do not forget to do good and to share with others, for with such sacrifices God is pleased.

l) Selfish Ambition

2 Cor 2 [17]Unlike so many, we do not peddle the word of God for profit. On the contrary, in Christ we speak before God with sincerity, like men sent from God.

Phil 1 [15]It is true that some preach Christ out of envy and rivalry, but others out of goodwill. [16]The latter do so in love, knowing that I am put here for the defense of the gospel. [17]The former preach Christ out of selfish ambition, not sincerely, supposing that they can stir up trouble for me while I am in chains. [18]But what does it matter? The important thing is that in every way, whether from false motives or true, Christ is preached. And because of this I rejoice.

Yes, and I will continue to rejoice. . . .

1 Tim 6 [3]If anyone teaches false doctrines and does not agree to the sound instruction of our Lord Jesus Christ and to godly teaching, [4]he is conceited and understands nothing. He has an unhealthy interest in controversies and quarrels about words that result in envy, strife, malicious talk, evil suspicions [5]and constant friction between men of corrupt mind, who have been robbed of the truth and who think that godliness is a means to financial gain. . . .

[10]For the love of money is a root of all kinds of evil. Some people, eager for money, have wandered from the faith and pierced themselves with many griefs.

3 John [9]I wrote to the church, but Diotrephes, who loves to be first, will have nothing to do with us. [10]So if I come, I will call attention to what he is doing, gossiping maliciously about us. Not satisfied with that, he refuses to welcome the brothers. He also stops those who want to do so and puts them out of the church.

m) Spiritual Ignorance, Misdirection, and Weakness

1 Thess 5 [14]And we urge you, brothers, warn those who are idle, encourage the timid, help the weak, be patient with everyone.

Heb 2 [18]Because he himself suffered when he was tempted, he is able to help those who are being tempted.

Heb 4 [15]For we do not have a high priest who is unable to sympathize with our weaknesses, but we have one who has been tempted in every way, just as we are—yet was without sin.

Heb 5 [2]He is able to deal gently with those who are ignorant and are going astray, since he himself is subject to weakness.

n) Spiritual and Theological Immaturity

Eph 4 [13]until we all reach unity in the faith and in the knowledge of the Son of God and become mature, attaining to the whole measure of the fullness of Christ.

[14]Then we will no longer be infants, tossed back and forth by the waves, and blown here and there by every wind of teaching and by the cunning and craftiness of men in their deceitful scheming. [15]Instead, speaking the truth in love, we will in all things grow up into him who is the Head, that is, Christ.

Heb 5 [11]We have much to say about this, but it is hard to explain because you are slow to learn. [12]In fact, though by this time you ought to be teachers, you need someone to teach you the elementary truths of God's word all over again. You need milk, not solid food! [13]Anyone who lives on milk, being still an infant, is not acquainted with the teaching about righteousness. [14]But solid food is for the mature, who by constant use have trained themselves to distinguish good from evil.

Rev 3 [2]"Wake up! Strengthen what remains and is about to die, for I have not found your deeds complete in the sight of my God. [3]Remember, therefore, what you have received and heard; obey it, and repent. But if you do not wake up, I will come like a thief, and you will not know at what time I will come to you."

2. External and Objective Spiritual Problems

a) Abused Governmental Authority

Rev 13 [11]Then I saw another beast, coming out of the earth. He had two horns like a lamb, but he spoke like a dragon. [12]He exercised all the authority of the first beast on his behalf, and made the earth and its inhabitants worship the first beast, whose fatal wound had been healed. [13]And he performed great and miraculous signs, even causing fire to come down from heaven to earth in full view of men. [14]Because of the signs he was given power to do on behalf of the first beast, he deceived the inhabitants of the earth. He ordered them to set up an image in honor of the beast who was wounded by the sword and yet lived. [15]He was given power to give breath to the image of the first beast, so that it could speak and cause all who refused to worship the image to be killed. [16]He also forced everyone, small and great, rich and poor, free and slave, to receive a mark on his right hand or on his forehead, [17]so that no one could buy or sell unless he had the mark, which is the name of the beast or the number of his name.

[18]This calls for wisdom. If anyone has insight, let him calculate the number of the beast, for it is man's number. His number is 666.

b) Antichrist(s)

2 Thess 2 [1]Concerning the coming of our Lord Jesus Christ and our being gathered to him, we ask you, brothers, [2]not to become easily unsettled or alarmed by some prophecy, report or letter supposed to have come from us, saying that the day of the Lord has already come. [3]Don't let anyone deceive you in any way, for that day will not come until the rebellion occurs and the man of lawlessness is revealed, the man doomed to destruction. [4]He will oppose and will exalt himself over everything that is called God or is worshiped, so that he sets himself up in God's temple, proclaiming himself to be God.

[5]Don't you remember that when I was with you I used to tell you these things? [6]And now you know what is holding him back, so that he may be revealed at the proper time. [7]For the secret power of lawlessness is already at work; but the one who now holds it back will continue to do so till he is taken out of the way. [8]And then the lawless one will be revealed, whom the Lord Jesus will overthrow with the breath of his mouth and destroy by the splendor of his coming. [9]The coming of the lawless one will be in accordance with the work of Satan displayed in all kinds of counterfeit miracles, signs and wonders, [10]and in every sort of evil that deceives those who are perishing. They perish because they refused to love the truth and so be saved.

1 John 2 [18]Dear children, this is the last hour; and as you have heard that the antichrist is coming, even now many antichrists have come. This is how we know it is the last hour.

1 John 4 [3]but every spirit that does not acknowledge Jesus is not from God. This is the spirit of the antichrist, which you have heard is coming and even now is already in the world.

c) Evil Spiritual Powers

Rom 8 [37]No, in all these things we are more than conquerors through him who loved us. [38]For I am convinced that neither death nor life, neither angels nor demons, neither the present nor the future, nor any powers, [39]neither height nor depth, nor anything else in all creation, will be able to separate us from the love of God that is in Christ Jesus our Lord.

1 Cor 10 [20]No, but the sacrifices of pagans are offered to demons, not to God, and I do not want you to be participants with demons. [21]You cannot drink the cup of the Lord and the cup of demons too; you cannot have a part in both the Lord's table and the table of demons. [22]Are we trying to arouse the Lord's jealousy? Are we stronger than he?

Eph 6 [10]Finally, be strong in the Lord and in his mighty power. [11]Put on the full armor of God so that you can take your stand against the devil's schemes. [12]For our struggle is not against flesh and blood, but against the rulers, against the authorities, against the powers of this dark world and against the spiritual forces of evil in the heavenly realms.

Col 2 [18]Do not let anyone who delights in false humility and the worship of angels disqualify you for the prize. Such a person goes into great detail about what he has seen, and his unspiritual mind puffs him up with idle notions.

d) False Brothers, Apostles, and Teachers

2 Cor 11 [3]But I am afraid that just as Eve was deceived by the serpent's cunning, your minds may somehow be led astray from your sincere and pure devotion to Christ. [4]For if someone comes to you and preaches a Jesus other than the Jesus we preached, or if you receive a different spirit from the one you received, or a different gospel from the one you accepted, you put up with it easily enough. . . .

[12]And I will keep on doing what I am doing in order to cut

the ground from under those who want an opportunity to be considered equal with us in the things they boast about.

[13]For such men are false apostles, deceitful workmen, masquerading as apostles of Christ. [14]And no wonder, for Satan himself masquerades as an angel of light. [15]It is not surprising, then, if his servants masquerade as servants of righteousness. Their end will be what their actions deserve.

Gal 2 [4]This matter arose because some false brothers had infiltrated our ranks to spy on the freedom we have in Christ Jesus and to make us slaves.

1 Tim 1 [6]Some have wandered away from these and turned to meaningless talk. [7]They want to be teachers of the law, but they do not know what they are talking about or what they so confidently affirm.

2 Tim 3 [12]In fact, everyone who wants to live a godly life in Christ Jesus will be persecuted, [13]while evil men and impostors will go from bad to worse, deceiving and being deceived.

2 Pet 2 [1]But there were also false prophets among the people, just as there will be false teachers among you. They will secretly introduce destructive heresies, even denying the sovereign Lord who bought them—bringing swift destruction on themselves. [2]Many will follow their shameful ways and will bring the way of truth into disrepute. [3]In their greed these teachers will exploit you with stories they have made up. Their condemnation has long been hanging over them, and their destruction has not been sleeping. . . .

[10]This is especially true of those who follow the corrupt desire of the sinful nature and despise authority.

Bold and arrogant, these men are not afraid to slander celestial beings; [11]yet even angels, although they are stronger and more powerful, do not bring slanderous accusations against such beings in the presence of the Lord. [12]But these men blaspheme in matters they do not understand. They are like brute beasts, creatures of instinct, born only to be caught and destroyed, and like beasts they too will perish.

[13]They will be paid back with harm for the harm they have done. Their idea of pleasure is to carouse in broad daylight. They are blots and blemishes, reveling in their pleasures while they feast with you. [14]With eyes full of adultery, they never stop sinning; they seduce the unstable; they are experts in greed—an accursed brood! [15]They have left the straight way and wandered off to follow the way of Balaam son of Beor, who loved the wages of wickedness. [16]But he was rebuked for his wrongdoing by a donkey—a beast without speech—who spoke with a man's voice and restrained the prophet's madness.

[17]These men are springs without water and mists driven by a storm. Blackest darkness is reserved for them. [18]For they mouth empty, boastful words and, by appealing to the lustful desires of sinful human nature, they entice people who are just escaping from those who live in error. [19]They promise them freedom, while they themselves are slaves of depravity—for a man is a slave to whatever has mastered him. [20]If they have escaped the corruption of the world by knowing our Lord and Savior Jesus Christ and are again entangled in it and overcome, they are worse off at the end than they were at the beginning. [21]It would have been better for them not to have known the way of righteousness, than to have known it and then to turn their backs on the sacred command that was passed on to them. [22]Of them the proverbs are true: "A dog returns to its vomit," and, "A sow that is washed goes back to her wallowing in the mud."

Jude [4]For certain men whose condemnation was written about long ago have secretly slipped in among you. They are godless men, who change the grace of our God into a license for immorality and deny Jesus Christ our only Sovereign and Lord. . . .

[8]In the very same way, these dreamers pollute their own bodies, reject authority and slander celestial beings. [9]But even the archangel Michael, when he was disputing with the devil about the body of Moses, did not dare to bring a slanderous accusation against him, but said, "The Lord rebuke you!" [10]Yet these men speak abusively against whatever they do not understand; and what things they do understand by instinct, like unreasoning animals—these are the very things that destroy them.

[11]Woe to them! They have taken the way of Cain; they have rushed for profit into Balaam's error; they have been destroyed in Korah's rebellion.

[12]These men are blemishes at your love feasts, eating with you without the slightest qualm—shepherds who feed only themselves. They are clouds without rain, blown along by the wind; autumn trees, without fruit and uprooted—twice dead. [13]They are wild waves of the sea, foaming up their shame; wandering stars, for whom blackest darkness has been reserved forever. . . . [16]These men are grumblers and faultfinders; they follow their own evil desires; they boast about themselves and flatter others for their own advantage.

e) Satanic Opposition

Acts 5 [3]Then Peter said, "Ananias, how is it that Satan has so filled your heart that you have lied to the Holy Spirit and have kept for yourself some of the money you received for the land?"

1 Cor 7 [5]Do not deprive each other except by mutual consent and for a time, so that you may devote yourselves to prayer. Then come together again so that Satan will not tempt you because of your lack of self-control.

2 Cor 2 [10]If you forgive anyone, I also forgive him. And what I have forgiven—if there was anything to forgive—I have forgiven in the sight of Christ for your sake, [11]in order that Satan might not outwit us. For we are not unaware of his schemes.

2 Cor 11 [14]And no wonder, for Satan himself masquerades as an angel of light. [15]It is not surprising, then, if his servants masquerade as servants of righteousness. Their end will be what their actions deserve.

2 Cor 12 [7]To keep me from becoming conceited because of these surpassingly great revelations, there was given me a thorn in my flesh, a messenger of Satan, to torment me.

1 Thess 2 [18]For we wanted to come to you—certainly I, Paul, did, again and again—but Satan stopped us.

1 Tim 5 [15]Some have in fact already turned away to follow Satan.

1 Pet 5 [8]Be self-controlled and alert. Your enemy the devil prowls around like a roaring lion looking for someone to devour. [9]Resist him, standing firm in the faith, because you know that your brothers throughout the world are undergoing the same kind of sufferings.

Rev 2 [10]"Do not be afraid of what you are about to suffer. I tell you, the devil will put some of you in prison to test you, and you will suffer persecution for ten days. Be faithful, even to the point of death, and I will give you the crown of life."

F. Theological Problems in the Church

1. Excessive Behavior Resulting from Theological Ideas

a) Asceticism and Self-Denial

Col 2 [20]Since you died with Christ to the basic principles of this world, why, as though you still belonged to it, do you submit to its rules: [21]"Do not handle! Do not taste! Do not touch!"? [22]These are all destined to perish with use, because they are based on human commands and teachings. [23]Such regulations indeed have an appearance of wisdom, with their self-imposed worship, their false humility and their harsh treatment of the body, but they lack any value in restraining sensual indulgence.

1 Tim 4 [1]The Spirit clearly says that in later times some will abandon the faith and follow deceiving spirits and things taught by demons. [2]Such teachings come through hypocritical liars, whose consciences have been seared as with a hot iron. [3]They forbid people to marry and order them to abstain from certain foods, which God created to be received with thanksgiving by those who believe and who know the truth. [4]For everything God created is good, and nothing is to be rejected if it is received with thanksgiving, [5]because it is consecrated by the word of God and prayer.

b) The Eating of Food Sacrificed to Idols

Rev 2 [14]"Nevertheless, I have a few things against you: You have people there who hold to the teaching of Balaam, who taught Balak to entice the Israelites to sin by eating food sacrificed to idols and by committing sexual immorality. [15]Likewise

you also have those who hold to the teaching of the Nicolaitans."
Rev 2 20"Nevertheless, I have this against you: You tolerate that woman Jezebel, who calls herself a prophetess. By her teaching she misleads my servants into sexual immorality and the eating of food sacrificed to idols."
See also The Misuse of Christian Freedom

c) Idolatry

1 Cor 10 7Do not be idolaters, as some of them were; as it is written: "The people sat down to eat and drink and got up to indulge in pagan revelry." . . .
14Therefore, my dear friends, flee from idolatry.
1 John 5 21Dear children, keep yourselves from idols.

d) The Misuse of Christian Freedom

1 Cor 8 1Now about food sacrificed to idols: We know that we all possess knowledge. Knowledge puffs up, but love builds up. 2The man who thinks he knows something does not yet know as he ought to know. 3But the man who loves God is known by God.

4So then, about eating food sacrificed to idols: We know that an idol is nothing at all in the world and that there is no God but one. 5For even if there are so-called gods, whether in heaven or on earth (as indeed there are many "gods" and many "lords"), 6yet for us there is but one God, the Father, from whom all things came and for whom we live; and there is but one Lord, Jesus Christ, through whom all things came and through whom we live.

7But not everyone knows this. Some people are still so accustomed to idols that when they eat such food they think of it as having been sacrificed to an idol, and since their conscience is weak, it is defiled. 8But food does not bring us near to God; we are no worse if we do not eat, and no better if we do.

9Be careful, however, that the exercise of your freedom does not become a stumbling block to the weak. 10For if anyone with a weak conscience sees you who have this knowledge eating in an idol's temple, won't he be emboldened to eat what has been sacrificed to idols? 11So this weak brother, for whom Christ died, is destroyed by your knowledge. 12When you sin against your brothers in this way and wound their weak conscience, you sin against Christ. 13Therefore, if what I eat causes my brother to fall into sin, I will never eat meat again, so that I will not cause him to fall.

e) Ritual Abuses

Col 2 4I tell you this so that no one may deceive you by fine-sounding arguments. . . .

8See to it that no one takes you captive through hollow and deceptive philosophy, which depends on human tradition and the basic principles of this world rather than on Christ. . . .

16Therefore do not let anyone judge you by what you eat or drink, or with regard to a religious festival, a New Moon celebration or a Sabbath day. 17These are a shadow of the things that were to come; the reality, however, is found in Christ. 18Do not let anyone who delights in false humility and the worship of angels disqualify you for the prize. Such a person goes into great detail about what he has seen, and his unspiritual mind puffs him up with idle notions. 19He has lost connection with the Head, from whom the whole body, supported and held together by its ligaments and sinews, grows as God causes it to grow.

f) Sexual Excess

1 Cor 5 1It is actually reported that there is sexual immorality among you, and of a kind that does not occur even among pagans: A man has his father's wife. 2And you are proud! Shouldn't you rather have been filled with grief and have put out of your fellowship the man who did this?
1 Cor 6 12"Everything is permissible for me"—but not everything is beneficial. "Everything is permissible for me"—but I will not be mastered by anything. 13"Food for the stomach and the stomach for food"—but God will destroy them both. The body is not meant for sexual immorality, but for the Lord, and the Lord for the body. 14By his power God raised the Lord from the dead, and he will raise us also. 15Do you not know that your bodies are members of Christ himself? Shall I then take the members of Christ and unite them with a prostitute? Never! 16Do you not know that he who unites himself with a prostitute is one with her in body? For it is said, "The two will become one flesh." 17But he who unites himself with the Lord is one with him in spirit.

18Flee from sexual immorality. All other sins a man commits are outside his body, but he who sins sexually sins against his own body. 19Do you not know that your body is a temple of the Holy Spirit, who is in you, whom you have received from God? You are not your own; 20you were bought at a price. Therefore honor God with your body.
Rev 2 14"Nevertheless, I have a few things against you: You have people there who hold to the teaching of Balaam, who taught Balak to entice the Israelites to sin by eating food sacrificed to idols and by committing sexual immorality."
Rev 2 20"Nevertheless, I have this against you: You tolerate that woman Jezebel, who calls herself a prophetess. By her teaching she misleads my servants into sexual immorality and the eating of food sacrificed to idols. 21I have given her time to repent of her immorality, but she is unwilling. 22So I will cast her on a bed of suffering, and I will make those who commit adultery with her suffer intensely, unless they repent of her ways."

2. Doctrinal Errors

a) Arguments about Myths and Genealogies

1 Tim 1 3As I urged you when I went into Macedonia, stay there in Ephesus so that you may command certain men not to teach false doctrines any longer 4nor to devote themselves to myths and endless genealogies. These promote controversies rather than God's work—which is by faith. 5The goal of this command is love, which comes from a pure heart and a good conscience and a sincere faith. 6Some have wandered away from these and turned to meaningless talk. 7They want to be teachers of the law, but they do not know what they are talking about or what they so confidently affirm.
2 Tim 2 14Keep reminding them of these things. Warn them before God against quarreling about words; it is of no value, and only ruins those who listen.
2 Tim 2 23Don't have anything to do with foolish and stupid arguments, because you know they produce quarrels.

b) Circumcision Is Necessary for Salvation

Acts 15 1Some men came down from Judea to Antioch and were teaching the brothers: "Unless you are circumcised, according to the custom taught by Moses, you cannot be saved." 2This brought Paul and Barnabas into sharp dispute and debate with them. So Paul and Barnabas were appointed, along with some other believers, to go up to Jerusalem to see the apostles and elders about this question. . . . 4When they came to Jerusalem, they were welcomed by the church and the apostles and elders, to whom they reported everything God had done through them.

5Then some of the believers who belonged to the party of the Pharisees stood up and said, "The Gentiles must be circumcised and required to obey the law of Moses."
Gal 6 12Those who want to make a good impression outwardly are trying to compel you to be circumcised. The only reason they do this is to avoid being persecuted for the cross of Christ. 13Not even those who are circumcised obey the law, yet they want you to be circumcised that they may boast about your flesh. 14May I never boast except in the cross of our Lord Jesus Christ, through which the world has been crucified to me, and I to the world. 15Neither circumcision nor uncircumcision means anything; what counts is a new creation. 16Peace and mercy to all who follow this rule, even to the Israel of God.
Phil 3 2Watch out for those dogs, those men who do evil, those mutilators of the flesh. 3For it is we who are the circumcision, we who worship by the Spirit of God, who glory in Christ Jesus, and who put no confidence in the flesh. . . .

c) False Teaching in General

2 Thess 2 1Concerning the coming of our Lord Jesus Christ and our being gathered to him, we ask you, brothers, 2not to become easily unsettled or alarmed by some prophecy, report or letter supposed to have come from us, saying that the day of the Lord has already come. [3]Don't let anyone deceive you in any way, for that day will not come until the rebellion occurs and the man of lawlessness is revealed, the man doomed to destruction.

1 Tim 6 [3]If anyone teaches false doctrines and does not agree to the sound instruction of our Lord Jesus Christ and to godly teaching, [4]he is conceited and understands nothing. He has an unhealthy interest in controversies and quarrels about words that result in envy, strife, malicious talk, evil suspicions [5]and constant friction between men of corrupt mind, who have been robbed of the truth and who think that godliness is a means to financial gain.

1 Tim 6 [20]Timothy, guard what has been entrusted to your care. Turn away from godless chatter and the opposing ideas of what is falsely called knowledge, [21]which some have professed and in so doing have wandered from the faith. Grace be with you.

2 Tim 4 [3]For the time will come when men will not put up with sound doctrine. Instead, to suit their own desires, they will gather around them a great number of teachers to say what their itching ears want to hear. [4]They will turn their ears away from the truth and turn aside to myths.

2 Pet 2 [1]But there were also false prophets among the people, just as there will be false teachers among you. They will secretly introduce destructive heresies, even denying the sovereign Lord who bought them—bringing swift destruction on themselves.

2 Pet 3 [15]Bear in mind that our Lord's patience means salvation, just as our dear brother Paul also wrote you with the wisdom that God gave him. [16]He writes the same way in all his letters, speaking in them of these matters. His letters contain some things that are hard to understand, which ignorant and unstable people distort, as they do the other Scriptures, to their own destruction.

d) Incipient Docetism

1 John 1 [1]That which was from the beginning, which we have heard, which we have seen with our eyes, which we have looked at and our hands have touched—this we proclaim concerning the Word of life. [2]The life appeared; we have seen it and testify to it, and we proclaim to you the eternal life, which was with the Father and has appeared to us. [3]We proclaim to you what we have seen and heard, so that you also may have fellowship with us. And our fellowship is with the Father and with his Son, Jesus Christ. [4]We write this to make our joy complete.

1 John 4 [1]Dear friends, do not believe every spirit, but test the spirits to see whether they are from God, because many false prophets have gone out into the world. [2]This is how you can recognize the Spirit of God: Every spirit that acknowledges that Jesus Christ has come in the flesh is from God, [3]but every spirit that does not acknowledge Jesus is not from God. This is the spirit of the antichrist, which you have heard is coming and even now is already in the world.

e) Legalism

Gal 2 [4]This matter arose because some false brothers had infiltrated our ranks to spy on the freedom we have in Christ Jesus and to make us slaves. [5]We did not give in to them for a moment, so that the truth of the gospel might remain with you.

Gal 3 [1]You foolish Galatians! Who has bewitched you? Before your very eyes Jesus Christ was clearly portrayed as crucified. [2]I would like to learn just one thing from you: Did you receive the Spirit by observing the law, or by believing what you heard? [3]Are you so foolish? After beginning with the Spirit, are you now trying to attain your goal by human effort? [4]Have you suffered so much for nothing—if it really was for nothing? [5]Does God give you his Spirit and work miracles among you because you observe the law, or because you believe what you heard?

Gal 4 [8]Formerly, when you did not know God, you were slaves to those who by nature are not gods. [9]But now that you know God—or rather are known by God—how is it that you are turning back to those weak and miserable principles? Do you wish to be enslaved by them all over again? [10]You are observing special days and months and seasons and years! [11]I fear for you, that somehow I have wasted my efforts on you. . . . [17]Those people are zealous to win you over, but for no good. What they want is to alienate you from us, so that you may be zealous for them.

f) Occult Teachings

Rev 2 [24]"Now I say to the rest of you in Thyatira, to you who do not hold to her teaching and have not learned Satan's so-called deep secrets (I will not impose any other burden on you). . . ."

g) The Resurrection Has Already Occurred

2 Tim 2 [17]Their teaching will spread like gangrene. Among them are Hymenaeus and Philetus, [18]who have wandered away from the truth. They say that the resurrection has already taken place, and they destroy the faith of some.

h) There Is No Resurrection of the Dead

1 Cor 15 [12]But if it is preached that Christ has been raised from the dead, how can some of you say that there is no resurrection of the dead? [13]If there is no resurrection of the dead, then not even Christ has been raised. [14]And if Christ has not been raised, our preaching is useless and so is your faith. [15]More than that, we are then found to be false witnesses about God, for we have testified about God that he raised Christ from the dead. But he did not raise him if in fact the dead are not raised. [16]For if the dead are not raised, then Christ has not been raised either. [17]And if Christ has not been raised, your faith is futile; you are still in your sins. [18]Then those also who have fallen asleep in Christ are lost. [19]If only for this life we have hope in Christ, we are to be pitied more than all men.

i) Those Who Die Miss the Resurrection

1 Thess 4 [13]Brothers, we do not want you to be ignorant about those who fall asleep, or to grieve like the rest of men, who have no hope. [14]We believe that Jesus died and rose again and so we believe that God will bring with Jesus those who have fallen asleep in him. [15]According to the Lord's own word, we tell you that we who are still alive, who are left till the coming of the Lord, will certainly not precede those who have fallen asleep. [16]For the Lord himself will come down from heaven, with a loud command, with the voice of the archangel and with the trumpet call of God, and the dead in Christ will rise first. [17]After that, we who are still alive and are left will be caught up together with them in the clouds to meet the Lord in the air. And so we will be with the Lord forever. [18]Therefore encourage each other with these words.

j) The Worship of Angels

Col 2 [18]Do not let anyone who delights in false humility and the worship of angels disqualify you for the prize. Such a person goes into great detail about what he has seen, and his unspiritual mind puffs him up with idle notions.

G. Problems Arising from Church Order and Practice

1. The Abuse of Giving

Acts 5 [1]Now a man named Ananias, together with his wife Sapphira, also sold a piece of property. [2]With his wife's full knowledge he kept back part of the money for himself, but brought the rest and put it at the apostles' feet.

2. The Abuse of the Lord's Supper

1 Cor 11 [20]When you come together, it is not the Lord's Supper you eat, [21]for as you eat, each of you goes ahead without waiting for anybody else. One remains hungry, another gets drunk. [22]Don't you have homes to eat and drink in? Or do you despise the church of God and humiliate those who have nothing? What shall I say to you? Shall I praise you for this? Certainly not!

3. A Desired Misuse of Apostolic Authority

Acts 8 [18]When Simon saw that the Spirit was given at the laying on of the apostles' hands, he offered them money 19and said, "Give me also this ability so that everyone on whom I lay my hands may receive the Holy Spirit."

4. The Improper Care of Widows

Acts 6 1In those days when the number of disciples was increasing, the Grecian Jews among them complained against the Hebraic Jews because their widows were being overlooked in the daily distribution of food.
1 Tim 5 3Give proper recognition to those widows who are really in need. 4But if a widow has children or grandchildren, these should learn first of all to put their religion into practice by caring for their own family and so repaying their parents and grandparents, for this is pleasing to God. 5The widow who is really in need and left all alone puts her hope in God and continues night and day to pray and to ask God for help. 6But the widow who lives for pleasure is dead even while she lives. 7Give the people these instructions, too, so that no one may be open to blame. 8If anyone does not provide for his relatives, and especially for his immediate family, he has denied the faith and is worse than an unbeliever.

5. The Misuse of Spiritual Gifts

1 Cor 14 1Follow the way of love and eagerly desire spiritual gifts, especially the gift of prophecy. 2For anyone who speaks in a tongue does not speak to men but to God. Indeed, no one understands him; he utters mysteries with his spirit. 3But everyone who prophesies speaks to men for their strengthening, encouragement and comfort. 4He who speaks in a tongue edifies himself, but he who prophesies edifies the church. 5I would like every one of you to speak in tongues, but I would rather have you prophesy. He who prophesies is greater than one who speaks in tongues, unless he interprets, so that the church may be edified.

6Now, brothers, if I come to you and speak in tongues, what good will I be to you, unless I bring you some revelation or knowledge or prophecy or word of instruction? . . .

18I thank God that I speak in tongues more than all of you. 19But in the church I would rather speak five intelligible words to instruct others than ten thousand words in a tongue.

20Brothers, stop thinking like children. In regard to evil be infants, but in your thinking be adults.

6. Unruly Services

1 Cor 14 23So if the whole church comes together and everyone speaks in tongues, and some who do not understand or some unbelievers come in, will they not say that you are out of your mind? . . . 40But everything should be done in a fitting and orderly way.

V
Corrective Measures Taken by the Church

A. The Church Appealed to OT Scriptures

1. The OT Explained Their Behavior

Acts 2 14Then Peter stood up with the Eleven, raised his voice and addressed the crowd: "Fellow Jews and all of you who live in Jerusalem, let me explain this to you; listen carefully to what I say. 15These men are not drunk, as you suppose. It's only nine in the morning! 16No, this is what was spoken by the prophet Joel: 17'In the last days, God says, I will pour out my Spirit on all people. Your sons and daughters will prophesy, your young men will see visions, your old men will dream dreams. 18Even on my servants, both men and women, I will pour out my Spirit in those days, and they will prophesy. 19I will show wonders in the heaven above and signs on the earth below, blood and fire and billows of smoke. 20The sun will be turned to darkness and the moon to blood before the coming of the great and glorious day of the Lord. 21And everyone who calls on the name of the Lord will be saved.'"

2. The OT Provided Moral Guidance

1 Cor 10 1For I do not want you to be ignorant of the fact, brothers, that our forefathers were all under the cloud and that they all passed through the sea. 2They were all baptized into Moses in the cloud and in the sea. 3They all ate the same spiritual food 4and drank the same spiritual drink; for they drank from the spiritual rock that accompanied them, and that rock was Christ. 5Nevertheless, God was not pleased with most of them; their bodies were scattered over the desert.

6Now these things occurred as examples to keep us from setting our hearts on evil things as they did. 7Do not be idolaters, as some of them were; as it is written: "The people sat down to eat and drink and got up to indulge in pagan revelry." 8We should not commit sexual immorality, as some of them did—and in one day twenty-three thousand of them died. 9We should not test the Lord, as some of them did—and were killed by snakes. 10And do not grumble, as some of them did—and were killed by the destroying angel.

11These things happened to them as examples and were written down as warnings for us, on whom the fulfillment of the ages has come. 12So, if you think you are standing firm, be careful that you don't fall! 13No temptation has seized you except what is common to man. And God is faithful; he will not let you be tempted beyond what you can bear. But when you are tempted, he will also provide a way out so that you can stand up under it.

14Therefore, my dear friends, flee from idolatry.
2 Cor 6 14Do not be yoked together with unbelievers. For what do righteousness and wickedness have in common? Or what fellowship can light have with darkness? 15What harmony is there between Christ and Belial? What does a believer have in common with an unbeliever? 16What agreement is there between the temple of God and idols? For we are the temple of the living God. As God has said: "I will live with them and walk among them, and I will be their God, and they will be my people."

17"Therefore come out from them and be separate, says the Lord. Touch no unclean thing, and I will receive you." 18"I will be a Father to you, and you will be my sons and daughters, says the Lord Almighty."

7 1Since we have these promises, dear friends, let us purify ourselves from everything that contaminates body and spirit, perfecting holiness out of reverence for God.

3. The OT Helped Them Understand Spiritual Gifts

1 Cor 14 21In the Law it is written: "Through men of strange tongues and through the lips of foreigners I will speak to this people, but even then they will not listen to me," says the Lord. 22Tongues, then, are a sign, not for believers but for unbelievers; prophecy, however, is for believers, not for unbelievers. 23So if the whole church comes together and everyone speaks in tongues, and some who do not understand or some unbelievers come in, will they not say that you are out of your mind? 24But if an unbeliever or someone who does not understand comes in while everybody is prophesying, he will be convinced by all that he is a sinner and will be judged by all, 25and the secrets of his heart will be laid bare. So he will fall down and worship God, exclaiming, "God is really among you!"

26What then shall we say, brothers? When you come together, everyone has a hymn, or a word of instruction, a revelation, a tongue or an interpretation. All of these must be done for the strengthening of the church. 27If anyone speaks in a tongue, two—or at the most three—should speak, one at a time, and someone must interpret. 28If there is no interpreter, the speaker should keep quiet in the church and speak to himself and God. . . .

39Therefore, my brothers, be eager to prophesy, and do not forbid speaking in tongues. 40But everything should be done in a fitting and orderly way.

4. The OT Resolved the Faith–Law Controversy in Galatia

Gal 3 [6]Consider Abraham: "He believed God, and it was credited to him as righteousness." [7]Understand, then, that those who believe are children of Abraham. [8]The Scripture foresaw that God would justify the Gentiles by faith, and announced the gospel in advance to Abraham: "All nations will be blessed through you." [9]So those who have faith are blessed along with Abraham, the man of faith.

[10]All who rely on observing the law are under a curse, for it is written: "Cursed is everyone who does not continue to do everything written in the Book of the Law." [11]Clearly no one is justified before God by the law, because, "The righteous will live by faith." [12]The law is not based on faith; on the contrary, "The man who does these things will live by them." [13]Christ redeemed us from the curse of the law by becoming a curse for us, for it is written: "Cursed is everyone who is hung on a tree." [14]He redeemed us in order that the blessing given to Abraham might come to the Gentiles through Christ Jesus, so that by faith we might receive the promise of the Spirit.

5. The OT Furnished Illustrations of Perseverance

Heb 4 [1]Therefore, since the promise of entering his rest still stands, let us be careful that none of you be found to have fallen short of it. [2]For we also have had the gospel preached to us, just as they did; but the message they heard was of no value to them, because those who heard did not combine it with faith. [3]Now we who have believed enter that rest, just as God has said, "So I declared on oath in my anger, 'They shall never enter my rest.'" And yet his work has been finished since the creation of the world. [4]For somewhere he has spoken about the seventh day in these words: "And on the seventh day God rested from all his work." [5]And again in the passage above he says, "They shall never enter my rest."

[6]It still remains that some will enter that rest, and those who formerly had the gospel preached to them did not go in, because of their disobedience. [7]Therefore God again set a certain day, calling it Today, when a long time later he spoke through David, as was said before: "Today, if you hear his voice, do not harden your hearts." [8]For if Joshua had given them rest, God would not have spoken later about another day. [9]There remains, then, a Sabbath-rest for the people of God; [10]for anyone who enters God's rest also rests from his own work, just as God did from his. [11]Let us, therefore, make every effort to enter that rest, so that no one will fall by following their example of disobedience.

B. The Church Relied on God

Acts 4 [29]"Now, Lord, consider their threats and enable your servants to speak your word with great boldness. [30]Stretch out your hand to heal and perform miraculous signs and wonders through the name of your holy servant Jesus."

[31]After they prayed, the place where they were meeting was shaken. And they were all filled with the Holy Spirit and spoke the word of God boldly.

C. The Church Underwent Divine Discipline

Acts 5 [3]Then Peter said, "Ananias, how is it that Satan has so filled your heart that you have lied to the Holy Spirit and have kept for yourself some of the money you received for the land? [4]Didn't it belong to you before it was sold? And after it was sold, wasn't the money at your disposal? What made you think of doing such a thing? You have not lied to men but to God."

[5]When Ananias heard this, he fell down and died. And great fear seized all who heard what had happened. [6]Then the young men came forward, wrapped up his body, and carried him out and buried him.

[7]About three hours later his wife came in, not knowing what had happened. [8]Peter asked her, "Tell me, is this the price you and Ananias got for the land?"

"Yes," she said, "that is the price."

[9]Peter said to her, "How could you agree to test the Spirit of the Lord? Look! The feet of the men who buried your husband are at the door, and they will carry you out also."

[10]At that moment she fell down at his feet and died. Then the young men came in and, finding her dead, carried her out and buried her beside her husband. [11]Great fear seized the whole church and all who heard about these events.

Heb 12 [7]Endure hardship as discipline; God is treating you as sons. For what son is not disciplined by his father? [8]If you are not disciplined (and everyone undergoes discipline), then you are illegitimate children and not true sons. [9]Moreover, we have all had human fathers who disciplined us and we respected them for it. How much more should we submit to the Father of our spirits and live! [10]Our fathers disciplined us for a little while as they thought best; but God disciplines us for our good, that we may share in his holiness. [11]No discipline seems pleasant at the time, but painful. Later on, however, it produces a harvest of righteousness and peace for those who have been trained by it.

Rev 3 [18]"I counsel you to buy from me gold refined in the fire, so you can become rich; and white clothes to wear, so you can cover your shameful nakedness; and salve to put on your eyes, so you can see.

[19]"Those whom I love I rebuke and discipline. So be earnest, and repent."

D. Peter Experienced Divine Deliverance from Prison

Acts 12 [5]So Peter was kept in prison, but the church was earnestly praying to God for him.

[6]The night before Herod was to bring him to trial, Peter was sleeping between two soldiers, bound with two chains, and sentries stood guard at the entrance. [7]Suddenly an angel of the Lord appeared and a light shone in the cell. He struck Peter on the side and woke him up. "Quick, get up!" he said, and the chains fell off Peter's wrists.

[8]Then the angel said to him, "Put on your clothes and sandals." And Peter did so. "Wrap your cloak around you and follow me," the angel told him. [9]Peter followed him out of the prison, but he had no idea that what the angel was doing was really happening; he thought he was seeing a vision. [10]They passed the first and second guards and came to the iron gate leading to the city. It opened for them by itself, and they went through it. When they had walked the length of one street, suddenly the angel left him.

[11]Then Peter came to himself and said, "Now I know without a doubt that the Lord sent his angel and rescued me from Herod's clutches and from everything the Jewish people were anticipating."

E. The Church Considered Persecution as Being from God

1. Persecution Is Sometimes God's Will

Eph 6 [19]Pray also for me, that whenever I open my mouth, words may be given me so that I will fearlessly make known the mystery of the gospel, [20]for which I am an ambassador in chains. Pray that I may declare it fearlessly, as I should.

Phil 1 [29]For it has been granted to you on behalf of Christ not only to believe on him, but also to suffer for him, [30]since you are going through the same struggle you saw I had, and now hear that I still have.

Col 4 [18]I, Paul, write this greeting in my own hand. Remember my chains. Grace be with you.

1 Thess 3 [4]In fact, when we were with you, we kept telling you that we would be persecuted. And it turned out that way, as you well know.

2 Tim 3 [12]In fact, everyone who wants to live a godly life in Christ Jesus will be persecuted. . . .

1 Pet 4 [12]Dear friends, do not be surprised at the painful trial you are suffering, as though something strange were happening to you. [13]But rejoice that you participate in the sufferings of

Christ, so that you may be overjoyed when his glory is revealed. [14]If you are insulted because of the name of Christ, you are blessed, for the Spirit of glory and of God rests on you. [15]If you suffer, it should not be as a murderer or thief or any other kind of criminal, or even as a meddler. [16]However, if you suffer as a Christian, do not be ashamed, but praise God that you bear that name. . . .

[19]So then, those who suffer according to God's will should commit themselves to their faithful Creator and continue to do good.

2. God Uses Persecution to Show the Direction the Gospel Should Go

Acts 18 [9]One night the Lord spoke to Paul in a vision: "Do not be afraid; keep on speaking, do not be silent. [10]For I am with you, and no one is going to attack and harm you, because I have many people in this city." [11]So Paul stayed for a year and a half, teaching them the word of God.

Acts 20 [1]When the uproar had ended, Paul sent for the disciples and, after encouraging them, said good-by and set out for Macedonia. [2]He traveled through that area, speaking many words of encouragement to the people, and finally arrived in Greece, [3]where he stayed three months. Because the Jews made a plot against him just as he was about to sail for Syria, he decided to go back through Macedonia.

Acts 23 [11]The following night the Lord stood near Paul and said, "Take courage! As you have testified about me in Jerusalem, so you must also testify in Rome."

3. God Works Persecution for Good

Rom 8 [28]And we know that in all things God works for the good of those who love him, who have been called according to his purpose.

4. God Uses Hardship for Discipline That Produces Holiness

Heb 12 [7]Endure hardship as discipline; God is treating you as sons. For what son is not disciplined by his father? [8]If you are not disciplined (and everyone undergoes discipline), then you are illegitimate children and not true sons. [9]Moreover, we have all had human fathers who disciplined us and we respected them for it. How much more should we submit to the Father of our spirits and live! [10]Our fathers disciplined us for a little while as they thought best; but God disciplines us for our good, that we may share in his holiness. [11]No discipline seems pleasant at the time, but painful. Later on, however, it produces a harvest of righteousness and peace for those who have been trained by it.

5. Sufferings Prove Genuine Faith

1 Pet 1 [6]In this you greatly rejoice, though now for a little while you may have had to suffer grief in all kinds of trials. [7]These have come so that your faith—of greater worth than gold, which perishes even though refined by fire—may be proved genuine and may result in praise, glory and honor when Jesus Christ is revealed.

6. Persecution Produces Perseverance

Rom 5 [3]Not only so, but we also rejoice in our sufferings, because we know that suffering produces perseverance; [4]perseverance, character; and character, hope.

2 Cor 1 [3]Praise be to the God and Father of our Lord Jesus Christ, the Father of compassion and the God of all comfort, [4]who comforts us in all our troubles, so that we can comfort those in any trouble with the comfort we ourselves have received from God. [5]For just as the sufferings of Christ flow over into our lives, so also through Christ our comfort overflows. [6]If we are distressed, it is for your comfort and salvation; if we are comforted, it is for your comfort, which produces in you patient endurance of the same sufferings we suffer. [7]And our hope for you is firm, because we know that just as you share in our sufferings, so also you share in our comfort.

Phil 4 [13]I can do everything through him who gives me strength.

2 Thess 1 [4]Therefore, among God's churches we boast about your perseverance and faith in all the persecutions and trials you are enduring.

James 1 [2]Consider it pure joy, my brothers, whenever you face trials of many kinds, [3]because you know that the testing of your faith develops perseverance. [4]Perseverance must finish its work so that you may be mature and complete, not lacking anything. . . .

[12]Blessed is the man who perseveres under trial, because when he has stood the test, he will receive the crown of life that God has promised to those who love him.

7. Christ Is the Believer's Model in Suffering

1 Pet 2 [19]For it is commendable if a man bears up under the pain of unjust suffering because he is conscious of God. [20]But how is it to your credit if you receive a beating for doing wrong and endure it? But if you suffer for doing good and you endure it, this is commendable before God. [21]To this you were called, because Christ suffered for you, leaving you an example, that you should follow in his steps.

[22]"He committed no sin, and no deceit was found in his mouth." [23]When they hurled their insults at him, he did not retaliate; when he suffered, he made no threats. Instead, he entrusted himself to him who judges justly.

8. Believers Rejoiced in Sharing in Christ's Suffering

Acts 5 [41]The apostles left the Sanhedrin, rejoicing because they had been counted worthy of suffering disgrace for the Name.

Col 1 [24]Now I rejoice in what was suffered for you, and I fill up in my flesh what is still lacking in regard to Christ's afflictions, for the sake of his body, which is the church.

1 Thess 1 [6]You became imitators of us and of the Lord; in spite of severe suffering, you welcomed the message with the joy given by the Holy Spirit.

9. Believers Considered It Blessed to Suffer for Doing Right

1 Pet 3 [14]But even if you should suffer for what is right, you are blessed. "Do not fear what they fear; do not be frightened." [15]But in your hearts set apart Christ as Lord. Always be prepared to give an answer to everyone who asks you to give the reason for the hope that you have. But do this with gentleness and respect, [16]keeping a clear conscience, so that those who speak maliciously against your good behavior in Christ may be ashamed of their slander. [17]It is better, if it is God's will, to suffer for doing good than for doing evil.

10. Believers Are Not to Be Discouraged or Ashamed When Persecuted

Eph 3 [13]I ask you, therefore, not to be discouraged because of my sufferings for you, which are your glory.

2 Tim 1 [7]For God did not give us a spirit of timidity, but a spirit of power, of love and of self-discipline.

[8]So do not be ashamed to testify about our Lord, or ashamed of me his prisoner. But join with me in suffering for the gospel, by the power of God. . . .

11. Believers Are to Bless Those Who Persecute Them

Rom 12 [14]Bless those who persecute you; bless and do not curse.

12. Believers Should Not Retaliate

Rom 12 [19]Do not take revenge, my friends, but leave room for God's wrath, for it is written: "It is mine to avenge; I will repay," says the Lord. [20]On the contrary: "If your enemy is hungry, feed him; if he is thirsty, give him something to drink. In doing this, you will heap burning coals on his head." [21]Do not be overcome by evil, but overcome evil with good.

13. Present Suffering Is Minor Compared to the Coming Glory

Rom 8 [17]Now if we are children, then we are heirs—heirs of God and co-heirs with Christ, if indeed we share in his sufferings in order that we may also share in his glory.

[18]I consider that our present sufferings are not worth comparing with the glory that will be revealed in us.

14. Believers Ultimately Are More Than Conquerors

Rom 8 [35]Who shall separate us from the love of Christ? Shall trouble or hardship or persecution or famine or nakedness or danger or sword? [36]As it is written: "For your sake we face death all day long; we are considered as sheep to be slaughtered." [37]No, in all these things we are more than conquerors through him who loved us. [38]For I am convinced that neither death nor life, neither angels nor demons, neither the present nor the future, nor any powers, [39]neither height nor depth, nor anything else in all creation, will be able to separate us from the love of God that is in Christ Jesus our Lord.

F. The Church Created Ministry Positions to Meet Needs

Acts 6 [2]So the Twelve gathered all the disciples together and said, "It would not be right for us to neglect the ministry of the word of God in order to wait on tables. [3]Brothers, choose seven men from among you who are known to be full of the Spirit and wisdom. We will turn this responsibility over to them [4]and will give our attention to prayer and the ministry of the word."

[5]This proposal pleased the whole group. They chose Stephen, a man full of faith and of the Holy Spirit; also Philip, Procorus, Nicanor, Timon, Parmenas, and Nicolas from Antioch, a convert to Judaism. [6]They presented these men to the apostles, who prayed and laid their hands on them.

G. The Church Rebuked Indiscretions

1. Simon Was Rebuked for His Selfish Ambition

Acts 8 [20]Peter answered: "May your money perish with you, because you thought you could buy the gift of God with money! [21]You have no part or share in this ministry, because your heart is not right before God. [22]Repent of this wickedness and pray to the Lord. Perhaps he will forgive you for having such a thought in your heart. [23]For I see that you are full of bitterness and captive to sin."

2. Elymas Was Rebuked for Opposing the Gospel

Acts 13 [9]Then Saul, who was also called Paul, filled with the Holy Spirit, looked straight at Elymas and said, [10]"You are a child of the devil and an enemy of everything that is right! You are full of all kinds of deceit and trickery. Will you never stop perverting the right ways of the Lord? [11]Now the hand of the Lord is against you. You are going to be blind, and for a time you will be unable to see the light of the sun."

Immediately mist and darkness came over him, and he groped about, seeking someone to lead him by the hand.

3. The Corinthian Church Was Rebuked for Its Doctrinal Error

1 Cor 15 [29]Now if there is no resurrection, what will those do who are baptized for the dead? If the dead are not raised at all, why are people baptized for them? [30]And as for us, why do we endanger ourselves every hour? [31]I die every day—I mean that,brothers—just as surely as I glory over you in Christ Jesus our Lord. [32]If I fought wild beasts in Ephesus for merely human reasons, what have I gained? If the dead are not raised, "Let us eat and drink, for tomorrow we die."

[33]Do not be misled: "Bad company corrupts good character." [34]Come back to your senses as you ought, and stop sinning; for there are some who are ignorant of God—I say this to your shame.

4. The Galatian Church Was Rebuked for Its Doctrinal Error

Gal 1 [6]I am astonished that you are so quickly deserting the one who called you by the grace of Christ and are turning to a different gospel—[7]which is really no gospel at all. Evidently some people are throwing you into confusion and are trying to pervert the gospel of Christ. [8]But even if we or an angel from heaven should preach a gospel other than the one we preached to you, let him be eternally condemned! [9]As we have already said, so now I say again: If anybody is preaching to you a gospel other than what you accepted, let him be eternally condemned!

Gal 3 [1]You foolish Galatians! Who has bewitched you? Before your very eyes Jesus Christ was clearly portrayed as crucified. [2]I would like to learn just one thing from you: Did you receive the Spirit by observing the law, or by believing what you heard? [3]Are you so foolish? After beginning with the Spirit, are you now trying to attain your goal by human effort? [4]Have you suffered so much for nothing—if it really was for nothing? [5]Does God give you his Spirit and work miracles among you because you observe the law, or because you believe what you heard?

5. Believers Were Rebuked for Yielding to False Teaching

Titus 1 [13]This testimony is true. Therefore, rebuke them sharply, so that they will be sound in the faith [14]and will pay no attention to Jewish myths or to the commands of those who reject the truth.

H. Peter Was Divinely Instructed through a Vision

Acts 10 [27]Talking with him, Peter went inside and found a large gathering of people. [28]He said to them: "You are well aware that it is against our law for a Jew to associate with a Gentile or visit him. But God has shown me that I should not call any man impure or unclean." . . .

[34]Then Peter began to speak: "I now realize how true it is that God does not show favoritism [35]but accepts men from every nation who fear him and do what is right. [36]You know the message God sent to the people of Israel, telling the good news of peace through Jesus Christ, who is Lord of all. [37]You know what has happened throughout Judea, beginning in Galilee after the baptism that John preached—[38]how God anointed Jesus of Nazareth with the Holy Spirit and power, and how he went around doing good and healing all who were under the power of the devil, because God was with him."

Acts 11 [4]Peter began and explained everything to them precisely as it had happened: [5]"I was in the city of Joppa praying, and in a trance I saw a vision. I saw something like a large sheet being let down from heaven by its four corners, and it came down to where I was. [6]I looked into it and saw four-footed animals of the earth, wild beasts, reptiles, and birds of the air. [7]Then I heard a voice telling me, 'Get up, Peter. Kill and eat.'

[8]"I replied, 'Surely not, Lord! Nothing impure or unclean has ever entered my mouth.'

[9]"The voice spoke from heaven a second time, 'Do not call anything impure that God has made clean.' [10]This happened three times, and then it was all pulled up to heaven again.

[11]"Right then three men who had been sent to me from Caesarea stopped at the house where I was staying. [12]The Spirit told me to have no hesitation about going with them. These six brothers also went with me, and we entered the man's house. [13]He told us how he had seen an angel appear in his house and say, 'Send to Joppa for Simon who is called Peter. [14]He will

bring you a message through which you and all your household will be saved.'

[15]"As I began to speak, the Holy Spirit came on them as he had come on us at the beginning. [16]Then I remembered what the Lord had said: 'John baptized with water, but you will be baptized with the Holy Spirit.' [17]So if God gave them the same gift as he gave us, who believed in the Lord Jesus Christ, who was I to think that I could oppose God?"

[18]When they heard this, they had no further objections and praised God, saying, "So then, God has granted even the Gentiles repentance unto life."

I. The Church Helped Needy Believers

Acts 11 [29]The disciples, each according to his ability, decided to provide help for the brothers living in Judea. [30]This they did, sending their gift to the elders by Barnabas and Saul.
Rom 15 [26]For Macedonia and Achaia were pleased to make a contribution for the poor among the saints in Jerusalem. [27]They were pleased to do it, and indeed they owe it to them. For if the Gentiles have shared in the Jews' spiritual blessings, they owe it to the Jews to share with them their material blessings. [28]So after I have completed this task and have made sure that they have received this fruit, I will go to Spain and visit you on the way.
2 Cor 8 [1]And now, brothers, we want you to know about the grace that God has given the Macedonian churches. [2]Out of the most severe trial, their overflowing joy and their extreme poverty welled up in rich generosity. [3]For I testify that they gave as much as they were able, and even beyond their ability. Entirely on their own, [4]they urgently pleaded with us for the privilege of sharing in this service to the saints. [5]And they did not do as we expected, but they gave themselves first to the Lord and then to us in keeping with God's will.
2 Cor 9 [12]This service that you perform is not only supplying the needs of God's people but is also overflowing in many expressions of thanks to God. [13]Because of the service by which you have proved yourselves, men will praise God for the obedience that accompanies your confession of the gospel of Christ, and for your generosity in sharing with them and with everyone else.

J. The Church Related Theology to Life

1. Christians Sought to Imitate God

Eph 5 [1]Be imitators of God, therefore, as dearly loved children [2]and live a life of love, just as Christ loved us and gave himself up for us as a fragrant offering and sacrifice to God.

[3]But among you there must not be even a hint of sexual immorality, or of any kind of impurity, or of greed, because these are improper for God's holy people. [4]Nor should there be obscenity, foolish talk or coarse joking, which are out of place, but rather thanksgiving. [5]For of this you can be sure: No immoral, impure or greedy person—such a man is an idolater—has any inheritance in the kingdom of Christ and of God. . . .

[15]Be very careful, then, how you live—not as unwise but as wise, [16]making the most of every opportunity, because the days are evil. [17]Therefore do not be foolish, but understand what the Lord's will is. [18]Do not get drunk on wine, which leads to debauchery. Instead, be filled with the Spirit. [19]Speak to one another with psalms, hymns and spiritual songs. Sing and make music in your heart to the Lord, [20]always giving thanks to God the Father for everything, in the name of our Lord Jesus Christ.

[21]Submit to one another out of reverence for Christ.

2. Christians Sought to Be Like Christ

Rom 12 [1]Therefore, I urge you, brothers, in view of God's mercy, to offer your bodies as living sacrifices, holy and pleasing to God—this is your spiritual act of worship. [2]Do not conform any longer to the pattern of this world, but be transformed by the renewing of your mind. Then you will be able to test and approve what God's will is—his good, pleasing and perfect will.
Rom 13 [14]Rather, clothe yourselves with the Lord Jesus Christ, and do not think about how to gratify the desires of the sinful nature.
1 John 2 [6]Whoever claims to live in him must walk as Jesus did.
1 John 2 [28]And now, dear children, continue in him, so that when he appears we may be confident and unashamed before him at his coming.

3. Christians Sought to Become Mature in Christ

Heb 6 [1]Therefore let us leave the elementary teachings about Christ and go on to maturity, not laying again the foundation of repentance from acts that lead to death, and of faith in God, [2]instruction about baptisms, the laying on of hands, the resurrection of the dead, and eternal judgment. [3]And God permitting, we will do so.

4. Christians Sought to Be Holy

1 Pet 1 [13]Therefore, prepare your minds for action; be self-controlled; set your hope fully on the grace to be given you when Jesus Christ is revealed. [14]As obedient children, do not conform to the evil desires you had when you lived in ignorance. [15]But just as he who called you is holy, so be holy in all you do; [16]for it is written: "Be holy, because I am holy." . . .

[22]Now that you have purified yourselves by obeying the truth so that you have sincere love for your brothers, love one another deeply, from the heart.

5. Christians Sought to Stand Firm against Evil and Sin

Acts 14 [21]They preached the good news in that city and won a large number of disciples. Then they returned to Lystra, Iconium and Antioch, [22]strengthening the disciples and encouraging them to remain true to the faith. "We must go through many hardships to enter the kingdom of God," they said.
Acts 20 [28]"Keep watch over yourselves and all the flock of which the Holy Spirit has made you overseers. Be shepherds of the church of God, which he bought with his own blood. [29]I know that after I leave, savage wolves will come in among you and will not spare the flock. [30]Even from your own number men will arise and distort the truth in order to draw away disciples after them. [31]So be on your guard! Remember that for three years I never stopped warning each of you night and day with tears."
Rom 16 [17]I urge you, brothers, to watch out for those who cause divisions and put obstacles in your way that are contrary to the teaching you have learned. Keep away from them. [18]For such people are not serving our Lord Christ, but their own appetites. By smooth talk and flattery they deceive the minds of naive people. [19]Everyone has heard about your obedience, so I am full of joy over you; but I want you to be wise about what is good, and innocent about what is evil.
1 Cor 16 [13]Be on your guard; stand firm in the faith; be men of courage; be strong.
2 Cor 4 [16]Therefore we do not lose heart. Though outwardly we are wasting away, yet inwardly we are being renewed day by day. [17]For our light and momentary troubles are achieving for us an eternal glory that far outweighs them all. [18]So we fix our eyes not on what is seen, but on what is unseen. For what is seen is temporary, but what is unseen is eternal.
Gal 5 [1]It is for freedom that Christ has set us free. Stand firm, then, and do not let yourselves be burdened again by a yoke of slavery.
Eph 6 [10]Finally, be strong in the Lord and in his mighty power. [11]Put on the full armor of God so that you can take your stand against the devil's schemes. [12]For our struggle is not against flesh and blood, but against the rulers, against the authorities, against the powers of this dark world and against the spiritual forces of evil in the heavenly realms. [13]Therefore put on the full armor of God, so that when the day of evil comes, you may be able to stand your ground, and after you have done everything,

to stand. [14]Stand firm then, with the belt of truth buckled around your waist, with the breastplate of righteousness in place, [15]and with your feet fitted with the readiness that comes from the gospel of peace. [16]In addition to all this, take up the shield of faith, with which you can extinguish all the flaming arrows of the evil one. [17]Take the helmet of salvation and the sword of the Spirit, which is the word of God. [18]And pray in the Spirit on all occasions with all kinds of prayers and requests. With this in mind, be alert and always keep on praying for all the saints.

2 Thess 2 [15]So then, brothers, stand firm and hold to the teachings we passed on to you, whether by word of mouth or by letter.

1 Tim 4 [14]Do not neglect your gift, which was given you through a prophetic message when the body of elders laid their hands on you.

[15]Be diligent in these matters; give yourself wholly to them, so that everyone may see your progress. [16]Watch your life and doctrine closely. Persevere in them, because if you do, you will save both yourself and your hearers.

Heb 10 [19]Therefore, brothers, since we have confidence to enter the Most Holy Place by the blood of Jesus, [20]by a new and living way opened for us through the curtain, that is, his body, [21]and since we have a great priest over the house of God, [22]let us draw near to God with a sincere heart in full assurance of faith, having our hearts sprinkled to cleanse us from a guilty conscience and having our bodies washed with pure water. [23]Let us hold unswervingly to the hope we profess, for he who promised is faithful. [24]And let us consider how we may spur one another on toward love and good deeds. [25]Let us not give up meeting together, as some are in the habit of doing, but let us encourage one another—and all the more as you see the Day approaching. . . .

[32]Remember those earlier days after you had received the light, when you stood your ground in a great contest in the face of suffering. [33]Sometimes you were publicly exposed to insult and persecution; at other times you stood side by side with those who were so treated. [34]You sympathized with those in prison and joyfully accepted the confiscation of your property, because you knew that you yourselves had better and lasting possessions.

[35]So do not throw away your confidence; it will be richly rewarded. [36]You need to persevere so that when you have done the will of God, you will receive what he has promised. [37]For in just a very little while, "He who is coming will come and will not delay. [38]But my righteous one will live by faith. And if he shrinks back, I will not be pleased with him."

[39]But we are not of those who shrink back and are destroyed, but of those who believe and are saved.

Heb 12 [1]Therefore, since we are surrounded by such a great cloud of witnesses, let us throw off everything that hinders and the sin that so easily entangles, and let us run with perseverance the race marked out for us. [2]Let us fix our eyes on Jesus, the author and perfecter of our faith, who for the joy set before him endured the cross, scorning its shame, and sat down at the right hand of the throne of God. [3]Consider him who endured such opposition from sinful men, so that you will not grow weary and lose heart. . . .

[12]Therefore, strengthen your feeble arms and weak knees.

James 5 [7]Be patient, then, brothers, until the Lord's coming. See how the farmer waits for the land to yield its valuable crop and how patient he is for the autumn and spring rains. [8]You too, be patient and stand firm, because the Lord's coming is near. [9]Don't grumble against each other, brothers, or you will be judged. The Judge is standing at the door!

[10]Brothers, as an example of patience in the face of suffering, take the prophets who spoke in the name of the Lord. [11]As you know, we consider blessed those who have persevered. You have heard of Job's perseverance and have seen what the Lord finally brought about. The Lord is full of compassion and mercy.

1 Pet 5 [8]Be self-controlled and alert. Your enemy the devil prowls around like a roaring lion looking for someone to devour. [9]Resist him, standing firm in the faith, because you know that your brothers throughout the world are undergoing the same kind of sufferings.

1 John 3 [7]Dear children, do not let anyone lead you astray. He who does what is right is righteous, just as he is righteous.

1 John 4 [1]Dear friends, do not believe every spirit, but test the spirits to see whether they are from God, because many false prophets have gone out into the world. [2]This is how you can recognize the Spirit of God: Every spirit that acknowledges that Jesus Christ has come in the flesh is from God, [3]but every spirit that does not acknowledge Jesus is not from God. This is the spirit of the antichrist, which you have heard is coming and even now is already in the world.

2 John [7]Many deceivers, who do not acknowledge Jesus Christ as coming in the flesh, have gone out into the world. Any such person is the deceiver and the antichrist. [8]Watch out that you do not lose what you have worked for, but that you may be rewarded fully. [9]Anyone who runs ahead and does not continue in the teaching of Christ does not have God; whoever continues in the teaching has both the Father and the Son. [10]If anyone comes to you and does not bring this teaching, do not take him into your house or welcome him. [11]Anyone who welcomes him shares in his wicked work.

6. Christians Sought to Teach Sound Doctrine

Titus 2 [1]You must teach what is in accord with sound doctrine.

7. Christians Sought to Imitate Faithful Believers

1 Cor 4 [14]I am not writing this to shame you, but to warn you, as my dear children. [15]Even though you have ten thousand guardians in Christ, you do not have many fathers, for in Christ Jesus I became your father through the gospel. [16]Therefore I urge you to imitate me. [17]For this reason I am sending to you Timothy, my son whom I love, who is faithful in the Lord. He will remind you of my way of life in Christ Jesus, which agrees with what I teach everywhere in every church.

1 Cor 10 [31]So whether you eat or drink or whatever you do, do it all for the glory of God. [32]Do not cause anyone to stumble, whether Jews, Greeks or the church of God—[33]even as I try to please everybody in every way. For I am not seeking my own good but the good of many, so that they may be saved.

11 [1]Follow my example, as I follow the example of Christ.

Gal 4 [12]I plead with you, brothers, become like me, for I became like you. You have done me no wrong. [13]As you know, it was because of an illness that I first preached the gospel to you. [14]Even though my illness was a trial to you, you did not treat me with contempt or scorn. Instead, you welcomed me as if I were an angel of God, as if I were Christ Jesus himself.

Phil 3 [17]Join with others in following my example, brothers, and take note of those who live according to the pattern we gave you.

Heb 6 [11]We want each of you to show this same diligence to the very end, in order to make your hope sure. [12]We do not want you to become lazy, but to imitate those who through faith and patience inherit what has been promised.

Heb 13 [7]Remember your leaders, who spoke the word of God to you. Consider the outcome of their way of life and imitate their faith.

8. Christians Sought to Do Good

Titus 3 [14]Our people must learn to devote themselves to doing what is good, in order that they may provide for daily necessities and not live unproductive lives.

9. Christians Sought to Support Each Other in Love

Rom 15 [1]We who are strong ought to bear with the failings of the weak and not to please ourselves. [2]Each of us should please his neighbor for his good, to build him up. . . .

[7]Accept one another, then, just as Christ accepted you, in order to bring praise to God.

2 Cor 2 [5]If anyone has caused grief, he has not so much grieved me as he has grieved all of you, to some extent—not to put it too severely. [6]The punishment inflicted on him by the majority is sufficient for him. [7]Now instead, you ought to forgive and comfort him, so that he will not be overwhelmed by excessive sorrow. [8]I urge you, therefore, to reaffirm your love for him.

Gal 5 [13]You, my brothers, were called to be free. But do not use your freedom to indulge the sinful nature; rather, serve one another in love. [14]The entire law is summed up in a single command: "Love your neighbor as yourself."

Gal 6 [1]Brothers, if someone is caught in a sin, you who are spiritual should restore him gently. But watch yourself, or you also may be tempted. [2]Carry each other's burdens, and in this way you will fulfill the law of Christ. . . . [4]Each one should test his own actions. Then he can take pride in himself, without comparing himself to somebody else, [5]for each one should carry his own load. . . .

[10]Therefore, as we have opportunity, let us do good to all people, especially to those who belong to the family of believers.

2 Tim 2 [24]And the Lord's servant must not quarrel; instead, he must be kind to everyone, able to teach, not resentful. [25]Those who oppose him he must gently instruct, in the hope that God will grant them repentance leading them to a knowledge of the truth, [26]and that they will come to their senses and escape from the trap of the devil, who has taken them captive to do his will.

Heb 3 [13]But encourage one another daily, as long as it is called Today, so that none of you may be hardened by sin's deceitfulness.

Heb 13 [1]Keep on loving each other as brothers. . . . [3]Remember those in prison as if you were their fellow prisoners, and those who are mistreated as if you yourselves were suffering.

1 Pet 4 [8]Above all, love each other deeply, because love covers over a multitude of sins.

1 John 3 [11]This is the message you heard from the beginning: We should love one another.

1 John 4 [7]Dear friends, let us love one another, for love comes from God. Everyone who loves has been born of God and knows God. . . . [21]And he has given us this command: Whoever loves God must also love his brother.

Jude [20]But you, dear friends, build yourselves up in your most holy faith and pray in the Holy Spirit. [21]Keep yourselves in God's love as you wait for the mercy of our Lord Jesus Christ to bring you to eternal life. [22]Be merciful to those who doubt; [23]snatch others from the fire and save them; to others show mercy, mixed with fear—hating even the clothing stained by corrupted flesh.

10. Christians Sought to Live in Harmony

Rom 12 [9]Love must be sincere. Hate what is evil; cling to what is good. [10]Be devoted to one another in brotherly love. Honor one another above yourselves. [11]Never be lacking in zeal, but keep your spiritual fervor, serving the Lord. [12]Be joyful in hope, patient in affliction, faithful in prayer. [13]Share with God's people who are in need. Practice hospitality. . . .

[15]Rejoice with those who rejoice; mourn with those who mourn. [16]Live in harmony with one another. Do not be proud, but be willing to associate with people of low position. Do not be conceited.

[17]Do not repay anyone evil for evil. Be careful to do what is right in the eyes of everybody. [18]If it is possible, as far as it depends on you, live at peace with everyone. . . . [21]Do not be overcome by evil, but overcome evil with good.

1 Cor 16 [14]Do everything in love.

2 Cor 13 [11]Finally, brothers, good-by. Aim for perfection, listen to my appeal, be of one mind, live in peace. And the God of love and peace will be with you.

Eph 4 [1]As a prisoner for the Lord, then, I urge you to live a life worthy of the calling you have received. [2]Be completely humble and gentle; be patient, bearing with one another in love. [3]Make every effort to keep the unity of the Spirit through the bond of peace.

1 Thess 5 [12]Now we ask you, brothers, to respect those who work hard among you, who are over you in the Lord and who admonish you. [13]Hold them in the highest regard in love because of their work. Live in peace with each other. [14]And we urge you, brothers, warn those who are idle, encourage the timid, help the weak, be patient with everyone. [15]Make sure that nobody pays back wrong for wrong, but always try to be kind to each other and to everyone else.

[16]Be joyful always; [17]pray continually; [18]give thanks in all circumstances, for this is God's will for you in Christ Jesus.

[19]Do not put out the Spirit's fire; [20]do not treat prophecies with contempt. [21]Test everything. Hold on to the good. [22]Avoid every kind of evil.

Heb 12 [14]Make every effort to live in peace with all men and to be holy; without holiness no one will see the Lord.

1 Pet 2 [11]Dear friends, I urge you, as aliens and strangers in the world, to abstain from sinful desires, which war against your soul. [12]Live such good lives among the pagans that, though they accuse you of doing wrong, they may see your good deeds and glorify God on the day he visits us. . . .

[17]Show proper respect to everyone: Love the brotherhood of believers, fear God, honor the king.

1 Pet 3 [8]Finally, all of you, live in harmony with one another; be sympathetic, love as brothers, be compassionate and humble. [9]Do not repay evil with evil or insult with insult, but with blessing, because to this you were called so that you may inherit a blessing.

11. Christians Sought to Consider the Weaker Believer

Rom 14 [1]Accept him whose faith is weak, without passing judgment on disputable matters. [2]One man's faith allows him to eat everything, but another man, whose faith is weak, eats only vegetables. [3]The man who eats everything must not look down on him who does not, and the man who does not eat everything must not condemn the man who does, for God has accepted him. . . .

[13]Therefore let us stop passing judgment on one another. Instead, make up your mind not to put any stumbling block or obstacle in your brother's way. [14]As one who is in the Lord Jesus, I am fully convinced that no food is unclean in itself. But if anyone regards something as unclean, then for him it is unclean. [15]If your brother is distressed because of what you eat, you are no longer acting in love. Do not by your eating destroy your brother for whom Christ died. [16]Do not allow what you consider good to be spoken of as evil. [17]For the kingdom of God is not a matter of eating and drinking, but of righteousness, peace and joy in the Holy Spirit, [18]because anyone who serves Christ in this way is pleasing to God and approved by men.

[19]Let us therefore make every effort to do what leads to peace and to mutual edification. [20]Do not destroy the work of God for the sake of food. All food is clean, but it is wrong for a man to eat anything that causes someone else to stumble. [21]It is better not to eat meat or drink wine or to do anything else that will cause your brother to fall.

[22]So whatever you believe about these things keep between yourself and God. Blessed is the man who does not condemn himself by what he approves. [23]But the man who has doubts is condemned if he eats, because his eating is not from faith; and everything that does not come from faith is sin.

1 Cor 8 [9]Be careful, however, that the exercise of your freedom does not become a stumbling block to the weak. [10]For if anyone with a weak conscience sees you who have this knowledge eating in an idol's temple, won't he be emboldened to eat what has been sacrificed to idols? [11]So this weak brother, for whom Christ died, is destroyed by your knowledge. [12]When you sin against your brothers in this way and wound their weak conscience, you sin against Christ. [13]Therefore, if what I eat causes my brother to fall into sin, I will never eat meat again, so that I will not cause him to fall.

12. Christians Sought to Avoid Immoral Believers

1 Cor 5 [9]I have written you in my letter not to associate with sexually immoral people—[10]not at all meaning the people of this world who are immoral, or the greedy and swindlers, or idolaters. In that case you would have to leave this world. [11]But now I am writing you that you must not associate with anyone who calls himself a brother but is sexually immoral or greedy, an idolater or a slanderer, a drunkard or a swindler. With such a man do not even eat.

13. Christians Sought to Practice Rightly the Lord's Supper

1 Cor 11 20When you come together, it is not the Lord's Supper you eat, 21for as you eat, each of you goes ahead without waiting for anyone else. One remains hungry, another gets drunk. 22Don't you have homes to eat and drink in? Or do you despise the church of God and humiliate those who have nothing? What shall I say to you? Shall I praise you for this? Certainly not! . . .

27Therefore, whoever eats the bread or drinks the cup of the Lord in an unworthy manner will be guilty of sinning against the body and blood of the Lord. 28A man ought to examine himself before he eats of the bread and drinks of the cup. 29For anyone who eats and drinks without recognizing the body of the Lord eats and drinks judgment on himself. 30That is why many among you are weak and sick, and a number of you have fallen asleep. 31But if we judged ourselves, we would not come under judgment. 32When we are judged by the Lord, we are being disciplined so that we will not be condemned with the world.

33So then, my brothers, when you come together to eat, wait for each other. 34If anyone is hungry, he should eat at home, so that when you meet together it may not result in judgment.

And when I come I will give further directions.

K. The Church Reconciled Racial Differences

Acts 15 6The apostles and elders met to consider this question. 7After much discussion, Peter got up and addressed them: "Brothers, you know that some time ago God made a choice among you that the Gentiles might hear from my lips the message of the gospel and believe. 8God, who knows the heart, showed that he accepted them by giving the Holy Spirit to them, just as he did to us. 9He made no distinction between us and them, for he purified their hearts by faith. 10Now then, why do you try to test God by putting on the necks of the disciples a yoke that neither we nor our fathers have been able to bear? 11No! We believe it is through the grace of our Lord Jesus that we are saved, just as they are."

12The whole assembly became silent as they listened to Barnabas and Paul telling about the miraculous signs and wonders God had done among the Gentiles through them. 13When they finished, James spoke up: "Brothers, listen to me. 14Simon has described to us how God at first showed his concern by taking from the Gentiles a people for himself. 15The words of the prophets are in agreement with this, as it is written: 16'After this I will return and rebuild David's fallen tent. Its ruins I will rebuild, and I will restore it, 17that the remnant of men may seek the Lord, and all the Gentiles who bear my name, says the Lord, who does these things' 18that have been known for ages.

19"It is my judgment, therefore, that we should not make it difficult for the Gentiles who are turning to God. 20Instead we should write to them, telling them to abstain from food polluted by idols, from sexual immorality, from the meat of strangled animals and from blood. 21For Moses has been preached in every city from the earliest times and is read in the synagogues on every Sabbath."

22Then the apostles and elders, with the whole church, decided to choose some of their own men and send them to Antioch with Paul and Barnabas. They chose Judas (called Barsabbas) and Silas, two men who were leaders among the brothers. 23With them they sent the following letter:

The apostles and elders, your brothers,

To the Gentile believers in Antioch, Syria and Cilicia: Greetings.

24We have heard that some went out from us without our authorization and disturbed you, troubling your minds by what they said. 25So we all agreed to choose some men and send them to you with our dear friends Barnabas and Paul—26men who have risked their lives for the name of our Lord Jesus Christ. 27Therefore we are sending Judas and Silas to confirm by word of mouth what we are writing. 28It seemed good to the Holy Spirit and to us not to burden you with anything beyond the following requirements: 29You are to abstain from food sacrificed to idols, from blood, from the meat of strangled animals and from sexual immorality. You will do well to avoid these things. Farewell.

30The men were sent off and went down to Antioch, where they gathered the church together and delivered the letter. 31The people read it and were glad for its encouraging message. 32Judas and Silas, who themselves were prophets, said much to encourage and strengthen the brothers. 33After spending some time there, they were sent off by the brothers with the blessing of peace to return to those who had sent them.

L. The Church Prayed for One Another

Rom 15 30I urge you, brothers, by our Lord Jesus Christ and by the love of the Spirit, to join me in my struggle by praying to God for me. 31Pray that I may be rescued from the unbelievers in Judea and that my service in Jerusalem may be acceptable to the saints there, 32so that by God's will I may come to you with joy and together with you be refreshed.

Eph 1 16I have not stopped giving thanks for you, remembering you in my prayers. 17I keep asking that the God of our Lord Jesus Christ, the glorious Father, may give you the Spirit of wisdom and revelation, so that you may know him better. 18I pray also that the eyes of your heart may be enlightened in order that you may know the hope to which he has called you, the riches of his glorious inheritance in the saints, 19and his incomparably great power for us who believe. That power is like the working of his mighty strength. . . .

Eph 3 14For this reason I kneel before the Father, 15from whom his whole family in heaven and on earth derives its name. 16I pray that out of his glorious riches he may strengthen you with power through his Spirit in your inner being, 17so that Christ may dwell in your hearts through faith. And I pray that you, being rooted and established in love, 18may have power, together with all the saints, to grasp how wide and long and high and deep is the love of Christ, 19and to know this love that surpasses knowledge—that you may be filled to the measure of all the fullness of God.

20Now to him who is able to do immeasurably more than all we ask or imagine, according to his power that is at work within us, 21to him be glory in the church and in Christ Jesus throughout all generations, for ever and ever! Amen.

Phil 1 3I thank my God every time I remember you. 4In all my prayers for all of you, I always pray with joy 5because of your partnership in the gospel from the first day until now, 6being confident of this, that he who began a good work in you will carry it on to completion until the day of Christ Jesus. . . .

9And this is my prayer: that your love may abound more and more in knowledge and depth of insight, 10so that you may be able to discern what is best and may be pure and blameless until the day of Christ, 11filled with the fruit of righteousness that comes through Jesus Christ—to the glory and praise of God.

Col 1 9For this reason, since the day we heard about you, we have not stopped praying for you and asking God to fill you with the knowledge of his will through all spiritual wisdom and understanding. 10And we pray this in order that you may live a life worthy of the Lord and may please him in every way: bearing fruit in every good work, growing in the knowledge of God, 11being strengthened with all power according to his glorious might so that you may have great endurance and patience, and joyfully 12giving thanks to the Father, who has qualified you to share in the inheritance of the saints in the kingdom of light.

Col 4 12Epaphras, who is one of you and a servant of Christ Jesus, sends greetings. He is always wrestling in prayer for you, that you may stand firm in all the will of God, mature and fully assured.

2 Thess 1 11With this in mind, we constantly pray for you, that our God may count you worthy of his calling, and that by his power he may fulfill every good purpose of yours and every act prompted by your faith. 12We pray this so that the name of our

Lord Jesus may be glorified in you, and you in him, according to the grace of our God and the Lord Jesus Christ.
1 Tim 2 [1]I urge, then, first of all, that requests, prayers, intercession and thanksgiving be made for everyone. . . .

[8]I want men everywhere to lift up holy hands in prayer, without anger or disputing.
Heb 13 [18]Pray for us. We are sure that we have a clear conscience and desire to live honorably in every way. [19]I particularly urge you to pray so that I may be restored to you soon.
James 5 [13]Is any one of you in trouble? He should pray. Is anyone happy? Let him sing songs of praise. [14]Is any one of you sick? He should call the elders of the church to pray over him and anoint him with oil in the name of the Lord. [15]And the prayer offered in faith will make the sick person well; the Lord will raise him up. If he has sinned, he will be forgiven. [16]Therefore confess your sins to each other and pray for each other so that you may be healed. The prayer of a righteous man is powerful and effective.

[17]Elijah was a man just like us. He prayed earnestly that it would not rain, and it did not rain on the land for three and a half years. [18]Again he prayed, and the heavens gave rain, and the earth produced its crops.

M. Paul Encouraged His Many Converts

Acts 16 [40]After Paul and Silas came out of the prison, they went to Lydia's house, where they met with the brothers and encouraged them. Then they left.
Acts 18 [23]After spending some time in Antioch, Paul set out from there and traveled from place to place throughout the region of Galatia and Phrygia, strengthening all the disciples.
Acts 20 [1]When the uproar had ended, Paul sent for the disciples and, after encouraging them, said good-by and set out for Macedonia.
Gal 3 [26]You are all sons of God through faith in Christ Jesus, [27]for all of you who were baptized into Christ have clothed yourselves with Christ. [28]There is neither Jew nor Greek, slave nor free, male nor female, for you are all one in Christ Jesus. [29]If you belong to Christ, then you are Abraham's seed, and heirs according to the promise.

N. The Church Handed Some Unrepentant Sinners Over to Satan for Discipline

1 Cor 5 [4]When you are assembled in the name of our Lord Jesus and I am with you in spirit, and the power of our Lord Jesus is present, [5]hand this man over to Satan, so that the sinful nature may be destroyed and his spirit saved on the day of the Lord.
1 Tim 1 [20]Among them are Hymenaeus and Alexander, whom I have handed over to Satan to be taught not to blaspheme.

VI
The Mission, Ministry, and Activities of the Church

A. Commissioning Leaders in the Church

See p. 725a, The Organization and Officers of the Church

B. Commissioning Missionaries in the Church

Acts 13 [2]While they were worshiping the Lord and fasting, the Holy Spirit said, "Set apart for me Barnabas and Saul for the work to which I have called them."
Acts 15 [40]but Paul chose Silas and left, commended by the brothers to the grace of the Lord.

C. Communicating with Other Local Churches

Acts 15 [2]This brought Paul and Barnabas into sharp dispute and debate with them. So Paul and Barnabas were appointed, along with some other believers, to go up to Jerusalem to see the apostles and elders about this question.
Acts 18 [27]When Apollos wanted to go to Achaia, the brothers encouraged him and wrote to the disciples there to welcome him. On arriving, he was a great help to those who by grace had believed.
Rom 16 [1]I commend to you our sister Phoebe, a servant of the church in Cenchrea.
2 Cor 3 [1]Are we beginning to commend ourselves again? Or do we need, like some people, letters of recommendation to you or from you?

D. Disciple-making in the Church

Matt 28 [19]"Therefore go and make disciples of all nations, baptizing them in the name of the Father and of the Son and of the Holy Spirit, [20]and teaching them to obey everything I have commanded you. And surely I am with you always, to the very end of the age."
Mark 1 [17]"Come, follow me," Jesus said, "and I will make you fishers of men."
Acts 6 [1]In those days when the number of disciples was increasing, the Grecian Jews among them complained against the Hebraic Jews because their widows were being overlooked in the daily distribution of food. [2]So the Twelve gathered all the disciples together and said, "It would not be right for us to neglect the ministry of the word of God in order to wait on tables. [3]Brothers, choose seven men from among you who are known to be full of the Spirit and wisdom. We will turn this responsibility over to them [4]and will give our attention to prayer and the ministry of the word."

[5]This proposal pleased the whole group. They chose Stephen, a man full of faith and of the Holy Spirit; also Philip, Procorus, Nicanor, Timon, Parmenas, and Nicolas from Antioch, a convert to Judaism. [6]They presented these men to the apostles, who prayed and laid their hands on them.

[7]So the word of God spread. The number of disciples in Jerusalem increased rapidly, and a large number of priests became obedient to the faith.
Acts 14 [21]They preached the good news in that city and won a large number of disciples. Then they returned to Lystra, Iconium and Antioch, [22]strengthening the disciples and encouraging them to remain true to the faith. "We must go through many hardships to enter the kingdom of God," they said.
Acts 18 [23]After spending some time in Antioch, Paul set out from there and traveled from place to place throughout the region of Galatia and Phrygia, strengthening all the disciples.
Acts 20 [1]When the uproar had ended, Paul sent for the disciples and, after encouraging them, said good-by and set out for Macedonia. [2]He traveled through that area, speaking many words of encouragement to the people, and finally arrived in Greece. . . .

E. Discipline in the Church

Matt 18 [15]"If your brother sins against you, go and show him his fault, just between the two of you. If he listens to you, you have won your brother over. [16]But if he will not listen, take one or two others along, so that 'every matter may be established by the testimony of two or three witnesses.' [17]If he refuses to listen to them, tell it to the church; and if he refuses to listen even to the church, treat him as you would a pagan or a tax collector.

[18]"I tell you the truth, whatever you bind on earth will be bound in heaven, and whatever you loose on earth will be loosed in heaven."
John 20 [23]"If you forgive anyone his sins, they are forgiven; if you do not forgive them, they are not forgiven."
Acts 5 [1]Now a man named Ananias, together with his wife Sapphira, also sold a piece of property. [2]With his wife's full

knowledge he kept back part of the money for himself, but brought the rest and put it at the apostles' feet.

3Then Peter said, "Ananias, how is it that Satan has so filled your heart that you have lied to the Holy Spirit and have kept for yourself some of the money you received for the land? 4Didn't it belong to you before it was sold? And after it was sold, wasn't the money at your disposal? What made you think of doing such a thing? You have not lied to men but to God."

5When Ananias heard this, he fell down and died. And great fear seized all who heard what had happened. 6Then the young men came forward, wrapped up his body, and carried him out and buried him.

7About three hours later his wife came in, not knowing what had happened. 8Peter asked her, "Tell me, is this the price you and Ananias got for the land?"

"Yes," she said, "that is the price."

9Peter said to her, "How could you agree to test the Spirit of the Lord? Look! The feet of the men who buried your husband are at the door, and they will carry you out also."

10At that moment she fell down at his feet and died. Then the young men came in and, finding her dead, carried her out and buried her beside her husband.

Rom 14 1Accept him whose faith is weak, without passing judgment on disputable matters.

Rom 15 1We who are strong ought to bear with the failings of the weak and not to please ourselves.

Rom 16 17I urge you, brothers, to watch out for those who cause divisions and put obstacles in your way that are contrary to the teaching you have learned. Keep away from them.

1 Cor 4 19But I will come to you very soon, if the Lord is willing, and then I will find out not only how these arrogant people are talking, but what power they have. . . . 21What do you prefer? Shall I come to you with a whip, or in love and with a gentle spirit?

1 Cor 5 1It is actually reported that there is sexual immorality among you, and of a kind that does not occur even among pagans: A man has his father's wife. 2And you are proud! Shouldn't you rather have been filled with grief and have put out of your fellowship the man who did this? 3Even though I am not physically present, I am with you in spirit. And I have already passed judgment on the one who did this, just as if I were present. 4When you are assembled in the name of our Lord Jesus and I am with you in spirit, and the power of our Lord Jesus is present, 5hand this man over to Satan, so that the sinful nature may be destroyed and his spirit saved on the day of the Lord.

6Your boasting is not good. Don't you know that a little yeast works through the whole batch of dough? 7Get rid of the old yeast that you may be a new batch without yeast—as you really are. For Christ, our Passover lamb, has been sacrificed. . . .

11But now I am writing you that you must not associate with anyone who calls himself a brother but is sexually immoral or greedy, an idolater or a slanderer, a drunkard or a swindler. With such a man do not even eat.

12What business is it of mine to judge those outside the church? Are you not to judge those inside? 13God will judge those outside. "Expel the wicked man from among you."

2 Cor 2 5If anyone has caused grief, he has not so much grieved me as he has grieved all of you, to some extent—not to put it too severely. 6The punishment inflicted on him by the majority is sufficient for him. 7Now instead, you ought to forgive and comfort him, so that he will not be overwhelmed by excessive sorrow. 8I urge you, therefore, to reaffirm your love for him. 9The reason I wrote you was to see if you would stand the test and be obedient in everything. 10If you forgive anyone, I also forgive him. And what I have forgiven—if there was anything to forgive—I have forgiven in the sight of Christ for your sake, 11in order that Satan might not outwit us. For we are not unaware of his schemes.

2 Cor 7 8Even if I caused you sorrow by my letter, I do not regret it. Though I did regret it—I see that my letter hurt you, but only for a little while. . . .

2 Cor 13 1This will be my third visit to you. "Every matter must be established by the testimony of two or three witnesses." 2I already gave you a warning when I was with you the second time. I now repeat it while absent: On my return I will not spare those who sinned earlier or any of the others. . . .

10This is why I write these things when I am absent, that when I come I may not have to be harsh in my use of authority—the authority the Lord gave me for building you up, not for tearing you down.

Gal 5 10I am confident in the Lord that you will take no other view. The one who is throwing you into confusion will pay the penalty, whoever he may be. . . . 12As for those agitators, I wish they would go the whole way and emasculate themselves!

Gal 6 1Brothers, if someone is caught in a sin, you who are spiritual should restore him gently. But watch yourself, or you also may be tempted.

1 Thess 5 14And we urge you, brothers, warn those who are idle, encourage the timid, help the weak, be patient with everyone.

2 Thess 3 6In the name of the Lord Jesus Christ, we command you, brothers, to keep away from every brother who is idle and does not live according to the teaching you received from us. . . .

14If anyone does not obey our instruction in this letter, take special note of him. Do not associate with him, in order that he may feel ashamed. 15Yet do not regard him as an enemy, but warn him as a brother.

1 Tim 1 19holding on to faith and a good conscience. Some have rejected these and so have shipwrecked their faith. 20Among them are Hymenaeus and Alexander, whom I have handed over to Satan to be taught not to blaspheme.

1 Tim 5 1Do not rebuke an older man harshly, but exhort him as if he were your father. Treat younger men as brothers, 2older women as mothers, and younger women as sisters, with absolute purity.

1 Tim 5 19Do not entertain an accusation against an elder unless it is brought by two or three witnesses. 20Those who sin are to be rebuked publicly, so that the others may take warning.

1 Tim 6 3If anyone teaches false doctrines and does not agree to the sound instruction of our Lord Jesus Christ and to godly teaching, 4he is conceited and understands nothing. He has an unhealthy interest in controversies and quarrels about words that result in envy, strife, malicious talk, evil suspicions 5and constant friction between men of corrupt mind, who have been robbed of the truth and who think that godliness is a means to financial gain.

2 Tim 4 2Preach the Word; be prepared in season and out of season; correct, rebuke and encourage—with great patience and careful instruction.

Titus 1 10For there are many rebellious people, mere talkers and deceivers, especially those of the circumcision group. 11They must be silenced, because they are ruining whole households by teaching things they ought not to teach—and that for the sake of dishonest gain. . . . 13This testimony is true. Therefore, rebuke them sharply, so that they will be sound in the faith. . . .

Titus 3 10Warn a divisive person once, and then warn him a second time. After that, have nothing to do with him. 11You may be sure that such a man is warped and sinful; he is self-condemned.

2 John 9Anyone who runs ahead and does not continue in the teaching of Christ does not have God; whoever continues in the teaching has both the Father and the Son. 10If anyone comes to you and does not bring this teaching, do not take him into your house or welcome him. 11Anyone who welcomes him shares in his wicked work.

Jude 22Be merciful to those who doubt; 23snatch others from the fire and save them; to others show mercy, mixed with fear—hating even the clothing stained by corrupted flesh.

F. Encouragement in the Church

1 Sam 23 16And Saul's son Jonathan went to David at Horesh and helped him find strength in God.

Luke 22 32"But I have prayed for you, Simon, that your faith

may not fail. And when you have turned back, strengthen your brothers."
Acts 15 [32]Judas and Silas, who themselves were prophets, said much to encourage and strengthen the brothers.
Rom 1 [11]I long to see you so that I may impart to you some spiritual gift to make you strong—[12]that is, that you and I may be mutually encouraged by each other's faith.
1 Cor 14 [3]But everyone who prophesies speaks to men for their strengthening, encouragement and comfort. [4]He who speaks in a tongue edifies himself, but he who prophesies edifies the church. [5]I would like every one of you to speak in tongues, but I would rather have you prophesy. He who prophesies is greater than one who speaks in tongues, unless he interprets, so that the church may be edified. . . .

[26]What then shall we say, brothers? When you come together, everyone has a hymn, or a word of instruction, a revelation, a tongue or an interpretation. All of these must be done for the strengthening of the church. . . . [31]For you can all prophesy in turn so that everyone may be instructed and encouraged.
Col 3 [16]Let the word of Christ dwell in you richly as you teach and admonish one another with all wisdom, and as you sing psalms, hymns and spiritual songs with gratitude in your hearts to God.
Col 4 [8]I am sending him to you for the express purpose that you may know about our circumstances and that he may encourage your hearts.
1 Thess 3 [2]We sent Timothy, who is our brother and God's fellow worker in spreading the gospel of Christ, to strengthen and encourage you in your faith. . . .
1 Thess 4 [18]Therefore encourage each other with these words.
1 Thess 5 [11]Therefore encourage one another and build each other up, just as in fact you are doing.
Titus 2 [15]These, then, are the things you should teach. Encourage and rebuke with all authority. Do not let anyone despise you.
Heb 3 [13]But encourage one another daily, as long as it is called Today, so that none of you may be hardened by sin's deceitfulness.
Heb 10 [24]And let us consider how we may spur one another on toward love and good deeds.

G. Fellowship in the Church

Ps 55 [13]But it is you, a man like myself, my companion, my close friend, [14]with whom I once enjoyed sweet fellowship as we walked with the throng at the house of God.
Ps 119 [63]I am a friend to all who fear you, to all who follow your precepts.
Ps 133 [1]How good and pleasant it is when brothers live together in unity! [2]It is like precious oil poured on the head, running down on the beard, running down on Aaron's beard, down upon the collar of his robes. [3]It is as if the dew of Hermon were falling on Mount Zion. For there the LORD bestows his blessing, even life forevermore.
Matt 23 [8]"But you are not to be called 'Rabbi,' for you have only one Master and you are all brothers."
Mark 10 [42]Jesus called them together and said, "You know that those who are regarded as rulers of the Gentiles lord it over them, and their high officials exercise authority over them. [43]Not so with you. Instead, whoever wants to become great among you must be your servant, [44]and whoever wants to be first must be slave of all. [45]For even the Son of Man did not come to be served, but to serve, and to give his life as a ransom for many."
Luke 24 [13]Now that same day two of them were going to a village called Emmaus, about seven miles from Jerusalem. [14]They were talking with each other about everything that had happened. [15]As they talked and discussed these things with each other, Jesus himself came up and walked along with them. . . .
John 13 [34]"A new command I give you: Love one another. As I have loved you, so you must love one another. [35]By this all men will know that you are my disciples, if you love one another."
John 15 [12]"My command is this: Love each other as I have loved you."
Acts 17 [4]Some of the Jews were persuaded and joined Paul and Silas, as did a large number of God-fearing Greeks and not a few prominent women.
Acts 20 [35]"In everything I did, I showed you that by this kind of hard work we must help the weak, remembering the words the Lord Jesus himself said: 'It is more blessed to give than to receive.'"
Rom 12 [15]Rejoice with those who rejoice; mourn with those who mourn.
1 Cor 16 [19]The churches in the province of Asia send you greetings. Aquila and Priscilla greet you warmly in the Lord, and so does the church that meets at their house. [20]All the brothers here send you greetings. Greet one another with a holy kiss.
2 Cor 6 [14]Do not be yoked together with unbelievers. For what do righteousness and wickedness have in common? Or what fellowship can light have with darkness? [15]What harmony is there between Christ and Belial? What does a believer have in common with an unbeliever? [16]What agreement is there between the temple of God and idols? For we are the temple of the living God. As God has said: "I will live with them and walk among them, and I will be their God, and they will be my people."

[17]"Therefore come out from them and be separate, says the Lord. Touch no unclean thing, and I will receive you." [18]"I will be a Father to you, and you will be my sons and daughters, says the Lord Almighty."
2 Cor 13 [14]May the grace of the Lord Jesus Christ, and the love of God, and the fellowship of the Holy Spirit be with you all.
Gal 2 [9]James, Peter and John, those reputed to be pillars, gave me and Barnabas the right hand of fellowship when they recognized the grace given to me. They agreed that we should go to the Gentiles, and they to the Jews.
Gal 6 [2]Carry each other's burdens, and in this way you will fulfill the law of Christ.
Phil 1 [3]I thank my God every time I remember you. [4]In all my prayers for all of you, I always pray with joy, [5]because of your partnership in the gospel from the first day until now. . . .
Phil 2 [1]If you have any encouragement from being united with Christ, if any comfort from his love, if any fellowship with the Spirit, if any tenderness and compassion, [2]then make my joy complete by being like-minded, having the same love, being one in spirit and purpose.
Col 2 [2]My purpose is that they may be encouraged in heart and united in love, so that they may have the full riches of complete understanding, in order that they may know the mystery of God, namely, Christ. . . .
1 Thess 4 [18]Therefore encourage each other with these words.
Heb 13 [1]Keep on loving each other as brothers.
1 Pet 2 [17]Show proper respect to everyone: Love the brotherhood of believers, fear God, honor the king.
1 John 1 [3]We proclaim to you what we have seen and heard, so that you also may have fellowship with us. And our fellowship is with the Father and with his Son, Jesus Christ. [4]We write this to make our joy complete.

[5]This is the message we have heard from him and declare to you: God is light; in him there is no darkness at all. [6]If we claim to have fellowship with him yet walk in the darkness, we lie and do not live by the truth. [7]But if we walk in the light, as he is in the light, we have fellowship with one another, and the blood of Jesus, his Son, purifies us from all sin.
1 John 3 [14]We know that we have passed from death to life, because we love our brothers. Anyone who does not love remains in death.
1 John 4 [7]Dear friends, let us love one another, for love comes from God. Everyone who loves has been born of God and knows God. [8]Whoever does not love does not know God, because God is love. . . . [11]Dear friends, since God so loved us, we also ought to love one another. [12]No one has ever seen God; but if we love one another, God lives in us and his love is made complete in us.

[13]We know that we live in him and he in us, because he has given us of his Spirit.

H. Giving in the Church

Mark 9 [41]"I tell you the truth, anyone who gives you a cup of water in my name because you belong to Christ will certainly not lose his reward."

Luke 3 [11]John answered, "The man with two tunics should share with him who has none, and the one who has food should do the same."

Acts 2 [44]All the believers were together and had everything in common. [45]Selling their possessions and goods, they gave to anyone as he had need.

Acts 4 [32]All the believers were one in heart and mind. No one claimed that any of his possessions was his own, but they shared everything they had. [33]With great power the apostles continued to testify to the resurrection of the Lord Jesus, and much grace was upon them all. [34]There were no needy persons among them. For from time to time those who owned lands or houses sold them, brought the money from the sales [35]and put it at the apostles' feet, and it was distributed to anyone as he had need.

[36]Joseph, a Levite from Cyprus, whom the apostles called Barnabas (which means Son of Encouragement), [37]sold a field he owned and brought the money and put it at the apostles' feet.

Acts 11 [29]The disciples, each according to his ability, decided to provide help for the brothers living in Judea. [30]This they did, sending their gift to the elders by Barnabas and Saul.

Acts 28 [10]They honored us in many ways and when we were ready to sail, they furnished us with the supplies we needed.

Rom 12 [6]We have different gifts, according to the grace given us. If a man's gift is prophesying, let him use it in proportion to his faith. [7]If it is serving, let him serve; if it is teaching, let him teach; [8]if it is encouraging, let him encourage; if it is contributing to the needs of others, let him give generously; if it is leadership, let him govern diligently; if it is showing mercy, let him do it cheerfully.

Rom 15 [25]Now, however, I am on my way to Jerusalem in the service of the saints there. [26]For Macedonia and Achaia were pleased to make a contribution for the poor among the saints in Jerusalem. [27]They were pleased to do it, and indeed they owe it to them. For if the Gentiles have shared in the Jews' spiritual blessings, they owe it to the Jews to share with them their material blessings.

1 Cor 16 [1]Now about the collection for God's people: Do what I told the Galatian churches to do. [2]On the first day of every week, each one of you should set aside a sum of money in keeping with his income, saving it up, so that when I come no collections will have to be made. [3]Then, when I arrive, I will give letters of introduction to the men you approve and send them with your gift to Jerusalem.

2 Cor 8 [1]And now, brothers, we want you to know about the grace that God has given the Macedonian churches. [2]Out of the most severe trial, their overflowing joy and their extreme poverty welled up in rich generosity. [3]For I testify that they gave as much as they were able, and even beyond their ability. Entirely on their own, [4]they urgently pleaded with us for the privilege of sharing in this service to the saints. [5]And they did not do as we expected, but they gave themselves first to the Lord and then to us in keeping with God's will. [6]So we urged Titus, since he had earlier made a beginning, to bring also to completion this act of grace on your part. [7]But just as you excel in everything—in faith, in speech, in knowledge, in complete earnestness and in your love for us—see that you also excel in this grace of giving.

[8]I am not commanding you, but I want to test the sincerity of your love by comparing it with the earnestness of others. [9]For you know the grace of our Lord Jesus Christ, that though he was rich, yet for your sakes he became poor, so that you through his poverty might become rich. [10]And here is my advice about what is best for you in this matter: Last year you were the first not only to give but also to have the desire to do so. [11]Now finish the work, so that your eager willingness to do it may be matched by your completion of it, according to your means. [12]For if the willingness is there, the gift is acceptable according to what one has, not according to what he does not have.

[13]Our desire is not that others might be relieved while you are hard pressed, but that there might be equality. [14]At the present time your plenty will supply what they need, so that in turn their plenty will supply what you need. Then there will be equality, [15]as it is written: "He who gathered much did not have too much, and he who gathered little did not have too little."

2 Cor 9 [1]There is no need for me to write to you about this service to the saints. [2]For I know your eagerness to help, and I have been boasting about it to the Macedonians, telling them that since last year you in Achaia were ready to give; and your enthusiasm has stirred most of them to action. [3]But I am sending the brothers in order that our boasting about you in this matter should not prove hollow, but that you may be ready, as I said you would be. [4]For if any Macedonians come with me and find you unprepared, we—not to say anything about you—would be ashamed of having been so confident. [5]So I thought it necessary to urge the brothers to visit you in advance and finish the arrangements for the generous gift you had promised. Then it will be ready as a generous gift, not as one grudgingly given.

[6]Remember this: Whoever sows sparingly will also reap sparingly, and whoever sows generously will also reap generously. [7]Each man should give what he has decided in his heart to give, not reluctantly or under compulsion, for God loves a cheerful giver. [8]And God is able to make all grace abound to you, so that in all things at all times, having all that you need, you will abound in every good work. [9]As it is written: "He has scattered abroad his gifts to the poor; his righteousness endures forever." [10]Now he who supplies seed to the sower and bread for food will also supply and increase your store of seed and will enlarge the harvest of your righteousness. [11]You will be made rich in every way so that you can be generous on every occasion, and through us your generosity will result in thanksgiving to God.

[12]This service that you perform is not only supplying the needs of God's people but is also overflowing in many expressions of thanks to God. [13]Because of the service by which you have proved yourselves, men will praise God for the obedience that accompanies your confession of the gospel of Christ, and for your generosity in sharing with them and with everyone else.

Eph 4 [28]He who has been stealing must steal no longer, but must work, doing something useful with his own hands, that he may have something to share with those in need.

Phil 4 [18]I have received full payment and even more; I am amply supplied, now that I have received from Epaphroditus the gifts you sent. They are a fragrant offering, an acceptable sacrifice, pleasing to God.

1 Tim 5 [16]If any woman who is a believer has widows in her family, she should help them and not let the church be burdened with them, so that the church can help those widows who are really in need.

1 Tim 6 [17]Command those who are rich in this present world not to be arrogant nor to put their hope in wealth, which is so uncertain, but to put their hope in God, who richly provides us with everything for our enjoyment. [18]Command them to do good, to be rich in good deeds, and to be generous and willing to share. [19]In this way they will lay up treasure for themselves as a firm foundation for the coming age, so that they may take hold of the life that is truly life.

Heb 13 [16]And do not forget to do good and to share with others, for with such sacrifices God is pleased.

James 2 [15]Suppose a brother or sister is without clothes and daily food. [16]If one of you says to him, "Go, I wish you well; keep warm and well fed," but does nothing about his physical needs, what good is it?

1 John 3 [17]If anyone has material possessions and sees his brother in need but has no pity on him, how can the love of God be in him?

I. Hospitality in the Church

Acts 16 [15]When she and the members of her household were baptized, she invited us to her home. "If you consider me a believer in the Lord," she said, "come and stay at my house." And she persuaded us.

Acts 16 [31]They replied, "Believe in the Lord Jesus, and you will be saved—you and your household." [32]Then they spoke the word of the Lord to him and to all the others in his house. [33]At

that hour of the night the jailer took them and washed their wounds; then immediately he and all his family were baptized. [34]The jailer brought them into his house and set a meal before them; he was filled with joy because he had come to believe in God—he and his whole family.
Acts 18 [1]After this, Paul left Athens and went to Corinth. [2]There he met a Jew named Aquila, a native of Pontus, who had recently come from Italy with his wife Priscilla, because Claudius had ordered all the Jews to leave Rome. Paul went to see them, [3]and because he was a tentmaker as they were, he stayed and worked with them.
Acts 21 [4]Finding the disciples there, we stayed with them seven days. Through the Spirit they urged Paul not to go on to Jerusalem. [5]But when our time was up, we left and continued on our way. All the disciples and their wives and children accompanied us out of the city, and there on the beach we knelt to pray. [6]After saying good-by to each other, we went aboard the ship, and they returned home.
Acts 21 [7]We continued our voyage from Tyre and landed at Ptolemais, where we greeted the brothers and stayed with them for a day. [8]Leaving the next day, we reached Caesarea and stayed at the house of Philip the evangelist, one of the Seven.
Acts 21 [15]After this, we got ready and went up to Jerusalem. [16]Some of the disciples from Caesarea accompanied us and brought us to the home of Mnason, where we were to stay. He was a man from Cyprus and one of the early disciples.
Rom 12 [13]Share with God's people who are in need. Practice hospitality.
Rom 15 [23]But now that there is no more place for me to work in these regions, and since I have been longing for many years to see you, [24]I plan to do so when I go to Spain. I hope to visit you while passing through and to have you assist me on my journey there, after I have enjoyed your company for a while.
Rom 16 [23]Gaius, whose hospitality I and the whole church here enjoy, sends you his greetings. Erastus, who is the city's director of public works, and our brother Quartus send you their greetings.
1 Cor 16 [6]Perhaps I will stay with you awhile, or even spend the winter, so that you can help me on my journey, wherever I go. [7]I do not want to see you now and make only a passing visit; I hope to spend some time with you, if the Lord permits.
1 Cor 16 [10]If Timothy comes, see to it that he has nothing to fear while he is with you, for he is carrying on the work of the Lord, just as I am. [11]No one, then, should refuse to accept him. Send him on his way in peace so that he may return to me. I am expecting him along with the brothers.
Titus 3 [13]Do everything you can to help Zenas the lawyer and Apollos on their way and see that they have everything they need. [14]Our people must learn to devote themselves to doing what is good, in order that they may provide for daily necessities and not live unproductive lives.
Philem [22]And one thing more: Prepare a guest room for me, because I hope to be restored to you in answer to your prayers.
Heb 13 [2]Do not forget to entertain strangers, for by so doing some people have entertained angels without knowing it.
1 Pet 4 [9]Offer hospitality to one another without grumbling.
3 John [5]Dear friend, you are faithful in what you are doing for the brothers, even though they are strangers to you. [6]They have told the church about your love. You will do well to send them on their way in a manner worthy of God. [7]It was for the sake of the Name that they went out, receiving no help from the pagans. [8]We ought therefore to show hospitality to such men so that we may work together for the truth.

J. Meetings in the Church

Acts 2 [46]Every day they continued to meet together in the temple courts. They broke bread in their homes and ate together with glad and sincere hearts, [47]praising God and enjoying the favor of all the people. And the Lord added to their number daily those who were being saved.
Acts 4 [31]After they prayed, the place where they were meeting was shaken. And they were all filled with the Holy Spirit and spoke the word of God boldly.
Acts 20 [7]On the first day of the week we came together to break bread. Paul spoke to the people and, because he intended to leave the next day, kept on talking until midnight. [8]There were many lamps in the upstairs room where we were meeting. [9]Seated in a window was a young man named Eutychus, who was sinking into a deep sleep as Paul talked on and on. When he was sound asleep, he fell to the ground from the third story and was picked up dead. [10]Paul went down, threw himself on the young man and put his arms around him. "Don't be alarmed," he said. "He's alive!" [11]Then he went upstairs again and broke bread and ate. After talking until daylight, he left. [12]The people took the young man home alive and were greatly comforted.
Heb 10 [25]Let us not give up meeting together, as some are in the habit of doing, but let us encourage one another—and all the more as you see the Day approaching.

K. Performing Miracles in the Church

Acts 5 [12]The apostles performed many miraculous signs and wonders among the people. And all the believers used to meet together in Solomon's Colonnade.
Acts 6 [8]Now Stephen, a man full of God's grace and power, did great wonders and miraculous signs among the people.
Acts 8 [6]When the crowds heard Philip and saw the miraculous signs he did, they all paid close attention to what he said. [7]With shrieks, evil spirits came out of many, and many paralytics and cripples were healed. [8]So there was great joy in that city.

L. Prayer in the Church

2 Chron 7 [14]". . . if my people, who are called by my name, will humble themselves and pray and seek my face and turn from their wicked ways, then will I hear from heaven and will forgive their sin and will heal their land."
Ps 145 [18]The LORD is near to all who call on him, to all who call on him in truth. [19]He fulfills the desires of those who fear him; he hears their cry and saves them.
Isa 56 [6]"And foreigners who bind themselves to the LORD to serve him, to love the name of the LORD, and to worship him, all who keep the Sabbath without desecrating it and who hold fast to my covenant—[7]these I will bring to my holy mountain and give them joy in my house of prayer. Their burnt offerings and sacrifices will be accepted on my altar; for my house will be called a house of prayer for all nations."
Zech 8 [21]". . . and the inhabitants of one city will go to another and say, 'Let us go at once to entreat the LORD and seek the LORD Almighty. I myself am going.' [22]And many peoples and powerful nations will come to Jerusalem to seek the LORD Almighty and to entreat him."
Matt 18 [19]"Again, I tell you that if two of you on earth agree about anything you ask for, it will be done for you by my Father in heaven. [20]For where two or three come together in my name, there am I with them."
Luke 18 [1]Then Jesus told his disciples a parable to show them that they should always pray and not give up.
Acts 1 [14]They all joined together constantly in prayer, along with the women and Mary the mother of Jesus, and with his brothers.
Acts 2 [42]They devoted themselves to the apostles' teaching and to the fellowship, to the breaking of bread and to prayer.
Acts 4 [31]After they prayed, the place where they were meeting was shaken. And they were all filled with the Holy Spirit and spoke the word of God boldly.
Rom 8 [26]In the same way, the Spirit helps us in our weakness. We do not know what we ought to pray for, but the Spirit himself intercedes for us with groans that words cannot express.
Eph 6 [18]And pray in the Spirit on all occasions with all kinds of prayers and requests. With this in mind, be alert and always keep on praying for all the saints.

[19]Pray also for me, that whenever I open my mouth, words may be given me so that I will fearlessly make known the mystery of the gospel. . . .
Phil 4 [6]Do not be anxious about anything, but in everything, by

prayer and petition, with thanksgiving, present your requests to God.

Col 4 [2]Devote yourselves to prayer, being watchful and thankful.

1 Thess 5 [17]pray continually; [18]give thanks in all circumstances, for this is God's will for you in Christ Jesus.

1 Tim 2 [8]I want men everywhere to lift up holy hands in prayer, without anger or disputing.

Heb 4 [16]Let us then approach the throne of grace with confidence, so that we may receive mercy and find grace to help us in our time of need.

James 4 [8]Come near to God and he will come near to you. Wash your hands, you sinners, and purify your hearts, you double-minded. . . . [10]Humble yourselves before the Lord, and he will lift you up.

James 5 [16]Therefore confess your sins to each other and pray for each other so that you may be healed. The prayer of a righteous man is powerful and effective.

1 John 3 [21]Dear friends, if our hearts do not condemn us, we have confidence before God [22]and receive from him anything we ask, because we obey his commands and do what pleases him.

1 John 5 [14]This is the confidence we have in approaching God: that if we ask anything according to his will, he hears us. [15]And if we know that he hears us—whatever we ask—we know that we have what we asked of him.

Jude [20]But you, dear friends, build yourselves up in your most holy faith and pray in the Holy Spirit.

Rev 5 [8]And when he had taken it, the four living creatures and the twenty-four elders fell down before the Lamb. Each one had a harp and they were holding golden bowls full of incense, which are the prayers of the saints.

Rev 8 [3]Another angel, who had a golden censer, came and stood at the altar. He was given much incense to offer, with the prayers of all the saints, on the golden altar before the throne. [4]The smoke of the incense, together with the prayers of the saints, went up before God from the angel's hand.

M. Preaching the Gospel in the Church

Acts 5 [42]Day after day, in the temple courts and from house to house, they never stopped teaching and proclaiming the good news that Jesus is the Christ.

Acts 6 [7]So the word of God spread. The number of disciples in Jerusalem increased rapidly, and a large number of priests became obedient to the faith.

N. Reading of Scripture in the Church

Exod 24 [7]Then he took the Book of the Covenant and read it to the people. They responded, "We will do everything the LORD has said; we will obey."

Josh 8 [34]Afterward, Joshua read all the words of the law—the blessings and the curses—just as it is written in the Book of the Law. [35]There was not a word of all that Moses had commanded that Joshua did not read to the whole assembly of Israel, including the women and children, and the aliens who lived among them.

2 Kings 23 [1]Then the king called together all the elders of Judah and Jerusalem. [2]He went up to the temple of the LORD with the men of Judah, the people of Jerusalem, the priests and the prophets—all the people from the least to the greatest. He read in their hearing all the words of the Book of the Covenant, which had been found in the temple of the LORD. [3]The king stood by the pillar and renewed the covenant in the presence of the LORD—to follow the LORD and keep his commands, regulations and decrees with all his heart and all his soul, thus confirming the words of the covenant written in this book. Then all the people pledged themselves to the covenant.

Neh 8 [7]The Levites—Jeshua, Bani, Sherebiah, Jamin, Akkub, Shabbethai, Hodiah, Maaseiah, Kelita, Azariah, Jozabad, Hanan and Pelaiah—instructed the people in the Law while the people were standing there. [8]They read from the Book of the Law of God, making it clear and giving the meaning so that the people could understand what was being read.

Neh 9 [3]They stood where they were and read from the Book of the Law of the LORD their God for a quarter of the day, and spent another quarter in confession and in worshiping the LORD their God.

1 Tim 4 [13]Until I come, devote yourself to the public reading of Scripture, to preaching and to teaching.

2 Tim 3 [15]and how from infancy you have known the holy Scriptures, which are able to make you wise for salvation through faith in Christ Jesus. [16]All Scripture is God-breathed and is useful for teaching, rebuking, correcting and training in righteousness, [17]so that the man of God may be thoroughly equipped for every good work.

Rev 1 [3]Blessed is the one who reads the words of this prophecy, and blessed are those who hear it and take to heart what is written in it, because the time is near.

O. Sacraments in the Church

See p. 732a, The Sacraments/Ordinances of the Church

P. Service in the Church

Rom 12 [10]Be devoted to one another in brotherly love. Honor one another above yourselves. [11]Never be lacking in zeal, but keep your spiritual fervor, serving the Lord.

1 Cor 12 [5]There are different kinds of service, but the same Lord.

1 Cor 16 [15]You know that the household of Stephanas were the first converts in Achaia, and they have devoted themselves to the service of the saints. I urge you, brothers, [16]to submit to such as these and to everyone who joins in the work, and labors at it.

Eph 4 [11]It was he who gave some to be apostles, some to be prophets, some to be evangelists, and some to be pastors and teachers, [12]to prepare God's people for works of service, so that the body of Christ may be built up. . . .

1 Pet 4 [10]Each one should use whatever gift he has received to serve others, faithfully administering God's grace in its various forms. [11]If anyone speaks, he should do it as one speaking the very words of God. If anyone serves, he should do it with the strength God provides, so that in all things God may be praised through Jesus Christ. To him be the glory and the power for ever and ever. Amen.

Rev 2 [2]"I know your deeds, your hard work and your perseverance. I know that you cannot tolerate wicked men, that you have tested those who claim to be apostles but are not, and have found them false."

Rev 2 [19]"I know your deeds, your love and faith, your service and perseverance, and that you are now doing more than you did at first."

Q. Teaching in the Church

Deut 6 [4]Hear, O Israel: The LORD our God, the LORD is one. [5]Love the LORD your God with all your heart and with all your soul and with all your strength. [6]These commandments that I give you today are to be upon your hearts. [7]Impress them on your children. Talk about them when you sit at home and when you walk along the road, when you lie down and when you get up. [8]Tie them as symbols on your hands and bind them on your foreheads. [9]Write them on the doorframes of your houses and on your gates.

2 Chron 17 [7]In the third year of his reign he sent his officials Ben-Hail, Obadiah, Zechariah, Nethanel and Micaiah to teach in the towns of Judah. [8]With them were certain Levites—Shemaiah, Nethaniah, Zebadiah, Asahel, Shemiramoth, Jehonathan, Adonijah, Tobijah and Tob-Adonijah—and the priests Elishama and Jehoram. [9]They taught throughout Judah, taking with them the Book of the Law of the LORD; they went around to all the towns of Judah and taught the people.

Ezra 7 [10]For Ezra had devoted himself to the study and observance of the Law of the LORD, and to teaching its decrees and laws in Israel.

Acts 5 [42]Day after day, in the temple courts and from house to

house, they never stopped teaching and proclaiming the good news that Jesus is the Christ.
Acts 11 26and when he found him, he brought him to Antioch. So for a whole year Barnabas and Saul met with the church and taught great numbers of people. The disciples were called Christians first at Antioch.
Rom 15 14I myself am convinced, my brothers, that you yourselves are full of goodness, complete in knowledge and competent to instruct one another.
1 Cor 14 31For you can all prophesy in turn so that everyone may be instructed and encouraged.
Eph 5 19Speak to one another with psalms, hymns and spiritual songs. Sing and make music in your heart to the Lord. . . .
Col 1 28We proclaim him, admonishing and teaching everyone with all wisdom, so that we may present everyone perfect in Christ.
Col 3 16Let the word of Christ dwell in you richly as you teach and admonish one another with all wisdom, and as you sing psalms, hymns and spiritual songs with gratitude in your hearts to God.
1 Tim 4 11Command and teach these things.
2 Tim 2 25Those who oppose him he must gently instruct, in the hope that God will grant them repentance leading them to a knowledge of the truth. . . .
2 Tim 4 2Preach the Word; be prepared in season and out of season; correct, rebuke and encourage—with great patience and careful instruction.
Heb 5 12In fact, though by this time you ought to be teachers, you need someone to teach you the elementary truths of God's word all over again. You need milk, not solid food!

R. Testing Prophets and Teachers in the Church

Rev 2 2"I know your deeds, your hard work and your perseverance. I know that you cannot tolerate wicked men, that you have tested those who claim to be apostles but are not, and have found them false."

S. Worship in the Church

Neh 8 6Ezra praised the LORD, the great God; and all the people lifted their hands and responded, "Amen! Amen!" Then they bowed down and worshiped the LORD with their faces to the ground.
Neh 9 3They stood where they were and read from the Book of the Law of the LORD their God for a quarter of the day, and spent another quarter in confession and in worshiping the LORD their God.
Ps 5 7But I, by your great mercy, will come into your house; in reverence will I bow down toward your holy temple.
Ps 22 22I will declare your name to my brothers; in the congregation I will praise you.
Ps 24 3Who may ascend the hill of the LORD? Who may stand in his holy place? 4He who has clean hands and a pure heart, who does not lift up his soul to an idol or swear by what is false. 5He will receive blessing from the LORD and vindication from God his Savior. 6Such is the generation of those who seek him, who seek your face, O God of Jacob.
Ps 29 2Ascribe to the LORD the glory due his name; worship the LORD in the splendor of his holiness.
Ps 35 18I will give you thanks in the great assembly; among throngs of people I will praise you.
Ps 89 7In the council of the holy ones God is greatly feared; he is more awesome than all who surround him.
Ps 95 6Come, let us bow down in worship, let us kneel before the LORD our Maker; 7for he is our God and we are the people of his pasture, the flock under his care. Today, if you hear his voice . . .
Ps 100 1Shout for joy to the LORD, all the earth. 2Worship the LORD with gladness; come before him with joyful songs. 3Know that the LORD is God. It is he who made us, and we are his; we are his people, the sheep of his pasture. 4Enter his gates with thanksgiving and his courts with praise; give thanks to him and praise his name.
Ps 107 31Let them give thanks to the LORD for his unfailing love and his wonderful deeds for men. 32Let them exalt him in the assembly of the people and praise him in the council of the elders.
Ps 122 1I rejoiced with those who said to me, "Let us go to the house of the LORD."
Ps 132 7"Let us go to his dwelling place; let us worship at his footstool—8arise, O LORD, and come to your resting place, you and the ark of your might. 9May your priests be clothed with righteousness; may your saints sing for joy." 10For the sake of David your servant, do not reject your anointed one.

11The LORD swore an oath to David, a sure oath that he will not revoke: "One of your own descendants I will place on your throne—12if your sons keep my covenant and the statutes I teach them, then their sons will sit on your throne for ever and ever."

13For the LORD has chosen Zion, he has desired it for his dwelling: 14"This is my resting place for ever and ever; here I will sit enthroned, for I have desired it—15I will bless her with abundant provisions; her poor will I satisfy with food. 16I will clothe her priests with salvation, and her saints will ever sing for joy.

17"Here I will make a horn grow for David and set up a lamp for my anointed one. 18I will clothe his enemies with shame, but the crown on his head will be resplendent."
Ps 149 1Praise the LORD. Sing to the LORD a new song, his praise in the assembly of the saints.

2Let Israel rejoice in their Maker; let the people of Zion be glad in their King. 3Let them praise his name with dancing and make music to him with tambourine and harp. 4For the LORD takes delight in his people; he crowns the humble with salvation. 5Let the saints rejoice in this honor and sing for joy on their beds.
Ps 150 1Praise the LORD. Praise God in his sanctuary; praise him in his mighty heavens. 2Praise him for his acts of power; praise him for his surpassing greatness. 3Praise him with the sounding of the trumpet, praise him with the harp and lyre, 4praise him with tambourine and dancing, praise him with the strings and flute, 5praise him with the clash of cymbals, praise him with resounding cymbals.

6Let everything that has breath praise the LORD. Praise the LORD.
Isa 2 3Many peoples will come and say, "Come, let us go up to the mountain of the LORD, to the house of the God of Jacob. He will teach us his ways, so that we may walk in his paths." The law will go out from Zion, the word of the LORD from Jerusalem.
Isa 12 4In that day you will say: "Give thanks to the LORD, call on his name; make known among the nations what he has done, and proclaim that his name is exalted. 5Sing to the LORD, for he has done glorious things; let this be known to all the world. 6Shout aloud and sing for joy, people of Zion, for great is the Holy One of Israel among you."
Isa 25 9In that day they will say, "Surely this is our God; we trusted in him, and he saved us. This is the LORD, we trusted in him; let us rejoice and be glad in his salvation."
Isa 30 29And you will sing as on the night you celebrate a holy festival; your hearts will rejoice as when people go up with flutes to the mountain of the LORD, to the Rock of Israel.
Isa 38 20The LORD will save me, and we will sing with stringed instruments all the days of our lives in the temple of the LORD.
Isa 52 9Burst into songs of joy together, you ruins of Jerusalem, for the LORD has comforted his people, he has redeemed Jerusalem.
Jer 31 11"For the LORD will ransom Jacob and redeem them from the hand of those stronger than they. 12They will come and shout for joy on the heights of Zion; they will rejoice in the bounty of the LORD—the grain, the new wine and the oil, the young of the flocks and herds. They will be like a well-watered garden, and they will sorrow no more. 13Then maidens will dance and be glad, young men and old as well. I will turn their mourning into gladness; I will give them comfort and joy instead of sorrow. 14I will satisfy the priests with abundance, and my people will be filled with my bounty," declares the LORD.
John 4 23"Yet a time is coming and has now come when the

true worshipers will worship the Father in spirit and truth, for they are the kind of worshipers the Father seeks. 24God is spirit, and his worshipers must worship in spirit and in truth."
Acts 2 46Every day they continued to meet together in the temple courts. They broke bread in their homes and ate together with glad and sincere hearts, 47praising God and enjoying the favor of all the people. And the Lord added to their number daily those who were being saved.
Acts 13 2While they were worshiping the Lord and fasting, the Holy Spirit said, "Set apart for me Barnabas and Saul for the work to which I have called them."
Eph 5 19Speak to one another with psalms, hymns and spiritual songs. Sing and make music in your heart to the Lord, 20always giving thanks to God the Father for everything, in the name of our Lord Jesus Christ.
Phil 3 3For it is we who are the circumcision, we who worship by the Spirit of God, who glory in Christ Jesus, and who put no confidence in the flesh. . . .
Heb 12 28Therefore, since we are receiving a kingdom that cannot be shaken, let us be thankful, and so worship God acceptably with reverence and awe. . . .
1 Pet 2 5you also, like living stones, are being built into a spiritual house to be a holy priesthood, offering spiritual sacrifices acceptable to God through Jesus Christ.
Rev 4 10the twenty-four elders fall down before him who sits on the throne, and worship him who lives for ever and ever. They lay their crowns before the throne and say: 11"You are worthy, our Lord and God, to receive glory and honor and power, for you created all things, and by your will they were created and have their being."
Rev 5 14The four living creatures said, "Amen," and the elders fell down and worshiped.
Rev 7 11All the angels were standing around the throne and around the elders and the four living creatures. They fell down on their faces before the throne and worshiped God. . . .
Rev 11 1I was given a reed like a measuring rod and was told, "Go and measure the temple of God and the altar, and count the worshipers there."
Rev 19 4The twenty-four elders and the four living creatures fell down and worshiped God, who was seated on the throne. And they cried: "Amen, Hallelujah!"

VII The Organization and Officers of the Church

A. Ministers in General

1. The Existence of Leaders

Exod 3 1Now Moses was tending the flock of Jethro his father-in-law, the priest of Midian, and he led the flock to the far side of the desert and came to Horeb, the mountain of God. 2There the angel of the LORD appeared to him in flames of fire from within a bush. Moses saw that though the bush was on fire it did not burn up. 3So Moses thought, "I will go over and see this strange sight—why the bush does not burn up."

4When the LORD saw that he had gone over to look, God called to him from within the bush, "Moses! Moses!" And Moses said, "Here I am."

5"Do not come any closer," God said. "Take off your sandals, for the place where you are standing is holy ground." 6Then he said, "I am the God of your father, the God of Abraham, the God of Isaac and the God of Jacob." At this, Moses hid his face, because he was afraid to look at God.

7The LORD said, "I have indeed seen the misery of my people in Egypt. I have heard them crying out because of their slave drivers, and I am concerned about their suffering. 8So I have come down to rescue them from the hand of the Egyptians and to bring them up out of that land into a good and spacious land, a land flowing with milk and honey—the home of the Canaanites, Hittites, Amorites, Perizzites, Hivites and Jebusites. 9And now the cry of the Israelites has reached me, and I have seen the way the Egyptians are oppressing them. 10So now, go. I am sending you to Pharaoh to bring my people the Israelites out of Egypt."
Exod 28 1"Have Aaron your brother brought to you from among the Israelites, along with his sons Nadab and Abihu, Eleazar and Ithamar, so they may serve me as priests."
Num 3 5The LORD said to Moses, 6"Bring the tribe of Levi and present them to Aaron the priest to assist him. 7They are to perform duties for him and for the whole community at the Tent of Meeting by doing the work of the tabernacle. 8They are to take care of all the furnishings of the Tent of Meeting, fulfilling the obligations of the Israelites by doing the work of the tabernacle. 9Give the Levites to Aaron and his sons; they are the Israelites who are to be given wholly to him. 10Appoint Aaron and his sons to serve as priests; anyone else who approaches the sanctuary must be put to death."

11The LORD also said to Moses, 12"I have taken the Levites from among the Israelites in place of the first male offspring of every Israelite woman. The Levites are mine, 13for all the firstborn are mine. When I struck down all the firstborn in Egypt, I set apart for myself every firstborn in Israel, whether man or animal. They are to be mine. I am the LORD."
Num 16 9"Isn't it enough for you that the God of Israel has separated you from the rest of the Israelite community and brought you near himself to do the work at the LORD's tabernacle and to stand before the community and minister to them?"
1 Sam 3 1The boy Samuel ministered before the LORD under Eli. In those days the word of the LORD was rare; there were not many visions.

2One night Eli, whose eyes were becoming so weak that he could barely see, was lying down in his usual place. 3The lamp of God had not yet gone out, and Samuel was lying down in the temple of the LORD, where the ark of God was. 4Then the LORD called Samuel.

Samuel answered, "Here I am." 5And he ran to Eli and said, "Here I am; you called me."

But Eli said, "I did not call; go back and lie down." So he went and lay down.

6Again the LORD called, "Samuel!" And Samuel got up and went to Eli and said, "Here I am; you called me."

"My son," Eli said, "I did not call; go back and lie down."

7Now Samuel did not yet know the LORD: The word of the LORD had not yet been revealed to him.

8The LORD called Samuel a third time, and Samuel got up and went to Eli and said, "Here I am; you called me."

Then Eli realized that the LORD was calling the boy. 9So Eli told Samuel, "Go and lie down, and if he calls you, say, 'Speak, LORD, for your servant is listening.'" So Samuel went and lay down in his place.

10The LORD came and stood there, calling as at the other times, "Samuel! Samuel!"

Then Samuel said, "Speak, for your servant is listening."
1 Kings 19 16"Also, anoint Jehu son of Nimshi king over Israel, and anoint Elisha son of Shaphat from Abel Meholah to succeed you as prophet. . . ."

19So Elijah went from there and found Elisha son of Shaphat. He was plowing with twelve yoke of oxen, and he himself was driving the twelfth pair. Elijah went up to him and threw his cloak around him. 20Elisha then left his oxen and ran after Elijah. "Let me kiss my father and mother good-by," he said, "and then I will come with you."

"Go back," Elijah replied. "What have I done to you?"

21So Elisha left him and went back. He took his yoke of oxen and slaughtered them. He burned the plowing equipment to cook the meat and gave it to the people, and they ate. Then he set out to follow Elijah and became his attendant.
1 Chron 23 13The sons of Amram: Aaron and Moses. Aaron was set apart, he and his descendants forever, to consecrate the most holy things, to offer sacrifices before the LORD, to minister before him and to pronounce blessings in his name forever.
2 Chron 29 11"My sons, do not be negligent now, for the LORD has chosen you to stand before him and serve him, to minister before him and to burn incense."
Ezra 7 1After these things, during the reign of Artaxerxes king of Persia, Ezra son of Seraiah, the son of Azariah, the son of Hilkiah . . . 5the son of Abishua, the son of Phinehas, the son of

Eleazar, the son of Aaron the chief priest—6this Ezra came up from Babylon. He was a teacher well versed in the Law of Moses, which the LORD, the God of Israel, had given. The king had granted him everything he asked, for the hand of the LORD his God was on him. . . .

21Now I, King Artaxerxes, order all the treasurers of Trans-Euphrates to provide with diligence whatever Ezra the priest, a teacher of the Law of the God of heaven, may ask of you. . . .

Ps 99 6Moses and Aaron were among his priests, Samuel was among those who called on his name; they called on the LORD and he answered them.

Isa 6 8Then I heard the voice of the LORD saying, "Whom shall I send? And who will go for us?" And I said, "Here am I. Send me!"

Jer 1 5"Before I formed you in the womb I knew you, before you were born I set you apart; I appointed you as a prophet to the nations."

Ezek 2 1He said to me, "Son of man, stand up on your feet and I will speak to you." 2As he spoke, the Spirit came into me and raised me to my feet, and I heard him speaking to me.

3He said: "Son of man, I am sending you to the Israelites, to a rebellious nation that has rebelled against me; they and their fathers have been in revolt against me to this very day. 4The people to whom I am sending you are obstinate and stubborn. Say to them, 'This is what the Sovereign LORD says.' 5And whether they listen or fail to listen—for they are a rebellious house—they will know that a prophet has been among them. 6And you, son of man, do not be afraid of them or their words. Do not be afraid, though briers and thorns are all around you and you live among scorpions. Do not be afraid of what they say or terrified by them, though they are a rebellious house."

Amos 2 11"I also raised up prophets from among your sons and Nazirites from among your young men. Is this not true, people of Israel?" declares the LORD.

Jon 1 1The word of the LORD came to Jonah son of Amittai: 2"Go to the great city of Nineveh and preach against it, because its wickedness has come up before me."

Mark 1 16As Jesus walked beside the Sea of Galilee, he saw Simon and his brother Andrew casting a net into the lake, for they were fishermen. 17"Come, follow me," Jesus said, "and I will make you fishers of men." 18At once they left their nets and followed him.

19When he had gone a little farther, he saw James son of Zebedee and his brother John in a boat, preparing their nets. 20Without delay he called them, and they left their father Zebedee in the boat with the hired men and followed him.

Mark 2 14As he walked along, he saw Levi son of Alphaeus sitting at the tax collector's booth. "Follow me," Jesus told him, and Levi got up and followed him.

Luke 10 1After this the Lord appointed seventy-two others and sent them two by two ahead of him to every town and place where he was about to go. 2He told them, "The harvest is plentiful, but the workers are few. Ask the Lord of the harvest, therefore, to send out workers into his harvest field."

John 1 43The next day Jesus decided to leave for Galilee. Finding Philip, he said to him, "Follow me."

44Philip, like Andrew and Peter, was from the town of Bethsaida. 45Philip found Nathanael and told him, "We have found the one Moses wrote about in the Law, and about whom the prophets also wrote—Jesus of Nazareth, the son of Joseph."

46"Nazareth! Can anything good come from there?" Nathanael asked.

"Come and see," said Philip. 47When Jesus saw Nathanael approaching, he said of him, "Here is a true Israelite, in whom there is nothing false."

48"How do you know me?" Nathanael asked.

Jesus answered, "I saw you while you were still under the fig tree before Philip called you."

49Then Nathanael declared, "Rabbi, you are the Son of God; you are the King of Israel."

50Jesus said, "You believe because I told you I saw you under the fig tree. You shall see greater things than that." 51He then added, "I tell you the truth, you shall see heaven open, and the angels of God ascending and descending on the Son of Man."

Acts 11 30This they did, sending their gift to the elders by Barnabas and Saul.

Acts 13 1In the church at Antioch there were prophets and teachers: Barnabas, Simeon called Niger, Lucius of Cyrene, Manaen (who had been brought up with Herod the tetrarch) and Saul. 2While they were worshiping the Lord and fasting, the Holy Spirit said, "Set apart for me Barnabas and Saul for the work to which I have called them." 3So after they had fasted and prayed, they placed their hands on them and sent them off.

Acts 14 23Paul and Barnabas appointed elders for them in each church and, with prayer and fasting, committed them to the Lord, in whom they had put their trust.

Acts 15 22Then the apostles and elders, with the whole church, decided to choose some of their own men and send them to Antioch with Paul and Barnabas. They chose Judas (called Barsabbas) and Silas, two men who were leaders among the brothers.

Acts 20 17From Miletus, Paul sent to Ephesus for the elders of the church.

Acts 26 14"We all fell to the ground, and I heard a voice saying to me in Aramaic, 'Saul, Saul, why do you persecute me? It is hard for you to kick against the goads.'

15"Then I asked, 'Who are you, Lord?'

"'I am Jesus, whom you are persecuting,' the Lord replied. 16'Now get up and stand on your feet. I have appeared to you to appoint you as a servant and as a witness of what you have seen of me and what I will show you. 17I will rescue you from your own people and from the Gentiles. I am sending you to them 18to open their eyes and turn them from darkness to light, and from the power of Satan to God, so that they may receive forgiveness of sins and a place among those who are sanctified by faith in me.'"

Rom 1 1Paul, a servant of Christ Jesus, called to be an apostle and set apart for the gospel of God. . . .

1 Cor 1 1Paul, called to be an apostle of Christ Jesus by the will of God, and our brother Sosthenes. . . .

2 Cor 5 18All this is from God, who reconciled us to himself through Christ and gave us the ministry of reconciliation: 19that God was reconciling the world to himself in Christ, not counting men's sins against them. And he has committed to us the message of reconciliation. 20We are therefore Christ's ambassadors, as though God were making his appeal through us. We implore you on Christ's behalf: Be reconciled to God.

Eph 4 10(He who descended is the very one who ascended higher than all the heavens, in order to fill the whole universe.) 11It was he who gave some to be apostles, some to be prophets, some to be evangelists, and some to be pastors and teachers, 12to prepare God's people for works of service, so that the body of Christ may be built up. . . .

Col 1 24Now I rejoice in what was suffered for you, and I fill up in my flesh what is still lacking in regard to Christ's afflictions, for the sake of his body, which is the church. 25I have become its servant by the commission God gave me to present to you the word of God in its fullness—26the mystery that has been kept hidden for ages and generations, but is now disclosed to the saints. 27To them God has chosen to make known among the Gentiles the glorious riches of this mystery, which is Christ in you, the hope of glory.

28We proclaim him, admonishing and teaching everyone with all wisdom, so that we may present everyone perfect in Christ. 29To this end I labor, struggling with all his energy, which so powerfully works in me.

Col 4 17Tell Archippus: "See to it that you complete the work you have received in the Lord."

1 Tim 1 12I thank Christ Jesus our Lord, who has given me strength, that he considered me faithful, appointing me to his service. 13Even though I was once a blasphemer and a persecutor and a violent man, I was shown mercy because I acted in ignorance and unbelief. 14The grace of our Lord was poured out on me abundantly, along with the faith and love that are in Christ Jesus.

1 Tim 2 7And for this purpose I was appointed a herald and an apostle—I am telling the truth, I am not lying—and a teacher of the true faith to the Gentiles.

Heb 5 [4]No one takes this honor upon himself; he must be called by God, just as Aaron was.
1 Pet 5 [1]To the elders among you, I appeal as a fellow elder, a witness of Christ's sufferings and one who also will share in the glory to be revealed. . . .

2. Qualifications for Leaders

Lev 10 [3]Moses then said to Aaron, "This is what the LORD spoke of when he said: 'Among those who approach me I will show myself holy; in the sight of all the people I will be honored.'" Aaron remained silent.

[4]Moses summoned Mishael and Elzaphan, sons of Aaron's uncle Uzziel, and said to them, "Come here; carry your cousins outside the camp, away from the front of the sanctuary." [5]So they came and carried them, still in their tunics, outside the camp, as Moses ordered.

[6]Then Moses said to Aaron and his sons Eleazar and Ithamar, "Do not let your hair become unkempt, and do not tear your clothes, or you will die and the LORD will be angry with the whole community. But your relatives, all the house of Israel, may mourn for those the LORD has destroyed by fire. [7]Do not leave the entrance to the Tent of Meeting or you will die, because the LORD's anointing oil is on you." So they did as Moses said.

[8]Then the LORD said to Aaron, [9]"You and your sons are not to drink wine or other fermented drink whenever you go into the Tent of Meeting, or you will die. This is a lasting ordinance for the generations to come. [10]You must distinguish between the holy and the common, between the unclean and the clean, [11]and you must teach the Israelites all the decrees the LORD has given them through Moses."
Lev 21 [5]"'Priests must not shave their heads or shave off the edges of their beards or cut their bodies. [6]They must be holy to their God and must not profane the name of their God. Because they present the offerings made to the LORD by fire, the food of their God, they are to be holy.'"
Josh 1 [8]"Do not let this Book of the Law depart from your mouth; meditate on it day and night, so that you may be careful to do everything written in it. Then you will be prosperous and successful."
1 Sam 2 [35]"'I will raise up for myself a faithful priest, who will do according to what is in my heart and mind. I will firmly establish his house, and he will minister before my anointed one always.'"
2 Chron 6 [41]"Now arise, O LORD God, and come to your resting place, you and the ark of your might. May your priests, O LORD God, be clothed with salvation, may your saints rejoice in your goodness."
Ezra 7 [10]For Ezra had devoted himself to the study and observance of the Law of the LORD, and to teaching its decrees and laws in Israel.
Isa 52 [11]Depart, depart, go out from there! Touch no unclean thing! Come out from it and be pure, you who carry the vessels of the LORD.
Jer 1 [7]But the LORD said to me, "Do not say, 'I am only a child.' You must go to everyone I send you to and say whatever I command you. [8]Do not be afraid of them, for I am with you and will rescue you," declares the LORD.
Jer 3 [14]"Return, faithless people," declares the LORD, "for I am your husband. I will choose you—one from a town and two from a clan—and bring you to Zion. [15]Then I will give you shepherds after my own heart, who will lead you with knowledge and understanding."
Jer 20 [8]Whenever I speak, I cry out proclaiming violence and destruction. So the word of the LORD has brought me insult and reproach all day long. [9]But if I say, "I will not mention him or speak any more in his name," his word is in my heart like a fire, a fire shut up in my bones. I am weary of holding it in; indeed, I cannot.
Mal 2 [6]True instruction was in his mouth and nothing false was found on his lips. He walked with me in peace and uprightness, and turned many from sin.

[7]"For the lips of a priest ought to preserve knowledge, and from his mouth men should seek instruction—because he is the messenger of the LORD Almighty."
Matt 10 [16]"I am sending you out like sheep among wolves. Therefore be as shrewd as snakes and as innocent as doves.

[17]"Be on your guard against men; they will hand you over to the local councils and flog you in their synagogues. [18]On my account you will be brought before governors and kings as witnesses to them and to the Gentiles. [19]But when they arrest you, do not worry about what to say or how to say it. At that time you will be given what to say, [20]for it will not be you speaking, but the Spirit of your Father speaking through you.

[21]"Brother will betray brother to death, and a father his child; children will rebel against their parents and have them put to death. [22]All men will hate you because of me, but he who stands firm to the end will be saved. [23]When you are persecuted in one place, flee to another. I tell you the truth, you will not finish going through the cities of Israel before the Son of Man comes.

[24]"A student is not above his teacher, nor a servant above his master. [25]It is enough for the student to be like his teacher, and the servant like his master. If the head of the house has been called Beelzebub, how much more the members of his household!"
Matt 20 [25]Jesus called them together and said, "You know that the rulers of the Gentiles lord it over them, and their high officials exercise authority over them. [26]Not so with you. Instead, whoever wants to become great among you must be your servant, [27]and whoever wants to be first must be your slave—[28]just as the Son of Man did not come to be served, but to serve, and to give his life as a ransom for many."
Matt 23 [8]"But you are not to be called 'Rabbi,' for you have only one Master and you are all brothers. [9]And do not call anyone on earth 'father,' for you have one Father, and he is in heaven. [10]Nor are you to be called 'teacher,' for you have one Teacher, the Christ. [11]The greatest among you will be your servant."
Luke 12 [42]The Lord answered, "Who then is the faithful and wise manager, whom the master puts in charge of his servants to give them their food allowance at the proper time? [43]It will be good for that servant whom the master finds doing so when he returns. [44]I tell you the truth, he will put him in charge of all his possessions."
Luke 24 [49]"I am going to send you what my Father has promised; but stay in the city until you have been clothed with power from on high."
John 10 [2]"The man who enters by the gate is the shepherd of his sheep. [3]The watchman opens the gate for him, and the sheep listen to his voice. He calls his own sheep by name and leads them out. [4]When he has brought out all his own, he goes on ahead of them, and his sheep follow him because they know his voice. [5]But they will never follow a stranger; in fact, they will run away from him because they do not recognize a stranger's voice." . . .

[11]"I am the good shepherd. The good shepherd lays down his life for the sheep. [12]The hired hand is not the shepherd who owns the sheep. So when he sees the wolf coming, he abandons the sheep and runs away. Then the wolf attacks the flock and scatters it. [13]The man runs away because he is a hired hand and cares nothing for the sheep.

[14]"I am the good shepherd; I know my sheep and my sheep know me—[15]just as the Father knows me and I know the Father—and I lay down my life for the sheep. [16]I have other sheep that are not of this sheep pen. I must bring them also. They too will listen to my voice, and there shall be one flock and one shepherd."
John 13 [13]"You call me 'Teacher' and 'Lord,' and rightly so, for that is what I am. [14]Now that I, your Lord and Teacher, have washed your feet, you also should wash one another's feet. [15]I have set you an example that you should do as I have done for you. [16]I tell you the truth, no servant is greater than his master, nor is a messenger greater than the one who sent him. [17]Now that you know these things, you will be blessed if you do them."
John 17 [15]"My prayer is not that you take them out of the world but that you protect them from the evil one. [16]They are not of the world, even as I am not of it. [17]Sanctify them by the truth; your word is truth. [18]As you sent me into the world, I have sent them into the world. [19]For them I sanctify myself, that they too may be truly sanctified.

20"My prayer is not for them alone. I pray also for those who will believe in me through their message. . . ."

Acts 4 8Then Peter, filled with the Holy Spirit, said to them: "Rulers and elders of the people! . . ."

31After they prayed, the place where they were meeting was shaken. And they were all filled with the Holy Spirit and spoke the word of God boldly.

Rom 2 21you, then, who teach others, do you not teach yourself? You who preach against stealing, do you steal? 22You who say that people should not commit adultery, do you commit adultery? You who abhor idols, do you rob temples? 23You who brag about the law, do you dishonor God by breaking the law?

1 Cor 2 2For I resolved to know nothing while I was with you except Jesus Christ and him crucified.

1 Cor 3 5What, after all, is Apollos? And what is Paul? Only servants, through whom you came to believe—as the Lord has assigned to each his task. 6I planted the seed, Apollos watered it, but God made it grow. 7So neither he who plants nor he who waters is anything, but only God, who makes things grow. 8The man who plants and the man who waters have one purpose, and each will be rewarded according to his own labor. 9For we are God's fellow workers; you are God's field, God's building.

1 Cor 4 1So then, men ought to regard us as servants of Christ and as those entrusted with the secret things of God. 2Now it is required that those who have been given a trust must prove faithful. . . .

10We are fools for Christ, but you are so wise in Christ! We are weak, but you are strong! You are honored, we are dishonored! 11To this very hour we go hungry and thirsty, we are in rags, we are brutally treated, we are homeless. 12We work hard with our own hands. When we are cursed, we bless; when we are persecuted, we endure it; 13when we are slandered, we answer kindly. Up to this moment we have become the scum of the earth, the refuse of the world.

1 Cor 9 16Yet when I preach the gospel, I cannot boast, for I am compelled to preach. Woe to me if I do not preach the gospel! 17If I preach voluntarily, I have a reward; if not voluntarily, I am simply discharging the trust committed to me. 18What then is my reward? Just this: that in preaching the gospel I may offer it free of charge, and so not make use of my rights in preaching it.

19Though I am free and belong to no man, I make myself a slave to everyone, to win as many as possible. 20To the Jews I became like a Jew, to win the Jews. To those under the law I became like one under the law (though I myself am not under the law), so as to win those under the law. 21To those not having the law I became like one not having the law (though I am not free from God's law but am under Christ's law), so as to win those not having the law. 22To the weak I became weak, to win the weak. I have become all things to all men so that by all possible means I might save some. 23I do all this for the sake of the gospel, that I may share in its blessings.

2 Cor 2 15For we are to God the aroma of Christ among those who are being saved and those who are perishing. 16To the one we are the smell of death; to the other, the fragrance of life. And who is equal to such a task? 17Unlike so many, we do not peddle the word of God for profit. On the contrary, in Christ we speak before God with sincerity, like men sent from God.

2 Cor 4 1Therefore, since through God's mercy we have this ministry, we do not lose heart. 2Rather, we have renounced secret and shameful ways; we do not use deception, nor do we distort the word of God. On the contrary, by setting forth the truth plainly we commend ourselves to every man's conscience in the sight of God. 3And even if our gospel is veiled, it is veiled to those who are perishing. 4The god of this age has blinded the minds of unbelievers, so that they cannot see the light of the gospel of the glory of Christ, who is the image of God. 5For we do not preach ourselves, but Jesus Christ as Lord, and ourselves as your servants for Jesus' sake. 6For God, who said, "Let light shine out of darkness," made his light shine in our hearts to give us the light of the knowledge of the glory of God in the face of Christ.

7But we have this treasure in jars of clay to show that this all-surpassing power is from God and not from us. 8We are hard pressed on every side, but not crushed; perplexed, but not in despair; 9persecuted, but not abandoned; struck down, but not destroyed. 10We always carry around in our body the death of Jesus, so that the life of Jesus may also be revealed in our body. 11For we who are alive are always being given over to death for Jesus' sake, so that his life may be revealed in our mortal body.

2 Cor 6 3We put no stumbling block in anyone's path, so that our ministry will not be discredited. 4Rather, as servants of God we commend ourselves in every way: in great endurance; in troubles, hardships and distresses; 5in beatings, imprisonments and riots; in hard work, sleepless nights and hunger; 6in purity, understanding, patience and kindness; in the Holy Spirit and in sincere love; 7in truthful speech and in the power of God; with weapons of righteousness in the right hand and in the left; 8through glory and dishonor, bad report and good report; genuine, yet regarded as impostors; 9known, yet regarded as unknown; dying, and yet we live on; beaten, and yet not killed; 10sorrowful, yet always rejoicing; poor, yet making many rich; having nothing, and yet possessing everything.

Gal 6 17Finally, let no one cause me trouble, for I bear on my body the marks of Jesus.

1 Thess 2 3For the appeal we make does not spring from error or impure motives, nor are we trying to trick you. 4On the contrary, we speak as men approved by God to be entrusted with the gospel. We are not trying to please men but God, who tests our hearts. 5You know we never used flattery, nor did we put on a mask to cover up greed—God is our witness. 6We were not looking for praise from men, not from you or anyone else.

As apostles of Christ we could have been a burden to you, 7but we were gentle among you, like a mother caring for her little children. 8We loved you so much that we were delighted to share with you not only the gospel of God but our lives as well, because you had become so dear to us. 9Surely you remember, brothers, our toil and hardship; we worked night and day in order not to be a burden to anyone while we preached the gospel of God to you.

10You are witnesses, and so is God, of how holy, righteous and blameless we were among you who believed. 11For you know that we dealt with each of you as a father deals with his own children, 12encouraging, comforting and urging you to live lives worthy of God, who calls you into his kingdom and glory.

1 Tim 6 11But you, man of God, flee from all this, and pursue righteousness, godliness, faith, love, endurance and gentleness. 12Fight the good fight of the faith. Take hold of the eternal life to which you were called when you made your good confession in the presence of many witnesses. 13In the sight of God, who gives life to everything, and of Christ Jesus, who while testifying before Pontius Pilate made the good confession, I charge you 14to keep this command without spot or blame until the appearing of our Lord Jesus Christ. . . .

2 Tim 1 13What you heard from me, keep as the pattern of sound teaching, with faith and love in Christ Jesus. 14Guard the good deposit that was entrusted to you—guard it with the help of the Holy Spirit who lives in us.

2 Tim 2 1You then, my son, be strong in the grace that is in Christ Jesus. 2And the things you have heard me say in the presence of many witnesses entrust to reliable men who will also be qualified to teach others. 3Endure hardship with us like a good soldier of Christ Jesus. 4No one serving as a soldier gets involved in civilian affairs—he wants to please his commanding officer. 5Similarly, if anyone competes as an athlete, he does not receive the victor's crown unless he competes according to the rules. 6The hardworking farmer should be the first to receive a share of the crops. 7Reflect on what I am saying, for the Lord will give you insight into all this. . . .

15Do your best to present yourself to God as one approved, a workman who does not need to be ashamed and who correctly handles the word of truth. . . .

20In a large house there are articles not only of gold and silver, but also of wood and clay; some are for noble purposes and some for ignoble. 21If a man cleanses himself from the latter, he will be an instrument for noble purposes, made holy, useful to the Master and prepared to do any good work.

22Flee the evil desires of youth, and pursue righteousness, faith, love and peace, along with those who call on the Lord out of a pure heart. 23Don't have anything to do with foolish and stupid arguments, because you know they produce quarrels.

[24]And the Lord's servant must not quarrel; instead, he must be kind to everyone, able to teach, not resentful. [25]Those who oppose him he must gently instruct, in the hope that God will grant them repentance leading them to a knowledge of the truth, [26]and that they will come to their senses and escape from the trap of the devil, who has taken them captive to do his will.
2 Tim 3 [14]But as for you, continue in what you have learned and have become convinced of, because you know those from whom you learned it. . . .
Titus 2 [1]You must teach what is in accord with sound doctrine. . . .
[7]In everything set them an example by doing what is good. In your teaching show integrity, seriousness [8]and soundness of speech that cannot be condemned, so that those who oppose you may be ashamed because they have nothing bad to say about us.
James 3 [13]Who is wise and understanding among you? Let him show it by his good life, by deeds done in the humility that comes from wisdom.
1 Pet 4 [10]Each one should use whatever gift he has received to serve others, faithfully administering God's grace in its various forms. [11]If anyone speaks, he should do it as one speaking the very words of God. If anyone serves, he should do it with the strength God provides, so that in all things God may be praised through Jesus Christ. To him be the glory and the power for ever and ever. Amen.

3. Duties of Ministers

a) Ministers Lead God's People

Isa 62 [6]I have posted watchmen on your walls, O Jerusalem; they will never be silent day or night. You who call on the LORD, give yourselves no rest, [7]and give him no rest till he establishes Jerusalem and makes her the praise of the earth.
Jer 23 [4]"I will place shepherds over them who will tend them, and they will no longer be afraid or terrified, nor will any be missing," declares the LORD.
Ezek 34 [2]"Son of man, prophesy against the shepherds of Israel; prophesy and say to them: 'This is what the Sovereign LORD says: Woe to the shepherds of Israel who only take care of themselves! Should not shepherds take care of the flock?'"
John 21 [15]When they had finished eating, Jesus said to Simon Peter, "Simon son of John, do you truly love me more than these?"
"Yes, Lord," he said, "you know that I love you."
Jesus said, "Feed my lambs."
[16]Again Jesus said, "Simon son of John, do you truly love me?"
He answered, "Yes, Lord, you know that I love you."
Jesus said, "Take care of my sheep."
[17]The third time he said to him, "Simon son of John, do you love me?"
Peter was hurt because Jesus asked him the third time, "Do you love me?" He said, "Lord, you know all things; you know that I love you."
Jesus said, "Feed my sheep."
1 Thess 5 [12]Now we ask you, brothers, to respect those who work hard among you, who are over you in the Lord and who admonish you.

b) Ministers Speak God's Word

Exod 4 [12]"Now go; I will help you speak and will teach you what to say."
Jer 1 [17]"Get yourself ready! Stand up and say to them whatever I command you. Do not be terrified by them, or I will terrify you before them. [18]Today I have made you a fortified city, an iron pillar and a bronze wall to stand against the whole land—against the kings of Judah, its officials, its priests and the people of the land. [19]They will fight against you but will not overcome you, for I am with you and will rescue you," declares the LORD.
Jer 15 [19]Therefore this is what the LORD says: "If you repent, I will restore you that you may serve me; if you utter worthy, not worthless, words, you will be my spokesman. Let this people turn to you, but you must not turn to them."
Jer 26 [2]"This is what the LORD says: Stand in the courtyard of the LORD's house and speak to all the people of the towns of Judah who come to worship in the house of the LORD. Tell them everything I command you; do not omit a word."
Ezek 2 [7]"You must speak my words to them, whether they listen or fail to listen, for they are rebellious."
Ezek 3 [11]"Go now to your countrymen in exile and speak to them. Say to them, 'This is what the Sovereign LORD says,' whether they listen or fail to listen."
Joel 2 [17]Let the priests, who minister before the LORD, weep between the temple porch and the altar. Let them say, "Spare your people, O LORD. Do not make your inheritance an object of scorn, a byword among the nations. Why should they say among the peoples, 'Where is their God?'"
Hab 2 [2]Then the LORD replied: "Write down the revelation and make it plain on tablets so that a herald may run with it."
Mal 2 [7]"For the lips of a priest ought to preserve knowledge, and from his mouth men should seek instruction—because he is the messenger of the LORD Almighty."
John 3 [34]"For the one whom God has sent speaks the words of God, for God gives the Spirit without limit."

c) Ministers Teach Godly Living

Lev 10 [11]". . . and you must teach the Israelites all the decrees the LORD has given them through Moses."
Deut 32 [1]Listen, O heavens, and I will speak; hear, O earth, the words of my mouth. [2]Let my teaching fall like rain and my words descend like dew, like showers on new grass, like abundant rain on tender plants.
[3]I will proclaim the name of the LORD. Oh, praise the greatness of our God!
2 Kings 17 [27]Then the king of Assyria gave this order: "Have one of the priests you took captive from Samaria go back to live there and teach the people what the god of the land requires." [28]So one of the priests who had been exiled from Samaria came to live in Bethel and taught them how to worship the LORD.
Ezek 44 [23]"'They are to teach my people the difference between the holy and the common and show them how to distinguish between the unclean and the clean.'"
Matt 28 [19]"Therefore go and make disciples of all nations, baptizing them in the name of the Father and of the Son and of the Holy Spirit, [20]and teaching them to obey everything I have commanded you. And surely I am with you always, to the very end of the age."
2 Thess 3 [4]We have confidence in the Lord that you are doing and will continue to do the things we command.
2 Pet 1 [12]So I will always remind you of these things, even though you know them and are firmly established in the truth you now have. [13]I think it is right to refresh your memory as long as I live in the tent of this body, [14]because I know that I will soon put it aside, as our Lord Jesus Christ has made clear to me. [15]And I will make every effort to see that after my departure you will always be able to remember these things.

d) Ministers Exercise God's Authority

1 Sam 12 [7]"Now then, stand here, because I am going to confront you with evidence before the LORD as to all the righteous acts performed by the LORD for you and your fathers."
Matt 18 [18]"I tell you the truth, whatever you bind on earth will be bound in heaven, and whatever you loose on earth will be loosed in heaven."
John 20 [23]"If you forgive anyone his sins, they are forgiven; if you do not forgive them, they are not forgiven."

e) Ministers Bear Witness of Christ

Luke 24 [46]He told them, "This is what is written: The Christ will suffer and rise from the dead on the third day, [47]and repentance and forgiveness of sins will be preached in his name to all nations, beginning at Jerusalem. [48]You are witnesses of these things."
John 15 [26]"When the Counselor comes, whom I will send to you from the Father, the Spirit of truth who goes out from the Father, he will testify about me. [27]And you also must testify, for you have been with me from the beginning."
Acts 1 [21]"Therefore it is necessary to choose one of the men who have been with us the whole time the Lord Jesus went in and out among us, [22]beginning from John's baptism to the time

when Jesus was taken up from us. For one of these must become a witness with us of his resurrection."

Acts 10 39"We are witnesses of everything he did in the country of the Jews and in Jerusalem. They killed him by hanging him on a tree, 40but God raised him from the dead on the third day and caused him to be seen. 41He was not seen by all the people, but by witnesses whom God had already chosen—by us who ate and drank with him after he rose from the dead. 42He commanded us to preach to the people and to testify that he is the one whom God appointed as judge of the living and the dead."

Acts 20 24"However, I consider my life worth nothing to me, if only I may finish the race and complete the task the Lord Jesus has given me—the task of testifying to the gospel of God's grace."

f) Ministers Preach the Message of Salvation

Prov 11 30The fruit of the righteous is a tree of life, and he who wins souls is wise.

Acts 5 20"Go, stand in the temple courts," he said, "and tell the people the full message of this new life."

Acts 10 42"He commanded us to preach to the people and to testify that he is the one whom God appointed as judge of the living and the dead. 43All the prophets testify about him that everyone who believes in him receives forgiveness of sins through his name."

Acts 18 9One night the Lord spoke to Paul in a vision: "Do not be afraid; keep on speaking, do not be silent. 10For I am with you, and no one is going to attack and harm you, because I have many people in this city."

Rom 1 14I am obligated both to Greeks and non-Greeks, both to the wise and the foolish. 15That is why I am so eager to preach the gospel also to you who are at Rome.

Eph 3 8Although I am less than the least of all God's people, this grace was given me: to preach to the Gentiles the unsearchable riches of Christ, 9and to make plain to everyone the administration of this mystery, which for ages past was kept hidden in God, who created all things.

2 Tim 4 2Preach the Word; be prepared in season and out of season; correct, rebuke and encourage—with great patience and careful instruction.

g) Ministers Resist Evil

Isa 57 14And it will be said: "Build up, build up, prepare the road! Remove the obstacles out of the way of my people."

Isa 58 1"Shout it aloud, do not hold back. Raise your voice like a trumpet. Declare to my people their rebellion and to the house of Jacob their sins."

Jon 1 2"Go to the great city of Nineveh and preach against it, because its wickedness has come up before me."

2 Tim 2 14Keep reminding them of these things. Warn them before God against quarreling about words; it is of no value, and only ruins those who listen. . . . 23Don't have anything to do with foolish and stupid arguments, because you know they produce quarrels.

2 Tim 3 1But mark this: there will be terrible times in the last days. 2People will be lovers of themselves, lovers of money, boastful, proud, abusive, disobedient to their parents, ungrateful, unholy, 3without love, unforgiving, slanderous, without self-control, brutal, not lovers of the good, 4treacherous, rash, conceited, lovers of pleasure rather than lovers of God—5having a form of godliness but denying its powers. Have nothing to do with them.

h) Ministers Edify God's People

Isa 40 1Comfort, comfort my people, says your God. 2Speak tenderly to Jerusalem, and proclaim to her that her hard service has been completed, that her sin has been paid for, that she has received from the LORD's hand double for all her sins.

3A voice of one calling: "In the desert prepare the way for the LORD; make straight in the wilderness a highway for our God." . . .

9You who bring good tidings to Zion, go up on a high mountain. You who bring good tidings to Jerusalem, lift up your voice with a shout, lift it up, do not be afraid; say to the towns of Judah, "Here is your God!"

Luke 22 32"But I have prayed for you, Simon, that your faith may not fail. And when you have turned back, strengthen your brothers."

2 Cor 10 8For even if I boast somewhat freely about the authority the Lord gave us for building you up rather than pulling you down, I will not be ashamed of it.

2 Cor 12 19Have you been thinking all along that we have been defending ourselves to you? We have been speaking in the sight of God as those in Christ; and everything we do, dear friends, is for your strengthening.

2 Cor 13 10This is why I write these things when I am absent, that when I come I may not have to be harsh in my use of authority—the authority the Lord gave me for building you up, not for tearing you down.

1 Thess 3 2We sent Timothy, who is our brother and God's fellow worker in spreading the gospel of Christ, to strengthen and encourage you in your faith. . . .

B. Bishops/Elders

1. The Existence of Bishops/Elders

Acts 11 30This they did, sending their gift to the elders by Barnabas and Saul.

Acts 14 23Paul and Barnabas appointed elders for them in each church and, with prayer and fasting, committed them to the Lord, in whom they had put their trust.

Acts 20 17From Miletus, Paul sent to Ephesus for the elders of the church.

Acts 21 18The next day Paul and the rest of us went to see James, and all the elders were present.

Phil 1 1Paul and Timothy, servants of Christ Jesus,

To all the saints in Christ Jesus at Philippi, together with the overseers and deacons. . . .

Titus 1 5The reason I left you in Crete was that you might straighten out what was left unfinished and appoint elders in every town, as I directed you.

2 John 1The elder,

To the chosen lady and her children, whom I love in the truth—and not I only, but also all who know the truth. . . .

3 John 1The elder,

To my dear friend Gaius, whom I love in the truth.

2. Qualifications for Bishops/Elders

1 Tim 3 1Here is a trustworthy saying: If anyone sets his heart on being an overseer, he desires a noble task. 2Now the overseer must be above reproach, the husband of but one wife, temperate, self-controlled, respectable, hospitable, able to teach, 3not given to drunkenness, not violent but gentle, not quarrelsome, not a lover of money. 4He must manage his own family well and see that his children obey him with proper respect. 5(If anyone does not know how to manage his own family, how can he take care of God's church?) 6He must not be a recent convert, or he may become conceited and fall under the same judgment as the devil. 7He must also have a good reputation with outsiders, so that he will not fall into disgrace and into the devil's trap.

Titus 1 6An elder must be blameless, the husband of but one wife, a man whose children believe and are not open to the charge of being wild and disobedient. 7Since an overseer is entrusted with God's work, he must be blameless—not overbearing, not quick-tempered, not given to drunkenness, not violent, not pursuing dishonest gain. 8Rather he must be hospitable, one who loves what is good, who is self-controlled, upright, holy and disciplined.

3. Duties of Bishops/Elders

a) Elders Oversee God's People

Acts 20 28"Keep watch over yourselves and all the flock of which the Holy Spirit has made you overseers. Be shepherds of the church of God, which he bought with his own blood. 29I know that after I leave, savage wolves will come in among you and will not spare the flock. 30Even from your own number men will arise and distort the truth in order to draw away disciples after them. 31So be on your guard! Remember that for three years I never stopped warning each of you night and day with tears.

32"Now I commit you to God and to the word of his grace, which can build you up and give you an inheritance among all those who are sanctified."

1 Thess 5 12Now we ask you, brothers, to respect those who work hard among you, who are over you in the Lord and who admonish you. 13Hold them in the highest regard in love because of their work. Live in peace with each other.

Heb 13 17Obey your leaders and submit to their authority. They keep watch over you as men who must give an account. Obey them so that their work will be a joy, not a burden, for that would be of no advantage to you.

1 Pet 5 1To the elders among you, I appeal as a fellow elder, a witness of Christ's sufferings and one who also will share in the glory to be revealed: 2Be shepherds of God's flock that is under your care, serving as overseers—not because you must, but because you are willing, as God wants you to be; not greedy for money, but eager to serve; 3not lording it over those entrusted to you, but being examples to the flock.

b) Elders Teach Doctrine

1 Tim 5 17The elders who direct the affairs of the church well are worthy of double honor, especially those whose work is preaching and teaching.

Titus 1 6An elder must be blameless, the husband of but one wife, a man whose children believe and are not open to the charge of being wild and disobedient. . . . 9He must hold firmly to the trustworthy message as it has been taught, so that he can encourage others by sound doctrine and refute those who oppose it.

Heb 13 7Remember your leaders, who spoke the word of God to you. Consider the outcome of their way of life and imitate their faith.

c) Elders Resolve Differences

Acts 15 1Some men came down from Judea to Antioch and were teaching the brothers: "Unless you are circumcised, according to the custom taught by Moses, you cannot be saved." 2This brought Paul and Barnabas into sharp dispute and debate with them. So Paul and Barnabas were appointed, along with some other believers, to go up to Jerusalem to see the apostles and elders about this question. 3The church sent them on their way, and as they traveled through Phoenicia and Samaria, they told how the Gentiles had been converted. This news made all the brothers very glad. 4When they came to Jerusalem, they were welcomed by the church and the apostles and elders, to whom they reported everything God had done through them.

5Then some of the believers who belonged to the party of the Pharisees stood up and said, "The Gentiles must be circumcised and required to obey the law of Moses."

6The apostles and elders met to consider this question. 7After much discussion, Peter got up and addressed them: "Brothers, you know that some time ago God made a choice among you that the Gentiles might hear from my lips the message of the gospel and believe. 8God, who knows the heart, showed that he accepted them by giving the Holy Spirit to them, just as he did to us. 9He made no distinction between us and them, for he purified their hearts by faith. 10Now then, why do you try to test God by putting on the necks of the disciples a yoke that neither we nor our fathers have been able to bear? 11No! We believe it is through the grace of our Lord Jesus that we are saved, just as they are."

12The whole assembly became silent as they listened to Barnabas and Paul telling about the miraculous signs and wonders God had done among the Gentiles through them. 13When they finished, James spoke up: "Brothers, listen to me. 14Simon has described to us how God at first showed his concern by taking from the Gentiles a people for himself. 15The words of the prophets are in agreement with this, as it is written: 16'After this I will return and rebuild David's fallen tent. Its ruins I will rebuild, and I will restore it, 17that the remnant of men may seek the Lord, and all the Gentiles who bear my name, says the Lord, who does these things' 18that have been known for ages.

19"It is my judgment, therefore, that we should not make it difficult for the Gentiles who are turning to God. 20Instead we should write to them, telling them to abstain from food polluted by idols, from sexual immorality, from the meat of strangled animals and from blood. 21For Moses has been preached in every city from the earliest times and is read in the synagogues on every Sabbath."

22Then the apostles and elders, with the whole church, decided to choose some of their own men and send them to Antioch with Paul and Barnabas. They chose Judas (called Barsabbas) and Silas, two men who were leaders among the brothers. 23With them they sent the following letter:

The apostles and elders, your brothers,

To the Gentile believers in Antioch, Syria and Cilicia: Greetings.

24We have heard that some went out from us without our authorization and disturbed you, troubling your minds by what they said. 25So we all agreed to choose some men and send them to you with our dear friends Barnabas and Paul—26men who have risked their lives for the name of our Lord Jesus Christ. 27Therefore we are sending Judas and Silas to confirm by word of mouth what we are writing. 28It seemed good to the Holy Spirit and to us not to burden you with anything beyond the following requirements: 29You are to abstain from food sacrificed to idols, from blood, from the meat of strangled animals and from sexual immorality. You will do well to avoid these things. Farewell.

Acts 16 4As they traveled from town to town, they delivered the decisions reached by the apostles and elders in Jerusalem for the people to obey.

d) Elders Commission Leaders

1 Tim 4 14Do not neglect your gift, which was given you through a prophetic message when the body of elders laid their hands on you.

e) Elders Minister to the Sick

James 5 14Is any one of you sick? He should call the elders of the church to pray over him and anoint him with oil in the name of the Lord. 15And the prayer offered in faith will make the sick person well; the Lord will raise him up. If he has sinned, he will be forgiven.

C. Deacons and Deaconesses

1. The Existence of Deacons

Acts 6 1In those days when the number of disciples was increasing, the Grecian Jews among them complained against the Hebraic Jews because their widows were being overlooked in the daily distribution of food. 2So the twelve gathered all the disciples together and said, "It would not be right for us to neglect the ministry of the word of God in order to wait on tables. 3Brothers, choose seven men from among you who are known to be full of the Spirit and wisdom. We will turn this responsibility over to them 4and will give our attention to prayer and the ministry of the word."

5This proposal pleased the whole group. They chose Stephen, a man full of faith and of the Holy Spirit; also Philip, Procorus, Nicanor, Timon, Parmenas, and Nicolas from Antioch, a convert to Judaism. 6They presented these men to the apostles, who prayed and laid their hands on them.

Rom 16 1I commend to you our sister Phoebe, a servant of the church in Cenchrea. 2I ask you to receive her in the Lord in a way worthy of the saints and to give her any help she may need from you, for she has been a great help to many people, including me.

Phil 1 1Paul and Timothy, servants of Christ Jesus,

To all the saints in Christ Jesus at Philippi, together with the overseers and deacons. . . .

2. Qualifications for Deacons

1 Tim 3 8Deacons, likewise, are to be men worthy of respect, sincere, not indulging in much wine, and not pursuing dishonest gain. 9They must keep hold of the deep truths of the faith with a clear conscience. 10They must first be tested; and then if there is nothing against them, let them serve as deacons.

[11]In the same way, their wives are to be women worthy of respect, not malicious talkers but temperate and trustworthy in everything.

[12]A deacon must be the husband of but one wife and must manage his children and his household well. [13]Those who have served well gain an excellent standing and great assurance in their faith in Christ Jesus.

[14]Although I hope to come to you soon, I am writing you these instructions so that, [15]if I am delayed, you will know how people ought to conduct themselves in God's household, which is the church of the living God, the pillar and foundation of the truth.

3. Duties of Deacons

Acts 6 [1]In those days when the number of disciples was increasing, the Grecian Jews among them complained against the Hebraic Jews because their widows were being overlooked in the daily distribution of food. [2]So the Twelve gathered all the disciples together and said, "It would not be right for us to neglect the ministry of the word of God in order to wait on tables. [3]Brothers, choose seven men from among you who are known to be full of the Spirit and wisdom. We will turn this responsibility over to them [4]and will give our attention to prayer and the ministry of the word."

D. Charismatic Offices

See p. 156a, Gifts of the Spirit

VIII
The Sacraments/Ordinances of the Church

A. The Ordinance of Baptism

1. Examples of Baptism

a) Jesus Was Baptized

Matt 3 [13]Then Jesus came from Galilee to the Jordan to be baptized by John. [14]But John tried to deter him, saying, "I need to be baptized by you, and do you come to me?"

[15]Jesus replied, "Let it be so now; it is proper for us to do this to fulfill all righteousness." Then John consented.

[16]As soon as Jesus was baptized, he went up out of the water. At that moment heaven was opened, and he saw the Spirit of God descending like a dove and lighting on him. [17]And a voice from heaven said, "This is my Son, whom I love; with him I am well pleased."

b) Believers at Pentecost Were Baptized

Acts 2 [41]Those who accepted his message were baptized, and about three thousand were added to their number that day.

c) Samaritans Were Baptized

Acts 8 [9]Now for some time a man named Simon had practiced sorcery in the city and amazed all the people of Samaria. He boasted that he was someone great, [10]and all the people, both high and low, gave him their attention and exclaimed, "This man is the divine power known as the Great Power." [11]They followed him because he had amazed them for a long time with his magic. [12]But when they believed Philip as he preached the good news of the kingdom of God and the name of Jesus Christ, they were baptized, both men and women.

d) Simon Was Baptized

Acts 8 [13]Simon himself believed and was baptized. And he followed Philip everywhere, astonished by the great signs and miracles he saw.

e) The Ethiopian Eunuch Was Baptized

Acts 8 [36]As they traveled along the road, they came to some water and the eunuch said, "Look, here is water. Why shouldn't I be baptized?" [38]And he gave orders to stop the chariot. Then both Philip and the eunuch went down into the water and Philip baptized him.

f) Paul Was Baptized

Acts 9 [18]Immediately, something like scales fell from Saul's eyes, and he could see again. He got up and was baptized. . . .

g) Cornelius, His Family, and His Friends Were Baptized

Acts 10 [24]The following day he arrived in Caesarea. Cornelius was expecting them and had called together his relatives and close friends. . . .

[44]While Peter was still speaking these words, the Holy Spirit came on all who heard the message. [45]The circumcised believers who had come with Peter were astonished that the gift of the Holy Spirit had been poured out even on the Gentiles. [46]For they heard them speaking in tongues and praising God.

Then Peter said, [47]"Can anyone keep these people from being baptized with water? They have received the Holy Spirit just as we have." [48]So he ordered that they be baptized in the name of Jesus Christ. Then they asked Peter to stay with them for a few days.

h) Lydia and Her Household Were Baptized

Acts 16 [13]On the Sabbath we went outside the city gate to the river, where we expected to find a place of prayer. We sat down and began to speak to the women who had gathered there. [14]One of those listening was a woman named Lydia, a dealer in purple cloth from the city of Thyatira, who was a worshiper of God. The Lord opened her heart to respond to Paul's message. [15]When she and the members of her household were baptized, she invited us to her home. "If you consider me a believer in the Lord," she said, "come and stay at my house." And she persuaded us.

i) The Philippian Jailer and His Household Were Baptized

Acts 16 [33]At that hour of the night the jailer took them and washed their wounds; then immediately he and all his family were baptized.

j) Corinthian Believers Were Baptized

Acts 18 [8]Crispus, the synagogue ruler, and his entire household believed in the Lord; and many of the Corinthians who heard him believed and were baptized.

k) Disciples of John Were Baptized

Acts 19 [1]While Apollos was at Corinth, Paul took the road through the interior and arrived at Ephesus. There he found some disciples [2]and asked them, "Did you receive the Holy Spirit when you believed?"

They answered, "No, we have not even heard that there is a Holy Spirit."

[3]So Paul asked, "Then what baptism did you receive?"

"John's baptism," they replied.

[4]Paul said, "John's baptism was a baptism of repentance. He told the people to believe in the one coming after him, that is, in Jesus." [5]On hearing this, they were baptized into the name of the Lord Jesus.

l) Crispus and Gaius Were Baptized

1 Cor 1 [14]I am thankful that I did not baptize any of you except Crispus and Gaius, [15]so no one can say that you were baptized into my name.

m) The Household of Stephanas Was Baptized

1 Cor 1 [16](Yes, I also baptized the household of Stephanas; beyond that, I don't remember if I baptized anyone else.)

2. The Nature of Baptism

a) Baptism Is from Heaven

Matt 21 [25]"John's baptism—where did it come from? Was it from heaven, or from men?"

They discussed it among themselves and said, "If we say,

'From heaven,' he will ask, 'Then why didn't you believe him?' 26But if we say, 'From men'—we are afraid of the people, for they all hold that John was a prophet."

Luke 7 29(All the people, even the tax collectors, when they heard Jesus' words, acknowledged that God's way was right, because they had been baptized by John. 30But the Pharisees and experts in the law rejected God's purpose for themselves, because they had not been baptized by John.)

John 1 24Now some Pharisees who had been sent 25questioned him, "Why then do you baptize if you are not the Christ, nor Elijah, nor the Prophet?"

26"I baptize with water," John replied, "but among you stands one you do not know. 27He is the one who comes after me, the thongs of whose sandals I am not worthy to untie."

28This all happened at Bethany on the other side of the Jordan, where John was baptizing.

29The next day John saw Jesus coming toward him and said, "Look, the Lamb of God, who takes away the sin of the world! 30This is the one I meant when I said, 'A man who comes after me has surpassed me because he was before me.' 31I myself did not know him, but the reason I came baptizing with water was that he might be revealed to Israel."

32Then John gave this testimony: "I saw the Spirit come down from heaven as a dove and remain on him. 33I would not have known him, except that the one who sent me to baptize with water told me, 'The man on whom you see the Spirit come down and remain is he who will baptize with the Holy Spirit.' 34I have seen and I testify that this is the Son of God."

b) Baptism Signifies Repentance and Forgiveness of Sins

Matt 3 11"I baptize you with water for repentance. But after me will come one who is more powerful than I, whose sandals I am not fit to carry. He will baptize you with the Holy Spirit and with fire."

Mark 1 4And so John came, baptizing in the desert region and preaching a baptism of repentance for the forgiveness of sins. 5The whole Judean countryside and all the people of Jerusalem went out to him. Confessing their sins, they were baptized by him in the Jordan River.

Acts 2 38Peter replied, "Repent and be baptized, every one of you, in the name of Jesus Christ for the forgiveness of your sins. And you will receive the gift of the Holy Spirit."

Acts 13 24Before the coming of Jesus, John preached repentance and baptism to all the people of Israel.

Acts 22 16"'And now what are you waiting for? Get up, be baptized and wash your sins away, calling on his name.'"

Heb 6 1Therefore let us leave the elementary teachings about Christ and go on to maturity, not laying again the foundation of repentance from acts that lead to death, and of faith in God, 2instruction about baptisms, the laying on of hands, the resurrection of the dead, and eternal judgment.

c) Baptism Identifies Believers with Christ

Mark 10 38"You don't know what you are asking," Jesus said. "Can you drink the cup I drink or be baptized with the baptism I am baptized with?"

39"We can," they answered.

Jesus said to them, "You will drink the cup I drink and be baptized with the baptism I am baptized with. . . ."

Rom 6 3Or don't you know that all of us who were baptized into Christ Jesus were baptized into his death? 4We were therefore buried with him through baptism into death in order that, just as Christ was raised from the dead through the glory of the Father, we too may live a new life.

5If we have been united with him like this in his death, we will certainly also be united with him in his resurrection. 6For we know that our old self was crucified with him so that the body of sin might be done away with, that we should no longer be slaves to sin—7because anyone who has died has been freed from sin.

8Now if we died with Christ, we believe that we will also live with him.

1 Cor 1 13Is Christ divided? Was Paul crucified for you? Were you baptized into the name of Paul?

Gal 3 26You are all sons of God through faith in Christ Jesus, 27for all of you who were baptized into Christ have clothed yourselves with Christ.

Eph 4 4There is one body and one Spirit—just as you were called to one hope when you were called—5one Lord, one faith, one baptism; 6one God and Father of all, who is over all and through all and in all.

Col 2 11In him you were also circumcised, in the putting off of the sinful nature, not with a circumcision done by the hands of men but with the circumcision done by Christ, 12having been buried with him in baptism and raised with him through your faith in the power of God, who raised him from the dead.

1 Pet 3 21and this water symbolizes baptism that now saves you also—not the removal of dirt from the body but the pledge of a good conscience toward God. It saves you by the resurrection of Jesus Christ. . . .

d) Baptism Testifies to the Indwelling Presence of the Holy Spirit

Matt 3 11"I baptize you with water for repentance. But after me will come one who is more powerful than I, whose sandals I am not fit to carry. He will baptize you with the Holy Spirit and with fire."

Acts 1 5"For John baptized with water, but in a few days you will be baptized with the Holy Spirit."

1 Cor 12 13For we were all baptized by one Spirit into one body—whether Jews or Greeks, slave or free—and we were all given the one Spirit to drink.

e) Baptism Is Commanded of Believers

Matt 28 19"Therefore go and make disciples of all nations, baptizing them in the name of the Father and of the Son and of the Holy Spirit. . . ."

Acts 2 38Peter replied, "Repent and be baptized, every one of you, in the name of Jesus Christ for the forgiveness of your sins. And you will receive the gift of the Holy Spirit."

3. Modes of Baptism

a) Baptism by Washing with Water

Ezek 36 24"'For I will take you out of the nations; I will gather you from all the countries and bring you back into your own land. 25I will sprinkle clean water on you, and you will be clean; I will cleanse you from all your impurities and from all your idols. 26I will give you a new heart and put a new spirit in you; I will remove from you your heart of stone and give you a heart of flesh. 27And I will put my Spirit in you and move you to follow my decrees and be careful to keep my laws. 28You will live in the land I gave your forefathers; you will be my people, and I will be your God. 29I will save you from all your uncleanness. I will call for the grain and make it plentiful and will not bring famine upon you. . . .

33"'This is what the Sovereign LORD says: On the day I cleanse you from all your sins, I will resettle your towns, and the ruins will be rebuilt.'"

Heb 9 10They are only a matter of food and drink and various ceremonial washings—external regulations applying until the time of the new order. . . .

13The blood of goats and bulls and the ashes of a heifer sprinkled on those who are ceremonially unclean sanctify them so that they are outwardly clean. 14How much more, then, will the blood of Christ, who through the eternal Spirit offered himself unblemished to God, cleanse our consciences from acts that lead to death, so that we may serve the living God!

Heb 10 22let us draw near to God with a sincere heart in full assurance of faith, having our hearts sprinkled to cleanse us from a guilty conscience and having our bodies washed with pure water.

b) Baptism by Immersing in Water

Matt 3 6Confessing their sins, they were baptized by him in the Jordan River.

Mark 1 9At that time Jesus came from Nazareth in Galilee and was baptized by John in the Jordan.

John 3 23Now John also was baptizing at Aenon near Salim, because there was plenty of water, and people were constantly coming to be baptized.

John 10 40Then Jesus went back across the Jordan to the place where John had been baptizing in the early days. Here he stayed. . . .

4. Exceptional Cases of Baptism: Baptism for the Dead

1 Cor 15 29Now if there is no resurrection, what will those do who are baptized for the dead? If the dead are not raised at all, why are people baptized for them?

B. The Ordinance of the Lord's Supper

1. The Institution and Meaning of the Lord's Supper

Matt 26 17On the first day of the Feast of Unleavened Bread, the disciples came to Jesus and asked, "Where do you want us to make preparations for you to eat the Passover?"

18He replied, "Go into the city to a certain man and tell him, 'The Teacher says: My appointed time is near. I am going to celebrate the Passover with my disciples at your house.'" 19So the disciples did as Jesus had directed them and prepared the Passover.

20When evening came, Jesus was reclining at the table with the Twelve. 21And while they were eating, he said, "I tell you the truth, one of you will betray me."

22They were very sad and began to say to him one after the other, "Surely not I, Lord?"

23Jesus replied, "The one who has dipped his hand into the bowl with me will betray me. 24The Son of Man will go just as it is written about him. But woe to that man who betrays the Son of Man! It would be better for him if he had not been born."

25Then Judas, the one who would betray him, said, "Surely not I, Rabbi?"

Jesus answered, "Yes, it is you."

26While they were eating, Jesus took bread, gave thanks and broke it, and gave it to his disciples, saying, "Take and eat; this is my body."

27Then he took the cup, gave thanks and offered it to them, saying, "Drink from it, all of you. 28This is my blood of the covenant, which is poured out for many for the forgiveness of sins. 29I tell you, I will not drink of this fruit of the vine from now on until that day when I drink it anew with you in my Father's kingdom."

30When they had sung a hymn, they went out to the Mount of Olives.

Mark 14 17When evening came, Jesus arrived with the Twelve. 18While they were reclining at the table eating, he said, "I tell you the truth, one of you will betray me—one who is eating with me."

19They were saddened, and one by one they said to him, "Surely not I?"

20"It is one of the Twelve," he replied, "one who dips bread into the bowl with me. 21The Son of Man will go just as it is written about him. But woe to that man who betrays the Son of Man! It would be better for him if he had not been born."

22While they were eating, Jesus took bread, gave thanks and broke it, and gave it to his disciples, saying, "Take it; this is my body."

23Then he took the cup, gave thanks and offered it to them, and they all drank from it.

24"This is my blood of the covenant, which is poured out for many," he said to them. 25"I tell you the truth, I will not drink again of the fruit of the vine until that day when I drink it anew in the kingdom of God."

26When they had sung a hymn, they went out to the Mount of Olives.

Luke 22 14When the hour came, Jesus and his apostles reclined at the table. 15And he said to them, "I have eagerly desired to eat this Passover with you before I suffer. 16For I tell you, I will not eat it again until it finds fulfillment in the kingdom of God."

17After taking the cup, he gave thanks and said, "Take this and divide it among you. 18For I tell you I will not drink again of the fruit of the vine until the kingdom of God comes."

19And he took bread, gave thanks and broke it, and gave it to them, saying, "This is my body given for you; do this in remembrance of me."

20In the same way, after the supper he took the cup, saying, "This cup is the new covenant in my blood, which is poured out for you."

1 Cor 10 16Is not the cup of thanksgiving for which we give thanks a participation in the blood of Christ? And is not the bread that we break a participation in the body of Christ? 17Because there is one loaf, we, who are many, are one body, for we all partake of the one loaf.

1 Cor 11 23For I received from the Lord what I also passed on to you: The Lord Jesus, on the night he was betrayed, took bread, 24and when he had given thanks, he broke it and said, "This is my body, which is for you; do this in remembrance of me." 25In the same way, after supper he took the cup, saying, "This cup is the new covenant in my blood; do this, whenever you drink it, in remembrance of me." 26For whenever you eat this bread and drink this cup, you proclaim the Lord's death until he comes.

2. Spiritual Preparation for the Lord's Supper

1 Cor 5 7Get rid of the old yeast that you may be a new batch without yeast—as you really are. For Christ, our Passover lamb, has been sacrificed. 8Therefore let us keep the Festival, not with the old yeast, the yeast of malice and wickedness, but with bread without yeast, the bread of sincerity and truth.

1 Cor 11 20When you come together, it is not the Lord's Supper you eat, 21for as you eat, each of you goes ahead without waiting for anybody else. One remains hungry, another gets drunk. 22Don't you have homes to eat and drink in? Or do you despise the church of God and humiliate those who have nothing? What shall I say to you? Shall I praise you for this? Certainly not! . . .

27Therefore, whoever eats the bread or drinks the cup of the Lord in an unworthy manner will be guilty of sinning against the body and blood of the Lord. 28A man ought to examine himself before he eats of the bread and drinks of the cup.

3. Judgment for Abusing the Lord's Supper

1 Cor 10 3They all ate the same spiritual food 4and drank the same spiritual drink; for they drank from the spiritual rock that accompanied them, and that rock was Christ. 5Nevertheless, God was not pleased with most of them; their bodies were scattered over the desert.

1 Cor 10 16Is not the cup of thanksgiving for which we give thanks a participation in the blood of Christ? And is not the bread that we break a participation in the body of Christ? 17Because there is one loaf, we, who are many, are one body, for we all partake of the one loaf.

18Consider the people of Israel: Do not those who eat the sacrifices participate in the altar? 19Do I mean then that a sacrifice offered to an idol is anything, or that an idol is anything? 20No, but the sacrifices of pagans are offered to demons, not to God, and I do not want you to be participants with demons. 21You cannot drink the cup of the Lord and the cup of demons too; you cannot have a part in both the Lord's table and the table of demons. 22Are we trying to arouse the Lord's jealousy? Are we stronger than he?

1 Cor 11 29For anyone who eats and drinks without recognizing the body of the Lord eats and drinks judgment on himself. 30That is why many among you are weak and sick, and a number of you have fallen asleep. 31But if we judged ourselves, we would not come under judgment. 32When we are judged by the Lord, we are being disciplined so that we will not be condemned with the world.

33So then, my brothers, when you come together to eat, wait for each other. 34If anyone is hungry, he should eat at home, so that when you meet together it may not result in judgment.

And when I come I will give further directions.

4. Frequency of Celebrating the Lord's Supper

Acts 2 [42]They devoted themselves to the apostles' teaching and to the fellowship, to the breaking of bread and to prayer.

Acts 2 [46]Every day they continued to meet together in the temple courts. They broke bread in their homes and ate together with glad and sincere hearts. . . .

Acts 20 [7]On the first day of the week we came together to break bread. Paul spoke to the people and, because he intended to leave the next day, kept on talking until midnight.

15

Eschatology

I
Death

A. The Fact of Death

1. Metaphors That Depict Death and the Subsequent State

1) Being Cut Off

Job 24 [24]"For a little while they are exalted, and then they are gone; they are brought low and gathered up like all others; they are cut off like heads of grain."

2) Being Gathered to One's People

Num 20 [23]At Mount Hor, near the border of Edom, the Lord said to Moses and Aaron, [24]"Aaron will be gathered to his people. He will not enter the land I give the Israelites, because both of you rebelled against my command at the waters of Meribah. [25]Get Aaron and his son Eleazar and take them up Mount Hor.

[26]Remove Aaron's garments and put them on his son Eleazar, for Aaron will be gathered to his people; he will die there."
Deut 32 [48]On that same day the LORD told Moses, [49]"Go up into the Abarim Range to Mount Nebo in Moab, across from Jericho, and view Canaan, the land I am giving the Israelites as their own possession. [50]There on the mountain that you have climbed you will die and be gathered to your people, just as your brother Aaron died on Mount Hor and was gathered to his people."

3) The Breaking of the Golden Bowl

Eccles 12 [6]Remember him—before the silver cord is severed, or the golden bowl is broken; before the pitcher is shattered at the spring, or the wheel broken at the well. . . .

4) Breathing One's Last

Gen 25 [17]Altogether, Ishmael lived a hundred and thirty-seven years. He breathed his last and died, and he was gathered to his people.
Gen 35 [29]Then he breathed his last and died and was gathered to his people, old and full of years. And his sons Esau and Jacob buried him.
Gen 49 [33]When Jacob had finished giving instructions to his sons, he drew his feet up into the bed, breathed his last and was gathered to his people.
Job 14 [10]"But man dies and is laid low; he breathes his last and is no more."

5) The Broken Wheel

Eccles 12 [6]Remember him—before the silver cord is severed, or the golden bowl is broken; before the pitcher is shattered at the spring, or the wheel broken at the well. . . .

6) The Company of the Dead

Prov 21 [16]A man who strays from the path of understanding comes to rest in the company of the dead.

7) Departing

Ps 39 [13]"Look away from me, that I may rejoice again before I depart and am no more."
Eccles 5 [15]Naked a man comes from his mother's womb, and as he comes, so he departs. He takes nothing from his labor that he can carry in his hand.
Phil 1 [23]I am torn between the two: I desire to depart and be with Christ, which is better by far. . . .
2 Tim 4 [6]For I am already being poured out like a drink offering, and the time has come for my departure.
2 Pet 1 [15]And I will make every effort to see that after my departure you will always be able to remember these things.

8) Destruction

Job 26 [6]"Death is naked before God; Destruction lies uncovered."
Ps 88 [11]Is your love declared in the grave, your faithfulness in Destruction?
Prov 15 [11]Death and Destruction lie open before the LORD—how much more the hearts of men!
Prov 27 [20]Death and Destruction are never satisfied, and neither are the eyes of man.

9) Dismissal

Luke 2 [29]"Sovereign Lord, as you have promised, you now dismiss your servant in peace."

10) The Earthly Tent Being Destroyed

2 Cor 5 [1]Now we know that if the earthly tent we live in is destroyed, we have a building from God, an eternal house in heaven, not built by human hands.

11) Glory

Ps 73 [24]You guide me with your counsel, and afterward you will take me into glory.

12) Going Down to Silence

Ps 115 [17]It is not the dead who praise the LORD, those who go down to silence. . . .

13) The Grave

Gen 37 [35]All his sons and daughters came to comfort him, but he refused to be comforted. "No," he said, "in mourning will I go down to the grave to my son." So his father wept for him.
Job 10 [19]"If only I had never come into being, or had been carried straight from the womb to the grave!"
Job 17 [1]"My spirit is broken, my days are cut short, the grave awaits me."
Job 17 [13]"If the only home I hope for is the grave, if I spread out my bed in darkness . . ."
Ps 18 [5]The cords of the grave coiled around me; the snares of death confronted me.
Ps 55 [15]Let death take my enemies by surprise; let them go down alive to the grave, for evil finds lodging among them.
Ps 88 [3]For my soul is full of trouble and my life draws near the grave. [4]I am counted among those who go down to the pit; I am like a man without strength. [5]I am set apart with the dead, like the slain who lie in the grave, whom you remember no more, who are cut off from your care.

14) The Journey of No Return

Job 16 [22]"Only a few years will pass before I go on the journey of no return."

15) The Land of Deepest Night

Job 10 [22]". . . to the land of deepest night, of deep shadow and disorder, where even the light is like darkness."

16) The Land of Deep Shadow and Disorder

Job 10 [22]". . . to the land of deepest night, of deep shadow and disorder, where even the light is like darkness."

17) The Land of Gloom and Deep Shadow

Job 10 [21]". . . before I go to the place of no return, to the land of gloom and deep shadow . . ."

18) The Land of Oblivion

Ps 88 [12]Are your wonders known in the place of darkness, or your righteous deeds in the land of oblivion?

19) The Last Sleep

Ps 76 [5]Valiant men lie plundered, they sleep their last sleep; not one of the warriors can lift his hands.

20) Lying Down in the Dust

Job 7 [21]"Why do you not pardon my offenses and forgive my sins? For I will soon lie down in the dust; you will search for me, but I will be no more."

21) Marching Off to the King of Terrors

Job 18 [14]"He is torn from the security of his tent and marched off to the king of terrors."

22) The Night

John 9 [4]"As long as it is day, we must do the work of him who sent me. Night is coming, when no one can work."

23) One's Life Being Demanded by God

Luke 12 [20]"But God said to him, 'You fool! This very night your life will be demanded from you. Then who will get what you have prepared for yourself?'"

24) Paradise

Luke 23 [43]Jesus answered him, "I tell you the truth, today you will be with me in paradise."

25) Passing Away

Job 34 [20]"They die in an instant, in the middle of the night; the people are shaken and they pass away; the mighty are removed without human hand."

26) The Pit

Ps 30 [9]"What gain is there in my destruction, in my going down into the pit? Will the dust praise you? Will it proclaim your faithfulness?"
Isa 14 [15]But you are brought down to the grave, to the depths of the pit.

27) The Place Appointed for All the Living

Job 30 [23]"I know you will bring me down to death, to the place appointed for all the living."

28) The Place of Darkness

Ps 88 [12]Are your wonders known in the place of darkness, or your righteous deeds in the land of oblivion?

29) The Place of No Return

Job 10 [21]". . . before I go to the place of no return, to the land of gloom and deep shadow . . ."

30) Putting Aside the Tent of This Body

2 Pet 1 [13]I think it is right to refresh your memory as long as I live in the tent of this body, [14]because I know that I will soon put it aside, as our Lord Jesus Christ has made clear to me.

31) Removal without Human Hand

Job 34 [20]"They die in an instant, in the middle of the night; the people are shaken and they pass away; the mighty are removed without human hand."

32) Resting with One's Fathers

Deut 31 [16]And the Lord said to Moses: "You are going to rest with your fathers, and these people will soon prostitute themselves to the foreign gods of the land they are entering. They will forsake me and break the covenant I made with them."

33) Returning to Dust

Gen 3 [19]"By the sweat of your brow you will eat your food until you return to the ground, since from it you were taken; for dust you are and to dust you will return."

Ps 104 [29]When you hide your face, they are terrified; when you take away their breath, they die and return to the dust.

34) The Severing of the Silver Cord

Eccles 12 [6]Remember him—before the silver cord is severed, or the golden bowl is broken; before the pitcher is shattered at the spring, or the wheel broken at the well. . . .

35) The Shattered Pitcher

Eccles 12 [6]Remember him—before the silver cord is severed, or the golden bowl is broken; before the pitcher is shattered at the spring, or the wheel broken at the well. . . .

36) Sleep

Job 14 [12]". . . so man lies down and does not rise; till the heavens are no more, men will not awake or be roused from their sleep."

Ps 13 [3]Look on me and answer, O Lord my God. Give light to my eyes, or I will sleep in death. . . .

Jer 51 [56]"A destroyer will come against Babylon; her warriors will be captured, and their bows will be broken. For the Lord is a God of retribution; he will repay in full. [57]I will make her officials and wise men drunk, her governors, officers and warriors as well; they will sleep forever and not awake," declares the King, whose name is the Lord Almighty.

Dan 12 [2]"Multitudes who sleep in the dust of the earth will awake: some to everlasting life, others to shame and everlasting contempt."

John 11 [11]After he had said this, he went on to tell them, "Our friend Lazarus has fallen asleep; but I am going there to wake him up."

[12]His disciples replied, "Lord, if he sleeps, he will get better." [13]Jesus had been speaking of his death, but his disciples thought he meant natural sleep.

[14]So then he told them plainly, "Lazarus is dead, [15]and for your sake I am glad I was not there, so that you may believe. But let us go to him."

Acts 7 [59]While they were stoning him, Stephen prayed, "Lord Jesus, receive my spirit." [60]Then he fell on his knees and cried out, "Lord, do not hold this sin against them." When he had said this, he fell asleep.

Acts 13 [36]"For when David had served God's purpose in his own generation, he fell asleep; he was buried with his fathers and his body decayed."

1 Cor 15 [6]After that, he appeared to more than five hundred of the brothers at the same time, most of whom are still living, though some have fallen asleep.

37) A Tempest

Job 27 [20]"Terrors overtake him like a flood; a tempest snatches him away in the night."

38) A Vanishing Cloud

Job 7 [9]"As a cloud vanishes and is gone, so he who goes down to the grave does not return."

James 4 [14]Why, you do not even know what will happen tomorrow. What is your life? You are a mist that appears for a little while and then vanishes.

39) Water Spilled on the Ground

2 Sam 14 [14]"Like water spilled on the ground, which cannot be recovered, so we must die. But God does not take away life; instead, he devises ways so that a banished person may not remain estranged from him."

40) A Way of All the Earth

Josh 23 [14]"Now I am about to go the way of all the earth. You know with all your heart and soul that not one of all the good promises the Lord your God gave you has failed. Every promise has been fulfilled; not one has failed."

1 Kings 2 [1]When the time drew near for David to die, he gave a charge to Solomon his son.

[2]"I am about to go the way of all the earth," he said. "So be strong, show yourself a man. . . ."

41) Withering Away

Job 14 [2]"He springs up like a flower and withers away; like a fleeting shadow, he does not endure."

Ps 90 [5]You sweep men away in the sleep of death; they are like the new grass of the morning—[6]though in the morning it springs up new, by evening it is dry and withered.

Ps 102 [11]My days are like the evening shadow; I wither away like grass.

James 1 [10]But the one who is rich should take pride in his low position, because he will pass away like a wild flower. [11]For the sun rises with scorching heat and withers the plant; its blossom falls and its beauty is destroyed. In the same way, the rich man will fade away even while he goes about his business.

2. Examples of the Fact of Death

a) Aaron

Num 20 [27]Moses did as the Lord commanded: They went up Mount Hor in the sight of the whole community. [28]Moses removed Aaron's garments and put them on his son Eleazar. And Aaron died there on top of the mountain. Then Moses and Eleazar came down from the mountain, [29]and when the whole community learned that Aaron had died, the entire house of Israel mourned for him thirty days.

b) Abraham

Gen 25 [7]Altogether, Abraham lived a hundred and seventy-five years. [8]Then Abraham breathed his last and died at a good old age, an old man and full of years; and he was gathered to his people.

c) David

1 Kings 2 [10]Then David rested with his fathers and was buried in the City of David. [11]He had reigned forty years over Israel—seven years in Hebron and thirty-three in Jerusalem.

1 Chron 29 [26]David son of Jesse was king over all Israel. [27]He ruled over Israel forty years—seven in Hebron and thirty-three in Jerusalem. [28]He died at a good old age, having enjoyed long life, wealth and honor. His son Solomon succeeded him as king.

d) Eli

1 Sam 4 [18]When he mentioned the ark of God, Eli fell backward off his chair by the side of the gate. His neck was broken and he died, for he was an old man and heavy. He had led Israel forty years.

e) Gideon

Judg 8 [32]Gideon son of Joash died at a good old age and was buried in the tomb of his father Joash in Ophrah of the Abiezrites.

f) Isaac

Gen 35 [28]Isaac lived a hundred and eighty years. [29]Then he breathed his last and died and was gathered to his people, old and full of years. And his sons Esau and Jacob buried him.

g) Ishmael

Gen 25 [17]Altogether, Ishmael lived a hundred and thirty-seven years. He breathed his last and died, and he was gathered to his people.

h) Jacob

Gen 49 [33]When Jacob had finished giving instructions to his sons, he drew his feet up into the bed, breathed his last and was gathered to his people.

i) Jehoiada

2 Chron 24 [15]Now Jehoiada was old and full of years, and he died at the age of a hundred and thirty. [16]He was buried with the kings in the City of David, because of the good he had done in Israel for God and his temple.

j) Joseph

Gen 50 [22]Joseph stayed in Egypt, along with all his father's family. He lived a hundred and ten years [23]and saw the third generation of Ephraim's children. Also the children of Makir son of Manasseh were placed at birth on Joseph's knees.

[24]Then Joseph said to his brothers, "I am about to die. But God will surely come to your aid and take you up out of this land to the land he promised on oath to Abraham, Isaac and Jacob." [25]And Joseph made the sons of Israel swear an oath and said, "God will surely come to your aid, and then you must carry my bones up from this place."

[26]So Joseph died at the age of a hundred and ten. And after they embalmed him, he was placed in a coffin in Egypt.

k) Joshua

Josh 24 [29]After these things, Joshua son of Nun, the servant of the LORD, died at the age of a hundred and ten. [30]And they buried him in the land of his inheritance, at Timnath Serah in the hill country of Ephraim, north of Mount Gaash.

l) Moses

Deut 34 [1]Then Moses climbed Mount Nebo from the plains of Moab to the top of Pisgah, across from Jericho. There the LORD showed him the whole land—from Gilead to Dan, [2]all of Naphtali, the territory of Ephraim and Manasseh, all the land of Judah as far as the western sea, [3]the Negev and the whole region from the Valley of Jericho, the City of Palms, as far as Zoar. [4]Then the LORD said to him, "This is the land I promised on oath to Abraham, Isaac and Jacob when I said, 'I will give it to your descendants.' I have let you see it with your eyes, but you will not cross over into it."

[5]And Moses the servant of the LORD died there in Moab, as the LORD had said. [6]He buried him in Moab, in the valley opposite Beth Peor, but to this day no one knows where his grave is. [7]Moses was a hundred and twenty years old when he died, yet his eyes were not weak nor his strength gone. [8]The Israelites grieved for Moses in the plains of Moab thirty days, until the time of weeping and mourning was over.

m) Paul

2 Tim 4 [6]For I am already being poured out like a drink offering, and the time has come for my departure.

n) Peter

2 Pet 1 [13]I think it is right to refresh your memory as long as I live in the tent of this body, [14]because I know that I will soon put it aside, as our Lord Jesus Christ has made clear to me. [15]And I will make every effort to see that after my departure you will always be able to remember these things.

o) Sarah

Gen 23 [1]Sarah lived to be a hundred and twenty-seven years old. [2]She died at Kiriath Arba (that is, Hebron) in the land of Canaan, and Abraham went to mourn for Sarah and to weep over her.

p) Solomon

1 Kings 11 [41]As for the other events of Solomon's reign—all he did and the wisdom he displayed—are they not written in the book of the annals of Solomon? [42]Solomon reigned in Jerusalem over all Israel forty years. [43]Then he rested with his fathers and was buried in the city of David his father. And Rehoboam his son succeeded him as king.

B. The Nature of Death

1. Death Is a Consequence of Human Sin

Gen 2 [17]". . . but you must not eat from the tree of the knowledge of good and evil, for when you eat of it you will surely die."

Gen 3 [17]To Adam he said, "Because you listened to your wife and ate from the tree about which I commanded you, 'You must not eat of it,' Cursed is the ground because of you; through painful toil you will eat of it all the days of your life. [18]It will produce thorns and thistles for you, and you will eat the plants of the field. [19]By the sweat of your brow you will eat your food until you return to the ground, since from it you were taken; for dust you are and to dust you will return."

Jer 9 [17]This is what the LORD Almighty says: "Consider now! Call for the wailing women to come; send for the most skillful of them. [18]Let them come quickly and wail over us till our eyes overflow with tears and water streams from our eyelids. [19]The sound of wailing is heard from Zion: 'How ruined we are! How great is our shame! We must leave our land because our houses are in ruins.'"

[20]Now, O women, hear the word of the LORD; open your ears to the words of his mouth. Teach your daughters how to wail; teach one another a lament. [21]Death has climbed in through our windows and has entered our fortresses; it has cut off the children from the streets and the young men from the public squares.

[22]Say, "This is what the LORD declares: 'The dead bodies of men will lie like refuse on the open field, like cut grain behind the reaper, with no one to gather them.'" . . .

[25]"The days are coming," declares the LORD, "when I will punish all who are circumcised only in the flesh—[26]Egypt, Judah, Edom, Ammon, Moab and all who live in the desert in distant places. For all these nations are really uncircumcised, and even the whole house of Israel is uncircumcised in heart."

Rom 5 [12]Therefore, just as sin entered the world through one man, and death through sin, and in this way death came to all men, because all sinned—[13]for before the law was given, sin was in the world. But sin is not taken into account when there is no law. [14]Nevertheless, death reigned from the time of Adam to the time of Moses, even over those who did not sin by breaking a command, as did Adam, who was a pattern of the one to come.

[15]But the gift is not like the trespass. For if the many died by the trespass of the one man, how much more did God's grace and the gift that came by the grace of the one man, Jesus Christ, overflow to the many! [16]Again, the gift of God is not like the result of the one man's sin: The judgment followed one sin and brought condemnation, but the gift followed many trespasses and brought justification. [17]For if, by the trespass of the one man, death reigned through that one man, how much more will those who receive God's abundant provision of grace and of the gift of righteousness reign in life through the one man, Jesus Christ.

[18]Consequently, just as the result of one trespass was condemnation for all men, so also the result of one act of righteousness was justification that brings life for all men. [19]For just as through the disobedience of the one man the many were made sinners, so also through the obedience of the one man the many will be made righteous.

[20]The law was added so that the trespass might increase. But where sin increased, grace increased all the more, [21]so that, just as sin reigned in death, so also grace might reign through righteousness to bring eternal life through Jesus Christ our Lord.

Rom 6 [23]For the wages of sin is death, but the gift of God is eternal life in Christ Jesus our Lord.

2. Death Is Separation from Earthly Existence

2 Sam 12 [23]"But now that he is dead, why should I fast? Can I bring him back again? I will go to him, but he will not return to me."

Job 3 [13]"For now I would be lying down in peace; I would be asleep and at rest [14]with kings and counselors of the earth, who built for themselves places now lying in ruins, [15]with rulers who had gold, who filled their houses with silver. . . . [17]There the wicked cease from turmoil, and there the weary are at rest. [18]Captives also enjoy their ease; they no longer hear the slave driver's shout. [19]The small and the great are there, and the slave is freed from his master."
Job 7 [9]"As a cloud vanishes and is gone, so he who goes down to the grave does not return. [10]He will never come to his house again; his place will know him no more."
Ps 6 [5]No one remembers you when he is dead. Who praises you from the grave?
Ps 49 [16]Do not be overawed when a man grows rich, when the splendor of his house increases; [17]for he will take nothing with him when he dies, his splendor will not descend with him.
Ps 88 [10]Do you show your wonders to the dead? Do those who are dead rise up and praise you? [11]Is your love declared in the grave, your faithfulness in Destruction? [12]Are your wonders known in the place of darkness, or your righteous deeds in the land of oblivion?
Ps 115 [17]It is not the dead who praise the LORD, those who go down to silence. . . .
Eccles 9 [5]For the living know that they will die, but the dead know nothing; they have no further reward, and even the memory of them is forgotten. [6]Their love, their hate and their jealousy have long since vanished; never again will they have a part in anything that happens under the sun. . . . [10]Whatever your hand finds to do, do it with all your might, for in the grave, where you are going, there is neither working nor planning nor knowledge nor wisdom.
Isa 38 [18]For the grave cannot praise you, death cannot sing your praise; those who go down to the pit cannot hope for your faithfulness.
1 Tim 6 [7]For we brought nothing into the world, and we can take nothing out of it.

3. Death Is Universal for All Humankind

1 Kings 2 [2]"I am about to go the way of all the earth," he said. "So be strong, show yourself a man. . . ."
Job 4 [18]"'If God places no trust in his servants, if he charges his angels with error, [19]how much more those who live in houses of clay, whose foundations are in the dust, who are crushed more readily than a moth! [20]Between dawn and dusk they are broken to pieces; unnoticed, they perish forever. [21]Are not the cords of their tent pulled up, so that they die without wisdom?'"
Job 9 [22]"It is all the same; that is why I say, 'He destroys both the blameless and the wicked.'"
Job 21 [22]"Can anyone teach knowledge to God, since he judges even the highest? [23]One man dies in full vigor, completely secure and at ease, [24]his body well nourished, his bones rich with marrow. [25]Another man dies in bitterness of soul, never having enjoyed anything good. [26]Side by side they lie in the dust, and worms cover them both."
Job 30 [23]"I know you will bring me down to death, to the place appointed for all the living."
Ps 49 [7]No man can redeem the life of another or give to God a ransom for him—[8]the ransom for a life is costly, no payment is ever enough—[9]that he should live on forever and not see decay.

[10]For all can see that wise men die; the foolish and the senseless alike perish and leave their wealth to others. [11]Their tombs will remain their houses forever, their dwellings for endless generations, though they had named lands after themselves.

[12]But man, despite his riches, does not endure; he is like the beasts that perish.
Ps 82 [6]"I said, 'You are "gods"; you are all sons of the Most High.' [7]But you will die like mere men; you will fall like every other ruler."

[8]Rise up, O God, judge the earth, for all the nations are your inheritance.
Ps 89 [48]What man can live and not see death, or save himself from the power of the grave?

Ps 146 [3]Do not put your trust in princes, in mortal men, who cannot save. [4]When their spirit departs, they return to the ground; on that very day their plans come to nothing.
Eccles 1 [4]Generations come and generations go, but the earth remains forever.
Eccles 2 [14]The wise man has eyes in his head, while the fool walks in the darkness; but I came to realize that the same fate overtakes them both.

[15]Then I thought in my heart, "The fate of the fool will overtake me also. What then do I gain by being wise?" I said in my heart, "This too is meaningless." [16]For the wise man, like the fool, will not be long remembered; in days to come both will be forgotten. Like the fool, the wise man too must die!
Eccles 3 [19]"Man's fate is like that of the animals; the same fate awaits them both: As one dies, so dies the other. All have the same breath; man has no advantage over the animal. Everything is meaningless. [20]All go to the same place; all come from dust, and to dust all return. [21]Who knows if the spirit of man rises upward and if the spirit of the animal goes down into the earth?"
Eccles 6 [6]even if he lives a thousand years twice over but fails to enjoy his prosperity. Do not all go to the same place?
Eccles 8 [8]No man has power over the wind to contain it; so no one has power over the day of his death. As no one is discharged in time of war, so wickedness will not release those who practice it.
Eccles 9 [3]This is the evil in everything that happens under the sun: The same destiny overtakes all. The hearts of men, moreover, are full of evil and there is madness in their hearts while they live, and afterward they join the dead.
Heb 9 [27]Just as man is destined to die once, and after that to face judgment . . .

4. The Duration of Life

a) The Duration of Life Is in God's Hands

Deut 32 [39]"See now that I myself am He! There is no god besides me. I put to death and I bring to life, I have wounded and I will heal, and no one can deliver out of my hand."
1 Sam 2 [6]"The LORD brings death and makes alive; he brings down to the grave and raises up."
2 Kings 8 [9]Hazael went to meet Elisha, taking with him as a gift forty camel-loads of all the finest wares of Damascus. He went in and stood before him, and said, "Your son Ben-Hadad king of Aram has sent me to ask, 'Will I recover from this illness?'"

[10]Elisha answered, "Go and say to him, 'You will certainly recover'; but the LORD has revealed to me that he will in fact die."
Job 7 [1]"Does not man have hard service on earth? Are not his days like those of a hired man? [2]Like a slave longing for the evening shadows, or a hired man waiting eagerly for his wages, [3]so I have been allotted months of futility, and nights of misery have been assigned to me."
Job 14 [5]"Man's days are determined; you have decreed the number of his months and have set limits he cannot exceed."
Job 24 [22]"But God drags away the mighty by his power; though they become established, they have no assurance of life. [23]He may let them rest in a feeling of security, but his eyes are on their ways. [24]For a little while they are exalted, and then they are gone; they are brought low and gathered up like all others; they are cut off like heads of grain."
Job 34 [14]"If it were his intention and he withdrew his spirit and breath, [15]all mankind would perish together and man would return to the dust."
Ps 90 [1]Lord, you have been our dwelling place throughout all generations. [2]Before the mountains were born or you brought forth the earth and the world, from everlasting to everlasting you are God.

[3]You turn men back to dust, saying, "Return to dust, O sons of men." [4]For a thousand years in your sight are like a day that has just gone by, or like a watch in the night.
Ps 104 [24]How many are your works, O LORD! In wisdom you made them all; the earth is full of your creatures. . . . [29]When

you hide your face, they are terrified; when you take away their breath, they die and return to the dust.
Eccles 3 [2]a time to be born and a time to die, a time to plant and a time to uproot . . .
Eccles 12 [5]when men are afraid of heights and of dangers in the streets; when the almond tree blossoms and the grasshopper drags himself along and desire no longer is stirred. Then man goes to his eternal home and mourners go about the streets. [7]. . . and the dust returns to the ground it came from, and the spirit returns to God who gave it.
Isa 38 [4]Then the word of the LORD came to Isaiah: [5]"Go and tell Hezekiah, 'This is what the LORD, the God of your father David, says: I have heard your prayer and seen your tears; I will add fifteen years to your life.'"
Dan 5 [23]"Instead, you have set yourself up against the Lord of heaven. You had the goblets from his temple brought to you, and you and your nobles, your wives and your concubines drank wine from them. You praised the gods of silver and gold, of bronze, iron, wood and stone, which cannot see or hear or understand. But you did not honor the God who holds in his hand your life and all your ways."
Matt 6 [26]"Look at the birds of the air; they do not sow or reap or store away in barns, and yet your heavenly Father feeds them. Are you not much more valuable than they? [27]Who of you by worrying can add a single hour to his life?"
Acts 17 [24]"The God who made the world and everything in it is the Lord of heaven and earth and does not live in temples built by hands. . . . [26]From one man he made every nation of men, that they should inhabit the whole earth; and he determined the times set for them and the exact places where they should live. . . . [28]'For in him we live and move and have our being.' As some of your own poets have said, 'We are his offspring.'"
Rev 1 [18]"I am the Living One; I was dead, and behold I am alive for ever and ever! And I hold the keys of death and Hades."

b) The Duration of Life Is Unknown to People

Gen 27 [2]Isaac said, "I am now an old man and don't know the day of my death."
Job 38 [16]"Have you journeyed to the springs of the sea or walked in the recesses of the deep? [17]Have the gates of death been shown to you? Have you seen the gates of the shadow of death? [18]Have you comprehended the vast expanses of the earth? Tell me, if you know all this."
Ps 39 [4]"Show me, O LORD, my life's end and the number of my days; let me know how fleeting is my life."
Prov 27 [1]Do not boast about tomorrow, for you do not know what a day may bring forth.
Eccles 3 [22]So I saw that there is nothing better for a man than to enjoy his work, because that is his lot. For who can bring him to see what will happen after him?
Luke 16 [19]"There was a rich man who was dressed in purple and fine linen and lived in luxury every day. [20]At his gate was laid a beggar named Lazarus, covered with sores [21]and longing to eat what fell from the rich man's table. Even the dogs came and licked his sores.

[22]"The time came when the beggar died and the angels carried him to Abraham's side. The rich man also died and was buried."
James 4 [13]Now listen, you who say, "Today or tomorrow we will go to this or that city, spend a year there, carry on business and make money." [14]Why, you do not even know what will happen tomorrow. What is your life? You are a mist that appears for a little while and then vanishes.

c) Life Is Short

Gen 47 [9]And Jacob said to Pharaoh, "The years of my pilgrimage are a hundred and thirty. My years have been few and difficult, and they do not equal the years of the pilgrimage of my fathers."
1 Sam 20 [3]But David took an oath and said, "Your father knows very well that I have found favor in your eyes, and he has said to himself, 'Jonathan must not know this or he will be grieved.' Yet as surely as the LORD lives and as you live, there is only a step between me and death."
1 Chron 29 [15]"We are aliens and strangers in your sight, as were all our forefathers. Our days on earth are like a shadow, without hope."
Job 7 [6]"My days are swifter than a weaver's shuttle, and they come to an end without hope. [7]Remember, O God, that my life is but a breath; my eyes will never see happiness again."
Job 8 [9]". . . for we were born only yesterday and know nothing, and our days on earth are but a shadow."
Job 9 [25]"My days are swifter than a runner; they fly away without a glimpse of joy. [26]They skim past like boats of papyrus, like eagles swooping down on their prey."
Job 10 [20]"Are not my few days almost over? Turn away from me so I can have a moment's joy. . . ."
Job 14 [1]"Man born of woman is of few days and full of trouble. [2]He springs up like a flower and withers away; like a fleeting shadow, he does not endure."
Ps 39 [5]"You have made my days a mere handbreadth; the span of my years is as nothing before you. Each man's life is but a breath. [6]Man is a mere phantom as he goes to and fro: He bustles about, but only in vain; he heaps up wealth, not knowing who will get it."
Ps 89 [47]Remember how fleeting is my life. For what futility you have created all men!
Ps 90 [10]The length of our days is seventy years—or eighty, if we have the strength; yet their span is but trouble and sorrow, for they quickly pass, and we fly away.
Ps 102 [11]My days are like the evening shadow; I wither away like grass.
Ps 103 [15]As for man, his days are like grass, he flourishes like a flower of the field; [16]the wind blows over it and it is gone, and its place remembers it no more.
Ps 144 [4]Man is like a breath; his days are like a fleeting shadow.
Isa 40 [6]A voice says, "Cry out." And I said, "What shall I cry?"

"All men are like grass, and all their glory is like the flowers of the field. [7]The grass withers and the flowers fall, because the breath of the LORD blows on them. Surely the people are grass. [8]The grass withers and the flowers fall, but the word of our God stands forever."
Zech 1 [5]"Where are your forefathers now? And the prophets, do they live forever?"
James 4 [14]Why, you do not even know what will happen tomorrow. What is your life? You are a mist that appears for a little while and then vanishes.

C. The Believer and Death

1. Death Brings Intimate Communion with God in Christ

Luke 23 [39]One of the criminals who hung there hurled insults at him: "Aren't you the Christ? Save yourself and us!"

[40]But the other criminal rebuked him. "Don't you fear God," he said, "since you are under the same sentence? [41]We are punished justly, for we are getting what our deeds deserve. But this man has done nothing wrong."

[42]Then he said, "Jesus, remember me when you come into your kingdom."

[43]Jesus answered him, "I tell you the truth, today you will be with me in paradise."
Acts 7 [59]While they were stoning him, Stephen prayed, "Lord Jesus, receive my spirit."
2 Cor 5 [1]Now we know that if the earthly tent we live in is destroyed, we have a building from God, an eternal house in heaven, not built by human hands. [2]Meanwhile we groan, longing to be clothed with our heavenly dwelling, [3]because when we are clothed, we will not be found naked. [4]For while we are in this tent, we groan and are burdened, because we do not wish to be unclothed but to be clothed with our heavenly dwelling, so that what is mortal may be swallowed up by life. [5]Now it is God who has made us for this very purpose and has given us the Spirit as a deposit, guaranteeing what is to come.

[6]Therefore we are always confident and know that as long as we are at home in the body we are away from the Lord. [7]We

live by faith, not by sight. [8]We are confident, I say, and would prefer to be away from the body and at home with the Lord.

Phil 1 [21]For to me, to live is Christ and to die is gain. [22]If I am to go on living in the body, this will mean fruitful labor for me. Yet what shall I choose? I do not know! [23]I am torn between the two: I desire to depart and be with Christ, which is better by far; [24]but it is more necessary for you that I remain in the body.

Heb 12 [22]But you have come to Mount Zion, to the heavenly Jerusalem, the city of the living God. You have come to thousands upon thousands of angels in joyful assembly, [23]to the church of the firstborn, whose names are written in heaven. You have come to God, the judge of all men, to the spirits of righteous men made perfect, [24]to Jesus the mediator of a new covenant, and to the sprinkled blood that speaks a better word than the blood of Abel.

2. Death Brings Peace and Rest

2 Kings 22 [19]"'Because your heart was responsive and you humbled yourself before the LORD when you heard what I have spoken against this place and its people, that they would become accursed and laid waste, and because you tore your robes and wept in my presence, I have heard you, declares the LORD. [20]Therefore I will gather you to your fathers, and you will be buried in peace. Your eyes will not see all the disaster I am going to bring on this place.'"

So they took her answer back to the king.

Isa 57 [1]The righteous perish, and no one ponders it in his heart; devout men are taken away, and no one understands that the righteous are taken away to be spared from evil. [2]Those who walk uprightly enter into peace; they find rest as they lie in death.

Dan 12 [13]"As for you, go your way till the end. You will rest, and then at the end of the days you will rise to receive your allotted inheritance."

Luke 2 [29]"Sovereign Lord, as you have promised, you now dismiss your servant in peace."

Luke 16 [22]"The time came when the beggar died and the angels carried him to Abraham's side. The rich man also died and was buried. . . .

[25]"But Abraham replied, 'Son, remember that in your lifetime you received your good things, while Lazarus received bad things, but now he is comforted here and you are in agony.'"

Rev 14 [13]Then I heard a voice from heaven say, "Write: Blessed are the dead who die in the Lord from now on."

"Yes," says the Spirit, "they will rest from their labor, for their deeds will follow them."

3. Death Is Precious in God's Sight

Ps 116 [15]Precious in the sight of the LORD is the death of his saints.

4. The Believer's Attitude toward Death

a) Death Drives Us to God Who Has Power over Death

Ps 49 [13]This is the fate of those who trust in themselves, and of their followers, who approve their sayings. [14]Like sheep they are destined for the grave, and death will feed on them. The upright will rule over them in the morning; their forms will decay in the grave, far from their princely mansions. [15]But God will redeem my life from the grave; he will surely take me to himself.

John 11 [9]Jesus answered, "Are there not twelve hours of daylight? A man who walks by day will not stumble, for he sees by this world's light. [10]It is when he walks by night that he stumbles, for he has no light."

[11]After he had said this, he went on to tell them, "Our friend Lazarus has fallen asleep; but I am going there to wake him up." . . .

[14]So then he told them plainly, "Lazarus is dead. . . ."

John 14 [19]"Before long, the world will not see me anymore, but you will see me. Because I live, you also will live."

Rom 14 [7]For none of us lives to himself alone and none of us dies to himself alone. [8]If we live, we live to the Lord; and if we die, we die to the Lord. So, whether we live or die, we belong to the Lord.

[9]For this very reason, Christ died and returned to life so that he might be the Lord of both the dead and the living.

1 Cor 15 [20]But Christ has indeed been raised from the dead, the firstfruits of those who have fallen asleep. [21]For since death came through a man, the resurrection of the dead comes also through a man. [22]For as in Adam all die, so in Christ all will be made alive. [23]But each in his own turn: Christ, the firstfruits; then, when he comes, those who belong to him.

1 Cor 15 [50]I declare to you, brothers, that flesh and blood cannot inherit the kingdom of God, nor does the perishable inherit the imperishable. [51]Listen, I tell you a mystery: We will not all sleep, but we will all be changed—[52]in a flash, in the twinkling of an eye, at the last trumpet. For the trumpet will sound, the dead will be raised imperishable, and we will be changed. [53]For the perishable must clothe itself with the imperishable, and the mortal with immortality. [54]When the perishable has been clothed with the imperishable, and the mortal with immortality, then the saying that is written will come true: "Death has been swallowed up in victory." [55]"Where, O death, is your victory? Where, O death, is your sting?" [56]The sting of death is sin, and the power of sin is the law. [57]But thanks be to God! He gives us the victory through our Lord Jesus Christ.

1 Thess 4 [13]Brothers, we do not want you to be ignorant about those who fall asleep, or to grieve like the rest of men, who have no hope. [14]We believe that Jesus died and rose again and so we believe that God will bring with Jesus those who have fallen asleep in him.

1 Thess 5 [9]For God did not appoint us to suffer wrath but to receive salvation through our Lord Jesus Christ. [10]He died for us so that, whether we are awake or asleep, we may live together with him.

2 Tim 1 [10]but it has now been revealed through the appearing of our Savior, Christ Jesus, who has destroyed death and has brought life and immortality to light through the gospel.

2 Tim 4 [18]The Lord will rescue me from every evil attack and will bring me safely to his heavenly kingdom. To him be glory for ever and ever. Amen.

Rev 1 [17]When I saw him, I fell at his feet as though dead. Then he placed his right hand on me and said: "Do not be afraid. I am the First and the Last. [18]I am the Living One; I was dead, and behold I am alive for ever and ever! And I hold the keys of death and Hades."

b) Death Teaches Us to Live Wisely

Ps 90 [12]Teach us to number our days aright, that we may gain a heart of wisdom.

John 9 [4]"As long as it is day, we must do the work of him who sent me. Night is coming, when no one can work."

James 4 [13]Now listen, you who say, "Today or tomorrow we will go to this or that city, spend a year there, carry on business and make money." [14]Why, you do not even know what will happen tomorrow. What is your life? You are a mist that appears for a little while and then vanishes. [15]Instead, you ought to say, "If it is the Lord's will, we will live and do this or that."

1 Pet 1 [17]Since you call on a Father who judges each man's work impartially, live your lives as strangers here in reverent fear.

c) Death Teaches Us to Live with Heaven in View

Job 19 [25]"I know that my Redeemer lives, and that in the end he will stand upon the earth. [26]And after my skin has been destroyed, yet in my flesh I will see God; [27]I myself will see him with my own eyes—I, and not another. How my heart yearns within me!"

Ps 73 [24]You guide me with your counsel, and afterward you will take me into glory. [25]Whom have I in heaven but you? And earth has nothing I desire besides you. [26]My flesh and my heart may fail, but God is the strength of my heart and my portion forever.

Hos 13 [14]"I will ransom them from the power of the grave; I will redeem them from death. Where, O death, are your plagues? Where, O grave, is your destruction?"

1 Cor 3 21So then, no more boasting about men! All things are yours, 22whether Paul or Apollos or Cephas or the world or life or death or the present or the future—all are yours, 23and you are of Christ, and Christ is of God.
2 Cor 1 9Indeed, in our hearts we felt the sentence of death. But this happened that we might not rely on ourselves but on God, who raises the dead.
1 Thess 4 13Brothers, we do not want you to be ignorant about those who fall asleep, or to grieve like the rest of men, who have no hope. 14We believe that Jesus died and rose again and so we believe that God will bring with Jesus those who have fallen asleep in him. 15According to the Lord's own word, we tell you that we who are still alive, who are left till the coming of the Lord, will certainly not precede those who have fallen asleep. 16For the Lord himself will come down from heaven, with a loud command, with the voice of the archangel and with the trumpet call of God, and the dead in Christ will rise first. 17After that, we who are still alive and are left will be caught up together with them in the clouds to meet the Lord in the air. And so we will be with the Lord forever. 18Therefore encourage each other with these words.
2 Tim 4 6For I am already being poured out like a drink offering, and the time has come for my departure. 7I have fought the good fight, I have finished the race, I have kept the faith. 8Now there is in store for me the crown of righteousness, which the Lord, the righteous Judge, will award to me on that day—and not only to me, but also to all who have longed for his appearing.
Heb 11 13All these people were still living by faith when they died. They did not receive the things promised; they only saw them and welcomed them from a distance. And they admitted that they were aliens and strangers on earth. 14People who say such things show that they are looking for a country of their own. 15If they had been thinking of the country they had left, they would have had opportunity to return. 16Instead, they were longing for a better country—a heavenly one. Therefore God is not ashamed to be called their God, for he has prepared a city for them.
Heb 13 14For here we do not have an enduring city, but we are looking for the city that is to come.
2 Pet 1 10Therefore, my brothers, be all the more eager to make your calling and election sure. For if you do these things, you will never fall, 11and you will receive a rich welcome into the eternal kingdom of our Lord and Savior Jesus Christ.

d) Death Holds No Fear, for It Is Conquered

Ps 23 4Even though I walk through the valley of the shadow of death, I will fear no evil, for you are with me; your rod and your staff, they comfort me.
Ps 103 13As a father has compassion on his children, so the LORD has compassion on those who fear him; 14for he knows how we are formed, he remembers that we are dust. 15As for man, his days are like grass, he flourishes like a flower of the field; 16the wind blows over it and it is gone, and its place remembers it no more. 17But from everlasting to everlasting the LORD's love is with those who fear him, and his righteousness with their children's children—18with those who keep his covenant and remember to obey his precepts.
Prov 14 32When calamity comes, the wicked are brought down, but even in death the righteous have a refuge.
Matt 10 28"Do not be afraid of those who kill the body but cannot kill the soul. Rather, be afraid of the One who can destroy both soul and body in hell."
Phil 1 20I eagerly expect and hope that I will in no way be ashamed, but will have sufficient courage so that now as always Christ will be exalted in my body, whether by life or by death.
Heb 2 14Since the children have flesh and blood, he too shared in their humanity so that by his death he might destroy him who holds the power of death—that is, the devil—15and free those who all their lives were held in slavery by their fear of death.
Rev 21 4"He will wipe every tear from their eyes. There will be no more death or mourning or crying or pain, for the old order of things has passed away."

II
The Intermediate State

A. The Intermediate State Is Continued Conscious Existence

Eccles 12 7and the dust returns to the ground it came from, and the spirit returns to God who gave it.
Matt 17 1After six days Jesus took with him Peter, James and John the brother of James, and led them up a high mountain by themselves. 2There he was transfigured before them. His face shone like the sun, and his clothes became as white as the light. 3Just then there appeared before them Moses and Elijah, talking with Jesus.

4Peter said to Jesus, "Lord, it is good for us to be here. If you wish, I will put up three shelters—one for you, one for Moses and one for Elijah."
Mark 9 2After six days Jesus took Peter, James and John with him and led them up a high mountain, where they were all alone. There he was transfigured before them. 3His clothes became dazzling white, whiter than anyone in the world could bleach them. 4And there appeared before them Elijah and Moses, who were talking with Jesus.
Luke 9 28About eight days after Jesus said this, he took Peter, John and James with him and went up onto a mountain to pray. 29As he was praying, the appearance of his face changed, and his clothes became as bright as a flash of lightning. 30Two men, Moses and Elijah, 31appeared in glorious splendor, talking with Jesus. They spoke about his departure, which he was about to bring to fulfillment at Jerusalem. 32Peter and his companions were very sleepy, but when they became fully awake, they saw his glory and the two men standing with him. 33As the men were leaving Jesus, Peter said to him, "Master, it is good for us to be here. Let us put up three shelters—one for you, one for Moses and one for Elijah." (He did not know what he was saying.)
Luke 16 19"There was a rich man who was dressed in purple and fine linen and lived in luxury every day. 20At his gate was laid a beggar named Lazarus, covered with sores 21and longing to eat what fell from the rich man's table. Even the dogs came and licked his sores.

22"The time came when the beggar died and the angels carried him to Abraham's side. The rich man also died and was buried. 23In hell, where he was in torment, he looked up and saw Abraham far away, with Lazarus by his side. 24So he called to him, 'Father Abraham, have pity on me and send Lazarus to dip the tip of his finger in water and cool my tongue, because I am in agony in this fire.'

25"But Abraham replied, 'Son, remember that in your lifetime you received your good things, while Lazarus received bad things, but now he is comforted here and you are in agony. 26And besides all this, between us and you a great chasm has been fixed, so that those who want to go from here to you cannot, nor can anyone cross over from there to us.'

27"He answered, 'Then I beg you, father, send Lazarus to my father's house, 28for I have five brothers. Let him warn them, so that they will not also come to this place of torment.'

29"Abraham replied, 'They have Moses and the Prophets; let them listen to them.'

30"'No, father Abraham,' he said, 'but if someone from the dead goes to them, they will repent.'

31"He said to him, 'If they do not listen to Moses and the Prophets, they will not be convinced even if someone rises from the dead.'"

B. The Intermediate State Is Isolation from Earthly Existence

2 Sam 12 15After Nathan had gone home, the LORD struck the child that Uriah's wife had borne to David, and he became ill. 16David pleaded with God for the child. He fasted and went into his house and spent the nights lying on the ground. 17The elders of his household stood beside him to get him up from the ground, but he refused, and he would not eat any food with them.

18On the seventh day the child died. David's servants were afraid to tell him that the child was dead, for they thought, "While the child was still living, we spoke to David but he would not listen to us. How can we tell him the child is dead? He may do something desperate."

19David noticed that his servants were whispering among themselves and he realized the child was dead. "Is the child dead?" he asked.

"Yes," they replied, "he is dead."

20Then David got up from the ground. After he had washed, put on lotions and changed his clothes, he went into the house of the LORD and worshiped. Then he went to his own house, and at his request they served him food, and he ate.

21His servants asked him, "Why are you acting this way? While the child was alive, you fasted and wept, but now that the child is dead, you get up and eat!"

22He answered, "While the child was still alive, I fasted and wept. I thought, 'Who knows? The LORD may be gracious to me and let the child live.' 23But now that he is dead, why should I fast? Can I bring him back again? I will go to him, but he will not return to me."

Ps 6 5No one remembers you when he is dead. Who praises you from the grave?

Ps 88 10Do you show your wonders to the dead? Do those who are dead rise up and praise you? 11Is your love declared in the grave, your faithfulness in Destruction? 12Are your wonders known in the place of darkness, or your righteous deeds in the land of oblivion?

Eccles 9 4Anyone who is among the living has hope—even a live dog is better off than a dead lion!

5For the living know that they will die, but the dead know nothing; they have no further reward, and even the memory of them is forgotten. 6Their love, their hate and their jealousy have long since vanished; never again will they have a part in anything that happens under the sun.

C. *The Intermediate State Foreshadows the Final State of Humanity*

1. The Intermediate State for the Righteous

a) Fellowship with Christ

Luke 23 43Jesus answered him, "I tell you the truth, today you will be with me in paradise."

Acts 7 59While they were stoning him, Stephen prayed, "Lord Jesus, receive my spirit."

2 Cor 5 1Now we know that if the earthly tent we live in is destroyed, we have a building from God, an eternal house in heaven, not built by human hands. 2Meanwhile we groan, longing to be clothed with our heavenly dwelling, 3because when we are clothed, we will not be found naked. 4For while we are in this tent, we groan and are burdened, because we do not wish to be unclothed but to be clothed with our heavenly dwelling, so that what is mortal may be swallowed up by life. 5Now it is God who has made us for this very purpose and has given us the Spirit as a deposit, guaranteeing what is to come.

6Therefore we are always confident and know that as long as we are at home in the body we are away from the Lord. 7We live by faith, not by sight. 8We are confident, I say, and would prefer to be away from the body and at home with the Lord. 9So we make it our goal to please him, whether we are at home in the body or away from it. 10For we must all appear before the judgment seat of Christ, that each one may receive what is due him for the things done while in the body, whether good or bad.

Phil 1 23I am torn between the two: I desire to depart and be with Christ, which is better by far. . . .

1 Thess 5 10He died for us so that, whether we are awake or asleep, we may live together with him.

b) Fellowship with God

Ps 17 15And I—in righteousness I will see your face; when I awake, I will be satisfied with seeing your likeness.

Ps 73 24You guide me with your counsel, and afterward you will take me into glory. 25Whom have I in heaven but you? And earth has nothing I desire besides you. 26My flesh and my heart may fail, but God is the strength of my heart and my portion forever.

Rev 7 9After this I looked and there before me was a great multitude that no one could count, from every nation, tribe, people and language, standing before the throne and in front of the Lamb. They were wearing white robes and were holding palm branches in their hands. . . .

13Then one of the elders asked me, "These in white robes—who are they, and where did they come from?"

14I answered, "Sir, you know."

And he said, "These are they who have come out of the great tribulation; they have washed their robes and made them white in the blood of the Lamb. 15Therefore, they are before the throne of God and serve him day and night in his temple; and he who sits on the throne will spread his tent over them. 16Never again will they hunger; never again will they thirst. The sun will not beat upon them, nor any scorching heat. 17For the Lamb at the center of the throne will be their shepherd; he will lead them to springs of living water. And God will wipe away every tear from their eyes."

c) Final Glory

Ps 49 15But God will redeem my life from the grave; he will surely take me to himself.

Dan 12 2"Multitudes who sleep in the dust of the earth will awake: some to everlasting life, others to shame and everlasting contempt. 3Those who are wise will shine like the brightness of the heavens, and those who lead many to righteousness, like the stars for ever and ever."

Matt 25 31"When the Son of Man comes in his glory, and all the angels with him, he will sit on his throne in heavenly glory. 32All the nations will be gathered before him, and he will separate the people one from another as a shepherd separates the sheep from the goats. 33He will put the sheep on his right and the goats on his left.

34"Then the King will say to those on his right, 'Come, you who are blessed by my Father; take your inheritance, the kingdom prepared for you since the creation of the world. 35For I was hungry and you gave me something to eat, I was thirsty and you gave me something to drink, I was a stranger and you invited me in, 36I needed clothes and you clothed me, I was sick and you looked after me, I was in prison and you came to visit me.'

37"Then the righteous will answer him, 'Lord, when did we see you hungry and feed you, or thirsty and give you something to drink? 38When did we see you a stranger and invite you in, or needing clothes and clothe you? 39When did we see you sick or in prison and go to visit you?'

40"The King will reply, 'I tell you the truth, whatever you did for one of the least of these brothers of mine, you did for me.'"

John 5 28"Do not be amazed at this, for a time is coming when all who are in their graves will hear his voice 29and come out—those who have done good will rise to live, and those who have done evil will rise to be condemned."

1 Thess 4 13Brothers, we do not want you to be ignorant about those who fall asleep, or to grieve like the rest of men, who have no hope. 14We believe that Jesus died and rose again and so we believe that God will bring with Jesus those who have fallen asleep in him. 15According to the Lord's own word, we tell you that we who are still alive, who are left till the coming of the Lord, will certainly not precede those who have fallen asleep. 16For the Lord himself will come down from heaven, with a loud command, with the voice of the archangel and with the trumpet call of God, and the dead in Christ will rise first. 17After that, we who are still alive and are left will be caught up together with them in the clouds to meet the Lord in the air. And so we will be with the Lord forever. 18Therefore encourage each other with these words.

Heb 9 27Just as man is destined to die once, and after that to face judgment, 28so Christ was sacrificed once to take away the sins of many people; and he will appear a second time, not to bear sin, but to bring salvation to those who are waiting for him.

d) Rest

Luke 16 [25]"But Abraham replied, 'Son, remember that in your lifetime you received your good things, while Lazarus received bad things, but now he is comforted here and you are in agony.'"

Rev 14 [13]Then I heard a voice from heaven say, "Write: Blessed are the dead who die in the Lord from now on."

"Yes," says the Spirit, "they will rest from their labor, for their deeds will follow them."

2. The Intermediate State for the Wicked

a) Anguish

Luke 16 [22]"The time came when the beggar died and the angels carried him to Abraham's side. The rich man also died and was buried. [23]In hell, where he was in torment, he looked up and saw Abraham far away, with Lazarus by his side. [24]So he called to him, 'Father Abraham, have pity on me and send Lazarus to dip the tip of his finger in water and cool my tongue, because I am in agony in this fire.'

[25]"But Abraham replied, 'Son, remember that in your lifetime you received your good things, while Lazarus received bad things, but now he is comforted here and you are in agony.'"

b) Final Condemnation

Dan 12 [2]"Multitudes who sleep in the dust of the earth will awake: some to everlasting life, others to shame and everlasting contempt."

Matt 25 [31]"When the Son of Man comes in his glory, and all the angels with him, he will sit on his throne in heavenly glory. [32]All the nations will be gathered before him, and he will separate the people one from another as a shepherd separates the sheep from the goats. [33]He will put the sheep on his right and the goats on his left. . . .

[41]"Then he will say to those on his left, 'Depart from me, you who are cursed, into the eternal fire prepared for the devil and his angels. [42]For I was hungry and you gave me nothing to eat, I was thirsty and you gave me nothing to drink, [43]I was a stranger and you did not invite me in, I needed clothes and you did not clothe me, I was sick and in prison and you did not look after me.'

[44]"They also will answer, 'Lord, when did we see you hungry or thirsty or a stranger or needing clothes or sick or in prison, and did not help you?'

[45]"He will reply, 'I tell you the truth, whatever you did not do for one of the least of these, you did not do for me.'

[46]"Then they will go away to eternal punishment, but the righteous to eternal life."

John 5 [28]"Do not be amazed at this, for a time is coming when all who are in their graves will hear his voice [29]and come out—those who have done good will rise to live, and those who have done evil will rise to be condemned."

Heb 9 [27]Just as man is destined to die once, and after that to face judgment . . .

Jude [5]Though you already know all this, I want to remind you that the Lord delivered his people out of Egypt, but later destroyed those who did not believe. [6]And the angels who did not keep their positions of authority but abandoned their own home—these he has kept in darkness, bound with everlasting chains for judgment on the great Day. [7]In a similar way, Sodom and Gomorrah and the surrounding towns gave themselves up to sexual immorality and perversion. They serve as an example of those who suffer the punishment of eternal fire.

Rev 20 [11]Then I saw a great white throne and him who was seated on it. Earth and sky fled from his presence, and there was no place for them. [12]And I saw the dead, great and small, standing before the throne, and books were opened. Another book was opened, which is the book of life. The dead were judged according to what they had done as recorded in the books. [13]The sea gave up the dead that were in it, and death and Hades gave up the dead that were in them, and each person was judged according to what he had done. [14]Then death and Hades were thrown into the lake of fire. The lake of fire is the second death. [15]If anyone's name was not found written in the book of life, he was thrown into the lake of fire.

III
The Second Coming of Jesus

A. Signs of Jesus' Second Coming

1. Apostasy

Matt 24 [3]As Jesus was sitting on the Mount of Olives, the disciples came to him privately. "Tell us," they said, "when will this happen, and what will be the sign of your coming and of the end of the age?" . . .

[10]"At that time many will turn away from the faith and will betray and hate each other. . . ."

2 Tim 4 [3]For the time will come when men will not put up with sound doctrine. Instead, to suit their own desires, they will gather around them a great number of teachers to say what their itching ears want to hear. [4]They will turn their ears away from the truth and turn aside to myths.

2. Appearance of Antichrist

Matt 24 [5]"For many will come in my name, claiming, 'I am the Christ,' and will deceive many. . . . [23]At that time if anyone says to you, 'Look, here is the Christ!' or, 'There he is!' do not believe it. [24]For false Christs and false prophets will appear and perform great signs and miracles to deceive even the elect—if that were possible. . . .

[26]"So if anyone tells you, 'There he is, out in the desert,' do not go out; or, 'Here he is, in the inner rooms,' do not believe it."

Luke 21 [8]He replied: "Watch out that you are not deceived. For many will come in my name, claiming, 'I am he,' and, 'The time is near.' Do not follow them."

2 Thess 2 [1]Concerning the coming of our Lord Jesus Christ and our being gathered to him, we ask you, brothers, [2]not to become easily unsettled or alarmed by some prophecy, report or letter supposed to have come from us, saying that the day of the Lord has already come. [3]Don't let anyone deceive you in any way, for that day will not come until the rebellion occurs and the man of lawlessness is revealed, the man doomed to destruction. [4]He will oppose and will exalt himself over everything that is called God or is worshiped, so that he sets himself up in God's temple, proclaiming himself to be God.

[5]Don't you remember that when I was with you I used to tell you these things? [6]And now you know what is holding him back, so that he may be revealed at the proper time. [7]For the secret power of lawlessness is already at work; but the one who now holds it back will continue to do so till he is taken out of the way. [8]And then the lawless one will be revealed, whom the Lord Jesus will overthrow with the breath of his mouth and destroy by the splendor of his coming. [9]The coming of the lawless one will be in accordance with the work of Satan displayed in all kinds of counterfeit miracles, signs and wonders, [10]and in every sort of evil that deceives those who are perishing. They perish because they refused to love the truth and so be saved.

1 John 2 [18]Dear children, this is the last hour; and as you have heard that the antichrist is coming, even now many antichrists have come. This is how we know it is the last hour. [19]They went out from us, but they did not really belong to us. For if they had belonged to us, they would have remained with us; but their going showed that none of them belonged to us.

[20]But you have an anointing from the Holy One, and all of you know the truth. [21]I do not write to you because you do not know the truth, but because you do know it and because no lie comes from the truth. [22]Who is the liar? It is the man who denies that Jesus is the Christ. Such a man is the antichrist—he denies the Father and the Son. [23]No one who denies the Son has the Father; whoever acknowledges the Son has the Father also.

1 John 4 [3]but every spirit that does not acknowledge Jesus is

not from God. This is the spirit of the antichrist, which you have heard is coming and even now is already in the world.
2 John [7]Many deceivers, who do not acknowledge Jesus Christ as coming in the flesh, have gone out into the world. Any such person is the deceiver and the antichrist.
Rev 13 [1]And the dragon stood on the shore of the sea.

And I saw a beast coming out of the sea. He had ten horns and seven heads, with ten crowns on his horns, and on each head a blasphemous name. [2]The beast I saw resembled a leopard, but had feet like those of a bear and a mouth like that of a lion. The dragon gave the beast his power and his throne and great authority. [3]One of the heads of the beast seemed to have had a fatal wound, but the fatal wound had been healed. The whole world was astonished and followed the beast. [4]Men worshiped the dragon because he had given authority to the beast, and they also worshiped the beast and asked, "Who is like the beast? Who can make war against him?"

[5]The beast was given a mouth to utter proud words and blasphemies and to exercise his authority for forty-two months. [6]He opened his mouth to blaspheme God, and to slander his name and his dwelling place and those who live in heaven. [7]He was given power to make war against the saints and to conquer them. And he was given authority over every tribe, people, language and nation. [8]All inhabitants of the earth will worship the beast—all whose names have not been written in the book of life belonging to the Lamb that was slain from the creation of the world.
Rev 19 [20]But the beast was captured, and with him the false prophet who had performed the miraculous signs on his behalf. With these signs he had deluded those who had received the mark of the beast and worshiped his image. The two of them were thrown alive into the fiery lake of burning sulfur.

3. Betrayal

Mark 13 [3]As Jesus was sitting on the Mount of Olives opposite the temple, Peter, James, John and Andrew asked him privately, [4]"Tell us, when will these things happen? And what will be the sign that they are all about to be fulfilled?". . .

[12]"Brother will betray brother to death, and a father his child. Children will rebel against their parents and have them put to death."
Luke 21 [16]"You will be betrayed even by parents, brothers, relatives and friends, and they will put some of you to death."

4. Earthquakes

Matt 24 [7]"Nation will rise against nation, and kingdom against kingdom. There will be famines and earthquakes in various places."
Mark 13 [8]"Nation will rise against nation, and kingdom against kingdom. There will be earthquakes in various places, and famines. These are the beginning of birth pains."

5. False Christs

Matt 24 [24]"For false Christs and false prophets will appear and perform great signs and miracles to deceive even the elect—if that were possible. [25]See, I have told you ahead of time."
Mark 13 [5]Jesus said to them: "Watch out that no one deceives you. [6]Many will come in my name, claiming, 'I am he,' and will deceive many. . . . [21]At that time if anyone says to you, 'Look, here is the Christ!' or, 'Look, there he is!' do not believe it. [22]For false Christs and false prophets will appear and perform signs and miracles to deceive the elect—if that were possible. [23]So be on your guard; I have told you everything ahead of time."
Luke 21 [8]He replied: "Watch out that you are not deceived. For many will come in my name, claiming, 'I am he,' and, 'The time is near.' Do not follow them."

6. False Prophets

Matt 24 [11]". . . and many false prophets will appear and deceive many people."
Mark 13 [6]"Many will come in my name, claiming, 'I am he,' and will deceive many. . . . [21]At that time if anyone says to you, 'Look, here is the Christ!' or, 'Look, there he is!' do not believe it. [22]For false Christs and false prophets will appear and perform signs and miracles to deceive the elect—if that were possible. [23]So be on your guard; I have told you everything ahead of time."

7. False Signs and Miracles

Matt 24 [24]"For false Christs and false prophets will appear and perform great signs and miracles to deceive even the elect—if that were possible."
Mark 13 [22]"For false Christs and false prophets will appear and perform signs and miracles to deceive the elect—if that were possible."
Luke 21 [8]He replied: "Watch out that you are not deceived. For many will come in my name, claiming, 'I am he,' and, 'The time is near.' Do not follow them."
2 Thess 2 [9]The coming of the lawless one will be in accordance with the work of Satan displayed in all kinds of counterfeit miracles, signs and wonders, [10]and in every sort of evil that deceives those who are perishing. They perish because they refused to love the truth and so be saved.
Rev 19 [20]But the beast was captured, and with him the false prophet who had performed the miraculous signs on his behalf. With these signs he had deluded those who had received the mark of the beast and worshiped his image. The two of them were thrown alive into the fiery lake of burning sulfur.

8. Famines

Matt 24 [7]"Nation will rise against nation, and kingdom against kingdom. There will be famines and earthquakes in various places."
Mark 13 [8]"Nation will rise against nation, and kingdom against kingdom. There will be earthquakes in various places, and famines. These are the beginning of birth pains."
Rev 6 [5]When the Lamb opened the third seal, I heard the third living creature say, "Come!" I looked, and there before me was a black horse! Its rider was holding a pair of scales in his hand. [6]Then I heard what sounded like a voice among the four living creatures, saying, "A quart of wheat for a day's wages, and three quarts of barley for a day's wages, and do not damage the oil and the wine!"

9. Increase of Evil

Matt 24 [12]"Because of the increase of wickedness, the love of most will grow cold. . . ."
2 Tim 3 [1]But mark this: There will be terrible times in the last days. [2]People will be lovers of themselves, lovers of money, boastful, proud, abusive, disobedient to their parents, ungrateful, unholy, [3]without love, unforgiving, slanderous, without self-control, brutal, not lovers of the good, [4]treacherous, rash, conceited, lovers of pleasure rather than lovers of God—[5]having a form of godliness but denying its power. Have nothing to do with them.
2 Pet 3 [3]First of all, you must understand that in the last days scoffers will come, scoffing and following their own evil desires. [4]They will say, "Where is this 'coming' he promised? Ever since our fathers died, everything goes on as it has since the beginning of creation."

10. International Strife

Matt 24 [7]"Nation will rise against nation, and kingdom against kingdom. There will be famines and earthquakes in various places."
Mark 13 [8]"Nation will rise against nation, and kingdom against kingdom. There will be earthquakes in various places, and famines. These are the beginning of birth pains."
Luke 21 [10]Then he said to them: "Nation will rise against nation, and kingdom against kingdom."
Rev 6 [3]When the Lamb opened the second seal, I heard the second living creature say, "Come!" [4]Then another horse came

out, a fiery red one. Its rider was given power to take peace from the earth and to make men slay each other. To him was given a large sword.

11. Persecution of Believers

Matt 24 [8]"All these are the beginning of birth pains.

[9]"Then you will be handed over to be persecuted and put to death, and you will be hated by all nations because of me."

Mark 13 [9]"You must be on your guard. You will be handed over to the local councils and flogged in the synagogues. On account of me you will stand before governors and kings as witnesses to them. [10]And the gospel must first be preached to all nations. [11]Whenever you are arrested and brought to trial, do not worry beforehand about what to say. Just say whatever is given you at the time, for it is not you speaking, but the Holy Spirit. . . . [13]All men will hate you because of me, but he who stands firm to the end will be saved."

Luke 21 [12]"But before all this, they will lay hands on you and persecute you. They will deliver you to synagogues and prisons, and you will be brought before kings and governors, and all on account of my name. [13]This will result in your being witnesses to them. [14]But make up your mind not to worry beforehand how you will defend yourselves. [15]For I will give you words and wisdom that none of your adversaries will be able to resist or contradict. [16]You will be betrayed even by parents, brothers, relatives and friends, and they will put some of you to death. [17]All men will hate you because of me. [18]But not a hair of your head will perish. [19]By standing firm you will gain life."

2 Tim 3 [1]But mark this: There will be terrible times in the last days. [2]People will be lovers of themselves, lovers of money, boastful, proud, abusive, disobedient to their parents, ungrateful, unholy, [3]without love, unforgiving, slanderous, without self-control, brutal, not lovers of the good, [4]treacherous, rash, conceited, lovers of pleasure rather than lovers of God—[5]having a form of godliness but denying its power. Have nothing to do with them. . . .

[10]You, however, know all about my teaching, my way of life, my purpose, faith, patience, love, endurance, [11]persecutions, sufferings—what kinds of things happened to me in Antioch, Iconium and Lystra, the persecutions I endured. Yet the Lord rescued me from all of them. [12]In fact, everyone who wants to live a godly life in Christ Jesus will be persecuted, [13]while evil men and impostors will go from bad to worse, deceiving and being deceived.

Rev 6 [9]When he opened the fifth seal, I saw under the altar the souls of those who had been slain because of the word of God and the testimony they had maintained. [10]They called out in a loud voice, "How long, Sovereign Lord, holy and true, until you judge the inhabitants of the earth and avenge our blood?" [11]Then each of them was given a white robe, and they were told to wait a little longer, until the number of their fellow servants and brothers who were to be killed as they had been was completed.

Rev 12 [17]Then the dragon was enraged at the woman and went off to make war against the rest of her offspring—those who obey God's commandments and hold to the testimony of Jesus.

Rev 20 [4]I saw thrones on which were seated those who had been given authority to judge. And I saw the souls of those who had been beheaded because of their testimony for Jesus and because of the word of God. They had not worshiped the beast or his image and had not received his mark on their foreheads or their hands. They came to life and reigned with Christ a thousand years.

12. Pestilence

Luke 21 [11]"There will be great earthquakes, famines and pestilences in various places, and fearful events and great signs from heaven."

Rev 6 [7]When the Lamb opened the fourth seal, I heard the voice of the fourth living creature say, "Come!" [8]I looked, and there before me was a pale horse! Its rider was named Death, and Hades was following close behind him. They were given power over a fourth of the earth to kill by sword, famine and plague, and by the wild beasts of the earth.

13. Unparalleled Distress

Matt 24 [21]"For then there will be great distress, unequaled from the beginning of the world until now—and never to be equaled again."

Mark 13 [17]"How dreadful it will be in those days for pregnant women and nursing mothers! [18]Pray that this will not take place in winter, [19]because those will be days of distress unequaled from the beginning, when God created the world, until now—and never to be equaled again."

Luke 21 [23]"How dreadful it will be in those days for pregnant women and nursing mothers! There will be great distress in the land and wrath against this people."

14. Wars and Rumors of Wars

Matt 24 [6]"You will hear of wars and rumors of wars, but see to it that you are not alarmed. Such things must happen, but the end is still to come."

Mark 13 [7]"When you hear of wars and rumors of wars, do not be alarmed. Such things must happen, but the end is still to come."

Luke 21 [9]"When you hear of wars and revolutions, do not be frightened. These things must happen first, but the end will not come right away."

15. Worldwide Proclamation of the Gospel

Matt 24 [14]"And this gospel of the kingdom will be preached in the whole world as a testimony to all nations, and then the end will come."

Mark 13 [10]"And the gospel must first be preached to all nations."

Rev 14 [6]Then I saw another angel flying in midair, and he had the eternal gospel to proclaim to those who live on the earth—to every nation, tribe, language and people. [7]He said in a loud voice, "Fear God and give him glory, because the hour of his judgment has come. Worship him who made the heavens, the earth, the sea and the springs of water."

B. Events and Beings That Accompany Jesus' Second Coming

1. Angels

Matt 25 [31]"When the Son of Man comes in his glory, and all the angels with him, he will sit on his throne in heavenly glory."

Mark 8 [38]"If anyone is ashamed of me and my words in this adulterous and sinful generation, the Son of Man will be ashamed of him when he comes in his Father's glory with the holy angels."

2 Thess 1 [7]and give relief to you who are troubled, and to us as well. This will happen when the Lord Jesus is revealed from heaven in blazing fire with his powerful angels.

2. Armies of Heaven

Rev 19 [11]I saw heaven standing open and there before me was a white horse, whose rider is called Faithful and True. With justice he judges and makes war. . . . [14]The armies of heaven were following him, riding on white horses and dressed in fine linen, white and clean.

3. Blazing Fire

2 Thess 1 [7]and give relief to you who are troubled, and to us as well. This will happen when the Lord Jesus is revealed from heaven in blazing fire with his powerful angels.

4. Clouds of Heaven

Dan 7 [13]"In my vision at night I looked, and there before me was one like a son of man, coming with the clouds of heaven. He approached the Ancient of Days and was led into his presence."

Matt 24 [30]"At that time the sign of the Son of Man will appear in the sky, and all the nations of the earth will mourn. They will see the Son of Man coming on the clouds of the sky, with power and great glory."

Matt 26 [64]"Yes, it is as you say," Jesus replied. "But I say to all of you: In the future you will see the Son of Man sitting at the right hand of the Mighty One and coming on the clouds of heaven."

Acts 1 [9]After he said this, he was taken up before their very eyes, and a cloud hid him from their sight.

[10]They were looking intently up into the sky as he was going, when suddenly two men dressed in white stood beside them. [11]"Men of Galilee," they said, "why do you stand here looking into the sky? This same Jesus, who has been taken from you into heaven, will come back in the same way you have seen him go into heaven."

Rev 1 [7]Look, he is coming with the clouds, and every eye will see him, even those who pierced him; and all the peoples of the earth will mourn because of him. So shall it be! Amen.

5. Cosmic Phenomena

Matt 24 [29]"Immediately after the distress of those days 'the sun will be darkened, and the moon will not give its light; the stars will fall from the sky, and the heavenly bodies will be shaken.'"

Mark 13 [24]"But in those days, following that distress, 'the sun will be darkened, and the moon will not give its light; [25]the stars will fall from the sky, and the heavenly bodies will be shaken.'"

Luke 21 [25]"There will be signs in the sun, moon and stars. On the earth, nations will be in anguish and perplexity at the roaring and tossing of the sea. [26]Men will faint from terror, apprehensive of what is coming on the world, for the heavenly bodies will be shaken."

Acts 2 [19]"'I will show wonders in the heaven above and signs on the earth below, blood and fire and billows of smoke. [20]The sun will be turned to darkness and the moon to blood before the coming of the great and glorious day of the Lord.'"

2 Pet 3 [10]But the day of the Lord will come like a thief. The heavens will disappear with a roar; the elements will be destroyed by fire, and the earth and everything in it will be laid bare.

Rev 6 [12]I watched as he opened the sixth seal. There was a great earthquake. The sun turned black like sackcloth made of goat hair, the whole moon turned blood red, [13]and the stars in the sky fell to earth, as late figs drop from a fig tree when shaken by a strong wind. [14]The sky receded like a scroll, rolling up, and every mountain and island was removed from its place.

6. The Gathering of the Saints unto Jesus

Matt 24 [31]"And he will send his angels with a loud trumpet call, and they will gather his elect from the four winds, from one end of the heavens to the other."

Mark 13 [27]"And he will send his angels and gather his elect from the four winds, from the ends of the earth to the ends of the heavens."

1 Cor 15 [50]I declare to you, brothers, that flesh and blood cannot inherit the kingdom of God, nor does the perishable inherit the imperishable. [51]Listen, I tell you a mystery: We will not all sleep, but we will all be changed—[52]in a flash, in the twinkling of an eye, at the last trumpet. For the trumpet will sound, the dead will be raised imperishable, and we will be changed. [53]For the perishable must clothe itself with the imperishable, and the mortal with immortality. [54]When the perishable has been clothed with the imperishable, and the mortal with immortality, then the saying that is written will come true: "Death has been swallowed up in victory." [55]"Where, O death, is your victory? Where, O death, is your sting?" [56]The sting of death is sin, and the power of sin is the law. [57]But thanks be to God! He gives us the victory through our Lord Jesus Christ.

1 Thess 4 [16]For the Lord himself will come down from heaven, with a loud command, with the voice of the archangel and with the trumpet call of God, and the dead in Christ will rise first. [17]After that, we who are still alive and are left will be caught up together with them in the clouds to meet the Lord in the air. And so we will be with the Lord forever.

Rev 19 [6]Then I heard what sounded like a great multitude, like the roar of rushing waters and like loud peals of thunder, shouting: "Hallelujah! For our Lord God Almighty reigns. [7]Let us rejoice and be glad and give him glory! For the wedding of the Lamb has come, and his bride has made herself ready. [8]Fine linen, bright and clean, was given her to wear." (Fine linen stands for the righteous acts of the saints.)

[9]Then the angel said to me, "Write: 'Blessed are those who are invited to the wedding supper of the Lamb!'" And he added, "These are the true words of God."

7. A Loud Command

1 Thess 4 [16]For the Lord himself will come down from heaven, with a loud command, with the voice of the archangel and with the trumpet call of God, and the dead in Christ will rise first.

8. A Multitude of Holy Followers

1 Thess 3 [13]May he strengthen your hearts so that you will be blameless and holy in the presence of our God and Father when our Lord Jesus comes with all his holy ones.

Jude [14]Enoch, the seventh from Adam, prophesied about these men: "See, the Lord is coming with thousands upon thousands of his holy ones. . . ."

9. The Trumpet Call of God

1 Cor 15 [52]in a flash, in the twinkling of an eye, at the last trumpet. For the trumpet will sound, the dead will be raised imperishable, and we will be changed.

1 Thess 4 [16]For the Lord himself will come down from heaven, with a loud command, with the voice of the archangel and with the trumpet call of God, and the dead in Christ will rise first.

10. The Voice of the Archangel

1 Thess 4 [16]For the Lord himself will come down from heaven, with a loud command, with the voice of the archangel and with the trumpet call of God, and the dead in Christ will rise first.

C. Theological Aspects of Jesus' Second Coming

1. It Is Glorious

Matt 16 [27]"For the Son of Man is going to come in his Father's glory with his angels, and then he will reward each person according to what he has done."

Matt 24 [30]"At that time the sign of the Son of Man will appear in the sky, and all the nations of the earth will mourn. They will see the Son of Man coming on the clouds of the sky, with power and great glory."

Titus 2 [13]while we wait for the blessed hope—the glorious appearing of our great God and Savior, Jesus Christ . . .

2. It Is Holy and Just

Rev 19 [11]I saw heaven standing open and there before me was a white horse, whose rider is called Faithful and True. With justice he judges and makes war. [12]His eyes are like blazing fire, and on his head are many crowns. He has a name written on him that no one knows but he himself. [13]He is dressed in a robe dipped in blood, and his name is the Word of God. . . . [15]Out of his mouth comes a sharp sword with which to strike down the nations. "He will rule them with an iron scepter." He treads the winepress of the fury of the wrath of God Almighty. [16]On his robe and on his thigh he has this name written: KING OF KINGS AND LORD OF LORDS.

3. It Is Personal

Mark 8 [38]"If anyone is ashamed of me and my words in this adulterous and sinful generation, the Son of Man will be ashamed of him when he comes in his Father's glory with the holy angels."

John 21 [20]Peter turned and saw that the disciple whom Jesus loved was following them. (This was the one who had leaned back against Jesus at the supper and had said, "Lord, who is going to betray you?") 21When Peter saw him, he asked, "Lord, what about him?"

22Jesus answered, "If I want him to remain alive until I return, what is that to you? You must follow me."

Acts 1 10They were looking intently up into the sky as he was going, when suddenly two men dressed in white stood beside them. 11"Men of Galilee," they said, "why do you stand here looking into the sky? This same Jesus, who has been taken from you into heaven, will come back in the same way you have seen him go into heaven."

1 Cor 4 5Therefore judge nothing before the appointed time; wait till the Lord comes. He will bring to light what is hidden in darkness and will expose the motives of men's hearts. At that time each will receive his praise from God.

1 Thess 2 19For what is our hope, our joy, or the crown in which we will glory in the presence of our Lord Jesus when he comes? Is it not you? 20Indeed, you are our glory and joy.

4. It Is Powerful

Matt 24 30"At that time the sign of the Son of Man will appear in the sky, and all the nations of the earth will mourn. They will see the Son of Man coming on the clouds of the sky, with power and great glory."

2 Pet 3 10But the day of the Lord will come like a thief. The heavens will disappear with a roar; the elements will be destroyed by fire, and the earth and everything in it will be laid bare.

5. It Is Visible

Mark 13 26"At that time men will see the Son of Man coming in clouds with great power and glory."

Acts 1 11"Men of Galilee," they said, "why do you stand here looking into the sky? This same Jesus, who has been taken from you into heaven, will come back in the same way you have seen him go into heaven."

Rev 1 7Look, he is coming with the clouds, and every eye will see him, even those who pierced him; and all the peoples of the earth will mourn because of him. So shall it be! Amen.

D. The Time of Jesus' Second Coming

1. It Is as the Coming of a Bridegroom

Matt 25 1"At that time the kingdom of heaven will be like ten virgins who took their lamps and went out to meet the bridegroom. 2Five of them were foolish and five were wise. 3The foolish ones took their lamps but did not take any oil with them. 4The wise, however, took oil in jars along with their lamps. 5The bridegroom was a long time in coming, and they all became drowsy and fell asleep.

6"At midnight the cry rang out: 'Here's the bridegroom! Come out to meet him!'

7"Then all the virgins woke up and trimmed their lamps. 8The foolish ones said to the wise, 'Give us some of your oil; our lamps are going out.'

9"'No,' they replied, 'there may not be enough for both us and you. Instead, go to those who sell oil and buy some for yourselves.'

10"But while they were on their way to buy the oil, the bridegroom arrived. The virgins who were ready went in with him to the wedding banquet. And the door was shut.

11"Later the others also came. 'Sir! Sir!' they said. 'Open the door for us!'

12"But he replied, 'I tell you the truth, I don't know you.'

13"Therefore keep watch, because you do not know the day or the hour."

2. It Is as the Destruction of Sodom

Luke 17 28"It was the same in the days of Lot. People were eating and drinking, buying and selling, planting and building. 29But the day Lot left Sodom, fire and sulfur rained down from heaven and destroyed them all.

30"It will be just like this on the day the Son of Man is revealed."

3. It Is as Lightning

Matt 24 27"For as lightning that comes from the east is visible even in the west, so will be the coming of the Son of Man."

4. It Is as Noah's Flood

Matt 24 37"As it was in the days of Noah, so it will be at the coming of the Son of Man. 38For in the days before the flood, people were eating and drinking, marrying and giving in marriage, up to the day Noah entered the ark; 39and they knew nothing about what would happen until the flood came and took them all away. That is how it will be at the coming of the Son of Man. 40Two men will be in the field; one will be taken and the other left. 41Two women will be grinding with a hand mill; one will be taken and the other left."

Luke 17 26"Just as it was in the days of Noah, so also will it be in the days of the Son of Man. 27People were eating, drinking, marrying and being given in marriage up to the day Noah entered the ark. Then the flood came and destroyed them all. . . .

30"It will be just like this on the day the Son of Man is revealed."

5. It Is as a Thief in the Night

Matt 24 42"Therefore keep watch, because you do not know on what day your Lord will come. 43But understand this: If the owner of the house had known at what time of night the thief was coming, he would have kept watch and would not have let his house be broken into. 44So you also must be ready, because the Son of Man will come at an hour when you do not expect him."

1 Thess 5 2for you know very well that the day of the Lord will come like a thief in the night. 3While people are saying, "Peace and safety," destruction will come on them suddenly, as labor pains on a pregnant woman, and they will not escape.

2 Pet 3 10But the day of the Lord will come like a thief. The heavens will disappear with a roar; the elements will be destroyed by fire, and the earth and everything in it will be laid bare.

Rev 16 15"Behold, I come like a thief! Blessed is he who stays awake and keeps his clothes with him, so that he may not go naked and be shamefully exposed."

6. It Is at the Final Consummation of History

1 Cor 1 8He will keep you strong to the end, so that you will be blameless on the day of our Lord Jesus Christ.

1 Pet 1 5who through faith are shielded by God's power until the coming of the salvation that is ready to be revealed in the last time.

7. It Is Coming Very Soon

Heb 10 37For in just a very little while, "He who is coming will come and will not delay."

James 5 8You too, be patient and stand firm, because the Lord's coming is near. 9Don't grumble against each other, brothers, or you will be judged. The Judge is standing at the door!

Rev 22 7"Behold, I am coming soon! Blessed is he who keeps the words of the prophecy in this book.". . .

20He who testifies to these things says, "Yes, I am coming soon."

Amen. Come, Lord Jesus.

8. It Is Known Only by God

Matt 24 36"No one knows about that day or hour, not even the angels in heaven, nor the Son, but only the Father. 37As it was in the days of Noah, so it will be at the coming of the Son of Man. 38For in the days before the flood, people were eating and drinking, marrying and giving in marriage, up to the day Noah entered the ark; 39and they knew nothing about what would happen until the flood came and took them all away. That is how it will be at the coming of the Son of Man. 40Two men will be in the field; one will be taken and the other left. [41]Two women will be grinding with a hand mill; one will be taken and the other left."

Acts 1 [6]So when they met together, they asked him, "Lord, are you at this time going to restore the kingdom to Israel?"

[7]He said to them: "It is not for you to know the times or dates the Father has set by his own authority."

1 Tim 6 [14]to keep this command without spot or blame until the appearing of our Lord Jesus Christ, [15]which God will bring about in his own time—God, the blessed and only Ruler, the King of kings and Lord of lords. . . .

9. It Is Sudden

Mark 13 [33]"Be on guard! Be alert! You do not know when that time will come. [34]It's like a man going away: He leaves his house and puts his servants in charge, each with his assigned task, and tells the one at the door to keep watch.

[35]"Therefore keep watch because you do not know when the owner of the house will come back—whether in the evening, or at midnight, or when the rooster crows, or at dawn. [36]If he comes suddenly, do not let him find you sleeping."

1 Thess 5 [2]for you know very well that the day of the Lord will come like a thief in the night. [3]While people are saying, "Peace and safety," destruction will come on them suddenly, as labor pains on a pregnant woman, and they will not escape.

10. It Is Unexpected

Matt 24 [44]"So you also must be ready, because the Son of Man will come at an hour when you do not expect him."

Luke 12 [35]"Be dressed ready for service and keep your lamps burning, [36]like men waiting for their master to return from a wedding banquet, so that when he comes and knocks they can immediately open the door for him. [37]It will be good for those servants whose master finds them watching when he comes. I tell you the truth, he will dress himself to serve, will have them recline at the table and will come and wait on them. [38]It will be good for those servants whose master finds them ready, even if he comes in the second or third watch of the night. [39]But understand this: If the owner of the house had known at what hour the thief was coming, he would not have let his house be broken into. [40]You also must be ready, because the Son of Man will come at an hour when you do not expect him."

11. It Is Unknown to People

Matt 24 [36]"No one knows about that day or hour, not even the angels in heaven, nor the Son, but only the Father. . . .

[42]"Therefore keep watch, because you do not know on what day your Lord will come."

Luke 12 [40]"You also must be ready, because the Son of Man will come at an hour when you do not expect him."

E. The Significance of Jesus' Second Coming

1. Its Significance for the Created Order

Acts 3 [19]"Repent, then, and turn to God, so that your sins may be wiped out, that times of refreshing may come from the Lord, [20]and that he may send the Christ, who has been appointed for you—even Jesus. [21]He must remain in heaven until the time comes for God to restore everything, as he promised long ago through his holy prophets."

Rom 8 [18]I consider that our present sufferings are not worth comparing with the glory that will be revealed in us. [19]The creation waits in eager expectation for the sons of God to be revealed. [20]For the creation was subjected to frustration, not by its own choice, but by the will of the one who subjected it, in hope [21]that the creation itself will be liberated from its bondage to decay and brought into the glorious freedom of the children of God.

[22]We know that the whole creation has been groaning as in the pains of childbirth right up to the present time.

2. Its Significance for Humanity in General

a) Defeat of Evil

Rev 19 [17]And I saw an angel standing in the sun, who cried in a loud voice to all the birds flying in midair, "Come, gather together for the great supper of God, [18]so that you may eat the flesh of kings, generals, and mighty men, of horses and their riders, and the flesh of all people, free and slave, small and great."

[19]Then I saw the beast and the kings of the earth and their armies gathered together to make war against the rider on the horse and his army. [20]But the beast was captured, and with him the false prophet who had performed the miraculous signs on his behalf. With these signs he had deluded those who had received the mark of the beast and worshiped his image. The two of them were thrown alive into the fiery lake of burning sulfur. [21]The rest of them were killed with the sword that came out of the mouth of the rider on the horse, and all the birds gorged themselves on their flesh.

b) Judgment of All People

Matt 16 [27]"For the Son of Man is going to come in his Father's glory with his angels, and then he will reward each person according to what he has done."

Matt 24 [45]"Who then is the faithful and wise servant, whom the master has put in charge of the servants in his household to give them their food at the proper time? [46]It will be good for that servant whose master finds him doing so when he returns. [47]I tell you the truth, he will put him in charge of all his possessions. [48]But suppose that servant is wicked and says to himself, 'My master is staying away a long time,' [49]and he then begins to beat his fellow servants and to eat and drink with drunkards. [50]The master of that servant will come on a day when he does not expect him and at an hour he is not aware of. [51]He will cut him to pieces and assign him a place with the hypocrites, where there will be weeping and gnashing of teeth."

Matt 25 [14]"Again, it will be like a man going on a journey, who called his servants and entrusted his property to them. [15]To one he gave five talents of money, to another two talents, and to another one talent, each according to his ability. Then he went on his journey. [16]The man who had received the five talents went at once and put his money to work and gained five more. [17]So also, the one with the two talents gained two more. [18]But the man who had received the one talent went off, dug a hole in the ground and hid his master's money.

[19]"After a long time the master of those servants returned and settled accounts with them. [20]The man who had received the five talents brought the other five. 'Master,' he said, 'you entrusted me with five talents. See, I have gained five more.'

[21]"His master replied, 'Well done, good and faithful servant! You have been faithful with a few things; I will put you in charge of many things. Come and share your master's happiness!'

[22]"The man with the two talents also came. 'Master,' he said, 'you entrusted me with two talents; see, I have gained two more.'

[23]"His master replied, 'Well done, good and faithful servant! You have been faithful with a few things; I will put you in charge of many things. Come and share your master's happiness!'

[24]"Then the man who had received the one talent came. 'Master,' he said, 'I knew that you are a hard man, harvesting where you have not sown and gathering where you have not scattered seed. [25]So I was afraid and went out and hid your talent in the ground. See, here is what belongs to you.'

[26]"His master replied, 'You wicked, lazy servant! So you knew that I harvest where I have not sown and gather where I have not scattered seed? [27]Well then, you should have put my money on deposit with the bankers, so that when I returned I would have received it back with interest.

[28]"'Take the talent from him and give it to the one who has the ten talents. [29]For everyone who has will be given more, and he will have an abundance. Whoever does not have, even what he has will be taken from him. [30]And throw that worthless ser-

vant outside, into the darkness, where there will be weeping and gnashing of teeth.'"

Matt 25 31"When the Son of Man comes in his glory, and all the angels with him, he will sit on his throne in heavenly glory. 32All the nations will be gathered before him, and he will separate the people one from another as a shepherd separates the sheep from the goats. 33He will put the sheep on his right and the goats on his left.

34"Then the King will say to those on his right, 'Come, you who are blessed by my Father; take your inheritance, the kingdom prepared for you since the creation of the world. 35For I was hungry and you gave me something to eat, I was thirsty and you gave me something to drink, I was a stranger and you invited me in, 36I needed clothes and you clothed me, I was sick and you looked after me, I was in prison and you came to visit me.'

37"Then the righteous will answer him, 'Lord, when did we see you hungry and feed you, or thirsty and give you something to drink? 38When did we see you a stranger and invite you in, or needing clothes and clothe you? 39When did we see you sick or in prison and go to visit you?'

40"The King will reply, 'I tell you the truth, whatever you did for one of the least of these brothers of mine, you did for me.'

41"Then he will say to those on his left, 'Depart from me, you who are cursed, into the eternal fire prepared for the devil and his angels. 42For I was hungry and you gave me nothing to eat, I was thirsty and you gave me nothing to drink, 43I was a stranger and you did not invite me in, I needed clothes and you did not clothe me, I was sick and in prison and you did not look after me.'

44"They also will answer, 'Lord, when did we see you hungry or thirsty or a stranger or needing clothes or sick or in prison, and did not help you?'

45"He will reply, 'I tell you the truth, whatever you did not do for one of the least of these, you did not do for me.'

46"Then they will go away to eternal punishment, but the righteous to eternal life."

1 Cor 4 5Therefore judge nothing before the appointed time; wait till the Lord comes. He will bring to light what is hidden in darkness and will expose the motives of men's hearts. At that time each will receive his praise from God.

2 Thess 1 7and give relief to you who are troubled, and to us as well. This will happen when the Lord Jesus is revealed from heaven in blazing fire with his powerful angels. 8He will punish those who do not know God and do not obey the gospel of our Lord Jesus. 9They will be punished with everlasting destruction and shut out from the presence of the Lord and from the majesty of his power. . . .

2 Tim 4 1In the presence of God and of Christ Jesus, who will judge the living and the dead, and in view of his appearing and his kingdom, I give you this charge. . . .

Jude 14Enoch, the seventh from Adam, prophesied about these men: "See, the Lord is coming with thousands upon thousands of his holy ones 15to judge everyone, and to convict all the ungodly of all the ungodly acts they have done in the ungodly way, and of all the harsh words ungodly sinners have spoken against him."

Rev 11 18"The nations were angry; and your wrath has come. The time has come for judging the dead, and for rewarding your servants the prophets and your saints and those who reverence your name, both small and great—and for destroying those who destroy the earth."

c) Reign of Christ

Job 19 25"I know that my Redeemer lives, and that in the end he will stand upon the earth."

Isa 24 23The moon will be abashed, the sun ashamed; for the LORD Almighty will reign on Mount Zion and in Jerusalem, and before its elders, gloriously.

Dan 7 13"In my vision at night I looked, and there before me was one like a son of man, coming with the clouds of heaven. He approached the Ancient of Days and was led into his presence. 14He was given authority, glory and sovereign power; all peoples, nations and men of every language worshiped him. His dominion is an everlasting dominion that will not pass away, and his kingdom is one that will never be destroyed."

Rev 11 15The seventh angel sounded his trumpet, and there were loud voices in heaven, which said: "The kingdom of the world has become the kingdom of our Lord and of his Christ, and he will reign for ever and ever."

d) Universal Recognition of Christ

Rev 1 7Look, he is coming with the clouds, and every eye will see him, even those who pierced him; and all the peoples of the earth will mourn because of him. So shall it be! Amen.

3. Its Significance for Believers

a) Believers Will Be Awarded Crowns of Glory

2 Tim 4 8Now there is in store for me the crown of righteousness, which the Lord, the righteous Judge, will award to me on that day—and not only to me, but also to all who have longed for his appearing.

1 Pet 5 4And when the Chief Shepherd appears, you will receive the crown of glory that will never fade away.

b) Believers Will Be Found Blameless

1 Cor 1 8He will keep you strong to the end, so that you will be blameless on the day of our Lord Jesus Christ.

1 Thess 3 13May he strengthen your hearts so that you will be blameless and holy in the presence of our God and Father when our Lord Jesus comes with all his holy ones.

1 Thess 5 23May God himself, the God of peace, sanctify you through and through. May your whole spirit, soul and body be kept blameless at the coming of our Lord Jesus Christ.

c) Believers Will Be Praised

1 Pet 1 7 These have come so that your faith—of greater worth than gold, which perishes even though refined by fire—may be proved genuine and may result in praise, glory and honor when Jesus Christ is revealed.

d) Believers Will Be Preserved

Phil 1 6being confident of this, that he who began a good work in you will carry it on to completion until the day of Christ Jesus.

1 Thess 5 23May God himself, the God of peace, sanctify you through and through. May your whole spirit, soul and body be kept blameless at the coming of our Lord Jesus Christ. 24The one who calls you is faithful and he will do it.

1 Pet 1 3Praise be to the God and Father of our Lord Jesus Christ! In his great mercy he has given us new birth into a living hope through the resurrection of Jesus Christ from the dead, 4and into an inheritance that can never perish, spoil or fade—kept in heaven for you, 5who through faith are shielded by God's power until the coming of the salvation that is ready to be revealed in the last time.

Jude 24To him who is able to keep you from falling and to present you before his glorious presence without fault and with great joy . . .

e) Believers Will Be Resurrected Bodily to Redemption

Rom 8 23Not only so, but we ourselves, who have the firstfruits of the Spirit, groan inwardly as we wait eagerly for our adoption as sons, the redemption of our bodies.

Phil 3 20But our citizenship is in heaven. And we eagerly await a Savior from there, the Lord Jesus Christ, 21who, by the power that enables him to bring everything under his control, will transform our lowly bodies so that they will be like his glorious body.

f) Believers Will Be Transformed to the Likeness of Christ

1 John 3 2Dear friends, now we are children of God, and what we will be has not yet been made known. But we know that when he appears, we shall be like him, for we shall see him as he is.

g) Believers Will Have Confidence

1 John 4 17In this way, love is made complete among us so that we will have confidence on the day of judgment, because in this world we are like him.

h) Believers Will Have Fellowship with Christ

John 14 2"In my Father's house are many rooms; if it were not so, I would have told you. I am going there to prepare a place for you. 3And if I go and prepare a place for you, I will come back and take you to be with me that you also may be where I am."

i) Believers Will Not Be Ashamed

1 John 2 28And now, dear children, continue in him, so that when he appears we may be confident and unashamed before him at his coming.

j) Believers Will Reign with Christ

Dan 7 27"'Then the sovereignty, power and greatness of the kingdoms under the whole heaven will be handed over to the saints, the people of the Most High. His kingdom will be an everlasting kingdom, and all rulers will worship and obey him.'"

2 Tim 2 12if we endure, we will also reign with him. If we disown him, he will also disown us. . . .

Rev 5 9And they sang a new song: "You are worthy to take the scroll and to open its seals, because you were slain, and with your blood you purchased men for God from every tribe and language and people and nation. 10You have made them to be a kingdom and priests to serve our God, and they will reign on the earth."

k) Believers Will Share in Christ's Glory

Col 3 4When Christ, who is your life, appears, then you also will appear with him in glory.

l) Christ Will Be Glorified in His People

2 Thess 1 9They will be punished with everlasting destruction and shut out from the presence of the Lord and from the majesty of his power 10on the day he comes to be glorified in his holy people and to be marveled at among all those who have believed. This includes you, because you believed our testimony to you.

m) Death Will Be Defeated

1 Cor 15 51Listen, I tell you a mystery: We will not all sleep, but we will all be changed—52in a flash, in the twinkling of an eye, at the last trumpet. For the trumpet will sound, the dead will be raised imperishable, and we will be changed. 53For the perishable must clothe itself with the imperishable, and the mortal with immortality. 54When the perishable has been clothed with the imperishable, and the mortal with immortality, then the saying that is written will come true: "Death has been swallowed up in victory." 55"Where, O death, is your victory? Where, O death, is your sting?" 56The sting of death is sin, and the power of sin is the law. 57But thanks be to God! He gives us the victory through our Lord Jesus Christ.

1 Thess 4 15According to the Lord's own word, we tell you that we who are still alive, who are left till the coming of the Lord, will certainly not precede those who have fallen asleep. 16For the Lord himself will come down from heaven, with a loud command, with the voice of the archangel and with the trumpet call of God, and the dead in Christ will rise first. 17After that, we who are still alive and are left will be caught up together with them in the clouds to meet the Lord in the air. And so we will be with the Lord forever.

n) Salvation Will Be Completed

Heb 9 27Just as man is destined to die once, and after that to face judgment, 28so Christ was sacrificed once to take away the sins of many people; and he will appear a second time, not to bear sin, but to bring salvation to those who are waiting for him.

1 Pet 1 3Praise be to the God and Father of our Lord Jesus Christ! In his great mercy he has given us new birth into a living hope through the resurrection of Jesus Christ from the dead, 4and into an inheritance that can never perish, spoil or fade—kept in heaven for you, 5who through faith are shielded by God's power until the coming of the salvation that is ready to be revealed in the last time.

4. The Binding of Satan

See p. 769a, The Binding of Satan

5. The Destruction of Antichrist

Rev 19 20But the beast was captured, and with him the false prophet who had performed the miraculous signs on his behalf. With these signs he had deluded those who had received the mark of the beast and worshiped his image. The two of them were thrown alive into the fiery lake of burning sulfur.

F. The Attitude of Believers toward Jesus' Second Coming

1. Believers Should Be Alert and Watchful

Matt 24 42"Therefore keep watch, because you do not know on what day your Lord will come. 43But understand this: If the owner of the house had known at what time of night the thief was coming, he would have kept watch and would not have let his house be broken into. 44So you also must be ready, because the Son of Man will come at an hour when you do not expect him."

Mark 13 33"Be on guard! Be alert! You do not know when that time will come. 34It's like a man going away: He leaves his house and puts his servants in charge, each with his assigned task, and tells the one at the door to keep watch.

35"Therefore keep watch because you do not know when the owner of the house will come back—whether in the evening, or at midnight, or when the rooster crows, or at dawn. 36If he comes suddenly, do not let him find you sleeping. 37What I say to you, I say to everyone: 'Watch!'"

Luke 12 35"Be dressed ready for service and keep your lamps burning, 36like men waiting for their master to return from a wedding banquet, so that when he comes and knocks they can immediately open the door for him. 37It will be good for those servants whose master finds them watching when he comes. I tell you the truth, he will dress himself to serve, will have them recline at the table and will come and wait on them. 38It will be good for those servants whose master finds them ready, even if he comes in the second or third watch of the night. 39But understand this: If the owner of the house had known at what hour the thief was coming, he would not have let his house be broken into. 40You also must be ready, because the Son of Man will come at an hour when you do not expect him."

1 Thess 5 4But you, brothers, are not in darkness so that this day should surprise you like a thief. 5You are all sons of the light and sons of the day. We do not belong to the night or to the darkness. 6So then, let us not be like others, who are asleep, but let us be alert and self-controlled.

Rev 16 15"Behold, I come like a thief! Blessed is he who stays awake and keeps his clothes with him, so that he may not go naked and be shamefully exposed."

2. Believers Should Be Motivated to Godly Living

Matt 24 45"Who then is the faithful and wise servant, whom the master has put in charge of the servants in his household to give them their food at the proper time? 46It will be good for that servant whose master finds him doing so when he returns. 47I tell you the truth, he will put him in charge of all his possessions. 48But suppose that servant is wicked and says to himself, 'My master is staying away a long time,' 49and he then begins to beat his fellow servants and to eat and drink with drunkards. 50The master of that servant will come on a day when he does not expect him and at an hour he is not aware of. 51He will cut him to pieces and assign him a place with the hypocrites, where there will be weeping and gnashing of teeth."

1 Pet 1 13Therefore, prepare your minds for action; be self-controlled; set your hope fully on the grace to be given you when Jesus Christ is revealed. 14As obedient children, do not conform to the evil desires you had when you lived in ignorance. 15But just as he who called you is holy, so be holy in all you do. . . .

2 Pet 3 11Since everything will be destroyed in this way, what kind of people ought you to be? You ought to live holy and godly lives 12as you look forward to the day of God and speed its coming. That day will bring about the destruction of the heavens by fire, and the elements will melt in the heat. . . .

14So then, dear friends, since you are looking forward to this, make every effort to be found spotless, blameless and at peace with him.

1 John 2 28And now, dear children, continue in him, so that when he appears we may be confident and unashamed before him at his coming.

3. Believers Should Consider It Is Coming Very Soon

Rom 13 11And do this, understanding the present time. The hour has come for you to wake up from your slumber, because our salvation is nearer now than when we first believed. 12The night is nearly over; the day is almost here. So let us put aside the deeds of darkness and put on the armor of light.

Phil 4 5Let your gentleness be evident to all. The Lord is near.

James 5 8You too, be patient and stand firm, because the Lord's coming is near. 9Don't grumble against each other, brothers, or you will be judged. The Judge is standing at the door!

1 Pet 4 7The end of all things is near. Therefore be clear minded and self-controlled so that you can pray.

4. Believers Should Eagerly Await It

1 Cor 1 7Therefore you do not lack any spiritual gift as you eagerly wait for our Lord Jesus Christ to be revealed.

Phil 3 20But our citizenship is in heaven. And we eagerly await a Savior from there, the Lord Jesus Christ. . . .

Titus 2 11For the grace of God that brings salvation has appeared to all men. 12It teaches us to say "No" to ungodliness and worldly passions, and to live self-controlled, upright and godly lives in this present age, 13while we wait for the blessed hope—the glorious appearing of our great God and Savior, Jesus Christ. . . .

5. Believers Should Hope and Should Encourage One Another

Rom 8 23Not only so, but we ourselves, who have the firstfruits of the Spirit, groan inwardly as we wait eagerly for our adoption as sons, the redemption of our bodies. 24For in this hope we were saved. But hope that is seen is no hope at all. Who hopes for what he already has? 25But if we hope for what we do not yet have, we wait for it patiently.

1 Thess 4 13Brothers, we do not want you to be ignorant about those who fall asleep, or to grieve like the rest of men, who have no hope. 14We believe that Jesus died and rose again and so we believe that God will bring with Jesus those who have fallen asleep in him. 15According to the Lord's own word, we tell you that we who are still alive, who are left till the coming of the Lord, will certainly not precede those who have fallen asleep. . . . 17After that, we who are still alive and are left will be caught up together with them in the clouds to meet the Lord in the air. And so we will be with the Lord forever. 18Therefore encourage each other with these words.

6. Believers Should Long for It

2 Tim 4 8Now there is in store for me the crown of righteousness, which the Lord, the righteous Judge, will award to me on that day—and not only to me, but also to all who have longed for his appearing.

2 Pet 3 12as you look forward to the day of God and speed its coming. That day will bring about the destruction of the heavens by fire, and the elements will melt in the heat.

Rev 22 20He who testifies to these things says, "Yes, I am coming soon."

Amen. Come, Lord Jesus.

7. Believers Should Persevere

Matt 24 12"Because of the increase of wickedness, the love of most will grow cold, 13but he who stands firm to the end will be saved."

1 Cor 1 7Therefore you do not lack any spiritual gift as you eagerly wait for our Lord Jesus Christ to be revealed. 8He will keep you strong to the end, so that you will be blameless on the day of our Lord Jesus Christ. 9God, who has called you into fellowship with his Son Jesus Christ our Lord, is faithful.

2 Thess 3 5May the Lord direct your hearts into God's love and Christ's perseverance.

1 Tim 6 12Fight the good fight of the faith. Take hold of the eternal life to which you were called when you made your good confession in the presence of many witnesses. 13In the sight of God, who gives life to everything, and of Christ Jesus, who while testifying before Pontius Pilate made the good confession, I charge you 14to keep this command without spot or blame until the appearing of our Lord Jesus Christ. . . .

James 5 7Be patient, then, brothers, until the Lord's coming. See how the farmer waits for the land to yield its valuable crop and how patient he is for the autumn and spring rains. 8You too, be patient and stand firm, because the Lord's coming is near.

IV
The Resurrection of the Dead

A. General Statements about the Resurrection

Job 19 25"I know that my Redeemer lives, and that in the end he will stand upon the earth. 26And after my skin has been destroyed, yet in my flesh I will see God; 27I myself will see him with my own eyes—I, and not another. How my heart yearns within me!"

Ps 17 15And I—in righteousness I will see your face; when I awake, I will be satisfied with seeing your likeness.

Ps 49 15But God will redeem my life from the grave; he will surely take me to himself.

Ps 71 20Though you have made me see troubles, many and bitter, you will restore my life again; from the depths of the earth you will again bring me up.

Luke 20 37"But in the account of the bush, even Moses showed that the dead rise, for he calls the Lord 'the God of Abraham, and the God of Isaac, and the God of Jacob.' 38He is not the God of the dead, but of the living, for to him all are alive."

John 11 21"Lord," Martha said to Jesus, "if you had been here, my brother would not have died. 22But I know that even now God will give you whatever you ask."

23Jesus said to her, "Your brother will rise again."

24Martha answered, "I know he will rise again in the resurrection at the last day."

Acts 23 6Then Paul, knowing that some of them were Sadducees and the others Pharisees, called out in the Sanhedrin, "My brothers, I am a Pharisee, the son of a Pharisee. I stand on trial because of my hope in the resurrection of the dead."

Acts 24 15". . . and I have the same hope in God as these men, that there will be a resurrection of both the righteous and the wicked."

Acts 24 21". . . unless it was this one thing I shouted as I stood in their presence: 'It is concerning the resurrection of the dead that I am on trial before you today.'"

Heb 11 19Abraham reasoned that God could raise the dead, and figuratively speaking, he did receive Isaac back from death.

B. The Resurrection of Jesus as Exemplar

See p. 466b, The Fact of the Resurrection of Christ

C. *The Resurrection of the Righteous*

1. Description of the Resurrection of the Righteous

a) *The Resurrection Forms Part of the Gospel Message*

John 11 [25]Jesus said to her, "I am the resurrection and the life. He who believes in me will live, even though he dies; [26]and whoever lives and believes in me will never die. Do you believe this?"

Acts 4 [2]They were greatly disturbed because the apostles were teaching the people and proclaiming in Jesus the resurrection of the dead.

Acts 17 [18]A group of Epicurean and Stoic philosophers began to dispute with him. Some of them asked, "What is this babbler trying to say?" Others remarked, "He seems to be advocating foreign gods." They said this because Paul was preaching the good news about Jesus and the resurrection.

1 Cor 15 [12]But if it is preached that Christ has been raised from the dead, how can some of you say that there is no resurrection of the dead? [13]If there is no resurrection of the dead, then not even Christ has been raised. [14]And if Christ has not been raised, our preaching is useless and so is your faith. [15]More than that, we are then found to be false witnesses about God, for we have testified about God that he raised Christ from the dead. But he did not raise him if in fact the dead are not raised. [16]For if the dead are not raised, then Christ has not been raised either. [17]And if Christ has not been raised, your faith is futile; you are still in your sins. [18]Then those also who have fallen asleep in Christ are lost. [19]If only for this life we have hope in Christ, we are to be pitied more than all men.

[20]But Christ has indeed been raised from the dead, the firstfruits of those who have fallen asleep. [21]For since death came through a man, the resurrection of the dead comes also through a man. [22]For as in Adam all die, so in Christ all will be made alive. [23]But each in his own turn: Christ, the firstfruits; then, when he comes, those who belong to him.

1 Thess 4 [14]We believe that Jesus died and rose again and so we believe that God will bring with Jesus those who have fallen asleep in him. [15]According to the Lord's own word, we tell you that we who are still alive, who are left till the coming of the Lord, will certainly not precede those who have fallen asleep. [16]For the Lord himself will come down from heaven, with a loud command, with the voice of the archangel and with the trumpet call of God, and the dead in Christ will rise first. [17]After that, we who are still alive and are left will be caught up together with them in the clouds to meet the Lord in the air. And so we will be with the Lord forever.

2 Tim 1 [8]So do not be ashamed to testify about our Lord, or ashamed of me his prisoner. But join with me in suffering for the gospel, by the power of God, [9]who has saved us and called us to a holy life—not because of anything we have done but because of his own purpose and grace. This grace was given us in Christ Jesus before the beginning of time, [10]but it has now been revealed through the appearing of our Savior, Christ Jesus, who has destroyed death and has brought life and immortality to light through the gospel.

Heb 11 [35]Women received back their dead, raised to life again. Others were tortured and refused to be released, so that they might gain a better resurrection. [36]Some faced jeers and flogging, while still others were chained and put in prison. [37]They were stoned; they were sawed in two; they were put to death by the sword. They went about in sheepskins and goatskins, destitute, persecuted and mistreated—[38]the world was not worthy of them. They wandered in deserts and mountains, and in caves and holes in the ground.

[39]These were all commended for their faith, yet none of them received what had been promised. [40]God had planned something better for us so that only together with us would they be made perfect.

b) *Resurrection Is Accomplished by God, Christ, and the Holy Spirit*

Ps 49 [15]But God will redeem my life from the grave; he will surely take me to himself.

Mark 12 [26]"Now about the dead rising—have you not read in the book of Moses, in the account of the bush, how God said to him, 'I am the God of Abraham, the God of Isaac, and the God of Jacob'? [27]He is not the God of the dead, but of the living. You are badly mistaken!"

John 2 [19]Jesus answered them, "Destroy this temple, and I will raise it again in three days."

[20]The Jews replied, "It has taken forty-six years to build this temple, and you are going to raise it in three days?" [21]But the temple he had spoken of was his body. [22]After he was raised from the dead, his disciples recalled what he had said. Then they believed the Scripture and the words that Jesus had spoken.

John 5 [19]Jesus gave them this answer: "I tell you the truth, the Son can do nothing by himself; he can do only what he sees his Father doing, because whatever the Father does the Son also does. [20]For the Father loves the Son and shows him all he does. Yes, to your amazement he will show him even greater things than these. [21]For just as the Father raises the dead and gives them life, even so the Son gives life to whom he is pleased to give it. . . . [25]I tell you the truth, a time is coming and has now come when the dead will hear the voice of the Son of God and those who hear will live. [26]For as the Father has life in himself, so he has granted the Son to have life in himself. [27]And he has given him authority to judge because he is the Son of Man."

John 6 [39]"And this is the will of him who sent me, that I shall lose none of all that he has given me, but raise them up at the last day. [40]For my Father's will is that everyone who looks to the Son and believes in him shall have eternal life, and I will raise him up at the last day."

Rom 4 [17]As it is written: "I have made you a father of many nations." He is our father in the sight of God, in whom he believed—the God who gives life to the dead and calls things that are not as though they were.

Rom 8 [11]And if the Spirit of him who raised Jesus from the dead is living in you, he who raised Christ from the dead will also give life to your mortal bodies through his Spirit, who lives in you.

1 Cor 6 [14]By his power God raised the Lord from the dead, and he will raise us also.

2 Cor 1 [9]Indeed, in our hearts we felt the sentence of death. But this happened that we might not rely on ourselves but on God, who raises the dead.

2 Cor 4 [14]because we know that the one who raised the Lord Jesus from the dead will also raise us with Jesus and present us with you in his presence.

c) *The Resurrection Is Included in Christian Teaching*

2 Tim 2 [15]Do your best to present yourself to God as one approved, a workman who does not need to be ashamed and who correctly handles the word of truth. [16]Avoid godless chatter, because those who indulge in it will become more and more ungodly. [17]Their teaching will spread like gangrene. Among them are Hymenaeus and Philetus, [18]who have wandered away from the truth. They say that the resurrection has already taken place, and they destroy the faith of some.

Heb 6 [1]Therefore let us leave the elementary teachings about Christ and go on to maturity, not laying again the foundation of repentance from acts that lead to death, and of faith in God, [2]instruction about baptisms, the laying on of hands, the resurrection of the dead, and eternal judgment. [3]And God permitting, we will do so.

d) *Resurrection Will Be Bodily, Yet Spiritual*

Luke 24 [39]"Look at my hands and my feet. It is I myself! Touch me and see; a ghost does not have flesh and bones, as you see I have."

John 20 [19]On the evening of that first day of the week, when the disciples were together, with the doors locked for fear of the Jews, Jesus came and stood among them and said, "Peace be with you!" [20]After he said this, he showed them his hands and side. The disciples were overjoyed when they saw the Lord.

John 20 [26]A week later his disciples were in the house again, and Thomas was with them. Though the doors were locked,

Jesus came and stood among them and said, "Peace be with you!" [27]Then he said to Thomas, "Put your finger here; see my hands. Reach out your hand and put it into my side. Stop doubting and believe."

[28]Thomas said to him, "My Lord and my God!"

1 Cor 15 [35]But someone may ask, "How are the dead raised? With what kind of body will they come?" [36]How foolish! What you sow does not come to life unless it dies. [37]When you sow, you do not plant the body that will be, but just a seed, perhaps of wheat or of something else. [38]But God gives it a body as he has determined, and to each kind of seed he gives its own body. [39]All flesh is not the same: Men have one kind of flesh, animals have another, birds another and fish another. [40]There are also heavenly bodies and there are earthly bodies; but the splendor of the heavenly bodies is one kind, and the splendor of the earthly bodies is another. [41]The sun has one kind of splendor, the moon another and the stars another; and star differs from star in splendor.

[42]So will it be with the resurrection of the dead. The body that is sown is perishable, it is raised imperishable; [43]it is sown in dishonor, it is raised in glory; it is sown in weakness, it is raised in power; [44]it is sown a natural body, it is raised a spiritual body.

If there is a natural body, there is also a spiritual body. [45]So it is written: "The first man Adam became a living being"; the last Adam, a life-giving spirit. [46]The spiritual did not come first, but the natural, and after that the spiritual. [47]The first man was of the dust of the earth, the second man from heaven. [48]As was the earthly man, so are those who are of the earth; and as is the man from heaven, so also are those who are of heaven. [49]And just as we have borne the likeness of the earthly man, so shall we bear the likeness of the man from heaven.

e) Resurrection Will Be Universal

Dan 12 [2]"Multitudes who sleep in the dust of the earth will awake: some to everlasting life, others to shame and everlasting contempt."

John 5 [28]"Do not be amazed at this, for a time is coming when all who are in their graves will hear his voice [29]and come out—those who have done good will rise to live, and those who have done evil will rise to be condemned."

Acts 24 [14]"However, I admit that I worship the God of our fathers as a follower of the Way, which they call a sect. I believe everything that agrees with the Law and that is written in the Prophets, [15]and I have the same hope in God as these men, that there will be a resurrection of both the righteous and the wicked."

Rev 20 [4]I saw thrones on which were seated those who had been given authority to judge. And I saw the souls of those who had been beheaded because of their testimony for Jesus and because of the word of God. They had not worshiped the beast or his image and had not received his mark on their foreheads or their hands. They came to life and reigned with Christ a thousand years. [5](The rest of the dead did not come to life until the thousand years were ended.) This is the first resurrection.

f) Resurrection Will Defeat Death

Isa 25 [7]On this mountain he will destroy the shroud that enfolds all peoples, the sheet that covers all nations; [8]he will swallow up death forever. The Sovereign LORD will wipe away the tears from all faces; he will remove the disgrace of his people from all the earth. The LORD has spoken.

Hos 13 [14]"I will ransom them from the power of the grave; I will redeem them from death. Where, O death, are your plagues? Where, O grave, is your destruction?"

1 Cor 15 [26]The last enemy to be destroyed is death.

1 Cor 15 [54]When the perishable has been clothed with the imperishable, and the mortal with immortality, then the saying that is written will come true: "Death has been swallowed up in victory." [55]"Where, O death, is your victory? Where, O death, is your sting?" [56]The sting of death is sin, and the power of sin is the law. [57]But thanks be to God! He gives us the victory through our Lord Jesus Christ.

1 Thess 4 [15]According to the Lord's own word, we tell you that we who are still alive, who are left till the coming of the Lord, will certainly not precede those who have fallen asleep. [16]For the Lord himself will come down from heaven, with a loud command, with the voice of the archangel and with the trumpet call of God, and the dead in Christ will rise first.

g) Resurrection Will Exclude Marriage Bonds

Matt 22 [23]That same day the Sadducees, who say there is no resurrection, came to him with a question. [24]"Teacher," they said, "Moses told us that if a man dies without having children, his brother must marry the widow and have children for him. [25]Now there were seven brothers among us. The first one married and died, and since he had no children, he left his wife to his brother. [26]The same thing happened to the second and third brother, right on down to the seventh. [27]Finally, the woman died. [28]Now then, at the resurrection, whose wife will she be of the seven, since all of them were married to her?"

[29]Jesus replied, "You are in error because you do not know the Scriptures or the power of God. [30]At the resurrection people will neither marry nor be given in marriage; they will be like the angels in heaven. [31]But about the resurrection of the dead—have you not read what God said to you, [32]'I am the God of Abraham, the God of Isaac, and the God of Jacob'? He is not the God of the dead but of the living."

2. The Righteous Are Resurrected at Christ's Coming

a) They Are Resurrected to Blessing

Dan 12 [13]"As for you, go your way till the end. You will rest, and then at the end of the days you will rise to receive your allotted inheritance."

Luke 14 [12]Then Jesus said to his host, "When you give a luncheon or dinner, do not invite your friends, your brothers or relatives, or your rich neighbors; if you do, they may invite you back and so you will be repaid. [13]But when you give a banquet, invite the poor, the crippled, the lame, the blind, [14]and you will be blessed. Although they cannot repay you, you will be repaid at the resurrection of the righteous."

b) They Are Resurrected to Christ-likeness

1 John 3 [2]Dear friends, now we are children of God, and what we will be has not yet been made known. But we know that when he appears, we shall be like him, for we shall see him as he is.

c) They Are Resurrected to Eternal Life

Dan 12 [1]"At that time Michael, the great prince who protects your people, will arise. There will be a time of distress such as has not happened from the beginning of nations until then. But at that time your people—everyone whose name is found written in the book—will be delivered. [2]Multitudes who sleep in the dust of the earth will awake: some to everlasting life, others to shame and everlasting contempt. [3]Those who are wise will shine like the brightness of the heavens, and those who lead many to righteousness, like the stars for ever and ever."

John 11 [25]Jesus said to her, "I am the resurrection and the life. He who believes in me will live, even though he dies; [26]and whoever lives and believes in me will never die. Do you believe this?"

1 Thess 4 [17]After that, we who are still alive and are left will be caught up together with them in the clouds to meet the Lord in the air. And so we will be with the Lord forever.

d) They Are Resurrected to Redemption of the Body

Isa 26 [19]But your dead will live; their bodies will rise. You who dwell in the dust, wake up and shout for joy. Your dew is like the dew of the morning; the earth will give birth to her dead.

Rom 8 [19]The creation waits in eager expectation for the sons of God to be revealed. [21]. . . that the creation itself will be liberated from its bondage to decay and brought into the glorious freedom of the children of God.

[22]We know that the whole creation has been groaning as in the pains of childbirth right up to the present time. [23]Not only so, but we ourselves, who have the firstfruits of the Spirit, groan inwardly as we wait eagerly for our adoption as sons, the redemption of our bodies.

1 Cor 15 [35]But someone may ask, "How are the dead raised?

With what kind of body will they come?" 36How foolish! What you sow does not come to life unless it dies. 37When you sow, you do not plant the body that will be, but just a seed, perhaps of wheat or of something else. 38But God gives it a body as he has determined, and to each kind of seed he gives its own body. 39All flesh is not the same: Men have one kind of flesh, animals have another, birds another and fish another. 40There are also heavenly bodies and there are earthly bodies; but the splendor of the heavenly bodies is one kind, and the splendor of the earthly bodies is another. 41The sun has one kind of splendor, the moon another and the stars another; and star differs from star in splendor.

42So will it be with the resurrection of the dead. The body that is sown is perishable, it is raised imperishable; 43it is sown in dishonor, it is raised in glory; it is sown in weakness, it is raised in power; 44it is sown a natural body, it is raised a spiritual body.

If there is a natural body, there is also a spiritual body. 45So it is written: "The first man Adam became a living being"; the last Adam, a life-giving spirit. 46The spiritual did not come first, but the natural, and after that the spiritual. 47The first man was of the dust of the earth, the second man from heaven. 48As was the earthly man, so are those who are of the earth; and as is the man from heaven, so also are those who are of heaven. 49And just as we have borne the likeness of the earthly man, so shall we bear the likeness of the man from heaven.

50I declare to you, brothers, that flesh and blood cannot inherit the kingdom of God, nor does the perishable inherit the imperishable. 51Listen, I tell you a mystery: We will not all sleep, but we will all be changed—52in a flash, in the twinkling of an eye, at the last trumpet. For the trumpet will sound, the dead will be raised imperishable, and we will be changed. 53For the perishable must clothe itself with the imperishable, and the mortal with immortality.

2 Cor 5 1Now we know that if the earthly tent we live in is destroyed, we have a building from God, an eternal house in heaven, not built by human hands. 2Meanwhile we groan, longing to be clothed with our heavenly dwelling, 3because when we are clothed, we will not be found naked. 4For while we are in this tent, we groan and are burdened, because we do not wish to be unclothed but to be clothed with our heavenly dwelling, so that what is mortal may be swallowed up by life. 5Now it is God who has made us for this very purpose and has given us the Spirit as a deposit, guaranteeing what is to come.

Eph 4 30And do not grieve the Holy Spirit of God, with whom you were sealed for the day of redemption.

Phil 3 20But our citizenship is in heaven. And we eagerly await a Savior from there, the Lord Jesus Christ, 21who, by the power that enables him to bring everything under his control, will transform our lowly bodies so that they will be like his glorious body.

e) They Are Resurrected to Rule and Reign with Christ

Rev 20 6Blessed and holy are those who have part in the first resurrection. The second death has no power over them, but they will be priests of God and of Christ and will reign with him for a thousand years.

3. The Value of the Resurrection

a) It Gives Hope to Believers

Acts 26 6"And now it is because of my hope in what God has promised our fathers that I am on trial today. 7This is the promise our twelve tribes are hoping to see fulfilled as they earnestly serve God day and night. O king, it is because of this hope that the Jews are accusing me. 8Why should any of you consider it incredible that God raises the dead?"

b) It Motivates Believers to Godly Living

Rom 6 1What shall we say, then? Shall we go on sinning so that grace may increase? 2By no means! We died to sin; how can we live in it any longer? 3Or don't you know that all of us who were baptized into Christ Jesus were baptized into his death? 4We were therefore buried with him through baptism into death in order that, just as Christ was raised from the dead through the glory of the Father, we too may live a new life.

5If we have been united with him like this in his death, we will certainly also be united with him in his resurrection. 6For we know that our old self was crucified with him so that the body of sin might be done away with, that we should no longer be slaves to sin—7because anyone who has died has been freed from sin.

8Now if we died with Christ, we believe that we will also live with him. 9For we know that since Christ was raised from the dead, he cannot die again; death no longer has mastery over him. 10The death he died, he died to sin once for all; but the life he lives, he lives to God.

1 Cor 15 29Now if there is no resurrection, what will those do who are baptized for the dead? If the dead are not raised at all, why are people baptized for them? 30And as for us, why do we endanger ourselves every hour? 31I die every day—I mean that, brothers—just as surely as I glory over you in Christ Jesus our Lord. 32If I fought wild beasts in Ephesus for merely human reasons, what have I gained? If the dead are not raised, "Let us eat and drink, for tomorrow we die." 33Do not be misled: "Bad company corrupts good character." 34Come back to your senses as you ought, and stop sinning; for there are some who are ignorant of God—I say this to your shame.

c) It Produces Eager Anticipation

Rom 8 23Not only so, but we ourselves, who have the firstfruits of the Spirit, groan inwardly as we wait eagerly for our adoption as sons, the redemption of our bodies.

Phil 3 10I want to know Christ and the power of his resurrection and the fellowship of sharing in his sufferings, becoming like him in his death, 11and so, somehow, to attain to the resurrection from the dead.

D. The Resurrection of the Unrighteous

Dan 12 2"Multitudes who sleep in the dust of the earth will awake: some to everlasting life, others to shame and everlasting contempt."

John 5 28"Do not be amazed at this, for a time is coming when all who are in their graves will hear his voice 29and come out—those who have done good will rise to live, and those who have done evil will rise to be condemned."

Acts 24 14"However, I admit that I worship the God of our fathers as a follower of the Way, which they call a sect. I believe everything that agrees with the Law and that is written in the Prophets, 15and I have the same hope in God as these men, that there will be a resurrection of both the righteous and the wicked."

Rev 20 11Then I saw a great white throne and him who was seated on it. Earth and sky fled from his presence, and there was no place for them. 12And I saw the dead, great and small, standing before the throne, and books were opened. Another book was opened, which is the book of life. The dead were judged according to what they had done as recorded in the books. 13The sea gave up the dead that were in it, and death and Hades gave up the dead that were in them, and each person was judged according to what he had done. 14Then death and Hades were thrown into the lake of fire. The lake of fire is the second death. 15If anyone's name was not found written in the book of life, he was thrown into the lake of fire.

V
The Last Judgment

A. General Descriptions of the Last Judgment

1. The Fact of the Last Judgment

Ps 9 7The LORD reigns forever; he has established his throne for judgment. 8He will judge the world in righteousness; he will govern the peoples with justice.

Ps 96 10Say among the nations, "The LORD reigns." The world is firmly established, it cannot be moved; he will judge the peoples with equity. 11Let the heavens rejoice, let the earth be glad;

let the sea resound, and all that is in it; [12]let the fields be jubilant, and everything in them. Then all the trees of the forest will sing for joy; [13]they will sing before the LORD, for he comes, he comes to judge the earth. He will judge the world in righteousness and the peoples in his truth.
Eccles 3 [17]I thought in my heart, "God will bring to judgment both the righteous and the wicked, for there will be a time for every activity, a time for every deed."
Eccles 11 [9]Be happy, young man, while you are young, and let your heart give you joy in the days of your youth. Follow the ways of your heart and whatever your eyes see, but know that for all these things God will bring you to judgment.
Eccles 12 [14]For God will bring every deed into judgment, including every hidden thing, whether it is good or evil.
Heb 9 [27]Just as man is destined to die once, and after that to face judgment . . .
Heb 10 [26]If we deliberately keep on sinning after we have received the knowledge of the truth, no sacrifice for sins is left, [27]but only a fearful expectation of judgment and of raging fire that will consume the enemies of God.

2. Features of the Last Judgment

a) Believers Participate in It

1 Cor 6 [2]Do you not know that the saints will judge the world? And if you are to judge the world, are you not competent to judge trivial cases? [3]Do you not know that we will judge angels? How much more the things of this life!

b) It Is According to the Light Given

Matt 11 [20]Then Jesus began to denounce the cities in which most of his miracles had been performed, because they did not repent. [21]"Woe to you, Korazin! Woe to you, Bethsaida! If the miracles that were performed in you had been performed in Tyre and Sidon, they would have repented long ago in sackcloth and ashes. [22]But I tell you, it will be more bearable for Tyre and Sidon on the day of judgment than for you. [23]And you, Capernaum, will you be lifted up to the skies? No, you will go down to the depths. If the miracles that were performed in you had been performed in Sodom, it would have remained to this day. [24]But I tell you that it will be more bearable for Sodom on the day of judgment than for you."
Luke 12 [48]"But the one who does not know and does things deserving punishment will be beaten with few blows. From everyone who has been given much, much will be demanded; and from the one who has been entrusted with much, much more will be asked."
John 9 [41]Jesus said, "If you were blind, you would not be guilty of sin; but now that you claim you can see, your guilt remains."
John 15 [22]"If I had not come and spoken to them, they would not be guilty of sin. Now, however, they have no excuse for their sin."

c) It Is an Aspect of Christian Doctrine

Acts 24 [24]Several days later Felix came with his wife Drusilla, who was a Jewess. He sent for Paul and listened to him as he spoke about faith in Christ Jesus. [25]As Paul discoursed on righteousness, self-control and the judgment to come, Felix was afraid and said, "That's enough for now! You may leave. When I find it convenient, I will send for you."
Heb 6 [1]Therefore let us leave the elementary teachings about Christ and go on to maturity, not laying again the foundation of repentance from acts that lead to death, and of faith in God, [2]instruction about baptisms, the laying on of hands, the resurrection of the dead, and eternal judgment. [3]And God permitting, we will do so.

d) It Is Based on Truth

Ps 96 [13]they will sing before the LORD, for he comes, he comes to judge the earth. He will judge the world in righteousness and the peoples in his truth.
Rom 2 [1]You, therefore, have no excuse, you who pass judgment on someone else, for at whatever point you judge the other, you are condemning yourself, because you who pass judgment do the same things. [2]Now we know that God's judgment against those who do such things is based on truth.

e) It Is Carried Out by God's Spoken Word

2 Pet 3 [3]First of all, you must understand that in the last days scoffers will come, scoffing and following their own evil desires. [4]They will say, "Where is this 'coming' he promised? Ever since our fathers died, everything goes on as it has since the beginning of creation." [5]But they deliberately forget that long ago by God's word the heavens existed and the earth was formed out of water and by water. [6]By these waters also the world of that time was deluged and destroyed. [7]By the same word the present heavens and earth are reserved for fire, being kept for the day of judgment and destruction of ungodly men.

f) It Is Future

(1) A Day Is Appointed for It

Acts 17 [31]"For he has set a day when he will judge the world with justice by the man he has appointed. He has given proof of this to all men by raising him from the dead."
Rom 2 [16]This will take place on the day when God will judge men's secrets through Jesus Christ, as my gospel declares.

(2) It Is at the Second Coming of Christ

Matt 25 [31]"When the Son of Man comes in his glory, and all the angels with him, he will sit on his throne in heavenly glory."
2 Tim 4 [1]In the presence of God and of Christ Jesus, who will judge the living and the dead, and in view of his appearing and his kingdom, I give you this charge. . . .

(3) It Is Coming Very Soon

Zeph 1 [7]"Be silent before the Sovereign LORD, for the day of the LORD is near. The LORD has prepared a sacrifice; he has consecrated those he has invited."
Zeph 1 [14]"The great day of the LORD is near—near and coming quickly. Listen! The cry on the day of the LORD will be bitter, the shouting of the warrior there."
Luke 21 [34]"Be careful, or your hearts will be weighed down with dissipation, drunkenness and the anxieties of life, and that day will close on you unexpectedly like a trap. [35]For it will come upon all those who live on the face of the whole earth. [36]Be always on the watch, and pray that you may be able to escape all that is about to happen, and that you may be able to stand before the Son of Man."

g) It Is Impartial

Ezek 18 [19]"Yet you ask, 'Why does the son not share the guilt of his father?' Since the son has done what is just and right and has been careful to keep all my decrees, he will surely live. [20]The soul who sins is the one who will die. The son will not share the guilt of the father, nor will the father share the guilt of the son. The righteousness of the righteous man will be credited to him, and the wickedness of the wicked will be charged against him. . . . [29]Yet the house of Israel says, 'The way of the Lord is not just.' Are my ways unjust, O house of Israel? Is it not your ways that are unjust?"
Acts 10 [34]Then Peter began to speak: "I now realize how true it is that God does not show favoritism. . . ."
Rom 2 [5]But because of your stubbornness and your unrepentant heart, you are storing up wrath against yourself for the day of God's wrath, when his righteous judgment will be revealed. [6]God "will give to each person according to what he has done." . . . [11]For God does not show favoritism.
Col 3 [25]Anyone who does wrong will be repaid for his wrong, and there is no favoritism.
1 Pet 1 [17]Since you call on a Father who judges each man's work impartially, live your lives as strangers here in reverent fear.
See also p. 57b, God Is Impartial

h) It Is Just

Acts 17 [31]"For he has set a day when he will judge the world with justice by the man he has appointed. He has given proof of this to all men by raising him from the dead."
Heb 2 [2]For if the message spoken by angels was binding, and every violation and disobedience received its just punishment, [3]how shall we escape if we ignore such a great salvation? This salvation, which was first announced by the Lord, was confirmed to us by those who heard him.
See also p. 57b, God Is Just

i) It Is Righteous

Ps 96 [13]they will sing before the LORD, for he comes, he comes to judge the earth. He will judge the world in righteousness and the peoples in his truth.
Ps 98 [9]let them sing before the LORD, for he comes to judge the earth. He will judge the world in righteousness and the peoples with equity.
Rom 2 [3]So when you, a mere man, pass judgment on them and yet do the same things, do you think you will escape God's judgment? [4]Or do you show contempt for the riches of his kindness, tolerance and patience, not realizing that God's kindness leads you toward repentance?

[5]But because of your stubbornness and your unrepentant heart, you are storing up wrath against yourself for the day of God's wrath, when his righteous judgment will be revealed.
See also p. 63a, God Is Righteous

j) It Is Thorough

Jer 17 [10]"I the LORD search the heart and examine the mind, to reward a man according to his conduct, according to what his deeds deserve."
Rom 2 [16]This will take place on the day when God will judge men's secrets through Jesus Christ, as my gospel declares.

k) It Is Universal

Amos 8 [8]"Will not the land tremble for this, and all who live in it mourn? The whole land will rise like the Nile; it will be stirred up and then sink like the river of Egypt.

[9]"In that day," declares the Sovereign LORD, "I will make the sun go down at noon and darken the earth in broad daylight."
Matt 25 [31]"When the Son of Man comes in his glory, and all the angels with him, he will sit on his throne in heavenly glory. [32]All the nations will be gathered before him, and he will separate the people one from another as a shepherd separates the sheep from the goats."
Rom 2 [5]But because of your stubbornness and your unrepentant heart, you are storing up wrath against yourself for the day of God's wrath, when his righteous judgment will be revealed. [6]God "will give to each person according to what he has done."
Heb 12 [23]to the church of the firstborn, whose names are written in heaven. You have come to God, the judge of all men, to the spirits of righteous men made perfect. . . .
1 Pet 4 [5]But they will have to give account to him who is ready to judge the living and the dead.
Jude [14]Enoch, the seventh from Adam, prophesied about these men: "See, the Lord is coming with thousands upon thousands of his holy ones [15]to judge everyone, and to convict all the ungodly of all the ungodly acts they have done in the ungodly way, and of all the harsh words ungodly sinners have spoken against him."
Rev 20 [12]And I saw the dead, great and small, standing before the throne, and books were opened. Another book was opened, which is the book of life. The dead were judged according to what they had done as recorded in the books.

l) None Can Stand in It without Divine Grace

Ps 130 [3]If you, O LORD, kept a record of sins, O Lord, who could stand?
Ps 143 [2]Do not bring your servant into judgment, for no one living is righteous before you.
Rom 3 [19]Now we know that whatever the law says, it says to those who are under the law, so that every mouth may be silenced and the whole world held accountable to God. . . .

[21]But now a righteousness from God, apart from law, has been made known, to which the Law and the Prophets testify. [22]This righteousness from God comes through faith in Jesus Christ to all who believe. There is no difference, [23]for all have sinned and fall short of the glory of God, [24]and are justified freely by his grace through the redemption that came by Christ Jesus.

3. Designations for the Last Judgment

a) Day

1 Cor 3 [13]his work will be shown for what it is, because the Day will bring it to light. It will be revealed with fire, and the fire will test the quality of each man's work.
2 Tim 4 [8]Now there is in store for me the crown of righteousness, which the Lord, the righteous Judge, will award to me on that day—and not only to me, but also to all who have longed for his appearing.

b) Day of Judgment, the Judgment

Matt 10 [15]"I tell you the truth, it will be more bearable for Sodom and Gomorrah on the day of judgment than for that town."
Matt 11 [21]"Woe to you, Korazin! Woe to you, Bethsaida! If the miracles that were performed in you had been performed in Tyre and Sidon, they would have repented long ago in sackcloth and ashes. [22]But I tell you, it will be more bearable for Tyre and Sidon on the day of judgment than for you. [23]And you, Capernaum, will you be lifted up to the skies? No, you will go down to the depths. If the miracles that were performed in you had been performed in Sodom, it would have remained to this day. [24]But I tell you that it will be more bearable for Sodom on the day of judgment than for you."
Matt 12 [39]He answered, "A wicked and adulterous generation asks for a miraculous sign! But none will be given it except the sign of the prophet Jonah. [40]For as Jonah was three days and three nights in the belly of a huge fish, so the Son of Man will be three days and three nights in the heart of the earth. [41]The men of Nineveh will stand up at the judgment with this generation and condemn it; for they repented at the preaching of Jonah, and now one greater than Jonah is here. [42]The Queen of the South will rise at the judgment with this generation and condemn it; for she came from the ends of the earth to listen to Solomon's wisdom, and now one greater than Solomon is here."
2 Pet 3 [7]By the same word the present heavens and earth are reserved for fire, being kept for the day of judgment and destruction of ungodly men.
1 John 4 [17]In this way, love is made complete among us so that we will have confidence on the day of judgment, because in this world we are like him.

c) Day of the Lord

Isa 2 [10]Go into the rocks, hide in the ground from dread of the LORD and the splendor of his majesty! [11]The eyes of the arrogant man will be humbled and the pride of men brought low; the LORD alone will be exalted in that day.

[12]The LORD Almighty has a day in store for all the proud and lofty, for all that is exalted (and they will be humbled), [13]for all the cedars of Lebanon, tall and lofty, and all the oaks of Bashan, [14]for all the towering mountains and all the high hills, [15]for every lofty tower and every fortified wall, [16]for every trading ship and every stately vessel. [17]The arrogance of man will be brought low and the pride of men humbled; the LORD alone will be exalted in that day, [18]and the idols will totally disappear.

[19]Men will flee to caves in the rocks and to holes in the ground from dread of the LORD and the splendor of his majesty, when he rises to shake the earth. [20]In that day men will throw away to the rodents and bats their idols of silver and idols of gold, which they made to worship. [21]They will flee to caverns in the rocks and to the overhanging crags from dread of the LORD and the splendor of his majesty, when he rises to shake the earth.
Amos 5 [18]Woe to you who long for the day of the LORD! Why do you long for the day of the LORD? That day will be darkness, not light. [19]It will be as though a man fled from a lion only to meet a bear, as though he entered his house and rested his hand on the wall only to have a snake bite him. [20]Will not the day of the LORD be darkness, not light—pitch-dark, without a ray of brightness?
Zeph 1 [7]"Be silent before the Sovereign LORD, for the day of the LORD is near. The LORD has prepared a sacrifice; he has consecrated those he has invited. [8]On the day of the LORD's sacrifice I will punish the princes and the king's sons and all those clad in foreign clothes. [9]On that day I will punish all who avoid

stepping on the threshold, who fill the temple of their gods with violence and deceit.

10"On that day," declares the LORD, "a cry will go up from the Fish Gate, wailing from the New Quarter, and a loud crash from the hills. 11Wail, you who live in the market district; all your merchants will be wiped out, all who trade with silver will be ruined. 12At that time I will search Jerusalem with lamps and punish those who are complacent, who are like wine left on its dregs, who think, 'The LORD will do nothing, either good or bad.' 13Their wealth will be plundered, their houses demolished. They will build houses but not live in them; they will plant vineyards but not drink the wine.

14"The great day of the LORD is near—near and coming quickly. Listen! The cry on the day of the LORD will be bitter, the shouting of the warrior there. 15That day will be a day of wrath, a day of distress and anguish, a day of trouble and ruin, a day of darkness and gloom, a day of clouds and blackness, 16a day of trumpet and battle cry against the fortified cities and against the corner towers. 17I will bring distress on the people and they will walk like blind men, because they have sinned against the LORD. Their blood will be poured out like dust and their entrails like filth. 18Neither their silver nor their gold will be able to save them on the day of the LORD's wrath. In the fire of his jealousy the whole world will be consumed, for he will make a sudden end of all who live in the earth."

d) Day of Our Lord Jesus Christ

1 Cor 1 7Therefore you do not lack any spiritual gift as you eagerly wait for our Lord Jesus Christ to be revealed. 8He will keep you strong to the end, so that you will be blameless on the day of our Lord Jesus Christ.

e) Day of (God's) Wrath

Zeph 1 18"Neither their silver nor their gold will be able to save them on the day of the LORD's wrath. In the fire of his jealousy the whole world will be consumed, for he will make a sudden end of all who live in the earth."

Rom 2 5But because of your stubbornness and your unrepentant heart, you are storing up wrath against yourself for the day of God's wrath, when his righteous judgment will be revealed.

Rev 6 15Then the kings of the earth, the princes, the generals, the rich, the mighty, and every slave and every free man hid in caves and among the rocks of the mountains. 16They called to the mountains and the rocks, "Fall on us and hide us from the face of him who sits on the throne and from the wrath of the Lamb! 17For the great day of their wrath has come, and who can stand?"

f) End of the Age

Matt 13 37He answered, "The one who sowed the good seed is the Son of Man. 38The field is the world, and the good seed stands for the sons of the kingdom. The weeds are the sons of the evil one, 39and the enemy who sows them is the devil. The harvest is the end of the age, and the harvesters are angels.

40"As the weeds are pulled up and burned in the fire, so it will be at the end of the age. . . . 49This is how it will be at the end of the age. The angels will come and separate the wicked from the righteous 50and throw them into the fiery furnace, where there will be weeping and gnashing of teeth."

g) Great Day

Jude 6And the angels who did not keep their positions of authority but abandoned their own home—these he has kept in darkness, bound with everlasting chains for judgment on the great Day.

h) Last Day

John 12 48"There is a judge for the one who rejects me and does not accept my words; that very word which I spoke will condemn him at the last day."

4. Parables about the Last Judgment

a) Parable of the Net

latt 13 47"Once again, the kingdom of heaven is like a net that as let down into the lake and caught all kinds of fish. 48When vas full, the fishermen pulled it up on the shore. Then they sat down and collected the good fish in baskets, but threw the bad away. 49This is how it will be at the end of the age. The angels will come and separate the wicked from the righteous 50and throw them into the fiery furnace, where there will be weeping and gnashing of teeth."

b) Parable of the Sheep and Goats

Matt 25 31"When the Son of Man comes in his glory, and all the angels with him, he will sit on his throne in heavenly glory. 32All the nations will be gathered before him, and he will separate the people one from another as a shepherd separates the sheep from the goats. 33He will put the sheep on his right and the goats on his left.

34"Then the King will say to those on his right, 'Come, you who are blessed by my Father; take your inheritance, the kingdom prepared for you since the creation of the world. 35For I was hungry and you gave me something to eat, I was thirsty and you gave me something to drink, I was a stranger and you invited me in, 36I needed clothes and you clothed me, I was sick and you looked after me, I was in prison and you came to visit me.'

37"Then the righteous will answer him, 'Lord, when did we see you hungry and feed you, or thirsty and give you something to drink? 38When did we see you a stranger and invite you in, or needing clothes and clothe you? 39When did we see you sick or in prison and go to visit you?'

40"The King will reply, 'I tell you the truth, whatever you did for one of the least of these brothers of mine, you did for me.'

41"Then he will say to those on his left, 'Depart from me, you who are cursed, into the eternal fire prepared for the devil and his angels. 42For I was hungry and you gave me nothing to eat, I was thirsty and you gave me nothing to drink, 43I was a stranger and you did not invite me in, I needed clothes and you did not clothe me, I was sick and in prison and you did not look after me.'

44"They also will answer, 'Lord, when did we see you hungry or thirsty or a stranger or needing clothes or sick or in prison, and did not help you?'

45"He will reply, 'I tell you the truth, whatever you did not do for one of the least of these, you did not do for me.'

46"Then they will go away to eternal punishment, but the righteous to eternal life."

c) Parable of the Weeds

Matt 13 24Jesus told them another parable: "The kingdom of heaven is like a man who sowed good seed in his field. 25But while everyone was sleeping, his enemy came and sowed weeds among the wheat, and went away. 26When the wheat sprouted and formed heads, then the weeds also appeared.

27"The owner's servants came to him and said, 'Sir, didn't you sow good seed in your field? Where then did the weeds come from?'

28"'An enemy did this,' he replied.

"The servants asked him, 'Do you want us to go and pull them up?'

29"'No,' he answered, 'because while you are pulling the weeds, you may root up the wheat with them. 30Let both grow together until the harvest. At that time I will tell the harvesters: First collect the weeds and tie them in bundles to be burned; then gather the wheat and bring it into my barn.'" . . .

36Then he left the crowd and went into the house. His disciples came to him and said, "Explain to us the parable of the weeds in the field."

37He answered, "The one who sowed the good seed is the Son of Man. 38The field is the world, and the good seed stands for the sons of the kingdom. The weeds are the sons of the evil one, 39and the enemy who sows them is the devil. The harvest is the end of the age, and the harvesters are angels.

40"As the weeds are pulled up and burned in the fire, so it will be at the end of the age. 41The Son of Man will send out his angels, and they will weed out of his kingdom everything that causes sin and all who do evil. 42They will throw them into the fiery furnace, where there will be weeping and gnashing of teeth. 43Then the righteous will shine like the sun in the kingdom of their Father. He who has ears, let him hear."

5. Agents of Judgment

a) Believers to Judge

Luke 22 29“And I confer on you a kingdom, just as my Father conferred one on me, 30so that you may eat and drink at my table in my kingdom and sit on thrones, judging the twelve tribes of Israel.”

b) Christ and Christ’s Word as Judge

Isa 11 1A shoot will come up from the stump of Jesse; from his roots a Branch will bear fruit. 2The Spirit of the LORD will rest on him—the Spirit of wisdom and of understanding, the Spirit of counsel and of power, the Spirit of knowledge and of the fear of the LORD—3and he will delight in the fear of the LORD.

He will not judge by what he sees with his eyes, or decide by what he hears with his ears; 4but with righteousness he will judge the needy, with justice he will give decisions for the poor of the earth. He will strike the earth with the rod of his mouth; with the breath of his lips he will slay the wicked. 5Righteousness will be his belt and faithfulness the sash around his waist.

Matt 16 27“For the Son of Man is going to come in his Father’s glory with his angels, and then he will reward each person according to what he has done.”

Matt 25 31“When the Son of Man comes in his glory, and all the angels with him, he will sit on his throne in heavenly glory. 32All the nations will be gathered before him, and he will separate the people one from another as a shepherd separates the sheep from the goats. 33He will put the sheep on his right and the goats on his left.”

John 5 22“Moreover, the Father judges no one, but has entrusted all judgment to the Son. . . . 26For as the Father has life in himself, so he has granted the Son to have life in himself. 27And he has given him authority to judge because he is the Son of Man.”

John 12 47“As for the person who hears my words but does not keep them, I do not judge him. For I did not come to judge the world, but to save it. 48There is a judge for the one who rejects me and does not accept my words; that very word which I spoke will condemn him at the last day. 49For I did not speak of my own accord, but the Father who sent me commanded me what to say and how to say it.”

Acts 10 36“You know the message God sent to the people of Israel, telling the good news of peace through Jesus Christ, who is Lord of all. . . . 42He commanded us to preach to the people and to testify that he is the one whom God appointed as judge of the living and the dead.”

Acts 17 31“For he has set a day when he will judge the world with justice by the man he has appointed. He has given proof of this to all men by raising him from the dead.”

Rom 2 16This will take place on the day when God will judge men’s secrets through Jesus Christ, as my gospel declares.

1 Cor 4 4My conscience is clear, but that does not make me innocent. It is the Lord who judges me. 5Therefore judge nothing before the appointed time; wait till the Lord comes. He will bring to light what is hidden in darkness and will expose the motives of men’s hearts. At that time each will receive his praise from God.

2 Tim 4 1In the presence of God and of Christ Jesus, who will judge the living and the dead, and in view of his appearing and his kingdom, I give you this charge. . . .

c) God as Judge

Gen 18 25“Far be it from you to do such a thing—to kill the righteous with the wicked, treating the righteous and the wicked alike. Far be it from you! Will not the Judge of all the earth do right?”

Ps 7 8let the LORD judge the peoples. Judge me, O LORD, according to my righteousness, according to my integrity, O Most High.

Ps 9 1I will praise you, O LORD, with all my heart; I will tell of all your wonders. . . . 4For you have upheld my right and my cause; you have sat on your throne, judging righteously.

Ps 50 6And the heavens proclaim his righteousness, for God himself is judge.

Ps 58 11Then men will say, “Surely the righteous still are rewarded; surely there is a God who judges the earth.”

Ps 98 7Let the sea resound, and everything in it, the world, and all who live in it. 8Let the rivers clap their hands, let the mountains sing together for joy; 9let them sing before the LORD, for he comes to judge the earth. He will judge the world in righteousness and the peoples with equity.

Acts 17 30“In the past God overlooked such ignorance, but now he commands all people everywhere to repent. 31For he has set a day when he will judge the world with justice by the man he has appointed. He has given proof of this to all men by raising him from the dead.”

Rom 2 2Now we know that God’s judgment against those who do such things is based on truth.

Rev 11 15The seventh angel sounded his trumpet, and there were loud voices in heaven, which said: “The kingdom of the world has become the kingdom of our Lord and of his Christ, and he will reign for ever and ever.” 16And the twenty-four elders, who were seated on their thrones before God, fell on their faces and worshiped God, 17saying: “We give thanks to you, Lord God Almighty, the One who is and who was, because you have taken your great power and have begun to reign. 18The nations were angry; and your wrath has come. The time has come for judging the dead, and for rewarding your servants the prophets and your saints and those who reverence your name, both small and great—and for destroying those who destroy the earth.”

B. The Judgment of the Righteous

1. Descriptions of the Judgment

a) Judgment Seat of Christ

2 Cor 5 10For we must all appear before the judgment seat of Christ, that each one may receive what is due him for the things done while in the body, whether good or bad.

b) Judgment Seat of God

Rom 14 10You, then, why do you judge your brother? Or why do you look down on your brother? For we will all stand before God’s judgment seat.

2. The Nature of the Judgment

a) All Believers Will Stand before God

Rom 14 9For this very reason, Christ died and returned to life so that he might be the Lord of both the dead and the living. 10You, then, why do you judge your brother? Or why do you look down on your brother? For we will all stand before God’s judgment seat. 11It is written: “‘As surely as I live,’ says the Lord, ‘every knee will bow before me; every tongue will confess to God.’” 12So then, each of us will give an account of himself to God.

2 Cor 5 10For we must all appear before the judgment seat of Christ, that each one may receive what is due him for the things done while in the body, whether good or bad.

b) All Works Will Be Tried by Fire

1 Cor 3 10By the grace God has given me, I laid a foundation as an expert builder, and someone else is building on it. But each one should be careful how he builds. 11For no one can lay any foundation other than the one already laid, which is Jesus Christ. 12If any man builds on this foundation using gold, silver, costly stones, wood, hay or straw, 13his work will be shown for what it is, because the Day will bring it to light. It will be revealed with fire, and the fire will test the quality of each man’s work. 14If what he has built survives, he will receive his reward. 15If it is burned up, he will suffer loss; he himself will be saved, but only as one escaping through the flames.

3. Results of the Judgment

a) Blessing

Matt 13 40“As the weeds are pulled up and burned in the fire, so it will be at the end of the age. 41The Son of Man will send out his angels, and they will weed out of his kingdom everything that causes sin and all who do evil. 42They will throw them into the fiery furnace, where there will be weeping and gnashing of teeth. 43Then the righteous will shine like the sun in the kingdom of their Father. He who has ears, let him hear.”

Matt 25 31“When the Son of Man comes in his glory, and all the angels with him, he will sit on his throne in heavenly glory. . . .

34"Then the King will say to those on his right, 'Come, you who are blessed by my Father; take your inheritance, the kingdom prepared for you since the creation of the world.'"

b) Crowns

1 Cor 9 25Everyone who competes in the games goes into strict training. They do it to get a crown that will not last; but we do it to get a crown that will last forever.
2 Tim 4 8Now there is in store for me the crown of righteousness, which the Lord, the righteous Judge, will award to me on that day—and not only to me, but also to all who have longed for his appearing.
James 1 12Blessed is the man who perseveres under trial, because when he has stood the test, he will receive the crown of life that God has promised to those who love him.
1 Pet 5 4And when the Chief Shepherd appears, you will receive the crown of glory that will never fade away.
Rev 2 10"Do not be afraid of what you are about to suffer. I tell you, the devil will put some of you in prison to test you, and you will suffer persecution for ten days. Be faithful, even to the point of death, and I will give you the crown of life."

c) Eternal Life

Matt 25 31"When the Son of Man comes in his glory, and all the angels with him, he will sit on his throne in heavenly glory. . . .
46"Then they will go away to eternal punishment, but the righteous to eternal life."
John 5 28"Do not be amazed at this, for a time is coming when all who are in their graves will hear his voice 29and come out—those who have done good will rise to live, and those who have done evil will rise to be condemned."

d) Glory, Honor, and Peace

Rom 2 5But because of your stubbornness and your unrepentant heart, you are storing up wrath against yourself for the day of God's wrath, when his righteous judgment will be revealed.
. . . 9There will be trouble and distress for every human being who does evil: first for the Jew, then for the Gentile; 10but glory, honor and peace for everyone who does good: first for the Jew, then for the Gentile.

e) Praise from God

1 Cor 4 5Therefore judge nothing before the appointed time; wait till the Lord comes. He will bring to light what is hidden in darkness and will expose the motives of men's hearts. At that time each will receive his praise from God.

f) Reward

1 Cor 3 8The man who plants and the man who waters have one purpose, and each will be rewarded according to his own labor. . . . 14If what he has built survives, he will receive his reward.
Gal 6 7Do not be deceived: God cannot be mocked. A man reaps what he sows. 8The one who sows to please his sinful nature, from that nature will reap destruction; the one who sows to please the Spirit, from the Spirit will reap eternal life.
9Let us not become weary in doing good, for at the proper time we will reap a harvest if we do not give up. 10Therefore, as we have opportunity, let us do good to all people, especially to those who belong to the family of believers.
Eph 6 8because you know that the Lord will reward everyone for whatever good he does, whether he is slave or free.
Col 3 23Whatever you do, work at it with all your heart, as working for the Lord, not for men, 24since you know that you will receive an inheritance from the Lord as a reward. It is the Lord Christ you are serving.
Rev 22 12"Behold, I am coming soon! My reward is with me, and I will give to everyone according to what he has done."

4. The Scope of the Judgment

a) Actions

62 12and that you, O Lord, are loving. Surely you will ard each person according to what he has done.
t 16 27"For the Son of Man is going to come in his Father's glory with his angels, and then he will reward each person according to what he has done."
Matt 25 31"When the Son of Man comes in his glory, and all the angels with him, he will sit on his throne in heavenly glory. 32All the nations will be gathered before him, and he will separate the people one from another as a shepherd separates the sheep from the goats. 33He will put the sheep on his right and the goats on his left.
34"Then the King will say to those on his right, 'Come, you who are blessed by my Father; take your inheritance, the kingdom prepared for you since the creation of the world. 35For I was hungry and you gave me something to eat, I was thirsty and you gave me something to drink, I was a stranger and you invited me in, 36I needed clothes and you clothed me, I was sick and you looked after me, I was in prison and you came to visit me.'
37"Then the righteous will answer him, 'Lord, when did we see you hungry and feed you, or thirsty and give you something to drink? 38When did we see you a stranger and invite you in, or needing clothes and clothe you? 39When did we see you sick or in prison and go to visit you?'
40"The King will reply, 'I tell you the truth, whatever you did for one of the least of these brothers of mine, you did for me.'"
Rom 2 7To those who by persistence in doing good seek glory, honor and immortality, he will give eternal life.
Eph 6 7Serve wholeheartedly, as if you were serving the Lord, not men, 8because you know that the Lord will reward everyone for whatever good he does, whether he is slave or free.
Col 3 25Anyone who does wrong will be repaid for his wrong, and there is no favoritism.
Heb 6 10God is not unjust; he will not forget your work and the love you have shown him as you have helped his people and continue to help them. 11We want each of you to show this same diligence to the very end, in order to make your hope sure.
Rev 2 23"I will strike her children dead. Then all the churches will know that I am he who searches hearts and minds, and I will repay each of you according to your deeds."

b) Thoughts

Jer 17 10"I the LORD search the heart and examine the mind, to reward a man according to his conduct, according to what his deeds deserve."
1 Cor 4 1So then, men ought to regard us as servants of Christ and as those entrusted with the secret things of God. 2Now it is required that those who have been given a trust must prove faithful. 3I care very little if I am judged by you or by any human court; indeed, I do not even judge myself. 4My conscience is clear, but that does not make me innocent. It is the Lord who judges me. 5Therefore judge nothing before the appointed time; wait till the Lord comes. He will bring to light what is hidden in darkness and will expose the motives of men's hearts. At that time each will receive his praise from God.
Rev 2 23"I will strike her children dead. Then all the churches will know that I am he who searches hearts and minds, and I will repay each of you according to your deeds."

c) Words

Matt 12 35"The good man brings good things out of the good stored up in him, and the evil man brings evil things out of the evil stored up in him. 36But I tell you that men will have to give account on the day of judgment for every careless word they have spoken. 37For by your words you will be acquitted, and by your words you will be condemned."

C. The Judgment of the Lost

1. Descriptions of the Judgment

a) It Is Awesome and Terrible

Rev 6 15Then the kings of the earth, the princes, the generals, the rich, the mighty, and every slave and every free man hid in caves and among the rocks of the mountains. 16They called to the mountains and the rocks, "Fall on us and hide us from the face of him who sits on the throne and from the wrath of the

Lamb! [17]For the great day of their wrath has come, and who can stand?"

Rev 20 [11]Then I saw a great white throne and him who was seated on it. Earth and sky fled from his presence, and there was no place for them.

b) It Is Bitter

Zeph 1 [14]"The great day of the LORD is near—near and coming quickly. Listen! The cry on the day of the LORD will be bitter, the shouting of the warrior there. [15]That day will be a day of wrath, a day of distress and anguish, a day of trouble and ruin, a day of darkness and gloom, a day of clouds and blackness, [16]a day of trumpet and battle cry against the fortified cities and against the corner towers. [17]I will bring distress on the people and they will walk like blind men, because they have sinned against the LORD. Their blood will be poured out like dust and their entrails like filth. [18]Neither their silver nor their gold will be able to save them on the day of the LORD's wrath. In the fire of his jealousy the whole world will be consumed, for he will make a sudden end of all who live in the earth."

c) It Is Certain

1 Thess 5 [3]While people are saying, "Peace and safety," destruction will come on them suddenly, as labor pains on a pregnant woman, and they will not escape.

2 Pet 3 [3]First of all, you must understand that in the last days scoffers will come, scoffing and following their own evil desires. [4]They will say, "Where is this 'coming' he promised? Ever since our fathers died, everything goes on as it has since the beginning of creation." [5]But they deliberately forget that long ago by God's word the heavens existed and the earth was formed out of water and by water. [6]By these waters also the world of that time was deluged and destroyed. [7]By the same word the present heavens and earth are reserved for fire, being kept for the day of judgment and destruction of ungodly men.

d) It Is Dreadful

Heb 10 [25]Let us not give up meeting together, as some are in the habit of doing, but let us encourage one another—and all the more as you see the Day approaching. . . . [30]For we know him who said, "It is mine to avenge; I will repay," and again, "The Lord will judge his people." [31]It is a dreadful thing to fall into the hands of the living God.

e) It Is Retribution

Isa 13 [9]See, the day of the LORD is coming—a cruel day, with wrath and fierce anger—to make the land desolate and destroy the sinners within it. [10]The stars of heaven and their constellations will not show their light. The rising sun will be darkened and the moon will not give its light. [11]I will punish the world for its evil, the wicked for their sins. I will put an end to the arrogance of the haughty and will humble the pride of the ruthless. [12]I will make man scarcer than pure gold, more rare than the gold of Ophir. [13]Therefore I will make the heavens tremble; and the earth will shake from its place at the wrath of the LORD Almighty, in the day of his burning anger.

f) It Is Righteous

Rom 2 [5]But because of your stubbornness and your unrepentant heart, you are storing up wrath against yourself for the day of God's wrath, when his righteous judgment will be revealed.

g) It Is without Hope

Amos 5 [20]Will not the day of the LORD be darkness, not light—pitch-dark, without a ray of brightness?

2. Historical Foreshadowings of the Judgment

a) Disobedient Angels

2 Pet 2 [4]For if God did not spare angels when they sinned, but sent them to hell, putting them into gloomy dungeons to be held for judgment . . .

Jude [6]And the angels who did not keep their positions of authority but abandoned their own home—these he has kept in darkness, bound with everlasting chains for judgment on the great Day.

b) The Flood

2 Pet 2 [5]if he did not spare the ancient world when he brought the flood on its ungodly people, but protected Noah, a preacher of righteousness, and seven others . . .

c) Sodom and Gomorrah

2 Pet 2 [6]if he condemned the cities of Sodom and Gomorrah by burning them to ashes, and made them an example of what is going to happen to the ungodly . . .

Jude [7]In a similar way, Sodom and Gomorrah and the surrounding towns gave themselves up to sexual immorality and perversion. They serve as an example of those who suffer the punishment of eternal fire.

d) Wilderness Wanderings

Jude [5]Though you already know all this, I want to remind you that the Lord delivered his people out of Egypt, but later destroyed those who did not believe.

3. The Nature of the Judgment

1 Pet 4 [4]They think it strange that you do not plunge with them into the same flood of dissipation, and they heap abuse on you. [5]But they will have to give account to him who is ready to judge the living and the dead.

Jude [14]Enoch, the seventh from Adam, prophesied about these men: "See, the Lord is coming with thousands upon thousands of his holy ones [15]to judge everyone, and to convict all the ungodly of all the ungodly acts they have done in the ungodly way, and of all the harsh words ungodly sinners have spoken against him."

4. Results of the Judgment

a) Anguish

Matt 13 [41]"The Son of Man will send out his angels, and they will weed out of his kingdom everything that causes sin and all who do evil. [42]They will throw them into the fiery furnace, where there will be weeping and gnashing of teeth."

b) Being Cast into the Lake of Fire

Matt 25 [41]"Then he will say to those on his left, 'Depart from me, you who are cursed, into the eternal fire prepared for the devil and his angels.'"

Rev 20 [14]Then death and Hades were thrown into the lake of fire. The lake of fire is the second death. [15]If anyone's name was not found written in the book of life, he was thrown into the lake of fire.

c) Condemnation

Matt 12 [36]"But I tell you that men will have to give account on the day of judgment for every careless word they have spoken. [37]For by your words you will be acquitted, and by your words you will be condemned."

John 5 [28]"Do not be amazed at this, for a time is coming when all who are in their graves will hear his voice [29]and come out—those who have done good will rise to live, and those who have done evil will rise to be condemned."

d) Destruction

Phil 1 [28]without being frightened in any way by those who oppose you. This is a sign to them that they will be destroyed, but that you will be saved—and that by God.

Phil 3 [18]For, as I have often told you before and now say again even with tears, many live as enemies of the cross of Christ. [19]Their destiny is destruction, their god is their stomach, and their glory is in their shame. Their mind is on earthly things.

e) Eternal Punishment

Matt 25 [46]"Then they will go away to eternal punishment, but the righteous to eternal life."

2 Thess 1 [6]God is just: He will pay back trouble to those who trouble you [7]and give relief to you who are troubled, and to us as well. This will happen when the Lord Jesus is revealed from heaven in blazing fire with his powerful angels. [8]He will punish those who do not know God and do not obey the gospel of our Lord Jesus. [9]They will be punished with everlasting destruction and shut out from the presence of the Lord and from the majesty of his power. . . .

f) Separation from God's Presence

2 Thess 1 [8]He will punish those who do not know God and do not obey the gospel of our Lord Jesus. [9]They will be punished with everlasting destruction and shut out from the presence of the Lord and from the majesty of his power. . . .

g) Separation from the Righteous

Matt 13 [47]"Once again, the kingdom of heaven is like a net that was let down into the lake and caught all kinds of fish. [48]When it was full, the fishermen pulled it up on the shore. Then they sat down and collected the good fish in baskets, but threw the bad away. [49]This is how it will be at the end of the age. The angels will come and separate the wicked from the righteous. . . ."
Matt 25 [32]"All the nations will be gathered before him, and he will separate the people one from another as a shepherd separates the sheep from the goats. [33]He will put the sheep on his right and the goats on his left. . . .

[41]"Then he will say to those on his left, 'Depart from me, you who are cursed, into the eternal fire prepared for the devil and his angels.'"

h) Trouble and Distress

Rom 2 [9]There will be trouble and distress for every human being who does evil: first for the Jew, then for the Gentile. . . .

5. The Scope of the Judgment

a) Actions

Eccles 12 [14]For God will bring every deed into judgment, including every hidden thing, whether it is good or evil.
Jer 32 [18]"You show love to thousands but bring the punishment for the fathers' sins into the laps of their children after them. O great and powerful God, whose name is the LORD Almighty, [19]great are your purposes and mighty are your deeds. Your eyes are open to all the ways of men; you reward everyone according to his conduct and as his deeds deserve."
Rom 2 [8]But for those who are self-seeking and who reject the truth and follow evil, there will be wrath and anger.
Rev 20 [12]And I saw the dead, great and small, standing before the throne, and books were opened. Another book was opened, which is the book of life. The dead were judged according to what they had done as recorded in the books. [13]The sea gave up the dead that were in it, and death and Hades gave up the dead that were in them, and each person was judged according to what he had done.

b) Thoughts

Ps 94 [11]The LORD knows the thoughts of man; he knows that they are futile.
Prov 15 [26]The LORD detests the thoughts of the wicked, but those of the pure are pleasing to him.
Prov 24 [12]If you say, "But we knew nothing about this," does not he who weighs the heart perceive it? Does not he who guards your life know it? Will he not repay each person according to what he has done?
Rom 2 [16]This will take place on the day when God will judge men's secrets through Jesus Christ, as my gospel declares.

c) Words

Matt 12 [33]"Make a tree good and its fruit will be good, or make a tree bad and its fruit will be bad, for a tree is recognized by its fruit. [34]You brood of vipers, how can you who are evil say anything good? For out of the overflow of the heart the mouth speaks. [35]The good man brings good things out of the good stored up in him, and the evil man brings evil things out of the evil stored up in him. [36]But I tell you that men will have to give account on the day of judgment for every careless word they have spoken. [37]For by your words you will be acquitted, and by your words you will be condemned."
Jude [14]Enoch, the seventh from Adam, prophesied about these men: "See, the Lord is coming with thousands upon thousands of his holy ones [15]to judge everyone, and to convict all the ungodly of all the ungodly acts they have done in the ungodly way, and of all the harsh words ungodly sinners have spoken against him." [16]These men are grumblers and faultfinders; they follow their own evil desires; they boast about themselves and flatter others for their own advantage.

D. The Times of Judgment

1. The Judgment as Past

a) Christ's Cross Was a Judgment

Rom 3 [21]But now a righteousness from God, apart from law, has been made known, to which the Law and the Prophets testify. [22]This righteousness from God comes through faith in Jesus Christ to all who believe. There is no difference, [23]for all have sinned and fall short of the glory of God, [24]and are justified freely by his grace through the redemption that came by Christ Jesus. [25]God presented him as a sacrifice of atonement, through faith in his blood. He did this to demonstrate his justice, because in his forbearance he had left the sins committed beforehand unpunished—[26]he did it to demonstrate his justice at the present time, so as to be just and the one who justifies those who have faith in Jesus.
Rom 8 [1]Therefore, there is now no condemnation for those who are in Christ Jesus, [2]because through Christ Jesus the law of the Spirit of life set me free from the law of sin and death. . . .

[31]What, then, shall we say in response to this? If God is for us, who can be against us? [32]He who did not spare his own Son, but gave him up for us all—how will he not also, along with him, graciously give us all things? [33]Who will bring any charge against those whom God has chosen? It is God who justifies. [34]Who is he that condemns? Christ Jesus, who died—more than that, who was raised to life—is at the right hand of God and is also interceding for us.

b) Satan and Demonic Forces Were Judged

John 12 [31]"Now is the time for judgment on this world; now the prince of this world will be driven out. [32]But I, when I am lifted up from the earth, will draw all men to myself." [33]He said this to show the kind of death he was going to die.
Col 2 [15]And having disarmed the powers and authorities, he made a public spectacle of them, triumphing over them by the cross.

2. The Judgment as Present

a) It Punishes the Wicked

Ps 7 [9]O righteous God, who searches minds and hearts, bring to an end the violence of the wicked and make the righteous secure.
Ps 7 [11]God is a righteous judge, a God who expresses his wrath every day.
Rom 1 [28]Furthermore, since they did not think it worthwhile to retain the knowledge of God, he gave them over to a depraved mind, to do what ought not to be done. [29]They have become filled with every kind of wickedness, evil, greed and depravity. They are full of envy, murder, strife, deceit and malice. They are gossips, [30]slanderers, God-haters, insolent, arrogant and boastful; they invent ways of doing evil; they disobey their parents; [31]they are senseless, faithless, heartless, ruthless. [32]Although they know God's righteous decree that those who do such things deserve death, they not only continue to do these very things but also approve of those who practice them.
2 Pet 2 [1]But there were also false prophets among the people, just as there will be false teachers among you. They will secretly introduce destructive heresies, even denying the sovereign Lord who bought them—bringing swift destruction on themselves. [2]Many will follow their shameful ways and will bring the way of truth into disrepute. [3]In their greed these teachers will exploit you with stories they have made up. Their condemnation has long been hanging over them, and their destruction has not been sleeping.

[4]For if God did not spare angels when they sinned, but sent them to hell, putting them into gloomy dungeons to be held for judgment; [5]if he did not spare the ancient world when he brought the flood on its ungodly people, but protected Noah, a

preacher of righteousness, and seven others; [6]if he condemned the cities of Sodom and Gomorrah by burning them to ashes, and made them an example of what is going to happen to the ungodly; [7]and if he rescued Lot, a righteous man, who was distressed by the filthy lives of lawless men [8](for that righteous man, living among them day after day, was tormented in his righteous soul by the lawless deeds he saw and heard)—[9]if this is so, then the Lord knows how to rescue godly men from trials and to hold the unrighteous for the day of judgment, while continuing their punishment. [10]This is especially true of those who follow the corrupt desire of the sinful nature and despise authority.

Bold and arrogant, these men are not afraid to slander celestial beings; [11]yet even angels, although they are stronger and more powerful, do not bring slanderous accusations against such beings in the presence of the Lord. [12]But these men blaspheme in matters they do not understand. They are like brute beasts, creatures of instinct, born only to be caught and destroyed, and like beasts they too will perish.

b) It Purifies Believers

1 Pet 4 [12]Dear friends, do not be surprised at the painful trial you are suffering, as though something strange were happening to you. [13]But rejoice that you participate in the sufferings of Christ, so that you may be overjoyed when his glory is revealed. [14]If you are insulted because of the name of Christ, you are blessed, for the Spirit of glory and of God rests on you. [15]If you suffer, it should not be as a murderer or thief or any other kind of criminal, or even as a meddler. [16]However, if you suffer as a Christian, do not be ashamed, but praise God that you bear that name. [17]For it is time for judgment to begin with the family of God; and if it begins with us, what will the outcome be for those who do not obey the gospel of God? [18]And, "If it is hard for the righteous to be saved, what will become of the ungodly and the sinner?"

[19]So then, those who suffer according to God's will should commit themselves to their faithful Creator and continue to do good.

3. The Judgment as Future

See p. 758b, It Is Future

VI
The Millennium

A. The Reign of Christ

1. He Crushes Wickedness

Isa 2 [2]In the last days the mountain of the LORD's temple will be established as chief among the mountains; it will be raised above the hills, and all nations will stream to it.

[3]Many peoples will come and say, "Come, let us go up to the mountain of the LORD, to the house of the God of Jacob. He will teach us his ways, so that we may walk in his paths." The law will go out from Zion, the word of the LORD from Jerusalem. [4]He will judge between the nations and will settle disputes for many peoples. They will beat their swords into plowshares and their spears into pruning hooks. Nation will not take up sword against nation, nor will they train for war anymore. . . . [9]So man will be brought low and mankind humbled—do not forgive them.

[10]Go into the rocks, hide in the ground from dread of the LORD and the splendor of his majesty! [11]The eyes of the arrogant man will be humbled and the pride of men brought low; the LORD alone will be exalted in that day.

[12]The LORD Almighty has a day in store for all the proud and lofty, for all that is exalted (and they will be humbled), [13]for all the cedars of Lebanon, tall and lofty, and all the oaks of Bashan, [14]for all the towering mountains and all the high hills, [15]for every lofty tower and every fortified wall, [16]for every trading ship and every stately vessel. [17]The arrogance of man will be brought low and the pride of men humbled; the LORD alone will be exalted in that day, [18]and the idols will totally disappear.

[19]Men will flee to caves in the rocks and to holes in the ground from dread of the LORD and the splendor of his majesty, when he rises to shake the earth. [20]In that day men will throw away to the rodents and bats their idols of silver and idols of gold, which they made to worship. [21]They will flee to caverns in the rocks and to the overhanging crags from dread of the LORD and the splendor of his majesty, when he rises to shake the earth.

Isa 24 [1]See, the LORD is going to lay waste the earth and devastate it; he will ruin its face and scatter its inhabitants—[2]it will be the same for priest as for people, for master as for servant, for mistress as for maid, for seller as for buyer, for borrower as for lender, for debtor as for creditor. [3]The earth will be completely laid waste and totally plundered. The LORD has spoken this word.

[4]The earth dries up and withers, the world languishes and withers, the exalted of the earth languish. [5]The earth is defiled by its people; they have disobeyed the laws, violated the statutes and broken the everlasting covenant. [6]Therefore a curse consumes the earth; its people must bear their guilt. Therefore earth's inhabitants are burned up, and very few are left. [7]The new wine dries up and the vine withers; all the merrymakers groan. [8]The gaiety of the tambourines is stilled, the noise of the revelers has stopped, the joyful harp is silent. [9]No longer do they drink wine with a song; the beer is bitter to its drinkers. [10]The ruined city lies desolate; the entrance to every house is barred. [11]In the streets they cry out for wine; all joy turns to gloom, all gaiety is banished from the earth. [12]The city is left in ruins, its gate is battered to pieces. [13]So will it be on the earth and among the nations, as when an olive tree is beaten, or as when gleanings are left after the grape harvest. . . . [16]From the ends of the earth we hear singing: "Glory to the Righteous One."

But I said, "I waste away, I waste away! Woe to me! The treacherous betray! With treachery the treacherous betray!" [17]Terror and pit and snare await you, O people of the earth. [18]Whoever flees at the sound of terror will fall into a pit; whoever climbs out of the pit will be caught in a snare.

The floodgates of the heavens are opened, the foundations of the earth shake. [19]The earth is broken up, the earth is split asunder, the earth is thoroughly shaken. [20]The earth reels like a drunkard, it sways like a hut in the wind; so heavy upon it is the guilt of its rebellion that it falls—never to rise again.

[21]In that day the LORD will punish the powers in the heavens above and the kings on the earth below. [22]They will be herded together like prisoners bound in a dungeon; they will be shut up in prison and be punished after many days. [23]The moon will be abashed, the sun ashamed; for the LORD Almighty will reign on Mount Zion and in Jerusalem, and before its elders, gloriously.

Isa 26 [20]Go, my people, enter your rooms and shut the doors behind you; hide yourselves for a little while until his wrath has passed by. [21]See, the LORD is coming out of his dwelling to punish the people of the earth for their sins. The earth will disclose the blood shed upon her; she will conceal her slain no longer.

2. He Restores His People Israel

Isa 25 [7]On this mountain he will destroy the shroud that enfolds all peoples, the sheet that covers all nations; [8]he will swallow up death forever. The Sovereign LORD will wipe away the tears from all faces; he will remove the disgrace of his people from all the earth. The LORD has spoken.

Isa 30 [26]The moon will shine like the sun, and the sunlight will be seven times brighter, like the light of seven full days, when the LORD binds up the bruises of his people and heals the wounds he inflicted.

Isa 51 [1]"Listen to me, you who pursue righteousness and who seek the LORD: Look to the rock from which you were cut and to the quarry from which you were hewn; [2]look to Abraham, your father, and to Sarah, who gave you birth. When I called him he was but one, and I blessed him and made him many. [3]The LORD will surely comfort Zion and will look with compassion on all her ruins; he will make her deserts like Eden, her wastelands like the garden of the LORD. Joy and gladness will be found in her, thanksgiving and the sound of singing.

[4]“Listen to me, my people; hear me, my nation: The law will go out from me; my justice will become a light to the nations. [5]My righteousness draws near speedily, my salvation is on the way, and my arm will bring justice to the nations. The islands will look to me and wait in hope for my arm. [6]Lift up your eyes to the heavens, look at the earth beneath; the heavens will vanish like smoke, the earth will wear out like a garment and its inhabitants die like flies. But my salvation will last forever, my righteousness will never fail.

[7]“Hear me, you who know what is right, you people who have my law in your hearts: Do not fear the reproach of men or be terrified by their insults. [8]For the moth will eat them up like a garment; the worm will devour them like wool. But my righteousness will last forever, my salvation through all generations.”

[9]Awake, awake! Clothe yourself with strength, O arm of the LORD; awake, as in days gone by, as in generations of old. Was it not you who cut Rahab to pieces, who pierced that monster through? [10]Was it not you who dried up the sea, the waters of the great deep, who made a road in the depths of the sea so that the redeemed might cross over? [11]The ransomed of the LORD will return. They will enter Zion with singing; everlasting joy will crown their heads. Gladness and joy will overtake them, and sorrow and sighing will flee away.

[12]“I, even I, am he who comforts you. Who are you that you fear mortal men, the sons of men, who are but grass, [13]that you forget the LORD your Maker, who stretched out the heavens and laid the foundations of the earth, that you live in constant terror every day because of the wrath of the oppressor, who is bent on destruction? For where is the wrath of the oppressor? [14]The cowering prisoners will soon be set free; they will not die in their dungeon, nor will they lack bread. [15]For I am the LORD your God, who churns up the sea so that its waves roar—the LORD Almighty is his name. [16]I have put my words in your mouth and covered you with the shadow of my hand—I who set the heavens in place, who laid the foundations of the earth, and who say to Zion, ‘You are my people.’”

Isa 52 [1]Awake, awake, O Zion, clothe yourself with strength. Put on your garments of splendor, O Jerusalem, the holy city. The uncircumcised and defiled will not enter you again. [2]Shake off your dust; rise up, sit enthroned, O Jerusalem. Free yourself from the chains on your neck, O captive Daughter of Zion.

[3]For this is what the LORD says: “You were sold for nothing, and without money you will be redeemed.”

[4]For this is what the Sovereign LORD says: “At first my people went down to Egypt to live; lately, Assyria has oppressed them.

[5]“And now what do I have here?” declares the LORD. “For my people have been taken away for nothing, and those who rule them mock,” declares the LORD. “And all day long my name is constantly blasphemed. [6]Therefore my people will know my name; therefore in that day they will know that it is I who foretold it. Yes, it is I.”

[7]How beautiful on the mountains are the feet of those who bring good news, who proclaim peace, who bring good tidings, who proclaim salvation, who say to Zion, “Your God reigns!” [8]Listen! Your watchmen lift up their voices; together they shout for joy. When the LORD returns to Zion, they will see it with their own eyes. [9]Burst into songs of joy together, you ruins of Jerusalem, for the LORD has comforted his people, he has redeemed Jerusalem. [10]The LORD will lay bare his holy arm in the sight of all the nations, and all the ends of the earth will see the salvation of our God.

[11]Depart, depart, go out from there! Touch no unclean thing! Come out from it and be pure, you who carry the vessels of the LORD. [12]But you will not leave in haste or go in flight; for the LORD will go before you, the God of Israel will be your rear guard.

Isa 65 [17]“Behold, I will create new heavens and a new earth. The former things will not be remembered, nor will they come to mind. [18]But be glad and rejoice forever in what I will create, for I will create Jerusalem to be a delight and its people a joy. [19]I will rejoice over Jerusalem and take delight in my people; the sound of weeping and of crying will be heard in it no more.”

Ezek 36 [24]“‘For I will take you out of the nations; I will gather you from all the countries and bring you back into your own land. [25]I will sprinkle clean water on you, and you will be clean; I will cleanse you from all your impurities and from all your idols. [26]I will give you a new heart and put a new spirit in you; I will remove from you your heart of stone and give you a heart of flesh. [27]And I will put my Spirit in you and move you to follow my decrees and be careful to keep my laws. [28]You will live in the land I gave your forefathers; you will be my people, and I will be your God. [29]I will save you from all your uncleanness. I will call for the grain and make it plentiful and will not bring famine upon you. [30]I will increase the fruit of the trees and the crops of the field, so that you will no longer suffer disgrace among the nations because of famine. [31]Then you will remember your evil ways and wicked deeds, and you will loathe yourselves for your sins and detestable practices. [32]I want you to know that I am not doing this for your sake, declares the Sovereign LORD. Be ashamed and disgraced for your conduct, O house of Israel!

[33]“‘This is what the Sovereign LORD says: On the day I cleanse you from all your sins, I will resettle your towns, and the ruins will be rebuilt. [34]The desolate land will be cultivated instead of lying desolate in the sight of all who pass through it. [35]They will say, “This land that was laid waste has become like the garden of Eden; the cities that were lying in ruins, desolate and destroyed, are now fortified and inhabited.” [36]Then the nations around you that remain will know that I the LORD have rebuilt what was destroyed and have replanted what was desolate. I the LORD have spoken, and I will do it.’

[37]“This is what the Sovereign LORD says: Once again I will yield to the plea of the house of Israel and do this for them: I will make their people as numerous as sheep, [38]as numerous as the flocks for offerings at Jerusalem during her appointed feasts. So will the ruined cities be filled with flocks of people. Then they will know that I am the LORD.”

Ezek 37 [1]The hand of the LORD was upon me, and he brought me out by the Spirit of the LORD and set me in the middle of a valley; it was full of bones. [2]He led me back and forth among them, and I saw a great many bones on the floor of the valley, bones that were very dry. [3]He asked me, “Son of man, can these bones live?”

I said, “O Sovereign LORD, you alone know.”

[4]Then he said to me, “Prophesy to these bones and say to them, ‘Dry bones, hear the word of the LORD! [5]This is what the Sovereign LORD says to these bones: I will make breath enter you, and you will come to life. [6]I will attach tendons to you and make flesh come upon you and cover you with skin; I will put breath in you, and you will come to life. Then you will know that I am the LORD.’”

[7]So I prophesied as I was commanded. And as I was prophesying, there was a noise, a rattling sound, and the bones came together, bone to bone. [8]I looked, and tendons and flesh appeared on them and skin covered them, but there was no breath in them.

[9]Then he said to me, “Prophesy to the breath; prophesy, son of man, and say to it, ‘This is what the Sovereign LORD says: Come from the four winds, O breath, and breathe into these slain, that they may live.’” [10]So I prophesied as he commanded me, and breath entered them; they came to life and stood up on their feet—a vast army.

[11]Then he said to me: “Son of man, these bones are the whole house of Israel. They say, ‘Our bones are dried up and our hope is gone; we are cut off.’ [12]Therefore prophesy and say to them: ‘This is what the Sovereign LORD says: O my people, I am going to open your graves and bring you up from them; I will bring you back to the land of Israel. [13]Then you, my people, will know that I am the LORD, when I open your graves and bring you up from them. [14]I will put my Spirit in you and you will live, and I will settle you in your own land. Then you will know that I the LORD have spoken, and I have done it, declares the LORD.’”

[15]The word of the LORD came to me: [16]“Son of man, take a stick of wood and write on it, ‘Belonging to Judah and the Israelites associated with him.’ Then take another stick of

wood, and write on it, 'Ephraim's stick, belonging to Joseph and all the house of Israel associated with him.' 17Join them together into one stick so that they will become one in your hand.

18"When your countrymen ask you, 'Won't you tell us what you mean by this?' 19say to them, 'This is what the Sovereign LORD says: I am going to take the stick of Joseph—which is in Ephraim's hand—and of the Israelite tribes associated with him, and join it to Judah's stick, making them a single stick of wood, and they will become one in my hand.' 20Hold before their eyes the sticks you have written on 21and say to them, 'This is what the Sovereign LORD says: I will take the Israelites out of the nations where they have gone. I will gather them from all around and bring them back into their own land. 22I will make them one nation in the land, on the mountains of Israel. There will be one king over all of them and they will never again be two nations or be divided into two kingdoms. 23They will no longer defile themselves with their idols and vile images or with any of their offenses, for I will save them from all their sinful backsliding, and I will cleanse them. They will be my people, and I will be their God.

24"'My servant David will be king over them, and they will all have one shepherd. They will follow my laws and be careful to keep my decrees. 25They will live in the land I gave to my servant Jacob, the land where your fathers lived. They and their children and their children's children will live there forever, and David my servant will be their prince forever. 26I will make a covenant of peace with them; it will be an everlasting covenant. I will establish them and increase their numbers, and I will put my sanctuary among them forever. 27My dwelling place will be with them; I will be their God, and they will be my people. 28Then the nations will know that I the LORD make Israel holy, when my sanctuary is among them forever.'"

Hos 2 16"In that day," declares the LORD, "you will call me 'my husband'; you will no longer call me 'my master.' 17I will remove the names of the Baals from her lips; no longer will their names be invoked. . . . 19I will betroth you to me forever; I will betroth you in righteousness and justice, in love and compassion. 20I will betroth you in faithfulness, and you will acknowledge the LORD.

21"In that day I will respond," declares the LORD—"I will respond to the skies, and they will respond to the earth; 22and the earth will respond to the grain, the new wine and oil, and they will respond to Jezreel. 23I will plant her for myself in the land; I will show my love to the one I called 'Not my loved one.' I will say to those called 'Not my people,' 'You are my people'; and they will say, 'You are my God.'"

Zeph 3 11"On that day you will not be put to shame for all the wrongs you have done to me, because I will remove from this city those who rejoice in their pride. Never again will you be haughty on my holy hill. 12But I will leave within you the meek and humble, who trust in the name of the LORD. 13The remnant of Israel will do no wrong; they will speak no lies, nor will deceit be found in their mouths. They will eat and lie down and no one will make them afraid."

Zech 9 11As for you, because of the blood of my covenant with you, I will free your prisoners from the waterless pit. 12Return to your fortress, O prisoners of hope; even now I announce that I will restore twice as much to you. 13I will bend Judah as I bend my bow and fill it with Ephraim. I will rouse your sons, O Zion, against your sons, O Greece, and make you like a warrior's sword.

14Then the LORD will appear over them; his arrow will flash like lightning. The Sovereign LORD will sound the trumpet; he will march in the storms of the south, 15and the LORD Almighty will shield them. They will destroy and overcome with slingstones. They will drink and roar as with wine; they will be full like a bowl used for sprinkling the corners of the altar. 16The LORD their God will save them on that day as the flock of his people. They will sparkle in his land like jewels in a crown. 17How attractive and beautiful they will be! Grain will make the young men thrive, and new wine the young women.

Rom 11 25I do not want you to be ignorant of this mystery, brothers, so that you may not be conceited: Israel has experienced a hardening in part until the full number of the Gentiles has come in. 26And so all Israel will be saved, as it is written: "The deliverer will come from Zion; he will turn godlessness away from Jacob. 27And this is my covenant with them when I take away their sins."

3. He Is Supreme in All the Earth

Ps 68 31Envoys will come from Egypt; Cush will submit herself to God.

32Sing to God, O kingdoms of the earth, sing praise to the Lord. . . .

Ps 110 1The LORD says to my Lord: "Sit at my right hand until I make your enemies a footstool for your feet."

2The LORD will extend your mighty scepter from Zion; you will rule in the midst of your enemies. 3Your troops will be willing on your day of battle. Arrayed in holy majesty, from the womb of the dawn you will receive the dew of your youth.

Isa 2 1This is what Isaiah son of Amoz saw concerning Judah and Jerusalem: 2In the last days the mountain of the LORD's temple will be established as chief among the mountains; it will be raised above the hills, and all nations will stream to it.

Isa 52 10The LORD will lay bare his holy arm in the sight of all the nations, and all the ends of the earth will see the salvation of our God.

Dan 2 31"You looked, O king, and there before you stood a large statue—an enormous, dazzling statue, awesome in appearance. 32The head of the statue was made of pure gold, its chest and arms of silver, its belly and thighs of bronze, 33its legs of iron, its feet partly of iron and partly of baked clay. 34While you were watching, a rock was cut out, but not by human hands. It struck the statue on its feet of iron and clay and smashed them. 35Then the iron, the clay, the bronze, the silver and the gold were broken to pieces at the same time and became like chaff on a threshing floor in the summer. The wind swept them away without leaving a trace. But the rock that struck the statue became a huge mountain and filled the whole earth.

36"This was the dream, and now we will interpret it to the king. 37You, O king, are the king of kings. The God of heaven has given you dominion and power and might and glory; 38in your hands he has placed mankind and the beasts of the field and the birds of the air. Wherever they live, he has made you ruler over them all. You are that head of gold.

39"After you, another kingdom will rise, inferior to yours. Next, a third kingdom, one of bronze, will rule over the whole earth. 40Finally, there will be a fourth kingdom, strong as iron—for iron breaks and smashes everything—and as iron breaks things to pieces, so it will crush and break all the others. 41Just as you saw that the feet and toes were partly of baked clay and partly of iron, so this will be a divided kingdom; yet it will have some of the strength of iron in it, even as you saw iron mixed with clay. 42As the toes were partly iron and partly clay, so this kingdom will be partly strong and partly brittle. 43And just as you saw the iron mixed with baked clay, so the people will be a mixture and will not remain united, any more than iron mixes with clay.

44"In the time of those kings, the God of heaven will set up a kingdom that will never be destroyed, nor will it be left to another people. It will crush all those kingdoms and bring them to an end, but it will itself endure forever. 45This is the meaning of the vision of the rock cut out of a mountain, but not by human hands—a rock that broke the iron, the bronze, the clay, the silver and the gold to pieces.

"The great God has shown the king what will take place in the future. The dream is true and the interpretation is trustworthy."

Mic 4 1In the last days the mountain of the LORD's temple will be established as chief among the mountains; it will be raised above the hills, and peoples will stream to it.

Hab 2 3"For the revelation awaits an appointed time; it speaks of the end and will not prove false. Though it linger, wait for it; it will certainly come and will not delay. . . . 14For the earth will be filled with the knowledge of the glory of the LORD, as the waters cover the sea."

Zech 14 9The LORD will be king over the whole earth. On that day there will be one LORD, and his name the only name.

4. He Produces Worship of God by All Peoples

Ps 22 [27]All the ends of the earth will remember and turn to the LORD, and all the families of the nations will bow down before him, [28]for dominion belongs to the LORD and he rules over the nations.

[29]All the rich of the earth will feast and worship; all who go down to the dust will kneel before him—those who cannot keep themselves alive. [30]Posterity will serve him; future generations will be told about the Lord. [31]They will proclaim his righteousness to a people yet unborn—for he has done it.

Ps 68 [32]Sing to God, O kingdoms of the earth, sing praise to the Lord. . . .

Ps 86 [9]All the nations you have made will come and worship before you, O LORD; they will bring glory to your name.

Isa 2 [3]Many peoples will come and say, "Come, let us go up to the mountain of the LORD, to the house of the God of Jacob. He will teach us his ways, so that we may walk in his paths." The law will go out from Zion, the word of the LORD from Jerusalem.

Isa 24 [14]They raise their voices, they shout for joy; from the west they acclaim the LORD's majesty. [15]Therefore in the east give glory to the LORD; exalt the name of the LORD, the God of Israel, in the islands of the sea. [16]From the ends of the earth we hear singing: "Glory to the Righteous One."

But I said, "I waste away, I waste away! Woe to me! The treacherous betray! With treachery the treacherous betray!"

Isa 66 [22]"As the new heavens and the new earth that I make will endure before me," declares the LORD, "so will your name and descendants endure. [23]From one New Moon to another and from one Sabbath to another, all mankind will come and bow down before me," says the LORD.

Jer 4 [2]". . . and if in a truthful, just and righteous way you swear, 'As surely as the LORD lives,' then the nations will be blessed by him and in him they will glory."

Mic 4 [2]Many nations will come and say, "Come, let us go up to the mountain of the LORD, to the house of the God of Jacob. He will teach us his ways, so that we may walk in his paths." The law will go out from Zion, the word of the LORD from Jerusalem.

Mic 7 [16]Nations will see and be ashamed, deprived of all their power. They will lay their hands on their mouths and their ears will become deaf. [17]They will lick dust like a snake, like creatures that crawl on the ground. They will come trembling out of their dens; they will turn in fear to the LORD our God and will be afraid of you.

Zech 14 [1]A day of the LORD is coming when your plunder will be divided among you. . . .

[16]Then the survivors from all the nations that have attacked Jerusalem will go up year after year to worship the King, the LORD Almighty, and to celebrate the Feast of Tabernacles. [17]If any of the peoples of the earth do not go up to Jerusalem to worship the King, the LORD Almighty, they will have no rain. [18]If the Egyptian people do not go up and take part, they will have no rain. The LORD will bring on them the plague he inflicts on the nations that do not go up to celebrate the Feast of Tabernacles. [19]This will be the punishment of Egypt and the punishment of all the nations that do not go up to celebrate the Feast of Tabernacles.

[20]On that day HOLY TO THE LORD will be inscribed on the bells of the horses, and the cooking pots in the LORD's house will be like the sacred bowls in front of the altar. [21]Every pot in Jerusalem and Judah will be holy to the LORD Almighty, and all who come to sacrifice will take some of the pots and cook in them. And on that day there will no longer be a Canaanite in the house of the LORD Almighty.

B. Widespread Conversion

Ps 22 [27]All the ends of the earth will remember and turn to the LORD, and all the families of the nations will bow down before him, [28]for dominion belongs to the LORD and he rules over the nations.

Isa 4 [2]In that day the Branch of the LORD will be beautiful and glorious, and the fruit of the land will be the pride and glory of the survivors in Israel. [3]Those who are left in Zion, who remain in Jerusalem, will be called holy, all who are recorded among the living in Jerusalem. [4]The Lord will wash away the filth of the women of Zion; he will cleanse the bloodstains from Jerusalem by a spirit of judgment and a spirit of fire. [5]Then the LORD will create over all of Mount Zion and over those who assemble there a cloud of smoke by day and a glow of flaming fire by night; over all the glory will be a canopy. [6]It will be a shelter and shade from the heat of the day, and a refuge and hiding place from the storm and rain.

Isa 10 [20]In that day the remnant of Israel, the survivors of the house of Jacob, will no longer rely on him who struck them down but will truly rely on the LORD, the Holy One of Israel. [21]A remnant will return, a remnant of Jacob will return to the Mighty God.

Isa 59 [20]"The Redeemer will come to Zion, to those in Jacob who repent of their sins," declares the LORD.

Jer 31 [31]"The time is coming," declares the LORD, "when I will make a new covenant with the house of Israel and with the house of Judah. [32]It will not be like the covenant I made with their forefathers when I took them by the hand to lead them out of Egypt, because they broke my covenant, though I was a husband to them," declares the LORD. [33]"This is the covenant I will make with the house of Israel after that time," declares the LORD. "I will put my law in their minds and write it on their hearts. I will be their God, and they will be my people. [34]No longer will a man teach his neighbor, or a man his brother, saying, 'Know the LORD,' because they will all know me, from the least of them to the greatest," declares the LORD. "For I will forgive their wickedness and will remember their sins no more."

[35]This is what the LORD says, he who appoints the sun to shine by day, who decrees the moon and stars to shine by night, who stirs up the sea so that its waves roar—the LORD Almighty is his name: [36]"Only if these decrees vanish from my sight," declares the LORD, "will the descendants of Israel ever cease to be a nation before me."

[37]This is what the LORD says: "Only if the heavens above can be measured and the foundations of the earth below be searched out will I reject all the descendants of Israel because of all they have done," declares the LORD.

Joel 3 [17]"Then you will know that I, the LORD your God, dwell in Zion, my holy hill. Jerusalem will be holy; never again will foreigners invade her.

[18]"In that day the mountains will drip new wine, and the hills will flow with milk; all the ravines of Judah will run with water. A fountain will flow out of the LORD's house and will water the valley of acacias. [19]But Egypt will be desolate, Edom a desert waste, because of violence done to the people of Judah, in whose land they shed innocent blood. [20]Judah will be inhabited forever and Jerusalem through all generations. [21]Their bloodguilt, which I have not pardoned, I will pardon."

The LORD dwells in Zion!

Rom 11 [11]Again I ask: Did they stumble so as to fall beyond recovery? Not at all! Rather, because of their transgression, salvation has come to the Gentiles to make Israel envious. [12]But if their transgression means riches for the world, and their loss means riches for the Gentiles, how much greater riches will their fullness bring!

[13]I am talking to you Gentiles. Inasmuch as I am the apostle to the Gentiles, I make much of my ministry [14]in the hope that I may somehow arouse my own people to envy and save some of them. [15]For if their rejection is the reconciliation of the world, what will their acceptance be but life from the dead? [16]If the part of the dough offered as firstfruits is holy, then the whole batch is holy; if the root is holy, so are the branches.

[17]If some of the branches have been broken off, and you, though a wild olive shoot, have been grafted in among the others and now share in the nourishing sap from the olive root, [18]do not boast over those branches. If you do, consider this: You do not support the root, but the root supports you. [19]You will say then, "Branches were broken off so that I could be grafted in." [20]Granted. But they were broken off because of unbelief, and you stand by faith. Do not be arrogant, but be afraid. [21]For if God did not spare the natural branches, he will not spare you either.

[22]Consider therefore the kindness and sternness of God: sternness to those who fell, but kindness to you, provided that you continue in his kindness. Otherwise, you also will be cut off. [23]And if they do not persist in unbelief, they will be grafted in, for God is able to graft them in again. [24]After all, if you were cut out of an olive tree that is wild by nature, and contrary to nature were grafted into a cultivated olive tree, how much more readily will these, the natural branches, be grafted into their own olive tree!

[25]I do not want you to be ignorant of this mystery, brothers, so that you may not be conceited: Israel has experienced a hardening in part until the full number of the Gentiles has come in. [26]And so all Israel will be saved, as it is written: "The deliverer will come from Zion; he will turn godlessness away from Jacob. [27]And this is my covenant with them when I take away their sins."

[28]As far as the gospel is concerned, they are enemies on your account; but as far as election is concerned, they are loved on account of the patriarchs, [29]for God's gifts and his call are irrevocable. [30]Just as you who were at one time disobedient to God have now received mercy as a result of their disobedience, [31]so they too have now become disobedient in order that they too may now receive mercy as a result of God's mercy to you. [32]For God has bound all men over to disobedience so that he may have mercy on them all.

C. The Reigning of the Saints with God and Christ

Matt 19 [27]Peter answered him, "We have left everything to follow you! What then will there be for us?"

[28]Jesus said to them, "I tell you the truth, at the renewal of all things, when the Son of Man sits on his glorious throne, you who have followed me will also sit on twelve thrones, judging the twelve tribes of Israel."

Rev 2 [26]"To him who overcomes and does my will to the end, I will give authority over the nations—[27]'He will rule them with an iron scepter; he will dash them to pieces like pottery'—just as I have received authority from my Father."

Rev 3 [21]"To him who overcomes, I will give the right to sit with me on my throne, just as I overcame and sat down with my Father on his throne."

Rev 5 [9]And they sang a new song: "You are worthy to take the scroll and to open its seals, because you were slain, and with your blood you purchased men for God from every tribe and language and people and nation. [10]You have made them to be a kingdom and priests to serve our God, and they will reign on the earth."

Rev 20 [4]I saw thrones on which were seated those who had been given authority to judge. And I saw the souls of those who had been beheaded because of their testimony for Jesus and because of the word of God. They had not worshiped the beast or his image and had not received his mark on their foreheads or their hands. They came to life and reigned with Christ a thousand years. [5](The rest of the dead did not come to life until the thousand years were ended.) This is the first resurrection. [6]Blessed and holy are those who have part in the first resurrection. The second death has no power over them, but they will be priests of God and of Christ and will reign with him for a thousand years.

Rev 22 [5]There will be no more night. They will not need the light of a lamp or the light of the sun, for the Lord God will give them light. And they will reign for ever and ever.

D. The Binding of Satan

Rev 20 [1]And I saw an angel coming down out of heaven, having the key to the Abyss and holding in his hand a great chain. [2]He seized the dragon, that ancient serpent, who is the devil, or Satan, and bound him for a thousand years. [3]He threw him into the Abyss, and locked and sealed it over him, to keep him from deceiving the nations anymore until the thousand years were ended. After that, he must be set free for a short time.

E. Universal Peace and Blessing

Ps 46 [8]Come and see the works of the LORD, the desolations he has brought on the earth. [9]He makes wars cease to the ends of the earth; he breaks the bow and shatters the spear, he burns the shields with fire.

Isa 2 [4]He will judge between the nations and will settle disputes for many peoples. They will beat their swords into plowshares and their spears into pruning hooks. Nation will not take up sword against nation, nor will they train for war anymore.

Isa 9 [5]Every warrior's boot used in battle and every garment rolled in blood will be destined for burning, will be fuel for the fire. [6]For to us a child is born, to us a son is given, and the government will be on his shoulders. And he will be called Wonderful Counselor, Mighty God, Everlasting Father, Prince of Peace. [7]Of the increase of his government and peace there will be no end. He will reign on David's throne and over his kingdom, establishing and upholding it with justice and righteousness from that time on and forever. The zeal of the LORD Almighty will accomplish this.

Isa 11 [6]The wolf will live with the lamb, the leopard will lie down with the goat, the calf and the lion and the yearling together; and a little child will lead them. [7]The cow will feed with the bear, their young will lie down together, and the lion will eat straw like the ox. [8]The infant will play near the hole of the cobra, and the young child put his hand into the viper's nest. [9]They will neither harm nor destroy on all my holy mountain, for the earth will be full of the knowledge of the LORD as the waters cover the sea.

Isa 35 [1]The desert and the parched land will be glad; the wilderness will rejoice and blossom. Like the crocus, [2]it will burst into bloom; it will rejoice greatly and shout for joy. The glory of Lebanon will be given to it, the splendor of Carmel and Sharon; they will see the glory of the LORD, the splendor of our God.

[3]Strengthen the feeble hands, steady the knees that give way; [4]say to those with fearful hearts, "Be strong, do not fear; your God will come, he will come with vengeance; with divine retribution he will come to save you."

[5]Then will the eyes of the blind be opened and the ears of the deaf unstopped. [6]Then will the lame leap like a deer, and the mute tongue shout for joy. Water will gush forth in the wilderness and streams in the desert. [7]The burning sand will become a pool, the thirsty ground bubbling springs. In the haunts where jackals once lay, grass and reeds and papyrus will grow.

[8]And a highway will be there; it will be called the Way of Holiness. The unclean will not journey on it; it will be for those who walk in that Way; wicked fools will not go about on it. [9]No lion will be there, nor will any ferocious beast get up on it; they will not be found there. But only the redeemed will walk there, [10]and the ransomed of the LORD will return. They will enter Zion with singing; everlasting joy will crown their heads. Gladness and joy will overtake them, and sorrow and sighing will flee away.

Isa 55 [9]"As the heavens are higher than the earth, so are my ways higher than your ways and my thoughts than your thoughts. [10]As the rain and the snow come down from heaven, and do not return to it without watering the earth and making it bud and flourish, so that it yields seed for the sower and bread for the eater, [11]so is my word that goes out from my mouth: It will not return to me empty, but will accomplish what I desire and achieve the purpose for which I sent it. [12]You will go out in joy and be led forth in peace; the mountains and hills will burst into song before you, and all the trees of the field will clap their hands. [13]Instead of the thornbush will grow the pine tree, and instead of briers the myrtle will grow. This will be for the LORD's renown, for an everlasting sign, which will not be destroyed."

Isa 65 [20]"Never again will there be in it an infant who lives but a few days, or an old man who does not live out his years; he who dies at a hundred will be thought a mere youth; he who fails to reach a hundred will be considered accursed. [21]They will build houses and dwell in them; they will plant vineyards and eat their fruit. [22]No longer will they build houses and others live in them, or plant and others eat. For as the days of a tree, so will be the days of my people; my chosen ones will long enjoy the works of their hands. [23]They will not toil in vain or bear children doomed to misfortune; for they will be a people blessed by the LORD, they and their descendants with them. [24]Before they call I will answer; while they are still speaking I will hear. [25]The wolf and the lamb will feed together, and the lion will eat straw like the ox, but dust will be the serpent's food. They will neither harm nor destroy on all my holy mountain," says the LORD.

Hos 2 [18]"In that day I will make a covenant for them with the beasts of the field and the birds of the air and the creatures that move along the ground. Bow and sword and battle I will abolish from the land, so that all may lie down in safety."

Joel 3 [17]"Then you will know that I, the LORD your God, dwell in Zion, my holy hill. Jerusalem will be holy; never again will foreigners invade her.

[18]"In that day the mountains will drip new wine, and the hills will flow with milk; all the ravines of Judah will run with water. A fountain will flow out of the LORD's house and will water the valley of acacias. . . . [20]Judah will be inhabited forever and Jerusalem through all generations. [21]Their bloodguilt, which I have not pardoned, I will pardon."

The LORD dwells in Zion!

Amos 9 [11]"In that day I will restore David's fallen tent. I will repair its broken places, restore its ruins, and build it as it used to be, [12]so that they may possess the remnant of Edom and all the nations that bear my name," declares the LORD, who will do these things.

[13]"The days are coming," declares the LORD, "when the reaper will be overtaken by the plowman and the planter by the one treading grapes. New wine will drip from the mountains and flow from all the hills. [14]I will bring back my exiled people Israel; they will rebuild the ruined cities and live in them. They will plant vineyards and drink their wine; they will make gardens and eat their fruit. [15]I will plant Israel in their own land, never again to be uprooted from the land I have given them," says the LORD your God.

Mic 4 [1]In the last days the mountain of the LORD's temple will be established as chief among the mountains; it will be raised above the hills, and peoples will stream to it.

[2]Many nations will come and say, "Come, let us go up to the mountain of the LORD, to the house of the God of Jacob. He will teach us his ways, so that we may walk in his paths." The law will go out from Zion, the word of the LORD from Jerusalem. [3]He will judge between many peoples and will settle disputes for strong nations far and wide. They will beat their swords into plowshares and their spears into pruning hooks. Nation will not take up sword against nation, nor will they train for war anymore. [4]Every man will sit under his own vine and under his own fig tree, and no one will make them afraid, for the LORD Almighty has spoken. [5]All the nations may walk in the name of their gods; we will walk in the name of the LORD our God for ever and ever.

Zeph 3 [9]"Then will I purify the lips of the peoples, that all of them may call on the name of the LORD and serve him shoulder to shoulder. [10]From beyond the rivers of Cush my worshipers, my scattered people, will bring me offerings. [11]On that day you will not be put to shame for all the wrongs you have done to me, because I will remove from this city those who rejoice in their pride. Never again will you be haughty on my holy hill. [12]But I will leave within you the meek and humble, who trust in the name of the LORD. [13]The remnant of Israel will do no wrong; they will speak no lies, nor will deceit be found in their mouths. They will eat and lie down and no one will make them afraid."

[14]Sing, O Daughter of Zion; shout aloud, O Israel! Be glad and rejoice with all your heart, O Daughter of Jerusalem! [15]The LORD has taken away your punishment, he has turned back your enemy. The LORD, the King of Israel, is with you; never again will you fear any harm. [16]On that day they will say to Jerusalem, "Do not fear, O Zion; do not let your hands hang limp. [17]The LORD your God is with you, he is mighty to save. He will take great delight in you, he will quiet you with his love, he will rejoice over you with singing."

[18]"The sorrows for the appointed feasts I will remove from you; they are a burden and a reproach to you. [19]At that time I will deal with all who oppressed you; I will rescue the lame and gather those who have been scattered. I will give them praise and honor in every land where they were put to shame. [20]At that time I will gather you; at that time I will bring you home. I will give you honor and praise among all the peoples of the earth when I restore your fortunes before your very eyes," says the LORD.

Zech 9 [10]I will take away the chariots from Ephraim and the war-horses from Jerusalem, and the battle bow will be broken. He will proclaim peace to the nations. His rule will extend from sea to sea and from the River to the ends of the earth. [11]As for you, because of the blood of my covenant with you, I will free your prisoners from the waterless pit.

Zech 14 [6]On that day there will be no light, no cold or frost. [7]It will be a unique day, without daytime or nighttime—a day known to the LORD. When evening comes, there will be light.

[8]On that day living water will flow out from Jerusalem, half to the eastern sea and half to the western sea, in summer and in winter.

[9]The LORD will be king over the whole earth. On that day there will be one LORD, and his name the only name. . . .

[20]On that day HOLY TO THE LORD will be inscribed on the bells of the horses, and the cooking pots in the LORD's house will be like the sacred bowls in front of the altar. [21]Every pot in Jerusalem and Judah will be holy to the LORD Almighty, and all who come to sacrifice will take some of the pots and cook in them. And on that day there will no longer be a Canaanite in the house of the LORD Almighty.

F. Final Rebellion and Judgment

Ezek 38 [1]The word of the LORD came to me: [2]"Son of man, set your face against Gog, of the land of Magog, the chief prince of Meshech and Tubal; prophesy against him [3]and say: 'This is what the Sovereign LORD says: I am against you, O Gog, chief prince of Meshech and Tubal. [4]I will turn you around, put hooks in your jaws and bring you out with your whole army—your horses, your horsemen fully armed, and a great horde with large and small shields, all of them brandishing their swords. [5]Persia, Cush and Put will be with them, all with shields and helmets, [6]also Gomer with all its troops, and Beth Togarmah from the far north with all its troops—the many nations with you.

[7]"'Get ready; be prepared, you and all the hordes gathered about you, and take command of them. [8]After many days you will be called to arms. In future years you will invade a land that has recovered from war, whose people were gathered from many nations to the mountains of Israel, which had long been desolate. They had been brought out from the nations, and now all of them live in safety. [9]You and all your troops and the many nations with you will go up, advancing like a storm; you will be like a cloud covering the land.

[10]"'This is what the Sovereign LORD says: On that day thoughts will come into your mind and you will devise an evil scheme. [11]You will say, "I will invade a land of unwalled villages; I will attack a peaceful and unsuspecting people—all of them living without walls and without gates and bars. [12]I will plunder and loot and turn my hand against the resettled ruins and the people gathered from the nations, rich in livestock and goods, living at the center of the land." [13]Sheba and Dedan and the merchants of Tarshish and all her villages will say to you, "Have you come to plunder? Have you gathered your hordes to loot, to carry off silver and gold, to take away livestock and goods and to seize much plunder?"'

[14]"Therefore, son of man, prophesy and say to Gog: 'This is what the Sovereign LORD says: In that day, when my people Israel are living in safety, will you not take notice of it? [15]You will come from your place in the far north, you and many nations with you, all of them riding on horses, a great horde, a mighty army. [16]You will advance against my people Israel like a cloud that covers the land. In days to come, O Gog, I will bring you against my land, so that the nations may know me when I show myself holy through you before their eyes.

17"'This is what the Sovereign LORD says: Are you not the one I spoke of in former days by my servants the prophets of Israel? At that time they prophesied for years that I would bring you against them. 18This is what will happen in that day: When Gog attacks the land of Israel, my hot anger will be aroused, declares the Sovereign LORD. 19In my zeal and fiery wrath I declare that at that time there shall be a great earthquake in the land of Israel. 20The fish of the sea, the birds of the air, the beasts of the field, every creature that moves along the ground, and all the people on the face of the earth will tremble at my presence. The mountains will be overturned, the cliffs will crumble and every wall will fall to the ground. 21I will summon a sword against Gog on all my mountains, declares the Sovereign LORD. Every man's sword will be against his brother. 22I will execute judgment upon him with plague and bloodshed; I will pour down torrents of rain, hailstones and burning sulfur on him and on his troops and on the many nations with him. 23And so I will show my greatness and my holiness, and I will make myself known in the sight of many nations. Then they will know that I am the LORD.'

39 1"Son of man, prophesy against Gog and say: 'This is what the Sovereign LORD says: I am against you, O Gog, chief prince of Meshech and Tubal. 2I will turn you around and drag you along. I will bring you from the far north and send you against the mountains of Israel. 3Then I will strike your bow from your left hand and make your arrows drop from your right hand. 4On the mountains of Israel you will fall, you and all your troops and the nations with you. I will give you as food to all kinds of carrion birds and to the wild animals. 5You will fall in the open field, for I have spoken, declares the Sovereign LORD. 6I will send fire on Magog and on those who live in safety in the coastlands, and they will know that I am the LORD.

7"'I will make known my holy name among my people Israel. I will no longer let my holy name be profaned, and the nations will know that I the LORD am the Holy One in Israel. 8It is coming! It will surely take place, declares the Sovereign LORD. This is the day I have spoken of. . . .

11"'On that day I will give Gog a burial place in Israel, in the valley of those who travel east toward the Sea. It will block the way of travelers, because Gog and all his hordes will be buried there. So it will be called the Valley of Hamon Gog.'"

Rev 20 7When the thousand years are over, Satan will be released from his prison 8and will go out to deceive the nations in the four corners of the earth—Gog and Magog—to gather them for battle. In number they are like the sand on the seashore. 9They marched across the breadth of the earth and surrounded the camp of God's people, the city he loves. But fire came down from heaven and devoured them. 10And the devil, who deceived them, was thrown into the lake of burning sulfur, where the beast and the false prophet had been thrown. They will be tormented day and night for ever and ever.

VII
Heaven

A. Descriptions of Heaven

1. Barn

Matt 3 11"I baptize you with water for repentance. But after me will come one who is more powerful than I, whose sandals I am not fit to carry. He will baptize you with the Holy Spirit and with fire. 12His winnowing fork is in his hand, and he will clear his threshing floor, gathering his wheat into the barn and burning up the chaff with unquenchable fire."

Matt 13 24Jesus told them another parable: "The kingdom of heaven is like a man who sowed good seed in his field. 25But while everyone was sleeping, his enemy came and sowed weeds among the wheat, and went away. 26When the wheat sprouted and formed heads, then the weeds also appeared.

27"The owner's servants came to him and said, 'Sir, didn't you sow good seed in your field? Where then did the weeds come from?'

28"'An enemy did this,' he replied.

"The servants asked him, 'Do you want us to go and pull them up?'

29"'No,' he answered, 'because while you are pulling the weeds, you may root up the wheat with them. 30Let both grow together until the harvest. At that time I will tell the harvesters: First collect the weeds and tie them in bundles to be burned; then gather the wheat and bring it into my barn.'"

2. Better and Lasting Possession

Heb 10 34You sympathized with those in prison and joyfully accepted the confiscation of your property, because you knew that you yourselves had better and lasting possessions.

3. City of the Living God

Heb 12 22But you have come to Mount Zion, to the heavenly Jerusalem, the city of the living God. You have come to thousands upon thousands of angels in joyful assembly. . . .

4. City of My God

Rev 3 12"Him who overcomes I will make a pillar in the temple of my God. Never again will he leave it. I will write on him the name of my God and the name of the city of my God, the new Jerusalem, which is coming down out of heaven from my God; and I will also write on him my new name."

5. Eternal Inheritance

Heb 9 15For this reason Christ is the mediator of a new covenant, that those who are called may receive the promised eternal inheritance—now that he has died as a ransom to set them free from the sins committed under the first covenant.

6. Father's House

John 14 1"Do not let your hearts be troubled. Trust in God; trust also in me. 2In my Father's house are many rooms; if it were not so, I would have told you. I am going there to prepare a place for you. 3And if I go and prepare a place for you, I will come back and take you to be with me that you also may be where I am. 4You know the way to the place where I am going."

7. Glory

Ps 73 24You guide me with your counsel, and afterward you will take me into glory.

2 Cor 4 17For our light and momentary troubles are achieving for us an eternal glory that far outweighs them all. 18So we fix our eyes not on what is seen, but on what is unseen. For what is seen is temporary, but what is unseen is eternal.

1 Thess 2 11For you know that we dealt with each of you as a father deals with his own children, 12encouraging, comforting and urging you to live lives worthy of God, who calls you into his kingdom and glory.

1 Pet 1 11trying to find out the time and circumstances to which the Spirit of Christ in them was pointing when he predicted the sufferings of Christ and the glories that would follow.

8. Heaven

Matt 6 19"Do not store up for yourselves treasures on earth, where moth and rust destroy, and where thieves break in and steal. 20But store up for yourselves treasures in heaven, where moth and rust do not destroy, and where thieves do not break in and steal. 21For where your treasure is, there your heart will be also."

Luke 10 20"However, do not rejoice that the spirits submit to you, but rejoice that your names are written in heaven."

Acts 7 55But Stephen, full of the Holy Spirit, looked up to heaven and saw the glory of God, and Jesus standing at the right hand of God. 56"Look," he said, "I see heaven open and the Son of Man standing at the right hand of God."

2 Cor 5 1Now we know that if the earthly tent we live in is destroyed, we have a building from God, an eternal house in heaven, not built by human hands.

9. Heavenly Country

Heb 11 [13]All these people were still living by faith when they died. They did not receive the things promised; they only saw them and welcomed them from a distance. And they admitted that they were aliens and strangers on earth. [14]People who say such things show that they are looking for a country of their own. [15]If they had been thinking of the country they had left, they would have had opportunity to return. [16]Instead, they were longing for a better country—a heavenly one. Therefore God is not ashamed to be called their God, for he has prepared a city for them.

10. Heavenly Jerusalem

Heb 12 [22]But you have come to Mount Zion, to the heavenly Jerusalem, the city of the living God. You have come to thousands upon thousands of angels in joyful assembly. . . .

11. Holy City

Rev 21 [1]Then I saw a new heaven and a new earth, for the first heaven and the first earth had passed away, and there was no longer any sea. [2]I saw the Holy City, the new Jerusalem, coming down out of heaven from God, prepared as a bride beautifully dressed for her husband.

12. Home of Righteousness

2 Pet 3 [13]But in keeping with his promise we are looking forward to a new heaven and a new earth, the home of righteousness.

13. Kingdom of God and Christ

Matt 25 [34]"Then the King will say to those on his right, 'Come, you who are blessed by my Father; take your inheritance, the kingdom prepared for you since the creation of the world.'"
Luke 22 [29]"And I confer on you a kingdom, just as my Father conferred one on me, [30]so that you may eat and drink at my table in my kingdom and sit on thrones, judging the twelve tribes of Israel."
Acts 14 [22]strengthening the disciples and encouraging them to remain true to the faith. "We must go through many hardships to enter the kingdom of God," they said.
Eph 5 [5]For of this you can be sure: No immoral, impure or greedy person—such a man is an idolater—has any inheritance in the kingdom of Christ and of God.
1 Thess 2 [11]For you know that we dealt with each of you as a father deals with his own children, [12]encouraging, comforting and urging you to live lives worthy of God, who calls you into his kingdom and glory.
2 Thess 1 [5]All this is evidence that God's judgment is right, and as a result you will be counted worthy of the kingdom of God, for which you are suffering.

14. Kingdom of Light

Col 1 [12]giving thanks to the Father, who has qualified you to share in the inheritance of the saints in the kingdom of light.

15. Kingdom That Cannot Be Shaken

Heb 12 [28]Therefore, since we are receiving a kingdom that cannot be shaken, let us be thankful, and so worship God acceptably with reverence and awe. . . .

16. Mount Zion

Heb 12 [22]But you have come to Mount Zion, to the heavenly Jerusalem, the city of the living God. You have come to thousands upon thousands of angels in joyful assembly. . . .
Rev 14 [1]Then I looked, and there before me was the Lamb, standing on Mount Zion, and with him 144,000 who had his name and his Father's name written on their foreheads. [2]And I heard a sound from heaven like the roar of rushing waters and like a loud peal of thunder. The sound I heard was like that of harpists playing their harps. [3]And they sang a new song before the throne and before the four living creatures and the elders. No one could learn the song except the 144,000 who had been redeemed from the earth.

17. New Jerusalem

Rev 3 [11]"I am coming soon. Hold on to what you have, so that no one will take your crown. [12]Him who overcomes I will make a pillar in the temple of my God. Never again will he leave it. I will write on him the name of my God and the name of the city of my God, the new Jerusalem, which is coming down out of heaven from my God; and I will also write on him my new name."
Rev 21 [1]Then I saw a new heaven and a new earth, for the first heaven and the first earth had passed away, and there was no longer any sea. [2]I saw the Holy City, the new Jerusalem, coming down out of heaven from God, prepared as a bride beautifully dressed for her husband. [3]And I heard a loud voice from the throne saying, "Now the dwelling of God is with men, and he will live with them. They will be his people, and God himself will be with them and be their God. [4]He will wipe every tear from their eyes. There will be no more death or mourning or crying or pain, for the old order of things has passed away."

[5]He who was seated on the throne said, "I am making everything new!" Then he said, "Write this down, for these words are trustworthy and true."

[6]He said to me: "It is done. I am the Alpha and the Omega, the Beginning and the End. To him who is thirsty I will give to drink without cost from the spring of the water of life. [7]He who overcomes will inherit all this, and I will be his God and he will be my son. [8]But the cowardly, the unbelieving, the vile, the murderers, the sexually immoral, those who practice magic arts, the idolaters and all liars—their place will be in the fiery lake of burning sulfur. This is the second death."

[9]One of the seven angels who had the seven bowls full of the seven last plagues came and said to me, "Come, I will show you the bride, the wife of the Lamb." [10]And he carried me away in the Spirit to a mountain great and high, and showed me the Holy City, Jerusalem, coming down out of heaven from God. [11]It shone with the glory of God, and its brilliance was like that of a very precious jewel, like a jasper, clear as crystal. [12]It had a great, high wall with twelve gates, and with twelve angels at the gates. On the gates were written the names of the twelve tribes of Israel. [13]There were three gates on the east, three on the north, three on the south and three on the west. [14]The wall of the city had twelve foundations, and on them were the names of the twelve apostles of the Lamb.

[15]The angel who talked with me had a measuring rod of gold to measure the city, its gates and its walls. [16]The city was laid out like a square, as long as it was wide. He measured the city with the rod and found it to be 12,000 stadia in length, and as wide and high as it is long. [17]He measured its wall and it was 144 cubits thick, by man's measurement, which the angel was using. [18]The wall was made of jasper, and the city of pure gold, as pure as glass. [19]The foundations of the city walls were decorated with every kind of precious stone. The first foundation was jasper, the second sapphire, the third chalcedony, the fourth emerald, [20]the fifth sardonyx, the sixth carnelian, the seventh chrysolite, the eighth beryl, the ninth topaz, the tenth chrysoprase, the eleventh jacinth, and the twelfth amethyst. [21]The twelve gates were twelve pearls, each gate made of a single pearl. The great street of the city was of pure gold, like transparent glass.

[22]I did not see a temple in the city, because the Lord God Almighty and the Lamb are its temple. [23]The city does not need the sun or the moon to shine on it, for the glory of God gives it light, and the Lamb is its lamp. [24]The nations will walk by its light, and the kings of the earth will bring their splendor into it. [25]On no day will its gates ever be shut, for there will be no night there. [26]The glory and honor of the nations will be brought into it. [27]Nothing impure will ever enter it, nor will anyone who does what is shameful or deceitful, but only those whose names are written in the Lamb's book of life.

22 [1]Then the angel showed me the river of the water of life, as clear as crystal, flowing from the throne of God and of the Lamb [2]down the middle of the great street of the city. On each side of the river stood the tree of life, bearing twelve crops of fruit, yielding its fruit every month. And the leaves of the tree are for the healing of the nations. [3]No longer will there be any curse. The throne of God and of the Lamb will be in the city, and his servants will serve him. [4]They will see his face, and his name will be on their foreheads. [5]There will be no more night. They will not need the light of a lamp or the light of the sun, for the Lord God will give them light. And they will reign for ever and ever.

18. Paradise of God

Rev 2 [7]"He who has an ear, let him hear what the Spirit says to the churches. To him who overcomes, I will give the right to eat from the tree of life, which is in the paradise of God."

19. Rest

Heb 4 [1]Therefore, since the promise of entering his rest still stands, let us be careful that none of you be found to have fallen short of it. [2]For we also have had the gospel preached to us, just as they did; but the message they heard was of no value to them, because those who heard did not combine it with faith. [3]Now we who have believed enter that rest, just as God has said, "So I declared on oath in my anger, 'They shall never enter my rest.'" And yet his work has been finished since the creation of the world. [4]For somewhere he has spoken about the seventh day in these words: "And on the seventh day God rested from all his work." [5]And again in the passage above he says, "They shall never enter my rest."

[6]It still remains that some will enter that rest, and those who formerly had the gospel preached to them did not go in, because of their disobedience. [7]Therefore God again set a certain day, calling it Today, when a long time later he spoke through David, as was said before: "Today, if you hear his voice, do not harden your hearts." [8]For if Joshua had given them rest, God would not have spoken later about another day. [9]There remains, then, a Sabbath-rest for the people of God; [10]for anyone who enters God's rest also rests from his own work, just as God did from his. [11]Let us, therefore, make every effort to enter that rest, so that no one will fall by following their example of disobedience.

B. The Nature of Heaven

1. Heaven Is Where God Dwells

See p. 38a, God Dwells in Heaven

2. Heaven Is Where Angels Dwell

See p. 283a, Angels Live in Heaven

3. Heaven Is Where Believers Will Dwell

a) It Is Eternal Life

John 3 [15]". . . that everyone who believes in him may have eternal life.

[16]"For God so loved the world that he gave his one and only Son, that whoever believes in him shall not perish but have eternal life."

John 10 [28]"I give them eternal life, and they shall never perish; no one can snatch them out of my hand. [29]My Father, who has given them to me, is greater than all; no one can snatch them out of my Father's hand."

Acts 13 [48]When the Gentiles heard this, they were glad and honored the word of the Lord; and all who were appointed for eternal life believed.

Rom 6 [22]But now that you have been set free from sin and have become slaves to God, the benefit you reap leads to holiness, and the result is eternal life. [23]For the wages of sin is death, but the gift of God is eternal life in Christ Jesus our Lord.

Titus 3 [7]so that, having been justified by his grace, we might become heirs having the hope of eternal life.

1 John 5 [11]And this is the testimony: God has given us eternal life, and this life is in his Son. [12]He who has the Son has life; he who does not have the Son of God does not have life.

[13]I write these things to you who believe in the name of the Son of God so that you may know that you have eternal life.

Jude [21]Keep yourselves in God's love as you wait for the mercy of our Lord Jesus Christ to bring you to eternal life.

b) It Is Everlasting

2 Cor 4 [17]For our light and momentary troubles are achieving for us an eternal glory that far outweighs them all. [18]So we fix our eyes not on what is seen, but on what is unseen. For what is seen is temporary, but what is unseen is eternal.

2 Cor 5 [1]Now we know that if the earthly tent we live in is destroyed, we have a building from God, an eternal house in heaven, not built by human hands.

c) It Is the Home of Believers

Matt 8 [10]When Jesus heard this, he was astonished and said to those following him, "I tell you the truth, I have not found anyone in Israel with such great faith. [11]I say to you that many will come from the east and the west, and will take their places at the feast with Abraham, Isaac and Jacob in the kingdom of heaven."

2 Cor 5 [6]Therefore we are always confident and know that as long as we are at home in the body we are away from the Lord. . . . [8]We are confident, I say, and would prefer to be away from the body and at home with the Lord.

Phil 3 [20]But our citizenship is in heaven. And we eagerly await a Savior from there, the Lord Jesus Christ. . . .

Rev 7 [9]After this I looked and there before me was a great multitude that no one could count, from every nation, tribe, people and language, standing before the throne and in front of the Lamb. They were wearing white robes and were holding palm branches in their hands. [10]And they cried out in a loud voice: "Salvation belongs to our God, who sits on the throne, and to the Lamb."

d) It Is Inconceivable

1 Cor 2 [9]However, as it is written: "No eye has seen, no ear has heard, no mind has conceived what God has prepared for those who love him.". . .

2 Cor 4 [17]For our light and momentary troubles are achieving for us an eternal glory that far outweighs them all.

e) It Is the Inheritance of Believers

Rom 8 [16]The Spirit himself testifies with our spirit that we are God's children. [17]Now if we are children, then we are heirs—heirs of God and co-heirs with Christ, if indeed we share in his sufferings in order that we may also share in his glory.

Gal 3 [18]For if the inheritance depends on the law, then it no longer depends on a promise; but God in his grace gave it to Abraham through a promise.

Eph 1 [13]And you also were included in Christ when you heard the word of truth, the gospel of your salvation. Having believed, you were marked in him with a seal, the promised Holy Spirit, [14]who is a deposit guaranteeing our inheritance until the redemption of those who are God's possession—to the praise of his glory. . . . [18]I pray also that the eyes of your heart may be enlightened in order that you may know the hope to which he has called you, the riches of his glorious inheritance in the saints. . . .

Eph 3 [6]This mystery is that through the gospel the Gentiles are heirs together with Israel, members together of one body, and sharers together in the promise in Christ Jesus.

James 2 [5]Listen, my dear brothers: Has not God chosen those who are poor in the eyes of the world to be rich in faith and to inherit the kingdom he promised those who love him?

1 Pet 1 [3]Praise be to the God and Father of our Lord Jesus Christ! In his great mercy he has given us new birth into a living hope through the resurrection of Jesus Christ from the dead, [4]and into an inheritance that can never perish, spoil or fade—kept in heaven for you. . . .

Rev 21 [6]He said to me: "It is done. I am the Alpha and the Omega, the Beginning and the End. To him who is thirsty I will give to drink without cost from the spring of the water of life.

[7]He who overcomes will inherit all this, and I will be his God and he will be my son."

f) It Is Life (to Come)

Matt 19 [17]"Why do you ask me about what is good?" Jesus replied. "There is only One who is good. If you want to enter life, obey the commandments."
Acts 11 [18]When they heard this, they had no further objections and praised God, saying, "So then, God has granted even the Gentiles repentance unto life."
1 Tim 4 [8]For physical training is of some value, but godliness has value for all things, holding promise for both the present life and the life to come.
1 Tim 6 [19]In this way they will lay up treasure for themselves as a firm foundation for the coming age, so that they may take hold of the life that is truly life.

g) It Is a Place of Reward

Matt 5 [12]"Rejoice and be glad, because great is your reward in heaven, for in the same way they persecuted the prophets who were before you."
Mark 10 [21]Jesus looked at him and loved him. "One thing you lack," he said. "Go, sell everything you have and give to the poor, and you will have treasure in heaven. Then come, follow me."
Luke 18 [22]When Jesus heard this, he said to him, "You still lack one thing. Sell everything you have and give to the poor, and you will have treasure in heaven. Then come, follow me."
1 Pet 1 [3]Praise be to the God and Father of our Lord Jesus Christ! In his great mercy he has given us new birth into a living hope through the resurrection of Jesus Christ from the dead, [4]and into an inheritance that can never perish, spoil or fade—kept in heaven for you. . . .

h) It Is Separation from the Wicked

1 Cor 6 [9]Do you not know that the wicked will not inherit the kingdom of God? Do not be deceived: Neither the sexually immoral nor idolaters nor adulterers nor male prostitutes nor homosexual offenders [10]nor thieves nor the greedy nor drunkards nor slanderers nor swindlers will inherit the kingdom of God. [11]And that is what some of you were. But you were washed, you were sanctified, you were justified in the name of the Lord Jesus Christ and by the Spirit of our God.
Gal 5 [19]The acts of the sinful nature are obvious: sexual immorality, impurity and debauchery; [20]idolatry and witchcraft; hatred, discord, jealousy, fits of rage, selfish ambition, dissensions, factions [21]and envy; drunkenness, orgies, and the like. I warn you, as I did before, that those who live like this will not inherit the kingdom of God.
Eph 5 [5]For of this you can be sure: No immoral, impure or greedy person—such a man is an idolater—has any inheritance in the kingdom of Christ and of God.
Rev 22 [14]"Blessed are those who wash their robes, that they may have the right to the tree of life and may go through the gates into the city. [15]Outside are the dogs, those who practice magic arts, the sexually immoral, the murderers, the idolaters and everyone who loves and practices falsehood."

C. Heaven Is Promised to Believers in Christ

1. It Is Promised to Those Who Are Righteous

Matt 25 [34]"Then the King will say to those on his right, 'Come, you who are blessed by my Father; take your inheritance, the kingdom prepared for you since the creation of the world. [35]For I was hungry and you gave me something to eat, I was thirsty and you gave me something to drink, I was a stranger and you invited me in, [36]I needed clothes and you clothed me, I was sick and you looked after me, I was in prison and you came to visit me.'

[37]"Then the righteous will answer him, 'Lord, when did we see you hungry and feed you, or thirsty and give you something to drink? [38]When did we see you a stranger and invite you in, or needing clothes and clothe you? [39]When did we see you sick or in prison and go to visit you?'

[40]"The King will reply, 'I tell you the truth, whatever you did for one of the least of these brothers of mine, you did for me.' . . .

[46]"Then they will go away to eternal punishment, but the righteous to eternal life."

2. It Is Promised to Those Who Are Spiritually Minded

Gal 6 [8]The one who sows to please his sinful nature, from that nature will reap destruction; the one who sows to please the Spirit, from the Spirit will reap eternal life.

3. It Is Promised to Those Who Die to Sin

Matt 18 [8]"If your hand or your foot causes you to sin, cut it off and throw it away. It is better for you to enter life maimed or crippled than to have two hands or two feet and be thrown into eternal fire. [9]And if your eye causes you to sin, gouge it out and throw it away. It is better for you to enter life with one eye than to have two eyes and be thrown into the fire of hell."
Rom 6 [8]Now if we died with Christ, we believe that we will also live with him. [9]For we know that since Christ was raised from the dead, he cannot die again; death no longer has mastery over him. [10]The death he died, he died to sin once for all; but the life he lives, he lives to God.

[11]In the same way, count yourselves dead to sin but alive to God in Christ Jesus.
2 Tim 2 [11]Here is a trustworthy saying: If we died with him, we will also live with him. . . .

4. It Is Promised to Those Who Endure

Matt 10 [22]"All men will hate you because of me, but he who stands firm to the end will be saved."
2 Tim 2 [10]Therefore I endure everything for the sake of the elect, that they too may obtain the salvation that is in Christ Jesus, with eternal glory.

[11]Here is a trustworthy saying: If we died with him, we will also live with him; [12]if we endure, we will also reign with him. If we disown him, he will also disown us. . . .

5. It Is Promised to Those Who Follow Christ

Matt 10 [37]"Anyone who loves his father or mother more than me is not worthy of me; anyone who loves his son or daughter more than me is not worthy of me; [38]and anyone who does not take his cross and follow me is not worthy of me. [39]Whoever finds his life will lose it, and whoever loses his life for my sake will find it."
Matt 19 [28]Jesus said to them, "I tell you the truth, at the renewal of all things, when the Son of Man sits on his glorious throne, you who have followed me will also sit on twelve thrones, judging the twelve tribes of Israel. [29]And everyone who has left houses or brothers or sisters or father or mother or children or fields for my sake will receive a hundred times as much and will inherit eternal life."
John 12 [26]"Whoever serves me must follow me; and where I am, my servant also will be. My Father will honor the one who serves me."
Rev 14 [4]These are those who did not defile themselves with women, for they kept themselves pure. They follow the Lamb wherever he goes. They were purchased from among men and offered as firstfruits to God and the Lamb. [5]No lie was found in their mouths; they are blameless.

6. It Is Promised to Those Who Have Been Redeemed

Rev 22 [14]"Blessed are those who wash their robes, that they may have the right to the tree of life and may go through the gates into the city."

7. It Is Promised to Those Who Love God

James 1 [12]Blessed is the man who perseveres under trial, because when he has stood the test, he will receive the crown of life that God has promised to those who love him.

8. It Is Promised to Those Who Obey God

Matt 19 [16]Now a man came up to Jesus and asked, "Teacher, what good thing must I do to get eternal life?"

[17]"Why do you ask me about what is good?" Jesus replied. "There is only One who is good. If you want to enter life, obey the commandments."

John 12 [47]"As for the person who hears my words but does not keep them, I do not judge him. For I did not come to judge the world, but to save it. [48]There is a judge for the one who rejects me and does not accept my words; that very word which I spoke will condemn him at the last day. . . . [50]I know that his command leads to eternal life. So whatever I say is just what the Father has told me to say."

9. It Is Promised to Those Who Overcome

Rev 2 [7]"He who has an ear, let him hear what the Spirit says to the churches. To him who overcomes, I will give the right to eat from the tree of life, which is in the paradise of God."

Rev 2 [11]"He who has an ear, let him hear what the Spirit says to the churches. He who overcomes will not be hurt at all by the second death."

Rev 2 [17]"He who has an ear, let him hear what the Spirit says to the churches. To him who overcomes, I will give some of the hidden manna. I will also give him a white stone with a new name written on it, known only to him who receives it."

Rev 3 [5]"He who overcomes will, like them, be dressed in white. I will never blot out his name from the book of life, but will acknowledge his name before my Father and his angels."

Rev 3 [12]"Him who overcomes I will make a pillar in the temple of my God. Never again will he leave it. I will write on him the name of my God and the name of the city of my God, the new Jerusalem, which is coming down out of heaven from my God; and I will also write on him my new name."

Rev 3 [21]"To him who overcomes, I will give the right to sit with me on my throne, just as I overcame and sat down with my Father on his throne."

Rev 21 [2]I saw the Holy City, the new Jerusalem, coming down out of heaven from God, prepared as a bride beautifully dressed for her husband. . . . [7]"He who overcomes will inherit all this, and I will be his God and he will be my son."

10. It Is Promised to Those Who Persevere

Rom 2 [7]To those who by persistence in doing good seek glory, honor and immortality, he will give eternal life.

11. It Is Promised to Those Who Repent

Acts 11 [18]When they heard this, they had no further objections and praised God, saying, "So then, God has granted even the Gentiles repentance unto life."

12. It Is Promised to Those Who Seek Godliness

1 Tim 4 [8]For physical training is of some value, but godliness has value for all things, holding promise for both the present life and the life to come.

13. It Is Promised to Those Who Serve God

Rom 6 [22]But now that you have been set free from sin and have become slaves to God, the benefit you reap leads to holiness, and the result is eternal life.

D. The Benefits of Heaven to Believers

1. Absence of Death

Isa 25 [8]he will swallow up death forever. The Sovereign LORD will wipe away the tears from all faces; he will remove the disgrace of his people from all the earth. The LORD has spoken.

1 Cor 15 [54]When the perishable has been clothed with the imperishable, and the mortal with immortality, then the saying that is written will come true: "Death has been swallowed up in victory."

2 Tim 1 [10]but it has now been revealed through the appearing of our Savior, Christ Jesus, who has destroyed death and has brought life and immortality to light through the gospel.

Rev 21 [4]"He will wipe every tear from their eyes. There will be no more death or mourning or crying or pain, for the old order of things has passed away."

2. Christ-likeness

Rom 8 [29]For those God foreknew he also predestined to be conformed to the likeness of his Son, that he might be the firstborn among many brothers.

Eph 5 [25]Husbands, love your wives, just as Christ loved the church and gave himself up for her [26]to make her holy, cleansing her by the washing with water through the word, [27]and to present her to himself as a radiant church, without stain or wrinkle or any other blemish, but holy and blameless.

1 John 3 [2]Dear friends, now we are children of God, and what we will be has not yet been made known. But we know that when he appears, we shall be like him, for we shall see him as he is.

3. Complete Moral Purity

Phil 3 [20]But our citizenship is in heaven. And we eagerly await a Savior from there, the Lord Jesus Christ, [21]who, by the power that enables him to bring everything under his control, will transform our lowly bodies so that they will be like his glorious body.

4. Complete Perfection

Rev 22 [3]No longer will there be any curse. The throne of God and of the Lamb will be in the city, and his servants will serve him.

5. Divine Sustenance

Luke 14 [15]When one of those at the table with him heard this, he said to Jesus, "Blessed is the man who will eat at the feast in the kingdom of God."

Luke 22 [29]"And I confer on you a kingdom, just as my Father conferred one on me, [30]so that you may eat and drink at my table in my kingdom and sit on thrones, judging the twelve tribes of Israel."

Rev 2 [17]"He who has an ear, let him hear what the Spirit says to the churches. To him who overcomes, I will give some of the hidden manna. I will also give him a white stone with a new name written on it, known only to him who receives it."

6. Drinking of the Water of Life

Rev 21 [6]He said to me: "It is done. I am the Alpha and the Omega, the Beginning and the End. To him who is thirsty I will give to drink without cost from the spring of the water of life."

Rev 22 [1]Then the angel showed me the river of the water of life, as clear as crystal, flowing from the throne of God and of the Lamb [2]down the middle of the great street of the city. On each side of the river stood the tree of life, bearing twelve crops of fruit, yielding its fruit every month. And the leaves of the tree are for the healing of the nations.

7. Eating from the Tree of Life

Rev 2 [7]"He who has an ear, let him hear what the Spirit says to the churches. To him who overcomes, I will give the right to eat from the tree of life, which is in the paradise of God."

8. A Glorified Body

2 Cor 5 [1]Now we know that if the earthly tent we live in is destroyed, we have a building from God, an eternal house in heaven, not built by human hands. [2]Meanwhile we groan, long-

ing to be clothed with our heavenly dwelling, 3because when we are clothed, we will not be found naked. 4For while we are in this tent, we groan and are burdened, because we do not wish to be unclothed but to be clothed with our heavenly dwelling, so that what is mortal may be swallowed up by life. 5Now it is God who has made us for this very purpose and has given us the Spirit as a deposit, guaranteeing what is to come.
Phil 3 20But our citizenship is in heaven. And we eagerly await a Savior from there, the Lord Jesus Christ, 21who, by the power that enables him to bring everything under his control, will transform our lowly bodies so that they will be like his glorious body.

9. Immortality

1 Cor 15 53For the perishable must clothe itself with the imperishable, and the mortal with immortality. 54When the perishable has been clothed with the imperishable, and the mortal with immortality, then the saying that is written will come true: "Death has been swallowed up in victory."
2 Tim 1 10but it has now been revealed through the appearing of our Savior, Christ Jesus, who has destroyed death and has brought life and immortality to light through the gospel.
Rev 2 11"He who has an ear, let him hear what the Spirit says to the churches. He who overcomes will not be hurt at all by the second death."

10. Intimate Fellowship with God and Christ

Isa 60 19"The sun will no more be your light by day, nor will the brightness of the moon shine on you, for the LORD will be your everlasting light, and your God will be your glory. 20Your sun will never set again, and your moon will wane no more; the LORD will be your everlasting light, and your days of sorrow will end."
John 12 26"Whoever serves me must follow me; and where I am, my servant also will be. My Father will honor the one who serves me."
John 14 3"And if I go and prepare a place for you, I will come back and take you to be with me that you also may be where I am."
John 17 24"Father, I want those you have given me to be with me where I am, and to see my glory, the glory you have given me because you loved me before the creation of the world."
2 Cor 5 6Therefore we are always confident and know that as long as we are at home in the body we are away from the Lord. 7We live by faith, not by sight. 8We are confident, I say, and would prefer to be away from the body and at home with the Lord.
Phil 1 23I am torn between the two: I desire to depart and be with Christ, which is better by far. . . .
1 Thess 4 17After that, we who are still alive and are left will be caught up together with them in the clouds to meet the Lord in the air. And so we will be with the Lord forever.
Rev 3 4"Yet you have a few people in Sardis who have not soiled their clothes. They will walk with me, dressed in white, for they are worthy. 5He who overcomes will, like them, be dressed in white. I will never blot out his name from the book of life, but will acknowledge his name before my Father and his angels."
Rev 3 12"Him who overcomes I will make a pillar in the temple of my God. Never again will he leave it. I will write on him the name of my God and the name of the city of my God, the new Jerusalem, which is coming down out of heaven from my God; and I will also write on him my new name."
Rev 19 6Then I heard what sounded like a great multitude, like the roar of rushing waters and like loud peals of thunder, shouting: "Hallelujah! For our Lord God Almighty reigns. 7Let us rejoice and be glad and give him glory! For the wedding of the Lamb has come, and his bride has made herself ready. 8Fine linen, bright and clean, was given her to wear." (Fine linen stands for the righteous acts of the saints.)

9Then the angel said to me, "Write: 'Blessed are those who are invited to the wedding supper of the Lamb.'" And he added, "These are the true words of God."

11. Joyfulness

Ps 16 11You have made known to me the path of life; you will fill me with joy in your presence, with eternal pleasures at your right hand.
Isa 35 10and the ransomed of the LORD will return. They will enter Zion with singing; everlasting joy will crown their heads. Gladness and joy will overtake them, and sorrow and sighing will flee away.
Rev 21 4"He will wipe every tear from their eyes. There will be no more death or mourning or crying or pain, for the old order of things has passed away."

12. Perfect Knowledge

1 Cor 13 12Now we see but a poor reflection as in a mirror; then we shall see face to face. Now I know in part; then I shall know fully, even as I am fully known.

13. Physical Well-being

Isa 33 24No one living in Zion will say, "I am ill"; and the sins of those who dwell there will be forgiven.
Rev 21 4"He will wipe every tear from their eyes. There will be no more death or mourning or crying or pain, for the old order of things has passed away."

14. Salvation

1 Pet 1 3Praise be to the God and Father of our Lord Jesus Christ! In his great mercy he has given us new birth into a living hope through the resurrection of Jesus Christ from the dead, 4and into an inheritance that can never perish, spoil or fade—kept in heaven for you, 5who through faith are shielded by God's power until the coming of the salvation that is ready to be revealed in the last time. . . . 8Though you have not seen him, you love him; and even though you do not see him now, you believe in him and are filled with an inexpressible and glorious joy, 9for you are receiving the goal of your faith, the salvation of your souls.
Rev 2 11"He who has an ear, let him hear what the Spirit says to the churches. He who overcomes will not be hurt at all by the second death."

15. Satisfaction of All Needs

Rev 7 16"Never again will they hunger; never again will they thirst. The sun will not beat upon them, nor any scorching heat. 17For the Lamb at the center of the throne will be their shepherd; he will lead them to springs of living water. And God will wipe away every tear from their eyes."

16. Sharing in Christ's Glory

Matt 13 40"As the weeds are pulled up and burned in the fire, so it will be at the end of the age. 41The Son of Man will send out his angels, and they will weed out of his kingdom everything that causes sin and all who do evil. . . . 43Then the righteous will shine like the sun in the kingdom of their Father. He who has ears, let him hear."
Rom 8 17Now if we are children, then we are heirs—heirs of God and co-heirs with Christ, if indeed we share in his sufferings in order that we may also share in his glory.
Col 3 4When Christ, who is your life, appears, then you also will appear with him in glory.
2 Tim 2 10Therefore I endure everything for the sake of the elect, that they too may obtain the salvation that is in Christ Jesus, with eternal glory.
1 Pet 5 1To the elders among you, I appeal as a fellow elder, a witness of Christ's sufferings and one who also will share in the glory to be revealed. . . .

17. Sinlessness

Eph 1 4For he chose us in him before the creation of the world to be holy and blameless in his sight. . . . 9And he made known to us the mystery of his will according to his good pleasure, which he purposed in Christ, 10to be put into effect when the

times will have reached their fulfillment—to bring all things in heaven and on earth together under one head, even Christ.
Jude [24]To him who is able to keep you from falling and to present you before his glorious presence without fault and with great joy . . .
Rev 14 [1]Then I looked, and there before me was the Lamb, standing on Mount Zion, and with him 144,000 who had his name and his Father's name written on their foreheads. . . . [5]No lie was found in their mouths; they are blameless.

E. Activities in Heaven

1. Praising God and Christ

Rev 4 [8]Each of the four living creatures had six wings and was covered with eyes all around, even under his wings. Day and night they never stop saying: "Holy, holy, holy is the Lord God Almighty, who was, and is, and is to come."
Rev 5 [8]And when he had taken it, the four living creatures and the twenty-four elders fell down before the Lamb. Each one had a harp and they were holding golden bowls full of incense, which are the prayers of the saints. [9]And they sang a new song: "You are worthy to take the scroll and to open its seals, because you were slain, and with your blood you purchased men for God from every tribe and language and people and nation. [10]You have made them to be a kingdom and priests to serve our God, and they will reign on the earth."

[11]Then I looked and heard the voice of many angels, numbering thousands upon thousands, and ten thousand times ten thousand. They encircled the throne and the living creatures and the elders. [12]In a loud voice they sang: "Worthy is the Lamb, who was slain, to receive power and wealth and wisdom and strength and honor and glory and praise!"

[13]Then I heard every creature in heaven and on earth and under the earth and on the sea, and all that is in them, singing: "To him who sits on the throne and to the Lamb be praise and honor and glory and power, for ever and ever!"
Rev 7 [9]After this I looked and there before me was a great multitude that no one could count, from every nation, tribe, people and language, standing before the throne and in front of the Lamb. They were wearing white robes and were holding palm branches in their hands. [10]And they cried out in a loud voice: "Salvation belongs to our God, who sits on the throne, and to the Lamb."
Rev 14 [2]And I heard a sound from heaven like the roar of rushing waters and like a loud peal of thunder. The sound I heard was like that of harpists playing their harps. [3]And they sang a new song before the throne and before the four living creatures and the elders. No one could learn the song except the 144,000 who had been redeemed from the earth.
Rev 15 [1]I saw in heaven another great and marvelous sign: seven angels with the seven last plagues—last, because with them God's wrath is completed. [2]And I saw what looked like a sea of glass mixed with fire and, standing beside the sea, those who had been victorious over the beast and his image and over the number of his name. They held harps given them by God [3]and sang the song of Moses the servant of God and the song of the Lamb: "Great and marvelous are your deeds, Lord God Almighty. Just and true are your ways, King of the ages. [4]Who will not fear you, O Lord, and bring glory to your name? For you alone are holy. All nations will come and worship before you, for your righteous acts have been revealed."
Rev 19 [1]After this I heard what sounded like the roar of a great multitude in heaven shouting: "Hallelujah! Salvation and glory and power belong to our God, [2]for true and just are his judgments. He has condemned the great prostitute who corrupted the earth by her adulteries. He has avenged on her the blood of his servants."

[3]And again they shouted: "Hallelujah! The smoke from her goes up for ever and ever."
Rev 19 [6]Then I heard what sounded like a great multitude, like the roar of rushing waters and like loud peals of thunder, shouting: "Hallelujah! For our Lord God Almighty reigns. [7]Let us rejoice and be glad and give him glory! For the wedding of the Lamb has come, and his bride has made herself ready. [8]Fine linen, bright and clean, was given her to wear." (Fine linen stands for the righteous acts of the saints.)

2. Serving God and Christ

Rev 1 [4]John, To the seven churches in the province of Asia: Grace and peace to you from him who is, and who was, and who is to come, and from the seven spirits before his throne, [5]and from Jesus Christ, who is the faithful witness, the firstborn from the dead, and the ruler of the kings of the earth.

To him who loves us and has freed us from our sins by his blood, [6]and has made us to be a kingdom and priests to serve his God and Father—to him be glory and power for ever and ever! Amen.

[7]Look, he is coming with the clouds, and every eye will see him, even those who pierced him; and all the peoples of the earth will mourn because of him. So shall it be! Amen.
Rev 7 [14]I answered, "Sir, you know."

And he said, "These are they who have come out of the great tribulation; they have washed their robes and made them white in the blood of the Lamb. [15]Therefore, they are before the throne of God and serve him day and night in his temple; and he who sits on the throne will spread his tent over them."
Rev 22 [3]No longer will there be any curse. The throne of God and of the Lamb will be in the city, and his servants will serve him. [4]They will see his face, and his name will be on their foreheads. [5]There will be no more night. They will not need the light of a lamp or the light of the sun, for the Lord God will give them light. And they will reign for ever and ever.

3. Worshiping God and Christ

Rev 4 [9]Whenever the living creatures give glory, honor and thanks to him who sits on the throne and who lives for ever and ever, [10]the twenty-four elders fall down before him who sits on the throne, and worship him who lives for ever and ever. They lay their crowns before the throne and say: [11]"You are worthy, our Lord and God, to receive glory and honor and power, for you created all things, and by your will they were created and have their being."
Rev 5 [14]The four living creatures said, "Amen," and the elders fell down and worshiped.
Rev 7 [11]All the angels were standing around the throne and around the elders and the four living creatures. They fell down on their faces before the throne and worshiped God, [12]saying: "Amen! Praise and glory and wisdom and thanks and honor and power and strength be to our God for ever and ever. Amen!"
Rev 11 [16]And the twenty-four elders, who were seated on their thrones before God, fell on their faces and worshiped God, [17]saying: "We give thanks to you, Lord God Almighty, the One who is and who was, because you have taken your great power and have begun to reign. [18]The nations were angry; and your wrath has come. The time has come for judging the dead, and for rewarding your servants the prophets and your saints and those who reverence your name, both small and great—and for destroying those who destroy the earth."
Rev 19 [4]The twenty-four elders and the four living creatures fell down and worshiped God, who was seated on the throne. And they cried: "Amen, Hallelujah!"

[5]Then a voice came from the throne, saying: "Praise our God, all you his servants, you who fear him, both small and great!"

VIII
Hell

A. Depictions of Hell

1. Prefigurations of Hell in Divine Wrath

a) Blazing Fire

2 Thess 1 [6]God is just: He will pay back trouble to those who trouble you [7]and give relief to you who are troubled, and to us as well. This will happen when the Lord Jesus is revealed from heaven in blazing fire with his powerful angels.

b) Burning Sulfur

Gen 19 [24]Then the LORD rained down burning sulfur on Sodom and Gomorrah—from the LORD out of the heavens.
Ps 11 [6]On the wicked he will rain fiery coals and burning sulfur; a scorching wind will be their lot.
Ezek 38 [22]"'I will execute judgment upon him with plague and bloodshed; I will pour down torrents of rain, hailstones and burning sulfur on him and on his troops and on the many nations with him.'"

c) Consuming Fire

Lev 10 [2]So fire came out from the presence of the LORD and consumed them, and they died before the LORD.
Deut 4 [24]For the LORD your God is a consuming fire, a jealous God.
2 Kings 1 [9]Then he sent to Elijah a captain with his company of fifty men. The captain went up to Elijah, who was sitting on the top of a hill, and said to him, "Man of God, the king says, 'Come down!'"

[10]Elijah answered the captain, "If I am a man of God, may fire come down from heaven and consume you and your fifty men!" Then fire fell from heaven and consumed the captain and his men.

[11]At this the king sent to Elijah another captain with his fifty men. The captain said to him, "Man of God, this is what the king says, 'Come down at once!'"

[12]"If I am a man of God," Elijah replied, "may fire come down from heaven and consume you and your fifty men!" Then the fire of God fell from heaven and consumed him and his fifty men.

[13]So the king sent a third captain with his fifty men. This third captain went up and fell on his knees before Elijah. "Man of God," he begged, "please have respect for my life and the lives of these fifty men, your servants! [14]See, fire has fallen from heaven and consumed the first two captains and all their men. But now have respect for my life!"
Ps 18 [7]The earth trembled and quaked, and the foundations of the mountains shook; they trembled because he was angry. [8]Smoke rose from his nostrils; consuming fire came from his mouth, burning coals blazed out of it. [9]He parted the heavens and came down; dark clouds were under his feet. [10]He mounted the cherubim and flew; he soared on the wings of the wind. [11]He made darkness his covering, his canopy around him—the dark rain clouds of the sky. [12]Out of the brightness of his presence clouds advanced, with hailstones and bolts of lightning. [13]The LORD thundered from heaven; the voice of the Most High resounded. [14]He shot his arrows and scattered the enemies, great bolts of lightning and routed them. [15]The valleys of the sea were exposed and the foundations of the earth laid bare at your rebuke, O LORD, at the blast of breath from your nostrils.
Ps 97 [3]Fire goes before him and consumes his foes on every side.
Isa 10 [17]The Light of Israel will become a fire, their Holy One a flame; in a single day it will burn and consume his thorns and his briers. [18]The splendor of his forests and fertile fields it will completely destroy, as when a sick man wastes away. [19]And the remaining trees of his forests will be so few that a child could write them down.
Isa 30 [27]See, the Name of the LORD comes from afar, with burning anger and dense clouds of smoke; his lips are full of wrath, and his tongue is a consuming fire. [28]His breath is like a rushing torrent, rising up to the neck. He shakes the nations in the sieve of destruction; he places in the jaws of the peoples a bit that leads them astray. . . . [30]The LORD will cause men to hear his majestic voice and will make them see his arm coming down with raging anger and consuming fire, with cloudburst, thunderstorm and hail.
Isa 33 [14]The sinners in Zion are terrified; trembling grips the godless: "Who of us can dwell with the consuming fire? Who of us can dwell with everlasting burning?"
Jer 5 [14]Therefore this is what the LORD God Almighty says: "Because the people have spoken these words, I will make my words in your mouth a fire and these people the wood it consumes."
Ezek 15 [6]"Therefore this is what the Sovereign LORD says: As I have given the wood of the vine among the trees of the forest as fuel for the fire, so will I treat the people living in Jerusalem. [7]I will set my face against them. Although they have come out of the fire, the fire will yet consume them. And when I set my face against them, you will know that I am the LORD. [8]I will make the land desolate because they have been unfaithful, declares the Sovereign LORD."
Obad [17]"But on Mount Zion will be deliverance; it will be holy, and the house of Jacob will possess its inheritance. [18]The house of Jacob will be a fire and the house of Joseph a flame; the house of Esau will be stubble, and they will set it on fire and consume it. There will be no survivors from the house of Esau." The LORD has spoken.
Heb 12 [29]for our "God is a consuming fire."

d) Destroying Fire

2 Pet 3 [10]But the day of the Lord will come like a thief. The heavens will disappear with a roar; the elements will be destroyed by fire, and the earth and everything in it will be laid bare.

[11]Since everything will be destroyed in this way, what kind of people ought you to be? You ought to live holy and godly lives [12]as you look forward to the day of God and speed its coming. That day will bring about the destruction of the heavens by fire, and the elements will melt in the heat.

e) Devouring Fire

Num 26 [8]The son of Pallu was Eliab, [9]and the sons of Eliab were Nemuel, Dathan and Abiram. The same Dathan and Abiram were the community officials who rebelled against Moses and Aaron and were among Korah's followers when they rebelled against the LORD. [10]The earth opened its mouth and swallowed them along with Korah, whose followers died when the fire devoured the 250 men. And they served as a warning sign.
Deut 9 [3]But be assured today that the LORD your God is the one who goes across ahead of you like a devouring fire. He will destroy them; he will subdue them before you. And you will drive them out and annihilate them quickly, as the LORD has promised you.
Deut 32 [22]"For a fire has been kindled by my wrath, one that burns to the realm of death below. It will devour the earth and its harvests and set afire the foundations of the mountains."
Ps 50 [3]Our God comes and will not be silent; a fire devours before him, and around him a tempest rages. [4]He summons the heavens above, and the earth, that he may judge his people. . . .
Isa 29 [5]But your many enemies will become like fine dust, the ruthless hordes like blown chaff. Suddenly, in an instant, [6]the LORD Almighty will come with thunder and earthquake and great noise, with windstorm and tempest and flames of a devouring fire.
Amos 5 [6]Seek the LORD and live, or he will sweep through the house of Joseph like a fire; it will devour, and Bethel will have no one to quench it.
Rev 20 [7]When the thousand years are over, Satan will be released from his prison [8]and will go out to deceive the nations in the four corners of the earth—Gog and Magog—to gather them for battle. In number they are like the sand on the seashore. [9]They marched across the breadth of the earth and surrounded the camp of God's people, the city he loves. But fire came down from heaven and devoured them.

f) Everlasting Burning

Isa 33 [14]The sinners in Zion are terrified; trembling grips the godless: "Who of us can dwell with the consuming fire? Who of us can dwell with everlasting burning?"

g) Fiery Furnace

Ps 21 [8]Your hand will lay hold on all your enemies; your right hand will seize your foes. [9]At the time of your appearing you will make them like a fiery furnace. In his wrath the LORD will swallow them up, and his fire will consume them.
Mal 4 [1]"Surely the day is coming; it will burn like a furnace. All the arrogant and every evildoer will be stubble, and that day

that is coming will set them on fire," says the LORD Almighty. "Not a root or a branch will be left to them."

h) Fire

Ps 89 [46]How long, O LORD? Will you hide yourself forever? How long will your wrath burn like fire?

Isa 47 [14]"Surely they are like stubble; the fire will burn them up. They cannot even save themselves from the power of the flame. Here are no coals to warm anyone; here is no fire to sit by."

Isa 66 [14]When you see this, your heart will rejoice and you will flourish like grass; the hand of the LORD will be made known to his servants, but his fury will be shown to his foes. [15]See, the LORD is coming with fire, and his chariots are like a whirlwind; he will bring down his anger with fury, and his rebuke with flames of fire. [16]For with fire and with his sword the LORD will execute judgment upon all men, and many will be those slain by the LORD.

Jer 48 [45]"In the shadow of Heshbon the fugitives stand helpless, for a fire has gone out from Heshbon, a blaze from the midst of Sihon; it burns the foreheads of Moab, the skulls of the noisy boasters."

Lam 1 [13]"From on high he sent fire, sent it down into my bones. He spread a net for my feet and turned me back. He made me desolate, faint all the day long."

Lam 2 [4]Like an enemy he has strung his bow; his right hand is ready. Like a foe he has slain all who were pleasing to the eye; he has poured out his wrath like fire on the tent of the Daughter of Zion.

Ezek 39 [6]"'I will send fire on Magog and on those who live in safety in the coastlands, and they will know that I am the LORD.'"

Nah 1 [5]The mountains quake before him and the hills melt away. The earth trembles at his presence, the world and all who live in it. [6]Who can withstand his indignation? Who can endure his fierce anger? His wrath is poured out like fire; the rocks are shattered before him.

i) Flames of Fire

Isa 66 [15]See, the LORD is coming with fire, and his chariots are like a whirlwind; he will bring down his anger with fury, and his rebuke with flames of fire. [16]For with fire and with his sword the LORD will execute judgment upon all men, and many will be those slain by the LORD.

j) Plague and Pestilence

Ezek 38 [22]"'I will execute judgment upon him with plague and bloodshed; I will pour down torrents of rain, hailstones and burning sulfur on him and on his troops and on the many nations with him.'"

Hab 3 [5]Plague went before him; pestilence followed his steps. [6]He stood, and shook the earth; he looked, and made the nations tremble. The ancient mountains crumbled and the age-old hills collapsed. His ways are eternal.

k) Raging Fire

Heb 10 [26]If we deliberately keep on sinning after we have received the knowledge of the truth, no sacrifice for sins is left, [27]but only a fearful expectation of judgment and of raging fire that will consume the enemies of God.

l) Refiner's Fire

Mal 3 [2]But who can endure the day of his coming? Who can stand when he appears? For he will be like a refiner's fire or a launderer's soap.

m) Storms, Thunder, Lightning, and Hail

Exod 9 [23]When Moses stretched out his staff toward the sky, the LORD sent thunder and hail, and lightning flashed down to the ground. So the LORD rained hail on the land of Egypt; [24]hail fell and lightning flashed back and forth. It was the worst storm in all the land of Egypt since it had become a nation.

Ezek 38 [22]"'I will execute judgment upon him with plague and bloodshed; I will pour down torrents of rain, hailstones and burning sulfur on him and on his troops and on the many nations with him.'"

n) Unquenchable Fire

Jer 4 [4]"Circumcise yourselves to the LORD, circumcise your hearts, you men of Judah and people of Jerusalem, or my wrath will break out and burn like fire because of the evil you have done—burn with no one to quench it."

Jer 17 [27]"'But if you do not obey me to keep the Sabbath day holy by not carrying any load as you come through the gates of Jerusalem on the Sabbath day, then I will kindle an unquenchable fire in the gates of Jerusalem that will consume her fortresses.'"

Jer 21 [12]"'O house of David, this is what the LORD says: Administer justice every morning; rescue from the hand of his oppressor the one who has been robbed, or my wrath will break out and burn like fire because of the evil you have done—burn with no one to quench it.'"

Ezek 20 [47]"Say to the southern forest: 'Hear the word of the LORD. This is what the Sovereign LORD says: I am about to set fire to you, and it will consume all your trees, both green and dry. The blazing flame will not be quenched, and every face from south to north will be scorched by it. [48]Everyone will see that I the LORD have kindled it; it will not be quenched.'"

Amos 5 [6]Seek the LORD and live, or he will sweep through the house of Joseph like a fire; it will devour, and Bethel will have no one to quench it.

o) Vengeance

Isa 35 [4]say to those with fearful hearts, "Be strong, do not fear; your God will come, he will come with vengeance; with divine retribution he will come to save you."

Heb 10 [30]For we know him who said, "It is mine to avenge; I will repay," and again, "The Lord will judge his people." [31]It is a dreadful thing to fall into the hands of the living God.

2. Descriptions of Hell

a) Abyss

Rev 9 [1]The fifth angel sounded his trumpet, and I saw a star that had fallen from the sky to the earth. The star was given the key to the shaft of the Abyss. [2]When he opened the Abyss, smoke rose from it like the smoke from a gigantic furnace. The sun and sky were darkened by the smoke from the Abyss. [3]And out of the smoke locusts came down upon the earth and were given power like that of scorpions of the earth. [4]They were told not to harm the grass of the earth or any plant or tree, but only those people who did not have the seal of God on their foreheads. [5]They were not given power to kill them, but only to torture them for five months. And the agony they suffered was like that of the sting of a scorpion when it strikes a man. [6]During those days men will seek death, but will not find it; they will long to die, but death will elude them.

[7]The locusts looked like horses prepared for battle. On their heads they wore something like crowns of gold, and their faces resembled human faces. [8]Their hair was like women's hair, and their teeth were like lions' teeth. [9]They had breastplates like breastplates of iron, and the sound of their wings was like the thundering of many horses and chariots rushing into battle. [10]They had tails and stings like scorpions, and in their tails they had power to torment people for five months. [11]They had as king over them the angel of the Abyss, whose name in Hebrew is Abaddon, and in Greek, Apollyon.

b) Burning Sulfur

Rev 14 [10]". . . he, too, will drink of the wine of God's fury, which has been poured full strength into the cup of his wrath. He will be tormented with burning sulfur in the presence of the holy angels and of the Lamb."

c) Condemnation

Matt 23 [33]"You snakes! You brood of vipers! How will you escape being condemned to hell?"

Mark 16 [16]"Whoever believes and is baptized will be saved, but whoever does not believe will be condemned."

John 3 [18]"Whoever believes in him is not condemned, but whoever does not believe stands condemned already because he has not believed in the name of God's one and only Son."

John 5 [29]". . . and come out—those who have done good will

rise to live, and those who have done evil will rise to be condemned."
2 Pet 2 [3]In their greed these teachers will exploit you with stories they have made up. Their condemnation has long been hanging over them, and their destruction has not been sleeping.

d) Darkness

Matt 8 [10]When Jesus heard this, he was astonished and said to those following him, "I tell you the truth, I have not found anyone in Israel with such great faith. [11]I say to you that many will come from the east and the west, and will take their places at the feast with Abraham, Isaac and Jacob in the kingdom of heaven. [12]But the subjects of the kingdom will be thrown outside, into the darkness, where there will be weeping and gnashing of teeth."
Matt 22 [13]"Then the king told the attendants, 'Tie him hand and foot, and throw him outside, into the darkness, where there will be weeping and gnashing of teeth.'"
Matt 25 [29]"For everyone who has will be given more, and he will have an abundance. Whoever does not have, even what he has will be taken from him. [30]And throw that worthless servant outside, into the darkness, where there will be weeping and gnashing of teeth.'"
Jude [4]For certain men whose condemnation was written about long ago have secretly slipped in among you. They are godless men, who change the grace of our God into a license for immorality and deny Jesus Christ our only Sovereign and Lord. . . . [13]They are wild waves of the sea, foaming up their shame; wandering stars, for whom blackest darkness has been reserved forever.

e) Destruction

Matt 7 [13]"Enter through the narrow gate. For wide is the gate and broad is the road that leads to destruction, and many enter through it."
Rom 9 [22]What if God, choosing to show his wrath and make his power known, bore with great patience the objects of his wrath—prepared for destruction?
Phil 3 [18]For, as I have often told you before and now say again even with tears, many live as enemies of the cross of Christ. [19]Their destiny is destruction, their god is their stomach, and their glory is in their shame. Their mind is on earthly things.
1 Thess 5 [2]for you know very well that the day of the Lord will come like a thief in the night. [3]While people are saying, "Peace and safety," destruction will come on them suddenly, as labor pains on a pregnant woman, and they will not escape.

f) Eternal Fire

Matt 18 [8]"If your hand or your foot causes you to sin, cut it off and throw it away. It is better for you to enter life maimed or crippled than to have two hands or two feet and be thrown into eternal fire."
Matt 25 [41]"Then he will say to those on his left, 'Depart from me, you who are cursed, into the eternal fire prepared for the devil and his angels.'"
Jude [7]In a similar way, Sodom and Gomorrah and the surrounding towns gave themselves up to sexual immorality and perversion. They serve as an example of those who suffer the punishment of eternal fire.

g) Eternal Punishment

Matt 25 [46]"Then they will go away to eternal punishment, but the righteous to eternal life."

h) Everlasting Destruction

2 Thess 1 [8]He will punish those who do not know God and do not obey the gospel of our Lord Jesus. [9]They will be punished with everlasting destruction and shut out from the presence of the Lord and from the majesty of his power. . . .

i) Fiery Furnace

Matt 13 [42]"They will throw them into the fiery furnace, where there will be weeping and gnashing of teeth."

j) Fire

Matt 3 [10]"The ax is already at the root of the trees, and every tree that does not produce good fruit will be cut down and thrown into the fire."

k) Hell

Matt 5 [22]"But I tell you that anyone who is angry with his brother will be subject to judgment. Again, anyone who says to his brother, 'Raca,' is answerable to the Sanhedrin. But anyone who says, 'You fool!' will be in danger of the fire of hell."
Matt 5 [29]"If your right eye causes you to sin, gouge it out and throw it away. It is better for you to lose one part of your body than for your whole body to be thrown into hell. [30]And if your right hand causes you to sin, cut it off and throw it away. It is better for you to lose one part of your body than for your whole body to go into hell."
Matt 10 [28]"Do not be afraid of those who kill the body but cannot kill the soul. Rather, be afraid of the One who can destroy both soul and body in hell."
Matt 18 [8]"If your hand or your foot causes you to sin, cut it off and throw it away. It is better for you to enter life maimed or crippled than to have two hands or two feet and be thrown into eternal fire. [9]And if your eye causes you to sin, gouge it out and throw it away. It is better for you to enter life with one eye than to have two eyes and be thrown into the fire of hell."
Matt 23 [33]"You snakes! You brood of vipers! How will you escape being condemned to hell?"
Mark 9 [43]"If your hand causes you to sin, cut it off. It is better for you to enter life maimed than with two hands to go into hell, where the fire never goes out."

l) Judgment

1 Tim 5 [24]The sins of some men are obvious, reaching the place of judgment ahead of them; the sins of others trail behind them.
Heb 6 [2]instruction about baptisms, the laying on of hands, the resurrection of the dead, and eternal judgment.
2 Pet 2 [4]For if God did not spare angels when they sinned, but sent them to hell, putting them into gloomy dungeons to be held for judgment; [5]if he did not spare the ancient world when he brought the flood on its ungodly people, but protected Noah, a preacher of righteousness, and seven others; [6]if he condemned the cities of Sodom and Gomorrah by burning them to ashes, and made them an example of what is going to happen to the ungodly; [7]and if he rescued Lot, a righteous man, who was distressed by the filthy lives of lawless men [8](for that righteous man, living among them day after day, was tormented in his righteous soul by the lawless deeds he saw and heard)—[9]if this is so, then the Lord knows how to rescue godly men from trials and to hold the unrighteous for the day of judgment, while continuing their punishment.
Jude [6]And the angels who did not keep their positions of authority but abandoned their own home—these he has kept in darkness, bound with everlasting chains for judgment on the great Day.

m) Lake of Burning Sulfur

Rev 19 [20]But the beast was captured, and with him the false prophet who had performed the miraculous signs on his behalf. With these signs he had deluded those who had received the mark of the beast and worshiped his image. The two of them were thrown alive into the fiery lake of burning sulfur.
Rev 20 [10]And the devil, who deceived them, was thrown into the lake of burning sulfur, where the beast and the false prophet had been thrown. They will be tormented day and night for ever and ever.

n) Lake of Fire

Rev 20 [14]Then death and Hades were thrown into the lake of fire. The lake of fire is the second death. [15]If anyone's name was not found written in the book of life, he was thrown into the lake of fire.

o) Second Death

Rev 20 [14]Then death and Hades were thrown into the lake of fire. The lake of fire is the second death.

Rev 21 [8]"But the cowardly, the unbelieving, the vile, the murderers, the sexually immoral, those who practice magic arts, the idolaters and all liars—their place will be in the fiery lake of burning sulfur. This is the second death."

p) Unquenchable Fire

Matt 3 [12]"His winnowing fork is in his hand, and he will clear his threshing floor, gathering his wheat into the barn and burning up the chaff with unquenchable fire."

Luke 3 [17]"His winnowing fork is in his hand to clear his threshing floor and to gather the wheat into his barn, but he will burn up the chaff with unquenchable fire."

B. The Nature of Hell

1. It Is Everlasting

Matt 12 [32]"Anyone who speaks a word against the Son of Man will be forgiven, but anyone who speaks against the Holy Spirit will not be forgiven, either in this age or in the age to come."

Mark 9 [47]"And if your eye causes you to sin, pluck it out. It is better for you to enter the kingdom of God with one eye than to have two eyes and be thrown into hell, [48]where 'their worm does not die, and the fire is not quenched.'"

Rev 14 [11]"And the smoke of their torment rises for ever and ever. There is no rest day or night for those who worship the beast and his image, or for anyone who receives the mark of his name."

Rev 20 [10]And the devil, who deceived them, was thrown into the lake of burning sulfur, where the beast and the false prophet had been thrown. They will be tormented day and night for ever and ever.

2. It Is Exclusion from God's Presence

Matt 25 [31]"When the Son of Man comes in his glory, and all the angels with him, he will sit on his throne in heavenly glory. [32]All the nations will be gathered before him, and he will separate the people one from another as a shepherd separates the sheep from the goats. [33]He will put the sheep on his right and the goats on his left. . . .

[41]"Then he will say to those on his left, 'Depart from me, you who are cursed, into the eternal fire prepared for the devil and his angels. [42]For I was hungry and you gave me nothing to eat, I was thirsty and you gave me nothing to drink, [43]I was a stranger and you did not invite me in, I needed clothes and you did not clothe me, I was sick and in prison and you did not look after me.'

[44]"They also will answer, 'Lord, when did we see you hungry or thirsty or a stranger or needing clothes or sick or in prison, and did not help you?'

[45]"He will reply, 'I tell you the truth, whatever you did not do for one of the least of these, you did not do for me.'

[46]"Then they will go away to eternal punishment, but the righteous to eternal life."

Luke 13 [24]"Make every effort to enter through the narrow door, because many, I tell you, will try to enter and will not be able to. [25]Once the owner of the house gets up and closes the door, you will stand outside knocking and pleading, 'Sir, open the door for us.'

"But he will answer, 'I don't know you or where you come from.'

[26] "Then you will say, 'We ate and drank with you, and you taught in our streets.'

[27]"But he will reply, 'I don't know you or where you come from. Away from me, all you evildoers!'

[28]"There will be weeping there, and gnashing of teeth, when you see Abraham, Isaac and Jacob and all the prophets in the kingdom of God, but you yourselves thrown out."

2 Thess 1 [8]He will punish those who do not know God and do not obey the gospel of our Lord Jesus. [9]They will be punished with everlasting destruction and shut out from the presence of the Lord and from the majesty of his power. . . .

3. It Is a Place of Suffering

Matt 8 [12]"But the subjects of the kingdom will be thrown outside, into the darkness, where there will be weeping and gnashing of teeth."

Matt 10 [28]"Do not be afraid of those who kill the body but cannot kill the soul. Rather, be afraid of the One who can destroy both soul and body in hell."

Luke 16 [19]"There was a rich man who was dressed in purple and fine linen and lived in luxury every day. [20]At his gate was laid a beggar named Lazarus, covered with sores [21]and longing to eat what fell from the rich man's table. Even the dogs came and licked his sores.

[22]"The time came when the beggar died and the angels carried him to Abraham's side. The rich man also died and was buried. [23]In hell, where he was in torment, he looked up and saw Abraham far away, with Lazarus by his side. [24]So he called to him, 'Father Abraham, have pity on me and send Lazarus to dip the tip of his finger in water and cool my tongue, because I am in agony in this fire.'

[25]"But Abraham replied, 'Son, remember that in your lifetime you received your good things, while Lazarus received bad things, but now he is comforted here and you are in agony. [26]And besides all this, between us and you a great chasm has been fixed, so that those who want to go from here to you cannot, nor can anyone cross over from there to us.'

[27]"He answered, 'Then I beg you, father, send Lazarus to my father's house, [28]for I have five brothers. Let him warn them, so that they will not also come to this place of torment.'

[29]"Abraham replied, 'They have Moses and the Prophets; let them listen to them.'

[30]"'No, father Abraham,' he said, 'but if someone from the dead goes to them, they will repent.'

[31]"He said to him, 'If they do not listen to Moses and the Prophets, they will not be convinced even if someone rises from the dead.'"

Rev 14 [9]A third angel followed them and said in a loud voice: "If anyone worships the beast and his image and receives his mark on the forehead or on the hand, [10]he, too, will drink of the wine of God's fury, which has been poured full strength into the cup of his wrath. He will be tormented with burning sulfur in the presence of the holy angels and of the Lamb. [11]And the smoke of their torment rises for ever and ever. There is no rest day or night for those who worship the beast and his image, or for anyone who receives the mark of his name."

4. It Is Separation from the Righteous

Matt 13 [47]"Once again, the kingdom of heaven is like a net that was let down into the lake and caught all kinds of fish. [48]When it was full, the fishermen pulled it up on the shore. Then they sat down and collected the good fish in baskets, but threw the bad away. [49]This is how it will be at the end of the age. The angels will come and separate the wicked from the righteous [50]and throw them into the fiery furnace, where there will be weeping and gnashing of teeth."

Matt 25 [31]"When the Son of Man comes in his glory, and all the angels with him, he will sit on his throne in heavenly glory. [32]All the nations will be gathered before him, and he will separate the people one from another as a shepherd separates the sheep from the goats. [33]He will put the sheep on his right and the goats on his left."

Matt 25 [46]"Then they will go away to eternal punishment, but the righteous to eternal life."

C. The Occupants of Hell

1. The Beast and the False Prophet

Rev 19 [19]Then I saw the beast and the kings of the earth and their armies gathered together to make war against the rider on the horse and his army. [20]But the beast was captured, and with him the false prophet who had performed the miraculous signs on his behalf. With these signs he had deluded those who had received the mark of the beast and worshiped his image. The two of them were thrown alive into the fiery lake of burning sulfur.

Rev 20 [10]And the devil, who deceived them, was thrown into the lake of burning sulfur, where the beast and the false prophet had been thrown. They will be tormented day and night for ever and ever.

2. Death and Hades

Rev 20 [13]The sea gave up the dead that were in it, and death and Hades gave up the dead that were in them, and each person was judged according to what he had done. [14]Then death and Hades were thrown into the lake of fire. The lake of fire is the second death.

3. The Devil

Matt 25 [41]"Then he will say to those on his left, 'Depart from me, you who are cursed, into the eternal fire prepared for the devil and his angels.'"
Rev 20 [10]And the devil, who deceived them, was thrown into the lake of burning sulfur, where the beast and the false prophet had been thrown. They will be tormented day and night for ever and ever.

4. Evildoers

Matt 7 [19]"Every tree that does not bear good fruit is cut down and thrown into the fire. . . .

[21]"Not everyone who says to me, 'Lord, Lord,' will enter the kingdom of heaven, but only he who does the will of my Father who is in heaven. [22]Many will say to me on that day, 'Lord, Lord, did we not prophesy in your name, and in your name drive out demons and perform many miracles?' [23]Then I will tell them plainly, 'I never knew you. Away from me, you evildoers!'"
Matt 13 [38]"The field is the world, and the good seed stands for the sons of the kingdom. The weeds are the sons of the evil one. . . .

[40]"As the weeds are pulled up and burned in the fire, so it will be at the end of the age. [41]The Son of Man will send out his angels, and they will weed out of his kingdom everything that causes sin and all who do evil."
Matt 23 [29]"Woe to you, teachers of the law and Pharisees, you hypocrites! You build tombs for the prophets and decorate the graves of the righteous. [30]And you say, 'If we had lived in the days of our forefathers, we would not have taken part with them in shedding the blood of the prophets.' [31]So you testify against yourselves that you are the descendants of those who murdered the prophets. [32]Fill up, then, the measure of the sin of your forefathers!

[33]"You snakes! You brood of vipers! How will you escape being condemned to hell?"
1 Cor 6 [9]Do you not know that the wicked will not inherit the kingdom of God? Do not be deceived: Neither the sexually immoral nor idolaters nor adulterers nor male prostitutes nor homosexual offenders [10]nor thieves nor the greedy nor drunkards nor slanderers nor swindlers will inherit the kingdom of God.
Gal 5 [19]The acts of the sinful nature are obvious: sexual immorality, impurity and debauchery; [20]idolatry and witchcraft; hatred, discord, jealousy, fits of rage, selfish ambition, dissensions, factions [21]and envy; drunkenness, orgies, and the like. I warn you, as I did before, that those who live like this will not inherit the kingdom of God.
Eph 5 [5]For of this you can be sure: No immoral, impure or greedy person—such a man is an idolater—has any inheritance in the kingdom of Christ and of God.
2 Thess 2 [9]The coming of the lawless one will be in accordance with the work of Satan displayed in all kinds of counterfeit miracles, signs and wonders, [10]and in every sort of evil that deceives those who are perishing. They perish because they refused to love the truth and so be saved. [11]For this reason God sends them a powerful delusion so that they will believe the lie [12]and so that all will be condemned who have not believed the truth but have delighted in wickedness.
Heb 6 [4]It is impossible for those who have once been enlightened, who have tasted the heavenly gift, who have shared in the Holy Spirit, . . . [6]if they fall away, to be brought back to repentance, because to their loss they are crucifying the Son of God all over again and subjecting him to public disgrace. . . . [8]But land that produces thorns and thistles is worthless and is in danger of being cursed. In the end it will be burned.
Rev 21 [7]"He who overcomes will inherit all this, and I will be his God and he will be my son. [8]But the cowardly, the unbelieving, the vile, the murderers, the sexually immoral, those who practice magic arts, the idolaters and all liars—their place will be in the fiery lake of burning sulfur. This is the second death."
Rev 22 [14]"Blessed are those who wash their robes, that they may have the right to the tree of life and may go through the gates into the city. [15]Outside are the dogs, those who practice magic arts, the sexually immoral, the murderers, the idolaters and everyone who loves and practices falsehood."

5. The Lawless One

2 Thess 2 [8]And then the lawless one will be revealed, whom the Lord Jesus will overthrow with the breath of his mouth and destroy by the splendor of his coming.

6. Unbelievers

Luke 8 [11]"This is the meaning of the parable: The seed is the word of God. [12]Those along the path are the ones who hear, and then the devil comes and takes away the word from their hearts, so that they may not believe and be saved."
John 3 [18]"Whoever believes in him is not condemned, but whoever does not believe stands condemned already because he has not believed in the name of God's one and only Son."
John 3 [36]"Whoever believes in the Son has eternal life, but whoever rejects the Son will not see life, for God's wrath remains on him."
1 Cor 1 [18]For the message of the cross is foolishness to those who are perishing, but to us who are being saved it is the power of God. . . . [21]For since in the wisdom of God the world through its wisdom did not know him, God was pleased through the foolishness of what was preached to save those who believe. [22]Jews demand miraculous signs and Greeks look for wisdom, [23]but we preach Christ crucified: a stumbling block to Jews and foolishness to Gentiles. . . .
Heb 3 [12]See to it, brothers, that none of you has a sinful, unbelieving heart that turns away from the living God. [13]But encourage one another daily, as long as it is called Today, so that none of you may be hardened by sin's deceitfulness. [14]We have come to share in Christ if we hold firmly till the end the confidence we had at first. [15]As has just been said: "Today, if you hear his voice, do not harden your hearts as you did in the rebellion."

[16]Who were they who heard and rebelled? Were they not all those Moses led out of Egypt? [17]And with whom was he angry for forty years? Was it not with those who sinned, whose bodies fell in the desert? [18]And to whom did God swear that they would never enter his rest if not to those who disobeyed? [19]So we see that they were not able to enter, because of their unbelief.
Heb 4 [1]Therefore, since the promise of entering his rest still stands, let us be careful that none of you be found to have fallen short of it. [2]For we also have had the gospel preached to us, just as they did; but the message they heard was of no value to them, because those who heard did not combine it with faith. [3]Now we who have believed enter that rest, just as God has said, "So I declared on oath in my anger, 'They shall never enter my rest.'" And yet his work has been finished since the creation of the world.
1 John 5 [12]He who has the Son has life; he who does not have the Son of God does not have life.
Jude [5]Though you already know all this, I want to remind you that the Lord delivered his people out of Egypt, but later destroyed those who did not believe.

7. Wicked Angels

Matt 25 [41]"Then he will say to those on his left, 'Depart from me, you who are cursed, into the eternal fire prepared for the devil and his angels.'"

IX
The New Heavens and the New Earth

A. The Old Heavens and Earth Will Perish

Ps 102 25“In the beginning you laid the foundations of the earth, and the heavens are the work of your hands. 26They will perish, but you remain; they will all wear out like a garment. Like clothing you will change them and they will be discarded.”
Isa 51 6“Lift up your eyes to the heavens, look at the earth beneath; the heavens will vanish like smoke, the earth will wear out like a garment and its inhabitants die like flies. But my salvation will last forever, my righteousness will never fail.”
Matt 5 18“I tell you the truth, until heaven and earth disappear, not the smallest letter, not the least stroke of a pen, will by any means disappear from the Law until everything is accomplished.”
Matt 24 35“Heaven and earth will pass away, but my words will never pass away.”
Heb 1 10He also says, “In the beginning, O Lord, you laid the foundations of the earth, and the heavens are the work of your hands. 11They will perish, but you remain; they will all wear out like a garment. 12You will roll them up like a robe; like a garment they will be changed. But you remain the same, and your years will never end.”
2 Pet 3 7By the same word the present heavens and earth are reserved for fire, being kept for the day of judgment and destruction of ungodly men.

8But do not forget this one thing, dear friends: With the Lord a day is like a thousand years, and a thousand years are like a day. 9The Lord is not slow in keeping his promise, as some understand slowness. He is patient with you, not wanting anyone to perish, but everyone to come to repentance.

10But the day of the Lord will come like a thief. The heavens will disappear with a roar; the elements will be destroyed by fire, and the earth and everything in it will be laid bare.

11Since everything will be destroyed in this way, what kind of people ought you to be? You ought to live holy and godly lives 12as you look forward to the day of God and speed its coming. That day will bring about the destruction of the heavens by fire, and the elements will melt in the heat. 13But in keeping with his promise we are looking forward to a new heaven and a new earth, the home of righteousness.

B. The New Heavens and Earth Will Be Established

Isa 65 17“Behold, I will create new heavens and a new earth. The former things will not be remembered, nor will they come to mind.”
Isa 66 22“As the new heavens and the new earth that I make will endure before me,” declares the LORD, “so will your name and descendants endure.”
Matt 19 28Jesus said to them, “I tell you the truth, at the renewal of all things, when the Son of Man sits on his glorious throne, you who have followed me will also sit on twelve thrones, judging the twelve tribes of Israel.”
Acts 3 21“He must remain in heaven until the time comes for God to restore everything, as he promised long ago through his holy prophets.”
Rom 8 18I consider that our present sufferings are not worth comparing with the glory that will be revealed in us. 19The creation waits in eager expectation for the sons of God to be revealed. 20For the creation was subjected to frustration, not by its own choice, but by the will of the one who subjected it, in hope 21that the creation itself will be liberated from its bondage to decay and brought into the glorious freedom of the children of God.

22We know that the whole creation has been groaning as in the pains of childbirth right up to the present time.
1 Cor 15 22For as in Adam all die, so in Christ all will be made alive. 23But each in his own turn: Christ, the firstfruits; then, when he comes, those who belong to him. 24Then the end will come, when he hands over the kingdom to God the Father after he has destroyed all dominion, authority and power. 25For he must reign until he has put all his enemies under his feet. 26The last enemy to be destroyed is death. 27For he “has put everything under his feet.” Now when it says that “everything” has been put under him, it is clear that this does not include God himself, who put everything under Christ. 28When he has done this, then the Son himself will be made subject to him who put everything under him, so that God may be all in all.
Eph 1 9And he made known to us the mystery of his will according to his good pleasure, which he purposed in Christ, 10to be put into effect when the times will have reached their fulfillment—to bring all things in heaven and on earth together under one head, even Christ.
Rev 21 1Then I saw a new heaven and a new earth, for the first heaven and the first earth had passed away, and there was no longer any sea. 2I saw the Holy City, the new Jerusalem, coming down out of heaven from God, prepared as a bride beautifully dressed for her husband. 3And I heard a loud voice from the throne saying, “Now the dwelling of God is with men, and he will live with them. They will be his people, and God himself will be with them and be their God. 4He will wipe every tear from their eyes. There will be no more death or mourning or crying or pain, for the old order of things has passed away.”

5He who was seated on the throne said, “I am making everything new!” Then he said, “Write this down, for these words are trustworthy and true.”

6He said to me: “It is done. I am the Alpha and the Omega, the Beginning and the End. To him who is thirsty I will give to drink without cost from the spring of the water of life. 7He who overcomes will inherit all this, and I will be his God and he will be my son. 8But the cowardly, the unbelieving, the vile, the murderers, the sexually immoral, those who practice magic arts, the idolaters and all liars—their place will be in the fiery lake of burning sulfur. This is the second death.”

Subject Index

Subject Index

Scripture Index

Deuteronomy

Joshua

Judges

Psalms

Proverbs

Ecclesiastes

Song of Songs

Isaiah

Daniel

Hosea

Mark

Luke

John

Romans

1 Corinthians

2 Corinthians

Galatians

Ephesians

Philippians

Colossians

1 Thessalonians

2 Thessalonians

1 Timothy

2 Timothy

Titus